1933 — Inez Beverly Prosser becomes the first African-American woman to receive a doctoral degree in psychology from a U.S institution (Ph.D., University of Cincinnati).

1935 — Christiana Morgan and Henry Murray introduce the Thematic Apperception Test to elicit fantasies from people undergoing psychoanalysis.

1936 — Egas Moniz, Portuguese physician, publishes work on the first frontal lobotomies performed on humans.

1938 — B. F. Skinner publishes *The Behavior of Organisms*, which describes operant conditioning of animals.

In *Primary Mental Abilities*, Louis L. Thurstone proposes seven such abilities.

Ugo Cerletti and Lucino Bini use electroshock treatment with a human patient.

1939 — David Wechsler publishes the Wechsler-Bellevue intelligence test, forerunner of the Wechsler Intelligence Scale for Children (WISC) and the Wechsler Adult Intelligence Scale (WAIS).

Marnie Phipps Clark (pictured) receives a master's degree from Howard University. In collaboration with Kenneth B. Clark, she later extends her thesis, "The Development of Consciousness of Self in Negro Preschool Children," providing joint research cited in the U.S. Supreme Court's **1954** decision to end racial segregation in public schools.

Edward Alexander Bott helps found the Canadian Psychological Association. He becomes its first president in **1940**.

1943 — World War II provides many opportunities for psychologists to enhance the popularity and influence of psychology, especially in applied areas.

Psychologist Starke Hathaway and physician J. Charnley McKinley publish the Minnesota Multiphasic Personality Inventory (MMPI).

1945 — Karen Horney, who criticized Freud's theory of female sexual development, publishes *Our Inner Conflicts*.

1946 — Benjamin Spock's first edition of *The Commonsense Book of Baby and Child Care* appears; the book will influence rearing in North America for several decades.

1948 — Alfred Kinsey and his colleagues publish *Sexual B... Human Male*, and they publish *Sexual Behavior in... Female* in **1953**.

B. F. Skinner's novel, *Walden Two*, describes a Uto... nity based on positive reinforcement, which bec... call for applying psychological principles in ever... especially communal living.

1949 — Ernest R. Hilgard publishes *Theories of Learning*, ... required reading for several generations of psych... in North America.

Raymond B. Cattell publishes the Sixteen Personality Factor Questionnaire (16PF).

Continued on inside back cover

1869 — Francis Galton, Charles Darwin's cousin, publishes *Hereditary Genius*, in which he claims that intelligence is inherited. In **1876** he coins the expression "nature and nurture" to correspond with "heredity and environment."

1874 — Carl Wernicke, a German neurologist and psychiatrist, shows that damage to a specific area in the left temporal lobe (now called Wernicke's area) disrupts ability to comprehend or produce spoken or written language.

1878 — G. Stanley Hall receives from Harvard University's Department of Philosophy the first U.S. Ph.D. degree based on psychological research.

1879 — Wilhelm Wundt establishes at the University of Leipzig, Germany, the first psychology laboratory, which becomes a Mecca for psychology students from all over the world.

1883 — G. Stanley Hall, student of Wilhelm Wundt, establishes the first formal U.S. psychology laboratory at Johns Hopkins University.

1885 — Hermann Ebbinghaus publishes *On Memory*, summarizing his extensive research on learning and memory, including the "forgetting curve."

1886 — Joseph Jastrow receives from Johns Hopkins University the first Ph.D. degree in psychology awarded by a Department of Psychology in the United States.

1889 — Alfred Binet and Henri Beaunis establish the first psychology laboratory in France at the Sorbonne, and the first International Congress of Psychology meets in Paris.

1890 — William James, Harvard University philosopher and psychologist, publishes *The Principles of Psychology*, describing psychology as "the science of mental life."

1891 — James Mark Baldwin establishes the first psychology laboratory in the British Commonwealth at the University of Toronto.

1892 — G. Stanley Hall spearheads the founding of the American Psychological Association (APA) and becomes its first president.

1893 — Mary Whiton Calkins (pictured) and Christine Ladd-Franklin are the first women elected to membership in the APA.

1894 — Margaret Floy Washburn is the first woman to receive a Ph.D. degree in psychology (Cornell University).

1896 — Harvard University denies Mary Whiton Calkins admission to doctoral candidacy because of her gender, despite Hugo Münsterberg's claim that she was the best student he had ever had there.

John Dewey publishes "The Reflex Arc Concept in Psychology," helping to formalize the school of psychology called functionalism.

1898 — In "Animal Intelligence," Edward L. Thorndike, Columbia University, describes his learning experiments with cats in "puzzle boxes." In **1905**, he proposes the "law of effect."

1900 — Sigmund Freud publishes *The Interpretation of Dreams*, his major theoretical work on psychoanalysis.

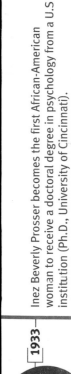

PSYCHOLOGY
NINTH EDITION IN MODULES

PSYCHOLOGY
NINTH EDITION IN MODULES

David G. Myers

Hope College
Holland, Michigan

WORTH PUBLISHERS

Senior Publisher: Catherine Woods
Senior Acquisitions Editor: Kevin Feyen
Executive Marketing Manager: Katherine Nurre
Development Editors: Trish Morgan, Christine Brune, Nancy Fleming
Media Editor: Sharon Prevost
Photo Editor: Bianca Moscatelli
Photo Researcher: Donna Ranieri
Art Director: Babs Reingold
Interior Designer: Lissi Sigillo
Layout Designers: Paul Lacy and Lee Ann McKevitt
Cover Designer: Lyndall Culbertson
Associate Managing Editor: Tracey Kuehn
Project Editor: Dana Kasowitz
Illustration Coordinator: Bill Page
Illustrations: TSI Graphics, Keith Kasnot
Production Manager: Sarah Segal
Composition: TSI Graphics
Printing and Binding: RR Donnelley
Cover Painting: *Illustration of Tree Losing Leaves in Autumn*
©Andrew Judd

Library of Congress Control Number: 2009931721

ISBN-13: 978-1-4292-1638-8
ISBN-10: 1-4292-1638-7

Printed in the United States of America

Fourth printing

All royalties from the sale of this book are assigned to the David and Carol Myers Foundation, which exists to receive and distribute funds to other charitable organizations.

Worth Publishers
41 Madison Avenue
New York, NY 10010
www.worthpublishers.com

FOR BETTY PROBERT,

with gratitude for 27 years of loyal friendship and superb editorial
support in creating this book and its teaching supplements

About the Author

David Myers received his psychology Ph.D. from the University of Iowa. He has spent his career at Hope College, Michigan, where he has taught dozens of introductory psychology sections. Hope College students have invited him to be their commencement speaker and voted him "outstanding professor."

Myers' scientific articles have, with support from National Science Foundation grants, appeared in more than two dozen scientific periodicals, including *Science, American Scientist, Psychological Science,* and the *American Psychologist.* In addition to his scholarly writing and his textbooks for introductory and social psychology, he also digests psychological science for the general public. His writings have appeared in four dozen magazines, from *Today's Education* to *Scientific American.* He also has authored five general audience books, including *The Pursuit of Happiness* and *Intuition: Its Powers and Perils.*

David Myers has chaired his city's Human Relations Commission, helped found a thriving assistance center for families in poverty, and spoken to hundreds of college and community groups. Drawing on his experience, he also has written articles and a book *(A Quiet World)* about hearing loss, and he is advocating a transformation in American assistive listening technology (see hearingloop.org).

He bikes to work year-round and plays daily pickup basketball. David and Carol Myers have raised two sons and a daughter.

Brief Contents

Preface   ix

Introduction to the History and Science of Psychology 3

MODULE 1   The Story of Psychology   2

MODULE 2   Thinking Critically With Psychological Science   14

MODULE 3   Research Strategies: How Psychologists Ask and Answer Questions   25

The Biology of Mind 45

MODULE 4   Neural and Hormonal Systems   46

MODULE 5   Tools of Discovery and Older Brain Structures   58

MODULE 6   The Cerebral Cortex and Our Divided Brain   67

Consciousness and the Two-Track Mind 83

MODULE 7   The Brain and Consciousness   85

MODULE 8   Sleep and Dreams   91

MODULE 9   Hypnosis   108

MODULE 10   Drugs and Consciousness   113

Nature, Nurture, and Human Diversity 131

MODULE 11   Behavior Genetics and Evolutionary Psychology   132

MODULE 12   Environmental Influences on Behavior   148

Developing Through the Life Span 169

MODULE 13   Prenatal Development and the Newborn   170

MODULE 14   Infancy and Childhood   174

MODULE 15   Adolescence   195

MODULE 16   Adulthood, and Reflections on Developmental Issues   206

Sensation and Perception 225

MODULE 17   Introduction to Sensation and Perception   226

MODULE 18   Vision   233

MODULE 19   Hearing   243

MODULE 20   Other Senses   251

MODULE 21   Perceptual Organization   262

MODULE 22   Perceptual Interpretation   272

Learning 289

MODULE 23   Classical Conditioning   290

MODULE 24   Operant Conditioning   301

MODULE 25   Learning by Observation   315

Memory 323

MODULE 26   Introduction to Memory   324

MODULE 27   Encoding: Getting Information In   327

MODULE 28   Storage: Retaining Information   336

MODULE 29   Retrieval: Getting Information Out   346

MODULE 30   Forgetting, Memory Construction, and Improving Memory   351

Thinking, Language, and Intelligence 369

MODULE 31 Thinking 370

MODULE 32 Language and Thought 384

MODULE 33 Introduction to Intelligence 404

MODULE 34 Assessing Intelligence 416

MODULE 35 Genetic and Environmental Influences on Intelligence 428

Motivation and Work 443

MODULE 36 Introduction to Motivation 444

MODULE 37 Hunger 448

MODULE 38 Sexual Motivation and the Need to Belong 466

MODULE 39 Motivation at Work 484

Emotions, Stress, and Health 499

MODULE 40 Introduction to Emotion 500

MODULE 41 Expressed Emotion 510

MODULE 42 Experienced Emotion 517

MODULE 43 Stress and Health 530

MODULE 44 Promoting Health 542

Personality 557

MODULE 45 The Psychoanalytic Perspective 558

MODULE 46 The Humanistic Perspective 570

MODULE 47 Contemporary Research on Personality 574

Psychological Disorders 597

MODULE 48 Introduction to Psychological Disorders 599

MODULE 49 Anxiety Disorders 610

MODULE 50 Dissociative, Personality, and Somatoform Disorders 618

MODULE 51 Mood Disorders 625

MODULE 52 Schizophrenia 637

Therapy 645

MODULE 53 The Psychological Therapies 646

MODULE 54 Evaluating Psychotherapies 660

MODULE 55 The Biomedical Therapies 671

Social Psychology 681

MODULE 56 Social Thinking 682

MODULE 57 Social Influence 690

MODULE 58 Antisocial Relations 703

MODULE 59 Prosocial Relations 719

Appendix A: Careers in Psychology A-1

Appendix B: Answers to *Test Yourself* Questions B-1

Contents

Preface ix

Introduction to the History and Science of Psychology 3

MODULE 1 The Story of Psychology 2

What Is Psychology? 2

Contemporary Psychology 6

CLOSE-UP: Tips for Studying Psychology 12

MODULE 2 Thinking Critically With Psychological Science 14

The Need for Psychological Science 14

Frequently Asked Questions About Psychology 19

MODULE 3 Research Strategies: How Psychologists Ask and Answer Questions 25

How *Do* Psychologists Ask and Answer Questions? 25

Statistical Reasoning in Everyday Life 37

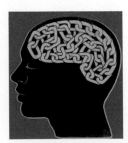

The Biology of Mind 45

MODULE 4 Neural and Hormonal Systems 46

Neural Communication 46

The Nervous System 52

The Endocrine System 56

MODULE 5 Tools of Discovery and Older Brain Structures 58

The Tools of Discovery: Having Our Head Examined 58

Older Brain Structures 60

MODULE 6 The Cerebral Cortex and Our Divided Brain 67

The Cerebral Cortex 67

Our Divided Brain 74

Right-Left Differences in the Intact Brain 77

Consciousness and the Two-Track Mind ... 83

MODULE 7 The Brain and Consciousness 85

Cognitive Neuroscience 85

Dual Processing 86

MODULE 8 Sleep and Dreams 91

Biological Rhythms and Sleep 91

Why Do We Sleep? 96

Sleep Disorders 100

Dreams 102

MODULE 9 Hypnosis 108

Facts and Falsehoods 108

Explaining the Hypnotized State 110

MODULE 10 Drugs and Consciousness 113

Dependence and Addiction 113

Psychoactive Drugs 115

CLOSE-UP: Near-Death Experiences 123

Influences on Drug Use 125

Nature, Nurture, and Human Diversity 131

MODULE 11 Behavior Genetics and Evolutionary Psychology 132

Behavior Genetics: Predicting Individual Differences 132

Evolutionary Psychology: Understanding Human Nature 141

MODULE 12 Environmental Influences on Behavior 148

Parents and Peers 148

Cultural Influences 151

Gender Development 157

Reflections on Nature and Nurture 164

Developing Through the Life Span 169

MODULE 13 Prenatal Development and the Newborn 170

Conception 170

Prenatal Development 170

The Competent Newborn 172

MODULE 14 Infancy and Childhood 174

Physical Development 174

Cognitive Development 176

CLOSE-UP: Autism and "Mind-Blindness" 182

Social Development 185

MODULE 15 Adolescence 195

Physical Development 195

Cognitive Development 198

Social Development 200

Emerging Adulthood 204

MODULE 16 Adulthood, and Reflections on Developmental Issues 206

Physical Development 206

Cognitive Development 212

Social Development 215

Reflections on Two Major Developmental Issues 221

Sensation and Perception 225

MODULE 17 Introduction to Sensation and Perception 226

Thresholds 227

Sensory Adaption 230

MODULE 18 Vision 233

The Stimulus Input: Light Energy 233

The Eye 234

Visual Information Processing 237

Color Vision 240

MODULE 19 Hearing 243

The Stimulus Input: Sound Waves 243

The Ear 244

Hearing Loss and Deaf Culture 247

CLOSE-UP: Living in a Silent World 249

MODULE 20 Other Senses 251

Touch 251

Pain 253

Taste 257

Smell 259

MODULE 21 Perceptual Organization 262

Form Perception 262

Depth Perception 264

Motion Perception 267

Perceptual Constancy 267

MODULE 22 Perceptual Interpretation 272

Sensory Deprivation and Restored Vision 272

Perceptual Adaptation 273

Perceptual Set 274

Perception and the Human Factor 279

Is There Extrasensory Perception? 281

Learning 287

MODULE 23 Classical Conditioning 290

Pavlov's Experiments 290

Extending Pavlov's Understanding 295

Pavlov's Legacy 298

CLOSE-UP: Trauma as Classical Conditioning 299

MODULE 24 Operant Conditioning 301

Skinner's Experiments 301

Extending Skinner's Understanding 308

Skinner's Legacy 310

CLOSE-UP: Training Our Partners 312

Contrasting Classical and Operant Conditioning 313

MODULE 25 Learning by Observation 315

Mirrors in the Brain 316

Bandura's Experiments 317

Applications of Observational Learning 318

Memory 323

MODULE 26 Introduction to Memory 324

The Phenomenon of Memory 324

Studying Memory: Information-Processing Models 325

MODULE 27 Encoding: Getting Information In 327

How We Encode 327

What We Encode 330

MODULE 28 Storage: Retaining Information 336

Sensory Memory 336

Working/Short-Term Memory 337

Long-Term Memory 338

Storing Memories in the Brain 339

MODULE 29 Retrieval: Getting Information Out 346

Retrieval Cues 347

MODULE 30 Forgetting, Memory Construction, and Improving Memory 351

Forgetting 351

CLOSE-UP: Retrieving Passwords 355

Memory Construction 357

Improving Memory 365

Thinking, Language, and Intelligence 369

MODULE 31 Thinking 370

Concepts 370

Solving Problems 371

Making Decisions and Forming Judgments 374

THINKING CRITICALLY ABOUT: The Fear Factor—Do We Fear the Right Things? 378

MODULE 32 Language and Thought 384

Language Structure 385

Language Development 386

The Brain and Language 391

Thinking and Language 393

Animal Thinking and Language 397

CLOSE-UP: Talking Hands 400

MODULE 33 Introduction to Intelligence 404

Is Intelligence One General Ability or Several Specific Abilities? 405

Intelligence and Creativity 409

Emotional Intelligence 411

Is Intelligence Neurologically Measurable? 412

MODULE 34 Assessing Intelligence 416

The Origins of Intelligence Testing 416

Modern Tests of Mental Abilities 418

Principles of Test Construction 420

The Dynamics of Intelligence 422

MODULE 35 Genetic and Environmental Influences on Intelligence 428

Twin and Adoption Studies 428

Heritability 430

Environmental Influences 430

Group Differences in Intelligence Test Scores 432

The Question of Bias 438

Motivation and Work 443

MODULE 36 Introduction to Motivation 444

Instincts and Evolutionary Psychology 444

Drives and Incentives 445

Optimum Arousal 445

A Hierarchy of Motives 446

MODULE 37 Hunger 448

The Physiology of Hunger 448

The Psychology of Hunger 451

Obesity and Weight Control 456

CLOSE-UP: Waist Management 463

MODULE 38 Sexual Motivation and the Need to Belong 466

The Physiology of Sex 466

The Psychology of Sex 468

Adolescent Sexuality 470

Sexual Orientation 472

Sex and Human Values 479

The Need to Belong 479

MODULE 39 Motivation at Work 484

CLOSE-UP: I/O Psychology at Work 485

Personnel Psychology 486

CLOSE-UP: Discovering Your Strengths 487

Organizational Psychology: Motivating Achievement 490

CLOSE-UP: Doing Well While Doing Good: "The Great Experiment" 492

Emotions, Stress, and Health 499

MODULE 40 Introduction to Emotion 500

Theories of Emotion 500

Embodied Emotion 501

THINKING CRITICALLY ABOUT: Lie Detection 504

MODULE 41 Expressed Emotion 510

Detecting Emotion 510

Gender, Emotion, and Nonverbal Behavior 511

Culture and Emotional Expression 513

The Effects of Facial Expressions 515

MODULE 42 Experienced Emotion 517

Fear 518

Anger 520

Happiness 521

CLOSE-UP: How to Be Happier 527

MODULE 43 Stress and Health 530

Stress and Illness 530

Stress and the Heart 535

Stress and Susceptibility to Disease 537

MODULE 44 Promoting Health 542

Coping With Stress 542

CLOSE-UP: Pets Are Friends, Too 546

Managing Stress 547

THINKING CRITICALLY ABOUT: Complementary and
Alternative Medicine 550

CLOSE-UP: The Relaxation Response 551

Personality 557

MODULE 45 The Psychoanalytic Perspective 558

Exploring the Unconscious 558

The Neo-Freudian and Psychodynamic Theorists 562

Assessing Unconscious Processes 563

Evaluating the Psychoanalytic Perspective 565

MODULE 46 The Humanistic Perspective 570

Abraham Maslow's Self-Actualizing Person 570

Carl Rogers' Person-Centered Perspective 570

Assessing the Self 571

Evaluating the Humanistic Perspective 572

MODULE 47 Contemporary Research on
Personality 574

The Trait Perspective 574

THINKING CRITICALLY ABOUT: How to Be a "Successful"
Astrologer or Palm Reader 578

The Social-Cognitive Perspective 583

CLOSE-UP: Toward a More Positive Psychology 588

Exploring the Self 590

Psychological Disorders 597

ᗰ᱐ᗪᑌᒪᕮ 48 Introduction to Psychological Disorders 599

Defining Psychological Disorders 599

THINKING CRITICALLY ABOUT: ADHD—Normal High Energy or Genuine Disorder? 600

Understanding Psychological Disorders 601

Classifying Psychological Disorders 602

CLOSE-UP: The "un-DSM": A Diagnostic Manual of Human Strengths 604

Labeling Psychological Disorders 605

THINKING CRITICALLY ABOUT: Insanity and Responsibility 606

Rates of Psychological Disorders 606

ᗰ᱐ᗪᑌᒪᕮ 49 Anxiety Disorders 610

Generalized Anxiety Disorder 610

Panic Disorder 611

Phobias 611

Obsessive-Compulsive Disorder 612

Post-Traumatic Stress Disorder 612

Understanding Anxiety Disorders 614

ᗰ᱐ᗪᑌᒪᕮ 50 Dissociative, Personality, and Somatoform Disorders 618

Dissociative Disorders 618

Personality Disorders 620

Somatoform Disorders 622

ᗰ᱐ᗪᑌᒪᕮ 51 Mood Disorders 625

Major Depressive Disorder 625

Bipolar Disorder 626

Understanding Mood Disorders 627

CLOSE-UP: Suicide 630

ᗰ᱐ᗪᑌᒪᕮ 52 Schizophrenia 637

Symptoms of Schizophrenia 637

Onset and Development of Schizophrenia 638

Understanding Schizophrenia 639

Therapy 645

ᗰ᱐ᗪᑌᒪᕮ 53 The Psychological Therapies 646

Psychoanalysis 646

Humanistic Therapies 649

Behavior Therapies 650

Cognitive Therapies 654

Group and Family Therapies 657

ᗰ᱐ᗪᑌᒪᕮ 54 Evaluating Psychotherapies 660

Is Psychotherapy Effective? 660

THINKING CRITICALLY ABOUT: "Regressing" From Unusual to Usual 662

The Relative Effectiveness of Different Therapies 663

Evaluating Alternative Therapies 665

Commonalities Among Psychotherapies 666

CLOSE-UP: A Consumer's Guide to Psychotherapists 667

Culture and Values in Psychotherapy 668

CLOSE-UP: Preventing Psychological Disorders 669

ᗰ᱐ᗪᑌᒪᕮ 55 The Biomedical Therapies 671

Drug Therapies 671

Brain Stimulation 675

Psychosurgery 677

Therapeutic Life-Style Change 678

Social Psychology 681

MODULE 56 Social Thinking 682

Attributing Behavior to Persons or to Situations 682

Attitudes and Actions 684

CLOSE-UP: Abu Ghraib Prison: An "Atrocity-Producing Situation"? 687

MODULE 57 Social Influence 690

Conformity and Obedience 690

Group Influence 697

The Power of Individuals 701

MODULE 58 Antisocial Relations 703

Prejudice 703

CLOSE-UP: Automatic Prejudice 705

Aggression 709

CLOSE-UP: Parallels Between Smoking Effects and Media Violence Effects 716

MODULE 59 Prosocial Relations 719

Attraction 719

CLOSE-UP: Online Matchmaking and Speed Dating 720

Altruism 726

Peacemaking 729

Appendix A: Careers in Psychology A-1

Preparing for a Career in Psychology A-1

The Bachelor's Degree A-1

Postgraduate Degrees A-3

Subfields of Psychology A-4

Preparing Early for Graduate Study in Psychology A-9

For More Information A-10

Appendix B: Answers to Test Yourself Questions B-1

Glossary G-1

References R-1

Name Index NI-1

Subject Index SI-1

Preface

With each new edition, I've found myself traveling a familiar path. When it is first published, I am relieved after many months of intense effort, and I am thrilled—sure that it is my best effort yet. But before long, as new research appears, and as thoughtful instructors and students begin writing with suggestions for improvement, and then when commissioned reviews and survey results start coming in, I have second thoughts about the current edition's seeming perfection. As my storage cubbies begin fattening with new materials, my eagerness for the next edition grows. By the time the new edition is ready to come out, I grimace when reminded of people using the old edition, which once seemed so perfect!

This new *Psychology, Ninth Edition in Modules* is no exception—it is so much improved over the previous work! I am delighted to offer the following changes:

▶ some **1300 new research citations** representing the most exciting and important new discoveries in our field,

▶ **organizational changes** based on changes in the field (for example, the heavily revised Consciousness unit, which now follows The Biology of Mind unit and is titled Consciousness and the Two-Track Mind to reflect the dual processing and cognitive neuroscience themes),

▶ **fine-tuned writing** with countless small and large improvements in the way concepts are presented, supported by the input and creative ideas of hundreds of contributing instructors and students, and from my longtime editors,

▶ a sharp **new art program** and **new pedagogy** that teaches more effectively,

▶ continually improving coverage of **cultural and gender diversity issues,** and

▶ **44 fewer pages.**

I find myself fascinated by today's psychology, with its studies of the neuroscience of our moods and memories, the reach of our adaptive unconscious, and the shaping power of the social and cultural context. Psychological science is increasingly attuned to the relative effects of nature and nurture, to gender and cultural diversity, to our conscious and unconscious information processing, and to the biology that underlies our behavior. (See **TABLES** 1 and 2 on the next page.)

I am grateful for the privilege of assisting with the teaching of this mind-expanding discipline to so many students, in so many countries, through so many different languages. To be entrusted with discerning and communicating psychology's insights is both an exciting honor and a great responsibility.

The thousands of instructors and millions of students across the globe who have studied this book have contributed immensely to its development. Much of this has occurred spontaneously, through correspondence and conversations. For this edition, we also formally involved over 300 researchers and teaching psychologists, along with many students. This input was part of our effort to gather accurate and up-to-date information about the field of psychology and the content, pedagogy, and supplements needs of instructors and students in the introductory course. We look forward to continuing feedback as we strive, over future editions, to create an ever better book and supplements package.

TABLE 1 Evolutionary Psychology and Behavior Genetics

In addition to the coverage found in Modules 11–12, the **evolutionary perspective** *is covered on the following pages:*

Aging, p. 208
Anxiety disorders, pp. 615–616
Attraction, p. 720
Biological predispositions
  in learning, pp. 295–298
  in operant conditioning,
    pp. 309–310
Brainstem, p. 61
Consciousness, p. 85
Darwin, Charles, pp. 3, 6–7, 416
Depression, p. 678
  and light exposure therapy, p. 666
Emotional expression, p. 514
  effects of facial expressions, 515
Emotion-detecting ability, p. 433
Evolutionary perspective,
  defined, p. 9
Exercise, p. 548
Fear, pp. 378–379
  function of, 519
Feature detection, p. 238
Hearing, p. 243

Hunger and taste preference, p. 452
Instincts, pp. 444–445
Intelligence, pp. 405, 416, 435–438
Language, pp. 384, 388–389
Love, p. 217
Math and spatial ability, p. 434
Mating preferences, pp. 145–146
Menopause, p. 207
Need to belong, p. 480
Obesity, p. 456
Overconfidence, p. 377
Perceptual adaptation, pp. 274–275
Puberty, onset of, pp. 204–205
Sensation, pp. 226–227
Sensory adaptation, pp. 230–231
Sexual orientation, p. 476
Sexuality, pp. 145–146, 466
Signal detection theory,
  pp. 227–228
Sleep, pp. 92, 99
Smell, p. 261
Taste, p. 257

In addition to the coverage found in Modules 11–12, **behavior genetics** *is covered on the following pages:*

Abuse, intergenerational
  transmission of, p. 319
Aggression, p. 710
Depth perception, p. 264
Drives and incentives, p. 445
Drug dependence, p. 126
Drug use, pp. 125–126
Eating disorders, p. 454
Fear, pp. 519–520
Happiness, pp. 528–529
Hunger and taste preference,
  p. 452
Intelligence, pp. 428–430
  brain size, p. 412
  Down syndrome, p. 425
Language, pp. 388–389
Learning, pp. 295–297, 309–310
Memory, pp. 345, 346
Motor development, p. 175
Obesity and weight control,
  p. 460
Perception, p. 272

Personality traits, pp. 576–580
Psychological disorders:
  ADHD, p. 600
  anxiety disorders, p. 616
  biopsychosocial approach, p. 602
  mood disorders, p. 629
  personality disorders,
    pp. 621–622
  schizophrenia, pp. 641–642
Romantic love, p. 217
Sexual orientation, pp. 475–476
Sexuality, p. 466
Smell, pp. 259–260
Stress:
  AIDS, pp. 539–540
  benefits of exercise, p. 548
  cancer, p. 540
  personality and illness,
    pp. 535–537
  psychoneuroimmunology,
    pp. 537–539
Traits, pp. 576, 577–580

TABLE 2 Neuroscience

In addition to the coverage found in Modules 4–6, **neuroscience** *can be found on the following pages:*

ADHD and the brain, p. 600
Aggression, pp. 710–711
Aging: physical exercise and the
  brain, pp. 210–211
Animal language, p. 397
Antisocial personality disorder,
  p. 621
Autism, pp. 182–183
Biofeedback, p. 549
Brain activity and:
  aging, pp. 210, 352
  dementia and Alzheimer's,
    pp. 211–212, 346
  disease, p. 248
  dreams, pp. 102–105
  emotion, pp. 197, 346–348,
    503–504, 507–508, 513
  sleep, pp. 91–96
Brain development:
  adolescence, p. 197
  experience and, pp. 148–149
  infancy and childhood, p. 174
  sexual differentiation in utero,
    p. 161
Cognitive neuroscience, pp. 5, 85
Drug dependence, p. 126
Emotion and cognition,
  pp. 506–508
Emotional intelligence and brain
  damage, p. 411
ESP and fMRI testing, p. 284
Fear-learning, p. 616
Fetal alcohol syndrome and brain
  abnormalities, p. 171

Hallucinations and:
  hallucinogens, pp. 122–124
  near-death experiences, p. 123
  sleep, p. 105
Hormones and:
  abuse, p. 190
  development, pp. 160–161,
    195–197
  emotion, pp. 500–501
  gender, pp. 160–161
  memory, pp. 346–348
  sex, p. 207
  sexual behavior, pp. 467–468
  stress, pp. 502, 532, 538, 544, 546
  weight control, pp. 449–451
Hunger, pp. 449–451
Insight, pp. 371–372
Intelligence, pp. 412–414
  and creativity, p. 409
  and twins, p. 428
Language, pp. 388–393
  and statistical learning, p. 390
  and thinking in images,
    pp. 395–396
Light-exposure therapy:
  brain scans, p. 666
Limbic system and fear,
  pp. 519–520
Meditation, p. 552
Memory:
  physical storage of, pp. 345–346
    implicit/explicit memories,
      pp. 348–351
  sleep, pp. 99–100, 105–106

Mirror neurons, pp. 316–317
Neuroscience perspective, defined,
  p. 9
Neurostimulation therapy:
  deep-brain stimulation, p. 677
  magnetic stimulation,
    pp. 676–677
Neurotransmitters and:
  anxiety disorders, pp. 616, 672
  biomedical therapy:
    depression, pp. 632, 673–674
    ECT, pp. 675–676
    schizophrenia, pp. 639, 672
  child abuse, p. 190
  cognitive-behavior therapy for
    obsessive-compulsive
    disorder, pp. 656–657
  curare, 50
  depression, pp. 630–632
  drugs, pp. 113, 115–122
  exercise, pp. 548–549
  narcolepsy, p. 101
  schizophrenia, pp. 639–640, 642
Optimum arousal: rewards, p. 446
Orgasm, pp. 466–467
Pain, pp. 254–255
  phantom limb pain, pp. 255–257
Parallel vs. serial processing,
  pp. 239–240
Perception:
  brain damage and, pp. 238, 239
  color vision, pp. 240–242
  feature detection, p. 238

transduction, p. 233
visual information processing,
  pp. 233, 235–238
Perceptual organization,
  pp. 262–270
Personality and brain-imaging,
  p. 576
PET scans and obsessive-
  compulsive disorder, p. 678
Post-traumatic stress disorder and
  the limbic system, p. 613
Prejudice (automatic) and the
  amygdala, p. 705
Psychosurgery: lobotomy,
  pp. 677–678
Schizophrenia and brain
  abnormalities, pp. 640, 642
Sensation:
  body position and movement,
    p. 253
  deafness, pp. 248–249
  hearing, pp. 243–245, 247
  sensory adaptation, p. 231
  smell, pp. 259–261
  taste, p. 258
  touch, p. 252
Sexual orientation, pp. 475–477
Sleep:
  hypnotized brain and, p. 111
  memory and, pp. 99–100
  recuperation during, p. 99
Smell and emotion, pp. 262–263
Unconscious mind, p. 566

Why a Modular Book?

This 59-module text has been a longtime wish come true for me. It breaks out of the box by restructuring the material into a buffet of (a) short, digestible chapters (called modules) that (b) can be selected and assigned in any order.

Have we not all heard the familiar student complaint: "The chapters are too long!" A text's typical 30- to 50-page chapters cannot be read in a single sitting before the eyes grow weary and the mind wanders. So why not parse the material into readable units? Ask your students whether they would prefer a 700-page book to be organized as fourteen 50-page chapters or as fifty 14-page chapters. You may be surprised at their overwhelming support for shorter chapters. Indeed, students digest material better when they process it in smaller chunks—as "spaced" rather than massed practice.

I have equally often heard from instructors bemoaning the fact that they "just can't get to everything" in the book. Sometimes instructors want to cover certain sections in a traditional, long chapter but not others. For example, in the typical Consciousness chapter, someone may want to cover Sleep and Hypnosis but not Drugs. In *Psychology, Ninth Edition in Modules,* instructors could easily choose to cover Module 8, Sleep and Dreams, and Module 9, Hypnosis, but not Module 10, Drugs and Consciousness.

How Is This Different From Psychology, Ninth Edition?

The primary differences between this book and my *Psychology,* Ninth Edition text are organization and module independence.

Organization

This book really IS *Psychology,* Ninth Edition—just in a different format. So, this modular version contains all the updated research and innovative new coverage from *Psychology,* Ninth Edition. A very few sections have moved around to accommodate the modular structure. For example, Rates of Psychological Disorders is a separate section at the end of the Psychological Disorders chapter in *Psychology,* Ninth Edition, but it is covered in the first of the Psychological Disorders modules in this modular version.

The Modules Are Independent

Each module in this book is self-standing rather than dependent upon the others for understanding. Cross references to other parts of the book have been replaced with brief explanations. In some cases, illustrations or key terms are repeated to avoid possible confusion. No assumptions are made about what students have read prior to each module. This independence gives instructors ultimate flexibility in deciding which modules to use, and in what order. Connections among psychology's subfields and findings are still made—they are just made in a way that does not assume knowledge of other parts of the book.

What Continues, and What's New Since Psychology, Eighth Edition in Modules?

Throughout its nine editions, my overall vision for *Psychology* has not wavered: *to merge rigorous science with a broad human perspective in a book that engages both mind and heart.* My aim has been to create a state-of-the-art introduction to psychology, written with sensitivity to students' needs and interests. I aspire to help students understand and appreciate the wonder of important phenomena in their lives. I also want to convey the inquisitive spirit with which psychologists *do* psychology. The study of psychology, I believe, enhances our abilities to restrain intuition with critical thinking, judgmentalism with compassion, and illusion with understanding.

Believing with Thoreau that "Anything living is easily and naturally expressed in popular language," I seek to communicate psychology's scholarship with crisp narrative and vivid storytelling. Writing as a solo author, I hope to tell psychology's story in a way that is warmly personal as well as rigorously scientific. I love to reflect on connections between psychology and other realms, such as literature, philosophy, history, sports, religion, politics, and popular culture. And I love to provoke thought, to play with words, and to laugh.

Eight Guiding Principles

Despite all the exciting changes, this new edition does retain its predecessors' voice, as well as much of the content and organization. It also retains the goals—the guiding principles—that have animated the previous eight editions:

1. ***To exemplify the process of inquiry*** I strive to show students not just the outcome of research, but how the research process works. Throughout, the book tries to excite the reader's curiosity. It invites readers to imagine themselves as participants in classic experiments. Several modules introduce research stories as mysteries that progressively unravel as one clue after another falls into place. (See, for example, the historical story of research on the brain's processing of language on pages 388–390.)

2. ***To teach critical thinking*** By presenting research as intellectual detective work, I exemplify an inquiring, analytical mindset. Whether students are studying development, cognition, or statistics, they will become involved in, and see the rewards of, critical reasoning. Moreover, they will discover how an empirical approach can help them evaluate competing ideas and claims for highly publicized phenomena—ranging from subliminal persuasion, ESP, and alternative therapies, to astrology, hypnotic regression, and repressed and recovered memories.

3. ***To put facts in the service of concepts*** My intention is not to fill students' intellectual file drawers with facts, but to reveal psychology's major concepts—to teach students how to think, and to offer psychological ideas worth thinking about. In each module I place emphasis on those concepts I hope students will carry with them long after they complete the course. Always, I try to follow Albert Einstein's dictum that "Everything should be made as simple as possible, but not simpler." Test Yourself questions at the end of each module reinforce the take-home message from that section.

4. ***To be as up-to-date as possible*** Few things dampen students' interest as quickly as the sense that they are reading stale news. While retaining psychology's classic studies and concepts, I also present the discipline's most important recent developments. More than 600 references in this edition are dated 2007 or 2008.

5. ***To integrate principles and applications*** Throughout—by means of anecdotes, case histories, and the posing of hypothetical situations—I relate the findings of basic research to their applications and implications. Where psychology can illuminate pressing human issues—be they racism and sexism, health and happiness, or violence and war—I have not hesitated to shine its light. Ask Yourself questions at the end of each module encourage students to apply the concepts to their own lives to help make the material more meaningful, and memorable.

6. ***To enhance comprehension by providing continuity*** Because the book has a single author, many significant issues—such as cognitive neuroscience, dual processing, cultural and gender diversity, behavior genetics, the bold thinking of intellectual pioneers, human rationality and irrationality, empathy for and understanding of troubled lives—weave throughout the whole book, and students hear a consistent voice. "The uniformity of a work," observed Edward Gibbon, "denotes the hand of a single artist."

7. ***To reinforce learning at every step*** Everyday examples and rhetorical questions encourage students to process the material actively. Concepts are presented and then frequently applied to reinforce learning. Learning objective questions, self-tests, a marginal glossary, and end-of-module key terms lists help students master important concepts and terminology.

8. *To convey respect for human unity and diversity* Throughout the book, readers will see evidence of our human kinship—our shared biological heritage, our common mechanisms of seeing and learning, hungering and feeling, loving and hating. They will also better understand the dimensions of our diversity—our *individual* diversity in development and aptitudes, temperament and personality, and disorder and health; and our *cultural* diversity in attitudes and expressive styles, child-rearing and care for older people, and life priorities.

Continually Improving Cultural and Gender Diversity Coverage

This edition presents an even more thoroughly cross-cultural perspective on psychology (**TABLE 3**)—reflected in research findings, and text and photo examples. Coverage of the psychology of women and men is thoroughly integrated (see **TABLE 4** on the next page).

TABLE 3 Culture and Multicultural Experience

*From Module 1 to Module 59, coverage of **culture and multicultural experience** can be found on the following pages:*

Aggression, p. 713
Aging population, p. 208
AIDS, pp. 381, 539–540
Anger, p. 520
Animal research ethics, p. 21
Attraction:
  love and marriage, p. 725
  speed-dating, p. 720
Attractiveness, pp. 145–146, 731
Attribution, political effects of, p. 684
Behavioral effects of culture, pp. 183–189
Body ideal, pp. 454–455
Categorization, p. 370
Complementary/alternative medicine, p. 550
Conformity, pp. 690–691, 693
Corporal punishment practices, p. 307
Cultural norms, pp. 152–153, 162, 164–165
Culture:
  context effects, p. 277
  definition, pp. 151–152
  and the self, pp. 154–155
  shock, pp. 153, 534, 586
Deaf culture, pp. 73, 77, 247–249, 387, 388, 390, 399–400
Development:
  adolescence, p. 195
  attachment, pp. 188, 191
  child-rearing, p. 156
  cognitive development, p. 185
  moral development, p. 199
  similarities, pp. 156–157
  social development, p. 188
Drugs:
  psychological effects of, pp. 114, 117
  use of, 127

Eating disorders: Western culture and, p. 139
Emotion:
  emotion-detecting ability, pp. 510–511
  experiencing, pp. 517, 520
  expressing, pp. 512, 513–515
Enemy perceptions, p. 731
Fear, p. 379
Flow, p. 484
Flynn effect, pp. 420–421
Fundamental attribution error, p. 682
Gender:
  roles, pp. 162–163
  social power, p. 158
Grief, expressing, p. 221
Happiness, p. 528
Hindsight bias, p. 15
History of psychology, pp. 2–6
Homosexuality, views on, p. 27
Human diversity/kinship, pp. 19–20, 151–153
Identity, forming a social, p. 201
Individualism/collectivism, pp. 154–155
Intelligence, pp. 404, 416, 418, 420–421, 433–434, 435–438
  bias, pp. 438–439
  nutrition and, p. 436
Language, pp. 152, 384–387, 388, 392–395
  monolingual/bilingual, p. 395
Leaving the nest, pp. 204–205
Life satisfaction, pp. 524–526
Life-expectancy, p. 208
Life-span and well-being, p. 219
Loop systems, pp. 280–281
Management styles, pp. 495–496
Marriage, p. 217
Mating preferences, p. 145–146

Meditation, p. 552
Memory, encoding, pp. 333, 352
Menopause, p. 207
Mental illness rate, p. 607
Molecular genetics: "missing women," p. 141
Motivation: hierarchy of needs, p. 447
Need to belong, pp. 479–481
Neurotransmitters: curare, p. 50
Obesity, pp. 456–457, 460–462
Obesity guidance/counseling, p. 457
Observational learning:
  attachment and television viewing, p. 191
  television and aggression, p. 319
Optimism and health, p. 544
Organ donation, p. 382
Pace of life, pp. 29, 153
Pain, perception of, p. 256
Parapsychology, p. 281
Parent and peer relationships, pp. 202–203
Participative management, p. 496
Peacemaking:
  conciliation, p. 734
  contact, p. 731
  cooperation, pp. 732–733
Peer influence, p. 151
Personal space, p. 153
Personality, p. 584
Prejudice prototypes, p. 371
Prejudice, pp. 23, 36, 703–709
Psychoanalysis, p. 648
Psychological disorders:
  antisocial personality disorder, p. 622
  cultural norms, p. 599
  depression, pp. 628, 634

dissociative personality disorder, p. 619
eating disorders, pp. 454–455, 602
  rates of, p. 597
schizophrenia, pp. 602, 640–641
somatoform, p. 622
suicide, p. 630
susto, p. 602
taijin-kyofusho, p. 602
Psychotherapy:
  culture and values in, pp. 668–669
  EMDR training, p. 665
Puberty and adult independence, pp. 204–205
Self-esteem, p. 528
Self-serving bias, pp. 592–593, 594
Sex drive, p. 144
Sexual orientation, pp. 472–473
Similarities, pp. 142–143
Social clock, p. 216
Social loafing, p. 698
Social-cultural perspective, p. 9
Spirituality: Israeli kibbutz communities, pp. 552–554
Stress:
  adjusting to a new culture, p. 534
  racism and, p. 535
Taste preferences, p. 452
Teen sexuality, pp. 470–472
Testing bias, pp. 439–440
Theory of mind: internalizing language, p. 184
Weight control, p. 453

See also Modules 56–59, Social Psychology, pp. 681–734

TABLE 4 The Psychology of Men and Women

*Coverage of the **psychology of men and women** can be found on the following pages:*

ADHD, p. 600

Adulthood: physical changes, pp. 206–207

Aggression, pp. 711–715
  pornography, pp. 714–715
  rape, pp. 712, 714–715

Alcohol:
  addiction and, p. 116
  use, p. 115
  sexual aggression, p. 117

Altruism: help-receiving, p. 728

Antisocial personality disorder, p. 620

Attraction, pp. 720–722

Autism, p. 182

Behavioral effects of gender, p. 20

Biological predispositions, and the color red, pp. 296–297

Biological sex/gender, pp. 160–161

Bipolar disorder, p. 627

Body image, pp. 454–455

Classical conditioning and trauma/rape, p. 299

Color vision, p. 241

Conformity: obedience, p. 694

Dating, p. 720

Depression, pp. 625, 627, 632–633

Dream content, p. 103

Drug use:
  biological influences, p. 126
  methamphetamines, p. 118
  psychological/social-cultural influences, p. 126

Eating disorders, pp. 453–455

Emotion-detecting ability, pp. 433, 511–513

Empty nest, p. 218

Father care, pp. 188, 472

Freud's views:
  evaluating, p. 565
  identification/gender identity, pp. 560–561
  Oedipus/Electra complexes, p. 560
  penis envy, p. 562

Gender:
  and anxiety, p. 610
  and child-rearing, pp. 163, 454
  development, pp. 157–164
  prejudice, pp. 703–704
  roles, pp. 162–163
  similarities/differences, pp. 157–160

Gendered brain, pp. 160–161, 469–470, 478

Generic pronoun "he," p. 394

Grief, p. 220

Group polarization, p. 699

Happiness, p. 529

Hormones and:
  aggression, p. 711
  sexual behavior, pp. 467–468
  sexual development, pp. 160–161, 195–197
  testosterone-replacement therapy, p. 468

Intelligence, pp. 432–435
  bias, p. 439
  low extreme, p. 425

Leadership: transformational, p. 495

Life expectancy, p. 208

Losing weight, p. 462

Marriage, pp. 217–218, 545

Maturation, pp. 195–197

Menarche, p. 196

Menopause, p. 207

Midlife crisis, p. 216

Molecular genetics: "missing women," p. 141

Obesity:
  genetic factors, p. 460
  guidance/counseling, p. 457
  health risks, p. 457
  ingested calories, p. 461
  weight discrimination, pp. 457–458

Observational learning:
  sexually violent media, p. 321
  TV's influence, p. 319

Pornography, p. 469

Post-traumatic stress disorder: development of, p. 614

Prejudice, pp. 371, 703–706

Psychological disorders, rates of, p. 607

Rape, p. 709

Religiosity and: life expectancy, pp. 552–553

REM sleep, arousal in, pp. 94–95

Romantic love, pp. 724–726

Savant syndrome, p. 406

Schizophrenia, pp. 638–639

Sense of smell, p. 260

Sexual abuse, p. 143

Sexual attraction, pp. 144–146

Sexual disorders, p. 467

Sexual fantasies, p. 470

Sexual orientation, pp. 472–479

Sexuality, pp. 466–472
  adolescent, pp. 470–472
  evolutionary explanation, pp. 143–146
  external stimuli, p. 469

Sleep, p. 97

Stereotyping, p. 277

Stress:
  and depression, p. 537
  and heart disease, pp. 535–536
  and HIV, p. 539
  and the immune system, p. 538
  and health and sexual abuse, p. 546
  response, p. 532

Suicide, pp. 630–631

Women in psychology, p. 4

In addition, I am working to offer a world-based psychology for our worldwide student readership. Thus, I continually search the world for research findings and text and photo examples, conscious that readers may be in Melbourne, Sheffield, Vancouver, or Nairobi. North American and European examples come easily, given that I reside in the United States, maintain contact with friends and colleagues in Canada, subscribe to several European periodicals, and live periodically in the U.K. This edition, for example, offers 61 explicit Canadian and 151 British examples, and 72 mentions of Australia and New Zealand. We are all citizens of a shrinking world, thanks to increased migration and the global economy. Thus, American students, too, benefit from information and examples that internationalize their world-consciousness. And if psychology seeks to explain *human* behavior (not just American or Canadian or Australian behavior), the broader the scope of studies presented, the more accurate is our picture of this world's people. My aim is to expose all students to the world beyond their own culture, and I continue to welcome input and suggestions from all readers.

Discussion of the relevance of cultural and gender diversity begins on the first page of the first module and continues throughout the text. Modules 11 and 12 provide focused coverage, encouraging students to appreciate cultural and gender differences and commonalities, and to consider the interplay of nature and nurture.

Emphasis on the Biological-Psychological-Social/Cultural Levels of Analysis Approach in Psychology

Psychology, Ninth Edition in Modules explores the biological, psychological, and social-cultural influences on our behavior. A significant section in Module 1 introduces the levels-of-analysis approach, setting the stage for discussion in other modules, and levels-of-analysis figures in several modules help students understand concepts in the biopsychosocial context.

Increasing Sensitivity to the Clinical Perspective

With helpful guidance from clinical psychologist colleagues, I have become more mindful of the clinical angle on various concepts within psychology, which has sensitized and improved the Personality, Psychological Disorders, and Therapy units, among others. For example, I cover problem-focused and emotion-focused coping strategies in Module 44, Promoting Health, and Module 34, Assessing Intelligence, describes how psychologists use intelligence tests in clinical settings.

Strong Critical Thinking Coverage

I aim to introduce students to critical thinking throughout the book. New learning objective questions at the beginning of main sections, and Review sections at the end of each module, encourage critical reading to glean an understanding of important concepts. This ninth edition also includes the following opportunities for students to learn or practice their critical thinking skills.

▶ *Module 2, Thinking Critically With Psychological Science,* introduces students to psychology's research methods, emphasizing the fallacies of our everyday intuition and common sense and, thus, the need for psychological science. Critical thinking is introduced as a key term in this module (p. 18). The Statistical Reasoning discussion in Module 3 encourages students to "focus on thinking smarter by applying simple statistical principles to everyday reasoning" (pp. 37–41).

▶ *"Thinking Critically About . . ." boxes* are found throughout the book, modeling for students a critical approach to some key issues in psychology. For example, see the updated box "Thinking Critically About: The Fear Factor—Do We Fear the Right Things?" (pp. 378–379).

▶ *Detective-style stories* throughout the narrative get students thinking critically about psychology's key research questions.

▶ *"Apply this"* and *"Think about it"*-style discussions keep students active in their study of each module.

▶ *Critical examinations of pop psychology* spark interest and provide important lessons in thinking critically about everyday topics.

See **TABLE 5** on the next page for a complete list of this text's coverage of critical thinking topics and Thinking Critically About boxes.

Stellar Teaching and Learning Resources

Our supplements and media have been celebrated for their quality, abundance, and connectivity. The package available for *Psychology, Ninth Edition in Modules* raises the bar even higher with **PsychPortal,** which includes an interactive eBook, a suite of interactive components, the powerful Online Study Center, the Student Video Tool Kit for Introductory Psychology, and the Scientific American News Feed. See page xxv for details.

APA Learning Goals and Outcomes for Psychology Majors

In March 2002, an American Psychological Association (APA) Task Force created a set of Learning Goals and Outcomes for students graduating with psychology majors from four-year schools (www.apa.org/ed/pcue/).

TABLE 5 Critical Thinking and Research Emphasis

Critical thinking coverage, and in-depth stories of psychology's **scientific research** process, can be found on the following pages:

Thinking Critically About . . . boxes:

The Fear Factor—Do We Fear the Right Things?, pp. 378–379

Lie Detection, pp. 504–505

Complementary and Alternative Medicine, p. 550

How to Be a "Successful" Astrologer or Palm Reader, pp. 578–579

ADHD—Normal High Energy or Genuine Disorder?, p. 600

Insanity and Responsibility, p. 606

"Regressing" from Unusual to Usual, p. 662

Critical Examinations of Pop Psychology:

The need for psychological science, p. 14

Perceiving order in random events, pp. 33–34

Do we use only 10 percent of our brains?, p. 72

Can hypnosis enhance recall? Coerce action? Be therapeutic? Alleviate pain?, pp. 109–110

Has the concept of "addiction" been stretched too far?, pp. 114–115

Near-death experiences, p. 123

Critiquing the evolutionary perspective, p. 146

How much credit (or blame) do parents deserve?, p. 150

Is there extrasensory perception?, pp. 281–283

How valid is the Rorschach test?, pp. 564–565

Is repression a myth?, p. 566

Is Freud credible?, pp. 565–568

Is psychotherapy effective?, pp. 660–664

Evaluating alternative therapies, pp. 665–666

Do video games teach or release violence?, pp. 715–717

Thinking Critically with Psychological Science:

The limits of intuition and common sense, pp. 14–15

The scientific attitude, pp. 17–19

"Critical thinking" introduced as a key term, p. 18

The scientific method, pp. 25–26

Correlation and causation, pp. 31–32

Illusory correlation, pp. 32–33

Exploring cause and effect, p. 34

Random assignment, pp. 34–35

Independent and dependent variables, pp. 35–36

Statistical reasoning, pp. 37–41

Describing data, pp. 37–40

Making inferences, pp. 40–41

Scientific Detective Stories:

Is breast milk better than formula?, pp. 34–36

Our divided brains, pp. 74–77

Why do we sleep?, pp. 96–100

Why do we dream?, pp. 104–106

Is hypnosis an extension of normal consciousness or an altered state?, pp. 110–112

Twin and adoption studies, pp. 133–137

How a child's mind develops, pp. 176–185

Aging and intelligence, pp. 213–215

Parallel processing, pp. 239–240

How do we see in color?, pp. 240–242

How do we store memories in our brains?, pp. 345–351

How are memories constructed?, pp. 357–365

Do animals exhibit language?, pp. 399–402

Why do we feel hunger?, pp. 448–451

What determines sexual orientation?, pp. 472–479

The pursuit of happiness: Who is happy, and why?, pp. 521–529

Why—and in whom—does stress contribute to heart disease?, pp. 535–537

How and why is social support linked with health?, pp. 545–547

Self-esteem versus self-serving bias, pp. 592–594

What causes mood disorders?, pp. 627–635

Do prenatal viral infections increase risk of schizophrenia?, pp. 640–641

Is psychotherapy effective?, pp. 660–663

Why do people fail to help in emergencies?, pp. 726–728

Psychology departments in many schools have since used these goals and outcomes to help them establish their own benchmarks.

Some instructors are eager to know whether a given text for the introductory course helps students get a good start at achieving these goals. *Psychology, Ninth Edition in Modules* will work nicely to help you begin to address these goals in your department. See www.worthpublishers.com/myers for a detailed guide to how *Psychology, Ninth Edition in Modules* corresponds to the APA Learning Goals and Outcomes.

A Thoroughly Considered Pedagogical Program

This edition includes the following study aids.

▶ *Numbered Questions* establish learning objectives for each significant section of text (around 3 to 7 per module) and direct student reading.

▶ *Review sections,* found at the end of each module, repeat the numbered objective questions and address them with a narrative summary followed by page-referenced *Terms and Concepts to Remember.*

▶ The module-ending Review sections also include *Ask Yourself questions,* which encourage students to apply new concepts to their own experiences, and *Test Yourself questions* (with answers in an appendix) that assess student mastery and encourage big-picture thinking.

Thoroughly Updated

Despite the overarching continuity, there is change on every page. There are updates everywhere and some 1300 new references—comprising nearly 30 percent of the bibliography! Psychology as a field is moving, and this new edition reflects much of that exciting progress.

Streamlined Coverage

My teaching colleagues have asked for a somewhat shorter length to help the book better fit the course. I worked judiciously to reduce the length, often by removing repetitive research examples (it is sometimes very hard to choose among all the great options!) and with lean, clean rewriting. The result is a text that is about 44 pages shorter.

Consciousness and the Two-Track Mind

New Module 7, The Brain and Consciousness, contains coverage of cognitive neuroscience and dual processing, establishing both more firmly as key ideas in psychology. In order to help students make the connection to neuroscience in The Biology of Mind unit (Modules 4 through 6), the Consciousness modules now follow (Modules 7 through 10). Module 7 previews the new evidence of the enormity of our automatic, out-of-sight information processing, including our implicit memories and attitudes.

Exciting New Art Program

We worked carefully with talented artists to create all new anatomical and "people" art throughout the text. The result is pedagogically more effective, and visually more appealing.

Innovative Multimedia Supplements Package

Psychology, Ninth Edition in Modules boasts impressive electronic and print supplements titles. For more information about any of these titles, visit Worth Publishers' online catalog at www.worthpublishers.com.

PsychPortal

Integrating the best online material that Worth has to offer, PsychPortal is an innovative learning space that combines a powerful quizzing engine with unparalleled media resources (see **FIGURE 1**). PsychPortal conveniently offers all the functionality

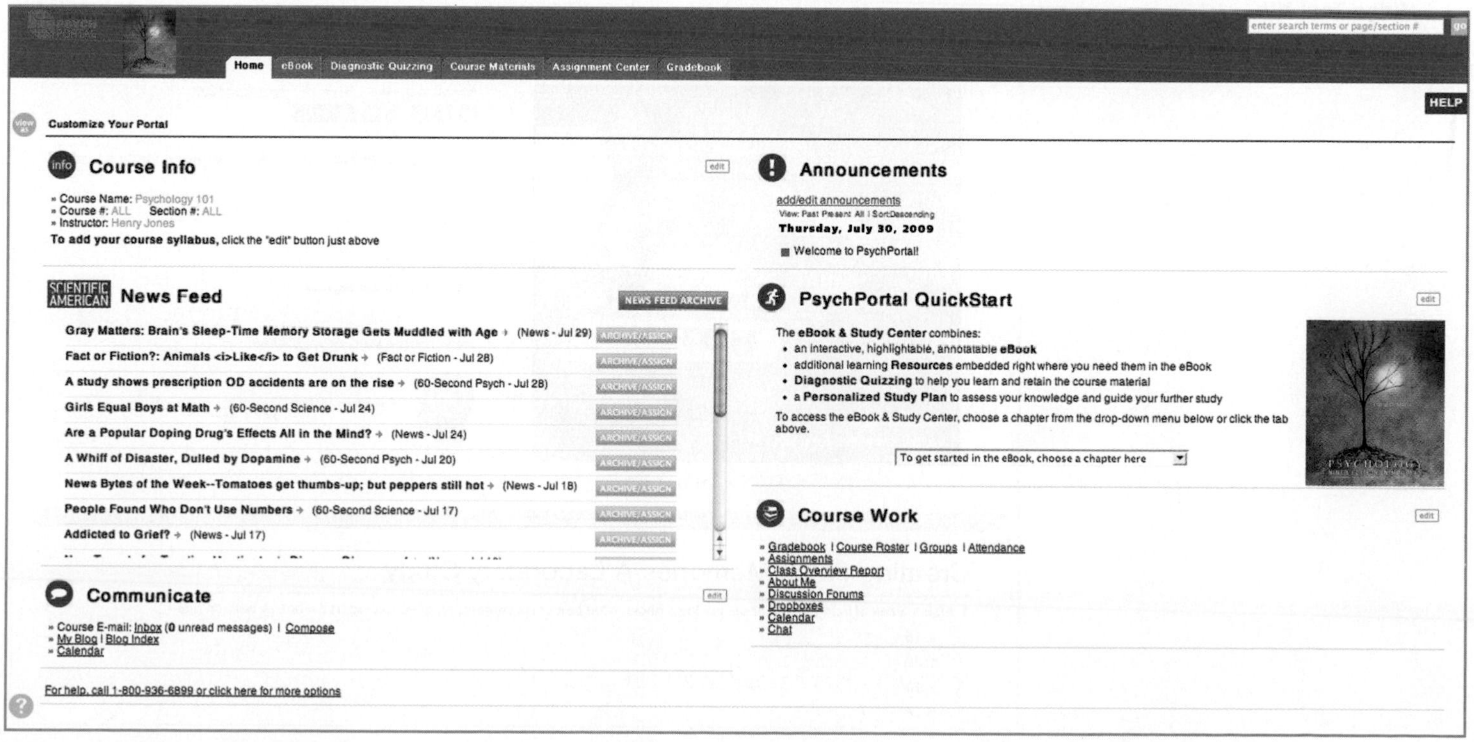

FIGURE 1 **PsychPortal opening page**

you need to support your online or hybrid course, yet it is flexible, customizable, and simple enough to enhance your traditional course. The following interactive learning materials contained within PsychPortal make it truly unique:

▶ *An interactive eBook* allows students to highlight, bookmark, and make their own notes just as they would with a printed textbook.

▶ Tom Ludwig's (Hope College) suite of interactive media—*PsychSim 5.0, PsychInquiry,* and the new *Concepts in Action*—bring key concepts to life.

▶ *The Online Study Center* combines PsychPortal's powerful assessment engine with Worth's unparalleled collection of interactive study resources. Based on their quiz results, students receive Personalized Study Plans that direct them to sections in the book and also to simulations, animations, links, and tutorials that will help them succeed in mastering the concepts. Instructors can access reports indicating their students' strengths and weaknesses (based on class quiz results) and browse suggestions for helpful presentation materials (from Worth's renowned videos and demonstrations) to focus their teaching efforts accordingly.

▶ *The Student Video Tool Kit for Introductory Psychology* includes more than 110 engaging video modules that instructors can easily assign, assess, and customize for their students (**FIGURE 2**). Videos cover classic experiments, current news footage, and cutting-edge research, all of which are sure to spark discussion and encourage critical thinking.

▶ *Scientific American News Feed* highlights current behavioral research.

Additional Student Media

▶ Book Companion Site
▶ Worth eBook for *Psychology, Ninth Edition in Modules*
▶ The Online Study Center
▶ Psych2Go (audio downloads for study and review)

FIGURE 2 Sample of our Student Video Tool Kit

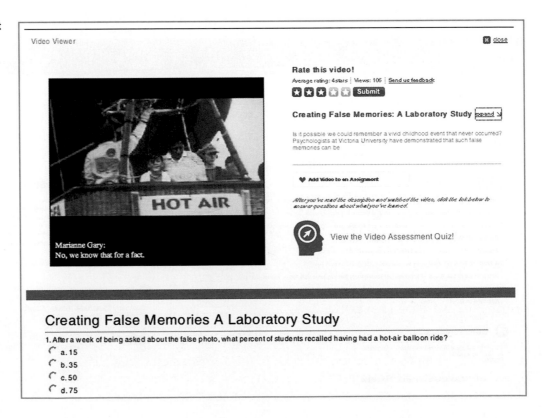

▶ PsychSim 5.0 (on CD-ROM)
▶ Student Video Tool Kit for Introductory Psychology
  (online and on CD-ROM)

Course Management

▶ Enhanced Course Management Solutions

Assessment

▶ Printed Test Bank, Volumes 1 and 2
▶ Diploma Computerized Test Bank
▶ i•Clicker Radio Frequency Classroom Response System

Presentation

▶ ActivePsych: Classroom Activities Project and Video Teaching Modules (including
  Worth's Digital Media Archive, Second Edition, and *Scientific American*
  Frontiers Video Collection, Third Edition)
▶ Instructor's Resource CD-ROM
▶ Worth's Image and Lecture Gallery at www.worthpublishers.com/ilg

Video and DVD

▶ Instructor Video Tool Kit for Introductory Psychology
▶ Digital Media Archive, Second Edition (available within ActivePsych and on
  closed-captioned DVD)
▶ *Scientific American* Frontiers Video Collection, Third Edition (available within Ac-
  tivePsych and on closed-captioned DVD)
▶ Worth Digital Media Archive
▶ *Scientific American* Frontiers Video Collection, Second Edition
▶ The Mind Video Teaching Modules, Second Edition
▶ The Brain Video Teaching Modules, Second Edition
▶ Psychology: The Human Experience Teaching Modules
▶ Moving Images: Exploring Psychology Through Film
▶ The Many Faces of Psychology Video

Print Resources

▶ Instructor's Resources and Lecture Guides
▶ Instructor's Media Guide for Introductory Psychology
▶ Study Guide
▶ *Pursuing Human Strengths: A Positive Psychology Guide*
▶ *Critical Thinking Companion,* Second Edition

Scientific American Resources

▶ *Scientific American Mind*
▶ *Scientific American Reader to Accompany Myers*
▶ *Improving the Mind and Brain: A Scientific American Special Issue*
▶ *Scientific American Explores the Hidden Mind: A Collector's Edition*

In Appreciation

If it is true that "whoever walks with the wise becomes wise" then I am wiser for all
the wisdom and advice received from my colleagues. Aided by over a thousand consultants and reviewers over the last two decades, this has become a better, more accurate book than one author alone (this author, at least) could write. As my editors and
I keep reminding ourselves, all of us together are smarter than any one of us.

My indebtedness continues to each of the teacher-scholars whose influence I have acknowledged in previous editions, to the innumerable researchers who have been so willing to share their time and talent to help me accurately report their research, and to the 191 instructors who took the time to respond to our early information-gathering survey. I also appreciated having detailed input from three of Rick Maddigan's (Memorial University) students—Charles Collier, Alex Penney, and Megan Freake.

My gratitude extends to the colleagues who contributed criticism, corrections, and creative ideas related to the content, pedagogy, and format of this new edition and its supplements package. For their expertise and encouragement, and the gifts of their time to the teaching of psychology, I thank the reviewers and consultants listed below.

Richard Alexander,
Muskegon Community College

Carol Anderson,
Bellevue Community College

Aaron Ashly,
Weber State University

John Baker,
University of Wisconsin, Stephens Point

Dave Baskind,
Delta College

Beth Lanes Battinelli,
Union County College

Alan Beauchamp,
Northern Michigan University

Brooke Bennett,
Florida State University

Sylvia Beyer,
University of Wisconsin, Parkside

Patricia Bishop,
Cleveland State Community College

James Bodle,
College of Mount Saint Joseph

Linda Bradford,
Community College of Aurora

Steve Brasel,
Moody Bible Institute

June Breninger,
Cascade College

Tom Brothen,
University of Minnesota

Eric L. Bruns,
Campbellsville University

David Campell,
Humboldt State University

LeeAnn Cardaciotto,
La Salle University

Jill Carlivati,
George Washington University

Kenneth Carter,
Oxford College

Lorelei Carvajal,
Triton College

Sarah Caverly,
George Mason University

Clara Cheng,
American University

Jennifer Cina,
Barnard College

Virgil Davis,
Ashland Community and Technical College

Joyce C. Day,
Naugatuck Valley Community College

Dawn Delaney,
Madison Area Technical College

G. William Domhoff,
University of California, Santa Cruz

Darlene Earley-Hereford,
Southern Union State Community College, Opelika

Kimberly Fairchild,
Rutgers University, Livingston

Pam Fergus,
Inver Hills Community College

Christopher J. Ferguson,
Texas A&M International University

Faith Florer,
New York University

Jocelyn Folk,
Kent State University

Patricia Foster,
Austin Community College, Northridge

Lauren Fowler,
Weber State University

Daniel J. Fox,
Sam Houston State University

Ron Friedman,
Rochester University

Stan Friedman,
Southwest Texas State University

Sandra Geer,
Northeastern University

Sandra Gibbs,
Muskegon Community College

Bryan Gibson,
Central Michigan University

Carl Granrud,
University of Northern Colorado

Laura Gruntmeir,
Redlands Community College

R. Mark Hamilton,
Chippewa Valley Technical College

Lora Harpster,
Salt Lake Community College

Susan Harris-Mitchell,
College of DuPage

Lesley Hathorn,
University of Nevada, Las Vegas

Paul Hillock,
Algonquin College

Herman Huber,
College of Saint Elizabeth

Linda Jackson,
Michigan State University

Andrew Johnson,
Park University

Deanna Julka,
University of Portland

Regina Kakhnovets,
Alfred University

Paul Kasenow,
Henderson Community College

Teresa King,
Bridgewater State College

Kristina Klassen,
North Idaho College

Chris Koch,
George Fox University

Daniel Kretchman,
University of Rhode Island, Providence

Jean Kubek,
New York City College of Technology, CUNY

Priya Lalvani,
William Patterson University

Claudia Lampman,
University of Alaska, Anchorage

Deb LeBlanc,
Bay Mills Community College

Don Lucas,
Northwest Vista College

Angelina MacKewn,
University of Tennessee, Martin

Marion Mason,
Bloomsburg University of Pennsylvania

Sal Massa,
Marist College

Christopher May,
Carroll College

Paul Mazeroff,
McDaniel College

Donna McEwen,
Friends University

Brian Meier,
Gettysburg College

Michelle Merwin,
University of Tennessee, Martin

Dinah Meyer,
Muskingum College

Antoinette Miller,
Clayton State University

Robin Morgan,
Indiana University, Southeast

Jeffrey Nicholas,
Bridgewater State College

Dan Patanella,
John Jay College of Criminal Justice, CUNY

Shirley Pavone,
Sacred Heart University

Andrew Peck,
Penn State University

Tom Peterson,
Grand View College

Brady Phelps,
South Dakota State University

Michelle Pilati,
Rio Hondo College

Ron Ponsford,
North Nazarene University

Diane Quartarolo,
Sierra College

Sharon Rief,
Logan View High School, and Northeast Community College

Alan Roberts,
Indiana University, Bloomington

June Rosenberg,
Lyndon State College

Nicole Rossi,
Augusta State University

Wade Rowatt,
Baylor University

Michelle Ryder,
Ashland University

Patrick Saxe,
SUNY, New Paltz

Sherry Schnake,
Saint Mary-of-the-Woods College

Cindy Selby,
California State University, Chico

Dennis Shaffer,
Ohio State University

Mark Sibicky,
Marietta College

Randy Simonson,
College of Southern Idaho

David B. Simpson,
Valparaiso College

David D. Simpson,
Carroll College

Jeff Skowronek,
University of Tampa

Todd Smith,
Lake Superior State University

Bettina Spencer,
Saint Mary's College

O'Ann Steere,
College of DuPage

Barry Stennett,
Gainesville State College

Bruce Stevenson,
North Island College

Colleen Stevenson,
Muskingum College

Jaine Strauss,
Macalester College

Cynthia Symons,
Houghton College

Rachelle Tannenbaum,
Anne Arundel Community College

Sarah Ting,
Cerritos College

Barbara Van Horn,
Indian River Community College

Michael Verro,
Champlain College

Craig Vickio,
Bowling Green State University

Denise Vinograde,
LaGuardia Community College, CUNY

Joan Warmbold,
Oakton Community College

Eric Weiser,
Curry College

Diane Wille,
Indiana University Southeast

Paul Young,
Houghton College

At Worth Publishers a host of people played key roles in creating this new edition.

Although the information gathering is never ending, the formal planning began as the author-publisher team gathered for a two-day retreat in June 2007. This happy and creative gathering included John Brink, Martin Bolt, Thomas Ludwig, Richard Straub, and me from the author team, along with my assistants Kathryn Brownson and Sara Neevel. We were joined by Worth Publishers executives Tom Scotty, Elizabeth Widdicombe, and Catherine Woods; editors Christine Brune, Kevin Feyen, Nancy Fleming, Tracey Kuehn, Betty Probert, and Peter Twickler; artistic director Babs Reingold; and sales and marketing colleagues Kate Nurre, Tom Kling, Guy Geraghty, Sandy Manly, Amy Shefferd, Rich Rosenlof, and Brendan Baruth. The input and brainstorming during this meeting of minds gave birth, among other things, to the new pedagogy in this edition, and to new Module 7, The Brain and Consciousness.

Christine Brune, chief editor for the last seven editions, is a wonder worker. She offers just the right mix of encouragement, gentle admonition, attention to detail, and passion for excellence. An author could not ask for more.

Development editor Nancy Fleming is one of those rare editors who is gifted both at "thinking big" while also applying her sensitive, graceful, line-by-line touches.

Editor Trish Morgan has repeatedly amazed me with her wide-ranging knowledge, meticulous focus, and deft editing.

Senior Psychology Acquisitions Editor Kevin Feyen has become a valued team leader, thanks to his dedication, creativity, and sensitivity. Publisher Catherine Woods helped construct and execute the plan for this text and its supplements. Catherine was also a trusted sounding board as we faced a seemingly unending series of discrete decisions along the way. Sharon Prevost coordinated production of the huge supplements package for this edition. Betty Probert efficiently edited and produced the print supplements and, in the process, also helped fine-tune the whole book. Lorraine Klimowich, with help from Greg Bennetts and Emily Ernst, provided invaluable support in commissioning and organizing the multitude of reviews, mailing information to professors, and handling numerous other daily tasks related to the book's development and production. Lee McKevitt did a splendid job of laying out each page. Bianca Moscatelli and Donna Ranieri worked together to locate the myriad photos.

Associate Managing Editor Tracey Kuehn and Project Editor Dana Kasowitz displayed tireless tenacity, commitment, and impressive organization in leading Worth's gifted artistic production team and coordinating editorial input throughout the production process. Production Manager Sarah Segal masterfully kept the book to its tight schedule, and Babs Reingold skillfully directed creation of the beautiful new design and art program. Production Manager Stacey Alexander, along with supplements production editor Jenny Chiu, did their usual excellent work of producing the many supplements.

To achieve our goal of supporting the teaching of psychology, this teaching package not only must be authored, reviewed, edited, and produced, but also made available to teachers of psychology. For their exceptional success in doing that, our author team is grateful to Worth Publishers' professional sales and marketing team. We are especially grateful to Executive Marketing Manager Kate Nurre, Marketing Manager Amy Shefferd, and National Psychology and Economics Consultant Tom Kling for their tireless efforts to inform our teaching colleagues of our efforts to assist their teaching, and for the joy of working with them.

At Hope College, the supporting team members for this edition included Kathryn Brownson, who researched countless bits of information and proofed hundreds of pages. Kathryn has become a knowledgeable and sensitive adviser on many matters, and Sara Neevel has become our high-tech manuscript developer, par excellence. Kathryn Brownson updated, with page citations, all the cross-referenced Preface tables.

Again, I gratefully acknowledge the influence and editing assistance of my writing coach, poet Jack Ridl, whose influence resides in the voice you will be hearing in the pages that follow. He, more than anyone, cultivated my delight in dancing with the language, and taught me to approach writing as a craft that shades into art.

After hearing countless dozens of people say that this book's supplements have taken their teaching to a new level, I reflect on how fortunate I am to be a part of a team in which everyone has produced on-time work marked by the highest professional standards. For their remarkable talents, their long-term dedication, and their friendship, I thank Martin Bolt (Instructor's Manual), John Brink (Test Bank), Thomas Ludwig (PsychPortal), and Richard Straub (Study Guide).

Finally, my gratitude extends to the many students and instructors who have written to offer suggestions, or just an encouraging word. It is for them, and those about to begin their study of psychology, that I have done my best to introduce the field I love.

The day this book went to press was the day I started gathering information and ideas for the tenth edition. Your input will again influence how this book continues to evolve. So, please, do share your thoughts.

Hope College
Holland, Michigan 49422-9000 USA

Introduction to the History and Science of Psychology

MODULES

1
The Story of Psychology

2
Thinking Critically With Psychological Science

3
Research Strategies: How Psychologists Ask and Answer Questions

Harvard astronomer Owen Gingerich (2006) reports that there are more than 100 billion galaxies. Just one of these, our own relative speck of a galaxy, has some 200 billion stars, many of which, like our Sun-star, are circled by planets. On the scale of outer space, we are less than a single grain of sand on all the oceans' beaches, and our lifetime but a relative nanosecond.

Yet there is nothing more awe inspiring and absorbing than our own inner space. Our brain, adds Gingerich, "is by far the most complex physical object known to us in the entire cosmos" (p. 29). Our consciousness—mind somehow arising from matter—remains a profound mystery. Our thinking, emotions, and actions (and their interplay with others' thinking, emotions, and actions) fascinate us. Outer space staggers us with its enormity, but inner space enthralls us. Enter psychological science.

For people whose exposure to psychology comes from popular books, magazines, TV, and the Internet, psychologists analyze personality, offer counseling, and dispense child-rearing advice. Do they? Yes, and much more. Consider some of psychology's questions that from time to time you may wonder about:

▶ Have you ever found yourself reacting to something as one of your biological parents would—perhaps in a way you vowed you never would—and then wondered how much of your personality you inherited? *To what extent are person-to-person differences in personality predisposed by our genes? To what extent by the home and community environments?*

▶ Have you ever worried about how to act among people of a different culture, race, or gender? *In what ways are we alike as members of the human family? How do we differ?*

▶ Have you ever awakened from a nightmare and, with a wave of relief, wondered why you had such a crazy dream? *How often, and why, do we dream?*

▶ Have you ever played peekaboo with a 6-month-old and wondered why the baby finds the game so delightful? The infant reacts as though, when you momentarily move behind a door, you actually disappear—only to reappear later out of thin air. *What do babies actually perceive and think?*

▶ Have you ever wondered what leads to school and work success? Are some people just born smarter? *Does sheer intelligence explain why some people get richer, think more creatively, or relate more sensitively?*

▶ Have you ever become depressed or anxious and wondered whether you'll ever feel "normal"? *What triggers our bad moods—and our good ones?*

Such questions provide grist for psychology's mill, because psychology is a science that seeks to answer all sorts of questions about us all—how and why we think, feel, and act as we do. In Module 1, we trace psychology's roots and survey its scope. In Module 2, we consider how psychological science can help you to think critically in everyday life and to understand some dangers in relying too heavily on intuition and common sense. In Module 3, we survey psychology's methods—how psychologists ask and answer questions.

"I have made a ceaseless effort not to ridicule, not to bewail, not to scorn human actions, but to understand them."

Benedict Spinoza, *A Political Treatise*, 1677

A smile is a smile the world around Throughout this book, you will see examples not only of our cultural and gender diversity but also of the similarities that define our shared human nature. People in different cultures vary in when and how often they smile, but a naturally happy smile *means* the same thing anywhere in the world.

John Lund/Sam Dephuis/Blend Images/Corbis

Megapress/Alamy

Ariadne Van Zandbl/Lonely Planet Images

MODULE 1

The Story of Psychology

▶‖ What Is Psychology?

Psychology's Roots

Once upon a time, on a planet in this neighborhood of the universe, there came to be people. Soon thereafter, these creatures became intensely interested in themselves and in one another: *"Who are we? What produces our thoughts? Our feelings? Our actions? And how are we to understand and manage those around us?"*

Psychological Science Is Born

1-1 When and how did psychological science begin?

To be human is to be curious about ourselves and the world around us. Before 300 B.C., the Greek naturalist and philosopher Aristotle theorized about learning and memory, motivation and emotion, perception and personality. Today we chuckle at some of his guesses, like his suggestion that a meal makes us sleepy by causing gas and heat to collect around the source of our personality, the heart. But credit Aristotle with asking the right questions.

Philosophers' thinking about thinking continued until the birth of psychology as we know it, on a December day in 1879, in a small, third-floor room at Germany's University of Leipzig. There, two young men were helping an austere, middle-aged professor, Wilhelm Wundt, create an experimental apparatus. Their machine measured the time lag between people's hearing a ball hit a platform and their pressing a telegraph key (Hunt, 1993). Curiously, people responded in about one-tenth of a second when asked to press the key as soon as the sound occurred—and in about two-tenths of a second when asked to press the key as soon as they were consciously aware of perceiving the sound. (To be aware of one's awareness takes a little longer.) Wundt was seeking to measure "atoms of the mind"—the fastest and simplest mental processes. Thus began what many consider psychology's first experiment, launching the first psychological laboratory, staffed by Wundt and psychology's first graduate students.

Before long, this new science of psychology became organized into different branches, or schools of thought, each promoted by pioneering thinkers. These early schools included *structuralism* and *functionalism,* described here, and three schools described in other modules: Gestalt psychology, behaviorism, and psychoanalysis.

Thinking About the Mind's Structure

Soon after receiving his Ph.D. in 1892, Wundt's student Edward Bradford Titchener joined the Cornell University faculty and introduced **structuralism.** As physicists and chemists discerned the structure of matter, so Titchener aimed to discover the

Wilhelm Wundt Wundt (far left) established the first psychology laboratory at the University of Leipzig, Germany.

Monika Suteski

"The rose is smooth-petaled, sweetly aromatic,..."

Edward Bradford Titchener
Titchener used <u>introspection</u> to search for the mind's structural elements.

Monika Suteski

structural elements of mind. His method was to engage people in self-reflective *intro-spection* (looking inward), training them to report elements of their experience as they looked at a rose, listened to a metronome, smelled a scent, or tasted a substance. What were their immediate sensations, their images, their feelings? And how did these relate to one another? Titchener shared with the English essayist C. S. Lewis the view that "there is one thing, and only one in the whole universe which we know more about than we could learn from external observation." That one thing, Lewis said, is ourselves. "We have, so to speak, inside information" (1960, pp. 18–19).

Alas, introspection required smart, verbal people. It also proved somewhat unreliable, its results varying from person to person and experience to experience. Moreover, we often just don't know why we feel what we feel and do what we do. Recent studies indicate that people's recollections frequently err. So do their self-reports about what, for example, has caused them to help or hurt another (Myers, 2002). As introspection waned, so did structuralism.

Thinking About the Mind's Functions

Unlike those hoping to assemble the structure of mind from simple elements—which was rather like trying to understand a car by examining its disconnected parts—philosopher-psychologist William James thought it more fruitful to consider the evolved *functions* of our thoughts and feelings. Smelling is what the nose does; thinking is what the brain does. But why do the nose and brain do these things? Under the influence of evolutionary theorist Charles Darwin, James assumed that thinking, like smelling, developed because it was *adaptive*—it contributed to our ancestors' survival. Consciousness serves a function. It enables us to consider our past, adjust to our present circumstances, and plan our future. As a **functionalist,** James encouraged explorations of down-to-earth emotions, memories, willpower, habits, and moment-to-moment streams of consciousness.

James' greatest legacy, however, came less from his laboratory than from his Harvard teaching and his writing. When not plagued by ill health and depression, James was an impish, outgoing, and joyous man, who once recalled that "the first lecture on psychology I ever heard was the first I ever gave." During one of his wise-cracking lectures, a student interrupted and asked him to get serious (Hunt, 1993). He was reportedly one of the first American professors to solicit end-of-course student evaluations of his teaching. He loved his students, his family, and the world of ideas, but he tired of painstaking chores such as proofreading. "Send me no proofs!" he once told an editor. "I will return them unopened and never speak to you again" (Hunt, 1993, p. 145).

"You don't know your own mind."
Jonathan Swift, *Polite Conversation*, 1738

structuralism an early school of psychology that used introspection to explore the structural elements of the human mind.

functionalism a school of psychology that focused on how our mental and behavioral processes function—how they enable us to adapt, survive, and flourish.

William James and Mary Whiton Calkins James, legendary teacher-writer, mentored Calkins, who became a pioneering memory researcher and the first woman to be president of the American Psychological Association.

James displayed the same spunk in 1890, when—over the objections of Harvard's president—he admitted Mary Calkins into his graduate seminar (Scarborough & Furumoto, 1987). (In those years women lacked even the right to vote.) When Calkins joined, the other students (all men) dropped out. So James tutored her alone. Later, she finished all the requirements for a Harvard Ph.D., outscoring all the male students on the qualifying exams. Alas, Harvard denied her the degree she had earned, offering her instead a degree from Radcliffe College, its undergraduate sister school for women. Calkins resisted the unequal treatment and refused the degree. (More than a century later, psychologists and psychology students were lobbying Harvard to posthumously award the Ph.D. she earned [*Feminist Psychologist,* 2002].) Calkins nevertheless went on to become a distinguished memory researcher and the American Psychological Association's (APA's) first female president in 1905.

When Harvard denied Calkins the claim to being psychology's first female psychology Ph.D., that honor fell to Margaret Floy Washburn, who later wrote an influential book, *The Animal Mind,* and became the second female APA president in 1921.

Although Washburn's thesis was the first foreign study Wundt published in his journal, her gender meant she was barred from joining the organization of experimental psychologists founded by Titchener, her own graduate adviser (Johnson, 1997). (What a different world from the recent past—1996 to 2009—when women claimed two-thirds or more of new psychology Ph.D.s and were 6 of the 13 elected presidents of the science-oriented Association for Psychological Science. In Canada and Europe, too, most recent psychology doctorates have been earned by women.)

James' influence reached even further through his dozens of well-received articles, which moved the publisher Henry Holt to offer a contract for a textbook of the new science of psychology. James agreed and began work in 1878, with an apology for requesting two years to finish his writing. The text proved an unexpected chore and actually took him 12 years. (Why am I not surprised?) More than a century later, people still read the resulting *Principles of Psychology* and marvel at the brilliance and elegance with which James introduced psychology to the educated public.

Margaret Floy Washburn The first woman to receive a psychology Ph.D., Washburn synthesized animal behavior research in *The Animal Mind.*

Psychological Science Develops

1-2 How did psychology continue to develop from the 1920s through today?

The young science of psychology developed from the more established fields of philosophy and biology. Wundt was both a philosopher and a physiologist. James was an American philosopher. Ivan Pavlov, who pioneered the study of learning, was a Russian physiologist. Sigmund Freud, who developed an influential theory of personality, was an Austrian physician. Jean Piaget, the last century's most influential observer of children, was a Swiss biologist. This list of pioneering psychologists—"Magellans of the mind," as Morton Hunt (1993) has called them—illustrates psychology's origins in many disciplines and countries.

The rest of the story of psychology—the subject of this book—develops at many levels. With activities ranging from the study of nerve cell activity to the study of international conflicts, *psychology* is not easily defined.

In psychology's early days, Wundt and Titchener focused on inner sensations, images, and feelings. James, too, engaged in introspective examination of the stream of consciousness and of emotion. Freud emphasized the ways emotional responses to childhood experiences and our unconscious thought processes affect our behavior. Thus, until the 1920s, *psychology* was defined as "the science of mental life."

From the 1920s into the 1960s, American psychologists, initially led by flamboyant and provocative John B. Watson and later by the equally provocative B. F. Skinner, dismissed introspection and redefined *psychology* as "the scientific study of observable behavior." After all, said these **behaviorists,** science is rooted in observation. You cannot observe a sensation, a feeling, or a thought, but you *can* observe and record people's *behavior* as they respond to different situations.

Humanistic psychology rebelled against Freudian psychology and behaviorism. Pioneers Carl Rogers and Abraham Maslow found behaviorism's focus on learned behaviors too mechanistic. Rather than focusing on the meaning of early childhood memories, as a psychoanalyst might, the humanistic psychologists emphasized the importance of current environmental influences on our growth potential, and the importance of having our needs for love and acceptance satisfied.

In the 1960s, another movement emerged as psychology began to recapture its initial interest in mental processes. This *cognitive revolution* supported ideas developed by earlier psychologists, such as the importance of how our mind processes and retains information. But cognitive psychology and more recently **cognitive neuroscience** (the study of brain activity linked with mental activity) have expanded upon those ideas to explore scientifically the ways we perceive, process, and remember information. This

Sigmund Freud The controversial ideas of this famed personality theorist and therapist have influenced humanity's self-understanding.

behaviorism the view that psychology (1) should be an objective science that (2) studies behavior without reference to mental processes. Most research psychologists today agree with (1) but not with (2).

humanistic psychology historically significant perspective that emphasized the growth potential of healthy people and the individual's potential for personal growth.

cognitive neuroscience the interdisciplinary study of the brain activity linked with cognition (including perception, thinking, memory, and language).

John B. Watson and Rosalie Rayner Working with Rayner, Watson championed psychology as the science of behavior and demonstrated conditioned responses on a baby who became famous as "Little Albert."

B. F. Skinner A leading behaviorist, Skinner rejected introspection and studied how consequences shape behavior.

approach has been especially beneficial in helping to develop new ways to understand and treat disorders such as depression.

To encompass psychology's concern with observable behavior *and* with inner thoughts and feelings, today we define **psychology** as the *science of behavior and mental processes.*

Let's unpack this definition. *Behavior* is anything an organism *does*—any action we can observe and record. Yelling, smiling, blinking, sweating, talking, and questionnaire marking are all observable behaviors. *Mental processes* are the internal, subjective experiences we infer from behavior—sensations, perceptions, dreams, thoughts, beliefs, and feelings.

The key word in psychology's definition is *science.* Psychology, as I will emphasize throughout this book, is less a set of findings than a way of asking and answering questions. My aim, then, is not merely to report results but also to show you how psychologists play their game. You will see how researchers evaluate conflicting opinions and ideas. And you will learn how all of us, whether scientists or simply curious people, can think smarter when describing and explaining the events of our lives.

▶‖ Contemporary Psychology

Like its pioneers, today's psychologists are citizens of many lands. The International Union of Psychological Science has 69 member nations, from Albania to Zimbabwe. Nearly everywhere, membership in psychological societies is mushrooming—from 4183 American Psychological Association members and affiliates in 1945 to nearly 150,000 today, with similarly rapid growth in the British Psychological Society (from 1100 to 45,000). In China, the first university psychology department began in 1978; in 2008 there were 200 (Tversky, 2008). Worldwide, some 500,000 people have been trained as psychologists, and 130,000 of them belong to European psychological organizations (Tikkanen, 2001). Moreover, thanks to international publications, joint meetings, and the Internet, collaboration and communication cross borders now more than ever. "We are moving rapidly toward a single world of psychological science," reported Robert Bjork (2000). Psychology is *growing* and it is *globalizing.*

Across the world, psychologists are debating enduring issues, viewing behavior from the differing perspectives offered by the subfields in which they teach, work, and do research.

Psychology's Biggest Question

1-3   What is psychology's historic big issue?

During its short history, psychology has wrestled with some issues that will reappear throughout this book. The biggest and most persistent is the **nature-nurture issue**—*the controversy over the relative contributions of biology and experience.* The origins of this debate are ancient. Do our human traits develop through experience, or are we born with them? The Greek philosopher Plato (428–348 B.C.) assumed that character and intelligence are largely inherited and that certain ideas are inborn. Aristotle (384–322 B.C.) countered that there is nothing in the mind that does not first come in from the external world through the senses. In the 1600s, European philosophers rekindled the debate. John Locke rejected the notion of inborn ideas, suggesting that the mind is a blank sheet on which experience writes. René Descartes disagreed, believing that some ideas are innate.

Two centuries later, Descartes' views gained support from a curious naturalist. In 1831, an indifferent student but ardent collector of beetles, mollusks, and shells set sail on what was to prove a historic round-the-world journey. The 22-year-old voyager was Charles Darwin, and for some time afterward, he pondered the incredible

---

psychology   the science of behavior and mental processes.

nature-nurture issue   the longstanding controversy over the relative contributions that genes and experience make to the development of psychological traits and behaviors. Today's science sees traits and behaviors arising from the interaction of nature and nurture.

natural selection   the principle that, among the range of inherited trait variations, those contributing to reproduction and survival will most likely be passed on to succeeding generations.

Charles Darwin Darwin argued that natural selection shapes behaviors as well as bodies.

Monika Su esk

species variation he had encountered, including tortoises on one island that differed from those on other islands of the region. Darwin's 1859 *On the Origin of Species* explained this diversity of life by proposing the evolutionary process of **natural selection:** From among chance variations, nature selects the traits that best enable an organism to survive and reproduce in a particular environment. Darwin's principle of natural selection—"the single best idea anyone has ever had," said philosopher Daniel Dennett (1996)—is still with us nearly 150 years later as an organizing principle of biology. Evolution also has become an important principle for twenty-first-century psychology. This would surely have pleased Darwin, for he believed his theory explained not only animal structures (such as a polar bear's white coat) but also animal behaviors (such as the emotional expressions associated with human lust and rage).

The nature-nurture debate weaves a thread from the ancient Greeks' time to our own. Today's psychologists explore the issue by asking, for example:

▶ How are we humans alike (because of our common biology and evolutionary history) and diverse (because of our differing environments)?

▶ Are gender differences biologically predisposed or socially constructed?

▶ Is children's grammar mostly innate or formed by experience?

▶ How are differences in intelligence and personality influenced by heredity and by environment?

▶ Are sexual behaviors more "pushed" by inner biology or "pulled" by external incentives?

▶ Should we treat psychological disorders—depression, for example—as disorders of the brain, disorders of thought, or both?

Mitch Diamond/Alamy

Gary Parker/Photo Researchers Inc.

A nature-made nature-nurture experiment Because identical twins have the same genes, they are ideal participants in studies designed to shed light on hereditary and environmental influences on intelligence, personality, and other traits. Studies of identical and fraternal twins provide a rich array of findings that underscore the importance of both nature and nurture.

levels of analysis the differing complementary views, from biological to psychological to social-cultural, for analyzing any given phenomenon.

biopsychosocial approach an integrated approach that incorporates biological, psychological, and social-cultural levels of analysis.

Such debates continue. Yet over and over again we will see that in contemporary science the nature-nurture tension dissolves: *Nurture works on what nature endows.* Our species is biologically endowed with an enormous capacity to learn and adapt. Moreover, every psychological event (every thought, every emotion) is simultaneously a biological event. Thus depression can be *both* a brain disorder *and* a thought disorder.

Psychology's Three Main Levels of Analysis

1-4 What are psychology's levels of analysis and related perspectives?

Each of us is a complex system that is part of a larger social system. But each of us is also composed of smaller systems, such as our nervous system and body organs, which are composed of still smaller systems—cells, molecules, and atoms.

These tiered systems suggest different **levels of analysis,** which offer complementary outlooks. It's like explaining why grizzly bears hibernate. Is it because hibernation helped their ancestors to survive and reproduce? Because their inner physiology drives them to do so? Because cold environments hinder food gathering during winter? Such perspectives are complementary because "everything is related to everything else" (Brewer, 1996). Together, different levels of analysis form an integrated **biopsychosocial approach,** which considers the influences of biological, psychological, and social-cultural factors (**FIGURE** 1.1).

Each level provides a valuable vantage point for looking at behavior, yet each by itself is incomplete. Like different academic disciplines, psychology's varied perspectives ask different questions and have their own limits. One perspective may stress the biological, psychological, or social-cultural level more than another, but the different perspectives described in **TABLE** 1.1 complement one another. Consider, for example, how they shed light on anger.

▶ Someone working from a *neuroscience perspective* might study brain circuits that cause us to be "red in the face" and "hot under the collar."

▶ Someone working from the *evolutionary perspective* might analyze how anger facilitated the survival of our ancestors' genes.

▶ Someone working from the *behavior genetics perspective* might study how heredity and experience influence our individual differences in temperament.

FIGURE 1.1 Biopsychosocial approach
This integrated viewpoint incorporates various levels of analysis and offers a more complete picture of any given behavior or mental process.

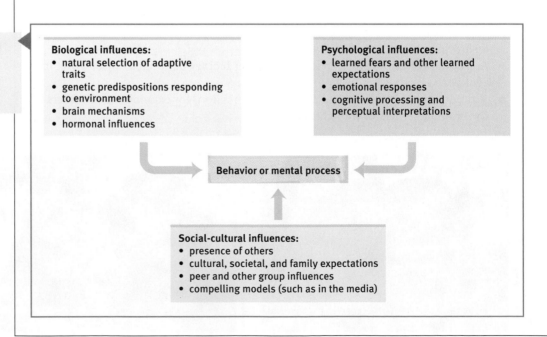

Biological influences:
- natural selection of adaptive traits
- genetic predispositions responding to environment
- brain mechanisms
- hormonal influences

Psychological influences:
- learned fears and other learned expectations
- emotional responses
- cognitive processing and perceptual interpretations

Behavior or mental process

Social-cultural influences:
- presence of others
- cultural, societal, and family expectations
- peer and other group influences
- compelling models (such as in the media)

TABLE 1.1 Psychology's Current Perspectives

Perspective	Focus	Sample Questions
Neuroscience	How the body and brain enable emotions, memories, and sensory experiences	How are messages transmitted within the body? How is blood chemistry linked with moods and motives?
Evolutionary	How the natural selection of traits promoted the survival of genes	How does evolution influence behavior tendencies?
Behavior genetics	How much our genes and our environment influence our individual differences	To what extent are psychological traits such as intelligence, personality, sexual orientation, and vulnerability to depression attributable to our genes? To our environment?
Psychodynamic	How behavior springs from unconscious drives and conflicts	How can someone's personality traits and disorders be explained in terms of sexual and aggressive drives or as the disguised effects of unfulfilled wishes and childhood traumas?
Behavioral	How we learn observable responses	How do we learn to fear particular objects or situations? What is the most effective way to alter our behavior, say, to lose weight or stop smoking?
Cognitive	How we encode, process, store, and retrieve information	How do we use information in remembering? Reasoning? Solving problems?
Social-cultural	How behavior and thinking vary across situations and cultures	How are we humans alike as members of one human family? As products of different environmental contexts, how do we differ?

▶ Someone working from the *psychodynamic perspective* might view an outburst as an outlet for unconscious hostility.

▶ Someone working from the *behavioral perspective* might attempt to determine which external stimuli trigger angry responses or aggressive acts.

▶ Someone working from the *cognitive perspective* might study how our interpretation of a situation affects our anger and how our anger affects our thinking.

▶ Someone working from the *social-cultural perspective* might explore how expressions of anger vary across cultural contexts.

The point to remember: Like two-dimensional views of a three-dimensional object, each of psychology's perspectives is helpful. But each by itself fails to reveal the whole picture.

So bear in mind psychology's limits. Don't expect it to answer the ultimate questions, such as those posed by Russian novelist Leo Tolstoy (1904): "Why should I live? Why should I do anything? Is there in life any purpose which the inevitable death that awaits me does not undo and destroy?" Instead, expect that psychology will help you understand why people think, feel, and act as they do. Then you should find the study of psychology fascinating and useful.

Psychology's Subfields

1-5 What are psychology's main subfields?

Picturing a chemist at work, you probably envision a white-coated scientist surrounded by glassware and high-tech equipment. Picture a psychologist at work and you would be right to envision

▶ a white-coated scientist probing a rat's brain.

▶ an intelligence researcher measuring how quickly an infant shows boredom by looking away from a familiar picture.

Views of anger How would each of psychology's levels of analysis explain what's going on here?

"I'm a social scientist, Michael. That means I can't explain electricity or anything like that, but if you ever want to know about people I'm your man."

basic research   pure science that aims to increase the scientific knowledge base.

applied research   scientific study that aims to solve practical problems.

counseling psychology   a branch of psychology that assists people with problems in living (often related to school, work, or marriage) and in achieving greater well-being.

clinical psychology   a branch of psychology that studies, assesses, and treats people with psychological disorders.

psychiatry   a branch of medicine dealing with psychological disorders; practiced by physicians who sometimes provide medical (for example, drug) treatments as well as psychological therapy

▶ an executive evaluating a new "healthy life-styles" training program for employees.

▶ someone at a computer keyboard analyzing data on whether adopted teens' temperaments more closely resemble those of their adoptive parents or their biological parents.

▶ a therapist listening carefully to a client's depressed thoughts.

▶ a traveler visiting another culture and collecting data on variations in human values and behaviors.

▶ a teacher or writer sharing the joy of psychology with others.

The cluster of subfields we call psychology has less unity than most other sciences. But there is a payoff: Psychology is a meeting ground for different disciplines. "Psychology is a hub scientific discipline," said Association for Psychological Science president John Cacioppo (2007). Thus, it's a perfect home for those with wide-ranging interests. In their diverse activities, from biological experimentation to cultural comparisons, the tribe of psychology is united by a common quest: describing and explaining behavior and the mind underlying it.

Some psychologists conduct **basic research** that builds psychology's knowledge base. In the pages that follow we will meet a wide variety of such researchers, including

▶ *biological psychologists* exploring the links between brain and mind.

▶ *developmental psychologists* studying our changing abilities from womb to tomb.

▶ *cognitive psychologists* experimenting with how we perceive, think, and solve problems.

▶ *personality psychologists* investigating our persistent traits.

▶ *social psychologists* exploring how we view and affect one another.

These psychologists also may conduct **applied research** that tackles practical problems. So do other psychologists, including *industrial-organizational psychologists,* who use psychology's concepts and methods in the workplace to help organizations and companies select and train employees, boost morale and productivity, design products, and implement systems.

Although most psychology textbooks focus on psychological science, psychology is also a helping profession devoted to such practical issues as how to have a happy marriage, how to overcome anxiety or depression, and how to raise thriving children. As a science, psychology at its best bases such interventions on evidence of effectiveness. **Counseling psychologists** help people to cope with challenges and crises (including academic, vocational, and marital issues) and to improve their personal and social functioning. **Clinical psychologists** assess and treat mental, emotional, and behavior disorders (APA, 2003). Both counseling and clinical psychologists administer and interpret tests, provide counseling and therapy, and sometimes conduct basic and applied research. By contrast, **psychiatrists,** who also often provide psychotherapy, are medical doctors licensed to prescribe drugs and otherwise treat physical causes of psychological disorders. (Some clinical psychologists are lobbying for a similar right to prescribe mental-health–related drugs, and in 2002 and 2004 New Mexico and Louisiana became the first states to grant that right to specially trained and licensed psychologists.)

With perspectives ranging from the biological to the social, and

I see you! A biological psychologist might view this child's delighted response as evidence of brain maturation. A cognitive psychologist might see it as a demonstration of the baby's growing knowledge of his surroundings. For a cross-cultural psychologist, the role of grandparents in different societies might be the issue of interest. As you will see throughout this book, these and other perspectives offer complementary views of behavior.

Laura Dwight

with settings from the laboratory to the clinic, psychology relates to many fields, ranging from mathematics to biology to sociology to philosophy. And more and more, psychology's methods and findings aid other disciplines. Psychologists teach in medical schools, law schools, and theological seminaries, and they work in hospitals, factories, and corporate offices. They engage in interdisciplinary studies, such as psychohistory (the psychological analysis of historical characters), psycholinguistics (the study of language and thinking), and psychoceramics (the study of crackpots).[1]

Psychology also influences modern culture. Knowledge transforms us. Learning about the solar system and the germ theory of disease alters the way people think and act. Learning psychology's findings also changes people: They less often judge psychological disorders as moral failings, treatable by punishment and ostracism. They less often regard and treat women as men's mental inferiors. They less often view and rear children as ignorant, willful beasts in need of taming. "In each case," notes Morton Hunt (1990, p. 206), "knowledge has modified attitudes, and, through them, behavior." Once aware of psychology's well-researched ideas—about how body and mind connect, how a child's mind grows, how we construct our perceptions, how we remember (and misremember) our experiences, how people across the world differ (and are alike)—your mind may never again be quite the same.

Psychology: A science and a profession Psychologists experiment with, observe, test, and treat behavior. Here we see psychologists testing a child, measuring emotion-related physiology, and doing face-to-face therapy.

|| Want to learn more? See Appendix A, Careers in Psychology, at the end of this book for more information about psychology's subfields and to learn about the many interesting options available to those with bachelor's, master's, and doctoral degrees in psychology. ||

"Once expanded to the dimensions of a larger idea, [the mind] never returns to its original size."
Oliver Wendell Holmes, 1809–1894

---

[1]Confession: I wrote the last part of this sentence on April Fools' Day.

Tips for Studying Psychology

1-6   How can psychological principles help you as a student?

The investment you are making in studying psychology should enrich your life and enlarge your vision. Although many of life's significant questions are beyond psychology, some very important ones are illuminated by even a first psychology course. Through painstaking research, psychologists have gained insights into brain and mind, dreams and memories, depression and joy. Even the unanswered questions can enrich us, by renewing our sense of mystery about "things too wonderful" for us yet to understand. Your study of psychology can also help teach you *how to ask and answer important questions*—how to think critically as you evaluate competing ideas and claims.

Having your life enriched and your vision enlarged (and getting a decent grade) requires effective study. To master information you must *actively process it*. Your mind is not like your stomach, something to be filled passively; it is more like a muscle that grows stronger with exercise. Countless experiments reveal that people learn and remember best when they put material in their own words, rehearse it, and then review and rehearse it again.

The **SQ3R** study method incorporates these principles (Robinson, 1970). SQ3R is an acronym for its five steps: *Survey, Question, Read, Rehearse, Review.*

To study a module, first *survey,* taking a bird's-eye view. Scan the headings, and notice how the module is organized.

As you prepare to read each section, use its heading or learning objective to form your own *question* to answer. For this section, you might have asked, "How can I most effectively and efficiently master the information in this book?"

Then *read,* actively searching for the answer. Usually a single module—sometimes just a main section within a module—will be as much as you can absorb without tiring. Read actively and critically. Ask questions. Make notes. Consider implications: How does what you've read relate to your own life? Does it support or challenge your assumptions? How convincing is the evidence?

Having read a section, *rehearse* in your own words what you read. Test yourself by trying to answer your question, rehearsing what you can recall, then glancing back over what you can't recall.

Finally, *review:* Read over any notes you have taken, again with an eye on the module's organization, and quickly review the whole module.

Survey, question, read, rehearse, review. I have organized this book's modules to facilitate your use of the SQ3R study system. Each module begins with an outline that aids your *survey.* Headings and learning objective *questions* suggest issues and concepts you should consider as you *read.* The material is organized into sections of readable length. The Test Yourself and Ask Yourself questions at the end of each module help you *rehearse* what you know. The module *Review* also provides answers to the learning objective questions, and the list of key terms helps you check your mastery of important concepts. Survey, question, read . . .

Five additional study tips may further boost your learning:

Distribute your study time. One of psychology's oldest findings is that *spaced practice* promotes better retention than *massed practice.* You'll remember material better if you space your time over several study periods—perhaps one hour a day, six days a week—rather than cram it into one long study blitz. For example, rather than trying to read an entire module in a single sitting, read just one main section and then turn to something else.

Spacing your study sessions requires a disciplined approach to managing your time. (Richard O. Straub explains time management in the helpful *Study Guide* that accompanies this text.)

Learn to think critically. Whether you are reading or in class, note people's assumptions and values. What perspective or bias underlies an argument? Evaluate evidence. Is it anecdotal? Correlational? Experimental? Assess conclusions. Are there alternative explanations?

In class, listen actively. Listen for the main ideas and sub-ideas of a lecture. *Write them down.* Ask questions during and after class. In class, as in your private study, process the information actively and you will understand and retain it better. As psychologist William James urged a century ago, *"No reception without reaction, no impression without . . . expression."*

Overlearn. Psychology tells us that overlearning improves retention. We are prone to overestimating how much we know. You may understand a module as you read it, but by devoting extra study time to testing yourself and reviewing what you think you know, you will retain your new knowledge long into the future.

Be a smart test-taker. If a test contains both multiple-choice questions and an essay question, turn first to the essay. Read the question carefully, noting exactly what the instructor is asking. On the back of a page, pencil in a list of points you'd like to make and then organize them. Before writing, put aside the essay and work through the multiple-choice questions. (As you do so, your mind may continue to mull over the essay question. Sometimes the learning objective questions will bring pertinent thoughts to mind.) Then reread the essay question, rethink your answer, and start writing. When you finish, proofread your answer to eliminate spelling and grammatical errors that make you look less competent than you are. When reading multiple-choice questions, don't confuse yourself by trying to imagine how each choice might be the right one. Instead, try to answer each question as if it were a fill-in-the-blank question. First cover the answers and form a sentence in your mind, recalling what you know to complete the sentence. Then read the answers on the test and find the alternative that best matches your own answer.

While exploring psychology, you will learn much more than effective study techniques. Psychology deepens our appreciation for how we humans perceive, think, feel, and act. By so doing it can indeed enrich our lives and enlarge our vision. Through this book I hope to help guide you toward that end. As educator Charles Eliot said a century ago: "Books are the quietest and most constant of friends, and the most patient of teachers."

SQ3R   a study method incorporating five steps: *Survey, Question, Read, Rehearse, Review.*

REVIEW

The Story of Psychology

1-1 **When and how did psychological science begin?** Psychological science had its modern beginning with the first psychological laboratory, founded in 1879 by German philosopher and physiologist Wilhelm Wundt, and from the later work of other scholars from several disciplines and many countries.

1-2 **How did psychology continue to develop from the 1920s through today?** Having begun as a "science of mental life," psychology evolved in the 1920s into the "scientific study of observable behavior." After rediscovering the mind, *psychology* since the 1960s has been widely defined as the *science of behavior and mental processes*.

1-3 **What is psychology's historic big issue?** Psychology's biggest and most enduring issue concerns the relative contributions and interplay between the influences of *nature* (genes) and *nurture* (all other influences, from conception to death). Today's science emphasizes the interaction of genes and experiences in specific environments.

1-4 **What are psychology's levels of analysis and related perspectives?** The *biopsychosocial approach* integrates information from the biological, psychological, and social-cultural *levels of analysis*. Psychologists study human behaviors and mental processes from many different perspectives (including the neuroscientific, evolutionary, behavior genetics, psychodynamic, behavioral, cognitive, and social-cultural perspectives).

1-5 **What are psychology's main subfields?** Psychology's subfields encompass *basic research* (often done by biological, developmental, cognitive, personality, and social psychologists), *applied research* (sometimes conducted by industrial-organizational psychologists), and clinical science and applications (the work of *counseling psychologists* and *clinical psychologists*). Clinical psychologists study, assess, and treat (with psychotherapy) people with psychological disorders. *Psychiatrists* also study, assess, and treat people with disorders, but as medical doctors, they may prescribe drugs in addition to psychotherapy.

1-6 **How can psychological principles help you as a student?** Research has shown that learning and memory are enhanced by active study. The *SQ3R* study method—survey, question, read, rehearse, and review—applies the principles derived from this research.

Terms and Concepts to Remember

structuralism, p. 2
functionalism, p. 3
behaviorism, p. 5
humanistic psychology, p. 5
cognitive neuroscience, p. 5
psychology, p. 6
nature-nurture issue, p. 6
natural selection, p. 7

levels of analysis, p. 8
biopsychosocial approach, p. 8
basic research, p. 10
applied research, p. 10
counseling psychology, p. 10
clinical psychology, p. 10
psychiatry, p. 10
SQ3R, p. 12

Test Yourself*

1. What event defined the founding of scientific psychology?
2. What are psychology's major levels of analysis?

Ask Yourself**

1. How do you think psychology might change as more people from non-Western countries contribute their ideas to the field?
2. When you signed up for this course, what did you think psychology would be all about?

∞ WEB

Multiple-choice self-tests and more may be found at www.worthpublishers.com/myers

*The Test Yourself questions offer you a handy self-test on the material you have just read. Answers to these questions can be found in Appendix B at the end of the book.

**The Ask Yourself questions will help you reflect on key issues and connect them to your own life. Making these issues personally meaningful will make them memorable.

MODULE 2

Thinking Critically With Psychological Science

Hoping to satisfy their curiosity about people and to remedy their own woes, millions turn to "psychology." They listen to talk-radio counseling, read articles on psychic powers, attend stop-smoking hypnosis seminars, and absorb self-help Web sites and books on the meaning of dreams, the path to ecstatic love, and the roots of personal happiness.

Others, intrigued by claims of psychological truth, wonder: Do mothers and infants bond in the first hours after birth? Should we trust childhood sexual abuse memories that get "recovered" in adulthood—and prosecute the alleged predators? Are first-born children more driven to achieve? Does psychotherapy heal?

In working with such questions, how can we separate uninformed opinions from examined conclusions? *How can we best use psychology to understand why people think, feel, and act as they do?*

▶‖ The Need for Psychological Science

2-1 Why are the answers that flow from the scientific approach more reliable than those based on intuition and common sense?

Some people suppose that psychology merely documents and dresses in jargon what people already know: "So what else is new—you get paid for using fancy methods to prove what my grandmother knew?" Others place their faith in human intuition: "Buried deep within each and every one of us, there is an instinctive, heart-felt awareness that provides—if we allow it to—the most reliable guide," offered Prince Charles (2000). "I know there's no evidence that shows the death penalty has a deterrent effect," George W. Bush (1999) reportedly said as Texas governor, "but I just feel in my gut it must be true." "I'm a gut player. I rely on my instincts," said the former president in explaining to Bob Woodward (2002) his decision to launch the Iraq war.

Prince Charles and former President Bush have much company. A long list of pop psychology books encourage us toward "intuitive managing," "intuitive trading," "intuitive healing," and much more. Today's psychological science does document a vast intuitive mind. As we will see, our thinking, memory, and attitudes operate on two levels, conscious and unconscious, with the larger part operating automatically, off-screen. Like jumbo jets, we fly mostly on autopilot.

So, are we smart to listen to the whispers of our inner wisdom, to simply trust "the force within"? Or should we more often be subjecting our intuitive hunches to skeptical scrutiny?

This much seems certain. Intuition is important, but we often underestimate its perils. My geographical intuition tells me that Reno is east of Los Angeles, that Rome is south of New York, that Atlanta is east of Detroit. But I am wrong, wrong, and wrong.

Experiments have found people greatly overestimating their lie detection accuracy, their eyewitness recollections, their interviewee assessments, their risk predictions, and their stock-picking talents. "The first principle," said Richard Feynman (1997), "is that you must not fool yourself—and you are the easiest person to fool."

The limits of intuition Personnel interviewers tend to be overconfident of their gut feelings about job applicants. Their confidence stems partly from their recalling cases where their favorable impression proved right, and partly from their ignorance about rejected applicants who succeeded elsewhere.

Chris Ryan/Ojo Images/Getty Images

Indeed, observed Madeleine L'Engle, "The naked intellect is an extraordinarily inaccurate instrument" (1973). Two phenomena—hindsight bias and judgmental overconfidence—illustrate why we cannot rely solely on intuition and common sense.

Did We Know It All Along? Hindsight Bias

How easy it is to seem astute when drawing the bull's eye after the arrow has struck. After the first New York World Trade Center tower was hit on September 11, 2001, commentators said people in the second tower *should* have immediately evacuated. (It became obvious only later that the strike was not an accident.) After the U.S. occupation of Iraq led to a bloody civil war rather than a peaceful democracy, commentators saw the result as inevitable. *Before* the invasion was launched, these results seemed anything but obvious: In voting to allow the Iraq invasion, most U.S. senators did not anticipate the chaos that would seem so predictable in hindsight. Finding that something has happened makes it seem inevitable, a tendency we call **hindsight bias** (also known as the *I-knew-it-all-along phenomenon*).

This phenomenon is easy to demonstrate: Give half the members of a group some purported psychological finding, and give the other half an opposite result. Tell the first group, "Psychologists have found that separation weakens romantic attraction. As the saying goes, 'Out of sight, out of mind.'" Ask them to imagine why this might be true. Most people can, and nearly all will then regard this true finding as unsurprising.

Tell the second group the opposite, "Psychologists have found that separation strengthens romantic attraction. As the saying goes, 'Absence makes the heart grow fonder.'" People given this untrue result can also easily imagine it, and they overwhelmingly see it as unsurprising common sense. Obviously, when both a supposed finding and its opposite seem like common sense, there is a problem.

Such errors in our recollections and explanations show why we need psychological research. Just asking people how and why they felt or acted as they did can sometimes be misleading—*not* because common sense is usually wrong, but because common sense more easily describes what *has* happened than what *will* happen. As physicist Neils Bohr reportedly said, "Prediction is very difficult, especially about the future."

Hindsight bias is widespread. Some 100 studies have observed it in various countries and among both children and adults (Blank et al., 2007). Nevertheless, Grandma's intuition is often right. As Yogi Berra once said, "You can observe a lot by watching." (We have Berra to thank for other gems, such as "Nobody ever comes here—it's too crowded," and "If the people don't want to come out to the ballpark, nobody's gonna stop 'em.") Because we're all behavior watchers, it would be surprising if many of psychology's findings had *not* been foreseen. Many people believe that love breeds happiness, and they are right, according to researchers who have found we have a "deep need to belong" to others. Indeed, note Daniel Gilbert, Brett Pelham, and Douglas Krull (2003), "good ideas in psychology usually have an oddly familiar quality, and the moment we encounter them we feel certain that we once came close to thinking the same thing ourselves and simply failed to write it down." Good ideas are like good inventions; once created, they seem obvious. (Why did it take so long for someone to invent suitcases on wheels and Post-it Notes?)

But sometimes Grandma's intuition, informed by countless casual observations, has it wrong. Research has overturned popular ideas—that familiarity breeds contempt, that dreams predict the future, and that emotional reactions coincide with menstrual

"He who trusts in his own heart is a fool."
Proverbs 28:26

"Life is lived forwards, but understood backwards."
Philosopher Søren Kierkegaard, 1813–1855

hindsight bias the tendency to believe, after learning an outcome, that one would have foreseen it. (Also known as the *I-knew-it-all-along phenomenon*.)

"Anything seems commonplace, once explained."
Dr. Watson to Sherlock Holmes

Hindsight bias *After* the 2007 Virginia Tech massacre of 32 people, it seemed obvious that school officials should have locked down the school (despite its having the population of a small city) after the first two people were murdered. With 20/20 hindsight, everything seems obvious.

AP Photo/*The Roanoke Times*, Matt Gentry

TABLE 2.1 True or False?

Psychological research has either confirmed or refuted each of these statements (adapted, in part, from Furnham et al., 2003). Can you predict which of these popular ideas have been confirmed and which refuted? (Check your answers at the bottom of this table.)

1. If you want to teach a habit that persists, reward the desired behavior every time, not just intermittently.
2. Patients whose brains are surgically split down the middle survive and function much as they did before the surgery.
3. Traumatic experiences, such as sexual abuse or surviving the Holocaust, are typically "repressed" from memory.
4. Most abused children do *not* become abusive adults.
5. Most infants recognize their own reflection in a mirror by the end of their first year.
6. Adopted siblings usually do not develop similar personalities, even though they are reared by the same parents.
7. Fears of harmless objects, such as flowers, are just as easy to acquire as fears of potentially dangerous objects, such as snakes.
8. Lie detection tests often lie.
9. Most of us use only about 10 percent of our brains.
10. The brain remains active during sleep.

Answers: 1. F, 2. T, 3. F, 4. T, 5. F, 6. T, 7. F, 8. T, 9. F, 10. T.

phase. (See also **TABLE 2.1.**) We will also see how it has surprised us with discoveries about how the brain's chemical messengers control our moods and memories, about other animals' abilities, and about the effects of stress on our capacity to fight disease.

Overconfidence

We humans tend to be overconfident. We tend to think we know more than we do. Asked how sure we are of our answers to factual questions (Is Boston north or south of Paris?), we tend to be more confident than correct.[1] Or consider these three anagrams, which Richard Goranson (1978) asked people to unscramble:

> WREAT → WATER
> ETRYN → ENTRY
> GRABE → BARGE

About how many seconds do you think it would have taken you to unscramble each of these?

Once people know the answer, hindsight makes it seem obvious—so much so that they become overconfident. They think they would have seen the solution in only 10 seconds or so, when in reality the average problem solver spends 3 minutes, as you also might, given a similar anagram without the solution: OCHSA.[2]

Are we any better at predicting our social behavior? To find out, Robert Vallone and his associates (1990) had students predict at the beginning of the school year whether they would drop a course, vote in an upcoming election, call their parents more than twice a month, and so forth. On average, the students felt 84 percent confident in making these self-predictions. Later quizzes about their actual behavior showed their predictions were only 71 percent correct. Even when students were 100 percent sure of themselves, their self-predictions erred 15 percent of the time.

[1]Boston is south of Paris.
[2]Solution to anagram: CHAOS.

‖ Fun anagram solutions from Wordsmith.org:
Elvis = lives
Dormitory = dirty room
Slot machines = cash lost in 'em ‖

"We don't like their sound. Groups of guitars are on their way out."
Decca Records, in turning down a recording contract with the Beatles in 1962

"Computers in the future may weigh no more than 1.5 tons."
Popular Mechanics, 1949

It's not just collegians. Ohio State University psychologist Philip Tetlock (1998, 2005) has collected more than 27,000 expert predictions of world events, such as the future of South Africa or whether Quebec would separate from Canada. His repeated finding: These predictions, which experts made with 80 percent confidence on average, were right less than 40 percent of the time. Nevertheless, even those who erred maintained their confidence by noting they were "almost right." "The Québécois separatists *almost* won the secessionist referendum."

The point to remember: Hindsight bias and overconfidence often lead us to overestimate our intuition. But scientific inquiry can help us sift reality from illusion.

The Scientific Attitude

2-2   What are three main components of the scientific attitude?

Underlying all science is, first, a hard-headed *curiosity,* a passion to explore and understand without misleading or being misled. Some questions (Is there life after death?) are beyond science. To answer them in any way requires a leap of faith. With many other ideas (Can some people demonstrate ESP?), the proof is in the pudding. No matter how sensible or crazy an idea sounds, the critical thinker's question is *Does it work?* When put to the test, can its predictions be confirmed?

This scientific approach has a long history. As ancient a figure as Moses used such an approach. How do you evaluate a self-proclaimed prophet? His answer: Put the prophet to the test. If the predicted event "does not take place or prove true," then so much the worse for the prophet (Deuteronomy 18:22). By letting the facts speak for themselves, Moses was using what we now call an *empirical approach.* Magician James Randi uses this approach when testing those claiming to see auras around people's bodies:

   Randi: Do you see an aura around my head?
Aura-seer: Yes, indeed.
   Randi: Can you still see the aura if I put this magazine in front of my face?
Aura-seer: Of course.
   Randi: Then if I were to step behind a wall barely taller than I am, you could determine my location from the aura visible above my head, right?

Randi has told me that no aura-seer has agreed to take this simple test.

When subjected to such scrutiny, crazy-sounding ideas sometimes find support. During the 1700s, scientists scoffed at the notion that meteorites had extraterrestrial origins. When two Yale scientists dared to deviate from the conventional opinion, Thomas Jefferson jeered, "Gentlemen, I would rather believe that those two Yankee Professors would lie than to believe that stones fell from heaven." Sometimes scientific inquiry turns jeers into cheers.

More often, science becomes society's garbage disposal by sending crazy-sounding ideas to the waste heap, atop previous claims of perpetual motion machines, miracle cancer cures, and out-of-body travels into centuries past. Today's "truths" sometimes become tomorrow's fallacies. To sift reality from fantasy, sense from nonsense, therefore requires a scientific attitude: being skeptical but not cynical, open but not gullible.

"To believe with certainty," says a Polish proverb, "we must begin by doubting." As scientists, psychologists approach the world of behavior with a *curious skepticism,* persistently asking two questions: *What do you mean? How do you know?*

When ideas compete, skeptical testing can reveal which ones best match the facts. Do parental behaviors determine children's sexual orientation? Can astrologers predict your future based on the position of the planets at your birth? As we will see, putting such claims to the test has led psychological scientists to doubt them.

"The telephone may be appropriate for our American cousins, but not here, because we have an adequate supply of messenger boys."
British expert group evaluating the invention of the telephone

"They couldn't hit an elephant at this distance."
General John Sedgwick just before being killed during a U.S. Civil War battle, 1864

"The scientist . . . must be free to ask any question, to doubt any assertion, to seek for any evidence, to correct any errors."
Physicist J. Robert Oppenheimer, *Life,* October 10, 1949

"A skeptic is one who is willing to question any truth claim, asking for clarity in definition, consistency in logic, and adequacy of evidence."
Philosopher Paul Kurtz, *The Skeptical Inquirer,* 1994

The Amazing Randi The magician James Randi exemplifies skepticism. He has tested and debunked a variety of psychic phenomena.

Courtesy of the James Randi Education Foundation

Non Sequitur

THE IRRESISTIBLE FORCE MEETS THE IMMOVABLE OBJECT

THE FACTS AS THEY ARE

THE TRUTH AS I SEE IT

WLEY 5-16

Putting a scientific attitude into practice requires not only skepticism but also *humility*—an awareness of our own vulnerability to error and an openness to surprises and new perspectives. In the last analysis, what matters is not my opinion or yours, but the truths nature reveals in response to our questioning. If people or other animals don't behave as our ideas predict, then so much the worse for our ideas. This humble attitude was expressed in one of psychology's early mottos: "The rat is always right."

Historians of science tell us that these three attitudes—curiosity, skepticism, and humility—helped make modern science possible. Many of its founders, including Copernicus and Newton, were people whose religious convictions made them humble before nature and skeptical of mere human authority (Hooykaas, 1972; Merton, 1938). Some deeply religious people today may view science, including psychological science, as a threat. Yet, notes sociologist Rodney Stark (2003a,b), the scientific revolution was led mostly by deeply religious people acting on the idea that "in order to love and honor God, it is necessary to fully appreciate the wonders of his handiwork."

Of course, scientists, like anyone else, can have big egos and may cling to their preconceptions. We all view nature through the spectacles of our preconceived ideas. Nevertheless, the ideal that unifies psychologists with all scientists is the curious, skeptical, humble scrutiny of competing ideas. As a community, scientists check and recheck one another's findings and conclusions.

Critical Thinking

The scientific attitude prepares us to think smarter. Smart thinking, called **critical thinking,** examines assumptions, discerns hidden values, evaluates evidence, and assesses conclusions. Whether reading a news report or listening to a conversation, critical thinkers ask questions. Like scientists, they wonder, How do they know that? What is this person's agenda? Is the conclusion based on anecdote and gut feelings, or on evidence? Does the evidence justify a cause-effect conclusion? What alternative explanations are possible?

Has psychology's critical inquiry been open to surprising findings? The answer is plainly yes. Believe it or not . . .

▶ massive losses of brain tissue early in life may have minimal long-term effects.
▶ within days, newborns can recognize their mother's <u>odor</u> and <u>voice</u>.
▶ brain damage can leave a person able to learn new skills yet unaware of such learning.
▶ diverse groups—men and women, old and young, rich and middle class, those with disabilities and without—report roughly comparable levels of personal happiness.
▶ electroconvulsive therapy (delivering an electric shock to the brain) is often a very effective treatment for <u>severe depression</u>.

"My deeply held belief is that if a god anything like the traditional sort exists, our curiosity and intelligence are provided by such a god. We would be unappreciative of those gifts . . . if we suppressed our passion to explore the universe and ourselves."

Carl Sagan, *Broca's Brain,* 1979

"The real purpose of the scientific method is to make sure Nature hasn't misled you into thinking you know something you don't actually know."

Robert M. Pirsig, *Zen and the Art of Motorcycle Maintenance,* 1974

critical thinking thinking that does not blindly accept arguments and conclusions. Rather, it examines assumptions, discerns hidden values, evaluates evidence, and assesses conclusions.

And has critical inquiry convincingly debunked popular presumptions? The answer is again yes. The evidence indicates that . . .

▶ sleepwalkers are _not_ acting out their dreams.

▶ our past experiences are _not_ all recorded verbatim in our brains; with brain stimulation or hypnosis, one _cannot_ simply "hit the replay button" and relive long-buried or repressed memories.

▶ most people do _not_ suffer from unrealistically low self-esteem, and high self-esteem is not all good.

▶ opposites do _not_ generally attract.

In each of these instances and more, what has been learned is not what is widely believed.

▶‖ Frequently Asked Questions About Psychology

You are now prepared to think critically about psychological matters. Yet, even knowing this much, you may still be approaching psychology with a mixture of curiosity and apprehension. So before we plunge in, let's entertain some frequently asked questions.

2-3 Can laboratory experiments illuminate everyday life?

When you see or hear about psychological research, do you ever wonder whether people's behavior in the lab will predict their behavior in real life? For example, does detecting the blink of a faint red light in a dark room have anything useful to say about flying a plane at night? After viewing a violent, sexually explicit film, does an aroused man's increased willingness to push buttons that he thinks will electrically shock a woman really say anything about whether violent pornography makes a man more likely to abuse a woman?

Before you answer, consider: The experimenter _intends_ the laboratory environment to be a simplified reality—one that simulates and controls important features of everyday life. Just as a wind tunnel lets airplane designers re-create airflow forces under controlled conditions, a laboratory experiment lets psychologists re-create psychological forces under controlled conditions.

An experiment's purpose is not to re-create the exact behaviors of everyday life but to test _theoretical principles_ (Mook, 1983). In aggression studies, deciding whether to push a button that delivers a shock may not be the same as slapping someone in the face, but the principle is the same. _It is the resulting principles—not the specific findings—that help explain everyday behaviors._

When psychologists apply laboratory research on aggression to actual violence, they are applying theoretical principles of aggressive behavior, principles they have refined through many experiments. Similarly, it is the principles of the visual system, developed from experiments in artificial settings (such as looking at red lights in the dark), that we apply to more complex behaviors such as night flying. And many investigations show that principles derived in the laboratory do typically generalize to the everyday world (Anderson et al., 1999).

The point to remember: Psychologists' concerns lie less with particular behaviors than with the general principles that help explain many behaviors.

2-4 Does behavior depend on one's culture and gender?

What can psychological studies done in one time and place, often with White Europeans or North Americans, really tell us about people in general? As we will see time and again, **culture**—shared ideas and behaviors that one generation passes on to the next—matters. Our culture shapes our behavior. It influences our standards of

culture the enduring behaviors, ideas, attitudes, and traditions shared by a group of people and transmitted from one generation to the next.

Ami Vitale/Getty Images

A cultured greeting Because culture shapes people's understanding of social behavior, actions that seem ordinary to us may seem quite odd to visitors from far away. Yet underlying these differences are powerful similarities. Supporters of newly elected leaders everywhere typically greet them with pleased deference, though not necessarily with bows and folded hands, as in India. Here influential and popular politician Sonia Gandhi greets some of her constituents shortly after her election.

"All people are the same; only their habits differ."

Confucius, 551–479 B.C.

"Rats are very similar to humans except that they are not stupid enough to purchase lottery tickets."

Dave Barry, July 2, 2002

promptness and frankness, our attitudes toward premarital sex and varying body shapes, our tendency to be casual or formal, our willingness to make eye contact, our conversational distance, and much, much more. Being aware of such differences, we can restrain our assumptions that others will think and act as we do. Given the growing mixing and clashing of cultures, our need for such awareness is urgent.

It is also true, however, that our shared biological heritage unites us as a universal human family. The same underlying processes guide people everywhere:

▶ People diagnosed with dyslexia, a reading disorder, exhibit the same brain malfunction whether they are Italian, French, or British (Paulesu et al., 2001).

▶ Variation in languages may impede communication across cultures. Yet all languages share deep principles of grammar, and people from opposite hemispheres can communicate with a smile or a frown.

▶ People in different cultures vary in feelings of loneliness. But across cultures, loneliness is magnified by shyness, low self-esteem, and being unmarried (Jones et al., 1985; Rokach et al., 2002).

We are each in certain respects like all others, like some others, and like no other. Studying people of all races and cultures helps us discern our similarities and our differences, our human kinship and our diversity.

You will see throughout this book that gender matters, too. Researchers report gender differences in what we dream, in how we express and detect emotions, and in our risk for alcohol dependence, depression, and eating disorders. Gender differences fascinate us, and studying them is potentially beneficial. For example, many researchers believe that women carry on conversations more readily to build relationships, while men talk more to give information and advice (Tannen, 1990). Knowing this difference can help us prevent conflicts and misunderstandings in everyday relationships.

But again, psychologically as well as biologically, women and men are overwhelmingly similar. Whether female or male, we learn to walk at about the same age. We experience the same sensations of light and sound. We feel the same pangs of hunger, desire, and fear. We exhibit similar overall intelligence and well-being.

The point to remember: Even when specific attitudes and behaviors vary by gender or across cultures, as they often do, the underlying processes are much the same.

2-5 Why do psychologists study animals, and is it ethical to experiment on animals?

Many psychologists study animals because they find them fascinating. They want to understand how different species learn, think, and behave. Psychologists also study animals to learn about people, by doing experiments permissible only with animals. Human physiology resembles that of many other animals. We humans are not *like* animals; we *are* animals. Animal experiments have therefore led to treatments for human diseases—insulin for diabetes, vaccines to prevent polio and rabies, transplants to replace defective organs.

Likewise, the same processes by which humans see, exhibit emotion, and become obese are present in rats and monkeys. To discover more about the basics of human learning, researchers even study sea slugs. To understand how a combustion engine works, you would do better to study a lawn mower's engine than a Mercedes'. Like Mercedes engines, human nervous systems are complex. But the simplicity of the sea slug's nervous system is precisely what makes it so revealing of the neural mechanisms of learning.

If we share important similarities with other animals, then should we not respect them? "We cannot defend our scientific work with animals on the basis of the similarities between them and ourselves and then defend it morally on the basis of differences," noted Roger Ulrich (1991). The animal protection movement protests the use of animals in psychological, biological, and medical research. Researchers remind us that the animals used worldwide each year in research are but a fraction of 1 percent of the billions of animals killed annually for food. And yearly, for every dog or cat used in an experiment and cared for under humane regulations, 50 others are killed in humane animal shelters (Goodwin & Morrison, 1999).

Some animal protection organizations want to replace experiments on animals with naturalistic observation. Many animal researchers respond that this is not a question of good versus evil but of compassion for animals versus compassion for people. How many of us would have attacked Louis Pasteur's experiments with rabies, which caused some dogs to suffer but led to a vaccine that spared millions of people (and dogs) from agonizing death? And would we really wish to have deprived ourselves of the animal research that led to effective methods of training children with mental disorders; of understanding aging; and of relieving fears and depression? The answers to such questions vary by culture. In Gallup surveys in Canada and the United States, about 60 percent of adults deem medical testing on animals "morally acceptable." In Britain, only 37 percent do (Mason, 2003).

Out of this heated debate, two issues emerge. The basic one is whether it is right to place the well-being of humans above that of animals. In experiments on stress and cancer, is it right that mice get tumors in the hope that people might not? Should some monkeys be exposed to an HIV-like virus in the search for an AIDS vaccine? Is our use and consumption of other animals as natural as the behavior of carnivorous hawks, cats, and whales? Defenders of research on animals argue that anyone who has eaten a hamburger, worn leather shoes, tolerated hunting and fishing, or supported the extermination of crop-destroying or plague-carrying pests has already agreed that, yes, it is sometimes permissible to sacrifice animals for the sake of human well-being.

Scott Plous (1993) notes, however, that our compassion for animals varies, as does our compassion for people—based on their perceived similarity to us. We feel more attraction, give more help, and act less aggressively toward similar others. Likewise, we value animals according to their perceived kinship with us. Thus, primates and companion pets get top priority. (Western people raise or trap mink and foxes for their fur, but not dogs or cats.) Other mammals occupy the second rung on the privilege ladder, followed by birds, fish, and reptiles on the third rung, with insects at the bottom. In deciding which animals have rights, we each draw our own cut-off line somewhere across the animal kingdom.

If we give human life first priority, the second issue is the priority we give to the well-being of animals in research. What safeguards should protect them? Most researchers today feel ethically obligated to enhance the well-being of captive animals and protect them from needless suffering. In one survey of animal researchers, 98 percent or more supported government regulations protecting primates, dogs, and cats, and 74 percent supported regulations providing for the humane care of rats and mice (Plous & Herzog, 2000). Many professional associations and funding agencies already have such guidelines. For example, British Psychological Society guidelines call for housing animals under reasonably natural living conditions, with companions for social animals (Lea, 2000). American Psychological Association (2002) guidelines mandate ensuring the "comfort, health, and humane treatment" of animals, and of minimizing "infection, illness, and pain of animal subjects." Humane care also leads to more effective science, because pain and stress would distort the animals' behavior during experiments.

"I believe that to prevent, cripple, or needlessly complicate the research that can relieve animal and human suffering is profoundly inhuman, cruel, and immoral."
Psychologist Neal Miller, 1983

"Please do not forget those of us who suffer from incurable diseases or disabilities who hope for a cure through research that requires the use of animals."
Psychologist Dennis Feeney, 1987

"The righteous know the needs of their animals."
Proverbs 12:10

Animal research benefiting animals Thanks partly to research on the benefits of novelty, control, and stimulation, these gorillas are enjoying an improved quality of life in New York's Bronx Zoo.

Ami Vitale/Getty Images

"The greatness of a nation can be judged by the way its animals are treated."

Mahatma Gandhi, 1869–1948

Animals have themselves benefited from animal research. One Ohio team of research psychologists measured stress hormone levels in samples of millions of dogs brought each year to animal shelters. They devised handling and stroking methods to reduce stress and ease the dogs' transition to adoptive homes (Tuber et al., 1999). In New York, formerly listless and idle Bronx Zoo animals now stave off boredom by working for their supper, as they would in the wild (Stewart, 2002). Other studies have helped improve care and management in animals' natural habitats. By revealing our behavioral kinship with animals and the remarkable intelligence of chimpanzees, gorillas, and other animals, experiments have also led to increased empathy and protection for them. At its best, a psychology concerned for humans and sensitive to animals serves the welfare of both.

2-6   Is it ethical to experiment on people?

If the image of researchers delivering supposed electric shocks troubles you, you may be relieved to know that in most psychological studies, especially those with human participants, blinking lights, flashing words, and pleasant social interactions are more common.

Occasionally, though, researchers do temporarily stress or deceive people, but only when they believe it is essential to a justifiable end, such as understanding and controlling violent behavior or studying mood swings. Such experiments wouldn't work if the participants knew all there was to know about the experiment beforehand. Wanting to be helpful, the participants might try to confirm the researcher's predictions.

Ethical principles developed by the American Psychological Association (1992), by the British Psychological Society (1993), and by psychologists internationally (Pettifor, 2004), urge investigators to (1) obtain the informed consent of potential participants, (2) protect them from harm and discomfort, (3) treat information about individual participants confidentially, and (4) fully explain the research afterward. Moreover, most universities today screen research proposals through an ethics committee that safeguards the well-being of every participant.

The ideal is for a researcher to be sufficiently informative *and* considerate that participants will leave feeling at least as good about themselves as when they came in. Better yet, they should be repaid by having learned something. If treated respectfully, most participants enjoy or accept their engagement (Epley & Huff, 1998; Kimmel, 1998). Indeed, say psychology's defenders, professors provoke much greater anxiety by giving and returning course exams than do researchers in the typical experiment.

Much research occurs outside of university laboratories, in places where there may be no ethics committees. For example, retail stores routinely survey people, photograph their purchasing behavior, track their buying patterns, and test the effectiveness of advertising. Curiously, such research attracts less attention than the scientific research done to advance human understanding.

2-7 Is psychology free of value judgments?

Psychology is definitely not value-free. Values affect what we study, how we study it, and how we interpret results. Researchers' values influence their choice of topics. Should we study worker productivity or worker morale? Sex discrimination or gender differences? Conformity or independence? Values can also color "the facts." As we noted earlier, our preconceptions can bias our observations and interpretations; sometimes we see what we want or expect to see (**FIGURE 2.1**).

Even the words we use to describe something can reflect our values. Are the sex acts that an individual does not practice "perversions" or "sexual variations"? Both in and out of psychology, labels describe and labels evaluate: The same holds true in everyday speech. One person's "rigidity" is another's "consistency." One person's "faith" is another's "fanaticism." Our labeling someone as "firm" or "stubborn," "careful" or "picky," "discreet" or "secretive" reveals our feelings.

Popular applications of psychology also contain hidden values. If you defer to "professional" guidance about how to live—how to raise children, how to achieve self-fulfillment, what to do with sexual feelings, how to get ahead at work—you are accepting value-laden advice. A science of behavior and mental processes can certainly help us reach our goals, but it cannot decide what those goals should be.

If some people see psychology as merely common sense, others have a different concern—that it is becoming dangerously powerful. Is it an accident that astronomy is the oldest science and psychology the youngest? To some people, exploring the external universe seems far safer than exploring our own inner universe. Might psychology, they ask, be used to manipulate people?

Knowledge, like all power, can be used for good or evil. Nuclear power has been used to light up cities—and to demolish them. Persuasive power has been used to educate people—and to deceive them. Although psychology does indeed have the power to deceive, its purpose is to enlighten. Every day, psychologists are exploring ways to enhance learning, creativity, and compassion. Psychology speaks to many of our world's great problems—war, overpopulation, prejudice, family crises, crime—all of which involve attitudes and behaviors. Psychology also speaks to our deepest longings—for nourishment, for love, for happiness. Psychology cannot address all of life's great questions, but it speaks to some mighty important ones.

FIGURE 2.1 **What do you see?** People interpret ambiguous information to fit their preconceptions. Did you see a duck or a rabbit? Before showing some friends this image, ask them if they can see the duck lying on its back (or the bunny in the grass). (From Shepard, 1990.)

"It is doubtless impossible to approach any human problem with a mind free from bias." Simone de Beauvoir, *The Second Sex*, 1953

Psychology speaks In making its historic 1954 school desegregation decision, the U.S. Supreme Court cited the expert testimony and research of psychologists Kenneth Clark and Mamie Phipps Clark (1947). The Clarks reported that, when given a choice between Black and White dolls, most African-American children chose the White doll, which seemingly indicated internalized anti-Black prejudice.

REVIEW

Thinking Critically With Psychological Science

2-1 **Why are the answers that flow from the scientific approach more reliable than those based on intuition and common sense?** Although common sense often serves us well, we are prone to *hindsight bias* (also called the "I-knew-it-all-along phenomenon"), the tendency to believe, after learning an outcome, that we would have foreseen it. We also are routinely overconfident of our judgments, thanks partly to our bias to seek information that confirms them. Although limited by the testable questions it can address, scientific inquiry can help us sift reality from illusion and restrain the biases of our unaided intuition.

2-2 **What are three main components of the scientific attitude?** The three components of the scientific attitude are (1) a curious eagerness to (2) skeptically scrutinize competing ideas and (3) an open-minded humility before nature. This attitude carries into everyday life as *critical thinking,* which examines assumptions, discerns hidden values, evaluates evidence, and assesses outcomes. Putting ideas, even crazy-sounding ideas, to the test helps us winnow sense from nonsense.

2-3 **Can laboratory experiments illuminate everyday life?** By intentionally creating a controlled, artificial environment in the lab, researchers aim to test theoretical principles. These general principles help explain everyday behaviors.

2-4 **Does behavior depend on one's culture and gender?** Attitudes and behaviors vary across *cultures,* but the underlying principles vary much less because of our human kinship. Although gender differences tend to capture attention, it is important to remember our greater gender similarities.

2-5 **Why do psychologists study animals, and is it ethical to experiment on animals?** Some psychologists are primarily interested in animal behavior. Others study animals to better understand the physiological and psychological processes shared by humans. Under ethical and legal guidelines, animals used in experiments rarely experience pain. Nevertheless, animal rights groups raise an important issue: Even if it leads to the relief of human suffering, is an animal's temporary suffering justified?

2-6 **Is it ethical to experiment on people?** Researchers may temporarily stress or deceive people in order to learn something important. Professional ethical standards provide guidelines concerning the treatment of both human and animal participants.

2-7 **Is psychology free of value judgments?** Psychologists' values influence their choice of research topics, their theories and observations, their labels for behavior, and their professional advice. Applications of psychology's principles have been used mainly in the service of humanity.

Terms and Concepts to Remember

hindsight bias, p. 15   culture, p. 19
critical thinking, p. 18

Test Yourself

1. What is the scientific attitude, and why is it important for critical thinking?

2. How are human and animal research subjects protected?

(Answers to the Test Yourself questions can be found in Appendix B at the end of the book.)

Ask Yourself

1. How might critical thinking help us assess someone's interpretations of people's dreams or their claims to communicate with the dead?

2. Were any of the Frequently Asked Questions your questions? Do you have other questions or concerns about psychology?

∞ WEB

Multiple-choice self-tests and more may be found at
www.worthpublishers.com/myers

MODULE 3

Research Strategies: How Psychologists Ask and Answer Questions

▶‖ How *Do* Psychologists Ask and Answer Questions?

Psychologists arm their scientific attitude with the *scientific method.* Psychological science evaluates competing ideas with careful observation and rigorous analysis. In its attempt to describe and explain human nature, it welcomes hunches and plausible-sounding theories. And it puts them to the test. If a theory works—if the data support its predictions—so much the better for that theory. If the predictions fail, the theory will be revised or rejected.

The Scientific Method

3-1 How do theories advance psychological science?

In everyday conversation, we often use *theory* to mean "mere hunch." In science, however, theory is linked with observation. A scientific **theory** *explains* through an integrated set of principles that *organizes* observations and *predicts* behaviors or events. By organizing isolated facts, a theory *simplifies*. There are too many facts about behavior to remember them all. By linking facts and bridging them to deeper principles, a theory offers a useful summary. As we connect the observed dots, a coherent picture emerges.

A good theory of depression, for example, helps us organize countless depression-related observations into a short list of principles. Imagine that we observe over and over that people with depression describe their past, present, and future in gloomy terms. We might therefore theorize that at the heart of depression lies low self-esteem. So far so good: Our self-esteem principle neatly summarizes a long list of facts about people with depression.

Yet no matter how reasonable a theory may sound—and low self-esteem seems a reasonable explanation of depression—we must put it to the test. A good theory produces testable predictions, called **hypotheses.** By enabling us to test and to reject or revise the theory, such predictions give direction to research. They specify what results would support the theory and what results would disconfirm it. To test our self-esteem theory of depression, we might assess people's self-esteem by having them respond to statements such as "I have good ideas" and "I am fun to be with." Then we could see whether, as we hypothesized, people who report poorer self-images also score higher on a depression scale (**FIGURE 3.1** on the next page).

In testing our theory, we should be aware that it can bias subjective observations. Having theorized that depression springs from low self-esteem, we may see what we expect. We may perceive depressed people's neutral comments as self-disparaging. The urge to see what we expect is an ever-present temptation, in the laboratory and outside of it. According to the bipartisan U.S. Senate Select Committee on Intelligence (2004), preconceived expectations that Iraq had weapons of mass destruction

theory an explanation using an integrated set of principles that organizes observations and predicts behaviors or events.

hypothesis a testable prediction, often implied by a theory.

FIGURE 3.1 The scientific method A self-correcting process for asking questions and observing nature's answers.

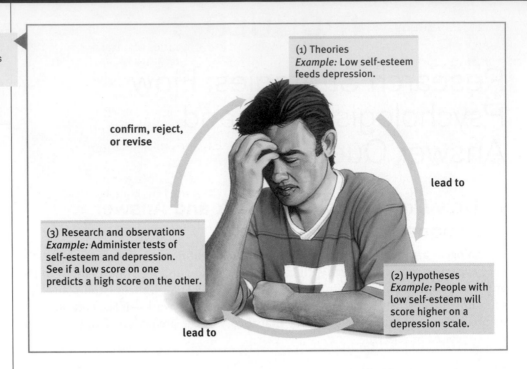

(1) Theories
Example: Low self-esteem feeds depression.

lead to

(2) Hypotheses
Example: People with low self-esteem will score higher on a depression scale.

lead to

(3) Research and observations
Example: Administer tests of self-esteem and depression. See if a low score on one predicts a high score on the other.

confirm, reject, or revise

led intelligence analysts to wrongly interpret ambiguous observations as confirming that theory, and this theory-driven conclusion then led to the preemptive U.S. invasion of Iraq.

As a check on their biases, psychologists report their research with precise **operational definitions** of procedures and concepts. *Hunger,* for example, might be defined as "hours without eating," *generosity* as "money contributed." Such carefully worded statements should allow others to **replicate** (repeat) the original observations. If other researchers re-create a study with different participants and materials and get similar results, then our confidence in the finding's reliability grows. The first study of hindsight bias aroused psychologists' curiosity. Now, after many successful replications with differing people and questions, we feel sure of the phenomenon's power.

In the end, our theory will be useful if it (1) effectively *organizes* a range of self-reports and observations, and (2) implies clear *predictions* that anyone can use to check the theory or to derive practical applications. (If we boost people's self-esteem, will their depression lift?) Eventually, our research will probably lead to a revised theory that better organizes and predicts what we know about depression.

As we will see next, we can test our hypotheses and refine our theories using *descriptive* methods (which describe behaviors, often using case studies, surveys, or naturalistic observations), *correlational* methods (which associate different factors), and *experimental* methods (which manipulate factors to discover their effects). To think critically about popular psychology claims, we need to recognize these methods and know what conclusions they allow.

Description

3-2   How do psychologists observe and describe behavior?

The starting point of any science is description. In everyday life, all of us observe and describe people, often drawing conclusions about why they behave as they do. Professional psychologists do much the same, though more objectively and systematically.

|| Good theories explain by

1. organizing and linking observed facts.

2. implying hypotheses that offer testable predictions and, sometimes, practical applications. ||

operational definition a statement of the procedures (operations) used to define research variables. For example, *human intelligence* may be operationally defined as what an intelligence test measures.

replication repeating the essence of a research study, usually with different participants in different situations, to see whether the basic finding extends to other participants and circumstances.

case study an observation technique in which one person is studied in depth in the hope of revealing universal principles.

survey a technique for ascertaining the self-reported attitudes or behaviors of a particular group, usually by questioning a representative, random sample of the group.

The Case Study

Among the oldest research methods, the **case study** examines one individual in depth in hopes of revealing things true of us all. Some examples: Much of our early knowledge about the brain came from case studies of individuals who suffered a particular impairment after damage to a certain brain region. Jean Piaget taught us about children's thinking after carefully observing and questioning only a few children. Studies of only a few chimpanzees have revealed their capacity for understanding and language. Intensive case studies are sometimes very revealing.

Case studies often suggest directions for further study, and they show us what *can* happen. But individual cases may mislead us if the individual being studied is atypical. Unrepresentative information can lead to mistaken judgments and false conclusions. Indeed, anytime a researcher mentions a finding ("Smokers die younger: 95 percent of men over 85 are nonsmokers") someone is sure to offer a contradictory anecdote ("Well, I have an uncle who smoked two packs a day and lived to be 89"). Dramatic stories and personal experiences (even psychological case examples) command our attention, and they are easily remembered. Which of the following do you find more memorable? (1) "In one study of 1300 dream reports concerning a kidnapped child, only 5 percent correctly envisioned the child as dead (Murray & Wheeler, 1937)." (2) "I know a man who dreamed his sister was in a car accident, and two days later she died in a head-on collision!" Numbers can be numbing, but the plural of *anecdote* is not *evidence*. As psychologist Gordon Allport (1954, p. 9) said, "Given a thimbleful of [dramatic] facts we rush to make generalizations as large as a tub."

The point to remember: Individual cases can suggest fruitful ideas. What's true of all of us can be glimpsed in any one of us. But to discern the general truths that cover individual cases, we must answer questions with other research methods.

The Survey

The **survey** method looks at many cases in less depth. A survey asks people to report their behavior or opinions. Questions about everything from sexual practices to political opinions are put to the public. Harris and Gallup polls have revealed that 72 percent of Americans think there is too much TV violence, 89 percent favor equal job opportunities for homosexual people, 89 percent are facing high stress, and 96 percent would like to change something about their appearance. In Britain, seven in ten 18- to 29-year-olds support gay marriage; among those over 50, about the same percentage oppose it (a generation gap found in many Western countries). But asking questions is tricky, and the answers often depend on the ways questions are worded and respondents are chosen.

Wording Effects Even subtle changes in the order or wording of questions can have major effects. Should cigarette ads or pornography be allowed on television? People are much more likely to approve "not allowing" such things than "forbidding" or "censoring" them. In one national survey, only 27 percent of Americans approved of "government censorship" of media sex and violence, though 66 percent approved of "more restrictions on what is shown on television" (Lacayo, 1995). People are similarly much more approving of "aid to the needy" than of "welfare," of "affirmative action" than of "preferential treatment," and of "revenue enhancers" than of "taxes." Because wording is such a delicate matter, critical thinkers will reflect on how the phrasing of a question might affect people's expressed opinions.

Random Sampling We can describe human experience by drawing on memorable anecdotes and personal experience. But for an accurate picture of a whole population's attitudes and experience, there's only one game in town—the representative sample.

The case of the conversational chimpanzee In case studies of chimpanzees, psychologists have asked whether language is uniquely human. Here Nim Chimpsky signs *hug* as his trainer, psychologist Herbert Terrace, shows him the puppet Ernie. But is Nim really using language?

"'Well my dear,' said Miss Marple, 'human nature is very much the same everywhere, and of course, one has opportunities of observing it at closer quarters in a village.'"
Agatha Christie, *The Tuesday Club Murders,* 1933

"How would you like me to answer that question? As a member of my ethnic group, educational class, income group, or religious category?"

This Modern World by Tom Tomorrow © 1991.

|| With very large samples, estimates become quite reliable. *E* is estimated to represent 12.7 percent of the letters in written English. *E*, in fact, is 12.3 percent of the 925,141 letters in Melville's *Moby Dick*, 12.4 percent of the 586,747 letters in Dickens' *A Tale of Two Cities*, and 12.1 percent of the 3,901,021 letters in 12 of Mark Twain's works (Chance News, 1997). ||

We can extend this point to everyday thinking, as we generalize from samples we observe, especially vivid cases. Given (a) a statistical summary of a professor's student evaluations and (b) the vivid comments of two irate students, an administrator's impression of the professor may be influenced as much by the two unhappy students as by the many favorable evaluations in the statistical summary. The temptation to generalize from a few vivid but unrepresentative cases is nearly irresistible.

The point to remember: The best basis for generalizing is from a representative sample of cases.

So how do you obtain a representative sample—say, of the students at your college or university? How could you choose a group that would represent the total student **population,** the whole group you want to study and describe? Typically, you would choose a **random sample,** in which every person in the entire group has an equal chance of participating. This means you would not send each student a questionnaire. (The conscientious people who return it would not be a random sample.) Rather, you might number the names in the general student listing and then use a random number generator to pick the participants for your survey. Large representative samples are better than small ones, but a small representative sample of 100 is better than an unrepresentative sample of 500.

Political pollsters sample voters in national election surveys just this way. Using only 1500 randomly sampled people, drawn from all areas of a country, they can provide a remarkably accurate snapshot of the nation's opinions. Without random sampling, large samples—including call-in phone samples and TV or Web site polls—often merely give misleading results.

The point to remember: Before accepting survey findings, think critically: Consider the sample. You cannot compensate for an unrepresentative sample by simply adding more people.

Naturalistic Observation

A third descriptive method records behavior in natural environments. These **naturalistic observations** range from watching chimpanzee societies in the jungle, to unobtrusively videotaping (and later systematically analyzing) parent-child interactions in different cultures, to recording racial differences in students' self-seating patterns in the lunchroom at school.

Like the case study and survey methods, naturalistic observation does not *explain* behavior. It *describes* it. Nevertheless, descriptions can be revealing. We once thought, for example, that only humans use tools. Then naturalistic observation revealed that chimpanzees sometimes insert a stick in a termite mound and withdraw it, eating the stick's load of termites. Such unobtrusive naturalistic observations paved the way for later studies of animal thinking, language, and emotion, which further expanded our understanding of our fellow animals. "Observations, made in the natural habitat, helped to show that the societies and behavior of animals are far more complex than previously supposed," notes chimpanzee observer Jane Goodall (1998). For example, chimpanzees and baboons have been observed using deception. Psychologists Andrew Whiten and Richard Byrne (1988) repeatedly saw one young baboon pretending to have been attacked by another as a tactic to get its mother to drive the other baboon away from its food. Moreover, the more developed a primate species' brain, the more likely it is that the animals will display deceptive behaviors (Byrne & Corp, 2004).

Naturalistic observations also illuminate human behavior. Here are three findings you might enjoy.

▶ *A funny finding.* We humans laugh 30 times more often in social situations than in solitary situations. (Have you noticed how seldom you laugh when alone?) As we laugh, 17 muscles contort our mouth and squeeze our eyes, and we emit a series of 75-millisecond vowel-like sounds that are spaced about one-fifth of a second apart (Provine, 2001).

▶ *Sounding out students.* What, really, are introductory psychology students saying and doing during their everyday lives? To find out, Matthias Mehl and James Pennebaker (2003) equipped 52 such students from the University of Texas with electronically activated belt-worn tape recorders. For up to four days, the recorders captured 30 seconds of the students' waking hours every 12.5 minutes, thus enabling the researchers to eavesdrop on more than 10,000 half-minute life slices by the end of the study. On what percentage of the slices do you suppose they found the students talking with someone? What percentage captured the students at a computer keyboard? The answers: 28 and 9 percent. (What percentage of *your* waking hours are spent in these activities?)

▶ *Culture, climate, and the pace of life.* Naturalistic observation also enabled Robert Levine and Ara Norenzayan (1999) to compare the pace of life in 31 countries. (Their operational definition of *pace of life* included walking speed, the speed with which postal clerks completed a simple request, and the accuracy of public clocks.) Their conclusion: Life is fastest paced in Japan and Western Europe, and slower paced in economically less-developed countries. People in colder climates also tend to live at a faster pace (and are more prone to die from heart disease).

Photo by Jack Kearse, Emory University for Yerkes National Primate Research Center

A natural observer Chimpanzee researcher Frans de Waal (2005) reports that "I am a born observer. . . . When picking a seat in a restaurant I want to face as many tables as possible. I enjoy following the social dynamics—love, tension, boredom, antipathy—around me based on body language, which I consider more informative than the spoken word. Since keeping track of others is something I do automatically, becoming a fly on the wall of an ape colony came naturally to me."

Courtesy of Matthias Mehl

An EAR for naturalistic observation Psychologists Matthias Mehl and James Pennebaker have used Electronically Activated Recorders (EAR) to sample naturally occurring slices of daily life.

Naturalistic observation offers interesting snapshots of everyday life, but it does so without controlling for all the factors that may influence behavior. It's one thing to observe the pace of life in various places, but another to understand what makes some people walk faster than others. Yet naturalistic observation, like surveys, can provide data for correlational research, which we consider next.

Correlation

3-3 What are positive and negative correlations, and why do they enable prediction but not cause-effect explanation?

Describing behavior is a first step toward predicting it. Surveys and naturalistic observations often show us that one trait or behavior is related to another. In such cases, we say the two **correlate.** A statistical measure (the **correlation coefficient**) helps us figure how closely two things vary together, and thus how well either one *predicts* the other. Knowing how much aptitude test scores *correlate* with school success tells us how well the scores *predict* school success.

population all the cases in a group being studied, from which samples may be drawn. (*Note:* Except for national studies, this does *not* refer to a country's whole population.)

random sample a sample that fairly represents a population because each member has an equal chance of inclusion.

naturalistic observation observing and recording behavior in naturally occurring situations without trying to manipulate and control the situation.

correlation a measure of the extent to which two factors vary together, and thus of how well either factor predicts the other.

correlation coefficient a statistical index of the relationship between two things (from −1 to +1).

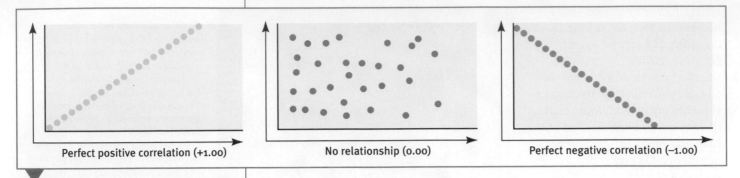

Perfect positive correlation (+1.00)   No relationship (0.00)   Perfect negative correlation (−1.00)

FIGURE 3.2 Scatterplots, showing patterns of correlation Correlations can range from +1.00 (scores on one measure increase in direct proportion to scores on another) to −1.00 (scores on one measure decrease precisely as scores rise on the other).

TABLE 3.1 Height and Temperament of 20 Men

Person	Height in Inches	Temperament
1	80	75
2	63	66
3	61	60
4	79	90
5	74	60
6	69	42
7	62	42
8	75	60
9	77	81
10	60	39
11	64	48
12	76	69
13	71	72
14	66	57
15	73	63
16	70	75
17	63	30
18	71	57
19	68	84
20	70	39

Throughout this book we will often ask how strongly two things are related: For example, how closely related are the personality scores of identical twins? How well do intelligence test scores predict achievement? How closely is stress related to disease?

FIGURE 3.2 contains three **scatterplots,** illustrating the range of possible correlations from a perfect positive to a perfect negative. (Perfect correlations rarely occur in the "real world.") Each dot in a scatterplot represents the scattered values of two variables. A correlation is positive if two sets of scores, such as height and weight, tend to rise or fall together. Saying that a correlation is "negative" says nothing about its strength or weakness. A correlation is negative if two sets of scores relate inversely, one set going up as the other goes down. Tooth brushing and decay correlate negatively. As brushing goes up from zero, tooth decay goes down. A weak correlation, indicating little relationship, has a coefficient near zero.

Here are four news reports of correlational research, some derived from surveys or natural observations. Can you spot which are reporting positive correlations, which negative? (Check your answers at the bottom of this page.)

1. The more young children watch TV, the less they read (Kaiser, 2003).
2. The more sexual content teens see on TV, the more likely they are to have sex (Collins et al., 2004).
3. The longer children are breast-fed, the greater their later academic achievement (Horwood & Fergusson, 1998).
4. The more often adolescents eat breakfast, the lower their body mass (Timlin et al., 2008).[1]

Statistics can help us see what the naked eye sometimes misses. To demonstrate this for yourself, try an imaginary project. Wondering if tall men are more or less easygoing, you collect two sets of scores: men's heights and men's temperaments. You measure the heights of 20 men, and you have someone else independently assess their temperaments (from zero for extremely calm to 100 for highly reactive).

With all the relevant data right in front of you (**TABLE 3.1**), can you tell whether there is (1) a positive correlation between height and reactive temperament, (2) very little or no correlation, or (3) a negative correlation?

Comparing the columns in Table 3.1, most people detect very little relationship between height and temperament. In fact, the correlation in this imaginary example is moderately positive, +0.63, as we can see if we display the data as a scatterplot. In **FIGURE 3.3,** moving from left to right, the upward, oval-shaped slope of the cluster of points shows that our two imaginary sets of scores (height and reactivity) tend to rise together.

If we fail to see a relationship when data are presented as systematically as in Table 3.1, how much less likely are we to notice them in everyday life? To see what is right in front of us, we sometimes need statistical illumination. We can easily see

[1] Answers to correlation questions: 1. negative, 2. positive, 3. positive, 4. negative.

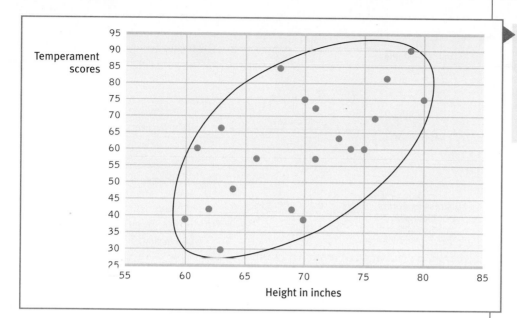

FIGURE 3.3 Scatterplot for height and temperament This display of data from 20 imagined people (each represented by a data point) reveals an upward slope, indicating a positive correlation. The considerable scatter of the data indicates the correlation is much lower than +1.0.

evidence of gender discrimination when given statistically summarized information about job level, seniority, performance, gender, and salary. But we often see no discrimination when the same information dribbles in, case by case (Twiss et al., 1989).

The point to remember: A correlation coefficient helps us see the world more clearly by revealing the extent to which two things relate.

Correlation and Causation

Correlations help us predict. Low self-esteem correlates with (and therefore predicts) depression. (This correlation might be indicated by a correlation coefficient, or just by a finding that people who score on the lower half of a self-esteem scale have an elevated depression rate.) So, does low self-esteem *cause* depression? If, based on the correlational evidence, you assume that it does, you have much company. A nearly irresistible thinking error is assuming that an association, sometimes presented as a correlation coefficient, proves causation. But no matter how strong the relationship, it does not *prove* anything!

As options 2 and 3 in **FIGURE 3.4** on the next page show, we'd get the same negative correlation between low self-esteem and depression if depression caused people to be down on themselves, or if some third factor—such as heredity or brain chemistry—caused both low self-esteem and depression. Among men, for example, length of marriage correlates positively with hair loss—because both are associated with a third factor, age.

This point is so important—so basic to thinking smarter with psychology—that it merits one more example, from a survey of over 12,000 adolescents. The study found that the more teens feel loved by their parents, the less likely they are to behave in unhealthy ways—having early sex, smoking, abusing alcohol and drugs, exhibiting violence (Resnick et al., 1997). "Adults have a powerful effect on their children's behavior right through the high school years," gushed an Associated Press (AP) story reporting the finding. But this correlation comes with no built-in cause-effect arrow. Said differently (turn the volume up here), *association does not prove causation.*[2] Thus, the AP could as well have reported, "Well-behaved teens feel their parents' love and approval; out-of-bounds teens more often think their parents are disapproving jerks."

scatterplots a graphed cluster of dots, each of which represents the values of two variables. The slope of the points suggests the direction of the relationship between the two variables. The amount of scatter suggests the strength of the correlation (little scatter indicates high correlation).

Correlation need not mean causation Length of marriage correlates with hair loss in men. Does this mean that marriage causes men to lose their hair (or that balding men make better husbands)? In this case, as in many others, a third factor obviously explains the correlation: Golden anniversaries and baldness both accompany aging.

[2]Because many associations are stated as correlations, the famously worded principle is "Correlation does not prove causation." That's true, but it's also true of associations verified by other nonexperimental statistics (Hatfield et al., 2006).

FIGURE 3.4 Three possible cause-effect relationships People low in self-esteem are more likely to report depression than are those high in self-esteem. One possible explanation of this negative correlation is that a bad self-image causes depressed feelings. But, as the diagram indicates, other cause-effect relationships are possible.

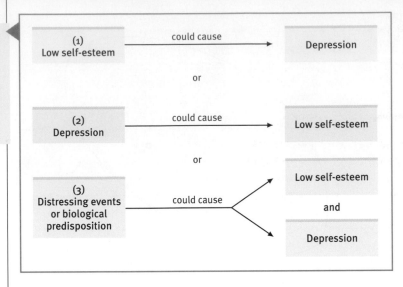

(1) Low self-esteem	could cause → Depression
	or
(2) Depression	could cause → Low self-esteem
	or
(3) Distressing events or biological predisposition	could cause → Low self-esteem and Depression

The point to remember: Correlation indicates the possibility of a cause-effect relationship, but it does not prove causation. Knowing that two events are associated need not tell us anything about causation. Remember this principle and you will be wiser as you read and hear news of scientific studies.

Illusory Correlations

3-4 What are illusory correlations?

Correlation coefficients make visible the relationships we might otherwise miss. They also restrain our "seeing" relationships that actually do not exist. A perceived but nonexistent correlation is an **illusory correlation.** When we *believe* there is a relationship between two things, we are likely to *notice* and *recall* instances that confirm our belief (Trolier & Hamilton, 1986).

Because we are sensitive to dramatic or unusual events, we are especially likely to notice and remember the occurrence of two such events in sequence—say, a premonition of an unlikely phone call followed by the call. When the call does not follow the premonition, we are less likely to note and remember the nonevent. Illusory correlations help explain many superstitious beliefs, such as the presumption that infertile couples who adopt become more likely to conceive (Gilovich, 1991). Couples who conceive after adopting capture our attention. We're less likely to notice those who adopt and never conceive, or those who conceive without adopting. In other words, illusory correlations occur when we over-rely on the top left cell of **FIGURE 3.5**, ignoring equally essential information in the other cells.

|| A study reported in the *British Medical Journal* found that youths who identify with the goth subculture attempt, more often than other young people, to harm or kill themselves (Young et al., 2006). Can you imagine multiple possible explanations for this association? ||

|| A *New York Times* writer reported a massive survey showing that "adolescents whose parents smoked were 50 percent more likely than children of nonsmokers to report having had sex." He concluded (would you agree?) that the survey indicated a causal effect—that "to reduce the chances that their children will become sexually active at an early age" parents might "quit smoking" (O'Neil, 2002). ||

FIGURE 3.5 Illusory correlation in everyday life Many people believe infertile couples become more likely to conceive a child after adopting a baby. This belief arises from their attention being drawn to such cases. The many couples who adopt without conceiving or conceive without adopting grab less attention. To determine whether there actually is a correlation between adoption and conception, we need data from all four cells in this figure. (From Gilovich, 1991.)

	Conceive	Do not conceive
Adopt	confirming evidence	disconfirming evidence
Do not adopt	disconfirming evidence	confirming evidence

Michael Newman Jr./PhotoEdit

Such illusory thinking helps explain why for so many years people believed (and many still do) that sugar makes children hyperactive, that getting chilled and wet causes people to catch a cold, and that changes in the weather trigger arthritis pain. We are, it seems, prone to perceiving patterns, whether they're there or not.

The point to remember: When we notice random coincidences, we may forget that they are random and instead see them as correlated. Thus, we can easily deceive ourselves by seeing what is not there.

Perceiving Order in Random Events

In our natural eagerness to make sense of our world—what poet Wallace Stevens called our "rage for order"—we look for order even in random data. And we usually find it, because—here's a curious fact of life—*random sequences often don't look random.* Consider a random coin flip: If someone flipped a coin six times, which of the following sequences of heads (H) and tails (T) would be most likely: HHHTTT or HTTHTH or HHHHHH?

Daniel Kahneman and Amos Tversky (1972) found that most people believe HTTHTH would be the most likely random sequence. Actually, all three are equally likely (or, you might say, equally unlikely). A bridge or poker hand of 10 through ace, all of hearts, would seem extraordinary; actually, it would be no more or less likely than any other specific hand of cards (**FIGURE 3.6**).

In actual random sequences, patterns and streaks (such as repeating digits) occur more often than people expect. To demonstrate this phenomenon for myself (as you can do), I flipped a coin 51 times, with these results:

1. H	11. T	21. T	31. T	41. H	51. T
2. T	12. H	22. T	32. T	42. H	
3. T	13. H	23. H	33. T	43. H	
4. T	14. T	24. T	34. T	44. H	
5. H	15. T	25. T	35. T	45. T	
6. H	16. H	26. T	36. H	46. H	
7. H	17. T	27. H	37. T	47. H	
8. T	18. T	28. T	38. T	48. T	
9. T	19. H	29. H	39. H	49. T	
10. T	20. H	30. T	40. T	50. T	

Looking over the sequence, patterns jump out: Tosses 10 to 22 provided an almost perfect pattern of pairs of tails followed by pairs of heads. On tosses 30 to 38 I had a "cold hand," with only one head in eight tosses. But my fortunes immediately reversed with a "hot hand"—seven heads out of the next nine tosses. Similar streaks happen, about as often as one would expect in random sequences, in basketball shooting, baseball hitting, and mutual fund stock pickers' selections (Gilovich et al., 1985; Malkiel, 1989, 1995; Myers, 2002). These sequences often don't look random, and so get overinterpreted ("When you're hot, you're hot!").

What explains these streaky patterns? Was I exercising some sort of paranormal control over my coin? Did I snap out of my tails funk and get in a heads groove? No such explanations are needed, for these are the sorts of streaks found in any random data. Comparing each toss to the next, 24 of the 50 comparisons yielded a changed result—just the sort of near 50-50 result we expect from coin tossing. Despite seeming patterns, the outcome of one toss gives no clue to the outcome of the next.

illusory correlation the perception of a relationship where none exists.

FIGURE 3.6 Two random sequences Your chances of being dealt either of these hands are precisely the same: 1 in 2,598,960.

BIZARRE SEQUENCE OF COMPUTER-GENERATED RANDOM NUMBERS

© 1990 by Sidney Harris/American Scientist magazine.

Bizarre-looking, perhaps. But actually no more unlikely than any other number sequence.

Given enough random events, something weird will happen Angelo and Maria Gallina were the beneficiaries of one of those extraordinary chance events when they won two California lottery games on the same day.

|| On March 11, 1998, Utah's Ernie and Lynn Carey gained three new grandchildren when three of their daughters gave birth—on the same day (*Los Angeles Times*, 1998). ||

"The really unusual day would be one where nothing unusual happens."
Statistician Persi Diaconis, 2002

Jerry Telfer/San Francisco Chronicle

However, some happenings seem so extraordinary that we struggle to conceive an ordinary, chance-related explanation (as applies to our coin tosses). In such cases, statisticians often are less mystified. When Evelyn Marie Adams won the New Jersey lottery *twice*, newspapers reported the odds of her feat as 1 in 17 trillion. Bizarre? Actually, 1 in 17 trillion are indeed the odds that a given person who buys a single ticket for two New Jersey lotteries will win both times. But statisticians Stephen Samuels and George McCabe (1989) reported that, given the millions of people who buy U.S. state lottery tickets, it was "practically a sure thing" that someday, somewhere, someone would hit a state jackpot twice. Indeed, said fellow statisticians Persi Diaconis and Frederick Mosteller (1989), "with a large enough sample, any outrageous thing is likely to happen." An event that happens to but 1 in 1 billion people every day occurs about six times a day, 2000 times a year.

Experimentation

3-5 How do experiments, powered by random assignment, clarify cause and effect?

Happy are they, remarked the Roman poet Virgil, "who have been able to perceive the causes of things." To isolate cause and effect, psychologists can statistically control for other factors. For example, researchers have found that breast-fed infants grow up with somewhat higher intelligence scores than do infants bottle-fed with cow's milk (Angelsen et al., 2001; Mortensen et al., 2002; Quinn et al., 2001). They have also found that breast-fed British babies have been more likely than their bottle-fed counterparts to eventually move into a higher social class (Martin et al., 2007). But the "breast is best" intelligence effect shrinks when researchers compare breast-fed and bottle-fed children from the same families (Der et al., 2006).

So, does this mean that smarter mothers (who in modern countries more often breast-feed) have smarter children? Or, as some researchers believe, do the nutrients of mother's milk contribute to brain development? To help answer this question, researchers have "controlled for" (statistically removed differences in) certain other factors, such as maternal age, education, and income. And they have found that in infant nutrition, mother's milk correlates modestly but positively with later intelligence.

Correlational research cannot control for all possible factors. But researchers can isolate cause and effect with an **experiment.** Experiments enable a researcher to focus on the possible effects of one or more factors by (1) *manipulating the factors of interest* and (2) *holding constant ("controlling") other factors*. With parental permission, a British research team randomly assigned 424 hospital preterm infants either to standard infant formula feedings or to donated breast milk feedings (Lucas et al., 1992). On intelligence tests taken at age 8, the children nourished with breast milk had significantly higher intelligence scores than their formula-fed counterparts.

Random Assignment

No single experiment is conclusive, of course. But by **randomly assigning** infants to one feeding group or the other, researchers were able to hold constant all factors except nutrition. This eliminated alternative explanations and supported the conclusion that breast is indeed best for developing intelligence (at least for preterm infants).

experiment a research method in which an investigator manipulates one or more factors (independent variables) to observe the effect on some behavior or mental process (the dependent variable). By *random assignment* of participants, the experimenter aims to control other relevant factors.

random assignment assigning participants to experimental and control groups by chance, thus minimizing preexisting differences between those assigned to the different groups.

If a behavior (such as test performance) changes when we vary an experimental factor (such as infant nutrition), then we infer the factor is having an effect. *The point to remember:* Unlike correlational studies, which uncover naturally occurring relationships, an experiment manipulates a factor to determine its effect.

Consider, too, how we might assess a therapeutic intervention. Our tendency to seek new remedies when we are ill or emotionally down can produce misleading testimonies. If three days into a cold we start taking vitamin C tablets and find our cold symptoms lessening, we may credit the pills rather than the cold naturally subsiding. If, after nearly failing the first exam, we listen to a "peak learning" subliminal CD and then improve on the next exam, we may credit the CD rather than conclude that our performance has returned to our average. In the 1700s, blood-letting *seemed* effective. Sometimes people improved after the treatment; when they didn't, the practitioner inferred the disease was just too advanced to be reversed. (We, of course, now know that usually blood-letting is a *bad* treatment.) So, whether or not a remedy is truly effective, enthusiastic users will probably endorse it. To find out whether it actually is effective, we must experiment.

And that is precisely how investigators evaluate new drug treatments and new methods of psychological therapy. The participants in these studies are randomly assigned to the research groups and are often *blind* (uninformed) about what treatment, if any, they are receiving. One group receives a treatment (such as medication or other therapy). The other group receives a pseudotreatment—an inert *placebo* (perhaps a pill with no drug in it). If the study is using a **double-blind procedure,** neither the participants nor the research assistants collecting the data will know which group is receiving the treatment. In such studies, researchers can check a treatment's actual effects apart from the participants' belief in its healing powers and the staff's enthusiasm for its potential. Just *thinking* you are getting a treatment can boost your spirits, relax your body, and relieve your symptoms. This **placebo effect** is well documented in reducing pain, depression, and anxiety (Kirsch & Sapirstein, 1998). And the more expensive the placebo, the more "real" it seems to us—a fake pill that costs US$2.50 works better than one costing 10 cents (Waber et al., 2008). To know how effective a therapy really is, researchers must control for a possible placebo effect.

The double-blind procedure is one way to create an **experimental group,** in which people receive the treatment, and a contrasting **control group** that does not receive the treatment. By randomly assigning people to these conditions, researchers can be fairly certain the two groups are otherwise identical. Random assignment roughly equalizes the two groups in age, attitudes, and every other characteristic. With random assignment, as occurred with the infants in the breast milk experiment, we also can conclude that any later differences between people in the experimental and control groups will usually be the result of the treatment.

Independent and Dependent Variables

Here is an even more potent example: The drug Viagra was approved for use after 21 clinical trials. One trial was an experiment in which researchers randomly assigned 329 men with erectile dysfunction to either an experimental group (Viagra takers) or a control group (placebo takers). It was a double-blind procedure—neither the men nor the person who gave them the pills knew which drug they were receiving. The result: At peak doses, 69 percent of Viagra-assisted attempts at intercourse were successful, compared with 22 percent for men receiving the placebo (Goldstein et al., 1998). Viagra worked.

This simple experiment manipulated just one factor: the drug dosage (none versus peak dose). We call this experimental factor the **independent variable** because we can vary it *independently* of other factors, such as the men's age, weight, and personality (which random assignment should control). Experiments examine the effect of one or more independent variables on some measurable behavior, called the

"If I don't think it's going to work, will it still work?"

double-blind procedure an experimental procedure in which both the research participants and the research staff are ignorant (blind) about whether the research participants have received the treatment or a placebo. Commonly used in drug-evaluation studies.

placebo [pluh-SEE-bo; Latin for "I shall please"] **effect** experimental results caused by expectations alone; any effect on behavior caused by the administration of an inert substance or condition, which the recipient assumes is an active agent.

experimental group in an experiment, the group that is exposed to the treatment, that is, to one version of the independent variable.

control group in an experiment, the group that is *not* exposed to the treatment; contrasts with the experimental group and serves as a comparison for evaluating the effect of the treatment.

independent variable the experimental factor that is manipulated; the variable whose effect is being studied.

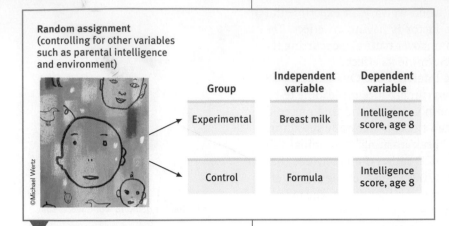

Random assignment (controlling for other variables such as parental intelligence and environment)

Group	Independent variable	Dependent variable
Experimental	Breast milk	Intelligence score, age 8
Control	Formula	Intelligence score, age 8

©Michael Wertz

FIGURE 3.7 Experimentation To discern causation, psychologists may randomly assign some participants to an experimental group, others to a control group. Measuring the dependent variable (intelligence score in later childhood) will determine the effect of the independent variable (type of milk).

‖ Note the distinction between random sampling in surveys (discussed earlier in relation to surveys) and random assignment in experiments (depicted in Figure 3.7). *Random sampling* helps us generalize to a larger population. *Random assignment* controls extraneous influences, which helps us infer cause and effect. ‖

dependent variable because it can vary *depending* on what takes place during the experiment. Both variables are given precise *operational definitions,* which specify the procedures that manipulate the independent variable (the precise drug dosage and timing in this study) or measure the dependent variable (the questions that assessed the men's responses). These definitions answer the "What do you mean?" question with a level of precision that enables others to repeat the study. (See **FIGURE 3.7** for the breast milk experiment's design.)

Let's pause to check your understanding using a simple psychology experiment: To test the effect of perceived ethnicity on the availability of a rental house, Adrian Carpusor and William Loges (2006) sent identically worded e-mail inquiries to 1115 Los Angeles-area landlords. The researchers varied the ethnic connotation of the sender's name and tracked the percentage of positive replies (invitations to view the apartment in person). "Patrick McDougall," "Said Al-Rahman," and "Tyrell Jackson" received, respectively, 89 percent, 66 percent, and 56 percent invitations. In this experiment, what was the independent variable? The dependent variable?[3]

Experiments can also help us evaluate social programs. Do early childhood education programs boost impoverished children's chances for success? What are the effects of different anti-smoking campaigns? Do school sex-education programs reduce teen pregnancies? To answer such questions, we can experiment: If an intervention is welcomed but resources are scarce, we could use a lottery to randomly assign some people (or regions) to experience the new program and others to a control condition. If later the two groups differ, the intervention's effect will be confirmed (Passell, 1993).

Let's recap. A *variable* is anything that can vary (infant nutrition, intelligence, TV exposure—anything within the bounds of what is feasible and ethical). Experiments aim to *manipulate* an *independent* variable, *measure* the *dependent* variable, and *control* all other variables. An experiment has at least two different groups: an *experimental group* and a *comparison* or *control group*. *Random assignment* works to equate the groups before any treatment effects. In this way, an experiment tests the effect of at least one independent variable (what we manipulate) on at least one dependent variable (the outcome we measure). **TABLE 3.2** compares the features of psychology's research methods.

[3]The independent variable, which the researchers manipulated, was the ethnicity-related names. The dependent variable, which they measured, was the positive response rate.

TABLE 3.2 Comparing Research Methods

Research Method	Basic Purpose	How Conducted	What Is Manipulated	Weaknesses
Descriptive	To observe and record behavior	Do case studies, surveys, or naturalistic observations	Nothing	No control of variables; single cases may be misleading
Correlational	To detect naturally occurring relationships; to assess how well one variable predicts another	Compute statistical association, sometimes among survey responses	Nothing	Does not specify cause and effect
Experimental	To explore cause and effect	Manipulate one or more factors; use random assignment	The independent variable(s)	Sometimes not feasible; results may not generalize to other contexts; not ethical to manipulate certain variables

▶∥ Statistical Reasoning in Everyday Life

In descriptive, correlational, and experimental research, statistics are tools that help us see and interpret what the unaided eye might miss. But statistical understanding benefits more than just researchers. To be an educated person today is to be able to apply simple statistical principles to everyday reasoning. One needn't memorize complicated formulas to think more clearly and critically about data.

Off-the-top-of-the-head estimates often misread reality and then mislead the public. Someone throws out a big, round number. Others echo it, and before long the big, round number becomes public misinformation. A few examples:

▶ *Ten percent of people are lesbians or gay men.* Or is it 2 to 3 percent, as suggested by various national surveys?

▶ *We ordinarily use but 10 percent of our brain.* Or is it closer to 100 percent?

▶ *The human brain has 100 billion nerve cells.* Or is it more like 40 billion, as suggested by extrapolation from sample counts?

The point to remember: Doubt big, round, undocumented numbers. Rather than swallowing top-of-the-head estimates, focus on thinking smarter by applying simple statistical principles to everyday reasoning.

Describing Data

3-6 How can we describe data with measures of central tendency and variation?

Once researchers have gathered their data, they must organize them in some meaningful way. One way to do this is to convert the data into a simple *bar graph,* as in **FIGURE 3.8**, which displays a distribution of different brands of trucks still on the road after a decade. When reading statistical graphs such as this, take care. It's easy to design a graph to make a difference look big (**FIGURE 3.8a**) or small (**FIGURE 3.8b**). The secret lies in how you label the vertical scale (the Y-axis).

The point to remember: Think smart. When viewing figures in magazines and on television, read the scale labels and note their range.

"Figures can be misleading—so I've written a song which I think expresses the real story of the firm's performance this quarter."

dependent variable the outcome factor; the variable that may change in response to manipulations of the independent variable.

FIGURE 3.8 Read the scale labels An American truck manufacturer offered graph (a)—with actual brand names included—to suggest the much greater durability of its trucks. Note, however, how the apparent difference shrinks as the vertical scale changes (graph b).

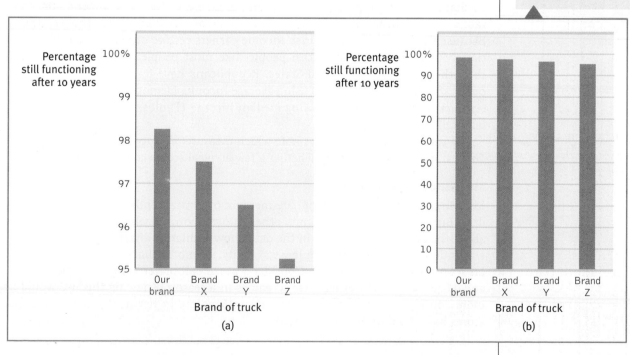

(a)

(b)

Measures of Central Tendency

The next step is to summarize the data using some *measure of central tendency,* a single score that represents a whole set of scores. The simplest measure is the **mode,** the most frequently occurring score or scores. The most commonly reported is the **mean,** or arithmetic average—the total sum of all the scores divided by the number of scores. On a divided highway, the median is the middle. So, too, with data: The **median** is the midpoint—the 50th percentile. If you arrange all the scores in order from the highest to the lowest, half will be above the median and half will be below it.

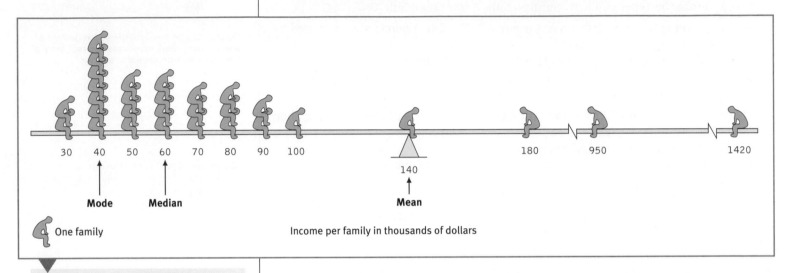

FIGURE 3.9 A skewed distribution
This graphic representation of the distribution of a village's incomes illustrates the three measures of central tendency—mode, median, and mean. Note how just a few high incomes make the mean—the fulcrum point that balances the incomes above and below—deceptively high.

|| The average person has one ovary and one testicle. ||

Measures of central tendency neatly summarize data. But consider what happens to the mean when a distribution is lopsided or *skewed.* With income data, for example, the mode, median, and mean often tell very different stories (**FIGURE 3.9**). This happens because the mean is biased by a few extreme scores. When Microsoft co-founder Bill Gates sits down in an intimate café, its average (mean) customer instantly becomes a billionaire. But the customer's median wealth remains unchanged. Understanding this, you can see how a British newspaper could accurately run the headline "Income for 62% Is Below Average" (Waterhouse, 1993). Because the bottom *half* of British income earners receive only a *quarter* of the national income cake, most British people, like most people everywhere, make less than the mean. In the United States, Republicans have tended to tout the economy's solid growth since 2000 using average income; Democrats have lamented the economy's lackluster growth using median income (Paulos, 2006). Mean and median tell different true stories.

The point to remember: Always note which measure of central tendency is reported. Then, if it is a mean, consider whether a few atypical scores could be distorting it.

Measures of Variation

Knowing the value of an appropriate measure of central tendency can tell us a great deal. But the single number omits other information. It helps to know something about the amount of *variation* in the data—how similar or diverse the scores are. Averages derived from scores with low variability are more reliable than averages based on scores with high variability. Consider a basketball player who scored between 13 and 17 points in each of her first 10 games in a season. Knowing this, we would be more confident that she would score near 15 points in her next game than if her scores had varied from 5 to 25 points.

The **range** of scores—the gap between the lowest and highest scores—provides only a crude estimate of variation because a couple of extreme scores in an otherwise uniform group, such as the $950,000 and $1,420,000 incomes in Figure 3.9, will create a deceptively large range.

The more useful standard for measuring how much scores deviate from one another is the **standard deviation.** It better gauges whether scores are packed together or dispersed, because it uses information from each score (**TABLE 3.3**). The computation assembles information about how much individual scores differ from the mean. If your college or university attracts students of a certain ability level, their intelligence scores will have a relatively small standard deviation compared with the more diverse community population outside your school.

You can grasp the meaning of the standard deviation if you consider how scores tend to be distributed in nature. Large numbers of data—heights, weights, intelligence scores, grades (though not incomes)—often form a symmetrical, bell-shaped distribution. Most cases fall near the mean, and fewer cases fall near either extreme. This bell-shaped distribution is so typical that we call the curve it forms the **normal curve.**

"The poor are getting poorer, but with the rich getting richer it all averages out in the long run."

mode the most frequently occurring score(s) in a distribution.

mean the arithmetic average of a distribution, obtained by adding the scores and then dividing by the number of scores.

median the middle score in a distribution; half the scores are above it and half are below it.

range the difference between the highest and lowest scores in a distribution.

standard deviation a computed measure of how much scores vary around the mean score.

normal curve (*normal distribution*) a symmetrical, bell-shaped curve that describes the distribution of many types of data; most scores fall near the mean (68 percent fall within one standard deviation of it) and fewer and fewer near the extremes.

TABLE 3.3 Standard Deviation Is Much More Informative Than Mean Alone

Note that the test scores in Class A and Class B have the same mean (80), but very different standard deviations, which tell us more about how the students in each class are really faring.

Test Scores in Class A			Test Scores in Class B		
Score	Deviation from the Mean	Squared Deviation	Score	Deviation from the Mean	Squared Deviation
72	−8	64	60	−20	400
74	−6	36	60	−20	400
77	−3	9	70	−10	100
79	−1	1	70	−10	100
82	+2	4	90	+10	100
84	+4	16	90	+10	100
85	+5	25	100	+20	400
87	+7	49	100	+20	400
Total = 640		Sum of (deviations)² = 204	Total = 640		Sum of (deviations)² = 2000
Mean = 640 ÷ 8 = 80			Mean = 640 ÷ 8 = 80		

Standard deviation =

$$\sqrt{\frac{Sum\ of\ (deviations)^2}{Number\ of\ scores}} = \sqrt{\frac{204}{8}} = 5.0$$

Standard deviation =

$$\sqrt{\frac{Sum\ of\ (deviations)^2}{Number\ of\ scores}} = \sqrt{\frac{2000}{8}} = 15.8$$

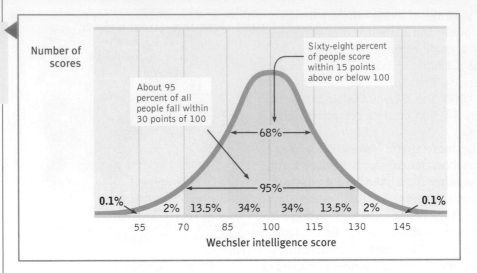

FIGURE 3.10 The normal curve Scores on aptitude tests tend to form a normal, or bell-shaped, curve. For example, the Wechsler Adult Intelligence Scale calls the average score 100.

As **FIGURE 3.10** shows, a useful property of the normal curve is that roughly 68 percent of the cases fall within one standard deviation on either side of the mean. About 95 percent of cases fall within two standard deviations. Thus, about 68 percent of people taking an intelligence test will score within ±15 points of 100. About 95 percent will score within ±30 points.

Making Inferences

3-7   What principles can guide our making generalizations from samples and deciding whether differences are significant?

Data are "noisy." The average score in one group (breast-fed babies) could conceivably differ from the average score in another group (formula-fed babies) not because of any real difference but merely because of chance fluctuations in the people sampled. How confidently, then, can we infer that an observed difference accurately estimates the true difference? For guidance, we can ask how reliable and significant the differences are.

When Is an Observed Difference Reliable?

In deciding when it is safe to generalize from a sample, we should keep three principles in mind.

1. **Representative samples are better than biased samples.** The best basis for generalizing is not from the exceptional and memorable cases one finds at the extremes but from a representative sample of cases. Research never randomly samples the whole human population. Thus, it pays to keep in mind what population a study has sampled.

2. **Less-variable observations are more reliable than those that are more variable.** As we noted in the example of the basketball player whose game-to-game points were consistent, an average is more reliable when it comes from scores with low variability.

3. **More cases are better than fewer.** An eager prospective student visits two university campuses, each for a day. At the first, the student randomly attends two classes and discovers both instructors to be witty and engaging. At the next campus, the two sampled instructors seem dull and uninspiring.

Returning home, the student (discounting the small sample size of only two teachers at each institution) tells friends about the "great teachers" at the first school, and the "bores" at the second. Again, we know it but we ignore it: *Averages based on many cases are more reliable* (less variable) than averages based on only a few cases.

The point to remember: Don't be overly impressed by a few anecdotes. Generalizations based on a few unrepresentative cases are unreliable.

When Is a Difference Significant?

Statistical tests also help us determine whether differences are meaningful. Here is the underlying logic: When averages from two samples are each reliable measures of their respective populations (as when each is based on many observations that have small variability), then their *difference* is likely to be reliable as well. (Example: The less the variability in women's and in men's aggression scores, the more confidence we would have that any observed gender difference is reliable.) And when the difference between the sample averages is *large,* we have even more confidence that the difference between them reflects a real difference in their populations.

In short, when the sample averages are reliable, and when the difference between them is relatively large, we say the difference has **statistical significance.** This means that the observed difference is probably not due to chance variation between the samples.

In judging statistical significance, psychologists are conservative. They are like juries who must presume innocence until guilt is proven. For most psychologists, proof beyond a reasonable doubt means not making much of a finding unless the odds of its occurring by chance are less than 5 percent (an arbitrary criterion).

PEANUTS

When reading about research, you should remember that, given large enough or homogeneous enough samples, a difference between them may be "statistically significant" yet have little practical significance. For example, comparisons of intelligence test scores among hundreds of thousands of first-born and later-born individuals indicate a highly significant tendency for first-born individuals to have higher average scores than their later-born siblings (Kristensen & Bjerkedal, 2007; Zajonc & Markus, 1975). But because the scores differ by only one to three points, the difference has little practical importance. Such findings have caused some psychologists to advocate alternatives to significance testing (Hunter, 1997). Better, they say, to use other ways to express a finding's *effect size*—its magnitude and reliability.

The point to remember: Statistical significance indicates the *likelihood* that a result will happen by chance. But this does not say anything about the *importance* of the result.

REVIEW

Research Strategies: How Psychologists Ask and Answer Questions

3-1   How do theories advance psychological science? Psychological *theories* organize observations and imply predictive *hypotheses*. After constructing precise *operational definitions* of their procedures, researchers test their hypotheses, validate and refine the theory, and, sometimes, suggest practical applications. If other researchers can *replicate* the study with similar results, we can then place greater confidence in the conclusion.

3-2   How do psychologists observe and describe behavior? Psychologists observe and describe behavior using individual *case studies, surveys* among *random samples* of a *population,* and *naturalistic observations.* In generalizing from observations, remember: Representative samples are a better guide than vivid anecdotes.

3-3   What are positive and negative correlations, and why do they enable prediction but not cause-effect explanation? *Scatterplots* help us to see *correlations.* A positive correlation (ranging from 0 to +1.00) indicates the extent to which two factors rise together. In a negative correlation (ranging from 0 to −1.00), one item rises as the other falls. An association (sometimes stated as a *correlation coefficient*) indicates the possibility of a cause-effect relationship, but it does not prove the direction of the influence, or whether an underlying third factor may explain the correlation.

3-4   What are illusory correlations? *Illusory correlations* are random events that we notice and falsely assume are related. Patterns or sequences occur naturally in sets of random data, but we tend to interpret these patterns as meaningful connections, perhaps in an attempt to make sense of the world around us.

3-5   How do experiments, powered by random assignment, clarify cause and effect? To discover cause-effect relationships, psychologists conduct *experiments,* manipulating one or more factors of interest and controlling other factors. *Random assignment* minimizes preexisting differences between the *experimental group* (exposed to the treatment) and the *control group* (given a placebo or different version of the treatment). The *independent variable* is the factor you manipulate to study its effect. The *dependent variable* is the factor you measure to discover any changes that occur in response to these manipulations. Studies may use a *double-blind procedure* to avoid the *placebo effect* and researcher's bias.

3-6   How can we describe data with measures of central tendency and variation? Three measures of central tendency are the *median* (the middle score in a group of data), the *mode* (the most frequently occurring score), and the *mean* (the arithmetic average). Measures of variation tell us how similar or diverse data are. A *range* describes the gap between the highest and lowest scores. The more useful measure, the *standard deviation,* states how much scores vary around the mean, or average, score. The *normal curve* is a bell-shaped curve that describes the distribution of many types of data.

3-7   What principles can guide our making generalizations from samples and deciding whether differences are significant? Three principles are worth remembering: (1) Representative samples are better than biased samples. (2) Less-variable observations are more reliable than those that are more variable. (3) More cases are better than fewer.

When averages from two samples are each reliable measures of their own populations, and the difference between them is relatively large, we can assume that the result is *statistically significant*—that it did not occur by chance alone.

Terms and Concepts to Remember

theory, p. 25

hypothesis, p.25

operational definition, p. 26

replication, p. 26

case study, p. 27

survey, p. 27

population, p. 28

random sample, p. 28

naturalistic observation, p. 28

correlation, p. 29

correlation coefficient, p. 29

scatterplots, p. 30

illusory correlation, p. 32

experiment, p. 34

random assignment, p. 34

double-blind procedure, p. 35

placebo effect, p. 35

experimental group, p. 35

control group, p. 35

independent variable, p.35

dependent variable, p. 36

mode, p. 38

mean, p. 38

median, p. 38

range, p. 39

standard deviation, p. 39

normal curve, p. 39

statistical significance, p. 41

Test Yourself

1. Why, when testing a new drug to control blood pressure, would we learn more about its effectiveness from giving it to half of the participants in a group of 1000 than to all 1000 participants?

2. Consider a question posed by Christopher Jepson, David Krantz, and Richard Nisbett (1983) to University of Michigan introductory psychology students:

   The registrar's office at the University of Michigan has found that usually about 100 students in Arts and Sciences have perfect marks at the end of their first term at the University. However, only about 10 to 15 students graduate with perfect marks. What do you think is the most likely explanation for the fact that there are more perfect marks after one term than at graduation?

(Answers to the Test Yourself questions can be found in Appendix B at the end of the book.)

Ask Yourself

1. If you were to become a research psychologist, what questions would you like to explore with experiments?

2. Find a graph in a popular magazine ad. How does the advertiser use (or abuse) statistics to make a point?

∞ WEB

Multiple-choice self-tests and more may be found at www.worthpublishers.com/myers

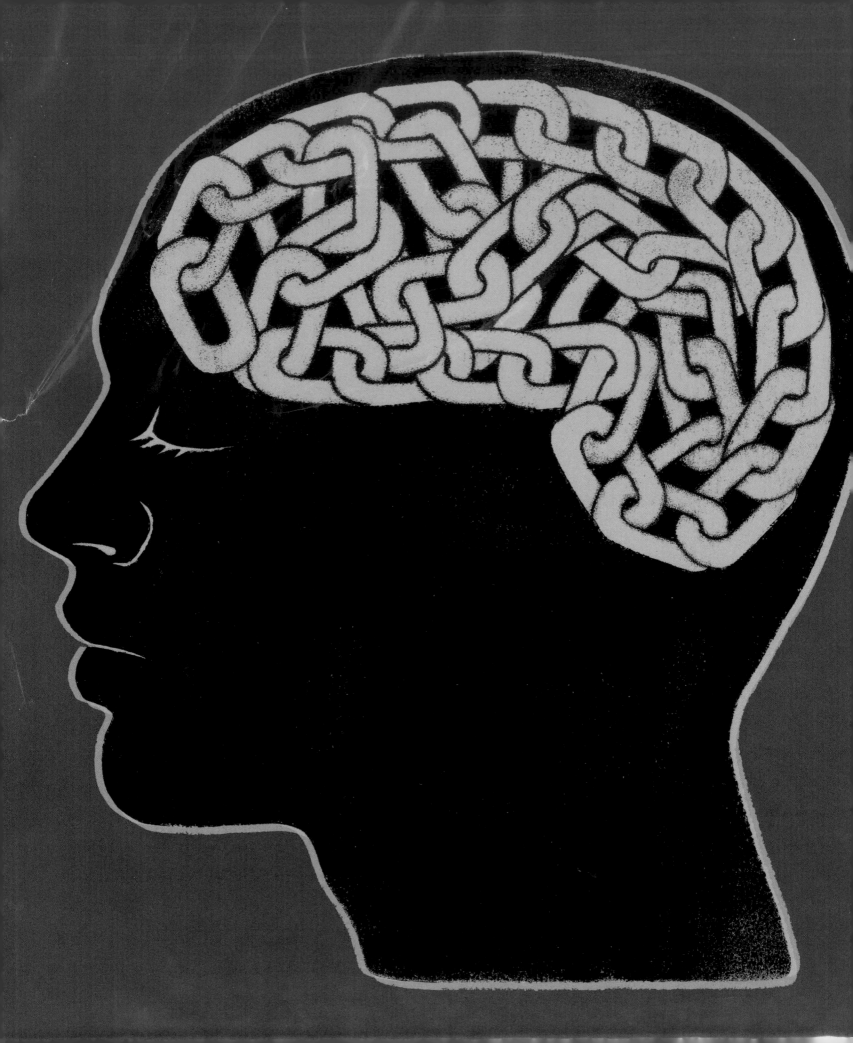

The Biology of Mind

MODULES

4
Neural and Hormonal Systems

5
Tools of Discovery and Older Brain Structures

6
The Cerebral Cortex and Our Divided Brain

No principle is more central to today's psychology, or to this book, than this: *Everything psychological is simultaneously biological.* Your every idea, every mood, every urge is a biological happening. You love, laugh, and cry with your body. Without your body—your genes, your brain, your appearance—you are, indeed, nobody. Although we find it convenient to talk separately of biological and psychological influences on behavior, we need to remember: To think, feel, or act without a body would be like running without legs.

Today's science is riveted on our body's most amazing parts—the brain, its component neural systems, and their genetic instructions. The brain's ultimate challenge? To understand itself. How does the brain organize and communicate with itself? How do heredity and experience together wire the brain? How does the brain process the information we need to shoot a basketball? To delight in a guitarist's notes? To remember our first kiss?

Our understanding of how the brain gives birth to the mind has come a long way. The ancient Greek philosopher Plato correctly located the mind in the spherical head—his idea of the perfect form. His student, Aristotle, believed the mind was in the heart, which pumps warmth and vitality to the body. The heart remains our symbol for love, but science has long since overtaken philosophy on this issue. It's your brain, not your heart, that falls in love.

We have come far since the early 1800s, when the German physician Franz Gall invented *phrenology,* a popular but ill-fated theory that claimed bumps on the skull could reveal our mental abilities and our character traits. At one point, Britain had 29 phrenological societies, and phrenologists traveled North America giving skull readings (Hunt, 1993). Using a false name, humorist Mark Twain put one famous phrenologist to the test. "He found a cavity [and] startled me by saying that that cavity represented the total absence of the sense of humor!" Three months later, Twain sat for a second reading, this time identifying himself. Now "the cavity was gone, and in its place was . . . the loftiest bump of humor he had ever encountered in his life-long experience!" (Lopez, 2002). Phrenology did, however, correctly focus attention on the idea that various brain regions have particular functions.

You and I enjoy a privilege Gall did not have. We are living in a time when discoveries about the interplay of our biology and our behavior and mental processes are occurring at an exhilarating pace. Within little more than the last century, as we will see in Modules 4 through 6, researchers seeking to understand the biology of the mind have discovered that

▶ the body is composed of cells (Module 4).
▶ among these are nerve cells that conduct electricity and "talk" to one another by sending chemical messages across a tiny gap that separates them (Module 4).
▶ specific brain systems serve specific functions—though not the functions Gall supposed (Module 5).
▶ we integrate information processed in these different brain systems to construct our experience of sights and sounds, meanings and memories, pain and passion (Module 6).
▶ our adaptive brain is wired by our experience (Module 6).

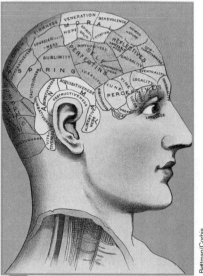

Bettmann/Corbis

A wrongheaded theory Despite initial acceptance of Franz Gall's speculations, bumps on the skull tell us nothing about the brain's underlying functions. Nevertheless, some of Gall's assumptions have held true. Different parts of the brain do control different aspects of behavior.

MODULE 4

Neural and Hormonal Systems

"If I were a college student today, I don't think I could resist going into neuroscience."

Novelist Tom Wolfe, 2004

biological psychology a branch of psychology concerned with the links between biology and behavior. (Some biological psychologists call themselves *behavioral neuroscientists, neuropsychologists, behavior geneticists, physiological psychologists,* or *biopsychologists.*)

neuron a nerve cell; the basic building block of the nervous system.

sensory neurons neurons that carry incoming information from the sensory receptors to the brain and spinal cord.

motor neurons neurons that carry outgoing information from the brain and spinal cord to the muscles and glands.

interneurons neurons within the brain and spinal cord that communicate internally and intervene between the sensory inputs and motor outputs.

dendrite the bushy, branching extensions of a neuron that receive messages and conduct impulses toward the cell body.

axon the extension of a neuron, ending in branching terminal fibers, through which messages pass to other neurons or to muscles or glands.

myelin [MY-uh-lin] **sheath** a layer of fatty tissue segmentally encasing the fibers of many neurons; enables vastly greater transmission speed of neural impulses as the impulse hops from one node to the next.

action potential a neural impulse; a brief electrical charge that travels down an axon.

▶‖ Neural Communication

By studying the links between biological activity and psychological events, **biological psychologists** continue to expand our understanding of sleep and dreams, depression and schizophrenia, hunger and sex, stress and disease.

We have also realized that we are each a system composed of subsystems that are in turn composed of even smaller subsystems. Tiny cells organize to form such body organs as the stomach, heart, and brain. These organs in turn form larger systems for digestion, circulation, and information processing. And those systems are part of an even larger system—the individual, who in turn is a part of a family, culture, and community. Thus, we are *biopsychosocial* systems, and to understand our behavior, we need to study how these biological, psychological, and social-cultural systems work and interact.

In this book we start small and build from the bottom up—from nerve cells up to the brain, and to the environmental and cultural influences that interact with our biology. We will also work from the top down, as we consider how our thinking and emotions influence our brain and our health. At all levels, psychologists examine how we process information—how we take in information; how we organize, interpret, and store it; and how we use it.

The body's information system handling all these tasks is built from billions of interconnected cells called *neurons*. To fathom our thoughts and actions, memories and moods, we must first understand how neurons work and communicate.

For scientists, it is a happy fact of nature that the information systems of humans and other animals operate similarly—so similarly, in fact, that you could not distinguish between small samples of brain tissue from a human and a monkey. This similarity allows researchers to study relatively simple animals, such as squids and sea slugs, to discover how our neural systems operate. It allows them to study other mammals' brains to understand the organization of our own. Cars differ, but all have engines, accelerators, steering wheels, and brakes. A Martian could study any one of them and grasp the operating principles. Likewise, animals differ, yet their nervous systems operate similarly. Though the human brain is more complex than a rat's, both follow the same principles.

Neurons

4-1 What are neurons, and how do they transmit information?

Our body's neural information system is complexity built from simplicity. Its building blocks are **neurons,** or nerve cells. **Sensory neurons** carry messages from the body's tissues and sensory organs inward to the brain and spinal cord, for processing. The brain and spinal cord then send instructions out to the body's tissues via the **motor neurons.** Between the sensory input and motor output, information is processed in the brain's internal communication system via its **interneurons.** Our complexity resides mostly in our interneuron systems. Our nervous system has a few million sensory neurons, a few million motor neurons, and billions and billions of interneurons.

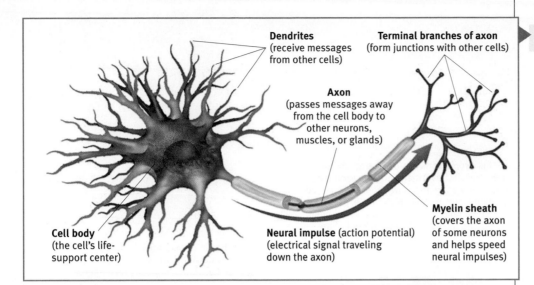

Dendrites
(receive messages
from other cells)

Terminal branches of axon
(form junctions with other cells)

Axon
(passes messages away
from the cell body to
other neurons,
muscles, or glands)

Cell body
(the cell's life-
support center)

Neural impulse (action potential)
(electrical signal traveling
down the axon)

Myelin sheath
(covers the axon
of some neurons
and helps speed
neural impulses)

FIGURE 4.1 A motor neuron

All are variations on the same theme (**FIGURE 4.1**). Each consists of a *cell body* and its branching fibers. The bushy **dendrite** fibers receive information and conduct it toward the cell body. From there, the cell's **axon** passes the message along to other neurons or to muscles or glands. Axons speak. Dendrites listen.

Unlike the short dendrites, axons are sometimes very long, projecting several feet through the body. A motor neuron carrying orders to a leg muscle, for example, has a cell body and axon roughly on the scale of a basketball attached to a rope 4 miles long. Much as home electrical wire is insulated, so a layer of fatty tissue, called the **myelin sheath,** insulates the axons of some neurons and helps speed their impulses. As myelin is laid down up to about age 25, neural efficiency, judgment, and self-control grows (Fields, 2008). If the myelin sheath degenerates, *multiple sclerosis* results: Communication to muscles slows, with eventual loss of muscle control.

Depending on the type of fiber, a neural impulse travels at speeds ranging from a sluggish 2 miles per hour to a breakneck 200 or more miles per hour. But even this top speed is 3 million times slower than that of electricity through a wire. We measure brain activity in milliseconds (thousandths of a second) and computer activity in nanoseconds (billionths of a second). Thus, unlike the nearly instantaneous reactions of a high-speed computer, your reaction to a sudden event, such as a child darting in front of your car, may take a quarter-second or more. Your brain is vastly more complex than a computer, but slower at executing simple responses.

Neurons transmit messages when stimulated by signals from our senses or when triggered by chemical signals from neighboring neurons. At such times, a neuron fires an impulse, called the **action potential**—a brief electrical charge that travels down its axon.

Neurons, like batteries, generate electricity from chemical events. The chemistry-to-electricity process involves the exchange of *ions,* electrically charged atoms. The fluid interior of a resting axon has an excess of negatively charged ions, while the fluid outside the axon membrane has more positively charged ions. This positive-outside/negative-inside state is called the *resting potential.* Like a tightly guarded facility, the axon's surface is very selective about what it allows in. We say the axon's surface is *selectively permeable.* For example, a resting axon has gates that block positive sodium ions.

When a neuron fires, however, the security parameters change: The first bit of the axon opens its gates, rather like sewer covers flipping open, and the positively charged

"I sing the body electric."
Walt Whitman, "Children of Adam" (1855)

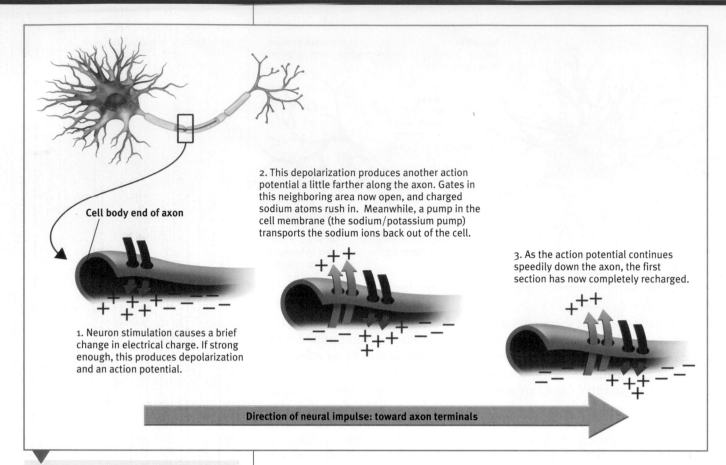

2. This depolarization produces another action potential a little farther along the axon. Gates in this neighboring area now open, and charged sodium atoms rush in. Meanwhile, a pump in the cell membrane (the sodium/potassium pump) transports the sodium ions back out of the cell.

3. As the action potential continues speedily down the axon, the first section has now completely recharged.

Cell body end of axon

1. Neuron stimulation causes a brief change in electrical charge. If strong enough, this produces depolarization and an action potential.

Direction of neural impulse: toward axon terminals

FIGURE 4.2 Action potential

"What one neuron tells another neuron is simply how much it is excited."

Francis Crick, *The Astonishing Hypothesis,* 1994

threshold the level of stimulation required to trigger a neural impulse.

sodium ions flood through the membrane (**FIGURE 4.2**). This *depolarizes* that section of the axon, causing the axon's next channel to open, and then the next, like dominoes falling, each one tripping the next. During a resting pause (the *refractory period,* rather like a camera flash pausing to recharge), the neuron pumps the positively charged sodium ions back outside. Then it can fire again. (In myelinated neurons, as in Figure 4.1, the action potential speeds up by hopping from one myelin "sausage" to the next.) The mind boggles when imagining this electrochemical process repeating up to 100 or even 1000 times a second. But this is just the first of many astonishments.

Each neuron is itself a miniature decision-making device performing complex calculations as it receives signals from hundreds, even thousands, of other neurons. Most of these signals are *excitatory,* somewhat like pushing a neuron's accelerator. Others are *inhibitory,* more like pushing its brake. If excitatory signals minus inhibitory signals exceed a minimum intensity, or **threshold,** the combined signals trigger an action potential. (Think of it this way: If the excitatory party animals outvote the inhibitory party poopers, the party's on.) The action potential then travels down the axon, which branches into junctions with hundreds or thousands of other neurons and with the body's muscles and glands.

Increasing the level of stimulation above the threshold, however, will not increase the neural impulse's intensity. The neuron's reaction is an *all-or-none response:* Like guns, neurons either fire or they don't. How then do we detect the intensity of a stimulus? How do we distinguish a gentle touch from a big hug? A strong stimulus—a slap rather than a tap—can trigger *more* neurons to fire, and to fire more often. But it does not affect the action potential's strength or speed. Squeezing a trigger harder won't make a bullet go faster.

How Neurons Communicate

4-2 How do nerve cells communicate with other nerve cells?

Neurons interweave so intricately that even with a microscope you would have trouble seeing where one neuron ends and another begins. Scientists once believed that the axon of one cell fused with the dendrites of another in an uninterrupted fabric. Then British physiologist Sir Charles Sherrington (1857–1952) noticed that neural impulses were taking an unexpectedly long time to travel a neural pathway. Inferring that there must be a brief interruption in the transmission, Sherrington called the meeting point between neurons a **synapse.**

We now know that the axon terminal of one neuron is in fact separated from the receiving neuron by a *synaptic gap* (or *synaptic cleft*) less than a millionth of an inch wide. Spanish anatomist Santiago Ramón y Cajal (1852–1934) marveled at these near-unions of neurons, calling them "protoplasmic kisses." "Like elegant ladies air-kissing so as not to muss their makeup, dendrites and axons don't quite touch," notes poet Diane Ackerman (2004). How do the neurons execute this protoplasmic kiss, sending information across the tiny synaptic gap? The answer is one of the important scientific discoveries of our age.

When an action potential reaches the knoblike terminals at an axon's end, it triggers the release of chemical messengers, called **neurotransmitters** (**FIGURE 4.3**).

synapse [SIN-aps] the junction between the axon tip of the sending neuron and the dendrite or cell body of the receiving neuron. The tiny gap at this junction is called the *synaptic gap* or *synaptic cleft*.

neurotransmitters chemical messengers that cross the synaptic gaps between neurons. When released by the sending neuron, neurotransmitters travel across the synapse and bind to receptor sites on the receiving neuron, thereby influencing whether that neuron will generate a neural impulse.

"All information processing in the brain involves neurons 'talking to' each other at synapses."
Neuroscientist Solomon H. Snyder (1984)

FIGURE 4.3 How neurons communicate

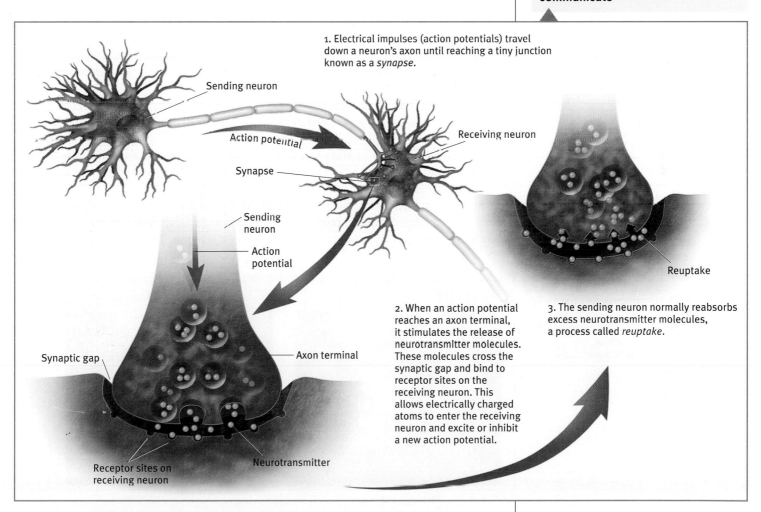

1. Electrical impulses (action potentials) travel down a neuron's axon until reaching a tiny junction known as a *synapse*.

Sending neuron

Action potential

Receiving neuron

Synapse

Sending neuron

Action potential

Synaptic gap

Axon terminal

Receptor sites on receiving neuron

Neurotransmitter

Reuptake

2. When an action potential reaches an axon terminal, it stimulates the release of neurotransmitter molecules. These molecules cross the synaptic gap and bind to receptor sites on the receiving neuron. This allows electrically charged atoms to enter the receiving neuron and excite or inhibit a new action potential.

3. The sending neuron normally reabsorbs excess neurotransmitter molecules, a process called *reuptake*.

Within 1/10,000th of a second, the neurotransmitter molecules cross the synaptic gap and bind to receptor sites on the receiving neuron—as precisely as a key fits a lock. For an instant, the neurotransmitter unlocks tiny channels at the receiving site, and electrically charged atoms flow in, exciting or inhibiting the receiving neuron's readiness to fire. Then, in a process called **reuptake,** the sending neuron reabsorbs the excess neurotransmitters.

How Neurotransmitters Influence Us

4-3 How do neurotransmitters influence behavior, and how do drugs and other chemicals affect neurotransmission?

In their quest to understand neural communication, researchers have discovered dozens of different neurotransmitters and almost as many new questions: Are certain neurotransmitters found only in specific places? How do they affect our moods, memories, and mental abilities? Can we boost or diminish these effects through drugs or diet?

In other modules we examine neurotransmitter influences on depression and euphoria, hunger and thinking, addictions and therapy. For now, let's glimpse how neurotransmitters influence our motions and our emotions. A particular pathway in the brain may use only one or two neurotransmitters (**FIGURE 4.4**), and particular neurotransmitters may have particular effects on behavior and emotions. (**TABLE 4.1** offers examples.) *Acetylcholine (ACh)* is one of the best-understood neurotransmitters. In addition to its role in learning and memory, ACh is the messenger at every junction between a motor neuron and skeletal muscle. When ACh is released to our muscle cell receptors, the muscle contracts. If ACh transmission is blocked, as happens during some kinds of anesthesia, the muscles cannot contract and we are paralyzed.

Candace Pert and Solomon Snyder (1973) made an exciting discovery about neurotransmitters when they attached a radioactive tracer to morphine, showing where it was taken up in an animal's brain. The morphine, an opiate drug that elevates mood and eases pain, bound to receptors in areas linked with mood and pain sensations. But why would the brain have these "opiate receptors"? Why would it have a chemical lock, unless it also had a natural key to open it?

Researchers soon confirmed that the brain does indeed produce its own naturally occurring opiates. Our body releases several types of neurotransmitter molecules similar to morphine in response to pain and vigorous exercise. These **endorphins** (short

"When it comes to the brain, if you want to see the action, follow the neurotransmitters."

Neuroscientist Floyd Bloom (1993)

FIGURE 4.4 Neurotransmitter pathways Each of the brain's differing chemical messengers has designated pathways where it operates, as shown here for the neurotransmitters serotonin and dopamine (Carter, 1998).

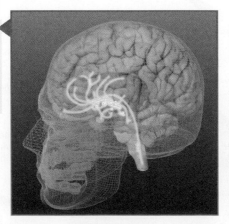

Seratonin pathways

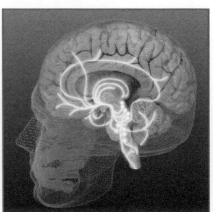

Dopamine pathways

Both photos from *Mapping the Mind*, Rita Carter, © 1989 University of California Press

TABLE 4.1 Some Neurotransmitters and Their Functions

Neurotransmitter	Function	Examples of Malfunctions
Acetylcholine (ACh)	Enables muscle action, learning, and memory.	With Alzheimer's disease, ACh-producing neurons deteriorate.
Dopamine	Influences movement, learning, attention, and emotion.	Excess dopamine receptor activity is linked to schizophrenia. Starved of dopamine, the brain produces the tremors and decreased mobility of Parkinson's disease.
Serotonin	Affects mood, hunger, sleep, and arousal.	Undersupply linked to depression. Prozac and some other antidepressant drugs raise serotonin levels.
Norepinephrine	Helps control alertness and arousal.	Undersupply can depress mood.
GABA (gamma-aminobutyric acid)	A major inhibitory neurotransmitter.	Undersupply linked to seizures, tremors, and insomnia.
Glutamate	A major excitatory neurotransmitter; involved in memory.	Oversupply can overstimulate brain, producing migraines or seizures (which is why some people avoid MSG, monosodium glutamate, in food).

reuptake a neurotransmitter's reabsorption by the sending neuron.

endorphins [en-DOR-fins] "morphine within"—natural, opiatelike neurotransmitters linked to pain control and to pleasure.

for *endogenous* [produced within] *morphine*), as we now call them, help explain good feelings such as the "runner's high," the painkilling effects of acupuncture, and the indifference to pain in some severely injured people. But once again, new knowledge led to new questions.

How Drugs and Other Chemicals Alter Neurotransmission

If indeed the endorphins lessen pain and boost mood, why not flood the brain with artificial opiates, thereby intensifying the brain's own "feel-good" chemistry? One problem is that when flooded with opiate drugs such as heroin and morphine, the brain may stop producing its own natural opiates. When the drug is withdrawn, the brain may then be deprived of any form of opiate, causing intense discomfort. For suppressing the body's own neurotransmitter production, nature charges a price.

Drugs and other chemicals affect brain chemistry at synapses, often by either amplifying or blocking a neurotransmitter's activity. An *agonist* molecule may be similar enough to a neurotransmitter to mimic its effects (**FIGURE 4.5b** on the next page) or it may block the neurotransmitter's reuptake. Some opiate drugs, for example, produce a temporary "high" by amplifying normal sensations of arousal or pleasure. Not so pleasant are the effects of black widow spider venom, which floods synapses with ACh. The result? Violent muscle contractions, convulsions, and possible death.

Antagonists block a neurotransmitter's functioning. Botulin, a poison that can form in improperly canned food, causes paralysis by blocking ACh release. (Small injections of botulin—Botox—smooth wrinkles by paralyzing the underlying facial muscles.) Other antagonists are enough like the natural neurotransmitter to occupy its receptor site and block its effect, as in Figure 4.5c, but are not similar enough to stimulate the receptor (rather like foreign coins that fit into, but won't operate, a soda or candy machine). Curare, a poison certain South American Indians have applied to hunting-dart tips, occupies and blocks ACh receptor sites, leaving the neurotransmitter unable to affect the muscles. Struck by one of these darts, an animal becomes paralyzed.

Physician Lewis Thomas, on the endorphins: "There it is, a biologically universal act of mercy. I cannot explain it, except to say that I would have put it in had I been around at the very beginning, sitting as a member of a planning committee."
The Youngest Science, 1983

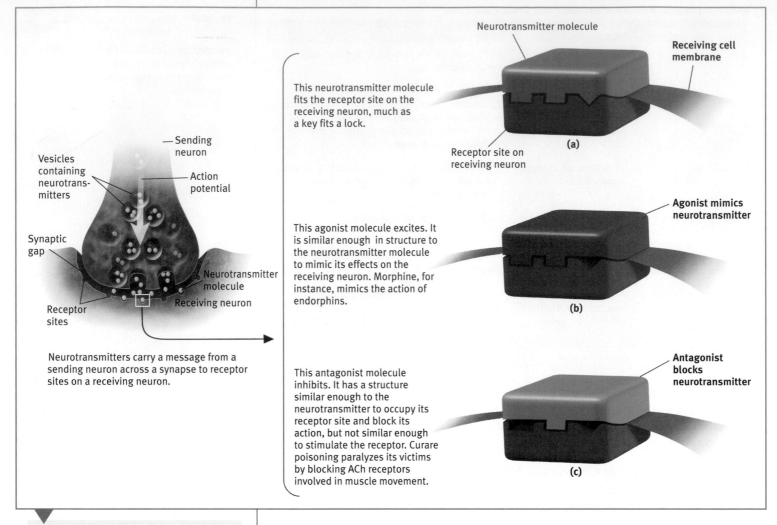

Neurotransmitter molecule

Receiving cell membrane

This neurotransmitter molecule fits the receptor site on the receiving neuron, much as a key fits a lock.

(a)

Receptor site on receiving neuron

This agonist molecule excites. It is similar enough in structure to the neurotransmitter molecule to mimic its effects on the receiving neuron. Morphine, for instance, mimics the action of endorphins.

Agonist mimics neurotransmitter

(b)

This antagonist molecule inhibits. It has a structure similar enough to the neurotransmitter to occupy its receptor site and block its action, but not similar enough to stimulate the receptor. Curare poisoning paralyzes its victims by blocking ACh receptors involved in muscle movement.

Antagonist blocks neurotransmitter

(c)

— Sending neuron

Vesicles containing neurotrans- mitters

— Action potential

Synaptic gap

Neurotransmitter molecule

Receptor sites

Receiving neuron

Neurotransmitters carry a message from a sending neuron across a synapse to receptor sites on a receiving neuron.

FIGURE 4.5 Agonists and antagonists

nervous system the body's speedy, electrochemical communication network, consisting of all the nerve cells of the peripheral and central nervous systems.

central nervous system (CNS) the brain and spinal cord.

peripheral nervous system (PNS) the sensory and motor neurons that con- nect the central nervous system (CNS) to the rest of the body.

nerves bundled axons that form neural "cables" connecting the central nervous system with muscles, glands, and sense organs.

somatic nervous system the division of the peripheral nervous system that controls the body's skeletal muscles. Also called the *skeletal nervous system*.

▶‖ The Nervous System

4-4 What are the functions of the nervous system's main divisions?

To live is to take in information from the world and the body's tissues, to make deci- sions, and to send back information and orders to the body's tissues. All this happens thanks to our body's speedy electrochemical communications network, our **nervous system** (FIGURE 4.6). The brain and spinal cord form the **central nervous system (CNS),** which communicates with the body's sensory receptors, muscles, and glands via the **peripheral nervous system (PNS).**

Neurons are the nervous system's building blocks. PNS information travels through axons that are bundled into the electrical cables we know as **nerves.** The optic nerve, for example, bundles a million axon fibers into a single cable carrying the messages each eye sends to the brain (Mason & Kandel, 1991). As noted earlier, in- formation travels in the nervous system through sensory neurons, motor neurons, and interneurons.

The Peripheral Nervous System

Our peripheral nervous system has two components—somatic and autonomic. Our **somatic nervous system** enables voluntary control of our skeletal muscles. As you

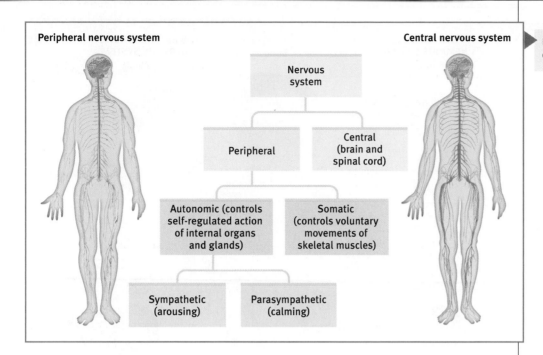

Peripheral nervous system

Central nervous system

FIGURE 4.6 The functional divisions of the human nervous system

reach the bottom of this page, your somatic nervous system will report to your brain the current state of your skeletal muscles and carry instructions back, triggering your hand to turn the page.

Our **autonomic nervous system** controls our glands and the muscles of our internal organs, influencing such functions as glandular activity, heartbeat, and digestion. Like an automatic pilot, this system may be consciously overridden, but usually it operates on its own (autonomously).

The autonomic nervous system serves two important, basic functions (**FIGURE 4.7** on the next page). The **sympathetic nervous system** arouses and expends energy. If something alarms, enrages, or challenges you, your sympathetic system will accelerate your heartbeat, raise your blood pressure, slow your digestion, raise your blood sugar, and cool you with perspiration, making you alert and ready for action. When the stress subsides, your **parasympathetic nervous system** produces opposite effects. It conserves energy as it calms you by decreasing your heartbeat, lowering your blood sugar, and so forth. In everyday situations, the sympathetic and parasympathetic nervous systems work together to keep you in a steady internal state.

The Central Nervous System

From the simplicity of neurons "talking" to other neurons arises the complexity of the central nervous system's brain and spinal cord.

It is the brain that enables our humanity—our thinking, feeling, and acting. Tens of billions of neurons, each communicating with thousands of other neurons, yield an ever-changing wiring diagram that dwarfs a powerful computer. With some 40 billion neurons, each having roughly 10,000 contacts with other neurons, we end up with perhaps 400 trillion synapses—places where neurons meet and greet their neighbors (de Courten-Myers, 2005). A grain-of-sand–sized speck of your brain contains some 100,000 neurons and one billion "talking" synapses (Ramachandran & Blakeslee, 1998).

The brain's neurons cluster into work groups called *neural networks*. To understand why, Stephen Kosslyn and Olivier Koenig (1992, p. 12) invite us to "think about why cities exist; why don't people distribute themselves more evenly across the countryside?"

autonomic [aw-tuh-NAHM-ik] **nervous system** the part of the peripheral nervous system that controls the glands and the muscles of the internal organs (such as the heart). Its sympathetic division arouses; its parasympathetic division calms.

sympathetic nervous system the division of the autonomic nervous system that arouses the body, mobilizing its energy in stressful situations.

parasympathetic nervous system the division of the autonomic nervous system that calms the body, conserving its energy.

© Tom Swick

"The body is made up of millions and millions of crumbs."

Stephen Colbert: "How does the brain work? Five words or less."
Steven Pinker: "Brain cells fire in patterns."
The Colbert Report, February 8, 2007

FIGURE 4.7 The dual functions of the autonomic nervous system The autonomic nervous system controls the more autonomous (or self-regulating) internal functions. Its sympathetic division arouses and expends energy. Its parasympathetic division calms and conserves energy, allowing routine maintenance activity. For example, sympathetic stimulation accelerates heartbeat, whereas parasympathetic stimulation slows it.

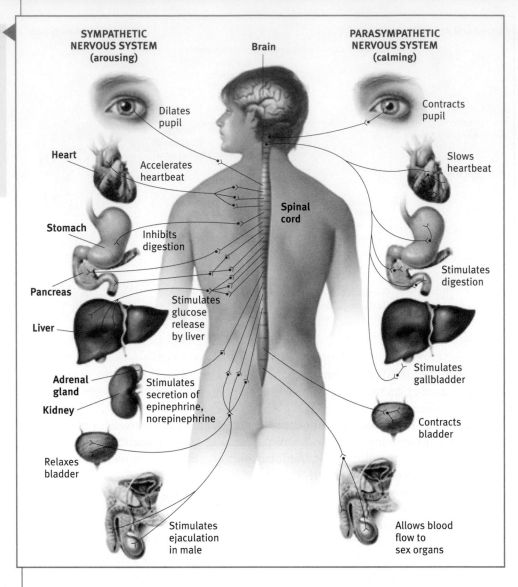

SYMPATHETIC NERVOUS SYSTEM (arousing)

Brain

PARASYMPATHETIC NERVOUS SYSTEM (calming)

Dilates pupil

Contracts pupil

Heart

Accelerates heartbeat

Slows heartbeat

Spinal cord

Stomach

Inhibits digestion

Stimulates digestion

Pancreas

Stimulates glucose release by liver

Liver

Stimulates gallbladder

Adrenal gland

Stimulates secretion of epinephrine, norepinephrine

Kidney

Contracts bladder

Relaxes bladder

Stimulates ejaculation in male

Allows blood flow to sex organs

reflex a simple, automatic response to a sensory stimulus, such as the knee-jerk response.

Like people networking with people, neurons network with nearby neurons with which they can have short, fast connections. As in **FIGURE 4.8**, the cells in each layer of a neural network connect with various cells in the next layer. Learning occurs as feedback strengthens connections. Learning to play the violin, for example, builds neural connections. Neurons that fire together wire together.

The *spinal cord* is an information highway connecting the peripheral nervous system to the brain. Ascending neural fibers send up sensory information, and descending fibers send back motor-control information. The neural pathways governing our **reflexes,** our automatic responses to stimuli, illustrate the spinal cord's work. A simple spinal reflex pathway is composed of a single sensory neuron and a single motor neuron. These often communicate through an interneuron. The knee-jerk response, for example, involves one such simple pathway. A headless warm body could do it.

Another such pathway enables the pain reflex (**FIGURE 4.9**). When your finger touches a flame, neural activity excited by the heat travels via sensory neurons to interneurons in your spinal cord. These interneurons respond by activating motor neurons leading to the muscles in your arm. Because the simple pain reflex pathway runs through the spinal cord and right back out, your hand jerks away from the

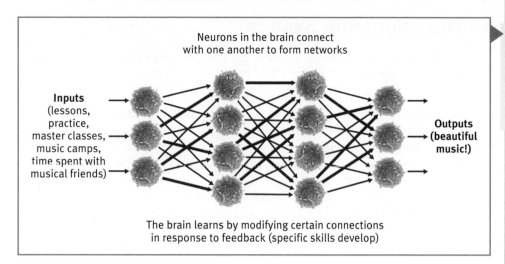

Neurons in the brain connect
with one another to form networks

Inputs
(lessons,
practice,
master classes,
music camps,
time spent with
musical friends)

**Outputs
(beautiful
music!)**

The brain learns by modifying certain connections
in response to feedback (specific skills develop)

FIGURE 4.8 A simplified neural network: learning to play the violin Neurons network with nearby neurons. Encoded in these networks of interrelating neurons is your own enduring identity (as a musician, an athlete, a devoted friend)—your sense of self that extends across the years.

candle's flame *before* your brain receives and responds to the information that causes you to feel pain. That's why it feels as if your hand jerks away not by your choice, but on its own.

Information travels to and from the brain by way of the spinal cord. Were the top of your spinal cord severed, you would not feel pain from your body below. Nor would you feel pleasure. With your brain literally out of touch with your body, you would lose all sensation and voluntary movement in body regions with sensory and motor connections to the spinal cord below its point of injury. You would exhibit the knee-jerk without feeling the tap. When the brain center keeping the brakes on erections is severed, men paralyzed below the waist may be capable of an erection (a simple reflex) if their genitals are stimulated (Goldstein, 2000). Females similarly paralyzed may respond with vaginal lubrication. But, depending on where and how completely the spinal cord is severed, they may be genitally unresponsive to erotic images and have no genital feeling (Kennedy & Over, 1990; Sipski & Alexander, 1999). To produce bodily pain or pleasure, the sensory information must reach the brain.

"If the nervous system be cut off between the brain and other parts, the experiences of those other parts are nonexistent for the mind. The eye is blind, the ear deaf, the hand insensible and motionless."

William James, *Principles of Psychology*, 1890

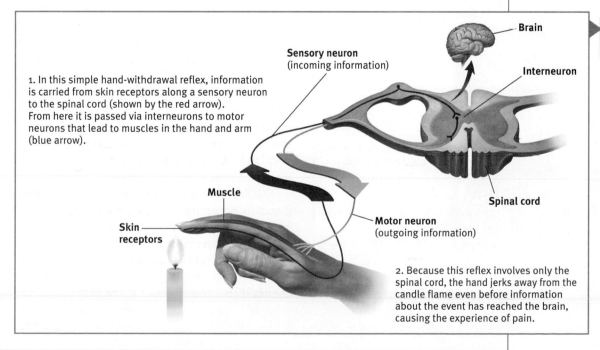

1. In this simple hand-withdrawal reflex, information is carried from skin receptors along a sensory neuron to the spinal cord (shown by the red arrow). From here it is passed via interneurons to motor neurons that lead to muscles in the hand and arm (blue arrow).

Sensory neuron (incoming information)

Brain

Interneuron

Spinal cord

Muscle

Skin receptors

Motor neuron (outgoing information)

2. Because this reflex involves only the spinal cord, the hand jerks away from the candle flame even before information about the event has reached the brain, causing the experience of pain.

FIGURE 4.9 A simple reflex

endocrine [EN-duh-krin] **system** the body's "slow" chemical communication system; a set of glands that secrete hormones into the bloodstream.

hormones chemical messengers that are manufactured by the endocrine glands, travel through the bloodstream, and affect other tissues.

adrenal [ah-DREEN-el] **glands** a pair of endocrine glands that sit just above the kidneys and secrete hormones (epinephrine and norepinephrine) that help arouse the body in times of stress.

pituitary gland the endocrine system's most influential gland. Under the influence of the hypothalamus, the pituitary regulates growth and controls other endocrine glands.

▶❙ The Endocrine System

4-5 How does the endocrine system—the body's slower information system—transmit its messages?

So far we have focused on the body's speedy electrochemical information system. Interconnected with your nervous system is a second communication system, the **endocrine system** (**FIGURE 4.10**). The endocrine system's glands secrete another form of chemical messengers, **hormones,** which travel through the bloodstream and affect other tissues, including the brain. When they act on the brain, they influence our interest in sex, food, and aggression.

Some hormones are chemically identical to neurotransmitters (those chemical messengers that diffuse across a synapse and excite or inhibit an adjacent neuron). The endocrine system and nervous system are therefore close relatives: Both produce molecules that act on receptors elsewhere. Like many relatives, they also differ. The speedy nervous system zips messages from eyes to brain to hand in a fraction of a second. Endocrine messages trudge along in the bloodstream, taking several seconds or more to travel from the gland to the target tissue. If the nervous system's communication delivers messages rather like e-mail, the endocrine system is the body's snail mail. But slow and steady sometimes wins the race. Endocrine messages tend to outlast the effects of neural messages. That helps explain why upset feelings may linger, sometimes beyond our thinking about what upset us. It takes time for us to "simmer down." In a moment of danger, for example, the autonomic nervous system orders the **adrenal glands** on top of the kidneys to release *epinephrine* and *norepinephrine* (also called *adrenaline* and *noradrenaline*). These hormones increase heart rate, blood pressure, and blood sugar, providing us with a surge of energy. When the emergency passes, the hormones—and the feelings of excitement—linger a while. The endocrine system's hormones influence many aspects of our lives—growth, reproduction, metabolism, mood—working with our nervous system to keep everything in balance while we respond to stress, exertion, and our own thoughts.

The most influential endocrine gland is the **pituitary gland,** a pea-sized structure located in the core of the brain, where it is controlled by an adjacent brain area, the hypothalamus. The pituitary releases hormones that influence growth, and its secretions also influence the release of hormones by other endocrine glands. The pituitary, then, is a sort of master gland (whose own master is the hypothalamus). For example, under the brain's influence, the pituitary triggers your sex glands to release sex hormones. These in turn influence your brain and behavior.

This feedback system (brain → pituitary → other glands → hormones → brain) reveals the intimate connection of the nervous and endocrine systems. The nervous system directs endocrine secretions, which then affect the nervous system. Conducting and coordinating this whole electrochemical orchestra is that maestro we call the brain.

FIGURE 4.10 The endocrine system

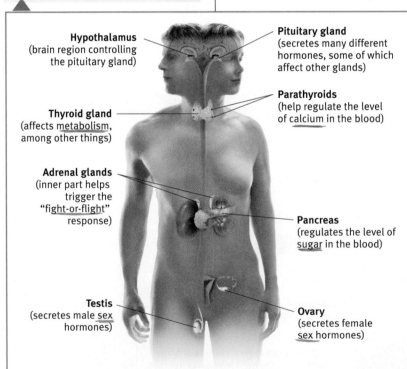

Hypothalamus (brain region controlling the pituitary gland)

Pituitary gland (secretes many different hormones, some of which affect other glands)

Parathyroids (help regulate the level of calcium in the blood)

Thyroid gland (affects metabolism, among other things)

Adrenal glands (inner part helps trigger the "fight-or-flight" response)

Pancreas (regulates the level of sugar in the blood)

Testis (secretes male sex hormones)

Ovary (secretes female sex hormones)

REVIEW

Neural and Hormonal Systems

4-1 **What are neurons, and how do they transmit information?** *Neurons* are the elementary components of the nervous system, the body's speedy electrochemical information system. *Sensory neurons* carry incoming information from sense receptors to the brain and spinal cord, and *motor neurons* carry information from the brain and spinal cord out to the muscles and glands. *Interneurons* communicate within the brain and spinal cord and between sensory and motor neurons. A neuron sends signals through its *axons*, and receives signals through its branching *dendrites*. If the combined signals are strong enough, the neuron fires, transmitting an electrical impulse (the *action potential*) down its axon by means of a chemistry-to-electricity process. The neuron's reaction is an all-or-none process.

4-2 **How do nerve cells communicate with other nerve cells?** When action potentials reach the end of an axon (the axon terminals), they stimulate the release of *neurotransmitters*. These chemical messengers carry a message from the sending neuron across a *synapse* to receptor sites on a receiving neuron. The sending neuron, in a process called *reuptake*, then normally absorbs the excess neurotransmitter molecules in the synaptic gap. The receiving neuron, if the signals from that neuron and others are strong enough, generates its own action potential and relays the message to other cells.

4-3 **How do neurotransmitters influence behavior, and how do drugs and other chemicals affect neurotransmission?** Each neurotransmitter travels a designated path in the brain and has a particular effect on behavior and emotions. Acetylcholine affects muscle action, learning, and memory. *Endorphins* are natural opiates released in response to pain and exercise. Drugs and other chemicals affect communication at the synapse. Agonists excite by mimicking particular neurotransmitters or by blocking their reuptake. Antagonists inhibit a particular neurotransmitter's release or block its effect.

4-4 **What are the functions of the nervous system's main divisions?** One major division of the *nervous system* is the *central nervous system (CNS)*, the brain and spinal cord. The other is the *peripheral nervous system (PNS)*, which connects the CNS to the rest of the body by means of *nerves*. The peripheral nervous system has two main divisions. The *somatic nervous system* enables voluntary control of the skeletal muscles. The *autonomic nervous system*, through its *sympathetic* and *parasympathetic* divisions, controls involuntary muscles and glands. Neurons cluster into working networks.

4-5 **How does the endocrine system—the body's slower information system—transmit its messages?** The *endocrine system* is a set of glands that secrete *hormones* into the bloodstream, where they travel through the body and affect other tissues, including the brain. The endocrine system's master gland, the *pituitary*, influences hormone release by other glands. In an intricate feedback system, the brain's hypothalamus influences the pituitary gland, which influences other glands, which release hormones, which in turn influence the brain.

Terms and Concepts to Remember

biological psychology, p. 46

neuron, p. 46

sensory neurons, p. 46

motor neurons, p. 46

interneurons, p. 46

dendrite, p. 47

axon, p. 47

myelin [MY-uh-lin] sheath, p. 47

action potential, p. 47

threshold, p. 48

synapse [SIN-aps], p. 49

neurotransmitters, p. 49

reuptake, p. 50

endorphins [en-DOR-fins], p. 50

nervous system, p. 52

central nervous system (CNS), p. 52

peripheral nervous system (PNS), p. 52

nerves, p. 52

somatic nervous system, p. 52

autonomic [aw-tuh-NAHM-ik] nervous system, p. 53

sympathetic nervous system, p. 53

parasympathetic nervous system, p. 53

reflex, p. 54

endocrine [EN-duh-krin] system, p. 56

hormones, p. 56

adrenal [ah-DREEN-el] glands, p. 56

pituitary gland, p. 56

Test Yourself

1. How do neurons communicate with one another?

2. How does information flow through your nervous system as you pick up a fork? Can you summarize this process?

3. Why is the pituitary gland called the "master gland"?

(Answers to the Test Yourself questions can be found in Appendix B at the end of the book.)

Ask Yourself

1. Can you recall a time when the endorphin response may have protected you from feeling extreme pain?

2. Does our nervous system's design—with its synaptic gaps that chemical messenger molecules cross in an imperceptibly brief instant—surprise you? Would you have designed yourself differently?

3. Can you remember feeling an extended period of discomfort after some particularly stressful event? How long did those feelings last?

∞ WEB

Multiple-choice self-tests and more may be found at www.worthpublishers.com/myers

MODULE 5

Tools of Discovery and Older Brain Structures

"You're certainly a lot less fun since the operation."

In a jar on a display shelf in Cornell University's psychology department resides the well-preserved brain of Edward Bradford Titchener, a great turn-of-the-century experimental psychologist and proponent of the study of consciousness. Imagine yourself gazing at that wrinkled mass of grayish tissue, wondering if in any sense Titchener is still there.[1]

You might answer that, without the living whir of electrochemical activity, there could be nothing of Titchener in his preserved brain. Consider then an experiment about which the inquisitive Titchener himself might have daydreamed. Imagine that just moments before his death, someone removed Titchener's brain from his body and kept it alive by floating it in a tank of cerebral fluid while feeding it enriched blood. Would Titchener still be in there? Further imagine that someone then transplanted the still-living brain into the body of a person with severe brain damage. To whose home should the recovered patient return?

That we can imagine such questions illustrates how convinced we are that we live "somewhere north of the neck" (Fodor, 1999). And for good reason: The brain enables the mind—seeing, hearing, smelling, feeling, remembering, thinking, speaking, dreaming. The brain is what poet Diane Ackerman (2004, p. 3) calls "that shiny mound of being . . . that dream factory . . . that huddle of neurons calling all the plays . . . that fickle pleasuredrome."

Moreover, it is the brain that self-reflectively analyzes the brain. When we're thinking *about* our brain, we're thinking *with* our brain—by firing countless millions of synapses and releasing billions of neurotransmitter molecules. The effect of hormones on experiences such as love reminds us that we would not be of the same mind if we were a bodiless brain. Brain + body = mind. Nevertheless, say neuroscientists, the *mind is what the brain does*. If all your organs were transplanted, you would still be much the same person, unless, as psychologist Jonathan Haidt has said, one of those organs was the brain. But precisely where and how are the mind's functions tied to the brain? Let's first see how scientists explore such questions.

"I am a brain, Watson. The rest of me is a mere appendix."

Sherlock Holmes, in Arthur Conan Doyle's "The Adventure of the Mazarin Stone"

▶‖ The Tools of Discovery: Having Our Head Examined

5-1 How do neuroscientists study the brain's connections to behavior and mind?

For centuries, we had no tools high-powered yet gentle enough to explore the living human brain. Clinical observations revealed some brain-mind connections. Physicians noted, for example, that damage to one side of the brain often caused numbness or paralysis on the body's opposite side, suggesting that the body's right side is wired to the brain's left side, and vice versa. Others noticed that damage to the back of the brain disrupted vision, and that damage to the left-front part of the brain produced speech difficulties. Gradually, these early explorers were mapping the brain.

[1]Carl Sagan's *Broca's Brain* (1979) inspired this question.

Banking brains Francine Benes, director of McLean Hospital's Brain Bank, sees the collection as a valuable database.

Now, within a lifetime, the whole brain-mapping process has changed. The known universe's most amazing organ is being probed and mapped by a new generation of neural cartographers. Whether in the interests of science or medicine, they can selectively **lesion** (destroy) tiny clusters of normal or defective brain cells, leaving the surrounding tissue unharmed. Such studies have revealed, for example, that damage to one area of the hypothalamus in a rat's brain reduces eating, causing the rat to starve unless force-fed. Damage in another area produces *over*eating.

Today's scientists can also electrically, chemically, or magnetically stimulate various parts of the brain and note the effects; snoop on the messages of individual neurons and eavesdrop on the chatter of billions of neurons; and see color representations of the brain's energy-consuming activity. These techniques for peering into the thinking, feeling brain are doing for psychology what the microscope did for biology and the telescope did for astronomy. Let's look at a few of them and see how neuroscientists study the working brain.

Recording the Brain's Electrical Activity

Right now, your mental activity is giving off telltale electrical, metabolic, and magnetic signals that would enable neuroscientists to observe your brain at work. The tips of modern microelectrodes are so small they can detect the electrical pulse in a single neuron. For example, we can now detect exactly where the information goes in a cat's brain when someone strokes its whisker.

Electrical activity in the brain's billions of neurons sweeps in regular waves across its surface. An **electroencephalogram (EEG)** is an amplified read-out of such waves. Studying an EEG of the brain's activity is like studying a car engine by listening to its hum. By presenting a stimulus repeatedly and having a computer filter out brain activity unrelated to the stimulus, one can identify the electrical wave evoked by the stimulus (**FIGURE 5.1**).

FIGURE 5.1 An electro-encephalograph providing amplified tracings of waves of electrical activity in the brain Here it is displaying the brain activity of this 4-year-old who has epilepsy.

lesion [LEE-zhuhn] tissue destruction. A brain lesion is a naturally or experimentally caused destruction of brain tissue.

electroencephalogram (EEG) an amplified recording of the waves of electrical activity that sweep across the brain's surface. These waves are measured by electrodes placed on the scalp.

FIGURE 5.2 The PET scan To obtain a PET scan, researchers inject volunteers with a low and harmless dose of a short-lived radioactive sugar. Detectors around the person's head pick up the release of gamma rays from the sugar, which has concentrated in active brain areas. A computer then processes and translates these signals into a map of the brain at work.

Courtesy of Brookhaven National Laboratories

Neuroimaging Techniques

"You must look into people, as well as at them," advised Lord Chesterfield in a 1746 letter to his son. Newer windows into the brain give us that Supermanlike ability to see inside the living brain. One such tool, the **PET (positron emission tomography) scan** (FIGURE 5.2), depicts brain activity by showing each brain area's consumption of its chemical fuel, the sugar glucose. Active neurons are glucose hogs. After a person receives temporarily radioactive glucose, the PET scan detects where this "food for thought" goes by locating the radioactivity. Rather like weather radar showing rain activity, PET scan "hot spots" show which brain areas are most active as the person performs mathematical calculations, looks at images of faces, or daydreams.

In **MRI (magnetic resonance imaging)** brain scans, the head is put in a strong magnetic field, which aligns the spinning atoms of brain molecules. Then a radio wave pulse momentarily disorients the atoms. When the atoms return to their normal spin, they release signals that provide a detailed picture of the brain's soft tissues. (MRI

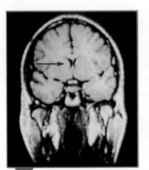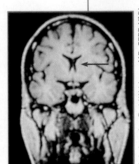

Both photos from Daniel Weinberger, M.D., CBDB, NIMH

scans are also used to scan other body parts.) MRI scans have revealed a larger-than-average neural area in the left hemisphere of musicians who display perfect pitch (Schlaug et al., 1995). They have also revealed enlarged fluid-filled brain areas in some patients who have schizophrenia, a disabling psychological disorder (FIGURE 5.3).

A special application of MRI—**fMRI (functional MRI)**—can reveal the brain's functioning as well as its structure. Where the brain is especially active, blood goes. By comparing MRI scans taken less than a second apart, researchers can watch the brain "light up" (with increased oxygen-laden bloodflow) as a person performs different mental functions. As the person looks at a scene, for example, the fMRI machine detects blood rushing to the back of the brain, which processes visual information. Such snapshots of the brain's changing activity provide new insights into how the brain divides its labor.

To be learning about the neurosciences now is like studying world geography while Magellan was exploring the seas. This truly is the golden age of brain science.

FIGURE 5.3 MRI scan of a healthy individual (left) and a person with schizophrenia (right) Note the enlarged fluid-filled brain region in the image on the right.

PET (positron emission tomography) scan a visual display of brain activity that detects where a radioactive form of glucose goes while the brain performs a given task.

MRI (magnetic resonance imaging) a technique that uses magnetic fields and radio waves to produce computer-generated images of soft tissue. MRI scans show brain anatomy.

fMRI (functional MRI) a technique for revealing bloodflow and, therefore, brain activity by comparing successive MRI scans. fMRI scans show brain function.

▶‖ Older Brain Structures

5-2 What are the functions of important lower-level brain structures?

If you could open the skull and look inside, the first thing you might note is the brain's size. In dinosaurs, the brain represents 1/100,000th of the body's weight; in whales, 1/10,000th; in elephants, 1/600th; in humans, 1/45th. It looks as though a principle is emerging. But read on. In mice, the brain is 1/40th of the body's weight, and in marmosets, 1/25th. So there are exceptions to the rule that the ratio of brain to body weight provides a clue to a species' intelligence.

Indicators about an animal's capacities come from its brain structures. In primitive animals, such as sharks, a not-so-complex brain primarily regulates basic survival functions: breathing, resting, and feeding. In lower mammals, such as rodents, a more complex brain enables emotion and greater memory. In advanced mammals, such as humans, a brain that processes more information enables foresight as well.

This increasing complexity arises from new brain systems built on top of the old, much as the Earth's landscape covers the old with the new. Digging down, one discovers the fossil remnants of the past—brainstem components performing for us much as they did for our distant ancestors. Let's start with the brain's basement and work up to the newer systems.

The Brainstem

The brain's oldest and innermost region is the **brainstem.** It begins where the spinal cord swells slightly after entering the skull. This slight swelling is the **medulla** (**FIGURE 5.4**). Here lie the controls for your heartbeat and breathing. Just above the medulla sits the *pons,* which helps coordinate movements. If a cat's brainstem is severed from the rest of the brain above it, the animal will still breathe and live—and even run, climb, and groom (Klemm, 1990). But cut off from the brain's higher regions, it won't purposefully run or climb to get food.

The brainstem is a crossover point, where most nerves to and from each side of the brain connect with the body's opposite side. This peculiar cross-wiring is but one of the brain's many surprises.

Inside the brainstem, between your ears, lies the **reticular** ("netlike") **formation,** a finger-shaped network of neurons that extends from the spinal cord right up to the thalamus. As the spinal cord's sensory input travels up to the thalamus, some of it travels through the reticular formation, which filters incoming stimuli and relays important information to other areas of the brain.

In 1949, Giuseppe Moruzzi and Horace Magoun discovered that electrically stimulating the reticular formation of a sleeping cat almost instantly produced an awake, alert animal. When Magoun *severed* a cat's reticular formation from higher brain regions, without damaging the nearby sensory pathways, the effect was equally dramatic: The cat lapsed into a coma from which it never awakened. Magoun could clap his hands by the cat's ear, even pinch it; still, no response. The conclusion? The reticular formation is involved in arousal.

brainstem the oldest part and central core of the brain, beginning where the spinal cord swells as it enters the skull; the brainstem is responsible for automatic survival functions.

medulla [muh-DUL-uh] the base of the brainstem; controls heartbeat and breathing.

reticular formation a nerve network in the brainstem that plays an important role in controlling arousal.

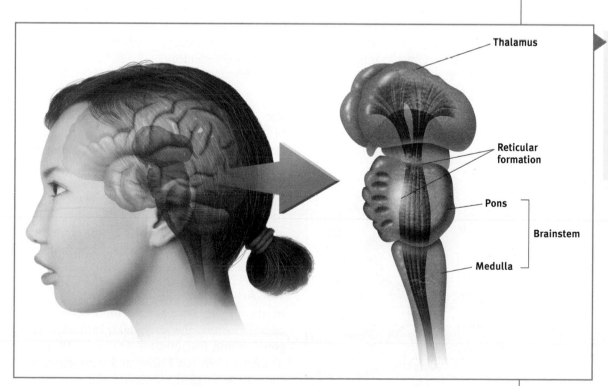

Thalamus

Reticular formation

Pons

Brainstem

Medulla

FIGURE 5.4 The brainstem and thalamus The brainstem, including the pons and medulla, is an extension of the spinal cord. The thalamus is attached to the top of the brainstem. The reticular formation passes through both structures.

The Thalamus

Sitting at the top of the brainstem is the **thalamus** (Figure 5.4). This joined pair of egg-shaped structures acts as the brain's sensory switchboard. It receives information from all the senses except smell and routes it to the higher brain regions that deal with seeing, hearing, tasting, and touching. Think of the thalamus as being to sensory input what London is to England's trains: a hub through which traffic passes en route to various destinations. The thalamus also receives some of the higher brain's replies, which it then directs to the medulla and to the cerebellum.

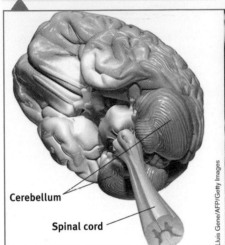

FIGURE 5.5 The brain's organ of agility Hanging at the back of the brain, the cerebellum coordinates our voluntary movements, as when David Beckham directs the ball precisely.

Cerebellum

Spinal cord

Lluis Gene/AFP/Getty Images

"Consciousness is a small part of what the brain does."

Neuroscientist Joseph LeDoux, in "Mastery of Emotions," 2006

The Cerebellum

Extending from the rear of the brainstem is the baseball-sized **cerebellum,** meaning "little brain," which is what its two wrinkled halves resemble (**FIGURE 5.5**). The cerebellum enables one type of nonverbal learning and memory. It helps us judge time, modulate our emotions, and discriminate sounds and textures (Bower & Parsons, 2003). It also coordinates voluntary movement. When soccer great David Beckham fires the ball into the net with a perfectly timed kick, give his cerebellum some credit. If you injured your cerebellum, you would have difficulty walking, keeping your balance, or shaking hands. Your movements would be jerky and exaggerated. Under alcohol's influence on the cerebellum, walking may lack coordination, as many a driver has learned after being pulled over and given a roadside test.

Note: These older brain functions all occur without any conscious effort. This illustrates another of our recurring themes: *Our brain processes most information outside of our awareness.* We are aware of the *results* of our brain's labor (say, our current visual experience) but not of *how* we construct the visual image. Likewise, whether we are asleep or awake, our brainstem manages its life-sustaining functions, freeing our newer brain regions to think, talk, dream, or savor a memory.

The Limbic System

At the border ("limbus") between the brain's older parts and the *cerebral hemispheres*—the two halves of the brain—is the **limbic system** (**FIGURE 5.6**). One limbic system component, the *hippocampus,* processes memory. (If animals or humans lose their hippocampus to surgery or injury, they become unable to process new memories of facts and episodes.) For now, let's look at the limbic system's links to emotions (such as fear and anger) and to basic motives (such as those for food and sex).

FIGURE 5.6 The limbic system This neural system sits between the brain's older parts and its cerebral hemispheres. The limbic system's hypothalamus controls the nearby pituitary gland.

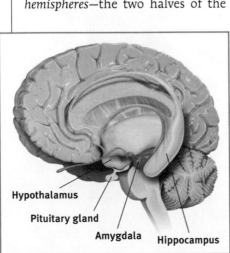

Hypothalamus

Pituitary gland

Amygdala   Hippocampus

The Amygdala

In the limbic system, two lima bean–sized neural clusters, the **amygdala,** influence aggression and fear (**FIGURE 5.7**). In 1939, psychologist Heinrich Klüver and neurosurgeon Paul Bucy surgically lesioned the part of a

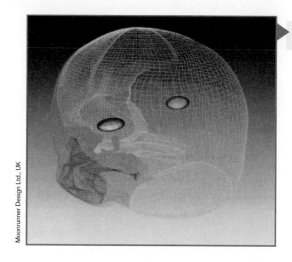

Moonrunner Design Ltd, UK

> **FIGURE 5.7 The amygdala**

thalamus [THAL-uh-muss]   the brain's sensory switchboard, located on top of the brainstem; it directs messages to the sensory receiving areas in the cortex and transmits replies to the cerebellum and medulla.

cerebellum [sehr-uh-BELL-um]   the "little brain" at the rear of the brainstem; functions include processing sensory input and coordinating movement output and balance.

limbic system   neural system (including the *hippocampus, amygdala,* and *hypothalamus*) located below the cerebral hemispheres; associated with emotions and drives.

amygdala [uh-MIG-duh-la]   two lima bean–sized neural clusters in the limbic system; linked to emotion.

hypothalamus [hi-po-THAL-uh-muss] a neural structure lying below *(hypo)* the thalamus; it directs several maintenance activities (eating, drinking, body temperature), helps govern the endocrine system via the pituitary gland, and is linked to emotion and reward.

rhesus monkey's brain that included the amygdala. The result? The normally ill-tempered monkey turned into the most mellow of creatures. Poke it, pinch it, do virtually anything that normally would trigger a ferocious response, and still the animal remained placid. In later studies with other wild animals, including the lynx, wolverine, and wild rat, researchers noted the same effect. What then might happen if we electrically stimulated the amygdala in a normally placid domestic animal, such as a cat? Do so in one spot and the cat prepares to attack, hissing with its back arched, its pupils dilated, its hair on end. Move the electrode only slightly within the amygdala, cage the cat with a small mouse, and now it cowers in terror.

These experiments confirm the amygdala's role in rage and fear, including the perception of these emotions and the processing of emotional memories (Anderson & Phelps, 2000; Poremba & Gabriel, 2001). Still, we must be careful. The brain is not neatly organized into structures that correspond to our categories of behavior. Aggressive and fearful behavior involves neural activity in many brain levels. Even within the limbic system, stimulating structures other than the amygdala can evoke such behavior. If you charge your car's dead battery, you can activate the engine. Yet the battery is merely one link in an integrated system that makes a car go.

Frank Siteman/Stock, Boston

> **Aggression as a brain state** Back arched and fur fluffed, this fierce cat is ready to attack. Electrical stimulation of a cat's amygdala provokes reactions such as the one shown here, suggesting its role in emotions like rage. Which division of the autonomic nervous system is activated by such stimulation? (Answer below.)
>
> The cat would be aroused via its sympathetic nervous system.

The Hypothalamus

Just below *(hypo)* the thalamus is the **hypothalamus** (**FIGURE 5.8** on the next page), an important link in the chain of command governing bodily maintenance. Some neural clusters in the hypothalamus influence hunger; others regulate thirst, body temperature, and sexual behavior.

The hypothalamus both monitors blood chemistry and takes orders from other parts of the brain. For example, thinking about sex (in your brain's cerebral cortex) can stimulate your hypothalamus to secrete hormones. These hormones in turn trigger the adjacent "master gland," the pituitary (see Figure 5.6), to influence hormones released by other glands. (Note the interplay between the nervous and endocrine systems: The brain influences the endocrine system, which in turn influences the brain.)

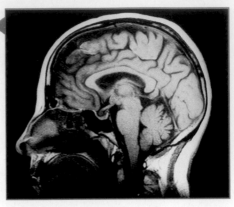

FIGURE 5.8 The hypothalamus This small but important structure, colored yellow/orange in this MRI scan photograph, helps keep the body's internal environment in a steady state.

A remarkable discovery about the hypothalamus illustrates how progress in science often occurs—when curious, open-minded investigators make an unexpected observation. Two young McGill University neuropsychologists, James Olds and Peter Milner (1954), were trying to implant an electrode in a rat's reticular formation when they made a magnificent mistake: They incorrectly placed the electrode in what they later discovered was a region of the rat's hypothalamus (Olds, 1975). Curiously, as if seeking more stimulation, the rat kept returning to the location where it had been stimulated by this misplaced electrode. On discovering their mistake, Olds and Milner alertly realized they had stumbled upon a brain center that provides a pleasurable reward.

In a meticulous series of experiments, Olds (1958) went on to locate other "pleasure centers," as he called them. (What the rats actually experience only they know, and they aren't telling. Rather than attribute human feelings to rats, today's scientists refer to *reward centers,* not "pleasure centers.") When allowed to press pedals to trigger their own stimulation in these areas, rats would sometimes do so at a feverish pace—up to 7000 times per hour—until they dropped from exhaustion. Moreover, to get this stimulation, they would even cross an electrified floor that a starving rat would not cross to reach food (**FIGURE 5.9**).

Similar reward centers in or near the hypothalamus were later discovered in many other species, including goldfish, dolphins, and monkeys. In fact, animal research has revealed both a general reward system that triggers the release of the neurotransmitter dopamine, and specific centers associated with the pleasures of eating, drinking, and sex. Animals, it seems, come equipped with built-in systems that reward activities essential to survival.

Experimenters have found new ways of using limbic stimulation to control animals' actions. By using brain stimulation to reward rats for turning left or right, Sanjiv Talwar and his colleagues (2002) trained previously caged rats to navigate natural environments (**FIGURE 5.10**). By pressing buttons on a laptop, the researchers

"If you were designing a robot vehicle to walk into the future and survive, . . . you'd wire it up so that behavior that ensured the survival of the self or the species—like sex and eating—would be naturally reinforcing."

Candace Pert (1986)

FIGURE 5.9 Rat with an implanted electrode With an electrode implanted in a reward center of its hypothalamus, the rat readily crosses an electrified grid, accepting the painful shocks, to press a pedal that sends electrical impulses to that center.

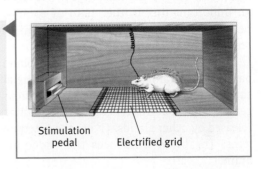

Stimulation pedal   Electrified grid

FIGURE 5.10 Ratbot on a pleasure cruise When stimulated by remote control, this rat could be guided to navigate across a field and even up a tree.

can direct a rat—which carries a receiver, power source, and video camera on a backpack—to turn on cue, climb trees, scurry along branches, and turn around and come back down. Their work suggests future applications in search-and-rescue operations.

Do we humans also have limbic centers for pleasure? Indeed we do. To calm violent patients, one neurosurgeon implanted electrodes in such areas. Stimulated patients reported mild pleasure; however, unlike Olds' rats, they were not driven to a frenzy (Deutsch, 1972; Hooper & Teresi, 1986). Some researchers believe that addictive disorders, such as alcohol dependence, drug abuse, and binge eating, may stem from a *reward deficiency syndrome*—a genetically disposed deficiency in the natural brain systems for pleasure and well-being that leads people to crave whatever provides that missing pleasure or relieves negative feelings (Blum et al., 1996).

FIGURE 5.11 locates the brain areas discussed in this module.

FIGURE 5.11 Brain structures and their functions

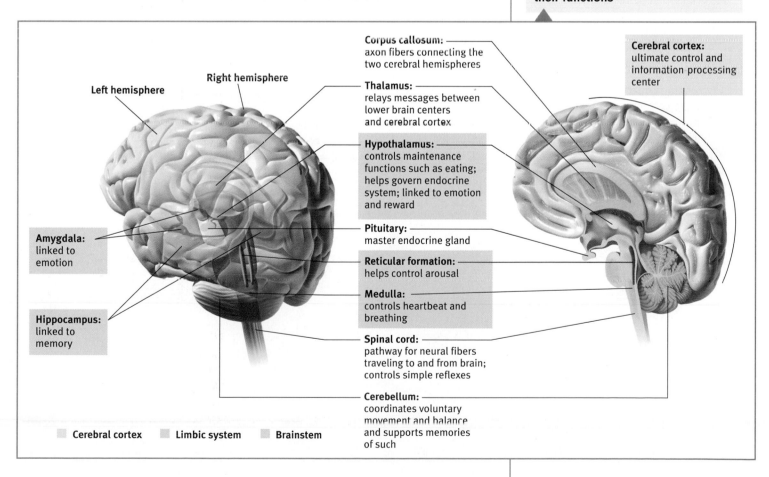

Left hemisphere

Right hemisphere

Corpus callosum: axon fibers connecting the two cerebral hemispheres

Cerebral cortex: ultimate control and information-processing center

Thalamus: relays messages between lower brain centers and cerebral cortex

Hypothalamus: controls maintenance functions such as eating; helps govern endocrine system; linked to emotion and reward

Amygdala: linked to emotion

Pituitary: master endocrine gland

Reticular formation: helps control arousal

Medulla: controls heartbeat and breathing

Hippocampus: linked to memory

Spinal cord: pathway for neural fibers traveling to and from brain; controls simple reflexes

Cerebellum: coordinates voluntary movement and balance and supports memories of such

Cerebral cortex   Limbic system   Brainstem

REVIEW

Tools of Discovery and Older Brain Structures

5-1 **How do neuroscientists study the brain's connections to behavior and mind?** Clinical observations and *lesioning* reveal the general effects of brain damage. *MRI* scans now reveal brain structures, and EEG, *PET,* and *fMRI (functional MRI)* recordings reveal brain activity.

5-2 **What are the functions of important lower-level brain structures?** The *brainstem* is the oldest part of the brain and is responsible for automatic survival functions. Its components are the *medulla* (which controls heartbeat and breathing), the *pons* (which helps coordinate movements), and the *reticular formation* (which affects arousal). The *thalamus,* the brain's sensory switchboard, sits above the brainstem. The *cerebellum,* attached to the rear of the brainstem, coordinates muscle movement and helps process sensory information.

The *limbic system* is linked to emotions, memory, and drives. Its neural centers include the *amygdala* (involved in responses of aggression and fear) and the *hypothalamus* (involved in various bodily maintenance functions, pleasurable rewards, and the control of the hormonal system). The hypothalamus also controls the pituitary, which influences other glands to release hormones. The hippocampus processes memory.

Terms and Concepts to Remember

lesion [LEE-zhuhn], p. 59

electroencephalogram (EEG), p. 59

PET (positron emission tomography) scan, p. 60

MRI (magnetic resonance imaging), p. 60

fMRI (functional MRI), p. 60

brainstem, p. 61

medulla [muh-DUL-uh], p. 61

reticular formation, p. 61

thalamus [THAL-uh-muss], p. 62

cerebellum [sehr-uh-BELL-um], p. 62

limbic system, p. 62

amygdala [uh-MIG-duh-la], p. 62

hypothalamus [hi-po-THAL-uh-muss], p. 63

Test Yourself

1. Within what brain region would damage be most likely to disrupt your ability to skip rope? Your ability to sense tastes or sounds? In what brain region would damage perhaps leave you in a coma? Without the very breath and heartbeat of life?

(Answers to the Test Yourself questions can be found in Appendix B at the end of the book.)

Ask Yourself

1. How do you feel about the idea of using selective lesioning or electrical stimulation to reduce aggression in those convicted of violent acts? How about for reducing appetite in those who are overweight?

○○ WEB

Multiple-choice self-tests and more may be found at www.worthpublishers.com/myers

The Cerebral Cortex and Our Divided Brain

The Cerebral Cortex

Our Divided Brain

Right-Left Differences in the Intact Brain

▶‖ The Cerebral Cortex

6-1 What functions are served by the various cerebral cortex regions?

Older brain networks sustain basic life functions and enable memory, emotions, and basic drives. Newer neural networks within the *cerebrum*—the two large hemispheres that contribute 85 percent of the brain's weight—form specialized work teams that enable our perceiving, thinking, and speaking. Covering those hemispheres, like bark on a tree, is the **cerebral cortex,** a thin surface layer of interconnected neural cells. It is your brain's thinking crown, your body's ultimate control and information-processing center.

As we move up the ladder of animal life, the cerebral cortex expands, tight genetic controls relax, and the organism's adaptability increases. Frogs and other amphibians with a small cortex operate extensively on preprogrammed genetic instructions. The larger cortex of mammals offers increased capacities for learning and thinking, enabling them to be more adaptable. What makes us distinctively human mostly arises from the complex functions of our cerebral cortex.

Structure of the Cortex

If you opened a human skull, exposing the brain, you would see a wrinkled organ, shaped somewhat like the meat of an oversized walnut. Without these wrinkles, a flattened cerebral cortex would require triple the area—roughly that of a very large pizza. The brain's ballooning left and right hemispheres are filled mainly with axons connecting the cortex to the brain's other regions. The cerebral cortex—that thin surface layer—contains some 20 to 23 billion nerve cells and 300 trillion synaptic connections (de Courten-Myers, 2005). Being human takes a lot of nerve.

Supporting these billions of nerve cells are nine times as many spidery **glial cells** ("glue cells"). Neurons are like queen bees; on their own they cannot feed or sheathe themselves. Glial cells are worker bees. They provide nutrients and insulating myelin, guide neural connections, and mop up ions and neurotransmitters. Glia may also play a role in learning and thinking. By "chatting" with neurons they may participate in information transmission and memory (Miller, 2005).

Moving up the ladder of animal life, the proportion of glia to neurons increases. A recent postmortem analysis of Einstein's brain did not find more or larger-than-usual neurons, but it did reveal a much greater concentration of glial cells than found in an average Albert's head (Fields, 2004).

Stepping back to consider the whole cortex, each hemisphere is divided into four *lobes,* geographic subdivisions separated by prominent *fissures,* or folds (**FIGURE 6.1** on the next page). Starting at the front of your brain and moving over the top, there are the **frontal lobes** (behind your forehead), the **parietal lobes** (at the top and to the rear), and the **occipital lobes** (at the back of your head). Reversing direction and moving forward, just above your ears, you find the **temporal lobes.** Each of the four lobes carries out many functions, and many functions require the interplay of several lobes.

‖ The people who first dissected and labeled the brain used the language of scholars—Latin and Greek. Their words are actually attempts at graphic description: For example, *cortex* means "bark," *cerebellum* is "little brain," and *thalamus* is "inner chamber." ‖

cerebral [seh-REE-bruhl] **cortex** the intricate fabric of interconnected neural cells covering the cerebral hemispheres; the body's ultimate control and information-processing center.

glial cells (glia) cells in the nervous system that support, nourish, and protect neurons.

frontal lobes portion of the cerebral cortex lying just behind the forehead; involved in speaking and muscle movements and in making plans and judgments.

parietal [puh-RYE-uh-tuhl] **lobes** portion of the cerebral cortex lying at the top of the head and toward the rear; receives sensory input for touch and body position.

occipital [ahk-SIP-uh-tuhl] **lobes** portion of the cerebral cortex lying at the back of the head; includes areas that receive information from the visual fields.

temporal lobes portion of the cerebral cortex lying roughly above the ears; includes the auditory areas, each receiving information primarily from the opposite ear.

FIGURE 6.1 The cortex and its basic subdivisions

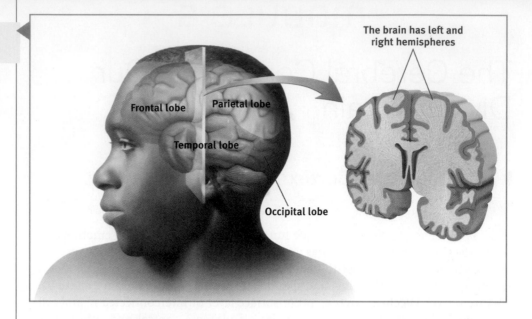

Functions of the Cortex

More than a century ago, autopsies of people who had been partially paralyzed or speechless revealed damaged cortical areas. But this rather crude evidence did not convince researchers that specific parts of the cortex perform specific complex functions. After all, if control of speech and movement were diffused across the cortex, damage to almost any area might produce the same effect. A television with its power cord cut would go dead, but we would be fooling ourselves if we thought we had "localized" the picture in the cord.

Motor Functions

Scientists had better luck in localizing simpler brain functions. For example, in 1870, when German physicians Gustav Fritsch and Eduard Hitzig applied mild electrical stimulation to parts of a dog's cortex, they made an important discovery: They could make parts of its body move. The effects were selective: Stimulation caused movement only when applied to an arch-shaped region at the back of the frontal lobe, running roughly ear-to-ear across the top of the brain. Moreover, stimulating parts of this region in the left or right hemisphere caused movements of specific body parts on the *opposite* side of the body. Fritsch and Hitzig had discovered what is now called the **motor cortex** (FIGURE 6.2).

Mapping the Motor Cortex Lucky for brain surgeons and their patients, the brain has no sensory receptors. Knowing this, Otfrid Foerster and Wilder Penfield were able to map the motor cortex in hundreds of wide-awake patients by stimulating different cortical areas and observing the body's responses. They discovered that body areas requiring precise control, such as the fingers and mouth, occupied the greatest amount of cortical space.

Spanish neuroscientist José Delgado repeatedly demonstrated the mechanics of motor behavior. In one human patient, he stimulated a spot on the left motor cortex that triggered the right hand to make a fist. Asked to keep the fingers open during the next stimulation, the patient, whose fingers closed despite his best efforts, remarked, "I guess, Doctor, that your electricity is stronger than my will" (Delgado, 1969, p. 114).

‖ *Demonstration:* Try moving your right hand in a circular motion, as if polishing a table. Now start your right foot doing the same motion synchronized with the hand. Now reverse the foot motion (but not the hand). Tough, huh? But easier if you try moving the *left* foot opposite to the right hand. The left and right limbs are controlled by opposite sides of the brain. So their opposed activities interfere less with each other. ‖

motor cortex   an area at the rear of the frontal lobes that controls voluntary movements.

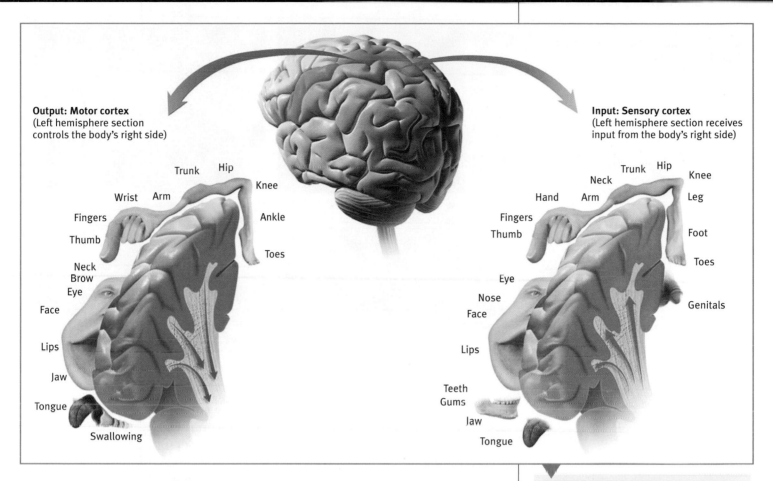

Output: Motor cortex
(Left hemisphere section controls the body's right side)

Trunk · Hip · Knee · Arm · Wrist · Ankle · Fingers · Thumb · Toes · Neck · Brow · Eye · Face · Lips · Jaw · Tongue · Swallowing

Input: Sensory cortex
(Left hemisphere section receives input from the body's right side)

Trunk · Hip · Neck · Knee · Hand · Arm · Leg · Fingers · Thumb · Foot · Toes · Eye · Nose · Face · Genitals · Lips · Teeth · Gums · Jaw · Tongue

FIGURE 6.2 Left hemisphere tissue devoted to each body part in the motor cortex and the sensory cortex As you can see from this classic though inexact representation, the amount of cortex devoted to a body part is not proportional to that part's size. Rather, the brain devotes more tissue to sensitive areas and to areas requiring precise control. Thus, the fingers have a greater representation in the cortex than does the upper arm.

More recently, scientists have been able to predict a monkey's arm motion a tenth of a second before it moves—by repeatedly measuring motor cortex activity preceding specific arm movements (Gibbs, 1996). Such findings, some researchers believe, have opened the door to a new generation of *prosthetics* (artificial body part replacements).

Neural Prosthetics By similarly eavesdropping on the brain, could we enable someone—perhaps a paralyzed person—to move a robotic limb or command a cursor to write an e-mail or surf the Net? To find out, Brown University brain researchers implanted 100 tiny recording electrodes in the motor cortexes of three monkeys (Nicolelis & Chapin, 2002; Serruya et al., 2002). As the monkeys used a joystick to move a cursor to follow a moving red target (to gain rewards), the researchers matched the brain signals with the arm movements. Then they programmed a computer to monitor the signals and operate the joystick without the monkey's help. When a monkey merely thought about a move, the mind-reading computer moved the cursor with nearly the same proficiency as had the reward-seeking monkey. In a follow-up experiment, two monkeys were trained to control a robot arm that could reach for and grab food (Velliste et al., 2008).

Research has also recorded messages not from the motor neurons that directly control a monkey's arm, but from a brain area involved in planning and intention (Musallam et al., 2004). While the monkeys awaited a cue that told them to reach toward a spot (to get a juice reward) that had flashed on a screen in one of up to eight locations, a computer program recorded activity in this planning-intention brain area. By matching this neural brain activity to the monkey's subsequent

Mind over matter Guided by a tiny, 100-electrode brain implant, monkeys learned to control a mechanical arm that can grab snacks and put them in their mouth (Velliste et al., 2008). Implantable electrode grids are not yet permanently effective, but such research raises hopes that people with paralyzed limbs may someday be able to use their own brain signals to control computers and robotic prosthetic limbs.

Motorlab, University of Pittsburgh School of Medicine

pointing, the mind-reading researchers could now program a cursor to move in response to the monkey's thinking. Monkey think, computer do.

If this technique works with motor brain areas, why not use it to capture the words a person can think but cannot say (for example, after a stroke)? Cal Tech neuroscientist Richard Andersen (2004, 2005) speculates that researchers could implant electrodes in speech areas, "ask a patient to think of different words and observe how the cells fire in different ways. So you build up your database, and then when the patient thinks of the word, you compare the signals with your database, and you can predict the words they're thinking. Then you take this output and connect it to a speech synthesizer. This would be identical to what we're doing for motor control."

In 2004, the U.S. Food and Drug Administration approved the first clinical trial of neural prosthetics with paralyzed humans (Pollack, 2004, 2006). The first patient, a paralyzed 25-year-old man, was able to mentally control a television, draw shapes on a computer screen, and play video games—all thanks to an aspirin-sized chip with 100 microelectrodes recording activity in his motor cortex (Hochberg et al., 2006).

Sensory Functions

If the motor cortex sends messages out to the body, where does the cortex receive the incoming messages? Penfield also identified the cortical area that specializes in receiving information from the skin senses and from the movement of body parts. This area at the front of the parietal lobes, parallel to and just behind the motor cortex, we now call the **sensory cortex** (Figure 6.2). Stimulate a point on the top of this band of tissue and a person may report being touched on the shoulder; stimulate some point on the side and the person may feel something on the face.

The more sensitive the body region, the larger the sensory cortex area devoted to it (Figure 6.2). Your supersensitive lips project to a larger brain area than do your toes, which is one reason we kiss with our lips rather than touch toes. Rats have a large area of the brain devoted to their whisker sensations, and owls to their hearing sensations.

sensory cortex area at the front of the parietal lobes that registers and processes body touch and movement sensations.

association areas areas of the cerebral cortex that are not involved in primary motor or sensory functions; rather, they are involved in higher mental functions such as learning, remembering, thinking, and speaking.

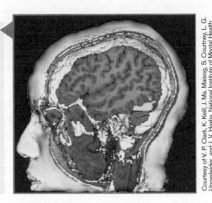

FIGURE 6.3 New technology shows the brain in action This fMRI (functional MRI) scan shows the visual cortex in the occipital lobes activated (color representation of increased bloodflow) as a research participant looks at a photo. When the person stops looking, the region instantly calms down.

Courtesy of V. P. Clark, K. Keill, J. Ma. Maisog, S. Courtney, L. G. Ungerleider, and J. V. Haxby, National Institute of Mental Health

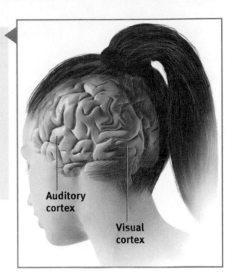

FIGURE 6.4 The visual cortex and auditory cortex The visual cortex of the occipital lobes at the rear of your brain receives input from your eyes. The auditory cortex, in your temporal lobes—above your ears—receives information from your ears.

Auditory cortex

Visual cortex

Scientists have identified additional areas where the cortex receives input from senses other than touch. At this moment, you are receiving visual information in the visual cortex in your occipital lobes, at the very back of your brain (**FIGURES 6.3** and **6.4**). A bad enough bash there would make you blind. Stimulated there, you might see flashes of light or dashes of color. (In a sense, we *do* have eyes in the back of our head!) From your occipital lobes, visual information goes to other areas that specialize in tasks such as identifying words, detecting emotions, and recognizing faces.

Any sound you now hear is processed by your auditory cortex in your temporal lobes (Figure 6.4). (If you think of your clenched fist as your brain, and hold it in front of you, your thumb would roughly correspond to one of your temporal lobes.) Most of this auditory information travels a circuitous route from one ear to the auditory receiving area above your opposite ear. If stimulated there, you might hear a sound. MRI scans of people with schizophrenia reveal active auditory areas in the temporal lobes during auditory hallucinations (Lennox et al., 1999). Even the phantom ringing sound experienced by people with hearing loss is—if heard in one ear—associated with activity in the temporal lobe on the brain's opposite side (Muhlnickel, 1998).

Association Areas

So far, we have pointed out small areas of the cortex that either receive sensory input or direct muscular output. In humans, that leaves a full three-fourths of the thin, wrinkled layer, the cerebral cortex, uncommitted to sensory or muscular activity. What, then, goes on in this vast region of the brain? Neurons in these **association areas** (the peach-colored areas in **FIGURE 6.5**) integrate information. They link sensory inputs with stored memories—a very important part of thinking.

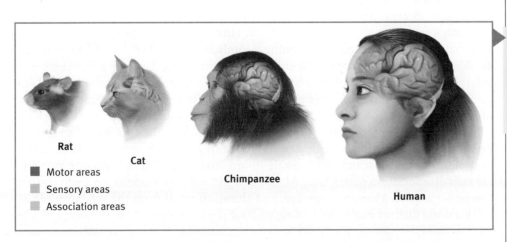

Rat

Cat

Chimpanzee

Human

■ Motor areas
■ Sensory areas
■ Association areas

FIGURE 6.5 Areas of the cortex in four mammals More intelligent animals have increased "uncommitted" or association areas of the cortex. These vast areas of the brain are responsible for integrating and acting on information received and processed by sensory areas.

Electrically probing the association areas doesn't trigger any observable response. So, unlike the sensory and motor areas, association area functions cannot be neatly mapped. Their silence has led to what Donald McBurney (1996, p. 44) calls "one of the hardiest weeds in the garden of psychology": the claim that we ordinarily use only 10 percent of our brains. (If true, wouldn't this imply a 90 percent chance that a bullet to your brain would land in an unused area?) Surgically lesioned animals and brain-damaged humans bear witness that association areas are not dormant. Rather, these areas interpret, integrate, and act on information processed by the sensory areas.

Association areas are found in all four lobes. In the frontal lobes, they enable judgment, planning, and processing of new memories. People with damaged frontal lobes may have intact memories, high scores on intelligence tests, and great cake-baking skills. Yet they would not be able to plan ahead to *begin* baking a cake for a birthday party (Huey et al., 2006).

FIGURE 6.6 Phineas Gage reconsidered Using measurements of his skull (which was kept as a medical record) and modern neuroimaging techniques, researcher Hanna Damasio and her colleagues (1994) have reconstructed the probable path of the rod through Gage's brain.

Frontal lobe damage also can alter personality, removing a person's inhibitions. Consider the classic case of railroad worker Phineas Gage. One afternoon in 1848, Gage, then 25 years old, was packing gunpowder into a rock with a tamping iron. A spark ignited the gunpowder, shooting the rod up through his left cheek and out the top of his skull, leaving his frontal lobes massively damaged (**FIGURE 6.6**). To everyone's amazement, he was immediately able to sit up and speak, and after the wound healed he returned to work. But the affable, soft-spoken Phineas Gage was now irritable, profane, and dishonest. Although his mental abilities and memories were intact, his personality was not. This person, said his friends, was "no longer Gage." He eventually lost his job and ended up earning his living as a fairground exhibit.

With his frontal lobes ruptured, Gage's moral compass had disconnected from his behavior. Similar impairments to moral judgment have appeared in more recent studies of people with damaged frontal lobes. Not only may they become less inhibited (without the frontal lobe brakes on their impulses), but their moral judgments seem unrestrained by normal emotions. Would you advocate pushing someone in front of a runaway boxcar to save five others? Most people do not, but those with damage to a brain area behind the eyes often do (Koenigs et al., 2007).

Association areas also perform other mental functions. In the parietal lobes, parts of which were large and unusually shaped in Einstein's normal-weight brain, they enable mathematical and spatial reasoning (Witelson et al., 1999). An area on the underside of the right temporal lobe enables us to recognize faces. If a stroke or head injury destroyed this area of your brain, you would still be able to describe facial features and to recognize someone's gender and approximate age, yet be strangely unable to identify the person as, say, Jack Black, or even your grandmother.

Nevertheless, we should be wary of using pictures of brain "hot spots" to create a new phrenology that locates complex functions in precise brain areas (Uttal, 2001). Complex mental functions don't reside in any one place. There is no one spot in a rat's small association cortex that, when damaged, will obliterate its ability to learn or remember a maze. Memory, language, and attention result from the synchronized activity among distinct brain areas (Knight, 2007).

The Brain's Plasticity

6-2 To what extent can a damaged brain reorganize itself?

Our brains are sculpted not only by our genes but also by our experiences. MRI scans show that well-practiced pianists have a larger-than-usual auditory cortex area that encodes piano sounds (Bavelier et al., 2000; Pantev et al., 1998). Other modules focus more on how experience molds the brain, but for now, let's turn to evidence from studies of the brain's **plasticity,** its ability to modify itself after some types of damage.

Unlike cut skin, severed neurons usually do not regenerate (if your spinal cord were severed, you would probably be permanently paralyzed). And some very specific brain functions seem preassigned to particular areas. One newborn who suffered damage to the facial recognition areas on both temporal lobes never regained a normal ability to recognize faces (Farah et al., 2000). But there is good news: Some neural tissue can *reorganize* in response to damage. It happens within all of us, as the brain repairs itself after little mishaps.

Our brains are most plastic when we are young children (Kolb, 1989; see also **FIGURE 6.7**). *Constraint-induced therapy* aims to rewire brains by restraining a fully functioning limb and forcing use of the "bad hand" or the uncooperative leg. Gradually, the therapy reprograms the brain, improving the dexterity of a brain-damaged child or even an adult stroke victim (Taub, 2004). One stroke victim, a surgeon in his fifties, was put to work cleaning tables, with his good arm and hand restrained. Slowly, the bad arm recovered its skills. As the damaged brain functions migrated to other brain regions, he gradually learned to write again and even to play tennis (Doidge, 2007).

The brain's plasticity is good news for those blind or deaf. Blindness or deafness makes unused brain areas available for other uses (Amedi et al., 2005). If a blind person uses one finger to read Braille, the brain area dedicated to that finger expands as the sense of touch invades the visual cortex that normally helps people see (Barinaga, 1992a; Sadato et al., 1996). Temporarily "knock out" the visual cortex with magnetic stimulation, and a lifelong-blind person will make more errors on a *language* task (Amedi et al., 2004). In Deaf people whose native language is sign, the temporal lobe area normally dedicated to hearing waits in vain for stimulation. Finally, it looks for other signals to process, such as those from the visual system. That helps explain why some studies find that Deaf people have enhanced peripheral vision (Bosworth & Dobkins, 1999).

Plasticity is especially evident after serious damage. If a slow-growing left hemisphere tumor disrupts language, the right hemisphere may compensate (Thiel et al., 2006). Lose a finger and the sensory cortex that received its input will begin to receive input from the adjacent fingers, which then become more sensitive (Fox, 1984). Lost fingers also feature in another mysterious phenomenon. As Figure 6.2 shows, the hand is between the sensory cortex's face and arm regions. When stroking the arm of someone whose hand had been amputated, V. S. Ramachandran found the person felt the sensations not only on the area stroked but also on the nonexistent ("phantom") fingers. Sensory fibers that terminate on adjacent areas had invaded the brain area vacated by the hand.

plasticity the brain's ability to change, especially during childhood, by reorganizing after damage or by building new pathways based on experience.

Joe McNally/Joe McNally Photography

FIGURE 6.7 Brain plasticity If surgery or an injury destroys one part of a child's brain or, as in the case of this 6-year-old, even an entire *hemisphere* (removed to eliminate seizures), the brain will compensate by putting other areas to work. One Johns Hopkins medical team reflected on the child hemispherectomies they had performed. Although use of the opposite hand is compromised, they reported being "awed" by how well children retain their memory, personality, and humor after removal of either brain hemisphere (Vining et al., 1997). The younger the child, the greater the chance that the remaining hemisphere can take over the functions of the one that was surgically removed (Choi, 2008).

neurogenesis the formation of <u>new</u> neurons.

corpus callosum [KOR-pus kah-LOW-sum] the large band of neural fibers connecting the two brain hemispheres and carrying messages between them.

Note, too, that the toes region is adjacent to the genitals. So what do you suppose was the sexual intercourse experience of another Ramachandran patient whose lower leg had been amputated? "I actually experience my orgasm in my foot. And there it's much bigger than it used to be because it's no longer just confined to my genitals" (Ramachandran & Blakeslee, 1998, p. 36).

Although brain modification often takes the form of reorganization, evidence suggests that, contrary to long-held belief, adult mice and humans can also generate new brain cells (Jessberger et al., 2008). Monkey brains illustrate **neurogenesis** by forming thousands of new neurons each day. These baby neurons originate deep in the brain and may then migrate elsewhere and form connections with neighboring neurons (Gould, 2007). Master stem cells that can develop into any type of brain cell have also been discovered in the human embryo. If mass-produced in a lab and injected into a damaged brain, might neural stem cells turn themselves into replacements for lost brain cells? Might we someday be able to rebuild damaged brains, much as we reseed damaged lawns? Might new drugs spur the production of new nerve cells? Stay tuned. Today's biotech companies are hard at work on such possibilities (Gage, 2003). In the meantime, we can all benefit from other natural promoters of neurogenesis, such as exercise, sleep, and nonstressful but stimulating environments (Iso et al., 2007; Pereira et al., 2007; Stranahan et al., 2006).

▶‖ Our Divided Brain

6-3 What do split brains reveal about the functions of our two brain hemispheres?

For more than a century, clinical evidence has shown that the brain's two sides serve differing functions. This hemispheric specialization (or *lateralization*) is apparent after brain damage. Accidents, strokes, and tumors in the left hemisphere can impair reading, writing, speaking, arithmetic reasoning, and understanding. Similar lesions in the right hemisphere seldom have such dramatic effects.

By 1960, many interpreted these differences as evidence that the left hemisphere is the "dominant" or "major" hemisphere, and its silent companion to the right is the "subordinate" or "minor" hemisphere. Then researchers found that the "minor" right hemisphere was not so limited after all. The story of this discovery is a fascinating chapter in psychology's history.

Splitting the Brain

In 1961, two Los Angeles neurosurgeons, Philip Vogel and Joseph Bogen, speculated that major epileptic seizures were caused by an amplification of abnormal brain activity bouncing back and forth between the two cerebral hemispheres. If so, they wondered, could they put an end to this biological tennis game by severing the **corpus callosum** (**FIGURE 6.8**), the wide band of axon fibers connecting the two hemispheres and carrying messages between them?

Vogel and Bogen knew that psychologists Roger Sperry, Ronald Myers, and Michael Gazzaniga had divided the brains of cats and monkeys in this manner, with no serious ill effects. So the surgeons operated. The result? The seizures were all but eliminated. Moreover, the

FIGURE 6.8 The corpus callosum This large band of neural fibers connects the two brain hemispheres. To photograph the half brain shown at left, a surgeon separated the hemispheres by cutting through the corpus callosum and lower brain regions. In the view on the right, brain tissue has been cut back to expose the corpus callosum and bundles of fibers coming out from it.

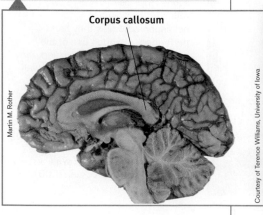

Corpus callosum

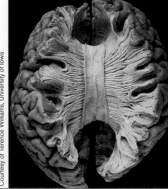

patients with these **split brains** were surprisingly normal, their personality and intellect hardly affected. Waking from surgery, one even joked that he had a "splitting headache" (Gazzaniga, 1967).

Sperry and Gazzaniga's studies of people with split brains provide a key to understanding the two hemispheres' complementary functions. As **FIGURE 6.9** explains, the peculiar nature of our visual wiring enabled the researchers to send information to a patient's left or right hemisphere. As the person stared at a spot, they flashed a stimulus to its right or left. They could do this with you, too, but in your intact brain, the hemisphere receiving the information would instantly pass the news to its partner across the valley. Not so in patients who had undergone split-brain surgery. The phone cables responsible for transmitting messages from one hemisphere to the other—the corpus callosum—had been severed. This enabled the researchers to quiz each hemisphere separately.

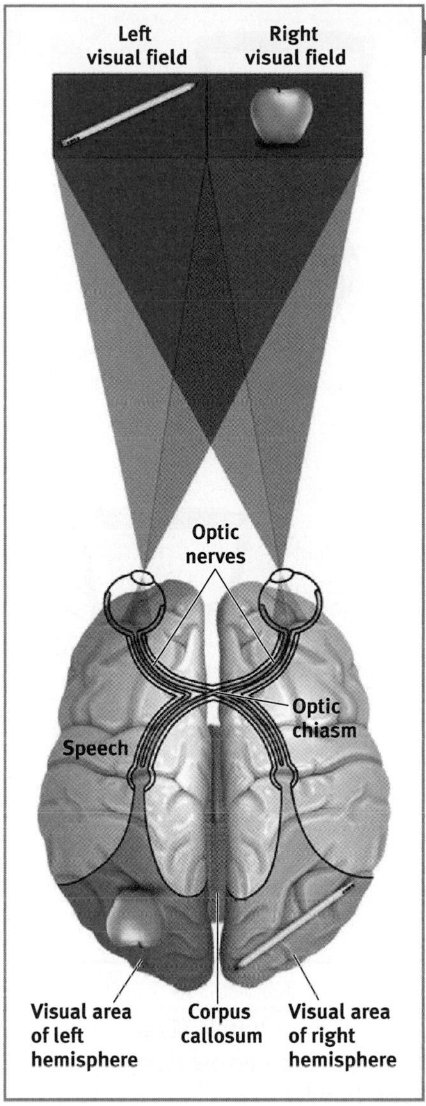

In an early experiment, Gazzaniga (1967) asked these patients to stare at a dot as he flashed HE·ART on a screen (**FIGURE 6.10** on the next page). Thus, HE appeared in their left visual field (which transmits to the right hemisphere) and ART in the right field (which transmits to the left hemisphere). When he then asked what they had seen, the patients said they had seen ART. But when asked to point to the word, they were startled when their left hand (controlled by the right hemisphere) pointed to HE. Given an opportunity to express itself, each hemisphere reported what it had seen. The right hemisphere (controlling the left hand) intuitively knew what it could not verbally report.

When a picture of a spoon was flashed to their right hemisphere, the patients could not *say* what they had viewed. But when asked to *identify* what they had viewed by feeling an assortment of hidden objects with their left hand, they readily selected the spoon. If the experimenter said, "Right!" the patient might reply, "What? Right? How could I possibly pick out the right object when I don't know what I saw?" It is, of course, the left hemisphere doing the talking here, bewildered by what the nonverbal right hemisphere knows.

A few people who have had split-brain surgery have been for a time bothered by the unruly independence of their left hand, which might unbutton a shirt while the right hand buttoned it, or put grocery store items back on the shelf after the right hand put them in the cart. It was as if each hemisphere was thinking "I've half a mind to wear my green (blue) shirt today." Indeed, said Sperry (1964), split-brain surgery leaves people "with two separate minds." With a split brain, both hemispheres can comprehend and follow an instruction to copy—*simultaneously*—different figures with the

FIGURE 6.9 The information highway from eye to brain Information from the left half of your field of vision goes to your right hemisphere, and information from the right half of your visual field goes to your left hemisphere, which usually controls speech. (Note, however, that each eye receives sensory information from both the right and left visual fields.) Data received by either hemisphere are quickly transmitted to the other across the corpus callosum. In a person with a severed corpus callosum, this information sharing does not take place.

split brain a condition resulting from surgery that isolates the brain's two hemispheres by cutting the fibers (mainly those of the corpus callosum) connecting them.

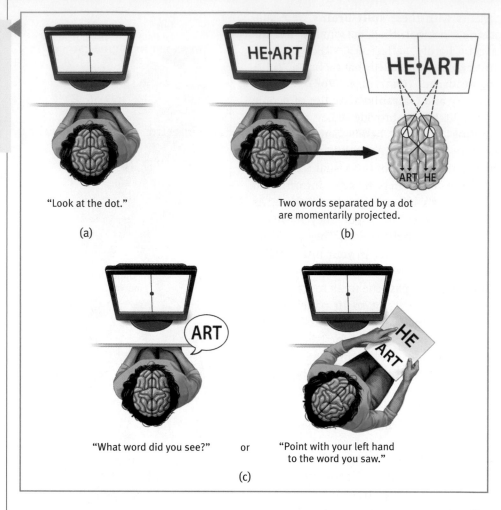

FIGURE 6.10 Testing the divided brain When an experimenter flashes the word HEART across the visual field, a woman with a split brain reports seeing the portion of the word transmitted to her left hemisphere. However, if asked to indicate with her left hand what she saw, she points to the portion of the word transmitted to her right hemisphere. (From Gazzaniga, 1983.)

"Look at the dot."

(a)

Two words separated by a dot are momentarily projected.

(b)

"What word did you see?"   or   "Point with your left hand to the word you saw."

(c)

left and right hands (Franz et al., 2000; see also **FIGURE 6.11**). (Reading these reports, I fantasize a person enjoying a solitary game of "rock, paper, scissors"—left versus right hand.)

When the "two minds" are at odds, the left hemisphere does mental gymnastics to rationalize reactions it does not understand. If a patient follows an order sent to the

FIGURE 6.11 Try this! Joe, who has had split-brain surgery, can simultaneously draw two different shapes.

BBC

right hemisphere ("Walk"), a strange thing happens. Unaware of the order, the left hemisphere doesn't know why the patient begins walking. Yet, when asked why, the patient doesn't say "I don't know." Instead, the interpretive left hemisphere improvises—"I'm going into the house to get a Coke." Thus, Michael Gazzaniga (1988), who considers these patients "The most fascinating people on earth," concludes that the conscious left hemisphere is an "interpreter" or press agent that instantly constructs theories to explain our behavior.

These studies reveal that the left hemisphere is more active when a person deliberates over decisions (Rogers, 2003). When the rational left brain is active, people more often discount disagreeable information (Drake, 1993). The right hemisphere understands simple requests, easily perceives objects, and is more engaged when quick, intuitive responses are needed. The right side of the brain also surpasses the left at copying drawings and at recognizing faces. The right hemisphere is skilled at perceiving emotion and at portraying emotions through the more expressive left side of the face (**FIGURE 6.12**). Right-hemisphere damage therefore more greatly disrupts emotion processing and social conduct (Tranel et al., 2002).

Most of the body's paired organs—kidneys, lungs, breasts—perform identical functions, providing a backup system should one side fail. Not so the brain's two halves, which can simultaneously carry out different functions with minimal duplication of effort. The result is a biologically odd but smart couple, each seemingly with a mind of its own.

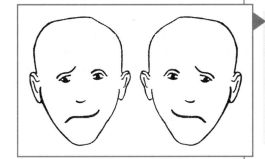

FIGURE 6.12 Which one is happier? Look at the center of one face, then the other. Does one appear happier? Most people say the right face does. Some researchers think this is because the right hemisphere, which is skilled in emotion processing, receives information from the left half of each face (when looking at its center).

|| *Question:* If we flashed a red light to the right hemisphere of a person with a split brain and flashed a green light to the left hemisphere, would each observe its own color? Would the person be aware that the colors differ? What would the person verbally report seeing? (Answers below.)||

Answers: Yes. No. Green.

▶|| Right-Left Differences in the Intact Brain

So, what about the 99.99+ percent of us with undivided brains? Does each of *our* hemispheres also perform distinct functions? Several different types of studies indicate they do.

When a person performs a *perceptual* task, for example, brain waves, bloodflow, and glucose consumption reveal increased activity in the *right* hemisphere. When the person speaks or calculates, activity increases in the *left* hemisphere.

A dramatic demonstration of hemispheric specialization happens before some types of brain surgery. To check the location of language centers, the surgeon injects a sedative into the neck artery feeding blood to the left hemisphere. Before the injection, the patient is lying down, arms in the air, chatting with the doctor. You can probably predict what happens when the drug flows into the artery going to the left hemisphere: Within seconds, the person's right arm falls limp. The patient also usually becomes speechless until the drug wears off. When the drug enters the artery to the right hemisphere, the *left* arm falls limp, but the person can still speak.

Which hemisphere would you suppose enables sign language among deaf people? The right, because of its visual-spatial superiority? Or the left, because it typically processes language? Studies reveal that, just as hearing people usually use the left hemisphere to process speech, deaf people use the left hemisphere to process sign language (Corina et al., 1992; Hickok et al., 2001). A stroke in the left hemisphere will disrupt a deaf person's signing, much as it would disrupt a hearing person's speaking. The same brain area is similarly involved in both spoken and signed speech production (Corina, 1998). To the brain, language is language, whether spoken or signed.

Although the left hemisphere is adept at making quick, literal interpretations of language, the right hemisphere excels in making inferences (Beeman & Chiarello, 1998;

Bowden & Beeman, 1998; Mason & Just, 2004). Primed with the flashed word *foot*, the left hemisphere will be especially quick to recognize the closely associated word *heel*. But if primed with *foot*, *cry*, and *glass*, the right hemisphere will more quickly recognize another word distantly related to all three *(cut)*. And if given an insightlike problem— "What word goes with *boot, summer,* and *ground?*"—the right hemisphere more quickly than the left recognizes the solution—*camp*. As one patient explained after a right-hemisphere stroke, "I understand words, but I'm missing the subtleties."

The right hemisphere also helps us modulate our speech to make meaning clear— as when we ask "What's that in the road ahead?" instead of "What's that in the road, a head?" (Heller, 1990).

The right hemisphere also seems to help orchestrate our sense of self. People who suffer partial paralysis will sometimes obstinately deny their impairment—strangely claiming they can move a paralyzed limb—if the damage is to the right hemisphere (Berti et al., 2005). With right brain damage, some patients have difficulty perceiving who other people are in relation to themselves, as in the case of a man who saw medical caretakers as family (Feinberg & Keenan, 2005). Others fail to recognize themselves in a mirror, or assign ownership of a limb to someone else ("that's my husband's arm"). The power of the right brain appeared in an experiment in which people with normal brains viewed a series of images that progressively morphed from the face of a co-worker into their own face. As people recognized themselves, parts of their right brain displayed sudden activity. But when magnetic stimulation disrupted their normal right-brain activity, they had difficulty recognizing themselves in the morphed photos (Uddin et al., 2005, 2006).

Simply looking at the two hemispheres, so alike to the naked eye, who would suppose they contribute uniquely to the harmony of the whole? Yet a variety of observations—of people with split brains and people with normal brains—converge beautifully, leaving little doubt that we have unified brains with specialized parts.

Brain Organization and Handedness

6-4   How does handedness relate to brain organization?

Nearly 90 percent of us are primarily right-handed (Leask & Beaton, 2007; Medland et al., 2004; Peters et al., 2006). Some 10 percent of us (somewhat more among males, somewhat less among females) are left-handed. (A few people write with their

|| **Most people also kick with their right foot, look through a microscope with their right eye, and (had you noticed?) kiss the right way—with their head tilted right (Güntürkün, 2003).** ||

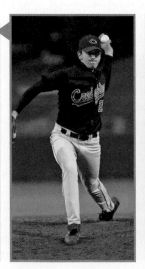

The rarest of baseball players: an ambidextrous pitcher Using a glove with two thumbs, Creighton University pitcher Pat Venditte, shown here in a 2008 game, pitched to right-handed batters with his right hand, then switched to face left-handed batters with his left hand. After one switch-hitter switched sides of the plate, Venditte switched pitching arms, which triggered the batter to switch again, and so on. The umpires ultimately ended the comedy routine by applying a little-known rule: A pitcher must declare which arm he will use before throwing his first pitch to a batter (Schwarz, 2007).

AP Photo/Nati Harnik, File

right hand and throw a ball with their left, or vice versa.) Almost all right-handers (96 percent) process speech primarily in the left hemisphere, which tends to be the slightly larger hemisphere (Hopkins, 2006). Left-handers are more diverse. Seven in ten process speech in the left hemisphere, as right-handers do. The rest either process language in the right hemisphere or use both hemispheres.

Is Handedness Inherited?

Judging from prehistoric human cave drawings, tools, and hand and arm bones, this veer to the right occurred long ago (Corballis, 1989; Steele, 2000). Right-handedness prevails in all human cultures. Moreover, it appears prior to culture's impact. Ultrasound observations of fetal thumb-sucking reveal that more than 9 in 10 fetuses suck the right hand's thumb (Hepper et al., 1990, 2004). This bias for the right hand is unique to humans and to the primates most like us: chimpanzees and bonobos (Hopkins, 2006). Other primates are more evenly divided between lefties and righties.

Observing 150 human babies during the first two days after their birth, George Michel (1981) found that two-thirds consistently preferred to lie with their heads turned to the right. When he again studied a sample of these babies at age 5 months, almost all of the "head-right" babies reached for things with their right hands, and almost all of the "head-left" babies reached with their left hands. Such findings, along with the universal prevalence of right-handers, indicate that either genes or some prenatal factors influence handedness.

So, Is It All Right to Be Left-Handed?

Judging by our everyday conversation, left-handedness is not all right. To be "coming out of left field" is hardly better than to be "gauche" (derived from the French word for "left"). On the other hand, right-handedness is "right on," which any "righteous" "right-hand man" "in his right mind" usually is.

Left-handers are more numerous than usual among those with reading disabilities, allergies, and migraine headaches (Geschwind & Behan, 1984). But in Iran, where students report which hand they write with when taking the university entrance exam, lefties outperform righties in all subjects (Noroozian et al., 2003). Left-handedness is also more common among musicians, mathematicians, professional baseball and cricket players, architects, and artists, including such luminaries as Michelangelo, Leonardo da Vinci, and Picasso.[1] Although left-handers must tolerate elbow jostling at the dinner table, right-handed desks, and awkward scissors, the pros and cons of being a lefty seem roughly equal.

* * *

We have glimpsed the truth of an overriding principle: Everything psychological is simultaneously biological. We have focused on how our thoughts, feelings, and actions arise from our specialized yet integrated brain. Elsewhere in this text, we further explore the significance of the biological revolution in psychology.

Today's neuroscience has come a long way, yet what is unknown still dwarfs what is known. We can describe the brain. We can learn the functions of its parts. We can study how the parts communicate. But how do we get mind out of meat? How does the electrochemical whir in a hunk of tissue the size of a head of lettuce give rise to elation, a creative idea, or that memory of Grandmother?

|| Evidence that challenges a genetic explanation of handedness: Handedness is one of but a few traits that genetically identical twins are not especially likely to share (Halpern & Coren, 1990). ||

[1]Strategic factors explain the higher-than-normal percentage of lefties in sports. For example, it helps a soccer team to have left-footed players on the left side of the field (Wood & Aggleton, 1989). In golf, however, no left-hander won the Masters tournament until Canadian Mike Weir did so in 2003.

Much as gas and air can give rise to something different—fire—so also, believed Roger Sperry, does the complex human brain give rise to something different: consciousness. The mind, he argued, emerges from the brain's dance of ions, yet is not reducible to it. Cells cannot be fully explained by the actions of atoms, nor minds by the activity of cells. Psychology is rooted in biology, which is rooted in chemistry, which is rooted in physics. Yet psychology is more than applied physics. As Jerome Kagan (1998) reminds us, the meaning of the Gettysburg Address is not reducible to neural activity. Sexual love is more than blood flooding to the genitals. Morality and responsibility become possible when we understand the mind as a "holistic system," said Sperry (1992) (**FIGURE 6.13**). We are not mere jabbering robots.

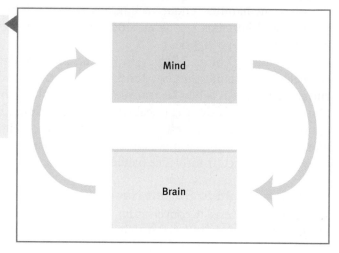

FIGURE 6.13 **Mind and brain as holistic system** In Roger Sperry's view, the brain creates and controls the emergent mind, which in turn influences the brain. (Think vividly about biting into a lemon and you may salivate.)

The mind seeking to understand the brain—that is indeed among the ultimate scientific challenges. And so it will always be. To paraphrase cosmologist John Barrow, a brain simple enough to be understood is too simple to produce a mind able to understand it.

REVIEW

The Cerebral Cortex and Our Divided Brain

6-1 **What functions are served by the various cerebral cortex regions?** In each hemisphere the *cerebral cortex* has four lobes, the *frontal, parietal, occipital,* and *temporal.* Each lobe performs many functions and interacts with other areas of the cortex. The *motor cortex* controls voluntary movements. The *sensory cortex* registers and processes body sensations. Body parts requiring precise control (in the motor cortex) or those that are especially sensitive (in the sensory cortex) occupy the greatest amount of space. Most of the brain's cortex—the major portion of each of the four lobes—is devoted to uncommitted *association areas,* which integrate information involved in learning, remembering, thinking, and other higher-level functions.

6-2 **To what extent can a damaged brain reorganize itself?** If one hemisphere is damaged early in life, the other will pick up many of its functions. This *plasticity* diminishes later in life. Some brain areas are capable of *neurogenesis* (forming new neurons).

6-3 **What do split brains reveal about the functions of our two brain hemispheres?** *Split-brain* research (experiments on people with a severed *corpus callosum*) has confirmed that in most people, the left hemisphere is the more verbal, and that the right hemisphere excels in visual perception and the recognition of emotion. Studies of healthy people with intact brains confirm that each hemisphere makes unique contributions to the integrated functioning of the brain.

6-4 **How does handedness relate to brain organization?** About 10 percent of us are left-handed. Almost all right-handers process speech in the left hemisphere, as do more than half of all left-handers.

Terms and Concepts to Remember

cerebral [seh-REE-bruhl] cortex, p. 67

glial cells (glia), p. 67

frontal lobes, p. 67

parietal [puh-RYE-uh-tuhl] lobes, p. 67

occipital [ahk-SIP-uh-tuhl] lobes, p. 67

temporal lobes, p. 67

motor cortex, p. 68

sensory cortex, p. 70

association areas, p. 71

plasticity, p. 73

neurogenesis, p. 74

corpus callosum [KOR-pus kah-LOW-sum], p. 74

split brain, p. 75

Test Yourself

1. What has split-brain research taught us about the intact brain?

2. What is the role of the corpus callosum in our brain?

(Answers to the Test Yourself questions can be found in Appendix B at the end of the book.)

Ask Yourself

1. Now that you have learned more about how our brains enable our minds, how has this affected your view of human nature?

∞ WEB

Multiple-choice self-tests and more may be found at www.worthpublishers.com/myers

Consciousness and the Two-Track Mind

MODULES

7
The Brain and Consciousness

8
Sleep and Dreams

9
Hypnosis

10
Drugs and Consciousness

Consciousness can be a funny thing. It offers us weird experiences, as when entering sleep or leaving a dream, and sometimes it leaves us wondering who is really in control. After putting me under the influence of nitrous oxide, my dentist tells me to turn my head to the left. My conscious mind resists: "No way," I silently say. "You can't boss me around!" Whereupon my robotic head, ignoring my conscious mind, turns obligingly under the dentist's control.

During my noontime pickup basketball games, I am sometimes mildly irritated as my body passes the ball while my conscious mind is saying, "No, stop, you fool! Peter is going to intercept!" Alas, my body completes the pass on its own. Other times, notes psychologist Daniel Wegner (2002) in *Illusion of Conscious Will*, people believe their consciousness is controlling their actions when it isn't. In one experiment, people co-controlled a computer mouse with a partner (who was actually the experimenter's accomplice). Even when the partner caused the mouse to stop on a predetermined square, the participants perceived that *they* had caused it to stop there.

And then there are those times when consciousness seems to split. Reading *Green Eggs and Ham* to one of my preschoolers for the umpteenth time, my obliging mouth could say the words while my mind wandered elsewhere. And if someone drops by my office while I'm typing this sentence, it's not a problem. My fingers can complete it as I strike up a conversation.

Was my drug-induced dental experience akin to people's experiences with other *psychoactive drugs* (mood- and perception-altering substances)? Was my automatic obedience to my dentist like people's responses to a hypnotist? Or does a split in consciousness, like those that we have when our mind goes elsewhere while reading or typing, explain people's behavior while under hypnosis? And during sleep, when and why do those weird dream experiences occur?

But first questions first: What is *consciousness?* Every science has concepts so fundamental they are nearly impossible to define. Biologists agree on what is alive but not on precisely what life is. In physics, *matter* and *energy* elude simple definition. To psychologists, consciousness is similarly a fundamental yet slippery concept.

At its beginning, *psychology* was "the description and explanation of states of consciousness" (Ladd, 1887). But during the first half of the twentieth century, the difficulty of scientifically studying consciousness led many psychologists—including those in the emerging school of *behaviorism*—to turn to direct observations of behavior. By the 1960s, psychology had nearly lost consciousness and was defining itself as "the science of behavior." Consciousness was likened to a car's speedometer: "It doesn't make the car go, it just reflects what's happening" (Seligman, 1991, p. 24).

After 1960, mental concepts began to reemerge. Advances in neuroscience made it possible to relate brain activity to sleeping, dreaming, and other mental states. Researchers began studying consciousness altered by hypnosis and drugs. Psychologists of all persuasions were affirming the importance of *cognition,* or mental processes. Psychology was regaining consciousness.

"Neither [psychologist] Steve Pinker nor I can explain human subjective consciousness. . . . We don't understand it."
Evolutionary biologist Richard Dawkins (1999)

"Psychology must discard all reference to consciousness."
Behaviorist John B. Watson (1913)

FIGURE 1 States of consciousness In addition to normal, waking awareness, consciousness comes to us in altered states, including daydreaming, sleeping, meditating, and drug-induced hallucinating.

Some states occur spontaneously	Daydreaming	Drowsiness	Dreaming
Some are physiologically induced	Hallucinations	Orgasm	Food or oxygen starvation
Some are psychologically induced	Sensory deprivation	Hypnosis	Meditation

Over the course of a day, a week, a month, we flit between various *states of consciousness,* from waking to sleeping and various other altered states (**FIGURE 1**). Module 7 focuses on the brain and consciousness in light of today's cognitive neuroscience and dual processing. Module 8 offers an in-depth look at sleep and dreams. Module 9 discusses various beliefs about hypnosis, including research support for some of the claims related to hypnosis. Module 10 details dependence, addiction, and the three main categories of psychoactive drugs.

MODULE 7

The Brain and Consciousness

7-1 What is the "dual processing" being revealed by today's cognitive neuroscience?

For most psychologists today, **consciousness** is our awareness of ourselves and our environment. Our spotlight of awareness allows us to assemble information from many sources as we reflect on our past and plan for our future. And it focuses our attention when we learn a complex concept or behavior—say, driving a car—making us aware of the car and the traffic. With practice, driving no longer requires our undivided attention, freeing us to focus our attention on other things.

In today's science, one of the most hotly pursued research quests is to understand the biology of consciousness. Evolutionary psychologists speculate that consciousness must offer a reproductive advantage (Barash, 2006). Perhaps consciousness helps us act in our long-term interests (by considering consequences) rather than merely seeking short-term pleasure and avoiding pain. Or perhaps consciousness promotes our survival by anticipating how we seem to others and helping us read their minds. ("He looks really angry! I'd better run!") Even so, that leaves us with the so-called "hard-problem": How do brain cells jabbering to one another create our awareness of the taste of a taco, the pain of a toothache, the feeling of fright?

▶‖ Cognitive Neuroscience

Scientists assume, in the words of neuroscientist Marvin Minsky (1986, p. 287), that "the mind is what the brain does." We just don't know *how* it does it. Even with all the world's chemicals, computer chips, and energy, we still don't have a clue *how* to make a conscious robot. Yet today's **cognitive neuroscience**—the interdisciplinary study of the brain activity linked with our mental processes—is taking the first small step by relating specific brain states to conscious experiences. We know, for example, that the upper brainstem contributes to consciousness because some children born without a cerebral cortex exhibit signs of consciousness (Merker, 2007).

Another stunning demonstration of some level of consciousness appeared in brain scans of a noncommunicative patient—a 23-year-old woman who had been in a car accident and showed no outward signs of conscious awareness (Owen et al., 2006). When researchers asked her to *imagine* playing tennis or moving around her home, fMRI scans revealed brain activity like that of healthy volunteers. As she imagined playing tennis, for example, an area of her brain controlling arm and leg movements became active (**FIGURE 7.1**). Even in a motionless body, the researchers concluded, the brain—and the mind—may still be active.

However, most cognitive neuroscientists are exploring and mapping the *conscious* functions of the cortex. Based on your cortical activation patterns, they can now, in some limited ways, read your mind. They can, for example, tell which of 10 similar objects (hammer, drill, and so forth) you are viewing (Shinkareva et al., 2008). Despite such advances, much disagreement remains. One research group theorizes that conscious experiences arise from specific neuron circuits firing in a specific manner. Another sees conscious experiences as produced by the synchronized activity of the whole brain (Koch & Greenfield, 2007). How the brain produces the mind remains a mystery.

consciousness our awareness of ourselves and our environment.

cognitive neuroscience the interdisciplinary study of the brain activity linked with cognition (including perception, thinking, memory, and language).

FIGURE 7.1 Evidence of awareness? When asked to imagine playing tennis or navigating her home, a vegetative patient's brain (top) exhibited activity similar to a healthy person's brain (bottom). Although the case may be an exception, researchers wonder if such fMRI scans might enable a "conversation" with unresponsive patients, by instructing them, for example, to answer *yes* to a question by imagining playing tennis, and *no* by imagining walking around their home.

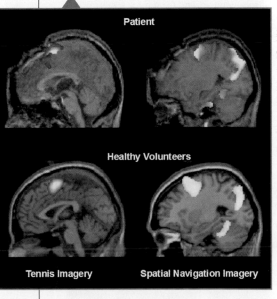

Patient

Healthy Volunteers

Tennis Imagery   Spatial Navigation Imagery

Courtesy: Adrian M. Owen, MRC Cognition and Brain Sciences Unit, University of Cambridge

dual processing the principle that information is often simultaneously processed on separate conscious and unconscious tracks.

▶‖ Dual Processing

Many cognitive neuroscience discoveries tell us of a particular brain region that becomes active with a particular conscious experience. Such findings strike many people as interesting but not mind-blowing. (If everything psychological is simultaneously biological, then our ideas, emotions, and spirituality must all, somehow, be embodied.) What *is* mind-blowing to many of us is the growing evidence that we have, so to speak, two minds, each supported by its own neural equipment.

At any moment, you and I are aware of little more than what's on the screen of our consciousness. But one of the grand ideas of recent cognitive neuroscience is that much of our brain work occurs off stage, out of sight. For example, fascinating studies of split-brain patients have revealed a conscious "left brain" and a more intuitive "right brain." Other modules explore our hidden mind at work in research on unconscious *priming,* on conscious *(explicit)* and unconscious *(implicit)* memories, on conscious versus automatic prejudices, and on the out-of-sight processing that enables sudden insights and creative moments. Perception, memory, thinking, language, and attitudes all operate on two levels—a conscious, deliberate "high road" and an unconscious, automatic "low road." Today's researchers call this **dual processing.** We know more than we know we know.

The Two-Track Mind

A scientific story illustrates the mind's two levels. Sometimes science-aided critical thinking confirms widely held beliefs. But sometimes, as this story illustrates, science is stranger than science fiction.

During my sojourns at Scotland's University of St. Andrews, I came to know cognitive neuroscientists Melvyn Goodale and David Milner (2004, 2006). A local woman, whom they call D. F., was overcome by carbon monoxide one day while showering. The resulting brain damage left her unable to recognize and discriminate objects visually. Yet she was only partly blind, for she would act as if she could see. Asked to slip a postcard into a vertical or horizontal mail slot, she could do so without error. Although unable to report the width of a block in front of her, she could grasp it with just the right finger-thumb distance.

How could this be? Don't we have one visual system? Goodale and Milner knew from animal research that the eye sends information simultaneously to different brain areas, which have different tasks. Sure enough, a scan of D. F.'s brain activity revealed normal activity in the area concerned with reaching for and grasping objects, but damage in the area concerned with consciously recognizing objects.

So, would the reverse damage lead to the opposite symptoms? Indeed, there are a few such patients—who can see and recognize objects but have difficulty pointing toward or grasping them.

How strangely intricate is this thing we call vision, conclude Goodale and Milner in their aptly titled book, *Sight Unseen.* We may think of our vision as one system that controls our visually guided actions, but it is actually a dual-processing system. A *visual perception track* enables us "to create the mental furniture that allows us to think about the world"—to recognize things and to plan future actions. A *visual action track* guides our moment-to-moment actions.

On rare occasions, the two conflict. Shown the *hollow face illusion,* people will mistakenly perceive the inside of a mask as a protruding face (**FIGURE 7.2**). Yet they will unhesitatingly and accurately reach into the inverted mask to flick off a buglike target stuck on the face. What their conscious mind doesn't know, their hand does.

This big idea—that much of our everyday thinking, feeling, and acting operates outside our conscious awareness—"is a difficult one for people to accept," report New York University psychologists John Bargh and Tanya Chartrand (1999). We

FIGURE 7.2 The hollow face illusion What you see (an illusory protruding face from a reverse mask, as in the box at upper right) may differ from what you do (reach for a speck on the face inside the mask).

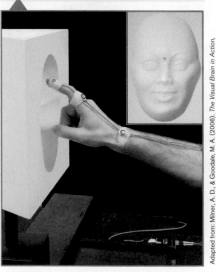

Adapted from: Milner, A. D., & Goodale, M. A. (2006). *The Visual Brain in Action,* 2nd Edition. Oxford University Press.

are understandably biased to believe that our own intentions and deliberate choices rule our lives. But in the mind's downstairs, there is much, much more to being human.

So, consciousness, though enabling us to exert voluntary control and to communicate our mental states to others, is but the tip of the information-processing iceberg. Beneath the surface, unconscious information processing occurs simultaneously on many parallel tracks. When we look at a bird flying, we are consciously aware of the result of our cognitive processing ("It's a hummingbird!") but not of our subprocessing of the bird's color, form, movement, distance, and identity.

Today's neuroscientists are identifying neural activity that precedes consciousness. In some provocative experiments, Benjamin Libet (1985, 2004) observed that when you move your wrist at will, you consciously experience the decision to move it about 0.2 seconds before the actual movement. No surprise there. But your brain waves jump about 0.35 seconds ahead of your conscious perception of your decision (**FIGURE 7.3**)! Thus, before you know it, your brain seems headed toward your decision to move your wrist. Likewise, if asked to press a button when you feel a tap, you can respond in 1/10th of a second—less time than it takes to become conscious that you have responded (Wegner, 2002). In a follow-up experiment, fMRI brain scans enabled researchers to predict—with 60 percent accuracy and up to 7 seconds ahead—participants' decisions to press a button with their left or right finger (Soon et al., 2008). The startling conclusion: Consciousness sometimes arrives late to the decision-making party.

All of this unconscious information processing occurs simultaneously on multiple parallel tracks. Traveling by car on a familiar route, your hands and feet do the driving while your mind rehearses your upcoming day. Running on automatic pilot allows your consciousness—your mind's CEO—to monitor the whole system and deal with new challenges, while many assistants automatically take care of routine business.

Serial conscious processing, though slower than parallel processing, is skilled at solving new problems, which require our focused attention. Try this: If you are right-handed, you can move your right foot in a smooth counterclockwise circle, and you can write the number 3 repeatedly with your right hand—but probably not at the same time. (If you are musically inclined, try something equally difficult: Tap a steady three times with your left hand while tapping four times with your right hand.) Both tasks require conscious attention, which can be in only one place at a time. If time is nature's way of keeping everything from happening at once, then consciousness is nature's way of keeping us from thinking and doing everything at once.

Selective Attention

7-2   How much information do we consciously attend to at once?

Through **selective attention,** your conscious awareness focuses, like a flashlight beam, on only a very limited aspect of all that you experience. By one estimate, your five senses take in 11,000,000 bits of information per second, of which you consciously process about 40 (Wilson, 2002). Yet your mind's unconscious track intuitively makes great use of the other 10,999,960 bits. Until reading this sentence, for example, you have been unaware that your shoes are pressing against your feet or that your nose is in your line of vision. Now, suddenly, your attentional spotlight shifts. Your feet feel encased, your nose stubbornly intrudes on the page before you. While attending to these words, you've also been blocking from awareness information coming from your peripheral vision. But you can change that. As you stare at the X on the next page, notice what surrounds the book (the edges of the page, your desktop, and so forth).

FIGURE 7.3 Is the brain ahead of the mind? In this study, volunteers watched a computer clock sweep through a full revolution every 2.56 seconds. They noted the time at which they decided to move their wrist. About one-third of a second before that decision, their brain wave activity jumped, indicating a *readiness potential* to move. Watching a slow-motion replay, the researchers were able to predict when a person was about to decide to move (following which, the wrist did move) (Libet, 1985, 2004).

selective attention the focusing of conscious awareness on a particular stimulus.

inattentional blindness failing to see visible objects when our attention is directed elsewhere.

change blindness failing to notice changes in the environment.

kchronicles.com—Keith Knight

X

Another example of selective attention, the *cocktail party effect,* is your ability to attend to only one voice among many. (Let another voice speak your name and your cognitive radar, operating on the mind's other track, will instantly bring that voice into consciousness.) This focused listening comes at a cost. Imagine hearing two conversations over a headset, one in each ear, and being asked to repeat the message in your left ear while it is spoken. When paying attention to what is being said in your left ear, you won't perceive what is said in your right. Asked later what language your right ear heard, you may draw a blank (though you could report the speaker's gender and loudness).

Selective Attention and Accidents

Talk on the phone while driving and your selective attention will shift back and forth from the road to the phone. But when a demanding situation requires your full attention, you'll probably stop talking. This process of switching attentional gears, especially when shifting to complex tasks, can entail a slight and sometimes fatal delay in coping (Rubenstein et al., 2001). The U.S. National Highway Traffic Safety Board (2006) estimates that almost 80 percent of vehicle crashes involve driver distraction. In University of Utah driving-simulation experiments, students conversing on cellphones were slower to detect and respond to traffic signals, billboards, and other cars (Strayer & Johnston, 2001; Strayer et al., 2003).

Because attention is selective, attending to a phone call (or a GPS navigation system or a DVD player) causes inattention to other things. Thus, when Suzanne McEvoy and her University of Sydney colleagues (2005, 2007) analyzed phone records for the moments before a car crash, they found that cellphone users (even with hands-free sets) were four times more at risk. Having a passenger increased risk only 1.6 times. This difference in risk also appeared in an experiment that asked drivers to pull off at a freeway rest stop 8 miles ahead. Of drivers conversing with a passenger, 88 percent did so. Of those talking on a cellphone, 50 percent drove on by (Strayer & Drews, 2007). Even hands-free cellphone talking is more distracting than a conversation with passengers, who can see the driving demands and pause the conversation.

Driven to distraction In driving-simulation experiments, people whose attention is diverted by cellphone conversation make more driving errors.

Walking while talking can also pose dangers, as one naturalistic observation of Ohio State University pedestrians found (Nasar et al., 2008). Half the people on cellphones and only a quarter without this distraction exhibited unsafe road crossing, such as by crossing when a car was approaching.

Selective Inattention

At the level of conscious awareness, we are "blind" to all but a tiny sliver of the immense array of visual stimuli constantly before us. Ulric Neisser (1979) and Robert Becklen and Daniel Cervone (1983) demonstrated this dramatically by showing people a one-minute video in which images of three black-shirted men tossing a basket-ball were superimposed over the images of three white-shirted players. The viewers' supposed task was to press a key every time a black-shirted player passed the ball. Most focused their attention so completely on the game that they failed to notice a young woman carrying an umbrella saunter across the screen midway through the video. When researchers replayed the video, viewers were astonished to see her. With their attention directed elsewhere, they exhibited **inattentional blindness** (Mack & Rock, 2000). In a recent repeat of

FIGURE 7.4 **Gorillas in our midst** When attending to one task (counting basketball passes by one of the three-person teams) about half the viewers displayed inattentional blindness by failing to notice a clearly visible gorilla passing through.

the experiment, smart-aleck researchers Daniel Simons and Christopher Chabris (1999) sent a gorilla-suited assistant through the swirl of players (**FIGURE 7.4**). During its 5- to 9-second cameo appearance, the gorilla paused to thump its chest. Still, half the conscientious pass-counting participants failed to see it.

In other experiments, people have also exhibited a blindness to change. After a brief visual interruption, a big Coke bottle may disappear, a railing may rise, clothing color may change, but, more often than not, viewers won't notice (Resnick et al., 1997; Simons, 1996; Simons & Ambinder, 2005). This form of inattentional blind-ness is called **change blindness.** It has occurred among people giving directions to a construction worker who, unnoticed by two-thirds of them, is replaced by another construction worker (**FIGURE 7.5**). Out of sight, out of mind. *Change deafness* can also occur. In one experiment, 40 percent of people focused on repeating a list of some-times challenging words failed to notice a change in the person speaking (Vitevitch, 2003).

An equally astonishing form of inattention is the *choice blindness* discovered by a Swedish research team. Petter Johansson and his colleagues (2005) showed 120 vol-unteers two female faces for 2 to 5 or more seconds and asked them which face was more attractive. The researchers then put the photos face down and handed viewers the one they had chosen, inviting them to explain their choice. But on 3 of 15 occa-sions, the tricky researchers used sleight-of-hand to switch the photos—showing viewers the face they had *not* chosen. Not only did people seldom notice the decep-tion (on only 13 percent of the switches), they readily explained why they preferred the face they had actually rejected. "I chose her because she smiled," said one person (after picking the solemn-faced one). Asked later whether they would notice such a

|| Magicians exploit our change blindness by selectively riveting our attention on one hand's dramatic act with inattention to the change accomplished by the other hand. ||

FIGURE 7.5 **Change blindness** While a man (white hair) provides directions to a construction worker, two experimenters rudely pass between them carrying a door. During this interruption, the original worker switches places with another person wearing different colored clothing. Most people, focused on their direction giving, do not notice the switch.

FIGURE 7.6
The pop-out phenomenon

switch in a "hypothetical experiment," 84 percent insisted they would. They exhibited a blindness the researchers call (can you see the twinkle in their eyes?) *choice-blindness blindness.*

Some stimuli, however, are so powerful, so strikingly distinct, that we experience *pop-out,* as with the only smiling face in **FIGURE 7.6**. We don't choose to attend to these stimuli; they draw our eye and demand our attention.

Our selective attention extends even into our sleep, when we are oblivious to most but not all of what is happening around us. We may feel "dead to the world," but we are not.

REVIEW

The Brain and Consciousness

7-1　**What is the "dual processing" being revealed by today's cognitive neuroscience?** *Cognitive neuroscientists* and others studying the brain mechanisms underlying *consciousness* and cognition have discovered a two-track human mind, each with its own neural processing. This *dual processing* affects our perception, memory, and attitudes at an explicit, conscious level and at an implicit, unconscious level.

7-2　**How much information do we consciously attend to at once?** We *selectively attend* to, and process, a very limited aspect of incoming information, blocking out most, often shifting the spotlight of our attention from one thing to another. The limits of our attention contribute to car and pedestrian accidents. We even display *inattentional blindness* to events and changes in our visual world.

Terms and Concepts to Remember

consciousness, p. 85
cognitive neuroscience, p. 85
dual processing, p. 86
selective attention, p. 87
inattentional blindness, p. 89
change blindness, p. 89

Test Yourself

1. What are the mind's two tracks, as revealed by studies of "dual processing"?

(Answers to the Test Yourself questions can be found in Appendix B at the end of the book.)

Ask Yourself

1. Can you recall a recent time when, your attention focused on one thing, you were oblivious to something else (perhaps to pain, to someone's approach, or to background music)?

∞ WEB

Multiple-choice self-tests and more may be found at www.worthpublishers.com/myers

MODULE 8

Sleep and Dreams

Biological Rhythms and Sleep

Why Do We Sleep?

Sleep Disorders

Dreams

Sleep—the irresistible tempter to whom we inevitably succumb. Sleep—the equalizer of presidents and peasants. Sleep—sweet, renewing, mysterious sleep.

Even when you are deeply asleep, your perceptual window is actually not completely shut. You move around on your bed, but you manage not to fall out. The occasional roar of passing vehicles may leave your deep sleep undisturbed, but a cry from a baby's nursery quickly interrupts it. So does the sound of your name. EEG recordings confirm that the brain's auditory cortex responds to sound stimuli even during sleep (Kutas, 1990). And when we are asleep, as when we are awake, we process most information outside our conscious awareness.

Many of sleep's mysteries are now being solved as some people sleep, attached to recording devices, while others observe. By recording brain waves and muscle movements, and by observing and occasionally waking sleepers, researchers are glimpsing things that a thousand years of common sense never told us. Perhaps you can anticipate some of their discoveries. Are the following statements true or false?

1. When people dream of performing some activity, their limbs often move in concert with the dream.
2. Older adults sleep more than young adults.
3. Sleepwalkers are acting out their dreams.
4. Sleep experts recommend treating insomnia with an occasional sleeping pill.
5. Some people dream every night; others seldom dream.

All these statements (adapted from Palladino & Carducci, 1983) are false. To see why, read on.

> "I love to sleep. Do you? Isn't it great? It really is the best of both worlds. You get to be alive and unconscious."
> Comedian Rita Rudner, 1993

|| Dolphins, porpoises, and whales sleep with one side of their brain at a time (Miller et al., 2008). ||

▶|| Biological Rhythms and Sleep

8-1 How do our biological rhythms influence our daily functioning and our sleep and dreams?

Like the ocean, life has its rhythmic tides. Over varying time periods, our bodies fluctuate, and with them, our minds. Let's look more closely at two of those biological rhythms—our 24-hour biological clock and our 90-minute sleep cycle.

Circadian Rhythm

The rhythm of the day parallels the rhythm of life—from our waking at a new day's birth to our nightly return to what Shakespeare called "death's counterfeit." Our bodies roughly synchronize with the 24-hour cycle of day and night through a biological clock called the **circadian rhythm** (from the Latin *circa,* "about," and *diem,* "day"). Body temperature rises as morning approaches, peaks during the day, dips for a time in early afternoon (when many people take siestas), and then begins to drop again before we go to sleep. Thinking is sharpest and memory most accurate when we are at our daily peak in circadian arousal. Pulling an all-nighter, we may feel groggiest about 4:00 A.M., and then we get a second wind after our normal wake-up time arrives.

Bright light in the morning tweaks the circadian clock by activating light-sensitive retinal proteins. These proteins control the circadian clock by triggering signals to the

circadian [ser-KAY-dee-an] **rhythm** the biological clock; regular bodily rhythms (for example, of temperature and wakefulness) that occur on a 24-hour cycle.

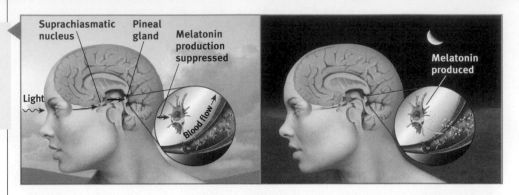

FIGURE 8.1 The biological clock
Light striking the retina signals the suprachiasmatic nucleus (SCN) to suppress the pineal gland's production of the sleep hormone melatonin. At night, the SCN quiets down, allowing the pineal gland to release melatonin into the bloodstream.

‖ At about age 20 (slightly earlier for women), we begin to shift from being evening-energized "owls" to being morning-loving "larks" (Roenneberg et al., 2004). Most 20-year-olds are owls, with performance improving across the day (May & Hasher, 1998). Most older adults are larks, with performance declining as the day wears on. Retirement homes are typically quiet by mid-evening; in university dorms, the day is far from over. ‖

‖ If our natural circadian rhythm were attuned to a 23-hour cycle, would we instead need to discipline ourselves to stay up later at night and sleep in longer in the morning? ‖

REM sleep   rapid eye movement sleep, a recurring sleep stage during which vivid dreams commonly occur. Also known as *paradoxical sleep,* because the muscles are relaxed (except for minor twitches) but other body systems are active.

alpha waves   the relatively slow brain waves of a relaxed, awake state.

brain's *suprachiasmatic nucleus (SCN)*—a pair of grain-of-rice-sized, 20,000-cell clusters in the hypothalamus (Foster, 2004). The SCN does its job in part by causing the brain's pineal gland to decrease its production of the sleep-inducing hormone *melatonin* in the morning or increase it in the evening (**FIGURE 8.1**).

Bright light at night helps delay sleep, thus resetting our biological clock when we stay up late and sleep in on weekends (Oren & Terman, 1998). Sleep often eludes those who sleep till noon on Sunday and then go to bed just 11 hours later in preparation for the new workweek. They are like New Yorkers whose biology is on California time. But what about North Americans who fly to Europe, and who need to be up when their circadian rhythm cries "Sleep!"? Studies in the laboratory and with shift workers find that bright light—spending the next day outdoors—helps reset the biological clock (Czeisler et al., 1986, 1989; Eastman et al., 1995).

Curiously—given that our ancestors' body clocks were attuned to the rising and setting sun of the 24-hour day—many of today's young adults adopt something closer to a 25-hour day, by staying up too late to get 8 hours of sleep. For this, we can thank (or blame) Thomas Edison, inventor of the light bulb. Being bathed in light disrupts our 24-hour biological clock (Czeisler et al., 1999; Dement, 1999). This helps explain why, until our later years, we must discipline ourselves to go to bed and force ourselves to get up. Most animals, too, when placed under unnatural constant illumination will exceed a 24-hour day. Artificial light delays sleep.

Sleep Stages

8-2   What is the biological rhythm of our sleep?

As sleep overtakes us and different parts of our brain's cortex stop communicating, consciousness fades (Massimini et al., 2005). But our still-active sleeping brain does not emit a constant dial tone, because sleep has its own biological rhythm. About every 90 minutes, we pass through a cycle of five distinct sleep stages. This elementary fact apparently was unknown until 8-year-old Armond Aserinsky went to bed one night in 1952. His father, Eugene, a University of Chicago graduate student, needed to test an electroencephalograph he had been repairing that day (Aserinsky, 1988; Seligman & Yellen, 1987). Placing electrodes near Armond's eyes to record the rolling eye movements then believed to occur during sleep, Aserinsky watched the machine go wild, tracing deep zigzags on the graph paper. Could the machine still be broken? As the night proceeded and the activity periodically recurred, Aserinsky finally realized that the fast, jerky eye movements were accompanied by energetic brain activity. Awakened during one such episode, Armond reported having a dream. Aserinsky had discovered what we now know as **REM sleep** (*rapid eye movement* sleep).

To find out if similar cycles occur during adult sleep, Nathaniel Kleitman (1960) and Aserinsky pioneered procedures that have now been used with thousands of volunteers.

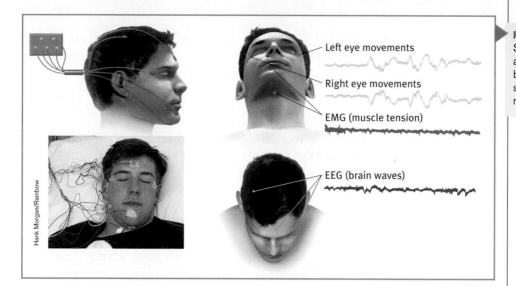

Left eye movements

Right eye movements

EMG (muscle tension)

EEG (brain waves)

Hank Morgan/Rainbow

FIGURE 8.2 Measuring sleep activity
Sleep researchers measure brain-wave activity, eye movements, and muscle tension by electrodes that pick up weak electrical signals from the brain, eye, and facial muscles. (From Dement, 1978.)

To appreciate their methods and findings, imagine yourself in their lab. As the hour grows late, you feel sleepy and you yawn in response to reduced brain metabolism. (Yawning, which can be socially contagious, stretches your neck muscles and increases your heart rate, which increases your alertness [Moorcroft, 2003]). When you are ready for bed, the researcher tapes electrodes to your scalp (to detect your brain waves), just outside the corners of your eyes (to detect eye movements), and on your chin (to detect muscle tension) (**FIGURE 8.2**). Other devices allow the researcher to record your heart rate, your respiration rate, and your genital arousal.

When you are in bed with your eyes closed, the researcher in the next room sees on the EEG the relatively slow **alpha waves** of your awake but relaxed state (**FIGURE 8.3**). As you adapt to all this equipment, you grow tired and, in an unremembered moment,

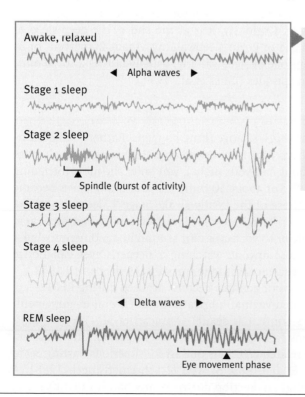

Awake, relaxed

◀ Alpha waves ▶

Stage 1 sleep

Stage 2 sleep

Spindle (burst of activity)

Stage 3 sleep

Stage 4 sleep

◀ Delta waves ▶

REM sleep

Eye movement phase

FIGURE 8.3 Brain waves and sleep stages The regular alpha waves of an awake, relaxed state are quite different from the slower, larger delta waves of deep Stage 4 sleep. Although the rapid REM sleep waves resemble the near-waking Stage 1 sleep waves, the body is more aroused during REM sleep than during Stage 1 sleep. (From Dement, 1978.)

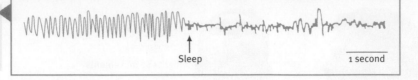

|| To catch your own hypnagogic experiences, you might use the "Repeat Snooze" alarm found on some alarm clocks. ||

sleep periodic, natural, reversible loss of consciousness—as distinct from unconsciousness resulting from a coma, general anesthesia, or hibernation. (Adapted from Dement, 1999.)

hallucinations false sensory experiences, such as seeing something in the absence of an external visual stimulus.

delta waves the large, slow brain waves associated with deep sleep.

slip into **sleep.** The transition is marked by the slowed breathing and the irregular brain waves of Stage 1 (**FIGURE 8.4**).

In one of his 15,000 research participants, William Dement (1999) observed the moment the brain's perceptual window to the outside world slammed shut. Dement asked this sleep-deprived young man, lying on his back with eyelids taped open, to press a button every time a strobe light flashed in his eyes (about every 6 seconds). After a few minutes the young man missed one. Asked why, he said, "Because there was no flash." But there was a flash. He missed it because (as his brain activity revealed) he had fallen asleep for 2 seconds. Unaware that he had done so, he had missed not only the flash 6 inches from his nose but also the abrupt moment of his entry into sleep.

During this brief Stage 1 sleep you may experience fantastic images, resembling **hallucinations**—sensory experiences that occur without a sensory stimulus. You may have a sensation of falling (at which moment your body may suddenly jerk) or of floating weightlessly. Such *hypnagogic* sensations may later be incorporated into memories. People who claim to have been abducted by aliens—often shortly after getting into bed—commonly recall being floated off or pinned down on their beds (Clancy, 2005).

You then relax more deeply and begin about 20 minutes of Stage 2 sleep, characterized by the periodic appearance of *sleep spindles*—bursts of rapid, rhythmic brain-wave activity (see Figure 8.3). Although you could still be awakened without too much difficulty, you are now clearly asleep. Sleeptalking—usually garbled or nonsensical—can occur during Stage 2 or any other sleep stage (Mahowald & Ettinger, 1990).

Then for the next few minutes you go through the transitional Stage 3 to the deep sleep of Stage 4. First in Stage 3, and increasingly in Stage 4, your brain emits large, slow **delta waves.** These two slow-wave stages last for about 30 minutes, during which you would be hard to awaken. Curiously, it is at the end of the deep sleep of Stage 4 that children may wet the bed or begin sleepwalking. About 20 percent of 3- to 12-year-olds have at least one episode of sleepwalking, usually lasting 2 to 10 minutes; some 5 percent have repeated episodes (Giles et al., 1994).

REM Sleep

About an hour after you first fall asleep, a strange thing happens. Rather than continuing in deep slumber, you ascend from your initial sleep dive. Returning through Stage 3 and Stage 2 (where you spend about half your night), you enter the most intriguing sleep phase—REM sleep (**FIGURE 8.5**). For about 10 minutes, your brain waves become rapid and saw-toothed, more like those of the nearly awake Stage 1 sleep. But unlike Stage 1 sleep, during REM sleep your heart rate rises, your breathing becomes rapid and irregular, and every half-minute or so your eyes dart around in a momentary burst of activity behind closed lids. Because anyone watching a sleeper's eyes can notice these REM bursts, it is amazing that science was ignorant of REM sleep until 1952.

Except during very scary dreams, your genitals become aroused during REM sleep, and you have an erection or increased vaginal lubrication and clitoral engorgement, regardless of whether the dream's content is sexual (Karacan et al., 1966). Men's common "morning erection" stems from the night's last REM period, often just before waking. In young men, sleep-related erections outlast REM periods, lasting 30 to 45 minutes on average (Karacan et al., 1983; Schiavi & Schreiner-Engel, 1988). A typical 25-year-old man therefore has an erection during nearly half his night's sleep,

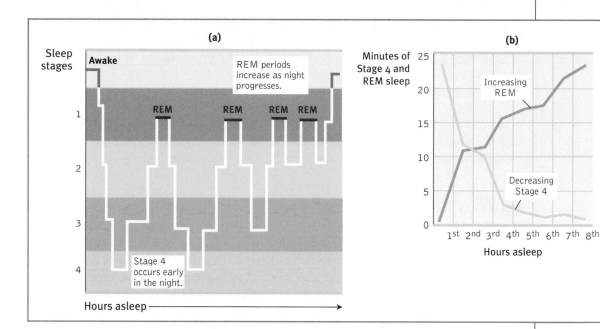

FIGURE 8.5 The stages in a typical night's sleep Most people pass through the five-stage sleep cycle (graph a) several times, with the periods of Stage 4 sleep and then Stage 3 sleep diminishing and REM sleep periods increasing in duration. Graph b plots this increasing REM sleep and decreasing deep sleep based on data from 30 young adults. (From Cartwright, 1978; Webb, 1992.)

a 65-year-old man for one-quarter. Many men troubled by *erectile dysfunction* (impotence) have sleep-related erections, suggesting the problem is not between their legs.

Although your brain's motor cortex is active during REM sleep, your brainstem blocks its messages, leaving muscles relaxed—so relaxed that, except for an occasional finger, toe, or facial twitch, you are essentially paralyzed. Moreover, you cannot easily be awakened. Thus, REM sleep is sometimes called *paradoxical* sleep, with the body internally aroused and externally calm.

More intriguing than the paradoxical nature of REM sleep is what the rapid eye movements announce: the beginning of a dream. Even those who claim they never dream will, more than 80 percent of the time, recall a dream after being awakened during REM sleep. Unlike the fleeting images of Stage 1 sleep ("I was thinking about my exam today," or "I was trying to borrow something from someone"), REM sleep dreams are often emotional, usually storylike, and more richly hallucinatory:

> My husband and I were at some friends' house, but our friends weren't there. Their TV had been left on, but otherwise it was very quiet. After we wandered around for a while, their dogs finally noticed us and barked and growled loudly, with bared teeth.

"Boy are my eyes tired! I had REM sleep all night long."

|| Horses, which spend 92 percent of each day standing and can sleep standing, must lie down for REM sleep (Morrison, 2003). ||

Some sleep deeply, some not The fluctuating sleep cycle enables safe sleep for these soldiers on the battlefield. One benefit of communal sleeping is that someone will probably be awake or easily roused in the event of a threat.

The sleep cycle repeats itself about every 90 minutes. As the night wears on, deep Stage 4 sleep gets progressively briefer and then disappears. The REM and Stage 2 sleep periods get longer (see Figure 8.5b). By morning, 20 to 25 percent of our average night's sleep—some 100 minutes—has been REM sleep. Thirty-seven percent of people report rarely or never having dreams "that you can remember the next morning" (Moore, 2004). Unknown to those people, they spend about 600 hours a year experiencing some 1500 dreams, or more than 100,000 dreams over a typical lifetime—dreams swallowed by the night but never acted out, thanks to REM's protective paralysis.

|| People rarely snore during dreams. When REM starts, snoring stops. ||

▶|| Why Do We Sleep?

The idea that "everyone needs 8 hours of sleep" is untrue. Newborns spend nearly two-thirds of their day asleep, most adults no more than one-third. Age-related differences in average sleeping time are rivaled by the differences among individuals at any age. Some people thrive with fewer than 6 hours per night; others regularly rack up 9 hours or more. Such sleep patterns may be genetically influenced. When Wilse Webb and Scott Campbell (1983) checked the pattern and duration of sleep among fraternal and identical twins, only the identical twins were strikingly similar.

Sleep patterns are also culturally influenced. In the United States and Canada, for example, adults average just over 8 hours per night (Hurst, 2008; Robinson & Martin, 2007). (The weeknight sleep of many students and workers falls short of this average [NSF, 2008].) North Americans are nevertheless sleeping less than their counterparts a century ago. Thanks to modern light bulbs, shift work, and social diversions, those who would have gone to bed at 9:00 P.M. are now up until 11:00 P.M. or later. Thomas Edison (1948, pp. 52, 178) was pleased to accept credit for this, believing that less sleep meant more productive time and greater opportunities:

> When I went through Switzerland in a motor-car, so that I could visit little towns and villages, I noted the effect of artificial light on the inhabitants. Where water power and electric light had been developed, everyone seemed normally intelligent. When these appliances did not exist, and the natives went to bed with the chickens, staying there till daylight, they were far less intelligent.

Allowed to sleep unhindered, most adults will sleep at least 9 hours a night, reports Stanley Coren (1996). With that much sleep, we awake refreshed, sustain better moods, and perform more efficient and accurate work. Compare that with a succession of 5-hour nights, when we accumulate a sleep debt that cannot be paid off by one long marathon sleep. "The brain keeps an accurate count of sleep debt for at least two weeks," says William Dement (1999, p. 64). With our body yearning for sleep, we will begin to feel terrible. Trying to stay awake, we will eventually lose. In the tiredness battle, sleep always wins.

Obviously, then, we need sleep. Sleep commands roughly one-third of our lives—some 25 years, on average. But why? It seems an easy question to answer: Just keep people awake for several days and note how they deteriorate. If you were a volunteer in such an experiment, how do you think it would affect your body and mind? You would, of course, become terribly drowsy—especially during the hours when your biological clock programs you to sleep. But could the lack of sleep physically damage you? Would it noticeably alter your biochemistry or body organs? Would you become emotionally disturbed? Mentally disoriented?

|| In 1989, Michael Doucette was named America's Safest Driving Teen. In 1990, while driving home from college, he fell asleep at the wheel and collided with an oncoming car, killing both himself and the other driver. Michael's driving instructor later acknowledged never having mentioned sleep deprivation and drowsy driving (Dement, 1999). ||

The Effects of Sleep Loss

8-3 How does sleep loss affect us?

Good news! Psychologists have discovered a treatment that strengthens memory, increases concentration, boosts mood, moderates hunger and obesity, fortifies the disease-fighting immune system, and lessens the risk of fatal accidents. Even better news: The treatment feels good, it can be self-administered, the supplies are limitless, and it's available free! If you are a typical university-age student, often going to bed near 2:00 A.M. and dragged out of bed six hours later by the dreaded alarm, the treatment is simple: Each night just add an hour to your sleep.

Reuters/China Daily (China)

Sleepless and suffering
These fatigued, sleep-deprived earthquake rescue workers in China may experience a depressed immune system, impaired concentration, and greater vulnerability to accidents.

The U.S. Navy and the National Institutes of Health have demonstrated the benefits of unrestricted sleep in experiments in which volunteers spent 14 hours daily in bed for at least a week. For the first few days, the volunteers averaged 12 hours of sleep a day or more, apparently paying off a sleep debt that averaged 25 to 30 hours. That accomplished, they then settled back to 7.5 to 9 hours nightly and, with no sleep debt, felt energized and happier (Dement, 1999). In one Gallup survey (Mason, 2005), 63 percent of adults who reported getting the sleep they need also reported being "very satisfied" with their personal life (as did only 36 percent of those needing more sleep). When Daniel Kahneman and his colleagues (2004) invited 909 working women to report on their daily moods, they were struck by what mattered little, such as money (so long as they were not battling poverty). And they were struck by what mattered a lot—less time pressure at work and a good night's sleep.

Unfortunately, many of us are suffering from patterns that not only leave us sleepy but also thwart our having an energized feeling of well-being (Mikulincer et al., 1989). Teens who typically need 8 or 9 hours of sleep now average less than 7 hours—nearly 2 hours less each night than did their counterparts of 80 years ago (Holden, 1993; Maas, 1999). In one survey, 28 percent of high school students acknowledged falling asleep in class at least once a week (Sleep Foundation, 2006). When the going gets boring, the students start snoring.

Even when awake, students often function below their peak. And they know it: Four in five American teens and three in five 18- to 29-year-olds wish they could get more sleep on weekdays (Mason, 2003, 2005). Yet that teen who staggers glumly out of bed in response to an unwelcome alarm, yawns through morning classes, and feels half-depressed much of the day may be energized at 11 P.M. and mindless of the next day's looming sleepiness (Carskadon, 2002).

Sleep researcher William Dement (1997) reports that at Stanford University, 80 percent of students are "dangerously sleep deprived. . . . Sleep deprivation [entails] difficulty studying, diminished productivity, tendency to make mistakes, irritability, fatigue." A large sleep debt "makes you stupid," says Dement (1999, p. 231).

It can also make you fatter. Sleep deprivation increases the hunger-arousing hormone ghrelin and decreases its hunger-suppressing partner, leptin. It also increases the stress hormone cortisol, which stimulates the body to make fat. Sure enough, children and adults who sleep less than normal are fatter than those who sleep more (Chen et al., 2008; Knutson et al., 2007; Schoenborn & Adams, 2008). And experimental sleep deprivation of adults increases appetite and eating (Nixon et al., 2008; Patel et al., 2006; Spiegel et al., 2004; Van Cauter et al., 2007). This may help explain

‖ In a 2001 Gallup poll, 61 percent of men, but only 47 percent of women, said they got enough sleep. ‖

"Tiger Woods said that one of the best things about his choice to leave Stanford for the professional golf circuit was that he could now get enough sleep."
Stanford sleep researcher William Dement, 1997

‖ To test whether you are one of the many sleep-deprived students, see Table 8.1 on the next page. ‖

TABLE 8.1

Cornell University psychologist James Maas reports that most students suffer the consequences of sleeping less than they should. To see if you are in that group, answer the following true-false questions:

True	False	
____	____	1. I need an alarm clock in order to wake up at the appropriate time.
____	____	2. It's a struggle for me to get out of bed in the morning.
____	____	3. Weekday mornings I hit the snooze bar several times to get more sleep.
____	____	4. I feel tired, irritable, and stressed out during the week.
____	____	5. I have trouble concentrating and remembering.
____	____	6. I feel slow with critical thinking, problem solving, and being creative.
____	____	7. I often fall asleep watching TV.
____	____	8. I often fall asleep in boring meetings or lectures or in warm rooms.
____	____	9. I often fall asleep after heavy meals or after a low dose of alcohol.
____	____	10. I often fall asleep while relaxing after dinner.
____	____	11. I often fall asleep within five minutes of getting into bed.
____	____	12. I often feel drowsy while driving.
____	____	13. I often sleep extra hours on weekend mornings.
____	____	14. I often need a nap to get through the day.
____	____	15. I have dark circles around my eyes.

If you answered "true" to three or more items, you probably are not getting enough sleep. To determine your sleep needs, Maas recommends that you "go to bed 15 minutes earlier than usual every night for the next week—and continue this practice by adding 15 more minutes each week—until you wake without an alarm clock and feel alert all day." (Quiz reprinted with permission from James B. Maas, *Power sleep: The revolutionary program that prepares your mind and body for peak performance* [New York: HarperCollins, 1999].)

the common weight gain among sleep-deprived students (although a review of 11 studies reveals that the mythical "freshman 15" is, on average, closer to a "first-year 4" [Hull et al., 2007]).

In addition to making us more vulnerable to obesity, sleep deprivation can suppress immune cells that fight off viral infections and cancer (Motivala & Irwin, 2007). This may help explain why people who sleep 7 to 8 hours a night tend to outlive those who are chronically sleep deprived, and why older adults who have no difficulty falling or staying asleep tend to live longer than their sleep-deprived agemates (Dement, 1999; Dew et al., 2003). When infections do set in, we typically sleep more, boosting our immune cells.

Chronic sleep debt also alters metabolic and hormonal functioning in ways that mimic aging and are conducive to hypertension and memory impairment (Spiegel et al., 1999; Taheri, 2004). Other effects include irritability, slowed performance, and impaired creativity, concentration, and communication (Harrison & Horne, 2000). Reaction times slow and errors increase on visual tasks similar to those involved in airport baggage screening, performing surgery, and reading X-rays (Horowitz et al., 2003).

Sleep deprivation can be devastating for driving, piloting, and equipment operating. Driver fatigue contributes to an estimated 20 percent of American traffic accidents (Brody, 2002) and to some 30 percent of Australian highway deaths (Maas, 1999). Consider the timing of the 1989 *Exxon Valdez* oil spill; Union Carbide's 1984 Bhopal, India, disaster; and the 1979 Three Mile Island and 1986 Chernobyl nuclear accidents—all occurred after midnight, when operators in charge were likely to be

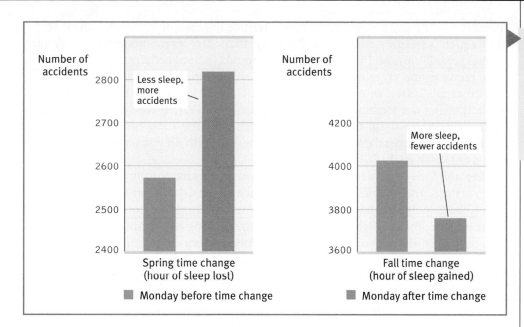

FIGURE 8.6 Canadian traffic accidents
On the Monday after the spring time change, when people lose one hour of sleep, accidents increased as compared with the Monday before. In the fall, traffic accidents normally increase because of greater snow, ice, and darkness, but they diminished after the time change. (Adapted from Coren, 1996.)

drowsiest and unresponsive to signals that require an alert response. When sleepy frontal lobes confront an unexpected situation, misfortune often results.

Stanley Coren capitalized on what is, for many North Americans, a semi-annual sleep-manipulation experiment—the "spring forward" to "daylight savings" time and "fall backward" to "standard" time. Searching millions of records, Coren found that in both Canada and the United States, accidents increase immediately after the time change that shortens sleep (**FIGURE 8.6**).

But let's put all this positively: To manage your life with enough sleep to awaken naturally and well rested is to be more alert, productive, happy, healthy, and safe.

Sleep Theories

8-4 What is sleep's function?

So, nature charges us for our sleep debt. But why do we have this need for sleep?

We have very few answers, but sleep may have evolved for five reasons: First, *sleep protects.* When darkness precluded our distant ancestors' hunting and food gathering and made travel treacherous, they were better off asleep in a cave, out of harm's way. Those who didn't try to navigate around rocks and cliffs at night were more likely to leave descendants. This fits a broader principle: A species' sleep pattern tends to suit its ecological niche. Animals with the most need to graze and the least ability to hide tend to sleep less. Elephants and horses sleep 3 to 4 hours a day, gorillas 12 hours, and cats 14 hours. For bats and eastern chipmunks, both of which sleep 20 hours, to live is hardly more than to eat and to sleep (Moorcroft, 2003). (Would you rather be like a giraffe and sleep 2 hours a day or a bat and sleep 20?)

Second, *sleep helps us recuperate.* It helps restore and repair brain tissue. Bats and other animals with high waking metabolism burn a lot of calories, producing a lot of *free radicals,* molecules that are toxic to neurons. Sleeping a lot gives resting neurons time to repair themselves, while allowing unused connections to weaken (Siegel, 2003; Vyazovski et al., 2008). Think of it this way: When consciousness leaves your house, brain construction workers come in for a makeover.

But sleep is not just for keeping us safe and for repairing our brain. New research reveals that *sleep is for making memories*—for restoring and rebuilding our fading

"Drowsiness is red alert!"
William Dement, *The Promise of Sleep*, 1999

"Sleep faster, we need the pillows."
Yiddish proverb

"Corduroy pillows make headlines."
Anonymous

insomnia recurring problems in falling or staying asleep.

narcolepsy a sleep disorder characterized by uncontrollable sleep attacks. The sufferer may lapse directly into REM sleep, often at inopportune times.

sleep apnea a sleep disorder characterized by temporary cessations of breathing during sleep and repeated momentary awakenings.

"The lion and the lamb shall lie down together, but the lamb will not be very sleepy."

Woody Allen, in the movie *Love and Death*, 1975

off the mark.com   by Mark Parisi

LET ME GET THIS STRAIGHT, IT'S BEEN TWO CONSECUTIVE HOURS SINCE YOU'VE SLEPT?

WHEN CATS EXPERIENCE INSOMNIA

"Sleep is like love or happiness. If you pursue it too ardently it will elude you."

Wilse Webb, *Sleep: The Gentle Tyrant*, 1992 (p. 170)

memories of the day's experiences. People trained to perform tasks recall them better after a night's sleep, or even after a short nap, than after several hours awake (Walker & Stickgold, 2006). And in both humans and rats, neural activity during slow-wave sleep reenacts and promotes recall of prior novel experiences (Peigneux et al., 2004; Ribeiro et al., 2004). In one experiment, people were exposed to the scent of roses while learning the locations of various picture cards. When reexposed to the scent during slow-wave sleep, their memory scratch-pad—the hippocampus—was reactivated, and they remembered the picture placements with almost perfect accuracy the next day (Rasch et al., 2007).

Sleep also feeds creative thinking. On occasion, dreams have inspired noteworthy literary, artistic, and scientific achievements, such as the dream that clued chemist August Kekulé to the structure of benzene (Ross, 2006). More commonplace is the boost that a complete night's sleep gives to our thinking and learning. After working on a task, then sleeping on it, people solve problems more insightfully than do those who stay awake (Wagner et al., 2004). They can also, after sleep, better discern connections among different novel pieces of information (Ellenbogen et al., 2007). Even 15-month-olds, if retested after a nap, better recall relationships among novel words (Gómez et al., 2006). To think smart and see connections, it often pays to sleep on it.

Finally, *sleep may play a role in the growth process.* During deep sleep, the pituitary gland releases a growth hormone. As we age, we release less of this hormone and spend less time in deep sleep (Pekkanen, 1982). Such discoveries are beginning to solve the ongoing riddle of sleep.

▶‖ Sleep Disorders

8-5 What are the major sleep disorders?

No matter what their normal need for sleep, 1 in 10 adults, and 1 in 4 older adults, complain of **insomnia**—not an occasional inability to sleep when anxious or excited, but persistent problems in falling or staying asleep (Irwin & others, 2006).

From middle age on, sleep is seldom uninterrupted. Being occasionally awakened becomes the norm, not something to fret over or treat with medication. And some people do fret unnecessarily about their sleep (Coren, 1996). In laboratory studies, insomnia complainers do sleep less than others, but they typically overestimate—by about double—how long it takes them to fall asleep. They also underestimate by nearly half how long they actually have slept. Even if we have been awake only an hour or two, we may *think* we have had very little sleep because it's the waking part we remember.

The most common quick fixes for true insomnia—sleeping pills and alcohol—can aggravate the problem, reducing REM sleep and leaving the person with next-day blahs. Relying on sleeping pills—sales of which soared 60 percent from 2000 to 2006 (Saul, 2007)—the person may need increasing doses to get an effect. Then, when the drug is discontinued, the insomnia can worsen.

Scientists are searching for natural chemicals that are abundant during sleep, hoping they might be synthesized as a sleep aid without side effects. In the meantime, sleep experts offer other natural alternatives:

▶ Exercise regularly but not in the late evening. (Late afternoon is best.)
▶ Avoid all caffeine after early afternoon, and avoid rich foods before bedtime. Instead, try a glass of milk, which provides raw materials for the manufacture of serotonin, a neurotransmitter that facilitates sleep.
▶ Relax before bedtime, using dimmer light.

Dwayne Newton/PhotoEdit

Stress robs sleep Urban police officers, especially those under stress, report poorer sleep quality and less sleep than average (Neylan et al., 2002).

▶ Sleep on a regular schedule (rise at the same time even after a restless night) and avoid naps. Sticking to a schedule boosts daytime alertness, too, as shown in an experiment in which University of Arizona students averaged 7.5 hours of sleep a night on either a varying or consistent schedule (Manber et al., 1996).

▶ Hide the clock face so you aren't tempted to check it repeatedly.

▶ Reassure yourself that a temporary loss of sleep causes no great harm.

▶ Realize that for any stressed organism, being vigilant is natural and adaptive. A personal conflict during the day often means a fitful sleep that night (Åkerstedt et al., 2007; Brisette & Cohen, 2002). Managing your stress levels will enable more restful sleeping.

▶ If all else fails, settle for less sleep, either going to bed later or getting up earlier.

Rarer but also more troublesome than insomnia are the sleep disorders *narcolepsy, sleep apnea, night terrors,* and *sleepwalking.*

Narcolepsy (from *narco,* "numbness," and *lepsy,* "seizure") sufferers experience periodic, overwhelming sleepiness. Attacks usually last less than 5 minutes but sometimes occur at the most inopportune times, perhaps just after taking a terrific swing at a softball or when laughing loudly, shouting angrily, or having sex (Dement, 1978, 1999). In severe cases, the person may collapse directly into a brief period of REM sleep, with its accompanying loss of muscular tension. People with narcolepsy—1 in 2000 of us, estimates the Stanford University Center for Narcolepsy (2002)—must therefore live with extra caution. As a traffic menace, "snoozing is second only to boozing," says the American Sleep Disorders Association, and those with narcolepsy are especially at risk (Aldrich, 1989).

At the twentieth century's end, researchers discovered a gene causing narcolepsy in dogs (Lin et al., 1999; Taheri, 2004). Genes help sculpt the brain, and neuroscientists are searching the brain for abnormalities linked with narcolepsy. One team of researchers discovered a relative absence of a hypothalamic neural center that produces *orexin* (also called hypocretin), a neurotransmitter linked to alertness (Taheri et al., 2002; Thannickal et al., 2000). (That discovery has led to the clinical testing of a new sleeping pill that works by blocking orexin's arousing activity.) Narcolepsy, it is now clear, is a brain disease; it is not just "in your mind." And this gives hope that narcolepsy might be effectively relieved by a drug that mimics the missing orexin and can sneak through the blood-brain barrier (Fujiki et al., 2003; Siegel, 2000). In the meantime, physicians are prescribing other drugs to relieve narcolepsy's sleepiness in humans.

Sleep apnea also puts millions of people at increased risk of traffic accidents (Teran-Santos et al., 1999). Although 1 in 20 of us has this disorder, it was unknown

"In 1757 Benjamin Franklin gave us the axiom, 'Early to bed, early to rise, makes a man healthy, wealthy, and wise.' It would be more accurate to say 'consistently to bed and consistently to rise . . .'"

James B. Maas, *Power Sleep,* 1999

Did Brahms need his own lullabies? Cranky, overweight, and nap-prone, Johannes Brahms exhibited common symptoms of sleep apnea (Margolis, 2000).

Archivo Iconografico, S.A./Corbis

before modern sleep research. *Apnea* means "with no breath," and people with this condition intermittently stop breathing during sleep. After an airless minute or so, decreased blood oxygen arouses them and they wake up enough to snort in air for a few seconds, in a process that repeats hundreds of times each night, depriving them of slow-wave sleep. Apart from complaints of sleepiness and irritability during the day—and their mate's complaints about their loud "snoring"—apnea sufferers are often unaware of their disorder. The next morning they have no recall of these episodes, and may just report feeling fatigued and depressed (Peppard et al., 2006).

Sleep apnea is associated with obesity, and as the number of obese people in the United States has increased, so has this disorder, particularly among overweight men, including some football players (Keller, 2007). Anyone who snores at night, feels tired during the day, and possibly has high blood pressure as well (increasing the risk of a stroke or heart attack) should be checked for apnea (Dement, 1999). A physician may prescribe a masklike device with an air pump that keeps the sleeper's airway open and breathing regular. If one doesn't mind looking a little goofy in the dark (imagine a snorkeler at a slumber party), the treatment can effectively treat both the apnea and associated depressed energy and mood.

Unlike sleep apnea, **night terrors** target mostly children, who may sit up or walk around, talk incoherently, experience a doubling of heart and breathing rates, and appear terrified (Hartmann, 1981). They seldom wake up fully during an episode and recall little or nothing the next morning—at most, a fleeting, frightening image. Night terrors are not nightmares (which, like other dreams, typically occur during early morning REM sleep); night terrors usually occur during the first few hours of Stage 4.

Children also are most prone to *sleepwalking*—another Stage 4 sleep disorder—and to *sleeptalking,* conditions that run in families. Finnish twin studies reveal that occasional childhood sleepwalking occurs for about one-third of those with a sleepwalking fraternal twin and half of those with a sleepwalking identical twin. The same is true for sleeptalking (Hublin et al., 1997, 1998). Sleepwalking is usually harmless and unrecalled the next morning. Sleepwalkers typically return to bed on their own or are guided there by a family member. Young children, who have the deepest and lengthiest Stage 4 sleep, are the most likely to experience both night terrors and sleepwalking. As we grow older and deep Stage 4 sleep diminishes, so do night terrors and sleepwalking. After being sleep deprived, people sleep more deeply, which increases any tendency to sleepwalk (Zadra et al., 2008).

▶‖ Dreams

8-6 What do we dream?

Now playing at an inner theater near you: the premiere showing of a sleeping person's vivid dream. This never-before-seen mental movie features captivating characters wrapped in a plot so original and unlikely, yet so intricate and so seemingly real, that the viewer later marvels at its creation.

Waking from a troubling dream, wrenched by its emotions, who among us has not wondered about this weird state of consciousness? How can our brain so creatively, colorfully, and completely construct this alternative, conscious world? In the shadowland between our dreaming and waking consciousness, we may even wonder for a moment which is real.

Discovering the link between REM sleep and dreaming opened a new era in dream research. Instead of relying on someone's hazy recall hours or days after having a dream, researchers could catch dreams as they happened. They could awaken people during or within 3 minutes after a REM sleep period and hear a vivid account.

night terrors a sleep disorder characterized by high arousal and an appearance of being terrified; unlike nightmares, night terrors occur during Stage 4 sleep, within two or three hours of falling asleep, and are seldom remembered.

dream a sequence of images, emotions, and thoughts passing through a sleeping person's mind. Dreams are notable for their hallucinatory imagery, discontinuities, and incongruities, and for the dreamer's delusional acceptance of the content and later difficulties remembering it.

manifest content according to Freud, the remembered story line of a dream (as distinct from its latent, or hidden, content).

What We Dream

REM **dreams**—"hallucinations of the sleeping mind"(Loftus & Ketcham, 1994, p. 67)—are vivid, emotional, and bizarre. They are unlike daydreams, which tend to involve the familiar details of our life—perhaps picturing ourselves explaining to an instructor why a paper will be late, or replaying in our minds personal encounters we relish or regret. The dreams of REM sleep are so vivid we may confuse them with reality. Awakening from a nightmare, a 4-year-old may be sure there is a bear in the house.

We spend six years of our life in dreams, many of which are anything but sweet. For both women and men, 8 in 10 dreams are marked by at least one negative event or emotion (Domhoff, 2007). People commonly dream of repeatedly failing in an attempt to do something; of being attacked, pursued, or rejected; or of experiencing misfortune (Hall et al., 1982). Dreams with sexual imagery occur less often than you might think. In one study, only 1 dream in 10 among young men and 1 in 30 among young women had sexual overtones (Domhoff, 1996). More commonly, the story line of our dreams—what Sigmund Freud called their **manifest content**—incorporates traces of previous days' nonsexual experiences and preoccupations (De Koninck, 2000):

▶ After suffering a trauma, people commonly report nightmares (Levin & Nielsen, 2007). One sample of Americans who were recording their dreams during September 2001 reported an increase in threatening dreams following the 9/11 attack (Propper et al., 2007).

▶ After playing the computer game *Tetris* for seven hours and then being awakened repeatedly during their first hour of sleep, 3 in 4 people reported experiencing images of the game's falling blocks (Stickgold et al., 2000).

▶ People in hunter-gatherer societies often dream of animals; urban Japanese rarely do (Mestel, 1997).

▶ Compared with nonmusicians, musicians report twice as many dreams of music (Uga et al., 2006).

Sensory stimuli in our sleeping environment may also intrude. A particular odor or the telephone's ringing may be instantly and ingeniously woven into the dream story. In a classic experiment, William Dement and Edward Wolpert (1958) lightly sprayed cold water on dreamers' faces. Compared with sleepers who did not get the cold-water treatment, these people were more likely to dream about a waterfall, a leaky roof, or even about being sprayed by someone. Even while in REM sleep, focused on internal stimuli, we maintain some awareness of changes in our external environment.

"I do not believe that I am now dreaming, but I cannot prove that I am not."
Philosopher Bertrand Russell (1872-1970)

‖ Would you suppose that people dream if blind from birth? Studies of blind people in France, Hungary, Egypt, and the United States all found them dreaming of using their nonvisual senses—hearing, touching, smelling, tasting (Buquet, 1988; Taha, 1972; Vckassy, 1977). ‖

"For what one has dwelt on by day, these things are seen in visions of the night."
Menander of Athens (342-292 B.C.), *Fragments*

‖ A popular sleep myth: If you dream you are falling and hit the ground (or if you dream of dying), you die. (Unfortunately, those who could confirm these ideas are not around to do so. Some people, however, have had such dreams and are alive to report them.) ‖

MAXINE

So, could we learn a foreign language by hearing it played while we sleep? If only it were so easy. While sleeping we can learn to associate a sound with a mild electric shock (and to react to the sound accordingly). But we do not remember recorded information played while we are soundly asleep (Eich, 1990; Wyatt & Bootzin, 1994). In fact, anything that happens during the 5 minutes just before we fall asleep is typically lost from memory (Roth et al., 1988). This explains why sleep apnea patients, who repeatedly awaken with a gasp and then immediately fall back to sleep, do not recall the episodes. It also explains why dreams that momentarily awaken us are mostly forgotten by morning. To remember a dream, get up and stay awake for a few minutes.

Why We Dream

8-7 What is the function of dreams?

Dream theorists have proposed several explanations of why we dream, including these:

To satisfy our own wishes. In 1900, in his landmark book *The Interpretation of Dreams,* Freud offered what he thought was "the most valuable of all the discoveries it has been my good fortune to make": Dreams provide a psychic safety valve that discharges otherwise unacceptable feelings. According to Freud, a dream's *manifest* (apparent) *content* is a censored, symbolic version of its **latent content,** which consists of unconscious drives and wishes that would be threatening if expressed directly. Although most dreams have no overt sexual imagery, Freud nevertheless believed that most adult dreams can be "traced back by analysis to erotic wishes." Thus, a gun might be a disguised representation of a penis.

Freud considered dreams the key to understanding our inner conflicts. However, his critics say it is time to wake up from Freud's dream theory, which is a scientific nightmare. Based on the accumulated science, "there is no reason to believe any of Freud's specific claims about dreams and their purposes," notes dream researcher William Domhoff (2003). Some contend that even if dreams are symbolic, they could be interpreted any way one wished. Others maintain that dreams hide nothing. A dream about a gun is a dream about a gun. Legend has it that even Freud, who loved to smoke cigars, acknowledged that "sometimes, a cigar is just a cigar." Freud's wish-fulfillment theory of dreams has in large part given way to other theories.

To file away memories. Researchers who see dreams as *information processing* believe that dreams may help sift, sort, and fix the day's experiences in our memory. As we noted earlier, people tested the next day generally improve on a learned task after a night of memory consolidation. Even after two nights of recovery sleep, those who have been deprived of both slow-wave and REM sleep don't do as well as those who sleep undisturbed on their new learning (Stickgold et al., 2000, 2001). People who hear unusual phrases or learn to find hidden visual images before bedtime remember less the next morning if awakened every time they begin REM sleep than they do if awakened during other sleep stages (Empson & Clarke, 1970; Karni & Sagi, 1994).

Brain scans confirm the link between REM sleep and memory. The brain regions that buzz as rats learn to navigate a maze, or as people learn to perform a visual-discrimination task, buzz again during later REM sleep (Louie & Wilson, 2001; Maquet, 2001). So precise are these activity patterns that scientists can tell where in the maze the rat would be if awake.

Some researchers are unpersuaded by these studies (Siegel, 2001; Vertes & Siegel, 2005). They note that memory consolidation may occur independent of dreaming, including during non-REM sleep. But this much seems true: A night of solid sleep (and

"Follow your dreams, except for that one where you're naked at work."
Attributed to Henny Youngman

"When people interpret [a dream] as if it were meaningful and then sell those interpretations, it's quackery."
Sleep researcher J. Allan Hobson (1995)

latent content according to Freud, the underlying meaning of a dream (as distinct from its manifest content).

dreaming) has an important place in our lives. To sleep, perchance to remember. This is important news for students, many of whom, researcher Robert Stickgold (2000) believes, suffer from a kind of sleep bulimia—binge-sleeping on the weekend. "If you don't get good sleep and enough sleep after you learn new stuff, you won't integrate it effectively into your memories," he warns. That helps explain why secondary students with high grades average 25 minutes more sleep a night and go to bed 40 minutes earlier than their lower-achieving classmates (Wolfson & Carskadon, 1998).

To develop and preserve neural pathways. Some researchers speculate that dreams may also serve a *physiological* function. Perhaps the brain activity associated with REM sleep provides the sleeping brain with periodic stimulation. This theory makes developmental sense. We know that stimulating experiences develop and preserve the brain's neural pathways. Infants, whose neural networks are fast developing, spend much of their abundant sleep time in REM sleep (**FIGURE 8.7**).

To make sense of neural static. Other theories propose that dreams erupt from neural activity spreading upward from the brainstem (Antrobus, 1991; Hobson, 2003, 2004). According to one version—the *activation-synthesis* theory—this neural activity is random, and dreams are the brain's attempt to make sense of it. Much as a neurosurgeon can produce hallucinations by stimulating different parts of a patient's cortex, so can stimulation originating within the brain. These internal stimuli activate brain areas that process visual images, but not the visual cortex area, which receives raw input from the eyes. As Freud might have expected, PET scans of sleeping people also reveal increased activity in the emotion-related limbic system (in the amygdala) during REM sleep. In contrast, frontal lobe regions responsible for inhibition and logical thinking seem to idle, which may explain why our dreams are less inhibited than we are (Maquet et al., 1996). Add the limbic system's emotional tone to the brain's visual bursts and—Voila!—we dream. Damage either the limbic system or the visual centers active during dreaming, and dreaming itself may be impaired (Domhoff, 2003).

To reflect cognitive development. Some dream researchers dispute both the Freudian and activation-synthesis theories, preferring instead to see dreams as part of brain maturation and cognitive development (Domhoff, 2003; Foulkes, 1999). For

‖ Rapid eye movements also stir the liquid behind the cornea; this delivers fresh oxygen to corneal cells, preventing their suffocation. ‖

‖ ***Question:*** Does eating spicy foods cause one to dream more?
Answer: Any food that causes you to awaken more increases your chance of recalling a dream (Moorcroft, 2003). ‖

FIGURE 8.7 Sleep across the life span As we age, our sleep patterns change. During our first few months, we spend progressively less time in REM sleep. During our first 20 years, we spend progressively less time asleep. (Adapted from Snyder & Scott, 1972.)

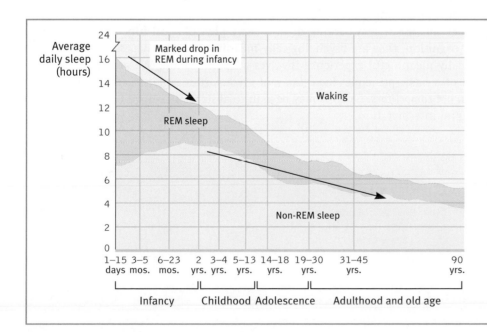

TABLE 8.2 Dream Theories

Theory	Explanation	Critical Considerations
Freud's wish-fulfillment	Dreams provide a "psychic safety valve"—expressing otherwise unacceptable feelings; contain manifest (remembered) content and a deeper layer of latent content—a hidden meaning.	Lacks any scientific support; dreams may be interpreted in many different ways.
Information-processing	Dreams help us sort out the day's events and consolidate our memories.	But why do we sometimes dream about things we have not experienced?
Physiological function	Regular brain stimulation from REM sleep may help develop and preserve neural pathways.	This may be true, but it does not explain why we experience *meaningful* dreams.
Activation-synthesis	REM sleep triggers neural activity that evokes random visual memories, which our sleeping brain weaves into stories.	The individual's brain is weaving the stories, which still tells us something about the dreamer.
Cognitive development	Dream content reflects dreamers' cognitive development—their knowledge and understanding.	Does not address the neuroscience of dreams.

example, prior to age 9, children's dreams seem more like a slide show and less like an active story in which the dreamer is an actor. Dreams overlap with waking cognition and feature coherent speech. They draw on our concepts and knowledge. **TABLE 8.2** compares major dream theories.

Although sleep researchers debate dreams' function—and some are skeptical that dreams serve any function—there is one thing they agree on: We need REM sleep. Deprived of it by repeatedly being awakened, people return more and more quickly to the REM stage after falling back to sleep. When finally allowed to sleep undisturbed, they literally sleep like babies—with increased REM sleep, a phenomenon called **REM rebound.** Withdrawing REM-suppressing sleeping medications also increases REM sleep, but with accompanying nightmares.

Most other mammals also experience REM rebound, suggesting that the causes and functions of REM sleep are deeply biological. That REM sleep occurs in mammals—and not in animals such as fish, whose behavior is less influenced by learning—also fits the information-processing theory of dreams.

So does this mean that because dreams serve physiological functions and extend normal cognition, they are psychologically meaningless? Not necessarily. Every psychologically meaningful experience involves an active brain. We are once again reminded of a basic principle: *Biological and psychological explanations of behavior are partners, not competitors.* Dreams may be akin to abstract art—open to more than one meaningful interpretation.

REM rebound the tendency for REM sleep to increase following REM sleep deprivation (created by repeated awakenings during REM sleep).

REVIEW

Sleep and Dreams

8-1 **How do our biological rhythms influence our daily functioning and our sleep and dreams?** Our internal biological rhythms create periodic physiological fluctuations. The *circadian rhythm's* 24-hour cycle regulates our daily schedule of sleeping and waking, in part in response to light on the retina, triggering alterations in the level of sleep-inducing melatonin. Shifts in schedules can reset our biological clock.

8-2 **What is the biological rhythm of our sleep?** We cycle through five *sleep* stages in about 90 minutes. Leaving the *alpha waves* of the awake, relaxed stage, we descend into transitional Stage 1 sleep, often with the sensation of falling or floating. Stage 2 sleep (in which we spend the most time) follows about 20 minutes later, with its characteristic sleep spindles. Then follow Stages 3 and 4, together lasting about 30 minutes, with large, slow *delta waves*. Reversing course, we retrace our path, but with one difference: About an hour after falling asleep, we begin periods of *REM (rapid eye movement) sleep*. Most dreaming occurs in this fifth stage (also known as paradoxical sleep) of internal arousal but outward paralysis. During a normal night's sleep, periods of Stages 3 and 4 sleep shorten and REM sleep lengthens.

8-3 **How does sleep loss affect us?** Sleep deprivation causes fatigue and impairs concentration, creativity, and communication. It also can lead to obesity, hypertension, a suppressed immune system, irritability, and slowed performance (with greater vulnerability to accidents).

8-4 **What is sleep's function?** Sleep may have played a protective role in human evolution by keeping people safe during potentially dangerous periods. Sleep also gives the brain time to heal, as it restores and repairs damaged neurons. During sleep, we restore and rebuild memories of the day's experiences. A good night's sleep promotes creative problem-solving the next day. Finally, sleep encourages growth; the pituitary gland secretes a growth hormone in Stage 4 sleep.

8-5 **What are the major sleep disorders?** The disorders of sleep include *insomnia* (recurring wakefulness), *narcolepsy* (sudden uncontrollable sleepiness or lapsing into REM sleep), *sleep apnea* (the stopping of breathing while asleep), *night terrors* (high arousal and the appearance of being terrified), sleepwalking, and sleeptalking. Sleep apnea mainly targets overweight men. Children are most prone to night terrors, sleepwalking, and sleeptalking.

8-6 **What do we dream?** We usually *dream* of ordinary events and everyday experiences, most involving some anxiety or misfortune. Fewer than 10 percent (and less among women) of dreams have any sexual content. Most dreams occur during REM sleep; those that happen during non-REM sleep tend to be vague fleeting images.

8-7 **What is the function of dreams?** There are five major views of the function of dreams. (1) Freudian: to provide a safety valve, with *manifest content* (or story line) acting as a censored version of *latent content* (some underlying meaning that gratifies our unconscious wishes). (2) The information-processing perspective: to sort out the day's experiences and fix them in memory. (3) Brain stimulation: to preserve neural pathways in the brain. (4) The activation-synthesis explanation: to make sense of neural static our brain tries to weave into a story line. (5) The brain-maturation/cognitive-development perspective: Dreams represent the dreamer's level of development, knowledge, and understanding. Most sleep theorists agree that REM sleep and its associated dreams serve an important function, as shown by the *REM rebound* that occurs following REM deprivation.

Terms and Concepts to Remember

circadian [ser-KAY-dee-an] rhythm, p. 91	narcolepsy, p. 101
	sleep apnea, p. 101
REM sleep, p. 92	night terrors, p. 102
alpha waves, p. 93	dream, p. 103
sleep, p. 94	manifest content, p. 103
hallucinations, p. 94	latent content, p. 104
delta waves, p. 94	REM rebound, p. 106
insomnia, p. 100	

Test Yourself

1. Are you getting enough sleep? What might you ask yourself to answer this question?

(Answers to the Test Yourself questions can be found in Appendix B at the end of the book.)

Ask Yourself

1. In some countries, such as Britain, the school day for teenagers runs from about 9:00 A.M. to 4:00 P.M. In other countries, such as the United States, the teen school day often runs from 8:00 A.M. to 3:00 P.M. or even 7:30 A.M. to 2:30 P.M. Early to rise isn't making kids wise, say critics—it's making them sleepy. For optimal alertness and well-being, teens need 8 to 9 hours of sleep a night. So, should early-start schools move to a later start time, even if it requires buying more buses or switching start times with elementary schools? Or is this impractical, and would it do little to remedy the tired-teen problem?

∞ WEB

Multiple-choice self-tests and more may be found at www.worthpublishers.com/myers

MODULE 9

Hypnosis

9-1 What is hypnosis, and what powers does a hypnotist have over a hypnotized subject?

Imagine you are about to be hypnotized. The hypnotist invites you to sit back, fix your gaze on a spot high on the wall, and relax. In a quiet voice the hypnotist suggests, "Your eyes are growing tired. . . . Your eyelids are becoming heavy . . . now heavier and heavier. . . . They are beginning to close. . . . You are becoming more deeply relaxed. . . . Your breathing is now deep and regular. . . . Your muscles are becoming more and more relaxed. Your whole body is beginning to feel like lead."

After a few minutes of this *hypnotic induction,* you may experience **hypnosis.** When the hypnotist suggests, "Your eyelids are shutting so tight that you cannot open them even if you try," it may indeed seem beyond your control to open your eyelids. Told to forget the number 6, you may be puzzled when you count 11 fingers on your hands. Invited to smell a sensuous perfume that is actually ammonia, you may linger delightedly over its pungent odor. Told that you cannot see a certain object, such as a chair, you may indeed report that it is not there, although you manage to avoid the chair when walking around.

But is hypnosis really an *altered* state of consciousness? Let's start with some agreed-upon facts.

▶‖ Facts and Falsehoods

Those who study hypnosis have agreed that its power resides not in the hypnotist but in the subject's openness to suggestion (Bowers, 1984). Hypnotists have no magical mind-control power; they merely engage people's ability to focus on certain images or behaviors. But how open to suggestions are we?

Can Anyone Experience Hypnosis?

To some extent, we are all open to suggestion. When people stand upright with their eyes closed and are told that they are swaying back and forth, most will indeed sway a little. In fact, *postural sway* is one of the items assessed on the Stanford Hypnotic Susceptibility Scale. People who respond to such suggestions without hypnosis are the same people who respond with hypnosis (Kirsch & Braffman, 2001).

After giving a brief hypnotic induction, a hypnotist suggests a series of experiences ranging from easy (your outstretched arms will move together) to difficult (with eyes open, you will see a nonexistent person). Highly hypnotizable people—say, the 20 percent who can carry out a suggestion not to smell or react to a bottle of ammonia held under their nose—are those who easily become deeply absorbed in imaginative activities (Barnier & McConkey, 2004; Silva & Kirsch, 1992). Typically, they have rich fantasy lives and become absorbed in the imaginary events of a novel or movie. (Perhaps you can recall being riveted by a movie into a trancelike state, oblivious to the people or noise surrounding you.) Many researchers refer to hypnotic "susceptibility" as hypnotic *ability*—the ability to focus attention totally on a task, to become imaginatively absorbed in it, to entertain fanciful possibilities.

Indeed, anyone who can turn attention inward and imagine is able to experience some degree of hypnosis—because that's what hypnosis is. And virtually anyone will experience hypnotic responsiveness if led to *expect* it. Imagine being asked to stare at a

hypnosis a social interaction in which one person (the hypnotist) suggests to another (the subject) that certain perceptions, feelings, thoughts, or behaviors will spontaneously occur.

posthypnotic suggestion a suggestion, made during a hypnosis session, to be carried out after the subject is no longer hypnotized; used by some clinicians to help control undesired symptoms and behaviors.

high spot and then hearing that "your eyes are growing tired . . . your eyelids are becoming heavy." With such strain, anyone's eyes would get tired. (Try looking up for 30 seconds.) But you likely would attribute your heavy eyelids to the hypnotist's abilities and then become more open to other suggestions.

Can Hypnosis Enhance Recall of Forgotten Events?

Can hypnotic procedures enable people to recall kindergarten classmates? To retrieve forgotten or suppressed details of a crime? Should testimony obtained under hypnosis be admissible in court?

Most people wrongly believe that our experiences are all "in there," recorded in our brain and available for recall if only we can break through our own defenses (Loftus, 1980). In one community survey, 3 in 4 people agreed with the inaccurate statement that hypnosis enables people to "recover accurate memories as far back as birth" (Johnson & Hauck, 1999). But 60 years of research disputes such claims of *age regression*—the supposed ability to relive childhood experiences. Age-regressed people act as they believe children would, but they typically miss the mark by outperforming real children of the specified age (Silverman & Retzlaff, 1986). They may, for example, *feel* childlike and print much as they know a 6-year-old would. But they sometimes do so with perfect spelling and typically without any change in their adult brain waves, reflexes, and perceptions.

"Hypnotically refreshed" memories combine fact with fiction. Without either person being aware of what is going on, a hypnotist's hints—"Did you hear loud noises?"—can plant ideas that become the subject's pseudomemory. Thus, American, Australian, and British courts generally ban testimony from witnesses who have been hypnotized (Druckman & Bjork, 1994; Gibson, 1995; McConkey, 1995).

Other striking examples of memories created under hypnosis come from the thousands of people who since 1980 have reported being abducted by UFOs. Most such reports have come from people who are predisposed to believe in aliens, are highly hypnotizable, and have undergone hypnosis (Newman & Baumeister, 1996; Nickell, 1996).

Can Hypnosis Force People to Act Against Their Will?

Researchers have induced hypnotized people to perform an apparently dangerous act: plunging one hand briefly into fuming "acid," then throwing the "acid" in a researcher's face (Orne & Evans, 1965). Interviewed a day later, these people exhibited no memory of their acts and emphatically denied they would ever follow such orders.

Had hypnosis given the hypnotist a special power to control others against their will? To find out, researchers Martin Orne and Frederich Evans unleashed that enemy of so many illusory beliefs—the control group. Orne asked other individuals to *pretend* they were hypnotized. Laboratory assistants, unaware that those in the experiment's control group had not been hypnotized, treated both groups the same. The result? All the *un*hypnotized participants (perhaps believing that the laboratory context assured safety) performed the same acts as those who were hypnotized.

Such studies illustrate a principle that social psychologist Stanley Milgram (1974) demonstrated: *An authoritative person in a legitimate context can induce people—hypnotized or not—to perform some unlikely acts.* Hypnosis researcher Nicholas Spanos (1982) put it directly: "The overt behaviors of hypnotic subjects are well within normal limits."

Can Hypnosis Be Therapeutic?

Hypnotherapists try to help patients harness their own healing powers (Baker, 1987). **Posthypnotic suggestions** have helped alleviate headaches, asthma, and stress-related skin disorders. One woman, who for more than 20 years suffered from open

"Hypnosis is not a psychological truth serum and to regard it as such has been a source of considerable mischief."
Researcher Kenneth Bowers (1987)

"It wasn't what I expected. But facts are facts, and if one is proved to be wrong, one must just be humble about it and start again."
Agatha Christie's Miss Marple

sores all over her body, was asked to imagine herself swimming in shimmering, sunlit liquids that would cleanse her skin, and to experience her skin as smooth and unblemished. Within three months her sores had disappeared (Bowers, 1984).

In one statistical digest of 18 studies, the average client whose therapy was supplemented with hypnosis showed greater improvement than 70 percent of other therapy patients (Kirsch et al., 1995, 1996). Hypnosis seemed especially helpful for the treatment of obesity. However, drug, alcohol, and smoking addictions have not responded well to hypnosis (Nash, 2001). In controlled studies, hypnosis speeds the disappearance of warts, but so do the same positive suggestions given without hypnosis (Spanos, 1991, 1996).

Can Hypnosis Alleviate Pain?

Yes, hypnosis *can* relieve pain (Druckman & Bjork, 1994; Patterson, 2004). When unhypnotized people put their arm in an ice bath, they feel intense pain within 25 seconds. When hypnotized people do the same after being given suggestions to feel no pain, they indeed report feeling little pain. As some dentists know, even light hypnosis can reduce fear, thus reducing hypersensitivity to pain.

Nearly 10 percent of us can become so deeply hypnotized that we can even undergo major surgery without anesthesia. Half of us can gain at least some pain relief from hypnosis. In surgical experiments, hypnotized patients have required less medication, recovered sooner, and left the hospital earlier than unhypnotized controls, thanks to the inhibition of pain-related brain activity (Askay & Patterson, 2007; Spiegel, 2007). The surgical use of hypnosis has flourished in Europe, where one Belgian medical team has performed more than 5000 surgeries with a combination of hypnosis, local anesthesia, and a mild sedative (Song, 2006).

▶❙❙ Explaining the Hypnotized State

9-2   Is hypnosis an extension of normal consciousness or an altered state?

We have seen that hypnosis involves heightened suggestibility. We have also seen that hypnotic procedures do not endow a person with special powers. But they can sometimes help people overcome stress-related ailments and cope with pain. So, just what *is* hypnosis?

Hypnosis as a Social Phenomenon

Some researchers believe that hypnotic phenomena reflect the workings of normal consciousness and the power of social influence (Lynn et al., 1990; Spanos & Coe, 1992). They point out how powerfully our interpretations and attentional spotlight influence our ordinary perceptions.

Does this mean that people are consciously faking hypnosis? No—like actors caught up in their roles, subjects begin to feel and behave in ways appropriate for "good hypnotic subjects." The more they like and trust the hypnotist, the more they allow that person to direct their attention and fantasies (Gfeller et al., 1987). "The hypnotist's ideas become the subject's thoughts," explained Theodore Barber (2000), "and the subject's thoughts produce the hypnotic experiences and behaviors." If told to scratch their ear later when they hear the word *psychology,* subjects will likely do so only if they think the experiment is still under way (and scratching is therefore expected). If an experimenter eliminates their motivation for acting hypnotized—by stating that hypnosis reveals their "gullibility"—subjects become unresponsive.

Based on such findings, advocates of the *social influence theory* contend that hypnotic phenomena—like the behaviors associated with other supposed altered states, such as dissociative identity disorder ("multiple personalities") and spirit or demon possession—are an extension of everyday social behavior, not something unique to hypnosis (Spanos, 1994, 1996).

Hypnosis as Divided Consciousness

Most hypnosis researchers grant that normal social and cognitive processes play a part in hypnosis, but they nevertheless believe hypnosis is more than inducing someone to play the role of "good subject." For one thing, hypnotized subjects will sometimes carry out suggested behaviors on cue, even when they believe no one is watching (Perugini et al., 1998). Moreover, distinctive brain activity accompanies hypnosis. When deeply hypnotized people in one experiment were asked to imagine a color, areas of their brain lit up as if they were really seeing the color. Mere imagination had become—to the hypnotized person's brain—a compelling hallucination (Kosslyn et al., 2000). Another experiment invited hypnotizable or nonhypnotizable people to say the color of letters—an easy task that slows if, say, green letters form the conflicting word RED (Raz et al., 2005). When given a suggestion to focus on the color and to perceive the letters as irrelevant gibberish, easily hypnotized people became much less slowed by the word-color conflict. (Brain areas that decode words and detect conflict remained inactive.)

These results would not have surprised famed researcher Ernest Hilgard (1986, 1992), who believed hypnosis involves not only social influence but also a special state of **dissociation**—a split between different levels of consciousness. Hilgard viewed hypnotic dissociation as a vivid form of everyday mind splits—similar to doodling while listening to a lecture or keying in the end of a sentence while starting a conversation. Hilgard felt that when, for example, hypnotized people lower their arm into an ice bath, as in **FIGURE 9.1**, that hypnosis dissociates the sensation of the pain stimulus (of which the subjects are still aware) from the emotional suffering that defines their experience of pain. The ice water therefore feels cold—very cold—but not painful.

Hypnotic pain relief may also result from another form of dual processing—*selective attention*—as when an injured athlete, caught up in the competition, feels little or no pain until the game ends. Support for this view comes from PET scans showing that hypnosis reduces brain activity in a region that processes painful stimuli, but not in the sensory cortex, which receives the raw sensory input (Rainville et al., 1997). Hypnosis does not block sensory input, but it may block our *attention* to those stimuli.

dissociation a split in consciousness, which allows some thoughts and behaviors to occur simultaneously with others.

"The total possible consciousness may be split into parts which co-exist but mutually ignore each other."

William James, *Principles of Psychology*, 1890

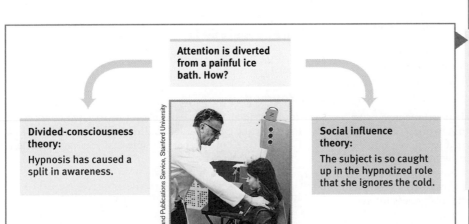

Attention is diverted from a painful ice bath. How?

Divided-consciousness theory:
Hypnosis has caused a split in awareness.

Social influence theory:
The subject is so caught up in the hypnotized role that she ignores the cold.

Courtesy of News and Publications Service, Stanford University

FIGURE 9.1 Dissociation or role-playing? This hypnotized woman tested by Ernest Hilgard exhibited no pain when her arm was placed in an ice bath. But asked to press a key if some part of her felt the pain, she did so. To Hilgard, this was evidence of dissociation, or divided consciousness. Proponents of social influence theory, however, maintain that people responding this way are caught up in playing the role of "good subject."

FIGURE 9.2 **Levels of analysis for hypnosis** Using a biopsychosocial approach, researchers explore hypnosis from complementary perspectives.

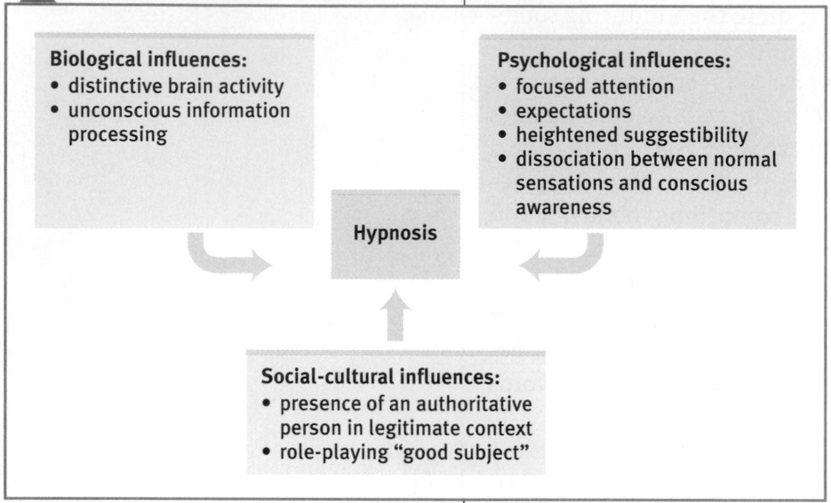

Biological influences:
• distinctive brain activity
• unconscious information processing

Psychological influences:
• focused attention
• expectations
• heightened suggestibility
• dissociation between normal sensations and conscious awareness

Hypnosis

Social-cultural influences:
• presence of an authoritative person in legitimate context
• role-playing "good subject"

Although the divided-consciousness theory of hypnosis is controversial, this much seems clear: There is, without doubt, much more to thinking and acting than we are conscious of. Our information processing, which starts with selective attention, is divided into simultaneous conscious and nonconscious realms. In hypnosis as in life, *much of our behavior occurs on autopilot.* We have two-track minds.

Yet, there is also little doubt that social influences do play an important role in hypnosis. So, might the two views—social influence and divided consciousness—be bridged? Researchers John Kihlstrom and Kevin McConkey (1990) believe there is no contradiction between the two approaches, which are converging toward a *unified account of hypnosis.* Hypnosis, they suggest, is an extension *both* of normal principles of social influence *and* of everyday dissociations between our conscious awareness and our automatic behaviors. Hypnosis researchers are moving beyond the "hypnosis is social influence" *versus* "hypnosis is divided consciousness" debate (Killeen & Nash, 2003; Woody & McConkey, 2003). They are instead exploring how brain activity, attention, and social influences interact to affect hypnotic phenomena (**FIGURE 9.2**).

REVIEW

Hypnosis

9-1 **What is hypnosis, and what powers does a hypnotist have over a hypnotized subject?** *Hypnosis* is a social interaction in which one person suggests to another that certain perceptions, feelings, thoughts, or behaviors will spontaneously occur. Hypnotized people are no more vulnerable to acting against their will than unhypnotized people are, and hypnosis does not enhance recall of forgotten events (it may even evoke false memories). Hypnotized people, like unhypnotized people, may perform unlikely acts when told to do so by an authoritative person. *Posthypnotic suggestions* have helped people harness their own healing powers but have not been very effective in treating addiction. Hypnosis can help relieve pain.

9-2 **Is hypnosis an extension of normal consciousness or an altered state?** Many psychologists believe that hypnosis is a form of normal social influence and that hypnotized people act out the role of "good subject." Other psychologists view hypnosis as a *dissociation*—a split between normal sensations and conscious awareness. A unified account of hypnosis melds these two views and studies how brain activity, attention, and social influences interact in hypnosis.

Terms and Concepts to Remember
hypnosis, p. 108
posthypnotic suggestion, p. 109
dissociation, p. 111

Test Yourself
1. When is the use of hypnosis potentially harmful, and when can hypnosis be used to help?

(Answers to the Test Yourself questions can be found in Appendix B at the end of the book.)

Ask Yourself
1. You've read about two examples of dissociated consciousness: talking while typing, and doodling while listening to a lecture. Can you think of another example that you have experienced?

∞ WEB
Multiple-choice self-tests and more may be found at www.worthpublishers.com/myers

MODULE 10

Dependence and Addiction

Psychoactive Drugs

Influences on Drug Use

Drugs and Consciousness

There is little dispute that some drugs alter consciousness. **Psychoactive drugs** are chemicals that change perceptions and moods through their actions at the neural synapses. Let's imagine a day in the life of a legal-drug user. It begins with a wake-up latte. By midday, several cigarettes have calmed frazzled nerves before an appointment at the plastic surgeon's office for wrinkle-smoothing Botox injections. A diet pill before dinner helps stem the appetite, and its stimulating effects can later be partially offset with a glass of wine and two Tylenol PMs. And if performance needs enhancing, there are beta blockers for onstage performers, Viagra for middle-aged men, hormone-delivering "libido patches" for middle-aged women, and Adderall for students hoping to focus their concentration. Before drifting off into REM-depressed sleep, our hypothetical drug user is dismayed by news reports of pill-sharing, pill-popping college students and of celebrity deaths (Anna Nicole Smith, Heath Ledger) attributed to accidental overdoses of lethal drug combinations.

"Just tell me where you kids got the idea to take so many drugs."

▶‖ Dependence and Addiction

10-1 What are tolerance, dependence, and addiction, and what are some common misconceptions about addiction?

Why might a person who rarely drinks alcohol get tipsy on one can of beer, but an experienced drinker show few effects until the second six-pack? Continued use of alcohol and other psychoactive drugs produces **tolerance.** As the user's brain adapts its chemistry to offset the drug effect (a process called *neuroadaptation*), the user requires larger and larger doses to experience the same effect (**FIGURE 10.1**). Despite the connotations of alcohol "tolerance," the brain, heart, and liver of a person addicted to alcohol suffer damage from the excessive alcohol being "tolerated."

Users who stop taking psychoactive drugs may experience the undesirable side effects of **withdrawal.** As the body responds to the drug's absence, the user may feel physical pain and intense cravings, indicating **physical dependence.** People can also

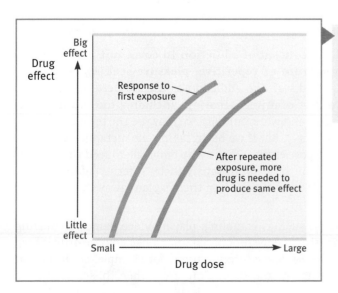

FIGURE 10.1 Drug tolerance In most cases, with repeated exposure to a psychoactive drug, the drug's effect lessens. Thus, it takes bigger doses to get the desired effect.

psychoactive drug a chemical substance that alters perceptions and moods.

tolerance the diminishing effect with regular use of the same dose of a drug, requiring the user to take larger and larger doses before experiencing the drug's effect.

withdrawal the discomfort and distress that follow discontinuing the use of an addictive drug.

physical dependence a physiological need for a drug, marked by unpleasant withdrawal symptoms when the drug is discontinued.

psychological dependence a psychological need to use a drug, such as to relieve negative emotions.

addiction compulsive drug craving and use, despite adverse consequences.

|| The odds of getting hooked after trying various drugs:

Marijuana: 9 percent

Alcohol: 15 percent

Heroin: 23 percent

Tobacco: 32 percent

Source: National Academy of Science, Institute of Medicine (Brody, 2003). ||

"About 70 percent of Americans have tried illicit drugs, but . . . only a few percent have done so in the last month. . . . Past age 35, the casual use of illegal drugs virtually ceases." Having sampled the pleasures and their aftereffects, "most people eventually walk away."

Neuropsychologist Michael Gazzaniga (1997)

develop **psychological dependence,** particularly for stress-relieving drugs. Such drugs, although not physically addictive, can become an important part of the user's life, often as a way of relieving negative emotions. With either physical or psychological dependence, the user's primary focus may be obtaining and using the drug.

Misconceptions About Addiction

An **addiction** is a compulsive craving for a substance despite adverse consequences and often with physical symptoms such as aches, nausea, and distress following sudden withdrawal. Worldwide, reports the World Health Organization (2008), 90 million people suffer from such problems related to alcohol and other drugs.

In recent pop psychology, the supposedly irresistible seduction of addiction has been extended to cover many behaviors formerly considered bad habits or even sins. Has the concept been stretched too far? Are addictions as irresistible as commonly believed? Many drug researchers believe the following three myths about addiction are *false:*

Myth 1. Addictive drugs quickly corrupt; for example, morphine taken to control pain is powerfully addictive and often leads to heroin abuse. People given morphine to control pain rarely develop the cravings of the addict who uses morphine as a mood-altering drug (Melzack, 1990). But some people—perhaps 10 percent—do indeed have a hard time using a psychoactive drug in moderation or stopping altogether. Even so, controlled, occasional users of drugs such as alcohol and marijuana far outnumber those addicted to these substances (Gazzaniga, 1988; Siegel, 1990). "Even for a very addictive drug like cocaine, only 15 to 16 percent of people become addicted within 10 years of first use," report Terry Robinson and Kent Berridge (2003). Much the same is true for rats, only some of which become compulsively addicted to cocaine (Deroche-Garmonet et al., 2004).

Myth 2. Addictions cannot be overcome voluntarily; therapy is required. Addictions can be powerful, and some addicts do benefit from treatment programs. Alcoholics Anonymous, for example, has supported many people in overcoming their alcohol dependence. But the recovery rates of treated and untreated groups differ less than one might suppose. Helpful as therapy or group support may be, people often recover on their own.

Moreover, viewing addiction as a disease, as diabetes is a disease, can undermine self-confidence and the will to change cravings that, without treatment, "one cannot fight." And that, critics say, would be unfortunate, for many people do voluntarily stop using addictive drugs, without treatment. Most of America's 41 million ex-smokers kicked the habit on their own, usually after prior failed efforts or treatments.

Myth 3. We can extend the concept of addiction to cover not just drug dependencies, but a whole spectrum of repetitive, pleasure-seeking behaviors. We can, and we have, but should we? The addiction-as-disease-needing-treatment idea has been suggested for a host of driven behaviors, including too much eating, shopping, exercise, sex, gambling, and work. Initially, we may use the term metaphorically ("I'm a science fiction addict"), but if we begin taking the metaphor as reality, addiction can become an all-purpose excuse. Those who embezzle to feed their "gambling addiction," surf the Web half the night to satisfy their "Internet addiction," or abuse or betray to indulge their "sex addiction" can then explain away their behavior as an illness.

Sometimes, though, behaviors such as gambling, playing video games, or surfing the Internet do become compulsive and dysfunctional, much like abusive drug taking (Griffiths, 2001; Hoeft et al., 2008). Some Internet users, for example, do display an apparent inability to resist logging on, and staying on, even when this excessive use impairs their work and relationships (Ko et al., 2005). So, there may be justification for stretching the addiction concept to cover certain social behaviors. Debates over the addiction-as-disease model continue.

▶‖ Psychoactive Drugs

The three major categories of psychoactive drugs—*depressants, stimulants,* and *hallucinogens*—all do their work at the brain's synapses. They stimulate, inhibit, or mimic the activity of the brain's own chemical messengers, the neurotransmitters. Our culturally influenced expectations also play a role in the way these drugs affect us (Ward, 1994). If one culture assumes that a particular drug produces euphoria (or aggression or sexual arousal) and another does not, each culture may find its expectations fulfilled.

Depressants

10-2 What are depressants, and what are their effects?

Depressants are drugs such as alcohol, barbiturates (tranquilizers), and opiates that calm neural activity and slow body functions.

Alcohol

True or false? In large amounts, alcohol is a depressant; in small amounts, it is a stimulant. *False.* Low doses of alcohol may, indeed, enliven a drinker, but they do so by slowing brain activity that controls judgment and inhibitions. Alcohol lowers our inhibitions, slows neural processing, disrupts memory formation, and reduces self-awareness.

Disinhibition Alcohol is an equal-opportunity drug: It increases harmful tendencies—as when angered people become aggressive after drinking. And it increases helpful tendencies—as when tipsy restaurant patrons leave extravagant tips (M. Lynn, 1988). *The urges you would feel if sober are the ones you will more likely act upon when intoxicated.*

Slowed Neural Processing Low doses of alcohol relax the drinker by slowing sympathetic nervous system activity. In larger doses, alcohol can become a staggering problem: Reactions slow, speech slurs, skilled performance deteriorates. Paired with sleep

"That is not one of the seven habits of highly effective people."

Ray Ng/Time & Life Pictures/Getty Images

Drawing by D. Fradon: © 1983 The New Yorker Magazine, Inc.

Dangerous disinhibition Alcohol consumption leads to feelings of invincibility, which become especially dangerous behind the wheel of a car, such as this one totaled by a teenage drunk driver. This Colorado University Alcohol Awareness Week exhibit prompted many students to post their own anti-drinking pledges (white flags).

deprivation, alcohol is a potent sedative. (Although either sleep deprivation or drinking can put a driver at risk, their combination is deadlier yet.) These physical effects, combined with lowered inhibitions, contribute to alcohol's worst consequences—the several hundred thousand lives claimed worldwide each year in alcohol-related accidents and violent crime. Car accidents occur despite most drinkers' belief (when sober) that driving under the influence of alcohol is wrong and despite their insisting that they would not do so. Yet, as blood-alcohol levels rise and moral judgments falter, people's qualms about drinking and driving lessen. Virtually all will drive home from a bar, even if given a breathalyzer test and told they are intoxicated (Denton & Krebs, 1990; MacDonald et al., 1995).

Memory Disruption Alcohol also disrupts the processing of recent experiences into long-term memories. Thus, heavy drinkers may not recall people they met the night before or what they said or did while intoxicated. These blackouts result partly from the way alcohol suppresses REM sleep, which helps fix the day's experiences into permanent memories.

The effects of heavy drinking on the brain and cognition can be long-term. In rats, at a development period corresponding to human adolescence, binge-drinking diminishes the genesis of nerve cells, impairs the growth of synaptic connections, and contributes to nerve cell death (Crews et al., 2006, 2007). MRI scans show another way prolonged and excessive drinking can affect cognition (**FIGURE 10.2**). It can shrink the brain, especially in women, who have less of a stomach enzyme that digests alcohol (Wuethrich, 2001). Girls and young women can also become addicted to alcohol more quickly than boys and young men do, and they are at risk for lung, brain, and liver damage at lower consumption levels (CASA, 2003).

FIGURE 10.2 Alcohol dependence shrinks the brain MRI scans show brain shrinkage in women with alcohol dependence (left) compared with women in a control group (right).

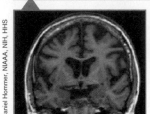
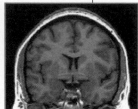

Scan of woman with   Scan of woman without
alcohol dependence   alcohol dependence

Daniel Hommer, NIAAA, NIH, HHS

Reduced Self-Awareness and Self-Control Alcohol not only impairs judgment and memory, it also reduces self-awareness (Hull et al., 1986). This may help explain why people who want to suppress their awareness of failures or shortcomings are more likely to drink than are those who feel good about themselves. Losing a business deal, a game, or a romantic partner sometimes elicits a drinking binge. Excess drinking is especially common when people with low self-esteem experience pain in a romantic relationship (DeHart et al., 2008). By focusing attention on the immediate situation and away from any future consequences, alcohol also lessens impulse control (Steele & Josephs, 1990). In surveys of rapists, more than half acknowledge drinking before committing their offense (Seto & Barbaree, 1995).

Expectancy Effects As with other psychoactive drugs, alcohol's behavioral effects stem not only from its alteration of brain chemistry but also from the user's expectations. When people believe that alcohol affects social behavior in certain ways, and believe, rightly or wrongly, that they have been drinking alcohol, they will behave accordingly (Leigh, 1989). David Abrams and Terence Wilson (1983) demonstrated this in a now-classic experiment. They gave Rutgers University men who volunteered for a study on "alcohol and sexual stimulation" either an alcoholic or a nonalcoholic drink. (Both had strong tastes that masked any alcohol.) In each group, half the participants thought they were drinking alcohol and half thought they were not. After watching an erotic movie clip, the men who *thought* they had consumed alcohol were more likely to report having strong sexual fantasies and feeling guilt-free. Being able to *attribute* their sexual responses to alcohol released their inhibitions—whether they actually had drunk alcohol or not. If, as commonly believed, liquor is the quicker pick-her-upper, the effect lies partly in that powerful sex organ, the mind.

Alcohol + Sex = The Perfect Storm Alcohol's effects on self-control and social expectations often converge in sexual situations. More than 600 studies have explored the link between drinking and risky sex, with "the overwhelming majority" finding the two correlated (Cooper, 2006). But of course correlations do not come with causal arrows attached. In this case, three factors appear to influence the correlation.

1. Underlying "third variables," such as sensation-seeking and peer influences, simultaneously push people toward both drinking and risky sex.
2. The desire for sex leads people to drink and to get their partners to drink. Sexually coercive college men, for example, may lower their dates' sexual inhibitions by getting them to drink (Abbey, 1991; Mosher & Anderson, 1986).
3. Drinking disinhibits, and when sexually aroused, men become more disposed to sexual aggression, and men and women more disposed to casual sex (Davis et al., 2006; Grello et al., 2006). University women under alcohol's influence find an attractive but sexually promiscuous man a more appealing potential date than they do when sober. It seems, surmise Sheila Murphy and her colleagues (1998), "that when people have been drinking, the restraining forces of reason may weaken and yield under the pressure of their desires."

Barbiturates

The **barbiturate** drugs, or *tranquilizers,* mimic the effects of alcohol. Because they depress nervous system activity, barbiturates such as Nembutal, Seconal, and Amytal are sometimes prescribed to induce sleep or reduce anxiety. In larger doses, they can lead to impaired memory and judgment or even death. If combined with alcohol—as sometimes happens when people take a sleeping pill after an evening of heavy drinking—the total depressive effect on body functions can be lethal.

Opiates

The **opiates**—opium and its derivatives, morphine and heroin—also depress neural functioning. Pupils constrict, breathing slows, and lethargy sets in, as blissful pleasure replaces pain and anxiety. But for this short-term pleasure the user may pay a long-term price: a gnawing craving for another fix, a need for progressively larger doses, and the extreme discomfort of withdrawal. When repeatedly flooded with an artificial opiate, the brain eventually stops producing its own opiates, the *endorphins.* If the artificial opiate is then withdrawn, the brain lacks the normal level of these painkilling neurotransmitters. Those who cannot or choose not to tolerate this state may pay an ultimate price—death by overdose.

Stimulants

10-3 What are stimulants, and what are their effects?

Stimulants such as caffeine and nicotine temporarily excite neural activity and arouse body functions. People use these substances to stay awake, lose weight, or boost mood or athletic performance. This category of drugs also includes **amphetamines,** and the even more powerful cocaine, Ecstasy, and **methamphetamine** ("speed"), which is chemically related to its parent drug, *amphetamine* (NIDA, 2002, 2005). All strong stimulants increase heart and breathing rates and cause pupils to dilate, appetite to diminish (because blood sugar increases), and energy and self-confidence to rise. And, as with other drugs, the benefits of stimulants come with a price. These substances can be addictive and may induce an aftermath crash into fatigue, headaches, irritability, and depression (Silverman et al., 1992).

Methamphetamine

Methamphetamine has even greater effects, which can include eight hours or so of heightened energy and euphoria. The drug triggers the release of the neurotransmitter dopamine, which stimulates brain cells that enhance energy and mood. In response

|| A University of Illinois campus survey showed that before sexual assaults, 80 percent of the male assailants and 70 percent of the female victims had been drinking (Camper, 1990). Another survey of 89,874 American collegians found alcohol or drugs involved in 79 percent of unwanted sexual intercourse experiences (Presley et al., 1997). ||

barbiturates drugs that depress the activity of the central nervous system, reducing anxiety but impairing memory and judgment.

opiates opium and its derivatives, such as morphine and heroin; they depress neural activity, temporarily lessening pain and anxiety.

stimulants drugs (such as caffeine, nicotine, and the more powerful amphetamines, cocaine, and Ecstasy) that excite neural activity and speed up body functions.

amphetamines drugs that stimulate neural activity, causing speeded-up body functions and associated energy and mood changes.

methamphetamine a powerfully addictive drug that stimulates the central nervous system, with speeded-up body functions and associated energy and mood changes; over time, appears to reduce baseline dopamine levels.

Dramatic drug-induced decline This woman's methamphetamine addiction led to obvious physical changes. Her decline is evident in these two photos, taken at age 36 (left) and, after four years of addiction, at age 40 (right).

 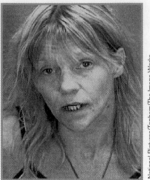

National Pictures/Topham/The Image Works

to a typical amphetamine dose, men show a higher rate of dopamine release than do women, which helps explain their higher addiction rate (Munro et al., 2006).

Over time, methamphetamine may reduce baseline dopamine levels, leaving the user with permanently depressed functioning. This drug is highly addictive, and its possible aftereffects include irritability, insomnia, hypertension, seizures, social isolation, depression, and occasional violent outbursts (Homer et al., 2008). The British government now classifies *crystal meth,* the highly addictive crystalized form of methamphetamine, alongside cocaine and heroin as one of the most dangerous drugs (BBC, 2006).

Caffeine

Caffeine, the world's most widely consumed psychoactive substance, can now be found not only in coffee, tea, and soda but also in fruit juices, mints, energy drinks, bars, and gels—and even in soap. Coffees and teas vary in their caffeine content, with a cup of drip coffee surprisingly having more caffeine than a shot of espresso, and teas having less. A mild dose of caffeine typically lasts three or four hours, which—if taken in the evening—may be long enough to impair sleep. Like other drugs, caffeine used regularly and in heavy doses produces tolerance: Its stimulating effects lessen. And discontinuing heavy caffeine intake often produces withdrawal symptoms, including fatigue and headache.

Nicotine

Imagine that cigarettes were harmless—except, once in every 25,000 packs, an occasional innocent-looking one is filled with dynamite instead of tobacco. Not such a bad risk of having your head blown off. But with 250 million packs a day consumed worldwide, we could expect more than 10,000 gruesome daily deaths (more than three times the 9/11 fatalities each and every day)—surely enough to have cigarettes banned everywhere.[1]

The lost lives from these dynamite-loaded cigarettes approximate those from today's actual cigarettes. Each year throughout the world, tobacco kills nearly 5.4 million of its 1.3 billion customers, reports the World Health Organization (WHO). (Imagine the outrage if terrorists took down an equivalent of 25 loaded jumbo jets today, let alone tomorrow and every day thereafter.) And by 2030, annual deaths will increase to 8 million, according to WHO predictions. That means that *1 billion* (say that number slowly) twenty-first-century people may be killed by tobacco (WHO, 2008).

A teen-to-the-grave smoker has a 50 percent chance of dying from the habit, and the death is often agonizing and premature, as the Philip Morris company acknowledged in 2001. Responding to Czech Republic complaints about the health-care costs of tobacco, Philip Morris reassured the Czechs that there was actually a net "health-care cost savings due to early mortality" and the resulting savings on pensions and elderly housing (Herbert, 2001).

"There is an overwhelming medical and scientific consensus that cigarette smoking causes lung cancer, heart disease, emphysema, and other serious diseases in smokers. Smokers are far more likely to develop serious diseases, like lung cancer, than nonsmokers."

Philip Morris Companies Inc., 1999

|| Smoke a cigarette and nature will charge you 12 minutes—ironically, just about the length of time you spend smoking it (*Discover,* 1996). ||

[1]This analogy, adapted here with world-based numbers, was suggested by mathematician Sam Saunders, as reported by K. C. Cole (1998).

Eliminating smoking would increase life expectancy more than any other preventive measure. Why, then, do so many people smoke?

Smoking usually begins during early adolescence. (If you are in college or university, and if by now the cigarette manufacturers haven't attracted your business, they almost surely never will.) Adolescents, self-conscious and often thinking the world is watching their every move, are vulnerable to smoking's allure. They may first light up to imitate glamorous celebrities, or to project a mature image, or to get the social reward of being accepted by other smokers (Cin et al., 2007; Tickle et al., 2006). Mindful of these tendencies, cigarette companies have effectively modeled smoking with themes that appeal to youths: sophistication, independence, adventure-seeking, social approval. Typically, teens who start smoking also have friends who smoke, who suggest its pleasures, and who offer them cigarettes (Eiser, 1985; Evans et al., 1988; Rose et al., 1999). Among teens whose parents and best friends are nonsmokers, the smoking rate is close to zero (Moss et al., 1992; also see **FIGURE 10.3**).

Those addicted to nicotine find it very hard to quit because tobacco products are as powerfully and quickly addictive as heroin and cocaine. As with other addictions, a smoker becomes dependent; each year fewer than one of every seven smokers who want to quit will do so. Smokers also develop tolerance, eventually needing larger and larger doses to get the same effect. Quitting causes nicotine-withdrawal symptoms, including craving, insomnia, anxiety, and irritability. Even attempts to quit within the first weeks of smoking often fail as nicotine cravings set in (DiFranza, 2008). And all it takes to relieve this aversive state is a cigarette—a portable nicotine dispenser.

Nicotine, like other addictive drugs, is not only compulsive and mood-altering, it is also reinforcing. Smoking delivers its hit of nicotine within 7 seconds, triggering the release of epinephrine and norepinephrine, which in turn diminish appetite and boost alertness and mental efficiency (**FIGURE 10.4** on the next page). At the same time, nicotine stimulates the central nervous system to release neurotransmitters that calm anxiety and reduce sensitivity to pain. For example, nicotine stimulates the release of dopamine and (like heroin and morphine) opioids (Nowak, 1994; Scott et al., 2004). These rewards keep people smoking even when they wish they could stop—indeed, even when they know they are committing slow-motion suicide (Saad, 2002). An informative exception: Brain-injured patients who have lost a prune-size frontal lobe region called the *insula*—an area that lights up when people crave drugs—are able to give up cigarettes instantly (Naqvi et al., 2007).

Nic-A-Teen "A cigarette in the hands of a Hollywood star on screen is a gun aimed at a 12- or 14-year-old." Screenwriter Joe Eszterhas, 2002

© WinStar Cinema/Courtesy: Everett Collection

Humorist Dave Barry (1995) recalling why he smoked his first cigarette the summer he turned 15: "Arguments against smoking: 'It's a repulsive addiction that slowly but surely turns you into a gasping, gray-skinned, tumor-ridden invalid, hacking up brownish gobs of toxic waste from your one remaining lung.' Arguments for smoking: 'Other teenagers are doing it.' Case closed! Let's light up!"

‖ Asked "If you had to do it all over again, would you start smoking?" more than 85 percent of adult smokers answer *No* (Slovic et al., 2002). ‖

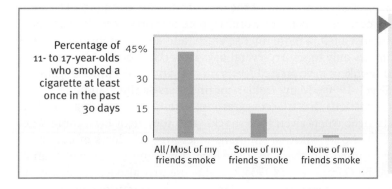

FIGURE 10.3 Peer influence Kids don't smoke if their friends don't (Philip Morris, 2003). A correlation-causation question: Does the close link between teen smoking and friends' smoking reflect peer influence? Teens seeking similar friends? Or both?

**FIGURE 10.4 Where there's smoke . . . :
The physiological effects of nicotine**
Nicotine reaches the brain within 7 seconds,
twice as fast as intravenous heroin. Within
minutes, the amount in the blood soars.

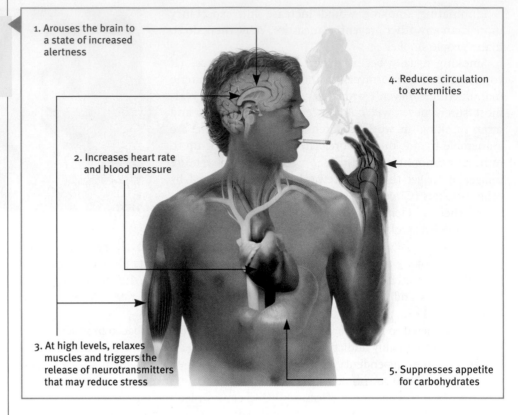

1. Arouses the brain to a state of increased alertness

4. Reduces circulation to extremities

2. Increases heart rate and blood pressure

3. At high levels, relaxes muscles and triggers the release of neurotransmitters that may reduce stress

5. Suppresses appetite for carbohydrates

"To cease smoking is the easiest thing I ever did; I ought to know because I've done it a thousand times."
Mark Twain, 1835–1910

Nevertheless, half of all Americans who have ever smoked have quit, and 81 percent of those who haven't yet quit wish to (Jones, 2007). For those who endure, the acute craving and withdrawal symptoms gradually dissipate over the ensuing six months (Ward et al., 1997). These nonsmokers may live not only healthier but also happier. Smoking correlates with higher rates of depression, chronic disabilities, and divorce (Doherty & Doherty, 1998; Vita et al., 1998). Healthy living seems to add both years to life and life to years.

Cocaine

Cocaine use offers a fast track from euphoria to crash. When sniffed ("snorted"), and especially when injected or smoked ("free-based"), cocaine enters the bloodstream quickly. The result: a "rush" of euphoria that depletes the brain's supply of the neurotransmitters dopamine, serotonin, and norepinephrine (**FIGURE 10.5**). Within 15 to 30 minutes, a crash of agitated depression follows as the drug's effect wears off.

|| The recipe for Coca-Cola originally included an extract of the coca plant, creating a cocaine tonic for tired older people. Between 1896 and 1905, Coke was indeed "the real thing." ||

In national surveys, 4 percent of U.S. high school seniors and 5 percent of British 18- to 24-year-olds reported having tried cocaine during the past year (Home Office, 2003; Johnston et al., 2009). Nearly half of the drug-using seniors had smoked *crack,* a crystallized form of cocaine. This faster-working, potent form of the drug produces a briefer but more intense high, a more intense crash, and a craving for more, which wanes after several hours only to return several days later (Gawin, 1991).

Cocaine-addicted monkeys have pressed levers more than 12,000 times to gain one cocaine injection (Siegel, 1990). Many regular cocaine users—animal and human—do become addicted. In situations that trigger aggression, ingesting cocaine may heighten reactions. Caged rats fight when given foot shocks, and they fight even more when given cocaine and foot shocks. Likewise, humans ingesting high doses of cocaine in laboratory experiments impose higher shock levels on a presumed opponent than do those receiving a placebo (Licata et al., 1993). Cocaine use may also lead to emotional disturbances, suspiciousness, convulsions, cardiac arrest, or respiratory failure.

"Cocaine makes you a new man. And the first thing that new man wants is more cocaine."
Comedian George Carlin (1937–2008)

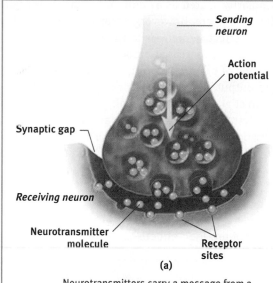
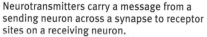

(a)

Neurotransmitters carry a message from a sending neuron across a synapse to receptor sites on a receiving neuron.

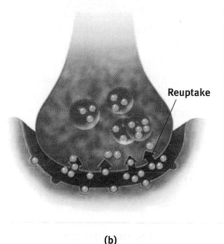

(b)

The sending neuron normally reabsorbs excess neurotransmitter molecules, a process called reuptake.

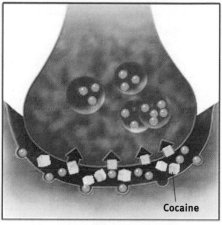

(c)

By binding to the sites that normally reabsorb neurotransmitter molecules, cocaine blocks reuptake of dopamine, norepinephrine, and serotonin (Ray & Ksir, 1990). The extra neurotransmitter molecules therefore remain in the synapse, intensifying their normal mood-altering effects and producing a euphoric rush. When the cocaine level drops, the absence of these neurotransmitters produces a crash.

FIGURE 10.5 Cocaine euphoria and crash

As with all psychoactive drugs, cocaine's psychological effects depend not only on the dosage and form consumed but also on the situation and the user's expectations and personality. Given a placebo, cocaine users who *think* they are taking cocaine often have a cocainelike experience (Van Dyke & Byck, 1982).

Ecstasy

Ecstasy, a street name for **MDMA** (methylenedioxymethamphetamine), is both a stimulant and a mild hallucinogen. As an amphetamine derivative, it triggers dopamine release. But its major effect is releasing stored serotonin and blocking its reabsorption, thus prolonging serotonin's feel-good flood (Braun, 2001). About a half-hour after taking an Ecstasy pill, users enter a three- to four-hour period of feelings of emotional elevation and, given a social context, connectedness with those around them ("I love everyone").

AP Photo/Dale Sparks

The hug drug MDMA, known as Ecstasy, produces a euphoric high and feelings of intimacy. But repeated use destroys serotonin-producing neurons and may permanently deflate mood and impair memory.

Ecstasy (MDMA) a synthetic stimulant and mild hallucinogen. Produces euphoria and social intimacy, but with short-term health risks and longer-term harm to serotonin-producing neurons and to mood and cognition.

During the late 1990s, Ecstasy's popularity soared as a "club drug" taken at night clubs and all-night raves (Landry, 2002). There are, however, reasons not to be ecstatic about Ecstasy. One is its dehydrating effect, which—when combined with prolonged dancing—can lead to severe overheating, increased blood pressure, and death. Another is that long-term, repeated leaching of brain serotonin can damage serotonin-producing neurons, leading to decreased output and increased risk of permanently depressed mood (Croft et al., 2001; McCann et al., 2001; Roiser et al., 2005). Ecstasy also suppresses the disease-fighting immune system, impairs memory and other cognitive functions, and disrupts sleep by interfering with serotonin's control of the circadian clock (Laws & Kokkalis, 2007; Pacifici et al., 2001; Schilt et al., 2007). Ecstasy delights for the night but dispirits the morrow.

Hallucinogens

10-4 What are hallucinogens, and what are their effects?

Hallucinogens distort perceptions and evoke sensory images in the absence of sensory input (which is why these drugs are also called *psychedelics,* meaning "mind-manifesting"). Some, such as LSD and MDMA (Ecstasy), are synthetic. Others, including the mild hallucinogen marijuana, are natural substances.

LSD

In 1943, Albert Hofmann reported perceiving "an uninterrupted stream of fantastic pictures, extraordinary shapes with intense, kaleidoscopic play of colors" (Siegel, 1984). Hofmann, a chemist, created—and on one Friday afternoon in April 1943 accidentally ingested—**LSD** (lysergic acid diethylamide). The result reminded him of a childhood mystical experience that had left him longing for another glimpse of "a miraculous, powerful, unfathomable reality" (Smith, 2006).

LSD and other powerful hallucinogens are chemically similar to (and therefore block the actions of) a subtype of the neurotransmitter serotonin (Jacobs, 1987). The emotions of an LSD trip vary from euphoria to detachment to panic. The user's current mood and expectations color the emotional experience, but the perceptual distortions and hallucinations have some commonalities. Psychologist Ronald Siegel (1982) reports that whether you provoke your brain to hallucinate by drugs, loss of oxygen, or extreme sensory deprivation, "it will hallucinate in basically the same way." The experience typically begins with simple geometric forms, such as a lattice, a cobweb, or a spiral. The next phase consists of more meaningful images; some may be superimposed on a tunnel or funnel, others may be replays of past emotional experiences. As the hallucination peaks, people frequently feel separated from their body and experience dreamlike scenes so real that they may become panic-stricken or harm themselves. (Some researchers have pointed out similarities between these experiences and the near-death phenomenon. See Close-Up: Near-Death Experiences.)

Marijuana

Marijuana consists of the leaves and flowers of the hemp plant, which for 5000 years has been cultivated for its fiber. Whether smoked or eaten, marijuana's major active ingredient, **THC** (delta-9-tetrahydrocannabinol), produces a mix of effects. (Smoking gets the drug into the brain in about 7 seconds, producing a greater effect than does eating the drug, which causes its peak concentration to be reached at a slower, unpredictable rate.) Like alcohol, marijuana relaxes, disinhibits, and may produce a euphoric high. But marijuana is also a mild hallucinogen, amplifying sensitivity to colors, sounds, tastes, and smells. And unlike alcohol, which the body eliminates within hours, THC and its by-products linger in the body for a month or more. Thus, contrary to the usual tolerance phenomenon, regular users may achieve a high with smaller amounts of the drug than occasional users would need to get the same effect.

hallucinogens psychedelic ("mind-manifesting") drugs, such as LSD, that distort perceptions and evoke sensory images in the absence of sensory input.

LSD a powerful hallucinogenic drug; also known as acid *(lysergic acid diethylamide).*

THC the major active ingredient in marijuana; triggers a variety of effects, including mild hallucinations.

Near-Death Experiences

10-5 What are near-death experiences, and what is the controversy over their explanation?

A man . . . hears himself pronounced dead by his doctor. He begins to hear an uncomfortable noise, a loud ringing or buzzing, and at the same time feels himself moving very rapidly through a long dark tunnel. After this, he suddenly finds himself outside of his own physical body . . . and sees his own body from a distance, as though he is a spectator. . . . Soon other things begin to happen. Others come to meet and to help him. He glimpses the spirits of relatives and friends who have already died, and a loving, warm spirit of a kind he has never encountered before—a being of light—appears before him. . . . He is overwhelmed by intense feelings of joy, love, and peace. Despite his attitude, though, he somehow reunites with his physical body and lives. (Moody, 1976, pp. 23, 24.)

This is a composite description of a **near-death experience.** In studies of those who have come close to death through cardiac arrest or other physical traumas, 12 to 40 percent recalled a near-death experience (Gallup, 1982; Ring,

"My entire vision for the future passed before my eyes."

1980; Schnaper, 1980; Van Lommel et al., 2001).

Did the description of the near-death experience sound familiar? The parallels with Ronald Siegel's (1977) descriptions of the typical hallucinogenic experience are striking: replay of old memories, out-of-body sensations, and visions of tunnels or funnels and bright lights or beings of light (**FIGURE 10.6**). After being resuscitated from apparent death—with no breathing or pulse for more than 30 seconds—many children, too, offer near-death recollections (Morse, 1994). And worldwide, people near death have sometimes reported visions of another world, though the content of that vision often depends on the culture (Kellehear, 1996).

Patients who have experienced temporal lobe seizures have reported profound mystical experiences, sometimes similar to those of near-death experiences. When researchers stimulated the crucial temporal lobe area of one such patient, she reported a sensation of "floating" near the ceiling and seeing herself, from above, lying in bed (Blanke et al., 2002, 2004). Solitary sailors and polar explorers have had out-of-body sensations while enduring monotony, isolation, and cold (Suedfeld & Mocellin, 1987). Oxygen deprivation can produce such hallucinations, complete with tunnel vision (Woerlee, 2004, 2005). As oxygen deprivation turns off the brain's inhibitory cells, neural activity increases in the visual cortex (Blackmore, 1991, 1993). In the oxygen-starved brain, the result is a growing patch of light, which looks much like what you would see as you moved through a tunnel. The near-death experience, argued Siegel (1980), is best understood as "hallucinatory activity of the brain."

Some near-death investigators object. People who have experienced both hallucinations and the near-death phenomenon typically deny their similarity. Moreover, a near-death experience may change people in ways that a drug trip does not. Those who have been "embraced by the light" may become kinder, more

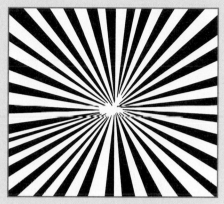

FIGURE 10.6 Near-death vision or hallucination? Psychologist Ronald Siegel (1977) reported that people under the influence of hallucinogenic drugs often see "a bright light in the center of the field of vision. . . . The location of this point of light create[s] a tunnel-like perspective."

spiritual, more believing in life after death. And they tend to handle stress well, often by addressing a stressful situation directly rather than becoming traumatized (Britton & Bootzin, 2004). Skeptics reply that these effects stem from the death-related context of the experience.

* * *

The debates over the significance of near-death experiences are an aspect of a wider debate over dreams, fantasy, hypnotic states, and drug-induced hallucinations. In all these cases, science informs our wondering about human consciousness and human nature. Although there remain questions that it cannot answer, science nevertheless helps fashion our image of who we are—of our human potentials and our human limits.

near-death experience an altered state of consciousness reported after a close brush with death (such as through cardiac arrest); often similar to drug-induced hallucinations.

A user's experience can vary with the situation. If the person feels anxious or depressed, using marijuana may intensify these feelings. And studies controlling for other drug use and personal traits have found that the more one uses marijuana, the greater one's risk of anxiety, depression, or possibly schizophrenia (Hall, 2006; Murray et al., 2007; Patton et al., 2002). Daily use bodes a worse outcome than infrequent use.

The National Academy of Sciences (1982, 1999) and National Institute on Drug Abuse (2004) have identified other marijuana consequences. Like alcohol, marijuana impairs the motor coordination, perceptual skills, and reaction time necessary for safely operating an automobile or other machine. "THC causes animals to misjudge events," reported Ronald Siegel (1990, p. 163). "Pigeons wait too long to respond to buzzers or lights that tell them food is available for brief periods; and rats turn the wrong way in mazes." Marijuana also disrupts memory formation and interferes with immediate recall of information learned only a few minutes before. Such cognitive effects outlast the period of smoking (Messinis et al., 2007). Prenatal exposure through maternal marijuana use also impairs brain development (Berghuis et al., 2007; Huizink & Mulder, 2006). Heavy adult use for over 20 years is associated with a shrinkage of brain areas that process memories and emotions (Yücel et al., 2008).

Scientists have shed light on marijuana's cognitive, mood, and motor effects with the discovery of concentrations of THC-sensitive receptors in the brain's frontal lobes, limbic system, and motor cortex (Iversen, 2000). As the 1970s discovery of receptors for morphine put researchers on the trail of morphinelike neurotransmitters (the endorphins), so the recent discovery of *cannabinoid receptors* has led to a successful hunt for naturally occurring THC-like molecules that bind with cannabinoid receptors. These molecules may naturally control pain. If so, this may help explain why marijuana can be therapeutic for those who suffer the pain, nausea, and severe weight loss associated with AIDS (Watson et al., 2000). Such uses have motivated legislation in some states to make the drug legally available for medical purposes. To avoid the toxicity of marijuana smoke—which, like cigarette smoke, can cause cancer, lung damage, and pregnancy complications—the Institute of Medicine recommends medical inhalers to deliver the THC.

* * *

Despite their differences, the psychoactive drugs summarized in **TABLE 10.1** share a common feature: They trigger negative aftereffects that offset their immediate positive

TABLE 10.1 A Guide to Selected Psychoactive Drugs

Drug	Type	Pleasurable Effects	Adverse Effects
Alcohol	Depressant	Initial high followed by relaxation and disinhibition	Depression, memory loss, organ damage, impaired reactions
Heroin	Depressant	Rush of euphoria, relief from pain	Depressed physiology, agonizing withdrawal
Caffeine	Stimulant	Increased alertness and wakefulness	Anxiety, restlessness, and insomnia in high doses; uncomfortable withdrawal
Methamphet-amine	Stimulant	Euphoria, alertness, energy	Irritability, insomnia, hypertension, seizures
Cocaine	Stimulant	Rush of euphoria, confidence, energy	Cardiovascular stress, suspiciousness, depressive crash
Nicotine	Stimulant	Arousal and relaxation, sense of well-being	Heart disease, cancer
Ecstasy (MDMA)	Stimulant; mild hallucinogen	Emotional elevation, disinhibition	Dehydration, overheating, depressed mood, impaired cognitive and immune functioning
Marijuana	Mild hallucinogen	Enhanced sensation, relief of pain, distortion of time, relaxation	Impaired learning and memory, increased risk of psychological disorders, lung damage from smoke

effects and grow stronger with repetition. And that helps explain both tolerance and withdrawal. As the opposing, negative aftereffects grow stronger, it takes larger and larger doses to produce the desired high (tolerance), causing the aftereffects to worsen in the drug's absence (withdrawal). This in turn creates a need to switch off the withdrawal symptoms by taking yet more of the drug.

▶‖ Influences on Drug Use

10-6 Why do some people become regular users of consciousness-altering drugs?

Drug use by North American youth increased during the 1970s. Then, with increased drug education and a more realistic and deglamorized media depiction of taking drugs, drug use declined sharply. After the early 1990s, the cultural antidrug voice softened, and drugs for a time were again glamorized in some music and films. Consider these marijuana-related trends:

▶ In the University of Michigan's annual survey of 15,000 U.S. high school seniors, the proportion who believe there is "great risk" in regular marijuana use rose from 35 percent in 1978 to 79 percent in 1991, then retreated to 52 percent in 2008 (Johnston et al., 2009).

▶ After peaking in 1978, marijuana use by U.S. high school seniors declined through 1992, then rose, but has recently been tapering off (**FIGURE 10.7**). Among Canadian 15- to 24-year-olds, 23 percent report using marijuana monthly, weekly, or daily (Health Canada, 2007).

For some adolescents, occasional drug use represents thrill seeking. Why, though, do other adolescents become regular drug users? In search of answers, researchers have engaged biological, psychological, and social-cultural levels of analysis.

Biological Influences

Some people may be biologically vulnerable to particular drugs. For example, evidence accumulates that heredity influences some aspects of alcohol abuse problems, especially those appearing by early adulthood (Crabbe, 2002):

▶ Adopted individuals are more susceptible to alcohol dependence if one or both biological parents have a history of it.

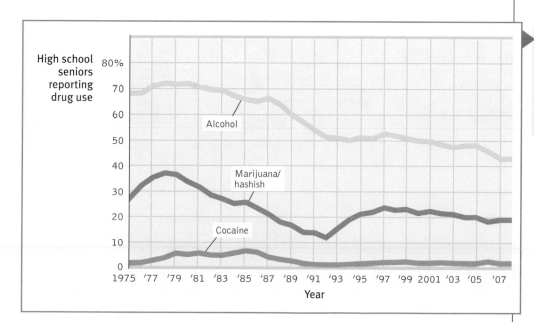

FIGURE 10.7 Trends in drug use The percentage of U.S. high school seniors who report having used alcohol, marijuana, or cocaine during the past 30 days declined from the late 1970s to 1992, when it partially rebounded for a few years. (From Johnston et al., 2009.)

|| Warning signs of alcohol dependence

- Drinking binges
- Regretting things done or said when drunk
- Feeling low or guilty after drinking
- Failing to honor a resolve to drink less
- Drinking to alleviate depression or anxiety
- Avoiding family or friends when drinking ||

▶ Having an identical rather than fraternal twin with alcohol dependence puts one at increased risk for alcohol problems (Kendler et al., 2002). (In marijuana use also, identical twins more closely resemble one another than do fraternal twins.)

▶ Boys who at age 6 are excitable, impulsive, and fearless (genetically influenced traits) are more likely as teens to smoke, drink, and use other drugs (Masse & Tremblay, 1997).

▶ Researchers have bred rats and mice that prefer alcoholic drinks to water. One such strain has reduced levels of the brain chemical NPY. Mice engineered to *overproduce* NPY are very sensitive to alcohol's sedating effect and drink little (Thiele et al., 1998).

▶ Researchers have identified genes that are more common among people and animals predisposed to alcohol dependency, and they are seeking genes that contribute to tobacco addiction (NIH, 2006; Nurnberger & Bierut, 2007). These culprit genes seemingly produce deficiencies in the brain's natural dopamine reward system, which is impacted by addictive drugs. When repeated, the drugs trigger dopamine-produced pleasure but also disrupt normal dopamine balance. Studies of how drugs reprogram the brain's reward systems raise hopes for anti-addiction drugs that might block or blunt the effects of alcohol and other drugs (Miller, 2008; Wilson & Kuhn, 2005).

Psychological and Social-Cultural Influences

Psychological and social-cultural influences also contribute to drug use (**FIGURE 10.8**). In their studies of youth and young adults, Michael Newcomb and L. L. Harlow (1986) found that one psychological factor is the feeling that one's life is meaningless and directionless, a common feeling among school dropouts who subsist without job skills, without privilege, and with little hope. When young unmarried adults leave home, alcohol and other drug use increases; when they marry and have children, it decreases (Bachman et al., 1997).

Heavy users of alcohol, marijuana, and cocaine often display other psychological influences. Many have experienced significant stress or failure and are depressed. Females with a history of depression, eating disorders, or sexual or physical abuse are at risk for substance addiction, as are those undergoing school or neighborhood transitions (CASA, 2003; Logan et al., 2002). Monkeys, too, develop a taste for alcohol when stressed by permanent separation from their mother at birth (Small, 2002). By

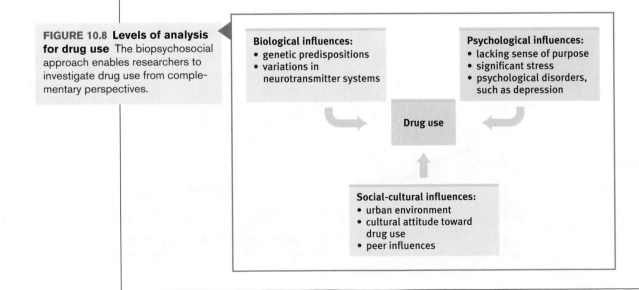

FIGURE 10.8 Levels of analysis for drug use The biopsychosocial approach enables researchers to investigate drug use from complementary perspectives.

Biological influences:
- genetic predispositions
- variations in neurotransmitter systems

Psychological influences:
- lacking sense of purpose
- significant stress
- psychological disorders, such as depression

Drug use

Social-cultural influences:
- urban environment
- cultural attitude toward drug use
- peer influences

temporarily dulling the pain of self-awareness, alcohol may offer a way to avoid coping with depression, anger, anxiety, or insomnia. The relief may be temporary, but behavior is often controlled more by its immediate consequences than by its later ones.

Especially for teenagers, drug use also has social roots. Most teen drinking is done for social reasons, not as a way to cope with problems (Kuntsche et al., 2005). Social influence also appears in the differing rates of drug use across cultural and ethnic groups. For example, a 2003 survey of 100,000 teens in 35 European countries found that marijuana use in the prior 30 days ranged from zero to 1 percent in Romania and Sweden to 20 to 22 percent in Britain, Switzerland, and France (ESPAD, 2003). Independent U.S. government studies of drug use in households nationwide and among high schoolers in all regions reveal that African-American teens have sharply lower rates of drinking, smoking, and cocaine use (Johnston et al., 2007). Alcohol and other drug addiction rates have also been extremely low in the United States among Orthodox Jews, Mormons, the Amish, and Mennonites (Trimble, 1994). Relatively drug-free small towns and rural areas tend to constrain any genetic predisposition to drug use, report Lisa Legrand and her colleagues (2005). For those whose genetic predispositions nudge them toward substance use, "cities offer more opportunities" and less supervision.

Whether in cities or rural areas, peers influence attitudes about drugs. They also throw the parties and provide the drugs. If an adolescent's friends use drugs, the odds are that he or she will, too. If the friends do not, the opportunity may not even arise. Teens who come from happy families, who do not begin drinking before age 14, and who do well in school tend not to use drugs, largely because they rarely associate with those who do (Bachman et al., 2007; Hingson et al., 2006; Oetting & Beauvais, 1987, 1990).

Peer influence, however, is not just a matter of what friends do and say but also of what adolescents *believe* friends are doing and favoring. In one survey of sixth graders in 22 U.S. states, 14 percent believed their friends had smoked marijuana, though only 4 percent acknowledged doing so (Wren, 1999). University students are not immune to such misperceptions: Drinking dominates social occasions partly because students overestimate their fellow students' enthusiasm for alcohol and underestimate their views of its risks (Prentice & Miller, 1993; Self, 1994) (**TABLE 10.2**).

People whose beginning use was influenced by their peers are more likely to stop using drugs when friends stop or the social network changes (Kandel & Raveis, 1989). One study that followed 12,000 adults over 32 years found that smokers tend to quit in clusters (Christakis & Fowler, 2008). Within a social network, the odds of a person's quitting increased when a spouse, friend, or co-worker stopped smoking. Similarly, most soldiers who became drug-addicted while in Vietnam ceased their drug use after returning home (Robins et al., 1974).

‖ In the real world, alcohol accounts for one-sixth or less of beverage use. In TV land, drinking alcohol occurs more often than the combined drinking of coffee, tea, soft drinks, and water (Gerbner, 1990). ‖

‖ **Culture and alcohol**
Percentage drinking weekly or more:

United States	30%
Canada	40%
Britain	58%

(Gallup Poll, from Moore, 2006) ‖

TABLE 10.2 Facts About "Higher" Education

College and university students drink more alcohol than their nonstudent peers and exhibit 2.5 times the general population's rate of substance abuse.
Fraternity and sorority members report nearly twice the binge drinking rate of nonmembers.
Since 1993, campus smoking rates have declined, alcohol use has been steady, and abuse of prescription opioids, stimulants, tranquilizers, and sedatives has increased, as has marijuana use.

Source: NCASA, 2007.

SNAPSHOTS

Once upon a time, peer pressure caused Bob to start smoking.

Twenty years later, it forces him to quit.

© Jason Love

As always with correlations, the traffic between friends' drug use and our own may be two-way: Our friends influence us. Social networks matter. But we also select as friends those who share our likes and dislikes.

What do the findings on drug use suggest for drug prevention and treatment programs? Three channels of influence seem possible:

▶ Educate young people about the long-term costs of a drug's temporary pleasures.
▶ Help young people find other ways to boost their self-esteem and purpose in life.
▶ Attempt to modify peer associations or to "inoculate" youths against peer pressures by training them in refusal skills.

People rarely abuse drugs if they understand the physical and psychological costs, feel good about themselves and the direction their lives are taking, and are in a peer group that disapproves of using drugs. These educational, psychological, and social factors may help explain why 42 percent of U.S. high school dropouts, but only 15 percent of college graduates, smoke (Ladd, 1998).

REVIEW

Drugs and Consciousness

10-1 What are tolerance, dependence, and addiction, and what are some common misconceptions about addiction? *Psychoactive drugs* alter perceptions and moods. Their continued use produces *tolerance* (requiring larger doses to achieve the same effect) and may lead to *physical* or *psychological dependence*. *Addiction* is compulsive drug craving and use. Three common misconceptions about addiction are that (1) addictive drugs quickly corrupt; (2) therapy is always required to overcome addiction; and (3) the concept of addiction can meaningfully be extended beyond chemical dependence to a wide range of other behaviors.

10-2 What are depressants, and what are their effects? *Depressants*, such as alcohol, *barbiturates*, and the *opiates*, dampen neural activity and slow body functions. Alcohol tends to disinhibit—it increases the likelihood that we will act on our impulses, whether harmful or helpful. Alcohol also slows nervous system activity and impairs judgment, disrupts memory processes by suppressing REM sleep, and reduces self-awareness. User expectations strongly influence alcohol's behavioral effects.

10-3 What are stimulants, and what are their effects? *Stimulants*—caffeine, nicotine, the *amphetamines*, cocaine, and *Ecstasy*—excite neural activity and speed up body functions. All are highly addictive. Nicotine's effects make smoking a difficult habit to kick, but the percentage of Americans who smoke is nevertheless decreasing. Continued use of *methamphetamine* may permanently reduce dopamine production. Cocaine gives users a 15- to 30-minute high, followed by a crash. Its risks include cardiovascular stress and suspiciousness. Ecstasy is a combined stimulant and mild hallucinogen that produces a euphoric high and feelings of intimacy. Its users risk immune system suppression, permanent damage to mood and memory, and (if taken during physical activity) dehydration and escalating body temperatures.

10-4 What are hallucinogens, and what are their effects? *Hallucinogens*—such as *LSD* and marijuana—distort perceptions and evoke hallucinations—sensory images in the absence of sensory input. The user's mood and expectations influence the effects of LSD, but common experiences are hallucinations and emotions varying from euphoria to panic. Marijuana's main ingredient, *THC*, may trigger feelings of disinhibition, euphoria, relaxation, relief from pain, and intense sensitivity to sensory stimuli. It may also increase feelings of depression or anxiety, impair motor coordination and reaction time, disrupt memory formation, and damage lung tissue (because of the inhaled smoke).

10-5 What are near-death experiences, and what is the controversy over their explanation? Many people who have survived a brush with death, such as through cardiac arrest, report *near-death experiences*. These sometimes involve out-of-body sensations and seeing or traveling toward a bright light. Some researchers believe that such experiences closely parallel reports of hallucinations and may be products of a brain under stress. Others reject this analysis.

10-6 Why do some people become regular users of consciousness-altering drugs? Psychological factors (such as stress, depression, and hopelessness) and social factors (such as peer pressure) combine to lead many people to experiment with—and sometimes become dependent on—drugs. Cultural and ethnic groups have differing rates of drug use. Some people may be biologically more likely to become dependent on drugs such as alcohol. Each type of influence—biological, psychological, and social-cultural—offers a possible path for drug prevention and treatment programs.

Terms and Concepts to Remember

psychoactive drug, p. 113
tolerance, p. 113
withdrawal, p. 113
physical dependence, p. 113
psychological dependence, p. 114
addiction, p. 114
depressants, p. 115
barbiturates, p. 117

opiates, p. 117
stimulants, p. 117
amphetamines, p. 117
metamphetamine, p. 117
Ecstasy (MDMA), p. 121
hallucinogens, p. 122
LSD, p. 122
THC, p. 122
near-death experience, p. 123

Test Yourself

1. In what ways are near-death experiences similar to drug-induced hallucinations?

2. A U.S. government survey of 27,616 current or former alcohol drinkers found that 40 percent of those who began drinking before age 15 grew dependent on alcohol. The same was true of only 10 percent of those who first imbibed at ages 21 or 22 (Grant & Dawson, 1998). What possible explanations might there be for this correlation between early use and later abuse?

(Answers to the Test Yourself questions can be found in Appendix B at the end of the book.)

Ask Yourself

1. Does your understanding of mind-brain science and your personal philosophy or faith incline you toward acceptance or denial of the "near death experience"?

2. Drinking dominates university parties when students overestimate other students' enthusiasm for alcohol. Do you think such misperceptions exist on your campus? How might you find out?

∞ WEB

Multiple-choice self-tests and more may be found at
www.worthpublishers.com/myers

Nature, Nurture, and Human Diversity

MODULES

11

Behavior Genetics and Evolutionary Psychology

12

Environmental Influences on Behavior

What makes you you? In important ways, we are each unique. We look different. We sound different. We have varying personalities, interests, and cultural and family backgrounds.

We are also the leaves of one tree. Our human family shares not only a common biological heritage—cut us and we bleed—but also common behavioral tendencies. Our shared brain architecture predisposes us to sense the world, develop language, and feel hunger through identical mechanisms. Whether we live in the Arctic or the tropics, we prefer sweet tastes to sour. We divide the color spectrum into similar colors. And we feel drawn to behaviors that produce and protect offspring.

Our kinship appears in our social behaviors as well. Whether named Wong, Nkomo, Smith, or Gonzales, we start fearing strangers at about eight months, and as adults we prefer the company of those with attitudes and attributes similar to our own. Coming from different parts of the globe, we know how to read one another's smiles and frowns. As members of one species, we affiliate, conform, return favors, punish offenses, organize hierarchies of status, and grieve a child's death. A visitor from outer space could drop in anywhere and find humans dancing and feasting, singing and worshiping, playing sports and games, laughing and crying, living in families and forming groups. Taken together, such universal behaviors define our human nature.

What causes our striking diversity, and also our shared human nature? How much are human differences shaped by our differing genes? And how much by our *environment*—by every external influence, from maternal nutrition while in the womb to social support while nearing the tomb? To what extent are we formed by our upbringing? By our culture? By our current circumstances? By people's reactions to our genetic dispositions? Modules 11 and 12 tell something of the complex story of how our genes *(nature)* and environments *(nurture)* define us.

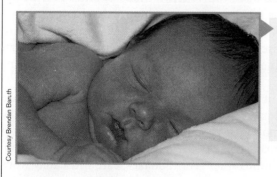

Courtesy Brendan Baruth

The nurture of nature Parents everywhere wonder: Will my baby grow up to be peaceful or aggressive? Homely or attractive? Successful or struggling at every step? What comes built in, and what is nurtured—and how? Research reveals that nature and nurture together shape our development—every step of the way.

MODULE 11

Behavior Genetics and Evolutionary Psychology

▶‖ Behavior Genetics: Predicting Individual Differences

11-1 What are genes, and how do behavior geneticists explain our individual differences?

If Jaden Agassi, son of tennis stars Andre Agassi and Stephanie Graf, grows up to be a tennis star, should we attribute his superior talent to his Grand Slam genes? To his growing up in a tennis-rich environment? To high expectations? Such questions intrigue **behavior geneticists,** who study our differences and weigh the effects and interplay of heredity and **environment.**

Genes: Our Codes for Life

Behind the story of our body and of our brain—surely the most awesome thing on our little planet—is the heredity that interacts with our experience to create both our universal human nature and our individual and social diversity. Barely more than a century ago, few would have guessed that every cell nucleus in your body contains the genetic master code for your entire body. It's as if every room in the Empire State Building had a book containing the architect's plans for the entire structure. The plans for your own book of life run to 46 chapters—23 donated by your mother (from her egg) and 23 by your father (from his sperm). Each of these 46 chapters, called a **chromosome,** is composed of a coiled chain of the molecule **DNA** (*deoxyribonucleic acid*). **Genes,** small segments of the giant DNA molecules, form the words of those chapters (**FIGURE 11.1**). All told, you have 30,000 or so gene words. Genes can be either active (*expressed*) or inactive. Environmental events "turn on" genes, rather like hot water enabling a tea bag to express its flavor. When turned on, genes provide the code for creating *protein molecules,* the building blocks of physical development.

Genetically speaking, every other human is close to being your identical twin. Human **genome** researchers have discovered the common sequence within human DNA. It is this shared genetic profile that makes us humans, rather than chimpanzees or tulips.

Actually, we aren't all that different from our chimpanzee cousins; with them we share about 96 percent of our DNA sequence (Mikkelsen et al., 2005). At "functionally important" DNA sites, reports one molecular genetics team, the human-chimpanzee DNA similarity is 99.4 percent (Wildman et al., 2003). Yet that wee difference matters. Despite some remarkable abilities, chimpanzees grunt. Shakespeare intricately wove some 24,000 words to form his literary masterpieces. And small differences matter among chimpanzees, too. Two species, common chimpanzees and bonobos, differ by much less than 1 percent of their genomes, yet they display markedly differing behaviors. Chimpanzees are aggressive and male-dominated. Bonobos are peaceable and female led.

Geneticists and psychologists are interested in the occasional variations found at particular gene sites in human DNA. Slight person-to-person variations from the common pattern give clues to our uniqueness—why one person has a disease that another does not, why one person is short and another tall, why one is outgoing and another shy.

"Thanks for almost everything, Dad."

"Your DNA and mine are 99.9 percent the same. . . . At the DNA level, we are clearly all part of one big worldwide family."

Francis Collins, Human Genome Project director, 2007

"We share half our genes with the banana."

Evolutionary biologist Robert May, president of Britain's Royal Society, 2001

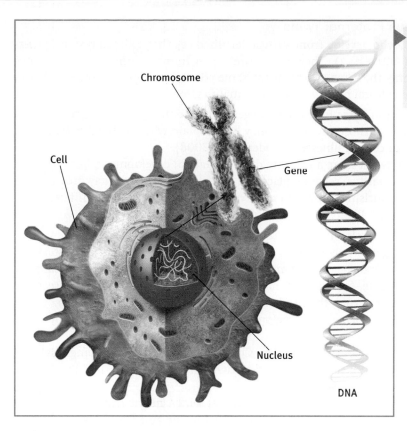

FIGURE 11.1 The human building blocks
The nucleus of every human cell contains chromosomes, each of which is made up of two strands of DNA connected in a double helix.

Most of our traits are influenced by many genes. How tall you are, for example, reflects the size of your face, vertebrae, leg bones, and so forth—each of which may be influenced by different genes interacting with your environment. Complex traits such as intelligence, happiness, and aggressiveness are similarly influenced by groups of genes. Thus our genetic predispositions—our genetically influenced traits—help explain both our shared human nature and our human diversity.

Twin and Adoption Studies

To scientifically tease apart the influences of environment and heredity, behavior geneticists would need to design two types of experiments. The first would control the home environment while varying heredity. The second would control heredity while varying the home environment. Such experiments with human infants would be unethical, but happily for our purposes, nature has done this work for us.

Fraternal Olsen twins The actresses Mary-Kate and Ashley Olsen have often been mistaken for identical twins. As babies and then preschoolers, they even played the same young character (trading places when one would tire or get fussy) in the late 1980s and early 1990s TV show *Full House*. But they are actually fraternal twins, having formed from two separate eggs, so they share no more genes than any other sibling pair.

behavior genetics the study of the relative power and limits of genetic and environmental influences on behavior.

environment every nongenetic influence, from prenatal nutrition to the people and things around us.

chromosomes threadlike structures made of DNA molecules that contain the genes.

DNA (*deoxyribonucleic acid*) a complex molecule containing the genetic information that makes up the chromosomes.

genes the biochemical units of heredity that make up the chromosomes; a segment of DNA capable of synthesizing a protein.

genome the complete instructions for making an organism, consisting of all the genetic material in that organism's chromosomes.

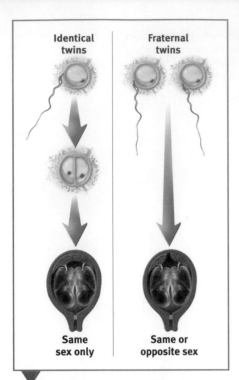

FIGURE 11.2 **Same fertilized egg, same genes; different eggs, different genes** Identical twins develop from a single fertilized egg, fraternal twins from two.

Identical twins

Fraternal twins

Same sex only

Same or opposite sex

"It will inevitably be revealed that there are strong genetic components associated with more aspects of what we attribute to human existence including personality subtypes, language capabilities, mechanical abilities, intelligence, sexual activities and preferences, intuitive thinking, quality of memory, willpower, temperament, athletic abilities, etc."

Genomics researcher J. Craig Venter, 2006

Identical Versus Fraternal Twins

Identical twins, who develop from a single fertilized egg that splits in two, are *genetically* identical (**FIGURE 11.2**). They are nature's own human clones—indeed, clones who share not only the same genes but the same conception, uterus, birth date, and usually the same cultural history. Two slight qualifications:

▶ Although identical twins have the same genes, they don't always have the same *number of copies* of those genes. That may help explain why one twin may be more at risk for certain illnesses (Bruder et al., 2008).

▶ Most identical twins share a placenta during prenatal development, but one of every three sets has two separate placentas. One twin's placenta may provide slightly better nourishment, which may contribute to identical twin differences (Davis et al., 1995; Phelps et al., 1997; Sokoll et al., 1995).

Fraternal twins develop from separate fertilized eggs. They share a fetal environment, but they are genetically no more similar than ordinary brothers and sisters.

Shared genes can translate into shared experiences. A person whose identical twin has Alzheimer's disease, for example, has a 60 percent risk of getting the disease; if the affected twin is fraternal, the risk is only 30 percent (Plomin et al., 1997).

Are identical twins, being genetic clones of one another, also behaviorally more similar than fraternal twins? Studies of thousands of twin pairs in Sweden, Finland, and Australia provide a consistent answer: On both extraversion (outgoingness) and neuroticism (emotional instability), identical twins are much more similar than fraternal twins.

If genes influence traits such as emotional instability, might they also influence the social effects of such traits? To find out, Matt McGue and David Lykken (1992) studied divorce rates among 1500 same-sex, middle-aged twin pairs. Their result: If you have a fraternal twin who has divorced, the odds of your divorcing go up 1.6 times (compared with having a not-divorced twin). If you have an identical twin who has divorced, the odds of your divorcing go up 5.5 times. From such data, McGue and Lykken estimate that people's differing divorce risks are about 50 percent attributable to genetic factors.

When John Loehlin and Robert Nichols (1976) gave a battery of questionnaires to 850 U.S. twin pairs, identical twins, more than fraternal twins, also reported being treated alike. So, did their experience rather than their genes account for their similarity? No, said Loehlin and Nichols; identical twins whose parents treated them alike were not psychologically more alike than identical twins who were treated less similarly. In explaining individual differences, genes matter.

More twins Curiously, twinning rates vary by race. The rate among Caucasians is roughly twice that of Asians and half that of Africans. In Africa and Asia, most twins are identical. In Western countries, most twins are fraternal, and fraternal twins are increasing with the use of fertility drugs (Hall, 2003; Steinhauer, 1999).

Separated Twins

Imagine the following science fiction experiment: A mad scientist decides to separate identical twins at birth, then rear them in differing environments. Better yet, consider a *true* story:

On a chilly February morning in 1979, some time after divorcing his first wife, Linda, Jim Lewis awoke in his modest home next to his second wife, Betty. Determined that this marriage would work, Jim made a habit of leaving love notes to Betty around the house. As he lay in bed he thought about others he had loved, including his son, James Alan, and his faithful dog, Toy.

Jim was looking forward to spending part of the day in his basement woodworking shop, where he had put in many happy hours building furniture, picture frames, and other items, including a white bench now circling a tree in his front yard. Jim also liked to spend free time driving his Chevy, watching stock-car racing, and drinking Miller Lite beer.

Jim was basically healthy, except for occasional half-day migraine headaches and blood pressure that was a little high, perhaps related to his chain-smoking habit. He had become overweight a while back but had shed some of the pounds. Having undergone a vasectomy, he was done having children.

What was extraordinary about Jim Lewis, however, was that at that same moment (I am not making this up) there existed another man—also named Jim—for whom all these things (right down to the dog's name) were also true.[1] This other Jim—Jim Springer—just happened, 38 years earlier, to have been his womb-mate. Thirty-seven days after their birth, these genetically identical twins were separated, adopted by blue-collar families, and reared with no contact or knowledge of each other's whereabouts until the day Jim Lewis received a call from his genetic clone (who, having been told he had a twin, set out to find him).

One month later, the brothers became the first twin pair tested by University of Minnesota psychologist Thomas Bouchard and his colleagues, beginning a study of separated twins that extends to the present (Holden, 1980a,b; Wright, 1998). Given tests measuring their personality, intelligence, heart rate, and brain waves, the Jim twins—despite 38 years of separation—were virtually as alike as the same person tested twice. Their voice intonations and inflections were so similar that, hearing a playback of an earlier interview, Jim Springer guessed "That's me." Wrong—it was his brother.

---

[1] Actually, this description of the two Jims errs in one respect: Jim Lewis named his son James Alan. Jim Springer named his James Allan.

Identical twins are people two Identical twins Jim Lewis and Jim Springer were separated shortly after birth and raised in different homes without awareness of each other. Research has shown remarkable similarities in the life choices of separated identical twins, lending support to the idea that genes influence personality.

©2006 Bob Sacha

|| Sweden has the world's largest national twin registry—140,000 living and dead twin pairs—which form part of a massive registry of 600,000 twins currently being sampled in the world's largest twin study (Wheelwright, 2004; www.genomeutwin.org). ||

|| Twins Lorraine and Levinia Christmas, driving to deliver Christmas presents to each other near Flitcham, England, collided (Shepherd, 1997). ||

|| Bouchard's famous twin research was, appropriately enough, conducted in Minneapolis, the "Twin City" (with St. Paul), and home to the Minnesota Twins baseball team. ||

identical twins twins who develop from a single fertilized egg that splits in two, creating two genetically identical organisms.

fraternal twins twins who develop from separate fertilized eggs. They are genetically no closer than brothers and sisters, but they share a fetal environment.

"In some domains it looks as though our identical twins reared apart are . . . just as similar as identical twins reared together. Now that's an amazing finding and I can assure you none of us would have expected that degree of similarity."

Thomas Bouchard (1981)

|| Coincidences are not unique to twins. Patricia Kern of Colorado was born March 13, 1941, and named Patricia Ann Campbell. Patricia DiBiasi of Oregon also was born March 13, 1941, and named Patricia Ann Campbell. Both had fathers named Robert, worked as bookkeepers, and at the time of this comparison had children ages 21 and 19. Both studied cosmetology, enjoyed oil painting as a hobby, and married military men, within 11 days of each other. They are not genetically related (from an AP report, May 2, 1983). ||

"We carry to our graves the essence of the zygote that was first us."

Mary Pipher, *Seeking Peace: Chronicles of the Worst Buddhist in the World*, 2009

Identical twins Oskar Stohr and Jack Yufe presented equally striking similarities. One was raised by his grandmother in Germany as a Catholic and a Nazi, while the other was raised by his father in the Caribbean as a Jew. Nevertheless, they shared traits and habits galore. They liked spicy foods and sweet liqueurs, fell asleep in front of the television, flushed the toilet before using it, stored rubber bands on their wrists, and dipped buttered toast in their coffee. Stohr was domineering toward women and yelled at his wife, as did Yufe before he and his wife separated. Both married women named Dorothy Jane Scheckelburger. Okay, the last item is a joke. But as Judith Rich Harris (2006) notes, it is hardly weirder than some other reported similarities.

Aided by publicity in magazine and newspaper stories, Bouchard and his colleagues (1990; DiLalla et al., 1996; Segal, 1999) located and studied 80 pairs of identical twins reared apart. They continued to find similarities not only of tastes and physical attributes but also of personality, abilities, attitudes, interests, and even fears.

In Sweden, Nancy Pedersen and her co-workers (1988) identified 99 separated identical twin pairs and more than 200 separated fraternal twin pairs. Compared with equivalent samples of identical twins reared together, the separated identical twins had somewhat less identical *personalities* (characteristic patterns of thinking, feeling, and acting). Still, separated twins were more alike if genetically identical than if fraternal. And separation shortly after birth (rather than, say, at age 8) did not amplify their personality differences.

Stories of startling twin similarities do not impress Bouchard's critics, who remind us that "the plural of *anecdote* is not *data*." They contend that if any two strangers were to spend hours comparing their behaviors and life histories, they would probably discover many coincidental similarities. If researchers created a control group of biologically unrelated pairs of the same age, sex, and ethnicity, who had not grown up together but who were as similar to one another in economic and cultural background as are many of the separated twin pairs, wouldn't these pairs also exhibit striking similarities (Joseph, 2001)? Bouchard replies that separated fraternal twins do not exhibit similarities comparable to those of separated identical twins. Twin researcher Nancy Segal (2000) notes that *virtual twins*—same-age, biologically unrelated siblings—are also much more dissimilar.

Even the more impressive data from personality assessments are clouded by the reunion of many of the separated twins some years before they were tested. Moreover, identical twins share an appearance, and the responses it evokes, and adoption agencies tend to place separated twins in similar homes. Despite these criticisms, the striking twin-study results helped shift scientific thinking toward a greater appreciation of genetic influences.

Biological Versus Adoptive Relatives

For behavior geneticists, nature's second type of real-life experiment—adoption—creates two groups: *genetic relatives* (biological parents and siblings) and *environmental relatives* (adoptive parents and siblings). For any given trait, we can therefore ask whether adopted children are more like their biological parents, who contributed their genes, or their adoptive parents, who contribute a home environment. While sharing that home environment, do adopted siblings also come to share traits?

The stunning finding from studies of hundreds of adoptive families is that people who grow up together, whether biologically related or not, do not much resemble one another in personality (McGue & Bouchard, 1998; Plomin et al., 1998; Rowe, 1990). In traits such as extraversion and agreeableness, adoptees are more similar to their biological parents than to their caregiving adoptive parents.

The finding is important enough to bear repeating: The environment shared by a family's children has virtually no discernible impact on their personalities. Two adopted children reared in the same home are no more likely to share personality traits with each other than with the child down the block. Heredity shapes other primates' personalities, too. Macaque monkeys raised by foster mothers exhibit social behaviors that resemble their biological, rather than foster, mothers (Maestripieri, 2003). Add all this to the similarity of identical twins, whether they grow up together or apart, and the effect of a shared rearing environment seems shockingly modest.

Sean Garnsworthy/Getty Images

Nature or nurture or both? When talent runs in families, as with the Williams sisters, how do heredity and environment together do their work?

What we have here is perhaps "the most important puzzle in the history of psychology," contends Steven Pinker (2002): Why are children in the same family so different? Why does shared family environment have so little effect on children's personalities? Is it because each sibling experiences unique peer influences and life events? Because sibling relationships ricochet off each other, amplifying their differences? Because siblings—despite sharing half their genes—have very different combinations of genes and may evoke very different kinds of parenting? Such questions fuel behavior geneticists' curiosity.

The minimal shared-environment effect does not, however, mean that adoptive parenting is a fruitless venture. The genetic leash may limit the family environment's influence on personality, but parents do influence their children's attitudes, values, manners, faith, and politics (Reifman & Cleveland, 2007). A pair of adopted children or identical twins *will,* especially during adolescence, have more similar religious beliefs if reared together (Kelley & De Graaf, 1997; Koenig et al., 2005; Rohan & Zanna, 1996). Parenting matters!

Moreover, in adoptive homes, child neglect and abuse and even parental divorce are rare. (Adoptive parents are carefully screened; natural parents are not.) So it is not surprising that, despite a somewhat greater risk of psychological disorder, most adopted children thrive, especially when adopted as infants (Loehlin et al., 2007; van IJzendoorn & Juffer, 2006; Wierzbicki, 1993). Seven in eight report feeling strongly attached to one or both adoptive parents. As children of self-giving parents, they grow up to be more self-giving and altruistic than average (Sharma et al., 1998). Many score higher than their biological parents on intelligence tests, and most grow into happier and more stable adults. In one Swedish study, infant adoptees grew up with fewer problems than were experienced by children whose biological mothers had initially registered them for adoption but then decided to raise the children themselves (Bohman & Sigvardsson, 1990). Regardless of personality differences between parents and their adoptees, children benefit from adoption.

Temperament and Heredity

As most parents will tell you after having their second child, babies differ even before gulping their first breath. Consider one quickly apparent aspect of personality. Infants' **temperaments** are their emotional excitability—whether reactive, intense, and fidgety, or easygoing, quiet, and placid. From the first weeks of life, *difficult* babies are more irritable, intense, and unpredictable. *Easy* babies are cheerful, relaxed, and predictable in feeding and sleeping. *Slow-to-warm-up* infants tend to resist or withdraw from new people and situations (Chess & Thomas, 1987; Thomas & Chess, 1977).

"Mom may be holding a full house while Dad has a straight flush, yet when Junior gets a random half of each of their cards his poker hand may be a loser."
David Lykken (2001)

‖ The greater uniformity of adoptive homes—mostly healthy, nurturing homes—helps explain the lack of striking differences when comparing child outcomes of different adoptive homes (Stoolmiller, 1999). ‖

temperament a person's characteristic emotional reactivity and intensity.

"Oh, he's cute, all right, but he's got the temperament of a car alarm."

Temperament differences tend to persist. Consider:

▶ The most emotionally reactive newborns tend also to be the most reactive 9-month-olds (Wilson & Matheny, 1986; Worobey & Blajda, 1989).

▶ Exceptionally inhibited and fearful 2-year-olds often are still relatively shy as 8-year-olds; about half will become introverted adolescents (Kagan et al., 1992, 1994).

▶ The most emotionally intense preschoolers tend to be relatively intense young adults (Larsen & Diener, 1987). In one study of more than 900 New Zealanders, emotionally reactive and impulsive 3-year-olds developed into somewhat more impulsive, aggressive, and conflict-prone 21-year-olds (Caspi, 2000).

Heredity predisposes temperament differences (Rothbart, 2007). As we have seen, identical twins have more similar personalities, including temperament, than do fraternal twins. Physiological tests reveal that anxious, inhibited infants have high and variable heart rates and a reactive nervous system, and that they become more physiologically aroused when facing new or strange situations (Kagan & Snidman, 2004). One form of a gene that regulates the neurotransmitter serotonin predisposes a fearful temperament and, in combination with unsupportive caregiving, an inhibited child (Fox et al., 2007). Such evidence adds to the emerging conclusion that our biologically rooted temperament helps form our enduring personality (McCrae et al., 2000, 2007; Rothbart et al., 2000).

Heritability

11-2 What is heritability, and how does it relate to individuals and groups?

Using twin and adoption studies, behavior geneticists can mathematically estimate the **heritability** of a trait—the extent to which variation among individuals can be attributed to their differing genes. If the heritability of intelligence is, say, 50 percent, this does *not* mean that *your* intelligence is 50 percent genetic. (If the heritability of height is 90 percent, this does not mean that a 60-inch-tall woman can credit her genes for 54 inches and her environment for the other 6 inches.) Rather, it means that genetic influence explains 50 percent of the observed variation *among people*. This point is so often misunderstood that I repeat: We can never say what percentage of an *individual's* personality or intelligence is inherited. It makes no sense to say that your personality is due *x* percent to your heredity and *y* percent to your environment. Heritability refers instead to the extent to which *differences among people* are attributable to genes.

Even this conclusion must be qualified, because heritability can vary from study to study. Consider humorist Mark Twain's (1835–1910) proposal to raise boys in barrels to age 12, feeding them through a hole. If we were to follow his suggestion, the boys would all emerge with lower-than-normal intelligence scores at age 12; yet, given their equal environments, their test score differences could be explained only by their heredity. In this case, heritability—differences due to genes—would be near 100 percent. As environments become more similar, heredity as a source of differences necessarily becomes more important. If all schools were of uniform quality, all families equally loving, and all neighborhoods equally healthy, then heritability would increase (because differences due to environment would decrease). At the other extreme, if all people had similar heredities but were raised in drastically different environments (some in barrels, some in luxury homes), heritability would be much lower.

Group Differences

If genetic influences help explain individual diversity in traits such as aggressiveness, can the same be said of group differences between men and women, or between people of different races? Not necessarily. Individual differences in height and weight, for example, are highly heritable; yet nutritional rather than genetic influences explain why, as a

"The title of my science project is 'My Little Brother: Nature or Nurture.'"

group, today's adults are taller and heavier than those of a century ago. The two groups differ, but not because human genes have changed in a mere century's eyeblink of time.

As with height and weight, so with personality and intelligence scores: Heritable individual differences need not imply heritable group differences. If some individuals are genetically disposed to be more aggressive than others, that needn't explain why some groups are more aggressive than others. Putting people in a new social context can change their aggressiveness. Today's peaceful Scandinavians carry many genes inherited from their Viking warrior ancestors.

Nature and Nurture

Among our similarities, the most important—the behavioral hallmark of our species—is our enormous adaptive capacity. Some human traits, such as having two eyes, develop the same in virtually every environment. But other traits are expressed only in particular environments. Go barefoot for a summer and you will develop toughened, callused feet—a biological adaptation to friction. Meanwhile, your shod neighbor will remain a tenderfoot. The difference between the two of you is, of course, an effect of environment. But it is also the product of a biological mechanism—adaptation. Our shared biology enables our developed diversity (Buss, 1991).

An analogy may help: Genes and environment—nature and nurture—work together like two hands clapping. Genes not only code for particular proteins, they also respond to environments. An African butterfly that is green in summer turns brown in fall, thanks to a temperature-controlled genetic switch. The genes that produce brown in one situation produce green in another. Thus, genes are *self-regulating*. Rather than acting as blueprints that lead to the same result no matter the context, genes react. People with identical genes but differing experiences therefore have similar though not identical minds. One twin may fall in love with someone quite different from the co-twin's love.

At least one known gene will, in response to major life stresses, code for a protein that controls a neurotransmitter involved in depression. By itself, the gene doesn't cause depression, but it is part of the recipe. Likewise, the research finding that breast feeding boosts later intelligence turns out to be true only for the 90 percent of infants with a gene that assists in breaking down fatty acids present in human milk (Caspi et al., 2007). Studies of 1037 New Zealand adults and 2232 English 12- and 13-year olds found no breast-feeding boost among those not carrying the gene. As so often happens, nature and nurture work together.

Thus, asking whether your personality is more a product of your genes or your environment is like asking whether the area of a field is more the result of its length or its width. We could, however, ask whether the differing areas of various fields are more the result of *differences* in their length or their width, and also whether person-to-person personality differences are influenced more by nature or nurture. Human differences result from both genetic and environmental influences. Thus, eating disorders are genetically influenced: Some individuals are more at risk than others. But culture also bends the twig, for eating disorders are primarily a contemporary Western cultural phenomenon.

Gene-Environment Interaction

To say that genes and experience are *both* important is true. But more precisely, they **interact.** Imagine two babies, one genetically predisposed to be attractive, sociable, and easygoing, the other less so. Assume further that the first baby attracts more affectionate and stimulating care than the second and so develops into a warmer and more outgoing person. As the two children grow older, the more naturally outgoing child more often seeks activities and friends that encourage further social confidence.

heritability the proportion of variation among individuals that we can attribute to genes. The heritability of a trait may vary, depending on the range of populations and environments studied.

interaction the interplay that occurs when the effect of one factor (such as environment) depends on another factor (such as heredity).

"Men's natures are alike; it is their habits that carry them far apart."
Confucius, *Analects*, 500 B.C.

Gene-environment interaction People respond differently to Rowan Atkinson (shown at left playing Mr. Bean) than to his fellow actor Zac Efron, right.

"Heredity deals the cards; environment plays the hand."

Psychologist Charles L. Brewer (1990)

What has caused their resulting personality differences? Neither heredity nor experience dances alone. Environments trigger gene activity. (Scientists are now exploring environmental influences on when particular genes generate proteins.) The other partner in the dance—our genetically influenced traits—also *evoke* significant responses in others. Thus, a child's impulsivity and aggression may evoke an angry response from a teacher who otherwise reacts warmly to the child's model classmates. Parents, too, may treat their own children differently; one child elicits punishment, another does not. In such cases, the child's nature and the parents' nurture interact. Neither operates apart from the other. Gene and scene dance together.

Evocative interactions may help explain why identical twins reared in different families recall their parents' warmth as remarkably similar—almost as similar as if they had had the same parents (Plomin et al., 1988, 1991, 1994). Fraternal twins have more differing recollections of their early family life—even if reared in the same family! "Children experience us as different parents, depending on their own qualities," noted Sandra Scarr (1990). Moreover, as we grow older we also *select* environments well suited to our natures.

So, from conception onward, we are the product of a cascade of interactions between our genetic predispositions and our surrounding environments. Our genes affect how people react to and influence us. Biological appearances have social consequences. So, forget nature *versus* nurture; think nature *via* nurture.

The New Frontier: Molecular Genetics

11-3 What is the promise of molecular genetics research?

Behavior geneticists have progressed beyond asking, "Do genes influence behavior?" The new frontier of behavior-genetics research draws on "bottom-up" **molecular genetics** as it seeks to identify *specific genes* influencing behavior.

As we have already seen, most human traits are influenced by teams of genes. For example, twin and adoption studies tell us that heredity influences body weight, but there is no single "obesity gene." More likely, some genes influence how quickly the stomach tells the brain, "I'm full." Others might dictate how much fuel the muscles need, how many calories are burned off by fidgeting, and how efficiently the body converts extra calories into fat (Vogel, 1999). The goal of *molecular behavior genetics* is to find some of the many genes that influence normal human traits, such as body weight, sexual orientation, and extraversion, and also to explore the mechanisms that control gene expression (Tsankova et al., 2007).

Genetic tests can now reveal at-risk populations for at least a dozen diseases. The search continues in labs worldwide, where molecular geneticists are teaming with psychologists to pinpoint genes that put people at risk for such genetically influenced disorders as learning disabilities, depression, schizophrenia, and alcohol dependence. Worldwide research efforts are under way to sleuth the genes that make people vulnerable to the emotional swings of bipolar disorder, formerly known as manic-depressive disorder. To tease out the implicated genes, molecular behavior geneticists seek links between certain genes or chromosome segments and specific disorders. First, they find families that have had the disorder across several generations. Then they draw blood or take cheek swabs from both affected and unaffected family members and examine their DNA, looking for differences. "The most powerful potential for DNA," note Robert Plomin and John Crabbe (2000), "is to predict risk so that steps can be taken to prevent problems before they happen."

Aided by inexpensive DNA-scanning techniques, medical personnel are becoming able to give would-be parents a readout on how their fetus' genes differ from the normal pattern and what this might mean. With this benefit come risks. Might labeling a fetus, for example, "at risk for a learning disorder" lead to discrimination? Prenatal screening poses ethical dilemmas. In China and India, where boys are highly valued, testing for an offspring's sex has enabled selective abortions resulting in millions—yes, millions—of "missing women."

Assuming it were possible, should prospective parents take their eggs and sperm to a genetics lab for screening before combining them to produce an embryo? Should we enable parents to screen their fertilized eggs for health—and for brains or beauty? Progress is a double-edged sword, raising both hopeful possibilities and difficult problems. By selecting out certain traits, we may deprive ourselves of future Handels and van Goghs, Churchills and Lincolns, Tolstoys and Dickinsons—troubled people all.

"I thought that sperm-bank donors remained anonymous."

▶‖ Evolutionary Psychology: Understanding Human Nature

11-4 How do evolutionary psychologists use natural selection to explain behavior tendencies?

Behavior geneticists explore the genetic and environmental roots of human differences. **Evolutionary psychologists** instead focus mostly on what makes us so much alike as humans. They use Darwin's principle of **natural selection** to understand the roots of behavior and mental processes. Richard Dawkins (2007) calls natural selection "arguably the most momentous idea ever to occur to a human mind." The idea, simplified, is this:

- ▶ Organisms' varied offspring compete for survival.
- ▶ Certain biological and behavioral variations increase their reproductive and survival chances in their environment.
- ▶ Offspring that survive are more likely to pass their genes to ensuing generations.
- ▶ Thus, over time, population characteristics may change.

To see these principles at work, let's consider a straightforward example in foxes.

Natural Selection and Adaptation

A fox is a wild and wary animal. If you capture a fox and try to befriend it, be careful. Stick your hand in the cage and, if the timid fox cannot flee, it may make a snack of your fingers. Dmitry Belyaev, of the Russian Academy of Science's Institute of Cytology and Genetics, wondered how our human ancestors had domesticated dogs from their equally

molecular genetics the subfield of biology that studies the molecular structure and function of genes.

evolutionary psychology the study of the evolution of behavior and the mind, using principles of natural selection.

natural selection the principle that, among the range of inherited trait variations, those that lead to increased reproduction and survival will most likely be passed on to succeeding generations.

L. N. Trut, *American Scientist* (1999) 87: 160–169

From wary to winsome More than 40 years into the fox-breeding experiment, most of the offspring are devoted, affectionate, and capable of forming strong bonds with people.

mutation a random error in gene replication that leads to a change.

wild wolf forebears. Might he, within a comparatively short stretch of time, accomplish a similar feat by transforming the fearful fox into a friendly fox?

To find out, Belyaev set to work with 30 male and 100 female foxes. From their offspring he selected and mated the tamest 5 percent of males and 20 percent of females. (He measured tameness by the foxes' responses to attempts to feed, handle, and stroke them.) Over more than 30 generations of foxes, Belyaev and his successor, Lyudmila Trut, repeated that simple procedure. Forty years and 45,000 foxes later, they had a new breed of foxes that, in Trut's (1999) words, are "docile, eager to please, and unmistakably domesticated. . . . Before our eyes, 'the Beast' has turned into 'beauty,' as the aggressive behavior of our herd's wild [ancestors] entirely disappeared." So friendly and eager for human contact are they, so inclined to whimper to attract attention and to lick people like affectionate dogs, that the cash-strapped institute seized on a way to raise funds—marketing its foxes to people as house pets.

When certain traits are *selected*—by conferring a reproductive advantage to an individual or a species—those traits, over time, will prevail. Dog breeders, as Robert Plomin and his colleagues (1997) remind us, have given us sheepdogs that herd, retrievers that retrieve, trackers that track, and pointers that point. Psychologists, too, have bred dogs, mice, and rats whose genes predispose them to be serene or reactive, quick learners or slow.

Does natural selection also explain our human tendencies? Nature has indeed selected advantageous variations from among the **mutations** (random errors in gene replication) and from the new gene combinations produced at each human conception. But the tight genetic leash that predisposes a dog's retrieving, a cat's pouncing, or an ant's nest building is looser on humans. The genes selected during our ancestral history provide more than a long leash; they endow us with a great capacity to learn and therefore to *adapt* to life in varied environments, from the tundra to the jungle. Genes and experience together wire the brain. Our adaptive flexibility in responding to different environments contributes to our *fitness*—our ability to survive and reproduce.

Evolutionary Success Helps Explain Similarities

Although human differences grab our attention, our deep similarities also demand explanation. And in the big picture, our lives are remarkably alike. Visit the international arrivals area at Amsterdam's Schiphol Airport, a world hub where arriving passengers meet their excited loved ones. There you will see the same delighted joy in the faces of Indonesian grandmothers, Chinese children, and homecoming Dutch. Evolutionary psychologist Steven Pinker (2002, p. 73) believes it is no wonder that our emotions, drives, and reasoning "have a common logic across cultures." Our shared human traits "were shaped by natural selection acting over the course of human evolution."

Our behavioral and biological similarities arise from our shared human genome. No more than 5 percent of the genetic differences among humans arise from population group differences. Some 95 percent of genetic variation exists within populations (Rosenberg et al., 2002). The typical genetic difference between two Icelandic villagers or between two Kenyans is much greater than the *average* difference between the two groups. Thus, noted geneticist Richard Lewontin (1982), if after a worldwide catastrophe only Icelanders or Kenyans survived, the human species would suffer only "a trivial reduction" in its genetic diversity.

And how did we develop this shared human genome? At the dawn of human history, our ancestors faced certain questions: Who is my ally, who my foe? What food should I eat? With whom should I mate? Some individuals answered those questions more successfully than others. For example, some women's experience of nausea in the critical first three months of pregnancy predisposes their avoiding certain bitter, strongly flavored, and novel foods. Avoiding such foods has survival value, since they are the very foods most often toxic to embryonic development (Schmitt & Pilcher, 2004). Early humans disposed to eat nourishing rather than poisonous food survived to contribute their genes to later generations. Those who deemed leopards "nice to pet" often did not.

Similarly successful were those whose mating helped them produce and nurture offspring. Over generations, the genes of individuals not so disposed tended to be lost from the human gene pool. As genes contributing to success continued to be selected, behavioral tendencies and thinking and learning capacities emerged that prepared our Stone Age ancestors to survive, reproduce, and send their genes into the future.

Outdated Tendencies

As inheritors of this prehistoric genetic legacy, we are predisposed to behave in ways that promoted our ancestors' surviving and reproducing. We love the taste of sweets and fats, which once were hard to come by but which prepared our ancestors to survive famines. With famine now rare in Western cultures, and sweets and fats beckoning us from store shelves, fast-food outlets, and vending machines, obesity has become a growing problem. Our natural dispositions, rooted deep in history, are mismatched with today's junk-food environment (Colarelli & Dettman, 2003). We are, in some ways, biologically prepared for a world that no longer exists.

|| Despite high infant mortality and rampant disease in past millennia, not one of your countless ancestors died childless. ||

Evolutionary Psychology Today

Charles Darwin's theory of evolution has been an organizing principle for biology for a long time. Jared Diamond (2001) notes that "virtually no contemporary scientists believe that Darwin was basically wrong." Today, Darwin's theory lives on in "the second Darwinian revolution": the application of evolutionary principles to psychology. In concluding *On the Origin of Species,* Darwin (1859, p. 346) anticipated this, foreseeing "open fields for far more important researches. Psychology will be based on a new foundation."

Evolutionary psychologists have addressed questions such as these:

▶ Why do infants start to fear strangers about the time they become mobile?

▶ Why are biological fathers so much less likely than unrelated boyfriends to abuse and murder the children with whom they share a home?

▶ Why do so many more people have phobias about spiders, snakes, and heights than about more dangerous threats, such as guns and electricity?

▶ Why do humans share some universal moral ideas?

▶ How are men and women alike? How and why do men's and women's sexuality differ?

To see how evolutionary psychologists think and reason, let's pause now to explore that last question.

|| Those who are troubled by an apparent conflict between scientific and religious accounts of human origins may find it helpful to recall that different perspectives of life can be complementary. For example, the scientific account attempts to tell us *when* and *how;* religious creation stories usually aim to tell about an ultimate *who* and *why.* As Galileo explained to the Grand Duchess Christina, "The Bible teaches how to go to heaven, not how the heavens go." ||

An Evolutionary Explanation of Human Sexuality

11-5 How might an evolutionary psychologist explain gender differences in mating preferences?

Having faced many similar challenges throughout history, men and women have adapted in similar ways. Whether male or female, we eat the same foods, avoid the same predators, and perceive, learn, and remember similarly. It is only in those domains where we have faced differing adaptive challenges—most obviously in behaviors related to reproduction—that we differ, say evolutionary psychologists.

"Not tonight, hon, I have a concussion."

"It's not that gay men are oversexed; they are simply men whose male desires bounce off other male desires rather than off female desires."

Steven Pinker, *How the Mind Works*, 1997

gender in psychology, the biologically and socially influenced characteristics by which people define *male* and *female*.

Gender Differences in Sexuality

Differ we do, report psychologists Roy Baumeister, Kathleen Catanese, and Kathleen Vohs (2001). They invite us to consider whether women or men have the stronger sex drive. Who desires more frequent sex, thinks more about sex, masturbates more often, initiates more sex, and sacrifices more to gain sex? The answers, they report, are *men, men, men, men,* and *men.* For example, in one BBC survey of more than 200,000 people in 53 nations, men everywhere more strongly agreed that "I have a strong sex drive" and "It doesn't take much to get me sexually excited" (Lippa, 2008).

Indeed, "with few exceptions anywhere in the world," report cross-cultural psychologist Marshall Segall and his colleagues (1990, p. 244), "males are more likely than females to initiate sexual activity." This is among the largest of **gender** differences in sexuality (Regan & Atkins, 2007). Consider:

▶ In a survey of 289,452 entering U.S. college students, 58 percent of men but only 34 percent of women agreed that "if two people really like each other, it's all right for them to have sex even if they've known each other for a very short time" (Pryor et al., 2005). "I can imagine myself being comfortable and enjoying 'casual' sex with different partners," agreed 48 percent of men and 12 percent of women in a survey of 4901 Australians (Bailey et al., 2000).

▶ In another survey of 3432 U.S. 18- to 59-year-olds, 48 percent of the women but only 25 percent of the men cited affection as a reason for first intercourse. And how often do they think about sex? "Every day" or "Several times a day," acknowledged 19 percent of the women and 54 percent of the men (Laumann et al., 1994). Ditto for the sexual thoughts of Canadians: "Several times a day," agreed 11 percent of women and 46 percent of men (Fischtein et al., 2007).

▶ In surveys, gay men (like straight men) report more interest in uncommitted sex, more responsiveness to visual sexual stimuli, and more concern with their partner's physical attractiveness than do lesbian women (Bailey et al., 1994; Doyle, 2005; Schmitt, 2007).

Gender differences in attitudes extend to differences in behavior. Gay male couples report having sex more often than do lesbian couples (Peplau & Fingerhut, 2007). And in the first year of Vermont's same-sex civil unions, men were only one-third of those electing this legal partnership (Rothblum, 2007).

Casual, impulsive sex is most frequent among males with traditional masculine attitudes (Pleck et al., 1993). Russell Clark and Elaine Hatfield (1989, 2003) observed this striking gender difference in 1978 when they sent some average-looking student research assistants strolling across the Florida State University quadrangle. Spotting an attractive person of the other sex, a researcher would approach and say, "I have been noticing you around campus and I find you to be very attractive. Would you go to bed with me tonight?" The women all declined, some obviously irritated ("What's wrong with you, creep? Leave me alone!"). But 75 percent of the men readily agreed, often replying with comments such as "Why do we have to wait until tonight?" (All were then truthfully told this was just an experiment.) Somewhat astonished by their result, Clark and Hatfield repeated their study in 1982 and twice more during the late 1980s, a high-risk AIDS time in the United States (Clark, 1990). Each time, virtually no women, but half or more of the men, agreed to go to bed with a stranger.

Men also have a lower threshold for perceiving warm responses as a sexual come-on. In study after study, men more often than women attribute a woman's friendliness to sexual interest (Abbey, 1987; Johnson et al., 1991). Misattributing women's cordiality as a come-on helps explain—but does not excuse—men's greater sexual assertiveness (Kolivas & Gross, 2007). The unfortunate results can range from sexual harassment to date rape.

Natural Selection and Mating Preferences

As biologists use natural selection to explain the mating behaviors of many species, so evolutionary psychologists use natural selection to explain a worldwide human sexuality difference: Women's approach to sex is usually more relational, and men's more recreational (Schmitt, 2005, 2007). The explanation goes like this: While a woman usually incubates and nurses one infant at a time, a male can spread his genes through other females. Our natural yearnings are our genes' way of reproducing themselves. In our ancestral history, women most often sent their genes into the future by pairing wisely, men by pairing widely. "Humans are living fossils—collections of mechanisms produced by prior selection pressures," says evolutionary psychologist David Buss (1995).

And what do heterosexual men and women find attractive in the other sex? Some aspects of attractiveness cross place and time. Men in a wide range of cultures, from Australia to Zambia (**FIGURE 11.3**), judge women as more attractive if they have a youthful appearance (Buss, 1994). Evolutionary psychologists say that men who were drawn to healthy, fertile-appearing women—women with smooth skin and a youthful shape suggesting many childbearing years to come—stood a better chance of sending their genes into the future. And sure enough, men feel most attracted to women whose waists are (or are surgically altered to be) roughly a third narrower than their hips—a sign of future fertility. Moreover, just as evolutionary psychology predicts, men are most attracted to women who, in the ancestral past (when ovulation began later than today), were at ages associated with peak fertility. Thus teen boys are most excited by a woman several years older than themselves, report Douglas Kenrick and his colleagues (in press). Mid-twenties men prefer women around their own age. And older men prefer younger women. This pattern, they report, consistently appears across European singles ads, Indian marital ads, and marriage records from North and South America, Africa, and the Philippines (Singh, 1993; Singh & Randall, 2007).

Women, in turn, prefer stick-around dads over likely cads. They are attracted to men who seem mature, dominant, bold, and affluent (Singh, 1995). They prefer mates with the potential for long-term mating and investment in their joint offspring (Gangestad & Simpson, 2000). Such attributes, say the evolutionary psychologists, connote a capacity to support and protect (Buss, 1996, 2000; Geary, 1998). In one experiment, women skillfully discerned which men most liked looking at baby pictures, and they rated those men higher as potential long-term mates (Roney et al., 2006).

"What about you, Walter—how do you feel about same-age marriage?"

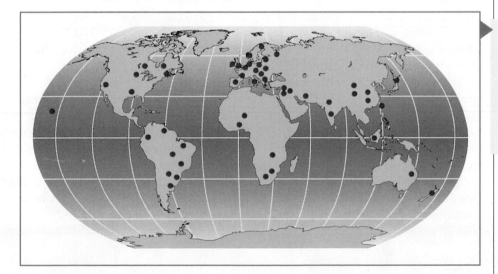

FIGURE 11.3 Worldwide mating preferences In a wide range of cultures studied (indicated by the red dots), men more than women preferred physical features suggesting youth and health—and reproductive potential. Women more than men preferred mates with resources and social status. Researchers credit (or blame) natural selection (Buss, 1994).

"I had a nice time, Steve. Would you like to come in, settle down, and raise a family?"

There is a principle at work here, say evolutionary psychologists: Nature selects behaviors that increase the likelihood of sending one's genes into the future. As mobile gene machines, we are designed to prefer whatever worked for our ancestors in their environments. They were predisposed to act in ways that would leave grandchildren—had they not been, we wouldn't be here. And as carriers of their genetic legacy, we are similarly predisposed.

Critiquing the Evolutionary Perspective

11-6   What are the key criticisms of evolutionary psychology?

Without disputing nature's selection of traits that enhance gene survival, critics see problems with evolutionary psychology. It often, they say, starts with an effect (such as the gender sexuality difference) and works backward to propose an explanation. So let's imagine a different observation and reason backward. If men were uniformly loyal to their mates, might we not reason that the children of these committed, supportive fathers would more often survive to perpetuate their genes? Might not men also be better off bonded to one woman—both to increase their odds of impregnation and to keep her from the advances of competing men? Might not a ritualized bond—a marriage—also spare women from chronic male harassment? Such suggestions are, in fact, evolutionary explanations for why humans tend to pair off monogamously. One can hardly lose at hindsight explanation, which is, said paleontologist Stephen Jay Gould (1997), mere "speculation [and] guesswork in the cocktail party mode."

Some also worry about the social consequences of evolutionary psychology. Does it suggest a genetic determinism that strikes at the heart of progressive efforts to remake society (Rose, 1999)? Does it undercut moral responsibility? Could it be used to rationalize "high-status men marrying a series of young, fertile women" (Looy, 2001)?

Much of who we are is *not* hard-wired, agree evolutionary psychologists. What's considered attractive does vary somewhat with time and place. The voluptuous Marilyn Monroe ideal of the 1950s has been replaced by the twenty-first-century, leaner, yet still curvy athletic image. Moreover, cultural expectations can bend the genders. If socialized to value lifelong commitment, men may sexually bond with one partner; if socialized to accept casual sex, women may willingly have sex with many partners.

Social expectations also shape gender differences in mate preferences. Show Alice Eagly and Wendy Wood (1999; Wood & Eagly, 2002, 2007) a culture with gender inequality—where men are providers and women are homemakers—and they will show you a culture where men strongly desire youth and domestic skill in their potential mates, and where women seek status and earning potential in their mates. Show Eagly and Wood a culture with gender equality, and they will show you a culture with smaller gender differences in mate preferences.

Evolutionary psychologists reassure us that the sexes, having faced similar adaptive problems, are far more alike than different. They stress that humans have a great capacity for learning and social progress. (We come equipped to adapt and survive, whether living in igloos or tree houses.) They point to the coherence and explanatory power of evolutionary principles, especially those offering testable predictions (for example, that we will favor others to the extent that they share our genes or can later reciprocate our favors). And they remind us that the study of how we came to be need not dictate how we *ought* to be. Understanding our propensities sometimes helps us overcome them.

REVIEW

Behavior Genetics and Evolutionary Psychology

11-1 **What are genes, and how do behavior geneticists explain our individual differences?** *Chromosomes* are coils of *DNA* containing *gene* segments that, when "turned on" (expressed), code for the proteins that form our body's building blocks. Most human traits are influenced by many genes acting together. *Behavior geneticists* seek to quantify genetic and *environmental* influences on our traits. Studies of *identical twins, fraternal twins,* and adoptive families help specify the influence of genetic nature and of environmental nurture, and the *interaction* between them (meaning that the effect of each depends on the other). The stability of *temperament* suggests a genetic predisposition.

11-2 **What is heritability, and how does it relate to individuals and groups?** *Heritability* describes the extent to which variation among members of a group can be attributed to genes. Heritable individual differences in traits such as height or intelligence need not explain group differences. Genes mostly explain why some are taller than others, but not why people today are taller than a century ago.

11-3 **What is the promise of molecular genetics research?** *Molecular geneticists* study the molecular structure and function of genes. Psychologists and molecular geneticists are cooperating to identify specific genes—or more often, teams of genes—that put people at risk for disorders.

11-4 **How do evolutionary psychologists use natural selection to explain behavior tendencies?** *Evolutionary psychologists* seek to understand how *natural selection* has shaped our traits and behavior tendencies. The principle of natural selection states that variations increasing the odds of reproducing and surviving are most likely to be passed on to future generations. Some variations arise from *mutations* (random errors in gene replication), others from new gene combinations at conception. Charles Darwin, whose theory of evolution has for a long time been an organizing principle in biology, anticipated the contemporary application of evolutionary principles in psychology.

11-5 **How might an evolutionary psychologist explain gender differences in mating preferences?** Men more than women approve of casual sex, think about sex, and misinterpret friendliness as sexual interest. Women more than men cite affection as a reason for first intercourse and have a relational view of sexual activity. Applying principles of natural selection, evolutionary psychologists reason that men's attraction to multiple healthy, fertile-appearing partners increases their chances of spreading their genes widely. Because women incubate and nurse babies, they increase their own and their children's chances of survival by searching for mates with the resources and the potential for long-term investment in their joint offspring.

11-6 **What are the key criticisms of evolutionary psychology?** Critics argue that evolutionary psychologists start with an effect and work backward to an explanation, that the evolutionary perspective gives too little emphasis to social influences, and that the evolutionary viewpoint absolves people from taking responsibility for their sexual behavior. Evolutionary psychologists respond that understanding our predispositions can help us overcome them. They also cite the value of testable predictions based on evolutionary principles, as well as the coherence and explanatory power of those principles.

Terms and Concepts to Remember

behavior genetics, p. 132

environment, p. 132

chromosomes, p. 132

DNA (*deoxyribonucleic acid*), p. 132

genes, p. 132

genome, p. 132

identical twins, p. 134

fraternal twins, p. 134

temperament, p. 137

heritability, p. 138

interaction, p. 139

molecular genetics, p. 140

evolutionary psychology, p. 141

natural selection, p. 141

mutation, p. 142

gender, p. 144

Test Yourself

1. What is *heritability*?

2. What are the three main criticisms of the evolutionary explanation of human sexuality?

(Answers to the Test Yourself questions can be found in Appendix B at the end of the book.)

Ask Yourself

1. Would you want genetic tests on your unborn offspring? What would you do if you knew your child would be destined for hemophilia? A learning disability? A high risk of depression? Do you think society would benefit or lose if such embryos were aborted?

2. Whose reasoning do you find most persuasive—that of evolutionary psychologists or their critics? Why?

∞ WEB

Multiple-choice self-tests and more may be found at www.worthpublishers.com/myers

Parents and Peers

Cultural Influences

Gender Development

Reflections on Nature and
Nurture

MODULE 12

Environmental Influences on Behavior

▶‖ Parents and Peers

12-1 To what extent are our lives shaped by early stimulation, by parents, and by peers?

Our genes, as expressed in specific environments, influence our developmental differences. We are not "blank slates," note Douglas Kenrick and his colleagues (in press). We are more like coloring books, with certain lines predisposed and experience filling in our picture. We are formed by nature *and* nurture. But what are the most influential components of our nurture? How do our early experiences, our family and peer relationships, and all our other experiences guide our development and contribute to our diversity?

Parents and Early Experiences

The formative nurture that conspires with nature begins at conception, with the prenatal environment in the womb, as embryos receive differing nutrition and varying levels of exposure to toxic agents. Nurture then continues outside the womb, where our early experiences foster brain development.

Experience and Brain Development

Our genes dictate our overall brain architecture, but experience fills in the details, developing neural connections and preparing our brain for thought and language and other later experiences. So how do early experiences leave their "marks" in the brain? Mark Rosenzweig and David Krech opened a window on that process when they raised some young rats in solitary confinement and others in a communal playground. When they later analyzed the rats' brains, those who died with the most toys had won. The rats living in the enriched environment, which simulated a natural environment, usually developed a heavier and thicker brain cortex (**FIGURE 12.1**).

Rosenzweig was so surprised by this discovery that he repeated the experiment several times before publishing his findings (Renner & Rosenzweig, 1987; Rosenzweig, 1984). So great are the effects that, shown brief video clips of rats, you could tell from

FIGURE 12.1 Experience affects brain development Mark Rosenzweig and David Krech raised rats either alone in an environment without playthings, or with other rats in an environment enriched with playthings changed daily. In 14 of 16 repetitions of this basic experiment, rats in the enriched environment developed significantly more cerebral cortex (relative to the rest of the brain's tissue) than did those in the impoverished environment.

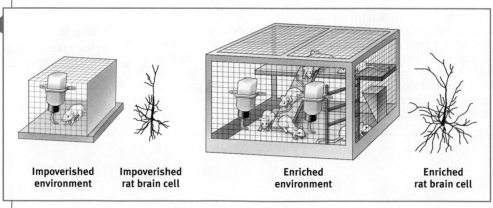

Impoverished environment

Impoverished rat brain cell

Enriched environment

Enriched rat brain cell

their activity and curiosity whether their environment had been impoverished or enriched (Renner & Renner, 1993). Bryan Kolb and Ian Whishaw (1998) noted extraordinary changes after 60 days in the enriched environment; the rats' brain weights increased 7 to 10 percent and the number of synapses mushroomed by about 20 percent.

Such results have motivated improvements in environments for laboratory, farm, and zoo animals—and for children in institutions. Stimulation by touch or massage also benefits infant rats and premature babies (Field et al., 2007). "Handled" infants of both species develop faster neurologically and gain weight more rapidly. By giving preemies massage therapy, neonatal intensive care units now help them to go home sooner (Field et al., 2006).

Both nature and nurture sculpt our synapses. After brain maturation provides us with an abundance of neural connections, our experiences trigger a *pruning process.* Sights and smells, touches and tugs activate connections and strengthen them. Unused neural pathways weaken and degenerate. Similar to pathways through a forest, popular paths are broadened and less-traveled paths gradually disappear. The result by puberty is a massive loss of unemployed connections.

Here at the juncture of nurture and nature is the biological reality of early childhood learning. During early childhood—while excess connections are still on call—youngsters can most easily master such skills as the grammar and accent of another language. Lacking any exposure to language before adolescence, a person will never master any language.

Likewise, lacking visual experience during the early years, people whose vision is restored by cataract removal never achieve normal perceptions. The brain cells normally assigned to vision have died or been diverted to other uses. For us to have optimum brain development, normal stimulation during the early years is critical. The maturing brain's rule: Use it or lose it.

The brain's development does not, however, end with childhood. Our neural tissue is ever changing. If a monkey is trained to push a lever with a finger several thousand times a day, the brain tissue controlling that finger will change to reflect the experience. Human brains work similarly (**FIGURE 12.2**). Whether learning to keyboard or skateboard, we perform with increasing skill as our brain incorporates the learning.

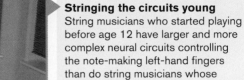

Courtesy cf C. Brune

Stringing the circuits young
String musicians who started playing before age 12 have larger and more complex neural circuits controlling the note-making left-hand fingers than do string musicians whose training started later (Elbert et al., 1995).

"Genes and experiences are just two ways of doing the same thing—wiring synapses."
Joseph LeDoux, *The Synaptic Self,* 2002

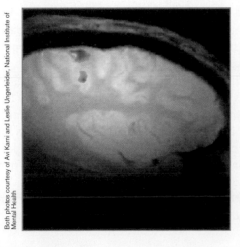
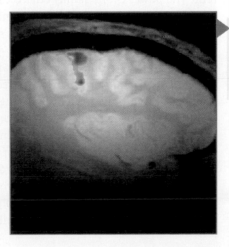

Both photos courtesy of Avi Karni and Leslie Ungerleider, National Institute of Mental Health

FIGURE 12.2 A trained brain A well-learned finger-tapping task activates more motor cortex neurons (orange area, right) than were active in the same brain before training (left). (From Karni et al., 1998.)

|| Even among chimpanzees, when one infant is hurt by another, the victim's mother will often attack the offender's mother (Goodall, 1968). ||

"So I blame you for everything—whose fault is that?"

"If you want to blame your parents for your own adult problems, you are entitled to blame the genes they gave you, but you are not entitled—by any facts I know—to blame the way they treated you. . . . We are not prisoners of our past."

Martin Seligman, *What You Can Change and What You Can't,* 1994

How Much Credit (or Blame) Do Parents Deserve?

In procreation, a woman and a man shuffle their gene decks and deal a life-forming hand to their child-to-be, who is then subjected to countless influences beyond their control. Parents, nonetheless, feel enormous satisfaction in their children's successes, and feel guilt or shame over their failures. They beam over the child who wins an award. They wonder where they went wrong with the child who is repeatedly called into the principal's office. Freudian psychiatry and psychology have been among the sources of such ideas, by blaming problems from asthma to schizophrenia on "bad mothering." Society reinforces such parent-blaming: Believing that parents shape their offspring as a potter molds clay, people readily praise parents for their children's virtues and blame them for their children's vices. Popular culture endlessly proclaims the psychological harm toxic parents inflict on their fragile children. No wonder that it can seem risky to have and raise children.

But do parents really produce future adults with an inner wounded child by being (take your pick from the toxic-parent lists) overbearing—or uninvolved? Pushy—or ineffectual? Overprotective—or distant? Are children really so easily wounded? If so, should we then blame our parents for our failings, and ourselves for our children's failings? Or does all the talk of wounding fragile children through normal parental mistakes trivialize the brutality of real abuse?

Peter Neubauer and Alexander Neubauer (1990, pp. 20–21) illustrate how, with hindsight, we may inappropriately credit or blame our parents:

> Identical twin men, now age 30, were separated at birth and raised in different countries by their respective adoptive parents. Both kept their lives neat—neat to the point of pathology. Their clothes were preened, appointments met precisely on time, hands scrubbed regularly to a raw, red color. When the first was asked why he felt the need to be so clean, his answer was plain.
>
> "My mother. When I was growing up she always kept the house perfectly ordered. She insisted on every little thing returned to its proper place, the clocks—we had dozens of clocks—each set to the same noonday chime. She insisted on this, you see. I learned from her. What else could I do?"
>
> The man's identical twin, just as much a perfectionist with soap and water, explained his own behavior this way: "The reason is quite simple. I'm reacting to my mother, who was an absolute slob."

Parents do matter. The power of parenting to shape our differences is clearest at the extremes—the abused who become abusive, the neglected who become neglectful, the loved but firmly handled children who become self-confident and socially competent. The power of the family environment also frequently shows up in children's political attitudes, religious beliefs, and personal manners. And it appears in the remarkable academic and vocational successes of children of the refugee "boat people" fleeing Vietnam and Cambodia—successes attributed to close-knit, supportive, even demanding families (Caplan et al., 1992).

Yet in personality measures, shared environmental influences—including, as we have seen, the home influences siblings share—typically account for less than 10 percent of children's differences. In the words of behavior geneticists Robert Plomin and Denise Daniels (1987), "Two children in the same family [are on average] as different from one another as are pairs of children selected randomly from the population." To developmental psychologist Sandra Scarr (1993), this implies that "parents should be given less credit for kids who turn out great and blamed less for kids who don't." Knowing children are not easily sculpted by parental nurture, perhaps parents can relax a bit more and love their children for who they are.

Peer Influence

As children mature, what other experiences do the work of nurturing? At all ages, but especially during childhood and adolescence, we seek to fit in with groups and are subject to group influences.

Consider the power of peers (Harris, 1998, 2000):

▶ Preschoolers who disdain a certain food often will eat that food if put at a table with a group of children who like it.

▶ Children who hear English spoken with one accent at home and another in the neighborhood and at school will invariably adopt the accent of their peers, not their parents. Accents (and slang) reflect culture, "and children get their culture from their peers," notes Harris (2007).

▶ Teens who start smoking typically have friends who model smoking, suggest its pleasures, and offer cigarettes (J. S. Rose et al., 1999; R. J. Rose et al., 2003). Part of this peer similarity may result from a *selection effect,* as kids seek out peers with similar attitudes and interests. Those who smoke (or don't) may select as friends those who also smoke (or don't).

Howard Gardner (1998) concludes that parents and peers are complementary:

Parents are more important when it comes to education, discipline, responsibility, orderliness, charitableness, and ways of interacting with authority figures. Peers are more important for learning cooperation, for finding the road to popularity, for inventing styles of interaction among people of the same age. Youngsters may find their peers more interesting, but they will look to their parents when contemplating their own futures. Moreover, parents [often] choose the neighborhoods and schools that supply the peers.

Ole Graf/zefa/Corbis

> "Men resemble the times more than they resemble their fathers."
> Ancient Arab proverb

▶ **Peer power** As we develop, we play, mate, and partner with peers. No wonder children and youths are so sensitive and responsive to peer influences.

As Gardner points out, parents can influence the culture that shapes the peer group, by helping to select their children's neighborhood and schools. And because neighborhood influences matter, parents may want to become involved in intervention programs for youth that aim at a whole school or neighborhood. If the vapors of a toxic climate are seeping into a child's life, that climate—not just the child—needs reforming. Even so, peers are but one medium of cultural influence.

> "It takes a village to raise a child."
> African proverb

▶‖ Cultural Influences

12-2 How do cultural norms affect our behavior?

Compared with the narrow path taken by flies, fish, and foxes, the road along which environment drives us is wider. The mark of our species—nature's great gift to us—is our ability to learn and adapt. We come equipped with a huge cerebral hard drive ready to receive many gigabytes of cultural software.

Culture is the behaviors, ideas, attitudes, values, and traditions shared by a group of people and transmitted from one generation to the next (Brislin, 1988). Human

culture the enduring behaviors, ideas, attitudes, values, and traditions shared by a group of people and transmitted from one generation to the next.

nature, notes Roy Baumeister (2005), seems designed for culture. We are social animals, but more. Wolves are social animals; they live and hunt in packs. Ants are incessantly social, never alone. But "culture is a better way of being social," notes Baumeister. Wolves function pretty much as they did 10,000 years ago. You and I enjoy things unknown to most of our century-ago ancestors, including electricity, indoor plumbing, antibiotics, and the Internet. Culture works.

Primates exhibit the rudiments of culture, with local customs of tool use, grooming, and courtship. Younger chimpanzees and macaque monkeys sometimes invent customs—potato washing, in one famous example—and pass them on to their peers and offspring. But human culture does more. It supports our species' survival and reproduction by enabling social and economic systems that give us an edge.

Thanks to our mastery of *language,* we humans enjoy the *preservation of innovation.* Within the span of this day, I have, thanks to my culture, made good use of Post-it Notes, Google, and a single-shot skinny latte. On a grander scale, we have culture's accumulated knowledge to thank for the last century's 30-year extension of the average life expectancy in most countries where this book is being read. Moreover, culture enables an efficient *division of labor.* Although one lucky person gets his name on this book's cover, the product actually results from the coordination and commitment of a team of women and men, no one of whom could produce it alone.

Across cultures, we differ in our language, our monetary systems, our sports, which fork—if any—we eat with, even which side of the road we drive on. But beneath these differences is our great similarity—our capacity for culture. Culture provides the shared and transmitted customs and beliefs that enable us to communicate, to exchange money for things, to play, to eat, and to drive with agreed-upon rules and without crashing into one another. This shared capacity for culture enables our striking group differences. Human nature manifests human diversity.

If we all lived in homogeneous ethnic groups in separate regions of the world, as some people still do, cultural diversity would be less relevant. In Japan, almost 99 percent of the country's 127 million people are of Japanese descent. Internal cultural differences are therefore minimal compared with those found in Los Angeles, where the public schools recently taught 82 different languages, or in Toronto or Vancouver, where minorities are one-third of the population and many are immigrants (as are 13.4 percent of all Canadians and 23 percent of Australians) (Axiss, 2007; Statistics Canada, 2002). I am ever mindful that the readers of this book are culturally diverse. You and your ancestors reach from Australia to Africa and from Singapore to Sweden.

Variation Across Cultures

We see our adaptability in cultural variations among our beliefs and our values, in how we raise our children and bury our dead, and in what we wear (or whether we wear anything at all). Riding along with a unified culture is like biking with the wind: As it carries us along, we hardly notice it is there. When we try riding *against* the wind we feel its force. Face to face with a different culture, we become aware of the cultural winds. Visiting Europe, most North Americans notice the smaller cars, the left-handed use of the fork, the uninhibited attire on the beaches. Stationed in Iraq, Afghanistan, and Kuwait, American and European soldiers alike realized how liberal their home cultures were. Arriving in North America, visitors from Japan and India struggle to understand why so many people wear their dirty *street* shoes in the house.

Each cultural group evolves its own **norms**—rules for accepted and expected behavior. Many South Asians, for example, use only the right hand's fingers for eating. The British have a norm for orderly waiting in line. Sometimes social expectations seem oppressive: "Why should it matter how I dress?" Yet, norms grease the social machinery and free us from self-preoccupation. Knowing when to clap or bow, which

norm an understood rule for accepted and expected behavior. Norms prescribe "proper" behavior.

fork to pick up first at a dinner party, and what sorts of gestures and compliments are appropriate—whether to greet people by shaking hands or kissing each cheek, for example—we can relax and enjoy one another without fear of embarrassment or insult.

When cultures collide, their differing norms often befuddle. For example, if someone invades our **personal space**—the portable buffer zone we like to maintain around our bodies—we feel uncomfortable. Scandinavians, North Americans, and the British have traditionally preferred more personal space than do Latin Americans, Arabs, and the French (Sommer, 1969). At a social gathering, a Mexican seeking a comfortable conversation distance may end up walking around a room with a backpedaling Canadian. (You can experience this at a party by playing Space Invader as you talk with someone.) To the Canadian, the Mexican may seem intrusive; to the Mexican, the Canadian may seem standoffish.

Cultures differ
Behavior seen as appropriate in one culture may violate the norms of another group. In Arab societies, but not in Western cultures, men often greet one another with a kiss.

Cultures also vary in their expressiveness. Those with roots in northern European culture have perceived people from Mediterranean cultures as warm and charming but inefficient. The Mediterraneans, in turn, have seen northern Europeans as efficient but cold and preoccupied with punctuality (Triandis, 1981).

Cultures vary in their pace of life, too. People from time-conscious Japan—where bank clocks keep exact time, pedestrians walk briskly, and postal clerks fill requests speedily—may find themselves growing impatient when visiting Indonesia, where clocks keep less accurate time and the pace of life is more leisurely (Levine & Norenzayan, 1999). In adjusting to their host countries, the first wave of U.S. Peace Corps volunteers reported that two of their greatest culture shocks, after the language differences, were the differing pace of life and the people's differing sense of punctuality (Spradley & Phillips, 1972).

Variation Over Time

Consider, too, how rapidly cultures may change over time. English poet Geoffrey Chaucer (1342–1400) is separated from a modern Briton by only 20 generations, but the two would converse with great difficulty. In the thin slice of history since 1960, most Western cultures have changed with remarkable speed. Middle-class people fly to places they once only read about, e-mail those they once snail-mailed, and work in air-conditioned comfort where they once sweltered. They enjoy the convenience of online shopping, anywhere-anytime electronic communication, and—enriched by doubled per-person real income—eating out more than twice as often as did their parents back in the culture of 1960. With greater economic independence, today's women are more likely to marry for love and less likely to endure abusive relationships out of economic need. Many minority groups enjoy expanded human rights.

But some changes seem not so wonderfully positive. Had you fallen asleep in the United States in 1960 and awakened today, you would open your eyes to a culture with more divorce, delinquency, and depression. You would also find North Americans—like their counterparts in Britain, Australia, and New Zealand—spending more hours at work, fewer hours sleeping, and fewer hours with friends and family (Frank, 1999; Putnam, 2000).

Whether we love or loathe these changes, we cannot fail to be impressed by their breathtaking speed. And we cannot explain them by changes in the human gene pool, which evolves far too slowly to account for high-speed cultural transformations. Cultures vary. Cultures change. And cultures shape our lives.

personal space the buffer zone we like to maintain around our bodies.

Culture and the Self

12-3 How do individualist and collectivist cultural influences affect people?

Cultures vary in the extent to which they give priority to the nurturing and expression of personal identity or group identity. To grasp the difference, imagine that someone were to rip away your social connections, making you a solitary refugee in a foreign land. How much of your identity would remain intact? The answer would depend in large part on whether you give greater priority to the independent self that marks **individualism** or to the interdependent self that marks **collectivism.**

If as our solitary traveler you pride yourself on your individualism, a great deal of your identity would remain intact—the very core of your being, the sense of "me," the awareness of your personal convictions and values. Individualists (often people from North America, Western Europe, Australia, or New Zealand) give relatively greater priority to personal goals and define their identity mostly in terms of personal attributes (Schimmack et al., 2005). They strive for personal control and individual achievement. In American culture, with its relatively big "I" and small "we," 85 percent of people say it is possible "to pretty much be who you want to be" (Sampson, 2000).

Individualists share the human need to belong. They join groups. But they are less focused on group harmony and doing their duty to the group (Brewer & Chen, 2007). Being more self-contained, individualists also move in and out of social groups more easily. They feel relatively free to switch places of worship, leave one job for another, or even leave their extended families and migrate to a new place. Marriage is often for as long as they both shall love.

If set adrift in a foreign land as a collectivist, you might experience a greater loss of identity. Cut off from family, groups, and loyal friends, you would lose the connections that have defined who you are. In a collectivist culture, group identifications provide a sense of belonging, a set of values, a network of caring individuals, an assurance of security. In return, collectivists have deeper, more stable attachments to their groups, often their family, clan, or company. In Korea, for example, people place less value on expressing a consistent, unique self-concept, and more on tradition and shared practices (Choi & Choi, 2002).

Valuing communal solidarity, people in collectivist cultures place a premium on preserving group spirit and making sure others never lose face. What people say reflects not only what they feel (their inner attitudes) but what they presume others

individualism giving priority to one's own goals over group goals and defining one's identity in terms of personal attributes rather than group identifications.

collectivism giving priority to goals of one's group (often one's extended family or work group) and defining one's identity accordingly.

Uniform requirements People in individualist Western cultures sometimes see traditional Japanese culture as confining. But from the Japanese perspective, the same tradition expresses a "serenity that comes to people who know exactly what to expect from each other" (Weisz et al., 1984).

feel (Kashima et al., 1992). Avoiding direct confrontation, blunt honesty, and uncomfortable topics, people often defer to others' wishes and display a polite, self-effacing humility (Markus & Kitayama, 1991). In new groups, they may be shy and more easily embarrassed than their individualist counterparts (Singelis et al., 1995, 1999). Compared with Westerners, people in Japanese and Chinese cultures, for example, exhibit greater shyness toward strangers and greater concern for social harmony and loyalty (Bond, 1988; Cheek & Melchior, 1990; Triandis, 1994). Elders and superiors receive respect, and duty to family may trump personal career preferences. When the priority is "we," not "me," that individualized latte—"decaf, single shot, skinny, extra hot"—that feels so good to a North American in a coffee shop might sound more like a selfish demand in Seoul (Kim & Markus, 1999).

To be sure, there is diversity within cultures. Even in the most individualistic countries, some people manifest collectivist values. And there are regional differences within cultures, such as the spirit of individualism in Japan's "northern frontier" island of Hokkaido (Kitayama et al., 2006). But in general, people (especially men) in competitive, individualist cultures have more personal freedom, are less geographically bound to their families, enjoy more privacy, and take more pride in personal achievements (**TABLE 12.1**). During the 2000 and 2002 Olympic games, U.S. gold medal winners and the U.S. media covering them attributed the achievements mostly to the athletes themselves (Markus et al., 2006). "I think I just stayed focused," explained swimming gold medalist Misty Hyman. "It was time to show the world what I could do. I am just glad I was able to do it." Japan's gold medalist in the women's marathon, Naoko Takahashi, had a different explanation: "Here is the best coach in the world, the best manager in the world, and all of the people who support me—all of these things were getting together and became a gold medal." Even when describing friends, Westerners tend to use trait-describing adjectives ("she is helpful"), whereas East Asians more often use verbs that describe behaviors in context ("she helps her friends") (Maass et al., 2006).

Individualism's benefits can come at the cost of more loneliness, more divorce, more homicide, and more stress-related disease (Popenoe, 1993; Triandis et al., 1988). People in individualist cultures demand more romance and personal fulfillment in marriage, subjecting the relationship to more pressure (Dion & Dion, 1993). In one survey, "keeping romance alive" was rated as important to a good marriage by 78 percent of U.S. women but only 29 percent of Japanese women (*American Enterprise*, 1992). In China, love songs often express enduring commitment and friendship (Rothbaum & Tsang, 1998). As one song put it, "We will be together from now on . . . I will never change from now to forever."

Interdependence This young man is helping a fellow student who became trapped in the rubble that was their school after a devastating earthquake shook China in 2008. By identifying strongly with family and other groups, Chinese people tend to have a collectivist sense of "we" and an accompanying support network of care, which may have helped them struggle through the aftermath of this disaster.

"One needs to cultivate the spirit of sacrificing the *little me* to achieve the benefits of the *big me*."
Chinese saying

TABLE 12.1 Value Contrasts Between Individualism and Collectivism

Concept	Individualism	Collectivism
Self	Independent (identity from individual traits)	Interdependent (identity from belonging)
Life task	Discover and express one's uniqueness	Maintain connections, fit in, perform role
What matters	Me—personal achievement and fulfillment; rights and liberties; self-esteem	Us—group goals and solidarity; social responsibilities and relationships; family duty
Coping method	Change reality	Accommodate to reality
Morality	Defined by individuals (self-based)	Defined by social networks (duty-based)
Relationships	Many, often temporary or casual; confrontation acceptable	Few, close and enduring; harmony valued
Attributing behavior	Behavior reflects one's personality and attitudes	Behavior reflects social norms and roles

Sources: Adapted from Thomas Schoeneman (1994) and Harry Triandis (1994).

Cultures vary In Scotland's Orkney Islands' town of Stromness, social trust has enabled parents to park their toddlers outside of shops.

Culture and Child-Rearing

Child-rearing practices reflect cultural values that vary across time and place. Do you prefer children who are independent or children who comply? If you live in a Westernized culture, the odds are you prefer independence. "You are responsible for yourself," Western families and schools tell their children. "Follow your conscience. Be true to yourself. Discover your gifts. Think through your personal needs." A half-century and more ago, Western cultural values placed greater priority on obedience, respect, and sensitivity to others (Alwin, 1990; Remley, 1988). "Be true to your traditions," parents then taught their children. "Be loyal to your heritage and country. Show respect toward your parents and other superiors." Cultures can change.

Many Asians and Africans live in cultures that value emotional closeness. Rather than being given their own bedrooms and entrusted to day care, infants and toddlers may sleep with their mothers and spend their days close to a family member (Morelli et al., 1992; Whiting & Edwards, 1988). These cultures encourage a strong sense of *family self*—a feeling that what shames the child shames the family, and what brings honor to the family brings honor to the self.

Children across place and time have thrived under various child-rearing systems. Upper-class British parents traditionally handed off routine caregiving to nannies, then sent their children off to boarding school at about age 10. These children generally grew up to be pillars of British society, just like their parents and their boarding-school peers. In the African Gusii society, babies nurse freely but spend most of the day on their mother's back—with lots of body contact but little face-to-face and language interaction. When the mother becomes pregnant, the toddler is weaned and handed over to someone else, often an older sibling. Westerners may wonder about the negative effects of this lack of verbal interaction, but then the African Gusii would in turn wonder about Western mothers pushing their babies around in strollers and leaving them in playpens and car seats (Small, 1997). Such diversity in child-rearing cautions us against presuming that our culture's way is the only way to rear children successfully.

Developmental Similarities Across Groups

Parental involvement promotes development Parents in every culture facilitate their children's discovery of their world, but cultures differ in what they deem important. Asian cultures place more emphasis on school and hard work than do North American cultures. This may help explain why Japanese and Taiwanese children get higher scores on mathematics achievement tests.

Mindful of how others differ from us, we often fail to notice the similarities predisposed by our shared biology. One 49-country study revealed that nation-to-nation differences in personality traits such as conscientiousness and extraversion are smaller than most people suppose (Terracciano et al., 2006). Australians see themselves as outgoing, German-speaking Swiss see themselves as conscientious, and Canadians see themselves as agreeable. Actually, these national stereotypes exaggerate differences that, although real, are modest. Compared with the person-to-person differences within groups, the differences between groups are small. Regardless of our culture, we humans are more alike than different. We share the same life cycle. We speak to our infants in similar ways and respond similarly to their coos and cries (Bornstein et al., 1992a,b). All over the world, the children of warm and supportive parents feel better about themselves and are less hostile than are the children of punitive and rejecting parents (Rohner, 1986; Scott et al., 1991).

Even differences *within* a culture, such as those sometimes attributed to race, are often easily explained by an interaction between our biology and our culture. David Rowe and his colleagues (1994, 1995) illustrate this with an analogy: Black men tend to have higher blood pressure than White men. Suppose that (1) in both groups salt consumption correlates with blood pressure, and (2) salt consumption is higher among Black men than among White men. The blood pressure "race difference" might then actually be, at least partly, a *diet* difference—a cultural preference for certain foods.

And that, say Rowe and his colleagues, parallels psychological findings. Although Latino, Asian, Black, White, and Native Americans differ in school achievement and delinquency, the differences are "no more than skin deep." To the extent that family structure, peer influences, and parental education predict behavior in one of these ethnic groups, they do so for the others as well.

So as members of different ethnic and cultural groups, we may differ in surface ways, but as members of one species we seem subject to the same psychological forces. Our languages vary, yet they reflect universal principles of grammar. Our tastes vary, yet they reflect common principles of hunger. Our social behaviors vary, yet they reflect pervasive principles of human influence. Cross-cultural research can help us appreciate both our cultural diversity *and* our human likeness.

▶‖ Gender Development

Cognitive psychologists have demonstrated that we humans share an irresistible urge to organize our worlds into simple categories. Among the ways we classify people—as tall or short, fat or slim, smart or dull—one stands out: At your birth, everyone wanted to know, "Boy or girl?" Our biological sex in turn helps define our *gender,* the biological and social characteristics by which people define male or female. In considering how nature and nurture together create social diversity, gender is the prime case example. Let's recap one of psychology's main themes—that nature and nurture together create our differences and commonalities—by considering gender variations.

Gender Similarities and Differences

12-4 What are some ways in which males and females tend to be alike and to differ?

Having faced similar adaptive challenges, we are in most ways alike. Men and women are not from different planets—Mars and Venus—but from the same planet Earth. Tell me whether you are male or female and you give me virtually no clues to your vocabulary, intelligence, and happiness, or to the mechanisms by which you see, hear, learn, and remember. Your "opposite" sex is, in reality, your very similar sex. And should we be surprised? Among your 46 chromosomes, 45 are unisex.

But males and females also differ, and differences command attention. Some much talked-about differences are actually quite modest, as Janet Hyde (2005) illustrated by graphically representing the gender difference in self-esteem scores, across many studies (**FIGURE 12.3**). Some differences are more striking. Compared with the average man, the average woman enters puberty two years sooner, lives five years longer, carries 70 percent more fat, has 40 percent less muscle, and is 5 inches shorter. Other gender differences appear throughout this book. Women can become sexually re-aroused immediately after orgasm. They smell fainter odors, express emotions more freely, and are offered help more often. They are doubly vulnerable to depression and anxiety, and their risk of developing eating disorders is 10 times greater. But then men are some 4 times more likely to commit suicide or suffer alcohol dependence. They are far more often diagnosed with autism, color-blindness, attention-deficit hyperactivity disorder (as children), and antisocial personality disorder (as adults). Choose your gender and pick your vulnerability.

"When [someone] has discovered why men in Bond Street wear black hats he will at the same moment have discovered why men in Timbuctoo wear red feathers."

G. K. Chesterton, *Heretics*, 1905

FIGURE 12.3 Much ado about a small difference Janet Hyde (2005) shows us two normal distributions that differ by the approximate magnitude (0.21 standard deviations) of the gender difference in self-esteem, averaged over all available samples. Moreover, though we can identify gender differences, the variation among individual women and among individual men greatly exceeds the difference between the average woman and man.

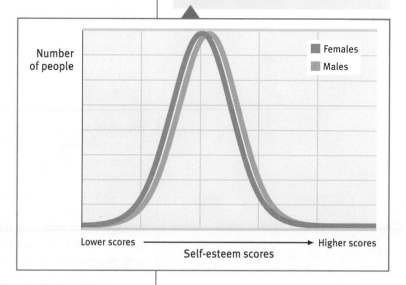

How much does biology bend the genders? What portion of our differences are socially constructed—by the gender roles our culture assigns us, and by how we are socialized as children? To answer those questions, let's look more closely at some average gender differences in aggression, social power, and social connectedness.

Gender and Aggression

In surveys, men admit to more **aggression** than do women, and experiments confirm that men tend to behave more aggressively, such as by administering what they believe are more painful electric shocks (Bettencourt & Kernahan, 1997). The aggression gender gap pertains to *physical* aggression (such as hitting) rather than verbal, *relational* aggression (such as excluding someone). The gender gap in physical aggression appears in everyday life at various ages and in various cultures, especially those with gender inequality (Archer, 2004, 2006). In dating relationships, violent acts (such as slaps and thrown objects) are often mutual (Straus, 2008). Violent crime rates more strikingly illustrate the gender difference. The male-to-female arrest ratio for murder, for example, is 10 to 1 in the United States and almost 7 to 1 in Canada (FBI, 2007; Statistics Canada, 2007).

Throughout the world, hunting, fighting, and warring are primarily men's activities (Wood & Eagly, 2002, 2007). Men also express more support for war. The Iraq war, for example, has consistently been supported more by American men than by American women (Newport et al., 2007).

Gender and Social Power

Around the world, from Nigeria to New Zealand, people have perceived men as more dominant, forceful, and independent, women as more deferential, nurturant, and affiliative (Williams & Best, 1990). Indeed, in most societies men *are* socially dominant. When groups form, whether as juries or companies, leadership tends to go to males (Colarelli et al., 2006). Men worldwide place more importance on power and achievement (Schwartz & Rubel, 2005). As leaders, men tend to be more directive, even autocratic; women tend to be more democratic, more welcoming of subordinates' participation in decision making (Eagly & Carli, 2007; van Engen & Willemsen, 2004). When people interact, men are more likely to utter opinions, women to express support (Aries, 1987; Wood, 1987). These differences carry into everyday behavior, where men are more likely to act as powerful people often do—talking assertively, interrupting, initiating touches, staring more, and smiling less (Hall, 1987; Leaper & Ayres, 2007; Major et al., 1990).

Such behaviors help sustain social power inequities. When political leaders are elected, they usually are men, who held 82 percent of the seats in the world's governing parliaments in 2008 (IPU, 2008). When salaries are paid, those in traditionally male occupations receive more.

|| Women's 2008 representations in national parliaments ranged from 9% in the Arab States to 17% in the United States and 24% in Canada to 41% in Scandinavia (IPU, 2008). ||

Gender and Social Connectedness

To Carol Gilligan and her colleagues (1982, 1990), the "normal" struggle to create a separate identity describes Western individualist males more than relationship-oriented females. Gilligan believes females tend to differ from males both in being less concerned with viewing themselves as separate individuals and in being more concerned with "making connections."

These gender differences in connectedness surface early in children's play, and they continue with age. Boys typically play in large groups with an activity focus and little intimate discussion (Rose & Rudolph, 2006). Girls usually play in smaller groups, often with one friend. Their play is less competitive than boys' and more imitative of social relationships. Both in play and other settings, females are more open and responsive to feedback than are males (Maccoby, 1990; Roberts, 1991). Asked

aggression physical or verbal behavior intended to hurt someone.

Every man for himself, or tend and befriend? Gender differences in the way we interact with others begin to appear at a very young age.

difficult questions—"Do you have any idea why the sky is blue?" "Do you have any idea why shorter people live longer?"—men are more likely than women to hazard answers rather than admit they don't know, a phenomenon Traci Giuliano and her colleagues (1998a,b) call the *male answer syndrome.*

Females are more *interdependent* than males. As teens, girls spend more time with friends and less time alone (Wong & Csikszentmihalyi, 1991). As late adolescents, they spend more time on social-networking Internet sites (Pryor et al., 2007). As adults, women take more pleasure in talking face-to-face, and they tend to use conversation more to explore relationships. Men enjoy doing activities side-by-side, and they tend to use conversation to communicate solutions (Tannen, 1990; Wright, 1989). The communication difference is apparent even in student e-mails, from which people in one New Zealand study could correctly guess the author's gender two-thirds of the time (Thomson & Murachver, 2001).

These gender differences are sometimes reflected in patterns of phone communication. In France, women make 63 percent of phone calls and, when talking to a woman, stay connected longer (7.2 minutes) than men do when talking to other men (4.6 minutes) (Smoreda & Licoppe, 2000). So, does this confirm the idea that women are just more talkative? To check that presumption, Matthias Mehl and his colleagues (2007) counted the number of words 396 college students spoke in the course of an average day. (How many words would you guess you speak a day?) They found that talkativeness varied enormously—by 45,000 words between their most and least talkative participants. But contrary to stereotypes of jabbering women, both men and women averaged about 16,000 words daily.

Women worldwide orient their interests and vocation more to people and less to things (Lippa, 2005, 2006, 2008). In the workplace, they often are less driven by money and status and are more likely to choose reduced work hours (Pinker, 2008). In the home, they provide most of the care to the very young and the very old. Women also purchase 85 percent of greeting cards (Time, 1997). Women's emphasis on caring helps explain another interesting finding: Although 69 percent of people say they have a close relationship with their father, 90 percent feel close to their mother (Hugick, 1989). When wanting understanding and someone with whom to share worries and hurts, both men and women usually turn to women, and both report their friendships with women to be more intimate, enjoyable, and nurturing (Rubin, 1985; Sapadin, 1988).

Bonds and feelings of support are even stronger among women than among men (Rossi & Rossi, 1993). Women's ties—as mothers, daughters, sisters, aunts, and

‖ *Question:* Why does it take 200 million sperm to fertilize one egg? *Answer:* Because they won't stop for directions. ‖

grandmothers—bind families together. As friends, women talk more often and more openly (Berndt, 1992; Dindia & Allen, 1992). And when they themselves must cope with stress, women more than men turn to others for support—they *tend and befriend* (Tamres et al., 2002; Taylor, 2002).

As empowered people generally do, men value freedom and self-reliance, which helps explain why men of all ages, worldwide, are less religious and pray less (Benson, 1992; Stark, 2002). Men also dominate the ranks of professional skeptics. All 10 winners and 14 runners-up on the *Skeptical Inquirer* list of outstanding twentieth-century rationalist skeptics were men. In the Science and the Paranormal section of the 2007 Prometheus Books catalog (from the leading publisher of skepticism), one can find 94 male and 4 female authors. In one Skeptics Society survey, nearly 4 in 5 respondents were men (Shermer, 1999). Women, it appears, are more open to spirituality (and are far more likely to author books on spirituality than on skepticism).

Gender differences in power, connectedness, and other traits peak in late adolescence and early adulthood—the very years most commonly studied (also the years of dating and mating). As teenagers, girls become progressively less assertive and more flirtatious; boys become more domineering and unexpressive. But by age 50, these differences have diminished. Men become more empathic and less domineering and women, especially if working, become more assertive and self-confident (Kasen et al., 2006; Maccoby, 1998).

"In the long years liker must they grow;
The man be more of woman, she of man."

Alfred Lord Tennyson, *The Princess*, 1847

The Nature of Gender

12-5 How do nature and nurture together form our gender?

What explains our gender diversity? Is biology destiny? Are we shaped by our cultures? A biopsychosocial view suggests it is both, thanks to the interplay among our biological dispositions, our developmental experiences, and our current situations (Wood & Eagly, 2002, 2007).

In domains where men and women have faced similar challenges—regulating heat with sweat, developing tastes that nourish, growing calluses where the skin meets friction—the sexes are similar. Even when describing the ideal mate, both men and women put traits such as "kind," "honest," and "intelligent" at the top of their lists. But in domains pertinent to mating, evolutionary psychologists contend, guys act like guys whether they are elephants or elephant seals, rural peasants or corporate presidents. Such gender differences may be influenced genetically, by our differing *sex chromosomes* and, physiologically, from our differing concentrations of *sex hormones.*

Males and females are variations on a single form. Seven weeks after conception, you were anatomically indistinguishable from someone of the other sex. Then your genes activated your biological sex, which was determined by your twenty-third pair of chromosomes, the two sex chromosomes. From your mother, you received an **X chromosome.** From your father, you received the one chromosome out of 46 that is not unisex—either another X chromosome, making you a girl, or a **Y chromosome,** making you a boy. The Y chromosome includes a single gene that throws a master switch triggering the testes to develop and produce the principal male hormone, **testosterone.** Females also have testosterone, but less of it. The male's greater output of testosterone starts the development of external male sex organs at about the seventh week.

Another key period for sexual differentiation falls during the fourth and fifth prenatal months, when sex hormones bathe the fetal brain and influence its wiring. Different patterns for males and females develop under the influence of the male's greater testosterone and the female's ovarian hormones (Hines,

Courtesy of Nick Downes.

2004; Udry, 2000). Recent research confirms male-female differences during development in brain areas with abundant sex hormone receptors (Cahill, 2005). In adulthood, parts of the frontal lobes, an area involved in verbal fluency, are reportedly thicker in women. Part of the parietal cortex, a key area for space perception, is thicker in men. Other studies report gender differences in the hippocampus, the amygdala, and the volume of brain *gray matter* (the neural bodies) versus *white matter* (the axons and dendrites).

Given sex hormones' influence on development, what do you suppose happens when glandular malfunction or hormone injections expose a female embryo to excess testosterone? These genetically female infants are born with masculine-appearing genitals, which can either be accepted or altered surgically. Until puberty, such females tend to act in more aggressive "tomboyish" ways than do most girls, and they dress and play in ways more typical of boys than of girls (Berenbaum & Hines, 1992; Ehrhardt, 1987). Given a choice of toys, they (like boys) are more likely to play with cars and guns than with dolls and crayons. Some develop into lesbians, but most—like nearly all girls with traditionally feminine interests—become heterosexual. Moreover, the hormones do not reverse their gender identity; they view themselves as girls, not boys (Berenbaum & Bailey, 2003).

Is the tomboyish behavior of these girls due to the prenatal hormones? If so, may we conclude that biological sex differences produce behavioral gender differences? Vervet monkeys seem to suggest one answer. Male vervets, like most little boys, will spend more time playing with "masculine" toys such as trucks, and female vervets, like most little girls, will choose "feminine" toys such as dolls (Hines, 2004). Moreover, experiments with many species, from rats to monkeys, confirm that female embryos given male hormones will later exhibit a typically masculine appearance and more aggressive behavior (Hines & Green, 1991). But a more complex picture emerges when we consider social influences. Girls who were prenatally exposed to excess testosterone frequently look masculine and are known to be "different," so perhaps people also treat them more like boys. Thus, the effect of early exposure to sex hormones is both direct, in the girl's biological appearance, and indirect, in the influence of social experiences that shape her. Like a sculptor's two hands shaping a lump of clay, nature and nurture work together.

Further evidence of biology's influence on gender development comes from studies of genetic males who, despite normal male hormones and testes, are born without penises or with very small ones. In one study of 14 who underwent early sex-reassignment surgery (which is now controversial) and were raised as girls, 6 later declared themselves as males, 5 were living as females, and 3 had an unclear sexual identity (Reiner & Gearhart, 2004). In one famous case, the parents of a Canadian boy who lost his penis to a botched circumcision followed advice to raise him as a girl rather than as a damaged boy. Alas, "Brenda" Reimer was not like most other girls. "She" didn't like dolls. She tore her dresses with rough-and-tumble play. At puberty she wanted no part of kissing boys. Finally, Brenda's parents explained what had happened, whereupon this young person immediately rejected the assigned female identity, got a haircut, and chose a male name, David. He ended up marrying a woman, becoming a stepfather, and, sadly, later committing suicide (Colapinto, 2000).

"Sex matters," concludes the National Academy of Sciences (2001). In combination with the environment, sex-related genes and physiology "result in behavioral and cognitive differences between males and females."

The Nurture of Gender

Although biologically influenced, gender is also socially constructed. What biology initiates, culture accentuates.

X chromosome the sex chromosome found in both men and women. Females have two X chromosomes; males have one. An X chromosome from each parent produces a female child.

Y chromosome the sex chromosome found only in males. When paired with an X chromosome from the mother, it produces a male child.

testosterone the most important of the male sex hormones. Both males and females have it, but the additional testosterone in males stimulates the growth of the male sex organs in the fetus and the development of the male sex characteristics during puberty.

"Genes, by themselves, are like seeds dropped onto pavement: powerless to produce anything."
Primatologist Frans B. M. de Waal (1999)

"Sex brought us together, but gender drove us apart."

role a set of expectations (norms) about a social position, defining how those in the position ought to behave.

gender role a set of expected behaviors for males or for females.

gender identity our sense of being male or female.

gender typing the acquisition of a traditional masculine or feminine role.

social learning theory the theory that we learn social behavior by observing and imitating and by being rewarded or punished.

Gender Roles

Sex indeed matters. But from a biopsychosocial perspective, culture and the immediate situation matter, too. *Culture,* as we noted earlier, is everything shared by a group and transmitted across generations. We can see culture's shaping power in the social expectations that guide men's and women's behavior. In psychology, as in the theater, a **role** refers to a cluster of prescribed actions—the behaviors we expect of those who occupy a particular social position. One set of norms defines our culture's **gender roles**—our expectations about the way men and women should behave. In the United States 30 years ago, it was standard for men to initiate dates, drive the car, and pick up the check, and for women to decorate the home, buy and care for the children's clothes, and select the wedding gifts.

Gender roles exist outside the home, too. Compared with employed women, employed men in the United States spend about an hour and a half more on the job each day and about one hour less on household activities and caregiving (Amato et al., 2007; Bureau of Labor Statistics, 2004; Fisher et al., 2006). I do not have to tell you which parent, about 90 percent of the time in two-parent U.S. families, has stayed home with a sick child, arranged for the baby-sitter, or called the doctor (Maccoby, 1995). In Australia, women devote 54 percent more time to unpaid household work and 71 percent more time to child care than do men (Trewin, 2001).

Gender roles can smooth social relations, saving awkward decisions about who does the laundry this week and who mows the lawn. But they often do so at a cost: If we deviate from such conventions, we may feel anxious.

Do gender roles reflect what is biologically natural for men and women? Or do cultures construct them? Gender-role diversity over time and space indicates that culture has a big influence. Nomadic societies of food-gathering people have only a minimal division of labor by sex. Boys and girls receive much the same upbringing. In agricultural societies, where women work in the fields close to home, and men roam more freely herding livestock, children typically socialize into more distinct gender roles (Segall et al., 1990; Van Leeuwen, 1978).

Among industrialized countries, gender roles and attitudes vary widely (UNICEF, 2006). Australia and the Scandinavian countries offer the greatest gender equity, Middle Eastern and North African countries the least (Social Watch, 2006). And consider: Would you say life is more satisfying when both spouses work for pay and share child care? If so, you would agree with most people in 41 of 44 countries, according to a Pew Global Attitudes survey (2003). Even so, the culture-to-culture differences were huge, ranging from Egypt, where people disagreed 2 to 1, to Vietnam, where people agreed 11 to 1.

The gendered tsunami In Sri Lanka, Indonesia, and India, the gendered division of labor helps explain the excess of female deaths from the 2004 tsunami. In some villages, 80 percent of those killed were women, who were mostly at home while the men were more likely to be at sea fishing or doing out-of-the-home chores (Oxfam, 2005).

© DPA/The Image Works

Attitudes about gender roles also vary over time. At the opening of the twentieth century, only one country—New Zealand—granted women the right to vote (Briscoe, 1997). By the late 1960s and early 1970s, with the flick of an apron, the number of U.S. college women hoping to be full-time homemakers had plunged. And in the three decades after 1976, the percentage of women in medical, law, and psychology programs roughly doubled (**FIGURE 12.4**).

Gender ideas vary not only across cultures and over time, but also across generations. When families emigrate from Asia to Canada and the United States, their children tend to grow up with peers from a new culture. Many immigrant children, especially girls, feel torn between the competing sets of gender-role norms presented by peers and parents (Dion & Dion, 2001).

FIGURE 12.4 Women and the professions Law, medicine, and psychology have been attracting more and more women. (Data from professional associations reported by A. Cynkar, 2007.)

Gender and Child-Rearing

As society assigns each of us to a gender, the social category of male or female, the inevitable result is our strong **gender identity,** our sense of *being* male or female. To varying extents, we also become **gender typed.** That is, some boys more than others exhibit traditionally masculine traits and interests, and some girls more than others become distinctly feminine.

Social learning theory assumes that children learn gender-linked behaviors by observing and imitating and by being rewarded or punished. "Nicole, you're such a good mommy to your dolls"; "Big boys don't cry, Alex." But parental modeling and rewarding of male-female differences aren't enough to explain gender typing (Lytton & Romney, 1991). In fact, even when their families discourage traditional gender typing, children usually organize themselves into "boy worlds" and "girl worlds," each guided by rules for what boys and girls do.

Cognition (thinking) also matters. In your own childhood, as you struggled to comprehend the world, you—like other children—formed *schemas,* or concepts that helped you make sense of your world. One of these was a schema for your own gender (Bem, 1987, 1993). Your *gender schema* then became a lens through which you viewed your experiences. Social learning shapes gender schemas. Before age 1, children begin to discriminate male and female voices and faces (Martin et al., 2002). After age 2, language forces children to begin organizing their worlds on the basis of gender. English, for example, uses the pronouns *he* and *she;* other languages classify objects as masculine ("*le train*") or feminine ("*la table*").

Young children are "gender detectives," explain Carol Lynn Martin and Diane Ruble (2004). Once they grasp that two sorts of people exist—and that they are of one sort—they search for clues about gender, and they find them in language, dress, toys, and songs. Girls, they may decide, are the ones with long hair. Having divided the human world in half, 3-year-olds will then like their own sex better and seek out their own kind for play. And having compared themselves with their concept of gender, they will adjust their behavior accordingly ("I am male—thus, masculine, strong, aggressive," or "I am female—therefore, feminine, sweet, and helpful"). The rigidity of boy-girl stereotypes peaks at about age 5 or 6. If the new neighbor is a boy, a 6-year-old girl may just assume he cannot share her interests. For young children, gender looms large.

"How is it gendered?"

San Diego Museum of Man, photograph by Rose Tyson

Culture matters As this exhibit at San Diego's Museum of Man illustrates, children learn their culture. A baby's foot can step into any culture.

▶‖ Reflections on Nature and Nurture

"There are trivial truths and great truths," reflected the physicist Niels Bohr on some of the paradoxes of modern science. "The opposite of a trivial truth is plainly false. The opposite of a great truth is also true." It appears true that our ancestral history helped form us as a species. Where there is variation, natural selection, and heredity, there will be evolution. The unique gene combination created when our mother's egg engulfed our father's sperm predisposed both our shared humanity and our individual differences. This is a great truth about human nature. Genes form us.

But it also is true that our experiences form us. In our families and in our peer relationships, we learn ways of thinking and acting. Differences initiated by our nature may be amplified by our nurture. If their genes and hormones predispose males to be more physically aggressive than females, culture may magnify this gender difference through norms that encourage males to be macho and females to be the kinder, gentler sex. If men are encouraged toward roles that demand physical power, and women toward more nurturing roles, each may then exhibit the actions expected of those who fill such roles and find themselves shaped accordingly. Roles remake their players. Presidents in time become more presidential, servants more servile. Gender roles similarly shape us.

But gender roles are converging. Brute strength has become increasingly irrelevant to power and status (think Bill Gates and Oprah Winfrey). Thus both women and men are now seen as "fully capable of effectively carrying out organizational roles at all levels," note Wendy Wood and Alice Eagly (2002). And as women's employment in formerly male occupations has increased, gender differences in traditional masculinity or femininity and in what one seeks in a mate have diminished (Twenge, 1997). As the roles we play change over time, we change with them.

* * *

If nature and nurture jointly form us, are we "nothing but" the product of nature and nurture? Are we rigidly determined?

We *are* the product of nature and nurture (**FIGURE 12.5**), but we are also an open system. Genes are all-pervasive but not all-powerful; people may defy their genetic

FIGURE 12.5 The biopsychosocial approach to development

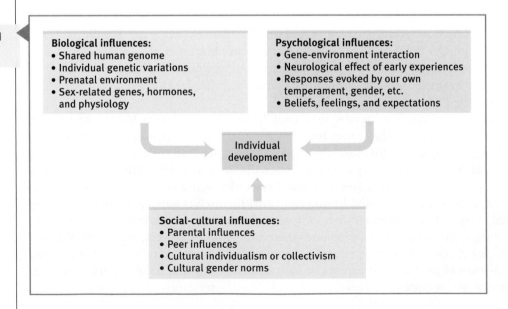

Biological influences:
• Shared human genome
• Individual genetic variations
• Prenatal environment
• Sex-related genes, hormones, and physiology

Psychological influences:
• Gene-environment interaction
• Neurological effect of early experiences
• Responses evoked by our own temperament, gender, etc.
• Beliefs, feelings, and expectations

Individual development

Social-cultural influences:
• Parental influences
• Peer influences
• Cultural individualism or collectivism
• Cultural gender norms

bent to reproduce, by electing celibacy. Culture, too, is all-pervasive but not all-powerful; people may defy peer pressures and do the opposite of the expected. To excuse our failings by blaming our nature and nurture is what philosopher-novelist Jean-Paul Sartre called "bad faith"—attributing responsibility for one's fate to bad genes or bad influences.

In reality, we are both the creatures and the creators of our worlds. We are—it is a great truth—the products of our genes and environments. Nevertheless (another great truth) the stream of causation that shapes the future runs through our present choices. Our decisions today design our environments tomorrow. Mind matters. The human environment is not like the weather—something that just happens. We are its architects. Our hopes, goals, and expectations influence our future. And that is what enables cultures to vary and to change so quickly.

* * *

I know from my mail and from public opinion surveys that some readers feel troubled by the naturalism and evolutionism of contemporary science. Readers from other nations bear with me, but in the United States there is a wide gulf between scientific and lay thinking about evolution. "The idea that human minds are the product of evolution is . . . unassailable fact," declared a 2007 editorial in *Nature,* a leading science magazine. That sentiment concurs with a 2006 statement of "evidence-based facts" about evolution jointly issued by the national science academies of 66 nations (IAP, 2006). In *The Language of God,* Human Genome Project director Francis Collins (2006, pp. 141, 146), a self-described evangelical Christian, compiles the "utterly compelling" evidence that leads him to conclude that Darwin's big idea is "unquestionably correct." Yet a 2007 Gallup survey reports that half of U.S. adults do not believe in evolution's role in "how human beings came to exist on Earth" (Newport, 2007). Many of those who dispute the scientific story worry that a science of behavior (and evolutionary science in particular) will destroy our sense of the beauty, mystery, and spiritual significance of the human creature. For those concerned, I offer some reassuring thoughts.

When Isaac Newton explained the rainbow in terms of light of differing wavelengths, the poet Keats feared that Newton had destroyed the rainbow's mysterious beauty. Yet, notes Richard Dawkins (1998) in *Unweaving the Rainbow,* Newton's analysis led to an even deeper mystery—Einstein's theory of special relativity. Moreover, nothing about Newton's optics need diminish our appreciation for the dramatic elegance of a rainbow arching across a brightening sky.

When Galileo assembled evidence that the Earth revolved around the Sun, not vice versa, he did not offer irrefutable proof for his theory. Rather, he offered a coherent explanation for a variety of observations, such as the changing shadows cast by the Moon's mountains. His explanation eventually won the day because it described and explained things in a way that made sense, that hung together. Darwin's theory of evolution likewise is a coherent view of natural history. It offers an organizing principle that unifies various observations.

Francis Collins is not the only person of faith to find the scientific idea of human origins congenial with his spirituality. In the fifth century, St. Augustine (quoted by Wilford, 1999) wrote, "The universe was brought into being in a less than fully formed state, but was gifted with the capacity to transform itself from unformed matter into a truly marvelous array of structures and life forms." Some 1600 years later, Pope John Paul II in 1996 welcomed a science-religion dialogue, finding it noteworthy that evolutionary theory "has been progressively accepted by researchers, following a series of discoveries in various fields of knowledge."

Meanwhile, many people of science are awestruck at the emerging understanding of the universe and the human creature. It boggles the mind—the entire universe

"Let's hope that it's not true; but if it is true, let's hope that it doesn't become widely known."

Lady Ashley, commenting on Darwin's theory

"Is it not stirring to understand how the world actually works—that white light is made of colors, that color measures light waves, that transparent air reflects light . . . ? It does no harm to the romance of the sunset to know a little about it."

Carl Sagan, *Skies of Other Worlds,* 1988

popping out of a point some 14 billion years ago, and instantly inflating to cosmological size. Had the energy of this Big Bang been the tiniest bit less, the universe would have collapsed back on itself. Had it been the tiniest bit more, the result would have been a soup too thin to support life. Astronomer Sir Martin Rees has described *Just Six Numbers* (1999), any one of which, if changed ever so slightly, would produce a cosmos in which life could not exist. Had gravity been a tad bit stronger or weaker, or had the weight of a carbon proton been a wee bit different, our universe just wouldn't have worked.

What caused this almost-too-good-to-be-true, finely tuned universe? Why is there something rather than nothing? How did it come to be, in the words of Harvard-Smithsonian astrophysicist Owen Gingerich (1999), "so extraordinarily right, that it seemed the universe had been expressly designed to produce intelligent, sentient beings"? Is there a benevolent superintelligence behind it all? Have there instead been an infinite number of universes born and we just happen to be the lucky inhabitants of one that, by chance, was exquisitely fine-tuned to give birth to us? Or does that idea violate *Occam's razor,* the principle that we should prefer the simplest of competing explanations? On such matters, a humble, awed, scientific silence is appropriate, suggested philosopher Ludwig Wittgenstein: "Whereof one cannot speak, thereof one must be silent."

Rather than fearing science, we can welcome its enlarging our understanding and awakening our sense of awe. In *The Fragile Species,* Lewis Thomas (1992) described his utter amazement that the Earth in time gave rise to bacteria and eventually to Bach's Mass in B Minor. In a short 4 billion years, life on Earth has come from nothing to structures as complex as a 6-billion-unit strand of DNA and the incomprehensible intricacy of the human brain. Atoms no different from those in a rock somehow formed dynamic entities that became conscious. Nature, says cosmologist Paul Davies (2007), seems cunningly and ingeniously devised to produce extraordinary, self-replicating, information-processing systems—us. Although we appear to have been created from dust, over eons of time, the end result is a priceless creature, one rich with potential beyond our imagining.

"The causes of life's history [cannot] resolve the riddle of life's meaning."
Stephen Jay Gould, *Rocks of Ages: Science and Religion in the Fullness of Life,* 1999

REVIEW

Environmental Influences on Behavior

12-1 **To what extent are our lives shaped by early stimulation, by parents, and by peers?** During maturation, a child's brain changes as neural connections increase in areas associated with stimulating activity, and unused synapses degenerate. Parents influence their children in areas such as manners and political and religious beliefs, but not in other areas, such as personality. Language and other behaviors are shaped by peer groups, as children adjust to fit in. By choosing their children's neighborhoods and schools, parents can exert some influence over peer group culture.

12-2 **How do cultural norms affect our behavior?** Cultural *norms* are rules for accepted and expected behaviors, ideas, attitudes, and values. Across places and over time *cultures* differ in their norms. Despite such cultural variations, we humans share many common forces that influence behavior.

12-3 **How do individualist and collectivist cultural influences affect people?** Cultures based on self-reliant *individualism,* like those of most of the United States, Canada, Australia, and Western Europe, value personal independence and individual achievement. Identity is defined in terms of self-esteem, personal goals and attributes, and personal rights and liberties. Cultures based on socially connected *collectivism,* like those of many parts of Asia and Africa, value interdependence, tradition, and harmony, and they define identity in terms of group goals and commitments and belonging to one's group. Within any culture, the degree of individualism or collectivism varies from person to person.

12-4 **What are some ways in which males and females tend to be alike and to differ?** Human males and females are more alike than different, thanks to their similar genetic makeup. Regardless of our gender, we see, hear, learn, and remember similarly. Males and females do differ in body fat, muscle, height, age of onset of puberty, and life expectancy; in vulnerability to certain disorders; and in *aggression,* social power, and social connectedness.

12-5 **How do nature and nurture together form our gender?** Biological sex is determined by the twenty-third pair of chromosomes, to which the mother contributes an *X chromosome* and the father either an X (producing a female) or a *Y chromosome* (producing a male). A Y chromosome triggers additional *testosterone* release and male sex organs. Gender refers to the characteristics, whether biologically or socially influenced, by which people define male and female. Sex-related genes and hormones influence gender differences in behavior, possibly by influencing brain development. We also learn *gender roles,* which vary with culture, across place and time. *Social learning theory* proposes that we learn *gender identity* as we learn other things—through reinforcement, punishment, and observation.

Terms and Concepts to Remember

culture, p. 151	Y chromosome, p. 160
norm, p. 152	testosterone, p. 160
personal space, p. 153	role, p. 162
individualism, p. 154	gender role, p. 162
collectivism, p. 154	gender identity, p. 163
aggression, p. 158	gender typing, p. 163
X chromosome, p. 160	social learning theory, p. 163

Test Yourself

1. To predict whether a teenager smokes, ask how many of the teen's friends smoke. One explanation for this correlation is peer influence. What's another?

2. How do individualist and collectivist cultures differ?

3. What are gender roles, and what do their variations tell us about our human capacity for learning and adaptation?

4. How does the biopsychosocial approach explain our individual development?

(Answers to the Test Yourself questions can be found in Appendix B at the end of the book.)

Ask Yourself

1. To what extent, and in what ways, have your peers and your parents helped shape who you are?

2. What concept best describes you—collectivist or individualist? Do you fit completely in either category, or are you sometimes a collectivist and sometimes an individualist?

3. Do you consider yourself strongly gender typed or *not* strongly gender typed? What factors do you think have contributed to your feelings of masculinity or femininity?

4. How have your heredity and your environment influenced who you are today? Can you recall an important time when you determined your own fate in a way that was at odds with pressure you felt from either your heredity or your environment?

∞ WEB

Multiple-choice self-tests and more may be found at www.worthpublishers.com/myers

Developing Through the Life Span

As we journey through life—from womb to tomb—when and how do we develop? Virtually all of us began walking around age 1 and talking by age 2. As children, we engaged in social play in preparation for life's work. As adults, we all smile and cry, love and loathe, and occasionally ponder the fact that someday we will die. As reflected in these modules, **developmental psychology** examines how people are continually developing—physically, cognitively, and socially—from infancy through old age. Much of its research centers on three major issues:

1. **Nature/nurture:** How do genetic inheritance (*our nature*) and experience (*the nurture we receive*) influence our development?

2. **Continuity/stages:** Is development a gradual, continuous process like riding an escalator, or does it proceed through a sequence of separate stages, like climbing rungs on a ladder?

3. **Stability/change:** Do our early personality traits persist through life, or do we become different persons as we age?

In other modules, we engage the nature/nurture issue. At the end of the modules in this part, we reflect on the continuity and stability issues throughout the life span.

MODULES

13
Prenatal Development and the Newborn

14
Infancy and Childhood

15
Adolescence

16
Adulthood, and Reflections on Developmental Issues

Courtesy of Christine Brune

"Nature is all that a man brings with him into the world; nurture is every influence that affects him after his birth."

Francis Galton,
English Men of Science, 1874

developmental psychology a branch of psychology that studies physical, cognitive, and social change throughout the life span.

Conception

Prenatal Development

The Competent Newborn

MODULE 13

Prenatal Development and the Newborn

13-1 How does life develop before birth?

▶‖ Conception

Nothing is more natural than a species reproducing itself. Yet nothing is more wondrous. With humans, the process starts when a woman's ovary releases a mature egg—a cell roughly the size of the period at the end of this sentence. The woman was born with all the immature eggs she would ever have, although only 1 in 5000 will ever mature and be released. A man, in contrast, begins producing sperm cells at puberty. For the rest of his life, 24 hours a day, he will be a nonstop sperm factory, although the rate of production—in the beginning more than 1000 sperm during the second it takes to read this phrase—will slow with age.

Like space voyagers approaching a huge planet, the 200 million or more deposited sperm begin their race upstream, approaching a cell 85,000 times their own size. The relatively few reaching the egg release digestive enzymes that eat away its protective coating (**FIGURE 13.1**). As soon as one sperm begins to penetrate and is welcomed in, the egg's surface blocks out the others. Before half a day elapses, the egg nucleus and the sperm nucleus fuse. The two have become one. Consider it your most fortunate of moments. Among 200 million sperm, the one needed to make you, in combination with that one particular egg, won the race.

FIGURE 13.1 Life is sexually transmitted (a) Sperm cells surround an ovum. (b) As one sperm penetrates the egg's jellylike outer coating, a series of chemical events begins that will cause sperm and egg to fuse into a single cell. If all goes well, that cell will subdivide again and again to emerge 9 months later as a 100-trillion-cell human being.

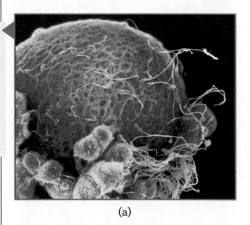
(a)

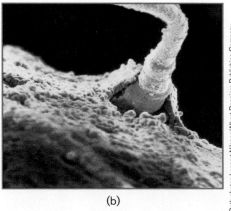
(b)

Both photos Lennart Nilsson/Albert Bonniers Publishing Company

▶‖ Prenatal Development

Fewer than half of all fertilized eggs, called **zygotes,** survive beyond the first 2 weeks (Grobstein, 1979; Hall, 2004). But for you and me, good fortune prevailed. One cell became 2, then 4—each just like the first—until this cell division produced a zygote of some 100 cells within the first week. Then the cells began to differentiate—to specialize in structure and function. How identical cells do this—as if one decides "I'll become a brain, you become intestines!"—is a puzzle that scientists are just beginning to solve.

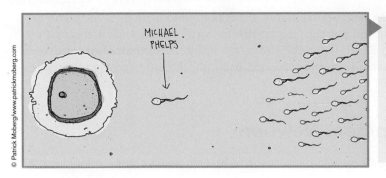

MICHAEL PHELPS

First known photo of Michael Phelps (If the playful cartoonist were to convey literal truth, a second arrow would also point to the egg that contributed the other half of Michael Phelps' genes.)

zygote the fertilized egg; it enters a 2-week period of rapid cell division and develops into an embryo.

embryo the developing human organism from about 2 weeks after fertilization through the second month.

fetus the developing human organism from 9 weeks after conception to birth.

teratogens agents, such as chemicals and viruses, that can reach the embryo or fetus during prenatal development and cause harm.

About 10 days after conception, the zygote attaches to the mother's uterine wall, beginning approximately 37 weeks of the closest human relationship. The zygote's inner cells become the **embryo** (**FIGURE 13.2a**). Over the next 6 weeks, organs begin to form and function. The heart begins to beat.

By 9 weeks after conception, the embryo looks unmistakably human (**FIGURE 13.2c**). It is now a **fetus** (Latin for "offspring" or "young one"). During the sixth month, organs such as the stomach have developed enough to allow a prematurely born fetus a chance of survival. At this point, the fetus is also responsive to sound (Hepper, 2005). Microphone readings taken inside the uterus have revealed that the fetus is exposed to the sound of its mother's muffled voice (Ecklund-Flores, 1992). Immediately after birth, when newborns emerge from living 38 or so weeks underwater, they prefer this voice to another woman's or to their father's voice (Busnel et al., 1992; DeCasper et al., 1984, 1986, 1994).

At each prenatal stage, genetic *and* environmental factors affect our development. The *placenta,* which formed as the zygote's outer cells attached to the uterine wall, transfers nutrients and oxygen from mother to fetus. The placenta also screens out many potentially harmful substances. But some substances slip by, including **teratogens,** which are harmful agents such as viruses and drugs. If the mother carries the HIV virus, her baby may also. If she is a heroin addict, her baby will be born a heroin addict. A pregnant woman never smokes alone; she and her fetus both experience reduced blood oxygen and a shot of nicotine. If she is a heavy smoker, her fetus may receive fewer nutrients and be born underweight and at risk for various problems (Pringle et al., 2005).

There is no known safe amount of alcohol during pregnancy. Alcohol enters the woman's bloodstream—and her fetus'—and depresses activity in both their central nervous systems. A pregnant mother's alcohol use may prime her offspring to like alcohol. Teens whose mothers drank when pregnant are at risk for heavy drinking and alcohol dependence. In experiments, when pregnant rats drink alcohol, their young offspring later display a liking for alcohol's odor (Youngentob et al., 2007). Even light

|| Prenatal development

zygote: conception to 2 weeks

embryo: 2 weeks through 8 weeks

fetus: 9 weeks to birth ||

FIGURE 13.2 Prenatal development (a) The embryo grows and develops rapidly. At 40 days, the spine is visible and the arms and legs are beginning to grow. (b) Five days later, the inch-long embryo's proportions have begun to change. The rest of the body is now bigger than the head, and the arms and legs have grown noticeably. (c) By the end of the second month, when the fetal period begins, facial features, hands, and feet have formed. (d) As the fetus enters the fourth month, its 3 ounces could fit in the palm of your hand.

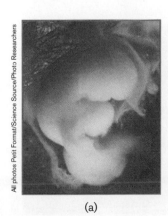

(a)

(b)

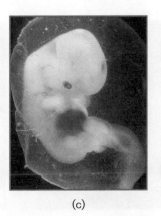

(c)

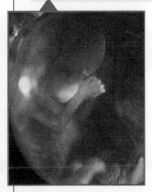

(d)

fetal alcohol syndrome (FAS) physical and cognitive abnormalities in children caused by a pregnant woman's heavy drinking. In severe cases, symptoms include noticeable facial misproportions.

habituation decreasing responsiveness with repeated stimulation. As infants gain familiarity with repeated exposure to a visual stimulus, their interest wanes and they look away sooner.

drinking can affect the fetal brain (Braun, 1996; Ikonomidou et al., 2000), and persistent heavy drinking will put the fetus at risk for birth defects and intellectual disability. For 1 in about 800 infants, the effects are visible as **fetal alcohol syndrome (FAS),** marked by a small, misproportioned head and lifelong brain abnormalities (May & Gossage, 2001).

▶‖ The Competent Newborn

13-2   What are some newborn abilities, and how do researchers explore infants' mental abilities?

Having survived prenatal hazards, we as newborns came equipped with automatic responses ideally suited for our survival. We withdrew our limbs to escape pain. If a cloth over our face interfered with our breathing, we turned our head from side to side and swiped at it.

New parents are often in awe of the coordinated sequence of reflexes by which their baby gets food. When something touches their cheek, babies turn toward that touch, open their mouth, and vigorously *root* for a nipple. Finding one, they automatically close on it and begin *sucking*—which itself requires a coordinated sequence of reflexive *tonguing, swallowing,* and *breathing.* Failing to find satisfaction, the hungry baby may *cry*—a behavior parents find highly unpleasant and very rewarding to relieve.

The pioneering American psychologist William James presumed that the newborn experiences a "blooming, buzzing confusion." Until the 1960s, few people disagreed. It was said that, apart from a blur of meaningless light and dark shades, newborns could not see. But then scientists discovered that babies can tell you a lot—if you know how to ask. To ask, you must capitalize on what babies can do—gaze, suck, turn their heads. So, equipped with eye-tracking machines and pacifiers wired to electronic gear, researchers set out to answer parents' age-old questions: What can my baby see, hear, smell, and think?

One technique developmental researchers use to answer such questions is a simple form of learning called **habituation**—a decrease in responding with repeated stimulation. A novel stimulus gets attention when first presented. But the more often the stimulus is presented, the weaker the response becomes. This seeming boredom with familiar stimuli gives us a way to ask infants what they see and remember.

Janine Spencer, Paul Quinn, and their colleagues (1997; Quinn, 2002) used a *novelty-preference procedure* to ask 4-month-olds how they recognize cats and dogs. The researchers first showed the infants a series of images of cats or dogs. Which of the two animals in **FIGURE 13.3** do you think the infants would find more novel (measured in

Prepared to feed and eat
Animals are predisposed to respond to their offsprings' cries for nourishment.

looking time) after seeing a series of cats? It was the hybrid animal with the dog's head (or with a cat's head, if they had previously viewed a series of dogs). This suggests that infants, like adults, focus first on the face, not the body.

Indeed, we are born preferring sights and sounds that facilitate social responsiveness. As newborns, we turn our heads in the direction of human voices. We gaze longer at a drawing of a facelike image (**FIGURE 13.4**) than at a bull's-eye pattern; yet we gaze more at a bull's-eye pattern—which has contrasts much like those of the human eye—than at a solid disk (Fantz, 1961). We prefer to look at objects 8 to 12 inches away. Wonder of wonders, that just happens to be the approximate distance between a nursing infant's eyes and its mother's (Maurer & Maurer, 1988).

Within days after birth, our brain's neural networks were stamped with the smell of our mother's body. Thus, a week-old nursing baby, placed between a gauze pad from its mother's bra and one from another nursing mother, will usually turn toward the smell of its own mother's pad (MacFarlane, 1978). At 3 weeks, if given a pacifier that sometimes turns on recordings of its mother's voice and sometimes that of a female stranger's, an infant will suck more vigorously when it hears its now-familiar mother's voice (Mills & Melhuish, 1974). So not only could we as young infants see what we needed to see, and smell and hear well, we were already using our sensory equipment to learn.

FIGURE 13.3 **Quick—which is the cat?** Researchers used cat-dog hybrid images such as these to test how infants categorize animals.

FIGURE 13.4 **Newborns' preference for faces** When shown these two stimuli with the same elements, Italian newborns spent nearly twice as many seconds looking at the facelike image (Johnson & Morton, 1991). Canadian newborns—average age 53 minutes in one study—display the same apparently inborn preference to look toward faces (Mondloch et al., 1999).

REVIEW

Prenatal Development and the Newborn

13-1 **How does life develop before birth?** *Developmental psychologists* study physical, mental, and social changes throughout the life span. The life cycle begins at conception, when one sperm cell unites with an egg to form a *zygote*. Attached to the uterine wall, the developing *embryo's* body organs begin to form and function. By 9 weeks, the *fetus* is recognizably human. *Teratogens* are potentially harmful agents that can pass through the placental screen and harm the developing embryo or fetus, as happens with *fetal alcohol syndrome*.

13-2 **What are some newborn abilities, and how do researchers explore infants' mental abilities?** Newborns are born with sensory equipment and reflexes that facilitate their survival and their social interactions with adults. For example, they quickly learn to discriminate their mother's smell and sound. Researchers use techniques that test *habituation,* such as the novelty-preference procedure, to explore infants' abilities.

Terms and Concepts to Remember

developmental psychology, p. 169

zygote, p. 170

embryo, p. 171

fetus, p. 171

teratogens, p. 171

fetal alcohol syndrome (FAS), p. 172

habituation, p. 172

Test Yourself

1. Your friend—a regular drinker—hopes to become pregnant soon and has stopped drinking. Why is this a good idea? What negative effects might alcohol consumed during pregnancy have on a developing fetus?

(Answers to the Test Yourself questions can be found in Appendix B at the end of the book.)

Ask Yourself

1. Are you surprised by the news of infants' competencies? Or did you "know it all along"?

∞ WEB

Multiple-choice self-tests and more may be found at www.worthpublishers.com/myers

MODULE 14

Infancy and Childhood

During infancy, a baby grows from newborn to toddler, and during childhood from toddler to teenager. We all traveled this path, developing physically, cognitively, and socially. From infancy on, brain and mind—neural hardware and cognitive software—develop together.

▶‖ Physical Development

14-1 During infancy and childhood, how do the brain and motor skills develop?

Brain Development

In your mother's womb, your developing brain formed nerve cells at the explosive rate of nearly one-quarter million per minute. The developing brain cortex actually overproduces neurons, with the number peaking at 28 weeks and then subsiding to a stable 23 billion or so at birth (Rabinowicz et al., 1996, 1999; de Courten-Myers, 2002). On the day you were born, you had most of the brain cells you would ever have. However, your nervous system was immature: After birth, the branching neural networks that eventually enabled you to walk, talk, and remember had a wild growth spurt (**FIGURE 14.1**). From ages 3 to 6, the most rapid growth was in your frontal lobes, which enable rational planning. This helps explain why preschoolers display a rapidly developing ability to control their attention and behavior (Garon et al., 2008).

The association areas—those linked with thinking, memory, and language—are the last cortical areas to develop. As they do, mental abilities surge (Chugani & Phelps, 1986; Thatcher et al., 1987). Fiber pathways supporting language and agility proliferate into puberty, after which a *pruning process* shuts down excess connections and strengthens others (Paus et al., 1999; Thompson et al., 2000).

As a flower unfolds in accord with its genetic instructions, so do we, in the orderly sequence of biological growth processes called **maturation.** Maturation decrees many of our commonalities—from standing before walking, to using nouns before adjectives. Severe deprivation or abuse can retard development, and ample parental experiences of talking and reading will help sculpt neural connections. Yet the genetic growth tendencies are inborn. Maturation sets the basic course of development; experience adjusts it.

maturation biological growth processes that enable orderly changes in behavior, relatively uninfluenced by experience.

FIGURE 14.1 Drawings of human cerebral cortex sections In humans, the brain is immature at birth. As the child matures, the neural networks grow increasingly more complex.

At birth   3 months   15 months

Motor Development

The developing brain enables physical coordination. As an infant's muscles and nervous system mature, more complicated skills emerge. With occasional exceptions, the sequence of physical (motor) development is universal. Babies roll over before they sit unsupported, and they usually creep on all fours before they walk (**FIGURE 14.2**). These behaviors reflect not imitation but a maturing nervous system; blind children, too, crawl before they walk.

There are, however, individual differences in timing. In the United States, for example, 25 percent of all babies walk by age 11 months, 50 percent within a week after their first birthday, and 90 percent by age 15 months (Frankenburg et al., 1992). The recommended infant *back-to-sleep position* (putting babies to sleep on their backs to reduce the risk of a smothering crib death) has been associated with somewhat later crawling but not with later walking (Davis et al., 1998; Lipsitt, 2003).

Genes play a major role in motor development. Identical twins typically begin sitting up and walking on nearly the same day (Wilson, 1979). Maturation—including the rapid development of the cerebellum at the back of the brain—creates our readiness to learn walking at about age 1. Experience before that time has a limited effect. This is true for other physical skills, including bowel and bladder control. Before necessary muscular and neural maturation, don't expect pleading or punishment to produce successful toilet training.

"This is the path to adulthood. You're here."

‖ In the eight years following the 1994 launch of a U.S. "Back to Sleep" educational campaign, the number of infants sleeping on their stomachs dropped from 70 to 11 percent—and SIDS (Sudden Infant Death Syndrome) deaths fell by half (Braiker, 2005). ‖

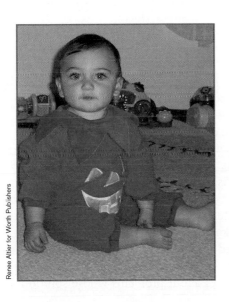

FIGURE 14.2 Triumphant toddlers
Sit, crawl, walk, run—the sequence of these motor development milestones is the same the world around, though babies reach them at varying ages.

Maturation and Infant Memory

Our earliest memories seldom predate our third birthday. We see this *infantile amnesia* in the memories of some preschoolers who experienced an emergency fire evacuation caused by a burning popcorn maker. Seven years later, they were able to recall the alarm and what caused it—*if* they were 4 to 5 years old at the time. Those experiencing the event as 3-year-olds could not remember the cause and usually misrecalled being already outside when the alarm sounded (Pillemer, 1995). Other studies confirm that the average age of earliest conscious memory is 3.5 years (Bauer, 2002). By 4 to 5 years, childhood amnesia is giving way to remembered experiences (Bruce et al., 2000). But even into adolescence, the brain areas underlying memory, such as the hippocampus and frontal lobes, continue to mature (Bauer, 2007).

Although we *consciously* recall little from before age 4, our memory was processing information during those early years. In 1965, while finishing her doctoral work, Carolyn Rovee-Collier observed an infant memory. She was also a new mom, whose

‖ Can you recall your first day of preschool (or your third birthday party)? ‖

Michael Newman/PhotoEdit

FIGURE 14.3 Infant at work Babies only 3 months old can learn that kicking moves a mobile, and they can retain that learning for a month. (From Rovee-Collier, 1989, 1997.)

"Who knows the thoughts of a child?"
Poet Nora Perry

"Childhood has its own way of seeing, thinking, and feeling, and there is nothing more foolish than the attempt to put ours in its place."
Philosopher Jean-Jacques Rousseau, 1798

cognition all the mental activities associated with thinking, knowing, remembering, and communicating.

schema a concept or framework that organizes and interprets information.

assimilation interpreting our new experience in terms of our existing schemas.

accommodation adapting our current understandings (schemas) to incorporate new information.

colicky 2-month-old, Benjamin, could be calmed by moving a crib mobile. Weary of bonking the mobile, she strung a cloth ribbon connecting the mobile to Benjamin's foot. Soon, he was kicking his foot to move the mobile. Thinking about her unintended home experiment, Rovee-Collier realized that, contrary to popular opinion at that time, babies are capable of learning. To know for sure that little Benjamin wasn't just a whiz kid, Rovee-Collier had to repeat the experiment with other infants (Rovee-Collier, 1989, 1999). Sure enough, they, too, soon kicked more when linked to a mobile, both on the day of the experiment and the day after. They had learned the link between moving legs and moving mobile. If, however, she hitched them to a different mobile the next day, the infants showed no learning. Their actions indicated that they remembered the original mobile and recognized the difference. Moreover, when tethered to a familiar mobile a month later, they remembered the association and again began kicking (**FIGURE 14.3**).

Evidence of early processing also appeared in a study in which 10-year-olds were shown photos of preschoolers and asked to spot their former classmates. Although they consciously recognized only 1 in 5 of their onetime compatriots, their physiological responses (measured as skin perspiration) were greater to their former classmates whether or not they consciously recognized them (Newcombe et al., 2000). What the conscious mind does not know and cannot express in words, the nervous system somehow remembers.

▶‖ Cognitive Development

14-2 From the perspective of Piaget and of today's researchers, how does a child's mind develop?

Cognition refers to all the mental activities associated with thinking, knowing, remembering, and communicating. Somewhere on your precarious journey "from egghood to personhood" (Broks, 2007), you became conscious. When was that, and how did your mind unfold from there? Developmental psychologist Jean Piaget (pronounced Pee-ah-ZHAY) spent his life searching for the answers to such questions. His interest began in 1920, when he was in Paris developing questions for children's intelligence tests. While administering the tests, Piaget became intrigued by children's *wrong* answers, which, he noted, were often strikingly similar among children of a given age. Where others saw childish mistakes, Piaget saw intelligence at work.

A half-century spent with children convinced Piaget that a child's mind is not a miniature model of an adult's. Thanks partly to his work, we now understand that children reason *differently,* in "wildly illogical ways about problems whose solutions are self-evident to adults" (Brainerd, 1996).

Bill Anderson/Photo Researchers, Inc.

Jean Piaget (1896–1980) "If we examine the intellectual development of the individual or of the whole of humanity, we shall find that the human spirit goes through a certain number of stages, each different from the other" (1930).

Both photos: Courtesy Judy DeLoache

FIGURE 14.4 Scale errors
Psychologists Judy DeLoache, David Uttal, and Karl Rosengren (2004) report that 18- to 30-month-old children may fail to take the size of an object into account when trying to perform impossible actions with it. At left, a 21-month-old attempts to slide down a miniature slide. At right, a 24-month-old opens the door to a miniature car and tries to step inside.

Piaget's studies led him to believe that a child's mind develops through a series of stages, in an upward march from the newborn's simple reflexes to the adult's abstract reasoning power. Thus, an 8-year-old can comprehend things a toddler cannot, such as the analogy that "getting an idea is like having a light turn on in your head," or that a miniature slide is too small for sliding, and a miniature car is much too small to get into (**FIGURE 14.4**). But our adult minds likewise engage in reasoning uncomprehended by 8-year-olds.

Piaget's core idea is that the driving force behind our intellectual progression is an unceasing struggle to make sense of our experiences: "Children are active thinkers, constantly trying to construct more advanced understandings of the world" (Siegler & Ellis, 1996). To this end, the maturing brain builds **schemas,** concepts or mental molds into which we pour our experiences (**FIGURE 14.5**). By adulthood we have built countless schemas, ranging from *cats* and *dogs* to our concept of *love.*

To explain how we use and adjust our schemas, Piaget proposed two more concepts. First, we **assimilate** new experiences—we interpret them in terms of our current understandings (schemas). Having a simple schema for *cow,* for example, a toddler may call all four-legged animals *cows.* But as we interact with the world, we also adjust, or **accommodate,** our schemas to incorporate information provided by new experiences. Thus, the child soon learns that the original *cow* schema is too broad and accommodates by refining the category (**FIGURE 14.6**).

FIGURE 14.5 An impossible object
Look carefully at the "devil's tuning fork" below. Now look away—no, better first study it some more—and then look away and draw it. . . . Not so easy, is it? Because this tuning fork is an impossible object, you have no schema for such an image.

FIGURE 14.6 Pouring experience into mental molds We use our existing schemas to *assimilate* new experiences. But sometimes we need to *accommodate* (adjust) our schemas to include new experiences.

Two-year-old Gabriella has learned the schema for *cow* from her picture books.

Gabriella sees a moose and calls it a "cow." She is trying to assimilate this new animal into an existing schema. Her mother tells her, "No, it's a moose."

Gabriella accommodates her schema for large, shaggy animals and continues to modify that schema to include "mommy moose," "baby moose," and so forth.

sensorimotor stage in Piaget's theory, the stage (from birth to about 2 years of age) during which infants know the world mostly in terms of their sensory impressions and motor activities.

object permanence the awareness that things continue to exist even when not perceived.

Piaget believed that as children construct their understandings while interacting with the world, they experience spurts of change, followed by greater stability as they move from one cognitive plateau to the next. He viewed these plateaus as forming stages. Let's consider Piaget's stages now, in the light of current thinking.

Piaget's Theory and Current Thinking

Piaget proposed that children progress through four stages of cognitive development, each with distinctive characteristics that permit specific kinds of thinking (TABLE 14.1).

TABLE 14.1 **Piaget's Stages of Cognitive Development**

Typical Age Range	Description of Stage	Developmental Phenomena
Birth to nearly 2 years	*Sensorimotor* Experiencing the world through senses and actions (looking, hearing, touching, mouthing, and grasping)	• Object permanence • Stranger anxiety
2 to about 6 or 7 years	*Preoperational* Representing things with words and images; using intuitive rather than logical reasoning	• Pretend play • Egocentrism
About 7 to 11 years	*Concrete operational* Thinking logically about concrete events; grasping concrete analogies and performing arithmetical operations	• Conservation • Mathematical transformations
About 12 through adulthood	*Formal operational* Abstract reasoning	• Abstract logic • Potential for mature moral reasoning

Milt and Patti Putnam/Corbis

Sensorimotor Stage

In the **sensorimotor stage,** from birth to nearly age 2, babies take in the world through their senses and actions—through looking, hearing, touching, mouthing, and grasping.

Very young babies seem to live in the present: Out of sight is out of mind. In one test, Piaget showed an infant an appealing toy and then flopped his beret over it. Before the age of 6 months, the infant acted as if it ceased to exist. Young infants lack **object permanence**—the awareness that objects continue to exist when not perceived (FIGURE 14.7). By 8 months, infants begin exhibiting memory for things no longer

FIGURE 14.7 Object permanence Infants younger than 6 months seldom understand that things continue to exist when they are out of sight. But for this infant, out of sight is definitely not out of mind.

Doug Goodman

seen. If you hide a toy, the infant will momentarily look for it. Within another month or two, the infant will look for it even after being restrained for several seconds.

But does object permanence in fact blossom at 8 months, much as tulips blossom in spring? Today's researchers see development as more continuous than Piaget did, and they believe object permanence unfolds gradually. Even young infants will at least momentarily look for a toy where they saw it hidden a second before (Wang et al., 2004).

Researchers believe Piaget and his followers underestimated young children's competence. Consider some simple experiments that demonstrate baby logic:

▶ Like adults staring in disbelief at a magic trick (the "Whoa!" look), infants look longer at an unexpected and unfamiliar scene of a car seeming to pass through a solid object, a ball stopping in midair, or an object violating object permanence by magically disappearing (Baillargeon, 1995, 2008; Wellman & Gelman, 1992). In another clever experiment, Sarah Shuwairi and her colleagues (2007) exposed 4-month-olds to a picture of a cube (**FIGURE 14.8**) with one small area covered. After the infants had habituated to this image, they stared longer when shown an impossible rather than possible version of the cube. Babies, it seems, have a more intuitive grasp of simple laws of physics than Piaget realized.

▶ Babies also have a head for numbers. Karen Wynn (1992, 2000) showed 5-month-olds one or two objects. Then she hid the objects behind a screen, and visibly removed or added one (**FIGURE 14.9**). When she lifted the screen, the infants sometimes did a double take, staring longer when shown a wrong number of objects. But were they just responding to a greater or smaller mass of objects, rather than a change in number (Feigenson et al., 2002)? Later experiments showed that babies' number sense extends to larger numbers and such things as drumbeats and motions (McCrink & Wynn, 2004; Spelke & Kinzler, 2007; Wynn et al., 2002). If accustomed to a Daffy Duck puppet jumping three times on stage, they show surprise if it jumps only twice. Clearly, infants are smarter than Piaget appreciated. Even as babies, we had a lot on our minds.

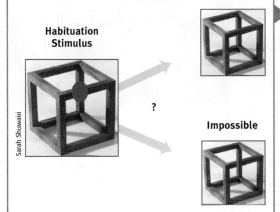

Sarah Shuwairi

FIGURE 14.8 Infants can discriminate between possible and impossible objects After habituating to the stimulus on the left, 4-month-olds stared longer if shown the impossible version of the cube—where one of the back vertical bars crosses over a front horizontal bar (Shuwairi et al., 2007).

FIGURE 14.9 Baby math Shown a numerically impossible outcome, 5-month-old infants stare longer. (From Wynn, 1992.)

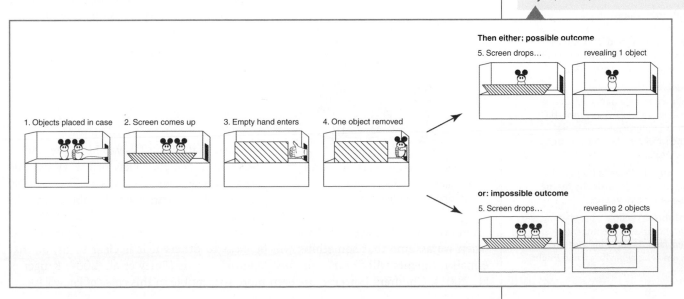

Preoperational Stage

Piaget believed that until about age 6 or 7, children are in a **preoperational stage**—too young to perform mental operations. For a 5-year-old, the milk that seems "too much" in a tall, narrow glass may become an acceptable amount if poured into a short, wide glass. Focusing only on the height dimension, this child cannot perform the operation of mentally pouring the milk back, because she lacks the concept of **conservation**—the principle that quantity remains the same despite changes in shape (**FIGURE 14.10**).

FIGURE 14.10 Piaget's test of conservation This preoperational child does not yet understand the principle of conservation of substance. When the milk is poured into a tall, narrow glass, it suddenly seems like "more" than when it was in the shorter, wider glass. In another year or so, she will understand that the volume stays the same.

|| Question: If most 2½-year-olds do not understand how miniature toys can symbolize real objects, should anatomically correct dolls be used when questioning such children about alleged physical or sexual abuse? Judy DeLoache (1995) reports that "very young children do not find it natural or easy to use a doll as a representation of themselves." ||

Piaget did not view the stage transitions as abrupt. Even so, symbolic thinking appears at an earlier age than he supposed. Judy DeLoache (1987) discovered this when she showed children a model of a room and hid a model toy in it (a miniature stuffed dog behind a miniature couch). The 2½-year-olds easily remembered where to find the miniature toy, but they could not use the model to locate an actual stuffed dog behind a couch in a real room. Three-year-olds—only 6 months older—usually went right to the actual stuffed animal in the real room, showing they *could* think of the model as a symbol for the room. Piaget probably would have been surprised.

Egocentrism

Piaget contended that preschool children are **egocentric:** They have difficulty perceiving things from another's point of view. Asked to "show Mommy your picture," 2-year-old Gabriella holds the picture up facing her own eyes. Three-year-old Gray makes himself "invisible" by putting his hands over his eyes, assuming that if he can't see his grandparents, they can't see him. Children's conversations also reveal their egocentrism, as one young boy demonstrated (Phillips, 1969, p. 61):

"Do you have a brother?"
"Yes."
"What's his name?"
"Jim."
"Does Jim have a brother?"
"No."

"It's too late, Roger—they've seen us."

Roger has not outgrown his early childhood egocentrism.

Like Gabriella, TV-watching preschoolers who block your view of the TV assume that you see what they see. They simply have not yet developed the ability to take another's viewpoint. Even as adults, we often overestimate the extent to which others share our opinions and perspectives, as when we assume that something will be clear to others if it is clear to us, or that e-mail recipients will "hear" our "just kidding" intent (Epley et al., 2004; Kruger et al., 2005). Children, however, are even more susceptible to this *curse of knowledge.*

preoperational stage in Piaget's theory, the stage (from 2 to about 6 or 7 years of age) during which a child learns to use language but does not yet comprehend the mental operations of concrete logic.

conservation the principle (which Piaget believed to be a part of concrete operational reasoning) that properties such as mass, volume, and number remain the same despite changes in the forms of objects.

egocentrism in Piaget's theory, the preoperational child's difficulty taking another's point of view.

theory of mind people's ideas about their own and others' mental states—about their feelings, perceptions, and thoughts, and the behaviors these might predict.

Theory of Mind

When Little Red Riding Hood realizes her "grandmother" is really a wolf, she swiftly revises her ideas about the creature's intentions and races away. Preschoolers, although still egocentric, develop this ability to infer others' mental states when they begin forming a **theory of mind** (a term first coined by psychologists David Premack and Guy Woodruff, to describe chimpanzees' seeming ability to read intentions).

As children's ability to take another's perspective develops, they seek to understand what made a playmate angry, when a sibling will share, and what might make a parent buy a toy. And they begin to tease, empathize, and persuade. Between about 3½ and 4½, children worldwide come to realize that others may hold false beliefs (Callaghan et al., 2005; Sabbagh et al., 2006). Jennifer Jenkins and Janet Astington (1996) showed Toronto children a Band-Aids box and asked them what was inside. Expecting Band-Aids, the children were surprised to discover that the box actually contained pencils. Asked what a child who had never seen the box would think was inside, 3-year-olds typically answered "pencils." By age 4 to 5, the children's theory of mind had leapt forward, and they anticipated their friends' false belief that the box would hold Band-Aids.

In a follow-up experiment, children see a doll named Sally leaving her ball in a red cupboard (**FIGURE 14.11**). Another doll, Anne, then moves the ball to a blue cupboard. Researchers then pose a question: When Sally returns, where will she look for the ball? Children with *autism* (see Close-Up: Autism, on the next page) have difficulty

|| Use your finger to trace a capital E on your forehead. When Adam Galinsky and his colleagues (2006) invited people to do that, they were more egocentric—less likely to draw it from the perspective of someone looking at them—if they were first made to feel powerful. Other studies confirm that feeling powerful reduces people's sensitivity to how others see, think, and feel. ||

Family Circus ® Bil Keane

"Don't you remember, Grandma? You were in it with me."

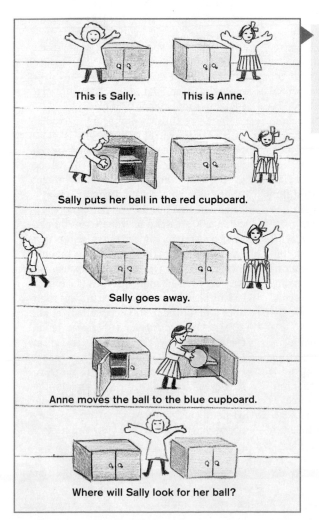

▶ **FIGURE 14.11 Testing children's theory of mind** This simple problem illustrates how researchers explore children's presumptions about others' mental states. (Inspired by Baron-Cohen et al., 1985.)

This is Sally.   This is Anne.

Sally puts her ball in the red cupboard.

Sally goes away.

Anne moves the ball to the blue cupboard.

Where will Sally look for her ball?

CLOSE-UP

Autism and "Mind-Blindness"

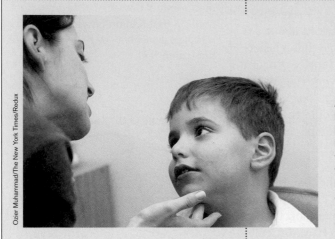

Ozier Muhammad/The New York Times/Redux

Autism This speech-language pathologist is helping a boy with autism learn to form sounds and words. Autism, which afflicts four boys for every girl, is marked by deficient social communication and difficulty in grasping others' states of mind.

Diagnoses of **autism,** a disorder marked by communication deficiencies and repetitive behaviors, have been increasing, according to recent estimates. Once believed to affect 1 in 2500 children, autism or a related disorder will now strike 1 in 150 American children and, in Britain's London area, 1 in 86 children (Baird et al., 2006; CDC, 2007; Lilienfeld & Arkowitz, 2007). Some people have attributed the modern "autism epidemic" to small amounts of mercury in childhood vaccines, leading nearly 5000 parents of children with autism to file a 2007 lawsuit against the U.S. government. But the mercury-laden ingredient was removed from vaccines in 2001, and autism rates have reportedly not dropped since then (Normand & Dallery, 2007; Schechter & Grether, 2008). Moreover, the increase in autism diagnoses has been offset by a decrease in the number of children considered "cognitively disabled" or "learning disabled," which suggests a relabeling of children's disorders (Gernsbacher et al., 2005; Grinker, 2007; Shattuck, 2006).

We do know that the underlying source of autism's symptoms seems to be poor communication among brain regions that normally work together to let us take another's viewpoint. This effect appears to result from an unknown number of autism-related genes interacting with the environment in as yet poorly understood ways (Blakeslee, 2005; Wiekelgren, 2005).

People with autism are therefore said to have an impaired theory of mind (Rajendran & Mitchell, 2007). They have difficulty inferring others' thoughts and feelings. They do not appreciate that playmates and parents might view things differently. Mindreading that most find intuitive (*Is that face conveying a happy smile, a self-satisfied smirk, or a contemptuous sneer?*) is difficult for those with autism. Most children learn that another child's pouting mouth signals sadness, and that twinkling eyes mean happiness or mischief. A child with autism fails to understand these signals (Frith & Frith, 2001).

To encompass the variations in autism, today's researchers refer to *Autism spectrum disorder.* One variation in this spectrum is *Asperger syndrome,* a "high-functioning" form of autism. Asperger syndrome is marked by normal intelligence, often accompanied by exceptional skill or talent in a specific area, but deficient social and communication skills (and thus an inability to form normal peer relationships).

Psychologist Simon Baron-Cohen (2008) proposes that autism, which afflicts four boys for every girl, represents an "extreme male brain." Girls are naturally predisposed to be "empathizers," he contends. They are better at reading facial expressions and gestures—a challenging task for those with autism. And, although the sexes overlap, boys are, he believes, better "systemizers": They understand things according to rules or laws, as in mathematical and mechanical systems.

"If two 'systemizers' have a child, this will increase the risk of the child having autism," Baron-Cohen theorizes. And because of *assortative mating*—people's tendency to seek spouses who share their interests—two systemizers will indeed often mate. "I do not discount environmental factors," he notes. "I'm just saying, don't forget about biology."

Biology's influence appears in studies of identical twins. If one twin is diagnosed with autism, the chances are 70 percent that the identical co-twin will be as well (Sebat et al., 2007). The younger sibling of a child with autism also is at a heightened risk of 15 percent or so (Sutcliffe, 2008). Random genetic mutations in sperm-producing cells may also play a role. As men age, these mutations become more frequent, which may help explain why an over-40 man has a much higher risk of fathering a child with autism than does a man under 30 (Reichenberg et al., 2007). Genetic influences appear to do their damage by altering brain synapses (Crawley, 2007; Garber, 2007).

Biology's role in autism also appears in studies comparing the brain's functioning in those with and without autism. People without autism often yawn after seeing others yawn. And as they view and imitate another's smiling or frowning, they feel something of what the other is feeling, thanks to their brain's *mirror neurons*. Not so among those with autism, who are less imitative and whose brain areas involved in mirroring others' actions are much less active (Dapretto et al., 2006; Perra et al., 2008; Senju et al., 2007). For example, when people with autism watch another person's hand movements, their brain displays less than normal mirroring activity (Oberman & Ramachandran, 2007; Théoret et al., 2005).

Such discoveries have launched explorations of treatments that might alleviate some of autism's symptoms by triggering mirror neuron activity (Ramachandran & Oberman, 2006). For example, seeking to "systemize empathy," Baron-Cohen and his Cambridge University colleagues (2007; Golan et al., 2007) collaborated with Britain's National Autistic Society and a film production company. Knowing that television shows with vehicles have been most popular for kids with autism, they created a series of animations that graft emotion-conveying faces onto toy tram, train, and tractor characters in a pretend boy's bedroom (**FIGURE 14.12**). After the boy leaves for school, the characters come to life and have experiences that lead them to display various emotions (which I predict you would enjoy viewing at www.thetransporters.com). The children expressed a surprising ability to generalize what they had learned to a new, real context. By the end of the intervention, their previously deficient ability to recognize emotions on real faces now equaled that of children without autism.

autism a disorder that appears in childhood and is marked by deficient communication, social interaction, and understanding of others' states of mind.

(a) Emotion-conveying faces grafted onto toy trains

© Crown copyright MMVI, www.thetransporters.com, courtesy Changing Media Development

(b) Matching new scenes and faces (and data for two trials)

"The neighbor's dog has bitten people before. He is barking at Louise."

Point to the face that shows how Louise is feeling.

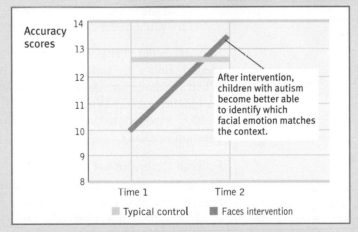

Accuracy scores

After intervention, children with autism become better able to identify which facial emotion matches the context.

Time 1   Time 2

■ Typical control   ■ Faces intervention

FIGURE 14.12 Transported into a world of emotion
(a) A research team at Cambridge University's Autism Research Centre introduced children with autism to emotions experienced and displayed by toy vehicles. (b) After four weeks of viewing animations, the children displayed a markedly increased ability to recognize emotions in human as well as the toy faces.

understanding that Sally's state of mind differs from their own—that Sally, not knowing the ball has been moved, will return to the red cupboard. They also have difficulty reflecting on their own mental states. They are, for example, less likely to use the personal pronouns *I* and *me*. Deaf children who have hearing parents and minimal communication opportunities have similar difficulty inferring others' states of mind (Peterson & Siegal, 1999).

Our abilities to perform mental operations, to think symbolically, and to take another's perspective are not absent in the preoperational stage and then miraculously present in later stages. Rather, these abilities begin to show up early and continue to develop gradually (Wellman et al., 2001). For example, we are able to appreciate others' perceptions and feelings before we can appreciate others' *beliefs* (Saxe & Powell, 2006).

By age 7, children become increasingly capable of thinking in words and of using words to work out solutions to problems. They do this, noted the Russian psychologist Lev Vygotsky (1896–1934), by internalizing their culture's language and relying on inner speech. Parents who say "No, no!" when pulling a child's hand away from a cake are giving the child a self-control tool. When later needing to resist temptation, the child may likewise say "No, no!" Second-graders who mutter to themselves while doing math problems grasp third-grade math better the following year (Berk, 1994). Whether out loud or inaudibly, talking to themselves helps children control their behavior and emotions and master new skills.

Concrete Operational Stage

By about 6 or 7 years of age, said Piaget, children enter the **concrete operational stage.** Given concrete materials, they begin to grasp conservation. Understanding that change in form does not mean change in quantity, they can mentally pour milk back and forth between glasses of different shapes. They also enjoy jokes that allow them to use this new understanding:

> Mr. Jones went into a restaurant and ordered a whole pizza for his dinner. When the waiter asked if he wanted it cut into 6 or 8 pieces, Mr. Jones said, "Oh, you'd better make it 6, I could never eat 8 pieces!" (McGhee, 1976)

Piaget believed that during the concrete operational stage, children fully gain the mental ability to comprehend mathematical transformations and conservation. When my daughter, Laura, was 6, I was astonished at her inability to reverse simple arithmetic. Asked, "What is 8 plus 4?" she required 5 seconds to compute "12," and another 5 seconds to then compute 12 minus 4. By age 8, she could answer a reversed question instantly.

Formal Operational Stage

By age 12, our reasoning expands from the purely concrete (involving actual experience) to encompass abstract thinking (involving imagined realities and symbols). As children approach adolescence, said Piaget, many become capable of solving hypothetical propositions and deducing consequences: *If* this, *then* that. Systematic reasoning, what Piaget called **formal operational** thinking, is now within their grasp.

Although full-blown logic and reasoning await adolescence, the rudiments of formal operational thinking begin earlier than Piaget realized. Consider this simple problem:

> If John is in school, then Mary is in school. John is in school. What can you say about Mary?

Formal operational thinkers have no trouble answering correctly. But neither do most 7-year-olds (Suppes, 1982).

concrete operational stage in Piaget's theory, the stage of cognitive development (from about 6 or 7 to 11 years of age) during which children gain the mental operations that enable them to think logically about concrete events.

formal operational stage in Piaget's theory, the stage of cognitive development (normally beginning about age 12) during which people begin to think logically about abstract concepts.

stranger anxiety the fear of strangers that infants commonly display, beginning by about 8 months of age.

Reflecting on Piaget's Theory

What remains of Piaget's ideas about the child's mind? Plenty—enough to merit his being singled out by *Time* magazine as one of the twentieth century's 20 most influential scientists and thinkers and rated in a survey of British psychologists as the greatest psychologist of that century (*Psychologist,* 2003). Piaget identified significant cognitive milestones and stimulated worldwide interest in how the mind develops. His emphasis was less on the ages at which children typically reach specific milestones than on their sequence. Studies around the globe, from aboriginal Australia to Algeria to North America, have confirmed that human cognition unfolds basically in the sequence Piaget described (Lourenco & Machado, 1996; Segall et al., 1990).

However, today's researchers see development as more continuous than did Piaget. By detecting the beginnings of each type of thinking at earlier ages, they have revealed conceptual abilities Piaget missed. Moreover, they see formal logic as a smaller part of cognition than he did. Piaget would not be surprised that today, as part of our own cognitive development, we are adapting his ideas to accommodate new findings.

Piaget's emphasis on how the child's mind grows through interaction with the physical environment is complemented by Vygotsky's emphasis on how the child's mind grows through interaction with the *social* environment. If Piaget's child was a young scientist, Vygotsky's was a young apprentice. By mentoring children and giving them new words, parents and others provide a temporary *scaffold* from which children can step to higher levels of thinking (Renninger & Granott, 2005). Language, an important ingredient of social mentoring, provides the building blocks for thinking, noted Vygotsky (who was born the same year as Piaget, but died prematurely of tuberculosis).

Implications for Parents and Teachers

Future parents and teachers remember: Young children are incapable of adult logic. Preschoolers who stand in the way or ignore negatively phrased instructions simply have not learned to take another's viewpoint. What seems simple and obvious to us— getting off a teeter-totter will cause a friend on the other end to crash—may be incomprehensible to a 3-year-old. Also remember that children are not passive receptacles waiting to be filled with knowledge. Better to build on what they already know, engaging them in concrete demonstrations and stimulating them to think for themselves. And, finally, accept children's cognitive immaturity as adaptive. It is nature's strategy for keeping children close to protective adults and providing time for learning and socialization (Bjorklund & Green, 1992).

▶‖ Social Development

14-3 How do parent-infant attachment bonds form?

From birth, babies in all cultures are social creatures, developing an intense bond with their caregivers. Infants come to prefer familiar faces and voices, then to coo and gurgle when given their mother's or father's attention. Soon after object permanence emerges and children become mobile, a curious thing happens. At about 8 months, they develop **stranger anxiety.** They may greet strangers by crying and reaching for familiar caregivers. "No! Don't leave me!" their distress seems to say. At about this age, children have schemas for familiar faces; when they cannot assimilate the new face into these remembered schemas, they become distressed (Kagan, 1984). Once again, we see an important principle: *The brain, mind, and social-emotional behavior develop together.*

"Assessing the impact of Piaget on developmental psychology is like assessing the impact of Shakespeare on English literature."

Developmental psychologist Harry Beilin (1992)

Lev Vygotsky (1895–1934) Vygotsky, a Russian developmental psychologist, pictured here with his daughter, studied how a child's mind feeds on the language of social interaction.

Stranger anxiety A newly emerging ability to evaluate people as unfamiliar and possibly threatening helps protect babies 8 months and older.

attachment an emotional tie with another person; shown in young children by their seeking closeness to the caregiver and showing distress on separation.

critical period an optimal period shortly after birth when an organism's exposure to certain stimuli or experiences produces proper development.

imprinting the process by which certain animals form attachments during a critical period very early in life.

Origins of Attachment

By 12 months, infants typically cling tightly to a parent when they are frightened or expect separation. Reunited after being separated, they shower the parent with smiles and hugs. No social behavior is more striking than this intense and mutual infant-parent bond. This **attachment** bond is a powerful survival impulse that keeps infants close to their caregivers. Infants become attached to those—typically their parents—who are comfortable and familiar. For many years, developmental psychologists reasoned that infants became attached to those who satisfied their need for nourishment. It made sense. But an accidental finding overturned this explanation.

Body Contact

During the 1950s, University of Wisconsin psychologists Harry Harlow and Margaret Harlow bred monkeys for their learning studies. To equalize the infant monkeys' experiences and to isolate any disease, they separated them from their mothers shortly after birth and raised them in sanitary individual cages, which included a cheesecloth baby blanket (Harlow et al., 1971). Then came a surprise: When their blankets were taken to be laundered, the monkeys became distressed.

The Harlows recognized that this intense attachment to the blanket contradicted the idea that attachment derives from an association with nourishment. But how could they show this more convincingly? To pit the drawing power of a food source against the contact comfort of the blanket, they created two artificial mothers. One was a bare wire cylinder with a wooden head and an attached feeding bottle, the other a cylinder wrapped with terry cloth.

When raised with both, the monkeys overwhelmingly preferred the comfy cloth mother (**FIGURE 14.13**). Like human infants clinging to their mothers, the monkeys would cling to their cloth mothers when anxious. When venturing into the environment, they used her as a secure base, as if attached to her by an invisible elastic band that stretched only so far before pulling them back. Researchers soon learned that other qualities—rocking, warmth, and feeding—made the cloth mother even more appealing.

Human infants, too, become attached to parents who are soft and warm and who rock, feed, and pat. Much parent-infant emotional communication occurs via touch (Hertenstein et al., 2006), which can be either soothing (snuggles) or arousing (tickles). Human attachment also consists of one person providing another with a safe haven when distressed and a secure base from which to explore. As we mature, our

FIGURE 14.13 The Harlows' mothers
Psychologists Harry Harlow and Margaret Harlow raised monkeys with two artificial mothers—one a bare wire cylinder with a wooden head and an attached feeding bottle, the other a cylinder with no bottle but covered with foam rubber and wrapped with terry cloth. The Harlows' discovery surprised many psychologists: The infants much preferred contact with the comfortable cloth mother, even while feeding from the nourishing mother.

Harlow Primate Laboratory, University of Wisconsin

secure base and safe haven shift—from parents to peers and partners (Cassidy & Shaver, 1999). But at all ages we are social creatures. We gain strength when someone offers, by words and actions, a safe haven: "I will be here. I am interested in you. Come what may, I will actively support you" (Crowell & Waters, 1994).

Familiarity

Contact is one key to attachment. Another is familiarity. In many animals, attachments based on familiarity likewise form during a **critical period**—an optimal period when certain events must take place to facilitate proper development (Bornstein, 1989). For goslings, ducklings, or chicks, that period falls in the hours shortly after hatching, when the first moving object they see is normally their mother. From then on, the young fowl follow her, and her alone.

Konrad Lorenz (1937) explored this rigid attachment process, called **imprinting.** He wondered: What would ducklings do if he was the first moving creature they observed? What they did was follow him around: Everywhere that Konrad went, the ducks were sure to go. Further tests revealed that although baby birds imprint best to their own species, they also will imprint to a variety of moving objects—an animal of another species, a box on wheels, a bouncing ball (Colombo, 1982; Johnson, 1992). And, once formed, this attachment is difficult to reverse.

Children—unlike ducklings—do not imprint. However, they do become attached to what they've known. *Mere exposure* to people and things fosters fondness. Children like to reread the same books, rewatch the same movies, reenact family traditions. They prefer to eat familiar foods, live in the same familiar neighborhood, attend school with the same old friends. Familiarity is a safety signal. Familiarity breeds content.

Attachment Differences

14-4 How have psychologists studied attachment differences, and what have they learned?

What accounts for children's attachment differences? Placed in a *strange situation* (usually a laboratory playroom), about 60 percent of infants display *secure attachment.* In their mother's presence they play comfortably, happily exploring their new environment. When she leaves, they are distressed; when she returns, they seek contact with her. Other infants avoid attachment or show *insecure attachment.* They are less likely to explore their surroundings; they may even cling to their mother. When she leaves, they either cry loudly and remain upset or seem indifferent to her departure and return (Ainsworth, 1973, 1989; Kagan, 1995; van IJzendoorn & Kroonenberg, 1988).

Mary Ainsworth (1979), who designed the strange situation experiments, studied attachment differences by observing mother-infant pairs at home during their first six months. Later she observed the 1-year-old infants in a strange situation without their mothers. Sensitive, responsive mothers—those who noticed what their babies were doing and responded appropriately—had infants who exhibited secure attachment. Insensitive, unresponsive mothers—mothers who attended to their babies when they felt like doing so but ignored them at other times—had infants who often became insecurely attached. The Harlows' monkey studies, with unresponsive artificial mothers, produced even more striking effects. When put in strange situations without their artificial mothers, the deprived infants were terrified (**FIGURE 14.14**).

|| Lee Kirkpatrick (1999) reports that for some people a perceived relationship with God functions as do other attachments, by providing a secure base for exploration and a safe haven when threatened. ||

Attachment When French pilot Christian Moullec took off in his microlight plane, his imprinted geese, which he had raised since their hatching, followed closely.

FIGURE 14.14 Social deprivation and fear Monkeys raised with artificial mothers were terror-stricken when placed in strange situations without their surrogate mothers. (Today's climate of greater respect for animal welfare prevents such primate studies.)

© Barry Hewlett

Fantastic father Among the Aka people of Central Africa, fathers form an especially close bond with their infants, even suckling the babies with their own nipples when hunger makes the child impatient for Mother's return. According to anthropologist Barry Hewlett (1991), fathers in this culture are holding or within reach of their babies 47 percent of the time.

Follow-up studies have confirmed that sensitive mothers—and fathers—tend to have securely attached infants (De Wolff & van IJzendoorn, 1997). But what explains the correlation? Is attachment style the *result* of parenting? Or is attachment style the result of genetically influenced *temperament*—a person's characteristic emotional reactivity and intensity? Shortly after birth, some babies are noticeably *difficult*—irritable, intense, and unpredictable. Others are *easy*—cheerful, relaxed, and feeding and sleeping on predictable schedules (Chess & Thomas, 1987). By neglecting such inborn differences, chides Judith Harris (1998), the parenting studies are like "comparing foxhounds reared in kennels with poodles reared in apartments." So, to separate nature and nurture, Dutch researcher Dymphna van den Boom (1990, 1995) varied parenting while controlling temperament. (Pause and think: If you were the researcher, how might you have done this?)

Van den Boom's solution was to randomly assign one hundred 6- to 9-month-old temperamentally difficult infants to either an experimental condition, in which mothers received personal training in sensitive responding, or to a control condition in which they did not. At 12 months of age, 68 percent of the experimental-condition infants were rated securely attached, as were only 28 percent of the control-condition infants. Other studies have also found that intervention programs can increase parental sensitivity and, to a lesser extent, infant attachment security (Bakermans-Kranenburg et al., 2003; Van Zeijl et al., 2006).

As these examples indicate, researchers have more often studied mother care than father care. Infants who lack a caring mother are said to suffer "maternal deprivation"; those lacking a father's care merely experience "father absence." This reflects a wider attitude in which "fathering a child" has meant impregnating, and "mothering" has meant nurturing. But fathers are more than just mobile sperm banks. Across nearly 100 studies worldwide, a father's love and acceptance have been comparable to a mother's love in predicting their offspring's health and well-being (Rohner & Veneziano, 2001). In one mammoth British study following 7259 children from birth to adulthood, those whose fathers were most involved in parenting (through outings, reading to them, and taking an interest in their education) tended to achieve more in school, even after controlling for many other factors, such as parental education and family wealth (Flouri & Buchanan, 2004).

Whether children live with one parent or two, are cared for at home or in a day-care center, live in North America, Guatemala, or the Kalahari Desert, their anxiety over separation from parents peaks at around 13 months, then gradually declines (**FIGURE 14.15**). Does this mean our need for and love of others also fades away? Hardly. Our capacity for love grows, and our pleasure in touching and holding those we love never ceases. The power of early attachment does nonetheless gradually relax,

FIGURE 14.15 Infants' distress over separation from parents In an experiment, groups of infants were left by their mothers in an unfamiliar room. In both groups, the percentage who cried when the mother left peaked at about 13 months. Whether the infant had experienced day care made little difference. (From Kagan, 1976.)

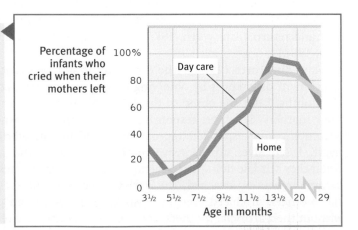

allowing us to move out into a wider range of situations, communicate with strangers more freely, and stay emotionally attached to loved ones despite distance.

Developmental theorist Erik Erikson (1902–1994), working in collaboration with his wife, Joan Erikson, said that securely attached children approach life with a sense of **basic trust**—a sense that the world is predictable and reliable. He attributed basic trust not to environment or inborn temperament, but to early parenting. He theorized that infants blessed with sensitive, loving caregivers form a lifelong attitude of trust rather than fear.

Although debate continues, many researchers now believe that our early attachments form the foundation for our adult relationships and our comfort with affection and intimacy (Birnbaum et al., 2006; Fraley, 2002). Adult styles of romantic love do tend to exhibit secure, trusting attachment; insecure, anxious attachment; or the avoidance of attachment (Feeney & Noller, 1990; Shaver & Mikulincer, 2007; Rholes & Simpson, 2004). Moreover, these adult attachment styles in turn affect relationships with our children, as avoidant people find parenting more stressful and unsatisfying (Rholes et al., 2006). Attachment style is also associated with motivation, note Andrew Elliot and Harry Reis (2003). Securely attached people exhibit less fear of failure and a greater drive to achieve.

Deprivation of Attachment

14-5 Do parental neglect, family disruption, or day care affect children's attachments?

If secure attachment nurtures social competence, what happens when circumstances prevent a child from forming attachments? In all of psychology, there is no sadder research literature. Babies reared in institutions without the stimulation and attention of a regular caregiver, or locked away at home under conditions of abuse or extreme neglect, are often withdrawn, frightened, even speechless. Those abandoned in Romanian orphanages during the 1980s looked "frighteningly like [the Harlows'] monkeys" (Carlson, 1995). If institutionalized more than 8 months, they often bore lasting emotional scars (Chisholm, 1998; Malinosky-Rummell & Hansen, 1993; Rutter et al., 1998).

The Harlows' monkeys bore similar scars if reared in total isolation, without even an artificial mother. As adults, when placed with other monkeys their age, they either cowered in fright or lashed out in aggression. When they reached sexual maturity, most were incapable of mating. If artificially impregnated, females often were neglectful, abusive, even murderous toward their first-born. A recent experiment with primates confirms the abuse-breeds-abuse phenomenon. Whether reared by biological or adoptive mothers, 9 of 16 females who were abused by their mothers became abusive parents, as did no female reared by a nonabusive mother (Maestripieri, 2005).

In humans, too, the unloved sometimes become the unloving. Most abusive parents—and many condemned murderers—report having been neglected or battered as children (Kempe & Kempe, 1978; Lewis et al., 1988). But does this mean that today's victim is predictably tomorrow's victimizer? No. Though most abusers were indeed abused, most abused children do *not* later become violent criminals or abusive parents. Most children growing up under adversity (as did the surviving children of the Holocaust) are *resilient;* they become normal adults (Helmreich, 1992; Masten, 2001).

But others, especially those who experience no sharp break from their abusive past, don't bounce back so readily. Some 30 percent of people who have been abused do abuse their children—a rate lower than that found in the primate study, but four

"Out of the conflict between trust and mistrust, the infant develops hope, which is the earliest form of what gradually becomes faith in adults."
Erik Erikson (1983)

"What is learned in the cradle, lasts to the grave."
French proverb

basic trust according to Erik Erikson, a sense that the world is predictable and trustworthy; said to be formed during infancy by appropriate experiences with responsive caregivers.

times the U.S. national rate of child abuse (Dumont et al., 2007; Kaufman & Zigler, 1987; Widom, 1989a,b).

Extreme early trauma seems to leave footprints on the brain. If repeatedly threatened and attacked while young, normally placid golden hamsters grow up to be cowards when caged with same-sized hamsters, or bullies when caged with weaker ones (Ferris, 1996). Such animals show changes in the brain chemical serotonin, which calms aggressive impulses. A similarly sluggish serotonin response has been found in abused children who become aggressive teens and adults. "Stress can set off a ripple of hormonal changes that permanently wire a child's brain to cope with a malevolent world," concludes abuse researcher Martin Teicher (2002).

Such findings help explain why young children terrorized through physical abuse or wartime atrocities (being beaten, witnessing torture, and living in constant fear) may suffer other lasting wounds—often nightmares, depression, and an adolescence troubled by substance abuse, binge eating, or aggression (Kendall-Tackett et al., 1993, 2004; Polusny & Follette, 1995; Trickett & McBride-Chang, 1995). Child sexual abuse, especially if severe and prolonged, places children at increased risk for health problems, psychological disorders, substance abuse, and criminality (Freyd et al., 2005; Tyler, 2002). Abuse victims are at considerable risk for depression *if* they carry a gene variation that spurs stress-hormone production (Bradley et al., 2008). As we will see again and again, behavior and emotion arise from a particular environment interacting with particular genes.

Disruption of Attachment

What happens to an infant when attachment is disrupted? Separated from their families, infants—both monkeys and humans—become upset and, before long, withdrawn and even despairing (Bowlby, 1973; Mineka & Suomi, 1978). Fearing that the stress of separation might cause lasting damage (and when in doubt, acting to protect parents' rights), courts are usually reluctant to remove children from their homes.

If placed in a more positive and stable environment, most infants recover from the separation distress. In studies of adopted children, Leon Yarrow and his co-workers (1973) found that when children between 6 and 16 months of age were removed from their foster mothers, they initially had difficulties eating, sleeping, and relating to their new mothers. But when these children were studied at age 10, little visible effect remained. Thus, they fared no worse than children placed before the age of 6 months (with little accompanying distress). Likewise, socially deprived but adequately nourished Romanian orphans who were adopted into a loving home during infancy or early childhood usually progressed rapidly, especially in their cognitive development. If removed and adopted after age 2, however, they were at risk for attachment problems. Foster care that prevents attachment by moving a child through a series of foster families can be very disruptive. So can repeated and prolonged removals from a mother.

We adults also suffer when our attachment bonds are severed. Whether through death or separation, a break produces a predictable sequence. Agitated preoccupation with the lost partner is followed by deep sadness and, eventually, the beginnings of emotional detachment and a return to normal living (Hazan & Shaver, 1994). Newly separated couples who have long ago ceased feeling affection are sometimes surprised at their desire to be near the former partner. Deep and longstanding attachments seldom break quickly. Detaching is a process, not an event.

Does Day Care Affect Attachment?

In the mid-twentieth century, when Mom-at-home was the social norm, researchers asked, "Is day care bad for children? Does it disrupt children's attachments to their parents?" For the high-quality day-care programs usually studied, the answer was *no.* In *Mother Care/Other Care,* developmental psychologist Sandra Scarr (1986) explained that children are "biologically sturdy individuals . . . who can thrive in a wide variety of life situations." Scarr spoke for many developmental psychologists, whose research has uncovered no major impact of maternal employment on children's development (Erel et al., 2000; Goldberg et al., 2008).

Research then shifted to the effects of differing quality of day care on different types and ages of children. Scarr (1997) explained: Around the world, "high-quality child care consists of warm, supportive interactions with adults in a safe, healthy, and stimulating environment. . . . Poor care is boring and unresponsive to children's needs." Newer research not only confirms that day-care quality matters, but also finds that family poverty often consigns children to lower-quality day care, as well as more family instability and turmoil, more authoritarian parenting (imposing strict rules and demanding obedience), more time in front of the television, and less access to books (Love et al., 2003; Evans, 2004).

An example of high-quality day care Research has shown that young children thrive socially and intellectually in safe, stimulating environments with a ratio of one caregiver for every three or four children.

One ongoing study in 10 American cities has followed 1100 children since the age of 1 month. The researchers found that at ages 4½ to 6, those children who had spent the most time in day care had slightly advanced thinking and language skills. They also had an increased rate of aggressiveness and defiance (NICHD, 2002, 2003, 2006). To developmental psychologist Eleanor Maccoby (2003), the positive correlation between increased rate of problem behaviors and time spent in child care suggests "some risk for some children spending extended time in some day-care settings as they're now organized." But the child's temperament, the parents' sensitivity, and the family's economic and educational level mattered more than time spent in day care.

To be a day-care researcher and "to follow the data" can be controversial, notes researcher Jay Belsky (2003). Both opponents and advocates of day care have strong feelings. "As a result," says Belsky, "the scientist who is willing to report unpopular results is all too frequently blamed for generating them." Just as weather forecasters can report rain but love sunshine, so scientists aim to reveal and report the way things are, even when they wish it were otherwise.

Children's ability to thrive under varied types of responsive caregiving should not surprise us, given cultural variations in attachment patterns. Westernized attachment features one or two caregivers and their offspring. In other cultures, such as the Efe of Zaire, multiple caregivers are the norm (Field, 1996; Whaley et al., 2002). Even before the mother holds her newborn, the baby is passed among several women. In the weeks to come, the infant will be constantly held (and fed) by other women. The result is strong multiple attachments. As an African proverb says, "It takes a village to raise a child."

There is little disagreement that the many preschool children left *alone* for part of their parents' working hours deserve better. So do the children who merely exist for 9 hours a day in minimally equipped, understaffed centers. What all children need is a consistent, warm relationship with people whom they can learn to trust. The importance of such relationships extends beyond the preschool years, as Finnish psychologist Lea Pulkkinen (2006) observed in her career-long study of 285 individuals tracked from age 8 to 42. Her observation that adult monitoring of children was associated with favorable outcomes led her to undertake, with support from Finland's parliament, a nationwide program of adult-supervised activities for all first and second graders (Pulkkinen, 2004; Rose, 2004).

self-concept our understanding and evaluation of who we are.

Self-Concept

14-6 How do children's self-concepts develop, and how are children's traits related to parenting styles?

Infancy's major social achievement is attachment. *Childhood's* major social achievement is a positive sense of self. By the end of childhood, at about age 12, most children have developed a **self-concept**—an understanding and assessment of who they are. Parents often wonder when and how this sense of self develops. "Is my baby girl aware of herself—does she know she is a person distinct from everyone else?"

Of course we cannot ask the baby directly, but we can again capitalize on what she can do—letting her *behavior* provide clues to the beginnings of her self-awareness. In 1877, biologist Charles Darwin offered one idea: Self-awareness begins when we recognize ourselves in a mirror. By this indicator, self-recognition emerges gradually over about a year, starting in roughly the sixth month as the child reaches toward the mirror to touch her image as if it were another child (Courage & Howe, 2002; Damon & Hart, 1982, 1988, 1992).

Self-awareness Mirror images fascinate infants from the age of about 6 months. Only at about 18 months, however, does the child recognize that the image in the mirror is "me."

But how can we know when the child recognizes that the girl in the mirror is indeed herself, not just an agreeable playmate? In a simple variation of the mirror procedure, researchers sneakily dabbed rouge on children's noses before placing them in front of the mirror. At about 15 to 18 months, children will begin to touch their own noses when they see the red spot in the mirror (Butterworth, 1992; Gallup & Suarez, 1986). Apparently, 18-month-olds have a schema of how their face should look, and they wonder, "What is that spot doing on *my* face?"

Beginning with this simple self-recognition, the child's self-concept gradually strengthens. By school age, children start to describe themselves in terms of their gender, group memberships, and psychological traits, and they compare themselves with other children (Newman & Ruble, 1988; Stipek, 1992). They come to see themselves as good and skillful in some ways but not others. They form a concept of which traits, ideally, they would like to have. By age 8 or 10, their self-image is quite stable.

As adolescents and adults, will our self-esteem be lower if we have experienced adoption? That's what Dutch researchers Femmie Juffer and Marinus van IJzendoorn (2007) predicted, given that some adopted children will have suffered early neglect or abuse, will know that their biological parents gave them up, and will often look different from their adoptive parents. To check their presumption, they mined data from 88 studies comparing the self-esteem scores of 10,977 adoptees and 33,862 nonadoptees. To their surprise, they found "no difference in self-esteem." This was true even for transracial and international adoptees. Many adoptees face challenges, the researchers acknowledge, but "supported by the large investment of adoptive families" they display resilience.

Children's views of themselves affect their actions. Children who form a positive self-concept are more confident, independent, optimistic, assertive, and sociable (Maccoby, 1980). This then raises important questions: How can parents encourage a positive yet realistic self-concept?

Self-aware animals After prolonged exposure to mirrors, several species—chimpanzees, orangutans, gorillas, dolphins, elephants, and magpies—have similarly demonstrated self-recognition of their mirror image (Gallup, 1970: Reiss & Marino, 2001; Prior et al., 2008). In an experiment by Joshua Plotnik and colleagues (2006), an Asian elephant, when facing a mirror, repeatedly used her trunk to touch an "X" painted above her eye (but not a similar mark above the other eye that was visible only under black light).

Parenting Styles

Some parents spank, some reason. Some are strict, some are lax. Some show little affection, some liberally hug and kiss. Do such differences in parenting styles affect children?

The most heavily researched aspect of parenting has been how, and to what extent, parents seek to control their children. Investigators have identified three parenting styles:

1. **Authoritarian** parents impose rules and expect obedience: "Don't interrupt." "Keep your room clean." "Don't stay out late or you'll be grounded." "Why? Because I said so."
2. **Permissive** parents submit to their children's desires. They make few demands and use little punishment.
3. **Authoritative** parents are both demanding and responsive. They exert control by setting rules and enforcing them, but they also explain the reasons for rules. And, especially with older children, they encourage open discussion when making the rules and allow exceptions.

Too hard, too soft, and just right, these styles have been called. Studies by Stanley Coopersmith (1967), Diana Baumrind (1996), and John Buri and others (1988) reveal that children with the highest self-esteem, self-reliance, and social competence usually have warm, concerned, *authoritative* parents. (Those with authoritarian parents tend to have less social skill and self-esteem, and those with permissive parents tend to be more aggressive and immature.) The participants in most studies have been middle-class White families, and some critics suggest that effective parenting may vary by culture. Yet studies with families of other races and in more than 200 cultures worldwide confirm the social and academic correlates of loving and authoritative parenting (Rohner & Veneziano, 2001; Sorkhabi, 2005; Steinberg & Morris, 2001). And the effects are stronger when children are embedded in *authoritative communities* with connected adults who model a good life (Commission on Children at Risk, 2003).

A word of caution: The association between certain parenting styles (being firm but open) and certain childhood outcomes (social competence) is correlational. *Correlation is not causation.* Here are two possible alternative explanations for this parenting-competence link. (Can you imagine others?)

▶ Children's traits may influence parenting more than vice versa. Parental warmth and control vary somewhat from child to child, even in the same family (Holden & Miller, 1999). So perhaps socially mature, agreeable, easygoing children *evoke* greater trust and warmth from their parents, and less competent and less cooperative children elicit less. Twin studies support this possibility (Kendler, 1996).

▶ Some underlying third factor may be at work. Perhaps, for example, competent parents and their competent children share genes that predispose social competence. Twin studies also support this possibility (South et al., 2008).

Parents struggling with conflicting advice and with the stresses of child-rearing should remember that *all advice reflects the advice-giver's values.* For those who prize unquestioning obedience from a child, an authoritarian style may have the desired effect. For those who value children's sociability and self-reliance, authoritative firm-but-open parenting is advisable.

The investment in raising a child buys many years not only of joy and love but of worry and irritation. Yet for most people who become parents, a child is one's biological and social legacy—one's personal investment in the human future. Remind young adults of their mortality and they will express increased desire for children (Wisman & Goldenberg, 2005). To paraphrase psychiatrist Carl Jung, we reach backward into our parents and forward into our children, and through their children into a future we will never see, but about which we must therefore care.

"You are the bows from which your children as living arrows are sent forth."
Kahlil Gibran, *The Prophet*, 1923

REVIEW

Infancy and Childhood

14-1 **During infancy and childhood, how do the brain and motor skills develop?** The brain's nerve cells are sculpted by heredity and experience; their interconnections multiply rapidly after birth. Our complex motor skills—sitting, standing, walking—develop in a predictable sequence whose timing is a function of individual *maturation* and culture. We lose conscious memories of experiences from before about age 3½, in part because major areas of the brain have not yet matured.

14-2 **From the perspective of Piaget and of today's researchers, how does a child's mind develop?** Piaget proposed that through *assimilation* and *accommodation,* children actively construct and modify their understanding of the world. They form *schemas* that help them organize their experiences. Progressing from the simplicity of the *sensorimotor stage* of the first two years, in which they develop *object permanence,* children move to more complex ways of thinking. In the *preoperational stage* they develop a *theory of mind* (absent in children with *autism*), but they are *egocentric* and unable to perform simple logical operations. At about age 6 or 7, they enter the *concrete operational stage* and can perform concrete operations, such as those required to comprehend the principle of *conservation.* By about age 12, children enter the *formal operational stage* and can reason systematically. Research supports the sequence Piaget proposed for the unfolding of human *cognition,* but it also shows that young children are more capable, and their development more continuous, than he believed.

14-3 **How do parent-infant attachment bonds form?** At about 8 months, infants separated from their caregivers display *stranger anxiety.* Infants form *attachments* not simply because parents gratify biological needs but, more important, because they are comfortable, familiar, and responsive. Ducks and other animals have a more rigid attachment process, called *imprinting,* that occurs during a *critical period.* Neglect or abuse can disrupt the attachment process. Infants' differing attachment styles reflect both their individual temperament and the responsiveness of their parents and child-care providers.

14-4 **How have psychologists studied attachment differences, and what have they learned?** Attachment has been studied in strange situation experiments, which show that some children are securely attached and others are insecurely attached. Sensitive, responsive parents tend to have securely attached children. Adult relationships seem to reflect the attachment styles of early childhood, lending support to Erikson's idea that *basic trust* is formed in infancy by our experiences with responsive caregivers.

14-5 **Do parental neglect, family disruption, or day care affect children's attachments?** Children are very resilient. But those who are moved repeatedly, severely neglected by their parents, or otherwise prevented from forming attachments by age 2 may be at risk for attachment problems. Quality day care, with responsive adults interacting with children in a safe and stimulating environment, does not appear to harm children's thinking and language skills. Some studies have linked extensive time in day care with increased aggressiveness and defiance, but other factors—the child's temperament, the parents' sensitivity, and the family's economic and educational levels and culture—also matter.

14-6 **How do children's self-concepts develop, and how are children's traits related to parenting styles?** *Self-concept,* a sense of one's identity and personal worth, emerges gradually. At 15 to 18 months, children recognize themselves in a mirror. By school age, they can describe many of their own traits, and by age 8 to 10 their self-image is stable. Parenting styles—authoritarian, permissive, and authoritative—reflect varying degrees of control. Children with high self-esteem tend to have authoritative parents and to be self-reliant and socially competent, but the direction of cause and effect in this relationship is not clear.

Terms and Concepts to Remember

maturation, p. 174

cognition, p. 176

schema, p. 177

assimilation, p. 177

accommodation, p. 177

sensorimotor stage, p. 178

object permanence, p. 178

preoperational stage, p. 180

conservation, p. 180

egocentrism, p. 180

theory of mind, p. 181

autism, p. 182

concrete operational stage, p. 184

formal operational stage, p. 184

stranger anxiety, p. 185

attachment, p. 186

critical period, p. 187

imprinting, p. 187

basic trust, p. 189

self-concept, p. 192

Test Yourself

1. Use Piaget's first three stages of cognitive development to explain why young children are not just miniature adults in the way they think.

(Answers to the Test Yourself questions can be found in Appendix B at the end of the book.)

Ask Yourself

1. Can you recall a time when you misheard some song lyrics because you *assimilated* them into your own *schema*? (For hundreds of examples of this phenomenon, visit www.kissthisguy.com.)

∞ WEB

Multiple-choice self-tests and more may be found at www.worthpublishers.com/myers

MODULE 15

Adolescence

Physical Development

Cognitive Development

Social Development

Emerging Adulthood

Many psychologists once believed that childhood sets our traits. Today's developmental psychologists see development as lifelong. At a five-year high school reunion, former soul mates may be surprised at their divergence; a decade later, they may have trouble sustaining a conversation.

As the life-span perspective emerged, psychologists began to look at how maturation and experience shape us not only in infancy and childhood, but also in adolescence and beyond. **Adolescence**—the years spent morphing from child to adult—starts with the physical beginnings of sexual maturity and ends with the social achievement of independent adult status (which means that in some cultures, where teens are self-supporting, adolescence hardly exists).

In industrialized countries, what are the teen years like? In Leo Tolstoy's *Anna Karenina,* the teen years were "that blissful time when childhood is just coming to an end, and out of that vast circle, happy and gay, a path takes shape." But another teenager, Anne Frank, writing in her diary while hiding from the Nazis, described tumultuous teen emotions:

> My treatment varies so much. One day Anne is so sensible and is allowed to know everything; and the next day I hear that Anne is just a silly little goat who doesn't know anything at all and imagines that she's learned a wonderful lot from books. . . . Oh, so many things bubble up inside me as I lie in bed, having to put up with people I'm fed up with, who always misinterpret my intentions.

G. Stanley Hall (1904), one of the first psychologists to describe adolescence, believed that this tension between biological maturity and social dependence creates a period of "storm and stress." Indeed, after age 30, many who grow up in independence-fostering Western cultures look back on their teenage years as a time they would not want to relive, a time when their peers' social approval was imperative, their sense of direction in life was in flux, and their feeling of alienation from their parents was deepest (Arnett, 1999; Macfarlane, 1964).

But for many, adolescence is a time of vitality without the cares of adulthood, a time of rewarding friendships, of heightened idealism and a growing sense of life's exciting possibilities.

‖ How will you look back on your life 10 years from now? Are you making choices that someday you will recollect with satisfaction? ‖

▶‖ Physical Development

15-1 What physical changes mark adolescence?

Adolescence begins with **puberty,** the time when we mature sexually. Puberty follows a surge of hormones, which may intensify moods and which trigger a two-year period of rapid physical development, usually beginning at about age 11 in girls and at about age 13 in boys. About the time of puberty, boys' growth propels them to greater height than their female counterparts (**FIGURE 15.1** on the next page). During this growth spurt, the **primary sex characteristics**—the reproductive organs and external genitalia—develop dramatically. So do **secondary sex characteristics,** the nonreproductive traits such as breasts and hips in girls, facial hair and deepened voice in boys,

adolescence the transition period from childhood to adulthood, extending from puberty to independence.

puberty the period of sexual maturation, during which a person becomes capable of reproducing.

primary sex characteristics the body structures (ovaries, testes, and external genitalia) that make sexual reproduction possible.

secondary sex characteristics nonreproductive sexual characteristics, such as female breasts and hips, male voice quality, and body hair.

FIGURE 15.1 **Height differences** Throughout childhood, boys and girls are similar in height. At puberty, girls surge ahead briefly, but then boys overtake them at about age 14. (Data from Tanner, 1978.) Recent studies suggest that sexual development and growth spurts are beginning somewhat earlier than was the case a half-century ago (Herman-Giddens et al., 2001).

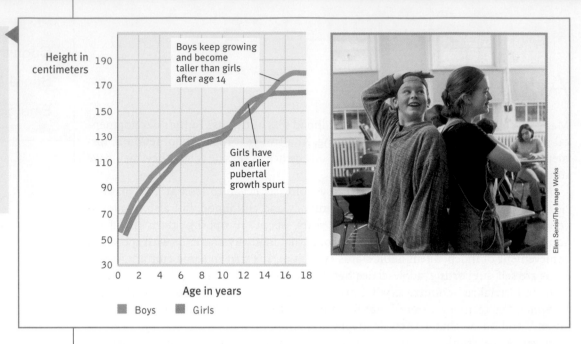

FIGURE 15.1 **Height differences** Throughout childhood, boys and girls are similar in height. At puberty, girls surge ahead briefly, but then boys overtake them at about age 14. (Data from Tanner, 1978.) Recent studies suggest that sexual development and growth spurts are beginning somewhat earlier than was the case a half-century ago (Herman-Giddens et al., 2001).

|| Menarche appears to occur a few months earlier, on average, for girls who have experienced stresses related to father absence or sexual abuse (Vigil et al., 2005; Zabin et al., 2005). ||

FIGURE 15.2 **Body changes at puberty** At about age 11 in girls and age 13 in boys, a surge of hormones triggers a variety of physical changes.

pubic and underarm hair in both sexes (**FIGURE 15.2**). A year or two before puberty, however, boys and girls often feel the first stirrings of attraction toward those of the other (or their own) sex (McClintock & Herdt, 1996).

In girls, puberty starts with breast development, which now often begins by age 10 (Brody, 1999). But puberty's landmarks are the first ejaculation in boys, usually by about age 14, and the first menstrual period in girls, usually within a year of age 12½ (Anderson et al., 2003). The first menstrual period, called **menarche** (meh-NAR-key), is a memorable event. Nearly all adult women recall it and remember experiencing a mixture of feelings—pride, excitement, embarrassment, and apprehension (Greif & Ulman, 1982; Woods et al., 1983). Girls who have been prepared for

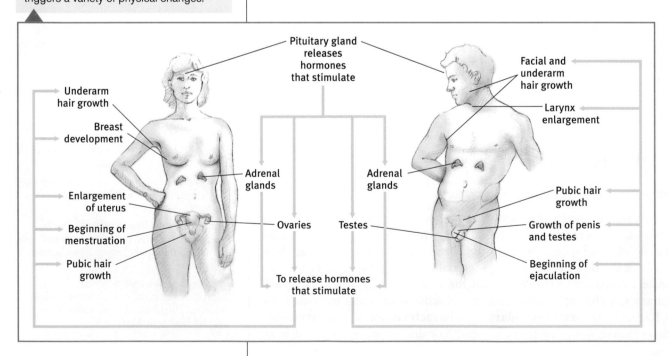

menarche usually experience it as a positive life transition. Most men similarly recall their first ejaculation *(spermarche),* which usually occurs as a nocturnal emission (Fuller & Downs, 1990).

Just as in the earlier life stages, the *sequence* of physical changes in puberty (for example, breast buds and visible pubic hair before menarche) is far more predictable than their *timing.* Some girls start their growth spurt at 9, some boys as late as age 16. Though such variations have little effect on height at maturity, they may have psychological consequences. For boys, early maturation pays dividends: Being stronger and more athletic during their early teen years, they tend to be more popular, self-assured, and independent, though also more at risk for alcohol use, delinquency, and premature sexual activity (Lynne et al., 2007; Steinberg & Morris, 2001). For girls, early maturation can be stressful (Mendle et al., 2007). If a young girl's body is out of sync with her own emotional maturity and her friends' physical development and experiences, she may begin associating with older adolescents or may suffer teasing or sexual harassment. It is not only when we mature that counts, but how people react to our genetically influenced physical development. Remember: *Heredity and environment interact.*

An adolescent's brain is also a work in progress. Until puberty, brain cells increase their connections, like trees growing more roots and branches. Then, during adolescence, comes a selective *pruning* of unused neurons and connections (Blakemore, 2008). What we don't use, we lose. It's rather like traffic engineers reducing congestion by eliminating certain streets and constructing new beltways that move traffic more efficiently.

As teens mature, their frontal lobes also continue to develop. The growth of *myelin,* the fatty tissue that forms around axons and speeds neurotransmission, enables better communication with other brain regions (Kuhn, 2006; Silveri et al., 2006). These developments bring improved judgment, impulse control, and the ability to plan for the long term.

Frontal lobe maturation lags the emotional limbic system. Puberty's hormonal surge and limbic system development help explain teens' occasional impulsiveness, risky behaviors, emotional storms—slamming doors and turning up the music (Casey et al., 2008). No wonder younger teens (whose unfinished frontal lobes aren't yet fully equipped for making long-term plans and curbing impulses) so often succumb to the lure of smoking, which most adult smokers could tell them they will later regret. Teens actually don't underestimate the risks of smoking—or driving fast or unprotected sex—they just, when reasoning from their gut, weigh the benefits more heavily (Reyna & Farley, 2006; Steinberg, 2007).

So, when Junior drives recklessly and academically self-destructs, should his parents reassure themselves that "he can't help it; his frontal cortex isn't yet fully grown"? They can at least take hope: The brain with which Junior begins his teens differs from the brain with which he will end his teens. Unless he slows his brain development with heavy drinking—leaving him prone to impulsivity and addiction—his frontal lobes will continue maturing until about age 25 (Beckman, 2004; Crews et al., 2007).

In 2004, the American Psychological Association joined seven other medical and mental health associations in filing U.S. Supreme Court briefs, arguing against the death penalty for 16- and 17-years-olds. The briefs documented the teen brain's immaturity "in areas that bear upon adolescent decision-making." Teens are "less guilty by reason of adolescence," suggested psychologist Laurence Steinberg and law professor Elizabeth Scott (2003). In 2005, by a 5-to-4 margin, the Court concurred, declaring juvenile death penalties unconstitutional.

"Young man, go to your room and stay there until your cerebral cortex matures."

"If a gun is put in the control of the prefrontal cortex of a hurt and vengeful 15-year-old, and it is pointed at a human target, it will very likely go off."

National Institutes of Health brain scientist Daniel R. Weinberger, "A Brain Too Young for Good Judgment," 2001

Drawing by Koren; © 1992 The New Yorker Magazine, Inc.

"Ben is in his first year of high school, and he's questioning all the right things."

▶‖ Cognitive Development

15-2 How did Piaget, Kohlberg, and later researchers describe adolescent cognitive and moral development?

As young teenagers become capable of thinking about their thinking, and of thinking about other people's thinking, they begin imagining what other people are thinking about *them*. (Adolescents might worry less if they understood their peers' similar preoccupation.) As their cognitive abilities mature, many begin to think about what is ideally possible and compare that with the imperfect reality of their society, their parents, and even themselves.

Developing Reasoning Power

During the early teen years, reasoning is often self-focused. Adolescents may think their private experiences are unique, something parents just could not understand: "But, Mom, *you* don't really know how it feels to be in love" (Elkind, 1978).

Gradually, though, most achieve the intellectual summit Jean Piaget called *formal operations,* and they become more capable of abstract reasoning. Adolescents ponder and debate human nature, good and evil, truth and justice. Having left behind the concrete images of early childhood, they may now seek a deeper conception of God and existence (Elkind, 1970; Worthington, 1989). The ability to reason hypothetically and deduce consequences also enables them to detect inconsistencies in others' reasoning and to spot hypocrisy. This can lead to heated debates with parents and silent vows never to lose sight of their own ideals (Peterson et al., 1986).

Demonstrating their reasoning ability Although on opposite sides of the Iraq war debate, these teens are demonstrating their ability to think logically about abstract topics. According to Piaget, they are in the final cognitive stage, formal operations.

William Thomas Cain/Getty Images

AP/Wide World Photos

Developing Morality

Two crucial tasks of childhood and adolescence are discerning right from wrong and developing character—the psychological muscles for controlling impulses. Much of our morality is rooted in gut-level reactions, for which the mind seeks rationalization (Haidt, 2006). Often, reason justifies passions such as disgust or liking. Yet to be a moral person is to *think* morally and *act* accordingly.

Piaget (1932) believed that children's moral judgments build on their cognitive development. Agreeing with Piaget, Lawrence Kohlberg (1981, 1984) sought to describe the development of *moral reasoning,* the thinking that occurs as we consider right and wrong. Kohlberg posed moral dilemmas (for example, whether a person should steal medicine to save a loved one's life) and asked children, adolescents, and adults if the action was right or wrong. He then analyzed their answers for evidence of stages of moral thinking.

AP Photo/Eric Gray

Moral reasoning New Orleans Hurricane Katrina victims were faced with a moral dilemma: Should they steal household necessities? Their reasoning likely reflected different levels of moral thinking, even if they behaved similarly.

His findings led him to believe that as we develop intellectually, we pass through three basic levels of moral thinking:

▸ ***Preconventional morality*** Before age 9, most children's morality focuses on self-interest: They obey rules either to avoid punishment or to gain concrete rewards.

▸ ***Conventional morality*** By early adolescence, morality focuses on caring for others and on upholding laws and social rules, simply because they are the laws and rules.

▸ ***Postconventional morality*** With the abstract reasoning of formal operational thought, people may reach a third moral level. Actions are judged "right" because they flow from people's rights or from self-defined, basic ethical principles.

Kohlberg claimed these levels form a moral ladder. As with all stage theories, the sequence is unvarying. We begin on the bottom rung and ascend to varying heights.

Research confirms that children in various cultures progress from Kohlberg's pre-conventional level into his conventional level (Gibbs et al., 2007). The postconventional level is more controversial. It appears mostly in the European and North American educated middle class, which prizes *individualism*—giving priority to one's own goals rather than to group goals (Eckensberger, 1994; Miller & Bersoff, 1995). Critics therefore contend that Kohlberg's theory is biased against the moral reasoning of members of collectivist societies such as China and India. Moreover, people's thinking about real-world moral choices also engages their emotions, and moral feelings don't easily fit into Kohlberg's neat stages (Krebs & Denton, 2005).

Moral Feeling

The mind makes moral judgments as it makes aesthetic judgments—quickly and automatically. We feel disgust when seeing people engaged in degrading or subhuman acts, and we feel *elevation*—a tingly, warm, glowing feeling in the chest—when seeing people display exceptional generosity, compassion, or courage.

One woman recalled driving through her snowy neighborhood with three young men as they passed "an elderly woman with a shovel in her driveway. I did not think much of it, when one of the guys in the back asked the driver to let him off there. . . . When I saw him jump out of the back seat and approach the lady, my mouth dropped in shock as I realized that he was offering to shovel her walk for her." Witnessing this unexpected goodness triggered elevation: "I felt like jumping out of the car and hugging this guy. I felt like singing and running, or skipping and laughing. I felt like saying nice things about people" (Haidt, 2000).

In Jonathan Haidt's (2002, 2007, 2008) *social intuitionist* account of morality, moral feelings precede moral reasoning. "Could human morality really be run by the moral

"I am a bit suspicious of any theory that says that the highest moral stage is one in which people talk like college professors."
James Q. Wilson, *The Moral Sense*, 1993

"This might not be ethical. Is that a problem for anybody?"

emotions," he wonders, "while moral reasoning struts about pretending to be in control?" Indeed, he surmises, "moral judgment involves quick gut feelings, or affectively laden intuitions, which then trigger moral reasoning." Moral reasoning—our mind's press secretary—aims to convince ourselves and others of what we intuitively feel.

The social intuitionist explanation of morality finds support from a study of moral paradoxes. Imagine seeing a runaway trolley headed for five people. All will certainly be killed unless you throw a switch that diverts the trolley onto another track, where it will kill one person. Should you throw the switch?

Most say *yes*. Kill one, save five. Now imagine the same dilemma, except that your opportunity to save the five requires you to push a large stranger onto the tracks, where he will die as his body stops the trolley. Kill one, save five?

The logic is the same, but most say *no*. Seeking to understand why, a Princeton research team led by Joshua Greene (2001) used brain imaging to spy on people's neural responses as they contemplated such dilemmas. Only when given the body-pushing type of moral dilemma did their brain's emotion areas light up. Despite the identical logic, the personal dilemma engaged emotions that altered moral judgment. Moral judgment is more than thinking; it is also gut-level feeling.

The gut feelings that drive our moral judgments turn out to be widely shared. To neuroscientist Marc Hauser (2006) this suggests that humans are hard-wired for moral feelings. Faced with moral choices, people across the world, with similar evolved brains, display similar moral intuitions. For example, is it acceptable to kill a healthy man who walks into a hospital that has five dying patients who could be saved by harvesting his organs? Most people say *no*. We all seem to unconsciously assume that harm caused by an action is worse than harm caused by failing to act (Cushman et al., 2006). With damage to a brain area that underlies emotions, however, people apply more coldly calculating reasoning to moral dilemmas (Koenigs et al., 2007).

Moral Action

Our moral thinking and feeling surely affect our moral talk. But sometimes talk is cheap and emotions are fleeting. Morality involves *doing* the right thing, and what we do also depends on social influences. As political theorist Hannah Arendt (1963) observed, many Nazi concentration camp guards during World War II were ordinary "moral" people who were corrupted by a powerfully evil situation.

Nevertheless, as our *thinking* matures, our *behavior* also becomes less selfish and more caring (Krebs & Van Hesteren, 1994; Miller et al., 1996). Today's character education programs therefore tend to focus both on moral issues and on *doing* the right thing. They teach children *empathy* for others' feelings, and also the self-discipline needed to restrain one's own impulses—to delay small gratifications now to enable bigger rewards later. Those who do learn to *delay gratification* become more socially responsible, academically successful, and productive (Funder & Block, 1989; Mischel et al., 1988, 1989). In service-learning programs, teens tutor, clean up their neighborhoods, and assist older people, and their sense of competence and desire to serve increase at the same time that their school absenteeism and drop-out rates diminish (Andersen, 1998; Piliavin, 2003). Moral action feeds moral attitudes.

On humanity's need to delay gratification in response to global climate change: "The benefits of strong early action considerably outweigh the costs."

The Economics of Climate Change, UK Government Economic Service, 2007

▶‖ Social Development

15-3   What are the social tasks and challenges of adolescence?

Theorist Erik Erikson (1963) contended that each stage of life has its own *psychosocial* task, a crisis that needs resolution. Young children wrestle with issues of *trust*, then *autonomy* (independence), then *initiative* (**TABLE 15.1**). School-age children strive for *competence*, feeling able and productive. The adolescent's task, said Erikson,

TABLE 15.1 Erikson's Stages of Psychosocial Development

Stage (approximate age)	Issue	Description of Task
Infancy (to 1 year)	Trust vs. mistrust	If needs are dependably met, infants develop a sense of basic trust.
Toddlerhood (1 to 3 years)	Autonomy vs. shame and doubt	Toddlers learn to exercise their will and do things for themselves, or they doubt their abilities.
Preschool (3 to 6 years)	Initiative vs. guilt	Preschoolers learn to initiate tasks and carry out plans, or they feel guilty about their efforts to be independent.
Elementary school (6 years to puberty)	Industry vs. inferiority	Children learn the pleasure of applying themselves to tasks, or they feel inferior.
Adolescence (teen years into 20s)	Identity vs. role confusion	Teenagers work at refining a sense of self by testing roles and then integrating them to form a single identity, or they become confused about who they are.
Young adulthood (20s to early 40s)	Intimacy vs. isolation	Young adults struggle to form close relationships and to gain the capacity for intimate love, or they feel socially isolated.
Middle adulthood (40s to 60s)	Generativity vs. stagnation	In middle age, people discover a sense of contributing to the world, usually through family and work, or they may feel a lack of purpose.
Late adulthood (late 60s and up)	Integrity vs. despair	Reflecting on his or her life, an older adult may feel a sense of satisfaction or failure.

Competence vs. inferiority

John Eastcott/Yves Momatiuk/The Image Works

Intimacy vs. isolation

Jeff Greenberg/PhotoEdit

is to synthesize past, present, and future possibilities into a clearer sense of self. Adolescents wonder, "Who am I as an individual? What do I want to do with my life? What values should I live by? What do I believe in?" Erikson called this quest the adolescent's *search for identity.*

As sometimes happens in psychology, Erikson's interests were bred by his own life experience. As the son of a Jewish mother and a Danish Gentile father, Erikson was "doubly an outsider," reports Morton Hunt (1993, p. 391). He was "scorned as a Jew in school but mocked as a Gentile in the synagogue because of his blond hair and blue eyes." Such episodes fueled his interest in the adolescent struggle for identity.

Forming an Identity

To refine their sense of identity, adolescents in individualistic cultures usually try out different "selves" in different situations. They may act out one self at home, another with friends, and still another at school or on Facebook. If two situations overlap—as when a teenager brings home friends—the discomfort can be considerable. The teen asks, "Which self should I be? Which is the real me?" The resolution is a self-definition that unifies the various selves into a consistent and comfortable sense of who one is—an **identity.**

For both adolescents and adults, group identities often form around how we differ from those around us. When living in Britain, I became conscious of my Americanness. When spending time with my daughter in Africa, I become conscious of my minority (White) race. When surrounded by women, I am mindful of my gender identity. For international students, for those of a minority ethnic group, for people with a disability, for those on a team, a **social identity** often forms around their distinctiveness.

identity our sense of self; according to Erikson, the adolescent's task is to solidify a sense of self by testing and integrating various roles.

social identity the "we" aspect of our self-concept; the part of our answer to "Who am I?" that comes from our group memberships.

"Self-consciousness, the recognition of a creature by itself as a 'self,' [cannot] exist except in contrast with an 'other,' a something which is not the self."

C. S. Lewis, *The Problem of Pain,* 1940

Who shall I be today? By varying the way they look, adolescents try out different "selves." Although we eventually form a consistent and stable sense of identity, the self we present may change with the situation.

"She says she's someone from your past who gave birth to you, and raised you, and sacrificed everything so you could have whatever you wanted."

But not always. Erikson noticed that some adolescents forge their identity early, simply by adopting their parents' values and expectations. (Traditional, less individualistic cultures inform adolescents about who they are, rather than encouraging them to decide on their own.) Other adolescents may adopt an identity defined in opposition to parents but in conformity with a particular peer group—jocks, preppies, geeks, goths.

Most young people do develop a sense of contentment with their lives. When American teens were asked whether a series of statements described them, 81 percent said *yes* to "I would choose my life the way it is right now." But others never quite seem to find themselves: The other 19 percent agreed with "I wish I were somebody else." In response to another question, 28 percent agreed that "I often wonder why I exist" (Lyons, 2004). Reflecting on their existence, 75 percent of American collegians say they "discuss religion/spirituality" with friends, "pray," and agree that "we are all spiritual beings" and "search for meaning/purpose in life" (Astin et al., 2004; Bryant & Astin, 2008). This would not surprise Stanford psychologist William Damon and his colleagues (2003), who contend that a key task of adolescent development is to achieve a purpose—a desire to accomplish something personally meaningful that makes a difference to the world beyond oneself.

The late teen years, when many people in industrialized countries begin attending college or working full time, provide new opportunities for trying out possible roles. Many college seniors have achieved a clearer identity and a more positive self-concept than they had as first-year students (Waterman, 1988). In several nationwide studies, researchers have given young Americans tests of self-esteem. (Sample item: "I am able to do things as well as most other people.") During the early to mid-teen years, self-esteem falls and, for girls, depression scores often increase, but then self-image rebounds during the late teens and twenties (Robins et al., 2002; Twenge & Campbell, 2001; Twenge & Nolen-Hoeksema, 2002).

Identity also becomes more personalized. Daniel Hart (1988) asked American youths of various ages to imagine a machine that would clone (a) what you think and feel, (b) your appearance, or (c) your relationships with friends and family. When he then asked which clone would be "closest to being you?" three-fourths of the seventh-graders chose (c), the clone with the same social network. In contrast, three-fourths of the ninth-graders chose (a), the one with their individual thoughts and feelings.

Erikson contended that the adolescent identity stage is followed in young adulthood by a developing capacity for **intimacy.** With a clear and comfortable sense of who you are, said Erikson, you are ready to form emotionally close relationships. Such relationships are, for most of us, a source of great pleasure. When Mihaly Csikszentmihalyi (pronounced chick-SENT-me-hi) and Jeremy Hunter (2003) used a beeper to sample the daily experiences of American teens, they found them unhappiest when alone and happiest when with friends. As Aristotle long ago recognized, we humans are "the social animal."

Parent and Peer Relationships

As adolescents in Western cultures seek to form their own identities, they begin to pull away from their parents (Shanahan et al., 2007). The preschooler who can't be close enough to her mother, who loves to touch and cling to her, becomes the 14-year-old who wouldn't be caught dead holding hands with Mom. The transition occurs gradually (**FIGURE 15.3**). By adolescence, arguments occur more often, usually

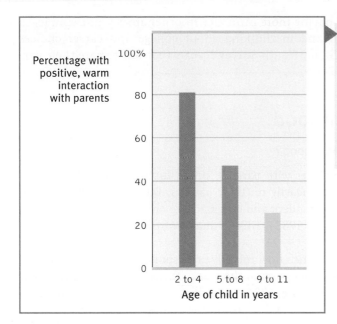

intimacy in Erikson's theory, the ability to form close, loving relationships; a primary developmental task in late adolescence and early adulthood.

over mundane things—household chores, bedtime, homework (Tesser et al., 1989). Parent-child conflict during the transition to adolescence tends to be greater with first-born than with second-born children (Shanahan et al., 2007).

For a minority of parents and their adolescents, differences lead to real splits and great stress (Steinberg & Morris, 2001). But most disagreements are at the level of harmless bickering. And most adolescents—6000 of them in 10 countries, from Australia to Bangladesh to Turkey—say they like their parents (Offer et al., 1988). "We usually get along but . . . ," adolescents often report (Galambos, 1992; Steinberg, 1987).

Positive parent-teen relations and positive peer relations often go hand-in-hand. High school girls who have the most affectionate relationships with their mothers tend also to enjoy the most intimate friendships with girlfriends (Gold & Yanof, 1985). And teens who feel close to their parents tend to be healthy and happy and to do well in school (Resnick et al., 1997). Of course, we can state this correlation the other way: Misbehaving teens are more likely to have tense relationships with parents and other adults.

Adolescence is typically a time of diminishing parental influence and growing peer influence. Asked in a survey if they had "ever had a serious talk" with their child about illegal drugs, 85 percent of American parents answered *yes*. But if the parents had indeed given this earnest advice, many teens apparently had tuned it out: Only 45 percent could recall such a talk (Morin & Brossard, 1997).

Heredity does much of the heavy lifting in forming individual differences in temperament and personality, and parent and peer influences do much of the rest. Most teens are herd animals. They talk, dress, and act more like their peers than their parents. What their friends are, they often become, and what "everybody's doing," they often do. In teen calls to hotline counseling services, peer relationships are the most discussed topic (Boehm et al., 1999). For those who feel excluded, the pain is acute. "The social atmosphere in most high schools is poisonously clique-driven and exclusionary," observed social psychologist Elliot Aronson (2001). Most excluded "students suffer in silence. . . . A small number act out in violent ways against their classmates." Those who withdraw are vulnerable to loneliness, low self-esteem, and depression (Steinberg & Morris, 2001). Peer approval matters.

"I love u guys."
Emily Keyes' final text message to her parents before dying in a Colorado school shooting, 2006

"How was my day? How was my day? Must you micromanage my life?"

Nine times out of ten, it's all about peer pressure.

Teens see their parents as having more influence in other areas—for example, in shaping their religious faith and in thinking about college and career choices (*Emerging Trends,* 1997). A Gallup Youth Survey reveals that most share their parent's political views (Lyons, 2005).

▶‖ Emerging Adulthood

15-4   What is emerging adulthood?

In young adulthood, emotional ties with parents loosen further. During their early twenties, many people still lean heavily on their parents. But by the late twenties, most feel more comfortably independent and better able to empathize with parents as fellow adults (Frank, 1988; White, 1983). This graduation from adolescence to adulthood is now taking longer.

In the Western world, adolescence now roughly corresponds to the teen years. At earlier times, and still today in other parts of the world, this slice of the life span has been much smaller (Baumeister & Tice, 1986). Shortly after sexual maturity, such societies bestowed adult responsibilities and status on the young person, often marking the event with an elaborate initiation—a public *rite of passage.* With society's blessing, the new adult would then work, marry, and have children.

When schooling became compulsory in many Western countries, independence began occurring later. In industrialized cultures from Europe to Australia, adolescents are now taking more time to finish college, leave the nest, and establish careers. In the United States, for example, the average age at first marriage varies by ethnic group but has increased more than 4 years since 1960 (to 27 for men, 25 for women).

While cultural traditions were changing, Western adolescents were also beginning to develop earlier. Today's earlier sexual maturity is related both to increased body fat (which can support pregnancy and nursing) and to weakened parent-child bonds, including absent fathers (Ellis, 2004). Together, delayed independence and earlier sexual maturity have widened the once-brief interlude between biological maturity and social independence (**FIGURE 15.4**).

Especially for those still in school, the time from 18 to the mid-twenties is an increasingly not-yet-settled phase of life, which some now call **emerging adulthood**

emerging adulthood for some people in modern cultures, a period from the late teens to early twenties, bridging the gap between adolescent dependence and full independence and responsible adulthood.

FIGURE 15.4 The transition to adulthood is being stretched from both ends In the 1890s, the average interval between a woman's first menstrual period and marriage, which typically marked a transition to adulthood, was about 7 years; in industrialized countries today it is about 12 years (Guttmacher, 1994, 2000). Although many adults are unmarried, later marriage combines with prolonged education and earlier menarche to help stretch out the transition to adulthood.

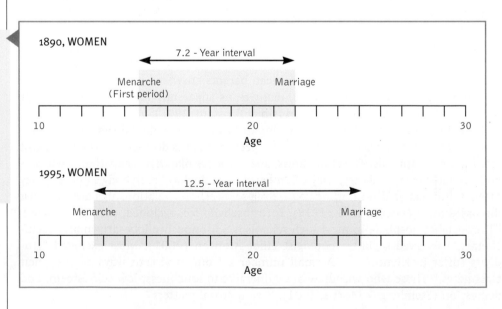

(Arnett, 2006, 2007; Reitzle, 2006). Unlike some other cultures with an abrupt transition to adulthood, Westerners typically ease their way into their new status. Those who leave home for college, for example, are separated from parents and, more than ever before, managing their time and priorities. Yet they may remain dependent on their parents' financial and emotional support and may return home for holidays. For many others, their parents' home may be the only affordable place to live. No longer adolescents, these emerging adults have not yet assumed full adult responsibilities and independence, and they feel "in between." But adulthood emerges gradually, and often with diminishing bouts of depression or anger and increased self-esteem (Galambos et al., 2006).

"When I was your age, I was an adult."

REVIEW

Adolescence

15-1 **What physical changes mark adolescence?** *Adolescence* is the transition period between *puberty* and social independence. During these years, both *primary* and *secondary sex characteristics* develop dramatically. Boys seem to benefit from "early" maturation, girls from "late" maturation. The brain's frontal lobes mature during adolescence and the early twenties, enabling improved judgment, impulse control, and long-term planning.

15-2 **How did Piaget, Kohlberg, and later researchers describe adolescent cognitive and moral development?** Piaget theorized that adolescents develop a capacity for formal operations and that this development is the foundation for moral judgment. Kohlberg proposed a stage theory of moral reasoning, from a pre-conventional morality of self-interest, to a conventional morality concerned with upholding laws and social rules, to (in some people) a postconventional morality of universal ethical principles. Kohlberg's critics note that morality lies in actions and emotions as well as thinking, and that his postconventional level represents morality from the perspective of individualist, middle-class males.

15-3 **What are the social tasks and challenges of adolescence?** Erikson theorized that a chief task of adolescence is solidifying one's sense of self—one's *identity*. This often means "trying on" a number of different roles. During adolescence, parental influence diminishes and peer influence increases.

15-4 **What is emerging adulthood?** The transition from adolescence to adulthood is now taking longer. *Emerging adulthood* is the period from age 18 to the mid-twenties, when many young people are not yet fully independent. But critics note that this stage is found mostly in today's Western cultures.

Terms and Concepts to Remember

adolescence, p. 195
puberty, p. 195
primary sex characteristics,
  p. 195
secondary sex characteristics,
  p. 195

menarche [meh-NAR-key],
  p. 196
identity, p. 201
social identity, p. 201
intimacy, p. 202
emerging adulthood, p. 204

Test Yourself

1. How has the transition from childhood to adulthood changed in Western cultures in the last century or so?

(Answers to the Test Yourself questions can be found in Appendix B at the end of the book.)

Ask Yourself

1. What are the most positive and negative things you remember about your own adolescence? And who do you credit or blame more—your parents or your peers?

∞ WEB

Multiple-choice self-tests and more may be found at www.worthpublishers.com/myers

Physical Development

Cognitive Development

Social Development

Reflections on Two Major
Developmental Issues

"I am still learning."
Michelangelo, 1560, at age 85

MODULE 16

Adulthood, and Reflections on Developmental Issues

At one time, psychologists viewed the center-of-life years between adolescence and old age as one long plateau. No longer. Those who follow the unfolding of people's adult lives now believe our development continues.

Adult abilities vary widely
Eighty-seven-year-olds: Don't try this. In 2002, George Blair became the world's oldest barefoot water skier, 18 days after his eighty-seventh birthday.

It is more difficult to generalize about adulthood stages than about life's early years. If you know that James is a 1-year-old and Jamal is a 10-year-old, you could say a great deal about each child. Not so with adults who differ by a similar number of years. The boss may be 30 or 60; the marathon runner may be 20 or 50; the 19-year-old may be a parent who supports a child or a child who receives an allowance. Yet our life courses are in some ways similar. Physically, cognitively, and especially socially, we are at age 50 different from our 25-year-old selves.

|| How old does a person have to be before you think of him or her as old? The average 18- to 29-year-old says 67. The average person 60 and over says 76 (Yankelovich, 1995). ||

▶|| Physical Development

16-1 What physical changes occur during middle and late adulthood?

Our physical abilities—muscular strength, reaction time, sensory keenness, and cardiac output—all crest by the mid-twenties. Like the declining daylight after the summer solstice, the decline of physical prowess begins imperceptibly. Athletes are often the first to notice. World-class sprinters and swimmers peak by their early twenties. Women—who mature earlier than men—also peak earlier. But most of us—especially those of us whose daily lives do not require top physical performance—hardly perceive the early signs of decline.

Physical Changes in Middle Adulthood

Middle-aged (post-40) athletes know all too well that physical decline gradually accelerates (**FIGURE 16.1**). As a 65-year-old who plays basketball, I now find myself occasionally wondering whether my team really needs me to run for that loose ball. But

"Happy fortieth. I'll take the muscle tone in your upper arms, the girlish timbre of your voice, your amazing tolerance for caffeine, and your ability to digest french fries. The rest of you can stay."

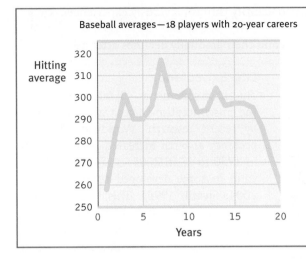

Baseball averages—18 players with 20-year careers

Hitting average

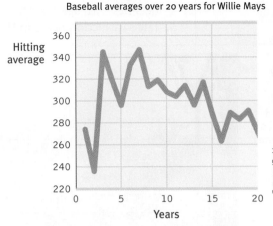

Baseball averages over 20 years for Willie Mays

Hitting average

Bettmann/Corbis

even diminished vigor is sufficient for normal activities. Moreover, during early and middle adulthood, physical vigor has less to do with age than with a person's health and exercise habits. Many of today's physically fit 50-year-olds run 4 miles with ease, while sedentary 25-year-olds find themselves huffing and puffing up two flights of stairs.

Aging also brings a gradual decline in fertility. For a 35- to 39-year-old woman, the chances of getting pregnant after a single act of intercourse are only half those of a woman 19 to 26 (Dunson et al., 2002). A woman's foremost biological sign of aging, the onset of **menopause,** ends her menstrual cycles, usually within a few years of age 50. Her expectations and attitudes will influence the emotional impact of this event. Does she see it as a sign that she is losing her femininity and growing old? Or does she view it as liberation from menstrual periods and fears of pregnancy? As is often the case, our expectations influence our perceptions.

Data from Africa support an evolutionary theory of menopause: Infants with a living maternal grandmother—typically a caring and invested family member without young children of her own—have had a greater chance of survival (Shanley et al., 2007).

Men experience no equivalent to menopause—no cessation of fertility, no sharp drop in sex hormones. They do experience a gradual decline in sperm count, testosterone level, and speed of erection and ejaculation. Some may also experience distress related to their perception of declining virility and physical capacities. But most age without such problems.

In a national survey of Canadians age 40 to 64, only 3 in 10 rated their sex life as less enjoyable than during their twenties (Wright, 2006). After middle age, most men and women remain capable of satisfying sexual activity. In another survey by the National Council on Aging, 39 percent of people over 60 expressed satisfaction with the amount of sex they were having and 39 percent said they wished for sex more frequently (Leary, 1998). And in an American Association of Retired Persons sexuality survey, it was not until age 75 or older that most women and nearly half of men reported little sexual desire (DeLamater & Sill, 2005).

Physical Changes in Later Life

Is old age "more to be feared than death" (Juvenal, *Satires*)? Or is life "most delightful when it is on the downward slope" (Seneca, *Epistulae ad Lucilium*)? What is it like to grow old? To gauge your own understanding, take the following true/false quiz:

1. Older people become more susceptible to short-term illnesses.
2. During old age many of the brain's neurons die.
3. If they live to be 90 or older, most people eventually become senile.

FIGURE 16.1 Gradually accelerating decline An analysis of aging and batting averages of all twentieth-century major league baseball players revealed a gradual but accelerating decline in players' later years (Schall & Smith, 2000). The career performance record of the great Willie Mays is illustrative.

"If the truth were known, we'd have to diagnose [older women] as having P.M.F.—Post-Menstrual Freedom." Social psychologist Jacqueline Goodchilds (1987)

"The things that stop you having sex with age are exactly the same as those that stop you riding a bicycle (bad health, thinking it looks silly, no bicycle)." Alex Comfort, *The Joy of Sex*, 2002

menopause the time of natural cessation of menstruation; also refers to the biological changes a woman experiences as her ability to reproduce declines.

4. Recognition memory—the ability to identify things previously experienced—declines with age.
5. Life satisfaction peaks in the fifties and then gradually declines after age 65.

Georges Gobet/AP Photo

World record for longevity?
French woman Jeanne Calment, the oldest human in history with authenticated age, died in 1998 at age 122. At age 100, she was still riding a bike. At age 114, she became the oldest film actor ever, by portraying herself in *Vincent and Me.*

Life Expectancy

The above statements—all false—are among the misconceptions about aging exploded by recent research. Worldwide, life expectancy at birth increased from 49 years in 1950 to 67 in 2004—and to 80 and beyond in some developed countries (PRB, 2004; Sivard, 1996). This increasing life expectancy (humanity's greatest achievement, say some) combines with decreasing birthrates to make older adults a bigger and bigger population segment, which provides an increasing demand for cruise ships, hearing aids, retirement villages, and nursing homes.

By 2050, about 35 percent of Europe's population likely will be over age 60 (Fernández-Ballesteros & Caprara, 2003). Clearly, countries that have depended on children to care for the aged are destined for a "demographic tsunami." Russia and Western Europe are also headed for depopulation—from 146 million to 104 million people in Russia by 2050, projects the United Nations (Brooks, 2005). "When an entire continent, healthier, wealthier, and more secure than ever before, fails to create the human future in the most elemental sense—by creating the next generation—something very serious is afoot," states George Weigel (2005).

Life expectancy differs for males and females; males are more prone to dying. Although 126 male embryos begin life for every 100 females who do so, the sex ratio is down to 105 males for every 100 females at birth (Strickland, 1992). During the first year, male infants' death rates exceed females' by one-fourth. Women outlive men by 4 years worldwide and by 5 to 6 years in Canada, the United States, and Australia. (Rather than marrying a man older than themselves, 20-year-old women who want a husband who shares their life expectancy should wait for the 15-year-old boys to mature.) By age 100, females outnumber males 5 to 1.

But few of us live to 100. Even if no one died before age 50, and cancer, heart disease, and infectious illness were eliminated, average life expectancy would still increase only to about 85 or a few years beyond (Barinaga, 1991). The body ages. Its cells stop reproducing. It becomes frail. It becomes vulnerable to tiny insults—hot weather, a fall, a mild infection—that at age 20 would have been trivial.

With age (especially when accentuated by smoking, obesity, or stress), people's chromosome tips, called *telomeres,* wear down, much as the tip of a shoelace frays. As these protective tips shorten, aging cells may die without being replaced with perfect genetic replicas (Blackburn et al., 2007; Valdes et al., 2005; Zhang et al., 2007).

Why do we eventually wear out? Why don't we, like the bristlecone pine trees, rockfish, and some social insect queens, grow older without withering? One theory, proposed by evolutionary biologists, speculates that the answer relates to our survival as a species: We pass on our genes most successfully when we raise our young and then stop consuming resources. Once we've fulfilled our gene-reproducing and nurturing task, there are no natural selection pressures against genes that cause degeneration in later life (Olshansky et al., 1993; Sapolsky & Finch, 1991).

The human spirit also affects life expectancy. For example, chronic anger and depression increase our risk of ill health and premature death. Researchers have even observed

Shoot, we'd better hurry up and figure this out.

Betsy Streeter

Aging researchers

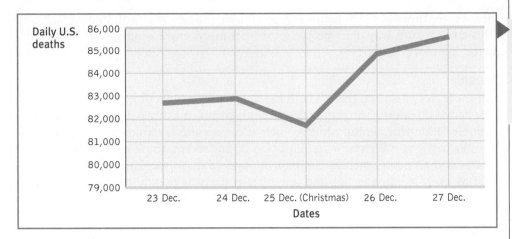

FIGURE 16.2 **Postponing a date with the grim reaper?** The total number of daily U.S. deaths from 1987 to 2002 increased on the days following Christmas. To researchers Mitsuru Shimizu and Brett Pelham (2008), this adds to the growing evidence of a death-deferral phenomenon.

an intriguing *death-deferral* phenomenon. For example, Mitsuru Shimizu and Brett Pelham (2008) report that, in one recent 15-year period, 2000 to 3000 more Americans died on the two days after Christmas than on Christmas and the two days before (**FIGURE 16.2**). And the death rate *increases* when people reach their birthdays, as it did for those who survived to the milestone first day of the new millennium.

Sensory Abilities

Although physical decline begins in early adulthood, we are not usually acutely aware of it until later life. Visual sharpness diminishes, and distance perception and adaptation to changes in light level are less acute. Muscle strength, reaction time, and stamina also diminish noticeably, as do vision, the sense of smell, and hearing (**FIGURE 16.3**). In later life, the stairs get steeper, the print gets smaller, and other people seem to mumble more. In Wales, teens' loitering around a convenience store has been discouraged by a device that emits an aversive high-pitched sound that almost no one over 30 can hear (Lyall, 2005). Some students use that pitch to their advantage with cellphone ringtones that their instructors cannot hear (Vitello, 2006).

With age, the eye's pupil shrinks and its lens becomes less transparent, reducing the amount of light reaching the retina. In fact, a 65-year-old retina receives only about one-third as much light as its 20-year-old counterpart (Kline & Schieber, 1985). Thus, to see as well as a 20-year-old when reading or driving, a 65-year-old

"For some reason, possibly to save ink, the restaurants had started printing their menus in letters the height of bacteria."
Dave Barry, *Dave Barry Turns Fifty*, 1998

FIGURE 16.3 **The aging senses** Sight, smell, and hearing all are less acute among those over age 70. (From Doty et al., 1984.)

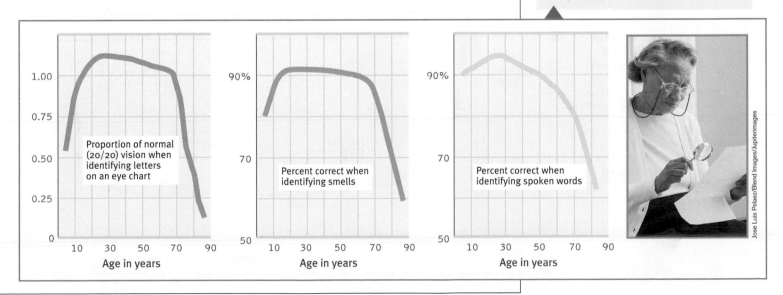

|| Most stairway falls taken by older people occur on the top step, precisely where the person typically descends from a window-lit hallway into the darker stairwell (Fozard & Popkin, 1978). Our knowledge of aging could be used to design environments that would reduce such accidents (National Research Council, 1990). ||

needs three times as much light—a reason for buying cars with untinted windshields. This also explains why older people sometimes ask younger people, "Don't you need better light for reading?"

Health

For those growing older, there is both bad and good news about health. The bad news: The body's disease-fighting immune system weakens, making older people more susceptible to life-threatening ailments such as cancer and pneumonia. The good news: Thanks partly to a lifetime's accumulation of antibodies, those over 65 suffer fewer short-term ailments, such as common flu and cold viruses. They are, for example, half as likely as 20-year-olds and one-fifth as likely as preschoolers to suffer upper respiratory flu each year (National Center for Health Statistics, 1990). This helps explain why older workers have lower absenteeism rates (Rhodes, 1983).

Aging levies a tax on the brain by slowing our neural processing. Up to the teen years, we process information with greater and greater speed (Fry & Hale, 1996; Kail, 1991). But compared with teens and young adults, older people take a bit more time to react, to solve perceptual puzzles, even to remember names (Bashore et al., 1997; Verhaeghen & Salthouse, 1997). The lag is greatest on complex tasks (Cerella, 1985; Poon, 1987). At video games, most 70-year-olds are no match for a 20-year-old. And, as **FIGURE 16.4** indicates, fatal accident rates per mile driven increase sharply after age 75. By age 85, they exceed the 16-year-old level. Nevertheless, because older people drive less, they account for fewer than 10 percent of crashes (Coughlin et al., 2004).

Brain regions important to memory begin to atrophy during aging (Schacter, 1996). In young adulthood, a small, gradual net loss of brain cells begins, contributing by age 80 to a brain-weight reduction of 5 percent or so. Late-maturing frontal lobes help account for teen impulsivity. Late in life, atrophy of the inhibition-controlling frontal lobes seemingly explains older people's occasional blunt questions ("Have you put on weight?") and frank comments (von Hippel, 2007).

In addition to enhancing muscles, bones, and energy and helping to prevent obesity and heart disease, exercising the body feeds the brain and helps compensate for cell loss (Coleman & Flood, 1986). Physical exercise stimulates brain cell development and neural connections, thanks perhaps to increased oxygen and nutrient flow (Kempermann et al., 1998; Pereira et al., 2007). That may explain why active older adults tend to be mentally quick older adults, and why, across 20 studies, sedentary older adults randomly assigned to aerobic exercise programs have exhibited enhanced

FIGURE 16.4 Age and driver fatalities Slowing reactions contribute to increased accident risks among those 75 and older, and their greater fragility increases their risk of death when accidents happen (NHTSA, 2000). Would you favor driver exams based on performance, not age, to screen out those whose slow reactions or sensory impairments indicate accident risk?

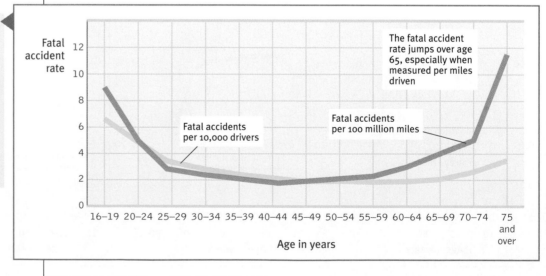

memory and sharpened judgment (Colcombe & Kramer, 2003; Colcombe et al., 2004; Weuve et al., 2004). Exercise also promotes neurogenesis (the birth of new nerve cells) in the hippocampus, a brain region important for memory (Pereira et al., 2007). And exercise helps maintain the telomeres protecting the ends of chromosomes (Cherkas et al., 2008). We are more likely to rust from disuse than to wear out from overuse.

Dementia and Alzheimer's Disease

Some adults do, unfortunately, suffer a substantial loss of brain cells. Up to age 95, the incidence of mental disintegration doubles roughly every 5 years (**FIGURE 16.5**). A series of small strokes, a brain tumor, or alcohol dependence can progressively damage the brain, causing that mental erosion we call *dementia*. So, too, can the feared brain ailment, *Alzheimer's disease,* which strikes 3 percent of the world's population by age 75. Alzheimer's symptoms are *not* normal aging. (Occasionally forgetting where you laid the car keys is no cause for alarm; forgetting how to get home may suggest Alzheimer's.)

Alzheimer's destroys even the brightest of minds. First memory deteriorates, then reasoning. Robert Sayre (1979) recalls his father shouting at his afflicted mother to "think harder," while his mother, confused, embarrassed, on the verge of tears, randomly searched the house for lost objects. A diminishing sense of smell is associated with the pathology that foretells Alzheimer's (Wilson et al., 2007). As the disease runs its course, after 5 to 20 years, the person becomes emotionally flat, then disoriented and disinhibited, then incontinent, and finally mentally vacant—a sort of living death, a mere body stripped of its humanity.

Underlying the symptoms of Alzheimer's is a loss of brain cells and deterioration of neurons that produce the neurotransmitter acetylcholine. Deprived of this vital chemical messenger, memory and thinking suffer. An autopsy reveals two telltale abnormalities in these acetylcholine-producing neurons: shriveled protein filaments in the cell body, and plaques (globs of degenerating tissue) at the tips of neuron branches. In one line of research, scientists are working to develop drugs that will block proteins from aggregating into plaques or that will lower the levels of the culprit protein, much as cholesterol-lowering drugs help prevent heart disease (Grady, 2007; Wolfe, 2006).

"We're keeping people alive so they can live long enough to get Alzheimer's disease."

Steve McConnell, Alzheimer's Association Vice President, 2007

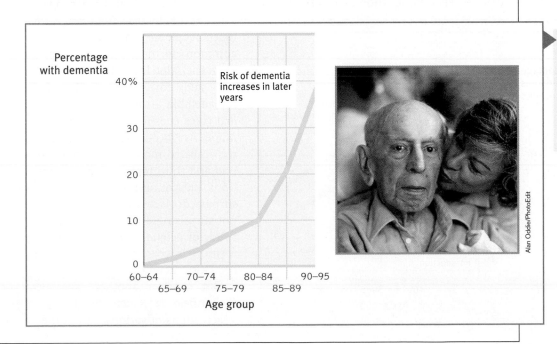

FIGURE 16.5 Incidence of dementia (mental disintegration) by age Risk of dementia due to Alzheimer's disease or a series of strokes doubles about every 5 years in later life. (From Jorm et al., 1987, based on 22 studies in industrial nations.)

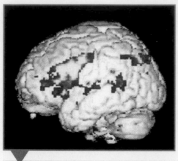

Susan Bookheimer

FIGURE 16.6 Predicting Alzheimer's disease During a memory test, MRI scans of the brains of people at risk for Alzheimer's (left) revealed more intense activity (yellow, followed by orange and red) when compared with normal brains (right). As brain scans and genetic tests make it possible to identify those likely to suffer Alzheimer's, would you want to be tested? At what age?

Researchers are gaining insights into the chemical, neural, and genetic roots of Alzheimer's (Gatz, 2007; Rogaeva et al., 2007). In people at risk for this disease, brain scans (**FIGURE 16.6**) reveal—before symptoms appear—the telltale degeneration of critical brain cells and diminished activity in brain areas affected by Alzheimer's (Apostolova et al., 2006; Johnson et al., 2006; Wu & Small, 2006). When the person is memorizing words, they also show diffuse brain activity, as if more exertion was required to achieve the same performance (Bookheimer et al., 2000). Physically active, nonobese people are less at risk for Alzheimer's (Abbott et al., 2004; Gustafson et al., 2003; Marx, 2005). So, too, are those with an active, challenged mind—often the mind of an educated, active reader (Wilson & Bennett, 2003). As with muscles, so with the brain: Those who use it, less often lose it.

▶‖ Cognitive Development

16-2 How do memory and intelligence change with age?

Among the most intriguing developmental psychology questions is whether adult cognitive abilities, such as memory, intelligence, and creativity, parallel the gradually accelerating decline of physical abilities.

Aging and Memory

‖ If you are within five years of 20, what experiences from your last year will you likely never forget? (This is the time of your life you may best remember when you are 50.) ‖

As we age, we remember some things well. Looking back in later life, people asked to recall the one or two most important events over the last half-century tend to name events from their teens or twenties (Conway et al., 2005; Rubin et al., 1998). Whatever people experience around this time of life—the Iraq war, the events of 9/11, the civil rights movement, World War II—becomes pivotal (Pillemer, 1998; Schuman & Scott, 1989). Our teens and twenties are a time of so many memorable "firsts"—first date, first job, first going to college or university, first meeting your parents-in-law.

Early adulthood is indeed a peak time for some types of learning and remembering. In one experiment, Thomas Crook and Robin West (1990) invited 1205 people to learn some names. Fourteen videotaped people said their names, using a common format: "Hi, I'm Larry." Then the same individuals reappeared and said, for example, "I'm from Philadelphia"—thus providing visual *and* voice cues for remembering their name. As **FIGURE 16.7** shows, everyone remembered more names after a second and third replay of the introductions, but younger adults consistently surpassed older adults. Perhaps it is not surprising, then, that nearly two-thirds of people over age 40 say their memory is worse than it was 10 years ago (KRC, 2001).

But consider another experiment (Schonfield & Robertson, 1966), in which adults of various ages learned a

FIGURE 16.7 Tests of recall Recalling new names introduced once, twice, or three times is easier for younger adults than for older ones. (Data from Crook & West, 1990.)

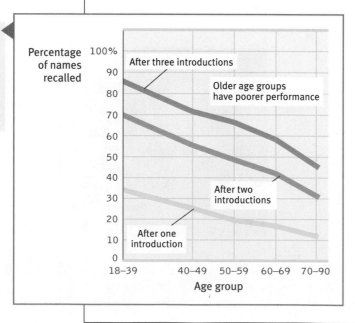

list of 24 words. Without giving any clues, the researchers then asked some to *recall* as many words as they could from the list, and others simply to *recognize* words, using multiple-choice questions. Although younger adults had better recall, no age-related memory decline appeared on the recognition tests (**FIGURE 16.8**). So, how well older people remember depends: Are they being asked simply to *recognize* what they have tried to memorize (minimal decline) or to *recall* it without clues (greater decline)?

Prospective memory ("Remember to . . .") remains strong when events help trigger memories, as when walking by a convenience store triggers a "Pick up milk!" memory. Time-based tasks ("Remember the 3:00 P.M. meeting") prove somewhat more challenging for older people. Habitual tasks, such as remembering to take medications three times daily, can be especially challenging (Einstein et al., 1990, 1995, 1998). Teens and young adults surpass both young children and 70-year-olds at remembering to do something (Zimmerman & Meier, 2006). To minimize problems associated with declining prospective memory, older adults rely more on time management and on using reminder cues, such as notes to themselves (Henry et al., 2004).

Those who study our capacity to learn and remember are aware of one other important complication: Right through our later years, we continue to diverge. Younger adults differ in their abilities to learn and remember, but 70-year-olds differ much more. "Differences between the most and least able 70-year-olds become much greater than between the most and least able 50-year-olds," reports Oxford researcher Patrick Rabbitt (2006). Some 70-year-olds perform below nearly all 20-year-olds; other 70-year-olds match or outdo the average 20-year-old.

But no matter how quick or slow we are, remembering seems also to depend on the type of information we are trying to retrieve. If the information is meaningless—nonsense syllables or unimportant events—then the older we are, the more errors we are likely to make. If the information is *meaningful,* older people's rich web of existing knowledge will help them to catch it, though they may take longer than younger adults to *produce* the words and things they know (Burke & Shafto, 2004). (Quick-thinking game show winners are usually younger to middle-aged adults.) Older people's capacity to learn and remember *skills* also declines less than their verbal recall (Graf, 1990; Labouvie-Vief & Schell, 1982; Perlmutter, 1983).

Aging and Intelligence

What happens to our broader intellectual powers as we age? Do they gradually decline, as does our ability to recall new material? Or do they remain constant, as does our ability to recognize meaningful material? The quest for answers to these questions makes an interesting research story, one that illustrates psychology's self-correcting process (Woodruff-Pak, 1989). This research developed in phases.

Phase I: Cross-Sectional Evidence for Intellectual Decline

In **cross-sectional studies,** researchers at one point in time test and compare people of various ages. When giving intelligence tests to representative samples of people, researchers consistently find that older adults give fewer correct answers than do younger adults. David Wechsler (1972), creator of the most widely used adult intelligence test, therefore concluded that "the decline of mental ability with age is part of the general [aging] process of the organism as a whole."

For a long time, this rather dismal view of mental decline went unchallenged. Many corporations established mandatory retirement policies, assuming the companies would benefit by replacing aging workers with younger, presumably more capable, employees. As everyone "knows," you can't teach an old dog new tricks.

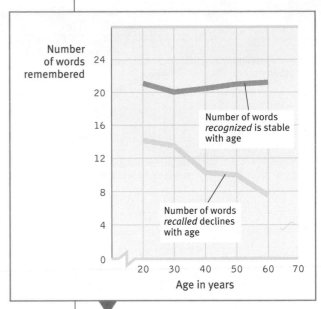

FIGURE 16.8 Recall and recognition in adulthood In this experiment, the ability to *recall* new information declined during early and middle adulthood, but the ability to *recognize* new information did not. (From Schonfield & Robertson, 1966.)

cross-sectional study a study in which people of different ages are compared with one another.

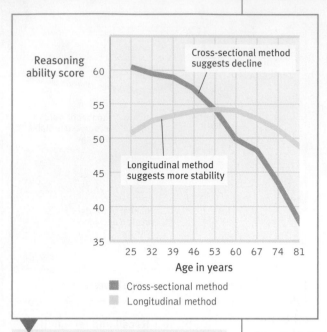

FIGURE 16.9 Cross-sectional versus longitudinal testing of intelligence at various ages In this test of one type of verbal intelligence (inductive reasoning), the cross-sectional method produced declining scores with age. The longitudinal method (in which the same people were retested over a period of years) produced a slight rise in scores well into adulthood. (Adapted from Schaie, 1994.)

|| Like older people, older gorillas process information more slowly (Anderson et al., 2005). ||

"In youth we learn, in age we understand."
Marie Von Ebner-Eschenbach, *Aphorisms,* 1883

Phase II: Longitudinal Evidence for Intellectual Stability

After colleges began giving intelligence tests to entering students about 1920, several psychologists saw their chance to study intelligence **longitudinally**—retesting the same people over a period of years. What they expected to find was a decrease in intelligence after about age 30 (Schaie & Geiwitz, 1982). What they actually found was a surprise: Until late in life, intelligence remained stable (**FIGURE 16.9**). On some tests, it even increased.

How then are we to account for the cross-sectional findings? In retrospect, researchers saw the problem. When cross-sectional studies compared 70-year-olds and 30-year-olds, it compared people not only of two different ages but of two different eras. It compared generally less-educated people (born, say, in the early 1900s) with better-educated people (born after 1950), people raised in large families with people raised in smaller families, people growing up in less affluent families with people raised in more affluent families.

According to this more optimistic view, the myth that intelligence sharply declines with age was laid to rest. At age 70, John Rock developed the birth control pill. At age 78, Grandma Moses took up painting, and she was still painting after age 100. At age 81—and 17 years from the end of his college football coaching career—Amos Alonzo Stagg was named coach of the year. At age 89, architect Frank Lloyd Wright designed New York City's Guggenheim Museum. As everyone "knows," given good health you're never too old to learn.

Phase III: It All Depends

With "everyone knowing" two different and opposing facts about age and intelligence, something was clearly wrong. As it turns out, longitudinal studies have their own potential pitfalls. Those who survive to the end of longitudinal studies may be bright, healthy people whose intelligence is least likely to decline. (Perhaps people who died younger and were removed from the study had declining intelligence.) Adjusting for the loss of participants, as did a study following more than 2000 people over age 75 in Cambridge, England, reveals a steeper intelligence decline. This is especially so as people age after 85 (Brayne et al., 1999).

Research is further complicated by the finding that intelligence is not a single trait, but rather several distinct abilities. Intelligence tests that assess speed of thinking may place older adults at a disadvantage because of their slower neural mechanisms for processing information. Meeting old friends on the street, names rise to the mind's surface more slowly—"like air bubbles in molasses," said David Lykken (1999). But slower processing need not mean less intelligent. When given tests that assess general vocabulary, knowledge, and ability to integrate information, older adults generally fare well (Craik, 1986). Older Canadians surpass younger Canadians at answering questions such as, "Which province was once called New Caledonia?" And in four studies in which players were given 15 minutes to fill in words in *New York Times* crossword puzzles, the highest average performance was achieved by adults in their fifties, sixties, and seventies (**FIGURE 16.10**).

German researcher Paul Baltes and his colleagues (1993, 1994, 1999) developed "wisdom" tests that assess "expert knowledge about life in general and good judgment and advice about how to conduct oneself in the face of complex, uncertain circumstances." Their results suggest that older adults more than hold their own on these tests, too. Thus, despite 30-year-olds' quick-thinking smarts, we usually select older-than-thirties people to be president of the company, the college, or the country. Age is sage. To paraphrase one 60-year-old, "Forty years ago I had a great memory, but I was a fool."

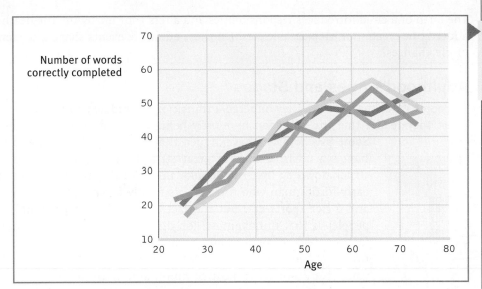

FIGURE 16.10 Word power grows with age In four studies summarized by Timothy Salthouse (2004), older crossword puzzle players excelled when given 15 minutes with a *New York Times* puzzle.

So the answers to our age-and-intelligence questions depend on what we assess and how we assess it. **Crystallized intelligence**—our accumulated knowledge as reflected in vocabulary and analogies tests—*increases* up to old age. **Fluid intelligence**—our ability to reason speedily and abstractly, as when solving novel logic problems—*decreases* slowly up to age 75 or so, then more rapidly, especially after age 85 (Cattell, 1963; Horn, 1982). We can see this pattern in the intelligence scores of a national sample of adults (Kaufman et al., 1989). After adjustments for education, verbal scores (reflecting crystallized intelligence) held relatively steady from ages 20 to 74. Nonverbal, puzzle-solving intelligence declined. With age we lose and we win. We lose recall memory and processing speed, but we gain vocabulary and knowledge (Park et al., 2002). Our decisions also become less distorted by negative emotions such as anxiety, depression, and anger (Blanchard-Fields, 2007; Carstensen & Mikels, 2005).

These cognitive differences help explain why mathematicians and scientists produce much of their most creative work during their late twenties or early thirties, whereas those in literature, history, and philosophy tend to produce their best work in their forties, fifties, and beyond, after accumulating more knowledge (Simonton, 1988, 1990). For example, poets (who depend on fluid intelligence) reach their peak output earlier than prose authors (who need a deeper knowledge reservoir), a finding observed in every major literary tradition, for both living and dead languages.

Despite age-related cognitive changes, studies in several countries indicate that age is only a modest predictor of abilities such as memory and intelligence. Mental ability more strongly correlates with proximity to death. Tell me whether someone is 70, 80, or 90, and you haven't told me much about the person's mental sharpness. But if you tell me whether someone is 8 months or 8 years from death, regardless of age, you'll give me a better clue to the person's mental ability. Especially in the last three or four years of life, cognitive decline typically accelerates (Wilson et al., 2007). Researchers call this near-death drop *terminal decline* (Backman & MacDonald, 2006).

▶‖ Social Development

16-3 What themes and influences mark our social journey from early adulthood to death?

Many differences between younger and older adults are created by significant life events. A new job means new relationships, new expectations, and new demands. Marriage brings the joy of intimacy and the stress of merging your life with another's.

longitudinal study research in which the same people are restudied and retested over a long period.

crystallized intelligence our accumulated knowledge and verbal skills; tends to increase with age.

fluid intelligence our ability to reason speedily and abstractly; tends to decrease during late adulthood.

The birth of a child introduces responsibilities and alters your life focus. The death of a loved one creates an irreplaceable loss. Do these adult life events shape a sequence of life changes?

Adulthood's Ages and Stages

As people enter their forties, they undergo a transition to middle adulthood, a time when they realize that life will soon be mostly behind instead of ahead of them.

Some psychologists have argued that for many the *midlife transition* is a crisis, a time of great struggle, regret, or even feeling struck down by life. The popular image of the midlife crisis is an early-forties man who forsakes his family for a younger girlfriend and a hot sports car. But the fact—reported by large samples of people—is that unhappiness, job dissatisfaction, marital dissatisfaction, divorce, anxiety, and suicide do *not* surge during the early forties (Hunter & Sundel, 1989; Mroczek & Kolarz, 1998). Divorce, for example, is most common among those in their twenties, suicide among those in their seventies and eighties. One study of emotional instability in nearly 10,000 men and women found "not the slightest evidence" that distress peaks anywhere in the midlife age range (**FIGURE 16.11**). For the 1 in 4 adults who do report experiencing a life crisis, the trigger is not age, but a major event, such as illness, divorce, or job loss (Lachman, 2004).

Life events trigger transitions to new life stages at varying ages. The **social clock**—the definition of "the right time" to leave home, get a job, marry, have children, and retire—varies from era to era and culture to culture. In Western Europe, fewer than 10 percent of men over 65 remain in the work force, as do 16 percent in the United States, 36 percent in Japan, and 69 percent in Mexico (Davies et al., 1991). And the once-rigid sequence for many Western women—of student to worker to wife to at-home mom to worker again—has loosened. Contemporary women occupy these roles in any order or all at once. The social clock still ticks, but people feel freer about being out of sync with it.

Even *chance events* can have lasting significance because they often deflect us down one road rather than another (Bandura, 1982). Romantic attraction, for example, is often influenced by chance encounters. Albert Bandura (2005) recalls the ironic true story of a book editor who came to one of Bandura's lectures on the "Psychology of Chance Encounters and Life Paths"—and ended up marrying the woman who happened to sit next to him. The sequence that led to my authoring this book (which was not my idea) began with my being seated near, and getting to know, a distinguished colleague at an international conference.

Thus, chance events, including romantic encounters, can change our lives. Consider one study of identical twins, who tend to make similar choices of friends, clothes, vacations, jobs, and so on. So, if your identical twin became engaged to someone, wouldn't you (being in so many ways the same as your twin) expect to also feel attracted to this person? Surprisingly, only half the identical twins recalled really liking their co-twin's selection, and only 5 percent said, "I could have fallen for my twin's partner." Researchers David Lykken and Auke Tellegen (1993) surmise that romantic love is rather like ducklings' imprinting: Given repeated exposure to someone after childhood, you may form a bond (infatuation) with almost any available person who has a roughly similar background and level of attractiveness and who reciprocates your affections.

> "The important events of a person's life are the products of chains of highly improbable occurrences."
>
> Joseph Traub, "Traub's Law," 2003

FIGURE 16.11 Early forties midlife crises? Among 10,000 people responding to a national health survey, there was no early forties increase in emotional instability ("neuroticism") scores. (From McCrae & Costa, 1990.)

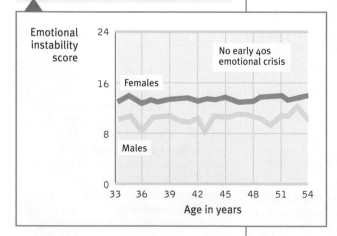

Adulthood's Commitments

Two basic aspects of our lives dominate adulthood. Erik Erikson called them *intimacy* (forming close relationships) and *generativity* (being productive and supporting future generations). Researchers have chosen various terms—*affiliation* and *achievement, attachment* and *productivity, commitment* and *competence*. Sigmund Freud (1935) put it most simply: The healthy adult, he said, is one who can *love* and *work*.

Love

We typically flirt, fall in love, and commit—one person at a time. "Pair-bonding is a trademark of the human animal," observed anthropologist Helen Fisher (1993). From an evolutionary perspective, relatively monogamous pairing makes sense: Parents who cooperated to nurture their children to maturity were more likely to have their genes passed along to posterity than were parents who didn't.

Adult bonds of love are most satisfying and enduring when marked by a similarity of interests and values, a sharing of emotional and material support, and intimate self-disclosure. Couples who seal their love with commitment—via (in one Vermont study) marriage for heterosexual couples and civil unions for homosexual couples—more often endure (Balsam et al., 2008). Marriage bonds are especially likely to last when couples marry after age 20 and are well educated. Compared with their counterparts of 40 years ago, people in Western countries *are* better educated and marrying later. Yet, ironically, they are nearly twice as likely to divorce. (Both Canada and the United States now have about one divorce for every two marriages [Bureau of the Census, 2007], and in Europe, divorce is only slightly less common.) The divorce rate partly reflects women's lessened economic dependence and men and women's rising expectations. We now hope not only for an enduring bond, but also for a mate who is a wage earner, caregiver, intimate friend, and warm and responsive lover.

Might test-driving life together in a "trial marriage" minimize divorce risk? In a 2001 Gallup survey of American twenty-somethings, 62 percent thought it would (Whitehead & Popenoe, 2001). In reality, in Europe, Canada, and the United States, those who cohabit before marriage have had *higher* rates of divorce and marital dysfunction than those who did not cohabit (Dush et al., 2003; Popenoe & Whitehead, 2002). The risk appears greatest for cohabiting prior to engagement (Kline et al., 2004).

Two factors help explain why American children born to cohabiting parents are about five times more likely to experience their parents' separation than are children born to married parents (Osborne et al., 2007). First, cohabiters tend to be initially less committed to the ideal of enduring marriage. Second, they become even less marriage-supporting while cohabiting.

Nonetheless, the institution of marriage endures. Worldwide, reports the United Nations, 9 in 10 heterosexual adults marry. And marriage is a predictor of happiness, health, sexual satisfaction, and income. National Opinion Research Center surveys of more than 40,000 Americans since 1972 reveal that 40 percent of married adults, though only 23 percent of unmarried adults, have reported being "very happy." Lesbian couples, too, report greater well-being than those who are alone (Peplau & Fingerhut, 2007; Wayment & Peplau, 1995). Moreover, neighborhoods with high marriage rates typically have low rates of social pathologies such as crime, delinquency, and emotional disorders among children (Myers & Scanzoni, 2005).

Marriages that last are not always devoid of conflict. Some couples fight but also shower one another with affection. Other couples never raise their voices yet also seldom praise one another or nuzzle. Both styles can last. After observing the interactions of 2000 couples, John Gottman (1994) reported one indicator of marital success: at least a five-to-one ratio of positive to negative interactions. Stable marriages provide five times more instances of smiling, touching, complimenting, and

"One can live magnificently in this world if one knows how to work and how to love."
Leo Tolstoy, 1856

Love Intimacy, attachment, commitment—love by whatever name—is central to healthy and happy adulthood.

‖ What do you think? Does marriage correlate with happiness because marital support and intimacy breed happiness, because happy people more often marry and stay married, or both? ‖

social clock the culturally preferred timing of social events such as marriage, parenthood, and retirement.

laughing than of sarcasm, criticism, and insults. So, if you want to predict which newlyweds will stay together, don't pay attention to how passionately they are in love. The couples who make it are more often those who refrain from putting down their partners. To prevent a cancerous negativity, successful couples learn to fight fair (to state feelings without insulting) and to steer conflict away from chaos with comments like "I know it's not your fault" or "I'll just be quiet for a moment and listen."

Often, love bears children. For most people, this most enduring of life changes is a happy event. "I feel an overwhelming love for my children unlike anything I feel for anyone else," said 93 percent of American mothers in a national survey (Erickson & Aird, 2005). Many fathers feel the same. A few weeks after the birth of my first child I was suddenly struck by a realization: "So *this* is how my parents felt about me!"

When children begin to absorb time, money, and emotional energy, satisfaction with the marriage itself may decline. This is especially likely among employed women who, more than they expected, carry the traditional burden of doing the chores at home. Putting effort into creating an equitable relationship can thus pay double dividends: a more satisfying marriage, which breeds better parent-child relations (Erel & Burman, 1995).

Although love bears children, children eventually leave home. This departure is a significant and sometimes difficult event. For most people, however, an empty nest is a happy place (Adelmann et al., 1989; Glenn, 1975). Compared with middle-aged women with children still at home, those living in an empty nest report greater happiness and greater enjoyment of their marriage. Many parents experience a "post-launch honeymoon," especially if they maintain close relationships with their children (White & Edwards, 1990). As Daniel Gilbert (2006) has said, "The only known symptom of 'empty nest syndrome' is increased smiling."

|| If you have left home, did your parents suffer the "empty nest syndrome"—a feeling of distress focusing on a loss of purpose and relationship? Did they mourn the lost joy of listening for you in the wee hours of Saturday morning? Or did they seem to discover a new freedom, relaxation, and (if still married) renewed satisfaction with their own relationship? ||

Work

For many adults, the answer to "Who are you?" depends a great deal on the answer to "What do you do?" For women and men, choosing a career path is difficult, especially in today's changing work environment. During the first two years of college or university, few students can predict their later careers. Most shift from their initially intended majors, many find their postcollege employment in fields not directly related to their majors, and most will change careers (Rothstein, 1980). In the end, happiness is about having work that fits your interests and provides you with a sense of competence and accomplishment. It is having a close, supportive companion who cheers your accomplishments (Gable et al., 2006). And for some, it includes having children who love you and whom you love and feel proud of.

Job satisfaction and life satisfaction
Work can provide us with a sense of identity and competence and opportunities for accomplishment. Perhaps this is why challenging and interesting occupations enhance people's happiness.

Well-Being Across the Life Span

To live is to grow older. This moment marks the oldest you have ever been and the youngest you will henceforth be. That means we all can look back with satisfaction or regret, and forward with hope or dread. When asked what they would have done differently if they could relive their lives, people's most common answer is "Taken my education more seriously and worked harder at it" (Kinnier & Metha, 1989; Roese & Summerville, 2005). Other regrets—"I should have told my father I loved him," "I regret that I never went to Europe"—also focus less on mistakes made than on the things one *failed* to do (Gilovich & Medvec, 1995).

From the teens to midlife, people typically experience a strengthening sense of identity, confidence, and self-esteem (Miner-Rubino et al., 2004; Robins & Trzesniewski, 2005). In later life, challenges arise: Income shrinks, work is often taken away, the body deteriorates, recall fades, energy wanes, family members and friends die or move away, and the great enemy, death, looms ever closer. Small wonder that most presume that happiness declines in later life (Lacey et al., 2006). But the over-65 years are not notably unhappy, as Ronald Inglehart (1990) discovered when he amassed interviews conducted during the 1980s with representative samples of nearly 170,000 people in 16 nations (**FIGURE 16.12**). Newer surveys of some 2 million people worldwide confirm that happiness is slightly higher among both young and older adults than among those middle-aged. Moreover, national studies in both Britain and Australia reveal that the risk of depression tapers off in later life (Blanchflower & Oswald, 2008; Troller et al., 2007).

If anything, positive feelings grow after midlife and negative feelings subside (Charles et al., 2001; Mroczek, 2001). Consider:

▶ Older adults increasingly use words that convey positive emotions (Pennebaker & Stone, 2003).

▶ Older adults attend less and less to negative information. For example, they are slower than younger adults to perceive negative faces (Carstensen & Mikels, 2005).

▶ The amygdala, a neural processing center for emotions, shows diminishing activity in older adults in response to negative events, but it maintains its responsiveness to positive events (Mather et al., 2004; Williams et al., 2006).

▶ Brain-wave reactions to negative images diminish with age (Kisley et al., 2007).

"I hope I die before I get old," sang rock star Pete Townshend—when he was 20.

"At twenty we worry about what others think of us. At forty we don't care what others think of us. At sixty we discover they haven't been thinking about us at all."
Anonymous

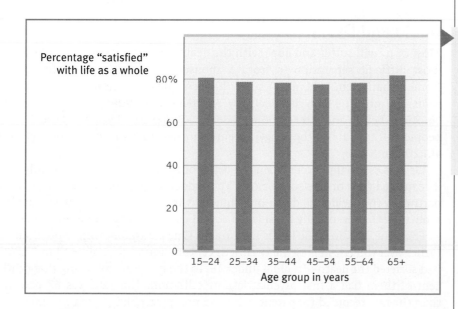

Percentage "satisfied" with life as a whole

Age group in years

FIGURE 16.12 Age and life satisfaction With the tasks of early adulthood behind them, many older adults have more time to pursue personal interests. No wonder their satisfaction with life remains high, and may even rise if they are healthy and active. As this graph, based on surveys of 170,000 people in 16 countries shows, age differences in life satisfaction are small. (Data from Inglehart, 1990.)

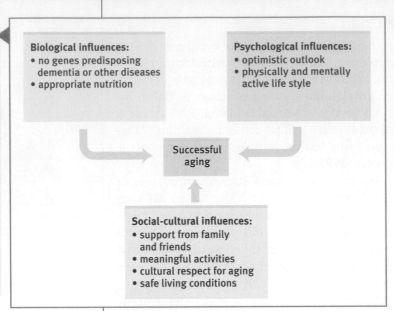

Biological influences:
• no genes predisposing dementia or other diseases
• appropriate nutrition

Psychological influences:
• optimistic outlook
• physically and mentally active life style

Successful aging

Social-cultural influences:
• support from family and friends
• meaningful activities
• cultural respect for aging
• safe living conditions

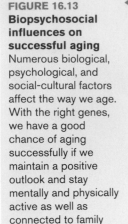

"The best thing about being 100 is *no peer pressure*."

Lewis W. Kuester, 2005, on turning 100

Moreover, at all ages, the bad feelings we associate with negative events fade faster than do the good feelings we associate with positive events (Walker et al., 2003). This contributes to most older people's sense that life, on balance, has been mostly good. Given that growing older is an outcome of living (an outcome nearly all of us prefer to early dying), the positivity of later life is comforting. More and more people flourish into later life, thanks to biological, psychological, and social-cultural influences (**FIGURE 16.13**).

The resilience of well-being across the life span obscures some interesting age-related emotional differences. Although life satisfaction does not decline with age, it often wanes in the terminal decline phase, as death approaches (Gerstorf et al., 2008). Also, as the years go by, feelings mellow (Costa et al., 1987; Diener et al., 1986). Highs become less high, lows less low. Thus, although we are less often depressed, and our *average* feeling level tends to remain stable, with age we also find ourselves less often feeling excited, intensely proud, and on top of the world. Compliments provoke less elation and criticisms less despair, as both become merely additional feedback atop a mountain of accumulated praise and blame.

Psychologists Mihaly Csikszentmihalyi and Reed Larson (1984) mapped people's emotional terrain by periodically signaling them with electronic beepers to report their current activities and feelings. They found that teenagers typically come down from elation or up from gloom in less than an hour. Adult moods are less extreme but more enduring. For most people, old age offers less intense joy but greater contentment and increased spirituality, especially for those who remain socially engaged (Harlow & Cantor, 1996; Wink & Dillon, 2002). As we age, life becomes less an emotional roller coaster.

Death and Dying

"Love—why, I'll tell you what love is: It's you at 75 and her at 71, each of you listening for the other's step in the next room, each afraid that a sudden silence, a sudden cry, could mean a lifetime's talk is over."

Brian Moore, *The Luck of Ginger Coffey*, 1960

Most of us will suffer and cope with the deaths of relatives and friends. Usually, the most difficult separation is from a spouse—a loss suffered by five times more women than men. When, as usually happens, death comes at an expected late-life time, the grieving may be relatively short-lived. (**FIGURE 16.14** shows the typical emotions before and after a spouse's death.) But even 20 years after losing a spouse, people still talk about the long-lost partner once a month on average (Carnelley et al., 2006).

Grief is especially severe when the death of a loved one comes suddenly and before its expected time on the social clock. The sudden illness that claims a 45-year-old life partner or the accidental death of a child may trigger a year or more of memory-laden mourning that eventually subsides to a mild depression (Lehman et al., 1987).

For some, however, the loss is unbearable. One study, following more than 1 million Danes over the last half of the twentieth century, found that more than 17,000 people had suffered the death of a child under 18. In the five years following that death, 3 percent of them had a first psychiatric hospitalization. This rate was 67 percent higher than the rate recorded for parents who had not lost a child (Li et al., 2005).

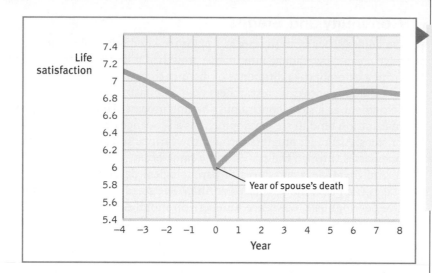

FIGURE 16.14 Life satisfaction before, during the year of, and after a spouse's death Richard Lucas and his collaborators (2003) examined longitudinal annual surveys of more than 30,000 Germans. The researchers identified 513 married people who experienced the death of a spouse and did not remarry. They found that life satisfaction began to dip during the prewidowhood year, dropped significantly during the year of the spouse's death, and then eventually rebounded to nearly the earlier level. (*Source:* Richard Lucas.)

Even so, the normal range of reactions to a loved one's death is wider than most suppose. Some cultures encourage public weeping and wailing; others hide grief. Within any culture, individuals differ. Given similar losses, some people grieve hard and long, others are more resilient (Ott et al., 2007). Contrary to popular misconceptions, however,

▶ terminally ill and bereaved people do not go through identical predictable stages, such as denial before anger (Nolen-Hoeksema & Larson, 1999). A Yale study following 233 bereaved individuals through time did, however, find that yearning for the loved one reached a high point four months after the loss, with anger peaking, on average, about a month later (Maciejewski et al., 2007).

▶ those who express the strongest grief immediately do not purge their grief more quickly (Bonanno & Kaltman, 1999; Wortman & Silver, 1989).

▶ bereavement therapy and self-help groups offer support, but there is similar healing power in the passing of time and the support of friends—and also in giving support and help to others (Brown et al., 2008). Grieving spouses who talk often with others or who receive grief counseling adjust about as well as those who grieve more privately (Bonanno, 2001, 2004; Genevro, 2003; Stroebe et al., 2001, 2002, 2005).

We can be grateful for the waning of death-denying attitudes. Facing death with dignity and openness helps people complete the life cycle with a sense of life's meaningfulness and unity—the sense that their existence has been good and that life and death are parts of an ongoing cycle. Although death may be unwelcome, life itself can be affirmed even at death. This is especially so for people who review their lives not with despair but with what Erik Erikson called a sense of *integrity*—a feeling that one's life has been meaningful and worthwhile.

"Donald is such a fatalist—he's convinced he's going to grow old and die."

"Consider, friend, as you pass by, as you are now, so once was I. As I am now, you too shall be. Prepare, therefore, to follow me."
Scottish tombstone epitaph

▶❙❙ Reflections on Two Major Developmental Issues

Any survey of developmental psychology must consider three pervasive issues. The first—how development is steered by genes and by experience—recurs throughout this text. But let's stop now and consider the second issue, whether development is a gradual, continuous process or a series of discrete stages, and the third, whether development is characterized more by stability over time or by change.

Stages of the life cycle

FIGURE 16.15 Comparing the stage theories (With thanks to Dr. Sandra Gibbs, Muskegon Community College, for inspiring this illustration.)

Continuity and Stages

Do adults differ from infants as a giant redwood differs from its seedling—a difference created by gradual, cumulative growth? Or do they differ as a butterfly differs from a caterpillar—a difference of distinct stages?

Generally speaking, researchers who emphasize experience and learning see development as a slow, continuous shaping process. Those who emphasize biological maturation tend to see development as a sequence of genetically predisposed stages or steps: Although progress through the various stages may be quick or slow, everyone passes through the stages in the same order.

Are there clear-cut stages of psychological development, as there are physical stages such as walking before running? The stage theories of Jean Piaget on cognitive development, Lawrence Kohlberg on moral development, and Erik Erikson on psychosocial development propose that such stages do exist (**FIGURE 16.15**). But some research casts doubt on the idea that life proceeds through neatly defined, age-linked stages. Young children have some abilities Piaget attributed to later stages. Kohlberg's work reflected a worldview characteristic of educated males in individualistic cultures and emphasized thinking over acting. Adult life does not progress through the fixed, predictable series of steps Erikson envisioned.

Nevertheless, the stage concept remains useful. The human brain does experience growth spurts during childhood and puberty that correspond roughly to Piaget's stages (Thatcher et al., 1987). And stage theories contribute a developmental perspective on the whole life span, by suggesting how people of one age think and act differently when they arrive at a later age.

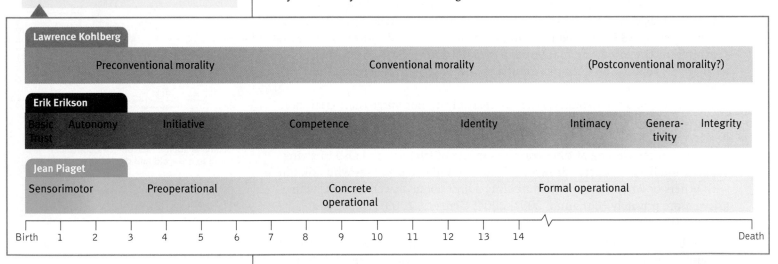

Stability and Change

This leads us to the final developmental issue: Over time, are people's personalities consistent, or do they change? If reunited with a long-lost grade school friend, would you instantly recognize that "it's the same old Andy"? Or does a person befriended during one period of life seem like a different person at a later period? (That was the experience of one male friend of mine who failed to recognize a former classmate at his 40-year college reunion. The aghast classmate to whom he spoke was his long-ago ex-wife.)

Researchers who have followed lives through time have found evidence for both stability and change. There is continuity to personality and yet, happily for troubled children and adolescents, life is a process of becoming: The struggles of the present may be laying a foundation for a happier tomorrow. More specifically, researchers generally agree on the following points:

1. The first two years of life provide a poor basis for predicting a person's eventual traits (Kagan et al., 1978, 1998). Older children and adolescents also change.

As adults grow older, there is continuity of self.

Although delinquent children have elevated rates of later work problems, substance abuse, and crime, many confused and troubled children have blossomed into mature, successful adults (Moffitt et al., 2002; Roberts et al., 2001; Thomas & Chess, 1986).

2. As people grow older, personality gradually stabilizes (Hampson & Goldberg, 2006; Johnson et al., 2005; Terracciano et al., 2006). Some characteristics, such as temperament, are more stable than others, such as social attitudes (Moss & Susman, 1980). When a research team led by Avshalom Caspi (2003) studied 1000 New Zealanders from age 3 to 26, they were struck by the consistency of temperament and emotionality across time.

3. In some ways, we all change with age. Most shy, fearful toddlers begin opening up by age 4, and most people become more self-disciplined, stable, agreeable, and self-confident in the years after adolescence (McCrae & Costa, 1994; Roberts et al., 2003, 2006, 2008). Many irresponsible 18-year-olds have matured into 40-year-old business or cultural leaders. (If you are the former, you aren't done yet.) Such changes can occur without changing a person's position *relative to others* of the same age. The hard-driving young adult may mellow by later life, yet still be a relatively hard-driving senior citizen.

Finally, we should remember that life requires *both* stability and change. Stability enables us to depend on others, provides our identity, and motivates our concern for the healthy development of children. Change motivates our concerns about present influences, sustains our hope for a brighter future, and lets us adapt and grow with experience.

> "As at 7, so at 70."
> Jewish proverb

> "At 70, I would say the advantage is that you take life more calmly. You know that 'this, too, shall pass!'"
> Eleanor Roosevelt, 1954

REVIEW

Adulthood, and Reflections on Developmental Issues

16-1 **What physical changes occur during middle and late adulthood?** Muscular strength, reaction time, sensory abilities, and cardiac output begin to decline in the late twenties and continue throughout middle and late adulthood. Around age 50, *menopause* ends women's period of fertility but usually does not trigger psychological problems or interfere with a satisfying sex life. Men do not undergo a similar sharp drop in hormone levels or fertility.

16-2 **How do memory and intelligence change with age?** As the years pass, recall begins to decline, especially for meaningless information, but recognition memory remains strong. *Cross-sectional* and *longitudinal studies* have shown that *fluid intelligence* declines in later life but *crystallized intelligence* does not.

16-3 **What themes and influences mark our social journey from early adulthood to death?** Adults do not progress through an orderly sequence of age-related social stages. More important are life events, and the loosening of strict dictates of the *social clock*—the culturally preferred timing of social events. The dominant themes of adulthood are love and work, which Erikson called intimacy and generativity. Life satisfaction tends to remain high across the life span.

Terms and Concepts to Remember

menopause, p. 207	crystallized intelligence, p. 215
cross-sectional study, p. 213	fluid intelligence, p. 215
longitudinal study, p. 214	social clock, p. 216

Test Yourself

1. Research has shown that living together before marriage predicts an increased likelihood of future divorce. Can you imagine two possible explanations for this correlation?

2. What findings in psychology support the concept of stages in development and the idea of stability in personality across the life span? What findings challenge these ideas?

(Answers to the Test Yourself questions can be found in Appendix B at the end of the book.)

Ask Yourself

1. As you reflect on your last few years—formative years if you are a young adult—what do you most regret? What do you feel best about?

2. Are you the same person you were as a preschooler? A 10-year-old? A mid-teen? How are you different? How are you the same?

⦿⦿ WEB

Multiple-choice self-tests and more may be found at www.worthpublishers.com/myers

Sensation and Perception

MODULES

17
Introduction to Sensation and Perception

18
Vision

19
Hearing

20
Other Senses

21
Perceptual Organization

22
Perceptual Interpretation

"I have perfect vision," explains my colleague, Heather Sellers, an acclaimed writer and writing teacher. Her vision may be fine, but there is a problem with her perception. She cannot recognize faces.

In her memoir, *Face First,* Sellers (2010) tells of awkward moments resulting from her lifelong *prosopagnosia*—face blindness.

> In college, on a date at the Spaghetti Station, I returned from the bathroom and plunked myself down in the wrong booth, facing the wrong man. I remained unaware he was not my date even as my date (a stranger to me) accosted Wrong Booth Guy, and then stormed out of the Station. I can't distinguish actors in movies and on television. I do not recognize myself in photos or video. I can't recognize my step-sons in the soccer pick-up line; I failed to determine which husband was mine at a party, in the mall, at the market.

Her inability to recognize acquaintances means that people sometimes perceive her as snobby or aloof. "Why did you walk past me?" someone might later ask. Similar to those of us with hearing loss who fake hearing during trite social conversation, Sellers sometimes fakes recognition. She often smiles at people she passes, in case she knows them. Or she pretends to know the person with whom she is talking. (To avoid the stress associated with such perception failures, people with serious hearing loss or with prosopagnosia often shy away from busy social situations.) But there is an upside: When encountering someone who previously irritated her, she typically won't feel ill will, because she doesn't recognize the person.

This curious mix of "perfect vision" and face blindness illustrates the distinction between *sensation* and *perception*. When Sellers looks at a friend, her sensation is normal: Her sensory receptors detect the same information yours would, and they transmit that information to her brain. And her perception—the organization and interpretation of sensory information that enables her to consciously recognize objects—is almost normal. Thus, she may recognize people from their hair, their gait, their voice, or their particular physique, just not their face. She can see the elements of their face—the nose, the eyes, and the chin—and yet, at a party, "[I introduce myself] to my colleague Gloria THREE TIMES." Her experience is much like the struggle you or I would have trying to recognize a specific penguin in a group of waddling penguins.

Thanks to an area on the underside of your brain's right hemisphere, you can recognize a human face (but not a penguin's) in one-seventh of a second. As soon as you detect a face, you recognize it (Jacques & Rossion, 2006).

How do you do it? Twenty-four hours a day, all kinds of stimuli from the outside world bombard your body. Meanwhile, in a silent, cushioned, inner world, your brain floats in utter darkness. By itself, it sees nothing. It hears nothing. It feels nothing. *So, how does the world out there get in?*

To phrase the question scientifically: How do we construct our representations of the external world? How do a campfire's flicker, crackle, and smoky scent activate neural connections? And how, from this living neurochemistry, do we create our conscious experience of the fire's motion and temperature, its aroma and beauty? In search of answers to such questions, let's look more closely at what psychologists have learned about how we sense and perceive the world around us. Module 17 outlines the basic principles of sensation and perception. Modules 18, 19, and 20 examine vision, hearing, and other senses. And Modules 21 and 22 explore perceptual organization and perceptual interpretation.

MODULE 17

Introduction to Sensation and Perception

17-1 What are sensation and perception? What do we mean by bottom-up processing and top-down processing?

In our everyday experiences, **sensation** and **perception** blend into one continuous process. Here, we slow down that process to study its parts.

We start with the sensory receptors and work up to higher levels of processing. Psychologists refer to sensory analysis that starts at the entry level as **bottom-up processing.** But our minds also *interpret* what our senses *detect*. We construct perceptions drawing both on sensations coming bottom-up to the brain and on our experience and expectations, which psychologists call **top-down processing.** For example, as our brain deciphers the information in **FIGURE 17.1**, bottom-up processing enables our sensory systems to detect the lines, angles, and colors that form the horses, rider, and surroundings. Using top-down processing we consider the painting's title, notice the apprehensive expressions, and then direct our attention to aspects of the painting that will give those observations meaning.

Nature's sensory gifts suit each recipient's needs. They enable each organism to obtain essential information. Consider:

▶ A frog, which feeds on flying insects, has eyes with receptor cells that fire only in response to small, dark, moving objects. A frog could starve to death knee-deep in motionless flies. But let one zoom by and the frog's "bug detector" cells snap awake.

▶ A male silkworm moth has receptors so sensitive to the female sex-attractant odor that a single female need release only a billionth of an ounce per second to attract every male silkworm moth within a mile. That is why there continue to be silkworms.

FIGURE 17.1 What's going on here? Our sensory and perceptual processes work together to help us sort out the complex images, including the hidden faces, in this Bev Doolittle painting, *The Forest Has Eyes*.

Detail, *The Forest Has Eyes* by Bev Doolittle © The Greenwich Workshop, Inc., Trumbull, CT.

▶ We are similarly equipped to detect the important features of our environment. Our ears are most sensitive to sound frequencies that include human voice consonants and a baby's cry.

We begin our exploration of our sensory gifts with a question that cuts across all our sensory systems: What stimuli cross our threshold for conscious awareness?

▶‖ Thresholds

17-2   What are the absolute and difference thresholds, and do stimuli below the absolute threshold have any influence?

We exist in a sea of energy. At this moment, you and I are being struck by X-rays and radio waves, ultraviolet and infrared light, and sound waves of very high and very low frequencies. To all of these we are blind and deaf. Other animals detect a world that lies beyond human experience (Hughes, 1999). Migrating birds stay on course aided by an internal magnetic compass. Bats and dolphins locate prey with sonar (bouncing echoing sound off objects). On a cloudy day, bees navigate by detecting polarized light from an invisible (to us) sun.

The shades on our own senses are open just a crack, allowing us only a restricted awareness of this vast sea of energy. Let's see what **psychophysics** has discovered about the physical energy we can detect and its effect on our psychological experience.

Absolute Thresholds

To some kinds of stimuli we are exquisitely sensitive. Standing atop a mountain on an utterly dark, clear night, most of us could see a candle flame atop another mountain 30 miles away. We could feel the wing of a bee falling on our cheek. We could smell a single drop of perfume in a three-room apartment (Galanter, 1962).

Our awareness of these faint stimuli illustrates our **absolute thresholds**—the minimum stimulation necessary to detect a particular light, sound, pressure, taste, or odor 50 percent of the time. To test your absolute threshold for sounds, a hearing specialist would expose each of your ears to varying sound levels. For each tone, the test would define where half the time you correctly detect the sound and half the time you do not. For each of your senses, that 50-50 recognition point defines your absolute threshold.

Absolute thresholds may vary with age. Sensitivity to high-pitched sounds declines with normal aging, leaving older ears in need of louder sound to hear a high-pitched cellphone ring. That fact of life has been exploited by some students wanting a ringtone their instructors are unlikely to hear, and by some Welsh shopkeepers broadcasting annoying sounds that help disperse loitering teens without repelling older adults.

Signal Detection

Detecting a weak stimulus, or signal, depends not only on the signal's strength (such as a hearing-test tone) but also on our psychological state—our experience, expectations, motivation, and alertness. **Signal detection theory** predicts when we will detect weak signals (measured as our ratio of "hits" to "false alarms"). Signal detection theorists seek to understand why people respond differently to the same stimuli, and why the same person's reactions vary as circumstances change. Exhausted parents will notice the faintest whimper from a newborn's cradle while failing to notice louder, unimportant sounds.

In a horror-filled wartime situation, failure to detect an intruder could be fatal. Mindful of many comrades' deaths, soldiers and police in Iraq probably became more likely to notice—and fire at—an almost imperceptible noise. With such heightened

sensation   the process by which our sensory receptors and nervous system receive and represent stimulus energies from our environment.

perception   the process of organizing and interpreting sensory information, enabling us to recognize meaningful objects and events.

bottom-up processing   analysis that begins with the sensory receptors and works up to the brain's integration of sensory information.

top-down processing   information processing guided by higher-level mental processes, as when we construct perceptions drawing on our experience and expectations.

psychophysics   the study of relationships between the physical characteristics of stimuli, such as their intensity, and our psychological experience of them.

absolute threshold   the minimum stimulation needed to detect a particular stimulus 50 percent of the time.

signal detection theory   a theory predicting how and when we detect the presence of a faint stimulus (*signal*) amid background stimulation (*noise*). Assumes there is no single absolute threshold and that detection depends partly on a person's experience, expectations, motivation, and alertness.

‖ Try out this old riddle on a couple of friends. "You're driving a bus with 12 passengers. At your first stop, 6 passengers get off. At the second stop, 3 get off. At the third stop, 2 more get off but 3 new people get on. What color are the bus driver's eyes?" Do your friends detect the signal—who is the bus driver?—amid the accompanying noise? ‖

Carol Lee/Tony Stone Images

Signal detection How soon would you notice the radar blips of an approaching object? Fairly quickly if (1) you expect an attack, (2) it is important that you detect it, and (3) you are alert.

responsiveness come more false alarms, as when the U.S. military fired on an approaching car that was rushing an Italian journalist to freedom, killing the Italian intelligence officer who had rescued her. In peacetime, when survival is not threatened, the same soldiers would require a stronger signal before sensing danger.

Signal detection can also have life-or-death consequences when people are responsible for watching an airport scanner for weapons, monitoring patients from an intensive-care nursing station, or detecting radar blips. Studies have shown, for example, that people's ability to catch a faint signal diminishes after about 30 minutes. But this diminishing response depends on the task, on the time of day, and even on whether the participants periodically exercise (Warm & Dember, 1986). To help motivate airport baggage screeners, the U.S. Transportation Security Administration periodically adds images of guns, knives, and other threatening objects into bag X-rays. When the signal is detected, the system congratulates the screener and the image disappears (Winerman, 2006). Experience matters, too. In one experiment, 10 hours of action video game playing—scanning for and instantly responding to any intrusion—increased novice players' signal detection skills (Green & Bavelier, 2003).

Subliminal Stimulation

Hoping to penetrate our unconscious, entrepreneurs offer recordings that supposedly speak directly to our brains to help us lose weight, stop smoking, or improve our memories. Masked by soothing ocean sounds, unheard messages ("I am thin," "Smoke tastes bad," or "I do well on tests. I have total recall of information") will, they say, influence our behavior. Such claims make two assumptions: (1) We can unconsciously sense **subliminal** (literally, "below threshold") stimuli, and (2) without our awareness, these stimuli have extraordinary suggestive powers. Can we? Do they?

Can we sense stimuli below our absolute thresholds? In one sense, the answer is clearly *yes*. Remember that an "absolute" threshold is merely the point at which we detect a stimulus *half the time* (**FIGURE 17.2**). At or slightly below this threshold, we will still detect the stimulus some of the time.

FIGURE 17.2 Absolute threshold What subtle differences can a person detect among these coffee samples? When stimuli are detectable less than 50 percent of the time, they are "subliminal." *Absolute threshold* is the intensity at which we can detect a stimulus half the time.

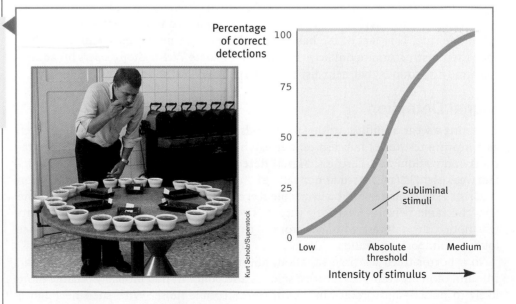

Kurt Scholz/Superstock

Can we be affected by stimuli so weak as to be unnoticed? Under certain conditions, the answer is *yes*. An invisible image or word can briefly **prime** your response to a later question. In a typical experiment, the image or word is quickly flashed, then replaced by a *masking stimulus* that interrupts the brain's processing before conscious perception. For example, one experiment subliminally flashed either emotionally positive scenes (kittens, a romantic couple) or negative scenes (a werewolf, a dead body) an instant before participants viewed slides of people (Krosnick et al., 1992). The participants consciously perceived either scene as only a flash of light. Yet the people somehow looked nicer if their image immediately followed unperceived kittens rather than an unperceived werewolf. Another experiment exposed people to subliminal pleasant, neutral, or unpleasant odors (Li et al., 2007). Despite having no awareness of the odors, the participants rated a neutral-expression face as more likable after exposure to pleasant rather than unpleasant smells.

This experiment illustrates an intriguing phenomenon: Sometimes we *feel* what we do not know and cannot describe. An imperceptibly brief stimulus often triggers a weak response that *can* be detected by brain scanning (Blankenburg et al., 2003; Haynes & Rees, 2005, 2006). The conclusion (turn up the volume here): *Much of our information processing occurs automatically, out of sight, off the radar screen of our conscious mind.*

But does the fact of subliminal *sensation* verify entrepreneurial claims of subliminal *persuasion*? Can advertisers really manipulate us with "hidden persuasion"? The near-consensus among researchers is *no*. Their verdict is similar to that of astronomers who say of astrologers, *yes*, they are right that stars and planets are out there; but *no*, the celestial bodies don't directly affect us. The laboratory research reveals a *subtle, fleeting* effect. Priming thirsty people with the subliminal word *thirst* might therefore, for a brief interval, make a thirst-quenching beverage ad more persuasive (Strahan et al., 2002). Likewise, priming thirsty people with Lipton Ice Tea may increase their choosing the primed brand (Karremans et al., 2006). But the subliminal-message hucksters claim something different: a *powerful, enduring* effect on behavior.

To test whether commercial subliminal recordings have an effect beyond that of a placebo (the effect of one's belief in them), Anthony Greenwald and his colleagues (1991, 1992) randomly assigned university students to listen daily for five weeks to commercial subliminal messages claiming to improve either self-esteem or memory. But the researchers played a very practical joke and switched half of the labels. Some students *thought* they were receiving affirmations of self-esteem when they actually were hearing the memory enhancement message. Others got the self-esteem message but thought their memory was being recharged.

Were the recordings effective? Students' scores on tests for both self-esteem and memory, taken before and after the five weeks, revealed no effects. And yet, those who *thought* they had heard a memory recording *believed* their memories had improved. A similar result occurred for those who thought they had heard a self-esteem recording. The recordings had no effects, yet the students *perceived* themselves receiving the benefits they *expected*. When reading this research, one hears echoes of the testimonies that ooze from the mail-order catalogs. Some customers, having bought what is not supposed to be heard (and having indeed not heard it!) offer testimonials like, "I really know that your tapes were invaluable in reprogramming my mind." Over a decade, Greenwald conducted 16 double-blind experiments evaluating subliminal self-help tapes. His results were uniform: Not one had any therapeutic effect (Greenwald, 1992). His conclusion: "Subliminal procedures offer little or nothing of value to the marketing practitioner" (Pratkanis & Greenwald, 1988).

subliminal below one's absolute threshold for conscious awareness.

priming the activation, often unconsciously, of certain associations, thus predisposing one's perception, memory, or response.

"The heart has its reasons which reason does not know."
Pascal, *Pensées*, 1670

Subliminal persuasion? Although subliminally presented stimuli *can* subtly influence people, experiments discount attempts at subliminal advertising and self-improvement. (The playful message here is not actually subliminal—because you can easily perceive it.)

Babs Reingold

The difference threshold In this computer-generated copy of the Twenty-third Psalm, each line of the typeface changes imperceptibly. How many lines are required for you to experience a just noticeable difference?

The LORD is my shepherd;
    I shall not want.
He maketh me to lie down
    in green pastures:
    he leadeth me
      beside the still waters.
He restoreth my soul:
    he leadeth me
    in the paths of righteousness
    for his name's sake.
Yea, though I walk through the valley
    of the shadow of death,
    I will fear no evil:
for thou art with me;
    thy rod and thy staff
    they comfort me.
Thou preparest a table before me
    in the presence of mine enemies:
    thou anointest my head with oil,
    my cup runneth over.
Surely goodness and mercy
    shall follow me
    all the days of my life:
and I will dwell
    in the house of the LORD
    for ever.

difference threshold the minimum difference between two stimuli required for detection 50 percent of the time. We experience the difference threshold as a *just noticeable difference* (or *jnd*).

Weber's law the principle that, to be perceived as different, two stimuli must differ by a constant minimum percentage (rather than a constant amount).

sensory adaptation diminished sensitivity as a consequence of constant stimulation.

"We need above all to know about changes; no one wants or needs to be reminded 16 hours a day that his shoes are on."
Neuroscientist David Hubel (1979)

"My suspicion is that the universe is not only queerer than we suppose, but queerer than we can suppose."
J. B. S. Haldane, *Possible Worlds,* 1927

Difference Thresholds

To function effectively, we need absolute thresholds low enough to allow us to detect important sights, sounds, textures, tastes, and smells. We also need to detect small differences among stimuli. A musician must detect minute discrepancies in an instrument's tuning. Parents must detect the sound of their own child's voice amid other children's voices. Even after living two years in Scotland, sheep *baa's* all sound alike to my ears. But not to those of ewes, which I have observed streaking, after shearing, directly to the *baa* of their lamb amid the chorus of other distressed lambs.

The **difference threshold,** also called the *just noticeable difference (jnd),* is the minimum difference a person (or sheep) can detect between any two stimuli half the time. That detectable difference increases with the size of the stimulus. Thus, if you add 1 ounce to a 10-ounce weight, you will detect the difference; add 1 ounce to a 100-ounce weight and you probably will not. More than a century ago, Ernst Weber noted something so simple and so widely applicable that we still refer to it as **Weber's law:** For their difference to be perceptible, two stimuli must differ by a constant *proportion*—not a constant amount. The exact proportion varies, depending on the stimulus. For the average person to perceive their differences, two lights must differ in intensity by 8 percent. Two objects must differ in weight by 2 percent. And two tones must differ in frequency by only 0.3 percent (Teghtsoonian, 1971).

▶‖ Sensory Adaptation

17-3   What is the function of sensory adaptation?

Entering your neighbors' living room, you smell a musty odor. You wonder how they can stand it, but within minutes you no longer notice it. **Sensory adaptation**—our diminishing sensitivity to an unchanging stimulus—has come to your rescue. (To experience this phenomenon, move your watch up your wrist an inch: You will feel it— but only for a few moments.) After constant exposure to a stimulus, our nerve cells fire less frequently.

Why, then, if we stare at an object without flinching, does it not vanish from sight? Because, unnoticed by us, our eyes are always moving, flitting from one spot to another enough to guarantee that stimulation on the eyes' receptors continually changes (**FIGURE 17.3**).

What if we actually could stop our eyes from moving? Would sights seem to vanish, as odors do? To find out, psychologists have devised ingenious instruments for maintaining a constant image on the eye's inner surface. Imagine that we have fitted a volunteer, Mary, with one of these instruments—a miniature projector mounted on a contact lens (**FIGURE 17.4a**). When Mary's eye moves, the image from the projector moves as well. So everywhere that Mary looks, the scene is sure to go.

If we project the profile of a face through such an instrument, what will Mary see? At first, she will see the complete profile. But within a few seconds, as her sensory system begins to fatigue, things will get weird. Bit by bit, the image will vanish, only later to reappear and then disappear—in recognizable fragments or as a whole (**FIGURE 17.4b**).

John M. Henderson

Although sensory adaptation reduces our sensitivity, it offers an important benefit: freedom to focus on *informative* changes in our environment without being distracted by the constant chatter of uninformative background stimulation. Our sensory receptors are alert to novelty; bore them with repetition and they free our attention for more important things. Stinky or heavily perfumed people don't notice their odor because, like you and me, they adapt to what's constant and detect only change. This reinforces a fundamental lesson: *We perceive the world not exactly as it is, but as it is useful for us to perceive it.*

Our sensitivity to changing stimulation helps explain television's attention-grabbing power. Cuts, edits, zooms, pans, sudden noises—all demand attention, even from TV researchers: During interesting conversations, notes Percy Tannenbaum (2002), "I cannot for the life of me stop from periodically glancing over to the screen."

Sensory thresholds and adaptation are only two of the commonalities shared by the senses. All our senses receive sensory stimulation, transform it into neural information, and deliver that information to the brain.

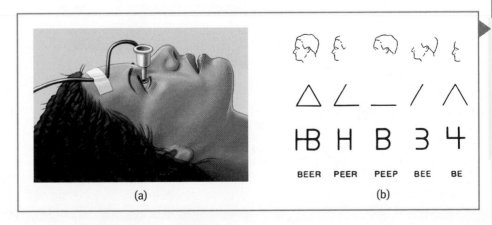

(a)   (b)

REVIEW

Introduction to Sensation and Perception

17-1 **What are sensation and perception? What do we mean by bottom-up processing and top-down processing?** *Sensation* is the process by which our sensory receptors and nervous system receive and represent stimulus energies from our environment. *Perception* is the process of organizing and interpreting this information. Although we view sensation and perception separately to analyze and discuss them, they are actually parts of one continuous process. *Bottom-up processing* is sensory analysis that begins at the entry level, with information flowing from the sensory receptors to the brain. *Top-down processing* is analysis that begins with the brain and flows down, filtering information through our experience and expectations to produce perceptions.

17-2 **What are the absolute and difference thresholds, and do stimuli below the absolute threshold have any influence?** Our *absolute threshold* for any stimulus is the minimum stimulation necessary for us to be consciously aware of it 50 percent of the time. *Signal detection theory* demonstrates that individual absolute thresholds vary, depending on the strength of the signal and also on our experience, expectations, motivation, and alertness. Our *difference threshold* (also called just noticeable difference, or jnd) is the barely noticeable difference we discern between two stimuli 50 percent of the time. *Priming* shows that we can process some information from stimuli below our absolute threshold for conscious awareness. But the effect is too fleeting to enable people to exploit us with *subliminal* messages. *Weber's law* states that two stimuli must differ by a constant proportion to be perceived as different.

17-3 **What is the function of sensory adaptation?** *Sensory adaptation* (our diminished sensitivity to constant or routine odors, sounds, and touches) focuses our attention on informative changes in our environment.

Terms and Concepts to Remember

sensation, p. 226
perception, p. 226
bottom-up processing, p. 226
top-down processing, p. 226
psychophysics, p. 227
absolute threshold, p. 227
signal detection theory, p. 227
subliminal, p. 228
priming, p. 229
difference threshold, p. 230
Weber's law, p. 230
sensory adaptation, p. 230

Test Yourself

1. What is the rough distinction between sensation and perception?

(Answers to the Test Yourself questions can be found in Appendix B at the end of the book.)

Ask Yourself

1. What types of sensory adaptation have you experienced in the last 24 hours?

∞ WEB

Multiple-choice self-tests and more may be found at
www.worthpublishers.com/myers

MODULE 18

Vision

The Stimulus Input:
Light Energy

The Eye

Visual Information Processing

Color Vision

18-1 What is the energy that we see as visible light?

One of nature's great wonders is neither bizarre nor remote, but commonplace: How does our material body construct our conscious visual experience? How do we transform particles of light energy into colorful sights?

Part of this genius is our ability to convert one sort of energy to another. Our eyes, for example, receive light energy and **transduce** (transform) it into neural messages that our brain then processes into what we consciously see. How does such a taken-for-granted yet remarkable thing happen?

▶‖ The Stimulus Input: Light Energy

Scientifically speaking, what strikes our eyes is not color but pulses of electromagnetic energy that our visual system perceives as color. What we see as visible light is but a thin slice of the whole spectrum of electromagnetic energy. As **FIGURE 18.1** illustrates, this *electromagnetic spectrum* ranges from imperceptibly short waves of gamma rays, to the narrow band we see as visible light, to the long waves of radio transmission and AC circuits. Other organisms are sensitive to differing portions of the spectrum. Bees, for instance, cannot see red but can see ultraviolet light.

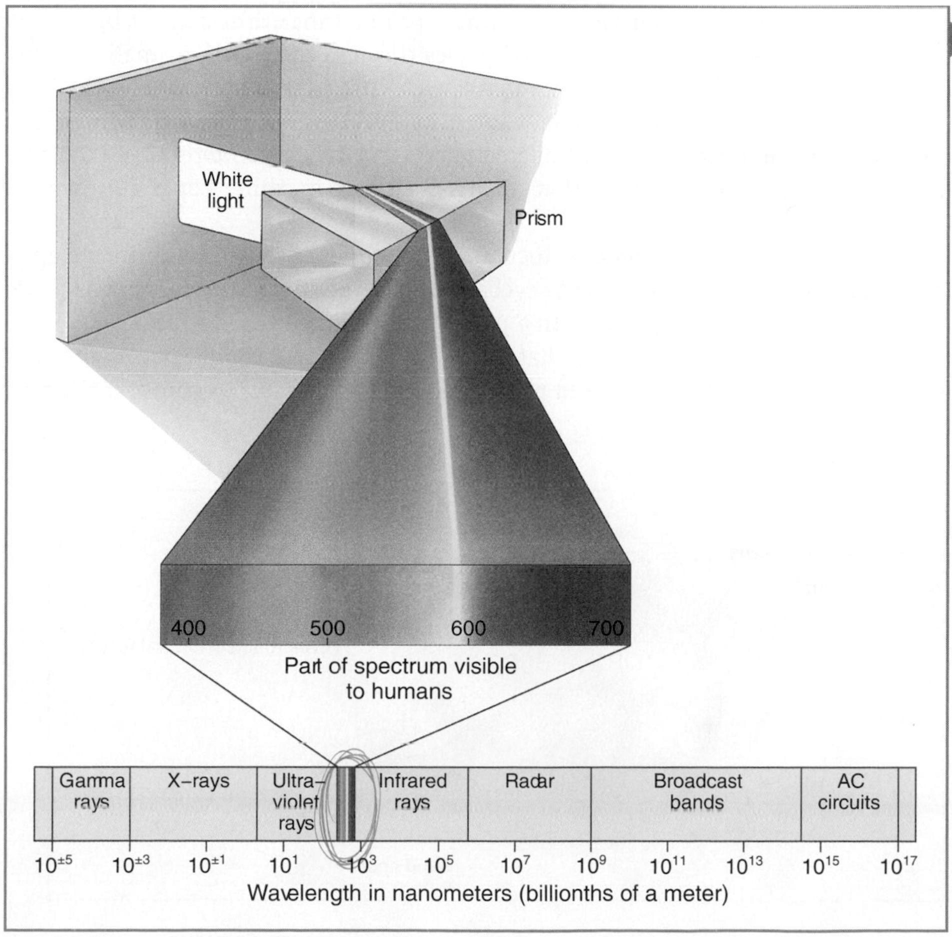

transduction conversion of one form of energy into another. In sensation, the transforming of stimulus energies, such as sights, sounds, and smells, into neural impulses our brains can interpret.

FIGURE 18.1 The spectrum of electromagnetic energy This spectrum ranges from gamma rays as short as the diameter of an atom to radio waves over a mile long. The narrow band of wavelengths visible to the human eye (shown enlarged) extends from the shorter waves of blue-violet light to the longer waves of red light.

White light

Prism

400   500   600   700
Part of spectrum visible to humans

| Gamma rays | X–rays | Ultra-violet rays | Infrared rays | Radar | Broadcast bands | AC circuits |

$10^{\pm5}$ $10^{\pm3}$ $10^{\pm1}$ 10^1 10^3 10^5 10^7 10^9 10^{11} 10^{13} 10^{15} 10^{17}

Wavelength in nanometers (billionths of a meter)

FIGURE 18.2 The physical properties of waves (a) Waves vary in wavelength (the distance between successive peaks). Frequency, the number of complete wavelengths that can pass a point in a given time, depends on the wavelength. The shorter the wavelength, the higher the frequency. (b) Waves also vary in amplitude (the height from peak to trough). Wave amplitude determines the intensity of colors.

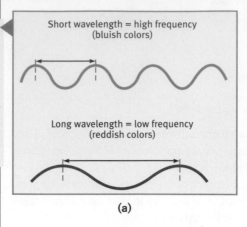
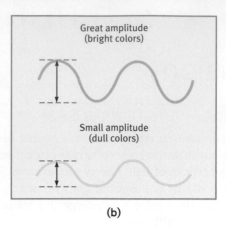

(a)   (b)

wavelength the distance from the peak of one light or sound wave to the peak of the next. Electromagnetic wavelengths vary from the short blips of cosmic rays to the long pulses of radio transmission.

hue the dimension of color that is determined by the wavelength of light; what we know as the color names *blue*, *green*, and so forth.

intensity the amount of energy in a light or sound wave, which we perceive as brightness or loudness, as determined by the wave's amplitude.

pupil the adjustable opening in the center of the eye through which light enters.

iris a ring of muscle tissue that forms the colored portion of the eye around the pupil and controls the size of the pupil opening.

lens the transparent structure behind the pupil that changes shape to help focus images on the retina.

retina the light-sensitive inner surface of the eye, containing the receptor rods and cones plus layers of neurons that begin the processing of visual information.

accommodation the process by which the eye's lens changes shape to focus near or far objects on the retina.

Two physical characteristics of light help determine our sensory experience of them. Light's **wavelength**—the distance from one wave peak to the next (**FIGURE 18.2a**)—determines its **hue** (the color we experience, such as blue or green). **Intensity,** the amount of energy in light waves (determined by a wave's *amplitude,* or height), influences brightness (**FIGURE 18.2b**). To understand *how* we transform physical energy into color and meaning, we first need to understand vision's window, the eye.

▶‖ The Eye

18-2 How does the eye transform light energy into neural messages?

Light enters the eye through the *cornea,* which protects the eye and bends light to provide focus (**FIGURE 18.3**). The light then passes through the **pupil,** a small adjustable opening surrounded by the **iris,** a colored muscle that adjusts light intake. The iris dilates or constricts in response to light intensity and even to inner emotions. (When we're feeling amorous, our telltale dilated pupils and dark eyes subtly signal our interest.) Each iris is so distinctive that an iris-scanning machine could confirm your identity.

Behind the pupil is a **lens** that focuses incoming light rays into an image on the **retina,** a multilayered tissue on the eyeball's sensitive inner surface. The lens focuses the rays by changing its curvature in a process called **accommodation.**

For centuries, scientists knew that when an image of a candle passes through a small opening, it casts an inverted mirror image on a dark wall behind. If the retina

FIGURE 18.3 The eye Light rays reflected from the candle pass through the cornea, pupil, and lens. The curvature and thickness of the lens change to bring either nearby or distant objects into focus on the retina. Rays from the top of the candle strike the bottom of the retina and those from the left side of the candle strike the right side of the retina. The candle's retinal image is thus upside-down and reversed.

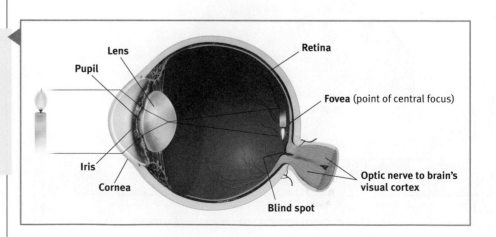

receives this sort of upside-down image, as in Figure 18.3, how can we see the world right side up? The ever-curious Leonardo da Vinci had an idea: Perhaps the eye's watery fluids bend the light rays, reinverting the image to the upright position as it reaches the retina. But then in 1604, the astronomer and optics expert Johannes Kepler showed that the retina does receive upside-down images of the world (Crombie, 1964). And how could we understand such a world? "I leave it," said the befuddled Kepler, "to natural philosophers."

Eventually, the answer became clear: The retina doesn't "see" a whole image. Rather, its millions of receptor cells convert particles of light energy into neural impulses and forward those to the brain. *There,* the impulses are reassembled into a perceived, upright-seeming image.

The Retina

If you could follow a single light-energy particle into your eye, you would first make your way through the retina's outer layer of cells to its buried receptor cells, the **rods** and **cones** (**FIGURE 18.4**). There, you would see the light energy trigger chemical changes that would spark neural signals, activating neighboring *bipolar cells*. The bipolar cells in turn would activate the neighboring *ganglion cells*. Following the particle's path, you would see axons from this network of ganglion cells converging, like the strands of a rope, to form the **optic nerve** that carries information to your brain (where the thalamus will receive and distribute the information). The optic nerve can send nearly 1 million messages at once through its nearly 1 million ganglion fibers. (The auditory nerve, which enables hearing, carries much less information through its mere 30,000 fibers.) Where the optic nerve leaves the eye there are no receptor cells—creating a **blind spot** (**FIGURE 18.5** on the next page). Close one eye and you won't see a black hole on your TV screen, however. Without seeking your approval, your brain fills in the hole.

rods retinal receptors that detect black, white, and gray; necessary for peripheral and twilight vision, when cones don't respond.

cones retinal receptor cells that are concentrated near the center of the retina and that function in daylight or in well-lit conditions. The cones detect fine detail and give rise to color sensations.

optic nerve the nerve that carries neural impulses from the eye to the brain.

blind spot the point at which the optic nerve leaves the eye, creating a "blind" spot because no receptor cells are located there.

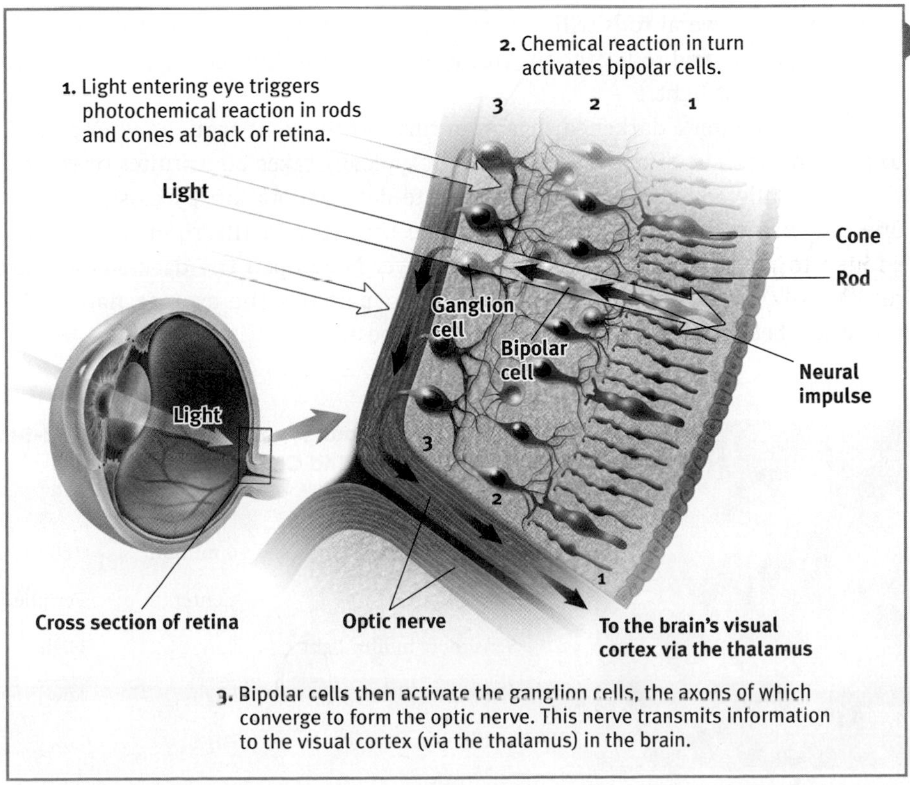

FIGURE 18.4 The retina's reaction to light

1. Light entering eye triggers photochemical reaction in rods and cones at back of retina.

2. Chemical reaction in turn activates bipolar cells.

Light

Cone

Rod

Ganglion cell

Bipolar cell

Neural impulse

Light

Cross section of retina

Optic nerve

To the brain's visual cortex via the thalamus

3. Bipolar cells then activate the ganglion cells, the axons of which converge to form the optic nerve. This nerve transmits information to the visual cortex (via the thalamus) in the brain.

FIGURE 18.5 The blind spot There are no receptor cells where the optic nerve leaves the eye (see Figure 18.4). This creates a blind spot in your vision. To demonstrate, close your left eye, look at the spot, and move the page to a distance from your face (about a foot) at which the car disappears. The blind spot does not normally impair your vision, because your eyes are moving and because one eye catches what the other misses.

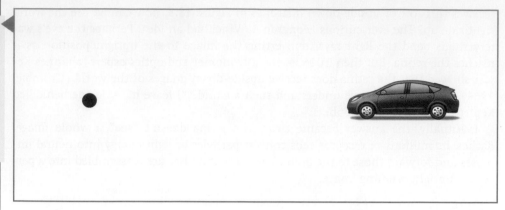

Rods and cones differ in their geography and in the tasks they handle (**TABLE 18.1**). Cones cluster in and around the **fovea,** the retina's area of central focus (see Figure 18.3). Many cones have their own hotline to the brain—bipolar cells that help relay the cone's individual message to the visual cortex, which devotes a large area to input from the fovea. These direct connections preserve the cones' precise information, making them better able to detect fine detail. Rods have no such hotline; they share bipolar cells with other rods, sending combined messages. To experience this difference in sensitivity to details, pick a word in this sentence and stare directly at it, focusing its image on the cones in your fovea. Notice that words a few inches off to the side appear blurred? Their image strikes the more peripheral region of your retina, where rods predominate. The next time you are driving or biking, note, too, that you can detect a car in your peripheral vision well before perceiving its details.

Cones also enable you to perceive color. In dim light they become ineffectual, so you see no colors. Rods, which enable black-and-white vision, remain sensitive in dim light, and several rods will funnel their faint energy output onto a single bipolar cell. Thus, cones and rods each provide a special sensitivity—cones to detail and color, and rods to faint light.

When you enter a darkened theater or turn off the light at night, your pupils dilate to allow more light to reach your retina. It typically takes 20 minutes or more before your eyes fully adapt. You can demonstrate dark adaptation by closing or covering one eye for up to 20 minutes. Then make the light in the room not quite bright enough to read this book with your open eye. Now open the dark-adapted eye and read (easily). This period of dark adaptation parallels the average natural twilight transition between the sun's setting and darkness.

Omikron/Photo Researchers, Inc.

TABLE 18.1 Receptors in the Human Eye: Rod-Shaped Rods and Cone-Shaped Cones

	Cones	Rods
Number	6 million	120 million
Location in retina	Center	Periphery
Sensitivity in dim light	Low	High
Color sensitivity	High	Low
Detail sensitivity	High	Low

Some nocturnal animals, such as toads, mice, rats, and bats, have retinas made up almost entirely of rods, allowing them to function well in dim light. These creatures probably have very poor color vision. Knowing just this much about the eye, can you imagine why a cat sees so much better at night than you do?[1]

▶‖ Visual Information Processing

18-3　How does the brain process visual information?

Visual information percolates through progressively more abstract levels. At the entry level, the retina processes information before routing it via the thalamus to the brain's cortex. The retina's neural layers—which are actually brain tissue that migrates to the eye during early fetal development—don't just pass along electrical impulses; they also help to encode and analyze the sensory information. The third neural layer in a frog's eye, for example, contains the "bug detector" cells that fire only in response to moving flylike stimuli.

After processing by your retina's nearly 130 million receptor rods and cones, information travels to your bipolar cells, then to your million or so ganglion cells, through their axons making up the optic nerve, to your brain. Any given retinal area relays its information to a corresponding location in the visual cortex, in the occipital lobe at the back of your brain (**FIGURE 18.6**).

The same sensitivity that enables retinal cells to fire messages can lead them to misfire as well. Turn your eyes to the left, close them, and then gently rub the right side of your right eyelid with your fingertip. Note the patch of light to the left, moving as your finger moves. Why do you see light? Why at the left?

---

[1]There are at least two reasons: (1) A cat's pupils can open much wider than yours, letting in more light; (2) a cat has a higher proportion of light-sensitive rods (Moser, 1987). But there is a trade-off: With fewer cones, a cat sees neither details nor color as well as you do.

fovea the central focal point in the retina, around which the eye's cones cluster

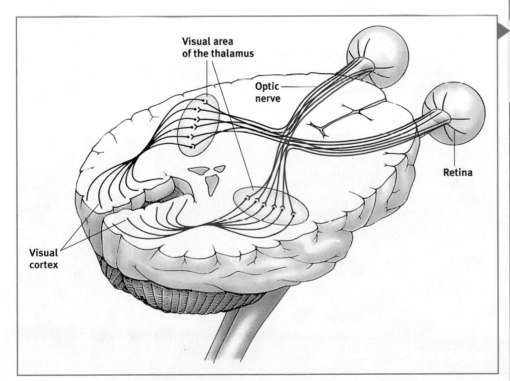

Visual area
of the thalamus

Optic
nerve

Retina

Visual
cortex

▶ **FIGURE 18.6 Pathway from the eyes to the visual cortex** Ganglion axons forming the optic nerve run to the thalamus, where they synapse with neurons that run to the visual cortex.

Your retinal cells are so responsive that even pressure triggers them. But your brain interprets their firing as light. Moreover, it interprets the light as coming from the left—the normal direction of light that activates the right side of the retina.

Feature Detection

Nobel prize winners David Hubel and Torsten Wiesel (1979) demonstrated that neurons in the occipital lobe's visual cortex receive information from individual ganglion cells in the retina. These **feature detector** cells derive their name from their ability to respond to a scene's specific features—to particular edges, lines, angles, and movements.

Feature detectors in the visual cortex pass such information to other cortical areas where teams of cells *(supercell clusters)* respond to more complex patterns. One temporal lobe area just behind your right ear, for example, enables you to perceive faces. If this region were damaged, you might recognize other forms and objects, but not familiar faces. Functional MRI (fMRI) scans show other brain areas lighting up when people view other object categories (Downing et al., 2001). Damage in these areas blocks other perceptions while sparing face recognition. Amazingly specific combinations of activity may appear (**FIGURE 18.7**). "We can tell if a person is looking at a shoe, a chair, or a face, based on the pattern of their brain activity," notes researcher James Haxby (2001).

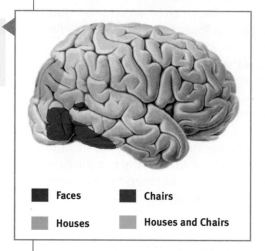

FIGURE 18.7 The telltale brain Looking at faces, houses, and chairs activates different brain areas in this right-facing brain.

■ Faces ■ Chairs
■ Houses ■ Houses and Chairs

Psychologist David Perrett and his colleagues (1988, 1992, 1994) reported that for biologically important objects and events, monkey brains (and surely ours as well) have a "vast visual encyclopedia" distributed as cells that specialize in responding to one type of stimulus—such as a specific gaze, head angle, posture, or body movement. Other supercell clusters integrate this information and fire only when the cues collectively indicate the direction of someone's attention and approach. This instant analysis, which aided our ancestors' survival, also helps a soccer goalie anticipate the direction of an impending kick, and a driver anticipate a pedestrian's next movement.

Well-developed supercells In this 2007 World Cup match, Brazil's Marta instantly processed visual information about the positions and movements of Australia's defenders and goalie (Melissa Barbieri) and somehow managed to get the ball around them all and into the net.

Reuters/Claro Cortes IV (China)

Parallel Processing

Unlike most computers, which do step-by-step *serial processing*, our brain engages in **parallel processing**: doing many things at once. The brain divides a visual scene into subdimensions, such as color, movement, form, and depth (**FIGURE 18.8**), and works on each aspect simultaneously (Livingstone & Hubel, 1988). We then construct our perceptions by integrating the separate but parallel work of these different visual teams.

To recognize a face, for example, the brain integrates information that the retina projects to several visual cortex areas, compares it to stored information, and enables you to recognize the image as, say, your grandmother. The whole process of facial recognition requires tremendous brain power—30 percent of the cortex (10 times the brain area devoted to hearing). If researchers temporarily disrupt the brain's face-processing areas with magnetic pulses, people are unable to recognize faces. They will, however, be able to recognize houses; the brain's face-perception process differs from its object-perception process (McKone et al., 2007; Pitcher et al., 2007).

Destroying or disabling the neural workstation for other visual subtasks produces different peculiar results, as happened to "Mrs. M." (Hoffman, 1998). Since a stroke damaged areas near the rear of both sides of her brain, she can no longer perceive movement. People in a room seem "suddenly here or there but I have not seen them moving." Pouring tea into a cup is a challenge because the fluid appears frozen—she cannot perceive it rising in the cup.

Others with stroke or surgery damage to their brain's visual cortex have experienced *blindsight,* a localized area of blindness in part of their field of vision (Weiskrantz, 1986). Shown a series of sticks in the blind field, they report seeing nothing. Yet when asked to guess whether the sticks are vertical or horizontal, their visual intuition typically offers the correct response. When told, "You got them all right," they are astounded. There is, it seems, a second "mind"—a parallel processing system—operating unseen. Our separate visual systems for perception and action illustrate *dual processing*—the two-track mind.

It's not just brain-injured people who have two visual information systems, as Jennifer Boyer and her colleagues (2005) showed in studies of people without such injuries. Using magnetic pulses to shut down the brain's primary visual cortex area, the researchers showed these temporarily disabled people a horizontal or vertical line, or a red or green dot. Although they reported seeing nothing, the participants were right 75 percent of the time in guessing the line orientation and 81 percent right in guessing the dot color.

A scientific understanding of visual information processing leaves many neuropsychologists awestruck. As Roger Sperry (1985) observed, the "insights of science give added, not lessened, reasons for awe, respect, and reverence." Think about it: As you look at someone, visual information is transduced and sent to your brain as millions of neural impulses, then constructed into its component features, and finally, in

feature detectors nerve cells in the brain that respond to specific features of the stimulus, such as shape, angle, or movement.

parallel processing the processing of many aspects of a problem simultaneously; the brain's natural mode of information processing for many functions, including vision. Contrasts with the step-by-step (serial) processing of most computers and of conscious problem solving.

| Color | Motion | Form | Depth |

FIGURE 18.8 Parallel processing Studies of patients with brain damage suggest that the brain delegates the work of processing color, motion, form, and depth to different areas. After taking a scene apart, how does the brain integrate these subdimensions into the perceived image? The answer to this question is the Holy Grail of vision research.

FIGURE 18.9 A simplified summary of visual information processing

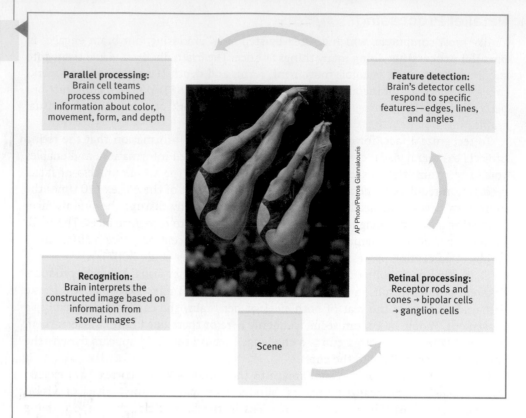

FIGURE 18.9 A simplified summary of visual information processing

Parallel processing: Brain cell teams process combined information about color, movement, form, and depth

Feature detection: Brain's detector cells respond to specific features—edges, lines, and angles

Recognition: Brain interprets the constructed image based on information from stored images

Retinal processing: Receptor rods and cones → bipolar cells → ganglion cells

Scene

AP Photo/Petros Giannakouris

some as-yet mysterious way, composed into a meaningful image, which you compare with previously stored images and recognize: "That's Sara!" Likewise, as you read this page, the printed squiggles are transmitted by reflected light rays onto your retina, which triggers a process that sends formless nerve impulses to several areas of your brain, which integrates the information and decodes meaning, thus completing the transfer of information across time and space from my mind to your mind. The whole process (**FIGURE 18.9**) is more complex than taking apart a car, piece by piece, transporting it to a different location, then having specialized workers reconstruct it. That all of this happens instantly, effortlessly, and continuously is indeed awesome.

"I am . . . wonderfully made."
King David, Psalm 139:14

"Only mind has sight and hearing; all things else are deaf and blind."
Epicharmus, *Fragments*, 550 B.C.

▶‖ Color Vision

18-4 What theories help us understand color vision?

We talk as though objects possess color: "A tomato is red." Perhaps you have pondered the old question, "If a tree falls in the forest and no one hears it, does it make a sound?" We can ask the same of color: If no one sees the tomato, is it red?

The answer is *no*. First, the tomato is everything *but* red, because it *rejects* (reflects) the long wavelengths of red. Second, the tomato's color is our mental construction. As Isaac Newton (1704) noted, "The [light] rays are not colored." Color, like all aspects of vision, resides not in the object but in the theater of our brains, as evidenced by our dreaming in color.

In the study of vision, one of the most basic and intriguing mysteries is how we see the world in color. How, from the light energy striking the retina, does the brain manufacture our experience of color—and of such a multitude of colors? Our difference threshold for colors is so low that we can discriminate some 7 million different color variations (Geldard, 1972).

At least most of us can. For about 1 person in 50, vision is color deficient—and that person is usually male, because the defect is genetically sex-linked. To understand why some people's vision is color deficient, it will help to first understand how normal color vision works.

Modern detective work on the mystery of color vision began in the nineteenth century when Hermann von Helmholtz built on the insights of an English physicist, Thomas Young. Knowing that any color can be created by combining the light waves of three primary colors—red, green, and blue—Young and von Helmholtz inferred that the eye must have three corresponding types of color receptors. Years later, researchers measured the response of various cones to different color stimuli and confirmed the **Young-Helmholtz trichromatic (three-color) theory,** which implies that the cones do their color magic in teams of three. Indeed, the retina has three types of color receptors, each especially sensitive to one of three colors. And those colors are, in fact, red, green, and blue. When we stimulate combinations of these cones, we see other colors. For example, there are no receptors especially sensitive to yellow. Yet when both red-sensitive and green-sensitive cones are stimulated, we see yellow.

Most people with color-deficient vision are not actually "colorblind." They simply lack functioning red- or green-sensitive cones, or sometimes both. Their vision—perhaps unknown to them, because their lifelong vision *seems* normal—is monochromatic (one-color) or dichromatic (two-color) instead of trichromatic, making it impossible to distinguish the red and green in **FIGURE 18.10** (Boynton, 1979). Dogs, too, lack receptors for the wavelengths of red, giving them only limited, dichromatic color vision (Neitz et al., 1989).

But trichromatic theory cannot solve all parts of the color vision mystery, as Ewald Hering soon noted. For example, we see yellow when mixing red and green light. But how is it that those blind to red and green can often still see yellow? And why does yellow appear to be a pure color and not a mixture of red and green, the way purple is of red and blue?

Hering, a physiologist, found a clue in the well-known occurrence of *afterimages*. When you stare at a green square for a while and then look at a white sheet of paper, you see red, green's *opponent color.* Stare at a yellow square and you will later see its opponent color, blue, on the white paper (as in the flag demonstration in **FIGURE 18.11**). Hering surmised that there must be two additional color processes, one responsible for red-versus-green perception, and one for blue-versus-yellow.

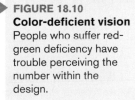

Young-Helmholtz trichromatic (three-color) theory the theory that the retina contains three different color receptors—one most sensitive to <u>red</u>, one to <u>green</u>, one to <u>blue</u>—which, when stimulated in combination, can produce the perception of <u>any color</u>.

FIGURE 18.10
Color-deficient vision People who suffer red-green deficiency have trouble perceiving the number within the design.

FIGURE 18.11 Afterimage effect Stare at the center of the flag for a minute and then shift your eyes to the dot in the white space beside it. What do you see? (After tiring your neural response to black, green, and yellow, you should see their opponent colors.) Stare at a white wall and note how the size of the flag grows with the projection distance!

opponent-process theory the theory that opposing retinal processes (red-green, yellow-blue, white-black) enable color vision. For example, some cells are stimulated by green and inhibited by red; others are stimulated by red and inhibited by green.

A century later, researchers confirmed Hering's **opponent-process theory.** As visual information leaves the receptor cells, we analyze it in terms of three sets of opponent colors: *red-green, yellow-blue,* and *white-black.* In the retina and in the thalamus (where impulses from the retina are relayed en route to the visual cortex), some neurons are turned "on" by red but turned "off" by green. Others are turned on by green but off by red (DeValois & DeValois, 1975).

Opponent processes explain afterimages, such as in the flag demonstration, in which we tire our green response by staring at green. When we then stare at white (which contains all colors, including red), only the red part of the green-red pairing will fire normally.

The present solution to the mystery of color vision is therefore roughly this: Color processing occurs in two stages. The retina's red, green, and blue cones respond in varying degrees to different color stimuli, as the Young-Helmholtz trichromatic theory suggested. Their signals are then processed by the nervous system's opponent-process cells, en route to the visual cortex.

REVIEW

Vision

18-1 What is the energy that we see as visible light? Each sense receives stimulation, transforms (*transduces*) it into neural signals, and sends these neural messages to the brain. In vision, the signals consist of light-energy particles from a thin slice of the broad spectrum of electromagnetic energy. The *hue* we perceive in a light depends on its *wavelength,* and its brightness depends on its *intensity.*

18-2 How does the eye transform light energy into neural messages? After entering the eye and being focused by a *lens,* light-energy particles strike the eye's inner surface, the *retina.* The retina's light-sensitive *rods* and color-sensitive *cones* convert the light energy into neural impulses which, after processing by bipolar and ganglion cells, travel through the *optic nerve* to the brain.

18-3 How does the brain process visual information? Impulses travel along the optic nerve, to the thalamus, and on to the visual cortex. In the visual cortex, *feature detectors* respond to specific features of the visual stimulus. Higher-level supercells integrate this pool of data for processing in other cortical areas. *Parallel processing* in the brain handles many aspects of a problem simultaneously, and separate neural teams work on visual subtasks (color, movement, depth, and form). Other neural teams integrate the results, comparing them with stored information, and enabling perceptions.

18-4 What theories help us understand color vision? The *Young-Helmholtz trichromatic (three-color) theory* proposed that the retina contains three types of color receptors. Contemporary research has found three types of cones, each most sensitive to the wavelengths of one of the three primary colors of light (red, green, or blue). Hering's *opponent-process theory* proposed three additional color processes (red-versus-green, blue-versus-yellow, black-versus-white). Contemporary research has confirmed that, en route to the brain, neurons in the retina and the thalamus code the color-related information from the cones into pairs of opponent colors. These two theories, and the research supporting them, show that color processing occurs in two stages.

Terms and Concepts to Remember

transduction, p. 233	cones, p. 235
wavelength, p. 234	optic nerve, p. 235
hue, p. 234	blind spot, p. 235
intensity, p. 234	fovea, p. 236
pupil, p. 234	feature detectors, p. 238
iris, p. 234	parallel processing, p. 239
lens, p. 234	Young-Helmholtz trichromatic
retina, p. 234	(three-color) theory, p. 241
accommodation, p. 234	opponent-process theory,
rods, p. 235	p. 242

Test Yourself

1. What is the rapid sequence of events that occurs when you see and recognize someone you know?

(Answers to the Test Yourself questions can be found in Appendix B at the end of the book.)

Ask Yourself

1. If you were forced to give up one sense, which would it be? Why?

∞ WEB

Multiple-choice self-tests and more may be found at www.worthpublishers.com/myers

MODULE 19

Hearing

The Stimulus Input: Sound Waves

The Ear

Hearing Loss and Deaf Culture

Among the mysterious but amazing aspects of our ordinary experience is the process by which we transduce air pressure waves into neural messages the brain interprets as a meaningful symphony of sound.

Like our other senses, our **audition,** or hearing, is highly adaptive. We hear a wide range of sounds, but we hear best those sounds with frequencies in a range corresponding to that of the human voice. We also are acutely sensitive to faint sounds, an obvious boon for our ancestors' survival when hunting or being hunted, or for detecting a child's whimper. (If our ears were much more sensitive, we would hear a constant hiss from the movement of air molecules.)

We are also remarkably attuned to variations in sounds. We easily detect differences among thousands of human voices: Answering the phone, we recognize a friend calling from the moment she says "Hi." A fraction of a second after such events stimulate receptors in the ear, millions of neurons have simultaneously coordinated in extracting the essential features, comparing them with past experience, and identifying the stimulus (Freeman, 1991). Let's start by considering the fundamental question: How do we do it?

▶‖ The Stimulus Input: Sound Waves

19-1 What are the characteristics of air pressure waves that we hear as sound?

Draw a bow across a violin, and the resulting stimulus energy is sound waves—jostling molecules of air, each bumping into the next, like a shove transmitted through a concert hall's crowded exit tunnel. The resulting waves of compressed and expanded air are like the ripples on a pond circling out from where a stone has been tossed. As we swim in our ocean of moving air molecules, our ears detect these brief air pressure changes. Exposed to a loud, low bass sound—perhaps from a bass guitar or a cello—we can also *feel* the vibration, and we hear by both air and bone conduction.

The sounds of music A violin's short, fast waves create a high pitch, a cello's longer, slower waves a lower pitch. Differences in the waves' height, or amplitude, also create differing degrees of loudness.

audition the sense or act of hearing.

243

FIGURE 19.1 The physical properties of waves (a) Waves vary in *wavelength*, the distance between successive peaks. *Frequency*, the number of complete wavelengths that can pass a point in a given time, depends on the wavelength. The shorter the wavelength, the higher the frequency. (b) Waves also vary in *amplitude*, the height from peak to trough. Wave amplitude determines the *intensity* of sounds.

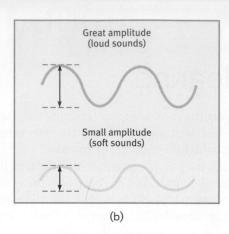

Short wavelength = high frequency (high-pitched sounds)

Long wavelength = low frequency (low-pitched sounds)

(a)

Great amplitude (loud sounds)

Small amplitude (soft sounds)

(b)

frequency the number of complete wavelengths that pass a point in a given time (for example, per second).

pitch a tone's experienced highness or lowness; depends on frequency.

middle ear the chamber between the eardrum and cochlea containing three tiny bones (hammer, anvil, and stirrup) that concentrate the vibrations of the eardrum on the cochlea's oval window.

cochlea [KOHK-lee-uh] a coiled, bony, fluid-filled tube in the inner ear through which sound waves trigger nerve impulses.

inner ear the innermost part of the ear, containing the cochlea, semicircular canals, and vestibular sacs.

The ears then transform the vibrating air into nerve impulses, which our brain decodes as sounds. The strength, or *amplitude,* of sound waves (**FIGURE 19.1**) determines their *loudness.* Waves also vary in length, and therefore in **frequency.** Their frequency determines the **pitch** we experience: Long waves have low frequency—and low pitch. Short waves have high frequency—and high pitch. A violin produces much shorter, faster sound waves than does a cello.

We measure sounds in decibels. The absolute threshold for hearing is arbitrarily defined as zero decibels. Every 10 decibels correspond to a tenfold increase in sound intensity. Thus, normal conversation (60 decibels) is 10,000 times more intense than a 20-decibel whisper. And a temporarily tolerable 100-decibel passing subway train is 10 billion times more intense than the faintest detectable sound.

▶‖ The Ear

19-2 How does the ear transform sound energy into neural messages?

To hear, we must somehow convert sound waves into neural activity. The human ear accomplishes this feat through an intricate mechanical chain reaction (**FIGURE 19.2**). First, the visible *outer ear* channels the sound waves through the auditory canal to the *eardrum,* a tight membrane that vibrates with the waves. The **middle ear** then transmits the eardrum's vibrations through a piston made of three tiny bones (the *hammer, anvil,* and *stirrup*) to the **cochlea,** a snail-shaped tube in the **inner ear.** The incoming vibrations cause the cochlea's membrane (the *oval window*) to vibrate, jostling the fluid that fills the tube. This motion causes ripples in the *basilar membrane,* bending the *hair cells* lining its surface, not unlike the wind bending a wheat field. Hair cell movement triggers impulses in the adjacent nerve cells, whose axons converge to form the *auditory nerve,* which sends neural messages (via the thalamus) to the temporal lobe's *auditory cortex.* From vibrating air to moving piston to fluid waves to electrical impulses to the brain: Voila! We hear.

My vote for the most intriguing part of the hearing process is the hair cells. A Howard Hughes Medical Institute (2008)

Be kind to your inner ear's hair cells When vibrating in response to sound, the hair cells shown here lining the cochlea produce an electrical signal.

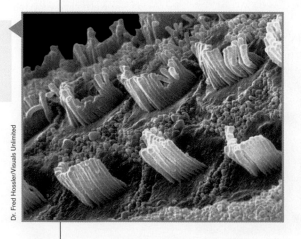

Dr. Fred Hossler/Visuals Unlimited

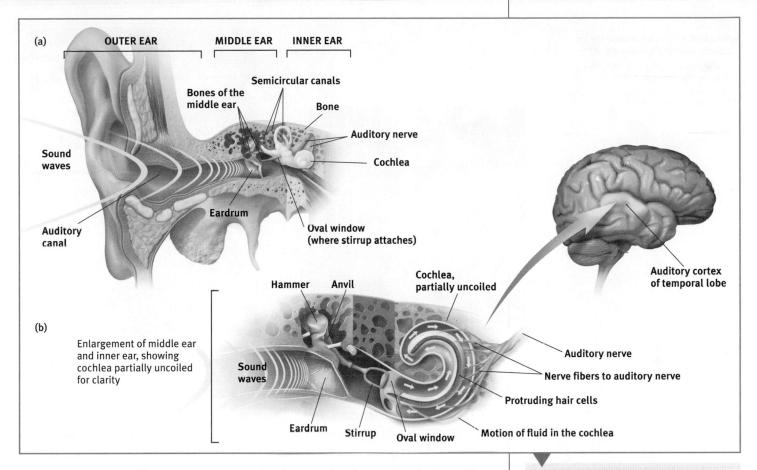

(a) OUTER EAR   MIDDLE EAR   INNER EAR

Semicircular canals

Bones of the
middle ear

Bone

Auditory nerve

Cochlea

Sound
waves

Eardrum

Auditory
canal

Oval window
(where stirrup attaches)

(b)

Enlargement of middle ear
and inner ear, showing
cochlea partially uncoiled
for clarity

Hammer   Anvil

Cochlea,
partially uncoiled

Auditory cortex
of temporal lobe

Sound
waves

Auditory nerve

Nerve fibers to auditory nerve

Protruding hair cells

Eardrum   Stirrup   Oval window

Motion of fluid in the cochlea

FIGURE 19.2 Hear here: How we transform sound waves into nerve impulses that our brain interprets (a) The outer ear funnels sound waves to the eardrum. The bones of the middle ear amplify and relay the eardrum's vibrations through the oval window into the fluid-filled cochlea. (b) As shown in this detail of the middle and inner ear, the resulting pressure changes in the cochlear fluid cause the basilar membrane to ripple, bending the hair cells on the surface. Hair cell movements trigger impulses at the base of the nerve cells, whose fibers converge to form the auditory nerve, which sends neural messages to the thalamus and on to the auditory cortex.

report on these "quivering bundles that let us hear" marvels at their "extreme sensitivity and extreme speed." A cochlea has 16,000 of them, which sounds like a lot until we compare that with an eye's 130 million or so photoreceptors. But consider their responsiveness. Deflect the tiny bundles of cilia on the tip of a hair cell by the width of an atom—the equivalent of displacing the top of the Eiffel Tower by half an inch—and the alert hair cell, thanks to a special protein at its tip, triggers a neural response (Corey et al., 2004).

Damage to hair cells accounts for most hearing loss. They have been likened to shag carpet fibers. Walk around on them and they will spring back with a quick vacuuming. But leave a heavy piece of furniture on them for a long time and they may never rebound. As a general rule, if we cannot talk over a noise, it is potentially harmful, especially if prolonged and repeated (Roesser, 1998). Such experiences are common when sound exceeds 100 decibels, as happens in venues from frenzied sports arenas to bagpipe bands to iPods playing near maximum volume (**FIGURE 19.3** on the next page). Ringing of the ears after exposure to loud machinery or music indicates that we have been bad to our unhappy hair cells. As pain alerts us to possible bodily harm, ringing of the ears alerts us to possible hearing damage. It is hearing's equivalent of bleeding.

Teen boys more than teen girls or adults blast themselves with loud volumes for long periods (Zogby, 2006). Males' greater noise exposure may help explain why men's hearing tends to be less acute than women's. But male or female, those who spend many hours in a loud nightclub, behind a power mower, or above a jackhammer should wear earplugs. "Condoms or, safer yet, abstinence," say sex educators. "Earplugs or walk away," say hearing educators.

FIGURE 19.3 **The intensity of some common sounds** At close range, the thunder that follows lightning has 120-decibel intensity.

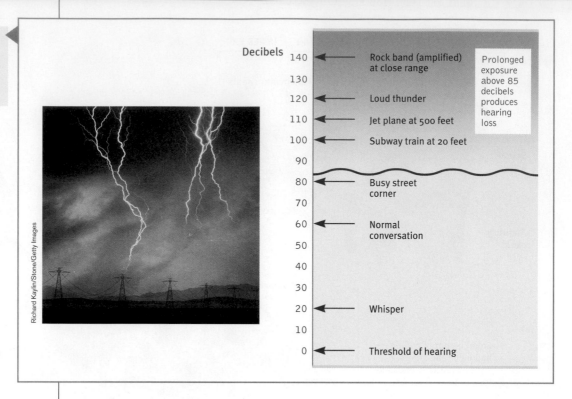

Perceiving Loudness

So, how do we detect loudness? It is not, as I would have guessed, from the intensity of a hair cell's response. Rather, a soft, pure tone activates only the few hair cells attuned to its frequency. Given louder sounds, its neighbor hair cells also respond. Thus, the brain can interpret loudness from the *number* of activated hair cells.

If a hair cell loses sensitivity to soft sounds, it may still respond to loud sounds. This helps explain another surprise: Really loud sounds may seem loud both to people with hearing loss and to those with normal hearing. As a person with hearing loss, I used to wonder when exposed to really loud music what it must sound like to people with normal hearing. Now I realize it can sound much the same; where we differ is in our sensation of soft sounds. This is why we hard-of-hearing people do not want *all* sounds (loud and soft) amplified. We like sound *compressed*—which means harder-to-hear sounds are amplified more than loud sounds (a feature of today's digital hearing aids).

Perceiving Pitch

19-3 What theories help us understand pitch perception?

How do we know whether a sound is the high-frequency, high-pitched chirp of a bird or the low-frequency, low-pitched roar of a truck? Current thinking on how we discriminate pitch combines two theories.

Hermann von Helmholtz's **place theory** presumes that we hear different pitches because different sound waves trigger activity at different places along the cochlea's basilar membrane. Thus, the brain determines a sound's pitch by recognizing the specific place (on the membrane) that is generating the neural signal. When Nobel laureate-to-be Georg von Békésy (1957) cut holes in the cochleas of guinea pigs and human cadavers and looked inside with a microscope, he discovered that the cochlea vibrated, rather like a shaken bedsheet, in response to sound. High frequencies produced large vibrations near the beginning of the cochlea's membrane, low frequencies near the end.

place theory in hearing, the theory that links the pitch we hear with the place where the cochlea's membrane is stimulated.

frequency theory in hearing, the theory that the rate of nerve impulses traveling up the auditory nerve matches the frequency of a tone, thus enabling us to sense its pitch.

conduction hearing loss hearing loss caused by damage to the mechanical system that conducts sound waves to the cochlea.

But there is a problem with place theory. It can explain how we hear high-pitched sounds, but not how we hear low-pitched sounds, because the neural signals generated by low-pitched sounds are not so neatly localized on the basilar membrane. **Frequency theory** suggests an alternative explanation: The brain reads pitch by monitoring the frequency of neural impulses traveling up the auditory nerve. The whole basilar membrane vibrates with the incoming sound wave, triggering neural impulses to the brain at the same rate as the sound wave. If the sound wave has a frequency of 100 waves per second, then 100 pulses per second travel up the auditory nerve.

Frequency theory can explain how we perceive low-pitched sounds. But it, too, is problematic: An individual neuron cannot fire faster than 1000 times per second. How, then, can we sense sounds with frequencies above 1000 waves per second (roughly the upper third of a piano keyboard)? Enter the *volley principle*: Like soldiers who alternate firing so that some can shoot while others reload, neural cells can alternate firing. By firing in rapid succession, they can achieve a *combined frequency* above 1000 waves per second.

Thus, place theory best explains how we sense high pitches, frequency theory best explains how we sense low pitches, and some combination of place and frequency seems to handle the pitches in the intermediate range.

Locating Sounds

19-4 How do we locate sounds?

Why don't we have one big ear—perhaps above our one nose? The better to hear you, as the wolf said to Red Riding Hood. As the placement of our eyes allows us to sense visual depth, so the placement of our two ears allows us to enjoy stereophonic ("three-dimensional") hearing.

Two ears are better than one for at least two reasons: If a car to the right honks, your right ear receives a more *intense* sound, and it receives sound slightly *sooner* than your left ear (**FIGURE 19.4**). Because sound travels 750 miles per hour and our ears are but 6 inches apart, the intensity difference and the time lag are extremely small. However, our supersensitive auditory system can detect such minute differences (Brown & Deffenbacher, 1979; Middlebrooks & Green, 1991). A just noticeable difference in the direction of two sound sources corresponds to a time difference of just 0.000027 second! To simulate what the ears experience with sound from varying locations, audio software can emit sound from two stereo speakers with varying time delays and intensity. The result: We may perceive a bee buzzing loudly in one ear, then flying around the room and returning to buzz near the other ear (Harvey, 2002).

So how well do you suppose we do at locating a sound that is equidistant from our two ears, such as those that come from directly ahead, behind, overhead, or beneath us? Not very well. Why? Because such sounds strike the two ears simultaneously. Sit with closed eyes while a friend snaps fingers around your head. You will easily point to the sound when it comes from either side, but you will likely make some mistakes when it comes from directly ahead, behind, above, or below. That is why, when trying to pinpoint a sound, you cock your head, so that your two ears will receive slightly different messages.

▶‖ Hearing Loss and Deaf Culture

19-5 What are the common causes of hearing loss, and why does controversy surround cochlear implants?

The ear's intricate and delicate structure makes it vulnerable to damage. Problems with the mechanical system that conducts sound waves to the cochlea cause **conduction hearing loss.** If the eardrum is punctured or if the tiny bones of the middle ear lose their ability to vibrate, the ear's ability to conduct vibrations diminishes.

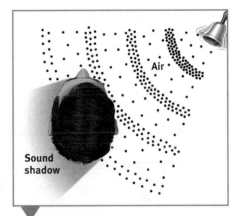

FIGURE 19.4 How we locate sounds Sound waves strike one ear sooner and more intensely than the other. From this information, our nimble brain computes the sound's location. As you might therefore expect, people who lose all hearing in one ear often have difficulty locating sounds.

"By placing my hand on a person's lips and throat, I gain an idea of many specific vibrations, and interpret them: a boy's chuckle, a man's 'Whew!' of surprise, the 'Hem!' of annoyance or perplexity, the moan of pain, a scream, a whisper, a rasp, a sob, a choke, and a gasp."
Helen Keller, 1908

sensorineural hearing loss hearing loss caused by damage to the cochlea's receptor cells or to the auditory nerves; also called <u>nerve deafness</u>.

cochlear implant a device for converting sounds into electrical signals and stimulating the auditory nerve through <u>electrodes</u> threaded into the <u>cochlea</u>.

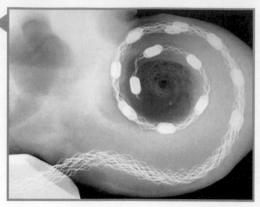

Hardware for hearing An X-ray image shows a cochlear implant's array of wires leading to 12 stimulation sites on the auditory nerve.

|| Experiments are also under way to restore vision—with a bionic retina (a 2-millimeter-diameter microchip with photoreceptors that stimulate damaged retinal cells), and with a video camera and computer that stimulate the visual cortex. In test trials, both devices have enabled blind people to gain partial sight (Boahen, 2005; Steenhuysen, 2002). ||

Damage to the cochlea's hair cell receptors or their associated nerves can cause the more common **sensorineural hearing loss** (or nerve deafness). Occasionally, disease causes sensorineural hearing loss, but more often the culprits are biological changes linked with heredity, aging, and prolonged exposure to ear-splitting noise or music. (See Close-Up: Living in a Silent World.)

For now, the only way to restore hearing for people with nerve deafness is a sort of bionic ear—a **cochlear implant.** This electronic device translates sounds into electrical signals that, wired into the cochlea's nerves, convey some information about sound to the brain. The implant helps children become proficient in oral communication (especially if they receive it as preschoolers or even before age 1) (Dettman et al., 2007; Schorr et al., 2005). The latest cochlear implants also can help restore hearing for most adults (though not for those whose adult brain never learned to process sound during childhood). By 2003, some 60,000 people worldwide had cochlear implants, and millions more were potential candidates (Gates & Miyamoto, 2003).

The use of cochlear implants is hotly debated. On the one side are the hearing parents of more than 90 percent of all deaf children. Most of these parents want their children to experience their world of sound and talk. If an implant is to be effective, they cannot delay the decision until their child reaches the age of consent. On the other side are Deaf culture advocates, who object to using the implants on children who were deaf prelingually—before developing language. The National Association of the Deaf, for example, argues that deafness is *not* a disability because native signers are not linguistically disabled. In his 1960 book *Sign Language Structure,* Gallaudet University linguist William Stokoe showed what even native signers had not fully understood: Sign is a complete language with its own grammar, syntax, and meanings.

|| Deaf culture advocates prefer capitalizing "Deaf" when referring to people with deafness, and to the Deaf community in general. In referring to children without hearing, "deaf" is usually lowercased because young children have not yet had the opportunity to make an informed decision about whether they are a part of the Deaf community. I have followed this style throughout my text. ||

Deaf culture advocates sometimes further contend that deafness could as well be considered "vision enhancement" as "hearing impairment." People who lose one channel of sensation do seem to compensate with a slight enhancement of their other sensory abilities (Backman & Dixon, 1992; Levy & Langer, 1992). Some examples:

▶ Blind musicians (think Stevie Wonder) are more likely than sighted ones to develop perfect pitch (Hamilton, 2000).

▶ With one ear plugged, blind people are also more accurate than sighted people at locating a sound source (Gougoux et al., 2005; Lessard et al., 1998).

▶ Close your eyes and with your hands indicate the width of a one-dozen egg carton. Blind individuals, report University of Otago researchers, can do this more accurately than sighted people (Smith et al., 2005).

Living in a Silent World

Signs of success Deaf participants in a spelling bee offer applause to a contestant.

The world's 500 million people who live with hearing loss are a diverse group (Phonak, 2007). Some are profoundly deaf; others have limited hearing. Some were deaf prelingually; others have known the hearing world. Some sign and identify with the language-based Deaf culture; more, especially those who lost their hearing postlingually, are "oral" and converse with the hearing world by reading lips or reading written notes. Still others move between the two cultures.

Despite its many variations, living without hearing poses challenges. When older people with hearing loss must expend effort to hear words, they have less remaining cognitive capacity available to remember and comprehend them (Wingfield et al., 2005). In several studies, people with hearing loss, especially if not wearing hearing aids, have also reported feeling sadder, being less socially engaged, and more often experiencing others' irritation (Chisolm et al., 2007; Fellinger et al., 2007; National Council on Aging, 1999).

Children who grow up around other Deaf people more often identify with Deaf culture and feel positive self-esteem. If raised in a signing household, whether by Deaf or hearing parents, they also express higher self-esteem and feel more accepted (Bat-Chava, 1993, 1994).

Separated from a supportive community, Deaf people face many challenges (Braden, 1994). Unable to communicate in customary ways, speaking and signing playmates may struggle to coordinate their play. And because academic subjects are rooted in *spoken* languages, signing students' school achievement may suffer. Adolescents may feel socially excluded, with a resulting low self-confidence.

Even adults whose hearing becomes impaired later in life may experience a sort of shyness. "It's almost universal among the deaf to want to cause hearing people as little fuss as possible," observed Henry Kisor (1990, p. 244), a Chicago newspaper editor and columnist who lost his hearing at age 3. "We can be self-effacing and diffident to the point of invisibility. Sometimes this tendency can be crippling. I must fight it all the time." Helen Keller, both blind and deaf, noted, "Blindness cuts people off from things. Deafness cuts people off from people."

I understand. My mother, with whom we communicated by writing notes on an erasable "magic pad," spent her last dozen years in a silent world, largely withdrawn from the stress and strain of trying to interact with people outside a small circle of family and old friends. With my own hearing declining on a trajectory toward hers, I find myself sitting front and center at plays and meetings, seeking quiet corners in restaurants, and asking my wife to make necessary calls to friends whose accents differ from ours. I do benefit from cool technology that, at the press of a button, can transform my hearing aids into in-the-ear loudspeakers for the broadcast of phone, TV, and public address system sound (see www.hearingloop.org). Yet I still experience frustration when, with or without hearing aids, I can't hear the joke everyone else is guffawing over; when, after repeated tries, I just can't catch that exasperated person's question and can't fake my way around it; when family members give up and say, "Oh, never mind" after trying three times to tell me something unimportant.

As she aged, my mother came to feel that seeking social interaction was simply not worth the effort. However, I share newspaper columnist Kisor's belief that communication is worth the effort (p. 246): "So, . . . I will grit my teeth and plunge ahead." To reach out, to connect, to communicate with others, even across a chasm of silence, is to affirm our humanity as social creatures.

▶ People who have been deaf from birth exhibit enhanced attention to their peripheral vision (Bavelier et al., 2006). Their auditory cortex, starved for sensory input, remains largely intact but becomes responsive to touch and to visual input (Emmorey et al., 2003; Finney et al., 2001; Penhune et al., 2003).

Close your eyes and immediately you, too, will notice your attention being drawn to your other senses. In one experiment, people who had spent 90 minutes sitting quietly blindfolded became more accurate in their location of sounds (Lewald, 2007). When kissing, lovers minimize distraction and increase their touch sensitivity by closing their eyes.

REVIEW

Hearing

19-1 **What are the characteristics of air pressure waves that we hear as sound?** Sound waves are bands of compressed and expanded air. Our ears detect these changes in air pressure and transform them into neural impulses, which the brain decodes as sound. Sound waves vary in *frequency,* which we experience as differing *pitch,* and amplitude, which we perceive as differing loudness.

19-2 **How does the ear transform sound energy into neural messages?** The outer ear is the visible portion of the ear. The *middle ear* is the chamber between the eardrum and *cochlea.* The *inner ear* consists of the cochlea, semicircular canals, and vestibular sacs. Through a mechanical chain of events, sound waves traveling through the auditory canal cause tiny vibrations in the eardrum. The bones of the middle ear amplify the vibrations and relay them to the fluid-filled cochlea. Rippling of the basilar membrane, caused by pressure changes in the cochlear fluid, causes movement of the tiny hair cells, triggering neural messages to be sent (via the thalamus) to the auditory cortex in the brain.

19-3 **What theories help us understand pitch perception?** *Place theory* proposes that our brain interprets a particular pitch by decoding the place where a sound wave stimulates the cochlea's basilar membrane. *Frequency theory* proposes that the brain deciphers the frequency of the pulses traveling to the brain. Place theory explains how we hear high-pitched sounds, but it cannot explain how we hear low-pitched sounds. Frequency theory explains how we hear low-pitched sounds, but it cannot explain how we hear high-pitched sounds. Some combination of the two helps explain how we hear sounds in the middle range.

19-4 **How do we locate sounds?** Sound waves strike one ear sooner and more intensely than the other. The brain analyzes the minute differences in the sounds received by the two ears and computes the sound's source.

19-5 **What are the common causes of hearing loss, and why does controversy surround cochlear implants?** *Conduction hearing loss* results from damage to the mechanical system that transmits sound waves to the cochlea. *Sensorineural hearing loss* (or nerve deafness) results from damage to the cochlea's hair cells or their associated nerves. Diseases and accidents can cause hearing loss, but age-related disorders and prolonged exposure to loud noises are more common causes. Artificial *cochlear implants* can restore hearing for some people, but members of the Deaf culture movement believe cochlear implants are unnecessary for people who have been Deaf from birth and who can speak their own language, sign.

Terms and Concepts to Remember

audition, p. 243

frequency, p. 244

pitch, p. 244

middle ear, p. 244

cochlea [KOHK-lee-uh], p. 244

inner ear, p. 244

place theory, p. 246

frequency theory, p. 247

conduction hearing loss, p. 247

sensorineural hearing loss, p. 248

cochlear implant, p. 248

Test Yourself

1. What are the basic steps in transforming sound waves into perceived sound?

(Answers to the Test Yourself questions can be found in Appendix B at the end of the book.)

Ask Yourself

1. If you are a hearing person, imagine that you had been born deaf. Do you think you would want to receive a cochlear implant? Does it surprise you that most lifelong Deaf adults do not desire implants for themselves or their children?

∞ WEB

Multiple-choice self-tests and more may be found at www.worthpublishers.com/myers

MODULE 20

Other Senses

Touch

Pain

Taste

Smell

Although our brains give seeing and hearing priority in the allocation of cortical tissue, extraordinary happenings occur within our four other senses—our senses of touch, body position and movement, taste, and smell. Sharks and dogs rely on their extraordinary sense of smell, aided by large brain areas devoted to this system. Without our own senses of touch, body position and movement, taste, and smell, we humans would also be seriously handicapped, and our capacities for enjoying the world would be devastatingly diminished.

▶‖ Touch

20-1 How do we sense touch and sense our body's position and movement? How do we experience pain?

Although not the first sense to come to mind, touch could be our priority sense. Right from the start, touch is essential to our development. Infant rats deprived of their mother's grooming produce less growth hormone and have a lower metabolic rate—a good way to keep alive until the mother returns, but a reaction that stunts growth if prolonged. Infant monkeys allowed to see, hear, and smell—but not touch—their mother become desperately unhappy; those separated by a screen with holes that allow touching are much less miserable. Premature human babies gain weight faster and go home sooner if they are stimulated by hand massage. As lovers, we yearn to touch—to kiss, to stroke, to snuggle. And even strangers, touching only their forearms and separated by a curtain, can communicate anger, fear, disgust, love, gratitude, and sympathy at well above chance levels (Hertenstein et al., 2006).

The precious sense of touch As William James wrote in his *Principles of Psychology* (1890), "Touch is both the alpha and omega of affection."

Humorist Dave Barry may be right to jest that your skin "keeps people from seeing the inside of your body, which is repulsive, and it prevents your organs from falling onto the ground." But skin does much more. Our "sense of touch" is actually a mix of distinct senses, with different types of specialized nerve endings within the skin. Touching various spots on the skin with a soft hair, a warm or cool wire, and the point of a pin reveals that some spots are especially sensitive to pressure, others to warmth, others to cold, still others to pain.

Surprisingly, there is no simple relationship between what we feel at a given spot and the type of specialized nerve ending found there. Only pressure has identifiable receptors. Other skin sensations are variations of the basic four (pressure, warmth, cold, and pain):

▶ Stroking adjacent pressure spots creates a tickle.
▶ Repeated gentle stroking of a pain spot creates an itching sensation.
▶ Touching adjacent cold and pressure spots triggers a sense of wetness, which you can experience by touching dry, cold metal.
▶ Stimulating nearby cold and warm spots produces the sensation of hot (**FIGURE 20.1**).

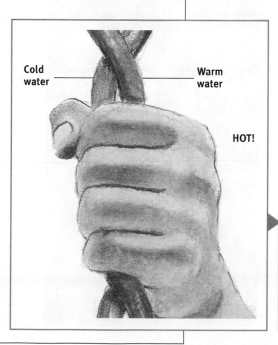

FIGURE 20.1 Warm + cold = hot When ice-cold water passes through one coil and comfortably warm water through another, we perceive the combined sensation as burning hot.

kinesthesis [kin-ehs-THEE-sehs] the system for sensing the position and movement of individual body parts.

vestibular sense the sense of body movement and position, including the sense of balance.

FIGURE 20.2 The rubber-hand illusion When Dublin researcher Deirdre Desmond simultaneously touches a volunteer's real and fake hands, the volunteer feels as though the seen fake hand is her own.

The intricate vestibular sense These Cirque du Soleil performers can thank their inner ears for the information that enables their brains to monitor their bodies' position so expertly.

Michal Cizek/AFP/Getty Images

Touch sensations involve more than tactile stimulation, however. A self-produced tickle produces less somatosensory cortex activation than the same tickle would from something or someone else (Blakemore et al., 1998). (The brain is wise enough to be most sensitive to unexpected stimulation.) This top-down influence on touch sensation also appears in the *rubber-hand illusion*. Imagine yourself looking at a realistic rubber hand while your own hand is hidden (**FIGURE 20.2**). If an experimenter simultaneously touches your fake and real hands, you likely will perceive the rubber hand as your own and sense it being touched. Even just "stroking" the fake hand with a laser light produces, for most people, an illusory sensation of warmth or touch in their unseen real hand (Durgin et al., 2007). Touch is not only a bottom-up property of your senses but also a top-down product of your brain and your expectations.

Important sensors in your joints, tendons, bones, and ears, as well as your skin sensors enable your **kinesthesis**—your sense of the position and movement of your body parts. By closing your eyes or plugging your ears you can momentarily imagine being without sight or sound. But what would it be like to live without touch or kinesthesis—without, therefore, being able to sense the positions of your limbs when you wake during the night? Ian Waterman of Hampshire, England, knows. In 1972, at age 19, Waterman contracted a rare viral infection that destroyed the nerves that enabled his sense of light touch and of body position and movement. People with this condition report feeling disembodied, as though their body is dead, not real, not theirs (Sacks, 1985). With prolonged practice, Waterman has learned to walk and eat—by visually focusing on his limbs and directing them accordingly. But if the lights go out, he crumples to the floor (Azar, 1998). Even for the rest of us, vision interacts with kinesthesis. Stand with your right heel in front of your left toes. Easy. Now close your eyes and you will probably wobble.

A companion **vestibular sense** monitors your head's (and thus your body's) position and movement. The biological gyroscopes for this sense of equilibrium are in your inner ear. The *semicircular canals,* which look like a three-dimensional pretzel (**FIGURE 20.3**), and the *vestibular sacs,* which connect the canals with the cochlea, contain fluid that moves when your head rotates or tilts. This movement stimulates hairlike receptors, which send messages to the cerebellum at the back of the brain, thus enabling you to sense your body position and to maintain your balance.

If you twirl around and then come to an abrupt halt, neither the fluid in your semicircular canals nor your kinesthetic receptors will immediately return to their neutral state. The dizzy aftereffect fools your brain with the sensation that you're still spinning. This illustrates a principle that underlies perceptual illusions: Mechanisms that normally give us an accurate experience of the world can, under special conditions, fool us. Understanding how we get fooled provides clues to how our perceptual system works.

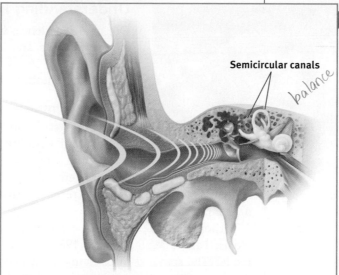

FIGURE 20.3
Semicircular canals in the inner ear

Semicircular canals

balance

w/ vestibular sacs.

▶‖ Pain

Be thankful for occasional pain. Pain is your body's way of telling you something has gone wrong. Drawing your attention to a burn, a break, or a sprain, pain orders you to change your behavior—"Stay off that turned ankle!" The rare people born without the ability to feel pain may experience severe injury or even die before early adulthood. Without the discomfort that makes us occasionally shift position, their joints fail from excess strain, and without the warnings of pain, the effects of unchecked infections and injuries accumulate (Neese, 1991).

More numerous are those who live with chronic pain, which is rather like an alarm that won't shut off. The suffering of such people, and of those with persistent or recurring backaches, arthritis, headaches, and cancer-related pain, prompts two questions: What is pain? How might we control it?

A pain-free, problematic life
Ashlyn Blocker (right), shown here with her mother and sister, has a rare genetic disorder. She feels neither pain nor extreme hot and cold. She must frequently be checked for accidentally self-inflicted injuries that she herself cannot feel. "Some people would say [that feeling no pain is] a good thing," says her mother. "But no, it's not. Pain's there for a reason. It lets your body know something's wrong and it needs to be fixed. I'd give anything for her to feel pain" (quoted by Bynum, 2004).

AP Photo/Stephen Morton

Tom Mihalek/AFP/Getty Images

Playing with pain In a 2008 NBA championship series game, Boston Celtic star Paul Pierce screamed in pain after an opposing player stepped on his right foot, causing his knee to twist and pop. After being carried off the court, he came back and played through the pain, which reclaimed his attention after the game's end.

"When belly with bad pains doth swell, It matters naught what else goes well."

Sadi, *The Gulistan*, 1258

Understanding Pain

Our pain experiences vary widely, depending on our physiology, our experiences and attention, and our surrounding culture (Gatchel et al., 2007). Thus, our feelings of pain combine both bottom-up sensations and top-down processes.

Biological Influences

The pain system, unlike vision, is not located in a simple neural cord running from a sensing device to a definable area in the brain. Moreover, there is no one type of stimulus that triggers pain (as light triggers vision). Instead, there are different *nociceptors*—sensory receptors that detect hurtful temperatures, pressure, or chemicals (**FIGURE 20.4**).

Although no theory of pain explains all available findings, Ronald Melzack and biologist Patrick Wall's (1965, 1983) classic **gate-control theory** provides a useful model. The spinal cord contains small nerve fibers that conduct most pain signals, and larger fibers that conduct most other sensory signals. Melzack and Wall theorized that the spinal cord contains a neurological "gate." When tissue is injured, the small fibers activate and open the gate, and you feel pain. Large-fiber activity closes the gate, blocking pain signals and preventing them from reaching the brain. Thus, one way to treat chronic pain is to stimulate (by massage, by electric stimulation, or by acupuncture) "gate-closing" activity in the large neural fibers (Wall, 2000). Rubbing the area around your stubbed toe will create competing stimulation that will block some pain messages.

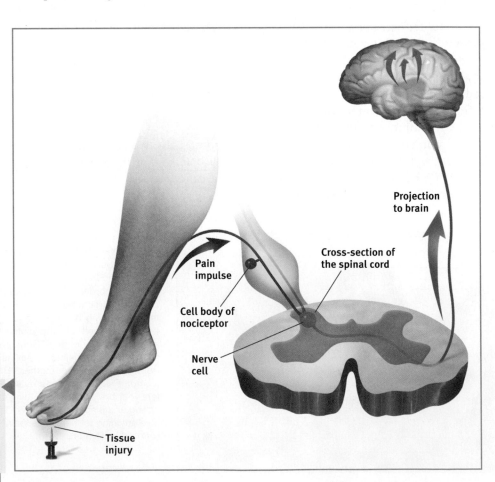

Pain impulse

Cell body of nociceptor

Nerve cell

Cross-section of the spinal cord

Projection to brain

Tissue injury

FIGURE 20.4 The pain circuit Sensory receptors (nociceptors) respond to potentially damaging stimuli by sending an impulse to the spinal cord, which passes the message to the brain, which interprets the signal as pain.

But pain is not merely a physical phenomenon of injured nerves sending impulses to the brain—like pulling on a rope to ring a bell. Melzack and Wall noted that brain-to-spinal-cord messages can also close the gate, helping to explain some striking influences on pain. When we are distracted from pain (a psychological influence) and soothed by the release of *endorphins,* our natural painkillers (a biological influence), our experience of pain may be greatly diminished. Sports injuries may go unnoticed until the after-game shower. People who carry a gene that boosts the availability of endorphins are less bothered by pain, and their brain is less responsive to pain (Zubieta et al., 2003). Others, who carry a mutated gene that disrupts pain circuit neurotransmission, may be unable to experience pain (Cox et al., 2006). Such discoveries may point the way toward new pain medications that mimic these genetic effects.

The brain can also create pain, as it does in people's experiences of *phantom limb sensations,* when it misinterprets the spontaneous central nervous system activity that occurs in the absence of normal sensory input. As the dreamer may see with eyes closed, so some 7 in 10 amputees may feel pain or movement in nonexistent limbs, notes psychologist Melzack (1992, 2005). (An amputee may also try to step off a bed onto a phantom limb or to lift a cup with a phantom hand.) Even those born without a limb sometimes perceive sensations from the absent arm or leg. The brain, Melzack (1998) surmises, comes prepared to anticipate "that it will be getting information from a body that has limbs."

A similar phenomenon occurs with other senses. People with hearing loss often experience the sound of silence: phantom sounds—a ringing-in-the-ears sensation known as *tinnitus.* Those who lose vision to glaucoma, cataracts, diabetes, or macular degeneration may experience phantom sights—nonthreatening hallucinations (Ramachandran & Blakeslee, 1998). Some with nerve damage have had taste phantoms, such as ice water seeming sickeningly sweet (Goode, 1999). Others have experienced phantom smells, such as nonexistent rotten food. The point to remember: *We feel, see, hear, taste, and smell with our brain,* which can sense even without functioning senses.

Psychological Influences

The psychological effects of distraction are clear in the stories of athletes who, focused on winning, play through the pain. Carrie Armel and Vilayanur Ramachandran (2003) cleverly illustrated psychological influences on pain with another version of the rubber-hand illusion. They bent a finger slightly backward on the unseen hands of 16 volunteers, while simultaneously "hurting" (severely bending) a finger on a visible fake rubber hand. The volunteers felt as if their real finger were being bent, and they responded with increased skin perspiration.

We also seem to edit our *memories* of pain, which often differ from the pain we actually experienced. In experiments, and after medical procedures, people overlook a pain's duration. Their memory snapshots instead record two factors: First, people tend to record pain's *peak* moment, which can lead them to recall variable pain, with peaks, as worse (Stone et al., 2005). Second, they register how much pain they felt at the *end,* as Daniel Kahneman and his co-researchers (1993) discovered when they asked people to immerse one hand in painfully cold water for 60 seconds, and then the other hand in the same painfully cold water for 60 seconds followed by a slightly less painful 30 seconds more. Which of these experiences would you expect to recall as most painful?

Curiously, when asked which trial they would prefer to repeat, most preferred the longer trial, with more net pain—but less pain at the end. A physician used this principle with patients undergoing colon exams—lengthening the discomfort by a minute, but lessening its intensity (Kahneman, 1999). Although the extended milder discomfort added to their net pain experience, patients experiencing this taper-down treatment later recalled the exam as less painful than did those whose pain ended abruptly.

gate-control theory the theory that the spinal cord contains a neurological "gate" that blocks pain signals or allows them to pass on to the brain. The "gate" is opened by the activity of pain signals traveling up small nerve fibers and is closed by activity in larger fibers or by information coming from the brain.

Biological influences:
• activity in spinal cord's large and small fibers
• genetic differences in endorphin production
• the brain's interpretation of CNS activity

Psychological influences:
• attention to pain
• learning based on experience
• expectations

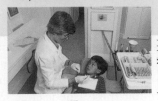

Social-cultural influences:
• presence of others
• empathy for others' pain
• cultural expectations

Personal experience of pain

FIGURE 20.5 Biopsychosocial approach to pain Our experience of pain is much more than neural messages sent to the brain.

Social-Cultural Influences

Our perception of pain also varies with our social situation and our cultural traditions. We tend to perceive more pain when others also seem to be experiencing pain (Symbaluk et al., 1997). This may help explain other apparent social aspects of pain, as when pockets of Australian keyboard operators during the mid-1980s suffered outbreaks of severe pain during typing or other repetitive work—without any discernible physical abnormalities (Gawande, 1998). Sometimes the pain in sprain is mainly in the brain—literally. When feeling empathy for another's pain, a person's own brain activity may partly mirror that of the other's brain in pain (Singer et al, 2004).

Thus, our perception of pain is a biopsychosocial phenomenon (**FIGURE 20.5**). Viewing pain this way can help us better understand how to cope with pain and treat it.

Controlling Pain

If pain is where body meets mind—if it is both a physical and a psychological phenomenon—then it should be treatable both physically and psychologically. Depending on the type of symptoms, pain control clinics select one or more therapies from a list that includes drugs, surgery, acupuncture, electrical stimulation, massage, exercise, hypnosis, relaxation training, and thought distraction.

Even an inert placebo can help, by dampening the brain's attention and responses to painful experiences—mimicking analgesic drugs (Wager, 2005). After being injected in the jaw with a stinging saltwater solution, men in one experiment were given a placebo that was said to relieve pain. They immediately felt better, a result associated with activity in a brain area that releases natural pain-killing opiates (Scott et al., 2007; Zubieta et al., 2005). Being given fake pain-killing chemicals caused the brain to dispense real ones. "Believing becomes reality," noted one commentator (Thernstrom, 2006), as "the mind unites with the body."

Another experiment pitted two placebos—fake pills and pretend acupuncture—against each other (Kaptchuk et al., 2006). People with persistent arm pain (270 of them) received either sham acupuncture (with trick needles that retracted without puncturing the skin) or blue cornstarch pills that looked like pills often prescribed for strain injury. A fourth of those receiving the nonexistent needle pricks and 31 percent of those receiving the pills complained of side effects, such as painful skin or dry mouth and fatigue. After two months, both groups were reporting less pain, with the fake acupuncture group reporting the greater pain drop.

Distracting people with pleasant images ("Think of a warm, comfortable environment") or drawing their attention away from the painful stimulation ("Count backward by 3's") is an especially effective way to increase pain tolerance (Fernandez & Turk, 1989; McCaul & Malott, 1984). A well-trained nurse may distract needle-shy patients by chatting with them and asking them to look away when inserting the needle. For burn victims receiving excruciating wound care, an even more effective

Seeking relief This acupuncturist is attempting to help this woman gain relief from back pain by using needles on points of the patient's hand.

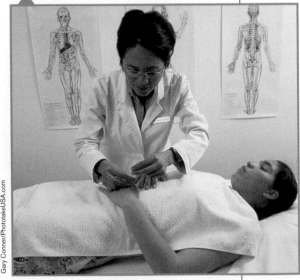

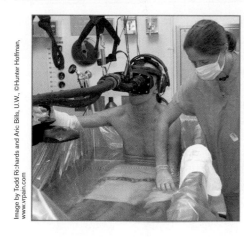

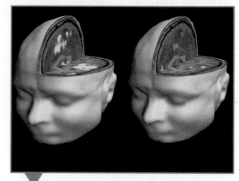

No distraction   Distraction

FIGURE 20.6 Virtual-reality pain control For burn victims undergoing painful skin repair, an escape into virtual reality can powerfully distract attention, thus reducing pain and the brain's response to painful stimulation. The MRI scans above illustrate a lowered pain response when the patient is distracted.

distraction comes from immersion in a computer-generated 3-D world, like the snow scene in **FIGURE 20.6**. Functional MRI (fMRI) scans reveal that playing in the virtual reality reduces the brain's pain-related activity (Hoffman, 2004). Because pain is in the brain, diverting the brain's attention may bring relief.

"Pain is increased by attending to it."
Charles Darwin, *Expression of Emotions in Man and Animals*, 1872

▶‖ Taste

20-2   How do we experience taste?

Like touch, our sense of taste involves several basic sensations. Taste's sensations were once thought to be sweet, sour, salty, and bitter, with all others stemming from mixtures of these four (McBurney & Gent, 1979). Then, as investigators searched for specialized nerve fibers for the four taste sensations, they encountered a receptor for what we now know is a fifth—the savory meaty taste of *umami,* best experienced as the flavor enhancer monosodium glutamate.

Tastes exist for more than our pleasure (see **TABLE 20.1**). Pleasureful tastes attracted our ancestors to energy- or protein-rich foods that enabled their survival. Aversive tastes deterred them from new foods that might be toxic. We see the inheritance of this biological wisdom in today's 2- to 6-year-olds, who are typically fussy eaters, especially when offered new meats or bitter-tasting vegetables, such as spinach and Brussels sprouts (Cooke et al., 2003). Meat and plant toxins were both potentially dangerous sources of food poisoning for our ancestors, especially for children. Given repeated small tastes of disliked new foods, children will, however, typically begin to accept them (Wardle et al., 2003).

Taste is a chemical sense. Inside each little bump on the top and sides of your tongue are 200 or more taste buds, each containing a pore that catches food chemicals. Into each taste bud pore, 50 to 100 taste receptor cells project antennalike hairs that sense food molecules. Some receptors respond mostly to sweet-tasting molecules, others to salty-, sour-, umami-, or bitter-tasting ones. It doesn't take much to trigger a response that alerts your brain's temporal lobe. If a stream of water is pumped across your tongue, the addition of a concentrated salty or sweet taste for but one-tenth of a second will get your attention (Kelling & Halpern, 1983). When a friend asks for "just a taste" of your soft drink, you can squeeze off the straw after a mere fraction of a second.

Taste receptors reproduce themselves every week or two, so if you burn your tongue with hot food it hardly matters. However, as you grow older, the number of taste buds decreases, as does taste sensitivity (Cowart, 1981). (No wonder adults enjoy strong-tasting foods that children resist.) Smoking and alcohol use accelerate these declines.

TABLE 20.1 The Survival Functions of Basic Tastes

Taste	Indicates
Sweet	Energy source
Salty	Sodium essential to physiological processes
Sour	Potentially toxic acid
Bitter	Potential poisons
Umami	Proteins to grow and repair tissue

(Adapted from Cowart, 2005.)

sensory interaction the principle that one sense may influence another, as when the smell of <u>food</u> influences its <u>taste</u>.

Those who lose their sense of taste report that food tastes like "straw" and is hard to swallow (Cowart, 2005).

Essential as taste buds are, there's more to taste than meets the tongue. As with other senses, your expectations influence your brain's response. When people are forewarned that an unpleasant taste is coming, their brain responds more actively to negative tastes, which they rate as very unpleasant. When led to believe that the *same taste* will be merely mildly unpleasant, the brain region that responds to aversive tastes is less active, and the participants rate the taste as less unpleasant (Nitschke et al., 2006). Likewise, being told that a wine costs $90 rather than its real $10 price makes an inexpensive wine taste better and triggers more activity in a brain area that responds to pleasant experiences (Plassmann et al., 2008). As happens with the pain placebo effect, the brain's thinking frontal lobes offer information that other brain regions act upon.

Sensory Interaction

Taste also illustrates another curious phenomenon. Hold your nose, close your eyes, and have someone feed you various foods. A slice of apple may be indistinguishable from a chunk of raw potato; a piece of steak may taste like cardboard; without their smells, a cup of cold coffee may be hard to distinguish from a glass of red wine. To savor a taste, we normally breathe the aroma through our nose—which is why eating is not much fun when you have a bad cold. Smell can also change our perception of taste: A drink's strawberry odor enhances our perception of its sweetness. This is **sensory interaction** at work—the principle that one sense may influence another. Smell plus texture plus taste equals flavor.

Sensory interaction similarly influences what we hear. If I (as a person with hearing loss) watch a video with simultaneous captioning, I have no trouble hearing the words I am seeing (and may therefore think I don't need the captioning). If I then turn off the captioning, I suddenly realize I need it (**FIGURE 20.7**). But what do you suppose happens if we *see* a speaker saying one syllable while *hearing* another? Surprise: We may perceive a third syllable that blends both inputs. Seeing the mouth movements for *ga* while hearing *ba* we may perceive *da*—a phenomenon known as the *McGurk effect,* after its discoverers, psychologist Harry McGurk and his assistant John MacDonald (1976).

Much the same is true with vision and touch. A weak flicker of light that we have trouble perceiving becomes more visible when accompanied by a short burst of sound (Kayser, 2007). In detecting events, the brain can combine simultaneous visual and touch signals, thanks to neurons projecting from the somatosensory cortex back to the visual cortex (Macaluso et al., 2000).

So, the senses interact: Seeing, hearing, touching, tasting, and smelling are not totally separate channels. In interpreting the world, the brain blends their inputs. In a few select individuals, the senses become joined in a phenomenon called *synaesthesia,* where one sort of sensation (such as hearing sound) produces another (such as seeing color). Thus, hearing music or seeing a specific number may activate color-sensitive cortex regions and trigger a sensation of color (Brang et al., 2008; Hubbard et al., 2005). Seeing the number 3 may evoke a taste sensation (Ward, 2003). For many people, an odor, perhaps of mint or chocolate, may evoke a sensation of taste (Stevenson & Tomiczek, 2007).

FIGURE 20.7 Sensory interaction When a hard-of-hearing listener sees an animated face forming the words being spoken at the other end of a phone line, the words become easier to understand (Knight, 2004).

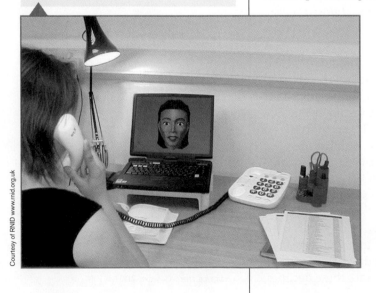

Courtesy of RNID www.rnid.org.uk

▶‖ Smell

20-3 How do we experience smell?

Inhale, exhale. Inhale, exhale. Breaths come in pairs—except at two moments: birth and death. Between those two moments, you will daily inhale and exhale nearly 20,000 breaths of life-sustaining air, bathing your nostrils in a stream of scent-laden molecules. The resulting experiences of smell *(olfaction)* are strikingly intimate: You inhale something of whatever or whoever it is you smell.

Like taste, smell is a chemical sense. We smell something when molecules of a substance carried in the air reach a tiny cluster of 5 million or more receptor cells at the top of each nasal cavity (**FIGURE 20.8**). These olfactory receptor cells, waving like sea anemones on a reef, respond selectively—to the aroma of a cake baking, to a wisp of smoke, to a friend's fragrance. Instantly, they alert the brain through their axon fibers.

Even nursing infants and their mothers have a literal chemistry to their relationship. They quickly learn to recognize each other's scents (McCarthy, 1986). Aided by smell, a mother fur seal returning to a beach crowded with pups will find her own. Our own sense of smell is less impressive than the acuteness of our seeing and hearing. Looking out across a garden, we see its forms and colors in exquisite detail and hear a variety of birds singing, yet we smell little of it without sticking our nose into the blossoms.

Odor molecules come in many shapes and sizes—so many, in fact, that it takes many different receptors to detect them. A large family of genes designs the 350 or so receptor proteins that recognize particular odor molecules (Miller, 2004). Richard

‖ Impress your friends with your new word for the day: People unable to see are said to experience blindness. People unable to hear experience deafness. People unable to smell experience *anosmia.* ‖

FIGURE 20.8 The sense of smell If you are to smell a flower, airborne molecules of its fragrance must reach receptors at the top of your nose. Sniffing swirls air up to the receptors, enhancing the aroma. The receptor cells send messages to the brain's olfactory bulb, and then onward to the temporal lobe's primary smell cortex and to the parts of the limbic system involved in memory and emotion.

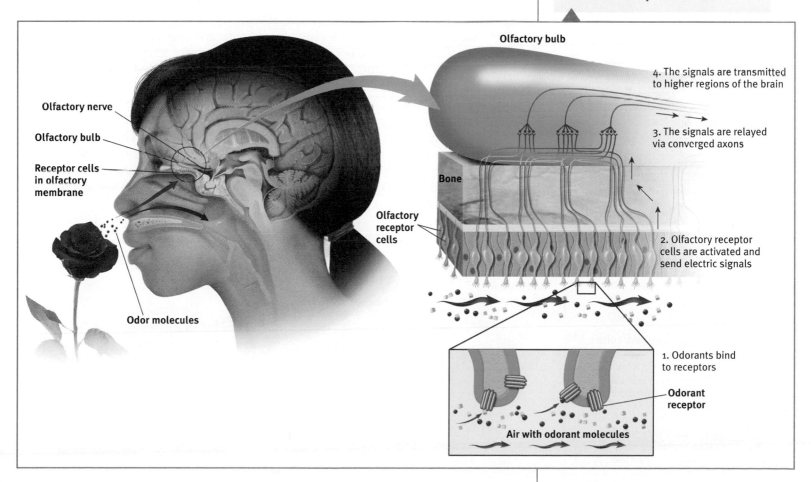

Olfactory bulb

Olfactory nerve

Olfactory bulb

Receptor cells in olfactory membrane

Bone

Olfactory receptor cells

Odor molecules

4. The signals are transmitted to higher regions of the brain

3. The signals are relayed via converged axons

2. Olfactory receptor cells are activated and send electric signals

1. Odorants bind to receptors

Odorant receptor

Air with odorant molecules

Axel and Linda Buck (1991) discovered (in work for which they received a 2004 Nobel prize) that these receptor proteins are embedded on the surface of nasal cavity neurons. As a key slips into a lock, so odor molecules slip into these receptors. Yet we don't seem to have a distinct receptor for each detectable odor. This suggests that some odors trigger a combination of receptors, in patterns that are interpreted by the olfactory cortex. As the English alphabet's 26 letters can combine to form many words, so odor molecules bind to different receptor arrays, producing the 10,000 odors we can detect (Malnic et al., 1999). It is the combinations of olfactory receptors, which activate different neuron patterns, that allow us to distinguish between the aromas of fresh-brewed and hours-old coffee (Zou et al., 2005).

The ability to identify scents peaks in early adulthood and gradually declines thereafter, with women's smelling ability tending to surpass men's (**FIGURE 20.9**). Despite our skill at discriminating scents, we aren't very good at describing them. Words more readily portray the sound of coffee brewing than its aroma. Compared with how we experience and remember sights and sounds, smells are almost primitive and certainly harder to describe and recall (Richardson & Zucco, 1989; Zucco, 2003).

As any dog or cat with a good nose could tell us, we each have our own identifiable chemical signature. (One noteworthy exception: A dog will follow the tracks of one identical twin as though they had been made by the other [Thomas, 1974].) Animals that have many times more olfactory receptors than we do also use their sense of smell to communicate and to navigate. Long before the shark can see its prey, or the moth its mate, odors direct their way. Migrating salmon follow faint olfactory cues back to their home stream. If exposed in a hatchery to one of two odorant chemicals, they will, when returning two years later, seek whichever stream near their release site is spiked with the familiar smell (Barinaga, 1999).

For humans, too, the attractiveness of smells depends on learned associations (Herz, 2001). Babies are not born with a built-in preference for the smell of their mother's breast; as they nurse, their preference builds. After a good experience becomes associated with a particular scent, people come to like that scent, which helps explain why people in the United States tend to like the smell of wintergreen (which they associate with candy and gum) more than do those in Great Britain (where it often is associated with medicine). In another example of odors evoking unpleasant emotions, Rachel Herz and her colleagues (2004) frustrated Brown University students with a rigged computer game in a scented room. Later, if exposed to the same odor while working on a verbal task, the students' frustration was rekindled and they gave up sooner than others exposed to a different odor or no odor.

"There could be a stack of truck tires burning in the living room, and I wouldn't necessarily smell it. Whereas my wife can detect a lone spoiled grape two houses away."
Dave Barry, 2005

|| Humans have 10 to 20 million olfactory receptors. A bloodhound has some 200 million (Herz, 2001). ||

"The smell and taste of things bears unfaltering, in the tiny and almost impalpable drop of their essence, the vast structure of recollection."
French novelist Marcel Proust, in *Remembrance of Things Past* (1913), describing how the aroma and flavor of a morsel of cake soaked in tea resurrected long-forgotten memories of the old family house.

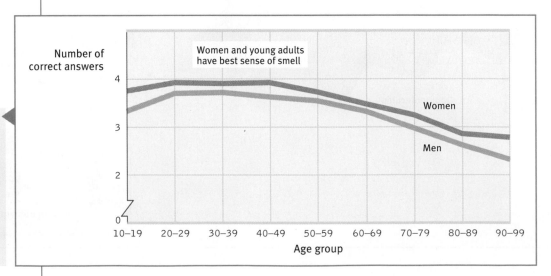

FIGURE 20.9 Age, sex, and sense of smell Among the 1.2 million people who responded to a *National Geographic* scratch-and-sniff survey, women and younger adults most successfully identified six sample odors (from Wysocki & Gilbert, 1989). Smokers and people with Alzheimer's, Parkinson's, or alcohol dependence typically experience a diminished sense of smell (Doty, 2001).

Though it's difficult to recall odors by name, we have a remarkable capacity to recognize long-forgotten odors and their associated memories (Engen, 1987; Schab, 1991). The smell of the sea, the scent of a perfume, or an aroma of a favorite relative's kitchen can bring to mind a happy time. It's a phenomenon understood by the British travel agent chain Lunn Poly. To evoke memories of lounging on sunny, warm beaches, the company once piped the aroma of coconut suntan oil into its shops (Fracassini, 2000).

Our brain's circuitry helps explain this power to evoke feelings and memories (**FIGURE 20.10**). A hotline runs between the brain area receiving information from the nose and the brain's ancient limbic centers associated with memory and emotion. Smell is primitive. Eons before the elaborate analytical areas of our cerebral cortex had fully evolved, our mammalian ancestors sniffed for food—and for predators.

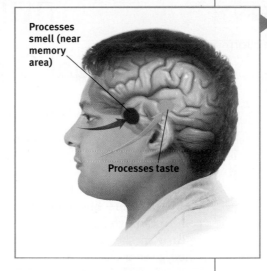

Processes smell (near memory area)

Processes taste

FIGURE 20.10 The olfactory brain Information from the taste buds (yellow arrow) travels to an area of the temporal lobe not far from where the brain receives olfactory information, which interacts with taste. The brain's circuitry for smell (red arrow) also connects with areas involved in memory storage, which helps explain why a smell can trigger a memory explosion.

REVIEW

Other Senses

20-1 How do we sense touch and sense our body's position and movement? How do we experience pain? Our sense of touch is actually several senses—pressure, warmth, cold, and pain—that combine to produce other sensations, such as "hot." Through *kinesthesis,* we sense the position and movement of body parts. We monitor the body's position and maintain our balance with our *vestibular sense.* Pain is an alarm system that draws our attention to some physical problem. One theory of pain is that a "*gate*" in the spinal cord either opens to permit pain signals traveling up small nerve fibers to reach the brain, or closes to prevent their passage. The biopsychosocial approach views pain as the sum of three sets of forces: biological influences, such as nerve fibers sending messages to the brain; psychological influences, such as our expectations; and social-cultural influences, such as the presence of others. Treatments to control pain often combine physiological and psychological elements.

20-2 How do we experience taste? Taste, a chemical sense, is a composite of five basic sensations—sweet, sour, salty, bitter, and umami—and of the aromas that interact with information from the taste receptor cells of the taste buds. The influence of smell on our sense of taste is an example of *sensory interaction,* the ability of one sense to influence another.

20-3 How do we experience smell? There are no basic sensations for smell. Smell is a chemical sense. Some 5 million olfactory receptor cells, with their approximately 350 different receptor proteins, recognize individual odor molecules. The receptor cells send messages to the brain's olfactory bulb, then to the temporal lobe and to parts of the limbic system. Odors can spontaneously evoke memories and feelings, due in part to the close connections between brain areas that process smell and memory.

Terms and Concepts to Remember

kinesthesis
   [kin-ehs-THEE-sehs], p. 252
vestibular sense, p. 252

gate-control theory, p. 254
sensory interaction, p. 258

Test Yourself

1. What are the similarities among our senses of touch (including the vestibular sense and kinesthesis), taste, and smell? What are the differences?

(Answers to the Test Yourself questions can be found in Appendix B at the end of the book.)

Ask Yourself

1. Can you recall a time when, with your attention focused on some activity, you felt no pain from a wound or injury?

⊙⊙ WEB

Multiple-choice self-tests and more may be found at www.worthpublishers.com/myers

Form Perception

Depth Perception

Motion Perception

Perceptual Constancy

MODULE 21

Perceptual Organization

21-1 How did the Gestalt psychologists understand perceptual organization?

Barring a disability, we all *sense* sights and sounds, touch and movement, tastes and smells. But how do we *perceive?* How do we see not just shapes and colors, but a rose in bloom, a loved one's face, a beautiful sunset? How do we hear not just a mix of pitches and rhythms, but a child's cry of pain, the hum of distant traffic, a symphony? In short, how do we organize and interpret our sensations so that they become meaningful perceptions?

Early in the twentieth century, a group of German psychologists noticed that when given a cluster of sensations, people tend to organize them into a **gestalt,** a German word meaning a "form" or a "whole." For example, look at the Necker cube in **FIGURE 21.1**. Note that the individual elements of the figure are really nothing but eight blue circles, each containing three converging white lines. When we view them all together, however, we see a *whole,* a cube. The Gestalt psychologists, who had wide-ranging interests, were fond of saying that in perception the whole may exceed the sum of its parts. Combine sodium, a corrosive metal, with chlorine, a poisonous gas, and something very different emerges—table salt. Likewise, a unique perceived form emerges from a stimulus' components (Rock & Palmer, 1990).

FIGURE 21.1 A Necker cube What do you see: circles with white lines, or a cube? If you stare at the cube, you may notice that it reverses location, moving the tiny X in the center from the front edge to the back. At times, the cube may seem to float in front of the page, with circles behind it; other times the circles may become holes in the page through which the cube appears, as though it were floating behind the page. There is far more to perception than meets the eye. (From Bradley et al., 1976.)

Over the years, the Gestalt psychologists provided compelling demonstrations and described principles by which we organize our sensations into perceptions. As you read further about these principles, keep in mind the fundamental truth they illustrate: *Our brain does more than register information about the world.* Perception is not just opening a shutter and letting a picture print itself on the brain. We constantly filter sensory information and infer perceptions in ways that make sense to us. Mind matters.

▶‖ Form Perception

21-2 How do figure-ground and grouping principles contribute to our perceptions?

Imagine designing a video/computer system that, like your eye/brain system, can recognize faces at a glance. What abilities would it need?

Figure and Ground

To start with, the system would need to recognize faces as distinct from their backgrounds. Likewise, our first perceptual task is to perceive any object (the figure) as distinct from its surroundings (the ground). Among the voices you hear at a party,

gestalt an organized whole. Gestalt psychologists emphasized our tendency to integrate pieces of information into meaningful wholes.

figure-ground the organization of the visual field into objects (the *figures*) that stand out from their surroundings (the *ground*).

grouping the perceptual tendency to organize stimuli into coherent groups.

the one you attend to becomes the figure; all others, part of the ground. As you read, the words are the figure; the white paper, the ground. In **FIGURE 21.2**, the **figure-ground** relationship continually reverses—but always we organize the stimulus into a figure seen against a ground. Such reversible figure-and-ground illustrations demonstrate again that the same stimulus can trigger more than one perception.

FIGURE 21.2 **Reversible figure and ground**

Grouping

Having discriminated figure from ground, we (and our video/computer system) now have to organize the figure into a meaningful form. Some basic features of a scene—such as color, movement, and light/dark contrast—we process instantly and automatically (Treisman, 1987). To bring order and form to these basic sensations, our minds follow certain rules for **grouping** stimuli together. These rules, identified by the Gestalt psychologists and applied even by infants, illustrate the idea that the perceived whole differs from the sum of its parts (Quinn et al., 2002; Rock & Palmer, 1990):

Proximity We group nearby figures together, as in **FIGURE 21.3**. We see three sets of two lines, not six separate lines.

Similarity We group similar figures together. We see the triangles and circles as vertical columns of similar shapes, not as horizontal rows of dissimilar shapes.

Continuity We perceive smooth, continuous patterns rather than discontinuous ones. The pattern in the lower-left corner of Figure 21.3 could be a series of alternating semicircles, but we perceive it as two continuous lines—one wavy, one straight.

Connectedness Because they are uniform and linked, we perceive each set of two dots and the line between them as a single unit.

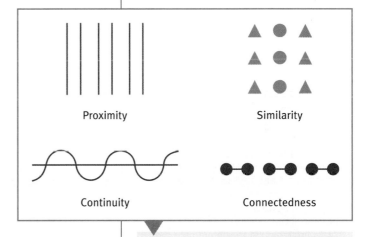

Proximity

Similarity

Continuity

Connectedness

FIGURE 21.3 **Organizing stimuli into groups** We could perceive the stimuli shown here in many ways, yet people everywhere see them similarly. The Gestalt psychologists believed this shows that the brain follows rules to order sensory information into wholes.

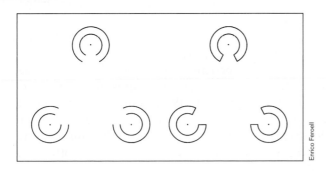

Closure We fill in gaps to create a complete, whole object. Thus we assume that the circles (above left) are complete but partially blocked by the (illusory) triangle. Add nothing more than little line segments that close off the circles (above right) and now your brain stops constructing a triangle.

depth perception the ability to see objects in three dimensions although the images that strike the retina are two-dimensional; allows us to judge distance.

visual cliff a laboratory device for testing depth perception in infants and young animals.

binocular cues depth cues, such as retinal disparity, that depend on the use of two eyes.

retinal disparity a binocular cue for perceiving depth: By comparing images from the retinas in the two eyes, the brain computes distance—the greater the disparity (difference) between the two images, the closer the object.

monocular cues depth cues, such as interposition and linear perspective, available to either eye alone.

FIGURE 21.4 Grouping principles What's the secret to this impossible doghouse? You probably perceive this doghouse as a gestalt—a whole (though impossible) structure. Actually, your brain imposes this sense of wholeness on the picture. As Figure 21.9 shows, Gestalt grouping principles such as closure and continuity are at work here.

Such principles usually help us construct reality. Sometimes, however, they lead us astray, as when we look at the doghouse in **FIGURE 21.4**.

▶‖ Depth Perception

21-3 How do we see the world in three dimensions?

From the two-dimensional images falling on our retinas, we somehow organize three-dimensional perceptions. **Depth perception,** seeing objects in three dimensions, enables us to estimate their distance from us. At a glance, we estimate the distance of an oncoming car or the height of a house. This ability is partly innate. Eleanor Gibson and Richard Walk (1960) discovered this using a miniature cliff with a drop-off covered by sturdy glass. Gibson's inspiration for these experiments occurred while she was picnicking on the rim of the Grand Canyon. She wondered: Would a toddler peering over the rim perceive the dangerous drop-off and draw back?

Back in their Cornell University laboratory, Gibson and Walk placed 6- to 14-month-old infants on the edge of a safe canyon—a **visual cliff** (**FIGURE 21.5**). When the infants' mothers then coaxed them to crawl out onto the glass, most refused to do so, indicating that they could perceive depth. Crawling infants come to the lab after lots of learning. Yet newborn animals with virtually no visual experience—including young kittens, a day-old goat, and newly hatched chicks—respond similarly. To Gibson and Walk, this suggested that mobile newborn animals come prepared to perceive depth.

Each species, by the time it is mobile, has the perceptual abilities it needs. But if biological maturation predisposes our wariness of heights, experience amplifies it. Infants' wariness increases with their experiences of crawling, no matter when they begin to crawl (Campos et al., 1992). And judging from what they will reach for, 7-month-olds use the cast shadow of a toy to perceive its distance, while 5-month-olds don't (Yonas & Granrud, 2006). This suggests that in human infants, depth perception grows with age.

How do we do it? How do we transform two differing two-dimensional retinal images into a single three-dimensional perception? The process begins with depth cues, some that depend on the use of two eyes, and others that are available to each eye separately.

FIGURE 21.5 Visual cliff Eleanor Gibson and Richard Walk devised this miniature cliff with a glass-covered drop-off to determine whether crawling infants and newborn animals can perceive depth. Even when coaxed, infants are reluctant to venture onto the glass over the cliff.

Binocular Cues

Try this: With both eyes open, hold two pens or pencils in front of you and touch their tips together. Now do so with one eye closed. With one eye, the task becomes noticeably more difficult, demonstrating the importance of **binocular cues** in judging the distance of nearby objects. Two eyes are better than one.

Because our eyes are about 2½ inches apart, our retinas receive slightly different images of the world. When the brain compares these two images, the difference between them—their **retinal disparity**—provides one important binocular cue to the relative distance of different objects. When you hold your fingers directly in front of your nose, your retinas receive quite different views. (You can see this if you close one eye and then the other, or create a finger sausage as in **FIGURE 21.6**.) At a greater distance—say, when you hold your fingers at arm's length—the disparity is smaller.

The creators of three-dimensional (3-D) movies simulate or exaggerate retinal disparity by photographing a scene with two cameras placed a few inches apart (a feature we might want to build into our seeing computer). When we view the movie through spectacles that allow the left eye to see the image from the left camera and the right eye the image from the right camera, the 3-D effect mimics or exaggerates normal retinal disparity. Similarly, twin cameras in airplanes can take photos of terrain for integration into 3-D maps.

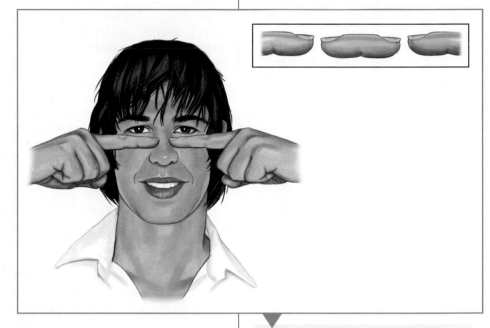

FIGURE 21.6 The floating finger sausage Hold your two index fingers about 5 inches in front of your eyes, with their tips a half-inch apart. Now look beyond them and note the weird result. Move your fingers out farther and the retinal disparity—and the finger sausage—will shrink.

Monocular Cues

How do we judge whether a person is 10 or 100 meters away? In both cases, retinal disparity while looking straight ahead is slight. At such distances, we depend on **monocular cues** (available to each eye separately). Monocular cues also influence our everyday perceptions. Is the St. Louis Gateway Arch (**FIGURE 21.7**)—the world's largest human-made illusion—taller than it is wide? Or wider than it is tall? To most of us, it appears taller. Actually, its height and width are equal. Relative height is a possible contributor to this unexplained *horizontal-vertical illusion*—our perceiving vertical dimensions as longer than identical horizontal dimensions. No wonder people (even experienced bartenders) pour less juice when given a tall, thin glass rather than a short, wide glass (Wansink & van Ittersum, 2003, 2005).

Another monocular depth cue, the light-and-shadow effect, may have contributed to several accidents when the steps of our new campus fieldhouse were unfortunately painted black on the step's edge (making it seem farther away) and bright silver on the flat surface of the step below (making it

FIGURE 21.7 The St. Louis Gateway Arch Which is greater: its height or width?

Rick Friedman/Black Star

seem closer). The seeming result was the misperception of no step-down, and (for some) sprained ankles and backs. FIGURE 21.8 illustrates relative height, light and shadow, and other monocular cues.

FIGURE 21.8 Monocular depth cues

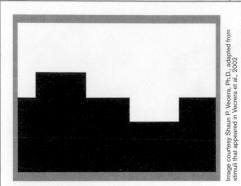

Relative height We perceive objects higher in our field of vision as farther away. Because we perceive the lower part of a figure-ground illustration as closer, we perceive it as figure (Vecera et al., 2002). Invert the illustration above and the black becomes ground, like a night sky.

Relative size If we assume two objects are similar in size, *most* people perceive the one that casts the smaller retinal image as farther away.

Light and shadow Nearby objects reflect more light to our eyes. Thus, given two identical objects, the dimmer one seems farther away. Shading, too, produces a sense of depth consistent with our assumption that light comes from above. Invert the illustration above and the hollow in the bottom row will become a hill.

■ Fixation point

Direction of passenger's motion ⟶

Relative motion As we move, objects that are actually stable may appear to move. If while riding on a bus you fix your gaze on some object—say, a house—the objects beyond the fixation point appear to move with you; objects in front of the fixation point appear to move backward. The farther those objects are from the fixation point, the faster they seem to move.

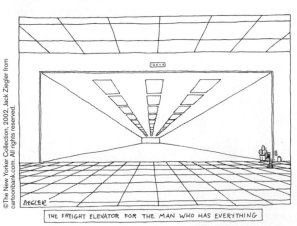

THE FREIGHT ELEVATOR FOR THE MAN WHO HAS EVERYTHING

Linear perspective Parallel lines, such as railroad tracks, appear to converge with distance. The more they converge, the greater their perceived distance.

Interposition If one object partially blocks our view of another, we perceive it as closer. The depth cues provided by interposition make this an impossible scene.

▶‖ Motion Perception

21-4 How do we perceive motion?

Imagine that you could perceive the world as having color, form, and depth but that you could not see motion. Not only would you be unable to bike or drive, you would have trouble writing, eating, and walking.

Normally your brain computes motion based partly on its assumption that shrinking objects are retreating (not getting smaller) and enlarging objects are approaching. But you are imperfect at motion perception. Large objects, such as trains, appear to move more slowly than smaller objects, such as cars moving at the same speed. (Perhaps at an airport you've noticed that jumbo jets seem to land more slowly than little jets.)

To catch a fly ball, softball or cricket players (unlike drivers) want to achieve a collision—with the ball that's flying their way. To accomplish that, they follow an unconscious rule—one they can't explain but know intuitively: Run to keep the ball at a constantly increasing angle of gaze (McBeath et al., 1995). A dog catching a Frisbee does the same (Shaffer et al., 2004).

The brain will also perceive continuous movement in a rapid series of slightly varying images (a phenomenon called *stroboscopic movement*). As film animation artists know well, you can create this illusion by flashing 24 still pictures a second. The motion we then see in popular action adventures is not in the film, which merely presents a superfast slide show. The motion is constructed in our heads. Marquees and holiday lights create another illusion of movement using the **phi phenomenon.** When two adjacent stationary lights blink on and off in quick succession, we perceive a single light moving back and forth between them. Lighted signs exploit the phi phenomenon with a succession of lights that creates the impression of, say, a moving arrow.

All of these illusions reinforce a fundamental lesson: Perception is not merely a projection of the world onto our brain. Rather, sensations are disassembled into information bits that the brain then reassembles into its own functional model of the external world. *Our brain constructs our perceptions.*

▶‖ Perceptual Constancy

21-5 How do perceptual constancies help us organize our sensations into meaningful perceptions?

So far, we have noted that our video/computer system must first perceive objects as we do—as having a distinct form, location, and perhaps motion. Its next task is to recognize objects without being deceived by changes in their shape, size, brightness, or color—an ability we call **perceptual constancy.** Regardless of our viewing angle, distance, and illumination, this top-down process lets us identify people and things in less time than it takes to draw a breath. This human perceptual feat, which has intrigued researchers for decades, provides a monumental challenge for our perceiving computer.

Shape and Size Constancies

Sometimes an object whose actual shape cannot change *seems* to change shape with the angle of our view (**FIGURE 21.10**). More often, thanks to *shape constancy,* we perceive the form of familiar objects, such as the door in **FIGURE 21.11** on the next page, as constant even while our retinal image of it changes.

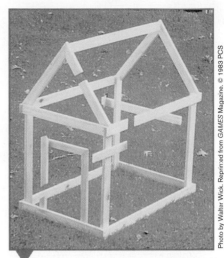

FIGURE 21.9 **The solution** Another view of the impossible doghouse in Figure 21.4 reveals the secrets of this illusion. From the photo angle in Figure 21.4, the grouping principle of closure leads us to perceive the boards as continuous.

phi phenomenon an illusion of movement created when two or more adjacent lights blink on and off in quick succession.

perceptual constancy perceiving objects as unchanging (having consistent shapes, size, lightness, and color) even as illumination and retinal images change.

FIGURE 21.10 **Perceiving shape** Do the tops of these tables have different dimensions? They appear to. But— believe it or not—they are identical. (Measure and see.) With both tables, we adjust our perceptions relative to our viewing angle.

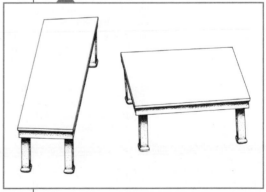

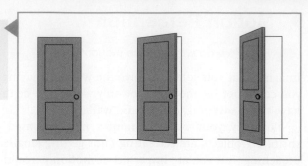

FIGURE 21.11 Shape constancy
A door casts an increasingly trapezoidal image on our retinas as it opens, yet we still perceive it as rectangular.

Thanks to *size constancy,* we perceive objects as having a constant size, even while our distance from them varies. We assume a car is large enough to carry people, even when we see its tiny image from two blocks away. This illustrates the close connection between perceived *distance* and perceived *size.* Perceiving an object's distance gives us cues to its size. Likewise, knowing its general size—that the object is a car—provides us with cues to its distance.

It is a marvel how effortlessly size perception occurs. Given an object's perceived distance and the size of its image on our retinas, we instantly and unconsciously infer the object's size. Although the monsters in **FIGURE 21.12a** cast the same retinal images, the linear perspective tells our brain that the monster in pursuit is farther away. We therefore perceive it as larger.

This interplay between perceived size and perceived distance helps explain several well-known illusions. For example, can you imagine why the Moon looks up to 50 percent larger when near the horizon than when high in the sky? For at least 22 centuries, scholars have debated this question (Hershenson, 1989). One reason for the *Moon illusion* is that cues to objects' distances make the horizon Moon—like the distant monster in Figure 21.12a and the distant bar in the *Ponzo illusion* in Figure 21.12b—appear farther away and therefore larger than the Moon high in the night sky (Kaufman & Kaufman, 2000). Take away these distance cues—by looking at the horizon Moon (or each monster or each bar) through a paper tube—and the object immediately shrinks.

Size-distance relationships also explain why in **FIGURE 21.13** the two same-age girls seem so different in size. As the diagram reveals, the girls are actually about the same

FIGURE 21.12 The interplay between perceived size and distance
(a) The monocular cues for distance (such as linear perspective and relative height) make the pursuing monster look larger than the pursued. It isn't.
(b) This visual trick, called the Ponzo illusion, is based on the same principle as the fleeing monsters. The two red bars cast identical-size images on our retinas. But experience tells us that a more distant object can create the same-size image as a nearer one only if it is actually larger. As a result, we perceive the bar that seems farther away as larger.

From Shepard (1990)

Alan Choisnet/The Image Bank

(a)   (b)

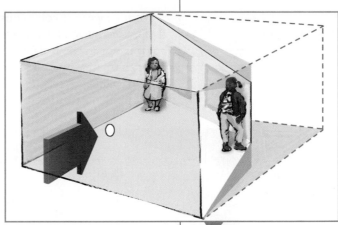

FIGURE 21.13 The illusion of the shrinking and growing girls This distorted room, designed by Adelbert Ames, appears to have a normal rectangular shape when viewed through a peephole with one eye. The girl in the right corner appears disproportionately large because we judge her size based on the false assumption that she is the same distance away as the girl in the far corner.

size, but the room is distorted. Viewed with one eye through a peephole, its trapezoidal walls produce the same images as those of a normal rectangular room viewed with both eyes. Presented with the camera's one-eyed view, the brain makes the reasonable assumption that the room *is* normal and each girl is therefore the same distance from us. And given the different sizes of their images on the retina, our brain ends up calculating that the girls are very different in size.

Our occasional misperceptions reveal the workings of our normally effective perceptual processes. The perceived relationship between distance and size is usually valid. But under special circumstances it can lead us astray—as when helping to create the Moon illusion and the Ames illusion.

Lightness Constancy

White paper reflects 90 percent of the light falling on it; black paper, only 10 percent. In sunlight, a black paper may reflect 100 times more light than does a white paper viewed indoors, but it still looks black (McBurney & Collings, 1984). This illustrates *lightness constancy* (also called *brightness constancy*); we perceive an object as having a constant lightness even while its illumination varies.

Perceived lightness depends on *relative luminance*—the amount of light an object reflects relative to its surroundings (**FIGURE 21.14**). If you view sunlit black paper through a narrow tube so nothing else is visible, it may look gray, because in bright sunshine it reflects a fair amount of light. View it without the tube and it is again black, because it reflects much less light than the objects around it.

Color Constancy

As light changes, a red apple in a fruit bowl retains its redness. This happens because our experience of color depends on something more than the wavelength information received by the cones in our retina. That something more is the surrounding *context*. If you view only part of a red apple, its color will seem to change as the light changes. But if you see the whole apple as one item in a bowl of fresh fruits, its color will remain roughly constant as the lighting and wavelengths shift—a phenomenon known as **color constancy.** Dorothea Jameson (1985) noted that a chip colored blue under indoor lighting matches the wavelengths reflected by a gold chip in sunlight. Yet bring a bluebird indoors and it won't look like a goldfinch. Likewise, a green leaf hanging from a brown branch may, when the illumination changes, reflect the same light energy that formerly came from the brown branch. Yet to us the leaf stays greenish and the branch stays brownish. Put on yellow-tinted ski goggles and the snow, after a second, looks as white as before.

FIGURE 21.14 Relative luminance Squares A and B are identical in color, believe it or not. (If you don't believe me, photocopy the illustration, cut out the squares, and compare.) But we perceive B as lighter, thanks to its surrounding context.

color constancy perceiving familiar objects as having consistent color, even if changing illumination alters the wavelengths reflected by the object.

Though we take color constancy for granted, the phenomenon is truly remarkable. It demonstrates that our experience of color comes not just from the object—the color is not in the isolated leaf—but from everything around it as well. You and I see color thanks to our brains' computations of the light reflected by any object *relative to its surrounding objects*. But only if we grew up with normal light, it seems. Monkeys raised under a restricted range of wavelengths later have great difficulty recognizing the same color when illumination varies (Sugita, 2004).

FIGURE 21.15 Color depends on context Believe it or not, these three blue disks are identical in color.

R. Beau Lotto at University College, London

In a context that does not vary, we maintain color constancy. But what if we change the context? Because the brain computes the color of an object relative to its context, the perceived color changes (as is dramatically apparent in **FIGURE 21.15**). This principle—that we perceive objects not in isolation but in their environmental context—matters to artists, interior decorators, and clothing designers. Our perception of the color of a wall or of a streak of paint on a canvas is determined not just by the paint in the can but by the surrounding colors. The take-home lesson: Comparisons govern perceptions.

* * *

Form perception, depth perception, motion perception, and perceptual constancy illuminate how we organize our visual experiences. Perceptual organization applies to other senses, too. It explains why we perceive a clock's steady tick not as a *tick-tick-tick* but as grouped sounds, say, *TICK-tick, TICK-tick*. Listening to an unfamiliar language, we have trouble hearing where one word stops and the next one begins. Listening to our own language, we automatically hear distinct words. This, too, reflects perceptual organization. But it is more, for we even organize a string of letters—THEDOGATEMEAT—into words that make an intelligible phrase, more likely "The dog ate meat" than "The do gate me at" (McBurney & Collings, 1984). This process involves not only the organization we've been discussing, but also interpretation—discerning meaning in what we perceive.

REVIEW

Perceptual Organization

21-1 **How did the Gestalt psychologists understand perceptual organization?** Gestalt psychologists searched for rules by which the brain organizes fragments of sensory data into *gestalts* (from the German word for "whole"), or meaningful forms. In pointing out that the whole is more than the sum of its parts, they noted that we filter sensory information and infer perceptions in ways that make sense to us.

21-2 **How do figure-ground and grouping principles contribute to our perceptions?** To recognize an object, we must first perceive it (see it as a *figure*) as distinct from its surroundings (the *ground*). We bring order and form to stimuli by organizing them into meaningful *groups,* following the rules of proximity, similarity, continuity, connectedness, and closure.

21-3 **How do we see the world in three dimensions?** *Depth perception* is our ability to see objects in three dimensions and judge distance. The *visual cliff* and other research demonstrates that many species perceive the world in three dimensions at, or very soon after, birth. *Binocular cues,* such as *retinal disparity,* are depth cues that rely on information from both eyes. *Monocular cues* (such as relative size, interposition, relative height, relative motion, linear perspective, and light and shadow) let us judge depth using information transmitted by only one eye.

21-4 **How do we perceive motion?** As objects move, we assume that shrinking objects are retreating and enlarging objects are approaching. But sometimes we miscalculate. A quick succession of images on the retina can create an illusion of movement, as in stroboscopic movement or the *phi phenomenon.*

21-5 **How do perceptual constancies help us organize our sensations into meaningful perceptions?** *Perceptual constancy* enables us to perceive objects as stable despite the changing image they cast on our retinas. Shape constancy is our ability to perceive familiar objects (such as an opening door) as unchanging in shape. Size constancy is perceiving objects as unchanging in size despite their changing retinal images. Knowing an object's size

gives us clues to its distance; knowing its distance gives clues about its size, but we sometimes misread monocular distance cues and reach the wrong conclusions, as in the Moon illusion. Lightness (or brightness) constancy is our ability to perceive an object as having a constant lightness even when its illumination—the light cast upon it—changes. The brain perceives lightness relative to surrounding objects. *Color constancy* is our ability to perceive consistent color in objects, even though the lighting and wavelengths shift. Our brain constructs our experience of the color of an object through comparisons with other surrounding objects.

Terms and Concepts to Remember

gestalt, p. 262	retinal disparity, p. 265
figure-ground, p. 263	monocular cues, p. 265
grouping, p. 263	phi phenomenon, p. 267
depth perception, p. 264	perceptual constancy, p. 267
visual cliff, p. 264	color constancy, p. 269
binocular cues, p. 265	

Test Yourself

1. What do we mean when we say that, in perception, the whole is greater than the sum of its parts?

(Answers to the Test Yourself questions can be found in Appendix B at the end of the book.)

Ask Yourself

1. Try drawing a realistic depiction of the scene from your window. How many monocular cues will you use in your drawing?

∞ WEB

Multiple-choice self-tests and more may be found at www.worthpublishers.com/myers

Sensory Deprivation and
Restored Vision

Perceptual Adaptation

Perceptual Set

Perception and
the Human Factor

Is There Extrasensory
Perception?

Perceptual Interpretation

Philosophers have debated whether our perceptual abilities should be credited to our nature or our nurture. To what extent do we *learn* to perceive? German philosopher Immanuel Kant (1724–1804) maintained that knowledge comes from our *inborn* ways of organizing sensory experiences. Indeed, we come equipped to process sensory information. But British philosopher John Locke (1632–1704) argued that through our experiences we also *learn* to perceive the world. Indeed, we learn to link an object's distance with its size. So, just how important is experience? How radically does it shape our perceptual interpretations?

"Let us then suppose the mind to be, as we say, white paper void of all characters, without any ideas: How comes it to be furnished? . . . To this I answer, in one word, from EXPERIENCE."

John Locke, *An Essay Concerning Human Understanding*, 1690

▶‖ Sensory Deprivation and Restored Vision

22-1 What does research on sensory restriction and restored vision reveal about the effects of experience?

Writing to John Locke, William Molyneux wondered whether "a man *born* blind, and now adult, taught by his *touch* to distinguish between a cube and a sphere" could, if made to see, visually distinguish the two. Locke's answer was *no*, because the man would never have *learned* to see the difference.

Molyneux' hypothetical case has since been put to the test with a few dozen adults who, though blind from birth, have gained sight (Gregory, 1978; von Senden, 1932). Most had been born with cataracts—clouded lenses that allowed them to see only diffused light, rather as you or I might see a diffuse fog through a Ping-Pong ball sliced in half. After cataract surgery, the patients could distinguish figure from ground and could sense colors—suggesting that these aspects of perception are innate. But much as Locke supposed, they often could not visually recognize objects that were familiar by touch.

Experience also influences our perception of faces. You and I perceive and recognize individual faces as a whole. Show us the same top half of a face paired with two different bottom halves (as in **FIGURE 22.1**), and the identical top halves will seem different. People deprived of visual experience during childhood surpass the rest of us at recognizing that the top halves are the same, because they didn't learn to process faces as a whole (Le Grand et al., 2004). One 43-year-old man whose sight was recently restored after 40 years of blindness could associate people with distinct features ("Mary's the one with red hair"). But he could not instantly recognize a face.

He also lacked perceptual constancy: As people walked away from him they seemed to be shrinking in size (Bower, 2003). Vision, such cases make clear, is partly an acquired sense.

Seeking to gain more control than is provided by clinical cases, researchers have conducted Molyneux' imaginary experiment with infant kittens and monkeys. In one experiment, they outfitted them with goggles through which the animals could see only diffuse, unpatterned light (Wiesel, 1982). After infancy, when their goggles were removed, these animals exhibited perceptual limitations much like those of humans born with cataracts. They could distinguish color and brightness, but not the form of a circle from that of a square. Their eyes had not degenerated; their retinas still relayed signals to their visual cortex. But lacking stimulation, the cortical cells had not developed

Learning to see At age 3, Mike May lost his vision in an explosion. On March 7, 2000, after a new cornea restored vision to his right eye, he got his first look at his wife and children. Alas, although signals were reaching his long dormant visual cortex, it lacked the experience to interpret them. Faces, apart from features such as hair, were not recognizable. Expressions eluded him. Yet he can see an object in motion and is gradually learning to navigate his world and to marvel at such things as dust floating in sunlight (Abrams, 2002).

Mike May, Allison Aliano Photography

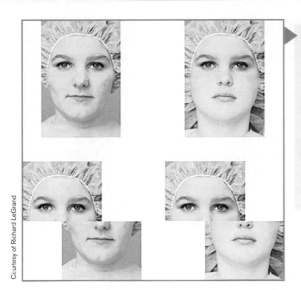

Courtesy of Richard LeGrand

FIGURE 22.1 Perceiving composite faces To most people, the top halves of these two faces in the top row, created by Richard Le Grand and his colleagues (2004), look different. Actually, they are the same, though paired with two different lower face halves. People deprived of visual experience early in life have more difficulty perceiving whole faces, which ironically enables their superiority at recognizing that the top halves of these faces are identical.

perceptual adaptation in vision, the ability to adjust to an artificially displaced or even inverted visual field.

normal connections. Thus, the animals remained functionally blind to shape. Experience guides, sustains, and maintains the brain's neural organization.

In both humans and animals, a similar period of sensory restriction does no permanent harm if it occurs later in life. Cover the eye of an animal for several months during adulthood, and its vision will be unaffected after the eye patch is removed. Remove cataracts that develop after early childhood, and a human, too, will enjoy normal vision.

The effects of visual experiences during infancy in cats, monkeys, and humans suggest there is a *critical period* shortly after birth—an optimal time when certain events must take place—for normal sensory and perceptual development. Likewise, cochlear implants given to congenitally deaf kittens and human infants seem to trigger an "awakening" of the pertinent brain area (Klinke et al., 1999; Sirenteanu, 1999). Nurture sculpts what nature has endowed.

Experiments on perceptual limitations and advantages produced by early sensory deprivation provide a partial answer to the enduring question about experience: Does the effect of early experience last a lifetime? For some aspects of visual and auditory perception, the answer is clearly *yes:* "Use it *soon* or lose it." We retain the imprint of early sensory experiences far into the future.

▶|| Perceptual Adaptation

22-2 How adaptable is our ability to perceive?

Given a new pair of glasses, we may feel slightly disoriented, even dizzy. Within a day or two, we adjust. Our **perceptual adaptation** to changed visual input makes the world seem normal again. But imagine a far more dramatic new pair of glasses—one that shifts the apparent location of objects 40 degrees to the left. When you first put them on and toss a ball to a friend, it sails off to the left. Walking forward to shake hands with the person, you veer to the left.

Could you adapt to this distorted world? Chicks cannot. When fitted with such lenses, they continue to peck where food grains *seem* to be (Hess, 1956; Rossi, 1968). But we humans adapt to distorting lenses quickly. Within a few minutes your throws would again be accurate, your stride on target. Remove the lenses and you would experience an aftereffect: At first your throws would err in the *opposite* direction, sailing off to the right; but again, within minutes you would readapt.

Perceptual adaptation "Oops, missed," thinks researcher Hubert Dolezal as he views the world through inverting goggles. Yet, believe it or not, kittens, monkeys, and humans can adapt to an inverted world.

Courtesy of Hubert Dolezal

perceptual set   a mental predisposition to perceive <u>one thing</u> and <u>not another.</u>

"The temptation to form premature theories upon insufficient data is the bane of our profession."

Sherlock Holmes, in Arthur Conan Doyle's *The Valley of Fear*, 1914

‖ When shown the phrase
  Mary had a
  a little lamb
many people perceive what they expect, and miss the repeated word. Did you? ‖

Indeed, given an even more radical pair of glasses—one that literally turns the world upside down—you could still adapt. Psychologist George Stratton (1896) experienced this when he invented, and for eight days wore, optical headgear that flipped left to right *and* up to down, making him the first person to experience a right-side-up retinal image while standing upright. The ground was up, the sky was down.

At first, Stratton felt disoriented. When he wanted to walk, he found himself searching for his feet, which were now "up." Eating was nearly impossible. He became nauseated and depressed. But Stratton persisted, and by the eighth day he could comfortably reach for something in the right direction and walk without bumping into things. When he finally removed the headgear, he readapted quickly.

Later experiments replicated Stratton's experience (Dolezal, 1982; Kohler, 1962). After a period of adjustment, people wearing the optical gear have even been able to ride a motorcycle, ski the Alps, and fly an airplane. Did they adjust by perceptually converting their strange worlds to "normal" views? No. Actually, the world around them still seemed above their heads or on the wrong side. But by actively moving about in these topsy-turvy worlds, they adapted to the context and learned to coordinate their movements.

▶‖ Perceptual Set

22-3   How do our expectations, contexts, and emotions influence our perceptions?

As everyone knows, to see is to believe. As we less fully appreciate, to believe is to see. Our experiences, assumptions, and expectations may give us a **perceptual set,** or mental predisposition, that greatly influences (top-down) what we perceive. People perceive an adult-child pair as looking more alike when told they are parent and child (Bressan & Dal Martello, 2002). And consider: Is the image in the center picture of **FIGURE 22.2** a man playing a saxophone or a woman's face? What we see in such a drawing can be influenced by first looking at either of the two unambiguous versions (Boring, 1930).

Once we have formed a wrong idea about reality, we have more difficulty seeing the truth. Everyday examples of perceptual set abound. In 1972, a British newspaper published genuine, unretouched photographs of a "monster" in Scotland's Loch Ness— "the most amazing pictures ever taken," stated the paper. If this information creates in you the same perceptual set it did in most of the paper's readers, you, too, will see the monster in the photo reproduced in **FIGURE 22.3a**. But when Steuart Campbell (1986) approached the photos with a different perceptual set, he saw a curved tree trunk—as had others the day the photo was shot. With this different perceptual set, you may now notice that the object is floating motionless, without any rippling water or wake around it—hardly what we would expect of a lively monster.

FIGURE 22.2 Perceptual set Show a friend either the left or right image. Then show the center image and ask, "What do you see?" Whether your friend reports seeing a saxophonist or a woman's face will likely depend on which of the other two drawings was viewed first. In each of those images, the meaning is clear, and it will establish perceptual expectations.

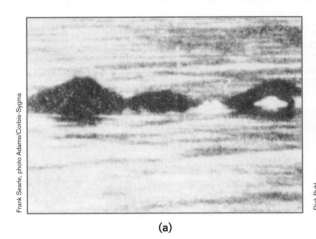

(a)   (b)

FIGURE 22.3 Believing is seeing What do you perceive in these photos? (a) Is this Nessie, the Loch Ness monster, or a log? (b) Are these flying saucers or clouds? We often perceive what we expect to see.

Perceptual set can similarly influence what we hear. Consider the kindly airline pilot who, on a takeoff run, looked over at his depressed co-pilot and said, "Cheer up." The co-pilot heard the usual "Gear up" and promptly raised the wheels—before they left the ground (Reason & Mycielska, 1982). Perceptual set also influenced some bar patrons invited to sample free beer (Lee et al., 2006). When researchers added a few drops of vinegar to a brand-name beer, the tasters preferred it—unless they had been told they were drinking vinegar-laced beer and thus expected, and usually experienced, a worse taste. Perceptual set also influences preschool children's taste preferences. By a 6 to 1 margin in one experiment, they judged french fries as tasting better when served in a McDonald's bag rather than a plain white bag (Robinson et al., 2007). Clearly, much of what we perceive comes not just from the world "out there" but also from what's behind our eyes and between our ears.

What determines our perceptual set? Through experience we form concepts, or *schemas,* that organize and interpret unfamiliar information. Our preexisting schemas for male saxophonists and women's faces, for monsters and tree trunks, for clouds and UFOs, all influence how we interpret ambiguous sensations with top-down processing.

Our schemas for faces prime us to see facial patterns even in random configurations, such as the Moon's landscape, clouds, rocks, or cinnamon buns. Kieran Lee, Graham Byatt, and Gillian Rhodes (2000) demonstrated how we recognize people by facial features that cartoonists can caricature. For but a fraction of a second they showed University of Western Australia students three versions of familiar faces—the actual face, a computer-created caricature that accentuated the differences between this face and the average face, and an "anticaricature" that muted the distinctive features. As **FIGURE 22.4** shows, the students more accurately recognized the caricatured faces than the actual ones. A caricatured Arnold Schwarzenegger is more recognizably Schwarzenegger than Schwarzenegger himself!

IT'S AMAZING HOW PEOPLE SLOW DOWN WHEN YOU POINT A HAIR DRYER AT THEM.

FIGURE 22.4 Recognizing faces When briefly flashed, a caricature of Arnold Schwarzenegger was more accurately recognized than Schwarzenegger himself. Ditto for other familiar male faces.

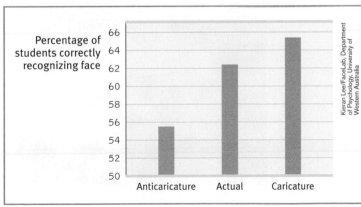

Percentage of students correctly recognizing face

| Anticaricature | Actual | Caricature |

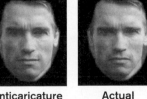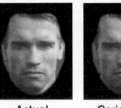

Anticaricature   Actual   Caricature

Context Effects

A given stimulus may trigger radically different perceptions, partly because of our differing set, but also because of the immediate context. Some examples:

▶ Imagine hearing a noise interrupted by the words "eel is on the wagon." Likely, you would actually perceive the first word as *wheel*. Given "eel is on the orange," you would hear *peel*. This curious phenomenon, discovered by Richard Warren, suggests that the brain can work backward in time to allow a later stimulus to determine how we perceive an earlier one. The context creates an expectation that, top-down, influences our perception as we match our bottom-up signal against it (Grossberg, 1995).

▶ Is the "magician's cabinet" in **FIGURE 22.5** sitting on the floor or hanging from the ceiling? How we perceive it depends on the context defined by the rabbits.

▶ How tall is the shorter player in **FIGURE 22.6**?

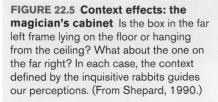

FIGURE 22.5 Context effects: the magician's cabinet Is the box in the far left frame lying on the floor or hanging from the ceiling? What about the one on the far right? In each case, the context defined by the inquisitive rabbits guides our perceptions. (From Shepard, 1990.)

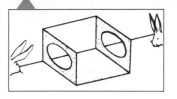  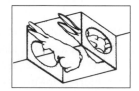 

Even hearing sad rather than happy music can predispose people to perceive a sad meaning in spoken homophonic words—*mourning* rather than *morning, die* rather than *dye, pain* rather than *pane* (Halberstadt et al., 1995).

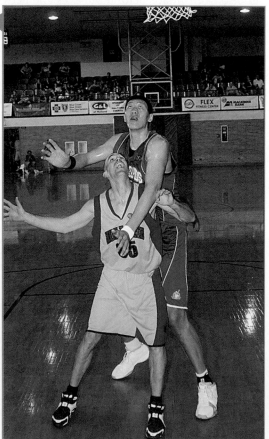

FIGURE 22.6 Big and "little" The "little guy" shown here is actually a 6'9" former Hope College basketball center who towers over me. But he seemed like a short player when matched in a semi-pro game against the world's tallest basketball player, 7'9" Sun Ming Ming from China.

Culture and context effects What is above the woman's head? In one study, nearly all the East Africans who were questioned said the woman was balancing a metal box or can on her head and that the family was sitting under a tree. Westerners, for whom corners and boxlike architecture are more common, were more likely to perceive the family as being indoors, with the woman sitting under a window. (Adapted from Gregory & Gombrich, 1973.)

The effects of perceptual set and context show how experience helps us construct perception. In everyday life, for example, stereotypes about gender (another instance of perceptual set) can color perception. Without the obvious cues of pink or blue, people will struggle over whether to call the new baby "he" or "she." But told an infant is "David," people (especially children) may perceive "him" as bigger and stronger than if the same infant is called "Diana" (Stern & Karraker, 1989). Some differences, it seems, exist merely in the eyes of their beholders.

"We hear and apprehend only what we already half know."

Henry David Thoreau, *Journal*, 1860

cathy®   **by Cathy Guisewite**

Given a perceptual set—"this is a girl"—people see a more feminine baby.

Emotion and Motivation

Perceptions are influenced, top-down, not only by our expectations and by the context, but also by our emotions. Dennis Proffitt (2006a,b) and others have demonstrated this with clever experiments showing that

▶ walking destinations look farther away to those who have been fatigued by prior exercise.

▶ a hill looks steeper to those wearing a heavy backpack or just exposed to sad, heavy classical music rather than light, bouncy music.

▶ a target seems farther away to those throwing a heavy rather than a light object at it.

Even a softball appears bigger when you are hitting well, observed Jessica Witt and Proffitt (2005), after asking players to choose a circle the size of the ball they had just hit well or poorly.

Motives also matter. In Cornell University experiments, students viewed ambiguous figures, such as the horse/seal in **FIGURE 22.7** on the next page. If rewards were linked with seeing one category of stimulus (such as a farm animal rather than a sea animal),

"When you're hitting the ball, it comes at you looking like a grapefruit. When you're not, it looks like a blackeyed pea."

Former major league baseball player George Scott

FIGURE 22.7 Ambiguous horse/seal figure If motivated to perceive farm animals, about 7 in 10 people immediately perceived a horse. If motivated to perceive a sea animal, about 7 in 10 perceived a seal.

"Ambiguity of form: Old and new" by G. H. Fisher, 1968, *Perception and Psychophysics*, 4, 189–192. Copyright 1968 by Psychonomic Society, Inc.

then, after just a one-second exposure to the drawing, viewers tended instantly to perceive an example of their hoped-for category (Balcetis & Dunning, 2006). (To confirm the participants' honesty in reporting their perceptions, the researchers in one experiment redefined the to-be-rewarded perception after the viewing. Still, people reported perceiving a stimulus from their originally hoped-for category.)

Emotions color our social perceptions, too. Spouses who feel loved and appreciated perceive less threat in stressful marital events—"He's just having a bad day" (Murray et al., 2003). Professional referees, if told a soccer team has a history of aggressive behavior, will assign more penalty cards after watching videotaped fouls (Jones et al., 2002). Lee Ross invites us to recall our own perceptions in different contexts: "Ever notice that when you're driving you hate pedestrians, the way they saunter through the crosswalk, almost daring you to hit them, but when you're walking you hate drivers?" (Jaffe, 2004).

To return to the question "Is perception innate or learned?" we can answer: It's both. The river of perception is fed by sensation, cognition, and emotion. And that is why we need multiple levels of analysis (**FIGURE 22.8**). "Simple" perceptions are the brain's creative products.

"Have you ever noticed that anyone driving slower than you is an idiot, and anyone going faster is a maniac?"

George Carlin, *George Carlin on Campus*, 1984

FIGURE 22.8
Perception is a biopsychosocial phenomenon
Psychologists study how we perceive with different levels of analysis, from the biological to the social-cultural.

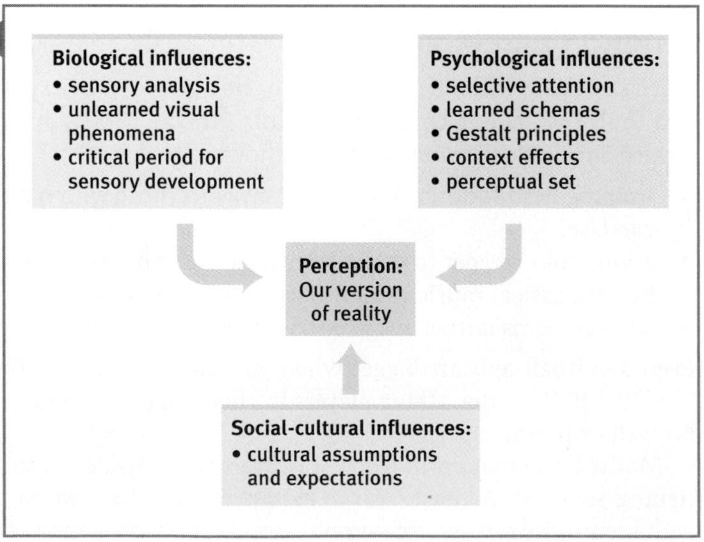

Biological influences:
• sensory analysis
• unlearned visual phenomena
• critical period for sensory development

Psychological influences:
• selective attention
• learned schemas
• Gestalt principles
• context effects
• perceptual set

Perception:
Our version of reality

Social-cultural influences:
• cultural assumptions and expectations

▶‖ Perception and the Human Factor

22-4 How do human factors psychologists work to create user-friendly machines and work settings?

Designs sometimes neglect the human factor. Psychologist Donald Norman, an MIT alumnus with a Ph.D., bemoaned the complexity of assembling his new high-definition TV, receiver, speakers, digital recorder, DVD player, VCR, and seven remotes into a usable home theater system: "I was VP of Advanced Technology at Apple. I can program dozens of computers in dozens of languages. I understand television, really, I do. . . . It doesn't matter: I am overwhelmed."

How much easier life might be if engineers would routinely work with **human factors psychologists** to test their designs and instructions on real people. Human factors psychologists help to design appliances, machines, and work settings that fit our natural perceptions and inclinations. ATM machines are internally more complex than VCRs ever were, yet, thanks to human factors psychologists working with engineers, ATMs are easier to operate. TiVo has solved the TV recording problem with a simple select-and-click menu system ("record that one"). Apple has similarly engineered easy usability with the iPod and iPhone.

Norman (2001) hosts a Web site (www.jnd.org) that illustrates good designs that fit people (see **FIGURE 22.9**). Human factors psychologists also work at designing safe and efficient environments. An ideal kitchen layout, researchers have found, stores needed items close to their usage point and near eye level. It locates work areas to enable doing tasks in order, such as with a refrigerator, stove, and sink in a triangle. It creates counters that enable hands to work at or slightly below elbow height (Boehm-Davis, 2005).

Understanding human factors can do more than enable us to design for reduced frustration; it can help prevent accidents and avoid disaster (Boehm-Davis, 2005). Two-thirds of commercial air accidents, for example, have been caused by human error (Nickerson, 1998). After beginning commercial flights in the late 1960s, the Boeing 727 was involved in several landing accidents caused by pilot error. Psychologist Conrad Kraft (1978) noted a common setting for these accidents: All took place at night, and all involved landing short of the runway after crossing a dark stretch of water or unilluminated ground. Kraft reasoned that, beyond the runway, city lights would project a larger retinal image if on a rising terrain. This would make the ground seem farther away than it was. By re-creating these conditions in flight simulations, Kraft discovered that pilots were deceived into thinking they were flying higher than their actual altitudes (**FIGURE 22.10** on the next page). Aided by Kraft's finding, the airlines began requiring the co-pilot to monitor the altimeter—calling out altitudes during the descent—and the accidents diminished.

human factors psychology a branch of psychology that explores how people and machines interact and how machines and physical environments can be made safe and easy to use.

The Ride On Carry On foldable chair attachment "designed by a flight attendant mom," enables a small suitcase to double as a stroller.

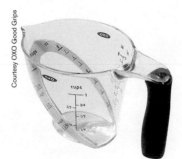

The Oxo measuring cup allows the user to see the quantity from above.

The Chatsford Tea Pot comes with a built-in strainer.

FIGURE 22.9 Designing products that fit people Human factors psychologist Donald Norman offers these and other examples of effectively designed new products.

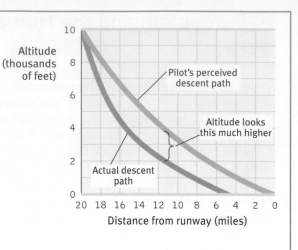

FIGURE 22.10 The human factor in accidents Lacking distance cues when approaching a runway from over a dark surface, pilots simulating a night landing tended to fly too low. (From Kraft, 1978.)

Altitude (thousands of feet)

Pilot's perceived descent path

Altitude looks this much higher

Actual descent path

Distance from runway (miles)

Later Boeing psychologists worked on other human factors problems (Murray, 1998): How should airlines best train and manage mechanics to reduce the maintenance errors that underlie about 50 percent of flight delays and 15 percent of accidents? What illumination and typeface would make on-screen flight data easiest to read? How could warning messages be most effectively worded—as an action statement ("Pull Up") rather than a problem statement ("Ground Proximity")?

In studying human factors issues, psychologists' most powerful tool is theory-aided research. If an organization wonders what sort of Web design (Emphasizing content? Speed? Graphics?) would most effectively draw in visitors and entice them to return, the psychologist will want to test responses to several alternatives. If NASA (National Aeronautics and Space Administration) wonders what sort of spacecraft design would best facilitate sleeping, work, and morale, their human factors psychologists will want to test the alternatives (**FIGURE 22.11**).

Consider, finally, the available *assistive listening* technologies in various theaters, auditoriums, and places of worship. One technology, commonly available in the United States, requires a headset attached to a pocket-size receiver that detects infrared or FM signals from the room's sound system. The well-meaning people who design, purchase, and install these systems correctly understand that the technology puts sound directly into the user's ears. Alas, few people with hearing loss undergo the hassle and embarrassment of locating, requesting, wearing, and returning a conspicuous headset. Most such units therefore sit in closets. Britain, the Scandinavian countries,

The human factor in safe landings Advanced cockpit design and rehearsed emergency procedures aided pilot Chesley "Sully" Sullenberger, a U.S. Air Force Academy graduate who studied psychology and human factors. In January 2009, Sullenberger's instantaneous decisions safely guided his disabled airliner onto New York City's Hudson River, where all 155 of the passengers and crew were safely evacuated.

AP Photo/Steven Day

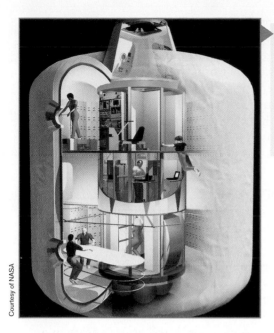

FIGURE 22.11 How not to go mad while going to Mars Future astronauts headed to Mars will be confined in conditions of monotony, stress, and weightlessness for months on end. To help design and evaluate a workable human environment, such as for this Transit Habitation (Transhab) Module, NASA engages human factors psychologists (Weed, 2001; Wichman, 1992).

Courtesy of NASA

extrasensory perception (ESP) the controversial claim that perception can occur apart from sensory input; includes telepathy, clairvoyance, and precognition.

parapsychology the study of paranormal phenomena, including ESP and psychokinesis.

and Australia have instead installed *loop systems* (see www.hearingloop.org) that broadcast customized sound directly through a person's own hearing aid. When suitably equipped, a hearing aid can be transformed by a discrete touch of a switch into an in-the-ear loudspeaker. Offered convenient, inconspicuous, personalized sound, many more people elect to use assistive listening.

Designs that enable safe, easy, and effective interactions between people and technology often seem obvious after the fact. Why, then, aren't they more common? Technology developers sometimes mistakenly assume that others share their expertise—that what's clear to them will similarly be clear to others (Camerer et al., 1989; Nickerson, 1999). When people rap their knuckles on a table to convey a familiar tune (try this with a friend), they often expect their listener to recognize it. But for the listener, this is a near-impossible task (Newton, 1991). When you know a thing, it's hard to mentally simulate what it's like not to know, and that is called the *curse of knowledge*.

The point to remember: Designers and engineers should consider human abilities and behaviors by designing things to fit people, user-testing their inventions before production and distribution, and being mindful of the curse of knowledge.

▶‖ Is There Extrasensory Perception?

22-5 What are the claims of ESP, and what have most research psychologists concluded after putting these claims to the test?

Can we perceive only what we sense? Or, as nearly half of Americans believe, are we capable of **extrasensory perception (ESP)** without sensory input (AP, 2007; Moore, 2005)?

Are there indeed people—any people—who can read minds, see through walls, or foretell the future? Five British universities have **parapsychology** units staffed by Ph.D. graduates of Edinburgh University's parapsychology program (Turpin, 2005). Sweden's Lund University, the Netherlands' Utrecht University, and Australia's University of Adelaide also have added faculty chairs or research units for parapsychology. Parapsychologists in such places do experiments that search for possible ESP and other paranormal phenomena. But other research psychologists and scientists—including 96

‖ There would also be some people, notes Michael Shermer (1999), who would have no need for caller ID, who would never lose at "rock, paper, scissors," and for whom we could never have a surprise party. ‖

SNAPSHOTS

© Jason Love

percent of the scientists in the U.S. National Academy of Sciences—are skeptical that such phenomena exist (McConnell, 1991). If ESP is real, we would need to overturn the scientific understanding that we are creatures whose minds are tied to our physical brains and whose perceptual experiences of the world are built of sensations. Sometimes new evidence does overturn our scientific preconceptions. Science, as we will see throughout this book, offers us various surprises—about the extent of the unconscious mind, about the effects of emotions on health, about what heals and what doesn't, and much more. Before we evaluate claims of ESP, let's review them.

Claims of ESP

Claims of paranormal phenomena ("psi") include astrological predictions, psychic healing, communication with the dead, and out-of-body experiences. But the most testable and (for a perception discussion) most relevant claims are for three varieties of ESP:

▶ *Telepathy,* or mind-to-mind communication—one person sending thoughts to another or perceiving another's thoughts.

▶ *Clairvoyance,* or perceiving remote events, such as sensing that a friend's house is on fire.

▶ *Precognition,* or perceiving future events, such as a political leader's death or a sporting event's outcome.

FIGURE 22.12 Parapsychological concepts

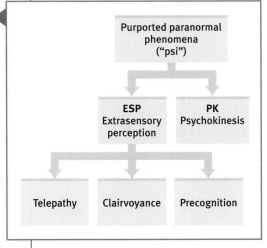

Closely linked with these are claims of *psychokinesis (PK),* or "mind over matter," such as levitating a table or influencing the roll of a die (**FIGURE 22.12**). (The claim is illustrated by the wry request, "Will all those who believe in psychokinesis please raise my hand?")

Premonitions or Pretensions?

Can psychics see into the future? Although one might wish for a psychic stock forecaster, the tallied forecasts of "leading psychics" reveal meager accuracy. No greedy—or charitable—psychic has been able to predict the outcome of a lottery jackpot, or to make billions on the stock market. During the 1990s, tabloid psychics were all wrong in predicting surprising events. (Madonna did not become a gospel singer, the Statue of Liberty did not lose both its arms in a terrorist blast, Queen Elizabeth did not abdicate her throne to enter a convent.) And the new-century psychics missed the big-news events, such as the horror of 9/11. (Where were the psychics on 9/10 when we needed them? Why, despite a $50 million reward offered, could none of them help locate Osama bin Laden after 9/11?) Gene Emery (2004), who has tracked annual psychic forecasts for 26 years, reports that almost never have unusual predictions come true, and virtually never have psychics anticipated any of the year's headline events.

Analyses of psychic visions offered to police departments reveal that these, too, are no more accurate than guesses made by others (Reiser, 1982). Psychics working with the police do, however, generate hundreds of predictions. This increases the odds of an occasional correct guess, which psychics can then report to the media. Moreover, vague predictions can later be interpreted ("retrofitted") to match events that provide a perceptual set for "understanding" them. Nostradamus, a sixteenth-century French psychic, explained in an unguarded moment that his ambiguous prophecies "could not possibly be understood till they were interpreted after the event and by it."

"A person who talks a lot is sometimes right."

Spanish proverb

Police departments are wise to all this. When Jane Ayers Sweat and Mark Durm (1993) asked the police departments of America's 50 largest cities whether they ever used psychics, 65 percent said they never had. Of those that had, not one had found it helpful.

Are the spontaneous "visions" of everyday people any more accurate? Consider our dreams. Do they foretell the future, as people often believe? Or do they only seem to do so because we are more likely to recall or reconstruct dreams that appear to have come true? Two Harvard psychologists (Murray & Wheeler, 1937) tested the prophetic power of dreams after aviator Charles Lindbergh's baby son was kidnapped and murdered in 1932, but before the body was discovered. When the researchers invited the public to report their dreams about the child, 1300 visionaries submitted dream reports. How many accurately envisioned the child dead? Five percent. And how many also correctly anticipated the body's location—buried among trees? Only 4 of the 1300. Although this number was surely no better than chance, to those 4 dreamers the accuracy of their apparent precognitions must have seemed uncanny.

Throughout the day, each of us imagines many events. Given the billions of events in the world each day, and given enough days, some stunning coincidences are sure to occur. By one careful estimate, chance alone would predict that more than a thousand times a day someone on Earth will think of someone and then within the ensuing five minutes will learn of the person's death (Charpak & Broch, 2004). With enough time and people, the improbable becomes inevitable.

That was the experience of comics writer John Byrne (2003). Six months after his Spider-Man story about a New York blackout appeared, New York suffered a massive blackout. A subsequent Spider-Man storyline involved a major earthquake in Japan. "And again," he recalled, "the real thing happened in the month the issue hit the stands." Later, when working on a Superman comic book, he "had the Man of Steel fly to the rescue when disaster beset the NASA space shuttle. The *Challenger* tragedy happened almost immediately thereafter" (with time for the issue to be redrawn). "Most recently, and chilling, came when I was writing and drawing Wonder Woman and did a story in which the title character was killed as a prelude to her becoming a goddess." The issue cover "was done as a newspaper front page, with the headline 'Princess Diana Dies.' (Diana is Wonder Woman's real name.) That issue went on sale on a Thursday. The following Saturday . . . I don't have to tell you, do I?"

Putting ESP to Experimental Test

In the past, there have been all kinds of strange ideas—that bumps on the head reveal character traits, that bloodletting is a cure-all, that each sperm cell contains a miniature person. Faced with such claims—or with claims of mind-reading or out-of-body travel or communication with the dead—how can we separate bizarre ideas from those that sound bizarre but are true? At the heart of science is a simple answer: *Test them to see if they work.* If they do, so much the better for the ideas. If they don't, so much the better for our skepticism.

This scientific attitude has led both believers and skeptics to agree that what parapsychology needs is a reproducible phenomenon and a theory to explain it. Parapsychologist Rhea White (1998) spoke for many in saying that "the image of parapsychology that comes to my mind, based on nearly 44 years in the field, is that of a small airplane [that] has been perpetually taxiing down the runway of the Empirical Science Airport since 1882 . . . its movement punctuated occasionally by lifting a few feet off the ground only to bump back down on the tarmac once again. It has never taken off for any sustained flight."

Seeking a reproducible phenomenon, how might we test ESP claims in a controlled experiment? An experiment differs from a staged demonstration. In the laboratory, the experimenter controls what the "psychic" sees and hears. On stage, the

"At the heart of science is an essential tension between two seemingly contradictory attitudes—an openness to new ideas, no matter how bizarre or counterintuitive they may be, and the most ruthless skeptical scrutiny of all ideas, old and new."
Carl Sagan (1987)

Testing psychic powers in the British population Hertfordshire University psychologist Richard Wiseman created a "mind machine" to see if people can influence or predict a coin toss. Using a touch-sensitive screen, visitors to festivals around the country were given four attempts to call heads or tails. Using a random-number generator, a computer then decided the outcome. When the experiment concluded in January 2000, nearly 28,000 people had predicted 110,972 tosses—with 49.8 percent correct.

Courtesy of Claire Cole

"A psychic is an actor playing the role of a psychic."

Psychologist-magician Daryl Bem (1984)

BIZARRO   By DAN PIRARO

HEY! WE WERE JUST THINKING ABOUT CALLING OUT FOR PIZZA!

I KNOW!

PSYCHIC PIZZA DELIVERED 15 MINUTES BEFORE YOU ORDER OR IT'S FREE!

The "Bizarro" cartoon by Dan Piraro is reprinted by permission of Chronicle Features.

Which supposed psychic ability does Psychic Pizza claim?

"People's desire to believe in the paranormal is stronger than all the evidence that it does not exist."

Susan Blackmore, "Blackmore's first law," 2004

psychic controls what the audience sees and hears. Time and again, skeptics note, so-called psychics have exploited unquestioning audiences with mind-blowing performances in which they *appeared* to communicate with the spirits of the dead, read minds, or levitate objects—only to have it revealed that their acts were nothing more than the illusions of stage magicians.

The search for a valid and reliable test of ESP has resulted in thousands of experiments. Some 380 of them have assessed people's efforts to influence computer-generated random sequences of ones and zeros. In some small experiments, the tally of the desired number has exceeded chance by 1 or 2 percent, an effect that disappears when larger experiments are added to the mix (Bösch et al., 2006a,b; Radin et al., 2006; Wilson & Shadish, 2006).

Another set of experiments has invited "senders" to telepathically transmit one of four visual images to "receivers" deprived of sensation in a nearby chamber (Bem & Honorton, 1994). The result? A reported 32 percent accurate response rate, surpassing the chance rate of 25 percent. But follow-up studies have (depending on who was summarizing the results) failed to replicate the phenomenon or produced mixed results (Bem et al., 2001; Milton & Wiseman, 2002; Storm, 2000, 2003).

If ESP nevertheless exists, might it subtly register in the brain? To find out, Harvard researchers Samuel Moulton and Stephen Kosslyn (2008) had a sender try to send one of two pictures telepathically to a receiver lying in an fMRI machine. In these pairs (mostly couples, friends, or twins), the receivers guessed the picture's content correctly at the level of chance (50.0 percent). Moreover, their brains responded no differently when later viewing the actual pictures "sent" by ESP. "These findings," concluded the researchers, "are the strongest evidence yet obtained against the existence of paranormal mental phenomena."

From 1998 to 2010, one skeptic, magician James Randi, offered $1 million "to anyone who proves a genuine psychic power under proper observing conditions" (Randi, 1999, 2008). French, Australian, and Indian groups have parallel offers of up to 200,000 euros to anyone with demonstrable paranormal abilities (CFI, 2003). Large as these sums are, the scientific seal of approval would be worth far more to anyone whose claims could be authenticated. To refute those who say there is no ESP, one need only produce a single person who can demonstrate a single, reproducible ESP phenomenon. (To refute those who say pigs can't talk would take but one talking pig.) So far, no such person has emerged. Randi's offer has been publicized for years and dozens of people have been tested, sometimes under the scrutiny of an independent panel of judges. Still, nothing.

* * *

To feel awe and to gain a deep reverence for life, we need look no further than our own perceptual system and its capacity for organizing formless nerve impulses into colorful sights, vivid sounds, and evocative smells. As Shakespeare's Hamlet recognized, "There are more things in Heaven and Earth, Horatio, than are dreamt of in your philosophy." Within our ordinary sensory and perceptual experiences lies much that is truly extraordinary—surely much more than has so far been dreamt of in our psychology.

The Cuigmans by Buddy Hickerson; © 1990, Los Angeles Times Syndicate. Reprinted with permission.

"So, how does the mind work? I don't know. You don't know. Pinker doesn't know. And, I rather suspect, such is the current state of the art, that if God were to tell us, we wouldn't understand."
Jerry Fodor, "Reply to Steven Pinker," 2005

REVIEW

Perceptual Interpretation

22-1 **What does research on sensory restriction and restored vision reveal about the effects of experience?** People who were born blind but regained sight after surgery lack the experience to recognize shapes, forms, and complete faces. Animals who have had severely restricted visual input suffer enduring visual handicaps when their visual exposure is returned to normal. There is a critical period for some aspects of sensory and perceptual development. Without early stimulation, the brain's neural organization does not develop normally.

22-2 **How adaptable is our ability to perceive?** *Perceptual adaptation* is evident when people are given glasses that shift the world slightly to the left or right, or even upside-down. People are initially disoriented, but they manage to adapt to their new context.

22-3 **How do our expectations, contexts, and emotions influence our perceptions?** *Perceptual set* is a mental predisposition that functions as a lens through which we perceive the world. Our learned concepts (schemas) prime us to organize and interpret ambiguous stimuli in certain ways. The surrounding context helps create expectations that guide our perceptions. Emotional context can color our interpretation of other people's behaviors, as well as our own.

22-4 **How do human factors psychologists work to create user-friendly machines and work settings?** *Human factors psychologists* contribute to human safety and improved design by encouraging developers and designers to consider human perceptual abilities, to avoid the curse of knowledge, and to test users to reveal perception-based problems.

22-5 **What are the claims of ESP, and what have most research psychologists concluded after putting these claims to the test?** The three most testable forms of *extrasensory perception (ESP)* are telepathy (mind-to-mind communication), clairvoyance

(perceiving remote events), and precognition (perceiving future events). Most research psychologists' skepticism focuses on two points. First, to believe in ESP, you must believe the brain is capable of perceiving without sensory input. Second, psychologists and *parapsychologists* have been unable to replicate (reproduce) ESP phenomena under controlled conditions.

Terms and Concepts to Remember

perceptual adaptation, p. 273
perceptual set, p. 274
human factors psychology, p. 279

extrasensory perception (ESP), p. 281
parapsychology, p. 281

Test Yourself

1. What type of evidence shows that, indeed, "there is more to perception than meets the senses"?

2. In the sports channel cartoon above, what psychic ability is being claimed?

(Answers to the Test Yourself questions can be found in Appendix B at the end of the book.)

Ask Yourself

1. Can you recall a time when your expectations have predisposed how you perceived a person (or group of people)?

2. Have you ever had what felt like an ESP experience? Can you think of an explanation other than ESP for that experience?

∞ WEB

Multiple-choice self-tests and more may be found at www.worthpublishers.com/myers

Learning

MODULES

23
Classical Conditioning

24
Operant Conditioning

25
Learning by Observation

When a chinook salmon first emerges from its egg in a stream's gravel bed, its genes provide most of the behavioral instructions it needs for life. It knows instinctively how and where to swim, what to eat, and how to protect itself. Following a built-in plan, the young salmon soon begins its trek to the sea. After some four years in the ocean, the mature salmon returns to its birthplace. It navigates hundreds of miles to the mouth of its home river and then, guided by the scent of its home stream, begins an upstream odyssey to its ancestral spawning ground. Once there, the salmon seeks out the best temperature, gravel, and water flow for breeding. It then mates and, its life mission accomplished, dies.

Unlike salmon, we are not born with a genetic plan for life. Much of what we do we learn from experience. Although we struggle to find the life direction a salmon is born with, our learning gives us more flexibility. We can learn how to build grass huts or snow shelters, submarines or space stations, and thereby adjust to almost any environment. Indeed, nature's most important gift to us may be our *adaptability*—our capacity to learn new behaviors that help us cope with changing circumstances.

Learning breeds hope. What is learnable we can potentially teach—a fact that encourages parents, educators, coaches, and animal trainers. What has been learned we can potentially change by new learning—an assumption that underlies counseling, psychotherapy, and rehabilitation programs. No matter how unhappy, unsuccessful, or unloving we are, that need not be the end of our story.

No topic is closer to the heart of psychology than learning, a *relatively permanent behavior change due to experience*. Psychologists study the learning of visual perceptions, of a drug's expected effect, of gender roles. They also consider how learning shapes our thought and language, our motivations and emotions, our personalities and attitudes. Modules 23 through 25 examine three types of learning: *classical conditioning, operant conditioning,* and *observational learning.*

> "Learning is the eye of the mind."
> Thomas Drake, *Bibliotheca Scholastica Instructissima*, 1633

▶|| How Do We Learn?

23-1 What are some basic forms of learning?

More than 200 years ago, philosophers such as John Locke and David Hume echoed Aristotle's conclusion from 2000 years earlier: We learn by *association*. Our minds naturally connect events that occur in sequence. Suppose you see and smell freshly baked bread, eat some, and find it satisfying. The next time you see and smell fresh bread, that experience will lead you to expect that eating it will once again be satisfying. So, too, with sounds. If you associate a sound with a frightening consequence, hearing the sound alone may trigger your fear. As one 4-year-old exclaimed after watching a TV character get mugged, "If I had heard that music, I wouldn't have gone around the corner!" (Wells, 1981).

Learned associations also feed our habitual behaviors (Wood & Neal, 2007). As we repeat behaviors in a given context—the sleeping posture we associate with bed, our walking routes on campus, our eating popcorn in a movie theater—the behaviors become associated with the contexts. Our next experience of the context then automatically triggers the habitual response. Such associations can make it hard to kick a

"Actually, sex just isn't that important to me."

Nature without appropriate nurture
Keiko—the killer whale of *Free Willy*
fame—had all the right genes for being
dropped right back into his Icelandic
home waters. But lacking life experience,
he required caregivers to his life's end in
a Norwegian fjord.

‖ Most of us would be unable to name
the order of the songs on our favorite
CD or playlist. Yet, hearing the end of
one piece cues (by association) an
anticipation of the next. Likewise, when
singing your national anthem, you
associate the end of each line with the
beginning of the next. (Pick a line out
of the middle and notice how much
harder it is to recall the *previous* line.) ‖

smoking habit; when back in the smoking context, the urge to light up can be power-ful (Siegel, 2005).

Other animals also learn by association. Disturbed by a squirt of water, the sea slug *Aplysia* protectively withdraws its gill. If the squirts continue, as happens natu-rally in choppy water, the withdrawal response diminishes. (The slug's response *ha-bituates.*) But if the sea slug repeatedly receives an electric shock just after being squirted, its withdrawal response to the squirt instead grows stronger. The animal re-lates the squirt to the impending shock. Complex animals can learn to relate their own behavior to its outcomes. Seals in an aquarium will repeat behaviors, such as slapping and barking, that prompt people to toss them a herring.

By linking two events that occur close together, both the sea slug and the seals ex-hibit *associative learning.* The sea slug associates the squirt with an impending shock; the seal associates slapping and barking with a herring treat. Each animal has learned something important to its survival: predicting the immediate future.

The significance of an animal's learning is illustrated by the challenges captive-bred animals face when introduced to the wild. After being bred and raised in captiv-ity, 11 Mexican gray wolves—extinct in the United States since 1977—were released in Arizona's Apache National Forest in 1998. Eight months later, a lone survivor was re-captured. The pen-reared wolves had learned how to hunt—and to move 100 feet away from people—but had not learned to run from a human with a gun. Their story is not unusual. Twentieth-century records document 145 reintroductions of 115 species. Of those, only 11 percent produced self-sustaining populations in the wild. Successful adaptation requires both nature (the needed genetic predispositions) and nurture (a history of appropriate learning).

Conditioning is the process of learning associations. In *classical conditioning,* the topic of Module 23, we learn to associate two stimuli and thus to anticipate events. We learn that a flash of lightning signals an impending crack of thunder, so when lightning flashes nearby, we start to brace ourselves (**FIGURE 1**).

In *operant conditioning,* Module 24's focus, we learn to associate a response (our be-havior) and its consequence and thus to repeat acts followed by good results (**FIGURE 2**) and avoid acts followed by bad results.

To simplify, we will explore these two types of associative learning separately in Modules 23 and 24. Often, though, they occur together, as on one Japanese cattle ranch, where the clever rancher outfitted his herd with electronic pagers, which he

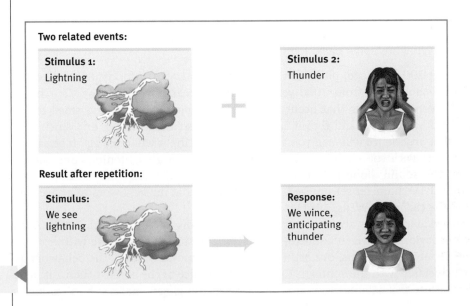

Two related events:

Stimulus 1:
Lightning

Stimulus 2:
Thunder

＋

Result after repetition:

Stimulus:
We see
lightning

Response:
We wince,
anticipating
thunder

FIGURE 1 Classical conditioning

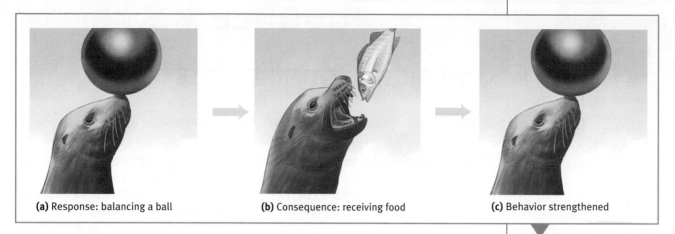

(a) Response: balancing a ball   **(b)** Consequence: receiving food   **(c)** Behavior strengthened

FIGURE 2 Operant conditioning

calls from his cellphone. After a week of training, the animals learn to associate two stimuli—the beep on their pager and the arrival of food (classical conditioning). But they also learn to associate their hustling to the food trough with the pleasure of eating (operant conditioning).

The concept of association by conditioning provokes questions: What principles influence the learning and the loss of associations? How can these principles be applied? And what really are the associations: Does the beep on a steer's pager evoke a mental representation of food, to which the steer responds by coming to the trough? Or does it make little sense to explain conditioned associations in terms of cognition? These questions are among the many being studied by researchers exploring how the brain stores and retrieves learning.

Conditioning is not the only form of learning. As Module 25 explains, we also learn from others' experiences through *observational learning.* Chimpanzees, too, may learn behaviors merely by watching others perform them. If one sees another solve a puzzle and gain a food reward, the observer may perform the trick more quickly.

By conditioning and by observation we humans learn and adapt to our environments. We learn to expect and prepare for significant events such as food or pain *(classical conditioning).* We also learn to repeat acts that bring good results and to avoid acts that bring bad results *(operant conditioning).* By watching others we learn new behaviors *(observational learning).* And through language, we also learn things we have neither experienced nor observed.

Pavlov's Experiments

Extending Pavlov's
Understanding

Pavlov's Legacy

MODULE 23

Classical Conditioning

23-2 What is classical conditioning, and how did Pavlov's work influence behaviorism?

Although **associative learning** had long generated philosophical discussion, only in the early twentieth century did psychology's most famous research verify it. For many people, the name Ivan Pavlov (1849–1936) rings a bell. His experiments are classics, and the phenomenon he explored we justly call **classical conditioning.**

Pavlov's work also laid the foundation for many of psychologist John B. Watson's ideas. In searching for laws underlying **learning,** Watson (1913) urged his colleagues to discard reference to inner thoughts, feelings, and motives. The science of psychology should instead study how organisms respond to stimuli in their environments, said Watson: "Its theoretical goal is the prediction and control of behavior. Introspection forms no essential part of its methods." Simply said, psychology should be an objective science based on observable behavior. This view, which influenced North American psychology during the first half of the twentieth century, Watson called **behaviorism.** Watson and Pavlov shared both a disdain for "mentalistic" concepts (such as consciousness) and a belief that the basic laws of learning were the same for all animals—whether dogs or humans. Few researchers today propose that psychology should ignore mental processes, but most now agree that classical conditioning is a basic form of learning by which all organisms adapt to their environment.

▶‖ Pavlov's Experiments

23-3 How does a neutral stimulus become a conditioned stimulus?

Pavlov was driven by a lifelong passion for research. After setting aside his initial plan to follow his father into the Russian Orthodox priesthood, Pavlov received a medical degree at age 33 and spent the next two decades studying the digestive system. This work earned him Russia's first Nobel prize in 1904. But it was his novel experiments on learning, to which he devoted the last three decades of his life, that earned this feisty scientist his place in history.

Pavlov's new direction came when his creative mind seized on an incidental observation. Without fail, putting food in a dog's mouth caused the animal to salivate. Moreover, the dog began salivating not only to the taste of the food, but also to the mere sight of the food, or the food dish, or the person delivering the food, or even the sound of that person's approaching footsteps. At first, Pavlov considered these "psychic secretions" an annoyance—until he realized they pointed to a simple but important form of learning.

Pavlov and his assistants tried to imagine what the dog was thinking and feeling as it drooled in anticipation of the food. This only led them into fruitless debates. So, to explore the phenomenon more objectively, they experimented. To eliminate other possible influences, they isolated the dog in a small room, secured it in a harness, and attached a device to divert its saliva to a measuring instrument. From the next room, they presented food—first by sliding in a food bowl, later by blowing meat powder into the dog's mouth at a precise moment. They then paired various *neutral events*—something the dog could see or hear but didn't associate with food—with food in the dog's mouth. If a sight or sound regularly signaled the arrival of food, would the dog learn the link? If so, would it begin salivating in anticipation of the food?

---

associative learning learning that certain events occur <u>together</u>. The events may be two <u>stimuli</u> (as in classical conditioning) or a <u>response</u> and its <u>consequences</u> (as in operant conditioning).

classical conditioning a type of learning in which one <u>learns</u> to link two or more stimuli and <u>anticipate events.</u>

learning a relatively permanent change in an organism's behavior due to <u>experience.</u>

behaviorism the view that psychology (1) should be an objective science that (2) studies behavior without reference to mental processes. Most research psychologists today agree with (1) but not with (2).

Ivan Pavlov "Experimental investigation . . . should lay a solid foundation for a future true science of psychology" (1927).

Sovfoto

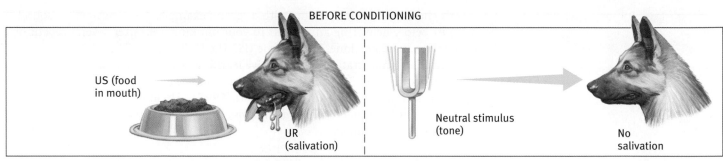

BEFORE CONDITIONING

US (food in mouth) → UR (salivation)

An unconditioned stimulus (US) produces an unconditioned response (UR).

Neutral stimulus (tone) → No salivation

A neutral stimulus produces no salivation response.

DURING CONDITIONING

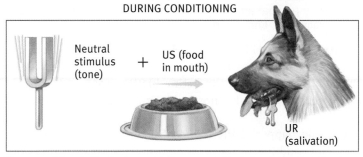

Neutral stimulus (tone) + US (food in mouth) → UR (salivation)

The unconditioned stimulus is repeatedly presented just after the neutral stimulus. The unconditioned stimulus continues to produce an unconditioned response.

AFTER CONDITIONING

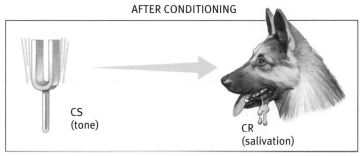

CS (tone) → CR (salivation)

The neutral stimulus alone now produces a conditioned response (CR), thereby becoming a conditioned stimulus (CS).

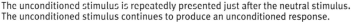

The answers proved to be *yes* and *yes.* Just before placing food in the dog's mouth to produce salivation, Pavlov sounded a tone. After several pairings of tone and food, the dog, anticipating the meat powder, began salivating to the tone alone. In later experiments, a buzzer, a light, a touch on the leg, even the sight of a circle set off the drooling.[1] (This procedure works with people, too. When hungry young Londoners viewed abstract figures before smelling peanut butter or vanilla, their brains soon were responding in anticipation to the abstract images alone [Gottfried et al., 2003]).

Because salivation in response to food in the mouth was unlearned, Pavlov called it an **unconditioned response (UR).** Food in the mouth automatically, *unconditionally,* triggers a dog's salivary reflex (**FIGURE 23.1**). Thus, Pavlov called the food stimulus an **unconditioned stimulus (US).**

Salivation in response to the tone was *conditional* upon the dog's learning the association between the tone and the food. Today we call this learned response the **conditioned response (CR).** The previously neutral (in this context) tone stimulus that now triggered the conditional salivation we call the **conditioned stimulus (CS).** Distinguishing these two kinds of stimuli and responses is easy: Conditioned = learned; *unconditioned* = *unlearned.*

FIGURE 23.1 Pavlov's classic experiment Pavlov presented a neutral stimulus (a tone) just before an unconditioned stimulus (food in mouth). The neutral stimulus then became a conditioned stimulus, producing a conditioned response.

unconditioned response (UR) in classical conditioning, the unlearned, naturally occurring response to the unconditioned stimulus (US), such as salivation when food is in the mouth.

unconditioned stimulus (US) in classical conditioning, a stimulus that unconditionally—naturally and automatically—triggers a response. *food*

conditioned response (CR) in classical conditioning, the learned response to a previously neutral (but now conditioned) stimulus (CS). *salivate*

conditioned stimulus (CS) in classical conditioning, an originally irrelevant stimulus that, after association with an unconditioned stimulus (US), comes to trigger a conditioned response. *bell*

PEANUTS

THE EARS HEAR THE CAN OPENER..

RIGHT AWAY THE STOMACH KNOWS THAT SUPPER IS COMING..

HOW DO THE EARS TELL THE STOMACH?

I'VE NEVER BEEN ABLE TO FIGURE THAT OUT..

[1]The "buzzer" (English translation) was perhaps Pavlov's supposed bell—a small electric bell (Tully, 2003).

Let's check your understanding with a second example. An experimenter sounds a tone just before delivering an air puff to your blinking eye. After several repetitions, you blink to the tone alone. What is the US? The UR? The CS? The CR?[2]

If Pavlov's demonstration of associative learning was so simple, what did he do for the next three decades? What discoveries did his research factory publish in his 532 papers on salivary conditioning (Windholz, 1997)? He and his associates explored five major conditioning processes: *acquisition, extinction, spontaneous recovery, generalization,* and *discrimination.*

Acquisition

23-4 In classical conditioning, what are the processes of acquisition, extinction, spontaneous recovery, generalization, and discrimination?

To understand the **acquisition,** or initial learning, of the stimulus-response relationship, Pavlov and his associates had to confront the question of timing: How much time should elapse between presenting the neutral stimulus (the tone, the light, the touch) and the unconditioned stimulus? In most cases, not much—half a second usually works well.

What do you suppose would happen if the food (US) appeared before the tone (CS) rather than after? Would conditioning occur?

Not likely. With but a few exceptions, conditioning doesn't happen when the CS follows the US. Remember, classical conditioning is biologically adaptive because it helps humans and other animals *prepare* for good or bad events. To Pavlov's dogs, the tone (CS) signaled an important biological event—the arrival of food (US). To deer in the forest, the snapping of a twig (CS) may signal a predator's approach (US). If the good or bad event had already occurred, the CS would not likely signal anything significant.

Michael Domjan (1992, 1994, 2005) showed how a CS can signal another important biological event, by conditioning the sexual arousal of male Japanese quail. Just before presenting an approachable female, the researchers turned on a red light. Over time, as the red light continued to herald the female's arrival, the light caused the male quail to become excited. They developed a preference for their cage's red-light district, and when a female appeared, they mated with her more quickly and released more semen and sperm (Matthews et al., 2007). All in all, the quail's capacity for classical conditioning gives it a reproductive edge. Again we see the larger lesson: *Conditioning helps an animal survive and reproduce—by responding to cues that help it gain food, avoid dangers, locate mates, and produce offspring* (Hollis, 1997).

In humans, too, objects, smells, and sights associated with sexual pleasure—even a geometric figure in one experiment—can become conditioned stimuli for sexual arousal (Byrne, 1982). Psychologist Michael Tirrell (1990) recalls: "My first girlfriend loved onions, so I came to associate onion breath with kissing. Before long, onion breath sent tingles up and down my spine. Oh what a feeling!" (**FIGURE 23.2**)

Through **higher-order conditioning,** a new neutral stimulus can become a new conditioned stimulus. All that's required is for it to become associated with a previously conditioned stimulus. If a tone regularly signals food and produces salivation, then a light that becomes associated with the tone may also begin to trigger salivation. Although this higher-order conditioning (also called *second-order conditioning*) tends to be weaker than first-stage conditioning, it influences our everyday lives. Imagine that something makes us very afraid (perhaps a pit bull dog associated with a previous dog bite). If something else, such as the sound of a barking dog, brings to mind that pit bull, the bark alone may make us feel a little afraid.

‖ Check yourself: If the aroma of cake baking sets your mouth to watering, what is the US? The CS? The CR? (Answers below.)

Remember:
US = **U**nconditioned **S**timulus
UR = **U**nconditioned **R**esponse
CS = **C**onditioned **S**timulus
CR = **C**onditioned **R**esponse ‖

The cake (and its taste) are the US. The associated aroma is the CS. Salivation to the aroma is the CR.

acquisition in classical conditioning, the initial stage, when one links a neutral stimulus and an unconditioned stimulus so that the neutral stimulus begins triggering the conditioned response. In operant conditioning, the strengthening of a reinforced response.

higher-order conditioning a procedure in which the conditioned stimulus in one conditioning experience is paired with a new neutral stimulus, creating a second (often weaker) conditioned stimulus. For example, an animal that has learned that a tone predicts food might then learn that a light predicts the tone and begin responding to the light alone. (Also called *second-order conditioning.*)

---

[2]US = air puff; UR = blink to air puff; CS = tone after procedure; CR = blink to tone

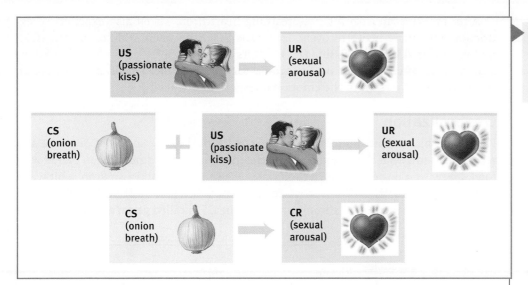

FIGURE 23.2 An unexpected CS
Onion breath does not usually produce sexual arousal. But when repeatedly paired with a passionate kiss, it can become a CS and do just that.

Associations can influence attitudes (De Houwer et al., 2001; Park et al., 2007). As Andy Field (2006) showed British children novel cartoon characters alongside either ice cream *(Yum!)* or Brussels sprouts *(Yuk!),* the children came to like best the ice-cream–associated characters. Michael Olson and Russell Fazio (2001) classically conditioned adults' attitudes, using little-known Pokémon characters. The participants, playing the role of a security guard monitoring a video screen, viewed a stream of words, images, and Pokémon characters. Their task, they were told, was to respond to one target Pokémon character by pressing a button. Unnoticed by the participants, when two other Pokémon characters appeared on the screen, one was consistently associated with various positive words and images (such as *awesome* or a hot fudge sundae); the other appeared with negative words and images (such as *awful* or a cockroach). Without any conscious memory for the pairings, the participants formed more gut-level positive attitudes for the characters associated with the positive stimuli.

Follow-up studies indicate that conditioned likes and dislikes are even stronger when people notice and are aware of the associations they have learned (De Houwer et al., 2005a,b; Pleyers et al., 2007). Cognition matters.

Extinction and Spontaneous Recovery

After conditioning, what happens if the CS occurs repeatedly without the US? Will the CS continue to elicit the CR? Pavlov discovered that when he sounded the tone again and again without presenting food, the dogs salivated less and less. Their declining salivation illustrates **extinction,** the diminished responding that occurs when the CS (tone) no longer signals an impending US (food).

Pavlov found, however, that if he allowed several hours to elapse before sounding the tone again, the salivation to the tone would reappear spontaneously (**FIGURE 23.3**). This **spontaneous recovery**—the reappearance of a (weakened) CR after a pause—suggested to Pavlov that extinction was suppressing the CR rather than eliminating it.

extinction the diminishing of a conditioned response; occurs in classical conditioning when an unconditioned stimulus (US) does not follow a conditioned stimulus (CS); occurs in operant conditioning when a response is no longer reinforced.

spontaneous recovery the reappearance, after a pause, of an extinguished conditioned response.

FIGURE 23.3 Idealized curve of acquisition, extinction, and spontaneous recovery The rising curve shows that the CR rapidly grows stronger as the CS and US are repeatedly paired *(acquisition),* then weakens as the CS is presented alone *(extinction).* After a pause, the CR reappears *(spontaneous recovery).*

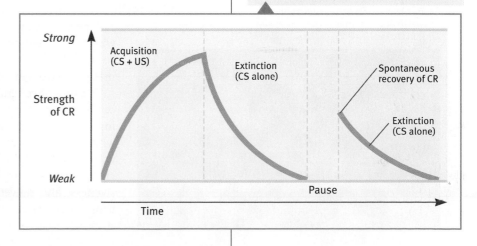

After breaking up with his fire-breathing heartthrob, Tirrell also experienced extinction and spontaneous recovery. He recalls that "the smell of onion breath (CS), no longer paired with the kissing (US), lost its ability to shiver my timbers. Occasionally, though, after not sensing the aroma for a long while, smelling onion breath awakens a small version of the emotional response I once felt."

Generalization

Pavlov and his students noticed that a dog conditioned to the sound of one tone also responded somewhat to the sound of a different tone that had never been paired with food. Likewise, a dog conditioned to salivate when rubbed would also drool a bit when scratched (Windholz, 1989) or when touched on a different body part (**FIGURE 23.4**). This tendency to respond to stimuli similar to the CS is called **generalization.**

Stimulus generalization

S. Gross

"I don't care if she's a tape dispenser. I love her."

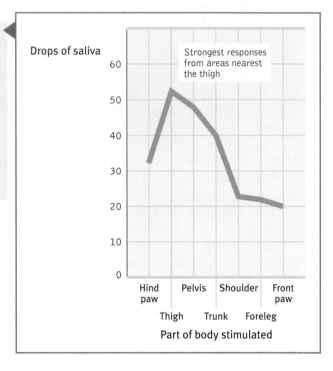

FIGURE 23.4 Generalization
Pavlov demonstrated generalization by attaching miniature vibrators to various parts of a dog's body. After conditioning salivation to stimulation of the thigh, he stimulated other areas. The closer a stimulated spot was to the dog's thigh, the stronger the conditioned response. (From Pavlov, 1927.)

Drops of saliva

Strongest responses from areas nearest the thigh

60

50

40

30

20

10

0

Hind paw   Pelvis   Shoulder   Front paw

Thigh   Trunk   Foreleg

Part of body stimulated

FIGURE 23.5 Child abuse leaves tracks in the brain Seth Pollak (University of Wisconsin–Madison) reports that abused children's sensitized brains react more strongly to angry faces. This generalized anxiety response may help explain why child abuse puts children at greater risk of psychological disorder.

Generalization can be adaptive, as when toddlers taught to fear moving cars also become afraid of moving trucks and motorcycles. So automatic is generalization that one Argentine writer who underwent torture still recoils with fear when he sees black shoes—his first glimpse of his torturers as they approached his cell. Generalization of anxiety reactions has been demonstrated in laboratory studies comparing abused with nonabused children (**FIGURE 23.5**). Shown an angry face on a computer screen, abused children's brain-wave responses are dramatically stronger and longer lasting (Pollak et al., 1998).

Because of generalization, stimuli similar to naturally disgusting or appealing objects will, by association, evoke some disgust or liking. Normally desirable foods, such as fudge, are unappealing when shaped to resemble dog feces (Rozin et al., 1986). Adults with childlike facial features (round face, large forehead, small chin, large eyes) are perceived as having childlike warmth, submissiveness, and naiveté (Berry & McArthur, 1986). In both cases, people's emotional reactions to one stimulus generalize to similar stimuli.

Discrimination

Pavlov's dogs also learned to respond to the sound of a particular tone and *not* to other tones. **Discrimination** is the learned ability to *distinguish* between a conditioned stimulus (which predicts the US) and other irrelevant stimuli. Being able to recognize differences is adaptive. Slightly different stimuli can be followed by vastly different consequences. Confronted by a pit bull, your heart may race; confronted by a golden retriever, it probably will not.

▶‖ Extending Pavlov's Understanding

23-5 Do cognitive processes and biological constraints affect classical conditioning?

In their dismissal of "mentalistic" concepts such as consciousness, Pavlov and Watson underestimated the importance of *cognitive processes* (thoughts, perceptions, expectations) and *biological constraints* on an organism's learning capacity.

Cognitive Processes

The early behaviorists believed that rats' and dogs' learned behaviors could be reduced to mindless mechanisms, so there was no need to consider cognition. But Robert Rescorla and Allan Wagner (1972) showed that an animal can learn the *predictability* of an event. If a shock always is preceded by a tone, and then may also be preceded by a light that accompanies the tone, a rat will react with fear to the tone but not to the light. Although the light is always followed by the shock, it adds no new information; the tone is a better predictor. The more predictable the association, the stronger the conditioned response. It's as if the animal learns an *expectancy,* an awareness of how likely it is that the US will occur.

Such experiments help explain why classical conditioning treatments that ignore cognition often have limited success. For example, people receiving therapy for alcohol dependency may be given alcohol spiked with a nauseating drug. Will they then associate alcohol with sickness? If classical conditioning were merely a matter of "stamping in" stimulus associations, we might hope so, and to some extent this does occur. However, the awareness that the nausea is induced by the drug, not the alcohol, often weakens the association between drinking alcohol and feeling sick. So, even in classical conditioning, it is (especially with humans) not simply the CS–US association but also the thought that counts.

Biological Predispositions

Ever since Charles Darwin, scientists have assumed that all animals share a common evolutionary history and thus commonalities in their makeup and functioning. Pavlov and Watson, for example, believed the basic laws of learning were essentially similar in all animals. So it should make little difference whether one studied pigeons or people. Moreover, it seemed that any natural response could be conditioned to any neutral stimulus. As learning researcher Gregory Kimble proclaimed in 1956, "Just about any activity of which the organism is capable can be conditioned and . . . these responses can be conditioned to any stimulus that the organism can perceive" (p. 195).

Twenty-five years later, Kimble (1981) humbly acknowledged that "half a thousand" scientific reports had proven him wrong. More than the early behaviorists realized, an animal's capacity for conditioning is constrained by its biology. Each species' predispositions prepare it to learn the associations that enhance its survival. Environments are not the whole story.

---

generalization the tendency, once a response has been conditioned, for stimuli <u>similar</u> to the conditioned stimulus to elicit similar responses. very similar

discrimination in classical conditioning, the learned ability to distinguish between a conditioned stimulus and stimuli that do not signal an unconditioned stimulus.

"All brains are, in essence, anticipation machines."

Daniel C. Dennett, *Consciousness Explained,* 1991

Courtesy of John Garcia

John Garcia As the laboring son of California farmworkers, Garcia attended school only in the off-season during his early childhood years. After entering junior college in his late twenties, and earning his Ph.D. in his late forties, he received the American Psychological Association's Distinguished Scientific Contribution Award "for his highly original, pioneering research in conditioning and learning." He was also elected to the National Academy of Sciences.

Taste aversion If you became violently ill after eating mussels, you probably would have a hard time eating them again. Their smell and taste would have become a CS for nausea. This learning occurs readily because our biology prepares us to learn taste aversions to toxic foods.

Colin Young-Wolff/PhotoEdit Inc.

John Garcia was among those who challenged the prevailing idea that all associations can be learned equally well. While researching the effects of radiation on laboratory animals, Garcia and Robert Koelling (1966) noticed that rats began to avoid drinking water from the plastic bottles in radiation chambers. Could classical conditioning be the culprit? Might the rats have linked the plastic-tasting water (a CS) to the sickness (UR) triggered by the radiation (US)?

To test their hunch, Garcia and Koelling gave the rats a particular taste, sight, or sound (CS) and later also gave them radiation or drugs (US) that led to nausea and vomiting (UR). Two startling findings emerged: First, even if sickened as late as several hours after tasting a particular novel flavor, the rats thereafter avoided that flavor. This appeared to violate the notion that for conditioning to occur, the US must immediately follow the CS.

Second, the sickened rats developed aversions to tastes but not to sights or sounds. This contradicted the behaviorists' idea that any perceivable stimulus could serve as a CS. But it made adaptive sense, because for rats the easiest way to identify tainted food is to taste it. (If sickened after sampling a new food, they thereafter avoid the food—which makes it difficult to eradicate a population of "bait-shy" rats by poisoning.)

Humans, too, seem biologically prepared to learn some associations rather than others. If you become violently ill four hours after eating contaminated mussels, you will probably develop an aversion to the taste of mussels but not to the sight of the associated restaurant, its plates, the people you were with, or the music you heard there. In contrast, birds, which hunt by sight, appear biologically primed to develop aversions to the *sight* of tainted food (Nicolaus et al., 1983). Organisms are predisposed to learn associations that help them adapt.

Remember those Japanese quail that were conditioned to get excited by a red light that signaled a receptive female's arrival? Michael Domjan and his colleagues (2004) report that such conditioning is even speedier, stronger, and more durable when the CS is *ecologically relevant*—something similar to stimuli associated with sexual activity in the natural environment, such as the stuffed head of a female quail. In the real world, observes Domjan (2005), conditioned stimuli have a natural association with the unconditioned stimuli they predict.

This may help explain why we humans seem to be naturally disposed to learn associations between the color red and women's sexuality, note Andrew Elliot and Daniela Niesta (2008). Female primates display red when nearing ovulation. In human females, enhanced bloodflow produces the red blush of flirtation and sexual excitation. Does the frequent pairing of red and sex—with Valentine's hearts, red-light districts, and red lipstick—naturally enhance men's attraction to women? Elliot and Niesta's experiments consistently suggest that, without men's awareness, it does (**FIGURE 23.6**).

Garcia's early findings on taste aversion were met with an onslaught of criticism. As the German philosopher Arthur Schopenhauer (1788–1860) once said, important ideas are first ridiculed, then attacked, and finally taken for granted. In Garcia's case, the leading journals refused to publish his work. The findings were impossible, said some critics. But, as often happens in science, Garcia and Koelling's taste-aversion research is now basic textbook material. It is also a good example of experiments that began with the discomfort of some laboratory animals and ended by enhancing the welfare of many others. In another conditioned taste-aversion study, coyotes and wolves that were tempted into eating sheep carcasses laced with a sickening poison developed an aversion to sheep meat (Gustavson et al., 1974, 1976). Two wolves later penned with a live sheep seemed actually to fear it. The study not only saved the sheep from their predators, but also saved the sheep-shunning coyotes and wolves from angry ranchers and farmers who had wanted to destroy them. Later applications of

Courtesy of Kathryn Brownson, Hope College

FIGURE 23.6 Romantic red In a series of experiments that controlled for other factors (such as the brightness of the image), men (but not women) found women more attractive and sexually desirable when framed in red (Elliot & Niesta, 2008).

Garcia and Koelling's findings have prevented baboons from raiding African gardens, raccoons from attacking chickens, and ravens and crows from feeding on crane eggs—all while preserving predators who occupy an important ecological niche (Garcia & Gustavson, 1997).

All these cases support Darwin's principle that natural selection favors traits that aid survival. Our ancestors who readily learned taste aversions were unlikely to eat the same toxic food again and were more likely to survive and leave descendants. Nausea, like anxiety, pain, and other bad feelings, serves a good purpose. Like a low-oil warning on a car dashboard, each alerts the body to a threat (Neese, 1991).

The discovery of biological constraints affirms the value of different levels of analysis, including the biological and cognitive (**FIGURE 23.7**), when we seek to understand phenomena such as learning. And once again, we see an important principle at work: *Learning enables animals to adapt to their environments.* Responding to stimuli that announce significant events, such as food or pain, is adaptive. So is a genetic predisposition to associate a CS with a US that follows predictably and immediately: Causes often immediately precede effects.

Often, but not always, as we saw in the taste-aversion findings. Adaptation also sheds light on this exception. The ability to discern that effect need not follow cause immediately—that poisoned food can cause sickness quite a while after it has been eaten—gives animals an adaptive advantage. Occasionally, however, our predispositions trick us. When chemotherapy triggers nausea and vomiting more than an hour following treatment, cancer patients may over time develop classically conditioned nausea (and sometimes anxiety) to the sights, sounds, and smells associated with the clinic (**FIGURE 23.8** on the next page) (Hall, 1997). Merely returning to the clinic's waiting room or seeing the nurses can provoke these conditioned feelings (Burish & Carey, 1986; Davey, 1992). Under normal circumstances, such revulsion to sickening stimuli would be adaptive.

"All animals are on a voyage through time, navigating toward futures that promote their survival and away from futures that threaten it. Pleasure and pain are the stars by which they steer."

Psychologists Daniel T. Gilbert and Timothy D. Wilson, "Prospection: Experiencing the Future," 2007

"Once bitten, twice shy."

G. F. Northall, *Folk-Phrases*, 1894

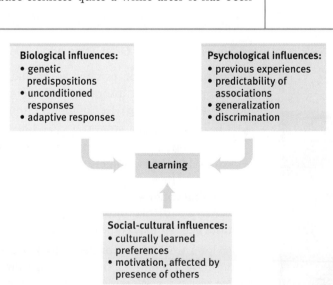

Biological influences:
• genetic predispositions
• unconditioned responses
• adaptive responses

Psychological influences:
• previous experiences
• predictability of associations
• generalization
• discrimination

Learning

Social-cultural influences:
• culturally learned preferences
• motivation, affected by presence of others

FIGURE 23.7
Biopsychosocial influences on learning Today's learning theorists recognize that our learning results not only from environmental experiences, but also from cognitive and biological influences.

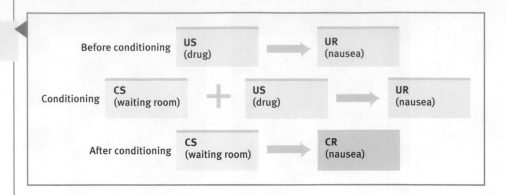

FIGURE 23.8 **Nausea conditioning in cancer patients**

Before conditioning   US (drug) → UR (nausea)

Conditioning   CS (waiting room) + US (drug) → UR (nausea)

After conditioning   CS (waiting room) → CR (nausea)

FIGURE 23.8 **Nausea conditioning in cancer patients**

> "[Psychology's] factual and theoretical developments in this century—which have changed the study of mind and behavior as radically as genetics changed the study of heredity—have all been the product of objective analysis—that is to say, behavioristic analysis."
>
> Psychologist Donald Hebb (1980)

John B. Watson Watson (1924) admitted to "going beyond my facts" when offering his famous boast: "Give me a dozen healthy infants, well-formed, and my own specified world to bring them up in and I'll guarantee to take any one at random and train him to become any type of specialist I might select— doctor, lawyer, artist, merchant-chief, and, yes, even beggar-man and thief, regardless of his talents, penchants, tendencies, abilities, vocations, and race of his ancestors."

▶‖ Pavlov's Legacy

23-6 Why is Pavlov's work important?

What, then, remains of Pavlov's ideas? A great deal. Most psychologists agree that classical conditioning is a basic form of learning. Judged by today's knowledge of cognitive processes and biological predispositions, Pavlov's ideas were incomplete. But if we see further than Pavlov did, it is because we stand on his shoulders.

Why does Pavlov's work remain so important? If he had merely taught us that old dogs can learn new tricks, his experiments would long ago have been forgotten. Why should we care that dogs can be conditioned to salivate at the sound of a tone? The importance lies first in this finding: *Many other responses to many other stimuli can be classically conditioned in many other organisms*—in fact, in every species tested, from earthworms to fish to dogs to monkeys to people (Schwartz, 1984). Thus, classical conditioning is one way that virtually all organisms learn to adapt to their environment.

Second, *Pavlov showed us how a process such as learning can be studied objectively.* He was proud that his methods involved virtually no subjective judgments or guesses about what went on in a dog's mind. The salivary response is a behavior measurable in cubic centimeters of saliva. Pavlov's success therefore suggested a scientific model for how the young discipline of psychology might proceed—by isolating the basic building blocks of complex behaviors and studying them with objective laboratory procedures.

Applications of Classical Conditioning

23-7 What have been some applications of classical conditioning?

In countless areas of psychology, including consciousness, motivation, emotion, health, psychological disorders, and therapy, Pavlov's principles of classical conditioning are now being used to improve human health and well-being. Two examples:

▶ Former drug users often feel a craving when they are again in the drug-using context—with people or in places they associate with previous highs. Thus, drug counselors advise addicts to steer clear of people and settings that may trigger these cravings (Siegel, 2005).

▶ Classical conditioning even works on the body's disease-fighting immune system. When a particular taste accompanies a drug that influences immune responses, the taste by itself may come to produce an immune response (Ader & Cohen, 1985).

Pavlov's work also provided a basis for John Watson's (1913) idea that human emotions and behaviors, though biologically influenced, are mainly a bundle of conditioned responses. Working with an 11-month-old named Albert, Watson and Rosalie Rayner (1920; Harris, 1979) showed how specific fears might be conditioned. Like most infants, "Little Albert" feared loud noises but not white rats. Watson and Rayner presented a white rat and, as Little Albert reached to touch it, struck a hammer against a steel bar just behind his head. After seven repeats of seeing the rat and hearing the frightening noise, Albert burst into tears at the mere sight of the rat (an ethically troublesome study by today's standards). What is more, five days later Albert showed generalization of his conditioned response by reacting with fear to a rabbit, a dog, and a sealskin coat, but not to dissimilar objects such as toys.

Although Little Albert's fate is unknown, Watson's is not. After losing his professorship at Johns Hopkins University over an affair with Rayner (whom he later married), he became the J. Walter Thompson advertising agency's resident psychologist. There he used his knowledge of associative learning to conceive many successful campaigns, including one for Maxwell House that helped make the "coffee break" an American custom (Hunt, 1993).

Some psychologists, noting that Albert's fear wasn't learned quickly, had difficulty repeating Watson and Rayner's findings with other children. Nevertheless, Little Albert's case has had legendary significance for many psychologists. Some have wondered if each of us might not be a walking repository of conditioned emotions (see Close-Up: Trauma as Classical Conditioning). Might extinction procedures or even new conditioning help us change our unwanted responses to emotion-arousing stimuli? One patient, who for 30 years had feared going into an elevator alone, did just that. Following his therapist's advice, he forced himself to enter 20 elevators a day. Within 10 days, his fear had nearly vanished (Ellis & Becker, 1982). This dramatic turnaround is but one example of how psychologists use behavioral techniques to treat emotional disorders and promote personal growth.

|| In Watson and Rayner's experiment, what was the US? The UR? The CS? The CR? (Answers below.) ||

The US was the loud noise; the UR was the startled fear response; the CS was the rat; the CR was fear.

CLOSE-UP

Trauma as Classical Conditioning

"A burnt child dreads the fire," says a medieval proverb. Experiments with dogs reveal that, indeed, if a painful stimulus is sufficiently powerful, a single event is sometimes enough to traumatize the animal when it again faces the situation. The human counterparts to these experiments can be tragic, as illustrated by one woman's experience of being attacked and raped, and conditioned to a period of fear. Her fear (CR) was most powerfully associated with particular locations and people (CS), but it generalized to other places and people. Note, too, how her traumatic experience robbed her of the normally relaxing associations with such stimuli as home and bed.

Four months ago I was raped. In the middle of the night I awoke to the sound of someone outside my bedroom. Thinking my housemate was coming home, I called out her name. Someone began walking slowly toward me, and then I realized. I screamed and fought, but there were two of them. One held my legs, while the other put a hand over my mouth and a knife to my throat and said, "Shut up, bitch, or we'll kill you." Never have I been so terrified and helpless. They both raped me, one brutally. As they then searched my room for money and valuables, my housemate came home. They brought her into my room, raped her, and left us both tied up on my bed.

We never slept another night in that apartment. We were too terrified. Still, when I go to bed at night—always with the bedroom light left on—the memory of them entering my room repeats itself endlessly. I was an independent person who had lived alone or with other women for four years; now I can't even think about spending a night alone. When I drive by our old apartment, or when I have to go into an empty house, my heart pounds and I sweat. I am afraid of strangers, especially men, and the more they resemble my attackers the more I fear them. My housemate shares many of my fears and is frightened when entering our new apartment. I'm afraid to stay in the same town, I'm afraid it will happen again, I'm afraid to go to bed. I dread falling asleep.

Eleven years later this woman could report—as do many trauma victims (Gluhoski & Wortman, 1996)—that her conditioned fears had mostly extinguished:

The frequency and intensity of my fears have subsided. Still, I remain cautious about personal safety and occasionally have nightmares about my experience. But more important is my renewed ability to laugh, love, and trust—both old friends and new. Life is once again joyful. I have survived.

(From personal correspondence, with permission.)

REVIEW

Classical Conditioning

23-1 **What are some basic forms of learning?** *Learning* is a relatively permanent change in an organism's behavior due to experience. In *associative learning,* we learn to associate two stimuli (as in classical conditioning) or a response and its consequences (as in operant conditioning). In observational learning, we learn by watching others' experiences and examples.

23-2 **What is classical conditioning, and how did Pavlov's work influence behaviorism?** *Classical conditioning* is a type of learning in which an organism comes to associate stimuli. Pavlov's work on classical conditioning laid the foundation for *behaviorism,* the view that psychology should be an objective science that studies behavior without reference to mental processes.

23-3 **How does a neutral stimulus become a conditioned stimulus?** In classical conditioning, a *UR* is an event that occurs naturally (such as salivation), in response to some stimulus. A *US* is something that naturally and automatically (without learning) triggers the unlearned response (as food in the mouth triggers salivation). A *CS* is a previously irrelevant stimulus (such as a bell) that, through learning, comes to be associated with some unlearned response (salivating). A *CR* is the learned response (salivating) to the originally irrelevant but now conditioned stimulus.

23-4 **In classical conditioning, what are the processes of acquisition, extinction, spontaneous recovery, generalization, and discrimination?** In classical conditioning, *acquisition* is associating a CS with the US. Acquisition occurs most readily when a CS is presented just before (ideally, about a half-second before) a US, preparing the organism for the upcoming event. This finding supports the view that classical conditioning is biologically adaptive. *Extinction* is diminished responding when the CS no longer signals an impending US. *Spontaneous recovery* is the appearance of a formerly extinguished response, following a rest period. *Generalization* is the tendency to respond to stimuli that are similar to a CS. *Discrimination* is the learned ability to distinguish between a CS and other irrelevant stimuli.

23-5 **Do cognitive processes and biological constraints affect classical conditioning?** The behaviorists' optimism that in any species, any response can be conditioned to any stimulus has been tempered. Conditioning principles, we now know, are cognitively and biologically constrained. In classical conditioning, animals learn when to expect a US, and they may be aware of the link between stimuli and responses. Moreover, because of biological predispositions, learning some associations is easier than learning others. Learning is adaptive: Each species learns behaviors that aid its survival.

23-6 **Why is Pavlov's work important?** Pavlov taught us that significant psychological phenomena can be studied objectively, and that classical conditioning is a basic form of learning that

applies to all species. Later research modified this finding somewhat by showing that in many species cognition and biological predispositions place some limits on conditioning.

23-7 **What have been some applications of classical conditioning?** Classical conditioning techniques are used in treatment programs for those recovering from drug abuse and to condition more appropriate responses in therapy for emotional disorders. The body's immune system also appears to respond to classical conditioning.

Terms and Concepts to Remember

associative learning, p. 290	conditioned stimulus (CS),
classical conditioning, p. 290	p. 291
learning, p. 290	acquisition, p. 292
behaviorism, p. 290	higher-order conditioning,
unconditioned response (UR),	p. 292
p. 291	extinction, p. 293
unconditioned stimulus (US),	spontaneous recovery, p. 293
p. 291	generalization, p. 294
conditioned response (CR),	discrimination, p. 295
p. 291	

Test Yourself

1. As we develop, we learn cues that lead us to expect and prepare for good and bad events. We learn to repeat behaviors that bring rewards. And we watch others and learn. What do psychologists call these three types of learning?

2. In slasher movies, sexually arousing images of women are sometimes paired with violence against women. Based on classical conditioning principles, what might be an effect of this pairing?

(Answers to the Test Yourself questions can be found in Appendix B at the end of the book.)

Ask Yourself

1. Can you remember some example from your childhood of learning through classical conditioning—perhaps salivating at the sound or smell of some delicious food cooking in your family kitchen? Can you remember an example of operant conditioning, when you repeated (or decided not to repeat) a behavior because you liked (or hated) its consequences? Can you recall watching someone else perform some act and later repeating or avoiding that act?

2. How have your emotions or behaviors been classically conditioned?

∞ WEB

Multiple-choice self-tests and more may be found at www.worthpublishers.com/myers

Operant Conditioning

Skinner's Experiments

Extending Skinner's Understanding

Skinner's Legacy

Contrasting Classical and Operant Conditioning

24-1 What is operant conditioning, and how does it differ from classical conditioning?

It's one thing to classically condition a dog to salivate at the sound of a tone, or a child to fear moving cars. To teach an elephant to walk on its hind legs or a child to say *please,* we must turn to another type of **associative learning**—*operant conditioning.*

Classical conditioning and operant conditioning are both forms of associative learning, yet their difference is straightforward:

▶ *Classical conditioning* forms associations between stimuli (a CS and the US it signals). It also involves **respondent behavior**—actions that are automatic responses to a stimulus (such as salivating in response to meat powder and later in response to a tone).

▶ In **operant conditioning,** organisms associate their own actions with consequences. Actions followed by reinforcers increase; those followed by punishers decrease. Behavior that *operates* on the environment to *produce* rewarding or punishing stimuli is called **operant behavior.**

We can therefore distinguish classical from operant conditioning by asking: *Is the organism learning associations between events it does not control* (classical conditioning)? *Or is it learning associations between its behavior and resulting events* (operant conditioning)?

▶‖ Skinner's Experiments

B. F. Skinner (1904–1990) was a college English major and an aspiring writer who, seeking a new direction, entered graduate school in psychology. He went on to become modern behaviorism's most influential and controversial figure. Skinner's work elaborated what psychologist Edward L. Thorndike (1874–1949) called the **law of effect:** Rewarded behavior is likely to recur (**FIGURE 24.1**). Using Thorndike's law of effect as a starting point, Skinner developed a *behavioral technology* that revealed principles of *behavior control.* These principles also enabled him to teach pigeons such unpigeonlike behaviors as walking in a figure 8, playing Ping-Pong, and keeping a missile on course by pecking at a screen target.

associative learning learning that certain events occur together. The events may be two stimuli (as in classical conditioning) or a response and its consequences (as in operant conditioning).

respondent behavior behavior that occurs as an automatic response to some stimulus. *CC*

operant conditioning a type of learning in which behavior is strengthened if followed by a reinforcer or diminished if followed by a punisher.

operant behavior behavior that operates on the environment, producing consequences. *OC*

law of effect Thorndike's principle that behaviors followed by favorable consequences become more likely, and that behaviors followed by unfavorable consequences become less likely.

FIGURE 24.1 Cat in a puzzle box
Thorndike (1898) used a fish reward to entice cats to find their way out of a puzzle box (right) through a series of maneuvers. The cats' performance tended to improve with successive trials (left), illustrating Thorndike's *law of effect.* (Adapted from Thorndike, 1898.)

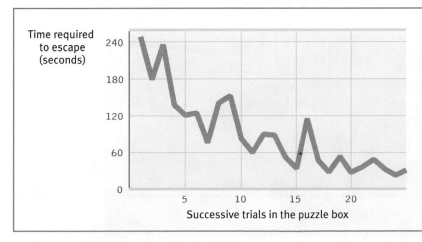

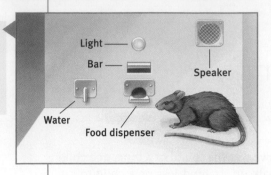

FIGURE 24.2 A Skinner box
Inside the box, the rat presses a bar for a food reward. Outside, a measuring device (not shown here) records the animal's accumulated responses.

Light
Bar
Speaker
Water
Food dispenser

For his pioneering studies, Skinner designed an **operant chamber,** popularly known as a *Skinner box* (**FIGURE 24.2**). The box has a bar or key that an animal presses or pecks to release a reward of food or water, and a device that records these responses. Operant conditioning experiments have done far more than teach us how to pull habits out of a rat. They have explored the precise conditions that foster efficient and enduring **learning.**

Shaping Behavior

In his experiments, Skinner used **shaping,** a procedure in which *reinforcers,* such as food, gradually guide an animal's actions toward a desired behavior. Imagine that you wanted to condition a hungry rat to press a bar. First, you would watch how the animal naturally behaves, so that you could build on its existing behaviors. You might give the rat a food reward each time it approaches the bar. Once the rat is approaching regularly, you would require it to move closer before rewarding it, then closer still. Finally, you would require it to touch the bar before you gave it the food. With this method of *successive approximations,* you reward responses that are ever-closer to the final desired behavior, and you ignore all other responses. By making rewards contingent on desired behaviors, researchers and animal trainers gradually shape complex behaviors.

Shaping rats to save lives A Gambian giant pouched rat, having been shaped to sniff out land mines, receives a bite of banana after successfully locating a mine during training in Mozambique.

Khamis Ramadhan/Panapress/Getty Images

Shaping can also help us understand what nonverbal organisms perceive. Can a dog distinguish red and green? Can a baby hear the difference between lower- and higher-pitched tones? If we can shape them to respond to one stimulus and not to another, then we know they can perceive the difference. Such experiments have even shown that some animals can form concepts. If an experimenter reinforces a pigeon for pecking after seeing a human face, but not after seeing other images, the pigeon learns to recognize human faces (Herrnstein & Loveland, 1964). In this experiment, a face is a *discriminative stimulus;* like a green traffic light, it signals that a response will be reinforced.

A discriminating creature University of Windsor psychologist Dale Woodyard uses a food reward to train this manatee to discriminate between objects of different shapes, colors, and sizes. Manatees remember such responses for a year or more.

Fred Bavendam/Peter Arnold, Inc.

After being trained to discriminate among flowers, people, cars, and chairs, pigeons can usually identify the category in which a new pictured object belongs (Bhatt et al., 1988; Wasserman, 1993). They have even been trained to discriminate between Bach's music and Stravinsky's (Porter & Neuringer, 1984).

In everyday life, we continually reward and shape others' behavior, said Skinner, but we often do so unintentionally. Billy's whining, for example, annoys his mystified parents, but look how they typically deal with Billy:

Billy:	Could you tie my shoes?
Father:	(Continues reading paper.)
Billy:	Dad, I need my shoes tied.
Father:	Uh, yeah, just a minute.
Billy:	DAAAAD! TIE MY SHOES!
Father:	How many times have I told you not to whine? Now, which shoe do we do first?

Billy's whining is reinforced, because he gets something desirable—his dad's attention. Dad's response is reinforced because it gets rid of something aversive—Billy's whining.

HI AND LOIS

Or consider a teacher who pastes gold stars on a wall chart after the names of children scoring 100 percent on spelling tests. As everyone can then see, some children consistently do perfect work. The others, who take the same test and may have worked harder than the academic all-stars, get no rewards. The teacher would be better advised to apply the principles of operant conditioning—to reinforce all spellers for gradual improvements (successive approximations toward perfect spelling of words they find challenging).

Types of Reinforcers

24-2 What are the basic types of reinforcers?

People often refer rather loosely to the power of "rewards." This idea gains a more precise meaning in Skinner's concept of a **reinforcer:** any event that strengthens (increases the frequency of) a preceding response. A reinforcer may be a tangible reward, such as food or money. It may be praise or attention—even being yelled at, for a child hungry for attention. Or it may be an activity—borrowing the family car after doing the dishes, or taking a break after an hour of study.

Although anything that serves to increase behavior is a reinforcer, reinforcers vary with circumstances. What's reinforcing to one person (rock concert tickets) may not be to another. What's reinforcing in one situation (food when hungry) may not be in another.

Up to now, we've really been discussing **positive reinforcement,** which strengthens a response by *presenting* a typically pleasurable stimulus after a response. But there are *two* basic kinds of reinforcement (**TABLE 24.1** on the next page). **Negative reinforcement** *strengthens* a response by *reducing or removing* something undesirable or unpleasant, as when an organism escapes an aversive situation. Taking aspirin may

operant chamber in operant conditioning research, a chamber (also known as a *Skinner box*) containing a bar or key that an animal can manipulate to obtain a food or water reinforcer; attached devices record the animal's rate of bar pressing or key pecking.

learning a relatively permanent change in an organism's behavior due to experience.

shaping an operant conditioning procedure in which reinforcers guide behavior toward closer and closer approximations of the desired behavior.

reinforcer in operant conditioning, any event that *strengthens* the behavior it follows.

positive reinforcement increasing behaviors by presenting positive stimuli, such as food. A positive reinforcer is any stimulus that, when presented after a response, strengthens the response.

negative reinforcement increasing behaviors by stopping or reducing negative stimuli, such as shock. A negative reinforcer is any stimulus that, when removed after a response, strengthens the response. (Note: negative reinforcement is not punishment.)

Positive reinforcement A heat lamp positively reinforces this Taronga Zoo meerkat's behavior during a cold snap in Sydney, Australia.

TABLE 24.1 Ways to Increase Behavior

Operant Conditioning Term	Description	Examples
Positive reinforcement	Add a desirable stimulus	Getting a hug; receiving a paycheck
Negative reinforcement	Remove an aversive stimulus	Fastening seatbelt to turn off beeping

relieve your headache, and pushing the snooze button will silence your annoying alarm. These welcome results (end of pain, end of alarm) provide negative reinforcement and increase the odds that you will repeat these behaviors. For drug addicts, the negative reinforcement of ending withdrawal pangs can be a compelling reason to resume using (Baker et al., 2004). Note that contrary to popular usage, *negative reinforcement is not punishment.* (*Advice:* Repeat the last five words in your mind, because this is one of psychology's most often misunderstood concepts.) Rather, negative reinforcement *removes* a punishing (aversive) event.

Sometimes negative and positive reinforcement coincide. Imagine a worried student who, after goofing off and getting a bad exam grade, studies harder for the next exam. This increased effort may be negatively reinforced by reduced anxiety, and positively reinforced by a better grade. Whether it works by reducing something aversive, or by giving something desirable, *reinforcement is any consequence that strengthens behavior.*

Primary and Conditioned Reinforcers

Primary reinforcers—getting food when hungry or having a painful headache go away—are unlearned. They are innately satisfying. **Conditioned reinforcers,** also called *secondary reinforcers,* get their power through learned association with primary reinforcers. If a rat in a Skinner box learns that a light reliably signals that food is coming, the rat will work to turn on the light. The light has become a conditioned reinforcer associated with food. Our lives are filled with conditioned reinforcers—money, good grades, a pleasant tone of voice—each of which has been linked with more basic rewards. If money is a conditioned reinforcer—if people's desire for money is derived from their desire for food—then hunger should also make people more money-hungry, reasoned one European research team (Briers et al., 2006). Indeed, in their experiments, people were less likely to donate to charity when food deprived, and less likely to share money with fellow participants when in a room with hunger-arousing aromas.

Immediate and Delayed Reinforcers

Let's return to the imaginary shaping experiment in which you were conditioning a rat to press a bar. Before performing this "wanted" behavior, the hungry rat will engage in a sequence of "unwanted" behaviors—scratching, sniffing, and moving around. If you present food immediately after any one of these behaviors, the rat will likely repeat that rewarded behavior. But what if the rat presses the bar while you are distracted, and you delay giving the reinforcer? If the delay lasts longer than 30 seconds, the rat will not learn to press the bar. You will have reinforced other incidental behaviors—more sniffing and moving—that intervened after the bar press.

Unlike rats, humans do respond to delayed reinforcers: the paycheck at the end of the week, the good grade at the end of the semester, the trophy at the end of the season. Indeed, to function effectively we must learn to delay gratification. In laboratory testing, some 4-year-olds show this ability. In choosing a candy, they prefer having a big reward tomorrow to munching on a small one right now. Learning to control our impulses in order to achieve more valued rewards is a big step toward maturity (Logue, 1998a,b). No wonder children who make such choices tend to become socially competent and high-achieving adults (Mischel et al., 1989).

|| Remember whining Billy? In that example, whose behavior was positively reinforced and whose was negatively reinforced? (Answer below.) ||

Billy's whining was *positively* reinforced, because Billy got something desirable—his father's attention. His dad's response to the whining (doing what Billy wanted) was *negatively* reinforced, because it got rid of Billy's annoying whining.

"Oh, not bad. The light comes on, I press the bar, they write me a check. How about you?"

But to our detriment, small but immediate consequences (the enjoyment of watching late-night TV, for example) are sometimes more alluring than big but delayed consequences (tomorrow's sluggishness). For many teens, the immediate gratification of risky, unprotected sex in passionate moments prevails over the delayed gratifications of safe sex or saved sex (Loewenstein & Furstenberg, 1991). And for too many of us, the immediate rewards of today's gas-guzzling vehicles, air travel, and air conditioning, have prevailed over the bigger future consequences of global climate change, rising seas, and extreme weather.

Reinforcement Schedules

24-3 How do different reinforcement schedules affect behavior?

So far, most of our examples have assumed **continuous reinforcement:** Reinforcing the desired response every time it occurs. Under such conditions, learning occurs rapidly, which makes continuous reinforcement preferable until a behavior is mastered. But extinction also occurs rapidly. When reinforcement stops—when we stop delivering food after the rat presses the bar—the behavior soon stops. If a normally dependable candy machine fails to deliver a chocolate bar twice in a row, we stop putting money into it (although a week later we may exhibit *spontaneous recovery* by trying again).

Real life rarely provides continuous reinforcement. Salespeople do not make a sale with every pitch, nor do anglers get a bite with every cast. But they persist because their efforts have occasionally been rewarded. This persistence is typical with **partial (intermittent) reinforcement** schedules, in which responses are sometimes reinforced, sometimes not. Although initial learning is slower, intermittent reinforcement produces greater *resistance to extinction* than is found with continuous reinforcement. Imagine a pigeon that has learned to peck a key to obtain food. When the experimenter gradually phases out the delivery of food until it occurs only rarely and unpredictably, pigeons may peck 150,000 times without a reward (Skinner, 1953). Slot machines reward gamblers in much the same way—occasionally and unpredictably. And like pigeons, slot players keep trying, time and time again. With intermittent reinforcement, hope springs eternal. Lesson for parents: Partial reinforcement also works with children. *Occasionally* giving in to children's tantrums for the sake of peace and quiet intermittently reinforces the tantrums. This is the very best procedure for making a behavior persist.

Skinner (1961) and his collaborators compared four schedules of partial reinforcement. Some are rigidly fixed, some unpredictably variable.

Fixed-ratio schedules reinforce behavior after a set number of responses. Just as coffee shops reward us with a free drink after every 10 purchased, laboratory animals may be reinforced on a fixed ratio of, say, one reinforcer for every 30 responses. Once conditioned, the animal will pause only briefly after a reinforcer and will then return to a high rate of responding (**FIGURE 24.3** on the next page).

Variable-ratio schedules provide reinforcers after an unpredictable number of responses. This is what slot-machine players and fly-casting anglers experience—unpredictable reinforcement—and what makes gambling and fly fishing so hard to extinguish even when both are getting nothing for something. Like the fixed-ratio schedule, the variable-ratio schedule produces high rates of responding, because reinforcers increase as the number of responses increases.

Fixed-interval schedules reinforce the first response after a fixed time period. Like people checking more frequently for the mail as the delivery time approaches, or checking to see if the Jell-O has set, pigeons on a fixed-interval schedule peck a key more frequently as the anticipated time for reward draws near, producing a choppy stop-start pattern (see Figure 24.3) rather than a steady rate of response.

primary reinforcer an innately reinforcing stimulus, such as one that satisfies a biological need.

conditioned reinforcer a stimulus that gains its reinforcing power through its association with a primary reinforcer; also known as a *secondary reinforcer*.

continuous reinforcement reinforcing the desired response every time it occurs.

partial (intermittent) reinforcement reinforcing a response only part of the time; results in slower acquisition of a response but much greater resistance to extinction than does continuous reinforcement.

fixed-ratio schedule in operant conditioning, a reinforcement schedule that reinforces a response only after a specified number of responses.

variable-ratio schedule in operant conditioning, a reinforcement schedule that reinforces a response after an unpredictable number of responses.

fixed-interval schedule in operant conditioning, a reinforcement schedule that reinforces a response only after a specified time has elapsed.

"The charm of fishing is that it is the pursuit of what is elusive but attainable, a perpetual series of occasions for hope."
Scottish author John Buchan (1875–1940)

‖ Door-to-door salespeople are reinforced by which schedule? People checking the oven to see if the cookies are done are on which schedule? Airline frequent-flyer programs that offer a free flight after every 25,000 miles of travel use which reinforcement schedule? (Answers below.) ‖

Door-to-door salespeople are reinforced on a variable-ratio schedule (after varying numbers of rings). Cookie checkers are reinforced on a fixed-interval schedule. Frequent-flyer programs use a fixed-ratio schedule.

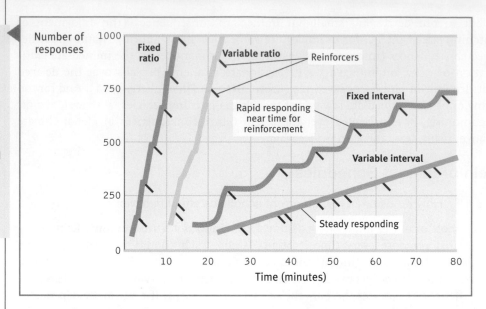

Variable-interval schedules reinforce the first response after *varying* time intervals. Like the "You've got mail" that finally rewards persistence in rechecking for e-mail, variable-interval schedules tend to produce slow, steady responding. This makes sense, because there is no knowing when the waiting will be over (**TABLE 24.2**).

TABLE 24.2 Schedules of Reinforcement

	Fixed	Variable
Ratio	*Every so many:* reinforcement after every *nth* behavior, such as buy 10 coffees, get 1 free, or pay per product unit produced	*After an unpredictable number:* reinforcement after a random number of behaviors, as when playing slot machines or fly-casting
Interval	*Every so often:* reinforcement for behavior after a fixed time, such as Tuesday discount prices	*Unpredictably often:* reinforcement for behavior after a random amount of time, as in checking for e-mail

Animal behaviors differ, yet Skinner (1956) contended that the reinforcement principles of operant conditioning are universal. It matters little, he said, what response, what reinforcer, or what species you use. The effect of a given reinforcement schedule is pretty much the same: "Pigeon, rat, monkey, which is which? It doesn't matter. . . . Behavior shows astonishingly similar properties."

Punishment

24-4 How does punishment affect behavior?

Reinforcement increases a behavior; **punishment** does the opposite. A *punisher* is any consequence that *decreases* the frequency of a preceding behavior (**TABLE 24.3**).

Swift and sure punishers can powerfully restrain unwanted behavior. The rat that is shocked after touching a forbidden object and the child who loses a treat after running into the street will learn not to repeat the behavior. Some punishments, though unintentional, are nevertheless quite effective: A dog that has learned to come running at the sound of an electric can opener will stop coming if its owner starts running the machine to attract the dog and banish it to the basement.

variable-interval schedule in operant conditioning, a reinforcement schedule that reinforces a response at unpredictable time intervals.

punishment an event that *decreases* the behavior that it follows.

TABLE 24.3 Ways to Decrease Behavior

Type of Punisher	Description	Possible Examples
Positive punishment	Administer an aversive stimulus	Spanking; a parking ticket
Negative punishment	Withdraw a desirable stimulus	Time-out from privileges (such as time with friends); revoked driver's license

Sureness and swiftness are also marks of effective criminal punishment, note John Darley and Adam Alter (in press). Studies show that criminal behavior, much of it impulsive, is not deterred by the threat of severe sentences. Thus, when Arizona introduced an exceptionally harsh sentence for first-time drunk drivers, it did not affect the drunk-driving rate. But when Kansas City started patrolling a high crime area to increase the sureness and swiftness of punishment, crime dropped dramatically.

So, how should we interpret the punishment studies in relation to parenting practices? Many psychologists and supporters of nonviolent parenting note four drawbacks of physically punishing children (Gershoff, 2002; Marshall, 2002).

1. **Punished behavior is suppressed, not forgotten.** This suppression, though temporary, may (negatively) reinforce parents' punishing behavior. The child swears, the parent swats, the parent hears no more swearing and feels the punishment successfully stopped the behavior. No wonder spanking is a hit with so many U.S. parents of 3- and 4-year-olds—more than 9 in 10 of whom acknowledge spanking their children (Kazdin & Benjet, 2003).

2. **Punishment teaches discrimination.** Was the punishment effective in putting an end to the swearing? Or did the child simply learn that it's not okay to swear around the house, but it is okay to swear elsewhere?

3. **Punishment can teach fear.** The child may associate fear not only with the undesirable behavior but also with the person who delivered the punishment or the place it occurred. Thus, children may learn to fear a punishing teacher and try to avoid school. For such reasons, most European countries now ban hitting children in schools and child-care institutions (Leach, 1993, 1994). Eleven countries, including those in Scandinavia, further outlaw hitting by parents, giving children the same legal protection given to spouses (EPOCH, 2000).

4. **Physical punishment may increase aggressiveness by modeling aggression as a way to cope with problems.** We know that many aggressive delinquents and abusive parents come from abusive families (Straus & Gelles, 1980; Straus et al., 1997). But some researchers note a problem with studies that find that spanked children are at increased risk for aggression (and depression and low self-esteem). Well, yes, they say, just as people who have undergone psychotherapy are more likely to suffer depression—because they had preexisting problems that triggered the treatments (Larzelere, 2000, 2004). Which is the chicken and which is the egg? The correlations don't hand us an answer.

If one adjusts for preexisting antisocial behavior, then an occasional single swat or two to misbehaving 2- to 6-year-olds looks more effective (Baumrind et al., 2002; Larzelere & Kuhn, 2005). That is especially so if the swat is used only as a backup when milder disciplinary tactics (such as a *time-out,* removing them from reinforcing surroundings) fail, and when the swat is combined with a generous dose of reasoning and reinforcing. Remember: *Punishment tells you what not to do; reinforcement tells you what to do.* This dual approach can be effective. When children with self-destructive behaviors bite themselves or bang their heads, they may be mildly punished (say, with

rat maze

cognitive map a mental representation of the layout of one's environment. For example, after exploring a maze, rats act as if they have learned a cognitive map of it.

latent learning learning that occurs but is not apparent until there is an incentive to <u>demonstrate</u> it.

intrinsic motivation a desire to perform a behavior effectively for its <u>own sake</u>.

extrinsic motivation a desire to perform a behavior to receive promised <u>rewards</u> or <u>avoid</u> threatened punishment.

a squirt of water in the face), but they may also be rewarded (with positive attention and food) when they behave well. In high school classrooms, teachers can give feedback on papers by saying, "No, but try this . . ." and "Yes, that's it!" Such responses reduce unwanted behavior while reinforcing more desirable alternatives.

Parents of delinquent youth are often unaware of how to achieve desirable behaviors without screaming or hitting their children (Patterson et al., 1982). Training programs can help reframe contingencies from dire threats to positive incentives—turning "You clean up your room this minute or no dinner!" to "You're welcome at the dinner table after you get your room cleaned up." When you stop to think about it, many threats of punishment are just as forceful, and perhaps more effective, if rephrased positively. Thus, "If you don't get your homework done, there'll be no car" would better be phrased as . . .

What punishment often teaches, said Skinner, is how to avoid it. Most psychologists now favor an emphasis on reinforcement: Notice people doing something right and affirm them for it.

▶‖ Extending Skinner's Understanding

24-5 Do cognitive processes and biological constraints affect operant conditioning?

Skinner granted the existence of private thought processes and the biological underpinnings of behavior. Nevertheless, many psychologists criticized him for discounting the importance of these influences.

Cognition and Operant Conditioning

A mere eight days before dying of leukemia, Skinner (1990) stood before the American Psychological Association convention for one final critique of "cognitive science," which he viewed as a throwback to early twentieth-century introspectionism. Skinner died resisting the growing belief that cognitive processes—thoughts, perceptions, expectations—have a necessary place in the science of psychology and even in our understanding of conditioning. (He regarded thoughts and emotions as behaviors that follow the same laws as other behaviors.) Yet we have seen several hints that cognitive processes might be at work in operant learning. For example, animals on a fixed-interval reinforcement schedule respond more and more frequently as the time approaches when a response will produce a reinforcer. Although a strict behaviorist would object to talk of "expectations," the animals behave as if they expected that repeating the response would soon produce the reward.

‖ For more information on animal behavior, see books by (I am not making this up) Robin Fox and Lionel Tiger. ‖

Latent learning Animals, like people, can learn from experience, with or without reinforcement. After exploring a maze for 10 days, rats received a food reward at the end of the maze. They quickly demonstrated their prior learning of the maze—by immediately completing it as quickly as (and even faster than) rats that had been reinforced for running the maze. (From Tolman & Honzik, 1930.)

Will and Deni McIntyre/Photo Researchers

Evidence of cognitive processes has also come from studying rats in mazes. Rats exploring a maze, with no obvious reward, are like people sightseeing in a new town. They seem to develop a **cognitive map,** a mental representation of the maze. When an experimenter then places food in the maze's goal box, the rats very soon run the maze as quickly as rats that have been reinforced with food for running the maze.

During their explorations, the rats have seemingly experienced **latent learning**—learning that becomes apparent only when there is some incentive to demonstrate it. Children, too, may learn from watching a parent but demonstrate the learning only much later, as needed. The point to remember: *There is more to learning than associating a response with a consequence; there is also cognition.* Psychologists have presented some striking evidence of animals' cognitive abilities in solving problems and in using aspects of language.

Intrinsic Motivation

The cognitive perspective has also led to an important qualification concerning the power of rewards: Promising people a reward for a task they already enjoy can backfire. Many think that offering tangible rewards will boost anyone's interest in an activity. Actually, in experiments, children promised a payoff for playing with an interesting puzzle or toy later play with the toy less than do their unpaid counterparts (Deci et al., 1999; Tang & Hall, 1995). It is as if the children think, "If I have to be bribed into doing this, it must not be worth doing for its own sake."

Excessive rewards can undermine **intrinsic motivation**—the desire to perform a behavior effectively and for its own sake. **Extrinsic motivation** is the desire to behave in certain ways to receive external rewards or avoid threatened punishment.

To sense the difference, think about your experience in this course. Are you feeling pressured to finish this reading before a deadline? Worried about your grade? Eager for rewards that depend on your doing well? If yes, then you are extrinsically motivated (as, to some extent, almost all students must be). Are you also finding the course material interesting? Does learning it make you feel more competent? If there were no grade at stake, might you be curious enough to want to learn the material for its own sake? If yes, intrinsic motivation also fuels your efforts. Intrinsically motivated people work and play in search of enjoyment, interest, self-expression, or challenge.

Youth sports coaches who aim to promote enduring interest in an activity, not just to pressure players into winning, should focus on the intrinsic joy of playing and of reaching one's potential, note motivation researchers Edward Deci and Richard Ryan (1985, 1992, 2002). Giving people choices also enhances their intrinsic motivation (Patall et al., 2008). Nevertheless, rewards can be effective if used neither to bribe nor to control but to signal a job well done (Boggiano et al., 1985). "Most improved player" awards, for example, can boost feelings of competence and increase enjoyment of a sport. Rightly administered, rewards can raise performance and spark creativity (Eisenberger & Rhoades, 2001; Henderlong & Lepper, 2002). And extrinsic rewards (such as the admissions scholarships and jobs that often follow good grades) are here to stay.

Biological Predispositions

As with classical conditioning, an animal's natural predispositions constrain its capacity for operant conditioning. Using food as a reinforcer, you can easily condition a hamster to dig or to rear up because these actions are among the animal's natural food-searching behaviors. But you won't be so successful if you use food as a reinforcer to shape other hamster behaviors, such as face washing, that aren't normally associated with food or hunger (Shettleworth, 1973). Similarly, you could easily teach pigeons to flap their wings to avoid being shocked, and to peck to obtain food, because fleeing with their wings and eating with their beaks are natural pigeon behaviors. However, they would have a hard time learning to peck to avoid a shock, or to flap their wings to obtain food (Foree & LoLordo, 1973). The principle: *Biological constraints predispose organisms to learn associations that are naturally adaptive.*

After witnessing the power of operant technology, Skinner's students Keller Breland and Marian Breland (1961; Bailey & Gillaspy, 2005) began training dogs, cats, chickens,

"Bathroom? Sure, it's just down the hall to the left, jog right, left, another left, straight past two more lefts, then right, and it's at the end of the third corridor on your right."

Tiger Woods' intrinsic motivation "I remember a daily ritual that we had: I would call Pop at work to ask if I could practice with him. He would always pause a second or two, keeping me in suspense, but he'd always say yes. . . . In his own way, he was teaching me initiative. You see, he never pushed me to play" (quoted in *USA Weekend*, 1997). Woods (shown here being consoled by his caddy, Steve Williams) reacted with strong emotion to his first tournament win after his father's death.

Natural athletes
Animals can most easily learn and retain behaviors that draw on their biological predispositions, such as cats' inborn tendency to leap high and land on their feet.

"Never try to teach a pig to sing. It wastes your time and annoys the pig."

Mark Twain (1835–1910)

parakeets, turkeys, pigs, ducks, and hamsters, and they eventually left their graduate studies to form an animal training company. Over the ensuing 47 years they trained over 15,000 animals from 140 species for movies, traveling shows, corporations, amusement parks, and the government. They also trained animal trainers, including Sea World's first director of training.

At first, the Brelands presumed that operant principles would work on almost any response an animal could make. But along the way, they confronted the constraints of biological predispositions. In one act, pigs trained to pick up large wooden "dollars" and deposit them in a piggy bank began to drift back to their natural ways. They would drop the coin, push it with their snouts as pigs are prone to do, pick it up again, and then repeat the sequence—delaying their food reinforcer. This *instinctive drift* occurred as the animals reverted to their biologically predisposed patterns.

▶‖ Skinner's Legacy

B. F. Skinner was one of the most controversial intellectual figures of the late twentieth century. He stirred a hornet's nest with his outspoken beliefs. He repeatedly insisted that external influences (not internal thoughts and feelings) shape behavior. And he urged people to use operant principles to influence others' behavior at school, work, and home. Knowing that behavior is shaped by its results, he said we should use rewards to evoke more desirable behavior.

Skinner's critics objected, saying that he dehumanized people by neglecting their personal freedom and by seeking to control their actions. Skinner's reply: External consequences already haphazardly control people's behavior. Why not administer those consequences toward human betterment? Wouldn't reinforcers be more humane than the punishments used in homes, schools, and prisons? And if it is humbling to think that our history has shaped us, doesn't this very idea also give us hope that we can shape our future?

Applications of Operant Conditioning

24-6   How might operant conditioning principles be applied at school, in sports, at work, and at home?

Psychologists are applying operant conditioning principles to help people with a variety of challenges, from moderating high blood pressure to gaining social skills. Reinforcement technologies are also at work in schools, sports, workplaces, and homes (Flora, 2004).

At School

A generation ago, Skinner and others worked toward a day when teaching machines and textbooks would shape learning in small steps, immediately reinforcing correct responses. Such machines and texts, they said, would revolutionize education and free teachers to focus on each student's special needs.

B. F. Skinner "I am sometimes asked, 'Do you think of yourself as you think of the organisms you study?' The answer is yes. So far as I know, my behavior at any given moment has been nothing more than the product of my genetic endowment, my personal history, and the current setting" (1983).

Stand in Skinner's shoes for a moment and imagine two math teachers, each with a class of students ranging from whiz kids to slow learners. Teacher A gives the whole class the same lesson, knowing that the bright kids will breeze through the math concepts, and the slower ones will be frustrated and fail. With so many different children, how could one teacher guide them individually? Teacher B, faced with a similar class, paces the material according to each student's rate of learning and provides prompt feedback, with positive reinforcement, to both the slow and the fast learners. Thinking as Skinner did, how might you achieve the individualized instruction of Teacher B?

Computers were Skinner's final hope. "Good instruction demands two things," he said. "Students must be told immediately whether what they do is right or wrong and, when right, they must be directed to the step to be taken next." Thus, the computer could be Teacher B—pacing math drills to the student's rate of learning, quizzing the student to find gaps in understanding, giving immediate feedback, and keeping flawless records. To the end of his life, Skinner (1986, 1988, 1989) believed his ideal was achievable. Although the predicted education revolution has not occurred, today's interactive student software, Web-based learning, and online testing bring us closer than ever before to achieving his ideal.

Computer-assisted learning
Computers have helped realize Skinner's goal of individually paced instruction with immediate feedback.

In Sports

Reinforcement principles can enhance athletic performance as well. Again, the key is to shape behavior, by first reinforcing small successes and then gradually increasing the challenge. Thomas Simek and Richard O'Brien (1981, 1988) applied these principles to teaching golf and baseball by starting with easily reinforced responses. Golf students learn putting by starting with very short putts. As they build mastery, they eventually step back farther and farther. Likewise, novice batters begin with half swings at an oversized ball pitched from 10 feet away, giving them the immediate pleasure of smacking the ball. As the hitters' confidence builds with their success and they achieve mastery at each level, the pitcher gradually moves back—to 15, then 22, 30, and 40.5 feet—and eventually introduces a standard baseball. Compared with children taught by conventional methods, those trained by this behavioral method show, in both testing and game situations, faster skill improvement.

At Work

Skinner's ideas have also shown up in the workplace. Knowing that reinforcers influence productivity, many organizations have invited employees to share the risks and rewards of company ownership. Others focus on reinforcing a job well done. Rewards are most likely to increase productivity if the desired performance has been well-defined and is achievable. The message for managers? *Reward specific, achievable behaviors, not vaguely defined "merit."* Even criticism triggers the least resentment and the greatest performance boost when specific and considerate (Baron, 1988).

Operant conditioning also reminds us that reinforcement should be *immediate.* IBM legend Thomas Watson understood. When he observed an achievement, he wrote the employee a check on the spot (Peters & Waterman, 1982). But rewards need not be material, or lavish. An effective manager may simply walk the floor and sincerely affirm people for good work, or write notes of appreciation for a completed project. As Skinner said, "How much richer would the whole world be if the reinforcers in daily life were more effectively contingent on productive work?"

OH! THAT WAS A WONDERFUL REPORT, BOB. A WONDERFUL, WONDERFUL REPORT.

THE VICE-PRESIDENT IN CHARGE OF SINCERITY

"I wrote another five hundred words. Can I have another cookie?"

At Home

As we have seen, parents can apply operant conditioning practices. Parent-training researchers remind us that parents who say "Get ready for bed" but cave in to protests or defiance reinforce whining and arguing (Wierson & Forehand, 1994). Exasperated, they may then yell or gesture menacingly. When the child, now frightened, obeys, that in turn reinforces the parents' angry behavior. Over time, a destructive parent-child relationship develops.

To disrupt this cycle, parents should remember the basic rule of shaping: *Notice people doing something right and affirm them for it.* Give children attention and other reinforcers when they are behaving *well* (Wierson & Forehand, 1994). Target a specific behavior, reward it, and watch it increase. When children misbehave or are defiant, don't yell at them or hit them. Simply explain the misbehavior and give them a time-out.

Finally, we can use operant conditioning in our own lives (see Close-Up: Training Our Partners). To reinforce your own desired behaviors and extinguish the undesired ones, psychologists suggest taking these steps:

1. **State your goal**—to stop smoking, eat less, or study or exercise more—in measurable terms, and announce it. You might, for example, aim to boost your study time by an hour a day and share that goal with some close friends.
2. **Monitor how often you engage in your desired behavior.** You might log your current study time, noting under what conditions you do and don't study. (When I began writing textbooks, I logged how I spent my time each day and was amazed to discover how much time I was wasting.)
3. **Reinforce the desired behavior.** To increase your study time, give yourself a reward (a snack or some activity you enjoy) only after you finish your extra hour of study. Agree with your friends that you will join them for weekend activities only if you have met your realistic weekly studying goal.
4. **Reduce the rewards gradually.** As your new behaviors become more habitual, give yourself a mental pat on the back instead of a cookie.

CLOSE-UP

Training Our Partners   By Amy Sutherland

For a book I was writing about a school for exotic animal trainers, I started commuting from Maine to California, where I spent my days watching students do the seemingly impossible: teaching hyenas to pirouette on command, cougars to offer their paws for a nail clipping, and baboons to skateboard.

I listened, rapt, as professional trainers explained how they taught dolphins to flip and elephants to paint. Eventually it hit me that the same techniques might work on that stubborn but lovable species, the American husband.

The central lesson I learned from exotic animal trainers is that I should reward behavior I like and ignore behavior I don't. After all, you don't get a sea lion to balance a ball on the end of its nose by nagging. The same goes for the American husband.

Back in Maine, I began thanking Scott if he threw one dirty shirt into the hamper. If he threw in two, I'd kiss him. Meanwhile, I would step over any soiled clothes on the floor without one sharp word, though I did sometimes kick them under the bed. But as he basked in my appreciation, the piles became smaller.

I was using what trainers call "approximations," rewarding the small steps toward learning a whole new behavior. . . . Once I started thinking this way, I couldn't stop. At the school in California, I'd be scribbling notes on how to walk an emu or have a wolf accept you as a pack member, but I'd be thinking, "I can't wait to try this on Scott. . . ."

After two years of exotic animal training, my marriage is far smoother, my husband much easier to love. I used to take his faults personally; his dirty clothes on the floor were an affront, a symbol of how he didn't care enough about me. But thinking of my husband as an exotic species gave me the distance I needed to consider our differences more objectively.

Excerpted with permission from Sutherland, A. (2006, June 25). What Shamu taught me about a happy marriage, *New York Times.*

▶‖ Contrasting Classical and Operant Conditioning

Both classical and operant conditioning are forms of associative learning, and both involve acquisition, extinction, spontaneous recovery, generalization, and discrimination. The similarities are sufficient to make some researchers wonder if a single stimulus-response learning process might explain them both (Donahoe & Vegas, 2004). Their procedural difference is this: Through classical (Pavlovian) conditioning, an organism associates different stimuli that it does not control and responds automatically (respondent behaviors) (**TABLE 24.4**). Through operant conditioning, an organism associates its operant behaviors—those that act on its environment to produce rewarding or punishing stimuli—with their consequences. Cognitive processes and biological predispositions influence both classical and operant conditioning.

"O! This learning, what a thing it is."
William Shakespeare, *The Taming of the Shrew*, 1597

TABLE 24.4 Comparison of Classical and Operant Conditioning

	Classical Conditioning	Operant Conditioning
Basic idea	Organism learns associations between events it doesn't control.	Organism learns associations between its behavior and resulting events.
Response	Involuntary, automatic.	Voluntary, operates on environment.
Acquisition	Associating events; CS announces US.	Associating response with a consequence (reinforcer or punisher).
Extinction	CR decreases when CS is repeatedly presented alone.	Responding decreases when reinforcement stops.
Spontaneous recovery	The reappearance, after a rest period, of an extinguished CR.	The reappearance, after a rest period, of an extinguished response.
Generalization	The tendency to respond to stimuli similar to the CS.	Organism's response to similar stimuli is also reinforced.
Discrimination	The learned ability to distinguish between a CS and other stimuli that do not signal a US.	Organism learns that certain responses, but not others, will be reinforced.
Cognitive processes	Organisms develop expectation that CS signals the arrival of US.	Organisms develop expectation that a response will be reinforced or punished; they also exhibit latent learning, without reinforcement.
Biological predispositions	Natural predispositions constrain what stimuli and responses can easily be associated.	Organisms best learn behaviors similar to their natural behaviors; unnatural behaviors instinctively drift back toward natural ones.

REVIEW

Operant Conditioning

24-1 **What is operant conditioning, and how does it differ from classical conditioning?** In *operant conditioning,* an organism learns associations between its own behavior and resulting events; this form of conditioning involves *operant behavior* (behavior that operates on the environment, producing consequences). In classical conditioning, the organism forms associations between stimuli—behaviors it does not control; this form of conditioning involves *respondent behavior* (automatic responses to some stimulus).

Expanding on Edward Thorndike's *law of effect,* B. F. Skinner and others found that the behavior of rats or pigeons placed in an *operant chamber* (Skinner box) can be *shaped* by using *reinforcers* to guide closer and closer approximations of the desired behavior.

24-2 **What are the basic types of reinforcers?** *Positive reinforcement* adds something desirable to increase the frequency of a behavior. *Negative reinforcement* removes something undesirable to increase the frequency of a behavior. *Primary reinforcers* (such as receiving food when hungry or having nausea end during an illness) are innately satisfying—no learning is required. *Conditioned* (or secondary) *reinforcers* (such as cash) are satisfying because we have learned to associate them with more basic rewards (such as the food or medicine we buy with them). Immediate reinforcers (such as unprotected sex) offer immediate payback; delayed reinforcers (such as a weekly paycheck) require the ability to delay gratification.

24-3 **How do different reinforcement schedules affect behavior?** In *continuous reinforcement* (reinforcing desired responses every time they occur), learning is rapid, but so is extinction if rewards cease. In *partial (intermittent) reinforcement,* initial learning is slower, but the behavior is much more resistant to extinction. *Fixed-ratio schedules* offer rewards after a set number of responses; *variable-ratio schedules,* after an unpredictable number. *Fixed-interval schedules* offer rewards after set time periods; *variable-interval schedules,* after unpredictable time periods.

24-4 **How does punishment affect behavior?** *Punishment* attempts to decrease the frequency of a behavior (a child's disobedience) by administering an undesirable consequence (such as spanking) or withdrawing something desirable (such as taking away a favorite toy). Undesirable side effects can include suppressing rather than changing unwanted behaviors, teaching aggression, creating fear, encouraging discrimination (so that the undesirable behavior appears when the punisher is not present), and fostering depression and feelings of helplessness.

24-5 **Do cognitive processes and biological constraints affect operant conditioning?** Skinner underestimated the limits that cognitive and biological constraints place on conditioning. Research on *cognitive mapping* and *latent learning* demonstrate the importance of cognitive processes in learning. Excessive rewards can undermine *intrinsic motivation.* Training that attempts to override biological constraints will probably not endure because the animals will revert to their predisposed patterns.

24-6 **How might operant conditioning principles be applied at school, in sports, at work, and at home?** At school, teachers can use shaping techniques to guide students' behaviors, and they can use interactive software and Web sites to provide immediate feedback. In sports, coaches can build players' skills and self-confidence by rewarding small improvements. At work, managers can boost productivity and morale by rewarding well-defined and achievable behaviors. At home, parents can reward behaviors they consider desirable, but not those that are undesirable. We can shape our own behaviors by stating our goals, monitoring the frequency of desired behaviors, reinforcing desired behaviors, and cutting back on incentives as behaviors become habitual.

Terms and Concepts to Remember

associative learning, p. 301

respondent behavior, p. 301

operant conditioning, p. 301

operant behavior, p. 301

law of effect, p. 301

operant chamber, p. 302

learning, p. 302

shaping, p. 302

reinforcer, p. 303

positive reinforcement, p 303

negative reinforcement, p. 303

primary reinforcer, p. 304

conditioned reinforcer, p. 304

continuous reinforcement, p. 305

partial (intermittent) reinforcement, p. 305

fixed-ratio schedule, p. 305

variable-ratio schedule, p. 305

fixed-interval schedule, p. 305

variable-interval schedule, p. 306

punishment, p. 306

cognitive map, p. 308

latent learning, p. 308

intrinsic motivation, p. 309

extrinsic motivation, p. 309

Test Yourself

1. *Positive reinforcement, negative reinforcement, positive punishment,* and *negative punishment* are tricky concepts for many students. Can you fit the right term in the three boxes in this table? I'll do the first one (positive reinforcement) for you.

Type of Stimulus	Give It	Take It Away
Desired (for example, a compliment)	*Positive reinforcement*	
Undesired/aversive (for example, an insult)		

(Answers to the Test Yourself questions can be found in Appendix B at the end of the book.)

Ask Yourself

1. Can you recall a time when a teacher, coach, family member, or employer helped you learn something by shaping your behavior in little steps until you achieved your goal?

∞ WEB

Multiple-choice self-tests and more may be found at www.worthpublishers.com/myers

MODULE 25

Learning by Observation

Mirrors in the Brain

Bandura's Experiments

Applications of Observational Learning

25-1 What is observational learning, and how is it enabled by mirror neurons?

From drooling dogs, running rats, and pecking pigeons we have learned much about the basic processes of **learning.** But conditioning principles don't tell us the whole story. Higher animals, especially humans, can learn without direct experience, through **observational learning,** by observing and imitating others. A child who sees his sister burn her fingers on a hot stove learns not to touch it. And a monkey watching another selecting certain pictures to gain treats learns to imitate that behavior (**FIGURE 25.1**). We learn all kinds of specific behaviors by observing and imitating models, a process called **modeling.** Lord Chesterfield (1694–1773) had the idea: "We are, in truth, more than half what we are by imitation."

learning a relatively permanent change in an organism's behavior due to experience.

observational learning learning by observing others.

modeling the process of observing and imitating a specific behavior.

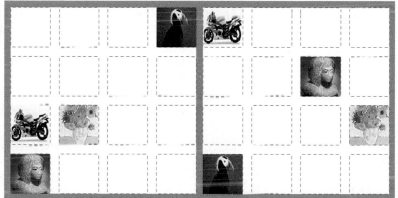

Monkey A's screen   Monkey B's screen

FIGURE 25.1 Cognitive imitation When Monkey A (left) sees Monkey B touch four pictures on a display screen in a certain order to gain a banana, Monkey A learns to imitate that order, even when shown a different configuration (Subiaul et al., 2004).

We can glimpse the roots of observational learning in other species. Rats, pigeons, crows, and gorillas all observe others and learn (Byrne & Russon, 1998; Dugatkin, 2002). So do monkeys. Rhesus macaque monkeys rarely make up quickly after a fight—unless they grow up with forgiving older macaques. Then, more often than not, their fights, too, are quickly followed by reconciliation (de Waal & Johanowicz, 1993). Monkey see, monkey do. Chimpanzees learn all sorts of foraging and tool use behaviors by observation, which then are transmitted across generations within their local culture (Hopper et al., 2008; Whiten et al., 2007).

Imitation is all the more striking in humans. Our catch-phrases, hem lengths, ceremonies, foods, traditions, vices, and fads all spread by one person copying another. Even as 2½-year-olds, when many of our mental abilities were near those of chimpanzees, we considerably surpassed chimps at social tasks such as imitating another's solution to a problem (Herrmann et al., 2007).

Children see, children do? Children who often experience physical punishment tend to display more aggression.

mirror neurons (frontal lobe neurons that fire when performing certain actions or when observing another doing so. The brain's mirroring of another's action may enable imitation and empathy.

"Children need models more than they need critics."

Joseph Joubert, *Pensées*, 1842

▶❙ Mirrors in the Brain

On a 1991 hot summer day in Parma, Italy, a lab monkey awaited its researchers' return from lunch. The researchers had implanted wires next to its motor cortex, in a frontal lobe brain region that enabled the monkey to plan and enact movements. When the monkey moved a peanut into its mouth, for example, the monitoring device would buzz. That day, as one of the researchers reentered the lab, ice cream cone in hand, the monkey stared at him. As the student raised the cone to lick it, the monkey's monitor again buzzed—as if the motionless monkey had itself moved (Blakeslee, 2006; Iacoboni, 2008).

Having earlier observed the same weird result when the monkey watched humans or other monkeys move peanuts to their mouths, the flabbergasted researchers, led by Giacomo Rizzolatti (2002, 2006), eventually surmised that they had stumbled onto a previously unknown type of neuron: **mirror neurons,** whose activity provides a neural basis for imitation and observational learning. When a monkey grasps, holds, or tears something, these neurons fire. And they likewise fire when the monkey observes another doing so. When one monkey sees, these neurons mirror what another monkey does.

It's not just monkey business. Imitation shapes even very young humans' behavior. Shortly after birth, a baby may imitate an adult who sticks out his tongue. By 8 to 16 months, infants imitate various novel gestures (Jones, 2007). By age 12 months, they begin looking where an adult is looking (Brooks & Meltzoff, 2005). And by age 14 months (**FIGURE 25.2**), children imitate acts modeled on TV (Meltzoff, 1988; Meltzoff & Moore, 1989, 1997). Children see, children do.

PET scans of different brain areas reveal that humans, like monkeys, have a mirror neuron system that supports empathy and imitation (Iacoboni, 2008). As we observe another's action, our brain generates an inner simulation, enabling us to experience the other's experience within ourselves. Mirror neurons help give rise to children's empathy and to their ability to infer another's mental state, an ability

FIGURE 25.2 Learning from observation This 14-month-old boy in Andrew Meltzoff's laboratory is imitating behavior he has seen on TV. In the top photo the infant leans forward and carefully watches the adult pull apart a toy. In the middle photo he has been given the toy. In the bottom photo he pulls the toy apart, imitating what he has seen the adult do.

Meltzoff, A. N. (1988). Imitation of televised models by infants. *Child Development, 59,* 1221–1229. Photos courtesy of A. N. Meltzoff and M. Hanuk.

known as *theory of mind.* People with autism, a developmental disorder, display reduced imitative yawning and mirror neuron activity—"broken mirrors," some have said (Ramachandran & Oberman, 2006; Senju et al., 2007; Williams et al., 2006).

For most of us, however, our mirror neurons make emotions contagious. We grasp others' states of mind—often feeling what they feel—by mental simulation. We find it harder to frown when viewing a smile than when viewing a frown (Dimberg et al., 2000, 2002). We find ourselves yawning after observing another's yawn, laughing when others laugh. When watching movies, a scorpion crawling up someone's leg makes us tighten up; observing a passionate kiss, we may notice our own lips puckering. Seeing a loved one's pain, our faces mirror their emotion. But as **FIGURE 25.3** shows, so do our brains. In this fMRI scan, the pain imagined by an empathic romantic partner has triggered some of the same brain activity experienced by the loved one actually having the pain (Singer et al., 2004). Even fiction reading may trigger such activity, as we mentally simulate the experiences described (Mar & Oatley, 2008). The bottom line: *Our brain's mirror neurons underlie our intensely social nature.*

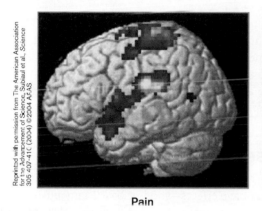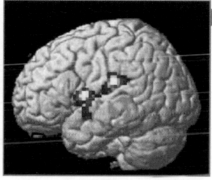

Pain   Empathy

FIGURE 25.3 Experienced and imagined pain in the brain Brain activity related to actual pain (left) is mirrored in the brain of an observing loved one (right). Empathy in the brain shows up in emotional brain areas, but not in the somatosensory cortex, which receives the physical pain input.

▶‖ Bandura's Experiments

Picture this scene from a famous experiment by Albert Bandura, the pioneering researcher of observational learning (Bandura et al., 1961). A preschool child works on a drawing. An adult in another part of the room is building with Tinkertoys. As the child watches, the adult gets up and for nearly 10 minutes pounds, kicks, and throws around the room a large inflated Bobo doll, yelling, "Sock him in the nose. . . . Hit him down. . . . Kick him."

The child is then taken to another room filled with appealing toys. Soon the experimenter returns and tells the child she has decided to save these good toys "for the other children." She takes the now-frustrated child to a third adjacent room containing a few toys, including a Bobo doll. Left alone, what does the child do?

Compared with children not exposed to the adult model, those who viewed the model's actions were much more likely to lash out at the doll. Apparently, observing the aggressive outburst lowered their inhibitions. But something more was also at work, for the children imitated the very acts they had observed and used the very words they had heard (**FIGURE 25.4** on the next page).

Albert Bandura "The Bobo doll follows me wherever I go. The photographs are published in every introductory psychology text and virtually every undergraduate takes introductory psychology. I recently checked into a Washington hotel. The clerk at the desk asked, 'Aren't you the psychologist who did the Bobo doll experiment?' I answered, 'I am afraid that will be my legacy.' He replied, 'That deserves an upgrade. I will put you in a suite in the quiet part of the hotel'" (2005).

Courtesy of Albert Bandura, Stanford University

FIGURE 25.4 The famous Bobo doll experiment Notice how the children's actions directly imitate the adult's.

What determines whether we will imitate a model? Bandura believes part of the answer is reinforcements and punishments—those received by the model as well as by the imitator. By watching, we learn to anticipate a behavior's consequences in situations like those we are observing. We are especially likely to imitate people we perceive as similar to ourselves, as successful, or as admirable.

▶‖ Applications of Observational Learning

The big news from Bandura's studies is that we look and we learn. Models—in one's family or neighborhood, or on TV—may have effects—good or bad. Many business organizations effectively use *behavior modeling* to train communications, sales, and customer service skills (Taylor et al., 2005). Trainees gain skills faster when they not only are told the needed skills but also are able to observe the skills being modeled effectively by experienced workers (or actors simulating them).

Prosocial Effects

25-2   What is the impact of prosocial modeling and of antisocial modeling?

The good news is that **prosocial** (positive, helpful) models can have prosocial effects. To encourage children to read, read to them and surround them with books and people who read. To increase the odds that your children will practice your religion, worship and attend religious activities with them. People who exemplify nonviolent, helpful behavior can prompt similar behavior in others. India's Mahatma Gandhi and America's Martin Luther King, Jr., both drew on the power of modeling, making nonviolent action a powerful force for social change in both countries. Parents are also powerful models. European Christians who risked their lives to rescue Jews from the Nazis usually had a close relationship with at least one parent who modeled a strong moral or humanitarian concern; this was also true for U.S. civil rights activists in the 1960s (London, 1970; Oliner & Oliner, 1988). The observational learning of morality begins early. Socially responsive toddlers who readily imitate their parents tend to become preschoolers with a strong internalized conscience (Forman et al., 2004).

A model grandma This boy is learning to cook by observing his grandmother. As the sixteenth-century proverb states, "Example is better than precept."

Bob Daemmrich/The Image Works

Models are most effective when their actions and words are consistent. Sometimes, however, models say one thing and do another. Many parents seem to operate according to the principle "Do as I *say,* not as I do." Experiments suggest that children learn to do both (Rice & Grusec, 1975; Rushton, 1975). Exposed to a hypocrite, they tend to imitate the hypocrisy by doing what the model did and saying what the model said.

Antisocial Effects

prosocial behavior positive, constructive, helpful behavior. The opposite of antisocial behavior.

The bad news is that observational learning may have *antisocial effects.* This helps us understand why abusive parents might have aggressive children, and why many men who beat their wives had wife-battering fathers (Stith et al., 2000). Critics note that being aggressive could be passed along by parents' genes. But with monkeys we know it can be environmental. In study after study, young monkeys separated from their mothers and subjected to high levels of aggression grew up to be aggressive themselves (Chamove, 1980). The lessons we learn as children are not easily unlearned as adults, and they are sometimes visited on future generations.

TV is a powerful source of observational learning. While watching TV, children may "learn" that bullying is an effective way to control others, that free and easy sex brings pleasure without later misery or disease, or that men should be tough and women gentle. And they have ample time to learn such lessons. During their first 18 years, most children in developed countries spend more time watching TV than they spend in school. In the United States, where 9 in 10 teens watch TV daily, someone who lives to age 75 will have spent 9 years staring at the tube (Gallup, 2002; Kubey & Csikszentmihalyi, 2002). With more than 1 billion TV sets playing in homes worldwide, CNN reaching 150 countries, and MTV broadcasting in 17 languages, television has created a global pop culture (Gundersen, 2001; Lippman, 1992).

‖ TV's greatest effect may stem from what it displaces. Children and adults who spend 4 hours a day watching TV spend 4 fewer hours in active pursuits—talking, studying, playing, reading, or socializing with friends. What would you have done with your extra time if you had never watched TV, and how might you therefore be different? ‖

Television viewers are learning about life from a rather peculiar storyteller, one that reflects the culture's mythology but not its reality. During the late twentieth century, the average child viewed some 8000 TV murders and 100,000 other acts of violence before finishing elementary school (Huston et al., 1992). If we include cable programming and video rentals, the violence numbers escalate. An analysis of more than 3000 network and cable programs aired in the 1996–1997 season revealed that nearly 6 in 10 featured violence, that 74 percent of the violence went unpunished, that 58 percent did not show the victims' pain, that nearly half the incidents involved "justified" violence, and that nearly half involved an attractive perpetrator. These conditions define the recipe for the *violence-viewing effect* described in many studies (Donnerstein, 1998).

How much are we affected by repeated exposure to violent programs? Was the judge who in 1993 tried two British 10-year-olds for their murder of a 2-year-old right to suspect that the pair had been influenced by "violent video films"? Were the American media right to think that the teen assassins who killed 13 of their Columbine High School classmates had been influenced by repeated exposure to *Natural Born Killers* and splatter games such as *Doom?* To understand whether violence viewing leads to violent behavior, researchers have done some 600 correlational and experimental studies (Anderson & Gentile, 2008; Comstock, 2008; Murray, 2008).

Correlational studies do support this link:

▶ In the United States and Canada, homicide rates doubled between 1957 and 1974, just when TV was introduced and spreading. Moreover, census regions with later dates for TV service also had homicide rates that jumped later.

▶ White South Africans were first introduced to TV in 1975. A similar near-doubling of the homicide rate began after 1975 (Centerwall, 1989).

▶ Elementary schoolchildren with heavy exposure to media violence (via TV, videos, and video games) also tend to get into more fights (**FIGURE 25.5** on the next page).

FIGURE 25.5 Media violence viewing predicts future aggressive behavior
Douglas Gentile and his colleagues (2004) studied more than 400 third to fifth graders. After controlling for existing differences in hostility and aggression, the researchers reported increased aggression in those heavily exposed to violent television, videos, and video games.

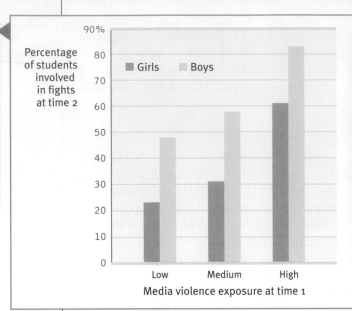

"Thirty seconds worth of glorification of a soap bar sells soap. Twenty-five minutes worth of glorification of violence sells violence."
U.S. Senator Paul Simon, Remarks to the Communitarian Network, 1993

‖ Gallup surveys asked American teens (Mazzuca, 2002): "Do you feel there is too much violence in the movies, or not?"
1977: 42 percent said yes.
1999: 23 percent said yes. ‖

But remember: *correlation does not imply causation.* So these studies do not prove that viewing violence causes aggression (Freedman, 1988; McGuire, 1986). Maybe aggressive children prefer violent programs. Maybe abused or neglected children are both more aggressive and more often left in front of the TV. Maybe violent programs simply reflect, rather than affect, violent trends.

To pin down causation, psychologists use experiments. In this case, researchers randomly assigned some viewers to observe violence and others to watch entertaining nonviolence. Does viewing cruelty prepare people, when irritated, to react more cruelly? To some extent, it does. "The consensus among most of the research community," reported the National Institute of Mental Health (1982), "is that violence on television does lead to aggressive behavior by children and teenagers who watch the programs." This is especially so when an attractive person commits seemingly justified, realistic violence that goes unpunished and causes no visible pain or harm (Donnerstein, 1998).

The violence-viewing effect seems to stem from at least two factors. One is *imitation* (Geen & Thomas, 1986). As we noted earlier, children as young as 14 months will imitate acts they observe on TV. As they watch, their mirror neurons simulate the behavior, and after this inner rehearsal they become more likely to act it out. One re-

Violence viewing leads to violent play
Research has shown that viewing media violence does lead to increased expression of aggression in the viewers, as with these boys imitating pro wrestlers.

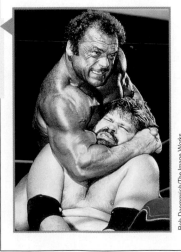

search team observed a sevenfold increase in violent play immediately after children viewed the "Power Rangers" (Boyatzis et al., 1995). These children, like those we saw earlier in the Bobo doll experiment, often precisely imitated the models' violent acts, including flying karate kicks. Imitation may also have played a role in the first eight days after the 1999 Columbine High School massacre, when every U.S. state except Vermont had to deal with copycat threats or incidents. Pennsylvania alone had 60 threats of school violence (Cooper, 1999).

Prolonged exposure to violence also *desensitizes* viewers; they become more indifferent to it when later viewing a brawl, whether on TV or in real life (Rule & Ferguson, 1986). Adult males who spent three evenings watching sexually violent movies became progressively less bothered by the rapes and slashings. Compared with those in a control group, the film watchers later expressed less sympathy for domestic violence victims, and they rated the victims' injuries as less severe (Mullin & Linz, 1995).

Indeed, suggested Edward Donnerstein and his co-researchers (1987), an evil psychologist could hardly imagine a better way to make people indifferent to brutality than to expose them to a graded series of scenes, from fights to killings to the mutilations in slasher movies. Watching cruelty fosters indifference.

* * *

Bandura's work—like that of Ivan Pavlov, John Watson, B. F. Skinner, and thousands of others who advanced our knowledge of learning principles—illustrates the impact that can result from single-minded devotion to a few well-defined problems and ideas. All of these researchers defined the issues and impressed on us the importance of learning. As their legacy demonstrates, intellectual history is often made by people who risk going to extremes in pushing ideas to their limits (Simonton, 2000).

"Don't you understand? This is life, this is what is happening. We can't switch to another channel."

REVIEW

Learning by Observation

25-1 **What is observational learning, and how is it enabled by mirror neurons?** In *observational learning,* we observe and imitate others. *Mirror neurons,* located in the brain's frontal lobes, demonstrate a neural basis for observational learning. They fire when we perform certain actions (such as responding to pain or moving our mouth to form words), or when we observe someone else performing those actions.

25-2 **What is the impact of prosocial modeling and of antisocial modeling?** Children tend to imitate what a model does and says, whether the behavior being *modeled* is *prosocial* (positive, constructive, and helpful) or antisocial. If a model's actions and words are inconsistent, children may imitate the hypocrisy they observe.

Terms and Concepts to Remember

learning, p. 315

observational learning, p. 315

modeling, p. 315

mirror neurons, p. 316

prosocial behavior, p. 318

Test Yourself

1. Jason's parents and older friends all smoke, but they advise him not to. Juan's parents and friends don't smoke, but they say nothing to deter him from doing so. Will Jason or Juan be more likely to start smoking?

(Answers to the Test Yourself questions can be found in Appendix B at the end of the book.)

Ask Yourself

1. Who has been a significant role model for you? For whom are you a model?

∞ WEB

Multiple-choice self-tests and more may be found at www.worthpublishers.com/myers

Memory

MODULES

26
Introduction to Memory

27
Encoding: Getting Information In

28
Storage: Retaining Information

29
Retrieval: Getting Information Out

30
Forgetting, Memory Construction, and Improving Memory

Be thankful for memory. We take it for granted, except when it malfunctions. But it is our memory that accounts for time and defines our life. It is our memory that enables us to recognize family, speak our language, find our way home, and locate food and water. It is our memory that enables us to enjoy an experience and then mentally replay and enjoy it again. Our shared memories help bind us together as Irish or Aussies, as Serbs or Albanians. And it is our memories that occasionally pit us against those whose offenses we cannot forget.

In large part, you are what you remember. Without memory, your storehouse of accumulated learning, there would be no savoring of past joys, no guilt or anger over painful recollections. You would instead live in an enduring present, each moment fresh. But each person would be a stranger, every language foreign, every task—dressing, cooking, biking—a new challenge. You would even be a stranger to yourself, lacking that continuous sense of self that extends from your distant past to your momentary present. "If you lose the ability to recall your old memories then you have no life," suggested memory researcher James McGaugh (2003). "You might as well be a rutabaga or a cabbage."

To think about memory, we first need a model of how it works. Module 26 introduces a modified version of Richard Atkinson and Richard Shiffrin's classic and influential three-stage model of memory. Modules 27 through 29 examine sensory memory, short-term/working memory, and long-term memory—thus reviewing how we move information into our memories, retain it, and later retrieve it. Module 30 looks at what happens when our memories fail us (as when we forget information, misremember it, or create false memories). That module concludes with some tips on how you can apply memory researchers' findings to your own education.

"Waiter, I'd like to order, unless I've eaten, in which case bring me the check."

MODULE 26

Introduction to Memory

▶‖ The Phenomenon of Memory

To a psychologist, **memory** is learning that has persisted over time, information that has been stored and can be retrieved.

Research on memory's extremes has helped us understand how memory works. At age 92, my father suffered a small stroke that had but one peculiar effect. His genial personality was intact. He was as mobile as before. He knew us and while poring over family photo albums could reminisce in detail about his past. But he had lost most of his ability to lay down new memories of conversations and everyday episodes. He could not tell me what day of the week it was. Told repeatedly of his brother-in-law's death, he expressed surprise each time he heard the news.

At the other extreme are people who would be medal winners in a memory Olympics, such as Russian journalist Shereshevskii, or S, who had merely to listen while other reporters scribbled notes (Luria, 1968). Where you and I could parrot back a string of about 7—maybe even 9—digits, S could repeat up to 70, provided they were read about 3 seconds apart in an otherwise silent room. Moreover, he could recall digits or words backward as easily as forward. His accuracy was unerring, even when recalling a list as much as 15 years later, after having memorized hundreds of others. "Yes, yes," he might recall. "This was a series you gave me once when we were in your apartment. . . . You were sitting at the table and I in the rocking chair. . . . You were wearing a gray suit and you looked at me like this. . . ."

Amazing? Yes, but consider your own pretty staggering capacity for remembering countless voices, sounds, and songs; tastes, smells, and textures; faces, places, and happenings. Imagine viewing more than 2500 slides of faces and places, for only 10 seconds each. Later you see 280 of these slides, paired with others not previously seen. If you are like the participants in this experiment by Ralph Haber (1970), you would recognize 90 percent of those you had seen before.

Or imagine yourself looking at a picture fragment, such as the one in **FIGURE 26.1**. Also imagine that you had seen the complete picture for a couple of seconds 17 years earlier. When David Mitchell (2006) gave people this experience, they were more likely to identify the previously seen objects than were members of a control group who had not seen the complete drawings. Moreover, like the cicada insect that reemerges every 17 years, the picture memory reappeared even for those who had no conscious recollection of participating in the long-ago experiment!

How do we accomplish such memory feats? How can we remember things we have not thought about for years, yet forget the name of someone we met a minute ago? How are memories stored in our brains? Why do some painful memories persist, like unwelcome houseguests, while other memories leave too quickly? How can two people's memories of the same event be so different? How can we improve our memories? These will be among the questions we consider as we review more than a century of research on memory.

FIGURE 26.1 What is this? People who had, 17 years earlier, seen the complete image (in Figure 26.3 when you turn the page) were more likely to recognize this fragment, even if they had forgotten the earlier experience (Mitchell, 2006).

▶‖ Studying Memory: Information-Processing Models

26-1 How do psychologists describe the human memory system?

A model of how memory works can help us think about how we form and retrieve memories. One model that has often been used is a computer's information-processing system, which is in some ways similar to human memory. To remember any event, we must *get information into our brain* (**encoding**), *retain* that information (**storage**), and later *get it back out* (**retrieval**). A computer also *encodes, stores,* and *retrieves* information. First, it translates input (keystrokes) into an electronic language, much as the brain encodes sensory information into a neural language. The computer permanently stores vast amounts of information on a drive, from which it can later be retrieved.

Like all analogies, the computer model has its limits. Our memories are less literal and more fragile than a computer's. Moreover, most computers process information speedily but sequentially, even while alternating between tasks. The brain is slower but does many things at once.

Psychologists have proposed several information-processing models of memory. One modern model, *connectionism,* views memories as emerging from interconnected neural networks. Specific memories arise from particular activation patterns within these networks. In an older but easier-to-picture model, Richard Atkinson and Richard Shiffrin (1968) proposed that we form memories in three stages:

1. We first record to-be-remembered information as a fleeting **sensory memory.**
2. From there, we process information into a **short-term memory** bin, where we encode it through *rehearsal.*
3. Finally, information moves into **long-term memory** for later retrieval.

Although historically important and helpfully simple, this three-step process is limited and fallible. In this text, we use a *modified version of the three-stage processing model of memory* (**FIGURE 26.2**). This updated model accommodates two important new concepts:

▶ Some information skips Atkinson and Shiffrin's first two stages and is processed directly and automatically into long-term memory, without our conscious awareness.

memory the persistence of learning over time through the storage and retrieval of information.

encoding the processing of information into the memory system—for example, by extracting meaning.

storage the retention of encoded information over time.

retrieval the process of getting information out of memory storage.

sensory memory the immediate, very brief recording of sensory information in the memory system.

short-term memory activated memory that holds a few items briefly, such as the seven digits of a phone number while dialing, before the information is stored or forgotten.

long-term memory the relatively permanent and limitless storehouse of the memory system. Includes knowledge, skills, and experiences.

FIGURE 26.2 A modified three-stage processing model of memory
Atkinson and Shiffrin's classic three-step model helps us to think about how memories are processed, but today's researchers recognize other ways long-term memories form. For example, some information slips into long-term memory via a "back door," without our consciously attending to it. And so much active processing occurs in the short-term memory stage that many now prefer the term *working memory.*

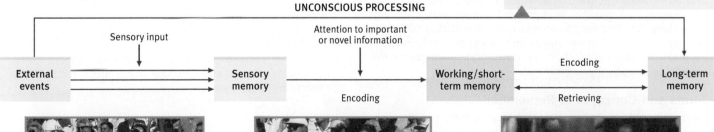

UNCONSCIOUS PROCESSING

External events → Sensory memory

Sensory input

Attention to important or novel information

Encoding

Working/short-term memory

Encoding

Retrieving

Long-term memory

Sensory memory registers incoming information, allowing your brain to capture for a moment a sea of faces.

We pay attention to and encode important or novel stimuli—in this case an angry face in the crowd.

If we stare at the face long enough (rehearsal), or if we're sufficiently disturbed by it (it's deemed "important"), we will encode it for long-term storage, and we may, an hour later, be able to call up an image of the face.

FIGURE 26.3 Now you know People who had seen this complete image were, 17 years later, more likely to recognize the fragment in Figure 26.1.

working memory a newer understanding of short-term memory that focuses on conscious, active processing of incoming auditory and visual-spatial information, and of information retrieved from long-term memory.

▶ **Working memory,** a newer understanding of Atkinson and Shiffrin's second stage, concentrates on the active processing of information in this intermediate stage. Because we cannot possibly focus on all the information bombarding our senses at once, we shine the flashlight beam of our attention on certain incoming stimuli—often those that are novel or important. We process these incoming stimuli, along with information we retrieve from long-term memory, in temporary working memory. Working memory associates new and old information and solves problems (Baddeley, 2001, 2002; Engle, 2002).

People's working memory capacity differs. Imagine being shown a letter of the alphabet, then asked a simple question, then being shown another letter, followed by another question, and so on. Those who can juggle the most mental balls—who can remember the most letters despite the interruptions—tend in everyday life to exhibit high intelligence and to better maintain their focus on tasks (Kane et al., 2007; Unsworth & Engle, 2007). When beeped to report in at various times, they are less likely than others to report that their mind was wandering from their current activity.

REVIEW

Introduction to Memory

26-1 How do psychologists describe the human memory system? *Memory* is the persistence of learning over time. The Atkinson-Shiffrin classic three-stage memory model (*encoding, storage,* and *retrieval*) suggests that we (1) register fleeting *sensory memories,* some of which are (2) processed into conscious *short-term memories,* a tiny fraction of which are (3) encoded for *long-term memory* and, possibly, later retrieval. Contemporary memory researchers note that we also register some information automatically, bypassing the first two stages. And they prefer the term *working memory* (rather than short-term memory) to emphasize the active processing in the second stage.

Terms and Concepts to Remember

memory, p. 324   sensory memory, p. 325
encoding, p. 325   short-term memory, p. 325
storage, p. 325   long-term memory, p. 325
retrieval, p. 325   working memory, p. 326

Test Yourself

1. Memory includes (in alphabetical order) long-term memory, sensory memory, and working/short-term memory. What's the correct order of these three memory stages?

(Answers to the Test Yourself questions can be found in Appendix B at the end of the book.)

Ask Yourself

1. How have you used the three parts of your memory system (encoding, storage, and retrieval) in learning something new today?

⊙⊙ WEB

Multiple-choice self-tests and more may be found at www.worthpublishers.com/myers

MODULE 27

Encoding: Getting Information In

27-1 What information do we encode automatically? What information do we encode effortfully, and how does the distribution of practice influence retention?

▶‖ How We Encode

We will use a modified version of Richard Atkinson and Richard Shiffrin's classic *three-stage processing model of memory* (1968) (**FIGURE 27.1**). We process some external stimuli consciously in our *sensory memory*, while other external events are processed beneath the radar of our conscious efforts. The events we notice and attend to are *encoded*, or processed in our *working memory* (which Atkinson and Shiffrin referred to as our *short-term memory*). Further processing and rehearsing encodes important parts of the event into our *long-term memory*, from which the information may later be retrieved. Here we will focus on the *encoding* part of that process. You encode some information, such as the route you walked to your last class, with great ease, freeing your memory system to focus on less familiar events. But to retain novel information, such as a friend's new cellphone number, you need to pay attention and try hard.

FIGURE 27.1 A modified three-stage processing model of memory Here we will focus on the encoding part of memory processing.

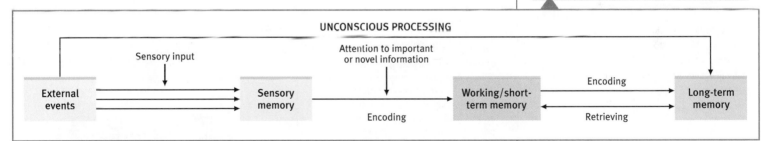

UNCONSCIOUS PROCESSING

Sensory input

Attention to important or novel information

Encoding

Retrieving

Encoding

External events → Sensory memory → Working/short-term memory → Long-term memory

Automatic Processing

Thanks to your brain's capacity for simultaneous activity (for parallel processing), an enormous amount of multitasking goes on without your conscious attention. For example, without conscious effort you **automatically process** information about

▶ *space.* While studying, you often encode the place on a page where certain material appears; later, when struggling to recall that information, you may visualize its location.

▶ *time.* While going about your day, you unintentionally note the sequence of the day's events. Later, when you realize you've left your coat somewhere, you can recreate that sequence and retrace your steps.

▶ *frequency.* You effortlessly keep track of how many times things happen, thus enabling you to realize "this is the third time I've run into her today."

automatic processing unconscious encoding of incidental information, such as space, time, and frequency, and of well-learned information, such as word meanings.

▶ *well-learned information.* For example, when you see words in your native language, perhaps on the side of a delivery truck, you cannot help but register their meanings. At such times, automatic processing is so effortless that it is difficult to shut it off.

Deciphering words was not always so easy. When you first learned to read, you sounded out individual letters to figure out what words they made. With effort, you plodded slowly through a mere 20 to 50 words on a page. Reading, like some other forms of processing, initially requires attention and effort, but with experience and practice becomes automatic. Imagine now learning to read reversed sentences like this:

.citamotua emoceb nac gnissecorp luftroffE

At first, this requires effort, but after enough practice, you would also perform this task much more automatically. We develop many skills in this way. We learn to drive, to text messages, to speak a new language first with great effort, then more automatically.

Effortful Processing

We encode and retain vast amounts of information automatically, but we remember other types of information, such as this module's concepts, only with effort and attention (**FIGURE 27.2**). **Effortful processing** often produces durable and accessible memories.

When learning novel information such as names, we can boost our memory through **rehearsal,** or conscious repetition. The pioneering researcher of verbal memory, German philosopher Hermann Ebbinghaus (1850–1909), showed this after becoming impatient with philosophical speculations about memory. Ebbinghaus decided he would scientifically study his own learning and forgetting of novel verbal materials.

|| Later in this module, I'll ask you to recall this sentence: The angry rioter threw the rock at the window. ||

effortful processing encoding that requires attention and conscious effort.

rehearsal the conscious repetition of information, either to maintain it in consciousness or to encode it for storage.

spacing effect the tendency for distributed study or practice to yield better long-term retention than is achieved through massed study or practice.

cramming

FIGURE 27.2 Automatic versus effortful processing Some information, such as where you ate dinner yesterday, you process automatically. Other information, such as this module's concepts, requires effort to encode and remember.

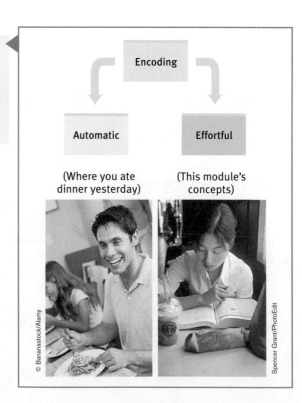

To create novel verbal material for his learning experiments, Ebbinghaus formed a list of all possible nonsense syllables by sandwiching one vowel between two consonants. He then randomly selected a sample of the syllables, practiced them, and tested himself. To get a feel for his experiments, rapidly read aloud, eight times over, the following list (from Baddeley, 1982). Then try to recall the items:

JIH, BAZ, FUB, YOX, SUJ, XIR, DAX, LEQ, VUM, PID, KEL, WAV, TUV, ZOF, GEK, HIW.

The day after learning such a list, Ebbinghaus could recall few of the syllables. But were they entirely forgotten? As **FIGURE 27.3** portrays, the more frequently he repeated the list aloud on day 1, the fewer repetitions he required to relearn the list on day 2. Here, then, was a simple beginning principle: *The amount remembered depends on the time spent learning.* Even after we learn material, additional rehearsal *(overlearning)* increases retention. *The point to remember:* For novel verbal information, practice—effortful processing—does indeed make perfect.

Later research revealed more about how to lay down enduring memories. To paraphrase Ebbinghaus (1885), those who learn quickly also forget quickly. We retain information better when our rehearsal is distributed over time (as when learning classmates' names), a phenomenon called the **spacing effect.** More than 300 experiments over the last century consistently reveal the benefits of spacing learning times (Cepeda et al., 2006). *Massed practice* (cramming) can produce speedy short-term learning and feelings of confidence. But *distributed study time* produces better long-term recall. After studying long enough to master the material, further study becomes inefficient, note Doug Rohrer and Harold Pashler (2007). Better to spend that extra reviewing time later—a day later if you need to remember something 10 days hence, or a month later if you need to remember something 6 months hence.

In a 9-year experiment, Harry Bahrick and three of his family members (1993) practiced foreign language word translations for a given number of times, at intervals ranging from 14 to 56 days. Their consistent finding: The longer the space between practice sessions, the better their retention up to 5 years later. The practical implication? Spreading out learning—over a semester or a year, rather than over a shorter

"He should test his memory by reciting the verses."

Abdur Rahman Abdul Khaliq, "Memorizing the Quran"

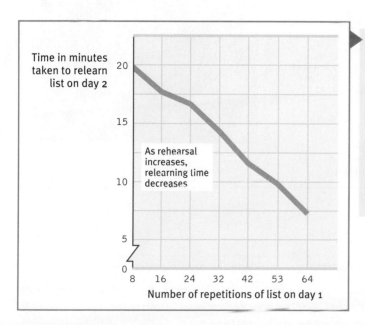

FIGURE 27.3

Ebbinghaus' retention curve Ebbinghaus found that the more times he practiced a list of nonsense syllables on day 1, the fewer repetitions he required to relearn it on day 2. Said simply, the more time we spend learning novel information, the more we retain. (From Baddeley, 1982.)

Time in minutes taken to relearn list on day 2

As rehearsal increases, relearning time decreases

Number of repetitions of list on day 1

term—should help you not only on comprehensive final exams, but also in retaining the information for a lifetime. Repeated quizzing of previously studied material also helps, a phenomenon that <u>Henry Roediger and Jeffrey Karpicke</u> (2006) call the <u>*testing effect*</u>, adding, "Testing is a powerful means of improving learning, not just assessing it." In one of their studies, students recalled the meaning of 40 previously learned Swahili words much better if tested repeatedly than if they spent the same time restudying the words (Karpicke & Roediger, 2008). *So here is another point to remember:* Spaced study and self-assessment beat cramming.

Another phenomenon, the **serial position effect,** further illustrates the benefits of rehearsal. As an everyday parallel, imagine it's your first day in a new job, and your manager is introducing co-workers. As you meet each one, you repeat (rehearse) all their names, starting from the beginning. By the time you meet the last person, you will have spent more time rehearsing the earlier names than the later ones; thus, the next day you will probably more easily recall the earlier names. Also, learning the first few names may interfere with your learning the later ones.

Experimenters have demonstrated the serial position effect by showing people a list of items (words, names, dates, even odors) and then immediately asking them to recall the items in any order (Reed, 2000). As people struggle to recall the list, they often remember the last and first items better than they do those in the middle (**FIGURE 27.4**). Perhaps because the last items are still in working memory, people briefly recall them especially quickly and well *(a recency effect)*. But after a delay— after they shift their attention from the last items—their recall is best for the first items *(a primacy effect)*.

Sometimes, however, rehearsal is not enough to store new information for later recall (Craik & Watkins, 1973; Greene, 1987). To understand why this happens, we need to know more about how we encode information for processing into long-term memory.

> "The mind is slow in unlearning what it has been long in learning."
> Roman philosopher Seneca (4 B.C.–A.D. 65)

FIGURE 27.4 The serial position effect Immediately after Australian Prime Minister Kevin Rudd introduces this long line of officials to Afghan President Hamid Karzai, President Karzai will probably recall the names of the last few people best. But later Karzai may recall the first few people best. (From Craik & Watkins, 1973.)

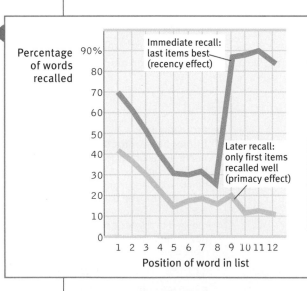

Percentage of words recalled

Immediate recall: last items best (recency effect)

Later recall: only first items recalled well (primacy effect)

Position of word in list

AP Photo/Musadeq Sadeq, Pool

▶‖ What We Encode

27-2   What effortful processing methods aid in forming memories?

Processing our sensory input is like sorting through e-mail. Some items we instantly discard. Others we open, read, and retain. We process information by encoding its meaning, encoding its image, or mentally organizing it.

Levels of Processing

When processing verbal information for storage, we usually encode its meaning, associating it with what we already know or imagine. Whether we hear *eye-screem* as "ice cream" or "I scream" depends on how the context and our experience guide us to interpret and encode the sounds. (Remember, our working memories interact with our long-term memories.)

Can you repeat the sentence about the rioter that I gave you at this module's beginning? ("The angry rioter threw . . .") Perhaps, like those in an experiment by William Brewer (1977), you recalled the rioter sentence by the meaning you encoded when you read it (for example, "The angry rioter threw the rock *through* the window") and not as it was written ("The angry rioter threw the rock *at* the window"). Referring to such recall, Gordon Bower and Daniel Morrow (1990) liken our minds to theater directors who, given a raw script, imagine a finished stage production. Asked later what we heard or read, we recall not the literal text but *what we encoded*. Thus, studying for an exam, you may remember your lecture notes rather than the lecture itself.

What kind of encoding do you think yields the best memory of verbal information? **Visual encoding** of images? **Acoustic encoding** of sounds? **Semantic encoding** of meaning? Each of these levels of processing has its own brain system (Poldrack & Wagner, 2004). And each can help. For example, acoustic encoding enhances the memorability and seeming truth of rhyming aphorisms. "What sobriety conceals, alcohol reveals" seems more accurate than "what sobriety conceals, alcohol unmasks" (McGlone & Tofighbakhsh, 2000). Attorney Johnnie Cochran's celebrated plea to O. J. Simpson's jury—"If the glove doesn't fit, you must acquit"—was also more easily remembered than had Cochran said, "If the glove doesn't fit, you must find him not guilty!"

To compare visual, acoustic, and semantic encoding, Fergus Craik and Endel Tulving (1975) flashed a word at people. Then they asked a question that required the viewers to process the words at one of three levels (1) visually (the appearance of the letters), (2) acoustically (the sound of the words), or (3) semantically (the meaning of the words). To experience the task yourself, rapidly answer the following questions:

Sample Questions to Elicit Processing	Word Flashed	Yes	No
1. Is the word in capital letters?	CHAIR	✓	___
2. Does the word rhyme with train?	brain	✓	___
3. Would the word fit in this sentence?			
The girl put the _____ on the table.	gun	✓	___

Which type of processing would best prepare you to recognize the words at a later time? In Craik and Tulving's experiment, the deeper, semantic processing—question 3—yielded much better memory than the "shallow processing" elicited by question 2 and especially by question 1 (**FIGURE 27.5** on the next page).

But given too raw a script, we have trouble creating a mental model. Put yourself in the place of the students who John Bransford and Marcia Johnson (1972) asked to remember the following recorded passage:

> The procedure is actually quite simple. First you arrange things into different groups. Of course, one pile may be sufficient depending on how much there is to do. . . . After the procedure is completed one arranges the materials into different groups again. Then they can be put into their appropriate places. Eventually they will be used once more and the whole cycle will then have to be repeated. However, that is part of life.

serial position effect our tendency to recall best the last and first items in a list.

visual encoding the encoding of picture images.

acoustic encoding the encoding of sound, especially the sound of words.

semantic encoding the encoding of meaning, including the meaning of words.

‖ How many *F*s are in the following sentence?
FINISHED FILES ARE THE RESULTS OF YEARS OF SCIENTIFIC STUDY COMBINED WITH THE EXPERIENCE OF YEARS. (Answer below.) ‖

Partly because your initial processing of the letters was primarily acoustic rather than visual, you probably missed some of the six *F*s, especially those that sound like a *V* rather than an *F*.

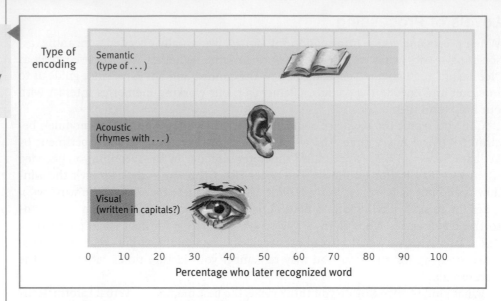

FIGURE 27.5 Levels of processing
Processing a word deeply—by its meaning (semantic encoding)—produces better recognition of it at a later time than does shallow processing by attending to its appearance or sound. (From Craik & Tulving, 1975.)

When the students heard the paragraph you have just read, without a meaningful context, they remembered little of it. When told the paragraph described washing clothes (something meaningful to them), they remembered much more of it—as you probably could now after rereading it. Processing a word deeply—by its meaning *(semantic encoding)*—produces better recognition later than does shallow processing, such as attending to its appearance *(visual encoding)* or sound *(acoustic encoding)* (Craik & Tulving, 1975).

Such research suggests the benefits of rephrasing what we read and hear into meaningful terms. People often ask actors how they learn "all those lines." They do it by first coming to understand the flow of meaning, report psychologist-actor team Helga Noice and Tony Noice (2006). "One actor divided a half-page of dialogue into three [intentions]: 'to flatter,' 'to draw him out,' and 'to allay his fears.'" With this meaningful sequence in mind, the actor more easily remembers the lines.

From his experiments on himself, Ebbinghaus estimated that, compared with learning nonsense material, learning meaningful material required one-tenth the effort. As memory researcher Wayne Wickelgren (1977, p. 346) noted, "The time you spend thinking about material you are reading and relating it to previously stored material is about the most useful thing you can do in learning any new subject matter." *The point to remember:* The amount remembered depends both on the time spent learning and on your making it meaningful.

We have especially good recall for information we can meaningfully relate to ourselves. Asked how well certain adjectives describe someone else, we often forget them; asked how well the adjectives describe us, we—especially those from individualistic Western cultures—remember the words well. This phenomenon is called the *self-reference effect* (Symons & Johnson, 1997; Wagar & Cohen, 2003). So, you will profit from taking time to find personal meaning in what you are studying. Information deemed "relevant to me" is processed more deeply and remains more accessible.

Visual Encoding

Why is it that we struggle to remember formulas, definitions, and dates, yet we can easily remember where we were yesterday, who was with us, where we sat, and what we wore? One difference is the greater ease of remembering mental pictures. Our earliest memories—probably of something that happened at age 3 or 4—involve visual **imagery.** We more easily remember concrete words, which lend themselves to visual mental images, than we do abstract, low-imagery words. (When I quiz you later, which three of these words—*typewriter, void, cigarette, inherent, fire, process*—will you most likely recall?) If you still recall the rock-throwing rioter sentence, it is probably not only because of the meaning you encoded but also because the sentence lent itself to a visual image. Memory for concrete nouns, such as "cigarette," is aided by encoding them *both* semantically and visually (Marschark et al., 1987; Paivio, 1986). Two codes are better than one.

Thanks to this durability of vivid images, our memory of an experience is often colored by its best or worst moment—the best moment of pleasure or joy, and the worst moment of pain or frustration (Fredrickson & Kahneman, 1993). Recalling the high points while forgetting the mundane may explain the phenomenon of *rosy retrospection* (Mitchell et al., 1997): People tend to recall events such as a camping holiday more positively than they judged them at the time. The muggy heat and long lines of that visit to Disney World fade in the glow of vivid surroundings, food, and rides.

Imagery is at the heart of many **mnemonic** (nih-MON-ik) devices (so named after the Greek word for "memory"). Ancient Greek scholars and orators developed mnemonics to help them retrieve lengthy memorized passages and speeches. Some modern mnemonic devices rely on both acoustic and visual codes. For example, the *peg-word system* requires you to memorize a jingle: *"One is a bun; two is a shoe; three is a tree; four is a door; five is a hive; six is sticks; seven is heaven; eight is a gate; nine is swine; ten is a hen."* Without much effort, you will soon be able to count by peg-words instead of numbers: *bun, shoe, tree* . . . and then to visually associate the peg-words with to-be-remembered items. Now you are ready to challenge anyone to give you a grocery list to remember. Carrots? Stick them into the imaginary bun. Milk? Fill the shoe with it. Paper towels? Drape them over the tree branch. Think *bun, shoe, tree* and you see their associated images: carrots, milk, paper towels. With few errors (Bugelski et al., 1968), you will be able to recall the items in any order and to name any given item. Memory whizzes understand the power of such systems. A study of star performers in the World Memory Championships showed them not to have exceptional intelligence, but rather to be superior at using spatial mnemonic strategies (Maguire et al., 2003).

Organizing Information for Encoding

Mnemonic devices can also help organize material for our later retrieval. When Bransford and Johnson's laundry paragraph became meaningful, we could mentally organize its sentences into a sequence. We process information more easily when we can organize it into meaningful units or structures.

Chunking

Glance for a few seconds at row 1 of **FIGURE 27.6**, then look away and try to reproduce what you saw. Impossible, yes? But you can easily reproduce the second row, which is no less complex. Similarly, you will probably find row 4 much easier to remember than row 3, although both contain the same letters. And you could remember the sixth cluster more easily than the fifth, although both contain the same words.

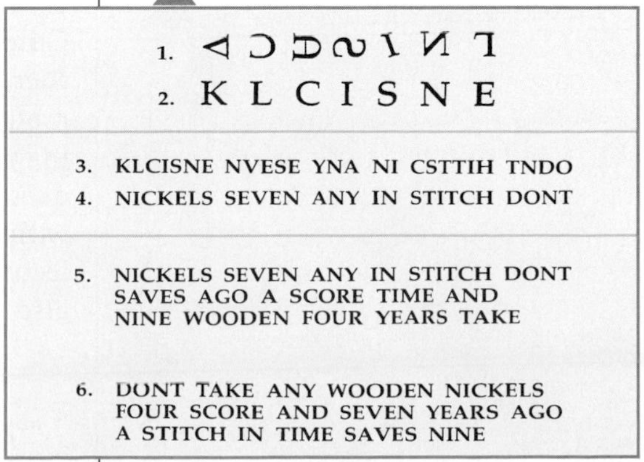

As these units demonstrate, we more easily recall information when we can organize it into familiar, manageable chunks. **Chunking** occurs so naturally that we take it for granted. If you are a native English speaker, you can reproduce perfectly the 150 or so line segments that make up the words in the three phrases of item 6 in Figure 27.6. It would astonish someone unfamiliar with the language.

I am similarly awed at the ability of someone literate in Chinese to glance at **FIGURE 27.7** and then to reproduce all of the strokes; or of a chess master

imagery mental pictures; a powerful aid to effortful processing, especially when combined with semantic encoding.

mnemonics [nih-MON-iks] memory aids, especially those techniques that use vivid imagery and organizational devices.

chunking organizing items into familiar, manageable units; often occurs automatically.

FIGURE 27.6 Effects of chunking on memory When we organize information into meaningful units, such as letters, words, and phrases, we recall it more easily. (From Hintzman, 1978.)

1. ◁ ⊃ ⊋ ⊌ ⋏ ⋈ ⊥
2. K L C I S N E
3. KLCISNE NVESE YNA NI CSTTIH TNDO
4. NICKELS SEVEN ANY IN STITCH DONT
5. NICKELS SEVEN ANY IN STITCH DONT SAVES AGO A SCORE TIME AND NINE WOODEN FOUR YEARS TAKE
6. **DONT TAKE ANY WOODEN NICKELS FOUR SCORE AND SEVEN YEARS AGO A STITCH IN TIME SAVES NINE**

|| In the discussion of encoding imagery, I gave you six words and told you I would quiz you about them later. How many of these words can you now recall? Of these, how many are high-imagery words? How many are low-imagery? (You can check your list against the six inverted words below.) ||

Typewriter, void, cigarette, inherent, fire, process

FIGURE 27.8 Organization benefits memory When we organize words or concepts into hierarchical groups, as illustrated here with concepts in this module, we remember them better than when we see them presented randomly.

who, after a 5-second look at the board during a game, can recall the exact positions of most of the pieces (Chase & Simon, 1973); or of a varsity basketball player who, given a 4-second glance at a basketball play, can recall the positions of the players (Allard & Burnett, 1985). We all remember information best when we can organize it into personally meaningful arrangements.

Chunking can also be used as a mnemonic technique to recall unfamiliar material. Want to remember the colors of the rainbow in order of wavelength? Think of the mnemonic ROY G. BIV (*red*, *orange*, *yellow*, *green*, *blue*, *indigo*, *violet*). Need to recall the names of North America's five Great Lakes? Just remember HOMES (*H*uron, *O*ntario, *M*ichigan, *E*rie, *S*uperior). In each case, we chunk information into a more familiar form by creating a word (called an *acronym*) from the first letters of the to-be-remembered items.

Hierarchies

When people develop expertise in an area, they process information not only in chunks but also in *hierarchies* composed of a few broad concepts divided and subdivided into narrower concepts and facts. This module, for example, aims not only to teach you the elementary facts of memory but also to help you organize these facts around broad principles, such as *encoding;* subprinciples, such as *automatic* and *effortful processing;* and still more specific concepts, such as *meaning, imagery,* and *organization* (**FIGURE 27.8**).

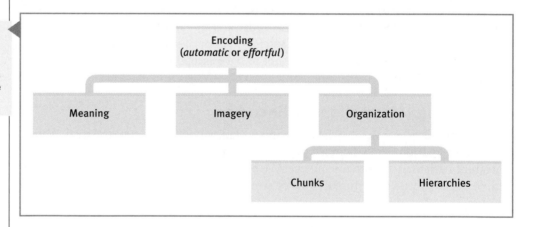

Organizing knowledge in hierarchies helps us retrieve information efficiently. Gordon Bower and his colleagues (1969) demonstrated this by presenting words either randomly or grouped into categories. When the words were organized into groups, recall was two to three times better. Such results show the benefits of organizing what you study—of paying special attention to module outlines, headings, preview questions, summaries, and self-test questions. If you can master a module's concepts within their overall organization, your recall should be effective at test time. Taking lecture and text notes in outline format—a type of hierarchical organization—may also prove helpful.

REVIEW

Encoding: Getting Information In

27-1 **What information do we encode automatically? What information do we encode effortfully, and how does the distribution of practice influence retention?** *Automatic processing* happens unconsciously, as we absorb information (space, time, frequency, well-learned material) in our environment. *Effortful processing* (of meaning, *imagery*, organization) requires conscious attention and deliberate effort. The *spacing effect* is our tendency to retain information more easily if we practice it repeatedly (spaced study) than if we practice it in one long session (massed practice, or cramming). The *serial position effect* is our tendency to recall the first item (the primacy effect) and the last item (the recency effect) in a long list more easily than we recall the intervening items.

27-2 **What effortful processing methods aid in forming memories?** *Visual encoding* (of images) and *acoustic encoding* (of sounds) engage shallower processing than *semantic encoding* (of meaning). We process verbal information best when we make it relevant to ourselves (the self-reference effect). Encoding imagery, as when using some *mnemonic* devices, also supports memory, because vivid images are memorable. *Chunking* and hierarchies help organize information for easier retrieval.

Terms and Concepts to Remember

automatic processing, p. 327

effortful processing, p. 328

rehearsal, p. 328

spacing effect, p. 329

serial position effect, p. 330

visual encoding, p. 331

acoustic encoding, p. 331

semantic encoding, p. 331

imagery, p. 332

mnemonics [nih-MON-iks], p. 333

chunking, p. 333

Test Yourself

1. What would be the most effective strategy to learn and retain a list of names of key historical figures for a week? For a year?

(Answers to the Test Yourself questions can be found in Appendix B at the end of the book.)

Ask Yourself

1. Can you think of three ways to employ the principles in this module to improve your own learning and retention of important ideas?

∞ WEB

Multiple-choice self-tests and more may be found at www.worthpublishers.com/myers

Sensory Memory

Working/Short-Term Memory

Long-Term Memory

Storing Memories in the Brain

MODULE 28

Storage: Retaining Information

At the heart of memory is storage. If you later recall something you experienced, you must, somehow, have stored and retrieved it. Anything stored in long-term memory lies dormant, waiting to be reconstructed by a cue. What is our memory storage capacity? Let's start with the first memory store noted in the *three-stage processing model* outlined in **FIGURE 28.1** (Atkinson & Shiffrin, 1968)—our fleeting *sensory memory.*

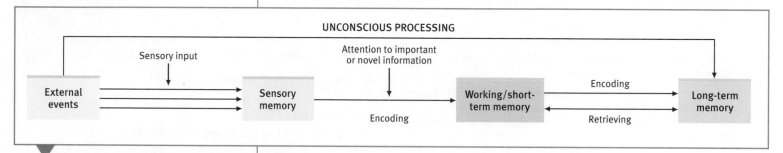

FIGURE 28.1 A modified three-stage processing model of memory Here we will focus on the storage aspects of our memory processing: sensory memory, working/short-term memory, and long-term memory.

▶|| Sensory Memory

28-1 What is sensory memory?

How much of this page could you sense and recall with less exposure than a lightning flash? Researcher George Sperling (1960) asked people to do something similar when he showed them, for only one-twentieth of a second, three rows of three letters each (**FIGURE 28.2**). After the nine letters disappeared, people could recall only about half of them.

Was it because they had insufficient time to glimpse them? No, Sperling cleverly demonstrated that people actually *could* see and recall all the letters, but only momentarily. Rather than ask them to recall all nine letters at once, Sperling sounded a high, medium, or low tone immediately *after* flashing the nine letters. This cue directed participants to report only the letters of the top, middle, or bottom row, respectively. Now they rarely missed a letter, showing that all nine letters were momentarily available for recall.

Sperling's experiment revealed that we have a fleeting photographic memory called **iconic memory.** For a few tenths of a second, our eyes register an exact representation

FIGURE 28.2 Momentary photographic memory When George Sperling flashed a group of letters similar to this for one-twentieth of a second, people could recall only about half the letters. But when signaled to recall a particular row immediately after the letters had disappeared, they could do so with near-perfect accuracy.

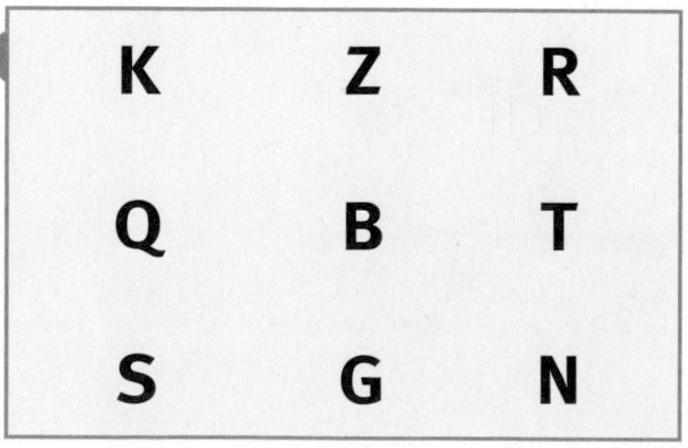

K   Z   R

Q   B   T

S   G   N

of a scene and we can recall any part of it in amazing detail. But if Sperling delayed the tone signal by more than half a second, the image faded and participants again recalled only about half the letters. Our visual screen clears quickly, as new images are superimposed over old ones.

We also have an impeccable, though fleeting, memory for auditory stimuli, called **echoic memory** (Cowan, 1988; Lu et al., 1992). Picture yourself in conversation, as your attention veers to the TV. If your mildly irked companion tests your attention by asking, "What did I just say?" you can recover the last few words from your mind's echo chamber. Auditory echoes tend to linger for 3 or 4 seconds. Experiments on echoic and iconic memory have helped us understand the initial recording of sensory information in the memory system.

▶‖ Working/Short-Term Memory

28-2   What are the duration and capacity of short-term and of long-term memory?

Among the vast amounts of information registered by our sensory memory, we illuminate some with our attentional flashlight. We also retrieve information from long-term storage for "on-screen" display. But unless our working memory meaningfully encodes or rehearses that information, it quickly disappears from our short-term store. During your finger's trip from phone book to phone, a telephone number may evaporate.

To find out how quickly a short-term memory will disappear, Lloyd Peterson and Margaret Peterson (1959) asked people to remember three-consonant groups, such as *CHJ*. To prevent rehearsal, the researchers asked them, for example, to start at 100 and count aloud backward by threes. After 3 seconds, people recalled the letters only about half the time; after 12 seconds, they seldom recalled them at all (**FIGURE 28.3**). Without active processing, short-term memories have a limited life.

Short-term memory is limited not only in duration but also in capacity, typically storing about seven bits of information (give or take two). George Miller (1956) enshrined this recall capacity as the *Magical Number Seven, plus or minus two*. Not surprisingly, when some phone companies began requiring all callers to dial a

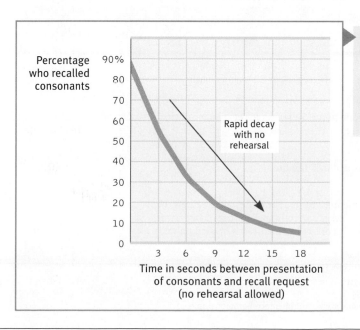

Percentage who recalled consonants

Time in seconds between presentation of consonants and recall request (no rehearsal allowed)

Rapid decay with no rehearsal

> **FIGURE 28.3 Short-term memory decay** Unless rehearsed, verbal information may be quickly forgotten. (From Peterson & Peterson, 1959; see also Brown, 1958.)

iconic memory   a <u>momentary</u> sensory memory of <u>visual</u> stimuli; a photographic or picture-image memory lasting no more than a <u>few tenths of a second</u>.

echoic memory   a <u>momentary</u> sensory memory of <u>auditory</u> stimuli; if attention is elsewhere, sounds and words can still be recalled <u>within 3 or 4 seconds</u>.

7 ±2

‖ The Magical Number Seven has become psychology's contribution to an intriguing list of magic sevens—the seven wonders of the world, the seven seas, the seven deadly sins, the seven primary colors, the seven musical scale notes, the seven days of the week—seven magical sevens. ‖

three-digit area code in addition to a seven-digit number, many people reported trouble retaining the just-looked-up number.

Our short-term recall is slightly better for random digits (as in a phone number) than for random letters, which may have similar sounds. It is slightly better for what we hear than for what we see. Both children and adults have short-term recall for roughly as many words as they can speak in 2 seconds (Cowan, 1994; Hulme & Tordoff, 1989). Compared with spoken English words, signs in American Sign Language take longer to articulate. And sure enough, short-term memory can hold fewer signs than spoken words (Wilson & Emmorey, 2006).

Without rehearsal, most of us actually retain in short-term memory only about four information chunks (for example, letters meaningfully grouped as BBC, FBI, KGB, CIA) (Cowan, 2001; Jonides et al., 2008). Suppressing rehearsal by saying *the, the, the* while hearing random digits also reduces memory to about four items. The basic principle: *At any given moment, we can consciously process only a very limited amount of information.*

▶‖ Long-Term Memory

In Arthur Conan Doyle's *A Study in Scarlet,* Sherlock Holmes offers a popular theory of memory capacity:

> I consider that a man's brain originally is like a little empty attic, and you have to stock it with such furniture as you choose. . . . It is a mistake to think that that little room has elastic walls and can distend to any extent. Depend upon it, there comes a time when for every addition of knowledge you forget something that you knew before.

Contrary to Holmes' belief, our capacity for storing long-term memories is essentially limitless. Our brains are *not* like attics, which once filled can store more items only if we discard old ones.

The point is vividly illustrated by those who have performed phenomenal memory feats (**TABLE 28.1**). Consider the 1990s tests of psychologist Rajan Mahadevan's memory.

Clark's nutcracker Among animals, one contender for champion memorist would be a mere birdbrain—the Clark's Nutcracker—which during winter and early spring can locate up to 6000 caches of pine seeds it had previously buried (Shettleworth, 1993).

TABLE 28.1 World Memory Championship Records

From world memory competitions, here are some current records, as of 2008:	
Contest/Description	**Record**
Speed cards Shortest time to memorize a shuffled pack of 52 playing cards	26 seconds
One-hour cards Most cards memorized in one hour (52 points for every pack correct; 26 points if 1 mistake)	1404 points
Speed numbers Most random digits memorized in 5 minutes	396 digits
Names and faces Most first and last names memorized in 15 minutes after being shown cards with faces (1 point for every correctly spelled first or last name; ½ point for every phonetically correct but incorrectly spelled name)	181 points
Binary digits Most binary digits (101101, etc.) memorized in 30 minutes when presented in rows of 30 digits	4140 digits

Sources: www.usamemoriad.com and www.worldmemorychampionship.com

Given a block of 10 digits from the first 30,000 or so digits of pi, Rajan, after a few moments of mental searching for the string, would pick up the series from there, firing numbers like a machine gun (Delaney et al., 1999; Thompson et al., 1993). He could also repeat 50 random digits—backward. It is not a genetic gift, he said; anyone could learn to do it. But given the genetic influence on so many human traits, and knowing that Rajan's father memorized Shakespeare's complete works, one wonders. We are reminded that many psychological phenomena, including memory capacity, can be studied by means of different levels of analysis, including the biological.

‖ Pi in the sky: In 2006, Japan's Akira Haraguchi reportedly recited the first 100,000 digits of pi, topping the world record by over 30,000 digits (Associated Press, 2006). ‖

▶‖ Storing Memories in the Brain

28-3   How does the brain store our memories?

I marveled at my aging mother-in-law, a retired pianist and organist. At age 88 her blind eyes could no longer read music. But let her sit at a keyboard and she would flawlessly play any of hundreds of hymns, including ones she had not thought of for 20 years. Where did her brain store those thousands of sequenced notes?

For a time, some surgeons and memory researchers believed that flashbacks triggered by brain stimulation during surgery indicated that our whole past, not just well-practiced music, is "in there," in complete detail, just waiting to be relived. But when Elizabeth Loftus and Geoffrey Loftus (1980) analyzed the vivid "memories" triggered by brain stimulation, they found that the seeming flashbacks appeared to have been invented, not relived. Psychologist Karl Lashley (1950) further demonstrated that memories do not reside in single, specific spots. He trained rats to find their way out of a maze, then cut out pieces of their cortexes and retested their memory. Amazingly, no matter which small brain section he removed, the rats retained at least a partial memory of how to navigate the maze. So, despite the brain's vast storage capacity, we do not store information as libraries store their books, in discrete, precise locations.

Synaptic Changes

Looking for clues to the brain's storage system, contemporary memory researchers have searched for a *memory trace.* Although the brain represents a memory in distributed groups of neurons, those nerve cells must communicate through their synapses (Tsien, 2007). Thus, the quest to understand the physical basis of memory—for how information becomes incarnated in matter—has sparked study of the synaptic meeting places where neurons communicate with one another via their neurotransmitter messengers.

We know that experience does modify the brain's neural networks; given increased activity in a particular pathway, neural interconnections form or strengthen. Eric Kandel and James Schwartz (1982) observed such changes in the sending neurons of a simple animal, the California sea slug, *Aplysia.* Its mere 20,000 or so nerve cells are unusually large and accessible, enabling the researchers to observe synaptic changes during learning. The sea slug can be classically conditioned (with electric shock) to reflexively withdraw its gills when squirted with water, much as a shell-shocked soldier jumps at the sound of a snapping twig. By observing the slug's neural connections before and after conditioning, Kandel and Schwartz pinpointed changes. When learning occurs, the slug releases more of the neurotransmitter *serotonin* at certain synapses. These synapses then become more efficient at transmitting signals.

Increased synaptic efficiency makes for more efficient neural circuits. In experiments, rapidly stimulating certain memory-circuit connections has increased their sensitivity for hours or even weeks to come. The sending neuron now needs less prompting to release its neurotransmitter, and the receiving neuron's receptor sites

Aplysia The California sea slug, which neuroscientist Eric Kandel studied for 45 years, has increased our understanding of the neural basis of learning.

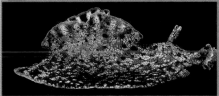

Jeff Rotman

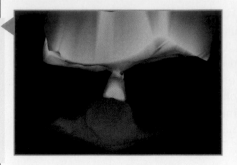
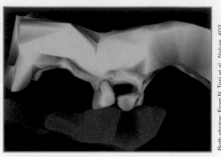

Both photos: From N. Toni et al., *Nature, 402,* Nov. 25, 1999. Courtesy of Dominique Muller

FIGURE 28.4 Doubled receptor sites
Electron microscope images show just one receptor site (gray) reaching toward a sending neuron before long-term potentiation (left) and two sites after LTP (right). A doubling of the receptor sites means that the receiving neuron has increased sensitivity for detecting the presence of the neurotransmitter molecules that may be released by the sending neuron. (From Toni et al., 1999.)

"The biology of the mind will be as scientifically important to this [new] century as the biology of the gene [was] to the twentieth century."

Eric Kandel, acceptance remarks for the 2000 Nobel prize

may increase (**FIGURE 28.4**). This prolonged strengthening of potential neural firing, called **long-term potentiation (LTP),** provides a neural basis for learning and remembering associations (Lynch, 2002; Whitlock et al., 2006). Several lines of evidence confirm that LTP is a physical basis for memory:

▶ Drugs that block LTP interfere with learning (Lynch & Staubli, 1991).
▶ Mutant mice engineered to lack an enzyme needed for LTP can't learn their way out of a maze (Silva et al., 1992).
▶ Rats given a drug that enhances LTP will learn a maze with half the usual number of mistakes (Service, 1994).
▶ Injecting rats with a chemical that blocks the preservation of LTP erases recent learning (Pastalkova et al., 2006).

Some memory-biology explorers have helped found pharmaceutical companies that are competing to develop and test memory-boosting drugs. Their target market includes millions of people with Alzheimer's disease, millions more with *mild cognitive impairment* that often becomes Alzheimer's, and countless millions who would love to turn back the clock on age-related memory decline. From expanding memories perhaps will come bulging profits.

One approach is developing drugs that boost production of the protein CREB, which can switch genes off or on. Genes code the production of protein molecules. With repeated neural firing, a nerve cell's genes produce synapse-strengthening proteins, enabling LTP (Fields, 2005). Boosting CREB production might lead to increased production of proteins that help reshape synapses and consolidate a short-term memory into a long-term memory. Sea slugs, mice, and fruit flies with enhanced CREB production have displayed enhanced memories.

Another approach is developing drugs that boost *glutamate,* a neurotransmitter that enhances synaptic communication (LTP). It remains to be seen whether such drugs can boost memory without nasty side effects and without cluttering our minds with trivia best forgotten. In the meantime, one effective, safe, and free memory enhancer is already available on college campuses: study followed by adequate sleep!

After long-term potentiation has occurred, passing an electric current through the brain won't disrupt old memories. But the current will wipe out very recent memories. Such is the experience both of laboratory animals and of depressed people given electroconvulsive therapy (ECT). A blow to the head can do the same. Football players and boxers momentarily knocked unconscious typically have no memory of events just before the knock-out (Yarnell & Lynch, 1970). Their working memory had no time to consolidate the information into long-term memory before the lights went out.

|| Although ECT for depression disrupts memory for recent experiences, it leaves most memories intact. ||

Stress Hormones and Memory

Researchers interested in the biology of the mind have also looked closely at the influence of emotions and stress hormones on memory. When we are excited or stressed, emotion-triggered stress hormones make more glucose energy available to fuel brain

Severe stress sears in memories Significantly stressful events, such as the disastrous 2007 California wildfires, may be an indelible part of the memories of those who experienced them.

Spencer Platt/Getty Images

long-term potentiation (LTP) an increase in a synapse's firing potential after brief, rapid stimulation. Believed to be a neural basis for learning and memory.

flashbulb memory a clear memory of an emotionally significant moment or event.

activity, signaling the brain that something important has happened. Moreover, the *amygdala,* two emotion-processing clusters in the limbic system, boosts activity and available proteins in the brain's memory-forming areas (Buchanan, 2007; Kensinger, 2007). The result? Arousal can sear certain events into the brain, while disrupting memory for neutral events around the same time (Birnbaum et al., 2004; Brewin et al., 2007).

"Stronger emotional experiences make for stronger, more reliable memories," says James McGaugh (1994, 2003). After traumatic experiences—a wartime ambush, a house fire, a rape—vivid recollections of the horrific event may intrude again and again. It is as if they were burned in. This makes adaptive sense. Memory serves to predict the future and to alert us to potential dangers.

Conversely, weaker emotion means weaker memories. People given a drug that blocks the effects of stress hormones will later have more trouble remembering the details of an upsetting story (Cahill, 1994). That connection is appreciated by those working to develop drugs that, when taken after a traumatic experience, might blunt intrusive memories. In one experiment, victims of car accidents, rapes, and other traumas received either one such drug, propranolol, or a placebo for 10 days following their horrific event. When tested three months later, half the placebo group but none of the drug-treated group showed signs of stress disorder (Pitman et al., 2002, 2005).

Emotion-triggered hormonal changes help explain why we long remember exciting or shocking events, such as our first kiss or our whereabouts when learning of a friend's death. In a 2006 Pew survey, 95 percent of American adults said they could recall exactly where they were or what they were doing when they first heard the news of the attack on 9/11. This perceived clarity of memories of surprising, significant events leads some psychologists to call them **flashbulb memories.** It's as if the brain commands, "Capture this!" The people who experienced a 1989 San Francisco earthquake did just that. A year and a half later, they had perfect recall of where they had been and what they were doing (verified by their recorded thoughts within a day or two of the quake). Others' memories for the circumstances under which they merely *heard* about the quake were more prone to errors (Neisser et al., 1991; Palmer et al., 1991). Flashbulb memories that people relive, rehearse, and discuss may also come to err (Talarico et al., 2003). Although our flashbulb memories are noteworthy for their vividness and the confidence with which we recall them, misinformation can seep into them (Talarico & Rubin, 2007).

There are other limits to stress-enhanced remembering. When *prolonged*—as in sustained abuse or combat—stress can act like acid, corroding neural connections and shrinking the brain area (the hippocampus) that is vital for laying down memories.

|| If you suffered a traumatic experience, would you want to take a drug to blunt that memory? ||

|| Which is more important—your experiences or your memories of them? ||

Moreover, when sudden stress hormones are flowing, older memories may be blocked. It is true for stressed rats trying to find their way to a hidden target (de Quervain et al., 1998). And it is true for those of us whose mind has gone blank while speaking in public.

Storing Implicit and Explicit Memories

A memory-to-be enters the cortex through the senses, then wends its way into the brain's depths. Precisely where it goes depends on the type of information, as dramatically illustrated by those who, as in the case of my father mentioned earlier, suffer from a type of **amnesia** in which they are unable to form new memories.

The most famous case, a patient known to every neuroscientist as H. M., experienced in 1953 the necessary surgical removal of a brain area involved in laying new conscious memories of facts and experiences. The brain tissue loss left his older memories intact. But converting new experiences to long-term storage was another matter. For example, over practice sessions H. M. became skilled at what is for anyone an initially difficult task: tracing the mirrored outline of a star. Yet, having no memory for doing the task he remarked to researcher Brenda Milner, after many practice trials, that "this was easier than I thought it would be" (Carey, 2009). "I've known H. M. since 1962, and he still doesn't know who I am," noted his longtime researcher Suzanne Corkin (Adelson, 2005).

Neurologist Oliver Sacks (1985, pp. 26–27) described another such patient, Jimmie, who had brain damage. Jimmie had no memories—thus, no sense of elapsed time—beyond his injury in 1945. Asked in 1975 to name the U.S. President, he replied, "FDR's dead. Truman's at the helm."

When Jimmie gave his age as 19, Sacks set a mirror before him: "Look in the mirror and tell me what you see. Is that a 19-year-old looking out from the mirror?"

Jimmie turned ashen, gripped the chair, cursed, then became frantic: "What's going on? What's happened to me? Is this a nightmare? Am I crazy? Is this a joke?" When his attention was diverted to some children playing baseball, his panic ended, the dreadful mirror forgotten.

Sacks showed Jimmie a photo from *National Geographic*. "What is this?" he asked. "It's the Moon," Jimmie replied.

"No, it's not," Sacks answered. "It's a picture of the Earth taken from the Moon."

"Doc, you're kidding? Someone would've had to get a camera up there!"

"Naturally."

"Hell! You're joking—how the hell would you do that?" Jimmie's wonder was that of a bright young man from 60 years ago reacting with amazement to his travel back to the future.

Careful testing of these unique people reveals something even stranger: Although incapable of recalling new facts or anything they have done recently, Jimmie and others with similar conditions can learn. Shown hard-to-find figures in pictures (in the *Where's Waldo?* series), they can quickly spot them again later. They can find their way to the bathroom, though without being able to tell you where it is. They can learn to read mirror-image writing or do a jigsaw puzzle, and they

amnesia the loss of memory.

implicit memory retention independent of conscious recollection. (Also called *nondeclarative memory*.)

explicit memory memory of facts and experiences that one can consciously know and "declare." (Also called *declarative memory*.)

hippocampus a neural center that is located in the limbic system; helps process explicit memories for storage.

"The most important patient in the history of brain science." So said the *New York Times* of H. M., revealed at his death in 2008 to be Henry Molaison. H. M. died at age 82 in a Connecticut nursing home.

http://www.nytimes.com/2008/12/05/us/05hm.html.

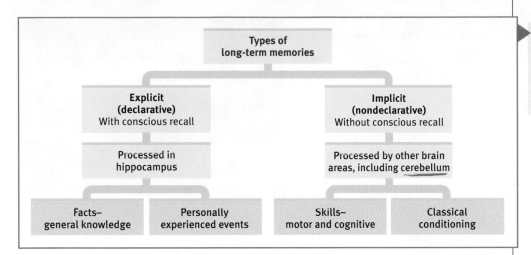

FIGURE 28.5 **Memory subsystems**
We process and store our explicit and implicit memories separately. Thus, one may lose explicit memory (becoming amnesic), yet display implicit memory for material one cannot consciously recall.

have even been taught complicated job skills (Schacter, 1992, 1996; Xu & Corkin, 2001). And they can be classically conditioned. However, *they do all these things with no awareness of having learned them.*

These amnesia victims are in some ways like people with brain damage who cannot consciously recognize faces but whose physiological responses to familiar faces reveal an implicit (unconscious) recognition. Their behaviors challenge the idea that memory is a single, unified, conscious system. Instead, we seem to have two memory systems operating in tandem (**FIGURE 28.6**). Whatever has destroyed *conscious* recall in these individuals with amnesia has not destroyed their *unconscious* capacity for learning. They can learn *how* to do something—called **implicit memory** *(nondeclarative memory)*. But they may not know and declare that they know—called **explicit memory** *(declarative memory)*.

Having read a story once, they will read it faster a second time, showing implicit memory. But there will be no explicit memory, for they cannot recall having seen the story before. If repeatedly shown the word *perfume,* they will not recall having seen it. But if asked the first word that comes to mind in response to the letters *per,* they say *perfume,* readily displaying their learning. Using such tasks, even Alzheimer's patients, whose explicit memories for people and events are lost, display an ability to form new implicit memories (Lustig & Buckner, 2004).

The Hippocampus

These remarkable stories provoke us to wonder: Do our explicit and implicit memory systems involve separate brain regions? Brain scans, such as PET scans of people recalling words (Squire, 1992), and autopsies of people who had amnesia, reveal that new explicit memories of names, images, and events are laid down via the **hippocampus,** a temporal lobe neural center that also forms part of the brain's limbic system (**FIGURE 28.6** on the next page; Anderson et al., 2007).

Damage to the hippocampus therefore disrupts some types of memory. Chickadees and other birds can store food in hundreds of places and return to these unmarked caches months later, but not if their hippocampus has been removed (Kamil & Cheng, 2001; Sherry & Vaccarino, 1989). Like the cortex, the hippocampus is lateralized. (You have two of them, one just above each ear and about an inch and a half straight in.) Damage to one or the other seems to produce different results. With left-hippocampus damage, people have trouble remembering verbal information, but they have no trouble recalling visual designs and locations. With right-hippocampus damage, the problem is reversed (Schacter, 1996).

off the mark.com   by Mark Parisi

THE BAD NEWS IS WE LEFT A CLAMP IN YOUR TEMPORAL LOBE... THE GOOD NEWS IS THAT YOU WON'T REMEMBER WHAT I JUST SAID...

offthemark.com

|| The two-track memory system reinforces an important principle of the way the brain handles information via parallel processing: Mental feats such as vision, thinking, and memory may seem to be single abilities, but they are not. Rather, we split information into different components for separate and simultaneous processing. ||

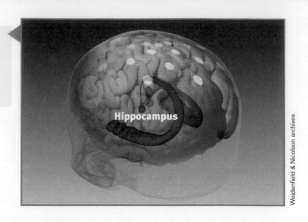

FIGURE 28.6 The hippocampus Explicit memories for facts and episodes are processed in the hippocampus and fed to other brain regions for storage.

Hippocampus

Weidenfield & Nicolson archives

New research also pinpoints the functions of subregions of the hippocampus. One part is active as people learn to associate names with faces (Zeineh et al., 2003). Another part is active as memory whizzes engage in spatial mnemonics (Maguire et al., 2003b). The rear area, which processes spatial memory, also grows bigger the longer a London cabbie has been navigating the maze of city streets (Maguire et al., 2003a).

The hippocampus is active during slow-wave sleep, as memories are processed and filed for later retrieval. The greater the hippocampus activity during sleep after a training experience, the better the next day's memory (Peigneux et al., 2004). But those memories are not permanently stored in the hippocampus. Instead, it seems to act as a loading dock where the brain registers and temporarily holds the elements of a remembered episode—its smell, feel, sound, and location. Then, like older files shifted to a basement storeroom, memories migrate for storage elsewhere. Removing the hippocampus 3 hours after rats learn the location of some tasty new food disrupts this process and prevents long-term memory formation; removal 48 hours later does not (Tse et al., 2007). Sleep supports this memory consolidation. During sleep, our hippocampus and brain cortex display simultaneous activity rhythms, as if they were having a dialogue (Euston et al., 2007; Mehta, 2007). Researchers suspect that the brain is replaying the day's experiences as it transfers them to the cortex for long-term storage.

Once stored, our mental encores of these past experiences activate various parts of the frontal and temporal lobes (Fink et al., 1996; Gabrieli et al., 1996; Markowitsch, 1995). Recalling a telephone number and holding it in working memory, for example, would activate a region of the left frontal cortex; calling up a party scene would more likely activate a region of the right hemisphere.

The Cerebellum

Although your hippocampus is a temporary processing site for your *explicit* memories, you could lose it and still lay down memories for skills and conditioned associations. Joseph LeDoux (1996) recounts the story of a brain-damaged patient whose amnesia left her unable to recognize her physician as, each day, he shook her hand and introduced himself. One day, after reaching for his hand, she yanked hers back, for the physician had pricked her with a tack in his palm. The next time he returned to introduce himself she refused to shake his hand but couldn't explain why. Having been classically conditioned, she just wouldn't do it.

The *cerebellum,* the brain region extending out from the rear of the brainstem, plays a key role in forming and storing the implicit memories created by classical conditioning. With a damaged cerebellum, people cannot develop certain conditioned reflexes, such as associating a tone with an impending puff of air—and thus do not blink in anticipation of the puff (Daum & Schugens, 1996; Green & Woodruff-Pak,

2000). By methodically disrupting the function of different pathways in the cortex and cerebellum of rabbits, researchers have shown that rabbits also fail to learn a conditioned eyeblink response when the cerebellum is temporarily deactivated (Krupa et al., 1993; Steinmetz, 1999). Implicit memory formation needs the cerebellum.

Our dual explicit-implicit memory system helps explain *infantile amnesia:* The implicit reactions and skills we learned during infancy reach far into our future, yet as adults we recall nothing (explicitly) of our first three years. Children's explicit memories have a seeming half-life. In one study, events experienced and discussed with one's mother at age 3 were 60 percent remembered at age 7 but only 34 percent remembered at age 9 (Bauer et al., 2007). As adults, our conscious memory of our first three years is blank because we index so much of our explicit memory by words that nonspeaking children have not learned, but also because the hippocampus is one of the last brain structures to mature.

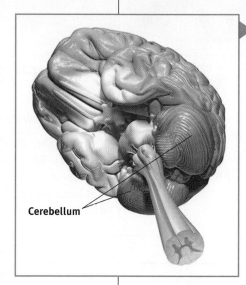

Cerebellum The cerebellum plays an important part in our forming and storing of implicit memories.

Cerebellum

REVIEW

Storage: Retaining Information

28-1 **What is sensory memory?** As information enters the memory system through our senses, we briefly register and store visual images via *iconic memory,* in which picture images last no more than a few tenths of a second. We register and store sounds via *echoic memory,* where echoes of auditory stimuli may linger as long as 3 or 4 seconds.

28-2 **What are the duration and capacity of short-term and of long-term memory?** At any given time, we can focus on and process only about seven items of information (either new or retrieved from our memory store). Without rehearsal, information disappears from short-term memory within seconds. Our capacity for storing information permanently in long-term memory is essentially unlimited.

28-3 **How does the brain store our memories?** Researchers are exploring memory-related changes within and between single neurons. *Long-term potentiation (LTP)* appears to be the neural basis of learning and memory. Stress triggers hormonal changes that arouse brain areas and can produce indelible memories. We are particularly likely to remember vivid events that form *flashbulb memories.* We have two memory systems. *Explicit (declarative) memories* of general knowledge, facts, and experiences are processed by the *hippocampus. Implicit (nondeclarative) memories* of skills and conditioned responses are processed by other parts of the brain, including the cerebellum.

Terms and Concepts to Remember

iconic memory, p. 336
echoic memory, p. 337
long-term potentiation (LTP),
  p. 340
flashbulb memory, p. 341

amnesia, p. 342
implicit memory, p. 343
explicit memory, p. 343
hippocampus, p. 343

Test Yourself

1. Your friend tells you that her father experienced brain damage in an accident. She wonders if psychology can explain why he can still play checkers very well but has a hard time holding a sensible conversation. What can you tell her?

(Answers to the Test Yourself questions can be found in Appendix B at the end of the book.)

Ask Yourself

1. Can you name an instance in which stress has helped you remember something, and another instance in which stress has interfered with remembering something?

∞ WEB

Multiple-choice self-tests and more may be found at www.worthpublishers.com/myers

MODULE 29

Retrieval: Getting Information Out

29-1 How do we get information out of memory?

To remember an event requires more than getting it in (encoding) and retaining it (storage). To most people, memory is **recall,** the ability to retrieve information not in conscious awareness. To a psychologist, memory is any sign that something learned has been retained. So **recognizing** or more quickly **relearning** information also indicates memory (**FIGURE 29.1**).

|| Later in this module, I'll ask you to recall this sentence: The fish attacked the swimmer. ||

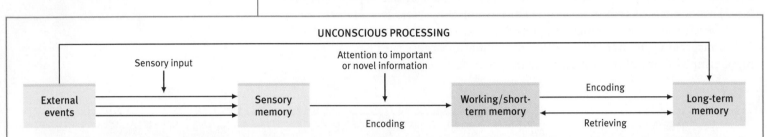

UNCONSCIOUS PROCESSING

Sensory input → Attention to important or novel information →

External events → Sensory memory → Working/short-term memory ⇄ Long-term memory

Encoding

Encoding · Retrieving

FIGURE 29.1 A modified three-stage processing model of memory Here we will focus on the retrieval aspects of our memory processing.

Long after you cannot recall most of the people in your high school graduating class, you may still be able to recognize their yearbook pictures from a photographic lineup and pick their names from a list of names. Harry Bahrick and his colleagues (1975) reported that people who had graduated 25 years earlier could not *recall* many of their old classmates, but they could *recognize* 90 percent of their pictures and names. If you are like most students, you, too, could likely recognize more names of the Seven Dwarfs than you could recall (Miserandino, 1991).

Our recognition memory is impressively quick and vast. "Is your friend wearing a new or old outfit?" "Old." "Is this five-second movie clip from a film you've ever seen?" "Yes." "Have you ever seen this person before—this minor variation on the same old human features (two eyes, one nose, and so on)?" "No." Before the mouth can form our answer to any of millions of such questions, the mind knows, and knows that it knows.

Our speed at relearning also reveals memory. If you once learned something and then forgot it, you probably will relearn it more quickly your second time around. When you study for a final exam or resurrect a language used in early childhood, the relearning is easier. Tests of recognition and of time spent relearning confirm the point: We remember more than we can recall.

recall a measure of memory in which the person must retrieve information learned earlier, as on a fill-in-the-blank test.

recognition a measure of memory in which the person need only identify items previously learned, as on a multiple-choice test.

relearning a measure of memory that assesses the amount of time saved when learning material for a second time.

Remembering things past Even if Oprah Winfrey and Brad Pitt had not become famous, their high school classmates would most likely still recognize their yearbook photos.

Both Photos: Spanky's Yearbook Archive

▶‖ Retrieval Cues

Imagine a spider suspended in the middle of her web, held up by the many strands extending outward from her in all directions to different points (perhaps a window sill, a tree branch, a leaf on a shrub). If you were to trace a pathway to the spider, you would first need to create a path from one of these anchor points and then follow the strand down into the web.

The process of retrieving a memory follows a similar principle, because memories are held in storage by a web of associations, each piece of information interconnected with others. When you encode into memory a target piece of information, such as the name of the person sitting next to you in class, you associate with it other bits of information about your surroundings, mood, seating position, and so on. These bits can serve as *retrieval cues,* anchor points you can use to access the target information when you want to retrieve it later. The more retrieval cues you have, the better your chances of finding a route to the suspended memory.

Mnemonic devices (memory aids that use vivid images or organizational devices) provide us with handy retrieval cues. But the best retrieval cues come from associations we form at the time we encode a memory. Tastes, smells, and sights often evoke our recall of associated episodes. To call up visual cues when trying to recall something, we may mentally place ourselves in the original context. After losing his sight, John Hull (1990, p. 174) described his difficulty recalling such details: "I knew I had been somewhere, and had done particular things with certain people, but where? I could not put the conversations . . . into a context. There was no background, no features against which to identify the place. Normally, the memories of people you have spoken to during the day are stored in frames which include the background."

The features Hull was mourning are the strands we activate to retrieve a specific memory from its web of associations. Philosopher-psychologist William James referred to this process, which we call **priming,** as the "wakening of associations." Often our associations are activated, or primed, without our awareness. As **FIGURE 29.2** indicates, seeing or hearing the word *rabbit* primes associations with *hare,* even though we may not recall having seen or heard *rabbit*.

Priming is often "memoryless memory"—invisible memory without explicit remembering. If, walking down a hallway, you see a poster of a missing child, you will then unconsciously be primed to interpret an ambiguous adult-child interaction as a

‖ Multiple-choice questions test our
a. recall.
b. recognition.
c. relearning.
Fill-in-the-blank questions test
our _____.
(Answers below.) ‖

Multiple-choice questions test recognition. Fill-in-the-blank questions test recall.

"Let me refresh your memory. It was the night before Christmas and all through the house not a creature was stirring until you landed a sled, drawn by reindeer, on the plaintiff's home, causing extensive damage to the roof and chimney."

‖ Ask a friend two rapid-fire questions: (a) How do you pronounce the word spelled by the letters *s-h-o-p*? (b) What do you do when you come to a green light? If your friend answers "stop" to the second question, you have demonstrated priming. ‖

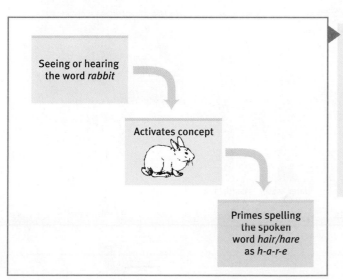

▶ **FIGURE 29.2**
Priming—awakening associations After seeing or hearing *rabbit,* we are later more likely to spell the spoken word as *h-a-r-e.* The spreading of associations unconsciously activates related associations. This phenomenon is called priming. (Adapted from Bower, 1986.)

Seeing or hearing the word *rabbit*

Activates concept

Primes spelling the spoken word *hair/hare* as *h-a-r-e*

priming   the activation, often unconsciously, of particular associations in memory.

déjà vu that eerie sense that "I've experienced this before." Cues from the current situation may subconsciously trigger retrieval of an earlier experience.

mood-congruent memory the tendency to recall experiences that are consistent with one's current good or bad mood.

possible kidnapping (James, 1986). Although you don't consciously remember the poster, it predisposes your interpretation. Meeting someone who reminds us of someone we've previously met can awaken our associated feelings about that earlier person, which may transfer into the new context (Andersen & Saribay, 2005; Lewicki, 1985). Even subliminal stimuli can briefly prime responses to later stimuli.

Context Effects

29-2 How do external contexts and internal emotions influence memory retrieval?

Putting yourself back in the context where you experienced something can prime your memory retrieval. Duncan Godden and Alan Baddeley (1975) discovered this when they had scuba divers listen to a list of words in two different settings, either 10 feet underwater or sitting on the beach. As **FIGURE 29.3** illustrates, the divers recalled more words when they were retested in the same place.

You may have experienced similar context effects. Consider this scenario: While taking notes from this book, you realize you need to sharpen your pencil. You get up and walk downstairs, but then you cannot remember why. After returning to your desk it hits you: "I wanted to sharpen this pencil!" What happens to create this frustrating experience? In one context (desk, reading psychology), you realize your pencil needs sharpening. When you go downstairs into a different context, you have few cues to lead you back to that thought. When you are once again at your desk, you are back in the context in which you encoded the thought "This pencil is dull."

In several experiments, Carolyn Rovee-Collier (1993) found that a familiar context can activate memories even in 3-month-olds. After infants learned that kicking a crib mobile would make it move (via a connecting ribbon from the ankle), the infants kicked more when tested again in the same crib with the same bumper than when in a different context.

Sometimes, being in a context similar to one we've been in before may trigger the experience of **déjà vu** (French for "already seen"). Two-thirds of us have experienced this fleeting, eerie sense that "I've been in this exact situation before," but it happens

FIGURE 29.3 The effects of context on memory Words heard underwater are best recalled underwater; words heard on land are best recalled on land. (Adapted from Godden & Baddeley, 1975.)

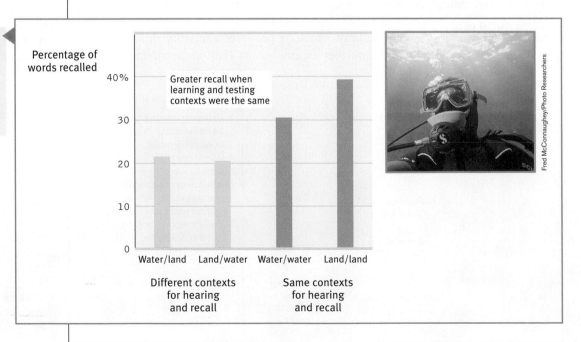

Percentage of words recalled

Greater recall when learning and testing contexts were the same

40%

30

20

10

0

| Water/land | Land/water | Water/water | Land/land |

Different contexts for hearing and recall — Same contexts for hearing and recall

Fred McConnaughey/Photo Researchers

most commonly to well-educated, imaginative young adults, especially when tired or stressed (Brown, 2003, 2004; McAneny, 1996). Some wonder, "How could I recognize a situation I'm experiencing for the first time?" Others may think of reincarnation ("I must have experienced this in a previous life") or precognition ("I viewed this scene in my mind before experiencing it").

Posing the question differently ("Why do I feel as though I recognize this situation?"), we can see how our memory system might produce déjà vu (Alcock, 1981). The current situation may be loaded with cues that unconsciously retrieve an earlier, similar experience. (We take in and retain vast amounts of information while hardly noticing and often forgetting where it came from.) Thus, if in a similar context you see a stranger who looks and walks like one of your friends, the similarity may give rise to an eerie feeling of recognition. Having awakened a shadow of that earlier experience, you may think, "I've seen that person in this situation before."

Or perhaps, suggests James Lampinen (2002), a situation seems familiar when moderately similar to several events. Imagine you briefly encounter my dad, my brothers, my sister, my children, and a few weeks later meet me. You might think, "I've been with this guy before." Although no one in my family looks or acts just like me (lucky them), their looks and gestures are somewhat like mine and I might form a "global match" to what you had experienced.

Yet another theory, among more than 50 proposed, attributes déjà vu to our dual processing. Recall that we assemble our perceptions from information processing that occurs simultaneously on multiple tracks. If there's a slight neural hiccup and one track's signal is delayed, perhaps it feels like a repeat of the earlier one, creating an illusion that we are now reexperiencing something (Brown, 2004b).

Moods and Memories

Associated words, events, and contexts are not the only retrieval cues. Events in the past may have aroused a specific *emotion* that later primes us to recall its associated events. Cognitive psychologist Gordon Bower (1983) explained it this way: "An emotion is like a library room into which we place memory records. We best retrieve those records by returning to that emotional room." What we learn in one state—be it drunk or sober—may be more easily recalled when we are again in that state, a subtle phenomenon called *state-dependent memory*. What people learn when drunk they don't recall well in *any* state (alcohol disrupts storage). But they recall it slightly better when again drunk. Someone who hides money when drunk may forget the location until drunk again.

Our mood states provide an example of memory's state dependence. Emotions that accompany good or bad events become retrieval cues (Fiedler et al., 2001). Thus, our memories are somewhat **mood-congruent.** If you've had a bad evening—your date never showed, your Toledo Mud Hens hat disappeared, your TV went out 10 minutes before the end of a mystery—your gloomy mood may facilitate recalling other bad times. Being depressed sours memories by priming negative associations, which we then use to explain our current mood. If put in a buoyant mood—whether under hypnosis or just by the day's events (a World Cup soccer victory for the German participants in one study)—people recall the world through rose-colored glasses (DeSteno et al., 2000; Forgas et al., 1984; Schwarz et al., 1987). They judge themselves competent and effective, other people benevolent, happy events more likely.

Knowing this mood-memory connection, we should not be surprised that in some studies *currently* depressed people recall their parents as rejecting, punitive, and guilt-promoting, whereas *formerly* depressed people describe their parents much as do those who have never suffered depression (Lewinsohn & Rosenbaum, 1987; Lewis,

"Do you ever get that strange feeling of vujà dé? Not déjà vu; vujà dé. It's the distinct sense that, somehow, something just happened that has never happened before. Nothing seems familiar. And then suddenly the feeling is gone. Vujà dé."

George Carlin (1937–2008), in *Funny Times*, December 2001

"I can't remember what we're arguing about, either. Let's keep yelling, and maybe it will come back to us."

"When a feeling was there, they felt as if it would never go; when it was gone, they felt as if it had never been; when it returned, they felt as if it had never gone."

George MacDonald, *What's Mine's Mine*, 1886

|| Moods influence not only our memories but also how we *interpret* other people's behavior. In a bad mood we read someone's look as a glare and feel even worse; in a good mood we encode the same look as interest and feel even better. Passions exaggerate. ||

|| Do you remember the gist of the sentence I asked you to remember at the beginning of this module? If not, does the word *shark* help? Experiments show that *shark* more readily cues the image you stored than does the sentence's actual word, *fish* (Anderson et al., 1976). ||

1992). Similarly, adolescents' ratings of parental warmth in one week give little clue to how they will rate their parents six weeks later (Bornstein et al., 1991). When teens are down, their parents seem inhuman; as their mood brightens, their parents morph from devils into angels. You and I may nod our heads knowingly. Yet, in a good or bad mood, we persist in attributing to reality our own changing judgments and memories.

Our mood's effect on retrieval helps explain why our moods persist. When happy, we recall happy events and therefore see the world as a happy place, which helps prolong our good mood. When depressed, we recall sad events, which darkens our interpretations of current events. For those of us with a predisposition to depression, this process can help maintain a vicious, dark cycle.

REVIEW

Retrieval: Getting Information Out

29-1 **How do we get information out of memory?** *Recall* is the ability to retrieve information not in conscious awareness; a fill-in-the-blank question tests recall. *Recognition* is the ability to identify items previously learned; a multiple-choice question tests recognition. *Relearning* is the ability to master previously stored information more quickly than you originally learned it. Retrieval cues catch our attention and tweak our web of associations, helping to move target information into conscious awareness. *Priming* is the process of activating associations (often unconsciously).

29-2 **How do external contexts and internal emotions influence memory retrieval?** The context in which we originally experienced an event or encoded a thought can flood our memories with retrieval cues, leading us to the target memory. In a different but similar context, such cues may trick us into retrieving a memory, a feeling known as *déjà vu*. Specific emotions can prime us to retrieve memories consistent with that state. *Mood-congruent memory,* for example, primes us to interpret others' behavior in ways consistent with our current emotions.

Terms and Concepts to Remember

recall, p. 346

recognition, p. 346

relearning, p. 346

priming, p. 347

déjà vu, p. 348

mood-congruent memory, p. 349

Test Yourself

1. You have just watched a movie that includes a chocolate factory. After the chocolate factory is out of mind, you nevertheless feel a strange urge for a chocolate bar. How do you explain this in terms of priming?

(Answers to the Test Yourself questions can be found in Appendix B at the end of the book.)

Ask Yourself

1. What sort of mood have you been in lately? How has your mood colored your memories, perceptions, and expectations?

⊙⊙ WEB

Multiple-choice self-tests and more may be found at www.worthpublishers.com/myers

MODULE 30

Forgetting, Memory Construction, and Improving Memory

Forgetting

Memory Construction

Improving Memory

▶‖ Forgetting

30-1 Why do we forget?

Amid all the applause for memory—all the efforts to understand it, all the books on how to improve it—have any voices been heard in praise of forgetting? William James (1890, p. 680) was such a voice: "If we remembered everything, we should on most occasions be as ill off as if we remembered nothing." To discard the clutter of useless or out-of-date information—where we parked the car yesterday, a friend's old phone number, restaurant orders already cooked and served—is surely a blessing. The Russian memory whiz Shereshevskii accumulated a junk heap of memories that haunted him. They dominated his consciousness. He had difficulty thinking abstractly—generalizing, organizing, evaluating. After reading a story, he could recite it but would struggle to summarize its gist.

A more recent case of a life overtaken by memory is "A. J.," whose experience has been studied and verified by a University of California at Irvine research team (Parker et al., 2006). A. J., who has identified herself as Jill Price, describes her memory as "like a running movie that never stops. It's like a split screen. I'll be talking to someone and seeing something else. . . . Whenever I see a date flash on the television (or anywhere for that matter) I automatically go back to that day and remember where I was, what I was doing, what day it fell on, and on and on and on and on. It is nonstop, uncontrollable, and totally exhausting." A good memory is helpful, but so is the ability to forget. If a memory-enhancing pill becomes available, it had better not be *too* effective.

More often, however, our memory dismays and frustrates us. Memories are quirky. My own memory can easily call up such episodes as that wonderful first kiss with the woman I love or trivial facts like the air mileage from London to Detroit. Then it abandons me when I discover I have failed to encode, store, or retrieve my new colleague's name or where I left my sunglasses. Memory researcher Daniel Schacter (1999) enumerates seven ways our memories fail us—the seven sins of memory, he calls them:

Three sins of forgetting:

▶ *Absent-mindedness*—inattention to details leads to encoding failure (our mind is elsewhere as we lay down the car keys).

▶ *Transience*—storage decay over time (after we part ways with former classmates, unused information fades).

▶ *Blocking*—inaccessibility of stored information (seeing an actor in an old movie, we feel the name on the tip of our tongue but experience retrieval failure—we cannot get it out).

Three sins of distortion:

▶ *Misattribution*—confusing the source of information (putting words in someone else's mouth or remembering a dream as an actual happening).

▶ *Suggestibility*—the lingering effects of misinformation (a leading question—"Did Mr. Jones touch your private parts?"—later becomes a young child's false memory).

"Amnesia seeps into the crevices of our brains, and amnesia heals."
Joyce Carol Oates, "Words Fail, Memory Blurs, Life Wins," 2001

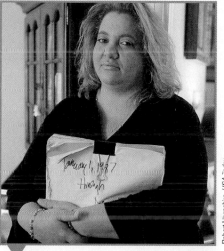

Robert Hanashiro, USA Today

The woman who can't forget "A. J." in real life is Jill Price, who, with writer Bart Davis, told her story in a 2008 published memoir. Price remembers every day of her life since age 14 with detailed clarity, including both the joys and the unforgotten hurts.

‖ Cellist Yo-Yo Ma forgot his 266-year-old, $2.5 million cello in a New York taxi. (He later recovered it.) ‖

"Oh, is that today?"

▶ *Bias*—belief-colored recollections (current feelings toward a friend may color our recalled initial feelings).

One sin of intrusion:

▶ *Persistence*—unwanted memories (being haunted by images of a sexual assault).

Let's first consider the sins of forgetting, then those of distortion and intrusion.

Encoding Failure

Much of what we sense we never notice, and what we fail to encode, we will never remember (**FIGURE 30.1**). Age can affect encoding efficiency. The brain areas that jump into action when young adults encode new information are less responsive in older adults. This slower encoding helps explain age-related memory decline (Grady et al., 1995).

FIGURE 30.1 Forgetting as encoding failure We cannot remember what we have not encoded.

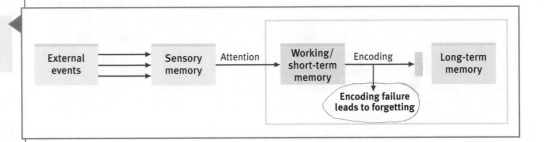

But no matter how young we are, we selectively attend to few of the myriad sights and sounds continually bombarding us. Consider this example: If you live in North America, Britain, or Australia, you have looked at thousands of pennies in your lifetime. You can surely recall their color and size, but can you recall what the side with the head looks like? If not, let's make the memory test easier: If you are familiar with U.S. coins, can you recognize the real thing in **FIGURE 30.2**? Most people cannot (Nickerson & Adams, 1979). Of the eight critical features (Lincoln's head, date, "In God we trust," and so on), the average person spontaneously remembers only three. Likewise, few British people can draw from memory the one-pence coin (Richardson, 1993). The details of these coins are not very meaningful—nor are they essential for distinguishing them from other coins—and few of us have made the effort to encode them. We encode some information—where we had dinner yesterday—automatically; other types of information—like the concepts in this module—require effortful processing. Without effort, many memories never form.

"Each of us finds that in [our] own life every moment of time is completely filled. [We are] bombarded every second by sensations, emotions, thoughts . . . ninetenths of which [we] must simply ignore. The past [is] a roaring cataract of billions upon billions of such moments: Any one of them too complex to grasp in its entirety, and the aggregate beyond all imagination. . . . At every tick of the clock, in every inhabited part of the world, an unimaginable richness and variety of 'history' falls off the world into total oblivion."

English novelist-critic C. S. Lewis (1967)

FIGURE 30.2 Test your memory Which one of these pennies is the real thing? (If you live outside the United States, try drawing one of your own country's coins.) (From Nickerson & Adams, 1979.) Answer below.

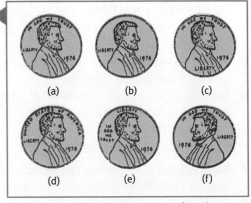

The first penny (a) is the real penny.

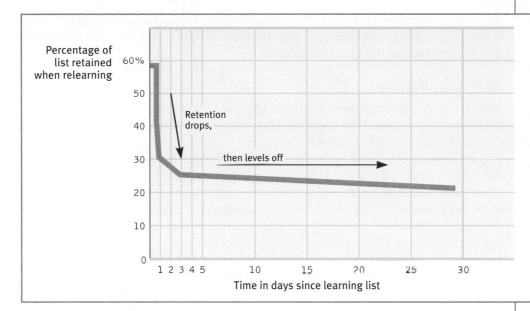

Percentage of list retained when relearning

Retention drops,

then levels off

Time in days since learning list

Hermann Ebbinghaus (1850–1909)

Storage Decay

Even after encoding something well, we sometimes later forget it. To study the durability of stored memories, German philosopher Hermann Ebbinghaus (1885) learned lists of nonsense syllables (for example, DAH) and measured how much he retained when relearning each list, from 20 minutes to 30 days later. The result, confirmed by later experiments, was his famous forgetting curve: The course of forgetting is initially rapid, then levels off with time (**FIGURE 30.3**; Wixted & Ebbesen, 1991). One such experiment was Harry Bahrick's (1984) study of the forgetting curve for Spanish vocabulary learned in school. Compared with those just completing a high school or college Spanish course, people 3 years out of school had forgotten much of what they had learned (**FIGURE 30.4**). However, what people remembered then, they still remembered 25 and more years later. Their forgetting had leveled off.

One explanation for these forgetting curves is a gradual fading of the physical memory trace. Cognitive neuroscientists are getting closer to solving the mystery of

FIGURE 30.3 Ebbinghaus' forgetting curve After learning lists of nonsense syllables, Ebbinghaus studied how much he retained up to 30 days later. He found that memory for novel information fades quickly, then levels out. (Adapted from Ebbinghaus, 1885.)

FIGURE 30.4 The forgetting curve for Spanish learned in school Compared with people just completing a Spanish course, those 3 years out of the course remembered much less. Compared with the 3-year group, however, those who studied Spanish even longer ago did not forget much more. (Adapted from Bahrick, 1984.)

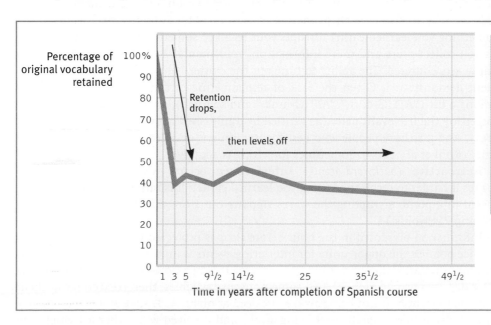

Percentage of original vocabulary retained

Retention drops,

then levels off

Time in years after completion of Spanish course

the physical storage of memory and are increasing our understanding of how memory storage could decay. But memories fade for other reasons, including the accumulation of learning that disrupts our retrieval.

Retrieval Failure

We have seen that forgotten events are like books you can't find in your campus library—some because they were never acquired (not encoded), others because they were discarded (stored memories decay).

But there is a third possibility: The book may be there but inaccessible because we don't have enough information to look it up and retrieve it. How frustrating when we know information is "in there," but we cannot get it out (**FIGURE 30.5**), as when a name lies poised on the tip of our tongue, waiting to be retrieved. Given retrieval cues ("It begins with an *M*"), we may easily retrieve the elusive memory. Retrieval problems contribute to the occasional memory failures of older adults, who more frequently are frustrated by tip-of-the-tongue forgetting (Abrams, 2008). Often, forgetting is not memories discarded but memories unretrieved.

|| Deaf persons fluent in sign language experience a parallel "tip of the fingers" phenomenon (Thompson et al., 2005). ||

FIGURE 30.5 Retrieval failure We store in long-term memory what's important to us or what we've rehearsed. But sometimes even stored information cannot be accessed, which leads to forgetting.

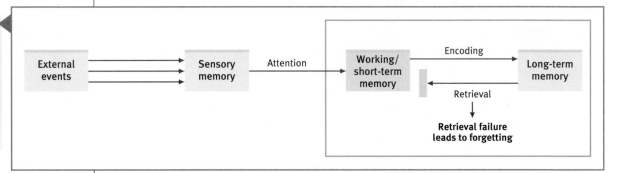

Interference

Learning some items may interfere with retrieving others, especially when the items are similar. If someone gives you a phone number, you may be able to recall it later. But if two more people give you their numbers, each successive number will be more difficult to recall. Likewise, if you buy a new combination lock, your memory of the old one may interfere. Such **proactive** *(forward-acting)* **interference** occurs when something you learned earlier disrupts your recall of something you experience later. As you collect more and more information, your mental attic never fills, but it certainly gets cluttered. The ability to tune out the clutter helps us focus, as one experiment demonstrated. Given the task of remembering certain new word pairs from among a list ("ATTIC-dust," "ATTIC-junk," and so forth), some people were better at forgetting the irrelevant pairs (as verified by diminished activity in a pertinent brain area). And it's those people who best focused on and recalled the to-be-remembered pairs (Kuhl et al., 2007). Sometimes forgetting is adaptive.

Retroactive *(backward-acting)* **interference** occurs when new information makes it harder to recall something you learned earlier. It is rather like a second stone tossed in a pond, disrupting the waves rippling out from a first. (See Close-Up: Retrieving Passwords.)

Information presented in the hour before sleep is protected from retroactive interference because the opportunity for interfering events is minimized. Researchers John Jenkins and Karl Dallenbach (1924) discovered this in a now-classic experiment. Day after day, two people each learned some nonsense syllables, then tried to recall them after up to eight hours of being awake or asleep at night. As **FIGURE 30.6** shows, forgetting occurred more rapidly after being awake and involved with other activities. The

proactive interference the disruptive effect of <u>prior</u> learning on the recall of <u>new</u> information.

retroactive interference the disruptive effect of <u>new</u> learning on the recall of <u>old</u> information.

investigators surmised that "forgetting is not so much a matter of the decay of old impressions and associations as it is a matter of interference, inhibition, or obliteration of the old by the new" (1924, p. 612). Later experiments have confirmed the benefits of sleep and found that the hour before a night's sleep is indeed a good time

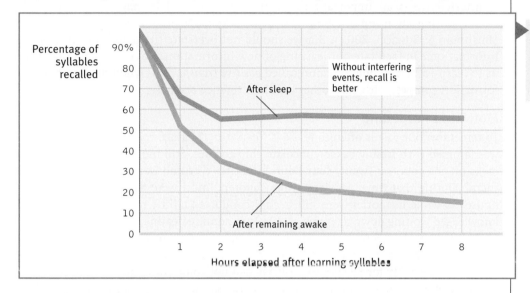

FIGURE 30.6 Retroactive interference More forgetting occurred when a person stayed awake and experienced other new material. (From Jenkins & Dallenbach, 1924.)

CLOSE-UP

Retrieving Passwords

There's something that you need lots of, and that your grandparents at your age didn't: passwords. To log into your e-mail, retrieve your voice mail, draw cash from a machine, access your phone card, use the copy machine, or persuade the keypad to open the building door, you need to remember your password. A typical student faces eight demands for passwords, report Alan Brown and his colleagues (2004).

With so many passwords needed, what's a person to do? As **FIGURE 30.7** illustrates, we are plagued by proactive interference from irrelevant old information and retroactive interference from other newly learned information.

Memory researcher Henry Roediger takes a simple approach to storing all the important phone, PIN, and code numbers in his life: "I have a sheet in my shirt pocket with all the numbers I need," says Roediger (2001), adding that he can't mentally store them all, so why bother? Other strategies may help those who do not want to lose their PINs in the wash. First, *duplicate*. The average student uses

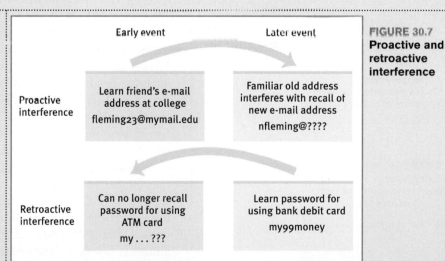

FIGURE 30.7 Proactive and retroactive interference

four different passwords to meet those eight needs. Second, *harness retrieval cues*. Surveys in Britain and the United States reveal that about half of our passwords harness a familiar name or date. Others often involve familiar phone or identification numbers.

Third, in online banking or other situations where security is essential, *use a*

mix of letters and numbers, advise Brown and his colleagues. After composing such a password, rehearse it, then rehearse it a day later, and continue rehearsing at increasing intervals. In such ways, long-term memories will form and be retrievable at the cash and copy machines.

repression in psychoanalytic theory, the basic defense mechanism that banishes from consciousness anxiety-arousing thoughts, feelings, and memories.

to commit information to memory (Benson & Feinberg, 1977; Fowler et al., 1973; Nesca & Koulack, 1994). But not the seconds just before sleep; information presented then is seldom remembered (Wyatt & Bootzin, 1994). Nor is recorded information played during sleep, although the ears do register it (Wood et al., 1992).

Interference is an important cause of forgetting, and it may explain why ads viewed during attention-grabbing violent or sexual TV programs are so forgettable (Bushman & Bonacci, 2002). But we should not overstate the point. Sometimes old information can facilitate our learning of new information. Knowing Latin may help us to learn French—a phenomenon called *positive transfer*. It is when old and new information compete with each other that interference occurs.

Motivated Forgetting

To remember our past is often to revise it. Years ago, the huge cookie jar in our kitchen was jammed with freshly baked chocolate chip cookies. Still more were cooling across racks on the counter. Twenty-four hours later, not a crumb was left. Who had taken them? During that time, my wife, three children, and I were the only people in the house. So while memories were still fresh, I conducted a little memory test. Andy acknowledged wolfing down as many as 20. Peter admitted eating 15. Laura guessed she had stuffed her then-6-year-old body with 15 cookies. My wife, Carol, recalled eating 6, and I remembered consuming 15 and taking 18 more to the office. We sheepishly accepted responsibility for 89 cookies. Still, we had not come close; there had been 160.

This would not have surprised Michael Ross and his colleagues (1981), who time and again showed that people unknowingly revise their own histories. One group of people, told the benefits of frequent tooth-brushing, then recalled (more than others did) having frequently brushed their teeth in the preceding two weeks.

Even memory researcher Ralph Haber has found his own memory sometimes unreliable. In one instance, his recollection was distorted by his motivation to see himself as boldly leaving home despite being loved by a mother who wanted him nearby.

FIGURE 30.8 When do we forget? Forgetting can occur at any memory stage. As we process information, we filter, alter, or lose much of it.

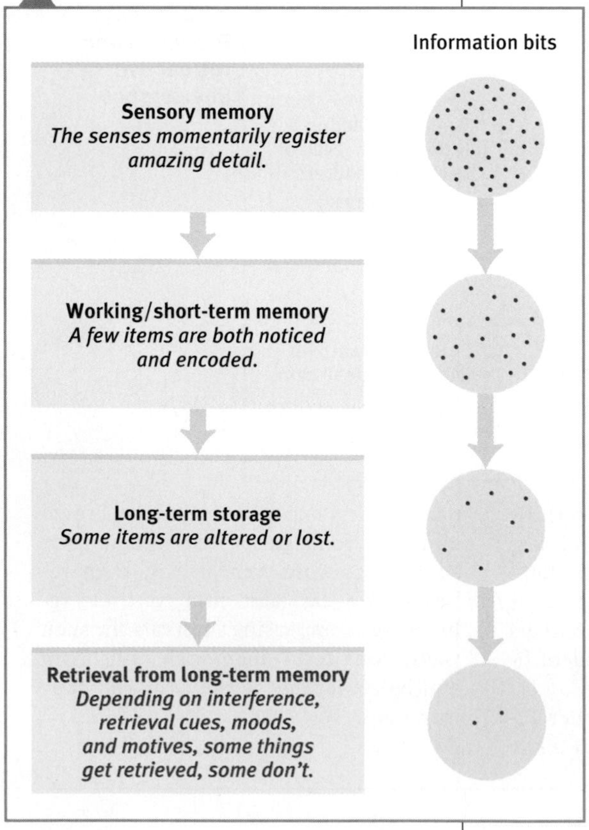

Information bits

Sensory memory
The senses momentarily register amazing detail.

Working/short-term memory
A few items are both noticed and encoded.

Long-term storage
Some items are altered or lost.

Retrieval from long-term memory
Depending on interference, retrieval cues, moods, and motives, some things get retrieved, some don't.

Thus, he recalled choosing to leave the University of Michigan to go to graduate school at Stanford. In his memory, he "leapt for joy" when the Stanford admission came, and he enthusiastically prepared to head west. Twenty-five years later he visited Michigan for his mother's eightieth birthday. Reading the letters he had sent her over the years, he was startled to discover himself explaining his decision to stay at Michigan, until yielding to his mother's passionate plea that he accept the Stanford offer. Sometimes, note Carol Tavris and Elliot Aronson (2007) in recording this story, memory is an "unreliable, self-serving historian" (pp. 6, 79).

Why do our memories fail us? Why did my family and I not remember the number of cookies each of us had eaten? As **FIGURE 30.8** reminds us, we automatically encode sensory information in amazing detail. So was it an encoding problem? Or a storage problem—might our memories of cookies, like Ebbinghaus' memory of nonsense syllables, have vanished almost as fast as the cookies themselves? Or was the information still intact but irretrievable because it would be embarrassing to remember?[1]

Sigmund Freud might have argued that our memory systems self-censored this information. He proposed that we **repress** painful memories to protect our self-concept and to minimize anxiety. But the submerged memory will linger, he believed, to be retrieved by some later cue or during therapy. Here is a sample case. A woman had an intense, unexplained fear of running water. One day her aunt whispered, "I have

---

[1]One of my cookie-scarfing sons, on reading this in his father's textbook years later, confessed he had fibbed "a little."

never told." Like relighting a blown-out candle, these words cued the woman's memory of an incident when, as a disobedient young child, she had wandered away from a family picnic and become trapped under a waterfall—until being rescued by her aunt, who promised not to tell her parents (Kihlstrom, 1990).

Repression was central to Freud's psychology and became part of psychology's lore. Most everyone—including 9 in 10 university students—believes that "memories for painful experiences are sometimes pushed into unconsciousness" (Brown et al., 1996). Therapists often assume it. Yet increasing numbers of memory researchers think repression rarely, if ever, occurs. People's efforts to intentionally forget neutral material often succeed, but not when the to-be-forgotten material is emotional (Payne & Corrigan, 2007). Thus, we may have intrusive memories of the very traumatic experiences we would most like to forget.

▶‖ Memory Construction

30-2 How do misinformation, imagination, and source amnesia influence our memory construction? How real-seeming are false memories?

Picture yourself having this experience:

> You go to a fancy restaurant for dinner. You are seated at a table with a white tablecloth. You study the menu. You tell the server you want prime rib, medium rare, a baked potato with sour cream, and a salad with blue cheese dressing. You also order some red wine from the wine list. A few minutes later the server returns with your salad. Later the rest of the meal arrives. You enjoy it all, except the prime rib is a bit overdone.

Were I immediately to quiz you on this paragraph (adapted from Hyde, 1983), you could surely retrieve considerable detail. For example, without looking back, answer the following questions:

1. What kind of salad dressing did you order?
2. Was the tablecloth red checked?
3. What did you order to drink?
4. Did the server give you a menu?

You were probably able to recall exactly what you ordered, and maybe even the tablecloth color. But did the server give you a menu? Not in the paragraph given. Nevertheless, many answer *yes*. We often construct our memories as we encode them, and we may also alter our memories as we withdraw them from our memory bank. Like scientists who infer a dinosaur's appearance from its remains, we infer our past from stored information plus what we later imagined, expected, saw, and heard. We don't just retrieve memories, we reweave them, notes Daniel Gilbert (2006, p. 79): "Information acquired after an event alters memory of the event."

"Memory isn't like reading a book; it's more like writing a book from fragmentary notes."

Psychologist John F. Kihlstrom (1994)

Misinformation and Imagination Effects

In more than 200 experiments, involving more than 20,000 people, Elizabeth Loftus has shown how eyewitnesses similarly reconstruct their memories when later questioned. In one classic experiment, Loftus and John Palmer showed a film of a traffic accident and then quizzed people about what they had seen (Loftus & Palmer, 1974). Those asked, "How fast were the cars going when they *smashed* into each other?" gave higher speed estimates than those asked, "How fast were the cars going when they *hit* each other?" A week later, the researchers asked both groups if they recalled seeing any broken glass. Those who had heard *smashed* were more than twice as likely to report seeing glass fragments (**FIGURE 30.9** on the next page). In fact, the film showed no broken glass.

FIGURE 30.9 Memory construction
When people who had seen the film of a car accident were later asked a leading question, they recalled a more serious accident than they had witnessed. (From Loftus, 1979.)

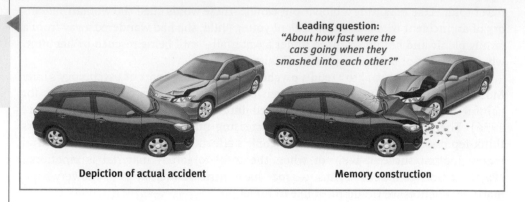

Leading question:
"About how fast were the cars going when they smashed into each other?"

Depiction of actual accident   **Memory construction**

In many follow-up experiments around the world, people have witnessed an event, received or not received misleading information about it, and then taken a memory test. The repeated result is a **misinformation effect:** After exposure to subtle misinformation, many people misremember. They have misrecalled a yield sign as a stop sign, hammers as screwdrivers, Coke cans as peanut cans, *Vogue* magazine as *Mademoiselle,* "Dr. Henderson" as "Dr. Davidson," breakfast cereal as eggs, and a clean-shaven man as a man with a mustache (Loftus et al., 1992). One experiment showed people digitally altered photos depicting themselves (pasted image from a childhood family album) taking a hot air balloon ride. After seeing this three times over two weeks, half the participants "remembered" the nonexistent experience, often in rich detail (Wade et al., 2002). The human mind comes with built-in Photoshopping software.

So unwitting is the misinformation effect that we may later find it nearly impossible to discriminate between our memories of real and suggested events (Schooler et al., 1986). Perhaps you can recall recounting an experience, and filling in memory gaps with plausible guesses and assumptions. We all do it, and after more retellings, we may recall the guessed details—now absorbed into our memories—as if we had actually observed them (Roediger et al., 1993). Others' vivid retelling of an event may also implant false memories.

Even repeatedly *imagining* nonexistent actions and events can create false memories. Students who repeatedly imagined simple acts such as breaking a toothpick or

"Memory is insubstantial. Things keep replacing it. Your batch of snapshots will both fix and ruin your memory. . . . You can't remember anything from your trip except the wretched collection of snapshots."

Annie Dillard, "To Fashion a Text," 1988

DOONESBURY

picking up a stapler later experienced this *imagination inflation;* they were more likely than others to think they had actually done such things during the experiment's first phase (Goff & Roediger, 1998; Seamon et al., 2006). Similarly, one in four American and British university students asked to imagine certain childhood events, such as breaking a window with their hand or having a skin sample removed from a finger, later recalled the imagined event as something that had really happened (Garry et al., 1996; Mazzoni & Memon, 2003). Imagination inflation occurs partly because visualizing something and actually perceiving it activate similar brain areas (Gonsalves et al., 2004).

Imagined events later seem more familiar, and familiar things seem more real. Thus, the more vividly we can imagine things, the more likely we are to inflate them into memories (Loftus, 2001; Porter et al., 2000). People who believe aliens transported them to spaceships for medical exams tend to have powerful imaginations and, in memory tests, to be more susceptible to false memories (Clancy, 2005). Those who believe they have recovered memories of childhood sexual abuse likewise tend to have vivid imaginations and to score high on false memory tests (Clancy et al., 2000; McNally, 2003).

To see how far the mind's search for a fact will go in creating a fiction, Richard Wiseman and his University of Hertfordshire colleagues (1999) staged eight seances, each attended by 25 curious people. During each session, the medium—actually a professional actor and magician—urged everyone to concentrate on the moving table. Although it never moved, he suggested it had: "That's good. Lift the table up. That's good. Keep concentrating. Keep the table in the air." When questioned two weeks later, 1 in 3 participants recalled actually having seen the table levitate.

Psychologists are not immune to memory construction. Famed child psychologist Jean Piaget was startled as an adult to learn that a vivid, detailed memory from his childhood—a nursemaid's thwarting his kidnapping—was utterly false. Piaget apparently constructed the memory from the many retellings of the story he had heard (which his nursemaid, after undergoing a religious conversion, later confessed had never happened).

Source Amnesia

Piaget remembered, but attributed his memory to the wrong sources (to his own experience rather than to his nursemaid's stories). Among the frailest parts of a memory is its source. Thus, we may recognize someone but have no idea where we have seen the person. We may dream an event and later be unsure whether it really happened. We may hear something and later recall seeing it (Henkel et al., 2000). In all these cases of **source amnesia** (also called *source misattribution*), we retain the memory of the event, but not of the context in which we acquired it.

Debra Poole and Stephen Lindsay (1995, 2001, 2002) demonstrated source amnesia among preschoolers. They had the children interact with "Mr. Science," who engaged them in activities such as blowing up a balloon with baking soda and vinegar. Three months later, on three successive days, their parents read them a story describing some things the children had experienced with Mr. Science and some they had not. When a new interviewer asked what Mr. Science had done with them—"Did Mr. Science have a machine with ropes to pull?"—4 in 10 children spontaneously recalled him doing things that had happened only in the story.

Discerning True and False Memories

Because memory is reconstruction as well as reproduction, we can't be sure whether a memory is real by how real it feels. Much as perceptual illusions may seem like real perceptions, unreal memories *feel* like real memories.

misinformation effect incorporating misleading information into one's memory of an event.

source amnesia attributing to the wrong source an event we have experienced, heard about, read about, or imagined. (Also called *source misattribution*.) Source amnesia, along with the misinformation effect, is at the heart of many false memories.

"It isn't so astonishing, the number of things I can remember, as the number of things I can remember that aren't so."
Mark Twain (1835–1910)

‖ Authors and songwriters sometimes suffer source amnesia. They think an idea came from their own creative imagination, when in fact they are unintentionally plagiarizing something they earlier read or heard. ‖

Indeed, note today's researchers, memories are akin to perceptions—perceptions of the past (Koriat et al., 2000). And as Jamin Halberstadt and Paul Niedenthal (2001) showed, people's initial interpretations influence their perceptual memories. They invited New Zealand university students to view morphed faces that expressed a mix of emotions, such as happiness and anger (**FIGURE 30.10a**), and to imagine and explain "why this person is feeling angry [or happy]." A half-hour later, the researchers asked the students to view a computer video showing a morphed transition from the angry to happy face, and to slide a bar to change the face's expression until it matched the expression they had seen earlier. Students who had explained anger ("This woman is angry because her best friend has cheated on her with her boyfriend") recalled the face as angrier (Figure 30.10b) than did those who had explained happiness ("This woman is very happy that everyone remembered her birthday").

So could we judge a memory's reality by its persistence? Again, the answer is *no*. Memory researchers Charles Brainerd and Valerie Reyna (Brainerd et al., 1995, 1998, 2002) note that memories we derive from experience have more detail than memories we derive from imagination. Memories of imagined experiences are more restricted to the *gist* of the supposed event—the associated meanings and feelings. Because gist memories are durable, children's false memories sometimes outlast their true memories, especially as children mature and become better able to process the gist (Brainerd & Poole, 1997). Thus, therapists or investigators who ask for the gist rather than the details run a greater risk of eliciting false memories.

False memories created by suggested misinformation and misattributed sources may *feel* as real as true memories and may be very persistent. Imagine that I were to read aloud a list of words such as *candy, sugar, honey,* and *taste.* Later, I ask you to recognize the presented words from a larger list. If you are at all like the people tested by Henry Roediger and Kathleen McDermott (1995), you would err three out of four times—by falsely remembering a nonpresented similar word, such as *sweet.* We more easily remember the gist than the words themselves.

In experiments on eyewitness testimony, researchers have repeatedly found that the most confident and consistent eyewitnesses are the most persuasive; however, they often are not the most accurate. Eyewitnesses, whether right or wrong, express roughly similar self-assurance (Bothwell et al., 1987; Cutler & Penrod, 1989; Wells & Murray, 1984).

Memory construction helps explain why 79 percent of 200 convicts exonerated by later DNA testing had been misjudged based on faulty eyewitness identification (Garrett, 2008). It explains why "hypnotically refreshed" memories of crimes so easily incorporate errors, some of which originate with the hypnotist's leading questions ("Did you hear loud noises?"). It explains why dating partners who fall in love *over*estimate their first impressions of one another ("It was love at first sight"), while

U.S. Senator John McCain on the Iraq war:

2007 (on MSNBC): "When I voted to support this war I knew it was probably going to be long and hard and tough."

2002 (on Larry King): "I believe that the operation will be relatively short [and] that the success will be fairly easy."

FIGURE 30.10 Our assumptions alter our perceptual memories Researchers showed people faces with computer-blended expressions, such as the angry/happy face in (a), then asked them to explain why the person was either angry or happy. Those asked to explain an "angry" expression later (when sliding a bar on a morphing movie to identify the earlier-seen face) remembered an angrier face, such as the one shown in (b).

(a)   (b)

© Simon Niedentha

those who break up *under*estimate their earlier liking ("We never really clicked") (McFarland & Ross, 1987). And it explains why people asked how they felt 10 years ago about marijuana or gender issues recall attitudes closer to their current views than to the views they had actually reported a decade earlier (Markus, 1986). How people feel today seems to be how they have always felt. What people know today seems to be what they have always known (Mazzoni & Vannucci, 2007; this is our tendency to experience *hindsight bias*).

One research team interviewed 73 ninth-grade boys and then reinterviewed them 35 years later. When asked to recall how they had reported their attitudes, activities, and experiences, most men recalled statements that matched their actual prior responses at a rate no better than chance. Only 1 in 3 now remembered receiving physical punishment, though as ninth-graders 82 percent had said they had (Offer et al., 2000). As George Vaillant (1977, p. 197) noted after following adult lives through time, "It is all too common for caterpillars to become butterflies and then to maintain that in their youth they had been little butterflies. Maturation makes liars of us all."

Australian psychologist Donald Thompson found his own work on memory distortion ironically haunting him when authorities brought him in for questioning about a rape. Although he was a near-perfect match to the victim's memory of the rapist, he had an airtight alibi. Just before the rape occurred, Thompson was being interviewed on live television. He could not possibly have made it to the crime scene. Then it came to light that the victim had been watching the interview—ironically about face recognition—and had experienced source amnesia, confusing her memories of Thompson with those of the rapist (Schacter, 1996).

Recognizing that the misinformation effect can occur as police and attorneys ask questions framed by their own understandings of an event, Ronald Fisher, Edward Geiselman, and their colleagues (1987, 1992) have trained police interviewers to ask less suggestive, more effective questions. To activate retrieval cues, the detective first asks witnesses to visualize the scene—the weather, time of day, lighting, sounds, smells, positions of objects, and their mood. Then the witness tells in detail, and without interruption, every point recalled, no matter how trivial. Only then does the detective ask evocative follow-up questions: "Was there anything unusual about the person's appearance or clothing?" When this *cognitive interview technique* is used, accurate recall increases (Wells et al., 2006).

Children's Eyewitness Recall

If memories can be sincere, yet sincerely wrong, might children's recollections of sexual abuse be prone to error? Stephen Ceci (1993) thinks "it would be truly awful to ever lose sight of the enormity of child abuse." Yet, as we have seen, interviewers who ask leading questions can plant false memories. Ceci and Maggie Bruck's (1993, 1995) studies of children's memories have sensitized them to children's suggestibility. For example, they asked 3-year-olds to show on anatomically correct dolls where a pediatrician had touched them. Fifty-five percent of the children who had not received genital examinations pointed to either genital or anal areas. And when the researchers used suggestive interviewing techniques, they found that most preschoolers and many older children could be induced to report false events, such as seeing a thief steal food in their day-care center (Bruck & Ceci, 1999, 2004). In another experiment, preschoolers merely *overheard* an erroneous remark that a magician's missing rabbit had gotten loose in their classroom. Later, when the children were suggestively questioned, 78 percent of them recalled actually seeing the rabbit (Principe et al., 2006).

In one study, Ceci and Bruck had a child choose a card from a deck of possible happenings and an adult then read from the card. For example, "Think real hard, and

|| In experiments with adults, suggestive questions ("In fresh water, do snakes swim upside down for about half the time?") are often misremembered as statements (Pandelaere & Dewitte, 2006). ||

"[The] research leads me to worry about the possibility of false allegations. It is not a tribute to one's scientific integrity to walk down the middle of the road if the data are more to one side."

Stephen Ceci (1993)

|| Like children (whose frontal lobes have not fully matured), older adults—especially those whose frontal lobe functioning has declined—are more susceptible than young adults to false memories. This makes older adults more vulnerable to scams, as when a repairperson overcharges by falsely claiming, "I told you it would cost x, and you agreed to pay" (Jacoby et al., 2005; Jacoby & Rhodes, 2006; Roediger & Geraci, 2007; Roediger & McDaniel, 2007). ||

tell me if this ever happened to you. Can you remember going to the hospital with a mousetrap on your finger?" After 10 weekly interviews, with the same adult repeatedly asking children to think about several real and fictitious events, a new adult asked the same question. The stunning result: 58 percent of preschoolers produced false (often vivid) stories regarding one or more events they had never experienced, as this little boy did (Ceci et al., 1994):

> My brother Colin was trying to get Blowtorch [an action figure] from me, and I wouldn't let him take it from me, so he pushed me into the wood pile where the mousetrap was. And then my finger got caught in it. And then we went to the hospital, and my mommy, daddy, and Colin drove me there, to the hospital in our van, because it was far away. And the doctor put a bandage on this finger.

Given such detailed stories, professional psychologists who specialize in interviewing children were often fooled. They could not reliably separate real memories from false ones. Nor could the children themselves. The above child, reminded that his parents had told him several times that the mousetrap incident never happened—that he had imagined it—protested, "But it really did happen. I remember it!"

Does this mean that children can never be accurate eyewitnesses? No. If questioned about their experiences in neutral words they understand, children often accurately recall what happened and who did it (Goodman, 2006; Howe, 1997; Pipe, 1996). When interviewers use less suggestive, more effective techniques, even 4- to 5-year-old children produce more accurate recall (Holliday & Albon, 2004; Pipe et al., 2004). Children are especially accurate when they have not talked with involved adults prior to the interview and when their disclosure is made in a first interview with a neutral person who asks nonleading questions.

Repressed or Constructed Memories of Abuse?

30-3   What is the controversy related to claims of repressed and recovered memories?

There are two tragedies related to adult recollections of child abuse. One is trauma survivors being disbelieved when telling their secret. The other is innocent people being falsely accused. What, then, shall we say about clinicians who have guided people in "recovering" memories of childhood abuse? Are they triggering false memories that damage innocent adults? Or are they uncovering the truth?

In one American survey, the average therapist estimated that 11 percent of the population—some 34 million people—have repressed memories of childhood sexual abuse (Kamena, 1998). In another survey, of British and American doctoral-level therapists, 7 in 10 said they had used techniques such as hypnosis or drugs to help clients recover suspected repressed memories of childhood sexual abuse (Poole et al., 1995).

Some have reasoned with patients that "people who've been abused often have your symptoms, so you probably were abused. Let's see if, aided by hypnosis or drugs, or helped to dig back and visualize your trauma, you can recover it." As we might expect from the research on source amnesia and the misinformation effect, patients exposed to such techniques may form an image of a threatening person. With further visualization, the image grows more vivid, leaving the patient stunned, angry, and ready to confront or sue the equally stunned and devastated parent, relative, or clergy member, who then vigorously denies the accusation. After 32 therapy sessions, one woman recalled her father abusing her when she was 15 months old.

Without questioning the professionalism of most therapists, critics have charged that clinicians who use "memory work" techniques such as "guided imagery," hypnosis, and dream analysis to recover memories "are nothing more than merchants of mental chaos, and, in fact, constitute a blight on the entire field of psychotherapy" (Loftus et al., 1995). "Thousands of families were cruelly ripped apart," with "previously loving adult daughters" suddenly accusing fathers, noted Martin Gardner (2006) in his commentary on North America's "greatest mental health scandal." Irate clinicians countered that those who dispute recovered memories of abuse add to abused people's trauma and play into the hands of child molesters.

In an effort to find a sensible common ground that might resolve this ideological battle—psychology's "memory war"—study panels have been convened and public statements made by the American Medical, American Psychological, and American Psychiatric Associations; the Australian Psychological Society; the British Psychological Society; and the Canadian Psychiatric Association. Those committed to protecting abused children and those committed to protecting wrongly accused adults agree on the following:

▶ *Sexual abuse happens.* And it happens more often than we once supposed. There is no characteristic "survivor syndrome" (Kendall-Tackett et al., 1993). However, sexual abuse is a traumatic betrayal that can leave its victims predisposed to problems ranging from sexual dysfunction to depression (Freyd et al., 2007).

▶ *Injustice happens.* Some innocent people have been falsely convicted. And some guilty people have evaded responsibility by casting doubt on their truth-telling accusers.

▶ *Forgetting happens.* Many of those actually abused were either very young when abused or may not have understood the meaning of their experience—circumstances under which forgetting is common. Forgetting isolated past events, both negative and positive, is an ordinary part of everyday life.

▶ *Recovered memories are commonplace.* Cued by a remark or an experience, we recover memories of long-forgotten events, both pleasant and unpleasant. What is debated is whether the unconscious mind sometimes *forcibly represses* painful experiences and, if so, whether these can be retrieved by certain therapist-aided techniques. (Memories that surface naturally are more likely to be corroborated than are therapist-assisted recollections [Geraerts et al., 2007].)

▶ *Memories of things happening before age 3 are unreliable.* People do not reliably recall happenings of any sort from their first three years—a phenomenon called *infantile amnesia*. Most psychologists—including most clinical and counseling psychologists—therefore doubt "recovered" memories of abuse during infancy (Gore-Felton et al., 2000; Knapp & VandeCreek, 2000). The older a child's age when suffering sexual abuse, and the more severe it was, the more likely it is to be remembered (Goodman et al., 2003).

▶ *Memories "recovered" under hypnosis or the influence of drugs are especially unreliable.* "Age-regressed" hypnotized subjects incorporate suggestions into their memories, even memories of "past lives."

▶ *Memories, whether real or false, can be emotionally upsetting.* Both the accuser and the accused may suffer when what was born of mere suggestion becomes, like an actual trauma, a stinging memory that drives bodily stress (McNally, 2003, 2007). People knocked unconscious in unremembered accidents have later developed stress disorders after being haunted by memories they constructed from photos, news reports, and friends' accounts (Bryant, 2001).

To more closely approximate therapist-aided recall, Elizabeth Loftus and her colleagues (1996) have experimentally implanted false memories of childhood traumas. In one study, she had a

"When memories are 'recovered' after long periods of amnesia, particularly when extraordinary means were used to secure the recovery of memory, there is a high probability that the memories are false."

Royal College of Psychiatrists Working Group on Reported Recovered Memories of Child Sexual Abuse (Brandon et al., 1998)

TODAY'S SPECIAL GUEST

BRUNDAGE MORNALD, OF BATTLE CREEK, MONTANA
UNDER HYPNOSIS, MR. MORNALD RECOVERED LONG-BURIED MEMORIES OF A PERFECTLY NORMAL, HAPPY CHILDHOOD.

Don Shrubshell

Elizabeth Loftus "The research findings for which I am being honored now generated a level of hostility and opposition I could never have foreseen. People wrote threatening letters, warning me that my reputation and even my safety were in jeopardy if I continued along these lines. At some universities, armed guards were provided to accompany me during speeches."
Elizabeth Loftus, on receiving the Association for Psychological Science's William James Fellow Award, 2001

|| Although scorned by some trauma therapists, Loftus has been elected president of the science-oriented Association for Psychological Science, awarded psychology's biggest prize ($200,000), and elected to the U.S. National Academy of Sciences and the Royal Society of Edinburgh. ||

trusted family member recall for a teenager three real childhood experiences and a false one—a vivid account of the child's being lost for an extended time in a shopping mall at age 5 until being rescued by an older person. Two days later, one participant, Chris, said, "That day I was so scared that I would never see my family again." Two days after that, he began to visualize the flannel shirt, bald head, and glasses of the old man who supposedly had found him. Told the story was made up, Chris was incredulous: "I thought I remembered being lost . . . and looking around for the guys. I do remember that, and then crying, and Mom coming up and saying, 'Where were you? Don't you . . . ever do that again.'" In other experiments, a third of participants have become wrongly convinced that they almost drowned as a child, and about half were led to falsely recall an awful experience, such as a vicious animal attack (Heaps & Nash, 2001; Porter et al., 1999).

Such is the memory construction process by which people can recall being abducted by aliens, victimized by a satanic cult, molested in a crib, or living a past life. Thousands of reasonable, normally functioning human beings, notes Loftus, "speak in terror-stricken voices about their experience aboard flying saucers. They *remember,* clearly and vividly, being abducted by aliens" (Loftus & Ketcham, 1994, p. 66).

Loftus knows firsthand the phenomenon she studies. At a family reunion, an uncle told her that at age 14 she found her mother's drowned body. Shocked, she denied it. But the uncle was adamant, and over the next three days she began to wonder if *she* had a repressed memory. "Maybe that's why I'm so obsessed with this topic." As the now-upset Loftus pondered her uncle's suggestion, she "recovered" an image of her mother lying in the pool, face down, and of herself finding the body. "I started putting everything into place. Maybe that's why I'm such a workaholic. Maybe that's why I'm so emotional when I think about her even though she died in 1959."

Then her brother called. Their uncle now remembered what other relatives also confirmed. Aunt Pearl, not Loftus, had found the body (Loftus & Ketcham, 1994; Monaghan, 1992).

Loftus also knows firsthand the reality of sexual abuse. A male baby-sitter molested her when she was 6 years old. She has not forgotten. And that makes her wary of those whom she sees as trivializing real abuse by suggesting uncorroborated traumatic experiences, then accepting them uncritically as fact. The enemies of the truly victimized are not only those who prey and those who deny, she says, but those whose writings and allegations "are bound to lead to an increased likelihood that society in general will disbelieve the genuine cases of childhood sexual abuse that truly deserve our sustained attention" (Loftus, 1993).

So, does repression ever occur? Psychologists continue to have heated debates on this topic, which is the cornerstone of Freud's theory and a recurring theme in much popular psychology. But this much now appears certain: The most common response to a traumatic experience (witnessing a parent's murder, experiencing the horrors of a Nazi death camp, being terrorized by a hijacker or a rapist, escaping the collapsing World Trade Center towers, surviving an Asian tsunami) is not banishment of the experience into the unconscious. Rather, such experiences are typically etched on the mind as vivid, persistent, haunting memories (Porter & Peace, 2007). Playwright Eugene O'Neill understood. As one of the characters in his *Strange Interlude* (1928) exclaimed, "The devil! . . . What beastly incidents our memories insist on cherishing!"

"Horror sears memory, leaving . . . the consuming memories of atrocity."
Robert Kraft, *Memory Perceived: Recalling the Holocaust*, 2002

▶‖ Improving Memory

30-4 How can an understanding of memory contribute to more effective study techniques?

Now and then we are dismayed at our forgetfulness—at our embarrassing inability to recall someone's name, at forgetting to bring up a point in conversation, at not bringing along something important, at finding ourselves standing in a room unable to recall why we are there (Herrmann, 1982). Is there anything we can do to minimize such memory misdeeds? Much as biology benefits medicine and botany benefits agriculture, so can the psychology of memory benefit education. Here for easy reference is a summary of concrete suggestions for improving memory. The SQ3R—Survey, Question, Read, Rehearse, Review—study technique used in this book incorporates several of these strategies.

Study repeatedly. To master material, use distributed (spaced) practice. To learn a concept, provide yourself with many separate study sessions. Take advantage of life's little intervals—riding on the bus, walking across campus, waiting for class to start. To memorize specific facts or figures, suggests Thomas Landauer (2001), "rehearse the name or number you are trying to memorize, wait a few seconds, rehearse again, wait a little longer, rehearse again, then wait longer still and rehearse yet again. The waits should be as long as possible without losing the information." New memories are weak; exercise them and

"I have discovered that it is of some use when you lie in bed at night and gaze into the darkness to repeat in your mind the things you have been studying. Not only does it help the understanding, but also the memory."
Leonardo da Vinci (1452-1519)

Thinking and memory
Most of what we know is not the result of efforts to memorize. We learn because we're curious and because we spend time thinking about our experiences. Actively thinking as we read, by rehearsing and relating ideas, yields the best retention.

"Knit each new thing on to some acquisition already there."

William James, *Principles of Psychology*, 1890

they will strengthen. Speed-reading (skimming) complex material—with minimal rehearsal—yields little retention. Rehearsal and critical reflection help more. It pays to study actively.

Make the material meaningful. To build a network of retrieval cues, take text and class notes in your own words. (Mindlessly repeating someone else's words is relatively ineffective.) To apply the concepts to your own life, form images, understand and organize information, relate the material to what you already know or have experienced, and put it in your own words. Increase retrieval cues by forming associations. Without such cues, you may find yourself stuck when a question uses phrasing different from the rote forms you memorized.

Activate retrieval cues. Mentally re-create the situation and the mood in which your original learning occurred. Return to the same location. Jog your memory by allowing one thought to cue the next.

Use mnemonic devices. Make up a story to associate items with memorable images or jingles. Vivid images or words in familiar rhymes can act as pegs on which you can "hang" items. Chunk information into acronyms by creating a word from the first letters of the to-be-remembered items. Create rhythmic rhymes ("i before e, except after c").

Minimize interference. Study before sleeping. Do not schedule back-to-back study times for topics that are likely to interfere with each other, such as Spanish and French.

Sleep more. During sleep, the brain organizes and consolidates information for long-term memory. Sleep-deprivation disrupts this process.

Test your own knowledge, both to rehearse it and to help determine what you do not yet know. Don't be lulled into overconfidence by your ability to recognize information. Test your recall using the preview questions. Outline sections on a blank page. Define the terms and concepts listed at each module's end before turning back to their definitions. Take practice tests; the study guides that accompany many texts, including this one, are a good source for such tests.

REVIEW

Forgetting, Memory Construction, and Improving Memory

30-1 **Why do we forget?** We may fail to encode information for entry into our memory system. Memories may fade after storage—rapidly at first, and then leveling off, a trend known as the forgetting curve. We may experience retrieval failure, when old and new material compete, when we don't have adequate retrieval cues, or possibly, in rare instances, because of motivated forgetting, or *repression*. In *proactive interference,* something learned in the past interferes with our ability to recall something recently learned. In *retroactive interference,* something recently learned interferes with something learned in the past.

30-2 **How do misinformation, imagination, and source amnesia influence our memory construction? How real-seeming are false memories?** If children or adults are subtly exposed to *misinformation* after an event, or if they repeatedly imagine and rehearse an event that never occurred, they may incorporate misleading details into their memory of what actually happened. When we reassemble a memory during retrieval, we may successfully retrieve something we have heard, read or imagined, but attribute it to the wrong source (*source amnesia*). False memories feel like true memories and are equally durable. Constructed memories are usually limited to the gist of the event.

30-3 **What is the controversy related to claims of repressed and recovered memories?** This controversy between memory researchers and some well-meaning therapists is related to whether most memories of early childhood abuse are repressed and can be recovered by means of leading questions and/or hypnosis during therapy. Psychologists now tend to agree that: (1) Abuse happens, and can leave lasting scars. (2) Some innocent people have been falsely convicted of abuse that never happened, and some true abusers have used the controversy over recovered memories to avoid punishment. (3) Forgetting isolated past events, good or bad, is an ordinary part of life. (4) Recovering good and bad memories, triggered by some memory cue, is commonplace. (5) Infantile amnesia—the inability to recall memories from the first three years of life—makes recovery of very early childhood memories unlikely. (6) Memories obtained under the influence of hypnosis or drugs or therapy are unreliable. (7) Both real and false memories cause stress and suffering.

30-4 **How can an understanding of memory contribute to more effective study techniques?** Research on memory suggests concrete strategies for improving memory. These include studying repeatedly, making material personally meaningful, activating retrieval cues, using mnemonic devices, minimizing interference, getting adequate sleep, and self-testing.

Terms and Concepts to Remember

proactive interference, p. 354
retroactive interference, p. 354
repression, p. 356

misinformation effect, p. 358
source amnesia, p. 359

Test Yourself

1. Can you offer an example of proactive interference?

2. Source amnesia occurs when we attribute to the wrong source an event we have experienced, heard about, read about, or imagined. What might life be like if we remembered all our waking experiences as well as all our dreams?

3. What are the recommended memory strategies you just read about? (One advised rehearsing to-be-remembered material. What were the others?)

(Answers to the Test Yourself questions can be found in Appendix B at the end of the book.)

Ask Yourself

1. Most people, especially as they grow older, wish for a better memory. Is that true of you? Or do you more often wish you could better discard old memories?

2. How would you feel about being an impartial jury member in a trial of a parent accused of sexual abuse based on a recovered memory, or of a therapist being sued for creating a false memory of abuse?

3. Which of the study and memory strategies suggested in this module will work best for you?

∞ WEB

Multiple-choice self-tests and more may be found at www.worthpublishers.com/myers

Thinking, Language, and Intelligence

MODULES

31
Thinking

32
Language and Thought

33
Introduction to Intelligence

34
Assessing Intelligence

35
Genetic and Environmental Influences on Intelligence

Throughout history, we humans have both bemoaned our foolishness and celebrated our wisdom. The poet T. S. Eliot was struck by "the hollow men . . . Headpiece filled with straw." But Shakespeare's Hamlet extolled the human species as "noble in reason! . . . infinite in faculties! . . . in apprehension how like a god!" Throughout this text, we likewise marvel at both our abilities and our errors.

We study the human brain—3 pounds of wet tissue the size of a small cabbage, yet containing circuitry more complex than the planet's telephone networks. We marvel at the competence of newborns. We relish our sensory system, which disassembles visual stimuli into millions of nerve impulses, distributes them for parallel processing, and then reassembles them into colorful perceptions. We ponder our memory's seemingly limitless capacity and the ease with which our two-track mind processes information, consciously and unconsciously. Little wonder that our species has had the collective genius to invent the camera, the car, and the computer; to unlock the atom and crack the genetic code; to travel out to space and into the oceans' depths.

Yet we also see that our species is kin to the other animals. We are influenced by the same principles that produce learning in rats and pigeons. As one pundit said, echoing Pavlov, "How like a dog!" We note that we assimilate reality into our preconceptions and succumb to perceptual illusions. We see how easily we deceive ourselves about pseudopsychic claims, hypnotic feats, and false memories.

In Modules 31 and 32, we encounter further instances of these two images of the human condition—the rational and the irrational. We will consider how our cognitive system uses all the information it has received, perceived, stored, and retrieved. We will look at our flair for language and consider how and why it develops. And we will reflect on how deserving we are of our name, *Homo sapiens*—wise human.

In Modules 33 through 35, we focus on an ongoing debate about *intelligence,* in which psychologists and others pick sides on two major questions: (1) Does each of us have an inborn general mental capacity (intelligence), and (2) can we quantify this capacity as a meaningful number?

Concepts

Solving Problems

Making Decisions and Forming Judgments

MODULE 31

Thinking

Thinking, or **cognition,** refers to all the mental activities associated with thinking, knowing, remembering, and communicating. *Cognitive psychologists* study these activities, including the logical and sometimes illogical ways in which we create concepts, solve problems, make decisions, and form judgments.

"The average newspaper boy in Pittsburgh knows more about the universe than did Galileo, Aristotle, Leonardo, or any of those other guys who were so smart they only needed one name."

Daniel Gilbert, *Stumbling on Happiness*, 2006

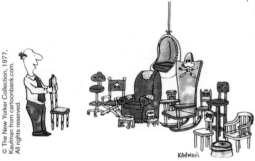

"Attention, everyone! I'd like to introduce the newest member of our family."

A bird and a . . . ? It takes a bit longer to conceptualize a penguin as a bird because it doesn't match our prototype of a small, feathered, flying creature.

▶‖ Concepts

31-1 What are the functions of concepts?

To think about the countless events, objects, and people in our world, we simplify things. We form **concepts**—mental groupings of similar objects, events, ideas, and people. The concept *chair* includes many items—a baby's high chair, a reclining chair, a dentist's chair—all of which are for sitting. Chairs vary, but it is their common features that define the concept of *chair*.

Imagine life without concepts. We would need a different name for every object and idea. We could not ask a child to "throw the ball" because there would be no concept of *ball* (or *throw*). Instead of saying, "They were angry," we would have to describe expressions, intensities, and words. Such concepts as *ball* and *anger* give us much information with little cognitive effort.

To further simplify things, we organize concepts into category *hierarchies*. Cab drivers organize their cities into geographical sectors, which subdivide into neighborhoods, and again into blocks. Once our categories exist, we use them efficiently. Shown a bird, car, or food, people need no more time to identify an item's category than to perceive that something is there. "As soon as you know it is there, you know what it is," report Kalanit Grill-Spector and Nancy Kanwisher (2005).

We form some concepts by *definition*. Told that a triangle has three sides, we thereafter classify all three-sided geometric forms as triangles. More often, however, we form our concepts by developing **prototypes**—a mental image or best example that incorporates all the features we associate with a category (Rosch, 1978). The more closely something matches our prototype of a concept, the more readily we recognize it as an example of the concept. A robin and a penguin both satisfy our definition of *bird:* a two-footed animal that has wings and feathers and hatches from an egg. Yet people agree more quickly that "a robin is a bird" than that "a penguin is a bird." For most of us, the robin is the birdier bird; it more closely resembles our bird prototype.

Once we place an item in a category, our memory of it later shifts toward the category prototype. Olivier Corneille and his colleagues (2004) found memory shifts after showing Belgian students ethnically mixed faces. For example, when shown a face that was a blend of 70 percent of the features of a Caucasian person and 30 percent of an Asian person, people categorized the face as Caucasian and later recalled having seen a more prototypically Caucasian person (Corneille et al., 2004). (They were more likely to recall an 80 percent Caucasian face than the 70 percent Caucasian they actually saw.) If shown a 70 percent Asian face, they later recalled a more prototypically Asian face (**FIGURE 31.1**). A follow-up study found the phenomenon with gender as well. Those shown 70 percent male faces categorized them as male (no surprise there), and then later misrecalled them as even more prototypically male (Huart et al., 2005).

370

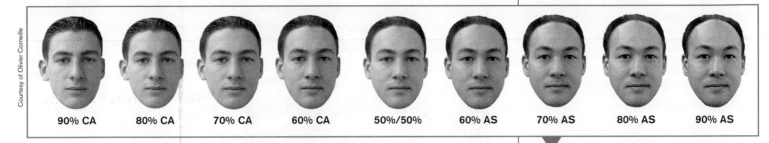

| 90% CA | 80% CA | 70% CA | 60% CA | 50%/50% | 60% AS | 70% AS | 80% AS | 90% AS |

FIGURE 31.1 Face categorization influences recollection For example, shown a face that was 70 percent Caucasian, people tended to classify the person as Caucasian and to recollect the face as more Caucasian than it was. (From Corneille et al., 2004.)

Move away from our prototypes, and category boundaries may blur. Is a tomato a fruit? Is a 17-year-old female a girl or a woman? Is a whale a fish or a mammal? Because this marine animal fails to match our prototype, we are slower to recognize it as a mammal. Similarly, we are slow to perceive an illness when our symptoms don't fit one of our disease prototypes (Bishop, 1991). People whose heart attack symptoms (shortness of breath, exhaustion, a dull weight in the chest) don't match their prototype of a heart attack (sharp chest pain) may not seek help. And when discrimination doesn't fit our prejudice prototypes—of White against Black, male against female, young against old—we often fail to notice it. People more easily detect male prejudice against females than female against males or female against females (Inman & Baron, 1996; Marti et al., 2000). So, concepts, like other mental shortcuts we will encounter, speed and guide our thinking. But they don't always make us wise.

▶‖ Solving Problems

31-2 What strategies assist our problem solving, and what obstacles hinder it?

One tribute to our rationality is our problem-solving skill in coping with novel situations. What's the best route around this traffic jam? How shall we handle a friend's criticism? How can we get in the house without our keys?

Some problems we solve through *trial and error*. Thomas Edison tried thousands of lightbulb filaments before stumbling upon one that worked. For other problems, we use **algorithms,** step-by-step procedures that guarantee a solution. But step-by-step algorithms can be laborious and exasperating. For example, to find another word using all the letters in *SPLOYOCHYG*, we could try each letter in each position, but we would need to generate and examine the 907,200 resulting permutations. In such cases, we often resort to simpler strategies called **heuristics** (see photo on next page). Thus, we might reduce the number of options in our *SPLOYOCHYG* example by excluding rare letter combinations, such as two Y's together. By using heuristics and then applying trial and error, we may hit upon the answer (which you can see by turning the page).

Sometimes, the problem-solving strategy seems to be no strategy at all. We puzzle over a problem, and suddenly, the pieces fall together as we perceive the solution in a sudden flash of **insight.** Ten-year-old Johnny Appleton displayed insight in solving a problem that had stumped construction workers: how to rescue a young robin that had fallen into a narrow 30-inch-deep hole in a cement-block wall. Johnny's solution: Slowly pour in sand, giving the bird enough time to keep its feet on top of the constantly rising sand (Ruchlis, 1990).

Teams of researchers have identified brain activity associated with sudden flashes of insight (Jung-Beeman et al., 2004; Sandkühler & Bhattacharya, 2008). They gave people a problem: Think of a word that will form a compound word or phrase with each of three words in a set (such as *pine, crab,* and *sauce*), and press a button to

cognition the mental activities associated with thinking, knowing, remembering, and communicating.

concept a mental grouping of similar objects, events, ideas, or people.

prototype a mental image or best example of a category. Matching new items to a prototype provides a quick and easy method for sorting items into categories (as when comparing feathered creatures to a prototypical bird, such as a robin).

algorithm a methodical, logical rule or procedure that guarantees solving a particular problem. Contrasts with the usually speedier—but also more error-prone—use of *heuristics*.

heuristic a simple thinking strategy that often allows us to make judgments and solve problems efficiently; usually speedier but also more error-prone than *algorithms*.

insight a sudden and often novel realization of the solution to a problem; it contrasts with strategy-based solutions.

Heuristic searching To search for guava juice, you could search every supermarket aisle (an algorithm), or check the bottled beverage, natural foods, and produce sections (heuristics). The heuristics approach is often speedier, but an algorithmic search guarantees you will find it eventually.

B₂M Productions/Digital Vision/Getty Images

sound a bell when you know the answer. (If you need a hint: The word is a fruit.[1]) All the while, the researchers mapped the problem solver's brain activity, using fMRIs (functional MRIs) or EEGs. In the first experiment, about half the solutions were by a sudden Aha! insight, which typically was preceded by frontal lobe activity involved in focusing attention and was accompanied by a burst of activity in the right temporal lobe, just above the ear (**FIGURE 31.2**).

As you perhaps experienced in solving the *pine-crab-sauce* problem, insight often pops into the mind with striking suddenness, with no prior sense that one is "getting warmer" or feeling close to the answer (Knoblich & Oellinger, 2006; Metcalfe, 1986). When the "Eureka moment" hits us, we feel a sense of satisfaction, a feeling of happiness. The joy of a joke may similarly lie in our sudden comprehension of an unexpected ending or a double meaning. See for yourself, with these 2 jokes rated funniest (among 2 million ratings of 40,000 submitted jokes) in an Internet humor study co-sponsored by Richard Wiseman (2002) and the British Association for the Advancement of Science. First, the runner-up:

> Sherlock Holmes and Dr. Watson are going camping. They pitch their tent under the stars and go to sleep. Sometime in the middle of the night Holmes wakes Watson up.
>
> Holmes: "Watson, look up at the stars, and tell me what you deduce."
> Watson: "I see millions of stars and even if a few of those have planets, it's quite likely there are some planets like Earth, and if there are a few planets like Earth out there, there might also be life. What does it tell you, Holmes?"
> Holmes: "Watson, you idiot, somebody has stolen our tent!"

And drum roll, please, for the winner:

> A couple of New Jersey hunters are out in the woods when one of them falls to the ground. He doesn't seem to be breathing, his eyes are rolled back in his head. The other guy whips out his cellphone and calls the emergency services. He gasps to the operator: "My friend is dead! What can I do?" The operator, in a calm, soothing voice says: "Just take it easy. I can help. First, let's make sure he's dead." There is a silence, then a shot is heard. The guy's voice comes back on the line: "OK, now what?"

Obstacles to Problem Solving

Inventive as we can be in solving problems, the correct answer may elude us. Two cognitive tendencies—*confirmation bias* and *fixation*—often lead us astray.

FIGURE 31.2 The Aha! moment A burst of right temporal lobe activity accompanies insight solutions to word problems (Jung-Beeman et al., 2004).

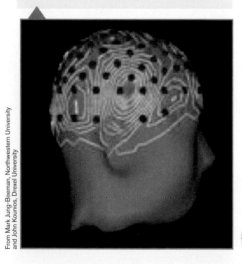

From Mark Jung-Beeman, Northwestern University and John Kounios, Drexel University

‖ Answer to SPLOYOCHYG anagram on previous page: PSYCHOLOGY. ‖

[1]The word is *apple:* pineapple, crabapple, applesauce.

Confirmation Bias

We seek evidence verifying our ideas more eagerly than we seek evidence that might refute them (Klayman & Ha, 1987; Skov & Sherman, 1986). This tendency, known as **confirmation bias,** is a major obstacle to problem solving. Peter Wason (1960) demonstrated the confirmation bias by giving British university students the three-number sequence 2-4-6 and asking them to guess the rule he had used to devise the series. (The rule was simple: any three ascending numbers.) Before submitting answers, students generated their own sets of three numbers, and Wason told them whether their sets conformed to his rule. Once they felt *certain* they had the rule, they were to announce it. The result? Seldom right but never in doubt. Most of Wason's students formed a wrong idea ("Maybe it's counting by twos") and then searched only for evidence confirming the wrong rule (by testing 6-8-10, 100-102-104, and so forth).

"Ordinary people," said Wason (1981), "evade facts, become inconsistent, or systematically defend themselves against the threat of new information relevant to the issue." The results are sometimes momentous. The United States launched its war against Iraq on the assumption that Saddam Hussein possessed weapons of mass destruction (WMD) that posed an immediate threat. When that assumption turned out to be false, confirmation bias was one of the flaws in the judgment process identified by the bipartisan U.S. Senate Select Committee on Intelligence (2004). Administration analysts "had a tendency to accept information which supported [their presumptions] . . . more readily than information which contradicted" them. Sources denying such weapons were deemed "either lying or not knowledgeable about Iraq's problems, while those sources who reported ongoing WMD activities were seen as having provided valuable information."

Fixation

Once we incorrectly represent a problem, it's hard to restructure how we approach it. If the solution to the matchstick problem in **FIGURE 31.3** eludes you, you may be experiencing **fixation**—the inability to see a problem from a fresh perspective. (See the solution in **FIGURE 31.5** on the next page.)

Two examples of fixation are *mental set* and *functional fixedness.* As a perceptual set predisposes what we perceive, a **mental set** predisposes how we think. Mental set refers to our tendency to approach a problem with the mind-set of what has worked for us previously. Indeed, solutions that worked in the past often do work on new problems. Consider:

Given the sequence *O-T-T-F-?-?-?*, what are the final three letters?

Most people have difficulty recognizing that the three final letters are *F*(ive), *S*(ix), and *S*(even). But solving this problem may make the next one easier:

Given the sequence *J-F-M-A-?-?-?*, what are the final three letters? (If you don't get this one, ask yourself what month it is.)

Sometimes, however, a mental set based on what worked in the past precludes our finding a new solution to a new problem. Our mental set from our past experiences with matchsticks predisposes our arranging them in two dimensions.

Another type of fixation—our tendency to think of only the familiar functions for objects, without imagining alternative uses—goes by the awkward but appropriate label **functional fixedness.** A person may ransack the house for a screwdriver when a coin would have turned the screw. As an example, try the candle-mounting problem in **FIGURE 31.4.** Did you experience functional fixedness? If so, see **FIGURE 31.6** (on the next page). Perceiving and relating familiar things in new ways is part of creativity.

"The human understanding, when any proposition has been once laid down . . . forces everything else to add fresh support and confirmation."

Francis Bacon, *Novum Organum*, 1620

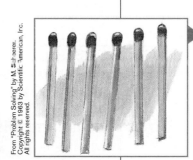

FIGURE 31.3
The matchstick problem
How would you arrange six matches to form four equilateral triangles?

FIGURE 31.4 The candle-mounting problem Using these materials, how would you mount the candle on a bulletin board? (From Duncker, 1945.)

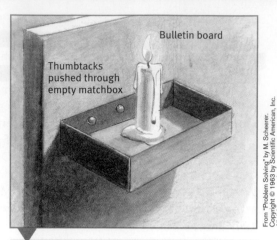

FIGURE 31.5 Solution to the matchstick problem To solve this problem, you must view it from a new perspective, breaking the fixation of limiting solutions to two dimensions.

FIGURE 31.6 Solution to the candle-mounting problem Solving this problem requires recognizing that a matchbox can have other functions besides holding matches. (From Duncker, 1945.)

▶‖ Making Decisions and Forming Judgments

31-3   How do heuristics, overconfidence, and belief perseverance influence our decisions and judgments?

When making each day's hundreds of judgments and decisions *(Is it worth the bother to take an umbrella? Can I trust this person? Should I shoot the basketball or pass to the player who's hot?)* we seldom take the time and effort to reason systematically. We just follow our intuition. After interviewing policymakers in government, business, and education, social psychologist Irving Janis (1986) concluded that they "often do not use a reflective problem-solving approach. How do they usually arrive at their decisions? If you ask, they are likely to tell you . . . they do it mostly by *the seat of their pants*."

Using and Misusing Heuristics

When we need to act quickly, those mental shortcuts we call heuristics often do help us overcome analysis paralysis. Thanks to our mind's automatic information processing, intuitive judgments are instantaneous. But the price we sometimes pay for this efficiency—quick but bad judgments—can be costly. Research by cognitive psychologists Amos Tversky and Daniel Kahneman (1974) on the *representativeness* and *availability* *heuristics* showed how these generally helpful shortcuts can lead even the smartest people into dumb decisions. (Their joint work on decision making received the 2002 Nobel prize, although sadly, only Kahneman was alive to receive the honor.)

The Representativeness Heuristic

To judge the likelihood of things in terms of how well they represent particular prototypes is to use the **representativeness heuristic.** To illustrate, consider:

> A stranger tells you about a person who is short, slim, and likes to read poetry, and then asks you to guess whether this person is more likely to be a professor of classics at an Ivy League university or a truck driver (adapted from Nisbett & Ross, 1980). Which would be the better guess?

Did you answer "professor"? Many people do, because the description seems more *representative* of Ivy League scholars than of truck drivers. The representativeness

representativeness heuristic judging the likelihood of things in terms of how well they seem to represent, or match, particular prototypes; may lead us to ignore other relevant information.

"In creating these problems, we didn't set out to fool people. All our problems fooled us, too."
Amos Tversky (1985)

"Intuitive thinking [is] fine most of the time. . . . But sometimes that habit of mind gets us in trouble."
Daniel Kahneman (2005)

availability heuristic estimating the likelihood of events based on their availability in memory; if instances come readily to mind (perhaps because of their vividness), we presume such events are common.

heuristic enabled you to make a snap judgment. But it also led you to ignore other relevant information. When I help people think through this question, the conversation goes something like this:

Question: First, let's figure out how many professors fit the description. How many Ivy League universities do you suppose there are?
Answer: Oh, about 10, I suppose.
Question: How many classics professors would you guess there are at each?
Answer: Maybe 4.
Question: Okay, that's 40 Ivy League classics professors. What fraction of these are short and slim?
Answer: Let's say half.
Question: And, of these 20, how many like to read poetry?
Answer: I'd say half—10 professors.
Question: Okay, now let's figure how many truck drivers fit the description. How many truck drivers do you suppose there are?
Answer: Maybe 400,000.
Question: What fraction are short and slim?
Answer: Not many—perhaps 1 in 8.
Question: Of these 50,000, what percentage like to read poetry?
Answer: Truck drivers who like poetry? Maybe 1 in 100—oh, oh, I get it—that leaves 500 short, slim, poetry-reading truck drivers.
Comment: Yup. So, even if we accept your stereotype that the description is more representative of classics professors than of truck drivers, the odds are 50 to 1 that this person is a truck driver.

The representativeness heuristic influences many of our daily decisions. To judge the likelihood of something, we intuitively compare it with our mental representation of that category—of, say, what truck drivers are like. If the two match, that fact usually overrides other considerations of statistics or logic.

The Availability Heuristic

The **availability heuristic** operates when we base our judgments on how mentally available information is. Anything that enables information to "pop into mind" quickly and with little effort—its recency, vividness, or distinctiveness—can increase its perceived availability, making it seem commonplace. Casinos entice us to gamble by signaling even small wins with bells and lights—making them vividly memorable—

"The problem is I can't tell the difference between a deeply wise, intuitive nudge from the Universe and one of my own bone-headed ideas!"

overconfidence the tendency to be more confident than correct—to over-estimate the accuracy of our beliefs and judgments.

belief perseverance clinging to one's initial conceptions after the basis on which they were formed has been discredited.

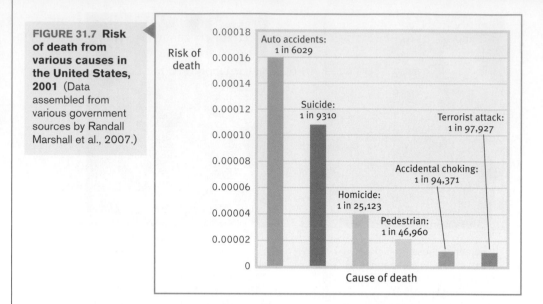

FIGURE 31.7 **Risk of death from various causes in the United States, 2001** (Data assembled from various government sources by Randall Marshall et al., 2007.)

"Don't believe everything you think."
Bumper sticker

"The human understanding is most excit-ed by that which strikes and enters the mind at once and suddenly, and by which the imagination is immediately filled and inflated. It then begins almost impercepti-bly to conceive and suppose that every-thing is similar to the few objects which have taken possession of the mind."
Francis Bacon, *Novum Organum*, 1620

while keeping big losses soundlessly invisible. And if someone from a particular eth-nic group commits a terrorist act, our readily available memory of the dramatic event may shape our impression of the whole group. When statistical reality is pitted against a single vivid case, the memorable case often wins. The mass killing of civil-ians may seem on the increase of late, thanks to memorably available terrorism and genocide. Actually, such horrors have declined sharply since the late 1980s (Pinker, 2007; U.S. Department of State, 2004).

Even during 9/11's horrific year, terrorist acts claimed comparatively few lives, note risk researchers (see **FIGURE 31.7**). Yet in 2007, a poll showed "terrorism" was Ameri-cans' top priority for Congress and the President, and that responding to global climate change—which some scientists regard as a future "Armageddon in slow motion"—was one of the lowest priorities (Pew, 2007). Emotion-laden images of terror exacerbate our fears of terrorism by harnessing the availability heuristic, notes political scientist Cass Sunstein (2007). We fear flying because we play in our heads a tape of 9/11 or some other air disaster. We fear letting our children walk to school because we play in our heads tapes of abducted and brutalized children. We fear swimming in ocean waters be-cause we replay *Jaws* in our heads. And so, thanks to these readily available images, we come to fear extremely rare events. Meanwhile, the lack of comparably available images of global climate change leaves most people little concerned. (For more on the power of vivid cases, turn the page to see Thinking Critically About: The Fear Factor.)

We reason emotionally and neglect probabilities, points out psychologist Paul Slovic (2007). We overfeel and underthink. In one experiment, Deborah Small, George Lowenstein, and Slovic (2007) found that donations to a starving 7-year-old child were greater when her image was *not* accompanied by statistical information about the millions of needy African children like her. "If I look at the mass I will never act," Mother Teresa reportedly said. "If I look at the one, I will."

Overconfidence

Our use of intuitive heuristics when forming judgments, our eagerness to confirm the beliefs we already hold, and our knack for explaining away failures combine to create **overconfidence,** a tendency to overestimate the accuracy of our knowledge and judgments. Across various tasks, people overestimate what their performance was, is, or will be (Metcalfe, 1998).

People are also more confident than correct when answering such questions as, "Is absinthe a liqueur or a precious stone?" (It's a licorice-flavored liqueur.) On questions where only 60 percent of people answer correctly, respondents typically feel 75 percent confident. Even those who feel 100 percent certain err about 15 percent of the time (Fischhoff et al., 1977).

Overconfidence plagues decisions outside the laboratory, too. It was an overconfident Lyndon Johnson who waged war with North Vietnam and an overconfident George W. Bush who marched into Iraq to eliminate supposed weapons of mass destruction. On a smaller scale, overconfidence drives stockbrokers and investment managers to market their ability to outperform stock market averages, despite overwhelming evidence to the contrary (Malkiel, 2004). A purchase of stock X, recommended by a broker who judges this to be the time to buy, is usually balanced by a sale made by someone who judges this to be the time to sell. Despite their confidence, buyer and seller cannot both be right.

Students are routinely overconfident about how quickly they can do assignments and write papers, typically expecting to finish ahead of schedule (Buehler et al., 1994). In fact, the projects generally take about twice the number of days predicted. Despite our painful underestimates, we remain overly confident of our next prediction. Moreover, anticipating how much we will accomplish, we then overestimate our future free time (Zauberman & Lynch, 2005). Believing we will have more free time next month than we do today, we happily accept invitations, only to discover we're just as busy when the day rolls around.

Failing to appreciate our potential for error can have serious consequences, but overconfidence does have adaptive value. People who err on the side of overconfidence live more happily, find it easier to make tough decisions, and seem more credible than those who lack self-confidence (Baumeister, 1989; Taylor, 1989). Moreover, given prompt and clear feedback—as weather forecasters receive after each day's predictions—we can learn to be more realistic about the accuracy of our judgments (Fischhoff, 1982). The wisdom to know when we know a thing and when we do not is born of experience.

The Belief Perseverance Phenomenon

Our readiness to fear the wrong things and to be overconfident in our judgments is startling. Equally startling is our tendency to cling to our beliefs in the face of contrary evidence. **Belief perseverance** often fuels social conflict, as it did in one study of people with opposing views of capital punishment (Lord et al., 1979). Those on both sides studied two supposedly new research findings, one supporting and the other refuting the claim that the death penalty deters crime. Each side was more impressed by the study supporting its own beliefs, and each readily disputed the other study. Thus, showing the pro- and anti–capital-punishment groups the *same* mixed evidence actually *increased* their disagreement.

If you want to rein in the belief perseverance phenomenon, a simple remedy exists: *Consider the opposite.* When Charles Lord and his colleagues (1984) repeated the capital-punishment study, they asked some participants to be "as *objective* and *unbiased* as possible." The plea did nothing to reduce biased evaluations of evidence. They asked another group to consider "whether you would have made the same high or low evaluations had exactly the same study produced results on the *other* side of the issue." Having imagined and pondered *opposite* findings, these people became much less biased in their evaluations of the evidence.

The more we come to appreciate why our beliefs might be true, the more tightly we cling to them. Once people have explained to themselves why they believe a child is "gifted" or "learning disabled," or why candidate X or Y will be a better commander-in-chief, or why company Z is a stock worth owning, they tend to ignore evidence undermining that belief. Prejudice persists. Once beliefs form and get justified, it takes more compelling evidence to change them than it did to create them.

Predict your own behavior When will you finish reading this module?

"When you know a thing, to hold that you know it; and when you do not know a thing, to allow that you do not know it; this is knowledge."
Confucius (551–479 B.C.), *Analects*

"As we know,
There are known knowns.
There are things we know we know.
We also know
There are known unknowns.
That is to say
We know there are some things
We do not know.
But there are also unknown unknowns,
The ones we don't know
We don't know."
Donald Rumsfeld, U.S. Department of Defense news briefing, 2002

"I'm happy to say that my final judgment of a case is almost always consistent with my prejudgment of the case."

Thinking Critically About

The Fear Factor—Do We Fear the Right Things?

"Most people reason dramatically, not quantitatively," said Oliver Wendell Holmes. After 9/11, many people feared flying more than driving. (In a 2006 Gallup survey, only 40 percent reported being "not afraid at all" to fly.) Yet Americans were—mile for mile—230 times more likely to die in an automobile crash than on a commercial flight in the months between 2003 and 2005 (National Safety Council, 2008). In a late-2001 essay, I calculated that if—because of 9/11—we flew 20 percent less and instead drove half those unflown miles, about 800 more people would die in traffic accidents in the year after 9/11 (Myers, 2001). In checking this estimate against actual accident data (why didn't I think of that?), German psychologist Gerd Gigerenzer (2004) found that the last three months of 2001 did indeed produce significantly more U.S. traffic fatalities than the three-month average in the previous five years (**FIGURE 31.8**). Long after 9/11, the dead terrorists were still killing Americans. As air travel gradually recovered during 2002 through 2005, U.S. commercial flights carried nearly 2.5 billion passengers, with no deaths on a major airline big jet (McMurray, 2006; Miller, 2005). Meanwhile, 172,000 Americans died in traffic accidents. For most people, the most dangerous aspect of airline flying is the drive to the airport.

Why do we fear the wrong things? Why do we judge terrorism to be a greater risk than accidents—which kill nearly as many per *week* in just the United States as did terrorism (2527 deaths worldwide) in all of the 1990s (Johnson, 2001)? Even with the horror of 9/11, more Americans in 2001 died of food poisoning (which scares few) than of terrorism (which scares many). Psychological science has identified four influences on our intuitions

FIGURE 31.8 Still killing Americans Images of 9/11 etched a sharper image in our minds than did the millions of fatality-free flights on U.S. airlines during 2002 and after. Such dramatic events, being readily available to memory, shape our perceptions of risk. In the three months after 2001, those faulty perceptions led more people to travel, and some to die, by car. (Adapted from Gigerenzer, 2004.)

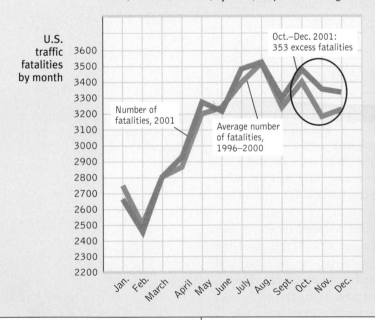

The Perils and Powers of Intuition

31-4   How do smart thinkers use intuition?

intuition an effortless, immediate, automatic feeling or thought, as contrasted with explicit, conscious reasoning.

We have seen how our irrational thinking can plague our efforts to solve problems, make wise decisions, form valid judgments, and reason logically. Intuition also feeds our gut fears and prejudices. Moreover, these perils of **intuition** appear even when people

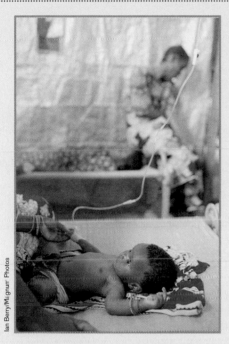

Ian Berry/Magnum Photos

Dramatic deaths in bunches breed concern and fear The memorable South Asian tsunami that killed some 300,000 people stirred an outpouring of concern and new tsunami-warning technology. Meanwhile, a "silent tsunami" of poverty-related malaria was killing about that many of the world's children every couple months, noted Jeffrey Sachs, the head of a United Nations project aiming to cut extreme poverty in half by 2015 (Dugger, 2005).

about risk. Together they explain why we sometimes fret over remote possibilities while ignoring much higher probabilities.

First, *we fear what our ancestral history has prepared us to fear.* Human emotions were road tested in the Stone Age. Our old brain prepares us to fear yesterday's risks: snakes, lizards, and spiders (which combined now kill relatively few in developed countries). And it prepares us to fear confinement and heights, and therefore flying.

Second, *we fear what we cannot control.* Driving we control, flying we do not.

Third, *we fear what is immediate.* Threats related to flying are mostly telescoped into the moments of takeoff and landing, while the dangers of driving are diffused across many moments to come, each trivially dangerous. Similarly, many smokers (whose habit shortens their lives, on average, by about five years) fret openly before flying (which, averaged across people, shortens life by one day). Smoking's toxicity kills in the distant future.

Fourth, *we fear what is most readily available in memory.* Powerful, available memories—like the image of United Flight 175 slicing into the World Trade Center—serve as our measuring rods as we intuitively judge risks. Thousands of safe car trips have extinguished our anxieties about driving.

Vivid events also distort our comprehension of risks and probable outcomes. We comprehend disasters that have killed people dramatically, in bunches. But we fear too little those threats that will claim lives undramatically, one by one, and in the distant future. As Bill Gates has noted, each year a half-million children worldwide—the equivalent of four 747s full of children every day—die quietly, one by one, from rotavirus, and we hear nothing of it (Glass, 2004). Dramatic outcomes make us gasp; probabilities we hardly grasp.

Nevertheless, we must "learn to protect ourselves and our families against future terrorist attacks," warns a U.S. Department of Homeland Security ad that appeared periodically in my local newspaper, advising us to buy and store the food supplies, duct tape, and battery-powered radios we'll need if "there's a terrorist attack on your city." With 4 in 10 Americans being at least somewhat worried "that you or someone in your family will become a victim of terrorism," the "Be afraid!" message—be afraid not just of a terrorist attack on somebody somewhere, but of one on you and your place—has been heard (Carroll, 2005).

The point to remember: It is perfectly normal to fear purposeful violence from those who hate us. When terrorists strike again, we will all recoil in horror. But smart thinkers will remember this: *Check your fears against the facts and resist those who serve their own purposes by cultivating a culture of fear.* By so doing, we can take away the terrorists' most omnipresent weapon: exaggerated fear.

"Fearful people are more dependent, more easily manipulated and controlled, more susceptible to deceptively simple, strong, tough measures and hard-line postures."

Media researcher George Gerbner to U.S. Congressional Subcommittee on Communications, 1981

are offered extra pay for thinking smart, even when they are asked to justify their answers, and even when they are expert physicians or clinicians (Shafir & LeBoeuf, 2002). From this you might conclude that our heads are indeed filled with straw.

But we must not abandon hope for human rationality. Today's cognitive scientists are also revealing intuition's powers, as you can see throughout this book (**TABLE 31.1** on the next page). For the most part, our cognition's instant, intuitive reactions enable us to react quickly and *usually* adaptively. They do so thanks, first, to our fast and frugal

TABLE 31.1 Intuition's Perils and Powers

Intuition's Dozen Deadly Sins	Evidence of Intuition's Powers
• *Hindsight bias*—looking back on events, we falsely surmise that we knew it all along. • *Illusory correlation*—intuitively perceiving a relationship where none exists. • *Memory construction*—influenced by our present moods and by misinformation, we may form false memories. • *Representativeness and availability heuristics*—fast and frugal heuristics become quick and dirty when leading us into illogical and incorrect judgments. • *Overconfidence*—our intuitive assessments of our own knowledge are often more confident than correct. • *Belief perseverance and confirmation bias*—thanks partly to our preference for confirming information, beliefs are often resilient, even after their foundation is discredited. • *Framing*—judgments flip-flop, depending on how the same issue or information is posed. • *Interviewer illusion*—inflated confidence in one's discernment based on interview alone. • *Mispredicting our own feelings*—we often mispredict the intensity and duration of our emotions. • *Self-serving bias*—in various ways, we exhibit inflated self-assessments. • *Fundamental attribution error*—overly attributing others' behavior to their dispositions by discounting unnoticed situational forces. • *Mispredicting our own behavior*—our intuitive self-predictions often go astray.	• *Blindsight*—brain-damaged persons' "sight unseen" as their bodies react to things and faces not consciously recognized. • *Right-brain thinking*—split-brain persons displaying knowledge they cannot verbalize. • *Infants' intuitive learning*—of language and physics. • *Moral intuition*—quick gut feelings that precede moral reasoning. • *Divided attention and priming*—unattended information processed by the mind's downstairs radar watchers. • *Everyday perception*—the instant parallel processing and integration of complex information streams. • *Automatic processing*—the cognitive autopilot that guides us through most of life. • *Implicit memory*—remembering *how* to do something without knowing *that* one knows. • *Heuristics*—those fast and frugal mental shortcuts that normally serve us well enough. • *Intuitive expertise*—phenomena of unconscious learning, expert learning, and physical genius. • *Creativity*—the sometimes-spontaneous appearance of novel and valuable ideas. • *Social and emotional intelligence*—the intuitive know-how to comprehend and manage ourselves in social situations and to perceive and express emotions. • *The wisdom of the body*—when instant responses are needed, the brain's emotional pathways bypass the cortex; hunches sometimes precede rational understanding. • *Thin slices*—detecting traits from mere seconds of behavior. • *Dual attitude system*—as we have two ways of knowing (unconscious and conscious) and two ways of remembering (implicit and explicit), we also have gut-level and rational attitude responses.

heuristics that enable us, for example, to intuitively assume that fuzzy-looking objects are far away, which they usually are (except on foggy mornings). Our learned associations also spawn the intuitions of our two-track mind. If a stranger looks like someone who previously harmed or threatened us, we may—without consciously recalling the earlier experience—react warily. (The learned association surfaces as a gut feeling.)

In showing how everyday heuristics usually make us smart (and only sometimes make us dumb), Gerd Gigerenzer (2004, 2007) asked both American and German university students, "Which city has more inhabitants: San Diego or San Antonio?" After thinking a moment, 62 percent of the Americans guessed right: San Diego. But German students, many of whom had not heard of San Antonio (apologies to our Texas friends), used a fast and frugal intuitive heuristic: Pick the one you recognize. With less knowledge but an adaptive heuristic, 100 percent of the German respondents answered correctly.

University of Amsterdam psychologist Ap Dijksterhuis and his colleagues (2006a,b) discovered the surprising powers of unconscious intuition in experiments that showed people complex information about potential apartments (or roommates or art posters). They invited some participants to state their immediate preference after reading a dozen pieces of information about each of four apartments. A second group, given several minutes to analyze the information, tended to make slightly smarter decisions. But wisest of all, in study after study, was a third group, whose attention was distracted for a time. This enabled their minds to process the complex information unconsciously and to arrive at a more satisfying result. Faced with complex decisions involving many factors, the best advice may indeed be to take our time—to "sleep on it"—and to await the intuitive result of our unconscious processing.

Intuition is huge. More than we realize, thinking occurs off-screen, with the results occasionally displayed on-screen. Intuition is adaptive. It feeds our expertise, our creativity, our love, and our spirituality. And intuition, smart intuition, is born of experience. Chess masters can look at a board and intuitively know the right move. Playing "blitz chess," where every move is made after barely more than a glance, they display a hardly diminished skill (Burns, 2004). Experienced chicken sexers can tell you a chick's sex at a glance, yet cannot tell you how they do it. In each case, the immediate insight describes acquired, speedy expertise that feels like instant intuition. Experienced nurses, firefighters, art critics, car mechanics, hockey players, and you, for anything in which you develop a deep and special knowledge, learn to size up many a situation in an eyeblink. Intuition is recognition, observed Nobel laureate psychologist-economist Herbert Simon (2001). It is analysis "frozen into habit."

So, intuition—fast, automatic, unreasoned feeling and thought—harvests our experience and guides our lives. Intuition is powerful, often wise, but sometimes perilous, and especially so when we overfeel and underthink, as we do when judging risks. Today's psychological science enhances our appreciation for intuition. But it also reminds us to check our intuitions against reality. Our two-track mind makes sweet harmony as smart, critical thinking listens to the creative whispers of our vast unseen mind, and builds upon it by evaluating evidence, testing conclusions, and planning for the future.

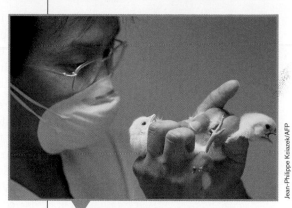

Chick sexing When acquired expertise becomes an automatic habit, as it is for experienced chick sexers, it feels like intuition. At a glance, they just know.

The Effects of Framing

31-5   What is framing?

A further test of rationality is whether the same issue, presented in two different but logically equivalent ways, will elicit the same answer. For example, one surgeon tells someone that 10 percent of people die while undergoing a particular surgery. Another tells someone that 90 percent survive. The information is the same. The effect is not. To both patients and physicians, the risk seems greater to those who hear that 10 percent will *die* (Marteau, 1989; McNeil et al., 1988; Rothman & Salovey, 1997).

The effects of **framing,** the way we present an issue, are sometimes striking. Nine in 10 college students rate a condom as effective if it has a supposed "95 percent success rate" in stopping the HIV virus that causes AIDS; only 4 in 10 think it successful given a "5 percent failure rate" (Linville et al., 1992). And people express more surprise when a 1-in-20 event happens than when an equivalent 10-in-200 event happens (Denes-Raj et al., 1995). To scare people, frame risks as numbers, not percentages. People told that a chemical exposure is projected to kill 10 of every 10 million people (imagine 10 dead people!) feel more frightened than if told the fatality risk is an infinitesimal .000001 (Kraus et al., 1992).

Consider how the framing effect influences political and business decisions. Politicians know to frame their position on public assistance as "aid to the needy" if they are for it and "welfare" if not. Merchants mark up their "regular prices" to appear to offer huge savings on "sale prices." A $100 coat marked down from $150 by Store X can seem like a better deal than the same coat priced regularly at $100 by Store Y (Urbany et al., 1988). And ground beef described as "75 percent lean" seems much more appealing than beef that is "25 percent fat" (Levin & Gaeth, 1988; Sanford et al.,

framing   the way an issue is posed; how an issue is framed can significantly affect decisions and judgments.

2002). Likewise, a price difference between gas purchased by credit card versus cash feels better if framed as a "cash discount" rather than a "credit card fee."

Framing research also finds a powerful application in the definition of options, which can be posed in ways that nudge people toward better decisions (Thaler & Sunstein, 2008).

▶ *Preferred portion size depends on framing.* If a restaurant offers a regular and an alternative "small-sized" menu option, most people will elect the larger option. If the restaurant makes the small portion the default option and relabels the larger option as "supersized," more people will choose the smaller portion (Schwartz, 2007).

▶ *Why choosing to be an organ donor depends on where you live.* In many European countries as well as North America, people can decide whether they want to be organ donors when renewing their driver's license. In countries where the default option is *yes,* but people can opt out, nearly 100 percent agree to be donors. In the United States, Canada, Britain, and Germany, where the default option is *no* but people can "opt in," only about 1 in 4 agree to be donors (Johnson & Goldstein, 2003).

▶ *How to help employees decide to save for their retirement.* A 2006 U.S. pension law recognized the huge effect of framing options. Previously, employees who wanted to defer part of their compensation to a 401(k) retirement plan typically had to elect to lower their take-home pay, which most people are averse to doing. Now companies are being encouraged to enroll their employees automatically but to allow them to opt out (thereby raising their take-home pay). In both plans, the choice was the employee's. But under the "opt-out" rather than "opt-in" option, enrollments soared from 49 to 86 percent (Madrian & Shea, 2001).

The point to remember: Those who understand the power of framing can use it to influence our decisions.

* * *

Returning to our debate about how deserving we are of our name *Homo sapiens,* let's pause to issue an interim report card. On decision making and judgment, our error-prone species might rate a C+. On problem solving, where humans are inventive yet vulnerable to fixation, we would probably receive a better mark, perhaps a B. On cognitive efficiency, our fallible but quick heuristics earn us an A.

|| What time is it now? When I asked you (in the section on overconfidence) to estimate how quickly you would finish this module, did you underestimate or overestimate? ||

REVIEW

Thinking

31-1 **What are the functions of concepts?** *Cognition* is a term covering all the mental activities associated with thinking, knowing, remembering, and communicating. We use *concepts,* mental groupings of similar objects, events, ideas, or people, to simplify and order the world around us. In creating hierarchies, we subdivide these categories into smaller and more detailed units. We form some concepts, such as triangles, by definition (three-sided objects), but we form most around *prototypes,* or best examples of a category.

31-2 **What strategies assist our problem solving, and what obstacles hinder it?** An *algorithm* is a time-consuming but thorough set of rules or procedures (such as a step-by-step description for evacuating a building during a fire) that guarantees a solution to a problem. A *heuristic* is a simpler thinking strategy (such as running for an exit if you smell smoke) that may allow us to solve problems quickly, but sometimes leads us to incorrect solutions. *Insight* is not a strategy-based solution, but rather a sudden flash of inspiration that solves a problem.

Obstacles to successful problem solving are the *confirmation bias,* which predisposes us to verify rather than challenge our hypotheses, and *fixation,* such as *mental set* and *functional fixedness,* which may prevent us from taking the fresh perspective that would let us solve the problem.

31-3 **How do heuristics, overconfidence, and belief perseverance influence our decisions and judgments?** The *representativeness heuristic* leads us to judge the likelihood of things in terms of how they represent our prototype for a group of items. The *availability heuristic* leads us to judge the likelihood of things based on how readily they come to mind, which often leads us to fear the wrong things. We are often more confident than correct. Once we have formed a belief and explained it, the explanation may linger in our minds even if the belief gets discredited—the result is *belief perseverance.* A remedy for belief perseverance is to consider how we might have explained an opposite result.

31-4 **How do smart thinkers use intuition?** Although it sometimes leads us astray, human *intuition*—effortless, immediate, automatic feeling or thought—can give us instant help when we need it. Experts in a field grow adept at making quick, shrewd judgments.

Smart thinkers will welcome their intuitions but check them against available evidence.

31-5 **What is framing?** *Framing* is the way a question or statement is worded. Subtle wording differences can dramatically alter our responses.

Terms and Concepts to Remember

cognition, p. 370

concept, p. 370

prototype, p. 370

algorithm, p. 371

heuristic, p. 371

insight, p. 371

confirmation bias, p. 373

fixation, p. 373

mental set, p. 373

functional fixedness, p. 373

representativeness heuristic, p. 374

availability heuristic, p. 375

overconfidence, p. 376

belief perseverance, p. 377

intuition, p. 378

framing, p. 381

Test Yourself

1. The availability heuristic is a quick-and-easy but sometimes misleading guide to judging reality. What is the availability heuristic?

(Answers to the Test Yourself questions can be found in Appendix B at the end of the book.)

Ask Yourself

1. People's perception of risk, often biased by vivid images from movies or the news, are surprisingly unrelated to actual risks. (People may hide in the basement during thunderstorms but fail to buckle their seat belts in the car.) What are the things you fear? Are some of those fears out of proportion to statistical risk? Are you failing, in other areas of your life, to take reasonable precautions?

∞ WEB

Multiple-choice self-tests and more may be found at www.worthpublishers.com/myers

Language Structure

Language Development

The Brain and Language

Thinking and Language

Animal Thinking and
Language

MODULE 32

Language and Thought

The most tangible indication of our thinking power is **language**—our spoken, written, or signed words and the ways we combine them as we think and communicate. Humans have long and proudly proclaimed that language sets us above all other animals. "When we study human language," asserted linguist Noam Chomsky (1972), "we are approaching what some might call the 'human essence,' the qualities of mind that are, so far as we know, unique [to humans]." To cognitive scientist Steven Pinker (1990), language is "the jewel in the crown of cognition."

Imagine an alien species that could pass thoughts from one head to another merely by pulsating air molecules in the space between them. Perhaps these weird creatures could inhabit a future Spielberg movie? Actually, we are those creatures! When we speak, our brain and voice box conjure up air pressure waves that we send banging against another's eardrum—enabling us to transfer thoughts from our brain into theirs. As Pinker (1998) notes, we sometimes sit for hours "listening to other people make noise as they exhale, because those hisses and squeaks contain *information*." And thanks to all those funny sounds created in our heads from the air pressure waves we send out, adds Bernard Guerin (2003), we get people's attention, we get them to do things, and we maintain relationships. Depending on how you vibrate the air after opening your mouth, you may get slapped or kissed.

But language is more than vibrating air. As I create this paragraph, my fingers on a keyboard generate electronic binary numbers that get translated into squiggles of dried carbon pressed onto stretched wood pulp on the page in front of you. When transmitted by reflected light rays into your retina, the printed squiggles trigger formless nerve impulses that project to several areas of your brain, which integrates the information, compares it to stored information, and decodes meaning. Thanks to language, we have transferred meaning from one mind to another. Whether spoken, written, or signed, language enables us not only to communicate but to transmit civilization's accumulated knowledge across generations. Monkeys mostly know what they see. Thanks to language, we know much that we've never seen.

Language transmits culture Words and grammar differ from culture to culture. But in every society, language allows people to transmit their accumulated knowledge from one generation to the next. Here, a group of Ivory Coast boys listens as an elder retells a tribal legend.

M. & E. Bernheim/Woodfin Camp & Associates

language our spoken, written, or signed words and the ways we combine them to communicate meaning.

▶‖ Language Structure

32-1 What are the structural components of a language?

Consider how we might go about inventing a language. For a spoken language, we would need three building blocks.

Phonemes

First, we would need a set of basic sounds, which linguists call **phonemes.** To say *bat* we utter the phonemes *b, a,* and *t. Chat* also has three phonemes—*ch, a,* and *t.* Linguists surveying nearly 500 languages have identified 869 different phonemes in human speech (Holt, 2002; Maddieson, 1984). No one language uses all of them. English uses about 40; other languages, anywhere from half to more than twice that many.

Within a language, changes in phonemes produce changes in meaning. In English, varying the vowel sound between *b* and *t* creates 12 different meanings: *bait, bat, beat/beet, bet, bit, bite, boat, boot, bought, bout,* and *but* (Fromkin & Rodman, 1983). Generally, though, consonant phonemes carry more information than do vowel phonemes. The treth ef thes stetement shed be evedent frem thes bref demenstretien.

People who grow up learning one set of phonemes usually have difficulty pronouncing those of another language. The native English speaker may smile at the native German speaker's difficulties with the *th* sound, which can make *this* sound like *dis.* But the German speaker smiles back at the problems English speakers have rolling the German *r* or pronouncing the breathy *ch* in *ich,* the German word for *I.*

Sign language also has phonemelike building blocks defined by hand shapes and movements. Like speakers, native signers of one of the 200+ sign languages may have difficulty with the phonemes of another. Chinese native signers who come to America and learn sign usually sign with an accent, notes researcher Ursula Bellugi (1994).

Morphemes

But sounds alone do not make a language. The second building block is the **morpheme,** the smallest unit of language that carries meaning. In English, a few morphemes are also phonemes—the personal pronoun *I* and the article *a,* for instance. But most morphemes are combinations of two or more phonemes. Some, like *bat,* are words, but others are only parts of words. Morphemes include prefixes and suffixes, such as the *pre-* in *preview* or the *-ed* that shows past tense.

Grammar

Finally, our new language must have a **grammar,** a system of rules (*semantics* and *syntax*) in a given language that enables us to communicate with and understand others. **Semantics** is the set of rules we use to derive meaning from morphemes, words, and even sentences. In English, a semantic rule tells us that adding *-ed* to *laugh* means that it happened in the past. **Syntax** refers to the rules we use to order words into sentences. One rule of English syntax says that adjectives usually come before nouns, so we say *white house.* Spanish adjectives usually reverse this order, as in *casa blanca.* The English rules of syntax allow the sentence *They are hunting dogs.* Given the context, semantics will tell us whether it refers to dogs that seek animals or people who seek dogs.

In all 6000 human languages, the grammar is intricately complex. "There are 'Stone Age' societies, but they do not have 'Stone Age' languages" (Pinker, 1995). Contrary to the illusion that less-educated people speak ungrammatically, they simply speak a different dialect. To a linguist, "ain't got none" is grammatically equal to "doesn't have any." (It has the same syntax.)

phoneme in language, the smallest distinctive sound unit.

morpheme in a language, the smallest unit that carries meaning; may be a word or a part of a word (such as a prefix).

grammar in a language, a system of rules that enables us to communicate with and understand others.

semantics the set of rules by which we derive meaning from morphemes, words, and sentences in a given language; also, the study of meaning.

syntax the rules for combining words into grammatically sensible sentences in a given language.

‖ How many morphemes are in the word *cats*? How many phonemes? (Answer below.) ‖

Two morphemes—*cat* and *s,* and four phonemes—*c, a, t,* and *s.*

‖ Slightly more than half the world's 6000 languages are spoken by fewer than 10,000 people. And slightly more than half the world's population speaks one of the top 20 languages (Gibbs, 2002). ‖

From The Wall Street Journal—permission Cartoon Features Syndicate.

"Let me get this straight now. Is what you want to build a jean factory or a gene factory?"

|| Although you probably know between 60,000 and 80,000 words, you use only 150 words for about half of what you say. ||

Note, however, that language becomes increasingly more complex as you move from one level to the next. In English, for example, the relatively small number of 40 or so phonemes can be combined to form more than 100,000 morphemes, which alone or in combination produce the 616,500 word forms in the *Oxford English Dictionary* (including 290,500 main entries such as *meat* and 326,000 subentries such as *meat eater*). We can then use these words to create an infinite number of sentences, most of which (like this one) are original. Like life itself constructed from the genetic code's simple alphabet, language is complexity built of simplicity. I know that you can know why I worry that you think this sentence is starting to get too complex, but that complexity—and our capacity to communicate and comprehend it—is what distinguishes human language capacity (Hauser et al., 2002).

▶|| Language Development

Make a quick guess: How many words did you learn during the years between your first birthday and your high school graduation? The answer is about 60,000 (Bloom, 2000; McMurray, 2007). That averages (after age 1) to nearly 3500 words each year, or nearly 10 each day! How you did it—how the 3500 words a year you learned could so far outnumber the roughly 200 words a year that your schoolteachers consciously taught you—is one of the great human wonders.

Before you were able to add 2 + 2, you were creating your own original and grammatically appropriate sentences. Most of us would have trouble stating our language's rules for ordering words to form sentences. Yet as preschoolers, you comprehended and spoke with a facility that puts to shame your fellow college students now struggling to learn a foreign language.

We humans have an astonishing facility for language. With remarkable efficiency, we selectively sample tens of thousands of words in memory, effortlessly assemble them with near-perfect syntax, and spew them out at a rate of three words (with a dozen or so phonemes) a second (Vigliocco & Hartsuiker, 2002). Seldom do we form sentences in our minds before speaking them. Rather they organize themselves on the fly as we speak. And while doing all this, we also adapt our utterances to our social and cultural context, following rules for speaking *(How far apart should we stand?)* and listening *(Is it OK to interrupt?)*. Given how many ways there are to mess up, it's amazing that we can master this social dance. So, when and how does it happen?

When Do We Learn Language?

32-2   What are the milestones in language development?

Receptive Language

Children's language development moves from simplicity to complexity. Infants start without language (*in fantis* means "not speaking"). Yet by 4 months of age, babies can discriminate speech sounds (Stager & Werker, 1997). They can also read lips: They prefer to look at a face that matches a sound, so we know they can recognize that *ah* comes from wide open lips and *ee* from a mouth with corners pulled back (Kuhl & Meltzoff, 1982). This period marks the beginning of the development of babies' *receptive language*, their ability to comprehend speech. At seven months and beyond, babies grow in their power to do what you and and I find difficult when listening to an unfamiliar language: segmenting spoken sounds into individual words. Moreover, their adeptness at this task, as judged by their listening patterns, predicts their language abilities at ages 2 and 5 (Newman et al., 2006).

Productive Language

Babies' *productive language,* their ability to produce words, matures after their receptive language. Around 4 months of age, babies enter the **babbling stage,** in which they spontaneously utter a variety of sounds, such as *ah-goo.* Babbling is not an imitation of adult speech, for it includes sounds from various languages, even those not spoken in the household. From this early babbling, a listener could not identify an infant as being, say, French, Korean, or Ethiopian. Deaf infants who observe their Deaf parents signing begin to babble more with their hands (Petitto & Marentette, 1991). Before nurture molds our speech, nature enables a wide range of possible sounds. Many of these natural babbling sounds are consonant-vowel pairs formed by simply bunching the tongue in the front of the mouth (*da-da, na-na, ta-ta*) or by opening and closing the lips (*ma-ma*), both of which babies do naturally for feeding (MacNeilage & Davis, 2000).

By the time infants are about 10 months old, their babbling has changed so that a trained ear can identify the language of the household (de Boysson-Bardies et al., 1989). Sounds and intonations outside that language begin to disappear. Without exposure to other languages, babies become functionally deaf to speech sounds outside their native language (Pallier et al., 2001). This explains why adults who speak only English cannot discriminate certain Japanese sounds within speech, and why Japanese adults with no training in English cannot distinguish between the English *r* and *l.* Thus, *la-la-ra-ra* may, to a Japanese-speaking adult, sound like the same syllable repeated. A Japanese-speaking person told that the train station is "just after the next light" may wonder, "The next what? After the street veering right, or farther down, after the traffic light?"

Around their first birthday (the exact age varies from child to child), most children enter the **one-word stage.** They have already learned that sounds carry meanings, and if repeatedly trained to associate, say, *fish* with a picture of a fish, 1-year-olds will look at a fish when a researcher says "Fish, fish! Look at the fish!" (Schafer, 2005). Not surprisingly, they now begin to use sounds—usually only one barely recognizable syllable, such as *ma* or *da*—to communicate meaning. But family members quickly learn to understand, and gradually the infant's language conforms more to the family's language. At this one-word stage, an inflected word may equal a sentence. "Doggy!" may mean "Look at the dog out there!"

At about 18 months, children's word learning explodes from about a word per week to a word per day. By their second birthday, most have entered the **two-word stage.** They start uttering two-word sentences (**TABLE 32.1**) in **telegraphic speech:** Like the old-fashioned telegrams (TERMS ACCEPTED. SEND MONEY), this early form of speech contains mostly nouns and verbs (*Want juice*). Also like telegrams, it follows rules of syntax; the words are in a sensible order. English-speaking children typically place adjectives before nouns—*big doggy* rather than *doggy big.*

babbling stage beginning at about 4 months, the stage of speech development in which the infant spontaneously utters various sounds at first unrelated to the household language.

one-word stage the stage in speech development, from about age 1 to 2, during which a child speaks mostly in single words.

two-word stage beginning about age 2, the stage in speech development during which a child speaks mostly two-word statements.

telegraphic speech early speech stage in which a child speaks like a telegram— "go car"—using mostly nouns and verbs.

"Got idea. Talk better. Combine words. Make sentences."

© 1994 by Sidney Harris.

TABLE 32.1 Summary of Language Development

Month (approximate)	Stage
4	Babbles many speech sounds.
10	Babbling resembles household language.
12	One-word stage.
24	Two-word, telegraphic speech.
24+	Language develops rapidly into complete sentences.

Once children move out of the two-word stage, they quickly begin uttering longer phrases (Fromkin & Rodman, 1983). If they get a late start on learning a particular language, for example after receiving a cochlear implant or being an international adoptee, their language development still proceeds through the same sequence, although usually at a faster pace (Ertmer et al., 2007; Snedeker et al., 2007). By early elementary school, children understand complex sentences and begin to enjoy the humor conveyed by double meanings: "You never starve in the desert because of all the sand-which-is there."

Explaining Language Development

32-3   How do we learn language?

Attempts to explain how we acquire language have sparked a spirited intellectual controversy. The nature-nurture debate surfaces again and, here as elsewhere, appreciation for innate predisposition and the nature-nurture interaction has grown.

Skinner: Operant Learning

Behaviorist B. F. Skinner (1957) believed we can explain language development with familiar learning principles, such as *association* (of the sights of things with the sounds of words); *imitation* (of the words and syntax modeled by others); and *reinforcement* (with smiles and hugs when the child says something right). Thus, Skinner (1985) argued, babies learn to talk in many of the same ways that animals learn to peck keys and press bars: "Verbal behavior evidently came into existence when, through a critical step in the evolution of the human species, the vocal musculature became susceptible to operant conditioning." And it's not just humans. Song-learning birds also acquire their "language" aided by imitation (Haesler, 2007).

Chomsky: Inborn Universal Grammar

Linguist Noam Chomsky (1959, 1987) has likened Skinner's ideas to filling a bottle with water. But developing language is not just being "filled up" with the right kinds of experiences, Chomsky insisted. Children acquire untaught words and grammar at a rate too extraordinary to be explained solely by learning principles. They generate all sorts of sentences they have never heard, sometimes with novel errors. (No parent teaches the sentence, "I hate you, Daddy.") Moreover, many of the errors young children make result from overgeneralizing logical grammatical rules, such as adding *-ed* to form the past tense (de Cuevas, 1990):

> **Child:** My teacher holded the baby rabbits and we petted them.
> **Mother:** Did you say your teacher held the baby rabbits?
> **Child:** Yes.
> **Mother:** Did you say she held them tightly?
> **Child:** No, she holded them loosely.

Chomsky instead views language development much like "helping a flower to grow in its own way." Given adequate nurture, language will naturally occur. It just "happens to the child." And the reason it happens is that we come prewired with a sort of switch box—a *language acquisition device*. It is as if the switches need to be turned either "on" or "off" for us to understand and produce language. As we hear language, the switches get set for the language we are to learn.

Underlying human language, Chomsky says, is a *universal grammar*: All human languages therefore have the same grammatical building blocks, such as nouns and verbs, subjects and objects, negations and questions. Thus, we readily learn the specific grammar of whatever language we experience, whether spoken or signed (Bavelier et al., 2003). And no matter what that language is, we start speaking mostly in nouns (*kitty, da-da*) rather than verbs and adjectives (Bornstein et al., 2004). It happens so naturally—as naturally as birds learning to fly—that training hardly helps.

|| Under Chomsky's influence, some researchers also infer a "universal moral grammar"—an innate sense of right and wrong—that comes prewired by evolution and gets refined by culture (Hauser, 2006; Mikhail, 2007). ||

Creating a language Brought together as if on a desert island (actually a school), Nicaragua's young deaf children over time drew upon sign gestures from home to create their own Nicaraguan Sign Language, complete with words and intricate grammar. Our biological predisposition for language does not create language in a vacuum. But activated by a social context, nature and nurture work creatively together (Osborne, 1999; Sandler et al., 2005; Senghas & Coppola, 2001).

Many psychologists believe we benefit from both Skinner's and Chomsky's views. Children's genes design complex brain wiring that prepares them to learn language as they interact with their caregivers. Skinner's emphasis on learning helps explain how infants acquire their language as they interact with others. Chomsky's emphasis on our built-in readiness to learn grammar rules helps explain why preschoolers acquire language so readily and use grammar so well. Once again, we see biology and experience working together.

Statistical Learning and Critical Periods

Human infants display a remarkable ability to learn statistical aspects of human speech. When you or I listen to an unfamiliar language, the syllables all run together. Someone unfamiliar with English might, for example, hear *United Nations* as "Uneye Tednay Shuns." Well before our first birthday, our brains were not only discerning word breaks, they were statistically analyzing which syllables, as in "hap-py-ba-by," most often go together. Jenny Saffran and her colleagues (1996; in press) showed this by exposing 8-month-old infants to a computer voice speaking an unbroken, monotone string of nonsense syllables (*bidakupadotigolabubidaku . . .*). After just two minutes of exposure, the infants were able to recognize (as indicated by their attention) three-syllable sequences that appeared repeatedly.

A natural talent Human infants come with a remarkable capacity to soak up language. But the particular language they learn will reflect their unique interactions with others.

Other research offers further testimony to infants' surprising knack for soaking up language. For example, 7-month-old infants can learn simple sentence structures. After repeatedly hearing syllable sequences that follow one rule, such as *ga-ti-ga* and *li-na-li* (an ABA pattern), they listen longer to syllables in a different sequence, such as *wo-fe-fe* (an ABB pattern) rather than *wo-fe-wo*. Their detecting the difference between the two patterns supports the idea that babies come with a built-in readiness to learn grammatical rules (Marcus et al., 1999).

But are we capable of performing this same feat of statistical analysis throughout our life span? Many researchers believe not. Childhood seems to represent a *critical* (or "sensitive") *period* for mastering certain aspects of language (Hernandez & Li, 2007). Deaf children who gain hearing with cochlear implants by age 2 develop better oral speech than do those who receive implants after age 4 (Greers, 2004). And whether children are deaf or hearing, later-than-usual exposure to language (at age 2

"Childhood is the time for language, no doubt about it. Young children, the younger the better, are good at it; it is child's play. It is a onetime gift to the species."
Lewis Thomas, *The Fragile Species*, 1992

No means no—no matter how you say it! Deaf children of Deaf-signing parents and hearing children of hearing parents have much in common. They develop language skills at about the same rate, and they are equally effective at opposing parental wishes and demanding their way.

George Ancona

"Children can learn multiple languages without an accent and with good grammar, if they are exposed to the language before puberty. But after puberty, it's very difficult to learn a second language so well. Similarly, when I first went to Japan, I was told not even to bother trying to bow, that there were something like a dozen different bows and I was always going to 'bow with an accent.'"

Psychologist Stephen M. Kosslyn, "The World in the Brain," 2008

or 3) unleashes their brain's idle language capacity, producing a rush of language. But children who have not been exposed to either a spoken or a signed language during their early years (by about age 7) gradually lose their ability to master *any* language. Natively deaf children who learn sign language after age 9 never learn it as well as those who become deaf at age 9 after learning English. They also never learn English as well as other natively deaf children who learned sign in infancy (Mayberry et al., 2002). The striking conclusion: When a young brain does not learn *any* language, its language-learning capacity never fully develops.

After the window for learning language closes, even learning a second language seems more difficult. People who learn a second language as adults usually speak it with the accent of their first. Grammar learning is similarly more difficult. Jacqueline Johnson and Elissa Newport (1991) asked Korean and Chinese immigrants to identify whether each of 276 English sentences (*"Yesterday the hunter shoots a deer"*) was grammatically correct or incorrect. Some test-takers had arrived in the United States in early childhood, others as adults, but all had been in the country for approximately 10 years. Nevertheless, as **FIGURE 32.1** reveals, those who learned their second language early learned it best. The older the age at which one emigrates to a new country, the harder it is to learn its language (Hakuta et al., 2003).

The impact of early experiences is also evident in language learning in the 90+ percent of deaf children born to hearing-nonsigning parents. These children typically do not experience language during their early years. Compared with children exposed to sign language from birth, those who learn to sign as teens or adults are like immigrants who learn English after childhood. They can master the basic words and learn to order them, but they never become as fluent as native signers in producing and comprehending subtle grammatical differences (Newport, 1990). Moreover, the late-learners show less brain activity in right hemisphere regions that are active as native signers read sign language (Newman et al., 2002). As a flower's growth will be stunted without nourishment, so, too, children will typically become linguistically stunted if isolated from language during the critical period for its acquisition. The altered brain activity in those deprived of early language raises a question: How does the maturing brain normally process language?

FIGURE 32.1 New language learning gets harder with age Young children have a readiness to learn language. Ten years after coming to the United States, Asian immigrants took a grammar test. Although there is no sharply defined critical period for second language learning, those who arrived before age 8 understood American English grammar as well as native speakers did. Those who arrived later did not. (From Johnson & Newport, 1991.)

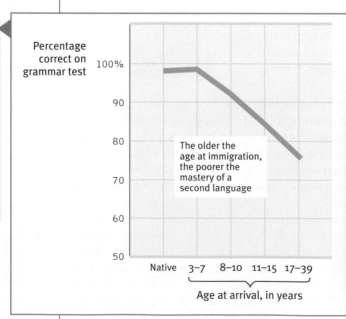

Percentage correct on grammar test

The older the age at immigration, the poorer the mastery of a second language

Native   3–7   8–10   11–15   17–39

Age at arrival, in years

▶‖ The Brain and Language

32-4 What brain areas are involved in language processing?

We think of speaking and reading, or writing and reading, or singing and speaking as merely different examples of the same general ability—language. But consider this curious finding: **Aphasia,** an impaired use of language, can result from damage to any one of several cortical areas. Even more curious, some people with aphasia can speak fluently but cannot read (despite good vision), while others can comprehend what they read but cannot speak. Still others can write but not read, read but not write, read numbers but not letters, or sing but not speak. What does this tell us about the mystery of how we use language, and how did researchers solve this mystery?

> *Clue 1* In 1865, French physician Paul Broca reported that after damage to a specific area of the left frontal lobe (later called **Broca's area**) a person would struggle to speak words while still being able to sing familiar songs and comprehend speech. Damage to Broca's area disrupts speaking.
>
> *Clue 2* In 1874, German investigator Carl Wernicke discovered that after damage to a specific area of the left temporal lobe (**Wernicke's area**) people could speak only meaningless words. Asked to describe a picture that showed two boys stealing cookies behind a woman's back, one patient responded: "Mother is away her working her work to get her better, but when she's looking the two boys looking the other part. She's working another time" (Geschwind, 1979). Damage to Wernicke's area also disrupts understanding.
>
> *Clue 3* A third brain area, the *angular gyrus,* is involved in reading aloud. It receives visual information from the visual area and recodes it into an auditory form, which Wernicke's area uses to derive its meaning. Damage to the angular gyrus leaves a person able to speak and understand, but unable to read.
>
> *Clue 4* Nerve fibers interconnect these brain areas.

A century after Broca's and Wernicke's findings, Norman Geschwind assembled these and other clues into an explanation of how we use language (**FIGURES 32.2** and **32.3**). When you read aloud, the words (1) register in the visual area, (2) are relayed to

aphasia impairment of language, usually caused by left hemisphere damage either to Broca's area (impairing speaking) or to Wernicke's area (impairing understanding).

Broca's area controls language expression—an area, usually in the left frontal lobe, that directs the muscle movements involved in speech.

Wernicke's area controls language reception—a brain area involved in language comprehension and expression; usually in the left temporal lobe.

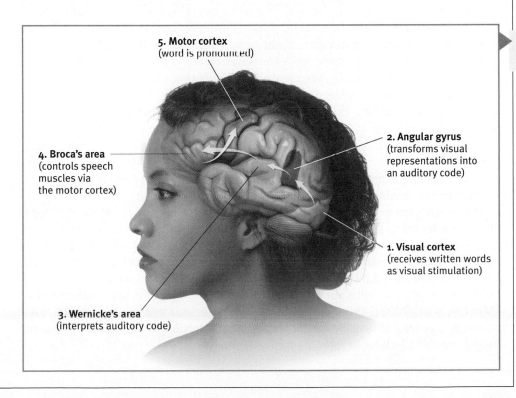

5. Motor cortex (word is pronounced)

4. Broca's area (controls speech muscles via the motor cortex)

2. Angular gyrus (transforms visual representations into an auditory code)

1. Visual cortex (receives written words as visual stimulation)

3. Wernicke's area (interprets auditory code)

FIGURE 32.2 A simplified model of brain areas involved in language processing

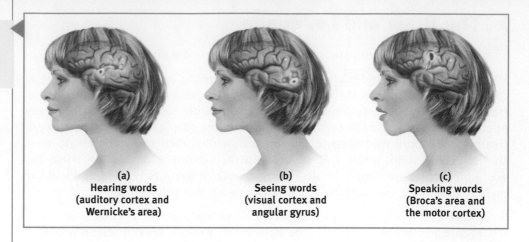

FIGURE 32.3 **Brain activity when hearing, seeing, and speaking words** PET scans such as these detect the activity of different areas of the brain.

(a)
Hearing words
(auditory cortex and
Wernicke's area)

(b)
Seeing words
(visual cortex and
angular gyrus)

(c)
Speaking words
(Broca's area and
the motor cortex)

a second brain area, the *angular gyrus,* which transforms the words into an auditory code that (3) is received and understood in the nearby Wernicke's area, and (4) is sent to Broca's area, which (5) controls the motor cortex as it creates the pronounced word. Depending on which link in this chain is damaged, a different form of aphasia occurs.

Today's neuroscience continues to enrich our understanding of language processing. We now know that more sites are involved than those portrayed in Figure 32.3, and that the "map" can vary from person to person. Moreover, fMRI scans reveal that different neural networks are activated by nouns and verbs, and by one's native language and a second language learned later in life (Perani & Abutalebi, 2005; Shapiro et al., 2006). For example, adults who learned a second language early in life use the *same* patch of frontal lobe tissue when recounting an event in either the native or the second language. Those who learned their second tongue after childhood display activity in an adjacent brain area while using their second language (Kim et al., 1997).

Still, the big point to remember is this: *In processing language, as in other forms of information processing, the brain operates by dividing its mental functions—speaking, perceiving, thinking, remembering—into subfunctions.* Your conscious experience of reading this page *seems* indivisible, but your brain is computing each word's form, sound, and meaning using different neural networks (Posner & Carr, 1992). We can also see this division of processing in vision. Right now, assuming you have sight, you are experiencing a whole visual scene as if your eyes were video cameras projecting the scene into your brain. Actually, your brain is breaking that scene into specialized subtasks, such as discerning color, depth, movement, and form. And in vision as in language, a localized trauma that destroys one of these neural work teams may cause people to lose just one aspect of processing, as when a stroke destroys the ability to perceive movement. In both systems, each specialized neural network, having simultaneously done its own thing, then feeds its information to higher-level networks that combine the atoms of experience and relay them to progressively higher-level association areas, enabling us to recognize a face as "Grandmother."

This helps explain another funny finding. Functional MRI scans show that jokes playing on meaning ("Why don't sharks bite lawyers? . . . Professional courtesy") are processed in a different brain area than jokes playing on words ("What kind of lights did Noah use on the ark? . . . Flood lights") (Goel & Dolan, 2001). Scientists have even been able to predict, from the brain's response to various concrete nouns (things we experience with our senses), the brain's response to other concrete nouns (Mitchell et al., 2008). Think about it: *What you experience as a continuous, indivisible stream of experience is actually but the visible tip of a subdivided information-processing iceberg, most of which lies beneath the surface of your awareness.*

To sum up, the mind's subsystems are localized in particular brain regions, yet the brain acts as a unified whole. Moving your hand; recognizing faces; perceiving scenes; comprehending language—all depend on specific neural networks. Yet complex functions such as listening, learning, and loving involve the coordination of many brain areas. Together, these two principles—specialization and integration—describe the brain's functioning.

▶‖ Thinking and Language

32-5 What is the relationship between language and thinking?

Thinking and language intricately intertwine. Asking which comes first is one of psychology's chicken-and-egg questions. Do our ideas come first and we wait for words to name them? Or are our thoughts conceived in words and therefore unthinkable without them?

Language Influences Thinking

Linguist Benjamin Lee Whorf contended that language determines the way we think. According to Whorf's (1956) **linguistic determinism** hypothesis, different languages impose different conceptions of reality: "Language itself shapes a man's basic ideas." The Hopi, Whorf noted, have no past tense for their verbs. Therefore, he contended, a Hopi could not so readily *think* about the past.

To say that language *determines* the way we think is much too strong. But to those who speak two dissimilar languages, such as English and Japanese, it seems obvious that a person may think differently in different languages (Brown, 1986). Unlike English, which has a rich vocabulary for self-focused emotions such as anger, Japanese has more words for interpersonal emotions such as sympathy (Markus & Kitayama, 1991). Many bilinguals report that they have different senses of self, depending on which language they are using (Matsumoto, 1994). They may even reveal different personality profiles when taking the same test in their two languages (Dinges & Hull, 1992). "Learn a new language and get a new soul," says a Czech proverb.

Michael Ross, Elaine Xun, and Anne Wilson (2002) demonstrated this by inviting China-born, bilingual University of Waterloo students to describe themselves in English or Chinese. English-language versions of self-descriptions fit typical Canadian profiles: Students expressed mostly positive self-statements and moods. Responding in Chinese, students gave typically Chinese self-descriptions: They reported more agreement with Chinese values and roughly equal positive and negative self-statements and moods. Their language use seemed to shape how they thought of themselves.

A similar personality change occurs as people shift between the cultural frames associated with English and Spanish. English speakers score higher than Spanish speakers on measures of extraversion, agreeableness, and conscientious. But is this a language effect? Nairán Ramírez-Esparza and her co-workers (2006) wondered. So they had samples of bicultural, bilingual Americans and Mexicans take the tests in each language. Sure enough, when using English they expressed their somewhat more extraverted, agreeable, and conscientious selves (and the differences were not due to how the questionnaires were translated).

So our words may not *determine* what we think, but they do *influence* our thinking (Hardin & Banaji, 1993; Özgen, 2004). We use our language in forming categories. In Brazil, the isolated Piraha tribespeople have words for the numbers *1* and *2*, but numbers above that are simply "many." Thus if shown *7* nuts in a row, they find it very difficult to lay out the same number from their own pile (Gordon, 2004).

"It is the way systems interact and have a dynamic interdependence that is—unless one has lost all sense of wonder—quite awe-inspiring."
Simon Conway Morris, "The Boyle Lecture," 2005

‖ Before reading on, use a pen or pencil to sketch this idea: "The girl pushes the boy." Now see the inverted margin note below. ‖

How did you illustrate "the girl pushes the boy"? Anne Maass and Aurore Russo (2003) report that people whose language reads from left to right mostly position the pushing girl on the left. Those who read and write Arabic, a right-to-left language, mostly place her on the right. This spatial bias appears only in those old enough to have learned their culture's writing system (Dobel et al., 2007).

linguistic determinism Whorf's hypothesis that language determines the way we think.

"All words are pegs to hang ideas on."
Henry Ward Beecher, *Proverbs from Plymouth Pulpit*, 1887

Words also influence our thinking about colors. Whether we live in New Mexico, New South Wales, or New Guinea, we *see* colors much the same, but we use our native language to *classify* and *remember* colors (Davidoff, 2004; Roberson et al., 2004, 2005). If that language is English, you might view three colors and call two of them "yellow" and one of them "blue." Later you would likely see and recall the yellows as being more similar. But if you were a member of Papua New Guinea's Berinmo tribe, which has words for two different shades of yellow, you would better recall the distinctions between the two yellows.

Perceived differences grow when we assign different names to colors. On the color spectrum, blue blends into green—until we draw a dividing line between the portions we call "blue" and "green." Although equally different on the color spectrum (**FIGURE 32.4**), two different "blues" (or two different "greens") that share the same name are harder to distinguish than two items with the different names "blue" and "green" (Özgen, 2004).

Given words' subtle influence on thinking, we do well to choose our words carefully. Does it make any difference whether I write, "A child learns language as *he* interacts with *his* caregivers" or "Children learn language as *they* interact with *their* caregivers"? Many studies have found that it does. When hearing the generic *he* (as in "the artist and *his* work") people are more likely to picture a male (Henley, 1989; Ng, 1990). If *he* and *his* were truly gender-free, we shouldn't skip a beat when hearing that "man, like other mammals, nurses his young."

To expand language is to expand the ability to think. In young children, thinking develops hand in hand with language (Gopnik & Meltzoff, 1986). Indeed, it is very difficult to think about or conceptualize certain abstract ideas (commitment, freedom, or rhyming) without language! And what is true for preschoolers is true for everyone: *It pays to increase your word power.* That's why most textbooks, including this one, introduce new words—to teach new ideas and new ways of thinking. And that is why psychologist Steven Pinker (2007) titled his book on language, *The Stuff of Thought.*

Increased word power helps explain what McGill University researcher Wallace Lambert (1992; Lambert et al., 1993) calls the *bilingual advantage.* Bilingual children, who learn to inhibit one language while using the other, are also better able to inhibit their attention to irrelevant information. If asked to say whether a sentence (*"Why is the cat barking so loudly?"*) is grammatically correct, they can more efficiently focus on the grammar alone (Bialystok, 2001; Carlson & Meltzoff, 2008).

Lambert helped devise a Canadian program that immerses English-speaking children in French. (From 1981 to 2001, the number of non-Quebec Canadian children immersed in French rose from 65,000 to 297,000 [Statistics Canada, 2007].) For most of their first three years in school, the English-speaking children are taught entirely in French, and thereafter gradually shift by the end of their schooling to classes mostly in English. Not surprisingly, the children attain a natural French fluency unrivaled by

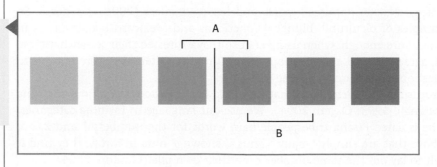

FIGURE 32.4 Language and perception
Emre Özgen (2004) reports that when people view blocks of equally different colors, they perceive those with different names as more different. Thus the "green" and "blue" in contrast A may appear to differ more than the two similarly different blues in contrast B.

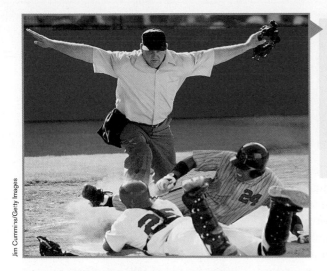

A safe sign We have outfielder William Hoy to thank for baseball sign language. The first deaf player to join the major leagues (1892), he invented hand signals for "Strike!" "Safe!" (shown here) and "Yerr Out!" (Pollard, 1992). Such gestures worked so well that referees in all sports now use invented signs, and fans are fluent in sports sign language.

other methods of language teaching. Moreover, compared with similarly capable children in control groups, they do so without detriment to their English fluency, and with increased aptitude scores, creativity, and appreciation for French-Canadian culture (Genesee & Gándara, 1999; Lazaruk, 2007).

Whether we are deaf or hearing, minority or majority, language links us to one another. Language also connects us to the past and the future. "To destroy a people, destroy their language," observed poet Joy Harjo.

Thinking in Images

When you are alone, do you talk to yourself? Is "thinking" simply conversing with yourself? Without a doubt, words convey ideas. But aren't there times when ideas precede words? To turn on the cold water in your bathroom, in which direction do you turn the handle? To answer this question, you probably thought not in words but with *nondeclarative* (procedural) memory—a mental picture of how you do it.

Indeed, we often think in images. Artists think in images. So do composers, poets, mathematicians, athletes, and scientists. Albert Einstein reported that he achieved some of his greatest insights through visual images and later put them into words. Pianist Liu Chi Kung showed the value of thinking in images. One year after placing second in the 1958 Tschaikovsky piano competition, Liu was imprisoned during China's cultural revolution. Soon after his release, after seven years without touching a piano, he was back on tour, the critics judging his musicianship better than ever. How did he continue to develop without practice? "I did practice," said Liu, "every day. I rehearsed every piece I had ever played, note by note, in my mind" (Garfield, 1986).

For someone who has learned a skill, such as ballet dancing, even *watching* the activity will activate the brain's internal simulation of it, reported one British research team after collecting fMRIs as people watched videos (Calvo-Merino et al., 2004). So, too, will imagining an activity. **FIGURE 32.5** on the next page shows an fMRI of a person imagining the experience of pain, activating neural networks that are active during actual pain (Grèzes & Decety, 2001).

Small wonder, then, that "mental practice has become a standard part of training" for Olympic athletes (Suinn, 1997). One experiment on mental practice and basketball foul shooting tracked the University of Tennessee women's team over 35 games (Savoy & Beitel, 1996). During that time, the team's free-throw shooting increased from approximately 52 percent in games following standard physical practice to some 65 percent after mental practice. Players had repeatedly imagined making foul shots

|| Many native English speakers, including most Americans, are monolingual. Most humans are bilingual or multilingual. Does monolingualism limit people's ability to comprehend the thinking of other cultures? ||

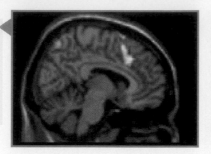
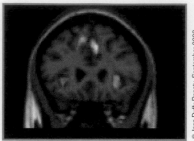

© Jean Duffy Decety, September 2003

FIGURE 32.5 The power of imagination Imagining a physical activity triggers action in the same brain areas that are triggered when actually performing that activity. These fMRIs show a person imagining the experience of pain, which activates some of the same areas in the brain as the actual experience of pain.

under various conditions, including being "trash-talked" by their opposition. In a dramatic conclusion, Tennessee won the national championship game in overtime, thanks in part to their foul shooting.

Mental rehearsal can also help you achieve an academic goal, as Shelley Taylor and her UCLA colleagues (1998) demonstrated with two groups of introductory psychology students facing a midterm exam one week later. (Scores of other students formed a control group, not engaging in any mental simulation.) The first group was told to spend five minutes each day visualizing themselves scanning the posted grade list, seeing their A, beaming with joy, and feeling proud. This daily *outcome simulation* had little effect, adding only 2 points to their exam-scores average. Another group spent five minutes each day visualizing themselves effectively studying—reading the chapters, going over notes, eliminating distractions, declining an offer to go out. This daily *process simulation* paid off—this second group began studying sooner, spent more time at it, and beat the others' average by 8 points. *The point to remember:* It's better to spend your fantasy time planning how to get somewhere than to dwell on the imagined destination.

Experiments on thinking without language bring up a recurring principle: Much of our information processing occurs outside of consciousness and beyond language. Inside our ever-active brain, many streams of activity flow in parallel, function automatically, are remembered implicitly, and only occasionally surface as conscious words.

* * *

What, then, should we say about the relationship between thinking and language? As we have seen, language does influence our thinking. But if thinking did not also affect language, there would never be any new words. And new words and new combinations of old words express new ideas. The basketball term *slam dunk* was coined after the act itself had become fairly common. So, let us say that *thinking affects our language, which then affects our thought* (**FIGURE 32.6**).

A thoughtful art Playing the piano engages thinking without language. In the absence of a piano, mental practice can sustain one's skill.

Courtesy Christine Brune

Psychological research on thinking and language mirrors the mixed views of our species by those in fields such as literature and religion. The human mind is simultaneously capable of striking intellectual failures and of striking intellectual power. Misjudgments are common and can have disastrous consequences. So we do well to appreciate our capacity for error. Yet our efficient heuristics—our snap judgment strategies—often serve us well. Moreover, our ingenuity at problem solving and our extraordinary power of language mark humankind as almost "infinite in faculties."

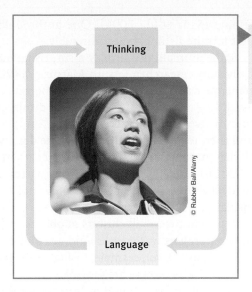

FIGURE 32.6 The interplay of thought and language The traffic runs both ways between thinking and language. Thinking affects our language, which affects our thought.

▶‖ Animal Thinking and Language

32-6 What do we know about animal thinking? Do other animals share our capacity for language?

If in our use of language we humans are, as the psalmist long ago rhapsodized, "little lower than God," where do other animals fit in the scheme of things? Are they "little lower than human"? Let's see what the research on animal thinking and language can tell us.

What Do Animals Think?

Animals are smarter than we often realize. A baboon knows everyone's voices within its 80-member troop (Jolly, 2007). Sheep can recognize and remember individual faces (Morell, 2008). A marmoset can learn from and imitate others. Great apes and even monkeys can *form concepts*. When monkeys learn to classify cats and dogs, certain frontal lobe neurons in their brains fire in response to new "catlike" images, others to new "doglike" images (Freedman et al., 2001). Even pigeons—mere birdbrains—can sort objects (pictures of cars, cats, chairs, flowers). Shown a picture of a never-before-seen chair, pigeons will reliably peck a key that represents the category "chairs" (Wasserman, 1995).

We also are not the only creatures to *display insight*, as psychologist Wolfgang Köhler (1925) demonstrated in an experiment with Sultan, a chimpanzee. Köhler placed a piece of fruit and a long stick well beyond Sultan's reach, and a short stick inside his cage. Spying the short stick, Sultan grabbed it and tried to reach the fruit. After several unsuccessful attempts, Sultan dropped the stick and seemed to survey the situation. Then suddenly, as if thinking "Aha!" he jumped up, seized the short stick again, and used it to pull in the longer stick—which he then used to reach the fruit. This evidence of animal cognition, said Köhler, showed that there is more to learning than conditioning. What is more, apes will even exhibit foresight, by storing a tool that they can use to retrieve food the next day (Mulcahy & Call, 2006).

Chimpanzees, like humans, are shaped by reinforcement when they solve problems. Forest-dwelling chimpanzees have become *natural tool users* (Boesch-Achermann & Boesch, 1993). They break off a reed or a stick, strip the twigs and leaves, carry it to a termite mound, fish for termites by twisting it just so, and then carefully remove it without scraping off many termites. They even select different tools for different purposes—a heavy stick to puncture holes, a light, flexible stick for fishing (Sanz et al., 2004). One anthropologist, trying to mimic the chimpanzee's deft termite fishing, failed miserably.

Some animals also display a surprising *numerical ability*. Over two decades, Kyoto University researcher Tetsuro Matsuzawa (2007) has studied chimpanzees' ability to remember and relate numbers. In one experiment, a chimpanzee named Ai taps, in ascending order, numbers randomly displayed on a computer screen (**FIGURE 32.7**). If four or five of the numbers between 1 and 9 are flashed for no more than a second, and then replaced by white boxes, she does what a human cannot. Remembering the flashed numbers, she again taps the boxes in numerical order.

Until his death in 2007, the grey parrot, Alex, also displayed a jaw-dropping numerical ability (Pepperberg, 2006). He not only could name and categorize objects, he displayed a comprehension of numbers up to 6. Thus, he could speak the number of objects, add two small clusters of objects and announce the sum, and indicate which of two numbers was greater. And he could answer when shown various groups of objects and asked, for example, "What color four?" (meaning "What's the color of the objects of which there are four?").

Researchers have found at least 39 local customs related to chimpanzee tool use, grooming, and courtship (Whiten & Boesch, 2001). One group may slurp ants directly from the stick, while another group plucks them off individually. One group may break nuts with a stone hammer, another with a wooden hammer. Or picture this actual laboratory experiment: Chimpanzee B observes Chimpanzee A as it obtains food, either by sliding or lifting a door. Then B follows the same lifting or sliding procedure. So does Chimpanzee C after observing B, and so forth. Chimp see, chimp do, unto the sixth generation (Bonnie et al., 2007; Horner et al., 2006).

To learn such customs, it helps to be a primate with a relatively large cortex (Whiten & van Schaik, 2007). But the chimpanzee group differences, along with differing dialects and hunting styles, seem not to be genetic. Rather, they are the chimpanzee equivalent of cultural diversity. Like humans, chimpanzees invent behaviors and *transmit cultural patterns* to their peers and offspring (**FIGURE 32.8a**). So do orangutans and capuchin monkeys (Dindo et al., 2008; van Schaik et al., 2003). And so do some Australian dolphins (**FIGURE 32.8b**), which have learned to break off sponges and wear them on their snouts while probing the sea floor for fish (Krützen et al., 2005).

Thus animals, and chimpanzees in particular, display remarkable talents. They form concepts, display insight, fashion tools, exhibit numerical abilities, and transmit local

FIGURE 32.7

Chimpanzee bests humans It is adaptive for chimpanzees to be able to monitor lots of information in their natural environment. This might explain how chimpanzee Ai can remember and tap numbers in ascending order, even after they are covered by white boxes.

Tetsuro Matsuzawa/Primate Research Institute, Kyoto University

(a)   (b)

FIGURE 32.8
Cultural transmission (a) On the western bank of one Ivory Coast river, a youngster watches as its mother uses a stone hammer to open a nut. On the river's other side, a few miles away, chimpanzees do not follow this custom. (b) This bottlenose dolphin in Shark Bay, Western Australia, is a member of a small group that uses marine sponges as protective gear when probing the sea floor for fish.

cultural behaviors. Chimpanzees and two species of monkeys can even read your intent. They would show more interest in a food container that you have intentionally grasped rather than one you flopped your hand on, as if by accident (Wood et al., 2007). Great apes, dolphins, and elephants have also demonstrated self-awareness (by recognizing themselves in a mirror). And as social creatures, chimpanzees have shown altruism, cooperation, and group aggression. But do they, like humans, exhibit language?

Do Animals Exhibit Language?

Without doubt, animals communicate. Vervet monkeys have different alarm cries for different predators: a barking call for a leopard, a cough for an eagle, and a chuttering for a snake. Hearing the leopard alarm, other vervets climb the nearest tree. Hearing the eagle alarm, they rush into the bushes. Hearing the snake chutter, they stand up and scan the ground (Byrne, 1991). Whales also communicate, with clicks and wails. Honeybees do a dance that informs other bees of the direction and distance of the food source.

Comprehending canine Rico, a border collie with a 200-word vocabulary, can infer that an unfamiliar sound refers to a novel object.

And what shall we say of dogs' ability to understand us? Border collie Rico knows and can fetch 200 items by name. Moreover, reports a team of psychologists at Leipzig's Max Planck Institute, if he is asked to retrieve a novel toy with a name he has never heard, Rico will pick out the novel item from among a group of familiar items (Kaminski et al., 2004). Hearing that novel word for the second time four weeks later, he as often as not retrieves the object. Such feats show animals' comprehension and communication. But is this language?

The Case of the Apes

The greatest challenge to our claim to be the only language-using species has come from one of our closest genetic relatives, the chimpanzees. Psychologists Allen Gardner and Beatrix Gardner (1969) aroused enormous scientific and public interest when they taught sign language to the chimpanzee Washoe (c. 1965–2007). After four years, Washoe could use 132 signs; by age 32, 181 signs (Sanz et al., 1998). One *New York Times* reporter, having learned sign language from his deaf parents, visited Washoe and exclaimed, "Suddenly I realized I was conversing with a member of another species in my native tongue."

"He says he wants a lawyer."

CLOSE-UP

Talking Hands

Chimpanzees' use of sign language builds upon their natural gestured words (such as a hand extended for "I want some"). Human language appears to have evolved from such gestured communications (Corballis, 2002, 2003; Pollick & de Waal, 2007). So, it's no wonder we talk and think with our hands:

- Gestures (pointing at a cup) pave the way for children's language (saying *cup,* while simultaneously pointing) (Iverson & Goldin-Meadow, 2005).
- Signed language readily develops among Deaf people.
- People gesture even when talking on the phone.
- Congenitally blind people, like sighted people, gesture (Iverson & Goldin-Meadow, 1998). (And they do so even when they believe their listener is also blind.)

- Prohibiting gestures disrupts speech with spatial content, as when people try to describe an apartment's layout.
- Gesturing lightens a speaker's "cognitive load" (Goldin-Meadow, 2006). People told not to gesture put more effort into communicating with words alone, and are less able to remember recently learned words or numbers.

Gestured communication For hearing people, today's gestures may be less central to communication than for those who first used hand signals. Yet gestures remain naturally associated with spontaneous speech, especially speech that has spatial content.

|| Gesture researcher Robert Krauss (1998) recalls his grandfather telling of two men walking on a bitter winter day. One chattered away while the second nodded, saying nothing. "Schmuel, why aren't you saying anything?" the first friend finally wondered. "Because," replied Schmuel, "I forgot my gloves." ||

|| Seeing a doll floating in her water, Washoe signed, "Baby in my drink." ||

Further evidence of gestured "ape language" surfaced during the 1970s (see Close-Up: Talking Hands). Usually apes sign just single words such as "that" or "gimme" (Bowman, 2003). But sometimes they string signs together to form intelligible sentences. Washoe signed, "You me go out, please." Apes even appear to combine words creatively. Washoe designated a swan as a "water bird." Koko, a gorilla trained by Francine Patterson (1978), reportedly described a long-nosed Pinocchio doll as an "elephant baby." Lana, a "talking" chimpanzee that punched a crude computer keyboard that translated her entries into English, wanted her trainer's orange. She had no word for *orange,* but she did know her colors and the word for *apple,* so she improvised: "?Tim give apple which-is orange" (Rumbaugh, 1977).

Granted, these vocabularies and sentences are simple, rather like those of a 2-year-old child (and nothing like your own 60,000 or so words, which you fluidly combine to create a limitless variety of sentences). Yet, as reports of ape language accumulated, it seemed that they might indeed be "little lower than human." Then, in the late 1970s, fascination with "talking apes" turned toward cynicism: Were the chimps language champs or were the researchers chumps? The ape language researchers were making monkeys of themselves, said the skeptics. Consider:

▶ Unlike speaking or signing children, who effortlessly soak up dozens of new words a week, apes gain their limited vocabularies only with great difficulty (Wynne, 2004, 2008). Saying that apes can learn language because they can sign words is like saying humans can fly because they can jump.

▶ Chimpanzees can make signs or push buttons in sequence to get a reward, but pigeons, too, can peck a sequence of keys to get grain (Straub et al., 1979). After training a chimpanzee he named Nim Chimsky, Herbert Terrace (1979) concluded that much of apes' signing is nothing more than aping their trainers' signs and learning that certain arm movements produce rewards.

▶ Presented with ambiguous information, people, thanks to their *perceptual set*, tend to see what they want or expect to see. Interpreting chimpanzee signs as language may be little more than the trainers' wishful thinking, claimed Terrace. (When Washoe signed *water bird,* she perhaps was separately naming *water* and *bird*.)

▶ "Give orange me give eat orange me eat orange . . ." is a far cry from the exquisite syntax of a 3-year-old (Anderson, 2004; Pinker, 1995). To the child, "you tickle" and "tickle you" communicate different ideas. A chimpanzee, lacking human syntax, might sign the phrases interchangeably.

But is this language? Chimpanzees' ability to express themselves in American Sign Language (ASL) raises questions about the very nature of language. Here, the trainer is asking, "What is this?" The sign in response is "Baby." Does the response constitute language?

In science as in politics, controversy can stimulate progress. Further evidence confirms chimpanzees' abilities to think and communicate. One surprising finding was of Washoe's training her adopted son in the signs she had learned. After her second infant died, Washoe became withdrawn when told, "Baby dead, baby gone, baby finished." Two weeks later, caretaker-researcher Roger Fouts (1992, 1997) signed better news: "I have baby for you." Washoe reacted with instant excitement, hair on end, swaggering and panting while signing over and again, "Baby, my baby." It took several hours for Washoe and the foster infant, Loulis, to warm to each other, whereupon she broke the ice by signing, "Come baby" and cuddling Loulis.

In the months that followed, Loulis picked up 68 signs simply by observing Washoe and three other language-trained chimpanzees. They now sign spontaneously, asking one another to *chase, tickle, hug, come,* or *groom.* People who sign are in near-perfect agreement about what the chimpanzees are saying, 90 percent of which pertains to social interaction, reassurance, or play (Fouts & Bodamer, 1987). The chimpanzees are even modestly bilingual; they can translate spoken English words into signs (Shaw, 1989–1990).

Even more stunning was the report by Sue Savage-Rumbaugh and her colleagues (1993) of pygmy chimpanzees learning to *comprehend syntax* in English spoken to them. Kanzi, a pygmy chimpanzee with the seeming grammatical abilities of a human 2-year-old, happened onto language while observing his adoptive mother during language training. Kanzi has behaved intelligently whether asked, "Can you show me the light?" or "Can you bring me the [flash]light?" or "Can you turn the light on?" Kanzi also knows many spoken words, such as *snake, bite,* and *dog.* Given stuffed animals and asked—for the first time—to "make the dog bite the snake," he put the snake to the dog's mouth. For chimpanzees as for humans, early life is a critical time for learning language.

"[Our] view that [we are] unique from all other forms of animal life is being jarred to the core."
Duane Rumbaugh and Sue Savage-Rumbaugh (1978)

"Although humans make sounds with their mouths and occasionally look at each other, there is no solid evidence that they actually communicate with each other."

Without early exposure to speech or word symbols, adults will not gain language competence (Rumbaugh & Savage-Rumbaugh, 1994).

The provocative claims that "apes share our capacity for language" and the skeptical counterclaims that "apes no use language" (as Washoe might have put it) have moved psychologists toward a greater appreciation of apes' remarkable abilities and of our own (Friend, 2004; Rumbaugh & Washburn, 2003). Most now agree that humans alone possess language, if by the term we mean verbal or signed expression of complex grammar. If we mean, more simply, an ability to communicate through a meaningful sequence of symbols, then apes are indeed capable of language.

Believing that animals could not think, Descartes and other philosophers argued that they were living robots without any moral rights. Animals, it has been said at one time or another, cannot plan, conceptualize, count, use tools, show compassion, or use language (Thorpe, 1974). Today, we know better. Animal researchers have shown us that primates exhibit insight, show family loyalty, communicate with one another, display altruism, transmit cultural patterns across generations, and comprehend the syntax of human speech. Accepting and working out the moral implications of all this is an unfinished task for our own thinking species.

"Chimps do not develop language. But that is no shame on them; humans would surely do no better if trained to hoot and shriek like chimps, to perform the waggle-dance of the bee, or any of the other wonderful feats in nature's talent show."

Steve Pinker (1995)

REVIEW

Language and Thought

32-1 **What are the structural components of a language?** *Phonemes* are a language's basic units of sound. *Morphemes* are the elementary units of meaning. *Grammar*—the system of rules that enables us to communicate—includes *semantics* (rules for deriving meaning) and *syntax* (rules for ordering words into sentences).

32-2 **What are the milestones in language development?** The timing varies from one child to another, but all children follow the same sequence. At about 4 months of age, infants *babble*, making sounds found in languages located all over the world. By about 10 months, their babbling contains only the sounds found in their household language. Around 12 months of age, children begin to speak in single words. This *one-word stage* evolves into *two-word (telegraphic)* utterances before their second birthday, after which they begin speaking in full sentences.

32-3 **How do we learn language?** Behaviorist B. F. Skinner proposed that we learn language by the familiar principles of association (of sights of things with sounds of words), imitation (of words and syntax modeled by others), and reinforcement (with smiles and hugs after saying something right). Linguist Noam Chomsky argues that we are born with a language acquisition device that biologically prepares us to learn language and that equips us with a universal grammar, which we use to learn a specific language. Cognitive researchers believe childhood is a critical period for learning spoken and signed language.

32-4 **What brain areas are involved in language processing?** When you read aloud, your brain's visual cortex registers words as visual stimuli, the angular gyrus transforms those visual representations into auditory codes, and *Wernicke's area* interprets those codes and sends the message to *Broca's area,* which controls the motor cortex as it creates the pronounced words. But we now know that language results from the integration of many specific neural networks performing specialized subtasks in many parts of the brain.

32-5 **What is the relationship between language and thinking?** Although Whorf's *linguistic determinism* hypothesis suggested that language determines thought, it is more accurate to say that language influences thought. Different languages embody different ways of thinking, and immersion in bilingual education can enhance thinking. We often think in images when we use procedural memory—our unconscious memory system for motor and cognitive skills and classically and operantly conditioned associations. Thinking in images can increase our skills when we mentally practice upcoming events.

32-6 **What do we know about animal thinking? Do other animals share our capacity for language?** Both humans and the great apes form concepts, display insight, use and create tools, exhibit numerical abilities, and transmit cultural innovations. A number of chimpanzees have learned to communicate with humans by signing or by pushing buttons wired to a computer, have developed vocabularies of nearly 200 words, have communicated by stringing these words together, and have taught their skills to younger animals. Only humans can master the verbal or signed expression of complex rules of syntax. Nevertheless, primates and other animals demonstrate impressive abilities to think and communicate.

Terms and Concepts to Remember

language, p. 384

phoneme, p. 385

morpheme, p. 385

grammar, p. 385

semantics, p. 385

syntax, p. 385

babbling stage, p. 387

one-word stage, p. 387

two-word stage, p. 387

telegraphic speech, p. 387

aphasia, p. 391

Broca's area, p. 391

Wernicke's area, p. 391

linguistic determinism, p. 393

Test Yourself

1. If children are not yet speaking, is there any reason to think they would benefit from parents and other caregivers reading to them?

2. To say that "words are the mother of ideas" assumes the truth of what concept?

3. If your dog barks at a stranger at the front door, does this qualify as language? What if the dog yips in a telltale way to let you know she needs to go out?

(Answers to the Test Yourself questions can be found in Appendix B at the end of the book.)

Ask Yourself

1. There has been controversy at some universities about allowing fluency in sign language to fulfill a second-language requirement for an undergraduate degree. What is your opinion?

2. Do you use certain words or gestures that only your family or closest circle of friends understand? Can you envision using these words or gestures to construct a language, as the Nicaraguan children did in building their version of sign?

3. Can you think of a time when you felt an animal was communicating with you? How might you put such intuition to a test?

∞ WEB

Multiple-choice self-tests and more may be found at www.worthpublishers.com/myers

Is Intelligence One General Ability or Several Specific Abilities?

Intelligence and Creativity

Emotional Intelligence

Is Intelligence Neurologically Measurable?

Introduction to Intelligence

School boards, courts, and scientists debate the use and fairness of tests that attempt to assess people's mental abilities and assign them a score. Is intelligence testing a constructive way to guide people toward suitable opportunities? Or is it a potent, discriminatory weapon camouflaged as science? First, some basic questions:

▶ What is intelligence?

▶ How can we best assess it?

▶ To what extent does it result from heredity rather than environment?

▶ What do test score differences among individuals and groups really mean? Should we use such differences to rank people, to admit them to colleges or universities, to hire them?

Psychologists debate: Should we consider intelligence as one aptitude or many? As linked to cognitive speed? As neurologically measurable? Yet, intelligence experts do agree on this: Although people have differing abilities, intelligence is a concept and not a "thing." When we refer to someone's "IQ" (short for *intelligence quotient*) as if it were a fixed and objectively real trait like height, we commit a reasoning error called *reification*—viewing an abstract, immaterial concept as if it were a concrete thing. To reify is to invent a concept, give it a name, and then convince ourselves that such a thing objectively exists in the world. When someone says, "She has an IQ of 120," they are reifying IQ; they are imagining IQ to be a thing this person *has,* rather than a score she once obtained on a particular **intelligence test.** Better to say, "She scored 120 on the intelligence test."

Intelligence is a socially constructed concept: Cultures deem "intelligent" whatever attributes enable success in those cultures (Sternberg & Kaufman, 1998). In the Amazon rain forest, intelligence may be understanding the medicinal qualities of local plants; in an Ontario high school, it may be superior performance on cognitive tasks. In each context, **intelligence** is the ability to learn from experience, solve problems, and use knowledge to adapt to new situations. In research studies, *intelligence* is what intelligence tests measure. Historically, as we will see, that has been the sort of problem solving displayed as "school smarts."

Hands-on healing The socially constructed concept of intelligence varies from culture to culture. This folk healer in Peru displays his intelligence in his knowledge about his medicinal plants and understanding of the needs of the people he is helping.

intelligence test a method for assessing an individual's mental aptitudes and comparing them with those of others, using numerical scores.

intelligence mental quality consisting of the ability to learn from experience, solve problems, and use knowledge to adapt to new situations.

▶‖ Is Intelligence One General Ability or Several Specific Abilities?

33-1 What arguments support intelligence as one general mental ability, and what arguments support the idea of multiple distinct abilities?

You probably know some people with talents in science, others who excel at the humanities, and still others gifted in athletics, art, music, or dance. You may also know a talented artist who is dumbfounded by the simplest mathematical problems, or a brilliant math student with little aptitude for literary discussion. Are all of these people intelligent? Could you rate their intelligence on a single scale? Or would you need several different scales?

Charles Spearman (1863–1945) believed we have one **general intelligence** (often shortened to **g**). He granted that people often have special abilities that stand out. Spearman had helped develop **factor analysis,** a statistical procedure that identifies clusters of related items. He had noted that those who score high in one area, such as verbal intelligence, typically score higher than average in other areas, such as spatial or reasoning ability. Spearman believed a common skill set, the g factor, underlies all of our intelligent behavior, from navigating the sea to excelling in school.

This idea of a general mental capacity expressed by a single intelligence score was controversial in Spearman's day, and it remains so in our own. One of Spearman's early opponents was L. L. Thurstone (1887–1955). Thurstone gave 56 different tests to people and mathematically identified seven clusters of primary mental abilities (word fluency, verbal comprehension, spatial ability, perceptual speed, numerical ability, inductive reasoning, and memory). Thurstone did not rank people on a single scale of general aptitude. But when other investigators studied the profiles of the people Thurstone had tested, they detected a persistent tendency: Those who excelled in one of the seven clusters generally scored well on the others. So, the investigators concluded, there was still some evidence of a g factor.

We might, then, liken mental abilities to physical abilities. Athleticism is not one thing but many. The ability to run fast is distinct from the strength needed for power lifting, which is distinct from the eye-hand coordination required to throw a ball on target. A champion weightlifter rarely has the potential to be a skilled ice skater. Yet there remains some tendency for good things to come packaged together—for running speed and throwing accuracy to correlate, thanks to general athletic ability. So, too, with intelligence. Several distinct abilities tend to cluster together and to correlate enough to define a small general intelligence factor.

Satoshi Kanazawa (2004) argues that general intelligence evolved as a form of intelligence that helps people solve *novel* problems—how to stop a fire from spreading, how to find food during a drought, how to reunite with one's band on the other side of a flooded river. More common problems—such as how to mate or how to read a stranger's face or how to find your way back to camp—require a different sort of intelligence. Kanazawa asserts that general intelligence scores *do* correlate with the ability to solve various novel problems (like those found in academic and many vocational situations) but do not much correlate with individuals' skills in *evolutionarily familiar* situations—such as marrying and parenting, forming close friendships, displaying social competence, and navigating without maps.

Theories of Multiple Intelligences

33-2 How do Gardner's and Sternberg's theories of multiple intelligences differ?

Since the mid-1980s some psychologists have sought to extend the definition of *intelligence* beyond Spearman's and Thurstone's academic smarts. They acknowledge that people who score well on one sort of cognitive test have some tendency to score well

"*g* is one of the most reliable and valid measures in the behavioral domain . . . and it predicts important social outcomes such as educational and occupational levels far better than any other trait."
Behavior geneticist Robert Plomin (1999)

general intelligence (g) a general intelligence factor that, according to Spearman and others, underlies specific mental abilities and is therefore measured by every task on an intelligence test.

factor analysis a statistical procedure that identifies clusters of related items (called *factors*) on a test; used to identify different dimensions of performance that underlie a person's total score.

savant syndrome a condition in which a person otherwise limited in mental ability has an exceptional specific skill, such as in computation or drawing.

on another. But maybe this occurs not because they express an underlying general intelligence but rather because, over time, different abilities interact and feed one another, rather as a speedy runner's throwing ability improves after being engaged in sports that develop both running and throwing abilities (van der Maas et al., 2006).

Gardner's Eight Intelligences

Howard Gardner (1983, 2006) views intelligence as multiple abilities that come in packages. Gardner finds evidence for this view in studies of people with diminished or exceptional abilities. Brain damage, for example, may destroy one ability but leave others intact. And consider people with **savant syndrome,** who often score low on intelligence tests but have an island of brilliance (Treffert & Wallace, 2002). Some have virtually no language ability, yet are able to compute numbers as quickly and accurately as an electronic calculator, or identify almost instantly the day of the week that corresponds to any given date in history, or render incredible works of art or musical performances (Miller, 1999). About 4 in 5 people with savant syndrome are males, and many also have autism, a developmental disorder.

Memory whiz Kim Peek, a savant who does not have autism, was the inspiration for the movie *Rain Man*. In 8 to 10 seconds, he can read and remember a page, and he has learned 9000 books, including Shakespeare and the Bible, by heart. He learns maps from the front of phone books, and he can provide MapQuest-like travel directions within any major U.S. city. Yet he cannot button his clothes. And he has little capacity for abstract concepts. Asked by his father at a restaurant to "lower your voice," he slid lower in his chair to lower his voice box. Asked for Lincoln's Gettysburg Address, he responded, "227 North West Front Street. But he only stayed there one night—he gave the speech the next day" (Treffert & Christensen, 2005).

Using such evidence, Gardner argues that we do not have *an* intelligence, but rather *multiple intelligences*. He identifies a total of eight (**TABLE 33.1**), including the verbal and mathematical aptitudes assessed by standard tests. Thus, the computer programmer, the poet, the street-smart adolescent who becomes a crafty executive, and the basketball team's point guard exhibit different kinds of intelligence (Gardner, 1998). He notes,

— If a person is strong (or weak) in telling stories, solving mathematical proofs, navigating around unfamiliar terrain, learning an unfamiliar song, mastering a new game that entails dexterity, understanding others, or understanding himself, one simply does not know whether comparable strengths (or weaknesses) will be found in other areas.

Islands of genius: Savant syndrome After a 30-minute helicopter ride and a visit to the top of a skyscraper, British savant artist Stephen Wiltshire began seven days of drawing that reproduced the Tokyo skyline.

© The Stephen Wiltshire Gallery

A general intelligence score is therefore like the overall rating of a city—which tells you something but doesn't give you much specific information about its schools, streets, or nightlife.

Wouldn't it be wonderful if the world were so just, responds intelligence researcher Sandra Scarr (1989). Wouldn't it be nice if being weak in one area would be compensated by genius in some other area? Alas, the world is not just. General intelligence scores predict performance on various complex tasks, in various jobs, and in varied countries; *g* matters (Bertua et al., 2005; Gottfredson, 2002a,b, 2003a,b; Rindermann, 2007). In two digests of more than 100 data sets, academic intelligence scores that predicted graduate school success also predicted later job success (Kuncel et al., 2004; Strenze, 2007; see also **FIGURE 33.1**).

TABLE 33.1 Gardner's Eight Intelligences

Aptitude	Exemplar
1. Linguistic	T. S. Eliot, poet
2. Logical-mathematical	Albert Einstein, scientist
3. Musical	Igor Stravinsky, composer
4. Spatial	Pablo Picasso, artist
5. Bodily-kinesthetic	Martha Graham, dancer
6. Intrapersonal (self)	Sigmund Freud, psychiatrist
7. Interpersonal (other people)	Mahatma Gandhi, leader
8. Naturalist	Charles Darwin, naturalist

|| Gardner (1998) has also speculated about a ninth possible intelligence— *existential intelligence*—the ability "to ponder large questions about life, death, existence." ||

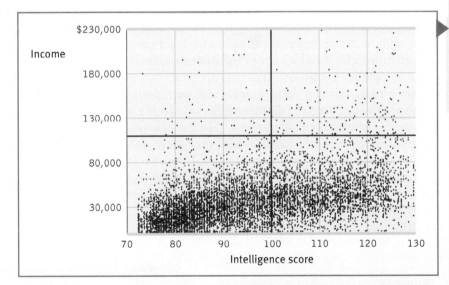

FIGURE 33.1 Smart and rich? Jay Zagorsky (2007) tracked 7403 participants in the U.S. National Longitudinal Survey of Youth across 25 years. As shown in this scatterplot, their intelligence scores correlated +.30, a moderate positive correlation, with their later income.

Even so, "success" is not a one-ingredient recipe. High intelligence may help you get into a profession (via the schools and training programs that take you there), but it won't make you successful once there. The recipe for success combines talent with *grit:* Those who become highly successful are also conscientious, well-connected, and doggedly energetic. Anders Ericsson (2002, 2007; Ericsson et al., 2007) reports a *10-year rule:* A common ingredient of expert performance in chess, dancing, sports, computer programming, music, and medicine is "about 10 years of intense, daily practice."

Spatial intelligence genius In 1998, World Checkers Champion Ron "Suki" King of Barbados set a new record by simultaneously playing 385 players in 3 hours and 44 minutes. Thus, while his opponents often had hours to plot their game moves, King could only devote about 35 seconds to each game. Yet he still managed to win all 385 games!

Sternberg's Three Intelligences

Robert Sternberg (1985, 1999, 2003) agrees that there is more to success than traditional intelligence. And he agrees with Gardner's idea of multiple intelligences. But he proposes a *triarchic theory* of three, not eight, intelligences:

▶ *Analytical (academic problem-solving) intelligence* is assessed by intelligence tests, which present well-defined problems having a single right answer. Such tests predict school grades reasonably well and vocational success more modestly.

▶ *Creative intelligence* is demonstrated in reacting adaptively to novel situations and generating novel ideas.

▶ *Practical intelligence* is required for everyday tasks, which may be ill-defined, with multiple solutions. Managerial success, for example, depends less on academic problem-solving skills than on a shrewd ability to manage oneself, one's tasks, and other people. Sternberg and Richard Wagner's (1993, 1995) test of practical managerial intelligence measures skill at writing effective memos, motivating people, delegating tasks and responsibilities, reading people, and promoting one's own career. Business executives who score relatively high on this test tend to earn high salaries and receive high performance ratings.

With support from the U.S. College Board (which administers the widely used SAT Reasoning Test to U.S. college and university applicants), Sternberg (2006, 2007) and a team of collaborators have developed new measures of creativity (such as thinking up a caption for an untitled cartoon) and practical thinking (such as figuring out how to move a large bed up a winding staircase). Their initial data indicate that these more comprehensive assessments improve prediction of American students' first-year college grades, and they do so with reduced ethnic-group differences.

Although Sternberg and Gardner differ on specific points, they agree that multiple abilities can contribute to life success. (Neither candidate in the 2000 U.S. presidential election had scored exceptionally high on college entrance aptitude tests, Sternberg [2000] noted, yet both became influential.) The two theorists also agree that the differing varieties of giftedness add spice to life and challenges for education. Under their influence, many teachers have been trained to appreciate the varieties of ability and to apply multiple intelligence theory in their classrooms. However we define *intelligence* (**TABLE 33.2**), one thing is clear: There's more to creativity than intelligence test scores.

"You have to be careful, if you're good at something, to make sure you don't think you're good at other things that you aren't necessarily so good at.... Because I've been very successful at [software development] people come in and expect that I have wisdom about topics that I don't."

Bill Gates (1998)

Street smarts This child selling candy on the streets of Manaus, Brazil, is developing practical intelligence at a very young age.

David R. Frazier Photolibrary, Inc./Alamy

TABLE 33.2 Comparing Theories of Intelligence

Theory	Summary	Strengths	Other Considerations
Spearman's general intelligence (*g*)	A basic intelligence predicts our abilities in varied academic areas.	Different abilities, such as verbal and spatial, do have some tendency to correlate.	Human abilities are too diverse to be encapsulated by a single general intelligence factor.
Thurstone's primary mental abilities	Our intelligence may be broken down into seven factors: word fluency, verbal comprehension, spatial ability, perceptual speed, numerical ability, inductive reasoning, and memory.	A single *g* score is not as informative as scores for seven primary mental abilities.	Even Thurstone's seven mental abilities show a tendency to cluster, suggesting an underlying *g* factor.
Gardner's multiple intelligences	Our abilities are best classified into eight independent intelligences, which include a broad range of skills beyond traditional school smarts.	Intelligence is more than just verbal and mathematical skills. Other abilities are equally important to our human adaptability.	Should all of our abilities be considered *intelligences*? Shouldn't some be called less vital *talents*?
Sternberg's triarchic	Our intelligence is best classified into three areas that predict real-world success: analytical, creative, and practical.	These three facets can be reliably measured.	1. These three facets may be less independent than Sternberg thought and may actually share an underlying *g* factor. 2. Additional testing is needed to determine whether these facets can reliably predict success.

▶‖ Intelligence and Creativity

33-3 What is creativity, and what fosters it?

Pierre de Fermat, a seventeenth-century mischievous genius, challenged mathematicians of his day to match his solutions to various number theory problems. His most famous challenge—*Fermat's last theorem*—baffled the greatest mathematical minds, even after a $2 million prize (in today's dollars) was offered in 1908 to whoever first created a proof.

Princeton mathematician Andrew Wiles had pondered the problem for more than 30 years and had come to the brink of a solution. Then, one morning, out of the blue, the final "incredible revelation" struck him. "It was so indescribably beautiful; it was so simple and so elegant. I couldn't understand how I'd missed it and I just stared at it in disbelief for 20 minutes. Then during the day I walked around the department, and I'd keep coming back to my desk looking to see if it was still there. It was still there. I couldn't contain myself, I was so excited. It was the most important moment of my working life" (Singh, 1997, p. 25).

Wiles' incredible moment illustrates **creativity**—the ability to produce ideas that are both novel and valuable. Studies suggest that a certain level of aptitude—a score of about 120 on a standard intelligence test—is necessary but not sufficient for creativity. Exceptionally creative architects, mathematicians, scientists, and engineers usually score no higher on intelligence tests than do their less creative peers (MacKinnon & Hall, 1972; Simonton, 2000). So, clearly there is more to creativity than what intelligence tests reveal. Indeed, the two kinds of thinking engage different brain areas. Intelligence tests, which demand a single correct answer, require *convergent thinking*. Creativity tests (*How many uses can you think of for a brick?*) require *divergent thinking*. Injury to the left parietal lobe damages the convergent thinking required by intelligence test scores and for school success. Injury to certain areas of the frontal lobes can leave reading, writing, and arithmetic skills intact but destroy imagination (Kolb & Whishaw, 2006).

creativity the ability to produce novel and valuable ideas.

Sternberg and his colleagues have identified five components of creativity (Sternberg, 1988, 2003; Sternberg & Lubart, 1991, 1992):

1. **Expertise,** a well-developed base of knowledge, furnishes the ideas, images, and phrases we use as mental building blocks. "Chance favors only the prepared mind," observed Louis Pasteur. The more blocks we have, the more chances we have to combine them in novel ways. Wiles' well-developed base of knowledge put the needed theorems and methods at his disposal.

2. **Imaginative thinking skills** provide the ability to see things in novel ways, to recognize patterns, and to make connections. Having mastered a problem's basic elements, we redefine or explore it in a new way. Copernicus first developed expertise regarding the solar system and its planets, and then creatively defined the system as revolving around the Sun, not the Earth. Wiles' imaginative solution combined two partial solutions.

3. **A venturesome personality** seeks new experiences, tolerates ambiguity and risk, and perseveres in overcoming obstacles. Inventor Thomas Edison tried countless substances before finding the right one for his lightbulb filament. Wiles said he labored in near-isolation from the mathematics community partly to stay focused and avoid distraction. Venturing encounters with different cultures also fosters creativity (Leung et al., 2008).

4. **Intrinsic motivation** is being driven more by interest, satisfaction, and challenge than by external pressures (Amabile & Hennessey, 1992). Creative people focus less on extrinsic motivators—meeting deadlines, impressing people, or making money—than on the pleasure and stimulation of the work itself. Asked how he solved such difficult scientific problems, Isaac Newton reportedly answered, "By thinking about them all the time." Wiles concurred: "I was so obsessed by this problem that for eight years I was thinking about it all the time—when I woke up in the morning to when I went to sleep at night" (Singh & Riber, 1997).

5. **A creative environment** sparks, supports, and refines creative ideas. After studying the careers of 2026 prominent scientists and inventors, Dean Keith Simonton (1992) noted that the most eminent among them were mentored, challenged, and supported by their relationships with colleagues. Many have the *emotional intelligence* needed to network effectively with peers. Even Wiles stood on the shoulders of others and wrestled his problem with the collaboration of a former student. Creativity-fostering environments often support contemplation. After Jonas Salk solved a problem that led to the polio vaccine while in a monastery, he designed the Salk Institute to provide contemplative spaces where scientists could work without interruption (Sternberg, 2006).

"If you would allow me any talent, it's simply this: I can, for whatever reason, reach down into my own brain, feel around in all the mush, find and extract something from my persona, and then graft it onto an idea."
Cartoonist Gary Larson, *The Complete Far Side*, 2003

Imaginative thinking Cartoonists often display creativity as they see things in new ways or make unusual connections.

"For the love of God, is there a doctor in the house?"

Everyone held up their crackers as David threw the cheese log into the ceiling fan.

▶‖ Emotional Intelligence

33-4 What makes up emotional intelligence?

emotional intelligence the ability to perceive, understand, manage, and use emotions.

Also distinct from academic intelligence is *social intelligence*—the know-how involved in comprehending social situations and managing oneself successfully. The concept was first proposed in 1920 by psychologist Edward Thorndike, who noted, "The best mechanic in a factory may fail as a foreman for lack of social intelligence" (Goleman, 2006, p. 83). Like Thorndike, later psychologists have marveled that high-aptitude people are "not, by a wide margin, more effective . . . in achieving better marriages, in successfully raising their children, and in achieving better mental and physical well-being" (Epstein & Meier, 1989). Others have explored the difficulty that some rationally smart people have in processing and managing social information (Cantor & Kihlstrom, 1987; Weis & Süß, 2007). This idea is especially significant for an aspect of social intelligence that John Mayer, Peter Salovey, and David Caruso (2002, 2008) have called **emotional intelligence.** They have developed a test that assesses four emotional intelligence components, which are the abilities to

"You're wise, but you lack tree smarts."

▶ *perceive* emotions (to recognize them in faces, music, and stories).
▶ *understand* emotions (to predict them and how they change and blend).
▶ *manage* emotions (to know how to express them in varied situations).
▶ *use* emotions to enable adaptive or creative thinking.

Mindful of popular misuses of their concept, Mayer, Salovey, and Caruso caution against stretching "emotional intelligence" to include varied traits such as self-esteem and optimism, although emotionally intelligent people are self-aware. In both the United States and Germany, those scoring high on managing emotions enjoy higher-quality interactions with friends (Lopes et al., 2004). They avoid being hijacked by overwhelming depression, anxiety, or anger. They can read others' emotions and know what to say to soothe a grieving friend, encourage a colleague, and manage a conflict. Such findings may help explain why, across 69 studies in many countries, those scoring high in emotional intelligence also exhibit modestly better job performance (Van Rooy & Viswesvaran, 2004; Zeidner et al., 2008). They can delay gratification in pursuit of long-range rewards, rather than being overtaken by immediate impulses. Simply said, they are emotionally in tune with others, and thus they often succeed in career, marriage, and parenting situations where academically smarter (but emotionally less intelligent) people fail (Ciarrochi et al., 2006).

Brain damage reports have provided extreme examples of the results of diminished emotional intelligence in people with high general intelligence. Neuroscientist Antonio Damasio (1994) tells of Elliot, who had a brain tumor removed: "I never saw a tinge of emotion in my many hours of conversation with him, no sadness, no impatience, no frustration." Shown disturbing pictures of injured people, destroyed communities, and natural disasters, Elliot showed—and realized he felt—no emotion. He knew but he could not feel. Unable to intuitively adjust his behavior in response to others' feelings, Elliot lost his job. He went bankrupt. His marriage collapsed. He remarried and divorced again. At last report, he was dependent on custodial care from a sibling and a disability check.

Some scholars, however, are concerned that emotional intelligence stretches the concept of intelligence too far. Multiple-intelligence man Howard Gardner (1999) welcomes our stretching the concept into the realms of space, music, and information about ourselves and others. But let us also, he says, respect emotional sensitivity, creativity, and motivation as important but different. Stretch "intelligence" to include everything we prize and it will lose its meaning.

"I worry about [intelligence] definitions that collapse assessments of our cognitive powers with statements about the kind of human beings we favor."

Howard Gardner, "Rethinking the Concept of Intelligence," 2000

▶‖ Is Intelligence Neurologically Measurable?

33-5 To what extent is intelligence related to brain anatomy and neural processing speed?

Using today's neuroscience tools, might we link differences in people's intelligence test performance to dissimilarities in the heart of smarts—the brain? Might we anticipate a future brain test of intelligence?

Brain Size and Complexity

‖ A sperm whale's brain is about 6 times heavier than your brain. ‖

After the brilliant English poet Lord Byron died in 1824, doctors discovered that his brain was a massive 5 pounds, not the normal 3 pounds. Three years later, Beethoven died and his brain was found to have exceptionally numerous and deep convolutions. Such observations set brain scientists off studying the brains of other geniuses at their wits' end (Burrell, 2005). Do people with big brains have big smarts?

‖ Correlations do not indicate cause-effect, but they do tell us whether two things are associated in some way. A correlation of −1.0 represents perfect disagreement between two sets of scores—as one score goes up, the other goes down. A correlation of zero represents no association. The highest correlation, +1.0, represents perfect agreement—as the first score goes up, so does the second. ‖

Alas, some geniuses had small brains, and some dim-witted criminals had brains like Byron's. More recent studies that directly measure brain volume using MRI scans do reveal correlations of about +.33 between brain size (adjusted for body size) and intelligence score (Carey, 2007; McDaniel, 2005). Moreover, as adults age, brain size and nonverbal intelligence test scores fall in concert (Bigler et al., 1995).

One review of 37 brain-imaging studies revealed associations between intelligence and brain size and activity in specific areas, especially within the frontal and parietal lobes (Jung & Haier, 2007). Sandra Witelson would not have been surprised. With the brains of 91 Canadians as a comparison base, Witelson and her colleagues (1999) seized an opportunity to study Einstein's brain. Although not notably heavier or larger in total size than the typical Canadian's brain, Einstein's brain was 15 percent larger in the parietal lobe's lower region—which just happens to be a center for processing mathematical and spatial information. Certain other areas were a tad smaller than average. With different mental functions competing for the brain's real estate, these observations may offer a clue to why Einstein, like some other great physicists such as Richard Feynman and Edward Teller, was slow in learning to talk (Pinker, 1999).

If intelligence does modestly correlate with brain size, the cause could be differing genes, nutrition, environmental stimulation, some combination of these, or perhaps something else. We now know that experience alters the brain. Rats raised in a stimulating rather than deprived environment develop thicker, heavier cortexes. And learning leaves detectable traces in the brain's neural connections. "Intelligence is due to the development of neural connections in response to the environment," notes University of Sydney psychologist Dennis Garlick (2003).

Postmortem brain analyses reveal that highly educated people die with more synapses—17 percent more in one study—than their less-educated counterparts (Orlovskaya et al., 1999). This does not tell us whether people grow synapses with education, or people with more synapses seek more education, or both. But other evidence suggests that highly intelligent people differ in their *neural plasticity*—their ability during childhood and adolescence to adapt and grow neural connections in response to their environment (Garlick, 2002, 2003).

One study repeatedly scanned the brains of 307 children and teens ages 5 to 19. The surprising result: Kids with average intelligence scores showed modest cortex thickening and thinning—with a peak thickness at age 8, suggesting a short developmental window (Shaw et al., 2006). The most intelligent 7-year-olds had a *thinner* brain cortex, which progressively thickened to age 11 to 13, before thinning with the natural pruning of unused connections. Agile minds came with agile brains.

Efforts to link brain structure with cognition continue. One research team, led by psychologist Richard Haier (2004; Colom et al., 2006), correlated intelligence scores from 47 adult volunteers with scans that measured their volume of *gray matter* (neural cell bodies) and *white matter* (axons and dendrites) in various brain regions. Higher intelligence scores were linked with more gray matter in areas known to be involved in memory, attention, and language (**FIGURE 33.2**).

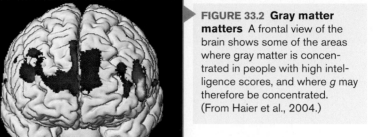

FIGURE 33.2 Gray matter matters A frontal view of the brain shows some of the areas where gray matter is concentrated in people with high intelligence scores, and where *g* may therefore be concentrated. (From Haier et al., 2004.)

Brain Function

Even if the modest correlations between brain anatomy and intelligence prove reliable, they only begin to explain intelligence differences. Searching for other explanations, neuroscientists are studying the brain's functioning.

As people contemplate a variety of questions like those found on intelligence tests, a frontal lobe area just above the outer edge of the eyebrows becomes especially active—in the left brain for verbal questions, and on both sides for spatial questions (Duncan et al., 2000). Information from various brain areas seems to converge in this spot, suggesting to researcher John Duncan (2000) that it may be a "global workspace for organizing and coordinating information" and that some people may be "blessed with a workspace that functions very, very well."

Are more intelligent people literally more quick-witted, much as today's speedier computer chips enable more powerful computing than did their predecessors? On some tasks they seem to be. Earl Hunt (1983) found that verbal intelligence scores are predictable from the speed with which people retrieve information from memory. Those who recognize quickly that *sink* and *wink* are different words, or that *A* and *a* share the same name, tend to score high in verbal ability. Extremely precocious 12- to 14-year-old college students are especially quick in responding to such tasks (Jensen, 1989). To try to define *quick-wittedness,* researchers are taking a close look at speed of perception and speed of neural processing of information.

Perceptual Speed

Across many studies, the correlation between intelligence score and the speed of taking in perceptual information tends to be about +.3 to +.5 (Deary & Der, 2005; Sheppard & Vernon, 2008). A typical experiment flashes an incomplete stimulus, as in **FIGURE 33.3**, then a *masking image*—another image that overrides the lingering afterimage of the incomplete stimulus. The researcher then asks participants whether the long side appeared on the right or left. How much stimulus inspection time do you think you would need to answer correctly 80 percent of the time? Perhaps .01 second? Or .02 second? Those who perceive very quickly tend to score somewhat higher on intelligence tests, particularly on tests based on perceptual rather than verbal problem solving.

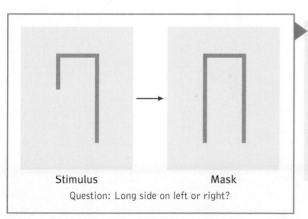

Stimulus   Mask

Question: Long side on left or right?

FIGURE 33.3 An inspection time task A stimulus is flashed before being overridden by a masking image. How long would you need to glimpse the stimulus at the left to answer the question? People who can perceive the stimulus very quickly tend to score somewhat higher on intelligence tests. (Adapted from Deary & Stough, 1996.)

Neurological Speed

Do the quicker processing and perceptions of highly intelligent people reflect greater neural processing speed? Repeated studies have found that their brain waves do register a simple stimulus (such as a flash of light or a beeped tone) more quickly and with greater complexity (Caryl, 1994; Deary & Caryl, 1993; Reed & Jensen, 1992). The evoked brain response also tends to be slightly faster when people with high rather than low intelligence scores perform a simple task, such as pushing a button when an *X* appears on a screen (McGarry-Roberts et al., 1992).

Neural processing speed on a simple task seems far removed from the untimed responses to complex intelligence test items, such as, "In what way are *wool* and *cotton* alike?" As yet, notes intelligence expert Nathan Brody (1992, 2001), we have no firm understanding of *why* fast reactions on simple tasks should predict intelligence test performance, though he suspects they reflect one's "core information processing ability." Philip Vernon (1983) has speculated that "faster cognitive processing may allow more information to be acquired." Perhaps people who more quickly process information accumulate more information—about wool, cotton, and millions of other things. Or perhaps, as one Australian-Dutch research team has found, processing speed and intelligence may correlate not because one causes the other but because they share an underlying genetic influence (Luciano et al., 2005).

The neurological approach to understanding intelligence (and so many other things in psychology) is currently in its heyday. Will this new research reduce what we now call the *g* factor to simple measures of underlying brain activity? Or are these efforts totally wrongheaded because what we call intelligence is not a single general trait but several culturally adaptive skills? The controversies surrounding the nature of intelligence are a long way from resolution.

REVIEW

Introduction to Intelligence

33-1 **What arguments support intelligence as one general mental ability, and what arguments support the idea of multiple distinct abilities?** *Factor analysis* is a statistical procedure that has revealed some underlying commonalities in different mental abilities. Spearman named this common factor the *g* factor. Thurstone argued against defining intelligence so narrowly as just one score. He identified seven different clusters of mental abilities. Yet there remained a tendency for high scorers in one of his clusters to score high in other clusters as well. Our *g* scores seem most predictive in novel situations and do not much correlate with skills in evolutionarily familiar situations.

33-2 **How do Gardner's and Sternberg's theories of multiple intelligences differ?** Gardner proposes eight independent intelligences: linguistic, logical-mathematical, musical, spatial, bodily-kinesthetic, intrapersonal, interpersonal, and naturalist. Sternberg's theory has proposed three intelligence domains: analytical (academic problem-solving), creative, and practical. (For more on the single-intelligence/multiple intelligences debate, see Table 33.2).

33-3 **What is creativity, and what fosters it?** *Creativity* is the ability to produce novel and valuable ideas. It correlates somewhat with intelligence, but beyond a score of 120, that correlation dwindles. It also correlates with expertise, imaginative thinking skills, a venturesome personality, intrinsic motivation, and the support offered by a creative environment.

33-4 **What makes up emotional intelligence?** *Emotional intelligence* is the ability to perceive, understand, manage, and use emotions. Those with higher emotional intelligence achieve greater personal and professional success. However, critics question whether we stretch the idea of intelligence too far when we apply it to emotions.

33-5 **To what extent is intelligence related to brain anatomy and neural processing speed?** Recent studies indicate some correlation (about +.33) between brain size (adjusted for body size) and intelligence score. Highly educated or intelligent people exhibit an above-average volume of synapses and gray matter. People who score high on *intelligence tests* tend also to have speedy brains that retrieve information and perceive stimuli quickly.

Terms and Concepts to Remember

intelligence test, p. 404	savant syndrome, p. 406
intelligence, p. 404	creativity, p. 409
general intelligence (*g*), p. 405	emotional intelligence, p. 411
factor analysis, p. 405	

Test Yourself

1. Joseph, a Harvard Law School student, has a straight-A average, writes for the *Harvard Law Review*, and will clerk for a Supreme Court justice next year. His grandmother, Judith, is very proud of him, saying that he is way more intelligent than she ever was. But Joseph is also very proud of Judith: As a young woman, she was imprisoned by the Nazis. When the war ended, she walked out of Germany, contacted an agency helping refugees, and began a new life in the United States as an assistant chef in her cousin's restaurant. According to the definition of *intelligence* in this module, is Joseph the only intelligent person in this story? Why or why not?

(Answers to the Test Yourself questions can be found in Appendix B at the end of the book.)

Ask Yourself

1. The modern concept of multiple intelligences (as proposed by Gardner and Sternberg) assumes that the analytical school smarts measured by traditional intelligence tests are important abilities but that other abilities are also important. Different people have different gifts. What are yours?

∞ WEB

Multiple-choice self-tests and more may be found at www.worthpublishers.com/myers

The Origins of
Intelligence Testing

Modern Tests of
Mental Abilities

Principles of Test
Construction

The Dynamics of Intelligence

Assessing Intelligence

How do we assess intelligence? In simple terms, *intelligence* is whatever **intelligence tests** measure. So, what are these tests, and what makes a test credible? Answering those questions begins with a look at why psychologists created tests of mental abilities and how they have used those tests.

▶‖ The Origins of Intelligence Testing

34-1 When and why were intelligence tests created?

intelligence test a method for assessing an individual's mental aptitudes and comparing them with those of others, using numerical scores.

Some societies concern themselves with promoting the collective welfare of the family, community, and society. Other societies emphasize individual opportunity. Plato, a pioneer of the individualist tradition, wrote more than 2000 years ago in *The Republic* that "no two persons are born exactly alike; but each differs from the other in natural endowments, one being suited for one occupation and the other for another." As heirs to Plato's individualism, people in Western societies have pondered how and why individuals differ in mental ability.

Western attempts to assess such differences began in earnest more than a century ago. The English scientist Francis Galton (1822–1911) had a fascination with measuring human traits. When his cousin Charles Darwin proposed that nature selects successful traits through the survival of the fittest, Galton wondered if it might be possible to measure "natural ability" and to encourage those of high ability to mate with one another. At the 1884 London Exposition, more than 10,000 visitors received his assessment of their "intellectual strengths" based on such things as reaction time, sensory acuity, muscular power, and body proportions. But alas, on these measures, eminent adults and high-achieving students did not outscore those supposedly not so bright. Nor did the measures correlate with each other.

Although Galton's quest for a simple intelligence measure failed, he gave us some statistical techniques that we still use (as well as the phrase "nature and nurture"). And his persistent belief in the inheritance of eminence and genius—reflected in the title of his book *Hereditary Genius*—illustrates an important lesson from both the history of intelligence research and the history of science: Although science itself strives for objectivity, individual scientists are affected by their own assumptions and attitudes.

Alfred Binet "Some recent philosophers have given their moral approval to the deplorable verdict that an individual's intelligence is a fixed quantity, one which cannot be augmented. We must protest and act against this brutal pessimism" (Binet, 1909, p. 141).

Alfred Binet: Predicting School Achievement

The modern intelligence-testing movement began at the turn of the twentieth century, when France passed a law requiring that all children attend school. Some children, including many newcomers to Paris, seemed incapable of benefiting from the regular school curriculum and in need of special classes. But how could the schools objectively identify children with special needs?

The French government hesitated to trust teachers' subjective judgments of children's learning potential. Academic slowness might merely reflect inadequate prior education. Also, teachers might prejudge children on the basis of their social backgrounds. To minimize bias, France's minister of public education in 1904 commissioned Alfred Binet (1857–1911) and others to study the problem.

Binet and his collaborator, Théodore Simon, began by assuming that all children follow the same course of intellectual development but that some develop more

National Library of Medicine

rapidly. On tests, therefore, a "dull" child should perform as does a typical younger child, and a "bright" child as does a typical older child. Thus, their goal became measuring each child's **mental age,** the level of performance typically associated with a certain chronological age. The average 9-year-old, for example, has a mental age of 9. Children with below-average mental ages, such as 9-year-olds who perform at the level of a typical 7-year-old, would struggle with schoolwork considered normal for their age.

To measure mental age, Binet and Simon theorized that mental aptitude, like athletic aptitude, is a general capacity that shows up in various ways. After testing a variety of reasoning and problem-solving questions on Binet's two daughters, and then on "bright" and "backward" Parisian schoolchildren, Binet and Simon identified items that would predict how well French children would handle their schoolwork.

Note that Binet and Simon made no assumptions concerning *why* a particular child was slow, average, or precocious. Binet personally leaned toward an environmental explanation. To raise the capacities of low-scoring children, he recommended "mental orthopedics" that would train them to develop their attention span and self-discipline. He believed his intelligence test did not measure inborn intelligence as a meter stick measures height. Rather, it had a single practical purpose: to identify French schoolchildren needing special attention. Binet hoped his test would be used to improve children's education, but he also feared it would be used to label children and limit their opportunities (Gould, 1981).

Lewis Terman: The Innate IQ

Binet's fears were realized soon after his death in 1911, when others adapted his tests for use as a numerical measure of inherited intelligence. This began when Stanford University professor Lewis Terman (1877–1956) found that the Paris-developed questions and age norms worked poorly with California schoolchildren. Adapting some of Binet's original items, adding others, and establishing new age norms, Terman extended the upper end of the test's range from teenagers to "superior adults." He also gave his revision the name it retains today—the **Stanford-Binet.**

From such tests, German psychologist William Stern derived the famous **intelligence quotient,** or **IQ.** The IQ was simply a person's mental age divided by chronological age and multiplied by 100 to get rid of the decimal point:

$$IQ = \frac{mental\ age}{chronological\ age} \times 100$$

Thus, an average child, whose mental and chronological ages are the same, has an IQ of 100. But an 8-year-old who answers questions as would a typical 10-year-old has an IQ of 125.

The original IQ formula worked fairly well for children but not for adults. (Should a 40-year-old who does as well on the test as an average 20-year-old be assigned an IQ of only 50?) Most current intelligence tests, including the Stanford-Binet, no longer compute an IQ (though the term *IQ* still lingers in everyday vocabulary as a shorthand expression for "intelligence test score"). Instead, they represent the test-taker's performance *relative* to the *average performance of others the same age.* This average performance is arbitrarily assigned a score of 100, and about two-thirds of all test-takers fall between 85 and 115.

Terman promoted the widespread use of intelligence testing. His motive was to "take account of the inequalities of children in original endowment" by assessing their "vocational fitness." In sympathy with *eugenics*—a much-criticized nineteenth-century movement that proposed measuring human traits and using the results to encourage only smart and fit people to reproduce—Terman (1916, pp. 91–92) envisioned that

mental age a measure of intelligence test performance devised by Binet; the chronological age that most typically corresponds to a given level of performance. Thus, a child who does as well as the average 8-year-old is said to have a mental age of 8.

Stanford-Binet the widely used American revision (by Terman at Stanford University) of Binet's original intelligence test.

intelligence quotient (IQ) defined originally as the ratio of mental age (*ma*) to chronological age (*ca*) multiplied by 100 (thus, IQ = *ma/ca* × 100). On contemporary intelligence tests, the average performance for a given age is assigned a score of 100.

"The IQ test was invented to predict academic performance, nothing else. If we wanted something that would predict life success, we'd have to invent another test completely." Social psychologist Robert Zajonc (1984b)

Mrs. Randolph takes mother's pride too far.

achievement tests a test designed to assess what a person has learned.

aptitude tests a test designed to predict a person's future performance; *aptitude* is the capacity to learn.

Wechsler Adult Intelligence Scale (WAIS) the WAIS is the most widely used intelligence test; contains verbal and performance (nonverbal) subtests.

the use of intelligence tests would "ultimately result in curtailing the reproduction of feeble-mindedness and in the elimination of an enormous amount of crime, pauperism, and industrial inefficiency" (p. 7).

With Terman's help, the U.S. government developed new tests to evaluate both newly arriving immigrants and World War I army recruits—the world's first mass administration of an intelligence test. To some psychologists, the results indicated the inferiority of people not sharing their Anglo-Saxon heritage. Such findings were part of the cultural climate that led to a 1924 immigration law that reduced Southern and Eastern European immigration quotas to less than a fifth of those for Northern and Western Europe.

Binet probably would have been horrified that his test had been adapted and used to draw such conclusions. Indeed, such sweeping judgments did become an embarrassment to most of those who championed testing. Even Terman came to appreciate that test scores reflected not only people's innate mental abilities but also their education and their familiarity with the culture assumed by the test. Nevertheless, abuses of the early intelligence tests serve to remind us that science can be value-laden. Behind a screen of scientific objectivity, ideology sometimes lurks.

▶‖ Modern Tests of Mental Abilities

34-2 What's the difference between aptitude and achievement tests, and how can we develop and evaluate them?

By this point in your life, you've faced dozens of ability tests: school tests of basic reading and math skills, course exams, intelligence tests, and driver's license exams, to name just a few. Psychologists classify such tests as either **achievement tests,** intended to *reflect* what you have learned, or **aptitude tests,** intended to *predict* your ability to learn a new skill. Exams covering what you have learned in this course are achievement tests. A college entrance exam, which seeks to predict your ability to do college work, is an aptitude test—a "thinly disguised intelligence test," says Howard Gardner (1999). Indeed, report Meredith Frey and Douglas Detterman (2004), total scores on the U.S. SAT Reasoning Test (formerly called the U.S. Scholastic Aptitude Test) correlated +.82 with general intelligence scores in a national sample of 14- to 21-year-olds (**FIGURE 34.1**).

FIGURE 34.1 Close cousins: Aptitude and intelligence scores A scatterplot shows the close correlation between intelligence scores and verbal and quantitative SAT scores. (From Frey and Detterman, 2004.)

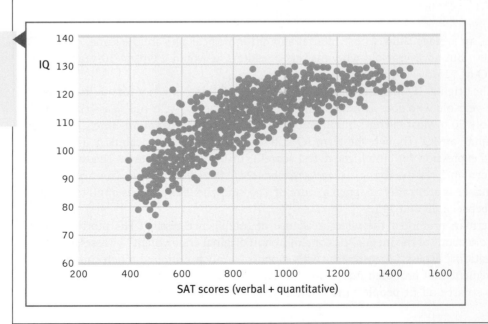

IQ (y-axis): 60, 70, 80, 90, 100, 110, 120, 130, 140

SAT scores (verbal + quantitative) (x-axis): 200, 400, 600, 800, 1000, 1200, 1400, 1600

Actually, the differences between achievement and aptitude tests are not so clear-cut. Your *achieved* vocabulary influences your score on most aptitude tests. Similarly, your *aptitudes* for learning and test-taking influence your grades on achievement tests. Most tests, whether labeled achievement or aptitude, assess both ability and its development. Practically speaking, however, achievement tests assess current performance and aptitude tests predict future performance.

Psychologist David Wechsler created what is now the most widely used intelligence test, the **Wechsler Adult Intelligence Scale (WAIS),** with a version for school-age children (the *Wechsler Intelligence Scale for Children [WISC]*), and another for preschool children. As illustrated in **FIGURE 34.2**, the WAIS consists of 11 subtests broken into verbal and performance areas. It yields not only an overall intelligence score, as does the Stanford-Binet, but also separate scores for verbal comprehension, perceptual organization, working memory, and processing speed. Striking differences among these scores can provide clues to cognitive strengths or weaknesses that teachers or therapists can build upon. For example, a low verbal comprehension score combined with high scores on other subtests could indicate a reading or language disability. Other comparisons can help a psychologist or psychiatrist establish a rehabilitation plan for a stroke patient. Such uses are possible, of course, only when we can trust the test results.

Matching patterns Block design puzzles test the ability to analyze patterns. Wechsler's individually administered intelligence test comes in forms suited for adults (WAIS) and children (WISC).

FIGURE 34.2 Sample items from the Wechsler Adult Intelligence Scale (WAIS) subtests (Adapted from Thorndike & Hagen, 1977.)

VERBAL

General Information
What day of the year is Independence Day?

Similarities
In what way are *wool* and *cotton* alike?

Arithmetic Reasoning
If eggs cost 60 cents a dozen, what does 1 egg cost?

Vocabulary
Tell me the meaning of corrupt.

Comprehension
Why do people buy fire insurance?

Digit Span
Listen carefully, and when I am through, say the numbers right after me.

7   3   4   1   8   6

Now I am going to say some more numbers, but I want you to say them backward.

3   8   4   1   6

PERFORMANCE

Picture Completion
I am going to show you a picture with an important part missing. Tell me what is missing.

'85

SUN	MON	TUE	WED	THU	FRI	SAT
1	2	3	4	5	6	7
8	9	10	11	12	13	14
15	16	17	18	19	20	21
22	23	24	25	26	27	28
29	30					

Picture Arrangement
The pictures below tell a story. Put them in the right order to tell the story.

Block Design
Using the four blocks, make one just like this.

Object Assembly
If these pieces are put together correctly, they will make something. Go ahead and put them together as quickly as you can.

Digit-Symbol Substitution

Code

△	○	⧄	✕	◇
1	2	3	4	5

Test

1	5	4	2	1	3	5	4	1	5

standardization defining meaningful scores by comparison with the performance of a pretested group.

normal curve the symmetrical bell-shaped curve that describes the distribution of many physical and psychological attributes. Most scores fall near the average, and fewer and fewer scores lie near the extremes.

▶‖ Principles of Test Construction

To be widely accepted, psychological tests must meet three criteria: They must be *standardized, reliable,* and *valid.* The Stanford-Binet and Wechsler tests meet these requirements.

Standardization

The number of questions you answer correctly on an intelligence test would tell us almost nothing. To evaluate your performance, we need a basis for comparing it with others' performance. To enable meaningful comparisons, test-makers first give the test to a representative sample of people. When you later take the test following the same procedures, your score can be compared with the sample's scores to determine your position relative to others. This process of defining meaningful scores relative to a pretested group is called **standardization.**

Group members' scores typically are distributed in a bell-shaped pattern that forms the **normal curve** shown in **FIGURE 34.3**. No matter what we measure—heights, weights, or mental aptitudes—people's scores tend to form this roughly symmetrical shape. On an intelligence test, we call the midpoint, the average score, 100. Moving out from the average, toward either extreme, we find fewer and fewer people. For both the Stanford-Binet and the Wechsler tests, a person's score indicates whether that person's performance fell above or below the average. As Figure 34.3 shows, a performance higher than all but 2 percent of all scores earns an intelligence score of 130. A performance lower than 98 percent of all scores earns an intelligence score of 70.

To keep the average score near 100, the Stanford-Binet and the Wechsler scales are periodically restandardized. If you took the WAIS Third Edition recently, your performance was compared with a standardization sample who took the test during 1996, not to David Wechsler's initial 1930s sample. If you compared the performance of the most recent standardization sample with that of the 1930s sample, do you suppose you would find rising or declining test performance? Amazingly—given that college entrance aptitude scores were dropping during the 1960s and 1970s—intelligence test performance has been improving. This worldwide phenomenon is called the *Flynn effect,* in honor of New Zealand researcher James Flynn (1987, 2007), who first calculated its magnitude. As **FIGURE 34.4** indicates, the average person's intelligence test score 80 years ago was—by today's standard—only a 76! Such rising performance has been observed in 20 countries, from Canada to rural Australia (Daley et al., 2003). Although the gains have recently reversed in Scandinavia, the historic increase is now widely accepted as an important phenomenon (Sundet et al., 2004; Teasdale & Owen, 2005, 2008).

FIGURE 34.3 The normal curve Scores on aptitude tests tend to form a normal, or bell-shaped, curve around an average score. For the Wechsler scale, for example, the average score is 100.

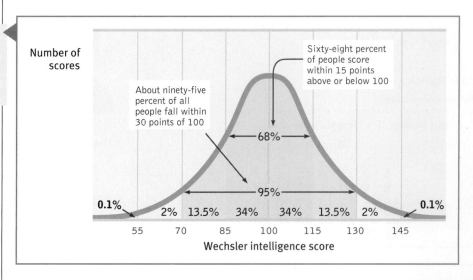

Number of scores

Sixty-eight percent of people score within 15 points above or below 100

About ninety-five percent of all people fall within 30 points of 100

68%

95%

0.1%   2%   13.5%   34%   34%   13.5%   2%   0.1%

55   70   85   100   115   130   145

Wechsler intelligence score

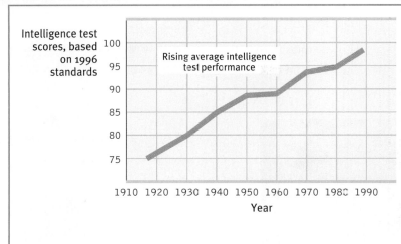

Intelligence test scores, based on 1996 standards

Rising average intelligence test performance

FIGURE 34.4 Getting smarter? In every country studied, intelligence test performance rose during the twentieth century, as shown here with American Wechsler and Stanford-Binet test performance between 1918 and 1989. In Britain, test scores have risen 27 points since 1942. (From Hogan, 1995.) Very recent data indicate this trend may have leveled off or may even be reversing.

The Flynn effect's cause is a mystery (Neisser, 1997a, 1998). Did it result from greater test sophistication? (But the gains began before testing was widespread.) Better nutrition? As the nutrition explanation would predict, people have gotten not only smarter but taller. Moreover, the increases have been greatest at the lowest economic levels, which have gained the most from improved nutrition (Colom et al., 2005). Or did the Flynn effect stem from more education? More stimulating environments? Less childhood disease? Smaller families and more parental investment?

Regardless of what combination of factors explains the rise in intelligence test scores, the phenomenon counters one concern of some hereditarians—that the higher twentieth-century birthrates among those with lower scores would shove human intelligence scores downward (Lynn & Harvey, 2008). Seeking to explain the rising scores, and mindful of global mixing, one scholar has even speculated about the influence of a genetic phenomenon comparable to "hybrid vigor," which occurs in agriculture when cross-breeding produces corn or livestock superior to the parent plants or animals (Mingroni, 2004, 2007).

Reliability

Knowing where you stand in comparison to a standardization group still won't tell us much about your intelligence unless the test has **reliability**—unless it yields dependably consistent scores. To check a test's reliability, researchers retest people. They may use the same test or they may split the test in half and see whether odd-question scores and even-question scores agree. If the two scores generally agree, or *correlate,* the test is reliable. The higher the correlation between the *test-retest* or the *split-half* scores, the higher the test's reliability. The tests we have considered so far—the Stanford-Binet, the WAIS, and the WISC—all have reliabilities of about +.9, which is very high. When retested, people's scores generally match their first score closely.

Validity

High reliability does not ensure a test's **validity**—the extent to which the test actually measures or predicts what it promises. If you use an inaccurate tape measure to measure people's heights, your height report would have high reliability (consistency) but low validity. It is enough for some tests that they have **content validity,** meaning the test taps the pertinent behavior, or *criterion.* The road test for a driver's license has content validity because it samples the tasks a driver routinely faces. Course exams have content validity if they assess one's mastery of a representative sample of course material. But we expect intelligence tests to have **predictive validity:** They should predict the criterion of future performance, and to some extent they do.

reliability the extent to which a test yields consistent results, as assessed by the consistency of scores on two halves of the test, or on retesting.

validity the extent to which a test measures or predicts what it is supposed to. (See also *content validity* and *predictive validity.*)

content validity the extent to which a test samples the behavior that is of interest.

predictive validity the success with which a test predicts the behavior it is designed to predict; it is assessed by computing the correlation between test scores and the criterion behavior. (Also called *criterion-related validity.*)

FIGURE 34.5 Diminishing predictive power Let's imagine a correlation between football linemen's body weight and their success on the field. Note how insignificant the relationship becomes when we narrow the range of weight to 280 to 320 pounds. As the range of data under consideration narrows, its predictive power diminishes.

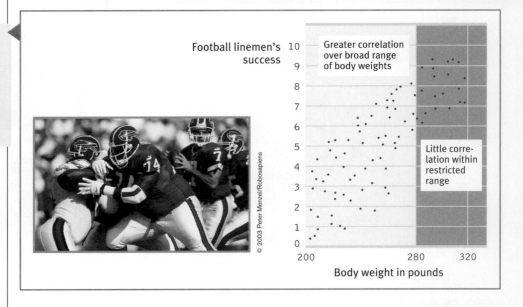

Are general aptitude tests as predictive as they are reliable? As critics are fond of noting, the answer is plainly *no*. The predictive power of aptitude tests is fairly strong in the early school years, but later it weakens. Academic aptitude test scores are reasonably good predictors of achievement for children ages 6 to 12, where the correlation between intelligence score and school performance is about +.6 (Jensen, 1980). Intelligence scores correlate even more closely with scores on *achievement tests*—+.81 in one comparison of 70,000 English children's intelligence scores at age 11 to their academic achievement in national exams at age 16 (Deary et al., 2007). The SAT, used in the United States as a college entrance exam, is less successful in predicting first-year college grades; here, the correlation is less than +.5 (Willingham et al., 1990). By the time we get to the Graduate Record Examination (GRE; an aptitude test similar to the SAT but for those applying to graduate school), the correlation with graduate school performance is an even more modest but still significant +.4 (Kuncel & Hezlett, 2007).

Why does the predictive power of aptitude scores diminish as students move up the educational ladder? Consider a parallel situation: Among all American or Canadian football linemen, body weight correlates with success. A 300-pound player tends to overwhelm a 200-pound opponent. But within the narrow 280- to 320-pound range typically found at the professional level, the correlation between weight and success becomes negligible (**FIGURE 34.5**). The narrower the *range* of weights, the lower the predictive power of body weight becomes. If an elite university takes only those students who have very high aptitude scores, those scores cannot possibly predict much. This will be true even if the test has excellent predictive validity with a more diverse sample of students. So, when we validate a test using a wide range of people but then use it with a restricted range of people, it loses much of its predictive validity.

▶‖ The Dynamics of Intelligence

We now can address some age-old questions about the dynamics of human intelligence—about its stability over the life span, and about the extremes of intelligence.

Stability or Change?

34-3 How stable are intelligence scores over the life span?

If we retested people periodically throughout their lives, would their intelligence scores be stable?

This question has led to a search for indicators of infants' later intelligence that has left few stones unturned. Unable to talk with infants, developmental psychologists have assessed what they can observe—everything from birth weight, to the relative lengths of different toes, to age of sitting up alone. None of these measures provides any useful prediction of intelligence scores at much later ages (Bell & Waldrop, 1989; Broman, 1989). Perhaps, as developmental psychologist Nancy Bayley reflected in 1949, "we have not yet found the right tests." Someday, she speculated, we might find "infant behaviors which are characteristic of underlying intellectual functions" and which will predict later intelligence. Some studies have found that infants who quickly grow bored with a picture—who, given a choice, prefer to look at a new one—score higher on tests of brain speed and intelligence up to 21 years later, but the prediction is crude (Fagan et al., 2007; Kavsek, 2004; Tasbihsazan et al., 2003).

So, new parents who are wondering about their baby's intelligence and anxiously comparing their baby to others can relax. Except for extremely impaired or very precocious children, casual observation and intelligence tests before age 3 only modestly predict children's future aptitudes (Humphreys & Davey, 1988; Tasbihsazan et al., 2003). For example, children who are early talkers—speaking in sentences typical of 3-year-olds by age 20 months—are not especially likely to be reading by age 4½ (Crain-Thoreson & Dale, 1992). (A better predictor of early reading is having parents who have read lots of stories to their child.) Remember that even Albert Einstein was slow in learning to talk (Quasha, 1980).

By age 4, however, children's performance on intelligence tests begins to predict their adolescent and adult scores. Moreover, high-scoring adolescents tend to have been early readers. One study surveyed the parents of 187 American seventh- and eighth-graders who had taken a college aptitude test as part of a seven-state talent search and had scored considerably higher than most high school seniors. If their parents' memories can be trusted, more than half of this precocious group of adolescents began reading by age 4 and more than 80 percent were reading by age 5 (Van Tassel-Baska, 1983). Not surprisingly, then, intelligence tests given to 5-year-olds do predict school achievement (Tramontana et al., 1988).

After about age 7, intelligence test scores, though certainly not fixed, stabilize (Bloom, 1964). Thus, the consistency of scores over time increases with the age of the child. The remarkable stability of aptitude scores by late adolescence is seen in a U.S. Educational Testing Service study of 23,000 students who took the SAT and then later took the GRE (Angoff, 1988). On either test, verbal scores correlated only modestly with math scores—revealing that these two aptitudes are distinct. Yet scores on the SAT verbal test correlated +.86 with the scores on the GRE verbal tests taken four to five years later. An equally astonishing +.86 correlation occurred between the two math tests. Given the time lapse and differing educational experiences of these 23,000 students, the stability of their aptitude scores is remarkable.

Ian Deary and his colleagues (2004) recently set a record for long-term follow-up. Their amazing study was enabled by their country, Scotland, doing something that no nation has done before or since. On Monday morning, June 1, 1932, essentially every child in the country who had been born in 1921—87,498 children at ages 10½ to 11½—was given an intelligence test. The aim was to identify working-class children who would benefit from further education. Sixty-five years later to the day, Patricia Whalley, the wife of Deary's co-worker, Lawrence Whalley, discovered the test results on dusty storeroom shelves at the Scottish Council for Research in Education, not far from Deary's Edinburgh University office. "This will change our lives," Deary replied when Whalley told him the news.

And so it has, with dozens of studies of the stability and the predictive capacity of these early test results. For example, when the intelligence test administered to 11-year-old Scots in 1932 was readministered to 542 survivors as turn-of-the-millennium

"My dear Adele, I am 4 years old and I can read any English book. I can say all the Latin substantives and adjectives and active verbs besides 52 lines of Latin poetry."
Francis Galton, letter to his sister, 1827

‖ Ironically, SAT and GRE scores correlate better with each other than either does with its intended criterion, school achievement. Thus, their reliability far exceeds their predictive validity. If either test was much affected by coaching, luck, or how one feels on the test day (as so many people believe), such reliability would be impossible. ‖

FIGURE 34.6 Intelligence endures When Ian Deary and his colleagues (2004) retested 80-year-old Scots, using an intelligence test they had taken as 11-year-olds, their scores across seven decades correlated +.66.

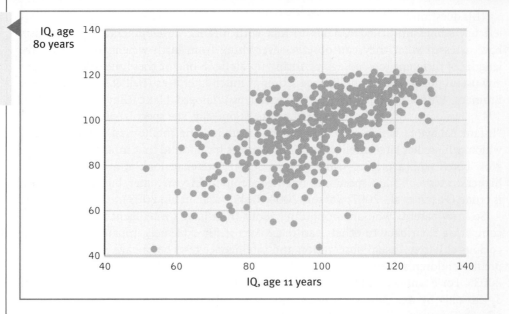

"Whether you live to collect your old-age pension depends in part on your IQ at age 11."

Ian Deary, "Intelligence, Health, and Death," 2005

80-year-olds, the correlation between the two sets of scores—after some 70 years of varied life experiences—was striking (**FIGURE 34.6**). High-scoring 11-year-olds also were more likely to be living independently as 77-year-olds and were less likely to have suffered late-onset Alzheimer's disease (Starr et al., 2000; Whalley et al., 2000). Among girls scoring in the highest 25 percent, 70 percent were still alive at age 76—as were only 45 percent of those scoring in the lowest 25 percent (**FIGURE 34.7**). (World War II prematurely ended the lives of many of the male test-takers.) Another study that followed 93 nuns confirmed that those exhibiting less verbal ability in essays written when entering their convent in their teens were more at risk for Alzheimer's disease after age 75 (Snowdon et al., 1996).

FIGURE 34.7 Living smart Women scoring in the highest 25 percent on the Scottish national intelligence test at age 11 tended to live longer than those who scored in the lowest 25 percent. (From Whalley & Deary, 2001.)

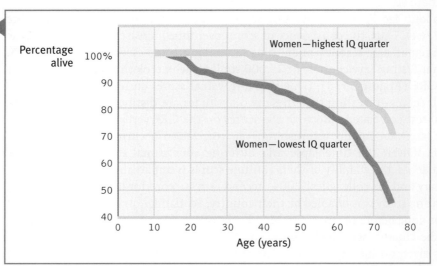

Extremes of Intelligence

34-4 What are the traits of those at the low and high intelligence extremes?

One way to glimpse the validity and significance of any test is to compare people who score at the two extremes of the normal curve. The two groups should differ noticeably, and they do.

The Low Extreme

At one extreme of the normal curve are those whose intelligence test scores fall at 70 or below. To be labeled as having an **intellectual disability** (formerly referred to as *mental retardation*), a child must have both a low test score and difficulty adapting to the normal demands of independent living. Only about 1 percent of the population meets both criteria, with males outnumbering females by 50 percent (American Psychiatric Association, 1994). As TABLE 34.1 indicates, most individuals with intellectual disabilities can, with support, live in mainstream society.

Intellectual disabilities sometimes have a known physical cause. **Down syndrome,** for example, is a disorder of varying severity caused by an extra chromosome 21 in the person's genetic makeup.

During the last two centuries, the pendulum of opinion about how best to care for Americans with intellectual disabilities has made a complete swing. Until the mid-nineteenth century, they were cared for at home. Many of those with the most severe disabilities died, but people with less significant challenges often found a place in a farm-based society. Then, residential schools for slow learners were established. By the twentieth century, many of these institutions had become warehouses, providing residents little attention, no privacy, and no hope. Parents often were told to separate themselves permanently from their impaired child before they became attached.

In the last half of the twentieth century, the pendulum swung back to normalization—encouraging people to live in their own communities as normally as their functioning permits. Children with mild disabilities are educated in less restrictive environments, and many are integrated, or *mainstreamed,* into regular classrooms. Most grow up with their own families, then move into a protected living arrangement, such as a group home. The hope, and often the reality, is a happier and more dignified life.

But think about another reason people diagnosed with mild intellectual disabilities—those just below the 70 score on an intelligence test used to draw the line on who has a disability—might be better able to live independently today than many decades ago. Recall that, thanks to the Flynn effect, the tests have been periodically restandardized. When that happens, individuals who scored near 70 suddenly lose about 6 IQ points, and two people with the same ability level could thus be classified differently depending on when they were tested (Kanaya et al., 2003). As the number of people diagnosed with an intellectual disability suddenly jumps, more people become eligible for special education and for Social Security payments for those with an intellectual disability. And in the United States (one of only a few countries with the

intellectual disability (formerly referred to as *mental retardation*) a condition of limited mental ability, indicated by an intelligence score of 70 or below and difficulty in adapting to the demands of life; varies from mild to profound.

Down syndrome a condition of intellectual disability and associated physical disorders caused by an extra copy of chromosome 21.

TABLE 34.1 Degrees of Intellectual Disability

Level	Approximate Intelligence Scores	Adaptation to Demands of Life
Mild	50–70	May learn academic skills up to sixth-grade level. Adults may, with assistance, achieve self-supporting social and vocational skills.
Moderate	35–50	May progress to second-grade level academically. Adults may contribute to their own support by laboring in sheltered workshops.
Severe	20–35	May learn to talk and to perform simple work tasks under close supervision but are generally unable to profit from vocational training.
Profound	Below 20	Require constant aid and supervision.

Source: Reprinted with permission from the *Diagnostic and Statistical Manual of Mental Disorders,* Fourth Edition, text revision. Copyright 2000 American Psychiatric Association.

death penalty), fewer people are eligible for execution—the U.S. Supreme Court ruled in 2002 that the execution of people with intellectual disabilities is "cruel and unusual punishment." For people near that score of 70, intelligence testing can be a high-stakes competition.

The High Extreme

In one famous project begun in 1921, Lewis Terman studied more than 1500 California schoolchildren with IQ scores over 135. Contrary to the popular notion that intellectually gifted children are frequently maladjusted because they are "in a different world" from their nongifted peers, Terman's high-scoring children, like those in later studies, were healthy, well-adjusted, and unusually successful academically (Lubinski & Benbow, 2006; Stanley, 1997). When restudied over the next seven decades, most people in Terman's group had attained high levels of education (Austin et al., 2002; Holahan & Sears, 1995). They included many doctors, lawyers, professors, scientists, and writers, but no Nobel prize winners.

A more recent study of precocious youths who aced the math SAT at age 13—by scoring in the top quarter of 1 percent of their age group—were at age 33 twice as likely to have patents as were those in the bottom quarter of the top 1 percent (Wai et al., 2005). And they were more likely to have earned a Ph.D.—1 in 3, compared with 1 in 5 from the lower part of the top 1 percent. Compared with the math aces, 13-year-olds scoring high on verbal aptitude were more likely to have become humanities professors or written a novel (Park et al., 2007).

These whiz kids remind me of Jean Piaget, who by age 7 was devoting his free time to studying birds, fossils, and machines; who by age 15 was publishing scientific articles on mollusks; and who later went on to become the twentieth century's most famous developmental psychologist (Hunt, 1993). Children with extraordinary academic gifts are sometimes more isolated, introverted, and in their own worlds (Winner, 2000). But most thrive.

There are critics who question many of the assumptions of currently popular "gifted child" programs, such as the belief that only 3 to 5 percent of children are gifted and that it pays to identify and "track" these special few—segregating them in special classes and giving them academic enrichment not available to the other 95 percent. Critics note that tracking by aptitude sometimes creates a self-fulfilling prophecy: Those implicitly labeled "ungifted" may be influenced to become so (Lipsey & Wilson, 1993; Slavin & Braddock, 1993). Denying lower-ability students opportunities for enriched education can widen the achievement gap between ability groups and increase their social isolation from one another (Carnegie, 1989; Stevenson & Lee, 1990). Because minority and low-income youth are more often placed in lower academic groups, tracking can also promote segregation and prejudice—hardly, note critics, a healthy preparation for working and living in a multicultural society.

Critics and proponents of gifted education do, however, agree on this: Children have differing gifts. Some are especially good at math, others at verbal reasoning, others at art, still others at social leadership. Educating children as if all were alike is as naive as assuming that giftedness is something, like blue eyes, that you either have or do not have. One need not hang labels on children to affirm their special talents and to challenge them all at the frontiers of their own ability and understanding. By providing *appropriate developmental placement* suited to each child's talents, we can promote both equity and excellence for all (Colangelo et al., 2004; Lubinski & Benbow, 2000; Sternberg & Grigorenko, 2000).

|| Terman did test two future Nobel laureates in physics but they failed to score above his gifted sample cutoff (Hulbert, 2005). ||

"Joining Mensa means that you are a genius. . . . I worried about the arbitrary 132 cutoff point, until I met someone with an IQ of 131 and, honestly, he was a bit slow on the uptake."
Steve Martin, 1997

The extremes of intelligence Sho Yano was playing Mozart by age 4, aced the SAT at age 8, and graduated summa cum laude from Loyola University at age 12, at which age he began combined Ph.D.–M.D. studies at the University of Chicago.

AP Photo/Anne Ryan

REVIEW

Assessing Intelligence

34-1 **When and why were intelligence tests created?** In France in 1904, Alfred Binet started the modern intelligence-testing movement by developing questions that helped predict children's future progress in the Paris school system. Lewis Terman of Stanford University revised Binet's work for use in the United States. Terman believed his *Stanford-Binet* could help guide people toward appropriate opportunities, but more than Binet, he believed intelligence is inherited. During the early part of the twentieth century, intelligence tests were sometimes used to "document" scientists' assumptions about the innate inferiority of certain ethnic and immigrant groups.

34-2 **What's the difference between aptitude and achievement tests, and how can we develop and evaluate them?** *Aptitude tests* are designed to predict what you *can learn*. *Achievement tests* are designed to assess what you *have learned*. The WAIS (*Wechsler Adult Intelligence Scale*), an aptitude test, is the most widely used intelligence test for adults. Such tests must be *standardized*, by giving the test to a representative sample of future test-takers to establish a basis for meaningful score comparisons. The distribution of test scores often forms a *normal,* bell-shaped *curve*. Tests must also be *reliable*, by yielding consistent scores (on two halves of the test, or when people are retested). And they must be *valid*. A valid test measures or predicts what it is supposed to. *Content validity* is the extent to which a test samples the pertinent behavior (as a driving test measures driving ability). *Predictive validity* is the extent to which the test predicts a behavior it is designed to predict (aptitude tests have predictive ability if they can predict future achievements).

34-3 **How stable are intelligence scores over the life span?** The stability of intelligence test scores increases with age. By age 4, scores fluctuate somewhat but begin to predict adolescent and adult scores. At about age 7, scores become fairly stable and consistent.

34-4 **What are the traits of those at the low and high intelligence extremes?** Those with intelligence test scores below 70, the cut-off mark for the diagnosis of an *intellectual disability* (formerly referred to as mental retardation), vary from near-normal to those requiring constant aid and supervision. *Down syndrome* is a form of intellectual disability with a physical cause—an extra copy of chromosome 21. High-scoring people, contrary to popular myths, tend to be healthy and well-adjusted, as well as unusually success-ful academically. Schools sometimes "track" such children, separating them from those with lower scores. Such programs can become self-fulfilling prophecies as children live up to—or down to—others' perceptions of their ability.

Terms and Concepts to Remember

intelligence test, p. 416

mental age, p. 417

Stanford-Binet, p. 417

intelligence quotient (IQ), p. 417

achievement tests, p. 418

aptitude tests, p. 418

Wechsler Adult Intelligence Scale (WAIS), p. 419

standardization, p. 420

normal curve, p. 420

reliability, p. 421

validity, p. 421

content validity, p. 421

predictive validity, p. 421

intellectual disability, p. 425

Down syndrome, p. 425

Test Yourself

1. What was the purpose of Binet's pioneering intelligence test?

2. The Smiths have enrolled their 2-year-old son in a special program that promises to assess his IQ and, if he places in the top 5 percent of test-takers, to create a plan that will guarantee his admission to a top university at age 18. Why is this endeavor of questionable value?

(Answers to the Test Yourself questions can be found in Appendix B at the end of the book.)

Ask Yourself

1. Are you working to the potential reflected in your college entrance exam scores? What, other than your aptitude, is affecting your college performance?

2. How do you feel about mainstreaming children of all ability levels in the same classroom? What evidence are you using to support your view?

⊙⊙ WEB

Multiple-choice self-tests and more may be found at www.worthpublishers.com/myers

Twin and Adoption Studies

Heritability

Environmental Influences

Group Differences in
Intelligence Test Scores

The Question of Bias

MODULE 35

Genetic and Environmental Influences on Intelligence

35-1 What does evidence reveal about hereditary and environmental influences on intelligence?

Intelligence runs in families. But why? Are our intellectual abilities mostly inherited? Or are they molded by our environment?

Few issues arouse such passion or have such serious political implications. Consider: If we mainly inherit our differing mental abilities, and if success reflects those abilities, then people's socioeconomic standing will correspond to their inborn differences. This could lead to those on top believing their intellectual birthright justifies their social positions.

But if mental abilities are primarily nurtured by the environments that raise and inform us, then children from disadvantaged environments can expect to lead disadvantaged lives. In this case, people's standing will result from their unequal opportunities.

For now, as best we can, let's set aside such political implications and examine the evidence.

▶‖ Twin and Adoption Studies

Do people who share the same genes also share comparable mental abilities? As you can see from **FIGURE 35.1**, which summarizes many studies, the answer is clearly *yes*. In support of the genetic contribution to intelligence, researchers cite three sets of findings:

▶ The intelligence test scores of identical twins reared together are virtually as similar as those of the same person taking the same test twice (Lykken, 1999; Plomin, 2001). (The scores of fraternal twins, who typically share only half their genes, are much less similar.) Likewise, the test scores of identical twins reared separately are similar enough to have led twin researcher Thomas Bouchard (1996a) to estimate that "about 70 percent" of intelligence test score variation "can be attributed to genetic variation." Other estimates range from 50 to 75 percent (Devlin et al., 1997; Neisser et al., 1996; Plomin, 2003). For simple reaction time tasks that measure processing speed, estimates range from 30 to 50 percent (Beaujean, 2005).

▶ Brain scans reveal that identical twins have very similar gray matter volume, and that their brains (unlike those of fraternal twins) are virtually the same in areas associated with verbal and spatial intelligence (Thompson et al., 2001).

▶ Are there genes for genius? Today's researchers have identified chromosomal regions important to intelligence, and they have pinpointed specific genes that seemingly influence variations in intelligence and learning disabilities (Dick et al., 2007; Plomin & Kovas, 2005; Posthuma & deGeus, 2006). Intelligence appears to be *polygenetic,* meaning many genes seem to be involved, with each gene accounting for much less than 1 percent of intelligence variations (Butcher et al., 2008).

But other evidence points to the effects of environment. Studies show that adoption enhances the intelligence scores of mistreated or neglected children (van IJzendoorn & Juffer, 2005, 2006). And fraternal twins, who are genetically no more alike than any other siblings—but who are treated more alike because they are the same age—tend to score more alike than other siblings. So if shared environment matters, do children in adoptive families share similar aptitudes?

"There are more studies addressing the genetics of *g* [general intelligence] than any other human characteristic."
Robert Plomin (1999)

"I told my parents that if grades were so important they should have paid for a smarter egg donor."

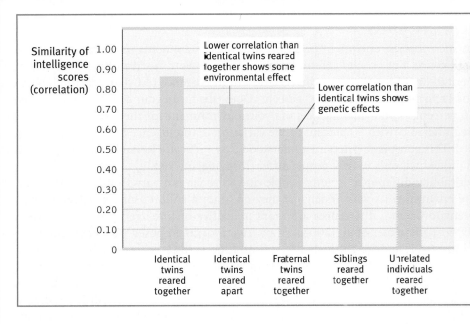

FIGURE 35.1 **Intelligence: Nature and nurture** The most genetically similar people have the most similar intelligence scores. Remember: 1.0 indicates a perfect correlation; zero indicates no correlation at all. (Data from McGue et al., 1993.)

Seeking to disentangle genes and environment, researchers have compared the intelligence test scores of adopted children with those of their adoptive siblings and with those of (a) their biological parents, the providers of their genes, and (b) their adoptive parents, the providers of their home environment. During childhood, the intelligence test scores of adoptive siblings correlate modestly. Over time, adopted children accumulate experience in their differing adoptive families. So would you expect the family environment effect to grow with age and the genetic legacy effect to shrink?

If you would, behavior geneticists have a surprise for you. Mental similarities between adopted children and their adoptive families wane with age, until the correlation approaches zero by adulthood (McGue et al., 1993). This is even true of "virtual twins"—same age, biologically unrelated siblings reared together from infancy (Segal et al., 2007). Genetic influences—not environmental ones—become more apparent as we accumulate life experience (Bouchard, 1995, 1996b). Identical twins' similarities, for example, continue or increase into their eighties (McClearn et al., 1997; Plomin et al., 1997). Similarly, adopted children's intelligence scores over time become more like those of their biological parents (**FIGURE 35.2**).

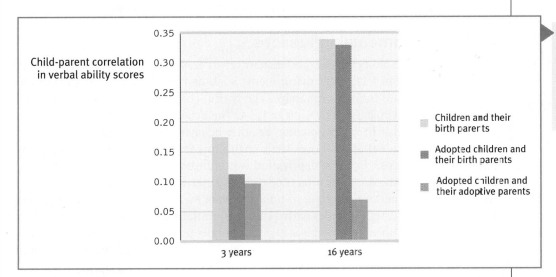

FIGURE 35.2 **Who do adopted children resemble?** As the years went by in their adoptive families, children's verbal ability scores became modestly more like their *biological* parents' scores. (Adapted from Plomin & DeFries, 1998.)

heritability the proportion of variation among individuals that we can attribute to genes. The heritability of a trait may vary, depending on the range of populations and environments studied.

|| A check on your understanding of heritability: If environments become more equal, the heritability of intelligence would

a. increase.

b. decrease.

c. be unchanged.

(Answer below.) ||

Heritability—variation explained by genetic influences—will *increase* as environmental variation decreases.

"Selective breeding has given me an aptitude for the law, but I still love fetching a dead duck out of freezing water."

▶|| Heritability

Given such studies, one might be tempted to make statements about the heritability of intelligence. But be very careful how you use the word **heritability.** Estimates of the heritability of intelligence—the variation in intelligence test scores attributable to genetic factors—put it at about 50 percent. Does this mean your genes are responsible for 50 percent of your intelligence and your environment for the rest? No. It means we credit heredity with 50 percent of the variation in intelligence among people being studied. This point is so often misunderstood that I repeat: Heritability never pertains to an individual, only to why people differ from one another.

Heritability differences among people due to genes can vary from study to study. Where environments vary widely, as they do among children of less-educated parents, environmental differences are more predictive of intelligence scores (Rowe et al., 1999; Turkheimer et al., 2003). Mark Twain once proposed that boys should be raised in barrels and fed through a hole until they were 12 years old. Given the boys' equal environments, differences in their individual intelligence test scores at age 12 could be explained only by their heredity. Thus, heritability for their differences would be nearly 100 percent. But if we raise people with similar heredities in drastically different environments (barrels versus advantaged homes), the environment effect will be huge, and heritability will therefore be lower. In a world of clones, heritability would be zero.

Remember, too, that genes and environment work together. If you try out for a basketball team and are just slightly taller and quicker than others, notes James Flynn (2003, 2007), you will more likely be picked, play more, and get more coaching. The same would be true for your separated identical twin—who might, *not just for genetic reasons,* also come to excel at basketball. Likewise, if you have a natural aptitude for academics, you will more likely stay in school, read books, and ask questions—all of which will amplify your cognitive brain power. Thanks to such gene-environment interaction, modest genetic advantages can be socially multiplied into big performance advantages. Our genes shape the experiences that shape us.

▶|| Environmental Influences

Genes make a difference. Even if we were all raised in the same intellectually stimulating environment, we would have differing aptitudes. But life experiences also matter. Human environments are rarely as impoverished as the dark and barren cages inhabited by deprived rats that develop thinner-than-normal brain cortexes (Rosenzweig et al., 1984). Yet severe deprivation does leave footprints on the brain.

Early Environmental Influences

We have seen that biology and experience intertwine. Nowhere is this more apparent than in impoverished human environments such as J. McVicker Hunt (1982) observed in a destitute Iranian orphanage. The typical child Hunt observed there could not sit up unassisted at age 2 or walk at age 4. The little care the infants received was not in response to their crying, cooing, or other behaviors, so the children developed little sense of personal control over their environment. They were instead becoming passive "glum lumps." Extreme deprivation was bludgeoning native intelligence.

Aware of both the dramatic effects of early experiences and the impact of early intervention, Hunt began a program of *tutored human enrichment.* He trained caregivers to play language-fostering games with 11 infants, imitating the babies' babbling, then engaging them in vocal follow-the-leader, and finally teaching them sounds from the Persian language. The results were dramatic. By 22 months of age, the infants could name more than 50 objects and body parts and so charmed visitors that most were adopted—an unprecedented success for the orphanage. (Institutionalized Romanian orphans also have benefited cognitively if transferred early to more enriched home care [Nelson et al., 2007].)

Hunt's findings are an extreme case of a more general finding: Among the poor, environmental conditions can override genetic differences, depressing cognitive development. Unlike children of affluence, siblings within impoverished families have more similar intelligence scores (Turkheimer et al., 2003). Schools with lots of poverty-level children often have less-qualified teachers, as one study of 1450 Virginia schools found. And even after controlling for poverty, having less-qualified teachers predicted lower achievement scores (Tuerk, 2005). Malnutrition also plays a role. Relieve infant malnutrition with nutritional supplements, and poverty's effect on physical and cognitive development lessens (Brown & Pollitt, 1996).

Do studies of such early interventions indicate that providing an "enriched" environment can "give your child a superior intellect," as some popular books claim? Most experts are doubtful (Bruer, 1999). Although malnutrition, sensory deprivation, and social isolation can retard normal brain development, there is no environmental recipe for fast-forwarding a normal infant into a genius. All babies should have normal exposure to sights, sounds, and speech. Beyond that, Sandra Scarr's (1984) verdict still is widely shared: "Parents who are very concerned about providing special educational lessons for their babies are wasting their time."

Still, explorations of intelligence promotion continue. One widely publicized but now-discounted finding, dubbed the "Mozart effect," suggested that listening to classical music boosted cognitive ability. Other research has, however, revealed small but enduring cognitive benefits to either keyboard or vocal music training (Schellenberg, 2005, 2006). The music-training effect appears unexplained by the greater parental income and education of music-trained children; it may result from improved attention focus or abstract thinking ability. Other researchers hold out hope that *targeted training* of specific abilities (rather like a body builder doing curls to strengthen biceps and sit-ups to strengthen abdominal muscles) might build mental muscles (Kosslyn, 2007).

Devastating neglect Romanian orphans who had minimal interaction with caregivers, such as this child in the Lagunul Pentro Copii orphanage in 1990, suffered delayed development.

"There is a large body of evidence indicating that there is little if anything to be gained by exposing middle-class children to early education."

Developmental psychologist
Edward F. Zigler (1987)

Schooling and Intelligence

Later in childhood, schooling is one intervention that pays dividends reflected in intelligence scores. Schooling and intelligence interact, and both enhance later income (Ceci & Williams, 1997). Hunt was a strong believer in the ability of education to boost children's chances for success by developing their cognitive and social skills. Indeed, his 1961 book, *Intelligence and Experience,* helped launch Project Head Start in 1965. Head Start, a U.S. government-funded preschool program, serves more than 900,000 children, most of whom come from families below the poverty level (Head Start, 2005).

Does it succeed? Researchers study Head Start and other preschool programs such as Sure Start in Britain by comparing children who experience the program with their counterparts who don't. Quality programs, offering individual attention, increase children's school readiness, which decreases their likelihood of repeating a grade or being placed in special education. Generally, the aptitude benefits dissipate over time (reminding us that life experience *after* Head Start matters, too). Psychologist Edward Zigler, the program's first director, nevertheless believes there are long-term benefits (Ripple & Zigler, 2003; Zigler & Styfco, 2001). High-quality preschool programs can provide at least a small boost to emotional intelligence—creating better attitudes toward learning and reducing school dropouts and criminality (Reynolds et al., 2001).

Genes and experience together weave the intelligence fabric. But what we accomplish with our intelligence depends also on our own beliefs and motivation, reports

Getting a Head Start Project Head Start offers educational activities designed to increase readiness for schoolwork and expand children's notions of where school might lead them. Here children in a classroom learn about colors, and children on a field trip prepare for the annual Head Start parade in Boston.

"It is our choices . . . that show what we truly are, far more than our abilities."
Professor Dumbledore to Harry Potter in J. K. Rowling's *Harry Potter and the Chamber of Secrets*, 1999

|| Despite the gender equivalence in intelligence test scores, males are more likely than females to overestimate their own test scores. Both males and females tend to rate their father's scores higher than their mother's, their brothers' scores higher than their sisters', and their sons' scores higher than their daughters' (Furnham, 2001; Furnham et al., 2002a,b, 2004a,b,c). ||

Carol Dweck (2006, 2007). Those who believe that intelligence is biologically fixed and unchanging tend to focus on proving and defending their identity. Those who instead believe that intelligence is changeable will focus more on learning and growing. Seeing that it pays to have a "growth mindset" rather than a "fixed mindset," Dweck has developed interventions that effectively teach early teens that the brain is like a muscle that grows stronger with use as neuron connections grow. Indeed, superior achievements in fields from sports to science to music arise from disciplined effort and sustained practice (Ericsson et al., 2007).

▶|| Group Differences in Intelligence Test Scores

35-2 How and why do gender and racial groups differ in mental ability scores?

If there were no group differences in aptitude scores, psychologists could politely debate hereditary and environmental influences in their ivory towers. But there are group differences. What are they? And what shall we make of them?

Gender Similarities and Differences

In science, as in everyday life, differences, not similarities, excite interest. Compared with the anatomical and physiological similarities between men and women, our differences are relatively minor. Yet it is the differences we find exciting. Similarly, in the psychological domain, gender similarities vastly outnumber gender differences. We are all so much alike. In a 1932 testing of all Scottish 11-year-olds, for example, girls' average intelligence score was 100.6 and boys' was 100.5 (Deary et al., 2003). On a 2001 to 2003 Cognitive Ability Test administered to 324,000 British 11- and 12-year-olds, boys averaged 99.1 and girls a similar 99.9 (Strand et al., 2006). So far as *general intelligence (g)* is concerned, boys and girls, men and women, are the same species. Yet, most people find differences more newsworthy. And here they are:

Spelling Females are better spellers: At the end of high school, only 30 percent of U.S. males spell better than the average female (Lubinski & Benbow, 1992).

Verbal ability Females excel at verbal fluency and remembering words (Halpern et al., 2007). And, year after year, among nearly 200,000 students taking Germany's Test for Medical Studies, young women have surpassed men in remembering facts from short medical cases (Stumpf & Jackson, 1994). (My wife, who remembers many of my experiences for me, tells me that if she died I'd be a man without a past.)

Nonverbal memory Females have an edge in remembering and locating objects (Voyer et al., 2007). In studies of more than 100,000 American adolescents, girls also modestly surpassed boys in memory for picture associations (Hedges & Nowell, 1995).

Sensation Females are more sensitive to touch, taste, and odor.

Emotion-detecting ability Females are better emotion detectors. Robert Rosenthal, Judith Hall, and their colleagues (1979; McClure, 2000) discovered this while studying sensitivity to emotional cues (an aspect of emotional intelligence). They showed hundreds of people brief film clips of portions of a person's emotionally expressive face or body, sometimes with a garbled voice added. For example, after showing a 2-second scene revealing only the face of an upset woman, the researchers asked people to guess whether the woman was criticizing someone for being late or was talking about her divorce. Rosenthal and Hall found that some people, many of them women, are much better emotion detectors than others. Such skills may explain women's somewhat greater responsiveness in both positive and negative emotional situations.

Could this ability also have helped our ancestral mothers read emotions in their infants and would-be lovers, in turn fueling cultural tendencies to encourage women's empathic skills? Some evolutionary psychologists believe so.

Math and spatial aptitudes On math tests given to more than 3 million representatively sampled people in 100 independent studies, males and females obtained nearly identical average scores (Hyde et al., 1990, 2008). But again—despite greater diversity within the genders than between them—group differences make the news. In 20 of 21 countries, females displayed an edge in math computation, but males scored higher in math problem solving (Bronner, 1998; Hedges & Nowell, 1995). In Western countries, virtually all math prodigies participating in the International Mathematics Olympiad have been males. (More female math prodigies have, however, reached the top levels in non-Western countries, such as China [Halpern, 1991]).

The score differences are sharpest at the extremes. Among 12- to 14-year-olds scoring extremely high on SAT math, boys have outnumbered girls 13 to 1, and within that precocious group, the boys more often went on to earn a degree in the inorganic sciences and engineering (Benbow et al., 2000). In the United States, males also have an edge in the annual physics and computer science Advanced Placement exams (Stumpf & Stanley, 1998).

Men are 99 percent of the world's chess grandmasters, a difference attributable to the much greater number of boys beginning to play competitive chess. Understanding *why* boys more than girls enter competitive chess is a challenge for future research (Chabris & Glickman, 2006).

‖ In the first 56 years of the college Putnam Mathematical Competition, all of the nearly 300 awardees were men (Arenson, 1997). In 1997, a woman broke the male grip by joining 5 men in the winner's circle. In 1998, Melanie Wood became the first female member of a U.S. math Olympics team (Shulman, 2000). Her training began at an early age: When mall-shopping with her then-4-year-old daughter, Melanie's mother would alleviate her child's boredom by giving her linear equations to solve. ‖

Robert Strawn/National Academy of Sciences/Einstein Statue, sculptor, Robert Berks

World Math Olympics champs After outscoring thousands of their U.S. peers, these young people became the U.S. Math Team in 2002 and placed third in the worldwide competition.

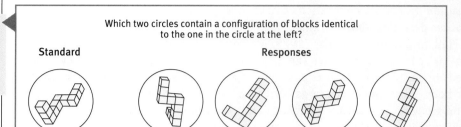

FIGURE 35.3 The mental rotation test
This is a test of spatial abilities. (From Vandenberg & Kuse, 1978.) (Answer below.)

The first and fourth alternatives.

|| Among entering American collegians, 22 percent of men and 4 percent of women report having played video/computer games six or more hours a week (Pryor et al., 2006). ||

The average male edge seems most reliable in spatial ability tests like the one shown in **FIGURE 35.3**, which involves speedily rotating three-dimensional objects in one's mind (Collins & Kimura, 1997; Halpern, 2000). Exposure to high levels of male sex hormones during the prenatal period does enhance spatial abilities (Berenbaum et al., 1995). So, one recent experiment indicates, does action video game playing (Feng et al., 2007). Spatial abilities skills help when fitting suitcases into a car trunk, playing chess, or doing certain types of geometry problems.

From an evolutionary perspective (Geary, 1995, 1996; Halpern et al., 2007), those same skills helped our ancestral fathers track prey and make their way home. The survival of our ancestral mothers may have benefited more from a keen memory for the location of edible plants—a legacy that lives today in women's superior memory for objects and their location.

Evolutionary psychologist Steven Pinker (2005) argues that biological as well as social influences appear to affect gender differences in life priorities (women's greater interest in people versus men's in money and things), in risk-taking (with men more reckless), and in math reasoning and spatial abilities. Such differences are, he notes, observed across cultures, stable over time, influenced by prenatal hormones, and observed in genetic boys raised as girls. Other researchers are exploring a brain basis for male-female cognitive differences (Halpern et al., 2007).

Elizabeth Spelke (2005), however, urges caution in charting male-female intellectual worlds. It oversimplifies to say that women have more "verbal ability" and men more "math ability." Women excel at verbal fluency, men at verbal analogies. Women excel at rapid math calculations, men at rapid math reasoning. Women excel at remembering objects' spatial positions, men at remembering geometric layouts.

Nature or nurture? At this 2005 Google Inc.-sponsored computer coding competition, programmers competed for cash prizes and possible jobs. What do you think accounted for the fact that only one of the 100 finalists was female?

AP Photo/Paul Sakuma

Other critics urge us to remember that social expectations and divergent opportunities shape boys' and girls' interests and abilities (Crawford et al., 1995; Eccles et al., 1990). Gender-equal cultures, such as Sweden and Iceland, exhibit little of the gender math gap found in gender-unequal cultures, such as Turkey and Korea (Guiso et al., 2008). In the United States, the male edge in math problem solving is detectable only after elementary school. Traditionally, math and science have been considered masculine subjects, but as more parents encourage their daughters to develop their abilities in math and science, the gender gap is narrowing (Nowell & Hedges, 1998). In some fields, including psychology, women now earn most of the Ph.D.s. Yet, notes Diane Halpern (2005) with a twinkle in her eye, "no one has asked if men have the innate ability to succeed in those academic disciplines where *they* are underrepresented."

Greater male variability Finally, intelligence research consistently reports a peculiar tendency for males' mental

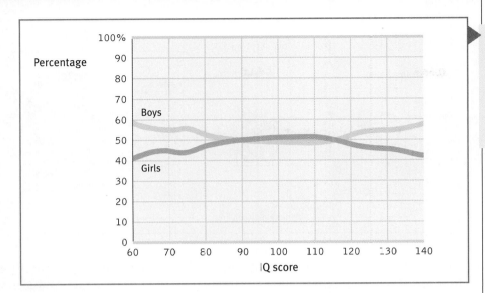

FIGURE 35.4 **Gender and variability**
When nearly 90,000 Scottish 11-year-olds were administered an intelligence test in 1932, the average IQ scores for girls and boys was essentially identical. But as other studies have found, boys were overrepresented at the low and high extremes. (Adapted from Deary et al., 2003.)

ability scores to vary more than females' (Halpern et al., 2007). Thus, boys outnumber girls at both the low extreme and the high extreme (Kleinfeld, 1998; Strand et al., 2006; also see **FIGURE 35.4**). Boys are, therefore, more often found in special education classes. They talk later. They stutter more.

Ethnic Similarities and Differences

Fueling the group-differences debate are two other disturbing but agreed-upon facts:

▶ Racial groups differ in their average intelligence test scores.
▶ High-scoring people (and groups) are more likely to attain high levels of education and income.

A statement by 52 intelligence researchers explained: "The bell curve for Whites is centered roughly around IQ 100; the bell curve for American Blacks roughly around 85; and those for different subgroups of Hispanics roughly midway between those for Whites and Blacks" (Avery et al., 1994). Comparable results come from other academic aptitude tests. In recent years, the Black-White difference has diminished somewhat, and among children has dropped to 10 points in some studies (Dickens & Flynn, 2006). Yet the test score gap stubbornly persists, and other studies suggest the gap stopped narrowing among those born after 1970 (Murray, 2006, 2007).

There are differences among other groups as well. New Zealanders of European descent outscore native Maori New Zealanders. Israeli Jews outscore Israeli Arabs. Most Japanese outscore the stigmatized Japanese minority, the Burakumin. And those who can hear outscore those born deaf (Braden, 1994; Steele, 1990; Zeidner, 1990).

Everyone further agrees that such *group* differences provide little basis for judging individuals. Women outlive men by six years, but knowing someone's sex doesn't tell us with any precision how long that person will live. Even Charles Murray and Richard Herrnstein (1994), whose writings drew attention to Black-White differences, reminded us that "millions of Blacks have higher IQs than the average White."

Swedes and Bantus differ in complexion and language. That first factor is genetic, the second environmental. So what about intelligence scores?

As we have seen, heredity contributes to individual differences in intelligence. Does that mean it also contributes to group differences? Some psychologists believe it does, perhaps because of the world's differing climates and survival challenges (Herrnstein & Murray, 1994; Lynn, 1991, 2001; Rushton & Jensen, 2005, 2006).

FIGURE 35.5 Group differences and environmental impact Even if the variation between members within a group reflects genetic differences, the average difference between groups may be wholly due to the environment. Imagine that seeds from the same mixture are sown in different soils. Although height differences *within* each window box will be genetic, the height difference *between* the two groups will be environmental. (From Lewontin, 1976.)

Variation within group

Variation within group

Seeds

Poor soil

Fertile soil

Difference between groups

|| In prosperous country X everyone eats all they want. In country Y the rich are well fed, but the semistarved poor are often thin. In which country will the heritability of body weight be greater? (Answer below.) ||

Heritability—differences due to genes—will be greater in country X, where environmental differences in nutrition are minimal.

|| Since 1830, the average Dutch man has grown from 5 feet 5 inches to nearly 6 feet. ||

But we have also seen that group differences in a heritable trait may be entirely environmental, as in our earlier barrel-versus-home–reared boys example. Consider one of nature's experiments: Allow some children to grow up hearing their culture's dominant language, while others, born deaf, do not. Then give both groups an intelligence test rooted in the dominant language, and (no surprise) those with expertise in that language will score highest. Although individual performance differences may be substantially genetic, the group difference is not (**FIGURE 35.5**).

Also consider: If each identical twin were exactly as tall as his or her co-twin, heritability would be 100 percent. Imagine that we then separated some young twins and gave only half of them a nutritious diet, and that the well-nourished twins all grew to be exactly 3 inches taller than their counterparts—an environmental effect comparable to that actually observed in both Britain and America, where adolescents are several inches taller than their counterparts were a half-century ago. What would the heritability of height now be for our well-nourished twins? Still 100 percent, because the variation in height within the group would remain entirely predictable from the heights of their malnourished identical siblings. So even perfect heritability within groups would not eliminate the possibility of a strong environmental impact on the group differences.

Might the racial gap be similarly environmental? Consider:

Genetics research reveals that under the skin, the races are remarkably alike (Cavalli-Sforza et al., 1994; Lewontin, 1982). Individual differences within a race are much

Nature's own morphing Nature draws no sharp boundaries between races, which blend gradually one into the next around the Earth. Thanks to the human urge to classify, however, people socially define themselves in racial categories, which become catch-all labels for physical features, social identity, and nationality.

© Paul Almasy/Corbis; © Rob Howard/Corbis; © Barbara Bannister, Gallo Images/Corbis; © David Turnley/Corbis; © Dave Bartruff/Corbis; © Haruyoshi Yamaguchi/Corbis; © Richard T. Nowitz/Corbis; © Owen Franken/Corbis; © Paul Almasy/Corbis; © John-Francis Bourke/zefa/Corbis

greater than differences between races. The average genetic difference between two Icelandic villagers or between two Kenyans greatly exceeds the group difference between Icelanders and Kenyans. Moreover, looks can deceive. Light-skinned Europeans and dark-skinned Africans are genetically closer than are dark-skinned Africans and dark-skinned Aboriginal Australians.

Race is not a neatly defined biological category. Some scholars argue that there is a reality to race, noting that there are genetic markers for race (the continent of one's ancestry) and that medical risks (such as skin cancer or high blood pressure) vary by race. Behavioral traits may also vary by race. "No runner of Asian or European descent—a majority of the world's population—has broken 10 seconds in the 100-meter dash, but dozens of runners of West African descent have done so," observes psychologist David Rowe (2005). Many social scientists, though, see race primarily as a social construction without well-defined physical boundaries (Helms et al., 2005; Smedley & Smedley, 2005; Sternberg et al., 2005). People with varying ancestry may categorize themselves in the same race. Moreover, with increasingly mixed ancestries, more and more people defy neat racial categorization. (What race is Tiger Woods?)

Asian students outperform North American students on math achievement and aptitude tests. But this difference appears to be a recent phenomenon and may reflect conscientiousness more than competence. Asian students also attend school 30 percent more days per year and spend much more time in and out of school studying math (Geary et al., 1996; Larson & Verma, 1999; Stevenson, 1992).

The intelligence test performance of today's better-fed, better-educated, and more test-prepared population exceeds that of the 1930s population—by the same margin that the intelligence test score of the average White today exceeds that of the average Black. No one attributes the generational group difference to genetics.

White and Black infants have scored equally well on an infant intelligence measure (preference for looking at novel stimuli—a crude predictor of future intelligence scores [Fagan, 1992]).

When Blacks and Whites have or receive the same pertinent knowledge, they exhibit similar information-processing skill. "The data support the view that cultural differences in the provision of information may account for racial differences in IQ," report researchers Joseph Fagan and Cynthia Holland (2007).

In different eras, different ethnic groups have experienced golden ages—periods of remarkable achievement. Twenty-five-hundred years ago, it was the Greeks and the Egyptians, then the Romans; in the eighth and ninth centuries, genius seemed to reside in

The culture of scholarship The children of Indochinese refugee families studied by Nathan Caplan, Marcella Choy, and James Whitmore (1992) typically excel in school. On weekday nights after dinner, the family clears the table and begins homework. Family cooperation is valued, and older siblings help younger ones.

Jason Goltz

the Arab world; 500 years ago it was the Aztec Indians and the peoples of Northern Europe. Today, people marvel at Asians' technological genius. Cultures rise and fall over centuries; genes do not. That fact makes it difficult to attribute a natural superiority to any race.

Moreover, consider the striking results of a national study that looked back over the mental test performances of White and Black young adults after graduation from college. From eighth grade through the early high school years, the average aptitude scores of the White students increased, while those of the Black students decreased—creating a gap that reached its widest point at about the time that high school students take college admissions tests. But during college, the Black students' scores increased "more than four times as much" as those of their White counterparts, thus greatly decreasing the aptitude gap. "It is not surprising," concluded researcher Joel Myerson and his colleagues (1998), "that as Black and White students complete more grades in high school environments that differ in quality, the gap in cognitive test scores widens. At the college level, however, where Black and White students are exposed to educational environments of comparable quality . . . many Blacks are able to make remarkable gains, closing the gap in test scores."

▶‖ The Question of Bias

35-3 Are intelligence tests inappropriately biased?

If one assumes that race is a meaningful concept, the debate over race differences in intelligence divides into three camps, note Earl Hunt and Jerry Carlson (2007):

▶ There are genetically disposed race differences in intelligence.
▶ There are socially influenced race differences in intelligence.
▶ There are race differences in test scores, but the tests are inappropriate or biased.

Are intelligence tests biased? The answer depends on which of two very different definitions of *bias* are used, and on an understanding of stereotypes.

Two Meanings of Bias

A test may be considered biased if it detects not only innate differences in intelligence but also performance differences caused by cultural experiences. This in fact happened to Eastern European immigrants in the early 1900s. Lacking the experience to answer questions about their new culture, many were classified as feeble-minded. David Wechsler, who entered the United States as a 6-year-old Romanian just before this group, designed the *Wechsler Adult Intelligence Scale (WAIS)*.

In this popular sense, intelligence tests are biased. They measure your developed abilities, which reflect, in part, your education and experiences. You may have read examples of intelligence test items that make middle-class assumptions (for example, that a cup goes with a saucer, or, as in one of the sample test items from the WAIS, that people buy insurance to protect the value of their homes and possessions). Do such items bias the test against those who do not use saucers or do not have enough possessions to make the cost of insurance relevant? Could such questions explain racial differences in test performance? If so, are tests a vehicle for discrimination, consigning potentially capable children to dead-end classes and jobs?

Defenders of aptitude testing note that racial group differences are at least as great on nonverbal items, such as counting digits backward (Jensen, 1983, 1998). Moreover, they add, blaming the test for a group's lower scores is like blaming a messenger for bad news. Why blame the tests for exposing unequal experiences and opportunities? If, because of malnutrition, people were to suffer stunted growth, would you blame the measuring stick that reveals it? If unequal past experiences predict unequal future achievements, a valid aptitude test will detect such inequalities.

The second meaning of *bias*—its *scientific* meaning—is different. It hinges on a test's validity—on whether it predicts future behavior only for some groups of test-takers. For example, if the U.S. SAT accurately predicted the college achievement of women but not that of men, then the test would be biased. In this statistical meaning of the term, the near-consensus among psychologists (as summarized by the U.S. National Research Council's Committee on Ability Testing and the American Psychological Association's Task Force on Intelligence) is that the major U.S. aptitude tests are *not* biased (Hunt & Carlson, 2007; Neisser et al., 1996; Wigdor & Garner, 1982). The tests' predictive validity is roughly the same for women and men, for Blacks and Whites, and for rich and poor. If an intelligence test score of 95 predicts slightly below average grades, that rough prediction usually applies equally to both genders and all ethnic and economic groups.

Test-Takers' Expectations

Throughout this text, we have seen that our expectations and attitudes can influence our perceptions and behaviors. Once again, we find this effect in intelligence testing. When Steven Spencer and his colleagues (1997) gave a difficult math test to equally capable men and women, women did not perform as well as men—except when they had been led to expect that women usually do as well as men on the test. Otherwise, the women apparently felt apprehensive, and it affected their performance. With Claude Steele and Joshua Aronson, Spencer (2002) also observed this self-fulfilling **stereotype threat** when Black students, taking verbal aptitude tests under conditions designed to make them feel threatened, performed at a lower level. Critics note that stereotype threat does not fully account for the Black-White aptitude score difference (Sackett et al., 2004, 2008). But it does help explain why Blacks have scored higher when tested by Blacks than when tested by Whites (Danso & Esses, 2001; Inzlicht & Ben-Zeev, 2000). And it gives us insight into why women have scored higher on math tests when no male test-takers were in the group, and why women's chess play drops sharply when they *think* they are playing a male rather than female opponent (Maass et al., 2008).

Steele (1995, 1997) concluded that telling students they probably won't succeed (as is sometimes implied by remedial "minority support" programs) functions as a stereotype that can erode test and school performance. Over time, such students may detach their self-esteem from academics and look for recognition elsewhere. Indeed, as African-American boys progress from eighth to twelfth grade, they tend to underachieve as the disconnect between their grades and their self-esteem becomes pronounced (Osborne, 1997). One experiment randomly assigned some African-American seventh-graders to write for 15 minutes about their most important values (Cohen et al., 2006). That simple exercise in self-affirmation had the apparent effect of boosting their semester grade point average by 0.26 in a first experiment and 0.34 in a replication. Minority students in university programs that challenge them to believe in their potential, or to focus on the idea that intelligence is malleable and not fixed, have likewise produced markedly higher grades and had lower dropout rates (Wilson, 2006).

What, then, can we realistically conclude about aptitude tests and bias? The tests do seem biased (appropriately so, some would say) in one sense—sensitivity to performance differences caused by cultural experience. But they are not biased in the scientific sense of making valid statistical predictions for different groups.

Bottom line: Are the tests discriminatory? Again, the answer can be *yes* or *no*. In one sense, *yes,* their purpose is to discriminate—to distinguish among individuals. In

"Math class is tough!"
"Teen talk" talking Barbie doll (introduced February 1992, recalled October 1992)

stereotype threat a self-confirming concern that one will be evaluated based on a negative stereotype.

Untestable compassion
Intelligence test scores are only one part of the picture of a whole person. They don't measure the abilities, talent, and commitment of, for example, people who devote their lives to helping others.

another sense, *no,* their purpose is to reduce discrimination by reducing reliance on subjective criteria for school and job placement—who you know, how you dress, or whether you are the "right kind of person." Civil service aptitude tests, for example, were devised to discriminate more fairly and objectively by reducing the political, racial, and ethnic discrimination that preceded their use. Banning aptitude tests would lead those who decide on jobs and admissions to rely more on other considerations, such as their personal opinions.

Perhaps, then, our goals for tests of mental abilities should be threefold. First, we should realize the benefits Alfred Binet, the founder of modern-day intelligence testing, foresaw—to enable schools to recognize who might profit most from early intervention. Second, we must remain alert to Binet's fear that intelligence test scores may be misinterpreted as literal measures of a person's worth and potential. And finally, we must remember that the competence that general intelligence tests sample is important; it helps enable success in some life paths. But it reflects only one aspect of personal competence. Our practical intelligence and emotional intelligence matter, too, as do other forms of creativity, talent, and character. The carpenter's spatial ability differs from the programmer's logical ability, which differs from the poet's verbal ability. Because there are many ways of being successful, our differences are variations of human adaptability.

"Almost all the joyful things of life are outside the measure of IQ tests."
Madeleine L'Engle, *A Circle of Quiet,* 1972

REVIEW

Genetic and Environmental Influences on Intelligence

35-1 **What does evidence reveal about hereditary and environmental influences on intelligence?** Studies of twins, family members, and adoptees together point to a significant hereditary contribution to intelligence scores. The search is under way for genes that together contribute to intelligence. Yet research also provides evidence of environmental influence. The intelligence test scores of fraternal twins raised together are more similar than those of other siblings, and the scores of identical twins raised apart are slightly less similar (though still very highly correlated) than the scores of identical twins raised together. Other studies, of children reared in extremely impoverished, enriched, or culturally different environments, indicate that life experiences can significantly influence intelligence test performance. *Heritability* of intelligence refers to the extent to which variation in intelligence test scores in a group of people being studied is attributable to genetic factors. Heritability never applies to an individual's intelligence, but only to differences among people.

35-2 **How and why do gender and racial groups differ in mental ability scores?** Males and females average the same in overall intelligence. There are, however, some small but intriguing gender differences in specific abilities. Girls are better spellers, more verbally fluent, better at locating objects, better at detecting emotions, and more sensitive to touch, taste, and color. Boys outperform girls at spatial ability and related mathematics, though girls outperform boys in math computation. Boys also outnumber girls at the low and high extremes of mental abilities. Psychologists debate evolutionary, brain-based, and cultural explanations of such gender differences. As a group, Whites score higher than their Hispanic and Black counterparts, though the gap is not as great as it was half a century and more ago. The evidence suggests that environmental differences are largely, perhaps entirely responsible for these group differences.

35-3 **Are intelligence tests inappropriately biased?** Aptitude tests aim to predict how well a test-taker will perform in a given situation. So they are necessarily "biased" in the sense that they are sensitive to performance differences caused by cultural experience. But bias can also mean what psychologists commonly mean by the term—that a test predicts less accurately for one group than for another. In this sense of the term, most experts consider the major aptitude tests unbiased. *Stereotype threat,* a self-confirming concern that one will be evaluated based on a negative stereotype, affects performance on all kinds of tests.

Terms and Concepts to Remember

heritability, p. 430   stereotype threat, p. 439

Test Yourself

1. As society succeeds in creating equality of opportunity, it will also increase the heritability of ability. The heritability of intelligence scores will be greater in a society marked by equal opportunity than in a society of peasants and aristocrats. Why?

(Answers to the Test Yourself questions can be found in Appendix B at the end of the book.)

Ask Yourself

1. How have genetic and environmental influences shaped your intelligence?

∞ WEB

Multiple-choice self-tests and more may be found at www.worthpublishers.com/myers

Motivation and Work

MODULES

36
Introduction
to Motivation

37
Hunger

38
Sexual Motivation and
the Need to Belong

39
Motivation at Work

"What's my motivation?" the actor asks the director. In our everyday conversation, "What motivated you to do *that*?" is a way of asking "What *caused* your behavior?" To psychologists, a *motivation* is a need or desire that *energizes* behavior and *directs* it toward a goal.

After an ill-fated Saturday morning in the spring of 2003, experienced mountaineer Aron Ralston understands the extent to which motivation can energize and direct behavior. Having bagged nearly all of Colorado's tallest peaks, many of them solo and in winter, Ralston ventured some solo canyon hiking that seemed so risk-free he didn't bother to tell anyone where he was going. In Utah's narrow Bluejohn Canyon, just 150 yards above his final rappel, he was climbing over an 800-pound rock when disaster struck: It shifted and pinned his right wrist and arm. He was, as the title of his recent book says, caught *Between a Rock and a Hard Place*.

Realizing no one would be rescuing him, Ralston tried with all his might to dislodge the rock. Then, with his dull pocket knife, he tried chipping away at the rock. When that, too, failed, he rigged up ropes to lift the rock. Alas, nothing worked. Hour after hour, then cold night after cold night, he was stuck.

By Tuesday, he had run out of food and water. On Wednesday, as thirst and hunger gnawed, he began saving and sipping his own urine. Using his video recorder, he said his good-byes to family and friends, for whom he now felt intense love: "So again love to everyone. Bring love and peace and happiness and beautiful lives into the world in my honor. Thank you. Love you."

On Thursday, surprised to find himself still alive, Ralston had a seemingly divine insight into his reproductive future, a vision of a preschool boy being scooped up by a one-armed man. With this inspiration, he summoned his remaining strength and his enormous will to live and, over the next hour, willfully broke his bones and then proceeded to use that dull knife to cut off his arm. The moment after putting on a tourniquet, chopping the last piece of skin, and breaking free— and before rappelling with his bleeding half-arm down a 65-foot cliff and hiking 5 miles until finding someone—he was, in his own words, "just reeling with this euphoria . . . having been dead and standing in my grave, leaving my last will and testament, etching 'Rest in peace' on the wall, all of that, gone and then replaced with having my life again. It was undoubtedly the sweetest moment that I will ever experience" (Ralston, 2004).

Ralston's thirst and hunger, his sense of belonging to others, and his brute will to live and become a father highlight motivation's energizing and directing power. In Modules 36 through 39, we explore motivation by focusing on four motives—hunger, sex, the need to belong, and achievement at work. Although other identifiable motives exist (including thirst and curiosity), a close look at these four reveals the interplay between nature (the physiological "push") and nurture (the cognitive and cultural "pulls"). Before considering specific motivations, we'll take time in Module 36 to see how psychologists have approached the study of motivation.

Motivation personified Aron Ralston's motivation to live and belong energized and directed his sacrificing half of his arm.

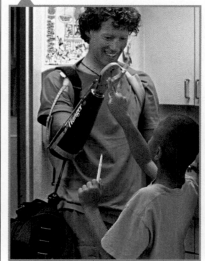

AP Photo/Rocky Mountain News, Judy Walgren

Instincts and Evolutionary Psychology

Drives and Incentives

Optimum Arousal

A Hierarchy of Motives

"What do you think . . . should we get started on that motivation research or not?"

MODULE 36

Introduction to Motivation

36-1 From what perspectives do psychologists view motivated behavior?

Psychologists today define **motivation** as a need or desire that energizes and directs behavior. In their attempt to understand motivated behaviors, psychologists have used four perspectives. *Instinct theory* (now replaced by the *evolutionary perspective*) focuses on genetically predisposed behaviors. *Drive-reduction theory* focuses on how our inner pushes and external pulls interact. *Arousal theory* focuses on finding the right level of stimulation. And Abraham Maslow's *hierarchy of needs* describes how some of our needs take priority over others.

▶‖ Instincts and Evolutionary Psychology

Early in the twentieth century, as the influence of Charles Darwin's evolutionary theory grew, it became fashionable to classify all sorts of behaviors as instincts. If people criticized themselves, it was because of their "self-abasement instinct." If they boasted, it reflected their "self-assertion instinct." After scanning 500 books, one sociologist compiled a list of 5759 supposed human instincts! Before long, this fad for naming instincts collapsed under its own weight. Rather than *explaining* human behaviors, the early instinct theorists were simply *naming* them. It was like "explaining" a bright child's low grades by labeling the child an "underachiever." To name a behavior is *not* to explain it.

To qualify as an **instinct,** a complex behavior must have a fixed pattern throughout a species and be unlearned (Tinbergen, 1951). Such behaviors are common in other species. Newly hatched ducks and geese form attachments to the first moving object they see. And mature salmon swim hundreds of miles upstream to reach the place they were born, where they will mate and then die. Human behavior, too, exhibits certain unlearned fixed patterns, including infants' innate reflexes for rooting and sucking. Most psychologists, though, view human behavior as directed both by physiological needs and by psychological wants.

Same motive, different wiring The more complex the nervous system, the more adaptable the organism. Both the people and the weaver bird satisfy their need for shelter in ways that reflect their inherited capacities. The people's behavior is flexible; they can learn whatever skills they need to build a house. The bird's behavior pattern is fixed; it can build only this kind of nest.

Although instinct theory failed to explain human motives, the underlying assumption that genes predispose species-typical behavior remains as strong as ever. Psychologists may apply this perspective, for example, in explanations of our human similarities, animals' biological predispositions to learn certain behaviors, and the influence of evolution on our phobias, our helping behaviors, and our romantic attractions.

▶‖ Drives and Incentives

When the original instinct theory of motivation collapsed, it was replaced by **drive-reduction theory**—the idea that a physiological need creates an aroused state that drives the organism to reduce the need by, say, eating or drinking. With few exceptions, when a physiological need increases, so does a psychological *drive*—an aroused, motivated state.

The physiological aim of drive reduction is **homeostasis**—the maintenance of a steady internal state. An example of homeostasis (literally "staying the same") is the body's temperature-regulation system, which works like a room thermostat. Both systems operate through feedback loops: Sensors feed room temperature to a control device. If the room temperature cools, the control device switches on the furnace. Likewise, if our body temperature cools, blood vessels constrict to conserve warmth, and we feel driven to put on more clothes or seek a warmer environment (**FIGURE 36.1**).

Not only are we *pushed* by our "need" to reduce drives, we also are *pulled* by **incentives**—positive or negative stimuli that lure or repel us. This is one way our individual learning histories influence our motives. Depending on our learning, the aroma of good food, whether fresh roasted peanuts or toasted ants, can motivate our behavior. So can the sight of those we find attractive or threatening.

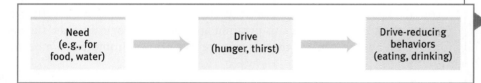

When there is both a need and an incentive, we feel strongly driven. The food-deprived person who smells baking bread feels a strong hunger drive. In the presence of that drive, the baking bread becomes a compelling incentive. For each motive, we can therefore ask, "How is it pushed by our inborn physiological needs and pulled by incentives in the environment?"

▶‖ Optimum Arousal

We are much more than homeostatic systems, however. Some motivated behaviors actually *increase* arousal. Well-fed animals will leave their shelter to explore and gain information, seemingly in the absence of any need-based drive. Curiosity drives monkeys to monkey around trying to figure out how to unlock a latch that opens nothing or how to open a window that allows them to see outside their room (Butler, 1954). It drives the 9-month-old infant who investigates every accessible corner of the house. It drives the scientists whose work this text discusses. And it drives explorers and adventurers such as Aron Ralston and George Mallory. Asked why he wanted to climb Mount Everest, Mallory answered, "Because it is there." Those who, like Mallory and Ralston, enjoy high arousal are most likely to enjoy intense music, novel foods, and risky behaviors (Zuckerman, 1979).

So, human motivation aims not to eliminate arousal but to seek optimum levels of arousal. Having all our biological needs satisfied, we feel driven to experience

motivation a need or desire that energizes and directs behavior.

instinct a complex behavior that is rigidly patterned throughout a species and is unlearned.

drive-reduction theory the idea that a physiological need creates an aroused tension state (a drive) that motivates an organism to satisfy the need.

homeostasis a tendency to maintain a balanced or constant internal state; the regulation of any aspect of body chemistry, such as blood glucose, around a particular level.

incentive a positive or negative environmental stimulus that motivates behavior.

FIGURE 36.1 Drive-reduction theory Drive-reduction motivation arises from *homeostasis*—an organism's natural tendency to maintain a steady internal state. Thus, if we are water deprived, our thirst drives us to drink and to restore the body's normal state.

Driven by curiosity Baby monkeys and young children are fascinated by things they've never handled before. Their drive to explore the relatively unfamiliar is one of several motives that do not fill any immediate physiological need.

stimulation and we hunger for information. We are "infovores," say neuroscientists Irving Biederman and Edward Vessel (2006), after identifying brain mechanisms that reward us for acquiring information. Lacking stimulation, we feel bored and look for a way to increase arousal to some optimum level. However, with too much stimulation comes stress, and we then look for a way to decrease arousal.

"Hunger is the most urgent form of poverty."
Alliance to End Hunger, 2002

▶‖ A Hierarchy of Motives

Some needs take priority over others. At this moment, with your needs for air and water hopefully satisfied, other motives—such as your desire to achieve—are energizing and directing your behavior. Let your need for water go unsatisfied and your thirst will preoccupy you. Just ask Aron Ralston. Deprived of air, your thirst would disappear.

Abraham Maslow (1970) described these priorities as a **hierarchy of needs** (**FIGURE 36.2**). At the base of this pyramid are our physiological needs, such as those for food and water. Only if these needs are met are we prompted to meet our need

FIGURE 36.2 Maslow's hierarchy of needs Once our lower-level needs are met, we are prompted to satisfy our higher-level needs. (From Maslow, 1970.) For survivors of the disastrous 2007 Bangladeshi flood, such as this man carefully carrying his precious load of clean water, satisfying very basic needs for water, food, and safety become top priority. Higher-level needs on Maslow's hierarchy, such as respect, self-actualization, and meaning, tend to become far less important during such times.

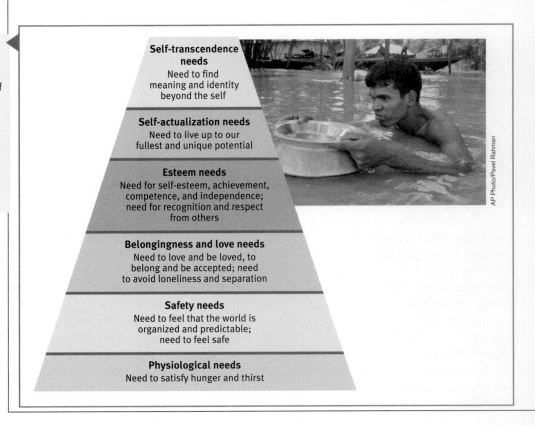

for safety, and then to satisfy the uniquely human needs to give and receive love and to enjoy self-esteem. Beyond this, said Maslow (1971), lies the need to actualize one's full potential.

Near the end of his life, Maslow proposed that some people also reach a level of self-transcendence. At the self-actualization level, people seek to realize their own potential. At the self-transcendence level, people strive for meaning, purpose, and communion that is beyond the self, that is *transpersonal* (Koltko-Rivera, 2006).

Maslow's hierarchy is somewhat arbitrary; the order of such needs is not universally fixed. People have starved themselves to make a political statement. Nevertheless, the simple idea that some motives are more compelling than others provides a framework for thinking about motivation. Life-satisfaction surveys in 39 nations support this basic idea (Oishi et al., 1999). In poorer nations that lack easy access to money and the food and shelter it buys, financial satisfaction more strongly predicts feelings of well-being. In wealthy nations, where most are able to meet basic needs, home-life satisfaction is a better predictor. Self-esteem matters most in individualist nations, whose citizens tend to focus more on personal achievements than on family and community identity.

> **hierarchy of needs** Maslow's pyramid of human needs, beginning at the base with physiological needs that must first be satisfied before higher-level safety needs and then psychological needs become active.

REVIEW

Introduction to Motivation

36-1 **From what perspectives do psychologists view motivated behavior?** The *instinct*/evolutionary perspective explores genetic influences on complex behaviors. *Drive-reduction theory* explores how physiological needs create aroused tension states (drives) that direct us to satisfy those needs. Arousal theory proposes a *motivation* for behaviors, such as curiosity-driven behaviors, that do not reduce physiological needs. Maslow's *hierarchy of needs* proposes a pyramid of human needs, from basic needs such as hunger and thirst up to higher-level needs such as actualization and transcendence.

Terms and Concepts to Remember

motivation, p. 444

instinct, p. 444

drive-reduction theory, p. 445

homeostasis, p. 445

incentive, p. 445

hierarchy of needs, p. 446

Test Yourself

1. While on a long road trip, you suddenly feel very hungry. You see a diner that looks pretty deserted and creepy, but you are *really* hungry, so you stop anyway. What motivational perspective would most easily explain this behavior, and why?

(Answers to the Test Yourself questions can be found in Appendix B at the end of the book.)

Ask Yourself

1. Consider your own experiences in relation to Maslow's hierarchy of needs. Have you ever experienced true hunger or thirst that displaced your concern for other, higher-level needs? Do you usually feel safe? Loved? Confident? How often do you feel you are able to address what Maslow called your "self-actualization" needs?

⊙⊙ WEB

Multiple-choice self-tests and more may be found at www.worthpublishers.com/myers

The Physiology of Hunger

The Psychology of Hunger

Obesity and Weight Control

MODULE 37

Hunger

A vivid demonstration of the supremacy of physiological needs came from starvation experiences in World War II prison camps. David Mandel (1983), a Nazi concentration camp survivor, recalled how a starving "father and son would fight over a piece of bread. Like dogs." One father, whose 20-year-old son stole his bread from under his pillow while he slept, went into a deep depression, asking over and over how his son could do such a thing. The next day the father died. "Hunger does something to you that's hard to describe," Mandel explained.

To learn more about the results of semistarvation, a research team led by physiologist Ancel Keys (1950), the creator of World War II Army K rations, fed 36 male volunteers—all conscientious objectors to the war—just enough to maintain their initial weight. Then, for six months, they cut this food level in half. The effects soon became visible. Without thinking about it, the men began conserving energy; they appeared listless and apathetic. After dropping rapidly, their body weights eventually stabilized at about 25 percent below their starting weights. Especially dramatic were the psychological effects. Consistent with Maslow's idea of a needs hierarchy, the men became food-obsessed. They talked food. They daydreamed food. They collected recipes, read cookbooks, and feasted their eyes on delectable forbidden foods. Preoccupied with their unfulfilled basic need, they lost interest in sex and social activities. As one participant reported, "If we see a show, the most interesting part of it is contained in scenes where people are eating. I couldn't laugh at the funniest picture in the world, and love scenes are completely dull."

The semistarved men's preoccupations illustrate the power of activated motives to hijack our consciousness. When we are hungry, thirsty, fatigued, or sexually aroused, little else may seem to matter. When you're not, food, water, sleep, or sex just don't seem like such big things in your life, now or ever. In University of Amsterdam studies, Loran Nordgren and his colleagues (2006, 2007) found that people in a motivational "hot" state (from fatigue, hunger, or sexual arousal) become more aware of having had such feelings in the past and more sympathetic to how fatigue, hunger, or sexual arousal might drive others' behavior. Similarly, if preschool children are made to feel thirsty (by eating salty pretzels), they understandably want water; but unlike children who are not thirsty, they also choose water over pretzels for "tomorrow" (Atance & Meltzoff, 2006). Motives matter mightily. Grocery shop with an empty stomach and you are more likely to think that those jelly-filled doughnuts are just what you've always loved and will be wanting tomorrow.

> "Nobody wants to kiss when they are hungry."
>
> Dorothea Dix, 1801–1887

> "The full person does not understand the needs of the hungry."
>
> Irish proverb

▶❙ The Physiology of Hunger

37-1 What physiological factors produce hunger?

Keys' semistarved volunteers felt their hunger in response to a homeostatic system designed to maintain normal body weight and an adequate nutrient supply. But what precisely triggers hunger? Is it the pangs of an empty stomach? That is how it feels. And so it seemed after A. L. Washburn, working with Walter Cannon (Cannon & Washburn, 1912), intentionally swallowed a balloon. When inflated to fill his stomach, the balloon transmitted his stomach contractions to a recording device

GARFIELD

(**FIGURE 37.1**). While his stomach was being monitored, Washburn pressed a key each time he felt hungry. The discovery: Washburn was indeed having stomach contractions whenever he felt hungry.

Would hunger persist without stomach pangs? To answer that question, researchers removed some rats' stomachs and attached their esophagi to their small intestines (Tsang, 1938). Did the rats continue to eat? Indeed they did. Some hunger persists similarly in humans whose ulcerated or cancerous stomachs have been removed.

If the pangs of an empty stomach are not the only source of hunger, what else matters?

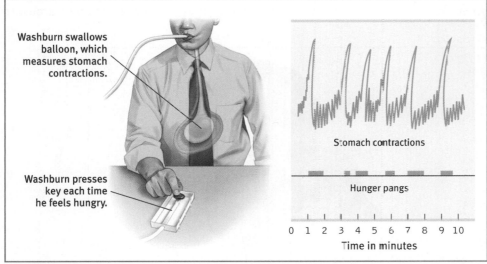

Washburn swallows balloon, which measures stomach contractions.

Washburn presses key each time he feels hungry.

Stomach contractions

Hunger pangs

0 1 2 3 4 5 6 7 8 9 10
Time in minutes

FIGURE 37.1 Monitoring stomach contractions Using this procedure, Washburn showed that stomach contractions (transmitted by the stomach balloon) accompany our feelings of hunger (indicated by a key press). (From Cannon, 1929.)

Body Chemistry and the Brain

People and other animals automatically regulate their caloric intake to prevent energy deficits and maintain a stable body weight. This suggests that somehow, somewhere, the body is keeping tabs on its available resources. One such resource is the blood sugar **glucose.** Increases in the hormone *insulin* (secreted by the pancreas) diminish blood glucose, partly by converting it to stored fat. If your blood glucose level drops, you won't consciously feel this change. But your brain, which is automatically monitoring your blood chemistry and your body's internal state, will trigger hunger. Signals from your stomach, intestines, and liver (indicating whether glucose is being deposited or withdrawn) all signal your brain to motivate eating or not.

glucose the form of sugar that circulates in the blood and provides the major source of energy for body tissues. When its level is low, we feel hunger.

FIGURE 37.2 The hypothalamus
The hypothalamus (colored red) performs various body maintenance functions, including control of hunger. Blood vessels supply the hypothalamus, enabling it to respond to our current blood chemistry as well as to incoming neural information about the body's state.

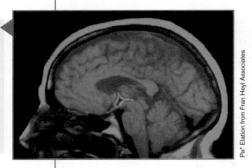

Pix' Elation from Fran Heyl Associates

Richard Howard

Evidence for the brain's control of eating A lesion near the ventromedial area of the hypothalamus caused this rat's weight to triple.

But how does the brain integrate and respond to these messages? More than a half-century ago, researchers began unraveling this puzzle when they located hunger controls within the *hypothalamus,* that small but complex neural traffic intersection deep in the brain (**FIGURE 37.2**).

Two distinct hypothalamic centers influence eating. Activity along the sides of the hypothalamus (the *lateral hypothalamus*) brings on hunger. If electrically stimulated there, well-fed animals begin to eat. (If the area is destroyed, even starving animals have no interest in food.) Recent research helps explain this behavior. When a rat is food-deprived, its blood sugar levels wane and the lateral hypothalamus churns out the hunger-triggering hormone *orexin.* When given orexin, rats become ravenously hungry (Sakurai et al., 1998).

Activity in the second center—the lower mid-hypothalamus (the *ventromedial hypothalamus*)—depresses hunger. Stimulate this area and an animal will stop eating; destroy it and the animal's stomach and intestines will process food more rapidly, causing it to become extremely fat (Duggan & Booth, 1986; Hoebel & Teitelbaum, 1966). This discovery helped explain why some patients with tumors near the base of the brain (in what we now realize is the hypothalamus) eat excessively and become very overweight (Miller, 1995). Rats with mid-hypothalamus lesions eat more often, produce more fat, and use less fat for energy, rather like a miser who runs every bit of extra money to the bank and resists taking any out (Pinel, 1993).

In addition to producing orexin, the hypothalamus monitors levels of the body's other appetite hormones (**FIGURE 37.3**). One of these is *ghrelin,* a hunger-arousing

FIGURE 37.3 The appetite hormones
Insulin: Secreted by pancreas; controls blood glucose.
Leptin: Secreted by fat cells; when abundant, causes brain to increase metabolism and decrease hunger.
Orexin: Hunger-triggering hormone secreted by hypothalamus.
Ghrelin: Secreted by empty stomach; sends "I'm hungry" signals to the brain.
Obestatin: Secreted by stomach; sends out "I'm full" signals to the brain.
PYY: Digestive tract hormone; sends "I'm *not* hungry" signals to the brain.

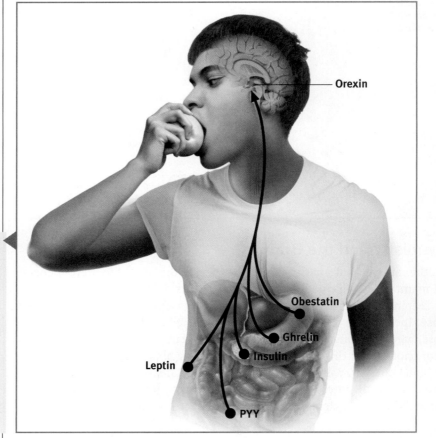

hormone secreted by an empty stomach. When people with severe obesity undergo by-pass surgery that seals off part of the stomach, the remaining stomach then produces much less ghrelin, and their appetite lessens (Lemonick, 2002). *Obestatin*, a sister hor-mone to ghrelin, is produced by the same gene, but obestatin sends out a fullness signal that suppresses hunger (Zhang et al., 2005). Other appetite-suppressants include *PYY*, a hormone secreted by the digestive tract, and *leptin*, a protein that is secreted by fat cells and acts to diminish the rewarding pleasure of food (Farooqi et al., 2007).

Experimental manipulation of appetite hormones has raised hopes for an appetite-reducing medication. Such a nose spray or skin patch might counteract the body's hunger-producing chemicals, or mimic or increase the levels of hunger-dampening chemicals. The recent ups and downs of excitement over PYY illustrate the intense search for a substance that might someday be a treatment, if not a magic bullet, for obesity. The initial report that PYY suppresses appetite in mice was followed by a skeptical statement from 12 laboratories reporting a big fat disappointment: The PYY finding did not replicate. But a few months later, this was followed by newer studies using different methods that *did* find at least a temporary appetite-suppressing effect (Gura, 2004).

The complex interaction of appetite hormones and brain activity may help explain the body's apparent predisposition to maintain itself at a particular weight level. When semistarved rats fall below their normal weight, this "weight thermostat" sig-nals the body to restore the lost weight: Hunger increases and energy expenditure de-creases. If body weight rises—as happens when rats are force-fed—hunger decreases and energy expenditure increases. This stable weight toward which semistarved and overstuffed rats return is their **set point** (Keesey & Corbett, 1983). In rats and hu-mans, heredity influences body type and set point.

Our bodies regulate weight through the control of food intake, energy output, and **basal metabolic rate**—the rate of energy expenditure for maintaining basic body functions when the body is at rest. By the end of their 24 weeks of semistarvation, the men who participated in Keys' experiment had stabilized at three-quarters of their normal weight, while taking in half of their previous calories. How did they manage this? By reducing their energy expenditure, partly through inactivity but partly be-cause of a 29 percent drop in their basal metabolic rate.

Some researchers, however, doubt that our bodies have a preset tendency to main-tain optimum weight (Assanand et al., 1998). They point out that slow, sustained changes in body weight can alter one's set point, and that psychological factors also sometimes drive our feelings of hunger. Given unlimited access to a wide variety of tasty foods, people and other animals tend to overeat and gain weight (Raynor & Epstein, 2001). For all these reasons, some researchers have abandoned the idea of a biologically fixed *set point*. They prefer the term *settling point* to indicate the level at which a person's weight settles in response to caloric intake and expenditure (which are influenced by environment as well as biology).

▶‖ The Psychology of Hunger

37-2 What psychological and cultural factors influence hunger?

Our eagerness to eat is indeed pushed by our physiological state—our body chemistry and hypothalamic activity. Yet there is more to hunger than meets the stomach. This was strikingly apparent when Paul Rozin and his trickster colleagues (1998) tested two patients with amnesia who had no memory for events occurring more than a minute ago. If, 20 minutes after eating a normal lunch, the patients were offered an-other, both readily consumed it . . . and usually a third meal offered 20 minutes after

"Never get a tattoo when you're drunk and hungry."

‖ Over the next 40 years you will eat about 20 tons of food. If, during those years, you increase your daily intake by just .01 ounce more than required for your energy needs, you will gain 24 pounds (Martin et al., 1991). ‖

set point the point at which an indi-vidual's "weight thermostat" is supposed-ly set. When the body falls below this weight, an increase in hunger and a low-ered metabolic rate may act to restore the lost weight.

basal metabolic rate the body's rest-ing rate of energy expenditure.

An acquired taste For Alaska Natives (left), but not for most other North Americans, whale blubber is a tasty treat. For these Campa Indians in Peru (right), roasted ants are similarly delicious. People everywhere learn to enjoy the foods prescribed by their culture.

the second was finished. This suggests that part of knowing when to eat is our memory of our last meal. As time passes since we last ate, we anticipate eating again and start feeling hungry.

Psychological influences on eating behavior are most striking when the desire to be thin overwhelms normal homeostatic pressures.

Taste Preferences: Biology and Culture

Body chemistry and environmental factors together influence not only when we feel hungry, but also what we hunger for—our taste preferences. When feeling tense or depressed, do you crave starchy, carbohydrate-laden foods? Carbohydrates help boost levels of the neurotransmitter serotonin, which has calming effects. When stressed, even rats find it extra rewarding to scarf Oreos (Artiga et al., 2007; Boggiano et al., 2005).

Our preferences for sweet and salty tastes are genetic and universal. Other taste preferences are conditioned, as when people given highly salted foods develop a liking for excess salt (Beauchamp, 1987), or when people who have been sickened by a food develop an aversion to it. (The frequency of children's illnesses provides many chances for them to learn food aversions.)

Culture affects taste, too. Bedouins enjoy eating the eye of a camel, which most North Americans would find repulsive. But then North Americans and Europeans shun horse, dog, and rat meat, all of which are prized elsewhere.

Rats themselves tend to avoid unfamiliar foods (Sclafani, 1995). So do we, especially those that are animal-based. In experiments, people have tried novel fruit drinks or ethnic foods. With repeated exposure, their appreciation for the new taste typically increases; moreover, exposure to one set of novel foods increases our willingness to try another (Pliner, 1982; Pliner et al., 1993). *Neophobia* (dislike of things unfamiliar) surely was adaptive for our ancestors, protecting them from potentially toxic substances.

Other taste preferences are also adaptive. For example, the spices most commonly used in hot-climate recipes—where food, especially meat, spoils more quickly—inhibit the growth of bacteria (**FIGURE 37.4**). Pregnancy-related nausea is another example of adaptive taste preferences. Its associated food aversions peak about the tenth week, when the developing embryo is most vulnerable to toxins.

FIGURE 37.4 Hot cultures like hot spices Countries with hot climates, in which food historically spoiled more quickly, feature recipes with more bacteria-inhibiting spices (Sherman & Flaxman, 2001). India averages nearly 10 spices per meat recipe; Finland, 2 spices.

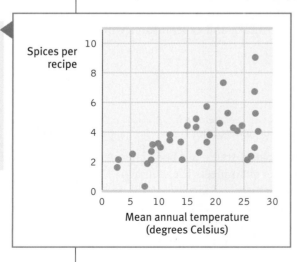

The Ecology of Eating

To a surprising extent, situations also control our eating. You perhaps have noticed one situational phenomenon, though you likely have underestimated its power: People eat more when eating with others (Herman et al., 2003; Hetherington et al., 2006). The presence of others tends to amplify our natural behavior tendencies (a phenomenon called *social facilitation,* which helps explain why, after a party or a feast, we may realize that we have overeaten).

Another aspect of the ecology of eating, which Andrew Geier and his colleagues (2006) call *unit bias,* occurs with similar mindlessness. In collaboration with researchers at France's National Center for Scientific Research, they explored a possible explanation of why French waistlines are smaller than American waistlines. From soda drinks to yogurt sizes, the French offer foods in smaller portion sizes. Does it matter? (One could as well order two small sandwiches as one large one.)

To find out, the investigators offered people varieties of free snacks. For example, in the lobby of an apartment house, they laid out either full or half pretzels, big or little Tootsie Rolls, or a big bowl of M&M's with either a small or large serving scoop. Their consistent result: Offered a supersized standard portion, people put away more calories. Another research team led by Brian Wansink (2006) invited some Americans to help themselves to ice cream. They, too, found a unit bias: Even nutrition experts took 31 percent more when given a big rather than small bowl, and 15 percent more when scooping it with a big scoop rather than a small one. For cultures struggling with rising obesity rates, the principle—that ecology influences eating—implies a practical message: Reduce standard portion sizes, and serve food with smaller bowls, plates, and utensils.

Eating Disorders

37-3 How do anorexia nervosa, bulimia nervosa, and binge-eating disorder demonstrate the influence of psychological forces on physiologically motivated behaviors?

Our bodies are naturally disposed to maintain a normal weight, including stored energy reserves for times when food becomes unavailable. Yet sometimes psychological influences overwhelm biological wisdom. This becomes painfully clear in three eating disorders.

▶ **Anorexia nervosa** typically begins as a weight-loss diet. People with anorexia—usually adolescents and 3 out of 4 times females—drop significantly (typically 15 percent or more) below normal weight. Yet they feel fat, fear gaining weight, and remain obsessed with losing weight. About half of those with anorexia display a binge-purge-depression cycle.

▶ **Bulimia nervosa** may also be triggered by a weight-loss diet, broken by gorging on forbidden foods. Binge-purge eaters—mostly women in their late teens or early twenties—eat the way some people with alcohol dependency drink—in spurts, sometimes influenced by friends who are bingeing (Crandall, 1988). In a cycle of repeating episodes, overeating is followed by compensatory purging (through vomiting or laxative use) or fasting or excessive exercise (Wonderlich et al., 2007). Preoccupied with food (craving sweet and high-fat foods), and fearful of becoming overweight, binge-purge eaters experience bouts of depression

anorexia nervosa an eating disorder in which a person (usually an adolescent female) diets and becomes significantly (15 percent or more) underweight, yet, still feeling fat, continues to starve.

bulimia nervosa an eating disorder characterized by episodes of overeating, usually of high-calorie foods, followed by vomiting, laxative use, fasting, or excessive exercise.

Dying to be thin Anorexia was identified and named in the 1870s, when it appeared among affluent adolescent girls (Brumberg, 2000). This 1930s photo illustrates the physical condition (left). Many modern-day celebrities have struggled publicly with eating disorders, as when actress Mary-Kate Olsen (right) was admitted to a rehabilitation clinic in Utah for six weeks in 2004 for treatment of anorexia.

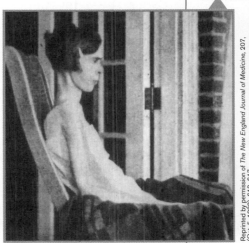

Reprinted by permission of *The New England Journal of Medicine,* 207, (Oct. 5, 1932), 613–617.

Reuters/Lucas Jackson (USA)

"Thanks, but we don't eat."

"Diana remained throughout a very inse-cure person at heart, almost childlike in her desire to do good for others, so she could release herself from deep feelings of unworthiness, of which her eating disor-ders were merely a symptom."

Charles, Ninth Earl of Spencer, eulogizing his sister Princess Diana, 1997

and anxiety, most severe during and following binges (Hinz & Williamson, 1987; Johnson et al., 2002). Unlike anorexia, bulimia is marked by weight fluc-tuations within or above normal ranges, making the condition easy to hide.

▶ Those who do significant binge eating, followed by remorse—but do not purge, fast, or exercise excessively—are said to have **binge-eating disorder.**

A national study funded by the U.S. National Institute of Mental Health reports that, at some point during their lifetimes, 0.6 percent of people meet the criteria for anorexia, 1 percent for bulimia, and 2.8 percent for binge-eating disorder (Hudson et al., 2007). So, how can we explain these disorders?

Eating disorders do *not* provide (as some have speculated) a telltale sign of child-hood sexual abuse (Smolak & Murnen, 2002; Stice, 2002). The family environment may provide a fertile ground for the growth of eating disorders in other ways, however.

▶ Mothers of girls with eating disorders tend to focus on their own weight and on their daughters' weight and appearance (Pike & Rodin, 1991).

▶ Families of bulimia patients have a higher-than-usual incidence of childhood obesity and negative self-evaluation (Jacobi et al., 2004).

▶ Families of anorexia patients tend to be competitive, high-achieving, and protec-tive (Pate et al., 1992; Yates, 1989, 1990).

Anorexia sufferers often have low self-evaluations, set perfectionist standards, fret about falling short of expectations, and are intensely concerned with how others per-ceive them (Pieters et al., 2007; Polivy & Herman, 2002; Striegel-Moore et al., 1993, 2007). Some of these factors also predict teen boys' pursuit of unrealistic muscularity (Ricciardelli & McCabe, 2004).

Genetics may influence susceptibility to eating disorders. Twins are somewhat more likely to share the disorder if they are identical rather than fraternal (Fairburn et al., 1999; Kaplan, 2004). In follow-up molecular studies, scientists are searching for culprit genes, which may influence the body's available serotonin and estrogen (Klump & Culbert, 2007).

But these disorders also have cultural and gender components. Body ideals vary across culture and time. In India, women students rate their ideals as close to their actual shape. In much of Africa—where plumpness means prosperous and thinness can signal poverty, AIDS, and hunger—bigger seems better (Knickmeyer, 2001).

Bigger does not seem better in Western cultures, where, according to 222 studies of 141,000 people, the rise in eating disorders over the last 50 years has coincided with a dramatic increase in women having a poor body image (Feingold & Mazzella, 1998). In one national survey, nearly one-half of all U.S. women reported feeling negative about their appearance and preoccupied with being or becoming overweight (Cash & Henry, 1995).

Gender differences in body image have surfaced in several stud-ies. In one study of New Zealand university students and 3500 British bank and university staff, men were more likely to *be* over-weight and women were more likely to *perceive* themselves as over-weight (Emslie et al., 2001; Miller & Halberstadt, 2005). In another study at the University of Michigan, men and women donned either a sweater or a swimsuit and completed a math test while alone in a changing room (Fredrickson et al., 1998). For the women but not the men, wearing the swimsuit triggered self-consciousness and shame that disrupted their math performance. That surely explains why a survey of 52,677 adults found that 16 percent of men and 31 percent of women avoid wearing a swimsuit in public (Frederick et al., 2006). In another informal survey of 60,000 people, 9 in 10 women said they would rather have a perfect body than have a mate with a perfect body; 6 of 10 men preferred the reverse (Lever, 2003).

"Gee, I had no idea you were married to a supermodel."

"Skeletons on parade" A recent article used this headline in criticizing superthin models. Do such models make self-starvation fashionable?

binge-eating disorder significant binge-eating episodes, followed by distress, disgust, or guilt, but without the compensatory purging, fasting, or excessive exercise that marks bulimia nervosa.

Those most vulnerable to eating disorders are also those (usually women) who most idealize thinness and have the greatest body dissatisfaction (Striegel-Moore & Bulik, 2007). Should it surprise us, then, that when women view real and doctored images of unnaturally thin models and celebrities, they often feel ashamed, depressed, and dissatisfied with their own bodies—the very attitudes that predispose eating disorders (Grabe et al., 2008)? Eric Stice and his colleagues (2001) tested this idea by giving some adolescent girls (but not others) a 15-month subscription to an American teen-fashion magazine. Compared with their counterparts who had not received the magazine, vulnerable girls—defined as those who were already dissatisfied, idealizing thinness, and lacking social support—exhibited increased body dissatisfaction and eating disorder tendencies. But even ultrathin models do not reflect the impossible standard of the classic Barbie doll, who had, when adjusted to a height of 5 feet 7 inches, a 32–16–29 figure (in centimeters, 82–41–73) (Norton et al., 1996).

It seems clear that the sickness of today's eating disorders lies in part within our weight-obsessed culture—a culture that says, in countless ways, "Fat is bad," that motivates millions of women to be "always dieting," and that encourages eating binges by pressuring women to live in a constant state of semistarvation. If cultural learning contributes to eating behavior (**FIGURE 37.5**), then might prevention programs increase acceptance of one's body? From their review of 66 prevention studies, Stice and his colleagues (2007) answer *yes*, and especially if the programs are interactive and focused on girls over age 15.

"Why do women have such low self-esteem? There are many complex psychological and societal reasons, by which I mean Barbie."
Dave Barry, 1999

Biological influences:
- hypothalamic centers in the brain monitoring appetite
- appetite hormones
- stomach pangs
- weight set/settling point
- attraction to sweet and salty tastes
- adaptive wariness toward novel foods

Psychological influences:
- sight and smell of food
- variety of foods available
- memory of time elapsed since last meal
- stress and mood
- food unit size

Eating behavior

Social-cultural influences:
- culturally learned taste preferences
- responses to cultural preferences for appearance

FIGURE 37.5 Levels of analysis for our hunger motivation Clearly, we are biologically driven to eat, yet psychological and social-cultural factors strongly influence what, when, and how much we eat.

▶‖ Obesity and Weight Control

37-4   What factors predispose some people to become and remain obese?

Why do some people gain weight while others eat the same amount and seldom add a pound? And why do so few overweight people win the battle of the bulge? Is there weight-loss hope for the 66 percent of Americans who, according to the Centers for Disease Control, are overweight?

Our bodies store fat for good reasons. Fat is an ideal form of stored energy—a high-calorie fuel reserve to carry the body through periods when food is scarce—a common occurrence in the feast-or-famine existence of our prehistoric ancestors. (Think of that spare tire around the middle as an energy storehouse—biology's counterpart to a hiker's waist-borne snack pack.) No wonder that in most developing societies today, as in Europe in earlier centuries—in fact, wherever people face famine—obesity signals affluence and social status (Furnham & Baguma, 1994).

In those parts of the world where food and sweets are now abundantly available, the rule that once served our hungry distant ancestors *(When you find energy-rich fat or sugar, eat it!)* has become dysfunctional.

Pretty much everywhere this book is being read, people have a growing problem. Worldwide, estimates the World Health Organization (WHO) (2007), more than 1 billion people are overweight, and 300 million of them are clinically *obese* (defined by WHO as a body mass index of 30 or more—see **FIGURE 37.6**). In the United States, the adult obesity rate has more than doubled in the last 40 years, reaching 34 percent, and child-teen obesity has quadrupled (CDC, 2007; NCHS, 2007). Australia classifies 54 percent of its population as overweight or obese, with Canada close behind at 49 percent, and France at 42 percent (Australian Bureau of Statistics, 2007; Statistics Canada, 2007). In all these and many other countries, rising obesity rates trail the

FIGURE 37.6 Obesity measured as body mass index (BMI) U.S. government guidelines encourage a BMI under 25. The World Health Organization and many countries define *obesity* as a BMI of 30 or more. The shading in this graph is based on BMI measurements for these heights and weights. BMI is calculated by using the following formula:

$$\frac{\text{Weight in kg (pounds} \times .45)}{\text{Squared height in meters (inches} \div 39.4)^2} = \text{BMI}$$

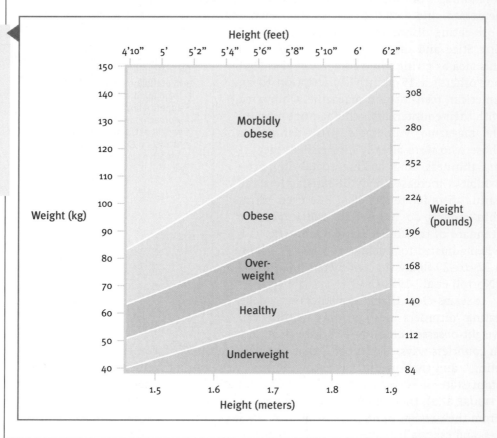

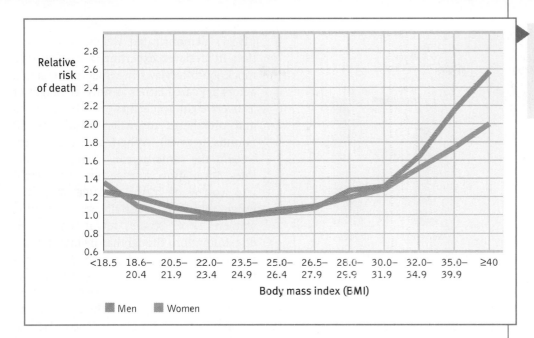

FIGURE 37.7 Obesity and mortality
Relative risk of death among healthy nonsmokers rises with extremely high or low body mass index. (Data from 14-year study of 1.05 million Americans, Calle et al., 1999.)

American rates by just a few years and are projected to increase further, resulting in a "global epidemic" of diabetes (Yach et al., 2006).

Being slightly overweight poses only modest health risks (Dolan et al., 2007; Gibbs, 2005). Fitness matters more than being a little overweight. But significant obesity increases the risk of diabetes, high blood pressure, heart disease, gallstones, arthritis, and certain types of cancer, thus shortening life expectancy (Olshansky et al., 2005). The risks are greater for apple-shaped people who carry their weight in pot bellies than for pear-shaped people with ample hips and thighs (Greenwood, 1989; Price et al., 2006). New research also has linked women's obesity to their risk of late-life Alzheimer's disease and brain tissue loss (Gustafson et al., 2003, 2004).

Not surprisingly, then, one study (Calle et al., 1999) that followed more than 1 million Americans over 14 years revealed that being significantly overweight can cut life short (**FIGURE 37.7**). Those overweight at age 40 die three years earlier than their slim counterparts, reports another long-term study (Peeters et al., 2003). The death rate is especially high among very overweight men. Understandably, in 2004 the U.S. Medicare system began recognizing obesity as an illness. And in 2008 in Japan, a new national law mandated waistline measurements as part of annual checkups for those ages 40 to 74, with dieting guidance and re-education for those persistently over 33.5 inches for men and 35.4 inches for women (Onishi, 2008).

The Social Effects of Obesity

Obesity can also be socially toxic, by affecting both how you are treated and how you feel about yourself. Obese people know the stereotype: slow, lazy, and sloppy (Crandall, 1994, 1995; Ryckman et al., 1989). Widen people's images on a video monitor (making them look fatter) and observers suddenly rate them as less sincere, less friendly, meaner, and more obnoxious (Gardner & Tockerman, 1994). The social effects of obesity were clear in a study that followed 370 obese 16- to 24-year-old women (Gortmaker et al., 1993). When restudied seven years later, two-thirds of the women were still obese. They also were making less money—$7000 a year less—than an equally intelligent comparison group of some 5000 nonobese women. And they were less likely to be married. In personal ads, men often state their preference for, and women often advertise, slimness (Miller et al., 2000; Smith et al., 1990).

"If we do nothing, in a few years the French will be as fat as Americans."
Olivier Andrault, food expert with the French Union of Consumers, 2007

Obesity stereotype: "The [obesity lawsuit] bill says, 'Don't run off and file a lawsuit if you are fat.' It says, 'Look in the mirror because you're the one to blame.'"
U.S. Senator F. James Sensenbrenner, 2004

FIGURE 37.8
Gender and weight discrimination When women applicants were made to look overweight, university students were less willing to think they would hire them. Among men applicants, weight mattered less. (Data from Pingitore et al., 1994.)

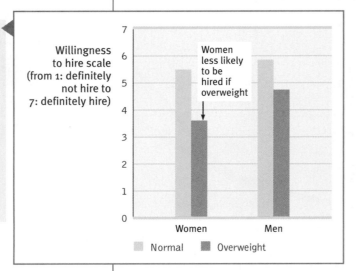

Willingness to hire scale (from 1: definitely not hire to 7: definitely hire)

Women less likely to be hired if overweight

Women   Men

☐ Normal   ☐ Overweight

"For fat students, the school experience is one of almost constant harassment."

Report on Size Discrimination, National Education Association, 1994

FIGURE 37.9 **Fat cells** We store energy in fat cells, which become larger and more numerous if we are obese, and smaller (but still more numerous) if we then lose weight. (Adapted from Jules Hirsch, 2003.)

Never obese   **Obese**   **Reduced obese**

Regina Pingitore and her colleagues (1994) demonstrated weight discrimination in a clever experiment. They filmed mock job interviews in which professional actors appeared either as normal-weight or as overweight applicants (wearing makeup and prostheses to make them look 30 pounds heavier). When appearing overweight, the same person—using the same lines, intonation, and gestures—was rated less worthy of hiring (**FIGURE 37.8**). The weight bias was especially strong against women. Other studies reveal that weight discrimination, though hardly discussed, is greater than race and gender discrimination. It occurs at every stage of the employment cycle—hiring, placement, promotion, compensation, discipline, and discharge—and is, indeed, much more likely to affect women (Roehling et al., 1999, 2007). Anti-fat prejudice even extends to applicants who are *seen* with an obese person (Hebl & Mannix, 2003)! This prejudice appears early. Children are disdainful of fat children, and they, too, may exhibit lessened liking of normal-weight children who are seen with an obese child (Penny & Haddock, 2007; Puhl & Latner, 2007).

In national studies of U.S. adults, obesity has been associated with lower psychological well-being, especially among women, and with a 25 percent increase in depression and anxiety (Bookwala & Boyar, 2008; Petry et al., 2008; Simon et al., 2006). Likewise, German and British people who feel overweight report lower than average psychological well-being (Oswald & Powdthavee, 2007). In studies of patients especially unhappy with their weight—those who had lost an average of 100 pounds after short-cutting digestion with intestinal bypass surgery—4 in 5 said their children had asked them not to attend school functions. And 9 in 10 said they would rather have a leg amputated than be obese again (Rand & Macgregor, 1990, 1991).

Why don't obese people drop their excess baggage and free themselves of all this pain? An answer lies in the physiology of fat.

The Physiology of Obesity

Research on the physiology of obesity challenges the stereotype of severely overweight people being weak-willed gluttons. First, consider the arithmetic of weight gain: People get fat by consuming more calories than they expend. The energy equivalent of a pound of fat is 3500 calories; therefore, dieters have been told they will lose a pound for every 3500-calorie reduction in their diet. Surprise: This conclusion is false. (Read on.)

Fat Cells

The immediate determinants of body fat are the size and number of fat cells. A typical adult has 30 to 40 billion of these miniature fuel tanks, half of which lie near the skin's surface. A fat cell can vary from relatively empty, like a deflated balloon, to overly full. In an obese person, fat cells may swell to two or three times their normal size and then divide or trigger nearby immature fat cells to divide—resulting in up to 75 billion fat cells (Hirsch, 2003). Once the number of fat cells increases—due to genetic predisposition, early childhood eating patterns, or adult overeating—it never decreases (**FIGURE 37.9**). On a diet, fat cells may shrink, but their number does not (Sjöstrum, 1980; Spalding et al., 2008).

Set Point and Metabolism

Once we become fat, we require less food to maintain our weight than we did to attain it. Why? Because compared with other tissue, fat has a lower metabolic rate—it takes less food energy to maintain. When an overweight person's body drops below its previous set point (or settling point), the person's hunger increases and metabolism decreases. Thus, the body adapts to starvation by burning off fewer calories.

In a classic month-long experiment (Bray, 1969), obese patients whose daily food intake was reduced from 3500 to 450 calories lost only 6 percent of their weight—partly because their bodies reacted as though they were being starved, and their metabolic rates dropped about 15 percent (**FIGURE 37.10**). That is why reducing your food intake by 3500 calories may not reduce your weight by 1 pound. That is also why further weight loss comes slowly following the rapid losses during the initial three weeks or so of a rigorous diet. And that is why amounts of food that worked to maintain weight before a diet began may increase it when a diet ends—the body is still conserving energy. Given two people who weigh and look the same, the formerly overweight one will likely need to eat fewer calories to maintain that weight than will the never-overweight one. (Who said life is fair?)

Thirty years after the Bray study, researchers performed a reverse experiment (Levine et al., 1999). They overfed volunteers an extra 1000 calories a day for eight weeks. Those who gained the least weight tended to spend the extra caloric energy by fidgeting more. Lean people are naturally disposed to fidget and move about more

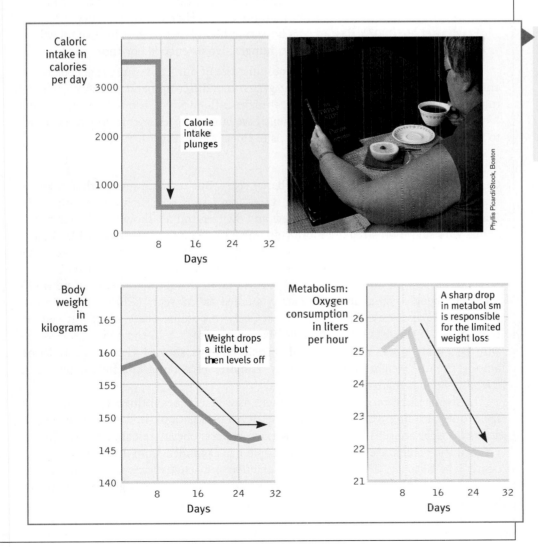

FIGURE 37.10 The effects of a severe diet on obese patients' body weight and metabolism After seven days on a 3500-calorie diet, six obese patients were given only 450 calories a day for the next 24 days. Body weight declined only 6 percent and then leveled off, because metabolism dropped about 15 percent. (From Bray, 1969.)

(and to burn more calories) than are energy-conserving overweight people who tend to sit still longer, report James Levine and his colleagues (2005). (How did the researchers know this? They outfitted people with undergarments that for 10 days monitored their movements every half-second.) These individual differences in resting metabolism help explain why two people of the same height, age, and activity level can maintain the same weight, even if one of them eats much less than the other does.

The Genetic Factor

Do our genes predispose us to fidget or sit still? Possibly. Studies do reveal a genetic influence on body weight. Consider:

▶ Despite shared family meals, adoptive siblings' body weights are uncorrelated with one another or with those of their adoptive parents. Rather, people's weights resemble those of their biological parents (Grilo & Pogue-Geile, 1991).

▶ Identical twins have closely similar weights, even when reared apart (Plomin et al., 1997; Stunkard et al., 1990). Across studies, their weight correlates +.74. The much lower +.32 correlation among fraternal twins suggests that genes explain two-thirds of our varying body mass (Maes et al., 1997).

▶ Given an obese parent, a boy is three times, and a girl six times, more likely to be obese than their counterparts with normal-weight parents (Carrière, 2003).

▶ Scientists have discovered many different genes that influence body weight. One gene scan of 40,000 people worldwide identified a variant of a gene called *FTO*, which nearly doubles the risk of becoming obese (Flier & Maratos-Flier, 2007; Frayling et al., 2007). Researchers hope that identifying such culprit genes will lead them to the trail of the protein hunger signals encoded by those genes.

So, the specifics of our genes predispose the size of our jeans. But the genetic influence is surely complex, with different genes, like differing band members, making music by playing together. Some genes might influence when our intestines signal "full," with others dictating how efficiently we burn calories or convert extra calories to fat, and, yes, still others prompting us to fidget or sit still.

The Food and Activity Factors

Genes tell an important part of the obesity story. But research reveals that environmental factors are mighty important, too. *Sleep loss* is one such factor. Studies in France, Japan, Spain, the United States, and Switzerland all show that children and adults who skimp on sleep are more vulnerable to obesity (Keith et al., 2006; Taheri, 2004a,b). With sleep deprivation, the levels of leptin (which reports body fat to the brain) fall and ghrelin (the stomach hormone that stimulates appetite) rise.

Social influence is another factor. One research team followed the social networks of 12,067 people whom they had closely studied for 32 years (Christakis & Fowler, 2007). Their discovery: People were most likely to become obese when a friend became obese. If the friend who became obese is a close friend, the odds of one's likewise becoming obese almost tripled. (Their analysis showed that the correlation among friends' weights was not simply a matter of seeking out similar people as friends.) Friends matter.

The strongest evidence that environment as well as genes influences weight comes from our fattening world. Although the developed nations lead the trend, people *across the globe* are getting heavier. In Mexico, reports obesity researcher Barry Popkin (2007), the percentage of overweight people has expanded from 1 in 10 in 1989, to nearly 7 in 10 today. Changing *food consumption* and *activity levels* are at work. Sugar-laden soft drinks and activity-inhibiting TV watching are spreading across the world. So are energy-rich cooking oils and energy-saving tools, trucks, and cars.

Too much food, and too little It is ironic that in a world where 800 million still live with hunger, obesity rates continue to rise in Western countries, endangering the lives of the severely overweight (Pinstrup-Andersen & Cheng, 2007; Popkin, 2007).

Western cultures especially have become like animal feedlots (where farmers fatten inactive animals). In a massive long-term study of 50,000 nurses, researchers found—even after controlling for exercise, smoking, age, and diet—that each two-hour increase in daily TV watching predicted a 23 percent obesity increase and a 7 percent diabetes increase (Hu et al., 2003). Other studies show that people living in walking-dependent communities such as Manhattan tend to weigh less than more sedentary folks in car-dependent suburbs (Ewing et al., 2003). Among Ontario's Old Order Amish, where farming and gardening is labor intensive and pedometers reveal that men walk nine miles a day and women seven miles, the obesity rate is one-seventh the U.S. rate (Bassett et al., 2004).

Inactivity is compounded by ever-larger food unit portions of high-calorie foods. Compared with our counterparts in the early 1900s, we are eating a higher-fat, higher-sugar diet, expending fewer calories, and suffering higher rates of diabetes at younger ages (Popkin, 2007). Just since 1971, women are eating 300 more calories a day and men nearly 200 calories more (O'Connor, 2004). And they are eating three times as many meals in fast-food restaurants (Farley & Cohen, 2001). Today's teens consume twice as much soda as milk—the reverse of a quarter-century ago (Brownell & Nestle, 2004).

On most North American college campuses, yesterday's cafeteria line with limited choices has been replaced by today's food buffet, with multiple serving stations offering all-you-can-eat entrees and make-your-own waffles washed down with limitless soft drinks (Brody, 2003). For many, the understandable result is the "freshman 15"—or, more typically, the "freshman 5" (Holm-Denoma et al., 2008). Small wonder that your parents and grandparents at age 30 likely weighed less than you did or will. Since 1960, the average adult American has grown one inch and gained 23 pounds (Ogden et al., 2004). Taken together, Big Macs, Double Whoppers, sugar-laden drinks, and inactivity form a weapon of mass destruction.

The "bottom" line: New stadiums, theaters, and subway cars are widening their own seats to accommodate this population growth (Hampson, 2000). Washington State Ferries abandoned a 50-year-old standard of 18 inches per person: "Eighteen-inch butts are a thing of the past," explained a spokesperson (Shepherd, 1999). New York City, facing a large problem with Big Apple bottoms, has mostly replaced 17.5-inch bucket-style subway seats with bucketless seats (Hampson, 2000). In the end, today's people need more room.

If the changing environment explains the expanding obesity problem, then environmental reform is part of the remedy, reasoned the 53 European health ministers who signed a new World Health Organization anti-obesity charter (Cheng, 2006). The charter beckons the private sector to "substantially reduce" its advertising of fatty, sugary foods to children and commits governments to increasing the availability of healthy foods and roadways that promote cycling and walking. In the United States, several states, including Arizona, California, and Kentucky, are now setting nutritional standards for school-provided food and drink (Tumulty, 2006).

Psychologist Kelly Brownell (2002) has been campaigning for these and other environmental reforms:

▶ Establish a fast-food–free zone around schools.

▶ Slap an extra tax on calorie-laden junk food and soft drinks. We're reducing smoking with increased cigarette taxes. Why not, for the same reason, institute a "Twinkie Tax"?

▶ Use the revenues to subsidize healthy foods and to finance health-supportive nutritional advertising.

Note how these findings reinforce a familiar lesson from the study of intelligence: There can be high levels of *heritability* (genetic influence on individual differences) without heredity explaining group differences. Genes mostly determine why one person today is heavier than another. Environment mostly determines why people today are heavier than their counterparts 50 years ago. Our eating behavior also demonstrates the now familiar interaction among biological, psychological, and social-cultural factors.

Losing Weight

Perhaps you are shaking your head: "Slim chance I have of becoming and staying thin. If I lose weight on a diet, my metabolism slows and my hungry fat cells cry out, 'Feed me!' I'm fated for fat!" Indeed, the condition of an obese person's body reduced to average weight is much like that of a semistarved body. Held under normal set point, the body "thinks" it is starving. Having lost weight, formerly obese people look normal, but their fat cells may be abnormally small, their metabolism slowed, and their minds obsessed with food.

The battle of the bulge rages on as intensely as ever, and it is most intense among those with two X chromosomes. Nearly two-thirds of women and half of men say they want to lose weight; about half of those women and men say they are "seriously trying" (Moore, 2006). Asked if they would rather "be five years younger or weigh 15 pounds less," 29 percent of men and 48 percent of women said they would prefer losing the weight (Responsive Community, 1996).

With fat cells, settling points, metabolism, and genetic and environmental factors all tirelessly conspiring against shedding excess pounds, what advice can psychology offer these people? Perhaps the most important point is that permanent weight loss is not easy. Millions can attest that it is possible to lose weight; they have done it lots of

"Some people daydream heroic deeds or sex scenes or tropical vacations. I daydream crab legs dipped in hot butter."

Judith Moore, *Fat Girl,* 2005

A losing battle
Ryan Benson lost 122 pounds to win the first season of the TV reality show *The Biggest Loser.* But then, like so many, he found maintaining the loss an even bigger challenge.

times. But short of drastic surgery to tie off part of the stomach and small intestine, most who succeed on a weight-loss program eventually regain the lost weight or more (Mann et al., 2007).

Those who do manage to keep pounds off set realistic and moderate goals, undertaking programs that modify their life-style and ongoing eating behavior. They realize that being moderately heavy is less risky than being extremely thin (Ernsberger & Koletsky, 1999). They lose weight gradually: "A reasonable time line for a 10 percent reduction in body weight is six months," advised the National Institutes of Health (1998). And they exercise regularly. For other helpful hints, see Close-Up: Waist Management.

CLOSE-UP

Waist Management

People struggling with obesity are well advised to seek medical evaluation and guidance. For others who wish to take off a few pounds, researchers have offered these tips.

Begin only if you feel motivated and self-disciplined. For most people, permanent weight loss requires making a career of staying thin—a lifelong change in eating habits combined with gradually increased exercise.

Minimize exposure to tempting food cues. Keep tempting foods out of the house or out of sight. Go to the supermarket only on a full stomach, and avoid the sweets and chips aisles. Eat simple meals, with only a few different foods; given more variety, people consume more.

Take steps to boost your metabolism. Inactive people are often overweight (**FIGURE 37.11**). In a 1980s study of 6671 young people 12 to 17 years old, and in a 1990s follow-up study of 4063 individuals 8 to 16 years old, obesity was more common among those who watched the most TV (Andersen et al., 1998; Dietz & Gortmaker, 1985). Of course, overweight people may avoid activity, preferring to sit and watch TV. But the association between TV watching and obesity remained when many other factors were controlled, suggesting that inactivity and snacking while watching TV do contribute to obesity. The good news is that one of the few predictors of successful long-term weight

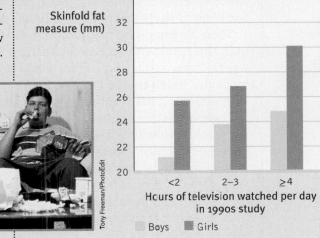

FIGURE 37.11 American idle: Couch potatoes beware—TV watching correlates with obesity As life-styles have become more sedentary and TV watching has increased, so has the percentage of overweight people in Britain, North America, and elsewhere. When California children were placed in a TV-reduction educational program, they watched less—and lost weight (Robinson, 1999).

loss is exercise, both during and after changing your eating patterns (Jeffery et al., 2000; McGuire et al., 1999; Wadden et al., 1998). Exercise, supported by 7 to 8 hours of sleep a night, empties fat cells, builds muscle, speeds up metabolism, and helps lower your settling point (Bennett, 1995; Kolata, 1987; Thompson et al., 1982).

Eat healthy foods. Whole grains, fruits, vegetables, and healthy fats such as those found in olive oil and fish help regulate appetite and artery-clogging cholesterol (Taubes, 2001, 2002). Better crispy greens than Krispy Kremes

Don't starve all day and eat one big meal at night. This eating pattern, common among overweight people, slows

metabolism. Moreover, those who eat a balanced breakfast are, by late morning, more alert and less fatigued (Spring et al., 1992).

Beware of the binge. Especially for men, eating more slowly leads to eating less (Martin et al., 2007). Among people who do consciously restrain their eating, drinking alcohol or feeling anxious or depressed can unleash the urge to eat (Herman & Polivy, 1980). So can being distracted from monitoring your eating (Ward & Mann, 2000). (Ever notice that you eat more when out with friends?) Once the diet is broken, the person often thinks "What the heck" and then binges (Polivy & Herman, 1985, 1987). A lapse need not become a full collapse: Remember, most people occasionally lapse.

A successful loser After losing 110 pounds, former Arkansas governor and U.S. presidential candidate Mike Huckabee poses with a girl who weighs what he lost. "Look at Huckabee," said his longtime adversary, former U.S. President Bill Clinton. "You've got to consume less and burn more. There is no other alternative. And to do that, you've got to change the culture."

"Fat! So?"
Popular T-shirt at the 1999 convention of the
National Association to Advance Fat Acceptance

Although mindful that preserving weight loss is a constant challenge, Stanley Schachter (1982) was less pessimistic than most of today's obesity researchers about the dieter's chances of success. He recognized the overwhelming rate of failure among those in structured weight-loss programs, but he also noted that these people are a special group who probably have been unable to help themselves. Moreover, the failure rates recorded for these programs are based on single attempts at weight loss. Perhaps when people try repeatedly to lose weight, more of them do eventually succeed. When Schachter interviewed people, he found that one-fourth had at one time been significantly overweight and had tried to slim down. Of these, 6 of 10 had *succeeded:* They weighed at least 10 percent less than their maximum prediet weight (an average loss of 35 pounds) and were no longer obese. A 1993 survey of 90,000 *Consumer Reports* readers found 25 percent of dieters claiming an enduring weight loss. Aided by media publicity, the National Weight Control Registry has identified more than 4000 people who have maintained significant weight loss for at least one year and are being studied over time. On average, these people have lost 60 pounds and kept it off for five years, virtually always with continued diet and exercise.

These findings hint that prospects for losing weight may be somewhat brighter than the dismal conclusions drawn from following patients who undergo a single weight-loss program. This pattern would be similar to the one found in stop-smoking programs, which tend to be (1) effective in the short run and (2) ineffective in the long run, even though (3) many people are former smokers.

There is another option for overweight people, and one chosen by 13 percent of the people Schachter interviewed: to accept one's weight. We all do well to note that researchers have *not* identified guilt, hostility, oral fixation, or any similar personality maladjustment as causes of obesity. Nor is obesity simply a matter of lack of willpower. Dieters are more likely to binge when under stress or after breaking their diets, which may be largely a consequence of their constant dieting. Indeed, the relentless pursuit of thinness puts people at risk not only for binge eating and food obsession, but also for weight fluctuations, malnutrition, smoking, depression, and harmful side effects of weight-loss drugs (Cogan & Ernsberger, 1999).

"Fat is not a four-letter world," proclaims the National Association to Advance Fat Acceptance, so "a waist is a terrible thing to mind." Such statements discount the health risks linked with significant obesity, but they do convey a valid point: It is surely better to accept oneself as a bit heavy than to diet and binge and feel continually out of control and guilty. Fans loved Oprah Winfrey before she lost 67 pounds. They loved her after she put them back on. They loved her when she shed them again. And they will love her still, chubby or not.

REVIEW

Hunger

37-1 **What physiological factors produce hunger?** Hunger pangs correspond to the stomach's contractions, but hunger also has other causes. Appetite hormones include insulin (controls blood *glucose*), leptin (secreted by fat cells), orexin (secreted by the hypothalamus), ghrelin (secreted by an empty stomach), obestatin (secreted by the stomach), and PYY (secreted by digestive tract). Two areas of the hypothalamus regulate the body's weight by affecting feelings of hunger and satiety. The body may have a *set point* (a biologically fixed tendency to maintain an optimum weight) or a looser settling point (also influenced by the environment).

37-2 **What psychological and cultural factors influence hunger?** Hunger also reflects learning, our memory of when we last ate, and our expectation of when we should eat again. Humans as a species prefer certain tastes (such as sweet and salty) but we satisfy those preferences with specific foods prescribed by our situation and our culture. Some taste preferences, such as the avoidance of new foods or of foods that have made us ill, have survival value.

37-3 **How do anorexia nervosa, bulimia nervosa, and binge-eating disorder demonstrate the influence of psychological forces on physiologically motivated behaviors?** In these eating disorders, psychological factors may overwhelm the homeostatic drive to maintain a balanced internal state. People with *anorexia nervosa* (usually adolescent females) starve themselves but continue to diet because they view themselves as fat. Those with *bulimia nervosa* binge and purge in secret (primarily females in their teens and twenties). Those with *binge-eating disorder* binge but do not purge. Cultural pressures, low self-esteem, and negative emotions interact with stressful life experiences to produce eating disorders. Twin research also indicates, however, that these disorders may have a genetic component.

37-4 **What factors predispose some people to become and remain obese?** The lack of exercise combined with the abundance of high-calorie food has led to increased rates of obesity, showing the influence of environment. Twin and adoption studies indicate that body weight is also genetically influenced (in the number of fat cells and *basal metabolic rate*). Thus, genes and environment interact to produce obesity. Those wishing to lose weight are advised to make a lifelong change in habits, minimize exposure to tempting food cues, boost energy expenditure through exercise, eat healthy foods, space meals throughout the day, beware of the binge, and forgive the occasional lapse.

Terms and Concepts to Remember

glucose, p. 449

set point, p. 451

basal metabolic rate, p. 451

anorexia nervosa, p. 453

bulimia nervosa, p. 453

binge-eating disorder, p. 454

Test Yourself

1. You are traveling and have not eaten anything in eight hours. As your long-awaited favorite dish is placed in front of you, your mouth waters. Even imagining this may set your mouth to watering. What triggers this anticipatory drooling?

(Answers to the Test Yourself questions can be found in Appendix B at the end of the book.)

Ask Yourself

1. Do you feel in touch with your body's hunger signals? Do you eat when your body needs food? Or do you tend to be more externally influenced by enticing foods even when you're full?

∞ WEB

Multiple-choice self-tests and more may be found at www.worthpublishers.com/myers

The Physiology of Sex

The Psychology of Sex

Adolescent Sexuality

Sexual Orientation

Sex and Human Values

The Need to Belong

"It is a near-universal experience, the invisible clause on one's birth certificate stipulating that one will, upon reaching maturity, feel the urge to engage in activities often associated with the issuance of more birth certificates."

Science writer Natalie Angier, 2007

"I love the idea of there being two sexes, don't you?"

|| A nonsmoking 50-year-old male has about a 1-in-a-million chance of a heart attack during any hour. This increases to merely 2-in-a-million during the hour following sex (with no increase for those who exercise regularly). Compared with risks associated with heavy exertion or anger, this risk seems not worth losing sleep (or sex) over (Muller et al., 1996). ||

MODULE 38

Sexual Motivation and the Need to Belong

Sex is part of life. Had this not been so for all your ancestors, you would not be reading this book. Sexual motivation is nature's clever way of making people procreate, thus enabling our species' survival. When two people feel attracted, they hardly stop to think of themselves as guided by their genes. As the pleasure we take in eating is nature's inventive method of getting our body nourishment, so the desires and pleasure of sex is our genes' way of preserving and spreading themselves. Life is sexually transmitted.

▶|| The Physiology of Sex

Sexual arousal depends on the interplay of internal and external stimuli. To understand sexual motivation, we must consider both.

The Sexual Response Cycle

38-1 What stages mark the human sexual response cycle?

In the 1960s, gynecologist-obstetrician William Masters and his collaborator Virginia Johnson (1966) made headlines by recording the physiological responses of volunteers who masturbated or had intercourse. With the help of 382 female and 312 male volunteers—a somewhat atypical sample, consisting only of people able and willing to display arousal and orgasm while being observed in a laboratory—Masters and Johnson monitored or filmed more than 10,000 sexual "cycles." Their description of the **sexual response cycle** identified four stages, similar in men and women. During the initial *excitement phase,* the genital areas become engorged with blood, a woman's vagina expands and secretes lubricant, and her breasts and nipples may enlarge.

In the *plateau phase,* excitement peaks as breathing, pulse, and blood pressure rates continue to increase. The penis becomes fully engorged and some fluid—frequently containing enough live sperm to enable conception—may appear at its tip. Vaginal secretion continues to increase, the clitoris retracts, and orgasm feels imminent.

Masters and Johnson observed muscle contractions all over the body during *orgasm;* these were accompanied by further increases in breathing, pulse, and blood pressure rates. A woman's arousal and orgasm facilitate conception by helping propel semen from the penis, positioning the uterus to receive sperm, and drawing the sperm further inward. A woman's orgasm therefore not only reinforces intercourse, which is essential to natural reproduction, it also increases retention of deposited sperm (Furlow & Thornhill, 1996). In the excitement of the moment, men and women are hardly aware of all this as their rhythmic genital contractions create a pleasurable feeling of sexual release.

The feeling apparently is much the same for both sexes. In one study, a panel of experts could not reliably distinguish between descriptions of orgasm written by men and those written by women (Vance & Wagner, 1976). University of Groningen neuroscientist Gerg Holstege and his colleagues (2003a,b) understand why. They discovered that when men and women undergo PET scans while having orgasms, the same subcortical brain regions glow. And when people who are passionately in love undergo fMRI (functional MRI) scans while viewing photos of their beloved or of a stranger, men's and women's brain responses to their partner are pretty similar (Fisher et al., 2002).

After orgasm, the body gradually returns to its unaroused state as the engorged genital blood vessels release their accumulated blood—relatively quickly if orgasm has occurred, relatively slowly otherwise. (It's like the nasal tickle that goes away rapidly if you have sneezed, slowly otherwise.) During this *resolution phase,* the male enters a **refractory period,** lasting from a few minutes to a day or more, during which he is incapable of another orgasm. The female's much shorter refractory period may enable her to have more orgasms if restimulated during or soon after resolution.

Masters and Johnson sought not only to describe the human sexual response cycle but also to understand and treat the inability to complete it. **Sexual disorders** are problems that consistently impair sexual arousal or functioning. Some involve sexual motivation, especially lack of sexual energy and arousability. For men, others include *premature ejaculation* and *erectile dysfunction* (inability to have or maintain an erection). For women, the problem may be *orgasmic dysfunction* (infrequently or never experiencing orgasm). Most women who experience sexual distress relate it to their emotional relationship with the partner during sex, not to physical aspects of the activity (Bancroft et al., 2003). A study of several hundred Australian identical and fraternal twins reveals that women's orgasm frequency is also genetically influenced (Dawood et al., 2005). But the genetic factor that accounted for 51 percent of the variation in frequency of orgasm via masturbation could account for only 31 percent of the variation in frequency of orgasm via intercourse. When there's a partner, emotional closeness, security, and intimacy also matter.

Men or women with sexual disorders can often be helped by receiving therapy. In behaviorally oriented therapy, for example, men learn ways to control their urge to ejaculate, and women are trained to bring themselves to orgasm. Starting with the introduction of Viagra in 1998, erectile dysfunction has been routinely treated by taking a pill.

Hormones and Sexual Behavior

38-2 Do hormones influence human sexual motivation?

Sex hormones have two effects: They direct the physical development of male and female sex characteristics, and (especially in nonhuman animals) they activate sexual behavior. In most mammals, nature neatly synchronizes sex with fertility. The female becomes sexually receptive ("in heat") when secretion of the female hormones, the **estrogens** (such as estradiol), peak during ovulation. In experiments, researchers can stimulate receptivity by injecting female animals with estrogen. Male hormone levels are more constant, and researchers cannot so easily manipulate the sexual behavior of male animals with hormones (Feder, 1984). Nevertheless, castrated male rats—having lost their testes, which manufacture the male sex hormone **testosterone**—gradually lose much of their interest in receptive females. They gradually regain it if injected with testosterone.

In humans, hormones more loosely influence sexual behavior, although sexual desire rises slightly at ovulation among women with mates (Pillsworth et al., 2004). One study invited partnered women not at risk for pregnancy to keep a diary of their sexual activity. (These women were either using intrauterine devices or had undergone surgery to prevent pregnancy.) On the days around ovulation, intercourse was 24 percent more frequent (Wilcox et al., 2004). Other studies find that women fantasize more about sex with desirable partners and wear more sexually attractive clothing around ovulation (Haselton et al., 2006; Pillsworth & Haselton, 2006; Sheldon et al. 2006). In a study of 5300 strip-club lap dancers, their hourly tips almost doubled on the days near ovulation, compared with days during menstruation (Miller et al., 2007).

---

sexual response cycle the four stages of sexual responding described by Masters and Johnson—excitement, plateau, orgasm, and resolution.

refractory period a resting period after orgasm, during which a man cannot achieve another orgasm.

sexual disorder a problem that consistently impairs sexual arousal or functioning.

estrogens sex hormones, such as estradiol, secreted in greater amounts by females than by males and contributing to female sex characteristics. In nonhuman female mammals, estrogen levels peak during ovulation, promoting sexual receptivity.

testosterone the most important of the male sex hormones. Both males and females have it, but the additional testosterone in males stimulates the growth of the male sex organs in the fetus and the development of the male sex characteristics during puberty.

‖ In a National Center for Health Statistics survey of adult Americans, using computer-assisted self-interviews that guaranteed privacy, nearly 98 percent of 30- to 59-year-olds reported having had sex (Fryar et al., 2007). ‖

"Fill'er up with testosterone."

Women's sexuality differs from that of other mammalian females in being more responsive to testosterone level than to estrogen levels (Meston & Frohlich, 2000; Reichman, 1998). If a woman's natural testosterone level drops, as happens with removal of the ovaries or adrenal glands, her sexual interest may wane. But testosterone-replacement therapy sometimes restores diminished sexual appetite. That is the finding of experiments with hundreds of surgically or naturally menopausal women, for whom a testosterone-replacement patch restored sexual activity, arousal, and desire more than did a placebo (Braunstein et al., 2005; Buster et al., 2005; Davis et al., 2003; Kroll et al., 2004).

In men, normal fluctuations in testosterone levels, from man to man and hour to hour, have little effect on sexual drive (Byrne, 1982). Indeed, fluctuations in male hormones are partly a *response* to sexual stimulation. When James Dabbs and his colleagues (1987, 2000) had heterosexual male collegians converse separately with another male student and with a female student, the men's testosterone levels rose with the social arousal, but especially after talking with the female. Thus, sexual arousal can be a cause as well as a consequence of increased testosterone levels. At the other end of the mating spectrum, studies in both North America and China find that married fathers tend to have lower testosterone levels than those found in bachelors and married men without children (Gray et al., 2006).

Although normal short-term hormonal changes have little effect on men's and women's desire, large hormonal shifts over the life span have a greater effect. A person's interest in dating and sexual stimulation usually increases with the pubertal surge in sex hormones, as happens with male testosterone levels during puberty. If the hormonal surge is precluded—as it was during the 1600s and 1700s for prepubertal boys who were castrated to preserve their soprano voices for Italian opera—the normal development of sex characteristics and sexual desire does not occur (Peschel & Peschel, 1987). When adult men are castrated, sex drive typically falls as testosterone levels decline (Hucker & Bain, 1990). Male sex offenders taking Depo-Provera, a drug that reduces testosterone level to that of a prepubertal boy, similarly lose much of their sexual urge (Money et al., 1983).

In later life, as sex hormone levels decline, the frequency of sexual fantasies and intercourse declines as well (Leitenberg & Henning, 1995). For men with abnormally low testosterone levels, testosterone-replacement therapy often increases sexual desire and also energy and vitality (Yates, 2000).

To summarize: We might compare human sex hormones, especially testosterone, to the fuel in a car. Without fuel, a car will not run. But if the fuel level is minimally adequate, adding more fuel to the gas tank won't change how the car runs. The analogy is imperfect, because hormones and sexual motivation interact. However, the analogy correctly suggests that biology is a necessary but not sufficient explanation of human sexual behavior. The hormonal fuel is essential, but so are the psychological stimuli that turn on the engine, keep it running, and shift it into high gear.

▶‖ The Psychology of Sex

38-3   How do internal and external stimuli influence sexual motivation?

Hunger and sex are different sorts of motivations. Hunger responds to a *need*. If we do not eat, we die. Sex is not in this sense a need. If we do not have sex, we may feel like dying, but we do not. Nevertheless, there are similarities between hunger and sexual motivation. Both depend on internal physiological factors. And both are influenced by external and imagined stimuli, as well as cultural expectations (**FIGURE 38.1**). Thus,

Biological influences:
• sexual maturity
• sex hormones, especially testosterone
• sexual orientation

Psychological influences:
• exposure to stimulating conditions
• sexual fantasies

Sexual motivation

Social-cultural influences:
• family and society values
• religious and personal values
• cultural expectations
• media

FIGURE 38.1 Levels of analysis for sexual motivation Compared with our motivation for eating, our sexual motivation is less influenced by biological factors. Psychological and social-cultural factors play a bigger role.

despite the shared biology that underlies sexual motivation, the 281 expressed reasons for having sex (at last count) range from "to get closer to God" to "to get my boyfriend to shut up" (Buss, 2008 Meston & Buss, 2007).

External Stimuli

Many studies confirm that men become aroused when they see, hear, or read erotic material. Surprising to many (because sexually explicit materials are sold mostly to men) is that most women—at least the less-inhibited women who volunteer to participate in such studies—report or exhibit nearly as much arousal to the same stimuli (Heiman, 1975; Stockton & Murnen, 1992). (Their brains do, however, respond differently, with fMRI scans revealing a more active amygdala in men viewing erotica [Hamann et al., 2004].)

People may find such arousal either pleasing or disturbing. (Those who find it disturbing often limit their exposure to such materials, just as those wishing to control hunger limit their exposure to tempting cues.) With repeated exposure, the emotional response to any erotic stimulus often lessens, or *habituates*. During the 1920s, when Western women's hemlines first reached the knee, an exposed leg was a mildly erotic stimulus, as were modest (by today's standards) two-piece swimsuits and movie scenes of a mere kiss.

Can sexually explicit material have adverse effects? Research indicates that it can. Depictions of women being sexually coerced—and enjoying it—tend to increase viewers' acceptance of the false idea that women enjoy rape, and they tend to increase male viewers' willingness to hurt women (Malamuth & Check, 1981; Zillmann, 1989). Viewing images of sexually attractive women and men may also lead people to devalue their own partners and relationships. After male collegians view TV or magazine depictions of sexually attractive women, they often find an average woman, or their own girlfriend or wife, less attractive (Kenrick & Gutierres, 1980; Kenrick et al., 1989; Weaver et al., 1984). Viewing X-rated sex films similarly tends to diminish people's satisfaction with their own sexual partner (Zillmann, 1989). Some sex researchers suspect that reading or watching erotica may create expectations that few men and women can fulfill.

Imagined Stimuli

The brain, it has been said, is our most significant sex organ. The stimuli inside our heads—our imagination—can influence sexual arousal and desire. People who, because of a spinal cord injury, have no genital sensation can still feel sexual desire

"Ours is a society which stimulates interest in sex by constant titillation. . . . Cinema, television, and all the formidable array of our marketing technology project our very effective forms of titillation and our prejudices about man as a sexy animal into every corner of every hovel in the world."
Germaine Greer, 1984

(Willmuth, 1987). Consider, too, the erotic potential of dreams. Sleep researchers have discovered that genital arousal accompanies all types of dreams, even though most dreams have no sexual content. But in nearly all men and some 40 percent of women, dreams sometimes contain sexual imagery that leads to orgasm (Wells, 1986). In men, nighttime orgasm and nocturnal emissions ("wet dreams") are more likely when orgasm has not occurred recently.

Wide-awake people become sexually aroused not only by memories of prior sexual activities but also by fantasies. In one survey of masturbation-related fantasies (Hunt, 1974), 19 percent of women and 10 percent of men reported imagining being "taken" by someone overwhelmed with desire for them. Fantasy is not reality, however. To paraphrase Susan Brownmiller (1975), there's a big difference between fantasizing that Leonardo DiCaprio just won't take no for an answer and having a hostile stranger actually force himself on you.

About 95 percent of both men and women say they have had sexual fantasies. Men (whether gay or straight) fantasize about sex more often, more physically, and less romantically. They also prefer less personal and faster-paced sexual content in books and videos (Leitenberg & Henning, 1995). Fantasizing about sex does *not* indicate a sexual problem or dissatisfaction. If anything, sexually active people have more sexual fantasies.

> "There is no difference between being raped and being run over by a truck except that afterward men ask if you enjoyed it."
> Marge Piercy, "Rape Poem," 1976

▶‖ Adolescent Sexuality

38-4   What factors influence teen pregnancy and risk of sexually transmitted infections?

Adolescents' physical maturation fosters a sexual dimension to their emerging identity. Yet sexual expression varies dramatically with time and culture. Among American women born before 1900, a mere 3 percent had experienced premarital sex by age 18 (Smith, 1998). In 2005, 47 percent of high school students acknowledged having had sexual intercourse (CDC, 2006). Teen intercourse rates are roughly similar in Western Europe and in Latin America, but much lower in Arab and Asian countries and among North Americans of Asian descent (McLaughlin et al., 1997; Wellings et al., 2006). Given the wide variation across time and place, it's no surprise that a recent twin study found that environmental factors accounted for almost three-fourths of the individual variation in age of sexual initiation (Bricker et al., 2006). Family and cultural values matter.

Sex during the teen years is often unprotected, leading to risks of pregnancy and *sexually transmitted infections* (*STIs,* also called *STDs* for *sexually transmitted diseases*).

Teen Pregnancy

> "Will your child learn to multiply before she learns to subtract?"
> Anti–teen-pregnancy poster, Children's Defense Fund

Compared with European teens, American teens have a lower rate of contraceptive use and thus a higher rate of teen pregnancy and abortion (Call et al., 2002). Why?

Ignorance   One survey of Canadian teens revealed some real gaps in knowledge about sex and sexual health (Ipsos, 2006). Although 9 in 10 claimed to be knowledgeable, many were unaware that STIs can be transmitted through oral sex (which two-thirds had engaged in); only 19 percent had heard of HPV (human papillomavirus, a leading cause of genital warts and cervical cancer); and only 37 percent mentioned infertility as a possible result of chlamydia. Most teens also overestimate their peers' sexual activity, a misperception that may influence their own behavior (Child Trends, 2001). Countering ignorance with contraceptive sex education "does not increase adolescent sexual activity" (Surgeon General, 2001), but a World Health Organization report found that it does increase "intention to practice safer sex," and may even *delay* "rather than hasten the onset of sexual activity" (Wellings et al., 2006).

Minimal communication about birth control Many teenagers are uncomfortable discussing contraception with their parents, partners, and peers. Teens who talk freely with parents and are in an exclusive relationship with a partner with whom they communicate openly are more likely to use contraceptives (Aspy et al., 2007; Milan & Kilmann, 1987).

Guilt related to sexual activity In one survey, 72 percent of sexually active 12- to 17-year-old American girls said they regretted having had sex (Reuters, 2000). Sexual inhibitions or ambivalence can reduce sexual activity, but they may also reduce attempts at birth control if passion overwhelms intentions (Gerrard & Luus, 1995; MacDonald & Hynie, 2008).

Alcohol use Sexually active teens are typically alcohol-using teens (Albert et al., 2003; ASA, 2004), and those who use alcohol prior to sex are less likely to use condoms (Kotchick et al., 2001). By depressing the brain centers that control judgment, inhibition, and self-awareness, alcohol tends to break down normal restraints, a phenomenon well known to sexually coercive males.

Mass media norms of unprotected promiscuity Media help write the "social scripts" that affect our perceptions and actions. So what sexual scripts do today's media write on our minds? An average hour of prime-time television on the three major U.S. networks contains approximately 15 sexual acts, words, and innuendos. The partners are usually unmarried, with no prior romantic relationship, and few communicate any concern for birth control or sexually transmitted infections (Brown et al., 2002; Kunkel, 2001; Sapolsky & Tabarlet, 1991). The more sexual content adolescents view (even when controlling for other predictors of early sexual activity), the more likely they are to perceive their peers as sexually active, to develop sexually permissive attitudes, and to experience early intercourse (Escobar-Chaves et al., 2005; Martino et al., 2005; Ward & Friedman, 2006).

Sexually Transmitted Infections

Unprotected sex has led to increased rates of sexually transmitted infections. Two-thirds of new infections occur in people under 25 (CASA, 2004). Teenage girls, because of their not yet fully mature biological development and lower levels of protective antibodies, seem especially vulnerable (Dehne & Riedner, 2005; Guttmacher, 1994). A recent Centers for Disease Control study of sexually experienced 14- to 19-year-old U.S. females found 39.5 percent had STIs (Forhan et al., 2008).

To comprehend the mathematics of transmitting these infections, imagine this scenario: Over the course of a year, Pat has sex with 9 people, each of whom over the same period has sex with 9 other people, who in turn have sex with 9 others. How many "phantom" sex partners (past partners of partners) will Pat have? Laura Brannon and Timothy Brock (1993) report that the actual number—511—is more than five times the estimate given by the average student. Or consider this: If someone uses a method that is 98 percent effective in preventing pregnancy or infection, there is a 2 percent chance of failure in the first such use. Surprising to many people, given 30 such uses, the risk would accumulate to nearly a 50 percent chance of failure at some point. Moreover, when people feel drawn to a partner, they become motivated to underestimate risks (Knäuper el al., 2005).

Given these odds, the rapid spread of STIs is not surprising. Condoms offer little protection against certain skin-to-skin STIs (Medical Institute, 1994; NIH, 2001). Across the available studies, condoms have, however, been 80 percent effective in preventing transmission of HIV (human immunodeficiency virus—the virus that causes

"Condoms should be used on every conceivable occasion."

Anonymous

"All of us who make motion pictures are teachers, teachers with very loud voices."

Film producer George Lucas, Academy Award ceremonies, 1992

AIDS) from an infected partner (Weller & Davis-Beaty, 2002; WHO, 2003). The effects were clear when Thailand promoted 100 percent condom use by commercial sex workers. Over a four-year period, as condom use soared from 14 to 94 percent, the annual number of bacterial STIs plummeted from 410,406 to 27,362 (WHO, 2000).

In the United States, STI facts of life have led to another response: a greater emphasis on teen abstinence within some comprehensive sex-education programs. A National Longitudinal Study of Adolescent Health among 12,000 teens found several predictors of sexual restraint:

High intelligence Teens with high rather than average intelligence test scores more often delay sex, evidently because they appreciate possible negative consequences and are more focused on future achievement than on here-and-now pleasures (Halpern et al., 2000).

Religious engagement Actively religious teens and adults more often reserve sex for marital commitment (Rostosky et al., 2004; Smith, 1998).

Father presence In studies following hundreds of New Zealand and U.S. girls from age 5 to 18, a father's absence was linked to sexual activity before age 16 and teen pregnancy (Ellis et al., 2003). These associations held even after adjusting for other adverse influences, such as poverty.

Participation in service learning programs Several experiments have found lower pregnancy rates among teens volunteering as tutors or teachers' aides or participating in community projects, than found among comparable teens randomly assigned to control conditions (Kirby, 2002; O'Donnell et al., 2002). Researchers are unsure why. Does service learning promote a sense of personal competence, control, and responsibility? Does it encourage more future-oriented thinking? Or does it simply reduce opportunities for unprotected sex?

* * *

In recent history, the pendulum of sexual values has swung from the European eroticism of the early 1800s to the conservative Victorian era of the late 1800s, from the libertine flapper era of the 1920s to the family values period of the 1950s. The pendulum may have begun a new swing toward commitment in the twenty-first century, with declining teen birth rates since 1991. This decline reflects both increasing condom use among sexually active high school students (from 46 to 63 percent between 1991 and 2005) and decreasing sexual intercourse (from 54 to 47 percent) (CDC, 2006).

▶‖ Sexual Orientation

38-5 What has research taught us about sexual orientation?

To motivate is to energize and direct behavior. So far, we have considered the energizing of sexual motivation but not its direction. We express the direction of our sexual interest in our **sexual orientation**—our enduring sexual attraction toward members of our own sex (*homosexual orientation*) or the other sex (*heterosexual orientation*). Cultures vary in their attitudes toward homosexuality. In Chile, 32 percent of people say they think homosexuality "is never justified," as do 50 percent of people in the United States and 98 percent in Kenya and Nigeria (Pew, 2006). As far as we know, all cultures in all times have been predominantly heterosexual (Bullough, 1990). Whether a culture condemns or accepts homosexuality, heterosexuality prevails and homosexuality survives.

Gay men and lesbians often recall childhood play preferences like those of the other sex (Bailey & Zucker, 1995). But most homosexual people report not becoming aware of same-sex attraction until during or shortly after puberty, and not thinking of themselves as gay or lesbian (their socially influenced identity) until later in their

sexual orientation an enduring sexual attraction toward members of either one's own sex (homosexual orientation) or the other sex (heterosexual orientation).

teens or twenties (Garnets & Kimmel, 1990; Hammack, 2005). As adolescents, their friendship quality is similar to that of "straight" teenagers, and as adults, their partnerships are "remarkably similar" to heterosexual couples in love and satisfaction (Busseri et al., 2006; Peplau & Fingerhut, 2007).

Sexual Orientation Statistics

How many people are exclusively homosexual? About 10 percent, as the popular press has often assumed? A little more than 20 percent, as average Americans estimated in a 2002 Gallup survey (Robinson, 2002)? Not according to more than a dozen national surveys in the early 1990s, which explored sexual orientation in Europe and the United States, using methods that protected the respondents' anonymity. The most accurate figure seems to be about 3 or 4 percent of men and 1 or 2 percent of women (Laumann et al., 1994; Mosher et al., 2005; Smith, 1998). Estimates derived from the sex of unmarried partners reported in the 2000 U.S. Census suggest that 2.5 percent of the population is gay or lesbian (Tarmann, 2002). Fewer than 1 percent of survey respondents—for example, 12 people out of 7076 Dutch adults in one survey (Sandfort et al., 2001)—reported being actively bisexual. A larger number of adults in that study reported having had an isolated homosexual experience. And most people report having had an occasional homosexual fantasy. Health experts find it helpful to know sexual statistics, but numbers do not decide issues of human rights.

What does it feel like to be homosexual in a heterosexual culture? If you are heterosexual, one way to understand is to imagine how you would feel if you were ostracized or fired for openly admitting or displaying your feelings toward someone of the other sex; if you overheard people making crude jokes about heterosexual people; if most movies, TV shows, and advertisements portrayed (or implied) homosexuality; and if your family members were pleading with you to change your heterosexual lifestyle and to enter into a homosexual marriage.

Sexual orientation is not an indicator of mental health. "Homosexuality, in and of itself, is not associated with mental disorders or emotional or social problems," declares the American Psychological Association (2007). Moreover, same-sex civil unions provide emotional, social, and health benefits similar to those of heterosexual unions (Herek, 2006; King & Bartlett, 2006; Kurdek, 2005). But some homosexual individuals, especially during adolescence, struggle with their sexual attractions and are at increased risk for thinking about and attempting suicide (Balsam et al., 2005; Kitts, 2005; Plöderl & Fartacek, 2005). They may at first try to ignore or deny their desires, hoping they will go away. But they don't. Then they may try to change, through psychotherapy, willpower, or prayer. But the feelings typically persist, as do those of heterosexual people—who are similarly incapable of becoming homosexual (Haldeman, 1994, 2002; Myers & Scanzoni, 2005). Most of today's psychologists therefore view sexual orientation as neither willfully chosen nor willfully changed. Sexual orientation in some ways is like handedness: Most people are one way, some the other. A very few are truly ambidextrous. Regardless, the way one is endures.

This conclusion is most strongly established for men. Compared with men's sexual orientation, women's tends to be less strongly felt and potentially more fluid and changing (Chivers, 2005; Diamond, 2007; Peplau & Garnets, 2000). Men's lesser sexual variability is apparent in many ways, notes Roy Baumeister (2000). Across time, across cultures, across situations, and across differing levels of education, religious observance, and peer influence, adult women's sexual drive and interests are more flexible and varying than are adult men's. Women, more than men, for example, prefer to alternate periods of high sexual activity with periods of almost none, and are somewhat more likely than men to feel and act on bisexual attractions (Mosher et al., 2005).

|| In one British survey, of the 18,876 people contacted, 1 percent were seemingly asexual, having "never felt sexually attracted to anyone at all" (Bogaert, 2004, 2006). ||

|| In one study of self-described heterosexual, bisexual, and homosexual men, those who described themselves as bisexual responded as did homosexual men—with genital arousal primarily to same-sex erotic stimuli (Rieger et al., 2005). They also exhibit interests and traits more like gay than heterosexual men (Lippa, 2005). ||

|| Personal values affect sexual orientation less than they affect other forms of sexual behavior. Compared with people who rarely attend religious services, for example, those who attend regularly are one-third as likely to have cohabited before marriage, and they report having had many fewer sex partners. But (if male) they are just as likely to be homosexual (Smith, 1998). ||

In men, a high sex drive is associated with increased attraction to women (if heterosexual) or men (if homosexual). In women, a high sex drive is associated with increased attraction to both men and women (Lippa, 2006, 2007). When shown pictures of heterosexual couples, in either erotic or nonerotic contexts, heterosexual men look mostly at the woman while heterosexual women look more equally at both the man and the woman (Lykins et al., 2008). And when shown sexually explicit film clips, men's genital and subjective sexual arousal is mostly to preferred sexual stimuli (for heterosexual viewers, depictions of women). Women respond more nonspecifically to depictions of sexual activity involving males or females (Chivers et al., 2007). Baumeister calls this phenomenon the gender difference in *erotic plasticity*.

Origins of Sexual Orientation

If our sexual orientation is indeed something we do not choose and seemingly cannot change (most clearly so for males), then where do these preferences—heterosexual or homosexual—come from? See if you can anticipate the consensus that has emerged from hundreds of research studies by responding *yes* or *no* to the following questions:

1. Is homosexuality linked with problems in a child's relationships with parents, such as with a domineering mother and an ineffectual father, or a possessive mother and a hostile father?
2. Does homosexuality involve a fear or hatred of people of the other gender, leading individuals to direct their sexual desires toward members of their own sex?
3. Is sexual orientation linked with levels of sex hormones currently in the blood?
4. As children, were many homosexuals molested, seduced, or otherwise sexually victimized by an adult homosexual?

The answer to all these questions appears to be *no* (Storms, 1983). In interviews with nearly 1000 homosexuals and 500 heterosexuals, Kinsey Institute investigators assessed nearly every imaginable psychological cause of homosexuality—parental relationships, childhood sexual experiences, peer relationships, dating experiences (Bell et al., 1981; Hammersmith, 1982). Their findings: Homosexuals are no more likely than heterosexuals to have been smothered by maternal love, neglected by their father, or sexually abused. And consider this: If "distant fathers" were more likely to produce homosexual sons, then shouldn't boys growing up in father-absent homes more often be gay? (They are not.) And shouldn't the rising number of such homes have led to a noticeable increase in the gay population? (It has not.)

Homosexual people do, however, appear more often in certain populations. One study (Ludwig, 1995) of the biographies of 1004 eminent people found homosexual and bisexual people overrepresented, especially among poets (24 percent), fiction writers (21 percent), and artists and musicians (15 percent). Gay more than straight men also express interest in occupations that attract many women, such as decorator, florist, and flight attendant (Lippa, 2002). (Given that some 96 percent of men are not gay, most men in such occupations may nevertheless be straight.)

Men who have older brothers are also somewhat more likely to be gay, report Ray Blanchard (1997, 2008) and Anthony Bogaert (2003)—about one-third more likely for each additional older brother. If the odds of homosexuality are roughly 2 percent among first sons, they would rise to nearly 3 percent among second sons, 4 percent for third sons, and so on for each additional older brother (see **FIGURE 38.2**). The reason for this curious phenomenon—the *fraternal birth-order effect*—is unclear. Blanchard suspects a defensive maternal immune response to foreign substances produced by male fetuses. With each pregnancy with a male fetus, the maternal antibodies may become stronger and may prevent the fetus' brain from

‖ Note that the scientific question is not "What causes homosexuality?" (or "What causes heterosexuality?") but "What causes differing sexual orientations?" In pursuit of answers, psychological science compares the backgrounds and physiology of people whose sexual orientations *differ*. ‖

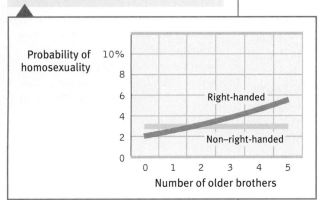

FIGURE 38.2 The fraternal birth-order effect Researcher Ray Blanchard (2008) offers these approximate curves depicting a man's likelihood of homosexuality as a function of his number of older brothers. This correlation has been found in several studies, but only among right-handed men.

developing in a male-typical pattern. Consistent with this biological explanation, the fraternal birth-order effect occurs only in men with older brothers from the same mother (whether reared together or not). Sexual orientation is unaffected by adoptive brothers (Bogaert, 2006). The birth-order effect on sexual orientation is not found among women with older sisters, women who were womb-mates of twin brothers, and men who are not right-handed (Rose et al., 2002).

So, what else might influence sexual orientation? One theory has proposed that people develop same-sex erotic attachments if segregated by gender at the time their sex drive matures (Storms, 1981). Indeed, gay men tend to recall going through puberty somewhat earlier, when peers are more likely to be all males (Bogaert et al., 2002). But even in tribal cultures in which homosexual behavior is expected of all boys before marriage, heterosexuality prevails (Hammack, 2005; Money, 1987). (As this illustrates, homosexual *behavior* does not always indicate a homosexual *orientation*.)

The bottom line from a half-century's theory and research: If there are environmental factors that influence sexual orientation, we do not yet know what they are. This reality has motivated researchers to consider more carefully the possible biological influences on orientation, including evidence of homosexuality in the animal world, and the influences of differing brain centers, genetics, and prenatal hormone exposure.

Same-Sex Attraction in Animals

At Coney Island's New York Aquarium, penguins Wendell and Cass spent several years as devoted same-sex partners. Central Park Zoo penguins Silo and Roy show similar devotion. Biologist Bruce Bagemihl (1999) has identified several hundred species in which at least occasional same-sex relations have been observed. Grizzlies, gorillas, monkeys, flamingos, and owls are all on the long list. Among rams, for example, some 6 to 10 percent—to sheep-breeding ranchers, the "duds"—display same-sex attraction by shunning ewes and seeking to mount other males (Perkins & Fitzgerald, 1997). Some degree of homosexuality seems to be a natural part of the animal world.

Juliet and Juliet Boston's beloved swan couple, "Romeo and Juliet," were discovered actually to be, as are many other animal partners, a same-sex pair.

The Brain and Sexual Orientation

Researcher Simon LeVay (1991) studied sections of the hypothalamus taken from deceased heterosexual and homosexual people. As a gay scientist, LeVay wanted to do "something connected with my gay identity." To avoid biasing the results, he did a *blind study,* not knowing which donors were gay. For nine months he peered through his microscope at a cell cluster he thought might be important. Then, one morning, he broke the codes: One cell cluster was reliably larger in heterosexual men than in women and homosexual men. "I was almost in a state of shock," LeVay said (1994). "I took a walk by myself on the cliffs over the ocean. I sat for half an hour just thinking what this might mean."

It should not surprise us that brains differ with sexual orientation, a finding confirmed by a recent discovery that gay men and straight women have brain hemispheres of similar size, whereas in lesbian women and straight men, the right hemisphere is larger (Savic & Lindström, 2008). Remember our maxim: *Everything psychological is simultaneously biological.* But when do such brain differences begin? At conception? In the womb? During childhood or adolescence? Does experience produce these differences? Or is it genes or prenatal hormones (or genes via prenatal hormones)?

LeVay does not view the hypothalamic center as a sexual orientation center; rather, he sees it as an important part of the neural pathway engaged in sexual behavior. He acknowledges that sexual behavior patterns may influence the brain's anatomy. In

"Gay men simply don't have the brain cells to be attracted to women."

Simon LeVay, *The Sexual Brain,* 1993

fish, birds, rats, and humans, brain structures vary with experience—including sexual experience, reports sex researcher Marc Breedlove (1997). But LeVay believes it more likely that brain anatomy influences sexual orientation. His hunch seems confirmed by the discovery of a similar hypothalamic difference between the 7 to 10 percent of male sheep that display same-sex attraction and the 90+ percent attracted to females (Larkin et al., 2002; Roselli et al., 2002, 2004). Moreover, report University of London psychologists Qazi Rahman and Glenn Wilson (2003), "the neuroanatomical correlates of male homosexuality differentiate very early postnatally, if not prenatally."

Responses to hormone-derived sexual scents also point to a brain difference (Savic et al., 2005). When straight women are given a whiff of a scent derived from men's sweat, their hypothalamus lights up in an area governing sexual arousal. Gay men's brains respond similarly to the men's scent. But straight men's brains show the arousal response only to a female hormone derivative. Gays and lesbians similarly differ from their straight counterparts in other studies of brain responses to sex-related sweat odors and to pictures of male and female faces (Kranz & Ishai, 2006; Martins et al., 2005).

Genes and Sexual Orientation

Are these sexuality-related brain differences genetically influenced? Evidence does indicate a genetic influence on sexual orientation. "First, homosexuality does appear to run in families," note Brian Mustanski and Michael Bailey (2003). "Second, twin studies have established that genes play a substantial role in explaining individual differences in sexual orientation." Identical twins are somewhat more likely than fraternal twins to share a homosexual orientation (Lángström et al., 2008). (Because sexual orientations differ in many identical twin pairs, especially female twins, we know that other factors besides genes are at work.)

Experimenters have also, by genetic manipulations, created female fruit flies that during courtship act like males (pursuing other females) and males that act like females (Demir & Dickson, 2005). "We have shown that a single gene in the fruit fly is sufficient to determine all aspects of the flies' sexual orientation and behavior," explained Barry Dickson (2005). With humans, it's likely that multiple genes, possibly in interaction with other influences, shape sexual orientation. One study financed by the U.S. National Institutes of Health is analyzing the genes of more than 1000 gay brothers in search of such genetic markers.

Researchers have speculated about possible reasons why "gay genes" might exist. Given that same-sex couples cannot naturally reproduce, how could such genes have survived in the human gene pool? One possible answer is kin selection. Evolutionary psychologists remind us that many of our genes also reside in our biological relatives. Perhaps, then, gay people's genes live on through their supporting the survival and reproductive success of their nieces, nephews, and other relatives (who also carry many of the same genes). Or perhaps, as now seems more likely, maternal genetics is at work (Bocklandt et al., 2006). Recent Italian studies (Camperio-Ciani et al., 2004, 2008) confirm what others have found—that homosexual men have more homosexual relatives on their mother's side than on their father's. And, compared with the maternal relatives of heterosexual men, the maternal relatives of homosexual men produce more offspring. Perhaps, surmise the researchers, the genes that make women more likely to have children (such as by strongly attracting them to men) also produce sons and nephews who are attracted to men.

Prenatal Hormones and Sexual Orientation

Elevated rates of homosexual orientation in identical *and* fraternal twins suggest that not just shared genetics but also a shared prenatal environment may be a factor. In animals and some exceptional human cases, abnormal prenatal hormone conditions have altered a fetus' sexual orientation. German researcher Gunter Dorner (1976, 1988) pioneered

"Studies indicate that male homosexuality is more likely to be transmitted from the mother's side of the family."

Robert Plomin, John DeFries, Gerald McClearn, and Michael Rutter, *Behavioral Genetics*, 1997

"Modern scientific research indicates that sexual orientation is . . . partly determined by genetics, but more specifically by hormonal activity in the womb."

Glenn Wilson and Qazi Rahman, *Born Gay: The Psychobiology of Sex Orientation*, 2005

research on the influence of prenatal hormones by manipulating a fetal rat's exposure to male hormones, thereby "inverting" its sexual orientation. In other studies, when pregnant sheep were injected with testosterone during a critical period of fetal development, their female offspring later showed homosexual behavior (Money, 1987).

A critical period for the human brain's neural-hormonal control system may exist between the middle of the second and fifth months after conception (Ellis & Ames, 1987; Gladue, 1990; Meyer-Bahlburg, 1995). Exposure to the hormone levels typically experienced by female fetuses during this time appears to predispose the person (whether female or male) to be attracted to males in later life.

On several traits, gays and lesbians appear to fall midway between straight females and males (**TABLE 38.1**). For example, lesbians' cochlea and hearing systems develop in a way that is intermediate between those of heterosexual females and heterosexual males, which seems attributable to prenatal hormonal influence (McFadden, 2002). Fingerprint ridge counts may also differ. Although most people have more fingerprint ridges on their right hand than on their left, some studies find a greater right-left difference in heterosexual males than in females and gay males (Hall & Kimura, 1994; Mustanski et al., 2002; Sanders et al., 2002). Given that fingerprint ridges are complete by the sixteenth fetal week, this difference may be due to prenatal hormones. Prenatal hormones also are a possible explanation for why data from 20 studies revealed that "homosexual participants had 39 percent greater odds of being non–right-handed" (Lalumière et al., 2000).

TABLE 38.1 Biological Correlates of Sexual Orientation

On average (the evidence is strongest for males), various biological and behavioral traits of gays and lesbians fall between those of straight men and straight women. Tentative findings—some in need of replication—include these:

Brain differences

- Brain asymmetry is greater in straight men and lesbian women.
- One hypothalamic cell cluster is larger in straight men than in women and gay men; same difference is found in male sheep displaying other-sex versus same-sex attraction.
- Gay men's hypothalamus reacts as does a straight woman's to the smell of sex-related hormones.

Genetic influences

- Shared sexual orientation is higher among identical twins than among fraternal twins.
- Sexual attraction in fruit flies can be genetically manipulated.

Prenatal hormonal influences

- Altered prenatal hormone exposure may lead to homosexuality in humans and other animals.
- Right-handed men with several older biological brothers are more likely to be gay.

These brain differences and genetic and prenatal influences may contribute to observed gay-straight differences in

- spatial abilities.
- fingerprint ridge counts.
- auditory system development.
- handedness.
- occupational preferences.
- relative finger lengths.
- gender nonconformity.
- age of onset of puberty in males.
- male body size.
- sleep length.
- physical aggression.
- male eating disorders.

Another you-never-would-have-guessed-it gay-straight difference appears in studies showing that gay men's spatial abilities resemble those typical of straight women (Cohen, 2002; Gladue, 1994; McCormick & Witelson, 1991; Sanders & Wright, 1997). On mental rotation tasks such as the one illustrated in **FIGURE 38.3**, straight men tend to outscore women. Studies by Qazi Rahman and colleagues (2003, 2008) find that, as on a number of other measures, the scores of gays and lesbians fall between those of heterosexual males and females. But straight women and gays both outperform straight men at remembering objects' spatial locations in tasks like those found in memory games (Hassan & Rahman, 2007).

Because the physiological evidence is preliminary and controversial, some scientists remain skeptical. Rather than specifying sexual orientation, they suggest, biological factors may predispose a *temperament* that influences sexuality "in the context of individual learning and experience" (Byne & Parsons, 1993). Daryl Bem (1996, 1998, 2000) has theorized that genes code for prenatal hormones and brain anatomy, which predispose temperaments that lead children to prefer gender-typical or gender-atypical activities and friends. These preferences may later lead children to feel attracted to whichever sex feels different from their own. The dissimilar-seeming sex (whether or not it conforms to one's own anatomy) becomes associated with anxiety and other forms of arousal, which are eventually transformed into romantic arousal. The exotic becomes erotic.

Regardless of the process, the consistency of the brain, genetic, and prenatal findings has swung the pendulum toward a biological explanation of sexual orientation (Rahman & Wilson, 2003). This helps explain why sexual orientation is so difficult to change, and why a BBC Internet study of more than 200,000 people found the same gay-straight differences in personality and interests worldwide (Lippa, 2007a,b, 2008).

Still, some people wonder: Should the cause of sexual orientation matter? Perhaps it shouldn't, but people's assumptions matter. Those who believe—as do 41 percent of Americans (up from 13 percent in 1977 [Gallup Polls]) and most gays and lesbians— that sexual orientation is biologically disposed also express more accepting attitudes toward homosexual people (Allen et al., 1996; Haslam & Levy, 2006; Kaiser, 2001; Whitley, 1990).

To gay and lesbian activists, the new biological research is a double-edged sword (Diamond, 1993). If sexual orientation, like skin color and sex, is genetically influenced, that offers a further rationale for civil rights protection. Moreover, it may

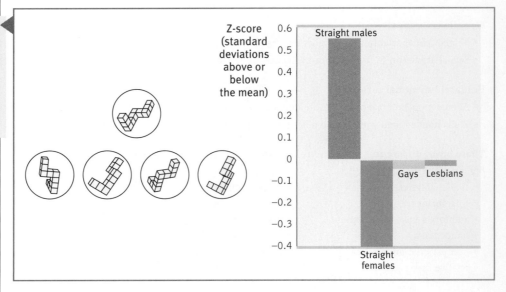

FIGURE 38.3 Spatial abilities and sexual orientation Which of the four figures can be rotated to match the target figure at the top? Straight males tend to find this an easier task than do straight females, with gays and lesbians intermediate. (From Rahman et al., 2003, with 60 people tested in each group.)

alleviate parents' concerns about their children being unduly influenced by gay teachers and role models. At the same time, this research raises the troubling possibility that genetic markers of sexual orientation could someday be identified through fetal testing, and a fetus could be aborted simply for being predisposed to an unwanted orientation.

▶‖ Sex and Human Values

38-6   Is scientific research on sexual motivation value free?

Recognizing that values are both personal and cultural, most sex researchers and educators strive to keep their writings on sexual behavior and its motivation value free. But the very words we use to describe behavior can reflect our personal values. Whether we label certain sexual behaviors as "perversions" or as part of an "alternative sexual life-style" depends on our attitude toward the behaviors. Labels describe, but they also evaluate.

Sex education separated from the context of human values may also give some students the idea that sexual intercourse is simply a recreational activity. Diana Baumrind (1982), a University of California child-rearing expert, has observed that an implication that adults are neutral about adolescent sexual activity is unfortunate, because "promiscuous recreational sex poses certain psychological, social, health, and moral problems that must be faced realistically."

Perhaps we can agree that the knowledge provided by sex research is preferable to ignorance, and yet also agree that researchers' values should be stated openly, enabling us to debate them and to reflect on our own values. We should remember that scientific research on sexual motivation does not aim to define the personal meaning of sex in our own lives. You could know every available fact about sex—that the initial spasms of male and female orgasm come at 0.8-second intervals, that the female nipples expand 10 millimeters at the peak of sexual arousal, that systolic blood pressure rises some 60 points and the respiration rate to 40 breaths per minute—but fail to understand the human significance of sexual intimacy.

Surely one significance of sexual intimacy is its expression of our profoundly social nature. Sex is a socially significant act. Men and women can achieve orgasm alone, yet most people find greater satisfaction—and experience a much greater surge in the prolactin hormone associated with sexual satisfaction and satiety—after intercourse and orgasm with their loved one (Brody & Tillmann, 2005). With the satisfaction of intimacy and relationship surpassing the satisfaction of self-stimulation, there is a yearning for closeness in sexual motivation. Sex at its human best is life-uniting and love-renewing.

▶‖ The Need to Belong

38-7   What evidence points to our human need to belong?

Separated from friends or family—isolated in prison, alone at a new school, living in a foreign land—most people feel keenly their lost connections with important others. We are what Aristotle called *the social animal.* "Without friends," wrote Aristotle in his *Nichomachean Ethics,* "no one would choose to live, though he had all other goods." We have a need to affiliate with others, even to become strongly attached to certain others in enduring, close relationships. Human beings, contended the personality theorist Alfred Adler, have an "urge to community" (Ferguson, 1989, 2001). Roy Baumeister and Mark Leary (1995) have assembled evidence for this deep *need to belong.*

A sharing of love For most adults, a sexual relationship fulfills not only a biological motive but also a social need for intimacy.

Aiding Survival

Social bonds boosted our ancestors' survival rate. By keeping children close to their caregivers, attachments served as a powerful survival impulse. As adults, those who formed attachments were more likely to reproduce and to co-nurture their offspring to maturity. To be "wretched" literally means, in its Middle English origin (*wrecche*), to be without kin nearby.

Survival also was enhanced by cooperation. In solo combat, our ancestors were not the toughest predators. But as hunters, they learned that six hands were better than two. As foragers, they gained protection from predators and enemies by traveling in groups. Those who felt a need to belong survived and reproduced most successfully, and their genes now predominate. We are innately social creatures. People in every society on Earth belong to groups and prefer and favor "us" over "them."

Do you have close friends—people with whom you freely disclose your ups and downs? People who feel supported by close relationships are not only happier, they also live with better health and at lower risk for psychological disorder and premature death than do those who lack social support. Married people, for example, are less at risk for depression, suicide, and early death than are unattached people.

Wanting to Belong

The need to belong colors our thoughts and emotions. We spend a great deal of time thinking about actual and hoped-for relationships. When relationships form, we often feel joy. Falling in mutual love, people have been known to feel their cheeks ache from their irrepressible grins. Asked, "What is necessary for your happiness?" or "What is it that makes your life meaningful?" most people mention—before anything else—close, satisfying relationships with family, friends, or romantic partners (Berscheid, 1985). Happiness hits close to home.

Pause a moment to consider: What was your most satisfying moment in the past week? Kennon Sheldon and his colleagues (2001) asked that question of American and South Korean collegians, then asked them to rate how much this peak experience had satisfied various needs. In both countries, the satisfaction of self-esteem and relatedness-belonging needs were the top two contributors to the peak moment. Another study found that *very* happy university students are not distinguished by their money but by their "rich and satisfying close relationships" (Diener & Seligman, 2002). The need to belong runs deeper, it seems, than any need to be rich. When our need for relatedness is satisfied in balance with two other basic psychological needs—*autonomy* and *competence*—the result is a deep sense of well-being (Deci & Ryan, 2002; Patrick et al., 2007; Sheldon & Niemiec, 2006). To feel connected, free, and capable is to enjoy a good life.

South Africans have a word for the human bonds that define us all. *Ubuntu* (oo-BOON-too), explained Desmond Tutu (1999), expresses the fact that "my humanity is caught up, is inextricably bound up, in yours." A Zulu maxim captures the idea: *Umuntu ngumuntu ngabantu*—"a person is a person through other persons."

When we feel included, accepted, and loved by those important to us, our self-esteem rides high. Indeed, say Mark Leary and his colleagues (1998), self-esteem is a gauge of how valued and accepted we feel. Much of our social behavior therefore aims to increase our belonging—our social acceptance and inclusion. To avoid rejection, we generally conform to group standards and seek to make favorable impressions. To win friendship and esteem, we monitor our behavior, hoping to create the right impressions. Seeking love and belonging, we spend billions on clothes, cosmetics, and diet and fitness aids—all motivated by our quest for acceptance. Two-thirds of entering American collegians report spending one to five or more hours per week on social networking sites such as Facebook and MySpace (Pryor et al., 2007).

"The only thing that really matters in life are your relationships to other people." George Vaillant, 2009, when asked what he had learned from his study following 238 Harvard University men from the 1930s to the end of their lives.

Separation amplifies the felt need to belong In the film *Cast Away*, Chuck Noland (played by Tom Hanks) combats social starvation by talking with his girlfriend's snapshot and a volleyball he names Wilson.

20TH Century Fox/Dreamworks/The Kobal Collection

Like sexual motivation, which feeds both love and exploitation, the need to belong feeds both deep attachments and menacing threats. Out of our need to define a "we" come loving families, faithful friendships, and team spirit, but also teen gangs, ethnic rivalries, and fanatic nationalism.

Sustaining Relationships

For most of us, familiarity breeds liking, not contempt. Thrown together in groups at school, at summer camp, on a vacation cruise, we later resist breaking those social bonds— we promise to call, to write, to come back for reunions. Parting, we feel distress. You don't need to look far to see people spending hours on smart phones and computers, sustaining their relationships with absent people by talking, text messaging, and e-mailing.

The need to connect Six days a week, women from the Philippines work as "domestic helpers" in 154,000 Hong Kong households. On Sundays, they throng to the central business district to picnic, dance, sing, talk, and laugh. "Humanity could stage no greater display of happiness," reported one observer (*Economist,* 2001).

When the fear of being alone seems worse than the pain of emotional or physical abuse, attachments can keep people in abusive relationships. Even when bad relationships break, people suffer. After separations, feelings of loneliness and anger— and sometimes even a strange desire to be near the former partner—linger. In one 16-nation survey, and repeated in U.S. surveys, separated and divorced people have been half as likely as married people to say they were "very happy" (Inglehart, 1990; NORC, 2007).

Our fear of being alone has some basis in reality. Children who move through a series of foster homes, with repeated disruption of budding attachments, may come to have difficulty forming deep attachments. And children reared in institutions without a sense of belonging to anyone, or locked away at home under extreme neglect, become pathetic creatures—withdrawn, frightened, speechless.

When something threatens or dissolves our social ties, negative emotions—anxiety, loneliness, jealousy, guilt—overwhelm us. The bereaved often feel life is empty, pointless. Even the first weeks living on a college campus away from home can be distressing. For immigrants and refugees moving alone to new places, the stress and loneliness can be depressing. But if feelings of acceptance and connection build, so do self-esteem, positive feelings, and desires to help rather than hurt others (Buckley & Leary, 2001). After years of placing individual refugee and immigrant families in isolated communities, U.S. policies today encourage *chain migration* (Pipher, 2002). The second refugee Sudanese family settling in a town generally has an easier adjustment than the first.

The Pain of Ostracism

Sometimes, though, the need to belong is denied. Perhaps you can recall such a time, when you felt excluded or ignored or shunned. Perhaps you received the silent treatment. Perhaps others avoided you, or averted their eyes in your presence, or even mocked you behind your back.

Social psychologist Kipling Williams (2007) and his colleagues have studied such experiences of *ostracism*—of social exclusion—in both natural and laboratory settings. Worldwide, humans control social behavior via the punishing effects of severe ostracism—of exile, imprisonment, and solitary confinement. For children, even a brief time-out in isolation can be punishing. Asked to describe personal episodes that made them feel especially good about themselves, people often think of some achievement. But asked what made them feel especially *bad* about themselves, they will—about four times in five—describe a relationship difficulty (Pillemer et al., 2007).

A violent response to social exclusion Most socially excluded teens do not commit violence, but some do. Charles "Andy" Williams, described by a classmate as someone his peers derided as "freak, dork, nerd, stuff like that," went on a shooting spree at his suburban California high school, killing 2 and wounding 13 (Bowles & Kasindorf, 2001).

|| Note: The researchers later debriefed and reassured the participants. ||

To be shunned—given the cold shoulder or the silent treatment, with others' eyes avoiding yours—is to have one's need to belong threatened (Williams & Zadro, 2001). "It's the meanest thing you can do to someone, especially if you know they can't fight back. I never should have been born," said Lea, a lifelong victim of the silent treatment by her mother and grandmother. Like Lea, people often respond to social ostracism with depressed moods, initial efforts to restore their acceptance, and then withdrawal. After two years of silent treatment by his employer, Richard reported, "I came home every night and cried. I lost 25 pounds, had no self-esteem and felt that I wasn't worthy."

To experience ostracism is to experience real pain, as Kipling Williams and his colleagues were surprised to discover in their studies of *cyber-ostracism* (Gonsalkorale & Williams, 2006). (Perhaps you can recall the feeling of being ignored in a chat room or having an e-mail go unanswered.) Such ostracism, they discovered, even by strangers or by a despised outgroup, such as the Australian branch of the KKK, takes a toll: It elicits increased activity in a brain area, the *anterior cingulate cortex,* that also activates in response to physical pain (Eisenberger et al., 2003). Psychologically, we seem to experience social pain with the same emotional unpleasantness that marks physical pain (MacDonald & Leary, 2005). And pain, whatever its source, focuses our attention and motivates corrective action.

Rejected and unable to remedy the situation, people may seek new friends—or they may turn nasty. In a series of experiments, Jean Twenge and her collaborators (2001, 2002, 2007; Baumeister et al., 2002; Maner et al., 2007) told some students (who had taken a personality test) that they were "the type likely to end up alone later in life," or that people they had met didn't want them in a group that was forming. They told other students that they would have "rewarding relationships throughout life," or that "everyone chose you as someone they'd like to work with." Those excluded became much more likely to engage in self-defeating behaviors and to underperform on aptitude tests. The rejection also interfered with their empathy for others and made them more likely to act in disparaging or aggressive ways against those who had excluded them (blasting them with noise, for example). "If intelligent, well-adjusted, successful university students can turn aggressive in response to a small laboratory experience of social exclusion," noted the research team, "it is disturbing to imagine the aggressive tendencies that might arise from a series of important rejections or chronic exclusion from desired groups in actual social life." Indeed, reports Williams (2007), ostracism "weaves through case after case of school violence."

REVIEW

Sexual Motivation and the Need to Belong

38-1 **What stages mark the human sexual response cycle?** Masters and Johnson described four stages in the human *sexual response cycle:* excitement, plateau, orgasm (which seems to involve similar feelings and brain activity in males and females), and resolution. During the resolution phase, males experience a *refractory period,* during which renewed arousal and orgasm are impossible. *Sexual disorders* (problems that consistently impair sexual arousal or functioning) can be successfully treated, often by behaviorally oriented therapy or drug therapy.

38-2 **Do hormones influence human sexual motivation?** The female *estrogen* and male *testosterone* hormones influence human sexual behavior less directly than they influence nonhuman animals. Unlike other mammalian females, women's sexuality is more responsive to testosterone level than to estrogen level. Short-term shifts in testosterone level are normal in men, partly in response to stimulation.

38-3 **How do internal and external stimuli influence sexual motivation?** Erotic material and other external stimuli can trigger sexual arousal in both men and women, although the activated brain areas differ somewhat. Men respond more specifically to sexual depictions involving their preferred sex. Sexually explicit material may lead people to perceive their partners as comparatively less appealing and to devalue their relationships. Sexually coercive material tends to increase viewers' acceptance of rape and violence toward women. Fantasies (imagined stimuli) also influence sexual arousal.

38-4 **What factors influence teen pregnancy and risk of sexually transmitted infections?** Rates of teen intercourse vary from culture to culture and era to era. Factors contributing to teen pregnancy include ignorance; minimal communication about contraception with parents, partners, and peers; guilt related to sexual activity; alcohol use; and mass media norms of unprotected and impulsive sexuality. STIs—sexually transmitted infections—have spread rapidly. Attempts to protect teens through comprehensive sex-education programs include contraceptive and abstinence education. High intelligence, religiosity, father presence, and participation in service learning programs are predictors of teen sexual restraint.

38-5 **What has research taught us about sexual orientation?** Surveys can tell us how many people (about 3 percent) are attracted to their own sex, but statistics cannot decide issues of human rights. There is no evidence that environmental influences deter-

mine *sexual orientation.* Evidence of biological influences may include the presence of same-sex behaviors in many animal species, straight-gay differences in body and brain characteristics, higher rates in certain families and in identical twins, and exposure to certain hormones during critical periods of prenatal development.

38-6 **Is scientific research on sexual motivation value free?** Scientific research on sexual motivation does not attempt to define the personal meaning of sex in our lives, but sex research and education are not value-free.

38-7 **What evidence points to our human need to belong?** Our need to affiliate or belong—to feel connected and identified with others—had survival value for our ancestors' chances, which may explain why humans in every society live in groups. Societies everywhere control behavior with the threat of ostracism—excluding or shunning others. When socially excluded, people may engage in self-defeating behaviors (performing below their ability) or in antisocial behaviors.

Terms and Concepts to Remember

sexual response cycle, p. 466	estrogens, p. 467
refractory period, p. 467	testosterone, p. 467
sexual disorder, p. 467	sexual orientation, p. 472

Test Yourself

1. What biological and psychological factors influence our sexual motivation and affiliation needs?

(Answers to the Test Yourself questions can be found in Appendix B at the end of the book.)

Ask Yourself

1. What do you think would be an effective strategy for reducing teen pregnancy?

2. Have there been times when you felt "out of the loop" with family and friends, or even ostracized by them? How did you respond?

∞ WEB

Multiple-choice self-tests and more may be found at www.worthpublishers.com/myers

MODULE 39

Motivation at Work

The healthy life, said Sigmund Freud, is filled by love and by work. For most of us, work is life's biggest single waking activity. To live is to work. Work helps satisfy several levels of need. Work supports us. Work connects us. Work defines us. Meeting someone for the first time, and wondering "Who are you?" we may ask, "So, what do you do?"

If we feel dissatisfied with our work-related pay, relationships, or identity, we may change where or for whom we work, as 16 percent of Australians did in just the year 2000 (Trewin, 2001). Most people therefore have neither a single vocation nor a predictable career path. Two decades from now, most of you reading this book will be doing work you cannot now imagine. To prepare you and others for this unknown future, many colleges and universities focus less on training your job skills and more on enlarging your capacities for understanding, thinking, and communicating in any work environment.

Amy Wrzesniewski and her colleagues (1997, 2001) have identified person-to-person variations in people's attitudes toward their work. Across various occupations, some people view their work as a *job*, an unfulfilling but necessary way to make money. Others view their work as a *career*, an opportunity to advance from one position to a better position. The rest—those who view their work as a *calling*, a fulfilling and socially useful activity—report the highest satisfaction with their work and with their lives.

This finding would not surprise Mihaly Csikszentmihalyi (1990, 1999), who has observed that people's quality of life increases when they are purposefully engaged. Between the anxiety of being overwhelmed and stressed, and the apathy of being underwhelmed and bored, lies a zone in which people experience **flow.** Csikszentmihalyi (chick-SENT-me-hi) formulated the flow concept after studying artists who spent hour after hour painting or sculpting with enormous concentration. Immersed in a project, they worked as if nothing else mattered, and then, when finished, they promptly forgot about it. The artists seemed driven less by the external rewards of producing art—money, praise, promotion—than by the intrinsic rewards of creating the work. Internet-related distractions can disrupt such flow. It takes time to refocus mental concentration after the distraction of an e-mail or instant message. Thus, Microsoft is developing an *attentional user interface* that aims to "detect when users are available for communication, or when the user is in a state of flow" (Ullman, 2005).

Csikszentmihalyi's later observations—of dancers, chess players, surgeons, writers, parents, mountain climbers, sailors, and farmers; of Australians, North Americans, Koreans, Japanese, and Italians; of people from their teens to their golden years—confirmed an overriding principle: It's exhilarating to flow with an activity that fully engages our skills. Flow experiences boost our sense of self-esteem, competence, and well-being. When the researchers beeped people at random intervals and asked them to report what they were doing and how much they were enjoying themselves, those who were vegetating usually reported little sense of flow and little satisfaction. People reported more positive feelings when interrupted while doing something active, something that engaged their skills, be it play or work. Other research indicates that in almost every industrialized nation, people have reported markedly lower well-being if unemployed (**FIGURE 39.1**). Idleness may sound like bliss, but purposeful work enriches our lives.

‖ Sometimes, notes Gene Weingarten (2002), a humor writer knows "when to just get out of the way." Here are some sample job titles from the U.S. Department of Labor *Dictionary of Occupational Titles:* Animal impersonator, human projectile, banana ripening-room supervisor, impregnator, impregnator helper, dope sprayer, finger waver, rug scratcher, egg smeller, bottom buffer, cookie breaker, brain picker, hand pouncer, bosom presser, and mother repairer. ‖

‖ Have you ever noticed that when you are immersed in an activity, time flies? And that when you are watching the clock, it seems to move more slowly? French researchers have confirmed that the more we attend to an event's duration, the longer it seems to last (Couli et al., 2004). ‖

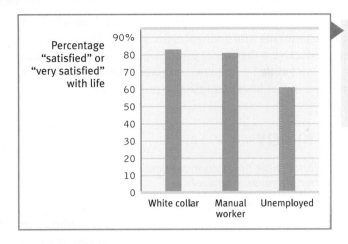

FIGURE 39.1 The bane of unemployment To want work but not have it is to feel less satisfied with life. These data are from 169,776 adults in 16 nations (Inglehart, 1990).

flow a completely involved, focused state of consciousness, with diminished awareness of self and time, resulting from optimal engagement of one's skills.

industrial-organizational (I/O) psychology the application of psychological concepts and methods to optimizing human behavior in workplaces.

personnel psychology a subfield of I/O psychology that focuses on employee recruitment, selection, placement, training, appraisal, and development.

In industrialized nations, work has been changing, from farming to manufacturing to *knowledge work*. More and more work is *outsourced* to temporary employees and consultants who communicate electronically from virtual workplaces in remote locations. (This book and its teaching package are developed and produced by a team of people in a dozen cities, from Alaska to Florida.) As work changes, will our attitudes toward our work also change? Will our satisfaction with work increase or decrease? Will the *psychological contract*—the subjective sense of mutual obligations between workers and employers—become more or less trusting and secure? These are among the questions that fascinate psychologists who study work-related behavior.

Industrial-organizational (I/O) psychology is a fast-growing profession that applies psychology's principles to the workplace (see Close-Up: I/O Psychology at Work). One of its subfields, *human factors psychology*, explores how machines and environments can be optimally designed to fit human abilities. Here we consider two other subfields: **personnel psychology,** which applies psychology's methods and

---

CLOSE-UP

I/O Psychology at Work

As scientists, consultants, and management professionals, industrial-organizational psychologists are found working in varied areas:

Personnel Psychology
Selecting and placing employees

- Developing and validating assessment tools for selecting, placing, and promoting workers
- Analyzing job content
- Optimizing worker placement

Training and developing employees

- Identifying needs

- Designing training programs
- Evaluating training programs

Appraising performance

- Developing criteria
- Measuring individual performance
- Measuring organizational performance

Organizational Psychology
Developing organizations

- Analyzing organizational structures
- Maximizing worker satisfaction and productivity
- Facilitating organizational change

Enhancing quality of worklife

- Expanding individual productivity
- Identifying elements of satisfaction
- Redesigning jobs

Human Factors (Engineering) Psychology

- Designing optimum work environments
- Optimizing person-machine interactions
- Developing systems technologies

Source: Adapted from the Society of Industrial and Organizational Psychology (www.siop.org).

organizational psychology a subfield of I/O psychology that examines organizational influences on worker satisfaction and productivity and facilitates organizational change.

principles to selecting and evaluating workers, and **organizational psychology,** which considers how work environments and management styles influence worker motivation, satisfaction, and productivity. Personnel psychologists match people with jobs, by identifying and placing well-suited candidates. Organizational psychologists modify jobs and supervision in ways that boost morale and productivity.

▶‖ Personnel Psychology

39-1 How do personnel psychologists help organizations with employee selection, work placement, and performance appraisal?

Psychologists can assist organizations at various stages of selecting and assessing employees. They may help identify needed job skills, decide upon selection methods, recruit and evaluate applicants, introduce and train new employees, and appraise their performance.

Harnessing Strengths

As a new AT&T human resource executive, psychologist Mary Tenopyr (1997) was assigned to solve a problem: Customer service representatives were failing at a high rate. After concluding that many of the hires were ill-matched to the demands of their new job, Tenopyr developed a new selection instrument:

1. She asked new applicants to respond to various questions (without as yet making any use of their responses).
2. She followed up later to assess which of the applicants excelled on the job.
3. She identified the individual items on the earlier test that best predicted who would succeed.

The happy result of her data-driven work was a new test that enabled AT&T to identify likely-to-succeed customer representatives. Personnel selection techniques such as this one aim to match people's strengths with work that enables them and their organization to flourish. Marry the strengths of people with the tasks of organizations and the result is often prosperity and profit.

Your strengths are any enduring qualities that can be productively applied. Are you naturally curious? Persuasive? Charming? Persistent? Competitive? Analytical? Empathic? Organized? Articulate? Neat? Mechanical? Any such trait, if matched with suitable work, can function as a strength (Buckingham, 2007). (See Close-Up: Discovering Your Strengths.)

Gallup researchers Marcus Buckingham and Donald Clifton (2001) have argued that the first step to a stronger organization is instituting a strengths-based selection system. Thus, as a manager, you would first identify a group of the most effective people in any role—the ones you would want to hire more of—and compare their strengths with those of a group of the least effective people in that role. In defining these groups, you would try to measure performance as objectively as possible. In one Gallup study of more than 5000 telecommunications customer-service representatives, those evaluated most favorably by their managers were strong in "harmony" and "responsibility," while those actually rated most effective by customers were strong in energy, assertiveness, and eagerness to learn.

An example: if you needed to hire new people in software development, and you had discovered that your best software developers are analytical, disciplined, and eager to learn, you would focus employment ads less on experience than on the identified strengths: "Do you take a logical and systematic approach to problem solving [*analytical*]? Are you a perfectionist who strives for timely completion of

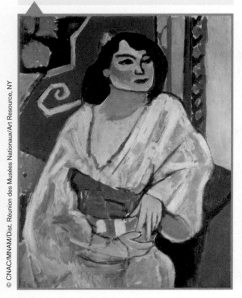

Artistic strengths At age 21, Henri Matisse was a sickly and often depressed lawyer's clerk. When his mother gave him a box of paints to cheer him up one day, he felt the darkness lift and his energy surge. He began to fill his days with painting and drawing and went on to art school and a life as one of the world's great painters. For Matisse, doing art felt like "a comfortable armchair." That is how exercising our strengths often feels.

Discovering Your Strengths

You can use some of the techniques personnel psychologists have developed to identify your own strengths and pinpoint types of work that will likely prove satisfying and successful. Buckingham and Clifton (2001) have suggested asking yourself:

- What activities give me pleasure? (Bringing order out of chaos? Playing host? Helping others? Challenging sloppy thinking?)

- What activities leave me wondering, "When can I do this again?" (Rather than "When will this be over?")

- What sorts of challenges do I relish? (And which do I dread?)

- What sorts of tasks do I learn easily? (And which do I struggle with?)

Some people find themselves in flow—their skills engaged and time flying—when teaching or selling or writing or cleaning or consoling or creating or repairing. If an activity feels good, if it comes easily, if you look forward to it, then look deeper and see your strengths at work.

Satisfied and successful people devote far less time to correcting their deficiencies than to accentuating their strengths. Top performers are "rarely well rounded," Buckingham and Clifton found (p. 26). Instead, they have sharpened their existing skills. Given the persistence of our traits and temperaments, we should focus not on our deficiencies, but rather on identifying and employing our talents. There may be limits to the benefits of assertiveness training if you are shy, for public speaking courses if you tend to be nervous and soft-spoken, or for drawing classes if you express your artistic side in stick figures.

But identifying your talents can help you recognize the activities you learn quickly and find absorbing. Knowing your strengths, you can develop them further.

As Robert Louis Stevenson said in *Familiar Studies of Men and Books* (1882), "To be what we are, and to become what we are capable of becoming, is the only end of life."

your projects *[disciplined]*? Do you want to learn to use Java, C++, and PHP *[eager to learn]*? If you can say *yes* to these questions, then please call . . ."

Identifying people's strengths and matching strengths to work is a first step toward workplace effectiveness. To assess applicants' strengths and decide who is best-suited to the job, personnel managers use various tools (Sackett & Lievens, 2008), including ability tests, personality tests, and behavioral observations in "assessment centers" that simulate job tasks. Here we focus on job interviews.

Do Interviews Predict Performance?

Interviewers tend to feel confident in their ability to predict long-term job performance from an unstructured, get-acquainted interview. What's therefore shocking is how error-prone those predictions are. Whether predicting job or graduate school success, interviewers' judgments are weak predictors. From their review of 85 years of personnel-selection research, I/O psychologists Frank Schmidt and John Hunter (1998; Schmidt, 2002) determined that for all but less-skilled jobs, general mental ability best predicts on-the-job performance. Subjective overall evaluations from informal interviews are more useful than handwriting analysis (which is worthless). But informal interviews are less informative than aptitude tests, work samples, job knowledge tests, and past job performance. If there's a contest between what our gut tells us about someone and what test scores, work samples, and past performance tell us, we should distrust our gut.

The Interviewer Illusion

Interviewers often overrate their discernment, a phenomenon psychologist Richard Nisbett (1987) has labeled the *interviewer illusion*. "I have excellent interviewing skills, so I don't need reference checking as much as someone who doesn't have my ability to read people," is a comment sometimes heard by I/O consultants. Four factors explain this gap between interviewers' intuition and the resulting reality:

"Interviews are a terrible predictor of performance."

Laszlo Bock, Google's Vice President, People Operations, 2007

"Between the idea and reality . . . falls the shadow."

T. S. Eliot, *The Hollow Men,* 1925

▶ *Interviews disclose the interviewee's good intentions, which are less revealing than habitual behaviors* (Ouellette & Wood, 1998). Intentions matter. People can change. But the best predictor of the person we will be is the person we have been. Wherever we go, we take ourselves along.

▶ *Interviewers more often follow the successful careers of those they have hired than the successful careers of those they have rejected and lost track of.* This missing feedback prevents interviewers from getting a reality check on their hiring ability.

▶ *Interviewers presume that people are what they seem to be in the interview situation.* When meeting others, we discount the enormous influence of varying situations and mistakenly presume that what we see is what we will get. But mountains of research on everything from chattiness to conscientiousness reveal that how we behave reflects not only our enduring traits, but also the details of the particular situation (such as wanting to impress in a job interview).

▶ *Interviewers' preconceptions and moods color how they perceive interviewees' responses* (Cable & Gilovich, 1998; Macan & Dipboye, 1994). If interviewers instantly like a person who perhaps is similar to themselves, they may interpret the person's assertiveness as indicating "confidence" rather than "arrogance." If told certain applicants have been prescreened, interviewers are disposed to judge them more favorably.

Traditional *unstructured interviews* do provide a sense of someone's personality—their expressiveness, warmth, and verbal ability, for example. But this information reveals less about the person's behavior toward others in different situations than most people suppose. Hoping to improve prediction and selection, personnel psychologists have put people in simulated work situations, scoured sources for information on past performance, aggregated evaluations from multiple interviews, administered tests, and developed job-specific interviews.

Structured Interviews

Unlike casual conversation aimed at getting a feel for someone, **structured interviews** offer a disciplined method of collecting information. A personnel psychologist may analyze a job, script questions, and train interviewers. The interviewers then put the same questions, in the same order, to all applicants, and rate each applicant on established scales.

In an unstructured interview, someone might ask, "How organized are you?" "How well do you get along with people?" or "How do you handle stress?" Street-smart applicants know how to score high: "Although I sometimes drive myself too hard, I handle stress by prioritizing and delegating, and by making sure I leave time for sleep and exercise."

By contrast, structured interviews pinpoint strengths (attitudes, behaviors, knowledge, and skills) that distinguish high performers in a particular line of work. The process includes outlining job-specific situations and asking candidates to explain how they would handle them, and how they handled similar situations in their prior employment. "Tell me about a time when you were caught between conflicting demands, without time to accomplish both. How did you handle that?"

To reduce memory distortions and bias, the interviewer takes notes and makes ratings as the interview proceeds and avoids irrelevant and follow-up questions. The structured interview therefore feels less warm, but that can be explained to the applicant: "This conversation won't typify how we relate to each other in this organization."

A review of 150 findings revealed that structured interviews had double the predictive accuracy of unstructured seat-of-the-pants interviews (Schmidt & Hunter, 1998; Wiesner & Cronshaw, 1988). Structured interviews also reduce bias, such as against overweight applicants (Kutcher & Bragger, 2004). Thanks partly to its greater reliability

structured interviews interview process that asks the same job-relevant questions of all applicants, each of whom is rated on established scales.

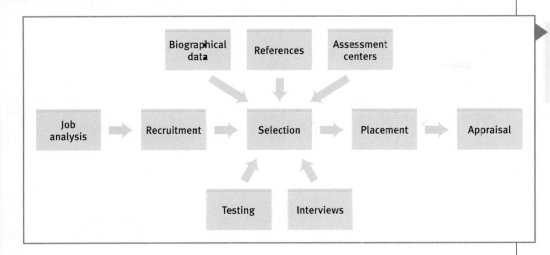

FIGURE 39.2 **Personnel psychologists' tasks** Personnel psychologists consult in human resources activities, from job definition to employee appraisal.

and partly to its job-analysis focus, the predictive power of one structured interview is roughly equal to that of the average judgment from three or four unstructured interviews (Huffcutt et al., 2001; Schmidt & Zimmerman, 2004).

If, instead, we let our intuitions bias the hiring process, notes Malcolm Gladwell (2000), then "all we will have done is replace the old-boy network, where you hired your nephew, with the new-boy network, where you hire whoever impressed you most when you shook his hand. Social progress, unless we're careful, can merely be the means by which we replace the obviously arbitrary with the not so obviously arbitrary."

To recap, personnel psychologists assist organizations in analyzing jobs, recruiting well-suited applicants, selecting and placing employees, and appraising their performance (**FIGURE 39.2**)—the topic we turn to next.

Appraising Performance

Performance appraisal serves organizational purposes: It helps decide who to retain, how to appropriately reward and pay people, and how to better harness employee strengths, sometimes with job shifts or promotions. Performance appraisal also serves individual purposes: Feedback affirms workers' strengths and helps motivate needed improvements.

Performance appraisal methods include

▶ *checklists* on which supervisors simply check specific behaviors that describe the worker ("always attends to customers' needs," "takes long breaks").

▶ *graphic rating scales* on which a supervisor checks, perhaps on a five-point scale, how often a worker is dependable, productive, and so forth.

▶ *behavior rating scales* on which a supervisor checks scaled behaviors that describe a worker's performance. If rating the extent to which a worker "follows procedures," the supervisor might mark the employee somewhere between "often takes shortcuts" and "always follows established procedures" (Levy, 2003).

In some organizations, performance feedback comes not only from supervisors but also from all organizational levels. If you join an organization that practices *360-degree feedback* (**FIGURE 39.3** on the next page), you will rate yourself, your manager, and your other colleagues, and you will be rated by your manager, other colleagues, and customers (Green, 2002). The net result is often more open communication and more complete appraisal.

Performance appraisal, like other social judgments, is vulnerable to bias (Murphy & Cleveland, 1995). *Halo errors* occur when one's overall evaluation of an employee,

achievement motivation a desire for significant accomplishment; for mastery of things, people, or ideas; for rapidly attaining a high standard.

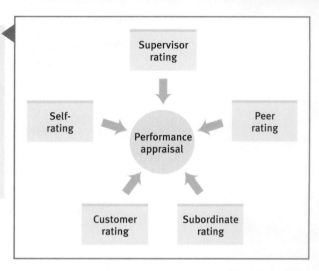

FIGURE 39.3 360-degree feedback With multisource 360-degree feedback, one's knowledge, skills, and behaviors are rated by self and surrounding others. Professors, for example, may be rated by their department chairs, their students, and their colleagues. After receiving all these ratings, professors discuss the 360-degree feedback with their department chair.

or of a personal trait such as their friendliness, biases ratings of their specific work-related behaviors, such as their reliability. *Leniency* and *severity errors* reflect evaluators' tendencies to be either too easy or too harsh on everyone. *Recency errors* occur when raters focus only on easily remembered recent behavior. By using multiple raters and developing objective, job-relevant performance measures, personnel psychologists seek to support their organizations while also helping employees perceive the appraisal process as fair.

▶‖ Organizational Psychology: Motivating Achievement

39-2   What is the role of organizational psychologists?

The appraisal of work and the matching of talents to work matter, but so does overall motivation. Before considering how organizational psychologists assist with efforts to motivate employees and keep them engaged, let's take a closer look at why any employee might want to pursue high standards or difficult goals.

Think of someone you know who strives to succeed by excelling at any task where evaluation is possible. Now think of someone who is less driven. Psychologist Henry Murray (1938) defined the first person's **achievement motivation** as a desire for significant accomplishment, for mastering skills or ideas, for control, and for rapidly attaining a high standard.

As you might expect from their persistence and eagerness for realistic challenges, people with high achievement motivation do achieve more. One study followed the lives of 1528 California children whose intelligence test scores were in the top 1 percent. Forty years later, when researchers compared those who were most and least successful professionally, they found a motivational difference. Those most successful were more ambitious, energetic, and persistent. As children, they had more active hobbies. As adults, they participated in more groups and favored being sports participants to being spectators (Goleman, 1980). Gifted children are able learners. Accomplished adults are tenacious doers.

In other studies of both secondary school and university students, self-discipline has been a better predictor of school performance, attendance, and graduation honors than intelligence scores have been. "Discipline outdoes talent," concluded researchers Angela Duckworth and Martin Seligman (2005, 2006), and it explains why girls get higher school grades than equally capable boys.

But discipline also refines talent. By their early twenties, top violinists have accumulated some 10,000 lifetime practice hours—double the practice time of other violin students aiming to be teachers (Ericsson et al., 2001, 2006, 2007). From his studies, Herbert Simon (1998), a psychologist who won the Nobel Prize in Economics, formed what has been called the *10-year rule:* That world-class experts in a field typically have invested "at least 10 years of hard work—say, 40 hours a week for 50 weeks a year." A study of outstanding scholars, athletes, and artists found that all were highly motivated and self-disciplined, willing to dedicate hours every day to the pursuit of their goals (Bloom, 1985). These superstar achievers were distinguished not so much by their extraordinary natural talent as by their extraordinary daily discipline. Great achievement, it seems, mixes a teaspoon of inspiration with a gallon of perspiration.

What distinguishes extremely successful individuals from their equally talented peers, note Duckworth and Seligman, is *grit*—passionate dedication to an ambitious, long-term goal. Although intelligence is distributed like a bell curve, achievements are not. That tells us that achievement involves much more than raw ability. And that is why organizational psychologists seek ways to engage and motivate ordinary people doing ordinary jobs.

Satisfaction and Engagement

Because work is such a big part of life, employee satisfaction is a priority concern for I/O psychologists. Satisfaction with work feeds satisfaction with life (see Close-Up: Doing Well While Doing Good on the next page). Moreover, studies confirm that decreased job stress feeds improved health.

Does employee satisfaction also contribute to successful organizations? Positive moods at work do contribute to creativity, persistence, and helpfulness (Brief & Weiss, 2002). But are engaged, happy workers also less often absent? Less likely to quit? Less prone to theft? More punctual? More productive? Conclusive evidence of satisfaction's benefits is, some have said, the holy grail of I/O psychology. Statistical digests of prior research have found a modest positive correlation between individual job satisfaction and performance (Judge et al., 2001; Parker et al., 2003). In one analysis of 4500 employees at 42 British manufacturing companies, the most productive workers tended to be those in satisfying work environments (Patterson et al., 2004). But does satisfaction *produce* better job performance? The debate continues, with one analysis of past research indicating that satisfaction

Disciplined motivation feeds achievement Aware that he was far behind other students when beginning his graduate education in psychology, B. F. Skinner devised a daily discipline of rising at 6:00 A.M., studying until breakfast, then going to classes, labs, and the library. After dinner he studied some more, leaving no more than 15 unscheduled minutes each day, and later continued a disciplined daily routine as he became one of the twentieth century's most influential psychologists.

"The only place success comes before work is in the dictionary."
Former Green Bay Packers football coach Vince Lombardi

Engaged employees facilitate organizational success Best Buy's electronic goods stores have nearly identical product layout and operations manuals. Yet some stores have had much more engaged employees—and more profitable performance. The store with the highest worker-engagement scores has been in the top tenth of stores in having profits beyond budget. And the store with the least-engaged employees has been in the bottom tenth (Buckingham, 2001).

Doing Well While Doing Good: "The Great Experiment"

At the end of the 1700s, the more than 1000 workers in the cotton mill at New Lanark, Scotland—many of them children drawn from Glasgow's poorhouses—worked 13-hour days and lived in grim conditions. Their education and sanitation were neglected, theft and drunkenness were commonplace, and most families occupied just one room.

On a visit to Glasgow, Welsh-born Robert Owen—an idealistic young cotton-mill manager—chanced to meet and fall in love with the mill owner's daughter. After their marriage, Owen, with several partners, purchased the mill and on the first day of the 1800s took control as its manager. Before long, he began what he said was "the most important experiment for the happiness of the human race that had yet been instituted at any time in any part of the world" (Owen, 1814). The exploitation of child and adult labor was, he observed, producing unhappy and inefficient workers. Believing that better working and living conditions could pay economic dividends, he undertook (with some resistance from his partners, whom he ultimately bought out) numerous innovations: a nursery for preschool children, education (with encouragement rather than corporal punishment), Sundays off, health care, paid sick days, unemployment pay for days when the mill could not operate, and a company store selling goods at reduced prices.

The great experiment New Lanark Mills, which today is preserved as a World Heritage Site, provided an influential demonstration of how industries could do well while doing good. In its heyday, New Lanark was visited by many European royals and reformers who came to observe its vibrant workforce and prosperous business. See www.newlanark.org for more information about this landmark.

Courtesy of New Lanark World Heritage Site

Owen also innovated a goals and worker-assessment program that included detailed records of daily productivity and costs. By each employee's workstation, one of four colored boards indicated that person's performance for the previous day. Owen could walk through the mill and at a glance see how individuals were performing. There was, he said, "no beating, no abusive language. . . . I merely looked at the person and then at the color. . . . I could at once see by the expression [which color] was shown."

The commercial success that followed was essential to sustaining what became a movement toward humanitarian reforms. By 1816, with decades of profitability still ahead, Owen believed he had demonstrated "that society may be formed so as to exist without crime, without poverty, with health greatly improved, with little if any misery, and with intelligence and happiness increased a hundredfold." Although his Utopian vision has not been fulfilled, Owen's great experiment did lay the groundwork for employment practices that have today become accepted in much of the world.

and performance correlate because both reflect job self-esteem ("I matter around here") and a sense that their efforts control their rewards (Bowling, 2007).

Nevertheless, some organizations do have a knack for cultivating more engaged and productive employees. In the United States, the *Fortune* "100 Best Companies to Work For" have also produced markedly higher-than-average returns for their investors (Fulmer et al., 2003). Other positive data come from the biggest-ever study, an analysis of Gallup data from more than 198,000 employees (**TABLE 39.**1) in nearly 8000 business units of 36 large companies (including some 1100 bank branches, 1200 stores, and 4200 teams or departments). James Harter, Frank Schmidt, and Theodore Hayes

TABLE 39.1 The Gallup Workplace Audit

Overall satisfaction—On a 5-point scale, where 5 is extremely satisfied and 1 is extremely dissatisfied, how satisfied are you with *(name of company)* as a place to work? _____
On a scale of 1 to 5, where 1 is strongly disagree and 5 is strongly agree,
please indicate your agreement with the following items.

1. I know what is expected from me at work.
2. I have the materials and equipment I need to do my work right.
3. At work, I have the opportunity to do what I do best every day.
4. In the last seven days, I have received recognition or praise for doing good work.
5. My supervisor, or someone at work, seems to care about me as a person.
6. There is someone at work who encourages my development.
7. At work, my opinions seem to count.
8. The mission/purpose of my company makes me feel my job is important.
9. My associates (fellow employees) are committed to doing quality work.
10. I have a best friend at work.
11. In the last six months, someone at work has talked to me about my progress.
12. This last year, I have had opportunities at work to learn and grow.

Note: These statements are proprietary and copyrighted by The Gallup Organization. They may not be printed or reproduced in any manner without the written consent of The Gallup Organization. Reprinted here by permission.

(2002) explored correlations between various measures of organizational success and *employee engagement*—the extent of workers' involvement, enthusiasm, and identification with their organizations. They found that engaged workers (compared with disengaged workers who are just putting in time) know what's expected of them, have what they need to do their work, feel fulfilled in their work, have regular opportunities to do what they do best, perceive that they are part of something significant, and have opportunities to learn and develop. They also found that business units with engaged employees have more loyal customers, less turnover, higher productivity, and greater profits. A follow-up analysis compared companies with top-quartile versus below-average employee engagement levels. Over a three-year period, earnings grew 2.6 times faster for the companies with highly engaged workers (Ott, 2007).

Managing Well

Every leader dreams of managing in ways that enhance people's satisfaction, engagement, and productivity and their organization's success. Effective leaders harness job-relevant strengths, set goals, and choose an appropriate leadership style.

Harnessing Job-Relevant Strengths

"The major challenge for CEOs over the next 20 years will be the effective deployment of human assets," observed Marcus Buckingham (2001). That challenge is "about psychology. It's about getting [individuals] to be more productive, more focused, more fulfilled than [they were] yesterday." To do so, he and others have maintained, effective leaders want first to select the right people. Then, they aim to discern their employees' natural talents, adjust their work roles to suit their talents, and develop those talents into great strengths (**FIGURE 39.4** on the next page). For example, should every professor at a given college or university be expected to teach the same load, advise the same number of students, serve on the same number of committees, and engage in the same amount of research? Or should each job description be tailored to harness a specific person's unique strengths?

|| **Three types of employees** (Crabtree, 2005):
Engaged: working with passion and feeling a profound connection to their company or organization.
Not-engaged: putting in the time, but investing little passion or energy into their work.
Actively disengaged: unhappy workers undermining what their colleagues accomplish. ||

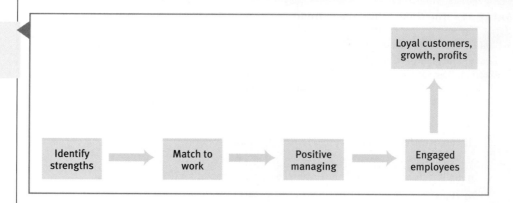

FIGURE 39.4 On the right path The Gallup Organization path to organizational success (adapted from Fleming, 2001).

Positive coaching Larry Brown, an adviser to the youth sports organization Positive Coaching Alliance, has been observed during practices to offer his players 4 to 5 positive comments for every negative comment (Insana, 2005). In 2004, his underdog Detroit Pistons won the National Basketball Association championship.

Ezra Shaw/Getty Images

As noted earlier in the discussion of personnel psychologists, our temperament and our traits tend to follow us throughout our lives. Managers who excel spend less time trying to instill talents that are not there and more time developing and drawing out what is there. Kenneth Tucker (2002) has noted that great managers

▶ start by helping people identify and measure their talents.
▶ match tasks to talents and then give people freedom to do what they do best.
▶ care how their people feel about their work.
▶ reinforce positive behaviors through recognition and reward.

Thus, rather than focusing on weaknesses and packing people off to training seminars to fix those problems, good managers focus training time on educating people about their strengths and building upon them (which means not promoting people into roles ill-suited to their strengths). In Gallup surveys, 77 percent of engaged workers, and only 23 percent of not-engaged workers, strongly agreed that "my supervisor focuses on my strengths or positive characteristics" (Krueger & Killham, 2005).

Celebrating engaged and productive employees in every organizational role builds upon a basic principle of *operant conditioning:* To teach a behavior, catch a person doing something right and reinforce it. It sounds simple, but many managers are like parents who, when a child returns home with perfect scores, focus on the one low score in a troublesome biology class and ignore the rest. "Sixty-five percent of Americans received NO praise or recognition in the workplace last year," reported the Gallup Organization (2004).

Setting Specific, Challenging Goals

In everyday life, our achievement goals sometimes involve approaching high levels of mastery or performance (perhaps mastering the material for this class and getting a high grade) and sometimes involve avoiding failure (Elliot & McGregor, 2001). In many situations, specific, challenging goals motivate achievement, especially when combined with progress reports (Johnson et al., 2006; Latham & Locke, 2007). Specific, measurable objectives, such as "finish gathering information for the history paper by Friday," serve to direct attention, promote effort, motivate persistence, and stimulate creative strategies.

When people state goals together with *subgoals* and *implementation intentions—* action plans that specify when, where, and how they will march toward achieving those goals—they become more focused in their work, and on-time completion becomes more likely (Burgess et al., 2004; Fishbach et al., 2006; Koestner et al., 2002). (Before beginning each new edition of this book, my editor, my associates, and I *manage by objectives*—we agree on target dates for the completion and editing of each draft manuscript.) So, to motivate high productivity, effective leaders work with people to define explicit goals, subgoals, and implementation plans, and then provide feedback on progress.

Choosing an Appropriate Leadership Style

Leadership varies from a boss-focused directive style to a democratic style that empowers workers in setting goals and strategies. Which works best may depend on the situation and the leader. The best leadership style for leading a discussion may not be the best style for leading troops on a charge (Fiedler, 1981). Moreover, different leaders are suited to different styles. Some excel at **task leadership**—setting standards, organizing work, and focusing attention on goals. Being goal-oriented, task leaders are good at keeping a group centered on its mission. Typically, they have a directive style, which can work well if the leader is bright enough to give good orders (Fiedler, 1987).

Other managers excel at **social leadership**—explaining decisions, mediating conflicts, and building high-achieving teams (Evans & Dion, 1991). Social leaders often have a democratic style: They delegate authority and welcome the participation of team members. Many experiments show that social leadership is good for morale. Subordinates usually feel more satisfied and motivated and perform better when they participate in decision making (Cawley et al., 1998; Pereira & Osburn, 2007).

Because effective leadership styles vary with the situation and the person, the once-popular *great person theory of leadership*—that all great leaders share certain traits—now seems overstated (Vroom & Jago, 2007; Wielkiewicz & Stelzner, 2005). The same coach may seem great or inferior depending on the strength of the team and its competition. But a leader's personality does matter (Zaccaro, 2007). Effective leaders tend to be neither extremely assertive (impairing social relationships) or unassertive (limiting task leadership) (Ames & Flynn, 2007). Effective leaders of laboratory groups, work teams, and large corporations also tend to exude *charisma* (House & Singh, 1987; Shamir et al., 1993). Their charisma blends a goal-based *vision,* clear *communication,* and optimism that *inspires* others to follow. In one study of 50 Dutch companies, the highest morale was at those firms with chief executives who most inspired their colleagues "to transcend their own self-interests for the sake of the collective" (de Hoogh et al., 2004). *Transformational leadership* of this kind motivates others to identify with and commit themselves to the group's mission. Transformational leaders, many of whom are natural extraverts, articulate high standards, inspire people to share their vision, and offer personal attention (Bono & Judge, 2004). The frequent result is more engaged, trusting, and effective workers (Turner et al., 2002). Women more than men tend to exhibit transformational leadership qualities. Alice Eagly (2007) believes this helps explain why companies with women in top management have recently tended to enjoy superior financial results, even after controlling for such variables as company size.

Peter Smith and Monir Tayeb (1989) compiled data from studies in India, Taiwan, and Iran indicating that effective managers—whether in coal mines, banks, or government offices—often exhibit a high degree of *both* task and social leadership. As achievement-minded people, effective managers certainly care about how well work is done, yet at the same time they are sensitive to their subordinates' needs. In one national survey of American

"Good leaders don't ask more than their constituents can give, but they often ask—and get—more than their constituents intended to give or thought it was possible to give."

John W. Gardner, *Excellence,* 1984

Sharing vision and decisions
As CEO, Jeffrey Bleustein helped Harley-Davidson thrive, in part by replacing the organization's command-and-control management style with one based on company-wide consensus planning and decision making.

Chris Kleponis/Zuma Press. © Chris Kleponis.

workers, those in family-friendly organizations offering flexible-time hours reported feeling greater loyalty to their employers (Roehling et al., 2001)

Many successful businesses have also increased employee participation in making decisions, a management style common in Sweden and Japan and increasingly elsewhere (Naylor, 1990; Sundstrom et al., 1990). Although managers often think better of work they have directly supervised, studies reveal a *voice effect*: If given a chance to voice their opinion during a decision-making process, people will respond more positively to the decision (van den Bos & Spruijt, 2002). And, as we noted earlier, positive engaged employees are a mark of thriving organizations.

The rags-to-riches Harley-Davidson story illustrates the potential of inviting workers to participate in decision making (Teerlink & Ozley, 2000). In 1987, the struggling company began transforming its *command-and-control* management process into a *joint-vision process*. The aim: "To push decision-making, planning, and strategizing from a handful of people at the top, down throughout the organization. We wanted all the employees to think every day about how to improve the company," reported CEO Jeffrey Bleustein (2002). In the mid-1990s, Harley signed a cooperative agreement with its unions that included them "in decision-making in virtually every aspect of the business." Consensus decision-making can take longer, but "when the decision is made, it gets implemented quickly and the commitment is by the group," says Bleustein. The result has been more engaged workers and also more satisfied stockholders. Every $1 of Harley-Davidson stock purchased at the end of 1986 was worth $60 at the end of 2008.

* * *

Identifiable physiological mechanisms drive some motives, such as hunger (though learned tastes and cultural expectations matter, too). Other motives, such as achievement at work, are more obviously driven by psychological factors, such as an intrinsic quest for mastery and the external rewards of recognition. What unifies all motives is their common effect: the energizing and directing of behavior.

REVIEW

Motivation at Work

39-1 **How do personnel psychologists help organizations with employee selection, work placement, and performance appraisal?** *Personnel psychologists* work with organizations to devise selection methods for new employees, recruit and evaluate applicants, design and evaluate training programs, identify people's strengths, analyze job content, and appraise individual and organizational performance. Subjective interviews foster the interviewer illusion; *structured interviews* pinpoint job-relevant strengths and are better predictors of performance. Checklists, graphic rating scales, and behavior rating scales are useful performance appraisal methods.

39-2 **What is the role of organizational psychologists?** *Organizational psychologists* examine influences on worker satisfaction and productivity and facilitate organizational change. Employee engagement tends to correlate with organizational success. Leadership style may be goal-oriented (*task leadership*), or group-oriented (*social leadership*), or some combination of the two.

Terms and Concepts to Remember

flow, p. 484

industrial-organizational
  (I/O) psychology, p. 485

personnel psychology, p. 485

organizational psychology,
  p. 486

structured interviews, p. 488

achievement motivation,
  p. 490

task leadership, p. 495

social leadership, p. 495

Test Yourself

1. A human resources director explains to you that "I don't bother with tests or references. I can pick employees by my gut." Based on I/O research, what concerns does this raise?

(Answers to the Test Yourself questions can be found in Appendix B at the end of the book.)

Ask Yourself

1. Are you highly motivated, or not highly motivated, to achieve in school? How has this affected your academic success? How might you improve upon your own achievement levels?

∞ WEB

Multiple-choice self-tests and more may be found at www.worthpublishers.com/myers

Emotions, Stress, and Health

MODULES

40
Introduction to Emotion

41
Expressed Emotion

42
Experienced Emotion

43
Stress and Health

44
Promoting Health

No one needs to tell you that feelings add color to your life, or that in times of stress they can disrupt your life or save it. Of all the species, we seem the most emotional (Hebb, 1980). More often than any other creature, we express fear, anger, sadness, joy, and love, and these psychological states often entail physical reactions. Nervous about an important encounter, we feel butterflies in our stomach. Anxious over speaking in public, we frequent the bathroom. Smoldering over a conflict with a family member, we get a splitting headache.

You can surely recall a time when you were overcome with emotion. I retain a flashbulb memory for the day I went to a huge store to drop off film and brought along Peter, my toddler first-born child. As I set Peter down on his feet and prepared to complete the paperwork, a passerby warned, "You'd better be careful or you'll lose that boy!" Not more than a few breaths later, after dropping the film in the slot, I turned and found no Peter beside me.

With mild anxiety, I peered around one end of the counter. No Peter in sight. With slightly more anxiety, I peered around the other end. No Peter there, either. Now, with my heart accelerating, I circled the neighboring counters. Still no Peter anywhere. As anxiety turned to panic, I began racing up and down the store aisles. He was nowhere to be found. Apprised of my alarm, the store manager used the public-address system to ask customers to assist in looking for a missing child. Soon after, I passed the customer who had warned me. "I told you that you were going to lose him!" he scorned. With visions of kidnapping (strangers routinely adored that beautiful child), I braced for the possibility that my negligence had caused me to lose what I loved above all else, and that I might have to return home and face my wife without our only child.

But then, as I passed the customer service counter yet again, there he was, having been found and returned by some obliging customer! In an instant, the arousal of terror spilled into ecstasy. Clutching my son, with tears suddenly flowing, I found myself unable to speak my thanks and stumbled out of the store awash in grateful joy.

Where do such emotions come from? Why do we have them? What are they made of? Emotions are our body's adaptive response. They exist not to give us interesting experiences but to enhance our survival. When we face challenges, emotions focus our attention and energize our action. Our heart races. Our pace quickens. All our senses go on high alert. Receiving unexpected good news, we may find our eyes tearing. We raise our hands triumphantly. We feel exuberance and a newfound confidence. Yet when prolonged and experienced as stress, emotions can also have a damaging effect on our health, as we will see.

So, how do psychologists think about and study emotions, stress, and health? In Module 40, we examine three classic theories of emotion that explore the interplay of physiological activation, expressive behavior, and conscious experience. Module 41 then turns to the topic of how we express our emotions. In Module 42, we focus on experiencing our emotions with an in-depth look at fear, anger, and happiness. Module 43 looks at a key question health psychologists ask: How do our emotions and personality influence our risk of disease? And Module 44 explores the attitudes and behaviors that may help prevent illness and promote health and well-being.

MODULE 40

Introduction to Emotion

▶‖ Theories of Emotion

40-1 What are the components of an emotion?

‖ Not only emotion, but most psychological phenomena (vision, sleep, memory, sex, and so forth) can be approached these three ways—physiologically, behaviorally, and cognitively. ‖

As my anguished search for Peter illustrates, **emotions** are a mix of (1) physiological arousal (heart pounding), (2) expressive behaviors (quickened pace), and (3) consciously experienced thoughts (is this a kidnapping?) and feelings (a sense of fear, and later joy). The puzzle for psychologists has been figuring out how these three pieces fit together.

There are two controversies over the interplay of our physiology, expressions, and experience in emotions. The first, a chicken-and-egg debate, is old: Does your physiological arousal precede or follow your emotional experience? (Did I first notice my heart racing and my faster step, and then feel anxious dread about losing Peter? Or did my sense of fear come first, stirring my heart and legs to respond?) The second controversy concerns the interaction between thinking and feeling: Does cognition always precede emotion? (Did I *think* about the kidnapping threat before reacting emotionally?)

Common sense tells most of us that we cry because we are sad, lash out because we are angry, tremble because we are afraid. First comes conscious awareness, then the physiological trimmings. But to pioneering psychologist William James, this common-sense view of emotion was backward. According to James, "We feel sorry because we cry, angry because we strike, afraid because we tremble" (1890, p. 1066). Perhaps you can recall a time when your car skidded on slick pavement. As it careened crazily, you countersteered and regained control. Just after the fishtail ended, you noticed your racing heart and then, shaking with fright, you felt the whoosh of emotion. Your feeling of fear *followed* your body's response. James' idea, also proposed by Danish physiologist Carl Lange, is called the **James-Lange theory.** First comes a distinct physiological response, then (as we observe that response) comes our experienced emotion.

This James-Lange theory struck U.S. physiologist Walter Cannon as implausible. Cannon thought the body's responses were not distinct enough to evoke the different emotions. Does a racing heart signal fear, anger, or love? Also, changes in heart rate, perspiration, and body temperature seemed too slow to trigger sudden emotion. Cannon, and later another physiologist, Philip Bard, concluded that our physiological arousal and our emotional experience occur *simultaneously:* The emotion-triggering stimulus is routed simultaneously to the brain's cortex, causing the subjective awareness of emotion, and to the sympathetic nervous system, causing the body's arousal. This **Cannon-Bard theory** implies that your heart begins pounding *as* you experience fear; one does not cause the other. Our physiological response and experienced emotion are separate.

Let's check your understanding of the James-Lange and Cannon-Bard theories. Imagine that your brain could not sense your heart pounding or your stomach churning. According to each theory, how would this affect your experienced emotions?

Cannon and Bard would have expected you to experience emotions normally because they believed emotions occur separately from (though simultaneously with) the body's arousal. James and Lange would have expected greatly diminished emotions because they believed that to experience emotion you must first perceive your body's arousal.

Joy expressed According to the James-Lange theory, we don't just smile because we share our teammates' joy. We also share the joy because we are smiling with them.

AP Photo/Charlie Neibergall

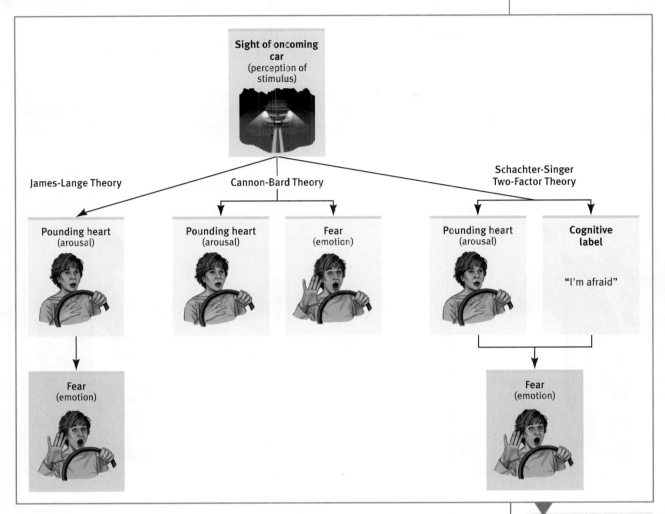

FIGURE 40.1
Theories of emotion

Stanley Schachter and Jerome Singer (1962) proposed a third theory: that our physiology and our cognitions—perceptions, memories, and interpretations—together create emotion. In their **two-factor theory,** emotions therefore have two ingredients: physical arousal and a cognitive label (**FIGURE 40.1**). Like James and Lange, Schachter and Singer presumed that our experience of emotion grows from our awareness of our body's arousal. Yet like Cannon and Bard, Schachter and Singer also believed that emotions are physiologically similar. Thus, in their view, an emotional experience requires a conscious interpretation of the arousal.

To assess the James-Lange, Cannon-Bard, and two-factor theories, we'll consider in the next section the answers researchers have gleaned to three questions:

▶ Does physiological arousal always precede emotional experience?
▶ Are different emotions marked by distinct physiological responses?
▶ What is the connection between what we *think* and how we *feel?*

▶‖ Embodied Emotion

Whether you are eagerly anticipating a long-awaited vacation, falling in love, or grieving a death, you need little convincing that emotions involve the body. Feeling without a body is like breathing without lungs. Some physical responses are easy to notice, others—many taking place at the level of brain neurons—happen without your awareness.

emotion a response of the whole organism, involving (1) physiological arousal, (2) expressive behaviors, and (3) conscious experience.

James-Lange theory the theory that our experience of emotion is our awareness of our physiological responses to emotion-arousing stimuli.

Cannon-Bard theory the theory that an emotion-arousing stimulus simultaneously triggers (1) physiological responses and (2) the subjective experience of emotion.

two-factor theory the Schachter-Singer theory that to experience emotion one must (1) be physically aroused and (2) cognitively label the arousal.

"Fear lends wings to his feet."
Virgil, *Aeneid*, 19 B.C.

Emotions and the Autonomic Nervous System

40-2   What is the link between emotional arousal and the autonomic nervous system?

In a crisis it is your *autonomic nervous system (ANS)* that mobilizes your body for action and calms it when the crisis passes (**FIGURE 40.2**). Without any conscious effort, your body's response to danger is wonderfully coordinated and adaptive—preparing you to *fight or flee*.

FIGURE 40.2 Emotional arousal Like a crisis control center, the autonomic nervous system arouses the body in a crisis and calms it when danger passes.

Autonomic Nervous System Controls Physiological Arousal

Sympathetic division (arousing)		Parasympathetic division (calming)
Pupils dilate	EYES	Pupils contract
Decreases	SALIVATION	Increases
Perspires	SKIN	Dries
Increases	RESPIRATION	Decreases
Accelerates	HEART	Slows
Inhibits	DIGESTION	Activates
Secrete stress hormones	ADRENAL GLANDS	Decrease secretion of stress hormones

FIGURE 40.3 Arousal and performance Performance peaks at lower levels of arousal for difficult tasks, and at higher levels for easy or well-learned tasks. Thus, runners excel when aroused by competition. But facing a difficult exam, high anxiety may disrupt performance. Teaching anxious students how to relax before an exam can therefore enable them to perform better (Hembree, 1988).

The *sympathetic division* of your ANS directs your adrenal glands to release the stress hormones epinephrine (adrenaline) and norepinephrine (noradrenaline). Influenced by this energy-enhancing hormonal surge, your liver pours extra sugar into your bloodstream. To help burn the sugar, your respiration increases to supply needed oxygen. Your heart rate and blood pressure increase. Your digestion slows, diverting blood from your internal organs to your muscles. With blood sugar driven into the large muscles, running becomes easier. Your pupils dilate, letting in more light. To cool your stirred-up body, you perspire. If wounded, your blood would clot more quickly.

When the crisis passes, the *parasympathetic division* of your ANS takes over, calming your body. Its neural centers inhibit further release of stress hormones, but those already in your bloodstream will linger awhile, so arousal diminishes gradually.

In many situations, arousal is adaptive. When you're taking an exam, for example, it pays to be moderately aroused—alert but not trembling with nervousness (**FIGURE 40.3**). But too little arousal (think sleepiness) can be disruptive, and prolonged high arousal can tax the body.

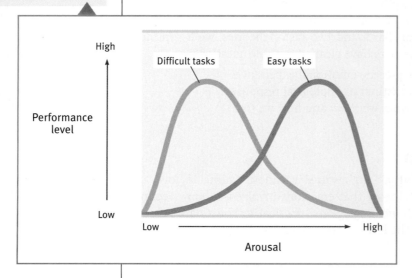

High

Difficult tasks   Easy tasks

Performance level

Low

Low ——————————→ High

Arousal

Physiological Similarities Among Specific Emotions

40-3 Do different emotions activate different physiological and brain-pattern responses?

Imagine conducting an experiment measuring the physiological responses of emotion. In each of four rooms, you have someone watching a movie: In the first, the person is viewing a horror show; in the second, an anger-provoking film; in the third, a sexually arousing film; in the fourth, an utterly boring movie. From the control center you monitor each person's physiological responses, measuring perspiration, breathing, and heart rates. Do you think you could tell who is frightened? Who is angry? Who is sexually aroused? Who is bored?

With training, you could probably pick out the bored viewer. But discerning physiological differences among fear, anger, and sexual arousal would be much more difficult (Barrett, 2006). Different emotions do not have sharply distinct biological signatures.

To you and me, sexual arousal, fear, and anger nevertheless *feel* different. And, despite similar arousal, emotions often *look* different. People may appear "paralyzed with fear" or "ready to explode." So, does research pinpoint any distinct physiological or brain-pattern indicators of each emotion? Sometimes. Read on.

Physiological Differences Among Specific Emotions

Researchers have found some real, though subtle, physiological distinctions among the emotions. The finger temperatures and hormone secretions that accompany fear and rage do sometimes differ (Ax, 1953; Levenson, 1992). And, though fear and joy can prompt similar increased heart rate, they stimulate different facial muscles. During fear, brow muscles tense. During joy, muscles in the cheeks and under the eyes pull into a smile (Witvliet & Vrana, 1995).

Emotions differ much more in the brain circuits they use (Panksepp, 2007). Compared with observers watching angry faces, those watching (and subtly mimicking) fearful faces show more activity in their amygdala, the emotional control center in the brain's limbic system (Whalen et al., 2001). (The amygdala also offers a shortcut for some of our emotional responses, as you'll see later in this module.) Brain scans and EEG recordings show that emotions also activate different areas of the brain's cortex, with some tendency for negative emotions to be linked to the right hemisphere and positive emotions to the left. Disgust, for example, triggers more activity in the right prefrontal cortex than in the left. Depression-prone people, and those with generally negative personalities, also show more right frontal activity (Harmon-Jones et al., 2002).

Positive moods tend to trigger more left frontal lobe activity. People with positive personalities—exuberant infants and alert, enthusiastic, energized, and persistently goal-directed adults—also show more activity in the left frontal lobe than in the right (Davidson, 2000, 2003; Urry et al., 2004). Indeed, the more a person's baseline frontal lobe activity tilts left—or is made to tilt left by perceptual activity—the more upbeat the person typically is (Drake & Myers, 2006). Brain injury can also tilt activity to the left. One man, having lost part of his right frontal lobe in brain surgery, became (his not-unhappy wife reported) less irritable and more affectionate (Goleman, 1995). After a right-hemisphere stroke at age 92, my father lived the last two years of his life with happy gratitude and nary a complaint or negative emotion.

The left frontal lobe's rich supply of dopamine receptors may help explain why a peppy left hemisphere predicts a perky personality. A neural pathway that increases dopamine levels runs from the frontal lobes to a nearby cluster of neurons, the *nucleus accumbens*. This small region lights up when people experience natural or drug-

AP Photo/HO

Emotional arousal Elated excitement and panicky fear involve similar physiological arousal. That allows us to flip rapidly between the two emotions.

"No one ever told me that grief felt so much like fear. I am not afraid, but the sensation is like being afraid. The same fluttering in the stomach, the same restlessness, the yawning. I keep on swallowing."

C. S. Lewis, *A Grief Observed*, 1961

|| In 1966, a young man named Charles Whitman killed his wife and mother and then climbed to the top of a tower at the University of Texas and shot 38 people. An autopsy later revealed a tumor pressing against his amygdala, which may have contributed to his violence. ||

Thinking Critically About

Lie Detection

Can polygraph tests like this identify liars? To learn more, read on.

The creators and users of the *lie detector,* or **polygraph,** have believed that our physical indicators of emotion can provide a telltale equivalent of Pinocchio's nose. Actually, polygraphs do not literally detect lies, and their accuracy has been questioned as our understanding of physiological measures of emotion has grown.

Polygraphs measure the changes in breathing, cardiovascular activity, and perspiration that accompany emotion. An examiner monitors these responses as you answer questions. Some items, called *control questions,* aim to make anyone a little

nervous. If asked, "In the last 20 years, have you ever taken something that didn't belong to you?" many people will tell a white lie and say *no,* and the polygraph will detect arousal. If your physiological reactions to *critical questions* ("Did you ever steal anything from your previous employer?") are weaker than to control questions, the examiner infers you are telling the truth.

But there are two problems: First, our physiological arousal is much the same from one emotion to another—anxiety, irritation, and guilt all prompt similar physiological reactivity. Second, these tests err about one-third of the time, especially when innocent people respond with heightened tension to the accusations implied by the critical questions (**FIGURE 40.4**). Many rape victims, for example, "fail" lie detector tests when reacting emotionally while telling the truth about their assailant (Lykken, 1991).

A 2002 U.S. National Academy of Sciences report noted that "no spy has ever

FIGURE 40.4 **How often do lie detectors lie?** Benjamin Kleinmuntz and Julian Szucko (1984) had polygraph experts study the polygraph data of 50 theft suspects who later confessed to being guilty and 50 suspects whose innocence was later established by someone's confession. Had the polygraph experts been the judges, more than one-third of the innocent would have been declared guilty, and almost one-fourth of the guilty would have been declared innocent.

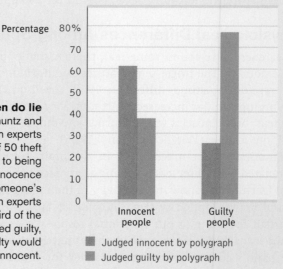

Percentage

- Judged innocent by polygraph
- Judged guilty by polygraph

induced pleasures. (When you're happy and you know it, your brain will surely show it.) In case studies, electrical stimulation of the nucleus accumbens of depressed patients has triggered smiles, laughter, and giddy euphoria (Okun et al., 2004).

* * *

We have seen that emotions as varied as fear, joy, and anger involve a similar general autonomic arousal (as in similar heart rate). We have also seen that there are real, if subtle, physiological and brain differences among the emotions. How does this new evidence affect the assessment of the James-Lange, Cannon-Bard, and two-factor theories of emotion? The evidence of real distinctions among the emotions makes the James-Lange theory plausible. Further support comes from observations of people with severed spinal cords. Psychologist George Hohmann (1966) asked 25 soldiers who suffered such injuries in World War II to recall emotion-arousing incidents that occurred before and after their spinal injuries. Those with lower-spine injuries, who had lost sensation only in their legs, reported little change in their emotions. But as James and Lange would have expected, those who could feel nothing below the neck

been caught [by] using the polygraph." It is not for lack of trying. The FBI, CIA, and Departments of Defense and Energy in the United States have spent millions of dollars testing tens of thousands of employees. Meanwhile Aldrich Ames, who enjoyed an unexplained lavish life-style as a Russian spy within the CIA, went undetected. Ames "took scores of polygraph tests and passed them all," noted Robert Park (1999). "Nobody thought to investigate the source of his sudden wealth—after all, he was passing the lie detector tests." The truth is, lie detectors can lie.

A more effective approach to lie detection uses the *guilty knowledge test*, which assesses a suspect's physiological responses to crime-scene details known only to the police and the guilty person (Ben-Shakhar & Elaad, 2003). If a camera and computer had been stolen, for example, presumably only a guilty person would react strongly to the specific brand names of these items. Given enough such specific probes, an innocent person will seldom be wrongly accused.

Several twenty-first-century research teams are exploring new ways to nab liars. Some are developing computer software that compares the language of truth tellers and of liars (who use fewer first-person pronouns and more negative-

James Salzano/OSalzano Photo

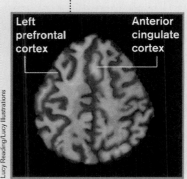
Lucy Reading/Lucy Illustrations

Left prefrontal cortex   Anterior cingulate cortex

FIGURE 40.5 Liar, liar, brain's on fire An fMRI scan identified two brain areas that became especially active when a participant lied about holding a five of clubs.

emotion words). Other software analyzes facial microexpressions linked with lying (Adelson, 2004; Newman et al., 2003). Psychologist Paul Ekman (2003) has run training seminars to teach law enforcement officers to detect the presumed fleeting signals of deceit in facial expressions.

Other researchers are going straight to the seat of deceit—the brain. EEG recordings have revealed brain waves indicating familiarity with crime scenes, and fMRI scans have shown liars' brains lighting up in places that honest people's brains do not (Langleben et al., 2002, 2005, 2006). Pinocchio's giveaway signal of lying may be not the length of his nose, but rather the telltale activity in places such as his

left frontal lobe and anterior cingulate cortex, which become active when the brain inhibits truth telling (**FIGURE 40.5**). A new US$10 million Law and Neuroscience Project, led by psychologist Michael Gazzaniga, aims to assess the new technology's appropriate uses by those seeking to identify terrorists, convict criminals, and protect the innocent (Dingfelder, 2007).

polygraph a machine, commonly used in attempts to detect lies, that measures several of the physiological responses accompanying emotion (such as perspiration and cardiovascular and breathing changes).

reported a considerable decrease in emotional intensity. The anger, as one man confessed, "just doesn't have the heat to it that it used to. It's a mental kind of anger." Those with high spinal-cord injury experienced their emotions more above the neck. They reported increases in weeping, lumps in the throat, and getting choked up when worshipping, saying good-bye, or watching a touching movie. Such evidence, some researchers believe, confirms the view that our feelings are "mostly shadows" of our bodily responses and behaviors (Damasio, 2003).

Does this mean that Cannon and Bard were wrong? No. Most researchers now agree that our experienced emotions also involve cognition, the topic we turn to next (Averill, 1993; Barrett, 2006). Whether we fear the man behind us on a dark street depends entirely on whether we interpret his actions as threatening or friendly. So, with James and Lange we can say that our body's reactions are an important ingredient of emotion. And with Cannon and Bard we can say that there is more to the experience of emotion than reading our body's responses. If that were not the case, lie detectors would be foolproof, which they are not (see Thinking Critically About Lie Detection).

Cognition and Emotion

40-4 To experience emotions, must we consciously interpret and label them?

What is the connection between what we *think* and how we *feel*? Which is the chicken and which the egg? Can we experience emotion apart from thinking? Or do we become what we think?

Reuters/Corbis

The spillover effect Arousal from a soccer match can fuel anger, which can descend into rioting or other violent confrontations.

"Feelings that one interprets as fear in the presence of a sheer drop may be interpreted as lust in the presence of a sheer blouse."

Daniel Gilbert, *Stumbling on Happiness*, 2006

Cognition Can Define Emotion

Sometimes our arousal response to one event spills over into our response to the next event. Imagine arriving home after an invigorating run and finding a message that you got a longed-for job. With arousal lingering from the run, would you feel more elated than if you received this news after awakening from a nap?

To find out whether this *spillover effect* exists, Stanley Schachter and Jerome Singer (1962) aroused college men with injections of the hormone epinephrine. Picture yourself as one of their participants: After receiving the injection, you go to a waiting room, where you find yourself with another person (actually an accomplice of the experimenters) who is acting either euphoric or irritated. As you observe this person, you begin to feel your heart race, your body flush, and your breathing become more rapid. If told to expect these effects from the injection, what would you feel? Schachter and Singer's volunteers felt little emotion—because they attributed their arousal to the drug. But if told the injection would produce no effects, what would you feel? Perhaps you would react, as another group of participants did, by "catching" the apparent emotion of the person you are with—becoming happy if the accomplice is acting euphoric, and testy if the accomplice is acting irritated.

This discovery—that a stirred-up state can be experienced as one emotion or another very different one, depending on how we interpret and label it—has been replicated in dozens of experiments. Insult people who have just been aroused by pedaling an exercise bike or watching rock videos and they will find it easy to misattribute their arousal to the provocation. Their anger will exceed that of people similarly provoked but not previously aroused. Likewise, sexually aroused people react with more hostility in anger-provoking situations. And, vice versa—the arousal that lingers after an intense argument or a frightening experience may intensify sexual passion (Palace, 1995). Just as the Schachter-Singer two-factor theory predicts, arousal + label = emotion. Emotional arousal may not be as undifferentiated as Schachter and Singer believed, but arousal from emotions as diverse as anger, fear, and sexual excitement can indeed spill from one emotion to another (Reisenzein, 1983; Sinclair et al., 1994; Zillmann, 1986). *The point to remember:* Arousal fuels emotion; cognition channels it.

Cognition Does Not Always Precede Emotion

Is the heart always subject to the mind? Robert Zajonc (pronounced ZI-yence; 1980, 1984a) has contended that we actually have many emotional reactions apart from, or even before, our interpretations of a situation. Imagine receiving some unsettling news. You discover that you've forgotten an important deadline, or that you've hurt someone's feelings. As the ongoing conversation distracts your attention, you lose awareness of the bad news. Yet the feeling still churns. You feel a little bad. You know there's a reason, but for the moment you can't put your finger on it. The arousal lingers, but without a label.

For example, when people repeatedly view stimuli flashed too briefly for them to interpret, much less label, they nevertheless come to prefer those stimuli. Without being consciously aware of having seen the stimuli, they rather like them. As a University of Amsterdam study confirms, we seem to have an acutely sensitive automatic radar for emotionally significant information (Zeelenberg et al., 2006). When researchers flashed a four-letter positive or negative word (such as *kiss* or *dead*), people more readily identified it than a similarly common neutral word (*fact*).

A subliminally flashed stimulus, such as a smiling or angry face or a disgusting scene, can also prime a mood or specific emotion and lead us to feel better or worse about a follow-up stimulus (Murphy et al., 1995; Ruys & Stapel, 2008). In one set of experiments, thirsty people were given a fruit-flavored drink after viewing a subliminally flashed (thus unperceived) face. Those exposed to a happy face drank about 50 percent more than those exposed to a neutral face (Berridge & Winkielman, 2003). Those flashed an angry face drank substantially less.

Neuroscience research helps us understand these surprising findings. Like speedy reflexes that operate apart from the brain's thinking cortex, some emotions take what Joseph LeDoux (2002) calls the "low road," via neural pathways that bypass the cortex (which offers the alternative "high road" pathway). One low-road pathway runs from the eye or ear via the thalamus to the amygdala, bypassing the cortex (**FIGURE 40.6**). This shortcut enables our greased-lightning emotional response before our intellect intervenes. So speedy is the amygdala reaction that we may be unaware of what's transpired (Dimberg et al., 2000). In one fascinating experiment, Paul Whalen and his colleagues (2004) used fMRI scans to observe the amygdala's response to subliminally presented fearful eyes (**FIGURE 40.7** on the next page). Compared with a control condition that presented the whites of happy eyes, the fearful eyes triggered increased amygdala activity (despite no one's being aware of seeing them).

The amygdala sends more neural projections up to the cortex than it receives back. This makes it easier for our feelings to hijack our thinking than for our thinking to rule our feelings, noted LeDoux and Jorge Armony (1999). In the forest, we jump at the sound of rustling bushes nearby, leaving the cortex to decide later whether the sound was made by a predator or just the wind. Such an experience supports Zajonc's belief that *some* of our emotional reactions involve no deliberate thinking.

Emotion researcher Richard Lazarus (1991, 1998) conceded that our brains process and react to vast amounts of information without our conscious awareness,

|| Can you recall liking something or someone immediately, without knowing why? ||

"Oh! ye'll tak' the high road and I'll tak' the low road, An' I'll be in Scotland afore ye." Traditional Scottish song "Bonnie Banks o' Loch Lomond"

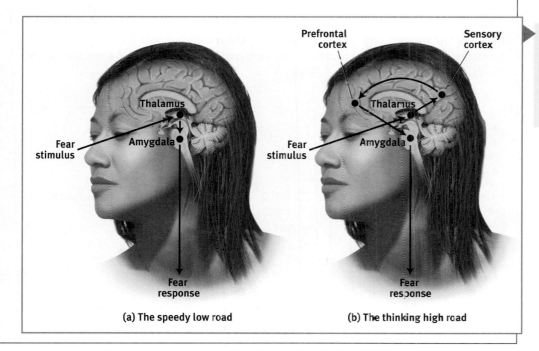

(a) The speedy low road

(b) The thinking high road

FIGURE 40.6 The brain's shortcut for emotions In the two-track brain, sensory input may be routed (a) directly to the amygdala (via the thalamus) for an instant emotional reaction or (b) to the cortex for analysis.

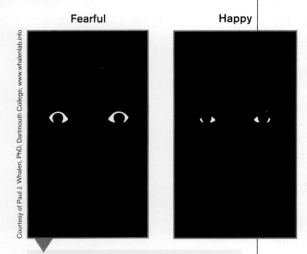

Fearful   Happy

FIGURE 40.7 The brain's sensitivity to threats Even when fearful eyes (left) were flashed too briefly for people to consciously perceive them, fMRI scans revealed that their hypervigilant amygdala was alerted (Whalen et al., 2004). The happy eyes on the right did not have this effect.

and he willingly granted that some emotional responses do not require *conscious* thinking. Much of our emotional life operates via the automatic, effortless, speedy low road. But, he noted, even instantaneously felt emotions require some sort of cognitive appraisal of the situation; otherwise, how would we *know* what we are reacting to? The appraisal may be effortless and we may not be conscious of it, but it is still a mental function. To know whether something is good or bad, the brain must have some idea of what it is (Storbeck et al., 2006). Thus, emotions arise when we *appraise* an event as beneficial or harmful to our well-being, whether we truly know it is or not. We appraise the sound of the rustling bushes as the presence of a threat. Later, we realize that it was "just the wind."

To sum up, as Zajonc and LeDoux have demonstrated, some emotional responses—especially simple likes, dislikes, and fears—involve no conscious thinking (**FIGURE 40.8**). We may fear a spider, even if we "know" it is harmless. Such responses are difficult to alter by changing our thinking.

The emotional brain even influences people's political decisions, leading many to vote for candidates they automatically *like* over a candidate expressing positions more like their own. When voters undergo brain imaging while watching candidates, their emotion circuits are more engaged than their rational frontal lobes (Westen, 2007).

But like other emotions—including moods such as depression and complex feelings such as hatred, guilt, happiness, and love—our feelings about politics are, as Lazarus, Schachter, and Singer predicted, greatly influenced by our memories, expectations, and interpretations. Highly emotional people are intense partly because of their interpretations. They may *personalize* events as being somehow directed at them, and they may *generalize* their experiences by blowing single incidents out of proportion (Larsen et al., 1987). In dealing with complex emotions, learning to *think* more positively can help people *feel* better. Even though the emotional low road functions automatically, the thinking high road allows us to retake some control over our emotional life.

A dramatic testimony to the interplay of emotion and cognition comes from the brain-damaged, seemingly emotionless patients studied by Antonio Damasio (1994, 2003). He devised a simple card-game task on which, over trials, people could make or lose money. Without brain damage, most people make money as the emotions generated by their unconscious brain figure things out ahead of their conscious reasoning. Without these feelings to inform their thinking, the emotionless patients typically *lose* money. This demonstrates once again that our two-track minds include a smart unconsciousness. Automatic emotion and conscious thinking together weave the fabric of our minds (Forgas, 2008).

FIGURE 40.8 Another example of dual processing: two routes to emotion Zajonc and LeDoux have emphasized that some emotional responses are immediate, before any conscious appraisal. Lazarus, Schachter, and Singer emphasized that our appraisal and labeling of events also determine our emotional responses.

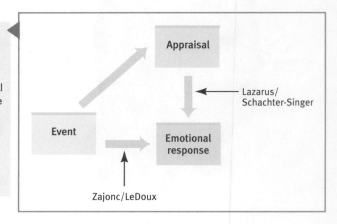

REVIEW

Introduction to Emotion

40-1 **What are the components of an emotion?** *Emotions* are psychological responses of the whole organism involving an interplay among (1) physiological arousal, (2) expressive behaviors, and (3) conscious experience (**FIGURE 40.9**).

Three theories support different combinations of these responses. The *James-Lange theory* maintains that our emotional feelings follow our body's response to the emotion-inducing stimuli. The *Cannon-Bard theory* proposes that our body responds to emotion at the same time that we experience the emotion (one does not cause the other). The *two-factor theory* holds that our emotions have two ingredients: physical arousal and a cognitive label.

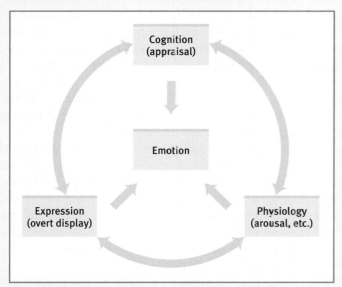

FIGURE 40.9 The ingredients of emotion From the interplay of physiology, expression, and cognition comes emotion.

40-2 **What is the link between emotional arousal and the autonomic nervous system?** Emotions are both psychological and physiological. Much of the physiological activity is controlled by the autonomic nervous system's sympathetic (arousing) and parasympathetic (calming) divisions. Our performance on a task is usually best when arousal is moderate, though this varies with the difficulty of the task.

40-3 **Do different emotions activate different physiological and brain-pattern responses?** Emotions may be similarly arousing, but there are some subtle physiological responses that distinguish them. More meaningful differences have been found in activity in the brain's cortical areas, in use of brain pathways, and in secretion of hormones associated with different emotions. *Polygraphs* measure several physiological indicators of emotion, but they are not accurate enough to justify their widespread use in business and law enforcement. The use of guilty knowledge questions and new forms of technology may produce better indications of lying.

40-4 **To experience emotions, must we consciously interpret and label them?** Schachter and Singer's two-factor theory of emotion contends that the cognitive labels we put on our states of arousal are an essential ingredient of emotion. Lazarus agreed that cognition is essential: Many important emotions arise from our interpretations or inferences. Zajonc and LeDoux, however, believe that some simple emotional responses occur instantly, not only outside our conscious awareness but before any cognitive processing occurs. The interplay between emotion and cognition again illustrates our dual-track mind.

Terms and Concepts to Remember

emotion, p. 500

James-Lange theory, p. 500

Cannon-Bard theory, p. 500

two-factor theory, p. 501

polygraph, p. 504

Test Yourself

1. Christine is holding her 8-month-old baby when a fierce dog appears out of nowhere and, with teeth bared, leaps for the baby's face. Christine immediately ducks for cover to protect the baby, screams at the dog, then notices that her heart is banging in her chest and she's broken out in a cold sweat. How would the James-Lange, Cannon-Bard, and two-factor theories explain Christine's emotional reaction?

2. How do the two divisions of the autonomic nervous system help us respond to and recover from a crisis, and why is this relevant to the study of emotions?

(Answers to the Test Yourself questions can be found in Appendix B at the end of the book.)

Ask Yourself

1. Can you remember a time when you began to feel upset or uneasy and only later labeled those feelings?

2. Can you think of a recent time when you noticed your body's reactions to an emotionally charged situation, such as a difficult social setting or perhaps even a test or game you were worrying about in advance? Did you perceive the situation as a challenge or a threat? How well did you do?

∞ WEB

Multiple-choice self-tests and more may be found at www.worthpublishers.com/myers

Detecting Emotion

Gender, Emotion, and Nonverbal Behavior

Culture and Emotional Expression

The Effects of Facial Expressions

MODULE 41

Expressed Emotion

41-1 How do we communicate nonverbally?

There is a simple method of deciphering people's emotions: We read their bodies, listen to their tone of voice, and study their faces. People's expressive behavior reveals their emotion. Does this nonverbal language vary with culture, or is it universal? And do our expressions influence our experienced emotions?

▶‖ Detecting Emotion

All of us communicate nonverbally as well as verbally. To Westerners, a firm handshake immediately conveys an outgoing, expressive personality (Chaplin et al., 2000). With a gaze, an averted glance, or a stare we can communicate intimacy, submission, or dominance (Kleinke, 1986). Among those passionately in love, gazing into each other's eyes is typically prolonged and mutual (Rubin, 1970). Joan Kellerman, James Lewis, and James Laird (1989) wondered if intimate gazes would stir such feelings between strangers. To find out, they asked unacquainted male-female pairs to gaze intently for two minutes either at each other's hands or into each other's eyes. After separating, the eye gazers reported feeling a tingle of attraction and affection.

Most of us are good enough at reading nonverbal cues to decipher the emotions in an old silent film. We are especially good at detecting threats. Even when hearing emotions conveyed in another language, people most readily detect anger (Scherer et al., 2001). When viewing subliminally flashed words, we more often sense the presence of a negative word, such as *snake* or *bomb* (Dijksterhuis & Aarts, 2003). And in a crowd of faces, a single angry face will "pop out" faster than a single happy one (Fox et al., 2000; Hansen & Hansen, 1988; Öhman et al., 2001).

Experience can sensitize us to particular emotions, as shown by experiments using a series of faces (like those in **FIGURE 41.1**) that morphed from anger to fear (or sadness). Viewing such faces, physically abused children are much quicker than other children to spot the signals of anger. Shown a face that is 40 percent anger and 60 percent fear, they are as likely to perceive anger as fear. Their perceptions become sensitively attuned to glimmers of danger that nonabused children miss.

Hard-to-control facial muscles reveal signs of emotions you may be trying to conceal. Lifting just the inner part of your eyebrows, which few people do consciously, reveals distress or worry. Eyebrows raised and pulled together signal fear. Activated muscles under the eyes and raised cheeks suggest a natural smile. A feigned smile, such as one we make for a photographer, often continues for more than 4 or 5 seconds. Most authentic expressions have faded by that time. Feigned smiles are also switched on and off more abruptly than is a genuine happy smile (Bugental, 1986).

Network Photographers/Alamy

A silent language of emotion Hindu classic dance uses the face and body to effectively convey 10 different emotions (Hejmadi et al., 2000).

FIGURE 41.1 Experience influences how we perceive emotions Viewing the morphed middle face, evenly mixing anger with fear, physically abused children were more likely than nonabused children to perceive the face as angry (Pollak & Kistler, 2002; Pollak & Tolley-Schell, 2003).

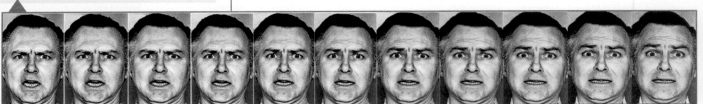

Used by permission of S. D. Pollack, D. J. Kistler, and the National Academy of Sciences

Our brains are rather amazing detectors of subtle expressions. Elisha Babad, Frank Bernieri, and Robert Rosenthal (1991) discovered just *how* amazing after filming teachers talking to unseen schoolchildren. A mere 10-second clip of either the teacher's voice or face provided enough clues for both young and old viewers to determine whether the teacher liked and admired the child he or she was addressing. In another experiment, a glimpse of a face for even one-tenth of a second was enough for people to judge someone's trustworthiness (Willis & Todorov, 2006). When researchers blur faces or hide them in distracting information, people still display remarkable skill at recognizing distinct emotions (Smith et al., 2005). Exposing different facial parts shows the eyes and mouth to be most revealing, with fear and anger read mostly from the eyes, and happiness from the mouth (Adolphs, 2006).

Despite our brain's emotion-detecting skill, we find it difficult to detect deceiving expressions (Porter & ten Brinke, 2008). People worldwide believe that one telltale sign of lying is averting one's gaze (Bond et al., 2006). Perhaps this is what former President George W. Bush had in mind when telling U.S. troops in Baghdad that he had come "to look at Prime Minister Maliki in the eyes and determine whether or not he is as dedicated to a free Iraq as you are"(Burns & Filkins, 2006). Yet in one digest of 206 studies of discerning truth from lies, people were just 54 percent accurate— barely better than a coin toss (Bond & DePaulo, 2006). Moreover, contrary to claims that some experts can spot lies, the available research indicates that virtually no one beats chance by much (Bond & DePaulo, 2008).

Some of us are, however, more sensitive than others to physical cues. Robert Rosenthal, Judith Hall, and their colleagues (1979) discovered this by showing hundreds of people brief film clips of portions of a person's emotionally expressive face or body, sometimes accompanied by a garbled voice. For example, after a 2-second scene revealing only the face of an upset woman, the researchers would ask whether the woman was criticizing someone for being late or was talking about her divorce. Rosenthal and Hall reported that, given such "thin slices," some people are much better than others at detecting emotion. Introverts tend to excel at reading others' emotions, although extraverts are generally easier to read (Ambady et al., 1995).

Gestures, facial expressions, and tones of voice are all absent in computer-based communication. E-mail communications sometimes include sideways *emoticons,* such as ;-) for a knowing wink and :-(for a frown. But e-mail messages and Internet discussions otherwise lack nonverbal cues to status, personality, and age. Nobody knows what you look or sound like, or anything about your background; you are judged solely on your words. When first meeting an e-mail pen pal face to face, people are often surprised at the person they encounter.

It's also easy to misread e-mailed communications, where the absence of expressive e-motion can make for ambiguous emotion. So can the absence of those vocal nuances by which we signal that a statement is serious, kidding, or sarcastic. Research by Justin Kruger and his colleagues (2005) shows that communicators often think their "just kidding" intent is equally clear, whether e-mailed or spoken. But they commonly exhibit egocentrism by not foreseeing misinterpretations in the absence of nonverbal cues.

Which of Paul Ekman's smiles is feigned, which natural? The smile on the right engages the facial muscles of a natural smile.

‖ Injected as part of the war on wrinkles, Botox paralyzes facial muscles that create wrinkles, allowing the overlying skin to relax and smooth. By erasing the subtle expressions of frown lines or smiling eyes, might this cosmetic procedure hide subtle emotions? ‖

▶‖ Gender, Emotion, and Nonverbal Behavior

Is women's intuition, as so many believe, superior to men's? Consider: As Jackie Larsen left her Grand Marais, Minnesota, church prayer group one April 2001 morning, she encountered Christopher Bono, a clean-cut, well-mannered youth. Bono's car had broken down, and he said he was looking for a ride to meet friends in Thunder

Bay. When Bono later appeared in Larsen's shop, where she had promised to help him phone his friends, she felt a pain in her stomach. Intuitively sensing that something was very wrong with this young man, she insisted that they talk outside on the sidewalk. "I said, 'I am a mother and I have to talk to you like a mother. . . . I can tell by your manners that you have a nice mother.'" At the mention of his mother, Bono's eyes fixed on her. "I don't know where my mother is," he said.

As the conversation ended, Larsen directed Bono back to the church to meet the pastor. She also called the police and suggested that they trace his license plates. The car was registered to his mother in southern Illinois. When police went to her apartment, they found blood all over and Lucia Bono dead in the bathtub. Christopher Bono, 16, was charged with first-degree murder (Biggs, 2001).

Was it a coincidence that Larsen, who saw through Bono's calm exterior, was a woman? Some psychologists would say *no*. In her analysis of 125 studies of sensitivity to nonverbal cues, Judith Hall (1984, 1987) discerned that, when given "thin slices," women generally surpass men at reading people's emotional cues. Women's nonverbal sensitivity also gives them an edge in spotting lies (DePaulo, 1994). And women have surpassed men in discerning whether a male-female couple is a genuine romantic couple or a posed phony couple, and in discerning which of two people in a photo is the other's supervisor (Barnes & Sternberg, 1989).

Women's nonverbal sensitivity helps explain their greater emotional literacy. Invited by Lisa Feldman Barrett and her colleagues (2000) to describe how they would feel in certain situations, men described simpler emotional reactions. You might like to try this yourself: Ask some people how they might feel when saying good-bye to friends after graduation. Barrett's work suggests you are more likely to hear men say, simply, "I'll feel bad," and to hear women express more complex emotions: "It will be bittersweet; I'll feel both happy and sad."

Women's skill at decoding others' emotions may also contribute to their greater emotional responsiveness in both positive and negative situations (Grossman & Wood, 1993; Sprecher & Sedikides, 1993; Stoppard & Gruchy, 1993). In studies of 23,000 people from 26 cultures around the world, women more than men reported themselves open to feelings (Costa et al., 2001). That helps explain the extremely strong perception that emotionality is "more true of women"—a perception expressed by nearly 100 percent of 18- to 29-year-old Americans (Newport, 2001).

One exception: Anger strikes most people as a more masculine emotion. Ask someone to imagine an angry face, then ask them: Is it male, as it seemed to be for three in four Arizona State University students (Becker et al., 2007)? The researchers also found that people are quicker to see anger on men's faces. And if a gender-neutral face is made to look angry, most people perceive it as male. If smiling, it's more likely to be perceived as female (**FIGURE 41.2**).

FIGURE 41.2 Angry = Male When Vaughn Becker and his colleagues (2007) manipulated a gender-neutral face, people were more likely to see it as a male when they gave it an angry expression.

 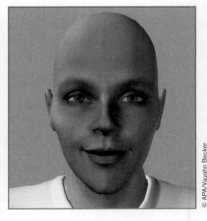

© APA/Vaughn Becker

When surveyed, women are also far more likely than men to describe themselves as empathic. If you have *empathy,* you identify with others and imagine what it must be like to walk in their shoes. You rejoice with those who rejoice and weep with those who weep. Physiological measures of empathy, such as one's heart rate while seeing another's distress, reveal a much smaller gender gap than is reported in surveys (Eisenberg & Lennon, 1983). Nevertheless, females are more likely to *express* empathy—to cry and to report distress when observing someone in distress. Ann Kring and Albert Gordon (1998) observed this gender difference in videotapes of men and women students watching film clips that were sad (children with a dying parent), happy (slapstick comedy), or frightening (a man nearly falling off the ledge of a tall building). As **FIGURE 41.3** shows, the women reacted more visibly to each film type. Women also tend to experience emotional events (such as viewing pictures of mutilation) more deeply—with more brain activation in areas sensitive to emotion—and then to remember the scenes better three weeks later (Canli et al., 2002).

In another exploration of gender and facial expression, Harold Hill and Alan Johnston (2001) animated an image of an average head with expressions (smirks, head tosses, raised eyebrows) that had been digitally captured from the faces of London University students as they read a joke. Despite having no anatomical clues to gender, observers could usually detect gender in the telltale expressions.

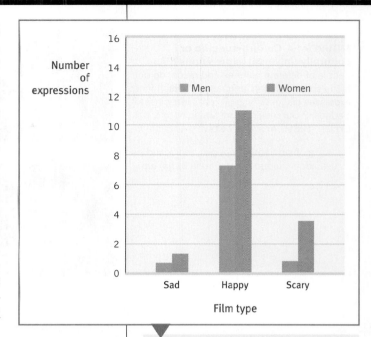

FIGURE 41.3 Gender and expressiveness Although male and female students did not differ dramatically in self-reported emotions or physiological responses while viewing emotional films, the women's faces *showed* much more emotion. (From Kring & Gordon, 1998.)

▶|| Culture and Emotional Expression

41-2 Are nonverbal expressions of emotion universally understood?

The meaning of gestures varies with the culture. Some years ago, psychologist Otto Klineberg (1938) observed that in Chinese literature people clapped their hands to express worry or disappointment, laughed a great "Ho-Ho" to express anger, and stuck out their tongues to show surprise. Similarly, the North American "thumbs up" and "A-OK" signs are considered insults in certain other cultures. (When former U.S. President Richard Nixon made the latter sign in Brazil, he didn't realize he was offering a crude insult.) Just how important cultural definitions of gestures can be was demonstrated in 1968, when North Korea publicized photos of supposedly happy officers from a captured U.S. Navy spy ship. In the photo, three of the men raised their middle fingers; they had told captors it was a "Hawaiian good luck sign" (Fleming & Scott, 1991).

Do facial expressions also have different meanings in different cultures? To find out, two investigative teams—one led by Paul Ekman, Wallace Friesen, and others (1975, 1987, 1994), the other by Carroll Izard (1977, 1994)—showed photographs of various facial expressions to people in different parts of the world and asked them to guess the emotion. You can try this matching task yourself by pairing the six emotions with the six faces of **FIGURE 41.4** on the next page.

Regardless of your cultural background, you probably did pretty well. A smile's a smile the world around. Ditto for anger, and to a lesser extent the other basic expressions (Elfenbein & Ambady, 1999). (There is no culture where people frown when they are happy.) Thus, a glimpse at competitors' spontaneous expressions following an Olympic judo competition gives a very good clue to who won, no matter their country (Matsumoto & Willingham, 2006).

FIGURE 41.4 Culture-specific or culturally universal expressions? As people of differing cultures and races, do our faces speak differing languages? Which face expresses disgust? Anger? Fear? Happiness? Sadness? Surprise? (From Matsumoto & Ekman, 1989.) Answers below.

From left to right, top to bottom: happiness, surprise, fear, sadness, anger, disgust.

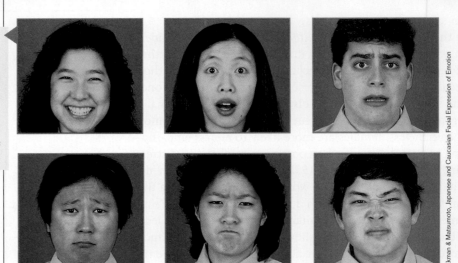

"For news of the heart, ask the face."
Guinean proverb

‖ While weightless, astronauts' internal bodily fluids move toward their upper body and their faces become puffy. This makes nonverbal communication more difficult, increasing the risks of misunderstanding, especially among multinational crews (Gelman, 1989). ‖

Do people from different cultures share these similarities because they share experiences, such as American movies or the BBC and CNN broadcasts? Apparently not. Ekman and his team asked isolated people in New Guinea to display various emotions in response to such statements as, "Pretend your child has died." When the researchers showed tapes of the New Guineans' facial reactions to North American collegians, the students read them easily.

Facial expressions do contain some nonverbal accents that provide clues to one's culture (Marsh et al., 2003). So it is not surprising that data from 182 studies show slightly enhanced accuracy when people judge emotions from their own culture (Elfenbein & Ambady, 2002, 2003a,b). Still, the telltale signs of emotion generally cross cultures. Even our emotional *display rules* (such as expressing more emotion to fellow group members than to outsiders) cross world cultures (Matsumoto et al., 2008).

Children's facial expressions—even those of blind children who have never seen a face—are also universal (Eibl-Eibesfeldt, 1971). People blind from birth spontaneously exhibit the common facial expressions associated with such emotions as joy, sadness, fear, and anger (Galati et al., 1997). The world over, children cry when distressed, shake their heads when defiant, and smile when they are happy.

The discovery that facial muscles speak a fairly universal language would not have surprised pioneering emotion researcher Charles Darwin (1809–1882). He speculated that in prehistoric times, before our ancestors communicated in words, their ability to convey threats, greetings, and submission with facial expressions helped them survive. That shared heritage, he believed, is why all humans express the basic emotions with similar facial expressions. A sneer, for example, retains elements of an animal baring its teeth in a snarl. Emotional expressions may enhance our survival in other ways, too. Surprise raises the eyebrows and widens the eyes, enabling us to take in more information. Disgust wrinkles the nose, closing it from foul odors.

Smiles, too, are social phenomena as well as emotional reflexes. Bowlers seldom smile when they score a strike—they smile when they turn to face their companions (Jones et al., 1991; Kraut & Johnston, 1979). Even euphoric winners of Olympic gold medals typically don't smile when they are awaiting their ceremony but do when interacting with officials and facing the crowd and cameras (Fernández-Dols & Ruiz-Belda, 1995).

It has been adaptive for us to interpret faces in particular contexts. People judge an angry face set in a frightening situation as afraid. They judge a fearful face set in a painful situation as pained (Carroll & Russell, 1996). Movie directors harness this phenomenon by creating contexts and soundtracks that amplify our perceptions of particular emotions.

Although cultures share a universal facial language for basic emotions, they differ in how much emotion they express. Cultures that encourage individuality, as in Western Europe, Australia, New Zealand, and North America, display mostly visible emotions (van Hemert et al., 2007). In Chinese culture, which encourages people to adjust to others, personal emotions are less visibly displayed (Tsai et al., 2007). Ditto Japan, where people infer emotion more from the surrounding context, and where the difficult-to-control eyes convey more emotion than the mouth, which is so expressive in North America (Masuda et al., 2008; Yuki et al., 2007). Eyes convey emotion in many ways. When someone asks you a question that requires some thinking, are you more likely to look up or down? In Japan, people typically look down, which displays respect for others. Canadians typically look up (McCarthy et al., 2006).

Cultural differences also exist within nations. The Irish and their Irish-American descendants tend to be more expressive than Scandinavians and their Scandinavian-American descendants (Tsai & Chentsova-Dutton, 2003). And that reminds us of a familiar lesson: Like most psychological events, emotion is best understood not only as a biological and cognitive phenomenon, but also as a social-cultural phenomenon (**FIGURE 41.5**).

Biological influences:	Psychological influences:
• physiological arousal	• cognitive labeling
• evolutionary adaptiveness	• gender differences
• brain pathways	
• spillover effect	

Emotion

Social-cultural influences:
• expressiveness
• presence of others
• cultural expectations

FIGURE 41.5 Levels of analysis for the study of emotion As with other psychological phenomena, researchers explore emotion at biological, psychological, and social-cultural levels.

▶‖ The Effects of Facial Expressions

41-3 Do our facial expressions influence our feelings?

As William James struggled with feelings of depression and grief, he came to believe that we can control emotions by going "through the outward movements" of any emotion we want to experience. "To feel cheerful," he advised, "sit up cheerfully, look around cheerfully, and act as if cheerfulness were already there."

Studies of emotional effects of facial expressions reveal precisely what James might have predicted. Expressions not only communicate emotion, they also amplify and regulate it. In his 1872 book, *The Expression of the Emotions in Man and Animals*, Darwin contended that "the free expression by outward signs of an emotion intensifies it. . . . He who gives way to violent gestures will increase his rage."

Was Darwin right? Let's test Darwin's hypothesis: Fake a big grin. Now scowl. Can you feel the "smile therapy" difference? Participants in dozens of experiments have felt a difference. For example, James Laird and his colleagues (1974, 1984, 1989) subtly induced students to make a frowning expression by asking them to "contract these muscles" and "pull your brows together" (supposedly to help the researchers attach facial electrodes). The results? The students reported feeling a little angry. People instructed to mold their faces in ways that express other basic emotions also experienced those emotions (**FIGURE 41.6**). For example, they reported feeling more fear than anger, disgust, or sadness when made to construct a fearful expression: "Raise your eyebrows. And open your eyes wide. Move your whole head back, so that your chin is tucked in a little bit, and let your mouth relax and hang open a little" (Duclos et al., 1989). The face is more than a billboard that displays our feelings; *it also feeds our feelings.*

In the absence of competing emotions, this *facial feedback* effect is subtle yet detectable. Students induced to smile have felt happier and recalled happier memories than did frowners. Just activating one of the smiling

"Whenever I feel afraid
I hold my head erect
And whistle a happy tune."
Richard Rodgers and Oscar Hammerstein, *The King and I*, 1958

FIGURE 41.6 How to make people frown without telling them to frown Randy Larsen, Margaret Kasimatis, and Kurt Frey's (1992) solution: Attach two golf tees above the eyebrows and ask the participants to make the tee tips touch. Participants felt sad while viewing scenes of war, sickness, and starvation, and even sadder with their "sad face" muscles activated.

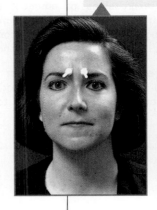

|| A request from your author: Smile often as you read this book. ||

muscles by holding a pen in the teeth (rather than with the lips, which activates a frowning muscle) is enough to make cartoons seem more amusing (Strack et al., 1988). A heartier smile—made not just with the mouth but with raised cheeks that crinkle the eyes—enhances positive feelings even more when you are reacting to something pleasant or funny (Soussignan, 2001). Smile warmly on the outside and you feel better on the inside. When smiling you will even more quickly understand sentences that describe pleasant events (Havas et al., 2007). Scowl and the whole world seems to scowl back.

Two new studies demonstrate the power of facial feedback. In one, Tiffany Ito and her colleagues (2006) used the pen-in-the-teeth procedure to induce happiness while people viewed pictures of faces. If they had viewed Black rather than White faces, they later, on an Implicit Attitude Test, exhibited lessened racial bias against Blacks. The good feeling had spread by association. Another study used Botox injections to paralyze the frowning muscles of 10 depressed patients (Finzi & Wasserman, 2006). Two months after the treatment, 9 of the 10 nonfrowning patients were no longer depressed. (This intriguing study awaits replication with an untreated control group.)

Sara Snodgrass and her associates (1986) observed the *behavior feedback* phenomenon with walking. You can duplicate the participants' experience: Walk for a few minutes with short, shuffling steps, keeping your eyes downcast. Now walk around taking long strides, with your arms swinging and your eyes looking straight ahead. Can you feel your mood shift? Going through the motions awakens the emotions.

One small way to become more empathic is to let your own face mimic another person's expression (Vaughn & Lanzetta, 1981). Acting as another acts helps us feel what another feels. Indeed, natural mimicry of others' emotions helps explain why emotions are contagious (Dimberg et al., 2000; Neumann & Strack, 2000). Blocking people's natural mimicry, for example, by having them bite a pencil with their teeth, impairs their ability to recognize others' emotions (Oberman et al., 2007).

REVIEW

Expressed Emotion

41-1 **How do we communicate nonverbally?** Much of our communication is through the silent language of the body. Even very thin (seconds-long) filmed slices of behavior can reveal feelings. Women tend to be better at reading people's emotional cues.

41-2 **Are nonverbal expressions of emotion universally understood?** Some gestures are culturally determined. Facial expressions, such as those of happiness and fear, are common the world over. Cultures differ in the amount of emotion they express.

41-3 **Do our facial expressions influence our feelings?** Expressions do more than communicate emotion to others. They also amplify the felt emotion and signal the body to respond accordingly.

Test Yourself

1. Who tends to express more emotion—men or women? How do we know the answer to that question?

(Answers to the Test Yourself questions can be found in Appendix B at the end of the book.)

Ask Yourself

1. Can you think of one situation in which you would like to change the way you feel, and create a simple plan for doing so? For instance, if you would like to feel more cheerful on your way to class tomorrow morning rather than dragging yourself there, you might try walking briskly—with head held high and a pleasant expression on your face.

MODULE 42

Fear

Anger

Happiness

Experienced Emotion

How many distinct emotions are there? Carroll Izard (1977) isolated 10 basic emotions (joy, interest-excitement, surprise, sadness, anger, disgust, contempt, fear, shame, and guilt), most of which are present in infancy (**FIGURE 42.1**). Jessica Tracey and Richard Robins (2004) believe that pride is also a distinct emotion, signaled by a small smile, head slightly tilted back, and an open posture. And Phillip Shaver and his colleagues (1996) believe that love, too, may be a basic emotion. But Izard has argued that other emotions are combinations of these 10, with love, for example, being a mixture of joy and interest-excitement.

(a) Joy (mouth forming smile, cheeks lifted, twinkle in eye)

(b) Anger (brows drawn together and downward, eyes fixed, mouth squarish)

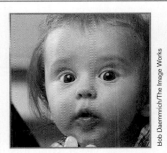

(c) Interest (brows raised or knitted, mouth softly rounded, lips may be pursed)

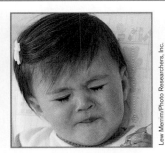

(d) Disgust (nose wrinkled, upper lip raised, tongue pushed outward)

(e) Surprise (brows raised, eyes widened, mouth rounded in oval shape)

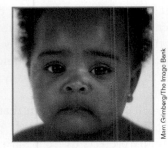

(f) Sadness (brow's inner corners raised, mouth corners drawn down)

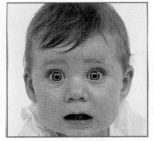

(g) Fear (brows level, drawn in and up, eyelids lifted, mouth corners retracted)

FIGURE 42.1 Infants' naturally occurring emotions To identify the emotions present from birth, Carroll Izard analyzed the facial expressions of infants.

The ingredients of emotion include not only physiology and expressive behavior but also our conscious experience. Varied people, including Estonians, Poles, Greeks, Chinese, and Canadians, place emotional experience along the two dimensions illustrated in **FIGURE 42.2** on the next page—pleasant/positive-versus-unpleasant/negative *valence,* and low-versus-high *arousal* (Russell et al., 1989, 1999a,b; Watson et al., 1999). On the valence and arousal dimensions, *terrified* is more frightened (more unpleasant and aroused) than *afraid, enraged* is angrier than *angry, delighted* is happier than *happy.*

Let's take a closer look at three of these emotions: fear, anger, and happiness. What functions do they serve? What influences our experience of each?

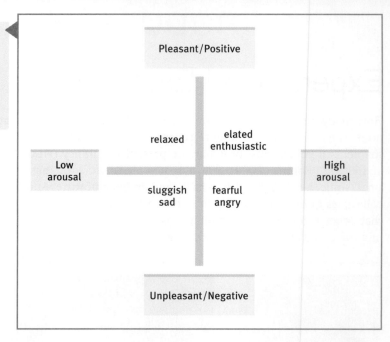

FIGURE 42.2 **Two dimensions of emotion** James Russell, David Watson, Auke Tellegen, and others describe emotions as variations on two dimensions—arousal (low versus high) and valence (pleasant versus unpleasant feeling).

▶‖ **Fear**

42-1 What is the function of fear, and how do we learn fears?

Fear can be poisonous. It can torment us, rob us of sleep, and preoccupy our thinking. People can be literally scared to death. Fear can also be contagious. In 1903, someone yelled "Fire!" as a fire broke out in Chicago's Iroquois Theater. Eddie Foy, the comedian on stage at the time, tried to reassure the crowd by calling out, "Don't get excited. There's no danger. Take it easy!" Alas, the crowd panicked. During the 10 minutes it took the fire department to arrive and quickly extinguish the flames, more than 500 people perished, most of them trampled or smothered in a stampede. Bodies were piled 7 or 8 feet deep in the stairways, and many of the faces bore heel marks (Brown, 1965).

More often, fear is adaptive. It's an alarm system that prepares our bodies to flee from danger. Fear of real or imagined enemies binds people together as families, tribes, and nations. Fear of injury protects us from harm. Fear of punishment or retaliation restrains our harming one another. Fear helps us focus on a problem and rehearse coping strategies. Fearful expressions improve peripheral vision and speed eye movements, thus boosting sensory input (Susskind et al., 2008).

‖ One explanation of sudden death caused by a voodoo "curse" is that the terrified person's parasympathetic nervous system, which calms the body, overreacts to the extreme arousal by slowing the heart to a stop (Seligman, 1974). ‖

Learning Fear

People can be afraid of almost anything—"afraid of truth, afraid of fortune, afraid of death, and afraid of each other," observed Ralph Waldo Emerson. The "politics of fear" builds upon people's fear—fear of terrorists, fear of immigrants, fear of criminals. Why so many fears? Behaviorists John B. Watson and Rosalie Rayner (1920) showed that infants can learn to fear furry objects associated with frightening noises. When infants begin to crawl, they learn from their falls and near-falls—and become increasingly afraid of heights (Campos et al., 1992). Through such conditioning, the short list of naturally painful and frightening events can multiply into a long list of human fears—fear of driving or flying, fear of mice or cockroaches, fear of closed or open spaces, fear of failure or success, fear of another race or nation.

Learning by observation extends the list. Susan Mineka (1985, 2002) sought to explain why nearly all monkeys reared in the wild fear snakes, yet lab-reared monkeys do not. Surely, most wild monkeys do not actually suffer snake bites. Do they learn their fear through observation? To find out, Mineka experimented with six monkeys reared in the wild (all strongly fearful of snakes) and their lab-reared offspring (virtually none of which feared snakes). After repeatedly observing their parents or peers refusing to reach for food in the presence of a snake, the younger monkeys developed a similar strong fear of snakes. When retested three months later, their learned fear persisted. Humans likewise learn fears by observing others (Olsson et al., 2007). This suggests that our fears include the fears we learn from our parents and friends.

The Biology of Fear

We may be biologically prepared to learn some fears more quickly than others. Monkeys learn to fear snakes even by watching tapes of monkeys reacting fearfully to a snake; but they *don't* learn to fear flowers when clever editing transposes the seemingly feared stimulus into a flower (Cook & Mineka, 1991). We humans quickly learn to fear snakes, spiders, and cliffs—fears that probably helped our ancestors survive (Öhman & Mineka, 2003). But our Stone Age fears leave us unprepared for high-tech dangers—cars, electricity, bombs, and global climate change—all of which are now far more dangerous.

One key to fear learning lies in the amygdala, that limbic system neural center deep in the brain (**FIGURE 42.3**). The amygdala plays a key role in associating various emotions, including fear, with certain situations (Baringa, 1992b; Reijmers et al., 2007). Rabbits learn to react with fear to a tone that predicts an impending small shock—unless their amygdala is damaged. If rats have their amygdala deactivated by a drug that blocks the strengthening of neural connections, they, too, show no fear learning.

The amygdala is similarly involved in human fears. If an experimenter repeatedly blasts people with a blaring horn after showing a blue slide, they will begin to react emotionally to the slide (as measured by the electricity conducted by their perspiring skin). If they have suffered damage to the nearby hippocampus, they still show the emotional reaction—an implicit memory—but they won't be able to remember why. If they have instead suffered amygdala damage, they will consciously remember the conditioning but will show no emotional effect of it (Schacter, 1996). Patients who have lost use of their amygdala are unusually trusting of scary-looking people (Adolphs et al., 1998).

Of course, there are people whose fears seem to fall outside the average range. Some, with *phobias*, have intense fears of specific objects (such as bugs) or situations (such as public speaking) that disrupt their ability to cope. Others—courageous heroes and remorseless criminals—are less fearful than most of us. Astronauts and adventurers who have "the right stuff"—who can keep their wits and function coolly and effectively in times of severe stress—seem to thrive on risk. So, too, do con artists and killers who calmly charm their intended victims. In laboratory tests, they exhibit little fear of a tone that predictably precedes a painful electric shock.

Experience helps shape such fearfulness or fearlessness, but so do our genes. Genes influence our temperament—our emotional reactivity. Among identical twins, one twin's level of fearfulness is similar to the other's—even when they have been reared separately (Lykken, 1982). Scientists have isolated a gene that influences the amygdala's response to frightening situations (Hariri et al., 2002). People with a

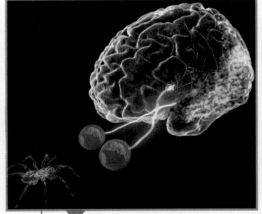

Courtesy of *National Geographic Magazine* and Laboratory of Neuro Imaging (LONI) at UCLA. Art and brain modeling by Amanda Hammond, Jacopo Annese, and Arthur Toga, LONI; spider art by Joon-Hyuck Kim.

FIGURE 42.3 The amygdala—a neural key to fear learning Nerves running out from these knots of neural tissue, one on either side of the brain's center, carry messages that control heart rate, sweating, stress hormones, attention, and other engines that rev up in threatening situations.

Hard-wired fears Entertainment businesses exploit our survival circuits. Although we can know that amusement park deaths are extremely rare, our fear alarm system nevertheless gives us an adrenaline rush and sweaty palms during a free-flying fair ride.

oote boe/Alamy

short version of this gene have less of a protein that speeds the reuptake of the neuro-transmitter serotonin. With more serotonin available to activate their amygdala neurons, people with this short gene exhibit a revved-up amygdala response to frightening pictures.

▶‖ Anger

42-2 What are the causes and consequences of anger?

Anger, the sages have said, is "a short madness" (Horace, 65–8 B.C.) that "carries the mind away" (Virgil, 70–19 B.C.) and can be "many times more hurtful than the injury that caused it" (Thomas Fuller, 1654–1734). But they have also said that "noble anger" (William Shakespeare, 1564–1616) "makes any coward brave" (Cato, 234–149 B.C.) and "brings back . . . strength" (Virgil).

What makes us angry? Sometimes anger is a response to a friend or loved one's perceived misdeeds, especially when the person's act seems willful, unjustified, and avoidable (Averill, 1983). But small hassles and blameless annoyances—foul odors, high temperatures, a traffic jam, aches and pains—also have the power to make us angry (Berkowitz, 1990).

Anger can harm us—chronic hostility is linked to heart disease (Smith & Ruiz, 2002; Williams 1993). How, then, can we rid ourselves of our anger? In a Gallup survey of teens, boys more than girls reported walking away from the situation or working it off with exercise; girls more often reported talking with a friend, listening to music, or writing (Ray, 2005). Popular books and articles on aggression at times advise that even releasing angry feelings as hostile outbursts can be better than internalizing them. When irritated, should we lash out at the offender? Are advice columnists right in urging us to teach children to vent their anger? Are "recovery" therapists right in encouraging us to rage at our dead parents, imaginatively curse the boss, or confront our childhood abuser?

Encouraging people to vent their rage is typical in individualized cultures, but it would seldom be heard in cultures where people's identity is centered more on the group. People who keenly sense their *inter*dependence see anger as a threat to group harmony (Markus & Kitayama, 1991). In Tahiti, for instance, people learn to be considerate and gentle. In Japan, from infancy on, angry expressions are less common than in Western cultures.

The Western "vent your anger" advice presumes that through aggressive action or fantasy we can achieve emotional release, or **catharsis.** Experimenters report that *sometimes* when people retaliate against a provoker, they may indeed calm down. But this tends to be true only *if* their counterattack is directed against the provoker, *if* their retaliation seems justifiable, and *if* their target is not intimidating (Geen & Quanty, 1977; Hokanson & Edelman, 1966). In short, expressing anger can be *temporarily* calming *if* it does not leave us feeling guilty or anxious.

However, despite the temporary afterglow, catharsis usually fails to cleanse one's rage. More often, expressing anger breeds more anger. For one thing, it may provoke further retaliation, thus escalating a minor conflict into a major confrontation. For another, expressing anger can magnify anger. As *behavior feedback* research indicates, acting angry can make us feel angrier. Ebbe Ebbesen and his colleagues (1975) saw this when they interviewed 100 frustrated engineers and technicians just laid off by an aerospace company. They asked some of the workers questions that released hostility, such as, "What instances can you think of where the company has not been fair

Wolfgang Kaehler

A cool culture Domestic violence is rare in Micronesia. This photo of community life on Pulap Island suggests one possible reason: Family life takes place in the open. Relatives and neighbors who witness angry outbursts can step in before the emotion escalates into child, spouse, or elder abuse.

SIX CHIX

© Isabella Bannerman. Distributed by King Features Syndicate.

The catharsis myth: Is it true?

with you?" When these people later filled out a questionnaire that assessed their attitudes toward the company, did this opportunity to "drain off" their hostility reduce it? Quite the contrary. Compared with those who had not vented their anger, those who had let it all out exhibited *more* hostility. Even when provoked people hit a punching bag *believing* it will be cathartic, the effect is the opposite—leading them to exhibit *more* cruelty (Bushman et al., 1999). And when they wallop a punching bag while ruminating about the person who angered them, they become even more aggressive when given a chance for revenge. "Venting to reduce anger is like using gasoline to put out a fire," concluded researcher Brad Bushman (2002).

When anger fuels physically or verbally aggressive acts we later regret, it becomes maladaptive. Anger primes prejudice. After 9/11, Americans who responded with anger more than fear displayed intolerance for immigrants and Muslims (DeSteno et al., 2004; Skitka et al., 2004). Angry outbursts that temporarily calm us are dangerous in another way: They may be reinforcing and therefore habit forming. If stressed managers find they can drain off some of their tension by berating an employee, then the next time they feel irritated and tense they may be more likely to explode again. Think about it: The next time you are angry you are likely to do whatever has relieved your anger in the past.

What, then, is the best way to handle our anger? Experts offer two suggestions. First, wait. You can bring down the level of physiological arousal of anger by waiting. "It is true of the body as of arrows," noted Carol Tavris (1982), "what goes up must come down. Any emotional arousal will simmer down if you just wait long enough." Second, deal with anger in a way that involves neither being chronically angry over every little annoyance, nor sulking and rehearsing your grievances. Ruminating inwardly about the causes of your anger serves only to increase it (Rusting & Nolen-Hoeksema, 1998). Calm yourself by exercising, playing an instrument, or talking it through with a friend.

Anger does communicate strength and competence (Tiedens, 2001). It can benefit a relationship when it expresses a grievance in ways that promote reconciliation rather than retaliation. Controlled expressions of anger are more adaptive than either hostile outbursts or pent-up angry feelings. When James Averill (1983) asked people to recall or keep careful records of their experiences with anger, they often recalled reacting assertively rather than hurtfully. Their anger frequently led them to talk things over with the offender, thereby lessening the aggravation. Civility means not only keeping silent about trivial irritations but also communicating important ones clearly and assertively. A nonaccusing statement of feeling—perhaps letting one's housemate know that "I get irritated when the dirty dishes are left for me to clean up"—can help resolve the conflicts that cause anger.

What if someone else's behavior really hurts you? Research commends the age-old response of forgiveness. Without letting the offender off the hook or inviting further harm, forgiveness releases anger and calms the body. To explore the bodily effects of forgiveness, Charlotte Witvliet and her co-researchers (2001) invited college students to recall an incident where someone had hurt them. As the students mentally rehearsed forgiveness, their negative feelings—and their perspiration, blood pressure, heart rate, and facial tension—all were lower than when they rehearsed their grudges.

▶‖ **Happiness**

42-3   What are the causes and consequences of happiness?

"How to gain, how to keep, how to recover happiness is in fact for most men at all times the secret motive for all they do," observed William James (1902, p. 76). Understandably so, for one's state of happiness or unhappiness colors everything. People

catharsis emotional release. In psychology, the catharsis hypothesis maintains that "releasing" aggressive energy (through action or fantasy) relieves aggressive urges.

"Anger will never disappear so long as thoughts of resentment are cherished in the mind."

The Buddha, 500 B.C.

who are happy perceive the world as safer, feel more confident, make decisions more easily, rate job applicants more favorably, are more cooperative and tolerant, and live healthier and more energized and satisfied lives (Briñol et al., 2007; Lyubomirsky et al., 2005; Pressman & Cohen, 2005). When your mood is gloomy and your thinking preoccupied, life as a whole seems depressing and meaningless. Let your mood brighten, and your thinking broadens and becomes more playful and creative (Amabile et al., 2005; Fredrickson, 2006; King et al., 2006). Your relationships, your self-image, and your hopes for the future also seem more promising. Positive emotions fuel upward spirals.

This helps explain why college students' happiness helps predict their life course. In one study, women who smiled happily (rather than smiling artificially or not at all) in 1950s college yearbook photos were more likely to be married, and happily so, in middle age (Harker & Keltner, 2001). In another study, which surveyed thousands of U.S. college students in 1976 and restudied them at age 37, happy students had gone on to earn significantly more money than their less-happy-than-average peers (Diener et al., 2002). Nonetheless, it's also true that social reforms are often launched, as well as great literature written, by those not extremely happy with how things are (Oishi et al., 2007).

Moreover—and this is one of psychology's most consistent findings—when we feel happy we more often help others. In study after study, a mood-boosting experience (finding money, succeeding on a challenging task, recalling a happy event) has made people more likely to give money, pick up someone's dropped papers, volunteer time, and do other good deeds. Psychologists call it the **feel-good, do-good phenomenon** (Salovey, 1990). Happiness doesn't just feel good, it does good. (Doing good also promotes good feeling, a phenomenon harnessed by some happiness coaches and instructors as they assign people to perform a daily "random act of kindness" and to record the results.)

Despite the significance of happiness, psychology throughout its history has more often focused on negative emotions. Since 1887, *Psychological Abstracts* (a guide to psychology's literature) has included, as of this writing, 14,889 articles mentioning anger, 93,371 mentioning anxiety, and 120,897 mentioning depression. For every 17 articles on these topics, only 1 dealt with the positive emotions of joy (1789), life satisfaction (6255), or happiness (5764). There is, of course, good reason to focus on negative emotions; they can make our lives miserable and drive us to seek help. But researchers are becoming increasingly interested in **subjective well-being,** assessed either as feelings of happiness (sometimes defined as a high ratio of positive to negative feelings) or as a sense of satisfaction with life. A new *positive psychology* is on the rise.

The Short Life of Emotional Ups and Downs

In their happiness research, psychologists have studied influences on both our temporary moods and our long-term life satisfaction. When studying people's hour-by-hour moods, David Watson (2000) and Daniel Kahneman and his colleagues (2004) discovered that positive emotion rises over the early to middle part of most days (**FIGURE 42.4**). Stressful events—an argument, a sick child, a car problem—trigger bad moods. No surprise there. But by the next day, the gloom nearly always lifts (Affleck et al., 1994; Bolger et al., 1989; Stone & Neale, 1984). If anything, people tend to rebound from a bad day to a *better*-than-usual good mood the following day. When in a bad mood, can you usually depend on rebounding within a day or two? Are your times of elation similarly hard to sustain? Over the long run, our emotional ups and downs tend to balance.

feel-good, do-good phenomenon people's tendency to be helpful when already in a good mood.

subjective well-being self-perceived happiness or satisfaction with life. Used along with measures of objective well-being (for example, physical and economic indicators) to evaluate people's quality of life.

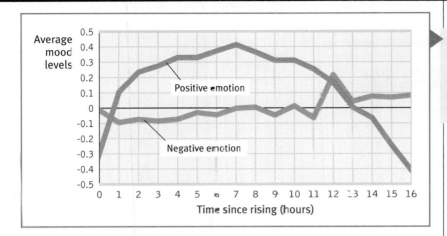

FIGURE 42.4 Moods across the day

When psychologist David Watson (2000) sampled nearly 4500 mood reports from 150 people, he found this pattern of variation from the average levels of positive and negative emotions.

Apart from prolonged grief over the loss of a loved one or lingering anxiety after a trauma (such as child abuse, rape, or the terrors of war), even tragedy is not permanently depressing:

▶ Learning that one is HIV-positive is devastating. But after five weeks of adapting to the grim news, those who have tested positive report feeling less emotionally distraught than they had expected (Sieff et al., 1999).

▶ Kidney dialysis patients recognize that their health is relatively poor, yet in their moment-to-moment experiences they report being just as happy as healthy non-patients (Riis et al., 2005).

▶ European 8- to 12-year-olds with cerebral palsy experience normal psychological well-being (Dickinson et al., 2007).

"If you are a paraplegic," explains Daniel Kahneman (2005), "you will gradually start thinking of other things, and the more time you spend thinking of other things the less miserable you are going to be." A major disability often leaves people less happy than average, yet happier than able-bodied people with depression (Kübler et al., 2005; Lucas, 2007a,b; Oswald & Powdthavee, 2006; Schwartz & Estrin, 2004). Even patients "locked-in" a motionless body "rarely want to die," report Eimar Smith and Mark Delargy (2005), which "counters a popular misconception that such patients would have been better off dead."

In less life-threatening contexts, the pattern continues. Faculty members up for tenure expect their lives would be deflated by a negative decision. Actually, 5 to 10 years later, those denied are not noticeably less happy than those who were awarded tenure, reported Daniel Gilbert and colleagues (1998). The same is true of romantic breakups, which feel devastating. The surprising reality: *We overestimate the duration of our emotions and underestimate our capacity to adapt.*

Positive emotions are similarly hard to sustain. In *Rethinking Happiness: The Science of Psychological Wealth,* Ed Diener and Robert Biswas-Diener (2009) illustrate the short life of most emotions with daily happiness reports of a 21-year-old student undergoing treatment for Hodgkins disease, a cancer of the immune system. Midway through his 80 daily reports, the young man learned the treatment had effectively wiped out his cancer. As **FIGURE 42.5** on the next page shows, on the day he received this wonderful news, he was elated. But although the ensuing month was relatively free of down-in-the-dumps days, his emotions soon returned to near their previous level, with fluctuations in response to daily events.

> "Weeping may tarry for the night, but joy comes with the morning."
> Psalm 30:5

Human resilience Seven weeks after her 1994 wedding, Anna Putt of South Midlands, England, shown here with her husband, Des, suffered a brainstem stroke that left her "locked-in." For months after, she recalls, "I was paralyzed from the neck down and was unable to communicate. These were VERY frightening times. But with encouragement from family, friends, faith, and medical staff, I tried to keep positive." In the ensuing three years, she became able to "talk" (by nodding at letters), to steer an electric wheelchair with her head, and to use a computer (by nodding while wearing spectacles that guide a cursor). Despite her paralysis, she reports that "I enjoy going out in the fresh air. My motto is 'Don't look back, move forward.' God would not want me to stop trying and I have no intention of doing so. Life is what you make of it!"

Courtesy of Anna Putt

FIGURE 42.5 The short life of strong emotions A university student's daily reports of negative and positive moods revealed day-to-day fluctuations, punctuated by temporary elation on the day he learned that he was now cancer free. (From Diener & Biswas-Diener, 2009.)

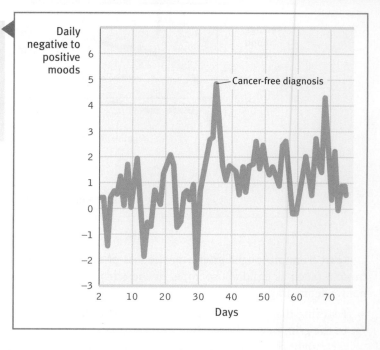

Wealth and Well-Being

"Do you think you would be happier if you made more money?" *Yes*, replied 73 percent of Americans in a 2006 Gallup poll. How important is "Being very well off financially?" In recent years, this has, for entering U.S. collegians, been ranked first or second among 21 possible objectives. Some 3 in 4 students rate their top two objectives—being "very well off" and "raising a family"—as "extremely important" or "essential" (**FIGURE 42.6**).

There is evidence that wealth, to a point, correlates with well-being. Consider:

▶ Within most countries, though especially in poor countries, individuals with lots of money are typically happier than those who struggle to afford life's basic needs (Diener & Biswas-Diener, 2009; Howell & Howell, 2008). They also often enjoy better health than those stressed by poverty and lack of control over their lives.

▶ People in rich countries are also somewhat happier than those in poor countries (Inglehart, 2009).

▶ Those who have experienced a recent windfall from a lottery, an inheritance, or a surging economy typically feel some elation (Diener & Oishi, 2000; Gardner & Oswald, 2007).

‖ In both World Values Surveys in 97 countries (Inglehart, 2008) and Gallup (2008) surveys in 130 countries, the highest self-reported happiness was found in Denmark. ‖

FIGURE 42.6 The changing materialism of entering collegians Surveys of more than 200,000 entering U.S. collegians per year have revealed an increasing desire for wealth after 1970. (From *The American Freshman* surveys, UCLA, 1966 to 2007.)

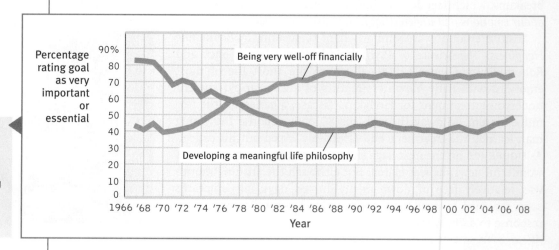

So, it seems that money enough to buy your way out of hunger and hopelessness also buys some happiness. But once one has enough money for comfort and security, piling up more and more matters less and less. This *diminishing returns* phenomenon is familiar to economists as *diminishing marginal utility* and to you as the second piece of dessert satisfying you less than the first. As Robert Cummins (2006) confirms with Australian data, the power of more money to increase happiness is significant at low incomes and diminishes as income rises. A $1000 annual wage increase does a lot more for the average person in Malawi than for the average person in Switzerland. This implies, he adds, that raising low incomes will do more to increase human well-being than raising high incomes.

The income-happiness correlation seemingly occurs because more income produces greater happiness. But perhaps, note John Cacioppo and his collaborators (2008), more happiness produces greater income. So it was among the middle-aged adults whom they studied over time: Today's happiness predicted tomorrow's income better than today's income predicted tomorrow's happiness. (Recall that after graduation, happy collegians likewise outearn their less happy fellow students.)

And consider this: During the last four decades, the average U.S. citizen's buying power almost tripled. Did this greater wealth—enabling twice as many cars per person, not to mention iPods, laptops, and camera cellphones—also buy more happiness? As **FIGURE 42.7** shows, the average American, though certainly richer, is not a bit happier. In 1957, some 35 percent said they were "very happy," as did slightly fewer—32 percent—in 2008. Much the same has been true of Europe, Australia, and Japan, where people enjoy better nutrition, health care, education, and science, and they are somewhat happier than those in very poor countries (Diener & Biswas-Diener, 2002, 2009; Speth, 2008). Yet their increasing real incomes have *not* produced increasing

"Money won't make you happy, Waldron. So instead of a raise, I'm giving a Prozac."

"Americans say that money doesn't bring happiness. But it helps you to live with misery in comfort."

Farah Pahlavi, exiled widow of the wealthy Shah of Iran, 2004

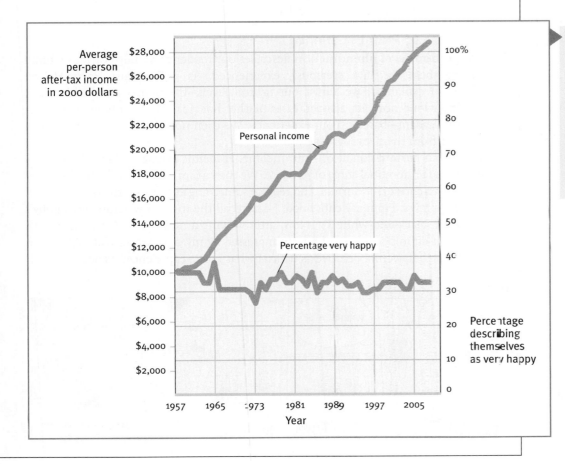

FIGURE 42.7 Does money buy happiness? It surely helps us to avoid certain types of pain. Yet, though buying power has almost tripled since the 1950s, the average American's reported happiness has remained almost unchanged. (Happiness data from National Opinion Research Center surveys; income data from *Historical Statistics of the United States* and *Economic Indicators.*)

happiness. This finding lobs a bombshell at modern materialism: *Economic growth in affluent countries has provided no apparent boost to morale or social well-being.*

Ironically, those who strive hardest for wealth tend to live with lower well-being, a finding that "comes through very strongly in every culture I've looked at," reported Richard Ryan (1999). This is especially so for those seeking money to prove themselves, gain power, or show off rather than support their families (Srivastava et al., 2001). Ryan's collaborator, Tim Kasser (2000, 2002), concluded from their studies that those who instead strive for "intimacy, personal growth, and contribution to the community" experience a higher quality of life.

If we are richer and healthier than were our grandparents at our age, but no happier, should our national priorities focus more on advancing psychological well-being? In Bhutan, King Jigme Singye Wangchuk said that "gross national happiness is more important than gross national product." Bhutan's prime minister framed his annual report in terms of Bhutan's four pillars of progress toward national happiness: "The promotion of equitable and sustainable socio-economic development, preservation and promotion of cultural values, conservation of the natural environment, and establishment of good governance" (Esty, 2004). Diener (2006), supported by 52 colleagues, has proposed ways in which nations might measure national well-being. "Policymakers should be interested in subjective well-being not only because of its inherent value to citizens, but also because individuals' subjective well-being can have positive spillover benefits for the society as a whole."

Two Psychological Phenomena: Adaptation and Comparison

Two psychological principles explain why, for those who are not poor, more money buys little more than a temporary surge of happiness and why our emotions seem attached to elastic bands that pull us back from highs or lows. In its own way, each principle suggests that happiness is relative.

Happiness and Prior Experience

The **adaptation-level phenomenon** describes our tendency to judge various stimuli relative to those we have previously experienced. As psychologist Harry Helson (1898–1977) explained, we adjust our *neutral* levels—the points at which sounds seem neither loud nor soft, temperatures neither hot nor cold, events neither pleasant nor unpleasant—based on our experience. We then notice and react to variations up or down from these levels.

Thus, if our current condition—our income, academic average, or social prestige—increases, we feel an initial surge of pleasure. We then adapt to this new level of achievement, come to consider it normal, and require something even better to give us another surge of happiness. From my childhood, I can recall the thrill of watching my family's first 12-inch, black-and-white TV. Now, after viewing a movie on a family member's 60-inch high-definition screen, I am unimpressed by my once wonderful 27-inch TV. Having adapted upward, I perceive as neutral what I once experienced as positive.

"But on the positive side, money can't buy happiness—so who cares?"

"No happiness lasts for long."
Seneca, *Agamemnon*, A.D. 60

"Continued pleasures wear off. . . . Pleasure is always contingent upon change and disappears with continuous satisfaction."
Dutch psychologist Nico Frijda (1988)

adaptation-level phenomenon our tendency to form judgments (of sounds, of lights, of income) relative to a neutral level defined by our prior experience.

HI & LOIS

CLOSE-UP

How to Be Happier

Happiness, like cholesterol level, is a genetically influenced trait. Yet as cholesterol is also influenced by diet and exercise, so our happiness is to some extent under our personal control. Here are some research-based suggestions for improving your mood and increasing your satisfaction with life.

1. **Realize that enduring happiness may not come from financial success.** People adapt to changing circumstances. Thus wealth is like health: Its utter absence breeds misery, but having it (or any circumstance we long for) doesn't guarantee happiness.

2. **Take control of your time.** Happy people feel in control of their lives. To master your use of time, set goals and break them into daily aims. Although we often overestimate how much we will accomplish in any given day (leaving us frustrated), we generally underestimate how much we can accomplish in a year, given just a little progress every day.

3. **Act happy.** We can sometimes act ourselves into a happier frame of mind. Manipulated into a smiling expression, people feel better; when they scowl, the whole world seems to scowl back. So put on a happy face.

Talk as *if* you feel positive self-esteem, are optimistic, and are outgoing. Going through the motions can trigger the emotions.

4. **Seek work and leisure that engage your skills.** Happy people often are in a zone called *flow*—absorbed in tasks that challenge but don't overwhelm them. The most expensive forms of leisure (sitting on a yacht) often provide less flow experience than gardening, socializing, or craft work. Take time to savor such pleasant experiences.

5. **Join the "movement" movement.** Aerobic exercise can relieve mild depression and anxiety and promote health and energy. Sound minds reside in sound bodies. Off your duffs, couch potatoes.

6. **Give your body the sleep it wants.** Happy people live active vigorous lives yet reserve time for renewing sleep and solitude. Many people suffer from sleep debt, with resulting fatigue, diminished alertness, and gloomy moods.

7. **Give priority to close relationships.** Intimate friendships with those who care deeply about you can help you weather difficult times. Confiding is

good for soul and body. Resolve to nurture your closest relationships by *not* taking your loved ones for granted, by displaying to them the sort of kindness you display to others, by affirming them, by playing together and sharing together.

8. **Focus beyond self.** Reach out to those in need. Happiness increases helpfulness (those who feel good do good). But doing good also makes one feel good.

9. **Count your blessings and record your gratitude.** Keeping a gratitude journal heightens well-being (Emmons, 2007; Seligman et al., 2005). Try pausing each day to record positive events and why they occurred. Express your gratitude to others.

10. **Nurture your spiritual self.** For many people, faith provides a support community, a reason to focus beyond self, and a sense of purpose and hope. That helps explain why people active in faith communities report greater-than-average happiness and often cope well with crisis.

Digested from David G. Myers, *The Pursuit of Happiness* (Harper, 1993).

So, could we ever create a permanent social paradise? Social psychologist Donald Campbell (1975) answered *no:* If you woke up tomorrow to your utopia—perhaps a world with no bills, no ills, perfect scores, someone who loves you unreservedly—you would feel euphoric, for a time. But then you would gradually recalibrate your adaptation level. Before long, you would again sometimes feel gratified (when achievements surpass expectations), sometimes feel deprived (when they fall below), and sometimes feel neutral. *The point to remember:* Satisfaction and dissatisfaction, success and failure—all are relative to our recent experience. Satisfaction, as Ryan (1999) said, "has a short half-life."

The point is not that, so far as long-term happiness goes, nothing really matters. Despite our remarkable adaptiveness and resilience, after being struck by a severe disability, we may not rebound all the way back to our former emotions (Diener et al., 2006). Moreover, there are some things we can do to enhance our happiness (see Close-Up: How to Be Happier).

"I have a 'fortune cookie maxim' that I'm very proud of: Nothing in life is quite as important as you think it is while you are thinking about it. So, nothing will ever make you as happy as you think it will."
Nobel laureate psychologist Daniel Kahneman, Gallup interview, "What Were They Thinking?" 2005

"Shortly after I realized I had plenty, I realized there was plenty more."

‖ The effect of comparison with others helps explain why students of a given level of academic ability tend to have a higher academic self-concept if they attend a school where most other students are not exceptionally able (Marsh & Parker, 1984). If you were near the top of your graduating class, you might feel inferior upon entering a college or university where all students were near the top of their class. ‖

"Researchers say I'm not happier for being richer, but do you know how much researchers make?"

‖ Studies of chimpanzees in zoos reveal that happiness in chimpanzees, as rated by 200 employees, is also genetically influenced (Weiss et al., 2000, 2002). ‖

relative deprivation the perception that one is worse off relative to those with whom one compares oneself.

Happiness and Others' Attainments

Happiness is relative not only to our past experience but also to our comparisons with others (Lyubomirsky, 2001). We are always comparing ourselves with others. And whether we feel good or bad depends on who those others are. We are slow-witted or clumsy only when others are smarter or more agile.

Two examples: To explain the frustration expressed by U.S. Air Corps soldiers during World War II, researchers formulated the concept of **relative deprivation**—the sense that we are worse off than others with whom we compare ourselves. Despite a relatively rapid promotion rate for the group, many soldiers were frustrated about their own promotion rates (Merton & Kitt, 1950). Apparently, seeing so many others being promoted inflated the soldiers' expectations. And when expectations soar above attainments, the result is disappointment. Alex Rodriguez's 10-year, $275 million baseball contract surely made him temporarily happy, but it likely also diminished other star players' satisfaction with their lesser, multimillion-dollar contracts. Likewise, the economic surge that has made some urban Chinese newly affluent appears to have fueled among others a sense of relative deprivation (Burkholder, 2005a,b).

Such comparisons help us understand why the middle- and upper-income people in a given country, who can compare themselves with the relatively poor, tend to be slightly more satisfied with life than their less fortunate compatriots. Nevertheless, once people reach a moderate income level, further increases buy little more happiness. Why? Because as people climb the ladder of success they mostly compare themselves with peers who are at or above their current level (Gruder, 1977; Suls & Tesch, 1978). "Beggars do not envy millionaires, though of course they will envy other beggars who are more successful," noted Bertrand Russell (1930, p. 90). Thus, "Napoleon envied Caesar, Caesar envied Alexander, and Alexander, I daresay, envied Hercules, who never existed. You cannot, therefore, get away from envy by means of success alone, for there will always be in history or legend some person even more successful than you are" (pp. 68–69).

Just as comparing ourselves with those who are better off creates envy, so counting our blessings as we compare ourselves with those worse off boosts our contentment. Marshall Dermer and his colleagues (1979) demonstrated this by asking University of Wisconsin-Milwaukee women to study others' deprivation and suffering. After viewing vivid depictions of how grim life was in Milwaukee in 1900, or after imagining and then writing about various personal tragedies, such as being burned and disfigured, the women expressed greater satisfaction with their own lives. Similarly, when mildly depressed people read about someone who is even more depressed, they feel somewhat better (Gibbons, 1986). "I cried because I had no shoes," states a Persian saying, "until I met a man who had no feet."

Predictors of Happiness

If, as the adaptation-level phenomenon implies, our emotions tend to rebound toward our normal, why are some people normally so joyful and others so gloomy? The answers vary somewhat by culture. Self-esteem matters more to individualistic Westerners, social acceptance matters more to those in communal cultures (Diener et al., 2003). But across many countries, research does reveal several predictors of happiness (TABLE 42.1).

Although tasks and relationships affect our happiness, genes matter, too. From their study of 254 identical and fraternal twins, David Lykken and Auke Tellegen (1996) estimated that 50 percent of the difference among people's happiness ratings is heritable. Other twin studies report similar or slightly less heritability (Lucas, 2008). Genes influence the personality traits that mark happy lives (Weiss et al., 2008). Thus even identical twins raised apart are often similarly happy.

But when researchers have followed thousands of lives over two decades, they observe that people's "happiness set point" is not fixed (Lucas & Donnellan, 2007). Satisfaction

TABLE 42.1 Happiness Is . . .

Researchers Have Found That Happy People Tend to	However, Happiness Seems Not Much Related to Other Factors, Such as
Have high self-esteem (in individualistic countries).	Age.
Be optimistic, outgoing, and agreeable.	Gender (women are more often depressed, but also more often joyful).
Have close friendships or a satisfying marriage.	Parenthood (having children or not).
Have work and leisure that engage their skills.	Physical attractiveness.
Have a meaningful religious faith.	
Sleep well and exercise.	

Sources: Summarized from DeNeve & Cooper (1998), Diener et al. (2003), Lucas et al. (2004), Myers (1993, 2000), Myers & Diener (1995, 1996), and Steel et al. (2008).

may rise or fall, and happiness can be influenced by factors that are under our control. A striking example: In a long-term study of people in Germany, married partners were as similarly satisfied with their lives as were identical twins (Schimmack & Lucas, 2007). Genes matter. But as this study hints, relationship quality matters too.

Our studies of happiness remind us that emotions combine physiological activation (left hemisphere especially), expressive behaviors (smiles), and conscious thoughts ("I was so ready for that test!") and feelings (pride, satisfaction). Fear, anger, happiness, and so much else have this in common: They are biopsychosocial phenomena. Our genetic predispositions, brain activity, outlooks, experiences, relationships, and cultures jointly form us.

"I could cry when I think of the years I wasted accumulating money, only to learn that my cheerful disposition is genetic."

REVIEW

Experienced Emotion

42-1 **What is the function of fear, and how do we learn fears?**
Fear has adaptive value because it helps us avoid threats and, when necessary, cope with them. We are predisposed to some fears, and we learn others through conditioning and observation.

42-2 **What are the causes and consequences of anger?**
Anger is most often evoked by events that not only are frustrating or insulting but also are interpreted as willful, unjustified, and avoidable. Blowing off steam (*catharsis*) may be temporarily calming, but in the long run it does not reduce anger. Expressing anger can actually make us angrier.

42-3 **What are the causes and consequences of happiness?**
A good mood boosts people's perceptions of the world and their willingness to help others (the *feel-good, do-good phenomenon*). The moods triggered by the day's good or bad events seldom last beyond that day. Even significant good events, such as a substantial rise in income, seldom increase happiness for long. We can explain the relativity of happiness with the *adaptation-level phenomenon* and the *relative deprivation* principle. Nevertheless, some people are usually happier than others, and researchers have identified factors that predict such happiness.

Terms and Concepts to Remember

catharsis, p. 520
feel-good, do-good phenomenon, p. 522
subjective well-being, p. 522
adaptation-level phenomenon, p. 526
relative deprivation, p. 528

Test Yourself

1. What things do (and do not) predict self-reported happiness?

(Answers to the Test Yourself questions can be found in Appendix B at the end of the book.)

Ask Yourself

1. If we learn our emotional responses, we may be able to learn new responses to replace old ones. Would you like to change any of your emotional responses? Do you feel you are too easily provoked to anger or fear, for instance? How might you go about changing your behavior or your thinking in order to change your emotional reactions?

MODULE 43

Stress and Health

How often do you experience stress in your daily life? Never? Rarely? Sometimes? Or frequently? When Gallup put that question to a national sample in late 2007, three in four said "sometimes" or "frequently." Slightly over half of those under age 55 also said they generally did not have enough time to do what they wanted to do (Carroll, 2008). And you?

For many students, and perhaps for you, the transition to college or university, with its new relationships and more demanding challenges, proves stressful. Debt piles up. Deadlines loom. Your favorite campus organization needs a volunteer, but you're already overbooked. Smoldering over a roommate or family conflict, you feel tense. Anxious over a big exam or a class presentation, you find yourself running to the bathroom. Then, stuck in traffic and late to class or work, your mood turns sour. It's enough to give you a headache or to disrupt sleep.

If such stress endures, it can also bring on (in those of us who are physiologically predisposed) skin rashes, asthma attacks, or high blood pressure (*hypertension*). It can also increase our risk for serious illness and death. To study how stress and healthy and unhealthy behaviors influence health and illness, psychologists and physicians created the interdisciplinary field of **behavioral medicine,** integrating behavioral and medical knowledge. **Health psychology** provides psychology's contribution to behavioral medicine. For psychologists, health is more than "merely the slowest possible rate at which one can die" (*Prairie Home Companion,* 1999). Health psychologists explore the influence of emotions, personality, and behaviors on health and well-being. To begin with, how do our perceptions of a situation determine the stress we feel? How can we reduce or control stress?

▶‖ Stress and Illness

43-1 What is stress?

You think roller coasters are scary? Imagine the stress of being 21-year-old Ben Carpenter on the world's wildest and fastest wheelchair ride. As he crossed an intersection on a sunny summer afternoon in 2007, the light changed. A large truck, whose driver didn't see him, started moving into the intersection. As they bumped, the wheelchair turned to face forward, its handles becoming stuck in the grille. And off they went, the driver unable to hear Ben's cries for help. As they sped down the highway about an hour from my home, passing motorists caught the bizarre sight of a truck pushing a wheelchair at 50 mph and started calling 911. (The first caller: "You are not going to believe this. There is a semi truck pushing a guy in a wheelchair on Red Arrow highway!") One passerby was an undercover police officer, who did a quick U-turn, followed the truck to its destination a couple of miles from where the incident started, and informed the disbelieving driver that he had a passenger hooked in his grille. "It was very scary," said Ben, who has muscular dystrophy.

Stress is a slippery concept. We sometimes use the word informally to describe threats or challenges ("Ben was under a lot of stress"), and at other times our responses ("Ben experienced acute stress"). To a psychologist, the dangerous truck ride was a *stressor.* Ben's physical and emotional responses were a *stress reaction.* And the process by which he related to the threat was *stress.*

behavioral medicine an interdisciplinary field that integrates behavioral and medical knowledge and applies that knowledge to health and disease.

health psychology a subfield of psychology that provides psychology's contribution to behavioral medicine.

stress the process by which we perceive and respond to certain events, called *stressors,* that we appraise as threatening or challenging.

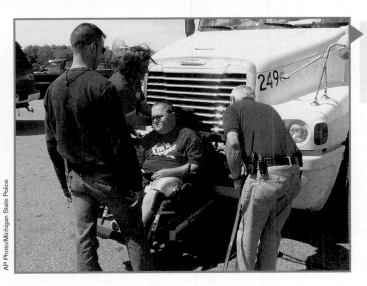

Extreme stress Ben Carpenter experienced the wildest of rides after his wheelchair got stuck in a truck's grille.

AP Photo/Michigan State Police

Thus, **stress** is not just a stimulus or a response. It is the process by which we appraise and cope with environmental threats and challenges (**FIGURE 43.1**). Stress arises less from events themselves than from how we appraise them (Lazarus, 1998). One person, alone in a house, dismisses its creaking sounds and experiences no stress; someone else suspects an intruder and becomes alarmed. One person regards a new job as a welcome challenge; someone else appraises it as risking failure.

When short-lived, or when perceived as challenges, stressors can have positive effects. A momentary stress can mobilize the immune system for fending off infections and healing wounds (Segerstrom, 2007). Stress also arouses and motivates us to conquer problems. Championship athletes, successful entertainers, and great teachers and leaders all thrive and excel when aroused by a challenge (Blascovich et al. 2004). Having conquered cancer or rebounded from a lost job, some people emerge with stronger self-esteem and a deepened spirituality and sense of purpose. Indeed, some stress early in life is conducive to later emotional resilience (Landauer & Whiting, 1979). Adversity can beget growth.

But stressors can also threaten us. And experiencing severe or prolonged stress may harm us. Children's physiological responses to severe child abuse put them at later risk of chronic disease (Repetti et al., 2002). Those who had post-traumatic stress reactions to heavy combat in the Vietnam war went on to suffer greatly elevated rates of circulatory, digestive, respiratory, and infectious diseases (Boscarino, 1997).

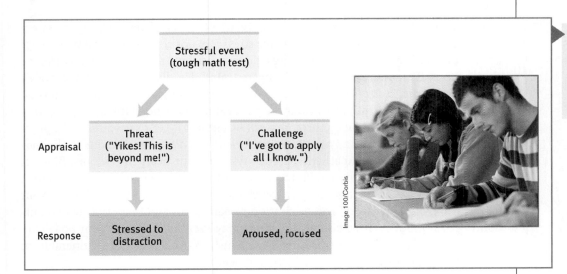

FIGURE 43.1 Stress appraisal The events of our lives flow through a psychological filter. How we appraise an event influences how much stress we experience and how effectively we respond.

general adaptation syndrome (GAS)
Selye's concept of the body's adaptive response to stress in three phases—alarm, resistance, exhaustion.

The Stress Response System

Medical interest in stress dates back to Hippocrates (460–377 B.C.). But it was not until the 1920s that Walter Cannon (1929) confirmed that the stress response is part of a unified mind-body system. He observed that extreme cold, lack of oxygen, and emotion-arousing incidents all trigger an outpouring of the stress hormones epinephrine and norepinephrine from the central core of the adrenal glands. This is but one part of the sympathetic nervous system's response. When alerted by any of a number of brain pathways, the sympathetic nervous system, as we have seen, increases heart rate and respiration, diverts blood from digestion to the skeletal muscles, dulls pain, and releases sugar and fat from the body's stores—all to prepare the body for the wonderfully adaptive response that Cannon called *fight or flight*.

Since Cannon's time, physiologists have identified an additional stress response system. On orders from the cerebral cortex (via the hypothalamus and pituitary gland), the outer part of the adrenal glands secrete *glucocorticoid* stress hormones such as *cortisol*. The two stress hormone systems work at different speeds, explains biologist Robert Sapolsky (2003): "In a fight-or-flight scenario, epinephrine is the one handing out guns; glucocorticoids are the ones drawing up blueprints for new aircraft carriers needed for the war effort." The epinephrine guns were firing at high speed during an experiment inadvertently conducted by British Airways on an April 23, 1999, flight from San Francisco to London. Three hours after takeoff, a mistakenly played message told passengers the plane was about to crash into the sea. Although the flight crew immediately recognized the error and tried to calm the terrified passengers, several required medical assistance (Associated Press, 1999). These passengers can empathize with those on a 2005 JetBlue flight as it circled Southern California for hours with faulty landing gear. Many of the plane's passengers became severely distressed, some crying, by the "surreal" experience of watching onboard satellite TV news broadcasts speculating on their fate (Nguyen, 2005).

There are alternatives to fight or flight. One is a common response to the stress of a loved one's death: Withdraw. Pull back. Conserve energy. Faced with an extreme disaster, such as a ship sinking, some people become paralyzed by fear. Another stress response, especially common among women, report Shelley Taylor and her colleagues (2000), is to seek and give support: *Tend and befriend*.

Facing stress, men more often than women tend to socially withdraw, turn to alcohol, or become aggressive. Women more often respond to stress by nurturing and banding together, which Taylor (2006) attributes partly to *oxytocin*, a stress-moderating hormone associated with pair-bonding in animals and released by cuddling, massage, and breast-feeding in humans.

Canadian scientist Hans Selye's (1936, 1976) 40 years of research on stress extended Cannon's findings and helped make stress a major concept in both psychology and medicine. Selye studied animals' reactions to various stressors, such as electric shock, surgical trauma, and immobilizing restraint. He discovered that the body's adaptive response to stress was so general—like a single burglar alarm that sounds no matter what intrudes—that he called it the **general adaptation syndrome (GAS).**

Selye saw the GAS as having three phases (**FIGURE 43.2**). Let's say you suffer a physical or emotional trauma. In Phase 1, you experience an *alarm reaction* due to the sudden activation of your sympathetic nervous system. Your heart rate zooms. Blood is diverted to your skeletal muscles. You feel the faintness of shock. With your resources mobilized, you are now ready to fight the challenge during Phase 2, *resistance*. Your temperature, blood pressure, and respiration remain high, and there is a sudden outpouring of hormones. If persistent, the stress may eventually deplete your body's reserves during Phase 3, *exhaustion*. With exhaustion, you are more vulnerable to illness or even, in extreme cases, collapse and death.

"You may be suffering from what's known as full-nest syndrome."

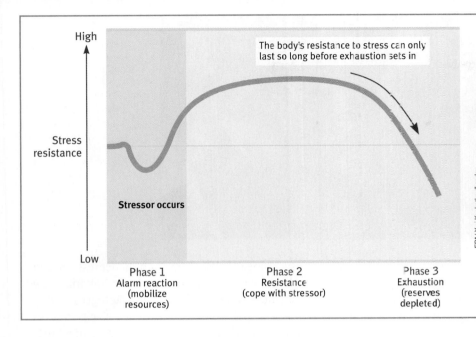

High

The body's resistance to stress can only last so long before exhaustion sets in

Stress resistance

Stressor occurs

Low

| Phase 1 | Phase 2 | Phase 3 |
| Alarm reaction (mobilize resources) | Resistance (cope with stressor) | Exhaustion (reserves depleted) |

EPA/ Yuri Kochetkov/Landow

FIGURE 43.2 Selye's general adaptation syndrome This girl being carried to freedom and medical attention managed to escape her terrorist captors in a three-day school holdup in North Ossetia in 2004. After such a trauma, the body enters an alarm phase of temporary shock. From this it rebounds, as stress resistance rises. If the stress is prolonged, as it was for the 400 school hostages and their waiting loved ones, wear and tear may lead to exhaustion.

Few medical experts today quarrel with Selye's basic point: Although the human body comes designed to cope with temporary stress, prolonged stress can produce physical deterioration. The brain's production of new neurons slows (Mirescu & Gould, 2006). In one study, women who suffered enduring stress as caregivers for children with serious disorders displayed a symptom that is a normal part of the aging process—shorter bits of DNA at the ends of their chromosomes (Epel et al., 2004). When these DNA pieces, called *telomeres,* get too short, the cell can no longer divide, and it ultimately dies. The most stressed women had cells that looked a decade older than their chronological age, which may help explain why severe stress seems to age people. Even fearful, easily stressed rats have been found to die sooner (after about 600 days) than their more confident siblings, which average 700-day life spans (Cavigelli & McClintock, 2003). Such findings serve as further incentives to today's health psychologists, as they ask: What causes stress? And how does stress affect us?

Stressful Life Events

43-2 What events provoke stress responses?

Research has focused on our responses to three types of stressors: catastrophes, significant life changes, and daily hassles.

Catastrophes

Catastrophes are unpredictable large-scale events, such as war and natural disasters, that nearly everyone appraises as threatening. Although people often provide one another with aid as well as comfort after such events, the health consequences can be significant. In the three weeks after the 9/11 terrorist attacks, two-thirds of Americans surveyed by University of Michigan researchers said they were having some trouble concentrating and sleeping (Wahlberg, 2001). In another national survey, New Yorkers were especially likely to report such symptoms (NSF, 2001). Sleeping pill prescriptions rose by a reported 28 percent in the New York area (HMHL, 2002).

Do other community disasters usually produce effects this great? After digesting data from 52 studies of catastrophic floods, hurricanes, and fires, Anthony Rubonis and Leonard Bickman (1991) found the typical effect more modest but nonetheless

Les Stone/Corbis

Toxic stress On the day of its 1994 earthquake, Los Angeles experienced a fivefold increase in sudden-death heart attacks—especially in the first two hours after the quake and near its epicenter. Physical exertion (running, lifting debris) was a factor in only 13 percent of the deaths, leaving stress as the likely trigger for the others (Muller & Verier, 1996).

genuine. In disaster's wake, rates of psychological disorders such as depression and anxiety rose an average 17 percent. In the four months after Hurricane Katrina, New Orleans reportedly experienced a tripled suicide rate (Saulny, 2006). Refugees fleeing their homeland also suffer increased rates of psychological disorders. Their stress is twofold: the trauma of uprooting and family separation, and the challenges of adjusting to a foreign culture's new language, ethnicity, climate, and social norms (Pipher, 2002; Williams & Berry, 1991). In years to come, relocations necessitated by climate change may also produce such effects.

Significant Life Changes

The second type of life-event stressor is a significant personal life change—the death of a loved one, the loss of a job, leaving home, a marriage, a divorce. Life transitions and insecurities are often keenly felt during young adulthood. That helps explain why, when 15,000 Canadian adults were asked whether "You are trying to take on too many things at once," responses indicated highest stress levels among the youngest adults. The same is true of Americans: Half of adults under age 50 report "frequent" stress, as do fewer than 30 percent of those over 50 (Saad, 2001).

Some psychologists study the health effects of life changes by following people over time to see if such events precede illnesses. Others compare the life changes recalled by those who have or have not suffered a specific health problem, such as a heart attack. A review of these studies commissioned by the U.S. National Academy of Sciences revealed that people recently widowed, fired, or divorced are more vulnerable to disease (Dohrenwend et al., 1982). A Finnish study of 96,000 widowed people confirmed the phenomenon: Their risk of death doubled in the week following their partner's death (Kaprio et al., 1987). Experiencing a cluster of crises puts one even more at risk.

Daily Hassles

As we noted earlier, our happiness stems less from enduring good fortune than from our response to daily events—a hoped-for medical result, a perfect exam score, a gratifying e-mail, your team's winning the big game.

This principle works for negative events, too. Everyday annoyances—rush-hour traffic, aggravating housemates, long lines at the store, too many things to do, e-mail spam, and obnoxious cellphone talkers—may be the most significant sources of stress (Kohn & Macdonald, 1992; Lazarus, 1990; Ruffin, 1993). Although some people can simply shrug off such hassles, others are "driven up the wall" by them. People's difficulties in letting go of unattainable goals is another everyday stressor with health consequences (Miller & Wrosch, 2007).

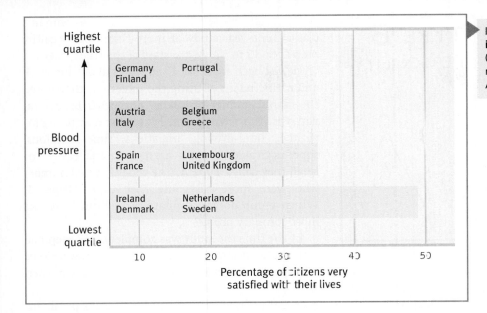

FIGURE 43.3 Where life satisfaction is high, hypertension rates are low (From data gleaned from European nations by David Blanchflower and Andrew Oswald, 2008.)

Over time, these little stressors can add up and take a toll on our health and well-being. Hypertension rates are high among residents of impoverished areas where the stresses that accompany inadequate income, unemployment, solo parenting, and overcrowding are part of daily life for many people. In Europe, hypertension rates are likewise highest in countries where people express the least satisfaction with their lives (**FIGURE 43.3**).

For minority populations, daily pressures may be compounded by racism, which—like other stressors—can have both psychological and physical consequences. Thinking that some of the people you encounter each day will distrust you, dislike you, or doubt your abilities makes daily life stressful. Such stress takes a toll on the health of many African-Americans, driving up blood pressure levels (Clark et al., 1999; Mays et al., 2007).

|| A 2009 Pew survey of 2969 American adults asked, "Is the recession causing stress in your family?"

Age	Yes responses
18–49	52%
50–64	58%
65+	38% ||

▶|| Stress and the Heart

43-3 Why are some of us more prone than others to coronary heart disease?

Elevated blood pressure is just one of the factors that increase the risk of **coronary heart disease,** the closing of the vessels that nourish the heart muscle. Although infrequent before 1900, this condition became by the 1950s North America's leading cause of death, and it remains so today. In addition to hypertension and a family history of the disease, many behavioral and physiological factors—smoking, obesity, a high-fat diet, physical inactivity, and an elevated cholesterol level—increase the risk of heart disease. The psychological factors of stress and personality also play a big role.

In a now-classic study, Meyer Friedman, Ray Rosenman, and their colleagues tested the idea that stress increases vulnerability to heart disease (Friedman & Ulmer, 1984). They measured the blood cholesterol level and clotting speed of 40 U.S. tax accountants. They found that from January through March, both of these coronary warning indicators were completely normal. Then, as the accountants began scrambling to finish their clients' tax returns before the April 15 filing deadline, their cholesterol and clotting measures rose to dangerous levels. In May and June, with the deadline past, the measures returned to normal. The researchers' hunch had paid off: Stress predicted heart attack risk.

coronary heart disease the clogging of the vessels that nourish the heart muscle; the leading cause of death in many developed countries.

|| In both India and America, Type A bus drivers are literally hard-driving: They brake, pass, and honk their horns more often than their more easygoing Type B colleagues (Evans et al., 1987). ||

"The fire you kindle for your enemy often burns you more than him."

Chinese proverb

Type A Friedman and Rosenman's term for competitive, hard-driving, impatient, verbally aggressive, and anger-prone people.

Type B Friedman and Rosenman's term for easygoing, relaxed people.

The stage was set for Friedman and Rosenman's classic nine-year study of more than 3000 healthy men aged 35 to 59. At the start of the study, they interviewed each man for 15 minutes about his work and eating habits. During the interview, they noted the man's manner of talking and other behavioral patterns. Those who seemed the most reactive, competitive, hard-driving, impatient, time-conscious, supermotivated, verbally aggressive, and easily angered they called **Type A.** The roughly equal number who were more easygoing they called **Type B.** Which group do you suppose turned out to be the most coronary prone?

By the time the study was complete, 257 men had suffered heart attacks; 69 percent of them were Type A. Moreover, not one of the "pure" Type Bs—the most mellow and laid-back of their group—had suffered a heart attack.

As often happens in science, this exciting discovery provoked enormous public interest. But after the honeymoon period, in which the finding seemed definitive and revolutionary, other researchers began asking: Is the finding reliable? If so, what is the toxic component of the Type A profile: Time-consciousness? Competitiveness? Anger?

More recent research has revealed that Type A's toxic core is negative emotions—especially the anger associated with an aggressively reactive temperament (Smith, 2006; Williams, 1993). Type A individuals are more often "combat ready." When we are harassed or challenged, our active sympathetic nervous system redistributes bloodflow to our muscles and away from internal organs such as the liver, which normally removes cholesterol and fat from the blood. Thus, a Type A person's blood may contain excess cholesterol and fat that later get deposited around the heart. Further stress—sometimes conflicts brought on by the person's own abrasiveness—may trigger the altered heart rhythms that, in those with weakened hearts, can cause sudden death (Kamarck & Jennings, 1991). Hostility also correlates with other risk factors, such as smoking, drinking, and obesity (Bunde & Suls, 2006). In important ways, people's minds and hearts interact.

The effect of an anger-prone personality appears most noticeably in studies in which interviewers assess verbal assertiveness and emotional intensity. (If you pause in the middle of a sentence, an intense, anger-prone person may jump in and finish it for you.) One study of young and middle-aged adults found that those who react with anger over little things are the most coronary-prone, and suppressing negative emotions only heightens the risk (Kupper & Denollet, 2007). Another study followed 13,000 middle-aged people for 5 years (Williams et al., 2000). Among those with normal blood pressure, people who had scored high on anger were three times more likely to have had heart attacks, even after researchers controlled for smoking and weight. The link between anger and heart attacks also appeared in a study that followed 1055 male medical students over an average of 36 years. Those who had reported being hot-tempered were five times more likely to have had a heart attack by age 55 (Chang et al., 2002). As Charles Spielberger and Perry London (1982) put it, rage "seems to lash back and strike us in the heart muscle."

Pessimism seems to be similarly toxic. Laura Kubzansky and her colleagues (2001) studied 1306 initially healthy men who a decade earlier had scored as optimists, pessimists, or neither. Even after other risk factors such as smoking had been ruled out, pessimists were more than twice as likely as optimists to develop heart disease (**FIGURE 43.4**).

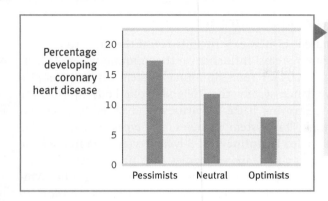

FIGURE 43.4 Pessimism and heart disease A Harvard School of Public Health team found that compared with optimistic men, pessimistic men have a more than doubled risk of developing heart disease over a 10-year period. (From Kubzansky et al., 2001.)

Depression, too, can be lethal. The accumulated evidence from 57 studies suggests that "depression substantially increases the risk of death, especially death by unnatural causes and cardiovascular disease" (Wulsin et al., 1999). One study of 7406 women age 67 or older found that among those with no depressive symptoms, 7 percent died within six years, as did 24 percent of those with six or more depressive symptoms (Whooley & Browner, 1998). In the years following a heart attack, people with high scores for depression are four times more likely than their low-scoring counterparts to develop further heart problems (Frasure-Smith & Lesperance, 2005). Depression is disheartening.

Recent research suggests that heart disease and depression may both result when chronic stress triggers persistent inflammation (Matthews, 2005; Miller & Blackwell, 2006). Stress, as we will see, disrupts the body's disease-fighting immune system, thus enabling the body to focus its energies on fleeing or fighting the threat. Yet stress hormones enhance one immune response, the production of proteins that contribute to the inflammation. Although inflammation helps fight infections, persistent inflammation can produce problems such as asthma or clogged arteries, and even, it now seems, depression (see **FIGURE 43.5**).

"A cheerful heart is a good medicine, but a downcast spirit dries up the bones."
Proverbs 17:22

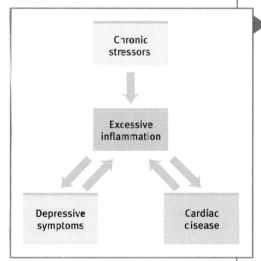

FIGURE 43.5 Stress→inflammation↔heart disease and depression Gregory Miller and Ekin Blackwell (2006) report that chronic stress leads to persistent inflammation, which heightens the risk of both depression and clogged arteries.

▶‖ Stress and Susceptibility to Disease

43-4 How does stress make us more vulnerable to disease?

Not so long ago, the term *psychosomatic* described psychologically caused physical symptoms. To laypeople, the term implied that the symptoms were unreal—"merely" psychosomatic. To avoid such connotations and to better describe the genuine physiological effects of psychological states, most experts today refer instead to stress-related **psychophysiological illnesses,** such as hypertension and some headaches. Stress also affects our resistance to disease, and this understanding has led to the burgeoning development of the field of **psychoneuroimmunology (PNI).** PNI studies how *psychological, neural,* and endocrine processes affect our *immune* system (psycho-neuro-immunology), and how all these factors influence our health and wellness.

psychophysiological illness literally, "mind-body" illness; any stress-related physical illness, such as hypertension and some headaches.

psychoneuroimmunology (PNI) the study of how psychological, neural, and endocrine processes together affect the immune system and resulting health.

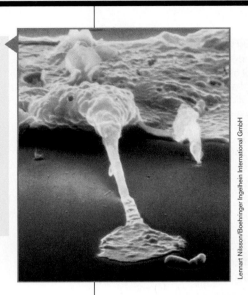

FIGURE 43.6 The immune system in action A large macrophage (at top) is about to trap and ingest a tiny bacterium (lower right). Macrophages constantly patrol our bodies in search of invaders—such as this *Escherichia coli* bacterium—and debris, such as worn-out red blood cells.

"In the eyes of God or biology or what have you, it is just very important to have women."

Immunologist Normal Talal (1995)

lymphocytes the two types of white blood cells that are part of the body's immune system: *B lymphocytes* form in the *bone* marrow and release antibodies that fight bacterial infections; *T lymphocytes* form in the *thymus* and other lymphatic tissue and attack cancer cells, viruses, and foreign substances.

"When the heart is at ease, the body is healthy."

Chinese proverb

Psychoneuroimmunology

Hundreds of new experiments reveal the nervous and endocrine systems' influence on the immune system (Sternberg, 2001). Your immune system is a complex surveillance system that defends your body by isolating and destroying bacteria, viruses, and other foreign substances. This system includes two types of white blood cells, called **lymphocytes.** *B lymphocytes* form in the *bone* marrow and release antibodies that fight bacterial infections. *T lymphocytes* form in the *thymus* and other lymphatic tissue and attack cancer cells, viruses, and foreign substances—even "good" ones, such as transplanted organs. Two other important agents of the immune system are the *macrophage* ("big eater"), which identifies, pursues, and ingests harmful invaders and worn-out cells (**FIGURE 43.6**), and the *natural killer cells* (NK cells), which pursue diseased cells (such as those infected by viruses or cancer). Age, nutrition, genetics, body temperature, and stress all influence the immune system's activity.

Your immune system can err in two directions. Responding too strongly, it may attack the body's own tissues, causing arthritis or an allergic reaction. Underreacting, it may allow a dormant herpes virus to erupt or cancer cells to multiply. Women are immunologically stronger than men, making them less susceptible to infections (Morell, 1995). But this very strength also makes them more susceptible to self-attacking diseases, such as lupus and multiple sclerosis.

Your immune system is not a headless horseman. The brain regulates the secretion of stress hormones, which lessens the disease-fighting lymphocytes. Thus, when animals are physically restrained, given unavoidable electric shocks, or subjected to noise, crowding, cold water, social defeat, or maternal separation, their immune systems become less active (Maier et al., 1994). One study monitored immune responses in 43 monkeys over six months (Cohen et al., 1992). Twenty-one were stressed by being housed with new roommates—three or four new monkeys—each month. (To empathize with the monkeys, recall the stress of leaving home to attend school or summer camp, and imagine having to repeat this experience monthly.) Compared with monkeys left in stable groups, the socially disrupted monkeys experienced weakened immune systems. Stress similarly depresses the immune system of humans. Consider some striking and consistent results:

▶ Surgical wounds heal more slowly in stressed animals and humans. In one experiment, dental students received punch wounds (precise small holes punched in the skin). Compared with wounds placed during summer vacation, those placed three days before a major exam healed 40 percent more slowly. In fact, reported Janice Kiecolt-Glaser and her co-researchers (1998), "no student healed as rapidly during this stressful period as during vacation."

▶ Compared with the healing of punch wounds in unstressed married couples, either the stress of a 30-minute marital spat or ongoing marital conflict caused punch wounds to take a day or two longer to heal (Kiecolt-Glaser et al., 2005).

▶ In another experiment, 47 percent of participants living stress-filled lives developed colds after a virus was dropped in their noses, as did only 27 percent of those living relatively free of stress (**FIGURE 43.7**). In follow-up research, the happiest and most relaxed people were likewise markedly less vulnerable to an experimentally delivered cold virus (Cohen et al., 2003, 2006).

▶ Managing stress may be life-sustaining. The one personality trait shared by 169 centenarians (people over 100) is their ability to manage stress well (Perls et al., 1999).

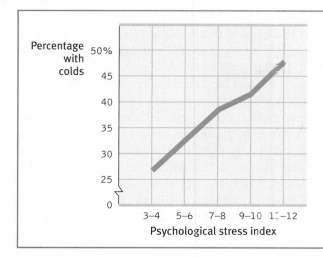

FIGURE 43.7 **Stress and colds** In an experiment by Sheldon Cohen and colleagues (1991), people with the highest life stress scores were also most vulnerable when exposed to an experimentally delivered cold virus.

The stress effect on immunity makes physiological sense (Maier et al., 1994). It takes energy to fight infections and maintain fevers. Thus, when diseased, our bodies reduce muscular energy output by inactivity and increased sleep. But stress creates a competing energy need. Stress triggers an aroused fight-or-flight response, diverting energy from the disease-fighting immune system to the muscles and brain, rendering us more vulnerable to illness. *The bottom line:* Stress does not make us sick, but it does alter our immune functioning, making us less able to resist infection and more prone to heart disease.

Stress and AIDS

AIDS has become the world's fourth leading cause of death and the number one killer in Africa. As its name tells us, AIDS is an immune disorder—an *acquired immune deficiency syndrome* caused by the *human immunodeficiency virus (HIV)*, which is spread by the exchange of bodily fluids, primarily semen and blood. If a disease spread by human contact kills slowly, as does AIDS, it ironically can be lethal to more people: Those who carry the virus have time to spread it, often without realizing they are infected. When the HIV infection manifests itself as AIDS, some years after the initial infection, the person has difficulty fighting off other diseases, such as pneumonia. Worldwide, reports the United Nations, more than 20 million people have died of AIDS (UNAIDS, 2008). (In the United States, where "only" a half-million of these fatalities have occurred, AIDS has killed more people than did combat in all the twentieth-century wars.) In 2007, worldwide some 2.7 million—half of them women—were infected with HIV, often without their awareness (UNAIDS, 2008).

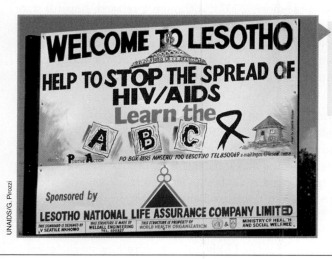

Africa is ground zero for AIDS In Lesotho, Uganda, and elsewhere, the "ABC" Campaign—Abstinence, Be faithful, and use Condoms—forms part of prevention efforts.

So if stress restrains the immune system's response to infections, could it also exacerbate the *course* of AIDS? Researchers have found that stress and negative emotions do correlate with (a) a progression from HIV infection to AIDS, and (b) the speed of decline in those infected (Bower et al., 1998; Kiecolt-Glaser & Glaser, 1995; Leserman et al., 1999). HIV-infected men faced with stressful life circumstances, such as the loss of a partner, exhibit somewhat greater immune suppression and a faster disease progression.

Would efforts to reduce stress help control the disease? Although the benefits are small compared with available drug treatments, the answer appears again to be *yes*. Educational initiatives, bereavement support groups, cognitive therapy, relaxation training, and exercise programs that reduce distress have all had positive consequences for HIV-positive individuals (Baum & Posluszny, 1999; McCain et al., 2008; Schneiderman, 1999). Better yet is preventing HIV infection, which is the focus of many educational programs, such as the ABC (*a*bstinence, *b*eing faithful, *c*ondom use) program used in many countries, with seeming success in Uganda (Altman, 2004; USAID, 2004).

Stress and Cancer

Stress and negative emotions have also been linked to cancer's rate of progression. To explore a possible connection between stress and cancer, experimenters have implanted tumor cells into rodents or given them *carcinogens* (cancer-producing substances). Those rodents also exposed to uncontrollable stress, such as inescapable shocks, were more prone to cancer (Sklar & Anisman, 1981). With immune systems weakened by stress, tumors developed sooner and grew larger.

Some investigators have reported that people are at increased risk for cancer within a year after experiencing depression, helplessness, or bereavement. One large Swedish study revealed that people with a history of workplace stress had 5.5 times greater risk of colon cancer than those who reported no such problems, a difference not attributable to differing age, smoking, drinking, or physical characteristics (Courtney et al., 1993). Other researchers have found no link between stress and human cancer (Edelman & Kidman, 1997; Fox, 1998; Petticrew et al., 1999, 2002). Concentration camp survivors and former prisoners of war, for example, have not exhibited elevated cancer rates.

One danger in hyping reports on attitudes and cancer is that some patients may then blame themselves for their illness—"If only I had been more expressive, relaxed, and hopeful." A corollary danger is a "wellness macho" among the healthy, who take credit for their "healthy character" and lay a guilt trip on the ill: "She has cancer? That's what you get for holding your feelings in and being so nice." Dying thus becomes the ultimate failure.

The emerging view seems to be that stress does *not* create cancer cells. At worst, it may affect their growth by weakening the body's natural defenses against proliferating malignant cells (Antoni & Lutgendorf, 2007). Although a relaxed, hopeful state may enhance these defenses, we should be aware of the thin line that divides science from wishful thinking. The powerful biological processes at work in advanced cancer or AIDS are not likely to be completely derailed by avoiding stress or maintaining a relaxed but determined spirit (Anderson, 2002; Kessler et al., 1991).

*   *   *

We can view the stress effect on our disease resistance as a price we pay for the benefits of stress (**FIGURE 43.8**). Stress invigorates our lives by arousing and motivating us. An unstressed life would hardly be challenging or productive. Moreover, it pays to spend our resources in fighting or fleeing an external threat. But we do so at the cost of diminished resources for fighting internal threats to health. When the stress is momentary, the cost is negligible. When uncontrollable aggravations persist, the cost may become considerable.

Behavioral medicine research provides yet another reminder of one of contemporary psychology's overriding themes: *Mind and body interact; everything psychological is*

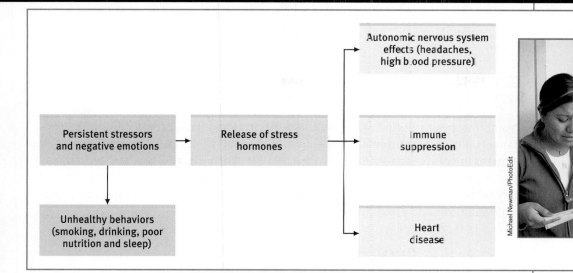

FIGURE 43.8
Stress can have a variety of health-related consequences This is especially so when experienced by "disease-prone" angry, depressed, or anxious persons.

Michael Newman/PhotoEdit

simultaneously physiological. Psychological states are physiological events that influence other parts of our physiological system. Just pausing to *think* about biting into an orange section—the sweet, tangy juice from the pulpy fruit flooding across your tongue—can trigger salivation. As the Indian sage Santi Parva recognized more than 4000 years ago, "Mental disorders arise from physical causes, and likewise physical disorders arise from mental causes." There is an interplay between our heads and our health. We are biopsychosocial systems.

REVIEW

Stress and Health

43-1 **What is stress?** Walter Cannon viewed *stress,* the process by which we appraise and respond to events that challenge or threaten us, as a "fight-or-flight" system. Hans Selye saw it as a three-phase (alarm-resistance-exhaustion) *general adaptation syndrome (GAS).*

43-2 **What events provoke stress responses?** Modern research on stress assesses the health consequences of catastrophic events, significant life changes, and daily hassles. The events that tend to provoke stress responses are those that we perceive as both negative and uncontrollable.

43-3 **Why are some of us more prone than others to coronary heart disease?** *Coronary heart disease,* North America's number one cause of death, has been linked with the competitive, hard-driving, impatient, and (especially) anger-prone *Type A* personality. Under stress, the body of a reactive, hostile person secretes more of the hormones that accelerate the buildup of plaque on the heart's artery walls. *Type B* personalities are more relaxed and easygoing. Chronic stress also contributes to persistent inflammation, which heightens the risk of clogged arteries and depression.

43-4 **How does stress make us more vulnerable to disease?** Stress diverts energy from the immune system, inhibiting the activities of its B and T *lymphocytes,* macrophages, and NK cells. Although stress does not cause diseases such as AIDS and cancer, it may influence their progression.

Terms and Concepts to Remember

behavioral medicine, p. 530
health psychology, p. 530
stress, p. 531
general adaptation syndrome (GAS), p. 532
coronary heart disease, p. 535
Type A, p. 536

Type B, p. 536
psychophysiological illness, p. 537
psychoneuroimmunology (PNI), p. 537
lymphocytes, p. 538

Test Yourself

1. What are the basic links in our stress response system?

(Answers to the Test Yourself questions can be found in Appendix B at the end of the book.)

Ask Yourself

1. What are the stresses in your own life? How intensely do you respond to them? Are there changes you could make to avoid the persistent stressors in your life?

∞ WEB

Multiple-choice self-tests and more may be found at www.worthpublishers.com/myers

MODULE 44

Promoting Health

Promoting health begins with implementing strategies that prevent illness and enhance wellness. Traditionally, people have thought about their health only when something goes wrong—visiting a physician for diagnosis and treatment. That, say health psychologists, is like ignoring a car's maintenance and going to a mechanic only when the car breaks down. Health maintenance includes alleviating stress, preventing illness, and promoting well-being.

▶‖ Coping With Stress

44-1 What factors affect our ability to cope with stress?

Stressors are unavoidable. This fact, coupled with the fact that persistent stress correlates with heart disease, depression, and lowered immunity, gives us a clear message. We need to learn to **cope** with the stress in our lives. We address some stressors directly, with **problem-focused coping.** For example, if our impatience leads to a family fight, we may go directly to that family member to work things out. If, despite our best efforts, we cannot get along with that family member, we may also incorporate an **emotion-focused coping,** such as reaching out to friends to help address our own emotional needs.

When challenged, some people tend to respond more with cool problem-focused coping, others with emotion-focused coping (Connor-Smith & Flachsbart, 2007). We tend to use problem-focused strategies when we feel a sense of control over a situation and think we can change the circumstances or change ourselves. We turn to emotion-focused strategies when we cannot—or *believe* we cannot—change a situation. We may, for example, seek emotional distance from a damaging relationship or keep busy with active hobbies to avoid thinking about an old addiction. Emotion-focused strategies can be nonadaptive, however, as when students worried about not keeping up with the reading in class go out to party to get it off their mind. Sometimes a problem-focused strategy (catching up with the reading) more effectively reduces stress and promotes long-term health and satisfaction.

Several factors affect our ability to cope successfully, including our feelings of personal control, our explanatory style, and our supportive connections.

Perceived Control

If two rats receive simultaneous shocks, but one can turn a wheel to stop the shocks (as illustrated in **FIGURE 44.1**), the helpless rat, but not the wheel turner, becomes more susceptible to ulcers and lowered immunity to disease (Laudenslager & Reite, 1984). In humans, too, uncontrollable threats trigger the strongest stress responses (Dickerson & Kemeny, 2004). For example, a bacterial infection often combines with uncontrollable stress to produce the most severe ulcers (Overmier & Murison, 1997). To cure the ulcer, kill the bug with antibiotics and control the stomach's acid secretions with reduced stress.

Perceiving a loss of control, we become more vulnerable to ill health. Elderly nursing home residents who have little perceived control over their activities tend to decline faster and die sooner than do those given more control over their activities (Rodin, 1986). Workers given control over their work environment—by being able to

coping alleviating stress using emotional, cognitive, or behavioral methods.

problem-focused coping attempting to alleviate stress directly—by changing the stressor or the way we interact with that stressor.

emotion-focused coping attempting to alleviate stress by avoiding or ignoring a stressor and attending to emotional needs related to one's stress reaction.

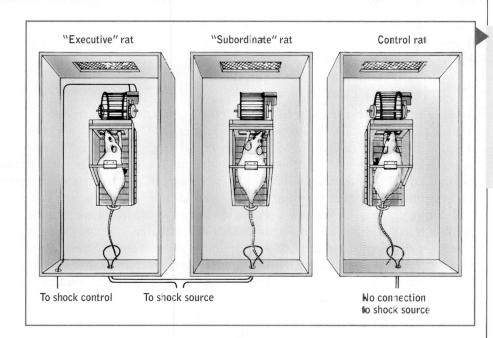

"Executive" rat   "Subordinate" rat   Control rat

To shock control   To shock source   No connection
                                              to shock source

FIGURE 44.1 Health consequences of a loss of control The "executive" rat at the left can switch off the tail shock by turning the wheel. Because it has control over the shock, it is no more likely to develop ulcers than is the unshocked control rat on the right. The "subordinate" rat in the center receives the same shocks as the executive rat, but with no control over the shocks. It is, therefore, more likely to develop ulcers. (Adapted from Weiss, 1977.)

adjust office furnishings and control interruptions and distractions—also experience less stress (O'Neill, 1993). This helps explain why British civil service workers at the executive grades outlive those at clerical or laboring grades, and why Finnish workers with low job stress are less than half as likely to die of cardiovascular disease (strokes or heart disease) as are those with a demanding job and little control. The more control workers have, the longer they live (Bosma et al., 1997, 1998; Kivimaki et al., 2002; Marmot et al., 1997).

Control may also help explain a well-established link between economic status and longevity. In one study of 843 grave markers in an old graveyard in Glasgow, Scotland, those with the costliest, highest pillars (indicating the most affluence) tended to have lived the longest (Carroll et al., 1994). Likewise, those living in Scottish regions with the least overcrowding and unemployment have the greatest longevity. There and elsewhere, high economic status predicts a lower risk of heart and respiratory diseases (Sapolsky, 2005). Wealthy predicts healthy among children, too (Chen, 2004). With higher economic status comes reduced risks of infant mortality, low birth weight, smoking, and violence. Even among other primates, those at the bottom of the social pecking order are more likely than their higher-status companions to become sick when exposed to a coldlike virus (Cohen et al., 1997). But for those high-status baboons and monkeys who frequently have to physically defend their dominant position, high status also entails stress (Sapolsky, 2005).

Researchers are debating the explanation for the income-health correlation, because poor health can lower income and because intelligence scores also correlate with both income and health (Kanazawa, 2006; Whalley & Deary, 2001). But this much seems clear: Poverty and diminished control entail physiologically measurable stress, even among children (Evans & Kim, 2007).

Why does perceived loss of control predict health problems? Animal studies show—and human studies confirm—that losing control provokes an outpouring of stress hormones. When rats cannot control shock or when primates or humans feel unable to control their environment, stress hormone levels rise, blood pressure increases, and immune responses drop (Rodin, 1986; Sapolsky, 2005). Captive animals therefore experience more stress and are more vulnerable to disease than are wild animals (Roberts, 1988). The crowding that occurs in high-density neighborhoods, prisons, and college and university dorms is another source of diminished feelings of control—and of elevated levels of stress hormones and blood pressure (Fleming et al., 1987; Ostfeld et al., 1987).

Optimism and Health

Another influence on our ability to cope with stress is whether our basic outlook is optimistic or pessimistic. Psychologists Michael Scheier and Charles Carver (1992) have reported that *optimists*—people who agree with statements such as, "In uncertain times, I usually expect the best"—perceive more control, cope better with stressful events, and enjoy better health. During the last month of a semester, students previously identified as optimistic report less fatigue and fewer coughs, aches, and pains. And during the stressful first few weeks of law school, those who are optimistic ("It's unlikely that I will fail") enjoy better moods and stronger infection-thwarting immune systems (Segerstrom et al., 1998). Optimists also respond to stress with smaller increases in blood pressure, and they recover more quickly from heart bypass surgery.

Consider the consistency and startling magnitude of the optimism and positive emotions factor in several other studies:

▶ One research team followed 941 Dutch people, ages 65 to 85, for nearly a decade (Giltay et al., 2004, 2007). Among those in the lowest optimism quartile, 57 percent died, as did only 30 percent of the top optimism quartile.

▶ When Finnish researchers followed 2428 men for up to a decade, the number of deaths among those with a bleak, hopeless outlook was more than double that found among their optimistic counterparts (Everson et al., 1996).

▶ Another study asked 795 Americans, ages 64 to 79, if they were "hopeful about the future." When the researchers checked up on these folks about 5 years later, 29 percent of those answering *no* had died—more than double the 11 percent of deaths among those who said *yes* (Stern et al., 2001).

▶ A now-famous study followed up on 180 Catholic nuns who had written brief autobiographies at about 22 years of age. Despite living thereafter with similar life-styles and status, those who had expressed happiness, love, and other positive feelings lived an average 7 years longer than their more dour counterparts (Danner et al., 2001). By age 80, some 54 percent of those expressing few positive emotions had died, as had only 24 percent of the most positive-spirited.

Those who manage to find humor in life's daily events also seem to benefit. Among 54,000 adult Norwegians, those scoring in the top quarter on humor appreciation were 35 percent more likely to be alive 7 years later, and the difference was even greater within a cancer-patient subgroup (Svebak et al., 2007). There is not yet

Laughter among friends is good medicine Laughter arouses us, massages muscles, and then leaves us feeling relaxed (Robinson, 1983).

Bob Daemmrich/Stock, Boston

enough consistent evidence to suggest that "laughter is the best medicine" (Martin, 2001, 2002). But some studies suggest that mirthful humor (not hostile sarcasm) may defuse stress and strengthen immune activity (Berk et al., 2001; Kimata, 2001). People who laugh a lot (which arouses, massages muscles, and relaxes the body [Robinson, 1983]) also have exhibited a lower incidence of heart disease (Clark et al., 2001). In one experiment, laughter in response to a hilarious movie clip caused the blood vessels' inner lining to respond with improved tone and increased bloodflow, the opposite of what happened after people viewed a stressful movie clip (Miller, 2005). Perhaps future research will confirm that, indeed, those who laugh, last.

Social Support

Social support also matters. That's what James Coan and his colleagues (2006) discovered when they subjected happily married women to the threat of electric shock to an ankle while lying in an fMRI machine. During the experiment, some of the women held their husband's hand. Others held the hand of an anonymous person or no hand at all. While awaiting the occasional shocks, the women's brains were less active in threat-responsive areas if they held their husband's hand. This soothing benefit was greatest for those reporting the highest-quality marriages.

For most of us, family relationships provide not only our greatest heartaches (even when well-meaning, family intrusions can be stressful) but also our greatest comfort and joy. Peter Warr and Roy Payne (1982) asked a representative sample of British adults what, if anything, had emotionally strained them the day before. Their most frequent answer? "Family." But asked what prompted yesterday's times of pleasure, the same British sample, by an even larger margin, again answered "Family."

Seven massive investigations, each following thousands of people for several years, revealed that close relationships predict health. Compared with those having few social ties, people are less likely to die prematurely if supported by close relationships with friends, family, fellow workers, members of a faith community, or other support groups (Cohen, 1988; House et al., 1988; Nelson, 1988).

Carefully controlled studies indicate that married people live longer, healthier lives than the unmarried (Kaplan & Kronick, 2006; Wilson & Oswald, 2002). The National Center for Health Statistics (2004) reports that regardless of people's age, sex, race, and income, they tend to be healthier if married. In a seven-decades-long Harvard study, a good marriage at age 50 predicted healthy aging better than did a low cholesterol level at 50 (Vaillant, 2002). But, as Coan's study indicated, marital *functioning* also matters. Conflict-laden marriages are not conducive to health; positive, happy, supportive ones are (De Vogli et al., 2007; Kiecolt-Glaser & Newton, 2001). Moreover, middle-aged and older adults who live alone are more likely to smoke, be obese, and have high-cholesterol—and to have a doubled risk of heart attacks (Nielsen et al., 2006).

How can we explain this link between social support and health? Is it because healthy people are more supportive and marriage-prone? Possibly. But people with supportive friends and marriage partners eat better, exercise more, sleep better, and smoke less, and therefore cope with stress more effectively (Helgeson et al., 1998). Supportive friends can also help buffer immediate threats. Humans aren't the only source of stress-buffering comfort. After stressful events, Medicare patients who have a dog or other companionable pet are less likely to visit their doctor (Siegel, 1990). (See Close-Up: Pets Are Friends, Too, on the next page.)

Environments that support our need to belong foster stronger immune functioning. Social ties and positive sociability even confer resistance to cold viruses. Sheldon Cohen and his colleagues (1997, 2004) demonstrated this by putting 276 healthy volunteers in quarantine for five days after administering nasal drops laden with a cold

CLOSE-UP

Pets Are Friends, Too

Have you ever wished for a friend who would love you just as you are, who is nonjudgmental, and who is always there for you, no matter your mood? For many tens of millions of people that friend exists, and it is a loyal dog or a friendly cat.

Many people describe their pet as a cherished family member who helps them feel calm, happy, and valued. Can pets also help people handle stress? If so, might pets have healing power? Karen Allen (2003) reports that, *yes*, pets have been found to increase the odds of survival after a heart attack, to relieve depression among AIDS patients, and to lower the level of blood lipids that contribute to cardiovascular risk. As nursing pioneer Florence Nightingale (1860) foresaw, "A small pet animal is often an

Frank Siteman/Jupiterimages

excellent companion for the sick." Allen reports from her own research that women's blood pressure rises as they struggle with challenging math problems in the presence of a best friend or even a

spouse, but much less so when accompanied by their dog.

So, would pets be good medicine for people who do not have pets? To find out, Allen studied a group of stockbrokers who lived alone, described their work as stressful, and had high blood pressure. She randomly selected half to adopt an animal shelter cat or dog. When later facing stress, these new pet owners exhibited less than half the blood pressure increase of their counterparts without pets. The effect was greatest for those with few social contacts or friends. Her conclusion: For lowering blood pressure, pets are no substitute for effective drugs and exercise. But for those who enjoy animals, and especially for those who live alone, they are a healthy pleasure.

"Woe to one who is alone and falls and does not have another to help."

Ecclesiastes 4:10

---

virus, and then repeating the experiment with 334 more volunteers. (In both experiments, the volunteers were paid $800 each to endure this experience.) The cold fact is that the effect of social ties is nothing to sneeze at. Age, race, sex, smoking, and other health habits being equal, those with the most social ties were least likely to catch a cold, and if they caught one, they produced less mucus. More sociability meant less susceptibility. More than 50 studies further reveal that social support calms the cardiovascular system, lowering blood pressure and stress hormones (Graham et al., 2006; Uchino et al., 1996, 1999).

Close relationships give us an opportunity to *confide* painful feelings, a social support component that has now been extensively studied (Frattaroli, 2006). In one study, health psychologists James Pennebaker and Robin O'Heeron (1984) contacted the surviving spouses of people who had committed suicide or died in car accidents. Those who bore their grief alone had more health problems than those who could express it openly. Talking about our troubles can be "open heart therapy."

Suppressing emotions can be detrimental to physical health. When Pennebaker surveyed more than 700 undergraduate women, he found that about 1 in 12 reported a traumatic sexual experience in childhood. Compared with women who had experienced nonsexual traumas, such as parental death or divorce, the sexually abused women—especially those who had kept their secret to themselves—reported more headaches and stomach ailments. Another study, of 437 Australian ambulance drivers, confirmed the ill effects of suppressing one's emotions after witnessing traumas (Wastell, 2002).

Even writing about personal traumas in a diary can help (Burton & King, 2008; Hemenover, 2003; Lyubomirsky et al., 2006). In one experiment, volunteers who did this had fewer health problems during the ensuing four to six months (Pennebaker, 1990). As one participant explained, "Although I have not talked with anyone about what I wrote, I was finally able to deal with it, work through the pain instead of trying to block it out. Now it doesn't hurt to think about it."

Talking about a stressful event can temporarily arouse people, but in the long run it calms them, by calming limbic system activity (Lieberman et al., 2007; Mendolia & Kleck, 1993). When Pennebaker and his colleagues (1989) invited 33 Holocaust survivors to spend two hours recalling their experiences, many did so in intimate detail never before disclosed. In the weeks following, most watched a tape of their recollections and showed it to family and friends. Those who were most self-disclosing had the most improved health 14 months later. Confiding is good for the body and the soul.

▶‖ Managing Stress

44-2 What tactics can we use to manage stress and reduce stress-related ailments?

Having a sense of control, developing more optimistic thinking, and building social support can help us *experience* less stress and thus improve our health. Moreover, these factors interrelate: People who are upbeat about themselves and their future tend also to enjoy health-promoting social ties (Stinson et al., 2008). But sometimes we cannot alleviate stress and simply need to *manage* our stress. Aerobic exercise, biofeedback, relaxation, meditation, and spirituality may help us gather inner strength and lessen stress effects.

"Is there anyone here who specializes in stress management?"

Aerobic Exercise

Aerobic exercise is sustained exercise that increases heart and lung fitness. Jogging, swimming, and biking are common examples. Such exercise strengthens the body. Does it also boost the spirit?

Exercise and Mood

Many studies suggest that aerobic exercise can reduce stress, depression, and anxiety. For example, 3 in 10 American and Canadian people, and 2 in 10 British people, who do aerobic exercise at least three times a week also manage stressful events better, exhibit more self-confidence, feel more vigor, and feel depressed and fatigued less often than those who exercise less (McMurray, 2004). In a Gallup survey, nonexercisers were twice as likely as exercisers to report being "not too happy" (Brooks, 2002). But if we state this observation the other way around—that stressed and depressed people exercise less—cause and effect become unclear.

Experiments have resolved this ambiguity by randomly assigning stressed, depressed, or anxious people either to aerobic exercise or to other treatments. In one such experiment, Lisa McCann and David Holmes (1984) assigned one-third of a group of mildly depressed female college students to a program of aerobic exercise, one-third to a treatment of relaxation exercises, and the remaining third (a control group) to no treatment. As **FIGURE 44.2** on the next page shows, 10 weeks later the women in the aerobic exercise program reported the greatest decrease in depression. Many of them had, quite literally, run away from their troubles. Vigorous exercise provides a "substantial" immediate mood boost, reports David Watson (2000) from his monitoring of university students. Even a 10-minute walk stimulates two hours of increased well-being by raising energy levels and lowering tension (Thayer, 1987, 1993).

Other studies confirm that exercise reduces depression and anxiety and is therefore a useful adjunct to antidepressant drugs and psychotherapy (Dunn et al., 2005; Stathopoulou et al., 2006). Not only is exercise about as effective as drugs, some research suggests it better prevents symptom recurrence (Babyak et al., 2000; Salmon, 2001).

aerobic exercise sustained exercise that increases heart and lung fitness; may also reduce stress, depression, and anxiety.

Kathryn Brownson

FIGURE 44.2 Aerobic exercise and depression Mildly depressed college women who participated in an aerobic exercise program showed markedly reduced depression, compared with those who did relaxation exercises or received no treatment. (From McCann & Holmes, 1984.)

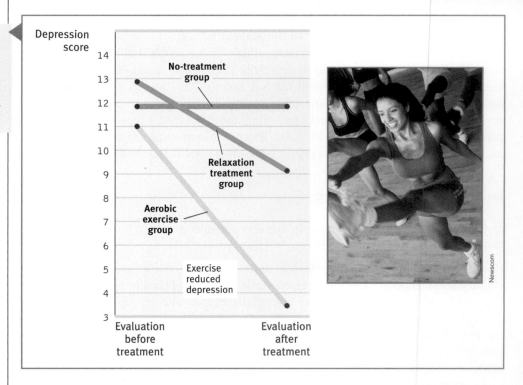

The mood boost When one's energy or spirits are sagging, few things reboot the day better than exercising (as I can confirm from my daily noontime basketball). Aerobic exercise appears to counteract depression partly by increasing arousal (replacing depression's low-arousal state) and by doing naturally what Prozac does—increasing the brain's serotonin activity.

Researchers are now wondering *why* aerobic exercise alleviates negative emotions. Exercise orders up mood-boosting chemicals from our body's internal pharmacy—neurotransmitters such as norepinephrine, serotonin, and the endorphins (Jacobs, 1994; Salmon, 2001). Perhaps the emotional benefits of exercise are also a side effect of increased warmth and body arousal (counteracting depression's low arousal state), or of the muscle relaxation and sounder sleep that occur afterward. Or perhaps a sense of accomplishment and an improved physique enhance one's emotional state.

Exercise and Health

Other research reveals that exercise not only boosts our mood, but also strengthens the heart, increases bloodflow, keeps blood vessels open, and lowers both blood pressure and the blood pressure reaction to stress (Ford, 2002; Manson, 2002). Compared with inactive adults, people who exercise suffer half as many heart attacks (Powell et al., 1987). Exercise makes the muscles hungry for the "bad fats" that, if not used by the muscles, contribute to clogged arteries (Barinaga, 1997). One study following adult Finnish twins for nearly 20 years revealed that, other things being equal, occasional exercise (compared with no exercise) reduced the risk of death by 29 percent. Daily conditioning exercise reduced death risk by 43 percent (Kujala et al., 1998). In later life, regular exercise also predicts better cognitive functioning and reduced risk of dementia and Alzheimer's disease (Kramer & Erickson, 2007).

The genes passed down to us from our distant ancestors were those that enabled the physical activity essential to hunting, foraging, and farming. In muscle cells, those genes, when activated by exercise, respond by producing proteins. In the modern inactive person, these genes produce lower quantities of proteins and leave us susceptible to more than 20 chronic diseases, such as type-2 diabetes, cardiovascular disease, and cancer (Booth & Neufer, 2005). Inactivity is thus potentially toxic.

With less physical activity demanded of us to provide food, shelter, and mobility (machines do much of the work for us), our more sedentary life-style contributes to today's high rate of depression. Less exercise means less brain activity in areas essential for reward, motivation, and effective coping (Ilardi et al., 2007; Lambert, 2005,

2008). More exercise has beneficial effects similar to those of antidepressant drugs: In mice, exercise causes their brains to produce a molecule that acts as a natural antidepressant by stimulating the production of new neurons (Hunsberger et al., 2007).

By one estimate, moderate exercise adds not only quality of life (more energy and better mood) but also quantity of life—two additional years, on average. "Perhaps God does not subtract the time spent exercising from your allotted time on Earth," jested Martin Seligman (1994, p. 193).

Biofeedback, Relaxation, and Meditation

Knowing the damaging effects of stress, could we train people to counteract stress, bringing their heart rate and blood pressure under conscious control? When a few psychologists started experimenting with this idea, many of their colleagues thought them foolish. After all, these functions are controlled by the autonomic ("involuntary") nervous system. Then, in the late 1960s, experiments by respected psychologists made the skeptics wonder. Neal Miller, for one, found that rats could modify their heartbeat if given pleasurable brain stimulation when their heartbeat increased or decreased. Later research revealed that some paralyzed humans could also learn to control their blood pressure (Miller & Brucker, 1979).

Miller was experimenting with **biofeedback,** a system of recording, amplifying, and feeding back information about subtle physiological responses. Biofeedback instruments mirror the results of a person's own efforts, thereby allowing the person to learn techniques for controlling a particular physiological response (**FIGURE 44.3**). After a decade of study, however, researchers decided the initial claims for biofeedback were overblown and oversold (Miller, 1985). A 1995 National Institutes of Health panel declared that biofeedback works best on tension headaches.

The years of rigorous testing and research on biofeedback exemplify the scientific attitude toward new but unproven health care treatment. (For more on this topic, see Thinking Critically About: Complementary and Alternative Medicine, on the next page).

Simple methods of relaxation, which require no expensive equipment, can produce many of the same results biofeedback once promised. For example, dozens of studies have found that relaxation procedures can help alleviate headaches, hypertension, anxiety, and insomnia (Nestoriuc et al., 2008; Stetter & Kupper, 2002). Such findings would not surprise Meyer Friedman and his colleagues. To find out whether teaching Type A heart attack victims to relax might reduce their risk of another attack, the researchers randomly assigned hundreds of middle-aged, male heart-attack

biofeedback a system for electronically recording, amplifying, and feeding back information regarding a subtle physiological state, such as blood pressure or muscle tension.

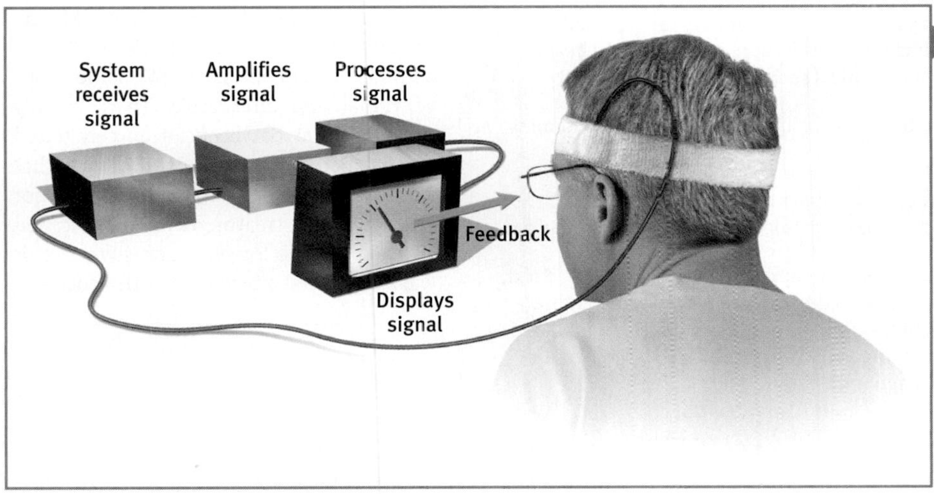

FIGURE 44.3 Biofeedback systems
Biofeedback systems—such as this one, which records tension in the forehead muscle of a headache sufferer—allow people to monitor their subtle physiological responses. As this man relaxes his forehead muscle, the pointer on the display screen (or a tone) may go lower.

Complementary and Alternative Medicine

One health care growth market is **complementary and alternative medicine (CAM),** which includes relaxation, acupuncture, massage therapy, homeopathy, spiritual healing, herbal remedies, chiropractic, and aromatherapy. In Germany, herbal remedies and homeopathy are enormously popular. In China, herbal therapies have long flourished, as have acupuncture and acupressure therapies that claim to correct "imbalances of energy flow" (called *Qi* or *Chi*) at identifiable points close to the skin. Andrew Weil's many books on alternative medicine have sold millions of copies, putting him on the cover of *Time* magazine.

Facing political pressure to explore these techniques, the U.S. National Institutes of Health (NIH) established the National Center for Complementary and Alternative Medicine, which the center defines as health care treatments not taught widely in medical schools, not usually reimbursed by insurance companies, and not used in hospitals (**TABLE 44.1**).

So what shall we make of CAM? Some aspects, such as life-style changes and stress management, have acknowledged validity.

And certain techniques have proved useful for specific ailments, such as acupuncture, massage therapy, and aromatherapy for pain relief in cancer patients (Fellowes et al., 2004). Do the other aspects offer, as some believe, a new medical paradigm?

Critics point out that people consult physicians for diagnosable, curable diseases and turn to CAM techniques for either incurable illnesses or when well but feeling subpar. Thus, an otherwise healthy person with a cold may try an herbal remedy and then credit the subsequent return to good health to CAM, rather than to the body's natural return to normal. CAM will seem especially effective with cyclical diseases, such as arthritis and allergies, as people seek therapy during the downturn and presume its effectiveness during the ensuing upturn. Add to this the healing power of belief—the *placebo effect*—plus the natural disappearance *(spontaneous remission)* of many diseases, and CAM practices are bound to seem effective, whether they are or not. One study of 302 migraine headache patients in Germany found that 51 percent of those receiving acupuncture treatment

found relief, as did only 15 percent of those in a waiting list control group. But among a third group that received "sham acupuncture" (needles inserted at non-acupuncture points), 53 percent enjoyed relief. Such results, the investigators suspected, may indicate "a powerful placebo effect" (Linde et al., 2005).

As always, the way to discern what works and what does not is to experiment: Randomly assign patients to receive the therapy or a placebo control. Then ask the critical question: When neither the therapist nor the patient knows who is getting the real therapy, is the real therapy effective?

Much of today's mainstream medicine began as yesterday's alternative medicine. Natural botanical life has given us digitalis (from purple foxglove), morphine (from the opium poppy), and penicillin (from penicillium mold). In each case, the active ingredient was verified in controlled trials. We have medical and public health science to thank for the antibiotics, vaccines, surgical procedures, sanitation, and emergency medicine that helped lengthen our life expectancy by three decades during the last century.

"CAM changes continually," notes the National Center for Complementary and Alternative Medicine (2006), "as those therapies that are proven to be safe and effective become adopted into conventional health care." Indeed, said *New England Journal of Medicine* editors Marcia Angell and Jerome Kassirer (1998), "There cannot be two kinds of medicine—conventional and alternative. There is only medicine that has been adequately tested and medicine that has not, medicine that works and medicine that may or may not work. Once a treatment has been tested rigorously, it no longer matters whether it was considered alternative at the outset."

"In God we trust. All others must have data."

George Lundberg, Editor, *Journal of the American Medical Association*, 1998

TABLE 44.1 Five Domains of Complementary and Alternative Medicine

Alternative medical systems	Therapies used in place of conventional medicine, including homeopathy in Western cultures and traditional Chinese medicine and Ayurveda in non-Western cultures.
Mind-body interventions	Techniques designed to enhance the mind's capacity to affect bodily function and symptoms, including meditation, prayer, mental healing, and therapies that use creative outlets such as art, music, or dance.
Biologically based therapies	Therapies using natural substances such as herbs, foods, and vitamins.
Manipulative and body-based methods	Based on manipulation and/or movement of one or more parts of the body, including chiropractic or osteopathic manipulation, and massage.
Energy therapies	Use presumed energy fields. Biofield therapies, such as qi gong, Reiki, and therapeutic touch, are intended to affect energy fields that purportedly surround and penetrate the human body. Bioelectromagnetic-based therapies involve the unconventional use of electromagnetic fields, such as pulsed or magnetic fields.

Source: Adapted from the National Center for Complementary and Alternative Medicine, NIH http://nccam.nih.gov/health/whatiscam.

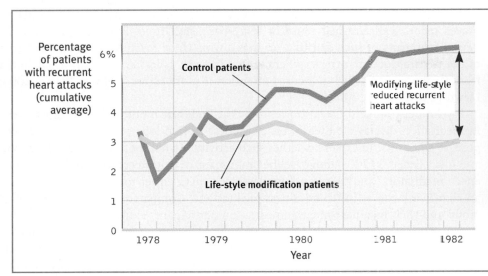

survivors to one of two groups. The first group received standard advice from cardiologists concerning medications, diet, and exercise habits. The second group received similar advice plus continuing counseling on modifying their life-styles—how to slow down and relax by walking, talking, and eating more slowly; by smiling at others and laughing at themselves; by admitting mistakes; by taking time to enjoy life; and by renewing their religious faith. As **FIGURE 44.4** indicates, during the ensuing three years, the second group experienced half as many repeat heart attacks as the first group. This, wrote the exuberant Friedman, was an unprecedented, spectacular reduction in heart-attack recurrence. A smaller-scale British study similarly divided heart-attack–prone people into control and life-style modification groups (Eysenck & Grossarth-Maticek, 1991). During the next 13 years, it also found a 50 percent reduction in death rate among those trained to alter their thinking and life-style. After suffering a heart attack at age 55, Friedman started taking his own behavioral medicine—and lived to age 90 (Wargo, 2007).

Cardiologist Herbert Benson (1996) became intrigued with meditative relaxation when he found that experienced meditators could decrease their blood pressure, heart rate, and oxygen consumption and raise their fingertip temperature. His study led him to what he calls the *relaxation response,* described in the Close-Up below.

FIGURE 44.4 Recurrent heart attacks and life-style modification The San Francisco Recurrent Coronary Prevention Project offered counseling from a cardiologist to survivors of heart attacks. Those who were also guided in modifying their Type A life-style suffered fewer repeat heart attacks. (From Friedman & Ulmer, 1984.)

complementary and alternative medicine (CAM) as yet unproven health care treatments intended to supplement (complement) or serve as alternatives to conventional medicine, and which typically are not widely taught in medical schools, used in hospitals, or reimbursed by insurance companies. When research shows a therapy to be safe and effective, it usually then becomes part of accepted medical practice.

CLOSE-UP

The Relaxation Response

The relaxation response is a state of calm marked by relaxed muscles, slowed breathing and heart rate, and decreased blood pressure. Advocates such as cardiologist Herbert Benson claim lasting stress-reducing benefits when relaxation is practiced once or twice daily.

To experience the relaxation response, the Benson-Henry Institute for Mind Body Medicine recommends these steps: Sit quietly in a comfortable position. Close your eyes. Relax your muscles, starting with your feet, then your calves, and upward through your thighs, shoulders, neck, and head. Breathe slowly. As you exhale each breath, repeat a focus word, phrase, or prayer—something drawn from your own belief system. When other thoughts intrude, don't worry. Just return to your repetition and continue for 10 to 20 minutes. When finished, sit quietly for another minute or two, then open your eyes and sit for a few more moments.

|| Meditation is a modern phenomenon with a long history: "Sit down alone and in silence. Lower your head, shut your eyes, breathe out gently, and imagine yourself looking into your own heart. . . . As you breathe out, say 'Lord Jesus Christ, have mercy on me.' . . . Try to put all other thoughts aside. Be calm, be patient, and repeat the process very frequently" (Gregory of Sinai, died 1346). ||

|| And then there are the mystics who seek to use the mind's power to enable novocaine-free cavity repair. Their aim: to transcend dental medication. ||

Tibetan Buddhists deep in meditation and Franciscan nuns deep in centering prayer report a diminished sense of self, space, and time. Brain scans reveal the neural footprints of such spiritual feelings during these mystical experiences: A part of the parietal lobe that tracks where we are in space is less active than usual, and a frontal lobe area involved in focused attention is more active (Cahn & Polich, 2006; Newberg & D'Aquili, 2001).

Psychologist Richard Davidson reports that Buddhist monks who are experienced in meditation display elevated levels of the left frontal lobe activity associated with positive emotions. To explore whether such activity is a *result* of meditation, Davidson and his colleagues (2003) ran baseline brain scans of volunteers who were *not* experienced meditators, and then randomly assigned them either to a control group or to an eight-week course in "mindfulness meditation." Compared with both the control group and their own baseline, the meditation participants exhibited noticeably more left-hemisphere activity, and also improved immune functioning after the training. Such effects may help explain the astonishing results of a study that randomly assigned 73 residents of homes for the elderly either to daily meditation or to none. After three years, one-fourth of the nonmeditators had died, but all the meditators were still alive (Alexander et al., 1989). A more recent study found that hypertension patients assigned to meditation training had (compared with other treatment groups) a 30 percent lower cardiovascular death rate over the ensuing 19-year study period (Schneider et al., 2005).

Spirituality and Faith Communities

As humans suffered ills and sought healing throughout history, two healing traditions —religion and medicine—have joined hands in caring for them. Often those hands belonged to the same person—the spiritual leader was also the healer. Maimonides was a twelfth-century rabbi and a renowned physician. Hospitals, which were first established in monasteries and then spread by missionaries, often carry the names of saints or faith communities.

As medical science matured, healing and religion diverged. Rather than asking God to spare their children from smallpox, people were able to vaccinate them. Rather than seeking a spiritual healer when burning with bacterial fever, they were able to use antibiotics. Recently, however, religion and healing are converging once again. In 1992, 4 percent of American medical schools offered spirituality and health courses; in 2005, 75 percent did (Koenig, 2002; Puchalski, 2005). A National Library of Medicine MEDLINE search of *religion* or *spirituality* reveals 8294 articles between 2000 and 2007, more than three times the articles in the database's prior 35 years.

More than a thousand studies have sought to correlate the *faith factor* with health and healing. For example, Jeremy Kark and his colleagues (1996) compared the death rates for 3900 Israelis either in one of 11 religiously orthodox or in one of 11 matched, nonreligious collective settlements (kibbutz communities). The researchers reported that over a 16-year period, "belonging to a religious collective was associated with a strong protective effect" not explained by age or economic differences. In every age group, religious community members were about half as likely to have died as were their nonreligious counterparts. This is roughly comparable to the gender difference in mortality.

In response to such findings, Richard Sloan and his skeptical colleagues (1999, 2000, 2002, 2005) remind us that mere correlations can leave many factors uncontrolled. Consider one obvious possibility: Women are more religiously active than men, and women outlive men. So perhaps religious involvement is merely an expression of the gender effect on longevity.

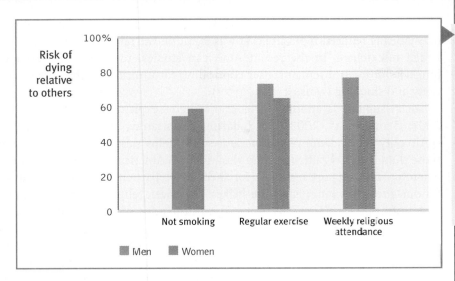

FIGURE 44.5 **Predictors of mortality: Not smoking, frequent exercise, and regular religious attendance** Epidemiologist William Strawbridge and his co-workers (1997, 1999; Oman et al., 2002) followed 5286 Alameda, California, adults over 28 years. After adjusting for age and education, the researchers found that not smoking, regular exercise, and religious attendance all predicted a lowered risk of death in any given year. Women attending weekly religious services, for example, were only 54 percent as likely to die in a typical study year as were nonattenders.

However, several new studies find the correlation between religious involvement and life expectancy among men alone, and even more strongly among women (McCullough et al., 2000, 2005). One study that followed 5286 Californians over 28 years found that, after controlling for age, gender, ethnicity, and education, frequent religious attenders were 36 percent less likely to have died in any year (**FIGURE 44.5**).

A U.S. National Health Interview Survey (Hummer et al., 1999) followed 21,204 people over 8 years. After controlling for age, sex, race, and region, researchers found that nonattenders were 1.87 times more likely to have died than were those attending more than weekly. This translated into a life expectancy at age 20 of 83 years for frequent attenders and 75 years for infrequent attenders (**FIGURE 44.6**).

These correlational findings do not indicate that nonattenders who start attending services and change nothing else will live 8 years longer. But they do indicate that as a *predictor* of health and longevity, religious involvement rivals nonsmoking and exercise effects. Such findings demand explanation. Can you imagine what intervening variables might account for the correlation?

First, religiously active people tend to have healthier life-styles; for example, they smoke and drink less (Lyons, 2002; Park, 2007; Strawbridge et al., 2001). Health-oriented, vegetarian Seventh Day Adventists have a longer-than-usual life expectancy (Berkel & de Waard, 1983). Religiously orthodox Israelis eat less fat than do their

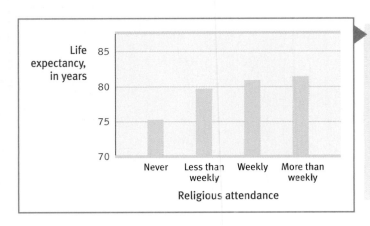

FIGURE 44.6 **Religious attendance and life expectancy** In a national health survey financed by the U.S. Centers for Disease Control and Prevention, religiously active people had longer life expectancies. (Data from Hummer et al., 1999.)

nonreligious compatriots. But such differences are not great enough to explain the dramatically reduced mortality that was found in the religious kibbutzim, argued the Israeli researchers. In the recent American studies, too, about 75 percent of the longevity difference remains after controlling for unhealthy behaviors such as inactivity and smoking (Musick et al., 1999).

Social support is another variable that helps explain the faith factor (Ai et al., 2007; George et al., 2002). For Judaism, Christianity, and Islam, faith is not solo spirituality but a communal experience that helps satisfy the need to belong. The more than 350,000 faith communities in North America and the millions more elsewhere provide support networks for their active participants—people who are there for one another when misfortune strikes. Moreover, religion encourages another predictor of health and longevity—marriage. In the religious kibbutzim, for example, divorce has been almost nonexistent.

But even after controlling for gender, unhealthy behaviors, social ties, and preexisting health problems, the mortality studies find much of the mortality reduction remaining (George et al., 2000; Powell et al., 2003). Researchers therefore speculate that a third set of intervening variables is the stress protection and enhanced well-being associated with a coherent worldview, a sense of hope for the long-term future, feelings of ultimate acceptance, and the relaxed meditation of prayer or Sabbath observance (**FIGURE 44.7**). These variables might also help to explain other recent findings among the religiously active, such as healthier immune functioning, fewer hospital admissions, and, for AIDS patients, fewer stress hormones and longer survival (Ironson et al., 2002; Koenig & Larson, 1998; Lutgendorf et al., 2004).

FIGURE 44.7 Possible explanations for the correlation between religious involvement and health/longevity

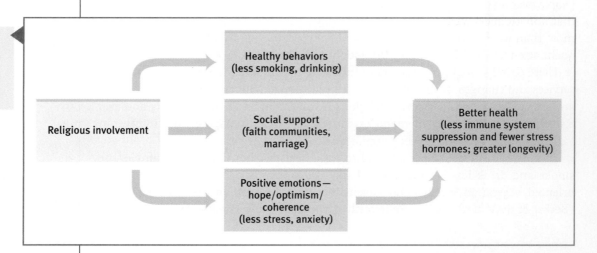

REVIEW

Promoting Health

44-1 **What factors affect our ability to cope with stress?** Having a sense of control, developing a more optimistic explanatory style, and building our base of social support can help us cope with stress emotionally, cognitively, or behaviorally. Direct, *problem-focused coping* strategies alleviate stress directly; *emotion-focused coping* tries to alleviate stress by attending to emotional needs. Optimists seem to cope more successfully with stress and enjoy better health.

44-2 **What tactics can we use to manage stress and reduce stress-related ailments?** Stress-management programs may include *aerobic exercise,* relaxation, and meditation. Learning to slow down and relax has helped lower rates of recurring heart attacks. Researchers are working toward understanding the active components of the religion-health correlation.

Terms and Concepts to Remember

coping, p. 542
problem-focused coping, p. 542
emotion-focused coping, p. 542
aerobic exercise, p. 547
biofeedback, p. 549
complementary and
  alternative medicine
  (CAM), p. 550

Test Yourself

1. How do problem-focused coping and emotion-focused coping differ?

(Answers to the Test Yourself questions can be found in Appendix B at the end of the book.)

Ask Yourself

1. Can you remember a time when you felt better about some worrisome problem after discussing it with a friend or family member, or even after playing with your pet? How did that interaction help you to cope?

∞ WEB

Multiple-choice self-tests and more may be found at www.worthpublishers.com/myers

Personality

MODULES

45
The Psychoanalytic Perspective

46
The Humanistic Perspective

47
Contemporary Research on Personality

Lord of the Rings hobbit-hero Frodo Baggins knew that throughout his difficult journey there was one who would never fail him—his loyal and ever-cheerful companion, Sam Gamgee. Even before they left their beloved hometown, Frodo warned Sam that the journey would not be easy.

"It is going to be very dangerous, Sam. It is already dangerous. Most likely neither of us will come back."

"If you don't come back, sir, then I shan't, that's certain," said Sam. "[The Elves told me] 'Don't you leave him!' Leave him! I said. I never mean to. I am going with him, if he climbs to the Moon; and if any of those Black Riders try to stop him, they'll have Sam Gamgee to reckon with." (J. R. R. Tolkien, *The Fellowship of the Ring*, p. 96)

And so they did! Later in the story, when it becomes clear that Frodo's path will lead him into the land of Mordor, it is Sam who insists he will be at Frodo's side, come what may. It is Sam who lifts Frodo's spirits with songs and stories from their boyhood. And it is Sam whom Frodo leans upon when he can barely take another step. When Frodo is overcome by the evil of the ring he carries, it is Sam who saves him. In the end, it is Sam who helps Frodo successfully reach the end of his journey. Sam Gamgee—cheerful, optimistic, emotionally stable—never falters in his faithfulness or his belief that they will overcome the threatening darkness.

As he appears and reappears throughout the series, Tolkien's Sam Gamgee exhibits the distinctive and enduring behaviors that define **personality**—a person's characteristic pattern of thinking, feeling, and acting. It is, suggest Dan McAdams and Jennifer Pals (2006), "an individual's unique variation on the general evolutionary design for human nature," which gets expressed in one's traits and cultural situation. Other modules focus on our shared paths—our similar ways of developing, perceiving, learning, remembering, thinking, and feeling. Modules 45 through 47 focus on what makes us unique.

Actually, much of psychology deals with personality. Across the field, psychologists study biological influences on personality; personality development across the life span; personality-related aspects of learning, motivation, emotion, and health; disorders of personality; and social influences on personality.

We begin with two grand theories that have become part of our cultural legacy. These historically significant perspectives helped establish the field of personality psychology and raised key issues still being addressed in today's research and clinical work.

▶ Sigmund Freud's *psychoanalytic* theory (Module 45) proposed that childhood sexuality and unconscious motivations influence personality.

▶ The *humanistic* approach (Module 46) focused on our inner capacities for growth and self-fulfillment.

These classic theories, which offer sweeping perspectives on human nature, are complemented by what Module 47 goes on to explore: today's more focused and down-to-earth scientific research of specific aspects of personality.

Today's personality researchers study the basic dimensions of personality, the biological roots of these basic dimensions, and the interaction of persons and environments. They also study self-esteem, self-serving bias, and cultural influences on one's sense of self. And they study the unconscious mind—with findings that probably would have surprised Freud himself.

personality an individual's characteristic pattern of thinking, feeling, and acting.

Exploring the Unconscious

The Neo-Freudian and Psychodynamic Theorists

Assessing Unconscious Processes

Evaluating the Psychoanalytic Perspective

Sigmund Freud, 1856–1939
"I was the only worker in a new field."

MODULE 45

The Psychoanalytic Perspective

45-1 What was Freud's view of personality and its development?

Love him or hate him, Sigmund Freud has profoundly influenced Western culture. Ask 100 people on the street to name a notable deceased psychologist, suggests Keith Stanovich (1996, p. 1), and "Freud would be the winner hands down." In the popular mind, he is to psychology's history what Elvis Presley is to rock music's history. Freud's influence lingers in literary and film interpretation, psychiatry, and clinical psychology. So, who was Freud, and what did he teach?

Long before entering the University of Vienna in 1873, a youthful Sigmund Freud showed signs of independence and brilliance. He had a prodigious memory and so loved reading plays, poetry, and philosophy that he once ran up a bookstore debt beyond his means. As a teen he often took his evening meal in his tiny bedroom in order to lose no time from his studies. After medical school he set up a private practice, specializing in nervous disorders. Before long, however, he faced patients whose disorders made no neurological sense. For example, a patient might have lost all feeling in a hand—yet there is no sensory nerve that, if damaged, would numb the entire hand and nothing else. Freud's search for a cause for such disorders set his mind running in a direction destined to change human self-understanding.

▶‖ Exploring the Unconscious

Might some neurological disorders have psychological causes? Observing patients led Freud to his "discovery" of the unconscious. He speculated that lost feeling in one's hand might be caused by a fear of touching one's genitals; that unexplained blindness or deafness might be caused by not wanting to see or hear something that aroused intense anxiety. Freud at first thought hypnosis might unlock the door to the unconscious, but his patients displayed an uneven capacity for hypnosis. He then turned to **free association,** in which he told the patient to relax and say whatever came to mind, no matter how embarrassing or trivial. Freud assumed that a line of mental dominoes had fallen from his patients' distant past to their troubled present. Free association, he believed, would allow him to retrace that line, following a chain of thought leading into the patient's unconscious, where painful unconscious memories, often from childhood, could be retrieved and released. Freud called his theory of personality and the associated treatment techniques **psychoanalysis.**

Basic to Freud's theory was his belief that the mind is mostly hidden (**FIGURE 45.1**). Our conscious awareness is like the part of an iceberg that floats above the surface. Beneath our awareness is the larger **unconscious** mind with its thoughts, wishes, feelings, and memories. Some of these thoughts we store temporarily in a *preconscious* area, from which we can retrieve them into conscious awareness. Of greater interest to Freud was the mass of unacceptable passions and thoughts that he believed we *repress,* or forcibly block from our consciousness because they would be too unsettling to acknowledge. Freud believed that, although we are not consciously aware of them, these troublesome feelings and ideas powerfully influence us, sometimes gaining expression in disguised forms—the work we choose, the beliefs we hold, our daily habits, our troubling symptoms.

"Good morning, beheaded—uh, I mean beloved."

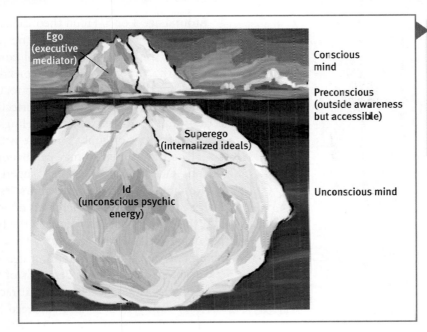

FIGURE 45.1 **Freud's idea of the mind's structure** Psychologists have used an iceberg image to illustrate Freud's idea that the mind is mostly hidden beneath the conscious surface. Note that the id is totally unconscious, but ego and superego operate both consciously and unconsciously. Unlike the parts of a frozen iceberg, however, the id, ego, and superego interact.

For Freud the determinist, nothing was ever accidental. He believed he could glimpse the unconscious seeping not only into people's free associations, beliefs, habits, and symptoms but also into slips of the tongue and pen. He illustrated with a financially stressed patient who, not wanting any large pills, said, "Please do not give me any bills, because I cannot swallow them." Similarly, Freud viewed jokes as expressions of repressed sexual and aggressive tendencies, and dreams as the "royal road to the unconscious." The remembered content of dreams (their *manifest content*) he believed to be a censored expression of the dreamer's unconscious wishes (the dream's *latent content*). In his dream analyses, Freud searched for patients' inner conflicts.

Personality Structure

In Freud's view, human personality—including its emotions and strivings—arises from a conflict between impulse and restraint—between our aggressive, pleasure-seeking biological urges and our internalized social controls over these urges. Freud believed personality is the result of our efforts to resolve this basic conflict—to express these impulses in ways that bring satisfaction without also bringing guilt or punishment. To understand the mind's dynamics during this conflict, Freud proposed three interacting systems: the *id*, *ego*, and *superego* (Figure 45.1).

The **id's** unconscious psychic energy constantly strives to satisfy basic drives to survive, reproduce, and aggress. The id operates on the *pleasure principle*: It seeks immediate gratification. To envision an id-dominated person, think of a newborn infant crying out for satisfaction, caring nothing for the outside world's conditions and demands. Or think of people with a present rather than future time perspective—those who often use tobacco, alcohol, and other drugs, and would sooner party now than sacrifice today's pleasure for future success and happiness (Keough et al., 1999)

As the **ego** develops, the young child responds to the real world. The ego, operating on the *reality principle*, seeks to gratify the id's impulses in realistic ways that will bring long-term pleasure. (Imagine what would happen if, lacking an ego, we expressed all our unrestrained sexual or aggressive impulses.) The ego contains our partly conscious perceptions, thoughts, judgments, and memories.

free association in psychoanalysis, a method of exploring the unconscious in which the person relaxes and says whatever comes to mind, no matter how trivial or embarrassing.

psychoanalysis Freud's theory of personality that attributes thoughts and actions to unconscious motives and conflicts; the techniques used in treating psychological disorders by seeking to expose and interpret unconscious tensions.

unconscious according to Freud, a reservoir of mostly unacceptable thoughts, wishes, feelings, and memories. According to contemporary psychologists, information processing of which we are unaware.

id contains a reservoir of unconscious psychic energy that, according to Freud, strives to satisfy basic sexual and aggressive drives. The id operates on the *pleasure principle*, demanding immediate gratification.

ego the largely conscious, "executive" part of personality that, according to Freud, mediates among the demands of the id, superego, and reality. The ego operates on the *reality principle*, satisfying the id's desires in ways that will realistically bring pleasure rather than pain.

superego the part of personality that, according to Freud, represents internalized ideals and provides standards for judgment (the conscience) and for future aspirations.

psychosexual stages the childhood stages of development (oral, anal, phallic, latency, genital) during which, according to Freud, the id's pleasure-seeking energies focus on distinct erogenous zones.

Oedipus [ED-uh-puss] **complex** according to Freud, a boy's sexual desires toward his mother and feelings of jealousy and hatred for the rival father.

identification the process by which, according to Freud, children incorporate their parents' values into their developing superegos.

"Fifty is plenty."   "Hundred and fifty."
The ego struggles to reconcile the demands of superego and id, said Freud.

Around age 4 or 5, Freud theorized, a child's ego recognizes the demands of the newly emerging **superego,** the voice of our moral compass (conscience) that forces the ego to consider not only the real but the *ideal*. The superego focuses on how we *ought* to behave. It strives for perfection, judging actions and producing positive feelings of pride or negative feelings of guilt. Someone with an exceptionally strong superego may be virtuous yet guilt-ridden; another with a weak superego may be wantonly self-indulgent and remorseless.

Because the superego's demands often oppose the id's, the ego struggles to reconcile the two. It is the personality "executive," mediating the impulsive demands of the id, the restraining demands of the superego, and the real-life demands of the external world. If chaste Jane feels sexually attracted to John, she may satisfy both id and superego by joining a volunteer organization that John attends regularly.

Personality Development

Analysis of his patients' histories convinced Freud that personality forms during life's first few years. He concluded that children pass through a series of **psychosexual stages,** during which the id's pleasure-seeking energies focus on distinct pleasure-sensitive areas of the body called *erogenous zones* (**TABLE 45.1**).

Freud believed that during the *phallic stage* boys seek genital stimulation, and they develop both unconscious sexual desires for their mother and jealousy and hatred for their father, whom they consider a rival. Given these feelings, boys supposedly also experience guilt and a lurking fear of punishment, perhaps by castration, from their father. Freud called this collection of feelings the **Oedipus complex** after the Greek legend of Oedipus, who unknowingly killed his father and married his mother. Some psychoanalysts in Freud's era believed that girls experienced a parallel *Electra complex*.

Children eventually cope with the threatening feelings, said Freud, by repressing them and by identifying with (trying to become like) the rival parent. It's as though something inside the child decides, "If you can't beat 'em [the parent of the same sex], join 'em." Through this **identification** process, children's superegos gain strength as they incorporate many of their parents' values. Freud believed that identification with

Identification Freud believed that children cope with threatening feelings of competition with their same-sex parent by identifying with that parent.

TABLE 45.1 Freud's Psychosexual Stages

Stage	Focus
Oral (0–18 months)	Pleasure centers on the mouth—sucking, biting, chewing
Anal (18–36 months)	Pleasure focuses on bowel and bladder elimination; coping with demands for control
Phallic (3–6 years)	Pleasure zone is the genitals; coping with incestuous sexual feelings
Latency (6 to puberty)	Dormant sexual feelings
Genital (puberty on)	Maturation of sexual interests

the same-sex parent provides what psychologists now call our *gender identity*—our sense of being male or female. Freud presumed that our early childhood relations—especially with parents and caregivers—influence our developing identity, personality, and frailties.

In Freud's view, conflicts unresolved during earlier psychosexual stages could surface as maladaptive behavior in the adult years. At any point in the oral, anal, or phallic stages, strong conflict could lock, or **fixate,** the person's pleasure-seeking energies in that stage. A person who had been either orally overindulged or deprived (perhaps by abrupt, early weaning) might fixate at the oral stage. This orally fixated adult could exhibit either passive dependence (like that of a nursing infant) or an exaggerated denial of this dependence (by acting tough or uttering biting sarcasm). Or the person might continue to seek oral gratification by smoking or excessive eating. In such ways, Freud suggested, the twig of personality is bent at an early age.

Defense Mechanisms

45-2 How did Freud think people defended themselves against anxiety?

Anxiety, said Freud, is the price we pay for civilization. As members of social groups, we must control our sexual and aggressive impulses, not act them out. But sometimes the ego fears losing control of this inner war between the id and superego. The presumed result is a dark cloud of unfocused anxiety that leaves us feeling unsettled but unsure why.

Freud proposed that the ego protects itself with **defense mechanisms**—tactics that reduce or redirect anxiety by distorting reality. Here are seven examples.

▶ **Repression** banishes anxiety-arousing wishes from consciousness. According to Freud, *repression underlies all the other defense mechanisms*, each of which disguises threatening impulses and keeps them from reaching consciousness. Freud believed that repression explains why we do not remember our childhood lust for our parent of the other sex. However, he also believed that repression is often incomplete, with repressed urges seeping out in dream symbols and slips of the tongue.

▶ **Regression** allows us to retreat to an earlier, more infantile stage of development. Facing the anxious first days of school, a child may regress to the oral comfort of thumb-sucking. Juvenile monkeys, when anxious, retreat to infantile clinging to their mothers or to one another (Suomi, 1987). Even homesick new college students may long for the security and comfort of home.

"Oh, for goodness' sake! Smoke!"

fixation according to Freud, a lingering focus of pleasure-seeking energies at an earlier psychosexual stage, in which conflicts were unresolved.

defense mechanisms in psychoanalytic theory, the ego's protective methods of reducing anxiety by unconsciously distorting reality.

repression in psychoanalytic theory, the basic defense mechanism that banishes anxiety-arousing thoughts, feelings, and memories from consciousness.

regression psychoanalytic defense mechanism in which an individual faced with anxiety retreats to a more infantile psychosexual stage, where some psychic energy remains fixated.

Regression Faced with a mild stressor, children and young orangutans will regress, retreating to the comfort of earlier behaviors.

"The lady doth protest too much, methinks."

William Shakespeare, *Hamlet*, 1600

reaction formation psychoanalytic defense mechanism by which the ego unconsciously switches unacceptable impulses into their opposites. Thus, people may express feelings that are the opposite of their anxiety-arousing unconscious feelings.

projection psychoanalytic defense mechanism by which people disguise their own threatening impulses by attributing them to others.

rationalization defense mechanism that offers self-justifying explanations in place of the real, more threatening, unconscious reasons for one's actions.

displacement psychoanalytic defense mechanism that shifts sexual or aggressive impulses toward a more acceptable or less threatening object or person, as when redirecting anger toward a safer outlet.

denial defense mechanism by which people refuse to believe or even to perceive painful realities.

"The female . . . acknowledges the fact of her castration, and with it, too, the superiority of the male and her own inferiority; but she rebels against this unwelcome state of affairs."

Sigmund Freud, *Female Sexuality*, 1931

▶ In **reaction formation,** the ego unconsciously makes unacceptable impulses look like their opposites. En route to consciousness, the unacceptable proposition "I hate him" becomes "I love him." Timidity becomes daring. Feelings of inadequacy become bravado.

▶ **Projection** disguises threatening impulses by attributing them to others. Thus, "He doesn't trust me" may be a projection of the actual feeling "I don't trust him" or "I don't trust myself." An El Salvadoran saying captures the idea: "The thief thinks everyone else is a thief."

▶ **Rationalization** occurs when we unconsciously generate self-justifying explanations to hide from ourselves the real reasons for our actions. Thus, habitual drinkers may say they drink with their friends "just to be sociable." Students who fail to study may rationalize, "All work and no play makes Jack [or Jill] a dull person."

▶ **Displacement** diverts sexual or aggressive impulses toward an object or person that is psychologically more acceptable than the one that aroused the feelings. Children who fear expressing anger against their parents may displace it by kicking the family pet. Students upset over an exam may snap at a roommate.

▶ **Denial** protects the person from real events that are painful to accept, either by rejecting a fact or its seriousness. Dying patients may deny the gravity of their illness. Parents may deny their child's misconduct. Spouses may deny evidence of their partner's affairs.

Note that all these defense mechanisms function indirectly and unconsciously, reducing anxiety by disguising some threatening impulse. Just as the body unconsciously defends itself against disease, so also, believed Freud, does the ego unconsciously defend itself against anxiety.

▶‖ The Neo-Freudian and Psychodynamic Theorists

45-3   Which of Freud's ideas did his followers accept or reject?

Freud's writings were controversial, but they soon attracted followers, mostly young, ambitious physicians who formed an inner circle around their strong-minded leader. These pioneering psychoanalysts and others, whom we now call *neo-Freudians,* accepted Freud's basic ideas: the personality structures of id, ego, and superego; the importance of the unconscious; the shaping of personality in childhood; and the dynamics of anxiety and the defense mechanisms. But they veered away from Freud in two important ways. First, they placed more emphasis on the conscious mind's role in interpreting experience and in coping with the environment. And second, they doubted that sex and aggression were all-consuming motivations. Instead, they tended to emphasize loftier motives and social interactions. The following examples illustrate.

Alfred Adler and Karen Horney [HORN-eye] agreed with Freud that childhood is important. But they believed that childhood *social,* not sexual, tensions are crucial for personality formation (Ferguson, 2003). Adler (who had proposed the still-popular idea of the *inferiority complex*) himself struggled to overcome childhood illnesses and accidents, and he believed that much of our behavior is driven by efforts to conquer childhood feelings of inferiority, feelings that trigger our strivings for superiority and power. Horney said childhood anxiety, caused by the dependent child's sense of helplessness, triggers our desire for love and security. Horney countered Freud's assumptions that women have weak superegos and suffer "penis envy," and she attempted to balance the bias she detected in this masculine view of psychology.

Alfred Adler "The individual feels at home in life and feels his existence to be worthwhile just so far as he is useful to others and is overcoming feelings of inferiority" (*Problems of Neurosis*, 1964).

Karen Horney "The view that women are infantile and emotional creatures, and as such, incapable of responsibility and independence is the work of the masculine tendency to lower women's self-respect" (*Feminine Psychology*, 1932).

Carl Jung "From the living fountain of instinct flows everything that is creative; hence the unconscious is the very source of the creative impulse" (*The Structure and Dynamics of the Psyche*, 1960).

Unlike other neo-Freudians, Carl Jung—Freud's disciple-turned-dissenter—placed less emphasis on social factors and agreed with Freud that the unconscious exerts a powerful influence. But to Jung (pronounced *Yoong*), the unconscious contains more than our repressed thoughts and feelings. He believed we also have a **collective unconscious,** a common reservoir of images derived from our species' universal experiences. Jung said that the collective unconscious explains why, for many people, spiritual concerns are deeply rooted and why people in different cultures share certain myths and images, such as mother as a symbol of nurturance. (Today's psychologists discount the idea of inherited experiences. But many do believe that our shared evolutionary history shaped some universal dispositions.)

Freud died in 1939. Since then, some of his ideas have been incorporated into *psychodynamic theory.* "Most contemporary dynamic theorists and therapists are not wedded to the idea that sex is the basis of personality," noted Drew Westen (1996). They "do not talk about ids and egos, and do not go around classifying their patients as oral, anal, or phallic characters." What they do assume, with Freud, is that much of our mental life is unconscious, that we often struggle with inner conflicts among our wishes, fears, and values, and that childhood shapes our personality and ways of becoming attached to others.

> **collective unconscious** Carl Jung's concept of a shared, inherited reservoir of memory traces from our species' history.

▶‖ Assessing Unconscious Processes

45-4 What are projective tests, and how are they used?

Personality assessment tools are useful to those who study personality or provide therapy. Such tools differ because they are tailored to specific theories. How might clinicians working in the Freudian tradition attempt to assess personality characteristics?

The first requirement would be some sort of a road into the unconscious, to track down residue from early childhood experiences—something to move beyond surface pretensions and reveal hidden conflicts and impulses. (Recall that Freud believed free association and dream interpretation could reveal the unconscious.) Objective assessment tools, such as agree-disagree or true-false questionnaires, would be inadequate because they would merely tap the conscious surface.

"The forward thrust of the antlers shows a determined personality, yet the small sun indicates a lack of self-confidence. . . ."

projective test a personality test, such as the Rorschach or TAT, that provides ambiguous stimuli designed to trigger projection of one's inner dynamics.

Thematic Apperception Test (TAT) a projective test in which people express their inner feelings and interests through the stories they make up about ambiguous scenes.

Rorschach inkblot test the most widely used projective test, a set of 10 inkblots, designed by Hermann Rorschach; seeks to identify people's inner feelings by analyzing their interpretations of the blots.

"We don't see things as they are; we see things as we are."
The Talmud

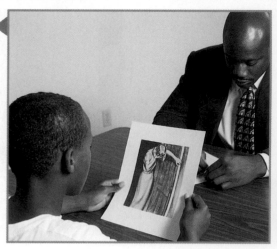

FIGURE 45.2 **The TAT** This clinician presumes that the hopes, fears, and interests expressed in this boy's descriptions of a series of ambiguous pictures in the Thematic Apperception Test (TAT) are projections of his inner feelings.

Lew Merrim/Photo Researchers, Inc.

Projective tests aim to provide this "psychological X-ray," by asking test-takers to describe an ambiguous stimulus or tell a story about it. Henry Murray introduced one such test, the **Thematic Apperception Test (TAT),** in which people view ambiguous pictures and then make up stories about them (**FIGURE 45.2**). One use of storytelling has been to assess achievement motivation. Shown a daydreaming boy, those who imagine he is fantasizing about an achievement are presumed to be projecting their own goals.

The most widely used projective test is the famous **Rorschach inkblot test,** in which people describe what they see in a series of inkblots (**FIGURE 45.3**). Swiss psychiatrist Hermann Rorschach [ROAR-shock] based it on a childhood game in which he and his friends dripped ink on a paper, folded it, and then said what they saw in the resulting blot (Sdorow, 2005). Do you see predatory animals or weapons? Perhaps you have aggressive tendencies. But is this a reasonable assumption?

Clinicians' and critics' answers differ. Some clinicians cherish the Rorschach, even offering Rorschach-based assessments of criminals' violence potential to judges. Others view it as a helpful diagnostic tool, a source of suggestive leads, or an icebreaker and a revealing interview technique. The Society for Personality Assessment (2005) commends "its responsible use" (which would *not* include inferring past child sexual abuse). And—in response to past criticisms of test scoring and interpretation

FIGURE 45.3 **The Rorschach test** In this projective test, people tell what they see in a series of symmetrical inkblots. Some who use this test are confident that the interpretation of ambiguous stimuli will reveal unconscious aspects of the test-taker's personality. Others use it as an icebreaker or to supplement other information.

Andy Warhol Foundation/Corbis

(Sechrest et al., 1998)—a research-based, computer-aided tool has been designed to improve agreement among raters and enhance the test's validity (Erdberg, 1990; Exner, 2003).

But the evidence is insufficient to its revilers, who insist the Rorschach is no emotional MRI. They argue that only a few of the many Rorschach-derived scores, such as ones for hostility and anxiety, have demonstrated validity (Wood, 2006). Moreover, they say, these tests are not reliable. Inkblot assessments diagnose many normal adults as pathological (Wood et al., 2003, 2006). Alternative projective assessment techniques fare little better. "Even seasoned professionals can be fooled by their intuitions and their faith in tools that lack strong evidence of effectiveness," warned Scott Lilienfeld, James Wood, and Howard Garb (2001). "When a substantial body of research demonstrates that old intuitions are wrong, it is time to adopt new ways of thinking." Freud himself might have agreed. He probably would have been more interested in the therapist-patient interactions that take place during the testing process.

▶‖ Evaluating the Psychoanalytic Perspective

Contradictory Evidence from Modern Research

45-5 How do contemporary psychologists view Freud and the unconscious?

We critique Freud from an early twenty-first-century perspective, a perspective that itself will be subject to revision. Freud did not have access to neurotransmitter or DNA studies, or to all that we have since learned about human development, thinking, and emotion. To criticize his theory by comparing it with current concepts, some say, is like criticizing Henry Ford's Model T by comparing it with today's hybrid cars. (How tempting it always is to judge people in the past from our perspective in the present.)

But both Freud's admirers and his critics agree that recent research contradicts many of his specific ideas. Today's developmental psychologists see our development as lifelong, not fixed in childhood. They doubt that infants' neural networks are mature enough to sustain as much emotional trauma as Freud assumed. Some think Freud overestimated parental influence and underestimated peer influence (and abuse). They also doubt that conscience and gender identity form as the child resolves the Oedipus complex at age 5 or 6. We gain our gender identity earlier and become strongly masculine or feminine even without a same-sex parent present. And they note that Freud's ideas about childhood sexuality arose from his skepticism of stories of childhood sexual abuse told by his female patients—stories that some scholars believe he attributed to their own childhood sexual wishes and conflicts (Esterson, 2001; Powell & Boer, 1994). Today, we understand how Freud's questioning might have created false memories of abuse, but we also know that childhood sexual abuse does happen.

New ideas about why we dream dispute Freud's belief that dreams disguise and fulfill wishes. And slips of the tongue can be explained as competition between similar verbal choices in our memory network. Someone who says "I don't want to do that—it's a lot of brothel" may simply be blending *bother* and *trouble* (Foss & Hakes, 1978). Researchers find little support for Freud's idea that defense mechanisms disguise sexual and aggressive impulses (though our cognitive gymnastics do indeed work to protect our self-esteem). History also has failed to support another of Freud's ideas—that suppressed sexuality causes psychological disorders. From Freud's time to ours, sexual inhibition has diminished; psychological disorders have not.

"The Rorschach Inkblot Test has been resoundingly discredited . . . I call it the Dracula of psychological tests, because no one has been able to drive a stake through the cursed thing's heart."
Carol Tavris, "Mind Games: Psychological Warfare Between Therapists and Scientists," 2003

"Many aspects of Freudian theory are indeed out of date, and they should be: Freud died in 1939, and he has been slow to undertake further revisions."
Psychologist Drew Westen (1998)

"For seven and a half years I've worked alongside President Reagan. We've had triumphs. Made some mistakes. We've had some sex . . . uh . . . setbacks."
George H. W. Bush, 1988

"I remember your name perfectly but I just can't think of your face."
Oxford professor W. A. Spooner, 1844–1930, famous for his linguistic flip-flops *(spoonerisms)*. Spooner rebuked one student for "fighting a liar in the quadrangle" and another who "hissed my mystery lecture," adding "You have tasted two worms."

Is Repression a Myth?

Freud's entire psychoanalytic theory rests on his assumption that the human mind often *represses* offending wishes, banishing them into the unconscious until they resurface, like long-lost books in a dusty attic. Recover and resolve childhood's conflicted wishes, and emotional healing should follow. Under Freud's influence, repression became a widely accepted concept, used to explain hypnotic phenomena and psychological disorders. Freud's followers extended repression to explain apparently lost and recovered memories of childhood traumas (Boag, 2006; Cheit, 1998; Erdelyi, 2006). In one survey, 88 percent of university students believed that painful experiences commonly get pushed out of awareness and into the unconscious (Garry et al., 1994).

Today's researchers acknowledge that we sometimes spare our egos by neglecting information that is threatening (Green et al., 2008). Yet, many contend that repression, if it ever occurs, is a rare mental response to terrible trauma. "Repression folklore is . . . partly refuted, partly untested, and partly untestable," says Elizabeth Loftus (1995). Even those who have witnessed a parent's murder or survived Nazi death camps retain their unrepressed memories of the horror (Helmreich, 1992, 1994; Malmquist, 1986; Pennebaker, 1990). "Dozens of formal studies have yielded not a single convincing case of repression in the entire literature on trauma," concludes personality researcher John Kihlstrom (2006). Ditto for the world's literature, report a Harvard team that offered $1000 to anyone who could provide a pre-1800 medical or even fictional example of a healthy person who had blocked out a specific traumatic event and retrieved it a year or more later (Pope et al., 2007). Surely, if such often occurred, someone would have noticed. But despite wide publicity, no such case was unearthed. (After their paper was published, one person did come up with a 1786 opera in which a woman apparently forgets discovering her dead lover after a duel [Pettus, 2008].)

Some researchers believe that extreme, prolonged stress, such as the stress some severely abused children experience, might disrupt memory by damaging the hippocampus (Schacter, 1996). But the far more common reality is that high stress and associated stress hormones enhance memory. Indeed, rape, torture, and other traumatic events haunt survivors, who experience unwanted flashbacks. They are seared onto the soul. "You see the babies," said Holocaust survivor Sally H. (1979). "You see the screaming mothers. You see hanging people. You sit and you see that face there. It's something you don't forget."

The Modern Unconscious Mind

Freud was right about at least one thing: We indeed have limited access to all that goes on in our minds (Erdelyi, 1985, 1988, 2006; Kihlstrom, 1990). In experiments, people have learned to anticipate the computer screen quadrant in which a character will appear next, even before being able to articulate the underlying rule (Lewicki, 1992, 1997). Research confirms the reality of unconscious *implicit learning* (Fletcher et al., 2005; Frensch & Rünger, 2003). Our two-track mind has a vast out-of-sight realm.

Nevertheless, the "iceberg" notion held by today's research psychologists differs from Freud's—so much so, argues Anthony Greenwald (1992), that it is time to abandon Freud's view of the unconscious. Many psychologists now think of the unconscious not as seething passions and repressive censoring but as cooler information processing that occurs without our awareness. To these researchers, the unconscious also involves

▶ the schemas that automatically control our perceptions and interpretations.
▶ the priming by stimuli to which we have not consciously attended.
▶ the right-hemisphere activity that enables the split-brain patient's left hand to carry out an instruction the patient cannot verbalize.
▶ the parallel processing of different aspects of vision and thinking.

"The overall findings . . . seriously challenge the classical psychoanalytic notion of repression."

Psychologist Yacov Rofé, "Does Repression Exist?" 2008

"During the Holocaust, many children . . . were forced to endure the unendurable. For those who continue to suffer [the] pain is still present, many years later, as real as it was on the day it occurred."

Eric Zillmer, Molly Harrower, Barry Ritzler, and Robert Archer, *The Quest for the Nazi Personality*, 1995

terror-management theory a theory of death-related anxiety; explores people's emotional and behavioral responses to reminders of their impending death.

▶ the implicit memories that operate without conscious recall, and even among those with amnesia.

▶ the emotions that activate instantly, before conscious analysis.

▶ the self-concept and stereotypes that automatically and unconsciously influence how we process information about ourselves and others.

More than we realize, we fly on autopilot. Our lives are guided by off-screen, out-of-sight, unconscious information processing. The unconscious mind is huge. This understanding of unconscious information processing is more like the pre-Freudian view of an underground, unattended stream of thought from which spontaneous behavior and creative ideas surface (Bargh & Morsella, 2008).

Recent research has also provided some support for Freud's idea of defense mechanisms (even if they don't work exactly as Freud supposed). For example, Roy Baumeister and his colleagues (1998) found that people tend to see their foibles and attitudes in others, a phenomenon that Freud called projection and that today's researchers call the *false consensus effect*, the tendency to overestimate the extent to which others share our beliefs and behaviors. People who cheat on their taxes or break speed limits tend to think many others do likewise. Supportive evidence is meager for other defenses, such as displacement, that are tied to instinctual energy. More evidence exists for defenses, such as reaction formation, that defend self-esteem. Defense mechanisms, Baumeister concluded, are motivated less by the seething impulses that Freud presumed than by our need to protect our self-image.

Finally, recent history has supported Freud's idea that we defend ourselves against anxiety. Again, however, the contemporary idea differs from Freud's. Jeff Greenberg, Sheldon Solomon, and Tom Pyszczynski (1997) have proposed that one source of anxiety is "the terror resulting from our awareness of vulnerability and death." More than 200 studies testing their **terror-management theory** show that thinking about one's mortality—for example, by writing a short essay on dying and its associated emotions—provokes various terror-management defenses. For example, death anxiety increases prejudice—contempt for others and esteem for oneself (Koole et al., 2006).

Faced with a threatening world, people act not only to enhance their self-esteem but also to adhere more strongly to worldviews that answer questions about life's meaning. The prospect of death promotes religious sentiments, and deep religious convictions enable people to be less defensive—less likely to rise in defense of their worldview—when reminded of death (Jonas & Fischer, 2006; Norenzayan & Hansen, 2006). Moreover, they cleave to close relationships (Mikulincer et al., 2003). The events of 9/11—a striking experience of the terror of death—led trapped World Trade Center occupants to spend their last moments calling loved ones, and led most Americans to reach out to family and friends.

Freud's Ideas as Scientific Theory

Psychologists also criticize Freud's theory for its scientific shortcomings, for falling short of the standard that good scientific theories explain observations and offer testable hypotheses. Freud's theory rests on few objective observations, and parts of it offer few testable hypotheses. (For Freud, his own recollections and interpretations of patients' free associations, dreams, and slips were evidence enough.)

What is the most serious problem with Freud's theory? It offers after-the-fact explanations of any characteristic (of one person's smoking, another's fear of horses, another's sexual orientation) yet fails to *predict* such behaviors and traits. If you feel angry at your mother's death, you illustrate his theory because "your unresolved childhood dependency needs are threatened." If you do not feel angry, you again illustrate his theory because "you are repressing your anger." That, said Calvin Hall and Gardner Lindzey (1978, p. 68), "is like betting on a horse after the race has been run." A good theory makes testable predictions.

"It says, 'Someday you will die.'"

"I don't want to attain immortality through my work; I want to attain immortality by not dying."
Woody Allen

"I sought the Lord, and he answered me and delivered me out of all my terror."
Psalm 34:4

"We are arguing like a man who should say, 'If there were an invisible cat in that chair, the chair would look empty; but the chair does look empty; therefore there is an invisible cat in it.'"
C. S. Lewis, *Four Loves*, 1958

For such reasons, some of Freud's critics offer harsh words. They see a decaying Freudian edifice built on the swamplands of childhood sexuality, repression, dream analysis, and after-the-fact speculation. "When we stand on [Freud's] shoulders, we only discover that we're looking further in the wrong direction," said John Kihlstrom (1997). To Freud's most searing critic, Frederick Crews (1998), what is original about Freud's ideas is not good, and what is good is not original (the unconscious mind is an idea that dates back to Plato).

So, should psychology post a "Do Not Resuscitate" order on this old theory? Freud's supporters object. To criticize Freudian theory for not making testable predictions is, they say, like criticizing baseball for not being an aerobic exercise, something it was never intended to be. Freud never claimed that psychoanalysis was predictive science. He merely claimed that, looking back, psychoanalysts could find meaning in our state of mind (Rieff, 1979).

Supporters also note that some of Freud's ideas *are* enduring. It was Freud who drew our attention to the unconscious and the irrational, to our self-protective defenses, to the importance of human sexuality, and to the tension between our biological impulses and our social well-being. It was Freud who challenged our self-righteousness, punctured our pretensions, and reminded us of our potential for evil.

In science, Darwin's legacy lives while Freud's is waning (Bornstein, 2001). Almost 9 in 10 American college courses that reference psychoanalysis are, according to one national survey, outside of psychology departments (Cohen, 2007). In the popular culture, Freud's legacy lives on. Some ideas that many people assume to be true—that childhood experiences mold personality, that dreams have meaning, that many behaviors have disguised motives—are part of that legacy. His early twentieth-century concepts penetrate our twenty-first-century language. Without realizing their source, we may speak of *ego, repression, projection, complex* (as in "inferiority complex"), *sibling rivalry, Freudian slips,* and *fixation.* "Freud's premises may have undergone a steady decline in currency within academia for many years," noted Martin Seligman (1994), "but Hollywood, the talk shows, many therapists, and the general public still love them."

REVIEW

The Psychoanalytic Perspective

45-1 **What was Freud's view of personality and its development?** Sigmund Freud's treatment of emotional disorders led him to believe that they spring from *unconscious* dynamics, which he sought to analyze through *free associations* and dreams. He referred to his theory and techniques as *psychoanalysis*. He saw *personality* as composed of pleasure-seeking psychic impulses (the *id*), a reality-oriented executive (the *ego*), and an internalized set of ideals (the *superego*). He believed that children develop through *psychosexual stages,* and that our personalities are influenced by how we have resolved conflicts associated with these stages and whether we have remained *fixated* at any stage.

45-2 **How did Freud think people defended themselves against anxiety?** Tensions between the demands of id and super-ego cause anxiety. The ego copes by using *defense mechanisms,* especially *repression*.

45-3 **Which of Freud's ideas did his followers accept or reject?** Neo-Freudians Alfred Adler, Karen Horney, and Carl Jung accepted many of Freud's ideas. But Adler and Horney argued that we have motives other than sex and aggression and that the ego's conscious control is greater than Freud supposed, and Jung proposed a *collective unconscious*. Psychodynamic theorists share Freud's view that unconscious mental processes, inner conflicts, and childhood experiences are important influences on personality.

45-4 **What are projective tests, and how are they used?** *Projective tests* attempt to assess personality by presenting ambiguous stimuli designed to reveal the unconscious. Although projective tests, such as the *Rorschach inkblots,* have questionable reliability and validity, many clinicians continue to use them.

45-5 **How do contemporary psychologists view Freud and the unconscious?** Today's research psychologists note that Freud's theory offers only after-the-fact explanations, and that repression rarely occurs. Current information-processing research confirms that our access to all that goes on in our mind is very limited, but it does not support Freud's view of the unconscious. Rather, the unconscious consists of schemas that control our perceptions; priming; parallel processing that occurs without our conscious knowledge; implicit memories of learned skills; instantly activated emotions; and self-concepts and stereotypes that filter information about ourselves and others. There is also little support for the idea of defense mechanisms. Psychology's false consensus effect (the tendency to overestimate the extent to which others share our beliefs and behaviors) does, however, bear a resemblance to Freud's *projection,* and *reaction formation* also seems to happen.

Nevertheless, Freud drew psychology's attention to the unconscious, to the struggle to cope with anxiety and sexuality, and to the conflict between biological impulses and social restraints. His cultural impact has been enormous.

Terms and Concepts to Remember

personality, p. 557	regression, p. 561
free association, p. 558	reaction formation, p. 562
psychoanalysis, p. 558	projection, p. 562
unconscious, p. 558	rationalization, p. 562
id, p. 559	displacement, p. 562
ego, p. 559	denial, p. 562
superego, p. 560	collective unconscious, p. 563
psychosexual stages, p. 560	projective test, p. 564
Oedipus [ED-uh-puss] complex, p. 560	Thematic Apperception Test (TAT), p. 564
identification, p. 560	Rorschach inkblot test, p. 564
fixation, p. 561	
defense mechanisms, p. 561	terror-management theory, p. 567
repression, p. 561	

Test Yourself

1. What, according to Freud, were some of the important defense mechanisms, and what do they defend against?

2. How does today's psychological science assess Freud's theory?

(Answers to the Test Yourself questions can be found in Appendix B at the end of the book.)

Ask Yourself

1. How would you describe *your* personality? What characteristics make up your typical patterns of thinking, feeling, and acting?

2. What understanding and impressions of Freud did you bring to this course? Have they changed in any way after reading this module?

∞ WEB

Multiple-choice self-tests and more may be found at www.worthpublishers.com/myers

Abraham Maslow's Self-Actualizing Person

Carl Rogers' Person-Centered Perspective

Assessing the Self

Evaluating the Humanistic Perspective

The Humanistic Perspective

46-1 How did humanistic psychologists view personality, and what was their goal in studying personality?

By the 1960s, some personality psychologists had become discontented with the negativity of Freudian theory and the mechanistic psychology of B. F. Skinner's behaviorism. In contrast to Freud's study of the base motives of "sick" people, these *humanistic psychologists* focused on the ways "healthy" people strive for self-determination and self-realization. In contrast to behaviorism's scientific objectivity, they studied people through their own self-reported experiences and feelings.

Two pioneering theorists—Abraham Maslow (1908–1970) and Carl Rogers (1902–1987)—offered a *third-force perspective* that emphasized human potential.

▶‖ Abraham Maslow's Self-Actualizing Person

Maslow proposed that we are motivated by a hierarchy of needs. If our physiological needs are met, we become concerned with personal safety; if we achieve a sense of security, we then seek to love, to be loved, and to love ourselves; with our love needs satisfied, we seek self-esteem. Having achieved self-esteem, we ultimately seek **self-actualization** (the process of fulfilling our potential) and *self-transcendence* (meaning, purpose, and communion beyond the self).

Maslow (1970) developed his ideas by studying healthy, creative people rather than troubled clinical cases. He based his description of self-actualization on a study of those who seemed notable for their rich and productive lives—among them, Abraham Lincoln, Thomas Jefferson, and Eleanor Roosevelt. Maslow reported that these people shared certain characteristics: They were self-aware and self-accepting, open and spontaneous, loving and caring, and not paralyzed by others' opinions. Secure in their sense of who they were, their interests were problem-centered rather than self-centered. They focused their energies on a particular task, one they often regarded as their mission in life. Most enjoyed a few deep relationships rather than many superficial ones. Many had been moved by spiritual or personal *peak experiences* that surpassed ordinary consciousness.

These, said Maslow, are mature adult qualities, ones found in those who have learned enough about life to be compassionate, to have outgrown their mixed feelings toward their parents, to have found their calling, to have "acquired enough courage to be unpopular, to be unashamed about being openly virtuous, etc." Maslow's work with college students led him to speculate that those likely to become self-actualizing adults were likable, caring, "privately affectionate to those of their elders who deserve it," and "secretly uneasy about the cruelty, meanness, and mob spirit so often found in young people."

▶‖ Carl Rogers' Person-Centered Perspective

Fellow humanistic psychologist Carl Rogers agreed with much of Maslow's thinking. Rogers believed that people are basically good and are endowed with self-actualizing tendencies. Unless thwarted by an environment that inhibits growth, each of us is like an acorn, primed for growth and fulfillment. Rogers (1980) believed that a growth-promoting climate required three conditions—genuineness, acceptance, and empathy.

self-actualization according to Maslow, one of the ultimate psychological needs that arises after basic physical and psychological needs are met and self-esteem is achieved; the motivation to fulfill one's potential.

unconditional positive regard according to Rogers, an attitude of total acceptance toward another person.

self-concept all our thoughts and feelings about ourselves, in answer to the question, "Who am I?"

Abraham Maslow "Any theory of motivation that is worthy of attention must deal with the highest capacities of the healthy and strong person as well as with the defensive maneuvers of crippled spirits" (*Motivation and Personality*, 1970).

Ted Polumbaum/Time Pix/Getty Images

According to Rogers, people nurture our growth by being *genuine*—by being open with their own feelings, dropping their facades, and being transparent and self-disclosing.

People also nurture our growth by being *accepting*—by offering us what Rogers called **unconditional positive regard.** This is an attitude of grace, an attitude that values us even knowing our failings. It is a profound relief to drop our pretenses, confess our worst feelings, and discover that we are still accepted. In a good marriage, a close family, or an intimate friendship, we are free to be spontaneous without fearing the loss of others' esteem.

Finally, people nurture our growth by being *empathic*—by sharing and mirroring our feelings and reflecting our meanings. "Rarely do we listen with real understanding, true empathy," said Rogers. "Yet listening, of this very special kind, is one of the most potent forces for change that I know."

Genuineness, acceptance, and empathy are the water, sun, and nutrients that enable people to grow like vigorous oak trees, according to Rogers. For "as persons are accepted and prized, they tend to develop a more caring attitude toward themselves" (Rogers, 1980, p. 116). As persons are empathically heard, "it becomes possible for them to listen more accurately to the flow of inner experiencings."

Writer Calvin Trillin (2006) recalls an example of parental genuineness and acceptance at a camp for children with severe disorders, where his wife, Alice, worked. L., a "magical child," had genetic diseases that meant she had to be tube-fed and could walk only with difficulty. Alice recalled,

> One day, when we were playing duck-duck-goose, I was sitting behind her and she asked me to hold her mail for her while she took her turn to be chased around the circle. It took her a while to make the circuit, and I had time to see that on top of the pile [of mail] was a note from her mom. Then I did something truly awful. . . . I simply had to know what this child's parents could have done to make her so spectacular, to make her the most optimistic, most enthusiastic, most hopeful human being I had ever encountered. I snuck a quick look at the note, and my eyes fell on this sentence: "If God had given us all of the children in the world to choose from, L., we would only have chosen you." Before L. got back to her place in the circle, I showed the note to Bud, who was sitting next to me. "Quick. Read this," I whispered. "It's the secret of life."

Maslow and Rogers would have smiled knowingly. For them a central feature of personality is one's **self-concept**—all the thoughts and feelings we have in response to the question, "Who am I?" If our self-concept is positive, we tend to act and perceive the world positively. If it is negative—if in our own eyes we fall far short of our *ideal self*—said Rogers, we feel dissatisfied and unhappy. A worthwhile goal for therapists, parents, teachers, and friends is therefore, he said, to help others know, accept, and be true to themselves.

▶‖ Assessing the Self

46-2 How did humanistic psychologists assess a person's sense of self?

Humanistic psychologists sometimes assessed personality by asking people to fill out questionnaires that would evaluate their self-concept. One questionnaire, inspired by Carl Rogers, asked people to describe themselves both as they would *ideally* like to be and as they *actually* are. When the ideal and the actual self are nearly alike, said Rogers, the self-concept is positive. Assessing his clients' personal growth during therapy, he looked for successively closer ratings of actual and ideal selves.

The picture of empathy Being open and sharing confidences is easier when the listener shows real understanding. Within such relationships people can relax and fully express their true selves.

A father *not* offering unconditional positive regard:

P. BYRNES.

"Just remember, son, it doesn't matter whether you win or lose—unless you want Daddy's love."

Some humanistic psychologists believed that any standardized assessment of personality, even a questionnaire, is depersonalizing. Rather than forcing the person to respond to narrow categories, these humanistic psychologists presumed that interviews and intimate conversation would provide a better understanding of each person's unique experiences.

▶‖ Evaluating the Humanistic Perspective

46-3   How has the humanistic perspective influenced psychology? What criticisms has it faced?

One thing said of Freud can also be said of the humanistic psychologists: Their impact has been pervasive. Maslow's and Rogers' ideas have influenced counseling, education, child-rearing, and management.

They have also influenced—sometimes in ways they did not intend—much of today's popular psychology. Is a positive self-concept the key to happiness and success? Do acceptance and empathy nurture positive feelings about oneself? Are people basically good and capable of self-improvement? Many people answer *yes, yes,* and *yes.* Responding to a 1992 *Newsweek* Gallup poll, 9 in 10 people rated self-esteem as very important for "motivating a person to work hard and succeed." Humanistic psychology's message has been heard.

The prominence of the humanistic perspective set off a backlash of criticism. First, said the critics, its concepts are vague and *subjective.* Consider Maslow's description of self-actualizing people as open, spontaneous, loving, self-accepting, and productive. Is this a scientific description? Isn't it merely a description of the theorist's own values and ideals? Maslow, noted M. Brewster Smith (1978), offered impressions of his own personal heroes. Imagine another theorist who began with a different set of heroes—perhaps Napoleon, John D. Rockefeller, Sr., and former U.S. Vice President Dick Cheney. This theorist would likely describe self-actualizing people as "undeterred by others' needs and opinions," "motivated to achieve," and "comfortable with power."

Critics also objected to the idea that, as Rogers put it, "The only question which matters is, 'Am I living in a way which is deeply satisfying to me, and which truly expresses me?'" (quoted by Wallach & Wallach, 1985). The *individualism* encouraged by humanistic psychology—trusting and acting on one's feelings, being true to oneself, fulfilling oneself—can, the critics have said, lead to self-indulgence, selfishness, and an erosion of moral restraints (Campbell & Specht, 1985; Wallach & Wallach, 1983). Indeed, it is those who focus beyond themselves who are most likely to experience social support, to enjoy life, and to cope effectively with stress (Crandall, 1984).

Humanistic psychologists reply that a secure, nondefensive self-acceptance is actually the first step toward loving others. Indeed, people who feel intrinsically liked and accepted—for who they are, not just for their achievements—exhibit less-defensive attitudes (Schimel et al., 2001).

A final accusation leveled against humanistic psychology is that it is *naive,* that it fails to appreciate the reality of our human capacity for evil. Faced with global climate change, overpopulation, terrorism, and the spread of nuclear weapons, we may become apathetic from either of two rationalizations. One is a naive optimism that denies the threat ("People are basically good; everything will work out"). The other is a dark despair ("It's hopeless; why try?"). Action requires enough realism to fuel concern and enough optimism to provide hope. Humanistic psychology, say the critics, encourages the needed hope but not the equally necessary realism about evil.

"We do pretty well when you stop to think that people are basically good."

REVIEW

The Humanistic Perspective

46-1 **How did humanistic psychologists view personality, and what was their goal in studying personality?** Humanistic psychologists sought to turn psychology's attention toward the growth potential of healthy people. Abraham Maslow believed that if basic human needs are fulfilled, people will strive toward *self-actualization*. To nurture growth in others, Carl Rogers advised being genuine, accepting, and empathic. In this climate of *unconditional positive regard*, he believed, people can develop a deeper self-awareness and a more realistic and positive *self-concept*.

46-2 **How did humanistic psychologists assess a person's sense of self?** Humanistic psychologists assessed personality through questionnaires on which people reported their self-concept and in therapy by seeking to understand others' subjective personal experiences.

46-3 **How has the humanistic perspective influenced psychology? What criticisms has it faced?** Humanistic psychology helped to renew psychology's interest in the concept of self. Nevertheless, humanistic psychology's critics complained that its concepts were vague and subjective, its values Western and self-centered, and its assumptions naively optimistic.

Terms and Concepts to Remember

self-actualization, p. 570   self-concept, p. 571
unconditional positive regard
   p. 571

Test Yourself

1. What does it mean to be "empathic"? To be "self-actualized"?

(Answers to the Test Yourself questions can be found in Appendix B at the end of the book.)

Ask Yourself

1. Have you had someone in your life who accepted you unconditionally? Do you think this person helped you to know yourself better and to develop a better image of yourself?

∞ WEB

Multiple-choice self-tests and more may be found at www.worthpublishers.com/myers

MODULE 47

Contemporary Research on Personality

▶‖ The Trait Perspective

47-1 How do psychologists use traits to describe personality?

In J. R. R. Tolkien's *Lord of the Rings,* Frodo Baggins' faithful companion, Sam Gamgee, is unwaveringly loyal and optimistic. In psychology, trait researchers attempt to define personality in terms of such stable and enduring behavior patterns. This perspective can be traced in part to a remarkable meeting in 1919, when Gordon Allport, a curious 22-year-old psychology student, interviewed Sigmund Freud in Vienna. Allport soon discovered just how preoccupied the founder of psychoanalysis was with finding hidden motives, even in Allport's own behavior during the interview. That experience ultimately led Allport to do what Freud did not do—to describe personality in terms of fundamental **traits**—people's characteristic behaviors and conscious motives (such as the curiosity that actually motivated Allport to see Freud). Meeting Freud, said Allport, "taught me that [psychoanalysis], for all its merits, may plunge too deep, and that psychologists would do well to give full recognition to manifest motives before probing the unconscious." Allport came to define personality in terms of identifiable behavior patterns. He was concerned less with *explaining* individual traits than with *describing* them.

Like Allport, Isabel Briggs Myers (1987) and her mother, Kathleen Briggs, wanted to describe important personality differences. They attempted to sort people according to Carl Jung's personality types, based on their responses to 126 questions. The *Myers-Briggs Type Indicator (MBTI),* available in 21 languages, is taken by more than 2 million people a year, mostly for counseling, leadership training, and work-team development (CPP, 2008). It offers choices, such as "Do you usually value sentiment more than logic, or value logic more than sentiment?" Then it counts the test-taker's preferences, labels them as indicating, say, a "feeling type," or "thinking type," and feeds them back to the person in complimentary terms. Feeling types, for example, are told they are sensitive to values and are "sympathetic, appreciative, and tactful"; thinking types are told they "prefer an objective standard of truth" and are "good at analyzing." (Every type has its strengths, so everyone is affirmed.)

Most people agree with their announced type profile, which mirrors their declared preferences. They may also accept their label as a basis for being matched with work partners and tasks that supposedly suit their temperaments. A National Research Council report noted, however, that despite the test's popularity in business and career counseling, its initial use outran research on its value as a predictor of job performance, and "the popularity of this instrument in the absence of proven scientific worth is troublesome" (Druckman & Bjork, 1991, p. 101; see also Pittenger, 1993). Although research on the MBTI has been accumulating since those cautionary words, the test remains mostly a counseling and coaching tool, not a research instrument.

Exploring Traits

Classifying people as one or another distinct personality type fails to capture their full individuality. We are each a unique complex of multiple traits. So how else

trait a characteristic pattern of behavior or a disposition to feel and act, as assessed by self-report inventories and peer reports.

could we describe our personalities? We might describe an apple by placing it along several trait dimensions—relatively large or small, red or yellow, sweet or sour. By placing people on several trait dimensions simultaneously, psychologists can describe countless individual personality variations, much as researchers can describe thousands of colors in terms of their variations on just three color dimensions—hue, saturation, and brightness.

What trait dimensions describe personality? If you had an upcoming blind date, what personality traits might give you an accurate sense of the person? Allport and his associate H. S. Odbert (1936) counted all the words in an unabridged dictionary with which one could describe people. How many were there? Almost 18,000! How, then, could psychologists condense the list to a manageable number of basic traits?

Jon Stewart: The extravert
Trait labels such as *extraversion* can describe our temperament and typical behaviors.

Factor Analysis

One way has been to propose traits, such as anxiety, that some theory regards as basic. A newer technique is *factor analysis,* a statistical procedure that has been used to identify clusters of test items that tap basic components of intelligence (such as spatial ability or verbal skill). Imagine that people who describe themselves as outgoing also tend to say that they like excitement and practical jokes and dislike quiet reading. Such a statistically correlated cluster of behaviors reflects a basic factor, or trait—in this case, *extraversion.*

British psychologists Hans Eysenck and Sybil Eysenck [EYE-zink] believed that we can reduce many of our normal individual variations to two or three dimensions, including *extraversion-introversion* and *emotional stability-instability* (**FIGURE 47.1**). People in 35 countries around the world, from China to Uganda to Russia, have taken

FIGURE 47.1 Two personality dimensions Mapmakers can tell us a lot by using two axes (north-south and east-west). Hans Eysenck and Sybil Eysenck used two primary personality factors—extraversion–introversion and stability–instability—as axes for describing personality variation. Varying combinations define other, more specific traits. (From Eysenck & Eysenck, 1963.)

UNSTABLE

INTROVERTED		EXTRAVERTED
Moody		Touchy
Anxious		Restless
Rigid		Aggressive
Sober		Excitable
Pessimistic		Changeable
Reserved		Impulsive
Unsociable		Optimistic
Quiet		Active
Passive		Sociable
Careful		Outgoing
Thoughtful		Talkative
Peaceful		Responsive
Controlled		Easygoing
Reliable		Lively
Even-tempered		Carefree
Calm		Leadership

STABLE

the *Eysenck Personality Questionnaire.* When their answers were analyzed, the extraversion and emotionality factors inevitably emerged as basic personality dimensions (Eysenck, 1990, 1992). The Eysencks believed that these factors are genetically influenced, and research supports this belief.

Biology and Personality

Brain-activity scans of extraverts add to the growing list of traits and mental states that have been explored with brain-imaging procedures. (That list includes intelligence, impulsivity, addictive cravings, lying, sexual attraction, aggressiveness, empathy, spiritual experience, and even racial and political attitudes [Olson, 2005].) Such studies indicate that extraverts seek stimulation because their normal *brain arousal* is relatively low. For example, PET scans show that a frontal lobe area involved in behavior inhibition is less active in extraverts than in introverts (Johnson et al., 1999). Dopamine and dopamine-related neural activity tend to be higher in extraverts (Wacker et al., 2006).

Our biology influences our personality in other ways as well. Our *genes* have much to say about the temperament and behavioral style that help define our personality. Jerome Kagan, for example, has attributed differences in children's shyness and inhibition to their *autonomic nervous system reactivity.* Given a reactive autonomic nervous system, we respond to stress with greater anxiety and inhibition. The fearless, curious child may become the rock-climbing or fast-driving adult.

Samuel Gosling and his colleagues (2003; Jones & Gosling, 2005) report that personality differences among dogs (in energy, affection, reactivity, and curious intelligence) are as evident, and as consistently judged, as personality differences among humans. Monkeys, chimpanzees, orangutans, and even birds have stable personalities (Weiss et al., 2006). Among the Great Tit (a European relative of the American chickadee), bold birds more quickly inspect new objects and explore trees (Groothuis & Carere, 2005; Verbeek et al., 1994). By selective breeding, researchers can produce bold or shy birds. Both have their place in natural history. In lean years, bold birds are more likely to find food; in abundant years, shy birds feed with less risk.

Assessing Traits

47-2 What are personality inventories, and what are their strengths and weaknesses as trait-assessment tools?

If stable and enduring traits guide our actions, can we devise valid and reliable tests of them? Several trait assessment techniques exist—some more valid than others (turn the page to see Thinking Critically About: How to Be a "Successful" Astrologer or Palm Reader). Some profile a person's behavior patterns—often providing quick assessments of a single trait, such as extraversion, anxiety, or self-esteem. **Personality inventories**—longer questionnaires covering a wide range of feelings and behaviors—are designed to assess several traits at once.

The classic personality inventory is the **Minnesota Multiphasic Personality Inventory (MMPI).** Although it assesses "abnormal" personality tendencies rather than normal personality traits, the MMPI illustrates a good way of developing a personality inventory. One of its creators, Starke Hathaway (1960), compared his effort to that of Alfred Binet, who developed the first intelligence test by selecting items that identified children who would probably have trouble progressing normally in French schools. The MMPI items, too, were **empirically derived.** That is, from a large pool of items, Hathaway and his colleagues selected those on which particular diagnostic groups differed. They then grouped the questions into 10 clinical scales, including scales that assess depressive tendencies, masculinity-femininity, and introversion-extraversion.

personality inventory a questionnaire (often with *true-false* or *agree-disagree* items) on which people respond to items designed to gauge a wide range of feelings and behaviors; used to assess selected personality traits.

Minnesota Multiphasic Personality Inventory (MMPI) the most widely researched and clinically used of all personality tests. Originally developed to identify emotional disorders (still considered its most appropriate use), this test is now used for many other screening purposes.

empirically derived test a test (such as the MMPI) developed by testing a pool of items and then selecting those that discriminate between groups.

Hathaway and others initially gave hundreds of true-false statements ("No one seems to understand me"; "I get all the sympathy I should"; "I like poetry") to groups of psychologically disordered patients and to "normal" people. They retained any statement—no matter how silly it sounded—on which the patient group's answer differed from that of the normal group. "Nothing in the newspaper interests me except the comics" may seem senseless, but it just so happened that depressed people were more likely to answer *True*. (Nevertheless, people have had fun spoofing the MMPI with their own mock items: "Weeping brings tears to my eyes," "Frantic screams make me nervous," and "I stay in the bathtub until I look like a raisin" [Frankel et al., 1983].) Today's MMPI-2 also has scales assessing, for instance, work attitudes, family problems, and anger.

In contrast to projective tests such as the Rorschach inkblots, personality inventories are scored objectively—so objectively that a computer can administer and score them. (The computer can also provide descriptions of people who previously responded similarly.) Objectivity does not, however, guarantee validity. For example, individuals taking the MMPI for employment purposes can give socially desirable answers to create a good impression. But in so doing they may also score high on a *lie scale* that assesses faking (as when people respond *False* to a universally true statement such as "I get angry sometimes"). The objectivity of the MMPI has contributed to its popularity and to its translation into more than 100 languages.

The Big Five Factors

47-3 Which traits seem to provide the most useful information about personality variation?

Today's trait researchers believe that simple trait factors, such as the Eysencks' introverted–extraverted and unstable–stable dimensions, are important, but they do not tell the whole story. A slightly expanded set of factors—dubbed the *Big Five*—does a better job (Costa & McCrae, 2006; John & Srivastava, 1999). If a test specifies where you are on the five dimensions (conscientiousness, agreeableness, neuroticism, openness, and extraversion; see **TABLE 47.1**), it has said much of what there is to

TABLE 47.1 The "Big Five" Personality Factors

(*Memory tip:* Picturing a **CANOE** will help you recall these.)

Trait Dimension	Endpoints of the Dimension		
Conscientiousness	Organized	⟷	Disorganized
	Careful	⟷	Careless
	Disciplined	⟷	Impulsive
Agreeableness	Soft-hearted	⟷	Ruthless
	Trusting	⟷	Suspicious
	Helpful	⟷	Uncooperative
Neuroticism (emotional stability vs. instability)	Calm	⟷	Anxious
	Secure	⟷	Insecure
	Self-satisfied	⟷	Self-pitying
Openness	Imaginative	⟷	Practical
	Preference for variety	⟷	Preference for routine
	Independent	⟷	Conforming
Extraversion	Sociable	⟷	Retiring
	Fun-loving	⟷	Sober
	Affectionate	⟷	Reserved

Source: Adapted from McCrae & Costa (1986, p. 1002).

How to Be a "Successful" Astrologer or Palm Reader

Can we discern people's traits from the alignment of the stars and planets at the time of their birth? From their handwriting? From lines on their palms?

Astronomers scoff at the naiveté of astrology—the constellations have shifted in the millennia since astrologers formulated their predictions (Kelly, 1997, 1998). Humorists mock it: "No offense," writes Dave Barry, "but if you take the horoscope seriously your frontal lobes are the size of Raisinets." Psychologists instead ask questions: Does it work? Can astrologers surpass chance when given someone's birth date and asked to identify the person from a short lineup of different personality descriptions? Can people pick out their own horoscopes from a lineup of horoscopes?

The consistent answers have been *no, no,* and *no* (British Psychological Society, 1993; Carlson, 1985; Kelly, 1997). For example, one researcher examined census data from 20 million married people in England and Wales and found that "astrological sign has no impact on the probability of marrying—and staying married to—someone of any other sign" (Voas, 2008).

Graphologists, who make predictions from handwriting samples, have similarly been found to do no better than chance when trying to discern people's

I SEE BY YOUR HANDWRITING YOU LIKE BANANAS.

©2000 by Rob Pudim

occupations from examining several pages of their handwriting (Beyerstein & Beyerstein, 1992; Dean et al., 1992). Nevertheless, graphologists—and introductory psychology students—will often *perceive* correlations between personality and handwriting even where there are none (King & Koehler, 2000).

If all these perceived correlations evaporate under close scrutiny, how do astrologers, palm readers, and crystal-ball gazers persuade millions of people worldwide to buy their services? Ray Hyman (1981), palm reader turned research psychologist, has revealed some of their suckering methods.

The first technique, the "stock spiel," builds on the observation that each of us is in some ways like no one else and in other ways just like everyone. That some things are true of us all enables the "seer" to offer statements that seem impressively accurate: "I sense that you worry about things more than you let on, even to your best friends." A number of such generally true statements can be combined into a personality description. Imagine that you take a personality test and then receive the following character sketch:

> You have a strong need for other people to like and to admire you. You have a tendency to be critical of yourself. . . . You pride yourself on being an independent thinker and do not accept other opinions without satisfactory proof. You have found it unwise to be too frank in revealing yourself to others. At times you are extraverted, affable, sociable; at other times you are introverted, wary, and reserved. Some of your aspirations tend to be pretty unrealistic (Davies, 1997; Forer, 1949).

In experiments, college students have received stock assessments like this one, drawn from statements in a newsstand astrology book. When they think the bogus, generic feedback was prepared just for them and when it is favorable, they nearly always rate the description

say about your personality. Around the world—across 56 nations and 29 languages in one study (Schmitt et al., 2007)—people describe others in terms roughly consistent with this list. The Big Five may not be the last word, but for now, at least, it is the winning number in the personality lottery. The Big Five—today's "common currency for personality psychology" (Funder, 2001)—has been the most active personality research topic since the early 1990s and is currently our best approximation of the basic trait dimensions.

The recent wave of Big Five research explores various questions:

▶ **How stable are these traits?** In adulthood, the Big Five traits are quite stable, with some tendencies (emotional instability, extraversion, and openness) waning a bit during early and middle adulthood, and others (agreeableness and

as either "good" or "excellent" (Davies, 1997). Even skeptics, given a flattering description attributed to an astrologer, begin to think that "maybe there's something to this astrology stuff after all" (Glick et al., 1989). An astrologer, it has been said, is someone "prepared to tell you what you think of yourself" (Jones, 2000).

French psychologist Michael Gauguelin offered a free personal horoscope in an ad he placed in a Paris newspaper. Ninety-four percent of those receiving the horoscope praised the description as accurate. Whose horoscope had they all received? That of France's Dr. Petiot, a notorious mass murderer (Kurtz, 1983). This acceptance of stock, positive descriptions is called the *Barnum effect,* named in honor of master showman P. T. Barnum's dictum, "There's a sucker born every minute."

A second technique used by seers is to "read" our clothing, physical features, nonverbal gestures, and reactions to what they are saying. Imagine yourself as the character reader visited by a young woman in her late twenties or early thirties. Hyman described the woman as "wearing expensive jewelry, a wedding band, and a black dress of cheap material. The observant reader noted that she was wearing shoes which were advertised for people with foot trouble." Do these clues suggest anything?

"Madame Zelinski can provide an even more accurate reading with your date of birth and Social Security number."

Drawing on these observations, the character reader proceeded to amaze his client with his insights. He assumed the woman had come to see him, as did most of his female customers, because of a love or financial problem. The black dress and the wedding band led him to reason that her husband had died recently. The expensive jewelry suggested she had been financially comfortable during the marriage, but the cheap dress suggested her husband's death had left her impoverished. The therapeutic shoes signified she was now on her feet more than she had been used to, implying that she had been working to support herself since her hus-

band's death. Based on these insights, the reader correctly guessed that the woman was wondering if she should remarry in hope of ending her economic hardship. No wonder, say the skeptics, that when mediums cannot see the person who has come to them, their clients cannot recognize the reading that was meant for them from among other readings (O'Keeffe & Wiseman, 2005).

If you are not as shrewd as this character reader, Hyman says it hardly matters. If people seek you out for a reading, start with some safe sympathy: "I sense you're having some problems lately. You seem unsure what to do. I get the feeling another person is involved." Then tell them what they want to hear. Memorize some Barnum statements from astrology and fortune-telling manuals and use them liberally. Tell people it is their responsibility to cooperate by relating your message to their specific experiences. Later they will recall that you predicted those specific details. Phrase statements as questions, and when you detect a positive response assert the statement strongly. Finally, be a good listener, and later, in different words, reveal to people what they earlier revealed to you. If you dupe them, they will come.

Better yet, beware of those who, by exploiting people with these techniques, are fortune takers rather than fortune tellers.

---

conscientiousness) rising (McCrae et al., 1999; Vaidya et al., 2002). Conscientiousness increases the most during people's twenties, as people mature and learn to manage their jobs and relationships. Agreeableness increases the most during people's thirties and continues to increase through their sixties (Srivastava et al., 2003).

▶ **How heritable are they?** *Heritability* of individual differences varies with the diversity of people studied, but it generally runs 50 percent or a tad more for each dimension, and genetic influences are similar in different nations (Loehlin et al., 1998; Yamagata et al., 2006).

▶ **Do the Big Five traits predict other personal attributes?** Yes, and here are some examples: Highly conscientious people earn better high school and university grades (Conard, 2006; Noftle & Robins, 2007). They also are more likely to be morning types (sometimes called "larks"); evening types ("owls") are marginally more extraverted (Jackson & Gerard, 1996). If one partner scores lower than the other on agreeableness, stability, and openness, marital and sexual satisfaction may suffer (Botwin et al., 1997; Donnellan et al., 2004).

By exploring such questions, Big Five research has sustained trait psychology and renewed appreciation for the importance of personality.

Evaluating the Trait Perspective

47-4   Does research support the consistency of personality traits over time and across situations?

Are our personality traits stable and enduring? Or does our behavior depend on where and with whom we find ourselves? J. R. R. Tolkien created characters, like the loyal Sam Gamgee, whose personality traits were consistent across various times and places. The Italian playwright Luigi Pirandello had a different view. For him, personality was ever-changing, tailored to the particular role or situation. In one of Pirandello's plays, Lamberto Laudisi describes himself: "I am really what you take me to be; though, my dear madam, that does not prevent me from also being really what your husband, my sister, my niece, and Signora Cini take me to be—because they also are absolutely right!" To which Signora Sirelli responds, "In other words you are a different person for each of us."

The Person-Situation Controversy

Who, then, typifies human personality, Tolkien's consistent Sam Gamgee or Pirandello's inconsistent Laudisi? Both. Our behavior is influenced by the interaction of our inner disposition with our environment. Still, the question lingers: Which is *more* important? Are we *more* as Tolkien or as Pirandello imagined us to be?

When we explore this *person-situation controversy,* we look for genuine personality traits that persist over time *and* across situations. Are some people dependably conscientious and others unreliable, some cheerful and others dour, some friendly and outgoing and others shy? If we are to consider friendliness a trait, friendly people must act friendly at different times and places. Do they?

In considering research that has followed lives through time, some scholars (especially those who study infants) are impressed with personality change; others are struck by personality stability during adulthood. As **FIGURE 47.2** illustrates, data from 152 long-term studies reveal that personality trait scores are positively correlated with scores obtained seven years later, and that as people grow older their personality stabilizes. Interests may change—the avid collector of tropical fish may become an avid

"There is as much difference between us and ourselves, as between us and others."
Michel de Montaigne, *Essays,* 1588

‖ Roughly speaking, the temporary, external influences on behavior are the focus of social psychology, and the enduring, inner influences are the focus of personality psychology. In actuality, behavior always depends on the interaction of persons with situations. ‖

‖ Change and consistency can co-exist. If all people were to become somewhat less shy with age, there would be personality change, but also relative stability and predictability. ‖

FIGURE 47.2 Personality stability With age, personality traits become more stable, as reflected in the correlation of trait scores with follow-up scores seven years later. (Data from Roberts & DelVecchio, 2000.)

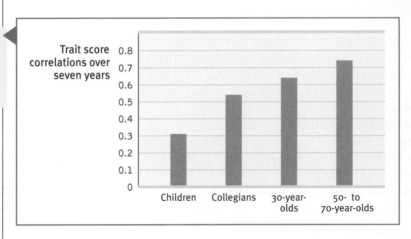

Trait score correlations over seven years

Children   Collegians   30-year-olds   50- to 70-year-olds

gardener. Careers may change—the determined salesperson may become a determined social worker. Relationships may change—the hostile spouse may start over with a new partner. But most people recognize their traits as their own, note Robert McCrae and Paul Costa (1994), "and it is well that they do. A person's recognition of the inevitability of his or her one and only personality is . . . the culminating wisdom of a lifetime." So most people—including most psychologists—would probably side with Tolkien's assumption of stability of personality traits. Moreover, our traits are socially significant. They influence our health, our thinking, and our job performance (Deary & Matthews, 1993; Hogan, 1998). Studies that follow lives through time show that personality traits rival socioeconomic status and cognitive ability as predictors of mortality, divorce, and occupational attainment (Roberts et al., 2007).

"Mr. Coughlin over there was the founder of one of the first motorcycle gangs."

Although our personality *traits* may be both stable and potent, the consistency of our specific *behaviors* from one situation to the next is another matter. As Walter Mischel (1968, 1984, 2004) has pointed out, people do not act with predictable consistency. Mischel's studies of college students' conscientiousness revealed but a modest relationship between a student's being conscientious on one occasion (say, showing up for class on time) and being similarly conscientious on another occasion (say, turning in assignments on time). Pirandello would not have been surprised. If you've noticed how outgoing you are in some situations and how reserved you are in others, perhaps you're not surprised either (though for certain traits, Mischel reports, you may accurately assess yourself as more consistent).

This inconsistency in behaviors also makes personality test scores weak predictors of behaviors. People's scores on an extraversion test, for example, do not neatly predict how sociable they actually will be on any given occasion. If we remember such results, says Mischel, we will be more cautious about labeling and pigeonholing individuals. Years in advance, science can tell us the phase of the Moon for any given date. A day in advance, meteorologists can often predict the weather. But we are much further from being able to predict how *you* will feel and act tomorrow.

However, people's *average* outgoingness, happiness, or carelessness over many situations is predictable (Epstein, 1983a,b). When rating someone's shyness or agreeableness, this consistency enables people who know someone well to agree on their ratings (Kenrick & Funder, 1988). By collecting snippets of people's daily experience via body-worn recording devices, Matthias Mehl and his colleagues (2006) confirmed that extraverts really do talk more. (I have repeatedly vowed to cut back on my jabbering and joking during my noontime pickup basketball games with friends. Alas, moments later, the irrepressible chatterbox inevitably reoccupies my body.) As our best friends can verify, we do have genetically influenced personality traits. And those traits even lurk, report Samuel Gosling and his colleagues in a series of studies, in our

▶ *music preferences*. Classical, jazz, blues, and folk music lovers tend to be open to experience and verbally intelligent; country, pop, and religious music lovers tend to be cheerful, outgoing, and conscientious (Rentfrow & Gosling, 2003, 2006). On first meeting, students often disclose their music preferences to each other; in doing so, they are swapping information about their personalities.

▶ *dorm rooms and offices*. Our personal spaces display our identity and leave a behavioral residue (in our scattered laundry or neat desktop). And that helps explain why just a few minutes' inspection of our living and working spaces can enable someone to assess with reasonable accuracy our conscientiousness, our openness to new experiences, and even our emotional stability (Gosling et al., 2002).

▶ *personal Web sites*. Is a personal Web site or a Facebook profile also a canvas for self-expression? Or is it an opportunity for people to present themselves in false or misleading ways? It's more the former (Gosling et al., 2007; Marcus et al., 2006; Vazire & Gosling, 2004). Visitors to personal Web sites quickly gain important clues to the owner's extraversion, conscientiousness, and openness to experience.

"I'm going to France—I'm a different person in France."

▶ *e-mail.* If you have ever felt you could detect someone's personality from the writing voice in their e-mail, you are right!! What a cool, exciting finding!!! (if you catch my drift). People's ratings of others' personalities based solely on their e-mails correlate with actual personality scores on measures such as extraversion and neuroticism (Gill et al., 2006; Oberlander & Gill, 2006). Extraverts, for example, use more adjectives.

In unfamiliar, formal situations—perhaps as a guest in the home of a person from another culture—our traits remain hidden as we carefully attend to social cues. In familiar, informal situations—just hanging out with friends—we feel less constrained, allowing our traits to emerge (Buss, 1989). In these informal situations, our expressive styles—our animation, manner of speaking, and gestures—are impressively consistent. That's why very thin slices of someone's behavior—even just three 2-second clips of a teacher—can be revealing (Ambady & Rosenthal, 1992, 1993).

Some people are naturally expressive (and therefore talented at pantomime and charades); others are less expressive (and therefore better poker players). To evaluate people's voluntary control over their expressiveness, Bella DePaulo and her colleagues (1992) asked people to *act* as expressive or inhibited as possible while stating opinions. Their remarkable findings: Inexpressive people, even when feigning expressiveness, were less expressive than expressive people acting naturally. Similarly, expressive people, even when trying to seem inhibited, were less inhibited than inexpressive people acting naturally. It's hard to be someone you're not, or not to be what you are.

Even our conversational word use expresses our personality. For example, in hour-long interviews, expressive, assertive people used more words expressing certainty, as in "I have *always* enjoyed computers and the Internet and that is *certainly* where I want to focus my attention" (Fast & Funder, 2008). The irrepressibility of expressiveness explains why we can size up how outgoing someone is within seconds. Picture this experiment by Maurice Levesque and David Kenny (1993). They seated groups of four university women around a table and asked each woman merely to state her name, year in school, hometown, and college residence. Judging from just these few seconds of verbal and nonverbal behavior, the women were then to guess one another's talkativeness. (How do you think you would do in guessing someone's talkativeness, based on such a small glimpse of their behavior?) When later correlated with how talkative each woman actually was during a series of one-on-one taped conversations, the snap judgments proved reasonably accurate. Despite situational variations in behavior, personality came shining through. Someone who seemed smart or outgoing in one situation tended to seem (to someone else) smart or outgoing in another. When we judge an expressive trait such as outgoingness, thin slices of behavior can be revealing.

Our spaces express our personalities Even at "zero acquaintance," people can discern something of others' personality from glimpsing their Web site, dorm room, or office. So, what is your read on University of Texas researcher Samuel Gosling?

To sum up, we can say that at any moment the immediate situation powerfully influences a person's behavior, especially when the situation makes clear demands. We can better predict drivers' behavior at traffic lights from knowing the color of the lights than from knowing the drivers' personalities. Thus, professors may perceive certain students as subdued (based on their classroom behavior), but friends may perceive them as pretty wild (based on their party behavior). Averaging our behavior across many occasions does, however, reveal distinct personality traits. Traits exist. We differ. And our differences matter.

▶‖ The Social-Cognitive Perspective

47-5 In the view of social-cognitive psychologists, what mutual influences shape an individual's personality?

Today's psychological science views individuals as biopsychosocial organisms. The **social-cognitive perspective** on personality proposed by Albert Bandura (1986, 2006, 2008) emphasizes the interaction of our traits with our situations. Much as nature and nurture always work together, so do individuals and their situations.

Social-cognitive theorists believe we learn many of our behaviors either through conditioning or by observing others and modeling our behavior after theirs. (That is the "social" part.) They also emphasize the importance of mental processes: What we *think* about our situations affects our behavior. (That is the "cognitive" part.) Instead of focusing solely on how our environment *controls* us (behaviorism), social-cognitive theorists focus on how we and our environment *interact*: How do we interpret and respond to external events? How do our schemas, our memories, and our expectations influence our behavior patterns?

Reciprocal Influences

Bandura (1986, 2006) views the person-environment interaction as **reciprocal determinism.** "Behavior, internal personal factors, and environmental influences," he said, "all operate as interlocking determinants of each other" (**FIGURE 47.3**). For example, children's TV-viewing habits (past behavior) influence their viewing preferences (internal factor), which influence how television (environmental factor) affects their current behavior. The influences are mutual.

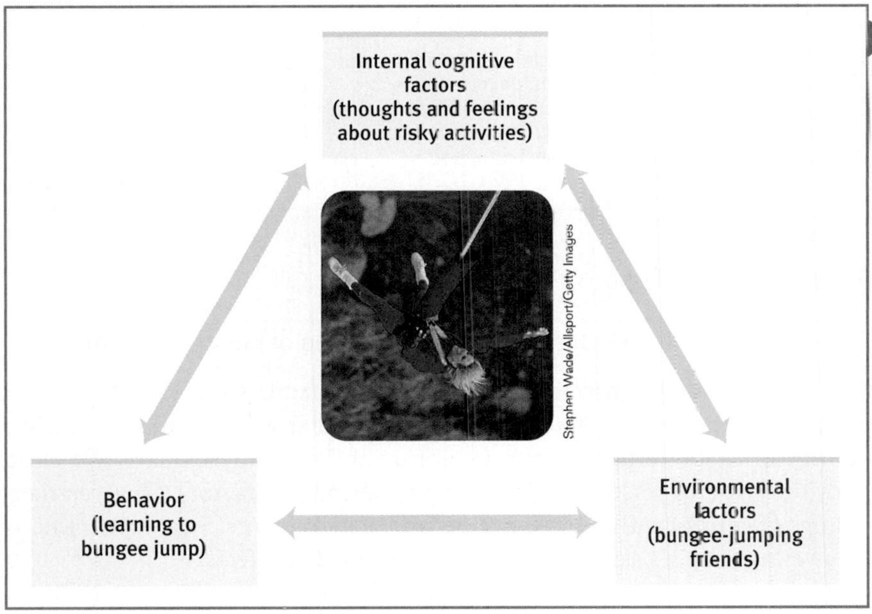

social-cognitive perspective views behavior as influenced by the interaction between people's traits (including their thinking) and their social context.

reciprocal determinism the interacting influences of behavior, internal cognition, and environment.

FIGURE 47.3 Reciprocal determinism The social-cognitive perspective proposes that our personalities are shaped by the interaction of our personal traits (including our thoughts and feelings), our environment, and our behaviors.

Internal cognitive factors
(thoughts and feelings
about risky activities)

Stephen Wade/Allsport/Getty Images

Behavior
(learning to
bungee jump)

Environmental
factors
(bungee-jumping
friends)

Consider three specific ways in which individuals and environments interact:

1. **Different people choose different environments.** The school you attend, the reading you do, the TV programs you watch, the music you listen to, the friends you associate with—all are part of an environment you have chosen, based partly on your dispositions (Ickes et al., 1997). You choose your environment and it then shapes you.

2. **Our personalities shape how we interpret and react to events.** Anxious people, for example, are attuned to potentially threatening events (Eysenck et al., 1987). Thus, they perceive the world as threatening, and they react accordingly.

3. **Our personalities help create situations to which we react.** Many experiments reveal that how we view and treat people influences how they in turn treat us. If we expect someone to be angry with us, we may give the person a cold shoulder, touching off the very anger we expect. If we have an easygoing, positive disposition, we will likely enjoy close, supportive friendships (Donnellan et al., 2005; Kendler, 1997).

In such ways, we are both the products and the architects of our environments.

If all this has a familiar ring, it may be because it parallels and reinforces a pervasive theme in psychology and in this book: *Behavior emerges from the interplay of external and internal influences.* Boiling water turns an egg hard and a potato soft. A threatening environment turns one person into a hero, another into a scoundrel. *At every moment, our behavior is influenced by our biology, our social and cultural experiences, and our cognition and dispositions* (**FIGURE 47.4**).

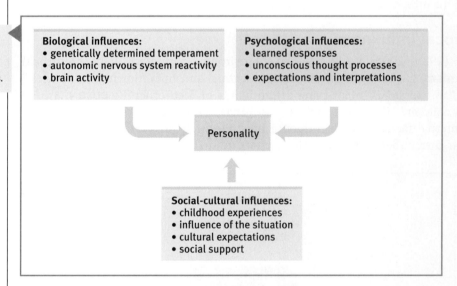

FIGURE 47.4 The biopsychosocial approach to the study of personality As with other psychological phenomena, personality is fruitfully studied at multiple levels.

Personal Control

47-6   What are the causes and consequences of personal control?

In studying how we interact with our environment, social-cognitive psychologists emphasize our sense of **personal control**—whether we learn to see ourselves as controlling, or as controlled by, our environment. Psychologists have two basic ways to study the effect of personal control (or any personality factor). One: *correlate* people's feelings of control with their behaviors and achievements. Two: *experiment,* by raising or lowering people's sense of control and noting the effects.

Internal Versus External Locus of Control

Consider your own feelings of control. Do you believe that your life is beyond your control? That the world is run by a few powerful people? That getting a good job depends mainly on being in the right place at the right time? Or do you more strongly believe that what happens to you is your own doing? That the average person can influence government decisions? That being a success is a matter of hard work?

Hundreds of studies have compared people who differ in their perceptions of control. On the one side are those who have what psychologist Julian Rotter called an **external locus of control**—the perception that chance or outside forces determine their fate. On the other are those who perceive an **internal locus of control,** who believe that they control their own destiny. In study after study, "internals" achieve more in school and work, act more independently, enjoy better health, and feel less depressed than do "externals" (Lefcourt, 1982; Ng et al., 2006). Moreover, they better delay gratification and cope with various stressors, including marital problems (Miller et al., 1986).

Depleting and Strengthening Self-Control

Self-control—the ability to control impulses and delay gratification—in turn predicts good adjustment, better grades, and social success, report June Tangney and her colleagues (2004). Students who plan their day's activities and then live out their day as planned are also at low risk for depression (Nezlek, 2001).

None of us experiences unvarying self-control. Like a muscle, self-control temporarily weakens after an exertion, replenishes with rest, and becomes stronger with exercise, report Roy Baumeister and Julia Exline (2000). Exercising willpower can deplete your mental energy and even the blood sugar and neural activity associated with mental focus (Inzlicht & Gutsell, 2007). In one experiment, hungry people who had resisted the temptation to eat chocolate chip cookies gave up sooner on a tedious task. People also become less restrained in their aggressive responses to provocation and in their sexuality after expending willpower on laboratory tasks, such as after stifling prejudice or saying the color of words (for example, "red" even if the red-colored word was *green*) (DeWall et al., 2007; Gaillot & Baumeister, 2007). But giving people energy-boosting sugar (in a naturally rather than an artificially sweetened lemonade)—as experimenters did in another experiment—strengthened their effortful thinking (Masicampo & Baumeister, 2008).

In the long run, self-control requires attention and energy. People who practice self-regulation through physical exercise and time-managed study programs can develop their self-regulation capacity. Strengthened self-control is seen both in their performance on laboratory tasks and in their improved self-management of eating, drinking, smoking, and household chores (Oaten & Cheng, 2006a,b). Develop your self-discipline in one area of your life and your strengthened self-control may spill over into other areas as well.

Learned Helplessness Versus Personal Control

People who feel helpless and oppressed often perceive control as external. This perception may then deepen their feelings of resignation. In fact, this is precisely what researcher Martin Seligman (1975, 1991) and others found in experiments with both animals and people. Dogs strapped in a harness and given repeated shocks, with no opportunity to avoid them, learned a sense of helplessness. Later placed in another situation where they *could* escape the punishment by simply leaping a hurdle, the dogs cowered as if without hope. In contrast, animals able to escape the first shocks learned personal control and easily escaped the shocks in the new situation.

People, too, when repeatedly faced with traumatic events over which they have no control, come to feel helpless, hopeless, and depressed. Psychologists call this passive resignation **learned helplessness** (FIGURE 47.5 on the next page).

personal control the extent to which people perceive control over their environment rather than feeling helpless.

external locus of control the perception that chance or outside forces beyond your personal control determine your fate.

internal locus of control the perception that you control your own fate.

learned helplessness the hopelessness and passive resignation an animal or human learns when unable to avoid repeated aversive events.

FIGURE 47.5 Learned helplessness When animals and people experience no control over repeated bad events, they often learn helplessness.

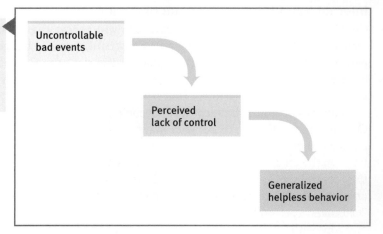

Uncontrollable bad events

Perceived lack of control

Generalized helpless behavior

Part of the shock we feel in an unfamiliar culture comes from a diminished sense of control when unsure how people in the new environment will respond (Triandis, 1994). Similarly, people given little control over their world in prisons, factories, colleges, and nursing homes experience lower morale and increased stress. Measures that increase control—allowing prisoners to move chairs and control room lights and the TV, having workers participate in decision making, offering nursing home patients choices about their environment—noticeably improve health and morale (Humphrey et al., 2007; Ruback et al., 1986; Wener et al., 1987). When Gallup pollsters asked workers whether they could personalize their workspace, those who answered *yes* were 55 percent more likely also to report high engagement with their work (Krueger & Killham, 2006). Telecommuters likewise tend to be both satisfied with their jobs and productive, especially when given control over their time (Gajendran & Harrison, 2007). (Those working from home three or more days a week do, however, feel more isolation from co-workers.)

In one famous study of nursing home patients, 93 percent of those encouraged to exert more control became more alert, active, and happy (Rodin, 1986). As researcher Ellen Langer (1983, p. 291) concluded, "perceived control is basic to human functioning." She recommended that "for the young and old alike," it is important that we create environments that enhance our sense of control and personal efficacy. No wonder so many people like their iPods and TiVos, which give them control of the content and timing of their entertainment.

Happy are those who choose their own path These happy East Berliners, crossing over to West Berlin after the wall came down in 1989, seem to personify this sentiment from the Roman philosopher Seneca.

Peter Turnley/Corbis

The verdict of these studies is reassuring: Under conditions of personal freedom and empowerment, people thrive. Small wonder that the citizens of stable democracies report higher levels of happiness (Inglehart, 1990, 2009). Shortly before the democratic revolution in the former East Germany, psychologists Gabriele Oettingen and Martin Seligman (1990) studied the telltale body language of working-class men in East and West Berlin bars. Compared with their counterparts on the other side of the Wall, the empowered West Berliners much more often laughed, sat upright rather than slumped, and had upward- rather than downward-turned mouths.

Some freedom and control is better than none, notes Barry Schwartz (2000, 2004). But does ever-increasing choice breed ever-happier lives? Actually not. Schwartz notes that the "excess of freedom" in today's Western cultures contributes to decreasing life satisfaction, increased depression, and sometimes paralysis. Increased consumer choices, as when buying a car or phone, are not an unmixed blessing. After choosing among 30 brands of jam or chocolate, people express less satisfaction than those choosing among a half-dozen options (Iyengar & Lepper, 2000). This *tyranny of choice* brings information overload and a greater likelihood that we will feel regret over some of the unchosen options.

Optimism Versus Pessimism

One measure of how helpless or effective you feel is where you stand on optimism-pessimism. How do you characteristically explain negative and positive events? Perhaps you have known students whose *attributional style* is pessimistic—who attribute poor performance to their lack of ability ("I can't do this") or to situations enduringly beyond their control ("There is nothing I can do about it"). Such students are more likely to persist in getting low grades than are students who adopt the more hopeful attitude that effort, good study habits, and self-discipline can make a difference (Noel et al., 1987; Peterson & Barrett, 1987). Mere fantasies do not fuel motivation and success, but realistic positive expectations do (Oettingen & Mayer, 2002).

Optimism and Health Health, too, benefits from a basic optimism. A depressed hopelessness dampens the body's disease-fighting immune system. In repeated studies, optimists have outlived pessimists or lived with fewer illnesses. When dating couples wrestle with conflicts, optimists and their partners see each other as engaging constructively. They tend then to feel more supported and satisfied with the resolution and with their relationship (Srivastava et al., 2006). Expect good things from others, and often you will get what you expect. Such studies helped point Seligman toward proposing a more positive psychology (see Close-Up: Toward a More Positive Psychology, on the next page).

Excessive Optimism If positive thinking in the face of adversity pays dividends, so, too, can a dash of realism (Schneider, 2001). Self-disparaging explanations of past failures can depress ambition, but realistic anxiety over possible *future* failures can fuel energetic efforts to avoid the dreaded fate (Goodhart, 1986; Norem, 2001; Showers, 1992). Students concerned about failing an upcoming exam may study thoroughly and outperform their equally able but more confident peers. Edward Chang (2001) reports that, compared with European-American students, Asian-American students express somewhat greater pessimism—which he suspects helps explain their impressive academic achievements. Success requires enough optimism to provide hope and enough pessimism to prevent complacency. We want our airline pilots to be mindful of worst-possible outcomes.

Excessive optimism can blind us to real risks. Neil Weinstein (1980, 1982, 1996) has shown how our natural positive-thinking bias can promote "an unrealistic optimism about future life events." Most late adolescents see themselves as much less vulnerable than their peers to the HIV virus that causes AIDS (Abrams, 1991). Most college students perceive themselves as less likely than their average classmate to develop drinking problems, drop out of school, or have a heart attack by age 40. Many credit-card users, unrealistically optimistic about how they will use their charge cards, elect cards with low fees and high interest (Yang et al., 2006). These and others who optimistically deny the effects of smoking, venture into ill-fated relationships, and outwit themselves in dozens of other ways, remind us that, like pride, blind optimism may go before a fall.

Our natural positive-thinking bias does seem to vanish, however, when we are bracing ourselves for feedback, such as exam results (Carroll et al., 2006). (Have you ever noticed that, as a game nears its end, the outcome seems more in doubt when your team is ahead than when it is behind?) Positive illusions also vanish after a traumatic personal experience—as they did for victims of a catastrophic California earthquake, who had to give up their illusions of being less vulnerable than others to earthquakes (Helweg-Larsen, 1999).

"O God, give us grace to accept with serenity the things that cannot be changed, courage to change the things which should be changed, and the wisdom to distinguish the one from the other."
Reinhold Niebuhr, "The Serenity Prayer," 1943

Positive expectations often motivate eventual success.

"We just haven't been flapping them hard enough."

CLOSE-UP

Toward a More Positive Psychology

During its first century, psychology understandably focused much of its attention on understanding and alleviating negative states. Psychologists have studied abuse and anxiety, depression and disease, prejudice and poverty. Since 1887, articles on selected negative emotions have outnumbered those on positive emotions by 17 to 1.

In ages past, notes American Psychological Association past-president Martin Seligman (2002), times of relative peace and prosperity have enabled cultures to turn their attention from repairing weakness and damage to promoting "the highest qualities of life." Prosperous fifth-century Athens nurtured philosophy and democracy. Flourishing fifteenth-century Florence nurtured great art. Victorian England, flush with the bounty of the British empire, nurtured honor, discipline, and duty. In this millennium, Seligman believes, thriving Western cultures have a parallel opportunity to create, as a "humane, scientific monument," a more **positive psychology**—a psychology concerned not only with weakness and damage but also with strength and virtue. Thanks to his own leadership and to some $30 million in funding, the new positive psychology movement has gained strength (Seligman, 2004).

Positive psychology shares with humanistic psychology an interest in advancing

Courtesy of Martin E. P. Seligman, Ph.D, Director, Positive Psychology Center/University of Pennsylvania

Martin E. P. Seligman "The main purpose of a positive psychology is to measure, understand, and then build the human strengths and the civic virtues."

human fulfillment, but its methodology is scientific. From these roots have grown not only the new studies of happiness and health, but also the shift in emphasis from learned helplessness and depression to optimism and thriving. "Positive psychology," say Seligman and colleagues (2005), "is an umbrella term for the study of positive emotions, positive character traits, and enabling institutions."

Taken together, satisfaction with the past, happiness with the present, and optimism about the future define the movement's first pillar: *positive emotions.* Happiness, Seligman argues, is a

by-product of a pleasant, engaged, and meaningful life.

Positive psychology is about building not just a pleasant life, says Seligman, but also a *good life* that engages one's skills, and a *meaningful life* that points beyond oneself. Thus, the second pillar, *positive character,* focuses on exploring and enhancing creativity, courage, compassion, integrity, self-control, leadership, wisdom, and spirituality. Current research examines the roots and fruits of such characteristics, sometimes by studying individuals who exemplify them in extraordinary ways.

The third pillar, *positive groups, communities, and cultures,* seeks to foster a positive social ecology, including healthy families, communal neighborhoods, effective schools, socially responsible media, and civil dialogue.

Will psychology have a more positive mission in this century? Without slighting the need to repair damage and cure disease, positive psychology's proponents hope so. With *American Psychologist* and *British Psychologist* special issues devoted to positive psychology, with lots of books, with networked scientists working in worldwide research groups, and with prizes, research awards, summer institutes, and a graduate program promoting positive psychology scholarship, these psychologists have reason to be positive.

---

positive psychology the scientific study of optimal human functioning; aims to discover and promote strengths and virtues that enable individuals and communities to thrive.

Blindness to One's Own Incompetence Ironically, people often are most overconfident when most incompetent. That's because it often takes competence to recognize competence, as Justin Kruger and David Dunning noted (1999). They found that most students scoring at the low end of grammar and logic tests believed they had scored in the top half. If you do not know what good grammar is, you may be unaware that your grammar is poor. This "ignorance of one's own incompetence" phenomenon has a parallel, as I can confirm, in hard-of-hearing people's difficulty recognizing their own hearing loss. We're not so much "in denial" as we are simply unaware of what we don't hear. If I fail to hear my friend calling my name, the friend notices my inattention. But for me it's a nonevent. I hear what I hear—which, to me, seems pretty normal.

The difficulty in recognizing one's own incompetence helps explain why so many low-scoring students are dumbfounded after doing badly on an exam. If you don't

DOONESBURY

know all the Scrabble word possibilities you've overlooked, you may feel pretty smart—until someone points them out. As Deanna Caputo and Dunning (2005) demonstrate in experiments that re-create this phenomenon, our ignorance of what we don't know helps sustain our confidence in our own abilities.

To judge one's competence and predict one's future performance, it often pays to invite others' assessments, notes Dunning (2006). Based on studies in which both individuals and their acquaintances predict their future, we can hazard some advice: If you're a junior doctor and want to predict how well you will do on a surgical skills exam, don't rate yourself—ask your peers for their candid prediction. If you're a Naval officer and need to assess your leadership ability—don't rate yourself, ask your fellow officers. And if you're in love and want to predict whether it will last, don't listen to your heart—ask your roommate.

Assessing Behavior in Situations

47-7 What underlying principle guides social-cognitive psychologists in their assessment of people's behavior and beliefs?

Social-cognitive psychologists explore how people interact with situations. To predict behavior, they often observe behavior in realistic situations.

The idea, though effective, is not new. One ambitious example was the U.S. Army's World War II strategy for assessing candidates for spy missions. Rather than using paper-and-pencil tests, Army psychologists subjected the candidates to simulated undercover conditions. They tested their ability to handle stress, solve problems, maintain leadership, and withstand intense interrogation without blowing their cover. Although time-consuming and expensive, this assessment of behavior in a realistic situation helped predict later success on actual spy missions (OSS Assessment Staff, 1948). Modern studies indicate that assessment center exercises are more revealing of some dimensions, such as communication ability, than others, such as achievement drive (Bowler & Woehr, 2006).

Military and educational organizations and many Fortune 500 companies are adopting assessment center strategies in their evaluations of hundreds of thousands of people each year (Bray et al., 1991, 1997; Thornton & Rupp 2005). AT&T has observed prospective managers doing simulated managerial work. Many colleges assess potential faculty members' teaching abilities by observing them teach, and assess

"The living-room [Scrabble] player is lucky. . . . He has no idea how miserably he fails with almost every turn, how many possible words or optimal plays slip by unnoticed."

Stefan Fatsis, *Word Freak*, 2001

Assessing behavior in situations Reality TV shows, such as Donald Trump's *The Apprentice,* may take "show me" job interviews to the extreme, but they do illustrate a valid point. Seeing how a potential employee behaves in a job-relevant situation helps predict job performance.

self in contemporary psychology, assumed to be the center of personality, the organizer of our thoughts, feelings, and actions.

|| A *New York Times* analysis of 100 rampage murders over the last half-century revealed that 55 of the killers had regularly exploded in anger and 63 had threatened violence (Goodstein & Glaberson, 2000). Most didn't, out of the blue, "just snap." ||

graduate students' potentials via internships and student teaching. Armies assess their soldiers by observing them during military exercises. Most American cities with populations of 50,000 or more have used assessment centers in evaluating police and fire officers (Lowry, 1997).

These procedures exploit the principle that the best means of predicting future behavior is neither a personality test nor an interviewer's intuition. Rather, it is the person's past behavior patterns in similar situations (Mischel, 1981; Ouellette & Wood, 1998; Schmidt & Hunter, 1998). As long as the situation and the person remain much the same, the best predictor of future job performance is past job performance; the best predictor of future grades is past grades; the best predictor of future aggressiveness is past aggressiveness; the best predictor of drug use in young adulthood is drug use in high school. If you can't check the person's past behavior, the next-best thing is to create an assessment situation that simulates the task so you can see how the person handles it.

Evaluating the Social-Cognitive Perspective

47-8 What has the social-cognitive perspective contributed to the study of personality, and what criticisms has it faced?

The social-cognitive perspective on personality sensitizes researchers to how situations affect, and are affected by, individuals. More than other perspectives, it builds from psychological research on learning and cognition.

Critics charge that the social-cognitive perspective focuses so much on the situation that it fails to appreciate the person's inner traits. Where is the person in this view of personality, ask the dissenters, and where are human emotions? True, the situation does guide our behavior. But, say the critics, in many instances our unconscious motives, our emotions, and our pervasive traits shine through. Personality traits have been shown to predict behavior at work, love, and play. Our biologically influenced traits really do matter. Consider Percy Ray Pridgen and Charles Gill. Each faced the same situation: They had jointly won a $90 million lottery jackpot (Harriston, 1993). When Pridgen learned of the winning numbers, he began trembling uncontrollably, huddled with a friend behind a bathroom door while confirming the win, then sobbed. When Gill heard the news, he told his wife and then went to sleep.

Possible selves By giving them a chance to try out many possible selves, pretend games offer children important opportunities to grow emotionally, socially, and cognitively. This young boy may or may not grow up to be a physician, but playing adult roles will certainly bear fruit in terms of an expanded vision of what he might become.

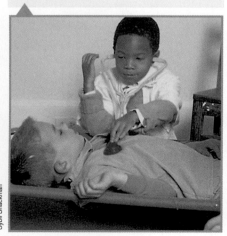

Sybil Shackman

▶|| Exploring the Self

47-9 Are we helped or hindered by high self-esteem?

Psychology's concern with people's sense of self dates back at least to William James, who devoted more than 100 pages of his 1890 *Principles of Psychology* to the topic. By 1943, Gordon Allport lamented that the self had become "lost to view." Although humanistic psychology's emphasis on the self did not instigate much scientific research, it did help renew the concept of self and keep it alive. Now, more than a century after James, the self is one of Western psychology's most vigorously researched topics. Every year, new studies galore appear on self-esteem, self-disclosure, self-awareness, self-schemas, self-monitoring, and so forth. Underlying this research is an assumption that the **self,** as organizer of our thoughts, feelings, and actions, is the center of personality.

One example of thinking about self is the concept of *possible selves* put forth by Hazel Markus and her colleagues (Cross & Markus, 1991; Markus & Nurius, 1986). Your possible selves include your visions of the self you dream of becoming—the rich self, the successful self, the loved and admired self. They also include the self you fear becoming—the unemployed self, the lonely self, the academically failed self. Such possible selves motivate us by laying out specific goals and calling forth the energy to work toward them. University of Michigan students in a combined undergraduate/medical school program earn higher grades if they undergo the program with a clear vision of themselves as successful doctors. Dreams do often give birth to achievements.

Our self-focused perspective may motivate us, but it can also lead us to presume too readily that others are noticing and evaluating us. Thomas Gilovich (1996) demonstrated this **spotlight effect** by having individual Cornell University students don Barry Manilow T-shirts before entering a room with other students. Feeling self-conscious, the T-shirt wearers guessed that nearly half their peers would take note of the shirt as they walked in. In reality, only 23 percent did. This absence of attention applies not only to our dorky clothes and bad hair but also to our nervousness, irritation, or attraction: Fewer people notice than we presume (Gilovich & Savitsky, 1999). Others are also less aware than we suppose of the variability—the ups and downs—of our appearance and performance (Gilovich et al., 2002). Even after a blunder (setting off a library alarm, showing up in the wrong clothes), we stick out like a sore thumb less than we imagine (Savitsky et al., 2001). Knowing about the spotlight effect can be empowering. Help public speakers to understand that their natural nervousness is not so apparent to their audience and their speaking performance improves (Savitsky & Gilovich, 2003).

The Benefits of Self-Esteem

How we feel about ourselves is also important. High **self-esteem**—a feeling of self-worth—pays dividends. People who feel good about themselves (who strongly agree with self-affirming questionnaire statements such as, "I am fun to be with") have fewer sleepless nights; succumb less easily to pressures to conform; are more persistent at difficult tasks; are less shy, anxious, and lonely; and are just plain happier (Greenberg, 2008; Leary, 1999; Murray et al., 2002; Watson et al., 2002). Moreover, today's self-esteem sometimes predicts tomorrow's achievements. In one study of 297 Finnish university students, self-esteem scores predicted employment, salary, and job satisfaction a decade later (Salmela-Aro & Nurmi, 2007).

Is high self-esteem really "the armor that protects kids" from life's problems? Some psychologists have their doubts (Baumeister, 2006; Dawes, 1994; Leary, 1999; Seligman, 1994, 2002). Although children's academic self-concept—their confidence that they can do well in a subject—predicts school achievement, general self-image does not (Marsh & Craven, 2006; Swann et al., 2007; Trautwein et al., 2006). Maybe self-esteem simply reflects reality. Maybe feeling good *follows* doing well. Maybe it's a side effect of meeting challenges and surmounting difficulties. Maybe self-esteem is a gauge that reads out the state of our relationships with others. If so, isn't pushing the gauge artificially higher akin to forcing a car's low fuel gauge to display "full"? And if problems and failures cause low self-esteem, won't the best boost therefore come not so much from our repeatedly telling children how wonderful they are as from their own effective coping and hard-won achievements?

However, experiments do reveal an *effect* of low self-esteem. Temporarily deflate people's self-image (say, by telling them they did poorly on an aptitude test or by disparaging their personality) and they will be more likely to disparage others or to express heightened racial prejudice (Ybarra, 1999). Those who are negative about themselves also tend to be thin-skinned and judgmental (Baumgardner et al., 1989; Pelham, 1993). In experiments, people made to feel insecure often become excessively critical, as if to impress others with their own brilliance (Amabile, 1983). Such findings are consistent with Maslow's and Rogers' presumptions that a healthy self-image pays dividends. Accept

spotlight effect overestimating others' noticing and evaluating our appearance, performance, and blunders (as if we presume a spotlight shines on us).

self-esteem one's feelings of high or low self-worth.

yourself and you'll find it easier to accept others. Disparage yourself and you will be prone to the floccinaucinihilipilification[1] of others. Said more simply, some "love their neighbors as themselves"; others loathe their neighbors as themselves. People who are down on themselves tend to be down on other things and people.

Self-Serving Bias

Humanist psychologist Carl Rogers (1958) once objected to the religious doctrine that humanity's problems arise from excessive self-love, or pride. He noted that most people he had known "despise themselves, regard themselves as worthless and unlovable." Mark Twain had a similar idea: "No man, deep down in the privacy of his heart, has any considerable respect for himself."

Actually, most of us have a good reputation with ourselves. In studies of self-esteem, even those who score low respond in the midrange of possible scores. (A low–self-esteem person responds to statements such as "I have good ideas" with qualifying adjectives such as *somewhat* or *sometimes*.) Moreover, one of psychology's most provocative and firmly established recent conclusions concerns our potent **self-serving bias**—our readiness to perceive ourselves favorably (Mezulis et al., 2004; Myers, 2008). Consider these findings:

People accept more responsibility for good deeds than for bad, and for successes than for failures. Athletes often privately credit their victories to their own prowess, and their losses to bad breaks, lousy officiating, or the other team's exceptional performance. After receiving poor grades on an exam, most students in a half-dozen studies criticized the exam, not themselves. On insurance forms, drivers have explained accidents in such words as: "An invisible car came out of nowhere, struck my car, and vanished." "As I reached an intersection, a hedge sprang up, obscuring my vision, and I did not see the other car." "A pedestrian hit me and went under my car." The question "What have I done to deserve this?" is one we usually ask of our troubles, not our successes—those, we assume we deserve.

PEANUTS

Most people see themselves as better than average. This is true for nearly any commonplace behavior that is subjectively assessed and socially desirable. In national surveys, most business executives say they are more ethical than their average counterpart. In several studies, 90 percent of business managers and more than 90 percent of college professors rated their performance as superior to that of their average peer. In Australia, 86 percent of people rate their job performance as above average, and only 1 percent as below average. The phenomenon, which reflects the overestimation of self rather than the underestimation of others (Epley & Dunning, 2000), is less striking in Asia, where people value modesty (Heine & Hamamura,

---

self-serving bias a readiness to perceive oneself favorably.

[1]I couldn't resist throwing that in. But don't worry, you won't be tested on floccinaucinihilipilification, which is the act of estimating something as worthless (and was the longest nontechnical word in the first edition of the *Oxford English Dictionary*).

2007). Yet self-serving biases have been observed worldwide: among Dutch, Australian, and Chinese students; Japanese drivers; Indian Hindus; and French people of most walks of life. In every one of 53 countries surveyed, people expressed self-esteem above the midpoint of the most widely used scale (Schmitt & Allik, 2005).

Ironically, people even see themselves as more immune than others to self-serving bias (Pronin, 2007). The world, it seems, is Garrison Keillor's Lake Wobegon writ large—a place where "all the women are strong, all the men are good-looking, and all the children are above average." And so are the pets. Three in four owners believe their pet is smarter than average (Nier, 2004).

Self-serving bias flies in the face of pop psychology. "All of us have inferiority complexes," wrote John Powell (1989, p. 15). "Those who seem not to have such a complex are only pretending." But additional findings remove any doubts (Myers, 2008):

▶ We remember and justify our past actions in self-enhancing ways.

▶ We exhibit an inflated confidence in our beliefs and judgments.

▶ We overestimate how desirably *we* would act in situations where most people behave less than admirably.

▶ We often seek out favorable, self-enhancing information.

▶ We are quicker to believe flattering descriptions of ourselves than unflattering ones, and we are impressed with psychological tests that make us look good.

▶ We shore up our self-image by *over*estimating the commonality of our foibles and by *under*estimating the commonality of our strengths.

▶ We see ourselves making better-than-average contributions to our groups (but so do our teammates, which explains why group members' self-contribution estimates usually total more than 100 percent).

▶ We exhibit group pride—a tendency to see our group (our school, our country, our race, our children, even our pets) as superior.

Moreover, pride, as religion and literature together remind us, does often go before a fall. Self-serving perceptions underlie conflicts ranging from blaming one's spouse for marital discord to arrogantly promoting one's own ethnic superiority. Finding their self-esteem threatened, people with large egos may do more than put others down; they may react violently. "Aryan pride" fueled Nazi atrocities. "These biases have the effect of making wars more likely to begin and more difficult to end," note Daniel Kahneman and Jonathan Renshon (2007).

We can see these tendencies even in children, where the recipe for frequent fighting mixes high self-esteem with social rejection. The most aggressive children tend to have high self-regard that gets punctured by other kids' dislike (van Boxtel et al., 2004). Similarly, an adolescent or adult with a swelled head that gets deflated by insult is potentially dangerous. Brad Bushman and Roy Baumeister (1998) experimented with this "dark side of high self-esteem." They had 540 undergraduate volunteers write a paragraph, in response to which another supposed student gave them either praise ("Great essay!") or stinging criticism ("One of the worst essays I have read!"). Then the essay writers played a reaction-time game against the other student. After wins, they could assault their opponent with noise of any intensity for any duration.

Can you anticipate the result? After criticism, those with unrealistically high self-esteem were "exceptionally aggressive." They delivered three times the auditory torture of those with normal self-esteem. Threatened egotism, more than low self-esteem, it seems, predisposes aggression. "Encouraging people to feel good about themselves when they haven't earned it" poses problems, Baumeister (2001)

TOO MUCH COFFEE MAN BY SHANNON WHEELER

AND GOD CREATED SELF-WORTH

"To love oneself is the beginning of a lifelong romance."
Oscar Wilde, *An Ideal Husband*, 1895

"The [self-]portraits that we actually believe, when we are given freedom to voice them, are dramatically more positive than reality can sustain."
Shelley Taylor, *Positive Illusions*, 1989

"The enthusiastic claims of the self-esteem movement mostly range from fantasy to hogwash. The effects of self-esteem are small, limited, and not all good."
Roy Baumeister (1996)

concluded. "Conceited, self-important individuals turn nasty toward those who puncture their bubbles of self-love."

After tracking self-importance across the last several decades, psychologist Jean Twenge (2006; Twenge et al., 2008) reports that today's new generation—Generation Me, she calls it—expresses more narcissism (by agreeing more often with statements such as, "If I ruled the world, it would be a better place," or "I think I am a special person"). Agreement with such statements correlates with materialism, the desire to be famous, inflated expectations, more hookups with fewer committed relationships, more gambling, and more cheating, all of which have been on the rise as narcissism has increased.

Despite the demonstrated perils of pride, many people reject the idea of self-serving bias, insisting it overlooks those who feel worthless and unlovable and seem to despise themselves. If self-serving bias prevails, why do so many people disparage themselves? For three reasons: Sometimes self-directed put-downs are subtly strategic: They elicit reassuring strokes. Saying "No one likes me" may at least elicit "But not everyone has met you!" Other times, such as before a game or an exam, self-disparaging comments prepare us for possible failure. The coach who extols the superior strength of the upcoming opponent makes a loss understandable, a victory noteworthy. And finally, self-disparagement also frequently pertains to one's old self. People are much more critical of their distant past selves than of their current selves—even when they have not changed (Wilson & Ross, 2001). "At 18, I was a jerk; today I'm more sensitive." In their own eyes, chumps yesterday, champs today.

Even so, it's true: All of us some of the time, and some of us much of the time, do feel inferior—especially when we compare ourselves with those who are a step or two higher on the ladder of status, looks, income, or ability. The deeper and more frequently we have such feelings, the more unhappy, even depressed, we are. But for most people, thinking has a naturally positive bias.

While recognizing the dark side of self-serving bias and self-esteem, some researchers prefer isolating the effects of two types of self-esteem—defensive and secure (Kernis, 2003; Lambird & Mann, 2006; Ryan & Deci, 2004). *Defensive self-esteem* is fragile. It focuses on sustaining itself, which makes failures and criticism feel threatening. Such egotism exposes one to perceived threats, which feed anger and disorder, note Jennifer Crocker and Lora Park (2004). Thus, like low self-esteem, defensive self-esteem correlates with aggressive and antisocial behavior (Donnellan et al., 2005).

Secure self-esteem is less fragile, because it is less contingent on external evaluations. To feel accepted for who we are, and not for our looks, wealth, or acclaim, relieves pressures to succeed and enables us to focus beyond ourselves. By losing ourselves in relationships and purposes larger than self, Crocker and Park add, we may achieve a more secure self-esteem and greater quality of life.

"If you compare yourself with others, you may become vain and bitter; for always there will be greater and lesser persons than yourself."

Max Ehrmann, "Desiderata," 1927

REVIEW

Contemporary Research on Personality

47-1 **How do psychologists use traits to describe personality?** Rather than explain the hidden aspects of personality, *trait* theorists attempt to describe our stable and enduring characteristics. Through factor analysis, researchers have isolated important dimensions of personality. Genetic predispositions influence many traits.

47-2 **What are personality inventories, and what are their strengths and weaknesses as trait-assessment tools?** *Personality inventories* (like the *MMPI*) are questionnaires on which people respond to items designed to gauge a wide range of feelings and behaviors. Items on the test are *empirically derived,* and the tests are objectively scored. But people can fake their answers to create a good impression, and the ease of computerized testing may lead to misuse of these tests.

47-3 **Which traits seem to provide the most useful information about personality variation?** The Big Five personality dimensions—conscientiousness, agreeableness, neuroticism (emotional stability vs. instability), openness, and extraversion—offer a reasonably comprehensive picture of personality.

47-4 **Does research support the consistency of personality traits over time and across situations?** Although people's traits persist over time, their behaviors vary widely from situation to situation. Despite these variations, a person's average behavior across different situations tends to be fairly consistent.

47-5 **In the view of social-cognitive psychologists, what mutual influences shape an individual's personality?** The *social-cognitive perspective* applies principles of learning, cognition, and social behavior to personality, with particular emphasis on the ways in which our personality influences and is influenced by our interaction with the environment. It assumes *reciprocal determinism*—that personal-cognitive factors interact with the environment to influence people's behavior.

47-6 **What are the causes and consequences of personal control?** By studying how people vary in their perceived *locus of control* (*external* or *internal*), researchers have found that a sense of *personal control* helps people to cope with life. Research on *learned helplessness* evolved into research on the effects of optimism and pessimism, which led to a broader *positive psychology* movement.

47-7 **What underlying principle guides social-cognitive psychologists in their assessment of people's behavior and beliefs?** Social-cognitive researchers study how people interact with their situations. They tend to believe that the best way to predict someone's behavior in a given situation is to observe that person's behavior in similar situations.

47-8 **What has the social-cognitive perspective contributed to the study of personality, and what criticisms has it faced?** Though faulted for underemphasizing the importance of unconscious dynamics, emotions, and inner traits, the social-cognitive perspective builds on psychology's well-established concepts of learning and cognition and reminds us of the power of social situations.

47-9 **Are we helped or hindered by high self-esteem?** In contemporary psychology, the *self* is assumed to be the center of personality, the organizer of our thoughts, feelings, and actions. Research confirms the benefits of high *self-esteem,* but it also warns of the dangers of unrealistically high self-esteem. The *self-serving bias* leads us to perceive ourselves favorably, often causing us to overestimate our abilities and underestimate our faults.

Terms and Concepts to Remember

trait, p. 574
personality inventory, p. 576
Minnesota Multiphasic
   Personality Inventory
   (MMPI), p. 576
empirically derived test, p. 576
social-cognitive perspective,
   p. 583
reciprocal determinism, p. 583
personal control, p. 584

external locus of control, p. 585
internal locus of control,
   p. 585
learned helplessness, p. 585
positive psychology, p. 588
self, p. 590
spotlight effect, p. 591
self-esteem, p. 591
self-serving bias, p. 592

Test Yourself

1. What is the person-situation controversy?

2. How do learned helplessness and optimism influence behavior?

3. In a 1997 Gallup poll, White Americans estimated 44 percent of their fellow White Americans to be high in prejudice (scoring them 5 or higher on a 10-point scale). How many rated themselves similarly high in prejudice? Just 14 percent. What phenomenon does this illustrate?

(Answers to the Test Yourself questions can be found in Appendix B at the end of the book.)

Ask Yourself

1. Where would you place yourself on the five personality dimensions—conscientiousness, agreeableness, neuroticism (emotional stability vs. instability), openness, and extraversion? Where might your family and friends place you?

2. Are you a pessimist? Do you tend to have low expectations and to attribute bad events to your inability or to circumstances beyond your control? Or are you an optimist, perhaps even being excessively optimistic at times? How did either tendency influence your choice of school or major?

3. What possible selves do you dream of—or fear—becoming? To what extent do these imagined selves motivate you now?

⊙ WEB

Multiple-choice self-tests and more may be found at www.worthpublishers.com/myers

Psychological Disorders

moDULes

48
Introduction to Psychological Disorders

49
Anxiety Disorders

50
Dissociative, Personality, and Somatoform Disorders

51
Mood Disorders

52
Schizophrenia

I felt the need to clean my room at home in Indianapolis every Sunday and would spend four to five hours at it. I would take every book out of the bookcase, dust and put it back. At the time I loved doing it. Then I didn't want to do it anymore, but I couldn't stop. The clothes in my closet hung exactly two fingers apart. . . . I made a ritual of touching the wall in my bedroom before I went out because something bad would happen if I didn't do it the right way. I had a constant anxiety about it as a kid, and it made me think for the first time that I might be nuts.

Marc, diagnosed with obsessive-compulsive disorder (from Summers, 1996)

Whenever I get depressed it's because I've lost a sense of self. I can't find reasons to like myself. I think I'm ugly. I think no one likes me. . . . I become grumpy and short-tempered. Nobody wants to be around me. I'm left alone. Being alone confirms that I am ugly and not worth being with. I think I'm responsible for everything that goes wrong.

Greta, diagnosed with depression (from Thorne, 1993, p. 21)

Voices, like the roar of a crowd, came. I felt like Jesus; I was being crucified. It was dark. . . . I just continued to huddle under the blanket, feeling weak, laid bare and defenseless in a cruel world I could no longer understand.

Stuart, diagnosed with schizophrenia (from Emmons et al., 1997)

People are fascinated by the exceptional, the unusual, the abnormal. "The sun shines and warms and lights us and we have no curiosity to know why this is so," observed Ralph Waldo Emerson, "but we ask the reason of all evil, of pain, and hunger, and [unusual] people." But why such fascination with disturbed people? Do we see in them something of ourselves? At various moments, all of us feel, think, or act the way disturbed people do much of the time. We, too, get anxious, depressed, withdrawn, suspicious, or deluded, just less intensely and more briefly. It's no wonder that studying psychological disorders may at times evoke an eerie sense of self-recognition, one that illuminates the dynamics of our own personality. "To study the abnormal is the best way of understanding the normal," proposed William James (1842–1910).

Another reason for our curiosity is that so many of us have felt, either personally or through friends or family, the bewilderment and pain of a psychological disorder that may bring unexplained physical symptoms, irrational fears, or a feeling that life is not worth living. Indeed, as members of the human family, most of us will at some point encounter a psychologically disturbed person.

The World Health Organization (WHO, 2008) reports that, worldwide, some 450 million people suffer from mental or behavioral disorders. These disorders account for 15.4 percent of the years of life lost due to death or disability—scoring slightly below cardiovascular conditions and slightly above cancer (Murray & Lopez, 1996). Rates and symptoms of psychological disorders vary by culture, but no known society is free of two terrible maladies: depression and schizophrenia (Baumeister & Härter, 2007; Draguns, 1990a,b, 1997).

Module 48 introduces psychological disorders, explaining the major perspectives, categories, and risks of labeling, and outlines the prevalence of the various disorders. Module 49 describes *anxiety disorders,* which are characterized by persistent distressing anxiety or maladaptive behaviors that reduce anxiety. Module 50 focuses on the rare and controversial *dissociative disorders,* the problematic *personality disorders* that impair social functioning, and the *somatoform disorders* that involve bodily symptoms in the absence of a physical cause. Module 51 examines in depth the emotional extremes of *mood disorders.* And Module 52 outlines the symptoms and characteristics of those suffering from *schizophrenia,* a frightening split from reality.

The normallity of occasional abnormality Many of us at times feel the bewilderment, pain, or sense of worthlessness that, if prolonged and disruptive, can define a disorder. Nearly half of collegians report feeling, at some point during the last school year, "so depressed it was difficult to function" (ACHA, 2006).

Ansgar/zefa/Corbis

MODULE 48

Introduction to Psychological Disorders

Defining Psychological Disorders

Understanding Psychological Disorders

Classifying Psychological Disorders

Labeling Psychological Disorders

Rates of Psychological Disorders

Most people would agree that someone who is too depressed to get out of bed for weeks at a time has a psychological disorder. But what about those who, having experienced a loss, are unable to resume their usual social activities? Where should we draw the line between sadness and depression? Between zany creativity and bizarre irrationality? Between normality and abnormality? Let's start with these questions:

▶ How should we *define* psychological disorders?

▶ How should we *understand* disorders—as sicknesses that need to be diagnosed and cured, or as natural responses to a troubling environment?

▶ How should we *classify* psychological disorders? And can we do so in a way that allows us to help people without stigmatizing them with *labels*?

▶ How *prevalent* are these disorders, and who is likely to experience them?

▶‖ Defining Psychological Disorders

48-1 How should we draw the line between normality and disorder?

Mental health workers view **psychological disorders** as patterns of thoughts, feelings, or behaviors that are deviant, distressful, and dysfunctional (Comer, 2004).

Being different *(deviant)* from most other people in one's culture is *part* of what it takes to define a psychological disorder. As the reclusive poet Emily Dickinson observed in 1862,

> *Assent—and you are sane—*
> *Demur—you're straightaway dangerous—*
> *and handled with a Chain.*

Standards for deviant behavior vary by context and by culture. In one context—wartime—mass killing may be viewed as normal and even heroic. In some contexts, people are presumed deranged when they hear voices. But in cultures practicing ancestor worship, people may claim to talk with the dead and not be seen as disordered because other people find them rational (Friedrich, 1987).

Standards for deviance also vary with time. From 1952 through December 9, 1973, homosexuality was classified as an illness. By day's end on December 10, it was not. The American Psychiatric Association had dropped homosexuality as a disorder because more and more of its members no longer viewed it as a psychological problem. (Later research has revealed that the stigma and stresses associated with being homosexual do, however, increase the risk of mental health problems [Meyer, 2003].) In this new century, controversy swirls over the frequent diagnosing of children with *attention-deficit hyperactivity disorder* (see Thinking Critically About ADHD—Normal High Energy or Genuine Disorder? on the next page).

But there is more to a disorder than being deviant. Olympic gold medalists deviate from the norm in their physical abilities, and society honors them. To be considered disordered, deviant behavior usually causes the person *distress.* Marc, Greta, and Stuart were all clearly distressed by their behaviors.

"Who in the rainbow can draw the line where the violet tint ends and the orange tint begins? Distinctly we see the difference of the colors, but where exactly does the one first blendingly enter into the other? So with sanity and insanity?"
Herman Melville, *Billy Budd, Sailor*, 1924

psychological disorder deviant, distressful, and dysfunctional patterns of thoughts, feelings, or behaviors.

Culture and normality Men of the West African Wodaabe tribe put on elaborate makeup and costumes to attract women. In Western society, the same behavior would break behavioral norms and might be judged abnormal.

Carol Beckwith

Thinking Critically About

ADHD—Normal High Energy or Genuine Disorder?

Eight-year-old Todd has always been energetic. At home, he chatters away and darts from one activity to the next, rarely settling down to read a book or focus on a game. At play, he is reckless and overreacts when playmates bump into him or take one of his toys. At school, his exasperated teacher complains that fidgety Todd doesn't listen, follow instructions, or stay in his seat and do his lessons.

If taken for a psychological evaluation, Todd may be diagnosed with **attention-deficit hyperactivity disorder (ADHD),** as are some 4 percent of children who display at least one of its key symptoms (extreme inattention, hyperactivity, and impulsivity) (NIMH, 2003).

To skeptics, being distractible, fidgety, and impulsive sounds like a "disorder" caused by a single genetic variation: a Y chromosome. And sure enough, ADHD is diagnosed two to three times more often in boys than in girls. Does energetic child + boring school = ADHD overdiagnosis? Is the label being applied to healthy schoolchildren who, in more natural outdoor environments, would seem perfectly normal?

Skeptics think so. In the decade after 1987, they note, the proportion of American children being treated for ADHD nearly quadrupled (Olfson et al., 2003). By 2005, a Gallup survey showed that 10 percent of American 13- to 17-year-olds were being medicated for ADHD (Mason, 2005). How commonplace the diagnosis is depends in part on teacher referrals. Some teachers refer lots of kids for ADHD assessment, others none. ADHD rates have varied by a factor of 10 in different counties of New York State (Carlson, 2000).

On the other side of the debate are those who argue that the more frequent diagnoses of ADHD today reflect increased awareness of the disorder, especially in those areas where rates are highest. They acknowledge that diagnoses can be subjective and sometimes inconsistent—ADHD is not as objectively defined as is a broken arm. Nevertheless, declared the World Federation for Mental Health (2005), "there is strong agreement among the international scientific community that ADHD is a real neurobiological disorder whose existence should no longer be debated." In neuroimaging studies, ADHD has associations with certain brain activity patterns, notes a consensus statement by 75 researchers (Barkley et al., 2002).

What, then, is known about ADHD's causes? It is not caused by too much sugar or poor schools. (Researchers have found, however, that toddlers who watch lots of TV are, at age 7, more likely than average to display ADHD symptoms [Christakis et al., 2004].) It often coexists with a learning disorder or with defiant and temper-prone behavior. The U.S. National Institute of Mental Health (1999, 2003) reports that ADHD is heritable, and research teams are sleuthing the culprit genes (Brookes et al., 2006). It is treatable with nonaddictive medications such as Ritalin and Adderall, which are stimulants but help calm hyperactivity and increase one's ability to sit and focus on a task. Psychological therapies, such as those focused on shaping behaviors in the classroom and at home, have also helped address the distress of ADHD.

New research is seeking not only more information on causes but also a more objective assessment of ADHD. Possibilities include a physical measure of fidgeting, an eye-tracking device that gauges ability to focus on and follow spots of light, and more detailed brain imaging (Ashtari et al., 2004; Pavlidis, 2005; Teicher, 2002).

Other research is targeting effects of long-term use of stimulant drugs. About 80 percent of children medicated for ADHD still require medication as teens, as do 50 percent or more as adults. People appear to tolerate long-term use with no increased risk of substance abuse (Biederman et al., 1999). However, one major long-term study found that medication benefits had disappeared after three years (Jensen et al., 2007). A possible explanation comes from another recent study that used brain imaging to observe the development of children diagnosed with ADHD (Shaw et al., 2007). Compared with their peers, these children's brain maturation was normal but lagged by about three years, with delayed thinning, or pruning, of the frontal cerebral cortex. Thus, many fidgety, hyperactive 5-year-olds mature into normal teens.

The bottom line: Extreme inattention, hyperactivity, and impulsivity can derail social, academic, and vocational achievements, and these symptoms can be treated with medication and other treatment. But the debate continues over whether normal rambunctiousness is too often diagnosed as a psychiatric disorder, and whether there is a cost to the long-term use of stimulant drugs in treating ADHD.

attention-deficit hyperactivity disorder (ADHD) a psychological disorder marked by the appearance by age 7 of one or more of three key symptoms: extreme inattention, hyperactivity, and impulsivity.

Deviant and distressful behaviors are more likely to be considered disordered when also judged to be a *harmful dysfunction* (Wakefield, 1992, 2006). Marc's distracting obsessive behaviors, for example, interfered with his work and leisure. By this measuring stick, even typical behaviors, such as the occasional despondency many college students feel, may signal a psychological disorder *if* they become disabling. Dysfunction is key to defining a disorder: An intense fear of spiders may be deviant, but if it doesn't impair your life it is not a disorder.

▶‖ Understanding Psychological Disorders

48-2 What perspectives can help us understand psychological disorders?

To explain puzzling behavior, people in earlier times often presumed that strange forces—the movements of the stars, godlike powers, or evil spirits—were at work. Had you lived during the Middle Ages, you might have said "The devil made him do it," and you might have approved of a cure to rid the evil force by exorcising the demon. Until the last two centuries, "mad" people were sometimes caged in zoolike conditions or given "therapies" appropriate to a demon: beatings, burning, or castration. In other times, therapy included trephination (drilling holes in the skull), pulling teeth, removing lengths of intestines, cauterizing the clitoris, or giving transfusions of animal blood (Farina, 1982).

The Medical Model

In opposition to brutal treatments, reformers, including Philippe Pinel (1745–1826) in France, insisted that madness is not demon possession but a sickness of the mind caused by severe stresses and inhumane conditions. For Pinel and others, "moral treatment" included boosting patients' morale by unchaining them and talking with them, and by replacing brutality with gentleness, isolation with activity, and filth with clean air and sunshine.

By the 1800s, the discovery that syphilis infects the brain and distorts the mind provided the impetus for further reform. Hospitals replaced asylums, and the medical world began searching for physical causes of mental disorders, and for treatments that would cure them. Today, this **medical model** is recognizable in the terminology of the mental *health* movement: A mental *illness* (also called a *psychopathology*) needs to be *diagnosed* on the basis of its *symptoms* and *cured* through *therapy,* which may include *treatment* in a psychiatric *hospital.*

The medical perspective has gained credibility from recent discoveries that genetically influenced abnormalities in brain structure and biochemistry contribute to many disorders. But as we will see, psychological factors, such as enduring or traumatic stress, also play an important role.

Yesterday's "therapy" In other times and places, psychologically disordered people sometimes received brutal treatments, including the trephination evident in this Stone Age skull. Drilling skull holes like these may have been an attempt to release evil spirits and cure those with mental disorders. Did this patient survive the "cure"?

"Moral treatment" Under Philippe Pinel's influence, hospitals sometimes sponsored patient dances, such as the "Lunatic Ball" depicted in this painting by George Bellows (*Dance in a Madhouse*).

medical model   the concept that diseases, in this case psychological disorders, have physical causes that can be *diagnosed, treated,* and, in most cases, *cured,* often through *treatment* in a hospital.

"It's no measure of health to be well adjusted to a profoundly sick society."
Krishnamurti, 1895–1986

|| In Malaysia, *amok* describes a sudden outburst of violent behavior (thus the phrase "run amok"). ||

The Biopsychosocial Approach

Today's psychologists contend that *all* behavior, whether called normal or disordered, arises from the interaction of nature (genetic and physiological factors) and nurture (past and present experiences). To presume that a person is "mentally ill," they say, attributes the condition to a "sickness" that must be found and cured. But instead or additionally, there may be a difficulty in the person's environment, in the person's current interpretations of events, or in the person's bad habits and poor social skills.

Evidence of such effects comes from links between specific disorders and cultures (Beardsley, 1994; Castillo, 1997). Cultures differ in their sources of stress, and they produce different ways of coping. The eating disorders anorexia nervosa and bulimia nervosa, for example, occur mostly in Western cultures. Latin America lays claim to *susto,* a condition marked by severe anxiety, restlessness, and a fear of black magic. *Taijinkyofusho,* social anxiety about one's appearance combined with a readiness to blush and a fear of eye contact, appears in Japan. Such disorders may share an underlying dynamic (such as anxiety) while differing in the symptoms (an eating problem or a type of fear) manifested in a particular culture. But not all disorders are culture-bound. As noted earlier, depression and schizophrenia occur worldwide. From Asia to Africa and across the Americas, schizophrenia's symptoms often include irrationality and incoherent speech.

To assess the whole set of influences—genetic predispositions and physiological states; inner psychological dynamics; and social and cultural circumstances—the biopsychosocial model helps (**FIGURE 48.1**). This approach recognizes that mind and body are inseparable. Negative emotions contribute to physical illness, and physical abnormalities contribute to negative emotions. We are mind embodied.

FIGURE 48.1 The biopsychosocial approach to psychological disorders Today's psychology studies how biological, psychological, and social-cultural factors interact to produce specific psychological disorders.

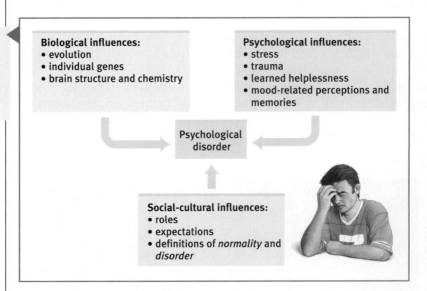

▶|| Classifying Psychological Disorders

48-3   How and why do clinicians classify psychological disorders?

In biology and the other sciences, classification creates order. To classify an animal as a "mammal" says a great deal—that it is warm-blooded, has hair or fur, and nourishes its young with milk. In psychiatry and psychology, too, classification orders and describes symptoms. To classify a person's disorder as "schizophrenia" suggests that the person talks incoherently; hallucinates or has delusions (bizarre beliefs); shows either little emotion or inappropriate emotion; or is socially withdrawn. "Schizophrenia" provides a handy shorthand for describing a complex disorder.

In psychiatry and psychology, diagnostic classification aims not only to describe a disorder but also to predict its future course, imply appropriate treatment, and stimulate research into its causes. Indeed, to study a disorder we must first name and describe it. A current authoritative scheme for classifying psychological disorders is the **DSM-IV-TR.** This volume is the American Psychiatric Association's *Diagnostic and Statistical Manual of Mental Disorders,* Fourth Edition, updated as a 2000 "text revision"; a more substantially revised DSM-V will appear in 2012. (A set of case illustrations accompanying DSM-IV-TR provides several of this book's case examples.) DSM-IV-TR was developed in coordination with the tenth edition of the World Health Organization's *International Classification of Diseases* (ICD-10), which covers both medical and psychological disorders.

Despite its medical terminology (*diagnosing, symptoms, illness*), most practitioners find the DSM-IV-TR a helpful and practical tool. It is also financially necessary: North American health insurance companies usually require an ICD diagnosis before they pay for therapy.

DSM-IV-TR defines a diagnostic process and 16 clinical syndromes (**TABLE 48.1**). Without presuming to explain their causes, it describes various disorders. To be helpful and useful, these categories and diagnostic guidelines must be reliable, and to a reasonable extent they are. If one psychiatrist or psychologist diagnoses someone as having, say, catatonic schizophrenia, the chances are good that another mental health worker will independently give the same diagnosis. Following these guidelines,

"I'm always like this, and my family was wondering if you could prescribe a mild depressant."

© 1992 by Sidney Harris.

TABLE 48.1 How Are Psychological Disorders Diagnosed?

Based on assessments, interviews, and observations, many clinicians diagnose by answering the following questions from the five levels, or *axes,* of the DSM-IV-TR.

Axis I Is a *Clinical Syndrome* present?
Using specifically defined criteria, clinicians may select none, one, or more syndromes from the following list:

- Disorders usually first diagnosed in infancy, childhood, and adolescence
- Delirium, dementia, amnesia, and other cognitive disorders
- Mental disorders due to a general medical condition
- Substance-related disorders
- Schizophrenia and other psychotic disorders
- Mood disorders
- Anxiety disorders
- Somatoform disorders
- Factitious disorders (intentionally faked)
- Dissociative disorders
- Eating disorders
- Sexual disorders and gender identity disorder
- Sleep disorders
- Impulse-control disorders not classified elsewhere
- Adjustment disorders
- Other conditions that may be a focus of clinical attention

Axis II Is a *Personality Disorder* or *Intellectual Disability* present?
Clinicians may or may not also select one of these two conditions.

Axis III Is a *General Medical Condition,* such as diabetes, hypertension, or arthritis, also present?

Axis IV Are *Psychosocial* or *Environmental Problems,* such as school or housing issues, also present?

Axis V What is the *Global Assessment* of this person's functioning?
Clinicians assign a code from 0–100.

DSM-IV-TR the American Psychiatric Association's *Diagnostic and Statistical Manual of Mental Disorders,* Fourth Edition, with an updated "text revision"; a widely used system for classifying psychological disorders.

clinicians answer a series of objective questions about observable behaviors, such as, "Is the person afraid to leave home?" In one study, 16 psychologists used this structured-interview procedure to diagnose 75 psychiatric patients as suffering from (1) depression, (2) generalized anxiety, or (3) some other disorder (Riskind et al., 1987). Without knowing the first psychologist's diagnosis, another psychologist viewed a videotape of each interview and offered a second opinion. For 83 percent of the patients, the two opinions agreed.

Some critics have faulted the manual for casting too wide a net and bringing "almost any kind of behavior within the compass of psychiatry" (Eysenck et al., 1983). Others note that as the number of disorder categories has swelled (from 60 in the 1950's DSM to 400 in today's), so has the number of adults who meet the criteria for at least one of them—26 percent in any year, according to the U.S. National Institute of Mental Health (2008), and 46 percent at some time in their lives (Kessler et al., 2005). The number of children diagnosed with psychological disorders has also mushroomed, tripling to 6 million children since the early 1990s, according to some reports (Carey, 2006). Today's adolescent mood swings are more often taken to be "bipolar disorder." Temper tantrums, arguing, touchiness, and spitefulness are more often taken to be "oppositional defiant disorder." Inattentive, impulsive, fidgety children are more often taken to have ADHD. As a complement to the DSM, some psychologists are offering a manual of human strengths and virtues (see Close-Up: The "un-DSM": A Diagnostic Manual of Human Strengths).

CLOSE-UP

The "un-DSM": A Diagnostic Manual of Human Strengths

Psychologists Christopher Peterson and Martin Seligman (2004) have noted the usefulness of the DSM-IV-TR in ordering and defining dysfunctions. Would it not also be useful, these researchers ask, to have a companion catalog of human strengths—the thinking-feeling-action tendencies that contribute to the *good* life, for self and others?

The result, *The Values in Action Classification of Strengths,* resembles the DSM-IV-TR in proposing a research-based common vocabulary. A questionnaire, which has been taken by some 1 million people worldwide (at viastrengths.org), assesses six clusters of 24 strengths:

- *Wisdom and knowledge*—curiosity; love of learning; critical judgment and open-mindedness; creativity; and perspective (wisdom)

Building strengths In their work for Habitat for Humanity, former U.S. President Jimmy Carter and First Lady Rosalynn Carter model strengths related to humaneness and justice.

- *Courage (overcoming opposition)*— bravery/valor; industry and perseverance; integrity and honesty; and vitality (zest and enthusiasm)

- *Humanity*—love; kindness; and social intelligence

- *Justice*—citizenship and teamwork; fairness and equity; and leadership

- *Temperance*—humility; self-control; prudence and caution; and forgiveness and mercy

- *Transcendence*—appreciation of beauty, awe/wonder; gratitude; hope and optimism; playfulness and humor; and spirituality and purpose

This classification of human strengths is an expression of the *positive psychology movement*. Psychological science seeks to understand and help alleviate human ills and evils, agree positive psychology advocates, but also to understand and promote human strengths and virtues.

▶|| Labeling Psychological Disorders

48-4   Why do some psychologists criticize the use of diagnostic labels?

The DSM has other critics who register a more fundamental complaint—that these labels are at best arbitrary and at worst value judgments masquerading as science. Once we label a person, we view that person differently (Farina, 1982). Labels create preconceptions that guide our perceptions and our interpretations.

In a now-classic study of the biasing power of labels, David Rosenhan (1973) and seven others went to hospital admissions offices, complaining of "hearing voices" saying *empty, hollow,* and *thud.* Apart from this complaint and giving false names and occupations, they answered questions truthfully. All eight normal people were misdiagnosed with disorders.

Should we be surprised? As one psychiatrist noted, if someone swallows blood, goes to an emergency room, and spits it up, should we fault the doctor for diagnosing a bleeding ulcer? Surely not. But what followed the diagnosis in the Rosenhan study was startling. Until being released an average of 19 days later, the "patients" exhibited no further symptoms. Yet after analyzing their (quite normal) life histories, clinicians were able to "discover" the causes of their disorders, such as reacting to mixed emotions about a parent. Even the routine behavior of taking notes was misinterpreted as a symptom.

Labels matter. When people watched videotaped interviews, those told the interviewees were job applicants perceived them as normal (Langer et al., 1974, 1980). Those who thought they were watching psychiatric or cancer patients perceived them as "different from most people." Therapists who thought an interviewee was a psychiatric patient perceived him as "frightened of his own aggressive impulses," a "passive, dependent type," and so forth. A label can, as Rosenhan discovered, have "a life and an influence of its own."

Surveys in Europe and North America have demonstrated the stigmatizing power of labels (Page, 1977). Getting a job or finding a place to rent can be a challenge for those known to be just released from prison—or a mental hospital. But as we are coming to understand that many psychological disorders are diseases of the brain, not failures of character, the stigma seems to be lifting (Solomon, 1996). Public figures are feeling freer to "come out" and speak with candor about their struggles with disorders such as depression. And the more contact people have with individuals with disorders, the more accepting their attitudes are (Kolodziej & Johnson, 1996).

Nevertheless, stereotypes linger in media portrayals of psychological disorders. Some are reasonably accurate and sympathetic. But too often people with disorders are portrayed as objects of humor or ridicule *(As Good as It Gets),* as homicidal maniacs (Hannibal Lecter in *Silence of the Lambs),* or as freaks (Nairn, 2007). Apart from the few who experience threatening delusions and hallucinated voices that command a violent act, mental disorders seldom lead to violence (Harris & Lurigio, 2007). In real life, people with disorders are more likely to be the victims of violence, rather than the perpetrators (Marley & Bulia, 2001). Indeed, reports the U.S. Surgeon General's Office (1999, p. 7), "There is very little risk of violence or harm to a stranger from casual contact with an individual who has a mental disorder." (Although most people with psychological disorders are not violent, those who are create a moral dilemma for society. For more on this topic, see Thinking Critically About: Insanity and Responsibility on the next page.)

Not only can labels bias perceptions, they can also change reality. When teachers are told certain students are "gifted," when students expect someone to be "hostile," or when interviewers check to see whether someone is "extraverted," they may act in

"One of the unpardonable sins, in the eyes of most people, is for a man to go about unlabeled. The world regards such a person as the police do an unmuzzled dog, not under proper control."

T. H. Huxley, *Evolution and Ethics,* 1893

Thinking Critically About

Insanity and Responsibility

"My brain . . . my genes . . . my bad up-bringing made me do it." Such defenses were anticipated by Shakespeare's *Hamlet*. If I wrong someone when not myself, he explained, "then Hamlet does it not, Hamlet denies it. Who does it then? His madness." Such is the essence of a legal insanity defense, created in 1843 after a deluded Scotsman tried to shoot the prime minister (who he thought was persecuting him) but killed an assistant by mistake. Like U.S. President Ronald Reagan's near-assassin, John Hinckley, Scotsman Daniel M'Naughten was sent to a mental hospital rather than to prison.

In both cases, the public was outraged. "Hinckley Insane, Public Mad," declared one headline. And they were mad again when a deranged Jeffrey Dahmer in 1991 admitted murdering 15 young men and eating parts of their bodies. They were mad in 1998 when 15-year-old Kip Kinkel, driven by "those voices in my head," killed his parents and 2 fellow Springfield, Oregon, students and wounded 25 others. And they were mad in 2002 when Andrea Yates, after being taken off her antipsychotic medication, was tried in Texas for drowning her five children. All

Jail or hospital? Two weeks after being taken off antipsychotic medication by her psychiatrist, Andrea Yates drowned her five children, ages 7, 5, 3, 2, and 6 months, in her bathtub, apparently believing she was sparing them "the fires of hell." Although she was psychotic, one jury rejected the insanity defense, believing Yates still could have discerned right from wrong. On retrial, a second jury found her not guilty by reason of insanity.

of these people were sent to jails, not hospitals, following their arrests (though later, after another trial, Yates was instead hospitalized).

Most people with psychological disorders are not violent. But what should society do with those who are? A 1999 U.S. Justice Department study found that about 16 percent of U.S. jail and prison inmates had severe mental disorders. This is roughly 100,000 more than the 183,000 psychiatric inpatients in all types of U.S. hospitals (Bureau of the Census, 2004; Butterfield, 1999). Many people who have been executed or are now on death row have been limited by intellectual disability or motivated by delusional voices. The State of Arkansas forcibly medicated one murderer with schizophrenia, Charles Singleton, with antipsychotic drugs—in order to make him mentally competent, so that he could then be put to death.

Which of Yates' two juries made the right decision? The first, which decided that people who commit such rare but terrible crimes should be held responsible? Or the second, which decided to blame the "madness" that clouds their vision? As we come to better understand the biological and environmental basis for all human behavior, from generosity to vandalism, when should we—and should we not—hold people accountable for their actions?

ways that elicit the very behavior expected (Snyder, 1984). Someone who was led to think you are nasty may treat you coldly, leading you to respond as a mean-spirited person would. Labels can serve as self-fulfilling prophecies.

But let us remember the *benefits* of diagnostic labels. Mental health professionals use labels to communicate about their cases, to comprehend the underlying causes, and to discern effective treatment programs.

"What's the use of their having names," the Gnat said, "if they won't answer to them?"
"No use to *them*," said Alice; "but it's useful to the people that name them, I suppose."
Lewis Carroll, *Through the Looking-Glass*, 1871

▶‖ Rates of Psychological Disorders

48-5 How many people suffer, or have suffered, from a psychological disorder?

Who is most vulnerable to psychological disorders? At what times of life? To answer such questions, various countries have conducted lengthy, structured interviews with representative samples of thousands of their citizens. After asking hundreds of questions that probed for symptoms—"Has there ever been a period of two weeks or more when you felt like you wanted to die?"—the researchers have estimated the current, prior-year, and lifetime prevalence of various disorders.

How many people have, or have had, a psychological disorder?
More than most of us suppose:

▶ The U.S. National Institute of Mental Health (2008, based on
Kessler et al., 2005) estimates that 26 percent of adult Ameri-
cans "suffer from a diagnosable mental disorder in a given year"
(**TABLE 48.2**).

▶ National population surveys reveal differing annual rates in
Australia (16 percent), Germany (31 percent), and the Netherlands (23 percent) (Baumeister & Härter, 2007).

▶ A twenty-first-century World Health Organization (2004) study—
based on 90-minute interviews of 60,463 people—estimated the
number of prior-year mental disorders in 20 countries. As **FIGURE
48.2** displays, the lowest rate of reported mental disorders was in
Shanghai, the highest rate in the United States. Moreover, immigrants to the United States from Mexico, Africa, and Asia average
better mental health than their native U.S. counterparts (Breslau
et al., 2007). For example, compared with people who have recently immigrated from Mexico, Mexican-Americans born in the
United States are at greater risk of mental disorder.

TABLE 48.2 Percentage of Americans Reporting Selected Psychological Disorders in the Past Year

Psychological Disorder	Percentage
Generalized anxiety	3.1
Social phobia	6.8
Phobia of specific object or situation	8.7
Mood disorder	9.5
Obsessive-compulsive disorder	1.0
Schizophrenia	1.1
Post-traumatic stress disorder (PTSD)	3.5
Attention-deficit hyperactivity disorder (ADHD)	4.1
Any mental disorder	26.2

Source: National Institute of Mental Health, 2008.

Who is most vulnerable to mental disorders? As we have seen, the answer varies
with the disorder. One predictor of mental disorder, poverty, crosses ethnic and gender lines. The incidence of serious psychological disorders is doubly high among those
below the poverty line (Centers for Disease Control,
1992). Like so many other correlations, the poverty-
disorder association raises a chicken-and-egg question: Does poverty cause disorders? Or do disorders
cause poverty? It is both, though the answer varies
with the disorder. Schizophrenia understandably
leads to poverty. Yet the stresses and demoralization
of poverty can also precipitate disorders, especially
depression in women and substance abuse in men
(Dohrenwend et al., 1992). In one natural experiment on the poverty-pathology link, researchers
tracked rates of behavior problems in North Carolina Native American children as economic development enabled a dramatic reduction in their
community's poverty rate. As the study began, children of poverty exhibited more deviant and aggressive behaviors. After four years, children whose
families had moved above the poverty line exhibited
a 40 percent decrease in the behavior problems,
while those who continued in their previous positions below or above the poverty line exhibited no
change (Costello et al., 2003).

As **TABLE 48.3** on the next page indicates, there is a
wide range of risk and protective factors for mental
disorders. At what times of life do disorders strike?
Usually by early adulthood. "Over 75 percent of our
sample with any disorder had experienced its first
symptoms by age 24," reported Lee Robins and
Darrel Regier (1991, p. 331). The symptoms of antisocial personality disorder and of phobias are among

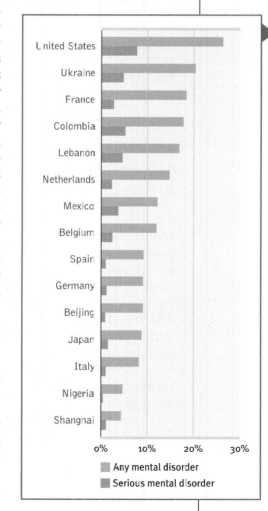

**FIGURE 48.2 Prior-year
prevalence of disorders in
selected areas** From World
Health Organization (2004)
interviews in 20 countries.

TABLE 48.3 Risk and Protective Factors for Mental Disorders

Risk Factors	Protective Factors
Academic failure	Aerobic exercise
Birth complications	Community offering empowerment, opportunity, and security
Caring for chronically ill or patients with dementia	Economic independence
Child abuse and neglect	Feelings of security
Chronic insomnia	Feelings of mastery and control
Chronic pain	Effective parenting
Family disorganization or conflict	Literacy
Low birth weight	Positive attachment and early bonding
Low socioeconomic status	Positive parent-child relationships
Medical illness	Problem-solving skills
Neurochemical imbalance	Resilient coping with stress and adversity
Parental mental illness	Self-esteem
Parental substance abuse	Social and work skills
Personal loss and bereavement	Social support from family and friends
Poor work skills and habits	
Reading disabilities	
Sensory disabilities	
Social incompetence	
Stressful life events	
Substance abuse	
Trauma experiences	

Source: World Health Organization (2004a,b).

the earliest to appear, at a median age of 8 and 10, respectively. Symptoms of alcohol dependency, obsessive-compulsive disorder, bipolar disorder, and schizophrenia appear at a median age near 20. Major depression often hits somewhat later, at a median age of 25. Such findings make clear the need for research and treatment to help the growing number of people, especially teenagers and young adults, who suffer the bewilderment and pain of a psychological disorder.

Although mindful of the pain, we can also be encouraged by the many successful people—including Leonardo da Vinci, Isaac Newton, and Leo Tolstoy—who pursued brilliant careers while enduring psychological difficulties. So have 18 U.S. presidents, including the periodically depressed Abraham Lincoln, according to one psychiatric analysis of their biographies (Davidson et al., 2006). The bewilderment, fear, and sorrow caused by psychological disorders are real. But hope, too, is real, as our understanding of these disorders continues to grow.

REVIEW

Introduction to Psychological Disorders

48-1 **How should we draw the line between normality and disorder?** Psychologists and psychiatrists consider behavior disordered when it is deviant, distressful, and dysfunctional. The definition of deviant varies with context and culture. It also varies with time; for example, some children who might have been judged rambunctious a few decades ago now are being diagnosed with *attention-deficit hyperactivity disorder*.

48-2 **What perspectives can help us understand psychological disorders?** The *medical model* assumes that *psychological disorders* are mental illnesses that can be diagnosed on the basis of their symptoms and cured through therapy, sometimes in a hospital. The biopsychosocial perspective assumes that disordered behavior, like other behavior, arises from genetic predispositions and physiological states; inner psychological dynamics; and social-cultural circumstances.

48-3 **How and why do clinicians classify psychological disorders?** The fourth edition (text revised) of the American Psychiatric Association's *Diagnostic and Statistical Manual of Mental Disorders (DSM-IV-TR)* provides diagnostic labels and descriptions that aid mental health professionals by providing a common language and shared concepts for communication and research. Most U.S. health insurance organizations require DSM-IV-TR diagnoses before they will pay for therapy.

48-4 **Why do some psychologists criticize the use of diagnostic labels?** Labels can create preconceptions that unfairly stigmatize people and can bias our perceptions of their past and present behavior. One label, "insanity"—used in some legal defenses—raises moral and ethical questions about how a society should treat people who have disorders and have committed crimes.

48-5 **How many people suffer, or have suffered, from a psychological disorder?** Mental health surveys in many countries provide varying estimates of the rates of psychological disorders. Poverty is a predictor of mental illness. Conditions and experiences associated with poverty contribute to the development of mental disorders, but some mental disorders, such as schizophrenia, can drive people into poverty. Among Americans who have ever experienced a psychological disorder, the three most common are phobias, alcohol dependency, and mood disorder.

Terms and Concepts to Remember

psychological disorder, p. 599   medical model, p. 601

attention-deficit hyperactivity   DSM-IV-TR, p. 603
   disorder (ADHD), p. 600

Test Yourself

1. What is the biopsychosocial perspective, and why is it important in our understanding of psychological disorders?

2. What is the relationship between poverty and psychological disorders?

(Answers to the Test Yourself questions can be found in Appendix B at the end of the book.)

Ask Yourself

1. How would you draw the line between sending disturbed criminals to prisons or to mental hospitals? Would the person's history (for example, having suffered child abuse) influence your decision?

2. Do you have a family member or friend who has experienced a psychological disorder? If so, has anything you have read in this module increased your understanding of the challenges that person has been facing?

∞ WEB

Multiple-choice self-tests and more may be found at www.worthpublishers.com/myers

Generalized Anxiety Disorder

Panic Disorder

Phobias

Obsessive-Compulsive Disorder

Post-Traumatic Stress Disorder

Understanding Anxiety Disorders

Snapshots

Obsessing about obsessive-compulsive disorder.

|| Gender and anxiety: Eight months after 9/11, more U.S. women (34 percent) than men (19 percent) told Gallup (2002) they were still less willing than before 9/11 to go into skyscrapers or fly on planes. In early 2003, more women (57 percent) than men (36 percent) were "somewhat worried" about becoming a terrorist victim (Jones, 2003). ||

MODULE 49

Anxiety Disorders

49-1 What are anxiety disorders, and how do they differ from ordinary worries and fears?

Anxiety is part of life. Speaking in front of a class, peering down from a ledge, or waiting to play in a big game, any one of us might feel anxious. At times we may feel enough anxiety to avoid making eye contact or talking with someone—"shyness," we call it. Fortunately for most of us, our uneasiness is not intense and persistent. If it becomes so, we may have one of the **anxiety disorders,** marked by distressing, persistent anxiety or dysfunctional anxiety-reducing behaviors. Let's consider these five:

▸ *Generalized anxiety disorder,* in which a person is unexplainably and continually tense and uneasy
▸ *Panic disorder,* in which a person experiences sudden episodes of intense dread
▸ *Phobias,* in which a person feels irrationally and intensely afraid of a specific object or situation
▸ *Obsessive-compulsive disorder,* in which a person is troubled by repetitive thoughts or actions
▸ *Post-traumatic stress disorder*, in which a person has lingering memories, nightmares, and other symptoms for weeks after a severely threatening, uncontrollable event

In its own way, each anxiety disorder harms quality of life (Olatunji et al., 2007).

▸|| Generalized Anxiety Disorder

For the past two years, Tom, a 27-year-old electrician, has been bothered by dizziness, sweating palms, heart palpitations, and ringing in his ears. He feels edgy and sometimes finds himself shaking. With reasonable success, he hides his symptoms from his family and co-workers. But he allows himself few other social contacts, and occasionally he has to leave work. His family doctor and a neurologist can find no physical problem.

Tom's unfocused, out-of-control, negative feelings suggest **generalized anxiety disorder.** The symptoms of this disorder are commonplace; their persistence is not. People with this condition (two-thirds are women) worry continually, and they are often jittery, agitated, and sleep-deprived. Concentration is difficult, as attention switches from worry to worry, and their tension and apprehension may leak out through furrowed brows, twitching eyelids, trembling, perspiration, or fidgeting.

One of the worst characteristics of this disorder is that the person cannot identify, and therefore cannot deal with or avoid, its cause. To use Sigmund Freud's term, the anxiety is *free-floating.* Generalized anxiety disorder is often accompanied by depressed mood, but even without depression it tends to be disabling (Hunt et al., 2004; Moffitt et al., 2007b). Moreover, it may lead to physical problems, such as high blood pressure.

Many people with generalized anxiety disorder were maltreated and inhibited as children (Moffitt et al., 2007a). As time passes, however, emotions tend to mellow, and by age 50, generalized anxiety disorder becomes rare (Rubio & López-Ibor, 2007).

▶‖ Panic Disorder

Panic disorder is an anxiety tornado. It strikes suddenly, wreaks havoc, and disappears. For the 1 person in 75 with this disorder, anxiety suddenly escalates into a terrifying *panic attack*—a minutes-long episode of intense fear that something horrible is about to happen. Heart palpitations, shortness of breath, choking sensations, trembling, or dizziness typically accompany the panic, which may be misperceived as a heart attack or other serious physical ailment. Smokers have at least a doubled risk of panic disorder (Zvolensky & Bernstein, 2005). Because nicotine is a stimulant, lighting up doesn't lighten up.

One woman recalled suddenly feeling "hot and as though I couldn't breathe. My heart was racing and I started to sweat and tremble and I was sure I was going to faint. Then my fingers started to feel numb and tingly and things seemed unreal. It was so bad I wondered if I was dying and asked my husband to take me to the emergency room. By the time we got there (about 10 minutes) the worst of the attack was over and I just felt washed out" (Greist et al., 1986).

▶‖ Phobias

Phobias are anxiety disorders in which an irrational fear causes the person to avoid some object, activity, or situation. Many people accept their phobias and live with them, but others are incapacitated by their efforts to avoid the feared situation. Marilyn, an otherwise healthy and happy 28-year-old, so fears thunderstorms that she feels anxious as soon as a weather forecaster mentions possible storms later in the week. If her husband is away and a storm is forecast, she may stay with a close relative. During a storm, she hides from windows and buries her head to avoid seeing the lightning.

Other *specific phobias* may focus on animals, insects, heights, blood, or close spaces (**FIGURE 49.1**). People avoid the stimulus that arouses the fear, hiding during thunderstorms or avoiding high places.

Not all phobias have such specific triggers. *Social phobia* is shyness taken to an extreme. Those with a social phobia, an intense fear of being scrutinized by others, avoid potentially embarrassing social situations, such as speaking up, eating out, or going to parties—or will sweat, tremble, or have diarrhea when doing so.

People who have experienced several panic attacks may come to fear the fear itself and avoid situations where the panic has struck before. If the fear is intense enough, it may become *agoraphobia,* fear or avoidance of situations in which escape might be difficult or help unavailable when panic strikes. Given such fear, people may avoid being outside the home, in a crowd, on a bus, or on an elevator.

anxiety disorders psychological disorders characterized by distressing, persistent anxiety or maladaptive behaviors that reduce anxiety.

generalized anxiety disorder an anxiety disorder in which a person is continually tense, apprehensive, and in a state of autonomic nervous system arousal.

panic disorder an anxiety disorder marked by unpredictable minutes-long episodes of intense dread in which a person experiences terror and accompanying chest pain, choking, or other frightening sensations.

phobia an anxiety disorder marked by a persistent, irrational fear and avoidance of a specific object or situation.

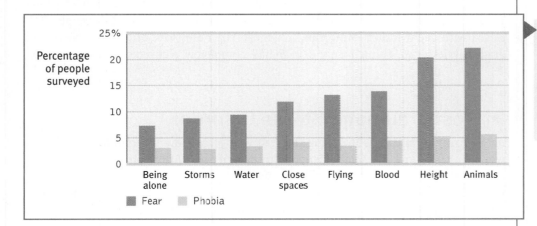

▶ **FIGURE 49.1 Some common and uncommon specific fears** This national interview study identified the commonality of various specific fears. A strong fear becomes a phobia if it provokes a compelling but irrational desire to avoid the dreaded object or situation. (From Curtis et al., 1998.)

OCD advocate Comedian and TV host Howie Mandel knows the reality of obsessive-compulsive disorder. He has used humor to deal with his own challenges and to help others understand the disorder. Mandel also suffers a germ phobia that prompted him to shave his head to "feel cleaner."

After spending five years sailing the world, Charles Darwin began suffering panic disorder at age 28. Because of the attacks, he moved to the country, avoided social gatherings, and traveled only in his wife's company. But the relative seclusion did free him to focus on developing his evolutionary theory. "Even ill health," he reflected, "has saved me from the distraction of society and its amusements" (quoted in Ma, 1997).

▶‖ Obsessive-Compulsive Disorder

As with generalized anxiety and phobias, we can see aspects of our own behavior in **obsessive-compulsive disorder (OCD).** We may at times be obsessed with senseless or offensive thoughts that will not go away. Or we may engage in compulsive behaviors, rigidly checking, ordering, and cleaning before guests arrive, or lining up books and pencils "just so" before studying.

Obsessive thoughts and compulsive behaviors cross the fine line between normality and disorder when they persistently interfere with everyday living and cause the person distress. Checking to see you locked the door is normal; checking 10 times is not. Washing your hands is normal; washing so often that your skin becomes raw is not. (**TABLE 49.1** offers more examples.) At some time during their lives, often during their late teens or twenties, 2 to 3 percent of people cross that line from normal preoccupations and fussiness to debilitating disorder (Karno et al., 1988). The obsessive thoughts become so haunting, the compulsive rituals so senselessly time-consuming, that effective functioning becomes impossible.

TABLE 49.1 Common Obsessions and Compulsions Among Children and Adolescents With Obsessive-Compulsive Disorder

Thought or Behavior	Percentage Reporting Symptom
Obsessions (*repetitive thoughts*)	
Concern with dirt, germs, or toxins	40
Something terrible happening (fire, death, illness)	24
Symmetry, order, or exactness	17
Compulsions (*repetitive behaviors*)	
Excessive hand washing, bathing, tooth brushing, or grooming	85
Repeating rituals (in/out of a door, up/down from a chair)	51
Checking doors, locks, appliances, car brakes, homework	46

Source: Adapted from Rapoport, 1989.

OCD is more common among teens and young adults than among older people (Samuels & Nestadt, 1997). A 40-year follow-up study of 144 Swedish people diagnosed with the disorder found that, for most, the obsessions and compulsions had gradually lessened, though only 1 in 5 had completely recovered (Skoog & Skoog, 1999).

▶‖ Post-Traumatic Stress Disorder

As an Army infantry scout during the Iraq war, Jesse "saw the murder of children, women. It was just horrible for anyone to experience." After calling in a helicopter strike on one house where he had seen ammunition crates carried in, he heard the screams of children from within. "I didn't know there were kids there," he recalls. Back home in Texas, he suffered "real bad flashbacks" (Welch, 2005).

Our memories exist in part to protect us in the future. So there is biological wisdom in not being able to forget our most emotional or traumatic experiences—our greatest embarrassments, our worst accidents, our most horrid experiences. But sometimes, for some of us, the unforgettable takes over our lives. The complaints of battled-scarred veterans such as Jesse—recurring haunting memories and nightmares, a numbed social withdrawal, jumpy anxiety, and insomnia—are typical of what once was called "shellshock" or "battle fatigue" and now is called **post-traumatic stress disorder (PTSD)** (Hoge et al., 2004; Kessler, 2000).

PTSD symptoms have also been reported by survivors of accidents, disasters, and violent and sexual assaults (including an estimated two-thirds of prostitutes) (Brewin et al., 1999; Farley et al., 1998; Taylor et al., 1998). A month after the 9/11 terrorist attacks, a survey of Manhattan residents indicated that 8.5 percent were suffering PTSD, most as a result of the attack (Galea et al., 2002). Among those living near the World Trade Center, 20 percent reported such telltale signs as nightmares, severe anxiety, and fear of public places (Susser et al., 2002).

To pin down the frequency of this disorder, the U.S. Centers for Disease Control (1988) compared 7000 Vietnam combat veterans with 7000 noncombat veterans who served during the same years. On average, according to a recent reanalysis, 19 percent of all Vietnam veterans reported PTSD symptoms. The rate varied from 10 percent among those who had never seen combat to 32 percent among those who had experienced heavy combat (Dohrenwend et al., 2006). Similar variations in rates have been found among people who have experienced a natural disaster or have been kidnapped, held captive, tortured, or raped (Brewin et al., 2000; Brody, 2000; Kessler, 2000; Stone, 2005).

The toll seems at least as high for veterans of the Iraq war, where 1 in 6 U.S. combat infantry personnel has reported symptoms of PTSD, depression, or severe anxiety in the months after returning home (Hoge et al., 2006, 2007). In one study of 103,788 veterans returning from Iraq and Afghanistan, 1 in 4 was diagnosed with a psychological disorder, most frequently PTSD (Seal et al., 2007). The extent of the PTSD problem was clear in the disability payments made to U.S. veterans in the decade following the mid-1990s: All forms of mental illness decreased, except PTSD, which nearly tripled, producing a $4.3 billion bill to taxpayers (Satel, 2006).

So what determines whether a person develops PTSD after a traumatic event? Research indicates that the greater one's emotional distress during a trauma, the higher the risk for post-traumatic symptoms (Ozer et al., 2003). Among New Yorkers who witnessed the 9/11 attacks, PTSD was doubled for survivors who were inside rather than outside the World Trade Center (Bonanno et al., 2006). And the more frequent an assault experience, the more adverse the long-term outcomes tend to be (Golding, 1999).

A sensitive limbic system seems to increase vulnerability, by flooding the body with stress hormones again and again as images of the traumatic experience erupt into consciousness (Kosslyn, 2005; Ozer & Weiss, 2004). Genes may also play a role. Some combat-exposed men have identical twins who did not experience combat. But these nonexposed co-twins tend to share their brother's risk for cognitive difficulties, such as unfocused attention. Such findings suggest that some PTSD symptoms may actually be genetically predisposed (Gilbertson et al., 2006).

Some psychologists believe that PTSD has been overdiagnosed, due partly to a broadening definition of *trauma* (which originally meant direct exposure to threatened death or serious injury, as during combat or rape [McNally, 2003]). PTSD is actually infrequent, say those critics, and well-intentioned attempts to have people relive the trauma may exacerbate their emotions and pathologize normal stress reactions (Wakefield & Spitzer, 2002). "Debriefing" survivors right after a trauma by getting them to revisit the experience and vent emotions has actually proven generally ineffective and sometimes harmful (Devilly et al., 2006; McNally et al., 2003; Rose et al. 2003).

AP Photo/Lawrence Journal-World, Thad Allender

Bringing the war home Many war veterans, such as this sergeant at a Veteran's Administration hospital, have recently been treated for post-traumatic stress disorder.

obsessive-compulsive disorder (OCD) an anxiety disorder characterized by unwanted repetitive thoughts (obsessions) and/or actions (compulsions).

post-traumatic stress disorder (PTSD) an anxiety disorder characterized by haunting memories, nightmares, social withdrawal, jumpy anxiety, and/or insomnia that lingers for four weeks or more after a traumatic experience.

Other researchers are interested in the impressive *survivor resiliency* of those who do *not* develop PTSD (Bonanno, 2004, 2005). About half of adults experience at least one traumatic event in their lifetime, but only about 1 in 10 women and 1 in 20 men develop PTSD (Olff et al., 2007; Ozer & Weiss, 2004; Tolin & Foa, 2006). More than 9 in 10 New Yorkers, although stunned and grief-stricken by 9/11, did *not* respond pathologically. By the following January, the stress symptoms of the rest had mostly subsided (Galea et al., 2002). Similarly, most combat-stressed veterans and most political dissidents who survive dozens of episodes of torture do not later exhibit PTSD (Mineka & Zinbarg, 1996).

Psychologist Peter Suedfeld (1998, 2000; Cassel & Suedfeld, 2006), who as a boy survived the Holocaust under deprived conditions while his mother died in Auschwitz, has documented the resilience of Holocaust survivors, most of whom lived productive lives. "It is not always true that 'What doesn't kill you makes you stronger,' but it is often true," he reports. And "what doesn't kill you may reveal to you just how strong you really are." Fellow Holocaust survivor Ervin Staub (Staub & Vollhardt, 2008) has described "altruism born of suffering." Although nothing justifies terror and victimization, those who have suffered, he reports, often develop a greater-than-usual sensitivity to suffering and empathy for others who suffer, an increased sense of responsibility, and an enlarged capacity for caring. Staub is a living example of his own work. After being spared from being sent to Auschwitz thanks to a heroic intervention, his lifelong mission has been to understand why some people perpetrate evil, some stand by, and some work to prevent it.

Indeed, suffering can lead to "benefit finding" (Helgeson et al., 2006), what Richard Tedeschi and Lawrence Calhoun (2004) call **post-traumatic growth.** Tedeschi and Calhoun have found that the struggle with challenging crises, such as facing cancer, often leads people later to report an increased appreciation for life, more meaningful relationships, increased personal strength, changed priorities, and a richer spiritual life. This idea—that suffering has transformative power—is also found in Judaism, Christianity, Hinduism, Buddhism, and Islam. Out of even our worst experiences some good can come. Like the body, the mind has great recuperative powers.

▶‖ Understanding Anxiety Disorders

49-2 What produces the thoughts and feelings that mark anxiety disorders?

Anxiety is both a feeling and a cognition, a doubt-laden appraisal of one's safety or social skill. How do these anxious feelings and cognitions arise? Freud's psychoanalytic theory proposed that, beginning in childhood, people *repress* intolerable impulses, ideas, and feelings and that this submerged mental energy sometimes produces mystifying symptoms, such as anxiety. Today's psychologists have turned to two contemporary perspectives—learning and biological.

The Learning Perspective

Fear Conditioning

When bad events happen unpredictably and uncontrollably, anxiety often develops (Field, 2006; Mineka & Zinbarg, 2006). Decades of research on conditioning show that dogs learn to fear neutral stimuli associated with shock and that infants come to fear furry objects associated with frightening noises. Using classical conditioning, researchers have also created chronically anxious, ulcer-prone rats by giving them unpredictable electric shocks (Schwartz, 1984). Like assault victims who report feeling anxious when returning to the scene of the crime, the rats become apprehensive in their lab environment. This link between conditioned fear and general anxiety helps

"'Tis an ill wind that blows no good."
English proverb

post-traumatic growth positive psychological changes as a result of struggling with extremely challenging circumstances and life crises.

explain why anxious people are hyperattentive to possible threats, and how panic-prone people come to associate anxiety with certain cues (Bar-Haim et al., 2007; Bouton et al., 2001). In one survey, 58 percent of those with social phobia experienced their disorder after a traumatic event (Ost & Hugdahl, 1981).

Through conditioning, the short list of naturally painful and frightening events can multiply into a long list of human fears. My car was once struck by another whose driver missed a stop sign. For months afterward, I felt a twinge of unease when any car approached from a side street. Marilyn's phobia may have been similarly conditioned during a terrifying or painful experience associated with a thunderstorm.

Two specific learning processes can contribute to such anxiety. The first, *stimulus generalization,* occurs, for example, when a person attacked by a fierce dog later develops a fear of *all* dogs. The second learning process, *reinforcement,* helps maintain our phobias and compulsions after they arise. Avoiding or escaping the feared situation reduces anxiety, thus reinforcing the phobic behavior. Feeling anxious or fearing a panic attack, a person may go inside and be reinforced by feeling calmer (Antony et al., 1992). Compulsive behaviors operate similarly. If washing your hands relieves your feelings of anxiety, you may wash your hands again when those feelings return.

Observational Learning

We may also learn fear through observational learning—by observing others' fears. As Susan Mineka (1985) demonstrated, wild monkeys transmit their fear of snakes to their watchful offspring. Human parents similarly transmit fears to their children. Moreover, just observing someone receiving a mild electric shock after a conditioned stimulus produces fear learning similar to that produced by direct experience (Olsson & Phelps, 2004).

The Biological Perspective

There is, however, more to anxiety than conditioning and observational learning. The biological perspective can help us understand why few people develop lasting phobias after suffering traumas, why we learn some fears more readily, and why some individuals are more vulnerable.

Natural Selection

We humans seem biologically prepared to fear threats faced by our ancestors. Our phobias focus on such specific fears: spiders, snakes, and other animals; close spaces and heights; storms and darkness. (Those fearless about these occasional threats were less likely to survive and leave descendants.) Thus, even in Britain, with only one poisonous snake species, people often fear snakes. And preschool children more speedily detect snakes in a scene than flowers, caterpillars, or frogs (LoBue & DeLoache, 2008). It is easy to condition and hard to extinguish fears of such stimuli (Davey, 1995; Öhman, 1986).

Our modern fears can also have an evolutionary explanation. For example, a fear of flying may come from our biological predisposition to fear confinement and heights. Moreover, consider what people tend *not* to learn to fear. World War II air raids produced remarkably few lasting phobias. As the air blitzes continued, the British, Japanese, and German populations became not more panicked, but rather more indifferent to planes outside their immediate neighborhoods (Mineka & Zinbarg, 1996). Evolution has not prepared us to fear bombs dropping from the sky.

Just as our phobias focus on dangers faced by our ancestors, our compulsive acts typically exaggerate behaviors that contributed to our species' survival. Grooming gone wild becomes hair pulling. Washing up becomes ritual hand washing. Checking territorial boundaries becomes rechecking an already locked door (Rapoport, 1989).

An emotional high Fearing heights is certainly an adaptive response. The biological perspective helps us understand why most people would be terrified in this situation, and why some individuals—like this construction worker—seem relatively free of that fear.

John Coletti/Stock, Boston

Genes

Some people more than others seem predisposed to anxiety. Genes matter. Pair a traumatic event with a sensitive, high-strung temperament and the result may be a new phobia.

Among monkeys, fearfulness runs in families. Individual monkeys react more strongly to stress if their close biological relatives are anxiously reactive (Suomi, 1986). In humans, vulnerability to anxiety disorder rises when an afflicted relative is an identical twin (Hettema et al., 2001; Kendler et al., 1992, 1999, 2002a,b). Identical twins also may develop similar phobias, even when raised separately (Carey, 1990; Eckert et al., 1981). One pair of 35-year-old female identical twins independently became so afraid of water that each would wade in the ocean backward and only up to the knees.

With the genetic contribution to anxiety disorders established, researchers are now sleuthing specific genes that put people at risk. One research team has identified 17 genes that appear to be expressed with typical anxiety disorder symptoms (Hovatta et al., 2005). Another team found genes associated specifically with OCD (Hu et al., 2006).

Genes influence disorders by regulating neurotransmitters. Some studies point to an *anxiety gene* that affects brain levels of serotonin, a neurotransmitter that influences sleep and mood (Canli, 2008). Other studies implicate genes that regulate the neurotransmitter *glutamate* (Lafleur et al., 2006; Welch et al., 2007). With too much glutamate, the brain's alarm centers become overactive.

The Brain

Generalized anxiety, panic attacks, PTSD, and even obsessions and compulsions are manifested biologically as an overarousal of brain areas involved in impulse control and habitual behaviors. When the disordered brain detects that something is amiss, it seems to generate a mental hiccup of repeating thoughts or actions (Gehring et al., 2000). Brain scans of people with OCD reveal elevated activity in specific brain areas during behaviors such as compulsive hand washing, checking, ordering, or hoarding (Mataix-Cols et al., 2004, 2005). As **FIGURE 49.2** shows, the *anterior cingulate cortex,* a brain region that monitors our actions and checks for errors, seems especially likely to be hyperactive in those with OCD (Ursu et al., 2003). Fear-learning experiences that traumatize the brain can also create fear circuits within the amygdala (Etkin & Wager, 2007; Kolassa & Elbert, 2007; Maren, 2007). Some antidepressant drugs dampen this fear-circuit activity and its associated obsessive-compulsive behavior.

The biological perspective cannot by itself explain all aspects of anxiety disorders, such as the sharp increase in the anxiety levels of both children and college students over the last half-century, which appears to be related to fraying social support accompanying family breakup (Twenge, 2006). It is nevertheless clear that biology underlies anxiety.

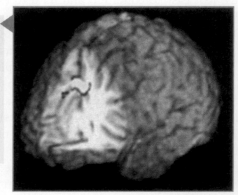

FIGURE 49.2 **An obsessive-compulsive brain** Neuroscientist Stefan Ursu and his colleagues (2003) used functional magnetic resonance imaging (fMRI) scans to compare the brains of those with and without OCD as they engaged in a challenging cognitive task. The fMRI scans showed elevated activity in the anterior cingulate cortex in the brain's frontal area of those with OCD.

S. Ursu, V. A. Stenger, M. K. Shear, M. R Jones, & C. S. Carter (2003). Overactive action monitoring in obsessive-compulsive disorder. *Psychological Science, 14*, 347–353.

REVIEW

Anxiety Disorders

49-1 **What are anxiety disorders, and how do they differ from ordinary worries and fears?** Anxiety is classified as a psychological disorder only when it becomes distressing or persistent, or is characterized by maladaptive behaviors intended to reduce it.

People with *generalized anxiety disorder* feel persistently and uncontrollably tense and apprehensive, for no apparent reason. In the more extreme *panic disorder,* anxiety escalates into periodic episodes of intense dread. Those with a *phobia* may be irrationally afraid of a specific object or situation. Persistent and repetitive thoughts (obsessions) and actions (compulsions) characterize *obsessive-compulsive disorder.* Symptoms of *post-traumatic stress disorder* include four or more weeks of haunting memories, nightmares, social withdrawal, jumpy anxiety, and sleep problems following some traumatic and uncontrollable event.

49-2 **What produces the thoughts and feelings that mark anxiety disorders?** Freud viewed anxiety disorders as the manifestation of mental energy associated with the discharge of repressed impulses. Psychologists working from the learning perspective view *anxiety disorders* as a product of fear conditioning, stimulus generalization, reinforcement of fearful behaviors, and observational learning of others' fear. Those working from the biological perspective consider the role that fears of life-threatening animals, objects, or situations played in natural selection and evolution; the genetic inheritance of a high level of emotional reactivity; and abnormal responses in the brain's fear circuits.

Terms and Concepts to Remember

anxiety disorders, p. 610
generalized anxiety disorder, p. 610
panic disorder, p. 611
phobia, p. 611
obsessive-compulsive disorder (OCD), p. 612
post-traumatic stress disorder (PTSD), p. 613
post-traumatic growth, p. 614

Test Yourself

1. How do generalized anxiety disorder, panic disorder, phobias, obsessive-compulsive disorder, and PTSD differ?

(Answers to the Test Yourself questions can be found in Appendix B at the end of the book.)

Ask Yourself

1. Can you recall a fear that you have learned? What role, if any, was played by fear conditioning and by observational learning?

∞ WEB

Multiple-choice self-tests and more may be found at www.worthpublishers.com/myers

Dissociative, Personality, and Somatoform Disorders

Dissociative Disorders

Personality Disorders

Somatoform Disorders

▶‖ Dissociative Disorders

50-1 What are dissociative disorders, and why are they controversial?

Among the most bewildering disorders are the rare **dissociative disorders.** These are disorders of consciousness, in which a person appears to experience a sudden loss of memory or change in identity, often in response to an overwhelmingly stressful situation. One Vietnam veteran who was haunted by his comrade's deaths, and who had left his World Trade Center office shortly before the 9/11 attack, disappeared en route to work one day and was discovered six months later in a Chicago homeless shelter, reportedly with no memory of his identity or family (Stone, 2006). In such cases, the person's conscious awareness is said to *dissociate* (become separated) from painful memories, thoughts, and feelings. (Note that this explanation presumes the existence of repressed memories, which have been questioned by memory researchers.)

Dissociation itself is not so rare. Now and then, many people may have a sense of being unreal, of being separated from their body, of watching themselves as if in a movie. Sometimes we may say, "I was not myself at the time." Perhaps you can recall getting in your car and driving to some unintended location while your mind was preoccupied elsewhere. Facing trauma, such detachment may actually protect a person from being overwhelmed by emotion.

Dissociative Identity Disorder

A massive dissociation of self from ordinary consciousness characterizes those with **dissociative identity disorder (DID),** in which two or more distinct identities are said to alternately control the person's behavior. Each personality has its own voice and mannerisms. Thus the person may be prim and proper one moment, loud and flirtatious the next. Typically, the original personality denies any awareness of the other(s).

People diagnosed with DID (formerly called *multiple personality disorder*) are usually not violent, but cases have been reported of dissociations into a "good" and a "bad" (or aggressive) personality—a modest version of the Dr. Jekyll/Mr. Hyde split immortalized in Robert Louis Stevenson's story. One unusual case involved Kenneth Bianchi, accused in the "Hillside Strangler" rapes and murders of 10 California women. During a hypnosis session with Bianchi, psychologist John Watkins (1984) "called forth" a hidden personality: "I've talked a bit to Ken, but I think that perhaps there might be another part of Ken that . . . maybe feels somewhat differently from the part that I've talked to. . . . Would you talk with me, Part, by saying, 'I'm here'?" Bianchi answered "Yes" and then claimed to be "Steve."

Speaking as Steve, Bianchi stated that he hated Ken because Ken was nice and that he (Steve), aided by a cousin, had murdered women. He also claimed Ken knew nothing about Steve's existence and was innocent of the murders. Was Bianchi's second personality a ruse, simply a way of disavowing responsibility for his actions? Indeed, Bianchi—a practiced liar who had read about multiple personality in psychology books—was later convicted.

The "Hillside Strangler" Kenneth Bianchi is shown here at his trial.

AP/Wide World Photos

Understanding Dissociative Identity Disorder

Skeptics question whether DID is a genuine disorder or an extension of our normal capacity for personality shifts. Nicholas Spanos (1986, 1994, 1996) asked college students to pretend they were accused murderers being examined by a psychiatrist. Given the same hypnotic treatment Bianchi received, most spontaneously expressed a second personality. This discovery made Spanos wonder: Are dissociative identities simply a more extreme version of our capacity to vary the "selves" we present—as when we display a goofy, loud self while hanging out with friends, and a subdued, respectful self around grandparents? Are clinicians who discover multiple personalities merely triggering role-playing by fantasy-prone people? Do these patients, like actors who commonly report "losing themselves" in their roles, then convince themselves of the authenticity of their own role enactments? Spanos was no stranger to this line of thinking. In a related research area, he had also raised these questions about the hypnotic state. Given that most DID patients are highly hypnotizable, whatever explains one condition—dissociation or role-playing—may help explain the other.

Skeptics also find it suspicious that the disorder is so localized in time and space. Between 1930 and 1960, the number of DID diagnoses in North America was 2 per decade. In the 1980s, when the DSM contained the first formal code for this disorder, the number of reported cases had exploded to more than 20,000 (McHugh, 1995a). The average number of displayed personalities also mushroomed—from 3 to 12 per patient (Goff & Simms, 1993). Outside North America, the disorder is much less prevalent, although in other cultures some people are said to be "possessed" by an alien spirit (Aldridge-Morris, 1989; Kluft, 1991). In Britain, DID—which some consider "a wacky American fad" (Cohen, 1995)—is rare. In India and Japan, it is essentially nonexistent.

Such findings, skeptics say, point to a cultural phenomenon—a disorder created by therapists in a particular social context (Merskey, 1992). Patients do not enter therapy saying "Allow me to introduce myselves." Rather, note skeptics some therapists—often practitioners of hypnosis (Goff, 1993; Piper, 1998)—go fishing for multiple personalities: "Have you ever felt like another part of you does things you can't control? Does this part of you have a name? Can I talk to the angry part of you?" Once patients permit a therapist to talk, by name, "to the part of you that says those angry things" they have begun acting out the fantasy. The result may be a real phenomenon, which vulnerable patients may experience as another self.

Other psychologists disagree, finding support for DID as a genuine disorder in the distinct brain and body states associated with differing personalities (Putnam, 1991). Handedness, for example, sometimes switches with personality (Henninger, 1992). Ophthalmologists have detected shifting visual acuity and eye-muscle balance as patients switched personalities, changes that did not occur among control group members trying to simulate DID (Miller et al., 1991). Dissociative disorder patients also have exhibited heightened activity in brain areas associated with the control and inhibition of traumatic memories (Elzinga et al., 2007).

Researchers and clinicians have interpreted DID symptoms from psychoanalytic and learning perspectives. Both views agree that the symptoms are ways of dealing with anxiety. Psychoanalysts see them as defenses against the anxiety caused by the eruption of unacceptable impulses; a wanton second personality enables the discharge of forbidden impulses. Learning theorists see dissociative disorders as behaviors reinforced by anxiety reduction.

Other clinicians include dissociative disorders under the umbrella of post-traumatic disorders—a natural, protective response to "histories of childhood trauma" (Putnam, 1995; Spiegel, 2008). Many DID patients recall suffering physical, sexual, or emotional abuse as children (Gleaves, 1996; Lilienfeld et al., 1999). In one

dissociative disorders disorders in which conscious awareness becomes separated (dissociated) from previous memories, thoughts, and feelings.

dissociative identity disorder (DID) a rare dissociative disorder in which a person exhibits two or more distinct and alternating personalities. Formerly called *multiple personality disorder.*

"Pretense may become reality."
Chinese proverb

Multiple personalities Chris Sizemore's story, *The Three Faces of Eve,* gave early visibility to what is now called *dissociative identity disorder.*

"Though this be madness, yet there is method in 't."
William Shakespeare, *Hamlet,* 1600

Antisocial personality? Dennis Rader, known as the "BTK killer" in Kansas, was convicted in 2005 of killing 10 people over a 30-year span. Rader exhibited the extreme lack of conscience that marks antisocial personality disorder.

study of 12 murderers diagnosed with DID, 11 had suffered severe, torturous child abuse (Lewis et al., 1997). One was set afire by his parents. Another was used in child pornography and was scarred from being made to sit on a stove burner. Some critics wonder, however, whether vivid imagination or therapist suggestion contribute to such recollections (Kihlstrom, 2005).

So the debate continues. On one side are those who believe multiple personalities are the desperate efforts of the traumatized to detach from a horrific existence. On the other are the skeptics who think DID is a condition contrived by fantasy-prone, emotionally vulnerable people, and constructed out of the therapist-patient interaction. If the skeptics' view wins, predicted psychiatrist Paul McHugh (1995b), "this epidemic will end in the way that the witch craze ended in Salem. The [multiple personality phenomenon] will be seen as manufactured."

▶‖ Personality Disorders

50-2   What characteristics are typical of personality disorders?

Some dysfunctional behavior patterns impair people's social functioning without depression or delusions. Among them are **personality disorders,** disruptive, inflexible, and enduring behavior patterns that impair one's social functioning. One cluster of these disorders expresses anxiety, such as a fearful sensitivity to rejection that predisposes the withdrawn *avoidant personality disorder*. A second cluster expresses eccentric behaviors, such as the emotionless disengagement of the *schizoid personality disorder*. A third cluster exhibits dramatic or impulsive behaviors, such as the attention-getting *histrionic personality disorder* and the self-focused and self-inflating *narcissistic personality disorder*. The personality disorders categories are not sharply distinguished, however, and likely will be revised in the next DSM revision (Clark, 2007; Widiger & Trull, 2007).

Antisocial Personality Disorder

The most troubling and heavily researched personality disorder is the **antisocial personality disorder.** The person (formerly called a *sociopath* or a *psychopath*) is typically a male whose lack of conscience becomes plain before age 15, as he begins to lie, steal, fight, or display unrestrained sexual behavior (Cale & Lilienfeld, 2002). About half of such children become antisocial adults—unable to keep a job, irresponsible as a spouse and parent, and assaultive or otherwise criminal (Farrington, 1991). When the antisocial personality combines a keen intelligence with amorality, the result may be a charming and clever con artist—or worse.

Despite their antisocial behavior, many criminals do not fit the description of antisocial personality disorder. Why? Because they actually show responsible concern

Many criminals, like this one, exhibit a sense of conscience and responsibility in other areas of their life, and thus do **not** exhibit antisocial personality disorder.

for their friends and family members. Antisocial personalities feel and fear little, and in extreme cases, the results can be horrifyingly tragic. Henry Lee Lucas confessed that during his 32 years of crime, he had bludgeoned, suffocated, stabbed, shot, or mutilated some 360 women, men, and children—the first (a woman) at age 13. During the last 6 years of his reign of terror, Lucas teamed with Elwood Toole, who reportedly slaughtered about 50 people he "didn't think was worth living anyhow." It ended when Lucas confessed to stabbing and dismembering his 15-year-old common-law wife, who was Toole's niece.

The antisocial personality expresses little regret over violating others' rights. "Once I've done a crime, I just forget it," said Lucas. Toole was equally matter-of-fact: "I think of killing like smoking a cigarette, like another habit" (Darrach & Norris, 1984).

"Thursday is out. I have jury duty."

Understanding Antisocial Personality Disorder

Antisocial personality disorder is woven of both biological and psychological strands. No single gene codes for a complex behavior such as crime, but twin and adoption studies reveal that biological relatives of those with antisocial and unemotional tendencies are at increased risk for antisocial behavior (Larsson et al., 2007; Livesley & Jang, 2008). The genetic vulnerability of people with antisocial and unemotional tendencies appears as a fearless approach to life. Awaiting aversive events, such as electric shocks or loud noises, they show little autonomic nervous system arousal (Hare, 1975; van Goozen et al., 2007). Even as youngsters, before committing any crime, they react with lower levels of stress hormones than do others their age (**FIGURE 50.1**).

Some studies have detected the early signs of antisocial behavior in children as young as ages 3 to 6 (Caspi et al., 1996; Tremblay et al., 1994). Boys who later became aggressive or antisocial adolescents tended, as young children, to have been impulsive, uninhibited, unconcerned with social rewards, and low in anxiety. If channeled in more productive directions, such fearlessness may lead to courageous heroism, adventurism, or star-level athleticism (Poulton & Milne, 2002). Lacking a sense of social responsibility, the same disposition may produce a cool con artist or killer (Lykken, 1995). The genes that put people at risk for antisocial behavior also put people at risk for dependence on alcohol and other drugs, which helps explain why these disorders often appear in combination (Dick, 2007).

Genetic influences help wire the brain. Adrian Raine (1999, 2005) compared PET scans of 41 murderers' brains with those from people of similar age and sex. Raine found reduced activity in the murderers' frontal lobes, an area of the cortex that helps control impulses (**FIGURE 50.2**). This reduction was especially apparent in those who murdered impulsively. In a follow-up study, Raine and his team (2000) found that violent repeat offenders had 11 percent less frontal lobe tissue than normal. This helps explain why people with antisocial personality disorder exhibit marked deficits in frontal lobe cognitive functions, such as planning, organization, and inhibition (Morgan & Lilienfeld, 2000). Compared with people who feel and display empathy, their brains also respond less to facial displays of others' distress (Deeley et al., 2006).

Perhaps a biologically based fearlessness, as well as early environment, helps explain the reunion of long-separated sisters Joyce Lott, 27, and Mary Jones, 29—in a South Carolina prison where both were sent on drug charges. After a newspaper story about their reunion, their long-lost half-brother Frank Strickland called. He explained it would be a while before he could come see them—because he, too, was in jail, on drug, burglary, and larceny charges (Shepherd et al., 1990). According to a 2004 U.S. Justice Department report, 48 percent of 2 million state prison inmates say they have had incarcerated relatives (Johnson, 2008).

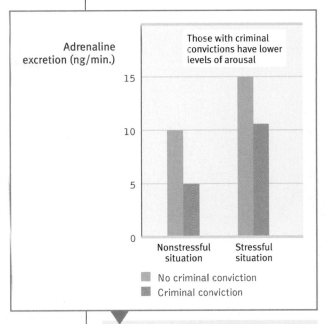

FIGURE 50.1 Cold-blooded arousability and risk of crime Levels of the stress hormone adrenaline were measured in two groups of 13-year-old Swedish boys. In both stressful and nonstressful situations, those later convicted of a crime (as 18- to 26-year-olds) showed relatively low arousal. (From Magnusson, 1990.)

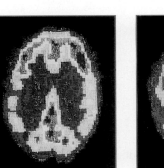 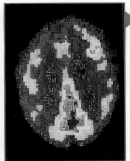

Normal   **Murderer**

FIGURE 50.2 Murderous minds These top-facing PET scans illustrate reduced activation (less red and yellow) in a murderer's frontal cortex—a brain area that helps brake impulsive, aggressive behavior. (From Raine, 1999.)

personality disorders psychological disorders characterized by inflexible and enduring behavior patterns that impair social functioning.

antisocial personality disorder a personality disorder in which the person (usually a man) exhibits a lack of conscience for wrongdoing, even toward friends and family members. May be aggressive and ruthless or a clever con artist.

Genetics alone is hardly the whole story of antisocial crime, however. Relative to 1960, the average American in 1995 (before the late 1990s crime decline) was twice as likely to be murdered, four times as likely to report being raped, four times as likely to report being robbed, and five times as likely to report being assaulted (FBI, *Uniform Crime Reports*). Violent crime was also surging in other Western nations. Yet the human gene pool had hardly changed. Or consider the British social experiment begun in 1787, exiling 160,000 criminals to Australia. The descendants of these exiles, carrying their ancestors' supposed "criminal genes," helped create a civilized democracy whose crime rate is similar to Britain's. Genetic predispositions do put some individuals more at risk for antisocial conduct than others; biological as well as environmental influences explain why 5 to 6 percent of offenders commit 50 to 60 percent of crimes (Lyman, 1996). But we must look to social-cultural factors to explain the modern epidemic of violence.

A study of criminal tendencies among young Danish men illustrates the usefulness of a complete biopsychosocial perspective. A research team led by Adrian Raine (1996) checked criminal records on nearly 400 men at ages 20 to 22, knowing that these men either had experienced biological risk factors at birth (such as premature birth) or came from family backgrounds marked by poverty and family instability. The researchers then compared each of these two groups with a third *biosocial* group whose lives were marked by *both* the biological and social risk factors. The biosocial group had double the risk of committing crime (**FIGURE 50.3**). Similar findings emerged from a famous study that followed 1037 children for a quarter-century: Two combined factors—childhood maltreatment and a gene that altered neurotransmitter balance—predicted antisocial problems (Caspi et al., 2002). Neither "bad" genes alone nor a "bad" environment alone predisposed later antisocial behavior. Rather, genes predisposed some children to be more sensitive to maltreatment. Within "genetically vulnerable segments of the population," environmental influences matter—for better or for worse (Belsky et al., 2007; Moffitt, 2005). With antisocial behavior, as with so much else, nature and nurture interact.

FIGURE 50.3
Biopsychosocial roots of crime Danish male babies whose backgrounds were marked both by obstetrical complications and social stresses associated with poverty were twice as likely to be criminal offenders by ages 20 to 22 as those in either the biological or social risk groups. (From Raine et al., 1996.)

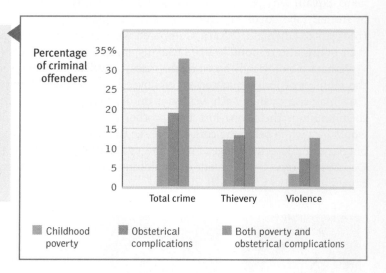

▶‖ Somatoform Disorders

50-3   What are somatoform disorders?

Among the most common problems bringing people into doctors' offices are "medically unexplained illnesses" (Johnson, 2008). Ellen becomes dizzy and nauseated in the late afternoon—shortly before she expects her husband home. Neither her primary care physician nor the neurologist he sent her to could identify a physical cause. They suspect her symptoms have an unconscious psychological origin, possibly triggered by her mixed feelings about her husband. In **somatoform disorders,** such as Ellen's, the distressing symptoms take a somatic (bodily) form without apparent physical causes. One person may have a variety of complaints—vomiting, dizziness, blurred vision, difficulty in swallowing. Another may experience severe and prolonged pain.

Culture has a big effect on people's physical complaints and how they explain them (Kirmayer & Sartorius, 2007). In China, psychological explanations of anxiety and depression are socially less acceptable than in many Western countries, and people less often express the emotional aspects of distress. The Chinese appear more sensitive to—and more willing to report—the physical symptoms of their distress (Ryder et al., 2008). Mr. Wu, a 36-year-old technician in Hunan, illustrates one of China's most common psychological disorders (Spitzer & Skodol, 2000). He finds work difficult because of his insomnia, fatigue, weakness, and headaches. Chinese herbs and Western medicines provide no relief. To his Chinese clinician, who treats the bodily symptoms, he seems not so much depressed as exhausted. Similar, generalized bodily complaints have often been observed in African cultures (Binitie, 1975).

Even to people in the West, somatic symptoms are familiar. To a lesser extent, we have all experienced inexplicable physical symptoms under stress. It is little comfort to be told that the problem is "all in your head." Although the symptoms may be psychological in origin, they are nevertheless genuinely felt.

One type of somatoform disorder, more common in Freud's day than in ours, is **conversion disorder,** so called because anxiety presumably is converted into a physical symptom. (Freud's effort to treat and understand psychological disorders stemmed from his puzzlement over ailments that had no physiological basis.) A patient with a conversion disorder might, for example, lose sensation in a way that makes no neurological sense. Yet the physical symptoms would be real; sticking pins in the affected area would produce no response. Other conversion disorder symptoms might be unexplained paralysis, blindness, or an inability to swallow. In each case, the person would be strangely indifferent to the problem.

As you can imagine, somatoform disorders send people not to a psychologist or psychiatrist but to a physician. This is especially true of those who experience **hypochondriasis.** In this relatively common somatoform disorder, people interpret normal sensations (a stomach cramp today, a headache tomorrow) as symptoms of a dreaded disease. Sympathy or temporary relief from everyday demands may reinforce such complaints. No amount of reassurance by any physician convinces the patient not to worry. So the patient moves on to another physician, seeking and receiving more medical attention—but failing to confront the disorder's psychological root.

somatoform disorder psychological disorder in which the symptoms take a somatic (bodily) form without apparent physical cause. (See *conversion disorder* and *hypochondriasis.*)

conversion disorder a rare somatoform disorder in which a person experiences very specific genuine physical symptoms for which no physiological basis can be found.

hypochondriasis a somatoform disorder in which a person interprets normal physical sensations as symptoms of a disease.

REVIEW

Dissociative, Personality, and Somatoform Disorders

50-1 **What are dissociative disorders, and why are they controversial?** *Dissociative disorders* are conditions in which conscious awareness seems to become separated from previous memories, thoughts, and feelings. Skeptics note that *dissociative identity disorder,* formerly known as multiple personality disorder, increased dramatically in the late twentieth century, that it is rarely found outside North America, and that it may reflect role-playing by people who are vulnerable to therapists' suggestions. Others view this disorder as a manifestation of feelings of anxiety, or as a response learned when behaviors are reinforced by reductions in feelings of anxiety.

50-2 **What characteristics are typical of personality disorders?** *Personality disorders* are enduring, maladaptive patterns of behavior that impair social functioning. *Antisocial personality disorder* is characterized by a lack of conscience and, sometimes, by aggressive and fearless behavior. Genetic predispositions may interact with environment to produce the altered brain activity associated with this disorder.

50-3 **What are somatoform disorders?** *Somatoform disorders* present a somatic (bodily) symptom—some physiologically unexplained but genuinely felt ailment. With *conversion disorder,* anxiety appears converted to a physical symptom that has no reasonable neurological basis. *Hypochondriasis* is the more common interpretation of normal sensations as a dreaded disorder.

Terms and Concepts to Remember

dissociative disorders, p. 618

dissociative identity disorder (DID), p. 618

personality disorders, p. 620

antisocial personality disorder, p. 620

somatoform disorder, p. 623

conversion disorder, p. 623

hypochondriasis, p. 623

Test Yourself

1. The psychoanalytic and learning perspectives agree that DID symptoms are ways of dealing with anxiety. How do their explanations differ?

2. Is antisocial personality disorder an inherited condition?

3. What does *somatoform* mean?

(Answers to the Test Yourself questions can be found in Appendix B at the end of the book.)

Ask Yourself

1. In a more normal way, do you ever flip between displays of different personalities?

2. Does research on antisocial personality disorder leave you with hope that parental education and training could help prevent the disorder?

3. Can you recall (as most people can) times when you have fretted needlessly over a normal bodily sensation?

∞ WEB

Multiple-choice self-tests and more may be found at www.worthpublishers.com/myers

Mood Disorders

Major Depressive Disorder

Bipolar Disorder

Understanding Mood Disorders

51-1 What are mood disorders, and what forms do they take?

The emotional extremes of **mood disorders** come in two principal forms: (1) *major depressive disorder,* with its prolonged hopelessness and lethargy, and (2) *bipolar disorder* (formerly called *manic-depressive disorder*), in which a person alternates between depression and mania, an overexcited, hyperactive state.

mood disorders psychological disorders characterized by emotional extremes. See *major depressive disorder, mania,* and *bipolar disorder.*

▶‖ Major Depressive Disorder

If you are like most college students, at some time during this year—more likely the dark months of winter than the bright days of summer—you will probably experience a few of depression's symptoms. You may feel deeply discouraged about the future, dissatisfied with your life, or socially isolated. You may lack the energy to get things done or even to force yourself out of bed; be unable to concentrate, eat, or sleep normally; or even wonder if you would be better off dead. Perhaps academic success came easily to you in high school, and now you find that disappointing grades jeopardize your goals. Maybe social stresses, such as feeling you don't belong or experiencing the end of a romance, have plunged you into despair. And maybe brooding has at times only worsened your self-torment. You are not alone. In one survey of 90,000 American college and university students, 44 percent reported that on one or more occasions within the last school year, they had felt "so depressed it was difficult to function" (ACHA, 2006).

Depression has been called the "common cold" of psychological disorders—an expression that effectively describes its pervasiveness but not its seriousness. Although phobias are more common, depression is the number-one reason people seek mental health services. At some point during their lifetime, depressive disorders have plagued 12 percent of Canadian adults and 13 percent of U.S. adults (Hasin et al., 2005; Patten et al., 2006). Moreover, it is the leading cause of disability worldwide (WHO, 2002). In any given year, a depressive episode plagues 5.8 percent of men and 9.5 percent of women, reports the World Health Organization.

As anxiety is a response to the threat of future loss, depressed mood is often a response to past and current loss. About one in four people diagnosed with depression is simply struggling with the normal emotional impact of a significant loss, such as a loved one's death, a ruptured marriage, a lost job (Wakefield et al., 2007). To feel bad in reaction to profoundly sad events is to be in touch with reality. In such times, depression is like a car's low–oil-pressure light—a signal that warns us to stop and take protective measures. Recall that, biologically speaking, life's purpose is not happiness but survival and reproduction. Coughing, vomiting, and various forms of pain protect the body from dangerous toxins. Similarly, depression is a sort of psychic hibernation: It slows us down, defuses aggression, and restrains risk taking (Allen & Badcock, 2003). To grind temporarily to a halt and ruminate, as depressed people do, is to reassess one's life when feeling threatened, and to redirect energy in more promising ways (Watkins, 2008). There is sense to suffering.

But when does this response become seriously maladaptive? Joy, contentment, sadness, and despair are different points on a continuum, points at which any of us may be found at any given moment. The difference between a blue mood after bad news and a mood disorder is like the difference between gasping for breath after a hard run and being chronically short of breath.

‖ For some people, recurring depression during winter's dark months constitutes a *seasonal affective disorder.* For others, winter darkness means more blue moods. When asked "Have you cried today?" Americans answered "Yes" more often in the winter.

	Percentage answering *yes*	
	Men	Women
August	4%	7%
December	8%	21%

Source: Time/CNN survey, 1994 ‖

"My life had come to a sudden stop. I was able to breathe, to eat, to drink, to sleep. I could not, indeed, help doing so; but there was no real life in me."
Leo Tolstoy, *My Confession*, 1887

"If someone offered you a pill that would make you permanently happy, you would be well advised to run fast and run far. Emotion is a compass that tells us what to do, and a compass that is perpetually stuck on NORTH is worthless."
Daniel Gilbert, "The Science of Happiness," 2006

major depressive disorder a mood disorder in which a person experiences, in the absence of drugs or a medical condition, two or more weeks of significantly depressed moods, feelings of worthlessness, and diminished interest or pleasure in most activities.

mania a mood disorder marked by a hyperactive, wildly optimistic state.

bipolar disorder a mood disorder in which the person alternates between the hopelessness and lethargy of depression and the overexcited state of mania. (Formerly called *manic-depressive disorder*.)

Major depressive disorder occurs when at least five signs of depression (including lethargy, feelings of worthlessness, or loss of interest in family, friends, and activities) last two or more weeks and are not caused by drugs or a medical condition. To sense what major depression feels like, suggest some clinicians, imagine combining the anguish of grief with the sluggishness of jet lag.

▶❙ Bipolar Disorder

With or without therapy, episodes of major depression usually end, and people temporarily or permanently return to their previous behavior patterns. However, some people rebound to, or sometimes start with, the opposite emotional extreme—the euphoric, hyperactive, wildly optimistic state of **mania.** If depression is living in slow motion, mania is fast forward. Alternating between depression and mania signals **bipolar disorder.**

Adolescent mood swings, from rage to bubbly, can, when prolonged, produce a bipolar diagnosis. Between 1994 and 2003, U.S. National Center for Health Statistics annual physician surveys revealed an astonishing 40-fold increase in diagnoses of bipolar disorder in those 19 and under—from an estimated 20,000 to 800,000 (Carey, 2007; Moreno et al., 2007). The new popularity of the diagnosis, given in two-thirds of the cases to boys, has been a boon to companies whose drugs are prescribed to lessen mood swings.

During the manic phase of bipolar disorder, the person is typically overtalkative, overactive, and elated (though easily irritated if crossed); has little need for sleep; and shows fewer sexual inhibitions. Speech is loud, flighty, and hard to interrupt. The person finds advice irritating. Yet they need protection from their own poor judgment, which may lead to reckless spending or unsafe sex.

To simulate mania's racing thoughts, such as you may have experienced when excited about a new idea, Emily Pronin and Daniel Wegner (2006) invited students to read a series of statements at either double or half the normal reading speed. Those who had just raced through the material reported feeling happier, more powerful, more energetic, and more creative. A racing mind arouses an upbeat mood.

In milder forms, mania's energy and free-flowing thinking does fuel creativity. George Frideric Handel (1685–1759), who may have suffered from a mild form of bipolar disorder, composed his nearly four-hour-long *Messiah* during three weeks of intense, creative energy (Keynes, 1980). Robert Schumann composed 51 musical works during two years of mania (1840 and 1849) and none during 1844, when he was severely depressed (Slater & Meyer, 1959). Those who rely on precision and logic, such as architects, designers, and journalists, suffer bipolar disorder less often than do those who rely on emotional expression and vivid imagery, reports Arnold Ludwig (1995). Composers, artists, poets, novelists, and entertainers seem especially prone (Jamison, 1993, 1995; Kaufman & Baer, 2002; Ludwig, 1995).

"All the people in history, literature, art, whom I most admire: Mozart, Shakespeare, Homer, El Greco, St. John, Chekhov, Gregory of Nyssa, Dostoevsky, Emily Brontë: not one of them would qualify for a mental-health certificate."
Madeleine L'Engle, *A Circle of Quiet,* 1972

Creativity and bipolar disorders
History has given us many creative artists, composers, and writers with bipolar disorder, including (left to right) Walt Whitman, Virginia Woolf, Samuel Clemens (Mark Twain), and Ernest Hemingway.

Bettmann/Corbis

George C. Beresford/Hulton Getty Pictures Library

The Granger Collection

Earl Theissen/Hulton Getty Pictures Library

It is as true of emotions as of everything else: What goes up comes down. Before long, the elated mood either returns to normal or plunges into a depression. Though bipolar disorder is much less common than major depressive disorder, it is often more dysfunctional, claiming twice as many lost workdays yearly (Kessler et al., 2006). In adults, it afflicts men and women about equally.

▶‖ Understanding Mood Disorders

51-2 What causes mood disorders, and what might explain the Western world's rising incidence of depression among youth and young adults?

In thousands of studies, psychologists have been accumulating evidence to help explain mood disorders and suggest more effective ways to treat and prevent them. Researcher Peter Lewinsohn and his colleagues (1985, 1998, 2003) have summarized the facts that any theory of depression must explain, including the following:

▶ *Many behavioral and cognitive changes accompany depression.* People trapped in a depressed mood are inactive and feel unmotivated. They are sensitive to negative happenings, more often recall negative information, and expect negative outcomes (my team will lose, my grades will fall, my love will fail). When the mood lifts, these behavioral and cognitive accompaniments disappear. Nearly half the time, people also exhibit symptoms of another disorder, such as anxiety or substance abuse.

▶ *Depression is widespread.* Its commonality suggests that its causes, too, must be common.

▶ *Compared with men, women are nearly twice as vulnerable to major depression* (**FIGURE 51.1**). This gender gap begins in adolescence; preadolescent girls are not more depression-prone than boys (Hyde et al., 2008). The factors that put women at risk for depression (genetic predispositions, child abuse, low self-esteem, marital problems, and so forth) similarly put men at risk (Kendler et al., 2006). Yet women are more vulnerable to disorders involving internalized states, such as depression, anxiety, and inhibited sexual desire. Men's disorders tend to be more external—alcohol abuse, antisocial conduct, lack of impulse control. When women get sad, they often get sadder than men do. When men get mad, they often get madder than women do.

▶ *Most major depressive episodes self-terminate.* Therapy tends to speed recovery, yet most people suffering major depression eventually return to normal even without professional help. The plague of depression comes and, a few weeks or months later, it goes, though it sometimes recurs (Burcusa & Iacono, 2007). About 50 percent of those who recover from depression will suffer another

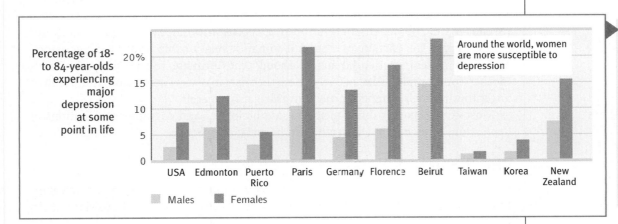

Around the world, women are more susceptible to depression

Males Females

FIGURE 51.1 Gender and major depression Interviews with 38,000 adults in 10 countries confirm what many smaller studies have found: Women's risk of major depression is nearly double that of men's. Lifetime risk of depression also varies by culture—from 1.5 percent in Taiwan to 19 percent in Beirut. (Data from Weissman et al., 1996.)

The emotional lives of men and women?

episode within two years. Recovery is more likely to be permanent the later the first episode strikes, the longer the person stays well, the fewer the previous episodes, the less stress experienced, and the more social support received (Belsher & Costello, 1988; Fergusson & Woodward, 2002; Kendler et al., 2001).

▶ ***Stressful events related to work, marriage, and close relationships often precede depression.*** A family member's death, a job loss, a marital crisis, or a physical assault increase one's risk of depression. If stress-related anxiety is a "crackling, menacing brushfire," notes biologist Robert Sapolsky (2003), "depression is a suffocating heavy blanket thrown on top of it." One long-term study (Kendler, 1998) tracked rates of depression in 2000 people. The risk of depression ranged from less than 1 percent among those who had experienced no stressful life event in the preceding month to 24 percent among those who had experienced three such events in that month. Major events such as Hurricane Katrina and 9/11 have increased anxiety and mood disorders (Galea et al., 2007; Person et al., 2006). But generally, depression results more often from a pileup of stresses than from a single loss or failure (Keller et al., 2007; van der Werf et al., 2006).

▶ ***With each new generation, depression is striking earlier (now often in the late teens) and affecting more people.*** This is true in Canada, the United States, England, France, Germany, Italy, Lebanon, New Zealand, Puerto Rico, and Taiwan (Collishaw et al., 2007; Cross-National Collaborative Group, 1992; Twenge et al., 2008). In one study, 12 percent of Australian adolescents reported symptoms of depression (Sawyer et al., 2000). Most hid it from their parents; almost 90 percent of those parents perceived their depressed teen as *not* suffering depression. In North America, today's young adults are three times more likely than their grandparents to report having recently—or ever—suffered depression (despite the grandparents' many more years of being at risk). The increase appears partly authentic, but it may also reflect today's young adults' greater willingness to disclose depression.

Researchers may accept these facts without agreeing how best to explain them. For example, proponents of Sigmund Freud's psychoanalytic theory (or the more modern psychodynamic approach) have an idea: Depression often occurs when significant losses, such as the breakup of a current romantic relationship, evoke feelings associated with losses experienced in childhood (the intimate relationship with one's mother, for example). Alternatively, these theorists may view depression as unresolved anger toward one's parents, turned inward against oneself.

Most contemporary researchers propose biological and cognitive explanations of depression, often combined in a biopsychosocial perspective.

The Biological Perspective

Most recent mental health research dollars have funded explorations of biological influences on mood disorders. Areas of interest have been genetic predispositions, brain activity, and biochemical imbalances.

"I see depression as the plague of the modern era."

Lewis Judd, former chief, National Institute of Mental Health, 2000

"Could bad cognitions be the hex, instead of conflicts over sex?"

Psychiatrist Robert L. Spitzer et al. (1982)

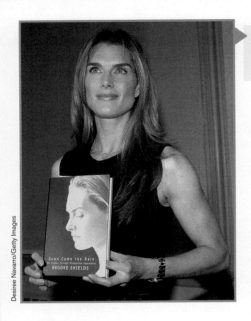

Down Came the Rain Actress Brooke Shields chronicled her disabling postpartum depression in this 2005 book.

Desiree Navarro/Getty Images

Genetic Influences

We have long known that mood disorders run in families. As one researcher noted, emotions are "postcards from our genes" (Plotkin, 1994). The risk of major depression and bipolar disorder increases if you have a parent or sibling with the disorder (Sullivan et al., 2000). If one identical twin is diagnosed with major depressive disorder, the chances are about 1 in 2 that at some time the other twin will be, too. If one identical twin has bipolar disorder, the chances are 7 in 10 that the other twin will at some point be diagnosed similarly. Among fraternal twins, the corresponding odds are just under 2 in 10 (Tsuang & Faraone, 1990). The greater similarity among identical twins holds even among twins reared apart (DiLalla et al., 1996). Summarizing the major twin studies, Kenneth Kendler and his co-researchers (2006) estimate that the heritability of major depression is 35 to 40 percent.

Moreover, adopted people who suffer a mood disorder often have close biological relatives who suffer mood disorders, become dependent on alcohol, or commit suicide (Wender et al., 1986). (Close-Up: Suicide, on the next page, reports other research findings on suicide.)

To tease out the genes that put people at risk for depression, some researchers have turned to *linkage analysis*. After finding families in which the disorder appears across several generations, geneticists examine DNA from affected and unaffected family members, looking for differences. Linkage analysis points us to a chromosome neighborhood, note behavior genetics researchers Robert Plomin and Peter McGuffin (2003); "a house-to-house search is then needed to find the culprit gene." Such studies are reinforcing the view that depression is a complex condition. Many genes probably work together, producing a mosaic of small effects that interact with other factors to put some people at greater risk. If the culprit gene variations can be identified, they may open the door to more effective drug therapy (Hu et al., 2007; McMahon et al., 2006; Paddock et al., 2007).

Jerry Irwin Photography

Gene-hunters' pursuit of bipolar-DNA links Linkage studies seek to identify aberrant genes in family members suffering a disorder. These Pennsylvania Amish family members—an isolated population sharing a common life-style and some vulnerability to bipolar disorder—have volunteered for such studies.

CLOSE-UP

Suicide

"But life, being weary of these worldly bars, Never lacks power to dismiss itself."
William Shakespeare, *Julius Caesar*, 1599

Each year nearly 1 million despairing people worldwide will elect a permanent solution to what might have been a temporary problem (WHO, 2008). Comparing the suicide rates of different groups, researchers have found

- *national differences:* Britain's, Italy's, and Spain's suicide rates are little more than half those of Canada, Australia, and the United States. Austria's and Finland's are about double (WHO, 2008). Within Europe, the most suicide-prone people (Lithuanians) have been 14 times more likely to kill themselves than the least (Greeks).

- *racial differences:* Within the United States, Whites are nearly twice as likely as Blacks to kill themselves (NIMH, 2002).

- *gender differences:* Women are much more likely than men to attempt suicide (WHO, 2008). But men are two to four times more likely (depending on the country) to succeed (**FIGURE 51.2**). Men use more lethal methods,

such as firing a bullet into the head, the method of choice in 6 of 10 U.S. suicides.

- *age differences and trends:* In late adulthood, rates increase, dramatically so among men (Figure 51.2). In the last half of the twentieth century, the global rate of annual suicide deaths rose from 10 to 18 per 100,000 (WHO, 2008).

- *other group differences:* Suicide rates are much higher among the rich, the nonreligious, and those who are single, widowed, or divorced (Hoyer & Lund, 1993; Stack, 1992; Stengel, 1981). Gay and lesbian youth much more often suffer distress and attempt suicide than do their heterosexual peers (Goldfried, 2001). Among 1.3 million Swedish military conscripts at age 18, the thinner men more often later committed suicide than their rounder age-mates (Magnusson et al., 2006). In England and Wales, there is a 17 percent increased risk of suicide among those born in the spring and early summer rather than autumn (Salib & Cortina-Borja, 2006).

The risk of suicide is at least five times greater for those who have been depressed than for the general population (Bostwick & Pankratz, 2000). People seldom commit

suicide while in the depths of depression, when energy and initiative are lacking. It is when they begin to rebound and become capable of following through that the risk increases. Compared with people who suffer no disorder, those with alcohol dependency are roughly 100 times more likely to commit suicide; some 3 percent of them do (Murphy & Wetzel, 1990). Even among people who have attempted suicide, those who abuse alcohol are five times more likely than others to kill themselves eventually (Beck & Steer, 1989). Teenage suicides are often linked with drug and alcohol abuse; the final act may follow a traumatic event, such as a romantic breakup or a guilt-provoking antisocial act (Fowler et al., 1986; Kolata, 1986). Because suicide is so often an impulsive act, environmental barriers (such as jump barriers on high bridges and the unavailability of loaded guns) can reduce suicides (Anderson, 2008). Although common sense might suggest that a determined person would simply find another way to complete the act, such restrictions give time for self-destructive impulses to subside.

Social suggestion may trigger suicide. Following highly publicized suicides and TV programs featuring suicide, known suicides increase. So do fatal auto and private airplane "accidents." One six-year study tracked suicide cases among all 1.2

The Depressed Brain

Using modern technology, researchers are also gaining insight into brain activity during depressed and manic states, and into the effects of certain neurotransmitters during these states. One study gave 13 elite Canadian swimmers the wrenching experience of watching a video of the swim in which they failed to make the Olympic team or failed at the Olympic games (Davis et al., 2008). Functional MRI (fMRI) scans showed the bummed-out swimmers experiencing brain activity patterns akin to those of patients with depressed moods.

Many studies have found less activity in the brain during slowed-down depressive states, and more activity during periods of mania (turn the page for **FIGURE 51.3**). The left frontal lobe, which is active during positive emotions, is likely to be inactive during depressed states (Davidson et al., 2002). In one study of people with severe depression, MRI scans found their frontal lobes 7 percent smaller than normal (Coffey et al., 1993). Other studies show that the *hippocampus,* the memory-

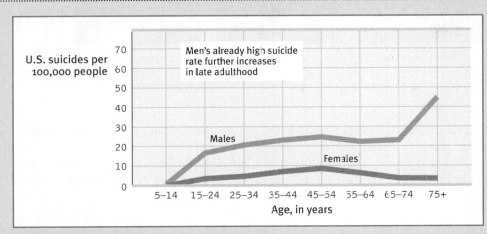

FIGURE 51.2 Suicide rates by gender and age
Worldwide suicide rates are higher among males than among females. The highest rates of all are found among older men. (From *Statistical Abstract,* 2008.)

million people who lived in metropolitan Stockholm at any time during the 1990s (Hedström et al., 2008). Men exposed to a family suicide were 8 times more likely to commit suicide than were nonexposed men. Although that phenomenon may be partly attributable to family genes, shared genetic predispositions do not explain why men exposed to a co-worker's suicide were 3.5 times more likely to commit suicide, compared with nonexposed men.

Suicide is not necessarily an act of hostility or revenge. The elderly sometimes choose death as an alternative to current or future suffering. In people of all ages, suicide may be a way of switching off unendurable pain and relieving a perceived burden on family members. "People desire death when two fundamental needs are frustrated to the point of extinction," notes Thomas Joiner (2006, p. 47): "The need to belong with or connect to others, and the need to feel effective with or to influence others."

In retrospect, families and friends may recall signs that they believe should have forewarned them—verbal hints, giving possessions away, or withdrawal and preoccupation with death. But few who talk of suicide or think suicidal thoughts (a number that includes one-third of all adolescents and college students) actually attempt suicide, and few of those who attempt it complete the act (Yip, 1998). U.S. hospital emergency rooms, for example, log a half-million visits as a result of attempted suicides each year (Surgeon General, 1999). But about 30,000 do succeed, one-third of whom have tried to kill themselves previously. Most discussed it beforehand. So, if a friend talks suicide to you, it's important to listen and to direct the person to professional help. Anyone who threatens suicide is at least sending a signal of feeling desperate or despondent.

"Don't let yourself mistake suicide—or suicidal thinking—for some kind of summary of a life. It's not. It's a lonely, private, furious moment that sometimes gets acted upon. But it's a moment of illness; it really isn't a report card."
Writer-broadcaster David Gilmour at the University of Toronto, 1999

processing center linked with the brain's emotional circuitry, is vulnerable to stress-related damage.

At least two neurotransmitter systems play a role in mood disorders. The first, *norepinephrine,* which increases arousal and boosts mood, is scarce during depression and overabundant during mania. (Drugs that alleviate mania reduce norepinephrine.) Most people with a history of depression also have a history of habitual smoking. This may indicate an attempt to self-medicate with inhaled nicotine, which can temporarily increase norepinephrine and boost mood (HMHL, 2002).

The second neurotransmitter, *serotonin,* is also scarce during depression. Some genes now under scrutiny provide codes for a protein that controls serotonin activity (Plomin & McGuffin, 2003). A widely publicized study of New Zealand young adults seemed to identify a serotonin-controlling gene that, in combination with significant stress, formed a recipe for depression (Caspi et al., 2003; Moffitt et al., 2006). Alas,

FIGURE 51.3 The ups and downs of bipolar disorder PET scans show that brain energy consumption rises and falls with the patient's emotional switches. Red areas are where the brain rapidly consumes glucose.

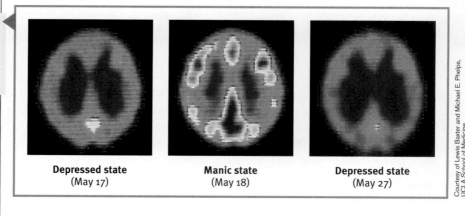

Depressed state
(May 17)

Manic state
(May 18)

Depressed state
(May 27)

other recent studies failed to replicate the finding (Risch et al., 2009). But stay tuned: science grows by fits and starts.

Drugs that relieve depression tend to increase norepinephrine or serotonin supplies by blocking either their reuptake (as Prozac, Zoloft, and Paxil do with serotonin) or their chemical breakdown. Repetitive physical exercise, such as jogging, reduces depression as it increases serotonin (Jacobs, 1994; Ilardi et al., 2007). Boosting serotonin may promote recovery from depression by stimulating hippocampus neuron growth (Airan et al., 2007; Jacobs et al., 2000).

The Social-Cognitive Perspective

Depression is a whole-body disorder. Biological influences contribute to depression but don't fully explain it. The social-cognitive perspective explores the roles of thinking and acting.

Depressed people view life through dark glasses. Their intensely negative assumptions about themselves, their situation, and their future lead them to magnify bad experiences and minimize good ones. Listen to Norman, a Canadian college professor, recalling his depression:

> I [despaired] of ever being human again. I honestly felt subhuman, lower than the lowest vermin. Furthermore, I was self-deprecatory and could not understand why anyone would want to associate with me, let alone love me. . . . I was positive that I was a fraud and a phony and that I didn't deserve my Ph.D. I didn't deserve to have tenure; I didn't deserve to be a Full Professor. . . . I didn't deserve the research grants I had been awarded; I couldn't understand how I had written books and journal articles. . . . I must have conned a lot of people. (Endler, 1982, pp. 45–49)

Research reveals how *self-defeating beliefs* and a *negative explanatory style* feed depression's vicious cycle.

Negative Thoughts and Negative Moods Interact

Self-defeating beliefs may arise from *learned helplessness*. Both dogs and humans act depressed, passive, and withdrawn after experiencing uncontrollable painful events. Learned helplessness is more common in women than in men, and they may respond more strongly to stress (Hankin & Abramson, 2001; Mazure et al., 2002; Nolen-Hoeksema, 2001, 2003). For example, 38 percent of women and 17 percent of men entering American colleges and universities report feeling "frequently overwhelmed by all I have to do" (Pryor et al., 2006). (Men report spending more of their time in "light anxiety" activities such as sports, TV watching, and partying, possibly avoiding activities that might make them feel overwhelmed.) This may help explain why, beginning in their early teens, women are nearly twice as vulnerable to depression (Kessler, 2001). Susan Nolen-Hoeksema (2003) believes women's higher risk of depression may also be related to what she describes as their tendency to *overthink,* to ruminate. Women often have vivid recall for both wonderful and horrid experiences; men more vaguely recall such experiences (Seidlitz & Diener, 1998). The gender difference in emotional memory may feed women's greater rumination over negative events and explain why fewer men than women report being frequently overwhelmed on entering college.

But why do life's unavoidable failures lead some people—women or men—and not others to become depressed? The answer lies partly in their *explanatory style*—who or what they blame for their failures. Think how you might feel if you failed a test. If you can externalize the blame (What an unfair test!), you are more likely to feel angry. But if you blame yourself, you probably will feel stupid and depressed.

So it is with depressed people, who tend to explain bad events in terms that are *stable* ("It's going to last forever"), *global* ("It's going to affect everything I do"), and *internal* ("It's all my fault") (**FIGURE 51.4**). Depression-prone people respond to bad events in an especially self-focused, self-blaming way (Mor & Winquist, 2002; Pyszczynski et al., 1991; Wood et al., 1990a,b). Their self-esteem fluctuates more rapidly up with boosts and down with threats (Butler et al., 1994).

The result of these pessimistic, overgeneralized, self-blaming attributions may be a depressing sense of hopelessness (Abramson et al., 1989; Panzarella et al., 2006). As Martin Seligman has noted, "A recipe for severe depression is preexisting pessimism encountering failure" (1991, p. 78). What then might we expect of new college students who are not depressed but do exhibit a pessimistic explanatory style? Lauren Alloy and her collaborators (1999) monitored Temple University and University of Wisconsin students every 6 weeks for 2.5 years. Among those identified as having a pessimistic thinking style, 17 percent had a first episode of major depression, as did only 1 percent of those who began college with an optimistic thinking style. Follow-up research has

Susan Nolen-Hoeksema "This epidemic of morbid meditation is a disease that women suffer much more than men. Women can ruminate about anything and everything—our appearance, our families, our career, our health." (*Women Who Think Too Much: How to Break Free of Overthinking and Reclaim Your Life,* 2003)

"I have learned to accept my mistakes by referring them to a personal history which was not of my making."
B. F. Skinner (1983)

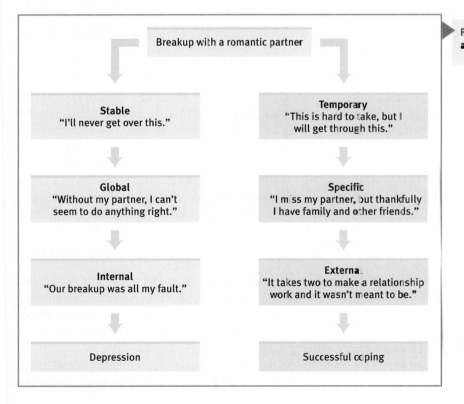

FIGURE 51.4 Explanatory style and depression

Breakup with a romantic partner

Stable "I'll never get over this."	**Temporary** "This is hard to take, but I will get through this."
Global "Without my partner, I can't seem to do anything right."	**Specific** "I miss my partner, but thankfully I have family and other friends."
Internal "Our breakup was all my fault."	**External** "It takes two to make a relationship work and it wasn't meant to be."
Depression	**Successful coping**

Might Charlie
Brown be helped
by an optimism-
training program?

found that students who exhibit optimism as they begin college develop more social support, which contributes to a lowered risk of depression (Brissette et al., 2002).

Seligman (1991, 1995) contends that depression is common among young Westerners because the rise of individualism and the decline of commitment to religion and family have forced young people to take personal responsibility for failure or rejection. In non-Western cultures, where close-knit relationships and cooperation are the norm, major depression is less common and less tied to self-blame over personal failure (WHO, 2004). In Japan, for example, depressed people instead tend to report feeling shame over letting others down (Draguns, 1990a).

|| From 1985 to 2004, Americans indeed reported fewer close relationships with co-workers, extended family, and neighbors, and thus had fewer people with whom they could discuss meaningful matters. The number of people with no confidantes increased from 10 to 25 percent (McPherson et al., 2006). ||

There is, however, a chicken-and-egg problem with the social-cognitive explanation of depression. Self-defeating beliefs, negative attributions, and self-blame surely do support depression. Peter Barnett and Ian Gotlib (1988) note that such cognitions *coincide* with a depressed mood and are *indicators* of depression. But do they *cause* depression, any more than a speedometer's reading of 70 mph causes a car's speed? Before or after being depressed, people's thoughts are less negative. Perhaps this is because, in a phenomenon known as *state-dependent memory,* a depressed mood triggers negative thoughts. If you temporarily put people in a bad or sad mood, their memories, judgments, and expectations suddenly become more pessimistic.

Joseph Forgas and his associates (1984) provided a striking demonstration of the mood effect. First, they filmed people talking to each other. The next day, they put those participants in a good or bad mood via hypnosis and had them watch the tape of themselves. The happy participants detected in their screen selves more positive than negative behaviors; the unhappy participants more often saw themselves behaving negatively.

"Man never reasons so much and becomes so introspective as when he suffers, since he is anxious to get at the cause of his sufferings."

Luigi Pirandello, *Six Characters in Search of an Author*, 1922

Depression's Vicious Cycle

Depression, as we have seen, is often brought on by stressful experiences—losing a job, getting divorced or rejected, suffering physical trauma—by anything that disrupts our sense of who we are and why we are worthy human beings. This disruption in turn leads to brooding, which amplifies negative feelings. But being withdrawn, self-focused, and complaining can by itself elicit rejection (Furr & Funder, 1998; Gotlib & Hammen, 1992). In one study, researchers Stephen Strack and James Coyne (1983) noted that "depressed persons induced hostility, depression, and anxiety in others and got rejected. Their guesses that they were not accepted were not a matter of cognitive distortion." Indeed, people in the throes of depression are at high risk for divorce, job loss, and other stressful life events. Weary of the person's fatigue, hopeless attitude, and lethargy, a spouse may threaten to leave or a boss may begin to question the person's competence. (This provides another example of genetic–environmental interaction: People genetically predisposed to depression more often experience depressing events.) The losses and stress only serve to compound the original depression. Rejection and depression feed each other. Misery may love another's company, but company does not love another's misery.

We can now assemble some of the pieces of the depression puzzle (**FIGURE 51.5**): (1) Negative, stressful events interpreted through (2) a ruminating, pessimistic

Reprinted by permission of United Feature Syndicate, Inc.

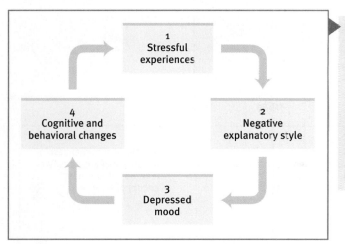

FIGURE 51.5 The vicious cycle of depressed thinking Cognitive therapists attempt to break this cycle by changing the way depressed people process events. Psychiatrists attempt to alter with medication the biological roots of persistently depressed moods.

explanatory style create (3) a hopeless, depressed state that (4) hampers the way the person thinks and acts. This, in turn, fuels (1) negative experiences such as rejection.

None of us is immune to the dejection, diminished self-esteem, and negative thinking brought on by rejection or defeat. As Edward Hirt and his colleagues (1992) demonstrated, even small losses can temporarily sour our thinking. They studied some avid Indiana University basketball fans who seemed to regard the team as an extension of themselves. After the fans watched their team lose or win, the researchers asked them to predict the team's future performance and their own. After a loss, the morose fans offered bleaker assessments not only of the team's future but also of their own likely performance at throwing darts, solving anagrams, and getting a date. When things aren't going our way, it may seem as though they never will.

It is a cycle we can all recognize. Bad moods feed on themselves: When we *feel* down, we *think* negatively and remember bad experiences. On the brighter side, we can break the cycle of depression at any of these points—by moving to a different environment, by reversing our self-blame and negative attributions, by turning our attention outward, or by engaging in more pleasant activities and more competent behavior.

Winston Churchill called depression a "black dog" that periodically hounded him. Poet Emily Dickinson was so afraid of bursting into tears in public that she spent much of her adult life in seclusion (Patterson, 1951). As each of these lives reminds us, people can and do struggle through depression. Most regain their capacity to love, to work, and even to succeed at the highest levels.

REVIEW

Mood Disorders

51-1 **What are mood disorders, and what forms do they take?** *Mood disorders* are characterized by emotional extremes. A person with *major depressive disorder* experiences two or more weeks of seriously depressed moods and feelings of worthlessness, takes little interest in most activities, and derives little pleasure from them. These feelings are not caused by drugs or a medical condition. People with the less common condition of *bipolar disorder* experience not only depression but also *mania,* episodes of hyperactive and wildly optimistic impulsive behavior.

51-2 **What causes mood disorders, and what might explain the Western world's rising incidence of depression among youth and young adults?** The biological perspective on depression focuses on genetic predispositions and on abnormalities in brain structures and functions (including those found in neurotransmitter systems). The social-cognitive perspective examines the influence of cyclic self-defeating beliefs, learned helplessness, negative attributions, and stressful experiences. The biopsychosocial approach considers influences interacting on many levels (**FIGURE 51.6**). Increased rates of depression among young Westerners may be due to the rise of individualism and the decline of commitment to religion and family, but this is a correlational finding, so the cause-effect relationship is not yet clear.

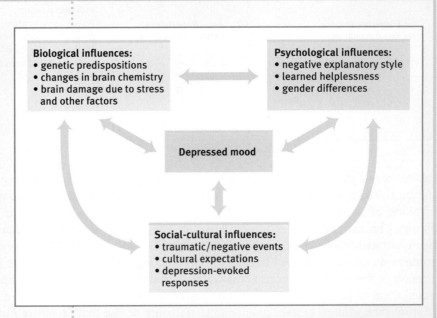

FIGURE 51.6 Biopsychosocial approach to depression
Seriously depressed moods result from a combination of interacting factors. Altering any one component can alter the others.

Terms and Concepts to Remember

mood disorders, p. 625

major depressive disorder,
   p. 626

mania, p. 626

bipolar disorder, p. 626

Test Yourself

1. What does it mean to say that "depression is the common cold of psychological disorders"?

(Answers to the Test Yourself questions can be found in Appendix B at the end of the book.)

Ask Yourself

1. Has your entry into student life been a challenging time for you? What advice would you have for others?

∞ WEB

Multiple-choice self-tests and more may be found at www.worthpublishers.com/myers

MODULE 52

Schizophrenia

Symptoms of Schizophrenia

Onset and Development
of Schizophrenia

Understanding Schizophrenia

52-1 What patterns of thinking, perceiving, feeling, and behaving characterize schizophrenia?

If depression is the common cold of psychological disorders, chronic schizophrenia is the cancer. Nearly 1 in 100 people will develop schizophrenia, joining the estimated 24 million across the world who suffer one of humanity's most dreaded disorders (WHO, 2008).

▶‖ Symptoms of Schizophrenia

Literally translated, **schizophrenia** means "split mind." It refers not to a multiple-personality split but rather to a split from reality that shows itself in disorganized thinking, disturbed perceptions, and inappropriate emotions and actions.

Disorganized Thinking

Imagine trying to communicate with Maxine, a young woman whose thoughts spill out in no logical order. Her biographer, Susan Sheehan (1982, p. 25), observed her saying aloud to no one in particular, "This morning, when I was at Hillside [Hospital], I was making a movie. I was surrounded by movie stars. . . . I'm Mary Poppins. Is this room painted blue to get me upset? My grandmother died four weeks after my eighteenth birthday."

As this strange monologue illustrates, the thinking of a person with schizophrenia is fragmented, bizarre, and often distorted by false beliefs called **delusions** ("I'm Mary Poppins"). Those with *paranoid* tendencies are particularly prone to delusions of persecution. Even within sentences, jumbled ideas may create what is called *word salad*. One young man begged for "a little more allegro in the treatment," and suggested that "liberationary movement with a view to the widening of the horizon" will "ergo extort some wit in lectures."

Disorganized thoughts may result from a breakdown in *selective attention*. We normally have a remarkable capacity for giving our undivided attention to one set of sensory stimuli while filtering out others. Those with schizophrenia cannot do this. Thus, irrelevant, minute stimuli, such as the grooves on a brick or the inflections of a voice, may distract their attention from a bigger event or a speaker's meaning. As one former patient recalled, "What had happened to me . . . was a breakdown in the filter, and a hodge-podge of unrelated stimuli were distracting me from things which should have had my undivided attention" (MacDonald, 1960, p. 218). This selective-attention difficulty is but one of dozens of cognitive differences associated with schizophrenia (Reichenberg & Harvey, 2007).

Disturbed Perceptions

A person with schizophrenia may have *hallucinations* (sensory experiences without sensory stimulation), seeing, feeling, tasting, or smelling things that are not there. Most often, however, the hallucinations are auditory, frequently voices making insulting remarks or giving orders. The voices may tell the patient that she is bad or that she must burn herself with a cigarette lighter. Imagine your own reaction if a dream broke into your waking consciousness. When the unreal seems real, the resulting perceptions are at best bizarre, at worst terrifying.

schizophrenia a group of severe disorders characterized by disorganized and delusional thinking, disturbed perceptions, and inappropriate emotions and actions.

delusions false beliefs, often of persecution or grandeur, that may accompany psychotic disorders.

August Natterer, *Witch's Head*. The Prinzhorn Collection, University of Heidelberg

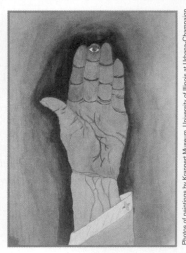

Photos of paintings by Krannert Museum, University of Illinois at Urbana-Champaign

"When someone asks me to explain schizophrenia I tell them, you know how sometimes in your dreams you are in them yourself and some of them feel like real nightmares? My schizophrenia was like I was walking through a dream. But everything around me was real. At times, today's world seems so boring and I wonder if I would like to step back into the schizophrenic dream, but then I remember all the scary and horrifying experiences."

Stuart Emmons, with Craig Geisler, Kalman J. Kaplan, and Martin Harrow, *Living With Schizophrenia*, 1997

Inappropriate Emotions and Actions

The emotions of schizophrenia are often utterly inappropriate, split off from reality. Maxine laughed after recalling her grandmother's death. On other occasions, she cried when others laughed, or became angry for no apparent reason. Others with schizophrenia lapse into an emotionless state of *flat affect*.

Motor behavior may also be inappropriate. Some perform senseless, compulsive acts, such as continually rocking or rubbing an arm. Others, who exhibit *catatonia*, may remain motionless for hours and then become agitated.

As you can imagine, such disorganized thinking, disturbed perceptions, and inappropriate emotions and actions profoundly disrupt social relationships and make it difficult to hold a job. During their most severe periods, those with schizophrenia live in a private inner world, preoccupied with illogical ideas and unreal images. Given a supportive environment, some eventually recover to enjoy a normal life or experience bouts of schizophrenia only intermittently. Others remain socially withdrawn and isolated throughout much of their lives.

▶‖ Onset and Development of Schizophrenia

Schizophrenia typically strikes as young people are maturing into adulthood. It knows no national boundaries, and it affects both males and females—though men tend to be struck earlier, more severely, and slightly more often (Aleman et al., 2003; Picchioni & Murray, 2007). Studies of Swedish and Danish male populations reveal that thin young men, and those who were not breast fed, are more vulnerable (Sørensen et al., 2005, 2006; Zammit et al., 2007).

For some, schizophrenia will appear suddenly, seemingly as a reaction to stress. For others, as was the case with Maxine, schizophrenia develops gradually, emerging from a long history of social inadequacy (which helps explain why those predisposed to schizophrenia often end up in the lower socioeconomic levels, or even homeless). We have thus far described schizophrenia as if it were a single disorder. Actually, it is a cluster of disorders. The subtypes share some common features, but they also have some distinguishing symptoms (**TABLE 52.1**). Schizophrenia patients with *positive symptoms* may experience hallucinations, talk in disorganized and deluded ways, and exhibit inappropriate laughter, tears, or rage. Those with *negative symptoms* have toneless voices, expressionless faces, or mute and rigid bodies. Thus, positive symptoms are the *presence* of inappropriate behaviors, and negative symptoms are the *absence* of appropriate behaviors. Because schizophrenia is a cluster of disorders, these varied symptoms could have more than one cause.

TABLE 52.1 **Subtypes of Schizophrenia**

Paranoid	Preoccupation with delusions or hallucinations, often with themes of persecution or grandiosity
Disorganized	Disorganized speech or behavior, or flat or inappropriate emotion
Catatonic	Immobility (or excessive, purposeless movement), extreme negativism, and/or parrotlike repeating of another's speech or movements
Undifferentiated	Many and varied symptoms
Residual	Withdrawal, after hallucinations and delusions have disappeared

One rule holds true around the world: When schizophrenia is a slow-developing process (called *chronic,* or *process, schizophrenia*), recovery is doubtful (WHO, 1979). Those with chronic schizophrenia often exhibit the persistent and incapacitating negative symptom of withdrawal (Kirkpatrick et al., 2006). Men, whose schizophrenia develops on average four years earlier than women's, more often exhibit negative symptoms and chronic schizophrenia (Räsänen et al., 2000). When previously well-adjusted people develop schizophrenia rapidly (called *acute,* or *reactive, schizophrenia*) following particular life stresses, recovery is much more likely. They more often have the positive symptoms that are more likely to respond to drug therapy (Fenton & McGlashan, 1991, 1994; Fowles, 1992).

▶‖ Understanding Schizophrenia

52-2 What causes schizophrenia?

Schizophrenia is not only the most dreaded psychological disorder but also one of the most heavily researched. Most of the new research studies link it with brain abnormalities and genetic predispositions. Schizophrenia is a disease of the brain exhibited in symptoms of the mind.

Brain Abnormalities

Might imbalances in brain chemistry underlie schizophrenia? Scientists have long known that strange behavior can have strange chemical causes. The saying "mad as a hatter" refers to the psychological deterioration of British hatmakers whose brains, it was later discovered, were slowly poisoned as they moistened the brims of mercury-laden felt hats with their lips (Smith, 1983). Scientists are clarifying the mechanism by which chemicals such as LSD produce hallucinations. These discoveries hint that schizophrenia symptoms might have a biochemical key.

Dopamine Overactivity

Researchers discovered one such key when they examined schizophrenia patients' brains after death and found an excess of receptors for *dopamine*—a sixfold excess for the so-called D4 dopamine receptor (Seeman et al., 1993; Wong et al., 1986). They speculate that such a high level may intensify brain signals in schizophrenia, creating positive symptoms such as hallucinations and paranoia. As we might therefore expect, drugs that block dopamine receptors often lessen these symptoms; drugs that increase dopamine levels, such as amphetamines and cocaine, sometimes intensify them (Swerdlow & Koob, 1987). Dopamine overactivity may underlie patients' overreactions to irrelevant external and internal stimuli.

Dopamine-blocking drugs have little effect on persistent negative symptoms of withdrawal. Researchers are exploring the excitatory neurotransmitter, glutamate. Impaired glutamate activity appears to be another source of schizophrenia symptoms (Javitt & Coyle, 2004). Drugs that interfere with glutamate receptors can produce schizophrenialike negative symptoms.

Abnormal Brain Activity and Anatomy

Modern brain-scanning techniques reveal that many people with chronic schizophrenia have abnormal activity in multiple brain areas. Some have abnormally low brain activity in the frontal lobes, which are critical for reasoning, planning, and problem solving (Morey et al., 2005; Pettegrew et al., 1993; Resnick, 1992). People diagnosed with schizophrenia also display a noticeable decline in the brain waves that reflect synchronized neural firing in the frontal lobes (Spencer et al., 2004; Symond et al., 2005). Out-of-sync neurons may disrupt the integrated functioning of neural networks, possibly contributing to schizophrenia symptoms.

One study took PET scans of brain activity while people were hallucinating (Silbersweig et al., 1995). When participants heard a voice or saw something, their brain became vigorously active in several core regions, including the thalamus, a structure deep in the brain that filters incoming sensory signals and transmits them to the cortex. Another PET scan study of people with paranoia found increased activity in the amygdala, a fear-processing center (Epstein et al., 1998).

Many studies have found enlarged, fluid-filled areas and a corresponding shrinkage of cerebral tissue in people with schizophrenia (Wright et al., 2000). Some studies have even found such abnormalities in the brains of people who would *later* develop this disorder and in their close relatives (Boos et al., 2007; Job et al., 2006). The greater the shrinkage, the more severe the thought disorder (Collinson et al., 2003; Nelson et al., 1998; Shenton, 1992). One smaller-than-normal area is the cortex. Another is the thalamus, which may explain why people with schizophrenia have difficulty filtering sensory input and focusing attention (Andreasen et al., 1994). The bottom line of various studies is that schizophrenia involves not one isolated brain abnormality but problems with several brain regions and their interconnections (Andreasen, 1997, 2001).

Naturally, scientists wonder what causes these abnormalities. Some suspect a mishap during prenatal development or delivery. Two known risk factors for schizophrenia are low birth weight and oxygen deprivation during delivery (Buka et al., 1999; Zornberg et al., 2000). Famine may also increase risks. People conceived during the peak of the Dutch wartime famine later displayed a doubled rate of schizophrenia, as did those conceived during the famine of 1959 to 1961 in eastern China (St. Clair et al., 2005; Susser et al., 1996).

Maternal Virus During Midpregnancy

Consider another possible culprit: a midpregnancy viral infection that impairs fetal brain development (Patterson, 2007). Can you imagine some ways to test this fetal-virus idea? Scientists have asked the following:

▶ *Are people at increased risk of schizophrenia if, during the middle of their fetal development, their country experienced a flu epidemic?* The repeated answer is *yes* (Mednick et al., 1994; Murray et al., 1992; Wright et al., 1995).

▶ *Are people born in densely populated areas, where viral diseases spread more readily, at greater risk for schizophrenia?* The answer, confirmed in a study of 1.75 million Danes, is *yes* (Jablensky, 1999; Mortensen, 1999).

▶ *Are those born during the winter and spring months—after the fall-winter flu season— also at increased risk?* The answer is again *yes*, at 5 to 8 percent increased risk (Torrey et al., 1997, 2002).

▶ *In the Southern Hemisphere, where the seasons are the reverse of the Northern Hemisphere, are the months of above-average schizophrenia births similarly reversed?*

‖ About 60 percent of schizophrenia patients smoke, often heavily. Nicotine apparently stimulates certain brain receptors, which helps focus attention (Javitt & Coyle, 2004). ‖

Studying the neurophysiology of schizophrenia Psychiatrist E. Fuller Torrey is collecting the brains of hundreds of those who died as young adults and suffered disorders such as schizophrenia and bipolar disorder. Torrey is making tissue samples available to researchers worldwide.

Chris Usher

Again, the answer is *yes,* though somewhat less so. In Australia, for example, people born between August and October are at greater risk—*unless* they migrated from the Northern Hemisphere, in which case their risk is greater if they were born between January and March (McGrath et al., 1995, 1999).

▶ *Are mothers who report being sick with influenza during pregnancy more likely to bear children who develop schizophrenia?* In one study of nearly 8000 women, the answer was *yes.* The schizophrenia risk increased from the customary 1 percent to about 2 percent—but only when infections occurred during the second trimester (Brown et al., 2000).

▶ *Does blood drawn from pregnant women whose offspring develop schizophrenia show higher-than-normal levels of antibodies that suggest a viral infection?* In one study of 27 women whose children later developed schizophrenia, the answer was *yes* (Buka et al., 2001). And the answer was again *yes* in a huge California study, which collected blood samples from some 20,000 pregnant women during the 1950s and 1960s. Some children born of those pregnancies were later diagnosed with schizophrenia. When antibodies in the mother's blood indicated she had been exposed to influenza during the first half of the pregnancy, the child's risk of developing schizophrenia tripled. Flu during the second half of the pregnancy produced no such increase (Brown et al., 2004).

These converging lines of evidence suggest that fetal-virus infections play a contributing role in the development of schizophrenia. They also strengthen the recommendation that "women who will be more than three months pregnant during the flu season" have a flu shot (CDC, 2003).

Why might a second-trimester maternal flu bout put fetuses at risk? Is it the virus itself? The mother's immune response to it? Medications taken? (Wyatt et al., 2001). Does the infection weaken the brain's supportive glial cells, leading to reduced synaptic connections (Moises et al., 2002)? In time, answers may become available.

Genetic Factors

Fetal-virus infections do appear to increase the odds that a child will develop schizophrenia. But this theory cannot tell us why some 98 percent of women who catch the flu during their second trimester of pregnancy bear children who do *not* develop schizophrenia. Might people also inherit a predisposition to this disorder? The evidence strongly suggests that, *yes,* some do. The nearly 1-in-100 odds of any person's being diagnosed with schizophrenia become about 1 in 10 among those whose sibling or parent has the disorder, and close to 1 in 2 if the affected sibling is an identical twin (**FIGURE 52.1**). And, although only a dozen or so such cases are on record, the co-twin of an identical twin with schizophrenia retains that 1-in-2 chance when the twins are reared apart (Plomin et al., 1997).

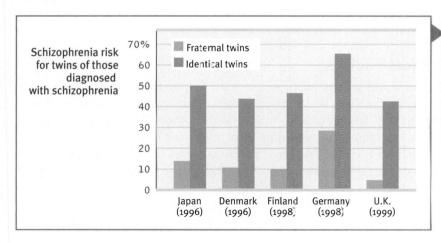

Schizophrenia risk for twins of those diagnosed with schizophrenia

FIGURE 52.1 Risk of developing schizophrenia The lifetime risk of developing schizophrenia varies with one's genetic relatedness to someone having this disorder. Across countries, barely more than 1 in 10 fraternal twins, but some 5 in 10 identical twins, share a schizophrenia diagnosis. (Adapted from Gottesman, 2001.)

No schizophrenia

Schizophrenia

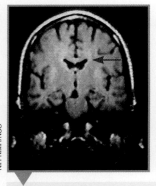

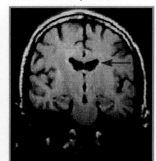

Both photos: Courtesy of Daniel R. Weinberger, M.D., NIH-NIMH/NSC

Schizophrenia in identical twins
When twins differ, only the one afflicted with schizophrenia typically has enlarged, fluid-filled cranial cavities (right) (Suddath et al., 1990). The difference between the twins implies some nongenetic factor, such as a virus, is also at work.

The Genain quadruplets The odds of any four people picked at random all being diagnosed with schizophrenia are 1 in 100 million. But genetically identical sisters Nora, Iris, Myra, and Hester Genain all have the disease. Two of the sisters have more severe forms of the disorder than the others, suggesting the influence of environmental as well as biological factors.

Courtesy of Genain family

Remember, though, that identical twins also share a prenatal environment. About two-thirds also share a placenta and the blood it supplies; the other one-third have two single placentas. If an identical twin has schizophrenia, the co-twin's chances of being similarly afflicted are 6 in 10 if they shared a placenta. If they had separate placentas, as do fraternal twins, the chances are only 1 in 10 (Davis et al., 1995a,b; Phelps et al., 1997). Twins who share a placenta are more likely to experience the same prenatal viruses. So it is possible that shared germs as well as shared genes produce identical twin similarities.

Adoption studies, however, confirm that the genetic link is real (Gottesman, 1991). Children adopted by someone who develops schizophrenia seldom "catch" the disorder. Rather, adopted children have an elevated risk if a biological parent is diagnosed with schizophrenia.

With the genetic factor established, researchers are now sleuthing specific genes that, in some combination, might predispose schizophrenia-inducing brain abnormalities (Marx, 2007; Millar et al., 2005; Williams et al., 2007). (It is not our genes but our brains that directly control our behavior.) Some of these genes influence the effects of dopamine and other neurotransmitters in the brain. Others affect the production of *myelin,* a fatty substance that coats the axons of nerve cells and lets impulses travel at high speed through neural networks.

Although the genetic contribution to schizophrenia is beyond question, the genetic formula is not as straightforward as the inheritance of eye color. A complex disorder such as schizophrenia is surely influenced by multiple genes with small effects, but identifying these genes has proven difficult (McClellan et al., 2007; Sanders et al., 2008; Walsh et al., 2008). And even within this context, other factors—such as the prenatal viral infections, nutritional deprivation, and oxygen deprivation at birth mentioned earlier—may somehow help to "turn on" the genes that predispose some of us to this disease. As we have so often seen, nature and nurture interact. Neither hand claps alone.

Our knowledge of human genetics and of genetic influences on maladies such as schizophrenia is exploding, thanks partly to millions of new U.S. National Institute of Mental Health dollars focused on solving the schizophrenia riddle. In 2007, one privately funded new research center announced its ambitious aim: "To unambiguously diagnose patients with psychiatric disorders based on their DNA sequence in 10 years' time" (Holden, 2007). So, can scientists develop genetic tests that reveal who is at risk? If so, will people in the future subject their embryos to genetic testing (and gene repair or abortion) if they are at risk for this or some other psychological or physical malady? Might they take their egg and sperm to a genetics lab for screening before combining them to produce an embryo? Or will children be tested for genetic risks and given appropriate preventive treatments? In this brave new twenty-first-century world, such questions await answers.

Psychological Factors

If prenatal viruses and genetic predispositions do not, by themselves, cause schizophrenia, neither do family or social factors alone. Psychologists who once attributed schizophrenia to cold and capricious "refrigerator mothers" have long since abandoned this idea. It remains true, as Susan Nicol and Irving Gottesman (1983) noted almost three decades ago, that "no environmental causes have been discovered that will invariably, or even with moderate probability, produce schizophrenia in persons who are not related to" a person with schizophrenia.

Hoping to identify environmental triggers of schizophrenia, several investigators are following the development of "high-risk" children, such as those born to a parent with schizophrenia or exposed to prenatal risks (Freedman et al., 1998; Olin & Mednick, 1996; Susser, 1999). One study followed 163 teens and early-twenties adults who had two relatives with schizophrenia. During the 2.5-year study, the 20 percent who developed schizophrenia displayed some tendency to withdraw socially and behave oddly before the onset of the disorder (Johnstone et al., 2005). By comparing the experiences of high-risk and low-risk children who do and do not develop schizophrenia, researchers have so far pinpointed the following possible early warning signs:

▶ A mother whose schizophrenia was severe and long-lasting
▶ Birth complications, often involving oxygen deprivation and low birth weight
▶ Separation from parents
▶ Short attention span and poor muscle coordination
▶ Disruptive or withdrawn behavior
▶ Emotional unpredictability
▶ Poor peer relations and solo play

* * *

Few of us can relate to the strange thoughts, perceptions, and behaviors of schizophrenia. Sometimes our thoughts do jump around, but we do not talk nonsensically. Occasionally we feel unjustly suspicious of someone, but we do not fear that the world is plotting against us. Often our perceptions err, but rarely do we see or hear things that are not there. We have felt regret after laughing at someone's misfortune, but we rarely giggle in response to bad news. At times we just want to be alone, but we do not live in social isolation. However, millions of people around the world do talk strangely, suffer delusions, hear nonexistent voices, see things that are not there, laugh or cry at inappropriate times, or withdraw into private imaginary worlds. The quest to solve the cruel puzzle of schizophrenia therefore continues, and more vigorously than ever.

REVIEW

Schizophrenia

52-1 **What patterns of thinking, perceiving, feeling, and behaving characterize schizophrenia?** *Schizophrenia* is a group of disorders that typically strike during late adolescence, affect men very slightly more than women, and seem to occur in all cultures. Symptoms of schizophrenia are disorganized and delusional thinking, disturbed perceptions, and inappropriate emotions and actions. *Delusions* are false beliefs; hallucinations are sensory experiences without sensory stimulation. Schizophrenia may emerge gradually from a chronic history of social inadequacy (in which case the outlook is dim) or suddenly in reaction to stress (in which case the prospects for recovery are brighter).

52-2 **What causes schizophrenia?** People with schizophrenia have increased receptors for the neurotransmitter dopamine, which may intensify the positive symptoms of schizophrenia. Brain abnormalities associated with schizophrenia include enlarged, fluid-filled cerebral cavities and corresponding decreases in the cortex. Brain scans reveal abnormal activity in the frontal lobes, thalamus, and amygdala. Malfunctions in multiple brain regions and their connections apparently interact to produce the symptoms of schizophrenia. Research support is mounting for the causal effects of a virus suffered in mid-pregnancy. Twin and adoption studies also point to a genetic predisposition that interacts with environmental factors to produce schizophrenia.

Terms and Concepts to Remember

schizophrenia, p. 637   delusions, p. 637

Test Yourself

1. What are the two main subtypes of schizophrenia?

(Answers to the Test Yourself questions can be found in Appendix B at the end of the book.)

Ask Yourself

1. Do you think the media accurately portrays the behavior of people suffering from schizophrenia? Why or why not?

∞ WEB

Multiple-choice self-tests and more may be found at www.worthpublishers.com/myers

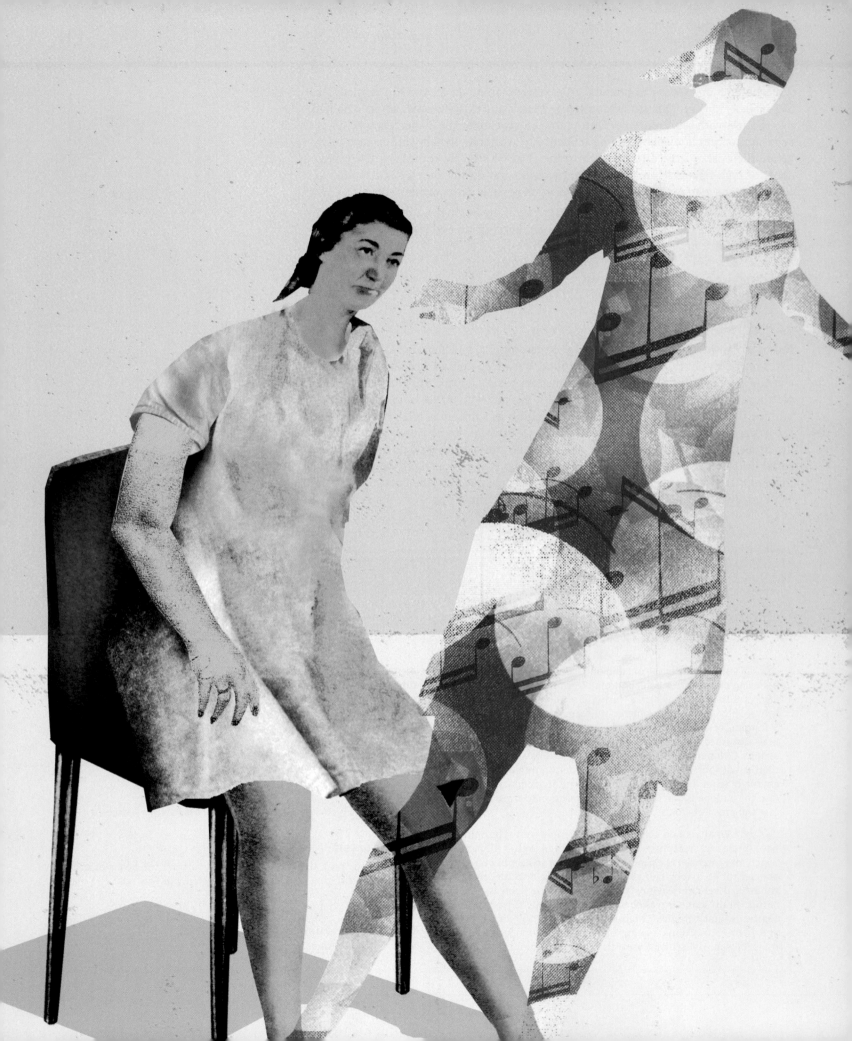

Therapy

MODULES

53
The Psychological Therapies

54
Evaluating Psychotherapies

55
The Biomedical Therapies

Today we comprehend deep outer space and can state with certainty the chemical composition of Jupiter's atmosphere. But in understanding and treating the disturbances of deep inner space—the psychological disorders that continue to plague humankind—we are only beginning to make real progress. In the 2200 years since Eratosthenes correctly estimated the Earth's circumference, we have charted the heavens, cracked the genetic code, and eliminated or found cures for all sorts of diseases. Meanwhile, we have treated psychological disorders with a bewildering array of harsh and gentle methods: by cutting holes in the head and by giving warm baths and massages; by restraining, bleeding, or "beating the devil" out of people and by placing them in sunny, serene environments; by administering drugs and electric shocks and by talking—talking about childhood experiences, about current feelings, about maladaptive thoughts and behaviors.

The transition from brutal to gentler treatments occurred thanks to the efforts of reformers such as Philippe Pinel in France and Dorothea Dix in the United States, Canada, and Scotland. Both advocated constructing mental hospitals to offer more humane methods of treatment. But times have once again changed, and the introduction of therapeutic drugs and community-based treatment programs has largely emptied mental health hospitals since the mid-1950s.

Today's mental health therapies can be classified into two main categories, and the favored treatment depends on both the disorder and the therapist's viewpoint. Learning-related disorders, such as phobias, are likely candidates for *psychotherapy* (Modules 53 and 54), in which a trained therapist uses psychological techniques to assist someone seeking to overcome difficulties or achieve personal growth. Biologically influenced disorders, such as schizophrenia, will often be treated with *biomedical therapy* (Module 55)—a prescribed medication or medical procedure that acts directly on the patient's nervous system.

Dorothea Dix (1802–1887) "I . . . call your attention to the state of the Insane Persons confined within this Commonwealth, in cages."

Culver Pictures

Psychoanalysis

Humanistic Therapies

Behavior Therapies

Cognitive Therapies

Group and Family Therapies

The Psychological Therapies

Among the dozens of types of **psychotherapy,** we will look at only the most influential. Each is built on one or more of psychology's major theories: psychoanalytic, humanistic, behavioral, and cognitive. Most of these techniques can be used one-on-one or in groups.

Depending on the client and the problem, some therapists—particularly the many using a biopsychosocial approach—draw from a variety of techniques. Many patients receive drug therapy in combination with psychotherapy. Half of all psychotherapists describe themselves as taking an **eclectic approach,** using a blend of therapies (Beitman et al., 1989; Castonguay & Goldfried, 1994). *Psychotherapy integration* attempts to combine a selection of assorted techniques into a single, coherent system.

The history of treatment As William Hogarth's (1697–1764) painting of London's St. Mary of Bethlehem hospital (commonly called Bedlam) depicts, visitors to eighteenth-century mental hospitals paid to gawk at patients, as though they were viewing zoo animals. Benjamin Rush (1746–1813), a founder of the movement for more humane treatment of the mentally ill, designed the chair on the far right "for the benefit of maniacal patients." He believed the restraints would help them regain their sensibilities.

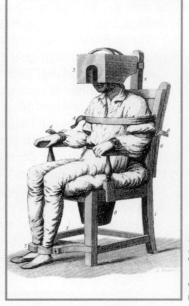

▶‖ Psychoanalysis

53-1 What are the aims and methods of psychoanalysis, and how have they been adapted in psychodynamic therapy?

Sigmund Freud's **psychoanalysis** was the first of the psychological therapies, and its terminology has crept into our modern vocabulary. Few clinicians today practice therapy as Freud did, but some of his techniques and assumptions survive, especially in the *psychodynamic therapies*.

Aims

Because Freud assumed that many psychological problems are fueled by childhood's residue of repressed impulses and conflicts, he and his students sought to bring these repressed feelings into patients' conscious awareness. By gaining insight into the origins of the disorder—by excavating their childhood's past and fulfilling the ancient

imperative to "know thyself" in a deep way—patients then work through the buried feelings and take responsibility for their own growth. Psychoanalytic theory presumes that healthier, less anxious living becomes possible when people release the energy they had previously devoted to id-ego-superego conflicts.

Methods

Psychoanalysis is historical reconstruction. Psychoanalytic theory emphasizes the formative power of childhood experiences, and thus aims to unearth the past in hope of unmasking the present. But how?

After trying hypnosis and discarding it as unreliable, Freud turned to *free association.* Imagine yourself as a patient using free association. First, you relax, perhaps by lying on a couch. To help you focus on your own thoughts and feelings, the psychoanalyst may sit out of your line of vision. You say aloud whatever comes to your mind, at one moment a childhood memory, at another a dream or recent experience. It sounds easy, but soon you notice how often you edit your thoughts as you speak, omitting what seems trivial, irrelevant, or shameful. Even in the safe presence of the analyst, you may pause momentarily before uttering an embarrassing thought. You may joke or change the subject to something less threatening. Sometimes your mind goes blank or you find yourself unable to remember important details.

To the psychoanalyst, these blocks in the flow of your free associations indicate **resistance.** They hint that anxiety lurks and you are defending against sensitive material. The analyst will note your resistances and then **interpret** their meaning, providing *insight* into your underlying wishes, feelings, and conflicts. If offered at the right moment, this interpretation—of, say, your not wanting to talk about your mother—may illuminate what you are avoiding and demonstrate how this resistance fits with other pieces of your psychological puzzle.

psychotherapy treatment involving psychological techniques; consists of interactions between a trained therapist and someone seeking to overcome psychological difficulties or achieve personal growth.

eclectic approach an approach to psychotherapy that, depending on the client's problems, uses techniques from various forms of therapy.

psychoanalysis Sigmund Freud's therapeutic technique. Freud believed the patient's free associations, resistances, dreams, and transferences—and the therapist's interpretations of them—released previously repressed feelings, allowing the patient to gain self-insight.

resistance in psychoanalysis, the blocking from consciousness of anxiety-laden material.

interpretation in psychoanalysis, the analyst's noting supposed dream meanings, resistances, and other significant behaviors and events in order to promote insight.

transference in psychoanalysis, the patient's transfer to the analyst of emotions linked with other relationships (such as love or hatred for a parent).

Edmund Engelman

Freud's consulting room Freud's office was rich with antiquities from around the world, including artwork related to his ideas about unconscious motives. His famous couch, piled high with pillows, placed patients in a comfortable reclining position facing away from him to help them focus inward.

Freud believed that another clue to unconscious conflicts is your dreams' *latent content*—their underlying but censored meaning. Thus, after inviting you to report a dream, the analyst may offer a *dream analysis,* suggesting its meaning.

During many such sessions you will probably disclose to your analyst more of yourself than you have ever revealed to anyone else, much of it pertaining to your earliest memories. You may find yourself experiencing strong positive or negative feelings for your analyst, who may suggest you are **transferring** to your analyst feelings you experienced in earlier relationships with family members or other important people. By exposing feelings you have previously defended against, such as dependency or mingled love and anger, transference will give you a belated chance to work through them, with your analyst's help. Examining your feelings may also give you insight into your current relationships, not just those of your past childhood.

"You say, 'Off with her head' but what I'm hearing is, 'I feel neglected.'"

"I haven't seen my analyst in 200 years. He was a strict Freudian. If I'd been going all this time, I'd probably almost be cured by now."

Woody Allen, after awakening from suspended animation in the movie *Sleeper*

"Look, making you happy is out of the question, but I can give you a compelling narrative for your misery."

Face-to-face therapy In this type of therapy session, the couch has disappeared. But the influence of psychoanalytic theory may not have, especially if the therapist probes for the origin of the patient's symptoms by seeking information from the patient's childhood.

Psychoanalysts acknowledge the criticism that their interpretations cannot be proven or disproven. But they insist that interpretations often are a great help to patients. Psychoanalysis, they say, is therapy, not science.

Traditional psychoanalysis takes time, up to several years of several sessions a week, and it is expensive. (Three times a week for just two years at more than $100 per hour comes to at least $30,000.) Outside of France, Germany, Quebec, and New York City, relatively few therapists offer it (Goode, 2003). In the United States, at least, this is not surprising, given that U.S. managed health care limits the types and length of insured mental health services.

Psychodynamic Therapy

Influenced by Freud, **psychodynamic therapists** try to understand a patient's current symptoms by focusing on themes across important relationships, including childhood experiences and the therapist relationship. They also help the person explore and gain perspective on defended-against thoughts and feelings. But these therapists may talk to the patient face to face (rather than out of the line of vision), once a week (rather than several times weekly), and for only a few weeks or months (rather than several years).

No brief excerpt can exemplify the way psychodynamic therapy interprets a patient's conflict. But the following interaction between therapist David Malan (1978, pp. 133–134) and a depressed patient illustrates the goal of enabling insight by looking for common, recurring themes, especially in relationships.

> **Malan:** I get the feeling that you're the sort of person who needs to keep active. If you don't keep active, then something goes wrong. Is that true?
>
> **Patient:** Yes.
>
> **Malan:** I get a second feeling about you and that is that you must, underneath all this, have an awful lot of very strong and upsetting feelings. Somehow they're there but you aren't really quite in touch with them. Isn't this right? I feel you've been like that as long as you can remember.
>
> **Patient:** For quite a few years, whenever I really sat down and thought about it I got depressed, so I tried not to think about it.
>
> **Malan:** You see, you've established a pattern, haven't you? You're even like that here with me, because in spite of the fact that you're in some trouble and you feel that the bottom is falling out of your world, the way you're telling me this is just as if there wasn't anything wrong.

Notice how Malan interpreted the woman's earlier remarks (when she did most of the talking) and suggested that her relationship with him reveals a characteristic pattern of behavior? He was suggesting insights into her problems.

Interpersonal psychotherapy, a brief (12- to 16-session) variation of psychodynamic therapy, has been effective in treating depression (Weissman, 1999). Interpersonal psychotherapy aims to help people gain insight into the roots of their difficulties, but its goal is symptom relief in the here and now, not overall personality change. Rather than focusing mostly on undoing past hurts and offering interpretations, the therapist focuses primarily on current relationships and on helping people improve their relationship skills.

The case of Anna (not her real name), a 34-year-old married professional, illustrates these goals. Five months after receiving a promotion, with accompanying increased responsibilities and longer hours, Anna experienced increased tensions with her husband over his wish for a second child. She began feeling depressed, had trouble sleeping, became irritable, and was gaining weight. A typical psychodynamic therapist might have helped Anna gain insight into her angry impulses and her defenses against anger. An interpersonal therapist similarly wanted Anna to gain these insights, but also engaged her thinking on more immediate issues—how she could balance work and home, resolve the dispute with her husband, and express her emotions more effectively (Markowitz et al., 1998).

▶❘❘ Humanistic Therapies

53-2 What are the basic themes of humanistic therapy such as Rogers' client-centered approach?

The humanistic perspective has emphasized people's inherent potential for self-fulfillment. Not surprisingly, humanistic therapists aim to boost self-fulfillment by helping people grow in self-awareness and self-acceptance. Like psychoanalytic therapies, humanistic therapies have attempted to reduce the inner conflicts that are impeding natural developmental growth by providing clients with new insights. Indeed, the psychoanalytic and humanistic therapies are often referred to as **insight therapies.** But humanistic therapists differ from psychoanalysts in focusing on

▶ the *present* and *future* more than the past. They explore feelings as they occur, rather than achieving insights into the childhood origins of the feelings.

▶ *conscious* rather than unconscious thoughts.

▶ taking immediate *responsibility* for one's feelings and actions, rather than uncovering hidden determinants.

▶ promoting growth instead of curing illness. Thus, those in therapy became "clients" rather than "patients" (a change many therapists have since adopted).

Carl Rogers (1902–1987) developed the widely used humanistic technique he called **client-centered therapy,** which focuses on the person's conscious self-perceptions. In this *nondirective therapy,* the therapist listens, without judging or interpreting, and seeks to refrain from directing the client toward certain insights.

Believing that most people already possess the resources for growth, Rogers (1961, 1980) encouraged therapists to exhibit *genuineness, acceptance,* and *empathy.* When therapists drop their facades and genuinely express their true feelings, when they enable their clients to feel unconditionally accepted, and when they empathically sense and reflect their clients' feelings, the clients may deepen their self-understanding and self-acceptance (Hill & Nakayama, 2000). As Rogers (1980, p. 10) explained,

> Hearing has consequences. When I truly hear a person and the meanings that are important to him at that moment, hearing not simply his words, but him, and when I let him know that I have heard his own private personal meanings, many things happen. There is first of all a grateful look. He feels released. He wants to tell me more about his world. He surges forth in a new sense of freedom. He becomes more open to the process of change.
>
> I have often noticed that the more deeply I hear the meanings of the person, the more there is that happens. Almost always, when a person realizes he has been deeply heard, his eyes moisten. I think in some real sense he is weeping for joy. It is as though he were saying, "Thank God, somebody heard me. Someone knows what it's like to be me."

"Hearing" refers to Rogers' technique of **active listening**—echoing, restating, and seeking clarification of what the person expresses (verbally or nonverbally) and acknowledging the expressed feelings. Active listening is now an accepted part of therapeutic counseling practices in many schools, colleges, and clinics. The counselor listens attentively and interrupts only to restate and confirm feelings, to accept what is being expressed, or to seek clarification. The following brief excerpt between Rogers and a male client illustrates how he sought to provide a psychological mirror that would help clients see themselves more clearly.

---

psychodynamic therapy therapy deriving from the psychoanalytic tradition that views individuals as responding to unconscious forces and childhood experiences, and that seeks to enhance self-insight.

insight therapies a variety of therapies which aim to improve psychological functioning by increasing the client's awareness of underlying motives and defenses.

client-centered therapy a humanistic therapy, developed by Carl Rogers, in which the therapist uses techniques such as active listening within a genuine, accepting, empathic environment to facilitate clients' growth. (Also called *person-centered therapy.*)

active listening empathic listening in which the listener echoes, restates, and clarifies. A feature of Rogers' client-centered therapy.

"We have two ears and one mouth that we may listen the more and talk the less."
Zeno, 335–263 B.C., *Diogenes Laertius*

Michael Rougier/*Life* Magazine © Time Warner, Inc.

Active listening Carl Rogers (right) empathized with a client during this group therapy session.

Rogers: Feeling that now, hm? That you're just no good to yourself, no good to anybody. Never will be any good to anybody. Just that you're completely worthless, huh?—Those really are lousy feelings. Just feel that you're no good at all, hm?

Client: Yeah. (*Muttering in low, discouraged voice*) That's what this guy I went to town with just the other day told me.

Rogers: This guy that you went to town with really told you that you were no good? Is that what you're saying? Did I get that right?

Client: M-hm.

Rogers: I guess the meaning of that if I get it right is that here's somebody that—meant something to you and what does he think of you? Why, he's told you that he thinks you're no good at all. And that just really knocks the props out from under you. (*Client weeps quietly.*) It just brings the tears. (*Silence of 20 seconds*)

Client: (*Rather defiantly*) I don't care though.

Rogers: You tell yourself you don't care at all, but somehow I guess some part of you cares because some part of you weeps over it.

(*Meador & Rogers, 1984, p. 167*)

Can a therapist be a perfect mirror, without selecting and interpreting what is reflected? Rogers conceded that one cannot be *totally* nondirective. Nevertheless, he believed that the therapist's most important contribution is to accept and understand the client. Given a nonjudgmental, grace-filled environment that provides **unconditional positive regard,** people may accept even their worst traits and feel valued and whole.

If you want to listen more actively in your own relationships, three hints may help:

1. *Paraphrase.* Rather than saying "I know how you feel," check your understandings by summarizing the speaker's words in your own words.

2. *Invite clarification.* "What might be an example of that?" may encourage the speaker to say more.

3. *Reflect feelings.* "It sounds frustrating" might mirror what you're sensing from the speaker's body language and intensity.

▶❙❙ Behavior Therapies

53-3 What are the assumptions and techniques of the behavior therapies?

The insight therapies assume that many psychological problems diminish as self-awareness grows. Traditional psychoanalysts expect problems to subside as people gain insight into their unresolved and unconscious tensions. Humanistic therapists

unconditional positive regard a caring, accepting, nonjudgmental attitude, which Carl Rogers believed to be conducive to developing self-awareness and self-acceptance.

expect problems to diminish as people get in touch with their feelings. Proponents of **behavior therapy,** however, doubt the healing power of self-awareness. (You can become aware of why you are highly anxious during exams and still be anxious.) They assume that problem behaviors *are* the problems, and the application of learning principles can eliminate them. Rather than delving deeply below the surface looking for inner causes, behavior therapists view maladaptive symptoms—such as phobias or sexual disorders—as learned behaviors that can be replaced by constructive behaviors.

Classical Conditioning Techniques

One cluster of behavior therapies derives from principles developed in Pavlov's early twentieth-century conditioning experiments. As Pavlov and others showed, we learn various behaviors and emotions through *classical conditioning.* Could maladaptive symptoms be examples of conditioned responses? If so, might reconditioning be a solution? Learning theorist O. H. Mowrer thought so and developed a successful conditioning therapy for chronic bed-wetters. The child sleeps on a liquid-sensitive pad connected to an alarm. Moisture on the pad triggers the alarm, waking the child. With sufficient repetition, this association of urinary relaxation with waking up stops the bed-wetting. In three out of four cases the treatment is effective, and the success provides a boost to the child's self-image (Christophersen & Edwards, 1992; Houts et al., 1994).

Another example: If a claustrophobic fear of elevators is a learned aversion to the stimulus of being in a confined space, then might one unlearn that association by undergoing another round of conditioning to replace the fear response? **Counterconditioning** pairs the trigger stimulus (in this case, the enclosed space of the elevator) with a new response (relaxation) that is incompatible with fear. And indeed, behavior therapists have successfully counterconditioned people with this fear. Two specific counterconditioning techniques—*exposure therapy* and *aversive conditioning*—replace unwanted responses.

Exposure Therapies

Picture this scene reported in 1924 by behaviorist psychologist Mary Cover Jones: Three-year-old Peter is petrified of rabbits and other furry objects. Jones plans to replace Peter's fear of rabbits with a conditioned response incompatible with fear. Her strategy is to associate the fear-evoking rabbit with the pleasurable, relaxed response associated with eating.

As Peter begins his midafternoon snack, Jones introduces a caged rabbit on the other side of the huge room. Peter, eagerly munching away on his crackers and drinking his milk, hardly notices. On succeeding days, she gradually moves the rabbit closer and closer. Within two months, Peter is tolerating the rabbit in his lap, even stroking it while he eats. Moreover, his fear of other furry objects subsides as well, having been *countered,* or replaced, by a relaxed state that cannot coexist with fear (Fisher, 1984; Jones, 1924).

Unfortunately for those who might have been helped by her counterconditioning procedures, Jones' story of Peter and the rabbit did not immediately become part of psychology's lore. It was more than 30 years later that psychiatrist Joseph Wolpe (1958; Wolpe & Plaud, 1997) refined Jones' technique into what are now the most widely used types of behavior therapies: **exposure therapies,** which expose people to what they normally avoid. As people can habituate to the sound of a train passing their new apartment, so, with repeated exposure, can they become less anxiously responsive to things that once petrified them (Deacon & Abramowitz, 2004).

behavior therapy therapy that applies learning principles to the elimination of unwanted behaviors.

counterconditioning a behavior therapy procedure that uses classical conditioning to evoke new responses to stimuli that are triggering unwanted behaviors; includes *exposure therapies* and *aversive conditioning.*

exposure therapies behavioral techniques, such as systematic desensitization, that treat anxieties by exposing people (in imagination or actuality) to the things they fear and avoid.

|| What might a psychoanalyst say about Mowrer's therapy for bed-wetting? How might a behavior therapist reply? ||

THE FAR SIDE By GARY LARSON

Professor Gallagher and his controversial technique of simultaneously confronting the fear of heights, snakes, and the dark.

systematic desensitization a type of exposure therapy that associates a pleasant relaxed state with gradually increasing anxiety-triggering stimuli. Commonly used to treat phobias.

virtual reality exposure therapy An anxiety treatment that progressively exposes people to simulations of their greatest fears, such as airplane flying, spiders, or public speaking.

One widely used exposure therapy is **systematic desensitization.** Wolpe assumed, as did Jones, that you cannot be simultaneously anxious and relaxed. Therefore, if you can repeatedly relax when facing anxiety-provoking stimuli, you can gradually eliminate your anxiety. The trick is to proceed gradually. Let's see how this might work with a common phobia. Imagine yourself afraid of public speaking. A behavior therapist might first ask for your help in constructing a hierarchy of anxiety-triggering speaking situations. Yours might range from mildly anxiety-provoking situations, perhaps speaking up in a small group of friends, to panic-provoking situations, such as having to address a large audience.

Next, using *progressive relaxation,* the therapist would train you to relax one muscle group after another, until you achieve a drowsy state of complete relaxation and comfort. Then the therapist would ask you to imagine, with your eyes closed, a mildly anxiety-arousing situation: You are having coffee with a group of friends and are trying to decide whether to speak up. If imagining the scene causes you to feel any anxiety, you would signal your tension by raising your finger, and the therapist would instruct you to switch off the mental image and go back to deep relaxation. This imagined scene is repeatedly paired with relaxation until you feel no trace of anxiety.

The therapist would progress up the constructed anxiety hierarchy, using the relaxed state to desensitize you to each imagined situation. After several sessions, you move to actual situations and practice what you had only imagined before, beginning with relatively easy tasks and gradually moving to more anxiety-filled ones. Conquering your anxiety in an actual situation, not just in your imagination, raises your self-confidence (Foa & Kozak, 1986; Williams, 1987). Eventually, you may even become a confident public speaker.

When an anxiety-arousing situation is too expensive, difficult, or embarrassing to re-create, **virtual reality exposure therapy** offers an efficient middle ground. Wearing a head-mounted display unit that projects a three-dimensional virtual world, you would view a lifelike series of scenes. As your head turns, motion sensors would adjust the scene. Experiments led by several research teams have treated many different people with many different fears—flying, heights, particular animals, and public speaking (Gregg & Tarrier, 2007; Powers & Emmelkamp, 2008; Rothbaum, 2006). People who fear flying, for example, can peer out a virtual window of a simulated plane, feel vibrations, and hear the engine roar as the plane taxis down the runway and takes off. In initial experiments, those experiencing virtual reality exposure therapy have had greater relief from their fears—in real life—than have those in control groups.

Developments in virtual reality therapy suggest the possibility of designing simulated worlds in which patients create an avatar (a computer representation of oneself), through which they can try out new behaviors in virtual environments (Gorini, 2007). For example, someone with a social phobia might visit a virtual party or group discussion, which others join over time.

Virtual reality exposure therapy Within the confines of a room, virtual reality technology exposes people to vivid simulations of feared stimuli, such as a plane's takeoff.

Bob Mahoney /The Image Works

Bob Mahoney /The Image Works

Aversive Conditioning

In systematic desensitization, the goal is substituting a positive (relaxed) response for a negative (fearful) response to a *harmless* stimulus. In **aversive conditioning,** the goal is substituting a negative (aversive) response for a positive response to a *harmful* stimulus (such as alcohol). Thus, aversive conditioning is the reverse of systematic desensitization—it seeks to condition an aversion to something the person *should* avoid.

The procedure is simple: It associates the unwanted behavior with unpleasant feelings. To treat nail biting, one can paint the fingernails with a nasty-tasting nail polish (Baskind, 1997). To treat alcohol dependency, an aversion therapist offers the client appealing drinks laced with a drug that produces severe nausea. By linking alcohol with violent nausea, the therapist seeks to transform the person's reaction to alcohol from positive to negative (**FIGURE 53.1**).

Does aversive conditioning work? In the short run it may. Arthur Wiens and Carol Menustix (1983) studied 685 patients with alcohol dependency who completed an aversion therapy program at a Portland, Oregon, hospital. One year later, after returning for several booster treatments of alcohol-sickness pairings, 63 percent were still successfully abstaining. But after three years, only 33 percent had remained abstinent.

The problem is that in therapy (as in research), cognition influences conditioning. People know that outside the therapist's office they can drink without fear of nausea. Their ability to discriminate between the aversive conditioning situation and all other situations can limit the treatment's effectiveness. Thus, therapists often use aversive conditioning in combination with other treatments.

Operant Conditioning

The work of B. F. Skinner and others teaches us a basic principle of *operant conditioning:* Voluntary behaviors are strongly influenced by their consequences. Knowing this, behavior therapists can practice *behavior modification*—reinforcing desired behaviors and withholding reinforcement for undesired behaviors or punishing them. Using operant conditioning to solve specific behavior problems has raised hopes for some otherwise hopeless cases. Children with an intellectual disability have been taught to care for themselves. Socially withdrawn children with autism have learned to interact. People with schizophrenia have been helped to behave more rationally in their hospital ward. In such cases, therapists use positive reinforcers to shape behavior in a step-by-step manner, rewarding closer and closer approximations of the desired behavior.

In extreme cases, treatment must be intensive. One study worked with 19 withdrawn, uncommunicative 3-year-olds with autism. Each participated in a 2-year program in which their parents spent 40 hours a week attempting to shape their behavior (Lovaas, 1987). The combination of positively reinforcing desired behaviors, and ignoring or punishing aggressive and self-abusive behaviors, worked wonders for some. By first grade, 9 of the 19 children were functioning successfully in school and exhibiting normal intelligence. In a group of 40 comparable children not undergoing this treatment (which involves sustained effort), only one showed similar improvement.

Rewards used to modify behavior vary. For some people, the reinforcing power of attention or praise is sufficient. Others require concrete rewards, such as food. In institutional settings, therapists may create a **token economy.** When people display appropriate behavior, such as getting out of bed, washing, dressing, eating, talking

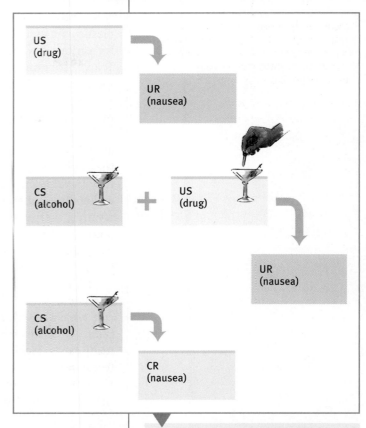

FIGURE 53.1 Aversion therapy for alcohol dependency After repeatedly imbibing an alcoholic drink mixed with a drug that produces severe nausea, some people with a history of alcohol abuse develop at least a temporary conditioned aversion to alcohol.

aversive conditioning a type of counterconditioning that associates an unpleasant state (such as nausea) with an unwanted behavior (such as drinking alcohol).

token economy an operant conditioning procedure in which people earn a token of some sort for exhibiting a desired behavior and can later exchange the tokens for various privileges or treats.

cognitive therapy therapy that teaches people new, more adaptive ways of thinking and acting; based on the assumption that thoughts intervene between events and our emotional reactions.

coherently, cleaning up their rooms, or playing cooperatively, they receive a token or plastic coin as a positive reinforcer. Later, they can exchange their accumulated tokens for various rewards, such as candy, TV time, trips to town, or better living quarters. Token economies have been successfully applied in various settings (homes, classrooms, hospitals, institutions for the delinquent) and among members of various populations (including disturbed children and people with schizophrenia and other mental disabilities).

Critics of behavior modification express two concerns. The first is practical: *How durable are the behaviors?* Will people become so dependent on extrinsic rewards that the appropriate behaviors will stop when the reinforcers stop, as may happen when they leave the institution? Proponents of behavior modification believe the behaviors will endure if therapists wean patients from the tokens by shifting them toward other rewards, such as social approval, more typical of life outside the institution. They also point out that the appropriate behaviors themselves can be intrinsically rewarding. For example, as a withdrawn person becomes more socially competent, the intrinsic satisfactions of social interaction may help the person maintain the behavior.

The second concern is ethical: *Is it right for one human to control another's behavior?* Those who set up token economies deprive people of something they desire and decide which behaviors to reinforce. To critics, this whole process has an authoritarian taint. Advocates reply that some patients request the therapy. Moreover, control already exists; rewards and punishers are already maintaining destructive behavior patterns. So why not reinforce adaptive behavior instead? Treatment with positive rewards is more humane than being institutionalized or punished, they argue, and the right to effective treatment and an improved life justifies temporary deprivation.

▶‖ Cognitive Therapies

53-4 What are the goals and techniques of the cognitive therapies?

We have seen how behavior therapists treat specific fears and problem behaviors. But how do they deal with major depression? Or with generalized anxiety, in which anxiety has no focus and developing a hierarchy of anxiety-triggering situations is difficult? Behavior therapists treating these less clearly defined psychological problems have had help from the same *cognitive revolution* that has profoundly changed other areas of psychology during the last five decades.

The **cognitive therapies** assume that our thinking colors our feelings (**FIGURE 53.2**). Between the event and our response lies the mind. Self-blaming and overgeneralized

Cognitive therapy for eating disorders aided by journaling Cognitive therapists guide people toward new ways of explaining their good and bad experiences. By recording each day's positive events and how one enabled them, for example, people may become more mindful of their self-control.

Lara Jo Regan/Gamma Liaison

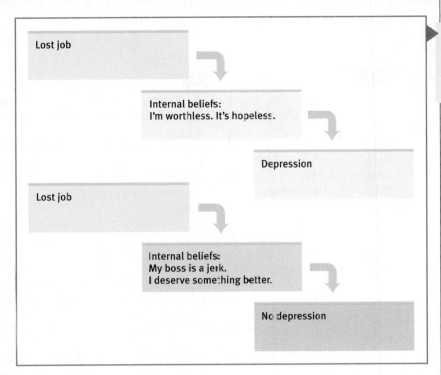

explanations of bad events are often an integral part of the vicious cycle of depression. The depressed person interprets a suggestion as criticism, disagreement as dislike, praise as flattery, friendliness as pity. Ruminating on such thoughts sustains the bad mood. If such thinking patterns can be learned, then surely they can be replaced. Cognitive therapists therefore try in various ways to teach people new, more constructive ways of thinking. If people are miserable, they can be helped to change their minds.

Beck's Therapy for Depression

Cognitive therapist Aaron Beck was originally trained in Freudian techniques. As Beck analyzed the dreams of depressed people, he found recurring negative themes of loss, rejection, and abandonment that extended into their waking thoughts. Such negativity even extends into therapy, as clients recall and rehearse their failings and worst impulses (Kelly, 2000). With cognitive therapy, Beck and his colleagues (1979) have sought to reverse clients' *catastrophizing* beliefs about themselves, their situations, and their futures. Gentle questioning seeks to reveal irrational thinking, and then to persuade the person to remove the dark glasses through which they view life (Beck et al., 1979, pp. 145–146):

> **Client:** I agree with the descriptions of me but I guess I don't agree that the way I think makes me depressed.
> **Beck:** How do you understand it?
> **Client:** I get depressed when things go wrong. Like when I fail a test.
> **Beck:** How can failing a test make you depressed?
> **Client:** Well, if I fail I'll never get into law school.
> **Beck:** So failing the test means a lot to you. But if failing a test could drive people into clinical depression, wouldn't you expect everyone who failed the test to have a depression? . . . Did everyone who failed get depressed enough to require treatment?
> **Client:** No, but it depends on how important the test was to the person.
> **Beck:** Right, and who decides the importance?
> **Client:** I do.

"Life does not consist mainly, or even largely, of facts and happenings. It consists mainly of the storm of thoughts that are forever blowing through one's mind."
Mark Twain, 1835–1910

cognitive-behavior therapy a popular integrative therapy that combines cognitive therapy (changing self-defeating thinking) with behavior therapy (changing behavior).

family therapy therapy that treats the family as a system. Views an individual's unwanted behaviors as influenced by, or directed at, other family members.

Beck: And so, what we have to examine is your way of viewing the test (or the way that you think about the test) and how it affects your chances of getting into law school. Do you agree?

Client: Right.

Beck: Do you agree that the way you interpret the results of the test will affect you? You might feel depressed, you might have trouble sleeping, not feel like eating, and you might even wonder if you should drop out of the course.

Client: I have been thinking that I wasn't going to make it. Yes, I agree.

Beck: Now what did failing mean?

Client: *(tearful)* That I couldn't get into law school.

Beck: And what does that mean to you?

Client: That I'm just not smart enough.

Beck: Anything else?

Client: That I can never be happy.

Beck: And how do these thoughts make you feel?

Client: Very unhappy.

Beck: So it is the meaning of failing a test that makes you very unhappy. In fact, believing that you can never be happy is a powerful factor in producing unhappiness. So, you get yourself into a trap—by definition, failure to get into law school equals "I can never be happy."

We often think in words. Therefore, getting people to change what they say to themselves is an effective way to change their thinking. Perhaps you can identify with the anxious students who before an exam make matters worse with self-defeating thoughts: "This exam's probably going to be impossible. All these other students seem so relaxed and confident. I wish I were better prepared. Anyhow, I'm so nervous I'll forget everything." To change such negative self-talk, Donald Meichenbaum (1977, 1985) has offered *stress inoculation training:* teaching people to restructure their thinking in stressful situations. Sometimes it may be enough simply to say more positive things to oneself: "Relax. The exam may be hard, but it will be hard for everyone else, too. I studied harder than most people. Besides, I don't need a perfect score to get a good grade." After being trained to dispute their negative thoughts, depression-prone children and college students exhibit a halved rate of future depression (Seligman, 2002). To a great extent, it *is* the thought that counts.

PEANUTS

Drawing by Charles Schulz; © 1956 Reprinted by permission of United Feature Syndicate, Inc.

"The trouble with most therapy is that it helps you to feel better. But you don't get better. You have to back it up with action, action, action."

Therapist Albert Ellis (1913–2007)

Cognitive-Behavior Therapy

Cognitive-behavior therapy, a widely practiced integrative therapy, aims not only to alter the way people think (cognitive therapy), but also to alter the way they act (behavior therapy). It seeks to make people aware of their irrational negative thinking, to replace it with new ways of thinking, *and to practice* the more positive approach in everyday settings. The anxiety and mood disorders share a common problem: emotion regulation. An effective treatment program for these emotional disorders trains people both to replace their catastrophizing thinking with more realistic appraisals, and to practice behaviors that are incompatible with their problem (Moses & Barlow, 2006). A person with a fear of social situations, for example, might learn new ways of thinking, but also practice approaching people.

In one study, people with obsessive-compulsive behaviors learned to relabel their compulsive thoughts (Schwartz et al., 1996). Feeling the urge to wash their hands again, they would tell themselves, "I'm having a compulsive urge," and attribute it to their brain's abnormal activity, as previously viewed in their PET scans. Instead of giving in to the urge, they would then spend 15 minutes in an enjoyable, alternative behavior, such as practicing an instrument, taking a walk, or gardening. This helped "unstick" the brain by shifting attention and engaging other brain areas. For two or three months, the weekly therapy sessions continued, with relabeling and refocusing practice at home. By the study's end, most participants' symptoms had diminished and their PET scans revealed normalized brain activity. Many other studies confirm cognitive-behavior therapy's effectiveness for those suffering anxiety or depression (Covin et al., 2008; Mitte, 2005; Norton & Price, 2007).

▶‖ Group and Family Therapies

53-5   What are the aims and benefits of group and family therapy?

Except for traditional psychoanalysis, most therapies may also occur in small groups. Group therapy does not provide the same degree of therapist involvement with each client. However, it saves therapists' time and clients' money—and it often is no less effective than individual therapy (Fuhriman & Burlingame, 1994). Therapists frequently suggest group therapy for people experiencing family conflicts or those whose behavior is distressing to others. For up to 90 minutes a week, the therapist guides the interactions of a group of people as they engage issues and react to one another.

Group sessions also offer a unique benefit: The social context allows people both to discover that others have problems similar to their own and to receive feedback as they try out new ways of behaving. It can be a relief to find that you are not alone—to learn that others, despite their apparent composure, share your problems and your troublesome feelings. It can also be reassuring to hear that you yourself look poised even though you feel anxious and self-conscious.

One special type of group interaction, **family therapy,** assumes that no person is an island, that we live and grow in relation to others, especially our families. We struggle to differentiate ourselves from our families, but we also need to connect with them emotionally. Some of our problem behaviors arise from the tension between these two tendencies, which can create family stress.

Unlike most psychotherapy, which focuses on what happens inside the person's own skin, family therapists work with family members to heal relationships and to mobilize family resources. They tend to view the family as a system in which each person's actions trigger reactions from others, and they help family members discover their role within their family's social system. A child's rebellion, for example, affects and is affected by other family tensions. Therapists also attempt—usually with some success, research suggests—to open up communication within the family or to help

Michael Newman/PhotoEdit

Family therapy This type of therapy often acts as a preventive mental health strategy. The therapist helps family members understand how their ways of relating to one another create problems. The treatment's emphasis is not on changing the individuals but on changing their relationships and interactions.

family members discover new ways of preventing or resolving conflicts (Hazelrigg et al., 1987; Shadish et al., 1993).

A wide range of people participate in self-help and support groups (Yalom, 1985). One analysis (Davison et al., 2000) of online support groups and more than 14,000 self-help groups reports that most support groups focus on stigmatized or hard-to-discuss illnesses. AIDS patients are 250 times more likely than hypertension patients to be in support groups. Those struggling with anorexia and alcohol dependency often join groups; those with migraines and ulcers do not. People with hearing loss have national organizations with local chapters; people with vision loss more often cope without such.

The grandparent of support groups, Alcoholics Anonymous (AA), reports having more than 2 million members in 114,000 groups worldwide. Its famous 12-step program, emulated by many other self-help groups, asks members to admit their powerlessness, to seek help from a higher power and from one another, and (the twelfth step) to take the message to others in need of it. In one eight-year, $27 million investigation, AA participants reduced their drinking sharply, although so did those assigned to cognitive-behavior therapy or to "motivational therapy" (Project Match, 1997). Other studies have similarly found that 12-step programs such as AA have helped reduce alcohol dependence comparably to other treatment interventions (Ferri et al., 2006; Moos & Moos, 2005). The more meetings patients attend, the greater their alcohol abstinence (Moos & Moos, 2006). In one study of 2300 veterans who sought treatment for alcohol dependency, a high level of AA involvement was followed by diminished alcohol problems (McKellar et al., 2003).

In an individualistic age, with more and more people living alone or feeling isolated, the popularity of support groups—for the addicted, the bereaved, the divorced, or simply those seeking fellowship and growth—seems to reflect a longing for community and connectedness. More than 100 million Americans belong to small religious, interest, or self-help groups that meet regularly—and 9 in 10 report that group members "support each other emotionally" (Gallup, 1994).

* * *

For a synopsis of the main forms of psychotherapy we've been discussing, see **TABLE 53.1**.

|| With over 2 million members worldwide, AA is said to be "the largest organization on Earth that nobody wanted to join" (Finlay, 2000). ||

TABLE 53.1 Comparison of a Sample of Major Psychotherapies

Therapy	Assumed Problem	Therapy Aims	Method
Psychodynamic	Unconscious forces and childhood experiences	Reduced anxiety through self-insight	Analysis and interpretation
Client-centered	Barriers to self-understanding and self-acceptance	Personal growth through self-insight	Active listening and unconditional positive regard
Behavior	Maladaptive behavior	Extinction and relearning	Counterconditioning, exposure, desensitization, aversive conditioning, and operant conditioning
Cognitive	Negative, self-defeating thinking	Healthier thinking and self-talk	Reveal and reverse self-blaming
Family	Stressful relationships	Relationship healing	Understanding family social system; exploring roles; improved communication

REVIEW

The Psychological Therapies

Psychotherapy consists of interactions between a trained therapist and someone seeking to overcome psychological difficulties or achieve personal growth. The major psychotherapies derive from the psychoanalytic, humanistic, behavioral, and cognitive perspectives on psychology. Today, many therapists combine aspects of these perspectives in an *eclectic approach* or psychotherapy integration, sometimes in a group setting.

53-1 **What are the aims and methods of psychoanalysis, and how have they been adapted in psychodynamic therapy?** Through *psychoanalysis,* Sigmund Freud and his students aimed to help people gain insight into the unconscious origins of their disorders, to work through the accompanying feelings, and to take responsibility for their own growth. Techniques included free association, dream analysis, and *interpretation* of *resistances* and *transference* to the therapist of long-repressed feelings. Contemporary *psychodynamic therapy* has been influenced by traditional psychoanalysis but is briefer and less expensive. It focuses on a patient's current conflicts and defenses by searching for themes common to many past and present important relationships. Interpersonal therapy (a brief 12- to 16-session form of psychodynamic therapy) deals primarily with current symptoms (such as depression) rather than the origins of unconscious conflicts.

53-2 **What are the basic themes of humanistic therapy, such as Rogers' client-centered approach?** Humanistic therapists have focused on clients' current conscious feelings and on their taking responsibility for their own growth. Carl Rogers' *client-centered therapy* proposed that therapists' most important contributions are to function as a psychological mirror through *active listening* and to provide a growth-fostering environment of *unconditional positive regard,* characterized by genuineness, acceptance, and empathy. The humanistic and psychoanalytic therapies are known as *insight therapies.*

53-3 **What are the assumptions and techniques of the behavior therapies?** *Behavior therapists* do not attempt to explain the origin of problems or to promote self-awareness. Instead, they attempt to modify the problem behaviors themselves. Thus, they may *countercondition* behaviors through *exposure therapies,* such as *systematic desensitization, virtual reality exposure therapy,* or *aversive conditioning.* Or they may apply operant conditioning principles with behavior modification techniques, such as *token economies.*

53-4 **What are the goals and techniques of the cognitive therapies?** The *cognitive therapies,* such as Aaron Beck's cognitive therapy for depression, aim to change self-defeating thinking by training people to look at themselves in new, more positive ways. The widely researched and practiced *cognitive-behavior therapy* also helps clients to regularly practice new ways of thinking and talking.

53-5 **What are the aims and benefits of group and family therapy?** Group therapy sessions can help more people and cost less per person than individual therapy would. Clients may benefit from knowing others have similar problems and from getting feedback and reassurance. *Family therapy* views a family as an interactive system and attempts to help members discover the roles they play and to learn to communicate more openly and directly.

Terms and Concepts to Remember

psychotherapy, p. 646
eclectic approach, p. 646
psychoanalysis, p. 646
resistance, p. 647
interpretation, p. 647
transference, p. 647
psychodynamic therapy, p. 648
insight therapies, p. 649
client-centered therapy, p. 649
active listening, p. 649
unconditional positive regard, p. 650
behavior therapy, p. 651

counterconditioning, p. 651
exposure therapies, p. 651
systematic desensitization, p. 652
virtual reality exposure therapy, p. 652
aversive conditioning, p. 653
token economy, p. 653
cognitive therapy, p. 654
cognitive-behavior therapy, p. 656
family therapy, p. 657

Test Yourself

1. What is the major distinction between the underlying assumption in insight therapies and in behavior therapies?

(Answers to the Test Yourself questions can be found in Appendix B at the end of the book.)

Ask Yourself

1. Critics say that behavior modification techniques, such as those used in token economies, are inhumane. Do you agree or disagree? Why?

∞ WEB

Multiple-choice self-tests and more may be found at www.worthpublishers.com/myers

Is Psychotherapy Effective?

The Relative Effectiveness
of Different Therapies

Evaluating Alternative
Therapies

Commonalities Among
Psychotherapies

Culture and Values
in Psychotherapy

MODULE 54

Evaluating Psychotherapies

Advice columnists frequently urge their troubled letter writers to get professional help: "Don't give up. Find a therapist who can help you. Make an appointment."

Therapists can verify that many Americans share this confidence in **psychotherapy's** effectiveness. Before 1950, psychiatrists were the primary providers of mental health care. Today, surging demands for psychotherapy also occupy the time and attention of clinical and counseling psychologists; clinical social workers; pastoral, marital, abuse, and school counselors; and psychiatric nurses. In 2004, for example, 7.4 percent of Americans reported "undergoing counseling for mental or emotional problems," a 25 percent increase since 1991 (Smith, 2005). With such an enormous outlay of time as well as money, effort, and hope, it is important to ask: Are the millions of people worldwide justified in placing such hope in psychotherapy?

▶‖ Is Psychotherapy Effective?

54-1 Does psychotherapy work? Who decides?

The question, though simply put, is not simply answered. Measuring therapy's effectiveness is not like taking your body's temperature to see if your fever has gone away. If you and I were to undergo psychotherapy, how would we assess its effectiveness? By how we feel about our progress? How our therapist feels about it? How our friends and family feel about it? How our behavior has changed?

Clients' Perceptions

If clients' testimonials were the only measuring stick, we could strongly affirm the effectiveness of psychotherapy. When 2900 *Consumer Reports* readers (1995; Kotkin et al., 1996; Seligman, 1995) related their experiences with mental health professionals, 89 percent said they were at least "fairly well satisfied." Among those who recalled feeling *fair* or *very poor* when beginning therapy, 9 in 10 now were feeling *very good, good,* or at least *so-so.* We have their word for it—and who should know better?

We should not dismiss these testimonials lightly. But for several reasons, client testimonials do not persuade psychotherapy's skeptics:

▶ *People often enter therapy in crisis.* When, with the normal ebb and flow of events, the crisis passes, people may attribute their improvement to the therapy.

▶ *Clients may need to believe the therapy was worth the effort.* To admit investing time and money in something ineffective is like admitting to having one's car serviced repeatedly by a mechanic who never fixes it. Self-justification is a powerful human motive.

▶ *Clients generally speak kindly of their therapists.* Even if the problems remain, say the critics, clients "work hard to find something positive to say. The therapist had been very understanding, the client had gained a new perspective, he learned to communicate better, his mind was eased, anything at all so as not to have to say treatment was a failure" (Zilbergeld, 1983, p. 117).

As research findings continue to document, we are prone to selective and biased recall and to making judgments that confirm our beliefs. Consider the testimonials gathered in a massive experiment with over 500 Massachusetts boys, aged 5 to 13 years, many of whom seemed bound for delinquency. By the toss of a coin, half the

psychotherapy treatment involving psychological techniques; consists of interactions between a trained therapist and someone seeking to overcome psychological difficulties or achieve personal growth.

boys were assigned to a 5-year treatment program. The treated boys were visited by counselors twice a month. They participated in community programs, and they received academic tutoring, medical attention, and family assistance as needed. Some 30 years later, Joan McCord (1978, 1979) located 485 participants, sent them questionnaires and checked public records from courts, mental hospitals, and other sources. Was the treatment successful?

Client testimonials yielded encouraging results, even glowing reports. Some men noted that, had it not been for their counselors, "I would probably be in jail," "My life would have gone the other way," or "I think I would have ended up in a life of crime." Court records offered apparent support: Even among the "difficult" boys in the treatment group, 66 percent had no official juvenile crime record.

But keep in mind psychology's most powerful tool for sorting reality from wishful thinking: the *control group*. For every boy in the treatment group, there was a similar boy in a control group, receiving no counseling. Of these untreated men, *70 percent* had no juvenile record. On several other measures, such as a record of having committed a second crime, alcohol dependence, death rate, and job satisfaction, the untreated men exhibited slightly *fewer* problems. The glowing testimonials of those treated had been unintentionally deceiving.

Clinicians' Perceptions

Do clinicians' perceptions give us any more reason to celebrate? Case studies of successful treatment abound. The problem is that clients justify entering psychotherapy by emphasizing their unhappiness, justify leaving by emphasizing their well-being, and stay in touch only if satisfied. Therapists treasure compliments from clients as they say good-bye or later express their gratitude, but they hear little from clients who experience only temporary relief and seek out new therapists for their recurring problems. Thus, the same person—with the same recurring anxieties, depression, or marital difficulty—may be a "success" story in several therapists' files.

Because people enter therapy when they are extremely unhappy, and usually leave when they are less extremely unhappy, most therapists, like most clients, testify to therapy's success—regardless of the treatment (see Thinking Critically About: "Regressing" From Unusual to Usual on the next page).

Outcome Research

How, then, can we objectively measure the effectiveness of psychotherapy if neither clients nor clinicians can tell us? How can we determine what types of people and problems are best helped, and by what type of psychotherapy?

In search of answers, psychologists have turned to controlled research studies. Similar research in the 1800s transformed the field of medicine. Physicians, skeptical of many of the fashionable treatments (bleeding, purging, infusions of plant and metal substances) began to realize that many patients got better on their own, without these treatments, and that others died in spite of them. Sorting fact from superstition required following patients with and without a particular treatment. Typhoid fever patients, for example, often improved after being bled, convincing most physicians that the treatment worked. Not until a control group was given mere bed rest—and 70 percent were observed to improve after five weeks of fever—did physicians learn, to their shock, that the bleeding was worthless (Thomas, 1992).

In psychology, the opening challenge to the effectiveness of psychotherapy was issued by British psychologist Hans Eysenck (1952). Launching a spirited debate, he summarized studies showing that two-thirds of those receiving psychotherapy for nonpsychotic disorders improved markedly. To this day, no one disputes that optimistic estimate.

"Regressing" From Unusual to Usual

"Once you become sensitized to it, you see regression everywhere."

Psychologist Daniel Kahneman (1985)

Clients' and therapists' perceptions of therapy's effectiveness are vulnerable to inflation from two phenomena. One is the *placebo effect*—the power of belief in a treatment. If you think a treatment is going to be effective, it just may be (thanks to the healing power of your positive expectation).

The second phenomenon is **regression toward the mean**—the tendency for unusual events (or emotions) to "regress" (return) to their average state. Thus, extraordinary happenings (feeling low) tend to be followed by more ordinary ones (a return to our more usual state). Indeed, when things hit bottom, whatever we try—going to a psychotherapist, starting yoga, doing aerobic exercise—is more likely to be

"The real purpose of [the] scientific method is to make sure Nature hasn't misled you into thinking you know something that you actually don't."

Robert Pirsig, *Zen and the Art of Motorcycle Maintenance*, 1974

followed by improvement than by further descent.

The point may seem obvious, yet we regularly miss it: We sometimes attribute what may be a normal regression (the expected return to normal) to something we have done. Consider:

- Students who score much lower or higher on an exam than they usually do are likely, when retested, to return toward their average.
- Unusual ESP subjects who defy chance when first tested nearly always lose their "psychic powers" when retested

(a phenomenon parapsychologists have called the *decline effect*).

- Coaches often yell at their players after an unusually bad first half. They may then feel rewarded for having done so when the team's performance improves (returns to normal) during the second half.

In each case, the cause-effect link may be genuine. More likely, however, is that each is an instance of the natural tendency for behavior to regress from the unusual to the more usual. And this defines the task for therapy-efficacy research: Does the client's improvement following a particular therapy exceed what could be expected from the placebo and regression effects alone, shown by comparison with control groups?

regression toward the mean the tendency for extreme or unusual scores to fall back (regress) toward their average.

"Fortunately, [psycho]analysis is not the only way to resolve inner conflicts. Life itself still remains a very effective therapist."

Karen Horney, *Our Inner Conflicts*, 1945

meta-analysis a procedure for statistically combining the results of many different research studies.

Why, then, are we still debating psychotherapy's effectiveness? Because Eysenck also reported similar improvement among *untreated* persons, such as those who were on waiting lists. With or without psychotherapy, he said, roughly two-thirds improved noticeably. Time was a great healer.

Later research revealed shortcomings in Eysenck's analyses; his sample was small (only 24 studies of psychotherapy outcomes in 1952). Today, hundreds of studies are available. The best are *randomized clinical trials,* in which researchers randomly assign people on a waiting list to therapy or to no therapy, and later evaluate everyone, using tests and the reports of people who don't know whether therapy was given. The results of many such studies are then digested by a means of **meta-analysis,** a statistical procedure that combines the conclusions of a large number of different studies. Simply said, meta-analyses give us the bottom-line results of lots of studies.

Psychotherapists welcomed the first meta-analysis of some 475 psychotherapy outcome studies (Smith et al., 1980). It showed that the average therapy client ends up better off than 80 percent of the untreated individuals on waiting lists (**FIGURE 54.1**). The claim is modest—by definition, about 50 percent of untreated people also are better off than the average untreated person. Nevertheless, Mary Lee Smith and her colleagues exulted that "psychotherapy benefits people of all ages as reliably as schooling educates them, medicine cures them, or business turns a profit" (p. 183).

More than five dozen subsequent summaries have now examined this question (Kopta et al., 1999; Shadish et al., 2000). Their verdict echoes the results of the earlier outcome studies: *Those not undergoing therapy often improve, but those undergoing therapy are more likely to improve.*

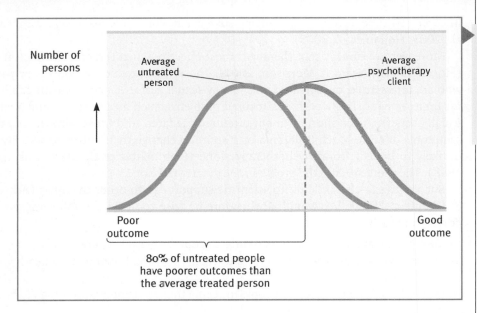

Number of persons

Average untreated person

Average psychotherapy client

Poor outcome

Good outcome

80% of untreated people have poorer outcomes than the average treated person

FIGURE 54.1 **Treatment versus no treatment** These two normal distribution curves based on data from 475 studies show the improvement of untreated people and psychotherapy clients. The outcome for the average therapy client surpassed that for 80 percent of the untreated people. (Adapted from Smith et al., 1980.)

Is psychotherapy also cost-effective? Again, the answer is *yes*. Studies show that when people seek psychological treatment, their search for other medical treatment drops—by 16 percent in one digest of 91 studies (Chiles et al., 1999). Given the staggering annual cost of psychological disorders and substance abuse—including crime, accidents, lost work, and treatment—this is a good investment, much like money spent on prenatal and well-baby care. Both *reduce* long-term costs. Boosting employees' psychological well-being, for example, can lower medical costs, improve work efficiency, and diminish absenteeism.

But note that the claim—that psychotherapy, *on average*, is somewhat effective—refers to no one therapy in particular. It is like reassuring lung-cancer patients that "on average," medical treatment of health problems is effective. What people want to know is the effectiveness of a *particular* treatment for their specific problems.

▶‖ The Relative Effectiveness of Different Therapies

54-2 Are some therapies more effective than others?

So what can we tell people considering therapy, and those paying for it, about *which* psychotherapy will be most effective for their problem? The statistical summaries and surveys fail to pinpoint any one type of therapy as generally superior (Smith et al., 1977, 1980). Clients seemed equally satisfied, *Consumer Reports* concluded, whether treated by a psychiatrist, psychologist, or social worker; whether seen in a group or individual context; whether the therapist had extensive or relatively limited training and experience (Seligman, 1995). Other studies concur. There is little if any connection between clinicians' experience, training, supervision, and licensing and their clients' outcomes (Luborsky et al., 2002; Wampold, 2007).

So, was the dodo bird in *Alice in Wonderland* right: "Everyone has won and all must have prizes"? Not quite. Some forms of therapy get prizes for particular problems. Behavioral conditioning therapies, for example, have achieved especially favorable results with specific behavior problems, such as bed-wetting, phobias, compulsions, marital problems, and sexual disorders (Bowers & Clum, 1988; Hunsley & DiGiulio, 2002; Shadish & Baldwin, 2005). And new studies confirm cognitive therapy's effectiveness

"Whatever differences in treatment efficacy exist, they appear to be extremely small, at best."

Bruce Wampold et al. (1997)

"Different sores have different salves."
English proverb

in coping with depression and reducing suicide risk (Brown et al., 2005; DeRubeis et al., 2005; Hollon et al., 2005).

Moreover, we can say that therapy is most effective when the problem is clear-cut (Singer, 1981; Westen & Morrison, 2001). Those who experience phobias or panic, who are unassertive, or who are frustrated by sexual performance problems can hope for improvement. Those with less-focused problems, such as depression and anxiety, usually benefit in the short term but often relapse later. And those with the negative symptoms of chronic schizophrenia or a desire to change their entire personality are unlikely to benefit from psychotherapy alone (Pfammatter et al., 2006; Zilbergeld, 1983). The more specific the problem, the greater the hope.

But no prizes—and little or no scientific support—go to other therapies (Arkowitz & Lilienfeld, 2006). We would all therefore be wise to avoid the following unsupported approaches.

▶ **Energy therapies** propose to manipulate people's invisible energy fields.
▶ **Recovered-memory therapies** aim to unearth "repressed memories" of early child abuse.
▶ **Rebirthing therapies** engage people in reenacting the supposed trauma of their birth.
▶ **Facilitated communication** has an assistant touch the typing hand of a child with autism.
▶ **Crisis debriefing** forces people to rehearse and "process" their traumatic experiences.

But this question—which therapies get prizes and which do not?—lies at the heart of a serious controversy some call psychology's civil war. To what extent should science guide both clinical practice and the willingness of health care providers and insurers to pay for psychotherapy? On the one side are research psychologists using scientific methods to extend the list of well-defined and validated therapies for various disorders. On the other side are nonscientist therapists who view their practices as more art than science, saying that people are too complex and therapy too intuitive to describe in a manual or test in an experiment. Between these two factions stand the science-oriented clinicians, who believe that by basing practice on evidence and making mental health professionals accountable for effectiveness, therapy will only gain in credibility. Moreover, the public will be protected from pseudotherapies, and therapists will be protected from accusations of sounding like snake-oil salespeople—"Trust me, I know it works, I've seen it work."

To encourage **evidence-based practice** in psychology, the American Psychological Association (2006; Spring, 2007) has followed the Institute of Medicine's lead, advocating that clinicians integrate the best available research with clinical expertise and patient preferences and characteristics. Available therapies "should be rigorously evaluated" and then applied by clinicians who are mindful of their skills and of each patient's unique situation (**FIGURE 54.2**). Increasingly, insurer and government support for mental health services requires evidence-based practice. In late 2007, for example, Britain's National Health Service announced that it would pour the equivalent of $600 million into training new mental health workers in evidence-based practices (such as cognitive-behavior therapy) and to disseminating information about such treatments (DeAngelis, 2008).

FIGURE 54.2
Evidence-based clinical decision-making The ideal clinical decision-making is a three-legged stool, upheld by research evidence, clinical expertise, and knowledge of the patient.

Clinical decision–making

Patient's values, characteristics, preferences, circumstances

Clinical expertise

Best available research evidence

▶‖ Evaluating Alternative Therapies

54-3 How do alternative therapies fare under scientific scrutiny?

evidence-based practice clinical decision-making that integrates the best available research with clinical expertise and patient characteristics and preferences.

The tendency of many abnormal states of mind to return to normal, combined with the placebo effect, creates fertile soil for pseudotherapies. Bolstered by anecdotes, heralded by the media, and praised on the Internet, alternative therapies can spread like wildfire. In one national survey, 57 percent of those with a history of anxiety attacks and 54 percent of those with a history of depression had used alternative treatments, such as herbal medicine, massage, and spiritual healing (Kessler et al., 2001).

Testimonials aside, what does the evidence say about alternative therapies? This is a tough question, because there is no evidence for or against most of them, though their proponents often feel personal experience is evidence enough. Some, however, have been the subject of controlled research. Let's consider two of them. As we do, remember that sifting sense from nonsense requires the scientific attitude: being skeptical but not cynical, open to surprises but not gullible.

Eye Movement Desensitization and Reprocessing (EMDR)

EMDR (eye movement desensitization and reprocessing) is a therapy adored by thousands and dismissed by thousands more as a sham—"an excellent vehicle for illustrating the differences between scientific and pseudoscientific therapy techniques," suggested James Herbert and seven others (2000). Francine Shapiro (1989, 2007) developed EMDR one day while walking in a park and observing that anxious thoughts vanished as her eyes spontaneously darted about. Offering her novel anxiety treatment to others, she had people imagine traumatic scenes while she triggered eye movements by waving her finger in front of their eyes, supposedly enabling them to unlock and reprocess previously frozen memories. After she tried this on 22 people haunted by old traumatic memories, and all reported marked reductions in their distress after just one therapeutic session, the extraordinary result evoked an enormous response from mental health professionals. To date, nearly 70,000 of them, from more than 75 countries, have undergone training (EMDR, 2008). Not since the similarly charismatic Franz Anton Mesmer introduced *animal magnetism* (hypnosis) more than two centuries ago (also after feeling inspired by an outdoor experience) has a new therapy attracted so many devotees so quickly.

Does it work? For 84 to 100 percent of single-trauma victims participating in four recent studies, the answer is *yes,* reports Shapiro (1999, 2002). (When EMDR did not fare well in other trials, Shapiro argued that the therapists were not properly trained.) Moreover, the treatment need take no more than three 90-minute sessions. The Society of Clinical Psychology task force on empirically validated treatments acknowledges that the treatment is "probably efficacious" for the treatment of nonmilitary post-traumatic stress disorder (Chambless et al.,1997; see also Bisson & Andrew, 2007; Seidler & Wagner, 2006). Encouraged by their seeming successes, EMDR therapists are now applying the technique to other anxiety disorders, such as panic disorder, and, with Shapiro's (1995, 2002) encouragement, to a wide range of complaints, including pain, grief, paranoid schizophrenia, rage, and guilt.

Why, wonder the skeptics, should rapidly moving one's eyes while recalling traumas be therapeutic? Indeed, it seems eye movements are *not* the therapeutic ingredient. In trials in which people imagined traumatic scenes and tapped a finger, or just stared straight ahead while the therapist's finger wagged, the therapeutic results were the same (Devilly, 2003). EMDR does work better than doing nothing, acknowledge the skeptics (Lilienfeld & Arkowitz, 2007), but many suspect that what is therapeutic is the combination of exposure therapy—repeatedly associating with

"Studies indicate that EMDR is just as effective with fixed eyes. If that conclusion is right, what's useful in the therapy (chiefly behavioral desensitization) is not new, and what's new is superfluous."

Harvard Mental Health Letter, 2002

traumatic memories a safe and reassuring context that provides some emotional distance from the experience—and a robust placebo effect. Had Mesmer's pseudo-therapy been compared with no treatment at all, it, too (thanks to the healing power of positive belief), could have been found "probably efficacious," observed Richard McNally (1999).

Light therapy To counteract winter depression, some people spend time each morning exposed to intense light that mimics natural outdoor light. Light boxes to counteract SAD are available from health supply and lighting stores.

Courtesy of Christine Brune

Light Exposure Therapy

Have you ever found yourself oversleeping, gaining weight, and feeling lethargic during the dark mornings and overcast days of winter? There likely was a survival advantage to your distant ancestors' slowing down and conserving energy during the dark days of winter. For some people, however, especially women and those living far from the equator, the wintertime blahs constitute a form of depression known as *seasonal affective disorder,* for which the appropriate acronym is SAD. To counteract these dark spirits, National Institute of Mental Health researchers in the early 1980s had an idea: Give SAD people a timed daily dose of intense light. Sure enough, people reported they felt better.

Was this a bright idea, or another dim-witted example of the placebo effect, attributable to people's expectations? Recent studies shed some light. One exposed some people with SAD to 90 minutes of bright light and others to a sham placebo treatment—a hissing "negative ion generator" about which the staff expressed similar enthusiasm (but which, unknown to the participants, was not turned on). After four weeks of treatment, 61 percent of those exposed to morning light had greatly improved, as had 50 percent of those exposed to evening light and 32 percent of those exposed to the placebo (Eastman et al., 1998). Other studies have found that 30 minutes of exposure to 10,000-lux white fluorescent light produced relief for more than half the people receiving morning light therapy and for one-third receiving evening light therapy (Terman et al., 1998, 2001). From 20 carefully controlled trials we have a verdict (Golden et al., 2005): Morning bright light does indeed dim SAD symptoms for many people. Moreover, it does so as effectively as taking antidepressant drugs or undergoing cognitive-behavior therapy (Lam et al., 2006; Rohan et al., 2007). The effects are clear in brain scans; this therapy sparks activity in a brain region that influences the body's arousal and hormones (Ishida et al., 2005).

▶‖ Commonalities Among Psychotherapies

54-4   What three elements are shared by all forms of psychotherapy?

The scientific attitude helps us sift sense from nonsense as we consider new forms of therapy. Might it also help explain why studies have found little correlation between therapists' training and experience and clients' outcomes? In search of some answers, Jerome Frank (1982), Marvin Goldfried (Goldfried & Padawer, 1982), Hans Strupp (1986), and Bruce Wampold (2001, 2007) have studied the common ingredients of various therapies. They suggest they all offer at least three benefits: *hope for demoralized people; a new perspective* on oneself and the world; and *an empathic, trusting, caring relationship.* (For those thinking about and seeking therapy, Close-Up: A Consumer's Guide to Psychotherapists offers some tips on when to seek help and how to start your search for a therapist who shares your perspectives and goals.)

CLOSE-UP

A Consumer's Guide to Psychotherapists

Life for everyone is marked by a mix of serenity and stress, blessing and bereavement, good moods and bad. So, when should we seek a mental health professional's help? The American Psychological Association offers these common trouble signals:

- Feelings of hopelessness
- Deep and lasting depression

- Self-destructive behavior, such as alcohol and drug abuse
- Disruptive fears
- Sudden mood shifts
- Thoughts of suicide
- Compulsive rituals, such as hand washing
- Sexual difficulties

In looking for a therapist, you may want to have a preliminary consultation with two or three. You can describe your problem and learn each therapist's treatment approach. You can ask questions about the therapist's values, credentials (**TABLE 54.1**), and fees. And, knowing the importance of the emotional bond between therapist and client, you can assess your own feelings about each of them.

TABLE 54.1 Therapists and Their Training

Type	Description
Counselors	Marriage and family counselors specialize in problems arising from family relations. Pastoral counselors provide counseling to countless people. Abuse counselors work with substance abusers and with spouse and child abusers and their victims.
Clinical or psychiatric social workers	A two-year master of social work graduate program plus postgraduate supervision prepares some social workers to offer psychotherapy, mostly to people with everyday personal and family problems. About half have earned the National Association of Social Workers' designation of clinical social worker.
Clinical psychologists	Most are psychologists with a Ph.D. or Psy.D. and expertise in research, assessment, and therapy, supplemented by a supervised internship and, often, post-doctoral training. About half work in agencies and institutions, half in private practice.
Psychiatrists	Psychiatrists are physicians who specialize in the treatment of psychological disorders. Not all psychiatrists have had extensive training in psychotherapy, but as M.D.s they can prescribe medications. Thus, they tend to see those with the most serious problems. Many have their own private practice.

Hope for Demoralized People

People seeking therapy typically feel anxious, depressed, devoid of self-esteem, and incapable of turning things around. What any therapy offers is the expectation that, with commitment from the therapy seeker, things can and will get better. This belief, apart from any therapeutic technique, may function as a placebo, improving morale, creating feelings of self-efficacy, and diminishing symptoms (Prioleau et al., 1983). Statistical analyses showing that improvement is greater for placebo-treated people than for untreated people suggest that one way therapies help is by harnessing the client's own healing powers. And that, says psychiatrist Jerome Frank, helps us understand why all sorts of treatments—including some folk healing rites that are powerless apart from the participants' belief—may in their own time and place produce cures.

A New Perspective

Every therapy also offers people a plausible explanation of their symptoms and an alternative way of looking at themselves or responding to their world. Armed with a believable fresh perspective, they may approach life with a new attitude, open to making changes in their behaviors and their views of themselves.

© 1994 by Sidney Harris—"Stress Test," Rutgers University Press.

"I utilize the best from Freud, the best from Jung, and the best from my Uncle Marty, a very smart fellow."

A caring relationship Effective therapists form a bond of trust with their patients.

Mary Kate Denny/PhotoEdit

An Empathic, Trusting, Caring Relationship

To say that therapy outcome is unrelated to training and experience is not to say all *therapists* are equally effective. No matter what therapeutic technique they use, effective therapists are empathic people who seek to understand another's experience; who communicate their care and concern to the client; and who earn the client's trust and respect through respectful listening, reassurance, and advice. Marvin Goldfried and his associates (1998) found these qualities in taped therapy sessions from 36 recognized master therapists. Some were cognitive-behavior therapists, others were psychodynamic-interpersonal therapists. Regardless, the striking finding was how *similar* they were during the parts of their sessions they considered most significant. At key moments, the empathic therapists of both persuasions would help clients evaluate themselves, link one aspect of their life with another, and gain insight into their interactions with others.

The emotional bond between therapist and client—the *therapeutic alliance*—is a key aspect of effective therapy (Klein et al., 2003; Wampold, 2001). One U.S. National Institute of Mental Health depression-treatment study confirmed that the most effective therapists were those who were perceived as most empathic and caring and who established the closest therapeutic bonds with their clients (Blatt et al., 1996). That all therapies offer hope through a fresh perspective offered by a caring person is what also enables paraprofessionals (briefly trained caregivers) to assist so many troubled people so effectively (Christensen & Jacobson, 1994).

These three common elements are also part of what the growing numbers of self-help and support groups offer their members. And they are part of what traditional healers have offered (Jackson, 1992). Healers everywhere—special people to whom others disclose their suffering, whether psychiatrists, witch doctors, or shamans—have listened in order to understand and to empathize, reassure, advise, console, interpret, or explain (Torrey, 1986). Such qualities may explain why people who feel supported by close relationships—who enjoy the fellowship and friendship of caring people—are less likely to need or seek therapy (Frank, 1982; O'Connor & Brown, 1984).

* * *

To recap, people who seek help usually improve. So do many of those who do not undergo psychotherapy, and that is a tribute to our human resourcefulness and our capacity to care for one another. Nevertheless, though the therapist's orientation and experience appear not to matter much, people who receive some psychotherapy usually improve more than those who do not. People with clear-cut, specific problems tend to improve the most.

▶‖ Culture and Values in Psychotherapy

54-5 How do culture and values influence the therapist-client relationship?

All therapies offer hope, and nearly all therapists attempt to enhance their clients' sensitivity, openness, personal responsibility, and sense of purpose (Jensen & Bergin, 1988). But in matters of cultural and moral diversity, therapists differ from one another and may differ from their clients (Delaney et al., 2007; Kelly, 1990).

These differences can become significant when a therapist from one culture meets a client from another. In North America, Europe, and Australia, for example, most therapists reflect their culture's individualism, which often gives priority to personal desires and identity. Clients who are immigrants from Asian countries, where people are mindful of others' expectations, may have trouble relating to therapies that require them to think only of their own well-being. Such differences help explain the reluctance of some minority populations to use mental health services (Sue, 2006). In one experiment, Asian-American clients matched with counselors who shared their cultural values (rather than mismatched with those who did not) perceived more counselor empathy and felt a stronger alliance with the counselor (Kim et al., 2005).

Recognizing that therapists and clients may differ in their values, communication styles, and language, many therapy training programs now provide training in cultural sensitivity and recruit members of underrepresented cultural groups.

Another area of potential value conflict is religion. Highly religious people may prefer and benefit from religiously similar therapists (Smith et al., 2007; Wade et al., 2006; Worthington et al., 1996). They may have trouble establishing an emotional bond with a therapist who does not share their values.

Albert Ellis, who advocated an aggressive *rational-emotive therapy,* and Allen Bergin, co-editor of the *Handbook of Psychotherapy and Behavior Change,* illustrated how sharply therapists can differ, and how those differences can affect their view of a healthy person. Ellis (1980) assumed that "no one and nothing is supreme," that "self-gratification" should be encouraged, and that "unequivocal love, commitment, service, and . . . *fidelity* to any interpersonal commitment, especially marriage, leads to harmful consequences." Bergin (1980) assumed the opposite—that "because God is supreme, humility and the acceptance of divine authority are virtues," that "self-control and committed love and self-sacrifice are to be encouraged," and that "*infidelity* to any interpersonal commitment, especially marriage, leads to harmful consequences."

Bergin and Ellis disagreed more radically than most therapists on what values are healthiest. In so doing, however, they agreed on a more general point: Psychotherapists' personal beliefs influence their practice. Because clients tend to adopt their therapists' values (Worthington et al., 1996), some psychologists believe therapists should divulge those values more openly. (For a social-cultural perspective on disorders and therapy, see Close-Up: Preventing Psychological Disorders.)

"It is better to prevent than to cure."
Peruvian folk wisdom

CLOSE-UP

Preventing Psychological Disorders

54-6 What is the rationale for preventive mental health programs?

Psychotherapies and biomedical therapies tend to locate the cause of psychological disorders within the person with the disorder. We infer that people who act cruelly must be cruel and that people who act "crazy" must be "sick." We attach labels to such people, thereby distinguishing them from "normal" folks. It follows, then, that we try to treat "abnormal" people by giving them insight into their problems, by changing their thinking, by helping them gain control with drugs.

There is an alternative viewpoint: We could interpret many psychological disorders as understandable responses to a disturbing and stressful society. According to this view, it is not just the person who needs treatment, but also the person's social context. Better to prevent a problem by reforming a sick situation and by developing people's coping competencies than to wait for a problem to arise and then treat it.

A story about the rescue of a drowning person from a rushing river illustrates this viewpoint: Having successfully administered first aid to the first victim, the rescuer spots another struggling person and pulls her out, too. After a half-dozen repetitions, the rescuer suddenly turns and starts running away while the river sweeps yet another floundering person into view. "Aren't you going to rescue that fellow?" asks a bystander. "Heck no," the rescuer replies. "I'm going upstream to find out what's pushing all these people in."

Preventive mental health is upstream work. It seeks to prevent psychological casualties by identifying and alleviating the conditions that cause them. As George Albee (1986) pointed out, there is abundant evidence that poverty, meaningless work, constant criticism, unemployment, racism, and sexism undermine people's sense of competence, personal control, and self-esteem. Such stresses increase their risk of depression, alcohol dependency, and suicide.

We who care about preventing psychological casualties should, Albee contended, support programs that alleviate these demoralizing situations. We eliminated smallpox not by treating the afflicted but by inoculating the unafflicted. We conquered yellow fever by controlling mosquitoes. Preventing psychological problems means empowering those who have learned an attitude of helplessness, changing environments that breed loneliness, renewing the disintegrating family, and bolstering parents' and teachers' skills at nurturing children's achievements and resulting self-esteem. Indeed, "Everything aimed at improving the human condition, at making life more fulfilling and meaningful, may be considered part of primary prevention of mental or emotional disturbance" (Kessler & Albee, 1975, p. 557). That includes the cognitive training that promotes positive thinking in children at risk for depression (Gillham et al., 2006).

REVIEW

Evaluating Psychotherapies

54-1 Does psychotherapy work? Who decides? Because the positive testimonials of clients and therapists cannot prove that therapy is actually effective, psychologists have conducted hundreds of outcome studies of *psychotherapy* using *meta-analyses*. Studies of randomized clinical trials indicate that people who remain untreated often improve, but those who receive psychotherapy are more likely to improve, regardless of the kind or duration of therapy. Placebo treatments or the sympathy and friendly counsel of paraprofessionals also tend to produce more improvement than no treatment at all.

54-2 Are some therapies more effective than others? No one type of psychotherapy is generally superior to all others. Therapy is most effective for those with clear-cut, specific problems. Some therapies—such as behavior conditioning for treating phobias and compulsions—are more effective for specific disorders. *Evidence-based practice* integrates the best available research with clinicians' expertise and patients' characteristics and preferences.

54-3 How do alternative therapies fare under scientific scrutiny? Controlled research has not supported the claims of eye movement and desensitization (EMDR) therapy. Light exposure therapy does seem to relieve the symptoms of seasonal affective disorder (SAD).

54-4 What three elements are shared by all forms of psychotherapy? All psychotherapies offer new hope for demoralized people; a fresh perspective; and (if the therapist is effective) an empathic, trusting, and caring relationship. A person seeking therapy may want to ask about the therapist's treatment approach, values, credentials, and fees.

54-5 How do culture and values influence the therapist-client relationship? Therapists differ in the values that influence their aims. These differences may create problems when therapists work with clients with different cultural or religious perspectives.

54-6 What is the rationale for preventive mental health programs? Preventive mental health programs are based on the idea that many psychological disorders could be prevented by changing oppressive, esteem-destroying environments into more benevolent, nurturing environments that foster individual growth and self-confidence.

Terms and Concepts to Remember

psychotherapy, p. 660

regression toward the mean, p. 662

meta-analysis, p. 662

evidence-based practice, p. 664

Test Yourself

1. How does the placebo effect bias clients' appraisals of the effectiveness of psychotherapies?

2. What is the difference between preventive mental health and psychological therapy?

(Answers to the Test Yourself questions can be found in Appendix B at the end of the book.)

Ask Yourself

1. Without trying to play therapist, how might you use the helping principles discussed in this module with a friend who is anxious?

2. Can you think of a specific way that improving the environment in your own community might prevent some psychological disorders among its residents?

∞ WEB

Multiple-choice self-tests and more may be found at www.worthpublishers.com/myers

MODULE 55

The Biomedical Therapies

Drug Therapies

Brain Stimulation

Psychosurgery

Therapeutic Life-Style Change

One way to treat psychological disorders is with *psychotherapy*, in which a trained therapist uses psychological techniques to assist someone seeking to overcome difficulties or achieve personal growth. The other, often used with serious disorders, is **biomedical therapy**—physically changing the brain's functioning by altering its chemistry with drugs, or affecting its circuitry with electroconvulsive shock, magnetic impulses, or psychosurgery. Psychologists can provide psychological therapies. But with a few exceptions, only psychiatrists (as medical doctors) offer biomedical therapies.

biomedical therapy prescribed medications or medical procedures that act directly on the patient's nervous system.

psychopharmacology the study of the effects of drugs on mind and behavior.

▶‖ Drug Therapies

55-1 What are the drug therapies? What criticisms have been leveled against drug therapies?

By far the most widely used biomedical treatments today are the drug therapies. Since the 1950s, discoveries in **psychopharmacology** (the study of drug effects on mind and behavior) have revolutionized the treatment of people with severe disorders, liberating hundreds of thousands from hospital confinement. Thanks to drug therapy—and to efforts to minimize involuntary hospitalization and to support people with community mental health programs—the resident population of U.S. state and county mental hospitals is a small fraction of what it was a half-century ago (**FIGURE 55.1**). For some unable to care for themselves, however, release from hospitals has meant homelessness, not liberation.

Almost any new treatment, including drug therapy, is greeted by an initial wave of enthusiasm as many people apparently improve. But that enthusiasm often diminishes after researchers subtract the rates of (1) normal recovery among untreated persons and (2) recovery due to the placebo effect, which arises from the positive expectations of patients and mental health workers alike. So, to evaluate the effectiveness of any new drug, researchers give half the patients the drug, and the other half a similar-appearing placebo. Because neither the staff nor the patients know who gets which, this is called a *double-blind procedure*. The good news: In double-blind studies, several types of drugs have proven useful in treating psychological disorders.

"The mentally ill were out of the hospital, but in many cases they were simply out on the streets, less agitated but lost, still disabled but now uncared for."

Lewis Thomas, *Late Night Thoughts on Listening to Mahler's Ninth Symphony*, 1983

FIGURE 55.1 The emptying of U.S. mental hospitals After the widespread introduction of antipsychotic drugs, starting in about 1955, the number of residents in state and county mental hospitals declined sharply. But in the rush to deinstitutionalize the mentally ill, many people who were ill-equipped to care for themselves were left homeless on city streets. (Data from the U.S. National Institute of Mental Health and Bureau of the Census, 2004.)

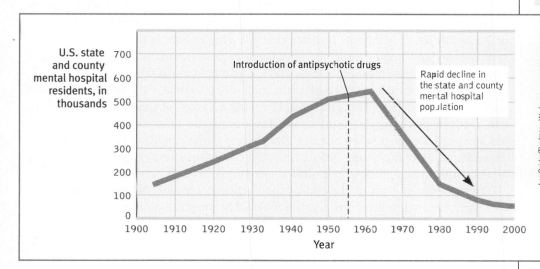

Loo Snider/The Image Works

Antipsychotic Drugs

The revolution in drug therapy for psychological disorders began with the accidental discovery that certain drugs, used for other medical purposes, calmed patients with *psychoses* (disorders in which hallucinations or delusions indicate some loss of contact with reality). These **antipsychotic drugs,** such as chlorpromazine (sold as Thorazine), dampened responsiveness to irrelevant stimuli. Thus, they provided the most help to patients experiencing positive symptoms of schizophrenia, such as auditory hallucinations and paranoia (Lehman et al., 1998; Lenzenweger et al., 1989).

The molecules of most conventional antipsychotic drugs are similar enough to molecules of the neurotransmitter dopamine to occupy its receptor sites and block its activity. This finding reinforces the idea that an overactive dopamine system contributes to schizophrenia. Antipsychotics are powerful drugs. Some can produce sluggishness, tremors, and twitches similar to those of Parkinson's disease, which is marked by too little dopamine (Kaplan & Saddock, 1989). Long-term use of these medications can also produce **tardive dyskinesia** with involuntary movements of the facial muscles (such as grimacing), tongue, and limbs.

Patients exhibiting the negative symptoms of schizophrenia, such as apathy and withdrawal, often do not respond well to conventional antipsychotic drugs. Newer *atypical antipsychotics,* such as clozapine (marketed since 1989 as Clozaril), target both dopamine and serotonin receptors. This helps alleviate negative symptoms, sometimes enabling "awakenings" in these individuals. Atypical antipsychotics may also help those who have positive symptoms but have not responded to other drugs.

Although not more effective in controlling schizophrenia symptoms, many of the newer antipsychotics have fewer conventional side effects. But they may increase the risk of obesity and diabetes (Lieberman et al., 2005, 2006). One new drug now undergoing testing stimulates receptors for the amino acid called glutamate. An initial trial has raised hopes that it may reduce schizophrenia symptoms with fewer side effects (Berenson, 2007).

Despite the drawbacks, antipsychotic drugs, combined with life-skills programs and family support, have enabled hundreds of thousands of people with schizophrenia who had been consigned to the back wards of mental hospitals to return to work and to near-normal lives (Leucht et al., 2003).

Antianxiety Drugs

Like alcohol, **antianxiety** agents, such as Xanax or Ativan, depress central nervous system activity (and so should not be used in combination with alcohol). Antianxiety drugs are often used in combination with psychological therapy. A new antianxiety drug, the antibiotic D-cycloserine, acts upon a receptor that facilitates the extinction of learned fears. Experiments indicate that the drug enhances the benefits of exposure therapy and helps relieve the symptoms of post-traumatic stress disorder and obsessive-compulsive disorder (Davis, 2005; Kushner et al., 2007).

A criticism sometimes made of antianxiety drugs is that they reduce symptoms without resolving underlying problems. "Popping a Xanax" at the first sign of tension can produce psychological dependence; the immediate relief reinforces a person's tendency to take drugs when anxious. Antianxiety drugs can also cause physiological dependence. After heavy use, people who stop taking them may experience increased anxiety, insomnia, and other withdrawal symptoms.

Over the dozen years at the end of the twentieth century, the rate of outpatient treatment for anxiety disorders nearly doubled. The proportion of psychiatric patients receiving medication during that time increased from 52 to 70 percent (Olfson et al., 2004). And the new standard drug treatment for anxiety disorders? Antidepressants.

‖ Perhaps you can guess an occasional side effect of L-dopa, a drug that raises dopamine levels for Parkinson's patients: hallucinations. ‖

‖ On U.S. college campuses, the 9 percent of counseling center visitors taking psychiatric medication in 1994 nearly tripled, to 24.5 percent in 2004 (Duenwald, 2004). ‖

antipsychotic drugs drugs used to treat schizophrenia and other forms of severe thought disorder.

tardive dyskinesia involuntary movements of the facial muscles, tongue, and limbs; a possible neurotoxic side effect of long-term use of antipsychotic drugs that target certain dopamine receptors.

antianxiety drugs drugs used to control anxiety and agitation.

antidepressant drugs drugs used to treat depression; also increasingly prescribed for anxiety. Different types work by altering the availability of various neurotransmitters.

Antidepressant Drugs

The **antidepressants** were named for their ability to lift people up from a state of depression, and this was their main use until recently. The label is a bit of a misnomer now that these drugs are increasingly being used to successfully treat anxiety disorders such as obsessive-compulsive disorder. They work by increasing the availability of norepinephrine or serotonin, neurotransmitters that elevate arousal and mood and appear scarce during depression. Fluoxetine, which tens of millions of users worldwide have known as Prozac, partially blocks the reabsorption and removal of serotonin from synapses (**FIGURE 55.2**). Because they slow the synaptic vacuuming up of serotonin, Prozac and its cousins Zoloft and Paxil are called *selective-serotonin-reuptake-inhibitors (SSRIs)*. Other antidepressants work by blocking the reabsorption or breakdown of both norepinephrine and serotonin. Though effective, these dual-action drugs have more potential side effects, such as dry mouth, weight gain, hypertension, or dizzy spells (Anderson, 2000; Mulrow, 1999). Administering them by means of a patch, bypassing the intestines and liver, helps reduce such side effects (Bodkin & Amsterdam, 2002).

After the introduction of SSRI drugs, the percentage of patients receiving medication for depression jumped dramatically, from 70 percent in 1987, the year before SSRIs were introduced, to 89 percent in 2001 (Olfson et al., 2003; Stafford et al., 2001). In the United States, 11 percent of women and 5 percent of men are now taking antidepressants (Barber, 2008).

Be advised: Patients with depression who begin taking antidepressants do not wake up the next day singing "Oh, what a beautiful morning!" Although the drugs begin to influence neurotransmission within hours, their full psychological effect often requires four weeks (and may involve a side effect of diminished sexual desire). One possible reason for the delay is that increased serotonin promotes *neurogenesis*—the birth of new brain cells, perhaps reversing stress-induced loss of neurons (Becker & Wojtowicz, 2007; Jacobs, 2004).

Antidepressant drugs are not the only way to give the body a lift. Aerobic exercise, which helps calm people who feel anxious and energize those who feel depressed, does about as much good for some people with mild to moderate depression, and has additional positive side effects. Cognitive therapy, by helping people reverse their habitual

"Our psychopharmacologist is a genius."

Drug or placebo effect? For many people, depression lifts while taking an antidepressant drug. But people given a placebo may experience the same effect. Double-blind clinical trials suggest that, especially for those with severe depression, antidepressant drugs do have at least a modest clinical effect.

|| One side effect of SSRI drugs can be decreased sexual appetite, which has led to their occasional prescription to control sexual behavior (Slater, 2000). ||

FIGURE 55.2 Biology of antidepressants Shown here is the action of Prozac, which partially blocks the reuptake of serotonin.

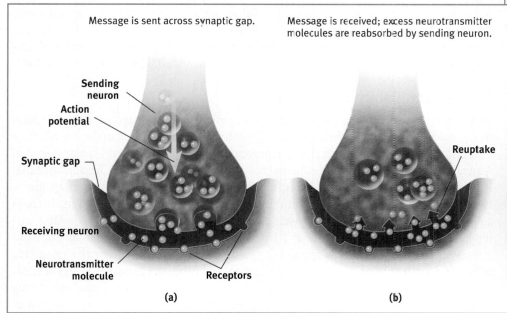

Message is sent across synaptic gap.

Message is received; excess neurotransmitter molecules are reabsorbed by sending neuron.

- Sending neuron
- Action potential
- Synaptic gap
- Receiving neuron
- Neurotransmitter molecule
- Receptors

(a)

(b)

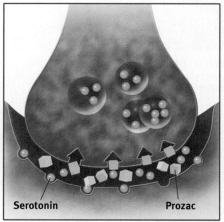

Prozac partially blocks normal reuptake of the neurotransmitter serotonin; excess serotonin in synapse enhances its mood-lifting effect.

- Reuptake
- Serotonin
- Prozac

(c)

negative thinking style, can boost the drug-aided relief from depression and reduce the post-treatment risk of relapse (Hollon et al., 2002; Keller et al., 2000; Vittengl et al., 2007). Better yet, some studies suggest, is to attack depression from both above and below (Goldapple et al., 2004; TADS, 2004). Use antidepressant drugs (which work, bottom-up, on the emotion-forming limbic system) in conjunction with cognitive-behavior therapy (which works, top-down, starting with changed frontal lobe activity).

Everyone agrees that people with depression often improve after a month on anti-depressants. But after allowing for natural recovery (the return to normal called *spontaneous recovery*) and the placebo effect, how big is the drug effect? Not big, report Irving Kirsch and his colleagues (1998, 2002). Their analyses of double-blind clinical trials indicate that placebos accounted for about 75 percent of the active drug's effect. In a follow-up review that included unpublished clinical trials, the antidepressant drug effect was again modest (Kirsch et al., 2008). The placebo effect was less for those with severe depression, which made the added benefit of the drug somewhat greater for them. "Given these results, there seems little reason to prescribe antide-pressant medication to any but the most severely depressed patients, unless alterna-tive treatments have failed," Kirsch concluded (BBC, 2008). For about 1 in 4 people who do not respond to a particular antidepressant, switching to another does bring relief (Rush et al., 2006). Scientists dream of a not-too-far-off day when patients may be screened for genetic variations that will indicate drugs to use or avoid.

Although the effects of drug therapy are less exciting than many TV ads suggest, they also are less frightening than other stories have warned. Some people taking Prozac, for example, have committed suicide, but their numbers seem fewer than we would expect from the millions of depressed people now taking that medication. Moreover, a large British study revealed that the ups and downs of adolescent SSRI prescriptions over time were unrelated to the adolescent suicide rate (Wheeler et al., 2008). Prozac users who commit suicide are like cellphone users who get brain can-cer. Given the millions of people taking Prozac and using cellphones, alarming anec-dotes tell us nothing.

The question critical thinkers want answered is this: Do these groups suffer an elevated *rate* of suicide and brain cancer? The answer in each case appears to be *no* (Grunebaum et al., 2004; Paulos, 1995; Tollefson et al., 1993, 1994). Some re-searchers have speculated that the start of drug therapy may give formerly inert peo-ple enough energy to act on their depression, which could make for a temporary heightened suicide risk. But three recent studies of between 70,000 and 439,000 pa-tients concur that, in the long run, patients attempt fewer suicides if treated with an-tidepressants (Gibbons et al., 2007; Simon & Savarino, 2007; Sønergård et al., 2006).

Mood-Stabilizing Medications

In addition to antipsychotic, antianxiety, and antidepressant drugs, psychiatrists have *mood-stabilizing drugs* in their arsenal. The simple salt *lithium* can be an effective mood stabilizer for those suffering the emotional highs and lows of bipolar disorder. Australian physician John Cade discovered this in the 1940s when he administered lithium to a patient with severe mania. Although Cade's reasoning was misguided—he thought lithium had calmed excitable guinea pigs when actually it had made them sick—his patient became perfectly well in less than a week (Snyder, 1986). After suf-fering mood swings for years, about 7 in 10 people with bipolar disorder benefit from a long-term daily dose of this cheap salt (Solomon et al., 1995). Their risk of suicide is but one-sixth that of bipolar patients not taking lithium (Tondo et al., 1997). Al-though we do not fully understand why, lithium works. And so does Depakote, a drug originally used to treat epilepsy and more recently found effective in the control of manic episodes associated with bipolar disorder.

"If this doesn't help you don't worry, it's a placebo."

"First of all I think you should know that last quarter's sales figures are interfering with my mood-stabilizing drugs."

"Lithium prevents my seductive but disas-trous highs, diminishes my depressions, clears out the wool and webbing from my disordered thinking, slows me down, gen-tles me out, keeps me from ruining my career and relationships, keeps me out of a hospital, alive, and makes psychotherapy possible."

Kay Redfield Jamison, *An Unquiet Mind*, 1995

▶‖ Brain Stimulation

55-2 How effective is electroconvulsive therapy, and what other brain-stimulation options may offer relief from severe depression?

Electroconvulsive Therapy

A more controversial brain manipulation occurs through shock treatment, or **electroconvulsive therapy (ECT).** When ECT was first introduced in 1938, the wide-awake patient was strapped to a table and jolted with roughly 100 volts of electricity to the brain, producing racking convulsions and brief unconsciousness. ECT therefore gained a barbaric image, one that lingers. Today, however, the patient receives a general anesthetic and a muscle relaxant (to prevent injury from convulsions) before a psychiatrist delivers 30 to 60 seconds of electrical current to the patient's brain (**FIGURE 55.3**). Within 30 minutes, the patient awakens and remembers nothing of the treatment or of the preceding hours. After three such sessions each week for two to four weeks, 80 percent or more of people receiving ECT improve markedly, showing some memory loss for the treatment period but no discernible brain damage. Study after study confirms that ECT is an effective treatment for severe depression in patients who have not responded to drug therapy (Pagnin et al., 2004; UK ECT Review Group, 2003). By 2001, confidence in ECT had further increased, with a leading medical journal concluding that "the results of ECT in treating severe depression are among the most positive treatment effects in all of medicine" (Glass, 2001).

How does ECT alleviate severe depression? After more than 50 years, no one knows for sure. One recipient likened ECT to the smallpox vaccine, which was saving lives before we knew how it worked. Perhaps the shock-induced seizures calm neural centers

‖ The medical use of electricity is an ancient practice. Physicians treated the Roman Emperor Claudius (10 B.C.–A.D. 54) for headaches by pressing electric eels to his temples. ‖

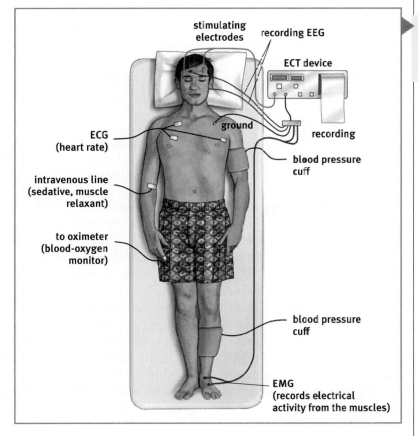

FIGURE 55.3 Electroconvulsive therapy Although controversial, ECT is often an effective treatment for depression that does not respond to drug therapy.

electroconvulsive therapy (ECT) a biomedical therapy for severely depressed patients in which a brief electric current is sent through the brain of an anesthetized patient.

ECT proponent In her book, *Shock: The Healing Power of Electroconvulsive Therapy* (2006), Kitty Dukakis writes, "I used to . . . be unable to shake the dread even when I was feeling good, because I knew the bad feelings would return. ECT has wiped away that foreboding. It has given me a sense of control, of hope."

where overactivity produces depression. ECT, like antidepressant drugs and exercise, also appears to boost the production of new brain cells (Bolwig & Madsen, 2007).

ECT reduces suicidal thoughts and is credited with saving many from suicide (Kellner et al., 2005). It is now administered with briefer pulses, sometimes only to the brain's right side and with less memory disruption (HMHL, 2007). Yet no matter how impressive the results, the idea of electrically shocking people into convulsions still strikes many as barbaric, especially given our ignorance about why ECT works. Moreover, about 4 in 10 ECT-treated patients relapse into depression within six months (Kellner et al., 2006). Nevertheless, in the minds of many psychiatrists and patients, ECT is a lesser evil than severe depression's misery, anguish, and risk of suicide. As research psychologist Norman Endler (1982) reported after ECT alleviated his deep depression, "A miracle had happened in two weeks."

Alternative Neurostimulation Therapies

Some patients with chronic depression have found relief through a chest implant that intermittently stimulates the vagus nerve, which sends signals to the brain's mood-related limbic system (Fitzgerald & Daskalakis, 2008; George & Belmaker, 2007; Marangell et al., 2007). Two other techniques—magnetic stimulation and deep-brain stimulation—are also raising hopes for gentler alternatives that jump-start neural circuits in the depressed brain.

Magnetic Stimulation

Depressed moods seem to improve when repeated pulses surge through a magnetic coil held close to a person's skull (**FIGURE 55.4**). Unlike deep-brain stimulation, the magnetic energy penetrates only to the brain's surface (though tests are under way with a higher energy field that penetrates more deeply). The painless procedure—called **repetitive transcranial magnetic stimulation (rTMS)**—is performed on wide-awake patients over several weeks. Unlike ECT, the rTMS procedure produces no seizures, memory loss, or other side effects.

In one double-blind experiment, 67 Israelis with major depression were randomly assigned to two groups (Klein et al., 1999). One group received rTMS daily for two weeks, while the other received sham treatments (without magnetic stimulation). At the end of the two weeks, half the stimulated patients showed at least a 50 percent improvement in their scores on a depression scale, as did only a quarter of the placebo group. One possible explanation is that the stimulation energizes depressed patients' relatively inactive left frontal lobe (Helmuth, 2001). When repeatedly stimulated, nerve cells can form functioning circuits through *long-term potentiation (LTP)*.

Other clinical experiments have had mixed results. Some have found little effect of rTMS treatment. However, several very recent studies using the latest techniques have produced significant relief from depression, as compared with sham treatments (George & Belmaker, 2007; Gross et al., 2007; O'Reardon et al., 2007).

repetitive transcranial magnetic stimulation (rTMS) the application of repeated pulses of magnetic energy to the brain; used to stimulate or suppress brain activity.

psychosurgery surgery that removes or destroys brain tissue in an effort to change behavior.

lobotomy a now-rare psychosurgical procedure once used to calm uncontrollably emotional or violent patients. The procedure cut the nerves connecting the frontal lobes to the emotion-controlling centers of the inner brain.

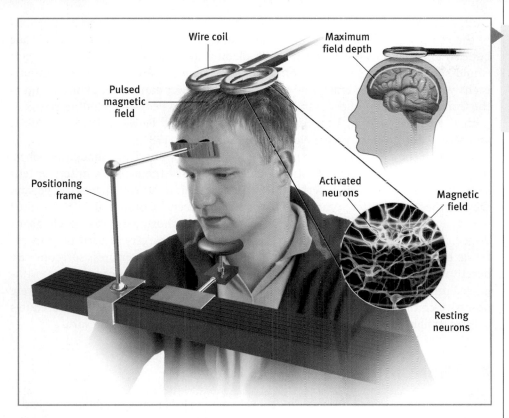

FIGURE 55.4 Magnets for the mind
Repetitive transcranial magnetic stimulation (rTMS) sends a painless magnetic field through the skull to the surface of the cortex. Pulses can be used to stimulate or dampen activity in various cortical areas. (From George, 2003.)

Deep-Brain Stimulation

Other patients whose depression has resisted both drugs that flood the body and ECT that jolts at least half the brain have benefited from an experimental treatment pinpointed at a brain depression center. Neuroscientist Helen Mayberg and her colleagues (2005, 2006, 2007; Dobbs, 2006) have been focusing on a cortex area that bridges the thinking frontal lobes to the limbic system. They have discovered that this area, which is overactive in the brain of a depressed or temporarily sad person, becomes calm when treated by ECT or antidepressants. To experimentally excite neurons that inhibit this negative emotion-feeding activity, Mayberg drew upon the deep-brain stimulation technology sometimes used to treat Parkinson's tremors. Among an initial 12 patients receiving implanted electrodes and a pacemaker stimulator, 8 experienced relief. Some felt suddenly more aware and became more talkative and engaged; others improved only slightly if at all. Future research will explore whether Mayberg has discovered a switch that can lift depression. Other researchers are following up on reports that deep-brain stimulation can offer relief to people with obsessive-compulsive disorder.

A depression switch? By comparing the brains of patients with and without depression, researcher Helen Mayberg identified a brain area that appears active in people who are depressed or sad, and whose activity may be calmed by deep-brain stimulation.

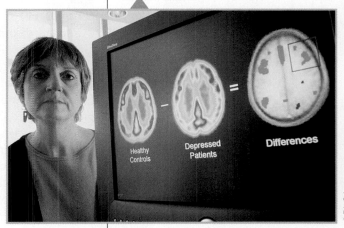

© Eric S. Lesser

▶❙❙ Psychosurgery

55-3 What is psychosurgery?

Because its effects are irreversible, **psychosurgery**—surgery that removes or destroys brain tissue—is the most drastic and the least-used biomedical intervention for changing behavior. In the 1930s, Portuguese physician Egas Moniz developed what became the best-known psychosurgical operation: the **lobotomy.** Moniz found that cutting the nerves connecting the frontal lobes with the emotion-controlling centers of the inner brain calmed uncontrollably emotional and violent patients. In a crude but easy and inexpensive procedure that took only about 10 minutes, a neurosurgeon would shock the patient into a coma, hammer an icepicklike instrument through each eye socket into the brain, and then wiggle it to sever connections running up to the frontal lobes. Tens of thousands of severely disturbed people—including President John F. Kennedy's sister, Rosemary—were "lobotomized" between 1936 and 1954, and Moniz was honored with a Nobel prize (Valenstein, 1986).

Although the intention was simply to disconnect emotion from thought, a lobotomy's effect was often more drastic: It usually decreased the person's misery or tension, but also produced a permanently lethargic, immature, uncreative person. During the 1950s, after some 35,000 people had been lobotomized in the United States alone, calming drugs became available and psychosurgery was largely abandoned. Today, lobotomies are history, and other psychosurgery is used only in extreme cases. For example, if a patient suffers uncontrollable seizures, surgeons can deactivate the specific nerve clusters that cause or transmit the convulsions. MRI-guided precision surgery is also occasionally done to cut the circuits involved in severe obsessive-compulsive disorder (Sachdev & Sachdev, 1997). Because these procedures are irreversible, however, neurosurgeons perform them only as a last resort.

▶|| Therapeutic Life-Style Change

55-4 How, by caring for their bodies with a healthy life-style, might people find some relief from depression?

The effectiveness of the biomedical therapies reminds us of a fundamental lesson: We find it convenient to talk of separate psychological and biological influences, but everything psychological is also biological (**FIGURE 55.5**). Every thought and feeling depends on the functioning brain. Every creative idea, every moment of joy or anger, every period of depression emerges from the electrochemical activity of the living brain. The influence is two-way: When psychotherapy relieves obsessive-compulsive behavior, PET scans reveal a calmer brain (Schwartz et al., 1996).

Anxiety disorders, major depression, bipolar disorder, and schizophrenia are all biological events. As we have seen over and again, *a human being is an integrated biopsychosocial system.* For years, we have trusted our bodies to physicians and our minds to psychiatrists and psychologists. That neat separation no longer seems valid. Stress affects body chemistry and health. And chemical imbalances, whatever their cause, can produce schizophrenia and depression.

That lesson is being applied by Stephen Ilardi and his colleagues (2008) in their training seminars promoting *therapeutic life-style change.* Human brains and bodies were designed for physical activity and social engagement, they note. Our ancestors hunted, gathered, and built in groups, with little evidence of disabling depression. Indeed, those whose way of life entails strenuous physical activity, strong community ties, sunlight exposure, and plenty of sleep (think of foraging bands in Papua New Guinea, or Amish farming communities in North America) rarely experience depression. "Simply put: humans were never designed for the sedentary, disengaged, socially isolated, poorly nourished, sleep-deprived pace of twenty-first-century American life."

The Ilardi team was also impressed by research showing that regular aerobic exercise rivals the healing power of antidepressant drugs, and that a complete night's sleep boosts mood and energy. So they invited small groups of people with depression to undergo a 12-week training program with the following goals:

▶ *Aerobic exercise,* 30 minutes a day, at least 3 times weekly (increases fitness and vitality, stimulates endorphins)

FIGURE 55.5 Mind-body interaction The biomedical therapies assume that mind and body are a unit: Affect one and you will affect the other.

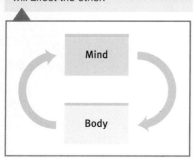

Mind

Body

▶ *Adequate sleep,* with a goal of 7 to 8 hours a night (increases energy and alertness, boosts immunity)

▶ *Light exposure,* at least 30 minutes each morning with a light box (amplifies arousal, influences hormones)

▶ *Social connection,* with less alone time and at least two meaningful social engagements weekly (satisfying the human need to belong)

▶ *Anti-rumination,* by identifying and redirecting negative thoughts (enhancing positive thinking)

▶ *Nutritional supplements,* including a daily fish oil supplement with omega-3 fatty acids (for healthy brain functioning)

In one study of 74 people, 77 percent of those who completed the program experienced relief from depressive symptoms, compared with a 19 percent rate in those assigned to a treatment-as-usual control condition. Future research will seek to replicate this striking result of life-style change, and also to identify which of the treatment components (additively or in some combination) produce the therapeutic effect. But there seems little reason to doubt the truth of the Latin adage, *Mens sana in corpore sano:* "A healthy mind in a healthy body."

REVIEW

The Biomedical Therapies

The *biomedical therapies* treat psychological disorders with medications or medical procedures that act directly on a patient's nervous system.

55-1 **What are the drug therapies? What criticisms have been leveled against drug therapies?** Drug therapy is the most widely used biomedical therapy. The *antipsychotic drugs,* used in treating schizophrenia, block dopamine activity. Some can have serious side effects, including *tardive dyskinesia* (with involuntary movements of facial muscles, tongue, and limbs) or increased risk of obesity and diabetes. *Antianxiety drugs,* which depress central nervous system activity, are used to treat anxiety disorders. These drugs can be physically and psychologically addictive. *Antidepressant drugs,* which increase the availability of serotonin and norepinephrine, are used for depression, with modest effectiveness beyond that of placebo drugs. Lithium and Depakote are mood stabilizers prescribed for those with bipolar disorder.

55-2 **How effective is electroconvulsive therapy, and what other brain-stimulation options may offer relief from severe depression?** *Electroconvulsive therapy (ECT),* in which a brief electric current is sent through the brain of an anesthetized patient, is an effective, last-resort treatment for severely depressed people who have not responded to other therapy. Newer alternative treatments for depression include *repetitive transcranial magnetic stimulation (rTMS)* and, in preliminary clinical experiments, deep-brain stimulation that calms an overactive brain region linked with negative emotions.

55-3 **What is psychosurgery?** *Psychosurgery* removes or destroys brain tissue in hopes of modifying behavior. Radical psychosurgical procedures such as *lobotomy* were once popular, but neurosurgeons now rarely perform brain surgery to change behavior or moods. Brain surgery is a treatment of last resort because its effects are irreversible.

55-4 **How, by caring for their bodies with a healthy life-style, might people find some relief from depression?** A healthy mind usually lives in a healthy body. Depressed people who undergo a program of aerobic exercise, adequate sleep, light exposure, social engagement, negative-thought reduction, and better nutrition often gain some relief.

Terms and Concepts to Remember

biomedical therapy, p. 671
psychopharmacology, p. 671
antipsychotic drugs, p. 672
tardive dyskinesia, p. 672
antianxiety drugs, p. 672
antidepressant drugs,
 p. 673

electroconvulsive therapy
 (ECT), p. 675
repetitive transcranial
 magnetic stimulation
 (rTMS), p. 676
psychosurgery, p. 677
lobotomy, p. 677

Test Yourself

1. How do researchers evaluate the effectiveness of particular drug therapies?

(Answers to the Test Yourself questions can be found in Appendix B at the end of the book.)

Ask Yourself

1. If a troubled friend asked, how would you summarize the available biomedical therapies?

◯◯ WEB

Multiple-choice self-tests and more may be found at www.worthpublishers.com/myers

Social Psychology

MODULES

56
Social Thinking

57
Social Influence

58
Antisocial Relations

59
Prosocial Relations

Although still young, this twenty-first century has dramatically reminded us that we are social animals whose lives and cultures revolve around how we think about, influence, and relate to one another.

On September 11, 2001, nineteen men with box cutters achieved a catastrophic violence that triggered fright, outrage, and a lust for revenge. But it also triggered an outpouring of compassion and care, including gifts of more money, food, clothing, and teddy bears than New Yorkers could possibly use. What drives people to feel such hatred that they would destroy thousands of innocent lives? And what motivates the heroic altruism of those who died trying to save others and of the many more who reached out to those coping with loss?

Echoes of these questions resurfaced after genocide plagued the Darfur region of Sudan beginning in 2003, and during the war in Iraq, where survey-based estimates of deaths ranged from 151,000 to more than 1 million from 2002 through 2006 (Iraq Family Study, 2008; ORB, 2008). What factors affect the decision making of our world leaders?

This century has also challenged Americans' preconceived notions about race, gender, and age. The unprecedented 2008 presidential contest involved a 60-year-old White woman (Hillary Clinton), a 46-year-old African-American man (Barack Obama), and a 71-year-old White man (John McCain). Knowing that a difference of but a few votes could change the course of history, donors contributed hundreds of millions of dollars in the hope of influencing people's opinions. How do we form our attitudes, and how do those attitudes affect our actions?

As each day's news has brought updates on acts of hate or heroism, defeats or victories, many of us have lived out our own experiences with love and loss. Why are we attracted to some people but not others, and what spurs friendship and romance?

Human connections are powerful and can be perilous. Yet "we cannot live for ourselves alone," remarked the novelist Herman Melville. "Our lives are connected by a thousand invisible threads." **Social psychologists** explore these connections by scientifically studying how we *think about, influence,* and *relate to* one another. In Modules 56 through 59, we consider these topics.

Social Thinking (Module 56) asks, How do we explain people's behavior? How do we form our beliefs and attitudes? What is the relationship between what we think and what we do? Social Influence (Module 57) asks, What invisible social threads pull us? How strong are they? How do they operate? Antisocial Relations (Module 58) asks, What makes us harm others? And in Prosocial Relations (Module 59): Why do we fall in love? And what can we do to transform the closed fists of aggression into the open arms of compassion?

social psychology the scientific study of how we think about, influence, and relate to one another.

MODULE 56

Social Thinking

Our social behavior arises from our social cognition. Especially when the unexpected occurs, we analyze why people act as they do. Does her warmth reflect romantic interest, or is that how she relates to everyone? Does his absenteeism signify illness? Laziness? A stressful work atmosphere? Was the horror of 9/11 the work of crazed people, or of ordinary people corrupted by life events? Such questions intrigue social psychologists. Just as personality psychologists study the enduring, inner determinants of behavior that help to explain why different people act differently in a given situation, so *social psychologists* study the social influences that help explain why the same person will act differently in different situations.

▶‖ Attributing Behavior to Persons or to Situations

56-1 How do we tend to explain others' behavior and our own?

After studying how people explain others' behavior, Fritz Heider (1958) proposed an **attribution theory.** Heider noted that people usually attribute others' behavior either to their internal dispositions or to their external situations. A teacher, for example, may wonder whether a child's hostility reflects an aggressive personality (a *dispositional attribution*) or a reaction to stress or abuse (a *situational attribution*).

In class, we notice that Juliette seldom talks; over coffee, Jack talks nonstop. Attributing their behaviors to their personal dispositions, we decide Juliette is shy and Jack is outgoing. Because people do have enduring personality traits, such attributions are sometimes valid. However, we often fall prey to the **fundamental attribution error,** by overestimating the influence of personality and underestimating the influence of situations. In class, Jack may be as quiet as Juliette. Catch Juliette at a party and you may hardly recognize your quiet classmate.

An experiment by David Napolitan and George Goethals (1979) illustrated the phenomenon. They had Williams College students talk, one at a time, with a young woman who acted either aloof and critical or warm and friendly. Beforehand, they told half the students that the woman's behavior would be spontaneous. They told the other half the truth—that she had been instructed to *act* friendly (or unfriendly). What do you suppose was the effect of being told the truth?

There was no effect. The students disregarded the information. If the woman acted friendly, they inferred she really was a warm person. If she acted unfriendly, they inferred she really was a cold person. In other words, they attributed her behavior to her personal disposition *even when told that her behavior was situational*—that she was merely acting that way for the purposes of the experiment. Although the fundamental attribution error occurs in all cultures studied, this tendency to attribute behavior to people's dispositions runs especially strong in individualistic Western countries. In East Asian cultures, for example, people are more sensitive to the power of the situation (Masuda & Kitayama, 2004).

You have surely committed the fundamental attribution error. In judging whether your psychology instructor is shy or outgoing, you have perhaps by now inferred that he or she has an outgoing personality. But you know your instructor only from the classroom, a situation that demands outgoing behavior. Catch the instructor in a

The fundamental attribution error If our new friend acts grouchy, we may decide she's a grouchy person. She may be more likely to explain her behavior as a result of losing sleep over a family worry, getting a flat tire on the way to work, or having a fight with her boyfriend.

Doug Mills/New York Times/Redux

Actor and observer perspectives make for differing attributions During their contentious U.S. presidential primaries in 2008, Barack Obama was criticized for seeming—in this camera perspective that faces him—to turn a cold shoulder to his opponent, Hillary Clinton. Obama later explained that he had greeted her earlier, and here was turning to speak to (as a picture shot from behind him might have shown) the unseen person to his left. In laboratory experiments, when a camera shows the actor's perspective, observers better appreciate the situation's influence.

different situation and you might be surprised. Outside their assigned roles, professors seem less professorial, presidents less presidential, servants less servile.

The instructor, on the other hand, observes his or her own behavior in many different situations—in the classroom, in meetings, at home—and so might say, "Me, outgoing? It all depends on the situation. In class or with good friends, yes, I'm outgoing. But at conventions I'm really rather shy." When explaining *our own* behavior, or the behavior of those we know well and see in varied situations, we are sensitive to how behavior changes with the situation (Idson & Mischel, 2001). (An important exception is our own intentional and admirable actions, which we more often attribute to our own good reasons than to situational causes [Malle, 2006; Malle et al., 2007].)

When explaining *others'* behavior, particularly the behavior of strangers we have observed in only one type of situation, we often commit the fundamental attribution error: We disregard the situation and leap to unwarranted conclusions about their personality traits. Many people initially assumed the 9/11 terrorists were obviously crazy, when actually they went unnoticed in their neighborhoods, health clubs, and favorite restaurants.

Researchers who have reversed the perspectives of actor and observer—by having each view a replay of the situation filmed from the other's perspective—have also reversed the attributions (Lassiter & Irvine, 1986; Storms, 1973). Seeing the world from the actor's perspective, the observers better appreciate the situation. (As you act, your eyes look outward; you see others' faces, not your own.) Taking the observer's point of view, the actors better appreciate their own personal style. Reflecting on our past selves of 5 or 10 years ago also switches our perspective. We now adopt an observer's perspective and attribute our behavior mostly to our traits (Pronin & Ross, 2006). Likewise, in another 5 or 10 years, our today's self may seem like another person.

The Effects of Attribution

In everyday life we often struggle to explain others' actions. A jury must decide whether a shooting was malicious or in self-defense. An interviewer must judge whether the applicant's geniality is genuine. A person must decide whether to attribute another's friendliness to sexual interest. When we make such judgments, our attributions—either to the person or to the situation—have important consequences (Fincham & Bradbury, 1993; Fletcher et al., 1990). Happily married couples attribute a spouse's tart-tongued remark to a temporary situation ("She must have had a bad day at work"). Unhappily married couples attribute the same remark to a mean disposition ("Why did I marry such a hostile person?").

attribution theory the theory that we explain someone's behavior by crediting either the situation or the person's disposition.

fundamental attribution error the tendency for observers, when analyzing another's behavior, to underestimate the impact of the situation and to overestimate the impact of personal disposition.

‖ Some 7 in 10 college women report having experienced a man misattributing her friendliness as a sexual come-on (Jacques-Tiura et al., 2007). ‖

An attribution question
Some people blamed the New Orleans residents for not evacuating before the predicted 2005 Hurricane Katrina. Others attributed their inaction to the situation—to their not having cars or not being offered bus transportation.

"Otis, shout at that man to pull himself together."

Or consider the political effects of attribution. How do you explain poverty or unemployment? Researchers in Britain, India, Australia, and the United States (Furnham, 1982; Pandey et al., 1982; Wagstaff, 1982; Zucker & Weiner, 1993) report that political conservatives tend to attribute such social problems to the personal dispositions of the poor and unemployed themselves: "People generally get what they deserve. Those who don't work are often freeloaders. Anybody who takes the initiative can still get ahead." "Society is not to blame for crime, criminals are," said one conservative U.S. presidential candidate (Dole, 1996). Political liberals (and social scientists) are more likely to blame past and present situations: "If you or I had to live with the same poor education, lack of opportunity, and discrimination, would we be any better off?" To understand and prevent terrorism, they say, consider the situations that breed terrorists. Better to drain the swamps than swat the mosquitoes.

Managers' attributions also have effects. In evaluating employees, they are likely to attribute poor performance to personal factors, such as low ability or lack of motivation. But remember the actor's viewpoint: Workers doing poorly on a job recognize situational influences, such as inadequate supplies, poor working conditions, difficult co-workers, or impossible demands (Rice, 1985).

The point to remember: Our attributions—to individuals' dispositions or to their situations—should be made carefully. They have real consequences.

▶‖ Attitudes and Actions

56-2 Does what we think affect what we do, or does what we do affect what we think?

Attitudes are feelings, often influenced by our beliefs, that predispose our reactions to objects, people, and events. If we *believe* someone is mean, we may *feel* dislike for the person and *act* unfriendly.

Attitudes Affect Actions

Our attitudes often predict our behavior. Al Gore's movie *An Inconvenient Truth* and the Alliance for Climate Protection it has spawned have a simple premise: Public opinion about the reality and dangers of global climate change can change, with effects on both personal behaviors and public policies. Indeed, by the end of 2007, an analysis of international opinion surveys by WorldPublicOpinion.org showed "widespread and growing concern about climate change. Large majorities believe that human activity causes climate change and favor policies designed to reduce emissions." Thanks to the mass persuasion campaign, many corporations, as well as campuses, are now going green.

This tidal wave of change has occurred as people have engaged scientific evidence and arguments and responded with favorable thoughts. Such **central route persuasion** occurs mostly when people are naturally analytical or involved in the issue. When issues don't engage systematic thinking, persuasion may occur through a faster **peripheral route,** as people respond to incidental cues, such as endorsements by respected people, and make snap judgments. Because central route persuasion is more thoughtful and less superficial, it is more durable and more likely to influence behavior.

Other factors, including the external situation, also influence behavior. Strong social pressures can weaken the attitude-behavior connection (Wallace et al., 2005). For example, the American public's overwhelming support for former President George W. Bush's preparation to attack Iraq motivated Democratic leaders to vote to support Bush's war plan, despite their private reservations (Nagourney, 2002). Nevertheless, attitudes do affect behavior when external influences are minimal, especially when the attitude is stable, specific to the behavior, and easily recalled (Glasman & Albarracín, 2006). One experiment used vivid, easily recalled information to persuade people that sustained tanning put them at risk for future skin cancer. One month later, 72 percent of the participants, and only 16 percent of those in a waiting list control group, had lighter skin (McClendon & Prentice-Dunn, 2001).

Actions Affect Attitudes

Now consider a more surprising principle: Not only will people sometimes stand up for what they believe, they will also come to believe in the idea they have supported. Many streams of evidence confirm that *attitudes follow behavior* (**FIGURE 56.1**).

The Foot-in-the-Door Phenomenon

Inducing people to act against their beliefs can affect their attitude. During the Korean war, many captured U.S. soldiers were imprisoned in war camps run by Chinese communists. Without using brutality, the captors secured the prisoners' collaboration in various activities. Some merely ran errands or accepted favors. Others made radio appeals and false confessions. Still others informed on fellow prisoners and divulged military information. When the war ended, 21 prisoners chose to stay with the communists. More returned home "brainwashed"—convinced that communism was a good thing for Asia.

attitude feelings, often influenced by our beliefs, that predispose us to respond in a particular way to objects, people, and events.

central route to persuasion occurs when interested people focus on the arguments and respond with favorable thoughts.

peripheral route to persuasion occurs when people are influenced by incidental cues, such as a speaker's attractiveness.

FIGURE 56.1 Attitudes follow behavior Cooperative actions, such as those performed by people on sports teams, feed mutual liking. Such attitudes, in turn, promote positive behavior.

Actions

Attitudes

D. MacDonald/PhotoEdit

foot-in-the-door phenomenon the tendency for people who have first agreed to a small request to comply later with a larger request.

role a set of explanations (norms) about a social position, defining how those in the position ought to behave.

"If the King destroys a man, that's proof to the King it must have been a bad man."
Thomas Cromwell, in Robert Bolt's *A Man for All Seasons*, 1960

"Fake it until you make it."
Alcoholics Anonymous saying

A key ingredient of the Chinese "thought-control" program was its effective use of the **foot-in-the-door phenomenon**—a tendency for people who agree to a small action to comply later with a larger one. The Chinese began with harmless requests but gradually escalated their demands (Schein, 1956). Having "trained" the prisoners to speak or write trivial statements, the communists then asked them to copy or create something more important—noting, perhaps, the flaws of capitalism. Then, perhaps to gain privileges, the prisoners participated in group discussions, wrote self-criticisms, or uttered public confessions. After doing so, they often adjusted their beliefs toward consistency with their public acts.

The point is simple: To get people to agree to something big, "start small and build," said Robert Cialdini (1993). Knowing this, you can be wary of those who would exploit you with the tactic. This chicken-and-egg spiral, of actions-feeding-attitudes-feeding-actions, enables behavior to escalate. A trivial act makes the next act easier. Succumb to a temptation and you will find the next temptation harder to resist.

Dozens of experiments have simulated part of the war prisoners' experience by coaxing people into acting against their attitudes or violating their moral standards. The nearly inevitable result: Doing becomes believing. When people are induced to harm an innocent victim—by making nasty comments or delivering electric shocks—they then begin to disparage their victim. If induced to speak or write on behalf of a position they have qualms about, they begin to believe their own words.

Fortunately, the attitudes-follow-behavior principle works as well for good deeds as for bad. The foot-in-the-door tactic has helped boost charitable contributions, blood donations, and product sales. In one experiment, researchers posing as safe-driving volunteers asked Californians to permit the installation of a large, poorly lettered "Drive Carefully" sign in their front yards. Only 17 percent consented. They approached other home owners with a small request first: Would they display a 3-inch-high "Be a Safe Driver" sign? Nearly all readily agreed. When reapproached two weeks later to allow the large, ugly sign in their front yards, 76 percent consented (Freedman & Fraser, 1966). To secure a big commitment, it often pays to put your foot in the door: Start small and build.

Racial attitudes likewise follow behavior. In the years immediately following the introduction of school desegregation in the United States and the passage of the Civil Rights Act of 1964, White Americans expressed diminishing racial prejudice. And as Americans in different regions came to act more alike—thanks to more uniform national standards against discrimination—they began to think more alike. Experiments confirm the observation: Moral action strengthens moral convictions.

Role-Playing Affects Attitudes

When you adopt a new **role**—when you become a college student, marry, or begin a new job—you strive to follow the social prescriptions. At first, your behaviors may feel phony, because you are *acting* a role. The first weeks in the military feel artificial—as if one is pretending to be a soldier. The first weeks of a marriage may feel like "playing house." Before long, however, what began as play-acting in the theater of life becomes *you*.

Researchers have confirmed this effect by assessing people's attitudes before and after they adopt a new role, sometimes in laboratory situations, sometimes in everyday situations, such as before and after taking a job. In one famous laboratory study, male college students volunteered to spend time in a simulated prison devised by psychologist Philip Zimbardo (1972). Some he randomly designated as guards; he gave them uniforms, billy clubs, and whistles and instructed them to enforce certain rules. The remainder became prisoners; they were locked in barren cells and forced to wear humiliating outfits. After a day or two in which the volunteers self-consciously "played" their roles, the simulation became real—too real. Most of the guards developed disparaging attitudes, and some devised cruel and degrading routines. One by one, the prisoners broke down, rebelled, or became passively resigned, causing Zimbardo to call off the study after only six days. More recently, similar situations have played themselves out in the real world—as in Iraq at the Abu Ghraib prison (see Close-Up: Abu Ghraib Prison: An "Atrocity-Producing Situation"?).

Greece's military junta during the early 1970s took advantage of the effects of role-playing to train men to become torturers (Staub, 1989). The men's indoctrination into their roles occurred in small steps. First, the trainee stood guard outside the interrogation cells—the "foot in the door." Next, he stood guard inside. Only then was he ready to become actively involved in the questioning and torture. As the nineteenth-century writer Nathaniel Hawthorne noted, "No man, for any considerable period, can wear one face to himself and another to the multitude without finally getting bewildered as to which may be true." What we do, we gradually become.

Psychologists add a cautionary note: In Zimbardo's prison simulation, at Abu Ghraib prison, and in other atrocity-producing situations, some people succumb to the situation and others do not (Carnahan & McFarland, 2007; Haslam & Reicher,

Philip G. Zimbardo, Inc.

The power of the situation In Philip Zimbardo's Stanford prison simulation, a toxic situation triggered degrading behaviors among those assigned to the guard role.

CLOSE-UP

Abu Ghraib Prison: An "Atrocity-Producing Situation"?

As the first photos emerged in 2004 from Iraq's Abu Ghraib prison, the civilized world was shocked. The photos showed U.S. military guards stripping prisoners naked, placing hoods on them, stacking them in piles, prodding them with electricity, taunting them with attack dogs, and subjecting them to sleep deprivation, humiliation, and extreme stress. Was the problem, as so many people initially supposed, a few bad apples—a few irresponsible or sadistic guards? That was the U.S. Army's seeming verdict when it court-martialed and imprisoned some of the guards, and then cleared four of the five top commanding officers responsible for Abu Ghraib's policies and operations. The lower-level military guards were "sick bastards," explained the defense attorney for one of the commanding officers (Tarbert, 2004).

Many social psychologists, however, reminded us that a toxic situation can make even good apples go bad (Fiske et al., 2004). "When ordinary people are put in a novel, evil place, such as most prisons, Situations Win, People Lose,"

Originally published in the *New Yorker*

Bad apples or bad barrels? Like the Stanford Prison Experiment in 1971, the real-life Abu Ghraib prison fiasco in 2004 was a powerfully toxic situation, contends social psychologist Philip Zimbardo.

offered Philip Zimbardo (2004), adding, "That is true for the majority of people in all the relevant social psychological research done over the past 40 years."

Consider the situation, explained Zimbardo. The guards, some of them model soldier-reservists with no prior criminal or sadistic history, were exhausted from working 12-hour shifts, seven days a week. They were dealing with an enemy, and their prejudices were heightened by fears of lethal attacks and by the violent deaths of many fellow soldiers. They were put in an understaffed guard role, with minimal training and supervision. They were then encouraged to "soften up" for interrogation detainees who had been denied access to the Red Cross. "When you put that set of horrendous work conditions and external factors together, it creates an evil barrel. You could put virtually anybody in it and you're going to get this kind of evil behavior" (Zimbardo, 2005). Atrocious behaviors often emerge in atrocious situations.

cognitive dissonance theory the theory that we act to reduce the discomfort (dissonance) we feel when two of our thoughts (cognitions) are inconsistent. For example, when our awareness of our attitudes and of our actions clash, we can reduce the resulting dissonance by changing our attitudes.

Regarding President Lyndon Johnson's commitment to the Vietnam war:
"A president who justifies his actions only to the public might be induced to change them. A president who has justified his actions to himself, believing that he has *the truth*, becomes impervious to self-correction."

Carol Tavris and Elliot Aronson, *Mistakes Were Made (But Not by Me)*, 2007

2007; Mastroianni & Reed, 2006; Zimbardo, 2007). Person and situation interact. Water has the power to dissolve some substances, notes John Johnson (2007), but not all. In a watery situation, salt dissolves, sand does not. So also, when put in with rotten apples, some people, but not others, become bad apples.

Cognitive Dissonance: Relief From Tension

So far we have seen that actions can affect attitudes, sometimes turning prisoners into collaborators, doubters into believers, mere acquaintances into friends, and compliant guards into abusers. But why? One explanation is that when we become aware that our attitudes and actions don't coincide, we experience tension, or *cognitive dissonance*. (I am aware of the threats posed by global climate change, and am aware, with some discomfort, that I often fly in CO_2-spewing planes—and thus appreciate airlines that let me reduce my dissonance by purchasing a carbon offset.) To relieve this tension, according to the **cognitive dissonance theory** proposed by Leon Festinger, we often bring our attitudes into line with our actions. It is as if we rationalize, "If I chose to do it (or say it), I must believe in it." The less coerced and more responsible we feel for a troubling act, the more dissonance we feel. The more dissonance we feel, the more motivated we are to find consistency, such as changing our attitudes to help justify the act.

The U.S. invasion of Iraq was mainly premised on the presumed threat of Saddam Hussein's weapons of mass destruction (WMD). As the war began, only 38 percent of Americans surveyed said the war was justified even if Iraq did not have WMD (Gallup, 2003). Nearly 80 percent believed such weapons would be found (Duffy, 2003; Newport et al., 2003). When no WMD were found, many Americans felt dissonance, which was heightened by their awareness of the war's financial and human costs, by scenes of chaos in Iraq, and by inflamed anti-American and pro-terrorist sentiments in some parts of the world.

To reduce dissonance, some people revised their memories of the main rationale for going to war, which then became liberating an oppressed people and promoting democracy in the Middle East. Before long, the once-minority opinion became the majority view: 58 percent of Americans said they supported the war even if there were no WMD (Gallup, 2003). "Whether or not they find weapons of mass destruction doesn't matter," explained Republican pollster Frank Luntz (2003), "because the rationale for the war changed." It was not until late 2004, when hopes for a flourishing peace waned, that Americans' support for the war dropped below 50 percent.

Dozens of experiments have explored cognitive dissonance by making people feel responsible for behavior that is inconsistent with their attitudes and that has foreseeable consequences. As a subject in one of these experiments, you might agree for a measly $2 to help a researcher by writing an essay that supports something you don't believe in (perhaps a tuition increase). Feeling responsible for the statements (which are not consistent with your attitudes), you would probably feel dissonance, especially if you thought an administrator would be reading your essay. How could you reduce the uncomfortable dissonance? One way would be to start believing your phony words. Your pretense would become your reality.

The attitudes-follow-behavior principle has a heartening implication: Although we cannot directly control all our feelings, we can influence them by altering our behavior. Facial expressions and body postures affect our emotions. If we are down in the dumps, we can do as cognitive therapists advise and talk in more positive, self-accepting

"Look, I have my misgivings, too, but what choice do we have except stay the course?"

ways with fewer self–put-downs. If we are unloving, we can become more loving by behaving as if we were so—by doing thoughtful things, expressing affection, giving affirmation. "Assume a virtue, if you have it not," says Hamlet to his mother. "For use can almost change the stamp of nature."

The point to remember: Cruel acts shape the self. But so do acts of good will. Act as though you like someone, and you soon will. Changing our behavior can change how we think about others and how we feel about ourselves.

> "Sit all day in a moping posture, sigh, and reply to everything with a dismal voice, and your melancholy lingers. . . . If we wish to conquer undesirable emotional tendencies in ourselves, we must . . . go through the outward movements of those contrary dispositions which we prefer to cultivate."
>
> William James, *Principles of Psychology*, 1890

REVIEW

Social Thinking

Social psychologists study how people think about, influence, and relate to one another.

56-1 **How do we tend to explain others' behavior and our own?** We generally explain people's behavior by *attributing* it to internal dispositions and/or to external situations. In committing the *fundamental attribution error,* we underestimate the influence of the situation on others' actions. When explaining our own behavior, we more often point to the situation. Our attributions influence our personal, legal, political, and workplace judgments.

56-2 **Does what we think affect what we do, or does what we do affect what we think?** *Attitudes* influence behavior when other influences are minimal, and when the attitude is stable, specific to the behavior, and easily recalled.

Studies of the *foot-in-the-door phenomenon* and of *role-playing* reveal that our actions (especially those we feel responsible for) can also modify our attitudes. *Cognitive dissonance theory* proposes that behavior shapes attitudes because we feel discomfort when our actions and attitudes differ. We reduce the discomfort by bringing our attitudes more into line with what we have done.

Terms and Concepts to Remember

social psychology, p. 681
attribution theory, p. 682
fundamental attribution error, p. 682
attitude, p. 684
central route to persuasion, p. 685
peripheral route to persuasion, p. 685
foot-in-the-door phenomenon, p. 686
role, p. 686
cognitive dissonance theory, p. 688

Test Yourself

1. Driving to school one snowy day, Marco narrowly misses a car that slides through a red light. "Slow down! What a terrible driver," he thinks to himself. Moments later, Marco himself slides through an intersection and yelps, "Wow! These roads are awful. The city plows need to get out here." What social psychology principle has Marco just demonstrated? Explain.

(Answers to the Test Yourself questions can be found in Appendix B at the end of the book.)

Ask Yourself

1. Do you have an attitude or tendency you would like to change? Using the attitudes-follow-behavior principle, how might you go about changing that attitude?

∞ WEB

Multiple-choice self-tests and more may be found at www.worthpublishers.com/myers

MODULE 57

Social Influence

Social psychology's great lesson is the enormous power of social influence. This influence can be seen in our conformity, our compliance, and our group behavior. Suicides, bomb threats, airplane hijackings, and UFO sightings all have a curious tendency to come in clusters. On campus, jeans are the dress code; on New York's Wall Street or London's Bond Street, dress suits are the norm. When we know how to act, how to groom, how to talk, life functions smoothly. Armed with social influence principles, advertisers, fund raisers, and campaign workers aim to sway our decisions to buy, to donate, to vote. Isolated with others who share their grievances, dissenters may gradually become rebels, and rebels may become terrorists. Let's examine the pull of these social strings. How strong are they? How do they operate?

▶‖ Conformity and Obedience

57-1 What do experiments on conformity and compliance reveal about the power of social influence?

Behavior is contagious. Consider:

- ▶ A cluster of people stand gazing upward, and passersby pause to do likewise.
- ▶ Baristas and street musicians know to "seed" their tip containers with money to suggest that others have given.
- ▶ One person laughs, coughs, or yawns, and others in the group soon do the same. Chimpanzees, too, are more likely to yawn after observing another chimpanzee yawn (Anderson et al., 2004).
- ▶ "Sickness" can also be psychologically contagious. In the anxious 9/11 aftermath, more than two dozen elementary and middle schools had outbreaks of children reporting red rashes, sometimes causing parents to wonder whether biological terrorism was at work (Talbot, 2002). Some cases may have been stress-related, but mostly, health experts concluded, people were just noticing normal early acne, insect bites, eczema, and dry skin from overheated classrooms.

We are natural mimics—an effect Tanya Chartrand and John Bargh (1999) have called the *chameleon effect*. Unconsciously mimicking others' expressions, postures, and voice tones helps us feel what they are feeling. This helps explain why we feel happier around happy people than around depressed ones, and why studies of groups of British nurses and accountants reveal *mood linkage*—sharing up and down moods (Totterdell et al., 1998). Just hearing someone reading a neutral text in either a happy- or sad-sounding voice creates "mood contagion" in listeners (Neumann & Strack, 2000).

Chartrand and Bargh demonstrated the chameleon effect when they had students work in a room alongside a confederate working for the experimenter. Sometimes the confederates rubbed their face; on other occasions, they shook their foot. Sure enough, participants tended to rub their own face when with the face-rubbing person and shake their own foot when with the foot-shaking person. Such automatic mimicry is part of empathy. Empathic people yawn more after seeing others yawn (Morrison, 2007). And empathic, mimicking people are liked more. Those most eager to fit in with a group seem intuitively to know this, for they are especially prone to unconscious mimicry (Lakin & Chartrand, 2003).

Niche conformity Are these students asserting their individuality or identifying themselves with others of the same microculture?

Yuriko Nakao/Reuters/Corbis

NON SEQUITUR   by WILEY

Sometimes the effects of suggestibility are more serious. In the eight days following the 1999 shooting rampage at Colorado's Columbine High School, every U.S. state except Vermont experienced threats of copycat violence. Pennsylvania alone recorded 60 such threats (Cooper, 1999). Sociologist David Phillips and his colleagues (1985, 1989) found that suicides, too, sometimes increase following a highly publicized suicide. In the wake of screen idol Marilyn Monroe's suicide on August 6, 1962, for example, the number of suicides in the United States exceeded the usual August count by 200. Within a one-year period, one London psychiatric unit experienced 14 patient suicides (Joiner, 1999). In the days after Saddam Hussein's widely publicized execution in Iraq, there were cases of boys in Turkey, Pakistan, Yemen, Saudi Arabia, and the United States who hung themselves, apparently accidently, after slipping nooses around their own heads (AP, 2007).

What causes suicide clusters? Do people act similarly because of their influence on one another? Or because they are simultaneously exposed to the same events and conditions? Seeking answers, social psychologists have conducted experiments on group pressure and conformity.

Group Pressure and Conformity

Suggestibility is a subtle type of **conformity**—adjusting our behavior or thinking toward some group standard. To study conformity, Solomon Asch (1955) devised a simple test. As a participant in what you believe is a study of visual perception, you arrive at the experiment location in time to take a seat at a table where five people are already seated. The experimenter asks which of three comparison lines is identical to a standard line (**FIGURE 57.1**). You see clearly that the answer is Line 2 and await your turn to say so after the others. Your boredom with this experiment begins to show when the next set of lines proves equally easy.

conformity adjusting one's behavior or thinking to coincide with a group standard.

FIGURE 57.1 Asch's conformity experiments Which of the three comparison lines is equal to the standard line? What do you suppose most people would say after hearing five others say, "Line 3"? In this photo from one of Asch's experiments, the student in the center shows the severe discomfort that comes from disagreeing with the responses of other group members (in this case, confederates of the experimenter).

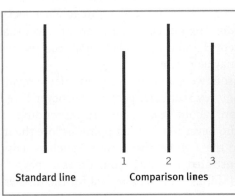

Standard line   Comparison lines

Now comes the third trial, and the correct answer seems just as clear-cut, but the first person gives what strikes you as a wrong answer: "Line 3." When the second person and then the third and fourth give the same wrong answer, you sit up straight and squint. When the fifth person agrees with the first four, you feel your heart begin to pound. The experimenter then looks to you for your answer. Torn between the unanimity of your five fellow respondents and the evidence of your own eyes, you feel tense and much less sure of yourself than you were moments ago. You hesitate before answering, wondering whether you should suffer the discomfort of being the oddball. What answer do you give?

In the experiments conducted by Asch and others after him, thousands of college students have experienced this conflict. Answering such questions alone, they erred less than 1 percent of the time. But the odds were quite different when several others—confederates working for the experimenter—answered incorrectly. Although most people told the truth even when others did not, Asch nevertheless was disturbed by his result: More than one-third of the time, these "intelligent and well-meaning" college-student participants were then "willing to call white black" by going along with the group.

Conditions That Strengthen Conformity

Asch's procedure became the model for later investigations. Although experiments have not always found so much conformity, they do reveal that conformity increases when

- one is made to feel incompetent or insecure.
- the group has at least three people.
- the group is unanimous. (The dissent of just one other person greatly increases social courage.)
- one admires the group's status and attractiveness.
- one has made no prior commitment to any response.
- others in the group observe one's behavior.
- one's culture strongly encourages respect for social standards.

Thus, we might predict the behavior of Austin, an enthusiastic but insecure new fraternity member: Noting that the 40 other members appear unanimous in their plans for a fund raiser, Austin is unlikely to voice his dissent.

Reasons for Conforming

Fish swim in schools. Birds fly in flocks. And humans, too, tend to go with their group, to think what it thinks and do what it does. Researchers have seen this in college residence halls, where over time students' attitudes become more similar to those living near them (Cullum & Harton, 2007). But why? Why do we clap when others clap, eat as others eat, believe what others believe, even see what others see? Frequently, it is to avoid rejection or to gain social approval. In such cases, we are responding to what social psychologists call **normative social influence.** We are sensitive to social norms—understood rules for accepted and expected behavior—because the price we pay for being different may be severe.

"I love the little ways you're identical to everyone else."

Respecting norms is not the only reason we conform: Groups may provide valuable information, and only an uncommonly stubborn person will never listen to others. When we accept others' opinions about reality, we are responding to **informational social influence.** "Those who never retract their opinions love themselves more than they love truth," observed the eighteenth-century French essayist, Joseph Joubert. As Rebecca Denton demonstrated in 2004, sometimes it pays to assume others are right and to follow their lead. Denton set a record for the furthest distance driven on the wrong side of a British divided highway—30 miles, with only

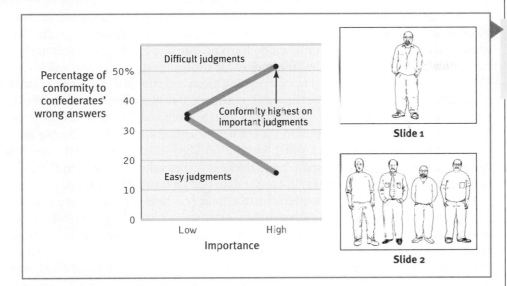

FIGURE 57.2 Informational influence
Sample task: After seeing Slides 1 and 2, participants judged which person in Slide 2 was the same as the person in Slide 1. (From Baron et al., 1996.)

one minor sideswipe, before the motorway ran out and police were able to puncture her tires. Denton later explained that she thought the hundreds of other drivers coming at her were all on the wrong side of the road (Woolcock, 2004).

Robert Baron and his colleagues (1996) cleverly demonstrated our openness to informational influence on tough, important judgments. They modernized the Asch experiment by showing University of Iowa students a slide of a stimulus person, followed by a slide of a four-person lineup (**FIGURE 57.2**). Their experiment made the task either easy (viewing the lineup for five seconds) or difficult (viewing the lineup for but half a second). It also led them to think their judgments were either unimportant (just a preliminary test of some eyewitness identification procedures) or important (establishing norms for an actual police procedure, with a $20 award to the most accurate participants). When the accuracy of their judgments seemed important, people rarely conformed when the task was easy, but they conformed half the time when the task was difficult. If we are unsure of what is right, and if being right matters, we are receptive to others' opinions.

Our view of social influence as bad or good depends on our values. When influence supports what we approve, we applaud those who are "open-minded" and "sensitive" enough to be "responsive." When influence supports what we disapprove, we scorn the "submissive conformity" of those who comply with others' wishes. Cultures vary in the extent to which they value individualism or collectivism. Western Europeans and people in most English-speaking countries tend to prize individualism more than conformity and obedience. These values are reflected in social influence experiments that have been conducted in 17 countries: In individualist cultures, conformity rates are lower (Bond & Smith, 1996). In the individualistic United States, university students tend to see themselves, in domains ranging from consumer purchases to political views, as less conforming than others (Pronin et al., 2007). We are, in our own eyes, individuals amid a crowd of sheep. Thus, tattoos, once a symbol of nonconformity, may lose their appeal if they become too popular.

Obedience

Social psychologist Stanley Milgram (1963, 1974), a student of Solomon Asch, knew that people often comply with social pressures. But how would they respond to outright commands? To find out, he undertook what have become social psychology's most famous and controversial experiments. Imagine yourself as one of the nearly 1000 participants in Milgram's 20 experiments.

normative social influence influence resulting from a person's desire to gain approval or avoid disapproval.

informational social influence influence resulting from one's willingness to accept others' opinions about reality.

Stanley Milgram (1933–1984)
This social psychologist's obedience experiments "belong to the self-understanding of literate people in our age" (Sabini, 1986).

Responding to an advertisement, you come to Yale University's psychology department to participate in an experiment. Professor Milgram's assistant explains that the study concerns the effect of punishment on learning. You and another person draw slips from a hat to see who will be the "teacher" (which your slip says) and who will be the "learner." The learner is then led to an adjoining room and strapped into a chair that is wired through the wall to an electric shock machine. You sit in front of the machine, which has switches labeled with voltages. Your task: to teach and then test the learner on a list of word pairs. You are to punish the learner for wrong answers by delivering brief electric shocks, beginning with a switch labeled "15 Volts—Slight Shock." After each of the learner's errors, you are to move up to the next higher voltage. With each flick of a switch, lights flash, relay switches click on, and an electric buzzing fills the air.

Complying with the experimenter's instructions, you hear the learner grunt when you flick the third, fourth, and fifth switches. After you activate the eighth switch (labeled "120 Volts—Moderate Shock"), the learner shouts that the shocks are painful. After the tenth switch ("150 Volts—Strong Shock"), he cries, "Get me out of here! I won't be in the experiment anymore! I refuse to go on!" Hearing these pleas, you draw back. But the experimenter prods you: "Please continue—the experiment requires that you continue." If you still resist, he insists, "It is absolutely essential that you continue," or "You have no other choice, you *must* go on."

Obeying, you hear the learner's protests escalate to shrieks of agony as you continue to raise the shock level with each succeeding error. After the 330-volt level, the learner refuses to answer and falls silent. Still, the experimenter pushes you toward the final, 450-volt switch, ordering you to ask the questions and, if no correct answer is given, to administer the next shock level.

How far do you think you would follow the experimenter's commands? In a survey Milgram conducted before the experiment, most people declared they would stop playing such a sadistic-seeming role soon after the learner first indicated pain and certainly before he shrieked in agony. This also was the prediction made by each of 40 psychiatrists Milgram asked to guess the outcome. When Milgram actually conducted the experiment with men aged 20 to 50, he was astonished to find that 63 percent complied fully—right up to the last switch. Ten later studies that included women found women's compliance rates were similar to men's (Blass, 1999).

Did the teachers figure out the hoax—that no shock was being delivered? Did they correctly guess the learner was a confederate who only pretended to feel the shocks? Did they realize the experiment was really testing their willingness to comply with commands to inflict punishment? No. The teachers typically displayed genuine distress: They perspired, trembled, laughed nervously, and bit their lips. In a recent virtual reality re-creation of these experiments, participants responded much as did Milgram's participants, including perspiration and racing heart, when shocking a virtual woman on a screen in front of them (Slater et al., 2006).

Milgram's use of deception and stress triggered a debate over his research ethics. In his own defense, Milgram pointed out that, after the participants learned of the deception and actual research purposes, virtually none regretted taking part (though perhaps by then the participants had reduced their dissonance). When 40 of the teachers who had agonized most were later interviewed by a psychiatrist, none appeared to be suffering emotional aftereffects. All in all, said Milgram, the experiments provoked less enduring stress than university students experience when facing and failing big exams (Blass, 1996).

Wondering whether the participants obeyed because the learners' protests were not convincing, Milgram repeated the experiment with 40 new teachers. This time his confederate mentioned a "slight heart condition" while being strapped into the chair, and then he complained and screamed more intensely as the shocks became more punishing. Still, 65 percent of the new teachers complied fully (**FIGURE 57.3**).

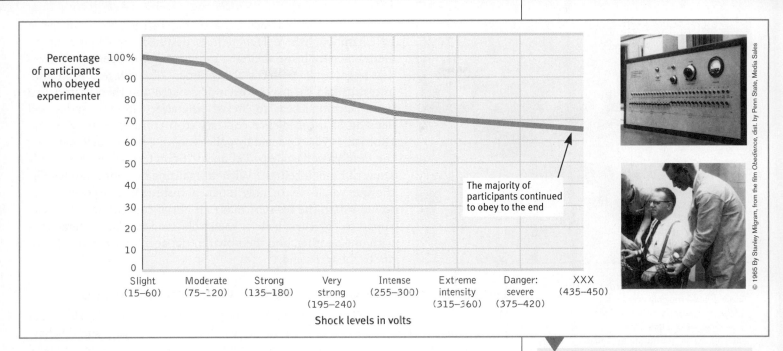

Percentage of participants who obeyed experimenter

Slight (15–60)	
Moderate (75–120)	
Strong (135–180)	
Very strong (195–240)	
Intense (255–300)	
Extreme intensity (315–360)	
Danger: severe (375–420)	
XXX (435–450)	

The majority of participants continued to obey to the end

Shock levels in volts

In later experiments, Milgram discovered that subtle details of a situation powerfully influence people. When he varied the social conditions, the proportion of fully compliant participants varied from 0 to 93 percent. Obedience was highest when

▶ the person giving the orders was close at hand and was perceived to be a legitimate authority figure. (Such was the case in 2005 when Temple University's basketball coach sent a 250-pound bench player, Nehemiah Ingram, into a game with instructions to commit "hard fouls." Following orders, Ingram fouled out in four minutes after breaking an opposing player's right arm.)

▶ the authority figure was supported by a prestigious institution. Compliance was somewhat lower when Milgram dissociated his experiments from Yale University.

▶ the victim was depersonalized or at a distance, even in another room. (Similarly, in combat with an enemy they can see, many soldiers either do not fire their rifles or do not aim them properly. Such refusals to kill are rare among those who operate more distant artillery or aircraft weapons [Padgett, 1989].)

▶ there were no role models for defiance; that is, no other participants were seen disobeying the experimenter.

The power of legitimate, close-at-hand authorities is dramatically apparent in stories of those who complied with orders to carry out the Holocaust atrocities, and those who didn't. Obedience alone does not explain the Holocaust; anti-Semitic ideology produced eager killers as well (Mastroianni, 2002). But obedience was a factor. In the summer of 1942, nearly 500 middle-aged German reserve police officers were dispatched to German-occupied Jozefow, Poland. On July 13, the group's visibly upset commander informed his recruits, mostly family men, that they had been ordered to round up the village's Jews, who were said to be aiding the enemy. Able-bodied men were to be sent to work camps, and all the rest were to be shot on the spot. Given a chance to refuse participation in the executions, only about a dozen immediately did so. Within 17 hours, the remaining 485 officers killed 1500 helpless women, children, and elderly by shooting them in the back of the head as they lay face down. Hearing the pleas of the victims, and seeing the gruesome results, some 20 percent of the officers did eventually dissent, managing either to miss their victims or to wander away and hide until the slaughter was over (Browning, 1992). But in real life, as in Milgram's experiments, the disobedient were the minority.

FIGURE 57.3 Milgram's follow-up obedience experiment In a repeat of the earlier experiment, 65 percent of the adult male "teachers" fully obeyed the experimenter's commands to continue. They did so despite the "learner's" earlier mention of a heart condition and despite hearing cries of protest after 150 volts and agonized protests after 330 volts. (Data from Milgram, 1974.)

"Drive off the cliff, James, I want to commit suicide."

Standing up for democracy Some individuals—roughly one in three in Milgram's experiments—resist social coercion, as did this unarmed man in Beijing, by single-handedly challenging an advancing line of tanks the day after the 1989 Tiananmen Square student uprising was suppressed.

"I was only following orders."

Adolf Eichmann, Director of Nazi deportation of Jews to concentration camps

"The normal reaction to an abnormal situation is abnormal behavior."

James Waller, *Becoming Evil: How Ordinary People Commit Genocide and Mass Killing,* 2007

Another story was being played out in the French village of Le Chambon, where French Jews destined for deportation to Germany were being sheltered by villagers who openly defied orders to cooperate with the "New Order." The villagers' Protestant ancestors had themselves been persecuted and their pastors had been teaching them to "resist whenever our adversaries will demand of us obedience contrary to the orders of the Gospel" (Rochat, 1993). Ordered by police to give a list of sheltered Jews, the head pastor modeled defiance: "I don't know of Jews, I only know of human beings." Without realizing how long and terrible the war would be, or how much punishment and poverty they would suffer, the resisters made an initial commitment to resist. Supported by their beliefs, their role models, their interactions with one another, and their own initial acts, they remained defiant to the war's end.

Lessons From the Conformity and Obedience Studies

What do the Asch and Milgram experiments teach us about ourselves? How does judging the length of a line or flicking a shock switch relate to everyday social behavior? This research, like all psychological experiments, aimed not to re-create the literal behaviors of everyday life but to capture and explore the underlying processes that shape those behaviors. Asch and Milgram devised experiments in which the participants had to choose between adhering to their own standards and being responsive to others, a dilemma we all face frequently.

In Milgram's experiments, participants were also torn between what they should respond to—the pleas of the victim or the orders of the experimenter. Their moral sense warned them not to harm another, yet it also prompted them to obey the experimenter and to be a good research participant. With kindness and obedience on a collision course, obedience usually won.

Such experiments demonstrate that strong social influences can make people conform to falsehoods or capitulate to cruelty. "The most fundamental lesson of our study," Milgram noted, is that "ordinary people, simply doing their jobs, and without any particular hostility on their part, can become agents in a terrible destructive process" (1974, p. 6). Milgram did not entrap his teachers by asking them first to zap learners with enough electricity to make their hair stand on end. Rather, he exploited the *foot-in-the-door* effect, beginning with a little tickle of electricity and escalating step by step. In the minds of those throwing the switches, the small action became justified, making the next act tolerable. In Jozefow, in Le Chambon, and in Milgram's experiments, those who resisted usually did so early. After the first acts of compliance or resistance, attitudes began to follow and justify behavior.

So it happens when people succumb, gradually, to evil. In any society, great evils sometimes grow out of people's compliance with lesser evils. The Nazi leaders suspected that most German civil servants would resist shooting or gassing Jews directly, but they found them surprisingly willing to handle the paperwork of the Holocaust (Silver & Geller, 1978). Likewise, when Milgram asked 40 men to administer the learning test while someone else did the shocking, 93 percent complied. Contrary to images of devilish villains, cruelty does not require monstrous characters; all it takes is ordinary people corrupted by an evil situation—ordinary soldiers who follow orders to torture prisoners, ordinary students who follow orders to haze initiates into their group, ordinary employees who follow orders to produce and market harmful products. Before leading the 9/11 attacks, Mohammed Atta reportedly was a sane, rational person who had been a "good boy" and an excellent student from a close-knit family— not someone who fits our image of a barbaric monster.

▶‖ Group Influence

How do groups affect our behavior? To find out, social psychologists study the various influences that operate in the simplest of groups—one person in the presence of another—and those that operate in more complex groups, such as families, teams, and committees.

Individual Behavior in the Presence of Others

57-2 How is our behavior affected by the presence of others or by being part of a group?

Appropriately, social psychology's first experiments focused on the simplest of all questions about social behavior: How are we influenced by people watching us or joining us in various activities?

Social Facilitation

Having noticed that cyclists' racing times were faster when they competed against each other than when they competed with a clock, Norman Triplett (1898) hypothesized that the presence of others boosts performance. To test his hypothesis, Triplett had adolescents wind a fishing reel as rapidly as possible. He discovered that they wound the reel faster in the presence of someone doing the same thing. This phenomenon of stronger performance in others' presence is called **social facilitation.** For example, after a light turns green, drivers take about 15 percent less time to travel the first 100 yards when another car is beside them at the intersection than when they are alone (Towler, 1986).

But on tougher tasks (learning nonsense syllables or solving complex multiplication problems), people perform *less* well when observers or others working on the same task are present. Further studies revealed why the presence of others sometimes helps and sometimes hinders performance (Guerin, 1986; Zajonc, 1965). When others observe us, we become aroused. This arousal strengthens the most *likely* response—the correct one on an easy task, an incorrect one on a difficult task. Thus, when we are being observed, we perform well-learned tasks more quickly and accurately, and unmastered tasks less quickly and accurately.

James Michaels and his associates (1982) found that expert pool players who made 71 percent of their shots when alone made 80 percent when four people came to watch them. Poor shooters, who made 36 percent of their shots when alone, made only 25 percent when watched. The energizing effect of an enthusiastic audience probably contributes to the home advantage enjoyed by various sports teams. Studies of more than 80,000 college and professional athletic events in Canada, the United States, and England reveal that home teams win about 6 in 10 games (somewhat fewer for baseball and football, somewhat more for basketball and soccer—see **TABLE 57.1**).

The point to remember: What you do well, you are likely to do even better in front of an audience, especially a friendly audience; what you normally find difficult may seem all but impossible when you are being watched.

Social facilitation also helps explain a funny effect of crowding: Comedy routines that are mildly amusing to people in an uncrowded room seem funnier in a densely packed room (Aiello et al., 1983; Freedman & Perlick, 1979). As comedians and actors know, a "good house" is a full one. The arousal triggered by crowding amplifies other reactions, too. If sitting close to one another, participants in experiments like a friendly person even more, an unfriendly person even less (Schiffenbauer & Schiavo, 1976; Storms & Thomas, 1977). The practical lesson: If choosing a room for a class or setting up chairs for a gathering, have barely enough seating.

social facilitation stronger responses on simple or well-learned tasks in the presence of others.

Courtesy Hope College Public Relations

Social facilitation Skilled athletes often find they are "on" before an audience. What they do well, they do even better when people are watching.

TABLE 57.1 Home Advantage in Major Team Sports

Sport	Games Studied	Home Team Winning Percentage
Baseball	23,034	53.5%
Football	2,592	57.3
Ice hockey	4,322	61.1
Basketball	13,596	64.4
Soccer	37,202	69.0

From Courneya & Carron (1992).

Social Loafing

Social facilitation experiments test the effect of others' presence on performance on an individual task, such as shooting pool. But what happens to performance when people perform the task as a group? In a team tug-of-war, for example, do you suppose your effort would be more than, less than, or the same as the effort you would exert in a one-on-one tug-of-war? To find out, Alan Ingham and his fellow researchers (1974) asked blindfolded University of Massachusetts students to "pull as hard as you can" on a rope. When Ingham fooled the students into believing three others were also pulling behind them, they exerted only 82 percent as much effort as when they knew they were pulling alone.

Bibb Latané and others (1981; Jackson & Williams, 1988) describe this diminished effort as **social loafing.** In 78 experiments conducted in the United States, India, Thailand, Japan, China, and Taiwan, social loafing occurred on various tasks, though it was especially common among men in individualistic cultures (Karau & Williams, 1993). In one of Latané's experiments, blindfolded people seated in a group clapped or shouted as loud as they could while listening through headphones to the sound of loud clapping or shouting. When told they were doing it with the others, the participants produced about one-third less noise than when they thought their individual efforts were identifiable.

Why this social loafing? First, people acting as part of a group feel less accountable and therefore worry less about what others think. Second, they may view their contribution as dispensable (Harkins & Szymanski, 1989; Kerr & Bruun, 1983). As many leaders of organizations know—and as you have perhaps observed on student group assignments—if group members share equally in the benefits regardless of how much they contribute, some may slack off. Unless highly motivated and identified with their group, they may free-ride on the other group members' efforts.

Deindividuation

So, the presence of others can arouse people (as in the social facilitation experiments) or can diminish their feelings of responsibility (as in the social loafing experiments). But sometimes the presence of others both arouses people *and* diminishes their sense of responsibility. The result can be uninhibited behavior ranging from a food fight in the dining hall or screaming at a basketball referee to vandalism or rioting. Abandoning normal restraints to the power of the group is termed **deindividuation.** To be deindividuated is to be less self-conscious and less restrained when in a group situation.

Deindividuation often occurs when group participation makes people feel aroused and anonymous. In one experiment, New York University women dressed in depersonalizing Ku Klux Klan–style hoods delivered twice as much electric shock to a victim as did identifiable women (Zimbardo, 1970). (As in all such experiments, the "victim" did not actually receive the shocks.) Similarly, tribal warriors who depersonalize themselves with face paints or masks are more likely than those with exposed faces to kill, torture, or mutilate captured enemies (Watson, 1973). Whether in a mob, at a rock concert, at a ballgame, or at worship, to lose self-consciousness (to become deindividuated) is to become more responsive to the group experience.

Effects of Group Interaction

57-3   What are group polarization and groupthink?

We have examined the conditions under which being in the *presence* of others can

▶ motivate people to exert themselves or tempt them to free-ride on the efforts of others.

▶ make easy tasks easier and difficult tasks harder.

▶ enhance humor or fuel mob violence.

Research shows that *interacting* with others can similarly have both bad and good effects.

social loafing the tendency for people in a group to exert less effort when pooling their efforts toward attaining a common goal than when individually accountable.

deindividuation the loss of self-awareness and self-restraint occurring in group situations that foster arousal and anonymity.

Group Polarization

Educational researchers have noted that, over time, initial differences between groups of college students tend to grow. If the first-year students at College X tend to be more intellectually oriented than those at College Y, that difference will probably be amplified by the time they are seniors. And if the political conservatism of students who join fraternities and sororities is greater than that of students who do not, the gap in the political attitudes of the two groups will probably widen as they progress through college (Wilson et al., 1975). Similarly, notes Eleanor Maccoby (2002) from her decades of observing gender development, girls talk more intimately than boys do and play and fantasize less aggressively—and these gender differences widen over time as they interact mostly with their own gender.

This enhancement of a group's prevailing tendencies—called **group polarization**—occurs when people within a group discuss an idea that most of them either favor or oppose. Group polarization can have beneficial results, as when it amplifies a sought-after spiritual awareness or reinforces the resolve of those in a self-help group, or strengthens feelings of tolerance in a low-prejudice group. But it can also have dire consequences. George Bishop and I discovered that when high-prejudice students discussed racial issues, they became *more* prejudiced (**FIGURE 57.4**). (Low-prejudice students became even more accepting.) The experiment's ideological separation and polarization finds a seeming parallel in the growing polarization of American politics. The percentage of landslide counties—voting 60 percent or more for one presidential candidate—increased from 26 percent in 1976 to 48 percent in 2004 (Bishop, 2004). More and more, people are living near and learning from others who think as they do. One experiment brought together small groups of citizens in liberal Boulder, Colorado, and other groups down in conservative Colorado Springs, to discuss global climate change, affirmative action, and same-sex unions. Although the discussions increased agreement within groups, those in Boulder generally moved further left and those in Colorado Springs moved further right (Schkade et al., 2006). Thus ideological separation + deliberation = polarization between groups.

The polarizing effect of interaction among the like-minded applies also to suicide terrorists. After analyzing terrorist organizations around the world, psychologists Clark McCauley and Mary Segal (1987; McCauley, 2002) noted that the terrorist mentality does not erupt suddenly. Rather, it usually arises among people who get

group polarization the enhancement of a group's prevailing inclinations through discussion within the group.

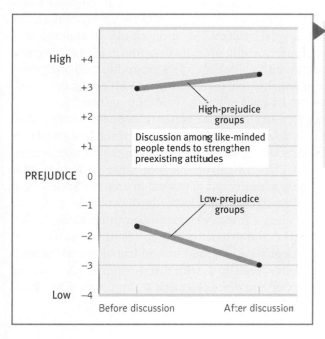

FIGURE 57.4 Group polarization If a group is like-minded, discussion strengthens its prevailing opinions. Talking over racial issues increased prejudice in a high-prejudice group of high school students and decreased it in a low-prejudice group (Myers & Bishop, 1970).

Discussion among like-minded people tends to strengthen preexisting attitudes

groupthink the mode of thinking that occurs when the desire for harmony in a decision-making group overrides a realistic appraisal of alternatives.

together because of a grievance and then become more and more extreme as they interact in isolation from any moderating influences. Increasingly, group members (who may be isolated with other "brothers" and "sisters" in camps) categorize the world as "us" against "them" (Moghaddam, 2005; Qirko, 2004). Suicide terrorism is virtually never done on a personal whim, reports researcher Ariel Merari (2002). The like-minded echo chamber will continue to polarize people, speculates the 2006 U.S. National Intelligence estimate: "We assess that the operational threat from self-radicalized cells will grow."

The Internet provides a medium for group polarization. Its tens of thousands of virtual groups enable bereaved parents, peacemakers, and teachers to find solace and support from kindred spirits. But the Internet also enables people who share interests in government conspiracy, extraterrestrial visitors, White supremacy, or citizen militias to find one another and to find support for their shared suspicions (McKenna & Bargh, 1998).

Groupthink

Does group interaction ever distort important decisions? Social psychologist Irving Janis began to think so as he read historian Arthur M. Schlesinger, Jr.'s account of how President John F. Kennedy and his advisers blundered into an ill-fated plan to invade Cuba with 1400 CIA-trained Cuban exiles. When the invaders were easily captured and soon linked to the U.S. government, Kennedy wondered in hindsight, "How could we have been so stupid?"

To find out, Janis (1982) studied the decision-making procedures that led to the fiasco. He discovered that the soaring morale of the recently elected president and his advisers fostered undue confidence in the plan. To preserve the good group feeling, any dissenting views were suppressed or self-censored, especially after President Kennedy voiced his enthusiasm for the scheme. Since no one spoke strongly against the idea, everyone assumed consensus support. To describe this harmonious but unrealistic group thinking, Janis coined the term **groupthink.**

Janis and others then examined other historical fiascos—the failure to anticipate the 1941 Japanese attack on Pearl Harbor, the escalation of the Vietnam war, the U.S. Watergate cover-up, the Chernobyl nuclear reactor accident (Reason, 1987), and the U.S. space shuttle *Challenger* explosion (Esser & Lindoerfer, 1989). They discovered that in these cases, too, groupthink was fed by overconfidence, conformity, self-justification, and group polarization.

Groupthink surfaced again, reported the bipartisan U.S. Senate Intelligence Committee (2004), when "personnel involved in the Iraq WMD [weapons of mass destruction] issue demonstrated several aspects of groupthink: examining few alternatives, selective gathering of information, pressure to conform within the group or withhold criticism, and collective rationalization." This groupthink led analysts to "interpret ambiguous evidence as conclusively indicative of a WMD program as well as ignore or minimize evidence that Iraq did not have [WMD] programs."

Despite such fiascos and tragedies, two heads are better than one in solving some types of problems. Knowing this, Janis also studied instances in which U.S. presidents and their advisers collectively made good decisions, such as when the Truman administration formulated the Marshall Plan, which offered assistance to Europe after World War II, and when the Kennedy administration worked to keep the Soviets from installing missiles in Cuba. In such instances—and in the business world, too, Janis believed—groupthink is prevented when a leader welcomes various opinions, invites experts' critiques of developing plans, and assigns people to identify possible problems. Just as the suppression of dissent bends a group toward bad decisions, so open debate often shapes good ones. This is especially so with diverse groups, whose varied perspectives enable creative or superior outcomes (Nemeth & Ormiston, 2007; Page, 2007). None of us is as smart as all of us.

"One's impulse to blow the whistle on this nonsense was simply undone by the circumstances of the discussion."
Arthur M. Schlesinger, Jr.,
A Thousand Days, 1965

"Truth springs from argument among friends."
Philosopher David Hume, 1711-1776

"If you have an apple and I have an apple and we exchange apples then you and I will still each have one apple. But if you have an idea and I have an idea and we exchange these ideas, then each of us will have two ideas."
Attributed to dramatist George Bernard Shaw, 1856-1950

▶❙❙ The Power of Individuals

57-4   How much power do we have as individuals? Can a minority sway a majority?

In affirming the power of social influence, we must not overlook our power as individuals. *Social control* (the power of the situation) and *personal control* (the power of the individual) interact. People aren't billiard balls. When feeling pressured, we may react by doing the opposite of what is expected, thereby reasserting our sense of freedom (Brehm & Brehm, 1981).

Three individual soldiers asserted their personal control at Iraq's notorious Abu Ghraib prison (O'Connor, 2004). Lt. David Sutton put an end to one incident, which he reported to his commanders. Navy dog-handler William Kimbro refused pressure to participate in improper interrogations using his attack dogs. Specialist Joseph Darby brought visual images of the horrors into the light of day, providing incontestable evidence of the atrocities. Each risked ridicule or even court-martial for not following orders.

As these three soldiers discovered, committed individuals can sway the majority and make social history. Were this not so, communism would have remained an obscure theory, Christianity would be a small Middle Eastern sect, and Rosa Parks' refusal to sit at the back of the bus would not have ignited the U.S. civil rights movement. Technological history, too, is often made by innovative minorities who overcome the majority's resistance to change. To many, the railroad was a nonsensical idea; some farmers even feared that train noise would prevent hens from laying eggs. People derided Robert Fulton's steamboat as "Fulton's Folly." As Fulton later said, "Never did a single encouraging remark, a bright hope, a warm wish, cross my path." Much the same reaction greeted the printing press, the telegraph, the incandescent lamp, and the typewriter (Cantril & Bumstead, 1960).

European social psychologists have sought to better understand *minority influence*—the power of one or two individuals to sway majorities (Moscovici, 1985). They investigated groups in which one or two individuals consistently expressed a controversial attitude or an unusual perceptual judgment. They repeatedly found that a minority that unswervingly holds to its position is far more successful in swaying the majority than is a minority that waffles. Holding consistently to a minority opinion will not make you popular, but it may make you influential. This is especially so if your self-confidence stimulates others to consider why you react as you do. Although people often follow the majority view publicly, they may privately develop sympathy for the minority view. Even when a minority's influence is not yet visible, it may be persuading some members of the majority to rethink their views (Wood et al., 1994). The powers of social influence are enormous, but so are the powers of the committed individual.

Gandhi As the life of Hindu nationalist and spiritual leader Mahatma Gandhi powerfully testifies, a consistent and persistent minority voice can sometimes sway the majority. Gandhi's nonviolent appeals and fasts were instrumental in winning India's independence from Britain in 1947.

REVIEW

Social Influence

57-1 **What do experiments on conformity and compliance reveal about the power of social influence?** Asch's conformity studies demonstrated that under certain conditions people will conform to a group's judgment even when it is clearly incorrect. We may *conform* either to gain social approval *(normative social influence)* or because we welcome the information that others provide *(informational social influence)*. In Milgram's famous experiments, people torn between obeying an experimenter and responding to another's pleas to stop the apparent shocks usually chose to obey orders. People most often obeyed when the person giving orders was nearby and was perceived as a legitimate authority figure; when the person giving orders was supported by a prestigious institution; when the victim was depersonalized or at a distance; and when no other person modeled defiance by disobeying.

57-2 **How is our behavior affected by the presence of others or by being part of a group?** *Social facilitation* experiments reveal that the presence of either observers or co-actors can arouse individuals, boosting their performance on easy tasks but hindering it on difficult ones. When people pool their efforts toward a group goal, *social loafing* may occur as individuals free-ride on others' efforts. *Deindividuation*—becoming less self-aware and self-restrained—may happen when people are both aroused and made to feel anonymous.

57-3 **What are group polarization and groupthink?** Discussions among like-minded members often produce *group polarization,* as prevailing attitudes are intensified. This is one cause of *groupthink,* the tendency to suppress unwelcome information and make unrealistic decisions for the sake of group harmony. To prevent groupthink, leaders can welcome a variety of opinions, invite experts' critiques, and assign people to identify possible problems in developing plans.

57-4 **How much power do we have as individuals? Can a minority sway a majority?** The power of the group is great, but even a small minority may sway group opinion, especially when the minority expresses its views consistently.

Terms and Concepts to Remember

conformity, p. 691	social facilitation, p. 697
normative social influence, p. 692	social loafing, p. 698
informational social influence, p. 692	deindividuation, p. 698
	group polarization, p. 699
	groupthink, p. 700

Test Yourself

1. You are organizing a Town Hall–style meeting of fiercely competitive political candidates. To add to the fun, friends have suggested handing out masks of the candidates' faces for supporters to wear. What phenomenon might these masks engage?

(Answers to the Test Yourself questions can be found in Appendix B at the end of the book.)

Ask Yourself

1. What two examples of social influence have you experienced this week? (Remember, influence may be informational.)

∞ WEB

Multiple-choice self-tests and more may be found at www.worthpublishers.com/myers

MODULE 58

Antisocial Relations

Social psychology studies how we think about and influence one another, and also how we *relate* to one another. What causes us to harm or to help or to fall in love? How can we move a destructive conflict toward a just peace? In this module we ponder insights into *antisocial* relations gleaned by researchers who have studied prejudice and aggression.

Prejudice

Aggression

▶‖ Prejudice

58-1 What is prejudice?

Prejudice means "prejudgment." It is an unjustifiable and usually negative attitude toward a group—often a different cultural, ethnic, or gender group. Like all attitudes, **prejudice** is a mixture of *beliefs* (in this case called **stereotypes**), *emotions* (hostility, envy, or fear), and predispositions to *action* (to discriminate). To *believe* that obese people are gluttonous, to *feel* dislike for an obese person, and to be hesitant to hire or date an obese person is to be prejudiced. Prejudice is a negative *attitude;* **discrimination** is a negative *behavior*.

How Prejudiced Are People?

To learn about levels of prejudice, we can assess what people say and what they do. Judging by what Americans say, gender and racial attitudes have changed dramatically in the last half-century. The one-third of Americans who in 1937 told Gallup they would vote for a qualified woman whom their party nominated for president soared to 89 percent in 2007. Support for all forms of racial contact, including interracial marriage (**FIGURE 58.1**), has also dramatically increased. Nearly everyone agrees that children of all races should attend the same schools and that women and men should receive the same pay for the same job.

prejudice an unjustifiable (and usually negative) attitude toward a group and its members. Prejudice generally involves stereotyped beliefs, negative feelings, and a predisposition to discriminatory action.

stereotype a generalized (sometimes accurate but often overgeneralized) belief about a group of people.

discrimination unjustifiable negative behavior toward a group and its members.

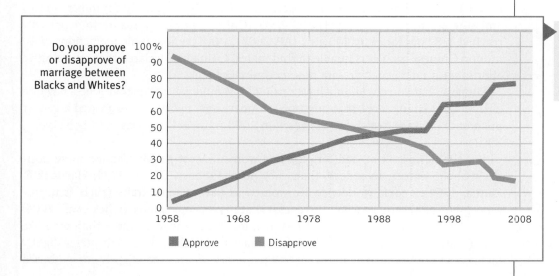

FIGURE 58.1 Prejudice over time Americans' approval of interracial marriage has soared over the past half-century. (Gallup surveys reported by Carroll, 2007.)

703

"Unhappily the world has yet to learn how to live with diversity."

Pope John Paul II, Address to the United Nations, 1995

|| In the aftermath of China's one-child social policy and sex-selective abortions, the looming excess of young Chinese men may impact Chinese society. Imbalanced population sex ratios have historically influenced gender roles. Places with a shortage of unmarried women have stressed sexual morality and traditional women's roles (Guttentag & Secord, 1983). Such places—with lots of unmarried men, as in some frontier towns, immigrant ghettos, and mining camps—have also tended to have high violence rates (Hvistendahl, 2008). ||

Yet as *overt* prejudice wanes, *subtle* prejudice lingers. Despite increased verbal support for interracial marriage, many people admit that in socially intimate settings (dating, dancing, marrying) they would feel uncomfortable with someone of another race. And in Western Europe, where many "guest workers" and refugees settled at the end of the twentieth century, "modern prejudice"—rejecting immigrant minorities as job applicants for supposedly nonracial reasons—has been replacing blatant prejudice (Jackson et al., 2001; Lester, 2004; Pettigrew, 1998, 2006). A slew of recent experiments illustrates that prejudice can be not only subtle but also automatic and unconscious (see Close-Up: Automatic Prejudice).

Nevertheless, overt prejudice still surfaces in public settings. In several U.S. states where Black motorists are a minority of the drivers and speeders on interstate highways, they have been the majority of those stopped and searched by state police (Lamberth, 1998; Staples, 1999a,b). In the Los Angeles area, 1115 landlords received identically worded e-mails from a would-be tenant (actually a researcher) expressing interest in vacant apartments advertised online. Encouraging replies came back to 56 percent of notes signed "Tyrell Jackson," to 66 percent signed "Said Al-Rahman," and to 89 percent of those signed "Patrick McDougall" (Carpusor & Loges, 2006).

In the aftermath of 9/11 and the Iraq war, 4 in 10 Americans acknowledged "some feelings of prejudice against Muslims," and about half of non-Muslims in Western Europe and the United States perceived Muslims as "violent" (Saad, 2006; Wike & Grim, 2007). Muslims reciprocated the negativity, with most in Jordan, Egypt, Turkey, and Britain seeing Westerners as "greedy" and "immoral."

In most places in the world, gays and lesbians cannot comfortably acknowledge who they are and whom they love. Gender prejudice and discrimination persist, too. Despite gender equality in intelligence scores, people tend to perceive their fathers as more intelligent than their mothers (Furnham & Rawles, 1995). In Saudi Arabia, women are not allowed to drive. In Western countries, we pay more to those (usually men) who drive machines that take care of our streets than to those (usually women) who take care of our children. Worldwide, women are more likely to live in poverty (Lipps, 1999), and their 69 percent literacy rate is well below men's 83 percent (PRB, 2002).

Female infants are no longer left out on a hillside to die of exposure, as was the practice in ancient Greece. Yet even today boys are often valued more than their sisters. With testing that enables sex-selective abortions, several south Asian countries, including certain regions of China and India, have experienced a shortfall in female births. Natural female mortality and the normal male-to-female newborn ratio (105-to-100) hardly explain the world's estimated 101 million (say that number slowly) "missing women" (Sen, 2003). In 2005, China's newborn sex ratio reportedly reached 118 boys for every 100 girls (AP, 2007). With demographic predictions of 40 million Chinese bachelors unable to find mates, China has declared that sex-selective abortions—gender genocide—are now a criminal offense.

Suppose that you could only have one child. Would you prefer that it be a boy or a girl? When Gallup asked that question of Americans, two-thirds expressed a gender preference, and for two-thirds of those—in 2003 as in 1941—it was for a boy (Lyons, 2003).

But the news isn't all bad for girls and women. Most people also *feel* more positively about women in general than they do about men (Eagly, 1994; Haddock & Zanna, 1994). People worldwide see women as having some traits (such as nurturance, sensitivity, and less aggressiveness) that most people prefer (Glick et al., 2004; Swim, 1994). That may explain why women tend to like women more than men like men (Rudman & Goodwin, 2004). And perhaps that is also why people prefer slightly feminized computer-generated faces—men's and women's—to slightly masculinized

CLOSE-UP

Automatic Prejudice

As we have seen throughout this book, we process information on two levels: conscious and unconscious. To some extent, our thinking, our memories, and our attitudes are explicit—on the radar screen of our awareness. And to an even greater extent, today's researchers believe, they are *implicit*—below the radar, out of sight. Modern studies of implicit, automatic attitudes indicate that prejudice is often more of an unthinking knee-jerk response than a decision. Consider these findings on U.S. racial prejudice:

Implicit racial associations When tapping computer keys, people more quickly associate positive words such as *happy* or *peace* with positive objects such as flowers, and negative words such as *rotten* or *ugly* with insects. Extending these Implicit Association Tests, Anthony Greenwald and his colleagues (1998) showed that even people who deny harboring racial prejudice may carry negative associations. For example, 9 in 10 White respondents took longer to identify pleasant words (such as *peace* and *paradise*) as "good" when presented with Black-sounding names (such as *Latisha* and *Darnell*) rather than White-sounding names (such as *Katie* and *Ian*). Moreover, people who more quickly associate good things with White names or faces also are the quickest to perceive anger and apparent threat in Black faces (Hugenberg & Bodenhausen, 2003). (By 2008, more than 6 million people had taken the Implicit Association Test, as you can at www.implicit.harvard.edu.)

Unconscious patronization Kent Harber (1998) asked White university women to evaluate a flawed essay said to be written by a Black or a White fellow student. When they believed the writer was Black, the women gave markedly higher ratings and never expressed the harsh criticisms they assigned to White-authored essays, such as "When I read college work this bad I just want to lay my head down on the table and cry." Did the evaluators calibrate their evaluations to their racial stereotypes, Harber wondered, leading them to patronize the Black writers with

less exacting standards? If used in real-world evaluations, such low expectations and the resulting "inflated praise and insufficient criticism" could hinder minority student achievement. (To preclude such bias, many teachers read essays while "blind" to their authors.)

Race-influenced perceptions Two research teams were interested in the shooting of an unarmed man in the doorway of his Bronx apartment building by officers who mistook his wallet for a gun. Each research team reenacted the situation with a video, asking viewers to press buttons quickly to "shoot" or not shoot men who suddenly appeared on screen holding either a gun or a harmless object such as a flashlight or bottle (Correll et al., 2002, 2007; Greenwald et al., 2003). People (both Blacks and Whites, in one of the studies) more often mistakenly shot targets who were Black. Priming people with a flashed Black rather than White face also makes them more likely then to misperceive a flashed tool as a gun (**FIGURE 58.2**).

Seeing Black Several studies show that the more a person's features are perceived as typical of their racial category, the more likely they are to elicit race-based responding (Maddox, 2004). In one study of 182 police officers, Jennifer Eberhardt and her collaborators (2004; 2006) found that "Black faces looked more criminal to police officers; the more Black, the more criminal." In a follow-up

study, they found people more willing to give the death sentence to Black defendants having the most stereotypically Black features.

Reflexive bodily responses Today's biopsychosocial approach has stimulated neuroscience studies that measure people's instant responses to viewing White and Black faces. These studies have detected implicit prejudice in people's facial-muscle responses and in the activation of their amygdala, the emotion-processing center (Cunningham et al., 2004; Eberhardt, 2005; Vanman et al., 2004). Even people who consciously express little prejudice may give off telltale signals as their body responds selectively to another's race.

If your own gut check sometimes reveals feelings you would rather not have about other people, be assured that you are not alone. It is what we do with our feelings that matters. By monitoring our feelings and actions, and by replacing old habits with new ones based on new friendships, we can work to free ourselves from prejudice.

> "There are still barriers and biases out there, often unconscious."
> Senator Hillary Rodham Clinton, 2008
> U.S. Presidential primary concession speech

FIGURE 58.2 Race primes perceptions In experiments by Keith Payne (2006), people viewed a White or Black face, immediately followed by a gun or hand tool, which was then followed by a visual mask. Participants were more likely to misperceive a tool as a gun when it was preceded by a Black rather than White face.

Paul Burns/Blend/Getty Images   Punchstock/Corbis   B. K. Payne (2006)

(a)   **(b)**

FIGURE 58.3 Who do you like best? Which one placed an ad seeking "a special lady to love and cherish forever"? (Answer below.)

Research suggests that subtly feminized features convey a likable image, which people tend to associate more with committed dads than with promiscuous cads. Thus, 66 percent of the women picked computer-generated face (b) in response to both of these questions.

faces. Researcher David Perrett and his colleagues (1998) speculate that a slightly feminized male face connotes kindness, cooperativeness, and other traits of a good father. When the British Broadcasting Corporation invited 18,000 women to guess which of the men in **FIGURE 58.3** was most likely to place a personal ad seeking a "special lady to love and cherish forever," which one do you think they picked?

Social Roots of Prejudice

58-2 What are the social and emotional roots of prejudice?

Why does prejudice arise? Inequalities, social divisions, and emotional scapegoating are partly responsible.

Social Inequalities

When some people have money, power, and prestige and others do not, the "haves" usually develop attitudes that justify things as they are. In the extreme case, slave "owners" perceived slaves as innately lazy, ignorant, and irresponsible—as having the very traits that "justified" enslaving them. More commonly, women have been perceived as unassertive but sensitive and therefore suited for the caretaking tasks they have traditionally performed (Hoffman & Hurst, 1990). In short, stereotypes rationalize inequalities.

Discrimination also increases stereotyping and prejudice through the reactions it provokes in its victims. In his classic 1954 book, *The Nature of Prejudice,* Gordon Allport noted that being a victim of discrimination can produce either self-blame or anger. Both reactions may create new grounds for prejudice through the classic *blame-the-victim* dynamic. If the circumstances of poverty breed a higher crime rate, someone can then use the higher crime rate to justify continuing the discrimination against those who live in poverty.

Us and Them: Ingroup and Outgroup

Thanks to our ancestral need to belong, we are a group-bound species. Our ancestors, living in a world where neighboring tribes occasionally raided and pillaged one another's camps, knew that there was safety in solidarity (those who didn't band together left fewer descendants). Whether hunting, defending, or attacking, 10 hands were better than 2. Dividing the world into "us" and "them" entails racism and war, but it also provides the benefits of communal solidarity. Thus we cheer for our groups, kill for them, die for them. Indeed, we define who we are—our identities—partly in terms of our groups. Australian psychologists John Turner (1987, 2007) and Michael Hogg (1996, 2006) note that through our *social identities* we associate ourselves with

ingroup "Us"—people with whom we share a common identity.

outgroup "Them"—those perceived as different or apart from our ingroup.

ingroup bias the tendency to favor our own group.

certain groups and contrast ourselves with others. When Ian identifies himself as a man, an Aussie, a Labourite, a University of Sydney student, a Catholic, and a MacGregor, he knows who he is, and so do we.

Ironically, we often reserve our most intense dislike for outgroup rivals most like us. Freud (1922, p. 42) long ago recognized that animosities formed around small differences: "Of two neighboring towns, each is the other's most jealous rival; every little canton looks down upon the others with contempt. Closely related races keep one another at arm's length; the South German cannot endure the North German, the Englishman casts every kind of aspersion upon the Scot, the Spaniard despises the Portuguese." In surveys, 7 in 10 Japanese express an unfavorable view of China, and 7 in 10 Chinese similarly dislike Japan (Pew, 2006). Hostilities between the Iraqi Sunni and Shia, the Rwandan Hutu and Tutsi, and the Northern Ireland Protestant and Catholic have pitted ingroups against outgroups who, on a world diversity scale, are much more alike than different.

French fury Members of France's marginalized ethnic groups reached the tipping point for tolerance in 2005, when they began destructive rioting.

As an occasional resident of Scotland, I've witnessed many examples of *The Xenophobe's Guide to the Scots* observation—that Scots divide non-Scots "into two main groups: (1) The English; (2) The Rest." As rabid Chicago Cubs fans are happy if either the Cubs win or the Chicago White Sox lose, so rabid fans of Scottish soccer rejoice in either a Scotland victory or an England defeat. "Phew! They lost," rejoiced one Scottish tabloid's front-page headline after England's 1996 Euro Cup defeat—by Germany, no less. Numerical minorities, such as the Scots in Britain, are especially conscious of their social identities. The 5 million Scots are more conscious of their national identity vis-à-vis the neighboring 51 million English than vice versa. Likewise, the 4 million New Zealanders are more conscious of their identity vis-à-vis the 21 million Australians, and they are more likely to root for Australia's sports opponents (Halberstadt et al., 2006).

The social definition of who we are also implies who we are not. Mentally drawing a circle that defines "us" (the **ingroup**) excludes "them" (the **outgroup**). Such group identifications typically promote an **ingroup bias**—a favoring of one's own group. Even arbitrarily creating an us-them distinction—by grouping people with the toss of a coin—leads people to show favoritism to their own group when dividing any rewards (Tajfel, 1982; Wilder, 1981).

The urge to distinguish enemies from friends and to have one's group be dominant predisposes prejudice against strangers (Whitley, 1999). To Greeks of the classical era, all non-Greeks were "barbarians." In our own era, most children believe their

The ingroup Scotland's famed "Tartan Army" soccer fans, shown here during a match against archrival England, share a social identity that defines "us" (the Scottish ingroup) and "them" (the English outgroup).

"All good people agree,
And all good people say
All nice people, like Us, are We
And every one else is They.
But if you cross over the sea
Instead of over the way
You may end by (think of it)
Looking on We
As only a sort of They."

Rudyard Kipling, "We and They," 1926

"If the Tiber reaches the walls, if the Nile does not rise to the fields, if the sky doesn't move or the Earth does, if there is famine, if there is plague, the cry is at once: 'The Christians to the lion!'"

Tertullian, *Apologeticus*, A.D. 197

‖ One seeming antidote to prejudice is intelligence. In a large national study, British children with high intelligence scores at age 10 typically expressed low prejudice at age 30 (Deary et al., 2008). ‖

scapegoat theory the theory that prejudice offers an outlet for anger by providing someone to blame.

other-race effect the tendency to recall faces of one's own race more accurately than faces of other races. Also called the *cross-race effect* and the *own-race bias.*

---

school is better than all other schools in town. Many high school students form cliques—jocks, goths, skaters, gangsters, freaks, geeks—and disparage those outside their own group. Even chimpanzees have been seen to wipe clean the spot where they were touched by a chimpanzee from another group (Goodall, 1986).

Emotional Roots of Prejudice

Prejudice springs not only from the divisions of society but also from the passions of the heart. Facing the terror of death tends to heighten patriotism and produce loathing and aggression toward "them"—those who threaten one's world (Pyszczynski et al., 2002). Recalling such terror may alter attitudes, as happened to participants when Mark Landau and eight others (2004) reminded them of their own mortality or of the terror of 9/11. This terror reminder led to their expressing increased support for then-President George W. Bush.

Prejudice may also express anger. According to the **scapegoat theory** of prejudice, finding someone to blame when things go wrong can provide a target for one's anger. In the late 1600s, New England settlers, after suffering devastating losses at the hands of Native Americans and their French allies, lashed out by hanging people as supposed witches (Norton, 2002). Following 9/11, some outraged people lashed out at innocent Arab-Americans, about whom negative stereotypes blossomed. Calls to eliminate Saddam Hussein, whom Americans had been grudgingly tolerating, also increased. "Fear and anger create aggression, and aggression against citizens of different ethnicity or race creates racism and, in turn, new forms of terrorism," noted Philip Zimbardo (2001).

Evidence for the scapegoat theory comes from high prejudice levels among economically frustrated people and from experiments in which a temporary frustration intensifies prejudice. In experiments, students who experience failure or are made to feel insecure will often restore their self-esteem by disparaging a rival school or another person (Cialdini & Richardson, 1980; Crocker et al., 1987). To boost our own sense of status, it helps to have others to denigrate. That is why a rival's misfortune sometimes provides a twinge of pleasure. By contrast, those made to feel loved and supported become more open to and accepting of others who differ (Mikulincer & Shaver, 2001).

Cognitive Roots of Prejudice

58-3 What are the cognitive roots of prejudice?

Prejudice springs from a culture's divisions, the heart's passions, and also from the mind's natural workings. Stereotyped beliefs are a by-product of how we cognitively simplify the world.

Categorization

One way we simplify our world is to categorize. A chemist categorizes molecules as organic and inorganic. A mental health professional categorizes psychological disorders by types. In categorizing people into groups, however, we often stereotype them, biasing our perceptions of their diversity. We recognize how greatly *we* differ from other individuals in *our* groups. But we overestimate the similarity of those within other groups. "They"—the members of some other group—seem to look and act alike, but "we" are diverse (Bothwell et al., 1989). To those in one ethnic group, members of another often seem more alike than they really are in appearance, personality, and attitudes. This greater recognition for own-race faces—called the **other-race effect,** or *own-race bias*—emerges during infancy, between 3 and 9 months of age (Kelly et al., 2007).

With experience, however, people get better at recognizing individual faces from another group. People of European descent, for example, more accurately identify individual African faces if they have watched a great deal of basketball on television, exposing them to many African-heritage faces (Li et al., 1996). And the longer Chinese people have resided in a Western country, the less they exhibit the other-race effect (Hancock & Rhodes, 2008).

Vivid Cases

We often judge the frequency of events by instances that readily come to mind. In a classic experiment, Myron Rothbart and his colleagues (1978) demonstrated this ability to overgeneralize from vivid, memorable cases. They divided University of Oregon student volunteers into two groups, then showed them information about 50 men. The first group's list included 10 men arrested for nonviolent crimes, such as forgery. The second group's list included 10 men arrested for violent crimes, such as assault. Later, when both groups recalled how many men on their list had committed any sort of crime, the second group overestimated the number. Vivid (violent) cases are readily available to our memory and therefore influence our judgments of a group (**FIGURE 58.4**).

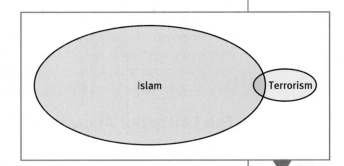

FIGURE 58.4 Vivid cases feed stereotypes The 9/11 Muslim terrorists created, in many minds, an exaggerated stereotype of Muslims as terror-prone. Actually, reported a U.S. National Research Council panel on terrorism, when offering the inexact illustration above, most terrorists are not Muslim and "the vast majority of Islamic people have no connection with and do not sympathize with terrorism" (Smelser & Mitchell, 2002).

The Just-World Phenomenon

As we noted earlier, people often justify their prejudice by blaming its victims. Bystanders, too, may blame victims by assuming the world is just and therefore "people get what they deserve." In experiments, merely observing someone receive painful shocks has led many people to think less of the victim (Lerner, 1980). This **just-world phenomenon** reflects an idea we commonly teach our children—that good is rewarded and evil is punished. From this it is but a short leap to assume that those who succeed must be good and those who suffer must be bad. Such reasoning enables the rich to see both their own wealth and the poor's misfortune as justly deserved. As one German civilian is said to have remarked when visiting the Bergen-Belsen concentration camp shortly after World War II, "What terrible criminals these prisoners must have been to receive such treatment."

Hindsight bias is also at work here (Carli & Leonard, 1989). Have you ever heard people say that rape victims, abused spouses, or people with AIDS got what they deserved? In some countries, women who have been raped have been sentenced to severe punishment for having violated a law against adultery (Mydans, 2002). An experiment by Ronnie Janoff-Bulman and her collaborators (1985) illustrates this phenomenon of blaming the victim. When given a detailed account of a date that ended with the woman being raped, people perceived the woman's behavior as at least partly to blame. In hindsight, they thought, "She should have known better." (Blaming the victim also serves to reassure people that it couldn't happen to them.) Others, given the same account with the rape ending deleted, did not perceive the woman's behavior as inviting rape.

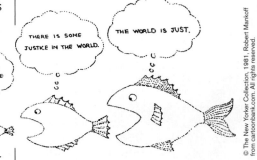

▶‖ Aggression

The most destructive force in our social relations is aggression. In psychology, *aggression* has a more precise meaning than it does in everyday usage. The assertive, persistent salesperson is not aggressive. Nor is the dentist who makes you wince with pain.

just-world phenomenon the tendency for people to believe the world is just and that people therefore get what they deserve and deserve what they get.

aggression any physical or verbal behavior intended to hurt or destroy.

‖ In the last 40 years in the United States, well over 1 million people— more than all deaths in all wars in American history—have been killed by firearms in nonwar settings. Compared with people of the same sex, race, age, and neighborhood, those who keep a gun in the home (ironically, often for protection) are nearly three times more likely to be murdered in the home— nearly always by a family member or close acquaintance. For every self- defense use of a gun in the home, there are 4 unintentional shootings, 7 criminal assaults or homicides, and 11 attempted or completed suicides (Kellermann et al., 1993, 1997, 1998). ‖

"It's a guy thing."

But the person who passes along a vicious rumor about you, the person who verbally assaults you, and the attacker who mugs you are aggressive. Thus, to a psychologist, **aggression** is any physical or verbal behavior intended to hurt or destroy, whether done reactively out of hostility or proactively as a calculated means to an end. Thus, murders and assaults that occurred as hostile outbursts are aggression. So were the 110 million war-related deaths that took place during the last century, many of which were cool and calculated.

Aggression research shows that behavior emerges from the interaction of biology and experience. For a gun to fire, the trigger must be pulled; with some people, as with hair-trigger guns, it doesn't take much to trip an explosion. Let us look first at biological factors that influence our thresholds for aggressive behavior, then at the psychological factors that pull the trigger.

The Biology of Aggression

58-4   What biological factors make us more prone to hurt one another?

Aggression varies too widely from culture to culture, era to era, and person to person to be considered an unlearned instinct. But biology does *influence* aggression. Stimuli that trigger aggressive behavior operate through our biological system. We can look for biological influences at three levels—genetic, neural, and biochemical. Our genes engineer our individual nervous systems, which operate electrochemically.

Genetic Influences

Animals have been bred for aggressiveness—sometimes for sport, sometimes for re- search. Pit bulls and cocker spaniels are formed by differing genes. Twin studies sug- gest that genes influence human aggression as well (Miles & Carey, 1997; Rowe et al., 1999). If one identical twin admits to "having a violent temper," the other twin will often independently admit the same. Fraternal twins are much less likely to respond similarly. Researchers are now searching for genetic markers found in those who commit the most violence. (One is already well known and is carried by half the human race: the Y chromosome.)

Neural Influences

Animal and human brains have neural systems that, when stimulated, either inhibit or produce aggressive behavior (Moyer, 1983). Consider:

▶ The domineering leader of a caged monkey colony had a radio-controlled elec- trode implanted in a brain area that, when stimulated, inhibits aggression. When researchers placed the button that activated the electrode in the colony's cage, one small monkey learned to push it every time the boss became threatening.

▶ A mild-mannered woman had an electrode implanted in her brain's limbic sys- tem (in the amygdala) by neurosurgeons seeking to diagnose a disorder. Because the brain has no sensory receptors, she was unable to feel the stimulation. But at the flick of a switch she snarled, "Take my blood pressure. Take it now," then stood up and began to strike the doctor.

▶ One intensive evaluation of 15 death-row inmates revealed that all 15 had suf- fered a severe head injury. Although most neurologically impaired people are not violent, researcher Dorothy Lewis and her colleagues (1986) inferred that unrec- ognized neurological disorders may be one ingredient in the violence recipe. Other studies of violent criminals have revealed diminished activity in the frontal lobes, which play an important role in controlling impulses (Amen et al., 1996; Davidson et al., 2000; Raine, 1999, 2005).

So, does the brain have a "violence center" that produces aggression when stimu- lated? Actually, no one spot in the brain controls aggression, because aggression is a complex behavior that occurs in particular contexts. Rather, the brain has neural systems that, given provocation, will *facilitate* aggression. And it has a frontal lobe system for inhibiting aggression, making aggression more likely if this system is damaged, inactive, disconnected, or not yet fully mature.

Biochemical Influences

Hormones, alcohol, and other substances in the blood influence the neural systems that control aggression. A raging bull will become a gentle Ferdinand when castration reduces its testosterone level. The same is true of castrated mice. When injected with testosterone, however, the castrated mice once again become aggressive.

Although humans are less sensitive to hormonal changes, violent criminals tend to be muscular young males with lower-than-average intelligence scores, low levels of the neurotransmitter serotonin, and higher-than-average testosterone levels (Dabbs et al., 2001a; Pendick, 1994). Drugs that sharply reduce their testosterone levels also subdue their aggressive tendencies. High testosterone correlates with irritability, assertiveness, impulsiveness, and low tolerance for frustration—qualities that predispose somewhat more aggressive responses to provocation (Dabbs et al., 2001b; Harris, 1999). Among both teenage boys and adult men, high testosterone levels correlate with delinquency, hard drug use, and aggressive-bullying responses to frustration (Berman et al., 1993; Dabbs & Morris, 1990; Olweus et al., 1988). With age, testosterone levels—and aggressiveness—diminish. Hormonally charged, aggressive 17-year-olds mature into hormonally quieter and gentler 70-year-olds.

The traffic between hormones and behavior is two-way. Testosterone heightens dominance and aggressiveness. But dominating behavior also boosts testosterone levels (Mazur & Booth, 1998). One study measured testosterone levels in the saliva of male college basketball fans before and after a big game. Testosterone levels swelled among the victorious fans and sank among the dejected ones (Bernhardt et al., 1998). Handling and describing a gun also has been found to increase testosterone in research participants' saliva and to increase the amount of hot sauce they put in water they believe another person will drink (Klinesmith et al., 2006).

For both biological and psychological reasons, alcohol unleashes aggressive responses to frustration (Bushman, 1993; Ito et al., 1996; Taylor & Chermack, 1993). Just *thinking* you've imbibed alcohol has some effect; but so, too, does unknowingly ingesting alcohol slipped into a drink. Unless people are distracted, alcohol tends to focus their attention on a provocation rather than on inhibitory cues (Giancola & Corman, 2007). Police data and prison surveys reinforce conclusions drawn from experiments on alcohol and aggression: Aggression-prone people are more likely to drink and to become violent when intoxicated (White et al., 1993). People who have been drinking commit 4 in 10 violent crimes and 3 in 4 acts of spousal abuse (Greenfeld, 1998).

"We could avoid two-thirds of all crime simply by putting all able-bodied young men in cryogenic sleep from the age of 12 through 28."

David T. Lykken, *The Antisocial Personalities*, 1995

Karl Ammann/Getty Images

A lean, mean fighting machine— the testosterone-laden female hyena
The hyena's unusual embryology pumps testosterone into female fetuses. The result is revved-up young female hyenas who seem born to fight.

Psychological and Social-Cultural Factors in Aggression

58-5 What psychological factors may trigger aggressive behavior?

Biological factors influence the ease with which aggression is triggered. But what psychological factors pull the trigger?

Aversive Events

Although suffering sometimes builds character, it may also bring out the worst in us. Studies in which animals or humans experience unpleasant events reveal that those made miserable often make others miserable (Berkowitz, 1983, 1989).

Being blocked short of a goal also increases people's readiness to aggress. This phenomenon is called the **frustration-aggression principle:** Frustration creates anger, which may in some people generate aggression, especially in the presence of an aggressive cue, such as a gun. One analysis of 27,667 hit-by-pitch major league baseball incidents between 1960 and 2004 found pitchers were most likely to hit batters when frustrated by the previous batter hitting a home run, by the current batter hitting a home run the last time at bat, or by a teammate's having been hit by a pitch in the previous half inning (Timmerman, 2007).

Organisms often respond to stress with a *fight-or-flight reaction*. After the frustration and stress of 9/11, Americans responded with a readiness to fight. Terrorism similarly may spring from a desire for revenge, sometimes after a friend or family member has been killed or injured. Contrary to the popular idea that poverty breeds terrorists, suicide bombers and those who support them actually tend to be neither uneducated nor desperately poor (Krueger, 2007). The 9/11 suicide bombers, for example, were mostly educated men from wealthy Saudi Arabia (McDermott, 2005). Frustration (and aggression) arise less from deprivation than from the gap between reality and expectations, which may rise with education and attainments.

Like frustration, other aversive stimuli—physical pain, personal insults, foul odors, hot temperatures, cigarette smoke, and a host of others—can also evoke hostility. For example, violent crime and spousal abuse rates are higher during hotter years, seasons, months, and days (**FIGURE 58.5**). When people get overheated, they think, feel, and act more aggressively. From the available data, Craig Anderson and his colleagues (2000) have projected that, other things being equal, global warming of 4 degrees Fahrenheit (about 2 degrees centigrade) would induce more than 50,000 additional assaults and murders in the United States alone.

FIGURE 58.5 Uncomfortably hot weather and aggressive reactions Between 1980 and 1982 in Houston, murders and rapes were more common on days over 91 degrees Fahrenheit (33 degrees centigrade), as shown in the graph. This finding is consistent with those from laboratory experiments in which people working in a hot room react to provocations with greater hostility. (From Anderson & Anderson, 1984.)

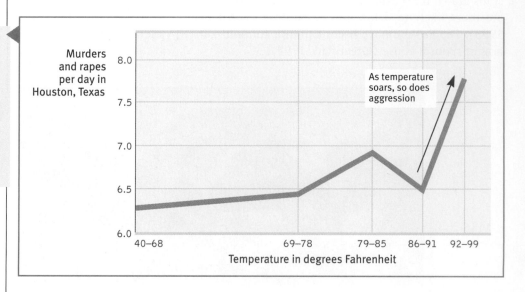

Social and Cultural Influences

Aggression may be a natural response to aversive events, but learning can alter natural reactions. Animals naturally eat when they are hungry. But if appropriately rewarded or punished, they can be taught either to overeat or to starve.

Our reactions are more likely to be aggressive in situations where experience has taught us that aggression pays. Children whose aggression successfully intimidates other children may become more aggressive. Animals that have successfully fought to get food or mates become increasingly ferocious.

Ostracism can also be a real pain. In a series of studies, Jean Twenge and her collaborators (2001, 2002, 2003) told some people that others whom they had met didn't want them in their group, or that a personality test indicated they "were likely to end up alone later in life." People led to feel socially excluded were later more likely to disparage or even deliver a blast of noise to someone who insulted them. This rejection-induced aggression brings to mind various North American and European school shootings, committed by youths who had been shunned, mocked, and sometimes bullied by peers, as reportedly was also the case in 2007 with Virginia Tech mass murderer Seung-Hui Cho. Other studies confirm that rejection often intensifies aggression (Catanese & Tice, 2005; Gaertner & Iuzzini, 2005).

Different cultures model, reinforce, and evoke different tendencies toward violence. For example, crime rates are higher (and average happiness is lower) in countries marked by a great disparity between rich and poor (Triandis, 1994). Richard Nisbett and Dov Cohen (1996) have shown how violence can vary by culture within a country. They analyzed violence among White Americans in southern towns settled by Scots-Irish herders whose tradition emphasized "manly honor," the use of arms to protect one's flock, and a history of coercive slavery. Their cultural descendants, Nisbett and Cohen found, have triple the homicide rates and are more supportive of physically punishing children, of warfare initiatives, and of uncontrolled gun ownership than are their White counterparts in New England towns settled by the more traditionally peaceful Puritan, Quaker, and Dutch farmer-artisans.

Social influence also appears in high violence rates among cultures and families that experience minimal father care (Triandis, 1994). Even after controlling for parental education, race, income, and teen motherhood, American male youths from father-absent homes have double their peers' incarceration rate (Harper & McLanahan, 2004).

It is important, however, to note how many people are leading gentle, even heroic lives amid social stresses, reminding us again that individuals differ. The person matters. That people differ over time and place reminds us that environments also differ, and situations matter. Yesterday's plundering Vikings have become today's peace-promoting Scandinavians. Like all behavior, aggression arises from the interaction of persons and situations.

Once established, however, aggressive behavior patterns are difficult to change. To foster a kinder, gentler world we had best model and reward sensitivity and cooperation from an early age, perhaps by training parents to discipline without modeling violence. Modeling violence—screaming and hitting—is precisely what exasperated parents often do. Parents of delinquent youngsters typically discipline with beatings, thus modeling aggression as a method of dealing with problems (Patterson et al., 1982, 1992). They also frequently cave into (reward) their children's tears and temper tantrums.

Parent-training programs advise a more positive approach. They encourage parents to reinforce desirable behaviors and to frame statements positively ("When you finish loading the dishwasher you can go play," rather than "If you don't load the dishwasher, there'll be no playing"). One *aggression-replacement program* has brought down re-arrest rates of juvenile offenders and gang members by teaching the youths and their parents communication skills, training them to control anger, and encouraging more thoughtful moral reasoning (Goldstein et al., 1998).

"Why do we kill people who kill people to show that killing people is wrong?"
National Coalition to Abolish the Death Penalty, 1992

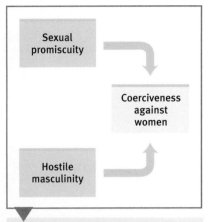

FIGURE 58.6 Men who sexually coerce women The recipe for coercion against women combines an impersonal approach to sex with a hostile masculinity. (Adapted from Malamuth, 1996.)

|| In follow-up studies, Zillmann (1989) found that after massive exposure to X-rated sexual films, men and women became more accepting of extramarital sex, of women's sexual submission to men, and of a man's seducing a 12-year-old girl. As people heavily exposed to televised crime perceive the world as more dangerous, so people heavily exposed to pornography see the world as more sexual. ||

Observing Models of Aggression

Parents are hardly the only aggression models. Observing TV violence tends to desensitize people to cruelty and prime them to respond aggressively when provoked. Does this media effect extend to sexual violence? We do know that sexually coercive men typically are sexually promiscuous and hostile in their relationships with women (**FIGURE 58.6**). We also know from surveys of American and Australian teens and university students that viewing X-rated films and Internet pornography is several times higher among males than among females (Carroll et al., 2008; Flood, 2007; Wolak et al., 2007). Might sexually explicit media models contribute to sexually aggressive tendencies?

Content analyses reveal that most X-rated films have depicted quick, casual sex between strangers, but that scenes of rape and sexual exploitation of women by men are also common (Cowan et al., 1988; NCTV, 1987; Yang & Linz, 1990). Rape scenes often portray the victim at first fleeing and resisting her attacker, but then becoming aroused and finally driven to ecstasy. In less graphic form, the same unrealistic script—she resists, he persists, she melts—is commonplace on TV and in romance novels. In *Gone With the Wind*, Scarlett O'Hara is carried to bed screaming and wakes up singing. Most rapists accept this *rape myth*—the idea that some women invite or enjoy rape and get "swept away" while being "taken" (Brinson, 1992). (In actuality, rape is traumatic, and it frequently harms women's reproductive and psychological health [Golding, 1996].) Compared with those who watch little television, men and women who watch a great deal are more likely to accept the rape myth (Kahlor & Morrison, 2007).

When interviewed, Canadian and U.S. sex offenders (rapists, child molesters, and serial killers) report a greater-than-usual appetite for sexually explicit and sexually violent materials—materials typically labeled as *pornography* (Marshall, 1989; Oddone-Paolucci et al., 2000; Ressler et al., 1988). For example, the Los Angeles Police Department has reported that pornography was "conspicuously present" in 62 percent of its extrafamilial child sexual abuse cases during the 1980s (Bennett, 1991). High pornography consumption also has predicted greater sexual aggressiveness among university men, even after controlling for other predictors of antisocial behavior (Vega & Malamuth, 2007). But are the sexual aggressors merely, as sex researcher John Money (1988) suspected, using pornography "as an alibi to explain to themselves and their captors what otherwise is inexplicable"?

Laboratory experiments reveal that repeatedly watching X-rated films (even if nonviolent) later makes one's own partner seem less attractive, makes a woman's friendliness seem more sexual, and makes sexual aggression seem less serious (Harris, 1994). In one such experiment, Dolf Zillmann and Jennings Bryant (1984) showed undergraduates six brief, sexually explicit films each week for six weeks. A control group viewed nonerotic films during the same six-week period. Three weeks later, both groups read a newspaper report about a man convicted but not yet sentenced for raping a hitchhiker. When asked to suggest an appropriate prison term, those who had viewed sexually explicit films recommended sentences half as long as those recommended by the control group.

Experiments cannot elicit actual sexual violence, but they can assess a man's willingness to hurt a woman. Often the research gauges the effect of violent versus nonviolent erotic films on men's willingness to deliver supposed electric shocks to women who had earlier provoked the men. These experiments suggest that it's not the eroticism but rather the depictions of sexual *violence* (whether in R-rated slasher films or X-rated films) that most directly affect men's acceptance and performance of aggression against women. A conference of 21 social scientists, including many of the researchers who conducted these experiments, produced a consensus (Surgeon General, 1986): "Pornography that portrays sexual aggression as pleasurable for the victim increases the acceptance of the use of coercion in sexual relations." Contrary to much popular opinion, viewing such depictions does not provide an outlet for bottled-up impulses. Rather, "in laboratory studies measuring short-term effects, exposure to violent pornography increases punitive behavior toward women."

Acquiring Social Scripts

Significant behaviors, such as violence, usually have many determinants, making any single explanation an oversimplification. Asking what causes violence is therefore like asking what causes cancer. Those who study the effects of asbestos exposure on cancer rates may remind us that asbestos is indeed a cancer cause, albeit only one among many. Likewise, report Neil Malamuth and his colleagues (1991, 1995), several factors can create a predisposition to sexual violence. They include the media but also dominance motives, disinhibition by alcohol, and a history of child abuse. Still, if media depictions of violence can disinhibit and desensitize; if viewing sexual violence fosters hostile, domineering attitudes and behaviors; and if viewing pornography leads viewers to trivialize rape, devalue their partners, and engage in uncommitted sex, then media influence is not a minor issue.

Social psychologists attribute the media's influence partly to the *social scripts* (mental tapes for how to act, provided by our culture) they portray. When we find ourselves in new situations, uncertain how to act, we rely on social scripts. After so many action films, youngsters may acquire a script that gets played when they face real-life conflicts. Challenged, they may "act like a man" by intimidating or eliminating the threat. Likewise, after viewing the multiple sexual innuendoes and acts found in most prime-time TV hours—often involving impulsive or short-term relationships—youths may acquire sexual scripts they later enact in real-life relationships (Kunkel et al., 2001; Sapolsky & Tabarlet, 1991). Music lyrics also write social scripts. In one set of experiments, German university men who listened to woman-hating song lyrics administered the most hot chili sauce to a woman and recalled more negative feelings and beliefs about women. Man-hating song lyrics had a similar effect on the aggressive behavior of women listeners (Fischer & Greitemeyer, 2006).

Might public consciousness be raised by making people aware of the information you have just been reading? (See also Close-Up: Parallels Between Smoking Effects and Media Violence Effects, on the next page.) In the 1940s, movies often depicted African-Americans as childlike superstitious buffoons. Today, we would not tolerate such images. In the 1960s and 1970s, some rock music and movies glamorized drug use. Responding to a tidal change in cultural attitudes, the entertainment industry now more often portrays the dark side of drug use. In response to growing public concern about violence in the media, television violence levels declined in the early 1990s (Gerbner et al., 1993). The growing sensitivity to violence has raised hopes that entertainers, producers, and audiences might someday look back with embarrassment on the days when movies "entertained" people with scenes of torture, mutilation, and sexual coercion.

Do Video Games Teach, or Release, Violence?

Violent video games became an issue for public debate after teen assassins in more than a dozen places seemed to mimic the carnage in the splatter games they had so often played (Anderson, 2004a). In 2002, two Grand Rapids, Michigan, teens and a man in his early twenties spent part of a night drinking beer and playing *Grand Theft Auto III*, using cars to run down simulated pedestrians, before beating them with fists and leaving a bloody body behind (Kolker, 2002). Then they went out on a real drive, spotted a 38-year-old man on a bicycle, ran him down with their car, got out, stomped and punched him, and returned home to play the game some more. (The man, a father of three, died six days later.)

Parallels Between Smoking Effects and Media Violence Effects

Researchers Brad Bushman and Craig Anderson (2001) note that the correlation between viewing violence and behaving aggressively nearly equals the correlation between smoking and lung cancer. They also note other parallels:

1. Not everyone who smokes gets lung cancer.

2. Smoking is only one cause of lung cancer, although an important one.

3. The first cigarette can nauseate, but the sickening effect lessens with repetition.

4. The short-term effect of one cigarette is minor and dissipates within an hour or so.

5. The long-term, cumulative effect of smoking can be severe.

6. Corporate interests have denied the smoking–lung cancer link.

1. Not everyone who watches violence becomes aggressive.

2. Viewing violence is only one cause of aggression, although an important one.

3. The first violence exposure can upset, but the upset lessens with repetition.

4. One violent TV program can prime aggressive thoughts and behaviors, but the effect dissipates within an hour or so.

5. The long-term, cumulative effect of viewing violence is increased likelihood of habitual aggression.

6. Corporate interests have denied the viewing violence–aggression link.

Interactive games transport the player into their own vivid reality. When youths play *Grand Theft Auto: San Andreas,* they can carjack vehicles; run down pedestrians; do drive-by shootings; pick up a prostitute, have sex with her, and then kill her. When youths play such games, do they learn social scripts?

Most abused children don't become abusive adults. Most social drinkers don't become alcohol dependent. And most youths who spend hundreds of hours in these mass murder simulators don't become teen assassins. Still, we wonder: If, as research has shown, passively viewing violence elevates aggressive responses to provocation and lowers sensitivity to cruelty, what will be the effect of actively role-playing aggression? Although very few will commit slaughter, how many will become desensitized to violence and more open to violent acts?

Thirty-eight studies of more than 7000 people offer some answers (Anderson et al., 2004). One study (Ballard & Wiest, 1998) observed a rising level of arousal and feelings of hostility in college men as they played *Mortal Kombat.* Other studies have found that video games can prime aggressive thoughts and increase aggression. Consider this report from Craig Anderson and Karen Dill (2000): University men who have spent the most hours playing violent video games tend to be the most physically aggressive (for example, to acknowledge having hit or attacked someone else). In one experiment, people randomly assigned to play a game involving bloody murders with groaning victims (rather than to play nonviolent *Myst*) became more hostile. On a follow-up task, they also were more likely to blast intense noise at a fellow student. Those with extensive experience in violent video gaming also display desensitization to violent images, as shown by blunted brain responses (Bartholow et al., 2006).

Studies of young adolescents by Douglas Gentile and his co-researchers (2004; 2007) further reveal that kids who play a lot of violent video games see the world as more hostile, get into more arguments and fights, and get worse grades (those hours

Desensitizing people to violence

Mark C. Burnett/Stock, Boston

aren't spent reading or studying). Ah, but is this merely because naturally hostile kids are drawn to such games? *No,* says Gentile. Even among violent-game players scoring low in hostility, 38 percent had been in fights. That figure is nearly 10 times the rate (4 percent) found among their nongaming counterparts. Moreover, over time, the nongamers became more likely to have fights only if they started playing the violent games. Anderson and his colleagues (2007) believe that, due partly to the more active participation and rewarded violence of game play, violent video games have even greater effects on aggressive behavior and cognition than do violent television and movies.

Although much remains to be learned, these studies disconfirm the *catharsis hypothesis*—the idea that we feel better if we "blow off steam" by venting our emotions. Playing violent video games *increases* aggressive thoughts, emotions, and behaviors. One video game company's CEO rationalizes that we are "violent by nature [and] need release valves." "It's a way to process violent feelings and anxieties through a fantasy medium," adds a prominent civil liberties lawyer in explaining her hunch that playing violent games calms violent tendencies (Heins, 2004). Actually, expressing anger breeds more anger, and practicing violence breeds more violence. Tomorrow's games may have even greater effects. Social psychologists Susan Persky and Jim Blascovich (2005) created a violent video game for students to play on either a desktop computer or by putting on a headset and stepping into a virtual reality. As they predicted, the virtual reality more dramatically heightened aggressive feelings and behavior during and after the play.

To sum up, research reveals biological, psychological, and social-cultural influences on aggressive behavior. Like so much else, aggression is a biopsychosocial phenomenon (**FIGURE 58.7**).

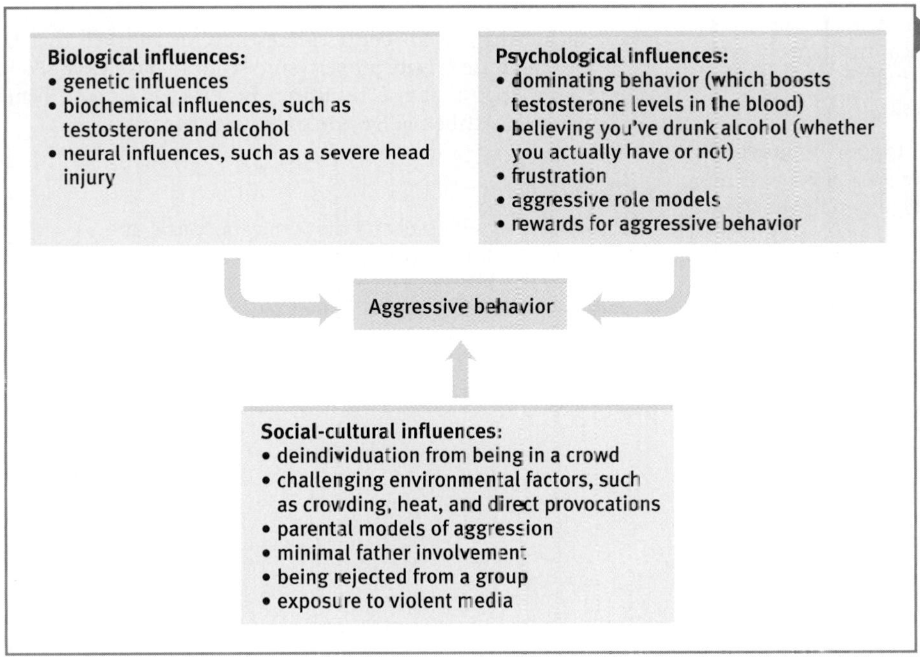

> "We are what we repeatedly do."
> Aristotle

FIGURE 58.7 Biopsychosocial understanding of aggression Because many factors contribute to aggressive behavior, there are many ways to change such behavior, including learning anger management and communication skills, and avoiding violent media and video games.

Biological influences:
• genetic influences
• biochemical influences, such as testosterone and alcohol
• neural influences, such as a severe head injury

Psychological influences:
• dominating behavior (which boosts testosterone levels in the blood)
• believing you've drunk alcohol (whether you actually have or not)
• frustration
• aggressive role models
• rewards for aggressive behavior

Aggressive behavior

Social-cultural influences:
• deindividuation from being in a crowd
• challenging environmental factors, such as crowding, heat, and direct provocations
• parental models of aggression
• minimal father involvement
• being rejected from a group
• exposure to violent media

REVIEW

Antisocial Relations

58-1 **What is prejudice?** *Prejudice* is a mixture of beliefs (often *stereotypes*), negative emotions, and predispositions to action. Prejudice may be overt (such as openly and consciously denying a particular ethnic group the right to vote) or subtle (such as feeling fearful when alone in an elevator with a stranger from a different racial or ethnic group).

58-2 **What are the social and emotional roots of prejudice?** Social and economic inequalities may trigger prejudice as people in power attempt to justify the status quo or develop an *ingroup bias*. Fear and anger feed prejudice, and, when frustrated, we may focus our anger on a *scapegoat*.

58-3 **What are the cognitive roots of prejudice?** In processing information, we tend to overestimate similarities when we categorize people, and to notice and remember vivid cases. Both trends help create stereotypes. Favored social groups often rationalize their higher status with the *just-world phenomenon*.

58-4 **What biological factors make us more prone to hurt one another?** *Aggression* is a complex behavior that results from an interaction between biology and experience. For example, genes influence our temperament, making us more or less likely to respond aggressively when frustrated in specific situations. Experiments stimulating portions of the brain (such as the amygdala and frontal lobes) have revealed neural systems in the brain that facilitate or inhibit aggression. Biochemical influences, such as testosterone and other hormones; alcohol (which disinhibits); and other substances also contribute to aggression.

58-5 **What psychological factors may trigger aggressive behavior?** Frustration and other aversive events (such as heat, crowding, and provocation) can evoke hostility, especially in those rewarded for aggression, those who have learned aggression from role models, and those who have been influenced by media violence.

Enacting violence in video games or viewing it in the media can desensitize people to cruelty and prime them to behave aggressively when provoked, or to view sexual aggression as more acceptable.

Terms and Concepts to Remember

prejudice, p. 703

stereotype, p. 703

discrimination, p. 703

ingroup, p. 707

outgroup, p. 707

ingroup bias, p. 707

scapegoat theory, p. 708

other-race effect, p. 708

just-world phenomenon, p. 709

aggression, p. 710

frustration-aggression principle, p. 712

Test Yourself

1. Kevin says, "I have no prejudice within me toward anyone. I believe everyone deserves equal opportunity in housing and employment." Even if Kevin indeed expresses no obvious prejudice, what sort of prejudice might nonetheless exist?

(Answers to the Test Yourself questions can be found in Appendix B at the end of the book.)

Ask Yourself

1. Imagine that recent court rulings have established that U.S. cities can seize private property and sell it to businesses. Policymakers hope that the resulting increased taxes will benefit collective well-being. Do you agree with the rulings?

∞ WEB

Multiple-choice self-tests and more may be found at www.worthpublishers.com/myers

MODULE 59

Attraction

Altruism

Peacemaking

Prosocial Relations

Social psychology studies how we think about and influence one another, and also how we *relate* to one another. Social psychologists focus not only on the dark side of social relationships, but also on the bright side, by studying *prosocial* behavior— behavior that intends to help or benefit someone. Our positive behaviors toward others are evident from explorations of attraction, altruism, and peacemaking.

▶‖ Attraction

Pause a moment and think about your relationships with two people—a close friend, and someone who stirs in you feelings of romantic love. What is the psychological chemistry that binds us together in these special sorts of attachments that help us cope with all other relationships? Social psychology suggests some answers.

The Psychology of Attraction

59-1 Why do we befriend or fall in love with some people but not with others?

We endlessly wonder how we can win others' affection and what makes our own affections flourish or fade. Does familiarity breed contempt, or does it intensify our affection? Do birds of a feather flock together, or do opposites attract? Is beauty only skin deep, or does attractiveness matter greatly? Consider three ingredients of our liking for one another: proximity, physical attractiveness, and similarity.

Proximity

Before friendships become close, they must begin. *Proximity*—geographic nearness—is friendship's most powerful predictor. Proximity provides opportunities for aggression, but much more often it breeds liking. Study after study reveals that people are most inclined to like, and even to marry, those who live in the same neighborhood, who sit nearby in class, who work in the same office, who share the same parking lot, who eat in the same dining hall. Look around. (For more on modern ways to connect people, see Close-Up: Online Matchmaking and Speed Dating, on the next page.)

Why is proximity so conducive to liking? Obviously, part of the answer is the greater availability of those we often meet. But there is more to it than that. For one thing, repeated exposure to novel stimuli—be they nonsense syllables, musical selections, geometric figures, Chinese characters, human faces, or the letters of our own name—increases our liking for them (Moreland & Zajonc, 1982; Nuttin, 1987; Zajonc, 2001). People are even somewhat more likely to marry someone whose familiar-sounding first or last name resembles their own (Jones et al., 2004).

This phenomenon is the **mere exposure effect.** Within certain limits (Bornstein, 1989, 1999), familiarity breeds fondness. Richard Moreland and Scott Beach (1992) demonstrated this by having four equally attractive women silently attend a 200-student class for zero, 5, 10, or 15 class sessions. At the end of the course, students were shown slides of each woman and asked to rate each one's attractiveness. The most attractive? The ones they'd seen most often. The phenomenon will come as no surprise to the young Taiwanese man who wrote more than 700 letters to his girl-friend, urging her to marry him. She did marry—the mail carrier (Steinberg, 1993).

mere exposure effect the phenomenon that repeated exposure to novel stimuli increases liking of them.

Familiarity breeds acceptance When this rare white penguin was born in the Sydney, Australia, zoo, his tuxedoed peers ostracized him. Zookeepers thought they would need to dye him black to gain acceptance. But after three weeks of contact, the other penguins came to accept him.

Rex USA

Online Matchmaking and Speed Dating

If you have not found a romantic partner in your immediate proximity, why not cast a wider net? In the United States, 16 million people have tried online dating and matchmaking services, as have an estimated 14 million more in China, 10 million in India, and tens of millions in other countries (Cullen & Masters, 2008).

Although published research on the effectiveness of Internet matchmaking services is sparse, this much seems well established: Some people dishonestly represent their age, attractiveness, occupation, or other details, and thus are not who they seem to be. Nevertheless, Katelyn McKenna and John Bargh and their colleagues have found that, on average, Internet-formed friendships and romantic relationships are more likely than relationships formed in person to last beyond two years (Bargh et al., 2002, 2004; McKenna & Bargh, 1998, 2000; McKenna et al., 2002). In one of their studies, people disclosed more, with less posturing, to those whom they met online. When conversing online with someone for 20 minutes, they felt more liking for that person than they did for someone they had met and talked with face to face. This was true even when (unknown to them) it was the same person! Small wonder that Internet friendships often feel as real and important to people as in-person relationships.

Speed dating is in-person matchmaking. People rotate through 3- to 8-minute conversations with a succession of prospective partners, deciding after each if they'd like to see the person again. Researchers report that 4 minutes is often enough for participants to form a feeling about the conversational partner and to register whether the partner likes them (Eastwick & Finkel, 2008a,b). It also is enough for researchers to have begun using speed dating as a vehicle for studying influences on people's first impressions of potential romantic partners.

No face is more familiar than one's own. And that helps explain an interesting finding from Lisa DeBruine's research (2004): Men liked other men, and women liked other women, when their faces incorporated some morphed features of their own. When DeBruine (2002) had McMaster University students play a game with a supposed other player, they also were more trusting and cooperative when the other person's image had some features of their own face morphed into it. In me I trust. (See also **FIGURE 59.1**.)

For our ancestors, the mere exposure effect was adaptive. What was familiar was generally safe and approachable. What was unfamiliar was more often dangerous and threatening. Evolution seems to have hard-wired into us the tendency to bond with those who are familiar and to be wary of those who are unfamiliar (Zajonc, 1998). Gut-level prejudice against those culturally different may thus be a primitive, automatic emotional response (Devine, 1995). It's what we do with our knee-jerk prejudice that matters, suggest researchers. Do we let those feelings control our behavior? Or do we monitor our feelings and act in ways that reflect our conscious valuing of human equality?

The mere exposure effect The mere exposure effect applies even to ourselves. Because the human face is not perfectly symmetrical, the face we see in the mirror is not the same as the one our friends see. Most of us prefer the familiar mirror image, while our friends like the reverse (Mita et al., 1977). The Bill Gates known to us all is at left. The person he sees in the mirror each morning is shown at right, and that's the photo he would probably prefer.

AP Photo/Jacques Brinon

Voter

George Bush

60:40 Blend

FIGURE 59.1 I like the candidate who looks a bit like dear old me Jeremy Bailenson and his colleagues (2005) incorporated morphed features of voters' faces into the faces of 2004 U.S. presidential candidates George Bush and John Kerry. Without conscious awareness of their own incorporated features, the participants became more likely to favor the candidate whose face incorporated some of their own features.

Physical Attractiveness

Once proximity affords you contact, what most affects your first impressions: The person's sincerity? Intelligence? Personality? Hundreds of experiments reveal that it is something far more superficial: Appearance. For people taught that "beauty is only skin deep" and that "appearances can be deceiving," the power of physical attractiveness is unnerving.

In one early study, Elaine Hatfield and her co-workers (Walster et al., 1966) randomly matched new University of Minnesota students for a Welcome Week dance. Before the dance, each student took a battery of personality and aptitude tests. On the night of the blind date, the couples danced and talked for more than two hours and then took a brief intermission to rate their dates. What determined whether they liked each other? As far as the researchers could determine, only one thing mattered: Physical attractiveness (which had been rated by the researchers beforehand). Both the men and the women liked good-looking dates best. Although women are more likely than men to say that another's looks don't affect them (Lippa, 2007), a man's looks do affect women's behavior (Feingold, 1990; Sprecher, 1989; Woll, 1986). Recent speed-dating experiments confirm that attractiveness influences first impressions for both sexes (Belot & Francesconi, 2006; Finkel & Eastwick, 2008).

People's physical attractiveness also predicts their frequency of dating, their feelings of popularity, and others' initial impressions of their personalities. We perceive attractive people to be healthier, happier, more sensitive, more successful, and more socially skilled, though not more honest or compassionate (Eagly et al., 1991; Feingold, 1992; Hatfield & Sprecher, 1986). Attractive, well-dressed people are more likely to make a favorable impression on potential employers and to enjoy occupational success (Cash & Janda, 1984; Langlois et al., 2000; Solomon, 1987). Income analyses show a penalty for plainness or obesity and a premium for beauty (Engemann & Owyang, 2005).

An analysis of 100 top-grossing films since 1940 found that attractive characters were portrayed as morally superior to unattractive characters (Smith et al., 1999). But Hollywood modeling doesn't explain why, to judge from their gazing times, even babies prefer attractive over unattractive faces (Langlois et al., 1987). So do some blind people, as University of Birmingham professor John Hull (1990, p. 23) discovered after going blind. A colleague's remarks on a woman's beauty would strangely affect his feelings. He found this "deplorable. . . . What can it matter to me what sighted men think of women . . . yet I do care what sighted men think, and I do not seem able to throw off this prejudice."

The importance of looks seems unfair and unenlightened. Why should it matter? Two thousand years ago the Roman statesman Cicero felt the same way: "The final good and the supreme duty of the wise person is to resist appearance." Cicero might be reassured by two other findings.

When Neanderthals fall in love.

"Personal beauty is a greater recommendation than any letter of introduction."
Aristotle, *Apothegems*, 330 B.C.

In the eye of the beholder
Conceptions of attractiveness vary by culture. Moreover, the current concept of attractiveness in Morocco, Kenya, and Scandinavia may well change in the future.

|| Percentage of Men and Women Who "Constantly Think About Their Looks"

	Men	Women
Canada	18%	20%
United States	17	27
Mexico	40	45
Venezuela	47	65

From Roper Starch survey, reported by McCool (1999). ||

|| *New York Times* columnist Maureen Dowd on liposuction (January 19, 2000): "Women in the 50's vacuumed. Women in the 00's are vacuumed. Our Hoovers have turned on us!" ||

|| Women have 91 percent of cosmetic procedures (ASAPS, 2008). Women also recall others' appearance better than do men (Mast & Hall, 2006). ||

FIGURE 59.2 Average is attractive
Which of these faces offered by University of St. Andrews psychologist David Perrett (2002) is most attractive? Most people say it's the face on the right—of a nonexistent person that is the average composite of these three plus 57 other actual faces.

First, people's attractiveness is surprisingly unrelated to their self-esteem and happiness (Diener et al., 1995; Major et al., 1984). One reason may be that, except after comparing themselves with superattractive people, few people (thanks, perhaps, to the mere exposure effect) view themselves as unattractive (Thornton & Moore, 1993). Another reason is that strikingly attractive people are sometimes suspicious that praise for their work may simply be a reaction to their looks. When less attractive people are praised, they are more likely to accept it as sincere (Berscheid, 1981).

Cicero might also find comfort in knowing that attractiveness judgments are relative. The standards by which judges crown Miss Universe hardly apply to the whole planet. Rather, beauty is in the eye of the culture—our standards for beauty reflect our time and place. Hoping to look attractive, people in different cultures have pierced their noses, lengthened their necks, bound their feet, and dyed or painted their skin and hair. They have gorged themselves to achieve a full figure or liposuctioned fat to achieve a slim one, applied chemicals hoping to rid themselves of unwanted hair or to regrow wanted hair, strapped on leather garments to make their breasts seem smaller or surgically filled their breasts with silicone and put on Wonderbras to make them look bigger.

For women in North America, the ultra-thin ideal of the Roaring Twenties gave way to the soft, voluptuous Marilyn Monroe ideal of the 1950s, only to be replaced by today's lean yet busty ideal. Americans now spend more on beauty supplies than on education and social services combined and, when still not satisfied, undergo 12 million cosmetic medical treatments each year, including plastic surgery, Botox skin smoothing, and laser hair removal—not even counting procedures for teeth capping or whitening (ASAPS, 2008). But the result of the beauty race since 1970 has been that more and more women feel *un*happy with their appearance (Feingold & Mazella, 1998).

Some aspects of attractiveness, however, do cross place and time (Cunningham et al., 2005; Langlois et al., 2000). Men in many cultures, from Australia to Zambia, judge women as more attractive if they have a youthful appearance. Women feel attracted to healthy-looking men, but especially to those who seem mature, dominant, and affluent.

People everywhere also seem to prefer physical features—noses, legs, physiques—that are neither unusually large nor small. An averaged face is attractive (**FIGURE 59.2**).

Extreme makeover In affluent, beauty-conscious cultures, increasing numbers of people, such as this woman from the American TV show *Extreme Makeover,* have turned to cosmetic surgery to improve their looks. If money were no concern, might you ever do the same?

In one clever demonstration of this, Judith Langlois and Lori Roggman (1990) digitized the faces of up to 32 college students and used a computer to average them. Students judged the averaged, composite faces as more attractive than 96 percent of the individual faces. One reason is that averaged faces are symmetrical, and people with symmetrical faces and bodies are more sexually attractive (Rhodes et al., 1999; Singh, 1995; Thornhill & Gangestad, 1994). Merge either half of your face with its mirror image and your symmetrical new face would boost your attractiveness a notch.

Beauty grows with mere exposure Herman Miller, Inc.'s famed Aeron chair initially received high comfort ratings but abysmal beauty ratings. To some it looked like "lawn furniture" or "a giant prehistoric insect" (Gladwell, 2005). But then, with design awards, media visibility, and imitators, the ugly duckling came to be the company's best-selling chair ever and to be seen as beautiful. With people, too, beauty lies partly in the beholder's eye and can grow with exposure.

Cultural standards aside, attractiveness also depends on our feelings about the person. If led to believe that someone has appealing traits (such as being honest, humorous, and polite rather than rude, unfair, and abusive) people perceive the person as more physically attractive (Lewandowski et al., 2007). In a Rodgers and Hammerstein musical, Prince Charming asks Cinderella, "Do I love you because you're beautiful, or are you beautiful because I love you?" Chances are it's both. As we see our loved ones again and again, their physical imperfections grow less noticeable and their attractiveness grows more apparent (Beaman & Klentz, 1983; Gross & Crofton, 1977). Shakespeare said it in *A Midsummer Night's Dream:* "Love looks not with the eyes, but with the mind." Come to love someone and watch beauty grow.

> "Love has ever in view the absolute loveliness of that which it beholds."
> George MacDonald, *Unspoken Sermons*, 1867

Similarity

Let's say that proximity has brought you into contact with someone and that your appearance has made an acceptable first impression. What now influences whether acquaintances develop into friends? For example, as you get to know someone better, is the chemistry better if you are opposites or if you are alike?

It makes a good story—extremely different types living in harmonious union: Rat, Mole, and Badger in *The Wind in the Willows,* Frog and Toad in Arnold Lobel's books. The stories delight us by expressing what we seldom experience, for we tend *not* to like dissimilar people (Rosenbaum, 1986). In real life, opposites retract. Birds that flock together usually *are* of a feather. Friends and couples are far more likely to share common attitudes, beliefs, and interests (and, for that matter, age, religion, race, education, intelligence, smoking behavior, and economic status) than are randomly paired people. Moreover, the more alike people are, the more their liking endures (Byrne, 1971). Journalist Walter Lippmann was right to suppose that love is best sustained "when the lovers love many things together, and not merely each other." Similarity breeds content. Dissimilarity often fosters disfavor, which helps explain many straight men's disapproval of gay men who are doubly dissimilar from themselves in sexual orientation and gender roles (Lehavot & Lambert, 2007).

Snapshots at jasonlove.com

Bill looked at Susan, Susan at Bill. Suddenly death didn't seem like an option. This was love at first sight.

|| In Italy and the United States, people also like political candidates who share their own self-perceived personality traits. In 2004, John Kerry was seen as open-minded and George Bush as loyal and sincere, and each was favored by voters who saw those traits in themselves (Caprara et al., 2007). ||

"I can't wait to see what you're like online."

passionate love an aroused state of intense positive absorption in another, usually present at the beginning of a love relationship.

companionate love the deep affectionate attachment we feel for those with whom our lives are intertwined.

equity a condition in which people receive from a relationship in proportion to what they give to it.

self-disclosure revealing intimate aspects of oneself to others.

Proximity, attractiveness, and similarity are not the only determinants of attraction. We also like those who like us. This is especially so when our self-image is low. When we believe someone likes us, we feel good and respond to them warmly, which leads them to like us even more (Curtis & Miller, 1986). To be liked is powerfully rewarding.

Indeed, a simple *reward theory of attraction*—that we will like those whose behavior is rewarding to us and that we will continue relationships that offer more rewards than costs—can explain all the findings we have considered so far. When a person lives or works in close proximity with someone else, it costs less time and effort to develop the friendship and enjoy its benefits. Attractive people are aesthetically pleasing, and associating with them can be socially rewarding. Those with similar views reward us by validating our own.

Romantic Love

59-2 How does romantic love typically change as time passes?

Occasionally, people move quickly from initial impressions, to friendship, to the more intense, complex, and mysterious state of romantic love. Elaine Hatfield (1988) distinguishes two types of love: temporary passionate love and a more enduring companionate love.

Passionate Love

Noting that arousal is a key ingredient of **passionate love,** Hatfield suggests that Stanley Schachter and Jerome Singer's two-factor theory of emotion can help us understand this intense positive absorption in another. The theory assumes that (1) emotions have two ingredients—physical arousal plus cognitive appraisal—and that (2) arousal from any source can enhance one emotion or another, depending on how we interpret and label the arousal.

In tests of this theory, college men have been aroused by fright, by running in place, by viewing erotic materials, or by listening to humorous or repulsive monologues. They were then introduced to an attractive woman and asked to rate her (or their girlfriend). Unlike unaroused men, those who were stirred up attributed some of their arousal to the woman or girlfriend and felt more attracted to her (Carducci et al., 1978; Dermer & Pyszczynski, 1978; White & Kight, 1984).

Outside the laboratory, Donald Dutton and Arthur Aron (1974, 1989) went to two bridges across British Columbia's rocky Capilano River. One, a swaying footbridge, was 230 feet above the rocks; the other was low and solid. An attractive young female accomplice intercepted men coming off each bridge, sought their help in filling out a short questionnaire, and then offered her phone number in case they wanted to hear more about her project. Far more of those who had just crossed the high bridge—which left their hearts pounding—accepted the number and later called the woman. To be revved up and to associate some of that arousal with a desirable person is to feel the pull of passion. Adrenaline makes the heart grow fonder.

Companionate Love

Although the spark of romantic love often endures, the intense absorption in the other, the thrill of the romance, the giddy "floating on a cloud" feeling typically fades. Does this mean the French are correct in saying that "love makes the time pass and time makes love pass"? Or can friendship and commitment keep a relationship going after the passion cools?

Hatfield reports that as love matures it becomes a steadier **companionate love**— a deep, affectionate attachment. There may be adaptive wisdom to this change from passion to attachment (Reis & Aron, 2008). Passionate love often produces children, whose survival is aided by the parents' waning obsession with one another. Social

HI & LOIS

I THINK I'M REALLY IN LOVE THIS TIME

HOW CAN YOU TELL?

WHENEVER I'M WITH HER, I GET ALL CLAMMY AND SWEATY AND NAUSEOUS AND DIZZY

YEP! THAT'S THE REAL THING

Reprinted with special permission of King Features Syndicate.

MATRIMONY

COURTSHIP

Courtship and Matrimony (From the collection of Werner Nekes)

Sometimes passionate love becomes enduring companionate love, sometimes not (invert the picture) What, in addition to similar attitudes and interests, predicts long-term loving attachment?

psychologist Ellen Berscheid and her colleagues (1984) noted that the failure to appreciate passionate love's limited half-life can doom a relationship: "If the inevitable odds against eternal passionate love in a relationship were better understood, more people might choose to be satisfied with the quieter feelings of satisfaction and contentment." Indeed, recognizing the short duration of passionate love, some societies have deemed such feelings an irrational reason for marrying. Better, such cultures say, to choose (or have someone choose for you) a partner with a compatible background and interests. Non-Western cultures, where people rate love less important for marriage, do have lower divorce rates (Levine et al., 1995).

One key to a gratifying and enduring relationship is **equity:** Both partners receive in proportion to what they give. When equity exists—when both partners freely give and receive, when they share decision making—their chances for sustained and satisfying companionate love are good (Gray-Little & Burks, 1983; Van Yperen & Buunk, 1990). In one national survey, "sharing household chores" ranked third, after "faithfulness" and a "happy sexual relationship," on a list of nine things people associated with successful marriages. "I like hugs. I like kisses. But what I really love is help with the dishes," summarized the Pew Research Center (2007).

Equity's importance extends beyond marriage. Mutually sharing self and possessions, giving and getting emotional support, promoting and caring about each other's welfare are at the core of every type of loving relationship (Sternberg & Grajek, 1984). It's true for lovers, for parent and child, and for intimate friends.

Another vital ingredient of loving relationships is **self-disclosure,** the revealing of intimate details about ourselves—our likes and dislikes, our dreams and worries, our proud and shameful moments. "When I am with my friend," noted the Roman statesman Seneca, "me thinks I am alone, and as much at liberty to speak anything as to think it." Self-disclosure breeds liking, and liking breeds self-disclosure (Collins & Miller, 1994). As one person reveals a little, the other reciprocates, the first then reveals more, and on and on, as friends or lovers move to deeper intimacy. Each increase in intimacy rekindles passion (Baumeister & Bratslavsky, 1999).

One experiment marched pairs of volunteer students through 45 minutes of increasingly self-disclosing conversation—from "When did you last sing to yourself?" to "When did you last cry in front of another person? By yourself?" By the experiment's end, those experiencing the escalating intimacy felt remarkably close to their conversation partner, much closer than others who had spent the time with small-talk questions, such as "What was your high school like?" (Aron et al., 1997). Given self-disclosing intimacy plus mutually supportive equality, the odds favor enduring companionate love.

"When two people are under the influence of the most violent, most insane, most delusive, and most transient of passions, they are required to swear that they will remain in that excited, abnormal, and exhausting condition continuously until death do them part."
George Bernard Shaw, "Getting Married," 1908

Love is an ancient thing In 2007, a 5000- to 6000-year-old "Romeo and Juliet" young couple was unearthed locked in an embrace, near Rome.

AP Photo/Archaeological Society SAP, ho

Intimacy can also grow from pausing to ponder and write our feelings. Richard Slatcher and James Pennebaker (2006) discovered this when they invited one person from each of 86 dating couples to spend 20 minutes a day over three days either writing their deepest thoughts and feelings about the relationship or writing merely about their daily activities. Those who wrote their feelings expressed more emotion in their instant messages with their partners in the days following, and 77 percent were still dating three months later (compared with 52 percent of those who had written about their activities).

▶‖ Altruism

59-3 When are we most—and least—likely to help?

Carl Wilkens, a Seventh Day Adventist missionary, was living with his family in Kigali, Rwanda, when Hutu militia began to slaughter the Tutsi in 1994. The U.S. government, church leaders, and friends all implored Wilkens to leave. He refused. After evacuating his family, and even after every other American had left Kigali, he alone stayed and contested the 800,000-person genocide. When the militia came to kill him and his Tutsi servants, Wilkens' Hutu neighbors deterred them. Despite repeated death threats, he spent his days running roadblocks to take food and water to orphanages and to negotiate, plead, and bully his way through the bloodshed, saving lives time and again. "It just seemed the right thing to do," he later explained (Kristof, 2004).

Elsewhere in Kigali, Paul Rusesabagina, a Hutu married to a Tutsi and the acting manager of a luxury hotel, was sheltering more than 1200 terrified Tutsis and moderate Hutus. When international peacemakers abandoned the city and hostile militia threatened his guests in the "Hotel Rwanda" (as it came to be called in a 2004 movie), the courageous Rusesabagina began cashing in past favors, bribing the militia, and telephoning influential persons abroad to bring pressure on local authorities, thereby sparing the lives of the hotel's occupants from the surrounding chaos.

Such selfless goodness exemplifies **altruism**—the unselfish regard for the welfare of others. Altruism became a major concern of social psychologists after an especially vile act of sexual violence. On March 13, 1964, a stalker repeatedly stabbed Kitty Genovese, then raped her as she lay dying outside her Queens, New York, apartment at 3:30 A.M. "Oh, my God, he stabbed me!" Genovese screamed into the early morning stillness. "Please help me!" Windows opened and lights went on as neighbors—38 of them, according to an initial *New York Times* report, though the number was later contested—heard her screams. Her attacker fled and then returned to stab and rape her again. Not until he had fled for good did anyone so much as call the police, at 3:50 A.M.

Bystander Intervention

Reflecting on the Genovese murder and other such tragedies, most commentators were outraged by the bystanders' "apathy" and "indifference." Rather than blaming the onlookers, social psychologists John Darley and Bibb Latané (1968b) attributed their inaction to an important situational factor—the presence of others. Given certain circumstances, they suspected, most of us might behave similarly.

After staging emergencies under various conditions, Darley and Latané assembled their findings into a decision scheme: We will help only if the situation enables us first to *notice* the incident, then to *interpret* it as an emergency, and finally to *assume responsibility* for helping (**FIGURE 59.3**). At each step, the presence of other bystanders turns people away from the path that leads to helping. In the laboratory and on the

"Probably no single incident has caused social psychologists to pay as much attention to an aspect of social behavior as Kitty Genovese's murder."

R. Lance Shotland (1984)

altruism unselfish regard for the welfare of others.

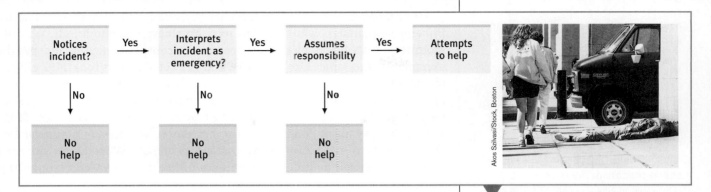

Akos Szilvasi/Stock, Boston

FIGURE 59.3 **The decision-making process for bystander intervention** Before helping, one must first notice an emergency, then correctly interpret it, and then feel responsible. (From Darley & Latané, 1968b.)

street, people in a group of strangers are more likely than solitary individuals to keep their eyes focused on what they themselves are doing or where they are going. If they notice an unusual situation, they may infer from the blasé reactions of the other passersby that the situation is not an emergency. "The person lying on the sidewalk must be drunk," they think, and move on.

But sometimes, as with the Genovese murder, the emergency is unambiguous and people still fail to help. The witnesses looking out through their windows noticed the incident, correctly interpreted the emergency, and yet failed to assume responsibility. Why? To find out, Darley and Latané (1968a) simulated a physical emergency in their laboratory. University students participated in a discussion over an intercom. Each student was in a separate cubicle, and only the person whose microphone was switched on could be heard. One of the students was an accomplice of the experimenters. When his turn came, he made sounds as though he were having an epileptic seizure and called for help.

How did the other students react? As **FIGURE 59.4** shows, those who believed only they could hear the victim—and therefore thought they bore total responsibility for helping him—usually went to his aid. Those who thought others also could hear were more likely to react as did Kitty Genovese's neighbors. When more people shared responsibility for helping—when there was a *diffusion of responsibility*—any single listener was less likely to help.

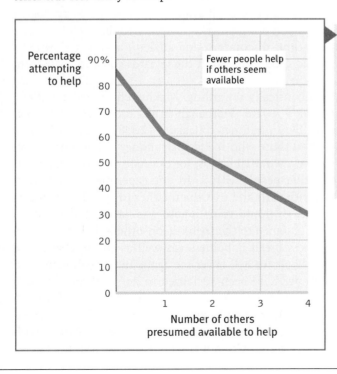

FIGURE 59.4 **Responses to a simulated physical emergency** When people thought they alone heard the calls for help from a person they believed to be having an epileptic seizure, they usually helped. But when they thought four others were also hearing the calls, fewer than a third responded. (From Darley & Latané, 1968a.)

"Oh, make us happy and you make us good!"

Robert Browning, *The Ring and the Book*, 1868

In hundreds of additional experiments, psychologists have studied the factors that influence bystanders' willingness to relay an emergency phone call, aid a stranded motorist, donate blood, pick up dropped books, contribute money, and give time. For example, Latané, James Dabbs (1975), and 145 collaborators took 1497 elevator rides in three cities and "accidentally" dropped coins or pencils in front of 4813 fellow passengers. The women coin droppers were more likely to receive help than were the men—a gender difference often reported by other researchers (Eagly & Crowley, 1986). But the major finding was the **bystander effect**—any particular bystander was less likely to give aid with other bystanders present. When alone with the person in need, 40 percent helped; in the presence of five other bystanders, only 20 percent helped.

From their observations of behavior in tens of thousands of such situations, altruism researchers have discerned some additional patterns. The *best* odds of our helping someone occur when

▶ the person appears to need and deserve help.
▶ the person is in some way similar to us.
▶ we have just observed someone else being helpful.
▶ we are not in a hurry.
▶ we are in a small town or rural area.
▶ we are feeling guilty.
▶ we are focused on others and not preoccupied.
▶ we are in a good mood.

This last result, that happy people are helpful people, is one of the most consistent findings in all of psychology. No matter how people are cheered—whether by being made to feel successful and intelligent, by thinking happy thoughts, by finding money, or even by receiving a posthypnotic suggestion—they become more generous and more eager to help (Carlson et al., 1988).

The Norms for Helping

Why do we help? One widely held view is that self-interest underlies all human interactions, that our constant goal is to maximize rewards and minimize costs. Accountants call it *cost-benefit analysis*. Philosophers call it *utilitarianism*. Social psychologists call it **social exchange theory.** If you are pondering whether to donate blood, you may weigh the costs of doing so (time, discomfort, and anxiety) against the benefits (reduced guilt, social approval, and good feelings). If the rewards you anticipate from helping exceed the costs, you will help.

For most people, helping is intrinsically rewarding. Making charitable donations activates brain areas associated with reward (Harbaugh et al., 2007). That helps explain some findings by Elizabeth Dunn and her colleagues (2008). People who give more money away are happier than those who spend their money almost entirely on themselves. Employees who receive a windfall bonus, for example, are later happier if they have done something for other people with it. In one experiment, researchers gave people an envelope with cash and told them either to spend it on themselves or on others. Which group do you suppose was happiest at the day's end? It was, indeed, those assigned to the spend-it-on-others condition.

But why does helpfulness breed happiness (as well as the reverse)? And why do we leave tips for people we will never see again and give directions to strangers? In part because we have been socialized to do so, through norms that prescribe how we *ought* to behave, often to our mutual benefit. Through socialization, we learn the **reciprocity norm,** the expectation that we should return help, not harm, to those who have helped us. In our relations with others of similar status, the reciprocity norm compels us to give (in favors,

gifts, or social invitations) about as much as we receive. We also learn a **social-responsibility norm:** that we should help those who need our help—young children and others who cannot give as much as they receive—even if the costs outweigh the benefits. In repeated Gallup surveys, people who each week attend religious services often exhibit the social responsibility norm: They report volunteering more than twice as many hours in helping the poor and infirm than do those who rarely or never attend religious services (Hodgkinson & Weitzman, 1992; Independent Sector, 2002). They also give away three times as much money.

A social responsibility norm was active on January 2, 2007, as construction worker Wesley Autry and his 6- and 4-year-old daughters were awaiting a New York City subway train. Before them a man collapsed in a seizure, got up, then stumbled to the platform's edge and fell onto the tracks. With train headlights approaching, "I had to make a split decision," Autry later recalled (Buckley, 2007). His decision, as his girls looked on in horror, was to leap from the platform, push the man off the tracks and into a foot-deep space between them, and lay atop him. As the train screeched to a halt, five cars traveled just above his head, leaving grease on his knit cap. When Autrey cried out, "I've got two daughters up there. Let them know their father is okay," the onlookers erupted into applause.

Subway hero Wesley Autrey: "I don't feel like I did something spectacular; I just saw someone who needed help."

▶‖ Peacemaking

59-4 How do social traps and mirror-image perceptions fuel social conflict?

We live in surprising times. With astonishing speed, late-twentieth-century democratic movements swept away totalitarian rule in Eastern European countries, and hopes for a new world order displaced the Cold War chill. And yet, the twenty-first century began with terrorist acts and war, and the world continued to spend $2 billion every day for arms and armies—money that could have been used for housing, nutrition, education, and health care. Knowing that wars begin in human minds, psychologists have wondered: What in the human mind causes destructive conflict? How might the perceived threats of social diversity be replaced by a spirit of cooperation?

To a social psychologist, a **conflict** is a perceived incompatibility of actions, goals, or ideas. The elements of conflict are much the same at all levels, from nations at war, to cultural disputes within a society, to individuals in a marital dispute. In each situation, people become enmeshed in a potentially destructive social process that can produce results no one wants. Among the destructive processes are social traps and distorted perceptions.

Social Traps

In some situations, we support our collective well-being by pursuing our personal interests. As capitalist Adam Smith wrote in *The Wealth of Nations* (1776), "It is not from the benevolence of the butcher, the brewer, or the baker that we expect our dinner, but from their regard to their own interest." In other situations, we harm our collective well-being by pursuing our personal interests. Such situations are **social traps.**

Consider the simple game matrix in **FIGURE 59.5**, which is similar to those used in experiments with countless thousands of people. Both sides can win or both can lose, depending on the players' individual choices. Pretend you are Person 1, and that you and Person 2 will each receive the amount shown after you separately choose either *A* or *B*. (You might invite someone to look at the matrix with you and take the role of Person 2.) Which do you choose—*A* or *B*?

FIGURE 59.5 Social-trap game matrix By pursuing our self-interest and not trusting others, we can end up losers. To illustrate this, imagine playing the game below. The peach triangles show the outcomes for Person 1, which depend on the choices made by both players. If you were Person 1, would you choose *A* or *B*? (This game is called a *non–zero-sum* game because the outcomes need not add up to zero; both sides can win or both can lose.)

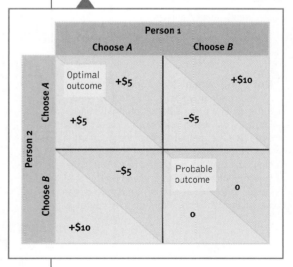

You and Person 2 are caught in a dilemma. If you both choose *A*, you both benefit, making $5 each. Neither of you benefits if you both choose *B*, for neither of you makes anything. Nevertheless, on any single trial you serve your own interests if you choose *B*: You can't lose, and you might make $10. But the same is true for the other person. Hence, the social trap: As long as you both pursue your own immediate best interest and choose *B*, you will both end up with nothing—the typical result—when you could have made $5.

Many real-life situations similarly pit our individual interests against our communal well-being. Individual whalers reasoned that the few whales they took would not threaten the species and that if they didn't take them others would anyway. The result: Some species of whales became endangered. Ditto for the buffalo hunters of yesterday and the elephant-tusk poachers of today. Individual car owners and home owners reason, "It would cost me comfort or money to buy a more fuel-efficient car and furnace. Besides, the fossil fuels I burn don't noticeably add to the greenhouse gases." When enough others reason similarly, the collective result threatens disaster—global climate change, rising seas, and more extreme weather.

Social traps challenge us to find ways of reconciling our right to pursue our personal well-being with our responsibility for the well-being of all. Psychologists are therefore exploring ways to convince people to cooperate for their mutual betterment—through agreed-upon *regulations,* through better *communication,* and through promoting *awareness* of our responsibilities toward community, nation, and the whole of humanity (Dawes, 1980; Linder, 1982; Sato, 1987). Given effective regulations, communication, and awareness, people more often cooperate, whether it be in playing a laboratory game or the real game of life.

Enemy Perceptions

Psychologists have noted that those in conflict have a curious tendency to form diabolical images of one another. These distorted images are ironically similar, so similar in fact that we call them **mirror-image perceptions:** As we see "them"—as untrustworthy and evil intentioned—so "they" see us. Each demonizes the other.

Mirror-image perceptions often feed a vicious cycle of hostility. If Juan believes Maria is annoyed with him, he may snub her, causing her to act in ways that justify his perception. As with individuals, so with countries. Perceptions can become self-fulfilling prophecies. They may confirm themselves by influencing the other country to react in ways that seem to justify them.

People in conflict also tend to see their own actions as responses to provocation, not as the causes of what happens next. When responding to a perceived provocation they often hit back harder, though perceiving themselves as merely returning tit for tat. In one experiment, University College London volunteers used a mechanical

Not in my ocean! Many people support alternative energy sources, including wind turbines. But proposals to construct wind farms in real-world neighborhoods elicit less support. One such proposal, for locating wind turbines off the coast of Massachusetts' Nantucket Island, produced heated debate over the future benefits of clean energy versus the costs of altering treasured ocean views and, possibly, migratory bird routes.

AP Photo/Lisa Poole

device to press on another volunteer's finger, after feeling pressure on their own finger. Although their task was to reciprocate with the same amount of pressure, they typically responded with about 40 percent more force than they had just experienced. Despite seeking to respond only in kind, their touches soon escalated to hard presses, much as when each child after a fight claims that "I just poked him, but he hit me harder" (Shergill et al., 2003).

In the early twenty-first century, many Americans came to loathe Saddam Hussein. Like the "evil" Saddam Hussein, "some of today's tyrants are gripped by an implacable hatred of the United States of America" declared then-President George W. Bush (2001). "They hate our friends, they hate our values, they hate democracy and freedom and individual liberty. Many care little for the lives of their own people." Hussein (2002) reciprocated the perception, seeing the United States as "an evil tyrant" that, with Satan as its protector, lusted for oil and aggressively attacked those who "defend what is right."

The point is not that truth must lie midway between two such views (one may be more accurate). The point is that enemy perceptions often form mirror images. Moreover, as enemies change, so do perceptions. In American minds and media, the "bloodthirsty, cruel, treacherous" Japanese of World War II later became our "intelligent, hardworking, self-disciplined, resourceful allies" (Gallup, 1972).

How can we make peace? Can contact, cooperation, communication, and conciliation transform the antagonisms fed by prejudice and conflicts into attitudes that promote peace? Research indicates that, in some cases, they can.

Contact

59-5 How can we transform feelings of prejudice, aggression, and conflict into attitudes that promote peace?

Does it help to put two conflicting parties into close contact? It depends. When such contact is noncompetitive and between parties of equal status, such as retail clerks working the same shift, it typically helps. Initially prejudiced co-workers of different races have, in such circumstances, usually come to accept one another.

This finding is confirmed by a statistical digest of more than 500 studies of face-to-face contact with outgroups (such as ethnic minorities, the elderly, and those with disabilities). Among the quarter-million people studied across 38 nations, contact has been correlated with, or in experimental studies has led to, more positive attitudes (Pettigrew & Tropp, 2006). Some examples:

▶ With interracial contact, South African Whites' and Blacks' "attitudes [have moved] into closer alignment" (Dixon et al., 2007).
▶ Heterosexuals' personal contact with gay people correlates with accepting attitudes. In one national survey, those who knowingly had a gay family member or close friend were twice as likely to support gay marriage as those who didn't—55 percent versus 25 percent (Neidorf & Morin, 2007).
▶ Even indirect contact with a member of an outgroup (via story reading or through a friend who has an outgroup friend) tends to reduce prejudice (Cameron & Rutland, 2006; Pettigrew et al., 2007).

However, mere contact is not always enough. In most desegregated schools, ethnic groups resegregate themselves in the lunchrooms and on the school grounds (Clack et al., 2005; Schofield, 1986). People in each group often think that they would welcome more contact with the other group, but they assume the other group does not reciprocate the wish (Richeson & Shelton, 2007). "I don't reach out to them, because I don't want to be rebuffed; they don't reach out to me, because they're just not interested." When such mirror-image misperceptions are corrected, friendships may then form and prejudices melt.

mirror-image perceptions mutual views often held by conflicting people, as when each side sees itself as ethical and peaceful and views the other side as evil and aggressive.

"You cannot shake hands with a clenched fist."
Indira Gandhi, 1971

superordinate goals shared goals that override differences among people and require their cooperation.

GRIT *Graduated* and *Reciprocated Initiatives in Tension-Reduction*—a strategy designed to decrease international tensions.

Cooperation

To see if enemies could overcome their differences, researcher Muzafer Sherif (1966) first instigated conflict. He placed 22 Oklahoma City boys in two separate areas of a Boy Scout camp. He then put the two groups through a series of competitive activities, with prizes going to the victors. Before long, each group became intensely proud of itself and hostile to the other group's "sneaky," "smart-alecky stinkers." Food wars broke out during meals. Cabins were ransacked. Fistfights had to be broken up by members of the camp staff. When Sherif brought the two groups together, they avoided one another, except to taunt and threaten.

Nevertheless, within a few days Sherif transformed these young enemies into jovial comrades. He gave them **superordinate goals**—shared goals that overrode their differences and that could be achieved only through cooperation. A planned disruption of the camp water supply necessitated that all 22 boys work together to restore water. Renting a movie in those pre-DVD days required their pooled resources. A stalled truck needed the combined force of all the boys pulling and pushing together to get it moving. Having used isolation and competition to make strangers into enemies, Sherif used shared predicaments and goals to reconcile the enemies and make them friends. What reduced conflict was not mere contact, but *cooperative* contact.

A shared predicament—a fearsome external threat and a superordinate desire to overcome it—likewise had a powerfully unifying effect in the weeks after 9/11. Patriotism soared as Americans felt that "we" were under attack. Gallup-surveyed approval of "our President" shot up from 51 percent the week before the attack to a highest-ever level of 90 percent 10 days after, just surpassing the previous approval-rating record of 89 percent enjoyed by his father, George Bush, at the climax of the 1991 Persian Gulf war (Newport, 2002). In chat groups and everyday speech, even the word *we* (relative to *I*) surged in the immediate aftermath (Pennebaker, 2002).

Cooperation has especially positive effects when it leads people to define a new, inclusive group that dissolves their former subgroups (Dovidio & Gaertner, 1999). Seat the members of two groups not on opposite sides, but alternately around the table. Give them a new, shared name. Have them work together. Such experiences change "us" and "them" into "we." Those once perceived as being in another group now are seen as part of one's own group. One 18-year-old New Jersey man would not be surprised. After 9/11, he explained a shift in his social identity: "I just thought of myself as Black. But now I feel like I'm an American, more than ever" (Sengupta, 2001). In one experiment, White Americans who read a newspaper article about a terrorist threat against all Americans subsequently expressed reduced prejudice against African-Americans (Dovidio et al., 2004).

During the 1970s, several teams of educational researchers simultaneously wondered: If cooperative contacts between members of rival groups encourage positive attitudes, could we apply this principle in multicultural schools? Could we promote interracial friendships by replacing competitive classroom situations with cooperative ones? And could cooperative learning maintain or even enhance student achievement? Many experiments with adolescents from 11 countries confirm that in all three cases, the answer is *yes* (Roseth, Johnson, & Johnson, 2008). Members of interracial groups who work together on projects and play together on athletic teams typically come to feel friendly toward those of another race. So do those who engage in cooperative classroom learning. So encouraging are these results that thousands of teachers have introduced interracial cooperative learning into their classrooms.

The power of cooperative activity to make friends of former enemies has led psychologists to urge increased international exchange and cooperation (Klineberg, 1984). As we engage in mutually beneficial trade, as we work to protect our common destiny on this fragile planet, and as we become more aware that our hopes and fears are shared, we can change misperceptions that feed conflict into a solidarity based on common interests.

"Most of us have overlapping identities which unite us with very different groups. We *can* love what we are, without hating what—and who—we are *not*. We can thrive in our own tradition, even as we learn from others."

Former U.N. Secretary-General Kofi Annan, Nobel prize lecture, 2001

Working toward shared goals enables diverse peoples to discover unity in their common values and superordinate identity. "Common values" are what we need, declared the chair of Britain's Commission for Racial Equality as ethnic tensions recently flared (Phillips, 2004). "There is no ethnicity here. We are all Rwandan," proclaimed Rwanda's government as it sought to resolve historic animosities between Tutsis and Hutus (Lacey, 2004). Western democracies have largely been spared ethnic tribal warfare because their different racial groups have shared so many of the very same goals, noted sociologist Amitai Etzioni (1999). In the United States, these shared goals include fair treatment for all, higher moral standards, and a wish that all high school graduates "understand the common history and ideas that tie all Americans together." Although diversity commands attention, we are—as working toward shared goals reminds us—more alike than different.

"We often forget how much unites all the members of humanity," declared President Ronald Reagan in 1987. "Perhaps we need some outside, universal threat to recognize this common bond." Echoing those words, climate protection advocate Al Gore (2007) noted, "We—all of us—now face a universal threat [which] requires us, in Reagan's phrase, to unite in recognition of our common bond."

Communication

When real-life conflicts become intense, a third-party mediator—a marriage counselor, labor mediator, diplomat, community volunteer—may facilitate much-needed communication (Rubin et al., 1994). Mediators help each party to voice its viewpoint and to understand the other's. By leading each side to think about the other's underlying needs and goals, the mediator aims to replace a competitive *win-lose* orientation with a cooperative *win-win* orientation that offers a mutually beneficial resolution. A classic example: Two friends, after quarreling over an orange, agreed to split it. One squeezed his half for juice. The other used the peel from her half to make a cake. If only the two had understood each other's motives, they could have hit on the win-win solution of one having all the juice, the other all the peel.

Such understanding and cooperative resolution is most needed, yet least likely, in times of anger or crisis (Bodenhausen et al., 1994; Tetlock, 1988).

Conciliation

When conflicts intensify, images become more stereotyped, judgments more rigid, and communication more difficult, or even impossible. Each party is likely to threaten, coerce, or retaliate. In the weeks before the Persian Gulf war, the first President George Bush threatened, in the full glare of publicity, to "kick Saddam's ass." Saddam Hussein communicated in kind, threatening to make Americans "swim in their own blood."

Under such conditions, is there an alternative to war or surrender? Social psychologist Charles Osgood (1962, 1980) advocated a strategy of *Graduated and Reciprocated Initiatives in Tension-Reduction,* nicknamed **GRIT.** In applying GRIT, one side first announces its recognition of mutual interests and its intent to reduce tensions. It then initiates one or more small, conciliatory acts. Without weakening one's retaliatory capability, this modest beginning opens the door for reciprocity by the other party. Should the enemy respond with hostility, one reciprocates in kind. But so, too, with any conciliatory response. Thus, U.S. President John Kennedy's gesture of stopping atmospheric nuclear tests began a series of reciprocated conciliatory acts that culminated in the 1993 atmospheric test-ban treaty.

In laboratory experiments, GRIT has been an effective strategy for increasing trust and cooperation (Lindskold et al., 1978, 1988). Even during intense personal conflict, when communication has been nonexistent, a small conciliatory gesture—a smile, a touch, a word of apology—may work wonders. Conciliations allow both

"I am prepared this day to declare myself a citizen of the world, and to invite everyone everywhere to embrace this broader vision of our interdependent world, our common quest for justice, and ultimately for Peace on Earth."

Father Theodore Hesburgh, *The Human Imperative,* 1974

Superordinate goals override differences Cooperative efforts to achieve shared goals are an effective way to break down social barriers.

Syracuse Newspapers/ The Image Works

"To begin with, I would like to express my sincere thanks and deep appreciation for the opportunity to meet with you. While there are still profound differences between us, I think the very fact of my presence here today is a major breakthrough."

parties to begin edging down the tension ladder to a safer rung where communication and mutual understanding can begin.

And how good that such can happen, for civilization advances not by cultural isolation—maintaining walls around ethnic enclaves—but by tapping the knowledge, the skills, and the arts that are each culture's legacy to the whole human race. Thomas Sowell (1991) observed that, thanks to cultural sharing, every modern society is enriched by a cultural mix. We have China to thank for paper and printing and for the magnetic compass that opened the great explorations. We have Egypt to thank for trigonometry. We have the Islamic world and India's Hindus to thank for our Arabic numerals. While celebrating and claiming these diverse cultural legacies, we can also welcome the enrichment of today's social diversity. We can view ourselves as instruments in a human orchestra. And we can therefore affirm our own culture's heritage while building bridges of communication, understanding, and cooperation across cultural traditions as we think about, influence, and relate to one another.

REVIEW

Prosocial Relations

59-1 Why do we befriend or fall in love with some people but not with others? Three factors are known to affect our liking for one another. Proximity—geographical nearness—is conducive to attraction, partly because *mere exposure* to novel stimuli enhances liking. Physical attractiveness increases social opportunities and influences the way we are perceived. As acquaintanceship moves toward friendship, similarity of attitudes and interests greatly increases liking.

59-2 How does romantic love typically change as time passes? *Passionate love* is an aroused state that we cognitively label as love. The strong affection of *companionate love,* which often emerges as passionate love subsides, is enhanced by an *equitable* relationship and by intimate *self-disclosure.*

59-3 When are we most—and least—likely to help? *Altruism* is unselfish regard for the well-being of others. We are less likely to help if others are present. This *bystander effect* is especially apparent in situations where the presence of others inhibits our noticing the event, interpreting it as an emergency, or assuming responsibility for offering help. Explanations of our willingness to help others focus on *social exchange theory* (the costs and benefits of helping); the intrinsic rewards of helping others; the *reciprocity norm* (we help those who help us); and the *social-responsibility norm* (we help those who need our help).

59-4 How do social traps and mirror-image perceptions fuel social conflict? Social *conflicts* are situations in which people perceive their actions, goals, or ideas to be incompatible. In *social traps,* two or more individuals engage in mutually destructive behavior by rationally pursuing their own self-interests. People in conflict tend to expect the worst of each other, producing *mirror-image* perceptions that can become self-fulfilling prophecies.

59-5 How can we transform feelings of prejudice, aggression, and conflict into attitudes that promote peace? Enemies some-times become friends, especially when the circumstances favor equal-status contact, cooperation to achieve *superordinate goals,* understanding through communication, and reciprocated conciliatory gestures.

Terms and Concepts to Remember

mere exposure effect, p. 719
passionate love, p. 724
companionate love, p. 724
equity, p. 725
self-disclosure, p. 725
altruism, p. 726
bystander effect, p. 728
social exchange theory, p. 728

reciprocity norm, p. 728
social-responsibility norm, p. 729
conflict, p. 729
social trap, p. 729
mirror-image perceptions, p. 730
superordinate goals, p. 732
GRIT, p. 733

Test Yourself

1. Why didn't anybody help Kitty Genovese? What social relations principle did this incident illustrate?

(Answers to the Test Yourself questions can be found in Appendix B at the end of the book.)

Ask Yourself

1. Do you regret not getting along with some friend or family member? How might you go about reconciling that relationship?

∞ WEB

Multiple-choice self-tests and more may be found at www.worthpublishers.com/myers

Careers in Psychology

Jennifer Zwolinski

University of San Diego

Preparing for a Career
in Psychology

  The Bachelor's Degree
  Postgraduate Degrees

Subfields of Psychology

Preparing Early for
Graduate Study in
Psychology

For More Information

What can you do with a degree in psychology? Lots!

As a psychology major, you will graduate with a scientific mind-set and an awareness of basic principles of human behavior (biological mechanisms, development, cognition, psychological disorders, social interaction). This background will prepare you for success in many areas, including business, the helping professions, health services, marketing, law, sales, and teaching. You may even go on to graduate school for specialized training to become a psychology professional. This appendix describes the various levels of psychology education and some jobs available at those levels; psychology's specialized subfields; and ways you can improve your chances of admission to graduate school.[1]

▶‖ Preparing for a Career in Psychology

Psychology is the second most popular major in the United States, second only to business (Princeton Review, 2005). Recent data show that more than 88,000 psychology majors graduate annually from U.S. colleges and universities (National Center for Education Statistics, 2007a,b). An undergraduate degree in psychology can prepare you for a broad array of jobs in numerous fields after graduation. For a career that is more closely related to the field of psychology, you will need a graduate degree.

The Bachelor's Degree

If you major in psychology, you will have several possible career paths to follow (Cannon, 2005). First, you might consider employment after graduation in a variety of professional settings. Most students who graduate with psychology majors find work in for-profit organizations, especially in management, sales, and administration. **TABLE A.1** on the next page shows the top 10 occupations that employ people with a bachelor's degree in psychology.[2] If you choose to work more directly in the field of psychology, a bachelor's degree will qualify you to work as an assistant to psychologists, researchers, or other professionals in community mental health centers, vocational rehabilitation offices, and correctional programs (U.S. Bureau of Labor Statistics, 2008). A second option for psychology majors after graduation is to pursue a graduate degree in psychology. Approximately 42 percent of U.S. psychology majors go on to graduate school in psychology (Fogg et al., 2004). A third option is to pursue advanced training in other disciplines such as law, business, education, or medicine.

    Clearly, psychology majors are marketable beyond the boundaries of psychology. Their sought-after skills include an ability to work and get along with others, a desire

---

[1] Although this text covers the world of psychology for students in many countries, this appendix draws primarily from available U.S. data. Its descriptions of psychology's subfields and its suggestions for preparing to enter the profession are, however, also applicable in many other countries.

[2] For a more comprehensive list of job titles, see Appleby (2006)

TABLE A.1 Top 10 U.S. Occupations That Employ People With a Bachelor's Degree in Psychology

1. Top- and mid-level managers, executives, administrators
2. Sales occupations, including retail
3. Social workers
4. Other management-related occupations
5. Personnel, training, labor relations specialists
6. Other administrative
7. Insurance, securities, real estate, business services
8. Other marketing and sales occupations
9. Registered nurses, pharmacists, therapists, physician assistants
10. Accountants, auditors, other financial specialists

Source: Fogg et al. (2004).

and willingness to learn new things, adaptability to changing situations, and a capacity for problem solving (Landrum, 2001). Psychology majors also have a number of methodological skills that result from the focus on the scientific study of human and animal behavior. The study of statistics and research methodology contributes to a scientific mind-set that emphasizes exploring and managing uncertainty, critical and analytical skills, and logical thinking abilities. The ability to analyze data using statistics, conduct database searches, and integrate multiple sources of information would be helpful in a number of professional settings. Prospective employers will also appreciate the excellent written and oral communication skills among students who present their research projects at conferences and master American Psychological Association (APA) style.

There are some things that all psychology majors can do to maximize success in the job market. Employers who hire people with only a bachelor's degree tend to favor individuals with strong interpersonal skills and practical experience as well as a good education (Cannon, 2005). Betsy Morgan and Ann Korschgen (1998) offer the following helpful tips for increasing your chances of getting a job after graduation. Many of these tools will benefit students who plan to apply to graduate school as well.

1. *Get to know your instructors.* Talk with them about the field of psychology and get their advice on your career plan. Ask them to support you on an independent study internship or research project. By learning more about your skills and future aims, faculty members can help you accomplish your goals. This may even result in an enthusiastic reference for future employment.

2. *Take courses that support your interests.* Although the psychology major offers a range of skills that will benefit you in the job market, don't assume the psychology curriculum will offer all the skills necessary to get a job in your area of interest. Add courses to increase your knowledge base and skills. This will also show prospective employers that your specific interests are in line with the demands of the job.

3. *Familiarize yourself with available resources, such as campus career services and alumni.* Career services can help you identify and market your job skills and emphasize the knowledge and abilities you have in your resume. They can also help you to network with other alumni who are working in your area of interest and who can help you to prepare for the career that you want.

4. *Participate in at least one internship experience.* Many employers want students to gain relevant experience outside the classroom. Internships are offered during

the school year as well as the summer break. Some are paid and others are not, but you may be able to earn course credit while completing your internship. In addition to gaining relevant work experience before you graduate, you will increase your support network of mentors who can provide supervision and support for your career goals as well as letters of support when you apply for jobs.

5. *Volunteer some of your time and talent to campus or community organizations, such as Psi Chi (the national honor society in psychology) or your school's psychology club.* In addition to showing that you are an active citizen in your department, you will gain important skills, such as meeting and event planning, how to work with a group, and improved communication skills, all of which enhance your marketability.

Postgraduate Degrees

A graduate degree in psychology will give you proficiency in an area of psychological specialization. According to the U.S. Bureau of Labor Statistics (2008), psychologists with advanced degrees held approximately 166,000 jobs in 2006. Employment for psychologists is expected to grow 15 percent from 2006 to 2016, which is faster than the average for all occupations. The work settings for psychologists vary somewhat by type of graduate degree. As shown in **FIGURE A.1**, psychologists with a doctorate work primarily in universities and colleges; most people with a master's degree work in other educational institutions (such as elementary and middle schools) and in for-profit companies. Among advanced degree recipients in 2005–2006, a total of 19,770 had master's degrees and 4921 earned doctoral degrees (National Center for Education Statistics, 2007a,b).

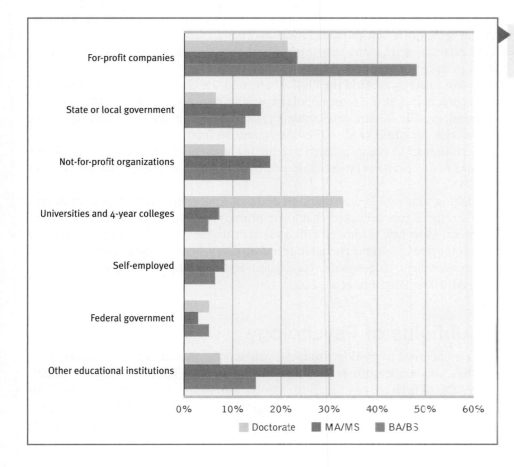

FIGURE A.1 Work settings for psychology-degree recipients
Source: Fogg et al., 2004.

The Master's Degree

A master's degree in psychology requires at least two years of full-time graduate study in a specific subfield of psychology. In addition to specialized course work in psychology, requirements usually include practical experience in an applied setting and/or a master's thesis reporting on an original research project. You might acquire a master's degree to do specialized work in psychology. As a graduate with a master's degree, you might handle research and data collection and analysis in a university, government, or private industry setting. You might work under the supervision of a psychologist with a doctorate, providing some clinical service such as therapy or testing. Or you might find a job in the health, government, industry, or education fields. You might also acquire a master's degree as a stepping stone for more advanced study in a doctoral program in psychology, which will considerably expand the number of employment opportunities available to you (Super & Super, 2001).

Doctoral Degrees

You will probably need five to seven years of graduate study in a specific subfield of psychology to get your doctoral degree. The degree you choose to pursue will depend on your career goals. You will probably choose to earn a doctor of philosophy (Ph.D.) in psychology if your career goals are geared toward conducting research, or a doctor of psychology (Psy.D.) if you are more interested in pursuing professional practice. Training for the Ph.D. culminates in a dissertation (an extensive research paper you will be required to defend orally) based on original research. Courses in quantitative research methods, which include the use of computer-based analysis, are an important part of graduate study and are necessary to complete the dissertation. Psy.D. training may be based on clinical (therapeutic) work and examinations rather than a dissertation. It is important to note, however, that psychologists with Psy.D. degrees are not the only ones who work in professional practice. Many psychologists who earn a Ph.D. in clinical or counseling psychology conduct research and work in professional settings. If you pursue clinical and counseling psychology programs, you should expect at least a one-year internship in addition to the regular course work, clinical practice, and research.

FIGURE A.2 lists by subfield the Ph.D.s earned in the United States in a recent year. Clinical psychology is the most popular specialty area among those with doctorates in psychology. The largest employment growth areas for doctoral graduates have been in the for-profit and self-employment sectors, including health services providers, industrial-organizational psychology, and educational psychology. About one-third of doctoral-level psychologists are employed in academic settings (Fogg et al., 2004).

In 2001, a total of 73 percent of new doctoral respondents and 55 percent of new master's respondents indicated that their primary occupational position was their first choice. Most new graduates with a master's degree or a Ph.D. are fairly satisfied with their current positions overall in terms of salary, benefits, opportunities for personal development, supervisors, colleagues, and working conditions (Kohout & Wicherski, 2004; Singleton et al., 2003).

▶‖ Subfields of Psychology

If you are like most psychology students, you may be unaware of the wide variety of specialties and work settings available in psychology (Terre & Stoddart, 2000). To date, the American Psychological Association (APA) has formed 56 divisions (**TABLE A.2** on page A-6). The following paragraphs (arranged alphabetically) describe some careers in the main specialty areas of psychology, most of which require a graduate degree in psychology.

Prescription privileges Many psychologists would like the opportunity to prescribe medicines (normally reserved for *physicians* only) in order to expand the scope of clinical practice and to meet the need for psychiatric services in many parts of the United States. Psychologists in the U.S. military and in the states of New Mexico and Louisiana currently have prescription privileges.

Tom Stewart/Corbis

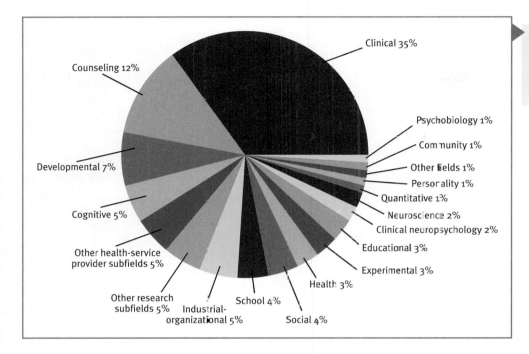

FIGURE A.2 **U.S. Ph.D.s by subfield, 2001** *Source:* National Science Foundation 2001 Survey of Doctorate Recipients. Compiled by the American Psychological Association.

Clinical psychologists promote psychological health in individuals, groups, and organizations. Some clinical psychologists specialize in specific psychological disorders. Others treat a range of disorders, from adjustment difficulties to severe psychopathology. Clinical psychologists might engage in research, teaching, assessment, and consultation. Some hold workshops and lectures on psychological issues for other professionals or for the public. Clinical psychologists work in a variety of settings, including private practice, mental health service organizations, schools, universities, industries, legal systems, medical systems, counseling centers, government agencies, and military services.

To become a clinical psychologist, you will need to earn a doctorate from a clinical psychology program. The APA sets the standards for clinical psychology graduate programs, offering accreditation (official recognition) to those who meet their standards. In all U.S. states, clinical psychologists working in independent practice must obtain a license to offer services such as therapy and testing.

Cognitive psychologists study thought processes and focus on such topics as perception, language, attention, problem solving, memory, judgment and decision making, forgetting, and intelligence. Recent areas of research interest include designing computer-based models of thought processes and identifying biological correlates of cognition. As a cognitive psychologist, you might work as a professor, industrial consultant, or human factors specialist in an educational or business setting.

Community psychologists move beyond focusing on specific individuals or families and deal with broad problems of mental health in community settings. These psychologists believe that human behavior is powerfully influenced by the interaction between people and their physical, social, political, and economic environments. They seek to improve individual functioning by enhancing environmental settings to promote psychological health. Community psychologists focus on prevention, promotion of positive mental health,

Cognitive consulting Cognitive psychologists may advise businesses on how to operate more effectively by understanding the human factors involved.

Karen Moskowitz/Getty Images

TABLE A.2 APA Divisions by Number and Name

1. Society for General Psychology
2. Society for the Teaching of Psychology
3. Experimental Psychology
4. There is no Division 4.
5. Evaluation, Measurement, and Statistics
6. Behavioral Neuroscience and Comparative Psychology
7. Developmental Psychology
8. Society for Personality and Social Psychology
9. Society for the Psychological Study of Social Issues (SPSSI)
10. Society for the Psychology of Aesthetics, Creativity, and the Arts
11. There is no Division 11.
12. Society of Clinical Psychology
13. Society of Consulting Psychology
14. Society for Industrial and Organizational Psychology
15. Educational Psychology
16. School Psychology
17. Society of Counseling Psychology
18. Psychologists in Public Service
19. Society for Military Psychology
20. Adult Development and Aging
21. Applied Experimental and Engineering Psychology
22. Rehabilitation Psychology
23. Society for Consumer Psychology
24. Society for Theoretical and Philosophical Psychology
25. Behavior Analysis
26. Society for the History of Psychology
27. Society for Community Research and Action: Division of Community Psychology
28. Psychopharmacology and Substance Abuse
29. Psychotherapy
30. Society of Psychological Hypnosis
31. State, Provincial, and Territorial Psychological Association Affairs
32. Society for Humanistic Psychology
33. Intellectual and Developmental Disabilities
34. Population and Environmental Psychology
35. Society for the Psychology of Women
36. Psychology of Religion
37. Society for Child and Family Policy and Practice
38. Health Psychology
39. Psychoanalysis
40. Clinical Neuropsychology
41. American Psychology-Law Society
42. Psychologists in Independent Practice
43. Society for Family Psychology
44. Society for the Psychological Study of Lesbian, Gay, and Bisexual Issues
45. Society for the Psychological Study of Ethnic Minority Issues
46. Media Psychology
47. Exercise and Sport Psychology
48. Society for the Study of Peace, Conflict, and Violence: Peace Psychology Division
49. Group Psychology and Group Psychotherapy
50. Addictions
51. Society for the Psychological Study of Men and Masculinity
52. International Psychology
53. Society of Clinical Child and Adolescent Psychology
54. Society of Pediatric Psychology
55. American Society for the Advancement of Pharmacotherapy
56. Trauma Psychology

Source: American Psychological Association.

and crisis intervention, with special attention to the problems of underserved groups and ethnic minorities. Given the shared emphasis on prevention, some community psychologists collaborate with professionals in other areas, such as public health. As a community psychologist, your work settings could include federal, state, and local departments of mental health, corrections, and welfare systems. You might conduct research or help evaluate research in health service settings, serve as an independent consultant for a private or government agency, or teach and consult as a college or university faculty member.

Counseling psychologists help people adjust to life transitions or make life-style changes. This field is very similar to clinical psychology, except that counseling psychologists typically help people with adjustment problems rather than severe psychopathology. Like clinical psychologists, counseling psychologists conduct therapy and provide assessments to individuals and groups. As a counseling psychologist, you would emphasize your clients' strengths, helping clients cope during a transitional time using their own skills, interests, and abilities. You might find yourself working in an academic setting as a faculty member or administrator or in a university counseling center, community mental health center, business, or private practice. As with clinical psychology, if you plan to work in independent practice you will need to obtain a state license to provide counseling services to the public.

Developmental psychologists conduct research in age-related behavioral changes and apply their scientific knowledge to educational, child care, policy, and related settings. As a developmental psychologist, you would in-

Coping with disaster After Peru's deadly August 2007 earthquake, this community psychologist working with Médecins Sans Frontières (Doctors Without Borders) helped survivors cope with the loss of their homes, and the deaths of family members and friends for many.

vestigate change across a broad range of topics, including the biological, social, psychological, and cognitive aspects of development. Developmental psychology informs a number of applied fields, including educational psychology, school psychology, child psychopathology, and gerontology. The field also informs public policy in areas such as education and child-care reform, maternal and child health, and attachment and adoption. You would probably specialize in behavior during infancy, childhood, adolescence, or middle or late adulthood. Your work setting could be an educational institution, day-care center, youth group program, or senior center.

Educational psychologists study the relationship between learning and our physical and social environments. They study the psychological processes involved in learning and develop strategies for enhancing the learning process. As an educational psychologist, you might work in a university—in a psychology department or a school of education. You might conduct basic research on topics related to learning or develop innovative methods of teaching to enhance the learning process. You might design effective tests including measures of aptitude and achievement. You might be employed by a school or government agency or charged with designing and implementing effective employee-training programs in a business setting.

Experimental psychologists are a diverse group of scientists who investigate a variety of basic behavioral processes in research involving humans and other animals. Prominent areas of study in experimental research include comparative methods of science, motivation, learning, thought, attention, memory, perception, and language. Most experimental psychologists identify with a particular subfield, such as cognitive psychology, depending on their area of study. It is also important to note that the experimental method for conducting research studies is not limited to the field of experimental psychology, as many other subfields rely on experimental methodology to conduct studies. As an experimental psychologist, you would most likely work in an academic setting, teaching courses and supervising students' research in addition to conducting your own research using experimental methodology. Or you might be employed by a research institution, zoo, business, industry affiliate, or government agency.

Forensic psychologists apply psychological principles to legal issues. They conduct research on the interface of law and psychology, help to create public policies related to mental health, help law-enforcement agencies in criminal investigations, or assist in forensic consultation involving jury selection and deliberation research. They also provide therapy and assessment to assist the legal community. Some forensic psychologists hold law degrees and provide clients with legal services as well. Although most forensic psychologists are clinical psychologists, they might have expertise in other areas of psychology, such as social or cognitive psychology. As a forensic psychologist,

Criminal profiling On the popular U.S. TV show *Law and Order: Special Victims Unit,* Dr. George Huang (played by B. D. Wong) is an FBI agent and psychiatrist who uses his background in forensic psychology to conduct criminal investigations.

you might work in a university psychology department, law school, research organization, community mental health agency, law-enforcement agency, court, or correctional setting.

Health psychologists are researchers and practitioners concerned with psychology's contribution to promoting health and preventing disease. As applied psychologists or clinicians, they may help individuals lead healthier lives by designing, conducting, and evaluating programs to stop smoking, lose weight, improve sleep, manage pain, treat associated psychosocial problems with chronic and terminal illness, or prevent the spread of sexually transmitted infections. As researchers and clinicians, they identify conditions and practices associated with health and illness to help create effective interventions. In public service, health psychologists study and work to improve government policies and health care systems. As a health psychologist, you could be employed in a hospital, medical school, rehabilitation center, public health agency, college or university, or, if you are also a clinical psychologist, in private practice.

Industrial-organizational (I/O) psychologists study the relationship between people and their working environments. They may develop new ways to increase productivity, improve personnel selection, or promote job satisfaction in a business setting. Their interests include organizational structure and change, consumer behavior, and personnel selection and training. As an I/O psychologist, you might conduct workplace training or provide organizational analysis and development. You may find yourself working in business, industry, the government, or a college or university. Or you may be self-employed as a consultant or work for a management consulting firm.

Neuropsychologists investigate the relationship between neurological processes (structure and function of the brain) and behavior. As a neuropsychologist you might assess, diagnose, or treat disorders related to the central nervous system, such as Alzheimer's disease or stroke. You might also evaluate individuals for evidence of head injuries, learning and developmental disabilities (such as autism), and other psychiatric disorders (including ADHD). If you are a ***clinical neuropsychologist,*** you might work in the neurology, neurosurgery, or psychiatric unit of a hospital. Neuropsychologists also work in academic settings, where they conduct research and teach.

Psychometric and ***quantitative psychologists*** study the methods and techniques used to acquire psychological knowledge. A psychometrician may update existing neurocognitive or personality tests or devise new tests for use in clinical and school settings or in business and industry. These psychologists also administer, score, and interpret such tests. Quantitative psychologists collaborate with researchers to design, analyze, and interpret the results of research programs. As a psychometric or quantitative psychologist, you will need to be well trained in research methods, statistics, and computer technology. You will most likely be employed by a university or college, testing company, private research firm, or government agency.

Rehabilitation psychologists are researchers and practitioners who work with people who have lost optimal functioning after an accident, illness, or other event. As a rehabilitation psychologist, you would probably work in a medical rehabilitation institution or hospital. You might also work in a medical school, university, state or federal vocational rehabilitation agency, or in private practice serving people with physical disabilities.

School psychologists are involved in the assessment of and intervention for children in educational settings. They diagnose and treat cognitive, social, and emotional problems that may negatively influence children's learning or overall functioning at school. As a school psychologist, you would collaborate with teachers, parents, and administrators, making recommendations to improve student learning. You would work in an academic setting, a federal or state government agency, a child guidance center, or a behavioral research laboratory.

Social psychologists are interested in our interactions with others. Social psychologists study how our beliefs, feelings, and behaviors are affected by and influence other people. They study topics such as attitudes, aggression, prejudice, interpersonal attraction, group behavior, and leadership. As a social psychologist, you would probably be a college or university faculty member. You might also work in organizational consultation, marketing research, or other applied psychology fields including social neuroscience. Some social psychologists work for hospitals, federal agencies, or businesses performing applied research.

As a **sport psychologist,** you would study the psychological factors that influence, and are influenced by, participation in sports and other physical activities. Professional activities of sports psychologists include coach education and athlete preparation, as well as research and teaching. Sports psychologists who also have a clinical or counseling degree can apply those skills to working with individuals with psychological problems such as anxiety or substance-abuse problems that might interfere with optimal performance. If you were not working in an academic or research setting, you would most likely work as part of a team or organization or in a private capacity.

▶‖ Preparing Early for Graduate Study in Psychology

Competition for the openings for advanced degrees in psychology is keen. If you choose to go to graduate school, there are a number of things you can do now to maximize your chances of gaining admission to the school of your choice.

If possible, begin preparing during your first year on campus to maximize opportunities and obtain the experience needed to gain admission to a competitive program. Kristy Arnold and Kelly Horrigan (2002) offer a number of suggestions to facilitate this process.

1. *Network.* Get to know faculty members and the psychology department by attending activities and meetings. This will be especially helpful when you apply to graduate school or for a professional position, because many applications require two to three letters of reference. Become involved in psychology clubs and in Psi Chi, the national honor society in psychology. These meetings connect students with similar interests and expose them to a broader study of the field.

2. *Become actively involved in research as early as possible.* Start by doing simple tasks such as data entry and data collection, and over time you will be prepared to conduct your own research project under the supervision of a research mentor. Consider applying for summer research positions through your university or from other organizations such as the American Psychological Association Summer Science Institute (SSI) or the National Science Foundation Research Experiences for Undergraduates (REU) Program to test your interest in academic careers and to build your skills for future study in psychology.

3. *Volunteer or get a job in a psychology-related field.* Getting involved will show your willingness to apply psychological concepts to real-world settings. Further, it will showcase your ability to juggle a number of tasks successfully, such as work and school—an important skill for graduate school success.

4. *Maintain good grades.* Demonstrate the ability to do well in graduate school with successful completion of challenging courses, especially those related to your interests. (See page 12 and pages 365–366 for tips on how to do well in this and other courses, and how to improve your retention of the information you are learning.)

Membership benefits Members of the Psi Chi Honor Society, such as those meeting here, enjoy educational and professional benefits. They may attend special Psi Chi sessions at psychological conventions, apply for research grants in psychology or other academic awards, and read about research advances in the society's journal *Eye on Psi Chi.* (See www.psichi.org for more information.)

Stephen Simpson/Getty Images

In your junior year, you should begin studying for the Graduate Record Exam (GRE), the standardized test that applicants to graduate school must complete. Many graduate programs in psychology require both the General GRE and the Psychology subject tests. If you start preparing early, you will be ready for success in your graduate school application and study.

* * *

So, the next time someone asks you what you will do with your psychology degree, tell them you have a lot of options. You might use your acquired skills and understanding to get a job and succeed in any number of fields, or you might pursue graduate school and then career opportunities in associated professions. In any case, what you have learned about behavior and mental processes will surely enrich your life (Hammer, 2003).

▶‖ For More Information

www.apa.org (Web site for the American Psychological Association)

Actkinson, T. R. (2000). Master's and myth. *Eye on Psi Chi, 4,* 19–25.

American Psychological Association (2003). *Careers for the twenty-first century.* Washington, DC: Author.

American Psychological Association (2005). *Graduate study in psychology.* Washington, DC: Author.

Appleby, D. C. (2002). *The savvy psychology major.* Dubuque, IA: Kendall/Hunt.

Appleby, D. C. (2006). Occupations of interest to psychology majors from the Dictionary of Occupational Titles. *Eye on Psi Chi, 10,* 28–29.

Arnold, K., & Horrigan, K. (2002). Gaining admission into the graduate program of your choice. *Eye on Psi Chi, 7, 1,* 30–33.

Aubrecht, L. (2001). What can you do with a BA in psychology? *Eye on Psi Chi, 5,* 29–31.

Cannon, J. (2005). Career planning and opportunities: The bachelor's degree in psychology, *Eye on Psi Chi, 9,* 26–28.

Huss, M. (1996). Secrets to standing out from the pile: Getting into graduate school. *Psi Chi Newsletter,* 6–7.

Koch, G. (2001). Utilizing Psi Chi's programs to maximize learning and success. *Eye on Psi Chi, 10,* 22.

Kracen, A. C., & Wallace, I. J. (Eds.) (2008). *Applying to graduate school in psychology: Advice from successful students and prominent psychologists.* Washington, DC: American Psychological Association.

Lammers, B. (2000). Quick tips for applying to graduate school in psychology. *Eye on Psi Chi, 4,* 40–42.

Landrum, E. (2001). I'm getting my bachelor's degree in psychology. What can I do with it? *Eye on Psi Chi, 6,* 22–24.

LaRoche, K. (2004). Advantages of undergraduate research: A student's perspective. *Eye on Psi Chi, 8,* 20–21.

Morgan, B., & Korschgen, A. (2001). Psychology career exploration made easy. *Eye on Psi Chi, 5,* 35–36.

Schultheiss, D. E. P. (2008). *Psychology as a major: Is it right for me and what can I do with my degree?* Washington, DC: American Psychological Association.

Sternberg, R. (Ed.) (2002). *Career paths in psychology: Where your degree can take you.* Washington, DC: American Psychological Association.

Answers to Test Yourself Questions

MODULE 1 The Story of Psychology

1. What event defined the founding of scientific psychology?

ANSWER: The founding of scientific psychology is often attributed to Wilhelm Wundt's opening of the University of Leipzig psychology laboratory in 1879. The new science of psychology was soon organized into different schools of thought, including structuralism (founded by Edward Bradford Titchener, using introspection to explore the elemental structure of the human mind) and functionalism (founded by William James, focusing on how mental and behavioral processes enable organisms to adapt, survive, and flourish). James also wrote an important psychology textbook, completed in 1890.

2. What are psychology's major levels of analysis?

ANSWER: Psychology's three major levels of analysis are the biological, psychological, and social-cultural. The complementary insights of psychologists studying behavior and mental processes from the neuroscience, evolutionary, behavior genetics, psychodynamic, behavioral, cognitive, and social-cultural perspectives offer a richer understanding than could usually be gained from any one viewpoint alone.

MODULE 2 Thinking Critically With Psychological Science

1. What is the scientific attitude, and why is it important for critical thinking?

ANSWER: The scientific attitude combines *skeptical* testing of various claims and ideas with *humility* about one's own unexamined presumptions. Examining assumptions, searching for hidden values, evaluating evidence, and assessing conclusions are essential parts of critical thinking.

2. How are human and animal research subjects protected?

ANSWER: Animal protection legislation, laboratory regulation and inspection, and local ethics committees serve to protect human and animal welfare.

MODULE 3 Research Strategies: How Psychologists Ask and Answer Questions

1. Why, when testing a new drug to control blood pressure, would we learn more about its effectiveness from giving it to half the participants in a group of 1000 than to all 1000 participants?

ANSWER: To determine whether this drug is medically effective—not just serving as a placebo—we must compare its effect on those randomly assigned to receive it (the experimental group) with those who receive a placebo (the control group). The only difference between the groups is whether they receive the actual drug. So, if blood pressure is lower in the experimental group, then we know that the drug itself has produced this effect, not just the participants' knowledge that they are being treated (placebo effect).

2. **Consider a question posed by Christopher Jepson, David Krantz, and Richard Nisbett (1983) to University of Michigan introductory psychology students:**
   The registrar's office at the University of Michigan has found that usually about 100 students in Arts and Sciences have perfect marks at the end of their first term at the University. However, only about 10 to 15 students graduate with perfect marks. What do you think is the most likely explanation for the fact that there are more perfect marks after one term than at graduation?
   ANSWER: Most students in the study came up with plausible causes for the drop in marks, such as, "Students tend to work harder at the beginning of their college careers than toward the end." Fewer than a third recognized the statistical phenomenon clearly at work: Averages based on fewer courses are more variable, which guarantees a greater number of extremely low and high marks at the end of the first term.

MODULE 4 Neural and Hormonal Systems

1. **How do neurons communicate with one another?**
   ANSWER: A neuron fires when excitatory inputs exceed inhibitory inputs by a sufficient threshold. When the resulting impulse reaches the axon's end, it triggers the release of chemical neurotransmitters. After crossing a tiny gap, these molecules activate receptor sites on neighboring neurons. So, the brief answer to how neurons communicate with one another is *chemically.*

2. **How does information flow through your nervous system as you pick up a fork? Can you summarize this process?**
   ANSWER: Your central nervous system's hungry brain activates and guides the muscles of your arm and hand via your peripheral nervous system's motor neurons. As you pick up the fork, your brain processes the information from your sensory nervous system, enabling it to continue to guide the fork to your mouth. The functional circle starts with sensory input, continues with interneuron processing by the central nervous system, and finishes with motor output.

3. **Why is the pituitary gland called the "master gland"?**
   ANSWER: The pituitary gland, responding to signals from the hypothalamus, releases hormones that act as triggers. In response, other endocrine glands release their own hormones, which in turn influence brain and behavior.

MODULE 5 Tools of Discovery and Older Brain Structures

1. **Within what brain region would damage be most likely to disrupt your ability to skip rope? Your ability to sense tastes or sounds? In what brain region would damage perhaps leave you in a coma? Without the very breath and heartbeat of life?**
   ANSWER: These regions are, respectively, the *cerebellum,* the *thalamus,* the *reticular formation,* and the *medulla.* These questions assess your understanding of the essential functions of the lower-level brain areas.

MODULE 6 The Cerebral Cortex and Our Divided Brain

1. **What has split-brain research taught us about the intact brain?**
   ANSWER: Split-brain research has verified that the right and left hemispheres have separate functions (with the left being more verbal and the right excelling in visual perception and the recognition of emotion). Messages from each hemisphere are carried through the corpus callosum, but this communication is not possible in people who have had split-brain surgery.

2. **What is the role of the corpus callosum in our brain?**

ANSWER: The corpus callosum acts as a bridge connecting the right and left hemispheres. Messages from each hemisphere are carried through the corpus callosum. This communication is not possible in people who have had split-brain surgery.

MODULE 7 The Brain and Consciousness

1. **What are the mind's two tracks, as revealed by studies of "dual processing"?**

ANSWER: The human brain has separate conscious and unconscious tracks that process information simultaneously. In vision, for example, the visual action track guides our conscious visual processing, while the visual perception track operates unconsciously, enabling our quick recognition of objects.

MODULE 8 Sleep and Dreams

1. **Are you getting enough sleep? What might you ask yourself to answer this question?**

ANSWER: You could start with the true/false questions in James Maas' sleep deprivation quiz in Table 8.1. Also, William Dement (1999, p. 73) has suggested considering these questions: "How often do you think about taking a quick snooze? How often do you rub your eyes and yawn during the day? How often do you feel like you really need some coffee?" Dement concluded that "each of these is a warning of a sleep debt that you ignore at your peril."

MODULE 9 Hypnosis

1. **When is the use of hypnosis potentially harmful, and when can hypnosis be used to help?**

ANSWER: Hypnosis is potentially harmful when therapists, seeking to "hypnotically refresh" memories, plant false memories. But posthypnotic suggestions have helped alleviate some ailments, and hypnosis can also help control pain.

MODULE 10 Drugs and Consciousness

1. **In what ways are near-death experiences similar to drug-induced hallucinations?**

ANSWER: Reports of near-death experiences and drug-induced hallucinations feature similar experiences: replay of old memories, out-of-body sensations, and visions of tunnels or funnels of bright light or beings of light.

2. **A U.S. government survey of 27,616 current or former alcohol drinkers found that 40 percent of those who began drinking before age 15 grew dependent on alcohol. The same was true of only 10 percent of those who first imbibed at ages 21 or 22 (Grant & Dawson, 1998). What possible explanations might there be for this correlation between early use and later abuse?**

ANSWER: Possible explanations include (1) a biological predisposition to both early use and later abuse, (2) brain changes and taste preferences induced by early use, and (3) enduring habits, attitudes, activities, and/or peer relationships that are conducive to alcohol use.

MODULE 11 Behavior Genetics and Evolutionary Psychology

1. **What is *heritability*?**

ANSWER: *Heritability* is the proportion of variation among individuals that we can attribute to genes. *Note:* Heritability is *not* the extent to which an *individual's* traits are genetically determined. Rather, it is the extent to which variation *among* individuals is due to their differing genes. For any trait, heritability can vary, depending on the population and range of environments studied.

2. **What are the three main criticisms of the evolutionary explanation of human sexuality?**

ANSWER: Critics of the evolutionary explanation of human sexuality point out that (1) it starts with an effect and works backward to propose an explanation; (2) unethical and immoral men could use such explanations to rationalize their behavior toward women; and (3) this explanation overlooks the effects of cultural expectations and socialization.

MODULE 12 Environmental Influences on Behavior

1. **To predict whether a teenager smokes, ask how many of the teen's friends smoke. One explanation for this correlation is peer influence. What's another?**

ANSWER: There may also be a *selection effect*. Adolescents tend to sort themselves into likeminded groups—the jocks, the geeks, the druggies, and so forth. Those who smoke may similarly seek out other teenagers who also smoke.

2. **How do individualist and collectivist cultures differ?**

ANSWER: A culture that favors individualism gives priority to personal goals over group goals; people in that culture will tend to define their identity in terms of their own personal attributes. A culture that favors collectivism gives priority to group goals over individual goals; people in collectivist cultures tend to define their identity in terms of group identifications. Cultures vary in the extent to which they favor individualism or collectivism.

3. **What are gender roles, and what do their variations tell us about our human capacity for learning and adaptation?**

ANSWER: *Gender roles* are social rules or norms for accepted and expected behavior for females and males. The norms associated with various roles, including gender roles, vary widely in different cultural contexts, which is proof that we are very capable of learning and adapting to the social demands of different environments.

4. **How does the biopsychosocial approach explain our individual development?**

ANSWER: The biopsychosocial approach considers all the factors that influence our individual development: biological factors (including evolution, genes, hormones, and brains), psychological factors (including our experiences, beliefs, feelings, and expectations), and social-cultural factors (including parental and peer influences, cultural individualism or collectivism, and gender norms).

MODULE 13 Prenatal Development and the Newborn

1. **Your friend—a regular drinker—hopes to become pregnant soon and has stopped drinking. Why is this a good idea? What negative effects might alcohol consumed during pregnancy have on a developing child?**

ANSWER: There is no known safe amount of alcohol during pregnancy, so your friend is wise to quit drinking before becoming pregnant. Harmful effects may occur even before a woman knows she is pregnant. If a woman drinks persistently and heavily during her pregnancy, the fetus may be at risk for physical or cognitive impairments (such as fetal alcohol syndrome).

MODULE 14 Infancy and Childhood

1. **Use Piaget's first three stages of cognitive development to explain why young children are not just miniature adults in the way they think.**

ANSWER: Infants in the *sensorimotor stage* tend to be focused only on their own perceptions of the world and may, for example, be unaware that objects continue to exist when unseen. A *preoperational* child is still egocentric and incapable of appreciating simple logic, such as the reversibility of operations. A preteen in the *concrete operational stage* is beginning to think logically about concrete events but not about abstract concepts.

MODULE 15 Adolescence

1. **How has the transition from childhood to adulthood changed in Western cultures in the last century or so?**

   ANSWER: In little more than a century, the gap between puberty and adult independence has widened from about 7 years to about 12 years. This tendency, known as emerging adulthood, may be limited to Western industrialized nations.

MODULE 16 Adulthood, and Reflections on Developmental Issues

1. **Research has shown that living together before marriage predicts an increased likelihood of future divorce. Can you imagine two possible explanations for this correlation?**

   ANSWER: William Axinn and Arland Thornton (1992) have reported data supporting two explanations. (1) The first explanation is an example of a *selection effect*—our tendency to seek out others who are similar to us. Cohabitation attracts people who are more open to terminating unsatisfying relationships. People who cohabit bring a more individualistic ethic to marriage, are more likely to see close relationships as temporary and fragile, are more accepting of divorce, and are about three times more likely after marriage to have an affair (Forste & Tanfer, 1996). (2) Axinn and Thornton's second explanation illustrates the *causal effect* of the experience of cohabitation. Over time, those who cohabit tend to become more approving of dissolving an unfulfilling union. This divorce-accepting attitude increases the odds of later divorce.

2. **What findings in psychology support the concept of stages in development and the idea of stability in personality across the life span? What findings challenge these ideas?**

   ANSWER: Stage theory is supported by the work of Piaget (cognitive development), Kohlberg (moral development), and Erikson (psychosocial development), but it is challenged by findings that change is more gradual and less culturally universal than these theorists supposed. Some traits, such as temperament, do exhibit remarkable stability across many years. But we do change in other ways, such as in our social attitudes, especially during life's early years.

MODULE 17 Introduction to Sensation and Perception

1. **What is the rough distinction between sensation and perception?**

   ANSWER: *Sensation* is the bottom-up process by which the physical sensory system receives and represents stimuli. *Perception* is the top-down mental process of organizing and interpreting sensory input. But in our everyday experiences, sensation and perception are different aspects of one continuous process.

MODULE 18 Vision

1. **What is the rapid sequence of events that occurs when you see and recognize someone you know?**

   ANSWER: Light waves reflect off the person and travel into your eye, where the rods and cones convert the light waves' energy into neural impulses sent to your brain. Your brain then processes the subdimensions of this visual input—including color, depth, movement, and form—separately but simultaneously, and integrates this information (along with previously stored information) into a conscious perception of the person you know.

MODULE 19 Hearing

1. **What are the basic steps in transforming sound waves into perceived sound?**
   ANSWER: A simple figure offers a synopsis:

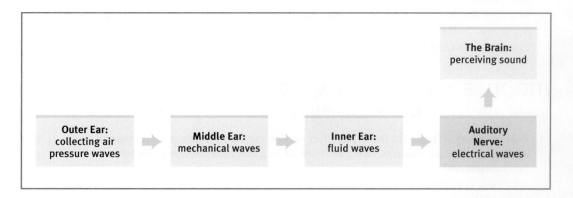

> **The Brain:** perceiving sound
>
> **Outer Ear:** collecting air pressure waves → **Middle Ear:** mechanical waves → **Inner Ear:** fluid waves → **Auditory Nerve:** electrical waves

MODULE 20 Other Senses

1. **What are the similarities among our senses of touch (including the vestibular sense and kinesthesis), taste, and smell? What are the differences?**
   ANSWER: Our senses of touch, taste, and smell all involve processing sensory input into information that our brains can interpret. These processes are influenced by both biological and psychological factors—the physiological input and our brain's interpretation of that input. Touch, taste, and smell are also all subject to sensory interaction: smell affects taste, and sight affects what we hear and what we feel (for example, the experience of pain can be diverted by distracting visuals). These three senses differ from each other as well. Touch involves several basic senses—pressure, warmth, cold, and pain. Taste involves five basic sensations—sweet, sour, salty, bitter, and umami. But there are no basic sensations for smell.

MODULE 21 Perceptual Organization

1. **What do we mean when we say that, in perception, the whole is greater than the sum of its parts?**
   ANSWER: Gestalt psychologists used this saying to describe our perceptual tendency to organize clusters of sensations into meaningful forms or coherent groups.

MODULE 22 Perceptual Interpretation

1. **What type of evidence shows that, indeed, "there is more to perception than meets the senses"?**
   ANSWER: We construct our perceptions based on both sensory input and—experiments show—on our assumptions, expectations, schemas, and perceptual sets, often influenced by the surrounding context.

2. **In the sports channel cartoon at left, what psychic ability is being claimed?**
   ANSWER: The psychic sports channel claims precognition—the ability to foresee future events.

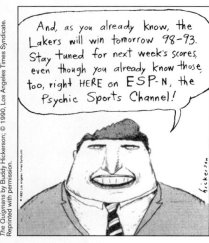

MODULE 23 Classical Conditioning

1. **As we develop, we learn cues that lead us to expect and prepare for good and bad events. We learn to repeat behaviors that bring rewards. And we watch others and learn. What do psychologists call these three types of learning?**

   ANSWER: Through *classical conditioning*, we learn cues that lead us to expect and prepare for good and bad events. Through *operant conditioning*, we learn to repeat behaviors that bring rewards. Through *observational learning*, we watch others and learn.

2. **In slasher movies, sexually arousing images of women are sometimes paired with violence against women. Based on classical conditioning principles, what might be an effect of this pairing?**

   ANSWER: If viewing an attractive nude or semi-nude woman (a US) elicits sexual arousal (a UR), then pairing the US with a new stimulus (violence) could turn the violence into a conditioned stimulus (CS) that also becomes sexually arousing, a conditioned response (CR).

MODULE 24 Operant Conditioning

1. *Positive reinforcement, negative reinforcement, positive punishment,* and *negative punishment* **are tricky concepts for many students. Can you fit the right term in the three boxes in this table? (I've done the first one—positive reinforcement—for you.)**

   ANSWER:

Type of Stimulus	Give It	Take It Away
Desired (for example, a compliment)	*Positive reinforcement*	*Negative punishment*
Undesired/aversive (for example, an insult)	*Positive punishment*	*Negative reinforcement*

MODULE 25 Learning by Observation

1. **Jason's parents and older friends all smoke, but they advise him not to. Juan's parents and friends don't smoke, but they say nothing to deter him from doing so. Will Jason or Juan be more likely to start smoking?**

   ANSWER: Although both saying and doing can influence people, experiments suggest that children more often do as others do and say as they say. Generalizing this finding to smoking, we can expect that Jason will be more likely to start smoking.

MODULE 26 Introduction to Memory

1. **Memory includes (in alphabetical order) long-term memory, sensory memory, and working/short-term memory. What's the correct order of these three memory stages?**

   ANSWER: Sensory memory, working (short-term) memory, long-term memory.

MODULE 27 Encoding: Getting Information In

1. **What would be the most effective strategy to learn and retain a list of names of key historical figures for a week? For a year?**

   ANSWER: For a week: Make the names personally meaningful. For a year: Overlearn the list and space out rehearsals over the course of several weeks.

MODULE 28 Storage: Retaining Information

1. **Your friend tells you that her father experienced brain damage in an accident. She wonders if psychology can explain why he can still play checkers very well but has a hard time holding a sensible conversation. What can you tell her?**
   ANSWER: Our *explicit* (declarable) memories differ from our *implicit* memories of skills and procedures, such as playing checkers. Our implicit memories are processed by more ancient brain areas, which apparently escaped damage during the accident.

MODULE 29 Retrieval: Getting Information Out

1. **You have just watched a movie that includes a chocolate factory. After the chocolate factory is out of mind, you nevertheless feel a strange urge for a chocolate bar. How do you explain this in terms of priming?**
   ANSWER: *Priming* is the activation (often without our awareness) of associations. Seeing a chocolate factory in a movie, for example, might temporarily predispose you to crave a chocolate treat. Although you might not consciously remember the chocolate factory, it may prime how you interpret or recall events.

MODULE 30 Forgetting, Memory Construction, and Improving Memory

1. **Can you offer an example of proactive interference?**
   ANSWER: Proactive (forward-acting) interference occurs when earlier learning disrupts your recall of a later experience. Proactive interference has occurred if learning names of new classmates in your first class makes it more difficult to learn the new names in your second class.

2. **Source amnesia occurs when we attribute to the wrong source an event we have experienced, heard about, read about, or imagined. What might life be like if we remembered all our waking experiences as well as all our dreams?**
   ANSWER: Real experiences would be confused with those we dreamed. When meeting someone, we might therefore be unsure whether we were reacting to something they previously did or to something we dreamed they did. William Dement (1999, p. 298) thinks this "would put a great burden on your sanity. . . . I truly believe that the wall of memory is a blessed protection."

3. **What are the recommended memory strategies you just read about? (One advised rehearsing to-be-remembered material. What were the others?)**
   ANSWER: Study repeatedly to boost long-term recall. Spend more time rehearsing or actively thinking about the material. Make the material personally meaningful. To remember a list of unfamiliar items, use mnemonic devices. Refresh your memory by activating retrieval cues. Recall events while they are fresh, before you encounter possible misinformation. Minimize interference. Test your own knowledge, both to rehearse it and to help determine what you do not yet know.

MODULE 31 Thinking

1. **The availability heuristic is a quick-and-easy but sometimes misleading guide to judging reality. What is the availability heuristic?**
   ANSWER: The *availability heuristic* is our tendency to judge the likeliness of an event by how easily we can recall instances of it. Like all heuristics, this guide is efficient. But it can mislead, as it does when we attempt to judge various risks (for example, of plane travel).

MODULE 32 Language and Thought

1. **If children are not yet speaking, is there any reason to think they would benefit from parents and other caregivers reading to them?**

   ANSWER: Indeed there is, because well before age one children are learning to detect words among the stream of spoken sounds and to discern grammatical rules. Before age one, they also are babbling with the phonemes of their own language. More than many parents realize, their infants are soaking up language. As researcher Peter Jusczyk reminds us, "Little ears are listening."

2. **To say that "words are the mother of ideas" assumes the truth of what concept?**

   ANSWER: This phrase supports the linguistic determinism hypothesis, which asserts that language determines thought. Research indicates that this position is too extreme, but language does *influence* what we perceive and think.

3. **If your dog barks at a stranger at the front door, does this qualify as language? What if the dog yips in a telltale way to let you know she needs to go out?**

   ANSWER: These are definitely communications. But if language consists of words and the grammatical rules we use to combine them to communicate meaning, few scientists would label a dog's barking and yipping as language.

MODULE 33 Introduction to Intelligence

1. **Joseph, a Harvard Law School student, has a straight-A average, writes for the *Harvard Law Review*, and will clerk for a Supreme Court justice next year. His grandmother, Judith, is very proud of him, saying that he is way more intelligent than she ever was. But Joseph is also very proud of Judith: As a young woman, she was imprisoned by the Nazis. When the war ended, she walked out of Germany, contacted an agency helping refugees, and began a new life in the United States as an assistant chef in her cousin's restaurant. According to the definition of *intelligence* in this module, is Joseph the only intelligent person in this story? Why or why not?**

   ANSWER: Joseph is not the only intelligent person in this story. Intelligence is the ability to learn, solve problems, and adapt to new situations. Judith certainly fits this description, given all that she has accomplished.

MODULE 34 Assessing Intelligence

1. **What was the purpose of Binet's pioneering intelligence test?**

   ANSWER: Binet's original test and those built upon it were designed to predict school achievement.

2. **The Smiths have enrolled their 2-year-old son in a special program that promises to assess his IQ and, if he places in the top 5 percent of test-takers, to create a plan that will guarantee his admission to a top university at age 18. Why is this endeavor of questionable value?**

   ANSWER: This is a waste of money at best. First, IQ tests given before age 3 are only modestly reliable predictors of adult intelligence. Second, admission to a top university depends on more than simple IQ. Third, there are no known training programs that could guarantee this result. The Smiths would do better to read to their child, which predicts early reading and love of reading.

MODULE 35 Genetic and Environmental Influences on Intelligence

1. **As society succeeds in creating equality of opportunity, it will also increase the heritability of ability. The heritability of intelligence scores will be greater in a**

society marked by equal opportunity than in a society of peasants and aristocrats. Why?

ANSWER: Perfect environmental equality would create 100 percent heritability—because genes alone would account for any remaining human differences.

MODULE 36 Introduction to Motivation

1. While on a long road trip, you suddenly feel very hungry. You see a diner that looks pretty deserted and creepy, but you are *really* hungry, so you stop anyway. What motivational perspective would most easily explain this behavior, and why?

ANSWER: *Drive-reduction theory*—the idea that physical needs create an aroused state that drives us to reduce the need—helps explain your behavior.

MODULE 37 Hunger

1. You are traveling and have not eaten anything in eight hours. As your long-awaited favorite dish is placed in front of you, your mouth waters. Even imagining this may set your mouth to watering. What triggers this anticipatory drooling?

ANSWER: You, like Pavlov's dogs, have learned through *classical conditioning* to respond to the cues—the sight and aroma—that signal the food about to enter your mouth. Both *physiological cues* (eight hours of deprivation have left you with low blood sugar) and *psychological cues* (the anticipation of the tasty meal) have heightened your experienced hunger.

MODULE 38 Sexual Motivation and the Need to Belong

1. What biological and psychological factors influence our sexual motivation and affiliation needs?

ANSWER: The female estrogens and male testosterone hormones biologically influence our sexual motivation and affiliation needs, which are also influenced by our evolutionary history. Societal factors and cultural influence are among the psychological factors, in that they affect what makes a person feel aroused and how a person meets affiliation needs.

MODULE 39 Motivation at Work

1. A human resources director explains to you that "I don't bother with tests or references. I can pick employees by my gut." Based on I/O research, what concerns does this raise?

ANSWER: Personnel interviewers feel very confident in their ability to predict long-term job performance from informal interviews. Unfortunately, this ability goes astray so often that I/O psychologists have labeled the gap between interviewers' intuition and workplace reality the *interviewer illusion*. Four factors contribute: (1) interviews disclose prospective workers' good intentions, not their habitual behaviors; (2) interviewers tend to track the successful careers of those they hire, not the successful careers of those they reject; (3) interviewers presume people are what they seem to be in interviews; and (4) interviewers' preconceptions and moods color how they perceive interviewees' responses.

MODULE 40 Introduction to Emotion

1. Christine is holding her 8-month-old baby when a fierce dog appears out of nowhere and, with teeth bared, leaps for the baby's face. Christine immediately ducks for cover to protect the baby, screams at the dog, then notices that her heart is banging in her chest and she's broken out in a cold sweat. How would the James-Lange, Cannon-Bard, and two-factor theories explain Christine's emotional reaction?

ANSWER: The James-Lange theory would say that Christine's emotional reaction consists of her awareness of her physiological responses to the dog attack. The Cannon-Bard theory would say that her fear experience happened simultaneously with her physiological arousal. Schacter's two-factor theory would presume that her emotional reaction stemmed from her interpreting and labeling the arousal.

2. **How do the two divisions of the autonomic nervous system help us respond to and recover from a crisis, and why is this relevant to the study of emotions?**

   ANSWER: The sympathetic division of the ANS arouses us, pumping out the stress hormones epinephrine and norepinephrine to prepare our body for fight or flight. The parasympathetic division of the ANS takes over when the crisis passes, restoring our body to a calm state.

MODULE 41 Expressed Emotion

1. **Who tends to express more emotion—men or women? How do we know the answer to that question?**

   ANSWER: Women tend to surpass men not only as emotion detectors but also at expressing certain emotions (though men have slightly surpassed women in conveying anger). Researchers discovered this by showing people brief, silent clips of men's and women's faces expressing various emotions and by observing who is most skilled at reading and sending emotions.

MODULE 42 Experienced Emotion

1. **What things do (and do not) predict self-reported happiness?**

   ANSWER: People's age, sex, and income give only modest clues to their happiness. Their personality traits, close relationships, "flow" in work and leisure, and religious faith do provide clues.

MODULE 43 Stress and Health

1. **What are the basic links in our stress response system?**

   ANSWER: When alerted to a threat (to negative, uncontrollable events), our sympathetic nervous system arouses us. Heart rate and respiration increase. Blood is diverted from digestion to the skeletal muscles. The body releases sugar and fat to prepare for fight or flight. Simultaneously, the brain (via the hypothalamus and adjacent pituitary gland) orders the adrenal glands to secrete the stress hormone cortisol. The system is wonderfully adaptive. But if stress is continuous, health consequences and exhaustion may result.

MODULE 44 Promoting Health

1. **How do problem-focused coping and emotion-focused coping differ?**

   ANSWER: Problem-focused coping attempts to alleviate stress directly, by changing the stressor or the way we interact with it. Emotion-focused coping attempts to alleviate stress indirectly, by avoiding or ignoring the stressor and dealing with the emotions generated during our stress reaction.

MODULE 45 The Psychoanalytic Perspective

1. **What, according to Freud, were some of the important defense mechanisms, and what do they defend against?**

   ANSWER: Freud believed repression to be the basic defense mechanism. Others include regression, reaction formation, projection, rationalization, and displacement. All supposedly serve to reduce anxiety. Modern research supports the phenomenon Freud called *projection* and current researchers call the *false consensus effect*. Some evidence also supports self-esteem defenses, such as reaction formation. But there is little support for the others.

2. How does today's psychological science assess Freud's theory?

ANSWER: Current research does not support Freud's view of the unconscious or of repression. It views the unconscious as part of our dual-track mind—the many types and instances of information processing that take place out of our awareness, such as priming, parallel processing of various aspects of vision, etc. Freudian theory does not enable predictions, and it tends to explain things after the fact.

MODULE 46 The Humanistic Perspective

1. What does it mean to be "empathic"? To be "self-actualized"?

ANSWER: To be *empathic* is to share and mirror another person's feelings. Carl Rogers believed that people nurture growth in others by being empathic. Abraham Maslow viewed *self-actualization* as the ultimate psychological need—the motivation to fulfill one's potential.

MODULE 47 Contemporary Research on Personality

1. What is the person-situation controversy?

ANSWER: The person-situation controversy is the question of whether personality traits are consistent over time and across situations. Traits do tend to be consistent, though specific behaviors may vary with time and place.

2. How do learned helplessness and optimism influence behavior?

ANSWER: Learned helplessness produces passive resignation after organisms find themselves unable to avoid aversive events. Concentration camps, prisons, and autocratic companies and countries have all been observed to produce symptoms of learned helplessness. Optimism has the opposite effect, leading to better moods, more persistence, and better health.

3. In a 1997 Gallup poll, White Americans estimated 44 percent of their fellow White Americans to be high in prejudice (scoring them 5 or higher on a 10-point scale). How many rated themselves similarly high in prejudice? Just 14 percent. What phenomenon does this illustrate?

ANSWER: This illustrates the general tendency to see oneself as superior to the average other, which is one example of the *self-serving bias.*

MODULE 48 Introduction to Psychological Disorders

1. What is the biopsychosocial perspective, and why is it important in our understanding of psychological disorders?

ANSWER: This contemporary perspective assumes that biological, psychological, and social-cultural influences combine to produce psychological disorders. Genes matter. The brain matters. Inner thoughts and feelings matter. Social and cultural influences matter. To get the whole integrated picture, a biopsychosocial perspective helps.

2. What is the relationship between poverty and psychological disorders?

ANSWER: Poverty-related stresses can help trigger disorders, but disabling disorders can also contribute to poverty. Thus, poverty and disorder are often a chicken-and-egg situation, and it's hard to know which came first.

MODULE 49 Anxiety Disorders

1. How do generalized anxiety disorder, panic disorder, phobias, obsessive-compulsive disorder, and PTSD differ?

ANSWER: *Generalized anxiety disorder* is unfocused tension, apprehension, and arousal. *Panic disorder* is marked by unpredictable episodes of intense dread accompanied by chest pain, choking, or other frightening sensations. *Phobias* focus anxiety on specific feared objects or situations. *Obsessive-compulsive disorders* express anxiety through unwanted repetitive thoughts (obsessions) or actions (compulsions). In *post-traumatic stress disorder (PTSD)*, anxiety may be accompanied by recurring memories and nightmares, social withdrawal, and insomnia for periods of four or more weeks after a traumatic event.

MODULE 50 Dissociative, Personality, and Somatoform Disorders

1. **The psychoanalytic and learning perspectives agree that DID symptoms are ways of dealing with anxiety. How do their explanations differ?**
ANSWER: The psychoanalytic explanation of DID symptoms is that they are defenses against anxiety generated by unacceptable urges. The learning perspective attempts to explain these symptoms as behaviors that have been reinforced by relieving anxiety in the past. Others attempt to explain DID symptoms as detachment resulting from horrific experiences, such as childhood abuse.

2. **Is antisocial personality disorder an inherited condition?**
ANSWER: *Antisocial personality disorder*—in which a person exhibits a lack of conscience for wrongdoing—seems to have both biological and psychological components. Twin and adoption studies show that biological relatives of people with this disorder are at increased risk for antisocial behavior. But the tendency to be fearless, when combined with a sense of social responsibility, can lead to heroism, adventurism, or athletic success.

3. **What does *somatoform* mean?**
ANSWER: Somatic symptoms are bodily symptoms. A somatoform disorder is one in which people express distress through physical complaints rather than psychological ones.

MODULE 51 Mood Disorders

1. **What does it mean to say that "depression is the common cold of psychological disorders"?**
ANSWER: This expression describes the frequency of depression, but it is not meant to minimize the seriousness of this condition.

MODULE 52 Schizophrenia

1. **What are the two main subtypes of schizophrenia?**
ANSWER: Chronic, or process, schizophrenia is a slow-developing disorder, often accompanied by negative symptoms. Acute, or reactive, schizophrenia is a rapid-onset disorder following specific life stresses. Those with the acute form often have positive symptoms, which are more responsive to drug therapy.

MODULE 53 The Psychological Therapies

1. **What is the major distinction between the underlying assumption in insight therapies and in behavior therapies?**
ANSWER: The insight therapies—psychoanalytic and humanistic therapies—seek to relieve problems by providing an understanding of their origins. Behavior therapies assume the problem behavior *is* the problem and treat it directly, paying less attention to its origins.

MODULE 54 Evaluating Psychotherapies

1. **How does the placebo effect bias clients' appraisals of the effectiveness of psychotherapies?**
ANSWER: The *placebo effect* is the healing power of *belief* in a treatment. Patients who expect a treatment to be effective may believe it was.

2. **What is the difference between preventive mental health and psychological therapy?**

ANSWER: Psychological therapies attempt to relieve people's suffering from psychological disorders. Preventive mental health attempts to prevent suffering by identifying and eliminating the conditions that cause disorders.

MODULE 55 The Biomedical Therapies

1. **How do researchers evaluate the effectiveness of particular drug therapies?**

ANSWER: Ideally, researchers assign people to treatment and no-treatment conditions to see if those who receive therapy improve more than those who don't. In many studies, the no-treatment comparison includes a placebo condition, which allows a double-blind controlled study. If neither the therapist nor the client knows for sure whether the client has received the experimental treatment (for example, a drug), then any difference between the treated and untreated groups will reflect the treatment's actual effect.

MODULE 56 Social Thinking

1. **Driving to school one snowy day, Marco narrowly misses a car that slides through a red light. "Slow down! What a terrible driver," he thinks to himself. Moments later, Marco himself slides through an intersection and yelps, "Wow! These roads are awful. The city plows need to get out here." What social psychology principle has Marco just demonstrated? Explain.**

ANSWER: By attributing the other person's behavior to the person ("he's a terrible driver") and his own to the situation ("these roads are awful"), Marco has exhibited the *fundamental attribution error*.

MODULE 57 Social Influence

1. **You are organizing a Town Hall–style meeting of fiercely competitive political candidates. To add to the fun, friends have suggested handing out masks of the candidates' faces for supporters to wear. What phenomenon might these masks engage?**

ANSWER: The anonymity provided by the masks, combined with the arousal of the contentious setting, might create *deindividuation* (lessened self-awareness and self-restraint).

MODULE 58 Antisocial Relations

1. **Kevin says, "I have no prejudice within me toward anyone. I believe everyone deserves equal opportunity in housing and employment." Even if Kevin indeed expresses no obvious prejudice, what sort of prejudice might nonetheless exist?**

ANSWER: Kevin exhibited no overt, conscious prejudice. He could nevertheless harbor implicit, unconscious prejudice that surfaces in subtle and automatic ways, including assumed racial associations, race-influenced perceptions, and telltale bodily responses to encountering someone of a different race.

MODULE 59 Prosocial Relations

1. **Why didn't anybody help Kitty Genovese? What social relations principle did this incident illustrate?**

ANSWER: The incident illustrated the *bystander effect*. This occurs because, in the presence of others, an individual is less likely to notice a situation, correctly interpret it as an emergency, and then take responsibility for offering help.

Glossary

absolute threshold the minimum stimulation needed to detect a particular stimulus 50 percent of the time. (p. 227)

accommodation adapting our current understandings (schemas) to incorporate new information. (p. 176)

accommodation the process by which the eye's lens changes shape to focus near or far objects on the retina. (p. 234)

achievement motivation a desire for significant accomplishment; for mastery of things, people, or ideas; for rapidly attaining a high standard. (p. 490)

achievement tests a test designed to assess what a person has learned. (p. 418)

acoustic encoding the encoding of sound, especially the sound of words. (p. 331)

acquisition in classical conditioning, the initial stage, when one links a neutral stimulus and an unconditioned stimulus so that the neutral stimulus begins triggering the conditioned response. In operant conditioning, the strengthening of a reinforced response. (p. 292)

action potential a neural impulse; a brief electrical charge that travels down an axon. (p. 47)

active listening empathic listening in which the listener echoes, restates, and clarifies. A feature of Rogers' client-centered therapy. (p. 649)

adaptation-level phenomenon our tendency to form judgments (of sounds, of lights, of income) relative to a neutral level defined by our prior experience. (p. 562)

addiction compulsive drug craving and use, despite adverse consequences. (p. 114)

adolescence the transition period from childhood to adulthood, extending from puberty to independence. (p. 195)

adrenal [ah-DREEN-el] **glands** a pair of endocrine glands that sit just above the kidneys and secrete hormones (epinephrine and norepinephrine) that help arouse the body in times of stress. (p. 56)

aerobic exercise sustained exercise that increases heart and lung fitness; may also reduce stress, depression, and anxiety. (p. 547)

aggression physical or verbal behavior intended to hurt someone. (pp. 158, 710)

algorithm a methodical, logical rule or procedure that guarantees solving a particular problem. Contrasts with the usually speedier—but also more error-prone—use of *heuristics*. (p. 371)

alpha waves the relatively slow brain waves of a relaxed, awake state. (p. 93)

altruism unselfish regard for the welfare of others. (p. 726)

amnesia the loss of memory. (p. 342)

amphetamines drugs that stimulate neural activity, causing speeded-up body functions and associated energy and mood changes. (p. 117)

amygdala [uh-MIG-duh-la] two lima bean–sized neural clusters in the limbic system; linked to emotion. (p. 62)

anorexia nervosa an eating disorder in which a person (usually an adolescent female) diets and becomes significantly (15 percent or more) underweight, yet, still feeling fat, continues to starve. (p. 453)

antianxiety drugs drugs used to control anxiety and agitation. (p. 672)

antidepressant drugs drugs used to treat depression; also increasingly prescribed for anxiety. Different types work by altering the availability of various neurotransmitters. (p. 673)

antipsychotic drugs drugs used to treat schizophrenia and other forms of severe thought disorder. (p. 672)

antisocial personality disorder a personality disorder in which the person (usually a man) exhibits a lack of conscience for wrongdoing, even toward friends and family members. May be aggressive and ruthless or a clever con artist. (p. 620)

anxiety disorders psychological disorders characterized by distressing, persistent anxiety or maladaptive behaviors that reduce anxiety. (p. 610)

aphasia impairment of language, usually caused by left hemisphere damage either to Broca's area (impairing speaking) or to Wernicke's area (impairing understanding). (p. 391)

applied research scientific study that aims to solve practical problems. (p. 10)

aptitude tests a test designed to predict a person's future performance; *aptitude* is the capacity to learn. (p. 418)

assimilation interpreting our new experience in terms of our existing schemas. (p. 177)

association areas areas of the cerebral cortex that are not involved in primary motor or sensory functions; rather, they are involved in higher mental functions such as learning, remembering, thinking, and speaking. (p. 71)

associative learning learning that certain events occur together. The events may be two stimuli (as in classical conditioning) or a response and its consequences (as in operant conditioning). (p. 290)

attachment an emotional tie with another person; shown in young children by their seeking closeness to the caregiver and showing distress on separation. (p. 186)

attention-deficit hyperactivity disorder (ADHD) a psychological disorder marked by the appearance by age 7 of one or more of three key symptoms: extreme inattention, hyperactivity, and impulsivity. (p. 600)

attitude feelings, often influenced by our beliefs, that predispose us to respond in a particular way to objects, people, and events. (p. 684)

attribution theory the theory that we explain someone's behavior by crediting either the situation or the person's disposition. (p. 682)

audition the sense or act of hearing. (p. 243)

autism a disorder that appears in childhood and is marked by deficient communication, social interaction, and understanding of others' states of mind. (p. 182)

automatic processing unconscious encoding of incidental information, such as space, time, and frequency, and of well-learned information, such as word meanings. (p. 327)

autonomic [aw-tuh-NAHM-ik] **nervous system** the part of the peripheral nervous system that controls the glands and the muscles of the internal organs (such as the heart). Its sympathetic division arouses; its parasympathetic division calms. (p. 53)

availability heuristic estimating the likelihood of events based on their availability in memory; if instances come readily to mind (perhaps because of their vividness), we presume such events are common. (p. 375)

aversive conditioning a type of counterconditioning that associates an unpleasant state (such as nausea) with an unwanted behavior (such as drinking alcohol). (p. 653)

axon the extension of a neuron, ending in branching terminal fibers, through which messages pass to other neurons or to muscles or glands. (p. 47)

babbling stage beginning at about 4 months, the stage of speech development in which the infant spontaneously utters various sounds at first unrelated to the household language. (p. 387)

barbiturates drugs that depress the activity of the central nervous system, reducing anxiety but impairing memory and judgment. (p. 117)

basal metabolic rate the body's resting rate of energy expenditure. (p. 451)

basic research pure science that aims to increase the scientific knowledge base. (p. 10)

basic trust according to Erik Erikson, a sense that the world is predictable and trustworthy; said to be formed during infancy by appropriate experiences with responsive caregivers. (p. 189)

behavior genetics the study of the relative power and limits of genetic and environmental influences on behavior. (p. 132)

behavior therapy therapy that applies learning principles to the elimination of unwanted behaviors. (p. 651)

behavioral medicine an interdisciplinary field that integrates behavioral and medical knowledge and applies that knowledge to health and disease. (p. 530)

behaviorism the view that psychology (1) should be an objective science that (2) studies behavior without reference to mental processes. Most research psychologists today agree with (1) but not with (2). (pp. 5, 290)

belief perseverance clinging to one's initial conceptions after the basis on which they were formed has been discredited. (p. 377)

binge-eating disorder significant binge-eating episodes, followed by distress, disgust, or guilt, but without the compensatory purging, fasting, or excessive exercise that marks bulimia nervosa. (p. 454)

binocular cues depth cues, such as retinal disparity, that depend on the use of two eyes. (p. 265)

biofeedback a system for electronically recording, amplifying, and feeding back information regarding a subtle physiological state, such as blood pressure or muscle tension. (p. 549)

biological psychology a branch of psychology concerned with the links between biology and behavior. (Some biological psychologists call themselves *behavioral neuroscientists, neuropsychologists, behavior geneticists, physiological psychologists,* or *biopsychologists.*) (p. 46)

biomedical therapy prescribed medications or medical procedures that act directly on the patient's nervous system. (p. 671)

biopsychosocial approach an integrated approach that incorporates biological, psychological, and social-cultural levels of analysis. (p. 8)

bipolar disorder a mood disorder in which the person alternates between the hopelessness and lethargy of depression and the overexcited state of mania. (Formerly called *manic-depressive disorder.*) (p. 626)

blind spot the point at which the optic nerve leaves the eye, creating a "blind" spot because no receptor cells are located there. (p. 235)

bottom-up processing analysis that begins with the sensory receptors and works up to the brain's integration of sensory information. (p. 226)

brainstem the oldest part and central core of the brain, beginning where the spinal cord swells as it enters the skull; the brainstem is responsible for automatic survival functions. (p. 61)

Broca's area controls language expression—an area, usually in the left frontal lobe, that directs the muscle movements involved in speech. (p. 391)

bulimia nervosa an eating disorder characterized by episodes of overeating, usually of high-calorie foods, followed by vomiting, laxative use, fasting, or excessive exercise. (p. 453)

bystander effect the tendency for any given bystander to be less likely to give aid if other bystanders are present. (p. 728)

Cannon-Bard theory the theory that an emotion-arousing stimulus simultaneously triggers (1) physiological responses and (2) the subjective experience of emotion. (p. 500)

case study an observation technique in which one person is studied in depth in the hope of revealing universal principles. (p. 27)

catharsis emotional release. In psychology, the catharsis hypothesis maintains that "releasing" aggressive energy (through action or fantasy) relieves aggressive urges. (p. 520)

central nervous system (CNS) the brain and spinal cord. (p. 52)

central route to persuasion occurs when interested people focus on the arguments and respond with favorable thoughts. (p. 685)

cerebellum [sehr-uh-BELL-um] the "little brain" at the rear of the brainstem; functions include processing sensory input and coordinating movement output and balance. (p. 62)

cerebral [seh-REE-bruhl] **cortex** the intricate fabric of interconnected neural cells covering the cerebral hemispheres; the body's ultimate control and information-processing center. (p. 67)

change blindness failing to notice changes in the environment. (p. 89)

chromosomes threadlike structures made of DNA molecules that contain the genes. (p. 132)

chunking organizing items into familiar, manageable units; often occurs automatically. (p. 333)

circadian [ser-KAY-dee-an] **rhythm** the biological clock; regular bodily rhythms (for example, of temperature and wakefulness) that occur on a 24-hour cycle. (p. 91)

classical conditioning a type of learning in which one learns to link two or more stimuli and anticipate events. (p. 290)

client-centered therapy a humanistic therapy, developed by Carl Rogers, in which the therapist uses techniques such as active listening within a genuine, accepting, empathic environment to facilitate clients' growth. (Also called *person-centered therapy*.) (p. 649)

clinical psychology a branch of psychology that studies, assesses, and treats people with psychological disorders. (p. 10)

cochlea [KOHK-lee-uh] a coiled, bony, fluid-filled tube in the inner ear through which sound waves trigger nerve impulses. (p. 244)

cochlear implant a device for converting sounds into electrical signals and stimulating the auditory nerve through electrodes threaded into the cochlea. (p. 248)

cognition all the mental activities associated with thinking, knowing, remembering, and communicating. (pp. 176, 370)

cognitive dissonance theory the theory that we act to reduce the discomfort (dissonance) we feel when two of our thoughts (cognitions) are inconsistent. For example, when our awareness of our attitudes and of our actions clash, we can reduce the resulting dissonance by changing our attitudes. (p. 688)

cognitive map a mental representation of the layout of one's environment. For example, after exploring a maze, rats act as if they have learned a cognitive map of it. (p. 308)

cognitive neuroscience the interdisciplinary study of the brain activity linked with cognition (including perception, thinking, memory, and language). (pp. 5, 85)

cognitive therapy therapy that teaches people new, more adaptive ways of thinking and acting; based on the assumption that thoughts intervene between events and our emotional reactions. (p. 654)

cognitive-behavior therapy a popular integrative therapy that combines cognitive therapy (changing self-defeating thinking) with behavior therapy (changing behavior). (p. 656)

collective unconscious Carl Jung's concept of a shared, inherited reservoir of memory traces from our species' history. (p. 563)

collectivism giving priority to goals of one's group (often one's extended family or work group) and defining one's identity accordingly. (p. 154)

color constancy perceiving familiar objects as having consistent color, even if changing illumination alters the wavelengths reflected by the object. (p. 269)

companionate love the deep affectionate attachment we feel for those with whom our lives are intertwined. (p. 724)

complementary and alternative medicine (CAM) as yet unproven health care treatments intended to supplement (complement) or serve as alternatives to conventional medicine, and which typically are not widely taught in medical schools, used in hospitals, or reimbursed by insurance companies. When research shows a therapy to be safe and effective, it usually then becomes part of accepted medical practice. (p. 550)

concept a mental grouping of similar objects, events, ideas, or people. (p. 370)

concrete operational stage in Piaget's theory, the stage of cognitive development (from about 6 or 7 to 11 years of age) during which children gain the mental operations that enable them to think logically about concrete events. (p. 184)

conditioned reinforcer a stimulus that gains its reinforcing power through its association with a primary reinforcer; also known as a *secondary reinforcer*. (p. 304)

conditioned response (CR) in classical conditioning, the learned response to a previously neutral (but now conditioned) stimulus (CS). (p. 291)

conditioned stimulus (CS) in classical conditioning, an originally irrelevant stimulus that, after association with an unconditioned stimulus (US), comes to trigger a conditioned response. (p. 291)

conduction hearing loss hearing loss caused by damage to the mechanical system that conducts sound waves to the cochlea. (p. 247)

cones retinal receptor cells that are concentrated near the center of the retina and that function in daylight or in well-lit conditions. The cones detect fine detail and give rise to color sensations. (p. 235)

confirmation bias a tendency to search for information that supports our preconceptions and to ignore or distort contradictory evidence. (p. 373)

conflict a perceived incompatibility of actions, goals, or ideas. (p. 729)

conformity adjusting one's behavior or thinking to coincide with a group standard. (p. 691)

consciousness our awareness of ourselves and our environment. (p. 85)

conservation the principle (which Piaget believed to be a part of concrete operational reasoning) that properties such as mass, volume, and number remain the same despite changes in the forms of objects. (p. 180)

content validity the extent to which a test samples the behavior that is of interest (such as a driving test that samples driving tasks). (p. 421)

continuous reinforcement reinforcing the desired response every time it occurs. (p. 305)

control group in an experiment, the group that is *not* exposed to the treatment; contrasts with the experimental group and serves as a comparison for evaluating the effect of the treatment. (p. 35)

conversion disorder a rare somatoform disorder in which a person experiences very specific genuine physical symptoms for which no physiological basis can be found. (p. 623)

coping alleviating stress using emotional, cognitive, or behavioral methods. (p. 542)

coronary heart disease the clogging of the vessels that nourish the heart muscle; the leading cause of death in many developed countries. (p. 535)

corpus callosum [KOR-pus kah-LOW-sum] the large band of neural fibers connecting the two brain hemispheres and carrying messages between them. (p. 74)

correlation a measure of the extent to which two factors vary together, and thus of how well either factor predicts the other. (p. 29)

correlation coefficient a statistical index of the relationship between two things (from −1 to +1). (p. 29)

counseling psychology a branch of psychology that assists people with problems in living (often related to school, work, or marriage) and in achieving greater well-being. (p. 10)

counterconditioning a behavior therapy procedure that uses classical conditioning to evoke new responses to stimuli that are triggering unwanted behaviors; includes *exposure therapies* and *aversive conditioning*. (p. 651)

creativity the ability to produce novel and valuable ideas. (p. 409)

critical period an optimal period shortly after birth when an organism's exposure to certain stimuli or experiences produces proper development. (p. 187)

critical thinking thinking that does not blindly accept arguments and conclusions. Rather, it examines assumptions, discerns hidden values, evaluates evidence, and assesses conclusions. (p. 18)

cross-sectional study a study in which people of different ages are compared with one another. (p. 213)

crystallized intelligence our accumulated knowledge and verbal skills; tends to increase with age. (p. 215)

culture the enduring behaviors, ideas, attitudes, and traditions shared by a group of people and transmitted from one generation to the next. (pp. 19, 167)

defense mechanisms in psychoanalytic theory, the ego's protective methods of reducing anxiety by unconsciously distorting reality. (p. 561)

deindividuation the loss of self-awareness and self-restraint occurring in group situations that foster arousal and anonymity. (p. 698)

déjà vu that eerie sense that "I've experienced this before." Cues from the current situation may subconsciously trigger retrieval of an earlier experience. (p. 348)

delta waves the large, slow brain waves associated with deep sleep. (p. 94)

delusions false beliefs, often of persecution or grandeur, that may accompany psychotic disorders. (p. 637)

dendrite the bushy, branching extensions of a neuron that receive messages and conduct impulses toward the cell body. (p. 47)

denial defense mechanism by which people refuse to believe or even to perceive painful realities. (p. 562)

dependent variable the outcome factor; the variable that may change in response to manipulations of the independent variable. (p. 36)

depressants drugs (such as alcohol, barbiturates, and opiates) that reduce neural activity and slow body functions. (p. 115)

depth perception the ability to see objects in three dimensions although the images that strike the retina are two-dimensional; allows us to judge distance. (p. 264)

developmental psychology a branch of psychology that studies physical, cognitive, and social change throughout the life span. (p. 169)

difference threshold the minimum difference between two stimuli required for detection 50 percent of the time. We experience the difference threshold as a *just noticeable difference* (or *jnd*). (p. 230)

discrimination in classical conditioning, the learned ability to distinguish between a conditioned stimulus and stimuli that do not signal an unconditioned stimulus. (p. 295)

discrimination unjustifiable negative behavior toward a group and its members. (p. 703)

displacement psychoanalytic defense mechanism that shifts sexual or aggressive impulses toward a more acceptable or less threatening object or person, as when redirecting anger toward a safer outlet. (p. 562)

dissociation a split in consciousness, which allows some thoughts and behaviors to occur simultaneously with others. (p. 111)

dissociative disorders disorders in which conscious awareness becomes separated (dissociated) from previous memories, thoughts, and feelings. (p. 618)

dissociative identity disorder (DID) a rare dissociative disorder in which a person exhibits two or more distinct and alternating personalities. Formerly called *multiple personality disorder*. (p. 618)

DNA (*deoxyribonucleic acid*) a complex molecule containing the genetic information that makes up the chromosomes. (p. 132)

double-blind procedure an experimental procedure in which both the research participants and the research staff are ignorant (blind) about whether the research participants have received the treatment or a placebo. Commonly used in drug-evaluation studies. (p. 35)

Down syndrome a condition of intellectual disability and associated physical disorders caused by an extra copy of chromosome 21. (p. 425)

dream a sequence of images, emotions, and thoughts passing through a sleeping person's mind. Dreams are notable for their hallucinatory imagery, discontinuities, and incongruities, and for the dreamer's delusional acceptance of the content and later difficulties remembering it. (p. 103)

drive-reduction theory the idea that a physiological need creates an aroused tension state (a drive) that motivates an organism to satisfy the need. (p. 445)

DSM-IV-TR the American Psychiatric Association's *Diagnostic and Statistical Manual of Mental Disorders,* fourth edition, with an updated "text revision"; a widely used system for classifying psychological disorders. (p. 603)

dual processing the principle that information is often simultaneously processed on separate conscious and unconscious tracks. (p. 86)

echoic memory a momentary sensory memory of auditory stimuli; if attention is elsewhere, sounds and words can still be recalled within 3 or 4 seconds. (p. 337)

eclectic approach an approach to psychotherapy that, depending on the client's problems, uses techniques from various forms of therapy. (p. 646)

Ecstasy (MDMA) a synthetic stimulant and mild hallucinogen. Produces euphoria and social intimacy, but with short-term health risks and longer-term harm to serotonin-producing neurons and to mood and cognition. (p. 121)

effortful processing encoding that requires attention and conscious effort. (p. 328)

ego the largely conscious, "executive" part of personality that, according to Freud, mediates among the demands of the id, superego, and reality. The ego operates on the *reality principle,* satisfying the id's desires in ways that will realistically bring pleasure rather than pain. (p. 559)

egocentrism in Piaget's theory, the preoperational child's difficulty taking another's point of view. (p. 180)

electroconvulsive therapy (ECT) a biomedical therapy for severely depressed patients in which a brief electric current is sent through the brain of an anesthetized patient. (p. 675)

electroencephalogram (EEG) an amplified recording of the waves of electrical activity that sweep across the brain's surface. These waves are measured by electrodes placed on the scalp. (p. 59)

embryo the developing human organism from about 2 weeks after fertilization through the second month. (p. 171)

emerging adulthood for some people in modern cultures, a period from the late teens to early twenties, bridging the gap between adolescent dependence and full independence and responsible adulthood. (p. 204)

emotion a response of the whole organism, involving (1) physiological arousal, (2) expressive behaviors, and (3) conscious experience. (p. 500)

emotion-focused coping attempting to alleviate stress by avoiding or ignoring a stressor and attending to emotional needs related to one's stress reaction. (p. 542)

emotional intelligence the ability to perceive, understand, manage, and use emotions. (p. 411)

empirically derived test a test (such as the MMPI) developed by testing a pool of items and then selecting those that discriminate between groups. (p. 576)

encoding the processing of information into the memory system—for example, by extracting meaning. (p. 325)

endocrine [EN-duh-krin] **system** the body's "slow" chemical communication system; a set of glands that secrete hormones into the bloodstream. (p. 56)

endorphins [en-DOR-fins] "morphine within"—natural, opiatelike neurotransmitters linked to pain control and to pleasure. (p. 50)

environment every nongenetic influence, from prenatal nutrition to the people and things around us. (p. 132)

equity a condition in which people receive from a relationship in proportion to what they give to it. (p. 725)

estrogens sex hormones, such as estradiol, secreted in greater amounts by females than by males and contributing to female sex characteristics. In nonhuman female mammals, estrogen levels peak during ovulation, promoting sexual receptivity. (p. 467)

evidence-based practice clinical decision-making that integrates the best available research with clinical expertise and patient characteristics and preferences. (p. 664)

evolutionary psychology the study of the evolution of behavior and the mind, using principles of natural selection. (p. 141)

experiment a research method in which an investigator manipulates one or more factors (independent variables) to observe the effect on some behavior or mental process (the dependent variable). By *random assignment* of participants, the experimenter aims to control other relevant factors. (p. 34)

experimental group in an experiment, the group that is exposed to the treatment, that is, to one version of the independent variable. (p. 35)

explicit memory memory of facts and experiences that one can consciously know and "declare." (Also called *declarative memory*.) (p. 343)

exposure therapies behavioral techniques, such as systematic desensitization, that treat anxieties by exposing people (in imagination or actuality) to the things they fear and avoid. (p. 651)

external locus of control the perception that chance or outside forces beyond your personal control determine your fate. (p. 585)

extinction the diminishing of a conditioned response; occurs in classical conditioning when an unconditioned stimulus (US) does not follow a conditioned stimulus (CS); occurs in operant conditioning when a response is no longer reinforced. (p. 293)

extrasensory perception (ESP) the controversial claim that perception can occur apart from sensory input; includes telepathy, clairvoyance, and precognition. (p. 281)

extrinsic motivation a desire to perform a behavior to receive promised rewards or avoid threatened punishment. (p. 309)

factor analysis a statistical procedure that identifies clusters of related items (called *factors*) on a test; used to identify different dimensions of performance that underlie a person's total score. (p. 405)

family therapy therapy that treats the family as a system. Views an individual's unwanted behaviors as influenced by, or directed at, other family members. (p. 657)

feature detectors nerve cells in the brain that respond to specific features of the stimulus, such as shape, angle, or movement. (p. 238)

feel-good, do-good phenomenon people's tendency to be helpful when already in a good mood. (p. 522)

fetal alcohol syndrome (FAS) physical and cognitive abnormalities in children caused by a pregnant woman's heavy drinking. In severe cases, symptoms include noticeable facial misproportions. (p. 172)

fetus the developing human organism from 9 weeks after conception to birth. (p. 171)

figure-ground the organization of the visual field into objects (the *figures*) that stand out from their surroundings (the *ground*). (p. 263)

fixation the inability to see a problem from a new perspective, by employing a different mental set. (p. 373)

fixation according to Freud, a lingering focus of pleasure-seeking energies at an earlier psychosexual stage, in which conflicts were unresolved. (p. 561)

fixed-interval schedule in operant conditioning, a reinforcement schedule that reinforces a response only after a specified time has elapsed. (p. 305)

fixed-ratio schedule in operant conditioning, a reinforcement schedule that reinforces a response only after a specified number of responses. (p. 305)

flashbulb memory a clear memory of an emotionally significant moment or event. (p. 341)

flow a completely involved, focused state of consciousness, with diminished awareness of self and time, resulting from optimal engagement of one's skills. (p. 484)

fluid intelligence our ability to reason speedily and abstractly; tends to decrease during late adulthood. (p. 215)

fMRI (functional MRI) a technique for revealing bloodflow and, therefore, brain activity by comparing successive MRI scans. fMRI scans show brain function. (p. 60)

foot-in-the-door phenomenon the tendency for people who have first agreed to a small request to comply later with a larger request. (p. 686)

formal operational stage in Piaget's theory, the stage of cognitive development (normally beginning about age 12) during which people begin to think logically about abstract concepts. (p. 184)

fovea the central focal point in the retina, around which the eye's cones cluster. (p. 236)

framing the way an issue is posed; how an issue is framed can significantly affect decisions and judgments. (p. 381)

fraternal twins twins who develop from separate fertilized eggs. They are genetically no closer than brothers and sisters, but they share a fetal environment. (p. 134)

free association in psychoanalysis, a method of exploring the unconscious in which the person relaxes and says whatever comes to mind, no matter how trivial or embarrassing. (p. 558)

frequency the number of complete wavelengths that pass a point in a given time (for example, per second). (p. 244)

frequency theory in hearing, the theory that the rate of nerve impulses traveling up the auditory nerve matches the frequency of a tone, thus enabling us to sense its pitch. (p. 247)

frontal lobes portion of the cerebral cortex lying just behind the forehead; involved in speaking and muscle movements and in making plans and judgments. (p. 67)

frustration-aggression principle the principle that frustration—the blocking of an attempt to achieve some goal—creates anger, which can generate aggression. (p. 712)

functional fixedness the tendency to think of things only in terms of their usual functions; an impediment to problem solving. (p. 373)

functionalism a school of psychology that focused on how our mental and behavioral processes function—how they enable us to adapt, survive, and flourish. (p. 3)

fundamental attribution error the tendency for observers, when analyzing another's behavior, to underestimate the impact of the situation and to overestimate the impact of personal disposition. (p. 682)

gate-control theory the theory that the spinal cord contains a neurological "gate" that blocks pain signals or allows them to pass on to the brain. The "gate" is opened by the activity of pain signals traveling up small nerve fibers and is closed by activity in larger fibers or by information coming from the brain. (p. 254)

gender in psychology, the biologically and socially influenced characteristics by which people define *male* and *female*. (p. 144)

gender identity our sense of being male or female. (p. 163)

gender role a set of expected behaviors for males or for females. (p. 162)

gender typing the acquisition of a traditional masculine or feminine role. (p. 163)

general adaptation syndrome (GAS) Selye's concept of the body's adaptive response to stress in three phases—alarm, resistance, exhaustion. (p. 532)

general intelligence (g) a general intelligence factor that, according to Spearman and others, underlies specific mental abilities and is therefore measured by every task on an intelligence test. (p. 405)

generalization the tendency, once a response has been conditioned, for stimuli similar to the conditioned stimulus to elicit similar responses. (p. 294)

generalized anxiety disorder an anxiety disorder in which a person is continually tense, apprehensive, and in a state of autonomic nervous system arousal. (p. 610)

genes the biochemical units of heredity that make up the chromosomes; a segment of DNA capable of synthesizing a protein. (p. 132)

genome the complete instructions for making an organism, consisting of all the genetic material in that organism's chromosomes. (p. 132)

gestalt an organized whole. Gestalt psychologists emphasized our tendency to integrate pieces of information into meaningful wholes. (p. 262)

glial cells (glia) cells in the nervous system that support, nourish, and protect neurons. (p. 67)

glucose the form of sugar that circulates in the blood and provides the major source of energy for body tissues. When its level is low, we feel hunger. (p. 449)

grammar in a language, a system of rules that enables us to communicate with and understand others. (p. 385)

GRIT Graduated and *R*eciprocated *I*nitiatives in *T*ension-Reduction— a strategy designed to decrease international tensions. (p. 732)

group polarization the enhancement of a group's prevailing inclinations through discussion within the group. (p. 699)

grouping the perceptual tendency to organize stimuli into coherent groups. (p. 263)

groupthink the mode of thinking that occurs when the desire for harmony in a decision-making group overrides a realistic appraisal of alternatives. (p. 700)

habituation decreasing responsiveness with repeated stimulation. As infants gain familiarity with repeated exposure to a visual stimulus, their interest wanes and they look away sooner. (p. 172)

hallucinations false sensory experiences, such as seeing something in the absence of an external visual stimulus. (p. 122)

hallucinogens psychedelic ("mind-manifesting") drugs, such as LSD, that distort perceptions and evoke sensory images in the absence of sensory input. (p. 94)

health psychology a subfield of psychology that provides psychology's contribution to behavioral medicine. (p. 530)

heritability the proportion of variation among individuals that we can attribute to genes. The heritability of a trait may vary, depending on the range of populations and environments studied. (p. 138)

heuristic a simple thinking strategy that often allows us to make judgments and solve problems efficiently; usually speedier but also more error-prone than *algorithms*. (p. 371)

hierarchy of needs Maslow's pyramid of human needs, beginning at the base with physiological needs that must first be satisfied before higher-level safety needs and then psychological needs become active. (p. 446)

higher-order conditioning a procedure in which the conditioned stimulus in one conditioning experience is paired with a new neutral stimulus, creating a second (often weaker) conditioned stimulus. For example, an animal that has learned that a tone predicts food might then learn that a light predicts the tone and begin responding to the light alone. (Also called *second-order conditioning*.) (p. 292)

hindsight bias the tendency to believe, after learning an outcome, that one would have foreseen it. (Also known as the *I-knew-it-all-along phenomenon*.) (p. 15)

hippocampus a neural center that is located in the limbic system and helps process explicit memories for storage. (p. 343)

homeostasis a tendency to maintain a balanced or constant internal state; the regulation of any aspect of body chemistry, such as blood glucose, around a particular level. (p. 445)

hormones chemical messengers that are manufactured by the endocrine glands, travel through the bloodstream, and affect other tissues. (p. 56)

hue the dimension of color that is determined by the wavelength of light; what we know as the color names *blue, green,* and so forth. (p. 234)

human factors psychology a branch of psychology that explores how people and machines interact and how machines and physical environments can be made safe and easy to use. (p. 279)

humanistic psychology historically significant perspective that emphasized the growth potential of healthy people and the individual's potential for personal growth. (p. 5)

hypnosis a social interaction in which one person (the hypnotist) suggests to another (the subject) that certain perceptions, feelings, thoughts, or behaviors will spontaneously occur. (p. 108)

hypochondriasis a somatoform disorder in which a person interprets normal physical sensations as symptoms of a disease. (p. 623)

hypothalamus [hi-po-THAL-uh-muss] a neural structure lying below (*hypo*) the thalamus; it directs several maintenance activities (eating, drinking, body temperature), helps govern the endocrine system via the pituitary gland, and is linked to emotion and reward. (p. 63)

hypothesis a testable prediction, often implied by a theory. (p. 25)

iconic memory a momentary sensory memory of visual stimuli; a photographic or picture-image memory lasting no more than a few tenths of a second. (p. 336)

id contains a reservoir of unconscious psychic energy that, according to Freud, strives to satisfy basic sexual and aggressive drives. The id operates on the *pleasure principle,* demanding immediate gratification. (p. 559)

identical twins twins who develop from a single fertilized egg that splits in two, creating two genetically identical organisms. (p. 134)

identification the process by which, according to Freud, children incorporate their parents' values into their developing superegos. (p. 560)

identity our sense of self; according to Erikson, the adolescent's task is to solidify a sense of self by testing and integrating various roles. (p. 201)

illusory correlation the perception of a relationship where none exists. (p. 32)

imagery mental pictures; a powerful aid to effortful processing, especially when combined with semantic encoding. (p. 332)

implicit memory retention independent of conscious recollection. (Also called *nondeclarative memory.*) (p. 343)

imprinting the process by which certain animals form attachments during a critical period very early in life. (p. 187)

inattentional blindness failing to see visible objects when our attention is directed elsewhere. (p. 89)

incentive a positive or negative environmental stimulus that motivates behavior. (p. 445)

independent variable the experimental factor that is manipulated; the variable whose effect is being studied. (p. 35)

individualism giving priority to one's own goals over group goals and defining one's identity in terms of personal attributes rather than group identifications. (p. 154)

industrial-organizational (I/O) psychology the application of psychological concepts and methods to optimizing human behavior in workplaces. (p. 485)

informational social influence influence resulting from one's willingness to accept others' opinions about reality. (p. 692)

ingroup "Us"—people with whom we share a common identity. (p. 707)

ingroup bias the tendency to favor our own group. (p. 707)

inner ear the innermost part of the ear, containing the cochlea, semicircular canals, and vestibular sacs. (p. 244)

insight a sudden and often novel realization of the solution to a problem; it contrasts with strategy-based solutions. (p. 371)

insight therapies a variety of therapies which aim to improve psychological functioning by increasing the client's awareness of underlying motives and defenses. (p. 649)

insomnia recurring problems in falling or staying asleep. (p. 100)

instinct a complex behavior that is rigidly patterned throughout a species and is unlearned. (p. 444)

intellectual disability (formerly referred to as *mental retardation*) a condition of limited mental ability, indicated by an intelligence score of 70 or below and difficulty in adapting to the demands of life; varies from mild to profound. (p. 425)

intelligence mental quality consisting of the ability to learn from experience, solve problems, and use knowledge to adapt to new situations. (p. 404)

intelligence quotient (IQ) defined originally as the ratio of mental age (*ma*) to chronological age (*ca*) multiplied by 100 (thus, IQ = *ma/ca* ? 100). On contemporary intelligence tests, the average performance for a given age is assigned a score of 100. (p. 417)

intelligence test a method for assessing an individual's mental aptitudes and comparing them with those of others, using numerical scores. (p. 416)

intensity the amount of energy in a light or sound wave, which we perceive as brightness or loudness, as determined by the wave's amplitude. (p. 234)

interaction the interplay that occurs when the effect of one factor (such as environment) depends on another factor (such as heredity). (p. 139)

internal locus of control the perception that you control your own fate. (p. 585)

interneurons neurons within the brain and spinal cord that communicate internally and intervene between the sensory inputs and motor outputs. (p. 46)

interpretation in psychoanalysis, the analyst's noting supposed dream meanings, resistances, and other significant behaviors and events in order to promote insight. (p. 647)

intimacy in Erikson's theory, the ability to form close, loving relationships; a primary developmental task in late adolescence and early adulthood. (p. 202)

intrinsic motivation a desire to perform a behavior effectively for its own sake. (p. 309)

intuition an effortless, immediate, automatic feeling or thought, as contrasted with explicit, conscious reasoning. (p. 378)

iris a ring of muscle tissue that forms the colored portion of the eye around the pupil and controls the size of the pupil opening. (p. 234)

James-Lange theory the theory that our experience of emotion is our awareness of our physiological responses to emotion-arousing stimuli. (p. 500)

just-world phenomenon the tendency for people to believe the world is just and that people therefore get what they deserve and deserve what they get. (p. 709)

kinesthesis [kin-ehs-THEE-sehs] the system for sensing the position and movement of individual body parts. (p. 252)

language our spoken, written, or signed words and the ways we combine them to communicate meaning. (p. 384)

latent content according to Freud, the underlying meaning of a dream (as distinct from its manifest content). (p. 104)

latent learning learning that occurs but is not apparent until there is an incentive to demonstrate it. (p. 308)

law of effect Thorndike's principle that behaviors followed by favorable consequences become more likely, and that behaviors followed by unfavorable consequences become less likely. (p. 301)

learned helplessness the hopelessness and passive resignation an animal or human learns when unable to avoid repeated aversive events. (p. 585)

learning a relatively permanent change in an organism's behavior due to experience. (pp. 290, 302)

lens the transparent structure behind the pupil that changes shape to help focus images on the retina. (p. 234)

lesion [LEE-zhuhn] tissue destruction. A brain lesion is a naturally or experimentally caused destruction of brain tissue. (p. 59)

levels of analysis the differing complementary views, from biological to psychological to social-cultural, for analyzing any given phenomenon. (p. 8)

limbic system neural system (including the *hippocampus, amygdala,* and *hypothalamus*) located below the cerebral hemispheres; associated with emotions and drives. (p. 62)

linguistic determinism Whorf's hypothesis that language determines the way we think. (p. 393)

lobotomy a now-rare psychosurgical procedure once used to calm uncontrollably emotional or violent patients. The procedure cut the nerves connecting the frontal lobes to the emotion-controlling centers of the inner brain. (p. 677)

long-term memory the relatively permanent and limitless storehouse of the memory system. Includes knowledge, skills, and experiences. (p. 325)

long-term potentiation (LTP) an increase in a synapse's firing potential after brief, rapid stimulation. Believed to be a neural basis for learning and memory. (p. 340)

longitudinal study research in which the same people are restudied and retested over a long period. (p. 214)

LSD a powerful hallucinogenic drug; also known as acid (*lysergic acid diethylamide*). (p. 122)

lymphocytes the two types of white blood cells that are part of the body's immune system: *B lymphocytes* form in the *b* one marrow and release antibodies that fight bacterial infections; *T lymphocytes* form in the *t* hymus and other lymphatic tissue and attack cancer cells, viruses, and foreign substances. (p. 538)

major depressive disorder a mood disorder in which a person experiences, in the absence of drugs or a medical condition, two or more weeks of significantly depressed moods, feelings of worthlessness, and diminished interest or pleasure in most activities. (p. 626)

mania a mood disorder marked by a hyperactive, wildly optimistic state. (p. 626)

manifest content according to Freud, the remembered story line of a dream (as distinct from its latent, or hidden, content). (p. 103)

maturation biological growth processes that enable orderly changes in behavior, relatively uninfluenced by experience. (p. 174)

mean the arithmetic average of a distribution, obtained by adding the scores and then dividing by the number of scores. (p. 38)

median the middle score in a distribution; half the scores are above it and half are below it. (p. 38)

medical model the concept that diseases, in this case psychological disorders, have physical causes that can be *diagnosed, treated,* and, in most cases, *cured,* often through *treatment* in a hospital. (p. 601)

medulla [muh-DUL-uh] the base of the brainstem; controls heartbeat and breathing. (p. 61)

memory the persistence of learning over time through the storage and retrieval of information. (p. 324)

menarche [meh-NAR-key] the first menstrual period. (p. 196)

menopause the time of natural cessation of menstruation; also refers to the biological changes a woman experiences as her ability to reproduce declines. (p. 207)

mental age a measure of intelligence test performance devised by Binet; the chronological age that most typically corresponds to a given level of performance. Thus, a child who does as well as the average 8-year-old is said to have a mental age of 8. (p. 417)

mental set a tendency to approach a problem in one particular way, often a way that has been successful in the past. (p. 373)

mere exposure effect the phenomenon that repeated exposure to novel stimuli increases liking of them. (p. 719)

meta-analysis a procedure for statistically combining the results of many different research studies. (p. 662)

methamphetamine a powerfully addictive drug that stimulates the central nervous system, with speeded-up body functions and associated energy and mood changes; over time, appears to reduce baseline dopamine levels. (p. 117)

middle ear the chamber between the eardrum and cochlea containing three tiny bones (hammer, anvil, and stirrup) that concentrate the vibrations of the eardrum on the cochlea's oval window. (p. 244)

Minnesota Multiphasic Personality Inventory (MMPI) the most widely researched and clinically used of all personality tests. Originally developed to identify emotional disorders (still considered its most appropriate use), this test is now used for many other screening purposes. (p. 576)

mirror neurons frontal lobe neurons that fire when performing certain actions or when observing another doing so. The brain's mirroring of another's action may enable imitation and empathy. (p. 316)

mirror-image perceptions mutual views often held by conflicting people, as when each side sees itself as ethical and peaceful and views the other side as evil and aggressive. (p. 730)

misinformation effect incorporating misleading information into one's memory of an event. (p. 358)

mnemonics [nih-MON-iks] memory aids, especially those techniques that use vivid imagery and organizational devices. (p. 333)

mode the most frequently occurring score(s) in a distribution. (p. 38)

modeling the process of observing and imitating a specific behavior. (p. 315)

molecular genetics the subfield of biology that studies the molecular structure and function of genes. (p. 140)

monocular cues depth cues, such as interposition and linear perspective, available to either eye alone. (p. 265)

mood disorders psychological disorders characterized by emotional extremes. See *major depressive disorder, mania,* and *bipolar disorder.* (p. 625)

mood-congruent memory the tendency to recall experiences that are consistent with one's current good or bad mood. (p. 349)

morpheme in a language, the smallest unit that carries meaning; may be a word or a part of a word (such as a prefix). (p. 385)

motivation a need or desire that energizes and directs behavior. (p. 444)

motor cortex an area at the rear of the frontal lobes that controls voluntary movements. (p. 68)

motor neurons neurons that carry outgoing information from the brain and spinal cord to the muscles and glands. (p. 46)

MRI (magnetic resonance imaging) a technique that uses magnetic fields and radio waves to produce computer-generated images of soft tissue. MRI scans show brain anatomy. (p. 60)

mutation a random error in gene replication that leads to a change. (p. 142)

myelin [MY-uh-lin] **sheath** a layer of fatty tissue segmentally encasing the fibers of many neurons; enables vastly greater transmission speed of neural impulses as the impulse hops from one node to the next. (p. 47)

narcolepsy a sleep disorder characterized by uncontrollable sleep attacks. The sufferer may lapse directly into REM sleep, often at inopportune times. (p. 101)

natural selection the principle that, among the range of inherited trait variations, those contributing to reproduction and survival will most likely be passed on to succeeding generations. (pp. 7, 141)

naturalistic observation observing and recording behavior in naturally occurring situations without trying to manipulate and control the situation. (p. 28)

nature-nurture issue the longstanding controversy over the relative contributions that genes and experience make to the development of psychological traits and behaviors. Today's science sees traits and behaviors arising from the interaction of nature and nurture. (p. 6)

near-death experience an altered state of consciousness reported after a close brush with death (such as through cardiac arrest); often similar to drug-induced hallucinations. (p. 123)

negative reinforcement increasing behaviors by stopping or reducing negative stimuli, such as shock. A negative reinforcer is any stimulus that, when *removed* after a response, strengthens the response. (Note: negative reinforcement is *not* punishment.) (p. 303)

nerves bundled axons that form neural "cables" connecting the central nervous system with muscles, glands, and sense organs. (p. 52)

nervous system the body's speedy, electrochemical communication network, consisting of all the nerve cells of the peripheral and central nervous systems. (p. 52)

neurogenesis the formation of new neurons. (p. 74)

neuron a nerve cell; the basic building block of the nervous system. (p. 46)

neurotransmitters chemical messengers that cross the synaptic gaps between neurons. When released by the sending neuron, neurotransmitters travel across the synapse and bind to receptor sites on the receiving neuron, thereby influencing whether that neuron will generate a neural impulse. (p. 49)

night terrors a sleep disorder characterized by high arousal and an appearance of being terrified; unlike nightmares, night terrors occur during Stage 4 sleep, within two or three hours of falling asleep, and are seldom remembered. (p. 102)

norm an understood rule for accepted and expected behavior. Norms prescribe "proper" behavior. (p. 152)

normal curve (*normal distribution*) a symmetrical, bell-shaped curve that describes the distribution of many types of data; most scores fall near the mean, or average (68 percent fall within one standard deviation of it), and fewer and fewer near the extremes. (pp. 39, 420)

normative social influence influence resulting from a person's desire to gain approval or avoid disapproval. (p. 692)

object permanence the awareness that things continue to exist even when not perceived. (p. 178)

observational learning learning by observing others. (p. 315)

obsessive-compulsive disorder (OCD) an anxiety disorder characterized by unwanted repetitive thoughts (obsessions) and/or actions (compulsions). (p. 612)

occipital [ahk-SIP-uh-tuhl] **lobes** portion of the cerebral cortex lying at the back of the head; includes areas that receive information from the visual fields. (p. 67)

Oedipus [ED-uh-puss] **complex** according to Freud, a boy's sexual desires toward his mother and feelings of jealousy and hatred for the rival father. (p. 560)

one-word stage the stage in speech development, from about age 1 to 2, during which a child speaks mostly in single words. (p. 387)

operant behavior behavior that operates on the environment, producing consequences. (p. 301)

operant chamber in operant conditioning research, a chamber (also known as a *Skinner box*) containing a bar or key that an animal can manipulate to obtain a food or water reinforcer; attached devices record the animal's rate of bar pressing or key pecking. (p. 302)

operant conditioning a type of learning in which behavior is strengthened if followed by a reinforcer or diminished if followed by a punisher. (p. 301)

operational definition a statement of the procedures (operations) used to define research variables. For example, *human intelligence* may be operationally defined as what an intelligence test measures. (p. 26)

opiates opium and its derivatives, such as morphine and heroin; they depress neural activity, temporarily lessening pain and anxiety. (p. 117)

opponent-process theory the theory that opposing retinal processes (red-green, yellow-blue, white-black) enable color vision. For example, some cells are stimulated by green and inhibited by red; others are stimulated by red and inhibited by green. (p. 242)

optic nerve the nerve that carries neural impulses from the eye to the brain. (p. 235)

organizational psychology a subfield of I/O psychology that examines organizational influences on worker satisfaction and productivity and facilitates organizational change. (p. 486)

other-race effect the tendency to recall faces of one's own race more accurately than faces of other races. Also called the *cross-race effect* and the *own-race bias*. (p. 708)

outgroup "Them"—those perceived as different or apart from our ingroup. (p. 707)

overconfidence the tendency to be more confident than correct—to overestimate the accuracy of our beliefs and judgments. (p. 376)

panic disorder an anxiety disorder marked by unpredictable minutes-long episodes of intense dread in which a person experiences terror and accompanying chest pain, choking, or other frightening sensations. (p. 611)

parallel processing the processing of many aspects of a problem simultaneously; the brain's natural mode of information processing for many functions, including vision. Contrasts with the step-by-step (serial) processing of most computers and of conscious problem solving. (p. 239)

parapsychology the study of paranormal phenomena, including ESP and psychokinesis. (p. 281)

parasympathetic nervous system the division of the autonomic nervous system that calms the body, conserving its energy. (p. 53)

parietal [puh-RYE-uh-tuhl] **lobes** portion of the cerebral cortex lying at the top of the head and toward the rear; receives sensory input for touch and body position. (p. 67)

partial (intermittent) reinforcement reinforcing a response only part of the time; results in slower acquisition of a response but much greater resistance to extinction than does continuous reinforcement. (p. 305)

passionate love an aroused state of intense positive absorption in another, usually present at the beginning of a love relationship. (p. 724)

perception the process of organizing and interpreting sensory information, enabling us to recognize meaningful objects and events. (p. 226)

perceptual adaptation in vision, the ability to adjust to an artificially displaced or even inverted visual field. (p. 273)

perceptual constancy perceiving objects as unchanging (having consistent shapes, size, lightness, and color) even as illumination and retinal images change. (p. 267)

perceptual set a mental predisposition to perceive one thing and not another. (p. 274)

peripheral nervous system (PNS) the sensory and motor neurons that connect the central nervous system (CNS) to the rest of the body. (p. 52)

peripheral route to persuasion occurs when people are influenced by incidental cues, such as a speaker's attractiveness. (p. 685)

personal control a sense of controlling your environment rather than feeling helpless. (p. 584)

personal space the buffer zone we like to maintain around our bodies. (p. 167)

personality an individual's characteristic pattern of thinking, feeling, and acting. (p. 557)

personality disorders psychological disorders characterized by inflexible and enduring behavior patterns that impair social functioning. (p. 620)

personality inventory a questionnaire (often with *true-false* or *agree-disagree* items) on which people respond to items designed to gauge a wide range of feelings and behaviors; used to assess selected personality traits. (p. 576)

personnel psychology a subfield of I/O psychology that focuses on employee recruitment, selection, placement, training, appraisal, and development. (p. 485)

PET (positron emission tomography) scan a visual display of brain activity that detects where a radioactive form of glucose goes while the brain performs a given task. (p. 60)

phi phenomenon an illusion of movement created when two or more adjacent lights blink on and off in quick succession. (p. 267)

phobia an anxiety disorder marked by a persistent, irrational fear and avoidance of a specific object or situation. (p. 611)

phoneme in language, the smallest distinctive sound unit. (p. 385)

physical dependence a physiological need for a drug, marked by unpleasant withdrawal symptoms when the drug is discontinued. (p. 113)

pitch a tone's experienced highness or lowness; depends on frequency. (p. 244)

pituitary gland the endocrine system's most influential gland. Under the influence of the hypothalamus, the pituitary regulates growth and controls other endocrine glands. (p. 56)

place theory in hearing, the theory that links the pitch we hear with the place where the cochlea's membrane is stimulated. (p. 246)

placebo [pluh-SEE-bo; Latin for "I shall please"] **effect** experimental results caused by expectations alone; any effect on behavior caused by the administration of an inert substance or condition, which the recipient assumes is an active agent. (p. 35)

plasticity the brain's ability to change, especially during childhood, by reorganizing after damage or by building new pathways based on experience. (p. 73)

polygraph a machine, commonly used in attempts to detect lies, that measures several of the physiological responses accompanying emotion (such as perspiration and cardiovascular and breathing changes). (p. 504)

population all the cases in a group being studied, from which samples may be drawn. (*Note:* Except for national studies, this does *not* refer to a country's whole population.) (p. 28)

positive psychology the scientific study of optimal human functioning; aims to discover and promote strengths and virtues that enable individuals and communities to thrive. (p. 588)

positive reinforcement increasing behaviors by presenting positive stimuli, such as food. A positive reinforcer is any stimulus that, when *presented* after a response, strengthens the response. (p. 303)

posthypnotic suggestion a suggestion, made during a hypnosis session, to be carried out after the subject is no longer hypnotized; used by some clinicians to help control undesired symptoms and behaviors. (p. 109)

post-traumatic growth positive psychological changes as a result of struggling with extremely challenging circumstances and life crises. (p. 614)

post-traumatic stress disorder (PTSD) an anxiety disorder characterized by haunting memories, nightmares, social withdrawal, jumpy anxiety, and/or insomnia that lingers for four weeks or more after a traumatic experience. (p. 613)

predictive validity the success with which a test predicts the behavior it is designed to predict; it is assessed by computing the correlation between test scores and the criterion behavior. (Also called *criterion-related validity*.) (p. 421)

prejudice an unjustifiable (and usually negative) attitude toward a group and its members. Prejudice generally involves stereotyped beliefs, negative feelings, and a predisposition to discriminatory action. (p. 703)

preoperational stage in Piaget's theory, the stage (from 2 to about 6 or 7 years of age) during which a child learns to use language but does not yet comprehend the mental operations of concrete logic. (p. 180)

primary reinforcer an innately reinforcing stimulus, such as one that satisfies a biological need. (p. 304)

primary sex characteristics the body structures (ovaries, testes, and external genitalia) that make sexual reproduction possible. (p. 195)

priming the activation, often unconsciously, of certain associations, thus predisposing one's perception, memory, or response. (p. 229)

priming the activation, often unconsciously, of particular associations in memory. (p. 347)

proactive interference the disruptive effect of prior learning on the recall of new information. (p. 354)

problem-focused coping attempting to alleviate stress directly—by changing the stressor or the way we interact with that stressor. (p. 542)

projection psychoanalytic defense mechanism by which people disguise their own threatening impulses by attributing them to others. (p. 562)

projective test a personality test, such as the Rorschach or TAT, that provides ambiguous stimuli designed to trigger projection of one's inner dynamics. (p. 564)

prosocial behavior positive, constructive, helpful behavior. The opposite of antisocial behavior. (p. 318)

prototype a mental image or best example of a category. Matching new items to a prototype provides a quick and easy method for sorting items into categories (as when comparing feathered creatures to a prototypical bird, such as a robin). (p. 370)

psychiatry a branch of medicine dealing with psychological disorders; practiced by physicians who sometimes provide medical (for example, drug) treatments as well as psychological therapy. (p. 10)

psychoactive drug a chemical substance that alters perceptions and moods. (p. 113)

psychoanalysis Freud's theory of personality and therapeutic technique that attributes thoughts and actions to unconscious motives and conflicts. Freud believed the patient's free associations, resistances, dreams, and transferences—and the therapist's interpretations of them—released previously repressed feelings, allowing the patient to gain self-insight. (pp. 558, 646)

psychodynamic therapy therapy deriving from the psychoanalytic tradition that views individuals as responding to unconscious forces and childhood experiences, and that seeks to enhance self-insight. (p. 648)

psychological dependence a psychological need to use a drug, such as to relieve negative emotions. (p. 114)

psychological disorder deviant, distressful, and dysfunctional patterns of thoughts, feelings, or behaviors. (p. 599)

psychology the science of behavior and mental processes. (p. 6)

psychoneuroimmunology (PNI) the study of how psychological, neural, and endocrine processes together affect the immune system and resulting health. (p. 537)

psychopharmacology the study of the effects of drugs on mind and behavior. (p. 671)

psychophysics the study of relationships between the physical characteristics of stimuli, such as their intensity, and our psychological experience of them. (p. 227)

psychophysiological illness literally, "mind-body" illness; any stress-related physical illness, such as hypertension and some headaches. (p. 537)

psychosexual stages the childhood stages of development (oral, anal, phallic, latency, genital) during which, according to Freud, the id's pleasure-seeking energies focus on distinct erogenous zones. (p. 560)

psychosurgery surgery that removes or destroys brain tissue in an effort to change behavior. (p. 677)

psychotherapy treatment involving psychological techniques; consists of interactions between a trained therapist and someone seeking to overcome psychological difficulties or achieve personal growth. (p. 646)

puberty the period of sexual maturation, during which a person becomes capable of reproducing. (p. 195)

punishment an event that *decreases* the behavior that it follows. (p. 306)

pupil the adjustable opening in the center of the eye through which light enters. (p. 234)

random assignment assigning participants to experimental and control groups by chance, thus minimizing preexisting differences between those assigned to the different groups. (p. 34)

random sample a sample that fairly represents a population because each member has an equal chance of inclusion. (p. 28)

range the difference between the highest and lowest scores in a distribution. (p. 39)

rationalization defense mechanism that offers self-justifying explanations in place of the real, more threatening, unconscious reasons for one's actions. (p. 562)

reaction formation psychoanalytic defense mechanism by which the ego unconsciously switches unacceptable impulses into their opposites. Thus, people may express feelings that are the opposite of their anxiety-arousing unconscious feelings. (p. 561)

recall a measure of memory in which the person must retrieve information learned earlier, as on a fill-in-the-blank test. (p. 346)

reciprocal determinism the interacting influences of behavior, internal cognition, and environment. (p. 583)

reciprocity norm an expectation that people will help, not hurt, those who have helped them. (p. 728)

recognition a measure of memory in which the person need only identify items previously learned, as on a multiple-choice test. (p. 346)

reflex a simple, automatic response to a sensory stimulus, such as the knee-jerk response. (p. 54)

refractory period a resting period after orgasm, during which a man cannot achieve another orgasm. (p. 467)

regression psychoanalytic defense mechanism in which an individual faced with anxiety retreats to a more infantile psychosexual stage, where some psychic energy remains fixated. (p. 561)

regression toward the mean the tendency for extreme or unusual scores to fall back (regress) toward their average. (p. 662)

rehearsal the conscious repetition of information, either to maintain it in consciousness or to encode it for storage. (p. 328)

reinforcer in operant conditioning, any event that *strengthens* the behavior it follows. (p. 303)

relative deprivation the perception that one is worse off relative to those with whom one compares oneself. (p. 528)

relearning a memory measure that assesses the amount of time saved when learning material for a second time. (p. 346)

reliability the extent to which a test yields consistent results, as assessed by the consistency of scores on two halves of the test, or on retesting. (p. 421)

REM rebound the tendency for REM sleep to increase following REM sleep deprivation (created by repeated awakenings during REM sleep). (p. 106)

REM sleep rapid eye movement sleep, a recurring sleep stage during which vivid dreams commonly occur. Also known as *paradoxical sleep,* because the muscles are relaxed (except for minor twitches) but other body systems are active. (p. 92)

repetitive transcranial magnetic stimulation (rTMS) the application of repeated pulses of magnetic energy to the brain; used to stimulate or suppress brain activity. (p. 676)

replication repeating the essence of a research study, usually with different participants in different situations, to see whether the basic finding extends to other participants and circumstances. (p. 26)

representativeness heuristic judging the likelihood of things in terms of how well they seem to represent, or match, particular prototypes; may lead us to ignore other relevant information. (p. 374)

repression in psychoanalytic theory, the basic defense mechanism that banishes anxiety-arousing thoughts, feelings, and memories from consciousness. (pp. 356, 561)

resistance in psychoanalysis, the blocking from consciousness of anxiety-laden material. (p. 647)

respondent behavior behavior that occurs as an automatic response to some stimulus. (p. 301)

reticular formation a nerve network in the brainstem that plays an important role in controlling arousal. (p. 61)

retina the light-sensitive inner surface of the eye, containing the receptor rods and cones plus layers of neurons that begin the processing of visual information. (p. 234)

retinal disparity a binocular cue for perceiving depth: By comparing images from the retinas in the two eyes, the brain computes distance—the greater the disparity (difference) between the two images, the closer the object. (p. 265)

retrieval the process of getting information out of memory storage. (p. 325)

retroactive interference the disruptive effect of new learning on the recall of old information. (p. 354)

reuptake a neurotransmitter's reabsorption by the sending neuron. (p. 50)

rods retinal receptors that detect black, white, and gray; necessary for peripheral and twilight vision, when cones don't respond. (p. 235)

role a set of expectations (norms) about a social position, defining how those in the position ought to behave. (pp. 162, 686)

Rorschach inkblot test the most widely used projective test, a set of 10 inkblots, designed by Hermann Rorschach; seeks to identify people's inner feelings by analyzing their interpretations of the blots. (p. 564)

savant syndrome a condition in which a person otherwise limited in mental ability has an exceptional specific skill, such as in computation or drawing. (p. 406)

scapegoat theory the theory that prejudice offers an outlet for anger by providing someone to blame. (p. 708)

scatterplots a graphed cluster of dots, each of which represents the values of two variables. The slope of the points suggests the direction of the relationship between the two variables. The amount of scatter suggests the strength of the correlation (little scatter indicates high correlation). (p. 30)

schema a concept or framework that organizes and interprets information. (p. 177)

schizophrenia a group of severe disorders characterized by disorganized and delusional thinking, disturbed perceptions, and inappropriate emotions and actions. (p. 637)

secondary sex characteristics nonreproductive sexual characteristics, such as female breasts and hips, male voice quality, and body hair. (p. 195)

selective attention the focusing of conscious awareness on a particular stimulus. (p. 87)

self in contemporary psychology, assumed to be the center of personality, the organizer of our thoughts, feelings, and actions. (p. 590)

self-actualization according to Maslow, one of the ultimate psychological needs that arises after basic physical and psychological needs are met and self-esteem is achieved; the motivation to fulfill one's potential. (p. 570)

self-concept all our thoughts and feelings about ourselves, in answer to the question, "Who am I?" (pp. 192, 571)

self-disclosure revealing intimate aspects of oneself to others. (p. 725)

self-esteem one's feelings of high or low self-worth. (p. 591)

self-serving bias a readiness to perceive oneself favorably. (p. 592)

semantic encoding the encoding of meaning, including the meaning of words. (p. 331)

semantics the set of rules by which we derive meaning from morphemes, words, and sentences in a given language; also, the study of meaning. (p. 385)

sensation the process by which our sensory receptors and nervous system receive and represent stimulus energies from our environment. (p. 226)

sensorimotor stage in Piaget's theory, the stage (from birth to about 2 years of age) during which infants know the world mostly in terms of their sensory impressions and motor activities. (p. 178)

sensorineural hearing loss hearing loss caused by damage to the cochlea's receptor cells or to the auditory nerves; also called nerve deafness. (p. 248)

sensory adaptation diminished sensitivity as a consequence of constant stimulation. (p. 230)

sensory cortex area at the front of the parietal lobes that registers and processes body touch and movement sensations. (p. 70)

sensory interaction the principle that one sense may influence another, as when the smell of food influences its taste. (p. 258)

sensory memory the immediate, very brief recording of sensory information in the memory system. (p. 325)

sensory neurons neurons that carry incoming information from the sensory receptors to the brain and spinal cord. (p. 40)

serial position effect our tendency to recall best the last and first items in a list. (p. 330)

set point the point at which an individual's "weight thermostat" is supposedly set. When the body falls below this weight, an increase in hunger and a lowered metabolic rate may act to restore the lost weight. (p. 451)

sexual disorder a problem that consistently impairs sexual arousal or functioning. (p. 467)

sexual orientation an enduring sexual attraction toward members of either one's own sex (homosexual orientation) or the other sex (heterosexual orientation). (p. 472)

sexual response cycle the four stages of sexual responding described by Masters and Johnson—excitement, plateau, orgasm, and resolution. (p. 466)

shaping an operant conditioning procedure in which reinforcers guide behavior toward closer and closer approximations of the desired behavior. (p. 302)

short-term memory activated memory that holds a few items briefly, such as the seven digits of a phone number while dialing, before the information is stored or forgotten. (p. 325)

signal detection theory a theory predicting how and when we detect the presence of a faint stimulus (*signal*) amid background stimulation (*noise*). Assumes there is no single absolute threshold and that detection depends partly on a person's experience, expectations, motivation, and alertness. (p. 227)

sleep periodic, natural, reversible loss of consciousness—as distinct from unconsciousness resulting from a coma, general anesthesia, or hibernation. (Adapted from Dement, 1999.) (p. 94)

sleep apnea a sleep disorder characterized by temporary cessations of breathing during sleep and repeated momentary awakenings. (p. 101)

social clock the culturally preferred timing of social events such as marriage, parenthood, and retirement. (p. 216)

social-cognitive perspective views behavior as influenced by the interaction between people's traits (including their thinking) and their social context. (p. 583)

social exchange theory the theory that our social behavior is an exchange process, the aim of which is to maximize benefits and minimize costs. (p. 728)

social facilitation stronger responses on simple or well-learned tasks in the presence of others. (p. 697)

social identity the "we" aspect of our self-concept; the part of our answer to "Who am I?" that comes from our group memberships. (p. 201)

social leadership group-oriented leadership that builds teamwork, mediates conflict, and offers support. (p. 495)

social learning theory the theory that we learn social behavior by observing and imitating and by being rewarded or punished. (p. 163)

social loafing the tendency for people in a group to exert less effort when pooling their efforts toward attaining a common goal than when individually accountable. (p. 698)

social psychology the scientific study of how we think about, influence, and relate to one another. (p. 681)

social-responsibility norm an expectation that people will help those dependent upon them. (p. 729)

social trap a situation in which the conflicting parties, by each rationally pursuing their self-interest, become caught in mutually destructive behavior. (p. 729)

somatic nervous system the division of the peripheral nervous system that controls the body's skeletal muscles. Also called the *skeletal nervous system*. (p. 52)

somatoform disorder psychological disorder in which the symptoms take a somatic (bodily) form without apparent physical cause. (See *conversion disorder* and *hypochondriasis*.) (p. 623)

source amnesia attributing to the wrong source an event we have experienced, heard about, read about, or imagined. (Also called *source misattribution*.) Source amnesia, along with the misinformation effect, is at the heart of many false memories. (p. 359)

spacing effect the tendency for distributed study or practice to yield better long-term retention than is achieved through massed study or practice. (p. 329)

split brain a condition resulting from surgery that isolates the brain's two hemispheres by cutting the fibers (mainly those of the corpus callosum) connecting them. (p. 75)

spontaneous recovery the reappearance, after a pause, of an extinguished conditioned response. (p. 293)

spotlight effect overestimating others' noticing and evaluating our appearance, performance, and blunders (as if we presume a spotlight shines on us). (p. 591)

SQ3R a study method incorporating five steps: Survey, Question, Read, Rehearse, Review. (p. 12)

standard deviation a computed measure of how much scores vary around the mean score. (p. 39)

standardization defining meaningful scores by comparison with the performance of a pretested group. (p. 420)

Stanford-Binet the widely used American revision (by Terman at Stanford University) of Binet's original intelligence test. (p. 417)

statistical significance a statistical statement of how likely it is that an obtained result occurred by chance. (p. 41)

stereotype a generalized (sometimes accurate but often overgeneralized) belief about a group of people. (p. 703)

stereotype threat a self-confirming concern that one will be evaluated based on a negative stereotype. (p. 439)

stimulants drugs (such as caffeine, nicotine, and the more powerful amphetamines, cocaine, and Ecstasy) that excite neural activity and speed up body functions. (p. 117)

storage the retention of encoded information over time. (p. 325)

stranger anxiety the fear of strangers that infants commonly display, beginning by about 8 months of age. (p. 185)

stress the process by which we perceive and respond to certain events, called *stressors*, that we appraise as threatening or challenging. (p. 531)

structuralism an early school of psychology that used introspection to explore the structural elements of the human mind. (p. 2)

structured interviews interview process that asks the same job-relevant questions of all applicants, each of whom is rated on established scales. (p. 488)

subjective well-being self-perceived happiness or satisfaction with life. Used along with measures of objective well-being (for example, physical and economic indicators) to evaluate people's quality of life. (p. 522)

subliminal below one's absolute threshold for conscious awareness. (p. 228)

superego the part of personality that, according to Freud, represents internalized ideals and provides standards for judgment (the conscience) and for future aspirations. (p. 560)

superordinate goals shared goals that override differences among people and require their cooperation. (p. 732)

survey a technique for ascertaining the self-reported attitudes or behaviors of a particular group, usually by questioning a representative, random sample of the group. (p. 27)

sympathetic nervous system the division of the autonomic nervous system that arouses the body, mobilizing its energy in stressful situations. (p. 53)

synapse [SIN-aps] the junction between the axon tip of the sending neuron and the dendrite or cell body of the receiving neuron. The tiny gap at this junction is called the *synaptic gap* or *synaptic cleft*. (p. 49)

syntax the rules for combining words into grammatically sensible sentences in a given language. (p. 385)

systematic desensitization a type of exposure therapy that associates a pleasant relaxed state with gradually increasing anxiety-triggering stimuli. Commonly used to treat phobias. (p. 652)

tardive dyskinesia involuntary movements of the facial muscles, tongue, and limbs; a possible neurotoxic side effect of long-term use of antipsychotic drugs that target certain dopamine receptors. (p. 672)

task leadership goal-oriented leadership that sets standards, organizes work, and focuses attention on goals. (p. 495)

telegraphic speech early speech stage in which a child speaks like a telegram—"go car"—using mostly nouns and verbs. (p. 387)

temperament a person's characteristic emotional reactivity and intensity. (p. 137)

temporal lobes portion of the cerebral cortex lying roughly above the ears; includes the auditory areas, each receiving information primarily from the opposite ear. (p. 67)

teratogens agents, such as chemicals and viruses, that can reach the embryo or fetus during prenatal development and cause harm. (p. 171)

terror-management theory a theory of death-related anxiety; explores people's emotional and behavioral responses to reminders of their impending death. (p. 567)

testosterone the most important of the male sex hormones. Both males and females have it, but the additional testosterone in males stimulates the growth of the male sex organs in the fetus and the development of the male sex characteristics during puberty. (pp. 160, 467)

thalamus [THAL-uh-muss] the brain's sensory switchboard, located on top of the brainstem; it directs messages to the sensory receiving areas in the cortex and transmits replies to the cerebellum and medulla. (p. 62)

THC the major active ingredient in marijuana; triggers a variety of effects, including mild hallucinations. (p. 122)

Thematic Apperception Test (TAT) a projective test in which people express their inner feelings and interests through the stories they make up about ambiguous scenes. (p. 564)

theory an explanation using an integrated set of principles that organizes observations and predicts behaviors or events. (p. 25)

theory of mind people's ideas about their own and others' mental states—about their feelings, perceptions, and thoughts, and the behaviors these might predict. (p. 181)

threshold the level of stimulation required to trigger a neural impulse. (p. 48)

token economy an operant conditioning procedure in which people earn a token of some sort for exhibiting a desired behavior and can later exchange the tokens for various privileges or treats. (p. 653)

tolerance the diminishing effect with regular use of the same dose of a drug, requiring the user to take larger and larger doses before experiencing the drug's effect. (p. 113)

top-down processing information processing guided by higher-level mental processes, as when we construct perceptions drawing on our experience and expectations. (p. 226)

trait a characteristic pattern of behavior or a disposition to feel and act, as assessed by self-report inventories and peer reports. (p. 574)

transduction conversion of one form of energy into another. In sensation, the transforming of stimulus energies, such as sights, sounds, and smells, into neural impulses our brains can interpret. (p. 233)

transference in psychoanalysis, the patient's transfer to the analyst of emotions linked with other relationships (such as love or hatred for a parent). (p. 647)

two-factor theory the Schachter-Singer theory that to experience emotion one must (1) be physically aroused and (2) cognitively label the arousal. (p. 501)

two-word stage beginning about age 2, the stage in speech development during which a child speaks mostly two-word statements. (p. 387)

Type A Friedman and Rosenman's term for competitive, hard-driving, impatient, verbally aggressive, and anger-prone people. (p. 536)

Type B Friedman and Rosenman's term for easygoing, relaxed people. (p. 536)

unconditional positive regard a caring, accepting, nonjudgmental attitude, which Carl Rogers believed to be conducive to developing self-awareness and self-acceptance. (pp. 571, 650)

unconditioned response (UR) in classical conditioning, the unlearned, naturally occurring response to the unconditioned stimulus (US), such as salivation when food is in the mouth. (p. 291)

unconditioned stimulus (US) in classical conditioning, a stimulus that unconditionally—naturally and automatically—triggers a response. (p. 291)

unconscious according to Freud, a reservoir of mostly unacceptable thoughts, wishes, feelings, and memories. According to contemporary psychologists, information processing of which we are unaware. (p. 558)

validity the extent to which a test measures or predicts what it is supposed to. (See also *content validity* and *predictive validity*.) (p. 421)

variable-interval schedule in operant conditioning, a reinforcement schedule that reinforces a response at unpredictable time intervals. (p. 306)

variable-ratio schedule in operant conditioning, a reinforcement schedule that reinforces a response after an unpredictable number of responses. (p. 305)

vestibular sense the sense of body movement and position, including the sense of balance. (p. 252)

virtual reality exposure therapy An anxiety treatment that progressively exposes people to simulations of their greatest fears, such as airplane flying, spiders, or public speaking. (p. 652)

visual cliff a laboratory device for testing depth perception in infants and young animals. (p. 264)

visual encoding the encoding of picture images. (p. 331)

wavelength the distance from the peak of one light or sound wave to the peak of the next. Electromagnetic wavelengths vary from the short blips of cosmic rays to the long pulses of radio transmission. (p. 234)

Weber's law the principle that, to be perceived as different, two stimuli must differ by a constant minimum percentage (rather than a constant amount). (p. 230)

Wechsler Adult Intelligence Scale (WAIS) the WAIS is the most widely used intelligence test; contains verbal and performance (nonverbal) subtests. (p. 419)

Wernicke's area controls language reception—a brain area involved in language comprehension and expression; usually in the left temporal lobe. (p. 391)

withdrawal the discomfort and distress that follow discontinuing the use of an addictive drug. (p. 113)

working memory a newer understanding of short-term memory that focuses on conscious, active processing of incoming auditory and visual-spatial information, and of information retrieved from long-term memory. (p. 326)

X chromosome the sex chromosome found in both men and women. Females have two X chromosomes; males have one. An X chromosome from each parent produces a female child. (p. 160)

Y chromosome the sex chromosome found only in males. When paired with an X chromosome from the mother, it produces a male child. (p. 160)

Young-Helmholtz trichromatic (three-color) theory the theory that the retina contains three different color receptors—one most sensitive to red, one to green, one to blue—which, when stimulated in combination, can produce the perception of any color. (p. 241)

zygote the fertilized egg; it enters a 2-week period of rapid cell division and develops into an embryo. (p. 170)

References

Abbey, A. (1987). Misperceptions of friendly behavior as sexual interest: A survey of naturally occurring incidents. *Psychology of Women Quarterly, 11,* 173–194. (p. 144)

Abbey, A. (1991). Acquaintance rape and alcohol consumption on college campuses: How are they linked? *Journal of American College Health, 39,* 165–169. (p. 117)

Abbott, R. D., White, L. R., Ross, G. W., Masaki, K. H., Curb, J. D., & Petrovitch, H. (2004). Walking and dementia in physically capable elderly men. *Journal of the American Medical Association, 292,* 1447–1453. (p. 212)

Abrams, D. B. (1991). AIDS: What young people believe and what they do. Paper presented at the British Association for the Advancement of Science conference. (p. 587)

Abrams, D. B., & Wilson, G. T. (1983). Alcohol, sexual arousal, and self-control. *Journal of Personality and Social Psychology, 45,* 188–198. (p. 116)

Abrams, L. (2008). Tip-of-the-tongue states yield language insights. *American Scientist, 96,* 234–239. (p. 354)

Abrams, M. (2002, June). Sight unseen—Restoring a blind man's vision is now a real possibility through stem-cell surgery. But even perfect eyes cannot see unless the brain has been taught to use them. *Discover, 23,* 54–60. (p. 272)

Abramson, L. Y., Metalsky, G. I., & Alloy, L. B. (1989). Hopelessness depression: A theory-based subtype. *Psychological Review, 96,* 358–372. (p. 633)

ACHA (2006). American College Health Association National College Health Assessment. Baltimore, MD: American College Health Association (acha-ncha.org). (pp. 598, 625)

Ackerman, D. (2004). *An alchemy of mind: The marvel and mystery of the brain.* New York: Scribner. (pp. 49, 58)

Actkinson, T. R. (2000). Master's and myth. *Eye on Psi Chi, 4,* 19–25. (p. A-10)

Adelmann, P. K., Antonucci, T. C., Crohan, S. F., & Coleman, L. M. (1989). Empty nest, cohort, and employment in the well-being of midlife women. *Sex Roles, 20,* 173–189. (p. 218)

Adelson, R. (2004, August). Detecting deception. *APA Monitor,* pp. 70–73. (p. 505)

Adelson, R. (2005, September). Lessons from H. M. *Monitor on Psychology,* p. 59. (p. 342)

Ader, R., & Cohen, N. (1985). CNS-immune system interactions: Conditioning phenomena. *Behavioral and Brain Sciences, 8,* 379–394. (p. 298)

Adolphs, R. (2006). Perception and emotion: How we recognize facial expressions. *Current Directions in Psychological Science, 15,* 222–226. (p. 511)

Adolphs, R., Tranel, D., & Damasio, A. R. (1998). The human amygdala in social judgment. *Nature, 393,* 470–474. (p. 519)

Affleck, G., Tennen, H., Urrows, S., & Higgins, P. (1994). Person and contextual features of daily stress reactivity: Individual differences in relations of undesirable daily events with mood disturbance and chronic pain intensity. *Journal of Personality and Social Psychology, 66,* 329–340. (p. 522)

Ai, A. L., Park, C. L., Huang, B., Rodgers, W., & Tice, T. N. (2007). Psychosocial mediation of religious coping styles: A study of short-term psychological distress following cardiac surgery. *Personality and Social Psychology Bulletin, 33,* 867–882. (p. 554)

Aiello, J. R., Thompson, D. D., & Brodzinsky, D. M. (1983). How funny is crowding anyway? Effects of room size, group size, and the introduction of humor. *Basic and Applied Social Psychology, 4,* 193–207. (p. 697)

Ainsworth, M. D. S. (1973). The development of infant-mother attachment. In B. Caldwell & H. Ricciuti (Eds.), *Review of child development research* (Vol. 3). Chicago: University of Chicago Press. (p. 187)

Ainsworth, M. D. S. (1979). Infant-mother attachment. *American Psychologist, 34,* 932–937. (p. 187)

Ainsworth, M. D. S. (1989). Attachments beyond infancy. *American Psychologist, 44,* 709–716. (p. 187)

Airan, R. D., Meltzer, L. A., Roy, M., Gong, Y., Chen, H., & Deisseroth, K. (2007). High-speed imaging reveals neurophysiological links to behavior in an animal model of depression. *Science, 317,* 819–823. (p. 632)

Åkerstedt, T., Kecklund, G., & Axelsson, J. (2007). Impaired sleep after bedtime stress and worries. *Biological Psychology, 76,* 170–173. (p. 101)

Albee, G. W. (1986). Toward a just society: Lessons from observations on the primary prevention of psychopathology. *American Psychologist, 41,* 891–898. (p. 669)

Albert, B., Brown, S., & Flanigan, C. M. (Eds.). (2003). *14 and younger: The sexual behavior of young adolescents.* Washington, DC: National Campaign to Prevent Teen Pregnancy. (p. 471)

Alcock, J. E. (1981). *Parapsychology: Science or magic?* Oxford: Pergamon. (p. 349)

Aldrich, M. S. (1989). Automobile accidents in patients with sleep disorders. *Sleep, 12,* 487–494. (p. 101)

Aldridge-Morris, R. (1989). *Multiple personality: An exercise in deception.* Hillsdale, NJ: Erlbaum. (p. 619)

Aleman, A., Kahn, R. S., & Selten, J-P. (2003). Sex differences in the risk of schizophrenia: Evidence from meta-analysis. *Archives of General Psychiatry, 60,* 565–571. (p. 638)

Alexander, C. N., Langer, E. J., Newman, R. I., Chandler, H. M., & Davies, J. L. (1989). Transcendental meditation, mindfulness, and longevity: An experimental study with the elderly. *Journal of Personality and Social Psychology, 57,* 950–964. (p. 552)

Allard, F., & Burnett, N. (1985). Skill in sport. *Canadian Journal of Psychology, 39,* 294–312. (p. 334)

Allen, J. B., Repinski, D. J., Ballard, J. C., & Griffin, B. W. (1996). Beliefs about the etiology of homosexuality may influence attitudes toward homosexuals. Paper presented to the American Psychological Society convention. (p. 478)

Allen, K. (2003). Are pets a healthy pleasure? The influence of pets on blood pressure. *Current Directions in Psychological Science, 12,* 236–239. (p. 546)

Allen, N. B., & Badcock, P. B. T. (2003). The social risk hypothesis of depressed mood: Evolutionary, psychosocial, and neurobiological perspectives. *Psychological Bulletin, 129,* 887–913. (p. 625)

Alloy, L. B., Abramson, L. Y., Whitehouse, W. G., Hogan, M. E., Tashman, N. A., Steinberg, D. L., Rose, D. T., & Donovan, P. (1999). Depressogenic cognitive styles: Predictive validity, information processing and personality characteristics, and developmental origins. *Behaviour Research and Therapy, 37,* 503–531. (p. 633)

Allport, G. W. (1954). *The nature of prejudice.* New York: Addison-Wesley. (pp. 27, 706)

Allport, G. W., & Odbert, H. S. (1936). Trait-names: A psycho-lexical study. *Psychological Monographs, 47*(1). (p. 575)

Altman, L. K. (2004, November 24). Female cases of HIV found rising worldwide. *New York Times* (www.nytimes.com). (p. 540)

Alwin, D. F. (1990). Historical changes in parental orientations to children. In N. Mandell (Ed.), *Sociological studies of child development* (Vol. 3). Greenwich, CT: JAI Press. (p. 156)

Amabile, T. M. (1983). *The social psychology of creativity.* New York: Springer-Verlag. (p. 591)

Amabile, T. M., Barsade, S. G., Mueller, J. S., & Staw, B. M. (2005). Affect and creativity at work. *Administrative Science Quarterly, 50,* 367–403. (p. 522)

Amabile, T. M., & Hennessey, B. A. (1992). The motivation for creativity in children. In A. K. Boggiano & T. S. Pittman (Eds.), *Achievement and motivation: A social-developmental perspective.* New York: Cambridge University Press. (p. 410)

Amato, P. R., Booth, A., Johnson, D. R., & Rogers, S. J. (2007). *Alone together: How marriage in America is changing.* Cambridge, MA: Harvard University Press. (p. 162)

Ambady, N., Hallahan, M., & Rosenthal, R. (1995). On judging and being judged accurately in zero-acquaintance situations. *Journal of Personality and Social Psychology, 69,* 518–529. (p. 511)

Ambady, N., & Rosenthal, R. (1992). Thin slices of expressive behavior as predictors of interpersonal consequences: A meta-analysis. *Psychological Bulletin, 111,* 256–274. (p. 582)

Ambady, N., & Rosenthal, R. (1993). Half a minute: Predicting teacher evaluations from thin slices of nonverbal behavior and physical attractiveness. *Journal of Personality and Social Psychology, 64,* 431–441. (p. 582)

Amedi, A., Floel, A., Knect, S., Zohary, E., & Cohen, L. (2004). Transcranial magnetic stimulation of the occipital pole interferes with verbal processing in blind subjects. *Nature Neuroscience, 7,* 1266–1270. (p. 73)

Amedi, A., Merabet, L. B., Bermpohl, F., & Pascual-Leone, A. (2005). The occipital cortex in the blind: Lessons about plasticity and vision. *Current Directions in Psychological Science, 14,* 306–311. (p. 73)

Amen, D. G., Stubblefield, M., Carmichael, B., & Thisted, R. (1996). Brain SPECT findings and aggressiveness. *Annals of Clinical Psychiatry, 8,* 129–137. (p. 710)

American Enterprise. (1992, January/February). Women, men, marriages & ministers. p. 106. (p. 155)

American Psychiatric Association. (1994). *Diagnostic and statistical manual of mental disorders* (4th ed.). Washington, DC: American Psychiatric Press. (p. 425)

American Psychological Association. (1992). Ethical principles of psychologists and code of conduct. *American Psychologist, 47,* 1597–1611. (p. 22)

American Psychological Association. (2002). *Ethical principles of psychologists and code of conduct.* Washington, DC: Author. (p. 21)

American Psychological Association. (2003). *Careers for the twenty-first century.* Washington, DC: Author. (p. A-10)

American Psychological Association. (2005). *Graduate study in psychology.* Washington, DC: Author. (p. A-10)

American Psychological Association. (2006). Evidence-based practice in psychology (from APA Presidential Task Force on Evidence-Based Practice). *American Psychologist, 61,* 271–285. (p. 664)

American Psychological Association. (2007). Answers to your questions about sexual orientation and homosexuality (www.apa.org. Accessed December 6, 2007). (p. 473)

Ames, D. R., & Flynn, F. J. (2007). What breaks a leader: The curvilinear relation between assertiveness and leadership. *Journal of Personality and Social Psychology, 92,* 307–324. (p. 495)

Andersen, R. A. (2005, October). Dialogue: A locksmith for the mind. *Discover* (www.discovermagazine.com). (p. 70)

Andersen, R. A., Burdick, J. W., Musallam, S., Pesaran, B., & Cham, J. G. (2004). Cognitive neural prosthetics. *Trends in Cognitive Sciences, 8,* 486–493. (p. 70)

Andersen, R. E., Crespo, C. J., Bartlett, S. J., Cheskin, L. J., & Pratt, M. (1998). Relationship of physical activity and television watching with body weight and level of fatness among children. *Journal of the American Medical Association, 279,* 938–942. (p. 463)

Andersen, S. M. (1998). *Service learning: A national strategy for youth development.* A position paper issued by the Task Force on Education Policy. Washington, DC: Institute for Communitarian Policy Studies, George Washington University. (p. 200)

Andersen, S. M., & Saribay, S. A. (2005). The relational self and transference: Evoking motives, self-regulation, and emotions through activation of mental representations of significant others. In M. W. Baldwin (Ed.), *Interpersonal cognition.* New York: Guilford. (p. 348)

Anderson, A. K., & Phelps, E. A. (2000). Expression without recognition: Contributions of the human amygdala to emotional communication. *Psychological Science, 11,* 106–111. (p. 63)

Anderson, B. L. (2002). Biobehavioral outcomes following psychological interventions for cancer patients. *Journal of Consulting and Clinical Psychology, 70,* 590–610. (p. 540)

Anderson, C. A. (2004). An update on the effects of playing violent video games. *Journal of Adolescence, 27,* 113–122. (p. 715)

Anderson, C. A., & Anderson, D. C. (1984). Ambient temperature and violent crime: Tests of the linear and curvilinear hypotheses. *Journal of Personality and Social Psychology, 46,* 91–97. (p. 712)

Anderson, C. A., Anderson, K. B., Dorr, N., DeNeve, K. M., & Flanagan, M. (2000). Temperature and aggression. In M. P. Zanna (Ed.), *Advances in Experimental Social Psychology.* San Diego: Academic Press. (p. 712)

Anderson, C. A., Carnagey, N. L., Flanagan, M., Benjamin, A. J., Jr., Eubanks, J., & Valentine, J. C. (2004). Violent video games: Specific effects of violent content on aggressive thoughts and behavior. *Advances in Experimental Social Psychology, 36,* 199–249. (p. 716)

Anderson, C. A., & Dill, K. E. (2000). Video games and aggressive thoughts, feelings, and behavior in the laboratory and in life. *Journal of Personality and Social Psychology, 78,* 772–790. (p. 716)

Anderson, C. A., & Gentile, D. A. (2008). Media violence, aggression, and public policy. In E. Borgida & S. Fiske (Eds.), *Beyond common sense: Psychological science in the courtroom.* Malden, MA: Blackwell. (p. 319)

Anderson, C. A., Gentile, D. A., & Buckley, K. E. (2007). *Violent video game effects on children and adolescents: Theory, research, and public policy.* New York: Oxford University Press. (pp. 343, 717)

Anderson, C. A., Lindsay, J. J., & Bushman, B. J. (1999). Research in the psychological laboratory: Truth or triviality? *Current Directions in Psychological Science, 8,* 3–9. (p. 19)

Anderson, I. M. (2000). Selective serotonin reuptake inhibitors versus tricyclic antidepressants: A meta-analysis of efficacy and tolerability. *Journal of Affective Disorders, 58,* 19–36. (p. 673)

Anderson, J. R., Myowa-Yamakoshi, M., & Matsuzawa, T. (2004). Contagious yawning in chimpanzees. *Biology Letters, 271,* S468–S470. (p. 690)

Anderson, R. C., Pichert, J. W., Goetz, E. T., Schallert, D. L., Stevens, K. V., & Trollip, S. R. (1976). Instantiation of general terms. *Journal of Verbal Learning and Verbal Behavior, 15,* 667–679. (pp. 347, 350)

Anderson, S. (2008, July 6). The urge to end it. *New York Times* (www.nytimes.com). (p. 630)

Anderson, S. E., Dallal, G. E., & Must, A. (2003). Relative weight and race influence average age at menarche: Results from two nationally representative surveys of U.S. girls studied 25 years apart. *Pediatrics, 111,* 844–850. (p. 196)

Anderson, S. R. (2004). *Doctor Dolittle's delusion: Animals and the uniqueness of human language.* New Haven: Yale University Press. (p. 401)

Anderson, U. S., Stoinski, T. S., Bloomsmith, M. A., Marr, M. J., Anderson, D., & Maple, T. L. (2005). Relative numerous judgment and summation in young and old western lowland gorillas. *Journal of Comparative Psychology, 119,* 285–295. (p. 214)

Andreasen, N. C. (1997). Linking mind and brain in the study of mental illnesses: A project for a scientific psychopathology. *Science, 275,* 1586–1593. (p. 640)

Andreasen, N. C. (2001). *Brave new brain: Conquering mental illness in the era of the genome.* New York: Oxford University Press. (p. 640)

Andreasen, N. C., Arndt, S., Swayze, V., II, Cizadlo, T., & Flaum, M. (1994). Thalamic abnormalities in schizophrenia visualized through magnetic resonance image averaging. *Science, 266,* 294–298. (p. 640)

Angell, M., & Kassirer, J. P. (1998). Alternative medicine: The risks of untested and unregulated remedies. *New England Journal of Medicine, 17,* 839–841. (p. 550)

Angelsen, N. K., Vik, T., Jacobsen, G., & Bakketeig, L. S. (2001). Breast feeding and cognitive development at age 1 and 5 years. *Archives of Disease in Childhood, 85,* 183–188. (p. 34)

Angoff, W. H. (1988, Winter). A philosophical discussion: The issues of test and item bias. *ETS Developments*, pp. 10–11. (p. 423)

Annan, K. A. (2001). We can love what we are, without hating who—and what—we are not. Nobel Peace Prize lecture. (p. 732)

Antoni, M. H., & Lutgendorf, S. (2007). Psychosocial factors and disease progression in cancer. *Current Directions in Psychological Science, 16*, 42–46. (p. 540)

Antony, M. M., Brown, T. A., & Barlow, D. H. (1992). Current perspectives on panic and panic disorder. *Current Directions in Psychological Science, 1*, 79–82. (p. 615)

Antrobus, J. (1991). Dreaming: Cognitive processes during cortical activation and high afferent thresholds. *Psychological Review, 98*, 96–121. (p. 105)

AP (2007). AP-Ipsos poll of 1,013 U.S. adults taken October 16-18, 2007 and distributed via Associated Press. (p. 281)

AP (2007). Kids copying execution accidentally hang selves. Associated Press, January 15, 2007 (*Grand Rapids Press*, p. A3). (p. 691)

AP (2007, January 12). China facing major gender imbalance. Associated Press release. (p. 704)

APA. (2003, November). *Psychology careers for the twenty-first century.* Washington, DC: American Psychological Association. (p. 10)

Apostolova, L. G., Dutton, R. A., Dinov, I. D., Hayashi, K. M., Toga, A. W., Cummings, J. L., Thompson, P. M. (2006). Conversion of mild cognitive impairment to Alzheimer disease predicted by hippocampal atrophy maps. *Archives of Neurology, 63*, 693–699. (p. 212)

Appleby, D. C. (2002). *The savvy psychology major.* Dubuque, IA: Kendall/Hunt. (p. A-10)

Appleby, D. C. (2006). Occupations of interest to psychology majors from the Dictionary of Occupational Titles. *Eye on Psi Chi, 10*, 28–29. (p. A-1)

Archer, J. (2004). Sex differences in aggression in real-world settings: A meta-analytic review. *Review of General Psychology, 8*, 291–322. (p. 158)

Archer, J. (2006). Cross-cultural differences in physical aggression between partners: A social-role analysis. *Personality and Social Psychology Review, 10*, 133–153. (p. 158)

Arendt, H. (1963). *Eichmann in Jerusalem: A report on the banality of evil.* New York: Viking Press. (p. 200)

Arenson, K. W. (1997, May 4). Romanian woman breaks male grip on top math prize. *New York Times* News Service (in *Grand Rapids Press*, p. A7). (p. 433)

Aries, E. (1987). Gender and communication. In P. Shaver & C. Henrick (Eds.), *Review of Personality and Social Psychology, 7*, 149–176. (p. 158)

Arkowitz, H., & Lilienfeld, S. O. (2006, April/May). Psychotherapy on trial. *Scientific American: Mind*, pp. 42–49. (p. 664)

Armel, K. C., & Ramachandran, V. S. (2003). Projecting sensations to external objects: Evidence from skin conductance response. *Proceedings of the Royal Society of London. Series B. Biological Sciences, 270*, 1499–1506. (p. 255)

Arnett, J. J. (1999). Adolescent storm and stress, reconsidered. *American Psychologist, 54*, 317–326. (p. 195)

Arnett, J. J. (2006). Emerging adulthood: Understanding the new way of coming of age. In J. J. Arnett & J. L. Tanner (Eds.), *Emerging adults in America: Coming of age in the 21st century.* Washington, DC: American Psychological Association. (p. 205)

Arnett, J. J. (2007). Socialization in emerging adulthood: From the family to the wider world, from socialization to self-socialization. In J. E. Grusec & P. D. Hastings (Eds.), *Handbook of socialization: Theory and research.* New York: Guilford Press. (p. 205)

Arnold, K., & Horrigan, K. (2002). Gaining admission into the graduate program of your choice. *Eye on Psi Chi, 30*–33. (pp. A-9, A-10)

Aron, A., Melinat, E., Aron, E. N., Vallone, R. D., & Bator, R. J. (1997). The experimental generation of interpersonal closeness: A procedure and some preliminary findings. *Personality and Social Psychology Bulletin, 23*, 363–377. (p. 725)

Aronson, E. (2001, April 13). Newsworthy violence. E-mail to SPSP discussion list, drawing from *Nobody Left to Hate*. New York: Freeman, 2000. (p. 203)

Artiga, A. I., Viana, J. B., Maldonado, C. R., Chandler-Laney, P. C., Oswald, K. D., & Boggiano, M. M. (2007). Body composition and endocrine status of long-term stress-induced binge-eating rats. *Physiology and Behavior, 91*, 424–431. (p. 452)

ASAPS. (2008). Cosmetic procedures in 2007. American Society for Aesthetic Plastic Surgery (www.surgery.org). (p. 722)

Asch, S. E. (1955). Opinions and social pressure. *Scientific American, 193*, 31–35. (p. 691)

Aserinsky, E. (1988, January 17). Personal communication. (p. 92)

ASHA. (2003). STD statistics. American Social Health Association (www.ashastd.org/stdfaqs/statistics.html). (p. 471)

Ashtari, M., Kumra, S., Clarke, T., Ardekani, B., Bhaskar, S., & Rhinewine, J (2004, November 29). Diffusion tensor imaging of children with attention deficit/hyperactivity disorder. Paper presented to the Radiological Society of North America convention. (p. 600)

Askay, S. W., & Patterson, D. R. (2007). Hypnotic analgesia. *Expert Review of Neurotherapeutics, 7*, 1675–1683. (p. 110)

Aspy, C. B., Vesely, S. K., Oman, R. F., Rodine, S., Marshall, L., & McLeroy, K. (2007). Parental communication and youth sexual behaviour. *Journal of Adolescence, 30*, 449–466. (p. 471)

Assanand, S., Pinel, J. P. J., & Lehman, D. R. (1998). Personal theories of hunger and eating. *Journal of Applied Social Psychology, 28*, 998–1015. (p. 451)

Associated Press. (1999, April 26). Airline passengers mistakenly told plane would crash. *Grand Rapids Press*, p. A3. (p. 532)

Associated Press. (2006, October 4). Man recites pi to 100,000 places. (p. 339)

Astin, A. W., Astin, H. S., & Lindholm, J. A. (2004). *Spirituality in higher education: A national study of college students' search for meaning and purpose.* Los Angeles: Higher Education Research Institute, UCLA. (p. 202)

Atance, C. M., & Meltzoff, A. N. (2006). Preschoolers' current desires warp their choices for the future. *Psychological Science, 17*, 583–587. (p. 448)

Atkinson, R. C., & Shiffrin, R. M. (1968). Human memory: A control system and its control processes. In K. Spence (Ed.), *The psychology of learning and motivation* (Vol. 2). New York: Academic Press. (pp. 325, 327, 336)

Aubrecht, L. (2001). What can you do with a BA in psychology? *Eye on Psi Chi, 5*, 29–31. (p. A-10)

Austin, E. J., Deary, I. J., Whiteman, M. C., Fowkes, F. G. R., Pedersen, N. L., Rabbitt, P., Bent, N., & McInnes, L. (2002). Relationships between ability and personality: Does intelligence contribute positively to personal and social adjustment? *Personality and Individual Differences, 32*, 1391–1411. (p 426)

Australian Bureau of Statistics (2007, July 8). Overweight and obesity (www.abs.gov.au). (p. 456)

Averill, J. R. (1983). Studies on anger and aggression: Implications for theories of emotion. *American Psychologist, 38*, 1145–1160. (pp. 520, 521)

Averill, J. R. (1993). William James's other theory of emotion. In M. E. Donnelly (Ed.), *Reinterpreting the legacy of William James*. Washington, DC: American Psychological Association. (p. 505)

Avery, R. D., & others. (1994, December 13). Mainstream science on intelligence. *Wall Street Journal*, p. A-18. (p. 435)

Ax, A. F. (1953). The physiological differentiation of fear and anger in humans. *Psychosomatic Medicine, 15*, 433–442. (p. 503)

Axinn, W. & Thornton, A. (1992). The relationship between cohabitation and divorce: Selectivity or causal influence? *Demography, 29*, 357–374. (p. B-6)

Axiss. (2007). Immigration and foreign population as percentage of total population: 1992 and 2003. Axiss Australia, Australian Government (www.axiss.gov.au). (p. 152)

Azar, B. (1998, June). Why can't this man feel whether or not he's standing up? *APA Monitor* (www.apa.org/monitor/jun98/touch.html). (p. 252)

Babad, E., Bernieri, F., & Rosenthal, R. (1991). Students as judges of teachers' verbal and nonverbal behavior. *American Educational Research Journal, 28*, 211–234. (p. 511)

Babyak, M., Blumenthal, J. A., Herman, S., Khatri, P., Doraiswamy, M., Moore, K., Craighead, W. W., Baldewics, T. T., & Krishnan, K. R. (2000). Exercise treatment for major depression: Maintenance of therapeutic benefit at ten months. *Psychosomatic Medicine, 62*, 633–638. (p. 547)

Bachman, J., O'Malley, P. M., Schulenberg, J. E., Johnston, L. D., Freedman-Doan, P., & Messersmith, E. E. (2007). The education-drug use connection: How successes and failures in school relate to adolescent smoking, drinking, drug use, and delinquency. Mahwah, NJ: Erlbaum. (p. 127)

Bachman, J., Wadsworth, K., O'Malley, P., Johnston, L., & Schulenberg, J. (1997). *Smoking, drinking, and drug use in young adulthood: The impact of new freedoms and new responsibilities.* Mahwah, NJ: Erlbaum. (p. 126)

Backman, L., & Dixon, R. A. (1992). Psychological compensation: A theoretical framework. *Psychological Bulletin, 112,* 259–283. (p. 248)

Backman, L., & MacDonald, S. W. S. (2006). Death and cognition: Synthesis and outlook. *European Psychologist, 11,* 224–235. (p. 215)

Baddeley, A. D. (1982). *Your memory: A user's guide.* New York: Macmillan. (p. 329)

Baddeley, A. D. (2001). Is working memory still working? *American Psychologist, 56,* 849–864. (p. 326)

Baddeley, A. D. (2002, June). Is working memory still working? *European Psychologist, 7,* 85–97. (p. 326)

Bagemihl, B. (1999). *Biological exuberance: Animal homosexuality and natural diversity.* New York: St. Martins. (p. 475)

Bahrick, H. P. (1984). Semantic memory content in permastore: 50 years of memory for Spanish learned in school. *Journal of Experimental Psychology: General, 111,* 1–29. (p. 353)

Bahrick, H. P., Bahrick, L. E., Bahrick, A. S., & Bahrick, P. E. (1993). Maintenance of foreign language vocabulary and the spacing effect. *Psychological Science, 4,* 316–321. (p. 329)

Bahrick, H. P., Bahrick, P. O., & Wittlinger, R. P. (1975). Fifty years of memory for names and faces: A cross-sectional approach. *Journal of Experimental Psychology: General, 104,* 54–75. (p. 346)

Bailenson, J. N., Iyengar, S., & Yee, N. (2005). Facial identity capture and presidential candidate preference. Paper presented at the Annual Conference of the International Communication Association. (p. 721)

Bailey, J. M., Gaulin, S., Agyei, Y., & Gladue, B. A. (1994). Effects of gender and sexual orientation on evolutionary relevant aspects of human mating psychology. *Journal of Personality and Social Psychology, 66,* 1081–1093. (p. 144)

Bailey, J. M., Kirk, K. M., Zhu, G., Dunne, M. P., & Martin, N. G. (2000). Do individual differences in sociosexuality represent genetic or environmentally contingent strategies? Evidence from the Australian twin registry. *Journal of Personality and Social Psychology, 78,* 537–545. (p. 144)

Bailey, J. M., & Zucker, K. J. (1995). Childhood sex-typed behavior and sexual orientation: A conceptual analysis and quantitative review. *Developmental Psychology, 31,* 43–55. (p. 472)

Bailey, R. E., & Gillaspy, J. A., Jr. (2005). Operant psychology goes to the fair: Marian and Keller Breland in the popular press, 1947–1966. *The Behavior Analyst, 28,* 143–159. (p. 309)

Baillargeon, R. (1995). A model of physical reasoning in infancy. In C. Rovee-Collier & L. P. Lipsitt (Eds.), *Advances in infancy research* (Vol. 9). Stamford, CT: Ablex. (p. 179)

Baillargeon, R. (1998). Infants' understanding of the physical world. In M. Sabourin, F. I. M. Craik, & M. Roberts (Eds.), *Advances in psychological science: Vol. 2. Biological and cognitive aspects.* Hove, England: Psychology Press. (p. 179)

Baird, G., Simonoff, E., Pickles, A., Chandler, S., Loucas, T., Meldrum, D., & Charman, T. (2006). Prevalence of disorders of the autism spectrum in a population cohort of children in South Thames: The special needs and autism project (SNAP). *Lancet, 368,* 210–215. (p. 182)

Baker, E. L. (1987). The state of the art of clinical hypnosis. *International Journal of Clinical and Experimental Hypnosis, 35,* 203–214. (p. 109)

Baker, T. B., Piper, M. E., McCarthy, D. E., Majeskie, M. R., & Fiore, M. C. (2004). Addiction motivation reformulated: An affective processing model of negative reinforcement. *Psychological Review, 111,* 33–51. (p. 304)

Bakermans-Kranenburg, M. J., van IJzendoorn, M. H., & Juffer, F. (2003). Less is more: Meta-analyses of sensitivity and attachment interventions in early childhood. *Psychological Bulletin, 129,* 195–215. (p. 188)

Balcetis, E., & Dunning, D. (2006). See what you want to see: Motivational influences on visual perception. *Journal of Personality and Social Psychology, 91,* 612–625. (p. 278)

Ballard, M. E., & Wiest, J. R. (1998). Mortal Kombat: The effects of violent videogame play on males' hostility and cardiovascular responding. *Journal of Applied Social Psychology, 26,* 717–730. (p. 716)

Balsam, K. F., Beauchaine, T. P., Mickey, R. M., & Rothblum, E. D. (2005). Mental health of lesbian, gay, bisexual, and heterosexual siblings: Effects of gender, sexual orientation, and family. *Journal of Abnormal Psychology, 114,* 471–476. (p. 473)

Balsam, K. F., Beauchaine, T. P., Rothblum, E. S., & Solomon, S. E. (2008). Three-year follow-up of same-sex couples who had civil unions in Vermont, same-sex couples not in civil unions, and heterosexual married couples. *Developmental Psychology, 44,* 102–116. (p. 217)

Baltes, P. B. (1993). The aging mind: Potential and limits. *The Gerontologist, 33,* 580–594. (p. 214)

Baltes, P. B. (1994). *Life-span developmental psychology: On the overall landscape of human development.* Invited address, American Psychological Association convention. (p. 214)

Baltes, P. B., & Baltes, M. M. (1999, September-October). Harvesting the fruits of age: Growing older, growing wise. *Science and the Spirit,* pp. 11–14. (p. 214)

Bancroft, J., Loftus, J., & Long, J. S. (2003). Distress about sex: A national survey of women in heterosexual relationships. *Archives of Sexual Behavior, 32,* 193–208. (p. 467)

Bandura, A. (1982). The psychology of chance encounters and life paths. *American Psychologist, 37,* 747–755. (p. 216)

Bandura, A. (1986). *Social foundations of thought and action: A social-cognitive theory.* Englewood Cliffs, NJ: Prentice-Hall. (p. 583)

Bandura, A. (2005). The evolution of social cognitive theory. In K. G. Smith & M. A. Hitt (Eds.), *Great minds in management: The process of theory development.* Oxford: Oxford University Press. (pp. 216, 317)

Bandura, A. (2006). Toward a psychology of human agency. *Perspectives on Psychological Science, 1,* 164–180. (p. 583)

Bandura, A. (2008). An agentic perspective on positive psychology. In S. J. Lopez (Ed.), *The science of human flourishing.* Westport, CT: Praeger. (p. 583)

Bandura, A., Ross, D., & Ross, S. A. (1961). Transmission of aggression through imitation of aggressive models. *Journal of Abnormal and Social Psychology, 63,* 575–582. (p. 317)

Barash, D. P. (2006, July 14). I am, therefore I think. *Chronicle of Higher Education,* pp. B9, B10. (p. 85)

Barber, C. (2008, February/March). The medicated American. *Scientific American Mind,* pp. 45–51. (p. 673)

Barber, T. X. (2000). A deeper understanding of hypnosis: Its secrets, its nature, its essence. *American Journal of Clinical Hypnosis, 42,* 208–272. (p. 110)

Bargh, J. A., & Chartrand, T. L. (1999). The unbearable automaticity of being. *American Psychologist, 54,* 462–479. (p. 86)

Bargh, J. A., & McKenna, K. Y. A. (2004). The Internet and social life. *Annual Review of Psychology, 55,* 573–590. (p. 720)

Bargh, J. A., McKenna, K. Y. A., & Fitzsimons, G. M. (2002). Can you see the real me? Activation and expression of the "true self" on the Internet. *Journal of Social Issues, 58,* 33–48. (p. 720)

Bargh, J. A., & Morsella, E. (2008). The unconscious mind. *Perspectives on Psychological Science, 3,* 73–79. (p. 567)

Bar-Haim, Y., Lamy, D., Pergamin, L., Bakermans-Kranenburg, M. J., & van IJzendoorn, M. H. (2007). Threat-related attentional bias in anxious and nonanxious individuals: A meta-analytic study. *Psychological Bulletin, 133,* 1–24. (p. 615)

Barinaga, M. (1991). How long is the human life-span? *Science, 254,* 936–938. (p. 208)

Barinaga, M. B. (1992a). The brain remaps its own contours. *Science, 258,* 216–218. (p. 73)

Barinaga, M. (1992b). How scary things get that way. *Science, 258,* 887–888. (p. 519)

Barinaga, M. (1999). Salmon follow watery odors home. *Science, 286,* 705–706. (p. 260)

Barinaga, M. B. (1997). How exercise works its magic. *Science, 276,* 1325. (p. 548)

Barkley, R. A., & 74 others. (2002). International consensus statement (January 2002). *Clinical Child and Family Psychology Review, 5,* 2. (p. 600)

Barnes, M. L., & Sternberg, R. J. (1989). Social intelligence and decoding of nonverbal cues. *Intelligence, 13,* 263–287. (p. 512)

Barnett, P. A., & Gotlib, I. H. (1988). Psychosocial functioning and depression: Distinguishing among antecedents, concomitants, and consequences. *Psychological Bulletin, 104,* 97–126. (p. 634)

Barnier, A. J., & McConkey, K. M. (2004). Defining and identifying the highly hypnotizable person. In M. Heap, R. J. Brown, & D. A. Oakley (Eds.),

High hypnotisability: Theoretical, experimental and clinical issues. London: Brunner-Routledge. (p. 108)

Baron, R. A. (1988). Negative effects of destructive criticism: Impact on conflict, self-efficacy, and task performance. *Journal of Applied Psychology, 73,* 199–207. (p. 311)

Baron, R. S., Vandello, J. A., & Brunsman, B. (1996). The forgotten variable in conformity research: Impact of task importance on social influence. *Journal of Personality and Social Psychology, 71,* 915–927. (p. 693)

Baron-Cohen, S. (2008). Autism, hypersystemizing, and truth. *Quarterly Journal of Experimental Psychology, 61,* 64–75. (p. 182)

Baron-Cohen, S., Golan, O., Chapman, E., & Granader, Y. (2007). Transported to a world of emotion. *The Psychologist, 20,* 76–77. (p. 183)

Baron-Cohen, S., Leslie, A. M., & Frith, U. (1985). Does the autistic child have a "theory of mind"? *Cognition, 21,* 37–46. (p. 181)

Barrett, L. F. (2006). Are emotions natural kinds? *Perspectives on Psychological Science, 1,* 28–58. (pp. 503, 505)

Barrett, L. F., Lane, R. D., Sechrest, L., & Schwartz, G. E. (2000). Sex differences in emotional awareness. *Personality and Social Psychology Bulletin, 26,* 1027–1035. (p. 512)

Barry, D. (1995, September 17). Teen smokers, too, get cool, toxic, waste-blackened lungs. *Asbury Park Press,* p. D3. (p. 119)

Bartholow, B. C., Bushman, B. J., & Sestir, M. A. (2006). Chronic violent video game exposure and desensitization to violence: Behavioral and event-related brain potential data. *Journal of Experimental Social Psychology, 42,* 532–539. (p. 716)

Bashore, T. R., Ridderinkhof, K. R., & van der Molen, M. W. (1997). The decline of cognitive processing speed in old age. *Current Directions in Psychological Science, 6,* 163–169. (p. 210)

Baskind, D. E. (1997, December 14). Personal communication, from Delta College. (p. 653)

Bassett, D. R., Schneider, P. L., & Huntington, G. E. (2004). Physical activity in an Old Order Amish community. *Medicine and Science in Sports and Exercise, 36,* 79–85. (p. 461)

Bat-Chava, Y. (1993). Antecedents of self-esteem in deaf people: A meta-analytic review. *Rehabilitation Psychology, 38*(4), 221–234. (p. 249)

Bat-Chava, Y. (1994). Group identification and self-esteem of deaf adults. *Personality and Social Psychology Bulletin, 20,* 494–502. (p. 249)

Bauer, P. J. (2002). Long-term recall memory: Behavioral and neurodevelopmental changes in the first 2 years of life. *Current Directions in Psychology, 11,* 137–141. (p. 175)

Bauer, P. J. (2007). Recall in infancy: A neurodevelopmental account. *Current Directions in Psychological Science, 16,* 142–146. (p. 175)

Bauer, P. J., Burch, M. M., Scholin, S. E., & Güler, O. E. (2007). Using cue words to investigate the distribution of autobiographical memories in childhood. *Psychological Science, 18,* 910–916. (p. 345)

Baum, A., & Posluszny, D. M. (1999). Health psychology: Mapping biobehavioral contributions to health and illness. *Annual Review of Psychology, 50,* 137–163. (p. 540)

Baumeister, H., & Härter, M. (2007). Prevalence of mental disorders based on general population surveys. *Social Psychiatry and Psychiatric Epidemiology, 42,* 537–546. (pp. 597, 607)

Baumeister, R. F. (1989). The optimal margin of illusion. *Journal of Social and Clinical Psychology, 8,* 176–189. (p. 377)

Baumeister, R. F. (1996). Should schools try to boost self-esteem? Beware the dark side. *American Educator, 20,* 43. (p. 593)

Baumeister, R. F. (2000). Gender differences in erotic plasticity: The female sex drive as socially flexible and responsive. *Psychological Bulletin, 126,* 347–374. (p. 473)

Baumeister, R. F. (2001, April). Violent pride: Do people turn violent because of self-hate, or self-love? *Scientific American,* pp. 96–101. (p. 593)

Baumeister, R. F. (2005). *The cultural animal: Human nature, meaning, and social life.* New York: Oxford University Press. (p. 152)

Baumeister, R. F. (2006, August/September). Violent pride. *Scientific American Mind,* pp. 54–59. (p. 591)

Baumeister, R. F., & Bratslavsky, E. (1999). Passion, intimacy, and time: Passionate love as a function of change in intimacy. *Personality and Social Psychology Review, 3,* 49–67. (p. 725)

Baumeister, R. F., Catanese, K. R., & Vohs, K. D. (2001). Is there a gender difference in strength of sex drive? Theoretical views, conceptual distinctions, and a review of relevant evidence. *Personality and Social Psychology Review, 5,* 242–273. (p. 144)

Baumeister, R. F., Dale, K., & Sommer, K. L. (1998). Freudian defense mechanisms and empirical findings in modern personality and social psychology: Reaction formation, projection, displacement, undoing, isolation, sublimation, and denial. *Journal of Personality, 66,* 1081–1125. (p. 567)

Baumeister, R. F., & Exline, J. J. (2000). Self-control, morality, and human strength. *Journal of Social and Clinical Psychology, 19,* 29–42. (p. 585)

Baumeister, R. F., & Leary, M. R. (1995). The need to belong: Desire for interpersonal attachments as a fundamental human motivation. *Psychological Bulletin, 117,* 497–529. (p. 479)

Baumeister, R. F., & Tice, D. M. (1986). How adolescence became the struggle for self: A historical transformation of psychological development. In J. Suls & A. G. Greenwald (Eds.), *Psychological perspectives on the self* (Vol. 3). Hillsdale, NJ: Erlbaum. (p. 204)

Baumeister, R. F., Twenge, J. M., & Nuss, C. K. (2002). Effects of social exclusion on cognitive processes: Anticipated aloneness reduces intelligent thought. *Journal of Personality and Social Psychology, 83,* 817–827. (p. 482)

Baumgardner, A. H., Kaufman, C. M., & Levy, P. E. (1989). Regulating affect interpersonally: When low esteem leads to greater enhancement. *Journal of Personality and Social Psychology, 56,* 907–921. (p. 591)

Baumrind, D. (1982). Adolescent sexuality: Comment on Williams' and Silka's comments on Baumrind. *American Psychologist, 37,* 1402–1403. (p. 479)

Baumrind, D. (1996). The discipline controversy revisited. *Family Relations, 45,* 405–414. (p. 193)

Baumrind, D., Larzelere, R. E., & Cowan, P. A. (2002). Ordinary physical punishment: Is it harmful? Comment on Gershoff (2002). *Psychological Bulletin, 128,* 602–611. (p. 307)

Bavelier, D., Dye, M. W. G., & Hauser, P. C. (2006). Do deaf individuals see better? *Trends in Cognitive Sciences, 10,* 512–518. (p. 249)

Bavelier, D., Newport, E. L., & Supalla, T. (2003). Children need natural languages, signed or spoken. *Cerebrum, 5*(1), 19–32. (p. 388)

Bavelier, D., Tomann, A., Hutton, C., Mitchell, T., Corina, D., Liu, G., & Neville, H. (2000). Visual attention to the periphery is enhanced in congenitally deaf individuals. *Journal of Neuroscience, 20,* 1–6. (p. 73)

Bayley, N. (1949). Consistency and variability in the growth of intelligence from birth to eighteen years. *Journal of Genetic Psychology, 75,* 165–196. (p. 423)

BBC (2006, June 14). Crystal meth to be Class A drug. BBC News (www.news.bbc.co.uk). (p. 118)

BBC (2008, February 26). Anti-depressants 'of little use.' BBC News (www.news.bbc.co.uk). (p. 674)

Beaman, A. L., & Klentz, B. (1983). The supposed physical attractiveness bias against supporters of the women's movement: A meta-analysis. *Personality and Social Psychology Bulletin, 9,* 544–550. (p. 723)

Beardsley, L. M. (1994). Medical diagnosis and treatment across cultures. In W. J. Lonner & R. Malpass (Eds.), *Psychology and culture.* Boston: Allyn & Bacon. (p. 602)

Beauchamp, G. K. (1987). The human preference for excess salt. *American Scientist, 75,* 27–33. (p. 452)

Beaujean, A. A. (2005). Heritability of cognitive abilities as measured by mental chronometric tasks: A meta-analysis. *Intelligence, 33,* 187–201. (p. 428)

Beck, A. T., Rush, A. J., Shaw, B. F., & Emery, G. (1979). *Cognitive therapy of depression.* New York: Guilford Press. (p. 655)

Beck, A. T., & Steer, R. A. (1989). Clinical predictors of eventual suicide: A 5- to 10-year prospective study of suicide attempters. *Journal of Affective Disorders, 17,* 203–209. (p. 630)

Becker, D. V., Kenrick, D. T., Neuberg, S. L., Blackwell, K. C., & Smith, D. M. (2007). The confounded nature of angry men and happy women. *Journal of Personality and Social Psychology, 92,* 179–190. (p. 512)

Becker, S., & Wojtowicz, J. M. (2007). A model of hippocampal neurogenesis in memory and mood disorders. *Trends in Cognitive Sciences, 11,* 70–76. (p. 673)

Becklen, R., & Cervone, D. (1983). Selective looking and the noticing of unexpected events. *Memory and Cognition, 11,* 601–608. (p. 88)

Beckman, M. (2004). Crime, culpability, and the adolescent brain. *Science, 305,* 596–599. (p. 197)

Beeman, M. J., & Chiarello, C. (1998). Complementary right- and left-hemisphere language comprehension. *Current Directions in Psychological Science, 7,* 2–8. (p. 77)

Beilin, H. (1992). Piaget's enduring contribution to developmental psychology. *Developmental Psychology, 28,* 191–204. (p. 185)

Beitman, B. D., Goldfried, M. R., & Norcross, J. C. (1989). The movement toward integrating the psychotherapies: An overview. *American Journal of Psychiatry, 146,* 138–147. (p. 646)

Bell, A. P., Weinberg, M. S., & Hammersmith, S. K. (1981). *Sexual preference: Its development in men and women.* Bloomington: Indiana University Press. (p. 474)

Bell, R. Q., & Waldrop, M. F. (1989). Achievement and cognitive correlates of minor physical anomalies in early development. In M. G. Bornstein & N. A. Krasnegor (Eds.), *Stability and continuity in mental development: Behavioral and biological perspectives.* Hillsdale, NJ: Erlbaum. (p. 423)

Bellugi, U. (1994, August). Quoted in P. Radetsky, Silence, signs, and wonder. *Discover,* pp. 60–68. (p. 385)

Belot, M., & Francesconi, M. (2006, November). *Can anyone be 'the one'? Evidence on mate selection from speed dating.* London: Centre for Economic Policy Research (www.cepr.org). (p. 721)

Belsher, G., & Costello, C. G. (1988). Relapse after recovery from unipolar depression: A critical review. *Psychological Bulletin, 104,* 84–96. (p. 628)

Belsky, J. (2003). The politicized science of day care: A personal and professional odyssey. *Family Policy Review 1*(2), 23–40. (2001). (p. 191)

Belsky, J., Bakermans-Kranenburg, M. J., & van IJzendoorn, M. H. (2007). For better *and* for worse: Differential susceptibility to environmental influences. *Current Directions in Psychological Science, 16,* 300–304. (p. 622)

Bem, D. J. (1984). Quoted in *The Skeptical Inquirer, 8,* 194. (p. 284)

Bem, D. J. (1996). Exotic becomes erotic: A developmental theory of sexual orientation. *Psychological Review, 103,* 320–335. (p. 478)

Bem, D. J. (1998). Is EBE theory supported by the evidence? Is it androcentric? A reply to Peplau et al. (1998). *Psychological Review, 105,* 395–398. (p. 478)

Bem, D. J. (2000). Exotic becomes erotic: Interpreting the biological correlates of sexual orientation. *Archives of Sexual Behavior, 29,* 531–548. (p. 478)

Bem, D. J., & Honorton, C. (1994). Does psi exist? Replicable evidence for an anomalous process of information transfer. *Psychological Bulletin, 115,* 4–18. (p. 284)

Bem, D. J., Palmer, J., & Broughton, R. S. (2001). Updating the Ganzfeld database: A victim of its own success? *Journal of Parapsychology, 65,* 207–218. (p. 284)

Bem, S. L. (1987). Masculinity and femininity exist only in the mind of the perceiver. In J. M. Reinisch, L. A. Rosenblum, & S. A. Sanders (Eds.), *Masculinity/femininity: Basic perspectives.* New York: Oxford University Press. (p. 163)

Bem, S. L. (1993). *The lenses of gender.* New Haven, CT: Yale University Press. (p. 163)

Benbow, C. P., Lubinski, D., Shea, D. L., & Eftekhari-Sanjani, H. (2000). Sex differences in mathematical reasoning ability at age 13: Their status 20 years later. *Psychological Science, 11,* 474–2000. (p. 433)

Bennett, R. (1991, February). *Pornography and extrafamilial child sexual abuse: Examining the relationship.* Unpublished manuscript, Los Angeles Police Department Sexually Exploited Child Unit. (p. 714)

Bennett, W. I. (1995). Beyond overeating. *New England Journal of Medicine, 332,* 673–674. (p. 463)

Ben-Shakhar, G., & Elaad, E. (2003). The validity of psychophysiological detection of information with the guilt knowledge test: A meta-analytic review. *Journal of Applied Psychology, 88,* 131–151. (p. 505)

Benson, H. (1996). *Timeless healing: The power and biology of belief.* New York: Scribner. (p. 551)

Benson, K., & Feinberg, I. (1977). The beneficial effect of sleep in an extended Jenkins and Dallenbach paradigm. *Psychophysiology, 14,* 375–384. (p. 356)

Benson, P. L. (1992, Spring). Patterns of religious development in adolescence and adulthood. *PIRI Newsletter,* pp. 2–9. (p. 160)

Berenbaum, S. A., & Bailey, J. M. (2003). Effects on gender identity of prenatal androgens and genital appearance: Evidence from girls with congenital adrenal hyperplasia. *Journal of Clinical Endocrinology and Metabolism, 88,* 1102–1106. (p. 161)

Berenbaum, S. A., & Hines, M. (1992). Early androgens are related to childhood sex-typed toy preferences. *Psychological Science, 3,* 203–206. (p. 161)

Berenbaum, S. A., Korman, K., & Leveroni, C. (1995). Early hormones and sex differences in cognitive abilities. *Learning and Individual Differences, 7,* 303–321. (p. 434)

Berenson, A. (2007, September 3). New schizophrenia drug shows promise in trials. *New York Times* (www.nytimes.com). (p. 672)

Berghuis, P., & 16 others (2007). Hardwiring the brain: Endocannabinoids shape neuronal connectivity. *Science, 316,* 1212–1216. (p. 124)

Bergin, A. E. (1980). Psychotherapy and religious values. *Journal of Consulting and Clinical Psychology, 48,* 95–105. (p. 669)

Berk, L. E. (1994, November). Why children talk to themselves. *Scientific American,* pp. 78–83. (p. 184)

Berk, L. S., Felten, D. L., Tan, S. A., Bittman, B. B., & Westengard, J. (2001). Modulation of neuroimmune parameters during the eustress of humor-associated mirthful laughter. *Alternative Therapies, 7,* 62–76. (p. 545)

Berkel, J., & de Waard, F. (1983). Mortality pattern and life expectancy of Seventh Day Adventists in the Netherlands. *International Journal of Epidemiology, 12,* 455–459. (p. 553)

Berkowitz, L. (1983). Aversively stimulated aggression: Some parallels and differences in research with animals and humans. *American Psychologist, 38,* 1135–1144. (p. 712)

Berkowitz, L. (1989). Frustration-aggression hypothesis: Examination and reformulation. *Psychological Bulletin, 106,* 59–73. (p. 712)

Berkowitz, L. (1990). On the formation and regulation of anger and aggression: A cognitive-neoassociationistic analysis. *American Psychologist, 45,* 494–503. (p. 520)

Berman, M., Gladue, B., & Taylor, S. (1993). The effects of hormones, Type A behavior pattern, and provocation on aggression in men. *Motivation and Emotion, 17,* 125–138. (p. 711)

Berndt, T. J. (1992). Friendship and friends' influence in adolescence. *Current Directions in Psychological Science, 1,* 156–159. (p. 160)

Bernhardt, P. C., Dabbs, J. M., Jr., Fielden, J. A., & Lutter, C. D. (1998). Testosterone changes during vicarious experiences of winning and losing among fans at sporting events. *Physiology and Behavior, 65,* 59–62. (p. 711)

Berridge, K. C., & Winkielman, P. (2003). What is an unconscious emotion? (The case of unconscious "liking"). *Cognition and Emotion, 17,* 181–211. (p. 507)

Berry, D. S., & McArthur, L. Z. (1986). Perceiving character in faces: The impact of age-related craniofacial changes on social perception. *Psychological Bulletin, 100,* 3–18. (p. 294)

Berscheid, E. (1981). An overview of the psychological effects of physical attractiveness and some comments upon the psychological effects of knowledge of the effects of physical attractiveness. In G. W. Lucker, K. Ribbens, & J. A. McNamara (Eds.), *Psychological aspects of facial form* (Craniofacial growth series). Ann Arbor: Center for Human Growth and Development, University of Michigan. (p. 722)

Berscheid, E. (1985). Interpersonal attraction. In G. Lindzey & E. Aronson (Eds.), *The handbook of social psychology.* New York: Random House. (p. 480)

Berscheid, E., Gangestad, S. W., & Kulakowski, D. (1984). Emotion in close relationships: Implications for relationship counseling. In S. D. Brown & R. W. Lent (Eds.), *Handbook of counseling psychology.* New York: Wiley. (p. 725)

Berti, A., Cottini, G., Gandola, M., Pia, L., Smania, N., Stracciari, A., Castiglioni, I., Vallar, G., & Paulesu, E. (2005). Shared cortical anatomy for motor awareness and motor control. *Science, 309,* 488–491. (p. 78)

Bertua, C., Anderson, N., & Salgado, J. F. (2005). The predictive validity of cognitive ability tests: A UK meta-analysis. *Journal of Occupational and Organizational Psychology, 78,* 387–409. (p. 407)

Bettencourt, B. A., & Kernahan, C. (1997). A meta-analysis of aggression in the presence of violent cues: Effects of gender differences and aversive provocation. *Aggressive Behavior, 23,* pp. 447–457. (p. 158)

Beyerstein, B., & Beyerstein, D. (Eds.). (1992). *The write stuff: Evaluations of graphology.* Buffalo, NY: Prometheus Books. (p. 578)

Bhatt, R. S., Wasserman, E. A., Reynolds, W. F., Jr., & Knauss, K. S. (1988). Conceptual behavior in pigeons: Categorization of both familiar and novel examples from four classes of natural and artificial stimuli. *Journal of Experimental Psychology: Animal Behavior Processes, 14*, 219–234. (p. 303)

Bialystok, E. (2001). *Bilingualism in development, language, literacy, and cognition.* New York: Cambridge University Press. (p. 394)

Biederman, I., & Vessel, E. A. (2006). Perceptual pleasure and the brain. *American Scientist, 94*, 247–253. (p. 446)

Biederman, J., Wilens, T., Mick, E., Spencer, T., & Faraone, S. V. (1999). Pharmacotherapy of attention-deficit/hyperactivity disorder reduces risk for substance use disorder. *Pediatrics, 104*, 1–5. (p. 600)

Biggs, V. (2001, April 13). Murder suspect captured in Grand Marais. *Cook County News-Herald.* (p. 512)

Bigler, E. D., Johnson, S. C., Jackson, C., & Blatter, D. D. (1995). Aging, brain size, and IQ. *Intelligence, 21*, 109–119. (p. 412)

Binet, A. (1909). *Les idées mordermes sur les enfants.* Paris: Flammarion (quoted by A. Clarke & A. Clarke, Born to be bright. *The Psychologist, 19*, 409). (p. 416)

Binitie, A. (1975). A factor-analytical study of depression across cultures (African and European). *British Journal of Psychiatry, 127*, 559–563. (p. 623)

Birnbaum, G. E., Reis, H. T., Mikulincer, M., Gillath, O., & Orpaz, A. (2006). When sex is more than just sex: Attachment orientations, sexual experience, and relationship quality. *Journal of Personality and Social Psychology, 91*, 929–943. (p. 189)

Birnbaum, S. G., Yuan, P. X., Wang, M., Vijayraghavan, S., Bloom, A. K., Davis, D. J., Gobeski, K. T., Sweatt, J. D., Manhi, H. K., & Arnsten, A. F. T. (2004). Protein kinase C overactivity impairs prefrontal cortical regulation of working memory. *Science, 306*, 882–884. (p. 341)

Bishop, G. (2004, November 22). Personal correspondence, and earlier articles on "The great divide" in the *Austin Statesman.* (p. 699)

Bishop, G. D. (1991). Understanding the understanding of illness: Lay disease representations. In J. A. Skelton & R. T. Croyle (Eds.), *Mental representation in health and illness.* New York: Springer-Verlag. (p. 371)

Bisson, J., & Andrew, M. (2007). Psychological treatment of post-traumatic stress disorder (PTSD). *Cochrane Database of Systematic Reviews 2007*, Issue 3. Art. No: CD003388. (p. 665)

Bjork, R. A. (2000, July/August). Toward one world of psychological science. *APS Observer*, p. 3. (p. 6)

Bjorklund, D. F., & Green, B. L. (1992). The adaptive nature of cognitive immaturity. *American Psychologist, 47*, 46–54. (p. 185)

Blackburn, E. H., Greider, C. W., & Szostak, J. W. (2007). Telomeres and telomerase: The path from maize, *Tetrahymena* and yeast to human cancer and aging. *Nature Medicine, 12*(10), vii–xii. (p. 208)

Blackmore, S. (1991, Fall). Near-death experiences: In or out of the body? *Skeptical Inquirer*, pp. 34–45. (p. 123)

Blackmore, S. (1993). *Dying to live.* Amherst, NY: Prometheus Books. (p. 123)

Blakemore, S-J. (2008). Development of the social brain during adolescence. *Quarterly Journal of Experimental Psychology, 61*, 40–49. (p. 197)

Blakemore, S-J., Wolpert, D. M., & Frith, C. D. (1998). Central cancellation of self-produced tickle sensation. *Nature Neuroscience, 1*, 635–640. (p. 252)

Blakeslee, S. (2005, February 8). Focus narrows in search for autism's cause. *New York Times* (www.nytimes.com). (p. 182)

Blakeslee, S. (2006, January 10). Cells that read minds. *New York Times* (www.nytimes.com). (p. 316)

Blanchard, R. (1997). Birth order and sibling sex ratio in homosexual versus heterosexual males and females. *Annual Review of Sex Research, 8*, 27–67. (p. 474)

Blanchard, R. (2008). Review and theory of handedness, birth order, and homosexuality in men. *Laterality, 13*, 51–70. (p. 474)

Blanchard-Fields, F. (2007). Everyday problem solving and emotion: An adult developmental perspective. *Current Directions in Psychological Science, 16*, 26–31. (p. 215)

Blanchflower, D. G., & Oswald, A. J. (2008). Hypertension and happiness across nations. *Journal of Health Economics, 27*, 218–233. (pp. 219, 535)

Blank, H., Musch, J., & Pohl, R. F. (2007). Hindsight bias: On being wise after the event. *Social Cognition, 25*, 1–9. (p. 15)

Blanke, O., Landis, T., & Spinelli, L. (2004). Out-of-body experience and autoscopy of neurological origin. *Brain: Journal of Neurology, 127*, 243–258 (p. 123)

Blanke, O., Ortigue, S., Landis, T., & Seeck, M. (2002). Stimulating illusory own-body perceptions. *Nature, 419*, 269–270. (p. 123)

Blankenburg, F., Taskin, B., Ruben, J., Moosmann, M., Ritter, P., Curio, G., & Villringer, A. (2003). Imperceptive stimuli and sensory processing impediment. *Science, 299*, 1864. (p. 229)

Blascovich, J., Seery, M. D., Mugridge, C. A., Norris, R. K., & Weisbuch, M. (2004). Predicting athletic performance from cardiovascular indexes of challenge and threat. *Journal of Experimental Social Psychology, 40*, 683–688. (p. 531)

Blass, T. (1996). Stanley Milgram: A life of inventiveness and controversy. In G. A. Kimble, C. A. Boneau, & M. Wertheimer (Eds.), *Portraits of pioneers in psychology* (Vol. II). Washington, DC and Mahwah, NJ: American Psychological Association and Lawrence Erlbaum Publishers. (p. 694)

Blass, T. (1999). The Milgram paradigm after 35 years: Some things we now know about obedience to authority. *Journal of Applied Social Psychology, 29*, 955–978. (p. 694)

Blatt, S. J., Sanislow, C. A., III, Zuroff, D. C., & Pilkonis, P. (1996). Characteristics of effective therapists: Further analyses of data from the National Institute of Mental Health Treatment of Depression Collaborative Research Program. *Journal of Consulting and Clinical Psychology, 64*, 1276–1284. (p. 668)

Bleustein, J. (2002, June 15). Quoted in "Harley retooled," by S. S. Smith, *American Way Magazine.* (p. 496)

Bloom, B. C. (Ed.). (1985). *Developing talent in young people.* New York: Ballantine. (p. 491)

Bloom, B. J. (1964). *Stability and change in human characteristics.* New York: Wiley. (p. 423)

Bloom, F. E. (1993, January/February). What's new in neurotransmitters. *BrainWork*, pp. 7–9. (p. 50)

Bloom, P. (2000). *How children learn the meanings of words.* Cambridge, MA: MIT Press. (p. 386)

Blum, K., Cull, J. G., Braverman, E. R., & Comings, D. E. (1996). Reward deficiency syndrome. *American Scientist, 84*, 132–145. (p. 65)

Boag, S. (2006). Freudian repression, the common view, and pathological science. *Review of General Psychology, 10*, 74–86. (p. 566)

Boahen, K. (2005, May). Neuromorphic microchips. *Scientific American*, pp. 56–63. (p. 248)

Bocklandt, S., Horvath, S., Vilain, E., & Hamer, D. H. (2006). Extreme skewing of X chromosome inactivation in mothers of homosexual men. *Human Genetics, 118*, 691–694. (p. 476)

Bodenhausen, G. V., Sheppard, L. A., & Kramer, G. P. (1994). Negative affect and social judgment: The differential impact of anger and sadness. *European Journal of Social Psychology, 24*, 45–62. (p. 733)

Bodkin, J. A., & Amsterdam, J. D. (2002). Transdermal selegiline in major depression: A double-blind, placebo-controlled, parallel-group study in outpatients. *American Journal of Psychiatry, 159*, 1869–1875. (p. 673)

Boehm, K. E., Schondel, C. K., Marlowe, A. L., & Manke-Mitchell, L. (1999). Teens' concerns: A national evaluation. *Adolescence, 34*, 523–528. (p. 203)

Boehm-Davis, D. A. (2005). Improving product safety and effectiveness in the home. In R. S. Nickerson (Ed.), *Reviews of human factors and ergonomics.* Volume 1 (pp. 219–253). Santa Monica, CA: Human Factors and Ergonomics Society, 219–253. (p. 279)

Boesch-Achermann, H., & Boesch, C. (1993). Tool use in wild chimpanzees: New light from dark forests. *Current Directions in Psychological Science, 2*, 18–21. (p. 397)

Bogaert, A. F. (2003). Number of older brothers and sexual orientation: New texts and the attraction/behavior distinction in two national probability samples. *Journal of Personality and Social Psychology, 84*, 644–652. (p. 474)

Bogaert, A. F. (2004). Asexuality: Prevalence and associated factors in a national probability sample. *Journal of Sex Research, 41*, 279–287. (p. 473)

Bogaert, A. F. (2006). Biological versus nonbiological older brothers and men's sexual orientation. *Proceedings of the National Academy of Sciences, 103*, 10771–10774. (p. 475)

Bogaert, A. F. (2006). Toward a conceptual understanding of asexuality. *Review of General Psychology, 10*, 241–250. (p. 473)

Bogaert, A. F., Friesen, C., & Klentrou, P. (2002). Age of puberty and sexual orientation in a national probability sample. *Archives of Sexual Behavior, 31*, 73–81. (p. 475)

Boggiano, A. K., Harackiewicz, J. M., Bessette, M. M., & Main, D. S. (1985). Increasing children's interest through performance-contingent reward. *Social Cognition, 3*, 400-411. (p. 309)

Boggiano, M. M., Chandler, P. C., Viana, J. B., Oswald, K. D., Maldonado, C. R., & Wauford, P. K. (2005). Combined dieting and stress evoke exaggerated responses to opioids in binge-eating rats. *Behavioral Neuroscience, 119*, 1207-1214. (p. 452)

Bohman, M., & Sigvardsson, S. (1990). Outcome in adoption: Lessons from longitudinal studies. In D. Brodzinsky & M. Schechter (Eds.), *The psychology of adoption.* New York: Oxford University Press. (p. 137)

Bolger, N., DeLongis, A., Kessler, R. C., & Schilling, E. A. (1989). Effects of daily stress on negative mood. *Journal of Personality and Social Psychology, 57*, 808-818. (p. 522)

Bolwig, T. G., & Madsen, T. M. (2007). Electroconvulsive therapy in melancholia: The role of hippocampal neurogenesis. *Acta Psychiatrica Scandinavica, 115*, 130-135. (p. 676)

Bonanno, G. A. (2001). Grief and emotion: Experience, expression, and dissociation. In M. Stroebe, W. Stroebe, R. O. Hansson, & H. Schut (Eds.), *New handbook of bereavement: Consciousness, coping, and care.* Cambridge: Cambridge University Press. (p. 221)

Bonanno, G. A. (2004). Loss, trauma, and human resilience: Have we underestimated the human capacity to thrive after extremely aversive events? *American Psychologist, 59*, 20-28. (pp. 221, 614)

Bonanno, G. A. (2005). Adult resilience to potential trauma. *Current Directions in Psychological Science, 14*, 135-137. (p. 614)

Bonanno, G. A., Galea, S., Bucciarelli, A., & Vlahov, D. (2006). Psychological resilience after disaster. *Psychological Science, 17*, 181-186. (p. 613)

Bonanno, G. A., & Kaltman, S. (1999). Toward an integrative perspective on bereavement. *Psychological Bulletin, 125*, 760-777. (p. 221)

Bond, C. F., Jr. & DePaulo, B. M. (2006). Accuracy of deception judgments. *Personality and Social Psychology Review, 10*, 214-234. (p. 511)

Bond, C. F., Jr. & DePaulo, B. M. (2008). Individual differences in detecting deception: Accuracy and bias. *Psychological Bulletin, 134*, 477-492. (p. 511)

Bond, C. F., Jr. & the 89 others on The Global Deception Research Team. (2006). A world of lies. *Journal of Cross-Cultural Psychology, 37*, 60-74. (p. 511)

Bond, M. H. (1988). Finding universal dimensions of individual variation in multi-cultural studies of values: The Rokeach and Chinese values surveys. *Journal of Personality and Social Psychology, 55*, 1009-1015. (p. 155)

Bond, R., & Smith, P. B. (1996). Culture and conformity: A meta-analysis of studies using Asch's (1952b, 1956) line judgment task. *Psychological Bulletin, 119*, 111-137. (p. 693)

Bonnie, K. E., Horner, V., Whiten, A., & de Waal, F. B. M. (2007). Spread of arbitrary conventions among chimpanzees: A controlled experiment. *Proceedings of the Royal Society, 274*, 367-372. (p. 398)

Bono, J. E., & Judge, T. A. (2004). Personality and transformational and transactional leadership: A meta-analysis. *Journal of Applied Psychology, 89*, 901-910. (p. 495)

Bookheimer, S. H., Strojwas, M. H., Cohen, M. S., Saunders, A. M., Pericak-Vance, M. A., Mazziotta, J. C., & Small, G. W. (2000). Patterns of brain activation in people at risk for Alzheimer's disease. *New England Journal of Medicine, 343*, 450-456. (p. 212)

Bookwala, J., & Boyar, J. (2008). Gender, excessive body weight, and psychological well-being in adulthood. *Psychology of Women Quarterly, 32*, 188-195. (p. 458)

Boos, H. B. M., Aleman, A., Cahn, W., Hulshoff, H., & Kahn, R. S. (2007). Brain volumes in relatives of patients with schizophrenia. *Archives of General Psychiatry, 64*, 297-304. (p. 640)

Booth, F. W., & Neufer, P. D. (2005). Exercise controls gene expression. *American Scientist, 93*, 28-35. (p. 548)

Boring, E. G. (1930). A new ambiguous figure. *American Journal of Psychology, 42*, 444-445. (p. 274)

Bornstein, M. H., Cote, L. R., Maital, S., Painter, K., Park, S-Y., Pascual, L., Pecheux, M-G., Ruel, J., Venute, P., & Vyt, A. (2004). Cross-linguistic analysis of vocabulary in young children: Spanish, Dutch, French, Hebrew, Italian, Korean, and American English. *Child Development, 75*, 1115-1139. (p. 388)

Bornstein, M. H., Tal, J., Rahn, C., Galperin, C. Z., Pecheux, M-G., Lamour, M., Toda, S., Azuma, H., Ogino, M., & Tamis-LeMonda, C. S. (1992a). Functional analysis of the contents of maternal speech to infants of 5 and 13 months in four cultures: Argentina, France, Japan, and the United States. *Developmental Psychology, 28*, 593-603. (p. 156)

Bornstein, M. H., Tamis-LeMonda, C. S., Tal, J., Ludemann, P., Toda, S., Rahn, C. W., Pecheux, M-G., Azuma, H., & Vardi, D. (1992b). Maternal responsiveness to infants in three societies: The United States, France, and Japan. *Child Development, 63*, 808-821. (p. 156)

Bornstein, R. F. (1989). Exposure and affect: Overview and meta-analysis of research, 1968-1987. *Psychological Bulletin, 106*, 265-289. (pp. 187, 719)

Bornstein, R. F. (1999). Source amnesia, misattribution, and the power of unconscious perceptions and memories. *Psychoanalytic Psychology, 16*, 155-178. (p. 719)

Bornstein, R. F. (2001). The impending death of psychoanalysis. *Psychoanalytic Psychology, 18*, 3-20. (p. 568)

Bornstein, R. F., Galley, D. J., Leone, D. R., & Kale, A. R. (1991). The temporal stability of ratings of parents: Test-retest reliability and influence of parental contact. *Journal of Social Behavior and Personality, 6*, 641-649. (p. 350)

Boscarino, J. A. (1997). Diseases among men 20 years after exposure to severe stress: Implications for clinical research and medical care. *Psychosomatic Medicine, 59*, 605-614. (p. 531)

Bösch, H., Steinkamp, F., & Boller, E. (2006a). Examining psychokinesis: The interaction of human intention with random number generators—A meta-analysis. *Psychological Bulletin, 132*, 497-523. (p. 284)

Bösch, H., Steinkamp, F., & Boller, E. (2006b). In the eye of beholder: Reply to Wilson and Shadish (2006) and Radin, Nelson, Dobyns, and Houtkooper (2006). *Psychological Bulletin, 132*, 533-537. (p. 284)

Bosma, H., Marmot, M. G., Hemingway, H., Nicolson, A. C., Brunner, E., & Stansfeld, S. A. (1997). Low job control and risk of coronary heart disease in Whitehall II (prospective cohort) study. *British Medical Journal, 314*, 558-565. (p. 543)

Bosma, H., Peter, R., Siegrist, J., & Marmot, M. (1998). Two alternative job stress models and the risk of coronary heart disease. *American Journal of Public Health, 88*, 68-74. (p. 543)

Bostwick, J. M., & Pankratz, V. S. (2000). Affective disorders and suicide risk: A re-examination. *American Journal of Psychiatry, 157*, 1925-1932. (p. 630)

Bosworth, R. G., & Dobkins, K. R. (1999). Left-hemisphere dominance for motion processing in deaf signers. *Psychological Science, 10*, 256-262. (p. 73)

Bothwell, R. K., Brigham, J. C., & Malpass, R. S. (1989). Cross-racial identification. *Personality and Social Psychology Bulletin, 15*, 19-25. (p. 708)

Bothwell, R. K., Deffenbacher, K. A., & Brigham, J. C. (1987). Correlation of eyewitness accuracy and confidence: Optimality hypothesis revised. *Journal of Applied Psychology, 72*, 691-695. (p. 360)

Botwin, M. D., Buss, D. M., & Shackelford, T. K. (1997). Personality and mate preferences: Five factors in mate selection and marital satisfaction. *Journal of Personality, 65*, 107-136. (p. 580)

Bouchard, T. J., Jr. (1981, December 6). Interview on Nova: Twins [program broadcast by the Public Broadcasting Service]. (p. 136)

Bouchard, T. J., Jr. (1995). Longitudinal studies of personality and intelligence: A behavior genetic and evolutionary psychology perspective. In D. H. Saklofske & M. Zeidner (Eds.), *International handbook of personality and intelligence.* New York: Plenum. (p. 429)

Bouchard, T. J., Jr. (1996a). IQ similarity in twins reared apart: Finding and responses to critics. In R. Sternberg & C. Grigorenko (Eds.), *Intelligence: Heredity and environment.* New York: Cambridge University Press. (p. 428)

Bouchard, T. J., Jr. (1996b). Behavior genetic studies of intelligence, yesterday and today: The long journey from plausibility to proof. *Journal of Biosocial Science, 28*, 527-555. (p. 429)

Bouchard, T. J., Jr., & McGue, M. (1990). Genetic and rearing environmental influences on adult personality: An analysis of adopted twins reared apart. *Journal of Personality, 58*, 263. (p. 136)

Bouton, M. E., Mineka, S., & Barlow, D. H. (2001). A modern learning theory perspective on the etiology of panic disorder. *Psychological Review, 108*, 4-32. (p. 615)

Bowden, E. M., & Beeman, M. J. (1998). Getting the right idea: Semantic activation in the right hemisphere may help solve insight problems. *Psychological Science, 9,* 435–440. (p. 78)

Bower, B. (2003, November 22). Vision seekers. *Science News, 164,* pp. 331, 332. (p. 272)

Bower, G. H. (1983). Affect and cognition. *Philosophical Transaction: Royal Society of London, Series B, 302,* 387–402. (p. 349)

Bower, G. H., Clark, M. C., Lesgold, A. M., & Winzenz, D. (1969). Hierarchical retrieval schemes in recall of categorized word lists. *Journal of Verbal Learning and Verbal Behavior, 8,* 323–343. (p. 334)

Bower, G. H., & Morrow, D. G. (1990). Mental models in narrative comprehension. *Science, 247,* 44–48. (p. 331)

Bower, J. E., Kemeny, M. E., Taylor, S. E., & Fahey, J. L. (1998). Cognitive processing, discovery of meaning, CD4 decline, and AIDS-related mortality among bereaved HIV-seropositive men. *Journal of Consulting and Clinical Psychology, 66,* 979–986. (p. 540)

Bower, J. M., & Parsons, L. M. (2003, August). Rethinking the "lesser brain." *Scientific American,* pp. 50–57. (p. 62)

Bowers, K. S. (1984). Hypnosis. In N. Endler & J. M. Hunt (Eds.), *Personality and behavioral disorders* (2nd ed.). New York: Wiley. (pp. 108, 110)

Bowers, K. S. (1987, July). Personal communication. (p. 109)

Bowers, T. G., & Clum, G. A. (1988). Relative contribution of specific and nonspecific treatment effects: Meta-analysis of placebo-controlled behavior therapy research. *Psychological Bulletin, 103,* 315–323. (p. 663)

Bowlby, J. (1973). *Separation: Anxiety and anger.* New York: Basic Books. (p. 190)

Bowler, M. C., & Woehr, D. J. (2006). A meta-analytic evaluation of the impact of dimension and exercise factors on assessment center ratings. *Journal of Applied Psychology, 91,* 1114–1124. (p. 589)

Bowles, S., & Kasindorf, M. (2001, March 6). Friends tell of picked-on but 'normal' kid. *USA Today,* p. 4A. (p. 482)

Bowling, N. A. (2007). Is the job satisfaction-job performance relationship spurious? A meta-analytic examination. *Journal of Vocational Behavior, 71,* 167–185. (p. 492)

Bowman, H. (2003, Fall). Interactions between chimpanzees and their human caregivers in captive settings: The effects of gestural communication on reciprocity. *Friends of Washoe, 25(1),* 7–16. (p. 400)

Boyatzis, C. J., Matillo, G. M., & Nesbitt, K. M. (1995). Effects of the "Mighty Morphin Power Rangers" on children's aggression with peers. *Child Study Journal, 25,* 45–55. (p. 321)

Boyer, J. L., Harrison, S., & Ro, T. (2005). Unconscious processing of orientation and color without primary visual cortex. *Proceedings of the National Academy of Sciences, 102,* 16875–16879 (www.pnas.org). (p. 239)

Boynton, R. M. (1979). *Human color vision.* New York: Holt, Rinehart & Winston. (p. 241)

Braden, J. P. (1994). *Deafness, deprivation, and IQ.* New York: Plenum. (pp. 249, 435)

Bradley, D. R., Dumais, S. T., & Petry, H. M. (1976). Reply to Cavonius. *Nature, 261,* 78. (p. 262)

Bradley, R. B., & 15 others (2008). Influence of child abuse on adult depression: Moderation by the corticotropin-releasing hormone receptor gene. *Archives of General Psychiatry, 65,* 190–200. (p. 190)

Braiker, B. (2005, October 18). A quiet revolt against the rules on SIDS. *New York Times* (www.nytimes.com). (p. 175)

Brainerd, C. J. (1996). Piaget: A centennial celebration. *Psychological Science, 7,* 191–195. (p. 176)

Brainerd, C. J., & Poole, D. A. (1997). Long-term survival of children's memories: A review. *Learning and Individual Differences, 9,* 125–151. (p. 360)

Brainerd, C. J., & Reyna, V. F. (1998). When things that were never experienced are easier to "remember" than things that were. *Psychological Science, 9,* 484–489. (p. 360)

Brainerd, C. J., & Reyna, V. F. (2002). Fuzzy-trace theory and false memory. *Current Directions in Psychological Science, 11,* 164–169. (p. 360)

Brainerd, C. J., Reyna, V. F., & Brandse, E. (1995). Are children's false memories more persistent than their true memories? *Psychological Science, 6,* 359–364. (p. 360)

Brandon, S., Boakes, J., Glaser, & Green, R. (1998). Recovered memories of childhood sexual abuse: Implications for clinical practice. *British Journal of Psychiatry, 172,* 294–307. (p. 363)

Brang, D., Edwards, L., Ramachandran, V. S., & Coulson, S. (2008). Is the sky 2? Contextual priming in grapheme-color synaesthesia. *Psychological Science, 19,* 421–428. (p. 258)

Brannon, L. A., & Brock, T. C. (1993). Comment on report of HIV infection in rural Florida: Failure of instructions to correct for gross underestimation of phantom sex partners in perception of AIDS risk. *New England Journal of Medicine, 328,* 1351–1352. (p. 471)

Bransford, J. D., & Johnson, M. K. (1972). Contextual prerequisites for understanding: Some investigations of comprehension and recall. *Journal of Verbal Learning and Verbal Behavior, 11,* 717–726. (p. 331)

Braun, S. (1996). New experiments underscore warnings on maternal drinking. *Science, 273,* 738–739. (p. 172)

Braun, S. (2001, Spring). Seeking insight by prescription. *Cerebrum,* pp. 10–21. (p. 121)

Braunstein, G. D., Sundwall, D. A., Katz, M., Shifren, J. L., Buster, J. E., Simon, J. A., Bachman, G., Aguirre, O. A., Lucas, J. D., Rodenberg, C., Buch, A., & Watts, N. B. (2005). Safety and efficacy of a testosterone patch for the treatment of hypoactive sexual desire disorder in surgically menopausal women: A randomized, placebo-controlled trial. *Archives of Internal Medicine, 165,* 1582–1589. (p. 468)

Bray, D. W., & Byham, W., interviewed by Mayes, B. T. (1997). Insights into the history and future of assessment centers: An interview with Dr. Douglas W. Bray and Dr. William Byham. *Journal of Social Behavior and Personality, 12,* 3–12. (p. 589)

Bray, D. W., & Byham, W. C. (1991, Winter). Assessment centers and their derivatives. *Journal of Continuing Higher Education,* pp. 8–11. (p. 589)

Bray, G. A. (1969). Effect of caloric restriction on energy expenditure in obese patients. *Lancet, 2,* 397–398. (p. 459)

Brayne, C., Spiegelhalter, D. J., Dufouil, C., Chi, L-Y., Dening, T. R., Paykel, E. S., O'Connor, D.W., Ahmed, A., McGee, M. A., & Huppert, F.A. (1999). Estimating the true extent of cognitive decline in the old old. *Journal of the American Geriatrics Society, 47,* 1283–1288. (p. 214)

Breedlove, S. M. (1997). Sex on the brain. *Nature, 389,* 801. (p. 476)

Brehm, S., & Brehm, J. W. (1981). *Psychological reactance: A theory of freedom and control.* New York: Academic Press. (p. 701)

Breland, K., & Breland, M. (1961). The misbehavior of organisms. *American Psychologist, 16,* 661–664. (p. 309)

Breslau, J., Aguilar-Gaxiola, S., Borges, G., Kendler, K. S., Su, M., & Kessler, R. C. (2007). Risk for psychiatric disorder among immigrants and their US-born descendants. *Journal of Nervous and Mental Disease, 195,* 189–195. (p. 607)

Bressan, P., & Dal Martello, M. F. (2002). Talis pater, talis filius: Perceived resemblance and the belief in genetic relatedness. *Psychological Science, 13,* 213–218. (p. 274)

Brewer, C. L. (1990). Personal correspondence. (p. 140)

Brewer, C. L. (1996). Personal communication. (p. 8)

Brewer, M. B., & Chen, Y-R. (2007). Where (who) are collectives in collectivism? Toward conceptual clarification of individualism and collectivism. *Psychological Review, 114,* 133–151. (p. 154)

Brewer, W. F. (1977). Memory for the pragmatic implications of sentences. *Memory & Cognition, 5,* 673–678. (p. 331)

Brewin, C. R., Andrews, B., Rose, S., & Kirk, M. (1999). Acute stress disorder and posttraumatic stress disorder in victims of violent crime. *American Journal of Psychiatry, 156,* 360–366. (p. 613)

Brewin, C. R., Andrews, B., & Valentine, J. D. (2000). Meta-analysis of risk factors for posttraumatic stress disorder in trauma-exposed adults. *Journal of Consulting and Clinical Psychology, 68,* 748–766. (p. 613)

Brewin, C. R., Kleiner, J. S., Vasterling J. J., & Field, A. P. (2007). Memory for emotionally neutral information in posttraumatic stress disorder: A meta-analytic investigation. *Journal of Abnormal Psychology, 116,* 448–463. (p. 341)

Bricker, J. B., Stallings, M. C., Corley, R. P., Wadsworth, S. J., Bryan, A., Timberlake, D. S., Hewitt, J. K., Caspi, A., Hofer, S. M., Rhea, S. A., & DeFries, J. C. (2006). Genetic and environmental influences on age at sexual initiation in the Colorado Adoption Project. *Behavior Genetics, 36,* 820–832. (p. 470)

Brief, A. P., & Weiss, H. M. (2002). Organizational behavior: Affect in the workplace. *Annual Review of Psychology, 53,* 279–307. (p. 491)

Briers, B., Pandelaere, M., Dewitte, S., & Warlop, L. (2006). Hungry for money: The desire for caloric resources increases the desire for financial resources and vice versa. *Psychological Science, 17,* 939–943. (p. 304)

Briñol, P., Petty, R. E., & Barden, J. (2007). Happiness versus sadness as a determinant of thought confidence in persuasion: A self-validation analysis. *Journal of Personality and Social Psychology, 93,* 711–727. (p. 522)

Brinson, S. L. (1992). The use and opposition of rape myths in prime-time television dramas. *Sex Roles, 27,* 359–375. (p. 714)

Briscoe, D. (1997, February 16). Women lawmakers still not in charge. *Grand Rapids Press,* p. A23. (p. 163)

Brislin, R. W. (1988). Increasing awareness of class, ethnicity, culture, and race by expanding on students' own experiences. In I. Cohen (Ed.), *The G. Stanley Hall Lecture Series.* Washington, DC: American Psychological Association. (p. 151)

Brissette, I., & Cohen, S. (2002). The contribution of individual differences in hostility to the associations between daily interpersonal conflict, affect, and sleep. *Personality and Social Psychology Bulletin, 28,* 1265–1274. (p. 101)

Brissette, I., Scheier, M. F., & Carver, C. S. (2002). The role of optimism in social network development, coping, and psychological adjustment during a life transition. *Journal of Personality and Social Psychology, 82,* 102–111. (p. 633)

British Psychological Society. (1993). Ethical principles for conducting research with human participants. *The Psychologist: Bulletin of the British Psychological Society, 6,* 33–36. (pp. 22, 578)

Britton, W. B., & Bootzin, R. R. (2004). Near-death experiences and the temporal lobe. *Psychological Science, 15,* 254–258. (p. 123)

Brody, J. E. (1999, November 30). Yesterday's precocious puberty is norm today. *New York Times* (www.nytimes.com). (p. 196)

Brody, J. E. (2000, March 21). When post-traumatic stress grips youth. *New York Times* (www.nytimes.com). (p. 613)

Brody, J. E. (2002, November 26). When the eyelids snap shut at 65 miles an hour. *New York Times* (www.nytimes.com). (p. 98)

Brody, J. E. (2003, December 23). Stampede of diabetes as U.S. races to obesity. *New York Times* (www.nytimes.com). (p. 461)

Brody, J. E. (2003, September). Addiction: A brain ailment, not a moral lapse. *New York Times* (www.nytimes.com). (p. 114)

Brody, N. (1992). *Intelligence* (2nd ed.). San Diego: Academic Press. (p. 414)

Brody, N. (2001). Inspection time: Past, present, and future. *Intelligence, 29,* 537–541. (p. 414)

Brody, S., & Tillmann, H. C. (2006). The post-orgasmic prolactin increase following intercourse is greater than following masturbation and suggests greater satiety. *Biological Psychology, 71,* 312–315. (p. 479)

Broks, P. (2007, April). The mystery of consciousness. *Prospect* (www.prospect-magazine.co.uk). (p. 176)

Broman, S. H. (1989). Infant physical status and later cognitive development. In M. G. Bornstein & N. A. Krasnegor (Eds.), *Stability and continuity in mental development: Behavioral and biological perspectives.* Hillsdale, NJ: Erlbaum. (p. 423)

Bronner, E. (1998, February 25). U.S. high school seniors among worst in math and science. *New York Times* (www.nytimes.com). (p. 433)

Brookes, K., & 61 others (2006). The analysis of 51 genes in DSM-IV combined type attention deficit hyperactivity disorder: Association signals in DRD4, DAT1 and 16 other genes. *Molecular Psychiatry, 11,* 935–953. (p. 600)

Brooks, D. (2005, April 28). Mourning Mother Russia. *New York Times* (www.nytimes.com). (p. 208)

Brooks, D. J. (2002, October 8). Running down the road to happiness. *Gallup Tuesday Briefing* (www.gallup.com). (p. 547)

Brooks, R., & Meltzoff, A. N. (2005). The development of gaze following and its relation to language. *Developmental Science, 8,* 535–543. (p. 316)

Brown, A. S. (2003). A review of the déjà vu experience. *Psychological Bulletin, 129,* 394–413. (p. 349)

Brown, A. S. (2004a). *The déjà vu experience.* East Sussex, England: Psychology Press. (p. 349)

Brown, A. S. (2004b). Getting to grips with déja vu. *The Psychologist, 17,* 694–696. (p. 349)

Brown, A. S., Begg, M. D., Gravenstein, S., Schaefer, C. A., Wyatt, R. J., Bresnahan, M., Babulas, V. P., & Susser, E. S. (2004). Serologic evidence of prenatal influenza in the etiology of schizophrenia. *Archives of General Psychiatry, 61,* 774–780. (p. 641)

Brown, A. S., Bracken, E., Zoccoli, S., & Douglas, K. (2004). Generating and remembering passwords. *Applied Cognitive Psychology, 18,* 641–651. (p. 355)

Brown, A. S., Schaefer, C. A., Wyatt, R. J., Goetz, R., Begg, M. D., Gorman, J. M., & Susser, E. S. (2000). Maternal exposure to respiratory infections and adult schizophrenia spectrum disorders: A prospective birth cohort study. *Schizophrenia Bulletin, 26,* 287–295. (p. 641)

Brown, E. L., & Deffenbacher, K. (1979). *Perception and the senses.* New York: Oxford University Press. (p. 247)

Brown, G. K., Ten Have, T., Henriques, G. R., Xie, S. X., Hollander, J. E., & Beck, A. T. (2005). Cognitive therapy for the prevention of suicide attempts. *Journal of the American Medical Association, 294,* 563–570. (p. 664)

Brown, J. A. (1958). Some tests of the decay theory of immediate memory. *Quarterly Journal of Experimental Psychology, 10,* 12–21. (p. 337)

Brown, J. D., Steele, J. R., & Walsh-Childers, K. (2002). *Sexual teens, sexual media: Investigating media's influence on adolescent sexuality.* Mahwah, NJ: Erlbaum. (p. 471)

Brown, J. L., & Pollitt, E. (1996, February). Malnutrition, poverty and intellectual development. *Scientific American,* pp. 38–43. (p. 431)

Brown, R. (1965). *Social psychology.* New York: Free Press. (p. 518)

Brown, R. (1986). Linguistic relativity. In S. H. Hulse & B. F. Green, Jr. (Eds.), *One hundred years of psychological research in America.* Baltimore: Johns Hopkins University Press. (p. 393)

Brown, S. L., Brown, R. M., House, J. S., & Smith, D. M. (2008). Coping with spousal loss: Potential buffering effects of self-reported helping behavior. *Personality and Social Psychology Bulletin, 34,* 849–861. (p. 221)

Brown, S. W., Garry, M., Loftus, E., Silver, B., DuBois, K., & DuBreuil, S. (1996). People's beliefs about memory: Why don't we have better memories? Paper presented at the American Psychological Society convention. (p. 357)

Brownell, K. D. (2002). Public policy and the prevention of obesity. In C. G. Fairburn & K. D. Brownell (Eds.), *Eating disorders and obesity: A comprehensive handbook* (2nd ed.). New York: Guilford. (p. 462)

Brownell, K. D., & Nestle, M. (2004, June 7). Are you responsible for your own weight? *Time,* p. 113. (p. 461)

Browning, C. (1992). Ordinary men: Reserve police battalion 101 and the final solution in Poland. New York: HarperCollins. (p. 695)

Brownmiller, S. (1975). *Against our will: Men, women, and rape.* New York: Simon & Schuster. (p. 470)

Bruce, D., Dolan, A., & Phillips-Grant, K. (2000). On the transition from childhood amnesia to the recall of personal memories. *Psychological Science, 11,* 360–364. (p. 175)

Bruck, M., & Ceci, S. (2004). Forensic developmental psychology: Unveiling four common misconceptions. *Current Directions in Psychological Science, 15,* 229–232. (p. 361)

Bruck, M., & Ceci, S. J. (1999). The suggestibility of children's memory. *Annual Review of Psychology, 50,* 419–439. (p. 361)

Bruder, C. E. G., & 22 others (2008). Phenotypically concordant and discordant monozygotic twins display different DNA copy-number-variation profiles. *American Journal of Human Genetics, 82,* 763–771. (p. 134)

Bruer, J. T. (1999). The myth of the first three years: A new understanding of early brain development and lifelong learning. New York: Free Press. (p. 431)

Brumberg, J. J. (2000). *Fasting girls: The history of anorexia nervosa.* New York: Vintage. (p. 453)

Bryant, A. N., & Astin, H. A. (2008). The correlates of spiritual struggle during the college years. *Journal of Higher Education, 79,* 1-27. (p. 202)

Bryant, R. A. (2001). Posttraumatic stress disorder and traumatic brain injury: Can they co-exist? *Clinical Psychology Review, 21,* 931–948. (p. 363)

Buchanan, T. W. (2007). Retrieval of emotional memories. *Psychological Bulletin, 133,* 761–779. (p. 341)

Buck, L. B., & Axel, R. (1991). A novel multigene family may encode odorant receptors: A molecular basis for odor recgnition. *Cell, 65,* 175–187. (p. 260)

Buckingham, M. (2001, August). Quoted by P. LaBarre, "Marcus Buckingham thinks your boss has an attitude problem." *The Magazine* (fastcompany.com/online/49/buckingham.html). (pp. 491, 493)

Buckingham, M. (2007). *Go put your strengths to work: 6 powerful steps to achieve outstanding performance.* New York: Free Press. (p. 486)

Buckingham, M., & Clifton, D. O. (2001). *Now, discover your strengths.* New York: Free Press. (pp. 486, 487)

Buckley, C. (2007, January 3). Man is rescued by stranger on subway tracks. *New York Times* (www.nytimes.com). (p. 729)

Buckley, K. E., & Leary, M. R. (2001). Perceived acceptance as a predictor of social, emotional, and academic outcomes. Paper presented at the Society of Personality and Social Psychology annual convention. (p. 481)

Buehler, R., Griffin, D., & Ross, M. (1994). Exploring the "planning fallacy": Why people underestimate their task completion times. *Journal of Personality and Social Psychology, 67,* 366-381. (p. 377)

Bugelski, B. R., Kidd, E., & Segmen, J. (1968). Image as a mediator in one-trial paired-associate learning. *Journal of Experimental Psychology, 76,* 69-73. (p. 333)

Bugental, D. B. (1986). Unmasking the "polite smile": Situational and personal determinants of managed affect in adult-child interaction. *Personality and Social Psychology Bulletin, 12,* 7-16. (p. 510)

Buka, S. L., Goldstein, J. M., Seidman, L. J., Zornberg, G., Donatelli, J-A. A., Denny, L. R., & Tsuang, M. T. (1999). Prenatal complications, genetic vulnerability, and schizophrenia: The New England longitudinal studies of schizophrenia. *Psychiatric Annals, 29,* 151-156. (p. 640)

Buka, S. L., Tsuang, M. T., Torrey, E. F., Klebanoff, M. A., Wagner, R. L., & Yolken, R. H. (2001). Maternal infections and subsequent psychosis among offspring. *Archives of General Psychiatry, 58,* 1032-1037. (p. 641)

Bullough, V. (1990). The Kinsey scale in historical perspective. In D. P. McWhirter, S. A. Sanders, & J. M. Reinisch (Eds.), *Homosexuality/heterosexuality: Concepts of sexual orientation.* New York: Oxford University Press. (p. 472)

Bunde, J., & Suls, J. (2006). A quantitative analysis of the relationship between the Cook-Medley Hostility Scale and traditional coronary artery disease risk factors. *Health Psychology, 25,* 493-500. (p. 536)

Buquet, R. (1988). Le reve et les deficients visuels [Dreams and the visually-impaired]. *Psychanalyse-a-l'Universite, 13,* 319-327. (p. 103)

Burcusa, S. L., & Iacono, W. G. (2007). Risk for recurrence in depression. *Clinical Psychology Review, 27,* 959-985. (p. 627)

Bureau of Labor Statistics. (2004, September 14). *American time-user survey summary.* Washington, DC: United States Department of Labor (www.bls.gov). (p. 162)

Bureau of the Census. (2004). *Statistical abstract of the United States 2004.* Washington, DC: U.S. Government Printing Office. (p. 606)

Bureau of the Census. (2007). *Statistical abstract of the United States 2007.* Washington, DC: U.S. Government Printing Office. (p. 217)

Burgess, M., Enzle, M. E., & Schmaltz, R. (2004). Defeating the potentially deleterious effects of externally imposed deadlines: Practitioners' rules-of-thumb. *Personality and Social Psychology Bulletin, 30,* 868-877. (p. 494)

Buri, J. R., Louiselle, P. A., Misukanis, T. M., & Mueller, R. A. (1988). Effects of parental authoritarianism and authoritativeness on self-esteem. *Personality and Social Psychology Bulletin, 14,* 271-282. (p. 193)

Burish, T. G., & Carey, M. P. (1986). Conditioned aversive responses in cancer chemotherapy patients: Theoretical and developmental analysis. *Journal of Counseling and Clinical Psychology, 54,* 593-600. (p. 297)

Burke, D. M., & Shafto, M. A. (2004). Aging and language production. *Current Directions in Psychological Science, 13,* 21-24. (p. 213)

Burkholder, R. (2005a, January 11). Chinese far wealthier than a decade ago—but are they happier? *Gallup Poll News Service* (www.gallup.com). (p. 528)

Burkholder, R. (2005b, January 18). China's citizens optimistic, yet not entirely satisfied. *Gallup Poll News Service* (www.gallup.com). (p. 528)

Burns, B. C. (2004). The effects of speed on skilled chess performance. *Psychological Science, 15,* 442-447. (p. 381)

Burns, J. F., & Filkins, D. (2006, June 14). Bush makes surprise visit to Iraq to press leadership. *New York Times* (www.nytimes.com). (p. 511)

Burrell, B. (2005). *Postcards from the brain museum: The improbable search for meaning in the matter of famous minds.* New York: Broadway Books. (p. 412)

Burris, C. T., & Branscombe, N. R. (2005). Distorted distance estimation induced by a self-relevant national boundary. *Journal of Experimental Social Psychology, 41,* 305-312. (p. 394)

Burton, C. M., & King, L. A. (2008). Effects of (very) brief writing on health: The two-minute miracle. *British Journal of Health Psychology, 13,* 9-14. (p. 546)

Bush, G. W. (1999). Quoted by M. Ivins, syndicated column, November 27, 1999. (p. 14)

Bush, G. W. (2001). Quoted in various places, including BBC News (bbc.co.uk), June 16, 2001. (p. 731)

Bushman, B. J. (1993). Human aggression while under the influence of alcohol and other drugs: An integrative research review. *Current Directions in Psychological Science, 2,* 148-152. (p. 711)

Bushman, B. J. (2002). Does venting anger feed or extinguish the flame? Catharsis, rumination, distraction, anger, and aggressive responding. *Personality and Social Psychology Bulletin, 28,* 724-731. (p. 521)

Bushman, B. J., & Anderson, C. A. (2001). Media violence and the American public: Scientific facts versus media misinformation. *American Psychologist, 56,* 477-489. (p. 716)

Bushman, B. J., & Baumeister, R. F. (1998). Threatened egotism, narcissism, self-esteem, and direct and displaced aggression: Does self-love or self-hate lead to violence? *Journal of Personality and Social Psychology, 75,* 219-229. (p. 593)

Bushman, B. J., Baumeister, R. F., & Stack, A. D. (1999). Catharsis, aggression, and persuasive influence: Self-fulfilling or self-defeating prophecies? *Journal of Personality and Social Psychology, 76,* 367-376. (p. 521)

Bushman, B. J., & Bonacci, A. M. (2002). Violence and sex impair memory for television ads. *Journal of Applied Psychology, 87,* 557-564. (p. 356)

Busnel, M. C., Granier-Deferre, C., & Lecanuet, J. P. (1992, October). Fetal audition. *New York Academy of Sciences, 662,* 118-134. (p. 171)

Buss, A. H. (1989). Personality as traits. *American Psychologist, 44,* 1378-1388. (p. 582)

Buss, D. (2008). Female sexual psychology. World Question Center 2008 (edge.org). (p. 469)

Buss, D. M. (1991). Evolutionary personality psychology. *Annual Review of Psychology, 42,* 459-491. (p. 139)

Buss, D. M. (1994). The strategies of human mating: People worldwide are attracted to the same qualities in the opposite sex. *American Scientist, 82,* 238-249. (p. 145)

Buss, D. M. (1995). Evolutionary psychology: A new paradigm for psychological science. *Psychological Inquiry, 6,* 1-30. (p. 145)

Buss, D. M. (1996). Sexual conflict: Evolutionary insights into feminism and the "battle of the sexes." In D. M. Buss & N. M. Malamuth (Eds.), *Sex, power, conflict: Evolutionary and feminist perspectives.* New York: Oxford University Press. (p. 145)

Buss, D. M. (2000). *The dangerous passion: Why jealousy is as necessary as love and sex.* New York: Free Press. (p. 145)

Busseri, M. A., Willoughby, T., Chalmers, H., & Bogaert, A. R. (2006). Same-sex attraction and successful adolescent development. *Journal of Youth and Adolescence, 35,* 563-575. (p. 473)

Buster, J. E., Kingsberg, S. A., Aguirre, O., Brown, C., Breaux, J. G., Buch, A., Rodenberg, C. A., Wekselman, K., & Casson, P. (2005). Testosterone patch for low sexual desire in surgically menopausal women: A randomized trial. *Obstetrics and Gynecology, 105*(5), 944-952. (p. 468)

Butcher, L. M., Davis, O. S. P., Craig, I. W., & Plomin, R. (2008). Genome-wide quantitative trait locus association scan of general cognitive ability using pooled DNA and 500K single nucleotide polymorphism microarrays. *Genes, Brain and Behavior, 7,* 435-446. (p. 428)

Butler, A. C., Hokanson, J. E., & Flynn, H. A. (1994). A comparison of self-esteem lability and low trait self-esteem as vulnerability factors for depression. *Journal of Personality and Social Psychology, 66,* 166-177. (p. 633)

Butler, R. A. (1954, February). Curiosity in monkeys. *Scientific American,* pp. 70-75. (p. 445)

Butterfield, F. (1999, July 12). Experts say study confirms prison's new role as mental hospital. *New York Times* (www.nytimes.com). (p. 606)

Butterworth, G. (1992). Origins of self-perception in infancy. *Psychological Inquiry, 3,* 103-111. (p. 192)

Byne, W., & Parsons, B. (1993). Human sexual orientation: The biologic theories reappraised. *Archives of General Psychiatry, 50,* 228-239. (p. 478)

Bynum, R. (2004, November 1). Associated Press article. (p. 253)

Byrne, D. (1971). *The attraction paradigm.* New York: Academic Press. (p. 723)

Byrne, D. (1982). Predicting human sexual behavior. In A. G. Kraut (Ed.), *The G. Stanley Hall Lecture Series* (Vol. 2). Washington, DC: American Psychological Association. (pp. 292, 468)

Byrne, J. (2003, September 21). From correspondence reported by Michael Shermer, E-Skeptic for September 21, 2003, from The Skeptics Society. (p. 283)

Byrne, R. W. (1991, May/June). Brute intellect. *The Sciences*, pp. 42-47. (p. 399)

Byrne, R. W., & Corp, N. (2004). Neocortex size predicts deception in primates. *Proceedings of the Royal Society B, 271,* 1693-1699. (p. 28)

Byrne, R. W., & Russon, A. E. (1998). Learning by imitation: A hierarchical approach. *Behavioral and Brain Sciences, 21,* 667-721. (p. 315)

Cable, D. M., & Gilovich, T. (1998). Looked over or overlooked? Prescreening decisions and postinterview evaluations. *Journal of Personality and Social Psychology, 83,* 501-508. (p. 488)

Cacioppo, J. T. (2007). Better interdisciplinary research through psychological science. *APS Observer, 20,* 3, 48-49. (p. 10)

Cacioppo, J. T., Hawkley, L. C., Kalil, A., Hughes, M. E., Waite, L., & Thisted, R. A. (2008). Happiness and the invisible threads of social connection: The Chicago Health, Aging, and Social Relations Study. In M. Eid & R. Larsen (Eds.), *The science of subjective well-being.* New York: Guilford. (p. 525)

Cahill, L. (1994). (Beta)-adrenergic activation and memory for emotional events. *Nature, 371,* 702-704. (p. 341)

Cahill, L. (2005, May). His brain, her brain. *Scientific American*, pp. 40-47. (p. 161)

Cahn, B. R., & Polich, J. (2006). Meditation states and traits: EEG, ERP, and neuroimaging studies. *Psychological Bulletin, 132,* 180-211. (p. 552)

Cale, E. M., & Lilienfeld, S. O. (2002). Sex differences in psychopathy and antisocial personality disorder: A review and integration. *Clinical Psychology Review, 22,* 1179-1207. (p. 620)

Call, K. T., Riedel, A. A., Hein, K., McLoyd, V., Petersen, A., & Kipke, M. (2002). Adolescent health and well-being in the twenty-first century: A global perspective. *Journal of Research on Adolescence, 12,* 69-98. (p. 470)

Callaghan, T., Rochat, P., Lillard, A., Claux, M. L., Odden, H., Itakura, S., Tapanya, S., & Singh, S. (2005). Synchrony in the onset of mental-state reasoning. *Psychological Science, 16,* 378-384. (p. 181)

Calle, E. E., Thun, M. J., Petrelli, J. M., Rodriguez, C., & Health, C. W., Jr. (1999). Body-mass index and mortality in a prospective cohort of U.S. adults. *New England Journal of Medicine, 341,* 1097-1105. (p. 457)

Calvo-Merino, B., Glaser, D. E., Grèzes, J., Passingham, R. E., & Haggard, P. (2004). Action observation and acquired motor skills: An fMRI study with expert dancers. *Cerebral Cortex, 15,* 1243-1249. (p. 395)

Camerer, C. F., Loewenstein, G., & Weber, M. (1989). The curse of knowledge in economic settings: An experimental analysis. *Journal of Political Economy, 97,* 1232-1254. (p. 281)

Campbell, D. T. (1975). On the conflicts between biological and social evolution and between psychology and moral tradition. *American Psychologist, 30,* 1103-1126. (p. 527)

Campbell, D. T., & Specht, J. C. (1985). Altruism: Biology, culture, and religion. *Journal of Social and Clinical Psychology, 3*(1), 33-42. (p. 572)

Campbell, S. (1986). *The Loch Ness Monster: The evidence.* Willingborough, Northamptonshire, U.K.: Acquarian Press. (p. 274)

Camper, J. (1990, February 7). Drop pompom squad, U. of I. rape study says. *Chicago Tribune*, p. 1. (p. 117)

Camperio-Ciani, A., Cermelli, P., & Zanzott, G. (2008). Sexually antagonistic selection in human male homosexuality. *PloS One, 3,* e2282, 1-8. (p. 476)

Camperio-Ciani, A., Corna, F., & Capiluppi, C. (2004). Evidence for maternally inherited factors favouring male homosexuality and promoting female fecundity. *Proceedings of the Royal Society of London B, 271,* 2217-2221. (p. 476)

Campos, J. J., Bertenthal, B. I., & Kermoian, R. (1992). Early experience and emotional development: The emergence of wariness and heights. *Psychological Science, 3,* 61-64. (pp. 264, 518)

Canli, T. (2008, February/March). The character code. *Scientific American Mind*, pp. 53-57. (p. 616)

Canli, T., Desmond, J. E., Zhao, Z., & Gabrieli, J. D. E. (2002). Sex differences in the neural basis of emotional memories. *Proceedings of the National Academy of Sciences, 99,* 10789-10794. (p. 513)

Cannon, J. (2005). Career planning and opportunities: The bachelor's degree in psychology. *Eye on Psi Chi, 9,* 26-28. (pp. A-1, A-2)

Cannon, W. B. (1929). *Bodily changes in pain, hunger, fear, and rage.* New York: Branford. (pp. 449, 532)

Cannon, W. B., & Washburn, A. (1912). An explanation of hunger. *American Journal of Physiology, 29,* 441-454. (p. 448)

Cantor, N., & Kihlstrom, J. F. (1987). *Personality and social intelligence.* Englewood Cliffs, NJ: Prentice-Hall. (p. 411)

Cantril, H., & Bumstead, C. H. (1960). *Reflections on the human venture.* New York: New York University Press. (p. 701)

Caplan, N., Choy, M. H., & Whitmore, J. K. (1992, February). Indochinese refugee families and academic achievement. *Scientific American*, pp. 36-42. (pp. 150, 437)

Caprara, G. V., Vecchione, M., Barbaranelli, C., & Fraley, R. C. (2007). When likeness goes with liking: The case of political preference. *Political Psychology, 28,* 609-632. (p. 724)

Caputo, D., & Dunning, D. (2005). What you don't know: The role played by errors of omission in imperfect self-assessments. *Journal of Experimental Social Psychology,* 488-505. (p. 589)

Carducci, B. J., Cosby, P. C., & Ward, D. D. (1978). Sexual arousal and interpersonal evaluations. *Journal of Experimental Social Psychology, 14,* 449-457. (p. 724)

Carey, B. (2006, November 11). What's wrong with a child? Psychiatrists often disagree. *New York Times* (www.nytimes.com). (p. 603)

Carey, B. (2007, September 4). Bipolar illness soars as a diagnosis for the young. *New York Times* (www.nytimes.com). (p. 626)

Carey, B. (2009, December 4). H. M., an unforgettable amnesiac, dies at 82. *New York Times* (www.nytimes.com). (p. 342)

Carey, D. P. (2007). Is bigger really better? The search for brain size and intelligence in the twenty-first century. In S. Della Sala (Ed.), *Tall tales about the mind and brain: Separating fact from fiction.* Oxford: Oxford University Press. (p. 412)

Carey, G. (1990). Genes, fears, phobias, and phobic disorders. *Journal of Counseling and Development, 68,* 628-632. (p. 616)

Carli, L. L., & Leonard, J. B. (1989). The effect of hindsight on victim derogation. *Journal of Social and Clinical Psychology, 8,* 331-343. (p. 709)

Carlson, C. L. (2000). ADHD is overdiagnosed. In R. L. Atkinson, R. C. Atkinson, E. E. Smith, D. J. Bem, & S. Nolen-Hoeksema (Eds.), *Hilgard's introduction to psychology* (13th ed.). Fort Worth: Harcourt. (p. 600)

Carlson, M. (1995, August 29). Quoted by S. Blakeslee, In brain's early growth, timetable may be crucial. *New York Times*, pp. C1, C3. (p. 189)

Carlson, M., Charlin, V., & Miller, N. (1988). Positive mood and helping behavior: A test of six hypotheses. *Journal of Personality and Social Psychology, 55,* 211-229. (p. 728)

Carlson, S. (1985). A double-blind test of astrology. *Nature, 318,* 419-425. (p. 578)

Carlson, S. M., & Meltzoff, A. N. (2008). Bilingual experience and executive functioning in young children. *Developmental Science, 11,* 282-298. (p. 394)

Carnahan, T., & McFarland, S. (2007). Revisiting the Stanford Prison Experiment: Could participant self-selection have led to the cruelty? *Personality and Social Psychology Bulletin, 33,* 603-614. (p. 687)

Carnegie Council on Adolescent Development. (1989, June). *Turning points: Preparing American youth for the 21st century.* (The report of the Task Force on Education of Young Adolescents.) New York: Carnegie Corporation. (p. 426)

Carnelley, K. B., Wortman, C. B., Bolger, N., & Burke, C. T. (2006). The time course of grief reactions to spousal loss: Evidence from a national probability sample. *Journal of Personality and Social Psychology, 91,* 476-492. (p. 220)

Carpusor, A., & Loges, W. E. (2006). Rental discrimination and ethnicity in names. *Journal of Applied Social Psychology, 36,* 934-952. (pp. 36, 704)

Carrière, G. (2003). Parent and child factors associated with youth obesity. *Statistics Canada, Catalogue 82-003,* Supplement to Health Reports, 2003. (p. 460)

Carroll, D., Davey Smith, G., & Bennett, P. (1994, March). Health and socio-economic status. *The Psychologist*, pp. 122–125. (p. 543)

Carroll, J. (2005, January 14). Terrorism concerns fade. *The Gallup Organization* (www.gallup.com). (p. 379)

Carroll, J. (2007, August 16). Most Americans approve of interracial marriages. *Gallup News Service* (www.gallup.com). (p. 703)

Carroll, J. (2008, January 2). Time pressures, stress common for Americans. Gallup Poll (www.gallup.com). (p. 530)

Carroll, J. M., & Russell, J. A. (1996). Do facial expressions signal specific emotions? Judging emotion from the face in context. *Journal of Personality and Social Psychology, 70*, 205–218. (p. 514)

Carroll, J. S., Padilla-Walker, L. M., Nelson, L. J., Olson, C. D., Barry, C. M., & Madsen, S. D. (2008). Generation XXX: Pornography acceptance and use among emerging adults. *Journal of Adolescent Research, 23*, 6–30. (p. 714)

Carroll, P., Sweeny, K., & Shepperd, J. A. (2006). Forsaking optimism. *Review of General Psychology, 10*, 56–73. (p. 587)

Carskadon, M. (2002). *Adolescent sleep patterns: Biological, social, and psychological influences.* New York: Cambridge University Press. (p. 97)

Carstensen, L. I., & Mikels, J. A. (2005). At the intersection of emotion and cognition: Aging and the positivity effect. *Current Directions in Psychological Science, 14*, 117–121. (pp. 215, 219)

Carter, R. (1998). *Mapping the mind.* Berkeley: University of California Press. (p. 50)

Cartwright, R. D. (1978). *A primer on sleep and dreaming.* Reading, MA: Addison-Wesley. (p. 95)

Caryl, P. G. (1994). Early event-related potentials correlate with inspection time and intelligence. *Intelligence, 18*, 15–46. (p. 414)

CASA. (2003). *The formative years: Pathways to substance abuse among girls and young women ages 8–22.* New York: National Center on Addiction and Substance Use, Columbia University. (pp. 116, 126)

CASA. (2004). CASA 2004 teen survey. National Center on Addiction and Substance Abuse, Columbia University (www.casacolumbia.org). (p. 471)

Casey, B. J., Getz, S., & Galvan, A. (2008). The adolescent brain. *Developmental Review, 28*, 62–77. (p. 197)

Cash, T., & Janda, L. H. (1984, December). The eye of the beholder. *Psychology Today*, pp. 46–52. (p. 721)

Cash, T. F., & Henry, P. E. (1995). Women's body images: The results of a national survey in the U.S.A. *Sex Roles, 33*, 19–28. (p. 454)

Caspi, A. (2000). The child is father of the man: Personality continuities from childhood to adulthood. *Journal of Personality and Social Psychology, 78*, 158–172. (p. 138)

Caspi, A., Harrington, H., Milne, B., Amell, J. W., Theodore, R. F., & Moffitt, T. E. (2003). Children's behavioral styles at age 3 are linked to their adult personality traits at age 26. *Journal of Personality, 71*, 496–513. (pp. 223, 631)

Caspi, A., McClay, J., Moffitt, T., Mill, J., Martin, J., Craig, I. W., Taylor, A., & Poulton, R. (2002). Role of genotype in the cycle of violence in maltreated children. *Science, 297*, 851–854. (p. 622)

Caspi, A., Moffitt, T. E., Newman, D. L., & Silva, P. A. (1996). Behavioral observations at age 3 years predict adult psychiatric disorders: Longitudinal evidence from a birth cohort. *Archives of General Psychiatry, 53*, 1033–1039. (p. 621)

Caspi, A., Williams, B., Kim-Cohen, J., Craig, I. W., Milne, B. J., Poulton, R., Schalkwyk, L. C., Taylor, A., Werts, H., & Moffitt, T. E. (2007). Moderation of breastfeeding effects on the IQ by genetic variation in fatty acid metabolism. *Proceedings of the National Academy of Sciences, 104*, 18860–18865. (p. 139)

Cassel, L., & Suedfeld, P. (2006). Salutogenesis and autobiographical disclosure among Holocaust survivors. *The Journal of Positive Psychology, 1*, 212–225. (p. 614)

Cassidy, J., & Shaver, P. R. (1999). *Handbook of attachment.* New York: Guilford. (p. 187)

Castillo, R. J. (1997). *Culture and mental illness: A client-centered approach.* Pacific Grove, CA: Brooks/Cole. (p. 602)

Castonguay, L. G., & Goldfried, M. R. (1994). Psychotherapy integration: An idea whose time has come. *Applied & Preventive Psychology, 3*, 159–172. (p. 646)

Catanese, K. R., & Tice, D. M. (2005). The effect of rejection on anti-social behaviors: Social exclusion produces aggressive behaviors. In K. D. Williams, J. P. Forgas, & W. Von Hippel (Eds.), *The social outcast: Ostracism, social exclusion, rejection, and bullying.* New York: Psychology Press. (p. 713)

Cattell, R. B. (1963). Theory of fluid and crystallized intelligence: A critical experiment. *Journal of Educational Psychology, 54*, 1–22. (p. 215)

Cavalli-Sforza, L., Menozzi, P., & Piazza, A. (1994). *The history and geography of human genes.* Princeton, NJ: Princeton University Press. (p. 436)

Cavigelli, S. A., & McClintock, M. K. (2003). Fear of novelty in infant rats predicts adult corticosterone dynamics and an early death. *Proceedings of the National Academy of Sciences, 100*, 16131–16136. (p. 533)

Cawley, B. D., Keeping, L. M., & Levy, P. E. (1998). Participation in the performance appraisal process and employee reactions: A meta-analytic review of field investigations. *Journal of Applied Psychology, 83*, 615–633. (p. 495)

CDC. (2002, September 27). Trends in sexual risk behaviors among high school students—United States, 1991–2002. *MMWR, 51*(38): 856–859 (www.cdc.gov/mmwr). (p. 472)

CDC. (2003). Who should get a flu shot (influenza vaccine). National Center for Infectious Diseases (http: //www.cdc.gov/ncidod/diseases/flu/who.htm). (p. 641)

CDC. (2006, June 9). Youth risk behavior surveillance: United States, 2005. *Morbidity and Mortality Weekly Report, 55*, No. SS-5, Centers for Disease Control and Prevention. (p. 470)

CDC. (2007, February 8). CDC releases new data on autism spectrum disorders (ASDs) from multiple communities in the United States. Centers for Disease Control and Prevention (www.cdc.gov). (p. 182)

CDC. (2007, November). Obesity among adults in the United States—No change since 2003–2004. NCHS Data Brief, Centers for Disease Control and Prevention (www.cdc.gov/nchs/data/databriefs/db01.pdf). (p. 456)

Ceci, S. J. (1993). Cognitive and social factors in children's testimony. Master lecture, American Psychological Association convention. (pp. 361, 362)

Ceci, S. J., & Bruck, M. (1993). Child witnesses: Translating research into policy. *Social Policy Report* (Society for Research in Child Development), *7*(3), 1–30. (p. 361)

Ceci, S. J., & Bruck, M. (1995). *Jeopardy in the courtroom: A scientific analysis of children's testimony.* Washington, DC: American Psychological Association. (p. 361)

Ceci, S. J., Huffman, M. L. C., Smith, E., & Loftus, E. F. (1994). Repeatedly thinking about a non-event: Source misattributions among preschoolers. *Consciousness and Cognition, 3*, 388–407. (p. 362)

Ceci, S. J., & Williams, W. M. (1997). Schooling, intelligence, and income. *American Psychologist, 52*, 1051–1058. (p. 431)

Centers for Disease Control. (1992, September 16). Serious mental illness and disability in the adult household population: United States, 1989. *Advance Data* No. 218 from *Vital and Health Statistics*, National Center for Health Statistics. (p. 607)

Centers for Disease Control Vietnam Experience Study. (1988). Health status of Vietnam veterans. *Journal of the American Medical Association, 259*, 2701–2709. (p. 613)

Centerwall, B. S. (1989). Exposure to television as a risk factor for violence. *American Journal of Epidemiology, 129*, 643–652. (p. 319)

Cepeda, N. J., Pashler, H., Vul, E., Wixted, J. T., & Rohrer, D. (2006). Distributed practice in verbal recall tasks: A review and quantitative synthesis. *Psychological Bulletin, 132*, 354–380. (p. 329)

Cerella, J. (1985). Information processing rates in the elderly. *Psychological Bulletin, 98*, 67–83. (p. 210)

CFI. (2003, July). International developments. Report. Amherst, NY: Center for Inquiry International. (p. 284)

Chabris, C. F., & Glickman, M. E. (2006). Sex differences in intellectual performance: Analysis of a large cohort of competitive chess players. *Psychological Science, 17*, 1040–1046. (p. 433)

Chambless, D. L., Baker, M. J., Baucom, D. H., Beutler, L. E., Calhoun, K. S., Crits-Christoph, P., Daiuto, A., DeRubeis, R., Detweiler, J., Haaga, D. A. F., Johnson, S. B., McCurry, S., Mueser, K. T., Pope, K. S., Sanderson, W. C., Shoham, V., Stickle, T., Williams, D. A., & Woody, S. R. (1997). Update on empirically validated therapies, II. *The Clinical Psychologist, 51*(1), 3–16. (p. 665)

Chamove, A. S. (1980). Nongenetic induction of acquired levels of aggression. *Journal of Abnormal Psychology, 89*, 469–488. (p. 319)

Chance News (1997, 25 November). More on the frequency of letters in texts. Dart.Chance@Dartmouth.edu. (p. 28)

Chang, E. C. (2001). Cultural influences on optimism and pessimism: Differences in Western and Eastern construals of the self. In E. C. Chang (Ed.), *Optimism and pessimism.* Washington, DC: APA Books. (p. 587)

Chang, P. P., Ford, D. E., Meoni, L. A., Wang, N-Y., & Klag, M. J. (2002). Anger in young men and subsequent premature cardiovascular disease: The precursors study. *Archives of Internal Medicine, 162,* 901–906. (p. 536)

Chaplin, W. F., Phillips, J. B., Brown, J. D., Clanton, N. R., & Stein, J. L. (2000). Handshaking, gender, personality, and first impressions. *Journal of Personality and Social Psychology, 79,* 110–117. (p. 510)

Charles, S. T., Reynolds, C. A., & Gatz, M. (2001). Age-related differences and change in positive and negative affect over 23 years. *Journal of Personality and Social Psychology, 80,* 136–151. (p. 219)

Charpak, G., & Broch, H. (2004). *Debunked! ESP, telekinesis, and other pseudoscience.* Baltimore, MD: Johns Hopkins University Press. (p. 283)

Chartrand, T. L., & Bargh, J. A. (1999). The chameleon effect: The perception-behavior link and social interaction. *Journal of Personality and Social Psychology, 76,* 893–910. (p. 690)

Chase, W. G., & Simon, H. A. (1973). Perception in chess. *Cognitive Psychology, 4,* 55–81. (p. 334)

Cheek, J. M., & Melchior, L. A. (1990). Shyness, self-esteem, and self-consciousness. In H. Leitenberg (Ed.), *Handbook of social and evaluation anxiety.* New York: Plenum. (p. 155)

Cheit, R. E. (1998). Consider this, skeptics of recovered memory. *Ethics & Behavior, 8,* 141–160. (p. 566)

Chen, E. (2004). Why socioeconomic status affects the health of children: A psychosocial perspective. *Current Directions in Psychological Science, 13,* 112–115. (p. 543)

Chen, X., Beydoun, M. A., & Wang, Y. (2008). Is sleep duration associated with childhood obesity? A systematic review and meta-analysis. *Obesity, 16,* 265–274. (p. 97)

Cheng, M. (2006, November 16). Europeans OK anti-obesity charter. Associated Press. (p. 461)

Cherkas, L. F., Hunkin, J. L., Kato, B. S., Richards, J. B., Gardner, J. P., Surdulescu, G. L., Kimura, M., Lu, X., Spector, T. D., & Aviv, A. (2008). The association between physical activity in leisure time and leukocyte telomere length. *Archives of Internal Medicine, 168,* 154–158. (p. 211)

Chess, S., & Thomas, A. (1987). *Know your child: An authoritative guide for today's parents.* New York: Basic Books. (pp. 72, 137, 188)

Child Trends. (2001, August). Facts at a glance. (www.childtrends.org). (p. 470)

Chiles, J. A., Lambert, M. J., & Hatch, A. L. (1999). The impact of psychological interventions on medical cost offset: A meta-analytic review. *Clinical Psychology: Science and Practice, 6,* 204–220. (p. 663)

Chisholm, K. (1998). A three year follow-up of attachment and indiscriminate friendliness in children adopted from Romanian orphanages. *Child Development, 69,* 1092–1106. (p. 189)

Chisolm, T. H., Johnson, C. E., Danhauer, J. L., Portz, L. J. P., Abrams, H. B., Lesner, S., McCarthy, P. A., & Newman, C. W. (2007). A systematic review of health-related quality of life and hearing aids: Final report of the American Academy of Audiology Task Force on the Health-Related Quality of Life Benefits of Amplification in Adults. *Journal of the American Academy of Audiology, 18,* 151–183. (p. 249)

Chivers, M. L. (2005). A brief review and discussion of sex differences in the specificity of sexual arousal. *Sexual and Relationship Therapy, 20,* 377–390. (p. 473)

Chivers, M. L., Seto, M. C., & Blanchard, R. (2007). Gender and sexual orientation differences in sexual response to sexual activities versus gender of actors in sexual films. *Journal of Personality and Social Psychology, 93,* 1108–1121. (p. 474)

Choi, C. Q. (2008, March). Do you need only half your brain? *Scientific American,* p. 104. (p. 73)

Choi, I., & Choi, Y. (2002). Culture and self-concept flexibility. *Personality and Social Psychology Bulletin, 28,* 1508–1517. (p. 154)

Chomsky, N. (1959). [Review of B. F. Skinner's *Verbal behavior*]. *Language, 35,* 26–58. (p. 388)

Chomsky, N. (1972). *Language and mind.* New York: Harcourt Brace. (p. 384)

Chomsky, N. (1987). *Language in a psychological setting* (Sophia Linguistic Working Papers in Linguistics, No. 22). Sophia University, Tokyo. (p. 388)

Christakis, D. S., Zimmerman, F. J., DiGiuseppe, D. L., & McCarty, C. A. (2004). Early television exposure and subsequent attentional problems in children. *Pediatrics, 113,* 708–713. (p. 600)

Christakis, N. A., & Fowler, J. H. (2007). The spread of obesity in a large social network over 32 years. *New England Journal of Medicine, 357,* 370–379. (pp. 127, 460)

Christensen, A., & Jacobson, N. S. (1994). Who (or what) can do psychotherapy: The status and challenge of nonprofessional therapies. *Psychological Science, 5,* 8–14. (p. 668)

Christophersen, E. R., & Edwards, K. J. (1992). Treatment of elimination disorders: State of the art 1991. *Applied & Preventive Psychology, 1,* 15–22. (p. 651)

Chugani, H. T., & Phelps, M. E. (1986). Maturational changes in cerebral function in infants determined by 18FDG positron emission tomography. *Science, 231,* 840–843. (p. 174)

Cialdini, R. B. (1993). *Influence: Science and practice* (3rd ed.). New York: HarperCollins. (p. 686)

Cialdini, R. B., & Richardson, K. D. (1980). Two indirect tactics of image management: Basking and blasting. *Journal of Personality and Social Psychology, 39,* 406–415. (p. 708)

Ciarrochi, J., Forgas, J. P., & Mayer, J. D. (2006). *Emotional intelligence in everyday life* (2nd ed.). New York: Psychology Press. (p. 411)

Cin, S. D., Gibson, B., Zanna, M. P., Shumate, R., & Fong, G. T. (2007). Smoking in movies, implicit associations of smoking with the self, and intentions to smoke. *Psychological Science, 18,* 559–563. (p. 119)

Clack, B., Dixon, J., & Tredoux, C. (2005). Eating together apart: Patterns of segregation in a multi-ethnic cafeteria. *Journal of Community and Applied Social Psychology, 15,* 1–16. (p. 731)

Clancy, S. A. (2005). *Abducted: How people come to believe they were kidnapped by aliens.* Cambridge, MA: Harvard University Press. (p. 359)

Clancy, S. A., Schacter, D. L., McNally, R. J., & Pitman, R. K. (2000). False recognition in women reporting recovered memories of sexual abuse. *Psychological Science, 11,* 26–31. (p. 359)

Clark, A., Seidler, A., & Miller, M. (2001). Inverse association between sense of humor and coronary heart disease. *International Journal of Cardiology, 80,* 87–88. (p. 545)

Clark, K. B., & Clark, M. P. (1947). Racial identification and preference in Negro children. In T. M. Newcomb & E. L. Hartley (Eds.), *Readings in social psychology.* New York: Holt. (p. 23)

Clark, L. A. (2007). Assessment and diagnosis of personality disorder: Perennial issues and an emerging reconceptualization. *Annual Review of Psychology, 58,* 227–257. (p. 620)

Clark, R., Anderson, N. B., Clark, V. R., & Williams, D. R. (1999). Racism as a stressor for African Americans: A biopsychosocial model. *American Psychologist, 54,* 805–816. (p. 535)

Clark, R. D. (1990, May). The impact of AIDS on gender differences in willingness to engage in casual sex. *Journal of Applied Social Psychology, 20,* 771–782. (p. 144)

Clark, R. D., III, & Hatfield, E. (1989). Gender differences in willingness to engage in casual sex. *Journal of Psychology and Human Sexuality, 2,* 39–55. (p. 144)

Clark, R. D., III, & Hatfield, E. (2003). Love in the afternoon. *Psychological Inquiry, 14,* 227–231. (p. 144)

Coan, J. A., Schaefer, H. S., & Davidson, R. J. (2006). Lending a hand: Social regulation of the neural response to threat. *Psychological Science, 17,* 1032–1039. (p. 545)

Coffey, C. E., Wilkinson, W. E., Weiner, R. D., Parashos, I. A., Djang, W. T., Webb, M. C., Figiel, G. S., & Spritzer, C. E. (1993). Quantitative cerebral anatomy in depression: A controlled magnetic resonance imaging study. *Archives of General Psychiatry, 50,* 7–16. (p. 630)

Cogan, J. C., & Ernsberger, P. (1999). Dieting, weight, and health: Reconceptualizing research and policy. *Journal of Social Issues, 55,* 187–205. (p. 464)

Cohen, D. (1995, June 17). Now we are one, or two, or three. *New Scientist*, pp. 14–15. (p. 619)

Cohen, K. M. (2002). Relationships among childhood sex-atypical behavior, spatial ability, handedness, and sexual orientation in men. *Archives of Sexual Behavior, 31*, 129–143. (p. 478)

Cohen, P. (2007, November 15). Freud is widely taught at universities, except in the psychology department. *New York Times* (www.nytimes.com). (p. 568)

Cohen, S. (1988). Psychosocial models of the role of social support in the etiology of physical disease. *Health Psychology, 7*, 269–297. (p. 545)

Cohen, S. (2004). Social relationships and health. *American Psychologist, 59*, 676–684. (p. 545)

Cohen, S., Alper, C. M., Doyle, W. J., Treanor, J. J., & Turner, R. B. (2006). Positive emotional style predicts resistance to illness after experimental exposure to rhinovuros or influenza A virus. *Psychosomatic Medicine, 68*, 809–815. (p. 538)

Cohen, S., Doyle, W. J., Skoner, D. P., Rabin, B. S., & Gwaltney, J. M., Jr. (1997). Social ties and susceptibility to the common cold. *Journal of the American Medical Association, 277*, 1940–1944. (p. 545)

Cohen, S., Doyle, W. J., Turner, R., Alper, C. M., & Skoner, D. P. (2003). Sociability and susceptibility to the common cold. *Psychological Science, 14*, 389–395. (p. 538)

Cohen, S., Kaplan, J. R., Cunnick, J. E., Manuck, S. B., & Rabin, B. S. (1992). Chronic social stress, affiliation, and cellular immune response in nonhuman primates. *Psychological Science, 3*, 301–304. (p. 538)

Cohen, S., Line, S., Manuck, S. B., Rabin, B. S., Heise, E. R., & Kaplan, J. R. (1997). Chronic social stress, social status, and susceptibility to upper respiratory infections in nonhuman primates. *Psychosomatic Medicine, 59*, 213–221. (p. 543)

Cohen, S., & Pressman, S. D. (2006). Positive affect and health. *Current Directions in Psychological Science, 15*, 122–125. (p. 439)

Cohen, S., Tyrrell, D. A. J., & Smith, A. P. (1991). Psychological stress and susceptibility to the common cold. *New England Journal of Medicine, 325*, 606–612. (p. 539)

Colangelo, N., Assouline, S. G., & Gross, M. U. M. (2004). *A nation deceived: How schools hold back America's brightest students* (Vols. I and II). (The Templeton National Report on Acceleration.) Iowa City, IA: College of Education, University of Iowa. (p. 426)

Colapinto, J. (2000). *As nature made him: The boy who was raised as a girl.* New York: HarperCollins. (p. 161)

Colarelli, S. M., & Dettman, J. R. (2003). Intuitive evolutionary perspectives in marketing. *Psychology and Marketing, 20*, 837–865. (p. 143)

Colarelli, S. M., Spranger, J. L., & Hechanova, M. R. (2006). Women, power, and sex composition in small groups: An evolutionary perspective. *Journal of Organizational Behavior, 27*, 163–184. (p. 158)

Colcombe, S., & Kramer, A. F. (2003). Fitness effects on the cognitive function of older adults: A meta-analytic study. *Psychological Science, 14*, 125–130. (p. 211)

Colcombe, S. J., Kramer, A. F., Erickson, K. I., Scalf, P., McAuley, E., Cohen, N. J., Webb, A., Jerome, G. J., Marquex, D. X., & Elavsky, S. (2004). Cardiovascular fitness, cortical plasticity, and aging. *Proceedings of the National Academy of Sciences, 101*, 3316–3321. (p. 211)

Cole, K. C. (1998). *The universe and the teacup: The mathematics of truth and beauty.* New York: Harcourt Brace. (p. 118)

Coleman, P. D., & Flood, D. G. (1986). Dendritic proliferation in the aging brain as a compensatory repair mechanism. In D. F. Swaab, E. Fliers, M. Mirmiram, W. A. Van Gool, & F. Van Haaren (Eds.), *Progress in brain research* (Vol. 20). New York: Elsevier. (p. 210)

Collins, D. W., & Kimura, D. (1997). A large sex difference on a two-dimensional mental rotation task. *Behavioral Neuroscience, 111*, 845–849. (p. 434)

Collins, F. (2006). *The language of God.* New York: Free Press. (p. 165)

Collins, N. L., & Miller, L. C. (1994). Self-disclosure and liking: A meta-analytic review. *Psychological Bulletin, 116*, 457–475. (p. 725)

Collins, R. L., Elliott, M. N., Berry, S. H., Danouse, D. E., Kunkel, D., Hunter, S. B., & Miu, A. (2004). Watching sex on television predicts adolescent initiation of sexual behavior. *Pediatrics, 114*, 280–289. (p. 30)

Collinson, S. L., MacKay, C. E., James, A. C., Quested, D. J., Phillips, T., Roberts, N., & Crow, T. J. (2003). Brain volume, asymmetry and intellectual impairment in relation to sex in early-onset schizophrenia. *British Journal of Psychiatry, 183*, 114–120. (p. 640)

Collishaw, S., Pickles, A., Natarajan, L., & Maughan, B. (2007, June). 20-year trends in depression and anxiety in England. Paper presented at the Thirteenth Scientific Meeting on The Brain and the Developing Child, London. (p. 628)

Colom, R., Jung, R. E., & Haier, R. J. (2006). Distributed brain sites for the g-factor of intelligence. *NeuroImage, 31*, 1359–1365. (p. 412)

Colom, R., Lluis-Font, J. M., & Andrés-Pueyo, A. (2005). The generational intelligence gains are caused by decreasing variance in the lower half of the distribution: Supporting evidence for the nutrition hypothesis. *Intelligence, 33*, 83–91. (p. 421)

Colombo, J. (1982). The critical period concept: Research, methodology, and theoretical issues. *Psychological Bulletin, 91*, 260–275. (p. 187)

Comer, R. J. (2004). *Abnormal psychology.* New York: Worth Publishers. (p. 599)

Commission on Children at Risk. (2003). *Hardwired to connect: The new scientific case for authoritative communities.* New York: Institute for American Values. (p. 193)

Comstock, G. (2008). A sociological perspective on television violence and aggression. *American Behavioral Scientist, 51*, 1184–1211. (p. 319)

Conard, M. A. (2006). Aptitude is not enough: How personality and behavior predict academic performance. *Journal of Research in Personality, 40*, 339–346. (p. 580)

Connor-Smith, J. K., & Flachsbart, C. (2007). Relations between personality and coping: A meta-analysis. *Journal of Personality and Social Psychology, 93*, 1080–1107. (p. 542)

Consumer Reports. (1995, November). Does therapy help? Pp. 734–739. (p. 660)

Conway, M. A., Wang, Q., Hanyu, K., & Haque, S. (2005). A cross-cultural investigation of autobiographical memory. On the universality and cultural variation of the reminiscence bump. *Journal of Cross-Cultural Psychology, 36*, 739–749. (p. 212)

Cook, M., & Mineka, S. (1991). Selective associations in the origins of phobic fears and their implications for behavior therapy. In P. Martin (Ed.), *Handbook of behavior therapy and psychological science: An integrative approach.* New York: Pergamon Press. (p. 519)

Cooke, L. J., Wardle, J., & Gibson, E. L. (2003). Relationship between parental report of food neophobia and everyday food consumption in 2–6-year-old children. *Appetite, 41*, 205–206. (p. 257)

Cooper, K. J. (1999, May 1). This time, copycat wave is broader. *Washington Post* (www.washingtonpost.com). (pp. 321, 691)

Cooper, M. L. (2006). Does drinking promote risky sexual behavior? A complex answer to a simple question. *Current Directions in Psychological Science, 15*, 19–23. (p. 117)

Coopersmith, S. (1967). *The antecedents of self-esteem.* San Francisco: Freeman. (p. 193)

Corballis, M. C. (1989). Laterality and human evolution. *Psychological Review, 96*, 492–505. (p. 79)

Corballis, M. C. (2002). *From hand to mouth: The origins of language.* Princeton, NJ: Princeton University Press. (p. 400)

Corballis, M. C. (2003). From mouth to hand: Gesture, speech, and the evolution of right-handedness. *Behavioral and Brain Sciences, 26*, 199–260. (p. 400)

Coren, S. (1996). *Sleep thieves: An eye-opening exploration into the science and mysteries of sleep.* New York: Free Press. (pp. 96, 99, 100)

Corey, D. P., & 15 others (2004). TRPA1 is a candidate for the mechanosensitive transduction channel of vertebrate hair cells. *Nature* (advance online publication, October 13, at www.nature.com). (p. 245)

Corina, D. P. (1998). The processing of sign language: Evidence from aphasia. In B. Stemmer & H. A. Whittaker (Eds.), *Handbook of neurolinguistics.* San Diego: Academic Press. (p. 77)

Corina, D. P., Vaid, J., & Bellugi, U. (1992). The linguistic basis of left hemisphere specialization. *Science, 255*, 1258–1260. (p. 77)

Corneille, O., Huart, J., Becquart, E., & Brédart, S. (2004). When memory shifts toward more typical category exemplars: Accentuation effects in the recollection of ethnically ambiguous faces. *Journal of Personality and Social Psychology, 86*, 236–250. (pp. 370, 371)

Correll, J., Park, B., Judd, C. M., & Wittenbrink, B. (2002). The police officer's dilemma: Using ethnicity to disambiguate potentially threatening individuals. *Journal of Personality and Social Psychology, 83*, 1314–1329. (p. 705)

Correll, J., Park, B., Judd, C. M., Wittenbrink, B., Sadler, M. S., & Keesee, T. (2007). Across the thin blue line: Police officers and racial bias in the decision to shoot. *Journal of Personality and Social Psychology, 92*, 1006–1023. (p. 705)

Costa, P. T., Jr., & McCrae, R. R. (2006). Trait and factor theories. In J. C. Thomas, D. L. Segal, & M. Hersen (Eds.), *Comprehensive handbook of personality and psychopathology: Vol. 1. Personality and everyday functioning.* Hoboken, NJ: Wiley. (p. 577)

Costa, P. T., Jr., Terracciano, A., & McCrae, R. R. (2001). Gender differences in personality traits across cultures: Robust and surprising findings. *Journal of Personality and Social Psychology, 81*, 322–331. (p. 512)

Costa, P. T., Jr., Zonderman, A. B., McCrae, R. R., Cornoni-Huntley, J., Locke, B. Z., & Barbano, H. E. (1987). Longitudinal analyses of psychological well-being in a national sample: Stability of mean levels. *Journal of Gerontology, 42*, 50–55. (p. 220)

Costello, E. J., Compton, S. N., Keeler, G., & Angold, A. (2003). Relationships between poverty and psychopathology: A natural experiment. *Journal of the American Medical Association, 290*, 2023–2029. (p. 607)

Coughlin, J. F., Mohyde, M., D'Ambrosio, L. A., & Gilbert, J. (2004). *Who drives older driver decisions?* Cambridge, MA: MIT Age Lab. (p. 210)

Couli, J. T., Vidal, F., Nazarian, B., & Macar, F. (2004). Functional anatomy of the attentional modulation of time estimation. *Science, 303*, 1506–1508. (p. 484)

Courage, M. L., & Howe, M. L. (2002). From infant to child: The dynamics of cognitive change in the second year of life. *Psychological Bulletin, 128*, 250–277. (p. 192)

Courneya, K. S., & Carron, A. V. (1992). The home advantage in sports competitions: A literature review. *Journal of Sport and Exercise Psychology, 14*, 13–27. (p. 697)

Courtney, J. G., Longnecker, M. P., Theorell, T., & de Verdier, M. G. (1993). Stressful life events and the risk of colorectal cancer. *Epidemiology, 4*, 407–414. (p. 540)

Covin, R., Ouimet, A. J., Seeds, P. M., & Dozois, D. J. A. (2008). A meta-analysis of CBT for pathological worry among clients with GAD. *Journal of Anxiety Disorders, 22*, 108–116. (p. 657)

Cowan, G., Lee, C., Levy, D., & Snyder, D. (1988). Dominance and inequality in X-rated videocassettes. *Psychology of Women Quarterly, 12*, 299–311. (p. 714)

Cowan, N. (1988). Evolving conceptions of memory storage, selective attention, and their mutual constraints within the human information-processing system. *Psychological Bulletin, 104*, 163–191. (p. 337)

Cowan, N. (1994). Mechanisms of verbal short-term memory. *Current Directions in Psychological Science, 3*, 185–189. (p. 338)

Cowan, N. (2001). The magical number 4 in short-term memory: A reconsideration of mental storage capacity. *Behavioral and Brain Sciences, 24*, 87–185. (p. 338)

Cowart, B. J. (1981). Development of taste perception in humans: Sensitivity and preference throughout the life span. *Psychological Bulletin, 90*, 43–73. (p. 257)

Cowart, B. J. (2005). Taste, our body's gustatory gatekeeper. *Cerebrum, 7*(2), 7–22. (pp. 257, 258)

Cox, J. J., & 18 others (2006). An *SCN9A* channelopathy causes congenital inability to experience pain. *Nature, 444*, 894–898. (p. 255)

CPP (2008). Myers-Briggs Type Indicator® assessment (MBTI®). CPP, Inc. (www.cpp.com). (p. 574)

Crabbe, J. C. (2002). Genetic contributions to addiction. *Annual Review of Psychology, 53*, 435–462. (p. 125)

Crabtree, S. (2005, January 13). Engagement keeps the doctor away. *Gallup Management Journal* (gmj.gallup.com). (p. 493)

Craik, F. I. M. (1986). A functional account of age differences in memory. In F. Klix & H. Hagendorf (Eds.), *Human memory and cognitive capabilities.* Amsterdam: Elsevier. (p. 214)

Craik, F. I. M., & Tulving, E. (1975). Depth of processing and the retention of words in episodic memory. *Journal of Experimental Psychology: General, 104*, 268–294. (p. 331, 332)

Craik, F. I. M., & Watkins, M. J. (1973). The role of rehearsal in short-term memory. *Journal of Verbal Learning and Verbal Behavior, 12*, 599–607. (p. 330)

Crain-Thoreson, C., & Dale, P. S. (1992). Do early talkers become early readers? Linguistic precocity, preschool language, and emergent literacy. *Developmental Psychology, 28*, 421–429. (p. 423)

Crandall, C. S. (1988). Social contagion of binge eating. *Journal of Personality and Social Psychology, 55*, 588–598. (p. 453)

Crandall, C. S. (1994). Prejudice against fat people: Ideology and self-interest. *Journal of Personality and Social Psychology, 66*, 882–894. (p. 457)

Crandall, C. S. (1995). Do parents discriminate against their heavyweight daughters? *Personality and Social Psychology Bulletin, 21*, 724–735. (p. 457)

Crandall, J. E. (1984). Social interest as a moderator of life stress. *Journal of Personality and Social Psychology, 47*, 164–174. (p. 572)

Crawford, M., Chaffin, R., & Fitton, L. (1995). Cognition in social context. Learning and Individual Differences, Special Issue: Psychological and psychobiological perspectives on sex differences in cognition: 1. *Theory and Research, 7*, 341–362. (p. 434)

Crawley, J. N. (2007). Testing hypotheses about autism. *Science, 318*, 56–57. (p. 182)

Crews, F. (Ed.). (1998). *Unauthorized Freud: Doubters confront a legend.* New York: Viking. (p. 568)

Crews, F., He, J., & Hodge, C. (2007). Adolescent cortical development: A critical period of vulnerability for addiction. *Pharmacology, Biochemistry and Behavior, 86*, 189–199. (pp. 116, 197)

Crews, F. T., Mdzinarishvilli, A., Kim, D., He, J., & Nixon, K. (2006). Neurogenesis in adolescent brain is potently inhibited by ethanol. *Neuroscience, 137*, 437–445. (p. 116)

Crocker, J., & Park, L. E. (2004). The costly pursuit of self-esteem. *Psychological Bulletin, 130*, 392–414. (p. 594)

Crocker, J., Thompson, L. L., McGraw, K. M., & Ingerman, C. (1987). Downward comparison, prejudice, and evaluation of others: Effects of self-esteem and threat. *Journal of Personality and Social Psychology, 52*, 907–916. (p. 708)

Croft, R. J., Klugman, A., Baldeweg, T., & Gruzelier, J. H. (2001). Electrophysiological evidence of serotonergic impairment in long-term MDMA ("Ecstasy") users. *American Journal of Psychiatry, 158*, 1687–1692. (p. 122)

Crombie, A. C. (1964, May). Early concepts of the senses and the mind. *Scientific American*, pp. 108–116. (p. 235)

Crook, T. H., & West, R. L. (1990). Name recall performance across the adult life-span. *British Journal of Psychology, 81*, 335–340. (p. 212)

Cross, S., & Markus, H. (1991). Possible selves across the life span. *Human Development, 34*, 230–255. (p. 590)

Cross-National Collaborative Group. (1992). The changing rate of major depression. *Journal of the American Medical Association, 268*, 3098–3105. (p. 628)

Crowell, J. A., & Waters, E. (1994). Bowlby's theory grown up: The role of attachment in adult love relationships. *Psychological Inquiry, 5*, 1–22. (p. 187)

Csikszentmihalyi, M. (1990). *Flow: The psychology of optimal experience.* New York: Harper & Row. (p. 484)

Csikszentmihalyi, M. (1999). If we are so rich, why aren't we happy? *American Psychologist, 54*, 821–827. (p. 484)

Csikszentmihalyi, M., & Hunter, J. (2003). Happiness in everyday life: The uses of experience sampling. *Journal of Happiness Studies, 4*, 185–199. (p. 202)

Csikszentmihalyi, M., & Larson, R. (1984). *Being adolescent: Conflict and growth in the teenage years.* New York: Basic Books. (p. 220)

Cullen, L. T., & Masters, C. (2008, January 28). We just clicked. *Time*, pp. 84–89. (p. 720)

Cullum, J., & Harton, H. C. (2007). Cultural evolution: Interpersonal influence, issue importance, and the development of shared attitudes in college residence halls. *Personality and Social Psychology Bulletin, 33*, 1327–1339. (p. 692)

Cummings, R. A. (2006, April 4). *Australian Unity Wellbeing Index: Survey 14.1.* (Report 14.1). Melbourne: Australian Centre on Quality of Life, Deakin University. (p. 525)

Cunningham, M. R., & others. (2005). "Their ideas of beauty are, on the whole, the same as ours": Consistency and variability in the cross-cultural perception of female physical attractiveness. *Journal of Personality and Social Psychology, 68*, 261–279. (p. 722)

Cunningham, W. A., Johnson, M. K., Raye, C. L., Gatenby, J. C., Gore, J. C., & Banaji, M. R. (2004). Separable neural components in the processing of Black and White faces. *Psychological Science, 15*, 806–313. (p. 705)

Curtis, G. C., Magee, W. J., Eaton, W. W., Wittchen, H-U., & Kessler, R. C. (1998). Specific fears and phobias: Epidemiology and classification. *British Journal of Psychiatry, 173*, 212–217. (p. 611)

Curtis, R. C., & Miller, K. (1986). Believing another likes or dislikes you: Behaviors making the beliefs come true. *Journal of Personality and Social Psychology, 51*, 284–290. (p. 724)

Cushman, F., Young, L., & Hauser, M. (2006). The role of conscious reasoning and intuition in moral judgment: Testing three principles of harm. *Psychological Science, 17*, 1082–1088. (p. 200)

Cutler, B. L., & Penrod, S. D. (1989). Forensically relevant moderators of the relation between eyewitness identification accuracy and confidence. *Journal of Applied Psychology, 74*, 650–652. (p. 360)

Cynkar, A. (2007, June). The changing gender composition of psychology. *Monitor on Psychology*, pp. 46–47. (p. 163)

Czeisler, C. A., Allan, J. S., Strogatz, S. H., Ronda, J. M., Sanchez, R., Rios, C. D., Freitag, W. O., Richardson, G. S., & Kronauer, R. E. (1986). Bright light resets the human circadian pacemaker independent of the timing of the sleep-wake cycle. *Science, 233*, 667–671. (p. 92)

Czeisler, C. A., Duffy, J. F., Shanahan, T. L., Brown, E. N., Mitchell, J. F., Rimmer, D. W., Ronda, J. M., Silva, E. J., Allan, J. S., Emens, J. S., Dijk, D-J., & Kronauer, R. E. (1999). Stability, precision, and near-24-hour period of the human circadian pacemaker. *Science, 284*, 2177–2181. (p. 92)

Czeisler, C. A., Kronauer, R. E., Allan, J. S., & Duffy, J. F. (1989). Bright light induction of strong (type O) resetting of the human circadian pacemaker. *Science, 244*, 1328–1333. (p. 92)

Dabbs, J. M., Jr. (2000). *Heroes, rogues, and lovers: Testosterone and behavior.* New York: McGraw-Hill. (p. 468)

Dabbs, J. M., Jr., Bernieri, F. J., Strong, R. K., Campo, R., & Milun, R. (2001b). Going on stage: Testosterone in greetings and meetings. *Journal of Research in Personality, 35*, 27–40. (p. 711)

Dabbs, J. M., Jr., & Morris, R. (1990). Testosterone, social class, and antisocial behavior in a sample of 4,462 men. *Psychological Science, 1*, 209–211. (p. 711)

Dabbs, J. M., Jr., Riad, J. K., & Chance, S. E. (2001a). Testosterone and ruthless homicide. *Personality and Individual Differences, 31*, 599–603. (p. 711)

Dabbs, J. M., Jr., Ruback, R. B., & Besch, N. F. (1987). Male saliva testosterone following conversations with male and female partners. Paper presented at the American Psychological Association convention. (p. 468)

Daley, T. C., Whaley, S. E., Sigman, M. D., Espinosa, M. P., & Neumann, C. (2003). IQ on the rise: The Flynn effect in rural Kenyan children. *Psychological Science, 14*, 215–219. (p. 420)

Damasio, A. (2003). *Looking for Spinoza: Joy, sorrow, and the feeling brain.* New York: Harcourt. (pp. 505, 508)

Damasio, A. R. (1994). *Descartes error: Emotion, reason, and the human brain.* New York: Grossett/Putnam & Sons. (pp. 411, 508)

Damasio, H., Grabowski, T., Frank, R., Galaburda, A. M., & Damasio, A. R. (1994). The return of Phineas Gage: Clues about the brain from the skull of a famous patient. *Science, 264*, 1102–1105. (p. 72)

Damon, W., & Hart, D. (1982). The development of self-understanding from infancy through adolescence. *Child Development, 53*, 841–864. (p. 192)

Damon, W., & Hart, D. (1988). *Self-understanding in childhood and adolescence.* Cambridge: Cambridge University Press. (p. 192)

Damon, W., & Hart, D. (1992). Self-understanding and its role in social and moral development. In M. H. Bornstein & M. E. Lamb (Eds.), *Developmental psychology: An advanced textbook* (3rd ed.). Hillsdale, NJ: Lawrence Erlbaum. (p. 192)

Damon, W., Menon, J., & Bronk, K. (2003). The development of purpose during adolescence. *Applied Developmental Science, 7*, 119–128. (p. 202)

Danner, D. D., Snowdon, D. A., & Friesen, W. V. (2001). Positive emotions in early life and longevity: Findings from the Nun Study. *Journal of Personality and Social Psychology, 80*, 804–813. (p. 544)

Danso, H., & Esses, V. (2001). Black experimenters and the intellectual test performance of white participants: The tables are turned. *Journal of Experimental Social Psychology, 37*, 158–165. (p. 439)

Dapretto, M., Davies, M. S., Pfeifer, J. H., Scott, A. A., Sigman, M., Bookheimer, S. Y., & Iacoboni, M. (2006). Understanding emotions in others: Mirror neuron dysfunction in children with autism spectrum disorders. *Nature Neuroscience, 9*, 28–30. (p. 183)

Darley, J., & Alter, A. (in press). Behavioral issues of punishment and deterrence. In E. Shafir (Ed.), *The behavioral foundations of policy*. Princeton, NJ: Princeton University Press and the Russell Sage Foundation. (p. 307)

Darley, J. M., & Latané, B. (1968a). Bystander intervention in emergencies: Diffusion of responsibility. *Journal of Personality and Social Psychology, 8*, 377–383. (p. 727)

Darley, J. M., & Latané, B. (1968b, December). When will people help in a crisis? *Psychology Today*, pp. 54–57, 70–71. (pp. 726, 727)

Darrach, B., & Norris, J. (1984, August). An American tragedy. *Life*, pp. 58–74. (p. 620)

Darwin, C. (1859). *On the origin of species by means of natural selection.* London: John Murray. (p. 143)

Daum, I., & Schugens, M. M. (1996). On the cerebellum and classical conditioning. *Psychological Science, 5*, 58–61. (p. 344)

Davey, G. C. L. (1992). Classical conditioning and the acquisition of human fears and phobias: A review and synthesis of the literature. *Advances in Behavior Research and Therapy, 14*, 29–66. (p. 297)

Davey, G. C. L. (1995). Preparedness and phobias: Specific evolved associations or a generalized expectancy bias? *Behavioral and Brain Sciences, 18*, 289–297. (p. 615)

Davidoff, J. (2004). Coloured thinking. *The Psychologist, 17*, 570–572. (p. 394)

Davidson, J. R. T., Connor, K. M., & Swartz, M. (2006). Mental illness in U.S. presidents between 1776 and 1974: A review of biographical sources. *Journal of Nervous and Mental Disease, 194*, 47–51. (p. 608)

Davidson, R. J. (2000). Affective style, psychopathology, and resilience: Brain mechanisms and plasticity. *American Psychologist, 55*, 1196–1209. (pp. 50, 710)

Davidson, R. J. (2003). Affective neuroscience and psychophysiology: Toward a synthesis. *Psychophysiology, 40*, 655–665. (p. 503)

Davidson, R. J., Kabat-Zinn, J., Schumacher, J., Rosenkranz, M., Muller, D., Santorelli, S. F., Urbanowski, F., Harrington, A., Bonus, K., & Sheridan, J. F. (2003). Alterations in brain and immune function produced by mindfulness meditation. *Psychosomatic Medicine, 65*, 564–570. (p. 552)

Davidson, R. J., Pizzagalli, D., Nitschke, J. B., & Putnam, K. (2002). Depression: Perspectives from affective neuroscience. *Annual Review of Psychology, 53*, 545–574. (p. 630)

Davies, D. R., Matthews, G., & Wong, C. S. K. (1991). Aging and work. *International Review of Industrial and Organizational Psychology, 6*, 149–211. (p. 216)

Davies, M. F. (1997). Positive test strategies and confirmatory retrieval processes in the evaluation of personality feedback. *Journal of Personality and Social Psychology, 73*, 574–583. (pp. 578, 579)

Davies, P. (2007). *Cosmic jackpot: Why our universe is just right for life.* Boston: Houghton Mifflin. (p. 166)

Davis, B. E., Moon, R. Y., Sachs, H. C., & Ottolini, M. C. (1998). Effects of sleep position on infant motor development. *Pediatrics, 102*, 1135–1140. (p. 175)

Davis, H., IV, Liotti, M., Ngan, E. T., Woodward, T. S., Van Sellenberg, J. X., van Anders, S. M., Smith, A., & Mayberg, H. S. (2008). FMRI BOLD signal changes in elite swimmers while viewing videos of personal failures. *Brain Imaging and Behavior, 2*, 94–104. (p. 630)

Davis, J. O., & Phelps, J. A. (1995a). Twins with schizophrenia: Genes or germs? *Schizophrenia Bulletin, 21*, 13–18. (p. 642)

Davis, J. O., Phelps, J. A., & Bracha, H. S. (1995b). Prenatal development of monozygotic twins and concordance for schizophrenia. *Schizophrenia Bulletin, 21*, 357–366. (pp. 134, 642)

Davis, K. C., Norris, J., George, W. H., Martell, J., & Heiman, J. R. (2006). Men's likelihood of sexual aggression: The influence of alcohol, sexual arousal, and violent pornography. *Aggressive Behavior, 32*, 581–589. (p. 117)

Davis, M. (2005). Searching for a drug to extinguish fear. *Cerebrum, 7*(3), 47-58. (p. 672)

Davis, S., Rees, M., Ribot, J., Moufarege, A., Rodenberg, C., & Purdie, D. (2003, October 1-15). Efficacy and safety of testosterone patches for the treatment of low sexual desire in surgically menopausal women. Paper presented to the American Society for Reproductive Medicine, San Antonio. (p. 468)

Davison, K. P., Pennebaker, J. W., & Dickerson, S. S. (2000). Who talks? The social psychology of illness support groups. *American Psychologist, 55,* 205-217. (p. 658)

Dawes, R. M. (1980). Social dilemmas. *Annual Review of Psychology, 31,* 169-193. (p. 730)

Dawes, R. M. (1994). *House of cards: Psychology and psychotherapy built on myth.* New York: Free Press. (p. 591)

Dawkins, R. (1998). *Unweaving the rainbow.* Boston: Houghton Mifflin. (p. 165)

Dawkins, R. (1999, April 8). Is science killing the soul (a discussion with Richard Dawkins and Steven Pinker). www.edge.org. (p. 83)

Dawkins, R. (2007, July 1). Inferior design. *New York Times* (www.nytimes.com). (p. 141)

Dawood, K., Kirk, K. M., Bailey, J. M., Andrews, P. W., & Martin, N. G. (2005). Genetic and environmental influences on the frequency of orgasm in women. *Twin Research, 8,* 27-33. (p. 467)

de Boysson-Bardies, B., Halle, P., Sagart, L., & Durand, C. (1989). A cross linguistic investigation of vowel formats in babbling. *Journal of Child Language, 16,* 1-17. (p. 387)

de Courten-Myers, G. M. (2002, May 9). Personal correspondence. (p. 174)

de Courten-Myers, G. M. (2005, February 4). Personal correspondence (estimating total brain neurons, extrapolating from her carefully estimated 20 to 23 billion cortical neurons). (pp. 53, 67)

de Cuevas, J. (1990, September-October). "No, she holded them loosely." *Harvard Magazine,* pp. 60-67. (p. 388)

de Hoogh, A. H. B., den Hartog, D. N., Koopman, P. L., Thierry, H., van den Berg, P. T., van der Weide, J. G., & Wilderom, C. P. M. (2004). Charismatic leadership, environmental dynamism, and performance. *European Journal of Work and Organisational Psychology, 13,* 447-471. (p. 495)

De Houwer, J., Baeyens, F., & Field, A. P. (2005a). Associative learning of likes and dislikes: Some current controversies and possible ways forward. *Cognition and Emotion, 19,* 161-174. (p. 293)

De Houwer, J., Thomas, S., & Baeyens, F. (2001). Associative learning of likes and dislikes: A review of 25 years of research on human evaluative conditioning. *Psychological Bulletin, 127,* 853-869. (p. 293)

De Houwer, J., Vandorpe, S., & Beckers, T. (2005b). On the role of controlled cognitive processes in human associative learning. In A. J. Wills (Ed.), *New directions in human associative learning.* Mahwah, NJ: Erlbaum. (p. 293)

De Koninck, J. (2000). Waking experiences and dreaming. In M. Kryger, T. Roth, & W. Dement (Eds.), *Principles and practice of sleep medicine* (3rd ed.). Philadelphia: Saunders. (p. 103)

de Quervain, D. J.-F., Roozendaal, B., & McGaugh, J. L. (1998). Stress and glucocorticoids impair retrieval of long-term spatial memory. *Nature, 394,* 787-790. (p. 342)

De Vogli, R., Chandola, T., & Marmot, M. G. (2007). Negative aspects of close relationships and heart disease. *Archives of Internal Medicine, 167,* 1951-1957. (p. 545)

de Waal, F. (2005, September 23). We're all Machiavellians. *Chronicle of Higher Education.* (p. 29)

de Waal, F. B. M. (1999, December). The end of nature versus nurture. *Scientific American,* pp. 94-99. (p. 161)

de Waal, F. B. M., & Johanowicz, D. L. (1993). Modification of reconciliation behavior through social experience: An experiment with two macaque species. *Child Development, 64,* 897-908. (p. 315)

De Wolff, M. S., & van IJzendoorn, M. H. (1997). Sensitivity and attachment: A meta-analysis on parental antecedents of infant attachment. *Child Development, 68,* 571-591. (p. 188)

Deacon, B. J., & Abramowitz, J. S. (2004). Cognitive and behavioral treatments for anxiety disorders: A review of meta-analytic findings. *Journal of Clinical Psychology, 60,* 429-441. (p. 651)

Dean, G. A., Kelly, I. W., Saklofske, D. H., & Furnham, A. (1992). Graphology and human judgment. In B. Beyerstein & D. Beyerstein (Eds.), *The write stuff: Evaluations of graphology.* Buffalo, NY: Prometheus Books. (p. 578)

DeAngelis, T. (2008, February). U.K. gives huge boost to psychologists. *Monitor on Psychology,* p. 51. (p. 664)

Deary, I. J., Batty, G. D., & Gale, C. R. (2008). Bright children become enlightened adults. *Psychological Science, 19,* 1-6. (p. 708)

Deary, I. J., & Caryl, P. G. (1993). Intelligence, EEG and evoked potentials. In P. A. Vernon (Ed.), *Biological approaches to the study of human intelligence.* Norwood, NJ: Ablex. (p. 414)

Deary, I. J., & Der, G. (2005). Reaction time explains IQ's association with death. *Psychological Science, 16,* 64-69. (p. 413)

Deary, I. J., & Matthews, G. (1993). Personality traits are alive and well. *The Psychologist: Bulletin of the British Psychological Society, 6,* 299-311. (p. 581)

Deary, I. J., & Stough, C. (1996). Intelligence and inspection time: Achievements, prospects, and problems. *American Psychologist, 51,* 599-608. (p. 413)

Deary, I. J., Strand, S., Smith, P., & Fernandes, C. (2007). Intelligence and educational achievement. *Intelligence, 35,* 13-21. (p. 422)

Deary, I. J., Thorpe, G., Wilson, V., Starr, J. M., & Whalley, L. J. (2003). Population sex differences in IQ at age 11: The Scottish mental survey 1932. *Intelligence, 31,* 533-541. (pp. 432, 435)

Deary, I. J., Whiteman, M. C., Starr, J. M., Whalley, L. J., & Fox, H. C. (2004). The impact of childhood intelligence on later life: Following up the Scottish mental surveys of 1932 and 1947. *Journal of Personality and Social Psychology, 86,* 130-147. (p. 423, 424)

DeBruine, L. M. (2002). Facial resemblance enhances trust. *Proceedings of the Royal Society of London, 269,* 1307-1312. (p. 720)

DeBruine, L. M. (2004). Facial resemblance increases the attractiveness of same-sex faces more than other-sex faces. *Proceedings of the Royal Society of London B, 271,* 2085-2090. (p. 720)

DeCasper, A. J., Lecanuet, J-P., Busnel, M-C., & others. (1994). Fetal reactions to recurrent maternal speech. *Infant Behavior and Development, 17,* 159-164. (p. 171)

DeCasper, A. J., & Prescott, P. A. (1984). Human newborns' perception of male voices: Preference, discrimination and reinforcing value. *Developmental Psychobiology, 17,* 481-491. (p. 171))

DeCasper, A. J., & Spence, M. J. (1986). Prenatal maternal speech influences newborns' perception of speech sounds. *Infant Behavior and Development, 9,* 133-150. (p. 171))

Deci, E. L., Koestner, R., & Ryan, R. M. (1999, November). A meta-analytic review of experiments examining the effects of extrinsic rewards on intrinsic motivation. *Psychological Bulletin, 125*(6), 627-668. (p. 309)

Deci, E. L., & Ryan, R. M. (1985). *Intrinsic motivation and self-determination in human behavior.* New York: Plenum Press. (p. 309)

Deci, E. L., & Ryan, R. M. (1992). The initiation and regulation of intrinsically motivated learning and achievement. In A. K. Boggiano & T. S. Pittman (Eds.), *Achievement and motivation: A social-developmental perspective.* New York: Cambridge University Press. (p. 309)

Deci, E. L., & Ryan, R. M. (Eds.). (2002). *Handbook of self-determination research.* Rochester, NY: University of Rochester Press. (pp. 309, 480)

Deeley, Q., Daly, E., Surguladze, S., Tunstall, N., Mezey, G., Beer, D., Ambikapathy, A., Robertson, D., Giampietro, V., Brammer, M. J., Clarke, A., Dowsett, J., Fahy, T., Phillips, M. L., & Murphy, D. G. (2006). Facial emotion processing in criminal psychopathy. *British Journal of Psychiatry, 189,* 533-539. (p. 621)

DeHart, T., Tennen, H., Armeli, S., Todd, M., & Affleck, G. (2008). Drinking to regulate negative romantic relationship interactions: The moderating role of self-esteem. *Journal of Experimental Social Psychology, 44,* 527-538. (p. 116)

Dehne, K. L., & Riedner, G. (2005). *Sexually transmitted infections among adolescents: The need for adequate health services.* Geneva: World Health Organization. (p. 471)

DeLamater, J. D., & Sill, M. (2005). Sexual desire in later life. *Journal of Sex Research, 42,* 138-149. (p. 207)

Delaney, H. D., Miller, W. R., & Bisonó, A. M. (2007). Religiosity and spirituality among psychologists: A survey of clinician members of the American Psychological Association. *Professional Psychology: Research and Practice, 38,* 538-546. (p. 668)

Delaney, P. F., Ericsson, K. A., Weaver, G. E., & Mahadevan, S. (1999). Accounts of the memorist Rajan's exceptional performance: Comparing three theoretical proposals. Paper presented to the American Psychological Society convention. (p. 339)

Delgado, J. M. R. (1969). Physical control of the mind: Toward a psychocivilized society. New York: Harper & Row. (p. 68)

DeLoache, J. S. (1987). Rapid change in the symbolic functioning of very young children. Science, 238, 1556-1557. (p. 180)

DeLoache, J. S. (1995). Early understanding and use of symbols: The model model. Current Directions in Psychological Science, 4, 109-113. (p. 180)

DeLoache, J. S., Uttal, D. H., & Rosengren, K. S. (2004). Scale errors offer evidence for a perception-action dissociation early in life. Science, 304, 1027-1029. (p. 177)

Dement, W. C. (1978). Some must watch while some must sleep. New York: Norton. (pp. 93, 101)

Dement, W. C. (1997, September). What all undergraduates should know about how their sleeping lives affect their waking lives. Stanford University: www.leland.stanford.edu/~dement/sleepless.html. (p. 97)

Dement, W. C. (1999). The promise of sleep. New York: Delacorte Press. (pp. 92, 94, 96, 97, 98, 99, 101, 102, B-2, B-10)

Dement, W. C., & Wolpert, E. A. (1958). The relation of eye movements, body mobility, and external stimuli to dream content. Journal of Experimental Psychology, 55, 543-553. (p. 103)

Demir, E., & Dickson, B. J. (2005). Fruitless splicing specifies male courtship behavior in Drosophila. Cell, 121, 785-794. (p. 476)

Denes-Raj, V., Epstein, S., & Cole, J. (1995). The generality of the ratio-bias phenomenon. Personality and Social Psychology Bulletin, 21, 1083-1092. (p. 381)

DeNeve, K. M., & Cooper, H. (1998). The happy personality: A meta-analysis of 137 personality traits and subjective well-being. Psychological Bulletin, 124, 197-229. (p. 529)

Dennett, D. (1996, September 9). Quoted by Ian Parker, Richard Dawkins' evolution. The New Yorker, pp. 41-45. (p. 7)

Dennett, D. C. (1991). Consciousness explained. Boston: Little, Brown. (p. 295)

Denton, K., & Krebs, D. (1990). From the scene to the crime: The effect of alcohol and social context on moral judgment. Journal of Personality and Social Psychology, 59, 242-248. (p. 116)

DePaulo, B. M. (1994). Spotting lies: Can humans learn to do better? Current Directions in Psychological Science, 3, 83-86. (p. 512)

DePaulo, B. M., Blank, A. L., Swaim, G. W., & Hairfield, J. G. (1992). Expressiveness and expressive control. Personality and Social Psychology Bulletin, 18, 276-285. (p. 582)

Der, G., Batty, G. D., & Deary, I. J. (2006). Effect of breast feeding on intelligence in children: Prospective study, sibling pairs analysis, and meta-analysis. British Medical Journal, 333, 945. (p. 34)

Dermer, M., Cohen, S. J., Jacobsen, E., & Anderson, E. A. (1979). Evaluative judgments of aspects of life as a function of vicarious exposure to hedonic extremes. Journal of Personality and Social Psychology, 37, 247-260. (p. 528)

Dermer, M., & Pyszczynski, T. A. (1978). Effects of erotica upon men's loving and liking responses for women they love. Journal of Personality and Social Psychology, 36, 1302-1309. (p. 724)

Deroche-Garmonet, V., Belin, D., & Piazza, P. V. (2004). Evidence for addiction-like behavior in the rat. Science, 305, 1014-1017. (p. 114)

DeRubeis, R. J., & 10 others. (2005). Cognitive therapy vs. medications in the treatment of moderate to severe depression. Archives of General Psychiatry, 62, 409-416. (p. 664)

DeSteno, D., Dasgupta, N., Bartlett, M. Y., & Cajdric, A. (2004). Prejudice from thin air: The effect of emotion on automatic intergroup attitudes. Psychological Science, 15, 319-324. (p. 521)

DeSteno, D., Petty, R. E., Wegener, D. T., & Rucker, D. D. (2000). Beyond valence in the perception of likelihood: The role of emotion specificity. Journal of Personality and Social Psychology, 78, 397-416. (p. 349)

Dettman, S. J., Pinder, D., Briggs, R. J. S., Dowell, R. C., & Leigh, J. R. (2007). Communication development in children who receive the cochlear implant younger than 12 months: Risk versus benefits. Ear and Hearing, 28(2), Supplement 11S-18S. (p. 248)

Deutsch, J. A. (1972, July). Brain reward: ESP and ecstasy. Psychology Today, 46-48. (p. 65)

DeValois, R. L., & DeValois, K. K. (1975). Neural coding of color. In E. C. Carterette & M. P. Friedman (Eds.), Handbook of perception: Vol. V. Seeing. New York: Academic Press. (p. 242)

Devilly, G. J. (2003). Eye movement desensitization and reprocessing: A chronology of its development and scientific standing. Scientific Review of Mental Health Practice, 1, 113-118. (p. 665)

Devilly, G. J., Gist, R., & Cotton, P. (2006). Ready! Fire! Aim! The status of psychological debriefing and therapeutic interventions: In the work place and after disasters. Review of General Psychology, 10, 318-345. (p. 613)

Devine, P. G. (1995). Prejudice and outgroup perception. In A. Tesser (Ed.), Advanced social psychology. New York: McGraw-Hill. (p. 720)

Devlin, B., Daniels, M., & Roeder, K. (1997). The heritability of IQ. Nature, 388, 468-471. (p. 428)

Dew, M. A., Hoch, C. C., Buysse, D. J., Monk, T. H., Begley, A. E., Houck, P. R., Hall, M., Kupfer, D. J., Reynolds, C. F., III (2003). Healthy older adults' sleep predicts all-cause mortality at 4 to 19 years of follow-up. Psychosomatic Medicine, 65, 63-73. (p. 98)

DeWall, C. N., Baumeister, R. F., Stillman, T. F., & Gaillot, M. T. (2007). Violence restrained: Effects of self-regulation and its depletion on aggression. Journal of Experimental Social Psychology, 43, 62-76. (p. 585)

Diaconis, P. (2002, August 11). Quoted by L. Belkin, The odds of that. New York Times (www.nytimes.com). (p. 34)

Diaconis, P., & Mosteller, F. (1989). Methods for studying coincidences. Journal of the American Statistical Association, 84, 853-861. (p. 34)

Diamond, J. (2001, February). A tale of two reputations: Why we revere Darwin and give Freud a hard time. Natural History, pp. 20-24. (p. 143)

Diamond, L. M. (2007). A dynamical systems approach to the development and expression of female same-sex sexuality. Perspectives on Psychological Science, 2, 142-161. (p. 473)

Diamond, R. (1993). Genetics and male sexual orientation (letter). Science, 261, 1258. (p. 478)

Dick, D. M. (2007). Identification of genes influencing a spectrum of externalizing psychopathology. Current Directions in Psychological Science, 16, 331-335. (p. 621)

Dick, D. M., & 14 others (2007). Association of CHRM2 with IQ: Converging evidence for a gene influencing intelligence. Behavior Genetics, 37, 265-272. (p. 428)

Dickens, W. T., & Flynn, J. R. (2006). Black Americans reduce the racial IQ gap: Evidence from standardization samples. Psychological Science, 17, 913-920. (p. 435)

Dickerson, S. S., & Kemeny, M. E. (2004). Acute stressors and cortisol responses: A theoretical integration and synthesis of laboratory research. Psychological Bulletin, 130, 355-391. (p. 542)

Dickinson, H. O., Parkinson, K. M., Ravens-Sieberer, U., Schirripa, G., Thyen, U., Arnaud, C., Beckung, E., Fauconnier, J., McManus, V., Michelsen, S. I., Parkes, J., & Colver, A. F. (2007). Self-reported quality of life of 8-12-year-old children with cerebral palsy: A cross-sectional European study. Lancet, 369, 2171-2178. (p. 523)

Dickson, B. J. (2005, June 3). Quoted in E. Rosenthal, For fruit flies, gene shift tilts sex orientation. New York Times (www.nytimes.com). (p. 476)

Diener, E. (2006). Guidelines of national indicators of subjective well-being and ill-being. Journal of Happiness Studies, 7, 397-404. (p. 526)

Diener, E., & Biswas-Diener, R. (2002). Will money increase subjective well-being? A literature review and guide to needed research. Social Indicators Research, 57, 119-169. (p. 525)

Diener, E., & Biswas-Diener, R. (2009). Rethinking happiness: The science of psychological wealth. Malden, MA: Wiley Blackwell. (pp. 523, 524, 525)

Diener, E., Emmons, R. A., & Sandvik, E. (1986). The dual nature of happiness: Independence of positive and negative moods. Unpublished manuscript, University of Illinois. (p. 220)

Diener, E., Lucas, R. E., & Scollon, C. N. (2006). Beyond the hedonic treadmill: Revising the adaptation theory of well-being. American Psychologist, 61, 305-314. (p. 527)

Diener, E., Nickerson, C., Lucas, R. E., & Sandvik, E. (2002). Dispositional affect and job outcomes. Social Indicators Research, 59, 229-259. (p. 522)

Diener, E., & Oishi, S. (2000). Money and happiness: Income and subjective well-being across nations. In E. Diener & E. M. Suh (Eds.), *Subjective well-being across cultures*. Cambridge, MA: MIT Press. (p. 524)

Diener, E., Oishi, S., & Lucas, R. E. (2003). Personality, culture, and subjective well-being: Emotional and cognitive evaluations of life. *Annual Review of Psychology, 54*, 403–425. (pp. 528, 529)

Diener, E., & Seligman, M. E. P. (2002). Very happy people. *Psychological Science, 13*, 81–84. (p. 480)

Diener, E., Wolsic, B., & Fujita, F. (1995). Physical attractiveness and subjective well-being. *Journal of Personality and Social Psychology, 69*, 120–129. (p. 722)

Dietz, W. H., Jr., & Gortmaker, S. L. (1985). Do we fatten our children at the television set? Obesity and television viewing in children and adolescents. *Pediatrics, 75*, 807–812. (p. 463)

DiFranza, J. R. (2008, May). Hooked from the first cigarette. *Scientific American*, pp. 82–87. (p. 119)

Dijksterhuis, A., & Aarts, H. (2003). On wildebeests and humans: The preferential detection of negative stimuli. *Psychological Science, 14*, 14–18. (p. 510)

Dijksterhuis, A., Bos, M. W., Nordgren, L. F., & van Baaren, R. B. (2006b). Complex choices better made unconsciously? *Science, 313*, 760–761. (p. 380)

Dijksterhuis, A., & Nordgren, L. F. (2006a). A theory of unconscious thought. *Perspectives on Psychological Science, 1*, 95–109. (p. 380)

DiLalla, D. L., Carey, G., Gottesman, I. I., & Bouchard, T. J., Jr. (1996). Heritability of MMPI personality indicators of psychopathology in twins reared apart. *Journal of Abnormal Psychology, 105*, 491–499. (pp. 136, 629)

Dimberg, U., Thunberg, M., & Elmehed, K. (2000). Unconscious facial reactions to emotional facial expressions. *Psychological Science, 11*, 86–89. (pp. 317, 507, 516)

Dimberg, U., Thunberg, M., & Grunedal, S. (2002). Facial reactions to emotional stimuli: Automatically controlled emotional responses. *Cognition and Emotion, 16*, 449–472. (p. 317)

Dindia, K., & Allen, M. (1992). Sex differences in self-disclosure: A meta-analysis. *Psychological Bulletin, 112*, 106–124. (p. 160)

Dindo, M., Thierry, B., & Whiten, A. (2008). Social diffusion of novel foraging skills in brown capuchin monkeys (*Cebus apella*). *Proceedings of the Royal Society. Series B. Biological Sciences, 275*, 187–193. (p. 398)

Dinges, N. G., & Hull, P. (1992). Personality, culture, and international studies. In D. Lieberman (Ed.), *Revealing the world: An interdisciplinary reader for international studies*. Dubuque, IA: Kendall-Hunt. (p. 393)

Dingfelder, S. (2007, December). $10 million project aims to integrate law and neuroscience. *Monitor on Psychology*, p. 11. (p. 505)

Dion, K. K., & Dion, K. L. (1993). Individualistic and collectivistic perspectives on gender and the cultural context of love and intimacy. *Journal of Social Issues, 49*, 53–69. (p. 155)

Dion, K. K., & Dion, K. L. (2001). Gender and cultural adaptation in immigrant families. *Journal of Social Issues, 57*, 511–521. (p. 163)

Discover (1996, May). A fistful of risks. Pp. 82–83. (p. 118)

Dixon, J., Durrheim, K., & Tredoux, C. (2007). Intergroup contact and attitudes toward the principle and practice of racial equality. *Psychological Science, 18*, 867–872. (p. 731)

Dobbs, D. (2006, August/September). Turning off depression. *Scientific American Mind*, pp. 26–31. (p. 677)

Dobel, C., Diesendruck, G., & Bölte, J. (2007). How writing system and age influence spatial representations of actions: A developments, cross-linguistic study. *Psychological Science, 18*, 487–491. (p. 393)

Doherty, E. W., & Doherty, W. J. (1998). Smoke gets in your eyes: Cigarette smoking and divorce in a national sample of American adults. *Families, Systems, and Health, 16*, 393–400. (p. 120)

Dohrenwend, B., Pearlin, L., Clayton, P., Hamburg, B., Dohrenwend, B. P., Riley, M., & Rose, R. (1982). Report on stress and life events. In G. R. Elliott & C. Eisdorfer (Eds.), *Stress and human health: Analysis and implications of research* (A study by the Institute of Medicine/National Academy of Sciences). New York: Springer. (p. 534)

Dohrenwend, B. P., Levav, I., Shrout, P. E., Schwartz, S., Naveh, G., Link, B. G., Skodol, A. E., & Stueve, A. (1992). Socioeconomic status and psychiatric disorders: The causation-selection issue. *Science, 255*, 946–952. (p. 607)

Dohrenwend, B. P., Turner, J. B., Turse, N. A., Adams, B. G., Koenen, K. C., & Marshall, R. (2006). The psychological risks of Vietnam for U.S. veterans: A revisit with new data and methods. *Science, 313*, 979–982. (p. 613)

Doidge, N. (2007). *The brain that changes itself*. New York: Viking. (p. 73)

Dolan, C. M., Kraemer, H., Browner, W., Ensrud, K., & Kelsey, J. L. (2007). Associations between body composition, anthropometry and mortality in women of age 65 and older. *American Journal of Public Health, 97*, 913–918. (p. 457)

Dole, R. (1996, April 20). Quoted by M. Duffy, Look who's talking. *Time*, p. 48. (p. 684)

Dolezal, H. (1982). *Living in a world transformed*. New York: Academic Press. (p. 274)

Domhoff, G. W. (1996). *Finding meaning in dreams: A quantitative approach*. New York: Plenum. (p. 103)

Domhoff, G. W. (2003). The scientific study of dreams: Neural networks, cognitive development, and content analysis. Washington, DC: APA Books. (pp. 104, 105)

Domhoff, G. W. (2007). Realistic simulations and bizarreness in dream content: Past findings and suggestions for future research. In D. Barrett & P. McNamara (Eds.), *The new science of dreaming: Content, recall, and personality characteristics*. Westport, CT: Praeger. (p. 103)

Domjan, M. (1992). Adult learning and mate choice: Possibilities and experimental evidence. *American Zoologist, 32*, 48–61. (p. 292)

Domjan, M. (1994). Formulation of a behavior system for sexual conditioning. *Psychonomic Bulletin & Review, 1*, 421–428. (p. 292)

Domjan, M. (2005). Pavlovian conditioning: A functional perspective. *Annual Review of Psychology, 56*. (pp. 292, 296)

Domjan, M., Cusato, B., & Krause, M. (2004). Learning with arbitrary versus ecological conditioned stimuli: Evidence from sexual conditioning. *Psychonomic Bulletin & Review, 11*, 232–246. (p. 296)

Donahoe, J. W., & Vegas, R. (2004). Pavlovian conditioning: The CS-UR relation. *Journal of Experimental Psychology: Animal Behavior, 30*, 17–33. (p. 313)

Donnellan, M. B., Conger, R. D., & Bryant, C. M. (2004). The Big Five and enduring marriages. *Journal of Research in Personality, 38*, 481–504. (p. 580)

Donnellan, M. B., Trzesniewski, K. H., Robins, R. W., Moffitt, T. E., & Caspi, A. (2005). Low self-esteem is related to aggression, antisocial behavior, and delinquency. *Psychological Science, 16*, 328–335. (pp. 584, 594)

Donnerstein, E. (1998). Why do we have those new ratings on television. Invited address to the National Institute on the Teaching of Psychology. (pp. 319, 320)

Donnerstein, E., Linz, D., & Penrod, S. (1987). *The question of pornography*. New York: Free Press. (p. 321)

Dorner, G. (1976). *Hormones and brain differentiation*. Amsterdam: Elsevier Scientific. (p. 476)

Dorner, G. (1988). Neuroendocrine response to estrogen and brain differentiation in heterosexuals, homosexuals, and transsexuals. *Archives of Sexual Behavior, 17*, 57–75. (p. 476)

Doty, R. L. (2001). Olfaction. *Annual Review of Psychology, 52*, 423–452. (p. 260)

Doty, R. L., Shaman, P., Applebaum, S. L., Giberson, R., Siksorski, L., & Rosenberg, L. (1984). Smell identification ability: Changes with age. *Science, 226*, 1441–1443. (p. 209)

Dovidio, J. F., & Gaertner, S. L. (1999). Reducing prejudice: Combating intergroup biases. *Current Directions in Psychological Science, 8*, 101–105. (p. 732)

Dovidio, J. F., ten Vergert, M., Stewart, T. L., Gaertner, S. L., Johnson, J. D., Esses, V. M., Riek, B. M., & Pearson, A. R. (2004). Perspective and prejudice: Antecedents and mediating mechanisms. *Personality and Social Psychology Bulletin, 30*, 1537–1549. (p. 732)

Downing, P. E., Jiang, Y., & Shuman, M. (2001). A cortical area selective for visual processing of the human body. *Science, 293*, 2470–2473. (p. 238)

Doyle, R. (2005, March). Gay and lesbian census. *Scientific American*, p. 28. (p. 144)

Draguns, J. G. (1990a). Normal and abnormal behavior in cross-cultural perspective: Specifying the nature of their relationship. *Nebraska Symposium on Motivation 1989, 37*, 235–277. (pp. 597, 634)

Draguns, J. G. (1990b). Applications of cross-cultural psychology in the field of mental health. In R. W. Brislin (Ed.), *Applied cross-cultural psychology*. Newbury Park, CA: Sage. (p. 597)

Draguns, J. G. (1997). Abnormal behavior patterns across cultures: Implications for counseling and psychotherapy. *International Journal of Intercultural Relations, 21*, 213–248. (p. 597)

Drake, R. A. (1993). Processing persuasive arguments: II. Discounting of truth and relevance as a function of agreement and manipulated activation asymmetry. *Journal of Research in Personality, 27*, 184–196. (p. 77)

Drake, R. A., & Myers, L. R. (2006). Visual attention, emotion, and action tendency: Feeling active or passive. *Cognition and Emotion, 20*, 608–622. (p. 503)

Druckman, D., & Bjork, R. A. (1991). *In the mind's eye: Enhancing human performance*. Washington, DC: National Academy Press. (p. 574)

Druckman, D., & Bjork, R. A. (Eds.). (1994). *Learning, remembering, believing: Enhancing human performance*. Washington, DC: National Academy Press. (pp. 109, 110)

Duckworth, A. L., & Seligman, M. E. P. (2005). Discipline outdoes talent: Self-discipline predicts academic performance in adolescents. *Psychological Science, 12*, 939–944. (p. 490)

Duckworth, A. L., & Seligman, M. E. P. (2006). Self-discipline gives girls the edge: Gender in self-discipline, grades, and achievement tests. *Journal of Educational Psychology, 98*, 198–208. (p. 490)

Duclos, S. E., Laird, J. D., Sexter, M., Stern, L., & Van Lighten, O. (1989). Emotion-specific effects of facial expressions and postures on emotional experience. *Journal of Personality and Social Psychology, 57*, 100–108. (p. 515)

Duenwald, M. (2004, October 26). The dorms may be great, but how's the counseling? *New York Times* (www.nytimes.com). (p. 672)

Duffy, M. (2003, June 9). Weapons of mass disappearance. *Time*, pp. 28–33. (p. 688)

Dugatkin, L. A. (2002, Winter). Watching culture shape even guppy love. *Cerebrum*, pp. 51–66. (p. 315)

Duggan, J. P., & Booth, D. A. (1986). Obesity, overeating, and rapid gastric emptying in rats with ventromedial hypothalamic lesions. *Science, 231*, 609–611. (p. 450)

Dugger, C. W. (2005, January 18). U.N. proposes doubling of aid to cut poverty. *New York Times* (www.nytimes.com). (p. 379)

Dumont, K. A., Widom, C. S., & Czaja, S. J. (2007). Predictors of resilience in abused and neglected children grown-up: The role of individual and neighborhood characteristics. *Child Abuse & Neglect, 31*, 255–274. (p. 190)

Duncan, J. (2000, July 21). Quoted by N. Angier, Study finds region of brain may be key problem solver. *New York Times* (www.nytimes.com). (p. 413)

Duncan, J., Seitz, R. J., Kolodny, J., Bor, D., Herzog, H., Ahmed, A., Newell, F. N., & Emslie, H. (2000). A neural basis of general intelligence. *Science, 289*, 457–460. (p. 413)

Duncker, K. (1945). On problem solving. *Psychological Monographs, 58* (Whole no. 270). (pp. 373, 374)

Dunn, A. L., Trivedi, M. H., Kampert, J. B., Clark, C. G., & Chambliss, H. O. (2005). Exercise treatment for depression: Efficacy and dose response. *American Journal of Preventive Medicine, 28*, 1–8. (p. 547)

Dunn, E. W., Aknin, L. B., & Norton, M. I. (2008). Spending money on others promotes happiness. *Science, 319*, 1687–1688. (p. 728)

Dunning, D. (2006). Strangers to ourselves? *The Psychologist, 19*, 600–603. (p. 589)

Dunson, D. B., Colombo, B., & Baird, D. D. (2002). Changes with age in the level and duration of fertility in the menstrual cycle. *Human Reproduction, 17*, 1399–1403. (p. 207)

Durgin, F. H., Evans, L., Dunphy, N., Klostermann, S., & Simmons, K. (2007). Rubber hands feel the touch of light. *Psychological Science, 18*, 152–157. (p. 252)

Dush, C. M. K, Cohan, C. L., & Amato, P. R. (2003). The relationship between cohabitation and marital quality and stability: Change across cohorts? *Journal of Marriage and Family, 65*, 539–549. (p. 217)

Dutton, D. G., & Aron, A. (1989). Romantic attraction and generalized liking for others who are sources of conflict-based arousal. *Canadian Journal of Behavioural Sciences, 21*, 246–257. (p. 724)

Dutton, D. G., & Aron, A. P. (1974). Some evidence for heightened sexual attraction under conditions of high anxiety. *Journal of Personality and Social Psychology, 30*, 510–517. (p. 724)

Dweck, C. S. (2006). *Mindset: The new psychology of success*. New York: Random House. (p. 432)

Dweck, C. S. (2007, November 28). The secret to raising smart kids. *Scientific American Mind*, pp. 36–43 (http://www.sciam.com). (p. 432)

Eagly, A., & Carli, L. (2007). *Through the labyrinth: The truth about how women become leaders*. Cambridge, MA: Harvard University Press. (p. 158)

Eagly, A. H. (1994). Are people prejudiced against women? Donald Campbell Award invited address, American Psychological Association convention. (p. 704)

Eagly, A. H. (2007). Female leadership advantage and disadvantage: Resolving the contradictions. *Psychology of Women Quarterly, 31*, 1–12. (p. 495)

Eagly, A. H., Ashmore, R. D., Makhijani, M. G., & Kennedy, L. C. (1991). What is beautiful is good, but . . .: A meta-analytic review of research on the physical attractiveness stereotype. *Psychological Bulletin, 110*, 109–128. (p. 721)

Eagly, A. H., & Crowley, M. (1986). Gender and helping behavior: A meta-analytic review of the social psychological literature. *Psychological Bulletin, 100*, 283–308. (p. 728)

Eagly, A. H., & Wood, W. (1999). The origins of sex differences in human behavior: Evolved dispositions versus social roles. *American Psychologist, 54*, 408–423. (p. 146)

Eastman, C. L., Boulos, Z., Terman, M., Campbell, S. S., Dijk, D-J., & Lewy, A. J. (1995). Light treatment for sleep disorders: Consensus report. VI. Shift work. *Journal of Biological Rhythms, 10*, 157–164. (p. 92)

Eastman, C. L., Young, M. A., Fogg, L. F., Liu, L., & Meaden, P. M. (1998). Bright light treatment of winter depression: A placebo-controlled trial. *Archives of General Psychiatry, 55*, 883–889. (p. 666)

Eastwick, P. W., & Finkel, E. J. (2008a). Speed-dating as a methodological innovation. *The Psychologist, 21*, 402–403. (p. 720)

Eastwick, P. W., & Finkel, E. J. (2008b). Sex differences in mate preferences revisited: Do people know what they initially desire in a romantic partner? *Journal of Personality and Social Psychology, 94*, 245–264. (p. 720)

Ebbesen, E. B., Duncan, B., & Konecni, V. J. (1975). Effects of content of verbal aggression on future verbal aggression: A field experiment. *Journal of Experimental Social Psychology, 11*, 192–204. (p. 520)

Ebbinghaus, H. (1885). Über das Gedächtnis. Leipzig: Duncker & Humblot. Cited in R. Klatzky (1980), *Human memory: Structures and processes*. San Francisco: Freeman. (p. 329)

Ebbinghaus, H. (1885/1964). *Memory: A contribution to experimental psychology* (H. A. Ruger & C. E. Bussenius, Trans.). New York: Dover. (p. 353)

Eberhardt, J. L. (2005). Imaging race. *American Psychologist, 60*, 181–190. (p. 705)

Eberhardt, J. L., Davies, P. G., Purdie-Vaughns, V. J., & Johnson, S. L. (2006). Looking deathworthy: Perceived stereotypicality of Black defendants predicts capital-sentencing outcomes. *Psychological Science, 17*, 383–386. (p. 705)

Eberhardt, J. L., Goff, P. A., Purdie, V. J., & Davies, P. G. (2004). Seeing Black: Race, crime, and visual processing. *Journal of Personality and Social Psychology, 87*, 876–893. (p. 705)

Eccles, J. S., Jacobs, J. E., & Harold, R. D. (1990). Gender role stereotypes, expectancy effects, and parents' socialization of gender differences. *Journal of Social Issues, 46*, 183–201. (p. 434)

Eckensberger, L. H. (1994). Moral development and its measurement across cultures. In W. J. Lonner & R. Malpass (Eds.), *Psychology and culture*. Boston: Allyn & Bacon. (p. 199)

Eckert, E. D., Heston, L. L., & Bouchard, T. J., Jr. (1981). MZ twins reared apart: Preliminary findings of psychiatric disturbances and traits. In L. Gedda, P. Paris, & W. D. Nance (Eds.), *Twin research: Vol. 3. Pt. B. Intelligence, personality, and development*. New York: Alan Liss. (p. 616)

Ecklund-Flores, L. (1992). The infant as a model for the teaching of introductory psychology. Paper presented to the American Psychological Association annual convention. (p. 171)

Economist. (2001, December 20). An anthropology of happiness. *The Economist* (www.economist.com/world/asia). (p. 481)

Edelman, S., & Kidman, A. D. (1997). Mind and cancer: Is there a relationship? A review of the evidence. *Australian Psychologist, 32,* 1–7. (p. 540)

Edison, T. A. (1948). *The diary and sundry observations of Thomas Alva Edison,* edited by D. D. Runes. New York: Philosophical Library. Cited by S. Coren (1996). *Sleep Thieves.* New York: Free Press. (p. 96)

Ehrhardt, A. A. (1987). A transactional perspective on the development of gender differences. In J. M. Reinisch, L. A. Rosenblum, & S. A. Sanders (Eds.), *Masculinity/femininity: Basic perspectives.* New York: Oxford University Press. (p. 161)

Eibl-Eibesfeldt, I. (1971). *Love and hate: The natural history of behavior patterns.* New York: Holt, Rinehart & Winston. (p. 514)

Eich, E. (1990). Learning during sleep. In R. B. Bootzin, J. F. Kihlstrom, & D. L. Schacter (Eds.), *Sleep and cognition.* Washington, DC: American Psychological Association. (p. 104)

Einstein, G. O., & McDaniel, M. A. (1990). Normal aging and prospective memory. *Journal of Experimental Psychology: Learning, Memory, and Cognition, 16,* 717–726. (p. 213)

Einstein, G. O., McDaniel, M. A., Richardson, S. L., Guynn, M. J., & Cunfer, A. R. (1995). Aging and prospective memory: Examining the influences of self-initiated retrieval processes. *Journal of Experimental Psychology: Learning, Memory, and Cognition, 21,* 996–1007. (p. 213)

Einstein, G. O., McDaniel, M. A., Smith, R. E., & Shaw, P. (1998). Habitual prospective memory and aging: Remembering intentions and forgetting actions. *Psychological Science, 9,* 284–288. (p. 213)

Eisenberg, N., & Lennon, R. (1983). Sex differences in empathy and related capacities. *Psychological Bulletin, 94,* 100–131. (p. 513)

Eisenberger, N. I., Lieberman, M. D., & Williams, K. D. (2003). Does rejection hurt? An fMRI study of social exclusion. *Science, 302,* 290–292. (p. 482)

Eisenberger, R., & Rhoades, L. (2001). Incremental effects of reward on creativity. *Journal of Personality and Social Psychology, 81,* 728–741. (p. 309)

Eiser, J. R. (1985). Smoking: The social learning of an addiction. *Journal of Social and Clinical Psychology, 3,* 446–457. (p. 119)

Ekman, P. (1994). Strong evidence for universals in facial expressions: A reply to Russell's mistaken critique. *Psychological Bulletin, 115,* 268–287. (p. 513)

Ekman, P. (2003). *Emotions revealed: Recognizing faces and feelings to improve communication and emotional life.* New York: Times Books. (p. 505)

Ekman, P., & Friesen, W. V. (1975). *Unmasking the face.* Englewood Cliffs, NJ: Prentice-Hall. (p. 513)

Ekman, P., Friesen, W. V., O'Sullivan, M., Chan, A., Diacoyanni-Tarlatzis, I., Heider, K., Krause, R., LeCompte, W. A., Pitcairn, T., Ricci-Bitti, P. E., Scherer, K., Tomita, M., & Tzavaras, A. (1987). Universals and cultural differences in the judgments of facial expressions of emotion. *Journal of Personality and Social Psychology, 53,* 712–717. (p. 513)

Elbert, T., Pantev, C., Wienbruch, C., Rockstroh, B., & Taub, E. (1995). Increased cortical representation of the fingers of the left hand in string players. *Science, 270,* 305–307. (p. 149)

Elfenbein, H. A., & Ambady, N. (1999). *Does it take one to know one? A meta-analysis of the universality and cultural specificity of emotion recognition.* Unpublished manuscript, Harvard University. (p. 513)

Elfenbein, H. A., & Ambady, N. (2002). On the universality and cultural specificity of emotion recognition: A meta-analysis. *Psychological Bulletin, 128,* 203–235. (p. 514)

Elfenbein, H. A., & Ambady, N. (2003a). When familiarity breeds accuracy: Cultural exposure and facial emotion recognition. *Journal of Personality and Social Psychology, 85,* 276–290. (p. 514)

Elfenbein, H. A., & Ambady, N. (2003b). Universals and cultural differences in recognizing emotions. *Current Directions in Psychological Science, 12,* 159–164. (p. 514)

Elkind, D. (1970). The origins of religion in the child. *Review of Religious Research, 12,* 35–42. (p. 198)

Elkind, D. (1978). *The child's reality: Three developmental themes.* Hillsdale, NJ: Erlbaum. (p. 198)

Ellenbogen, J. M., Hu, P. T., Payne, J. D., Titone, D., & Walker, M. P. (2007). Human relational memory requires time and sleep. *Proceedings of the National Academy of Sciences, 104,* 7723–7728. (p. 100)

Elliot, A. J., & McGregor, H. A. (2001). A 2x2 achievement goal framework. *Journal of Personality and Social Psychology, 80,* 501–519. (p. 494)

Elliot, A. J., & Niesta, D. (2008). Romantic red: Red enhances men's attraction to women. *Journal of Personality and Social Psychology, 95,* 1150–1164. (pp. 296, 297)

Elliot, A. J., & Reis, H. T. (2003). Attachment and exploration in adulthood. *Journal of Personality and Social Psychology, 85,* 317–331. (p. 189)

Ellis, A. (1980). Psychotherapy and atheistic values: A response to A. E. Bergin's "Psychotherapy and religious values." *Journal of Consulting and Clinical Psychology, 48,* 635–639. (p. 669)

Ellis, A., & Becker, I. M. (1982). *A guide to personal happiness.* North Hollywood, CA: Wilshire Book Co. (p. 299)

Ellis, B. J. (2004). Timing of pubertal maturation in girls: An integrated life history approach. *Psychological Bulletin, 130,* 920–958. (p. 204)

Ellis, B. J., Bates, J. E., Dodge, K. A., Fergusson, D. M., John, H. L., Pettit, G. S., & Woodward, L. (2003). Does father absence place daughters at special risk for early sexual activity and teenage pregnancy? *Child Development, 74,* 801–821. (p. 472)

Ellis, L., & Ames, M. A. (1987). Neurohormonal functioning and sexual orientation: A theory of homosexuality-heterosexuality. *Psychological Bulletin, 101,* 233–258. (p. 477)

Elzinga, B. M., Ardon, A. M., Heijnis, M. K., De Ruiter, M. B., Van Dyck, R., & Veltman, D. J. (2007). Neural correlates of enhanced working-memory performance in dissociative disorder: A functional MRI study. *Psychological Medicine, 37,* 235–245. (p. 619)

EMDR. (2008). E-mail correspondence from Robbie Dunton, EMDR Institute (www.emdr.org). (p. 665)

Emerging Trends. (1997, September). *Teens turn more to parents than friends on whether to attend church.* Princeton, NJ: Princeton Religion Research Center. (p. 204)

Emery, G. (2004). Psychic predictions 2004. Committee for the Scientific Investigation of Claims of the Paranormal (www.csicop.org). (p. 282)

Emmons, R. A. (2007). *Thanks! How the new science of gratitude can make you happier.* Boston: Houghton Mifflin. (p. 527)

Emmons, S., Geisler, C., Kaplan, K. J., & Harrow, M. (1997). *Living with schizophrenia.* Muncie, IN: Taylor and Francis (Accelerated Development). (pp. 597, 638)

Emmorey, K., Allen, J. S., Bruss, J., Schenker, N., & Damasio, H. (2003). A morphometric analysis of auditory brain regions in congenitally deaf adults. *Proceedings of the National Academy of Sciences, 100,* 10049–10054. (p. 249)

Empson, J. A. C., & Clarke, P. R. F. (1970). Rapid eye movements and remembering. *Nature, 227,* 287–288. (p. 104)

Emslie, C., Hunt, K., & Macintyre, S. (2001). Perceptions of body image among working men and women. *Journal of Epidemiology and Community Health, 55,* 406–407. (p. 454)

Endler, N. S. (1982). *Holiday of darkness: A psychologist's personal journey out of his depression.* New York: Wiley. (pp. 632, 676)

Engemann, K. M., & Owyang, M. T. (2005, April). So much for that merit raise: The link between wages and appearance. *Regional Economist* (www.stlouisfed.org). (p. 721)

Engen, T. (1987). Remembering odors and their names. *American Scientist, 75,* 497–503. (p. 261)

Engle, R. W. (2002). Working memory capacity as executive attention. *Current Directions in Psychological Science, 11,* 19–23. (p. 326)

Epel, E. S., Blackburn, E. H., Lin, J., Dhabhar, F. S., Adler, N. E., Morrow, J. D., & Cawthon, R. M. (2004). Accelerated telomere shortening in response to life stress. *Proceedings of the National Academy of Sciences, 101,* 17312–17315. (p. 533)

Epley, N., & Dunning, D. (2000). Feeling "holier than thou": Are self-serving assessments produced by errors in self- or social prediction? *Journal of Personality and Social Psychology, 79,* 861–875. (p. 592)

Epley, N., & Huff, C. (1998). Suspicion, affective response, and educational benefit as a result of deception in psychology research. *Personality and Social Psychology Bulletin, 24,* 759–768. (p. 22)

Epley, N., Keysar, B., Van Boven, L., & Gilovich, T. (2004). Perspective taking as egocentric anchoring and adjustment. *Journal of Personality and Social Psychology, 87,* 327–339. (p. 180)

EPOCH. (2000). Legal reforms: Corporal punishment of children in the family (www.stophitting.com/laws/legalReform.php). (p. 307)

Epstein, J., Stern, E., & Silbersweig, D. (1998). Mesolimbic activity associated with psychosis in schizophrenia: Symptom-specific PET studies. In J. F. McGinty (Ed.), *Advancing from the ventral striatum to the extended amygdala: Implications for neuropsychiatry and drug use: In honor of Lennart Heimer. Annals of the New York Academy of Sciences, 877,* 562–574. (p. 640)

Epstein, S. (1983a). Aggregation and beyond: Some basic issues on the prediction of behavior. *Journal of Personality, 51,* 360–392. (p. 581)

Epstein, S. (1983b). The stability of behavior across time and situations. In R. Zucker, J. Aronoff, & A. I. Rabin (Eds.), *Personality and the prediction of behavior.* San Diego: Academic Press. (p. 581)

Epstein, S., & Meier, P. (1989). Constructive thinking: A broad coping variable with specific components. *Journal of Personality and Social Psychology, 57,* 332–350. (p. 411)

Erdberg, P. (1990). Rorschach assessment. In G. Goldstein & M. Hersen (Eds.), *Handbook of psychological assessment* (2nd ed.). New York: Pergamon. (p. 565)

Erdelyi, M. H. (1985). *Psychoanalysis: Freud's cognitive psychology.* New York: Freeman. (p. 566)

Erdelyi, M. H. (1988). Repression, reconstruction, and defense: History and integration of the psychoanalytic and experimental frameworks. In J. Singer (Ed.), *Repression: Defense mechanism and cognitive style.* Chicago: University of Chicago Press. (p. 566)

Erdelyi, M. H. (2006). The unified theory of repression. *Behavioral and Brain Sciences, 29,* 499–551. (p. 566)

Erel, O., & Burman, B. (1995). Interrelatedness of marital relations and parent-child relations: A meta-analytic review. *Psychological Bulletin, 118,* 108–132. (p. 218)

Erel, O., Oberman, Y., & Yirmiya, N. (2000). Maternal versus nonmaternal care and seven domains of children's development. *Psychological Bulletin, 126,* 727–747. (p. 191)

Erickson, M. F., & Aird, E. G. (2005). *The motherhood study: Fresh insights on mothers' attitudes and concerns.* New York: The Motherhood Project, Institute for American Values. (p. 218)

Ericsson, K. A. (2001). Attaining excellence through deliberate practice: Insights from the study of expert performance. In M. Ferrari (Ed.), *The pursuit of excellence in education.* Hillsdale, NJ: Erlbaum. (p. 491)

Ericsson, K. A. (2002). Attaining excellence through deliberate practice: Insights from the study of expert performance. In C. Desforges & R. Fox (Eds.), *Teaching and learning: The essential readings.* Malden, MA: Blackwell Publishers. (p. 407)

Ericsson, K. A. (2006). The influence of experience and deliberate practice on the development of superior expert performance. In K. A. Ericsson, N. Charness, P. J. Feltovich, & R. R. Hoffman (Eds.), *The Cambridge handbook of expertise and expert performance.* Cambridge: Cambridge University Press. (p. 491)

Ericsson, K. A. (2007). Deliberate practice and the modifiability of body and mind: Toward a science of the structure and acquisition of expert and elite performance. *International Journal of Sport Psychology, 38,* 4–34. (p. 407)

Ericsson, K. A., Roring, R. W., & Nandagopal, K. (2007). Giftedness and evidence for reproducibly superior performance: An account based on the expert performance framework. *High Ability Studies, 18,* 3–56. (pp. 407, 432, 491)

Erikson, E. H. (1963). *Childhood and society.* New York: Norton. (p. 200)

Erikson, E. H. (1983, June). A conversation with Erikson (by E. Hall). *Psychology Today,* pp. 22–30. (p. 189)

Ernsberger, P., & Koletsky, R. J. (1999). Biomedical rationale for a wellness approach to obesity: An alternative to a focus on weight loss. *Journal of Social Issues, 55,* 221–260. (p. 463)

Ertmer, D. J., Young, N. M., & Nathani, S. (2007). Profiles of focal development in young cochlear implant recipients. *Journal of Speech, Language, and Hearing Research, 50,* 393–407. (p. 388)

Escobar-Chaves, S. L., Tortolero, S., Markham, C., Low, B., Eitel, P., & Thickstun, P. (2005). Impact of the media on adolescents attitudes and behaviors. *Pediatrics, 116,* 303–326. (p. 471)

ESPAD. (2003). Summary of the 2003 findings. European School Survey Project on Alcohol and Other Drugs (www.espad.org). (p. 127)

Esser, J. K., & Lindoerfer, J. S. (1989). Groupthink and the space shuttle Challenger accident: Toward a quantitative case analysis. *Journal of Behavioral Decision Making, 2,* 167–177. (p. 700)

Esterson, A. (2001). The mythologizing of psychoanalytic history: Deception and self-deception in Freud's accounts of the seduction theory episode. *History of Psychiatry, 12,* 329–352. (p. 565)

Esty, A. (2004). The new wealth of nations. *American Scientist, 92,* 513. (p. 526)

Eszterhas, J. (2002, August 9). Hollywood's responsibility for smoking deaths. *New York Times* (www.nytimes.com). (p. 119)

Etkin, A., & Wager, T. D. (2007). Functional neuroimaging of anxiety: A meta-analysis of emotional processing in PTSD, social anxiety disorder, and specific phobia. *American Journal of Psychiatry, 164,* 1476–1488. (p. 616)

Etzioni, A. (1999). The monochrome society. *The Public Interest, 137,* 42–55. (p. 733)

Euston, D. R., Tatsuno, M., & McNaughton, B. L. (2007). Fast-forward playback of recent memory sequences in prefrontal cortex during sleep. *Science, 318,* 1147–1150. (p. 344)

Evans, C. R., & Dion, K. L. (1991). Group cohesion and performance: A meta-analysis. *Small Group Research, 22,* 175–186. (p. 495)

Evans, G. W. (2004). The environment of childhood poverty. *American Psychologist, 59,* 77–92. (p. 191)

Evans, G. W., & Kim, P. (2007). Childhood poverty and health: Cumulative risk exposure and stress dysregulation. *Psychological Science, 18,* 953–957. (p. 543)

Evans, G. W., Palsane, M. N., & Carrere, S. (1987). Type A behavior and occupational stress: A cross-cultural study of blue-collar workers. *Journal of Personality and Social Psychology, 52,* 1002–1007. (p. 536)

Evans, R. I., Dratt, L. M., Raines, B. E., & Rosenberg, S. S. (1988). Social influences on smoking initiation: Importance of distinguishing descriptive versus mediating process variables. *Journal of Applied Social Psychology, 18,* 925–943. (p. 119)

Everson, S. A., Goldberg, D. E., Kaplan, G. A., Cohen, R. D., Pukkala, E., Tuomilehto, J., & Salonen, J. T. (1996). Hopelessness and risk of mortality and incidence of myocardial infarction and cancer. *Psychosomatic Medicine, 58,* 113–121. (p. 544)

Ewing, R., Schmid, T., Killingsworth, R., Zlot, A., & Raudenbush, S. (2003). Relationship between urban sprawl and physical activity, obesity, and morbidity. *American Journal of Health Promotion, 18,* 47–57. (p. 461)

Exner, J. E. (2003). *The Rorschach: A comprehensive system* (4th ed.). Hoboken, NJ: Wiley. (p. 565)

Eysenck, H. J. (1952). The effects of psychotherapy: An evaluation. *Journal of Consulting Psychology, 16,* 319–324. (p. 661)

Eysenck, H. J. (1990, April 30). An improvement on personality inventory. *Current Contents: Social and Behavioral Sciences, 22*(18), 20. (p. 576)

Eysenck, H. J. (1992). Four ways five factors are *not* basic. *Personality and Individual Differences, 13,* 667–673. (p. 576)

Eysenck, H. J., & Grossarth-Maticek, R. (1991). Creative novation behaviour therapy as a prophylactic treatment for cancer and coronary heart disease: Part II—Effects of treatment. *Behaviour Research and Therapy, 29,* 17–31. (p. 551)

Eysenck, H. J., Wakefield, J. A., Jr., & Friedman, A. F. (1983). Diagnosis and clinical assessment: The DSM-III. *Annual Review of Psychology, 34,* 167–193. (p. 603)

Eysenck, M. W., MacLeod, C., & Mathews, A. (1987). Cognitive functioning and anxiety. *Psychological Research, 49,* 189–195. (p. 584)

Eysenck, S. B. G., & Eysenck, H. J. (1963). The validity of questionnaire and rating assessments of extraversion and neuroticism, and their factorial stability. *British Journal of Psychology, 54,* 51–62. (p. 575)

Fagan, J. F., III. (1992). Intelligence: A theoretical viewpoint. *Current Directions in Psychological Science, 1,* 82–86. (p. 437)

Fagan, J. F., & Holland, C. R. (2007). Racial equality in intelligence: Predictions from a theory of intelligence as processing. *Intelligence, 35,* 319–334. (p. 437)

Fagan, J. F., Holland, C. R., & Wheeler, K. (2007). The prediction, from infancy, of adult IQ and achievement. *Intelligence, 35,* 225–231. (p. 423)

Fairburn, C. G., Cowen, P. J., & Harrison, P. J. (1999). Twin studies and the etiology of eating disorders. *International Journal of Eating Disorders, 26,* 349–358. (p. 454)

Fantz, R. L. (1961, May). The origin of form perception. *Scientific American,* pp. 66–72. (p. 173)

Farah, M. J., Rabinowitz, C., Quinn, G. E., & Liu, G. T. (2000). Early commitment of neural substrates for face recognition. *Cognitive Neuropsychology, 17,* 117–124. (p. 73)

Farina, A. (1982). The stigma of mental disorders. In A. G. Miller (Ed.), *In the eye of the beholder.* New York: Praeger. (pp. 601, 605)

Farley, M., Baral, I., Kiremire, M., & Sezgin, U. (1998). Prostitution in five countries: Violence and post-traumatic stress disorder. *Feminism and Psychology, 8,* 405–426. (p. 613)

Farley, T., & Cohen, D. (2001, December). Fixing a fat nation. *Washington Monthly* (www.washingtonmonthly.com/features/2001/0112.farley.cohen.html). (p. 461)

Farooqi, I. S., Bullmore, E., Keogh, J., Gillard, J., O'Rahilly, S., & Fletcher, P. C. (2007). Leptin regulates striatal regions and human eating behavior. *Science, 317,* 1355. (p. 451)

Farrington, D. P. (1991). Antisocial personality from childhood to adulthood. *The Psychologist: Bulletin of the British Psychological Society, 4,* 389–394. (p. 620)

Fast, L. A., & Funder, D. C. (2008). Personality as manifest in word use: Correlations with self-report, acquaintance report, and behavior. *Journal of Personality and Social Psychology, 94,* 334–346. (p. 582)

FBI. 2007. Crime in the United States, 2007. Murder offenders by age, sex, and race, 2006, Expanded homicide data, table 3 (www.fbi.gov/ucr/cius2006/offenses/expanded_information/data/shrtable_03.html). (p. 158)

Feder, H. H. (1984). Hormones and sexual behavior. *Annual Review of Psychology, 35,* 165–200. (p. 467)

Feeney, D. M. (1987). Human rights and animal welfare. *American Psychologist, 42,* 593–599. (p. 21)

Feeney, J. A., & Noller, P. (1990). Attachment style as a predictor of adult romantic relationships. *Journal of Personality and Social Psychology, 58,* 281–291. (p. 189)

Feigenson, L., Carey, S., & Spelke, E. (2002). Infants' discrimination of number vs. continuous extent. *Cognitive Psychology, 44,* 33–66. (p. 179)

Feinberg, T. E., & Keenan, J. P. (Eds.). (2005). *The lost self: Pathologies of the brain and identity.* New York: Oxford University Press. (p. 78)

Feingold, A. (1990). Gender differences in effects of physical attractiveness on romantic attraction: A comparison across five research paradigms. *Journal of Personality and Social Psychology, 59,* 981–993. (p. 721)

Feingold, A. (1992). Good-looking people are not what we think. *Psychological Bulletin, 111,* 304–341. (p. 721)

Feingold, A., & Mazzella, R. (1998). Gender differences in body image are increasing. *Psychological Science, 9,* 190–195. (pp. 454, 722)

Fellinger, J., Holzinger, D., Gerich, J., & Goldberg, D. (2007). Mental distress and quality of life in the hard of hearing. *Acta Psychiatrica Scandinavica, 115,* 243–245. (p. 249)

Fellowes, D., Barnes, K., & Wilkinson, S. (2004). Aromatherapy and massage for symptom relief in patients with cancer. *The Cochrane Library, 3,* Oxford, England: Update Software. (p. 550)

Feminist Psychologist. (2002, Winter). *Justice for Mary Whiton Calkins,* p. 11. (p. 4)

Feng, J., Spence, I., & Pratt, J. (2007). Playing an action video game reduces gender differences in spatial cognition. *Psychological Science, 18,* 850–855. (p. 434)

Fenton, W. S., & McGlashan, T. H. (1991). Natural history of schizophrenia subtypes: II. Positive and negative symptoms and long-term course. *Archives of General Psychiatry, 48,* 978–986. (p. 639)

Fenton, W. S., & McGlashan, T. H. (1994). Antecedents, symptom progression, and long-term outcome of the deficit syndrome in schizophrenia. *American Journal of Psychiatry, 151,* 351–356. (p. 639)

Ferguson, E. D. (1989). Adler's motivational theory: An historical perspective on belonging and the fundamental human striving. *Individual Psychology, 45,* 354–361. (p. 479)

Ferguson, E. D. (2001). Adler and Dreikurs: Cognitive-social dynamic innovators. *Journal of Individual Psychology, 57,* 324–341. (p. 479)

Ferguson, E. D. (2003). Social processes, personal goals, and their intertwining: Their importance in Adlerian theory and practice. *Journal of Individual Psychology, 59,* 136–144. (p. 562)

Fergusson, D. M., & Woodward, L. G. (2002). Mental health, educational, and social role outcomes of adolescents with depression. *Archives of General Psychiatry, 59,* 225–231. (p. 628)

Fernandez, E., & Turk, D. C. (1989). The utility of cognitive coping strategies for altering pain perception: A meta-analysis. *Pain, 38,* 123–135. (p. 256)

Fernández-Ballesteros, R., & Caprara, M. (2003). Psychology of aging in Europe. *European Psychologist, 8,* 129–130. (p. 208)

Fernandez-Dols, J-M., & Ruiz-Belda, M-A. (1995). Are smiles a sign of happiness? Gold medal winners at the Olympic Games. *Journal of Personality and Social Psychology, 69,* 1113–1119. (p. 514)

Ferri, M., Amato, L., & Davoli, M. (2006). Alcoholics Anonymous and other 12-step programmes for alcohol dependence. *Cochrane Database of Systematic Reviews,* Issue 3. Art. No.: CD005032. (p. 658)

Ferris, C. F. (1996, March). The rage of innocents. *The Sciences,* pp. 22–26. (p. 190)

Feynman, R. (1997). Quoted by E. Hutchings (Ed.), *"Surely you're joking, Mr. Feynman."* New York: Norton. (p. 14)

Fiedler, F. E. (1981). Leadership effectiveness. *American Behavioral Scientist, 24,* 619–632. (p. 495)

Fiedler, F. E. (1987, September). When to lead, when to stand back. *Psychology Today,* pp. 26–27. (p. 495)

Fiedler, K., Nickel, S., Muehlfriedel, T., & Unkelbach, C. (2001). Is mood congruency an effect of genuine memory or response bias? *Journal of Experimental Social Psychology, 37,* 201–214. (p. 349)

Field, A. P. (2006). I don't like it because it eats sprouts: Conditioning preferences in children. *Behaviour Research and Therapy, 44,* 439–455. (p. 293)

Field, A. P. (2006). Is conditioning a useful framework for understanding the development and treatment of phobias? *Clinical Psychology Review, 26,* 857–875. (p. 614)

Field, T. (1996). Attachment and separation in young children. *Annual Review of Psychology, 47,* 541–561. (p. 191)

Field, T., Diego, M., & Hernandez-Reif, M. (2007). Massage therapy research. *Developmental Review, 27,* 75–89. (p. 149)

Field, T., Hernandez-Reif, M., Feijo, L., & Freedman, J. (2006). Prenatal, perinatal and neonatal stimulation: A survey of neonatal nurseries. *Infant Behavior & Development, 29,* 24–31. (p. 149)

Fields, R. D. (2004, April). The other half of the brain. *Scientific American,* pp. 54–61. (p. 67)

Fields, R. D. (2005, February). Making memories stick. *Scientific American,* pp. 75–81. (p. 340)

Fields, R. D. (2008, March). White matter. *Scientific American,* pp. 54–61. (p. 47)

Fincham, F. D., & Bradbury, T. N. (1993). Marital satisfaction, depression, and attributions: A longitudinal analysis. *Journal of Personality and Social Psychology, 64,* 442–452. (p. 683)

Fink, G. R., Markowitsch, H. J., Reinkemeier, M., Bruckbauer, T., Kessler, J., & Heiss, W-D. (1996). Cerebral representation of one's own past: Neural networks involved in autobiographical memory. *Journal of Neuroscience, 16,* 4275–4282. (p. 344)

Finkel, E. J., & Eastwick, P. W. (2008). Speed-dating. *Current Directions in Psychological Science, 17,* 193–197. (p. 721)

Finlay, S. W. (2000). Influence of Carl Jung and William James on the origin of alcoholics anonymous. *Review of General Psychology, 4,* 3–12. (p. 658)

Finney, E. M., Fine, I., & Dobkins, K. R. (2001). Visual stimuli activate auditory cortex in the deaf. *Nature Neuroscience, 4,* 1171–1173. (p. 249)

Finzi, E., & Wasserman, E. (2006). Treatment of depression with botulinum toxin A: A case series. *Dermatological Surgery, 32,* 645–650. (p. 516)

Fischer, P., & Greitemeyer, T. (2006). Music and aggression: The impact of sexual-aggressive song lyrics on aggression-related thoughts, emotions, and behavior toward the same and the opposite sex. *Personality and Social Psychology Bulletin, 32,* 1165–1176. (p. 715)

Fischhoff, B. (1982). Debiasing. In D. Kahneman, P. Slovic, & A. Tversky (Eds.), *Judgment under uncertainty: Heuristics and biases.* New York: Cambridge University Press. (p. 377)

Fischhoff, B., Slovic, P., & Lichtenstein, S. (1977). Knowing with certainty: The appropriateness of extreme confidence. *Journal of Experimental Psychology: Human Perception and Performance, 3,* 552–564. (p. 377)

Fischtein, D. S., Herold, E. S., & Desmarais, S. (2007). How much does gender explain in sexual attitudes and behaviors? A survey of Canadian adults. *Archives of Sexual Behavior, 36,* 451–461. (p. 144)

Fishbach, A., Dhar, R., & Zhang, Y. (2006). Subgoals as substitutes or complements: The role of goal accessibility. *Journal of Personality and Social Psychology, 91,* 232–242. (p. 494)

Fisher, H. E. (1993, March/April). After all, maybe it's biology. *Psychology Today,* pp. 40–45. (p. 217)

Fisher, H. E., Aron, A., Mashek, D., Li, H., & Brown, L. L. (2002). Defining the brain systems of lust, romantic attraction, and attachment. *Archives of Sexual Behavior, 31,* 413–419. (p. 467)

Fisher, H. T. (1984). Little Albert and Little Peter. *Bulletin of the British Psychological Society, 37,* 269. (p. 651)

Fisher, K., Egerton, M., Gershuny, J. I., & Robinson, J. P. (2006). Gender convergence in the American Heritage Time Use Study (AHTUS). *Social Indicators Research, 82,* 1–33. (p. 162)

Fisher, R. P., & Geiselman, R. E. (1992). *Memory-enhancing techniques for investigative interviewing: The cognitive interview.* Springfield, IL: Charles C. Thomas. (p. 361)

Fisher, R. P., Geiselman, R. E., & Raymond, D. S. (1987). Critical analysis of police interview techniques. *Journal of Police Science and Administration, 15,* 177–185. (p. 361)

Fiske, S. T., Harris, L. T., & Cuddy, A. J. C. (2004). Why ordinary people torture enemy prisoners. *Science, 306,* 1482–1483. (p. 687)

Fitzgerald, P. B., & Daskalakis, Z. J. (2008). The use of repetitive transcranial magnetic stimulation and vagal nerve stimulation in the treatment of depression. *Current Opinion in Psychiatry, 21,* 25–29. (p. 676)

Fleming, I., Baum, A., & Weiss, L. (1987). Social density and perceived control as mediator of crowding stress in high-density residential neighborhoods. *Journal of Personality and Social Psychology, 52,* 899–906. (p. 544)

Fleming, J. H. (2001, Winter/Spring). Introduction to the special issue on linkage analysis. *The Gallup Research Journal,* pp. i–vi. (p. 494)

Fleming, J. H., & Scott, B. A. (1991). The costs of confession: The Persian Gulf War POW tapes in historical and theoretical perspective. *Contemporary Social Psychology, 15,* 127–138. (p. 513)

Fletcher, G. J. O., Fitness, J., & Blampied, N. M. (1990). The link between attributions and happiness in close relationships: The roles of depression and explanatory style. *Journal of Social and Clinical Psychology, 9,* 243–255. (p. 683)

Fletcher, P. C., Zafiris, O., Frith, C. D., Honey, R. A. E., Corlett, P. R., Zilles, K., & Fink, G. R. (2005). On the benefits of not trying: Brain activity and connectivity reflecting the interactions of explicit and implicit sequence learning. *Cerebral Cortex, 7,* 1002–1015. (p. 566)

Flier, J. S., & Maratos-Flier, E. (2007, September). What fuels fat. *Scientific American,* pp. 72–81. (p. 460)

Flood, M. (2007). Exposure to pornography among youth in Australia. *Journal of Sociology, 43,* 45–60. (p. 714)

Flora, S. R. (2004). *The power of reinforcement.* Albany, NJ: SUNY Press. (p. 310)

Flouri, E., & Buchanan, A. (2004). Early father's and mother's involvement and child's later educational outcomes. *British Journal of Educational Psychology, 74,* 141–153. (p. 188)

Flynn, J. R. (1987). Massive IQ gains in 14 nations: What IQ tests really measure. *Psychological Bulletin, 101,* 171–191. (p. 420)

Flynn, J. R. (2003). Movies about intelligence: The limitations of g. *Current Directions in Psychological Science, 12,* 95–99. (p. 430)

Flynn, J. R. (2007). *What is intelligence?* New York: Cambridge University Press. (pp. 420, 430)

Foa, E. B., & Kozak, M. J. (1986). Emotional processing of fear: Exposure to corrective information. *Psychological Bulletin, 99,* 20–35. (p. 652)

Fodor, J. D. (1999). Let your brain alone. *London Review of Books, 21* (www.lrb.co.uk). (p. 58)

Fogg, N. P., Harrington P. E., & Harrington T. F. (2004). *The college majors' handbook.* Indianapolis, IN: JIST Works, Inc. (pp. A-1, A-2, A-3, A-4)

Ford, E. S. (2002). Does exercise reduce inflammation? Physical activity and B-reactive protein among U.S. adults. *Epidemiology, 13,* 561–569. (p. 548)

Foree, D. D., & LoLordo, V. M. (1973). Attention in the pigeon: Differential effects of food-getting versus shock-avoidance procedures. *Journal of Comparative and Physiological Psychology, 85,* 551–558. (p. 309)

Forer, B. R. (1949). The fallacy of personal validation: A classroom demonstration of gullibility. *Journal of Abnormal and Social Psychology, 44,* 118–123. (p. 578)

Forgas, J. P. (2008). Affect and cognition. *Perspectives on Psychological Science, 3,* 94–101. (p. 508)

Forgas, J. P., Bower, G. H., & Krantz, S. E. (1984). The influence of mood on perceptions of social interactions. *Journal of Experimental Social Psychology, 20,* 497–513. (pp. 349, 634)

Forhan, S. E., Gottlieb, S. L., Sternberg, M. R., Xu, F., Datta, D., Berman, S., & Markowitz, L. (2008). Prevalence of sexually transmitted infections and bacterial vaginosis among female adolescents in the United States: Data from the National Health and Nutrition Examination Survey (NHANES) 2003–2004. Paper presented to the 2008 National STD Prevention Conference, Chicago, Illinois. (p. 471)

Forman, D. R., Aksan, N., & Kochanska, G. (2004). Toddlers' responsive imitation predicts preschool-age conscience. *Psychological Science, 15,* 699–704. (p. 318)

Forste, R., & Tanfer, K. (1996). Sexual exclusivity among dating, cohabiting, and married women. *Journal of Marriage and the Family, 58,* 33–47. (p. B-6)

Foss, D. J., & Hakes, D. T. (1978). *Psycholinguistics: An introduction to the psychology of language.* Englewood Cliffs, NJ: Prentice-Hall. (p. 565)

Foster, R. G. (2004). Are we trying to banish biological time? *Cerebrum, 6*(2), 7–26. (p. 92)

Foulkes, D. (1999). *Children's dreaming and the development of consciousness.* Cambridge, MA: Harvard University Press. (p. 105)

Fouts, R. (1997). *Next of kin: What chimpanzees have taught me about who we are.* New York: Morrow. (p. 401)

Fouts, R. S. (1992). Transmission of a human gestural language in a chimpanzee mother-infant relationship. *Friends of Washoe, 12/13,* pp. 2–8. (p. 401)

Fouts, R. S., & Bodamer, M. (1987). Preliminary report to the National Geographic Society on: "Chimpanzee intrapersonal signing." *Friends of Washoe, 7*(1), 4–12. (p. 401)

Fowler, M. J., Sullivan, M. J., & Ekstrand, B. R. (1973). Sleep and memory. *Science, 179,* 302–304. (p. 356)

Fowler, R. C., Rich, C. L., & Young, D. (1986). San Diego suicide study: II. Substance abuse in young cases. *Archives of General Psychiatry, 43,* 962–965. (p. 630)

Fowles, D. C. (1992). Schizophrenia: Diathesis-stress revisited. *Annual Review of Psychology, 43,* 303–336. (p. 639)

Fox, B. H. (1998). Psychosocial factors in cancer incidence and prognosis. In P. M. Cinciripini & others (Eds.), *Psychological and behavioral factors in cancer risk.* New York: Oxford University Press. (p. 540)

Fox, E., Lester, V., Russo, R., Bowles, R. J., Pichler, A., & Dutton, K. (2000). Facial expression of emotion: Are angry faces detected more efficiently? *Cognition and Emotion, 14,* 61–92. (p. 510)

Fox, J. L. (1984). The brain's dynamic way of keeping in touch. *Science, 225,* 820–821. (p. 73)

Fox, N. A., Hane, A. E., & Pine, D. S. (2007). Plasticity for affective neurocircuitry. *Current Directions in Psychological Science, 16,* 1–5. (p. 138)

Fozard, J. L., & Popkin, S. J. (1978). Optimizing adult development: Ends and means of an applied psychology of aging. *American Psychologist, 33,* 975–989. (p. 210)

Fracassini, C. (2000, August 27). Holidaymakers led by the nose in sales quest. *Scotland on Sunday.* (p. 261)

Fraley, R. C. (2002). Attachment stability from infancy to adulthood: Meta-analysis and dynamic modeling of developmental mechanisms. *Personality and Social Psychology Review, 6,* 123–151. (p. 189)

Frank, J. D. (1982). Therapeutic components shared by all psychotherapies. In J. H. Harvey & M. M. Parks (Eds.), *The Master Lecture Series: Vol. 1. Psychotherapy research and behavior change.* Washington, DC: American Psychological Association. (pp. 666, 668)

Frank, R. (1999). *Luxury fever: Why money fails to satisfy in an era of excess.* New York: Free Press. (p. 153)

Frank, S. J. (1988). Young adults' perceptions of their relationships with their parents: Individual differences in connectedness, competence, and emotional autonomy. *Developmental Psychology, 24,* 729–737. (p. 204)

Frankel, A., Strange, D. R., & Schoonover, R. (1983). CRAP: Consumer rated assessment procedure. In G. H. Scherr & R. Liebmann-Smith (Eds.), *The best of The Journal of Irreproducible Results.* New York: Workman Publishing. (p. 577)

Frankenburg, W., Dodds, J., Archer, P., Shapiro, H., & Bresnick, B. (1992). The Denver II: A major revision and restandardization of the Denver Developmental Screening Test. *Pediatrics, 89,* 91–97. (p. 175)

Franz, E. A., Waldie, K. E., & Smith, M. J. (2000). The effect of callosotomy on novel versus familiar bimanual actions: A neural dissociation between controlled and automatic processes? *Psychological Science, 11,* 82–85. (p. 76)

Frasure-Smith, N., & Lespérance, F. (2005). Depression and coronary heart disease: Complex synergism of mind, body, and environment. *Current Directions in Psychological Science, 14,* 39–43. (p. 537)

Frattaroli, J. (2006). Experimental disclosure and its moderators: A meta-analysis. *Psychological Bulletin, 132,* 823–865. (p. 546)

Frayling, T. M., & 41 others (2007, April 12). A common variant in the FTO gene is associated with body mass index and predisposes to childhood and adult obesity. *Science, 316,* 889–894. (p. 460)

Frederick, D. A., Peplau, L. A., & Lever, J. (2006). The swimsuit issue: Correlates of body image in a sample of 52,667 heterosexual adults. *Body Image, 3,* 413–419. (p. 454)

Fredrickson, B. L. (2006). The broaden-and-build theory of positive emotions. In M. Csikszentmihalyi & I. S. Csikszentmihalyi (Eds.), *A life worth living: Contributions to positive psychology.* New York: Oxford University Press. (p. 522)

Fredrickson, B. L., & Kahneman, D. (1993). Duration neglect in retrospective evaluations of affective episodes. *Journal of Personality and Social Psychology, 65,* 45–55. (p. 333)

Fredrickson, B. L., Roberts, T-A., Noll, S. M., Quinn, D. M., & Twenge, J. M. (1998). That swimsuit becomes you: Sex differences in self-objectification, restrained eating, and math performance. *Journal of Personality and Social Psychology, 75,* 269–284. (p. 454)

Freedman, D. J., Riesenhuber, M., Poggio, T., & Miller, E. K. (2001). Categorical representation of visual stimuli in the primate prefrontal cortex. *Science, 291,* 312–316. (p. 397)

Freedman, J. L. (1988). Television violence and aggression: What the evidence shows. In S. Oskamp (Ed.), *Television as a social issue.* Newbury Park, CA: Sage. (p. 320)

Freedman, J. L., & Fraser, S. C. (1966). Compliance without pressure: The foot-in-the-door technique. *Journal of Personality and Social Psychology, 4,* 195–202. (p. 686)

Freedman, J. L., & Perlick, D. (1979). Crowding, contagion, and laughter. *Journal of Experimental Social Psychology, 15,* 295–303. (p. 697)

Freedman, L. R., Rock, D., Roberts, S. A., Cornblatt, B. A., & Erlenmeyer-Kimling, L. (1998). The New York high-risk project: Attention, anhedonia and social outcome. *Schizophrenia Research, 30,* 1–9. (p. 643)

Freeman, W. J. (1991, February). The physiology of perception. *Scientific American,* pp. 78–85. (p. 243)

Frensch, P. A., & Rünger, D. (2003). Implicit learning. *Current Directions in Psychological Science, 12,* 13–18. (p. 566)

Freud, S. (1922/1975). *Group psychology and the analysis of the ego.* New York: Norton. (p. 707)

Freud, S. (1931; reprinted 1961). Female sexuality. In J. Strachey (Trans.), *The standard edition of the complete psychological works of Sigmund Freud.* London: Hogarth Press. (p. 562)

Freud, S. (1935; reprinted 1960). *A general introduction to psychoanalysis.* New York: Washington Square Press. (p. 217)

Frey, M. C., & Detterman, D. K. (2004). Scholastic assessment or g? The relationship between the Scholastic Assessment Test and general cognitive ability. *Psychological Science, 15,* 373–378. (p. 418)

Freyd, J. J., DePrince, A. P., & Gleaves, D. H. (2007). The state of betrayal trauma theory: Reply to McNally—Conceptual issues and future directions. *Memory, 15,* 295–311. (p. 363)

Freyd, J. J., Putnam, F. W., Lyon, T. D., Becker-Blease, K. A., Cheit, R. E., Siegel, N. B., & Pezdek, K. (2005). The science of child sexual abuse. *Science, 308,* 501. (p. 190)

Friedman, M., & Ulmer, D. (1984). *Treating Type A behavior—and your heart.* New York: Knopf. (pp. 535, 551)

Friedrich, O. (1987, December 7). New age harmonies. *Time,* pp. 62–72. (p. 599)

Friend, T. (2004). *Animal talk: Breaking the codes of animal language.* New York: Free Press. (p. 402)

Frijda, N. H. (1988). The laws of emotion. *American Psychologist, 43,* 349–358. (p. 526)

Frith, U., & Frith, C. (2001). The biological basis of social interaction. *Current Directions in Psychological Science, 10,* 151–155. (p. 182)

Fromkin, V., & Rodman, R. (1983). *An introduction to language* (3rd ed.). New York: Holt, Rinehart & Winston. (p. 385, 388)

Fry, A. F., & Hale, S. (1996). Processing speed, working memory, and fluid intelligence: Evidence for a developmental cascade. *Psychological Science, 7,* 237–241. (p. 210)

Fryar, C., Hirsch, R., Porter, K. S., Kottiri, B., Brody, D. J., & Louis, T. (2007, June 28). Drug use and sexual behavior reported by adults: United States, 1999–2002. *Advance Data: From Vital and Health Statistics,* Number 384 (Centers for Disease Control and Prevention). (p. 467)

Fuhriman, A., & Burlingame, G. M. (1994). Group psychotherapy: Research and practice. In A. Fuhriman & G. M. Burlingame (Eds.), *Handbook of group psychotherapy.* New York: Wiley. (p. 657)

Fujiki, N., Yoshida, Y., Ripley, B., Mignot, E., & Nishino, S. (2003). Effects of IV and ICV hypocretin-1 (Orexin A) in hypocretin receptor-2 gene mutated narcoleptic dogs and IV hypocretin-1 replacement therapy in a hypocretin-ligand-deficient narcoleptic dog. *Sleep, 26,* 953–959. (p. 101)

Fuller, M. J., & Downs, A. C. (1990). Spermarche is a salient biological marker in men's development. Poster presented at the American Psychological Society convention. (p. 197)

Fulmer, I. S., Gerhart, B., & Scott, K. S. (2003). Are the 100 best better? An empirical investigation of the relationship between being a "great place to work" and firm performance. *Personnel Psychology, 56,* 965–993. (p. 492)

Funder, D. C. (2001). Personality. *Annual Review of Psychology, 52,* 197–221. (p. 578)

Funder, D. C., & Block, J. (1989). The role of ego-control, ego-resiliency, and IQ in delay of gratification in adolescence. *Journal of Personality and Social Psychology, 57,* 1041–1050. (p. 200)

Furlow, F. B., & Thornhill, R. (1996, January/February). The orgasm wars. *Psychology Today,* pp. 42–46. (p. 466)

Furnham, A. (1982). Explanations for unemployment in Britain. *European Journal of Social Psychology, 12,* 335–352. (p. 684)

Furnham, A. (2001). Self-estimates of intelligence: Culture and gender difference in self and other estimates of both general (g) and multiple intelligences. *Personality and Individual Differences, 31,* 1381–1405. (p. 432)

Furnham, A., & Baguma, P. (1994). Cross-cultural differences in the evaluation of male and female body shapes. *International Journal of Eating Disorders, 15,* 81–89. (p. 456)

Furnham, A., Callahan, I., & Akande, D. (2004a). Self-estimates of intelligence: A study in two African countries. *Journal of Psychology, 138,* 265–285. (p. 432)

Furnham, A., Callahan, I., & Rawles, R. (2003). Adults' knowledge of general psychology. *European Psychologist, 8,* 101–116. (p. 16)

Furnham, A., Hosoe, T., & Tang, T. L.-P. (2002a). Male hubris and female humility? A cross-cultural study of ratings of self, parental, and sibling multiple intelligence in America, Britain, and Japan. *Intelligence, 30,* 101–115. (p. 432)

Furnham, A., & Mottabu, R. (2004b). Sex and culture differences in the estimates of general and multiple intelligence: A study comparing British and Egyptian students. *Individual Differences Research, 3,* 82–96. (p. 432)

Furnham, A., & Rawles, R. (1995). Sex differences in the estimation of intelligence. *Journal of Social Behavior and Personality, 10,* 741–748. (p. 704)

Furnham, A., Reeves, E., & Bughani, S. (2002b). Parents think their sons are brighter than their daughters: Sex differences in parental self-estimations and estimations of their children's multiple intelligences. *Journal of Genetic Psychology, 163,* 24–39. (p. 432)

Furnham, A., & Thomas, C. (2004c). Parents' gender and personality and estimates of their own and their children's intelligence. *Personality and Individual Differences, 37,* 887–903. (p. 432)

Furr, R. M., & Funder, D. C. (1998). A multimodal analysis of personal negativity. *Journal of Personality and Social Psychology, 74,* 1580-1591. (p. 634)

Gable, S. L., Gonzaga, G. C., & Strachman, A. (2006). Will you be there for me when things go right? Supportive responses to positive event disclosures. *Journal of Personality and Social Psychology, 91,* 904-917. (p. 218)

Gabrieli, J. D. E., Desmond, J. E., Demb, J. E., Wagner, A. D., Stone, M. V., Vaidya, C. J., & Glover, G. H. (1996). Functional magnetic resonance imaging of semantic memory processes in the frontal lobes. *Psychological Science, 7,* 278-283. (p. 344)

Gaertner, L., & Iuzzini, J. (2005). Rejection and entitativity: A synergistic model of mass violence. In K. D. Williams, J. P. Forgas, & W. von Hippel (Eds.). *The social outcast: Ostracism, social exclusion, rejection, and bullying.* New York: Psychology Press. (p. 713)

Gage, F. H. (2003, September). Repair yourself. *Scientific American,* pp. 46-53. (p. 74)

Gaillot, M. T., & Baumeister, R. F. (2007). Self-regulation and sexual restraint: Dispositionally and temporarily poor self-regulatory abilities contribute to failures at restraining sexual behavior. *Personality and Social Psychology Bulletin, 33,* 173-186. (p. 585)

Gajendran, R. S., & Harrison, D. A. (2007). The good, the bad, and the unknown about telecommunity: Meta-analysis of psychological mediators and individual consequences. *Journal of Applied Psychology, 92,* 1524-1541. (p. 586)

Galambos, N. L. (1992). Parent-adolescent relations. *Current Directions in Psychological Science, 1,* 146-149. (p. 203)

Galambos, N. L., Barker, E. T., & Krahn, H. J. (2006). Depression, self-esteem, and anger in emerging adulthood: Seven-year trajectories. *Developmental Psychology, 42,* 350-365. (p. 205)

Galanter, E. (1962). Contemporary psychophysics. In R. Brown, E. Galanter, E. H. Hess, & G. Mandler (Eds.), *New directions in psychology.* New York: Holt Rinehart & Winston. (p. 227)

Galati, D., Scherer, K. R., & Ricci-Bitti, P. E. (1997). Voluntary facial expression of emotion: Comparing congenitally blind with normally sighted encoders. *Journal of Personality and Social Psychology, 73,* 1363-1379. (p. 514)

Galea, S., Boscarino, J., Resnick, H., & Vlahov, D. (2002). Mental health in New York City after the September 11 terrorist attacks: Results from two population surveys. In R. W. Manderscheid & M. J. Henderson (Eds.), *Mental Health, United States, 2001.* Washington, DC: U.S. Government Printing Office. (pp. 613, 614, 628)

Gallup. (2001). Reported in "The gender gap: Sleeplessness." (www.gallup.com/poll/pollInsights), January 29, 2002. (p. 97)

Gallup. (2002, June 11). Poll insights: The gender gap—post Sept. 11th fear. The Gallup Organization (www.gallup.com/poll/pollInsights). (p. 610)

Gallup, G., Jr. (1982). *Adventures in immortality.* New York: McGraw-Hill. (p. 123)

Gallup, G., Jr. (2002, April 30). Education and youth. *Gallup Tuesday Briefing* (www.gallup.com/poll/tb/educaYouth/20020430.asp). (p. 319)

Gallup, G. G., Jr. (1970). Chimpanzees: Self-recognition. *Science, 167,* 86-87. (p. 192)

Gallup, G. G., Jr., & Suarez, S. D. (1986). Self-awareness and the emergence of mind in humans and other primates. In J. Suls & A. G. Greenwald (Eds.), *Psychological perspectives on the self* (Vol. 3.). Hillsdale, NJ: Erlbaum. (p. 192)

Gallup, G. H. (1972). *The Gallup poll: Public opinion 1935-1971* (Vol. 3). New York: Random House. (p. 731)

Gallup, G. H., Jr. (1994, October). Millions finding care and support in small groups. *Emerging Trends,* pp. 2-5. (p. 658)

Gallup Organization. (2003, July 8). American public opinion about Iraq. *Gallup Poll News Service* (www.gallup.com). (p. 688)

Gallup Organization. (2004, August 16). 65% of Americans receive NO praise or recognition in the workplace. E-mail from Tom Rath: bucketbook@gallup.com. (p. 494)

Gallup Poll. (2007, October 22). Denmark, New Zealand, Canada rank highest in well-being. (www.gallup.com). (p. 524)

Gangestad, S. W., & Simpson, J. A. (2000). The evolution of human mating: Trade-offs and strategic pluralism. *Behavioral and Brain Sciences, 23,* 573-587. (p. 145)

Garber, K. (2007). Autism's cause may reside in abnormalities at the synapse. *Science, 317,* 190-191. (p. 182)

Garcia, J., & Gustavson, A. R. (1997, January). Carl R. Gustavson (1946-1996): Pioneering wildlife psychologist. *APS Observer,* pp. 34-35. (p. 297)

Garcia, J., & Koelling, R. A. (1966). Relation of cue to consequence in avoidance learning. *Psychonomic Science, 4,* 123-124. (p. 296)

Gardner, H. (1983). *Frames of mind: The theory of multiple intelligences.* New York: Basic Books. (p. 406)

Gardner, H. (1998, March 19). An intelligent way to progress. *The Independent* (London), p. E4. (pp. 406, 407)

Gardner, H. (1998, November 5). Do parents count? *New York Review of Books* (www.nybooks.com). (p. 151)

Gardner, H. (1999). *Multiple views of multiple intelligence.* New York: Basic Books. (p. 411)

Gardner, H. (1999, February). Who owns intelligence? *Atlantic Monthly,* pp. 67-76. (p 418)

Gardner, H. (2006). *The development and education of the mind: The selected works of Howard Gardner.* New York: Routledge/Taylor & Francis. (p. 406)

Gardner, J., & Oswald, A. J. (2007). Money and mental well-being: A longitudinal study of medium-sized lottery wins. *Journal of Health Economics, 6,* 49-60. (p. 524)

Gardner, J. W. (1984). *Excellence: Can we be equal and excellent too?* New York: Norton. (p. 495)

Gardner, M. (2006, January/February). The memory wars, part one. *Skeptical Inquirer, 30,* 28-31. (p. 363)

Gardner, R. A., & Gardner, B. I. (1969). Teaching sign language to a chimpanzee. *Science, 165,* 664-672. (p. 399)

Gardner, R. M., & Tockerman, Y. R. (1994). A computer-TV video methodology for investigating the influence of somatotype on perceived personality traits. *Journal of Social Behavior and Personality, 9,* 555-563. (p. 457)

Garfield, C. (1986). *Peak performers: The new heroes of American business.* New York: Morrow. (p. 395)

Garlick, D. (2002). Understanding the nature of the general factor of intelligence: The role of individual differences in neural plasticity as an explanatory mechanism. *Psychological Review, 109,* 116-136. (p. 412)

Garlick, D. (2003). Integrating brain science research with intelligence research. *Current Directions in Psychological Science, 12,* 185-189. (p. 412)

Garnets, L., & Kimmel, D. (1990). Lesbian and gay dimensions in the psychological study of human diversity. Master lecture, American Psychological Association convention. (p. 473)

Garon, N., Bryson, S. E., & Smith, I. M. (2008). Executive function in preschoolers: A review using an integrative framework. *Psychological Bulletin, 134,* 31-60. (p. 174)

Garrett, B. L. (2008). Judging innocence. *Columbia Law Review, 108,* 55-142. (p. 360)

Garry, M., Loftus, E. F., & Brown, S. W. (1994). Memory: A river runs through it. *Consciousness and Cognition, 3,* 438-451. (p. 566)

Garry, M., Manning, C. G., Loftus, E. F., & Sherman, S. J. (1996). Imagination inflation: Imagining a childhood event inflates confidence that it occurred. *Psychonomic Bulletin & Review, 3,* 208-214. (p. 359)

Gatchel, R. J., Peng, Y. B., Peters, M. L., Fuchs, P. N., & Turk, D. C. (2007). The biopsychosocial approach to chronic pain: Scientific advances and future directions. *Psychological Bulletin, 133,* 581-624. (p. 254)

Gates, G. A., & Miyamoto, R. T. (2003). Cochlear implants. *New England Journal of Medicine, 349,* 421-423. (p. 248)

Gates, W. (1998, July 20). Charity begins when I'm ready (interview). *Fortune* (www.pathfinder.com/fortune/1998/980720/bil7.html). (p. 408)

Gatz, M. (2007). Genetics, dementia, and the elderly. *Current Directions in Psychological Science, 16,* 123-127. (p. 212)

Gawande, A. (1998, September 21). The pain perplex. *The New Yorker,* pp. 86-94. (p. 256)

Gawin, F. H. (1991). Cocaine addiction: Psychology and neurophysiology. *Science, 251,* 1580-1586. (p. 120)

Gazzaniga, M. S. (1967, August). The split brain in man. *Scientific American,* pp. 24-29. (p. 75)

Gazzaniga, M. S. (1983). Right hemisphere language following brain bisection: A 20-year perspective. *American Psychologist, 38,* 525–537. (p. 76)

Gazzaniga, M. S. (1988). Organization of the human brain. *Science, 245,* 947–952. (p. 77)

Gazzaniga, M. S. (1997). Brain, drugs, and society. *Science, 275,* 459. (p. 114)

Geary, D. C. (1995). Sexual selection and sex differences in spatial cognition. *Learning and Individual Differences, 7,* 289–301. (p. 434)

Geary, D. C. (1996). Sexual selection and sex differences in mathematical abilities. *Behavioral and Brain Sciences, 19,* 229–247. (p. 434)

Geary, D. C. (1998). *Male, female: The evolution of human sex differences.* Washington, DC: American Psychological Association. (p. 145)

Geary, D. C., Salthouse, T. A., Chen, G-P., & Fan, L. (1996). Are East Asian versus American differences in arithmetical ability a recent phenomenon? *Developmental Psychology, 32,* 254–262. (p. 437)

Geen, R. G., & Quanty, M. B. (1977). The catharsis of aggression: An evaluation of a hypothesis. In L. Berkowitz (Ed.), *Advances in experimental social psychology* (Vol. 10). New York: Academic Press. (p. 520)

Geen, R. G., & Thomas, S. L. (1986). The immediate effects of media violence on behavior. *Journal of Social Issues, 42*(3), 7–28. (p. 320)

Gehring, W. J., Wimke, J., & Nisenson, L. G. (2000). Action monitoring dysfunction in obsessive-compulsive disorder. *Psychological Science, 11*(1), 1–6. (p. 616)

Geier, A. B., Rozin, P., & Doros, G. (2006). Unit bias: A new heuristic that helps explain the effects of portion size on food intake. *Psychological Science, 17,* 521–525. (p. 453)

Geldard, F. A. (1972). *The human senses* (2nd ed.). New York: Wiley. (p. 240)

Gelman, D. (1989, May 15). Voyages to the unknown. *Newsweek,* pp. 66–69. (p. 514)

Genesee, F., & Gándara, P. (1999). Bilingual education programs: A cross-national perspective. *Journal of Social Issues, 55,* 665–685. (p. 395)

Genevro, J. L. (2003). *Report on bereavement and grief research.* Washington, DC: Center for the Advancement of Health. (p. 221)

Gentile, D. A., Lynch, P. J., Linder, J. R., & Walsh, D. A. (2004). The effects of violent video game habits on adolescent hostility, aggressive behaviors, and school performance. *Journal of Adolescence, 27,* 5–22. (pp. 320, 716)

Gentile, D. A., Saleem, M., & Anderson, C. A. (2007). Public policy and the effects of media violence on children. *Social Issues and Policy Review, 1,* 15–61. (p. 716)

George, L. K., Ellison, C. G., & Larson, D. B. (2002). Explaining the relationships between religious involvement and health. *Psychological Inquiry, 13,* 190–200. (p. 554)

George, L. K., Larson, D. B., Koenig, H. G., & McCullough, M. E. (2000). Spirituality and health: What we know, what we need to know. *Journal of Social and Clinical Psychology, 19,* 102–116. (p. 554)

George, M. S. (2003, September). Stimulating the brain. *Scientific American,* pp. 67–73. (p. 677)

George, M. S., & Belmaker, R. H. (Eds.). (2007). *Transcranial magnetic stimulation in clinical psychiatry.* Washington, DC: American Psychiatric Publishing. (p. 676)

Geraerts, E., Schooler, J. W., Merckelbach, H., Jelicic, M., Hauer, B. J. A., & Ambadar, Z. (2007). The reality of recovered memories: Corroborating continuous and discontinuous memories of childhood sexual abuse. *Psychological Science, 18,* 564–568. (p. 363)

Gerbner, G. (1990). Stories that hurt: Tobacco, alcohol, and other drugs in the mass media. In H. Resnik (Ed.), *Youth and drugs: Society's mixed messages.* Rockville, MD: Office for Substance Abuse Prevention, U.S. Department of Health and Human Services. (p. 127)

Gerbner, G., Morgan, M., & Signorielli, N. (1993). *Television violence profile No. 16: The turning point from research to action.* Philadelphia: Annenberg School for Communication, University of Pennsylvania. (p. 715)

Gernsbacher, M. A., Dawson, M., & Goldsmith, H. H. (2005). Three reasons not to believe in an autism epidemic. *Current Directions in Psychological Science, 14,* 55–58. (p. 182)

Gerrard, M., & Luus, C. A. E. (1995). Judgments of vulnerability to pregnancy: The role of risk factors and individual differences. *Personality and Social Psychology Bulletin, 21,* 160–171. (p. 471)

Gershoff, E. T. (2002). Parental corporal punishment and associated child behaviors and experiences: A meta-analytic and theoretical review. *Psychological Bulletin, 128,* 539–579. (p. 307)

Gerstorf, D., Ram, N., Röcke, C., Lindenberger, U., & Smith, J. (2008). Decline in life satisfaction in old age: Longitudinal evidence for links to distance-to-death. *Psychology and Aging, 23,* 154–168. (p. 220)

Geschwind, N. (1979, September). Specializations of the human brain. *Scientific American, 241,* 180–199. (p. 391)

Geschwind, N., & Behan, P. O. (1984). Laterality, hormones, and immunity. In N. Geschwind & A. M. Galaburda (Eds.), *Cerebral dominance: The biological foundations.* Cambridge, MA: Harvard University Press. (p. 79)

Gfeller, J. D., Lynn, S. J., & Pribble, W. E. (1987). Enhancing hypnotic susceptibility: Interpersonal and rapport factors. *Journal of Personality and Social Psychology, 52,* 586–595. (p. 110)

Giancola, P. R., & Corman, M. D. (2007). Alcohol and aggression: A test of the attention-allocation model. *Psychological Science, 18,* 649–655. (p. 711)

Gibbons, F. X. (1986). Social comparison and depression: Company's effect on misery. *Journal of Personality and Social Psychology, 51,* 140–148. (p. 528)

Gibbons, R. D., Brown, C. H., Hur, K., Marcus, S. M., Bhaumik, D. K., & Mann, J. J. (2007). Relationship between antidepressants and suicide attempts: An analysis of the Veterans Health Administration data sets. *American Journal of Psychiatry, 164,* 1044–1049. (p. 674)

Gibbs, J. C., Basinger, K. S., Grime, R. L., & Snarey, J. R. (2007). Moral judgment development across cultures: Revisiting Kohlberg's universality claims. *Developmental Review, 27,* 443–500. (p. 199)

Gibbs, W. W. (1996, June). Mind readings. *Scientific American,* pp. 34–36. (p. 69)

Gibbs, W. W. (2002, August). Saving dying languages. *Scientific American, 287,* 79–85. (p. 385)

Gibbs, W. W. (2005, June). Obesity: An overblown epidemic? *Scientific American,* pp. 70–77. (p. 457)

Gibson, E. J., & Walk, R. D. (1960, April). The "visual cliff." *Scientific American,* pp. 64–71. (p. 264)

Gibson, H. B. (1995, April). Recovered memories. *The Psychologist,* pp. 153–154. (p. 109)

Gigerenzer, G. (2004). Dread risk, September 11, and fatal traffic accidents. *Psychological Science, 15,* 286–287. (p. 378)

Gigerenzer, G. (2004). Fast and frugal heuristics: The tools of bounded rationality. In D. Koehler & N. Harvey (Eds.), *Handbook of judgment and decision making.* Oxford, England: Blackwell. (p. 380)

Gigerenzer, G. (2007). *Gut feelings: The intelligence of the unconscious.* New York: Viking. (p. 380)

Gilbert, D. T. (2006). *Stumbling on happiness.* New York: Knopf. (pp. 218, 357, 370, 506)

Gilbert, D. T., Pelham, B. W., & Krull, D. S. (2003). The psychology of good ideas. *Psychological Inquiry, 14,* 258–260. (p. 15)

Gilbert, D. T., Pinel, E. C., Wilson, T. D., Blumberg, S. J., & Wheatley, T. P. (1998). Immune neglect: A source of durability bias in affective forecasting. *Journal of Personality and Social Psychology, 75,* 617–638. (p. 523)

Gilbertson, M. W., Paulus, L. A., Williston, S. K., Gurvits, T. V., Lasko, N. B., Pitman, R. K., & Orr, S. P. (2006). Neurocognitive function in monozygotic twins discordant for combat exposure: Relationship to posttraumatic stress disorder. *Journal of Abnormal Psychology, 115,* 484–495. (p. 613)

Giles, D. E., Dahl, R. E., & Coble, P. A. (1994). Childbearing, developmental, and familial aspects of sleep. In J. M. Oldham & M. B. Riba (Eds.), *Review of psychiatry* (Vol. 13). Washington, DC: American Psychiatric Press. (p. 94)

Gill, A. J., Oberlander, J., & Austin, E. (2006). Rating e-mail personality at zero acquaintance. *Personality and Individual Differences, 40,* 497–507. (p. 582)

Gillham, J.E., Hamilton, J., Freres, D.R., Patton, K. & Gallop, R. (2006). Preventing depression among early adolescents in the primary care setting: A randomized controlled study of the Penn Resiliency Program. *Journal of Abnormal Child Psychology, 34,* 195–211. (p. 669)

Gilligan, C. (1982). *In a different voice: Psychological theory and women's development.* Cambridge, MA: Harvard University Press. (p. 158)

Gilligan, C., Lyons, N. P., & Hanmer, T. J. (Eds.). (1990). *Making connections: The relational worlds of adolescent girls at Emma Willard School.* Cambridge, MA: Harvard University Press. (p. 158)

Gilovich, T. (1991). *How we know what isn't so: The fallibility of human reason in everyday life.* New York: Free Press. (p. 32)

Gilovich, T., Kruger, J., & Medvec, V. H. (2002). The spotlight effect revisited: Overestimating the manifest variability of our actions and appearance. *Journal of Experimental Social Psychology, 38,* 93–99. (p. 591)

Gilovich, T., & Medvec, V. H. (1995). The experience of regret: What, when, and why. *Psychological Review, 102,* 379–395. (p. 219)

Gilovich, T., & Savitsky, K. (1999). The spotlight effect and the illusion of transparency: Egocentric assessments of how we are seen by others. *Current Directions in Psychological Science, 8,* 165–168. (p. 591)

Gilovich, T., Vallone, R., & Tversky, A. (1985). The hot hand in basketball: On the misperception of random sequences. *Cognitive Psychology, 17,* 295–314. (p. 33)

Gilovich, T. D. (1996). *The spotlight effect: Exaggerated impressions of the self as a social stimulus.* Unpublished manuscript, Cornell University. (p. 591)

Giltay, E. J., Geleijnse, J. M., Zitman, F. G., Buijsse, B., & Kromhout, D. (2007). Lifestyle and dietary correlates of dispositional optimism in men: The Zutphen Elderly Study. *Journal of Psychosomatic Research, 63,* 483–490. (p. 544)

Giltay, E. J., Geleijnse, J. M., Zitman, F. G., Hoekstra, T., & Schouten, E. G. (2004). Dispositional optimism and all-cause and cardiovascular mortality in a prospective cohort of elderly Dutch men and women. *Archives of General Psychiatry, 61,* 1126–1135. (p. 544)

Gingerich, O. (1999, February 6). Is there a role for natural theology today? *The Real Issue* (www.origins.org/real/n9501/natural.html). (p. 166)

Gingerich, O. (2006). *God's universe.* Cambridge, MA: Belknap Press of Harvard University Press. (p. 1)

Giuliano, T. A., Barnes, L. C., Fiala, S. E., & Davis D. M. (1998). An empirical investigation of male answer syndrome. Paper presented at the Southwestern Psychological Association convention. (p. 159)

Gladue, B. A. (1990). Hormones and neuroendocrine factors in atypical human sexual behavior. In J. R. Feierman (Ed.), *Pedophilia: Biosocial dimensions.* New York: Springer-Verlag. (p. 477)

Gladue, B. A. (1994). The biopsychology of sexual orientation. *Current Directions in Psychological Science, 3,* 150–154. (p. 478)

Gladwell, M. (2000, May 9). The new-boy network: What do job interviews really tell us? *New Yorker,* pp. 68–86. (p. 489)

Gladwell, M. (2005). *Blink: The power of thinking without thinking.* New York: Little, Brown. (p. 723)

Glasman, L. R., & Albarracin, D. (2006). Forming attitudes that predict future behavior: A meta-analysis of the attitude-behavior relation. *Psychological Bulletin, 132,* 778–822. (p. 685)

Glass, R. I. (2004). Perceived threats and real killers. *Science, 304,* 927. (p. 379)

Glass, R. M. (2001). Electroconvulsive therapy: Time to bring it out of the shadows. *Journal of the American Medical Association, 285,* 1346–1348. (p. 675)

Gleaves, D. H. (1996). The sociocognitive model of dissociative identity disorder: A reexamination of the evidence. *Psychological Bulletin, 120,* 42–59 (p. 619)

Glenn, N. D. (1975). Psychological well-being in the postparental stage: Some evidence from national surveys. *Journal of Marriage and the Family, 37,* 105–110. (p. 218)

Glick, P., & 15 others. (2004). Bad but bold: Ambivalent attitudes toward men predict gender inequality in 16 nations. *Journal of Personality and Social Psychology, 86,* 713–728. (p. 704)

Glick, P., Gottesman, D., & Jolton, J. (1989). The fault is not in the stars: Susceptibility of skeptics and believers in astrology to the Barnum effect. *Personality and Social Psychology Bulletin, 15,* 572–583. (p. 579)

Gluhoski, V. L., & Wortman, C. B. (1996). The impact of trauma on world views. *Journal of Social and Clinical Psychology, 15,* 417–429. (p. 299)

Godden, D. R., & Baddeley, A. D. (1975). Context-dependent memory in two natural environments: On land and underwater. *British Journal of Psychology, 66,* 325–331. (p. 348)

Goel, V., & Dolan, R. J. (2001). The functional anatomy of humor: Segregating cognitive and affective components. *Nature Neuroscience, 4,* 237–238. (p. 392)

Goff, D. C. (1993). Reply to Dr. Armstrong. *Journal of Nervous and Mental Disease, 181,* 604–605. (p. 619)

Goff, D. C., & Simms, C. A. (1993). Has multiple personality disorder remained consistent over time? *Journal of Nervous and Mental Disease, 181,* 595–600. (p. 619)

Goff, L. M., & Roediger, H. L., III. (1998). Imagination inflation for action events: Repeated imaginings lead to illusory recollections. *Memory and Cognition, 26,* 20–33. (p. 359)

Gold, M., & Yanof, D. S. (1985). Mothers, daughters, and girlfriends. *Journal of Personality and Social Psychology, 49,* 654–659. (p. 203)

Goldapple, K., Segal, Z., Garson, C., Lau, M., Bieling, P., Kennedy, S., & Mayberg, H. (2004). Modulation of cortical-limbic pathways in major depression. *Archives of General Psychiatry, 61,* 34–41. (p. 674)

Goldberg, W. A., Prause, J., Lucas-Thompson, R., & Himsel, A. (2008). Maternal employment and children's achievement in context: A meta-analysis of four decades of research. *Psychological Bulletin, 134,* 77–108. (p. 191)

Golden, R. N., Gaynes, B. N., Ekstrom, R. D., Hamer, R. M., Jacobsen, F. M., Suppes, T., Wisner, K. L., & Nemeroff, C. B. (2005). The efficacy of light therapy in the treatment of mood disorders: A review and meta-analysis of the evidence. *American Journal of Psychiatry, 162,* 656–662. (p. 666)

Goldfried, M. R. (2001). Integrating gay, lesbian, and bisexual issues into mainstream psychology. *American Psychologist, 56,* 977–988. (p. 630)

Goldfried, M. R., & Padawer, W. (1982). Current status and future directions in psychotherapy. In M. R. Goldfried (Ed.), *Converging themes in psychotherapy: Trends in psychodynamic, humanistic, and behavioral practice.* New York: Springer. (p. 666)

Goldfried, M. R., Raue, P. J., & Castonguay, L. G. (1998). The therapeutic focus in significant sessions of master therapists: A comparison of cognitive-behavioral and psychodynamic-interpersonal interventions. *Journal of Consulting and Clinical Psychology, 66,* 803–810. (p. 668)

Golding, J. M. (1996). Sexual assault history and women's reproductive and sexual health. *Psychology of Women Quarterly, 20,* 101–121. (p. 714)

Golding, J. M. (1999). Sexual-assault history and the long-term physical health problems: Evidence from clinical and population epidemiology. *Current Directions in Psychological Science, 8,* 191–194. (p. 613)

Goldin-Meadow, S. (2006). Talking and thinking with our hands. *Current Directions in Psychological Science, 15,* 34–39. (p. 400)

Goldstein, A. P., Glick, B., & Gibbs, J. C. (1998). *Aggression replacement training: A comprehensive intervention for aggressive youth* (rev. ed.). Champaign, IL: Research Press. (p. 713)

Goldstein, I. (2000, August). Male sexual circuitry. *Scientific American,* pp. 70–75. (p. 55)

Goldstein, I., Lue, T. F., Padma-Nathan, H., Rosen, R. C., Steers, W. D., & Wicker, P. A. (1998). Oral sildenafil in the treatment of erectile dysfunction. *New England Journal of Medicine, 338,* 1397–1404. (p. 35)

Goleman, D. (1980, February). 1,528 little geniuses and how they grew. *Psychology Today,* pp. 28–53. (p. 490)

Goleman, D. (1995). *Emotional intelligence.* New York: Bantam. (p. 503)

Goleman, D. (2006). *Social intelligence.* New York: Bantam Books. (p. 411)

Gómez, R. L., Bootzin, R. R., & Nadel, L. (2006). Naps promote abstraction in language-learning infants. *Psychological Science, 17,* 670–674. (p. 100)

Gonsalkorale, K., & Williams, K. D. (2006). The KKK would not let me play: Ostracism even by a despised outgroup hurts. *European Journal of Social Psychology, 36,* 1–11. (p. 482)

Gonsalves, B., Reber, P. J., Gitelman, D. R., Parrish, T. B., Mesulam, M.-M., & Paller, K. A. (2004). Neural evidence that vivid imagining can lead to false remembering. *Psychological Science, 15,* 655–659. (p. 359)

Goodale, M. A., & Milner, D. A. (2004). *Sight unseen: An exploration of conscious and unconscious vision.* Oxford: Oxford University Press. (p. 86)

Goodale, M. A., & Milner, D. A. (2006). One brain—two visual systems. *The Psychologist, 19,* 660–663. (p. 86)

Goodall, J. (1968). The behaviour of free-living chimpanzees in the Gombe Stream Reserve. *Animal Behaviour Monographs, 1,* 161–311. (p. 150)

Goodall, J. (1986). *The chimpanzees of Gombe: Patterns of behavior.* Cambridge, MA: Harvard University Press. (p. 708)

Goodall, J. (1998). Learning from the chimpanzees: A message humans can understand. *Science, 282,* 2184–2185. (p. 28)

Goodchilds, J. (1987). Quoted by Carol Tavris, Old age is not what it used to be. *The New York Times Magazine: Good Health Magazine*, September 27, pp. 24–25, 91–92. (p. 207)

Goode, E. (1999, April 13). If things taste bad, 'phantoms' may be at work. *New York Times* (www.nytimes.com). (p. 255)

Goode, E. (2003, January 28). Even in the age of Prozac, some still prefer the couch. *New York Times* (www.nytimes.com). (p. 648)

Goodhart, D. E. (1986). The effects of positive and negative thinking on performance in an achievement situation. *Journal of Personality and Social Psychology, 51,* 117–124. (p. 587)

Goodman, G. S. (2006). Children's eyewitness memory: A modern history and contemporary commentary. *Journal of Social Issues, 62,* 811–832. (p. 362)

Goodman, G. S., Ghetti, S., Quas, J. A., Edelstein, R. S., Alexander, K. W., Redlich, A. D., Cordon, I. M., & Jones, D. P. H. (2003). A prospective study of memory for child sexual abuse: New findings relevant to the repressed-memory controversy. *Psychological Science, 14,* 113–118. (p. 363)

Goodstein, L., & Glaberson, W. (2000, April 9). The well-marked roads to homicidal rage. *New York Times* (www.nytimes.com). (p. 590)

Goodwin, F. K., & Morrison, A. R. (1999). Scientists in bunkers: How appeasement of animal rights activism has failed. *Cerebrum, 1*(2), 50–62. (p. 21)

Gopnik, A., & Meltzoff, A. N. (1986). Relations between semantic and cognitive development in the one-word stage: The specificity hypothesis. *Child Development, 57,* 1040–1053. (p. 394)

Goranson, R. E. (1978). *The hindsight effect in problem solving.* Unpublished manuscript, cited by G. Wood (1984), Research methodology: A decision-making perspective. In A. M. Rogers & C. J. Scheirer (Eds.), *The G. Stanley Hall Lecture Series* (Vol. 4). Washington, DC. (p. 16)

Gordon, P. (2004). Numerical cognition without words: Evidence from Amazonia. *Science, 306,* 496–499. (p. 393)

Gore, A. (2007, July 1). Moving beyond Kyoto. *New York Times* (www.nytimes.com). (p. 733)

Gore-Felton, C., Koopman, C., Thoresen, C., Arnow, B., Bridges, E., & Spiegel, D. (2000). Psychologists' beliefs and clinical characteristics: Judging the veracity of childhood sexual abuse memories. *Professional Psychology: Research and Practice, 31,* 372–377. (p. 363)

Gortmaker, S. L., Must, A., Perrin, J. M., Sobol, A. M., & Dietz, W. H. (1993). Social and economic consequences of overweight in adolescence and young adulthood. *New England Journal of Medicine, 329,* 1008–1012. (p. 457)

Gosling, S. D., Gladdis, S., & Vazire, S. (2007). Personality impressions based on Facebook profiles. Paper presented to the Society for Personality and Social Psychology meeting. (p. 581)

Gosling, S. D., Ko, S. J., Mannarelli, T., & Morris, M. E. (2002). A room with a cue: Personality judgments based on offices and bedrooms. *Journal of Personality and Social Psychology, 82,* 379–398. (p. 581)

Gosling, S. D., Kwan, V. S. Y., & John, O. P. (2003). A dog's got personality: A cross-species comparative approach to personality judgments in dogs and humans. *Journal of Personality and Social Psychology, 85,* 1161–1169. (p. 576)

Gotlib, I. H., & Hammen, C. L. (1992). *Psychological aspects of depression: Toward a cognitive-interpersonal integration.* New York: Wiley. (p. 634)

Gottesman, I. I. (1991). *Schizophrenia genesis: The origins of madness.* New York: Freeman. (p. 642)

Gottesman, I. I. (2001). Psychopathology through a life span—genetic prism. *American Psychologist, 56,* 867–881. (p. 641)

Gottfredson, L. S. (2002a). Where and why g matters: Not a mystery. *Human Performance, 15,* 25–46. (p. 407)

Gottfredson, L. S. (2002b). g: Highly general and highly practical. In R. J. Sternberg & E. L. Grigorenko (Eds.), *The general factor of intelligence: How general is it?* Mahwah, NJ: Erlbaum. (p. 407)

Gottfredson, L. S. (2003a). Dissecting practical intelligence theory: Its claims and evidence. *Intelligence, 31,* 343–397. (p. 407)

Gottfredson, L. S. (2003b). On Sternberg's "Reply to Gottfredson." *Intelligence, 31,* 415–424. (p. 407)

Gottfried, J. A., O'Doherty, J., & Dolan, R. J. (2003). Encoding predictive reward value in human amygdala and orbitofrontal cortex. *Science, 301,* 1104–1108. (p. 291)

Gottman, J., with Silver, N. (1994). *Why marriages succeed or fail.* New York: Simon & Schuster. (p. 217)

Gougoux, F., Zatorre, R., Lassonde, M., Voss, P., & Lepore, F. (2005). A functional neuroimaging study of sound localization: Visual cortex activity predicts performance in early-blind individuals. *PloS Biology, 3*(2), e27. (p. 248)

Gould, E. (2007). How widespread is adult neurogenesis in mammals? *Nature Neuroscience, 8,* 481–488. (p. 74)

Gould, S. J. (1981). *The mismeasure of man.* New York: Norton. (p. 417)

Gould, S. J. (1997, June 12). Darwinian fundamentalism. *The New York Review of Books, XLIV*(10), 34–37. (p. 146)

Grabe, S., Ward, L. M., & Hyde, J. S. (2008). The role of the media in body image concerns among women: A meta-analysis of experimental and correlational studies. *Psychological Bulletin, 134,* 460–476. (p. 455)

Grady, C. L., McIntosh, A. R., Horwitz, B., Maisog, J. M., Ungeleider, L. G., Mentis, M. J., Pietrini, P., Schapiro, M. B., & Haxby, J. V. (1995). Age-related reductions in human recognition memory due to impaired encoding. *Science, 269,* 218–221. (p. 352)

Grady, D. (2007, December 26). Finding Alzheimer's before a mind fails. *New York Times* (www.nytimes.com). (p. 211)

Graf, P. (1990). Life-span changes in implicit and explicit memory. *Bulletin of the Psychonomic Society, 28,* 353–358. (p. 213)

Graham, J. E., Christian, L. M., & Kiecolt-Glaser, J. K. (2006). Marriage, health, and immune function. In S. R. H. Beach & others (Eds.), *Relational processes and DSM-V: Neuroscience, assessment, prevention, and treatment.* Washington, DC: American Psychiatric Association. (p. 546)

Grant, B. F., & Dawson, D. A. (1998). Age of onset of drug use and its association with DSM-IV drug abuse and dependence: Results from the national Longitudinal Alcohol Epidemiologic Survey. *Journal of Substance Abuse, 10,* 163–173. (pp. 129, B-6)

Gray, P. B., Yang, C-F. J., & Pope, Jr., H. G. (2006). Fathers have lower salivary testosterone levels than unmarried men and married non-fathers in Beijing, China. *Proceedings of the Royal Society, 273,* 333–339. (p. 468)

Gray-Little, B., & Burks, N. (1983). Power and satisfaction in marriage: A review and critique. *Psychological Bulletin, 93,* 513–538. (p. 725)

Green, B. (2002). Listening to leaders: Feedback on 360-degree feedback one year later. *Organizational Development Journal, 20,* 8–16. (p. 489)

Green, C. S., & Bavelier, D. (2003). Action video game modifies visual selective attention. *Nature, 423,* 534–537. (p. 228)

Green, J. D., Sedikides, C., & Gregg, A. P. (2008). Forgotten but not gone: The recall and recognition of self-threatening memories. *Journal of Experimental Social Psychology, 44,* 547–561. (p. 566)

Green, J. T., & Woodruff-Pak, D. S. (2000). Eyeblink classical conditioning: Hippocampal formation is for neutral stimulus associations as cerebellum is for association-response. *Psychological Bulletin, 126,* 138–158. (p. 345)

Greenberg, J. (2008). Understanding the vital human quest for self-esteem. *Perspectives on Psychological Science, 3,* 48–55. (p. 591)

Greenberg, J., Solomon, S., & Pyszczynski, T. (1997). Terror management theory of self-esteem and cultural worldviews: Empirical assessments and conceptual refinements. *Advances in Social Psychology, 29,* 61–142. (p. 567)

Greene, J., Sommerville, R. B., Nystrom, L. E., Darley, J. M., & Cohen, J. D. (2001). An fMRI investigation of emotional engagement in moral judgment. *Science, 293,* 2105. (p. 200)

Greene, R. L. (1987). Effects of maintenance rehearsal on human memory. *Psychological Bulletin, 102,* 403–413. (p. 330)

Greenfeld, L. A. (1998). *Alcohol and crime: An analysis of national data on the prevalence of alcohol involvement in crime.* Washington, DC: Document NCJ-168632, Bureau of Justice Statistics (www.ojp.usdoj.gov/bjs). (p. 711)

Greenwald, A. G. (1992). Subliminal semantic activation and subliminal snake oil. Paper presented to the American Psychological Association Convention, Washington, DC. (pp. 229, 566)

Greenwald, A. G., McGhee, D. E., & Schwartz, J. L. K. (1998). Measuring individual differences in implicit cognition: The implicit association test. *Journal of Personality and Social Psychology, 74,* 1464–1480. (p. 705)

Greenwald, A. G., Oakes, M. A., & Hoffman, H. (2003). Targets of discrimination: Effects of race on responses to weapons holders. *Journal of Experimental Social Psychology, 39,* 399. (p. 705)

Greenwald, A. G., Spangenberg, E. R., Pratkanis, A. R., & Eskenazi, J. (1991). Double-blind tests of subliminal self-help audiotapes. *Psychological Science, 2,* 119-122. (p. 229)

Greenwood, M. R. C. (1989). Sexual dimorphism and obesity. In A. J. Stunkard & A. Baum (Eds.). *Perspectives in behavioral medicine: Eating, sleeping, and sex.* Hillsdale, NJ: Erlbaum. (p. 457)

Greer, G. (1984, April). The uses of chastity and other paths to sexual pleasures. *MS,* pp. 53-60, 96. (p. 469)

Greers, A. E. (2004). Speech, language, and reading skills after early cochlear implantation. *Archives of Otolaryngology—Head & Neck Surgery, 130,* 634-638. (p. 389)

Gregory, R. L. (1978). *Eye and brain: The psychology of seeing* (3rd ed.). New York: McGraw-Hill. (p. 272)

Gregory, R. L., & Gombrich, E. H. (Eds.). (1973). *Illusion in nature and art.* New York: Charles Scribner's Sons. (pp. 254, 277)

Greif, E. B., & Ulman, K. J. (1982). The psychological impact of menarche on early adolescent females: A review of the literature. *Child Development, 53.* 1413-1430. (p. 196)

Greist, J. H., Jefferson, J. W., & Marks, I. M. (1986). *Anxiety and its treatment: Help is available.* Washington, DC: American Psychiatric Press. (p. 611)

Grello, C. M., Welsh, D. P., & Harper, M. S. (2006). No strings attached: The nature of casual sex in college students. *Journal of Sex Research, 43,* 255-267. (p. 117)

Grèzes, J., & Decety, J. (2001). Function anatomy of execution, mental simulation, observation, and verb generation of actions: A meta-analysis. *Human Brain Mapping, 12,* 1-19. (p. 395)

Griffiths, M. (2001). Sex on the Internet: Observations and implications for Internet sex addiction. *Journal of Sex Research, 38,* 333-342. (p. 114)

Grill-Spector, K., & Kanwisher, N. (2005). Visual recognition: As soon as you know it is there, you know what it is. *Psychological Science, 16,* 152-160. (p. 370)

Grilo, C. M., & Pogue-Geile, M. F. (1991). The nature of environmental influences on weight and obesity: A behavior genetic analysis. *Psychological Bulletin, 110,* 520-537. (p. 460)

Grinker, R. R. (2007). *Unstrange minds: Remapping the world of autism.* New York: Basic Books. (p. 182)

Grobstein, C. (1979, June). External human fertilization. *Scientific American,* pp. 57-67. (p. 170)

Groothuis, T. G. G., & Carere, C. (2005). Avian personalities: Characterization and epigenesis. *Neuroscience and Biobehavioral Reviews, 29,* 137-150. (p. 576)

Gross, A. E., & Crofton, C. (1977). What is good is beautiful. *Sociometry, 40,* 85-90. (p. 723)

Gross, M., Nakamura, L., Pascual-Leone, A., & Fregni, F. (2007). Has repetitive transcranial magnetic stimulation (rTMS) treatment for depression improved? A systematic review and meta-analysis comparing the recent vs. the earlier rTMS studies. *Acta Psychiatrica Scandinavica, 116,* 165-173. (p. 676)

Grossberg, S. (1995). The attentive brain. *American Scientist, 83,* 438-449. (p. 276)

Grossman, M., & Wood, W. (1993). Sex differences in intensity of emotional experience: A social role interpretation. *Journal of Personality and Social Psychology, 65,* 1010-1022. (p. 512)

Gruder, C. L. (1977). Choice of comparison persons in evaluating oneself. In J. M. Suls & R. L. Miller (Eds.), *Social comparison processes.* New York: Hemisphere. (p. 528)

Grunebaum, M. F., Ellis, S. P., Li, S., Oquendo, M. A., & Mann, J. J. (2004). Antidepressants and suicide risk in the United States, 1985-1999. *Journal of Clinical Psychiatry, 65,* 1456-1462. (p. 674)

Guerin, B. (1986). Mere presence effects in humans: A review. *Journal of Personality and Social Psychology, 22,* 38-77. (p. 697)

Guerin, B. (2003). Language use as social strategy: A review and an analytic framework for the social sciences. *Review of General Psychology, 7,* 251-298. (p. 384)

Guiso, L., Monte, F., Sapienza, P., & Zingales, L. (2008). Culture, gender, and math. *Science, 320,* 1164-1165. (p. 434)

Gundersen, E. (2001, August 1). MTV is a many splintered thing. *USA Today,* pp. D1, D2. (p. 319)

Güntürkün, O. (2003). Adult persistence of head-turning asymmetry. *Nature, 421,* 711. (p. 78)

Gura, T. (2000). Enzyme blocker prompts mice to shed weight. *Science, 288,* 2299-2300. (p. 451)

Gustafson, D., Lissner, L., Bengtsson, C., Björkelund, C., & Skoog, I. (2004). A 24-year follow-up of body mass index and cerebral atrophy. *Neurology, 63,* 1876-1881. (p. 457)

Gustafson, D., Rothenberg, E., Blennow, K., Steen, B., & Skoog, I. (2003). An 18-year follow-up of overweight and risk of Alzheimer disease. *Archives of Internal Medicine, 163,* 1524-1528. (pp. 212, 457)

Gustavson, C. R., Garcia, J., Hankins, W. G., & Rusiniak, K. W. (1974). Coyote predation control by aversive conditioning. *Science, 184,* 581-583. (p. 296)

Gustavson, C. R., Kelly, D. J., & Sweeney, M. (1976). Prey-lithium aversions I: Coyotes and wolves. *Behavioral Biology, 17,* 61-72. (p. 296)

Guttentag, M., & Secord, P. F. (1983). *Too many women? The sex ratio question.* Thousand Oaks, CA: Sage. (p. 704)

Guttmacher Institute. (1994). *Sex and America's teenagers.* New York: Alan Guttmacher Institute. (pp. 204, 471)

Guttmacher Institute. (2000). *Fulfilling the promise: Public policy and U.S. family planning clinics.* New York: Alan Guttmacher Institute. (p. 204)

H., Sally. (1979, August). Videotape recording number T-3, Fortunoff Video Archive of Holocaust Testimonies. New Haven, CT: Yale University Library. (p. 566)

Haber, R. N. (1970, May). How we remember what we see. *Scientific American,* pp. 104-112. (p. 324)

Haddock, G., & Zanna, M. P. (1994). Preferring "housewives" to "feminists." *Psychology of Women Quarterly, 18,* 25-52. (p. 704)

Haesler, S. (2007, June/July). Programmed for speech. *Scientific American Mind,* pp. 67-71. (p. 388)

Haidt, J. (2000). The positive emotion of elevation. *Prevention and Treatment, 3,* article 3 (journals.apa.org/prevention/volume3). (p. 199)

Haidt, J. (2002). The moral emotions. In R. J. Davidson, K. Scherer, & H. H. Goldsmith (Eds.), *Handbook of affective sciences.* New York: Oxford University Press. (p. 199)

Haidt, J. (2006). The happiness hypothesis: Finding modern truth in ancient wisdom. New York: Basic Books. (p. 198)

Haidt, J. (2007). The new synthesis in moral psychology. *Science, 316,* 998-1001. (p. 199)

Haidt, J. (2008). Morality. *Perspectives on Psychological Science, 3,* 65-72. (p. 199)

Haier, R. J., Jung, R. E., Yeo, R. A., Head, K., & Alkire, M. T. (2004). Structural brain variation and general intelligence. *NeuroImage, 23,* 425-433. (pp. 412, 413)

Hakuta, K., Bialystok, E., & Wiley, E. (2003). Critical evidence: A test of the critical-period hypothesis for second-language acquisition. *Psychological Science, 14,* 31-38. (p. 390)

Halberstadt, J. B., & Niedenthal, P. M. (2001). Effects of emotion concepts on perceptual memory for emotional expressions. *Journal of Personality and Social Psychology, 81,* 587-598. (p. 360)

Halberstadt, J. B., Niedenthal, P. M., & Kushner, J. (1995). Resolution of lexical ambiguity by emotional state. *Psychological Science, 6,* 278-281. (p. 276)

Halberstadt, J., O'Shea, R. P., & Forgas, J. (2006). Outgroup fanship in Australia and New Zealand. *Australian Journal of Psychology, 58,* 159-165. (p. 707)

Haldeman, D. C. (1994). The practice and ethics of sexual orientation conversion therapy. *Journal of Consulting and Clinical Psychology, 62,* 221-227. (p. 473)

Haldeman, D. C. (2002). Gay rights, patient rights: The implications of sexual orientation conversion therapy. *Professional Psychology: Research and Practice, 33,* 260-264. (p. 473)

Hall, C. S., Dornhoff, W., Blick, K. A., & Weesner, K. E. (1982). The dreams of college men and women in 1950 and 1980: A comparison of dream contents and sex differences. *Sleep, 5,* 188-194. (p. 103)

Hall, C. S., & Lindzey, G. (1978). *Theories of personality* (2nd ed.). New York: Wiley. (p. 567)

Hall, G. (1997). Context aversion, Pavlovian conditioning, and the psychological side effects of chemotherapy. *European Psychologist, 2,* 118–124. (p. 297)

Hall, G. S. (1904). Adolescence: Its psychology and its relations to physiology, anthropology, sex, crime, religion and education (Vol. I). New York: Appleton-Century-Crofts. (p. 195)

Hall, J. A. (1984). *Nonverbal sex differences: Communication accuracy and expressive style.* Baltimore: Johns Hopkins University Press. (p. 512)

Hall, J. A. (1987). On explaining gender differences: The case of nonverbal communication. In P. Shaver & C. Hendrick (Eds.), *Review of Personality and Social Psychology, 7,* 177–200. (pp. 158, 512)

Hall, J. A. Y., & Kimura, D. (1994). Dermatoglyphic assymetry and sexual orientation in men. *Behavioral Neuroscience, 108,* 1203–1206. (p. 477)

Hall, J. G. (2003). Twinning. *Lancet, 362,* 735–743. (p. 134)

Hall, S. S. (2004, May). The good egg. *Discover,* pp. 30–39. (p. 170)

Hall, W. (2006). The mental health risks of adolescent cannabis use. *PloS Medicine, 3*(2), e39. (p. 124)

Halpern, D. F. (1991). Cognitive sex differences: Why diversity is a critical research issue. Paper presented to the American Psychological Association convention. (p. 433)

Halpern, D. F. (2000). *Sex-related ability differences: Changing perspectives, changing minds.* Mahwah, NJ: Erlbaum. (pp. 434, 472)

Halpern, D. F. (2005, May 20). Response to Drs. Pinker and Spelke. www.edge.org. (p. 434)

Halpern, D. F., Benbow, C. P., Geary, D. C., Gur, R. C., Hyde, J. S., & Gernsbacher, M. A. (2007). The science of sex differences in science and mathematics. *Psychological Science in the Public Interest, 8,* 1–51. (pp. 432, 434, 435)

Halpern, D. F., & Coren, S. (1990). Laterality and longevity: Is left-handedness associated with a younger age at death? In S. Coren (Ed.), *Left-handedness: Behavioral implications and anomalies.* Amsterdam: North-Holland. (p. 79)

Hamann, S., Herman, R. A., Nolan, C. L., & Wallen, K. (2004). Men and women differ in amygdala response to visual sexual stimuli. *Nature Neuroscience, 7,* 411–416. (p. 469)

Hamilton, R. H. (2000, November). Increased prevalence of absolute pitch in blind musicians (Abstract 739.13). Society for Neuroscience meeting, New Orleans. (p. 248)

Hammack, P. L., (2005). The life course development of human sexual orientation: An integrative paradigm. *Human Development, 48,* 267–290. (pp. 473, 475)

Hammer, E. (2003). How lucky you are to be a psychology major. *Eye on Psi Chi,* 4–5. (p. A-9)

Hammersmith, S. K. (1982, August). Sexual preference: An empirical study from the Alfred C. Kinsey Institute for Sex Research. Paper presented at the meeting of the American Psychological Association, Washington, DC. (p. 474)

Hampson, R. (2000, April 10). In the end, people just need more room. *USA Today,* p. 19A. (p. 461)

Hampson, S. E., & Goldberg, L. R. (2006). A first large cohort study of personality trait stability over the years between elementary school and midlife. *Journal of Personality and Social Psychology, 91,* 763–779. (p. 223)

Hancock, K. J., & Rhodes, G. (2008). Contact, configural coding and the other-race effect in face recognition. *British Journal of Psychology, 99,* 45–56. (p. 709)

Hankin, B. L., & Abramson, L. Y. (2001). Development of gender differences in depression: An elaborated cognitive vulnerability-transactional stress theory. *Psychological Bulletin, 127,* 773–796. (p. 632)

Hansen, C. H., & Hansen, R. D. (1988). Finding the face-in-the-crowd: An anger superiority effect. *Journal of Personality and Social Psychology, 54,* 917–924. (p. 510)

Harbaugh, W. T., Mayr, U., & Burghart, D. R. (2007). Neural responses to taxation and voluntary giving reveal motives for charitable donations. *Science, 316,* 1622–1625. (p. 728)

Harber, K. D. (1998), Feedback to minorities: Evidence of a positive bias. *Journal of Personality and Social Psychology, 74,* 622–628. (p. 705)

Hardin, C., & Banaji, M. R. (1993). The influence of language on thought. *Social Cognition, 11,* 277–308. (p. 393)

Hare, R. D. (1975). Psychophysiological studies of psychopathy. In D. C. Fowles (Ed.), *Clinical applications of psychophysiology.* New York: Columbia University Press. (p. 621)

Hariri, A. R., Mattay, V. S., Tessitore, A., Kolachana, B., Fera, F., Goldman, D., Egan, M. F., & Weinberger, D. R. (2002). Serotonin transporter genetic variation and the response of the human amygdala. *Science, 297,* 400–403. (p. 519)

Harker, L. A., & Keltner, D. (2001). Expressions of positive emotion in women's college yearbook pictures and their relationship to personality and life outcomes across adulthood. *Journal of Personality and Social Psychology, 80,* 112–124. (p. 522)

Harkins, S. G., & Szymanski, K. (1989). Social loafing and group evaluation. *Journal of Personality and Social Psychology, 56,* 934–941. (p. 698)

Harlow, H. F., Harlow, M. K., & Suomi, S. J. (1971). From thought to therapy: Lessons from a primate laboratory. *American Scientist, 59,* 538–549. (p. 186)

Harlow, R. E., & Cantor, N. (1996). Still participating after all these years: A study of life task participation in later life. *Journal of Personality and Social Psychology, 71,* 1235–1249. (p. 220)

Harmon-Jones, E., Abramson, L. Y., Sigelman, J., Bohlig, A., Hogan, M. E., & Harmon-Jones, C. (2002). Proneness to hypomania/mania symptoms or depression symptoms and asymmetrical frontal cortical responses to an anger-evoking event. *Journal of Personality and Social Psychology, 82,* 610–618. (p. 503)

Harper, C., & McLanahan, S. (2004). Father absence and youth incarceration. *Journal of Research on Adolescence, 14,* 369–397. (p. 713)

Harris, A., & Lurigio, A. J. (2007). Mental illness and violence: A brief review of research and assessment strategies. *Aggression and Violent Behavior, 12,* 542–551. (p. 605)

Harris, B. (1979). Whatever happened to Little Albert? *American Psychologist, 34,* 151–160. (p. 298)

Harris, J. A. (1999). Review and methodological considerations in research on testosterone and aggression. *Aggression and Violent Behavior, 4,* 273–291. (p. 711)

Harris, J. R. (1998). *The nurture assumption.* New York: Free Press. (pp. 151, 181)

Harris, J. R. (2000). Beyond the nurture assumption: Testing hypotheses about the child's environment. In J. G. Borkowski & S. L. Ramey (Eds.), *Parenting and the child's world: Influences on academic, intellectual, and social-emotional development.* Washington, DC: APA Books. (p. 151)

Harris, J. R. (2006). No two are alike: Human nature and human individuality. New York: Norton. (p. 136)

Harris, J. R. (2007, August 8). Do pals matter more than parents? *The Times* (www.timesonline.co.uk). (p. 151)

Harris, R. J. (1994). The impact of sexually explicit media. In J. Brant & D. Zillmann (Eds.), *Media effects: Advances in theory and research.* Hillsdale, NJ: Erlbaum. (p. 714)

Harrison, Y., & Horne, J. A. (2000). The impact of sleep deprivation on decision making: A review. *Journal of Experimental Psychology: Applied, 6,* 236–249. (p. 98)

Harriston, K. A. (1993, December 24). 1 shakes, 1 snoozes: Both win $45 million. *Washington Post* release (in *Tacoma News Tribune,* pp. A1, A2). (p. 590)

Hart, D. (1988). The development of personal identity in adolescence: A philosophical dilemma approach. *Merrill-Palmer Quarterly, 34,* 105–114. (p. 202)

Harter, J. K., Schmidt, F. L., & Hayes, T. L. (2002). Business-unit-level relationship between employee satisfaction, employee engagement, and business outcomes: A meta-analysis. *Journal of Applied Psychology, 87,* 268–279. (p. 493)

Hartmann, E. (1981, April). The strangest sleep disorder. *Psychology Today,* pp. 14, 16, 18. (p. 102)

Harvard Mental Health Letter. (2002, February). EMDR (Eye movement and reprocessing). *Harvard Mental Health Letter, 18,* 4–5. (p. 665)

Harvey, F. (2002, February). Surrounded by sound. *Scientific American,* pp. 94–95. (p. 247)

Haselton, M. G., Mortezaie, M., Pillsworth, E. G., Bleske-Rechek, A., & Frederick, D. A. (2006). Ovulatory shifts in human female ornamentation: Near ovulation, women dress to impress. *Hormones and Behavior, 51,* 40–45. (p. 467)

Hasin, D. S., Goodwin, R. D., Stinson, F. S., & Grant, B. F. (2005). Epidemiology of major depressive disorder: Results from the National Epidemiologic Survey on Alcoholism and Related Conditions. *Archives of General Psychiatry, 62,* 1097-1106. (p. 625)

Haslam, N., & Levy, S. R. (2006). Essentialist beliefs about homosexuality: Structure and implications for prejudice. *Personality and Social Psychology Bulletin, 32,* 471-485. (p. 478)

Haslam, S. A., & Reicher, S. (2007). Beyond the banality of evil: Three dynamics of an interactionist social psychology of tyranny. *Personality and Social Psychology Bulletin, 33,* 615-622. (p. 688)

Hassan, B., & Rahman, Q. (2007). Selective sexual orientation-related differences in object location memory. *Behavioral Neuroscience, 121,* 625-633. (p. 478)

Hatfield, E. (1988). Passionate and companionate love. In R. J. Sternberg & M. L. Barnes (Eds.), *The psychology of love.* New Haven, CT: Yale University Press. (p. 724)

Hatfield, E., & Sprecher, S. (1986). *Mirror, mirror . . . The importance of looks in everyday life.* Albany: State University of New York Press. (p. 721)

Hatfield, J., Faunce, G. J., & Job, R. F. S. (2006). Avoiding confusion surrounding the phrase "correlation does not imply causation." *Teaching of Psychology, 33,* 49-51. (p. 31)

Hathaway, S. R. (1960). *An MMPI Handbook* (Vol. 1, Foreword). Minneapolis: University of Minnesota Press (rev. ed., 1972). (p. 576)

Hauser, M. (2006). *Moral minds: How nature designed our universal sense of right and wrong.* New York: Ecco. (pp. 200, 388)

Hauser, M. D., Chomsky, N., & Fitch, W. T. (2002). The faculty of language: What is it, who has it, and how did it evolve? *Science, 298,* 1569-1579. (p. 386)

Havas, D. A., Glenberg, A. M., & Rink, M. (2007). Emotion simulation during language comprehension. *Psychonomic Bulletin & Review, 14,* 436-441. (p. 516)

Haxby, J. V. (2001, July 7). Quoted by B. Bower, Faces of perception. *Science News,* pp. 10-12. See also J. V. Haxby, M. I. Gobbini, M. L. Furey, A. Ishai, J. L. Schouten & P. Pietrini, Distributed and overlapping representations of faces and objects in ventral temporal cortex. *Science, 293,* 2425-2430. (p. 238)

Haynes, J-D., & Rees, G. (2005). Predicting the orientation of invisible stimuli from activity in human primary visual cortex. *Nature Neuroscience, 8,* 686-691. (p. 229)

Haynes, J-D., & Rees, G. (2006). Decoding mental states from brain activity in humans. *Nature Reviews Neuroscience, 7,* 523-534. (p. 229)

Hazan, C., & Shaver, P. R. (1994). Attachment as an organizational framework for research on close relationships. *Psychological Inquiry, 5,* 1-22. (p. 190)

Hazelrigg, M. D., Cooper, H. M., & Borduin, C. M. (1987). Evaluating the effectiveness of family therapies: An integrative review and analysis. *Psychological Bulletin, 101,* 428-442. (p. 658)

Head Start. (2005). Head Start program fact sheet. www.acf.hhs.gov/programs//hsb/research/22005.htm. (p. 431)

Health Canada. (2007). *Canadian addiction survey: Substance use by Canadian youth.* Health Canada Publication 4946 (www.hc-sc.gc.ca). (p. 125)

Heaps, C. M., & Nash, M. (2001). Comparing recollective experience in true and false autobiographical memories. *Journal of Experimental Psychology: Learning, Memory, and Cognition, 27,* 920-930. (p. 364)

Hebb, D. O. (1980). *Essay on mind.* Hillsdale, NJ: Erlbaum. (pp. 298, 499)

Hebl, M. R., & Mannix, L. M. (2003). The weight of obesity in evaluating others: A mere proximity effect. *Personality and Social Psychology Bulletin, 29,* 28-38. (p. 458)

Hedges, L. V., & Nowell, A. (1995). Sex differences in mental test scores, variability, and numbers of high-scoring individuals. *Science, 269,* 41-45. (p. 432, 433)

Hedström, P., Liu, K-Y., & Nordvik, M. K. (2008). Interaction domains and suicides: A population-based panel study of suicides in the Stockholm metropolitan area, 1991-1999. *Social Forces,* in press. (p. 631)

Heider, F. (1958). *The psychology of interpersonal relations.* New York: Wiley. (p. 682)

Heiman, J. R. (1975, April). The physiology of erotica: Women's sexual arousal. *Psychology Today,* pp. 90-94. (p. 469)

Heine, S. J., & Hamamura, T. (2007). In search of East Asian self-enhancement. *Personality and Social Psychology Review, 11,* 4-27. (p. 593)

Heins, M. (2004, December 14). Quoted by B. Kloza, Violent Christmas games. *ScienCentralNews* (www.sciencecentral.com). (p. 717)

Hejmadi, A., Davidson, R. J., & Rozin, P. (2000). Exploring Hindu Indian emotion expressions: Evidence for accurate recognition by Americans and Indians. *Psychological Science, 11,* 183-187. (p. 510)

Helgeson, V. S., Cohen, S., & Fritz, H. L. (1998). Social ties and cancer. In P. M. Cinciripini & others (Eds.), *Psychological and behavioral factors in cancer risk.* New York: Oxford University Press. (p. 545)

Helgeson, V. S., Reynolds, K. A., & Tomich, P. L. (2006). A meta-analytic review of benefit finding and growth. *Journal of Consulting and Clinical Psychology, 74,* 797-816. (p. 614)

Heller, W. (1990, May/June). Of one mind: Second thoughts about the brain's dual nature. *The Sciences,* pp. 38-44. (p. 78)

Helmreich, W. B. (1992). *Against all odds: Holocaust survivors and the successful lives they made in America.* New York: Simon & Schuster. (pp. 189, 566)

Helmreich, W. B. (1994). Personal correspondence. Department of Sociology, City University of New York. (p. 566)

Helms, J. E., Jernigan, M., & Mascher, J. (2005). The meaning of race in psychology and how to change it: A methodological perspective. *American Psychologist, 60,* 27-36. (p. 437)

Helmuth, L. (2001). Boosting brain activity from the outside in. *Science, 292,* 1284-1286. (p. 676)

Helweg-Larsen, M. (1999). (The lack of) optimistic biases in response to the 1994 Northridge earthquake: The role of personal experience. *Basic and Applied Social Psychology, 21,* 119-129. (p. 587)

Hembree, R. (1988). Correlates, causes, effects, and treatment of test anxiety. *Review of Educational Research, 58,* 47-77. (p. 502)

Hemenover, S. H. (2003). The good, the bad, and the healthy: Impacts of emotional disclosure of trauma on resilient self-concept and psychological distress. *Personality and Social Psychology Bulletin, 29,* 1236-1244. (p. 546)

Henderlong, J., & Lepper, M. R. (2002). The effects of praise on children's intrinsic motivation: A review and synthesis. *Psychological Bulletin, 128,* 774-795. (p. 309)

Henderson, J. M. (2007). Regarding scenes. *Current Directions in Psychological Science, 16,* 219-222. (p. 231)

Henkel, L. A., Franklin, N., & Johnson, M. K. (2000, March). Cross-modal source monitoring confusions between perceived and imagined events. *Journal of Experimental Psychology: Learning, Memory, & Cognition, 26,* 321-335. (p. 359)

Henley, N. M. (1989). Molehill or mountain? What we know and don't know about sex bias in language. In M. Crawford & M. Gentry (Eds.), *Gender and thought: Psychological perspectives.* New York: Springer-Verlag. (p. 394)

Henninger, P. (1992). Conditional handedness: Handedness changes in multiple personality disordered subject reflect shift in hemispheric dominance. *Consciousness and Cognition, 1,* 265-287. (p. 619)

Henry, J. D., MacLeod, M. S., Phillips, L. H., & Crawford, J. R. (2004). A meta-analytic review of prospective memory and aging. *Psychology and Aging, 19,* 27-39. (p. 213)

Hepper, P. (2005). Unravelling our beginnings. *The Psychologist, 18,* 474-477. (p. 171)

Hepper, P. G., Shahidullah, S., & White, R. (1990). Origins of fetal handedness. *Nature, 347,* 431. (p. 79)

Hepper, P. G., Wells, D. L., & Lynch, C. (2004). Prenatal thumb sucking is related to postnatal handedness. *Neuropsychologia, 43,* 313-315. (p. 79)

Herbert, B. (2001, July 23). Economics 202 at Big Tobacco U. *New York Times* (www.nytimes.com). (p. 118)

Herbert, J. D., Lilienfeld, S. O., Lohr, J. M., Montgomery, R. W., O'Donohue, W. T., Rosen, G. M., & Tolin, D. F. (2000). Science and pseudoscience in the development of eye movement desensitization and reprocessing: Implications for clinical psychology. *Clinical Psychology Review, 20,* 945-971. (p. 665)

Herek, G. M. (2006). Legal recognition of same-sex relationships in the United States: A social science perspective. *American Psychologist, 61,* 607-621. (p. 473)

Herman, C. P., & Polivy, J. (1980). Restrained eating. In A. J. Stunkard (Ed.), *Obesity.* Philadelphia: Saunders. (p. 463)

Herman, C. P., Roth, D. A., & Polivy, J. (2003). Effects of the presence of others on food intake: A normative interpretation. *Psychological Bulletin, 129*, 873–886. (p. 453)

Herman-Giddens, M. E., Wang, L., & Koch, G. (2001). Secondary sexual characteristics in boys: Estimates from the National Health and Nutrition Examination Survey III, 1988–1994. *Archives of Pediatrics and Adolescent Medicine, 155*, 1022–1028. (p. 196)

Hernandez, A. E., & Li, P. (2007). Age of acquisition: Its neural and computational mechanisms. *Psychological Bulletin, 133*, 638–650. (p. 389)

Herrmann, D. (1982). Know thy memory: The use of questionnaires to assess and study memory. *Psychological Bulletin, 92*, 434–452. (p. 365)

Herrmann, E., Call, J., Hernández-Lloreda, M. V., Hare, B., & Tomasello, M. (2007). Humans have evolved specialized skills of social cognition: The cultural intelligence hypothesis. *Science, 317*, 1360–1365. (p. 315)

Herrnstein, R. J., & Loveland, D. H. (1964). Complex visual concept in the pigeon. *Science, 146*, 549–551. (p. 302)

Herrnstein, R. J., & Murray, C. A. (1994). *The bell curve: Intelligence and class structure in American life.* New York: Free Press. (p. 435)

Hershenson, M. (1989). *The moon illusion.* Hillsdale, NJ: Erlbaum. (p. 268)

Hertenstein, M. J., Keltner, D., App, B. Bulleit, B., & Jaskolka, A. (2006). Touch communicates distinct emotions. *Emotion, 6*, 528–533. (p. 186)

Hertenstein, M. J., Verkamp, J. M., Kerestes, A. M., & Holmes, R. M. (2006). The communicative functions of touch in humans, nonhumans primates, and rats: A review and synthesis of the empirical research. *Genetic, Social, and General Psychology Monographs, 132*, 5–94. (p. 251)

Herz, R. S. (2001). Ah sweet skunk! Why we like or dislike what we smell. *Cerebrum, 3*(4), 31–47. (p. 260)

Herz, R.S., Beland, S.L., & Hellerstein, M. (2004). Changing odor hedonic perception through emotional associations in humans. *International Journal of Comparative Psychology, 17*, 315–339. (p. 260)

Hess, E. H. (1956, July). Space perception in the chick. *Scientific American*, pp. 71–80. (p. 273)

Hetherington, M. M., Anderson, A. S., Norton, G. N. M., & Newson, L. (2006). Situational effects on meal intake: A comparison of eating alone and eating with others. *Physiology and Behavior, 88*, 498–505. (p. 453)

Hettema, J. M., Neale, M. C., & Kendler, K. S. (2001). A review and meta-analysis of the genetic epidemiology of anxiety disorders. *American Journal of Psychiatry, 158*, 1568–1578. (p. 616)

Hewlett, B. S. (1991). *Intimate fathers: The nature and context of Aka Pygmy.* Ann Arbor: University of Michigan Press. (p. 188)

Hickok, G., Bellugi, U., & Klima, E. S. (2001, June). Sign language in the brain. *Scientific American*, pp. 58–65. (p. 77)

Hilgard, E. R. (1986). *Divided consciousness: Multiple controls in human thought and action.* New York: Wiley. (p. 111)

Hilgard, E. R. (1992). Dissociation and theories of hypnosis. In E. Fromm & M. R. Nash (Eds.), *Contemporary hypnosis research.* New York: Guilford. (p. 111)

Hill, C. E., & Nakayama, E. Y. (2000). Client-centered therapy: Where has it been and where is it going? A comment on Hathaway. *Journal of Clinical Psychology, 56*, 961–875. (p. 649)

Hill, H., & Johnston, A. (2001). Categorizing sex and identity from the biological motion of faces. *Current Biology, 11*, 880–885. (p. 513)

Hines, M. (2004). *Brain gender.* New York: Oxford University Press. (p. 161)

Hines, M., & Green, R. (1991). Human hormonal and neural correlates of sex-typed behaviors. *Review of Psychiatry, 10*, 536–555. (p. 161)

Hingson, R. W., Heeren, T., & Winter, M. R. (2006). Age at drinking onset and alcohol dependence. *Archives of Pediatrics & Adolescent Medicine, 160*, 739–746. (p. 127)

Hintzman, D. L. (1978). *The psychology of learning and memory.* San Francisco: Freeman. (p. 333)

Hinz, L. D., & Williamson, D. A. (1987). Bulimia and depression: A review of the affective variant hypothesis. *Psychological Bulletin, 102*, 150–158. (p. 454)

Hirsch, J. (2003). Obesity: Matter over mind? *Cerebrum, 5*(1), 7–18. (p. 458)

Hirt, E. R., Zillmann, D., Erickson, G. A., & Kennedy, C. (1992). Costs and benefits of allegiance: Changes in fans' self-ascribed competencies after team victory versus defeat. *Journal of Personality and Social Psychology, 63*, 724–738. (p. 635)

HMHL. (2002, August). Smoking and depression. *Harvard Mental Health Letter*, pp. 6–7. (p. 631)

HMHL. (2002, January). Disaster and trauma. *Harvard Mental Health Letter*, pp. 1–5. (p. 533)

HMHL (2007, February). Electroconvulsive therapy. *Harvard Mental Health Letter*, Harvard Medical School, pp. 1–4. (p. 676)

Hobson, J. A. (1995, September). Quoted by C. H. Colt, The power of dreams. *Life*, pp. 36–49. (p. 104)

Hobson, J. A. (2003). *Dreaming: An introduction to the science of sleep.* New York: Oxford. (p. 105)

Hobson, J. A. (2004). *13 dreams Freud never had: The new mind science.* New York: Pi Press. (p. 105)

Hochberg, L. R., Serruya, M. D., Friehs, G. M., Mukand, J. A., Saleh, M., Caplan, A. H., Branner, A., Chen, D., Penn, R. D., & Donoghue, J. P. (2006). Neuronal ensemble control of prosthetic devices by a human with tetraplegia. *Nature, 442*, 164–171. (p. 70)

Hodgkinson, V. A., & Weitzman, M. S. (1992). *Giving and volunteering in the United States.* Washington, DC: Independent Sector. (p. 729)

Hoebel, B. G., & Teitelbaum, P. (1966). Effects of forcefeeding and starvation on food intake and body weight in a rat with ventromedial hypothalamic lesions. *Journal of Comparative and Physiological Psychology, 61*, 189–193. (p. 450)

Hoeft, F., Watson, C. L., Kesler, S. R., Bettinger, K. E., & Reiss, A. L. (2008). Gender differences in the mesocorticolimbic system during computer game-play. *Journal of Psychiatric Research, 42*, 253–258. (p. 114)

Hoffman, C., & Hurst, N. (1990). Gender stereotypes: Perception or rationalization? *Journal of Personality and Social Psychology, 58*, 197–208. (p. 706)

Hoffman, D. D. (1998). *Visual intelligence: How we create what we see.* New York: Norton. (p. 239)

Hoffman, H. G. (2004, August). Virtual-reality therapy. *Scientific American*, pp. 58–65. (p. 257)

Hogan, J. (1995, November). Get smart, take a test. *Scientific American*, pp. 12, 14. (p. 421)

Hogan, R. (1998). Reinventing personality. *Journal of Social and Clinical Psychology, 17*, 1–10. (p. 581)

Hoge, C. W., & Castro, C. A. (2006). Post-traumatic stress disorder in UK and U.S. forces deployed to Iraq. *Lancet, 368*, 837. (p. 613)

Hoge, C. W., Castro, C. A., Messer, S. C., McGurk, D., Cotting, D. I., & Koffman, R. L. (2004). Combat duty in Iraq and Afghanistan, mental health problems, and barriers to care. *New England Journal of Medicine, 351*, 13–22. (p. 613)

Hoge, C. W., Terhakopian, A., Castro, C. A., Messer, S. C., & Engel, C. C. (2007). Association of posttraumatic stress disorder with somatic symptoms, health care visits, and absenteeism among Iraq War veterans. *American Journal of Psychiatry, 164*, 150–153. (p. 613)

Hogg, M. A. (1996). Intragroup processes, group structure and social identity. In W. P. Robinson (Ed.), *Social groups and identities: Developing the legacy of Henri Tajfel.* Oxford: Butterworth Heinemann. (p. 706)

Hogg, M. A. (2006). Social identity theory. In P. J. Burke (Ed.), *Contemporary social psychological theories.* Stanford, CA: Stanford University Press. (p. 706)

Hohmann, G. W. (1966). Some effects of spinal cord lesions on experienced emotional feelings. *Psychophysiology, 3*, 143–156. (p. 504)

Hokanson, J. E., & Edelman, R. (1966). Effects of three social responses on vascular processes. *Journal of Personality and Social Psychology, 3*, 442–447. (p. 520)

Holahan, C. K., & Sears, R. R. (1995). *The gifted group in later maturity.* Stanford, CA: Stanford University Press. (p. 426)

Holden, C. (1980a). Identical twins reared apart. *Science, 207*, 1323–1325. (p. 135)

Holden, C. (1980b, November). Twins reunited. *Science, 80*, 55–59. (p. 135)

Holden, C. (1993). Wake-up call for sleep research. *Science, 259*, 305. (p. 97)

Holden, C. (2007). Mental illness: The next frontier. *Science, 317*, 23. (p. 642)

Holden, G. W., & Miller, P. C. (1999). Enduring and different: A meta-analysis of the similarity in parents' child rearing. *Psychological Bulletin, 125,* 223–254. (p. 193)

Holliday, R. E., & Albon, A. J. (2004). Minimizing misinformation effects in young children with cognitive interview mnemonics. *Applied Cognitive Psychology, 18,* 263–281. (p. 362)

Hollis, K. L. (1997). Contemporary research on Pavlovian conditioning: A "new" functional analysis. *American Psychologist, 52,* 956–965. (p. 292)

Hollon, S. D., & 10 others. (2005). Prevention of relapse following cognitive therapy vs. medications in moderate to severe depression. *Archives of General Psychiatry, 62,* 417–422. (p. 664)

Hollon, S. D., Thase, M. E., & Markowitz, J. C. (2002). Treatment and prevention of depression. *Psychological Science in the Public Interest, 3,* 39–77. (p. 674)

Holm-Denoma, J., Joiner, T., Vohs, K., & Heatherton, T. (2008). The "freshman fifteen" (the freshman five actually): Predictors and possible explanations. *Health Psychology, 27,* S3–S9. (p. 461)

Holstege, G., Georgiadis, J. R., Paans, A. M. J., Meiners, L. C., van der Graaf, F. H. C. E., & Reinders, A. A. T. S. (2003a). Brain activation during male ejaculation. *Journal of Neuroscience, 23,* 9185–9193. (p. 466)

Holstege, G., Reinders, A. A. T., Paans, A. M. J., Meiners, L. C., Pruim, J., & Georgiadis, J. R. (2003b). *Brain activation during female sexual orgasm. Program No. 727.7.* Washington, DC: Society for Neuroscience. (p. 466)

Holt, L. (2002, August). Reported in "Sounds of speech," p. 26, and in personal correspondence, July 18, 2002. (p. 385)

Home Office. (2003). *Prevalence of drug use: Key findings from the 2002/2003 British Crime Survey.* London: Research, Development and Statistics Directorate, Home Office. (p. 120)

Homer, B. D., Solomon, T. M., Moeller, R. W., Mascia, A., DeRaleau, L., & Halkitis, P. N. (2008). Methamphetamine abuse and impairment of social functioning: A review of the underlying neurophysiological causes and behavioral implications. *Psychological Bulletin, 134,* 301–310. (p. 118)

Hooper, J., & Teresi, D. (1986). *The three-pound universe.* New York: Macmillan. (p. 65)

Hooykaas, R. (1972). *Religion and the rise of modern science.* Grand Rapids, MI: Eerdmans. (p. 18)

Hopkins, W. D. (2006). Comparative and familial analysis of handedness in great apes. *Psychological Bulletin, 132,* 538–559. (p. 79)

Hopper, L. M., Lambeth, S. P., Schapiro, S. J., & Whiten, A. (2008). Observational learning in chimpanzees and children studied through 'ghost' conditions. *Proceedings of the Royal Society, 275,* 835–840. (p. 315)

Horn, J. L. (1982). The aging of human abilities. In J. Wolman (Ed.), *Handbook of developmental psychology.* Englewood Cliffs, NJ: Prentice-Hall. (p. 215)

Horner, V., Whiten, A., Flynn, E., & de Waal, F. B. M. (2006). Faithful replication of foraging techniques along cultural transmission chains by chimpanzees and children. *Proceedings of the National Academy of Sciences, 103,* 13878–13883. (p. 398)

Horowitz, T. S., Cade, B. E., Wolfe, J. M., & Czeisler, C. A. (2003). Searching night and day: A dissociation of effects of circadian phase and time awake on visual selective attention and vigilance. *Psychological Science, 14,* 549–557. (p. 98)

Horwood, L. J., & Fergusson, D. M. (1998). Breastfeeding and later cognitive and academic outcomes. *Pediatrics, 101*(1). (p. 30)

House, J. S., Landis, K. R., & Umberson, D. (1988). Social relationships and health. *Science, 241,* 540–545. (p. 545)

House, R. J., & Singh, J. V. (1987). Organizational behavior: Some new directions for I/O psychology. *Annual Review of Psychology, 38,* 669–718. (p. 495)

Houts, A. C., Berman, J. S., & Abramson, H. (1994). Effectiveness of psychological and pharmacological treatments for nocturnal enuresis. *Journal of Consulting and Clinical Psychology, 62,* 737–745. (p. 651)

Hovatta, I., Tennant, R. S., Helton, R., Marr, R. A., Singer, O., Redwine, J. M., Ellison, J. A., Schadt, E. E., Verma, I. M., Lockhart, D. J., & Barlow, C. (2005). Glyoxalase 1 and glutathione reductase 1 regulate anxiety in mice. *Nature, 438,* 662–666. (p. 616)

Howard Hughes Medication Institute. (2008). The quivering bundles that let us hear. (www.hhmi.org/senses/c120.html.), 244)

Howe, M. L. (1997). Children's memory for traumatic experiences. *Learning and Individual Differences, 9,* 153–174. (p. 362)

Howell, R. T., & Howell, C. J. (2008). The relation of economic status to subjective well-being in developing countries: A meta-analysis. *Psychological Bulletin, 134,* 536–560. (p. 524)

Hoyer, G., & Lund, E. (1993). Suicide among women related to number of children in marriage. *Archives of General Psychiatry, 50,* 134–137. (p. 630)

Hu, F. B., Li, T. Y., Colditz, G. A., Willett, W. C., & Manson, J. E. (2003). Television watching and other sedentary behaviors in relation to risk of obesity and type 2 diabetes mellitus in women. *Journal of the American Medical Association, 289,* 1785–1791. (p. 461)

Hu, X.-Z., & 13 others (2007). Association between a functional serotonin transporter promoter polymorphism and citalopram treatment in adult outpatients with major depression. *Archives of General Psychiatry, 64,* 783–792. (p. 629)

Hu, X.-Z., Lipsky, R. H., Zhu, G., Akhtar, L. A., Taubman, J., Greenberg, B. D., Xu, K., Arnold, P. D., Richter, M. A., Kennedy, J. L., Murphy, D. L., & Goldman, D. (2006). Serotonin transporter promoter gain-of-function genotypes are linked to obsessive-compulsive disorder. *American Journal of Human Genetics, 78,* 815–826. (p. 616)

Huart, J., Corneille, O., & Becquart, E. (2005). Face-based categorization, context-based categorization, and distortions in the recollection of gender ambiguous faces. *Journal of Experimental Social Psychology, 41,* 598–608. (p. 370)

Hubbard, E. M., Arman, A. C., Ramachandran, V. S., & Boynton, G. M. (2005). Individual differences among grapheme-color synesthetes: Brain-behavior correlations. *Neuron, 45,* 975–985. (p. 258)

Hubel, D. H. (1979, September). The brain. *Scientific American,* pp. 45–53. (p. 230)

Hubel, D. H., & Wiesel, T. N. (1979, September). Brian mechanisms of vision. *Scientific American,* pp. 150–162. (p. 238)

Hublin, C., Kaprio, J., Partinen, M., Heikkila, K., & Koskenvuo, M. (1997). Prevalence and genetics of sleepwalking—A population-based twin study. *Neurology, 48,* 177–181. (p. 102)

Hublin, C., Kaprio, J., Partinen, M., & Koskenvuo, M. (1998). Sleeptalking in twins: Epidemiology and psychiatric comorbidity. *Behavior Genetics, 28,* 289–298. (p. 102)

Hucker, S. J., & Bain, J. (1990). Androgenic hormones and sexual assault. In W. Marshall, R. Law, & H. Barbaree (Eds.), *The handbook on sexual assault.* New York: Plenum. (p. 468)

Hudson, J. I., Hiripi, E., Pope, H. G., & Kessler, R. C. (2007). The prevalence and correlates of eating disorders in the National Comorbidity Survey Replication. *Biological Psychiatry, 61,* 348–358. (p. 454)

Huey, E. D., Krueger, F., & Grafman, J. (2006). Representations in the human prefrontal cortex. *Current Directions in Psychological Science, 15,* 167–171. (p. 72)

Huffcutt, A. I., Conway, J. M., Roth, P. L., & Stone, N. J. (2001). Identification and meta-analytic assessment of psychological constructs measured in employment interviews. *Journal of Applied Psychology, 86,* 897–913. (p. 489)

Hugenberg, K., & Bodenhausen, G. V. (2003). Facing prejudice: Implicit prejudice and the perception of facial threat. *Psychological Science, 14,* 640–643. (p. 705)

Hughes, H. C. (1999). *Sensory exotica: A world beyond human experience.* Cambridge, MA: MIT Press. (p. 227)

Hugick, L. (1989, July). Women play the leading role in keeping modern families close. *Gallup Report, No. 286,* p. 27–34. (p. 159)

Huizink, A. C., & Mulder, E. J. (2006). Maternal smoking, drinking or cannabis use during pregnancy and neurobehavioral and cognitive functioning in human offspring. *Neuroscience and Biobehavioral Reviews, 30,* 24–41. (p. 124)

Hulbert, A. (2005, November 20). The prodigy puzzle. *New York Times Magazine* (www.nytimes.com). (p. 426)

Hull, H. R., Morrow, M. L., Dinger, M. K., Han, J. L., & Fields, D. A. (2007, November 20). Characterization of body weight and composition changes during the sophomore year of college. *BMC Women's Health, 7,* 21 (biomedcentral.com). (p. 98)

Hull, J. G., & Bond, C. F., Jr. (1986). Social and behavioral consequences of alcohol consumption and expectancy: A meta-analysis. *Psychological Bulletin, 99,* 347–360. (p. 116)

Hull, J. M. (1990). *Touching the rock: An experience of blindness.* New York: Vintage Books. (pp. 347, 721)

Hulme, C., & Tordoff, V. (1989). Working memory development: The effects of speech rate, word length, and acoustic similarity on serial recall. *Journal of Experimental Child Psychology, 47,* 72–87. (p. 338)

Hummer, R. A., Rogers, R. G., Nam, C. B., & Ellison, C. G. (1999). Religious involvement and U.S. adult mortality. *Demography, 36,* 273–285. (p. 553)

Humphrey, S. E., Nahrgang, J. D., & Morgeson, F. P. (2007). Integrating motivational, social, and contextual work design features: A meta-analytic summary and theoretical extension of the work design literature. *Journal of Applied Psychology, 92,* 1332-1356. (p. 586)

Humphreys, L. G., & Davey, T. C. (1988). Continuity in intellectual growth from 12 months to 9 years. *Intelligence, 12,* 183–197. (p. 423)

Hunsberger, J. G., Newton, S. S., Bennett, A. H., Duman, C. H., Russell, D. S., Salton, S. R., & Duman, R. S. (2007). Antidepressant actions of the exercise-regulated gene VGF. *Nature Medicine, 13,* 1476–1482. (p. 549)

Hunsley, J., & Di Giulio, G. (2002). Dodo bird, phoenix, or urban legend? The question of psychotherapy equivalence. *Scientific Review of Mental Health Practice, 1,* 11–22. (p. 663)

Hunt, C., Slade, T., & Andrews, G. (2004). Generalized anxiety disorder and major depressive disorder comorbidity in the National Survey of Mental Health and Well-Being. *Depression and Anxiety, 20,* 23–31. (p. 610)

Hunt, E. (1983). On the nature of intelligence. *Science, 219,* 141–146. (p. 413)

Hunt, E., & Carlson, J. (2007). Considerations relating to the study of group differences in intelligence. *Perspectives on Psychological Science, 2,* 194–213. (pp. 438, 439)

Hunt, J. M. (1982). Toward equalizing the developmental opportunities of infants and preschool children. *Journal of Social Issues, 38*(4), 163–191. (p. 430)

Hunt, M. (1974). *Sexual behavior in the 1970s.* Chicago: Playboy Press. (p. 470)

Hunt, M. (1990). *The compassionate beast: What science is discovering about the humane side of humankind.* New York: William Morrow. (pp. 4, 11)

Hunt, M. (1993). *The story of psychology.* New York: Doubleday. (pp. 2, 3, 4, 45, 201, 299, 426)

Hunter, J. E. (1997). Needed: A ban on the significance test. *Psychological Science, 8,* 3–7. (p. 41)

Hunter, S., & Sundel, M. (Eds.). (1989). *Midlife myths: Issues, findings, and practice implications.* Newbury Park, CA: Sage. (p. 216)

Hurst, M. (2008, April 22). Who gets any sleep these days? Sleep patterns of Canadians. *Canadian Social Trends.* Statistics Canada Catalogue No. 11-008. (p. 96)

Huss, M. (1996). Secrets to standing out from the pile: Getting into graduate school. *Psi Chi Newsletter,* 6–7. (p. A-10)

Hussein, S. (2002, July 17 and August 28). Speeches to the Iraqi people as reported by various media. (p. 731)

Huston, A. C., Donnerstein, E., Fairchild, H., Feshbach, N. D., Katz, P. A., & Murray, J. P. (1992). *Big world, small screen: The role of television in American society.* Lincoln: University of Nebraska Press. (p. 319)

Hvistendahl, M. (2008, July 9). No country for young men. *New Republic* (www.tnr.com). (p. 704)

Hyde, J. (2005). The gender similarities hypothesis. *American Psychologist, 60,* 581–592. (p. 157)

Hyde, J. S. (1983, November). Bem's gender schema theory. Paper presented at GLCA Women's Studies Conference, Rochester, IN. (p. 357)

Hyde, J. S., Fennema, E., & Lamon, S. J. (1990). Gender differences in mathematics performance: A meta-analysis. *Psychological Bulletin, 107,* 139–155. (p. 433)

Hyde, J. S., Mezulis, A. H., & Abramson, L. Y. (2008). The ABCs of depression: Integrating affective, biological, and cognitive models to explain the emergence of the gender difference in depression. *Psychological Review, 115,* 291–313. (pp. 433, 627)

Hyman, R. (1981). Cold reading: How to convince strangers that you know all about them. In K. Frazier (Ed.), *Paranormal borderlands of science.* Buffalo, NY: Prometheus. (p. 578)

Iacoboni, M. (2008). *Mirroring people: The new science of how we connect with others.* New York: Farrar, Straus & Giroux. (p. 316)

IAP. (2006, June 21). IAP statement on the teaching of evolution. *The Interacademy Panel on International Issues* (www.interacademies.net/iap). (p. 165)

Ickes, W., Snyder, M., & Garcia, S. (1997). Personality influences on the choice of situations. In R. Hogan, J. Johnson, & S. Briggs (Eds.). *Handbook of personality psychology.* San Diego, CA: Academic Press. (p. 584)

Idson, L. C., & Mischel, W. (2001). The personality of familiar and significant people: The lay perceiver as a social-cognitive theorist. *Journal of Personality and Social Psychology, 80,* 585–596. (p. 683)

Ikonomidou, C., Bittigau, P., Ishimaru, M. J., Wozniak, D. F., Koch, C., Genz, K., Price, M. T., Stefovska, V., Hoerster, F., Tenkova, T., Dikranian, K., & Olney, J. W. (2000). Ethanol-induced apoptotic neurodegeneration and fetal alcohol syndrome. *Science, 287,* 1056–1060. (p. 172)

Ilardi, S. S., Karwoski, L., Lehman, K. A., Stites, B. A., & Steidtmann, D. (2007). *We were never designed for this: The depression epidemic and the promise of therapeutic lifestyle change.* Unpublished manuscript, University of Kansas, in press. (pp. 548, 632, 678)

Independent Sector. (2002). Faith and philanthropy: The connection between charitable giving behavior and giving to religion. Washington, DC: Author. (p. 729)

Ingham, A. G., Levinger, G., Graves, J., & Peckham, V. (1974). The Ringelmann effect: Studies of group size and group performance. *Journal of Experimental Social Psychology, 10,* 371–384. (p. 698)

Inglehart, R. (1990). *Culture shift in advanced industrial society.* Princeton, NJ: Princeton University Press. (pp. 219, 481, 485, 586)

Inglehart, R. (2008, June 30). Subjective well-being in 97 countries based on reported happiness and life satisfaction, equally weighted. World Values Survey distributed by University of Michigan News Service: umich.edu/news/happy_08/HappyChart.pdf. (p. 524)

Inglehart, R. (2009). Cultural change and democracy in Latin America. In F. Hagopian (Ed.), *Contemporary Catholicism, religious pluralism and democracy in Latin America.* South Bend, IN: Notre Dame University Press, in press. (pp. 524, 586)

Inman, M. L., & Baron, R. S. (1996). Influence of prototypes on perceptions of prejudice. *Journal of Personality and Social Psychology, 70,* 727–739. (p. 371)

Insana, R. (2005, February 21). Coach says honey gets better results than vinegar (interview with Larry Brown). *USA Today,* p. 4B. (p. 494)

Inzlicht, M., & Ben-Zeev, T. (2000). A threatening intellectual environment: Why females are susceptible to experiencing problem-solving deficits in the presence of males. *Psychological Science, 11,* 365–371. (p. 439)

Inzlicht, M., & Gutsell, J. N. (2007). Running on empty: Neural signals for self-control failure. *Psychological Science, 18,* 933–937. (p. 585)

Ipsos. (2006, February 21). Sexual behaviour and lack of knowledge threaten health of Canadian teens. Ipsos Reid (www.ipsos-na.com). (p. 470)

IPU. (2008). Women in national parliaments: Situation as of 30 April 2008. International Parliamentary Union (www.ipu.org). (p. 158)

Iraq Family Health Survey Study Group. (2008). Violence-related mortality in Iraq from 2002 to 2006. *New England Journal of Medicine, 358,* 484–493. (p. 681)

Ironson, G., Solomon, G. F., Balbin, E. G., O'Cleirigh, C., George, A., Kumar, M., Larson, D., & Woods, T. E. (2002). The Ironson-Woods spiritual/religiousness index is associated with long survival, health behaviors, less distress, and low cortisol in people with HIV/AIDS. *Annals of Behavioral Medicine, 24,* 34–48. (p. 554)

Irwin, M. R., Cole, J. C., & Nicassio, P. M. (2006). Comparative meta-analysis of behavioral interventions for insomnia and their efficacy in middle-aged adults and in older adults 55+ years of age. *Health Psychology, 25,* 3-14. (p. 100)

Ishida, A., Mutoh, T., Ueyama, T., Brando, H., Masubuchi, S., Nakahara, D., Tsujimoto, G., & Okamura, H. (2005). Light activates the adrenal gland: Timing of gene expression and glucocorticoid release. *Cell Metabolism, 2,* 297–307. (p. 666)

Iso, H., Simoda, S., & Matsuyama, T. (2007). Environmental change during postnatal development alters behaviour. *Behavioural Brain Research, 179,* 90–98. (p. 74)

Ito, T. A., Chiao, K. W., Devine P. G., Lorig, T. S., & Cacioppo, J. T. (2006). The influence of facial feedback on race bias. *Psychological Science, 17,* 256–261. (p. 516)

Ito, T. A., Miller, N., & Pollock, V. E. (1996). Alcohol and aggression: A meta-analysis on the moderating effects of inhibitory cues, triggering events, and self-focused attention. *Psychological Bulletin, 120,* 60–82. (p. 711)

Iversen, L. L. (2000). *The science of marijuana.* New York: Oxford. (p. 124)

Iverson, J. M., & Goldin-Meadow, S. (1998). Why people gesture when they speak. *Nature, 396,* 228. (p. 400)

Iverson, J. M., & Goldin-Meadow, S. (2005). Gesture paves the way for language development. *Psychological Science, 16,* 367–371. (p. 400)

Iyengar, S. S., & Lepper, M. R. (2000). When choice is demotivating: Can one desire too much of a good thing? *Journal of Personality and Social Psychology, 79,* 995–1006. (p. 587)

Izard, C. E. (1977). *Human emotions.* New York: Plenum Press. (pp. 513, 517)

Izard, C. E. (1994). Innate and universal facial expressions: Evidence from developmental and cross-cultural research. *Psychological Bulletin, 114,* 288–299. (p. 513)

Jablensky, A. (1999). Schizophrenia: Epidemiology. *Current Opinion in Psychiatry, 12,* 19–28. (p. 640)

Jackson, J. M., & Williams, K. D. (1988). *Social loafing: A review and theoretical analysis.* Unpublished manuscript, Fordham University. (p. 698)

Jackson, J. S., Brown, K. T., Brown, T. N., & Marks, B. (2001). Contemporary immigration policy orientations among dominant-group members in western Europe. *Journal of Social Issues, 57,* 431–456. (p. 704)

Jackson, L. A., & Gerard, D. A. (1996). Diurnal types, the "Big Five" personality factors and other personal characteristics. *Journal of Social Behavior and Personality, 11,* 273–283. (p. 580)

Jackson, S. W. (1992). The listening healer in the history of psychological healing. *American Journal Psychiatry, 149,* 1623–1632. (p. 668)

Jacobi, C., Hayward, C., deZwaan, M., Kraemer, H. C., & Agras, W. S. (2004). Coming to terms with risk factors for eating disorders: Application of risk terminology and suggestions for a general taxonomy. *Psychological Bulletin, 130,* 19–65. (p. 454)

Jacobs, B., van Praag, H., & Gage, F. H. (2000). Adult brain neurogenesis and psychiatry: A novel theory of depression. *Molecular Psychiatry, 5,* 262–269. (p. 632)

Jacobs, B. L. (1987). How hallucinogenic drugs work. *American Scientist, 75,* 386–392. (p. 122)

Jacobs, B. L. (1994). Serotonin, motor activity, and depression-related disorders. *American Scientist, 82,* 456–463. (pp. 548, 632)

Jacobs, B. L. (2004). Depression: The brain finally gets into the act. *Current Directions in Psychological Science, 13,* 103–106. (p. 673)

Jacoby, L. L., Bishara, A. J., Hessels, S., & Toth, J. P. (2005). Aging, subjective experience, and cognitive control: Dramatic false remembering by older adults. *Journal of Experimental Psychology: General, 154,* 131–148. (p. 362)

Jacoby, L. L., & Rhodes, M. G. (2006). False remembering in the aged. *Current Directions in Psychological Science, 15,* 49–53. (p. 362)

Jacques, C., & Rossion, B. (2006). The speed of individual face categorization. *Psychological Science, 17,* 485–492. (p. 225)

Jacques-Tiura, A. J., Abbey, A., Parkhill, M. R., & Zawacki, T. (2007). Why do some men misperceive women's sexual intentions more frequently than others do? An application of the confluence model. *Personality and Social Psychology Bulletin, 33,* 1467–1480. (p. 684)

Jaffe, E. (2004, October). Peace in the Middle East may be impossible: Lee D. Ross on naive realism and conflict resolution. *APS Observer,* pp. 9–11. (p. 278)

James, K. (1986). Priming and social categorizational factors: Impact on awareness of emergency situations. *Personality and Social Psychology Bulletin, 12,* 462–467. (p. 348)

James, W. (1890). *The principles of psychology* (Vol. 2). New York: Holt. (pp. 55, 111, 251, 351, 366, 500, 689)

James, W. (1902; reprinted 1958). *Varieties of religious experience.* New York: Mentor Books. (p. 521)

Jameson, D. (1985). Opponent-colors theory in light of physiological findings. In D. Ottoson & S. Zeki (Eds.), *Central and peripheral mechanisms of color vision.* New York: Macmillan. (p. 269)

Jamison, K. R. (1993). *Touched with fire: Manic-depressive illness and the artistic temperament.* New York: Free Press. (p 626)

Jamison, K. R. (1995). *An unquiet mind.* New York: Knopf. (pp. 626, 674)

Janis, I. L. (1982). Groupthink: Psychological studies of policy decisions and fiascoes. Boston: Houghton Mifflin. (p. 700)

Janis, I. L. (1986). Problems of international crisis management in the nuclear age. *Journal of Social Issues, 42*(2), 201–220. (p. 374)

Janoff-Bulman, R., Timko, C., & Carli, L. L. (1985). Cognitive biases in blaming the victim. *Journal of Experimental Social Psychology, 21,* 161–177. (p. 709)

Javitt, D. C., & Coyle, J. T. (2004, January). Decoding schizophrenia. *Scientific American,* pp. 48–55. (p. 640)

Jeffery, R. W., Drewnowski, A., Epstein, L. H., Stunkard, A. J., Wilson, G. T., Wing, R. R., & Hill, D. R. (2000). Long-term maintenance of weight loss: Current status. *Health Psychology, 19,* No. 1 (Supplement), 5–16. (p. 463)

Jenkins, J. G., & Dallenbach, K. M. (1924). Obliviscence during sleep and waking. *American Journal of Psychology, 35,* 605–612. (pp. 354, 355)

Jenkins, J. M., & Astington, J. W. (1996). Cognitive factors and family structure associated with theory of mind development in young children. *Developmental Psychology, 32,* 70–78. (p. 181)

Jensen, A. R. (1980). *Bias in mental testing.* New York: Free Press. (p. 422)

Jensen, A. R. (1983, August). The nature of the Black-White difference on various psychometric tests: Spearman's hypothesis. Paper presented at the meeting of the American Psychological Association, Anaheim, CA. (p. 438)

Jensen, A. R. (1989). New findings on the intellectually gifted. *New Horizons, 30,* 73–80. (p. 413)

Jensen, A. R. (1998). *The g factor: The science of mental ability.* Westport, CT: Praeger/Greenwood. (p. 438)

Jensen, J. P., & Bergin, A. E. (1988). Mental health values of professional therapists: A national interdisciplinary survey. *Professional Psychology: Research and Practice, 19,* 290–297. (p. 668)

Jensen, P. S., & 20 others. (2007). 3-year follow-up of the NIMH MTA study. *Journal of the American Academy of Child and Adolescent Psychiatry, 46,* 989–1002. (p. 600)

Jepson, C., Krantz, D. H., & Nisbett, R. E. (1983). Inductive reasoning: Competence or skill. *The Behavioral and Brain Sciences, 3,* 494–501. (pp. 43, B-1)

Jessberger, S., Aimone, J. B., & Gage, F. H. (2008). Neurogenesis. In *Learning and memory: A comprehensive reference.* Oxford: Elsevier. (p. 74)

Job, D. E., Whalley, H. C., McIntosh, A. M., Owens, D. G. C., Johnstone, E. C., & Lawrie, S. M. (2006). Grey matter changes can improve the prediction of schizophrenia in subjects at high risk. *BMC Medicine, 4,* 29. (p. 640)

Johansson, P., Hall, L., Sikström, S., & Olsson, A. (2005). Failure to detect mismatches between intention and outcome in a simple decision task. *Science, 310,* 116–119. (p. 89)

John, O. P., & Srivastava, S. (1999). The Big Five trait taxonomy: History, measurement, and theoretical perspectives. In L. A. Pervin & O. P. John (Eds.), *Handbook of personality: Theory and research.* New York: Guilford. (p. 577)

Johnson, C. B., Stockdale, M. S., & Saal, F. E. (1991). Persistence of men's misperceptions of friendly cues across a variety of interpersonal encounters. *Psychology of Women Quarterly, 15,* 463–475. (p. 144)

Johnson, D. F. (1997). Margaret Floy Washburn. *Psychology of Women Newsletter,* pp. 17, 22. (p. 4)

Johnson, D. L., Wiebe, J. S., Gold, S. M., Andreasen, N. C., Hichwa, R. D., Watkins, G. L., & Ponto, L. L. B. (1999). Cerebral blood flow and personality: A positron emission tomography study. *American Journal of Psychiatry, 156,* 252–257. (p. 576)

Johnson, E. J., & Goldstein, D. (2003). Do defaults save lives? *Science, 302,* 1338–1339. (p. 382)

Johnson, J. A. (2007, June 26). Not so situational. Commentary on the SPSP listserv (spsp-discuss@stolaf.edu). (p. 688)

Johnson, J. G., Cohen, P., Kotler, L., Kasen, S., & Brook, J. S. (2002). Psychiatric disorders associated with risk for the development of eating disorders during adolescence and early adulthood. *Journal of Consulting and Clinical Psychology, 70,* 1119–1128. (p. 454)

Johnson, J. S., & Newport, E. L. (1991). Critical period affects on universal properties of language: The status of subjacency in the acquisition of a second language. *Cognition, 39,* 215–258. (p. 390)

Johnson, K. (2008, January 29). For many of USA's inmates, crime runs in the family. *USA Today*, pp. 1A, 2A. (p. 621)

Johnson, L. C. (2001, July 10). The declining terrorist threat. *New York Times* (www.nytimes.com). (p. 378)

Johnson, M. E., & Hauck, C. (1999). Beliefs and opinions about hypnosis held by the general public: A systematic evaluation. *American Journal of Clinical Hypnosis, 42*, 10–20. (p. 109)

Johnson, M. H. (1992). Imprinting and the development of face recognition: From chick to man. *Current Directions in Psychological Science, 1*, 52–55. (p. 187)

Johnson, M. H., & Morton, J. (1991). *Biology and cognitive development: The case of face recognition.* Oxford: Blackwell Publishing. (p. 173)

Johnson, R. E., Chang, C-H., & Lord, R. G. (2006). Moving from cognition to behavior: What the research says. *Psychological Bulletin, 132*, 381–415. (p. 494)

Johnson, S. C., & 13 others (2006). Activation of brain regions vulnerable to Alzheimer's disease: The effect of mild cognitive impairment. *Neurobiology of Aging, 27*, 1604–1612. (p. 212)

Johnson, S. K. (2008). *Medically unexplained illness: Gender and biopsychosocial implications.* Washington, DC: American Psychological Association. (p. 622)

Johnson, W., McGue, M., & Krueger, R. F. (2005). Personality stability in late adulthood: A behavioral genetic analysis. *Journal of Personality, 73*, 523–552. (p. 223)

Johnston, L. D., O'Malley, P. M., Bachman, J. G., & Schulenberg, J. E. (2007). *Monitoring the Future national results on adolescent drug use: Overview of key findings, 2006.* Bethesda, MD: National Institute on Drug Abuse. (p. 127)

Johnston, L. D., O'Malley, P. M., Bachman, J. G., & Schulenberg, J. E. (2008). *Monitoring the Future national results on adolescent drug use: Overview of key findings, 2007.* Bethesda, MD: National Institute on Drug Abuse. (pp. 120, 125)

Johnston, L. D., O'Malley, P. M., Bachman, J. G., & Schulenberg, J. E. (2009). *Monitoring the Future national results on adolescent drug use: Overview of key findings, 2008* (NIH Publication No. 09-7401). Bethesda, MD: National Institute on Drug Abuse.

Johnstone, E. C., Ebmeier, K. P., Miller, P., Owens, D. G. C., & Lawrie, S. M. (2005). Predicting schizophrenia: Findings from the Edinburgh High-Risk Study. *British Journal of Psychiatry, 186*, 18–25. (p. 643)

Joiner, T. (2006). *Why people die by suicide.* Cambridge, MA: Harvard University Press. (p. 631)

Joiner, T. E., Jr. (1999). The clustering and contagion of suicide. *Current Directions in Psychological Science, 8*, 89–92. (p. 691)

Jolly, A. (2007). The social origin of mind. *Science, 317*, 1326. (p. 397)

Jonas, E., & Fischer, P. (2006). Terror management and religion: Evidence that intrinsic religiousness mitigates worldview defense following mortality salience. *Journal of Personality and Social Psychology, 91*, 553–567. (p. 567)

Jones, A. C., & Gosling, S. D. (2005). Temperament and personality in dogs (*Canis familiaris*): A review and evaluation of past research. *Applied Animal Behaviour Science, 95*, 1–53. (p. 576)

Jones, J. M. (2003, February 12). Fear of terrorism increases amidst latest warning. *Gallup News Service* (www.gallup.com/releases/pr030212.asp). (p. 610)

Jones, J. M. (2007, July 25). Latest Gallup update shows cigarette smoking near historical lows. *Gallup Poll News Service* (poll.gallup.com). (p. 120)

Jones, J. T., Pelham, B. W., Carvallo, M., & Mirenberg, M. C. (2004). How do I love thee? Let me count the Js: Implicit egotism and interpersonal attraction. *Journal of Personality and Social Psychology, 87*, 665–683. (p. 719)

Jones, L. (2000, December). Skeptics New Year quiz. *Skeptical Briefs*, p. 11. (p. 579)

Jones, M. C. (1924). A laboratory study of fear: The case of Peter. *Journal of Genetic Psychology, 31*, 308–315. (p. 651)

Jones, M. V., Paull, G. C., & Erskine, J. (2002). The impact of a team's aggressive reputation on the decisions of association football referees. *Journal of Sports Sciences, 20*, 991–1000. (p. 278)

Jones, S. S. (2007). Imitation in infancy: The development of mimicry. *Psychological Science, 18*, 593–599. (p. 316)

Jones, S. S., Collins, K., & Hong, H.-W. (1991). An audience effect on smile production in 10-month-old infants. *Psychological Science, 2*, 45–49. (p. 514)

Jones, W. H., Carpenter, B. N., & Quintana, D. (1985). Personality and interpersonal predictors of loneliness in two cultures. *Journal of Personality and Social Psychology, 48*, 1503–1511. (p. 20)

Jonides, J., Lewis, R. L., Nee, D. E., Lustig, C. A., Berman, M. G., & Moore, K. S. (2008). The mind and brain of short-term memory. *Annual Review of Psychology, 59*, 193–224. (p. 338)

Jorm, A. F., Korten, A. E., & Henderson, A. S. (1987). The prevalence of dementia: A quantitative integration of the literature. *Acta Psychiatrica Scandinavica, 76*, 465–479. (p. 211)

Joseph, J. (2001). Separated twins and the genetics of personality differences: A critique. *American Journal of Psychology, 114*, 1–30. (p. 136)

Judge, T. A., Thoresen, C. J., Bono, J. E., & Patton, G. K. (2001). The job satisfaction/job performance relationship: A qualitative and quantitative review. *Psychological Bulletin, 127*, 376–407. (p. 491)

Juffer, F., & van IJzendoorn, M. H. (2007). Adoptees do not lack self-esteem: A meta-analysis of studies on self-esteem of transracial, international, and domestic adoptees. *Psychological Bulletin, 133*, 1067–1083. (p. 192)

Jung, R. E., & Haier, R. J. (2007). The Parieto-Frontal Integration Theory (P-FIT) of intelligence: Converging neuroimaging evidence. *Behavioral and Brain Sciences, 30*, 135–187. (p. 412)

Jung-Beeman, M., Bowden, E. M., Haberman, J., Frymiare, J. L., Arambel-Liu, S., Greenblatt, R., Reber, P. J., & Kounios, J. (2004). Neural activity when people solve verbal problems with insight. *PLoS Biology 2*(4), e111. (pp. 371, 372)

Kagan, J. (1976). Emergent themes in human development. *American Scientist, 64*, 186–196. (p. 188)

Kagan, J. (1984). *The nature of the child.* New York: Basic Books. (p. 185)

Kagan, J. (1995). On attachment. *Harvard Review of Psychiatry, 3*, 104–106. (p. 187)

Kagan, J. (1998). *Three seductive ideas.* Cambridge, MA: Harvard University Press. (pp. 80, 222)

Kagan, J., Arcus, D., Snidman, N., Feng, W. Y., Hendler, J., & Greene, S. (1994). Reactivity in infants: A cross-national comparison. *Developmental Psychology, 30*, 342–345. (p. 138)

Kagan, J., Lapidus, D. R., & Moore, M. (December, 1978). Infant antecedents of cognitive functioning: A longitudinal study. *Child Development, 49*(4), 1005–1023. (p. 222)

Kagan, J., & Snidman, N. (2004). *The long shadow of temperament.* Cambridge, MA: Belknap Press. (p. 138)

Kagan, J., Snidman, N., & Arcus, D. M. (1992). Initial reactions to unfamiliarity. *Current Directions in Psychological Science, 1*, 171–174. (p. 138)

Kahlor, L., & Morrison, D. (2007). Television viewing and rape myth acceptance among college women. *Sex Roles, 56*, 729–739. (p. 714)

Kahneman, D. (1985, June). Quoted by K. McKean, Decisions, decisions. *Discover*, pp. 22–31. (p. 662)

Kahneman, D. (1999). Assessments of objective happiness: A bottom-up approach. In D. Kahneman, E. Diener, & N. Schwartz (Eds.), *Understanding well-being: Scientific perspectives on enjoyment and suffering.* New York: Russell Sage Foundation. (p. 255)

Kahneman, D. (2005, January 13). What were they thinking? Q&A with Daniel Kahneman. *Gallup Management Journal* (gmj.gallup.com). (p. 375)

Kahneman, D. (2005, February 10). Are you happy now? *Gallup Management Journal* interview (www.gmj.gallup.com). (p. 523)

Kahneman, D., Fredrickson, B. L., Schreiber, C. A., & Redelmeier, D. A. (1993). When more pain is preferred to less: Adding a better end. *Psychological Science, 4*, 401–405. (p. 255)

Kahneman, D., Krueger, A. B., Schkade, D. A., Schwarz, N., & Stone, A. A. (2004). A survey method for characterizing daily life experience: The day reconstruction method. *Science, 306*, 1776–1780. (pp. 97, 522)

Kahneman, D., & Renshon, J. (2007, January/February). Why hawks win. *Foreign Policy* (www.foreignpolicy.com). (p. 593)

Kahneman, D., & Tversky, A. (1972). Subjective probability: A judgment of representativeness. *Cognitive Psychology, 3*, 430–454. (p. 33)

Kail, R. (1991). Developmental change in speed of processing during childhood and adolescence. *Psychological Bulletin, 109*, 490–501. (p. 210)

Kaiser. (2001). Inside-out: A report on the experiences of lesbians, gays and bisexuals in America and the public's views on issues and policies related to sexual orientation. The Henry J. Kaiser Foundation (www.kff.org). (p. 478)

Kaiser Family Foundation. (2003, October 28). New study finds children age zero to six spend as much time with TV, computers and video games as playing outside. www.kff.org/entmedia/entmedia102803nr.cfm. (p. 30)

Kamarck, T., & Jennings, J. R. (1991). Biobehavioral factors in sudden cardiac death. *Psychological Bulletin, 109,* 42–75. (p. 536)

Kamena, M. (1998). Repressed/false childhood sexual abuse memories: A survey of therapists. Paper presented to the Sexual Abuse memories Symposium at the American Psychological Association convention. (p. 362)

Kamil, A. C., & Cheng, K. (2001). Way-finding and landmarks: The multiple-bearings hypothesis. *Journal of Experimental Biology, 204,* 103–113. (p. 343)

Kaminski, J., Cali, J., & Fischer, J. (2004). Word learning in a domestic dog: Evidence for "fast mapping." *Science, 304,* 1682–1683. (p. 399)

Kanaya, T., Scullin, M. H., & Ceci, S. J. (2003). The Flynn effect and U.S. policies: The impact of rising IQ scores on American society via mental retardation diagnoses. *American Psychologist, 58,* 778–790. (p. 425)

Kanazawa, S. (2004). General intelligence as a domain-specific adaptation. *Psychological Review, 111,* 512–523. (p. 405)

Kanazawa, S. (2006). Mind the gap . . . in intelligence: Re-examining the relationship between inequality and health. *British Journal of Health Psychology, 11,* 623–642. (p. 543)

Kandel, D. B., & Raveis, V. H. (1989). Cessation of illicit drug use in young adulthood. *Archives of General Psychiatry, 46,* 109–116. (p. 127)

Kandel, E. R., & Schwartz, J. H. (1982). Molecular biology of learning Modulation of transmitter release. *Science, 218,* 433–443. (p. 339)

Kane, M. J., Brown, L. H., McVay, J. C., Silvia, P. J., Myin-Germeys, I., & Kwapil, T. R. (2007). For whom the mind wanders, and when: An experience-sampling study of working memory and executive control in daily life. *Psychological Science, 18,* 614–621. (p. 326)

Kaplan, A. (2004). Exploring the gene-environment nexus in anorexia, bulimia. *Psychiatric Times, 21* (www.psychiatrictimes.com/p040801b.html). (p. 454)

Kaplan, H. I., & Saddock, B. J. (Eds.). (1989). *Comprehensive textbook of psychiatry, V.* Baltimore, MD: Williams and Wilkins. (p. 672)

Kaplan, R. M., & Kronick, R. G. (2006). Marital status and longevity in the United States population. *Journal of Epidemiology and Community Health, 60,* 760–765. (p. 545)

Kaprio, J., Koskenvuo, M., & Rita, H. (1987). Mortality after bereavement: A prospective study of 95,647 widowed persons. *American Journal of Public Health, 77,* 283–287. (p. 534)

Kaptchuk, T. J., Stason, W. B., Davis, R. B., Legedza, A. R. T., Schnyer, R. N., Kerr, C. E., Stone, D. A., Nam, B. H., Kirsch, I., & Goldman, R. H. (2006). Sham device v inert pill: Randomised controlled trial of two placebo treatments. *British Medical Journal, 332,* 391–397. (p. 256)

Karacan, I., Aslan, C., & Hirshkowitz, M. (1983). Erectile mechanisms in man. *Science, 220,* 1080–1082. (p. 94)

Karacan, I., Goodenough, D. R., Shapiro, A., & Starker, S. (1966). Erection cycle during sleep in relation to dream anxiety. *Archives of General Psychiatry, 15,* 183–189. (p. 94)

Karau, S. J., & Williams, K. D. (1993). Social loafing: A meta-analytic review and theoretical integration. *Journal of Personality and Social Psychology, 65,* 681–706. (p. 698)

Kark, J. D., Shemi, G., Friedlander, Y., Martin, O., Manor, O., & Blondheim, S. H. (1996). Does religious observance promote health? Mortality in secular vs. religious kibbutzim in Israel. *American Journal of Public Health, 86,* 341–346. (p. 552)

Karni, A., Meyer, G., Rey-Hipolito, C., Jezzard, P., Adams, M. M., Turner, R., & Ungerleider, L. G. (1998). The acquisition of skilled motor performance: Fast and slow experience-driven changes in primary motor cortex. *Proceedings of the National Academy of Sciences, 95,* 861–868. (p. 149)

Karni, A., & Sagi, D. (1994). Dependence on REM sleep for overnight improvement of perceptual skills. *Science, 265,* 679–682. (p. 104)

Karno, M., Golding, J. M., Sorenson, S. B., & Burnam, A. (1988). The epidemiology of obsessive-compulsive disorder in five US communities. *Archives of General Psychiatry, 45,* 1094–1099. (p. 612)

Karpicke, J. D., & Roediger, H. L., III. (2008). The critical importance of retrieval for learning. *Science, 319,* 966–968. (p. 330)

Karremans, J. C., Stroebe, W., & Claus, J. (2006). Beyond Vicary's fantasies: The impact of subliminal priming and brand choice. *Journal of Experimental Social Psychology, 42,* 792–798. (p. 229)

Kasen, S., Chen, H., Sneed, J., Crawford, T., & Cohen, P. (2006). Social role and birth cohort influences on gender-linked personality traits in women: A 20-year longitudinal analysis. *Journal of Personality and Social Psychology, 91,* 944–958. (p. 160)

Kashima, Y. Siegal, M., Tanaka, K., & Kashima, E. S. (1992). Do people believe behaviours are consistent with attitudes? Towards a cultural psychology of attribution processes. *British Journal of Social Psychology, 31,* 111–124. (p. 155)

Kasser, T. (2000). Two version of the American dream: Which goals and values make for a high quality of life? In E. Diener (Ed.), *Advances in quality of life theory and research.* Dordrecht, Netherlands: Kluwer. (p. 526)

Kasser, T. (2002). *The high price of materialism.* Cambridge, MA: MIT Press. (p. 526)

Kaufman, A S., Reynolds, C. R., & McLean, J. E. (1989). Age and WAIS-R intelligence in a national sample of adults in the 20- to 74-year age range: A cross-sectional analysis with educational level controlled. *Intelligence, 13,* 235–253. (p. 215)

Kaufman, J. & Zigler, E. (1987). Do abused children become abusive parents? *American Journal of Orthopsychiatry, 57,* 186–192. (p. 190)

Kaufman, J. C., & Baer, J. (2002). I bask in dreams of suicide: Mental illness, poetry, and women. *Review of General Psychology, 6,* 271–286. (p. 626)

Kaufman, L. & Kaufman, J. H. (2000). Explaining the moon illusion. *Proceedings of the National Academy of Sciences, 97,* 500–505. (p. 268)

Kavsek, M. (2004). Predicting later IQ from infant visual habituation and dishabituation: A meta-analysis. *Journal of Applied Developmental Psychology, 25,* 369–393. (p. 423)

Kayser, C. (2007, April/May). Listening with your eyes. *Scientific American Mind,* pp. 24–29. (p. 258)

Kazdin, A. E. & Benjet, C. (2003). Spanking children: Evidence and issues. *Current Directions in Psychological Science, 12,* 99–103. (p. 307)

Keesey, R. E., & Corbett, S. W. (1983). Metabolic defense of the body weight set-point. In A. J. Stunkard & E. Stellar (Eds.), *Eating and its disorders.* New York: Raven Press. (p. 451)

Keith, S. W., & 19 others (2006). Putative contributors to the secular increase in obesity: Exploring the roads less traveled. *International Journal of Obesity, 30,* 1585–1594. (p. 460)

Kellehear, A. (1996). *Experiences near death: Beyond medicine and religion.* New York: Oxford University Press. (p. 123)

Keller, J. (2007, March 9). As football players get bigger, more of them risk a dangerous sleep disorder. *Chronicle of Higher Education,* pp. A43–A44. (p. 102)

Keller, M. B., McCullough, J. P., Klein, D. N., Arnow, B., Dunner, D. L., Gelenberg, A. J., Markowitz, J. C., Nemeroff, C. B., Russell, J. M., Thase, M. E., Trivedi, M. H., & Zajecka J. (2000). A comparison of nefazodone, the cognitive behavioral-analysis system of psychotherapy, and their combination for the treatment of chronic depression. *New England Journal of Medicine, 342,* 1462–1470. (p. 674)

Keller, M. C., Neale, M. C., & Kendler, K. S. (2007). Association of different adverse life events with distinct patterns of depressive symptoms. *American Journal of Psychiatry, 164,* 1521–1529. (p. 628)

Kellerman, J., Lewis, J., & Laird, J. D. (1989). Looking and loving: The effects of mutual gaze on feelings of romantic love. *Journal of Research in Personality, 23,* 145–161. (p. 510)

Kellermann, A. L. (1997). Comment: Gunsmoke—changing public attitudes toward smoking and firearms. *American Journal of Public Health, 87,* 910–913. (p. 710)

Kellermann, A. L., Rivara, F. P., Rushforth, N. B., Banton, H. G., Feay, D. T., Francisco, J. T., Locci, A. B., Prodzinski, J., Hackman, B. B., & Somes, G. (1993). Gun ownership as a risk factor for homicide in the home. *New England Journal of Medicine, 329,* 1084–1091. (p. 710)

Kellermann, A. L., Somes, G., Rivara, F. P., Lee, R. K., & Banton, J. G. (1998). Injuries and deaths due to firearms in the home. *Journal of Trauma, 45,* 263–267. (p. 710)

Kelley, J., & De Graaf, N. D. (1997). National context, parental socialization, and religious belief: Results from 15 nations. *American Sociological Review, 62,* 639–659. (p. 137)

Kelling, S. T., & Halpern, B. P. (1983). Taste flashes: Reaction times, intensity, and quality. *Science, 219,* 412–414. (p. 257)

Kellner, C. H., & 15 others. (2005). Relief of expressed suicidal intent by ECT: A consortium for research in ECT study. *American Journal of Psychiatry, 162,* 977–982. (p. 676)

Kellner, C. H., & 16 others (2006). Continuation electroconvulsive therapy vs. pharmacotherapy for relapse prevention in major depression: A multi-site study from the Consortium for Research in Electroconvulsive Therapy (CORE). *Archives of General Psychiatry, 63*, 1337-1344. (p. 676)

Kelly, A. E. (2000). Helping construct desirable identities: A self-presentational view of psychotherapy. *Psychological Bulletin, 126*, 475-494. (p. 655)

Kelly, D. J., Quinn, P. C., Slater, A. M., Lee, K., Ge, L., & Pascalis, O. (2007). The other-race effect develops during infancy: Evidence of perceptual narrowing. *Psychological Science, 18*, 1084-1089. (p. 708)

Kelly, I. W. (1997). Modern astrology: A critique. *Psychological Reports, 81*, 1035-1066. (p. 578)

Kelly, I. W. (1998). Why astrology doesn't work. *Psychological Reports, 82*, 527-546. (p. 578)

Kelly, T. A. (1990). The role of values in psychotherapy: A critical review of process and outcome effects. *Clinical Psychology Review, 10*, 171-186. (p. 668)

Kempe, R. S., & Kempe, C. C. (1978). *Child abuse.* Cambridge, MA: Harvard University Press. (p. 189)

Kempermann, G., Kuhn, H. G., & Gage, F. H. (May, 1998). Experience-induced neurogenesis in the senescent dentate gyrus. *Journal of Neuroscience, 18*(9), 3206-3212. (p. 210)

Kendall-Tackett, K. A. (Ed.). (2004). *Health consequences of abuse in the family: A clinical guide for evidence-based practice.* Washington, DC: American Psychological Association. (p. 190)

Kendall-Tackett, K. A., Williams, L. M., & Finkelhor, D. (1993). Impact of sexual abuse on children: A review and synthesis of recent empirical studies. *Psychological Bulletin, 113*, 164-180. (pp. 190, 363)

Kendler, K. S. (1996). Parenting: A genetic-epidemiologic perspective. *The American Journal of Psychiatry, 153*, 11-20. (p. 193)

Kendler, K. S. (1997). Social support: A genetic-epidemiologic analysis. *American Journal of Psychiatry, 154*, 1398-1404. (p. 584)

Kendler, K. S. (1998, January). Major depression and the environment: A psychiatric genetic perspective. *Pharmacopsychiatry, 31*(1), 5-9. (p. 628)

Kendler, K. S., Gardner, C. O., & Prescott, C. A. (2006). Toward a comprehensive developmental model for major depression in men. *American Journal of Psychiatry, 163*,115-124. (p. 627)

Kendler, K. S., Gatz, M., Gardner, C. O., & Pedersen, N. L. (2006). A Swedish national twin study of lifetime major depression. *American Journal of Psychiatry, 163*, 109-114. (p. 629)

Kendler, K. S., Jacobson, K. C., Myers, J., & Prescott, C. A. (2002a). Sex differences in genetic and environmental risk factors for irrational fears and phobias. *Psychological Medicine, 32*, 209-217. (p. 616)

Kendler, K. S., Karkowski, L. M., & Prescott, C. A. (1999). Fears and phobias: Reliability and heritability. *Psychological Medicine, 29*, 539-553. (p. 616)

Kendler, K. S., Myers, J., & Prescott, C. A. (2002b). The etiology of phobias: An evaluation of the stress-diathesis model. *Archives of General Psychiatry, 59*, 242-248. (p. 616)

Kendler, K. S., Neale, M. C., Kessler, R. C., Heath, A. C., & Eaves, L. J. (1992). Generalized anxiety disorder in women: A population-based twin study. *Archives of General Psychiatry, 49*, 267-272. (p. 616)

Kendler, K. S., Neale, M. C., Thornton, L. M., Aggen, S. H., Gilman, S. E., & Kessler, R. C. (2002). Cannabis use in the last year in a U.S. national sample of twin and sibling pairs. *Psychological Medicine, 32*, 551-554. (p. 126)

Kendler, K. S., Thornton, L. M., & Gardner, C. O. (2001). Genetic risk, number of previous depressive episodes, and stressful life events in predicting onset of major depression. *American Journal of Psychiatry, 158*, 582-586. (p. 628)

Kennedy, S., & Over, R. (1990). Psychophysiological assessment of male sexual arousal following spinal cord injury. *Archives of Sexual Behavior, 19*, 15-27. (p. 55)

Kenrick, D. T., & Funder, D. C. (1988). Profiting from controversy: Lessons from the person-situation debate. *American Psychologist, 43*, 23-34. (p. 581)

Kenrick, D. T., & Gutierres, S. E. (1980). Contrast effects and judgments of physical attractiveness: When beauty becomes a social problem. *Journal of Personality and Social Psychology, 38*, 131-140. (p. 469)

Kenrick, D. T., Gutierres, S. E., & Goldberg, L. L. (1989). Influence of popular erotica on judgments of strangers and mates. *Journal of Experimental Social Psychology, 25*, 159-167. (p. 469)

Kenrick, D. T., Nieuweboer, S., & Bunnk, A. P. (in press). Universal mechanisms and cultural diversity: Replacing the blank slate with a coloring book. In M. Schaller, S. Heine, A. Norenzayan, T. Yamagishi, & T. Kameda (Eds.), *Evolution, culture, and the human mind.* Mahwah, NJ: Erlbaum. (pp. 145, 148)

Kensinger, E. A. (2007). Negative emotion enhances memory accuracy: Behavioral and neuroimaging evidence. *Current Directions in Psychological Science, 16*, 213-218. (p. 341)

Keough, K. A., Zimbardo, P. G., & Boyd, J. N. (1999). Who's smoking, drinking, and using drugs? Time perspective as a predictor of substance use. *Basic and Applied Social Psychology, 2*, 149-164. (p. 559)

Kernis, M. H. (2003). Toward a conceptualization of optimal self-esteem. *Psychological Inquiry, 14*, 1-26. (p. 594)

Kerr, N. L., & Bruun, S. E. (1983). Dispensability of member effort and group motivation losses: Free-rider effects. *Journal of Personality and Social Psychology, 44*, 78-94. (p. 698)

Kessler, M., & Albee, G. (1975). Primary prevention. *Annual Review of Psychology, 26*, 557-591. (p. 669)

Kessler, R. C. (2000). Posttraumatic stress disorder: The burden to the individual and to society. *Journal of Clinical Psychiatry, 61*(suppl. 5), 4-12. (p. 613)

Kessler, R. C. (2001). Epidemiology of women and depression. *Journal of Affective Disorders, 74*, 5-1. (p. 632)

Kessler, R. C., Akiskal, H. S., Ames, M., Birnbaum, H., Greenberg, P., Hirschfeld, R. M. A., Jin, R., Merikangas, K. R., Simon, G. E., & Wang, P. S. (2006). Prevalence and effects of mood disorders on work performance in a nationally representative sample of U.S. workers. *American Journal of Psychiatry, 163*, 1561-1568. (p. 627)

Kessler, R. C., Berglund, P., Demler, O., Jin, R., Merikangos, K. R., & Walters, E. E. (2005). Lifetime prevalence and age-of-onset distributions of DSM-IV disorders in the National Comorbidity Survey Replication. *Archives of General Psychiatry, 62*, 593-602. (pp. 603, 607)

Kessler, R. C., Foster, C., Joseph, J., Ostrow, D., Wortman, C., Phair, J., & Chmiel, J. (1991). Stressful life events and symptom onset in HIV infection. *American Journal of Psychiatry, 148*, 733-738. (p. 540)

Kessler, R. C., Soukup, J., Davis, R. B., Foster, D. F., Wilkey, S. A., Van Rompay, M. I., & Eisenberg, D. M. (2001). The use of complementary and alternative therapies to treat anxiety and depression in the United States. *American Journal of Psychiatry, 158*, 289-294. (p. 665)

Keynes, M. (1980, December 20/27). Handel's illnesses. *Lancet,* pp. 1354-1355. (p. 626)

Keys, A., Brozek, J., Henschel, A., Mickelsen, O., & Taylor, H. L. (1950). *The biology of human starvation.* Minneapolis: University of Minnesota Press. (p. 448)

Kiecolt-Glaser, J. K., & Glaser, R. (1995). Psychoneuroimmunology and health consequences: Data and shared mechanisms. *Psychosomatic Medicine, 57*, 269-274. (p. 540)

Kiecolt-Glaser, J. K., Loving, T. J., Stowell, J. R., Malarkey, W. B., Lemeshow, S., Dickinson, S. L., & Glaser, R. (2005). Hostile marital interactions, proinflammatory cytokine production, and wound healing. *Archives of General Psychiatry, 62*, 1377-1384. (p. 538)

Kiecolt-Glaser, J. K., & Newton, T. L. (2001). Marriage and health: His and hers. *Psychological Bulletin, 127*, 472-503. (p. 545)

Kiecolt-Glaser, J. K., Page, G. G., Marucha, P. T., MacCallum, R. C., & Glaser, R. (1998). Psychological influences on surgical recovery: Perspectives from psychoneuroimmunology. *American Psychologist, 53*, 1209-1218. (p. 538)

Kihlstrom, J. F. (1990). The psychological unconscious. In L. A. Pervin (Ed.), *Handbook of personality: Theory and research.* New York: Guilford Press. (pp. 357, 566)

Kihlstrom, J. F. (1994). The social construction of memory. Paper presented at the American Psychological Society convention. (p. 357)

Kihlstrom, J. F. (1997, November 11). Freud as giant pioneer on whose shoulders we should stand. Social Psychology listserv posting (spsp@stolaf.edu). (p. 568)

Kihlstrom, J. F. (2005). Dissociative disorders. *Annual Review of Clinical Psychology, 1*, 227-253 (p. 620)

Kihlstrom, J. F. (2006). Repression: A unified theory of a will-o'-the-wisp. *Behavioral and Brain Sciences, 29*, 523. (p. 566)

Kihlstrom, J. F., & McConkey, K. M. (1990). William James and hypnosis: A centennial reflection. *Psychological Science, 1*, 174–177. (p. 112)

Killeen, P. R., & Nash, M. R. (2003). The four causes of hypnosis. *International Journal of Clinical and Experimental Hypnosis, 51*, 195–231. (p. 112)

Kim, B. S. K., Ng, G. F., & Ahn, A. J. (2005). Effects of client expectation for counseling success, client-counselor worldview match, and client adherence to Asian and European American cultural values on counseling process with Asian Americans. *Journal of Counseling Psychology, 52*, 67–76. (p. 668)

Kim, H., & Markus, H. R. (1999). Deviance or uniqueness, harmony or conformity? A cultural analysis. *Journal of Personality and Social Psychology, 77*, 785–800. (p. 155)

Kim, K. H. S., Relkin, N. R., Lee, K-M., & Hirsch, J. (1997). Distinct cortical areas associated with native and second languages. *Nature, 388*, 171–174. (p. 392)

Kimata, H. (2001). Effect of humor on allergen-induced wheal reactions. *Journal of the American Medical Association, 285*, 737. (p. 545)

Kimble, G. A. (1956). *Principles of general psychology*. New York: Ronald. (p. 295)

Kimble, G. A. (1981). *Biological and cognitive constraints on learning*. Washington, DC: American Psychological Association. (p. 295)

Kimmel, A. J. (1998). In defense of deception. *American Psychologist, 53*, 803–805. (p. 22)

King, L. A., Hicks, J. A., Krull, J. L., & Del Gaiso, A. K. (2006). Positive affect and the experience of meaning in life. *Journal of Personality and Social Psychology, 90*, 179–196. (p. 522)

King, M., & Bartlett, A. (2006). What same sex civil partnerships may mean for health. *Journal of Epidemiology and Community Health, 60*, 188–191. (p. 473)

King, R. N., & Koehler, D. J. (2000). Illusory correlations in graphological interference. *Journal of Experimental Psychology: Applied, 6*, 336–348. (p. 578)

Kinnier, R. T., & Metha, A. T. (1989). Regrets and priorities at three stages of life. *Counseling and Values, 33*, 182–193. (p. 219)

Kirby, D. (2002). Effective approaches to reducing adolescent unprotected sex, pregnancy, and childbearing. *Journal of Sex Research, 39*, 51–57. (p. 472)

Kirkpatrick, B., Fenton, W. S., Carpenter, W. T., Jr., & Marder, S. R. (2006). The NIMH-MATRICS consensus statement on negative symptoms. *Schizophrenia Bulletin, 32*, 214–219. (p. 639)

Kirkpatrick, L. (1999). Attachment and religious representations and behavior. In J. Cassidy & P. R. Shaver (Eds.), *Handbook of attachment*. New York: Guilford. (p. 187)

Kirmayer, L. J., & Sartorius, N. (2007). Cultural models and somatic syndromes. *Psychosomatic Medicine, 69*, 832–840. (p. 623)

Kirsch, I. (1996). Hypnotic enhancement of cognitive-behavioral weight loss treatments: Another meta-reanalysis. *Journal of Consulting and Clinical Psychology, 64*, 517–519. (p. 110)

Kirsch, I., & Braffman, W. (2001). Imaginative suggestibility and hypnotizability. *Current Directions in Psychological Science, 10*, 57–61. (p. 108)

Kirsch, I., Deacon, B. J., Huedo-Medina, T. B., Scoboria, A., Moore, T. J., & Johnson, B. T. (2008) Initial severity and antidepressant benefits: A meta-analysis of data submitted to the Food and Drug Administration. *Public Library of Science Medicine, 5*, e45. (p. 674)

Kirsch, I., & Lynn, S. J. (1995). The altered state of hypnosis. *American Psychologist, 50*, 846–858. (p. 110)

Kirsch, I., Moore, T. J., Scoboria, A., & Nicholls, S. S. (2002, July 15). New study finds little difference between effects of antidepressants and placebo. *Prevention and Treatment* (journals.apa.org/prevention). (p. 674)

Kirsch, I., & Sapirstein, G. (1998). Listening to Prozac but hearing placebo: A meta-analysis of antidepressant medication. *Prevention and Treatment, 1*, posted June 26 at (journals.apa.org/prevention/volume1). (pp. 35, 674)

Kisley, M. A., Wood, S., & Burrows, C. L. (2007). Looking at the sunny side of life: Age-related change in an event-related potential measure of the negativity bias. *Psychological Science, 18*, 838–843. (p. 219)

Kisor, H. (1990). *What's that pig outdoors*. New York: Hill and Wang. (p. 249)

Kitayama, S., Ishii, K., Imada, T., Takemura, K., & Ramaswamy, J. (2006). Voluntary settlement and the spirit of independence: Evidence from Japan's "northern frontier." *Journal of Personality and Social Psychology, 91*, 369–384. (p. 155)

Kitts, R. L. (2005). Gay adolescents and suicide: Understanding the association. *Adolescence, 40*, 621–628. (p. 473)

Kivimaki, M., Leino-Arjas, P., Luukkonen, R., Rihimaki, H., & Kirjonen, J. (2002). Work stress and risk of cardiovascular mortality: Prospective cohort study of industrial employees. *British Medical Journal, 325*, 857. (p. 543)

Klayman, J., & Ha, Y-W. (1987). Confirmation, disconfirmation, and information in hypothesis testing. *Psychological Review, 94*, 211–228. (p. 373)

Klein, D. N., & 16 others. (2003). Therapeutic alliance in depression treatment: Controlling for prior change and patient characteristics. *Journal of Consulting and Clinical Psychology, 71*, 997–1006. (p. 668)

Klein, E., Kreinin, I., Chistyakov, A., Koren, D., Mecz, L., Marmur, S., Ben-Shachar, D., & Feinsod, M. (1999). Therapeutic efficacy of right prefrontal slow repetitive transcranial magnetic stimulation in major depression. *Archives of General Psychiatry, 56*, 315–320. (p. 676)

Kleinfeld, J. (1998). *The myth that schools shortchange girls: Social science in the service of deception*. Washington, DC: Women's Freedom Network. Available from ERIC, Document ED423210, and via www.uaf.edu/northern/schools/myth.html. (p. 435)

Kleinke, C. L. (1986). Gaze and eye contact: A research review. *Psychological Bulletin, 1000*, 78–100. (p. 510)

Kleinmuntz, B., & Szucko, J. J. (1984). A field study of the fallibility of polygraph lie detection. *Nature, 308*, 449–450. (p. 504)

Kleitman, N. (1960, November). Patterns of dreaming. *Scientific American*, pp. 82–88. (p. 92)

Klemm, W. R. (1990). Historical and introductory perspectives on brain-stem-mediated behaviors. In W. R. Klemm & R. P. Vertes (Eds.), *Brainstem mechanisms of behavior*. New York: Wiley. (p. 61)

Kline, D., & Schieber, F. (1985). Vision and aging. In J. E. Birren & K. W. Schaie (Eds.), *Handbook of the psychology of aging*. New York: Van Nostrand Reinhold. (p. 209)

Kline, G. H., Stanley, S. M., Markman, J. H., Olmos-Gallo, P. A., St. Peters, M., Whitton, S. W., & Prado, L. M. (2004). Timing is everything: Pre-engagement cohabitation and increased risk for poor marital outcomes. *Journal of Family Psychology, 18*, 311–318. (p. 217)

Klineberg, O. (1938). Emotional expression in Chinese literature. *Journal of Abnormal and Social Psychology, 33*, 517–520. (p. 513)

Klineberg, O. (1984). Public opinion and nuclear war. *American Psychologist, 39*, 1245–1253. (p. 732)

Klinesmith, J., Kasser, T., & McAndrew, F. T. (2006). Guns, testosterone, and aggression: An experimental test of a mediational hypothesis. *Psychological Science, 17*, 568–576. (p. 711)

Klinke, R., Kral, A., Heid, S., Tillein, J., & Hartmann, R. (1999). Recruitment of the auditory cortex in congenitally deaf cats by long-term cochlear electrostimulation. *Science, 285*, 1729–1733. (p. 273)

Kluft, R. P. (1991). Multiple personality disorder. In A. Tasman & S. M. Goldfinger (Eds.), *Review of Psychiatry* (Vol. 10). Washington, DC: American Psychiatric Press. (p. 619)

Klump, K. L., & Culbert, K. M. (2007). Molecular genetic studies of eating disorders: Current status and future directions. *Current Directions in Psychological Science, 16*, 37–41. (p. 454)

Klüver, H., & Bucy, P. C. (1939). Preliminary analysis of functions of the temporal lobes in monkeys. *Archives of Neurology and Psychiatry, 42*, 979–1000. (p. 62)

Knapp, S., & VandeCreek, L. (2000, August). Recovered memories of childhood abuse: Is there an underlying professional consensus? *Professional Psychology: Research and Practice, 31*, 365–371. (p. 363)

Knäuper, B., Kornik, R., Atkinson, K., Guberman, C., & Aydin, C. (2005). Motivation influences the underestimation of cumulative risk. *Personality and Social Psychology Bulletin, 31*, 1511–1523. (p. 471)

Knickmeyer, E. (2001, August 7). In Africa, big is definitely better. *Seattle Times*, p. A7. (p. 454)

Knight, R. T. (2007). Neural networks debunk phrenology. *Science, 316*, 1578–1579. (p. 72)

Knight, W. (2004, August 2). Animated face helps deaf with phone chat. NewScientist.com. (p. 258)

Knoblich, G., & Oellinger, M. (2006, October/November). The Eureka moment. *Scientific American Mind*, pp. 38–43. (p. 372)

Knutson, K. L., Spiegel, K., Penev, P., & Van Cauter, E. (2007). The metabolic consequences of sleep deprivation. *Sleep Medicine Reviews, 11,* 163–178. (p. 97)

Ko, C-K., Yen, J-Y., Chen, C-C., Chen, S-H., & Yen, C-F. (2005). Proposed diagnostic criteria of Internet addiction for adolescents. *Journal of Nervous and Mental Disease, 193,* 728–733. (p. 115)

Koch, C., & Greenfield, S. (2007, October). How does consciousness happen? *Scientific American,* pp. 76–83. (p. 85)

Koch, G. (2001). Utilizing Psi Chi's programs to maximize learning and success. *Eye on Psi Chi, 10,* 22. (p. A-10)

Koenig, H. G. (2002, October 9). Personal communication, from Director of Center for the Study of Religion/Spirituality and Health, Duke University. (p. 552)

Koenig, H. G., & Larson, D. B. (1998). Use of hospital services, religious attendance, and religious affiliation. *Southern Medical Journal, 91,* 925–932. (p. 554)

Koenig, L. B., McGue, M., Krueger, R. F., & Bouchard, T. J., Jr. (2005). Genetic and environmental influences on religiousness: Findings for retrospective and current religiousness ratings. *Journal of Personality, 73,* 471–488. (p. 137)

Koenigs, M., Young, L., Adolphs, R., Tranel, D., Cushman, F., Hauser, M., & Damasio, A. (2007). Damage to the prefrontal cortex increases utilitarian moral judgements. *Nature, 446,* 908–911. (pp. 72, 200)

Koestner, R., Lekes, N., Powers, T. A., & Chicoine, E. (2002). Attaining personal goals: Self-concordance plus implementation intentions equals success. *Journal of Personality and Social Psychology, 83,* 231–244. (p. 494)

Kohlberg, L. (1981). *The philosophy of moral development: Essays on moral development* (Vol. I). San Francisco: Harper & Row. (p. 198)

Kohlberg, L. (1984). *The psychology of moral development: Essays on moral development* (Vol. II). San Francisco: Harper & Row. (p. 198)

Kohler, I. (1962, May). Experiments with goggles. *Scientific American,* pp. 62–72. (p. 274)

Köhler, W. (1925: reprinted 1957). *The mentality of apes.* London: Pelican. (p. 397)

Kohn, P. M., & Macdonald, J. E. (1992). The survey of recent life experiences: A decontaminated hassles scale for adults. *Journal of Behavioral Medicine, 15,* 221–236. (p. 534)

Kohout, J., & Wicherski, M. (2004). *2001 doctorate employment survey,* Washington, DC: American Psychological Association. (p. A-4)

Kolassa, I-T., & Elbert, T. (2007). Structural and functional neuroplasticity in relation to traumatic stress. *Current Directions in Psychological Science, 16,* 321–325. (p. 616)

Kolata, G. (1986). Youth suicide: New research focuses on a growing social problem. *Science, 233,* 839–841. (p. 630)

Kolata, G. (1987). Metabolic catch-22 of exercise regimens. *Science, 236,* 146–147. (p. 463)

Kolb, B. (1989). Brain development, plasticity, and behavior. *American Psychologist, 44,* 1203–1212. (p. 73)

Kolb, B., & Whishaw, I. Q. (1998). Brain plasticity and behavior. *Annual Review of Psychology, 49,* 43–64. (p. 149)

Kolb, B., & Whishaw, I. Q. (2006). *An introduction to brain and behavior* (2nd ed.). New York: Worth Publishers. (p. 409)

Kolivas, E. D., & Gross, A. M. (2007). Assessing sexual aggression: Addressing the gap between rape victimization and perpetration prevalence rates. *Aggression and Violent Behavior, 12,* 315–328. (p. 144)

Kolker, K. (2002, December 8). Video violence disturbs some: Others scoff at influence. *Grand Rapids Press,* pp. A1, A12. (p. 715)

Kolodziej, M. E., & Johnson, B. T. (1996). Interpersonal contact and acceptance of persons with psychiatric disorders: A research synthesis. *Journal of Consulting and Clinical Psychology, 64,* 1387–1396. (p. 605)

Koltko-Rivera, M. E. (2006). Rediscovering the later version of Maslow's hierarchy of needs: Self-transcendence and opportunities for theory, research, and unification. *Review of General Psychology, 10,* 302–317. (p. 447)

Koole, S. L., Greenberg, J., & Pyszczynski, T. (2006). Introducing science to the psychology of the soul. *Current Directions in Psychological Science, 15,* 212–216. (p. 567)

Kopta, S. M., Lueger, R. J., Saunders, S. M., & Howard, K. I. (1999). Individual psychotherapy outcome and process research: Challenges leading to greater turmoil or a positive transition? *Annual Review of Psychology, 30,* 441–469. (p. 662)

Koriat, A., Goldsmith, M., & Pansky, A. (2000). Toward a psychology of memory accuracy. *Annual Review of Psychology, 51,* 481–537. (p. 360)

Kosslyn, S. (2007). *Human intelligence can be increased, and can be increased dramatically.* World Question Center, The Edge (www.edge.org). (p. 431)

Kosslyn, S. M. (2005). Reflective thinking and mental imagery: A perspective on the development of posttraumatic stress disorder. *Development and Psychopathology, 17,* 851–863. (p. 613)

Kosslyn, S. M., & Koenig, O. (1992). *Wet mind: The new cognitive neuroscience.* New York: Free Press. (p. 53)

Kosslyn, S. M., Thompson, W. L., Costantini-Ferrando, M. F., Alpert, N. M., & Spiegel, D. (2000). Hypnotic visual illusion alters color processing in the brain. *American Journal of Psychiatry, 157,* 1279–1284. (p. 111)

Kotchick, B. A., Shaffer, A., & Forehand, R. (2001). Adolescent sexual risk behavior: A multi-system perspective. *Clinical Psychology Review, 21,* 493–519. (p. 471)

Kotkin, M., Daviet, C., & Gurin, J. (1996). The Consumer Reports mental health survey. *American Psychologist, 51,* 1080–1082. (p. 660)

Kracen, A. C., & Wallace, I. J. (Eds.). (2008). *Applying to graduate school in psychology: Advice from successful students and prominent psychologists.* Washington, DC: American Psychological Association. (p. A-10)

Kraft, C. (1978). A psychophysical approach to air safety: Simulator studies of visual illusions in night approaches. In H. L. Pick, H. W. Leibowitz, J. E. Singer, A. Steinschneider, & H. W. Stevenson (Eds.), *Psychology: From research to practice.* New York: Plenum Press. (pp. 279, 280)

Kraft, R. N. (2002). *Memory perceived: Recalling the Holocaust.* Westport, CT: Praeger. (p. 365)

Kramer, A. F., & Erickson, K. I. (2007). Capitalizing on cortical plasticity: Influence of physical activity on cognition and brain function. *Trends in Cognitive Sciences, 11,* 342–348. (p. 548)

Kranz, F., & Ishai, A. (2006). Face perception is modulated by sexual preference. *Current Biology, 16,* 63–68. (p. 476)

Kraus, N., Malmfors, T., & Slovic, P. (1992). Intuitive toxicology: Expert and lay judgments of chemical risks. *Risk Analysis, 12,* 215–232. (p. 381)

Krauss, R. M. (1998). Why do we gesture when we speak. *Current Directions in Psychology, 7,* 54–60. (p. 400)

Kraut, R. E., & Johnston, R. E. (1979). Social and emotional messages of smiling: An ethological approach. *Journal of Personality and Social Psychology, 37,* 1539–1553. (p. 514)

KRC Research & Consulting. (2001, August 7). Memory isn't quite what it used to be (survey for General Nutrition Centers). *USA Today,* p. D1. (p. 212)

Krebs, D. L., & Denton, K. (2005). Toward a more pragmatic approach to morality: A critical evaluation of Kohlberg's model. *Psychological Review, 112,* 629–649. (p. 199)

Kring, A. M., & Gordon, A. H. (1998). Sex differences in emotion: Expression, experience, and physiology. *Journal of Personality and Social Psychology, 74,* 686–703. (p. 513)

Kristensen, P., & Bjerkedal, T. (2007). Explaining the relation between birth order and intelligence. *Science, 316,* 1717. (p. 41)

Kristof, N. D. (2004, July 21). Saying no to killers. *New York Times* (www.nytimes.com). (p. 726)

Kroll, R., Danis, S., Moreau, M., Waldbaum, A., Shifren, J., & Wekselman, K. (2004, October). Testosterone transdermal patch (TPP) significantly improved sexual function in naturally menopausal women in a large Phase III study. Paper presented to the American Society of Reproductive Medicine annual meeting, Philadelphia. (p. 468)

Krosnick, J. A., Betz, A. L., Jussim, L. J., & Lynn, A. R. (1992). Subliminal conditioning of attitudes. *Personality and Social Psychology Bulletin, 18,* 152–162. (p. 229)

Krueger, A. (2007, November/December). What makes a terrorist. *The American* (www.american.com). (p. 712)

Krueger, J., & Killham, E. (2005, December 8). At work, feeling good matters. *Gallup Management Journal* (www.gmj.gallup.com). (p. 494)

Krueger, J., & Killham, E. (2006, March 9). Why Dilbert is right. Uncomfortable work environments make for disgruntled employees—just like the cartoon says. *Gallup Management Journal* (www.gmj.gallup.com). (p. 586)

Kruger, J., & Dunning, D. (1999). Unskilled and unaware of it: How difficulties in recognizing one's own incompetence lead to inflated self-assessments. *Journal of Personality and Social Psychology, 77,* 1121–1134. (p. 588)

Kruger, J., Epley, N., Parker, J., & Ng, Z-W. (2005). Egocentrism over e-mail: Can we communicate as well as we think? *Journal of Personality and Social Psychology, 89,* 925–936. (pp. 180, 511)

Krupa, D. J., Thompson, J. K., & Thompson, R. F. (1993). Localization of a memory trace in the mammalian brain. *Science, 260,* 989–991. (p. 345)

Krützen, M., Mann, J., Heithaus, M. R., Connor, R. C., Bejder, L., & Sherwin, W. B. (2005). Cultural transmission of tool use in bottlenose dolphins. *Proceedings of the National Academy of Sciences, 102,* 8939–8943. (p. 398)

Kubey, R., & Csikszentmihalyi, M. (2002, February). Television addiction is no mere metaphor. *Scientific American,* pp. 74–80. (p. 319)

Kübler, A., Winter, S., Ludolph, A. C., Hautzinger, M., & Birbaumer, N. (2005). Severity of depressive symptoms and quality of life in patients with amyotrophic lateral sclerosis. *Neurorehabilitation and Neural Repair, 19*(3), 182–193. (p. 523)

Kubzansky, L. D., Sparrow, D., Vokanas, P., & Kawachi, I. (2001). Is the glass half empty or half full? A prospective study of optimism and coronary heart disease in the normative aging study. *Psychosomatic Medicine, 63,* 910–916. (pp. 536, 537)

Kuhl, B. A., Dudukovic, N. M., Kahn, I., & Wagner, A. D. (2007). Decreased demands on cognitive control reveal the neural processing benefits of forgetting. *Nature Neuroscience, 10,* 908–914. (p. 354)

Kuhl, P. K., & Meltzoff, A. N. (1982). The bimodal perception of speech in infancy. *Science, 218,* 1138–1141. (p. 386)

Kuhn, D. (2006). Do cognitive changes accompany developments in the adolescent brain? *Perspectives on Psychological Science, 1,* 59–67. (p. 197)

Kujala, U. M., Kaprio, J., Sarna, S., & Koskenvuo, M. (1998). Relationship of leisure-time physical activity and mortality: The Finnish twin cohort. *Journal of the American Medical Association, 279,* 440–444. (p. 548)

Kuncel, N. R., & Hezlett, S. A. (2007). Standardized tests predict graduate students' success. *Science, 315,* 1080–1081. (p. 422)

Kuncel, N. R., Nezlett, S. A., & Ones, D. S. (2004). Academic performance, career potential, creativity, and job performance: Can one construct predict them all? *Journal of Personality and Social Psychology, 86,* 148–161. (p. 407)

Kunkel, D. (2001, February 4). *Sex on TV.* Menlo Park, CA: Henry J. Kaiser Family Foundation (www.kff.org). (p. 471)

Kunkel, D., Cope-Farrar, K., Biely, E., Farinola, W. J. M., & Donnerstein, E. (2001). *Sex on TV (2): A biennial report to the Kaiser Family Foundation.* Menlo Park, CA: Kaiser Family Foundation. (p. 715)

Kuntsche, E., Knibbe, R., Gmel, G., & Engels, R. (2005). Why do young people drink? A review of drinking motives. *Clinical Psychology Review, 25,* 841–861. (p. 127)

Kupper, N., & Denollet, J. (2007). Type D personality as a prognostic factor in heart disease: Assessment and mediating mechanisms. *Journal of Personality Assessment, 89,* 265–276. (p. 536)

Kurdek, L. A. (2005). What do we know about gay and lesbian couples? *Current Directions in Psychological Science, 14,* 251–254. (p. 473)

Kurtz, P. (1983, Spring). Stars, planets, and people. *The Skeptical Inquirer,* pp. 65–68. (p. 579)

Kushner, M. G., Kim, S. W., Conahue, C., Thuras, P., Adson, D., Kotlyar, M., McCabe, J., Peterson, J., & Foa, E. B. (2007). D-cycloserine augmented exposure therapy for obsessive-compulsive disorder. *Biological Psychiatry, 62,* 835–838. (p. 672)

Kutas, M. (1990). Event-related brain potential (ERP) studies of cognition during sleep: Is it more than a dream? In R. R. Bootzin, J. F. Kihlstrom, & D. Schacter (Eds.), *Sleep and cognition.* Washington, DC: American Psychological Association. (p. 91)

Kutcher, E. J., & Bragger, J. D. (2004). Selection interviews of overweight job applicants: Can structure reduce the bias? *Journal of Applied Social Psychology, 34,* 1993–2022. (p. 488)

L'Engle, M. (1973). *A Wind in the Door, 87.* New York: Farrar, Straus and Giroux. (p. 15)

Labouvie-Vief, G., & Schell, D. A. (1982). Learning and memory in later life. In B. B. Wolman (Ed.), *Handbook of developmental psychology.* Englewood Cliffs, NJ: Prentice-Hall. (p. 213)

Lacayo, R. (1995, June 12). Violent reaction. *Time Magazine,* pp. 25–39. (p. 27)

Lacey, H. P., Smith, D. M., & Ubel, P. A. (2006). Hope I die before I get old: Mispredicting happiness across the lifespan. *Journal of Happiness Studies, 7,* 167–182. (p. 219)

Lacey, M. (2004. April 9). A decade after massacres, Rwanda outlaws ethnicity. *New York Times* (www.nytimes.com). (p. 733)

Lachman, M. E. (2004). Development in midlife. *Annual Review of Psychology, 55,* 305–331. (p. 216)

Ladd, E. C. (1998, August/September). The tobacco bill and American public opinion. *The Public Perspective,* pp. 5–19. (p. 128)

Ladd, G. T. (1887). *Elements of physiological psychology.* New York: Scribner's. (p. 83)

Laird, J. D. (1974). Self-attribution of emotion: The effects of expressive behavior on the quality of emotional experience. *Journal of Personality and Social Psychology, 29,* 475–486. (p. 515)

Laird, J. D. (1984). The real role of facial response in the experience of emotion: A reply to Tourangeau and Ellsworth, and others. *Journal of Personality and Social Psychology, 47,* 909–917. (p. 515)

Laird, J. D., Cuniff, M., Sheehan, K., Shulman, D., & Strum, G. (1989). Emotion specific effects of facial expressions on memory for life events. *Journal of Social Behavior and Personality, 4,* 87–98. (p. 515)

Lakin, J. L., & Chartrand, T. L. (2003). Using nonconscious behavioral mimicry to create affiliation and rapport. *Psychological Science, 14,* 334–339. (p. 690)

Lalumière, M. L., Blanchard, R., & Zucker, K. J. (2000). Sexual orientation and handedness in men and women: A meta-analysis. *Psychological Bulletin, 126,* 575–592. (p. 477)

Lam, R. W., Levitt, A. J., Levitan, R. D., Enns, M. W., Morehouse, R., Michalak, E. E., & Tam, E. M. (2006). The Can-SAD study: A randomized controlled trial of the effectiveness of light therapy and fluoxetine in patients with winter seasonal affective disorder. *American Journal of Psychiatry, 163,* 805–812. (p. 666)

Lambert, K. (2008, August/September). Depressingly easy. *Scientific American Mind,* pp. 31–37. (p. 549)

Lambert, K. G. (2005). Rising rates of depression in today's society: Consideration of the roles of effort-based rewards and enhanced resilience in day-to-day functioning. *Neuroscience and Biobehavioral Reviews, 30,* 497–510. (p. 548)

Lambert, W. E. (1992). Challenging established views on social issues: The power and limitations of research. *American Psychologist, 47,* 533–542. (p. 394)

Lambert, W. E., Genesee, F., Holobow, N., & Chartrand, L. (1993). Bilingual education for majority English-speaking children. *European Journal of Psychology of Education, 8,* 3–22. (p. 394)

Lamberth, J. (1998, August 6). Driving while Black: A statistician proves that prejudice still rules the road. *Washington Post,* p. C1. (p. 704)

Lambird, K. H., & Mann, T. (2006). When do ego threats lead to self-regulation failure? Negative consequences of defensive high self-esteem. *Personality and Social Psychology Bulletin, 32,* 1177–1187. (p. 594)

Lammers, B. (2000). Quick tips for applying to graduate school in psychology. *Eye on Psi Chi, 4,* 40–42. (p. A-10)

Lampinen, J. M. (2002). What exactly is déjà vu? *Scientific American* (scieam.com/askexpert/biology/biology63). (p. 349)

Landau, M. J., Solomon, S., Greenberg, J., Cohen, F., Pyszczynski, T., Arndt, J., Miller, C. H., Ogilvie, D. M., & Cook, A. (2004). Deliver us from evil: The effects of mortality salience and reminders of 9/11 on support for President George W. Bush. *Personality and Social Psychology Bulletin, 30,* 1136–1150. (p. 708)

Landauer, T. (2001, September). Quoted by R. Herbert, You must remember this. *APS Observer,* p. 11. (p. 365)

Landauer, T. K., & Whiting, J. W. M. (1979). Correlates and consequences of stress in infancy. In R. Munroe, B. Munroe, & B. Whiting (Eds.), *Handbook of cross-cultural human development.* New York: Garland. (p. 531)

Landrum, E. (2001). I'm getting my bachelor's degree in psychology. What can I do with it? *Eye on Psi Chi, 6,* 22–24. (p. A-2)

Landry, M. J. (2002). MDMA: A review of epidemiologic data. *Journal of Psychoactive Drugs, 34,* 163–169. (p. 122)

Langer, E. J. (1983). *The psychology of control.* Beverly Hills, CA: Sage. (p. 586)

Langer, E. J., & Abelson, R. P. (1974). A patient by any other name . . .: Clinician group differences in labeling bias. *Journal of Consulting and Clinical Psychology, 42,* 4–9. (p. 605)

Langer, E. J., & Imber, L. (1980). The role of mindlessness in the perception of deviance. *Journal of Personality and Social Psychology, 39,* 360–367. (p. 605)

Langleben, D. D., Dattilio, F. M., & Gutheil, T. G. (2006). True lies: Delusions and lie-detection technology. *Journal of Psychiatry and Law, 34,* 351–370. (p. 505)

Langleben, D. D., Loughead, J. W., Bilker, W. B., & others. (2005). Telling truth from lie in individual subjects with fast event-related fMRI. *Human Brain Mapping, 26,* 262–273. (p. 505)

Langleben, D. D., Schroeder, L., Maldjian, J. A., Gur, R. C., McDonald, S., Ragland, J. D., O'Brien, C. P., & Childress, A. R. (2002). Brain activity during simulated deception: An event-related functional magnetic resonance study. *NeuroImage, 15,* 727–732. (p. 505)

Langlois, J. H., Kalakanis, L., Rubenstein, A. J., Larson, A., Hallam, M., & Smoot, M. (2000). Maxims or myths of beauty? A meta-analytic and theoretical review. *Psychological Bulletin, 126,* 390–423. (pp. 721, 722)

Langlois, J. H., & Roggman, L. A. (1990). Attractive faces are only average. *Psychological Science, 1,* 115–121. (p. 723)

Langlois, J. H., Roggman, L. A., Casey, R. J., Ritter, J. M., Rieser-Danner, L. A., & Jenkins, V. Y. (1987). Infant preferences for attractive faces: Rudiments of a stereotype? *Developmental Psychology, 23,* 363–369. (p. 721)

Lángström, N., Rahman, Q., Carlström, E., & Lichtenstein, P. (2008). Genetic and environmental effects on same-sex sexual behavior: A population study of twins in Sweden. *Archives of Sexual Behavior.* (p. 476)

Larkin, K., Resko, J. A., Stormshak, F., Stellflug, J. N., & Roselli, C. E. (2002). Neuroanatomical correlates of sex and sexual partner preference in sheep. Paper presented at Society for Neuroscience convention. (p. 476)

LaRoche, K. (2004). Advantages of undergraduate research: A student's perspective. *Eye on Psi Chi, 8,* 20–21. (p. A-10)

Larsen, R. J., & Diener, E. (1987). Affect intensity as an individual difference characteristic: A review. *Journal of Research in Personality, 21,* 1–39. (pp. 138, 508)

Larsen, R. J., Kasimatis, M., & Frey, K. (1992). Facilitating the furrowed brow: An unobtrusive test of the facial feedback hypothesis applied to unpleasant affect. *Cognition and Emotion, 6,* 321–338. (p. 515)

Larson, R. W., & Verma, S. (1999). How children and adolescents spend time across the world: Work, play, and developmental opportunities. *Psychological Bulletin, 125,* 701–736. (p. 437)

Larsson, H., Tuvblad, C., Rijsdijk, F. V., Andershed, H., Grann, M., & Lichetenstein, P. (2007). A common genetic factor explains the association between psychopathic personality and antisocial behavior. *Psychological Medicine, 37,* 15–26. (p. 621)

Larzelere, R. E. (2000). Child outcomes of non-abusive and customary physical punishment by parents: An updated literature review. *Clinical Child and Family Psychology Review, 3,* 199–221. (p. 307)

Larzelere, R. E., & Kuhn, B. R. (2005). Comparing child outcomes of physical punishment and alternative disciplinary tactics: A meta-analysis. *Clinical Child and Family Psychology Review, 8,* 1–37. (p. 307)

Larzelere, R. E., Kuhn, B. R., & Johnson, B. (2004). The intervention selection bias: An underrecognized confound in intervention research. *Psychological Bulletin, 130,* 289–303. (p. 307)

Lashley, K. S. (1950). In search of the engram. In *Symposium of the Society for Experimental Biology* (Vol. 4). New York: Cambridge University Press. (p. 339)

Lassiter, G. D., & Irvine, A. A. (1986). Video-taped confessions: The impact of camera point of view on judgments of coercion. *Journal of Personality and Social Psychology, 16,* 268–276. (p. 683)

Latané, B. (1981). The psychology of social impact. *American Psychologist, 36,* 343–356. (p. 698)

Latané, B., & Dabbs, J. M., Jr. (1975). Sex, group size and helping in three cities. *Sociometry, 38,* 180–194. (p. 728)

Latham, G. P., & Locke, E. A. (2007). New developments in and directions for goal-setting research. *European Psychologist, 12,* 290–300. (p. 494)

Laudenslager, M. L., & Reite, M. L. (1984). Losses and separations: Immunological consequences and health implications. *Review of Personality and Social Psychology, 5,* 285–312. (p. 542)

Laumann, E. O., Gagnon, J. H., Michael, R. T., & Michaels, S. (1994). *The social organization of sexuality: Sexual practices in the United States.* Chicago: University of Chicago Press. (pp. 144, 473)

Laws, K. R., & Kokkalis, J. (2007). Ecstasy (MDMA) and memory function: A meta-analytic update. *Human Psychopharmacology: Clinical and Experimental, 22,* 381–388. (p. 122)

Lazaruk, W. (2007). Linguistic, academic, and cognitive benefits of French immersion. *Canadian Modern Language Review, 63,* 605–628. (p. 395)

Lazarus, R. S. (1990). Theory-based stress measurement. *Psychological Inquiry, 1,* 3–13. (p. 534)

Lazarus, R. S. (1991). Progress on a cognitive-motivational-relational theory of emotion. *American Psychologist, 46,* 352–367. (p. 507)

Lazarus. R. S. (1998). Fifty years of the research and theory of R. S. Lazarus: An analysis of historical and perennial issues. Mahwah, NJ: Erlbaum. (pp. 507, 531)

Lea, S. E. G. (2000). Towards an ethical use of animals. *The Psychologist, 13,* 556–557. (p. 21)

Leach, P. (1993). Should parents hit their children? *The Psychologist: Bulletin of the British Psychological Society, 6,* 216–220. (p. 307)

Leach, P. (1994). *Children first.* New York: Knopf. (p. 307)

Leaper, C., & Ayres, M. M. (2007). A meta-analytic review of gender variations in adults' language use: Talkativeness, affiliative speech, and assertive speech. *Personality and Social Psychology Review, 11,* 328–363. (p. 158)

Leary, M. R. (1999). The social and psychological importance of self-esteem. In R. M. Kowalski & M. R. Leary (Eds.), *The social psychology of emotional and behavioral problems.* Washington, DC: APA Books. (p. 591)

Leary, M. R., Haupt, A. L., Strausser, K. S., & Chokel, J. T. (1998). Calibrating the sociometer: The relationship between interpersonal appraisals and state self-esteem. *Journal of Personality and Social Psychology, 74,* 1290–1299. (p. 480)

Leary, W. E. (1998, September 28). Older people enjoy sex, survey says. *New York Times* (www.nytimes.com). (p. 207)

Leask, S. J., & Beaton, A. A. (2007). Handedness in Great Britain. *Laterality, 12,* 559–572. (p. 78)

LeDoux, J. (1996). The emotional brain: The mysterious underpinnings of emotional life. New York: Simon & Schuster. (p. 344)

LeDoux, J. E. (2002). *The synaptic self.* London: Macmillan. (p. 507)

LeDoux, J. E., & Armony, J. (1999). Can neurobiology tell us anything about human feelings? In D. Kahneman, E. Diener, & N. Schwartz (Eds.), *Well-being: The foundations of hedonic psychology.* New York: Sage. (p. 507)

Lee, K., Byatt, G., & Rhodes, G. (2000). Caricature effects, distinctiveness, and identification: Testing the face-space framework. *Psychological Science, 11,* 379–385. (p. 275)

Lee, L., Frederick, S., & Ariely, D. (2006). Try it, you'll like it: The influence of expectation, consumption, and revelation on preferences for beer. *Psychological Science, 17,* 1054–1058. (p. 275)

Lefcourt, H. M. (1982). *Locus of control: Current trends in theory and research.* Hillsdale, NJ: Erlbaum. (p. 585)

Lefleur, D. L., Pittenger, C., Kelmendi, B., Gardner, T., Wasylink, S., Malison, R. T., Sanacora, G., Krystal, J. H., & Coric, V. (2006). N-acetyl-cysteine augmentation in serotonin reuptake inhibitor refractory obsessive-compulsive disorder. *Psychopharmacology, 184,* 254–256. (p. 616)

Legrand, L. N., Iacono, W. G., & McGue, M. (2005). Predicting addiction. *American Scientist, 93,* 140–147. (p. 127)

Le Grand, R., Mondloch, C. J., Maurer, D., & Brent, H. P. (2004). Impairment in holistic face processing following early visual deprivation. *Psychological Science, 15,* 762–768. (pp. 272, 273)

Lehavot, K., & Lambert, A. J. (2007). Toward a greater understanding of antigay prejudice: On the role of sexual orientation and gender role violation. *Basic and Applied Social Psychology, 29,* 279–292. (p. 723)

Lehman, A. F., Steinwachs, D. M., Dixon, L. B., Goldman, H. H., Osher, F., Postrado, L., Scott, J. E., Thompson, J. W., Fahey, M.,

Fischer, P., Kasper, J. A., Lyles, A., Skinner, E. A., Buchanan, R., Carpenter, W. T., Jr., Levine, J., McGlynn, E. A., Rosenheck, R., & Zito, J. (1998). Translating research into practice: The schizophrenic patient outcomes research team (PORT) treatment recommendations. *Schizophrenia Bulletin, 24*, 1–10. (p. 672)

Lehman, D. R., Wortman, C. B., & Williams, A. F. (1987). Long-term effects of losing a spouse or child in a motor vehicle crash. *Journal of Personality and Social Psychology, 52*, 218–231. (p. 220)

Leigh, B. C. (1989). In search of the seven dwarves: Issues of measurement and meaning in alcohol expectancy research. *Psychological Bulletin, 105*, 361–373. (p. 116)

Leitenberg, H., & Henning, K. (1995). Sexual fantasy. *Psychological Bulletin, 117*, 469–496. (pp. 468, 470)

Lemonick, M. D. (2002, June 3). Lean and hungrier. *Time*, p. 54. (p. 451)

L'Engle, M. (1972). *A wind in the door*. Bantam Doubleday Dell Books for Young Readers. (p. 15)

Lennox, B. R., Bert, S., Park, G., Jones, P. B., & Morris, P. G. (1999). Spatial and temporal mapping of neural activity associated with auditory hallucinations. *Lancet, 353*, 644. (p. 71)

Lenzenweger, M. F., Dworkin, R. H., & Wethington, E. (1989). Models of positive and negative symptoms in schizophrenia: An empirical evaluation of latent structures. *Journal of Abnormal Psychology, 98*, 62–70. (p. 672)

Lerner, M. J. (1980). *The belief in a just world: A fundamental delusion*. New York: Plenum Press. (p. 709)

Leserman, J., Jackson, E. D., Petitto, J. M., Golden, R. N., Silva, S. G., Perkins, D. O., Cai, J., Folds, J. D., & Evans, D. L. (1999). Progression to AIDS: The effects of stress, depressive symptoms, and social support. *Psychosomatic Medicine, 61*, 397–406. (p. 540)

Lessard, N., Pare, M., Lepore, F., & Lassonde, M. (1998). Early-blind human subjects localize sound sources better than sighted subjects. *Nature, 395*, 278–280. (p. 248)

Lester, W. (2004, May 26). AP polls: Nations value immigrant workers. Associated Press release. (p. 704)

Leucht, S., Barnes, T. R. E., Kissling, W., Engel, R. R., Correll, C., & Kane, J. M. (2003). Relapse prevention in schizophrenia with new-generation antipsychotics: A systematic review and exploratory meta-analysis of randomized, controlled trials. *American Journal of Psychiatry, 160*, 1209–1222. (p. 672)

Leung, A. K.-Y., Maddux, W. W., Galinsky, A. D., & Chiu, C.-Y. (2008). Multicultural experience enhances creativity: The when and how. *American Psychologist, 63*, 169–181. (p. 410)

LeVay, S. (1991). A difference in hypothalamic structure between heterosexual and homosexual men. *Science, 253*, 1034–1037. (p. 475)

LeVay, S. (1994, March). Quoted in D. Nimmons, Sex and the brain. *Discover*, p. 64–71. (p. 475)

Levenson, R. W. (1992). Autonomic nervous system differences among emotions. *Psychological Science, 3*, 23–27. (p. 503)

Lever, J. (2003, November 11). Personal correspondence reporting data responses volunteered to *Elle/MSNBC.com* survey of weight perceptions. (p. 454)

Levesque, M. J., & Kenny, D. A. (1993). Accuracy of behavioral predictions at zero acquaintance: A social relations analysis. *Journal of Personality and Social Psychology, 65*, 1178–1187. (p. 582)

Levin, I. P., & Gaeth, G. J. (1988). How consumers are affected by the framing of attribute information before and after consuming the product. *Journal of Consumer Research, 15*, 374–378. (p. 381)

Levin, R., & Nielsen, T. A. (2007). Disturbed dreaming, posttraumatic stress disorder, and affect distress: A review and neurocognitive model. *Psychological Bulletin, 133*, 482–528. (p. 103)

Levine, J. A., Eberhardt, N. L., & Jensen, M. D. (1999). Role of nonexercise activity thermogenesis in resistance to fat gain in humans. *Science, 283*, 212–214. (p. 459)

Levine, J. A., Lanningham-Foster, L. M., McCrady, S. K., Krizan, A. C., Olson, L. R., Kane, P. H., Jensen, M. D., & Clark, M. M. (2005). Interindividual variation in posture allocation: Possible role in human obesity. *Science, 307*, 584–586. (p. 460)

Levine, R., Sato, S., Hashimoto, T., & Verma, J. (1995). Love and marriage in eleven cultures. *Journal of Cross-Cultural Psychology, 26*, 554–571. (p. 725)

Levine, R. V., & Norenzayan, A. (1999). The pace of life in 31 countries. *Journal of Cross-Cultural Psychology, 30*, 178–205. (pp. 29, 153)

Levy, B., & Langer, E. (1992). Avoidance of the memory loss stereotype: Enhanced memory among the elderly deaf. Paper presented at American Psychological Association convention, Washington, DC. (p. 248)

Levy, P. E. (2003). Industrial/organizational psychology: Understanding the workplace. Boston: Houghton Mifflin. (p. 489)

Lewald, J. (2007). More accurate sound localisation induced by short-term light deprivation. *Neuropsychologia, 45*, 1215–1222. (p. 249)

Lewandowski, G. W., Jr., Aron, A., & Gee, J. (2007). Personality goes a long way: The malleability of opposite-sex physical attractiveness. *Personality Relationships, 14*, 571–585. (p. 723)

Lewicki, P. (1985). Nonconscious biasing effects of single instances on subsequent judgments. *Journal of Personality and Social Psychology, 48*, 563–574. (p. 348)

Lewicki, P., Hill, T., & Czyzewska, M. (1992). Nonconscious acquisition of information. *American Psychologist, 47*, 796–801. (p. 566)

Lewicki, P., Hill, T., & Czyzewska, M. (1997). Hidden covariation detection: A fundamental and ubiquitous phenomenon. *Journal of Experimental Psychology: Learning, Memory, and Cognition, 23*, 221–228. (p. 566)

Lewinsohn, P. M., Hoberman, H., Teri, L., & Hautziner, M. (1985). An integrative theory of depression. In S. Reiss & R. Bootzin (Eds.), *Theoretical issues in behavior therapy*. Orlando, FL: Academic Press. (p. 627)

Lewinsohn, P. M., Petit, J., Joiner, T. E., Jr., & Seeley, J. R. (2003). The symptomatic expression of major depressive disorder in adolescents and young adults. *Journal of Abnormal Psychology, 112*, 244–252. (p. 627)

Lewinsohn, P. M., Rohde, P., & Seeley, J. R. (1998). Major depressive disorder in older adolescents: Prevalence, risk factors, and clinical implications. *Clinical Psychology Review, 18*, 765–794. (p. 627)

Lewinsohn, P. M., & Rosenbaum, M. (1987). Recall of parental behavior by acute depressives, remitted depressives, and nondepressives. *Journal of Personality and Social Psychology, 52*, 611–619. (p. 349)

Lewis, C. S. (1960). *Mere Christianity*. New York: Macmillan. (p. 3)

Lewis, C. S. (1967). *Christian reflections*. Grand Rapids, MI: Eerdmans. (p. 352)

Lewis, D. O., Pincus, J. H., Bard, B., Richardson, E., Prichep, L. S., Feldman, M., & Yeager, C. (1988). Neuropsychiatric, psychoeducational, and family characteristics of 14 juveniles condemned to death in the United States. *American Journal of Psychiatry, 145*, 584–589. (p. 189)

Lewis, D. O., Pincus, J. H., Feldman, M., Jackson, L., & Bard, B. (1986). Psychiatric, neurological, and psychoeducational characteristics of 15 death row inmates in the United States. *American Journal of Psychiatry, 143*, 838–845. (p. 710)

Lewis, D. O., Yeager, C. A., Swica, Y., Pincus, J. H., & Lewis, M. (1997). Objective documentation of child abuse and dissociation in 12 murderers with dissociative identity disorder. *American Journal of Psychiatry, 154*, 1703–1710. (p. 620)

Lewis, M. (1992). Commentary. *Human Development, 35*, 44–51. (p. 350)

Lewontin, R. (1976). Race and intelligence. In N. J. Block & G. Dworkin (Eds.), *The IQ controversy: Critical readings*. New York: Pantheon. (p. 436)

Lewontin, R. (1982). *Human diversity*. New York: Scientific American Library. (pp. 142, 436)

Li, J. C., Dunning, D., & Malpass, R. L. (1996). Cross-racial identification among European-Americans basketball fandom and the contact hypothesis. Unpublished manuscript, Cornell University. (p. 709)

Li, J., Laursen, T. M., Precht, D. H., Olsen, J., & Mortensen, P. B. (2005). Hospitalization for mental illness among parents after the death of a child. *New England Journal of Medicine, 352*, 1190–1196. (p. 220)

Li, W., Moallem, I., Paller, K. A., & Gottfried, J. A. (2007). Subliminal smells can guide social preferences. *Psychological Science, 18*, 1044–1049. (p. 229)

Libet, B. (1985). Unconscious cerebral initiative and the role of conscious will in voluntary action. *Behavioral and Brain Sciences, 12*, 181–187. (p. 87)

Libet, B. (2004). *Mind time: The temporal factor in consciousness*. Cambridge, MA: Harvard University Press. (p. 87)

Licata, A., Taylor, S., Berman, M., & Cranston, J. (1993). Effects of cocaine on human aggression. *Pharmacology Biochemistry and Behavior, 45*, 549–552. (p. 120)

Lieberman, J. A. (2006). Comparative effectiveness of antipsychotic drugs. *Archives of General Psychiatry, 63,* 1069–1072. (p. 672)

Lieberman, J. A., & 11 others. (2005). Effectiveness of antipsychotic drugs in patients with chronic schizophrenia. *New England Journal of Medicine, 353,* 1209–1223. (p. 672)

Lieberman, M. D., Eisenberger, N. L., Crockett, M. J., Tom, S. M., Pfeifer, J. H., & Way, B. M. (2007). Putting feelings into words: Affect labeling disrupts amygdala activity in response to affective stimuli. *Psychological Science, 18,* 421–428. (p. 547)

Lilienfeld, S. O., & Arkowitz, H. (2007, April/May). Autism: An epidemic. *Scientific American Mind,* pp. 82–83. (p. 182)

Lilienfeld, S. O., & Arkowitz, H. (2007, December, 2006/January, 2007). Taking a closer look: Can moving your eyes back and forth help to ease anxiety? *Scientific American Mind,* pp. 80–81. (p. 665)

Lilienfeld, S. O., Lynn, S. J., Kirsch, I., Chaves, J. F., Sarbin, T. R., Ganaway, G. K., & Powell, R. A. (1999). Dissociative identity disorder and the sociocognitive model: Recalling the lessons of the past. *Psychological Bulletin, 125,* 507–523. (p. 619)

Lilienfeld, S. O., Wood, J. M., & Garb, H. N. (2001, May). What's wrong with this picture? *Scientific American,* pp. 81–87. (p. 565)

Lin, L., Faraco, J., Li, R., Kadotani, H., Rogers, W., Lin, X., Qiu, X., de Jong, P. J., Nishino, S., & Mignot E. (1999). The sleep disorder canine narcolepsy is caused by a mutation in the hypocretin (orexin) receptor 2 gene. *Cell, 98,* 365–376. (p. 101)

Linde, K., & 10 others. (2005). Acupuncture for patients with migraine: A randomized controlled trial. *Journal of the American Medical Association, 293,* 2118–2125. (p. 550)

Linder, D. (1982). Social trap analogs: The tragedy of the commons in the laboratory. In V. J. Derlega & J. Grzelak (Eds.), *Cooperative and helping behavior: Theories and research.* New York: Academic Press. (p. 730)

Lindskold, S. (1978). Trust development, the GRIT proposal, and the effects of conciliatory acts on conflict and cooperation. *Psychological Bulletin, 85,* 772–793. (p. 733)

Lindskold, S., & Han, G. (1988). GRIT as a foundation for integrative bargaining. *Personality and Social Psychology Bulletin, 14,* 335–345. (p. 733)

Linville, P. W., Fischer, G. W., & Fischhoff, B. (1992). AIDS risk perceptions and decision biases. In J. B. Pryor & G. D. Reeder (Eds.), *The social psychology of HIV infection.* Hillsdale, NJ: Erlbaum. (p. 381)

Lippa, R. A. (2002). Gender-related traits of heterosexual and homosexual men and women. *Archives of Sexual Behavior, 31,* 83–98. (p. 474)

Lippa, R. A. (2005). *Gender, nature, and nurture* (2nd ed.). Mahwah, NJ: Erlbaum. (p. 159)

Lippa, R. A. (2005). Sexual orientation and personality. *Annual Review of Sex Research, 16,* 119–153. (p. 473)

Lippa, R. A. (2006). Is high sex drive associated with increased sexual attraction to both sexes? It depends on whether you are male or female. *Psychological Science, 17,* 46–52. (p. 474)

Lippa, R. A. (2006). The gender reality hypothesis. *American Psychologist, 61,* 639–640. (p. 159)

Lippa, R. A. (2007a). The relation between sex drive and sexual attraction to men and women: A cross-national study of heterosexual, bisexual, and homosexual men and women. *Archives of Sexual Behavior, 36,* 209–222. (p. 478)

Lippa, R. A. (2007b). The preferred traits of mates in a cross-national study of heterosexual and homosexual men and women: An examination of biological and cultural influences. *Archives of Sexual Behavior, 36,* 193–208. (pp. 474, 478, 721)

Lippa, R. A. (2008) Sex differences and sexual orientation differences in personality: Findings from the BBC Internet survey. *Archives of Sexual Behavior, Special Issue: Biological research on sex-dimorphic behavior and sexual orientation, 37*(1), 173–187. (pp. 144, 159, 478)

Lippman, J. (1992, October 25). Global village is characterized by a television in every home. *Grand Rapids Press,* p. F9. (p. 319)

Lipps, H. M. (1999). *A new psychology of women: Gender, culture, and ethnicity.* Mountain View, CA: Mayfield Publishing. (p. 704)

Lipsey, M. W., & Wilson, D. B. (1993). The efficacy of psychological, educational, and behavioral treatment: Confirmation from meta-analyses. *American Psychologist, 48,* 1181–1209. (p. 426)

Lipsitt, L. P. (2003). Crib death: A biobehavioral phenomenon? *Current Directions in Psychological Science, 12,* 164–170. (p. 175)

Livesley, W. J., & Jang, K. L. (2008). The behavioral genetics of personality disorder. *Annual Review of Clinical Psychology, 4,* 247–274. (p. 621)

Livingstone, M., & Hubel, D. (1988). Segregation of form, color, movement, and depth: Anatomy, physiology, and perception. *Science, 240,* 740–749. (p. 239)

LoBue, V., & DeLoache, J. S. (2008). Detecting the snake in the grass: Attention to fear-relevant stimuli by adults and young children. *Psychological Science, 19,* 284–289. (p. 615)

Loehlin, J. C., Horn, J. M., & Ernst, J. L. (2007). Genetic and environmental influences on adult life outcomes: Evidence from the Texas adoption project. *Behavior Genetics, 37,* 463–476. (p. 137)

Loehlin, J. C., McCrae, R. R., & Costa, P. T., Jr. (1998). Heritabilities of common and measure-specific components of the Big Five personality factors. *Journal of Research in Personality, 32,* 431–453. (p. 579)

Loehlin, J. C., & Nichols, R. C. (1976). *Heredity, environment, and personality.* Austin: University of Texas Press. (p. 134)

Loewenstein, G., & Furstenberg, F. (1991). Is teenage sexual behavior rational? *Journal of Applied Social Psychology, 21,* 957–986. (p. 305)

Loftus, E. (1995, March/April). Remembering dangerously. *Skeptical Inquirer,* pp. 20–29. (p. 566)

Loftus, E. F. (1979). The malleability of human memory. *American Scientist, 67,* 313–320. (p. 358)

Loftus, E. F. (1980). Memory: Surprising new insights into how we remember and why we forget. Reading, MA: Addison-Wesley. (p. 109)

Loftus, E. F. (1993). The reality of repressed memories. *American Psychologist, 48,* 518–537. (p. 365)

Loftus, E. F. (2001, November). Imagining the past. *The Psychologist, 14,* 584–587. (p. 359)

Loftus, E. F., Coan, J., & Pickrell, J. E. (1996). Manufacturing false memories using bits of reality. In L. Reder (Ed.), *Implicit memory and metacognition.* Mahwah, NJ: Erlbaum. (p. 363)

Loftus, E. F., & Ketcham, K. (1994). *The myth of repressed memory.* New York: St. Martin's Press. (pp. 103, 364)

Loftus, E. F., Levidow, B., & Duensing, S. (1992). Who remembers best? Individual differences in memory for events that occurred in a science museum. *Applied Cognitive Psychology, 6,* 93–107. (p. 358)

Loftus, E. F., & Loftus, G. R. (1980). On the permanence of stored information in the human brain. *American Psychologist, 35,* 409–420. (p. 339)

Loftus, E. F., Milo, E. M., & Paddock, J. R. (1995). The accidental executioner: Why psychotherapy must be informed by science. *The Counseling Psychologist, 23,* 300–309. (p. 363)

Loftus, E. F., & Palmer, J. C. (October, 1974). Reconstruction of automobile destruction: An example of the interaction between language and memory. *Journal of Verbal Learning & Verbal Behavior, 13*(5), 585–589. (p. 357)

Logan, T. K., Walker, R., Cole, J., & Leukefeld, C. (2002). Victimization and substance abuse among women: Contributing factors, interventions, and implications. *Review of General Psychology, 6,* 325–397. (p. 126)

Logue, A. W. (1998a). Laboratory research on self-control: Applications to administration. *Review of General Psychology, 2,* 221–238. (p. 304)

Logue, A. W. (1998b). Self-control. In W. T. O'Donohue (Ed.), *Learning and behavior therapy.* Boston, MA: Allyn & Bacon. (p. 304)

London, P. (1970). The rescuers: Motivational hypotheses about Christians who saved Jews from the Nazis. In J. Macaulay & L. Berkowitz (Eds.), *Altruism and helping behavior.* New York: Academic Press. (p. 318)

Looy, H. (2001). Sex differences: Evolved, constructed, and designed. *Journal of Psychology and Theology, 29,* 301–313. (p. 146)

Lopes, P. N., Brackett, M. A., Nezlek, J. B., Schutz, A., Sellin, II, & Salovey, P. (2004). Emotional intelligence and social interaction. *Personality and Social Psychology Bulletin, 30,* 1018–1034. (p. 411)

Lopez, D. J. (2002, January/February). Snaring the fowler: Mark Twain debunks phrenology. *Skeptical Inquirer* (www.csicop.org). (p. 45)

Lord, C. G., Lepper, M. R., & Preston, E. (1984). Considering the opposite: A corrective strategy for social judgment. *Journal of Personality and Social Psychology, 47,* 1231–1247. (p. 377)

Lord, C. G., Ross, L., & Lepper, M. (1979). Biased assimilation and attitude polarization: The effects of prior theories on subsequently considered evidence. *Journal of Personality and Social Psychology, 37,* 2098–2109. (p. 377)

Lorenz, K. (1937). The companion in the bird's world. *Auk, 54,* 245–273. (p. 187)

Los Angeles Times. (1998, 14 March). Daughters give birth on same day. P. A15. (p. 34)

Louie, K., & Wilson, M. A. (2001). Temporally structured replay of awake hippocampal ensemble activity during rapid eye movement sleep. *Neuron, 29,* 145–156. (p. 104)

Lourenco, O., & Machado, A. (1996). In defense of Piaget's theory: A reply to 10 common criticisms. *Psychological Review, 103,* 143–164. (p. 185)

Lovaas, O. I. (1987). Behavioral treatment and normal educational and intellectual functioning in young autistic children. *Journal of Consulting and Clinical Psychology, 55,* 3–9. (p. 653)

Love, J. M., & 13 others (2003). Child care quality matters: How conclusions may vary with context. *Child Development, 74,* 1021–1033. (p. 191)

Lowry, P. E. (1997). The assessment center process: New directions. *Journal of Social Behavior and Personality, 12,* 53–62. (p. 590)

Lu, Z.-L., Williamson, S. J., & Kaufman, L. (1992). Behavioral lifetime of human auditory sensory memory predicted by physiological measures. *Science, 258,* 1668–1670. (p. 337)

Lubinski, D., & Benbow, C. P. (1992). Gender differences in abilities and preferences among the gifted: Implications for the math-science pipeline. *Current Directions in Psychological Science, 1,* 61–66. (p. 432)

Lubinski, D., & Benbow, C. P. (2000). States of excellence. *American Psychologist,* 137–150. (p. 426)

Lubinski, D., & Benbow, C. P. (2006). Study of mathematically precocious youth after 35 years: Uncovering antecedents for the development of math-science expertise. *Perspectives on Psychological Science, 1,* 316–345. (p. 426)

Luborsky, L., Rosenthal, R., Diguer, L., Andrusyna, T. P., Berman, J. S., Levitt, J. T., Seligman, D. A., & Krause, E. D. (2002). The dodo bird verdict is alive and well—mostly. *Clinical Psychology: Science and Practice, 9,* 2–34. (p. 663)

Lucas, A., Morley, R., Cole, T. J., Lister, G., & Leeson-Payne, C. (1992). Breast milk and subsequent intelligence quotient in children born preterm. *Lancet, 339,* 261–264. (p. 34)

Lucas, R. E. (2007a). Adaptation and the set-point model of subjective well-being. *Current Directions in Psychological Science, 16,* 75–79. (p. 523)

Lucas, R. E. (2007b). Long-term disability is associated with lasting changes in subjective well-being: Evidence from two nationally representative longitudinal studies. *Journal of Personality and Social Psychology, 92,* 717–730. (p. 523)

Lucas, R. E. (2008). Personality and subjective well-being. In M. Eid & R. Larsen (Eds.), *The science of subjective well-being.* New York: Guilford. (p. 528)

Lucas, R. E., Clark, A. E., Georgellis, Y., & Diener, E. (2003). Re-examining adaptation and the setpoint model of happiness: Reactions to changes in marital status. *Journal of Personality and Social Psychology, 84,* 527–539. (p. 221)

Lucas, R. E., Clark, A. E., Georgellis, Y., & Diener, E. (2004). Unemployment alters the set point for life satisfaction. *Psychological Science, 15,* 8–13. (p. 529)

Lucas, R. E., & Donnellan, M. B. (2007). How stable is happiness? Using the STARTS model to estimate the stability of life satisfaction. *Journal of Research in Personality, 41,* 1091–1098. (p. 528)

Luciano, M., Posthuma, D., Wright, M. J., de Geus, E. J. C., Smith, G. A., Geffen, G. M., Boomsma, D. I., & Martin, N. G. (2005). Perceptual speed does not cause intelligence, and intelligence does not cause perceptual speed. *Biological Psychology, 70,* 1–8. (p. 414)

Ludwig, A. M. (1995). *The price of greatness: Resolving the creativity and madness controversy.* New York: Guilford Press. (pp. 474, 626)

Luntz, F. (2003, June 10). Quoted by T. Raum, Bush insists banned weapons will be found. Associated Press (story.news.yahoo.com). (p. 688)

Luria, A. M. (1968). In L. Solotaroff (Trans.), *The mind of a mnemonist.* New York: Basic Books. (p. 324)

Lustig, C., & Buckner, R. L. (2004). Preserved neural correlates of priming in old age and dementia. *Neuron, 42,* 865–875. (p. 343)

Lutgendorf, S. K., Russell, D., Ullrich, P., Harris, T. B., & Wallace, R. (2004). Religious participation, interleukin-6, and mortality in older adults. *Health Psychology, 23,* 465–475. (p. 554)

Lyall, S. (2005, November 29). What's the buzz? Rowdy teenagers don't want to hear it. *New York Times* (www.nytimes.com). (p. 209)

Lykins, A. D., Meana, M., & Strauss, G. P. (2008). Sex differences in visual attention to erotic and non-erotic stimuli. *Archives of Sexual Behavior, 37,* 219–228. (p. 474)

Lykken, D. T. (1982, September). Fearlessness: Its carefree charm and deadly risks. *Psychology Today,* pp. 20–28. (p. 519)

Lykken, D. T. (1991). Science, lies, and controversy: An epitaph for the polygraph. Invited address upon receipt of the Senior Career Award for Distinguished Contribution to Psychology in the Public Interest, American Psychological Association convention. (p. 504)

Lykken, D. T. (1995). *The antisocial personalities.* Hillsdale, NJ: Erlbaum. (pp. 621, 711)

Lykken, D. T. (1999). *Happiness.* New York: Golden Books. (pp. 214, 428)

Lykken, D. T. (2001). Happiness—stuck with what you've got? *The Psychologist, 14,* 470–473. (p. 137)

Lykken, D. T., & Tellegen, A. (1993). Is human mating adventitious or the result of lawful choice? A twin study of mate selection. *Journal of Personality and Social Psychology, 65,* 56–68. (p. 216)

Lykken, D. T., & Tellegen, A. (1996). Happiness is a stochastic phenomenon. *Psychological Science, 7,* 186–189. (p. 528)

Lyman, D. R. (1996). Early identification of chronic offenders: Who is the fledgling psychopath? *Psychological Bulletin, 120,* 209–234. (p. 622)

Lynch, G. (2002). Memory enhancement: The search for mechanism-based drugs. *Nature Neuroscience, 5* (suppl.), 1035–1038. (p. 340)

Lynch, G., & Staubli, U. (1991). Possible contributions of long-term potentiation to the encoding and organization of memory. *Brain Research Reviews, 16,* 204–206. (p. 340)

Lynn, M. (1988). The effects of alcohol consumption on restaurant tipping. *Personality and Social Psychology Bulletin, 14,* 87–91. (p. 115)

Lynn, R. (1991, Fall/Winter). The evolution of racial differences in intelligence. *The Mankind Quarterly, 32,* 99–145. (p. 435)

Lynn, R. (2001). *Eugenics: A reassessment.* Westport, CT: Praeger/ Greenwood. (p. 435)

Lynn, R., & Harvey, J. (2008). The decline of the world's intelligence. *Intelligence, 36,* 112–120. (p. 421)

Lynn, S. J., Rhue, J. W., & Weekes, J. R. (1990). Hypnotic involuntariness: A social cognitive analysis. *Psychological Review, 97,* 169–184. (p. 110)

Lynne, S. D., Graber, J. A., Nichols, T. R., Brooks-Gunn, J., & Botvin, G. J. (2007). Links between pubertal timing, peer influences, and externalizing behaviors among urban students followed through middle school. *Journal of Adolescent Health, 40,* 181.e7–181.e13. (p. 197)

Lyons, L. (2002, June 25). Are spiritual teens healthier? *Gallup Tuesday Briefing,* Gallup Organization (www.gallup.com/poll/tb/religValue/20020625b.asp). (p. 553)

Lyons, L. (2003, September 23). Oh, boy: Americans still prefer sons. *Gallup Poll Tuesday Briefing* (www.gallup.com). (p. 704)

Lyons, L. (2004, February 3). Growing up lonely: Examining teen alienation. *Gallup Poll Tuesday Briefing* (www.gallup.com). (p. 202)

Lyons, L. (2005, January 4). Teens stay true to parents' political perspectives. *Gallup Poll News Service* (www.gallup.com). (p. 204)

Lytton, H., & Romney, D. M. (1991). Parents' differential socialization of boys and girls: A meta-analysis. *Psychological Bulletin, 109,* 267–296. (p. 163)

Lyubomirsky, S. (2001). Why are some people happier than others? The role of cognitive and motivational processes in well-being. *American Psychologist, 56,* 239–249. (p. 528)

Lyubomirsky, S., King, L., & Diener, E. (2005). The benefits of frequent positive affect: Does happiness lead to success? *Psychological Bulletin, 131,* 803–855. (p. 522)

Lyubomirsky, S., Sousa, L., & Dickerhoof, R. (2006). The costs and benefits of writing, talking, and thinking about life's triumphs and defeats. *Journal of Personality and Social Psychology,* in press. (p. 546)

Ma, L. (1997, September). On the origin of Darwin's ills. *Discover*, p. 27. (p. 612)

Maas, J. B. (1999). Power sleep. The revolutionary program that prepares your mind and body for peak performance. New York: HarperCollins. (pp. 97, 98, 101)

Maass, A., D'Ettole, C., & Cadinu, M. (2008). Checkmate? The role of gender stereotypes in the ultimate intellectual sport. *European Journal of Social Psychology, 38*, 231–245. (p. 439)

Maass, A., Karasawa, M., Politi, F., & Suga, S. (2006). Do verbs and adjectives play different roles in different cultures? A cross-linguistic analysis of person representation. *Journal of Personality and Social Psychology, 90*, 734–750. (p. 155)

Maass, A., & Russo, A. (2003). Directional bias in the mental representation of spatial events: Nature or culture? *Psychological Science, 14*, 296–301. (p. 393)

Macaluso, E., Frith, C. D., & Driver, J. (2000). Modulation of human visual cortex by crossmodal spatial attention. *Science, 289*, 1206–1208. (p. 258)

Macan, T. H., & Dipboye, R. L. (1994). The effects of the application on processing of information from the employment interview. *Journal of Applied Social Psychology, 24*, 1291. (p. 488)

Maccoby, E. (1980). *Social development: Psychological growth and the parent-child relationship.* New York: Harcourt Brace Jovanovich. (p. 192)

Maccoby, E. E. (1990). Gender and relationships: A developmental account. *American Psychologist, 45*, 513–520. (p. 158)

Maccoby, E. E. (1995). Divorce and custody: The rights, needs, and obligations of mothers, fathers, and children. *Nebraska Symposium on Motivation, 42*, 135–172. (p. 162)

Maccoby, E. E. (1998). *The paradox of gender.* Cambridge, MA: Harvard University Press. (p. 160)

Maccoby, E. E. (2002). Gender and group process: A developmental perspective. *Current Directions in Psychological Science, 11*, 54–58. (p. 699)

Maccoby, E. E. (2003, July 22). In Susan Gilbert, Turning a mass of data on child care into advice for parents. *New York Times* (www.nytimes.com). (p. 191)

MacDonald, G., & Leary, M. R. (2005). Why does social exclusion hurt? The relationship between social and physical pain. *Psychological Bulletin, 131*, 202–223. (p. 482)

MacDonald, N. (1960). Living with schizophrenia. *Canadian Medical Association Journal, 82*, 218–221. (p. 637)

MacDonald, T. K., & Hynie, M. (2008). Ambivalence and unprotected sex: Failure to predict sexual activity and decreased condom use. *Journal of Applied Social Psychology, 38*, 1092–1107. (p. 471)

MacDonald, T. K., Zanna, M. P., & Fong, G. T. (1995). Decision making in altered states: Effects of alcohol on attitudes toward drinking and driving. *Journal of Personality and Social Psychology, 68*, 973–985. (p. 116)

MacFarlane, A. (1978, February). What a baby knows. *Human Nature*, pp. 74–81. (p. 173)

Macfarlane, J. W. (1964). Perspectives on personality consistency and change from the guidance study. *Vita Humana, 7*, 115–126. (p. 195)

Maciejewski, P. K., Zhang, B., Block, S. D., & Prigerson, H. G. (2007). An empirical examination of the stage theory of grief. *Journal of the American Medical Association, 297*, 722–723. (p. 221)

Mack, A., & Rock, I. (2000). *Inattentional blindness.* Cambridge, MA: MIT Press. (p. 89)

MacKinnon, D. W., & Hall, W. B. (1972). Intelligence and creativity. In *Proceedings, XVIIth International Congress of Applied Psychology* (Vol. 2). Brussels: Editest. (p. 409)

MacNeilage, P. F., & Davis, B. L. (2000). On the origin of internal structure of word forms. *Science, 288*, 527–531. (p. 387)

Maddieson, I. (1984). *Patterns of sounds.* Cambridge: Cambridge University Press. (p. 385)

Maddox, K. B. (2004). Perspectives on racial phenotypicality bias. *Personality and Social Psychology Review, 8*, 383–401. (p. 705)

Madrian, B. C., & Shea, D. F. (2001). The power of suggestion: Inertia in 401(k) participation and savings behavior. *Quarterly Journal of Economics, 116*, 1149–1187. (p. 382)

Maes, H. H. M., Neale, M. C., & Eaves, L. J. (1997). Genetic and environmental factors in relative body weight and human adiposity. *Behavior Genetics, 27*, 325–351. (p. 460)

Maestripieri, D. (2003). Similarities in affiliation and aggression between cross-fostered rhesus macaque females and their biological mothers. *Developmental Psychobiology, 43*, 321–327. (p. 137)

Maestripieri, D. (2005). Early experience affects the intergenerational transmission of infant abuse in rhesus monkeys. *Proceedings of the National Academy of Sciences, 102*, 9726–9729. (p. 189)

Magnusson, D. (1990). Personality research—challenges for the future. *European Journal of Personality, 4*, 1–17. (p. 621)

Magnusson, P. E. E., Rasmussen, F., Lawlor, D. A., Tynelius, P., & Gunnell, D. (2006). Association of body mass index with suicide mortality: A prospective cohort study of more than one million men. *American Journal of Epidemiology, 163*, 1–8. (p. 630)

Maguire, E. A., Spiers, H. J., Good, C. D., Hartley, T., Frackowiak, R. S. J., & Burgess, N. (2003a). Navigation expertise and the human hippocampus: A structural brain imaging analysis. *Hippocampus, 13*, 250–259. (p. 344)

Maguire, E. A., Valentine, E. R., Wilding, J. M., & Kapur, N. (2003b). Routes to remembering: The brains behind superior memory. *Nature Neuroscience, 6*, 90–95. (pp. 333, 344)

Mahowald, M. W., & Ettinger, M. G. (1990). Things that go bump in the night: The parsomias revisted. *Journal of Clinical Neurophysiology, 7*, 119–143. (p. 94)

Maier, S. F., Watkins, L. R., & Fleshner, M. (1994). Psychoneuroimmunology: The interface between behavior, brain, and immunity. *American Psychologist, 49*, 1004–1017. (pp. 538, 539)

Major, B., Carrington, P. I., & Carnevale, P. J. D. (1984). Physical attractiveness and self-esteem: Attribution for praise from an other-sex evaluator. *Personality and Social Psychology Bulletin, 10*, 43–50. (p. 722)

Major, B., Schmidlin, A. M., & Williams, L. (1990). Gender patterns in social touch: The impact of setting and age. *Journal of Personality and Social Psychology, 58*, 634–643. (p. 158)

Malamuth, N. M. (1996). Sexually explicit media, gender differences, and evolutionary theory. *Journal of Communication, 46*, 8–31. (p. 714)

Malamuth, N. M., & Check, J. V. P. (1981). The effects of media exposure on acceptance of violence against women: A field experiment. *Journal of Research in Personality, 15*, 436–446. (p. 469)

Malamuth, N. M., Linz, D., Heavey, C. L., Barnes, G., & Acker, M. (1995). Using the confluence model of sexual aggression to predict men's conflict with women: A 10-year follow-up study. *Journal of Personality and Social Psychology, 69*, 353–369. (p. 715)

Malamuth, N. M., Sockloskie, R. J., Koss, M. P., & Tanaka, J. S. (1991). Characteristics of aggressors against women: Testing a model using a national sample of college students. *Journal of Consulting and Clinical Psychology, 59*, 670–681. (p. 715)

Malan, D. H. (1978). The case of the secretary with the violent father. In H. Davanloo (Ed.), *Basic principles and techniques in short-term dynamic psychotherapy.* New York: Spectrum. (p. 648)

Malinosky-Rummell, R., & Hansen, D. J. (1993). Long-term consequences of childhood physical abuse. *Psychological Bulletin, 114*, 68–79. (p. 189)

Malkiel, B. (2004). *A random walk down Wall Street* (8th ed.). New York: Norton. (p. 377)

Malkiel, B. G. (1989). Is the stock market efficient? *Science, 243*, 1313–1318. (p. 33)

Malkiel, B. G. (1995, June). Returns from investing in equity mutual funds 1971 to 1991. *Journal of Finance*, pp. 549–572. (p. 33)

Malle, B. F. (2006). The actor-observer asymmetry in attribution: A (surprising) meta-analysis. *Psychological Bulletin, 132*, 895–919. (p. 683)

Malle, B. F., Knobe, J. M., & Nelson, S. E. (2007). Actor-observe asymmetries in explanations of behavior: New answers to an old question. *Journal of Personality and Social Psychology, 93*, 491–514. (p. 683)

Malmquist, C. P. (1986). Children who witness parental murder: Posttraumatic aspects. *Journal of the American Academy of Child Psychiatry, 25*, 320–325. (p. 566)

Malnic, B., Hirono, J., Sato, T., & Buck, L. B. (1999). Combinatorial receptor codes for odors. *Cell, 96*, 713–723. (p. 260)

Manber, R., Bootzin, R. R., Acebo, C., & Carskadon, M. A. (1996). The effects of regularizing sleep-wake schedules on daytime sleepiness. *Sleep, 19*, 432–441. (p. 101)

Mandel, D. (1983, March 13). One man's holocaust: Part II. The story of David Mandel's journey through hell as told to David Kagan. *Wonderland Magazine* (*Grand Rapids Press*), pp. 2–7. (p. 448)

Maner, J. K., DeWall, C. N, Baumeister, R. F., & Schaller, M. (2007). Does social exclusion motivate interpersonal reconnection? Resolving the "porcupine problem." *Journal of Personality and Social Psychology, 92,* 42–55. (p. 482)

Mann, T., Tomiyama, A. J., Westling, E., Lew, A-M., Samuels, B., & Chatman, J. (2007). Medicare's search for effective obesity treatments: Diets are not the answer. *American Psychologist, 62,* 220–233. (p. 463)

Manson, J. E. (2002). Walking compared with vigorous exercise for the prevention of cardiovascular events in women. *New England Journal of Medicine, 347,* 716–725. (p. 548)

Maquet, P. (2001). The role of sleep in learning and memory. *Science, 294,* 1048–1052. (p. 104)

Maquet, P., Peters, J-M., Aerts, J., Delfiore, G., Degueldre, C., Luxen, A., & Franck, G. (1996). Functional neuroanatomy of human rapid-eye-movement sleep and dreaming. *Nature, 383,* 163–166. (p. 105)

Mar, R. A., & Oatley, K. (2008). The function of fiction is the abstraction and simulation of social experience. *Perspectives on Psychological Science, 3,* 173–192. (p. 317)

Marangell, L. B., Martinez, M., Jurdi, R. A., & Zboyan, H. (2007). Neurostimulation therapies in depression: A review of new modalities. *Acta Psychiatrica Scandinavica, 116,* 174–181. (p. 676)

Marcus, B., Machilek, F., & Schütz, A. (2006). Personality in cyberspace: Personal web sites as media for personality expressions and impressions. *Journal of Personality and Social Psychology, 90,* 1014–1031. (p. 581)

Marcus, G. F., Vijayan, S., Rao, S. B., & Vishton, P. M. (1999). Rule learning by seven-month-old infants. *Science, 283,* 77–80. (p. 389)

Maren, S. (2007). The threatened brain. *Science, 317,* 1043–1044. (p. 616)

Margolis, M. L. (2000). Brahms' lullaby revisited: Did the composer have obstructive sleep apnea? *Chest, 118,* 210–213. (p. 101)

Markowitsch, H. J. (1995). Which brain regions are critically involved in the retrieval of old episodic memory? *Brain Research Reviews, 21,* 117–127. (p. 344)

Markowitz, J. C., Svartberg, M., & Swartz, H. A. (1998). Is IPT time-limited psychodynamic psychotherapy? *Journal of Psychotherapy Practice and Research, 7,* 185–195. (p. 649)

Markus, G. B. (1986). Stability and change in political attitudes: Observe, recall, and "explain." *Political Behavior, 8,* 21–44. (p. 361)

Markus, H. R., & Kitayama, S. (1991). Culture and the self: Implications for cognition, emotion, and motivation. *Psychological Review, 98,* 224–253. (pp. 155, 393, 520)

Markus, H. R., & Nurius, P. (1986). Possible selves. *American Psychologist, 41,* 954–969. (p. 590)

Markus, H. R., Uchida, Y., Omoregie, H., Townsend, S. S. M., & Kitayama, S. (2006). Going for the gold: Models of agency in Japanese and American contexts. *Psychological Science, 17,* 103–112. (p. 155)

Marley, J., & Bulia, S. (2001). Crimes against people with mental illness: Types, perpetrators and influencing factors. *Social Work, 46,* 115–124. (p. 605)

Marmot, M. G., Bosma, H., Hemingway, H., Brunner, E., & Stansfeld, S. (1997). Contribution to job control and other risk factors to social variations in coronary heart disease incidents. *Lancet, 350,* 235–239. (p. 543)

Marschark, M., Richman, C. L., Yuille, J. C., & Hunt, R. R. (1987). The role of imagery in memory: On shared and distinctive information. *Psychological Bulletin, 102,* 28–41. (p. 333)

Marsh, A. A., Elfenbein, H. A., & Ambady, N. (2003). Nonverbal "accents": Cultural differences in facial expressions of emotion. *Psychological Science, 14,* 373–376. (p. 514)

Marsh, H. W., & Craven, R. G. (2006). Reciprocal effects of self-concept and performance from a multidimensional perspective: Beyond seductive pleasure and unidimensional perspectives. *Perspectives on Psychological Science, 1,* 133–163. (p. 591)

Marsh, H. W., & Parker, J. W. (1984). Determinants of student self-concept: Is it better to be a relatively large fish in a small pond even if you don't learn to swim as well? *Journal of Personality and Social Psychology, 47,* 213–231. (p. 528)

Marshall, M. J. (2002). *Why spanking doesn't work.* Springville, UT: Bonneville Books. (p. 307)

Marshall, R. D., Bryant, R. A., Amsel, L., Suh, E. J., Cook, J. M., & Neria, Y. (2007). The psychology of ongoing threat: Relative risk appraisal, the September 11 attacks, and terrorism-related fears. *American Psychologist, 62,* 304–316. (p. 376)

Marshall, W. L. (1989). Pornography and sex offenders. In D. Zillmann & J. Bryant (Eds.), *Pornography: Research advances and policy considerations.* Hillsdale, NJ: Erlbaum. (p. 714)

Marteau, T. M. (1989). Framing of information: Its influences upon decisions of doctors and patients. *British Journal of Social Psychology, 28,* 89–94. (p. 381)

Marti, M. W., Robier, D. M., & Baron, R. S. (2000). Right before our eyes: The failure to recognize non-prototypical forms of prejudice. *Group Processes and Intergroup Relations, 3,* 403–418. (p. 371)

Martin, C. K., Anton, S. D., Walden, H., Arnett, C., Greenway, F. L., & Williamson, D. A. (2007). Slower eating rate reduces the food intake of men, but not women: Implications for behavioural weight control. *Behaviour Research and Therapy, 45,* 2349–2359. (p. 463)

Martin, C. L., & Ruble, D. (2004). Children's search for gender cues. *Current Directions in Psychological Science, 13,* 67–70. (p. 163)

Martin, C. L., Ruble, D. N., & Szkrybalo, J. (2002). Cognitive theories of early gender development. *Psychological Bulletin, 128,* 903–933. (p. 163)

Martin, R. A. (2001). Humor, laughter, and physical health: Methodological issues and research findings. *Psychological Bulletin, 127,* 504–519. (p. 545)

Martin, R. A. (2002). Is laughter the best medicine? Humor, laughter, and physical health. *Current Directions in Psychological Science, 11,* 216–220. (p. 545)

Martin, R. J., White, B. D., & Hulsey, M. G. (1991). The regulation of body weight. *American Scientist, 79,* 528–541. (p. 451)

Martin, R. M., Goodall, S. H., Gunnell, D., & Smith, G. D. (2007). Breast feeding in infancy and social mobility: 60-year follow-up of the Boyd Orr cohort. *Archives of Disease in Childhood, 92,* 317–321. (p. 34)

Martino, S. C., Collins, R. L., Kanouse, D. E., Elliott, M., & Berry, S. H. (2005). Social cognitive processes mediating the relationship between exposure to television's sexual content and adolescents' sexual behavior. *Journal of Personality and Social Psychology, 89,* 914–924. (p. 471)

Martins, Y., Preti, G., Crabtree, C. R., & Wysocki, C. J. (2005). Preference for human body odors is influenced by gender and sexual orientation. *Psychological Science, 16,* 694–701. (p. 476)

Marx, J. (2005). Preventing Alzheimer's: A lifelong commitment? *Science, 309,* 864–866. (p. 212)

Marx, J. (2007). Evidence linking *DISC1* gene to mental illness builds. *Science, 318,* 1062–1063. (p. 642)

Masicampo, E. J., & Baumeister, R. F. (2008). Toward a physiology of dual-process reasoning and judgment: Lemonade, willpower, and the expensive rule-based analysis. *Psychological Science, 19,* 255–260. (p. 585)

Maslow, A. H. (1970). *Motivation and personality* (2nd ed.). New York: Harper & Row. (pp. 446, 570)

Maslow, A. H. (1971). *The farther reaches of human nature.* New York: Viking Press. (p. 447)

Mason, C., & Kandel, E. R. (1991). Central visual pathways. In E. R. Kandel, J. H. Schwartz, & T. M. Jessell (Eds.), *Principles of neural science* (3rd ed.). New York: Elsevier. (p. 52)

Mason, H. (2003, March 25). Wake up, sleepy teen. *Gallup Poll Tuesday Briefing* (www.gallup.com). (p. 97)

Mason, H. (2003, September 2). Americans, Britons at odds on animal testing. *Gallup Poll News Service* (www.gallup.com). (p. 21)

Mason, H. (2005, January 25). Who dreams, perchance to sleep? *Gallup Poll News Service* (www.gallup.com). (p. 97)

Mason, H. (2005, February 22). How many teens are on mood medication? *The Gallup Organization* (www.gallup.com). (p. 600)

Mason, R. A., & Just, M. A. (2004). How the brain processes causal inferences in text. *Psychological Science, 15,* 1–7. (p. 78)

Masse, L. C., & Tremblay, R. E. (1997). Behavior of boys in kindergarten and the onset of substance use during adolescence. *Archives of General Psychiatry, 54,* 62–68. (p. 126)

Massimini, M., Ferrarelli, F., Huber, R., Esser, S. K., Singh, H., & Tononi, G. (2005). Breakdown of cortical effective connectivity during sleep. *Science, 309,* 2228–2232. (p. 92)

Mast, M. S., & Hall, J. A. (2006). Women's advantage at remembering others' appearance: A systematic look at the why and when of a gender difference. *Personality and Social Psychology Bulletin, 32,* 353–364. (p. 722)

Masten, A. S. (2001). Ordinary magic: Resilience processes in development. *American Psychologist, 56,* 227–238. (p. 189)

Masters, W. H., & Johnson, V. E. (1966). *Human sexual response.* Boston: Little, Brown. (p. 466)

Mastroianni, G. R. (2002). Milgram and the Holocaust: A reexamination. *Journal of Theoretical and Philosophical Psychology, 22,* 158–173. (p. 695)

Mastroianni, G. R., & Reed, G. (2006). Apples, barrels, and Abu Ghraib. *Sociological Focus, 39,* 239–250. (p. 688)

Masuda, T., Ellsworth, P. C., Mesquita, B., Leu, J., Tanida, S., & Van de Veerdonk, E. (2008). Placing the face in context: Cultural differences in the perception of facial emotion. *Journal of Personality and Social Psychology, 94,* 365–381. (p. 515)

Masuda, T., & Kitayama, S. (2004). Perceiver-induced constraint and attitude attribution in Japan and the US: A case for the cultural dependence of the correspondence bias. *Journal of Experimental Social Psychology, 40,* 409–416. (p. 682)

Mataix-Cols, D., Rosario-Campos, M. C., & Leckman, J. F. (2005). A multidimensional model of obsessive-compulsive disorder. *American Journal of Psychiatry, 162,* 228–238. (p. 616)

Mataix-Cols, D., Wooderson, S., Lawrence, N., Brammer, M. J., Speckens, A., & Phillips, M. L. (2004). Distinct neural correlates of washing, checking, and hoarding symptom dimensions in obsessive-compulsive disorder. *Archives of General Psychiatry, 61,* 564–576. (p. 616)

Mather, M., Canli, T., English, T., Whitfield, S., Wais, P., Ochsner, K., Gabrieli, J. D. E., & Carstensen, L. L. (2004). Amygdala responses to emotionally valenced stimuli in older and younger adults. *Psychological Science, 15,* 259–263. (p. 219)

Matsumoto, D. (1994). *People: Psychology from a cultural perspective.* Pacific Grove, CA: Brooks/Cole. (p. 393)

Matsumoto, D., & Ekman, P. (1989). American-Japanese cultural differences in intensity ratings of facial expressions of emotion. *Motivation and Emotion, 13,* 143–157. (p. 514)

Matsumoto, D., & 60 others (2008). Mapping expressive differences around the world: The relationship between emotional display rules and individualism versus collectivism. *Journal of Cross-Cultural Psychology, 39,* 55–74. (p. 514)

Matsumoto, D., & Willingham, B. (2006). The thrill of victory and the agony of defeat: Spontaneous expressions of medal winners of the 2004 Athens Olympic Games. *Journal of Personality and Social Psychology, 91,* 568–581. (p. 513)

Matsuzawa, T. (2007). Comparative cognitive development. *Developmental Science, 10,* 97–103. (p. 398)

Matthews, K. A. (2005). Psychological perspectives on the development of coronary heart disease. *American Psychologist, 60,* 783–796. (p. 537)

Matthews, R. N., Domjan, M., Ramsey, M., & Crews, D. (2007). Learning effects on sperm competition and reproductive fitness. *Psychological Science, 18,* 758–762. (p. 292)

Maurer, D., & Maurer, C. (1988). *The world of the newborn.* New York: Basic Books. (p. 173)

May, C., & Hasher, L. (1998). Synchrony effects in inhibitory control over thought and action. *Journal of Experimental Psychology: Human Perception and Performance, 24,* 363–380. (p. 92)

May, P. A., & Gossage, J.P. (2001). Estimating the prevalence of fetal alcohol syndrome: A summary. *Alcohol Research and Health, 25,* 159–167. (p. 172)

Mayberg, H. S. (2006). Defining neurocircuits in depression: Strategies toward treatment selection based on neuroimaging phenotypes. *Psychiatric Annals, 36,* 259–268. (p. 677)

Mayberg, H. S. (2007). Defining the neural circuitry of depression: Toward a new nosology with therapeutic implications. *Biological Psychiatry, 61,* 729–730. (p. 677)

Mayberg, H. S., Lozano, A. M., Voon, V., McNeely, H. E., Seminowicz, D., Hamani, C., Schwalb, J. M., & Kennedy, S. H. (2005). Deep brain stimulation for treatment-resistant depression. *Neuron, 45,* 651–660. (p. 677)

Mayberry, R. I., Lock, E., & Kazmi, H. (2002). Linguistic ability and early language exposure. *Nature, 417,* 38. (p. 390)

Mayer, J. D., Salovey, P., & Caruso, D. (2002). *The Mayer-Salovey-Caruso emotional intelligence test (MSCEIT).* Toronto: Multi-Health Systems, Inc. (p. 411)

Mayer, J. D., Salovey, P., & Caruso, D. R. (2008). Emotional intelligence: New ability or eclectic traits? *American Psychologist, 63,* 503–517. (p. 411)

Mays, V. M., Cochran, S. D., & Barnes, N. W. (2007). Race, race-based discrimination, and health outcomes among African Americans. *Annual Review of Psychology, 58,* 201–225. (p. 535)

Mazur, A., & Booth, A. (1998). Testosterone and dominance in men. *Behavioral and Brain Sciences, 21,* 353–363. (p. 711)

Mazure, C., Keita, G., & Blehar, M. (2002). *Summit on women and depression: Proceedings and recommendations.* Washington, DC; American Psychological Association (www.apa.org/pi/wpo/women&depression.pdf). (p. 632)

Mazzoni, G., & Memon, A. (2003). Imagination can create false autobiographical memories. *Psychological Science, 14,* 186–188. (p. 359)

Mazzoni, G., & Vannucci, M. (2007). Hindsight bias, the misinformation effect, and false autobiographical memories. *Social Cognition, 25,* 203–220. (p. 361)

Mazzuca, J. (2002, August 20). Teens shrug off movie sex and violence. *Gallup Tuesday Briefing* (www.gallup.com/poll/tb/educayouth/20020820b.asp). (p. 320)

McAdams, D. P., & Pals, J. L. (2006). A new Big Five: Fundamental principles for an integrative science of personality. *American Psychologist, 61,* 204–217. (p. 557)

McAneny, L. (1996, September). Large majority think government conceals information about UFO's. *Gallup Poll Monthly,* pp. 23–26. (p. 349)

McBeath, M. K., Shaffer, D. M., & Kaiser, M. K. (1995). How baseball outfielders determine where to run to catch fly balls. *Science, 268,* 569–572. (p. 267)

McBurney, D. H. (1996). *How to think like a psychologist: Critical thinking in psychology.* Upper Saddle River, NJ: Prentice-Hall. (p. 72)

McBurney, D. H., & Collings, V. B. (1984). *Introduction to sensation and perception* (2nd ed.). Englewood Cliffs, NJ: Prentice-Hall. (pp. 269, 270)

McBurney, D. H., & Gent, J. F. (1979). On the nature of taste qualities. *Psychological Bulletin, 86,* 151–167. (p. 257)

McCain, N. L., Gray, D. P., Elswick, R. K., Jr., Robins, J. W., Tuck, I., Walter, J. M., Rausch, S. M., & Ketchum, J. M. (2008). A randomized clinical trial of alternative stress management interventions in persons with HIV infection. *Journal of Consulting and Clinical Psychology, 76,* 431–441. (p. 540)

McCann, I. L., & Holmes, D. S. (1984). Influence of aerobic exercise on depression. *Journal of Personality and Social Psychology, 46,* 1142–1147. (pp. 547, 548)

McCann, U. D., Eligulashvili, V., & Ricaurte, G. A. (2001). (+-)3,4-Methylenedioxymethamphetamine ('Ecstasy')-induced serotonin neurotoxicity: Clinical studies. *Neuropsychobiology, 42,* 11–16. (p. 122)

McCarthy, A., Lee, K., Itakura, S., & Muir, D. W. (2006). Cultural display rules drive eye gaze during thinking. *Journal of Cross-Cultural Psychology, 37,* 717–722. (p. 515)

McCarthy, P. (1986, July). Scent: The tie that binds? *Psychology Today,* pp. 6, 10. (p. 259)

McCaul, K. D., & Malott, J. M. (1984). Distraction and coping with pain. *Psychological Bulletin, 95,* 516–533. (p. 256)

McCauley, C. R. (2002). Psychological issues in understanding terrorism and the response to terrorism. In C. E. Stout (Ed.), *The psychology of terrorism* (Vol. 3). Westport, CT: Praeger/Greenwood. (p. 699)

McCauley, C. R., & Segal, M. E. (1987). Social psychology of terrorist groups. In C. Hendrick (Ed.), *Group processes and intergroup relations.* Beverly Hills, CA: Sage. (p. 699)

McClearn, G. E., Johansson, B., Berg, S., Pedersen, N. L., Ahern, F., Petrill, S. A., & Plomin, R. (1997). Substantial genetic influence on cognitive abilities in twins 80 or more years old. *Science, 276,* 1560–1563. (p. 429)

McClellan, J. M., Susser, E., & King, M.-C. (2007). Schizophrenia: A common disease caused by multiple rare alleles. *British Journal of Psychiatry, 190,* 194–199. (p. 642)

McClendon, B. T., & Prentice-Dunn, S. (2001). Reducing skin cancer risk: An intervention based on protection motivation theory. *Journal of Health Psychology, 6,* 321–328. (p. 685)

McClintock, M. K., & Herdt, G. (1996, December). Rethinking puberty: The development of sexual attraction. *Current Directions in Psychological Science, 5*(6), 178–183. (p. 196)

McClure, E. B. (2000). A meta-analytic review of sex differences in facial expression processing and their development in infants, children, and adolescents. *Psychological Bulletin, 126,* 424–453. (p. 433)

McConkey, K. M. (1995). Hypnosis, memory, and the ethics of uncertainty. *Australian Psychologist, 30,* 1–10. (p. 109)

McConnell, R. A. (1991). National Academy of Sciences opinion on parapsychology. *Journal of the American Society for Psychical Research, 85,* 333–365. (p. 282)

McCool, G. (1999, October 26). Mirror-gazing Venezuelans top of vanity stakes. *Toronto Star* (via web.lexis-nexis.com). (p. 722)

McCord, J. (1978). A thirty-year follow-up on treatment effects. *American Psychologist, 33,* 284–289. (p. 661)

McCord, J. (1979). Following up on Cambridge-Somerville. *American Psychologist, 34,* 727. (p. 661)

McCormick, C. M., & Witelson, S. F. (1991). A cognitive profile of homosexual men compared to heterosexual men and women. *Psychoneuroendocrinology, 16,* 459–473. (p. 478)

McCrae, R. R., & Costa, P. T., Jr. (1986). Clinical assessment can benefit from recent advances in personality psychology. *American Psychologist, 41,* 1001–1003. (p. 577)

McCrae, R. R., & Costa, P. T., Jr. (1990). *Personality in adulthood.* New York: Guilford. (p. 216)

McCrae, R. R., & Costa, P. T., Jr. (1994). The stability of personality: Observations and evaluations. *Current Directions in Psychological Science, 3,* 173–175. (pp. 223, 581)

McCrae, R. R., Costa, P. T., Jr., de Lirna, M. P., Simoes, A., Ostendorf, F., Angleitner, A., Marusic, I., Bratko, D., Caprara, G. V., Barbaranelli, C., Chae, J-H., & Piedmont, R. L. (1999). Age differences in personality across the adult life span: Parallels in five cultures. *Developmental Psychology, 35,* 466–477. (p. 579)

McCrae, R. R., Costa, P. T., Jr., Ostendorf, F., Angleitner, A., Hrebickova, M., Avia, M. D., Sanz, J., Sanchez-Bernardos, M. L., Kusdil, M. E., Woodfield, R., Saunders, P. R., & Smith, P. B. (2000). Nature over nurture: Temperament, personality, and life span development. *Journal of Personality and Social Psychology, 78,* 173–186. (p. 138)

McCrae, R. R., Terracciano, A., & Khoury, B. (2007). Dolce far niente: The positive psychology of personality stability and invariance. In A. D. Ong & M. H. Van Dulmen (Eds.), *Oxford handbook of methods in positive psychology.* New York: Oxford University Press. (p. 138)

McCrink, K., & Wynn, K. (2004). Large-number addition and subtraction by 9-month-old infants. *Psychological Science, 15,* 776–781. (p. 179)

McCullough, M. E., Hoyt, W. T., Larson, D. B., Koenig, H. G., & Thoresen, C. (2000). Religious involvement and mortality: A meta-analytic review. *Health Psychology, 19,* 211–222. (p. 553)

McCullough, M. E., & Laurenceau, J.-P. (2005). Religiousness and the trajectory of self-rated health across adulthood. *Personality and Social Psychology Bulletin, 31,* 560–573. (p. 553)

McDaniel, M. A. (2005). Big-brained people are smarter: A meta-analysis of the relationship between in vivo brain volume and intelligence. *Intelligence, 33,* 337–346. (p. 412)

McDermott, T. (2005). *Perfect soldiers: The 9/11 hijackers: Who they were, why they did it.* New York: HarperCollins. (p. 712)

McEvoy, S. P., Stevenson, M. R., McCartt, A. T., Woodward, M., Hawroth, C., Palamara, P., & Ceracelli, R. (2005). Role of mobile phones in motor vehicle crashes resulting in hospital attendance: A case-crossover study. *British Medical Journal, 33,* 428. (p. 88)

McEvoy, S. P., Stevenson, M. R., & Woodward, M. (2007). The contribution of passengers versus mobile phone use to motor vehicle crashes resulting in hospital attendance by the driver. *Accident Analysis and Prevention, 39,* 1170–1176. (p. 88)

McFadden, D. (2002). Masculinization effects in the auditory system. *Archives of Sexual Behavior, 31,* 99–111. (p. 477)

McFarland, C., & Ross, M. (1987). The relation between current impressions and memories of self and dating partners. *Psychological Bulletin, 13,* 228–238. (p. 361)

McGarry-Roberts, P. A., Stelmack, R. M., & Campbell, K. B. (1992). Intelligence, reaction time, and event-related potentials. *Intelligence, 16,* 289–313. (p. 414)

McGaugh, J. L. (1994). Quoted by B. Bower, Stress hormones hike emotional memories. *Science News, 146,* 262. (p. 341)

McGaugh, J. L. (2003). *Memory and emotion: The making of lasting memories.* New York: Columbia University Press. (pp. 323, 341)

McGhee, P. E. (June, 1976). Children's appreciation of humor: A test of the cognitive congruency principle. *Child Development, 47*(2), 420–426. (p. 184)

McGlone, M. S., & Tofighbakhsh, J. (2000). Birds of a feather flock conjointly (?): Rhyme as reason in aphorisms. *Psychological Science, 11,* 424–428. (p. 331)

McGrath, J., Welham, J., & Pemberton, M. (1995). Month of birth, hemisphere of birth and schizophrenia. *British Journal of Psychiatry, 167,* 783–785. (p. 641)

McGrath, J. J., & Welham, J. L. (1999). Season of birth and schizophrenia: A systematic review and meta-analysis of data from the Southern hemisphere. *Schizophrenia Research, 35,* 237–242. (p. 641)

McGue, M., & Bouchard, T. J., Jr. (1998). Genetic and environmental influences on human behavioral differences. *Annual Review of Neuroscience, 21,* 1–24. (p. 136)

McGue, M., Bouchard, T. J., Jr., Iacono, W. G., & Lykken, D. T. (1993). Behavioral genetics of cognitive ability: A life-span perspective. In R. Plomin & G. E. McClearn (Eds.), *Nature, nurture and psychology.* Washington, DC: American Psychological Association. (p. 429)

McGue, M., & Lykken, D. T. (1992). Genetic influence on risk of divorce. *Psychological Science, 3,* 368–373. (p. 134)

McGuire, M. T., Wing, R. R., Klem, M. L., Lang, W., & Hill, J. O. (1999). What predicts weight regain in a group of successful weight losers? *Journal of Consulting and Clinical Psychology, 67,* 177–185. (p. 463)

McGuire, W. J. (1986). The myth of massive media impact: Savings and salvagings. In G. Comstock (Ed.), *Public communication and behavior.* Orlando, FL: Academic Press. (p. 320)

McGurk, H., & MacDonald, J. (1976). Hearing lips and seeing voices. *Nature, 264,* 746–748. (p. 258)

McHugh, P. R. (1995a). Witches, multiple personalities, and other psychiatric artifacts. *Nature Medicine, 1*(2), 110–114. (p. 619)

McHugh, P. R. (1995b). Resolved: Multiple personality disorder is an individually and socially created artifact. *Journal of the American Academy of Child and Adolescent Psychiatry, 34,* 957–959. (p. 620)

McKellar, J., Stewart, E., & Humphreys, K. (2003). Alcoholics Anonymous involvement and positive alcohol-related outcomes: Cause, consequence, or just a correlate? A prospective 2-year study of 2,319 alcohol-dependent men. *Journal of Consulting and Clinical Psychology, 71,* 302–308. (p. 658)

McKenna, K. Y. A., & Bargh, J. A. (1998). Coming out in the age of the Internet: Identity "demarginalization" through virtual group participation. *Journal of Personality and Social Psychology, 75,* 681–694. (pp. 700, 720)

McKenna, K. Y. A., & Bargh, J. A. (2000). Plan 9 from cyberspace: The implications of the Internet for personality and social psychology. *Personality and Social Psychology Review, 4,* 57–75. (p. 720)

McKenna, K. Y. A., Green, A. S., & Gleason, M. E. J. (2002). What's the big attraction? Relationship formation on the Internet. *Journal of Social Issues, 58,* 9–31. (p. 720)

McKone, E., Kanwisher, N., & Duchaine, B. C. (2007). Can generic expertise explain special processing for faces? *Trends in Cognitive Sciences, 11,* 8–15. (p. 239)

McLaughlin, C. S., Chen, C., Greenberger, E., & Biermeier, C. (1997). Family, peer, and individual correlates of sexual experience among Caucasian and Asian American late adolescents. *Journal of Personality and Social Psychology: Journal of Research on Adolescence, 7,* 33–53. (p. 470)

McMahon, F. J., & 12 others (2006). Variation in the gene encoding the serotonin 2A receptor is associated with outcome of antidepressant treatment. *American Journal of Human Genetics, 78,* 804–814. (p. 629)

McMurray, B. (2007). Defusing the childhood vocabulary explosion. *Science, 317,* 631. (p. 386)

McMurray, C. (2004, January 13). U.S., Canada, Britain: Who's getting in shape? *Gallup Poll Tuesday Briefing* (www.gallup.com). (p. 547)

McMurray, J. (2006, August 28). Cause of deadly Comair crash probed. Associated Press release. (p. 378)

McNally, R. J. (1999). EMDR and Mesmerism: A comparative historical analysis. *Journal of Anxiety Disorders, 13,* 225–236. (p. 666)

McNally, R. J. (2003). *Remembering trauma.* Cambridge, MA: Harvard University Press. (pp. 359, 363, 613)

McNally, R. J. (2007). Betrayal trauma theory: A critical appraisal. *Memory, 15,* 280–294. (p. 363)

McNally, R. J., Bryant, R. A., & Ehlers, A. (2003). Does early psychological intervention promote recovery from posttraumatic stress? *Psychological Science in the Public Interest, 4,* 45–79. (p. 613)

McNeil, B. J., Pauker, S. G., & Tversky, A. (1988). On the framing of medical decisions. In D. E. Bell, H. Raiffa, & A. Tversky (Eds.), *Decision making: Descriptive, normative, and prescriptive interactions.* New York: Cambridge University Press. (p. 381)

McPherson, J. M., Smith-Lovin, L., & Brashears, M. E. (2006). Social isolation in America: Changes in core discussion networks over two decades. *American Sociological Review, 71,* 353–375. (p. 634)

Meador, B. D., & Rogers, C. R. (1984). Person-centered therapy. In R. J. Corsini (Ed.), *Current psychotherapies* (3rd ed.). Itasca, IL: Peacock. (p. 650)

Medical Institute for Sexual Health. (1994, April). Condoms ineffective against human papilloma virus. *Sexual Health Update,* p. 2. (p. 471)

Medland, S. E., Perelle, I., De Monte, V., & Ehrman, L. (2004). Effects of culture, sex, and age on the distribution of handedness: An evaluation of the sensitivity of three measures of handedness. *Laterality: Asymmetries of Body, Brain, and Cognition, 9,* 287–297. (p. 78)

Mednick, S. A., Huttunen, M. O., & Machon, R. A. (1994). Prenatal influenza infections and adult schizophrenia. *Schizophrenia Bulletin, 20,* 263–267. (p. 640)

Mehl, M. R., Gosling, S. D., & Pennebaker, J. W. (2006). Personality in its natural habitat: Manifestations and implicit folk theories of personality in daily life. *Journal of Personality and Social Psychology, 90,* 862–877. (p. 581)

Mehl, M. R., & Pennebaker, J. W. (2003). The sounds of social life: A psychometric analysis of students' daily social environments and natural conversations. *Journal of Personality and Social Psychology, 84,* 857–870. (p. 29)

Mehl, M. R., Vazire, S., Ramirez-Esparza, N., Slatcher, R. B., & Pennebaker, J. W. (2007). Are women really more talkative than men? *Science, 317,* 82. (p. 159)

Mehta, M. R. (2007). Cortico-hippocampal interaction during up-down states and memory consolidation. *Nature Neuroscience, 10,* 13–15. (p. 344)

Meichenbaum, D. (1977). *Cognitive-behavior modification: An integrative approach.* New York: Plenum Press. (p. 656)

Meichenbaum, D. (1985). *Stress inoculation training.* New York: Pergamon. (p. 656)

Meltzoff, A. N. (1988). Infant imitation after a 1-week delay: Long-term memory for novel acts and multiple stimuli. *Developmental Psychology, 24,* 470–476. (p. 316)

Meltzoff, A. N., & Moore, M. K. (1989). Imitation in newborn infants: Exploring the range of gestures imitated and the underlying mechanisms. *Developmental Psychology, 25,* 954–962. (p. 316)

Meltzoff, A. N., & Moore, M. K. (1997). Explaining facial imitation: A theoretical model. *Early Development and Parenting, 6,* 179–192. (p. 316)

Melzack, R. (1990, February). The tragedy of needless pain. *Scientific American,* pp. 27–33. (p. 114)

Melzack, R. (1992, April). Phantom limbs. *Scientific American,* pp. 120–126. (p. 255)

Melzack, R. (1998, February). Quoted in Phantom limbs. *Discover,* p. 20. (p. 255)

Melzack, R. (2005). Evolution of the neuromatrix theory of pain. *Pain Practice, 5,* 85–94. (p. 255)

Melzack, R., & Wall, P. D. (1965). Pain mechanisms: A new theory. *Science, 150,* 971–979. (p. 254)

Melzack, R., & Wall, P. D. (1983). *The challenge of pain.* New York: Basic Books. (p. 254)

Mendle, J., Turkheimer, E., & Emery, R. E. (2007). Detrimental psychological outcomes associated with early pubertal timing in adolescent girls. *Developmental Review, 27,* 151–171. (p. 197)

Mendolia, M., & Kleck, R. E. (1993). Effects of talking about a stressful event on arousal: Does what we talk about make a difference? *Journal of Personality and Social Psychology, 64,* 283–292. (p. 547)

Merari, A. (2002). Explaining suicidal terrorism: Theories versus empirical evidence. Invited address to the American Psychological Association. (p. 700)

Merker, B. (2007). Consciousness without a cerebral cortex: A challenge for neuroscience and medicine. *Behavioral and Brain Sciences, 30,* 63–134. (p. 85)

Merskey, H. (1992). The manufacture of personalities: The production of multiple personality disorder. *British Journal of Psychiatry, 160,* 327–340. (p. 619)

Merton, R. K. (1938; reprinted 1970). *Science, technology and society in seventeenth-century England.* New York: Fertig. (p. 18)

Merton, R. K., & Kitt, A. S. (1950). Contributions to the theory of reference group behavior. In R. K. Merton & P. F. Lazarsfeld (Eds.), *Continuities in social research: Studies in the scope and method of the American soldier.* Glencoe, IL: Free Press. (p. 528)

Messinis, L., Kyprianidou, A., Malefaki, S., & Papathanasopoulos, P. (2006). Neuropsychological deficits in long-term frequent cannabis users. *Neurology, 66,* 737–739. (p. 124)

Mestel, R. (1997, April 26). Get real, Siggi. *New Scientist* (www.newscientist.com/ns/970426/siggi.html). (p. 103)

Meston, C. M., & Buss, D. M. (2007). Why humans have sex. *Archives of Sexual Behavior, 36,* 477–507. (p. 469)

Meston, C. M., & Frohlich, P. F. (2000). The neurobiology of sexual function. *Archives of General Psychiatry, 57,* 1012–1030. (p. 468)

Metcalfe, J. (1986). Premonitions of *insight* predict impending error. *Journal of Experimental Psychology: Learning, Memory, and Cognition, 12,* 623–634. (p. 372)

Metcalfe, J. (1998). Cognitive optimism: Self-deception or memory-based processing heuristics. *Personality and Social Psychology Review, 2,* 100–110. (p. 376)

Meyer, I. H. (2003). Prejudice, social stress, and mental health in lesbian, gay, and bisexual populations: Conceptual issues and research evidence. *Psychological Bulletin, 129,* 674–697. (p. 599)

Meyer-Bahlburg, H. F. L. (1995). Psychoneuroendocrinology and sexual pleasure: The aspect of sexual orientation. In P. R. Abramson & S. D. Pinkerton (Eds.), *Sexual nature/sexual culture.* Chicago: University of Chicago Press. (p. 477)

Mezulis, A. M., Abramson, L. Y., Hyde, J. S., & Hankin, B. L. (2004). Is there a universal positivity bias in attributions? A meta-analytic review of individual, developmental, and cultural differences in the self-serving attributional bias. *Psychological Bulletin, 130,* 711–747. (p. 592)

Michaels, J. W., Bloomel, J. M., Brocato, R. M., Linkous, R. A., & Rowe, J. S. (1982). Social facilitation and inhibition in a natural setting. *Replications in Social Psychology, 2,* 21–24. (p. 697)

Michel, G. F. (1981). Right-handedness: A consequence of infant supine head-orientation preference? *Science, 212,* 685–687. (p. 79)

Middlebrooks, J. C., & Green, D. M. (1991). Sound localization by human listeners. *Annual Review of Psychology, 42,* 135–159. (p. 247)

Mikhail, J. (2007). Universal moral grammar: Theory, evidence and the future. *Trends in Cognitive Sciences, 11,* 143–152. (p. 388)

Mikkelsen, T. S., & 66 others. (2005). Initial sequence of the chimpanzee genome and comparison with the human genome. *Nature, 437,* 69–87. (p. 132)

Mikulincer, M., Babkoff, H., Caspy, T., & Sing, H. (1989). The effects of 72 hours of sleep loss on psychological variables. *British Journal of Psychology, 80,* 145–162. (p. 97)

Mikulincer, M., Florian, V., & Hirschberger, G. (2003). The existential function of close relationships: Introducing death into the science of love. *Personality and Social Psychology Review, 7,* 20–40. (p. 567)

Mikulincer, M., & Shaver, P. R. (2001). Attachment theory and intergroup bias: Evidence that priming the secure base schema attenuates negative reactions to out-groups. *Journal of Personality and Social Psychology, 81,* 97–115. (p. 708)

Milan, R. J., Jr., & Kilmann, P. R. (1987). Interpersonal factors in premarital contraception. *Journal of Sex Research, 23,* 289–321. (p. 471)

Miles, D. R., & Carey, G. (1997). Genetic and environmental architecture of human aggression. *Journal of Personality and Social Psychology, 72,* 207–217. (p. 710)

Milgram, S. (1963). Behavioral study of obedience. *Journal of Abnormal & Social Psychology, 67*(4), 371–378. (p. 693)

Milgram, S. (1974). *Obedience to authority.* New York: Harper & Row. (pp. 109, 693, 695, 696)

Millar, J. K., & 19 others. (2005). DISC1 and PDE4B are interacting genetic factors in schizophrenia that regulate cAMP signaling. *Science, 310,* 1187–1191. (p. 642)

Miller, E. J., & Halberstadt, J. (2005). Media consumption, body image and thin ideals in New Zealand men and women. *New Zealand Journal of Psychology, 34,* 189–195. (p. 454)

Miller, E. J., Smith, J. E., & Trembath, D. L. (2000). The "skinny" on body size requests in personal ads. *Sex Roles, 43,* 129–141. (p. 457)

Miller, G. (2004). Axel, Buck share award for deciphering how the nose knows. *Science, 306,* 207. (p. 259)

Miller, G. (2005). The dark side of glia. *Science, 308,* 778–781. (p. 67)

Miller, G. (2008). Tackling alcoholism with drugs. *Science, 320,* 168–170. (p. 126)

Miller, G., Tybur, J. M., & Jordan, B. D. (2007). Ovulatory cycle effects on tip earnings by lap dancers: Economic evidence for human estrus? *Evolution and Human Behavior, 28,* 375–381. (p. 467)

Miller, G. A. (1956). The magical number seven, plus or minus two: Some limits on our capacity for processing information. *Psychological Review, 63,* 81–97. (p. 337)

Miller, G. E., & Blackwell, E. (2006). Turning up the heat: Inflammation as a mechanism linking chronic stress, depression, and heart disease. *Current Directions in Psychological Science, 15,* 269–272. (p. 537)

Miller, G. E., & Wrosch, C. (2007). You've gotta know when to fold 'em. *Psychological Science, 18,* 773–777. (p. 534)

Miller, J. G., & Bersoff, D. M. (1995). Development in the context of everyday family relationships: Culture, interpersonal morality and adaptation. In M. Killen & D. Hart (Eds.), *Morality in everyday life: A developmental perspective.* New York: Cambridge University Press. (p. 199)

Miller, K. I., & Monge, P. R. (1986). Participation, satisfaction, and productivity: A meta-analytic review. *Academy of Management Journal, 29,* 727–753. (p. 585)

Miller, L. (2005, January 4). U.S. airlines have 34 deaths in 3 years. Associated Press. (p. 378)

Miller, L. K. (1999). The Savant Syndrome: Intellectual impairment and exceptional skill. *Psychological Bulletin, 125,* 31–46. (p. 406)

Miller, M. (2005, March 7). Effects of laughter and mental stress on endothelial function: Potential impact of entertainment. Paper presented to the Scientific Session of the American College of Cardiology, Orlando. (p. 545)

Miller, N. E. (1983). Understanding the use of animals in behavioral research: Some critical issues. *Annals of the New York Academy of Sciences, 406,* 113–118. (p. 21)

Miller, N. E. (1985, February). Rx: Biofeedback. *Psychology Today,* pp. 54–59. (p. 549)

Miller, N. E. (1995). Clinical-experimental interactions in the development of neuroscience: A primer for nonspecialists and lessons for young scientists. *American Psychologist, 50,* 901–911. (p. 450)

Miller, N. E., & Brucker, B. S. (1979). A learned visceral response apparently independent of skeletal ones in patients paralyzed by spinal lesions. In N. Birbaumer & H. D. Kimmel (Eds.), *Biofeedback and self-regulation.* Hillsdale, NJ: Erlbaum. (p. 549)

Miller, P. A., Eisenberg, N., Fabes, R. A., & Shell, R. (1996). Relations of moral reasoning and vicarious emotion to young children's prosocial behavior toward peers and adults. *Developmental Psychology, 32,* 210–219. (p. 200)

Miller, P. J. O., Aoki, K., Rendell, L. E., & Amano, M. (2008). Stereotypical resting behavior of the sperm whale. *Current Biology, 18,* R21–R23. (p. 91)

Miller, S. D., Blackburn, T., Scholes, G., White, G. L., & Mamalis, N. (1991). Optical differences in multiple personality disorder: A second look. *Journal of Nervous and Mental Disease, 179,* 132–135. (p. 619)

Mills, M., & Melhuish, E. (1974). Recognition of mother's voice in early infancy. *Nature, 252,* 123–124. (p. 173)

Milton, J., & Wiseman, R. (2002). A response to Storm and Ertel (2002). *Journal of Parapsychology, 66,* 183–185. (p. 284)

Mineka, S. (1985). The frightful complexity of the origins of fears. In F. R. Brush & J. B. Overmier (Eds.), *Affect, conditioning and cognition: Essays on the determinants of behavior.* Hillsdale, NJ: Erlbaum. (pp. 519, 615)

Mineka, S. (2002). Animal models of clinical psychology. In N. Smelser & P. Baltes (Eds.), *International encyclopedia of the social and behavioral sciences.* Oxford, England: Elsevier Science. (p. 519)

Mineka, S., & Suomi, S. J. (1978). Social separation in monkeys. *Psychological Bulletin, 85,* 1376–1400. (p. 190)

Mineka, S., & Zinbarg, R. (1996). Conditioning and ethological models of anxiety disorders: Stress-in-dynamic-context anxiety models. In D. Hope (Ed.), *Perspectives on anxiety, panic, and fear* (Nebraska Symposium on Motivation). Lincoln: University of Nebraska Press. (pp. 614, 615)

Mineka, S., & Zinbarg, R. (2006). A contemporary learning theory perspective on the etiology of anxiety disorders: It's not what you thought it was. *American Psychologist, 61,* 10–26. (p. 614)

Miner-Rubino, K., Winter, D. G., & Stewart, A. J. (2004). Gender, social class, and the subjective experience of aging: Self-perceived personality change from early adulthood to late midlife. *Personality and Social Psychology Bulletin, 30,* 1599–1610. (p. 219)

Mingroni, M. A. (2004). The secular rise in IQ: Giving heterosis a closer look. *Intelligence, 32,* 65–83. (p. 421)

Mingroni, M. A. (2007). Resolving the IQ paradox: Heterosis as a cause of the Flynn effect and other trends. *Psychological Review, 114,* 806–829. (p. 421)

Minsky, M. (1986). *The society of mind.* New York: Simon & Schuster. (p. 85)

Mirescu, C., & Gould, E. (2006). Stress and adult neurogenesis. *Hippocampus, 16,* 233–238. (p. 533)

Mischel, W. (1968). *Personality and assessment.* New York: Wiley. (p. 581)

Mischel, W. (1981). Current issues and challenges in personality. In L. T. Benjamin, Jr. (Ed.), *The G. Stanley Hall Lecture Series* (Vol. 1). Washington, DC: American Psychological Association. (p. 590)

Mischel, W. (1984). Convergences and challenges in the search for consistency. *American Psychologist, 39,* 351–364. (p. 581)

Mischel, W. (2004). Toward an integrative science of the person. *Annual Review of Psychology, 55,* 1–22. (p. 581)

Mischel, W., Shoda, Y., & Peake, P. K. (1988). The nature of adolescent competencies predicted by preschool delay of gratification. *Journal of Personality and Social Psychology, 54,* 687–696. (p. 200)

Mischel, W., Shoda, Y., & Rodriguez, M. L. (1989). Delay of gratification in children. *Science, 244,* 933–938. (pp. 200, 304)

Miserandino, M. (1991). Memory and the seven dwarfs. *Teaching of Psychology, 18,* 169–171. (p. 346)

Mita, T. H., Dermer, M., & Knight, J. (1977). Reversed facial images and the mere-exposure hypothesis. *Journal of Personality and Social Psychology, 35,* 597–601. (p. 720)

Mitchell, D. B. (2006). Nonconscious priming after 17 years: Invulnerable implicit memory? *Psychological Science, 17,* 925–929. (p. 324)

Mitchell, T. M., Shinkareva, S. V., Carlson, A., Chang, K-M., Malave, V. L., Mason, R. A., & Just, M. A. (2008). Predicting human brain activity associated with the meanings of nouns. *Science, 320,* 1191–1195. (p. 392)

Mitchell, T. R., Thompson, L., Peterson, E., & Cronk, R. (1997). Temporal adjustments in the evaluation of events: The "rosy view." *Journal of Experimental Social Psychology, 33,* 421–448. (p. 333)

Mitte, K. (2005). Meta-analysis of cognitive-behavioral treatments for generalized anxiety disorder: A comparison with pharmacotherapy. *Psychological Bulletin, 131,* 785–795. (p. 657)

Moffitt, T. E. (2005). The new look of behavioral genetics in developmental psychopathology: Gene-environment interplay in antisocial behaviors. *Psychological Bulletin, 131,* 533–554. (p. 622)

Moffitt, T. E., Caspi, A., Harrington, H., & Milne, B. J. (2002). Males on the life-course-persistent and adolescence-limited antisocial pathways: Follow-up at age 26 years. *Development and Psychopathology, 14,* 179–207. (p. 223)

Moffitt, T. E., Caspi, A., Harrington, H., Milne, B. J., Melchior, M., Goldberg, D., & Poulton, R. (2007a). Generalized anxiety disorder and depression: Childhood risk factors in a birth cohort followed to age 32. *Psychological Medicine, 37,* 441–452. (p. 610)

Moffitt, T. E., Caspi, A., & Rutter, M. (2006). Measured gene-environment interactions in psychopathology: Concepts, research strategies, and implications for research, intervention, and public understanding of genetics. *Perspectives on Psychological Science, 1,* 5–27. (p. 631)

Moffitt, T. E., Harrington, H., Caspi, A., Kim-Cohen, J., Goldberg, D., Gregory, A. M., & Poulton, R. (2007b). Depression and generalized anxiety disorder: Cumulative and sequential comorbidity in a birth cohort followed prospectively to age 32 years. *Archives of General Psychiatry, 64,* 651–660. (p. 610)

Moghaddam, F. M. (2005). The staircase to terrorism: A psychological exploration. *American Psychologist, 60,* 161–169. (p. 700)

Moises, H. W., Zoega, T., & Gottesman, I. I. (2002, July 3). The glial growth factors deficiency and synaptic destabilization hypothesis of schizophrenia. *BMC Psychiatry, 2*(8) (www.biomedcentral.com/1471-244X/2/8). (p. 641)

Monaghan, P. (1992, September 23). Professor of psychology stokes a controversy on the reliability and repression of memory. *Chronicle of Higher Education,* pp. A9–A10. (p. 364)

Mondloch, C. J., Lewis, T. L., Budreau, D. R., Maurer, D., Dannemiller, J. L., Stephens, B. R., & Kleiner-Gathercoal, K. A. (1999). Face perception during early infancy. *Psychological Science, 10,* 419–422. (p. 173)

Money, J. (1987). Sin, sickness, or status? Homosexual gender identity and psychoneuroendocrinology. *American Psychologist, 42,* 384–399. (pp. 475, 477)

Money, J. (1988). *Gay, straight, and in-between.* New York: Oxford University Press. (p. 714)

Money, J., Berlin, F. S., Falck, A., & Stein, M. (1983). *Antiandrogenic and counseling treatment of sex offenders.* Baltimore: Department of Psychiatry and Behavioral Sciences, The Johns Hopkins University School of Medicine. (p. 468)

Moody, R. (1976). *Life after life.* Harrisburg, PA: Stackpole Books. (p. 123)

Mook, D. G. (1983). In defense of external invalidity. *American Psychologist, 38,* 379–387. (p. 19)

Moorcroft, W. H. (2003). *Understanding sleep and dreaming.* New York: Kluwer/Plenum. (pp. 93, 99, 105)

Moore, D. W. (2004, December 17). Sweet dreams go with a good night's sleep. *Gallup News Service* (www.gallup.com). (p. 96)

Moore, D. W. (2005, June 16). Three in four Americans believe in paranormal. *Gallup New Service* (www.gallup.com). (p. 281)

Moore, D. W. (2006, February 6). Britons outdrink Canadians, Americans. *Gallup News Service* (poll.gallup.com). (p. 127)

Moore, D. W. (2006, March 10). Close to 6 in 10 Americans want to lose weight. *Gallup News Service* (poll.gallup.com). (p. 462)

Moos, R. H., & Moos, B. S. (2005). Sixteen-year changes and stable remission among treated and untreated individuals with alcohol use disorders. *Drug and Alcohol Dependence, 80,* 337–347. (p. 658)

Moos, R. H., & Moos, B. S. (2006). Participation in treatment and Alcoholics Anonymous: A 16-year follow-up of initially untreated individuals. *Journal of Clinical Psychology, 62,* 735–750. (p. 658)

Mor, N., & Winquist, J. (2002). Self-focused attention and negative affect: A meta-analysis. *Psychological Bulletin, 128,* 638–662. (p. 633)

Moreland, R. L., & Beach, S. R. (1992). Exposure effects in the classroom: The development of affinity among students. *Journal of Experimental Social Psychology, 28,* 255–276. (p. 719)

Moreland, R. L., & Zajonc, R. B. (1982). Exposure effects in person perception: Familiarity, similarity, and attraction. *Journal of Experimental Social Psychology, 18,* 395–415. (p. 719)

Morell, V. (1995). Zeroing in on how hormones affect the immune system. *Science, 269,* 773–775. (p. 538)

Morell, V. (2008, March). Minds of their own: Animals are smarter than you think. *National Geographic,* pp. 37–61. (p. 397)

Morelli, G. A., Rogoff, B., Oppenheim, D., & Goldsmith, D. (1992). Cultural variation in infants' sleeping arrangements: Questions of independence. *Developmental Psychology, 26,* 604–613. (p. 156)

Moreno, C., Laje, G., Blanco, C., Jiang, H., Schmidt, A. B., & Olfson, M. (2007). National trends in the outpatient diagnosis and treatment of bipolar disorder in youth. *Archives of General Psychiatry, 64,* 1032–1039. (p. 626)

Morey, R. A., Inan, S., Mitchell, T. V., Perkins, D. O., Lieberman, J. A., & Belger, A. (2005). Imaging frontostriatal function in ultra-high-risk, early, and chronic schizophrenia during executive processing. *Archives of General Psychiatry, 62,* 254–262. (p. 640)

Morgan, A. B., & Lilienfeld, S. O. (2000). A meta-analytic review of the relation between antisocial behavior and neuropsychological measures of executive function. *Clinical Psychology Review, 20,* 113–136. (p. 621)

Morgan, B., & Korschgen, A. (2001). Psychology career exploration made easy. *Eye on Psi Chi, 5,* 35–36. (p. A-2)

Morin, R., & Brossard, M. A. (1997, March 4). Communication breakdown on drugs. *Washington Post,* pp. A1, A6. (p. 203)

Morrison, A. R. (2003). The brain on night shift. *Cerebrum, 5*(3), 23–36. (p. 95)

Morrison, C. (2007). *What does contagious yawning tell us about the mind?* Unpublished manuscript, University of Leeds. (p. 690)

Morse, M. L. (1994). Near death experiences and death-related visions in children: Implications for the clinician. *Current Problems in Pediatrics, 24,* 55–83. (p. 123)

Mortensen, E. L., Michaelsen, K. F., Sanders, S. A., & Reinisch, J. M. (2002). The association between duration of breastfeeding and adult intelligence. *Journal of the American Medical Association, 287,* 2365–2371. (p. 34)

Mortensen, P. B. (1999). Effects of family history and place and season of birth on the risk of schizophrenia. *New England Journal of Medicine, 340,* 603–608. (p. 640)

Moscovici, S. (1985). Social influence and conformity. In G. Lindzey & E. Aronson (Eds.), *The handbook of social psychology* (3rd ed). Hillsdale, N.J.: Erlbaum. (p. 701)

Moser, P. W. (1987, May). Are cats smart? Yes, at being cats. *Discover,* pp. 77–88. (p. 237)

Moses, E. B., & Barlow, D. H. (2006). A new unified treatment approach for emotional disorders based on emotion science. *Current Directions in Psychological Science, 15,* 146–150. (p. 656)

Mosher, D. L., & Anderson, R. D. (1986). Macho personality, sexual aggression, and reactions to guided imagery of realistic rape. *Journal of Research in Personality, 20,* 77–94. (p. 117)

Mosher, W. D., Chandra, A., & Jones, J. (2005, September 15). Sexual behavior and selected health measures: Men and women 15–44 years of age, United States, 2002. *Advance Data from Vital and Health Statistics,* No. 362, National Center for Health Statistics, Centers for Disease Control and Prevention, U.S. Department of Health and Human Services. (p. 473)

Moss, A. J., Allen, K. F., Giovino, G. A., & Mills, S. L. (1992, December 2). Recent trends in adolescent smoking, smoking-update correlates, and expectations about the future. *Advance Data No. 221* (from Vital and Health Statistics of the Centers for Disease Control and Prevention). (p. 119)

Moss, H. A., & Susman, E. J. (1980). Longitudinal study of personality development. In O. G. Brim, Jr., & J. Kagan (Eds.), *Constancy and change in human development.* Cambridge, MA: Harvard University Press. (p. 223)

Motivala, S. J., & Irwin, M. R. (2007). Sleep and immunity: Cytokine pathways linking sleep and health outcomes. *Current Directions in Psychological Science, 16,* 21–25. (p. 98)

Moulton, S. T., & Kosslyn, S. M. (2008). Using neuroimaging to resolve the psi debate. *Journal of Cognitive Neuroscience, 20,* 182–192. (p. 284)

Moyer, K. E. (1983). The physiology of motivation: Aggression as a model. In C. J. Scheier & A. M. Rogers (Eds.), *G. Stanley Hall Lecture Series* (Vol. 3). Washington, DC: American Psychological Association. (p. 710)

Mroczek, D. K. (2001). Age and emotion in adulthood. *Current Directions in Psychological Science, 10,* 87–90. (p. 219)

Mroczek, D. K., & Kolarz, D. M. (1998). The effect of age on positive and negative affect: A developmental perspective on happiness. *Journal of Personality and Social Psychology, 75,* 1333–1349. (p. 216)

Muhlnickel, W. (1998). Reorganization of auditory cortex in tinnitus. *Proceedings of the National Academy of Sciences, 95,* 10340–10343. (p. 71)

Mulcahy, N. J., & Call, J. (2006). Apes save tools for future use. *Science, 312,* 1038–1040. (p. 397)

Muller, J. E., Mittleman, M. A., Maclure, M., Sherwood, J. B., & Tofler, G. H. (1996). Triggering myocardial infarction by sexual activity. *Journal of the American Medical Association, 275,* 1405–1409. (p. 466)

Muller, J. E., & Verier, R. L. (1996). Triggering of sudden death—Lessons from an earthquake. *New England Journal of Medicine, 334,* 461. (p. 534)

Mullin, C. R., & Linz, D. (1995). Desensitization and resensitization to violence against women: Effects of exposure to sexually violent films on judgments of domestic violence victims. *Journal of Personality and Social Psychology, 69*, 449–459. (p. 321)

Mulrow, C. D. (1999, March). Treatment of depression—newer pharmacotherapies, summary. *Evidence Report/Technology Assessment, 7.* Agency for Health Care Policy and Research, Rockville, MD. (http: //www.ahrq.gov/clinic/deprsumm.htm). (p. 673)

Munro, D. A., McCaul, M. E., Wong, D. F., Oswald, L. M., Zhou, Y., Brasic, J., Kuwabara, H., Kumar, A., Alexander, M., Ye, W., & Wand, G. S. (2006). Sex differences in striatal dopamine release in health adults. *Biological Psychiatry, 59*, 966–974. (p. 118)

Murphy, G. E., & Wetzel, R. D. (1990). The lifetime risk of suicide in alcoholism. *Archives of General Psychiatry, 47*, 383–392. (p. 630)

Murphy, K. R., & Cleveland, J. N. (1995). Understanding performance appraisal: Social, organizational, and goal-based perspectives. Thousand Oaks, CA: Sage. (p. 489)

Murphy, S. T., Monahan, J. L., & Miller, L. C. (1998). Inference under the influence: The impact of alcohol and inhibition conflict on women's sexual decision making. *Personality and Social Psychology Bulletin, 24*, 517–528. (p. 117)

Murphy, S. T., Monahan, J. L., & Zajonc, R. B. (1995). Additivity of nonconscious affect: Combined effects of priming and exposure. *Journal of Personality and Social Psychology, 69*, 589–602. (p. 507)

Murray, B. (1998, May). Psychology is key to airline safety at Boeing. *The APA Monitor*, p. 36. (p. 280)

Murray, C. (2006). Changes over time in the Black-White difference on mental tests: Evidence from the children of the 1979 cohort of the National Longitudinal Survey of Youth. *Intelligence, 34*, 527–540. (p. 435)

Murray, C. (2007). The magnitude and components of change in the Black-White IQ difference from 1920 to 1991: A birth cohort analysis of the Woodcock-Johnson standardizations. *Intelligence, 35*, 305–318. (p. 435)

Murray, C. A., & Herrnstein, R. J. (1994, October 31). Race, genes and I.Q.—An apologia. *New Republic*, pp. 27–37. (p. 435)

Murray, C. J., & Lopez, A. D. (Eds.). (1996). The global burden of disease: A comprehensive assessment of mortality and disability from diseases, injuries, and risk factors in 1990 and projected to 2020. Cambridge, MA: Harvard University Press. (p. 597)

Murray, H. (1938). *Explorations in personality.* New York: Oxford University Press. (p. 490)

Murray, H. A., & Wheeler, D. R. (1937). A note on the possible clairvoyance of dreams. *Journal of Psychology, 3*, 309–313. (pp. 27, 283)

Murray, J. P. (2008). Media violence: The effects are both real and strong. *American Behavioral Scientist, 51*, 1212–1230. (p. 319)

Murray, R., Jones, P., O'Callaghan, E., Takei, N., & Sham, P. (1992). Genes, viruses, and neurodevelopmental schizophrenia. *Journal of Psychiatric Research, 26*, 225–235. (p. 640)

Murray, R. M., Morrison, P. D., Henquet, C., & Di Forti, M. (2007). Cannabis, the mind and society: The hash realities. *Nature Reviews: Neuroscience, 8*, 885–895. (p. 124)

Murray, S. L., Bellavia, G. M., Rose, P., & Griffin, D. W. (2003). Once hurt, twice hurtful: How perceived regard regulates daily marital interactions. *Journal of Personality and Social Psychology, 84*, 126–147. (p. 278)

Murray, S. L., Rose, P., Bellavia, G. M., Holmes, J. G., & Kusche, A. G. (2002). When rejection stings: How self-esteem constrains relationship-enhancement processes. *Journal of Personality and Social Psychology, 83*, 556–573. (p. 591)

Musallam, S., Corneil, B. D., Greger, B., Scherberger, H., & Andersen, R. A. (2004). Cognitive control signals for neural prosthetics. *Science, 305*, 258–262. (p. 69)

Musick, M. A., Herzog, A. R., & House, J. S. (1999). Volunteering and mortality among older adults: Findings from a national sample. *Journals of Gerontology, 54B*, 173–180. (p. 554)

Mustanski, B. S., & Bailey, J. M. (2003). A therapist's guide to the genetics of human sexual orientation, *Sexual and Relationship Therapy, 18*, 1468–1479. (p. 476)

Mustanski, B. S., Bailey, J. M., & Kaspar, S. (2002). Dermatoglyphics, handedness, sex, and sexual orientation. *Archives of Sexual Behavior, 31*, 113–122. (p. 477)

Mydans, S. (2002, May 17). In Pakistan, rape victims are the 'criminals.' *New York Times* (www.nytimes.com). (p. 709)

Myers, D. G. (1993). *The pursuit of happiness.* New York: Harper. (p. 527)

Myers, D. G. (2000). *The American paradox: Spiritual hunger in an age of plenty.* New Haven, CT: Yale University Press. (p. 529)

Myers, D. G. (2001, December). Do we fear the right things? *American Psychological Society Observer*, p. 3. (p. 378)

Myers, D. G. (2002). *Intuition: Its powers and perils.* New Haven, CT: Yale University Press. (pp. 3, 33)

Myers, D. G. (2008). *Social psychology* (9th ed.). New York: McGraw-Hill. (pp. 592, 593)

Myers, D. G., & Bishop, G. D. (1970). Discussion effects on racial attitudes. *Science, 169*, 78–779. (p. 699)

Myers, D. G., & Diener, E. (1995). Who is happy? *Psychological Science, 6*, 10–19. (p. 529)

Myers, D. G., & Diener, E. (1996, May). The pursuit of happiness. *Scientific American.* (p. 529)

Myers, D. G., & Scanzoni, L. D. (2005). *What God has joined together?* San Francisco: HarperSanFrancisco. (pp. 217, 473)

Myers, I. B. (1987). Introduction to type: A description of the theory and applications of the Myers-Briggs Type Indicator. Palo Alto, CA: Consulting Psychologists Press. (p. 574)

Myerson, J., Rank, M. R., Raines, F. Q., & Schnitzler, M. A. (1998). Race and general cognitive ability: The myth of diminishing returns to education. *Psychological Science, 9*, 139–142. (p. 438)

Nagourney, A. (2002, September 25). For remarks on Iraq, Gore gets praise and scorn. *New York Times* (www.nytimes.com). (p. 685)

Nairn, R. G. (2007). Media portrayals of mental illness, or is it madness? A review. *Australian Psychologist, 42*, 138–146. (p. 605)

Napolitan, D. A., & Goethals, G. R. (1979). The attribution of friendliness. *Journal of Experimental Social Psychology, 15*, 105–113. (p. 682)

Naqvi, N. H., Rudrauf, D., Damasio, H., & Bechara, A. (2007). Damage to the insula disrupts addiction to cigarette smoking. *Science, 315*, 531–534. (p. 119)

Nasar, J., Hecht, P., & Wener, R. (2008). Mobile telephones, distracted attention, and pedestrian safety. *Accident Analysis and Prevention, 40*, 69–75. (p. 88)

Nash, M. R. (2001, July). The truth and the hype of hypnosis. *Scientific American*, pp. 47–55. (p. 110)

National Academy of Sciences. (1999). *Marijuana and medicine: Assessing the science base* (by J. A. Benson, Jr. & S. J. Watson, Jr.). Washington, DC: National Academy Press. (p. 124)

National Academy of Sciences. (2001). *Exploring the biological contributions to human health: Does sex matter?* Washington, DC: Institute of Medicine, National Academy Press. (p. 161)

National Academy of Sciences, Institute of Medicine. (1982). *Marijuana and health.* Washington, DC: National Academic Press. (p. 124)

National Center for Complementary and Alternative Medicine. (2006). What is complementary and alternative medicine. nccam.nih.gov/health/whatiscam. (p. 550)

National Center for Education Statistics (NCES) (U.S. Department of Education). (2007a). Digest of Education Statistics. (NCES 2008-022), table 261, data from U.S. Department of Education, NCES, 1990-91, 1995-96, and 2005-06 Integrated Postsecondary Education Data System, "Completions Survey" (IPEDS-C:91 and 96), and Fall 2006. (p. A-1)

National Center for Education Statistics (NCES) (U.S. Department of Education). (2007b). Digest of Education Statistics. (NCES 2008-022), tables 262, 263 and 270, data from U.S. Department of Education, NCES, 1990-91, 1995-96, and 2005-06 Integrated Postsecondary Education Data System, "Completions Survey" (IPEDS-C:91 and 96), and Fall 2006. (p. A-1)

National Center for Health Statistics. (1990). *Health, United States, 1989.* Washington, DC: U.S. Department of Health and Human Services. (p. 210)

National Center for Health Statistics. (2004, December 15). Marital status and health: United States, 1999-2002 (by Charlotte A. Schoenborn).

Advance Data from Vital and Human Statistics, number 351. Centers for Disease Control and Prevention. (p. 545)

National Council on Aging. (1999). *The consequences of untreated hearing loss in older persons.* Washington, DC: Author. (www.ncoa.org). (p. 249)

National Institute of Mental Health. (1982). *Television and behavior: Ten years of scientific progress and implications for the eighties.* Washington, DC: U. S. Government Printing Office. (p. 320)

National Institute of Mental Health. (1999). *ADHD: Attention deficity hyperactivity disorder.* Bethesda, MD: National Institute of Health Publication No. 96-3572, 1994, update July 1, 1999. (p. 600)

National Institute of Mental Health. (2003). *Attention deficit hyperactivity disorder.* Bethesda, MD: National Institute of Mental Health. (p. 600)

National Institute of Mental Health (2008). The numbers count: Mental disorders in America (nimh.nih.gov). (pp. 603, 607)

National Institute on Drug Abuse. (2004). NIDA InfoFacts: Marijuana. www.nida.nih.gov/Infofax/marijuana.html. (p. 124)

National Institutes of Health. (1998). Clinical guidelines on the identification evaluation and treatment of overweight and obesity in adults. Executive summary, Obesity Education Initiative, National Heart, Lung, and Blood Institute. (p. 463)

National Research Council. (1990). *Human factors research needs for an aging population.* Washington, DC: National Academy Press. effect. (p. 210)

National Safety Council (2008). Transportation mode comparisons, from *Injury Facts* (via correspondence with Kevin T. Fearn, Research & Statistical Services Department). (p. 378)

Naylor, T. H. (1990). Redefining corporate motivation, Swedish style. *Christian Century, 107,* 566-570. (p. 496)

NCASA (2007). *Wasting the best and the brightest: Substance abuse at America's colleges and universities.* New York: National Center on Addiction and Drug Abuse, Columbia University. (p. 127)

NCHS (2007). *Health, United States, 2007.* Hyattsville, MD: National Center for Health Statistics. (p. 456)

NCTV News. (1987, July-August). More research links harmful effects to non-violent porn, p. 12. (p. 714)

Neese, R. M. (1991, November/December). What good is feeling bad? The evolutionary benefits of psychic pain. *The Sciences,* pp. 30-37. (pp. 253, 297)

Neisser, U. (1979). The control of information pickup in selective looking. In A. D. Pick (Ed.), *Perception and its development: A tribute to Eleanor J. Gibson.* Hillsdale, NJ: Erlbaum. (p. 88)

Neisser, U. (1997). The ecological study of memory. *Philosophical Transactions of the Royal Society of London, 352,* 1697-1701. (p. 421)

Neisser, U. (1998). *The rising curve: Long-term gains in IQ and related measures.* Washington, DC: American Psychological Association. (p. 421)

Neisser, U., Boodoo, G., Bouchard, T. J., Jr., Boykin, A. W., Brody, N., Ceci, S. J., Halpern, D. F., Loehlin, J. C., Perloff, R., Sternberg, R. J., & Urbina, S. (1996). Intelligence: Knowns and unknowns. *American Psychologist, 51,* 77-101. (pp. 428, 439)

Neisser, U., Winograd, E., & Weldon, M. S. (1991). Remembering the earthquake: "What I experienced" vs. "How I heard the news." Paper presented to the Psychonomic Society convention. (p. 341)

Neitz, J., Geist, T., & Jacobs, G. H. (1989). Color vision in the dog. *Visual Neuroscience, 3,* 119-125. (p. 241)

Nelson, C. A., III, Zeanah, C. H., Fox, N. A., Marshall, P. J., Smyke, A. T., & Guthrie, D. (2007). Cognitive recovery in socially deprived young children: The Bucharest Early Intervention Project. *Science, 318,* 1937-1940. (p. 431)

Nelson, M. D., Saykin, A. J., Flashman, L. A., & Riordan, H. J. (1998). Hippocampal volume reduction in schizophrenia as assessed by magnetic resonance imaging. *Archives of General Psychiatry, 55,* 433-440. (p. 640)

Nelson, N. (1988). *A meta-analysis of the life-event/health paradigm: The influence of social support.* Unpublished doctoral dissertation, Temple University, Philadelphia. (p. 545)

Nemeth, C. J., & Ormiston, M. (2007). Creative idea generation: Harmony versus stimulation. *European Journal of Social Psychology, 37,* 524-535. (p. 700)

Nesca, M., & Koulack, D. (1994). Recognition memory, sleep and circadian rhythms. *Canadian Journal of Experimental Psychology, 48,* 359-379. (p. 356)

Nestoriuc, Y., Rief, W., & Martin, A. (2008). Meta-analysis of biofeedback for tension-type headache: Efficacy, specificity, and treatment moderators. *Journal of Consulting and Clinical Psychology, 76,* 379-396. (p. 549)

Neubauer, P. B., & Neubauer, A. (1990). *Nature's thumbprint: The new genetics of personality.* Reading, MA: Addison-Wesley. (p. 150)

Neumann, R., & Strack, F. (2000). "Mood contagion": The automatic transfer of mood between persons. *Journal of Personality and Social Psychology, 79,* 211-223. (pp. 516, 690)

Newberg, A., & D'Aquili, E. (2001). *Why God won't go away: Brain science and the biology of belief.* New York: Simon & Schuster. (p. 552)

Newcomb, M. D., & Harlow, L. L. (1986). Life events and substance use among adolescents: Mediating effects of perceived loss of control and meaninglessness in life. *Journal of Personality and Social Psychology, 51,* 564-577. (p. 126)

Newcombe, N. S., Drummey, A. B., Fox, N. A., Lie, E., & Ottinger-Alberts, W. (2000). Remembering early childhood: How much, how, and why (or why not). *Current Directions in Psychological Science, 9,* 55-58. (p. 176)

Newman, A. J., Bavelier, D., Corina, D., Jezzard, P., & Neville, H. J. (2002). A critical period for right hemisphere recruitment in American Sign Language processing. *Nature Neuroscience, 5,* 76-80. (p. 390)

Newman, L. S., & Baumeister, R. F. (1996). Toward an explanation of the UFO abduction phenomenon: Hypnotic elaboration, extraterrestrial sadomasochism, and spurious memories. *Psychological Inquiry, 7,* 99-126. (p. 109)

Newman, L. S., & Ruble, D. N. (1988). Stability and change in self-understanding: The early elementary school years. *Early Child Development and Care, 40,* 77-99. (p. 192)

Newman, M. L., Pennebaker, J. W., Berry, D. S., & Richards, J. M. (2003). Lying words: Predicting deception from linguistic style. *Personality and Social Psychology Bulletin, 29,* 665-675. (p. 505)

Newman, R., Ratner, N. B., Jusczyk, A. M., Jusczyk, P. W., & Dow, K. A. (2006). Infants' early ability to segment the conversational speech signal predicts later language development: A retrospective analysis. *Developmental Psychology, 42,* 643-655. (p. 386)

Newport, E. L. (1990). Maturational constraints on language learning. *Cognitive Science, 14,* 11-28. (p. 390)

Newport, F. (2001, February). Americans see women as emotional and affectionate, men as more aggressive. *The Gallup Poll Monthly,* pp. 34-38. (p. 512)

Newport, F. (2002, July 29). Bush job approval update. *Gallup News Service* (www.gallup.com/poll/releases/pr020729.asp). (p. 732)

Newport, F. (2007, June 11). Majority of Republicans doubt theory of evolution. *Gallup Poll* (www.galluppoll.com). (p. 165)

Newport, F., Jones, J. M., Saad, L., & Carroll, J. (2007, April 27). Gallup poll review: 10 key points about public opinion on Iraq. *The Gallup Poll* (www.gallluppoll.com). (p. 158)

Newport, F., Moore, D. W., Jones, J. M., & Saad, L. (2003, March 21). Special release: American opinion on the war. *Gallup Poll Tuesday Briefing* (www.gallup.com). (p. 688)

Newton, E. L. (1991). The rocky road from actions to intentions. *Dissertation Abstracts International, 51*(8-B), 4105. (p. 281)

Neylan, T. C., Metzler, T. J., Best, S. R., Weiss, D. S., Fagan, J. A., Liberman, A., Rogers, C., Vedantham, K., Brunet, A., Lipsey, T. L., & Marmar, C. R. (2002). Critical incident exposure and sleep quality in police officers. *Psychosomatic Medicine, 64,* 345-352. (p. 101)

Nezlek, J. B. (2001). Daily psychological adjustment and the planfulness of day-to-day behavior. *Journal of Social and Clinical Psychology, 20,* 452-475. (p. 585)

Ng, S. H. (1990). Androcentric coding of *man* and *his* in memory by language users. *Journal of Experimental Social Psychology, 26,* 455-464. (p. 394)

Ng, W. W. H., Sorensen, K. L., & Eby, L. T. (2006). Locus of control at work: A meta-analysis. *Journal of Organizational Behavior, 27,* 1057-1087. (p. 585)

Nguyen, D. (2005, September 22). JetBlue passengers watched news of drama. Associated Press release. (p. 532)

NHTSA. (2000). Traffic safety facts 1999: Older population. Washington, DC: National Highway Traffic Safety Administration (National Transportation Library: www.ntl.bts.gov). (p. 210)

NHTSA (2006, April). The 100-car naturalistic driving study phase II: Results of the 100-car field experiment. Washington, DC: National Highway Traffic Safety Administration (www.nhtsa.gov). (p. 88)

NICHD (2006). Child-care effect sizes for the NICHD study of early child care and youth development. *American Psychologist, 61,* 99–116. (p. 191)

NICHD Early Child Care Research Network. (2002). Structure/process/outcome: Direct and indirect effects of caregiving quality on young children's development. *Psychological Science, 13,* 199–206. (p. 191)

NICHD Early Child Care Research Network. (2003). Does amount of time spent in child care predict socioemotional adjustment during the transition to kindergarten? *Child Development, 74,* 976–1005. (p. 191)

Nickell, J. (1996, May/June). A study of fantasy proneness in the thirteen cases of alleged encounters in John Mack's abduction. *Skeptical Inquirer,* pp. 18–20, 54. (p. 109)

Nickerson, R. S. (1998). Applied experimental psychology. *Applied Psychology: An International Review, 47,* 155–173. (p. 279)

Nickerson, R. S. (1999). How we know—and sometimes misjudge—what others know: Imputing one's own knowledge to others. *Psychological Bulletin, 125,* 737–759. (p. 281)

Nickerson, R. S., & Adams, M. J. (1979). Long-term memory for a common object. *Cognitive Psychology, 11,* 287–307. (p. 352)

Nicol, S. E., & Gottesman, I. I. (1983). Clues to the genetics and neurobiology of schizophrenia. *American Scientist, 71,* 398–404. (p. 642)

Nicolaus, L. K., Cassel, J. F., Carlson, R. B., & Gustavson, C. R. (1983). Taste-aversion conditioning of crows to control predation on eggs. *Science, 220,* 212–214. (p. 296)

Nicolelis, M. A. L., & Chapin, J. K. (2002, October). Controlling robots with the mind. *Scientific American,* pp. 46–53. (p. 69)

NIDA. (2002). Methamphetamine abuse and addiction. *Research Report Series.* National Institute on Drug Abuse, NIH Publication Number 02-4210. (p. 117)

NIDA. (2005, May). Methamphetamine. *NIDA Info Facts.* National Institute on Drug Abuse. (p. 117)

Nielsen, K. M., Faergeman, O., Larsen, M. L., & Foldspang, A. (2006). Danish singles have a twofold risk of acute coronary syndrome: Data from a cohort of 138,290 persons. *Journal of Epidemiology and Community Health, 60,* 721–728. (p. 545)

Nier, J. A. (2004). Why does the "above average effect" exist? Demonstrating idiosyncratic trait definition. *Teaching of Psychology, 31,* 53–54. (p. 593)

Nightingale, F. (1860/1969). *Notes on nursing.* Mineola, NY: Dover. (p. 546)

NIH. (2001, July 20). Workshop summary: Scientific evidence on condom effectiveness for sexually transmitted disease (STD) prevention. Bethesda: National Institute of Allergy and Infectious Diseases, National Institutes of Health. (p. 471)

NIH (2006, December 4). NIDA researchers complete unprecedented scan of human genome that may help unlock the genetic contribution to tobacco addiction. *NIH News,* National Institutes of Health (www.nih.gov). (p. 126)

NIMH. (2002, April 26). U.S. suicide rates by age, gender, and racial group. National Institute of Mental Health (www.nimh.nih.gov/research/suichart.cfm). (p. 630)

NIMH. (2003). *Attention deficit hyperactivity disorder.* Bethesda, MD: National Institute of Mental Health. (p. 600)

Nisbett, R. E. (1987). Lay personality theory: Its nature, origin, and utility. In N. E. Grunberg, R. E. Nisbett, & others, *A distinctive approach to psychological research: The influence of Stanley Schachter.* Hillsdale, NJ: Erlbaum. (p. 487)

Nisbett, R. E., & Cohen, D. (1996). *Culture of honor: The psychology of violence in the South.* Boulder, CO: Westview Press. (p. 713)

Nisbett, R. E., & Ross, L. (1980). *Human inference: Strategies and shortcomings of social judgment.* Englewood Cliffs, NJ: Prentice-Hall. (p. 374)

Nitschke, J. B., Dixon, G. E., Sarinopoulos, I., Short, S. J., Cohen, J. D., Smith, E. E., Kosslyn, S. M., Rose, R. M., & Davidson, R. J. (2006). Altering expectancy dampens neural response to aversive taste in primary taste cortex. *Nature Neuroscience 9,* 435–442. (p. 258)

Nixon, G., M., Thompson, J. M. D., Han, D. Y., Becroft, D. M., Clark, P. M., Robinson, E., Waldie, K E., Wild, C. J., Black, P. N., & Mitchell, E. A. (2008). Short sleep duration in middle childhood: Risk factors and consequences. *Sleep, 31,* 71–78. (p. 97)

Noel, J. G., Forsyth, D. R., & Kelley, K. N. (1987). Improving the performance of failing students by overcoming their self-serving attributional biases. *Basic and Applied Social Psychology, 8,* 151–162. (p. 587)

Noftle, E. E., & Robins, R. W. (2007). Personality predictors of academic outcomes: Big Five correlates of GPA and SAT scores. *Journal of Personality and Social Psychology, 93,* 116–130. (p. 580)

Noice, H., & Noice, T. (2006). What studies of actors and acting can tell us about memory and cognitive functioning. *Current Directions in Psychological Science, 15,* 14–18. (p. 332)

Nolen-Hoeksema, S. (2001). Gender differences in depression. *Current Directions in Psychological Science, 10,* 173–176. (p. 632)

Nolen-Hoeksema, S. (2003). Women who think too much: How to break free of overthinking and reclaim your life. New York; Holt. (pp. 632, 633)

Nolen-Hoeksema, S., & Larson, J. (1999). *Coping with loss.* Mahwah, NJ: Erlbaum. (p. 221)

NORC. (2007). National Opinion Research Center (University of Chicago) General Social Survey data, 1972 through 2004, accessed via sda.berkeley.edu. (p. 481)

Nordgren, L. F., van der Pligt, J., & van Harreveld, F. (2006). Visceral drives in retrospect: Explanations about the inaccessible past. *Psychological Science, 17,* 635–640. (p. 448)

Nordgren, L. F., van der Pligt, J., & van Harreveld, F. (2007). Evaluating Eve: Visceral states influence the evaluation of impulsive behavior. *Journal of Personality and Social Psychology, 93,* 75–84. (p. 448)

Norem, J. K. (2001). The positive power of negative thinking: Using defensive pessimism to harness anxiety and perform at your peak. New York: Basic Books. (p. 587)

Norenzayan, A., & Hansen, I. G. (2006). Belief in supernatural agents in the face of death. *Personality and Social Psychology Bulletin, 32,* 174–187. (p. 567)

Norman, D. A. (2001). The perils of home theater (www.jnd.org/dn.mss/ProblemsOfHomeTheater.html). (p. 279)

Normand, M. P., & Dallery, J. (2007, June 20). Mercury rising: Exposing the vaccine-autism myth. *eSkeptic: The email newsletter of the Skeptics Society* (www.skeptic.com/eskep). (p. 182)

Noroozian, M., Lofti, J., Gassemzadeh, H., Emami, H., & Mehrabi, Y. (2003). Academic achievement and learning abilities in left-handers: Guilt or gift? *Cortex, 38,* 779–785. (p. 79)

Norton, K. L., Olds, T. S., Olive, S., & Dank, S. (1996). Ken and Barbie at life size. *Sex Roles, 34,* 287–294. (p. 455)

Norton, M. B. (2002, October 31). They called it witchcraft. *New York Times* (www.nytimes.com). (p. 708)

Norton, P. J., & Price, E. C. (2007). A meta-analytic review of adult cognitive-behavioral treatment outcome across the anxiety disorders. *Journal of Nervous and Mental Disease, 195,* 521–531. (p. 657)

Nowak, R. (1994). Nicotine scrutinized as FDA seeks to regulate cigarettes. *Science, 263,* 1555–1556. (p. 119)

Nowell, A., & Hedges, L. V. (1998). Trends in gender differences in academic achievement from 1960 to 1994: An analysis of differences in mean, variance, and extreme scores. *Sex Roles, 39,* 21–43. (p. 434)

NSF. (2001, October 24). Public bounces back after Sept. 11 attacks, national study shows. *NSF News,* National Science Foundation (www.nsf.gov/od/lpa/news/press/ol/pr0185.htm). (p. 533)

NSF. (2008). *2008 sleep in America poll.* National Sleep Foundation (sleepfoundation.org). (p. 96)

Nurnberger, J. I., Jr., & Bierut, L. J. (2007, April). Seeking the connections: Alcoholism and our genes. *Scientific American,* pp. 46–53. (p. 126)

Nuttin, J. M., Jr. (1987). Affective consequences of mere ownership: The name letter effect in twelve European languages. *European Journal of Social Psychology, 17,* 381–402. (p. 719)

Oaten, M., & Cheng, K. (2006a). Longitudinal gains in self-regulation from regular physical exercise. *British Journal of Health Psychology, 11,* 717–733. (p. 585)

Oaten, M., & Cheng, K. (2006b). Improved self-control: The benefits of a regular program of academic study. *Basic and Applied Social Psychology, 28,* 1–16. (p. 585)

Oberlander, J., & Gill, A. J. (2006). Language with character: A stratified corpus comparison of individual differences in e-mail communication. *Discourse Processes, 42,* 239–270. (p. 582)

Oberman, L. M., & Ramachandran, V. S. (2007). The simulating social mind: The role of the mirror neuron system and simulation in the social and communicative deficits of autism spectrum disorders. *Psychological Bulletin, 133,* 310–327. (p. 183)

Oberman, L. M., Winkielman, P., & Ramachandran. V. S. (2007). Face to face: Blocking facial mimicry can selectively impair recognition of emotional expressions. *Social Neuroscience, 2,* 167–178. (p. 516)

O'Connor, A. (2004, February 6). Study details 30-year increase in calorie consumption. *New York Times* (www.nytimes.com). (p. 461)

O'Connor, A. (2004, May 14). Pressure to go along with abuse is strong, but some soldiers find strength to refuse. *New York Times* (www.nytimes.com). (p. 701)

O'Connor, P., & Brown, G. W. (1984). Supportive relationships: Fact or fancy? *Journal of Social and Personal Relationships, 1,* 159–175. (p. 668)

Oddone-Paolucci, E., Genuis, M., & Violato, C. (2000). A meta-analysis of the published research on the effects of pornography. In C. Violato, E. Oddone-Paolucci, & M. Genuis (Eds.), *The changing family and child development.* Aldershot, England: Ashgate. (p. 714)

O'Donnell, L., Stueve, A., O'Donnell, C., Duran, R., San Doval, A., Wilson, R. F., Haber, D., Perry, E., & Pleck, J. H. (2002). Long-term reduction in sexual initiation and sexual activity among urban middle schoolers in the reach for health service learning program. *Journal of Adolescent Health, 31,* 93–100. (p. 472)

Oetting, E. R., & Beauvais, F. (1987). Peer cluster theory, socialization characteristics, and adolescent drug use: A path analysis. *Journal of Counseling Psychology, 34,* 205–213. (p. 127)

Oetting, E. R., & Beauvais, F. (1990). Adolescent drug use: Findings of national and local surveys. *Journal of Social and Personal Relationships, 1,* 159–175. (p. 127)

Oettingen, G., & Mayer, D. (2002). The motivating function of thinking about the future: Expectations versus fantasies. *Journal of Personality and Social Psychology, 83,* 1198–1212. (p. 587)

Oettingen, G., & Seligman, M. E. P. (1990). Pessimism and behavioural signs of depression in East versus West Berlin. *European Journal of Social Psychology, 20,* 207–220. (p. 586)

Offer, D., Kaiz, M., Howard, K. I., & Bennett, E. S. (2000). The altering of reported experiences. *Journal of the American Academy of Child and Adolescent Psychiatry, 39,* 735–742. (p. 361)

Offer, D., Ostrov, E., Howard, K. I., & Atkinson, R. (1988). *The teenage world: Adolescents' self-image in ten countries.* New York: Plenum. (p. 203)

Ogden, C. L., Fryar, C. D., Carroll, M. D., & Flegal, K. M. (2004, October 27). Mean body weight, heights, and body mass index, United States 1960–2002. *Advance Data from Vital and Health Statistics,* No. 347. (p. 461)

Öhman, A. (1986). Face the beast and fear the face: Animal and social fears as prototypes for evolutionary analyses of emotion. *Psychophysiology, 23,* 123–145. (p. 615)

Öhman, A., Lundqvist, D., & Esteves, F. (2001). The face in the crowd revisited: A threat advantage with schematic stimuli. *Journal of Personality and Social Psychology, 80,* 381–396. (p. 510)

Öhman, A., & Mineka, S. (2003). The malicious serpent: Snakes as a prototypical stimulus for an evolved module of fear. *Current Directions in Psychological Science, 12,* 5–9. (p. 519)

Oishi, S., Diener, E., & Lucas, R. E. (2007). The optimum level of well-being: Can people be too happy? *Perspectives on Psychological Science, 2,* 346–360. (p. 522)

Oishi, S., Diener, E. F., Lucas, R. E., & Suh, E. M. (1999). Cross-cultural variations in predictors of life satisfaction: Perspectives from needs and values. *Personality and Social Psychology Bulletin, 25,* 980–990. (p. 447)

O'Keeffe, C., & Wiseman, R. (2005). Testing alleged mediumship: Methods and results. *British Journal of Psychology, 96,* 165–179. (p. 579)

Okun, M. S., & 12 others. (2004). What's in a "smile"? Intra-operative observations of contralateral smiles induced by deep brain stimulation. *Neurocase, 10,* 271–279. (p. 504)

Olatunhi, B. O., Cisler, J. M., & Tolin, D. F. (2007). Quality of life in the anxiety disorders: A meta-analytic review. *Clinical Psychology Review, 27,* 572–581. (p. 610)

Olds, J. (1958). Self-stimulation of the brain. *Science, 127,* 315–324. (p. 64)

Olds, J. (1975). Mapping the mind onto the brain. In F. G. Worden, J. P. Swazey, & G. Adelman (Eds.), *The neurosciences: Paths of discovery.* Cambridge, MA: MIT Press. (p. 64)

Olds, J., & Milner, P. (1954). Positive reinforcement produced by electrical stimulation of the septal area and other regions of rat brain. *Journal of Comparative and Physiological Psychology, 47,* 419–427. (p. 64)

Olff, M., Langeland, W., Draijer, N., & Gersons, B. P. R. (2007). Gender differences in posttraumatic stress disorder. *Psychological Bulletin, 135,* 183–204. (p. 614)

Olfson, M., Gameroff, M. J., Marcus, S. C., & Jensen, P. S. (2003). National trends in the treatment of attention deficit hyperactivity disorder. *American Journal of Psychiatry, 160,* 1071–1077. (p. 600)

Olfson, M., Marcus, S. C., Wan, G. J., & Geissler, E. C. (2004). National trends in the outpatient treatment of anxiety disorders. *Journal of Clinical Psychiatry, 65,* 1166–1173. (p. 672)

Olfson, M., Shaffer, D., Marcus, S. C., & Greenberg, T. (2003). Relationship between antidepressant medication treatment and suicide in adolescents. *Archives of General Psychiatry, 60,* 978–982. (p. 673)

Olin, S. S., & Mednick, S. A. (1996). Risk factors of psychosis: Identifying vulnerable populations premorbidly. *Schizophrenia Bulletin, 22,* 223–240. (p. 643)

Oliner, S. P., & Oliner, P. M. (1988). *The altruistic personality: Rescuers of Jews in Nazi Europe.* New York: Free Press. (p. 318)

Olshansky, S. J., Carnes, B. A., & Cassel, C. K. (1993, April). The aging of the human species. *Scientific American,* pp. 46–52. (p. 208)

Olshansky, S. J., Passaro, D. J., Hershow, R. C., Layden, J., Carnes, B. A., Brody, J., Hayflick, L., Butler, R. N., Allison, D. B., & Ludwig, D. S. (2005). A potential decline in life expectancy in the United States in the 21st century. *New England Journal of Medicine, 352,* 1138–1145. (p. 457)

Olson, M. A., & Fazio, R. H. (2001). Implicit attitude formation through classical conditioning. *Psychological Science, 12,* 413–417. (p. 293)

Olson, S. (2005). Brain scans raise privacy concerns. *Science, 307,* 1548–1550. (p. 576)

Olsson, A., & Phelps, E. A. (2004). Learned fear of "unseen" faces after Pavlovian, observational, and instructed fear. *Psychological Science, 15,* 822–828. (p. 615)

Olsson, A., Nearing, K. I., & Phelps, E. A. (2007). Learning fears by observing others: The neural systems of social fear transmission. *Social Cognitive and Affective Neuroscience, 2,* 3–11. (p. 519)

Olweus, D., Mattsson, A., Schalling, D., & Low, H. (1988). Circulating testosterone levels and aggression in adolescent males: A causal analysis. *Psychosomatic Medicine, 50,* 261–272. (p. 711)

Oman, D., Kurata, J. H., Strawbridge, W. J., & Cohen, R. D. (2002). Religious attendance and cause of death over 31 years. *International Journal of Psychiatry in Medicine, 32,* 69–89. (p. 553)

O'Neil, J. (2002, September 3). Vital signs: Behavior: Parent smoking and teenage sex. *New York Times.* (p. 32)

O'Neill, M. J. (1993). The relationship between privacy, control, and stress responses in office workers. Paper presented to the Human Factors and Ergonomics Society convention. (p. 543)

Onishi, N. (2008, June 13). Japan, seeking trim waists, measures millions. *New York Times* (www.nytimes.com). (p. 457)

ORB (2008, January). Update on Iraqi casualty data. Opinion Research Business (London) (www.opinion.co.uk). (p. 681)

O'Reardon, J. P., & 12 others. (2007). Efficacy and safety of transcranial magnetic stimulation in the acute treatment of major depression: A multisite randomized controlled trial. *Biological Psychiatry, 62,* 1208–1216. (p. 676)

Oren, D. A., & Terman, M. (1998). Tweaking the human circadian clock with light. *Science, 279,* 333–334. (p. 92)

Orlovskaya, D. D., Uranova, N. A., Zimina, I. S., Kolomeets, N. S., Vikhreva, O. V., Rachmanova, V. I., Black, J. E., Klintsova, A. Y., & Greenough, W. T. (1999). Effect of professional status on the number of synapses per neuron in the prefrontal cortex of normal human and schizophrenic brain. *Society for Neuroscience Abstracts, 329.11, 25,* 818. (p. 412)

Orne, M. T., & Evans, F. J. (1965). Social control in the psychological experiment: Antisocial behavior and hypnosis. *Journal of Personality and Social Psychology, 1,* 189–200. (p. 109)

Osborne, C., Manning, W. D., & Smock, P. J. (2007). Married and cohabiting parents' relationship stability: A focus on race and ethnicity. *Journal of Marriage and Family, 69,* 1345–1366. (p. 217)

Osborne, J. W. (1997). Race and academic disidentification. *Journal of Educational Psychology, 89,* 728–735. (p. 439)

Osborne, L. (1999, October 27). A linguistic big bang. *New York Times Magazine* (www.nytimes.com). (p. 389)

Osgood, C. E. (1962). *An alternative to war or surrender.* Urbana: University of Illinois Press. (p. 733)

Osgood, C. E. (1980). GRIT: A strategy for survival in mankind's nuclear age? Paper presented at the Pugwash Conference on New Directions in Disarmament. (p. 733)

OSS Assessment Staff. (1948). *The assessment of men.* New York: Rinehart. (p. 589)

Ost, L. G., & Hugdahl, K. (1981). Acquisition of phobias and anxiety response patterns in clinical patients. *Behaviour Research and Therapy, 16,* 439–447. (p. 615)

Ostfeld, A. M., Kasl, S. V., D'Atri, D. A., & Fitzgerald, E. F. (1987). *Stress, crowding, and blood pressure in prison.* Hillsdale, NJ: Erlbaum. (p. 544)

Oswald, A. J., & Powdthavee, N. (2006). *Does happiness adapt? A longitudinal study of disability with implications for economists and judges* (Discussion Paper No. 2208). Bonn: Institute for the Study of Labor. (p. 523)

Oswald, A. J., & Powdthavee, N. (2007). Obesity, unhappiness, and *The challenge of affluence:* Theory and evidence. *Economic Journal.* (p. 458)

Ott, B. (2007, June 14). Investors, take note: Engagement boosts earnings. *Gallup Management Journal* (gmj.gallup.com). (p. 493)

Ott, C. H., Lueger, R. J., Kelber, S. T., & Prigerson, H. G. (2007). Spousal bereavement in older adults: Common, resilient, and chronic grief with defining characteristics. *Journal of Nervous and Mental Disease, 195,* 332–341. (p. 221)

Ouellette, J. A., & Wood, W. (1998). Habit and intention in everyday life: The multiple processes by which past behavior predicts future behavior. *Psychological Bulletin, 124,* 54–74. (pp. 488, 590)

Overmier, J. B., & Murison, R. (1997). Animal models reveal the "psych" in the psychosomatics of peptic ulcers. *Current Directions in Psychological Science, 6,* 180–184. (p. 542)

Owen, A. M., Coleman, M. R., Boly, M., Davis, M. H., Laureys, S., & Pickard, J. D. (2006). Detecting awareness in the vegetative state. *Science, 313,* 1402. (p. 85)

Owen, R. (1814). First essay in *New view of society or the formation of character.* Quoted in *The story of New Lamark.* New Lamark Mills, Lamark, Scotland: New Lamark Conservation Trust, 1993. (p. 492)

Oxfam. (2005, March 26). Three months on: New figures show tsunami may have killed up to four times as many women as men. Oxfam Press Release (www.oxfam.org.uk). (p. 162)

Ozer, E. J., Best, S. R., Lipsey, T. L., & Weiss, D. S. (2003). Predictors of posttraumatic stress disorder and symptoms in adults: A meta-analysis. *Psychological Bulletin, 129,* 52–73. (p. 613)

Ozer, E. J., & Weiss, D. S. (2004). Who develops posttraumatic stress disorder. *Current Directions in Psychological Science, 13,* 169–172. (pp. 613, 614)

Özgen, E. (2004). Language, learning, and color perception. *Current Directions in Psychological Science, 13,* 95–98. (p. 394)

Pacifici, R., Zuccaro, P., Farre, M., Pichini, S., Di Carlo, S., Roset, P. N., Ortuno, J., Pujadus, M., Bacosi, A., Menoyo, E., Segura, J., & de la Torre, R. (2001). Effects of repeated doses of MDMA ("Ecstasy") on cell-mediated immune response in humans. *Life Sciences, 69,* 2931–2941. (p. 122)

Paddock, S., Laje, G., Charney, D., Rush, A. J., Wilson, A. F., Sorant, A. J. M., Lipsky, R., Wisniewski, S. R., Manji, H., & McMahon, F. J. (2007). Association of GRIK4 with outcome of antidepressant treatment in the STAR*D cohort. *American Journal of Psychiatry, 164,* 1181–1188. (p. 629)

Padgett, V. R. (1989). Predicting organizational violence: An application of 11 powerful principles of obedience. Paper presented to the American Psychological Association convention. (p. 695)

Page, S. (1977). Effects of the mental illness label in attempts to obtain accommodation. *Canadian Journal of Behavioral Science, 9,* 84–90. (p. 605)

Page, S. E. (2007). *The difference: How the power of diversity creates better groups, firms, schools, and societies.* Princeton, NJ: Princeton University Press. (p. 700)

Pagnin, D., de Queiroz, V., Pini, S., & Cassano, G. B. (2004). Efficacy of ECT in depression: A meta-analytic review. *Journal of ECT, 20,* 13–20. (p. 675)

Paivio, A. (1986). *Mental representations: A dual coding approach.* New York: Oxford University Press. (p. 333)

Palace, E. M. (1995). Modification of dysfunctional patterns of sexual response through autonomic arousal and false physiological feedback. *Journal of Consulting and Clinical Psychology, 63,* 604–615. (p. 506)

Palladino, J. J., & Carducci, B. J. (1983). "Things that go bump in the night": Students' knowledge of sleep and dreams. Paper presented at the meeting of the Southeastern Psychological Association. (p. 91)

Pallier, C., Colomé, A., & Sebastián-Gallés, N. (2001). The influence of native-language phonology on lexical access: Exemplar-based versus abstract lexical entries. *Psychological Science, 12,* 445–448. (p. 387)

Palmer, S., Schreiber, C., & Box, C. (1991). Remembering the earthquake: "Flashbulb" memory for experienced vs. reported events. Paper presented to the Psychonomic Society convention. (p. 341)

Pandelaere, M., & Dewitte, S. (2006). Is this a question? Not for long. The statement bias. *Journal of Experimental Social Psychology, 42,* 525–531. (p. 362)

Pandey, J., Sinha, Y., Prakash, A., & Tripathi, R. C. (1982). Right-left political ideologies and attribution of the causes of poverty. *European Journal of Social Psychology, 12,* 327–331. (p. 684)

Panskepp, J. (2007). Neurologizing the psychology of affects: How appraisal-based constructivism and basic emotion theory can coexist. *Perspectives on Psychological Science, 2,* 281–295. (p. 503)

Pantev, C., Oostenveld, R., Engelien, A., Ross, B., Roberts, L. R., & Hoke, M. (1998). Increased auditory cortical representation in musicians. *Nature, 392,* 811–814. (p. 73)

Panzarella, C., Alloy, L. B., & Whitehouse, W. G. (2006). Expanded hopelessness theory of depression: On the mechanisms by which social support protects against depression. *Cognitive Theory and Research, 30,* 307–333. (p. 633)

Park, C. L. (2007). Religiousness/spirituality and health: A meaning systems perspective. *Journal of Behavioral Medicine, 30,* 319–328. (p. 553)

Park, D. C., Lautenschlager, G., Hedden, T., Davidson, N. S., Smith, A. D., & Smith, P. K. (2002). Models of visuospatial and verbal memory across the adult life span. *Psychology and Aging, 17,* 299–320. (p. 215)

Park, G., Lubinski, D., & Benbow, C. P. (2007). Contrasting intellectual patterns predict creativity in the arts and sciences. *Psychological Science, 18,* 948–952. (p. 426)

Park, J., Felix, K., & Lee, G. (2007). Implicit attitudes toward Arab-Muslims and the moderating effects of social information. *Basic and Applied Social Psychology, 29,* 35–45. (p. 293)

Park, R. L. (1999, July 12). Liars never break a sweat. *New York Times* (www.nytimes.com). (p. 505)

Parker, C. P., Baltes, B. B., Young, S. A., Huff, J. W., Altmann, R. A., LaCost, H. A., & Roberts, J. E. (2003). Relationships between psychological climate perceptions and work outcomes: A meta-analytic review. *Journal of Organizational Behavior, 24,* 389–416. (p. 491)

Parker, E. S., Cahill, L., & McGaugh, J. L. (2006). A case of unusual autobiographical remembering. *Neurocase, 12,* 35–49. (p. 351)

Passell, P. (1993, March 9). Like a new drug, social programs are put to the test *New York Times,* pp. C1, C10. (p. 36)

Patall, E. A., Cooper, H., & Robinson, J. C. (2008). The effects of choice on intrinsic motivation and related outcomes: A meta-analysis of research findings. *Psychological Bulletin, 134,* 270–300. (p. 309)

Pate, J. E., Pumariega, A. J., Hester, C., & Garner, D. M. (1992). Cross-cultural patterns in eating disorders: A review. *Journal of the American Academy of Child and Adolescent Psychiatry, 31,* 802–809. (p. 454)

Patel, S. R., Malhotra, A., White, D. P., Gottlieb, D. J., & Hu, F. B. (2006). Association between reduced sleep and weight gain in women. *American Journal of Epidemiology, 164,* 947–954. (p. 97)

Patrick, H., Knee, C. R., Canevello, A., & Lonsbary, C. (2007). The role of need fulfillment in relationship functioning and well-being: A self-determination theory perspective. *Journal of Personality and Social Psychology, 92,* 434–457. (p. 480)

Patten, S. B., Wang, J. L., Williams, J. V. A., Currie, S., Beck, C. A., Maxwell, C. J., & el-Guebaly, N. (2006). Descriptive epidemiology of major depression in Canada. *Canadian Journal of Psychiatry, 51,* 84–90. (p. 625)

Patterson, D. R. (2004). Treating pain with hypnosis. *Current Directions in Psychological Science, 13,* 252–255. (p. 110)

Patterson, F. (1978, October). Conversations with a gorilla. *National Geographic,* pp. 438–465. (p. 400)

Patterson, G. R., Chamberlain, P., & Reid, J. B. (1982). A comparative evaluation of parent training procedures. *Behavior Therapy, 13,* 638–650. (pp. 308, 713)

Patterson, G. R., Reid, J. B., & Dishion, T. J. (1992). *Antisocial boys.* Eugene, OR: Castalia. (p. 713)

Patterson, M., Warr, P., & West, M. (2004). Organizational climate and company productivity: The role of employee affect and employee level. *Journal of Occupational and Organizational Psychology, 77,* 193–216. (p. 491)

Patterson, P. H. (2007). Maternal effects on schizophrenia risk. *Science, 318,* 576–577. (p. 640)

Patterson, R. (1951). *The riddle of Emily Dickinson.* Boston: Houghton Mifflin. (p. 635)

Patton, G. C., Coffey, C., Carlin, J. B., Degenhardt, L., Lynskey, M., & Hall, W. (2002). Cannabis use and mental health of young people: Cohort study. *British Medical Journal, 325,* 1195–1198. (p. 124)

Paulesu, E., Demonet, J.-F., Fazio, F., McCrory, E., Chanoine, V., Brunswick, N., Cappa, S. F., Cossu, G., Habib, M., Frith, C. D., & Frith, U. (2001). Dyslexia: Cultural diversity and biological unity. *Science, 291,* 2165–2167. (p. 20)

Paulos, J. A. (1995). *A mathematician reads the newspaper.* New York: Basic Books. (p. 674)

Paulos, J. A. (2006, August 6). Who's counting: It's mean to ignore the median (www.ABCNews.com). (p. 38)

Paus, T., Zijdenbos, A., Worsley, K., Collins, D. L., Blumenthal, J., Giedd, J. N., Rapoport, J. L., & Evans, A. C. (1999). Structural maturation of neural pathways in children and adolescents: In vivo study. *Science, 283,* 1908–1911. (p. 174)

Pavlidis, G. T. (2005, January 17). Eye movements can diagnose preschoolers at high risk for attention deficit/hyperactivity disorder (ADHD). Press release, Brunel University (www.brunel.ac.uk). (p. 600)

Pavlov, I. (1927). Conditioned reflexes: An investigation of the physiological activity of the cerebral cortex. Oxford: Oxford University Press. (pp. 290, 294)

Payne, B. K. (2006). Weapon bias: Split-second decisions and unintended stereotyping. *Current Directions in Psychological Science, 15,* 287–291. (p. 705)

Payne, B. K., & Corrigan, E. (2007). Emotional constraints on intentional forgetting. *Journal of Experimental Social Psychology, 43,* 780–786. (p. 357)

Pedersen, N. L., Plomin, R., McClearn, G. E., & Friberg, L. (1988). Neuroticism, extraversion, and related traits in adult twins reared apart and reared together. *Journal of Personality and Social Psychology, 55,* 950–957. (p. 136)

Peeters, A., Barendregt, J. J., Willekens, F., Mackenbach, J. P., & Mamum, A. A. (2003). Obesity in adulthood and its consequences for life expectancy: A life-table analysis. *Annals of Internal Medicine, 138,* 24–32. (p. 457)

Peigneux, P., Laureys, S., Fuchs, S., Collette, F., Perrin, F., Reggers, J., Phillips, C., Degueldre, C., Del Fiore, G., Aerts, J., Luxen, A., & Maquet, P. (2004). Are spatial memories strengthened in the human hippocampus during slow wave sleep? *Neuron, 44,* 535–545. (pp. 100, 344)

Pekkanen, J. (1982, June). Why do we sleep? *Science, 82,* p. 86. (p. 100)

Pelham, B. W. (1993). On the highly positive thoughts of the highly depressed. In R. F. Baumeister (Ed.), *Self-esteem: The puzzle of low self-regard.* New York: Plenum. (p. 591)

Pendick, D. (1994, January/February). The mind of violence. *Brain Work: The Neuroscience Newsletter,* pp. 1–3, 5. (p. 711)

Penhune, V. B., Cismaru, R., Dorsaint-Pierre, R., Petitto, L-A., & Zatorre, R. J. (2003). The morphometry of auditory cortex in the congenitally deaf measured using MRI. *NeuroImage, 20,* 1215–1225. (p. 249)

Pennebaker, J. (1990). *Opening up: The healing power of confiding in others.* New York: William Morrow. (pp. 546, 566)

Pennebaker, J. W. (2002, January 28). Personal communication. (p. 732)

Pennebaker, J. W., Barger, S. D., & Tiebout, J. (1989). Disclosure of traumas and health among Holocaust survivors. *Psychosomatic Medicine, 51,* 577–589. (p. 547)

Pennebaker, J. W., & O'Heeron, R. C. (1984). Confiding in others and illness rate among spouses of suicide and accidental death victims. *Journal of Abnormal Psychology, 93,* 473–476. (p. 546)

Pennebaker, J. W., & Stone, L. D. (2003). Words of wisdom: Language use over the life span. *Journal of Personality and Social Psychology, 85,* 291–301. (p. 219)

Penny, H., & Haddock, G. (2007). Anti-fat prejudice among children: The "mere proximity" effect in 5-10 year olds. *Journal of Experimental Social Psychology, 43,* 678–683. (p. 458)

Peplau, L. A., & Fingerhut, A. W. (2007). The close relationships of lesbians and gay men. *Annual Review of Psychology, 58,* 405–424. (pp. 144, 217, 473)

Peplau, L. A., & Garnets, L. D. (2000). A new paradigm for understanding women's sexuality and sexual orientation. *Journal of Social Issues, 56,* 329–350. (p. 473)

Peppard, P. E., Szklo-Coxe, M., Hia, K. M., & Young, T. (2006). Longitudinal association of sleep-related breathing disorder and depression. *Archives of Internal Medicine, 166,* 1709–1715. (p. 102)

Pepperberg, I. M. (2006). Grey parrot numerical competence: A review. *Animal Cognition, 9,* 377–391. (p. 398)

Perani, D., & Abutalebi, J. (2005). The neural basis of first and second language processing. *Current Opinion in Neurobiology, 15,* 202–206. (p. 392)

Pereira, A. C., Huddleston, D. E., Brickman, A. M., Sosunov, A. A., Hen, R., McKhann, G. M., Sloan, R., Gage, F. H., Brown, T. R., & Small, S. A. (2007). An *in vivo* correlate of exercise-induced neurogenesis in the adult dentate gyrus. *Proceedings of the National Academic of Sciences, 104,* 5638–5643. (pp. 74, 211)

Pereira, G. M., & Osburn, H. G. (2007). Effects of participation in decision making on performance and employee attitudes: A quality circles meta-analysis. *Journal of Business Psychology, 22,* 145–153. (pp. 210, 495)

Perkins, A., & Fitzgerald, J. A. (1997). Sexual orientation in domestic rams: Some biological and social correlates. In L. Ellis & L. Ebertz (Eds.), *Sexual orientation: Toward biological understanding.* Westport, CT: Praeger Publishers. (p. 475)

Perlmutter, M. (1983). Learning and memory through adulthood. In M. W. Riley, B. B. Hess, & K. Bond (Eds.), *Aging in society: Selected reviews of recent research.* Hillsdale, NJ: Erlbaum. (p. 213)

Perls, T., & Silver, M. H., with Lauerman, J. F. (1999). *Living to 100: Lessons in living to your maximum potential.* Thorndike, ME: Thorndike Press. (p. 538)

Perra, O., Williams, J. H. G., Whiten, A., Fraser, L., Benzie, H., & Perrett, D. I. (2008). Imitation and 'theory of mind' competencies in discrimination of autism from other neurodevelopmental disorders. *Research in Autism Disorders, 2,* 456–468. (p. 183)

Perrett, D. (2002, October 1). Perception laboratory, Department of Psychology, University of St. Andrews, Scotland (www.perception.st-and.ac.uk). (p. 722)

Perrett, D. I., Harries, M., Misflin, A. J., & Chitty, A. J. (1988). Three stages in the classification of body movements by visual neurons. In H. B. Barlow, C. Blakemore, & M. Weston Smith (Eds.), *Images and understanding.* Cambridge: Cambridge University Press. (p. 238)

Perrett, D. I., Hietanen, J. K., Oram, M. W., & Benson, P. J. (1992). Organization and functions of cells responsive to faces in the temporal cortex. *Philosophical Transactions of the Royal Society of London: Series B, 335,* 23–30. (p. 238)

Perrett, D. I., Lee, K. J., Penton-Voak, I., Rowland, D., Yoshikawa, S., Burt, D. M., Henzi, S. P., Castles, D. L., & Akamatsu, S. (1998, August). Effects of sexual dimorphism on facial attractiveness. *Nature, 394,* 884–887. (p. 706)

Perrett, D. I., May, K. A., & Yoshikawa, S. (1994). Facial shape and judgments of female attractiveness. *Nature, 368,* 239–242. (p. 238)

Persky, S., & Blascovich, J. (2005). Consequences of playing violent video games in immersive virtual environments. In A. Axelsson & R. Schroeder (Eds.). *Work and play in shared virtual environments.* New York: Springer. (p. 717)

Person, C., Tracy, M., & Galea, S. (2006). Risk factors for depression after a disaster. *Journal of Nervous and Mental Disease, 194,* 659–666. (p. 628)

Pert, C. (1986). Quoted in J. Hooper & D. Teresi, *The three-pound universe.* New York: Macmillan. (p. 64)

Pert, C. B., & Snyder, S. H. (1973). Opiate receptor: Demonstration in nervous tissue. *Science, 179,* 1011–1014. (p. 50)

Perugini, E. M., Kirsch, I., Allen, S. T., Coldwell, E., Meredith, J., Montgomery, G. H., & Sheehan, J. (1998). Surreptitious observation of responses to hypnotically suggested hallucinations: A test of the compliance hypothesis. *International Journal of Clinical and Experimental Hypnosis, 46,* 191–203. (p. 111)

Peschel, E. R., & Peschel, R. E. (1987). Medical insights into the castrati in opera. *American Scientist, 75,* 578–583. (p. 468)

Peters, M., Reimers, S., & Manning, J. T. (2006). Hand preference for writing and associations with selected demographic and behavioral variables in 255,100 subjects: The BBC Internet study. *Brain and Cognition, 62,* 177–189. (p. 78)

Peters, T. J., & Waterman, R. H., Jr. (1982). *In search of excellence: Lessons from America's best-run companies.* New York: Harper & Row. (p. 311)

Peterson, C., & Barrett, L. C. (1987). Explanatory style and academic performance among university freshmen. *Journal of Personality and Social Psychology, 53,* 603–607. (p. 587)

Peterson, C., Peterson, J., & Skevington, S. (1986). Heated argument and adolescent development. *Journal of Social and Personal Relationships, 3,* 229–240. (p. 198)

Peterson, C., & Seligman, M. E. P. (2004). *Character strengths and virtues: A handbook and classification.* New York: Oxford University Press. (p. 603)

Peterson, C. C., & Siegal, M. (1999). Representing inner worlds: Theory of mind in autistic, deaf, and normal hearing children. *Psychological Science, 10,* 126–129. (p. 184)

Peterson, L. R., & Peterson, M. J. (1959). Short-term retention of individual verbal items. *Journal of Experimental Psychology, 58,* 193–198. (p. 337)

Petitto, L. A., & Marentette, P. F. (1991). Babbling in the manual mode: Evidence for the ontogeny of language. *Science, 251,* 1493–1496. (p. 387)

Petry, N. M., Barry, D., Pietrzak, R. H., & Wagner, J. A. (2008). Overweight and obesity are associated with psychiatric disorders: Results from the National Epidemiologic Survey on Alcohol and Related Conditions. *Psychosomatic Medicine, 70,* 288–297. (p. 458)

Pettegrew, J. W., Keshavan, M. S., & Minshew, N. J. (1993). 31P nuclear magnetic resonance spectroscopy: Neurodevelopment and schizophrenia. *Schizophrenia Bulletin, 19,* 35–53. (p. 640)

Petticrew, C., Bell, R., & Hunter, D. (2002). Influence of psychological coping on survival and recurrence in people with cancer: Systematic review. *British Medical Journal, 325,* 1066. (p. 540)

Petticrew, M., Fraser, J. M., & Regan, M. F. (1999). Adverse life events and risk of breast cancer: A meta-analysis. *British Journal of Health Psychology, 4,* 1–17. (p. 540)

Pettifor, J. P. (2004). Professional ethics across national boundaries. *European Psychologist, 9,* 264–272. (p. 22)

Pettigrew, T. F. (1998). Reactions toward the new minorities of western Europe. *Annual Review of Sociology, 24,* 77–103. (p. 704)

Pettigrew, T. F. (2006). A two-level approach to anti-immigrant prejudice and discrimination. In R. Mahalingam (Ed.), *Cultural psychology of immigrants.* Mahwah, NJ: Erlbaum. (p. 704)

Pettigrew, T. F., & Tropp, L. R. (2006). A meta-analytic test of intergroup contact theory. *Journal of Personality and Social Psychology, 90,* 751–783. (p. 731)

Pettus, A. (2008, January–February). A cultural symptom? Repressed memory. *Harvard Magazine* (www.harvardmagazine.com). (p. 566)

Pew. (2003). Views of a changing world 2003. The Pew Global Attitudes Project. Washington, DC: Pew Research Center for the People and the Press (http://people-press.org/reports/pdf/185.pdf). (p. 162)

Pew. (2006, September 21). Publics of Asian powers hold negative views of one another. Pew Global Attitudes Project Report, Pew Research Center (pewresearch.org). (p. 707)

Pew Research Center. (2006, November 14). Attitudes toward homosexuality in African countries (pewresearch.org). (p. 472)

Pew Research Center. (2007, July 18). Modern marriage: "I like hugs. I like kisses. But what I really love is help with the dishes." Pew Research Center (www.pewresearch.org). (p. 725)

Pfammatter, M., Junghan, U. M., Brenner, H. D. (2006). Efficacy of psychological therapy in schizophrenia: Conclusions from meta-analyses. *Schizophrenia Bulletin, 32,* S64–S80. (p. 664)

Phelps, J. A., Davis J. O., & Schartz, K. M. (1997). Nature, nurture, and twin research strategies. *Current Directions in Psychological Science, 6,* 117–120. (pp. 134, 642)

Philip Morris. (2003). Philip Morris USA youth smoking prevention. Teenage attitudes and behavior study, 2002. In "Raising kids who don't smoke," vol. 1(2). (p. 119)

Philip Morris Companies, Inc. (1999, October 13). Referenced in Myron Levin, Philip Morris' new campaign echoes medical experts, *Los Angeles Times.* (p. 118)

Phillips, D. P. (1985). Natural experiments on the effects of mass media violence on fatal aggression: Strengths and weaknesses of a new approach. In L. Berkowitz (Ed.), *Advances in experimental social psychology* (Vol. 19). Orlando, FL: Academic Press. (p. 691)

Phillips, D. P., Carstensen, L. L., & Paight, D. J. (1989). Effects of mass media news stories on suicide, with new evidence on the role of story content. In D. R. Pfeffer (Ed.), *Suicide among youth: Perspectives on risk and prevention.* Washington, DC: American Psychiatric Press. (p. 691)

Phillips, J. L. (1969). *Origins of intellect: Piaget's theory.* San Francisco: Freeman. (p. 180)

Phillips, T. (2004, April 3). Quoted by T. Baldwin & G. Rozenberg, Britain 'must scrap multiculturalism.' *The Times,* p. 1. (p. 733)

Phonak. (2007). Hear the world (www.hear-the-world.com). (p. 249)

Piaget, J. (1930). *The child's conception of physical causality.* London: Routledge & Kegan Paul. (p. 176)

Piaget, J. (1932). *The moral judgment of the child.* New York: Harcourt, Brace & World. (p. 198)

Picchioni, M. M., & Murray, R. M. (2007). Schizophrenia. *British Medical Journal, 335,* 91–95. (p. 638)

Pieters, G. L. M., de Bruijn, E. R. A., Maas, Y., Hultijn, W., Vandereycken, W., Peuskens, J., & Sabbe, B. G. (2007). Action monitoring and perfectionism in anorexia nervosa. *Brain and Cognition, 63,* 42–50. (p. 454)

Pike, K. M., & Rodin, J. (1991). Mothers, daughters, and disordered eating. *Journal of Abnormal Psychology, 100,* 198–204. (p. 454)

Piliavin, J. A. (2003). Doing well by doing good: Benefits for the benefactor. In C. L. M. Keyes & J. Haidt (Eds.), *Flourishing: Positive psychology and the life well-lived.* Washington, DC: American Psychological Association. (p. 200)

Pillemer, D. (1998). *Momentous events, vivid memories.* Cambridge, MA: Harvard University Press. (p. 212)

Pillemer, D. B., Ivcevic, Z., Gooze, R. A., & Collins, K. A. (2007). Self-esteem memories: Feeling good about achievement success, feeling bad about relationship distress. *Personality and Social Psychology Bulletin, 33,* 1292–1305. (p. 481)

Pillemer, D. G. (1995). *What is remembered about early childhood events?* Invited paper presentation to the American Psychological Society convention. (p. 175)

Pillsworth, E. G., & Haselton, M. G. (2006). Male sexual attractiveness predicts differential ovulatory shifts in female extra-pair attraction and male mate retention. *Evolution and Human Behavior, 27,* 247–258. (p. 467)

Pillsworth, M. G., Haselton, M. G., & Buss, D. M. (2004). Ovulatory shifts in female desire. *Journal of Sex Research, 41,* 55–65. (p. 467)

Pinel, J. P. J. (1993). *Biopsychology* (2nd ed). Boston: Allyn & Bacon. (p. 450)

Pingitore, R., Dugoni, B. L., Tindale, R. S., & Spring, B. (1994). Bias against overweight job applicants in a simulated employment interview. *Journal of Applied Psychology, 79,* 909–917. (p. 458)

Pinker, S. (1990, September–October). Quoted by J. de Cuevas, "No, she holded them loosely." *Harvard Magazine,* pp. 60–67. (p. 384)

Pinker, S. (1995). The language instinct. *The General Psychologist, 31,* 63–65. (pp. 385, 401, 402)

Pinker, S. (1998). Words and rules. *Lingua, 106,* 219–242. (p. 384)

Pinker, S. (1999, June 24). His brain measured up. *New York Times* (www.nytimes.com). (p. 412)

Pinker, S. (2002, September 9). A biological understanding of human nature: A talk with Steven Pinker. *The Edge Third Culture Mail List* (www.edge.org). (pp. 137, 142)

Pinker, S. (2005, April 22). The science of gender and science: A conversation with Elizabeth Spelke. Harvard University (www.edge.org). (p. 434)

Pinker, S. (2006, January 1). Groups of people may differ genetically in their average talents and temperaments. *The Edge* (www.edge.org). (p. 438)

Pinker, S. (2007). *The stuff of thought.* New York: Viking. (p. 394)

Pinker, S. (2007, March 19). A history of violence. *New Republic* (available at www.edge.org). (p. 376)

Pinker, S. (2008). The sexual paradox: Men, women, and the real gender gap. New York: Scribner. (p. 159)

Pinstrup-Andersen, P., & Cheng, F. (2007). Still hungry. *Scientific American, 297,* 96–103. (p. 461)

Pipe, M-E. (1996). Children's eyewitness memory. *New Zealand Journal of Psychology, 25,* 36–43. (p. 362)

Pipe, M.-E., Lamb, M. E., Orbach, Y., & Esplin, P. W. (2004). Recent research on children's testimony about experienced and witnessed events. *Developmental Review, 24,* 440–468. (p. 362)

Piper, A., Jr. (1998, Winter). Multiple personality disorder: Witchcraft survives in the twentieth century. *Skeptical Inquirer,* pp. 44–50. (p. 619)

Pipher, M. (2002). *The middle of everywhere: The world's refugees come to our town.* New York: Harcourt Brace. (pp. 481, 534)

Pitcher, D., Walssh, V., Yovel, G., & Duchaine, B. (2007). TMS evidence for the involvement of the right occipital face area in early face processing. *Current Biology, 17,* 1568–1573. (p. 239)

Pitman, R. K., & Delahanty, D. L. (2005). Conceptually driven pharmacologic approaches to acute trauma. *CNS Spectrums, 10*(2), 99–106. (p. 341)

Pitman, R. K., Sanders, K. M., Zusman, R. M., Healy, A. R., Cheema, F., Lasko, N. B., Cahill, L., & Orr, S. P. (2002). Pilot study of secondary prevention of posttraumatic stress disorder with propranolol. *Biological Psychiatry, 51,* 189–192. (p. 341)

Pittenger, D. J. (1993). The utility of the Myers-Briggs Type Indicator. *Review of Educational Research, 63,* 467–488. (p. 574)

Plassmann, H., O'Doherty, J., Shiv, B., & Rangel, A. (2008). Marketing actions can modulate neural representations of experienced pleasantness. *Proceedings of the National Academy of Sciences, 105,* 1050–1054. (p. 258)

Pleck, J. H., Sonenstein, F. L., & Ku, L. C. (1993). Masculinity ideology: Its impact on adolescent males' heterosexual relationships. *Journal of Social Issues, 49,* 11–29. (p. 144)

Pleyers, G., Corneille, O., Luminet, O., & Yzerbyt, V. (2007). Aware and (dis)liking: Item-based analyses reveal that valence acquisition via evaluative conditioning emerges only when there is contingency awareness. *Journal of Experimental Psychology: Learning, Memory, and Cognition, 33,* 130–144. (p. 293)

Pliner, P. (1982). The effects of mere exposure on liking for edible substances. *Appetite: Journal for Intake Research, 3,* 283–290. (p. 452)

Pliner, P., Pelchat, M., & Grabski, M. (1993). Reduction of neophobia in humans by exposure to novel foods. *Appetite, 20,* 111–123. (p. 452)

Plöderl, M., & Fartacek, R. (2005). Suicidality and associated risk factors among lesbian, gay, and bisexual compared to heterosexual Austrian adults. *Suicide and Life-Threatening Behavior, 35,* 661–670. (p. 473)

Plomin, R. (1999). Genetics and general cognitive ability. *Nature, 402* (Suppl), C25–C29. (pp. 405, 428)

Plomin, R. (2001). Genetics and behaviour. *The Psychologist, 14,* 134–139. (p. 428)

Plomin, R. (2003). General cognitive ability. In R. Plomin, J. C. DeFries, I. W. Craig, & P. McGuffin (Eds.), *Behavioral genetics in a postgenomic world.* Washington, DC: APA Books. (p. 428)

Plomin, R., & Bergeman, C. S. (1991). The nature of nurture: Genetic influence on "environmental" measures. *Behavioral and Brain Sciences, 14,* 373–427. (p. 140)

Plomin, R., Corley, R., Caspi, A., Fulker, D. W., & DeFries, J. (1998). Adoption results for self-reported personality: Evidence for nonadditive genetic effects? *Journal of Personality and Social Psychology, 75,* 211–219. (p. 136)

Plomin, R., & Crabbe, J. (2000). DNA. *Psychological Bulletin, 126,* 806–828. (p. 141)

Plomin, R., & Daniels, D. (1987). Why are children in the same family so different from one another? *Behavioral and Brain Sciences, 10,* 1–60. (p. 150)

Plomin, R., & DeFries, J. C. (1998, May). The genetics of cognitive abilities and disabilities. *Scientific American,* pp. 62–69. (p. 429)

Plomin, R., DeFries, J. C., McClearn, G. E., & Rutter, M. (1997). *Behavioral genetics.* New York: Freeman. (pp. 134, 142, 429, 476, 641)

Plomin, R., Fulker, D. W., Corley, R., & DeFries, J. C. (1997). Nature, nurture and cognitive development from 1 to 16 years: A parent-offspring adoption study. *Psychological Science, 8,* 442–447. (p. 460)

Plomin, R., & Kovas, Y. (2005). Generalist genes and learning disabilities. *Psychological Bulletin, 131,* 592–617. (p. 428)

Plomin, R., McClearn, G. E., Pedersen, N. L., Nesselroade, J. R., & Bergeman, C. S. (1988). Genetic influence on childhood family environment perceived retrospectively from the last half of the life span. *Developmental Psychology, 24,* 37–45. (p. 140)

Plomin, R., & McGuffin, P. (2003). Psychopathology in the postgenomic era. *Annual Review of Psychology, 54,* 205–228. (p. 631)

Plomin, R., Reiss, D., Hetherington, E. M., & Howe, G. W. (January, 1994). Nature and nurture: Genetic contributions to measures of the family environment. *Developmental Psychology, 30*(1), 32–43. (p. 140)

Plotkin, H. (1994). *Darwin machines and the nature of knowledge.* Cambridge, MA: Harvard University Press. (p. 629)

Plotnik, J. M., de Waal, F. B. M., & Reiss, D. (2006). Self-recognition in an Asian elephant. *Proceedings of the National Academy of Sciences, 103,* 17053–17057. (p. 192)

Plous, S. (1993). Psychological mechanisms in the human use of animals. *Journal of Social Issues, 49*(1), 11–52. (p. 21)

Plous, S., & Herzog, H. A. (2000). Poll shows researchers favor lab animal protection. *Science, 290,* 711. (p. 21)

Poastalkova, E., Serrano, P., Pinkhasova, D., Wallace, E., Fenton, A. A., & Sacktor, T. C. (2006). Storage of spatial information by the maintenance mechanism of LTP. *Science, 313,* 1141–1144. (p. 340)

Poldrack, R. A., & Wagner, A. D. (2004). What can neuroimaging tell us about the mind? *Current Directions in Psychological Science, 13,* 177–181. (p. 331)

Polivy, J., & Herman, C. P. (1985). Dieting and binging: A causal analysis. *American Psychologist, 40,* 193–201. (p. 463)

Polivy, J., & Herman, C. P. (1987). Diagnosis and treatment of normal eating. *Journal of Personality and Social Psychology, 55,* 635–644. (p. 463)

Polivy, J., & Herman, C. P. (2002). Causes of eating disorders. *Annual Review of Psychology, 53,* 187–213. (p. 454)

Pollack, A. (2004, April 13). With tiny brain implants, just thinking may make it so. *New York Times* (www.nytimes.com). (p. 70)

Pollack, A. (2006, July 13). Paralyzed man uses thoughts to move a cursor. *New York Times* (www.nytimes.com). (p. 70)

Pollak, S., Cicchetti, D., & Klorman, R. (1998). Stress, memory, and emotion: Developmental considerations from the study of child maltreatment. *Developmental Psychopathology, 10,* 811–828. (p. 294)

Pollak, S. D., & Kistler, D. J. (2002). Early experience is associated with the development of categorical representations for facial expressions of emotion. *Proceedings of the National Academy of Sciences, 99,* 9072–9076. (p. 510)

Pollak, S. D., & Tolley-Schell, S. A. (2003). Selective attention to facial emotion in physically abused children. *Journal of Abnormal Psychology, 112,* 323–328. (p. 510)

Pollard, R. (1992). 100 years in psychology and deafness: A centennial retrospective. Invited address to the American Psychological Association convention, Washington, DC. (p. 395)

Pollick, A. S., & de Waal, F. B. M. (2007). Ape gestures and language evolution. *Proceedings of the National Academic of Sciences, 104,* 8184–8189. (p. 400)

Polusny, M. A., & Follette, V. M. (1995). Long-term correlates of child sexual abuse: Theory and review of the empirical literature. *Applied & Preventive Psychology, 4,* 143–166. (p. 190)

Poole, D. A., & Lindsay, D. S. (1995). Interviewing preschoolers: Effects of nonsuggestive techniques, parental coaching and leading questions on reports of nonexperienced events. *Journal of Experimental Child Psychology, 60,* 129–154. (p. 359)

Poole, D. A., & Lindsay, D. S. (2001). Children's eyewitness reports after exposure to misinformation from parents. *Journal of Experimental Psychology: Applied, 7,* 27–50. (p. 359)

Poole, D. A., & Lindsay, D. S. (2002). Reducing child witnesses' false reports of misinformation from parents. *Journal of Experimental Child Psychology, 81,* 117–140. (p. 359)

Poole, D. A., Lindsay, D. S., Memon, A., & Bull, R. (1995). Psychotherapy and the recovery of memories of childhood sexual abuse: U.S. and British practitioners' opinions, practices, and experiences. *Journal of Consulting and Clinical Psychology, 63,* 426–437. (p. 362)

Poon, L. W. (1987). Myths and truisms: Beyond extant analyses of speed of behavior and age. Address to the Eastern Psychological Association convention. (p. 210)

Pope, H. G., Poliakoff, M. B., Parker, M. P., Boynes, M., & Hudson, J. I. (2007). Is dissociative amnesia a culture-bound syndrome? Findings from a survey of historical literature. *Psychological Medicine, 37,* 225–233. (p. 566)

Popenoe, D. (1993). The evolution of marriage and the problem of stepfamilies: A biosocial perspective. Paper presented at the National Symposium on Stepfamilies, Pennsylvania State University. (p. 155)

Popenoe, D., & Whitehead, B. D. (2002). *Should we live together?* (2nd ed.). New Brunswick, NJ: The National Marriage Project, Rutgers University. (p. 217)

Popkin, B. M. (2007, September). The world is fat. *Scientific American,* pp. 88–95. (pp. 460, 461)

Poremba, A., & Gabriel, M. (2001). Amygdalar efferents initiate auditory thalamic discriminative training-induced neuronal activity. *Journal of Neuroscience, 21,* 270–278. (p. 63)

Porter, D., & Neuringer, A. (1984). Music discriminations by pigeons. *Journal of Experimental Psychology: Animal Behavior Processes, 10,* 138–148. (p. 303)

Porter, S., Birt, A. R., Yuille, J. C., & Lehman, D. R. (2000, November). Negotiating false memories: Interviewer and rememberer characteristics relate to memory distortion. *Psychological Science, 11,* 507–510. (p. 359)

Porter, S., & Peace, K. A. (2007). The scars of memory: A prospective, longitudinal investigation of the consistency of traumatic and positive emotional memories in adulthood. *Psychological Science, 18,* 435–441. (p. 365)

Porter, S., & ten Brinke, L. (2008). Reading between the lies: Identifying concealed and falsified emotions in universal facial expressions. *Psychological Science, 19,* 508–514. (p. 511)

Porter, S., Yuille, J. C., & Lehman, D. R. (1999). The nature of real, implanted, and fabricated memories for childhood events: Implications for the recovered memory debate. *Law and Human Behavior, 23,* 517–537. (p. 364)

Posner, M. I., & Carr, T. H. (1992). Lexical access and the brain: Anatomical constraints on cognitive models of word recognition. *American Journal of Psychology, 105,* 1–26. (p. 392)

Posthuma, D., & de Geus, E. J. C. (2006). Progress in the molecular-genetic study of intelligence. *Current Directions in Psychological Science, 15,* 151–155. (p. 428)

Poulton, R., & Milne, B. J. (2002). Low fear in childhood is associated with sporting prowess in adolescence and young adulthood. *Behaviour Research and Therapy, 40,* 1191–1197. (p. 621)

Powell, J. (1989). *Happiness is an inside job.* Valencia, CA: Tabor. (p. 593)

Powell, K. E., Thompson, P. D., Caspersen, C. J., & Kendrick, J. S. (1987). Physical activity and the incidence of coronary heart disease. *Annual Review of Public Health, 8,* 253–287. (p. 548)

Powell, L. H., Schahabi, L., & Thoresen, C. E. (2003). Religion and spirituality: Linkages to physical health. *American Psychologist, 58,* 36–52. (p. 554)

Powell, R. A., & Boer, D. P. (1994). Did Freud mislead patients to confabulate memories of abuse? *Psychological Reports, 74,* 1283–1298. (p. 565)

Prairie Home Companion. (1999). *The Prairie Home Companion's pretty good joke book* (Vol. 4). St. Paul, MN: Prairie Home Companion. (p. 530)

Pratkanis, A. R., & Greenwald, A. G. (1988). Recent perspectives on unconscious processing: Still no marketing applications. *Psychology and Marketing, 5,* 337–353. (p. 229)

PRB. (2002). *2002 women of our world.* Population Reference Bureau (www.prb.org). (p. 704)

PRB. (2004). *2004 world population data sheet.* Washington, DC: Population Reference Bureau. (p. 208)

Prentice, D. A., & Miller, D. T. (1993). Pluralistic ignorance and alcohol use on campus: Some consequences of misperceiving the social norm. *Journal of Personality and Social Psychology, 64,* 243–256. (p. 127)

Presley, C. A., Meilman, P. W., & Lyerla, R. (1997). *Alcohol and drugs on American college campuses: Issues of violence and harrassment.* Carbondale: Core Institute, Southern Illinois University. (p. 117)

Pressman, S. D., & Cohen, S. (2005). Does positive affect influence health? *Psychological Bulletin, 131,* 925–971. (p. 522)

Price, G. M., Uauy, R., Breeze, E., Bulpitt, C. J., & Fletcher, A. E. (2006). Weight, shape, and mortality risk in older persons: Elevated waist-hip ratio, not high body mass index, is associated with a greater risk of death. *American Journal of Clinical Nutrition, 84,* 449–460. (p. 457)

Prince Charles (2000). BBC Reith Lecture. (p. 14)

Princeton Review. (2005). *Guide to college majors.* Princeton, NJ: Author. (p. A-1)

Principe, G. F., Kanaya, T., Ceci, S. J., & Singh, M. (2006). Believing is seeing: How rumors can engender false memories in preschoolers. *Psychological Science, 17,* 243–248. (p. 361)

Pringle, P. J., Geary, M. P., Rodeck, C. H., Kingdom, J. C., Kayamba-Kay's, S., & Hindmarsh, P. C. (2005). The influence of cigarette smoking on antenatal growth, birth size, and the insulin-like growth factor axis. *Journal of Clinical Endocrinology and Metabolism, 90,* 2556–2562. (p. 171)

Prioleau, L., Murdock, M., & Brody, N. (1983). An analysis of psychotherapy versus placebo studies. *The Behavioral and Brain Sciences, 6,* 275–310. (p. 667)

Prior, H., Schwarz, A., & Güntürkün, O. (2008). Mirror-induced behavior in the magpie (*Pica pica*): Evidence of self-recognition. *PloS Biology, 6,* 1642–1650. (p. 192)

Proffitt, D. R. (2006a). Embodied perception and the economy of action. *Perspectives on Psychological Science, 1,* 110–122. (p. 277)

Proffitt, D.R. (2006b). Distance perception. *Current Directions in Psychological Research, 15,* 131–135. (p. 277)

Project Match Research Group. (1997). Matching alcoholism treatments to client heterogeneity: Project MATCH posttreatment drinking outcomes. *Journal of Studies on Alcohol, 58,* 7–29. (p. 658)

Pronin, E. (2007). Perception and misperception of bias in human judgment. *Trends in Cognitive Sciences, 11,* 37–43. (pp. 593, 693)

Pronin, E., & Ross, L. (2006). Temporal differences in trait self-ascription: When the self is seen as an other. *Journal of Personality and Social Psychology, 90,* 197–209. (p. 683)

Pronin, E., & Wegner, D. M. (2006). Manic thinking: Independent effects of thought speed and thought content on mood. *Psychological Science, 17,* 807–813. (p. 626)

Propper, R. E., Stickgold, R., Keeley, R., & Christman, S. D. (2007). Is television traumatic? Dreams, stress, and media exposure in the aftermath of September 11, 2001. *Psychological Science, 18,* 334–340. (p. 103)

Provine, R. R. (2001). *Laughter: A scientific investigation.* New York: Penguin. (p. 29)

Pryor, J. H., Hurtado, S., Saenz, V. B., Korn, J. S., Santos, J. L., & Korn, W. S. (2006). *The American freshman: National norms for fall 2006.* Los Angeles: UCLA Higher Education Research Institute. (pp. 434, 632)

Pryor, J. H., Hurtado, S., Saenz, V. B., Lindholm, J. A., Korn, W. S., & Mahoney, K. M. (2005). *The American freshman: National norms for fall 2005.* Los Angeles: Higher Education Research Institute, UCLA. (p. 144)

Pryor, J. H., Hurtado, S., Sharkness, J., & Korn, W. S. (2007). *The American freshman: National norms for fall 2007.* Los Angeles: UCLA Higher Education Research Institute. (pp. 159, 480)

Psychologist. (2003, April). Who's the greatest? *The Psychologist, 16,* p. 17. (p. 185)

Puchalski, C. (2005, March 12). Personal correspondence from Director, George Washington Institute for Spirituality and Health. (p. 552)

Puhl, R. M., & Latner, J. D. (2007). Stigma, obesity, and the health of the nation's children. *Psychological Bulletin, 133,* 557–580. (p. 458)

Pulkkinen, L. (2004). A longitudinal study on social development as an impetus for school reform toward an integrated school day. *European Psychologist, 9,* 125–141. (p. 191)

Pulkkinen, L. (2006). The Jyväskylä longitudinal study of personality and social development (JYLS). In L. Pulkkinen, J. Kaprio, & R. J. Rose (Eds.),

Socioemotional development and health from adolescence to adulthood (Cambridge studies on child and adolescent health). New York: Cambridge University Press. (p. 191)

Putnam, F. W. (1991). Recent research on multiple personality disorder. *Psychiatric Clinics of North America, 14,* 489–502. (p. 619)

Putnam, F. W. (1995). Rebuttal of Paul McHugh. *Journal of the American Academy of Child and Adolescent Psychiatry, 34,* 963. (p. 619)

Putnam, R. (2000). *Bowling alone.* New York: Simon and Schuster. (p. 153)

Pyszczynski, T., Hamilton, J. C., Greenberg, J., & Becker, S. E. (1991). Self-awareness and psychological dysfunction. In C. R. Snyder & D. O. Forsyth (Eds.), *Handbook of social and clinical psychology: The health perspective.* New York; Pergamon. (p. 633)

Pyszczynski, T. A., Solomon, S., & Greenberg, J. (2002). *In the wake of 9/11: The psychology of terror.* Washington, DC: American Psychological Association. (p. 708)

Qirko, H. N. (2004). "Fictive kin" and suicide terrorism. *Science, 304,* 49–50. (p. 700)

Quasha, S. (1980). *Albert Einstein: An intimate portrait.* New York: Forest. (p. 423)

Quinn, P. C. (2002). Category representation in young infants. *Current Directions in Psychological Science, 11,* 66–70. (p. 172)

Quinn, P. C., Bhatt, R. S., Brush, D., Grimes, A., & Sharpnack, H. (2002). Development of form similarity as a Gestalt grouping principle in infancy. *Psychological Science, 13,* 320–328. (p. 263)

Quinn, P. J., Williams, G. M., Najman, J. M., Andersen, M. J., & Bor, W. (2001). The effect of breastfeeding on child development at 5 years: A cohort study. *Journal of Pediatrics & Child Health, 3,* 465–469. (p. 34)

Rabbitt, P. (2006). Tales of the unexpected: 25 years of cognitive gerontology. *The Psychologist, 19,* 674–676. (p. 213)

Rabinowicz, T., Dean, D. E., Petetot, J. M., & de Courten-Myers, G. M. (1999). Gender differences in the human cerebral cortex: More neurons in males; more processes in females. *Journal of Child Neurology, 14,* 98–107. (p. 174)

Rabinowicz, T., deCourten-Myers, G. M., Petetot, J. M., Xi, G., & de los Reyes, E. (1996). Human cortex development: Estimates of neuronal numbers indicate major loss late during gestation. *Journal of Neuropathology and Experimental Neurology, 55,* 320–328. (p. 174)

Radin, D., Nelson, R., Dobyns, Y., & Houtkooper, J. (2006). Reexamining psychokinesis: Comment on Bösch, Steinkamp, and Boller (2006). *Psychological Bulletin, 132,* 529–532. (p. 284)

Rahman, Q., & Wilson, G. D. (2003). Born gay? The psychobiology of human sexual orientation. *Personality and Individual Differences, 34,* 1337–1382. (pp. 476, 478)

Rahman, Q., Wilson, G. D., & Abrahams, S. (2003). Biosocial factors, sexual orientation and neurocognitive functioning. *Psychoneuroendocrinology, 29,* 867–881. (p. 478)

Raine, A. (1999). Murderous minds: Can we see the mark of Cain? *Cerebrum: The Dana Forum on Brain Science 1*(1), 15–29. (pp. 621, 710)

Raine, A. (2005). The interaction of biological and social measures in the explanation of antisocial and violent behavior. In D. M. Stoff & E. J. Susman (Eds.) *Developmental psychobiology of aggression.* New York: Cambridge University Press. (pp. 62, 710)

Raine, A., Brennan, P., Mednick, B., & Mednick, S. A. (1996). High rates of violence, crime, academic problems, and behavioral problems in males with both early neuromotor deficits and unstable family environments. *Archives of General Psychiatry, 53,* 544–549. (p. 622)

Raine, A., Lencz, T., Bihrle, S., LaCasse, L., & Colletti, P. (2000). Reduced prefrontal gray matter volume and reduced autonomic activity in antisocial personality disorder. *Archives of General Psychiatry, 57,* 119–127. (p. 621)

Rainville, P., Duncan, G. H., Price, D. D., Carrier, B., & Bushnell, M. C. (1997). Pain affect encoded in human anterior cingulate but not somatosensory cortex. *Science, 277,* 968–971. (p. 111)

Rajendran, G., & Mitchell, P. (2007). Cognitive theories of autism. *Developmental Review, 27,* 224–260. (p. 182)

Ralston, A. (2004). Enough rope. Interview for ABC TV, Australia, by Andrew Denton (www.abc.net.au/enoughrope/stories/s1227885.htm). (p. 443)

Ramachandran, V. S., & Blakeslee, S. (1998). *Phantoms in the brain: Probing the mysteries of the human mind.* New York: Morrow. (pp. 53, 74, 255)

Ramachandran, V. S., & Oberman, L. M. (2006, November). Broken mirrors: A theory of autism. *Scientific American,* pp. 63–69. (pp. 183, 317)

Ramirez-Esparza, N., Gosling, S. D., Benet-Martínez, V., Potter, J. P., & Pennebaker, J. W. (2006). Do bilinguals have two personalities? A special case of cultural frame switching. *Journal of Research in Personality, 40,* 99–120. (p. 393)

Rand, C. S. W., & Macgregor, A. M. C. (1990). Morbidly obese patients' perceptions of social discrimination before and after surgery for obesity. *Southern Medical Journal, 83,* 1390–1395. (p. 458)

Rand, C. S. W., & Macgregor, A. M. C. (1991). Successful weight loss following obesity surgery and perceived liability or morbid obesity. *Internal Journal of Obesity, 15,* 577–579. (p. 458)

Randi, J. (1999, February 4). 2000 club mailing list e-mail letter. (p. 284)

Randi, J. (2008). 'Twas Brillig . . . . Last chance to win the million-dollar challenge. *Skeptic, 14*(1), 6. (p. 284)

Rapoport, J. L. (1989, March). The biology of obsessions and compulsions. *Scientific American,* pp. 83–89. (pp. 612, 615)

Räsänen, S., Pakaslahti, A., Syvalahti, E., Jones, P. B., & Isohanni, M. (2000). Sex differences in schizophrenia: A review. *Nordic Journal of Psychiatry, 54,* 37–45. (p. 639)

Rasch, B., Büchel, C., Gais, S., & Born, J. (2007). Odor cues during slow-wave sleep prompt declarative memory consolidation. *Science, 315,* 1426–1429. (p. 100)

Ray, J. (2005, April 12). U.S. teens walk away from anger: Boys and girls manage anger differently. *The Gallup Organization* (www.gallup.com). (p. 520)

Ray, O., & Ksir, C. (1990). *Drugs, society, and human behavior* (5th ed.). St. Louis: Times Mirror/Mosby. (p. 121)

Raynor, H. A., & Epstein, L. H. (2001). Dietary variety, energy regulation, and obesity. *Psychological Bulletin, 127,* 325–341. (p. 451)

Raz, A., Fan, J., & Posner, M. I. (2005). Hypnotic suggestion reduces conflict in the human brain. *PNAS, 102,* 9978–9983. (p. 111)

Reason, J. (1987). The Chernobyl errors. *Bulletin of the British Psychological Society, 40,* 201–206. (p. 700)

Reason, J., & Mycielska, K. (1982). *Absent-minded? The psychology of mental lapses and everyday errors.* Englewood Cliffs, NJ: Prentice-Hall. (p. 275)

Reed, P. (2000). Serial position effects in recognition memory for odors. *Journal of Experimental Psychology: Learning, Memory, and Cognition, 26,* 411–422. (p. 330)

Reed, T. E., & Jensen, A. R. (1992). Conduction velocity in a brain nerve pathway of normal adults correlates with intelligence level. *Intelligence, 16,* 259–272. (p. 414)

Rees, M. (1999). *Just six numbers: The deep forces that shape the universe.* New York: Basic Books. (p. 166)

Regan, P. C., & Atkins, L. (2007). Sex differences and similarities in frequency and intensity of sexual desire. *Social Behavior and Personality, 34,* 95–102. (p. 144)

Reichenberg, A., Gross, R., Weiser, M., Bresnahan, M., Silverman, J., Harlap, S., Rabinoqitz, J., Shulman, C., Malaspina, D., Lubin, G., Knobler, H Y., Davidson, M., & Susser, E. (2007). Advancing paternal age and autism. *Archives of General Psychiatry, 63,* 1026–1032. (p. 182)

Reichenberg, A., & Harvey, P. D. (2007). Neuropsychological impairments in schizophrenia: Integration of performance-based and brain imaging findings. *Psychological Bulletin, 133,* 833–858. (p. 637)

Reichman, J. (1998). *I'm not in the mood: What every woman should know about improving her libido.* New York: Morrow. (p. 468)

Reifman, A., & Cleveland, H. H. (2007). Shared environment: A quantitative review. Paper presented to the Society for Research in Child Development, Boston, MA. (p. 137)

Reijmers, L. G., Perkins, B. L., Matsuo, N., & Mayford, M. (2007). Localization of a stable neural correlate of associative memory. *Science, 317,* 1230–1233. (p. 519)

Reiner, W. G., & Gearhart, J. P. (2004). Discordant sexual identity in some genetic males with cloacal exstrophy assigned to female sex at birth. *New England Journal of Medicine, 350,* 333–341. (p. 161)

Reis, D., & Marino, L. (2001). Mirror self-recognition in the bottlenose dolphin: A case of cognitive convergence. *PNAS, 98,* 5937–5942. (p. 192)

Reis, H. T., & Aron, A. (2008). Love: What is it, why does it matter, and how does it operate? *Perspectives on Psychological Science, 3,* 80–86. (p. 724)

Reisenzein, R. (1983). The Schachter theory of emotion: Two decades later. *Psychological Bulletin, 94,* 239–264. (p. 506)

Reiser, M. (1982). *Police psychology.* Los Angeles: LEHI. (p. 282)

Reitzle, M. (2006). The connections between adulthood transitions and the self-perception of being adult in the changing contexts of East and West Germany. *European Psychologist, 11,* 25–38. (p. 205)

Remley, A. (1988, October). From obedience to independence. *Psychology Today,* pp. 56–59. (p. 156)

Renner, M. J., & Renner, C. H. (1993). Expert and novice intuitive judgments about animal behavior. *Bulletin of the Psychonomic Society, 31,* 551–552. (p. 149)

Renner, M. J., & Rosenzweig, M. R. (1987). *Enriched and impoverished environments: Effects on brain and behavior.* New York: Springer-Verlag. (p. 148)

Renninger, K. A., & Granott, N. (2005). The process of scaffolding in learning and development. *New Ideas in Psychology, 23*(3), 111–114. (p. 185)

Rentfrow, P. J., & Gosling, S. D. (2003). The Do Re Mi's of everyday life: The structure and personality correlates of music preferences. *Journal of Personality and Social Psychology, 84,* 1236–1256. (p. 581)

Rentfrow, P. J., & Gosling, S. D. (2006). Message in a ballad: The role of music preferences in interpersonal perception. *Psychological Science, 17,* 236–242. (p. 581)

Repetti, R. L., Taylor, S. E., & Seeman, T. E. (2002). Risky families: Family social environments and the mental and physical health of offspring. *Psychological Bulletin, 128,* 330–366. (p. 531)

Rescorla, R. A., & Wagner, A. R. (1972). A theory of Pavlovian conditioning: Variations in the effectiveness of reinforcement and nonreinforcement. In A. H. Black & W. F. Perokasy (Eds.), *Classical conditioning II: Current theory.* New York: Appleton-Century-Crofts. (p. 295)

Resnick, M. D., Bearman, P. S., Blum, R. W., Bauman, K. E., Harris, K. M., Jones, J., Tabor, J., Beuhring, T., Sieving, R., Shew, M., Bearinger, L. H., & Udry, J. R. (1997). Protecting adolescents from harm: Findings from the National Longitudinal Study on Adolescent Health. *Journal of the American Medical Association, 278,* 823–832. (pp. 31, 203)

Resnick, R. A., O'Regan, J. K., & Clark, J. J. (1997). To see or not to see: The need for attention to perceive changes in scenes. *Psychological Science, 8,* 368–373. (p. 89)

Resnick, S. M. (1992). Positron emission tomography in psychiatric illness. *Current Directions in Psychological Science, 1,* 92–98. (p. 640)

Responsive Community. (1996, Fall). Age vs. weight. Page 83 (reported from a *Wall Street Journal* survey). (p. 462)

Ressler, R. K., Burgess, A. W., & Douglas, J. E. (1988). *Sexual homicide patterns.* Boston: Lexington Books. (p. 714)

Reuters. (2000, July 5). Many teens regret decision to have sex (National Campaign to Prevent Teen Pregnancy survey). www.washingtonpost.com. (p. 471)

Reyna, V. F., & Farley, F. (2006). Risk and rationality in adolescent decision making: Implications for theory, practice, and public policy. *Psychological Science in the Public Interest, 7*(1), 1–44. (p. 197)

Reynolds, A. J., Temple, J. A., Robertson, D. L., & Manri, E. A. (2001). Long-term effects of an early childhood intervention on educational achievement and juvenile arrest. *Journal of the American Medical Association, 285,* 2339–2346. (p. 431)

Rhodes, G., Sumich, A., & Byatt, G. (1999). Are average facial configurations attractive only because of their symmetry? *Psychological Science, 10,* 52–58. (p. 723)

Rhodes, S. R. (1983). Age-related differences in work attitudes and behavior: A review and conceptual analysis. *Psychological Bulletin, 93,* 328–367. (p. 210)

Rholes, W. S., & Simpson, J. A. (Eds.). (2004). *Adult attachment: Theory, research, and clinical implications.* New York: Guilford. (p. 189)

Rholes, W. S., Simpson, J. A., & Friedman, M. (2006). Avoidant attachment and the experience of parenting. *Personality and Social Psychology Bulletin, 32,* 275–285. (p. 189)

Ribeiro, R., Gervasoni, D., Soares, E. S., Zhou, Y., Lin, S.-C., Pantoja, J., Lavine, M., & Nicolelis, M. A. L. (2004). Long-lasting novelty-induced neuronal reverberation during slow-wave sleep in multiple forebrain areas. *PloS Biology, 2*(1), e37 (www.plosbiology.org). (p. 100)

Ricciardelli, L. A., & McCabe, M. P. (2004). A biopsychosocial model of disordered eating and the pursuit of muscularity in adolescent boys. *Psychological Bulletin, 130,* 179–205. (p. 454)

Rice, B. (1985, September). Performance review: The job nobody likes. *Psychology Today,* pp. 30–36. (p. 634)

Rice, M. E., & Grusec, J. E. (1975). Saying and doing: Effects on observer performance. *Journal of Personality and Social Psychology, 32,* 584–593. (p. 319)

Richardson, J. (1993). The curious case of coins: Remembering the appearance of familiar objects. *The Psychologist: Bulletin of the British Psychological Society, 6,* 360–366. (p. 352)

Richardson, J. T. E., & Zucco, G. M. (1989). Cognition and olfaction: A review. *Psychological Bulletin, 105,* 352–360. (p. 260)

Richeson, J. A., & Shelton, J. N. (2007). Negotiating interracial interactions. *Current Directions in Psychological Science, 16,* 316–320. (p. 731)

Rieff, P. (1979). *Freud: The mind of a moralist* (3rd ed.). Chicago: University of Chicago Press. (p. 568)

Rieger, G., Chivers, M. L., & Bailey, J. M. (2005). Sexual arousal patterns of bisexual men. *Psychological Science, 16,* 579–584. (p. 473)

Riis, J., Loewenstein, G., Baron, J., Jepson, C., Fagerlin, A., & Ubel, P. A. (2005). Ignorance of hedonic adaptation to hemodialysis: A study using ecological momentary assessment *Journal of Experimental Psychology: General, 134,* 3–9. (p. 523)

Rindermann, H. (2007). The g-factor of international cognitive ability comparisons: The homogeneity of results in PISA, TIMSS, PIRLS and IQ-tests across nations. *European Journal of Personality, 21,* 667–7006. (p. 407)

Ring, K. (1980). *Life at death: A scientific investigation of the near-death experience.* New York: Coward, McCann & Geoghegan. (p. 123)

Ripple, C. H., & Zigler, E. F. (2003). Research, policy, and the federal role in prevention initiatives for children. *American Psychologist, 58,* 482–490. (p. 431)

Risch, N., Herrell, R., Lehner, T., Liang, K.-Y., Eaves, L., Hoh, J., Griem, A., Kovacs, M., Ott, J., & Merkangas, R. (2009). Interaction between the serotonin transporter gene (5-HTTLPR), stressful life events, and risk of depression. *Journal of the American Medical Association, 301,* 2462–2471. (p. 632)

Riskind, J. H., Beck, A. T., Berchick, R. J., Brown, G., & Steer, R. A. (1987). Reliability of DSM-III diagnoses for major depression and generalized anxiety disorder using the structured clinical interview for DSM-III. *Archives of General Psychiatry, 44,* 817–820. (p. 603)

Rizzolatti, G., Fadiga, L., Fogassi, L., & Gallese, V. (2002). From mirror neurons to imitation: Facts and speculations. In A. N. Meltzoff & W. Prinz (Eds.), *The imitative mind: Development, evolution, and brain bases.* Cambridge: Cambridge University Press, 2002. (p. 316)

Rizzolatti, G., Fogassi, L., & Gallese, V. (2006, November). Mirrors in the mind. *Scientific American,* pp. 54–61. (p. 316)

Roberson, D., Davidoff, J., Davies, I. R. L., & Shapiro, L. R. (2004). The development of color categories in two languages: A longitudinal study. *Journal of Experimental Psychology: General, 133,* 554–571. (p. 394)

Roberson, D., Davies, I. R. L., Corbett, G. G., & Vandervyver, M. (2005). Free-sorting of colors across cultures: Are there universal grounds for grouping? *Journal of Cognition and Culture, 5,* 349–386. (p. 394)

Roberts, B. W., Caspi, A., & Moffitt, T. E. (2001). The kids are alright: Growth and stability in personality development from adolescence to adulthood. *Journal of Personality and Social Psychology, 81,* 670–683. (p. 223)

Roberts, B. W., Caspi, A., & Moffitt, T. E. (2003). Work experiences and personality development in young adulthood. *Journal of Personality and Social Psychology, 84,* 582–593. (p. 223)

Roberts, B. W., & DelVecchio, W. F. (2000). The rank-order consistency of personality traits from childhood to old age: A quantitative review of longitudinal studies. *Psychological Bulletin, 126,* 3–25. (p. 580)

Roberts, B. W., Kuncel, N. R., Shiner, R., Caspi, A., & Goldberg, L. R. (2007). The power of personality: The comparative validity of personality traits, socioeconomic status, and cognitive ability for predicting important life outcomes. *Perspectives on Psychological Science, 2,* 313–345. (p. 581)

Roberts, B. W., & Mroczek, D. (2008). Personality trait change in adulthood. *Current Directions in Psychological Science, 17,* 31–35. (p. 223)

Roberts, B. W., Walton, K. E., & Viechtbauer, W. (2006). Patterns of mean-level change in personality traits across the life course: A meta-analysis of longitudinal studies. *Psychological Bulletin, 132,* 1–25. (p. 223)

Roberts, L. (1988). Beyond Noah's ark: What do we need to know? *Science, 242,* 1247. (p. 543)

Roberts, T.-A. (1991). Determinants of gender differences in responsiveness to others' evaluations. *Dissertation Abstracts International, 51*(8–B). (p. 158)

Robins, L., & Regier, D. (Eds.). (1991). *Psychiatric disorders in America.* New York: Free Press. (p. 607)

Robins, L. N., Davis, D. H., & Goodwin, D. W. (1974). Drug use by U.S. Army enlisted men in Vietnam: A follow-up on their return home. *American Journal of Epidemiology, 99,* 235–249. (p. 127)

Robins, R. W., & Trzesniewski, K. H. (2005). Self-esteem development across the lifespan. *Current Directions in Psychological Science, 14*(3), 158–162. (p. 219)

Robins, R. W., Trzesniewski, K. H., Tracy, J. L., Gosling, S. D., & Potter, J. (2002). Global self-esteem across the lifespan. *Psychology and Aging, 17,* 423–434. (p. 202)

Robinson, F. P. (1970). *Effective study.* New York: Harper & Row. (p. 12)

Robinson, J. (2002, October 8). What percentage of the population is gay? *Gallup Tuesday Briefing* (www.gallup.com/poll/tb/religValue/20021008b.asp). (p. 473)

Robinson, J. P., & Martin, S. P. (2007, October). Not so deprived: Sleep in America, 1965–2005. *Public Opinion Pros* (www.publicopinionpros.com). (p. 96)

Robinson, T. E., & Berridge, K. C. (2003). Addiction. *Annual Review of Psychology, 54,* 25–53. (p. 114)

Robinson, T. N. (1999). Reducing children's television viewing to prevent obesity. *Journal of the American Medical Association, 282,* 1561–1567. (p. 463)

Robinson, T. N., Borzekowski, D. L. G., Matheson, D. M., & Kraemer, H. C. (2007). Effects of fast food branding on young children's taste preferences. *Archives of Pediatric and Adolescent Medicine, 161,* 792–797. (p. 275)

Robinson, V. M. (1983). Humor and health. In P. E. McGhee & J. H. Goldstein (Eds.), *Handbook of humor research: Vol. II. Applied studies.* New York: Springer-Verlag. (p. 544, 545)

Rochat, F. (1993). How did they resist authority? Protecting refugees in Le Chambon during World War II. Paper presented at the American Psychological Association convention. (p. 696)

Rock, I., & Palmer, S. (1990, December). The legacy of Gestalt psychology. *Scientific American,* pp. 84–90. (pp. 262, 263)

Rodin, J. (1986). Aging and health: Effects of the sense of control. *Science, 233,* 1271–1276. (pp. 542, 543, 586)

Roediger, H. (2001, September). Quoted by R. Herbert, Doing a number on memory. *APS Observer,* pp. 1, 7–11. (p. 355)

Roediger, H. L., & Karpicke, J. D. (2006). Test-enhanced learning: Taking memory tests improves long-term retention. *Psychological Science, 17,* 249–255. (p. 330)

Roediger, H. L., III, & Geraci, L. (2007). Aging and the misinformation effect: A neuropsychological analysis. *Journal of Experimental Psychology, 33,* 321–334. (p. 362)

Roediger, H. L., III, & McDaniel, M. A. (2007). Illusory recollection in older adults: Testing Mark Twain's conjecture. In M. Garry H. Hayne (Ed.), *Do justice and let the sky fall: Elizabeth F. Loftus and her contributions to science, law, and academic freedom.* Mahwah, NJ: Erlbaum. (p. 362)

Roediger, H. L., III, & McDermott, K. B. (1995). Creating false memories: Remembering words not presented in lists. *Journal of Experimental Psychology: Learning, Memory, and Cognition, 21,* 803–814. (p. 360)

Roediger, H. L., III, Wheeler, M. A., & Rajaram, S. (1993). Remembering, knowing, and reconstructing the past. In D. L. Medin (Ed.), *The psychology of learning and motivation: Advances in research and theory* (Vol. 30). Orlando, FL: Academic Press. (p. 358)

Roehling, M. V. (1999). Weight-based discrimination in employment: Psychological and legal aspects. *Personnel Psychology, 52,* 969–1016. (p. 458)

Roehling, M. V., Roehling, P. V., & Pichler, S. (2007). The relationship between body weight and perceived weight-related employment discrimination: The role of sex and race. *Journal of Vocational Behavior, 71,* 300–318. (p. 458)

Roehling, P. V., Roehling, M. V., & Moen, P. (2001). The relationship between work-life policies and practices and employee loyalty: A life course perspective. *Journal of Family and Economic Issues, 22,* 141–170. (p. 496)

Roenneberg, T., Kuehnle, T., Pramstaller, P. P., Ricken, J., Havel, M., Guth, A., Merrow, M. (2004). A marker for the end of adolescence. *Current Biology, 14,* R1038–R1039. (p. 92)

Roese, N. J., & Summerville, A. (2005). What we regret most . . . and why. *Personality and Social Psychology Bulletin, 31,* 1273–1285. (p. 219)

Roesser, R. (1998). What you should know about hearing conservation. *Better Hearing Institute* (www.betterhearing.org). (p. 245)

Rofé, Y. (2008). Does repression exist? Memory, pathogenic, unconscious and clinical evidence. *Review of General Psychology, 12,* 63–85. (p. 566)

Rogaeva, E., & 40 others. (2007). The neuronal sortilin-related receptor SORL1 is genetically associated with Alzehimer disease. *Nature Genetics, 39,* 168–177. (p. 212)

Rogers, C. R. (1958). Reinhold Niebuhr's *The self and the dramas of history:* A criticism. *Pastoral Psychology, 9,* 15–17. (p. 592)

Rogers, C. R. (1961). *On becoming a person: A therapist's view of psychotherapy.* Boston: Houghton Mifflin. (p. 649)

Rogers, C. R. (1980). *A way of being.* Boston: Houghton Mifflin. (pp. 570, 571, 649)

Rogers, L. J. (2003, Fall). Seeking the right answers about right brain-left brain. *Cerebrum, 5*(4), 55–68. (p. 77)

Rohan, K. J., Roecklein, K. A., Lindsey, K. T., Johnson, L. G., Lippy, R. D., Lacy, T. J., & Barton, F. B. (2007). A randomized controlled trial of cognitive-behavioral therapy, light therapy, and their combination for seasonal affective disorder. *Journal of Consulting and Clinical Psychology, 75,* 489–500. (p. 666)

Rohan, M. J., & Zanna, M. P. (1996). Value transmission in families. In C. Seligman, J. M. Olson, & M. P. Zanna (Eds.), *The psychology of values: The Ontario Symposium* (Vol. 8). Malwah, NJ: Erlbaum. (p. 137)

Rohner, R. P. (1986). *The warmth dimension: Foundations of parental acceptance-rejection theory.* Newbury Park, CA: Sage. (p. 156)

Rohner, R. P., & Veneziano, R. A. (2001). The importance of father love: History and contemporary evidence. *Review of General Psychology, 5,* 382–405. (pp. 188, 193)

Rohrer, D., & Pashler, H. (2007). Increasing retention without increasing study time. *Current Directions in Psychological Science, 16,* 183–186. (p. 329)

Roiser, J. P., Cook, L. J., Cooper, J. D., Rubinsztein, D. C., & Sahakian, B. J. (2005). Association of a functional polymorphism in the serotonin transporter gene with abnormal emotional processing in Ecstasy users. *American Journal of Psychiatry, 162,* 609–612. (p. 122)

Rokach, A., Orzeck, T., Moya, M., & Exposito, F. (2002). Causes of loneliness in North America and Spain. *European Psychologist, 7,* 70–79. (p. 20)

Roney, J. R., Hanson, K. N., Durante, K. M., & Maestripieri, D. (2006). Reading men's faces: Women's mate attractiveness judgments track men's testosterone and interest in infants. *Proceedings of the Royal Society B, 273,* 2169–2175. (p. 145)

Rosch, E. (1978). Principles of categorization. In E. Rosch & B. L. Lloyd (Eds.), *Cognition and categorization.* Hillsdale, NJ: Erlbaum. (p. 370)

Rose, A. J., & Rudolph, K. D. (2006). A review of sex differences in peer relationship processes: Potential trade-offs for the emotional and behavioral development of girls and boys. *Psychological Bulletin, 132,* 98–131. (p. 158)

Rose, J. S., Chassin, L., Presson, C. C., & Sherman, S. J. (1999). Peer influences on adolescent cigarette smoking: A prospective sibling analysis. *Merrill-Palmer Quarterly, 45,* 62–84. (pp. 119, 151)

Rose, R. J. (2004). Developmental research as impetus for school reform. *European Psychologist, 9,* 142–144. (p. 191)

Rose, R. J., Kaprio, J., Winter, T., Dick, D. M., Viken, R. J., Pulkkinen, L., & Koskenvuo, M. (2002). Femininity and fertility in sisters with twin brothers: Prenatal androgenization? Cross-sex socialization? *Psychological Science, 13,* 263–266. (p. 475)

Rose, R. J., Viken, R. J., Dick, D. M., Bates, J. E., Pulkkinen, L., & Kaprio, J. (2003). It *does* take a village: Nonfamiliar environments and children's behavior. *Psychological Science, 14,* 273–277. (p. 151)

Rose, S. (1999). Precis of lifelines: Biology, freedom, determinism. *Behavioral and Brain Sciences, 22,* 871–921. (p. 146)

Rose, S., Bisson, J., & Wessely, S. (2003). A systematic review of single-session psychological interventions ('debriefing') following trauma. *Psychotherapy and Psychosomatics, 72,* 176–184. (p. 613)

Roselli, C. E., Larkin, K., Schrunk, J. M., & Stormshak, F. (2004). Sexual partner preference, hypothalamic morphology and aromatase in rams. *Physiology and Behavior, 83,* 233–245. (p. 476)

Roselli, C. E., Resko, J. A., & Stormshak, F. (2002). Hormonal influences on sexual partner preference in rams. *Archives of Sexual Behavior, 31,* 43–49. (p. 476)

Rosenbaum, M. (1986). The repulsion hypothesis: On the nondevelopment of relationships. *Journal of Personality and Social Psychology, 51,* 1156–1166. (p. 723)

Rosenberg, N. A., Pritchard, J. K., Weber, J. L., Cann, H. M., Kidd, K. K., Zhivotosky, L. A., & Feldman, M. W. (2002). Genetic structure of human populations. *Science, 298,* 2381–2385. (p. 142)

Rosenhan, D. L. (1973). On being sane in insane places. *Science, 179,* 250–258. (p. 605)

Rosenthal, R., Hall, J. A., Archer, D., DiMatteo, M. R., & Rogers, P. L. (1979). The PONS test: Measuring sensitivity to nonverbal cues. In S. Weitz (Ed.), *Nonverbal communication* (2nd ed.). New York: Oxford University Press. (pp. 433, 511)

Rosenzweig, M. R. (1984). Experience, memory, and the brain. *American Psychologist, 39,* 365–376. (pp. 148, 430)

Roseth, C. J., Johnson, D. W., & Johnson, R. T. (2008). Promoting early adolescents' achievement and peer relationships: The effects of cooperative, competitive, and individualistic goal structures. *Psychological Bulletin, 134,* 223–246. (p. 732)

Ross, J. (2006, December). Sleep on a problem . . . it works like a dream. *The Psychologist, 19,* 738–740. (p. 100)

Ross, M., McFarland, C., & Fletcher, G. J. O. (1981). The effect of attitude on the recall of personal histories. *Journal of Personality and Social Psychology, 40,* 627–634. (p. 356)

Ross, M., Xun, W. Q. E., & Wilson, A. E. (2002). Language and the bicultural self. *Personality and Social Psychology Bulletin, 28,* 1040–1050. (p. 393)

Rossi, A. S., & Rossi, P. H. (1993). *Of human bonding: Parent-child relations across the life course.* Hawthorne, NY: Aldine de Gruyter. (p. 159)

Rossi, P. J. (1968). Adaptation and negative aftereffect to lateral optical displacement in newly hatched chicks. *Science, 160,* 430–432. (p. 273)

Rostosky, S. S., Wilcox, B. L., Wright, M. L. C., & Randall, B. A. (2004). The impact of religiosity on adolescent sexual behavior: A review of the evidence. *Journal of Adolescent Research, 19,* 677–697. (p. 472)

Roth, T., Roehrs, T., Zwyghuizen-Doorenbos, A., Stpeanski, E., & Witting, R. (1988). Sleep and memory. In I. Hindmarch & H. Ott (Eds.), *Benzodiazepine receptor ligans, memory and information processing.* New York: Springer-Verlag. (p. 104)

Rothbart, M., Fulero, S., Jensen, C., Howard, J., & Birrell, P. (1978). From individual to group impressions: Availability heuristics in stereotype formation. *Journal of Experimental Social Psychology, 14,* 237–255. (p. 709)

Rothbart, M. K. (2007). Temperament, development, and personality. *Current Directions in Psychological Science, 16,* 207–212. (p. 138)

Rothbart, M. K., Ahadi, S. A., & Evans, D. E. (2000). Temperament and personality: Origins and outcomes. *Journal of Personality and Social Psychology, 78,* 122–135. (p. 138)

Rothbaum, F., & Tsang, B. Y.-P. (1998). Lovesongs in the United States and China: On the nature of romantic love. *Journal of Cross-Cultural Psychology, 29,* 306–319. (p. 155)

Rothblum, E. D. (2007). *Same-sex couples in legalized relationships: I do, or do I?* Unpublished manuscript, Women's Studies Department, San Diego State University. (p. 144)

Rothman, A. J., & Salovey, P. (1997). Shaping perceptions to motivate healthy behavior: The role of message framing. *Psychological Bulletin, 121,* 3–19. (p. 381)

Rothstein, W. G. (1980). The significance of occupations in work careers: An empirical and theoretical review. *Journal of Vocational Behavior, 17,* 328–343. (p. 218)

Rovee-Collier, C. (1989). The joy of kicking: Memories, motives, and mobiles. In P. R. Solomon, G. R. Goethals, C. M. Kelley, & B. R. Stephens (Eds.), *Memory: Interdisciplinary approaches.* New York: Springer-Verlag. (p. 176)

Rovee-Collier, C. (1993). The capacity for long-term memory in infancy. *Current Directions in Psychological Science, 2,* 130–135. (p. 348)

Rovee-Collier, C. (1997). Dissociations in infant memory: Rethinking the development of implicit and explicit memory. *Psychological Review, 104,* 467–498. (p. 176)

Rovee-Collier, C. (1999). The development of infant memory. *Current Directions in Psychological Science, 8,* 80–85. (p. 176)

Rowe, D. C. (1990). As the twig is bent? The myth of child-rearing influences on personality development. *Journal of Counseling and Development, 68,* 606–611. (p. 136)

Rowe, D. C. (2005). Under the skin: On the impartial treatment of genetic and environmental hypotheses of racial differences. *American Psychologist, 60,* 60–70. (p. 437)

Rowe, D. C., Almeida, D. M., & Jacobson, K. C. (1999). School context and genetic influences on aggression in adolescence. *Psychological Science, 10,* 277–280. (p. 710)

Rowe, D. C., Jacobson, K. C., & Van den Oord, E. J. C. G. (1999). Genetic and environmental influences on vocabulary IQ: Parental education level as moderator. *Child Development, 70*(5), 1151–1162. (p. 430)

Rowe, D. C., Vazsonyi, A. T., & Flannery, D. J. (1994). No more than skin deep: Ethnic and racial similarity in developmental process. *Psychological Review, 101*(3), 396. (p. 156)

Rowe, D. C., Vazsonyi, A. T., & Flannery, D. J. (1995). Ethnic and racial similarity in developmental process: A study of academic achievement. *Psychological Science, 6,* 33–38. (p. 156)

Rozin, P., Dow, S., Mosovitch, M., & Rajaram, S. (1998). What causes humans to begin and end a meal? A role for memory for what has been eaten, as evidenced by a study of multiple meal eating in amnesic patients. *Psychological Science, 9,* 392–396. (p. 451)

Rozin, P., Millman, L., & Nemeroff, C. (1986). Operation of the laws of sympathetic magic in disgust and other domains. *Journal of Personality and Social Psychology, 50,* 703–712. (p. 294)

Ruback, R. B., Carr, T. S., & Hopper, C. H. (1986). Perceived control in prison: Its relation to reported crowding, stress, and symptoms. *Journal of Applied Social Psychology, 16,* 375–386. (p. 586)

Rubenstein, J. S., Meyer, D. E., & Evans, J. E. (2001). Executive control of cognitive processes in task switching. *Journal of Experimental Psychology: Human Perception and Performance, 27,* 763–797. (p. 88)

Rubin, D. C., Rahhal, T. A., & Poon, L. W. (1998). Things learned in early adulthood are remembered best. *Memory and Cognition, 26,* 3–19. (p. 212)

Rubin, J. Z., Pruitt, D. G., & Kim, S. H. (1994). *Social conflict: Escalation, stalemate, and settlement.* New York: McGraw-Hill. (p. 733)

Rubin, L. B. (1985). *Just friends: The role of friendship in our lives.* New York: Harper & Row. (p. 159)

Rubin, Z. (1970). Measurement of romantic love. *Journal of Personality and Social Psychology, 16,* 265–273. (p. 510)

Rubio, G., & López-Ibor, J. J. (2007). Generalized anxiety disorder: A 40-year follow-up study. *Acta Psychiatrica Scandinavica, 115,* 372–379. (p. 610)

Rubonis, A. V., & Bickman, L. (1991). Psychological impairment in the wake of disaster: The disaster-psychopathology relationship. *Psychological Bulletin, 109,* 384–399. (p. 533)

Ruchlis, H. (1990). *Clear thinking: A practical introduction.* Buffalo, NY: Prometheus Books. (p. 371)

Rudman, L. A., & Goodwin, S. A. (2004). Gender differences in automatic in-group bias: Why do women like women more than men like men? *Journal of Personality and Social Psychology, 87,* 494–509. (p. 704)

Ruffin, C. L. (1993). Stress and health—little hassles vs. major life events. *Australian Psychologist, 28,* 201–208. (p. 534)

Rule, B. G., & Ferguson, T. J. (1986). The effects of media violence on attitudes, emotions, and cognitions. *Journal of Social Issues, 42*(3), 29–50. (p. 321)

Rumbaugh, D. M. (1977). *Language learning by a chimpanzee: The Lana project.* New York: Academic Press. (p. 400)

Rumbaugh, D. M., & Savage-Rumbaugh, S. (1978). Chimpanzee language research: Status and potential. *Behavior Research Methods & Instrumentation, 10,* 119–131. (p. 401)

Rumbaugh, D. M., & Savage-Rumbaugh, S. (1994, January/February). Language and apes. *Psychology Teacher Network,* pp. 2–5, 9. (p. 402)

Rumbaugh, D. M., & Washburn, D. A. (2003). *Intelligence of apes and other rational beings.* New Haven, CT: Yale University Press. (p. 402)

Rush, A. J., & 12 others from the STAR*D Study team. (2006). Bupropion-SR, Sertaline, or Venlafaxine-XR after failure of SSRIs for depression. *New England Journal of Medicine, 354,* 1231–1242. (p. 674)

Rushton, J. P. (1975). Generosity in children: Immediate and long-term effects of modeling, preaching, and moral judgment. *Journal of Personality and Social Psychology, 31,* 459–466. (p. 319)

Rushton, J. P., & Jensen, A. R. (2005). Thirty years of research on race differences in cognitive ability. *Psychology, Public Policy, and Law, 11,* 235–294. (p. 435)

Rushton, J. P., & Jensen, A. R. (2006). The totality of available evidence shows the race IQ gap still remains. *Psychological Science, 17,* 921–922. (p. 435)

Russell, B. (1930/1985). *The conquest of happiness.* London: Unwin Paperbacks. (p. 528)

Russell, J. A., & Carroll, J. M. (January, 1999a). On the bipolarity of positive and negative affect. *Psychological Bulletin, 125,* 3–30. (p. 517)

Russell, J. A., & Carroll, J. M. (1999b). The phoenix of bipolarity: Reply to Watson and Tellegan (1999). *Psychological Bulletin, 125,* 611–614. (p. 517)

Russell, J. A., Lewicka, M., & Niit, T. (1989). A cross-cultural study of a circumplex model of affect. *Journal of Personality and Social Psychology, 57,* 848–856. (p. 517)

Rusting, C. L., & Nolen-Hoeksema, S. (1998). Regulating responses to anger: Effects of rumination and distraction on angry mood. *Journal of Personality and Social Psychology, 74,* 790–803. (p. 521)

Rutter, M., and the English and Romanian Adoptees (ERA) study team. (1998). Developmental catch-up, and deficit, following adoption after severe global early privation. *Journal of Child Psychology and Psychiatry, 39,* 465–476. (p. 189)

Ruys, K. I., & Stapel, D. A. (2008). The secret life of emotions. *Psychological Science, 19,* 385–391. (p. 507)

Ryan, R. (1999, February 2). Quoted by Alfie Kohn, In pursuit of affluence, at a high price. *New York Times* (www.nytimes.com). (pp. 526, 527)

Ryan, R. M., & Deci, E. L. (2004). Avoiding death or engaging life as accounts of meaning and culture: Comment on Pyszczynski et al. (2004). *Psychological Bulletin, 130,* 473–477. (p. 594)

Ryckman, R. M., Robbins, M. A., Kaczor, L. M., & Gold J. A. (1989). Male and female raters' stereotyping of male and female physiques. *Personality and Social Psychology Bulletin, 15,* 244–251. (p. 457)

Ryder, A. G., Yang, J., Zhu, X., Yao, S., Yi, J., Heine, S. J., & Bagby, R. M. (2008). The cultural shaping of depression: Somatic symptoms in China, psychological symptoms in North America? *Journal of Abnormal Psychology, 117,* 300–313. (p. 623)

Saad, L. (2001, December 17). Americans' mood: Has Sept. 11 made a difference? *Gallup Poll News* Service (www.gallup.com/poll/releases/pr011217.asp). (p. 534)

Saad, L. (2002, November 21). Most smokers wish they could quit. *Gallup News Service* (www.gallup.com). (p. 119)

Saad, L. (2006, August 10). Anti-Muslim sentiments fairly commonplace. *Gallup News Service* (poll.gallup.com). (p. 704)

Sabbagh, M. A., Xu, F., Carlson, S. M., Moses, L. J., & Lee, K. (2006). The development of executive functioning and theory of mind: A comparison of Chinese and U.S. preschoolers. *Psychological Science, 17,* 74–81. (p. 181)

Sabini, J. (1986). Stanley Milgram (1933–1984). *American Psychologist, 41,* 1378–1379. (p. 694)

Sachdev, P., & Sachdev, J. (1997). Sixty years of psychosurgery: Its present status and its future. *Australian and New Zealand Journal of Psychiatry, 31,* 457–464. (p. 678)

Sackett, P. R., Borneman, M. J., & Connelly, B. S. (2008). High-stakes testing in higher education and employment: Appraising the evidence for validity and fairness. *American Psychologist, 63,* 215–227. (p. 439)

Sackett, P. R., Hardison, C. M., & Cullen, M. J. (2004). On interpreting stereotype threat as accounting for African American-White differences on cognitive tests. *American Psychologist, 59,* 7–13. (p. 439)

Sackett, P. R., & Lievens, F. (2008). Personnel selection. *Annual Review of Psychology, 59,* 419–450. (p. 487)

Sacks, O. (1985). *The man who mistook his wife for a hat.* New York: Summit Books. (pp. 252, 342)

Sadato, N., Pascual-Leone, A., Grafman, J., Ibanez, V., Deiber, M-P., Dold, G., & Hallett, M. (1996). Activation of the primary visual cortex by Braille reading in blind subjects. *Nature, 380,* 526–528. (p. 73)

Saffran, J. R., Aslin, R. N., & Newport, E. L. (1996). Statistical learning by 8-month-old infants. *Science, 274,* 1926–1928. (p. 389)

Sagan, C. (1987, February 1). The fine art of baloney detection. *Parade.* (p. 283)

Sakurai, T., Amemiya, A., Ishii, M., Matsuzaki, I., Chemelli, R. M., Tanaka, H., Williams, S. C., Richardson, J. A., Kozlowski, G. P., Wilson, S., Arch, J. R. S., Buckingham, R. E., Haynes, A. C., Carr, S. A., Annan, R. S., McNulty, D. E., Liu, W.-S., Terrett, J. A., Elshourbagy, N. A., Bergsma, D. J., & Yanagisawa, M. (1998). Orexins and orexin receptors: A family of hypothalamic neuropeptides and G protein-coupled receptors that regulate feeding behavior. *Cell, 92,* 573–585. (p. 450)

Salib, E., & Cortina-Borja, M. (2006). Effect of month of birth on the risk of suicide. *British Journal of Psychiatry, 188,* 416–422. (p. 630)

Salmela-Aro, K., & Nurmi, J.-E. (2007). Self-esteem during university studies predicts career characteristics 10 years later. *Journal of Vocational Behavior, 70,* 463–477. (p. 591)

Salmon, P. (2001). Effects of physical exercise on anxiety, depression, and sensitivity to stress: A unifying theory. *Clinical Psychology Review, 21,* 33–61. (pp. 547, 548)

Salovey, P. (1990, January/February). Interview. *American Scientist,* pp. 25–29. (p. 522)

Salthouse, T. A. (2004). What and when of cognitive aging. *Current Directions in Psychological Science, 13,* 140–144. (p. 215)

Sampson, E. E. (2000). Reinterpreting individualism and collectivism: Their religious roots and monologic versus dialogic person–other relationship. *American Psychologist, 55,* 1425–1432. (p. 154)

Samuels, J., & Nestadt, G. (1997). Epidemiology and genetics of obsessive-compulsive disorder. *International Review of Psychiatry, 9,* 61–71. (p. 612)

Samuels, S., & McCabe, G. (1989). Quoted by P. Diaconis & F. Mosteller, Methods for studying coincidences. *Journal of the American Statistical Association, 84,* 853–861. (p. 34)

Sanders, A. R., & 22 others. (2008). No significant association of 14 candidate genes with schizophrenia in a large European ancestry sample: Implications for psychiatric genetics. *American Journal of Psychiatry, 165,* 497–506. (p. 642)

Sanders, G., Sjodin, M., & de Chastelaine, M. (2002). On the elusive nature of sex differences in cognition hormonal influences contributing to within-sex variation. *Archives of Sexual Behavior, 31,* 145–152. (p. 477)

Sanders, G., & Wright, M. (1997). Sexual orientation differences in cerebral asymmetry and in the performance of sexually dimorphic cognitive and motor tasks. *Archives of Sexual Behavior, 26,* 463–479. (p. 478)

Sandfort, T. G. M., de Graaf, R., Bijl, R., & Schnabel, P. (2001). Same-sex sexual behavior and psychiatric disorders. *Archives of General Psychiatry, 58,* 85–91. (p. 473)

Sandkühler, S., & Bhattacharya, J. (2008). Deconstructing insight: EEG correlates of insightful problem solving. *PloS ONE, 3,* e1459 (www.plosone.org). (p. 371)

Sandler, W., Meir, I., Padden, C., & Aronoff, M. (2005). The emergence of grammar: Systematic structure in a new language. *Proceedings of the National Academy of Sciences, 102,* 2261–2265. (p. 389)

Sanford, A. J., Fray, N., Stewart, A., & Moxey, L. (2002). Perspective in statements of quantity, with implications for consumer psychology. *Psychological Science, 13,* 130–134. (p. 382)

Sanz, C., Blicher, A., Dalke, K., Gratton-Fabri, L., McClure-Richards, T., & Fouts, R. (1998, Winter-Spring). Enrichment object use: Five chimpanzees' use of temporary and semi-permanent enrichment objects. *Friends of Washoe, 19*(1,2), 9–14. (p. 399)

Sanz, C., Morgan, D., & Gulick, S. (2004). New insights into chimpanzees, tools, and termites from the Congo Basin. *American Naturalist, 164,* 567–581. (p. 398)

Sapadin, L. A. (1988). Friendship and gender: Perspectives of professional men and women. *Journal of Social and Personal Relationships, 5,* 387–403. (p. 159)

Sapolsky, B. S., & Tabarlet, J. O. (1991). Sex in primetime television: 1979 versus 1989. *Journal of Broadcasting and Electronic Media, 35,* 505–516. (pp. 471, 715)

Sapolsky, R. (2003, September). Taming stress. *Scientific American*, pp. 87–95. (pp. 532, 628)

Sapolsky, R. (2005). The influence of social hierarchy on primate health. *Science, 308*, 648–652. (p. 543)

Sapolsky, R. M., & Finch, C. E. (1991, March/April). On growing old. *The Sciences*, pp. 30–38. (p. 208)

Satel, S. (2006, March 1). For some, the war won't end. *New York Times* (www.nytimes.com). (p. 613)

Sato, K. (1987). Distribution of the cost of maintaining common resources. *Journal of Experimental Social Psychology, 23*, 19–31. (p. 730)

Saul, S. (2007, March 15). F.D.A. warns of sleeping pills' strange effects. *New York Times* (www.nytimes.com). (p. 100)

Saulny, S. (2006, June 21). A legacy of the storm: Depression and suicide. *New York Times* (www.nytimes.com). (p. 534)

Savage-Rumbaugh, E. S., Murphy, J., Sevcik, R. A., Brakke, K. E., Williams, S. L., & Rumbaugh, D. M., with commentary by Bates, E. (1993). Language comprehension in ape and child. *Monographs of the Society for Research in Child Development, 58* (no. 233), 1–254. (p. 401)

Savic, I., Berglund, H., & Lindstrom, P. (2005). Brain response to putative pheromones in homosexual men. *Proceedings of the National Academy of Sciences, 102*, 7356–7361. (p. 476)

Savic, I., & Lindström, P. (2008). PET and MRI show differences in cerebral asymmetry and functional connectivity between homo- and heterosexual subjects. *Proceedings of the National Academy of Sciences, 105*, 9403–9408. (p. 475)

Savitsky, K., Epley, N., & Gilovich, T. (2001). Do others judge us as harshly as we think? Overestimating the impact of our failures, shortcomings, and mishaps. *Journal of Personality and Social Psychology, 81*, 44–56. (p. 591)

Savitsky, K., & Gilovich, T. (2003). The illusion of transparency and the alleviation of speech anxiety. *Journal of Experimental Social Psychology, 39*, 618–625. (p. 591)

Savoy, C., & Beitel, P. (1996). Mental imagery for basketball. *International Journal of Sport Psychology, 27*, 454–462. (p. 395)

Sawyer, M. G., Arney, F. M., Baghurst, P. A., Clark, J. J., Graetz, B. W., Kosky, R. J., Nurcombe, B., Patton, G. C., Prior, M. R., Raphael, B., Rey, J., Whaites, L. C., & Zubrick, S. R. (2000). *The mental health of young people in Australia*. Canberra: Mental Health and Special Programs Branch, Commonwealth Department of Health and Aged Care. (p. 628)

Saxe, R., & Powell, L. J. (2006). It's the thought that counts. *Psychological Science, 17*, 692–699. (p. 184)

Sayre, R. F. (1979). The parents' last lessons. In D. D. Van Tassel (Ed.) *Aging, death, and the completion of being*. Philadelphia: University of Pennsylvania Press. (p. 211)

Scarborough, E., & Furumoto, L. (1987). *Untold lives: The first generation of American women psychologists*. New York: Columbia University Press. (p. 4)

Scarr, S. (1984, May). What's a parent to do? A conversation with E. Hall. *Psychology Today*, pp. 58–63. (p. 431)

Scarr, S. (1986). *Mother care/other care*. New York: Basic Books. (p. 191)

Scarr, S. (1989). Protecting general intelligence: Constructs and consequences for interventions. In R. J. Linn (Ed.), *Intelligence: Measurement, theory, and public policy*. Champaign: University of Illinois Press. (p. 407)

Scarr, S. (1990). Back cover comments on J. Dunn & R. Plomin (1990), *Separate lives: Why siblings are so different*. New York: Basic Books. (p. 140)

Scarr, S. (1993, May/June). Quoted by *Psychology Today*, Nature's thumbprint: So long, superparents, p. 16. (p. 150)

Scarr, S. (1997). Why child care has little impact on most children's development. *Current Directions in Psychological Science, 6*, 143–148. (p. 191)

Schab, F. R. (1991). Odor memory: Taking stock. *Psychological Bulletin, 109*, 242–251. (p. 261)

Schachter, S. (1982). Recidivism and self-cure of smoking and obesity. *American Psychologist, 37*, 436–444. (p. 464)

Schachter, S., & Singer, J. E. (1962). Cognitive, social and physiological determinants of emotional state. *Psychological Review, 69*, 379–399. (pp. 501, 506)

Schacter, D. L. (1992). Understanding implicit memory: A cognitive neuroscience approach. *American Psychologist, 47*, 559–569. (p. 343)

Schacter, D. L. (1996). *Searching for memory: The brain, the mind, and the past*. New York: Basic Books. (pp. 210, 343, 361, 519, 566)

Schacter, D. L. (1999). The seven sins of memory: Insights from psychology and cognitive neuroscience. *American Psychologist, 54*, 182–201. (p. 351)

Schafer, G. (2005). Infants can learn decontextualized words before their first birthday. *Child Development, 76*, 87–96. (p. 387)

Schaie, K. W. (1994). The life course of adult intellectual abilities. *American Psychologist, 49*, 304–313. (p. 214)

Schaie, K. W., & Geiwitz, J. (1982). *Adult development and aging*. Boston: Little, Brown. (p. 214)

Schall, T., & Smith, G. (2000, Fall). Career trajectories in baseball. *Chance*, pp. 35–38. (p. 207)

Schechter, R., & Grether, J. K. (2008). Continuing increases in autism reported to California's developmental services system. *Archives of General Psychiatry, 65*, 19–24. (p. 182)

Scheier, M. F., & Carver, C. S. (1992). Effects of optimism on psychological and physical well-being: Theoretical overview and empirical update. *Cognitive Therapy and Research, 16*, 201–228. (p. 544)

Schein, E. H. (1956). The Chinese indoctrination program for prisoners of war: A study of attempted brainwashing. *Psychiatry, 19*, 149–172. (p. 686)

Schellenberg, E. G. (2005). Music and cognitive abilities. *Current Directions in Psychological Science, 14*, 317–320. (p. 431)

Schellenberg, E. G. (2006). Long-term positive associations between music lessons and IQ. *Journal of Educational Psychology, 98*, 457–468. (p. 431)

Scherer, K. R., Banse, R., & Wallbott, H. G. (2001). Emotion inferences from vocal expression correlate across languages and cultures. *Journal of Cross-Cultural Psychology, 32*, 76–92. (p. 510)

Schiavi, R. C., & Schreiner-Engel, P. (1988). Nocturnal penile tumescence in healthy aging men. *Journal of Gerontology: Medical Sciences, 43*, M146–M150. (p. 94)

Schiffenbauer, A., & Schiavo, R. S. (1976). Physical distance and attraction: An intensification effect. *Journal of Experimental Social Psychology, 12*, 274–282. (p. 697)

Schilt, T., de Win, M. M. L., Koeter, M., Jager, G., Korf, D. J., van den Brink, W., & Schmand, B. (2007). Cognition in novice Ecstasy users with minimal exposure to other drugs. *Archives of General Psychiatry, 64*, 728–736. (p. 122)

Schimel, J., Arndt, J., Pyszczynski, T., & Greenberg, J. (2001). Being accepted for who we are: Evidence that social validation of the intrinsic self reduces general defensiveness. *Journal of Personality and Social Psychology, 80*, 35–52. (p. 572)

Schimmack, U., & Lucas, R. (2007). Marriage matters: Spousal similarity in life satisfaction. *Schmollers Jahrbuch, 127*, 1–7. (p. 529)

Schimmack, U., Oishi, S., & Diener, E. (2005). Individualism: A valid and important dimension of cultural differences between nations. *Personality and Social Psychology Review, 9*, 17–31. (p. 154)

Schkade, D., Sunstein, C. R., & Hastie, R. (2006). *What happened on deliberation day?* (University of Chicago Law and Economics, Olin Working Paper No. 298.) (p. 699)

Schlaug, G., Jancke, L., Huang, Y., & Steinmetz, H. (1995). In vivo evidence of structural brain asymmetry in musicians. *Science, 267*, 699–701. (p. 60)

Schlesinger, A. M., Jr. (1965). *A thousand days*. Boston: Houghton Mifflin. (p. 700)

Schmidt, F. L. (2002). The role of general cognitive ability and job performance: Why there cannot be a debate. *Human Performance, 15*, 187–210. (p. 487)

Schmidt, F. L., & Hunter, J. E. (1998). The validity and utility of selection methods in personnel psychology: Practical and theoretical implications of 85 years of research findings. *Psychological Bulletin, 124*, 262–274. (pp. 487, 488, 590)

Schmidt, F. L., & Zimmerman, R. D. (2004). A counterintuitive hypothesis about employment interview validity and some supporting evidence. *Journal of Applied Psychology, 89*, 553–561. (p. 489)

Schmitt, D. P. (2005). Sociosexuality from Argentina to Zimbabwe: A 48-nation study of sex, culture, and strategies of human mating. *Behavioral and Brain Sciences, 28*, 247–311. (p. 145)

Schmitt, D. P. (2007). Sexual strategies across sexual orientations: How personality traits and culture relate to sociosexuality among gays, lesbians, bisexuals, and heterosexuals. *Journal of Psychology and Human Sexuality, 18*, 183–214. (pp. 144, 145)

Schmitt, D. P., & Allik, J. (2005). Simultaneous administration of the Rosenberg Self-esteem Scale in 53 nations: Exploring the universal and culture-specific features of global self-esteem. *Journal of Personality and Social Psychology, 89,* 623–642. (p. 593)

Schmitt, D. P., Allik, J., McCrae, R. R., & Benet-Martínez, V., with many others. (2007). The geographic distribution of Big Five personality traits: Patterns and profiles of human self-description across 56 nations. *Journal of Cross-Cultural Psychology, 38,* 173–212. (p. 578)

Schmitt, D. P., & Pilcher, J. J. (2004). Evaluating evidence of psychological adaptation: How do we know one when we see one? *Psychological Science, 15,* 643–649. (p. 143)

Schnaper, N. (1980). Comments germane to the paper entitled "The reality of death experiences" by Ernst Rodin. *Journal of Nervous and Mental Disease, 168,* 268–270. (p. 123)

Schneider, R. H., Alexander, C. N., Staggers, F., Rainforth, M., Salerno, J. W., Hartz, A., Arndt, S., Barnes, V. A., & Nidich, S. (2005). Long-term effects of stress reduction on mortality in persons > or = 55 years of age with systemic hypertension. *American Journal of Cardiology, 95,* 1060–1064. (p. 552)

Schneider, S. L. (2001). In search of realistic optimism: Meaning, knowledge, and warm fuzziness. *American Psychologist, 56,* 250–263. (p. 587)

Schneiderman, N. (1999). Behavioral medicine and the management of HIV/AIDS. *International Journal of Behavioral Medicine, 6,* 3–12. (p. 540)

Schoenborn, C. A., & Adams, P. F. (2008). Sleep duration as a correlate of smoking, alcohol use, leisure-time physical inactivity, and obesity among adults: United States, 2004–2006. Centers for Disease Control and Prevention (www.cdc.gov/nchs). (p. 97)

Schoeneman, T. J. (1994). Individualism. In V. S. Ramachandran (Ed.), *Encyclopedia of human behavior.* San Diego: Academic Press. (p. 155)

Schofield, J. W. (1986). Black-White contact in desegregated schools. In M. Hewstone & R. Brown (Eds.), *Contact and conflict in intergroup encounters.* Oxford: Basil Blackwell. (p. 731)

Schonfield, D., & Robertson, B. A. (1966). Memory storage and aging. *Canadian Journal of Psychology, 20,* 228–236. (pp. 212, 213)

Schooler, J. W., Gerhard, D., & Loftus, E. F. (1986). Qualities of the unreal. *Journal of Experimental Psychology: Learning, Memory, and Cognition, 12,* 171–181. (p. 358)

Schorr, E. A., Fox, N.A., van Wassenhove, V., & Knudsen, E.I. (2005). Auditory-visual fusion in speech perception in children with cochlear implants. *Proceedings of the National Academy of Sciences, 102,* 18748–18750. (p. 248)

Schultheiss, D. E. P. (2008). *Psychology as a major: Is it right for me and what can I do with my degree?* Washington, DC: American Psychological Association. (p. A-10)

Schuman, H., & Scott, J. (June, 1989). Generations and collective memories. *American Sociological Review, 54*(3), 359–381. (p. 212)

Schwartz, B. (1984). *Psychology of learning and behavior* (2nd ed.). New York: Norton. (pp. 298, 614)

Schwartz, B. (2000). Self-determination: The tyranny of freedom. *American Psychologist, 55,* 79–88. (p. 586)

Schwartz, B. (2004). *The paradox of choice: Why more is less.* New York: Ecco/HarperCollins. (p. 586)

Schwartz, B. (2007, April 12). Unnatural selections. *New York Times* (www.nytimes.com). (p. 382)

Schwartz, J., & Estrin, J. (2004, November 7). Living for today, locked in a paralyzed body. *New York Times* (www.nytimes.com). (p. 523)

Schwartz, J. M., Stoessel, P. W., Baxter, L. R., Jr., Martin, K. M., & Phelps, M. E. (1996). Systematic changes in cerebral glucose metabolic rate after successful behavior modification treatment of obsessive-compulsive disorder. *Archives of General Psychiatry, 53,* 109–113. (pp. 656, 678)

Schwartz, S. H., & Rubel, T. (2005). Sex differences in value priorities: Cross-cultural and multimethod studies. *Journal of Personality and Social Psychology, 89,* 1010–1028. (p. 158)

Schwarz, A. (2007, April 6). Throwing batters curves before throwing a pitch. *New York Times* (www.nytimes.com). (p. 78)

Schwarz, N., Strack, F., Kommer, D., & Wagner, D. (1987). Soccer, rooms, and the quality of your life: Mood effects on judgments of satisfaction with life in general and with specific domains. *European Journal of Social Psychology, 17,* 69–79. (p. 349)

Sclafani, A. (1995). How food preferences are learned: Laboratory animal models. *Proceedings of the Nutrition Society, 54,* 419–427. (p. 452)

Scott, D. J., & others. (2004, November 9). U-M team reports evidence that smoking affects human brain's natural "feel good" chemical system (press release by Kara Gavin). University of Michigan Medical School (www.med.umich.edu). (p. 119)

Scott, D. J., Stohler, C. S., Egnatuk, C. M., Wang, H., Koeppe, R. A., & Zubieta, J.-K. (2007). Individual differences in reward responding explain placebo-induced expectations and effects. *Neuron, 55,* 325–336. (p. 256)

Scott, W. A., Scott, R., & McCabe, M. (1991). Family relationships and children's personality: A cross-cultural, cross-source comparison. *British Journal of Social Psychology, 30,* 1–20. (p. 156)

Sdorow, L. M. (2005). The people behind psychology. In B. Perlman, L. McCann, & W. Buskist (Eds.), *Voices of experience: Memorable talks from the National Institute on the Teaching of Psychology.* Washington, DC: American Psychological Society. (p. 564)

Seal, K. H., Bertenthal, D., Miner, C. R., Sen, S., & Marmar, C. (2007). Bringing the war back home: Mental health disorders among 103,788 U.S. veterans returning from Iraq and Afghanistan seen at Department of Veterans Affairs facilities. *Archives of Internal Medicine, 167,* 467–482. (p. 613)

Seamon, J. G., Philbin, M. M., & Harrison, L. G. (2006). Do you remember proposing marriage to the Pepsi machine? False recollections from a campus walk. *Psychonomic Bulletin and Review, 13,* 752–756. (p. 359)

Sebat, J., & 31 others. (2007). Strong association of de novo copy number mutations with autism. *Science, 316,* 445–449. (p. 182)

Sechrest, L., Stickle, T. R., & Stewart, M. (1998). The role of assessment in clinical psychology. In A. Bellack, M. Hersen (series eds.), & C. R. Reynolds (vol. ed.), *Comprehensive clinical psychology: Vol. 4. Assessment.* New York: Pergamon. (p. 565)

Seeman, P., Guan, H.-C., & Van Tol, H. H. M. (1993). Dopamine D4 receptors elevated in schizophrenia. *Nature, 365,* 441–445. (p. 639)

Segal, N. L. (1999). *Entwined lives: Twins and what they tell us about human behavior.* New York: Dutton. (p. 136)

Segal, N. L. (2000). Virtual twins: New findings on within-family environmental influences on intelligence. *Journal of Educational Psychology, 92,* 442–448. (p. 136)

Segal, N. L., McGuire, S. A., Havlena, J., Gill, P., & Hershberger, S. L. (2007). Intellectual similarity of virtual twin pairs: Developmental trends. *Personality and Individual Differences, 42,* 1209–1219. (p. 429)

Segall, M. H., Dasen, P. R., Berry, J. W., & Poortinga, Y. H. (1990). *Human behavior in global perspective: An introduction to cross-cultural psychology.* New York: Pergamon. (pp. 144, 162, 185)

Segerstrom, S. C. (2007). Stress, energy, and immunity. *Current Directions in Psychological Science, 16,* 326–330. (p. 531)

Segerstrom, S. C., Taylor, S. E., Kemeny, M. E., & Fahey, J. L. (1998). Optimism is associated with mood, coping, and immune change in response to stress. *Journal of Personality and Social Psychology, 74,* 1646–1655. (p. 544)

Seidler, G. H., & Wagner, F. E. (2006). Comparing the efficacy of EMDR and trauma-focused cognitive-behavioral therapy in the treatment of PTSD: A meta-analytic study. *Psychological Medicine, 36,* 1515–1522. (p. 665)

Seidlitz, L., & Diener, E. (1998). Sex differences in the recall of affective experiences. *Journal of Personality and Social Psychology, 74,* 262–271. (p. 633)

Self, C. E. (1994). *Moral culture and victimization in residence halls.* Unpublished master's thesis. Bowling Green University. (p. 127)

Seligman, M. E. P. (1974, May). Submissive death: Giving up on life. *Psychology Today,* pp. 80–85. (p. 518)

Seligman, M. E. P. (1975). *Helplessness: On depression, development and death.* San Francisco: Freeman. (p. 585)

Seligman, M. E. P. (1991). *Learned optimism.* New York: Knopf. (pp. 83, 585, 633, 634)

Seligman, M. E. P. (1994). *What you can change and what you can't.* New York: Knopf. (pp. 150, 549, 568, 591)

Seligman, M. E. P. (1995). The effectiveness of psychotherapy: The Consumer Reports study. *American Psychologist, 50,* 965–974. (pp. 634, 660, 663)

Seligman, M. E. P. (2002). *Authentic happiness: Using the new positive psychology to realize your potential for lasting fulfillment.* New York: Free Press. (pp. 588, 591, 656)

Seligman, M. E. P. (2004). Eudaemonia, the good life. A talk with Martin Seligman. www.edge.org. (p. 588)

Seligman, M. E. P., Steen, T. A., Park, N., & Peterson, C. (2005). Positive psychology progress: Empirical validation of interventions. *American Psychologist, 60,* 410–421. (pp. 527, 588)

Seligman, M. E. P., & Yellen, A. (1987). What is a dream? *Behavior Research and Therapy, 25,* 1–24. (p. 92)

Sellers, H. (2010). *Face first.* New York: Riverhead Books. (p. 225)

Selye, H. (1936). A syndrome produced by diverse nocuous agents. *Nature, 138,* 32. (p. 532)

Selye, H. (1976). *The stress of life.* New York: McGraw-Hill. (p. 532)

Sen, A. (2003). Missing women—revisited. *British Medical Journal, 327,* 1297–1298. (p. 704)

Senghas, A., & Coppola, M. (2001). Children creating language How Nicaraguan Sign Language acquired a spatial grammar. *Psychological Science, 12,* 323–328. (p. 389)

Sengupta, S. (2001, October 10). Sept. 11 attack narrows the racial divide. *New York Times* (www.nytimes.com). (p. 732)

Senju, A., Maeda, M., Kikuchi, Y., Hasegawa, T., Tojo, Y., & Osanai, H. (2007). Absence of contagious yawning in children with autism spectrum disorder. *Biology Letters, 3,* 706–708. (pp. 183, 317)

Sensenbrenner, F. J. (2004, March 11). Quoted by C. Hulse, Vote in House offers a shield in obesity suits. *New York Times* (www.nytimes.com). (p. 457)

Serruya, M. D., Hatsopoulos, N. G., Paninski, L., Fellow, M. R., & Donoghue, J. P. (2002). Instant neural control of a movement signal. *Nature, 416,* 141–142. (p. 69)

Service, R. F. (1994). Will a new type of drug make memory-making easier? *Science, 266,* 218–219. (p. 340)

Seto, M. C., & Barbaree, H. E. (1995). The role of alcohol in sexual aggression. *Clinical Psychology Review, 15,* 545–566. (p. 116)

Shadish, W. R., & Baldwin, S. A. (2005). Effects of behavioral marital therapy: A meta-analysis of randomized controlled trials. *Journal of Consulting and Clinical Psychology, 73,* 6–14. (p. 663)

Shadish, W. R., Matt, G. E., Navarro, A. M., & Phillips, G. (2000). The effects of psychological therapies under clinically representative conditions: A meta-analysis. *Psychological Bulletin, 126,* 512–529. (p. 662)

Shadish, W. R., Montgomery, L. M., Wilson, P., Wilson, M. R., Bright, I., & Okwumabua, T. (1993). Effects of family and marital psychotherapies: A meta-analysis. *Journal of Consulting and Clinical Psychology, 61,* 992–1002. (p. 658)

Shaffer, D. M., Krauchunas, S. M., Eddy, M., & McBeath, M. K. (2004). How dogs navigate to catch Frisbees, *Psychological Science, 15,* 437–441. (p. 267)

Shafir, E., & LeBoeuf, R. A. (2002). Rationality. *Annual Review of Psychology, 53,* 491–517. Times, p. B1. (p. 379)

Shamir, B., House, R. J., & Arthur, M. B. (1993). The motivational effects of charismatic leadership: A self-concept based theory. *Organizational Science, 4*(4), 577–594. (p. 495)

Shanahan, L., McHale, S. M., Osgood, D. W., & Crouter, A. C. (2007). Conflict frequency with mothers and fathers from middle childhood to late adolescence: Within- and between-families comparisons. *Developmental Psychology, 43,* 539–550. (pp. 202, 203)

Shanley, D. P., Sear, R., Mace, R., & Kirkwood, T. B. L. (2007). Testing evolutionary theories of menopause. *Proceedings of the Royal Society, 274,* 2943–2949. (p. 207)

Shapiro, F. (1989). Efficacy of the eye movement desensitization procedure in the treatment of traumatic memories. *Journal of Traumatic Stress, 2,* 199–223. (p. 665)

Shapiro, F. (1995). *Eye movement desensitization and reprocessing: Basic principles, protocols, and procedures.* New York: Guilford. (p. 665)

Shapiro, F. (1999). Eye movement desensitization and reprocessing (EMDR) and the anxiety disorders: Clinical and research implications of an integrated psychotherapy treatment. *Journal of Anxiety Disorders, 13,* 35–67. (p. 665)

Shapiro, F. (Ed.). (2002). *EMDR as an integrative psychotherapy approach: Experts of diverse orientations explore the paradigm prism.* Washington, DC: APA Books. (p. 665)

Shapiro, F. (2007). EMDR and case conceptualization from an adaptive information processing perspective. In F. Shapiro, F. W. Kaslow, & L. Maxfield (Eds.), *Handbook of EMDR and family therapy processes.* Hoboken, NJ: Wiley. (p. 665)

Shapiro, K. A., Moo, L. R., & Caramazza, A. (2006). Cortical signatures of noun and verb production. *Proceedings of the National Academic of Sciences, 103,* 1644–1649. (p. 392)

Sharma, A. R., McGue, M. K., & Benson, P. L. (1998). The psychological adjustment of United States adopted adolescents and their nonadopted siblings. *Child Development, 69,* 791–802. (p. 137)

Shattuck, P. T. (2006). The contribution of diagnostic substitution to the growing administrative prevalence of autism in US special education. *Pediatrics, 117,* 1028–1037. (p. 182)

Shaver, P. R., & Mikulincer, M. (2007). Adult attachment strategies and the regulation of emotion. In J. J. Gross (Ed.), *Handbook of emotion regulation.* New York: Guilford Press. (p. 189)

Shaver, P. R., Morgan, H. J., & Wu, S. (1996). Is love a basic emotion? *Personal Relationships, 3,* 81–96. (p. 517)

Shaw, H. L. (1989–90). Comprehension of the spoken word and ASL translation by chimpanzees (Pan troglodytes). *Friends of Washoe, 9*(1/2), 8–19. (p. 401)

Shaw, P., Eckstrand, K., Sharp, W., Blumenthal, J., Lerch, J. P., Greenstein, D., Clasen, L., Evans, A., Giedd, J., & Rapoport, J. L. (2007). Attention-deficit/hyperactivity disorder is characterized by a delay in cortical maturation. *Proceedings of the National Academy of Sciences, 104,* 19649–19654. (p. 600)

Shaw, P., Greenstein, D., Lerch, J., Clasen, L., Lenroot, R., Gogtay, N., Evans, A., Rapoport, J., & Giedd, J. (2006). Intellectual ability and cortical development in children and adolescents. *Nature, 440,* 676–679. (p. 412)

Sheehan, S. (1982). *Is there no place on earth for me?* Boston: Houghton Mifflin. (p. 637)

Sheldon, K. M., Elliot, A. J., Kim, Y., & Kasser, T. (2001). What is satisfying about satisfying events? Testing 10 candidate psychological needs. *Journal of Personality and Social Psychology, 80,* 325–339. (p. 480)

Sheldon, K. M., & Niemiec, C. P. (2006). It's not just the amount that counts: Balanced need satisfaction also affects well-being. *Journal of Personality and Social Psychology, 91,* 331–341. (p. 480)

Sheldon, M. S., Cooper, M. L., Geary, D. C., Hoard, M., & DeSoto, M. C. (2006). Fertility cycle patterns in motives for sexual behavior. *Personality and Social Psychology Bulletin, 32,* 1659–1673. (p. 467)

Shenton, M. E. (1992). Abnormalities of the left temporal lobe and thought disorder in schizophrenia: A quantitative magnetic resonance imaging study. *New England Journal of Medicine, 327,* 604–612. (p. 640)

Shepard, R. N. (1990). *Mind sights.* New York: Freeman. (pp. 23, 276)

Shepherd, C. (1997, April). News of the weird. *Funny Times,* p. 15. (p. 135)

Shepherd, C. (1999, June). News of the weird. *Funny Times,* p. 21. (p. 461)

Shepherd, C., Kohut, J. J., & Sweet, R. (1990). *More news of the weird.* New York: Penguin/Plume Books. (p. 621)

Sheppard, L. D., & Vernon, P. A. (2008). Intelligence and speed of information-processing: A review of 50 years of research. *Personality and Individual Differences, 44,* 535–551. (p. 413)

Shergill, S. S., Bays, P. M., Frith, C. D., & Wolpert, D. M. (2003). Two eyes for an eye: The neuroscience of force escalation. *Science, 301,* 187. (p. 731)

Sherif, M. (1966). *In common predicament: Social psychology of intergroup conflict and cooperation.* Boston: Houghton Mifflin. (p. 732)

Sherman, P. W., & Flaxman, S. M. (2001). Protecting ourselves from food. *American Scientist, 89,* 142–151 (p. 452)

Shermer, M. (1999). *How we believe: The search for God in an age of science.* New York: Freeman. (p. 281)

Shermer, M. (1999). If that's true, what else would be true? *Skeptic, 7*(4), 192–193. (p. 160)

Sherry, D., & Vaccarino, A. L. (1989). Hippocampus and memory for food caches in black-capped chickadees. *Behavioral Neuroscience, 103,* 308–318. (p. 343)

Shettleworth, S. J. (1973). Food reinforcement and the organization of behavior in golden hamsters. In R. A. Hinde & J. Stevenson-Hinde (Eds.), *Constraints on learning.* London: Academic Press. (p. 309)

Shettleworth, S. J. (1993). Where is the comparison in comparative cognition? Alternative research programs. *Psychological Science, 4,* 179–184. (p. 338)

Shimizu, M., & Pelham, B. W. (2008). Postponing a date with the grim reaper. *Basic and Applied Social Psychology, 30,* 36–45. (p. 209)

Shinkareva, S. V., Mason, R. A., Malave, V. L., Wang, W., Mitchell, T. M., & Just, M. A. (2008, January 2). Using fMRI brain activation to identify cognitive states associated with perceptions of tools and dwellings. *PloS One 3*(1), 31394. (p. 85)

Shotland, R. L. (1984, March 12). Quoted in Maureen Dowd, 20 years after the murder of Kitty Genovese, the question remains: Why? *The New York Times,* p. B1. (p. 726)

Showers, C. (1992). The motivational and emotional consequences of considering positive or negative possibilities for an upcoming event. *Journal of Personality and Social Psychology, 63,* 474–484. (p. 587)

Shulman, P. (2000, June). The girl who loved math. *Discover,* pp. 67–70, (p. 433)

Shuwairi, S. M., Albert, M. K., & Johnson, S. P. (2007). Discrimination of possible and impossible objects in infancy. *Psychological Science, 18,* 303–307. (p. 179)

Sieff, E. M., Dawes, R. M., & Loewenstein, G. (1999). Anticipated versus actual reaction to HIV test results. *The American Journal of Psychology, 112,* 297–313. (p. 523)

Siegel, J. (2000, Winter). Recent developments in narcolepsy research: An explanation for patients and the general public. *Narcolepsy Network Newsletter,* pp. 1–2. (p. 101)

Siegel, J. (2001). The REM sleep-memory consolidation hypothesis. *Science, 294,* 1058–1063. (p. 104)

Siegel, J. M. (1990). Stressful life events and use of physician services among the elderly: The moderating role of pet ownership. *Journal of Personality and Social Psychology, 58,* 1081–1086. (p. 545)

Siegel, J. M. (2003, November). Why we sleep. *Scientific American,* pp. 92–97. (p. 99)

Siegel, R. K. (1977, October). Hallucinations. *Scientific American,* pp. 132–140. (p. 123)

Siegel, R. K. (1980). The psychology of life after death. *American Psychologist, 35,* 911–931. (p. 123)

Siegel, R. K. (1982, October). Quoted by J. Hooper, Mind tripping. *Omni,* pp. 72–82, 159–160. (p. 122)

Siegel, R. K. (1984, March 15). Personal communication. (p. 122)

Siegel, R. K. (1990). *Intoxication.* New York: Pocket Books. (pp. 114, 120, 124)

Siegel, S. (2005). Drug tolerance, drug addiction, and drug anticipation. *Current Directions in Psychological Science, 14,* 296–300. (pp. 288, 298)

Siegler, R. S., & Ellis, S. (1996). Piaget XE "Piaget, J." on childhood. *Psychological Science, 7,* 211–215. (p. 177)

Silbersweig, D. A., Stern, E., Frith, C., Cahill, C., Holmes, A., Grootoonk, S., Seaward, J., McKenna, P., Chua, S. E., Schnorr, L., Jones, T., & Frackowiak, R. S. J. (1995). A functional neuroanatomy of hallucinations in schizophrenia. *Nature, 378,* 176–179. (p. 640)

Silva, A. J., Stevens, C. F., Tonegawa, S., & Wang, Y. (1992). Deficient hippocampal long-term potentiation in alpha-calcium-calmodulin kinase II mutant mice. *Science, 257,* 201–206. (p. 340)

Silva, C. E., & Kirsch, I. (1992). Interpretive sets, expectancy, fantasy proneness, and dissociation as predictors of hypnotic response. *Journal of Personality and Social Psychology, 63,* 847–856. (p. 108)

Silver, M., & Geller, D. (1978). On the irrelevance of evil: The organization and individual action. *Journal of Social Issues, 34,* 125–136. (p. 696)

Silveri, M. M., Rohan, M. L., Pimental, P. J., Gruber, S. A., Rosso, I. M., & Yurgelun-Todd, D. A. (2006). Sex differences in the relationship between white matter microstructure and impulsivity in adolescents. *Magnetic Resonance Imaging, 24,* 833–841. (p. 197)

Silverman, K., Evans, S. M., Strain, E. C., & Griffiths, R. R. (1992). Withdrawal syndrome after the double-blind cessation of caffeine consumption. *New England Journal of Medicine, 327,* 1109–1114. (p. 117)

Silverman, P. S., & Retzlaff, P. D. (1986). Cognitive stage regression through hypnosis: Are earlier cognitive stages retrievable? *International Journal of Clinical and Experimental Hypnosis, 34,* 192–204. (p. 109)

Simek, T. C., & O'Brien, R. M. (1981). *Total golf: A behavioral approach to lowering your score and getting more out of your game.* Huntington, NY: B-MOD Associates. (p. 311)

Simek, T. C., & O'Brien, R. M. (1988). A chaining-mastery, discrimination training program to teach Little Leaguers to hit a baseball. *Human Performance, 1,* 73–84. (p. 311)

Simon, G. E., & Savarino, J. (2007). Suicide attempts among patients starting depression treatment with medications or psychotherapy. *American Journal of Psychiatry, 164,* 1029–1034. (p. 674)

Simon, G. E., Von Korff, M., Saunders, K., Miglioretti, D. L., Crane, P. K., van Belle, G., & Kessler, R. C. (2006). Association between obesity and psychiatric disorders in the U.S. population. *Archives of General Psychiatry, 63,* 824–830. (p. 458)

Simon, H. (1998, November 16). Flash of genius (interview with P. E. Ross). *Forbes,* pp. 98–104. (p. 491)

Simon, H. (2001, February). Quoted by A. M. Hayashi, When to trust your gut. *Harvard Business Review,* pp. 59–65. (p. 381)

Simons, D. J. (1996). In sight, out of mind: When object representations fail. *Psychological Science, 7,* 301–305. (p. 89)

Simons, D. J., & Ambinder, M. S. (2005). Change blindness: Theory and consequences. *Current Directions in Psychological Science, 14,* 44–48. (p. 89)

Simons, D. J., & Chabris, C. F. (1999). Gorillas in our midst: Sustained inattentional blindness for dynamic events. *Perception, 28,* 1059–1074. (p. 89)

Simonton, D. K. (1988). Age and outstanding achievement: What do we know after a century of research? *Psychological Bulletin, 104,* 251–267. (p. 215)

Simonton, D. K. (1990). Creativity in the later years: Optimistic prospects for achievement. *The Gerontologist, 30,* 626–631. (p. 215)

Simonton, D. K. (1992). The social context of career success and course for 2,026 scientists and inventors. *Personality and Social Psychology Bulletin, 18,* 452–463. (p. 410)

Simonton, D. K. (2000). Creativity: Cognitive, personal, developmental, and social aspects. *American Psychologist, 55,* 151–158. (p. 409)

Simonton, D. K. (2000). Methodological and theoretical orientation and the long-term disciplinary impact of 54 eminent psychologists. *Review of General Psychology, 4,* 13–24. (p. 321)

Sinclair, R. C., Hoffman, C., Mark, M. M., Martin, L. L., & Pickering, T. L. (1994). Construct accessibility and the misattribution of arousal: Schachter and Singer revisited. *Psychological Science, 5,* 15–18. (p. 506)

Singelis, T. M., Bond, M. H., Sharkey, W. F., & Lai, C. S. Y. (1999). Unpackaging culture's influence on self-esteem and embarrassability: The role of self-construals. *Journal of Cross-Cultural Psychology, 30,* 315–341. (p. 155)

Singelis, T. M., & Sharkey, W. F. (1995). Culture, self-construal, and embarrassability. *Cross-Cultural Psychology, 26,* 622–644. (p. 155)

Singer, J. L. (1981). Clinical intervention: New developments in methods and evaluation. In L. T. Benjamin, Jr. (Ed.), *The G. Stanley Hall Lecture Series* (Vol. 1). Washington, DC: American Psychological Association. (p. 664)

Singer, T., Seymour, B., O'Doherty, J., Kaube, H., Dolan, R. J., & Frith, C. (2004). Empathy for pain involves the affective but not sensory components of pain. *Science, 303,* 1157–1162. (pp. 256, 317)

Singh, D. (1993). Adaptive significance of female physical attractiveness: Role of waist-to-hip ratio. *Journal of Personality and Social Psychology, 65,* 293–307. (p. 145)

Singh, D. (1995). Female health, attractiveness, and desirability for relationships: Role of breast asymmetry and waist-to-hip ratio. *Ethology and Sociobiology, 16,* 465–481. (pp. 145, 723)

Singh, D., & Randall, P. K. (2007). Beauty is in the eye of the plastic surgeon: Waist-hip ration (WHR) and women's attractiveness. *Personality and Individual Differences, 43,* 329–340. (p. 145)

Singh, S. (1997). *Fermat's enigma: The epic quest to solve the world's greatest mathematical problem.* New York: Bantam Books. (p. 409)

Singh, S., & Riber, K. A. (1997, November). Fermat's last stand. *Scientific American,* pp. 68–73. (p. 410)

Singleton, D., Tate, A., & Kohout, J. (2003). *2002 Master's, specialist's, and related degrees employment survey.* Washington, DC: American Psychological Association. (p. A-4)

Sipski, M. L., & Alexander, C. J. (1999). Sexual response in women with spinal cord injuries: Implications for our understanding of the able bodied. *Journal of Sex and Marital Therapy, 25,* 11–22. (p. 55)

Sireteanu, R. (1999). Switching on the infant brain. *Science, 286,* 59, 61. (p. 273)

Sivard, R. L. (1996). *World military and social expenditures 1996* (16th ed.). Washington, DC: World Priorities. (p. 208)

Sjöstrum, L. (1980). Fat cells and body weight. In A. J. Stunkard (Ed.), *Obesity.* Philadelphia: Saunders. (p. 458)

Skinner, B. F. (1953). *Science and human behavior.* New York: Macmillan. (p. 305)

Skinner, B. F. (1956). A case history in scientific method. *American Psychologist, 11,* 221–233. (p. 306)

Skinner, B. F. (1957). *Verbal behavior.* Englewood Cliffs, NJ: Prentice-Hall. (p. 388)

Skinner, B. F. (1961, November). Teaching machines. *Scientific American,* pp. 91–102. (p. 305)

Skinner, B. F. (1983, September). Origins of a behaviorist. *Psychology Today,* pp. 22–33. (p. 310)

Skinner, B. F. (1985). *Cognitive science and behaviorism.* Unpublished manuscript, Harvard University. (p. 388)

Skinner, B. F. (1986). What is wrong with daily life in the Western world? *American Psychologist, 41,* 568–574. (p. 311)

Skinner, B. F. (1988). The school of the future. Address to the American Psychological Association convention. (p. 311)

Skinner, B. F. (1989). Teaching machines. *Science, 243,* 1535. (p. 311)

Skinner, B. F. (1990). Address to the American Psychological Association convention. (p. 308)

Skitka, L. J., Bauman, C. W., & Mullen, E. (2004). Political tolerance and coming to psychological closure following the September 11, 2001, terrorist attacks: An integrative approach. *Personality and Social Psychology Bulletin, 30,* 743–756. (p. 521)

Sklar, L. S., & Anisman, H. (1981). Stress and cancer. *Psychological Bulletin, 89,* 369–406. (p. 540)

Skoog, G., & Skoog, I. (1999). A 40-year follow-up of patients with obsessive-compulsive disorder. *Archives of General Psychiatry, 56,* 121–127. (p. 512)

Skov, R. B., & Sherman, S. J. (1986). Information-gathering processes: Diagnosticity, hypothesis-confirmatory strategies, and perceived hypothesis confirmation. *Journal of Experimental Social Psychology, 22,* 93–121. (p. 373)

Slatcher, R. B., & Pennebaker, J. W. (2006) How do I love thee? Let me count the words: The social effects of expressive writing, *Psychological Science, 17,* 660–664. (p. 726)

Slater, E., & Meyer, A. (1959). *Confinia psychiatra.* Basel: S. Karger AG. (p. 626)

Slater, L. (2000, November 19). How do you cure a sex addict? *New York Times Magazine* (www.nytimes.com). (p. 673)

Slater, M., Antley, A., Davison, A., Swapp, D., Guger, C., Barker C., Pistrang, N., & Sanchez-Vives, M. V. (2006). A virtual reprise of the Stanley Milgram obedience experiments. *PloS One, 1*(1): e39. Doi: 10.1371/journal.pone.0000039. (p. 694)

Slavin, R. E., & Braddock, J. H., III (1993, Summer). Ability grouping: On the wrong track. *The College Board Review,* pp. 11–18. (p. 426)

Sleep Foundation. (2006). The ABC's of back-to-school sleep schedules: The consequences of insufficient sleep. National Sleep Foundation (press release) (www.sleepfoundation.org). (p. 97)

Sloan, R. P. (2005). Field analysis of the literature on religion, spirituality, and health. Columbia University (available at www.metanexus.net/tarp). (p. 552)

Sloan, R. P., & Bagiella, E. (2002). Claims about religious involvement and health outcomes. *Annals of Behavioral Medicine, 24,* 14–21. (p. 552)

Sloan, R. P., Bagiella, E., & Powell, T. (1999). Religion, spirituality, and medicine. *Lancet, 353,* 664–667. (p. 552)

Sloan, R. P., Bagiella, E., VandeCreek, L., & Poulos, P. (2000). Should physicians prescribe religious activities? *New England Journal of Medicine, 342,* 1913–1917. (p. 552)

Slovic, P., Finucane, M., Peters, E., & MacGregor, D. G. (2002). The affect heuristic. In T. Gilovich, D. Griffin, & D. Kahneman (Eds.), *Intuitive judgment: Heuristics and biases.* New York: Cambridge University Press. (p. 119)

Small, M. F. (1997). Making connections. *American Scientist, 85,* 502–504. (p. 156)

Small, M. F. (2002, July). What you can learn from drunk monkeys. *Discover,* pp. 40–45. (p. 126)

Smedley, A., & Smedley, B. D. (2005). Race as biology is fiction, racism as a social problem is real: Anthropological and historical perspectives on the social construction of race. *American Psychologist, 60,* 16–26. (p. 437)

Smelser, N. J., & Mitchell, F. (Eds.). (2002). *Terrorism: Perspectives from the behavioral and social sciences.* Washington, DC: National Research Council, National Academies Press. (p. 709)

Smith, A. (1983). Personal correspondence. (p. 639)

Smith, C. (2006, January 7). Nearly 100, LSD's father ponders his "problem child." *New York Times* (www.nytimes.com). (pp. 122, 536)

Smith, E., & Delargy, M. (2005). Locked-in syndrome. *British Medical Journal, 330,* 406–409. (p. 523)

Smith, J. E., Waldorf, V. A., & Trembath, D. L. (1990). "Single white male looking for thin, very attractive . . ." *Sex Roles, 23,* 675–685. (p. 457)

Smith, M., Franz, E. A., Joy, S. M., & Whitehead, K. (2005). Superior performance of blind compared with sighted individuals on bimanual estimations of object size. *Psychological Science, 16,* 11–14. (p. 248)

Smith, M. B. (1978). Psychology and values. *Journal of Social Issues, 34,* 181–199. (p. 572)

Smith, M. L., Cottrell, G. W., Gosselin, F., & Schyns, P. G. (2005). Transmitting and decoding facial expressions. *Psychological Science, 16,* 184–189. (p. 511)

Smith, M. L., & Glass, G. V. (1977). Meta-analysis of psychotherapy outcome studies. *American Psychologist, 32,* 752–760. (p. 663)

Smith, M. L., Glass, G. V., & Miller, R. L. (1980). *The benefits of psychotherapy.* Baltimore: Johns Hopkins Press. (pp. 662, 663)

Smith, P. B., & Tayeb, M. (1989). Organizational structure and processes. In M. Bond (Ed.), *The cross-cultural challenge to social psychology.* Newbury Park, CA: Sage. (p. 495)

Smith, S. M., McIntosh, W. D., & Bazzini, D. G. (1999). Are the beautiful good in Hollywood? An investigation of the beauty-and-goodness stereotype on film. *Basic and Applied Social Psychology, 21,* 69–80. (p. 721)

Smith, T. B., Bartz, J., & Richards, P. S. (2007). Outcomes of religious and spiritual adaptations to psychotherapy: A meta-analytic review. *Psychotherapy Research, 17,* 643–655. (p. 669)

Smith, T. W. (1998, December). American sexual behavior: Trends, sociodemographic differences, and risk behavior (National Opinion Research Center GSS Topical Report No. 25). (pp. 470, 472, 473)

Smith, T. W. (2005). *Troubles in America: A study of negative life events across time and sub-groups* (GSS Topical Report No 40., National Opinion Research Center, University of Chicago). (p. 660)

Smith, T. W., & Ruiz, J. M. (2002). Psychosocial influences on the development and course of coronary heart disease: Current status and implications for research and practice. *Journal of Consulting and Clinical Psychology, 70,* 543–568. (p. 520)

Smolak, L., & Murnen, S. K. (2002). A meta-analytic examination of the relationship between child sexual abuse and eating disorders. *International Journal of Eating Disorders, 31,* 136–150. (p. 454)

Smoreda, Z., & Licoppe, C. (2000). Gender-specific use of the domestic telephone. *Social Psychology Quarterly, 63,* 238–252. (p. 159)

Snedeker, J., Geren, J., & Shafto, C. L. (2007). Starting over: International adoption as a natural experiment in language development. *Psychological Science, 18,* 79–86. (p. 388)

Snodgrass, S. E., Higgins, J. G., & Todisco, L. (1986). The effects of walking behavior on mood. Paper presented at the American Psychological Association convention. (p. 516)

Snowdon, D. A., Kemper, S. J., Mortimer, J. A., Greiner, L. H., Wekstein, D. R., & Markesbery, W. R. (1996). Linguistic ability in early life and cognitive function and Alzheimer's disease in late life: Finds from the Nun Study. *Journal of the American Medical Association, 275,* 528–532. (p. 424)

Snyder, F., & Scott, J. (1972). The psychophysiology of sleep. In N. S. Greenfield & R. A. Sterbach (Eds.), *Handbook of psychophysiology.* New York: Holt, Rinehart & Winston. (p. 105)

Snyder, M. (1984). When belief creates reality. In L. Berkowitz (Ed.), *Advances in experimental social psychology* (Vol. 18). New York: Academic Press. (p. 606)

Snyder, S. H. (1984). Neurosciences: An integrative discipline. *Science, 225,* 1255–1257. (p. 49)

Snyder, S. H. (1986). *Drugs and the brain.* New York: Scientific American Library. (p. 674)

Social Watch. (2006, March 8). No country in the world treats its women as well as its men (www.socialwatch.org). (p. 162)

Society for Personality Assessment. (2005). The status of the Rorschach in clinical and forensic practice: An official statement by the Board of Trustees of the Society for Personality Assessment. *Journal of Personality Assessment, 85,* 219–237. (p. 564)

Sokol, D. K., Moore, C. A., Rose, R. J., Williams, C. J., Reed, T., & Christian, J. C. (1995). Intrapair differences in personality and cognitive ability among young monozygotic twins distinguished by chorion type. *Behavior Genetics, 25,* 457–466. (p. 134)

Solomon, D. A., Keitner, G. I., Miller, I. W., Shea, M. T., & Keller, M. B. (1995). Course of illness and maintenance treatments for patients with bipolar disorder. *Journal of Clinical Psychiatry, 56,* 5–13. (p. 674)

Solomon, J. (1996, May 20). Breaking the silence. *Newsweek,* pp. 20–22. (p. 605)

Solomon, M. (1987, December). Standard issue. *Psychology Today,* pp. 30–31. (p. 721)

Sommer, R. (1969). *Personal space.* Englewood Cliffs, NJ: Prentice-Hall. (p. 153)

Söndergard, L., Kvist, K., Andersen, P. K., & Kessing, L. V. (2006). Do antidepressants prevent suicide? *International Clinical Psychopharmacology, 21,* 211–218. (p. 674)

Song, S. (2006, March 27). Mind over medicine. *Time,* p. 47. (p. 110)

Sontag, S. (1978). *Illness as metaphor.* New York: Farrar, Straus, & Giroux. (p. 540)

Soon, C. S., Brass, M., Heinze, H., & Haynes, J. (2008). Unconscious determinants of free decisions in the human brain. *Nature Neuroscience, 11,* 543–545. (p. 87)

Sørensen, H. J., Mortensen, E. L., Reinisch, J. M., & Mednick, S. A. (2005). Breastfeeding and risk of schizophrenia in the Copenhagen Perinatal Cohort. *Acta Psychiatrica Scandinavica, 112,* 26–29. (p. 638)

Sørensen, H. J., Mortensen, E. L., Reinisch, J. M., & Mednick, S. A. (2006). Height, weight, and body mass index in early adulthood and risk of schizophrenia. *Acta Psychiatrica Scandinavica, 114,* 49–54. (p. 638)

Sorkhabi, N. (2005). Applicability of Baumrind's parent typology to collective cultures: Analysis of cultural explanations of parent socialization effects. *International Journal of Behavioral Development, 29,* 552–563. (p. 193)

Soussignan, R. (2001). Duchenne smile, emotional experience, and autonomic reactivity: A test of the facial feedback hypothesis. *Emotion, 2,* 52–74. (p. 516)

South, S. C., Krueger, R. F., Johnson, W., & Iacono, W. G. (2008). Adolescent personality moderates genetic and environmental influences on relationships with parents. *Journal of Personality and Social Psychology, 94,* 899–912. (p. 193)

Sowell, T. (1991, May/June). Cultural diversity: A world view. *American Enterprise,* pp. 44–55. (p. 734)

Spalding, K. L., & 14 others. (2008). Dynamics of fat cell turnover in humans. *Nature, 453,* 783–787. (p. 458)

Spanos, N. P. (1982). A social psychological approach to hypnotic behavior. In G. Weary & H. L. Mirels (Eds.), *Integrations of clinical and social psychology.* New York: Oxford. (p. 109)

Spanos, N. P. (1986). Hypnosis, nonvolitional responding, and multiple personality: A social psychological perspective. *Progress in Experimental Personality Research, 14,* 1–62. (p. 619)

Spanos, N. P. (1991). Hypnosis, hypnotizability, and hypnotherapy. In C. R. Snyder & D. R. Forsyth (Eds.), *Handbook of social and clinical psychology: The health perspective.* New York: Pergamon Press. (p. 110)

Spanos, N. P. (1994). Multiple identity enactments and multiple personality disorder: A sociocognitive perspective. *Psychological Bulletin, 116,* 143–165. (pp. 111, 619)

Spanos, N. P. (1996). *Multiple identities and false memories: A sociocognitive perspective.* Washington, DC: American Psychological Association Books. (pp. 110, 111, 619)

Spanos, N. P., & Coe, W. C. (1992). A social-psychological approach to hypnosis. In E. Fromm & M. R. Nash (Eds.), *Contemporary hypnosis research.* New York: Guilford. (p. 110)

Spelke, E. (2005). Sex differences in intrinsic aptitude for mathematics and science? A critical review. *American Psychologist, 60,* 950–958. (p. 434)

Spelke, E. S., & Kinzler, K. D. (2007). Core knowledge. *Developmental Science, 10,* 89–96. (p. 179)

Spencer, J., Quinn, P. C., Johnson, M. H., & Karmiloff-Smith, A. (1997). Heads you win, tails you lose: Evidence for young infants categorizing mammals by head and facial attributes. *Early Development & Parenting, 6,* 113–126. (p. 172)

Spencer, K. M., Nestor, P. G., Perlmutter, R., Niznikiewicz, M. A., Klump, M. C., Frumin, M., Shenton, M. E., & McCarley, R. W. (2004). Neural synchrony indexes disordered perception and cognition in schizophrenia. *Proceedings of the National Academy of Sciences, 101,* 17288–17293. (p. 640)

Spencer, S. J., Steele, C. M., & Quinn, D. M. (1997). *Stereotype threat and women's math performance.* Unpublished manuscript, Hope College. (p. 439)

Sperling, G. (1960). The information available in brief visual presentations. *Psychological Monographs, 74* (Whole No. 498). (p. 336)

Sperry, R. W. (1964). Problems outstanding in the evolution of brain function. James Arthur Lecture, American Museum of Natural History, New York. Cited by R. Ornstein (1977), *The psychology of consciousness* (2nd ed.). New York: Harcourt Brace Jovanovich. (p. 75)

Sperry, R. W. (1985). Changed concepts of brain and consciousness: Some value implications. *Zygon, 20,* 41–57. (p. 239)

Sperry, R. W. (1992, Summer). Turnabout on consciousness: A mentalist view. *Journal of Mind & Behavior, 13*(3), 259–280. (p. 80)

Speth, J. G. (2008). Bridge at the edge of the world: Capitalism, the environment, and crossing from crisis to sustainability. New Haven, CT: Yale University Press. (p. 525)

Spiegel, D. (2007). The mind prepared: Hypnosis in surgery. *Journal of the National Cancer Institute, 99,* 1280–1281. (p. 110)

Spiegel, D. (2008, January 31). Coming apart: Trauma and the fragmentation of the self. Dana Foundation (www.dana.org). (p. 619)

Spiegel, K., Leproult, R., L'Hermite-Balériaux, M., Copinschi, G., Penev, P. D., & Van Cauter, E. (2004). Leptin levels are dependent on sleep duration: Relationships with sympathovagal balance, carbohydrate regulation, cortisol, and thyrotropin. *Journal of Clinical Endocrinology and Metabolism, 89,* 5762–5771. (p. 97)

Spiegel, K., Leproult, R., & Van Cauter, E. (1999). Impact of sleep debt on metabolic and endocrine function. *Lancet, 354,* 1435–1439. (p. 98)

Spielberger, C., & London, P. (1982). Rage boomerangs. *American Health, 1,* 52–56. (p. 536)

Spitzer, R. L., & Skodol, A. E. (2000). *DSM-IV-TR casebook: A learning companion to the Diagnostic and Statistical Manual of Mental Disorders, Fourth Edition, Text Revision.* Washington, DC: American Psychiatric Publications. (p. 623)

Spitzer, R. L., Skodol, A. E., & Gibbon, M. (1982). Reply. *Archives of General Psychiatry, 39,* 623–624. (p. 628)

Spradley, J. P., & Phillips, M. (1972). Culture and stress: A quantitative analysis. *American Anthropologist, 74,* 518–529. (p. 153)

Sprecher, S. (1989). The importance to males and females of physical attractiveness, earning potential, and expressiveness in initial attraction. *Sex Roles, 21,* 591–607. (p. 721)

Sprecher, S., & Sedikides, C. (1993). Gender differences in perceptions of emotionality: The case of close heterosexual relationships. *Sex Roles, 28,* 511–530. (p. 512)

Spring, B. (2007). Evidence-based practice in clinical psychology: Why it is, why it matters; what you need to know. *Journal of Clinical Psychology, 63,* 611–631. (p. 664)

Spring, B., Pingitore, R., Bourgeois, M., Kessler, K. H., & Bruckner, E. (1992). The effects and non-effects of skipping breakfast: Results of three studies. Paper presented at the American Psychological Association convention. (p. 463)

Squire, L. R. (1992). Memory and the hippocampus: A synthesis from findings with rats, monkeys, and humans. *Psychological Review, 99,* 195–231. (p. 343)

Srivastava, A., Locke, E. A., & Bartol, K. M. (2001). Money and subject well-being: It's not the money, it's the motives. *Journal of Personality and Social Psychology, 80,* 959–971. (p. 526)

Srivastava, S., John, O. P., Gosling, S. D., & Potter, J. (2003). Development of personality in early and middle adulthood: Set like plaster or persistent change? *Journal of Personality & Social Psychology, 84*, 1041–1053. (p. 579)

Srivastava, S., McGonigal, K. M., Richards, J. M., Butler, E. A., & Gross, J. J. (2006). Optimism in close relationships: How seeing things in a positive light makes them so. *Journal of Personality and Social Psychology, 91*, 143–153. (p. 587)

Stack, S. (1992). Marriage, family, religion, and suicide. In R. Maris, A. Berman, J. Maltsberger, & R. Yufit (Eds.), *Assessment and prediction of suicide.* New York: Guilford Press. (p. 630)

Stafford, R. S., MacDonald, E. A., & Finkelstein, S. N. (2001). National patterns of medication treatment for depression, 1987 to 2001. *Primary Care Companion Journal of Clinical Psychiatry, 3*, 232–235. (p. 673)

Stager, C. L., & Werker, J. F. (1997). Infants listen for more phonetic detail in speech perception than in word-learning tasks. *Nature, 388*, 381–382. (p. 386)

Stanford University Center for Narcolepsy. (2002). Narcolepsy is a serious medical disorder and a key to understanding other sleep disorders (www.med.stanford.edu/school/Psychiatry/narcolepsy). (p. 101)

Stanley, J. C. (1997). Varieties of intellectual talent. *Journal of Creative Behavior, 31*, 93–119. (p. 426)

Stanovich, K. (1996). *How to think straight about psychology.* New York: HarperCollins. (p. 558)

Staples, B. (1999a, May 2). When the 'paranoids' turn out to be right. *New York Times* (www.nytimes.com). (p. 704)

Staples, B. (1999b, May 24). Why 'racial profiling' will be tough to fight. *New York Times* (www.nytimes.com). (p. 704)

Stark, R. (2002). Physiology and faith: Addressing the "universal" gender difference in religious commitment. *Journal for the Scientific Study of Religion, 41*, 495–507. (p. 160)

Stark, R. (2003a). *For the glory of God: How monotheism led to reformations, science, witch-hunts, and the end of slavery.* Princeton, NJ: Princeton University Press. (p. 18)

Stark, R. (2003b, October–November). False conflict: Christianity is not only compatible with science—it created it. *American Enterprise,* pp. 27–33. (p. 18)

Starr, J. M., Deary, I. J., Lemmon, H., & Whalley, L. J. (2000). Mental ability age 11 years and health status age 77 years. *Age and Ageing, 29*, 523–528. (p. 424)

Stathopoulou, G., Powers, M. B., Berry, A. C., Smiths, J. A. J., & Otto, M. W. (2006). Exercise interventions for mental health: A quantitative and qualitative review. *Clinical Psychology: Science and Practice, 13*, 179–193. (p. 547)

Statistics Canada. (1999). *Statistical report on the health of Canadians.* Prepared by the Federal, Provincial and Territorial Advisory Committee on Population Health for the Meeting of Ministers of Health, Charlottetown, PEI, September 16–17, 1999. (p. 203)

Statistics Canada. (2002). (www.statcan.ca). (p. 152)

Statistics Canada (2007). Languages in Canada: 2001 Census (www.statcan.ca). (p. 394)

Statistics Canada (2007). Overweight and obesity, by province and territory, 2003 and 2005 (www.statcan.ca/english/freepub/16-253-XIE/2006000/t446_en.htm). (p. 456)

Staub, E. (1989). *The roots of evil: The psychological and cultural sources of genocide.* New York: Cambridge University Press. (p. 687)

Staub, E., & Vollhardt, J. (2008). Altruism born of suffering: The roots of caring and helping after experiences of personal and political victimization. *American Journal of Orthopsychiatry,* in press. (p. 614)

St. Clair, D., Xu, M., Wang, P., Yu, Y., Fang, Y., Zhang, F., Zheng, X., Gu, N., Feng, G., Sham, P., & He, L. (2005). Rates of adult schizophrenia following prenatal exposure to the Chinese famine of 1959–1961. *Journal of the American Medical Association, 294*, 557–562. (p. 640)

Steel, P., Schmidt, J., & Schultz, J. (2008). Refining the relationship between personality and subject well-being. *Psychological Bulletin, 134*, 138–161. (p. 529)

Steele, C. (1990, May). A conversation with Claude Steele. *APS Observer,* pp. 11–17. (p. 435)

Steele, C. M. (1995, August 31). Black students live down to expectations. *New York Times.* (p. 439)

Steele, C. M. (1997). A threat in the air: How stereotypes shape intellectual identity and performance. *American Psychologist, 52*, 613–629. (p. 439)

Steele, C. M., & Josephs, R. A. (1990). Alcohol myopia: Its prized and dangerous effects. *American Psychologist, 45*, 921–933. (p. 116)

Steele, C. M., Spencer, S. J., & Aronson, J. (2002). Contending with group image: The psychology of stereotype and social identity threat. *Advances in Experimental Social Psychology, 34*, 379–440. (p. 439)

Steele, J. (2000). Handedness in past human population: Skeletal markers. *Laterality, 5*, 193–220. (p. 79)

Steenhuysen, J. (2002, May 8). Bionic retina gives six patients partial sight. *Reuters News Service.* (See also www.optobionics.com/artificialretina.htm.) (p. 248)

Steinberg, L. (1987, September). Bound to bicker. *Psychology Today,* pp. 36–39. (p. 203)

Steinberg, L. (2007). Risk taking in adolescence: New perspectives from brain and behavioral science. *Current Directions in Psychological Science, 16*, 55–59. (p. 197)

Steinberg, L., & Morris, A. S. (2001). Adolescent development. *Annual Review of Psychology, 52*, 83–110. (pp. 193, 197, 203)

Steinberg, L., & Scott, E. S. (2003). Less guilty by reason of adolescence: Developmental immaturity, diminished responsibility, and the juvenile death penalty. *American Psychologist, 58*, 1009–1018. (p. 197)

Steinberg, N. (1993, February). Astonishing love stories (from an earlier United Press International report). *Games,* p. 47. (p. 719)

Steinhauer, J. (1999, November 29). Number of twins rises: So does parental stress. *New York Times* (www.nytimes.com). (p. 134)

Steinmetz, J. E. (1999). The localization of a simple type of learning and memory: The cerebellum and classical eyeblink conditioning. *Contemporary Psychology, 7*, 72–77. (p. 345)

Stengel, E. (1981). Suicide. In *The new Encyclopaedia Britannica, macropaedia* (Vol. 17, pp. 777–782). Chicago: Encyclopaedia Britannica. (p. 630)

Stern, M., & Karraker, K. H. (1989). Sex stereotyping of infants: A review of gender labeling studies. *Sex Roles, 20*, 501–522. (p. 277)

Stern, S. L., Dhanda, R., & Hazuda, H. P. (2001). Hopelessness predicts mortality in older Mexican and European Americans. *Psychosomatic Medicine, 63*, 344–351. (p. 544)

Sternberg, E. M. (2001). *The balance within: The science connecting health and emotions.* New York: Freeman. (p. 538)

Sternberg, E. M. (2006). A compassionate universe? *Science, 311*, 611–612. (p. 410)

Sternberg, R. J. (1985). *Beyond IQ: A triarchic theory of human intelligence.* New York: Cambridge University Press. (p. 408)

Sternberg, R. J. (1988). Applying cognitive theory to the testing and teaching of intelligence. *Applied Cognitive Psychology, 2*, 231–255. (p. 410)

Sternberg, R. J. (1999). The theory of successful intelligence. *Review of General Psychology, 3*, 292–316. (p. 408)

Sternberg, R. J. (2000). Presidential aptitude in science. (p. 408)

Sternberg, R. J. (Ed.). (2002). *Career paths in psychology: Where your degree can take you.* Washington, DC: American Psychological Association. (p. A-10)

Sternberg, R. J. (2003). Our research program validating the triarchic theory of successful intelligence: Reply to Gottfredson. *Intelligence, 31*, 399–413. (pp. 408, 410)

Sternberg, R. J. (2006). The Rainbow Project: Enhance the SAT through assessments of analytical, practical, and creative skills. *Intelligence, 34*, 321–350. (p. 408)

Sternberg, R. J. (2007, July 6). Finding students who are wise, practical, and creative. *The Chronicle Review* (www.chronicle.com). (p. 408)

Sternberg, R. J., & Grajek, S. (1984). The nature of love. *Journal of Personality and Social Psychology, 47*, 312–329. (p. 725)

Sternberg, R. J., & Grigorenko, E. L. (2000). Theme-park psychology: A case study regarding human intelligence and its implications for education. *Educational Psychology Review, 12*, 247–268. (p. 426)

Sternberg, R. J., Grigorenko, E. L., & Kidd, K. K. (2005). Intelligence, race, and genetics. *American Psychologist, 60*, 46–59. (p. 437)

Sternberg, R. J., & Kaufman, J. C. (1998). Human abilities. *Annual Review of Psychology, 49*, 479–502. (p. 404)

Sternberg, R. J., & Lubart, T. I. (1991). An investment theory of creativity and its development. *Human Development*, 1–31. (p. 410)

Sternberg, R. J., & Lubart, T. I. (1992). Buy low and sell high: An investment approach to creativity. *Psychological Science, 1*, 1–5. (p. 410)

Sternberg, R. J., & Wagner, R. K. (1993). The g-ocentric view of intelligence and job performance is wrong. *Current Directions in Psychological Science, 2*, 1–5. (p. 408)

Sternberg, R. J., Wagner, R. K., Williams, W. M., & Horvath, J. A. (1995). Testing common sense. *American Psychologist, 50*, 912–927. (p. 408)

Stetter, F., & Kupper, S. (2002). Autogenic training: A meta-analysis of clinical outcome studies. *Applied Psychophysiology and Biofeedback, 27*, 45–98. (p. 549)

Stevenson, H. W. (1992, December). Learning from Asian schools. *Scientific American*, pp. 70–76. (p. 437)

Stevenson, H. W., & Lee, S.-Y. (1990). Contexts of achievement: A study of American, Chinese, and Japanese children. *Monographs of the Society for Research in Child Development, 55* (Serial No. 221, Nos. 1–2). (p. 426)

Stevenson, R. J., & Tomiczek, C. (2007). Olfactory-induced synesthesias: A review and model. *Psychological Bulletin, 133*, 294–309. (p. 258)

Stewart, B. (2002, April 6). Recall of the wild. *New York Times* (www.nytimes.com). (p. 22)

Stice, E. (2002). Risk and maintenance factors for eating pathology: A meta-analytic review. *Psychological Bulletin, 128*, 825–848. (p. 454)

Stice, E., Shaw, H., & Marti, C. N. (2007). A meta-analytic review of eating disorder prevention programs: Encouraging findings. *Annual Review of Clinical Psychology, 3*, 233–257. (p. 455)

Stice, E., Spangler, D., & Agras, W. S. (2001). Exposure to media-portrayed thin-ideal images adversely affects vulnerable girls: A longitudinal experiment. *Journal of Social and Clinical Psychology, 20*, 270–288. (p. 455)

Stickgold, R. (2000, March 7). Quoted by S. Blakeslee, For better learning, researchers endorse "sleep on it" adage. *New York Times*, p. F2. (pp. 104, 105)

Stickgold, R., Hobson, J. A., Fosse, R., & Fosse, M. (2001). Sleep, learning, and dreams: Off-line memory processing. *Science, 294*, 1052–1057. (p. 104)

Stickgold, R., Malia, A., Maquire, D., Roddenberry, D., & O'Connor, M. (2000, October 13). Replaying the game: Hypnagogic images in normals and amnesics. *Science, 290*, 350–353. (p. 103)

Stinson, D. A., Logel, C., Zanna, M. P., Holmes, J. G., Camerson, J. J., Wood, J. V., & Spencer, S. J. (2008). The cost of lower self-esteem: Testing a self- and social-bonds model of health. *Journal of Personality and Social Psychology, 94*, 412–428. (p. 547)

Stipek, D. (1992). The child at school. In M. H. Bornstein & M. E. Lamb (Eds.), *Developmental psychology: An advanced textbook*. Hillsdale, NJ: Erlbaum. (p. 192)

Stith, S. M., Rosen, K. H., Middleton, K. A., Busch, A. L., Lunderberg, K., & Carlton, R. P. (2000). The intergenerational transmission of spouse abuse: A meta-analysis. *Journal of Marriage and the Family, 62*, 640–654. (p. 319)

Stockton, M. C., & Murnen, S. K. (1992). Gender and sexual arousal in response to sexual stimuli: A meta-analytic review. Paper presented at the American Psychological Society convention. (p. 469)

Stone, A. A., & Neale, J. M. (1984). Effects of severe daily events on mood. *Journal of Personality and Social Psychology, 46*, 137–144. (p. 522)

Stone, A. A., Schwartz, J. E., Broderick, J. E., & Shiffman, S. S. (2005). Variability of momentary pain predicts recall of weekly pain: A consequences of the peak (or salience) memory heuristic. *Personality and Social Psychology Bulletin, 31*, 1340–1346. (p. 255)

Stone, G. (2006, February 17). Homeless man discovered to be lawyer with amnesia. *ABC News* (abcnews.go.com). (p. 618)

Stone, R. (2005). In the wake: Looking for keys to posttraumatic stress. *Science, 310*, 1605. (p. 613)

Stoolmiller, M. (1999). Implications of the restricted range of family environments for estimates of heritability and nonshared environment in behavior-genetic adoption studies. *Psychological Bulletin, 125*, 392–409. (p. 137)

Stoppard, J. M., & Gruchy, C. D. G. (1993). Gender, context, and expression of positive emotion. *Personality and Social Psychology Bulletin, 19*, 143–150. (p. 512)

Storbeck, J., Robinson, M. D., & McCourt, M. E. (2006). Semantic processing precedes affect retrieval: The neurological case for cognitive primary in visual processing. *Review of General Psychology, 10*, 41–55. (p. 508)

Storm, L. (2000). Research note: Replicable evidence of psi: A revision of Milton's (1999) meta-analysis of the ganzfeld data bases. *Journal of Parapsychology, 64*, 411–416. (p. 284)

Storm, L. (2003). Remote viewing by committee: RV using a multiple agent/multiple percipient design. *Journal of Parapsychology, 67*, 325–342. (p. 284)

Storms, M. D. (1973). Videotape and the attribution process: Reversing actors' and observers' points of view. *Journal of Personality and Social Psychology, 27*, 165–175. (p. 683)

Storms, M. D. (1981). A theory of erotic orientation development. *Psychological Review, 88*, 340–353. (p. 475)

Storms, M. D. (1983). *Development of sexual orientation*. Washington, DC: Office of Social and Ethical Responsibility, American Psychological Association. (p. 474)

Storms, M. D., & Thomas, G. C. (1977). Reactions to physical closeness. *Journal of Personality and Social Psychology, 35*, 412–418. (p. 697)

Strack, F., Martin, L., & Stepper, S. (1988). Inhibiting and facilitating conditions of the human smile: A nonobtrusive test of the facial feedback hypothesis. *Journal of Personality and Social Psychology, 54*, 768–777. (p. 516)

Strack, S., & Coyne, J. C. (1983). Social confirmation of dysphoria: Shared and private reactions to depression. *Journal of Personality and Social Behavior, 44*, 798–806. (p. 634)

Strahan, E. J., Spencer, S. J., & Zanna, M. P. (2002). Subliminal priming and persuasion: Striking while the iron is hot. *Journal of Experimental Social Psychology, 38*, 556–568. (p. 229)

Stranahan, A. M., Khalil, D., & Gould, E. (2006). Social isolation delays the positive effects of running on adult neurogenesis. *Nature Neuroscience, 9*, 526–533. (p. 74)

Strand, S., Deary, I. J., & Smith, P. (2006). Sex differences in cognitive abilities test scores: A UK national picture. *British Journal of Educational Psychology, 76*, 463–480. (pp. 432, 435)

Stratton, G. M. (1896). Some preliminary experiments on vision without inversion of the retinal image. *Psychological Review, 3*, 611–617. (p. 274)

Straub, R. O., Seidenberg, M. S., Bever, T. G., & Terrace, H. S. (1979). Serial learning in the pigeon. *Journal of the Experimental Analysis of Behavior, 32*, 137–148. (p. 401)

Straus, M. A. (2008). Dominance and symmetry in partner violence by male and female university students in 32 nations. *Children and Youth Services Review, 30*, 252–275. (p. 158)

Straus, M. A., & Gelles, R. J. (1980). *Behind closed doors: Violence in the American family*. New York: Anchor/Doubleday. (p. 307)

Straus, M. A., Sugarman, D. B., & Giles-Sims, J. (1997). Spanking by parents and subsequent antisocial behavior of children. *Archives of Pediatric Adolescent Medicine, 151*, 761–767. (p. 307)

Strawbridge, W. J. (1999). Mortality and religious involvement: A review and critique of the results, the methods, and the measures. Paper presented at a Harvard University conference on religion and health, sponsored by the National Institute for Health Research and the John Templeton Foundation. (p. 553)

Strawbridge, W. J., Cohen, R. D., & Shema, S. J. (1997). Frequent attendance at religious services and mortality over 28 years. *American Journal of Public Health, 87*, 957–961. (p. 553)

Strawbridge, W. J., Shema, S. J., Cohen, R. D., & Kaplan, G. A. (2001). Religious attendance increases survival by improving and maintaining good health behaviors, mental health, and social relationships. *Annals of Behavioral Medicine, 23*, 68–74. (p. 553)

Strayer, D. L., & Drews, F. A. (2007). Cell-phone-induced driver distraction. *Current Directions in Psychological Science, 16*, 128–131. (p. 88)

Strayer, D. L., Drews, F. A., & Johnston, W. A. (2003). Cell phone-induced failures of visual attention during simulated driving. *Journal of Experimental Psychology: Applied, 9*, 23–32. (p. 88)

Strayer, D. L., & Johnston, W. A. (2001). Driven to distraction: Dual-task studies of simulated driving and conversing on a cellular telephone. *Psychological Science, 12*, 462–466. (p. 88)

Strenze, T. (2007). Intelligence and socioeconomic success: A meta-analytic review of longitudinal research. *Intelligence, 35*, 401–426. (p. 407)

Strickland, B. (1992, February 20). Gender differences in health and illness. Sigma Xi national lecture delivered at Hope College. (p. 208)

Striegel-Moore, R. H., Silberstein, L. R., & Rodin, J. (1993). The social self in bulimia nervosa: Public self-consciousness, social anxiety, and perceived fraudulence. *Journal of Abnormal Psychology, 102,* 297–303. (p. 454)

Striegel-Moore, R. M., & Bulik, C. M. (2007). Risk factors for eating disorders. *American Psychologist, 62,* 181–198. (pp. 454, 455)

Stroebe, M., Stroebe, W., & Schut, H. (2001). Gender differences in adjustment to bereavement: An empirical and theoretical review. *Review of General Psychology, 5,* 62–83. (p. 221)

Stroebe, M., Stroebe, W., Schut, H., Zech, E., & van den Bout, J. (2002). Does disclosure of emotions facilitate recovery from bereavement? Evidence from two prospective studies. *Journal of Consulting and Clinical Psychology, 70,* 169–178. (p. 221)

Stroebe, W., Schut, H., & Stroebe, M. S. (2005). Grief work, disclosure and counseling: Do they help the bereaved? *Clinical Psychology Review, 25,* 395–414. (p. 221)

Strupp, H. H. (1986). Psychotherapy: Research, practice, and public policy (How to avoid dead ends). *American Psychologist, 41,* 120–130. (p. 666)

Stumpf, H., & Jackson, D. N. (1994). Gender-related differences in cognitive abilities: Evidence from a medical school admissions testing program. *Personality and Individual Differences, 17,* 335–344. (p. 432)

Stumpf, H., & Stanley, J. C. (1998). Stability and change in gender-related differences on the College Board advanced placement and achievement tests. *Current Directions in Psychology, 7,* 192–196. (p. 433)

Stunkard, A. J., Harris, J. R., Pedersen, N. L., & McClearn, G. E. (1990). A separated twin study of the body mass index. *New England Journal of Medicine, 322,* 1483–1487. (p. 460)

Subiaul, F., Cantlon, J. F., Holloway, R. L., & Terrace, H. S. (2004). Cognitive imitation in rhesus macaques. *Science, 305,* 407–410. (p. 315)

Suddath, R. L., Christison, G. W., Torrey, E. F., Casanova, M. F., & Weinberger, D. R. (1990). Anatomical abnormalities in the brains of monozygotic twins discordant for schizophrenia. *New England Journal of Medicine, 322,* 789–794. (p. 642)

Sue, S. (2006). Research to address racial and ethnic disparities in mental health: Some lessons learned. In S. I. Donaldson, D. E. Berger, & K. Pezdek (Eds.), *Applied psychology: New frontiers and rewarding careers.* Mahwah, NJ: Erlbaum. (p. 668)

Suedfeld, P. (1998). Homo invictus: The indomitable species. *Canadian Psychology, 38,* 164–173. (p. 614)

Suedfeld, P. (2000). Reverberations of the Holocaust fifty years later: Psychology's contributions to understanding persecution and genocide. *Canadian Psychology, 41,* 1–9. (p. 614)

Suedfeld, P., & Mocellin, J. S. P. (1987). The "sensed presence" in unusual environments. *Environment and Behavior, 19,* 33–52. (p. 123)

Sugita, Y. (2004). Experience in early infancy is indispensable for color perception. *Current Biology. 14,* 1267–1271. (p. 270)

Suinn, R. M. (1997). Mental practice in sports psychology: Where have we been, where do we go? *Clinical Psychology: Science and Practice, 4,* 189–207. (p. 395)

Sullivan, P. F., Neale, M. C., & Kendler, K. S. (2000). Genetic epidemiology of major depression: Review and meta-analysis. *American Journal of Psychiatry, 157,* 1552–1562. (p. 629)

Suls, J. M., & Tesch, F. (1978). Students' preferences for information about their test performance: A social comparison study. *Journal of Experimental Social Psychology, 8,* 189–197. (p. 528)

Summers, M. (1996, December 9). Mister clean. *People Weekly,* pp. 139–142. (p. 597)

Sundet, J. M., Barlaug, D. G., & Torjussen, T. M. (2004). The end of the Flynn effect? A study of secular trends in mean intelligence test scores of Norwegian conscripts during half a century. *Intelligence, 32,* 349–362. (p. 420)

Sundstrom, E., De Meuse, K. P., & Futrell, D. (1990). Work teams: Applications and effectiveness. *American Psychologist, 45,* 120–133. (p. 496)

Suomi, S. J. (1986). Anxiety-like disorders in young nonhuman primates. In R. Gettleman (Ed.), *Anxiety disorders of childhood.* New York: Guilford Press. (p. 616)

Suomi, S. J. (1987). Genetic and maternal contributions to individual differences in rhesus monkey biobehavioral development. In N. A. Krasnegor &

others (Eds.), *Perinatal development: A psychobiological perspective.* Orlando, FL: Academic Press. (p. 561)

Super, C., & Super, D. (2001). *Education and training. Opportunities in psychology careers.* Chicago, IL: VGM Career Books. (p. A-4)

Suppes, P. (1982). Quoted by R. H. Ennis, Children's ability to handle Piaget XE "Piaget, J." 's propositional logic: A conceptual critique. In S. Modgil & C. Modgil (Eds.), *Jean Piaget: Consensus and controversy.* New York: Praeger. (p. 184)

Surgeon General. (1986). *The surgeon general's workshop on pornography and public health,* June 22–24. Report prepared by E. P. Mulvey & J. L. Haugaard and released by Office of the Surgeon General on August 4, 1986. (p. 714)

Surgeon General. (1999). *Mental health: A report of the surgeon general.* Rockville, MD: U.S. Department of Health and Human Services. (pp. 605, 631)

Surgeon General (2001). *The surgeon general's call to action to promote sexual health and responsible sexual behavior 2001.* Office of the Surgeon General (www.surgeongeneral.gov/library). (p. 470)

Susser, E. (1999). Life course cohort studies of schizophrenia. *Psychiatric Annals, 29,* 161–165. (p. 643)

Susser, E., Neugenbauer, R., Hoek, H. W., Brown, A. S., Lin, S., Labovitz, D., & Gorman, J. M. (1996). Schizophrenia after prenatal famine. *Archives of General Psychiatry, 53*(1), 25–31. (p. 640)

Susser, E. S., Herman, D. B., & Aaron, B. (2002, August). Combating the terror of terrorism. *Scientific American,* pp. 70–77. (p. 613)

Susskind, J. M., Lee, D. H., Cusi, A., Feiman, R., Grabski, W., & Anderson, A. K. (2008). Expressing fear enhances sensory acquisition. *Nature Neuroscience, 11,* 843–850. (p. 518)

Sutcliffe, J. S. (2008). Insights into the pathogenesis of autism. *Science, 321,* 208–209. (p. 182)

Sutherland, A. (2006). *Bitten and scratched: Life and lessons at the premier school for exotic animal trainers.* New York: Viking. (p. 312)

Svebak, S., Romundstad, S., & Holmen, J. (2007). Sense of humor and mortality: A seven-year prospective study of an unselected adult county population and a sub-population diagnosed with cancer. The Hunt study. Paper presented at the American Psychomatic Society 65th Annual Meeting, Budapest, Hungary. (p. 544)

Swann, Jr., W. B., Chang-Schneider, C., & McClarty, K. L. (2007). Do people's self-views matter: Self-concept and self-esteem in everyday life. *American Psychologist, 62,* 84–94. (p. 591)

Sweat, J. A., & Durm, M. W. (1993). Psychics: Do police departments really use them? *Skeptical Inquirer, 17,* 148–158. (p. 283)

Swerdlow, N. R., & Koob, G. F. (1987). Dopamine, schizophrenia, mania, and depression: Toward a unified hypothesis of cortico-stiato-pallido-thalamic function (with commentary). *Behavioral and Brain Sciences, 10,* 197–246. (p. 639)

Swim, J. K. (1994). Perceived versus meta-analytic effect sizes: An assessment of the accuracy of gender stereotypes. *Journal of Personality and Social Psychology, 66,* 21–36. (p. 704)

Symbaluk, D. G., Heth, C. D., Cameron, J., & Pierce, W. D. (1997). Social modeling, monetary incentives, and pain endurance: The role of self-efficacy and pain perception. *Personality and Social Psychology Bulletin, 23,* 258–269. (p. 256)

Symond, M. B., Harris, A. W. F., Gordon, E., & Williams, L. M. (2005). "Gamma synchrony" in first-episode schizophrenia: A disorder of temporal connectivity? *American Journal of Psychiatry, 162,* 459–465. (p. 640)

Symons, C. S., & Johnson, B. T. (1997). The self-reference effect in memory: A meta-analysis. *Psychological Bulletin, 121*(3), 371–394. (p. 332)

TADS (Treatment for Adolescents with Depression Study Team). (2004). Fluoxetine, cognitive-behavioral therapy, and their combination for adolescents with depression: Treatment for adolescents with depression study (TADS) randomized controlled trial. *Journal of the American Medical Association, 292,* 807–820. (p. 674)

Taha, F. A. (1972). A comparative study of how sighted and blind perceive the manifest content of dreams. *National Review of Social Sciences, 9*(3), 28. (p. 103)

Taheri, S. (2004). The genetics of sleep disorders. *Minerva Medica, 95,* 203–212. (pp. 98, 101)

Taheri, S. (2004a, 20 December). Does the lack of sleep make you fat? *University of Bristol Research News* (www.bristol.ac.uk). (p. 460)

Taheri, S., Lin, L., Austin, D., Young, T., & Mignot, E. (2004). Short sleep duration is associated with reduced leptin, elevated ghrelin, and increased body mass index. *PloS Medicine, 1*(3): e62. (p. 460)

Taheri, S., Zeitzer, J. M., & Mignot, E. (2002). The role of hypocretins (orexins) in sleep regulation and narcolepsy. *Annual Review of Neuroscience, 25*, 283-313. (p. 101)

Tajfel, H. (Ed.). (1982). *Social identity and intergroup relations.* New York: Cambridge University Press. (p. 707)

Talal, N. (1995). Quoted by V. Morell, Zeroing in on how hormones affect the immune system. *Science, 269*, 773-775. (p. 538)

Talarico, J. M., & Rubin, D. C. (2003). Confidence, not consistency, characterizes flashbulb memories. *Psychological Science, 14*, 455-461. (p. 341)

Talarico, J. M., & Rubin, D. C. (2007). Flashbulb memories are special after all; in phenomenology, not accuracy. *Applied Cognitive Psychology, 21*, 557-578. (p. 341)

Talbot, M. (2002, June 2). Hysteria hysteria. *New York Times* (www.nytimes.com). (p. 690)

Talwar, S. K., Xu, S., Hawley, E. S., Weiss, S. A., Moxon, K. A., & Chapin, J. K. (2002). Rat navigation guided by remote control. *Nature, 417*, 37-38. (p. 64)

Tamres, L. K., Janicki, D., & Helgeson, V. S. (2002). Sex differences in coping behavior: A meta-analytic review and an examination of relative coping. *Personality and Social Psychology Review, 6*, 2-30. (p. 160)

Tang, S-H., & Hall, V. C. (1995). The overjustification effect: A meta-analysis. *Applied Cognitive Psychology, 9*, 365-404. (p. 309)

Tangney, J. P., Baumeister, R. F., & Boone, A. L. (2004). High self-control predicts good adjustment, less pathology, better grades, and interpersonal success. *Journal of Personality, 72*, 271-324. (p. 585)

Tannen, D. (1990). *You just don't understand: Women and men in conversation.* New York: Morrow. (pp. 20, 159)

Tannenbaum, P. (2002, February). Quoted in R. Kubey & M. Csikszentmihalyi, Television addiction is no mere metaphor. *Scientific American*, pp. 74-80. (p. 231)

Tanner, J. M. (1978). *Fetus into man: Physical growth from conception to maturity.* Cambridge, MA: Harvard University Press. (p. 196)

Tarbert, J. (2004, May 14). Bad apples, bad command, or both? *Dart Center for Journalism and Trauma* (www.dartcenter.org). (p. 687)

Tarmann, A. (2002, May/June). Out of the closet and onto the Census long form. *Population Today, 30*, pp. 1, 6. (p. 473)

Tasbihsazan, R., Nettelbeck, T., & Kirby, N. (2003). Predictive validity of the Fagan test of infant intelligence. *British Journal of Developmental Psychology, 21*, 585-597. (p. 423)

Taub, E. (2004). Harnessing brain plasticity through behavioral techniques to produce new treatments in neurorehabilitation. *American Psychologist, 59*, 692-698. (p. 73)

Taubes, G. (2001). The soft science of dietary fat. *Science, 291*, 2536-2545. (p. 463)

Taubes, G. (2002, July 7). What if it's all been a big fat lie? *New York Times* (www.nytimes.com). (p. 463)

Tavris, C. (1982, November). Anger defused. *Psychology Today*, pp. 25-35. (p. 521)

Tavris, C., & Aronson, E. (2007). *Mistakes were made (but not by me).* Orlando, FL: Harcourt. (pp. 356, 688)

Taylor, P. J., Russ-Eft, D. F., & Chan, D. W. L. (2005). A meta-analytic review of behavior modeling training. *Journal of Applied Psychology, 90*, 692-709. (p. 318)

Taylor, S., Kuch, K., Koch, W. J., Crockett, D. J., & Passey, G. (1998). The structure of posttraumatic stress symptoms. *Journal of Abnormal Psychology, 107*, 154-160. (p. 613)

Taylor, S. E. (1989). *Positive illusions.* New York: Basic Books. (pp. 377, 593)

Taylor, S. E. (2002). *The tending instinct: How nurturing is essential to who we are and how we live.* New York: Times Books. (p. 160)

Taylor, S. E. (2006). Tend and befriend: Biobehavioral bases of affiliation under stress. *Current Directions in Psychological Science, 15*, 273-277. (p. 532)

Taylor, S. E., Cousino, L. K., Lewis, B. P., Gruenewald, T. L., Gurung, R. A. R., & Updegraff, J. A. (2000). Biobehavioral responses to stress in females: Tend-and-befriend, not fight-or-flight. *Psychological Review, 107*, 411-430. (p. 532)

Taylor, S. E., Pham, L. B., Rivkin, I. D., & Armor, D. A. (1998). Harnessing the imagination: Mental simulation, self-regulation, and coping. *American Psychologist, 53*, 429-439. (p. 396)

Taylor, S. P., & Chermack, S. T. (1993). Alcohol, drugs and human physical aggression. *Journal of Studies on Alcohol*, Supplement No. 11, 78-88. (p. 711)

Teasdale, T., & Owen, D. (2008). Secular declines in cognitive test scores: A reversal of the Flynn effect. *Intelligence, 36*, 121-126. (p. 420)

Teasdale, T. W., & Owen, D. R. (2005). A long-term rise and recent decline in intelligence test performance: The Flynn effect in reverse. *Personality and Individual Differences, 39*, 837-843. (p. 420)

Tedeschi, R. G., & Calhoun, L. G. (2004). Posttraumatic growth: Conceptual foundations and empirical evidence. *Psychological Inquiry, 15*, 1-18. (p. 614)

Teerlink, R., & Ozley, L. (2000). *More than a motorcycle: The leadership journey at Harley-Davidson.* Cambridge, MA: Harvard Business School Press. (p. 496)

Teghtsoonian, R. (1971). On the exponents in Stevens' law and the constant in Ekinan's law. *Psychological Review, 78*, 71-80. (p. 230)

Teicher, M. (2002). McLean motion and attention test (M-MAT): A new test to diagnose a troubling disorder. *McLean Hospital Annual Report* (www.mclean.harvard.edu). (p. 600)

Teicher, M. H. (2002, March). The neurobiology of child abuse. *Scientific American*, pp. 68-75. (p. 190)

Tenopyr, M. L. (1997). Improving the workplace: Industrial/organizational psychology as a career. In R. J. Sternberg (Ed.), *Career paths in psychology: Where your degree can take you.* Washington, DC: American Psychological Association. (p. 486)

Teran-Santos, J., Jimenez-Gomez, A., & Cordero-Guevara, J. (1999). The association between sleep apnea and the risk of traffic accidents. *New England Journal of Medicine, 340*, 847-851. (p. 101)

Terman, J. S., Terman, M., Lo, E.-S., & Cooper, T. B. (2001). Circadian time of morning light administration and therapeutic response in winter depression. *Archives of General Psychiatry, 58*, 69-73. (p. 666)

Terman, L. M. (1916). *The measurement of intelligence.* Boston: Houghton Mifflin. (p. 417)

Terman, M., Terman, J. S., & Ross, D. C. (1998). A controlled trial of timed bright light and negative air ionization for treatment of winter depression. *Archives of General Psychiatry, 55*, 875-882. (p. 666)

Terracciano, A., Costa, P. T., Jr., & McCrae, R. R. (2006). Personality plasticity after age 30. *Personality and Social Psychology Bulletin, 32*, 999-1009. (pp. 156, 223)

Terrace, H. S. (1979, November). How Nim Chimpsky changed my mind. *Psychology Today*, pp. 65-76. (p. 401)

Terre, L., & Stoddart, R. (2000). Cutting edge specialties for graduate study in psychology. *Eye on Psi Chi, 23-26.* (p. A-5)

Tesser, A., Forehand, R., Brody, G., & Long, N. (1989). Conflict: The role of calm and angry parent-child discussion in adolescent development. *Journal of Social and Clinical Psychology, 8*, 317-330. (p. 203)

Tetlock, P. E. (1988). Monitoring the integrative complexity of American and Soviet policy rhetoric: What can be learned? *Journal of Social Issues, 44*, 101-131. (p. 733)

Tetlock, P. E. (1998). Close-call counterfactuals and belief-system defenses: I was not almost wrong but I was almost right. *Journal of Personality and Social Psychology, 75*, 639-652. (p. 17)

Tetlock, P. E. (2005). *Expert political judgement: How good is it? How can we know?* Princeton, NJ: Princeton University Press. (p. 17)

Thaler, R. H., & Sunstein, C. R. (2008). *Nudge: Improving decisions about health, wealth, and happiness.* New Haven, CT: Yale University Press. (p. 382)

Thannickal, T. C., Moore, R. Y., Nienhuis, R., Ramanathan, L., Gulyani, S., Aldrich, M., Cornford, M., & Siegel, J. M. (2000). Reduced number of hypocretin neurons in human narcolepsy. *Neuron, 27*, 469-474. (p. 101)

Thatcher, R. W., Walker, R. A., & Giudice, S. (1987). Human cerebral hemispheres develop at different rates and ages. *Science, 236*, 1110-1113. (pp. 174, 222)

Thayer, R. E. (1987). Energy, tiredness, and tension effects of a sugar snack versus moderate exercise. *Journal of Personality and Social Psychology, 52,* 119–125. (p. 547)

Thayer, R. E. (1993). Mood and behavior (smoking and sugar snacking) following moderate exercise: A partial test of self-regulation theory. *Personality and Individual Differences, 14,* 97–104. (p. 547)

Théoret, H., Halligan, H., Kobayashi, M., Fregni, F., Tager-Flusberg, H., & Pascual-Leone, A. (2005). Impaired motor facilitation during action observation in individuals with autism spectrum disorder. *Current Biology, 15,* R84–R85. (p. 183)

Thernstrom, M. (2006, May 14). My pain, my brain. *New York Times* (www.nytimes.com). (p. 256)

Thiel, A., Hadedank, B., Herholz, K., Kessler, J., Winhuisen, L., Haupt, W. F., & Heiss, W.-D. (2006). From the left to the right: How the brain compensates progressive loss of language function. *Brain and Language, 98,* 57–65. (p. 73)

Thiele, T. E., Marsh, D. J., Ste. Marie, L., Bernstein, I. L., & Palmiter, R. D. (1998). Ethanol consumption and resistance are inversely related to neuropeptide Y levels. *Nature, 396,* 366–369. (p. 126)

Thomas, A., & Chess, S. (1977). *Temperament and development.* New York: Brunner/Mazel. (p. 137)

Thomas, A., & Chess, S. (1986). The New York Longitudinal Study: From infancy to early adult life. In R. Plomin & J. Dunn (Eds.), *The study of temperament: Changes, continuities, and challenges.* Hillsdale, NJ: Erlbaum. (p. 223)

Thomas, L. (1974). *The lives of a cell.* New York: Viking Press. (p. 260)

Thomas, L. (1983). *The youngest science: Notes of a medicine watcher.* New York: Viking Press. (p. 51)

Thomas, L. (1992). *The fragile species.* New York: Scribner's. (pp. 166, 389, 661)

Thompson, C. P., Frieman, J., & Cowan, T. (1993). Rajan's memory. Paper presented to the American Psychological Society convention. (p. 339)

Thompson, J. K., Jarvie, G. J., Lahey, B. B., & Cureton, K. J. (1982). Exercise and obesity: Etiology, physiology, and intervention. *Psychological Bulletin, 91,* 55–79. (p. 463)

Thompson, P. M., Cannon, T. D., Narr, K. L., van Erp, T., Poutanen, V.-P., Huttunen, M., Lönnqvist, J., Standerskjöld-Nordenstam, C.-G., Kaprio, J., Khaledy, M., Dail, R., Zoumalan, C. I., & Toga, A. W. (2001). Genetic influences on brain structure. *Nature Neuroscience, 4,* 1253–1258. (p. 428)

Thompson, P. M., Giedd, J. N., Woods, R. P., MacDonald, D., Evans, A. C., & Toga, A. W. (2000). Growth patterns in the developing brain detected by using continuum mechanical tensor maps. *Nature, 404,* 190–193. (p. 174)

Thompson, R., Emmorey, K., & Gollan, T. H. (2005). "Tip of the fingers" experiences by Deaf signers. *Psychological Science, 16,* 856–860. (p. 354)

Thomson, R., & Murachver, T. (2001). Predicting gender from electronic discourse. *British Journal of Social Psychology, 40,* 193–208 (and personal correspondence from T. Murachver, May 23, 2002). (p. 159)

Thorndike, A. L., & Hagen, E. P. (1977). *Measurement and evaluation in psychology and education.* New York: Macmillan. (p. 419)

Thorne, J., with Rothstein, L. (1993). *You are not alone: Words of experience and hope for the journey through depression.* New York: HarperPerennial. (p. 597)

Thornhill, R., & Gangestad, S. W. (1994). Human fluctuating asymmetry and sexual behavior. *Psychological Science, 5,* 297–302. (p. 723)

Thornton, B., & Moore, S. (1993). Physical attractiveness contrast effect: Implications for self-esteem and evaluations of the social self. *Personality and Social Psychology Bulletin, 19,* 474–480. (p. 722)

Thornton, G. C., III, & Rupp, D. E. (2005). *Assessment centers in human resource management: Strategies for prediction, diagnosis, and development.* Mahwah, NJ: Erlbaum. (p. 589)

Thorpe, W. H. (1974). *Animal nature and human nature.* London: Metheun. (p. 402)

Tickle, J. J., Hull, J. G., Sargent, J. D., Dalton, M. A., & Heatherton, T. F. (2006). A structural equation model of social influences and exposure to media smoking on adolescent smoking. *Basic and Applied Social Psychology, 28,* 117–129. (p. 119)

Tiedens, L. Z. (2001). Anger and advancement versus sadness and subjugation: The effect of negative emotion expressions on social status conferral. *Journal of Personality and Social Psychology, 80,* 86–94. (p. 521)

Tikkanen, T. (2001). Psychology in Europe: A growing profession with high standards and a bright future. *European Psychologist, 6,* 144–146. (p. 6)

Time. (1997, December 22). Greeting card association data, p. 19. (p. 159)

Time/CNN Survey. (1994, December 19). Vox pop: Happy holidays, *Time.* (p. 625)

Timlin, M. T., Pereira, M. A., Story, M., & Neumark-Sztainer, D. (2008). Breakfast eating and weight change in a 5-year prospective analysis of adolescents: Project EAT (Eating Among Teens). *Pediatrics, 121,* e638–e645. (p. 30)

Timmerman, T. A. (2007). "It was a thought pitch": Personal, situational, and target influences on hit-by-pitch events across time. *Journal of Applied Psychology, 92,* 876–884. (p. 712)

Tinbergen, N. (1951). *The study of instinct.* Oxford: Clarendon. (p. 444)

Tirrell, M. E. (1990). Personal communication. (p. 292)

Tolin, D. F., & Foa, E. B. (2006). Sex differences in trauma and posttraumatic stress disorder: A quantitative review of 25 years of research. *Psychological Bulletin, 132,* 959–992. (p. 614)

Tollefson, G. D., Fawcett, J., Winokur, G., Beasley, C. M., et al. (1993). Evaluation of suicidality during pharmacologic treatment of mood and nonmood disorders. *Annals of Clinical Psychiatry, 5*(4), 209–224. (p. 674)

Tollefson, G. D., Rampey, A. H., Beasley, C. M., & Enas, G. G. (1994). Absence of a relationship between adverse events and suicidality during pharmacotherapy for depression. *Journal of Clinical Psychopharmacology, 14,* 163–169. (p. 674)

Tolman, E. C., & Honzik, C. H. (1930). Introduction and removal of reward, and maze performance in rats. *University of California Publications in Psychology, 4,* 257–275. (p. 308)

Tolstoy, L. (1904). *My confessions.* Boston: Dana Estes. (p. 9)

Tondo, L., Jamison, K. R., & Baldessarini, R. J. (1997). Effect of lithium maintenance on suicidal behavior in major mood disorders. In D. M. Stoff & J. J. Mann (Eds.), *The neurobiology of suicide: From the bench to the clinic.* New York: New York Academy of Sciences. (p. 674)

Toni, N., Buchs, P.-A., Nikonenko, I., Bron, C. R., & Muller, D. (1999). LTP promotes formation of multiple spine synapses between a single axon terminal and a dendrite. *Nature, 402,* 421–442. (p. 340)

Torrey, E. F. (1986). *Witchdoctors and psychiatrists.* New York: Harper & Row. (p. 668)

Torrey, E. F., & Miller, J. (2002). *The invisible plague: The rise of mental illness from 1750 to the present.* New Brunswick, NJ: Rutgers University Press. (p. 640)

Torrey, E. F., Miller, J., Rawlings, R., & Yolken, R. H. (1997). Seasonality of births in schizophrenia and bipolar disorder: A review of the literature. *Schizophrenia Research, 28,* 1–38. (p. 640)

Totterdell, P., Kellett, S., Briner, R. B., & Teuchmann, K. (1998). Evidence of mood linkage in work groups. *Journal of Personality and Social Psychology, 74,* 1504–1515. (p. 690)

Towler, G. (1986). From zero to one hundred: Coaction in a natural setting. *Perceptual and Motor Skills, 62,* 377–378. (p. 697)

Tracey, J. L., & Robins, R. W. (2004). Show your pride: Evidence for a discrete emotion expression. *Psychological Science, 15,* 194–197. (p. 517)

Tramontana, M. G., Hooper, S. R., & Selzer, S. C. (1988). Research on the preschool prediction of later academic achievement: A review. *Developmental Review, 8,* 89–146. (p. 423)

Tranel, D., Bechara, A., & Denburg, N. L. (2002). Asymmetric functional roles of right and left ventromedial prefrontal cortices in social conduct, decision-making and emotional processing. *Cortex, 38,* 589–613. (p. 77)

Trautwein, U., Lüdtke, O., Köller, O., & Baumert, J. (2006). Self-esteem, academic self-concept, and achievement: How the learning environment moderates the dynamics of self-concept. *Journal of Personality and Social Psychology, 90,* 334–349. (p. 591)

Treffert, D. A., & Christensen, D. D. (2005, December). Inside the mind of a savant. *Scientific American.* (p. 406)

Treffert, D. A., & Wallace, G. L. (2002). Island of genius—The artistic brilliance and dazzling memory that sometimes accompany autism and other disorders hint at how all brains work. *Scientific American, 286,* 76–86. (p. 406)

Treisman, A. (1987). Properties, parts, and objects. In K. R. Boff, L. Kaufman, & J. P. Thomas (Eds.), *Handbook of perception and human performance.* New York: Wiley. (p. 263)

Tremblay, R. E., Pihl, R. O., Vitaro, F., & Dobkin, P. L. (1994). Predicting early onset of male antisocial behavior from preschool behavior. *Archives of General Psychiatry, 51,* 732–739. (p. 621)

Trewin, D. (2001). *Australian social trends 2001.* Canberra: Australian Bureau of Statistics. (pp. 162, 484)

Triandis, H. C. (1981). Some dimensions of intercultural variation and their implications for interpersonal behavior. Paper presented at the American Psychological Association convention. (p. 153)

Triandis, H. C. (1994). *Culture and social behavior.* New York: McGraw-Hill. (pp. 155, 586, 713)

Triandis, H. C., Bontempo, R., Villareal, M. J., Asai, M., & Lucca, N. (1988). Individualism and collectivism: Cross-cultural perspectives on self-ingroup relationships. *Journal of Personality and Social Psychology, 54,* 323–338. (p. 155)

Trickett, P. K., & McBride-Chang, C. (1995). The developmental impact of different forms of child abuse and neglect. *Developmental Review, 15,* 311–337. (p. 190)

Trillin, C. (2006, March 27). Alice off the page. *The New Yorker,* p. 44. (p. 571)

Trimble, J. E. (1994). Cultural variations in the use of alcohol and drugs. In W. J. Lonner & R. Malpass (Eds.), *Psychology and culture.* Boston: Allyn & Bacon. (p. 127)

Triplett, N. (1898). The dynamogenic factors in pacemaking and competition. *American Journal of Psychology, 9,* 507–533. (p. 697)

Trolier, T. K., & Hamilton, D. L. (1986). Variables influencing judgments of correlational relations. *Journal of Personality and Social Psychology, 50,* 879–888. (p. 32)

Troller, J. N., Anderson, T. M., Sachdev, P. S., Brodaty, H., & Andrews, G. (2007). Age shall not weary them: Mental health in the middle-aged and the elderly. *Australian and New Zealand Journal of Psychiatry, 41,* 581–589. (p. 219)

Trut, L. N. (1999). Early canid domestication: The farm-fox experiment. *American Scientist, 87,* 160–169. (p. 142)

Tsai, J. L., & Chentsova-Dutton, Y. (2003). Variation among European Americans in emotional facial expression. *Journal of Cross-Cultural Psychology, 34,* 650–657. (p. 515)

Tsai, J. L., Miao, F. F., Seppala, E., Fung, H. H., & Yeung, D. Y. (2007). Influence and adjustment goals: Sources of cultural differences in ideal affect. *Journal of Personality and Social Psychology, 92,* 1102–1117. (p. 515)

Tsang, Y. C. (1938). Hunger motivation in gastrectomized rats. *Journal of Comparative Psychology, 26,* 1–17. (p. 449)

Tsankova, N., Renthal, W., Kumar, A., & Nestler, E. J. (2007). Epigenetic regulation in psychiatric disorders. *Nature Reviews Neuroscience, 8,* 355–367. (p. 140)

Tse, D., Langston, R. F., Kakeyama, M., Bethus, I., Spooner P. A., Wood, E. R., Witter, M. P., & Morris, R. G. M. (2007). Schemas and memory consolidation. *Science, 316,* 76–82. (p. 344)

Tsien, J. Z. (2007, July). The memory code. *Scientific American,* pp. 52–59. (p. 339)

Tsuang, M. T., & Faraone, S. V. (1990). *The genetics of mood disorders.* Baltimore, MD: Johns Hopkins University Press. (p. 629)

Tuber, D. S., Miller, D. D., Caris, K. A., Halter, R., Linden, F., & Hennessy, M. B. (1999). Dogs in animal shelters: Problems, suggestions, and needed expertise. *Psychological Science, 10,* 379–386. (p. 22)

Tucker, K. A. (2002). I believe you can fly. *Gallup Management Journal* (www.gallupjournal.com/CA/st/20020520.asp). (p. 494)

Tuerk, P. W. (2005). Research in the high-stakes era: Achievement, resources, and No Child Left Behind. *Psychological Science, 16,* 419–425. (p. 431)

Tully, T. (2003). Reply: The myth of a myth. *Current Biology, 13,* R426. (p. 291)

Tumulty, K. (2006, March 27). The politics of fat. *Time,* pp. 40–43. (p. 462)

Turkheimer, E., Haley, A., Waldron, M., D'Onofrio, B., & Gottesman, I. I. (2003). Socioeconomic status modifies heritability of IQ in young children. *Psychological Science, 14,* 623–628. (pp. 430, 431)

Turner, J. C. (1987). *Rediscovering the social group: A self-categorization theory.* New York: Basil Blackwell. (p. 706)

Turner, J. C. (2007) Self-categorization theory. In R. Baumeister & K. Vohs (Eds.), *Encyclopedia of social psychology.* Thousand Oaks, CA: Sage. (p. 706)

Turner, N., Barling, J., & Zacharatos, A. (2002). Positive psychology at work. In C. R. Snyder & S. J. Lopez (Eds.), *The handbook of positive psychology.* New York: Oxford University Press. (p. 495)

Turpin, A. (2005, April 3). The science of psi. *FT Weekend,* pp. W1, W2. (p. 281)

Tutu, D. (1999). *No future without forgiveness.* New York: Doubleday. (p. 480)

Tversky, A. (1985, June). Quoted in K. McKean, Decisions, decisions. *Discover,* pp. 22–31. (p. 375)

Tversky, A., & Kahneman, D. (1974). Judgment under uncertainty: Heuristics and biases. *Science, 185,* 1124–1131. (p. 374)

Tversky, B. (2008, June/July). Glimpses of Chinese psychology: Reflections on the APS trip to China. *Observer,* pp. 13–14 (also at psychologicalscience.org/observer). (p. 6)

Twenge, J. (2006). *Generation me.* New York: Free Press. (pp. 594, 616)

Twenge, J. M. (1997). Changes in masculine and feminine traits over time: A meta-analysis. *Sex Roles 36*(5–6), 305–325. (p. 164)

Twenge, J. M., Baumeister, R. F., DeWall, C. N., Ciarocco, N. J., & Bartels, J. M. (2007). Social exclusion decreases prosocial behavior. *Journal of Personality and Social Psychology, 92,* 56–66. (p. 482)

Twenge, J. M., Baumeister, R. F., Tice, D. M., & Stucke, T. S. (2001). If you can't join them, beat them: Effects of social exclusion on aggressive behavior. *Journal of Personality and Social Psychology, 81,* 1058–1069. (pp. 482, 713)

Twenge, J. M., & Campbell, W. K. (2001). Age and birth cohort differences in self-esteem: A cross-temporal meta-analysis. *Personality and Social Psychology Review, 5,* 321–344. (p. 202)

Twenge, J. M., Catanese, K. R., & Baumeister, R. F. (2002). Social exclusion causes self-defeating behavior. *Journal of Personality and Social Psychology, 83,* 606–615. (pp. 482, 713)

Twenge, J. M., Catanese, K. R., & Baumeister, R. F. (2003). Social exclusion and the deconstructed state: Time perception, meaninglessness, lethargy, lack of emotion, and self-awareness. *Journal of Personality and Social Psychology, 85,* 409–423. (p. 713)

Twenge, J. M., Gentile, B., DeWall, C. D., Ma, D., & Lacefield, K. (2008). *A growing disturbance: Increasing psychopathology in young people 1938-2007 in a meta-analysis of the MMPI.* Unpublished manuscript, San Diego State University. (p. 628)

Twenge, J. M., Konrath, S., Foster, J. D., Campbell, W. K., & Bushman, B. J. (2008). Egos inflating over time: A cross-temporary meta-analysis of the Narcissistic Personality Inventory. *Journal of Personality, 76,* 875–902. (p. 594)

Twenge, J. M., & Nolen-Hoeksema, S. (2002). Age, gender, race, socioeconomic status, and birth cohort differences on the children's depression inventory: A meta-analysis. *Journal of Abnormal Psychology, 111,* 578–588. (p. 202)

Twiss, C., Tabb, S., & Crosby, F. (1989). Affirmative action and aggregate data: The importance of patterns in the perception of discrimination. In F. Blanchard & F. Crosby (Eds.), *Affirmative action: Social psychological perspectives.* New York: Springer-Verlag. (p. 31)

Tyler, K. A. (2002). Social and emotional outcomes of childhood sexual abuse: A review of recent research. *Aggression and Violent Behavior, 7,* 567–589. (p. 190)

Uchino, B. N., Cacioppo, J. T., & Kiecolt-Glaser, J. K. (1996). The relationship between social support and physiological processes: A review with emphasis on underlying mechanisms and implications for health. *Psychological Bulletin, 119,* 488–531. (p. 546)

Uchino, B. N., Uno, D., & Holt-Lunstad, J. (1999). Social support, physiological processes, and health. *Current Directions in Psychological Science, 8,* 145–148. (p. 546)

Uddin, L. Q., Kaplan, J. T., Molnar-Szakacs, I., Zaidel, E., & Iacoboni, M. (2005). Self-face recognition activates a frontoparietal "mirror" network in the right hemisphere: An event-related fMRI study. *NeuroImage, 25,* 926–935. (p. 78)

Uddin, L. Q., Molnar-Szakacs, II., Zaidel, E., & Iacoboni, M. (2006). rTMS to the right inferior parietal lobule disrupts self-other discrimination. *Social Cognitive Affective Neuroscience, 1,* 65–71. (p. 78)

Udry, J. R. (2000). Biological limits of gender construction. *American Sociological Review, 65,* 443–457. (p. 161)

Uga, V., Lemut, M. C., Zampi, C., Zilli, I., & Salzarulo, P. (2006). Music in dreams. *Consciousness and Cognition, 15,* 351–357. (p. 103)

UK ECT Review Group. (2003). Efficacy and safety of electroconvulsive therapy in depressive disorders: A systematic review and meta-analysis. *Lancet, 361,* 799–808. (p. 675)

Ullman, E. (2005, October 19). The boss in the machine. *New York Times* (www.nytimes.com). (p. 484)

Ulrich, R. E. (1991). Animal rights, animal wrongs and the question of balance. *Psychological Science, 2,* 197–201. (p. 21)

UNAIDS. (2005). *AIDS epidemic update, December 2005.* United Nations (www.unaids.org). (p. 540)

UNAIDS. (2008). *Report on the global AIDS epidemic.* United Nations (www.unaids.org). (p. 539)

UNICEF (2006). *The state of the world's children 2007.* New York: UNICEF. (p. 162)

Unsworth, N., & Engle, R. W. (2007). The nature of individual differences in working memory capacity: Active maintenance in primary memory and controlled search from secondary memory. *Psychological Review, 114,* 104–132. (p. 326)

Urbany, J. E., Bearden, W. O., & Weilbaker, D. C. (1988). The effect of plausible and exaggerated reference prices on consumer perceptions and price search. *Journal of Consumer Research, 15,* 95–110. (p. 381)

Urry, H. L., Nitschke, J. B., Dolski, I., Jackson, D. C., Dalton, K. M., Mueller, C. J., Rosenkranz, M. A., Ryff, C. D., Singer, B. H., & Davidson, R. J. (2004). Making a life worth living: Neural correlates of well-being. *Psychological Science, 15,* 367–372. (p. 503)

Ursu, S., Stenger, V. A., Shear, M. K., Jones, M. R., & Carter, C. S. (2003). Overactive action monitoring in obsessive-compulsive disorder: Evidence from functional magnetic resonance imaging. *Psychological Science, 14,* 347–353. (p. 616)

USAID. (2004, January). *The ABCs of HIV prevention.* www.usaid.gov. (p. 540)

U. S. Bureau of Labor Statistics (U.S. Department of Labor). (2008). *Occupational outlook handbook,* 2008–09 edition, Psychologists (http://www.bls.gov/oco/ocos056.htm). (pp. A-1, A-3)

U. S. Department of State (2004, April). *Patterns of global terrorism 2003: Appendix G.* (www.state.gov). (p. 376)

U. S. Senate Select Committee on Intelligence (2004, July 9). *Report of the U.S. intelligence community's prewar intelligence assessments on Iraq.* www.gpoaccess.gov/serialset/creports/iraq.html. (pp. 25, 373, 700)

Uttal, W. R. (2001). *The new phrenology: The limits of localizing cognitive processes in the brain.* Cambridge, MA: MIT Press. (p. 72)

Vaidya, J. G., Gray, E. K., Haig, J., & Watson, D. (2002). On the temporal stability of personality: Evidence for differential stability and the role of life experiences. *Journal of Personality and Social Psychology, 83,* 1469–1484. (p. 579)

Vaillant, G. E. (1977). *Adaptation to life.* New York: Little, Brown. (p. 361)

Vaillant, G. E. (2002). Aging well: Surprising guideposts to a happier life from the landmark Harvard study of adult development. Boston: Little, Brown. (p. 545)

Valdes, A. M., Andrew, T., Gardner, J. P., Kimura, M., Oelsner, E., Cherkas, L. F., Aviv, A., & Spector, T. D. (2005). Obesity, cigarette smoking, and telomere length in women. *Lancet, 366,* 662–664. (p. 208)

Valenstein, E. S. (1986). *Great and desperate cures: The rise and decline of psychosurgery.* New York: Basic Books. (p. 678)

Vallone, R. P., Griffin, D. W., Lin, S., & Ross, L. (1990). Overconfident prediction of future actions and outcomes by self and others. *Journal of Personality and Social Psychology, 58,* 582–592. (p. 16)

van Boxtel, H. W., Orobio de Castro, B., & Goossens, F. A. (2004). High self-perceived social competence in rejected children is related to frequent fighting. *European Journal of Developmental Psychology, 1,* 205–214. (p. 593)

Van Cauter, E., Holmback, U., Knutson, K., Leproult, R., Miller, A., Nedeltcheva, A., Pannain, S., Penev, P., Tasali, E., & Spiegel, K. (2007). Impact of sleep and sleep loss on neuroendocrine and metabolic function. *Hormone Research, 67*(1), Supp. 1: 2–9. (p. 97)

van den Boom, D. (1990). Preventive intervention and the quality of mother-infant interaction and infant exploration in irritable infants. In W. Koops, H. J. G. Soppe, J. L. van der Linden, P. C. M. Molenaar, & J. J. F. Schroots (Eds.), *Developmental psychology research in The Netherlands.* The Netherlands: Uitgeverij Eburon. Cited by C. Hazan & P. R. Shaver (1994). Deeper into attachment theory. *Psychological Inquiry, 5,* 68–79. (p. 188)

van den Boom, D. C. (1995). Do first-year intervention effects endure? Follow-up during toddlerhood of a sample of Dutch irritable infants. *Child Development, 66,* 1798–1816. (p. 188)

van den Bos, K., & Spruijt, N. (2002). Appropriateness of decisions as a moderator of the psychology of voice. *European Journal of Social Psychology, 32,* 57–72. (p. 496)

Van der Maas, H. L. J., Dolan, C. V., Raoul, P. P. P., Grasman, R. P. P. P., Wicherts, J. M., Huizenga, H. M., & Raijmakers, M. E. J. (2006). A dynamical model of general intelligence: The positive manifold of intelligence by mutualism. *Psychological Review, 113,* 842–861. (p. 406)

Van der Werf, S. Y., Kaptein, K. I., de Jonge, P., Spijker, J., de Graaf, R., & Korf, J. (2006). Major depressive episodes and random mood. *Archives of General Psychiatry, 63,* 509–518. (p. 628)

Van Dyke, C., & Byck, R. (1982, March). Cocaine. *Scientific American,* pp. 128–141. (p. 121)

van Engen, M. L., & Willemsen, T. M. (2004). Sex and leadership styles: A meta-analysis of research published in the 1990s. *Psychological Reports, 94,* 3–18. (p. 158)

Van Goozen, S. H. M., Fairchild, G., Snoek, H., & Harold, G. T. (2007). The evidence for a neurobiological model of childhood antisocial behavior. *Psychological Bulletin, 133,* 149–182. (p. 621)

van Hemert, D. A., Poortinga, Y. H., & van de Vijver, F. J. R. (2007). Emotion and culture: A meta-analysis. *Cognition and Emotion, 21,* 913–943. (p. 515)

Van IJzendoorn, M. H., & Juffer, F. (2005). Adoption is a successful natural intervention enhancing adopted children's IQ and school performance. *Current Directions in Psychological Science, 14,* 326–330. (p. 428)

Van IJzendoorn, M. H., & Juffer, F. (2006). The Emanual Miller Memorial Lecture 2006: Adoption as intervention. Meta-analytic evidence for massive catch-up and plasticity in physical, socio-emotional, and cognitive development. *Journal of Child Psychology and Psychiatry, 47,* 1228–1245. (pp. 137, 428)

van IJzendoorn, M. H., & Kroonenberg, P. M. (1988). Cross-cultural patterns of attachment: A meta-analysis of the strange situation. *Child Development, 59,* 147–156. (p. 187)

Van Leeuwen, M. S. (1978). A cross-cultural examination of psychological differentiation in males and females. *International Journal of Psychology, 13,* 87–122. (p. 162)

Van Lommel, P., van Wees, R., Meyers, V., & Elfferich, I. (2001). Near-death experience in survivors of cardiac arrest: A prospective study in the Netherlands. *Lancet, 358,* 2039–2045. (p. 123)

Van Rooy, D. L., & Viswesvaran, C. (2004). Emotional intelligence: A meta-analytic investigation of predictive validity and nomological net. *Journal of Vocational Behavior, 65,* 71–95. (p. 411)

van Schaik, C. P., Ancrenaz, M., Borgen, G., Galdikas, B., Knott, C. D., Singleton, I., Suzuki, A., Utami, S. S., & Merrill, M. (2003). Orangutan cultures and the evolution of material culture. *Science, 299,* 102–105. (p. 398)

Van Tassel-Baska, J. (1983). Profiles of precocity: The 1982 Midwest Talent Search finalists. *Gifted Child Quarterly, 27,* 139–145. (p. 423)

Van Yperen, N. W., & Buunk, B. P. (1990). A longitudinal study of equity and satisfaction in intimate relationships. *European Journal of Social Psychology, 20,* 287–309. (p. 725)

Van Zeijl, J., Mesman, J., Van IJzendoorn, M. H., Bakermans-Kranenburg, M. J., Juffer, F., Stolk, M. N., Koot, H. M., & Alink, L. R. A. (2006). Attachment-based intervention for enhancing sensitive discipline in mothers of 1- to 3-year-old children at risk for externalizing behavior problems: A randomized controlled trial. *Journal of Consulting and Clinical Psychology, 74,* 994–1005. (p. 188)

Vance, E. B., & Wagner, N. N. (1976). Written descriptions of orgasm: A study of sex differences. *Archives of Sexual Behavior, 5,* 87–98. (p. 466)

Vandenberg, S. G., & Kuse, A. R. (1978). Mental rotations: A group test of three-dimensional spatial visualization. *Perceptual and Motor Skills, 47,* 599–604. (p. 434)

Vanman, E. J., Saltz, J. L., Nathan, L. R., & Warren, J. A. (2004). Racial discrimination by low-prejudiced Whites. *Psychological Science, 15,* 711–714. (p. 705)

Vaughn, K. B., & Lanzetta, J. T. (1981). The effect of modification of expressive displays on vicarious emotional arousal. *Journal of Experimental Social Psychology, 17*, 16–30. (p. 516)

Vazire, S., & Gosling, S. D. (2004). e-Perceptions: Personality impressions based on personal websites. *Journal of Personality and Social Psychology, 87*, 123–132. (p. 581)

Vecera, S. P., Vogel, E. K., & Woodman, G. F. (2002). Lower region: A new cue for figure-ground assignment. *Journal of Experimental Psychology: General, 13*, 194–205. (p. 266)

Vega, V., & Malamuth, N. M. (2007). Predicting sexaul aggression: The role of pornography in the context of general and specific risk factors. *Aggressive Behavior, 33*, 104–117. (p. 714)

Vekassy, L. (1977). Dreams of the blind. *Magyar Pszichologiai Szemle, 34*, 478–491. (p. 103)

Velliste, M., Perel, S., Spalding, M. C., Whitford, A. S., & Schwartz, A. B. (2008). Cortical control of a prosthetic arm for self-feeding. *Nature, 453*, 1098–1101. (pp. 69, 70)

Verbeek, M. E. M., Drent, P. J., & Wiepkema, P. R. (1994). Consistent individual differences in early exploratory behaviour of male great tits. *Animal Behaviour, 48*, 1113–1121. (p. 576)

Verhaeghen, P., & Salthouse, T. A. (1997). Meta-analyses of age-cognition relations in adulthood: Estimates of linear and nonlinear age effects and structural models. *Psychological Bulletin, 122*, 231–249. (p. 210)

Vernon, P. A. (1983). Speed of information processing and general intelligence. *Intelligence, 7*, 53–70. (p. 414)

Vertes, R., & Siegel, J. (2005). Time for the sleep community to take a critical look at the purported role of sleep in memory processing. *Sleep, 28*, 1228–1229. (p. 104)

Vigil, J. M., Geary, D. C., & Byrd-Craven, J. (2005). A life history assessment of early childhood sexual abuse in women. *Developmental Psychology, 41*, 553–561. (p. 196)

Vigliocco, G., & Hartsuiker, R. J. (2002). The interplay of meaning, sound, and syntax in sentence production. *Psychological Bulletin, 128*, 442–472. (p. 386)

Vining, E. P. G., Freeman, J. M., Pillas, D. J., Uematsu, S., Carson, B. S., Brandt, J., Boatman, D., Pulsifer, M. B., & Zukerberg, A. (1997). Why would you remove half a brain? The outcome of 58 children after hemispherectomy—The Johns Hopkins Experience: 1968 to 1996. *Pediatrics, 100*, 163–171, (p. 73)

Vita, A. J., Terry, R. B., Hubert, H. B., & Fries, J. F. (1998). Aging, health risks, and cumulative disability. *New England Journal of Medicine, 338*, 1035–1041. (p. 120)

Vitello, P. (2006, June 12). A ring tone meant to fall on deaf ears. *New York Times* (www.nytimes.com). (p. 209)

Vitevitch, M. S. (2003). Change deafness: The inability to detect changes between two voices. *Journal of Experimental Psychology: Human Perception and Performance, 29*, 333–342. (p. 89)

Vittengl, J. R., Clark, L. A., Dunn, T. W., & Jarrett, R. B. (2007). Reducing relapse and recurrence in unipolar depression: A comparative meta-analysis of cognitive-behavioral therapy's effects. *Journal of Consulting and Clinical Psychology, 75*, 475–488. (p. 674)

Voas, D. (2008, March/April). Ten million marriages: An astrological detective story. *Skeptical Inquirer*, pp. 52–55. (p. 578)

Vogel, S. (1999). *The skinny on fat: Our obsession with weight control*. New York: W. H. Freeman. (p. 140)

von Békésy, G. (1957, August). The ear. *Scientific American*, pp. 66–78. (p. 246)

von Hippel, W. (2007). Aging, executive functioning, and social control. *Current Directions in Psychological Science, 16*, 240–244. (p. 210)

von Senden, M. (1932: *The perception of space and shape in the congenitally blind before and after operation*. Glencoe, IL: Free Press. (p. 272)

Voyer, D., Postma, A., Brake, B., & Imperato-McGinley, J. (2007). Gender differences in object location memory: A meta-analysis. *Psychonomic Bulletin & Review, 14*, 23–38. (p. 432)

Vroom, V. H., & Jago, A. G. (2007). The role of the situation in leadership. *American Psychologist, 62*, 17–24. (p. 495)

Vyazovskiy, V. V., Cirelli, C., Pfister-Genskow, M., Faraguna, U., & Tononi, G. (2008). Molecular and electrophysiological evidence for net synaptic potentiation in wake and depression in sleep. *Nature Neuroscience, 11*, 200–208. (p. 99)

Waber, R. L., Shiv, B., Carmon, & Ariely, D. (2008). Commercial features of placebo and therapeutic efficacy. *Journal of the American Medical Association, 299*, 1016–1017. (p. 35)

Wacker, J., Chavanon, M.-L., & Stemmler, G. (2006). Investigating the dopaminergic basis of extraversion in humans: A multilevel approach. *Journal of Personality and Social Psychology, 91*, 177–187. (p. 576)

Wadden, T. A., Vogt, R. A., Foster, G. D., & Anderson, D. A. (1998). Exercise and the maintenance of weight loss: 1-year follow-up of a controlled clinical trial. *Journal of Consulting and Clinical Psychology, 66*, 429–433. (p. 463)

Wade, K. A., Garry, M., Read, J. D., & Lindsay, D. S. (2002). A picture is worth a thousand lies: Using false photographs to create false childhood memories. *Psychonomic Bulletin & Review, 9*, 597–603. (p. 358)

Wade, N. G., Worthington, E. L., Jr., & Vogel, D. L. (2006). Effectiveness of religiously tailored interventions in Christian therapy. *Psychotherapy Research, 17*, 91–105. (p. 669)

Wagar, B. M., & Cohen, D. (2003). Culture, memory, and the self: An analysis of the personal and collective self in long-term memory. *Journal of Experimental Social Psychology, 39*, 458–475. (p. 332)

Wager, T. D. (2005). The neural bases of placebo effects in pain. *Current Directions in Psychological Science, 14*, 175–179. (p. 256)

Wagner, U., Gais, S., Haider, H., Verleger, R., & Born, J. (2004). Sleep inspires insight. *Nature, 427*, 352–355. (p. 100)

Wagstaff, G. (1982). Attitudes to rape: The "just world" strikes again? *Bulletin of the British Psychological Society, 13*, 275–283. (p. 684)

Wahlberg, D. (2001, October 11). We're more depressed, patriotic, poll finds. *Grand Rapids Press*, p. A15. (p. 533)

Wai, J., Lubinski, D., & Benbow, C. P. (2005). Creativity and occupational accomplishments among intellectually precocious youths: An age 13 to age 33 longitudinal study. *Journal of Educational Psychology, 97*, 484–492. (p. 426)

Wakefield, J. C. (1992). Disorder as a harmful dysfunction: A conceptual critique of DSM-III-R's definition of mental disorder. *Psychological Review, 99*, 232–247. (p. 600)

Wakefield, J. C. (2006). What makes a mental disorder mental? *Philosophy, Psychiatry, and Psychology, 13*, 123–131. (p. 600)

Wakefield, J. C., Schmitz, M.F., First, M. B., & Horwitz, A. V. (2007). Extending the bereavement exclusion for major depression to other losses: Evidence from the National Comorbidity Survey. *Archives of General Psychiatry, 64*, 433–440. (p. 625)

Wakefield, J. C., & Spitzer, R. L. (2002). Lowered estimates—but of what? *Archives of General Psychiatry, 59*, 129–130. (p. 613)

Walker, M. P., & Stickgold, R. (2006). Sleep, memory, and plasticity. *Annual Review of Psychology, 57*, 139–166. (p. 100)

Walker, W. R., Skowronski, J. J., & Thompson, C. P. (2003). Life is pleasant—and memory helps to keep it that way! *Review of General Psychology, 7*, 203–210. (p. 220)

Wall, P. D. (2000). *Pain: The science of suffering*. New York: Columbia University Press. (p. 254)

Wallace, D. S., Paulson, R. M., Lord, C. G., & Bond, C. F., Jr. (2005). Which behaviors do attitudes predict? Meta-analyzing the effects of social pressure and perceived difficulty. *Review of General Psychology, 9(3)*, 214–227. (p. 685)

Wallach, M. A., & Wallach, L. (1983). Psychology's sanction for selfishness: The error of egoism in theory and therapy. New York: Freeman. (p. 572)

Wallach, M. A., & Wallach, L. (1985, February). How psychology sanctions the cult of the self. *Washington Monthly*, pp. 46–56. (p. 572)

Walsh, T., & 35 others. (2008). Rare structural variants disrupt multiple genes in neurodevelopmental pathways in schizophrenia. *Science, 320*, 539–543. (p. 642)

Walster (Hatfield), E., Aronson, V., Abrahams, D., & Rottman, L. (1966). Importance of physical attractiveness in dating behavior. *Journal of Personality and Social Psychology, 4*, 508–516. (p. 721)

Wampold, B. E. (2001). *The great psychotherapy debate: Models, methods, and findings*. Mahwah, NJ: Erlbaum. (p. 666)

Wampold, B. E. (2007). Psychotherapy: The humanistic (and effective) treatment. *American Psychologist, 62*, 857–873. (pp. 663, 666)

Wampold, B. E., Mondin, G. W., Moody, M., & Ahn, H. (1997). The flat earth as a metaphor for the evidence for uniform efficacy of bona fide psychotherapies: Reply to Crits-Christoph (1997) and Howard et al. (1997). *Psychological Bulletin, 122,* 226–230. (p. 663)

Wang, S-H., Baillargeon, R., & Brueckner, L. (2004). Young infants' reasoning about hidden objects: Evidence from violation-of-expectation tasks with test trials only. *Cognition, 93,* 167–198. (p. 179)

Wansink, B., & van Ittersum, K. (2003). Bottoms up! The influence of elongation on pouring and consumption volume. *Journal of Consumer Research, 30,* 455–464. (p. 265)

Wansink, B., & van Ittersum, K. (2005). Shape of glass and amount of alcohol poured: Comparative study of effect of practice and concentration. *British Medical Journal, 331,* 1512–1514. (p. 265)

Wansink, B., van Ittersum, K., & Painter, J. E. (2006). Ice cream illusions: Bowls, spoons, and self-served portion sizes. *American Journal of Preventive Medicine, 31,* 240–243. (p. 453)

Ward, A., & Mann, T. (2000). Don't mind if I do: Disinhibited eating under cognitive load. *Journal of Personality and Social Psychology, 78,* 753–763. (p. 463)

Ward, C. (1994). Culture and altered states of consciousness. In W. J. Lonner & R. Malpass (Eds.), *Psychology and culture.* Boston: Allyn & Bacon. (p. 115)

Ward, J. (2003). State of the art synaesthesia. *The Psychologist, 16,* 196–199. (p. 258)

Ward, K. D., Klesges, R. C., & Halpern, M. T. (1997). Predictors of smoking cessation and state-of-the-art smoking interventions. *Journal of Social Issues, 53,* 129–145. (p. 120)

Ward, L. M., & Friedman, K. (2006). Using TV as a guide: Associations between television viewing and adolescents' sexual attitudes and behavior. *Journal of Research on Adolescence, 16,* 133–156. (p. 471)

Wardle, J., Cooke, L. J., Gibson, L., Sapochnik, M., Sheiham, A., & Lawson, M. (2003). Increasing children's acceptance of vegetables: A randomized trial of parent-led exposure. *Appetite, 40,* 155–162. (p. 257)

Wargo, E. (2007, December). Understanding the have-knots. *APS Observer,* pp. 18–21. (p. 551)

Warm, J. S., & Dember, W. N. (1986, April). Awake at the switch. *Psychology Today,* pp. 46–53. (p. 228)

Warr, P., & Payne, R. (1982). Experiences of strain and pleasure among British adults. *Social Science and Medicine, 16,* 1691–1697. (p. 545)

Wason, P. C. (1960). On the failure to eliminate hypotheses in a conceptual task. *Quarterly Journal of Experimental Psychology, 12,* 129–140. (p. 373)

Wason, P. C. (1981). The importance of cognitive illusions. *The Behavioral and Brain Sciences, 4,* 356. (p. 373)

Wasserman, E. A. (1993). Comparative cognition: Toward a general understanding of cognition in behavior. *Psychological Science, 4,* 156–161. (p. 303)

Wasserman, E. A. (1995). The conceptual abilities of pigeons. *American Scientist, 83,* 246–255. (p. 397)

Wastell, C. A. (2002). Exposure to trauma: The long-term effects of suppressing emotional reactions. *Journal of Nervous and Mental Disorders, 190,* 839–845. (p. 546)

Waterhouse, R. (1993, July 19). Income for 62 percent is below average pay. *The Independent,* p. 4. (p. 38)

Waterman, A. S. (1988). Identity status theory and Erikson's theory: Commonalities and differences. *Developmental Review, 8,* 185–208. (p. 202)

Watkins, E. R. (2008). Constructive and unconstructive repetitive thought. *Psychological Bulletin, 134,* 163–206. (p. 625)

Watkins, J. G. (1984). The Bianchi (L. A. Hillside Strangler) case: Sociopath or multiple personality? *International Journal of Clinical and Experimental Hypnosis, 32,* 67–101. (p. 618)

Watson, D. (2000). *Mood and temperament.* New York: Guilford Press. (pp. 522, 523, 547)

Watson, D., Suls, J., & Haig, J. (2002). Global self-esteem in relation to structural models of personality and affectivity. *Journal of Personality and Social Psychology, 83,* 185–197. (p. 591)

Watson, D., Wiese, D., Vaidya, J., & Tellegen, A. (1999). The two general activation systems of affect: Structured findings, evolutionary considerations, and psychobiological evidence. *Journal of Personality and Social Psychology, 76,* 820–838. (p. 517)

Watson, J. B. (1913). Psychology as the behaviorist views it. *Psychological Review, 20,* 158–177. (pp. 83, 290, 298)

Watson, J. B. (1924). The unverbalized in human behavior. *Psychological Review, 31,* 339–347. (p. 298)

Watson, J. B., & Rayner, R. (1920). Conditioned emotional reactions. *Journal of Experimental Psychology, 3,* 1–14. (pp. 298, 518)

Watson, R. I., Jr. (1973). Investigation into deindividuation using a cross-cultural survey technique. *Journal of Personality and Social Psychology, 25,* 342–345. (p. 698)

Watson, S. J., Benson, J. A., Jr., & Joy, J. E. (2000). NEWS AND VIEWS—Marijuana and medicine: Assessing the science base: A summary of the 1999 Institute of Medicine report. *Archives of General Psychiatry, 57,* 547–553. (p. 124)

Wayment, H. A., & Peplau, L. A. (1995). Social support and well-being among lesbian and heterosexual women: A structural modeling approach. *Personality and Social Psychology Bulletin, 21,* 1189–1199. (p. 217)

Weaver, J. B., Masland, J. L., & Zillmann, D. (1984). Effect of erotica on young men's aesthetic perception of their female sexual partners. *Perceptual and Motor Skills, 58,* 929–930. (p. 469)

Webb, W. B. (1992). *Sleep: The gentle tyrant.* Bolton, MA: Anker. (p. 95)

Webb, W. B., & Campbell, S. S. (1983). Relationships in sleep characteristics of identical and fraternal twins. *Archives of General Psychiatry, 40,* 1093–1095. (p. 96)

Wechsler, D. (1972). "Hold" and "Don't Hold" tests. In S. M. Chown (Ed.), *Human aging.* New York: Penguin. (p. 213)

Weed, W. S. (2001, May). Can we go to Mars without going crazy? *Discover,* pp. 31–43. (p. 281)

Wegner, D. M. (2002). *The illusion of conscious will.* Cambridge, MA: MIT Press. (pp. 83, 87)

Weigel, G. (2005, March-April). Is Europe dying? Notes on a crisis of civilizational morale. New Atlantic Initiative, American Enterprise Institute for Public Policy Research (www.aei.org/nai). (p. 208)

Weinberger, D. R. (2001, March 10). A brain too young for good judgment. *New York Times* (www.nytimes.com). (p. 197)

Weingarten, G. (2002, March 10). Below the beltway. *Washington Post,* p. WO3. (p. 484)

Weinstein, N. D. (1980). Unrealistic optimism about future life events. *Journal of Personality and Social Psychology, 39,* 806–820. (p. 587)

Weinstein, N. D. (1982). Unrealistic optimism about susceptibility to health problems. *Journal of Behavioral Medicine, 5,* 441–460. (p. 587)

Weinstein, N. D. (1996, October 4). 1996 optimistic bias bibliography. (weinstein_c@aesop.rutgers.edu). (p. 587)

Weis, S., & Suß, H.-M. (2007). Reviving the search for social intelligence: A multitrait-multimethod study of its structure and construct validity. *Personality and Individual Differences, 42,* 3–14. (p. 411)

Weiskrantz, L. (1986). *Blindsight: A case study and implications.* Oxford: Oxford University Press. (p. 239)

Weiss, A., Bates, T. C., & Luciano, M. (2008). Happiness is a personal(ity) thing. *Psychological Science, 19,* 205–210. (p. 528)

Weiss, A., King, J. E., & Enns, R. M. (2002). Subjective well-being is heritable and genetically correlated with dominance in chimpanzees (Pan troglodytes). *Journal of Personality and Social Psychology, 83,* 1141–1149. (p. 528)

Weiss, A., King, J. E., & Figueredo, A. J. (2000). The heritability of personality factors in chimpanzees (Pan troglodytes). *Behavior Genetics, 30,* 213–221. (p. 528)

Weiss, A., King, J. E., & Perkins, L. (2006). Personality and subjective well-being in orangutans (Pongo pygmaeus and Pongo abelii). *Journal of Personality and Social Psychology, 90,* 501–511. (p. 576)

Weiss, J. M. (1977). Psychological and behavioral influences on gastrointestinal lesions in animal models. In J. D. Maser & M. E. P. Seligman (Eds.), *Psychopathology: Experimental models.* San Francisco: Freeman. (p. 543)

Weissman, M. M. (1999). Interpersonal psychotherapy and the health care scene. In D. S. Janowsky (Ed.), *Psychotherapy indications and outcomes.* Washington, DC: American Psychiatric Press. (p. 648)

Weissman, M. M., Bland, R. C., Canino, G. J., Faravelli, C., Greenwald, S., Hwu, H.-G., Joyce, P. R., Karam, E. G., Lee, C.-K., Lellouch, J., Lepine, J.-P., Newman, S. C., Rubio-Stepic, M., Wells, J. E., Wickramaratne, P. J., Wittchen, H.-U., & Yeh, E.-K. (1996). Cross-national epidemiology of major depression and bipolar disorder. *Journal of the American Medical Association, 276,* 293–299. (p. 627)

Weisz, J. R., Rothbaum, F. M., & Blackburn, T. C. (1984). Standing out and standing in: The psychology of control in America and Japan. *American Psychologist, 39,* 955–969. (p. 154)

Welch, J. M., Lu, J., Rodriquiz, R. M., Trotta, N. C., Peca, J., Ding, J.-D., Feliciano, C., Chen, M., Adams, J. P., Luo, J., Dudek, S. M., Weinberg, R. J., Calakos, N., Wetsel, W. C., & Feng, G. (2007). Cortico-striatal synaptic defects and OCD-like behaviours in *Sapap3*-mutant mice. *Nature, 448,* 894–900. (p. 616)

Welch, W. W. (2005, February 28). Trauma of Iraq war haunting thousands returning home. *USA Today* (www.usatoday.com). (p. 612)

Weller, S., & Davis-Beaty, K. (2002). The effectiveness of male condoms in prevention of sexually transmitted diseases (protocol). *Cochrane Database of Systematic Reviews,* Issue 4, Art. No. CD004090. (p. 472)

Wellings, K., Collumbien, M., Slaymaker, E., Singh, S., Hodges, Z., Patel, D., & Bajos, N. (2006). Sexual behaviour in context: A global perspective. *Lancet, 368,* 1706–1728. (pp. 470, 471)

Wellman, H. M., Cross, D., & Watson, J. (2001). Meta-analysis of theory-of-mind development: The truth about false belief. *Child Development, 72,* 655–684. (p. 184)

Wellman, H. M., & Gelman, S. A. (1992). Cognitive development: Foundational theories of core domains. *Annual Review of Psychology, 43,* 337–375. (p. 179)

Wells, B. L. (1986). Predictors of female nocturnal orgasms: A multivariate analysis. *Journal of Sex Research, 22,* 421–437. (p. 470)

Wells, G. L. (1981). Lay analyses of causal forces on behavior. In J. Harvey (Ed.), *Cognition, social behavior and the environment.* Hillsdale, NJ: Erlbaum. (p. 287)

Wells, G. L., Memon, A., & Penrod, S. D. (2006). Eyewitness evidence: Improving its probative value. *Psychological Science in the Public Interest, 7,* 45–75. (p. 361)

Wells, G. L., & Murray, D. M. (1984). Eyewitness confidence. In G. L. Wells & E. F. Loftus (Eds.), *Eyewitness testimony: Psychological perspectives.* New York: Cambridge University Press. (p. 360)

Wender, P. H., Kety, S. S., Rosenthal, D., Schulsinger, F., Ortmann, J., & Lunde, I. (1986). Psychiatric disorders in the biological and adoptive families of adopted individuals with affective disorders. *Archives of General Psychiatry, 43,* 923–929. (p. 629)

Wener, R., Frazier, W., & Farbstein, J. (1987, June). Building better jails. *Psychology Today,* pp. 40–49. (p. 586)

Westen, D. (1996). Is Freud really dead? Teaching psychodynamic theory to introductory psychology. Presentation to the Annual Institute on the Teaching of Psychology, St. Petersburg Beach, FL. (p. 563)

Westen, D. (1998). The scientific legacy of Sigmund Freud: Toward a psychodynamically informed psychological science. *Psychological Bulletin, 124,* 333–371. (p. 565)

Westen, D. (2007). *The political brain: The role of emotion in deciding the fate of the nation.* New York: PublicAffairs. (p. 508)

Westen, D., & Morrison, K. (2001). A multidimensional meta-analysis of treatments for depression, panic, and generalized anxiety disorder: An empirical examination of the status of empirically supported therapies. *Journal of Consulting and Clinical Psychology, 69,* 875–899. (p. 664)

Weuve, J., Kang, J. H., Manson, J. E., Breteler, M. M. B., Ware, J. H., & Grodstein, F. (2004). Physical activity, including walking, and cognitive function in older women. *Journal of the American Medical Association, 292,* 1454–1460. (p. 211)

Whalen, P. J., Kagan, J., Cook, R. G., Davis, F. C., Kim, H., Polis, S., McLaren, D. G., Somerville, L. H., McLean, A. A., Maxwell, J. S., & Johnstone, T. (2004). Human amygdala responsibility to masked fearful eye whites. *Science, 302,* 2061. (pp. 507, 508)

Whalen, P. J., Shin, L. M., McInerney, S. C., Fisher, H., Wright, C. I., & Rauch, S. L. (2001). A functional MRI study of human amygdala responses to facial expressions of fear versus anger. *Emotion, 1,* 70–83. (p. 503)

Whaley, S. E., Sigman, M., Beckwith, L., Cohen, S. E., & Espinosa, M. P. (2002). Infant-caregiver interaction in Kenya and the United States: The importance of multiple caregivers and adequate comparison samples. *Journal of Cross-Cultural Psychology, 33,* 236–247. (p. 191)

Whalley, L., Starr, J. M., Athawes, R., Hunter, D., Pattie, A., & Deary, I. J. (2000). Childhood mental ability and dementia. *Neurology, 55,* 1455–1459. (p. 424)

Whalley, L. J., & Deary, I. J. (2001). Longitudinal cohort study of childhood IQ and survival up to age 76. *British Medical Journal, 322,* 1–5. (pp. 424, 543)

Wheeler, B. W., Gunnell, D., Metcalfe, C., Stephens, P., & Martin, R. M. (2008). The population impact on incidence of suicide and non-fatal self harm of regulatory action against the use of selective serotonin reuptake inhibitors in under 18s in the United Kingdom: Ecological study. *British Medical Journal, 336,* 542–545. (p. 674)

Wheelwright, J. (2004, August). Study the clones first. *Discover,* pp. 44–50. (p. 135)

White, G. L., & Kight, T. D. (1984). Misattribution of arousal and attraction: Effects of salience of explanations for arousal. *Journal of Experimental Social Psychology, 20,* 55–64. (p. 724)

White, H. R., Brick, J., & Hansell, S. (1993). A longitudinal investigation of alcohol use and aggression in adolescence. *Journal of Studies on Alcohol,* Supplement No. 11, 62–77. (p. 711)

White, K. M. (1983). Young adults and their parents: Individuation to mutuality. *New Directions for Child Development, 22,* 61–76. (p. 204)

White, L., & Edwards, J. (1990). Emptying the nest and parental well-being: An analysis of national panel data. *American Sociological Review, 55,* 235–242. (p. 218)

White, R. A. (1998). Intuition, heart knowledge, and parapsychology. *Journal of the American Society for Psychical Research, 92,* 158–171. (p. 283)

Whitehead, B. D., & Popenoe, D. (2001). *The state of our unions 2001: The social health of marriage in America.* Rutgers University: The National Marriage Project. (p. 217)

Whiten, A., & Boesch, C. (2001, January). Cultures of chimpanzees. *Scientific American,* pp. 60–67. (p. 398)

Whiten, A., & Byrne, R. W. (1988). Tactical deception in primates. *Behavioral and Brain Sciences, 11,* 233–244, 267–273. (p. 28)

Whiten, A., Spiteri, A., Horner, V., Bonnie, K. E., Lambeth, S. P., Schapiro, S. J., & de Waal, F. B. M. (2007). Transmission of multiple traditions within and between chimpanzee groups. *Current Biology, 17,* 1038–1043. (p. 315)

Whiten, A., & van Schaik, C. P. (2007). The evolution of animal 'cultures' and social intelligence. *Philosophical Transactions of the Royal Society, 362,* 603–620. (p. 398)

Whiting, B. B., & Edwards, C. P. (1988). *Children of different worlds: The formation of social behavior.* Cambridge, MA: Harvard University Press. (p. 156)

Whitley, B. E., Jr. (1990). The relationships of heterosexuals' attributions for the causes of homosexuality to attitudes toward lesbians and gay men. *Personality and Social Psychology Bulletin, 16,* 369–377. (p. 478)

Whitley, B. E., Jr. (1999). Right-wing authoritarianism, social dominance orientation, and prejudice. *Journal of Personality and Social Psychology, 77,* 126–134. (p. 707)

Whitlock, J. R., Heynen, A. L., Shuler, M. G., & Bear, M. F. (2006). Learning induces long-term potentiation in the hippocampus. *Science, 313,* 1093–1097. (p. 340)

WHO. (1979). *Schizophrenia: An international followup study.* Chicester, England: Wiley. (p. 639)

WHO. (2000). Effectiveness of male latex condoms in protecting against pregnancy and sexually transmitted infections. World Health Organization (www.who.int). (p. 472)

WHO. (2002). *The global burden of disease.* Geneva: World Health Organization (www.who.int/msa/mnh/ems/dalys/intro.htm). (p. 625)

WHO. (2003). *The male latex condom: Specification and guidelines for condom procurement.* Department of Reproductive Health and Research, Family and Community Health, World Health Organization. (p. 472)

WHO. (2004). Prevalence, severity, and unmet need for treatment of mental disorders in the World Health Organization World Mental Health Surveys. *Journal of the American Medical Association, 291,* 2581–2590. (pp. 607, 634)

WHO. (2008). *Mental health (nearly 1 million annual suicide deaths).* Geneva: World Health Organization (www.who.int/mental_health/en). (p. 630)

WHO. (2008). *Mental health and substance abuse: Facts and figures.* Geneva: World Health Organization (www.who.int). (pp. 114, 597)

WHO. (2008). *Schizophrenia.* Geneva: World Health Organization (www.who.int). (p. 637)

WHO. (2008). *Suicide rates per 100,000 by country, year and sex.* Geneva: World Health Organization (www.who.int). (p. 630)

WHO. (2008). *WHO report on the global tobacco epidemic, 2008.* Geneva: World Health Organization (www.who.int). (p. 118)

Whooley, M. A., & Browner, W. S. (1998). Association between depressive symptoms and mortality in older women. *Archives of Internal Medicine, 158,* 2129-2135. (p. 537)

Whorf, B. L. (1956). Science and linguistics. In J. B. Carroll (Ed.), *Language, thought, and reality: Selected writings of Benjamin Lee Whorf.* Cambridge, MA: MIT Press. (p. 393)

Wichman, H. (1992). *Human factors in the design of spacecraft.* Stony Brook: State University of New York Press. (p. 281)

Wickelgren, I. (2005). Autistic brains out of sync? *Science, 308,* 1856-1858. (p. 182)

Wickelgren, W. A. (1977). *Learning and memory.* Englewood Cliffs, NJ: Prentice-Hall. (p. 332)

Widiger, T. A., & Trull, T. J. (2007). Plate tectonics in the classification of personality disorder: Shifting to a dimensional model. *American Psychologist, 62,* 71-83. (p. 620)

Widom, C. S. (1989a). Does violence beget violence? A critical examination of the literature. *Psychological Bulletin, 106,* 3-28. (p. 190)

Widom, C. S. (1989b). The cycle of violence. *Science, 244,* 160-166. (p. 190)

Wielkiewicz, R. M., & Stelzner, S. P. (2005). An ecological perspective on leadership theory, research, and practice. *Review of General Psychology, 9,* 326-341. (p. 495)

Wiens, A. N., & Menustik, C. E. (1983). Treatment outcome and patient characteristics in an aversion therapy program for alcoholism. *American Psychologist, 38,* 1089-1096. (p. 653)

Wierson, M., & Forehand, R. (1994). Parent behavioral training for child noncompliance: Rationale, concepts, and effectiveness. *Current Directions in Psychological Science, 3,* 146-149. (p. 312)

Wierzbicki, M. (1993). Psychological adjustment of adoptees: A meta-analysis. *Journal of Clinical Child Psychology, 22,* 447-454. (p. 137)

Wiesel, T. N. (1982). Postnatal development of the visual cortex and the influence of environment. *Nature, 299,* 583-591. (p. 272)

Wiesner, W. H., & Cronshaw, S. P. (1988). A meta-analytic investigation of the impact of interview format and degree of structure on the validity of the employment interview. *Journal of Occupational Psychology, 61,* 275-290. (p. 488)

Wigdor, A. K., & Garner, W. R. (1982). *Ability testing: Uses, consequences, and controversies.* Washington, DC: National Academy Press. (p. 439)

Wike, R., & Grim, B. J. (2007, October 30). Widespread negativity: Muslims distrust Westerners more than vice versa. *Pew Research Center* (www.pewresearch.org). (p. 704)

Wilcox, A. J., Baird, D. D., Dunson, D. B., McConnaughey, D. R., Kesner, J. S., & Weinberg, C. R. (2004). On the frequency of intercourse around ovulation: Evidence for biological influences. *Human Reproduction, 19,* 1539-1543. (p. 467)

Wilder, D. A. (1981). Perceiving persons as a group: Categorization and intergroup relations. In D. L. Hamilton (Ed.), *Cognitive processes in stereotyping and intergroup behavior.* Hillsdale, NJ: Erlbaum. (p. 707)

Wildman, D. E., Uddin, M., Liu, G., Grossman, L. I., & Goodman, M. (2003). Implications of natural selection in shaping 99.4% nonsynonymous DNA identity between humans and chimpanzees: Enlarging genus Homo. *Proceedings of the National Academy of Sciences, 100,* 7181-7188.

Wilford, J. N. (1999, February 9). New findings help balance the cosmological books. *New York Times* (www.nytimes.com). (p. 165)

Williams, C. L., & Berry, J. W. (1991). Primary prevention of acculturative stress among refugees. *American Psychologist, 46,* 632-641. (p. 534)

Williams, H. J., Owen, M. J., & O'Donovan, M. C. (2007). Is COMT a susceptibility gene for schizophrenia? *Schizophrenia Bulletin, 33,* 635-641. (p. 642)

Williams, J. E., & Best, D. L. (1990). *Measuring sex stereotypes: A multinational study.* Newbury Park, CA: Sage. (p. 158)

Williams, J. E., Paton, C. C., Siegler, I. C., Eigenbrodt, M. L., Nieto, F. J., & Tyroler, H. A. (2000). Anger proneness predicts coronary heart disease risk: Prospective analysis from the artherosclerosis risk in communities (ARIC) study. *Circulation, 101*(17), 2034-2040. (p. 536)

Williams, J. H. G., Waister, G. D., Gilchrist, A., Perrett, D. I., Murray, A. D., & Whiten, A. (2006). Neural mechanisms of imitation and 'mirror neuron' functioning in autistic spectrum disorder. *Neuropsychogia, 44,* 610-621. (pp. 219, 317)

Williams, K. D. (2007). Ostracism. *Annual Review of Psychology, 58,* 425-452. (pp. 481, 482)

Williams, K. D., & Zadro, L. (2001). Ostracism: On being ignored, excluded and rejected. In M. Leary (Ed.), *Rejection.* New York: Oxford University Press. (p. 482)

Williams, R. (1993). *Anger kills.* New York: Times Books. (pp. 520, 536)

Williams, S. L. (1987). Self-efficacy and mastery-oriented treatment for severe phobias. Paper presented to the American Psychological Association convention. (p. 652)

Willingham, W. W., Lewis, C., Morgan, R., & Ramist, L. (1990). *Predicting college grades: An analysis of institutional trends over two decades.* Princeton, NJ: Educational Testing Service. (p. 422)

Willis, J., & Todorov, A. (2006). First impressions: Making up your mind after a 100-ms. exposure to a face. *Psychological Science, 17,* 592-598. (p. 511)

Willmuth, M. E. (1987). Sexuality after spinal cord injury: A critical review. *Clinical Psychology Review, 7,* 389-412. (p. 470)

Wilson, A. E., & Ross, M. (2001). From chump to champ: People's appraisals of their earlier and present selves. *Journal of Personality and Social Psychology, 80,* 572-584. (p. 594)

Wilson, C. M., & Oswald, A. J. (2002). *How does marriage affect physical and psychological health? A survey of the longitudinal evidence.* Working paper, University of York and Warwick University. (p. 545)

Wilson, D. B., & Shadish, W. R. (2006). On blowing trumpets to the tulips: To prove or not to prove the null hypothesis—Comment on Bösch, Steinkamp, and Boller (2006). *Psychological Bulletin, 132,* 524-528. (p. 284)

Wilson, J. Q. (1993). *The moral sense.* New York: Free Press. (p. 199)

Wilson, M., & Emmorey, K. (2006). Comparing sign language and speech reveals a universal limit on short-term memory capacity. *Psychological Science, 17,* 682-683. (p. 338)

Wilson, R. C., Gaft, J. G., Dienst, E. R., Wood, L., & Bavry, J. L. (1975). *College professors and their impact on students.* New York: Wiley. (p. 699)

Wilson, R. S. (1979). Analysis of longitudinal twin data: Basic model and applications to physical growth measures. *Acta Geneticae medicae et Gemellologiae, 28,* 93-105. (p. 175)

Wilson, R. S., Arnold, S. E., Schneider, J. A., Tang, Y., & Bennett, D. A. (2007). The relationship between cerebral Alzheimer's disease pathology and odour identification in old age. *Journal of Neurology, Neurosurgery, and Psychiatry, 78,* 30-35. (p. 211)

Wilson, R. S., Beck, T. L., Bienias, J. L., & Bennett, D. A. (2007). Terminal cognitive decline: Accelerated loss of cognition in the last years of life. *Psychosomatic Medicine, 69,* 131-137. (p. 215)

Wilson, R. S., & Bennett, D. A. (2003). Cognitive activity and risk of Alzheimer's disease. *Current Directions in Psychological Science, 12,* 87-91. (p. 212)

Wilson, R. S., & Matheny, A. P., Jr. (1986). Behavior-genetics research in infant temperament: The Louisville twin study. In R. Plomin & J. Dunn (Eds.), *The study of temperament: Changes, continuities, and challenges.* Hillsdale, NJ: Erlbaum. (p. 138)

Wilson, T. D. (2002). *Strangers to ourselves: Discovering the adaptive unconscious.* Cambridge, MA: Harvard University Press. (p. 87)

Wilson, T. D. (2006). The power of social psychological interventions. *Science, 313,* 1251-1252. (p. 439)

Wilson, W. A., & Kuhn, C. M. (2005). How addiction hijacks our reward system. *Cerebrum, 7*(2), 53-66. (p. 126)

Windholz, G. (1989, April-June). The discovery of the principles of reinforcement, extinction, generalization, and differentiation of conditional reflexes in Pavlov's laboratories. *Pavlovian Journal of Biological Science, 26,* 64-74. (p. 294)

Windholz, G. (1997). Ivan P. Pavlov: An overview of his life and psychological work. *American Psychologist, 52,* 941-946. (p. 292)

Winerman, L. (2006, January). Screening surveyed. *Monitor on Psychology,* pp. 28–29. (p. 228)

Wingfield, A., McCoy, S. L., Peelle, J. E., Tun, P. A., & Cox, L. C. (2005). Effects of adult aging and hearing loss on comprehension of rapid speech varying in syntactic complexity. *Journal of the American Academy of Audiology, 17,* 487–497. (p. 249)

Wink, P., & Dillon, M. (2002). Spiritual development across the adult life course: Findings from a longitudinal study. *Journal of Adult Development, 9,* 79–94. (p. 220)

Winner, E. (2000). The origins and ends of giftedness. *American Psychologist, 55,* 159–169. (p. 426)

Wiseman, R. (2002). *Laugh Lab—final results.* University of Hertfordshire (www.laughlab.co.uk). (p. 372)

Wiseman, R., Jeffreys, C., Smith, M., & Nyman, A. (1999). The psychology of the seance. *The Skeptical Inquirer, 23*(2), 30–33. (p. 359)

Wisman, A., & Goldenberg, J. L. (2005). From the grave to the cradle: Evidence that mortality salience engenders a desire for offspring. *Journal of Personality and Social Psychology, 89,* 46–61. (p. 193)

Witelson, S. F., Kigar, D. L., & Harvey, T. (1999). The exceptional brain of Albert Einstein. *Lancet, 353,* 2149–2153. (pp. 72, 412)

Witt, J. K., & Proffitt, D. R. (2005). See the ball, hit the ball: Apparent ball size is correlated with batting average. *Psychological Science, 16,* 937–938. (p. 277)

Witvliet, C. V. O., Ludwig, T., & Vander Laan, K. (2001). Granting forgiveness or harboring grudges: Implications for emotions, physiology, and health. *Psychological Science, 12,* 117–123. (p. 521)

Witvliet, C. V. O., & Vrana, S. R. (1995). Psychophysiological responses as indices of affective dimensions. *Psychophysiology, 32,* 436–443. (p. 503)

Wixted, J. T., & Ebbesen, E. B. (1991). On the form of forgetting. *Psychological Science, 2,* 409–415. (p. 353)

Woerlee, G. M. (2004, May/June). Darkness, tunnels, and light. *Skeptical Inquirer,* pp. 28–32. (p. 123)

Woerlee, G. M. (2005). *Mortal minds: The biology of near-death experiences.* Buffalo, NY: Prometheus Books. (p. 123)

Wolak, J., Mitchell, K., & Finkelhor, D. (2007). Unwanted and wanted exposure to online pornography in a national sample of youth Internet users. *Pediatrics, 119,* 247–257. (p. 714)

Wolfe, M. S. (2006, May). Shutting down Alzheimer's. *Scientific American,* pp. 73–79. (p. 211)

Wolfson, A. R., & Carskadon, M. A. (1998). Sleep schedules and daytime functioning in adolescents. *Child Development, 69,* 875–887. (p. 105)

Woll, S. (1986). So many to choose from: Decision strategies in videodating. *Journal of Social and Personal Relationships, 3,* 43–52. (p. 721)

Wolpe, J. (1958). *Psychotherapy by reciprocal inhibition.* Stanford, CA: Stanford University Press. (p. 651)

Wolpe, J., & Plaud, J. J. (1997). Pavlov's contributions to behavior therapy: The obvious and the not so obvious. *American Psychologist, 52,* 966–972. (p. 651)

Wonderlich, S. A., Joiner, T. E., Jr., Keel, P. K., Williamson, D. A., & Crosby, R. D. (2007). Eating disorder diagnoses: Empirical approaches to classification. *American Psychologist, 62,* 167–180. (p. 453)

Wong, D. F., Wagner, H. N., Tune, L. E., Dannals, R. F., et al. (1986). Positron emission tomography reveals elevated D_2 dopamine receptors in drug-naive schizophrenics. *Science, 234,* 1588–1593. (p. 639)

Wong, M. M., & Csikszentmihalyi, M. (1991). Affiliation motivation and daily experience: Some issues on gender differences. *Journal of Personality and Social Psychology, 60,* 154–164. (p. 159)

Wood, C. J, & Aggleton, J. P. (1989). Handedness in 'fast ball' sports: Do left-handers have an innate advantage? *British Journal of Psychology, 80,* 227–240. (p. 79)

Wood, J. M. (2003, May 19). Quoted by R. Mestel, Rorschach tested: Blot out the famous method? Some experts say it has no place in psychiatry. *Los Angeles Times* (www.latimes.com). (p. 565)

Wood, J. M. (2006, Spring). The controversy over Exner's Comprehensive System for the Rorschach: The critics speak. *Independent Practitioner* (works.bepress.com/james_wood/7). (p. 565)

Wood, J. M., Bootzin, R. R., Kihlstrom, J. F., & Schacter, D. L. (1992). Implicit and explicit memory for verbal information presented during sleep. *Psychological Science, 3,* 236–239. (p. 356)

Wood, J. M., Nezworski, M. T., Garb, H. N., & Lilienfeld, S. O. (2006). The controversy over the Exner Comprehensive System and the Society for Personality Assessment's white paper on the Rorschach. *Independent Practitioner, 26.* (p. 565)

Wood, J. N., Glynn, D. D., Phillips, B. C., & Hauser, M. C. (2007). The perception of rational, goal-directed action in nonhuman primates. *Science, 317,* 1402–1405. (p. 399)

Wood, J. V., Saltzberg, J. A., & Goldsamt, L. A. (1990a). Does affect induce self-focused attention? *Journal of Personality and Social Psychology, 58,* 899–908. (p. 633)

Wood, J. V., Saltzberg, J. A., Neale, J. M., Stone, A. A., & Rachmiel, T. B. (1990b). Self-focused attention, coping responses, and distressed mood in everyday life. *Journal of Personality and Social Psychology, 58,* 1027–1036. (p. 633)

Wood, W. (1987). Meta-analytic review of sex differences in group performance. *Psychological Bulletin, 102,* 53–71. (p. 158)

Wood, W., & Eagly, A. (2002). A cross-cultural analysis of the behavior of women and men: Implications for the origins of sex differences. *Psychological Bulletin, 128,* 699–727. (pp. 146, 158, 160, 164)

Wood, W., & Eagly, A. H. (2007). Social structural origins of sex differences in human mating. In S. W. Gagestad & J. A. Simpson (Eds.), *The evolution of mind: Fundamental questions and controversies.* New York: Guilford Press. (pp. 146, 158, 160)

Wood, W., Lundgren, S., Ouellette, J. A., Busceme, S., & Blackstone, T. (1994). Minority influence: A meta-analytic review of social influence processes. *Psychological Bulletin, 115,* 323–345. (p. 701)

Wood, W., & Neal, D. T. (2007, October). A new look at habits and the habit-goal interface. *Psychological Review, 114,* 843–863. (p. 287)

Woodruff-Pak, D. S. (1989). Aging and intelligence: Changing perspectives in the twentieth century. *Journal of Aging Studies, 3,* 91–118. (p. 213)

Woods, N. F., Dery, G. K., & Most, A. (1983). Recollections of menarche, current menstrual attitudes, and premenstrual symptoms. In S. Golub (Ed.), *Menarche: The transition from girl to woman.* Lexington, MA: Lexington Books. (p. 196)

Woodward, B. (2002). *Bush at war.* New York: Simon & Schuster. (p. 14)

Woody, E. Z., & McConkey, K. M. (2003). What we don't know about the brain and hypnosis, but need to: A view from the Buckhorn Inn. *International Journal of Clinical and Experimental Hypnosis, 51,* 309–338. (p. 112)

Woolcock, N. (2004, September 3). Driver thought everyone else was on wrong side. *The Times,* p. 22. (p. 693)

World Federation for Mental Health. (2005). ADHD: The hope behind the hype (www.wfmh.org). (p. 600)

World Health Organization. (2004a). *Prevention of mental disorders: Effective interventions and policy options. Summary report.* Geneva: World Health Organization, Department of Mental Health and Substance Abuse. (p. 607)

World Health Organization. (2004b). *Promoting mental health: Concepts, emerging evidence, practice. Summary report.* Geneva: World Health Organization, Department of Mental Health and Substance Abuse. (p. 608)

World Health Organization. (2007). Obesity and overweight (www.who.int/dietphysicalactivity/publications/facts/obesity/en/). (p. 456)

World Health Organization. (2008). The numbers count: Mental disorders in America (www.nimh.nih.gov). (p. 607)

Worobey, J., & Blajda, V. M. (1989). Temperament ratings at 2 weeks, 2 months, and 1 year: Differential stability of activity and emotionality. *Developmental Psychology, 25,* 257–263. (p. 138)

Worthington, E. L., Jr. (1989). Religious faith across the life span: Implications for counseling and research. *The Counseling Psychologist, 17,* 555–612. (p. 198)

Worthington, E. L., Jr., Kurusu, T. A., McCullogh, M. E., & Sandage, S. J. (1996). Empirical research on religion and psychotherapeutic processes and outcomes: A 10-year review and research prospectus. *Psychological Bulletin, 119,* 448–487. (p. 669)

Wortman, C. B., & Silver, R. C. (1989). The myths of coping with loss. *Journal of Consulting and Clinical Psychology, 57,* 349–357. (p. 221)

Wren, C. S. (1999, April 8). Drug survey of children finds middle school a pivotal time. *New York Times* (www.nytimes.com). (p. 127)

Wright, I. C., Rabe-Hesketh, S., Woodruff, P. W. R., David, A. S., Murray, R. M., & Bullmore, E. T. (2000). Meta-analysis of regional brain volumes in schizophrenia. *American Journal of Psychiatry, 157,* 16–25. (p. 640)

Wright, J. (2006, March 16). Boomers in the bedroom: Sexual attitudes and behaviours in the boomer generation. Ipsos Reid survey (www.ipsos-na.com). (p. 207)

Wright, P., Takei, N., Rifkin, L., & Murray, R. M. (1995). Maternal influenza, obstetric complications, and schizophrenia. *American Journal of Psychiatry, 152*, 1714-1720. (p. 640)

Wright, P. H. (1989). Gender differences in adults' same- and cross-gender friendships. In R. G. Adams & R. Blieszner (Eds.), *Older adult friendships: Structure and process.* Newbury Park, CA: Sage. (p. 159)

Wright, W. (1998). *Born that way: Genes, behavior, personality.* New York: Knopf. (p. 135)

Wrzesniewski, A., & Dutton, J. E. (2001). Crafting a job: Revisioning employees as active crafters of their work. *Academy of Management Review, 26*, 179-201. (p. 484)

Wrzesniewski, A., McCauley, C. R., Rozin, P., & Schwartz, B. (1997). Jobs, careers, and callings: People's relations to their work. *Journal of Research in Personality, 31*, 21-33. (p. 484)

Wu, W., & Small, S. A. (2006). Imaging the earliest stages of Alzheimer's disease. *Current Alzheimer Research, 3*, 529-539. (p. 212)

Wuethrich, B. (2001, March). Features—GETTING STUPID—Surprising new neurological behavioral research reveals that teenagers who drink too much may permanently damage their brains and seriously compromise their ability to learn. *Discover, 56*, 56-64. (p. 116)

Wulsin, L. R., Vaillant, G. E., & Wells, V. E. (1999). A systematic review of the mortality of depression. *Psychosomatic Medicine, 61*, 6-17. (p. 537)

Wyatt, J. K., & Bootzin, R. R. (1994). Cognitive processing and sleep: Implications for enhancing job performance. *Human Performance, 7*, 119-139. (pp. 104, 356)

Wyatt, R. J., Henter, I., & Sherman-Elvy, E. (2001). Tantalizing clues to preventing schizophrenia. *Cerebrum: The Dana Forum on Brain Science, 3*, pp. 15-30. (p. 641)

Wynn, K. (1992). Addition and subtraction by human infants. *Nature, 358*, 749-759. (p. 179)

Wynn, K. (2000). Findings of addition and subtraction in infants are robust and consistent: Reply to Wakeley, Rivera, and Langer. *Child Development, 71*, 1535-1536. (p. 179)

Wynn, K., Bloom, P., & Chiang, W-C. (2002). Enumeration of collective entities by 5-month-old infants. *Cognition, 83*, B55-B62. (p. 179)

Wynne, C. (2008). Aping language: A skeptical analysis of the evidence for nonhuman primate language. *Skeptic, 13*(4), 10-13. (p. 401)

Wynne, C. D. L. (2004). *Do animals think?* Princeton, NJ: Princeton University Press. (p. 401)

Wysocki, C. J., & Gilbert, A. N. (1989). *National Geographic* Survey: Effects of age are heterogeneous. *Annals of the New York Academy of Sciences, 561*, 12-28. (p. 260)

Xu, Y., & Corkin, S. (2001). H.M. revisits the Tower of Hanoi puzzle. *Neuropsychology, 15*, 69-79. (p. 343)

Yach, D., Struckler, D., & Brownell, K. D. (2006). Epidemiologic and economic consequences of the global epidemics of obesity and diabetes. *Nature Medicine, 12*, 62-66. (p. 457)

Yalom, I. D. (1985). *The theory and practice of group psychotherapy* (3rd ed.). New York: Basic Books. (p. 658)

Yamagata, S., & 11 others. (2006). Is the genetic structure of human personality universal? A cross-cultural twin study from North America, Europe, and Asia. *Journal of Personality and Social Psychology, 90*, 987-998. (p. 579)

Yang, N., & Linz, D. (1990). Movie ratings and the content of adult videos: The sex-violence ratio. *Journal of Communication, 40*(2), 28-42. (p. 714)

Yang, S., Markoczy, L., & Qi, M. (2006). Unrealistic optimism in consumer credit card adoption. *Journal of Economic Psychology, 28*, 170-185. (p. 587)

Yankelovich Partners. (1995, May/June). Growing old. *American Enterprise*, p. 108. (p. 206)

Yarnell, P. R., & Lynch, S. (1970, April 25). Retrograde memory immediately after concussion. *Lancet*, pp. 863-865. (p. 340)

Yarrow, L. J., Goodwin, M. S., Manheimer, H., & Milowe, I. D. (1973). Infancy experience and cognitive and personality development at ten years. In

L. J. Stone, H. T. Smith, & L. B. Murphy (Eds.), *The competent infant.* New York: Basic Books. (p. 190)

Yates, A. (1989). Current perspectives on the eating disorders: I. History, psychological and biological aspects. *Journal of the American Academy of Child and Adolescent Psychiatry, 28*, 813-828. (p. 454)

Yates, A. (1990). Current perspectives on the eating disorders: II. Treatment, outcome, and research directions. *Journal of the American Academy of Child and Adolescent Psychiatry, 29*, 1-9. (p. 454)

Yates, W. R. (2000). Testosterone in psychiatry. *Archives of General Psychiatry, 57*, 155-156. (p. 468)

Ybarra, O. (1999). Misanthropic person memory when the need to self-enhance is absent. *Personality and Social Psychology Bulletin, 25*, 261-269. (p. 591)

Yip, P. S. F. (1998). Age, sex, marital status and suicide: An empirical study of east and west. *Psychological Reports, 82*, 311-322. (p. 631)

Yonas, A., & Granrud, C. E. (2006). Infants' perception of depth from cast shadows. *Perception and Psychophysics, 68*, 154-160. (p. 264)

Young, R., Sweeting, H., & West, P. (2006). Prevalence of deliberate self harm and attempted suicide within contemporary Goth youth subculture: Longitudinal cohort study. *British Medical Journal, 332*, 1058-1061. (p. 32)

Youngentob, S. L., Kent, P. F., Scheehe, P. R., Molina, J. C., Spear, N. E., & Youngentob, L. M. (2007). Experience-induced fetal plasticity: The effect of gestational ethanol exposure on the behavioral and neurophysiologic olfactory response to ethanol odor in early postnatal and adult rats. *Behavioral Neuroscience, 121*, 1293-1305. (p. 171)

Yücel, M., Solowij, N., Respondek, C., Whittle, S., Fornito, A., Pantelis, C., & Lubman, D. I. (2008). Regional brain abnormalities associated with long-term cannabis use. *Archives of General Psychiatry, 65*, 694-701. (p. 124)

Yuki, M., Maddux, W. W., & Masuda. T. (2007). Are the windows to the soul the same in the East and West? Cultural differences in using the eyes and mouth as cues to recognize emotions in Japan and the United States. *Journal of Experimental Social Psychology, 43*, 303-311. (p. 515)

Zabin, L. S., Emerson, M. R., & Rowland, D. L. (2005). Child sexual abuse and early menarche: The direction of their relationship and its implications. *Journal of Adolescent Health, 36*, 393-400. (p. 196)

Zaccaro, S. J. (2007). Triat-based perspectives of leadership. *American Psychologist, 62*, 6-16. (p. 495)

Zadra, A., Pilon, M., & Montplairsir, J. (2008). Polysomnographic diagnosis of sleepwalking: Effects of sleep deprivation. *Annals of Neurology, 63*, 513-519. (p. 102)

Zagorsky, J. L. (2007). Do you have to be smart to be rich? The impact of IQ on wealth, income and financial distress. *Intelligence, 35*, 489-501. (p. 407)

Zajonc, R. B. (1965). Social facilitation. *Science, 149*, 269-274. (p. 697)

Zajonc, R. B. (1980). Feeling and thinking: Preferences need no inferences. *American Psychologist, 35*, 151-175. (p. 506)

Zajonc, R. B. (1984a). On the primacy of affect. *American Psychologist, 39*, 117-123. (p. 506)

Zajonc, R. B. (1984b, July 22). Quoted by D. Goleman, Rethinking IQ tests and their value. *The New York Times*, p. D22. (p. 417)

Zajonc, R. B. (1998). Emotions. In D. Gilbert, S. T. Fiske, & G. Lindzey (Eds.), *Handbook of social psychology* (4th ed.). New York: McGraw-Hill. (p. 720)

Zajonc, R. B. (2001). Mere exposure: A gateway to the subliminal. *Current Directions in Psychological Science, 10*, 224-228. (p. 719)

Zajonc, R. B., & Markus, G. B. (1975). Birth order and intellectual development. *Psychological Review, 82*, 74-88. (p. 41)

Zammit, S., Rasmussen, F., Farahmand, B., Gunnell, D., Lewis, G., Tynelius, P., & Brobert, G. P. (2007). Height and body mass index in young adulthood and risk of schizophrenia: A longitudinal study of 1,347,520 Swedish men. *Acta Psychiatrica Scandinavica, 116*, 378-385. (p. 638)

Zauberman, G., & Lynch, J. G., Jr. (2005). Resource slack and propensity to discount delayed investments of time versus money. *Journal of Experimental Psychology: General, 134*, 23-37. (p. 377)

Zeelenberg, R., Wagenmakers, E.-J., & Rotteveel, M. (2006). The impact of emotion on perception. *Psychological Science, 17*, 287-291. (p. 507)

Zeidner, M. (1990). Perceptions of ethnic group modal intelligence: Reflections of cultural stereotypes or intelligence test scores? *Journal of Cross-Cultural Psychology, 21*, 214–231. (p. 435)

Zeidner, M., Roberts, R. D., & Matthews, G. (2008). The science of emotional intelligence: Current consensus and controversies. *European Psychologist, 13*, 64–78. (p. 411)

Zeineh, M. M., Engel, S. A., Thompson, P. M., & Bookheimer, S. Y. (2003). Dynamics of the hippocampus during encoding and retrieval of face-name pairs. *Science, 299*, 577–580. (p. 344)

Zhang, J. V., Ren, P.-G., Avsian-Kretchmer, O., Luo, C.-W., Rauch, R., Klein, C., & Hsueh, A. J. W. (2005). Obestatin, a peptide encoded by the ghrelin gene, opposes ghrelin's effect on food intake. *Science, 310*, 996–999. (p. 451)

Zhang, P., Dilley, C., & Mattson, M. P. (2007). DNA damage responses in neural cells: Focus on the telomere. *Neuroscience, 145*, 1439–1448. (p. 208)

Zigler, E. F. (1987). Formal schooling for four-year-olds? No. *American Psychologist, 42*, 254–260. (p. 431)

Zigler, E. F., & Styfco, S. J. (2001). Extended childhood intervention prepared children for school and beyond. *Journal of the American Medical Association, 285*, 2378–2380. (p. 431)

Zilbergeld, B. (1983). *The shrinking of America: Myths of psychological change.* Boston: Little, Brown. (pp. 660, 664)

Zillmann, D. (1986). Effects of prolonged consumption of pornography. Background paper for *The surgeon general's workshop on pornography and public health,* June 22–24. Report prepared by E. P. Mulvey & J. L. Haugaard and released by Office of the Surgeon General on August 4, 1986. (p. 506)

Zillmann, D. (1989). Effects of prolonged consumption of pornography. In .D. Zillmann & J. Bryant (Eds.), *Pornography: Research advances and policy considerations.* Hillsdale, NJ: Erlbaum. (pp. 469, 714)

Zillmann, D., & Bryant, J. (1984). Effects of massive exposure to pornography. In N. Malamuth & E. Donnerstein (Eds.), *Pornography and sexual aggression.* Orlando, FL: Academic Press. (p. 714)

Zimbardo, P. G. (1970). The human choice: Individuation, reason, and order versus deindividuation, impulse, and chaos. In W. J. Arnold & D. Levine (Eds.), *Nebraska Symposium on Motivation, 1969.* Lincoln, NE: University of Nebraska Press. (p. 698)

Zimbardo, P. G. (1972, April). Pathology of imprisonment. *Transaction/Society,* pp. 4–8. (p. 686)

Zimbardo, P. G. (2001, September 16). Fighting terrorism by understanding man's capacity for evil. Op-ed essay distributed by spsp-discuss@stolaf.edu. (p. 708)

Zimbardo, P. G. (2004, May 25). *Journalist interview re: Abu Ghraib prison abuses: Eleven answers to eleven questions.* Unpublished manuscript, Stanford University. (p. 687)

Zimbardo, P. G. (2005, January 18). You can't be a sweet cucumber in a vinegar barrel. *The Edge* (www.edge.org). (p. 687)

Zimbardo, P. G. (2007, September). Person x situation x system dynamics. *The Observer* (Association for Psychological Science), p. 43. (p. 688)

Zimmermann, T. D., & Meier, B. (2006). The rise and decline of prospective memory performance across the lifespan. *Quarterly Journal of Experimental Psychology, 59*, 2040–2046. (p. 213)

Zogby, J. (2006, March). Survey of teens and adults about the use of personal electronic devices and head phones. *Zogby International.* (p. 245)

Zornberg, G. L., Buka, S. L., & Tsuang, M. T. (2000). At issue: The problem of obstetrical complications and schizophrenia. *Schizophrenia Bulletin, 26*, 249–256. (p. 640)

Zou, Z., Li, F., & Buck, L. B. (2005). From the cover: Odor maps in the olfactory cortex. *Proceedings of the National Academy of Sciences, 102*, 7724–7729. (p. 260)

Zubieta, J.-K., Bueller, J. A., Jackson, L. R., Scott, D. J., Xu, Y., Koeppe, R. A., Nichols, T. E., & Stohler, C. S. (2005). Placebo effects mediated by endogenous opioid activity on μ-opioid receptors. *Journal of Neuroscience, 25*, 7754–7762. (p. 256)

Zubieta, J.-K., Heitzeg, M. M., Smith, Y. R., Bueller, J. A., Xu, K., Xu, Y., Koeppe, R. A., Stohler, C. S., & Goldman, D. (2003). COMT val158met genotype affects μ-opioid neurotransmitter responses to a pain stressor. *Science, 299*, 1240–1243. (p. 255)

Zucco, G. M. (2003). Anomalies in cognition: Olfactory memory. *European Psychologist, 8*, 77–86. (p. 260)

Zucker, G. S., & Weiner, B. (1993). Conservatism and perceptions of poverty: An attributional analysis. *Journal of Applied Social Psychology, 23*, 925–943. (p. 684)

Zuckerman, M. (1979). *Sensation seeking: Beyond the optimal level of arousal.* Hillsdale, NJ: Erlbaum. (p. 445)

Zvolensky, M. J., & Bernstein, A. (2005). Cigarette smoking and panic psychopathology. *Current Directions in Psychological Science, 14*, 301–305. (p. 611)

Name Index

Aarts, H., 510
Abbey, A., 117, 144
Abbott, R. D., 212
Abramowitz, J. S., 651
Abrams, D. B., 116, 587
Abrams, L., 354
Abrams, M., 272
Abramson, L. Y., 632, 633
Abutalebi, J., 392
Ackerman, D., 49, 58
Actkinson, T. R., A-10
Adams, E. M., 34
Adams, M. J., 352
Adams, P. F., 97
Adelmann, P. K., 218
Adelson, R., 342, 505
Ader, R., 298
Adler, A., 479, 562, 563, 569
Adolphs, R., 511, 519
Affleck, G., 522
Agassi, A., 132
Agassi, J., 132
Aggleton, J. P., 79
Ai, A. L., 554
Aiello, J. R., 697
Ainsworth, M. D. S., 187
Airan, R. D., 632
Aird, E. G., 218
Åkerstedt, T., 101
Albarracín, D., 685
Albee, G. W., 669
Albert ("Little"), 5, 298, 299
Albert, B., 471
Albon, A. J., 362
Alcock, J. E., 349
Aldrich, M. S., 101
Aldridge-Morris, R., 619
Aleman, A., 638
Alexander the Great, 528
Alexander, C. J., 55
Alexander, C. N., 552
Allard, F., 334
Allen, J. B., 478
Allen, K., 546
Allen, M., 160
Allen, N. B., 625
Allen, W., 100, 567, 648
Allik, J., 593
Alloy, L. B., 633
Allport, G. W., 27, 574, 590, 706
Alter, A., 307

Altman, L. K., 540
Alwin, D. F., 156
Amabile, T. M., 410, 522, 591
Amato, P. R., 162
Abrams, D. B., 116, 587
Ambinder, M. S., 89
Amedi, A., 73
Amen, D. G., 710
Ames, A., 269, 505
Ames, D. R., 495
Ames, M. A., 477
Amsterdam, J. D., 673
Andersen, R. A., 70
Andersen, R. E., 463
Andersen, S. M., 200, 348
Anderson, A. K., 63
Anderson, B. L., 540
Anderson, C. A., 19, 319, 343,
    712, 715, 716, 717
Anderson, D. C., 712
Anderson, I. M., 673
Anderson, J. R., 690
Anderson, R. C., 347, 350
Anderson, R. D., 117
Anderson, S., 630
Anderson, S. E., 196
Anderson, S. R., 401
Anderson, U. S., 214
Andrault, O., 457
Andreasen, N. C., 640
Andrew, M., 665
Angell, M., 550
Angelsen, N. K., 34
Angier, N., 466
Angoff, W. H., 423
Anisman, H., 540
Annan, K. A., 732
Antoni, M. H., 540
Antony, M. M., 615
Antrobus, J., 105
Apostolova, L. G., 212
Appleby, D. C., A-1, A-10
Appleton, J., 371
Archer, J., 158
Archer, R., 566
Arendt, H., 200
Arenson, K. W., 433
Aries, E., 158
Aristotle, 2, 6, 45, 287, 370, 479,
    717, 721
Arkowitz, H., 182, 664, 665

Armel, K. C., 255
Armony, J., 507
Arnett, J. J., 195, 205
Arnold, K., A-9, A-10
Aron, A. P., 724, 725
Aronson, E., 203, 356, 688
Aronson, J., 439
Artiga, A. I., 452
Asch, S. E., 691, 692, 693, 696,
    702
Aserinsky, A., 92
Aserinsky, E., 92
Ashbery, J., 638
Ashley (Lady), 165
Ashtari, M., 600
Askay, S. W., 110
Aspy, C. B., 471
Assanand, S., 451
Astin, A. W., 202
Astin, H. A., 202
Astington, J. W., 181
Atance, C. M., 448
Atkins, L., 144
Atkinson, R., 140
Atkinson, R. C., 323, 325, 326,
    327, 336
Atta, M., 696
Aubrecht, L., A-10
Austin, E. J., 426
Autry, W., 729
Averill, J. R., 505, 520, 521
Avery, R. D., 435
Ax, A. F., 503
Axel, R., 260
Axinn, W., B-6
Ayres, M. M., 158
Azar, B., 252

Babad, E., 511
Babyak, M., 547
Bach, J. S., 166, 303
Bachman, J., 126, 127
Backman, L., 215, 248
Bacon, F., 373, 376
Badcock, P. B. T., 625
Baddeley, A. D., 326, 329, 348
Baer, J., 626
Bagemihl, B., 475
Baguma, P., 456
Bahrick, H. P., 329, 346, 353
Bailenson, J. N., 721

Bailey, J. M., 144, 161, 472, 476
Bailey, R. E., 309
Baillargeon, R., 179
Bain, J., 468
Baird, G., 182
Baker, E. L., 109
Baker, T. B., 304
Bakermans-Kranenburg, M. J.,
    188
Balcetis, E., 278
Baldwin, S. A., 663
Ballard, M. E., 716
Balsam, K. F., 217, 473
Baltes, P. B., 214
Banaji, M. R., 393
Bancroft, J., 467
Bandura, A., 216, 317, 318, 321,
    583
Barash, D. P., 85
Barbaree, H. E., 116
Barber, C., 673
Barber, T. X., 110
Barbieri, M., 238
Bard, P., 500, 501, 504, 505, 509
Bargh, J. A., 567, 690, 700, 720
Bar-Haim, Y., 615
Barinaga, M. B., 73, 208, 260,
    519, 548
Barkley, R. A., 600
Barlow, D. H., 656
Barnes, M. L., 512
Barnett, P. A., 634
Barnier, A. J., 108
Barnum, P. T., 579
Baron, R. A., 311
Baron, R. S., 371, 693
Baron-Cohen, S., 181, 182, 183
Barrett, L. C., 587
Barrett, L. F., 503, 505, 512
Barrow, J., 80
Barry, D., 20, 119, 209, 251, 260,
    455, 578
Bartholow, B. C., 716
Bartlett, A., 473
Bashore, T. R., 210
Baskind, D. E., 653
Bassett, D. R., 461
Bat-Chava, Y., 249
Bauer, P. J., 175, 345
Baum, A., 540
Baumeister, H., 597, 607

Baumeister, R. F., 109, 144, 152, 204, 377, 473, 474, 479, 482, 567, 585, 591, 593, 725
Baumgardner, A. H., 591
Baumrind, D., 193, 307, 479
Bavelier, D., 228, 249, 388, 73
Bayley, N., 423
Beach, S. R., 719
Beaman, A. L., 723
Beardsley, L. M., 602
Beatles (group), 16
Beaton, A. A., 78
Beauchamp, G. K., 452
Beaujean, A. A., 428
Beauvais, F., 127
Beck, A. T., 630, 655, 659
Becker, D. V., 512
Becker, I. M., 299
Becker, S., 673
Beckham, D., 62
Becklen, R., 88
Beckman, M., 197
Beecher, H. W., 394
Beeman, M. J., 77
Beethoven, L. (von), 412
Behan, P. O., 79
Beilin, H., 185
Beitel, P., 395
Beitman, B. D., 646
Bell, A. P., 474
Bell, R. Q., 423
Bellows, G., 601
Bellugi, U., 385
Belmaker, R. H., 676
Belot, M., 721
Belsher, G., 628
Belsky, J., 191, 622
Belyaev, D., 141, 142
Bem, D. J., 284, 478
Bem, S. L., 163
Benbow, C. P., 426, 432, 433
Benes, F., 59
Benjet, C., 307
Bennett, R., 714
Bennett, W. I., 463
Ben-Shakhar, G., 505
Benson, H., 551
Benson, K., 356
Benson, P. L., 160
Benson, R., 462
Ben-Zeev, T., 439
Berenbaum, S. A., 161, 434
Berenson, A., 672
Berghuis, P., 124
Bergin, A. E., 668, 669
Berk, L. E., 184
Berk, L. S., 545
Berkel, J., 553
Berkowitz, L., 520, 712
Berman, M., 711
Berndt, T. J., 160
Bernhardt, P. C., 711
Bernieri, F., 511
Bernstein, A., 611
Berra, Y., 15
Berridge, K. C., 114, 507
Berry, D. S., 294

Berry, J. W., 534
Berscheid, E., 480, 722, 725
Bersoff, D. M., 199
Berti, A., 78
Bertua, C., 407
Best, D. L., 158
Bettencourt, B. A., 158
Beyerstein, B., 578
Beyerstein, D., 578
Bhatt, R. S., 303
Bhattacharya, J., 371
Bialystok, E., 394
Bianchi, K., 618, 619
Bickman, L., 533
Biederman, I., 446
Biederman, J., 600
Bierut, L. J., 126
Biggs, V., 512
Bigler, E. D., 412
bin Laden, O., 282
Binet, A., 416, 417, 418, 419, 420, 427, 440, 576
Binitie, A., 623
Birnbaum, G. E., 189
Birnbaum, S. G., 341
Bishop, D. G., 699
Bishop, G. D., 371, 699
Bisson, J., 665
Biswas-Diener, R., 523, 524, 525
Bjerkedal, T., 41
Bjork, R. A., 6, 109, 110, 574
Bjorklund, D. F., 185
Black, J., 72
Blackburn, E. H., 208
Blackmore, S., 123, 284
Blackwell, E., 537
Blair, G., 206
Blajda, V. M., 138
Blakemore, S-J., 197, 252
Blakeslee, S., 53, 74, 182, 255, 316
Blanchard, R., 474
Blanchard-Fields, F., 215
Blanchflower, D. G., 219, 535
Blank, H., 15
Blanke, O., 123
Blankenburg, F., 229
Blascovich, J., 531, 717
Blass, T., 694
Blatt, S. J., 668
Bleustein, J., 496
Bliss, C., 172
Block, J., 200
Blocker, A., 253
Bloom, B. C., 491
Bloom, B. J., 423
Bloom, F., 50
Bloom, P., 386
Blum, K., 65
Boag, S., 566
Boahen, K., 248
Bock, L., 487
Bocklandt, S., 476
Bodenhausen, G. V., 705, 733
Bodkin, J. A., 673
Boehm, K. E., 203
Boehm-Davis, D. A., 279

Boer, D. P., 565
Boesch, C., 397, 398
Boesch-Achermann, H., 397
Bogaert, A. F., 473, 474, 475
Bogen, J., 74
Boggiano, A. K., 309
Boggiano, M. M., 452
Bohman, M., 137
Bohr, N., 15, 164
Bolger, N., 522
Bolt, R., 686
Bolwig, T. G., 676
Bonacci, A. M., 356
Bonanno, G. A., 221, 613, 614
Bonaparte, N., 528
Bond, Jr., C. F., 511
Bond, M. H., 155
Bond, R., 693
Bonnie, K. E., 398
Bono, C., 511, 512
Bono, J. E., 495
Bono, L., 512
Bookheimer, S. H., 212
Bookwala, J., 458
Boos, H. B. M., 640
Booth, A., 711
Booth, D. A., 450
Booth, F. W., 548
Bootzin, R. R., 104, 123, 356
Boring, E. G., 274
Bornstein, M. H., 156, 388
Bornstein, R. F., 187, 350, 568, 719
Boscarino, J. A., 531
Bösch, H., 284
Bosma, H., 543
Bostwick, J. M., 630
Bosworth, R. G., 73
Bothwell, R. K., 360, 708
Botwin, M. D., 580
Bouchard, T. J., Jr., 135, 136, 428, 429
Bouton, M. E., 615
Bowden, E. M., 78
Bower, B., 272
Bower, G. H., 331, 334, 349
Bower, J. E., 540
Bower, J. M., 62
Bowers, K. S., 108, 109, 110
Bowers, T. G., 663
Bowlby, J., 190
Bowler, M. C., 589
Bowles, S., 482
Bowling, N. A., 492
Bowman, H., 400
Boyar, J., 458
Boyatzis, C. J., 321
Boyer, J. L., 239
Boynton, R. M., 241
Bradbury, T. N., 683
Braddock, J. H., III, 426
Braden, J. P., 249, 435
Bradley, D. R., 262
Bradley, R. B., 190
Braffman, W., 108
Bragger, J. D., 488
Brahms, J., 101

Braiker, B., 175
Brainerd, C. J., 176, 360
Brandon, S., 363
Brang, D., 258
Brannon, L. A., 471
Branscombe, N. R., 394
Bransford, J. D., 331, 333
Bratslavsky, E., 725
Braun, S., 121, 172
Braunstein, G. D., 468
Bray, D. W., 589
Bray, G. A., 459
Brayne, C., 214
Breedlove, S. M., 476
Brehm, J. M., 701
Brehm, S., 701
Breland, K., 309
Breland, M., 309
Breslau, J., 607
Bressan, P., 274
Brewer, C. L., 8, 140
Brewer, M. B., 154
Brewer, W. F., 331
Brewin, C. R., 341, 613
Bricker, J. B., 470
Brief, A. P., 491
Briers, B., 304
Briggs, K., 574
Briñol, P., 522
Brinson, S. L., 714
Briscoe, D., 163
Brisette, I., 101
Brislin, R. W., 151
Brissette, I., 633
Britton, W. B., 123
Broca, P., 391, 392, 403
Broch, H., 283
Brock, T. C., 471
Brody, J. E., 98, 114, 196, 461, 613
Brody, N., 414
Brody, S., 479
Broks, P., 176
Broman, S. H., 423
Bronner, E., 433
Brontë, E., 626
Brookes, K., 600
Brooks, D., 208
Brooks, D. J., 547
Brooks, R., 316
Brossard, M. A., 203
Brown, A. S., 349, 355, 641
Brown, E. L., 247
Brown, G. K., 664
Brown, G. W., 668
Brown, J. A., 337
Brown, J. D., 471
Brown, J. L., 431
Brown, L., 494
Brown, R., 393, 518
Brown, S. L., 221
Brown, S. W., 357
Brownell, K. D., 461, 462
Browner, W. S., 537
Browning, C., 695
Browning, R., 728
Brownmiller, S., 470

Bruce, D., 175
Bruck, M., 361
Bruck, S. J., 361
Brucker, B. S., 549
Bruder, C. E. G., 134
Bruer, J. T., 431
Brumberg, J. J., 453
Bruun, S. E., 698
Bryant, A. N., 202
Bryant, J., 714
Bryant, R. A., 363
Buchan, J., 305
Buchanan, A., 188
Buchanan, T. W., 341
Buck, L. B., 260
Buckingham, M., 486, 487, 491, 493
Buckley, C., 729
Buckley, K. E., 481
Buckner, R. L., 343
Bucy, P. C., 62
Buddha, The, 521
Buehler, R., 377
Bugelski, B. R., 333
Bugental, D. B., 510
Buka, S. L., 640, 641
Bulia, S., 605
Bulik, C. M., 455
Bullough, V., 472
Bumstead, C. H., 701
Bunde, J., 536
Buquet, R., 103
Burcusa, S. L., 627
Burgess, M., 494
Buri, J. R., 193
Burish, T. G., 297
Burke, D. M., 213
Burkholder, R., 528
Burks, N., 725
Burlingame, G. M., 657
Burman, B., 218
Burnett, N., 334
Burns, B. C., 381
Burns, J. F., 511
Burrell, B., 412
Burris, C. T., 394
Burton, C. M., 546
Bush, G. H. W., 565, 732, 733
Bush, G. W., 14, 377, 511, 559, 685, 708, 721, 724, 731
Bushman, B. J., 356, 521, 593, 711, 716
Busnel, M. C., 171
Buss, A. H., 582
Buss, D. M., 139, 145, 469
Busseri, M. A., 473
Buster, J. E., 468
Butcher, L. M., 428
Butler, A. C., 633
Butler, R. A., 445
Butterfield, F., 606
Butterworth, G., 192
Buunk, B. P., 725
Byatt, G., 275
Byck, R., 121
Byne, W., 478
Bynum, R., 253

Byrne, D., 292, 468, 723
Byrne, J., 283
Byrne, R. W., 28, 315, 399
Byron, Lord, 412

Cable, D. M., 488
Cacioppo, J. T., 10, 525
Cade, J., 674
Caesar, J., 528 630
Cahill, L., 161, 341
Cahn, B. R., 552
Cale, E. M., 620
Calhoun, L. G., 614
Calkins, M. W., 4
Call, K. T., 470
Callaghan, T., 181
Calle, E. E., 457
Calment, J., 208
Calvo-Merino, B., 395
Camerer, C. F., 281
Campbell, D. T., 527, 572
Campbell, P. A., 136
Campbell, R., 136
Campbell, S., 274
Campbell, S. S., 96
Campbell, W. K., 202
Camper, J., 117
Camperio-Ciani, A., 476
Campos, J. J., 264, 518
Canli, T., 513, 616
Cannon, J., A-1, A-2
Cannon, W., 448, 449, 500, 501, 504, 505, 509, 532, 541
Cantor, N., 220, 411
Cantril, H., 701
Caplan, N., 150, 437
Caprara, G. V., 724
Caprara, M., 208
Caputo, D., 589
Carducci, B. J., 91, 724
Carere, C., 576
Carey, B., 342, 603, 626
Carey, D. P., 412
Carey, E., 34
Carey, G., 616, 710
Carey, L., 34
Carey, M. P., 297
Carli, L., 158
Carli, L. L., 709
Carlin, G., 120, 278, 349
Carlson, C. L., 600
Carlson, J., 438, 439
Carlson, M., 189, 728
Carlson, S., 578
Carlson, S. M., 394
Carnahan, T., 687
Carnelley, K. B., 220
Carpenter, B., 530, 531
Carpusor, A., 36, 704
Carr, T. H., 392
Carrière, G., 460
Carroll, D., 543
Carroll, J., 379, 530 703
Carroll, J. M., 514
Carroll, J. S., 714
Carroll, L., 606
Carroll, P., 587

Carron, A. V., 697
Carskadon, M. A., 97, 105
Carstensen, L. I., 215, 219
Carter, J., 604
Carter, R., 50, 604
Cartwright, R. D., 95
Caruso, D., 411
Carver, C. S., 544
Caryl, P. G., 414
Casey, B. J., 197
Cash, T. F., 454, 721
Caspi, A., 138, 139, 223, 621, 622, 631
Cassel, L., 614
Cassidy, J., 187
Castillo, R. J., 602
Castonguay, L. G., 646
Catanese, K. R., 144, 713
Cato, 520
Cattell, R. B., 215
Cavalli-Sforza, L., 436
Cavigelli, S. A., 533
Cawley, B. D., 495
Ceci, S. J., 361, 362, 431
Centerwall, B. S., 319
Cepeda, N. J., 329
Cerella, J., 210
Cervone, D., 88
Chabris, C. F., 89, 433
Chambless, D. L., 665
Chamove, A. S., 319
Chang, E. C., 587
Chang, P. P., 536
Chapin, J. K., 69
Chaplin, W. F., 510
Charles (Ninth Earl of Spencer), 14, 454
Charles, S. T., 219
Charpak, G., 283
Chartrand, T. L., 86, 690
Chase, W. G., 334
Chaucer, G., 153
Check, J. V. P., 469
Cheek, J. M., 155
Cheit, R. E., 566
Chekhov, A., 626
Chen, E., 543
Chen, X., 97
Chen, Y-R., 154
Cheney, R. (Dick), 572
Cheng, F., 461
Cheng, K., 343, 585
Cheng, M., 461
Chentsova-Dutton, Y., 515
Cherkas, L. F., 211
Chermack, S. T., 711
Chess, A., 223
Chess, S., 137, 188
Chesterfield (Lord), 60, 315
Chesterton, G. K., 157
Chiarello, C., 77
Chiles, J. A., 663
Chisholm, K., 189
Chisolm, T. H., 249
Chivers, M. L., 473, 474
Cho, S-H., 713
Choi, C. Q., 73

Choi, I., 154
Choi, Y., 154
Chomsky, N., 384, 388, 389, 403
Choy, M. H., 437
Christakis, D. S., 600
Christakis, N. A., 127, 460
Christensen, A., 668
Christensen, D. D., 406
Christie, A., 27, 109
Christina, Grand Duchess of Tuscany, 143
Christmas, L., 135
Christophersen, E. R., 651
Chugani, H., 174
Churchill, W., 141, 635
Cialdini, R. B., 686, 708
Ciarrochi, J., 411
Cicero, 438, 721, 722
Cin, S. D., 119
Clack, B., 731
Clancy, S. A., 94, 359
Clark, A., 545
Clark, K. B., 23
Clark, L. A., 620
Clark, M. P., 23
Clark, R., 535
Clark, R. D., 144
Clarke, P. R. F., 104
Claudius (Emperor), 675
Clemens, S., 626
Cleveland, H. H., 137
Cleveland, J. N., 489
Clifton, D. O., 486, 487
Clinton, H. R., 681, 683, 705
Clinton, W. (Bill), 464
Clum, G. A., 663
Coan, J. A., 545
Cochran, J., 331
Coe, W. C., 110
Coffey, C. E., 630
Cogan, J. C., 464
Cohen, D., 332, 461, 619, 713
Cohen, K. M., 478
Cohen, N., 298
Cohen, P., 568
Cohen, S., 101, 439, 522, 538, 539, 543, 545
Colangelo, N., 426
Colapinto, J., 161
Colarelli, S. M., 143, 158
Colbert, S., 53
Colcombe, S. J., 211
Cole, K. C., 118
Coleman, P. D., 210
Collings, V. B., 269, 270
Collins, D. W., 434
Collins, F., 132, 165
Collins, N. L., 725
Collins, R. L., 30
Collinson, S. L., 640
Collishaw, S., 628
Colom, R., 412, 421
Colombo, J., 187
Comer, R. J., 599
Comfort, A., 207
Comstock, G., 319
Conard, M. A., 580

Confucius, 20, 139, 377
Connor-Smith, J. K., 542
Conway, M. A., 212
Cook, M., 519
Cooke, L. J., 257
Cooper, H., 529
Cooper, K. J., 321, 691
Cooper, M. L., 117
Coopersmith, S., 193
Copernicus, 18, 410
Coppola, M., 389
Corballis, M. C., 79, 400
Corbett, S. W., 451
Coren, S., 79, 96, 99, 100
Corey, D. P., 245
Corina, D. P., 77
Corkin, S., 342, 343
Corman, M. D., 711
Corneille, O., 370, 371
Corp, N., 28
Correll, J., 705
Corrigan, E., 357
Costa, P. T., Jr., 216, 220, 223,
    512, 577, 581
Costello, C. G., 628
Costello, E. J., 607
Coughlin, J. F., 210
Couli, J. T., 484
Courage, M. L., 192
Courneya, K. S., 697
Courtney, J. G., 540
Covin, R., 657
Cowan, G., 714
Cowan, N., 337, 338
Cowart, B. J., 257, 258
Cox, J. J., 255
Coyle, J. T., 640
Coyne, J. C., 634
Crabbe, J. C., 125, 141
Crabtree, S., 493
Craik, F. I. M., 214, 330, 331, 332
Crain-Thoreson, C., 423
Crandall, C. S., 453, 457
Crandall, J. E., 572
Craven, R. G., 591
Crawford, M., 434
Crawley, J. N., 182
Crews, F., 568
Crews, F. T., 116, 197
Crick, F., 48
Crocker, J., 594, 708
Croft, R. J., 122
Crofton, C., 723
Crombie, A. C., 235
Cromwell, T., 686
Cronshaw, S. P., 488
Crook, T. H., 212
Cross, S., 590
Crowell, J. A., 187
Crowley, M., 728
Csikszentmihalyi, M., 159, 202,
    220, 319, 484
Culbert, K. M., 454
Cullen, L. T., 720
Cullum, J., 692
Cummings, R. A., 525
Cunningham, M. R., 722

Cunningham, W. A., 705
Curtis, G. C., 611
Curtis, R. C., 724
Cushman, F., 200
Cutler, B. L., 360
Cynkar, A., 163
Czeisler, C. A., 92

D'Aquili, E., 552
da Vinci, L., 79, 235, 365, 370,
    608
Dabbs, J. M., Jr., 468, 711, 728
Dahmer, J., 606
Dal Martello, M. F., 274
Dale, P. S., 423
Daley, T. C., 420
Dallenbach, K. M., 354
Dallery, J., 182
Damasio, A. R., 411, 505, 508
Damasio, H., 72
Damon, W., 192, 202
Daniels, D., 150
Danner, D. D., 544
Danso, H., 439
Dapretto, M., 183
Darby, J., 701
Darley, J., 307
Darley, J. M., 726, 727
Darrach, B., 620
Darwin, C., 3, 6, 7, 141, 143, 147,
    165, 192, 257, 295, 297, 407,
    416, 444, 514, 515, 568, 612
Daskalakis, Z. J., 676
Daum, I., 344
Davey, G. C. L., 297, 615
Davey, T. C., 423
David (King), 240
Davidoff, J., 394
Davidson, J. R. T., 608
Davidson, R. J., 503, 552, 630,
    710
Davies, D. R., 216
Davies, M. F., 578, 579
Davies, P., 166
Davis, B., 351
Davis, B. E., 175
Davis, B. L., 387
Davis, H., IV, 630
Davis, J. O., 134, 642
Davis, K. C., 117
Davis, M., 672
Davis, S., 468
Davis-Beaty, K., 472
Davison, K. P., 658
Dawes, R. M., 591, 730
Dawkins, R., 83, 141, 165
Dawood, K., 467
Dawson, D. A., 129, B-6
de Beauvoir, S., 23
de Boysson-Bardies, B., 387
de Courten-Myers, G. M., 53, 67,
    174
de Cuevas, J., 388
de Fermat, P., 409
de Geus, E. J. C., 428
De Graaf, N. S., 137
de Hoogh, A. H. B., 495

De Houwer, J., 293
De Koninck, J., 103
de Montaigne, M. E., 198, 580
de Quervain, D. J.-F., 342
De Vogli, R., 545
de Waal, F. B. M., 29, 161, 315,
    400
de Waard, F., 553
De Wolff, M. S., 188
Deacon, B. J., 651
Dean, G. A., 578
DeAngelis, T., 664
Deary, I. J., 413, 414, 422, 423,
    424, 432, 435., 543, 581, 708
DeBruine, L. M., 720
DeCasper, A. J., 171
Decety, J., 395
Deci, E. L., 309, 480, 594
Deeley, Q., 621
Deffenbacher, K., 247
DeFries, J. C., 429, 476
DeHart, T., 116
Dehne, K. L., 471
DeLamater, J. D., 207
Delaney, H. D., 668
Delaney, P. F., 339
Delargy, M., 523
Delgado, J. M. R., 68
DeLoache, J. S., 177, 180, 615
DelVecchio, W. F., 580
Dember, W. N., 228
Dement, W. C., 92, 93, 94, 96,
    97, 98, 99, 101, 102, 103,
    B-2, B-10
Demir, E., 476
Denes-Raj, V., 381
DeNeve, K. M., 529
Dennett, D. C., 7, 295
Denollet, J., 536
Denton, K., 116, 199
Denton, R., 692
DePaulo, B. M., 511, 512, 582
Der, G., 34, 413
Dermer, M., 528, 724
Deroche-Garmonet, V., 114
DeRubeis, R. J., 664
Descartes, R., 6, 402
Desmond, D., 252
DeSteno, D., 349, 521
Detterman, D. K., 418
Dettman, J. R., 143
Dettman, S. J., 248
Deutsch, J. A., 65
DeValois, K. K., 242
DeValois, R. L., 242
Devilly, G. J., 613, 665
Devine, P. G., 720
Devlin, B., 428
Dew, M. A., 98
DeWall, C. N., 585
Diaconis, P., 34
Diamond, J., 143
Diamond, L. M., 473
Diamond, R., 478
Diana (Princess), 283
DiBiasi, P., 136
DiCaprio, L., 470

Dick, D. M., 428, 621
Dickens, C., 28
Dickens, W. T., 435
Dickerson, S. S., 542
Dickinson, E., 141, 599, 635
Dickinson, H. O., 523
Dickson, B. J., 476
Diener, E., 138, 220, 480, 522,
    523, 524, 525, 526, 527, 528,
    529, 633, 722
Dietz, W. H., 463
DiFranza, J. R., 119
DiGiulio, G., 663
Dijksterhuis, A., 380, 510
DiLalla, D. L., 136, 629
Dill, K. E., 716
Dillard, A., 358
Dillon, M., 220
Dimberg, U., 317, 507, 516
Dindia, K., 160
Dindo, M., 398
Dinges, N. G., 393
Dingfelder, S., 505
Dion, K. K., 155, 163
Dion, K. L., 155, 163, 495
Dipboye, R. L., 488
Dix, D., 448, 645
Dixon, J., 731
Dixon, R. A., 248
Dobbs, D., 677
Dobel, C., 393
Dobkins, K. R., 73
Doherty, E. W., 120
Doherty, W. J., 120
Dohrenwend, B. P., 534, 607, 613
Doidge, N., 73
Dolan, C. M., 457
Dolan, R. J., 392
Dole, R., 684
Dolezal, H., 273, 274
Domhoff, G. W., 103, 104, 105
Domjan, M., 292, 296
Donahoe, J. W., 313
Donnellan, M. B., 528, 580, 584,
    594
Donnerstein, E., 319, 320, 321
Doolittle, B., 226
Dorner, G., 476
Dostoevsky, F., 626
Doty, R. L., 209, 260
Doucette, M., 96
Dovidio, J. F., 732
Dowd, M., 722
Downing, P. E., 238
Downs, A. C., 197
Doyle, A. C., 58, 274, 338
Doyle, R., 144
Draguns, J. G., 597, 634
Drake, R. A., 77, 503
Drake, T., 287
Drews, F. A., 88
Druckman, D., 109, 110, 574
Duckworth, A. L., 490
Duclos, S. E., 515
Duenwald, M., 672
Duffy, M., 688
Dugatkin, L. A., 315

Duggan, J. P., 450
Dugger, C. W., 379
Dukakis, K., 676
Dumont, K. A., 190
Duncan, J., 413
Duncker, K., 373, 374
Dunn, A. L., 547
Dunn, E. W., 728
Dunning, D., 278, 588, 589, 592
Dunson, D. B., 207
Durgin, F. H., 252
Durm, M. W., 283
Dush, C. M. K., 217
Dutton, D. G., 724
Dweck, C. S., 432

Eagly, A. H., 146, 158, 160, 164, 495, 704, 721, 728
Eastman, C. L., 92, 666
Eastwick, P. W., 720, 721
Ebbesen, E. B., 353, 520
Ebbinghaus, H., 328, 329, 332, 353, 356
Eberhardt, J. L., 705
Eccles, J. S., 434
Eckensberger, L. H., 199
Eckert, E. D., 616
Ecklund-Flores, L., 171
Edelman, M. W., 692
Edelman, R., 520
Edelman, S., 540
Edison, T. A., 92, 96, 371, 410
Edwards, C. P., 156
Edwards, J., 218
Edwards, K. J., 651
Efron, Z., 140
Ehrhardt, A. A., 161
Ehrmann, M., 594
Eibl-Eibesfeldt, I., 514
Eich, E., 104
Eichmann, A., 696
Einstein, A., 72, 165, 395, 407, 412, 423
Einstein, G. O., 213
Eisenberg, N., 513
Eisenberger, N. I., 482
Eisenberger, R., 309
Eiser, J. R., 119
Ekman, P., 505, 511, 513, 514
El Greco, 626
Elaad, E., 505
Elbert, T., 149, 616
Elfenbein, H. A., 513, 514
Eliot, C., 13
Eliot, T. S., 369, 407
Elizabeth (Queen), 282
Elkind, D., 198
Ellenbogen, J. M., 100
Elliot, A. J., 189, 296, 297, 494
Ellis, A., 299, 656, 669
Ellis, B. J., 204, 472
Ellis, L., 477
Ellis, S., 177
Elzinga, B. M., 619
Emerson, R. W., 518, 597
Emery, G., 282
Emmons, R. A., 527

Emmons, S., 597, 638
Emmorey, K., 249, 338
Empson, J. A. C., 104
Emslie, C., 454
Endler, N. S., 632, 676
Engemann, K. M., 721
Engen, T., 261
Engle, R. W., 326
Epel, E. S., 533
Epicharmus, 240
Epley, N., 22, 180, 592
Epstein, J., 640
Epstein, L. H., 451
Epstein, S., 411, 581
Eratosthenes, 645
Erdberg, P., 565
Erdelyi, M. H., 566
Erel, O., 191, 218
Erickson, K. I., 548
Erickson, M. F., 218
Ericsson, K. A., 407, 432, 491
Erikson, E. H., 189, 194, 200, 201, 202, 203, 205, 217, 221, 222, B-7
Erikson, J., 189
Ernsberger, P., 463, 464
Ertmer, D. J., 388
Escobar-Chaves, S. L., 471
Esser, J. K., 700
Esses, V., 439
Esterson, A., 565
Estrin, J., 523
Esty, A., 526
Eszterhas, J., 119
Etkin, A., 616
Ettinger, M. G., 94
Etzioni, A., 733
Euston, D. R., 344
Evans, C. R., 495
Evans, F. J., 109
Evans, G. W., 191, 536, 543
Evans, R. I., 119
Everson, S. A., 544
Ewing, R., 461
Exline, J. J., 585
Exner, J. E., 565
Eysenck, H. J., 551, 575, 576, 577, 603, 661, 662
Eysenck, M. W., 584
Eysenck, S. B. G., 575

Fagan, J. F., 423, 437
Fairburn, C. G., 454
Fantz, R. L., 173
Farah, M. J., 73
Faraone, S. V., 629
Farina, A., 601, 605
Farley, F., 197
Farley, M., 613
Farley, T., 461
Farooqi, I. S., 451
Farrington, D. P., 620
Fartacek, R., 473
Fast, L. A., 582
Fatsis, S., 589
Fazio, R. H., 293
Feder, H. H., 467

Feeney, D. M., 21
Feeney, J. A., 189
Feigenson, L., 179
Feinberg, I., 356
Feinberg, T. E., 78
Feingold, A., 454, 721, 722
Fellinger, J., 249
Fellowes, D., 550
Feng, J., 434
Fenton, W. S., 639
Ferguson, E. D., 479, 562
Ferguson, T. J., 321
Fergusson, D. M., 30, 628
Fernandez, E., 256
Fernández-Ballesteros, R., 208
Fernández-Dols, J-M., 514
Ferri, M., 658
Ferris, C. F., 190
Festinger, L., 688
Feynman, R., 14, 412
Fiedler, F. E., 495
Fiedler, K., 349
Field, A. P., 293, 614
Field, T., 149, 191
Fields, R. D., 47, 67, 340
Filkins, D., 511
Finch, C. E., 208
Fincham, F. D., 683
Fingerhut, A. W., 144, 217, 473
Fink, G. R., 344
Finkel, E. J., 720, 721
Finlay, S. W., 658
Finney, E. M., 249
Finzi, E., 516
Fischer, P., 567, 715
Fischhoff, B., 377
Fischtein, D. S., 144
Fishbach, A., 494
Fisher, H. E., 217, 467
Fisher, H. T., 651
Fisher, K., 162
Fisher, R. P., 361
Fiske, S. T., 687
Fitzgerald, J. A., 475
Fitzgerald, P. B., 676
Flachsbart, C., 542
Flaxman, S. M., 452
Fleming, I., 544
Fleming, J. H., 494, 513
Fletcher, G. J. O., 683
Fletcher, P. C., 566
Flier, J. S., 460
Flood, D. G., 210
Flood, M., 714
Flora, S. R., 310
Flouri, E., 188
Flynn, F. J., 495
Flynn, J. R., 420, 421, 425, 430, 435
Foa, E. B., 614, 652
Fodor, J. D., 58, 285
Foerster, O., 68
Fogg, N. P., A-1, A-2, A-3, A-4
Follette, V. M., 190
Ford, E. S., 548
Ford, H., 565
Foree, D. D., 309

Forehand, R., 312
Forer, B. R., 578
Forgas, J. P., 349, 508, 634
Forste, R., B-6
Forhan, S. E., 471
Forman, D. R., 318
Foss, D. J., 565
Foster, R. G., 92
Foulkes, D., 105
Fouts, R., 401
Fowler, J. H., 127, 460
Fowler, M. J., 356
Fowler, R. C., 630
Fowles, D. C., 639
Fox, B. H., 540
Fox, E., 510
Fox, J. L., 73
Fox, N. A., 138
Fox, R., 308
Foy, E., 518
Fozard, J. L., 210
Fracassini, C., 261
Fraley, R. C., 189
Francesconi, M., 721
Frank, A., 195
Frank, J. D., 666, 667, 668
Frank, R., 153
Frank, S. J., 204
Frankel, A., 577
Frankenburg, W., 175
Franklin, B., 101
Franz, E. A., 76
Fraser, S. C., 686
Frasure-Smith, N., 537
Frattaroli, J., 546
Frayling, T. M., 460
Frederick, D. A., 454
Fredrickson, B. L., 333, 454, 522
Freedman, D. J., 397
Freedman, J. L., 320, 686, 697
Freedman, L. R., 643
Freeman, W. J., 243
Frensch, P. A., 566
Freud, S., 4, 5, 102, 103, 104, 105, 106, 217, 356, 357, 365, 407, 484, 557, 558, 559, 560, 561, 562, 563, 565, 566, 567, 568, 569, 570, 572, 574, 610, 614, 617, 623, 628, 646, 647, 648, 659, 668, 707
Frey, K., 515
Frey, M. C., 418
Freyd, J. J., 190, 363
Friedman, K., 471
Friedman, M. A., 535, 536, 549, 551
Friedrich, O., 599
Friend, T., 402
Friesen, W. V., 513
Frijda, N., 526
Frith, C., 182
Frith, U., 182
Fritsch, G., 68
Frohlich, P. F., 468
Fromkin, V., 385, 388
Fry, A. F., 210
Fryar, C., 467

Fuhriman, A., 657
Fujiki, N., 101
Fuller, M. J., 197
Fuller, T., 520
Fulmer, I. S., 492
Fulton, R., 701
Funder, D. C., 200, 578, 581, 582, 634
Furlow, F. B., 466
Furnham, A., 16, 432, 456, 684, 704
Furr, R. M., 634
Furstenberg, F., 305
Furumoto, L., 4

Gable, S. L., 218
Gabriel, M., 63
Gabrieli, J. D. E., 344
Gaertner, L., 713
Gaertner, S. L., 732
Gaeth, G. J., 381
Gage, F. H., 74
Gage, P., 72
Gaillot, M. T., 585
Gajendran, R. S., 586
Galambos, N. L., 203, 205
Galanter, E., 227
Galati, D., 514
Galea, S., 613, 614, 628
Galileo, 143, 165, 370
Gall, F., 45
Gallina, A., 34
Gallina, M., 34
Gallup, G., Jr., 123, 319
Gallup, G. G., Jr., 192
Gallup, G. H., 731
Gallup, G. H., Jr., 658
Galton, F., 169, 416, 423
Gándara, P., 395
Gandhi, I., 731
Gandhi, M., 22, 318, 407, 701
Gandhi, S., 20
Gangestad, S. W., 145, 723
Garb, H. N., 565
Garber, K., 182
Garcia, J., 296, 297
Gardner, B. I., 399
Gardner, H., 151, 405, 406, 408, 409, 411, 415, 418
Gardner, J., 524
Gardner, J. W., 495
Gardner, M., 363
Gardner, R. A., 399
Gardner, R. M., 457
Garfield, C., 395
Garlick, D., 412
Garner, W. R., 439
Garnets, L. D., 473
Garon, N., 174
Garrett, B. L., 360
Garry, M., 359, 566
Gatchel, R. J., 254
Gates, G. A., 248
Gates, W. ("Bill"), 38, 164, 379, 408, 720
Gatz, M., 212
Gauguelin, M., 579

Gawande, A., 256
Gawin, F. H., 120
Gazzaniga, M. S., 74, 75, 76, 77, 114, 505
Gearhart, J. P., 161
Geary, D. C., 145, 434, 437
Geen, R. G., 320, 520
Gehring, W. J., 616
Geier, A. B., 453
Geiselman, R. E., 361
Geisler, C., 638
Geiwitz, J., 214
Geldard, F. A., 240
Geller, D., 696
Gelles, R. J., 307
Gelman, D., 514
Gelman, S. A., 179
Genain, H., 642
Genain, I., 642
Genain, M., 642
Genain, N., 642
Genesee, F., 395
Genevro, J. L., 221
Genovese, K., 726, 727
Gent, J. F., 257
Gentile, D. A., 319, 320, 716, 717
George, L. K., 554
George, M. S., 676, 677
Geraci, L., 362
Geraerts, E., 363
Gerard, D. A., 580
Gerbner, G., 127, 379, 715
Gernsbacher, M. A., 182
Gerrard, M., 471
Gershoff, E. T., 307
Gerstorf, D., 220
Geschwind, N., 79, 391
Gfeller, J. D., 110
Giancola, P. R., 711
Gibbons, F. X., 528
Gibbons, R. D., 674
Gibbs, J. C., 199
Gibbs, S., 222
Gibbs, W. W., 69, 385, 457
Gibran, K., 193
Gibson, E. J., 264
Gibson, H. B., 109
Gigerenzer, G., 378, 380
Gilbert, A. N., 260
Gilbert, D. T., 15, 218, 297, 357, 370, 506, 523, 625
Gilbertson, M. W., 613
Giles, D. E., 94
Gill, A. J., 582
Gill, C., 590
Gillaspy, J. A., Jr., 309
Gillham, J. E., 669
Gilligan, C., 158
Gilovich, T., 32, 33, 219, 488
Gilovich, T. D., 591
Giltay, E. J., 544
Gingerich, O., 1, 166
Giuliano, T. A., 159
Glaberson, W., 590
Gladue, B. A., 477, 478
Gladwell, M., 489, 723
Glaser, R., 540

Glasman, L. R., 685
Glass, R. I., 379
Glass, R. M., 675
Gleaves, D. H., 619
Glenn, N. D., 218
Glick, P., 579, 704
Glickman, M. E., 433
Gluhoski, V. L., 299
Godden, D. R., 348
Goel, V., 392
Goethals, G., 682
Goff, D. C., 619
Goff, L. M., 359
Gold, M., 203
Goldapple, K., 674
Goldberg, L. R., 223
Goldberg, W. A., 191
Golden, R. N., 666
Goldenberg, J. L., 193
Goldfried, M. R., 630, 646, 666, 668
Golding, J. M., 613, 714
Goldin-Meadow, S., 400
Goldstein, A. P., 713
Goldstein, D., 382
Goldstein, I., 35
Goldstein, L., 55
Goleman, D., 411, 490, 503
Gombrich, E. H., 277
Gómez, R. L., 100
Gonsalkorale, K., 482
Gonsalves, B., 359
Goodale, M. A., 86
Goodall, J., 28, 150, 708
Goodchilds, J., 207
Goode, E., 255, 648
Goodhart, D. E., 587
Goodman, G. S., 362, 363
Goodstein, L., 590
Goodwin, F. K., 21
Goodwin, S. A., 704
Gopnik, A., 394
Goranson, R. E., 16
Gordon, A. H., 513
Gordon, P., 393
Gore, A., 684, 733
Gore-Felton, C., 363
Gortmaker, S. L., 457, 463
Gosling, S. D., 576, 581
Gossage, J. P., 172
Gotlib, I. H., 634
Gottesman, I. I., 641, 642
Gottfredson, L. S., 407
Gottfried, J. A., 291
Gottman, J., 217
Gougoux, F., 248
Gould, E., 74, 533
Gould, S. J., 146, 166, 417
Grabe, S., 455
Grady, C. L., 352
Grady, D., 211
Graf, P., 213
Graf, S., 132
Graham, J. E., 546
Graham, M., 407
Grajek, S., 725
Granott, N., 185

Granrud, C. E., 264
Grant, B. F., 129, B-6
Gray, P. B., 468
Gray-Little, B., 725
Green, B., 489
Green, B. L., 185
Green, C. S., 228
Green, D. M., 247
Green, J. D., 566
Green, J. T., 344, 345
Green, R., 161
Greenberg, J., 567, 591
Greene, J., 200
Greene, R. L., 330
Greenfeld, L. A., 711
Greenfield, S., 85
Greenwald, A. G., 229, 566, 705
Greenwood, M. R. C., 457
Greer, G., 469
Greers, A. E., 389
Gregory of Nyssa, 626
Gregory of Sinai, 552
Gregory, R. L., 272, 277
Greif, E. B., 196
Greist, J. H., 611
Greitemeyer, T., 715
Grello, C. M., 117
Grether, J. K., 182
Grèzes, J., 395
Griffiths, M., 114
Grigorenko, E. L., 426
Grill-Spector, K., 370
Grilo, C. M., 460
Grim, B. J., 704
Grinker, R. R., 182
Grobstein, C., 170
Groothuis, T. G. G., 576
Gross, A. E., 723
Gross, A. M., 144
Gross, M., 676
Grossarth-Maticek, R., 551
Grossberg, S., 276
Grossman, M., 512
Gruchy, C. D. G., 512
Gruder, C. L., 528
Grunebaum, M. F., 674
Grusec, J. E., 319
Guerin, B., 384, 697
Guiso, L., 434
Gundersen, E., 319
Güntürkün, O., 78
Gura, T., 451
Gustafson, D., 212, 457
Gustavson, A. R., 297
Gustavson, C. R., 296
Gutierres, S. E., 469
Gutsell, J. N., 585
Guttentag, M., 704

H. M., 342
H., S., 566
Ha, Y-W., 373
Haber, R. N., 324, 356
Haddock, G., 458, 704
Haesler, S., 388
Hagen, E. P., 419
Haidt, J., 58, 198, 199

Haier, R. J., 412, 413
Hakes, D. T., 565
Hakuta, K., 390
Halberstadt, J., 454, 707
Halberstadt, J. B., 276, 360
Haldane, J. B. S., 230
Haldeman, D. C., 473
Hale, S., 210
Hall, C. S., 103, 567
Hall, G., 297
Hall, G. S., 195
Hall, J. A., 158, 433, 477, 511, 512, 722
Hall, J. G., 134
Hall, S. S., 170
Hall, V. C., 309
Hall, W., 124
Hall, W. B., 409
Halpern, B. P., 257
Halpern, D. F., 79, 432, 433, 434, 435, 472
Hamamura, T., 592, 593
Hamann, S., 469
Hamilton, D. L., 32
Hamilton, R. H., 248
Hammack, P. L., 473, 475
Hammen, C. L., 634
Hammer, E., A-9
Hammersmith, S. K., 474
Hammerstein, O., 515, 723
Hampson, R., 461
Hampson, S. E., 223
Hancock, K. J., 709
Handel, G. F., 141, 626
Hankin, B. L., 632
Hanks, T., 480
Hansen, C. H., 510
Hansen, I. G., 567
Hansen, R. D., 510
Haraguchi, A., 339
Harbaugh, W. T., 728
Harber, K. D., 705
Hardin, C., 393
Hare, R. D., 621
Hariri, A. R., 519
Harjo, J., 395
Harker, L. A., 522
Harkins, S. G., 698
Harlow, H. F., 186
Harlow, L. L., 126
Harlow, M. K., 186
Harlow, R. E., 220
Harmon-Jones, E., 503
Harper, C., 713
Harris, A., 605
Harris, B., 298
Harris, J. A., 711
Harris, J. R., 136, 151, 188
Harris, R. J., 714
Harrison, D. A., 586
Harrison, Y., 98
Harriston, K. A., 590
Harrow, M., 638
Harrower, M., 566
Hart, D., 192, 202
Harter, J. K., 492, 493
Härter, M., 597, 607

Hartmann, E., 102
Harton, H. C., 692
Hartsuiker, R. J., 386
Harvey, F., 247
Harvey, J., 421
Harvey, P. D., 637
Haselton, M. G., 467
Hasher, L., 92
Hasin, D. S., 625
Haslam, N., 478
Haslam, S. A., 687
Hassan, B., 478
Hatfield, E., 144, 721, 724
Hatfield, J., 31
Hathaway, S. R., 576, 577
Hauck, C., 109
Hauser, M. D., 200, 386, 388
Havas, D. A., 516
Hawking, S., 404
Hawthorne, N., 687
Haxby, J. V., 238
Hayes, T. L., 492
Haynes, J-D., 229
Hazan, C., 190
Hazelrigg, M. D., 558
Heaps, C. M., 364
Hebb, D. O., 298, 499
Hebl, M. R., 458
Hedges, L. V., 432, 433, 434
Hedström, P., 631
Heider, F., 682
Heiman, J. R., 469
Heine, S. J., 592, 593
Heins, M., 717
Hejmadi, A., 510
Helgeson, V. S., 545, 614
Heller, W., 78
Helmreich, W. B., 189, 566
Helms, J. E., 437
Helmuth, L., 676
Helson, H., 526
Helweg-Larsen, M., 587
Hembree, R., 502
Hemenover, S. H., 546
Hemingway, E., 626
Henderlong, J., 309
Henderson, J. M., 231
Henkel, L. A., 359
Henley, N. M., 394
Hennessey, B. A., 410
Henning, K., 468, 470
Henninger, P., 619
Henry, J. D., 213
Henry, P. E., 454
Hepper, P. G., 79, 171
Herbert, B., 118
Herbert, J. D., 665
Herek, G. M., 473
Hering, E., 241, 242
Herman, C. P., 453, 454, 463
Herman-Giddens, M. E., 196
Hernandez, A. E., 389
Herrmann, D., 365
Herrmann, E., 315
Herrnstein, R. J., 302, 435
Hershenson, M., 268
Hertenstein, M. J., 186, 251

Herz, R. S., 260
Herzog, H. A., 21
Hesburgh, T., 733
Hess, E. H., 273
Hetherington, M. M., 453
Hettema, J. M., 616
Hewlett, B., 188
Hezlett, S. A., 422
Hickok, G., 77
Hilgard, E. R., 111
Hill, C. E., 649
Hill, H., 513
Hinckley, J., 606
Hines, M., 160, 161
Hingson, R. W., 127
Hintzman, D. L., 333
Hinz, L. D., 454
Hippocrates, 532
Hirsch, J., 458
Hirt, E. R., 635
Hitzig, E., 68
Hobson, J. A., 104, 105
Hochberg, L. R., 70
Hodgkinson, V. A., 729
Hoebel, B. G., 450
Hoeft, F., 114
Hoffman, C., 706
Hoffman, D. D., 239
Hoffman, H. G., 257
Hofmann, A., 122
Hogan, J., 421
Hogan, R., 581
Hogarth, W., 646
Hoge, C. W., 613
Hogg, M. A., 706
Hohmann, G. W., 504
Hokanson, J. E., 520
Holahan, C. K., 426
Holden, C., 97, 135, 642
Holden, G. W., 193
Holland, C. R., 437
Holliday, R. E., 362
Hollis, K. L., 292
Hollon, S. D., 664, 674
Holm-Denoma, J., 461
Holmes, D. S., 547, 548
Holmes, O. W., 11, 378
Holstege, G., 466
Holt, H., 4
Holt, L., 385
Homer, 626
Homer, B. D., 118
Honorton, C., 284
Honzik, C. H., 308
Hooper, J., 65
Hooykaas, R., 18
Hopkins, W. D., 79
Hopper, L. M., 315
Horace, 520
Horn, J. L., 215
Horne, J. A., 98
Horner, V., 398
Horney, K., 562, 563, 569, 662
Horowitz, T. S., 98
Horrigan, K., A-9, A-10
Horwood, L. J., 30
House, J. S., 545

Herz, R. S., 260
House, R. J., 495
Houts, A. C., 651
Hovatta, I., 616
Howe, M. L., 192, 362
Howell, C. J., 524
Howell, R. T., 524
Hoy, W., 395
Hoyer, G., 630
Hu, F. B., 461
Hu, X-Z., 616, 629
Huart, J., 370
Hubbard, E. M., 258
Hubel, D. H., 230, 238, 239
Hublin, C., 102
Huckabee, M., 464
Hucker, S. J., 468
Hudson, J. I., 454
Huey, E. D., 72
Huff, C., 22
Huffcutt, A. I., 489
Hugdahl, K., 615
Hugenberg, K., 705
Hughes, H. C., 227
Hugick, L., 159
Huizink, A. C., 124
Hulbert, A., 426
Hull, H. R., 98
Hull, J. G., 116
Hull, J. M., 347, 721
Hull, P., 393
Hulme, C., 338
Hume, D., 287, 700
Hummer, R. A., 553
Humphrey, S. E., 586
Humphreys, L. G., 423
Hunsberger, J. G., 549
Hunsley, J., 663
Hunt, C., 610
Hunt, E., 413, 438, 439
Hunt, J. M., 430, 431
Hunt, M., 2, 3, 4, 11, 45, 201, 299, 426, 470
Hunter, J. E., 41, 487, 488, 590
Hunter, J., 202
Hunter, S., 216
Hurst, M., 96
Hurst, N., 706
Huss, M., A-10
Hussein, S., 373, 688, 691, 708, 731
Huston, A. C., 319
Huxley, T. H., 605
Hvistendahl, M., 704
Hyde, J. S., 157, 357, 433, 627
Hyman, M., 155
Hyman, R., 578, 579
Hynie, M., 471

Iacoboni, M., 316
Iacono, W. G., 627
Ickes, W., 584
Idson, L. C., 683
Ikonomidou, C., 172
Ilardi, S. S., 548, 632, 678
Ingham, A., 698
Inglehart, R., 219, 481, 485, 524, 586

Ingram, N., 695
Inman, M. L., 371
Insana, R., 494
Inzlicht, M., 439, 585
Ironson, G., 554
Irvine, A. A., 683
Irwin, M. R., 98, 100
Ishai, A., 476
Ishida, A., 666
Iso, H., 74
Ito, T. A., 516, 711
Iuzzini, J., 713
Iversen, L. L., 124
Iverson, J. M., 400
Iyengar, S. S., 587
Izard, C. E., 513, 517

Jablensky, A., 640
Jackson, D. N., 432
Jackson, J. M., 698
Jackson, J. S., 704
Jackson, L. A., 580
Jackson, S. W., 668
Jacobi, C., 454
Jacobs, B. L., 122, 548, 632, 673
Jacobson, N. S., 668
Jacoby, L. L., 362
Jacques, C., 225
Jacques-Tiura, A. J., 684
Jaffe, E., 278
Jago, A. G., 495
James, K., 348
James, W., 3, 4, 5, 12, 55, 111,
    172, 251, 347, 351, 366, 500,
    501, 504, 509, 515, 521, 590,
    597, 689
Jameson, D., 269
Jamison, K. R., 626, 674
Janda, L. H., 721
Jang, K. L., 621
Janis, I. L., 374, 700
Janoff-Bulman, R., 709
Javitt, D. C., 640
Jefferson, T., 17, 570
Jeffery, R. W., 463
Jenkins, J. G., 354, 355
Jenkins, J. M., 181
Jennings, J. R., 536
Jensen, A. R., 413, 414, 422, 435,
    438
Jensen, J. P., 668
Jensen, P. S., 600
Jepson, C., 43, B-1
Jessberger, S., 74
Job, D. E., 640
Johanowicz, D. L., 315
Johansson, P., 89
John Paul II, Pope, 704
John, O. P., 577
Johnson, B. T., 332, 605
Johnson, C. B., 144
Johnson, D. F., 4
Johnson, D. L., 576
Johnson, D. W., 732
Johnson, E. J., 382
Johnson, J. A., 688
Johnson, J. G., 454

Johnson, J. S., 390
Johnson, K., 621
Johnson, L. B., 377, 688
Johnson, L. C., 378
Johnson, M. E., 109
Johnson, M. H., 173, 187
Johnson, M. K., 331, 333
Johnson, R. E., 494
Johnson, R. T., 732
Johnson, S. C., 212
Johnson, S. K., 622
Johnson, V. E., 466, 467, 483
Johnson, W., 223
Johnston, A., 513
Johnston, L. D., 120, 125, 127
Johnston, R. E., 514
Johnston, W. A., 88
Johnstone, E. C., 643
Joiner, T. E., Jr., 631, 691
Jolly, A., 397
Jonas, E., 567
Jones, A. C., 576
Jones, J. M., 120, 610
Jones, J. T., 719
Jones, L., 579
Jones, M., 621
Jones, M. C., 651, 652
Jones, M. V., 278
Jones, S. S., 316, 514
Jones, W. H., 20
Jonides, J., 338
Jorm, A. F., 211
Joseph, J., 136
Josephs, R. A., 116
Joubert, J., 316, 692
Judd, L., 628
Judge, T. A., 491, 495
Juffer, F., 137, 192, 428
Jung, C., 193, 563, 569, 574, 668
Jung, R. E., 412
Jung-Beeman, M., 371, 372
Just, M. A., 78
Juvenal, 207

Kagan, J., 80, 138, 185, 187, 188,
    222, 576
Kahlor, L., 714
Kahneman, D., 33, 97, 255, 333,
    374, 375, 522, 523, 527, 593,
    662
Kail, R., 210
Kaltman, S., 221
Kamarck, T., 536
Kamena, M., 362
Kamil, A. C., 343
Kaminski, J., 399
Kanawaza, S., 543
Kanaya, T., 425
Kanazawa, S., 405
Kandel, D. B., 127
Kandel, E. R., 52, 339, 340
Kane, M. J., 326
Kant, I., 272
Kanwisher, N., 370
Kaplan, A., 454
Kaplan, H. I., 672
Kaplan, K. J., 638

Kaplan, R. M., 545
Kaprio, J., 534
Kaptchuk, T. J., 256
Karacan, I., 94
Karau, S. J., 698
Kark, J. D., 552
Karni, A., 104, 149
Karno, M., 612
Karpicke, J. D., 330
Karraker, K. H., 277
Karremans, J. C., 229
Kasen, S., 160
Kashima, Y., 155
Kasimatis, M., 515
Kasindorf, M., 482
Kasser, T., 526
Kassirer, J. P., 550
Kaufman, A. S., 215
Kaufman, J., 190
Kaufman, J. C., 404, 626
Kaufman, J. H., 268
Kaufman, L., 268
Kavsek, M., 423
Kayser, C., 258
Kazdin, A. E., 307
Keats, J., 165
Keenan, J. P., 78
Keesey, R. E., 451
Keillor, G., 593
Keith, S. W., 460
Kekulé, A., 100
Kellehear, A., 123
Keller, H., 174, 247, 249
Keller, J., 102
Keller, M. B., 674
Keller, M. C., 628
Kellerman, J., 510
Kellermann, A. L., 710
Kelley, J., 137
Kelling, S. T., 257
Kellner, C. H., 676
Kelly, A. E., 655
Kelly, D. J., 708
Kelly, I. W., 578
Kelly, T. A., 668
Keltner, D., 522
Kemeny, M. E., 542
Kempe, C. C., 189
Kempe, R. S., 189
Kempermann, G., 210
Kendall-Tackett, K. A., 190, 363
Kendler, K. S., 126, 193, 584, 616,
    627, 628, 629
Kennedy, J. F., 678, 700, 733
Kennedy, S., 55
Kenny, D. A., 582
Kenrick, D. T., 145 148, 469,
    581
Kensinger, E. A., 341
Keough, K. A., 559
Kepler, J., 235
Kern, P., 136
Kernahan, C., 158
Kernis, M. H., 594
Kerr, N. L., 698
Kerry, J., 721, 724
Kessler, M., 669

Kessler, R. C., 540, 603, 607, 613,
    627, 632, 665
Ketcham, K., 103, 364
Keyes, E., 203
Keynes, M., 626
Keys, A., 448, 451
Khaliq, A. (Abdur-Rahman), 329
Kidman, A. D., 540
Kiecolt-Glaser, J. K., 538, 540,
    545
Kierkegaard, S., 15
Kight, T. D., 724
Kihlstrom, J. F., 112, 357, 411,
    566, 568, 620
Killeen, P. R., 112
Killham, E., 494, 586
Kilmann, P. R., 471
Kim, B. S., 668
Kim, H., 155
Kim, K. A., 392
Kim, P., 543
Kimata, H., 545
Kimble, G., 295
Kimbro, W., 701
Kimmel, A. J., 22
Kimmel, D., 473, 434, 477
King, L., 360
King, L. A., 522, 546
King, M., 473
King, M. L., Jr., 318
King, R. N., 578
King, R. "Suki," 407
Kinkel, K., 606
Kinnier, R. T., 219
Kinzler, K. D., 179
Kipling, R., 708
Kirby, D., 472
Kirkpatrick, B., 639
Kirkpatrick, L., 187
Kirmayer, L. J., 623
Kirsch, I., 35, 108, 110, 674
Kisley, M. A., 219
Kisor, H., 249
Kistler, D. J., 510
Kitayama, S., 155, 393, 520, 682
Kitt, A. S., 528
Kitts, R. L., 473
Kivimaki, M., 543
Klayman, J., 373
Klein, D. N., 668
Klein, E., 676
Kleinfeld, J., 435
Kleinke, C. L., 510
Kleinmuntz, B., 504
Kleitman, N., 92
Klemm, W. R., 61
Klentz, B., 723
Kline, D., 209
Kline, G. H., 217
Klineberg, O., 513, 732
Klinesmith, J., 711
Klinke, R., 273
Kluft, R. P., 619
Klump, K. L., 454
Klüver, H., 62
Knapp, S., 363
Knäuper, B., 471

Knickmeyer, E., 454
Knight, R. T., 72
Knight, W., 258
Knoblich, G., 372
Knutson, K. L., 97
Ko, C-K., 115
Koch, C., 85
Koch, G., A-10
Koehler, D. J., 578
Koelling, R. A., 296, 297
Koenig, H. G., 552, 554
Koenig, L. B., 137
Koenig, O., 53
Koenigs, M., 72, 200
Koestner, R., 494
Kohlberg, L., 198, 199, 205, 222, B-7
Kohler, I., 274
Köhler, W., 397
Kohn, P. M., 534
Kohout, J., A-4
Kokkalis, J., 122
Kolarz, D. M., 216
Kolassa, I.-T., 616
Kolata, G., 463, 630
Kolb, B., 73, 149, 409
Koletsky, R. J., 463
Kolivas, E. D., 144
Kolker, K., 715
Kolodziej, M. E., 605
Koltko-Rivera, M. E., 447
Koob, G. F., 639
Koole, S. L., 567
Kopta, S. M., 662
Koriat, A., 360
Korschgen, A., A-2
Kosslyn, S. M., 53, 111, 284, 390, 431, 613
Kotchick, B. A., 471
Kotkin, M., 660
Kotkin, M., 356
Kovas, Y., 428
Kozak, M. J., 652
Kracen, A. C., A-10
Kraft, C., 279, 280
Kraft, R. N., 365
Kramer, A. F., 211, 548
Krantz, D. H., 43, B-1
Kranz, F., 476
Kraus, N., 381
Krauss, R. M., 400
Kraut, R. E., 514
Krebs, D. L., 116, 199, 200
Krech, D., 148
Kring, A. M., 513
Krishnamurti, 605
Kristensen, P., 41
Kristof, N. D., 726
Kroll, R., 468
Kronick, R. G., 545
Kroonenberg, P. M., 187
Krosnick, J. A., 229
Krueger, A., 712
Krueger, J., 494, 586
Kruger, J., 180, 511, 588
Krull, D. S., 15
Krupa, D. J., 345

Krützen, M., 398
Ksir, C., 121
Kubey, R., 319
Kübler, A., 523
Kubzansky, L. D., 536, 537
Kuester, L. W., 220
Kuhl, B. A., 354
Kuhl, P. K., 386
Kuhn, B. R., 307
Kuhn, C. M., 126
Kuhn, D., 197
Kujala, U. M., 548
Kuncel, C. R., 407
Kuncel, N. R., 422
Kung, L.-C., 395
Kunkel, D., 471, 715
Kuntsche, E., 127
Kupper, N., 536
Kupper, S., 549
Kurdek, L. A., 473
Kurtz, P., 17, 579
Kuse, A. R., 434
Kushner, M. G., 672
Kutas, M., 91
Kutcher, E. J., 488

L'Engle, M., 15, 440, 626
Labouvie-Vief, G., 213
Lacayo, R., 27
Lacey, H. P., 219
Lacey, M., 733
Lachman, M. E., 216
Ladd, E. C., 128
Ladd, G. T., 83
Lafleur, D. L., 616
Laird, J. D., 510, 515
Lakin, J. L., 690
Lalumière, M. L., 477
Lam, R. W., 666
Lambert, A. J., 723
Lambert, K. G., 548
Lambert, W. E., 394
Lamberth, J., 704
Lambird, K. H., 594
Lammers, B., A-10
Lampinen, J. M., 349
Landau, M. J., 708
Landauer, T., 365
Landauer, T. K., 531
Landrum, E., A-2
Landry, M. J., 122
Lange, C., 500, 501, 504, 509
Langer, E., 248
Langer, E. J., 586, 605
Langleben, D. D., 505
Langlois, J. H., 721, 722, 723
Lángström, N., 476
Lanzetta, J. T., 516
Larkin, K., 476
LaRoche, K., A-10
Larsen, J., 511, 512
Larsen, R. J., 138, 508, 515
Larson, D. B., 554
Larson, G., 410
Larson, J., 221
Larson, R. W., 220, 437
Larsson, H., 621

Larzelere, R. E., 307
Lashley, K. S., 339
Lassiter, G. D., 683
Latané, B., 698, 726, 727, 728
Latham, G. P., 494
Latner, J. D., 458
Laudenslager, M. L., 542
Laumann, E. O., 144, 473
Laws, K. R., 122
Lazaruk, W., 395
Lazarus, R. S., 507, 508, 509, 531, 534
Le Grand, R., 272, 273
Lea, S. E. G., 21
Leach, P., 307
Leaper, C., 158
Leary, M. R., 479, 480, 481, 482, 591
Leary, W. E., 207
Leask, S. J., 78
LeBoeuf, R. A., 379
Ledger, H., 113
LeDoux, J. E., 62, 149, 344, 507, 508, 509
Lee, K., 275
Lee, L., 275
Lee, S-Y., 426
Lefcourt, H. M., 585
Legrand, L. N., 127
Lehavot, K., 723
Lehman, A. F., 672
Lehman, D. R., 220
Leigh, B. C., 116
Leitenberg, H., 468, 470
Lemonick, M. D., 451
Lennon, R., 513
Lennox, B. R., 71
Lenzenweger, M. F., 672
Leonard, J. B., 709
Lepper, M. R., 309, 587
Lerner, M. J., 709
Leserman, J., 540
Lesperance, F., 537
Lessard, N., 248
Lester, W., 704
Leucht, S., 672
Leung, A. K-Y., 410
LeVay, S., 475, 476
Levenson, R. W., 503
Lever, J., 454
Levesque, M. J., 582
Levin, I. P., 381
Levin, R., 103
Levine, J. A., 459, 460
Levine, R. V., 29, 153, 725
Levy, B., 248
Levy, P. E., 489
Levy, S. R., 478
Lewald, J., 249
Lewandowski, G. W., Jr., 723
Lewicki, P., 348, 566
Lewinsohn, P. M., 349, 627
Lewis, B., 135
Lewis, C. S., 3, 201, 352, 503, 567
Lewis, D. O., 189, 620, 710
Lewis, J., 510
Lewis, J. A., 135

Lewis, L., 135
Lewis, M., 349, 350
Lewontin, R., 142, 436
Li, J., 220
Li, J. C., 709
Li, P., 389
Li, W., 229
Libet, B., 87
Licata, A., 120
Licoppe, C., 159
Lieberman, J. A., 672
Lieberman, M. D., 547
Lievens, F., 487
Lilienfeld, S. O., 182, 565, 619, 620, 621, 664, 665
Lin, L., 101
Lincoln, A., 141, 352, 406, 570, 608
Lindbergh, C., 283
Linde, K., 550
Linder, D., 730
Lindoerfer, J. S., 700
Lindsay, D. S., 359
Lindskold, S., 733
Lindström, P., 475
Lindzey, G., 567
Linville, P. W., 381
Linz, D., 321, 714
Lippa, R. A., 144, 159, 473, 474, 478, 721
Lippman, J., 319
Lippmann, W., 723
Lipps, H. M., 704
Lipsey, M. W., 426
Lipsitt, L. P., 175
Livesley, W. J., 621
Livingstone, M., 239
Lobel, A., 723
LoBue, V., 615
Locke, E. A., 494
Locke, J., 6, 272, 287
Loehlin, J. C., 134, 137, 579
Loewenstein, G., 305
Loftus, E. F., 103, 109, 339, 357, 358, 359, 363, 364, 365, 566
Loftus, G., 339
Logan, T. K., 126
Loges, W. E., 36, 704
Logue, A. W., 304
LoLordo, V. M., 309
Lombardi, V., 491
London, P., 318, 536
Looy, H., 146
Lopes, P. N., 411
Lopez, A. D., 597
Lopez, D. J., 45
López-Ibor, J. J., 610
Lord, C. G., 377
Lorenz, K., 187
Lott, J., 621
Louie, K., 104
Lourenco, O., 185
Lovaas, O. I., 653
Love, J. M., 191
Loveland, D. H., 302
Lowry, P. E., 590
Lu, Z-L., 337

Lubart, T. I., 410
Lubinski, D., 426, 432
Luborsky, L., 663
Lucas, A., 34
Lucas, G., 471
Lucas, H. L., 620
Lucas, R. E., 221, 523, 528, 529
Luciano, M., 414
Ludwig, A. M., 474, 626
Lund, E., 630
Lundberg, G., 550
Luntz, F., 688
Luria, A. M., 324
Lurigio, A. J., 605
Lustig, C., 343
Lutgendorf, S. K., 540, 554
Luus, C. A. E., 471
Lyall, S., 209
Lykins, A. D., 474
Lykken, D. T., 134, 137, 214, 216,
    428, 504, 519, 528, 621, 711
Lyman, D. R., 622
Lynch, G., 340
Lynch, J. G., Jr., 377
Lynch, S., 340
Lynn, M., 115
Lynn, R., 421, 435
Lynn, S. J., 110
Lynne, S. D., 197
Lyons, L., 202, 204, 553, 704
Lytton, H., 163
Lyubomirsky, S., 522, 528, 546

M'Naughten, D., 606
Ma, L., 612
Ma, Y.-Y., 351
Maas, J. B., 97, 98, 101
Maass, A., 155, 393, 439
Macaluso, E., 258
Macan, T. H., 488
Maccoby, E. E., 158, 160, 162,
    191, 192, 699
MacDonald, G., 349, 482, 723
MacDonald, J., 258
Macdonald, J. E., 534
MacDonald, N., 637
MacDonald, S. W., 215
MacDonald, T. K., 116, 471
MacFarlane, A., 173
Macfarlane, J. W., 195
Macgregor, A. M. C., 458
Machado, A., 185
Maciejewski, P. K., 221
Mack, A., 89
MacKinnon, D. W., 409
MacNeilage, P. F., 387
Maddieson, I., 385
Maddox, K. B., 705
Madonna, 282
Madrian, B. C., 382
Madsen, T. M., 676
Maes, H. H. M., 460
Maestripieri, D., 137, 189
Magellan, F., 60
Magnusson, D., 621
Magnusson, P. E. E., 630
Magoun, H. W., 61

Maguire, E. A., 333, 344
Mahadevan, R., 338, 339
Mahler, G., 671
Mahowald, M. W., 94
Maier, S. F., 538, 539
Maimonides, 552
Major, B., 158, 722
Malamuth, N. M., 469, 714, 715,
    714
Malan, D. H., 648
Maliki, J. (al-), 511
Malinosky-Rummell, R., 189
Malkiel, B. G., 33, 377
Malle, B. F., 683
Mallory, G., 445
Malmquist, C. P., 566
Malnic, B., 260
Malott, J. M., 256
Manber, R., 101
Mandel, D., 448
Mandel, H., 612
Maner, J. K., 482
Manilow, B., 591
Mann, T., 463, 594
Mannix, L. M., 458
Manson, J. E., 548
Maquet, P., 104, 105
Mar, R. A., 317
Marangell, L. B., 676
Maratos-Flier, E., 460
Marcus, B., 581
Marcus, G. F., 389
Maren, S., 616
Marentette, P. F., 387
Margolis, M. L., 101
Marino, L., 192
Markowitsch, H. J., 344
Markowitz, J. C., 649
Markus, G. B., 41, 361
Markus, H. R., 155, 393, 520, 590
Marley, J., 605
Marmot, M. G., 543
Marschark, M., 333
Marsh, A. A., 514
Marsh, H. W., 528, 591
Marshall, M. J., 307
Marshall, R. D., 376
Marshall, W. L., 714
Marta, 238
Marteau, T. M., 381
Marti, M. W., 371
Martin, C. K., 463
Martin, C. L., 163
Martin, R. A., 545
Martin, R. J., 451
Martin, R. M., 34
Martin, S., 426
Martin, S. P., 96
Martino, S. C., 471
Martins, Y., 476
Marx, J., 212, 642
Masicampo, E. J., 585
Maslow, A. H., 5, 44, 446, 447,
    448, 484, 570, 571, 572, 573,
    591
Mason, C., 52
Mason, H., 21, 97, 600

Mason, R. A., 78
Masse, L. C., 126
Massimini, M., 92
Mast, M. S., 722
Masten, A. S., 189
Masters, C., 720
Masters, W. H., 466, 467, 483
Mastroianni, G. R., 688, 695
Masuda, T., 515, 682
Mataix-Cols, D., 616
Matheny, A. P., Jr., 138
Mather, M., 219
Matisse, H., 486
Matsumoto, D., 393, 513, 514
Matsuzawa, T., 398
Matthews, G., 581
Matthews, K. A., 537
Matthews, R. N., 292
Maurer, C., 173
Maurer, D., 173
May, C., 92
May, M., 272
May, P. A., 172
May, R., 132
Mayberg, H. S., 677
Mayberry, R. I., 390
Mayer, D., 587
Mayer, J. D., 411
Mays, V. M., 535
Mays, W., 207
Mazella, R., 722
Mazur, A., 711
Mazure, C., 632
Mazzella, R., 454
Mazzoni, G., 359, 361
Mazzuca, J., 320
McAdams, D. P., 557
McAneny, L., 349
McArthur, L. Z., 294
McBeath, M. K., 267
McBride-Chang, C., 190
McBurney, D. H., 72, 257, 269,
    270
McCabe, G., 34
McCabe, M. P., 454
McCain, J., 360, 681
McCain, N. L., 540
McCann, I. L., 547, 548
McCann, U. D., 122
McCarthy, A., 515
McCarthy, P., 259
McCarty, O., 591
McCaul, K. D., 256
McCauley, C. R., 699
McClearn, G. E., 429, 476
McClellan, J. M., 642
McClendon, B. T., 685
McClintock, M. K., 196, 533
McClure, E. B., 433
McConkey, K. M., 108, 109, 112
McConnell, R. A., 282
McConnell, S., 211
McCool, G., 722
McCord, J., 661
McCormick, C. M., 478
McCrae, R. R., 138, 216, 223, 577,
    579, 581

McCrink, K., 179
McCullough, M. E., 553
McDaniel, M. A., 362, 412
McDermott, K. B., 360
McDermott, T., 712
McEvoy, S. P., 88
McFadden, D., 477
McFarland, C., 361
McFarland, S., 687
McGarry-Roberts, P. A., 414
McGaugh, J. L., 323, 341
McGhee, P. E., 184
McGlashan, T. H., 639
McGlone, M. S., 331
McGrath, J., 641
McGregor, H. A., 494
McGue, M., 134, 136, 429
McGuffin, P., 629, 631
McGuire, M. T., 463
McGuire, W. J., 320
McGurk, H., 258
McHugh, P. R., 619, 620
McKellar, J., 658
McKenna, K. Y. A., 700, 720
McKone, E., 239
McLanahan, S., 713
McLaughlin, C. S., 470
McMahon, F. J., 629
McMurray, B., 386
McMurray, C., 547
McMurray, J., 378
McNally, R. J., 359, 363, 613, 666
McNeil, B. J., 381
McPherson, J. M., 634
Meador, B. D., 650
Medland, S. E., 78
Mednick, S. A., 640, 643
Medvec, V. H., 219
Mehl, M. R., 29, 159, 581
Mehta, M. R., 344
Meichenbaum, D., 656
Meier, B., 213
Meier, P., 411
Melchior, L. A., 155
Melhuish, E., 173
Meltzoff, A. N., 316, 386, 394
Meltzoff, C. M., 448
Melville, H., 28, 599, 681
Melzack, R., 114, 254, 255
Memon, A., 359
Menander of Athens, 103
Mendle, J., 197
Mendolia, M., 547
Menustik, C. E., 653
Merari, A., 700
Merker, B., 85
Merskey, H., 619
Merton, R. K., 18, 528
Mesmer, F. A., 665, 666
Messinis, L., 124
Mestel, R., 103
Meston, C. M., 468, 469
Metcalfe, J., 372, 376
Metha, A. T., 219
Meyer, A., 626
Meyer, I. H., 599
Meyer-Bahlburg, H. F. L., 477

Mezulis, A. M., 592
Michaels, J. W., 697
Michel, G. F., 79
Michelangelo, 79, 206
Middlebrooks, J. C., 247
Mikels, J. A., 215, 219
Mikhail, J., 388
Mikkelsen, T. S., 132
Mikulincer, M., 97, 189, 567, 708
Milan, R. J., Jr., 471
Miles, D. R., 710
Milgram, S., 109, 693, 694, 695, 696, 702
Millar, J. K., 642
Miller, D. T., 127
Miller, E., 454
Miller, E. J., 457
Miller, G., 67, 126, 259,
Miller, G., 467
Miller, G. A., 337
Miller, G. E., 534, 537
Miller, J. G., 199
Miller, K., 724
Miller, K. I., 585
Miller, L., 378
Miller, L. C., 725
Miller, L. K., 406
Miller, M., 545
Miller, N. E., 21, 450, 549
Miller, P., 643
Miller, P. A., 200
Miller, P. C., 193
Miller, P. J. O., 91
Miller, S. D., 619
Mills, M., 173
Milne, B. J., 621
Milner, B., 342
Milner, D. A., 86
Milner, P., 64
Milton, J., 284
Mineka, S., 190, 519, 614, 615
Miner-Rubino, K., 219
Ming, S-M., 276
Mingroni, M. A., 421
Minsky, M., 85
Mirescu, C., 533
Mischel, W., 200, 304, 581, 590, 683
Miserandino, M., 346
Mita, T. H., 720
Mitchell, D. B., 324
Mitchell, F., 709
Mitchell, P., 182
Mitchell, T. M., 392
Mitchell, T. R., 333
Mitte, K., 657
Miyamoto, R. T., 248
Mocellin, J. S. P., 123
Moffitt, T. E., 223, 610, 622, 631
Moghaddam, F. M., 700
Moises, H. W., 641
Molaison, H., 342
Molyneux, W., 272
Monaghan, P., 364
Mondloch, C. J., 173
Money, J., 468, 475, 477, 714

Moniz, E., 677, 678
Monroe, M., 146, 691, 722
Moody, R., 123
Mook, D. G., 19
Moorcroft, W. H., 93, 99, 105
Moore, B., 220
Moore, D. W., 96, 127, 281, 462
Moore, J., 462
Moore, M. K., 316
Moore, S., 722
Moos, B. S., 658
Moos, R. H., 658
Mor, N., 633
Moreland, R. L., 719
Morell, V., 397, 538
Morelli, G. A., 156
Moreno, C., 626
Morey, R. A., 640
Morgan, A. B., 621
Morgan, B., A-2
Morin, R., 203
Morris, A. S., 193, 197, 203
Morris, R., 711
Morris, S. C., 393
Morrison, A. R., 21, 95
Morrison, C., 690
Morrison, D., 714
Morrison, K., 664
Morrow, D. G., 331
Morse, M. L., 123
Morsella, E., 567
Mortensen, E. L., 34
Mortensen, P. B., 640
Morton, J., 173
Moruzzi, G., 61
Moscovici, S., 701
Moser, P. W., 237
Moses, 17
Moses, E. B., 656
Moses (Grandma), 214
Mosher, D. L., 117
Mosher, W. D., 473
Moss, A. J., 119
Moss, H. A., 223
Mosteller, F., 34
Motivala, S. J., 98
Moullec, C., 187
Moulton, S. T., 284
Mowrer, O. H., 651
Moyer, K. E., 710
Mozart, W. A., 426, 431, 626
Mroczek, D. K., 216, 219
Muhlnickel, W., 71
Mulcahy, N. J., 397
Mulder, E. J., 124
Muller, J. E., 466, 534
Mullin, C. R., 321
Mulrow, C. D., 673
Munro, D. A., 118
Murachver, T., 159
Murison, R., 542
Murnen, S. K., 454, 469
Murphy, G. E., 630
Murphy, K. R., 489
Murphy, S. T., 117, 507
Murray, B., 280
Murray, C. A., 435

Murray, C. J., 597
Murray, D. M., 360
Murray, H., 490
Murray, H., 564
Murray, H. A., 27, 283
Murray, J. P., 319
Murray, R. M., 124, 638, 640
Murray, S. L., 278, 591
Musallam, S., 69
Musick, M. A., 554
Mustanski, B. S., 476, 477
Mycielska, K., 275
Mydans, S., 709
Myers, D. G., 3, 33, 217, 378, 473, 527, 529, 592, 593, 699
Myers, I. B., 574
Myers, L. R., 503
Myers, R., 74
Myerson, J., 438

Nagourney, A., 685
Nairn, R. G., 605
Nakayama, E. Y., 649
Napoleon, 572
Napolitan, D. A., 682
Naqvi, N. H., 119
Nasar, J., 88
Nash, M. R., 110, 112, 364
Naylor, T. H., 496
Neal, D. T., 287
Neale, J. M., 522
Neese, R. M., 253, 297
Neisser, U., 88, 341, 421, 428, 439
Neitz, J., 241
Nelson, C. A., 431
Nelson, M. D., 640
Nelson, N., 545
Nemeth, C. J., 700
Nesca, M., 356
Nestadt, G., 612
Nestle, M., 461
Nestoriuc, Y., 549
Neubauer, A., 150
Neubauer, P. B., 150
Neufer, P. D., 548
Neumann, R., 516, 690
Neuringer, A., 303
Newberg, A., 552
Newcomb, M. D., 126
Newcombe, N. S., 176
Newman, A. J., 390
Newman, L. S., 109, 192
Newman, M. L., 505
Newman, R., 386
Newport, E. L., 390
Newport, F., 158, 165, 512, 688, 732
Newton, E. L., 281
Newton, I., 18, 165, 18, 240, 410, 608
Newton, T. L., 545
Neylan, T. C., 101
Nezlek, J. B., 585
Ng, S. H., 394
Ng, W. W. H., 585

Nguyen, D., 532
Nichols, R. C., 134
Nickell, J., 109
Nickerson, R. S., 279, 281, 352
Nicol, S. E., 642
Nicolaus, L. K., 296
Nicolelis, M. A. L., 69
Niebuhr, R., 587
Niedenthal, P. M., 360
Nielsen, K. M., 545
Nielsen, T. A., 103
Niemiec, C. P., 480
Nier, J. A., 593
Niesta, D., 296, 297
Nightingale, F., 546
Nisbett, R. E., 43, 374, 487, 713, B-1
Nitschke, J. B., 258
Nixon, G. M., 97
Nixon, R. M., 513
Noel, J. G., 587
Noftle, E. E., 580
Noice, H., 332
Noice, T., 332
Nolen-Hoeksema, S., 202, 221, 521, 632, 633
Noller, P., 189
Nordgren, L. F., 448
Norem, J. K., 587
Norenzayan, A., 29, 153, 567
Norman, D. A., 279
Normand, M. P., 182
Noroozian, M., 79
Norris, J., 620
Northall, G. F., 297
Norton, K. L., 455
Norton, M. B., 708
Norton, P. J., 657
Nostradamus, 282
Nowak, R., 119
Nowell, A., 432, 433, 434
Nurius, P., 590
Nurmi, J-E., 591
Nurnberger, J. I., Jr., 126
Nuttin, J. M., Jr., 719

O'Brien, R. M., 311
O'Connor, A., 461, 701
O'Connor, P., 668
O'Donnell, L., 472
O'Heeron, R. C., 546
O'Keeffe, C., 579
O'Neil, J., 32
O'Neill, E., 365
O'Neill, M. J., 543
O'Reardon, J. P., 676
Oaten, M., 585
Oates, J. C., 351
Oatley, K., 317
Obama, B., 681, 683
Oberlander, J., 582
Oberman, L. M., 183, 317, 516
Odbert, H. S., 575
Oddone-Paolucci, E., 714
Oellinger, M., 372
Oetting, E. R., 127
Oettingen, G., 586, 587

Offer, D., 203, 361
Ogden, C. L., 461
Öhman, A., 510, 519, 615
Oishi, S., 447, 522, 524
Okun, M. S., 504
Olatunhi, B. O., 610
Olds, J., 64, 65
Olff, M., 614
Olfson, M., 600, 672, 673
Olin, S. S., 643
Oliner, P. M., 318
Oliner, S. P., 318
Olsen, A., 133
Olsen, M.-K., 133, 453
Olshansky, S. J., 208, 457
Olson, M. A., 293
Olson, S., 576
Olsson, A., 519, 615
Olweus, D., 711
Oman, D., 553
Onishi, N., 457
Oppenheimer, J. R., 17
Oren, D. A., 92
Orlovskaya, D. D., 412
Ormiston, M., 700
Orne, M. T., 109
Osborne, C., 217
Osborne, J. W., 439
Osborne, L., 389
Osburn, H. G., 495
Osgood, C. E., 733
Ost, L. G., 615
Ostfeld, A. M., 544
Oswald, A. J., 219, 458, 523, 524,
    535, 545
Ott, B., 493
Ott, C. H., 221
Ouellette, J. A., 488, 590
Over, R., 55
Overmier, J. B., 542
Owen, A. M., 85
Owen, D. R., 420
Owen, R., 492
Owyang, M. T., 721
Ozer, E. J., 613, 614
Özgen, E., 394
Ozley, L., 496

Pacifici, R., 122
Padawer, W., 666
Paddock, S., 629
Padgett, V. R., 695
Page, S., 605
Page, S. E., 700
Pagnin, D., 675
Pahlavi, F., 525
Palace, E. M., 506
Palladino, J. J., 91
Pallier, C., 387
Palmer, J. C., 357
Palmer, S., 262, 263, 341
Pals, J. L., 557
Pandelaere, M., 362
Pandey, J., 684
Pankratz, V. S., 630
Panksepp, J., 503
Pantev, C., 73

Panzarella, C., 633
Park, C. L., 553
Park, D. C., 215
Park, G., 426
Park, J., 293
Park, L. E., 594
Park, R. L., 505
Parker, C. P., 491
Parker, E. S., 351
Parker, J. W., 528
Parks, R., 701
Parsons, B., 478
Parsons, L. M., 62
Parva, S., 541
Pascal, 229
Pashler, H., 329
Passell, P., 36
Pastalkova, E., 340
Pasteur, L., 21, 410
Patall, E. A., 309
Pate, J. E., 454
Patel, S. R., 97
Patrick, H., 480
Patten, S. B., 625
Patterson, D. R., 110
Patterson, F., 400
Patterson, G. R., 308, 713
Patterson, M., 491
Patterson, P. H., 640
Patterson, R., 635
Patton, G. C., 124
Paulesu, E., 20
Paulos, J. A., 38, 674
Paus, T., 174
Pavlidis, G. T., 600
Pavlov, I., 4, 290, 291, 292, 293,
    294, 295, 298, 300, 321,
    369, 651
Payne, B. K., 357, 705
Payne, R., 545
Peace, K. A., 365
Pedersen, N., 136
Peek, K., 406
Peeters, A., 457
Peigneux, P., 100, 344
Pekkanen, J., 100
Pelham, B. W., 15, 209, 591
Pendick, D., 711
Penfield, W., 68
Penhune, V. B., 249
Pennebaker, J. W., 29, 219, 546,
    547, 566, 726, 732
Penny, H., 458
Penrod, S. D., 360
Peplau, L. A., 144, 217, 473
Peppard, P. E., 102
Pepperberg, I. M., 398
Perani, D., 392
Pereira, A. C., 74, 211
Pereira, G. M., 210, 495
Perkins, A., 475
Perlick, D., 697
Perlmutter, M., 213
Perls, T., 538
Perra, O., 183
Perrett, D. I., 238, 706, 722
Perry, N., 176

Persky, S., 717
Person, C., 628
Pert, C. B., 50, 64
Perugini, E. M., 111
Peschel, E. R., 468
Peschel, R. E., 468
Peters, M., 78
Peters, T. J., 311
Peterson, C., 184, 198, 587, 603
Peterson, L. R., 337
Peterson, M. J., 337
Petiot, M. (Dr.), 579
Petitto, L. A., 387
Petry, N. M., 458
Pettegrew, J. W., 640
Petticrew, C., 540
Petticrew, M., 540
Pettifor, J. P., 22
Pettigrew, T. F., 704, 731
Pettus, A., 566
Pfammatter, M., 664
Phelps, E. A., 63, 615
Phelps, J. A., 134, 642
Phelps, M., 171
Phelps, M. E., 174
Phillips, D. P., 691
Phillips, J. L., 180
Phillips, M., 153
Phillips, T., 733
Piaget, J., 4, 27, 176, 177, 178,
    179, 180, 184, 185, 194,
    198, 205, 222, 359, 426, B-7
Picasso, P., 79, 407
Picchioni, M. M., 638
Pierce, P., 254
Piercy, M., 470
Pieters, G. L. M., 454
Pike, K. M., 454
Pilcher, J. J., 143
Piliavin, J. A., 200
Pillemer, D. B., 481
Pillemer, D. G., 175, 212
Pillsworth, E. G., 467
Pillsworth, M. G., 467
Pinel, J. P. J., 450
Pinel, P., 601, 645
Pingitore, R., 458
Pinker, S., 53, 83, 137, 142,
    144, 159, 285, 376, 384,
    385, 394, 401, 402, 412, 434,
    438
Pinstrup-Andersen, P., 461
Pipe, M-E., 362
Piper, A., Jr., 619
Pipher, M., 136, 481, 534
Pirandello, L., 580, 581, 634
Pirsig, R. M., 18, 662
Pitcher, D., 239
Pitman, R. K., 341
Pitt, B., 346
Pittenger, D. J., 574
Planck, M., 399
Plassmann, H., 258
Plato, 6, 45, 125, 416, 568
Plaud, J. J., 651
Pleck, J. H., 144
Pleyers, G., 293

Pliner, P., 452
Plöderl, M., 473
Plomin, R., 134, 136, 140, 141,
    142, 150, 405, 428, 429, 460,
    476, 629, 631, 641
Plotkin, H., 629
Plotnik, J. M., 192
Plous, S., 21
Poastalkova, E., 340
Pogue-Geile, M. F., 460
Poldrack, R. A., 331
Polich, J., 552
Polivy, J., 454, 463
Pollack, A., 70
Pollak, S. D., 294, 510
Pollard, R., 395
Pollick, A. S., 400
Pollitt, E., 431
Polusny, M. A., 190
Poole, D. A., 359, 360, 362
Poon, L. W., 210
Pope John Paul II, 165
Pope, H. G., 566
Popenoe, D., 155, 217
Popkin, B. M., 460, 461
Popkin, S. J., 210
Poremba, A., 63
Porter, D., 303
Porter, S., 359, 364, 365, 511
Posluszny, D. M., 540
Posner, M. I., 392
Posthuma, D., 428
Poulton, R., 621
Powdthavee, N., 458, 523
Powell, J., 593
Powell, K. E., 548
Powell, L. H., 554
Powell, L. J., 184
Powell, R. A., 565
Pratkanis, A. R., 229
Premack, D., 181
Prentice, D. A., 127
Prentice-Dunn, S., 685
Presley, C. A., 117
Presley, E., 16, 558
Pressman, S. D., 522
Price, E. C., 657
Price, G. M., 457
Price, J., 351
Pridgen, P. R., 590
Principe, G. F., 361
Pringle, P. J., 171
Prioleau, L., 667
Prior, H., 192
Pritchard, R. M., 231
Proffitt, D. R., 277
Pronin, E., 593, 626, 683, 693
Propper, R. E., 103
Proust, M., 260
Provine, R. R., 29
Pryor, J. H., 144, 159, 434, 480,
    632
Puchalski, C., 552
Puhl, R. M., 458
Pulkkinen, L., 191
Putnam, F. W., 619
Putnam, R., 153

Putt, A., 523
Putt, D., 523
Pyszczynski, T. A., 567, 633, 708, 724

Qirko, H. N., 700
Quanty, M. B., 520
Quasha, S., 423
Quinn, P. C., 172, 263
Quinn, P. J., 34

Rabbitt, P., 213
Rabinowicz, T., 174
Rader, D., 620
Radin, D., 284
Rahman, Q., 476, 478
Raine, A., 621, 622, 710
Rainville, P., 111
Rajendran, G., 182
Ralston, A., 443, 445, 446
Ramachandran, V. S., 53, 73, 74, 183, 255, 317
Ramírez-Esparza, N., 393
Ramón y Cajal, S., 49
Rand, C. S., 458
Randall, P. K., 145
Randi, J., 17, 284
Rapoport, J. L., 612, 615
Räsänen, S., 639
Rasch, B., 100
Raveis, V. H., 127
Rawles, R., 704
Rawlings, J., 198
Ray, J., 520
Ray, O., 121
Rayner, R., 5, 298, 299, 518
Raynor, H. A., 451
Raz, A., 111
Reagan, R., 565, 606, 733
Reason, J., 275, 700
Reed, G., 688
Reed, P., 330
Reed, T. E., 414
Rees, G., 229
Rees, Martin (Sir), 166
Regan, P. C., 144
Regier, D., 607
Reichenberg, A., 182, 637
Reicher, S., 687
Reichman, J., 468
Reifman, A., 137
Reijmers, L. G., 519
Reimer, D., 161
Reiner, W. G., 161
Reis, D., 192
Reis, H. T., 189, 724
Reisenzein, R., 506
Reiser, M., 282
Reite, M. L., 542
Reitzle, M., 205
Remley, A., 156
Renner, C. H., 149
Renner, M. J., 148, 149
Renninger, K. A., 185
Renshon, J., 593
Rentfrow, P. J., 581
Repetti, R. L., 531

Rescorla, R. A., 295
Resnick, M. D., 31, 203
Resnick, R. A., 89
Resnick, S. M., 640
Ressler, R. K., 714
Retzlaff, P. D., 109
Reyna, V. F., 197, 360
Reynolds, A. J., 431
Rhoades, L., 309
Rhodes, G., 275, 709, 723
Rhodes, M. G., 362
Rhodes, S. R., 210
Rholes, W. S., 189
Ribeiro, R., 100
Riber, K. A., 410
Ricciardelli, L. A., 454
Rice, B., 684
Rice, M. E., 319
Richardson, J., 352
Richardson, J. T. E., 260
Richardson, K. D., 708
Richeson, J. A., 731
Riedner, G., 471
Rieff, P., 568
Rieger, G., 473
Riis, J., 523
Rindermann, H., 407
Ring, K., 123
Ripple, C. H., 431
Risch, N., 632
Riskind, J. H., 603
Ritzler, B., 566
Rizzolatti, G., 316
Roberson, D., 394
Roberts, B. W., 223, 580, 581
Roberts, L., 543
Roberts, T-A., 158
Robertson, B. A., 212, 213
Robins, L., 607
Robins, L. N., 127
Robins, R. W., 202, 219, 517, 580
Robinson, F. P., 12
Robinson, J., 473
Robinson, J. P., 96
Robinson, T. E., 114
Robinson, T. N., 275, 463
Robinson, V. M., 544, 545
Rochat, F., 696
Rock, I., 89, 262, 263
Rock, J., 214
Rockefeller, J. D., Sr., 572
Rodgers, R., 515, 723
Rodin, J., 454, 542, 543, 586
Rodman, R., 385, 388
Rodriguez, A., 528
Roediger, H. L., III, 330, 355, 358, 360, 362
Roehling, M. V., 458
Roehling, P. V., 496
Roenneberg, T., 92
Roese, N. J., 219
Roesser, R., 245
Rofé, Y., 566
Rogaeva, E., 212
Rogers, C. R., 5, 570, 571, 572, 573, 591, 592, 649, 650, 659
Rogers, L. J., 77

Roggman, L. A., 723
Rohan, K. J., 666
Rohan, M. J., 137
Rohner, R. P., 156, 138, 193
Rohrer, D., 329
Roiser, J. P., 122
Rokach, A., 20
Romney, D. M., 163
Roney, J. R., 145
Roosevelt, E., 223, 570
Roosevelt, F. D. (FDR), 342
Rorschach, H., 564, 565
Rosch, E., 370
Rose, A. J., 158
Rose, J. S., 119, 151
Rose, R. J., 151, 191, 475
Rose, S., 146, 613
Roselli, C. E., 476
Rosemary, R., 678
Rosenbaum, M., 349, 723
Rosenberg, N. A., 142
Rosengren, K. S., 177
Rosenhan, D. L., 605
Rosenman, R., 535, 536
Rosenthal, R., 433, 511, 582
Rosenzweig, M. R., 148, 430
Roseth, C. J., 732
Ross, J., 100
Ross, L., 278, 374, 683
Ross, M., 356, 361, 393, 594
Rossi, A. S., 159
Rossi, P. H., 159
Rossi, P. J., 273
Rossion, B., 225
Rostosky, S. S., 472
Roth, T., 104
Rothbart, M., 709
Rothbart, M. K., 138
Rothbaum, F., 155
Rothblum, E. D., 144
Rothman, A. J., 381
Rothstein, W. G., 213
Rotter, J., 585
Rousseau, J-J., 176
Rovee-Collier, C., 175, 176, 348
Rowe, D. C., 136, 156, 157, 430, 437, 710
Rowling, J. K., 432
Rozin, P., 294, 451
Ruback, R. B., 586
Rubel, T., 158
Rubenstein, J. S., 88
Rubin, D. C., 212, 341
Rubin, J. Z., 733
Rubin, L. B., 159
Rubin, Z., 510
Rubio, G., 610
Ruble, D. N., 163, 192
Rubonis, A. V., 533
Ruchlis, H., 371
Rudman, L. A., 704
Rudner, R., 91
Rudolph, K. D., 158
Ruffin, C. L., 534
Ruiz, J. M., 520
Ruiz-Belda, M-A., 514
Rule, B. G., 321

Rumbaugh, D. M., 400, 401, 402
Rumsfeld, D., 377
Rünger, D., 566
Rupp, D. E., 589
Rusesabagina, P., 726
Rush, A. J., 674
Rush, B., 646
Rushton, J. P., 319, 435
Russell, B., 103, 528
Russell, J. A., 514, 517, 518
Russo, A., 393
Russon, A. E., 315
Rusting, C. L., 521
Rutter, M., 189, 476
Ruys, K. I., 507
Ryan, R. M., 309, 480, 526, 527, 594
Ryckman, R. M., 457
Ryder, A. G., 623

S, 324
Saad, L., 119, 534, 704
Sabbagh, M. A., 181
Sabini, J., 694
Sachdev, J., 678
Sachdev, P., 678
Sachs, J., 379
Sackett, P. R., 439, 487
Sacks, O., 252, 342
Sadato, N., 73
Saddam, S., 733
Saddock, B. J., 672
Sadi, 254
Saffran, J. R., 389
Sagan, C., 18, 58, 165, 283
Sagi, D., 104
Sakurai, T., 450
Salib, E., 630
Salk, J., 410
Salmela-Aro, K., 591
Salmon, P., 547, 548
Salovey, P., 381, 411, 522
Salthouse, T. A., 210, 215
Sampson, E. E., 154
Samuels, J., 612
Samuels, S., 34
Sanders, A. R., 642
Sanders, G., 477, 478
Sandfort, T. G. M., 473
Sandkühler, S., 371
Sandler, W., 389
Sanford, A. J., 381, 382
Sanz, C., 398, 399
Sapadin, L. A., 159
Sapirstein, G., 35
Sapolsky, B. S., 471, 715
Sapolsky, R. M., 208, 532, 543, 628
Saribay, S. A., 348
Sartorius, N., 623
Sartre, J-P., 165
Satel, S., 613
Sato, K., 730
Saul, S., 100
Saulny, S., 534
Saunders, S., 118
Savage-Rumbaugh, S., 401, 402

Savarino, J., 674
Savic, I., 475, 476
Savitsky, K., 591
Savoy, C., 395
Sawyer, M. G., 628
Saxe, R., 184
Sayre, R. F., 211
Scanzoni, L. D., 217, 473
Scarborough, E., 4
Scarr, S., 140, 150, 191, 407, 431
Schab, F. R., 261
Schachter, S., 464, 501, 506, 508, 509, 724
Schacter, D. L., 210, 343, 351, 361, 519, 566
Schafer, G., 387
Schaie, K. W., 214
Schall, T., 207
Schechter, R., 182
Scheier, M. F., 544
Schein, E. H., 686
Schell, D. A., 213
Schellenberg, E. G., 431
Scherer, K. R., 510
Schiavi, R. C., 94
Schiavo, R. S., 697
Schieber, F., 209
Schiffenbauer, A., 697
Schilt, T., 122
Schimel, J., 572
Schimmack, U., 154, 529
Schkade, D., 699
Schlaug, G., 60
Schlesinger, A. M., Jr., 700
Schmidt, F. L., 487, 488, 489, 492, 590
Schmitt, D. P., 143, 144, 145, 578, 593
Schnaper, N., 123
Schneider, R. H., 552
Schneider, S. L., 587
Schneiderman, N., 540
Schoenborn, C. A., 97
Schoenema, T. J., 155
Schofield, J. W., 731
Schonfield, D., 212, 213
Schooler, J. W., 358
Schopenhauer, A., 296
Schorr, E. A., 248
Schreiner-Engel, P., 94
Schugens, M. M., 344
Schultheiss, D. E. P., A-10
Schuman, H., 212
Schumann, R., 626
Schwartz, B., 298, 382, 586, 614
Schwartz, J., 523
Schwartz, J. H., 339
Schwartz, J. M., 656, 678
Schwartz, S. H., 158
Schwarz, A., 78
Schwarz, N., 349
Schwarzenegger, A., 275
Sclafani, A., 452
Scott, B. A., 513
Scott, D. J., 119, 256
Scott, E. S., 197
Scott, G., 277

Scott, J., 105, 212
Scott, W. A., 156
Sdorow, L. M., 564
Seal, K. H., 613
Seamon, J. G., 359
Sears, R. R., 426
Sebat, J., 182
Sechrest, L., 565
Secord, P. F., 704
Sedgwick, J., 17
Sedikides, C., 512
Seeman, P., 639
Segal, M. E., 699
Segal, N. L., 136, 429
Segall, M. H., 144, 162, 185
Segerstrom, S. C., 531, 544
Seidler, G. H., 665
Seidlitz, L., 633
Self, C. E., 127
Seligman, M. E. P., 83, 92, 150, 480, 490, 518, 527, 549, 568, 585, 586, 587, 588, 591, 603, 633, 634, 656, 660, 663
Sellers, H., 225, 238
Selye, H., 532, 533, 541
Sen, A., 704
Seneca, 207, 330, 526, 586, 725
Senghas, A., 389
Sengupta, S., 732
Senju, A., 183, 317
Sensenbrenner, F. J., 457
Serruya, M. D., 69
Service, R. F., 340
Seto, M. C., 116
Seuss (Geisel, Theodor Seuss), 270
Shadish, W. R., 284, 658, 662, 663
Shaffer, D. M., 267
Shafir, E., 379
Shafto, M. A., 213
Shakespeare, W., 91, 132, 185, 285, 313, 339, 369, 406, 510, 520, 562, 606, 619, 626, 630, 723
Shamir, B., 495
Shanahan, L., 202, 203
Shanley, D. P., 207
Shapiro, F., 665
Shapiro, K. A., 392
Sharma, A. R., 137
Shattuck, P. T., 182
Shaver, P. R., 187, 189, 190, 517, 708
Shaw, G. B., 700, 725
Shaw, H. L., 401
Shaw, P., 412, 600
Shea, D. F., 382
Sheehan, S., 637
Sheldon, K. M., 480
Sheldon, M. S., 467
Shelton, J. N., 731
Shenton, M. E., 640
Shepard, R. N., 23, 276
Shepherd, C., 135, 461, 621
Sheppard, L. D., 413
Shereshevskii, 324, 351

Shergill, S. S., 731
Sherif, M., 732
Sherman, P. W., 452
Sherman, S. J., 373
Shermer, M., 160, 281
Sherrington, C., 49
Sherry, D., 343
Shettleworth, S. J., 309, 338
Shields, B., 629
Shiffrin, R. M., 323, 325, 326, 327, 336
Shimizu, M., 209
Shinkareva, S., 85
Shotland, R. L., 726
Showers, C., 587
Shulman, P., 433
Shuwairi, S. M., 179
Sieff, E. M., 523
Siegal, M., 184
Siegel, J. M., 99, 101, 104, 545
Siegel, R. K., 114, 120, 122, 123, 124
Siegel, S., 288, 298
Siegler, R. S., 177
Sigmund, B. B., 540
Sigvardsson, S., 137
Silbersweig, D. A., 640
Sill, M., 207
Silva, A. J., 340
Silva, C. E., 108
Silver, M., 696
Silver, R. C., 221
Silveri, M. M., 197
Silverman, K., 117
Silverman, P. S., 109
Simek, T. C., 311
Simms, C. A., 619
Simon, G. E., 458, 674
Simon, H., 381, 491
Simon, H. A., 334
Simon, P., 320
Simon, T., 416, 417
Simons, D. J., 89
Simonton, D. K., 215, 321, 409, 410
Simpson, J. A., 145, 189
Simpson, O. J., 331
Sinclair, R. C., 506
Singelis, T. M., 155
Singer, J. E., 501, 506, 508, 509, 724
Singer, J. L., 664
Singer, T., 256, 317
Singh, D., 145, 723
Singh, J. V., 495
Singh, S., 409, 410
Singleton, C., 606
Singleton, D., A-4
Sipski, M. L., 55
Sirenteanu, R., 273
Sivard, R. L., 208
Sizemore, C., 619
Sjöstrum, L., 458
Skinner, B. F., 5, 301, 303, 305, 306, 308, 310, 311, 314, 321, 388, 389, 403, 491, 570, 633, 653

Skitka, L. J., 521
Sklar, L. S., 540
Skodol, A. E., 623
Skoog, G., 612
Skoog, I., 612
Skov, R., 373
Slatcher, R. B., 726
Slater, E., 626
Slater, L., 673
Slater, M., 694
Slavin, R. E., 426
Sloan, R. P., 552
Slovic, P., 119
Small, M. F., 126, 156
Small, S. A., 212
Smedley, A., 437
Smedley, B. D., 437
Smelser, N. J., 709
Smith, A., 639
Smith, Adam, 729
Smith, A. N., 113
Smith, C., 122, 536
Smith, E., 523
Smith, G., 207
Smith, J. E., 457
Smith, M., 248
Smith, M. B., 572
Smith, M. L., 511, 662, 663
Smith, P. B., 495, 693
Smith, S. M., 721
Smith, T. B., 669
Smith, T. W., 470, 472, 473, 520, 660
Smolak, L., 454
Smoreda, Z., 159
Snedeker, J., 388
Snidman, N., 138
Snodgrass, S. E., 516
Snowdon, D. A., 424
Snyder, F., 105
Snyder, M., 606
Snyder, S. H., 49, 50, 674
Sokol, D. K., 134
Solomon, D., 404
Solomon, D. A., 674
Solomon, J., 605
Solomon, M., 721
Solomon, S., 567
Sommer, R., 153
Søndergård, L., 674
Song, S., 110
Sontag, S., 540
Soon, C. S., 87
Sørensen, H. J., 638
Sorkhabi, N., 193
Soussignan, R., 516
South, S. C., 193
Sowell, T., 734
Spalding, K. L., 458
Spanos, N. P., 109, 110, 111, 619
Spearman, C., 405, 409, 415
Specht, J. C., 572
Spelke, E. S., 179, 434
Spencer, D. (Princess of Wales), 454
Spencer, J., 172
Spencer, K. M., 640

Spencer, S. J., 439
Sperling, G., 336, 337
Sperry, R. W., 74, 75, 80, 239
Speth, J. G., 525
Spiegel, D., 110, 619
Spiegel, K., 97, 98
Spielberg, S., 384
Spielberger, C., 536
Spinoza, B., 1
Spitzer, R. L., 613, 623, 628
Spooner, W. A., 565
Spradley, J. P., 153
Sprecher, S., 512, 721
Spring, B., 463, 664
Springer, J. A., 135
Spruijt, N., 496
Squire, L. R., 343
Srivastava, A., 526
Srivastava, S., 577, 579, 587
St. Augustine, 165
St. Clair, D., 640
St. John, 626
Stack, S., 630
Stafford, R. S., 673
Stager, C. L., 386
Stagg, A. A., 214
Stanley, J. C., 426, 433
Stanovich, K., 558
Stapel, D. A., 507
Staples, B., 704
Stark, R., 18, 160
Starr, J. M., 424
Stathopoulou, G., 547
Staub, E., 614, 687
Staubli, U., 340
Steel, P., 529
Steele, C. M., 116, 439
Steele, J., 79
Steenhuysen, J., 248
Steer, R. A., 630
Steinberg, L., 193, 197, 203
Steinberg, N., 719
Steinhauer, J., 134
Steinmetz, J. E., 345
Stelzner, S. P., 495
Stengel, E., 630
Stern, M., 277
Stern, S. L., 544
Stern, W., 417
Sternberg, E. M., 410, 538
Sternberg, R. J., 404, 405, 408,
    409, 410, 415, 426, 437, 512,
    725, A-10
Stetter, F., 549
Stevens, W., 33
Stevenson, H. W., 426, 437
Stevenson, R. J., 258
Stevenson, R. L., 487, 618
Stewart, B., 22
Stewart, J., 575
Stice, E., 454, 455
Stickgold, R., 100, 103, 104, 105
Stinson, D. A., 547
Stipek, D., 192
Stith, S. M., 319
Stockton, M. C., 469
Stoddart, R., A-5

Stohr, O., 136
Stokoe, W., 248
Stone, A. A., 255, 522
Stone, G., 618
Stone, L. D., 219
Stone, R., 613
Stoolmiller, M., 137
Stoppard, J. M., 512
Storbeck, J., 508
Storm, L., 284
Storms, M. D., 474, 475, 683, 697
Stough, C., 413
Strack, F., 516, 690
Strack, S., 634
Strahan, E. J., 229
Stranahan, A. M., 74
Strand, S., 432, 435
Stratton, G. M., 274
Straub, R. O., 12, 401
Straus, M. A., 158, 307
Stravinsky, I., 303, 407
Strawbridge, W. J., 553
Strayer, D. L., 88
Strenze, T., 407
Strickland, B., 208
Strickland, F., 621
Striegel-Moore, R. H., 454, 455
Stroebe, M., 221
Stroebe, W., 221
Strupp, H. H., 666
Stumpf, H., 432, 433
Stunkard, A. J., 460
Styfco, S. J., 431
Suarez, S. D., 192
Subiaul, F., 315
Suddath, R. L., 642
Sue, S., 668
Suedfeld, P., 123, 614
Sugita, Y., 270
Suinn, R. M., 395
Sullenberger, C., 280
Sullivan, A., 174
Sullivan, P. F., 629
Suls, J., 536
Suls, J. M., 528
Summers, M., 597
Summerville, A., 219
Sundel, M., 216
Sundet, J. M., 420
Sundstrom, E., 496
Sunstein, C. R., 382
Suomi, S. J., 190, 561, 616
Super, C., A-4
Super, D., A-4
Suppes, P., 184
Susman, E. J., 223
Süß, H-M., 411
Susser, E., 640, 643
Susser, E. S., 613
Susskind, J. M., 518
Sutcliffe, J. S., 182
Sutherland, A., 312
Sutherland, S., 312
Sutton, D., 701
Svebak, S., 544
Swann, W. B., Jr., 591
Sweat, J. A., 283

Swerdlow, N. R., 639
Swift, J., 3
Swim, J. K., 704
Symbaluk, D. G., 256
Symond, M. B., 640
Symons, C. S., 332
Szucko, J. J., 504
Szymanski, K., 698

Tabarlet, J. O., 471, 715
Taha, F. A., 103
Taheri, S., 98, 101, 460
Tajfel, H., 707
Takahashi, N., 155
Talal, N., 538
Talarico, J. M., 341
Talbot, M., 690
Talwar, S. K., 64
Tamres, L. K., 160
Tanfer, K., B-6
Tang, S-H., 309
Tangney, J. P., 585
Tannen, D., 20, 159
Tannenbaum, P., 231
Tanner, J. M., 196
Tarbert, J., 687
Tarmann, A., 473
Tasbihsazan, R., 423
Taub, E., 73
Taubes, G., 463
Tavris, C., 356, 521, 565, 688
Tayeb, M., 495
Taylor, P. J., 318
Taylor, S. E., 160, 377, 396, 532,
    593, 613
Taylor, S. P., 711
Teasdale, T. W., 420
Tedeschi, R. G., 614
Teerlink, R., 496
Teghtsoonian, R., 230
Teicher, M. H., 190, 600
Teitelbaum, P., 450
Tellegen, A., 216, 518, 528
Teller, E., 412
ten Brinke, L., 511
Tennyson, A., 160
Tenopyr, M. L., 486
Teran-Santos, J., 101
Teresi, D., 65
Terman, J. S., 666
Terman, L. M., 417, 418, 426, 427
Terman, M., 92, 666
Terracciano, A., 156, 223
Terrace, H. S., 27, 401
Terre, L., A-5
Tertullian, 708
Tesch, F., 528
Tesser, A., 203
Tetlock, P. E., 17, 733
Thaler, R. H., 382
Thannickal, T., 101
Thatcher, R. W., 174, 222
Thayer, R. E., 547
Théoret, H., 183
Thernstrom, M., 256
Thiel, A., 73
Thiele, T. E., 126

Thomas, A., 137, 188, 223
Thomas, G. C., 697
Thomas, L., 51, 166, 260, 389,
    661, 671
Thomas, S. L., 320
Thompson, C. P., 339
Thompson, D., 361
Thompson, J. K., 463
Thompson, P. M., 174, 428
Thompson, R., 354
Thomson, R., 159
Thoreau, H. D., 277
Thorndike, A. L., 419
Thorndike, E. L., 301, 314, 411
Thorne, J., 597
Thornhill, R., 466, 723
Thornton, A., B-6
Thornton, B., 722
Thornton, G. C. III, 589
Thorpe, W. H., 402
Thurstone, L. L., 405, 409, 415
Tice, D. M., 204, 713
Tickle, J. J., 119
Tiedens, L. Z., 521
Tiger, L., 308
Tikkanen, T., 6
Tillmann, H. C., 479
Timlin, M. T., 30
Timmerman, T. A., 712
Tinbergen, N., 444
Tirrell, M. E., 292, 294
Titchener, E. B., 2, 3, 4, 5, 58
Tockerman, Y. R., 457
Todorov, A., 511
Tofighbakhsh, J., 331
Tolin, D. F., 614
Tolkien, J.R.R., 557, 580, 581
Tollefson, G. D., 674
Tolley-Schell, S. A., 510
Tolman, E. C., 308
Tolstoy, L., 9, 141, 195, 217, 608,
    625
Tomiczek, C., 258
Tondo, L., 674
Toni, N., 340
Toole, E., 620
Tordoff, V., 338
Torrey, E. F., 640, 668
Totterdell, P., 690
Towler, G., 697
Townshend, P., 219
Tracey, J. L., 517
Tramontana, M. G., 423
Tranel, D., 77
Traub, J., 216
Trautwein, U., 591
Treffert, D. A., 406
Treisman, A., 263
Tremblay, R. E., 126, 621
Trewin, D., 162, 484
Triandis, H. C., 153, 155, 586,
    713
Trickett, P. K., 190
Trillin, A., 571
Trillin, C., 571
Trimble, J. E., 127
Triplett, N., 697

Trolier, T. K., 32
Troller, J. N., 219
Trope, L. R., 731
Trull, T. J., 620
Truman, H. S., 342, 700
Trump, D., 589
Trut, L. N., 142
Trzesniewski, K. H., 219
Tsai, J. L., 515
Tsang, B. Y-P., 155
Tsang, Y, C., 449
Tsankova, N., 140
Tschaikovsky, P. I., 395
Tse, D., 344
Tsien, J. Z., 339
Tsuang, M. T., 629
Tuber, D. S., 22
Tucker, K. A., 494
Tuerk, P. W., 431
Tully, T., 291
Tulving, E., 331, 332
Tumulty, K., 462
Turk, D. C., 256
Turkheimer, E., 430, 431
Turner, J. C., 706
Turner, N., 495
Turpin, A., 281
Tutu, D., 480
Tversky, A., 33, 374, 375
Tversky, B., 6
Twain, M. (Samuel Clemens), 28, 45, 120, 138, 310, 359, 430, 592, 626, 655
Twenge, J.,
Twenge, J. M., 164, 202, 482, 594, 616, 628, 713
Twiss, C., 31
Tyler, K. A., 190

Uchino, B. N., 546
Uddin, L. Q., 78
Udry, J. R., 161
Uga, V., 103
Ullman, E., 484
Ulman, K. J., 196
Ulmer, D., 535, 551
Ulrich, R. E., 21
Unsworth, N., 326
Urbany, J. E., 381
Urry, H. L., 503
Ursu, S., 616
Uttal, D. H., 177
Uttal, W. R., 72

Vaccarino, A. L., 343
Vaidya, J. G., 579
Vaillant, G. E., 361, 480, 545
Valdes, A. M., 208
Valenstein, E. S., 678
Vallone, R. P., 16
van Boxtel, H. W., 593
Van Cauter, E., 97
van den Boom, D., 188
van den Bos, K., 496
van der Maas, H. L. J., 406
van der Werf, S. Y., 628
Van Dyke, C., 121

van Engen, M. L., 158
van Gogh, V., 141
van Goozen, S. H. M., 621
van Hemert, D., 515
Van Hesteren, F., 200
van IJzendoorn, M. H., 137, 187, 188, 192, 428
van Ittersum, K., 265
Van Leeuwen, M. S., 162
Van Lommel, P., 123
Van Rooy, D. L., 411
van Schaik, C. P., 398
Van Tassel-Baska, J., 423
Van Yperen, N. W., 725
Van Zeijl, J., 188
Vance, E. B., 466
VandeCreek, L., 363
Vandenberg, S. G., 434
Vanman, E. J., 705
Vannucci, M., 361
Vaughn, K. B., 516
Vazire, S., 581
Vecera, S. P., 266
Vega, V., 714
Vegas, R., 313
Vekassy, L., 103
Velliste, M., 69, 70
Venditte, P., 78
Veneziano, R. A., 188, 193
Venter, J. C., 134
Verbeek, M. E. M., 576
Verhaeghen, P., 210
Verier, R. L., 534
Verma, S., 437
Vernon, P. A., 413, 414
Vertes, R., 104
Vessel, E. A., 446
Vigil, J. M., 196
Vigliocco, G., 386
Vining, E. P. G., 73
Virgil, 34, 502, 520
Viswesvaran, C., 411
Vita, A. J., 120
Vitello, P., 209
Vitevitch, M. S., 89
Vittengl, J. R., 674
Voas, D., 578
Vogel, P., 74
Vogel, S., 140
Vohs, K. D., 144
Vollhardt, J., 614
von Békésy, G., 246
Von Ebner-Eschenbach, M., 214
von Helmholtz, H., 241, 246
von Hippel, W., 210
von Senden, M., 272
Voyer, D., 432
Vrana, S. R., 503
Vroom, V. H., 495
Vyazovski, V. V., 99
Vygotsky, L., 184, 185

Waber, R. L., 35
Wacker, J., 576
Wadden, T. A., 463
Wade, K. A., 358
Wade, N. G., 669

Wagar, B. M., 332
Wager, T. D., 256, 616
Wagner, A. D., 331
Wagner, A. R., 295
Wagner, F. E., 665
Wagner, N. N., 466
Wagner, R. K., 408
Wagner, U., 100
Wagstaff, G., 684
Wahlberg, D., 533
Wai, J., 426
Wakefield, J. C., 600, 613, 625
Waldrop, M. F., 423
Walk, R. D., 264
Walker, M. P., 100
Walker, W. R., 220
Wall, P. D., 254, 255
Wallace, D. S., 685
Wallace, G. L., 406
Wallace, I. J., A-10
Wallach, L., 572
Wallach, M. A., 572
Waller, J., 696
Walsh, T., 642
Walster (Hatfield), E., 721
Wampold, B. E., 663, 666, 668
Wang, S-H., 179
Wangchuk, J. S., 526
Wansink, B., 265, 453
Ward, A., 463
Ward, C., 115
Ward, J., 258
Ward, K. D., 120
Ward, L. M., 471
Wardle, J., 257
Wargo, E., 551
Warm, J. S., 228
Warr, P., 545
Warren, R., 276
Washburn, A. L., 448, 449
Washburn, D. A., 402
Washburn, M. F., 4
Wason, P. C., 373
Wasserman, E., 516
Wasserman, E. A., 303, 397
Wastell, C. A., 546
Waterhouse, R., 38
Waterman, A. S., 202
Waterman, I., 252
Waterman, R. H., Jr., 311
Waters, E., 187
Watkins, E. R., 625
Watkins, J. G., 618
Watkins, M. J., 330
Watson, D., 517, 518, 522, 523, 547, 591
Watson, J. B., 5, 83, 290, 295, 298, 299, 321, 518
Watson, R. I., Jr., 698
Watson, S. J., 124
Watson, T., 311
Wayment, H. A., 217
Weaver, J. B., 469
Webb, W. B., 95, 96, 100
Weber, E., 230, 232
Wechsler, D., 213, 418, 419, 420, 427, 438

Weed, W. S., 281
Wegner, D. M., 83, 87, 626
Weigel, G., 208
Weil, A., 550
Weinberger, D. R., 197
Weiner, B., 684
Weingarten, G., 484
Weinstein, N. D., 587
Weir, M., 79
Weis, S., 411
Weiskrantz, L., 239
Weiss, A., 528, 576
Weiss, D. S., 613, 614
Weiss, H. M., 491
Weiss, J. M., 543
Weissman, M. M., 627, 648
Weisz, J. R., 154
Weitzman, M. S., 729
Welch, J. M., 616
Welch, W. W., 612
Weller, S., 472
Wellings, K., 470, 471
Wellman, H. M., 179, 184
Wells, B. L., 470
Wells, G. L., 287, 360, 361
Wender, P. H., 629
Wener, R., 586
Werker, J. F., 386
Wernicke, C., 391, 392, 403
West, R. L., 212
Westen, D., 508, 563, 565, 664
Wetzel, R. D., 630
Weuve, J., 211
Whalen, P. J., 503, 507, 508
Whaley, S. E., 191
Whalley, L. J., 423, 424, 543
Whalley, P., 423
Wheeler, B. W., 674
Wheeler, D. R., 27, 283
Wheelwright, J., 135
Whishaw, I. Q., 149, 409
White, G. L., 724
White, H. R., 711
White, K. M., 204
White, L., 218
White, R. A., 283
Whitehead, B. D., 217
Whiten, A., 28, 315, 398
Whiting, B. B., 156
Whiting, J. W. M., 531
Whitley, B. E., Jr., 478, 707
Whitlock, J. R., 340
Whitman, C., 503
Whitman, W., 47, 626
Whitmore, J. K., 437
Whooley, M. A., 537
Whorf, B. L., 393, 403
Wicherski, M., A-4
Wichman, H., 281
Wickelgren, I., 182
Wickelgren, W. A., 3320
Widiger, T. A., 620
Widom, C. S., 190
Wiekelgren, I., 182
Wielkiewicz, R. M., 495
Wiens, A. N., 653
Wierson, M., 312

Wierzbicki, M., 137
Wiesel, T. N., 238, 272
Wiesner, W. H., 488
Wiest, J. R., 716
Wigdor, A. K., 439
Wike, R., 704
Wilcox, A. J., 467
Wilde, O., 593
Wilder, D. A., 707
Wildman, D. E., 132
Wiles, A., 409, 410
Wilford, J. N., 165
Wilkens, C., 726
Willemsen, T. M., 158
Williams, C. "Andy," 482
Williams, C. L., 534
Williams, H. J., 642
Williams, J. E., 158, 536
Williams, J. H. G., 219, 317
Williams, K. D., 481, 482, 698
Williams, R. E., 520, 536
Williams, Serena, 137
Williams, Steve, 309
Williams, S. L., 652
Williams, V., 137
Williams, W. M., 431
Williamson, D. A., 454
Willingham, B., 513
Willingham, W. W., 422
Willis, J., 511
Willmuth, M. E., 470
Wilson, A. E., 393, 594
Wilson, C. M., 545
Wilson, D. B., 284, 426
Wilson, G. D., 476, 478
Wilson, G. T., 116
Wilson, J. Q., 199
Wilson, M., 338
Wilson, M. A., 104
Wilson, R. C., 699
Wilson, R. S., 138, 175, 211, 212, 215
Wilson, T. D., 87, 297, 439
Wilson, W. A., 126

Wiltshire, S., 406
Windholz, G., 292, 294
Winerman, L., 228
Winfrey, O., 164, 346, 464
Wingfield, A., 249
Wink, P., 220
Winkielman, P., 507
Winner, E., 426
Winquist, J., 633
Wiseman, R., 284, 359, 372, 579
Wisman, A., 193
Witelson, S. F., 72, 412, 478
Witt, J. K., 277
Wittgenstein, L., 166
Witvliet, C. V. O., 503, 521
Wixted, J. T., 353
Woehr, D. J., 589
Woerlee, G. M., 123
Wojtowicz, J. M., 673
Wolak, J., 714
Wolfe, M. S., 211
Wolfe, T., 46
Wolfson, A. R., 105
Woll, S., 721
Wolpe, J., 651, 652
Wolpert, E. A., 103
Wonder, S., 248
Wonderlich, S. A., 453
Wong, D. F., 639
Wong, M. M., 159
Wood, C. J., 79
Wood, J. M., 356, 565
Wood, J. N., 399
Wood, J. V., 633
Wood, M., 433
Wood, W., 146, 158, 160, 164, 287, 488, 512, 590, 701
Woodruff, G., 181
Woodruff-Pak, D. S., 213, 344, 345
Woods, N. F., 196
Woods, T., 97, 309, 437
Woodward, B., 14

Woodward, L. G., 628
Woody, E. Z., 112
Woodyard, D., 302
Woolcock, N., 693
Woolf, V., 626
Worobey, J., 138
Worthington, E. L., Jr., 198, 669
Wortman, C. B., 221, 299
Wren, C. S., 127
Wright, F. L., 214
Wright, I. C., 640
Wright, J., 207
Wright, P., 640
Wright, P. H., 159
Wright, W., 135
Wrosch, C., 534
Wrzesniewski, A., 484
Wu, W., 212
Wuethrich, B., 116
Wulsin, L. R., 537
Wundt, W., 2, 4, 5, 14
Wyatt, J. K., 104, 356
Wyatt, R. J., 641
Wynn, K., 179
Wynne, C. D. L., 401
Wysocki, C. J., 260

Xu, Y., 343
Xun, W. Q. E., 393

Yach, D., 457
Yalom, I. D., 658
Yamagata, S., 579
Yang, N., 714
Yang, S., 587
Yano, S., 426
Yanof, D. S., 203
Yarnell, P. R., 340
Yarrow, L. J., 190
Yates, A., 454, 606
Yates, W. R., 468
Ybarra, O., 591
Yellen, A., 92

Yip, P. S. F., 631
Yonas, A., 264
Young, R., 32
Young, T., 241
Youngentob, S. L., 171
Youngman, H., 104
Yücel, M., 124
Yufe, J., 136
Yuki, M., 515

Zabin, L. S., 196
Zaccaro, S. J., 495
Zadra, A., 102
Zadro, L., 482
Zagorsky, J. L., 407
Zajonc, R. B., 41, 417, 506, 507, 508, 509, 697, 719, 720
Zammit, S., 638
Zanna, M. P., 137, 704
Zauberman, G., 377
Zeelenberg, R., 507
Zeidner, M., 411, 435
Zeineh, M. M., 344
Zeno, 649
Zhang, J. V., 451
Zhang, P., 208
Zigler, E. F., 190, 431
Zilbergeld, B., 660, 664
Zillmann, D., 469, 506, 714
Zillmer, E., 566
Zimbardo, P. G., 686, 687, 688, 698, 708
Zimmerman, R. D., 489
Zimmerman, T. D., 213
Zinbarg, R., 614, 615
Zogby, J., 245
Zornberg, G. L., 640
Zou, Z., 260
Zubieta, J-K., 255, 256
Zucco, G. M., 260
Zucker, G. S., 684
Zucker, K. J., 472
Zuckerman, M., 445
Zvolensky, M. J., 611

Subject Index

Absent-mindedness, forgetting and, 351
Absolute thresholds, 227
Abu Ghraib prison, 687
Abuse, repressed vs. constructed memories of, 362–365
Acceptance
    in client-centered therapy, 649
    in person-centered perspective, 571
Accidents
    alcohol and, 116
    selective attention and, 88
    sleep deprivation and, 97, 98–99, 101–102
Accommodation
    in cognitive development, 177
    visual, 234
Acetylcholine (ACh), 50, 51
Achievement motivation, 490–496
    effective leadership and, 493–496
    satisfaction and engagement and, 491–493
Achievement tests, 418, 419, 422
Acoustic encoding, 331–332
Acquired immunodeficiency syndrome (AIDS). See AIDS (acquired immunodeficiency syndrome)
Acquisition, in classical conditioning, 292–293
Acronyms, 334
Action, moral, 200
Action potentials, 47
Activation-synthesis theory of dreams, 105, 106
Active listening, in client-centered therapy, 649
Activity level. See also Exercise
    obesity and, 460
Acupuncture, 256
Adaptability, heritability and, 139
Adaptation
    dark, 236
    learning and, 287, 297
    natural selection and, 141–142
    neuroadaptation, 113
    sensory, 230–231
    taste preferences and, 452
Adaptation-level phenomenon, 526–527
Addiction
    definition of, 114
    misconceptions about, 114–115
ADHD (attention-deficit/hyperactivity disorder), 599, 600

Adolescence, 195–205
    brain development in, 197
    cognitive development in, 198–200
    drug use in. See Psychoactive drugs
    emerging adulthood and, 204–205
    mood swings in, 626
    physical development in, 195–197
    pregnancy in 470–471
    psychosocial development in, 201
    sexuality in, 470–472
    social development in, 200–204
Adoption studies, 136–137
    of intelligence, 429
    of schizophrenia, 642
Adrenal glands, 56
Adrenaline, 56
Adulthood, 206–221
    cognitive development in, 212–215
    commitments in, 217–218
    emerging, 204–205
    physical development in, 206–212
    psychosocial development in, 201
    social development in, 215–221
Advice, 193
Aerobic exercise
    depression and, 678
    stress management and, 547–549
Afterimages, 241
Age. See also Adolescence; Adulthood; Childhood; Infancy
    depression and, 628
    mental, 417
    psychological disorders and, 607–608
    sleeping time and, 96
    suicide and, 630, 631
Age regression, 109
Aggression, 709–717. See also Violence
    biology of, 710–711
    brain and, 62–63
    combating, 731
    cultural influences on, 713
    gender and, 158
    modeling of, 307
    psychological factors in, 712–717
    social influences on, 713
Aggression-replacement program, 713
Aging
    biopsychosocial perspective on, 220
    intelligence and, 213–215
    memory and, 212–213
Agonists, 51

Agoraphobia, 611
AIDS (acquired immunodeficiency syndrome)
    HIV transmission and, 471–472
    stress and, 539–540
Alarm reaction, 532
Alcohol, 115–117
    accidents and, 116
    aggression and, 711
    aversive conditioning and, 653
    disinhibition and, 115, 117
    expectancy effects and, 116
    memory and, 116, 349
    neural processing and, 115–116
    during pregnancy, 171–172
    self-awareness and self-control and, 116
    sexual behavior and, 116–117
    teen pregnancy and, 471
Alcoholics Anonymous, 114, 659
Algorithms, 371
All-or-none response, 48
Alpha waves, 93–94
Altered states of consciousness. See Consciousness; Hypnosis; Psychoactive drugs; Sleep
Altruism, 726–729
    bystander intervention and, 726–728
    social exchange theory and, 728–729
Alzheimer's disease, 211–212, 340
American Psychological Association (APA), female presidents of, 4
Amnesia, 342
    infantile, 175–176, 345
    source, 359
Amphetamines, 117
Amplitude
    of light waves, 234
    of sound waves, 244
Amygdala, 62–63, 65
    in adulthood, 219
    aggression and, 62–63
    emotion and, 503, 507, 519
    fear and, 62–63
    gender and, 161
    memory and, 341
    schizophrenia and, 640
Anal stage, 560
Analytical intelligence, 408
Anger, 520–521
    heart disease and, 536
    as masculine emotion, 512

Angular gyrus, 392
  language development and, 391
Animal(s)
  observational learning in, 315
  personality differences in, 576
  as pets, 21, 546, 593
  same-sex attraction in, 475
  thinking by, language and, 397–402
Animal experiments, 20–22
Animal magnetism, 665
The Animal Mind (Washburn), 4
Anorexia nervosa, 453
ANS. *See* Autonomic nervous system (ANS)
Antagonists, 51
Anterior cingulate gyrus
  in anxiety disorders, 616
  ostracism and, 482
Antianxiety drugs, 672
Antidepressant drugs, 632, 673–675
Antipsychotic drugs, 672
Anti-rumination, for depression, 679
Antisocial behavior, modeling of, 319–321
Antisocial personality disorder, 620–622
Antisocial relations, 703–718
  aggression and. *See* Aggression
  prejudice and, 703–709
Anvil (bone), 244
Anxiety. *See also* Fear; Phobias
  free-floating, 610
  stranger, 185
Anxiety disorders, 610–617
  biological perspective on, 615–616
  generalized, 610
  learning perspective on, 614–615
  obsessive-compulsive disorder, 610, 612
  panic disorder, 610, 611
  phobias, 610, 611–612
  post-traumatic stress disorder, 610, 612–614
  treatment of, 672
Anxiety gene, 616
APA (American Psychological Association),
    female presidents of, 4
Aphasia, 391–392
Appetite. *See also* Hunger
  hormones and, 450–451
  sleep deprivation and, 97–98
Applied research, 10
Appropriate developmental placement, 326
Aptitude tests, 418, 419
Arousal, optimum, 445–446
Asperger syndrome, 182
Assessment. *See also* Intelligence testing;
    Personality tests
  of behavior in situations, 589–590
  of self, 571–572
Assimilation, 177
Assistive listening technologies, 280–281
Association areas, 71–72
Associative learning, 287–289, 290, 301. *See
    also* Classical conditioning; Operant
    conditioning
  of language, 388
Assortative mating, 182
Astrology, 578–579
Athletic performance. *See also* Sports
  operant conditioning and, 311
  stimulant drugs and, 117

Attachment, 186–191
  day care and, 190–191
  deprivation of, 189–191
  differences in, 187–189
  disruption of, 190
  origins of, 186–187
Attention
  in schizophrenia, 640, 643
  selective, 87–90, 111, 637
Attentional user interfaces, 484
Attention-deficit/hyperactivity disorder
    (ADHD), 599, 600
Attitude(s), 684–689. *See also* Beliefs;
    Prejudice
  actions affected by, 684–685
  actions affecting, 685–689
  cognitive dissonance and, 688–689
  peacemaking and. *See* Peacemaking
  role-playing and, 686–688
  scientific, 17–18
Attraction, 719–726
  psychology of, 719–724
  reward theory of, 724
  romantic love and, 724–726
Attributional style, 587
Attribution theory, 682–684
Atypical antipsychotics, 672
Audition. *See* Deafness; Hearing; Hearing loss
Auditory cortex, 71, 244
Auditory nerve, 244
Authoritarian parents, 193
Authoritative communities, 193
Authoritative parents, 193
Autism, 182–183, 317
Autism spectrum disorder, 182
Automatic processes, closure and, 263
Automatic processing, 327–328
Autonomic nervous system (ANS), 53
  emotion and, 502
  personality and, 576
Autonomy vs. shame and doubt stage, 201
Availability heuristic, 375–376
Aversive conditioning, 653
Aversive events, aggression and, 712
Avoidant personality disorder, 620
Awareness. *See also* Consciousness
  emotion and, 507–508
  selective attention and, 87–90
  of self, 116, 192
Axons, 47

Babbling stage, 387
Back-to-sleep position, 175
Barbiturates, 117
Bar graphs, 37
Barnum effect, 579
Basal metabolic rate, 451
Basic research, 10
Basic trust, 189
Basilar membrane, 244
Beck's cognitive therapy for depression,
    655–656
Behavior
  culture and, 19–20
  definition of, 6
  experiments to explain, 19
  gender and, 20

Behavioral medicine, 530, 540–541, 551
Behavioral perspective, 9
Behavior control, 301
Behavior feedback, anger and, 520–521
Behavior genetics, 132–141. *See also* Nature-
    nurture issue
  adoption studies and, 136–137
  gene-environment interaction and,
    139–140
  genes and. *See* Gene(s)
  heritability and, 138–139
  molecular genetics and, 140–141
  temperament studies and, 137–138
  twin studies and, 133–136, 428–429,
    641–642
Behavior genetics perspective, 8, 9
Behaviorism, 5, 83, 290
Behavior modeling, 318
Behavior modification, 653–654
Behavior rating scales, for performance
    appraisal, 489
Behavior therapies, 650–654
  classical conditioning techniques in,
    651–653
  operant conditioning techniques in,
    653–654
Belief(s)
  catastrophizing, 655
  prejudice and, 703
  self-defeating, depression and, 632–634
Belief perseverance, 377
Belonging, need for, 479–482
  ostracism and, 481–482
  sustaining relationships and, 481
  thoughts and emotions and, 480–481
Between a Rock and a Hard Place (Ralston),
    443
Bias
  confirmation, 373
  forgetting and, 352
  hindsight, 15–16, 361, 709
  ingroup, 706–708
  in intelligence testing, 438–440
  labels and, 605
  own-race, 708
  positive-thinking, 587
  self-serving, 592–594
  unit, eating and, 453
Big Five personality factors, 577–580
Bilingual advantage, 394–395
Binge-eating disorder, 454
Binocular cues, 265
Biochemical influences. *See also* Hormones;
    Neurotransmitters; Psychoactive drugs;
    specific substances
  on aggression, 711
Biofeedback, 549
Biological clock, 91–92, 96
Biological influences. *See also*
    Biopsychosocial perspective; Genetic
    influences; Heritability; Levels of
    analysis; Nature-nurture issue; *specific
    biological influences*
  on aggression, 710–711
  on antisocial personality disorder, 621
  on anxiety disorders, 615–616
  in autism, 182–183

on depth perception, 264
on dissociative identity disorder, 619
on drug use, 125–126
on emotion, 501–509, 519–520
on gender, 160–161
medical model and, 601
on mood disorders, 628–632
on operant conditioning, 309–310
on pain, 254–255
on personality, 576
on sexual orientation, 476–479
on storage, 339–345
on stress, 532–533
on taste preferences, 452
Biological predispositions
classical conditioning and, 295–298
operant conditioning and, 309
Biological psychologists, 10, 46
Biological relatives, adoptive relatives vs., 136–137
Biological rhythms, 91–92
Biomedical therapies, 645, 671–679
brain stimulation, 675–677
drug therapies, 671–674
psychosurgery, 677–678
therapeutic life-style change, 678–679
Biopsychosocial perspective, 8–9. *See also* Biological influences; Culture; Psychological influences; Social-cultural influences; *specific biopsychosocial influences*
on aging, 220
on antisocial personality disorder, 622
on development, 164–165
on drug use, 125–128
interaction of components of, 45
on mind, 80
on neural communication, 46
on pain, 254–256
on personality, 584
on prejudice, 705
on psychological disorders, 602
on sexual orientation, 475–476
on social development, 185
on stress, 540–541
therapeutic life-style change and, 678
Bipolar cells, 235
Bipolar disorder, 626–627
Birth-order effect, fraternal, 474–475
Bitter taste, 257
Blame-the-victim dynamic, 706
Blindness
brain plasticity and, 73
change, 89
choice, 89
choice-blindness, 89
face, 225
inattentional, 89
to one's own incompetence, 588–589
restored vision and, 274
Blindsight, 239
Blind spot, 235
Blocking, forgetting and, 351
B lymphocytes, 538
Body contact, attachment and, 186–187
Body image, gender and, 454
Body weight. *See* Eating disorders; Obesity

Bottom-up processing, 226
Botulin, 51
Brain
activity preceding consciousness, 87
in adulthood, 210–211, 219
aggression and, 710–711
in anxiety disorders, 616
arousal of, 576, personality and, 576
autism and, 182–183, 317
cerebral cortex of. *See* Cerebral cortex
color constancy and, 270
complexity of, intelligence and, 412–413
consciousness and, 85–90
dementia and, 211–212
depression and, 630–632
development of. *See* Brain development
dissociative identity disorder and, 619
electrical activity of, recording, 59
electroencephalography and, 59, 91, 93–94
emotion and, 503–504, 507–508
exercise and, 210–211
experience and, 412
extrasensory perception and, 284
face recognition and, 225
feature detection and, 238
functioning of, intelligence and, 413
gray matter of, 161, 413
handedness and, 78–80
hemispheric specialization of. *See* Hemispheric specialization
hunger and, 449–451
imaging of, 60
information processing and. *See* Information processing
insight and, 371–372
intelligence and, 428
lack of awareness of function of, 62
language development and, 391–393
lateralization of. *See* Hemispheric specialization
lesioning, 59
lie detection and, 505
lobes of, 67, 68. *See also specific lobes*
mapping, 58–59, 68–69, 85
memory and, 175, 343–345
motion perception and, 267
observational learning and, 316–317
older structures of, 60–65
pain perception and, 254–255
perceptual organization and, 262
personality and, 72
plasticity of, 73–74
post-traumatic stress disorder and, 613
repair of, 73, 99
reward centers of, 64
schizophrenia and, 639–641
sex hormones and, 56, 160–161, 434
sexual orientation and, 475–476
sexual response cycle and, 467
size of, intelligence and, 412
sleep and, 91, 93–94
split-brain studies of, 74–77
storing memories in, 339–345
stress and, 533
study methods for, 58–60
taste sense and, 452
vision and, 86, 237

touch sense and, 252
white matter of, 161, 413
Brain development
in adolescence, 197
experience and, 148–149
gender and, 160–161
in infancy and childhood, 174
pruning process and, 149, 174, 197
Brainstem, 61, 65
Brain stimulation, 675–677
Breathing, 172
Brightness constancy, 269
Broca's area, 391, 392
Bulimia nervosa, 453–454
Bystander effect, 726–728

Caffeine, 118
Callings, 484
CAM (complementary and alternative medicine), 550
Cancer, stress and, 540
Cannabinoid receptors, 124
Cannon-Bard theory of emotion, 500
Carcinogens, 540
Careers, 484
Case studies, 26, 27
Catastrophes, 533–534
Catastrophizing beliefs, 655
Catatonia, 638
Catatonic schizophrenia, 639
Categorization
of faces, 370–371
racial, 437, 708–709
Catharsis, 520
Catharsis hypothesis, 717
Causation, correlation and, 31–32
Cell body, of neuron, 47
Central nervous system, 53–55. *See also* Brain; Spinal cord
Central route persuasion, 685
Central tendency measures, 38
Cerebellum, 62, 65
memory and, 344–345
Cerebral cortex, 67–74
emotion and, 503
functions of, 68–72
schizophrenia and, 640
structure of, 67, 68
Cerebral hemispheres, 62
Cerebrum, 67
Chain migration, 481
Chameleon effect, 690
Change, stability vs., 169, 222–223
Change blindness, 89
Change deafness, 89
Change events, 216
Charisma, 495
Checklists, for performance appraisal, 489
Childhood
antisocial personality disorder in, 621
attachment in, 186–191
bilingualism in, 394–395
brain development in, 174
cognitive development in, 176–185
eyewitness recall in, 361–362
language development in, 387–388, 389–390

Childhood (continued)
marriage and, 218
motor development in, 175
parents and. See Parent(s); Parenting
peer relationships in, 151
psychosocial development in, 200–201
repressed vs. constructed memories of
abuse and, 362–365
self-concept in, 192
social development in, 185–193
Child-rearing practices. See also Parenting
culture and, 156
gender and, 163
Choice, tyranny of, 587
Choice blindness, 89
Choice-blindness blindness, 90
Chromosomes, 132
Chunking, 333–334
Cigarette smoking, 118–120
Cingulate gyrus, anterior
in anxiety disorders, 616
ostracism and, 482
Circadian rhythm, 91–92
Clairvoyance, 282
Clarification, in client-centered therapy,
650
Classical conditioning, 288, 289,
290–300
applications of, 298–299
aversive, 653
in behavior therapies, 651
biological predispositions and, 295–298
cognitive processes and, 295
of fear, 614–615
operant conditioning vs., 301, 313
Pavlov's experiments on, 290–295,
298–299
trauma as, 299
Client-centered therapy, 649–650
Clinical psychologists, 10
Closure, grouping and, 263
Cocaine, 120–121
Cochlea, 244
Cochlear implants, 248
Cocktail party effect, 88
Cognition, 83, 176. See also Decision
making; Language; Memory;
Social-cognitive entries; Thinking
classical conditioning and, 295
concepts and, 370–371, 397
emotion and, 506–508
operant conditioning and, 308–309
prejudice and, 708–709
problem solving and, 371–374
Cognitive-behavior therapy, 656–657
Cognitive development
in adolescence, 198–200
in adulthood, 212–215
dreams and, 105–106
in infancy and childhood, 176–185
moral reasoning and, 198–200
Piaget's theory of, 178–181, 184–185
Cognitive dissonance, 688–689
Cognitive impairment, mild, 340
Cognitive interview technique, 361
Cognitive maps, 308
Cognitive neuroscience, 5–6, 85

Cognitive perspective, 9
Cognitive processes. See also Language;
Memory; Thinking
in classical conditioning, 295
Cognitive psychologists, 10
Cognitive revolution, 5, 654
Cognitive therapies, 654–657
of Beck, 655–656
cognitive-behavior therapy, 656–657
Collective unconscious, 563
Collectivism, 154–155
Color constancy, 269–270
Color vision, 240–242
Command-and-control management
process, 496
Commitments, in adulthood, 218
Communication. See also Language
facilitated, 664
neural. See Neural communication;
Neurotransmitters
nonverbal, 511–513
peacemaking and, 733
Companionate love, 724–726
Complementary and alternative medicine
(CAM), 550
Concept(s), 370–371
in animals, 397
Conception, 170
Conciliation, 733–734
Concrete operational stage, 178, 184
Conditioned reinforcers, 304
Conditioned response (CR), 291
Conditioned stimulus (CS), 291
Conditioning, 288–289. See also Classical
conditioning; Operant conditioning
of fear, 298–299, 518–519, 614–615
higher-order, 292
second-order, 292
Condoms, sexually transmitted infections
and, 471–472
Conductive hearing loss, 247–248
Cones, 235–237
Confirmation bias, 373
Conflict, 729
peacemaking and. See Peacemaking
Conformity, 690–693, 696
conditions strengthening, 692
group pressure and, 691–693
reasons for, 692–693
Connectedness, grouping and, 263
Connectionism model of memory, 325
Consciousness, 80, 83–129
altered states of. See Hypnosis;
Psychoactive drugs; Sleep
brain and, 85–90
cognitive neuroscience and, 85
definition of, 83
divided, hypnosis as, 111–112
dual processing and, 86–90
near-death experiences and, 124
psychoactive drugs and. See Psychoactive
drugs
states of, 84
Conservation, 180
Constraint-induced therapy, 73
Contact, peacemaking and, 731
Content validity, 421

Context effects, 276–277
retrieval and, 348–349
Continuity, grouping and, 263
Continuity/stages issue, 169, 222
Continuous reinforcement, 305
Control. See also Self-control
hypnotic, 109
locus of, 585
perceived, 542–544
personal, 584–589, 701
social, 701
Control group, 35
Conventional morality, 199
Convergent thinking, 409
Conversion disorder, 623
Cooperation, peacemaking and, 732–733
Coping with stress, 542–547
optimism and, 544–545
perceived control and, 542–544
social support and, 545–547
Cornea, 234
Coronary heart disease, stress and, 535–537
Corpus callosum, 74, 75
Correlation, 29–34
causation and, 31–32
illusory, 32–33
perceiving order in random events and,
33–34
of test scores, 421
Correlation coefficients, 29
Cortex, intelligence and, 412
Cortisol, 97, 532
Counseling psychologists, 10
Counterconditioning, 651
CR (conditioned response), 291
Cramming, 12, 329, 330
Creative intelligence, 408
Creativity
bipolar disorder and, 626
components of, 410
definition of, 409
intelligence and, 409–410
sleep and, 100
Crime
antisocial personality disorder and,
620–622
insanity defense and, 606
Crisis debriefing, 664
Critical periods, 187, 273
for language development, 389–390
Critical thinking, 12, 18–19
Cross-race effect, 708
Cross-sectional studies, 213
Crystallized intelligence, 215
Crystal meth, 118
CS (conditioned stimulus), 291
Culture, 151–157. See also Social-cultural
influences; Social-cultural perspective;
specific social-cultural influences
aggression and, 713
attractiveness and, 722
behavior and, 19–20
child rearing and, 156, 163
Deaf culture and, 248–249
developmental similarities across groups
and, 156–157
dissociative identity disorder and, 619

eating disorders and, 454
emotional expression and, 513–515
gender roles and, 162–163
globalization of psychology and, 6
happiness and wealth and, 524
hunger and, 452
individualist and collectivist, 154–155
intelligence and, 435
norms of, 151–157
pain and, 256
perception and, 277
in psychotherapy, 668–669
self and, 154–155
sleeping patterns and, 96
somatoform disorders and, 623
suicide and, 630
taste preferences and, 452
transmission of, in animals, 398
variation over time, 153
variations across, 152–153
Curiosity, 17
Curious skepticism, 17
Curse of knowledge, 281
Cyber-ostracism, 482

Daily hassles, 534–535
Danger, response to, 502
Dark adaptation, 236
Dating, speed, 720
Day care, attachment and, 190–191
Deaf culture, 248–249
Deafness. See also Hearing loss
    change, 89
Death, 220–221
    life expectancy and, 208–209
    near-death experiences and, 124
    suicide and, 630–631, 674, 676
    terminal decline and, 215
Death-deferral phenomenon, 209
Decay, of storage, 353–354
Decision making, 374–382
    belief perseverance and, 377
    framing and, 381–382
    heuristics and, 374–376
    intuition and, 378–381
    overconfidence and, 376–377
Declarative memory, 343
Deep-brain stimulation, 677
Defense mechanisms, 561–562
Defensive self-esteem, 594
Deindividuation, 698
Déjà vu, 348–349
Delayed gratification, 200
Delayed reinforcers, 304–305
Delta-9-tetrahydrocannabinol (THC), 122
Delta waves, 94
Delusions, 637
Dementia, 211–212
Dendrites, 47
Denial, 562
Deoxyribonucleic acid (DNA), 132, 133
    molecular genetics and, 140–141
    telomeres and, 208, 533
Dependence, on psychoactive drugs,
    113–114
Dependent variable, 36
Depolarization, 48

Depressants, 115–117
Depression. See also Mood disorders
    heart disease and, 537
    stress and, 628
    suicide and, 630–631
    treatment of, 673–676, 678–679
Depth perception, 264–266
Descriptive research, 26–29
    case studies and, 26, 27
    naturalistic observation and, 28–29
    surveys and, 26, 27–28
Descriptive statistics, 38–40
Desensitization, exposure to violence and,
    321
Development. See also Adolescence;
    Adulthood; Childhood; Infancy
    biopsychosocial perspective on, 164–165
    of brain. See Brain development
    cognitive. See Cognitive development
    continuity/stages issue in, 169
    gender. See Gender
    of language, 386–390
    moral, 198–200
    nature/nurture issue in, 169
    of personality, 560–561
    physical. See Physical development
    prenatal, 170–172
    similarities across groups, 156–157
    social. See Social development
    stability/change issue in, 169
Developmental psychologists, 10
Developmental psychology, 169
Diagnostic and Statistical Manual of Mental
    Disorders (DSM-IV-TR), 603
DID (dissociative identity disorder),
    618–620
Difference thresholds, 230
Difficult babies, 137, 189
Diffusion of responsibility, 727
Diminishing returns, 525
Discrimination (in conditioning), 295
    punishment and, 307
Discrimination (against others), prejudice
    and, 703, 704
Discriminative stimulus, 302–303
Disease. See Health entries; Illness
Disinhibition, alcohol and, 115
Disorganized schizophrenia, 639
Displacement, 562
Display rules, 514
Dispositional attribution, 682
Dissociation, 111
Dissociative disorders, 618–620
Dissociative identity disorder (DID),
    618–620
Distraction
    accidents and 88
    pain control and, 256–257
Distress, 599
Distributed practice, 329–330
Distributions
    normal, 39–40, 420
    skewed, 38
Divergent thinking, 409
Division of labor
    culture and, 152
    by sex, 162

DNA. See Deoxyribonucleic acid (DNA)
Dopamine, 51, 64
    personality and, 576
    schizophrenia and, 639–640
Double-blind procedure, 35, 671
Down syndrome, 425
Dream(s), 102–106
    content of, 103–104, 559, 647
    definition of, 103
    reasons for, 104–106
    REM sleep and, 95, 102
Dream analysis, 647
Drive-reduction theory, 445
Drugs. See Alcohol; Psychoactive drugs;
    Psychopharmacology
DSM-IV-TR (Diagnostic and Statistical
    Manual of Mental Disorders), 603
Dual processing, 86–90, 239
    selective attention and, 87–90
    two-track mind and, 86–87
Dying, 220–221

Ear, 244–247
Eardrum, 244
Early experiences, parents and, 148–150
Early intervention, intelligence and, 431
Eating. See also Appetite; Hunger
    ecology of, 453
    obesity and. See Obesity
    sleep deprivation and, 97–98
Eating disorders, 453–455
Echoic memory, 337
Eclectic approach, 646
Ecstasy (MDMA), 121–122
Education. See Early intervention; School
    entries
EEG. See Electroencephalogram (EEG)
Effective leaders, 493–496
Effortful processing, 328–330
Ego, 559
Egocentrism, in preschool children, 180
Ejaculation, premature, 467
Electra complex, 560
Electroconvulsive therapy, 675–676
Electroencephalogram (EEG), 59
    during sleep, 91, 93–94
Electromagnetic spectrum, 233
Embryo, 171
EMDR (eye movement desensitization and
    reprocessing), 665–666
Emerging adulthood, 204–205
Emoticons, 511
Emotion(s), 499–529
    ability to detect, gender and, 433
    autonomic nervous system and, 502
    brain and, 503–504, 507–508
    cognition and, 506–508
    culture and expression of, 513–515
    definition of, 500
    detecting, 510–511
    experienced, 500, 505, 517–529. See also
        specific emotions
    expressed, 510–516
    facial expressions and, 513–516
    gender and nonverbal behavior and,
        511–513
    inappropriate, in schizophrenia, 638

Emotion(s) (continued)
  in infancy, 517
  lie detection and, 504
  memory and, 349–350
  nonverbal behavior and, 511–513
  perceptual set and, 277–278
  physiological similarities among, 503–506
  prejudice and, 703
  theories of, 500–501
  valence of, 517–518
Emotional intelligence, 410, 411
Emotional stability-instability dimension,
      575–576
Emotion-focused coping, 542
Empathy, 200, 513
  in client-centered therapy, 649
  in person-centered perspective, 571
  psychotherapy and, 668
Empirical approach, 17
Empirically derived tests, 576
Employee engagement, 493
Employment interviews, 487–489
Empty nest syndrome, 218
Encoding, 325, 327–335
  acoustic, 331–332
  organizing information for, 333–334
  process of, 327–330
  semantic, 331–332
  visual, 331–333
Endocrine system, 56
Endorphins, 50–51, 117, 255
Enemy perceptions, 730–731
Energy therapies, 664
Environment, 132. See also Environmental
      influences; Nature-nurture issue
  adaptation to, learning and, 297
  interaction with genes, 139–140
Environmental influences. See also Nature-
      nurture issue; specific influences
  on antisocial personality disorder, 622
  on creativity, 410
  on immune function, 545–546
  on intelligence, 429–430, 436–438
  on obesity, 460–462
  on prenatal development, 171–172
  on puberty, 197
  sexual orientation and, 474–475
Environmental relatives, 136–137
Epinephrine, 56
Equity, love and, 725
Erikson's theory of psychosocial
      development, 189, 200–204, 217,
      219, 222
Erectile dysfunction, 95, 467
Erogenous zones, 560
Erotic plasticity, 474
Errors
  fundamental attribution, 682
  halo, 489–490
  recency, 490
  severity, 490
ESP. See Extrasensory perception (ESP)
Estrogens, sexual behavior and, 467, 468
Ethics, of research, 20–22
Ethnicity
  intelligence and, 435–438
  suicide and, 630

Eugenics, 417–418
Evidence-based practice, 664
Evolutionary perspective, 8, 9, 165–166
  on menopause, 207
Evolutionary psychology, 141–146
  contemporary, 143
  critique of, 146
  human sexuality and, 143–146
  instincts and, 444–445
  natural selection and, 141–142
  similarities explained by, 141–143
Excessive optimism, 587
Excitatory signals, 48
Excitement phase of sexual response cycle, 466
Exercise. See also Athletic performance;
      Sports
  brain and, 210–211
  depression and, 678
  stress management and, 547–549
Exhaustion, in general adaptation syndrome,
      532
Expectancy effects of alcohol, 116
Expectations
  alcohol and, 116
  intelligence testing and, 439–440
Experience. See also Learning; Nature-
      nurture issue
  brain and, 412
  depth perception and, 264
  intelligence and, 431–432
  peak experiences and, 570
Experienced emotion, 500, 505, 517–529
Experiment(s), 34–36
  animals as subjects for, 20–22
  humans as subjects of, 22
  independent and dependent variables and,
      35–36
  random assignment and, 34–35
Experimental group, 35
Expertise, creativity and, 410
Explanatory style, negative, depression and,
      632–634
Explicit memory, 343
Exposure therapies, 651–652
Expressed emotion, 510–516
External locus of control, 585
Extinction
  in classical conditioning, 293–294
  resistance to, 305
Extrasensory perception (ESP), 281–285
  claims of, 282
  experimental tests of, 282–285
  premonitions vs. pretensions and, 282–283
Extraversion-introversion dimension,
      575–576
Extrinsic motivation, 309
Eye, 234–237
Eye movement desensitization and
      reprocessing (EMDR), 665–666
Eyewitness recall, of children, 361–362
Eyewitness testimony, accuracy of, 360–361
Eysenck Personality Questionnaire, 576

Face(s), newborns' preference for, 173
Face blindness, 225
Face recognition, 225
  brain and, 72

information processing and, 239–240
  memory and, 346
  sensory deprivation and, 272–273
Facial expressions
  culture and, 513–515
  detecting emotion and, 510–511
  effects of, 515–516
  memories and, 360
Facial feedback, 515–516
Facilitated communication, 664
Factor analysis, 405, 575–576
Faith communities, stress management and,
      552–554
False consensus effect, 567
False memories, 359–361
Familiarity, attachment and, 187
Familiar Studies of Men and Books
      (Stevenson), 487
Family self, 156
Family therapy, 657–658
FAS (fetal alcohol syndrome), 172
Fat cells, 458
Fathers. See also Parent(s)
  presence of, sexual restraint and, 472
Fear. See also Anxiety entries; Phobias
  biology of, 519–520
  brain and, 62–63
  conditioning of, 614–615
  learning of, 298–299, 518–519, 614–615
  objects of, 378–379
  punishment and, 307
Feature detection, 238
Feedback
  behavior, anger and, 520–521
  biofeedback, 549
Feel-good, do-good phenomenon, 522
Feeling, moral, 199–200
Females. See Gender entries; Sexuality entries;
      Sexual orientation
Fermat's last theorem, 409
Fetal alcohol syndrome (FAS), 172
Fetus, 171
Fight-or-flight response, 502, 532, 712
Figure-ground relationship, 262–263
Fissures, in cerebral cortex, 67
Fixation, 373, 374, 561
Fixed-interval schedules, 305, 306
Fixed-ratio schedules, 305, 306
Flashbulb memories, 341
Flat affect, in schizophrenia, 638
Fluid intelligence, 215
Flynn effect, 420–421, 425
fMRI (functional MRI), 60
Food, obesity and, 460
Foot-in-the-door phenomenon, 685–686
Forgetting, 351–357. See also Amnesia
  encoding failure and, 352
  interference and, 354–357
  motivated, 356–357
  reasons for, 351–352
  retrieval failure and, 354–357
  storage decay and, 353–354
Forgiveness, 521
Formal operation(s), 198
Formal operational stage, 178, 184
Form perception, 262–264
Fovea, 236

The Fragile Species (Thomas), 166
Framing, 381–382
Fraternal birth-order effect, 474–475
Fraternal twins, 134
Free association, 558, 647
Free-floating anxiety, 610
Free radicals, sleep and, 99
Frequency, of sound waves, 244
Frequency theory, 247
Freudian theory. *See* Psychoanalytic perspective
Frontal lobes, 67, 68
  in adolescence, 197
  emotion and, 503
  intelligence and, 412
  personality and, 72, 576
  schizophrenia and, 640
Frustration-aggression principle, 712
Functional fixedness, 373
Functionalism, 3–4
Functional MRI (fMRI), 60
Fundamental attribution error, 682

g (general intelligence), 405
GABA (gamma-aminobutyric acid), 51
Ganglion cells, 235
GAS (general adaptation syndrome), 532–533
Gate-control theory of pain, 254
Gay men, 472. *See also* Sexual orientation
Gender, 157–163
  aggression and, 158
  behavior and, 20
  biological influences on, 160–161
  body image and, 454
  child-rearing and, 163
  cultural influences on, 161–163
  depression and, 627, 632–633
  differences in sexuality and, 144
  eating disorders and, 454
  emotion and, 511–513
  intelligence and, 432–435
  life expectancy and, 208
  prejudice and discrimination based on, 704
  religious involvement and, 552–553
  similarities and differences and, 157–160
  social connectedness and, 158–160
  social power and, 158
  suicide and, 630, 631
Gender identity, 163, 561
Gender roles, 162–163
Gender schemas, 163
Gender typing, 163
Gene(s), 132–133
  anxiety, 616
  interaction with environment, 139–140. *See also* Nature-nurture issue
  mutations of, 142
  self-regulation by, 139
General adaptation syndrome (GAS), 532–533
General intelligence (*g*), 405
Generalization, in classical conditioning, 294
Generalized anxiety disorder, 610
Generativity vs. stagnation stage, 201

Genetic influences. *See also* Behavior genetics; Heritability; Nature-nurture issue
  on aggression, 710
  on antisocial personality disorder, 621
  on anxiety disorders, 616
  on eating disorders, 454
  on fear, 519–520
  on handedness, 79
  on intelligence, 428–429, 436
  on life expectancy, 203
  on mood disorders, 629
  on motor development, 175
  on narcolepsy, 101
  on obesity, 460, 462
  on personality traits, 576
  on prenatal development, 171
  on puberty, 197
  on schizophrenia, 641–642
  on sexual orientation, 476
  storage and, 340
Genetic relatives, 136–137
Genetics. *See also* Genetic influences; Heritability; Nature-nurture issue
  behavior. *See* Behavior genetics
  molecular, 140–141
Genital stage, 560
Genome, 132
Genuineness
  in client-centered therapy, 649
  in person-centered perspective, 571
Gestalt, 262
Gestures, 400
  culture and, 513
Ghrelin, 97–98, 450–451, 460
Giftedness, 426
Glial cells, 67
Globalization of psychology, 6
Glucocorticoid stress hormones, 532
Glucose, hunger and, 449
Glutamate, 51
  in anxiety disorders, 616
  storage and, 340
Goals
  setting, 494–495
  superordinate, 732–733
Graduated and Reciprocated Initiatives in Tension-Reduction (GRIT), 733
Grammar, 385–386
  universal, 388–389
Graphic rating scales, for performance appraisal, 489
Graphologists, 578
Gratification, delayed, 200
Gray matter
  gender and, 161
  intelligence and, 413
Great person theory of leadership, 495
Grief, 220–221
GRIT (Graduated and Reciprocated Initiatives in Tension-Reduction), 733
Group differences, heritability and, 138–139
Group influence, 697–700
Grouping, 263–264
Group interaction, social influence and, 698–700
Group polarization, 699–700
Group pressure, conformity and, 691–693

Group therapy, 657–658
Groupthink, 700
Growth, sleep and, 100
Guilty knowledge test, 505

Habituation, 288
  in newborns, 172
  sexual behavior and, 469
Hair cells, of ear, 245
Hallucinations, 94, 637
Hallucinogens, 122, 124–125
Halo errors, 489–490
Hammer (bone), 244
Handbook of Psychotherapy and Behavior Change (Ellis and Bergin), 669
Handedness, 78–80
  factors influencing, 79
Happiness, 521–529. *See also* Optimism
  increasing, 527
  others' attainments and, 528
  predictors of, 528–529
Head Start program, 431, 432
Health. *See also* Illness
  in adulthood, 210–211
  exercise and, 548–549
  mental, 601
  optimism and, 587
  pets and, 546
  religious involvement and, 554
Health promotion, 542–555
  coping with stress and, 542–547
  stress management and, 547–554
Hearing, 243–250
  ear and, 244–247
  loss of. *See* Deafness
  loudness perception and, 246
  pitch perception and, 246–247
  sound localization and, 247
  sound waves and, 243–244
  tinnitus and, 255
Hearing loss, 245, 247–249
  assistive listening technologies and, 280–281
  brain plasticity and, 73
  conductive, 247–248
  Deaf culture and, 248–249
  language development and, 389, 390
  sensorineural, 248
Heart disease, stress and, 535–537
Height, relative, as depth cue, 266
Helping behavior. *See* Altruism
Helplessness, learned, 585–587
Hemispheric specialization, 74–77
  handedness and, 78–80
  right-left differences and, 77–80
  split-brain research and, 74–77
  study in intact brain, 77–80
Hereditary Genius (Galton), 416
Heritability, 138–139
  group differences and, 138–139
  of intelligence, 430
  interaction of nature and nurture and, 139
  of personality traits, 579
Heroin, 51, 114, 117, 118, 119, 120, 124, 171
Heterosexual orientation, 472. *See also* Sexual orientation

Heuristics, 371, 374–376
  availability, 375–376
  representativeness, 374–375
Hierarchies
  of needs, 446–447
  organizing information in, 334
Higher-order conditioning, 292
Hindsight bias, 15–16, 361, 709
Hippocampus, 62, 65
  depression and, 630
  exercise and, 211
  gender and, 161
  memory and, 343–344
Histrionic personality disorder, 620
HIV (human immunodeficiency virus),
  transmission of, 471–472
Hollow face illusion, 86
Homeostasis, 445
Homosexual orientation, 472. See also Sexual
  orientation
Hope, psychotherapy and, 667
Horizontal-vertical illusion, 265
Hormones, 56
  aggression and, 711
  appetite and, 450–451
  sex. See Sex hormones
  stress, 340–342, 542
Hue, of light, 234
Human experiments, 22
Human factors psychology, 279, 485
  perception and, 279–281
Human genome, 132
Human immunodeficiency virus (HIV),
  transmission of, 471–472
Humanistic perspective, 570–573
  assessment of self and, 571–572
  evaluation of, 572
  person-centered perspective and,
    570–571
  self-actualization and, 570
Humanistic psychology, 5
Humanistic therapies, 649–650
Human values, sexuality and, 479
Humility, 18
Hunger, 448–465. See also Appetite
  brain and, 63–65
  obesity and weight control and,
    456–464
  physiology of, 448–451
  psychology of, 451–455
  sleep deprivation and, 97–98
Hypertension, sleep deprivation and,
  98
Hypnagogic sensations, 94
Hypnosis, 108–112
  as divided consciousness, 111–112
  facts and myths about, 108–110
  induction of, 108
  as social phenomenon, 110–111
  unified account of, 112
Hypnotherapy, 109–110
Hypochondriasis, 623
Hypocretin, 101
Hypothalamus, 63–65
  hunger and, 450–451
  sexual orientation and, 476
Hypotheses, 25

ICD-10 (International Classification of
  Diseases), 603
Iconic memory, 336–337
Id, 559
Ideal self, 571
Identical twins, 134
Identification, in psychoanalytic perspective,
  560–561
Identity
  formation of, 201–202
  gender, 163, 561
  search for, 201
  social, 201–202, 706–708
Identity vs. role confusion stage, 201
I-knew-it-all-along phenomenon, 15–16
Illness. See also Health entries
  AIDS, 539–540
  cancer, 540
  coronary heart disease, 535–537
  maternal, schizophrenia and, 640–641
  mental, 601. See also Psychological
    disorders
  psychophysiological, 537–541
  sexually transmitted infections, 471–472
  stress and. See Stress
  susceptibility to, 537–541
Illusion(s)
  hollow face, 86
  horizontal-vertical, 265
  interviewer, 487–488
  moon, 268
  Ponzo, 268
  rubber-hand, 252
Illusion of Conscious Will (Wegner), 83
Illusory correlation, 32–33
Imagery, visual encoding and, 332–333
Images
  masking, 413
  thinking in, 395–396
Imagination
  creativity and, 410
  memory and, 358–359
Imagination effect, 358–359
Imaginative thinking, 410
Imagined stimuli, sexual motivation and,
  468, 469–470
Imitation. See also Observational learning
  language development and, 388
Immediate reinforcers, 304–305
Immune system
  environmental influences on, 545–546
  sleep deprivation and, 98
  stress and, 537–539
Implementation intentions, 494–495
Implicit learning, 566
Implicit memory, 343
Impotence, 95, 467
Imprinting, 187
Inattention, selective, 88–90
Inattentional blindness, 89
Incentives, 445
Incompetence, one's own, blindness to,
  588–589
Independent variable, 35–36
Individual differences
  behavior genetics and, 132–141
  body weight and, 460, 462

heritability of, 579
  in intelligence, 435, 436
  in motor development, 175
  in sexual orientation, 476
  in temperament and personality, 203, 579
Individualism, 154–155
  moral reasoning and, 199
Industrial-organizational psychologists, 10
Industrial-organizational (I/O) psychology,
  485–497. See also Achievement
  motivation; Organizational psychology
Industry vs. inferiority stage, 201
Infancy
  brain development in, 174
  cognitive development in, 176–179
  emotions in, 517
  environmental influences on intelligence
    and, 430–431
  indicators of later intelligence of, 423
  language development in, 387, 389
  memory in, 175–176, 345
  motor development in, 175
  newborns and, 172–173
  psychosocial development in, 201
  social development in, 185–191
  temperament of, 137–138
Infantile amnesia, 175–176, 345
Infections
  sexually transmitted, 471–472
  viral, during pregnancy, schizophrenia
    and, 640–641
Inferences, 40–41
Inferiority complex, 562
Influence. See Social influence
Informational social influence, 692–693
Information processing
  automatic, 327–328
  bottom-up, 226
  dreams as, 104–105, 106
  effortful, 328–330
  of language, 392
  levels of, 331–332
  memory and, 325–326
  organizing information for encoding and,
    333–334
  parallel, 239–240
  serial, 239
  speed of, intelligence and, 414
  top-down, 226
  unconscious, 86–87
  visual, 237–240
Ingroup, prejudice and, 706–708
Inhibitory signals, 48
Initiative vs. guilt stage, 201
Inner ear, 244
Inoculation training, 656
Innovation, preservation of, 152
Insanity defense, 606
Insecure attachment, 187
Insight
  in animals, 397
  problem solving and, 371–372
  in psychoanalysis, 647
Insight therapies, 649
Insomnia, 100–101
Instinct(s), 444–445
Instinctive drift, 310

Insulin, 449, 450
Integrity vs. despair stage, 201
Intellectual disability, 425–426
Intelligence, 404–415
aging and, 213–215
analytical, 408
assessment of. *See* Intelligence testing
brain and, 412–414, 428
creative, 408
creativity and, 409–410
crystallized, 215
definition of, 404
emotional, 410, 411
environmental influences on, 430–432, 436–438
ethnicity and, 435–438
extremes of, 424–426
fluid, 215
gender and, 432–435
general, 405
genetic influences on, 428–430, 436
heritability of, 430
high extreme of, 426
low extreme of, 425–426
multiple, 405–409
neurological measurement of, 412–414
practical, 408
sexual restraint and, 472
social, 411
stability vs. change and, 422–424
Intelligence and Experience (Hunt), 431
Intelligence quotient (IQ), 404, 417–418
Intelligence testing, 404, 416–422
bias and, 438–440
modern tests and, 418–419
origins of, 416–418
reliability and, 421
standardization and, 420–421
validity and, 421–422
Intensity, of light, 234
Interaction
of genes and environment, 139–140. *See also* Nature-nurture issue
sensory, 258
Interdependence, 155
gender and, 159
Interference
proactive, 354
retrieval failure and, 354–357
retroactive, 354
Intermittent reinforcement, 305
Internal locus of control, 585
International Classification of Diseases (ICD-10), 603
Interneurons, 46
Interpersonal psychotherapy, 648–649
Interposition, as depth cue, 266
Interpretation, in psychoanalysis, 647
The Interpretation of Dreams (Freud), 104
Interview(s), employment, 487–489
Interviewer illusion, 487–488
Intimacy, 202. *See also* Love
Intimacy vs. isolation stage, 201
Intrinsic motivation, 309
creativity and, 410
Introspection, 3

Intuition, 15–16, 378–331
of women, 511–512
Ions, 47
I/O psychology. *See* Industrial-organizational (I/O) psychology
IQ (intelligence quotient), 404, 417–418
Iris, 234

James-Lange theory of emotion, 500
jnd (just noticeable difference), 230
Job(s), 484
Job interviews, 487–489
Joint-vision process, 496
Judgments. *See also* Decision making
value, 23
Just noticeable difference (jnd), 230
Just Six Numbers (Rees), 166
Just-world phenomenon, 709

Kinesthesis, 252
Knee-jerk response, 54
Knowledge, curse of, 281
Knowledge work, 485

Labeling, of psychological disorders, 605–606
Language, 384–403
animal thinking and, 397–402
bilingual advantage and, 394–395
brain and, 391–393
development of, 386–390
human thinking and, 393–397
productive, learning of, 387–388
receptive, learning of, 386
statistical aspects of, learning of, 389–390
structure of, 385–386
timing of learning, 386–388
universal grammar and, 388–389
Language acquisition device, 388
The Language of God (Collins), 165
Latency stage, 560
Latent content, 104, 559, 647
Latent learning, 308–309
Lateral hypothalamus, 450–451
Lateralization. *See* Hemispheric specialization
Law of effect, 301
Leaders, effective, 493–496
Leadership styles, 495–496
Learned helplessness, 585–587
depression and, 632
Learning, 287–326, 315. *See also* Experience
associative, 287–289, 290, 301. *See also* Classical conditioning; Operant conditioning
definition of, 290
of fear, 298–299, 518–519, 614–615
implicit, 566
of language, 386–388
latent, 308–309
meaningfulness and, 332
observational. *See* Observational learning
process of, 287–289
Learning perspective, on anxiety disorders, 614–615
Leniency, 490
Lens, 234
Leptin, 97–98, 451, 460

Lesbians, 472. *See also* Sexual orientation
Lesions, 59
Levels of analysis, 8–9. *See also* Biological influences; Biopsychosocial *entries*; Psychological influences; Social-cultural influences
Levels of processing, 331–332
Lie detection, 504–505
Life events, stressful, 533–535
Life expectancy, 208–209
religious involvement and, 553–554
Life span, well-being across, 219–220
Life-style change, therapeutic, 678–679
Light-and-shadow effect, 265–266
Light energy, 233–234
Light exposure therapy, 666, 679
Lightness constancy, 269
Limbic system, 62–65
in adolescence, 197
post-traumatic stress disorder and, 613
Linear perspective, as depth cue, 266
Linguistic determinism, 393
Linkage analysis, 629
Listening
active, in client-centered therapy, 649
in class, 12
Lithium, 674
"Little Albert" experiment, 298–299, 518–519
Lobotomy, 677–678
Locus of control, 585
Longitudinal studies, 214
Long-term memory, 325, 327, 338–339
Long-term potentiation (LTP), 340, 676
Loop systems, 281
Loudness, 244
perception of, 246
Love
in adulthood, 217–218
companionate, 724–726
passionate, 724
romantic, 724–726
LSD (lysergic acid diethylamide), 122
LTP (long-term potentiation), 340, 676
Luminance, relative, 269
Lymphocytes, 538
Lysergic acid diethylamide (LSD), 122

Macrophages, 538
Magnetic resonance imaging (MRI), 60
Magnetic stimulation, 676, 677
Mainstreaming, 425
Major depressive disorder, 625–626
Male(s). *See* Gender *entries*; Sexuality *entries*; Sexual orientation
Male answer syndrome, 159
Management. *See also* Leaders; Leadership styles
by objectives, 495
Managing stress, 542–547
Mania, 626
Manifest content, 103, 104, 559
Mapping of brain, 58–59, 68–69, 85
Marijuana, 122, 124
Marriage, 217–218
coping with stress and, 545
operant conditioning applications in, 312

Masking images, 413
Masking stimulus, 229
Massed practice, 12, 329–330
Matchmaking, online, 720
Math ability, gender and, 433
Mating
    assortative, 182
    love and, 724–726
    online matchmaking and speed dating
        and, 720
Mating preferences, natural selection and,
    145–146
Maturation, 174
    of brain, in adolescence, 197
    infant memory and, 175–176
MBTI (Myers-Briggs Type Indicator), 574
McGurk effect, 258
MDMA (Ecstasy; methylenedioxymetham-
    phetamine), 121–122
Mean, 38
Meaningfulness
    learning and, 332
    memory and, 213
Median, 38
Medical model, 601
Medication, 551–552
Meditation
    morbid, 633
    for stress management, 550, 552, 554
Medulla, 61, 65
Melatonin, 92
Memory, 323–367
    of abuse, repressed vs. constructed,
        362–365
    aging and, 212–213
    alcohol and, 116, 349
    amnesia and. See Amnesia
    brain and, 62, 175
    children's eyewitness recall and, 361–362
    connectionism model of, 325
    definition of, 324
    discerning true and false memories and,
        359–361
    echoic, 337
    encoding and. See Encoding
    explicit (declarative), 343
    eyewitness recall of children and, 361–362
    flashbulb memories and, 341
    forgetting and. See Amnesia; Forgetting
    hippocampus and, 343–344
    hypnosis and, 109
    iconic, 336–337
    implicit (nondeclarative), 343
    improving, 365–366
    in infancy, 175–176
    information-processing models of,
        325–326
    long-term, 325, 327
    meaningfulness and, 213
    misinformation and imagination effects
        on, 357–359
    mood and, 349–350
    nonverbal, gender and, 432
    of pain, 255
    prospective, 213
    retrieval and, 325, 346–350
    sensory, 325, 327

short-term, 325, 327
sleep and, 99–100
sleep deprivation and, 98
source amnesia and, 359
state-dependent, 349, 634
storage and. See Storage
stress hormones and, 340–342
working, 326, 327
Memory construction, 357–365
    children's eyewitness recall and, 361–362
    discerning true and false memories and,
        359–361
    misinformation and imagination effects
        and, 357–359
    repressed vs. constructed memories of
        abuse and, 362–365
    source amnesia and, 359
Memory traces, 339, 353
Menarche, 196–197
Menopause, 207
Mental age, 417
Mental health movement, 601
Mental illness, 601. See also Psychological
    disorders
Mental processes
    definition of, 6
    unconscious. See Unconscious processes
Mental rehearsal, 395–396
Mental retardation, 425–426
Mental set, 373
Mere exposure effect, 187, 719, 720
Meta-analysis, 662
Metabolism, obesity and, 459–460
Methamphetamine, 117–118
Methylenedioxymethamphetamine
    (MDMA), 121–122
Middle ear, 244
Midlife transition, 216
Migration, chain, 481
Mild cognitive impairment, 340
Mind
    biopsychosocial perspective on, 80
    conscious. See Consciousness
    hidden, 86
    how brain produces, 85
    theory of, 181–184, 317
    two-track, 86–87
    unconscious. See Unconscious
Minnesota Multiphasic Personality Inventory
    (MMPI), 576–577
Minority influence, 701
Mirror-image perceptions, 730–731
Mirror neurons, 183
    observational learning and, 316–317
Misattribution
    forgetting and, 351
    source, 359
Misinformation effect, memory and,
    357–358
MMPI (Minnesota Multiphasic Personality
    Inventory), 576–577
Mnemonics, 333, 347
Mode, 38
Modeling, 315
    of aggression, 307
    of antisocial behavior, 319–321
    of prosocial behavior, 318–319

Molecular genetics, 140–141
Money, well-being and, 524–526
Monocular cues, 265–266
Mood(s). See also Emotion(s); specific
    emotions
    duration of, 522–523, 524
    exercise and, 547–548
    memory and, 349–350, 634
Mood-congruent memory, 349, 634
Mood disorders, 625–636
    biological perspective on, 628–632
    bipolar disorder, 626–627
    causes of, 627–635
    major depressive disorder, 625–626
    social-cognitive perspective on, 632–635
    treatment of, 674
Mood linkage, 690
Mood-stabilizing drugs, 674
Moon illusion, 268
Moral action, 200
Moral feeling, 199–200
Moral reasoning, development of, 198–200
Morphemes, 385
Mother Care/Other Care (Scarr), 191
Motion, relative, as depth cue, 266
Motion perception, 267
Motivated forgetting, 356–357
Motivation, 443–497
    achievement. See Achievement
        motivation
    belongingess need and, 479–482
    creativity and, 410
    definition of, 444
    drives and, 445
    evolutionary psychology and, 444–445
    extrinsic, 309
    hierarchy of motives and, 446–447
    hunger and. See Hunger
    incentives and, 445
    instincts and, 444–445
    intrinsic, 309
    optimum arousal and, 445–446
    perceptual set and, 277–278
    sexual. See Sexuality
    in workplace, 484–497. See also
        Achievement motivation;
        Organizational psychology
Motor cortex, 68–70
    mapping, 68–69
    neural prosthetics and, 69–70
Motor development, in infants and children,
    175
Motor neurons, 46
"Mozart effect," 431
MRI (magnetic resonance imaging), 60
Multiple intelligences, 405–409
Multiple personality disorder, 618–620
Multiple sclerosis, 47
Mutations, 142
Myelin, in schizophrenia, 642
Myelin sheath, 47
Myers-Briggs Type Indicator (MBTI), 574

Narcissistic personality disorder, 620
Narcolepsy, 101
Naturalistic observation, 28–29
Natural killer cells (NK cells), 538

Natural selection, 141–142
  anxiety disorders and, 615
  mating preferences and, 145–146
Nature-nurture issue, 6–8, 169. *See also*
    Behavior genetics; Biological influences;
    Culture; Environmental influences;
    Evolutionary psychology; Gender *entries;*
    Gene(s); Genetic influences; *specific
    influences*
  gene-environment interaction and,
    139–140
  heritability and, 139
The Nature of Prejudice (Allport), 706
Near-death experiences, 124
Necker cube, 262
Needs
  to belong, 479–482
  hierarchy of, 446–447
Negative explanatory style, depression and,
    632–634
Negative reinforcement, 303–304
Negative symptoms of schizophrenia, 638
Neo-Freudian theorists, 562–563
Neophobia, 452
Nervous system, 52–55
  autonomic, 53, 572, 576
  central, 53–55. *See also* Brain; Spinal cord
  parasympathetic, 53, 502
  peripheral, 52–53
  sympathetic, 53, 502
Neural communication, 46–52
  neurons and, 46–48, 53–54
  neurotransmitters and, 49–52
  process of, 49–50
Neural connections, pruning of, 149, 174,
    197
Neural firing, 47–48
  schizophrenia and, 640
Neural influences, aggression and, 710–711
Neural networks, 53–54
  of infant, 173
  pain and, 395
Neural pathways
  dreams and, 105, 106
  emotion and, 507
Neural processing
  in adulthood, 210
  alcohol and, 115–116
  speed of, intelligence and, 414
Neural prosthetics, 69–70
Neuroadaptation, 113
Neurogenesis, 74
Neuroimaging, 60
Neurological speed, intelligence and, 414
Neurons, 46–48
  communication between. *See* Neural
      communication; Neurotransmitters
  interneurons, 46
  mirror, 183, 316–317
  motor, 46
  pruning of, 149, 174, 197
  sensory, 46
Neuroscience perspective, 8, 9
Neurotransmitters, 49–52, 56
  actions of, 51–52
  aggression and, 711
  in anxiety disorders, 616

depression and, 631–632
hypothalamus and, 64
personality and, 576
in schizophrenia, 639–640
storage and, 339, 340
temperament and, 138
Newborn, 172–173
New perspective, psychotherapy and, 667
Nicaraguan Sign Language, 389
Nichomachean Ethics (Aristotle), 479
Nicotine, 118–120
Night terrors, 102
NK cells (natural killer cells), 538
Nociceptors, 254
Nondeclarative memory, 343
Nondirective therapy, 649–650
Nonverbal behavior, emotional expression
    and, 511–513
Norepinephrine (noradrenaline), 51, 56
  depression and, 631
Norm(s), 152–153
  reciprocity, 728
  social-responsibility, 729
Normal curve, 39–40, 420
Normative social influence, 692
Novelty-preference procedure, 172–173
Nucleus accumbens, emotion and,
    503–504
Numerical ability, in animals, 398
Nutritional supplements, for depression,
    679

Obedience, 693–696
Obesity, 451, 456–464
  physiology of, 458–462
  social effects of, 457–458
  weight loss and, 462–464
Obestatin, 451
Object permanence, 178–179
Observation, naturalistic, 28–29
Observational learning, 289, 315–321
  aggression and, 714–715
  antisocial effects of, 319–321
  applications of, 318–321
  Bandura's experiments in, 317–318
  of fear, 615
  mirror neurons and, 316–317
  prosocial effects of, 313–319
Obsessive-compulsive disorder (OCD), 610,
    612
Occam's razor, 166
Occipital lobes, 67, 68
OCD (obsessive-compulsive disorder), 610,
    612
Oedipus complex, 560
Olfaction, 259–261
One-word stage, 387
Online matchmaking, 720
On the Origin of Species (Darwin), 7, 143
Operant behavior, 301
Operant chambers, 302
Operant conditioning, 288, 289, 301–314
  applications of, 310–312
  in behavior therapies, 653–654
  biological predispositions and, 309
  classical conditioning vs., 301, 313
  cognition and, 308–309

language development and, 388
Skinner's experiments in, 301–308,
    310–312
Operational definitions, 26, 36
Opiates, 117
Opponent colors, 241–242
Opponent-process theory, 242
Optic nerve, 235
Optimism, 587
  excessive, 587
  health and, 544–545
Oral stage, 560
Orexin, 101
  hunger and, 450–451
Organizational psychology, 490–496
Orgasm, 466–467
Orgasmic dysfunction, 467
Ostracism, pain of, 481–482
Other-race effect, 708
Outcome research, 661–663
Outer ear, 244
Outgroup, prejudice and, 706–708
Outsourcing, 485
Oval window, 244
Overconfidence, 16–17
  blindness to one's own incompetence and,
    588–589
  groupthink and, 700
  in one's judgments, 376–377
Overlearning, 12
Own-race bias, 708

Pain, 253–257
  biological influences on, 254–255
  controlling, 256–257
  hypnosis to alleviate, 110, 111
  neural networks and, 395
  psychological influences on, 255
  social-cultural influences on, 256
Pain reflex, 54–55
Palm readers, 578–579
Panic attacks, 611
Panic disorder, 610, 611
Paradoxical sleep, 92, 94–96, 102
Parallel processing, 239–240
Parallel unconscious processing, 87
Paranoid schizophrenia, 639
Paranoid tendencies, 637
Paraphrasing, in client-centered therapy, 650
Parapsychology, 281
Parasympathetic nervous system, 53
  emotion and, 502
Parent(s). *See also* Child-rearing practices
  adolescents and, 202–204
  attachment and. *See* Attachment
  authoritarian, 193
  authoritative, 193
  cohabiting vs. married, 217
  early experiences and, 148–150
  permissive, 193
  sexual restraint and, 472
Parenting. *See also* Child-rearing practices
  adoptive, 137
  operant conditioning applications in, 312
  styles of, attachment and, 193
Parietal lobes, 67, 68
  intelligence and, 412

Partial reinforcement, 305
Passionate love, 724
Passwords, retrieval of, 355
Peacemaking, 729–734
  conciliation and, 733–734
  contact and, 731
  cooperation and, 732–733
  enemy perceptions and, 730–731
  social traps and, 729–730
Peak experiences, 570
Peers
  adolescents and, 203
  drug use and, 127
  influence on behavior, 151
"Penis envy," 562
Perceived control, 542–544
Perception
  adaptation of, 273–274
  definition of, 226
  of depth, 264–266
  disturbed, in schizophrenia, 637
  enemy, 730–731
  form, 262–264
  human factors and, 279–281
  interpretation of. See Perceptual
    interpretation
  of loudness, 246
  mirror-image perceptions and, 730–731
  of order in random events, 33–34
  organization of. See Perceptual organization
  perceptual constancy and, 267–270
  of pitch, 246–247
  sensation vs., 225
Perceptual adaptation, 273–274
Perceptual constancy, 267–270
Perceptual interpretation, 272–285
  extrasensory perception and, 281–285
  human factor and, 279–281
  perceptual adaptation and, 273–274
  perceptual set and, 274–278
  sensory deprivation and restored vision
    and, 272–273
Perceptual organization, 262–271
  depth perception and, 264–266
  form perception and, 262–264
  motion perception and, 267
  perceptual constancy and, 267–270
Perceptual set, 274–278
Perceptual speed, intelligence and, 413
Performance appraisal, 489–490
Peripheral nervous system, 52–53
Peripheral route persuasion, 685
Permissive parents, 193
Persistence, forgetting and, 352
Personal control, 584–589, 701
Personality, 557–595
  creativity and, 410
  definition of, 557
  frontal lobes and, 72
  humanistic perspective on, 570–573
  psychoanalytic perspective on, 558–569
  self and. See Self entries
  social-cognitive perspective on. See Social-
    cognitive perspective on personality
  trait perspective on. See Trait perspective
    on personality
  types A and B, 536

Personality disorders, 620–622
Personality inventories, 576–577
Personality psychologists, 10
Personality tests
  personality inventories, 576–577
  projective, 563–565
Personal space, 153
Person-centered perspective, 570–571
Personnel psychology, 486–490
  harnessing strengths and, 486–489
  performance appraisal and, 489–490
Person-situation controversy, 580–583
Perspective, linear, as depth cue, 266
Persuasion, 684–685
Pessimism, 587
PET (positron-emission tomography), 60
Pets, health and, 546
Phallic stage, 560
Phantom limb sensation, 255
Phi Phenomenon, 267
Phobias, 519, 610, 611–612
  specific, 611
Phonemes, 385
Phrenology, 45
Physical attractiveness, attraction and,
  721–723
Physical dependence, on psychoactive drugs,
  113
Physical development
  in adolescence, 195–197
  in adulthood, 206–212
  in infancy and childhood, 174–176
  prenatal, 170–172
Piaget's theory of cognitive development,
  178–181, 184–185
Pitch, 244
  perception of, 246–247
Pituitary gland, 56, 65
PK (psychokinesis), 282
Placebo effect, 35, 256, 662
Placenta, 171
Place theory, 246–247
Plasticity
  of brain, 73–74
  erotic, 474
Plateau phase of sexual response cycle, 466
Pleasure principle, 559
PNI (psychoneuroimmunology), 537–539
Polygraph, 504–505
Ponzo illusion, 268
Pop-out, 90
Population, 28
Positive psychology, 588
Positive reinforcement, 303
Positive symptoms of schizophrenia, 638
Positive transfer, 356
Positron-emission tomography (PET), 60
Possible selves, 590–591
Postconventional morality, 199
Posthypnotic suggestions, 109–110
Post-traumatic growth, 614
Post-traumatic stress disorder (PTSD), 610,
  612–614
Poverty, psychological disorders and, 607
Practical intelligence, 408
Practice, spaced and massed, 12, 329–330
Precognition, 282

Preconscious area, 558
Preconventional morality, 199
Predictive validity, 421–422
Pregnancy
  adolescent, 470–471
  conception and, 170
  with male fetuses, sexual orientation of
    offspring and, 474–475
  maternal virus during, schizophrenia and,
    640–641
  prenatal development during, 170–171
Prejudice, 703–709
  automatic, 705
  cognitive roots of, 708–709
  combating, 731
  definition of, 703
  emotional roots of, 708
  levels of, 703–704, 706
  against obese people, 457–458
  social roots of, 706–708
Premature ejaculation, 467
Prenatal development, 170–172. See also
  Pregnancy
  maternal virus during, schizophrenia and,
    640–641
  sexual orientation and, 476–479
Preoperational stage, 178, 180
Preservation of innovation, 152
Primacy effect, 330
Primary mental abilities, 405
Primary reinforcers, 304
Primary sex characteristics, 195
Priming, 86, 347–348
Principles of Psychology (James), 4, 590
Prison simulation, 687–688
Proactive interference, 354
Problem-focused coping, 542
Problem solving, 371–374
Productive language, development of, 387–388
Progressive relaxation, 652
Project Head Start, 431, 432
Projection, 562
Projective tests, 563–565
Prosocial behavior, modeling of, 318–319
Prosocial relations, 719–734
  altruism and, 726–729
  attraction and, 719–726
  peacemaking and, 729–734
Prosopagnosia, 225
Prospective memory, 213
Prosthetics, neural, 69–70
Protein synthesis, 132
Prototypes, 370
Proximity
  attraction and, 719–720
  grouping and, 263
Pruning process
  in adolescence, 174, 197
  in childhood, 149
Psychiatrists, 10
Psychics, 282–283
Psychoactive drugs, 83, 113–129
  dependence and addiction to, 113–115
  depressants, 115–117. See also Alcohol
  hallucinogens, 122, 124–125
  influences on use of, 125–128
  stimulants, 117–122

Psychoanalysis, 558, 646–649
  aims of, 646–647
  methods of, 647–648
  psychodynamic therapy and, 646, 648–649
Psychoanalytic perspective, 558–569. *See also* Unconscious
  evaluation of, 565–568
  neo-Freudian theorists and, 562–563
  personality development and, 560–561
  personality structure and, 559–560
  psychodynamic theorists and, 563
  shortcomings as theory, 567–568
  unconscious and, 558–562, 563–565
Psychodynamic perspective, 9
Psychodynamic theory, 563
Psychodynamic therapy, 646, 648–649
Psychokinesis (PK), 282
Psychological contracts, 485
Psychological dependence, on psychoactive drugs, 113–114
Psychological disorders, 597–643
  anxiety. *See* Anxiety disorders
  attention-deficit/hyperactivity disorder, 599, 600
  biopsychosocial approach to, 602
  classification of, 602–604
  defining, 599–600
  definition of, 599
  dissociative, 618–620
  insanity defense and, 606
  labeling, 605–606
  medical model of, 601
  mood. *See* Mood disorders
  personality disorders, 620–622
  prevention of, 669
  rates of, 606–608
  schizophrenia. *See* Schizophrenia
  somatoform, 622–623
  treatment of. *See* Biomedical therapies; Psychotherapies
Psychological influences. *See also* Biopsychosocial perspective; Levels of analysis; *specific psychological influences*
  on aggression, 712–717
  on antisocial personality disorder, 621
  on attraction, 719–724
  on drug use, 126–128
  on hunger, 451–455
  on hypnosis, 111–112
  on memory, 349–350
  on pain, 255
  on perception, 274–278
  on schizophrenia, 642–643
  on sexual behavior, 468–470
Psychological science, 14–24
  birth of, 2
  need for, 14–19
Psychology
  contemporary, 6–11
  definition of, 5, 6, 83
  development of field, 4–6
  frequently asked questions about, 19–23
  globalization of, 6
  levels of analysis in. *See* Levels of analysis
  roots of, 2–4
  as science, 6

subfields of, 9–11
  tips for studying, 12
  value judgments in, 23
Psychoneuroimmunology (PNI), 537–539
Psychopath(s), 620
Psychopathology, 601. *See also* Psychological disorders
Psychopharmacology, 671–674
  antianxiety drugs for, 672
  antidepressant drugs for, 632, 673–674
  antipsychotic drugs for, 672
  memory and, 341
  mood-stabilizing drugs for, 674
Psychophysics, 227
Psychophysiological illnesses, 537–541
Psychoses. *See also* Bipolar disorder; Schizophrenia
  treatment of, 672
Psychosocial development, Erikson's theory of, 189, 200–204, 217, 219, 222
Psychosexual stages, 560
Psychosocial tasks, 200
Psychosurgery, 677–678
Psychotherapies, 645–670
  alternative, evaluation of, 665–666
  behavior therapies, 650–654
  cognitive therapies, 654–657
  commonalities among approaches to, 666–668
  culture and values in, 668–669
  eclectic approach to, 646
  effectiveness of, 660–663
  group and family therapies, 657–658
  humanistic, 649–650
  interpersonal, 648–649
  psychoanalytic, 646–649
  relative effectiveness of different approaches and, 663–664
Psychotherapists, 667
  culture and values of, 668–669
Psychotherapy integration, 646
PTSD (post-traumatic stress disorder), 610, 612–614
Puberty, 195–197
Punishment, 304, 306–308
  reinforcement vs., 307
Pupil, 234
PYY, 451

Racial prejudice. *See* Prejudice
Rage. *See also* Anger
  brain and, 63
Random assignment, 34–35
Random events, perceiving order in, 33–34
Randomized clinical trials, 662
Random sampling, 27–28
Range, 39
Rating scales, for performance appraisal, 489
Rational-emotive therapy, 669
Rationalization, 562
Reaction formation, 562
Reality principle, 559
Reasoning
  development of, 198
  moral, 198–200
  statistical. *See* Statistical reasoning
Rebirthing therapies, 664

Recall. *See also* Memory
  aging and, 213, 215
  eyewitness, of children, 361–362
Recency effect, 330
Recency errors, 490
Receptive language, development of, 386
Reciprocal determinism, 583–584
Reciprocity norm, 728
Recognition, intelligence and, 213
Recovered-memory therapies, 664
Reflection, in client-centered therapy, 650
Reflexes, 54–55
Refractory period, 48, 467
Regression, 561
Regression toward the mean, 662
Rehearsal, 328–330
  mental, 395–396
Reification, 404
Reinforcement
  continuous, 305
  fear and, 615
  language development and, 388
  negative, 303–304
  partial (intermittent), 305
  positive, 303
  punishment vs., 307
Reinforcement schedules, 305–306
Reinforcers, 303–305
  conditioned, 304
  delayed, 304–305
  immediate, 304–305
  primary, 304
  secondary, 304
  shaping and, 302
Relationships
  conflict and, 729. *See also* Peacemaking
  coping with stress and, 545–547
  peer. *See* Peers
  sustaining, 481
  therapeutic, 668
Relative deprivation, 528
Relative height, as depth cue, 266
Relative luminance, 269
Relative motion, as depth cue, 266
Relative size, as depth cue, 266
Relaxation, 549, 551–552
  progressive, 652
Relearning, 346, 353
Reliability, of tests, 421
Religion. *See also* Spirituality
  psychotherapy and, 669
  sexual restraint and, 472
REM rebound, 106
REM sleep, 92, 94–96, 102
Repair, of brain, 73, 99
Repetitive transcranial magnetic stimulation (rTMS), 676, 677
Replication, 26
Representativeness heuristic, 374–375
Repressed memories, 362–365
Repression, 356–357, 558, 561
  contemporary views of, 566
Research
  adoption studies, 136–137, 429, 642
  application of, 19
  applied, 10
  basic, 10

Research (continued)
    correlation and, 29–34, 36
    cross-sectional studies, 213
    descriptive, 26–29, 36
    ethics of, 20–22
    experimental, 20–22, 34–36
    longitudinal studies, 214
    outcome, 661–663
    scientific method and, 25–26
    twin studies, 133–136
Residual schizophrenia, 639
Resilience, 189
Resiliency, survivor, 614
Resistance
    in general adaptation syndrome, 532
    in psychoanalysis, 647
Resolution phase of sexual response cycle,
        467
Respondent behavior, 301
Responses
    conditioned, 291
    to danger, 502
    fight-or-flight, 502, 532, 712
    unconditioned, 291
Responsibility, diffusion of, 727
Resting potential, 47
Rethinking Happiness: The Science of
        Psychological Wealth (Diener and
        Biswas-Diener), 523
Reticular formation, 61, 65
Retina, 234, 235–237
Retinal disparity, 265
Retrieval, 325, 346–350
    failure of, 354–357
    of passwords, 355
Retrieval cues, 347
Retroactive interference, 354
Reuptake, 50
Reward centers, 64
Reward deficiency syndrome, 65
Reward theory of attraction, 724
Risk taking, excessive optimism and, 587
Rites of passage, 204
Rods, 235–237
Role(s), 162
    gender, 162–163
Role-playing, attitudes and, 686–688
Romantic love, 724–726
Rorschach inkblot test, 564–565
Rosy retrospection, 333
rTMS (repetitive transcranial magnetic
        stimulation), 676, 677
Rubber-hand illusion, 252

SAD (seasonal affective disorder), 666
Salty taste, 257
Sampling, random, 27–28
Savant syndrome, 406
Scaffolding, 185
Scapegoat theory of prejudice, 708
Scatterplots, 30
Schemas, 177
    gender, 163
    perceptual set and, 275
Schizoid personality disorder, 620
Schizophrenia, 637–643
    brain abnormalities in, 639–641

definition of, 637
    genetic factors in, 641–642
    onset and development of, 638–639
    psychological factors in, 642–643
    subtypes of, 639
    symptoms of, 637–638
    treatment of, 672
School(s)
    appropriate developmental placement and,
        326
    intelligence and, 431–432
    mainstreaming in, 425
    operant conditioning applications in,
        310–311
School achievement, predicting, 416–417
Science, psychology as, 6. See also
        Psychological science
Scientific attitude, 17–18
Scientific method, 25–26
SCN (suprachiasmatic nucleus), 92
Scripts, social, aggression and, 715
Seasonal affective disorder (SAD), 666
Secondary reinforcers, 304
Secondary sex characteristics, 195–196
Second-order conditioning, 292
Secure attachment, 187
Secure self-esteem, 594
Selection effect, 151
Selective attention, 87–90, 111, 637
Selective inattention, 88–90
Selective permeability, 47
Selective serotonin reuptake inhibitors
        (SSRIs), 673
Self, 590–594
    definition of, 590
    family, 156
    ideal, 571
    individualist and collectivist cultures and,
        154–155
    possible selves and, 590–591
Self-actualization, 570
Self-awareness, 192
    alcohol and, 116
Self-concept, 571
    assessment of, 571–572
    development of, 192
Self-control
    alcohol and, 116
    depleting and strengthening, 585
Self-defeating beliefs, depression and,
        632–634
Self-disclosure, love and, 725
Self-esteem, 590–592
    benefits of, 591–592
    defensive, 594
    secure, 594
Self-recognition, 192
Self-reference effect, 332
Self-serving bias, 592–594
Self-transcendence, 547, 570
Semantic encoding, 331–332
Semantics, 385
Semicircular canals, 253
Sensation
    auditory. See Hearing
    definition of, 226
    gender and, 433

kinesthetic, 252
    pain. See Pain
    perception vs., 225
    sensory adaptation and, 230–231
    smell, 259–261
    taste, 257–258
    touch, 252
    visual. See Vision
Sensitive periods. See Critical periods
Sensorimotor stage, 178–179
Sensorineural hearing loss, 248
Sensory abilities, in adulthood, 209–210
Sensory adaptation, 230–231
Sensory cortex, 69, 70–71
Sensory deprivation, 272–273
Sensory interaction, 258
Sensory memory, 325, 327
Sensory neurons, 46
Serial conscious processing, 87
Serial position effect, 330
Serial processing, 239
Serotonin, 51
    aggression and, 711
    in anxiety disorders, 616
    depression and, 631–632
    storage and, 339
    temperament and, 138
Service learning programs, sexual restraint
        and, 472
Set point, 451
    obesity and, 459–460
Settling point, 451
Severity errors, 490
Sex characteristics
    primary, 195
    secondary, 195–196
Sex chromosomes, 160
Sex hormones, 160
    aggression and, 711
    prenatal, sexual orientation and, 476–479
    sexual behavior and, 467, 468
Sexual disorders, 467
Sexuality, 466–483
    adolescent, 470–472
    alcohol and sexual behavior and, 116–117
    evolutionary explanation of, 143–146
    hormones and, 467–468
    human values and, 479
    mating and. See Mating; Mating
        preferences
    psychology of, 468–470
    sexual orientation and. See Sexual
        orientation
    sexual response cycle and, 466–467
Sexually transmitted infections (STIs),
        471–472
Sexual orientation, 472–479
    in animals, 475
    origins of, 474–479
    statistics on, 473–474
Sexual response cycle, 466–467
Shape constancy, 267, 268
Shaping, 302–303
Short-term memory, 325, 327, 337–338
Sight Unseen (Goodale and Milner), 86
Signal detection theory, 227–228
Significance, statistical, 41

Significant life changes, 534
Sign language, 390
    animals' use of, 400–401
    Nicaraguan, 389
    structure of, 385
Sign Language Structure (Stokoe), 248
Similarity(ies)
    attraction and, 723–724
    explanation for, 142–143
    grouping and, 263
Situational attribution, 682
Size, relative, as depth cue, 266
Size constancy, 268
Size-distance relationships, 268–269
Skepticism, science and, 18
Skewed distributions, 38
Skinner box, 302
Sleep, 91–107
    circadian rhythm and, 91–92
    depression and, 679
    disorders of, 100–102
    dreams and. *See* Dream(s)
    loss of, obesity and, 460
    reasons for, 96–100
    REM (paradoxical), 92, 94–96
    stages of, 92–94
    theories of, 99–100
Sleep apnea, 101–102
Sleep cycle, 96
Sleep deprivation, 97–99, 101–102
Sleep spindles, 94
Sleeptalking, 94, 102
Sleepwalking, 94, 102
Slow-to-warm-up babies, 137
Smell sense, 259–261
Smoking, 118–120
Social clock, 216
Social-cognitive perspective on mood
        disorders, 632–635
Social-cognitive perspective on personality,
        583–590
    assessing behavior in situations and,
        589–590
    evaluation of, 590
    personal control and, 584–589
    reciprocal influences and, 583–584
Social connectedness, gender and, 158–160
Social control, 701
Social-cultural influences. *See also*
        Biopsychosocial perspective; Culture;
        Levels of analysis; *specific social-cultural*
        influences
    on aggression, 713
    on drug use, 126–128
    on emotion, 513–515
    on hypnosis, 110–111
    on pain, 256
    on prejudice, 706–708
Social-cultural perspective, 9
Social development
    in adolescence, 200–204
    in adulthood, 215–221
    in infants and children, 185–193
Social exchange theory, 728
Social facilitation, 697
    eating and, 453
Social identity, 201–202, 706–708

Social inequalities, prejudice and, 706
Social influence, 690–702
    conformity and, 690–693, 696
    group, 697–700
    group influence and, 697–700
    individuals and, 701
    informational, 692–693
    normative, 692
    obedience and, 693–696
    obesity and, 460
Social influence theory of hypnosis, 110–111
Social intelligence, 411
Social interaction, obesity and, 457–458
Social intuitionism, 199–200
Social leadership, 495
Social learning theory, gender and, 163
Social loafing, 698
Social phobia, 611
Social power, gender and, 158
Social psychologists, 10
Social psychology, 681–734. *See also*
        Aggression; Prejudice; Prosocial
        relations; Social influence; Social
        thinking
    definition of, 681
Social relationships. *See also* Relationships
    depression and, 679
Social-responsibility norm, 729
Social scripts, aggression and, 715
Social support
    coping with stress and, 545–547
    faith factor and, 555
Social thinking, 682–689
    attitudes and actions and, 684–689
    attribution and, 682–684
Social traps, 729–730
Sociopaths, 620
Somatoform disorders, 622–623
Sounds. *See* Hearing; Hearing loss
Sound waves, 243–244
Source amnesia, 359
Source misattribution, 359
Sour taste, 257
Spaced practice, 12
Spacing effect, 329–330
Spatial aptitude, gender and, 433–434
Specific phobias, 611
Speed dating, 720
Spelling ability, gender and, 432
Spermarche, 197
Spillover effects, 506
Spinal cord, 65
    pain perception and, 254
    reflexes and, 54–55
Spirituality. *See also* Religion
    life expectancy and, 208–209
    stress management and, 552–554
Split brains, 74–77
Split-half reliability, 421
Spontaneous recovery, 305, 674
    in classical conditioning, 293–294
Sports. *See also* Athletic performance
    operant conditioning applications in, 311
Spotlight effect, 591
SQ3R method, 12, 365–366
SSRIs (selective serotonin reuptake
        inhibitors), 673

Stability, of personality traits, 578–579
Stability/change issue, 169, 222–223
    intelligence and, 422–424
Stages
    of cognitive development, 178–181, 184
    continuity/stages issue and, 169, 222
    psychosexual, 560
    of sleep, 92–94
    three-stage processing model of memory
        and, 325–326, 327
Standard deviation, 39
Standardization, of tests, 420
Stanford-Binet test, 417, 420
Stanford prison simulation, 687
State-dependent memory, 349, 634
States of consciousness, 84
Statistical reasoning, 37–41
    central tendency measures and, 38
    inferences and, 40–41
    statistical differences and, 41
    variation measures and, 38–40
Statistical significance, 41
Stereotypes, prejudice and, 703
Stereotype threat, 439–440
Stigma, labels and, 605
Stimulants, 117–122
Stimulus(i)
    conditioned, 291
    discriminative, 302–303
    imagined, sexual behavior and, 469–470
    masking, 229
    sexual, 469–470
    subliminal, 228–229
    unconditioned, 291
Stimulus generalization, 615
Stirrup (bone), 244
STIs (sexually transmitted infections),
        471–472
Storage, 325, 336–345
    in brain, 339–345
    decay of, 353–354
    in long-term memory, 338–339
    in sensory memory, 336–337
Strange Interlude (O'Neill), 365
Stranger anxiety, 185
Strange situation, 187
Strengths, job-relevant, harnessing,
        486–489, 493–494
Stress, 530–555
    coping with, 542–547
    definition of, 530–531
    depression and, 628
    heart and, 535–537
    illness and, 530–535
    managing, 547–554
    post-traumatic stress disorder and, 610,
        612–614
    repression and, 566
    stress response system and, 532–533
    susceptibility to disease and, 537–541
Stress hormones, 532
    memory and, 340–342
Stressors, definition of, 530
Stress reactions, 530
Stroboscopic movement, 267
Structuralism, 2–3
Structured interviews, 488–489

Studying
    spaced and massed practice for, 12,
        329–330
    tips for, 12, 365–366
A Study in Scarlet (Doyle), 338
Subgoals, 494
Subjective well-being, 522
Subliminal stimulation, 228–229
Successive approximations, 302
Sucking, 172
Suggestibility, forgetting and, 351
Suicide, 630–631, 674, 676
Supercell clusters, 238
Superego, 559, 560
Superordinate goals, 732–733
Suppression, by punishment, 307
Suprachiasmatic nucleus (SCN), 92
Surveys, 26, 27–28
    random sampling and, 27–28
    wording effects on, 27
Survival, need to belong and, 480
Survivor resiliency, 614
Swallowing, 172
Sweet taste, 257
Sympathetic nervous system, 53
    emotion and, 502
Synaesthesia, 258
Synapses, 49
    intelligence and, 412
    storage and, 339–340
Synaptic gaps (clefts), 49
Syntax, 385
Systematic desensitization, 652

Taijin-kyofusho, 602
Tardive dyskinesia, 672
Task leadership, 495
Taste aversion, conditioning, 296, 297
Taste buds, 257
Taste preferences, 452
Taste sense, 257–258
TAT (Thematic Apperception Test), 564
Teen pregnancy, 470–471
Telegraphic speech, 387
Telepathy, 282
Telomeres, 208
    stress and, 533
Temperament
    attachment and, 189
    heredity and, 137–138
Temporal lobes, 67, 68
Teratogens, 171–172
Terminal decline, 215
Terrorism, fear of, 378–379
Terror-management theory, 567
Test(s). *See* Intelligence testing; Personality
    inventories; Projective tests
Testing effect, 330
Testosterone, 160
    aggression and, 711
    sexual behavior and, 467, 468
Test-retest reliability, 421
Test-taking tips, 12
Thalamus, 61, 62, 65
    schizophrenia and, 640
THC (delta-9-tetrahydrocannabinol), 122
Thematic Apperception Test (TAT), 564

Theory, 25
Theory of mind, 181–184
    in autism, 182–183, 317
    mirror neurons and, 317
Therapeutic alliance, 668
Therapeutic life-style change, 678–679
Therapists, 667
    culture and values of, 668–669
Therapy. *See* Biomedical therapies;
    Psychotherapies
Thinking, 370–383. *See also* Cognition;
    Cognitive *entries*
    animal, language and, 397–402
    concepts and, 370–371
    convergent, 409
    critical, 12, 18–19
    decision making and judgments and,
        374–382
    divergent, 409
    in images, 395–396
    imaginative, 410
    language and, 393–397
    problem solving and, 371–374
    sleep and, 100
    social. *See* Social thinking
360-degree feedback, 489
Three-stage processing model of memory,
    325–326, 327
Thresholds, 48, 227–230
    absolute, 227
    difference, 230
    signal detection and, 227–228
    subliminal stimulation and, 228–229
Time-out, 307
Tinnitus, 255
T lymphocytes, 538
Tobacco use, 118–120
Token economies, 653–654
Tolerance, to psychoactive drugs, 113
Tonguing, 172
Tool use, by animals, 397–398
Top-down processing, 226
Touch sense, 251–253
Trait(s), definition of, 574
Trait perspective on personality, 574–583
    Big Five factors and, 577–580
    biological factors and, 576
    evaluation of, 580–583
    factor analysis and, 575–576
    personality inventories and, 576–577
Tranquilizers, 117
Transcranial magnetic stimulation,
    repetitive, 676, 677
Transduction, 233
Transference, in psychoanalysis, 647
Transformational leadership, 495
Transience, forgetting and, 351
Trauma. *See also* Stress
    as classical conditioning, 299
    post-traumatic stress disorder and, 613
Trial and error, 371
Triarchic theory of intelligence, 408, 409
Trust
    basic, 189
    psychotherapy and, 668
Trust vs. mistrust stage, 201
Tutored human enrichment, 430–431

Twins
    fraternal, 134
    identical, 134
    separated, 135–136
    virtual, 136, 429
Twin studies, 133–136
    of intelligence, 428–429
    of schizophrenia, 641–642
Two-factor theory of emotion, 501
Two-track mind, 86–87, 369, 566. *See also*
    Dual processing; Unconscious
    cognition and emotion and, 508
    hypnosis and, 112
    intuition and, 380, 381
Two-word stage, 387
Type A personality, 536
Type B personality, 536

Ubuntu, 480
Umami, 257
Unconditional positive regard, 650
Unconditioned response (UR), 291
Unconditioned stimulus (US), 291
Unconscious, 558–562, 563–565. *See also*
    Psychoanalytic perspective
    collective, 563
    contemporary views of, 565
    defense mechanisms and, 561–562
    definition of, 558
    projective tests and, 563–565
Unconscious information processing, 86–87
Unconscious processes
    in amnesia, 342–343, 359
    automatic processing, 327–328
    in déjà vu, 348–349
    dual processing and, 86–90
    false memories, 359–361
    in hypnosis. *See* Hypnosis
    misinformation and imagination effects,
        357–359
    prejudice and, 705
    in psychoanalytic perspective. *See*
        Psychoanalytic perspective
    repression, 356–357, 558, 561, 566
    in selective attention, 87–90
    in sleep. *See* Dream(s); Sleep
Undifferentiated schizophrenia, 639
Unit bias, eating and, 453
Universal grammar, 388–389
Unstructured interviews, 488
Unweaving the rainbow (Newton), 165
UR (unconditioned response), 291
US (unconditioned stimulus), 291

Valence, of emotions, 517–518
Validity, of tests, 421–422
Value(s)
    advice giving and, 193
    human, sexuality and, 479
    in psychotherapy, 668–669
Value judgments, 23
*The Values in Action Classification of
    Strengths*, 604
Variable(s)
    independent and dependent, 35–36
    operational definitions of, 26, 36
Variable-interval schedules, 306

Variable-ratio schedules, 305, 306
Variation, measures of, 38–40
Ventromedial hypothalamus, 450–451
Venturesome personality, 410
Verbal ability, gender and, 432
Vestibular sacs, 253
Vestibular sense, 252–253
Video games, aggression and, 715–717
Violence. *See also* Aggression
   insanity defense and, 606
    media, aggression and, 715–717
Violence-viewing effect, 319–321
Viral infection
   HIV/AIDS, 471–472, 539–540
   during pregnancy, schizophrenia and,
    640–641
Virtual reality exposure therapy, 652
Virtual twins, 136, 429
Vision, 233–242
   color, 240–242
   as dual-processing system, 86
   eye and, 234–237
   information processing and, 237–240
   light energy and, 233–234
   loss of. *See* Blindness
   restored, 274
Visual cliff, 264

Visual cortex, 71
Visual encoding, 331–333
Visual perception track, 86
Vivid cases, prejudice and, 709
Voice effects, 496
Volley principle, 247

WAIS (Wechsler Adult Intelligence Scale),
   419, 420, 438
Wavelength, of light, 234
Wealth, well-being and, 524–526
Weber's law, 230
Wechsler Adult Intelligence Scale (WAIS),
   419, 420, 438
Wechsler Intelligence Scale for Children
   (WISC), 419, 420
Weight discrimination, 457–458
Weight loss, 462–464
Well-being. *See also* Happiness; Optimism
   across life span, 219–220
   wealth and, 524–526
Wernicke's area, 391, 392
White matter
   gender and, 161
   intelligence and, 413
WISC (Wechsler Intelligence Scale for
   Children), 419, 420

Wish fulfillment, dreams and, 104, 106
Withdrawal, from psychoactive drugs, 113
Women. *See also* Gender *entries;* Sexuality;
   Sexual orientation
   menarche and, 196–197
   menopause and, 207
   pregnancy and. *See* Pregnancy
   in psychology, 4
Women's intuition, 511–512
Wording, surveys and, 27
Word salad, 637
Work. *See also* Career *entries*
   in adulthood, 218
   job interviews and, 487–489
   operant conditioning applications in, 311
Working memory, 326, 327, 337–338
Workplace, motivation in, 484–497. *See also*
   Achievement motivation; Organizational
   psychology

X chromosome, 160

Yawning, 93, 182, 317, 690
Y chromosome, 160
Young-Helmholtz trichromatic theory, 241

Zygotes, 170

The Story of Psychology: A Timeline (continued from inside front cover)

1949 In *The Organization of Behavior: A Neuropsychological Theory,* Canadian psychologist Donald O. Hebb outlines a new and influential conceptualization of how the nervous system functions.

1950 Solomon Asch publishes studies of effects of conformity on judgments of line length.

1951 In *Childhood and Society,* Erik Erikson outlines his stages of psychosocial development.

Carl Rogers publishes *Client-Centered Therapy.*

1952 The American Psychiatric Association publishes the *Diagnostic and Statistical Manual of Mental Disorders,* an influential book that will be updated periodically.

1953 Eugene Aserinski and Nathaniel Kleitman describe rapid eye movements (REM) that occur during sleep.

Janet Taylor's Manifest Anxiety Scale appears in the *Journal of Abnormal Psychology.*

1954 In *Motivation and Personality,* Abraham Maslow proposes a hierarchy of motives ranging from physiological needs to self-actualization. (Maslow later updates the hierarchy to include self-transcendence needs.)

James Olds and Peter Milner, McGill University neuropsychologists, describe rewarding effects of electrical stimulation of the hypothalamus in rats.

Gordon Allport publishes *The Nature of Prejudice.*

1956 In his *Psychological Review* article titled "The Magical Number Seven, Plus or Minus Two: Some Limits on Our Capacity for Processing Information," George Miller coins the term *chunk* for memory researchers.

1957 Robert Sears, Eleanor Maccoby, and Harry Levin publish *Patterns of Child Rearing.*

Charles Ferster and B. F. Skinner publish *Schedules of Reinforcement.*

Noam Chomsky's critical review of B. F. Skinner's *Verbal Behavior* appears in the journal *Language.*

Eleanor Gibson and Richard Walk report their research on infants' depth perception in "The Visual Cliff."

Harry Harlow outlines "The Nature of Love," his work on attachment in monkeys.

1959 Lloyd Peterson and Margaret Peterson in the *Journal of Experimental Psychology* article, "Short-Term Retention of Individual Verbal Items," highlight the importance of rehearsal in memory.

John Thibaut and Harold Kelley publish *The Social Psychology of Groups.*

1969 In his APA presidential address, "Psychology as a Means of Promoting Human Welfare," George Miller emphasizes the importance of "giving psychology away."

1971 Kenneth B. Clark becomes the first African-American president of the American Psychological Association.

Albert Bandura publishes *Social Learning Theory.*

Allan Paivio publishes *Imagery and Verbal Processes.*

B. F. Skinner publishes *Beyond Freedom and Dignity.*

1972 Elliot Aronson publishes *The Social Animal.*

Fergus Craik and Robert Lockhart's "Levels of Processing: A Framework for Memory Research" appears in the *Journal of Verbal Learning and Verbal Behavior.*

Robert Rescorla and Allan Wagner publish their associative model of Pavlovian conditioning.

Under the leadership of Derald Sue and Stanley Sue, the Asian-American Psychological Association is founded.

1973 Ethologists Karl von Frisch, Konrad Lorenz, and Nikolaas Tinbergen receive the Nobel prize for their research on animal behavior.

1974 APA's Division 2 first publishes its journal, *Teaching of Psychology,* with Robert S. Daniel as editor.

Eleanor Maccoby (pictured) and Carol Jacklin publish *The Psychology of Sex Differences.*

1975 Biologist Edward O. Wilson's *Sociobiology* appears; it will be a controversial precursor to evolutionary psychology.

1976 Sandra Wood Scarr and Richard A. Weinberg publish "IQ Test Performance of Black Children Adopted by White Families" in *American Psychologist.*

1978 Psychologist Herbert A. Simon, Carnegie-Mellon University, wins a Nobel prize for pioneering research on computer simulations of human thinking and problem solving.

1979 James J. Gibson publishes *The Ecological Approach to Visual Perception.*

Elizabeth Loftus publishes *Eyewitness Testimony.*

1981 Ellen Langer is the first woman to be granted tenure in Harvard University's Department of Psychology.

David Hubel and Torsten Wiesel receive a Nobel prize for research on single-cell recordings that identified feature detector cells in the visual cortex .

Roger Sperry receives a Nobel prize for research on split-brain patients.